AF862219

McGraw Hill Education create™

Course

INFT124 - Computing Skills

BRYANT & STRATTON COLLEGE

create™

http://create.mheducation.com

ISBN-10: 1308888589 ISBN-13: 9781308888583

Contents

Credits

dedication

Bob and Lanita, thank you for generously allowing me to use the cabin where I completed much of the work on this book. Don and Jennie, thank you for teaching me the value of hard work and encouraging me throughout the years. Kelsey and Taylor, thank you for keeping me young at heart. Kelly, thank you for your daily love, support, and encouragement. I could not have done this without you. I'm looking forward to spending more time together on our tandem!

—Randy Nordell

Robert, thank you for your gift of quiet support as I worked on this book. Many thanks also to understanding family and friends who listened and offered encouragement, ideas, and suggestions.

—Kathleen Stewart

George, Timothy, and Amanda, thank you for your sacrifices. Your love sustains me, and your encouragement and support inspires me.

—Annette Easton

Brent, thank you for the many ways you have helped me while I worked on this book. Your love and support mean so much to me. I also appreciate my friends who shared their expertise and provided content for projects.

—Pat Graves

about the authors

RANDY NORDELL, Ed.D.

Randy Nordell is a professor of business technology at American River College in Sacramento, California. He has been an educator for over 25 years and has taught at the high school, community college, and university levels. He holds a bachelor's degree in business administration from California State University, Stanislaus, a single-subject teaching credential from Fresno State University, a master's degree in education from Fresno Pacific University, and a doctorate in education from Argosy University. Randy is the lead author of the *Microsoft Office 2013: In Practice* and *Microsoft Office 2016: In Practice* series of texts. He is also the author of *101 Tips for Online Course Success* and *Microsoft Outlook 2010.* Randy speaks regularly at conferences on the integration of technology into the curriculum. When not teaching and writing, he enjoys spending time with his family, cycling, skiing, swimming, backpacking, and enjoying the California weather and terrain.

KATHLEEN STEWART, M.S. Ed., M.B.A.

Kathleen Stewart is retired from her role as professor and department chairperson for the Information Management Systems Department at Moraine Valley Community College in Palos Hills, Illinois. She has a master's degree in occupational education from Southern Illinois University in Carbondale and an MBA from Loyola University in Chicago. She has authored Microsoft Office texts for many years for McGraw-Hill and has been involved in corporate training in the Chicago area. When not occupied by a writing project, she enjoys traveling, working on her golf game, literacy tutoring, and exploring cultural activities in the city.

ANNETTE EASTON, Ph.D.

Annette Easton is department chair and associate professor of management information systems at San Diego State University. She has been an educator for over 25 years at the university level and served as a School Board Trustee for eight years. She holds a bachelor's degree in business administration from California State University, Fresno, and a doctorate in management information systems from the University of Arizona. Annette has published articles on information technology education, electronic meeting systems, and integrating new technologies into the information systems curriculum. She co-authored *Cases for Modern Systems Development,* and she presents regularly at conferences. When not teaching, she enjoys spending time with her family, traveling, and cooking.

PAT GRAVES, Ed.D.

Pat Graves is a professor emeritus at Eastern Illinois University in Charleston, Illinois. She taught at the high school level before receiving her doctorate in education from the University of Memphis. At Eastern Illinois University, she taught in the School of Business for 20 years. Pat has been an author of PowerPoint textbooks for McGraw-Hill Education since 2002. When not writing, she travels, spends time with family and friends, enjoys the music city of Nashville, and appreciates the peacefulness of the Tennessee mountains.

preface

What We're About

We wrote *Microsoft Office 2016: In Practice* to meet the diverse needs of both students and instructors. Our approach focuses on presenting Office topics in a logical and structured manner, teaching concepts in a way that reinforces learning with practice projects that are transferrable, relevant, and engaging. Our pedagogy and content are based on the following beliefs.

Students Need to Learn and Practice Transferable Skills

Students must be able to transfer the concepts and skills learned in the text to a variety of projects, not simply follow steps in a textbook. Our material goes beyond the instruction of many texts. In our content, students practice the concepts in a variety of current and relevant projects *and* are able to transfer skills and concepts learned to different projects in the real world. To further increase the transferability of skills learned, this text is integrated with SIMnet so students also practice skills and complete projects in an online environment.

Your Curriculum Drives the Content

The curriculum in the classroom should drive the content of the text, not the other way around. This book is designed to allow instructors and students to cover all the material they need to in order to meet the curriculum requirements of their courses no matter how the courses are structured. *Microsoft Office 2016: In Practice* teaches the marketable skills that are key to student success. McGraw-Hill's Custom Publishing site, **Create,** can further tailor the content material to meet the unique educational needs of any school.

Integrated with Technology

Our text provides a fresh and new approach to an Office applications course. Topics integrate seamlessly with SIMnet with 1:1 content to help students practice and master concepts and skills using SIMnet's interactive learning philosophy. Projects in SIMnet allow students to practice their skills and receive immediate feedback. This integration with SIMnet meets the diverse needs of students and accommodates individual learning styles. Additional textbook resources found in SIMnet (Resources and Library sections) integrate with the learning management systems that are widely used in many online and onsite courses.

Reference Text

In addition to providing students with an abundance of real-life examples and practice projects, we designed this text to be used as a Microsoft Office 2016 reference source. The core material, uncluttered with exercises, focuses on real-world use and application. Our text provides clear step-by-step instructions on how readers can apply the various features available in Microsoft Office in a variety of contexts. At the same time, users have access to a variety of both online (SIMnet) and textbook practice projects to reinforce skills and concepts.

instructor walkthrough

Textbook Learning Approach

Microsoft Office 2016: In Practice uses the *T.I.P. approach:*

- **T**opic
- **I**nstruction
- **P**ractice

Topic

- Each Office application section begins with foundational skills and builds to more complex topics as the text progresses.
- Topics are logically sequenced and grouped by topics.
- Student Learning Outcomes (SLOs) are thoroughly integrated with and mapped to chapter content, projects, end-of-chapter review, and test banks.
- Reports are available within SIMnet for displaying how students have met these Student Learning Outcomes.

Instruction (How To)

- *How To* guided instructions about chapter topics provide transferable and adaptable instructions.
- Because *How To* instructions are not locked into single projects, this textbook functions as a reference text, not just a point-and-click textbook.
- Chapter content is aligned 1:1 with SIMnet.

Practice (Pause & Practice and End-of-Chapter Projects)

- Within each chapter, integrated Pause & Practice projects (three to five per chapter) reinforce learning and provide hands-on guided practice.
- In addition to Pause & Practice projects, each chapter has 10 comprehensive and practical practice projects: Guided Projects (three per chapter), Independent Projects (three per chapter), Improve It Project (one per chapter), and Challenge Projects (three per chapter). Additional projects can also be found in the Library or Resources section of SIMnet.
- Pause & Practice and end-of-chapter projects are complete content-rich projects, not small examples lacking context.
- Select auto-graded projects are available in SIMnet.

SIMnet
Keep IT SIMple!

Chapter Features

All chapters follow a consistent theme and instructional methodology. Below is an example of chapter structure.

Main headings are organized according to the ***Student Learning Outcomes (SLOs)***.

SLO 1.1

Creating, Saving, and Opening Documen

In Microsoft Word, you can create a variety of document types. Y
of Word enables you to create, edit, and customize high-quality a
ments. You can create Word documents from a new blank docum
plates, or from existing documents. Word allows you to save docu

amount of computer knowledge. This chapter covers the basics o
Word document.

STUDENT LEARNING OUTCOMES (SLOs)

After completing this chapter, you will be able to:

- **SLO 1.1** Create, save, and open a Word document (p. W1-3).
- **SLO 1.2** Customize a document by entering and selecting text, usi and using *AutoComplete*, *AutoCorrect*, and *AutoFormat* fe
- **SLO 1.3** Enhance a document using paragraph breaks, line breaks non-breaking spaces (p. W1-10).
- **SLO 1.4** Edit a document using cut, copy, paste, the *Clipboard*, an and repeat features. (p. W1-15).
- **SLO 1.5** Customize a document using different fonts, font sizes, ar (p. W1-18).
- **SLO 1.6** Enhance a document using text alignment and line and pa (p. W1-28).
- **SLO 1.7** Finalize a document using Word's research and proofing t
- **SLO 1.8** Apply custom document properties to a document (p. W1-

A list of Student Learning Outcomes begins each chapter. All chapter content, examples, and practice projects are organized according to the chapter SLOs.

WORD

CASE STUDY

Throughout this book you have the opportunity to put into practice the application features that you are learning. Each chapter begins with a case study that introduces you to the Pause & Practice projects in the chapter. These Pause & Practice projects give you a chance to apply and practice key skills realistic and practical context. Each chapter contains three to five Pause & Practice projects.

Placer Hills Real Estate (PHRE) is a real estate company with regional offices throughout central California. PHRE encourages agents to use standard formats for their business documents. This ensures consistency in document appearance while also allowing agents to personalize their correspondence to customers and colleagues. In the Pause & Practice projects in this chapter, you create a business document related to the real estate business.

The *Case Study* for each chapter is a scenario that establishes the theme for the entire chapter. Chapter content, examples, figures, Pause & Practice projects, SIMnet skills, and projects throughout the chapter closely related to this case study content. The three to five Pause & Practice projects in each chapter build upon each other and address key case study themes.

How To instructions enhance transferability of skills with concise steps and screen shots.

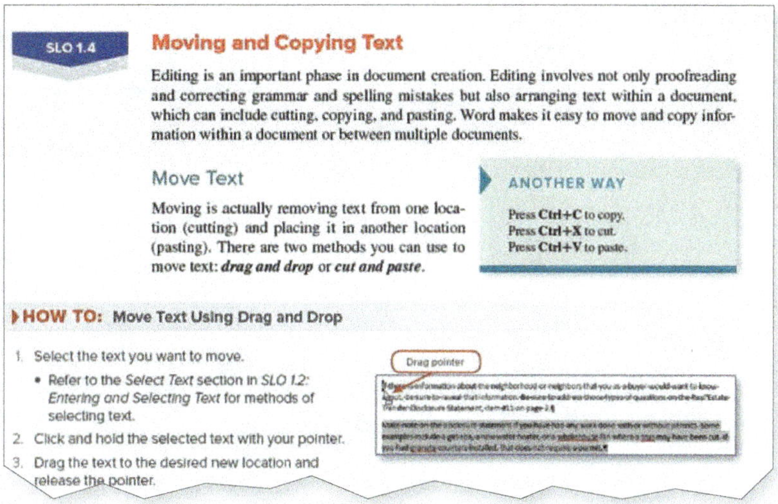
SLO 1.4

Moving and Copying Text

Editing is an important phase in document creation. Editing involves not only proofreading and correcting grammar and spelling mistakes but also arranging text within a document, which can include cutting, copying, and pasting. Word makes it easy to move and copy information within a document or between multiple documents.

Move Text

Moving is actually removing text from one location (cutting) and placing it in another location (pasting). There are two methods you can use to move text: ***drag and drop*** or ***cut and paste***.

ANOTHER WAY

Press **Ctrl+C** to copy.
Press **Ctrl+X** to cut.
Press **Ctrl+V** to paste.

HOW TO: Move Text Using Drag and Drop

1. Select the text you want to move.
   - Refer to the *Select Text* section in *SLO 1.2: Entering and Selecting Text* for methods of selecting text.
2. Click and hold the selected text with your pointer.
3. Drag the text to the desired new location and release the pointer.

Drag pointer

How To instructions are easy-to-follow concise steps. Screen shots and other figures fully illustrate How To topics.

Students can complete hands-on exercises in either the Office application or in SIMnet.

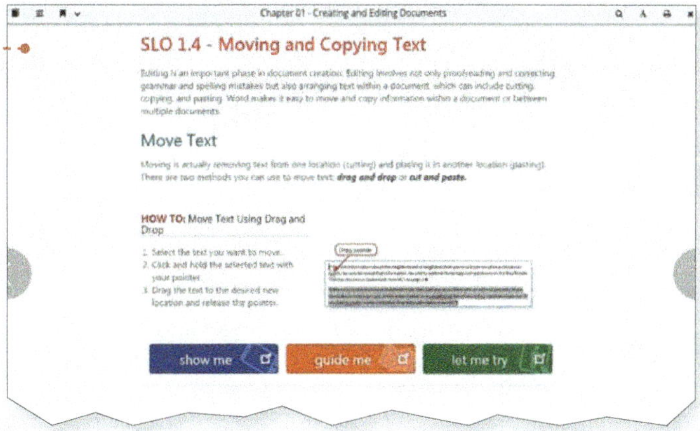

Pause & Practice 1-1: Create a business letter in block format with mixed punctuation.

Pause & Practice 1-2: Edit the business letter using copy, paste, and *Format Painter*. Modify the font, font size, color, style, and effects of selected text.

Pause & Practice 1-3: Finalize the business letter by modifying line spacing and paragraph spacing, changing paragraph alignment, translating text, using research and proofing tools, and adding document properties.

Pause & Practice projects, which each cover two to three of the student learning outcomes in the chapter, provide students with the opportunity to review and practice skills and concepts. Every chapter contains three to five Pause & Practice projects.

MORE INFO

The ***launcher*** (also referred to as the ***dialog box launcher***) is referred to throughout this text. Click the launcher in the bottom right corner of a group to open a dialog box or pane for additional options.

More Info provides readers with additional information about chapter content.

Another Way notations teach alternative methods of accomplishing the same task or feature such as keyboard shortcuts.

> **ANOTHER WAY**
> Press **Ctrl+Z** to undo.
> Press **Ctrl+Y** to redo or repeat.

Marginal notations present additional information and alternative methods.

End-of-Chapter Projects

Ten learning projects at the end of each chapter provide additional reinforcement and practice for students. Many of these projects are available in SIMnet for completion and automatic grading.

- ***Guided Projects (three per chapter):*** Guided Projects provide guided step-by-step instructions to apply Office features, skills, and concepts from the chapter. Screen shots guide students through the more challenging tasks. End-of-project screen shots provide a visual of the completed project.
- ***Independent Projects (three per chapter):*** Independent Projects provide students further opportunities to practice and apply skills, instructing students what to do, but not how to do it. These projects allow students to apply previously learned content in a different context.
- ***Improve It Project (one per chapter):*** In these projects, students apply their knowledge and skills to enhance and improve an existing document. These are independent-type projects that instruct students what to do, but not how to do it.
- ***Challenge Projects (three per chapter):*** Challenge Projects are open-ended projects that encourage creativity and critical thinking by integrating Office concepts and features into relevant and engaging projects.

Appendix

- ***Office 2016 Shortcuts:*** Appendix A covers the shortcuts available in Microsoft Office and within each of the specific Office applications. Information is in table format for easy access and reference.

Additional Resources in SIMnet

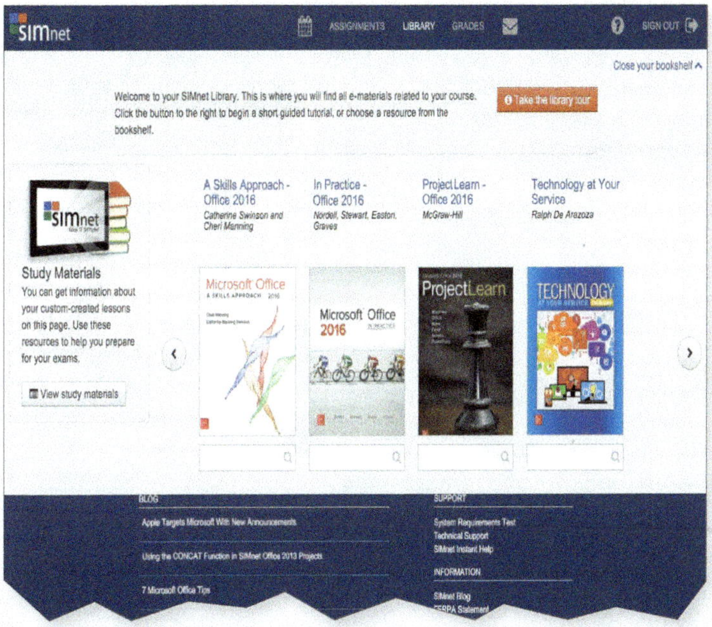

Students and instructors can find the following resources in the Library or Resources sections in SIMnet.

Student Resources

- ***Data Files:*** Files contain start files for all Pause & Practice, Capstone, and end-of-chapter projects.
- ***SIMnet Resources:*** Resources provide getting started and informational handouts for instructors and students.
- ***Check for Understanding:*** A combination of multiple choice, fill-in, matching, and short answer questions are available at the end of each SIMbook chapter in SIMnet to assist students in their review of the skills and concepts covered in the chapter.

Capstone Projects

- ***Integrating Applications:*** Projects provide students with the opportunity to learn, practice, and transfer skills using multiple Office applications.
- ***Integrating Skills:*** Projects provide students with a comprehensive and integrated review of all of the topics covered in each application (Word, Excel, Access, and PowerPoint). Available in individual application texts.

Appendices

- ***Business Document Formats:*** Appendix B is a guide to regularly used business document formatting and includes numerous examples and detailed instructions.

Instructor Resources

- ***Instructor's Manual:*** An Instructor's Manual provides teaching tips and lecture notes aligned with the PowerPoint presentations for each chapter. The manual also includes the solutions for online ***Check for Understanding*** questions.
- ***Test Bank:*** The extensive test bank integrates with learning management systems (LMSs) such as Blackboard, WebCT, Desire2Learn, and Moodle.
- ***PowerPoint Presentations:*** PowerPoint presentations for each chapter can be used in onsite course formats for lectures or can be uploaded to LMSs.
- ***SIMnet Resources:*** These resources provide getting started and informational handouts for instructors.
- ***Solution Files:*** Files contain solutions for all Pause & Practice, Capstone, Check for Understanding, and end-of-chapter projects.

acknowledgments

REVIEWERS

We would like to thank the following instructors, whose invaluable insights shaped the development of this series.

Scott Straub
College of Western Idaho

Jeremy Eason
West Georgia Technical College

Linda Johnsonius
Murray State University

Barbara West
Central Georgia Technical College

Yvonne Galusha
University of Iowa

Jean Finley
Asheville Buncombe Technical Community College

Candace S. Garrod
Red Rocks Community College

Marianne Dougherty
Middlesex County College

Adam Rosen
LIM College

Peter F. Meggison
Massasoit Community College

Robert Doyle
Dona Ana Community College

Pamela Silvers
Asheville-Buncombe Technical Community College

Lisa Cady
University of Arkansas - Fort Smith

Richard Johnsen
County College of Morris

Joan Butler
Manchester Community College

Robert Nichols
College of DuPage

Anna Tsipenyuk
LIM College

Brian Fox
Santa Fe College

Leilani Benoit
Dona Ana Community College

Uma Sridharan
Presbyterian College

Marianne Daugharthy
College of Western Idaho

Tom Moore
Kapiolani Community College

Diane Morris
Tyler Junior College

Brenda McFarland
Asheville-Buncombe Technical Community College

Mitch Pendleton
LDS Business College

Tony Hunnicutt
College of the Ouachitas

Jeanine Taylor
Bryan University

Darin Bell
Treasure Valley Community College

Martha Guzman
Taller San Jose

Mary Jean Blink
Mount St. Joseph University

Ralph Dickerson
The Atlanta Workforce Development Agency

Robert LaRocca
Keiser University

Jenna Dulak
Hilbert College

Carole Eustice
Clark College

Brad West
Sinclair Community College

Gwyn Ebie
Colorado Mountain College

Susan Paulsen
Community College of Vermont

Karen A. Myers
Fisher College

Gary Judd
Trinity Baptist College

Letty Barnes
Lake Washington Institute of Technology

Tiffinee Morgan
West Kentucky Community and Technical College

Carol Lee
Central Georgia Technical College

Ronald Creel
Troy University

John Sehloff
Bethany Lutheran College

Samuel Gabay
Chicago ORT Technical Institute

Bonnie Armendariz
Bakersfield College, Bakersfield California

Sherry E. Jacob
Jefferson Community and Technical College

Tuncay Bayrak
Western New England University

Mandy Burrell
Holmes community college

Denver Riffe
American National University

Dan Lowrance
LDS Business College

Velma Latson
Bowie State University

Marilyn Mendoza
Franklin Career Institute

Lisa McCool
Alfred State College

Pamela Sorensen
Santa Rosa Junior College

Peggy Batchelor
Furman University

Larry Fudella
Erie Community College

Chet Cunningham
Madisonville Community College

Lauri Smedley
Sacramento City College

Gary Ewen
Colorado Christian University

Amanda Hardin
Mississippi Delta Community College

Rob Durrance
Keiser University

Alli Vainshtein
Riverland Community College

George C. Holder
Cloud County Community College

Colin Onita
University of Akron

Melissa Nemeth
Indiana University Kelley School of Business

Keith Conn
Cleveland Institute of Electronics

Phil Young
Baylor University

Laura Earner
Saint Xavier University

Josanne Ford
Metropolitan Career Center Computer Technology Institute

Darla Hunt
Maysville Community and Technical College

Christopher VanOosterhout
Muskegon Community College

Mark Webb
Illinois Central College

David Raney
Cuyamaca College

Christine Wolfe
Ohio University Lancaster

Dan Guerra
Community Business College

Samuel Abraham
Siena Heights University

Sandra Carriker
North Shore Community College

Shelly Smith
Valley College- Beckley

Tahir Aziz
Long Beach City College

Kin Lam
Medgar Evers College/CUNY

Sherry Grosso
University of South Carolina

Regena Aye
Allen Community College

Paul Weaver
Bossier Parish Community College

Brian McDaniel
Palo Alto College

Stephen Arney
Washburn Institute of Technology

Lynn Wermers
North Shore Community College

Lois McWhorter
Somerset Community College

J. Kirk Atkinson
Western Kentucky University

Salina Chahal
UEI College

Dana Fellows
Whiteside Area Career Center

John Golofski
Everest Institute

Eileen Dewey
Rose State College

Nasser Tadayon
Southern Utah University

Tina Denmark
Montgomery College

Delores Vance
Hazard Community and Technical College

Brad Thomas
Olivet Nazareth University

Steven Mark Sachs
Los Angeles Valley College

Andrew Smith
Marian University

Nelly Delessy
Miami Dade COllege

Richard Patterson
Peirce College

Michael Goeken
Northwest Vista College

Janice Flegle
Thomas Edison State College

Sara Rutledge
Mount Aloysius College

Seyed Roosta
Albany State University

Jim Flannery
Central Carolina Community College

Lynn Krausse
Bakersfield College

Kay Hammond
Lindenwood University

Penny Pereira
Indiana University-Purdue University Fort Wayne

Kevin Lambert
Southeast Kentucky Community and Technical College

Adam Rosen
LIM College

Cheri Whalen
Odessa College

Karr Dyal
LIM College

Shirley Birenz
New York University College of Dentistry

Jose Valdes
IBMC College

Gary DeLorenzo
California University of Pennsylvania

Kristin Roberts
Grand Rapids Community College

Michael Gray
Lane Community College

Ed Jaramillo
Peninsula College

Debasish Banerjee
Western Carolina University

Jenny Elshtain
Indiana University East

Sarah Rencher
Coconino Community College

Debbi Dybevik
Washtenaw Community College

Ann Kiefer
Chippewa Valley Technical College

Keff Lagoditz
American International College

Barbara Lave
Clark College

Morris Pondfield
Towson University

Peter Meggison
Massasoit Community College

Anne Acker
Jacksonville University

Gary Mosley
Southern Wesleyan University

Patrick J. Nedry
Monroe County Community College

Wasim A. Alhamdani
Kentucky State University

Bruce Baginski
Craven Community College

Diane Kosharek
Madison Area Technical College (Madison College)

Christina Shaner
Evergreen Valley College

Thomas Magliolo
Alvin Community College

Dmitriy Kupis
St. Joseph's College

Craig Brigman
Liberty University

Janak Shah
Berkeley college

Gary McFall
Purdue University

Phil Feinberg
Palomar College

Sheila Sicilia
Onondaga Community College

Randy Hollifield
McDowell Technical Community College

Bala R. Subramanian
Kean University

Marie Schmitz
Erie Community College

Tamar Mosley
Meridian Community College

David Bell
Pacific Union College

Jack Tan
University of Wisconsin - Eau Claire

Richard Brown
Loyola University Maryland

Narcissus Shambare
College of Saint Mary

S. E. Rouse
University of Southern Mississippi

Robert Doyle
Dona Ana Community College

David Welch
Nashville State Community College

Chen Ye
Purdue University Calumet

Bahadir Akcam
Western New England University

Frank Lucente
Westmoreland County Community College

Ted Janicki
University of Mount Olive

Kenneth R. Mayer, Jr.
Lipscomb University

Tamar Mosley
Meridian Community College

Pat McMahon
South Suburban College

Maureen Greenbaum
Union County College

Paulinus Ozor-Ilo
Gadsden State Community College

Michael Haugrud
Minnesota State University Moorhead

John Finley
Columbus State University

Philip Reaves
University of West Georgia
Cerro Coso Community College

Michael Leih
Trevecca Nazarene University

Shahla Durany
Tarrant County College - South Campus

Gary Sibbitts
St. Louis Community College at Meramec

Sandro Marchegiani
University of Pittsburgh at Johnstown

Sambit Bhattacharya
Fayetteville State University

Christine Peterson
Saint Paul College

C. Steven Hunt
Morehead State University

Shirley Nagg
Everest College

Ruth Parker
Rowan-Cabarrus Community College

Cecil Lawson
Evergreen Valley College

Adnan Turkey
DeVry College of New York

Janet Nicolaus
Mitchell Technical Institute

Mohammad Morovati
College of Dupage

Anthony Kapolka
Wilkes University

Steven Singer
Kapi'olani Community College

Bill Mills
East Texas Baptist University

Michele Schutte
Delaware Technical Community College - Terry Campus

Mark Evans
American National University

Syed Raza
Talladega College

Pam Gilmore
Reedley College

Philip Kim
Walsh University

Jeanann Boyce
Montgomery College
MaryJo Slater
Community College of Beaver County
JoAnn Brannen
Abraham Baldwin Agricultural College
Robert Patrick Sheridan
Northeast Iowa Community College
Sherry Muse
American Institute
Marcus Lacher
Minnesota State Community and Technical College
John Hupp
Columbus State University
Bernard Ku
Austin Community College
Theresa Meza
James Sprunt Community College
Jeremy A. Pittman
Coahoma Community College
LeAnne Lovering
Augusta Technical College
Lois Ann ONeal
Rogers State University
Lucy DeCaro
College of the Sequoias
Fredrick Bsharah
Cape Cod Community College
Timothy Holston
Mississippi Valley State University
Robert Balicki
Wayne County Community College District
Anita Beecroft
Kwantlen Polytechnic University
Margaret Cooksey
Tallahassee Community College
Susan Jackson
University of New Mexico-Valencia Campus
Beverly Forney
Clackamas Community College
Yves Durand
Keiser University
Cindi Nadelman
New England College
Susan Mahon
Collin College
Anthony Cameron
Fayetteville Tech Comm College
W. Randy Somsen
Brigham Young University-Idaho
Leanne Ruff
Blue Ridge Community College
Jan Wilms
Union University
Diane Bigger
LDS Business College
Michael Kurhan
Burlington County College
Vincent Yip
Umpqua Community College
Cheryl Jordan
San Juan College
Md Manzoor Murshed
Upper Iowa University
Pengtao Li
California State University, Stanislaus
George Sweiss
Governors State University Ill
Sharon M. Hope
Maria College
Ann Konarski
Baker College - Port Huron
Saiid Ganjalizadeh
Metropolitan School of Professional Studies
Brittany Bright
University of Arkansas
Iftikhar Sikder
Cleveland State University
Robin Fuller
Mississippi Gulf Coast Community College
Trude Pang
Kapiolani Community College
Tanya Patrick
Clackamas Community College
Tom Sill
Northwest University
Diane Franklin
Uintah Basin Applied Technology College
Cameron Spears
Hillsborough Community College
Kristi Smith
Allegany College of Maryland
Philip H. Nielson
Salt Lake Community College
Angela Nino
Richland College
Rajkumar Kempaiah
College of Mount Saint Vincent
Jeff Hansen
Treasure Valley Community College
J. F. Pauer
Bowling Green State University Firelands Campus
Ryan Carter
Mayland Community College

Kungwen (Dave) Chu
Purdue University Calumet
Bruce Haft
Glendale College
Tahir Aziz
J. Sargeant Reynolds Community College
Mercedes N. Alafriz
University of Phoenix/WIU
Dusty Anderson
Bluefield College
Keith Grubb
Rowan-Cabarrus Community College
Denise Reimer
Iowa Lakes Community College
Michael Sisk
Cleveland Community College
Anna Beavers
Laney College
Ted Tedmon
North Idaho College
Paulette Bell
Santa Rosa Junior College
Kevin Wyzkiewicz
Delta College
Uma Sridharan
Presbyterian College
Frank Tatum
Patrick Henry Community College
Jean Welsh
Lansing Community College
Karen Poland
Bryant and Stratton College
Aaron Tenenbaum
Brooklyn College
Susan Burden
Moberly Area Community College
Jim Patterson
Paradise Valley Community College
Richard Johnsen
County College of Morris
Ann Henry
Opportunity Center, Inc., ServiceSource - Delaware
Cathy Urbanski
Chandler-Gilbert College
Panda Jones
Gwinnett Technical College
Roni Ettleman
Atchison High School
Georgia Vanderark
Stark State College
Kevin Bradford
Somerset Community College - KCTCS
Shan Bhagoji
Monroe College
Anita Laird
Schoolcraft College
Carmen M. Aponte
Ana G. Mendez University System
Roberto Ordonez
Southern Adventist University
Marni Ferner
University of North Carolina Wilmington
Alisa Kadenic-Newman
NHTI
Andrea Langford
Ohio Valley Goodwill Industries
Barbara Schwartz
Pine Manor College
Carolyn Hill
Tallahassee Community College
Tracy Richardson
Eastern Maine Community College
Steve Nichols
Metropolitan Community College
Adell Brooks
Hinds Community College
Don Gaber
University of Wisconsin - Eau Claire
Laurie Zouharis
Suffolk University
Jill Fisher
Indian Capital Technology Center—Bill Willis Campus
Daniel Lowrance
Salt Lake Community College
Dee Hobson
Richland College
Matthew Macarty
University of New Hampshire
Jackie Porter
El Centro College
Alton Tripp
Northern Virginia Community College
Jan Repnow
Minot State University
Muhammad Obeidat
Southern Poly State University
Kirk McLean
LIM College
Saiid Ganjalizadeh
Northern Virginia Community College
Masoud Naghedolfeizi
Fort Valley State University
Kevin Fishbeck
University of Mary

Judy Smith
University District of Columbia
Mary Williams
University of Akron
Lisa Cady
University of Arkansas - Fort Smith (UAFS)
Phyllis Hutson
Southern Arkansas University Tech
Madison Ngafeeson
Northern Michigan University
Mandy Reininger
Chemeketa Community College
Lennie Alice Cooper
Miami Dade College - North Campus
Robert Pavkovich
Fortis College
Augustine Brennan
Erie Community College South
Judy Paternite
Kent State University Geauga
Brian Bradley
College of DuPage
Wilma Andrews
Virginia Commonwealth University
Anna Fitzpatrick
Rowan College at Gloucester County
Abdul Sattar
Bridgewater State University
Annette Kerwin
College of DuPage
Carolyn Barren
Macomb Community College
Matthew Marie
Aquinas College
Michael C. Theiss
University of Wisconsin Colleges
Kimberly Campbell
Eastern Maine Community College
Kamiyar Maleky
American River College
Chris Cheske
Lakeshore Technical College
Teresa Ferguson
Seattle Vocational Institute
Candace S. Garrod
Red Rocks Community College
Amiya K. Samantray
Marygrove College
Alex Morgan
DeAnza College
Howard Divins
DuBois Business College
Reshma R. Tolani
Charter College
Melinda White
Seminole State College
Michelle Thompson
Hillsborough Community College
Roy Stewart
Harris-Stowe State University
Joan Butler
Manchester Community College
Gary Moore
Caldwell Community College and Technical Institute
Brian Downs
Century College
Mitch Pendleton
LDS Business College
Meg Stoner
Santa Rosa Junior College
Orletta E. Caldwell
Grand Rapids Community College
Julia Basham
Southern State Community College
Mary Ann Culbertson
Tarrant County College Northwest Campus
Michael Carrington
Northern Virginia Community College
Freddy Barton
Tampa Vocational Institute
Sandy Keeter
Seminole State College
Harold Gress, Jr.
Wilson College
Sujing Wang
Lamar University
Brent Nabors
Clovis Community College Center
Dennis Walpole
University of South Florida
LaToya Smith
Piedmont Community College
Kyu Lee
Saint Martin's University
Lacey Lormand
University of Louisiana at Lafayette
Rebecca Bullough
College of the Sequoias
Mark Vancleve
Terronez
Raj Parikh
Westwood College
Carolyn Carvalho
Kent State University

Gerry Young
Vance Granville Community College
Marie Hartlein
Montgomery County Community College
Doug Read
Ball State University
Marie Guest
North Florida Community College
Gloria Sabatelli
Butler County Community College
Rose Steimel
Kansas Wesleyan University
Ronald Johnson
Central Alabama Community College
Eddie Bannister
Keiser University-Pembroke Pines, FL
Gustavo Diaz
Broward College
Pamela Lewis
Wilson Community College
James Schaap
Grand Rapids Community College
Gregory Latterell
Alexandria Technical and Community College
David Lewis
Bryant and Stratton College
Pamela Van Nutt
American National University - Martinsville, VA
Cheryl Miller
Bay College
James Anderson
Bay College
Darryl Habeck
Milwaukee Area Technical College
Dorvin Froseth
United Tribes Technical College
Wade Graves
Grayson College
Brenda McFarland
Asheville-Buncombe Technical Community College
Cherie M. Stevens
South Florida State College
Sandra Tavegia
The Community College of Baltimore County
Robyn Barrett
St Louis Community College - Meramec
Sharon Breeding
Bluegrass Community and Technical College
Theodore Tielens
Mt. San Jacinto
Lynda Hodge
Guilford Technical Community College
James Graves
College of Southern Maryland
Mike Michaelson
Palomar College
Kristi Parker
Baptist Bible College
Cheri Broadway
Jacksonville University
Anna Tsipenyuk
LIM College
Pamela Silvers
Asheville-Buncombe Technical Community College
Clarence Stokes
American River College
Cheryl D. Green
Delgado Community College
Kenneth N. Bryant
Kentucky State University
James Cammack
Lamar State College Port Arthur
Bryan Moss
San Jacinto College
Becky McAfee
Hillsborough Community College
David Gomillion
Northern Michigan University
Steven Bale
Truckee Meadows Community College
Julie Craig
Scottsdale Community College
Ashley Harrier
Hillsborough Community College
Brian Fox
Santa Fe College
Alicen Flosi
Lamar University
Karl Smart
Central Michigan University
David Little
High Point University
Paula Gregory
Yavapai College
Gary Sorenson
Northwest Technical College, Bemidji
Linda Lau
Longwood University
Frank Clements
State College of Florida
Keith Hood
Indiana Purdue Fort Wayne
Timothy Ely
Harcum College

Deborah Sahrbeck
North Shore Community College, Danvers, MA
Barbara West
Central Georgia Technical College
Shondra Greene
Albany State University
Amy Giddens
Central Alabama Community College
Dishi Shrivastava
University of North Florida
Patricia Frederick
Del Mar College
Bill Hammerschlag
Brookhaven College
Vinzanna Leysath
Allen University
Robert Nichols
College of DuPage
Corrine Sweet
Darton State College
Michael Magro
Shenandoah University
Vijay K Agrawal
University of Nebraska at Kearney
Timothy Ely
Harcum College
Rosie L. Inwang
Olive-Harvey College
Milledge Mosby
Prince George's Community College
Michael Torguson
Rogue Community College
Linda Phelps
Northwest Arkansas Community College
Corey DeLaplain
Keiser University Online
Lisa Lopez
Southern Wesleyan University
John Marek
Houston Community College
Lori Krei
Iowa Lakes Community College
Sharon Sneed
Eastfield Community College
Michael C. Johnson
ACD Computer College
Ben Martz
Northern Kentucky University
Russ Dulaney
Rasmussen College
Linda Johnsonius
Murray State University
Ionie Pierce
LIM College
Jo Ann Koenig
Indiana University-Purdue University Indianapolis
James Reneau
Shawnee State University
Wanda Gibson
Consolidated School of Business
David Milazzo
Niagara County Community College
John S. Galliano
University of Maryland University College
Lee Janczak
Lackawanna College
Philip Raphan
Broward College North Campus

Larry Schulze
San Antonio College
David Easton
Waubonsee Community College
Doug Baker
Kent State University
Alanna Duley
College of Western Idaho
Helen Slack
Mahoning County Career and Technical Center
Carolyn Golden
Huston-Tillotson University
Terri Tiedeman
Southeast Community College
Edwin Harris
University of North Florida
Jeff Lehman
Huntington University
Aimee Durham
Rowan-Cabarrus Community College
Denise Askew
Rowan-Cabarrus Community College
Curby Simerson
Randolph Community College
Cindi Albrightson
Southwestern Oklahoma State University
Amanda Kaari
Central Georgia Tech
Ruben Ruiz
Morton College
Riza Marjadi
Murray State University
Annette Yauney
Herkimer Couny Community College
Donna Maxson
Lake Michigan College
Benjamin White
Bainbridge State College
Joy Flanders
Central Methodist University
Jill McCollum
Southern Arkansas University Tech
Sonya Sample
Greenville Technical College
Michelle Chappell
Henderson Community College
Shawn Brown
Ashland Community and Technical College
Sherry Cox
Broward College
Bonnie J. Tuggle-Ziglar
Brookstone College of Business
Fernando Wilches
Ana G. Mendez University System
Doreen Palucci
Wilmington University
Thomas Seeley
Urbana University
Victor Wotzkow
New Professions Technical Institute
Ahmed Kamel
Concordia College, Moorhead
Marie Campbell
Idaho State University-College of Technology
Sue McCrory
Missouri State University
Somone Washington
Broward College Online

Johnnie Nixon
King's College
Gloria Hensel
Matanuska-Susitna College University of Alaska Anchorage
Gary Cotton
American River College,
Kingsley Meyer
University of Rio Grande / Rio Grande Community College
Martha Merrill
Pellissippi State Community College
Olusade Ajayi
Germanna Community College
Pat Pettit
Millikin University
Mary Evens
Clark College
Michelle Masingill
North Idaho College
Mark Douglas
Our Lady of the Lake University
Rhonda Lucas
Spring Hill College
Anita Sutton
Germanna Community College
S. E. Beladi
Broward College
Ronda Thompson
Keene State College
Lyn Snyder
Owens Community College
Mark Connell
SUNY at Cortland
Guarionex Salivia
Minnesota State University
David Arevigian
Monroe County Community College
Verlan Erickson
Western Dakota Technical Institute
John Robinson
Cumberland County College
Allan Greenberg
New York University
Debra Adams
Mott Community College
Bobbie Hawkins
Southwest TN Community College
Nancy Stephens
Chemeketa Community College
Jeremy Harris
Evangel University
Kim Mangan
Manor College
Judith Scheeren
Westmoreland County Community College
Darrelyn Relyea
Grays Harbor College
Jay F. Miller
Union College, Barbourville
Deborah Franklin
Bryant and Stratton College
Nina Fontenot
South Louisiana Community College
Jim Speers
Southeastern Oklahoma State University
Jennifer Klenke
East Central College
Young Baek
Los Angeles City College

Carl Rebman
University of San Diego
Shelly Knittle
Alaska Career College
Natunya Johnson
Holmes Community College
Linda Lemley
Pensacola State College
Ranida Harris
Indiana University Southeast
Kelly Young
Lander University
Karin Stulz
Northern Michigan University
Cathie Phillips
Lamar State College-Orange
James Brown
Central Washington University
H. Roger Fulk
Rhodes State College
Dan Britton
Chemeketa Community College
Olivia Kerr
El Centro College
Michelle Dawson
Missouri Southern State University
Dianne Hargrove
College of Health Care Professions
Shannon Shoemaker
SUNY Delhi
Bruce Caraway
Lone Star College - University Park
Richard DiRose
Hillsborough Community College - South Shore

TECHNICAL EDITORS

Karen May
Blinn College
Andrea Nevill
College of Western Idaho
Richard Finn
Moraine Valley Community College
Chris Anderson
North Central Michigan College
Gena Casas
Florida State College
Leon Blue
Pensacola State College
Mary Carole Hollingsworth
Georgia Perimeter College
Amie Mayhall
Olney Central College
Julie Haar
Alexandria Technical and Community College
Diane Santurri
Johnson & Wales University
Ramona Santa Maria
Buffalo State College

Thank you to the wonderful team at McGraw-Hill for your confidence in us and support throughout this project. Alan, Wyatt, Tiffany, Debbie, Rick, and Julianna, we thoroughly enjoy working with you all! A special thanks to Debbie Hinkle for her thorough and insightful review of the series. Thank you to all of the reviewers and technical editors for your expertise and invaluable insight, which helped shape this book.

—Randy, Kathleen, Annette, and Pat

Intro Chapter

Windows 10, Office 2016, and File Management

OFFICE 2016

CHAPTER OVERVIEW

Microsoft Office 2016 and Windows 10 introduce many new features, including cloud storage for your files, Office file sharing, and enhanced online content. The integration of Office 2016 and Windows 10 means that files are more portable and accessible than ever when you use *OneDrive*, Microsoft's free online cloud storage. The new user interface for Office 2016 and Windows 10 allows you to work on tablet computers and smartphones in a consistent working environment that resembles that of your desktop or laptop computer.

STUDENT LEARNING OUTCOMES (SLOs)

After completing this chapter, you will be able to:

SLO Intro.1 Explore the features of Windows 10 (p. OI-2).

SLO Intro.2 Use the basic features of Office 2016 and navigate the Office 2016 working environment (p. OI-10).

SLO Intro.3 Create, save, close, and open Office files (p. OI-17).

SLO Intro.4 Customize the view and display size in Office applications and work with multiple Office files (p. OI-25).

SLO Intro.5 Print, share, and customize Office files (p. OI-28).

SLO Intro.6 Use the *Ribbon*, tabs, groups, dialog boxes, task panes, galleries, and the *Quick Access* toolbar (p. OI-33).

SLO Intro.7 Use context menus, mini toolbars, keyboard shortcuts, and function keys in Office applications (p. OI-37).

SLO Intro.8 Organize and customize Windows folders and Office files (p. OI-42).

CASE STUDY

Throughout this book you have the opportunity to put into practice the application features that you are learning. Each chapter begins with a case study that introduces you to the Pause & Practice projects in the chapter. These Pause & Practice projects give you a chance to apply and practice key skills in a realistic and practical context. Each chapter contains three to five Pause & Practice projects.

American River Cycling Club (ARCC) is a community cycling club that promotes fitness. ARCC members include recreational cyclists who enjoy the exercise and camaraderie as well as competitive cyclists who compete in road, mountain, and cyclocross races throughout the cycling season. In the Pause & Practice projects, you incorporate many of the topics covered in the chapter to create, save, customize, manage, and share Office 2016 files.

Pause & Practice Intro-1: Customize the Windows *Start* menu and *Taskbar*, create and save a PowerPoint presentation, create a folder, open and rename an Excel workbook, and use Windows 10 features.

Pause & Practice Intro-2: Modify the existing document, add document properties, customize the Quick Access toolbar, export the document as a PDF file, and share the document.

Pause & Practice Intro-3: Copy and rename files, create a folder, move files, create a zipped folder, and rename a zipped folder.

SLO INTRO. 1

Using Windows 10

Windows 10 is the ***operating system*** that controls computer functions and the working environment. Windows 10 uses the familiar ***Windows desktop***, ***Taskbar***, and ***Start menu***, and you can customize the working environment. You can install traditional applications (***apps***), such as Microsoft Office, to your computer. Also, you can add modern apps from the Microsoft Store similar to how you add an app to your smartphone. Your ***Microsoft account*** is used to store your Microsoft settings, download apps from the Microsoft Store, and connect you to Microsoft Office, *OneDrive*, and *Office Online*.

Windows 10

The Windows 10 operating system controls interaction with computer hardware and software applications. ***Windows 10*** has a revised user interface that utilizes an updated ***Start menu***, where you can select and open a program. Alternatively, you can use the *Taskbar* on the Windows desktop, which has the familiar look of previous versions of Windows. When you log in to Windows 10 using your Microsoft account, it synchronizes your Windows, Office, and ***OneDrive*** cloud storage among computers.

Microsoft Account

In Windows 10 and Office 2016, your files and account settings are portable. In other words, your Office settings and files can travel with you and be accessed from different computers. You are not restricted to a single computer. When you sign in to Windows 10 using your Microsoft account (user name and password), Microsoft uses this information to transfer your Windows and Office 2016 settings to the computer you are using. Your Microsoft account not only signs you in to Windows and Office but also to other free Microsoft online services, such as *OneDrive* and ***Office Online***. If you don't have a Microsoft account, you can create a free account at https://signup.live.com (Figure Intro-1).

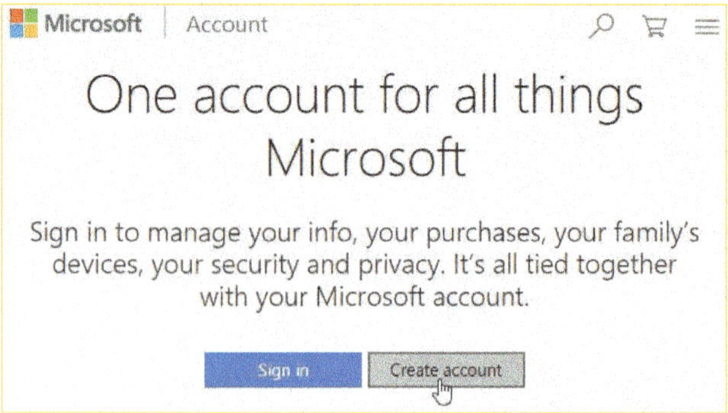

Intro-1 Create a Microsoft account

MORE INFO

You will use your Microsoft account for projects in this text.

Windows Desktop and Taskbar

The Windows desktop is the working area of Windows. When you log in to Windows, the desktop displays (Figure Intro-2). The *Taskbar* displays at the bottom of the desktop. You can open programs and folders from the *Taskbar* by clicking on an icon on the *Taskbar* (see Figure Intro-2). You can pin apps and other Windows items, such as the *Control Panel* or *File Explorer*, to the *Taskbar* (see "Customize the Taskbar" later in this section).

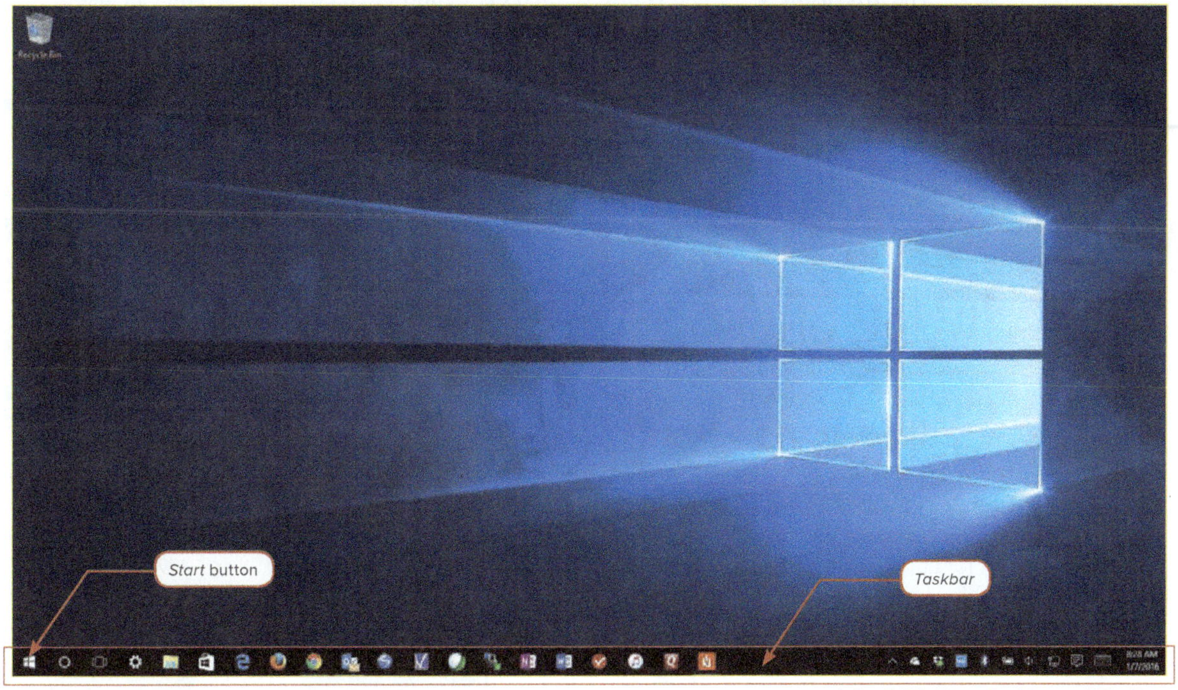

Intro-2 Windows desktop and *Taskbar*

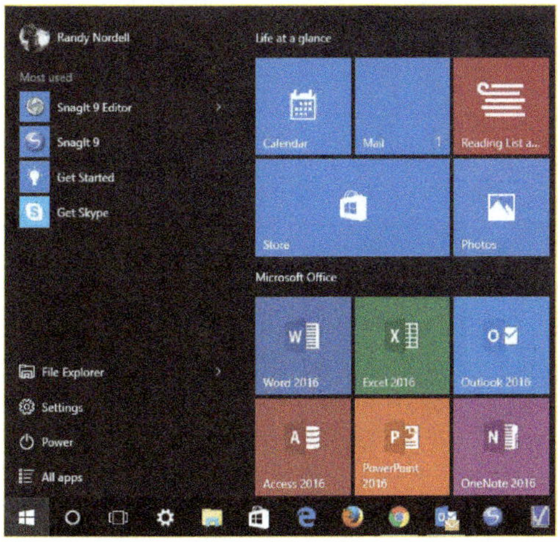

Intro-3 Windows *Start* menu

Start Menu

Windows 10 utilizes a redesigned *Start* menu (Figure Intro-3), that you open by clicking the ***Start button*** located in the bottom left of the *Taskbar*. From the *Start* menu, you can open programs, files, folders, or other Windows resources. The *Start* menu is divided into two main sections. The left side of the *Start* menu displays ***Most Used*** items, buttons to open the ***File Explorer*** and ***Settings*** windows, the ***Power*** button, and ***All apps***, which displays an alphabetical listing of all applications installed on your computer. The right side of the *Start* menu displays apps as tiles (large and small buttons) you can click to open an application or window.

You can customize which apps and items appear on either side of the *Start* menu, arrange and group apps on the *Start* menu, resize the *Start* menu, and display the *Start* menu as a ***Start* page** when you log in to Windows (similar to the *Start* page in Windows 8 and 8.1). See "Customize the Start Menu" later in this section for information about customizing the *Start* menu.

Add Apps

Windows 10 uses the term *apps* generically to refer to applications and programs. Apps include the Windows 10 Weather app, Microsoft Excel program, Control Panel, Google Chrome, or *File Explorer*. Many apps are preinstalled on a Windows 10 computer, and you can add apps to your computer. You can install an app such as Office 2016 or Quicken by downloading it from a web site or from a program DVD. These are referred to as ***traditional apps***.

The ***Microsoft Store*** app is preinstalled on Windows 10 computers. You can also install apps such as Netflix, Trip Advisor, and The Weather Channel from the Microsoft Store. These apps are referred to as ***modern apps*** and look and function similar to apps you install on your smartphone. Many apps in the Microsoft Store are free and others are available for purchase.

▸HOW TO: Add an App from the Microsoft Store

1. Click the **Start** button to open the *Start* menu.
2. Click the **Store** button (tile) to open the Microsoft Store app (Figure Intro-4).
   - If the *Store* tile is not available on the *Start* menu, click **All apps** on the *Start* menu, scroll down, and click **Store** in the alphabetic listing of all apps.
3. Select an app in the Microsoft Store (Figure Intro-5).
   - The Microsoft Store has different categories of apps.
   - You can search for apps by typing key words in the *Search* box in the upper right.
   - When you select an app, a description and screen shots of the app displays.
4. Click the **Free**, **Free trial**, or price button to install the app.
   - You must have a payment method stored in your Microsoft account to purchase apps from the Microsoft Store.
5. Click **Open** to open the installed app.
   - When you install an app, the app is listed in the *Recently added* area on the *Start* menu and *All apps* list of applications.

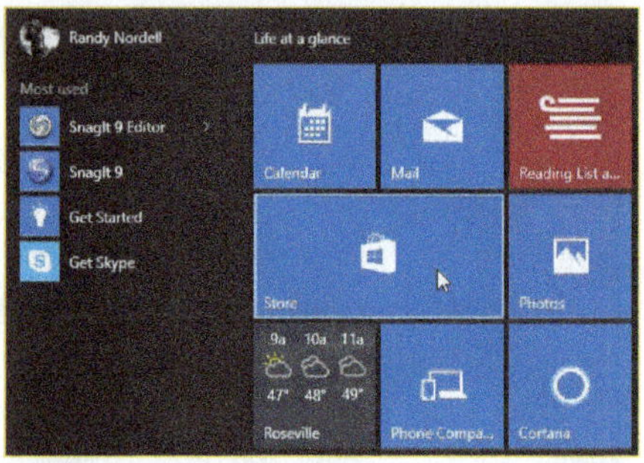

Intro-4 *Store* button on the *Start* menu

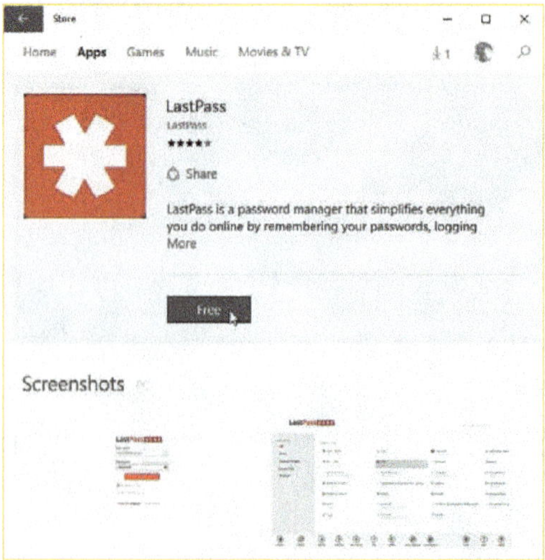

Intro-5 Install an app from the Microsoft Store

Customize the Start Menu

When you start using Windows 10 or after you have installed either traditional or modern apps, you can customize what appears on your *Start* menu and resize the *Start* menu. When you ***pin*** an app to the *Start* menu, the app tile remains on the right side of the *Start* menu. Pin the apps you most regularly use, unpin the apps you don't want to display on the *Start* menu, and rearrange and resize apps tiles to your preference.

HOW TO: Customize the Start Menu

1. Move an app tile by clicking and dragging the app tile to a new location on the *Start* menu. The other app tiles shuffle to accommodate the placement of the app tile.
2. Remove an app tile from the *Start* menu by right-clicking the app tile you want to remove and selecting **Unpin from Start** from the context menu (Figure Intro-6).
   - The app tile is removed from the *Start* menu, but the program or task is not removed from your computer.
3. Pin an app tile to the *Start* menu by clicking **All apps** at the bottom of the *Start* menu, right-clicking the app to pin, and selecting **Pin to Start** (Figure Intro-7).
   - Drag the newly added app tile to the desired location on the Start menu.
4. Resize an app tile by right-clicking the app tile, selecting **Resize**, and selecting **Small**, **Medium**, **Wide**, or **Large**.
   - Some apps only have *Small*, *Medium*, and *Wide* size options.
5. Turn on or off the live tile option by right-clicking the app tile and selecting **Turn live tile on** or **Turn live tile off**.
   - Live tile displays rotating graphics and options on the app tile. When this option is turned off, the name of the app displays on the tile.
6. Uninstall an app by right-clicking the app you want to uninstall and selecting **Uninstall**.
   - Unlike the unpin option, this option uninstalls the program from your computer, not just your *Start* menu.
7. Resize the *Start* menu by clicking and dragging the top or right edge of the *Start* menu.
8. Use a full screen *Start* menu by clicking the **Start** button to open the *Start* menu, selecting **Settings** to open the *Settings* window, clicking the **Personalization** button, clicking the **Start** option at the left, selecting **Use Start full screen**, and clicking the **X** in the upper right to close the *Settings* window (Figure Intro-8).
   - The *Start* menu expands to the full screen when opened.

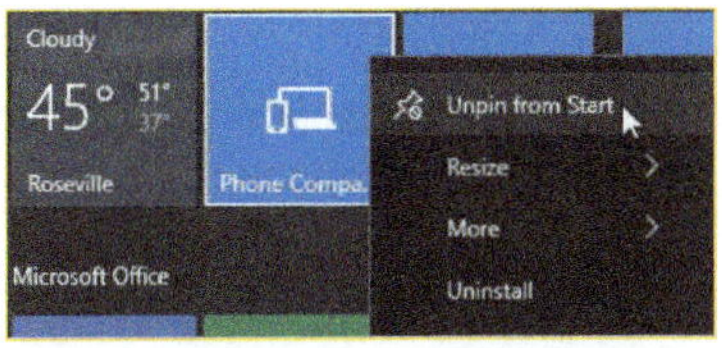

Intro-6 Unpin an app from the *Start* menu

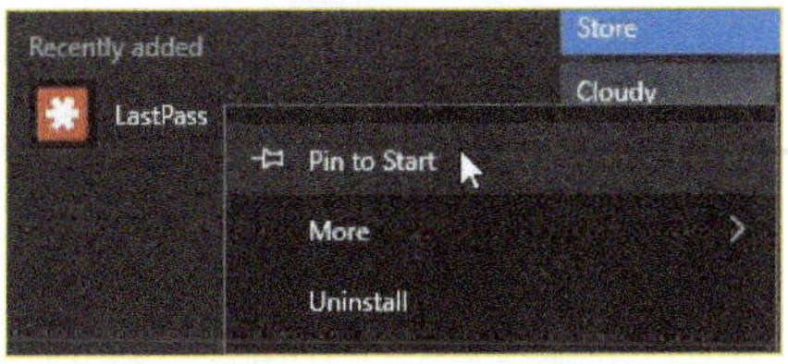

Intro-7 Pin an app to the *Start* menu

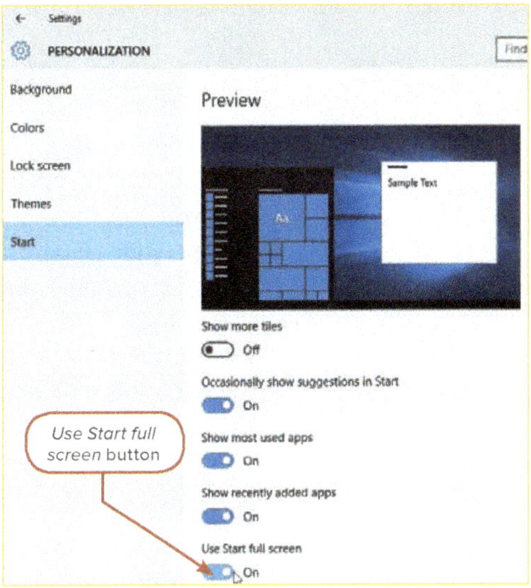

Intro-8 Use full screen *Start* menu

Customize the Taskbar

The *Taskbar* is located at the bottom of the Windows desktop, and you can quickly open an app by clicking a button on the *Taskbar* rather than opening it from the *Start* menu. You can customize the *Taskbar* by pinning, unpinning, and rearranging apps on the *Taskbar*.

HOW TO: Customize the Taskbar

1. Pin an app to the *Taskbar* by clicking the *Start* menu, right-clicking an app, clicking **More**, and selecting **Pin to taskbar** (Figure Intro-9).
   - You can also pin an app to the *Taskbar* from the *All apps* list in the *Start* menu.
2. Unpin an app from the *Taskbar* by right-clicking an app on the *Taskbar*, and selecting **Unpin from taskbar** (Figure Intro-10).
   - You can also unpin apps from the *Taskbar* by right-clicking the app in the *Start* menu, clicking **More**, and selecting **Unpin from taskbar**.
3. Rearrange apps on the *Taskbar* by clicking and dragging the app to the desired location on the *Taskbar* and release.

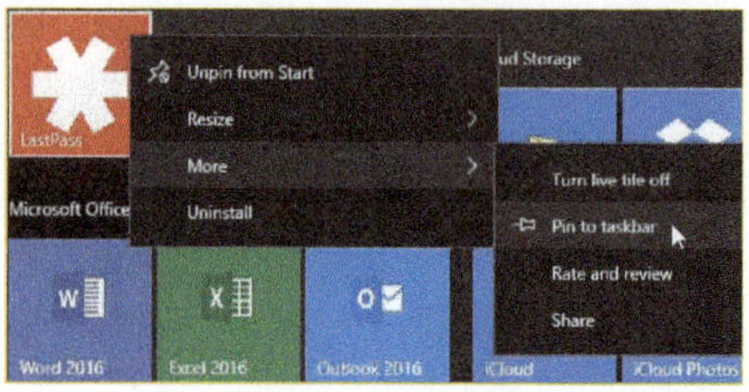

Intro-9 Pin an app to the *Taskbar*

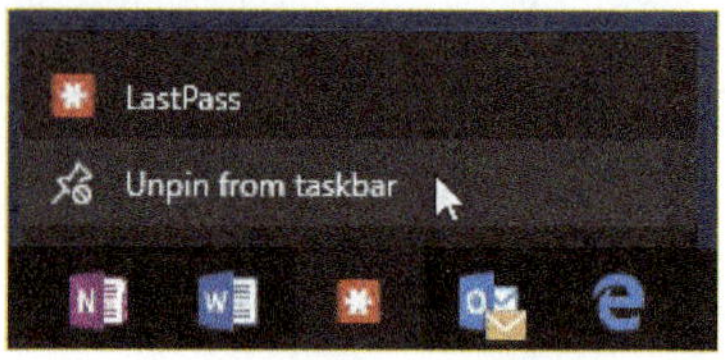

Intro-10 Unpin an app from the *Taskbar*

MORE INFO

If using a touch screen, you can press and hold an app on the *Start* menu or *Taskbar* to display the app options.

File Explorer

The redesigned *File Explorer* in Windows 10 is a window that opens on your desktop where you can browse for files stored on your computer (Figure Intro-11). You can open a file or folder, move or copy items, create folders, and delete files or folders. Click the **Start** button and select **File Explorer** to open a *File Explorer* window.

The *File Explorer* has different areas:

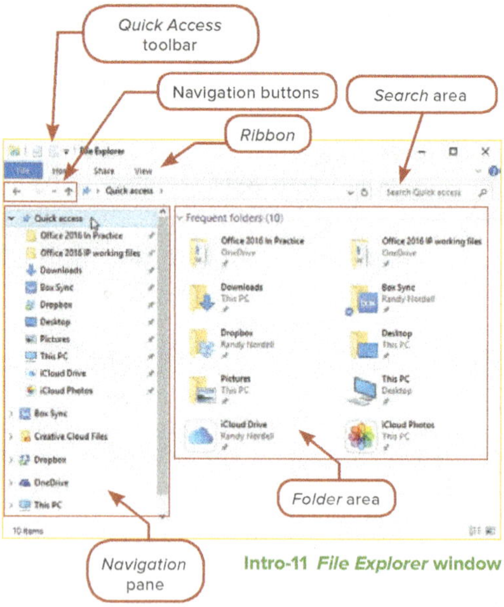

Intro-11 *File Explorer* window

- ***Navigation pane***: The *Navigation* pane displays folders on the left. The ***Quick access*** area at the top of the *Navigation* pane displays shortcuts to favorite folders. You can pin or unpin folders in the *Quick access* area of the *Navigation* pane.
- ***Navigation buttons***: The navigation buttons (*Back*, *Forward*, *Recent location*, and *Up*) are located directly above the *Navigation* pane and below the *Ribbon*. Use these buttons to navigate a File Explorer window.
- ***Folder pane***: When you select a folder in the *Navigation* pane, the contents of the folder displays in the *Folder* pane to the right of the *Navigation* pane. Double-click a folder or file in the *Folder* pane to open it.
- ***Ribbon***: The *Ribbon* at the top of the *File Explorer* is collapsed by default. When you click a tab on the *Ribbon*, it expands to display the options on the tab. The main tabs of

the *Ribbon* are ***File***, ***Home***, ***Share***, and ***View***. Other context-sensitive tabs open when you select certain types of files. For example, the *Picture Tool Manage* tab opens when you select a picture file.

- ***Quick Access toolbar***: The *Quick Access* toolbar is above the *Ribbon*. From the *Quick Access* toolbar, you can click the **New Folder** button to create a new folder or **Properties** to display the properties of a selected file or folder. You can add buttons, such as *Rename*, to the *Quick Access* toolbar.
- ***Search***: The *Search* text box is located on the right of the *File Explorer* window below the *Ribbon*. Type key words in the *Search* text box to find files or folders.

OneDrive

OneDrive is a cloud storage area where you can store files in a private and secure online location that you can access from any computer. When you store your files in *OneDrive*, the files are actually saved on both your computer and on the cloud. *OneDrive* synchronizes your files so when you change a file it is automatically updated on the *OneDrive* cloud.

With Windows 10, the ***OneDrive folder*** is one of your storage location folder options, similar to your *Documents* or *Pictures* folders (Figure Intro-12). You can save, open, and edit your *OneDrive* files from a *File Explorer* folder. Your *OneDrive* folder looks and functions similar to other Windows folders.

In addition to the *OneDrive* folder on your computer, you can also access your *OneDrive* files online using an Internet browser such as Microsoft Edge, Google Chrome, or Mozilla Firefox. When you access *OneDrive* online using a web browser, you can upload files, create folders, move and copy files and folders, and create Office files using *Office Online* (*Office Online* is discussed in *SLO Intro.2: Using Office 2016*).

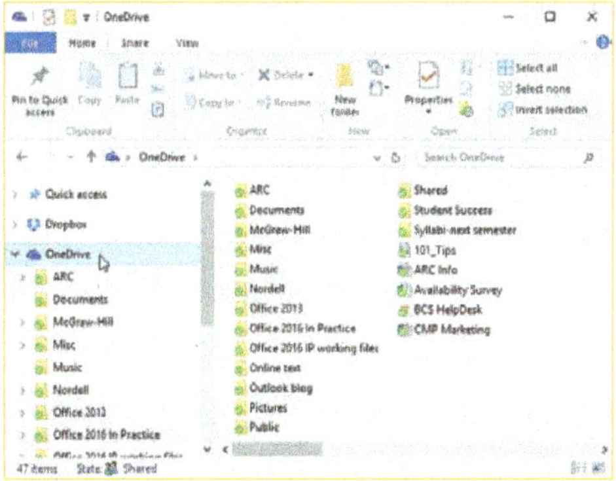

Intro-12 *OneDrive* folder in a *File Explorer* window

▸HOW TO: Use OneDrive Online

1. Open an Internet browser window and navigate to the *OneDrive* web site (www.onedrive.live.com), which takes you to the *OneDrive* sign in page.
   - You can use any Internet browser to access *OneDrive* (Microsoft Edge, Google Chrome, Mozilla Firefox).
2. Click the **Sign in** button, type your Microsoft account email address, and click **Next**.
3. Type your Microsoft account password and click **Sign in** (Figure Intro-13). You are taken to your *OneDrive* page.
   - If you are on your own computer, check the **Keep me signed in** box to stay signed in to *OneDrive* when you return to the page.

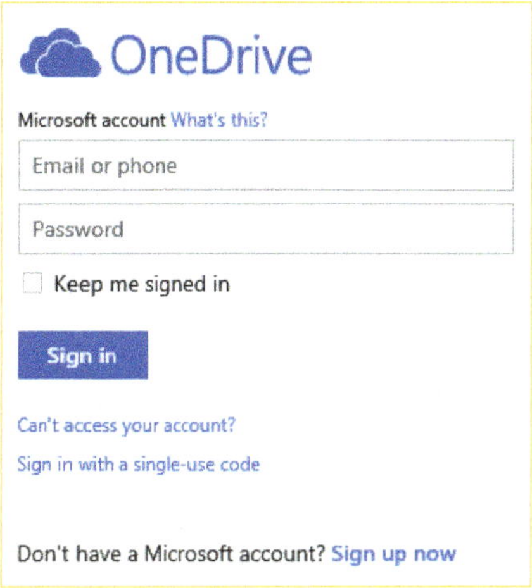

Intro-13 Log in to *OneDrive* online

- The different areas of *OneDrive* are listed under the *OneDrive* heading on the left (Figure Intro-14).
- Click **Files** to display your folders and files in the folder area.
- At the top of the page, buttons and drop-down menus list the different actions you can perform on selected files and folders.

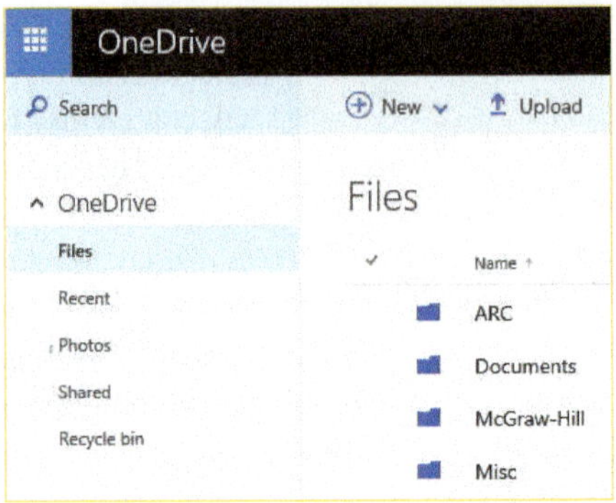

Intro-14 *OneDrive* online environment

Cortana

In addition to using the search tools in the *File Explorer*, you can also use ***Cortana***, which is new in Windows 10. While the search feature in the *File Explorer* searches only for content on your computer, *Cortana* searches for content on your computer, on the Internet, and in the Microsoft Store. You can either type key words for a search or use voice commands to search for content.

When you open *Cortana*, other content, such as weather, upcoming appointments, and popular news stories, displays in the *Cortana* pane.

HOW TO: Search Using Cortana

1. Click the **Cortana** button on the *Taskbar* to open the *Cortana* pane (Figure Intro-15).

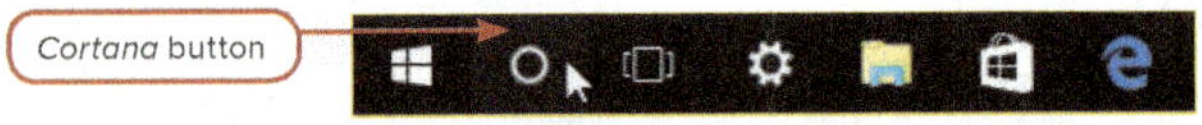

Intro-15 *Cortana* button on the *Taskbar*

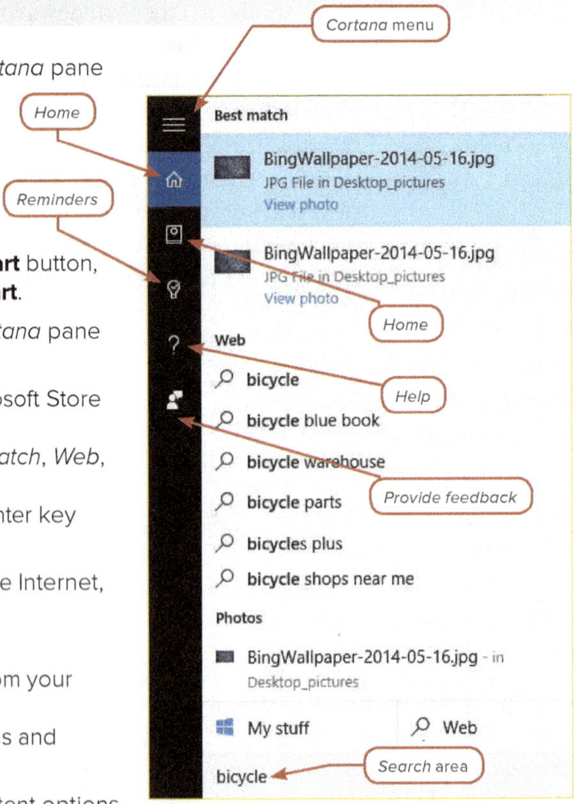

Intro-16 Use *Cortana* to search your computer, the Internet, and the Microsoft Store

   - If the *Cortana* button is not on the *Taskbar*, click the **Start** button, click **All apps**, right-click **Cortana**, and select **Pin to Start**.
2. Click the **Ask me anything** area at the bottom of the *Cortana* pane and type key words for your search.
   - Content from your computer, the Internet, and the Microsoft Store displays in the *Cortana* pane (Figure Intro-16).
   - The search results are grouped into categories: *Best match*, *Web*, and *Store*.
   - You can also click the microphone icon and speak to enter key words as the search.
3. Click a result in the *Cortana* pane to view a file, search the Internet, or view apps in the Microsoft Store.
   - Click **My stuff** or **Web** to refine your search.
   - If you click **My stuff**, *Cortana* displays search results from your computer.
   - If you click **Web**, the Microsoft Edge web browser opens and displays your search results.
4. Click the **Menu** button at the top left to display other content options in the *Cortana* pane (see Figure Intro-16).
   - The other content options are *Home*, *Notebook*, *Reminders*, *Help*, and *Feedback*.

Task View

A new feature to Windows 10 is ***Task View***. *Task View* displays all open apps and windows as tiles on your desktop, and you can choose which item to display or close. This feature is very helpful when you have multiple items open and want to select or close one.

HOW TO: Use Task View

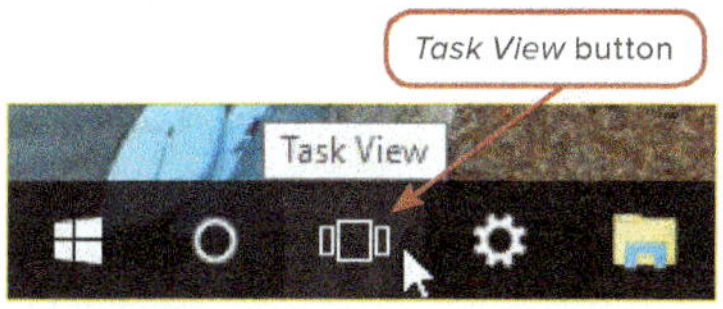

Intro-17 ***Task View*** **button on the** ***Taskbar***

1. Click the **Task View** button on the *Taskbar* (Figure Intro-17).
   - All open apps and windows display on the desktop (Figure Intro-18).

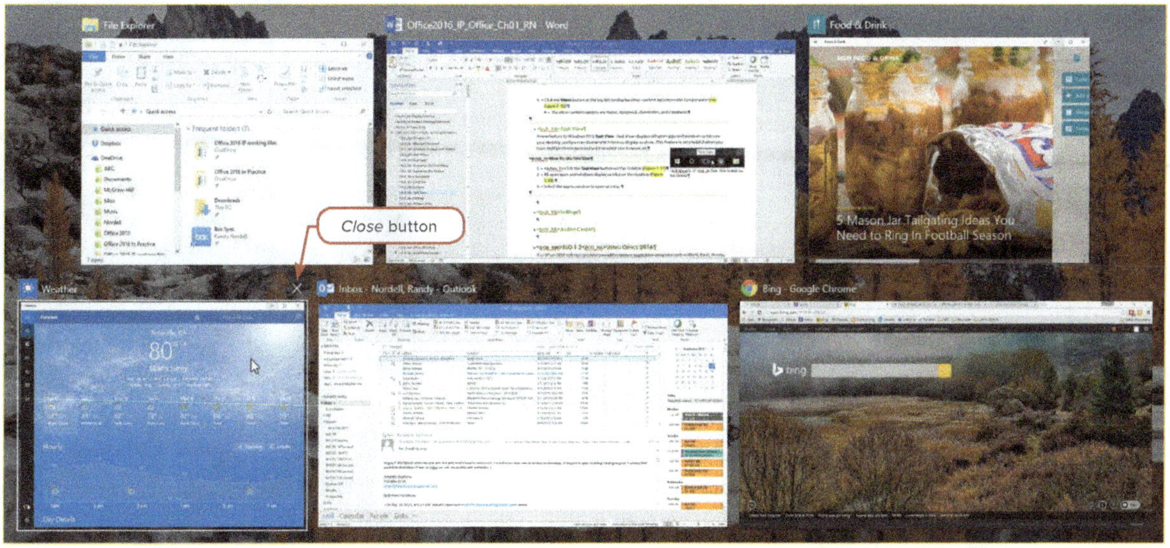

Intro-18 ***Task View*** **with open apps and windows displayed on the desktop**

2. Select the app or window to open or close.
   - Click a tile to open an app. The app opens and *Task View* closes.
   - Click the **X** in the upper right corner of an app to close an app. *Task View* remains open when you close an app.

Settings

In Windows 10, the ***Settings*** window is the redesigned *Control Panel* (although the *Control Panel* is still available). The *Settings* window is where you change global Windows settings, customize the Windows environment, add devices, and manage your Microsoft account. Click the **Settings** button on the *Taskbar* or *Start* menu to open the *Settings* window (Figure Intro-19). The following categories are available in the *Settings* window:

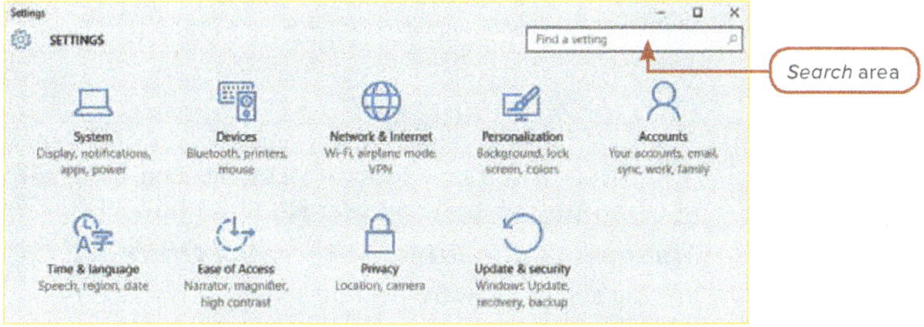

Intro-19 ***Settings*** **window**

- ***System***: Display, notifications, apps, and power
- ***Devices***: Bluetooth, printers, and mouse
- ***Network & Internet***: Wi-Fi, airplane mode, and VPN
- ***Personalization***: Background, lock screen, and colors
- ***Accounts***: Your account, sync settings, work, and family
- ***Time & Language***: Speech, region, and date
- ***Ease of Access***: Narrator, magnifier, and high contrast
- ***Privacy***: Location and camera
- ***Update & Security***: Windows Update, recovery, and backup

> **MORE INFO**
>
> If you can't find an item in *Settings*, use the *Search* dialog box (*Find a setting*) in the upper right corner and type key words. If *Settings* is not available on the *Taskbar*, you can find it in the *All apps* list on the *Start* menu.

Action Center

The ***Action Center*** in Windows 10 provides a quick glance of notifications and buttons to open other commonly used settings and features in Windows. The *Action Center* displays notifications such as emails and Windows update notifications. Or you can click an action button to turn on or off features or open other windows or apps such as the *Settings* menu (*All Settings* button) or OneNote (*Note* button). Click the **Action Center** button on the right side of the *Taskbar* to open the *Action Center* pane on the right side of your screen (Figure Intro-20).

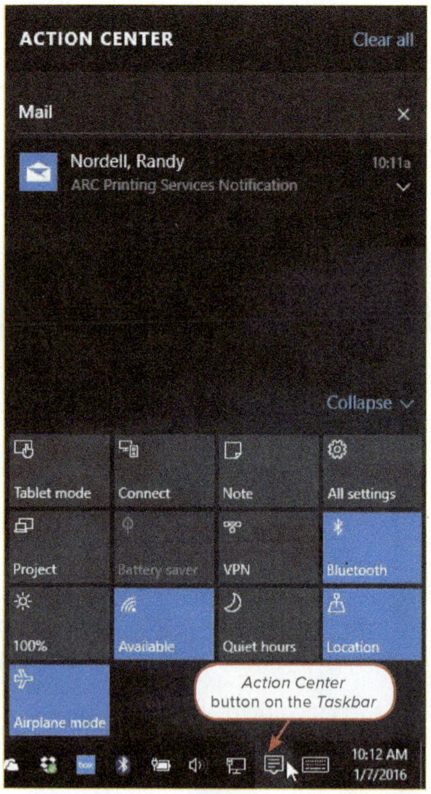

Intro-20 *Action Center*

SLO INTRO. 2

Using Office 2016

Office 2016 includes common software applications such as Word, Excel, Access, and PowerPoint. These applications give you the ability to work with word processing documents, spreadsheets, presentations, and databases in your personal and business projects.

Office 2016 and Office 365

Microsoft Office is a suite of personal and business software applications (Figure Intro-21). ***Microsoft Office 2016*** and ***Microsoft Office 365*** are the same software products; the difference is how you purchase the software. Office 2016 is

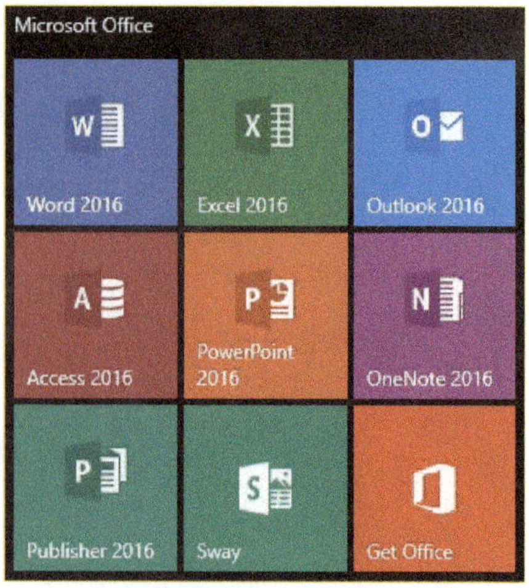

Intro-21 Microsoft Office application tiles on the *Start* menu

the traditional model of purchasing the software, and you own that software for as long as you want to use it. Office 365 is a subscription that you pay monthly or yearly, similar to how you purchase Netflix or Spotify. If you subscribe to Office 365, you automatically receive new versions of the software when they are released.

The common applications typically included in Microsoft Office 2016 and 365 are described in the following list:

- ***Microsoft Word***: Word processing software used to create, format, and edit documents such as reports, letters, brochures, and resumes.
- ***Microsoft Excel***: Spreadsheet software used to perform calculations on numerical data such as financial statements, budgets, and expense reports.
- ***Microsoft Access***: Database software used to store, organize, compile, and report information such as product information, sales data, client information, and employee records.
- ***Microsoft PowerPoint***: Presentation software used to graphically present information in slides such as a presentation on a new product or sales trends.
- ***Microsoft Outlook***: Email and personal management software used to create and send email and create and store calendar items, contacts, and tasks.
- ***Microsoft OneNote***: Note-taking software used to take and organize notes, which can be shared with other Office applications.
- ***Microsoft Publisher***: Desktop publishing software used to create professional-looking documents containing text, pictures, and graphics such as catalogs, brochures, and flyers.

Office Desktop Apps, Office Universal Apps, and Office Online

Office desktop apps are the full-function Office 2016 or 365 programs installed on your computer (PC or Mac). Both Office 2016 and Office 365 are considered Office desktop apps. Because of the increased popularity and capabilities of tablets and mobile devices, Office software is also available for both tablets and smartphones. ***Office universal apps*** are the Office 365 programs that can be installed on tablets or other mobile devices. Office universal apps do not have the full range of advanced features available in Office desktop applications, but Office universal apps provide users the ability to create, edit, save, and share Office files using many of the most common features in the Office suite of programs.

> **MORE INFO**
>
> Office universal apps are also referred to as ***Office mobile apps***.

Office Online is free online software from Microsoft that works in conjunction with your Microsoft account and *OneDrive* (Figure Intro-22). With *Office Online*, you can work with Office files online through a web browser, even on computers that do not have Office 2016 or 365 installed. This is a useful option when you use a computer at a computer lab or use a friend's computer that does not have Office installed.

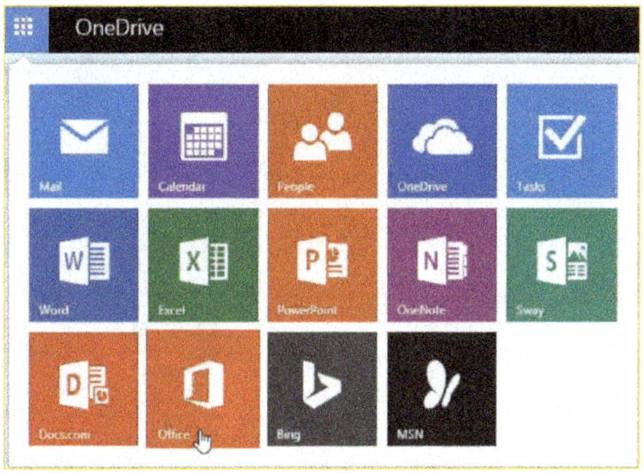

Intro-22 *Office Online*

You can access *Office Online* from your *OneDrive* web page to create and edit Word documents, Excel workbooks, PowerPoint presentations, and OneNote notebooks. *Office Online* is a scaled-down version of Office 2016/365 and not as robust in terms of features, but you can use it to create, edit, print, share, and collaborate on files. If you need more advanced features, you can open *Office Online* files in Office 2016.

> **MORE INFO**
>
> Microsoft Access is not available in *Office Online* or as an Office universal app.

HOW TO: Create an Office Online File

1. Open an Internet browser Window, navigate to the *OneDrive* web site (www.onedrive.live.com), and log in to *OneDrive*. If you are not already logged in to *OneDrive*, use the following steps.
   - Click the **Sign in** button, type your Microsoft account email address, and click **Next**.
   - Type your Microsoft account password and click **Sign in** to open your *OneDrive* page.
2. Click the **New** button and select the type of *Office Online* file to create (Figure Intro-23).
   - A new file is created and opens in the *Office Online* program.
   - The new file is saved in your *OneDrive* folder (both online and on your computer).
3. Rename the file by clicking on the file name at the top of the file, typing a new file name, and pressing **Enter** (Figure Intro-24).
   - You can also click the **File** tab to open the *Backstage* view, select *Save As*, and choose **Save As** or **Rename**.
   - Click the **OPEN IN *[OFFICE APPLICATION]*** button (for example **OPEN IN EXCEL**) to open the file in the Office desktop application (see Figure Intro-24).
4. Close the browser tab or window to close the file.
   - *Office Online* automatically saves the file as you make changes.

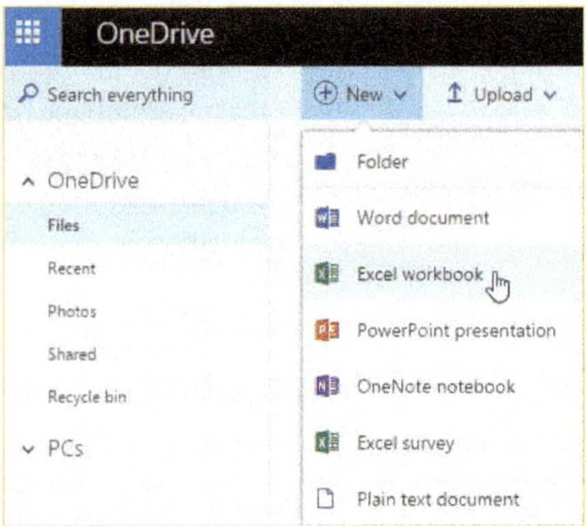

Intro-23 Create an Office Online file from your online *OneDrive* page

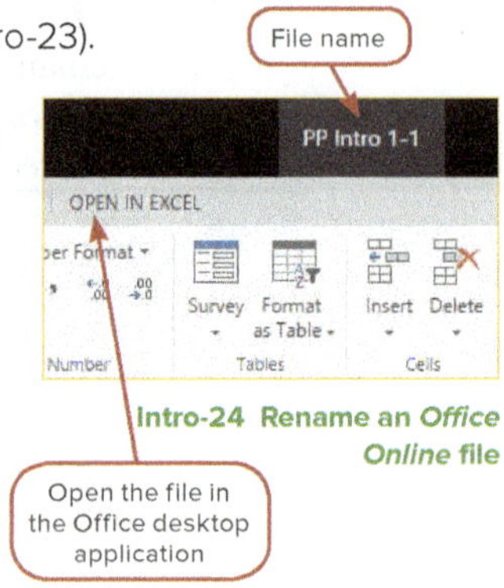

Intro-24 Rename an *Office Online* file

Open an Office Desktop Application

When using Windows 10, you open an Office desktop application by clicking the application tile on the *Start* menu or the application icon on the *Taskbar*. If your *Start* menu and *Taskbar* do not have the Office applications displayed, click the **Start** button, select **All apps**, and select **Word 2016**, **Excel 2016**, **Access 2016**, or **PowerPoint 2016** to launch the application (Figure Intro-25).

You can also use *Cortana* to quickly locate an Office desktop app (Figure Intro-26).

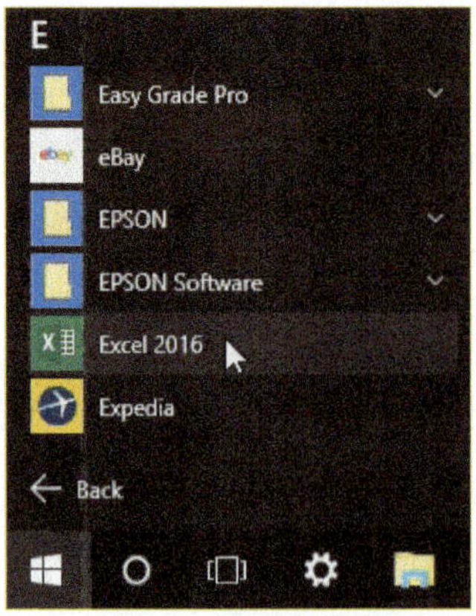

Intro-25 Open an Office desktop app from the *All apps* area on the *Start* menu

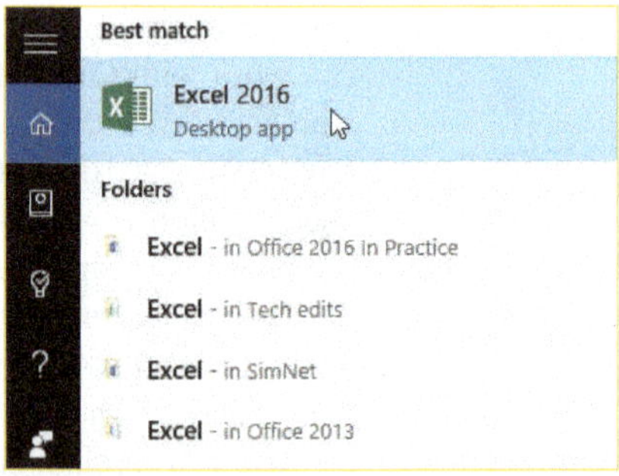

Intro-26 Use *Cortana* to find and open an app

> **MORE INFO**
>
> Add commonly used apps to your Windows *Start* menu and/or *Taskbar* to save you time. See the "Customize the *Start* Menu" and "Customize the *Taskbar*" sections in *SLO Intro.1: Using Windows 10.*

Office Start Page

Most of the Office applications (except Outlook and OneNote) display a ***Start page*** when you launch the application (Figure Intro-27). From this *Start* page, you can create a new blank file (for example a Word document, an Excel workbook, an Access database, or a PowerPoint presentation), create a file from an online template, search for an online template, open a recently used file, or open another file. These options vary depending on the Office application.

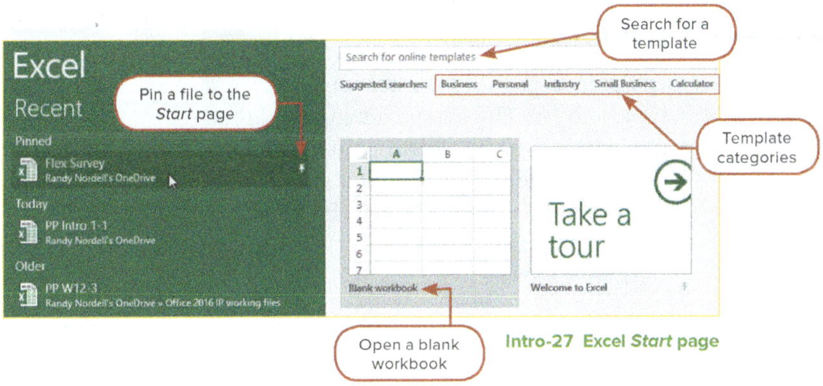

Intro-27 Excel *Start* page

HOW TO: Use the Office Start Page

1. Open a file listed in the *Recent* area on the left side of the *Start* menu by clicking the file to open. The file opens in the working area of the Office application.
   - The *Recent* area on the left side of the *Start* page lists files you have recently used and files that are pinned to the *Start* page.
2. Open a new blank file by clicking the **Blank *[file type]*** tile (*Blank workbook*, *Blank document*, etc.) to the right of the *Recent* area.
   - You can also press the **Esc** key to exit the *Start* page and open a new blank file.
3. Open an existing file that is not listed in the *Recent* area by clicking the **Open Other Workbooks** link (Figure Intro-28). The *Open* area on the *Backstage* view displays.
   - Click the **Browse** button to open the *Open* dialog box where you can locate and open a file.
   - You can also select a different location, *OneDrive* or *This PC*, and select a file to open.
4. Open a template by clicking a template file on the right or searching for templates.
   - Search for a template by typing key words in the *Search* area on the *Start* page.
   - Click a link to one of the categories below the *Search* area to display templates in that category.

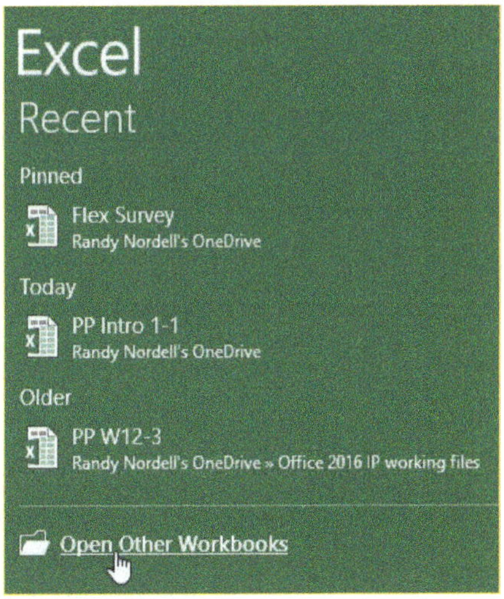

Intro-28 *Open Other Workbooks* link on the *Start* page

5. Pin a frequently used file to the *Start* page by clicking the **Pin** button.
    - The *Pin* button is on the right side of items listed in the *Recent* area and at the bottom right of templates displayed in the *Templates* area (to the right of the *Recent* area).
    - Pinned files display at the top of the *Recent* area.

MORE INFO

In Access, you have to open an existing database or create a new one to enter the program.

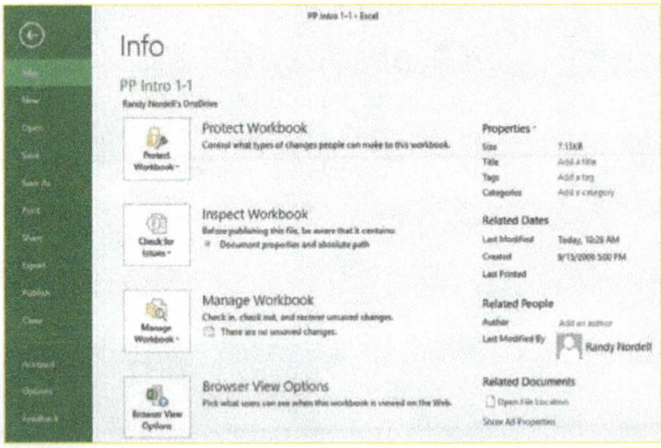

Intro-29 *Backstage* view in Excel

Backstage View

Office incorporates the ***Backstage view*** into all Office applications (including *Office Online* apps). Click the **File** tab on the *Ribbon* to open the *Backstage* view (Figure Intro-29). *Backstage* options vary on the different Office applications. The following list describes common tasks you can perform from the *Backstage* view:

- ***Info***: Displays document properties and other protection, inspection, and version options.
- ***New***: Creates a new blank file or a new file from a template or theme.
- ***Open***: Opens an existing file from a designated location or a recently opened file.
- ***Save***: Saves a file. If the file has not been named, the *Save As* dialog box opens when you select this option.
- ***Save As***: Opens the *Save As* dialog box.
- ***Print***: Prints a file, displays a preview of the file, or displays print options.
- ***Share***: Invites people to share a file or email a file.
- ***Export***: Creates a PDF file from a file or saves as a different file type.
- ***Close***: Closes an open file.
- ***Account***: Displays your Microsoft account information.
- ***Options***: Opens the *[Application] Options* dialog box (for example *Excel Options*).

Office Help—Tell Me

In all the Office 2016/365 applications, ***Tell Me*** is the new help feature (Figure Intro-30). This new help feature displays the commands in the Office application related to your search. The *Help* feature in older versions of Office displayed articles describing the feature and how to use it. The new *Tell Me* feature provides command options that take you directly to a command or dialog box. For example if you type *PivotTable* in the *Tell Me* search box in Excel, the results include the option to open the *Create PivotTable* dialog box, as well as other options such as *Recommended PivotTables* and *Summarize with PivotTable*.

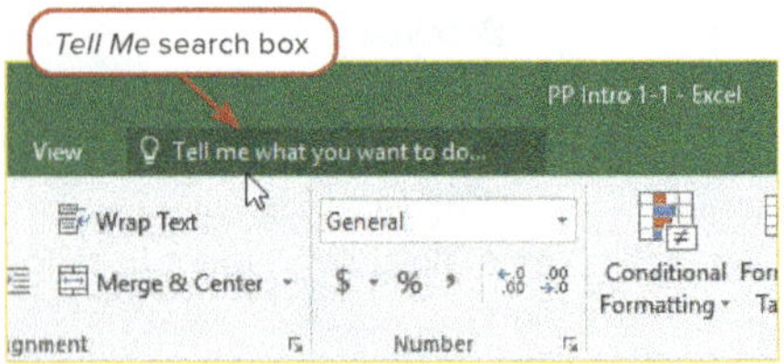

Intro-30 *Tell Me* search box

HOW TO: Use Tell Me

1. Place your insertion point in the **Tell Me** search box at the top of the *Ribbon* (see Figure Intro-30).
2. Type key words for the command or feature for which you are searching.
3. Select an option from the list of displayed search results (Figure Intro-31).
   - When you select a search result, it may apply a command, open a dialog box, or display a gallery of command choices.

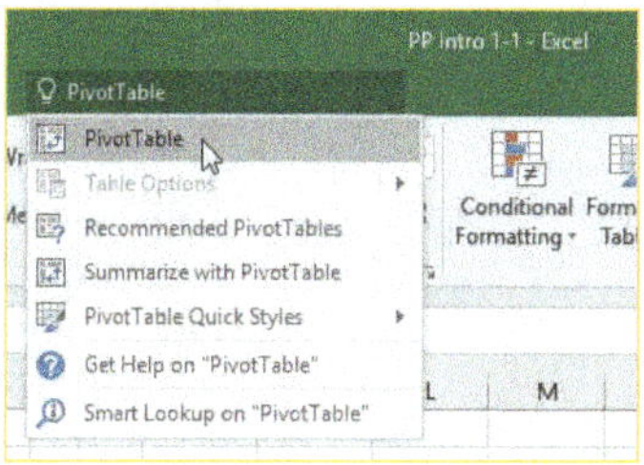

Intro-31 ***Tell Me* search results**

ANOTHER WAY

Alt+Q places the insertion point in the *Tell Me* dialog box.
The previous *Help* feature is still available in Office 2016/365. Press **F1** to open the *Help* dialog box.

Mouse and Pointers

If you are using Office on a desktop or laptop computer, use your mouse (or touch pad) to navigate around files, click tabs and buttons, select text and objects, move text and objects, and resize objects. The following table lists mouse and pointer terminology used in Office:

Mouse and Pointer Terminology

Term	Description
Pointer	When you move your mouse, the pointer moves on your screen. A variety of pointers are used in different contexts in Office applications. The following pointers are available in most of the Office applications (the appearance of these pointers varies depending on the application and the context used): • ***Selection pointer:*** Select text or an object. • ***Move pointer:*** Move text or an object. • ***Copy pointer:*** Copy text or an object. • ***Resize pointer:*** Resize objects or table columns or rows. • ***Crosshair:*** Draw a shape.
Insertion point	The vertical flashing line indicating where you type text in a file or text box. Click the left mouse button to position the insertion point.
Click	Click the left mouse button. Used to select an object or button or to place the insertion point in the selected location.
Double-click	Click the left mouse button twice. Used to select text.
Right-click	Click the right mouse button. Used to display the context menu and the mini toolbar.
Scroll	Use the scroll wheel on the mouse to scroll up and down through your file. You can also use the horizontal or vertical scroll bars at the bottom and right of an Office file window to move around in a file.

Touch Mode and Touch Screen Gestures

The new user interface in Windows 10 and Office 2016 has improved touch features to facilitate the use of Windows and the Office applications on a tablet computer or smartphone. On tablets and smartphones, you use a touch screen rather than using a mouse, so the process of selecting text and objects and navigating around a file is different from a computer without a touch screen.

In Office 2016/365, ***Touch mode*** optimizes the Office working environment when using a computer with a touch screen to provide more space between buttons and commands. Click the **Touch/Mouse Mode** button on the *Quick Access* toolbar (upper left of the Office app window) and select **Touch** from the drop-down list to enable *Touch* mode (Figure Intro-32). To turn off *Touch* mode, select **Mouse** from the *Touch/ Mouse Mode* drop-down list.

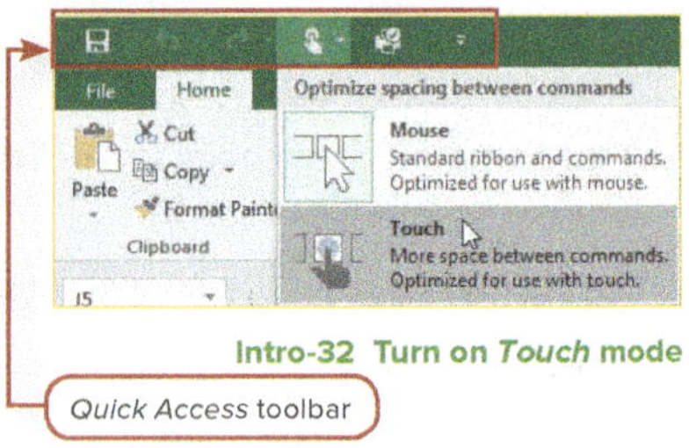

Intro-32 Turn on *Touch* mode

> **MORE INFO**
>
> The *Touch/Mouse Mode* button displays on the *Quick Access* toolbar when using a touch-screen computer.

The following table lists common gestures used when working on a tablet or smartphone (these gestures vary depending on the application used and the context):

Touch Screen Gestures

Gesture	Used To	How To
Tap	Select text or an object or position the insertion point. Double tap to edit text in an object or cell.	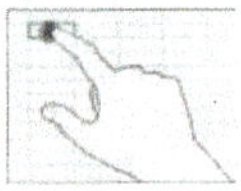
Pinch	Zoom in or resize an object.	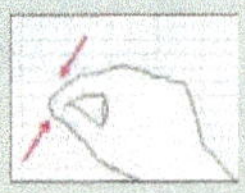
Stretch	Zoom out or resize an object.	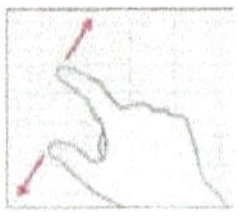
Slide	Move an object or selected text.	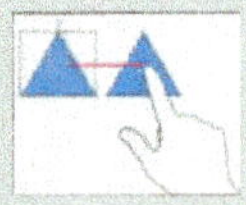
Swipe	Select text or multiple objects.	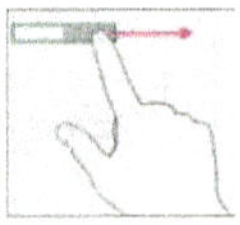

> **MORE INFO**
>
> Window 10 has a ***Tablet mode*** that optimizes all of Windows and apps for touch screens. When you turn on the *Tablet mode* feature in Windows, the *Touch mode* in Office apps turns on automatically. Click the **Action Center** button on the Windows *Taskbar* and click the **Tablet mode** button to turn on this feature in Windows.

SLO INTRO. 3

Creating, Saving, Closing, and Opening Files

Creating, saving, opening, and closing files is primarily done from the *Start* page or *Backstage* view of the Office application you are using. These areas provide you with many options and a central location to perform these tasks. You can also use shortcut commands to create, save, and open files.

Create a New File

When you create a new file in an Office application, you can create a new blank file or a new file based on a template (in PowerPoint, you can also create a presentation based on a theme). On the *Start* page, click **Blank [file type]** to create a new blank file in the application you are using (in Word, you begin with a blank document; in Excel, a blank workbook; in Access, a blank desktop database; and in PowerPoint, a blank presentation).

HOW TO: Create a New File from the Start Page

1. Open the Office application you want to use. The *Start* page displays when the application opens (Figure Intro-33).

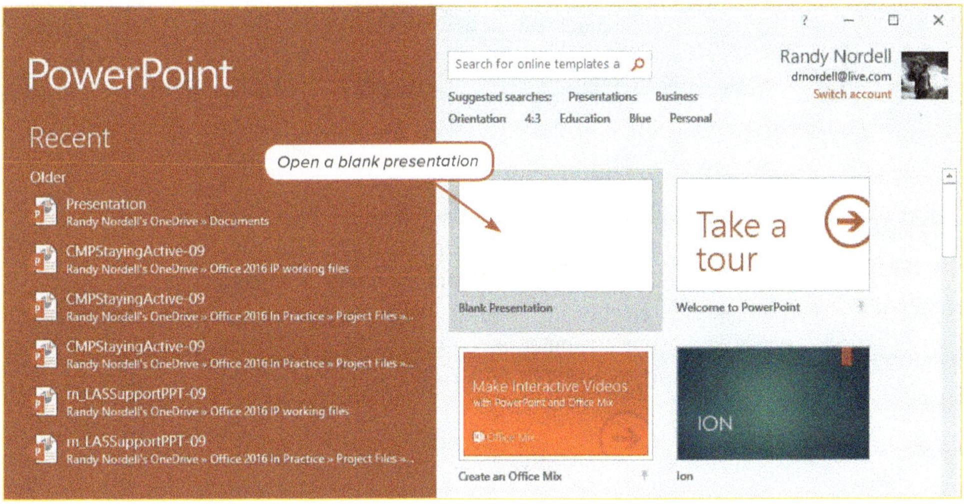

Intro-33 *Start* page in PowerPoint

2. Click **Blank [file type]** or select a template or theme to use for your new blank file. A new file opens in the application you are using.
   - The new file is given a generic file name (for example *Document1, Book1,* or *Presentation1*). You can name and save this file later.
   - When creating a new Access database, you are prompted to name the new file when you create it.
   - A variety of templates (and themes in PowerPoint only) display on the *Start* page, but you can search for additional online templates and themes using the *Search* text box at the top of the *Start* page.

MORE INFO

Esc closes the *Start* page and takes you into the Office application (except in Access).

If you have been using an application already and want to create a new file, you create it from the *Backstage* view. From the *Backstage* view, the new file options are available in the *New* area.

HOW TO: Create a New File from the Backstage View

1. Click the **File** tab to display the *Backstage* view.
2. Select **New** on the left to display the *New* area (Figure Intro-34).
3. Click **Blank [file type]** or select a template or theme to use in your new blank file. A new file opens in the application.
   - The new file is given a generic file name (*Document1, Book1,* or *Presentation1*). You can name and save this file later.
   - When you are creating a new Access database, you are prompted to name the new file when you create it.

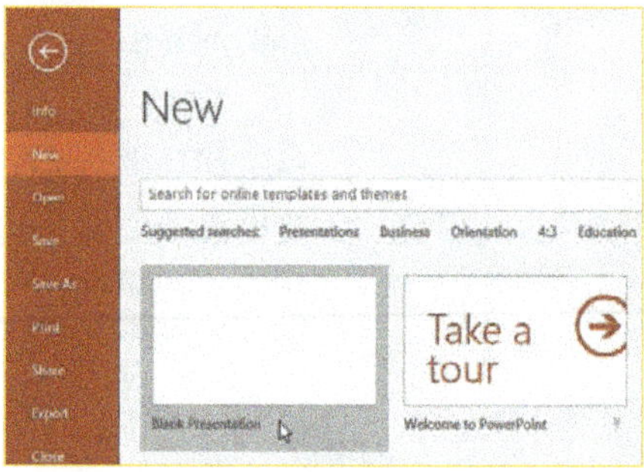

Intro-34 *New* area on the *Backstage* view in PowerPoint

> **ANOTHER WAY**
>
> **Ctrl+N** opens a new file from within an Office application. In Access, **Ctrl+N** opens the *New* area in the *Backstage* view.

Save a File

In Access, you name a file as you create it, but in Word, Excel, and PowerPoint, you name a file after you have created it. When you save a file, you type a name for the file and select the location to save the file. You can save a file on your computer, an online storage location such as *OneDrive*, or portable device, such as a USB drive.

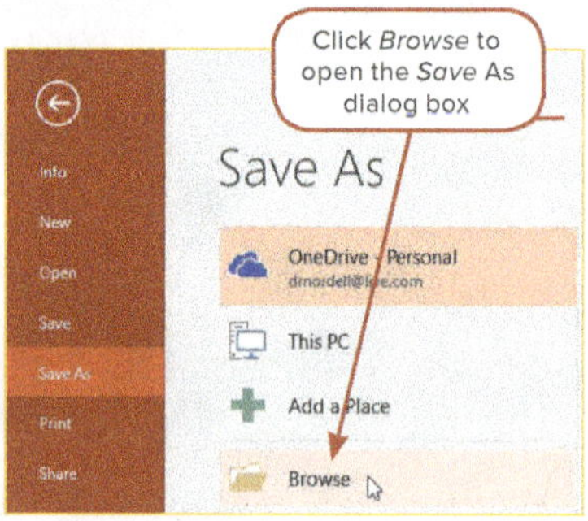

Intro-35 *Save As* area on the *Backstage* view in PowerPoint

HOW TO: Save a File

1. Click the **File** tab to display the *Backstage* view.
2. Select **Save** or **Save As** on the left to display the *Save As* area (Figure Intro-35).
   - If the file has not already been saved, clicking *Save* or *Save As* takes you to the *Save As* area on the *Backstage* view.
3. Click the **Browse** button to open the *Save As* dialog box (Figure Intro-36).
   - You can also select a different location (*OneDrive* or *This PC*) and select a folder from the list of folders at the right to open the *Save As* dialog box.
4. Select a location to save the file in the *Folder* list on the left.

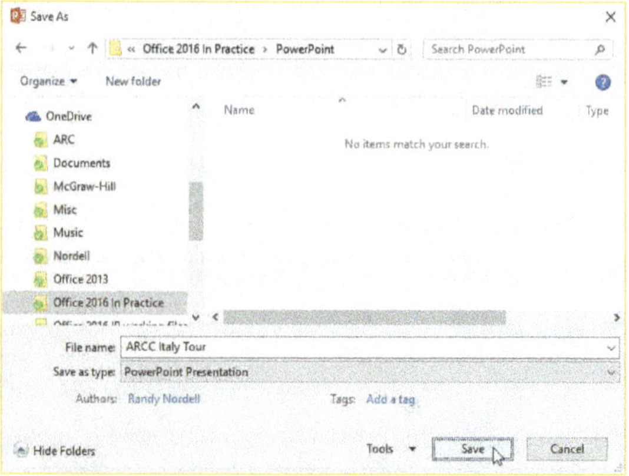

Intro-36 *Save As* dialog box

5. Type a name for the file in the *File name* area.
   - By default, Office selects the file type, but you can change the file type from the *Save as type* drop-down list.
6. Click **Save** to close the dialog box and save the file.

ANOTHER WAY

Ctrl+S opens the *Save As* area on the *Backstage* view when a file has not been named. If a file has already been named, **Ctrl+S** saves the file without opening the *Backstage* view.

MORE INFO

If you save a file in *OneDrive*, you have access to that file from any computer with Internet access. Also, you can share and collaborate on files stored in *OneDrive*. *OneDrive* is one of the folders in the *Save As* dialog box.

Create a New Folder When Saving a File

When saving files, it is a good idea to create folders to organize your files. Organizing your files in folders makes it easier to find your files and saves you time when you are searching for a specific file (see *SLO Intro.8: Organizing and Customizing Folders and Files* for more information on this topic). When you save an Office file, you can also create a folder in which to store that file.

HOW TO: Create a New Folder When Saving a File

1. Click the **File** tab to display the *Backstage* view.
2. Select **Save As** on the left to display the *Save As* area.
3. Click **Browse** to open the *Save As* dialog box.
4. Select a location to save the file in the *Folder* list on the left.
5. Click the **New Folder** button to create a new folder (Figure Intro-37).
6. Type a name for the new folder and press **Enter**.

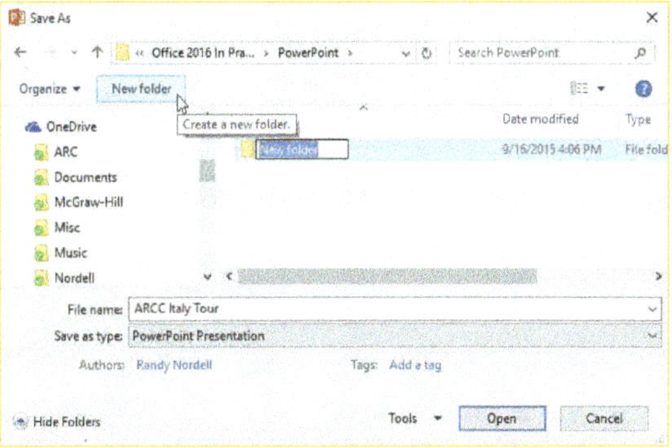

Intro-37 Create a new folder

ANOTHER WAY

F12 opens the *Save As* dialog box (except in Access). On a laptop, you might have to press **Fn+F12**. See more about the *Fn* (Function) key in *SLO Intro.7: Using Context Menus, the Mini Toolbars, and Keyboard Shortcuts*.

Save As a Different File Name

After you have saved a file, you can save it again with a different file name. If you do this, you have preserved the original file, and you can continue to revise the second file for a different purpose.

HOW TO: Save as a Different File Name

1. Click the **File** tab to display the *Backstage* view.
2. Select **Save As** on the left to display the *Save As* area.
3. Click the **Browse** button to open the *Save As* dialog box.
4. Select a location to save the file in the *Folder* list on the left.
5. Type a new name for the file in the *File name* area.
6. Click **Save** to close the dialog box and save the file.

Office 2016 File Types

When you save an Office file, by default Office saves the file in the most recent file format for that application. You also have the option of saving files in older versions of the Office application you are using. For example, you can save a Word document as an older version to share with or send to someone who uses an older version of Word. Each file has an extension at the end of the file name that determines the file type. The ***file name extension*** is automatically added to a file when you save it. The following table lists common file types used in the different Office applications:

Office File Types

File Type	Extension	File Type	Extension
Word Document	*.docx*	Access Database	*.accdb*
Word Template	*.dotx*	Access Template	*.accdt*
Word 97-2003 Document	*.doc*	Access Database (2000-2003 format)	*.mdb*
Rich Text Format	*.rtf*	PowerPoint Presentation	*.pptx*
Excel Workbook	*.xlsx*	PowerPoint Template	*.potx*
Excel Template	*.xltx*	PowerPoint 97-2003 Presentation	*.ppt*
Excel 97-2003 Workbook	*.xls*	Portable Document Format (PDF)	*.pdf*
Comma Separated Values (CSV)	*.csv*		

Close a File

You can close a file using the following different methods:

- Click the **File** tab and select **Close** on the left.
- Press **Ctrl+W**.
- Click the **X** in the upper right corner of the file window. This method closes the file and the program if only one file is open in the application.

When you close a file, you are prompted to save the file if it has not been named or if changes were made after the file was last saved (Figure Intro-38). Click **Save** to save and close the file or click **Don't Save** to close the file without saving. Click **Cancel** to return to the file.

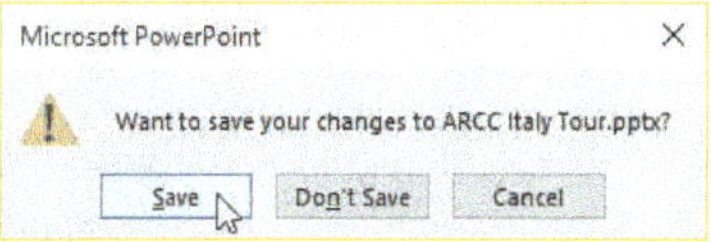

Intro-38 Prompt to save a document before closing

Open an Existing File

You can open an existing file from the *Start* page when you open an Office application or while you are working on another Office file.

HOW TO: Open a File from the Start Page

1. Open an Office application to display the *Start* page.
2. Select a file to open in the *Recent* area on the left (Figure Intro-39). The file opens in the Office application.
   - If you select a file in the *Recent* area that has been renamed, moved, or on a storage device not connected to the computer, you receive an error message.
3. Alternatively, click the **Open Other [file type]** (for example *Open Other Presentations*) (see Figure Intro-39) link to open the *Open* area of the *Backstage* view (Figure Intro-40).

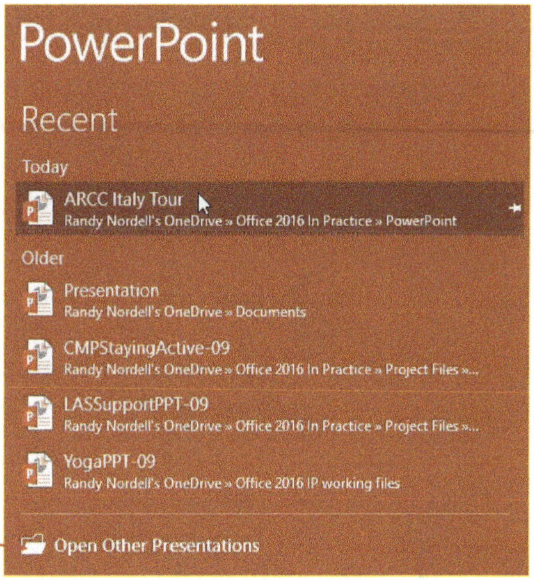

Intro-39 Open a file from the *Start* page

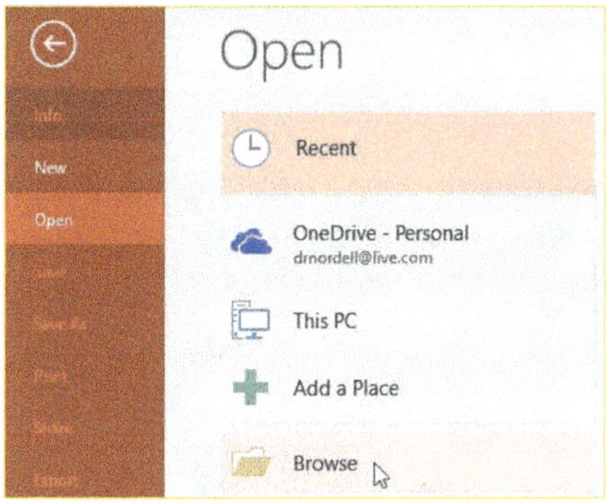

Intro-40 *Open* area on the *Backstage* view

4. Click the **Browse** button to open the *Open* dialog box (Figure Intro-41).
5. Select a location from the *Folder* list on the left.
6. Select the file to open and click the **Open** button.
   - If the file opens in *Protected View*, click the **Enable Editing** button to allow you to edit the file.

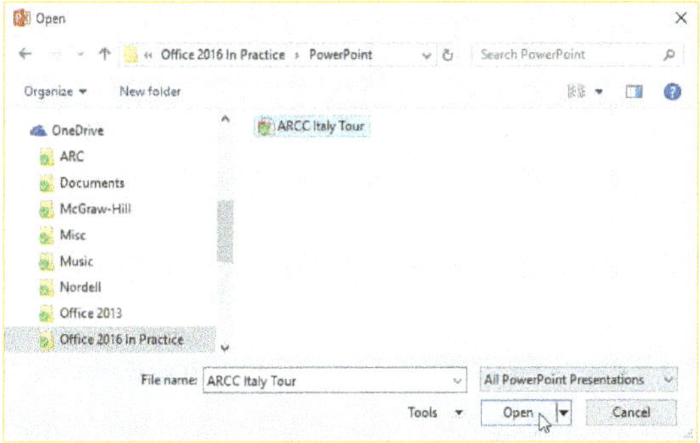

Intro-41 *Open* dialog box

When working on a file in an Office application, you might want to open another file. You can open an existing file from within an Office application from the *Open* area on the *Backstage* view.

MORE INFO

When opening a file from an online location, Office may open the file in *Protected* view. If the file opens in *Protected View*, click the **Enable Editing** button to allow you to edit the file.

HOW TO: Open a File from the Backstage View

1. Click the **File** tab from within an open Office application to open the *Backstage* view.
2. Click **Open** on the left to display the *Open* area on the *Backstage* view (see Figure Intro-40).
3. Click the **Browse** button to open the *Open* dialog box (see Figure Intro-41).
   - You can also select a file to open from the list of *Recent* files on the right of the *Open* area on the *Backstage* view.
4. Select a location from the *Folder* list on the left.
5. Select the file to open and click the **Open** button.
   - If the file opens in *Protected View*, click the **Enable Editing** button to allow you to edit the file.

ANOTHER WAY

Press **Ctrl+F12** to open the *Open* dialog box when you are in the working area of an Office application (except in Access). On some laptops, you might have to press **Fn+Ctrl+F12**.

You can also open a file from a *File Explorer* folder. When you double-click a file in a *File Explorer* folder, the file opens in the appropriate Office application. Windows recognizes the file name extension and launches the correct Office application.

PAUSE & PRACTICE: INTRO-1

For this project, you log in to Windows using your Microsoft account, customize the Windows *Start* menu and *Taskbar*, create and save a PowerPoint presentation, create a folder, open and rename an Excel workbook, and use Windows 10 features.

File Needed: ***ARCC2018Budget-Intro.xlsx*** *(Student data files are available in the* Library *of your SIMnet account)*
Completed Project File Names: ***[your initials] PP Intro-1a.pptx*** and ***[your initials] PP Intro-1b.xlsx***

1. Log in to Windows using your Microsoft account if you are not already logged in.
   a. If you don't have a Microsoft account, you can create a free account at https://signup.live.com.
   b. If you are using a computer on your college campus, you may be required to log in to the computer using your college user name and password.
2. Customize the *Start* menu to include Office 2016 apps. If these apps tiles are already on the *Start* menu, skip steps 2a–e. You can pin other apps of your choice to the *Start* menu.
   a. Click the **Start** button at the bottom left of your screen to open the *Start* menu.

b. Click **All apps** at the bottom left of the *Start* menu (Figure Intro-42). The list of apps installed on the computer displays on the left side of the *Start* menu.

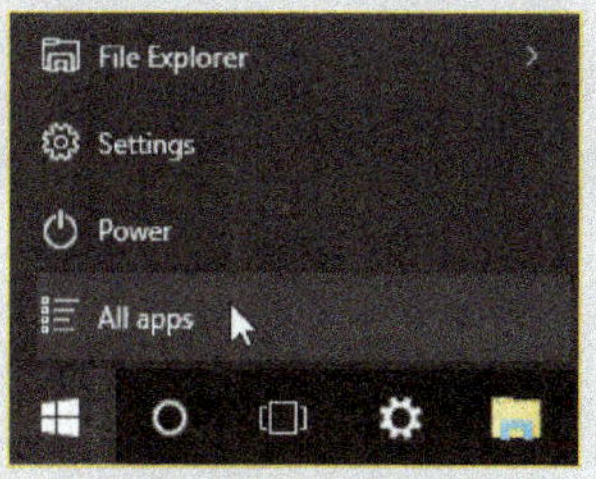

Intro-42 *All apps* button on the *Start* menu

c. Locate and right-click **Access 2016** and select **Pin to Start** (Figure Intro-43). The app displays as a tile on the right side of the *Start* menu.
d. Repeat step 2c to pin **Excel 2016**, **PowerPoint 2016**, and **Word 2016** apps to the *Start* menu.
e. Display the *Start* menu and drag these Office app tiles so they are close to each other.
f. Click the **Start** button (or press the **Esc** key) to close the *Start* menu.

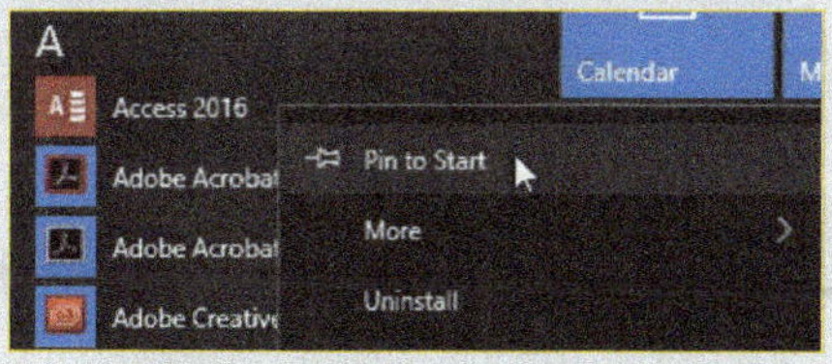

Intro-43 Pin Access 2016 app to *Start* menu

3. Use *Cortana* and the *Start* menu to pin Office 2016 apps to the *Taskbar*.
   a. Click the **Cortana** button (to the right of the *Start* button) on the *Taskbar* and type Access. *Cortana* displays content matching your search.
   b. Right-click the **Access 2016** option near the top of the *Cortana* pane and select **Pin to taskbar** (Figure Intro-44). The app pins to the *Taskbar*.
   c. Click the **Start** button to open the *Start* menu.
   d. Right-click the **Excel 2016** tile on the right side of the *Start* menu, click **More**, and select **Pin to taskbar**. The app pins to the *Taskbar*.
   e. Use either of the methods described above to pin the **PowerPoint 2016** and **Word 2016** apps to the *Taskbar*.
   f. Drag the Office apps on the *Taskbar* to rearrange them to your preference.

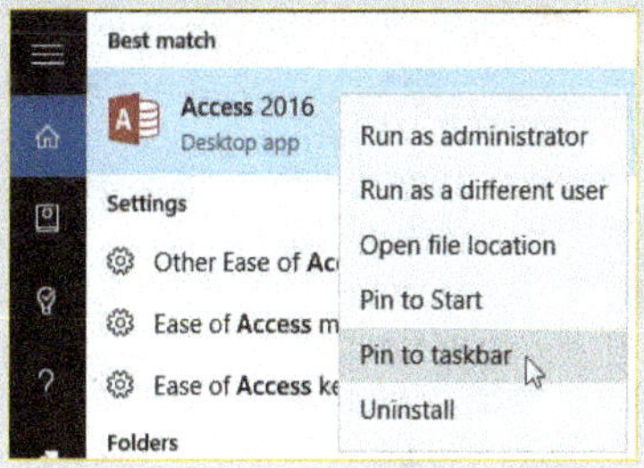

Intro-44 Use *Cortana* to find an Office app and pin it to the *Taskbar*

4. Create a PowerPoint presentation and save the presentation in a new folder.
   a. Click the **PowerPoint 2016** app tile on your *Start* menu to open the application.
   b. Click **Blank Presentation** on the PowerPoint *Start* page to create a new blank presentation.
   c. Click the **Click to add title** placeholder and type American River Cycling Club to replace the placeholder text.
   d. Click the **File** tab to open the *Backstage* view and click **Save As** on the left to display the *Save As* area.
   e. Click **Browse** to open the *Save As* dialog box (Figure Intro-45).

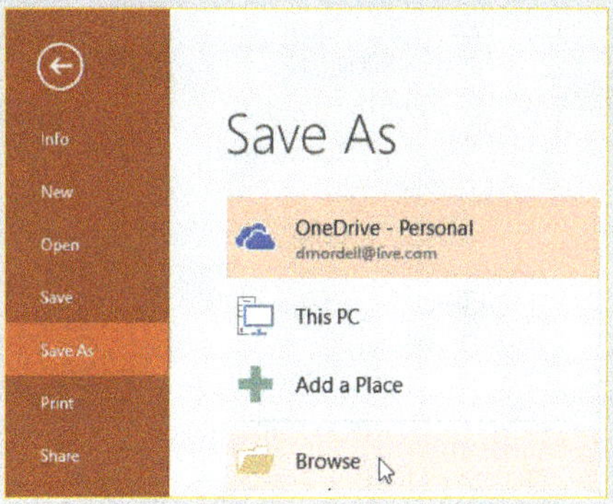

Intro-45 *Save As* area on the *Backstage* view in PowerPoint

   f. Select a location to save the file from the *Folder* list on the left. If the *OneDrive* folder is an option, select **OneDrive**. If it is not, select the **Documents** folder in the *This PC* folder. You can also save to a portable storage device if you have one.
   g. Click the **New Folder** button to create a new folder.
   h. Type American River Cycling Club as the name of the new folder and press **Enter** (Figure Intro-46).
   i. Double-click the **American River Cycling Club** folder to open it.

j. Type [your initials] PP Intro-1a in the *File name* area.
k. Click **Save** to close the dialog box and save the presentation. Leave the file and PowerPoint open.

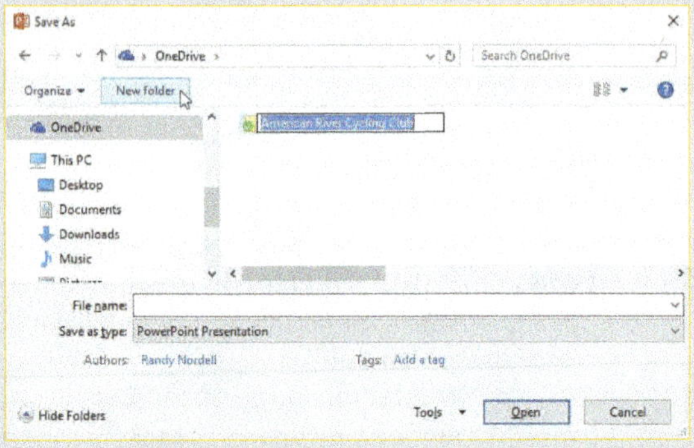

Intro-46 Create a new folder from the *Save As* dialog box

5. Open an Excel file and save as a different file name.
   a. Return to the Windows *Start* menu.
   b. Click the **Excel 2016** app button on the *Taskbar* to open it.
   c. Click the **Open Other Workbooks** link on the bottom left of the Excel *Start* page to display the *Open* area of the *Backstage* view.
   d. Click **Browse** to open the *Open* dialog box (Figure Intro-47).
   e. Browse to your student data files and select the ***ARCC2018Budget-Intro*** file.
   f. Click **Open** to open the workbook. If the file opens in *Protected View*, click the **Enable Editing** button.
   g. Click the **File** tab to open the *Backstage* view.
   h. Click **Save As** on the left to display the *Save As* area and click **Browse** to open the *Save As* dialog box.
   i. Locate the **American River Cycling Club** folder (created in step 4h) in the *Folder* list on the left and double-click the folder to open it.
   j. Type [your initials] PP Intro-1b in the *File name* area.
   k. Click **Save** to close the dialog box and save the workbook. Leave the file and Excel open.

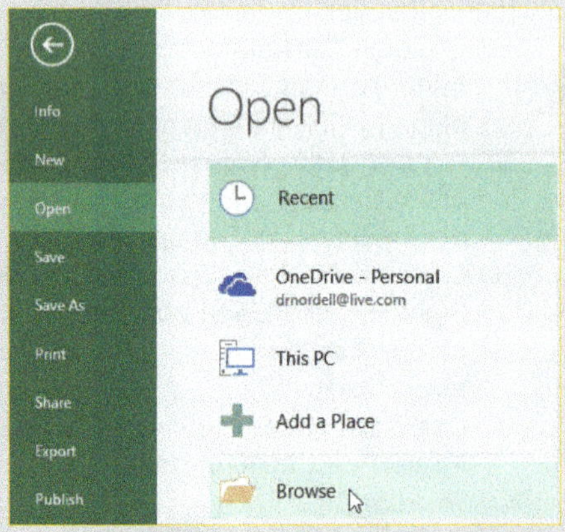

Intro-47 *Open* area on the *Backstage* view

6. Use the *Tell Me* feature in Excel to find a command.
   a. Click the **Tell Me** search box on the *Ribbon* of the Excel window and type PivotTable (Figure Intro-48).
   b. Click **PivotTable** to open the *Create PivotTable* dialog box.
   c. Click the **X** in the upper right corner of the *Create PivotTable* dialog box to close it.

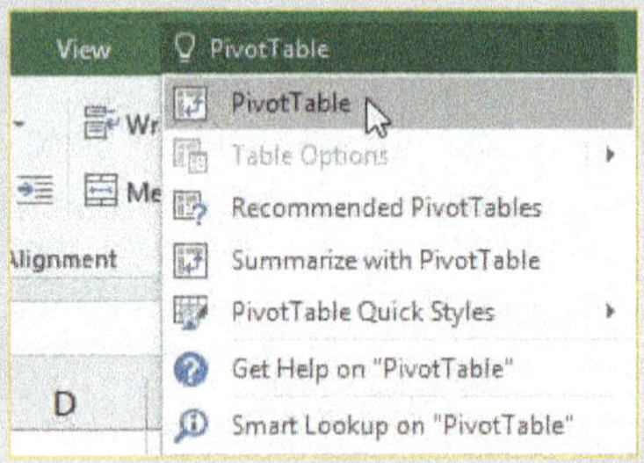

Intro-48 Use the *Tell Me* feature to find a command

7. Open the *Microsoft Store* app, the *Action Center*, and the *Settings* window.
   a. Click the **Cortana** button and type Microsoft Store.
   b. Click **Store** at the top of the *Cortana* pane to open the *Store* app.
   c. Click **Apps** in the top left and browse the available apps in the Microsoft Store.
   d. Click the **Minimize** button in the upper right corner of the *Store* window to minimize this app (Figure Intro-49). The app is still open, but it is minimized on the *Taskbar*.
   e. Click the **Action Center** button on the right side of the *Taskbar* to display the *Action Center* pane at the right (Figure Intro-50).

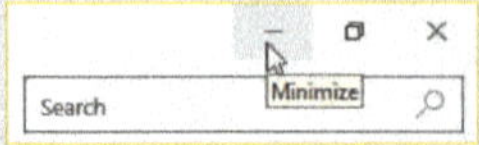

Intro-49 *Minimize* button on an app window

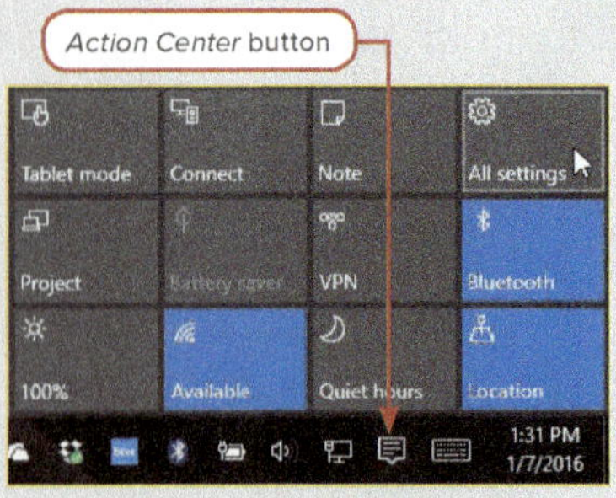

Intro-50 Windows 10 *Action Center*

f. Click **All settings** to open the *Settings* window.
g. Click the **Find a setting** search box, type Printer, and view the search results.
h. Click the **Minimize** button to minimize the *Settings* windows to the *Taskbar*.

8. Use the *Task View* feature to open and close apps and windows.
   a. Click the **Task View** button on the left side of the *Taskbar* (Figure Intro-51). All of the open apps and windows are tiled on the Windows desktop.
   b. Click the **Store** app to open it. *Task View* closes and the *Store* app displays on your Windows desktop.
   c. Click the **Task View** button again.
   d. Click the **X** in the upper right corner to close each open app and window. You may be prompted to save changes to a file.
   e. Click the **Task View** button again or press **Esc** to return to the desktop.

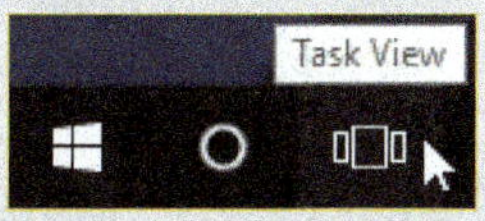

Intro-51 *Task View* button on the *Taskbar*

SLO INTRO. 4

Working with Files

When you work with Office files, a variety of display views are available. You can change how a file displays, adjust the display size, work with multiple files, and arrange the windows to view multiple files. Because most people work with multiple files at the same time, Office makes it easy and intuitive to move from one file to another or to display multiple document windows at the same time.

File Views

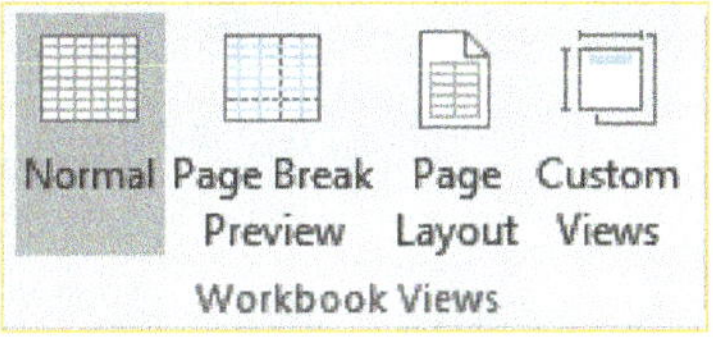

Intro-52 *Workbook Views* group on the *View* tab in Excel

Each of the different Office applications provides you with a variety of ways to view your document. In Word, Excel, and PowerPoint, the different views are available on the ***View tab*** (Figure Intro-52). You can also change views using the buttons on the right side of the ***Status bar*** at the bottom of the file window (Figure Intro-53). In Access, the different views for each object are available in the *Views* group on the *Home* tab.

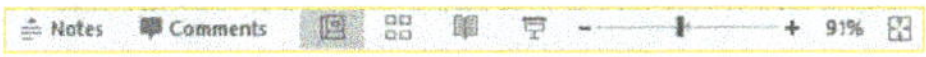

Intro-53 PowerPoint views on the *Status* bar

The following table lists the views that are available in each of the different Office applications:

File Views

Office Application	Views	Office Application	Views
Word	*Read Mode* *Print Layout* *Web Layout* *Outline* *Draft*	**Access** *(Access views vary depending on active object)*	*Layout View* *Design View* *Datasheet View* *Form View* *SQL View* *Report View* *Print Preview*
Excel	*Normal* *Page Break Preview* *Page Layout* *Custom Views*	**PowerPoint**	*Normal* *Outline View* *Slide Sorter* *Notes Page* *Reading View* *Presenter View*

Change Display Size

You can use the ***Zoom*** feature to increase or decrease the display size of your file. Using *Zoom* to change the display size does not change the actual size of text or objects in your file; it only changes the size of your display. For example, if you change the *Zoom* level to 120%, you increase the display of your file to 120% of its normal size (100%), but changing the display size does not affect the actual size of text and objects in your file. You could also decrease the *Zoom* level to 80% to display more of your file on the screen.

You can increase or decrease the *Zoom* level several different ways. Your *Zoom* options vary depending on the Office application you are using.

- ***Zoom level** on the Status* bar (Figure Intro-54): Click the + or – button to increase or decrease *Zoom* level in 10% increments.
- ***Zoom group** on the View tab* (Figure Intro-55): The *Zoom* group includes a variety of *Zoom* options. The options vary depending on the Office application.
- ***Zoom dialog box*** (Figure Intro-56): Click the **Zoom** button in the *Zoom* group on the *View* tab or click the **Zoom level** on the *Status* bar to open the *Zoom* dialog box.

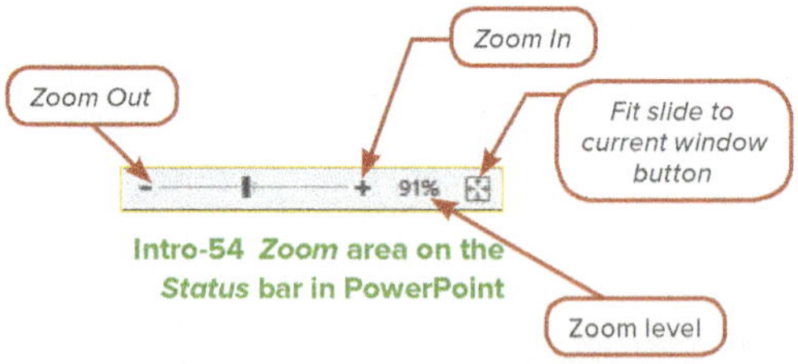

Intro-54 *Zoom* area on the *Status* bar in PowerPoint

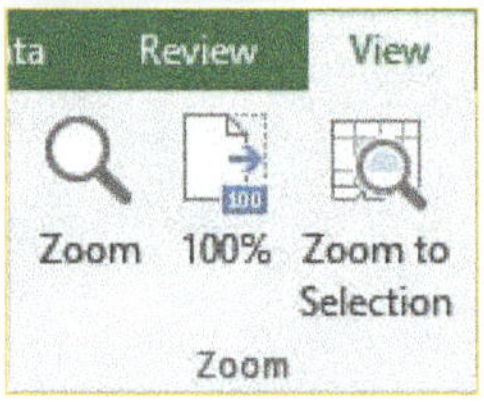

Intro-55 *Zoom* group in Excel

> **MORE INFO**
>
> The *Zoom* feature is only available in Access in *Print Preview* view when you are working with reports.

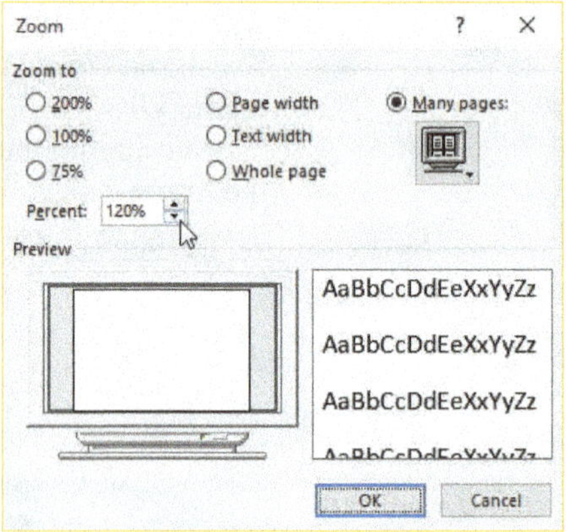

Intro-56 *Zoom* dialog box in Word

Manage Multiple Open Files and Windows

When you are working on multiple files in an Office application, each file is opened in a new window. You can ***minimize*** an open window to place the file on the Windows *Taskbar* (the bar at the bottom of the Windows desktop), ***restore down*** an open window so it does not fill the entire computer screen, or ***maximize*** a window so it fills the entire computer screen. The *Minimize*, *Restore Down/Maximize*, and *Close* buttons are in the upper right of a file window (Figure Intro-57).

> **MORE INFO**
>
> You can open only one Access file at a time. If you open another Access file, the first one closes.

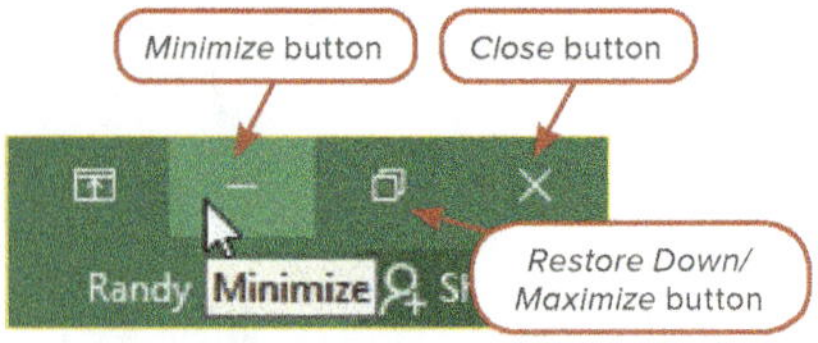

Intro-57 Window options buttons

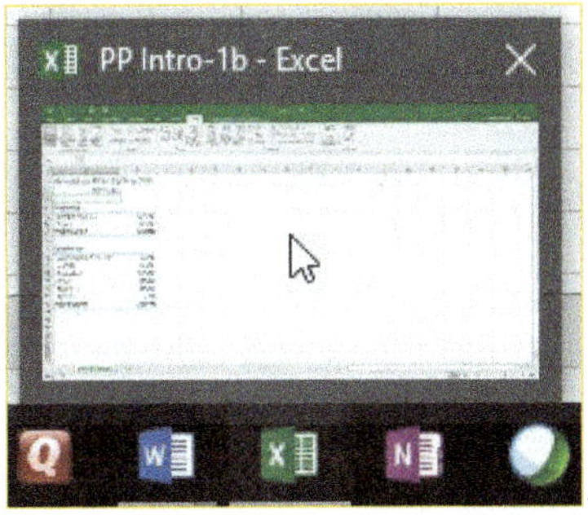

Intro-58 Display minimized file on the *Taskbar*

- ***Minimize***: Click the **Minimize** button (see Figure Intro-57) to hide the active window. When a document is minimized, it is not closed. It is minimized to the *Taskbar* so the window is not displayed on your screen. Place your pointer on the application icon on the Windows *Taskbar* to display thumbnails of open files. You can click an open file thumbnail to display the file (Figure Intro-58).
- ***Restore Down/Maximize***: Click the **Restore Down/ Maximize** (see Figure Intro-57) button to decrease the size of an open window or maximize the window to fill the entire screen. This button toggles between *Restore Down* and *Maximize*. When a window is restored down, you can change the size of a window by clicking and dragging a border of the window. You can also move the window by clicking and dragging the title bar at the top of the window.
- ***Close***: Click the **Close** button (see Figure Intro-57) to close the window. If there is only one open file, the Office application also closes when you click the *Close* button on the file.

You can switch between open files or arrange the open files to display more than one window at the same time. The following are several methods to do this:

- ***Switch Windows button***: Click the **Switch Windows** button [*View* tab, *Window* group] (not available in Access) to display a drop-down list of open files. Click a file from the drop-down list to display the file.

ANOTHER WAY

Click the Windows **Task View** button on the *Taskbar* to tile all open windows and apps on the desktop.

- ***Windows Taskbar***: Place your pointer on an Office application icon on the Windows *Taskbar* to display the open files in that application. Click a file thumbnail to display it (see Figure Intro-58).
- ***Arrange All button***: Click the **Arrange All** button [*View* tab, *Window* group] to display all windows in an application. You can resize or move the open file windows.

Snap Assist

The ***Snap Assist*** feature in Windows provides the ability to position an open window to the left or right side of your computer screen and fill half the screen. When you snap an open window to the left or right side of the screen, the other open windows tile on the opposite side where you can select another window to fill the opposite side of the computer screen (Figure Intro-59).

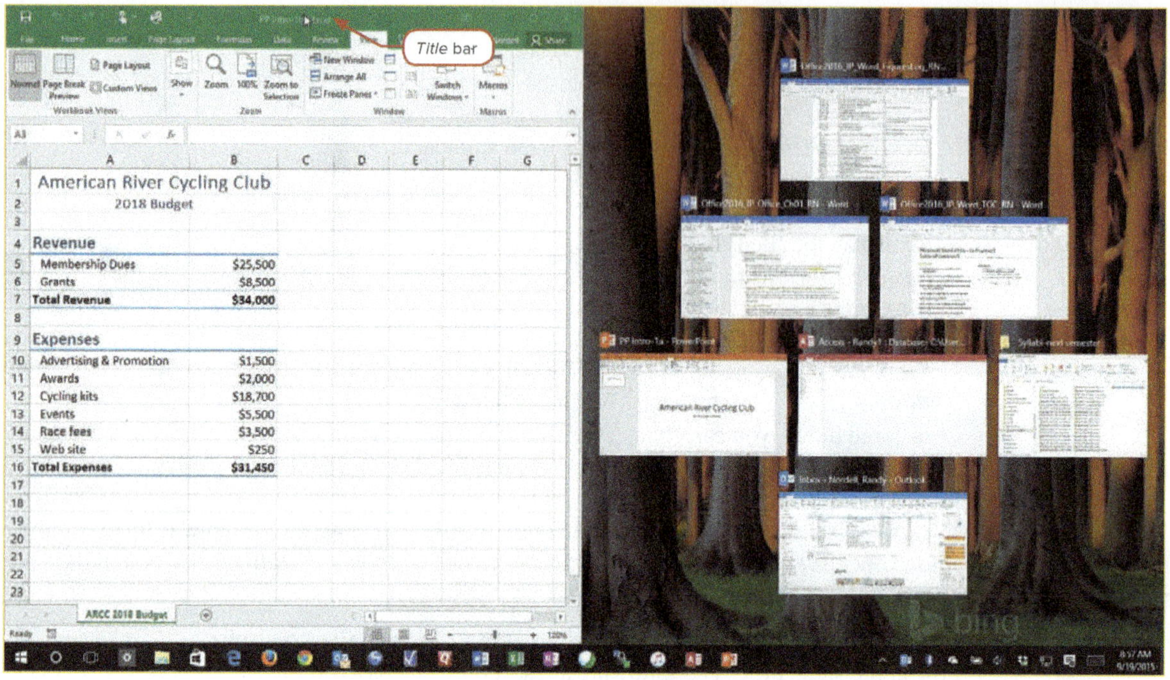

Intro-59 Windows *Snap Assist* feature

▶HOW TO: Use Snap Assist

1. Click the **title bar** of an open window.
2. Drag it to the left or right edge of the computer screen and release the pointer.
   - The window snaps to the side of the screen and fills half of the computer screen (see Figure Intro-59).
   - The other open windows and apps display as tiles on the opposite side.
   - If you're using a touch screen computer, you can use *Snap Assist* by pressing and holding the title bar of an open window and dragging to either side of the computer screen.
3. Select a tile of an open window or app to fill the other half of the screen.

MORE INFO

Snap Assist also allows you to snap a window to a quadrant (quarter rather than half) of your screen. Drag the **title bar** of an open window to one of the four corners of your computer screen.

SLO INTRO. 5

Printing, Sharing, and Customizing Files

On the *Backstage* view of any of the Office applications, you can print a file and customize how a file is printed. You can also export an Office file as a PDF file in most of the Office applications. In addition, you can add and customize document properties for an Office file and share a file in a variety of formats.

Print a File

You can print an Office file if you need a hard copy. The *Print* area on the *Backstage* view displays a preview of the open file and many print options. For example, you can choose which page or pages to print and change the margins of the file in the *Print* area. Print settings vary depending on the Office application you are using and what you are printing.

HOW TO: Print a File

1. Open the file you want to print from a Windows folder or within an Office program.
2. Click the **File** tab to open the *Backstage* view.
3. Click **Print** on the left to display the *Print* area (Figure Intro-60).
   - A preview of the file displays on the right. Click the **Show Margins** button to adjust margins or **Zoom to Page** button to change the view in the *Preview* area. The *Show Margins* button is only available in Excel.
4. Change the number of copies to print in the *Copies* area.
5. Click the **Printer** drop-down list to choose from available printers.
6. Customize what is printed and how it is printed in the *Settings* area.
   - The *Settings* options vary depending on the Office application you are using and what you are printing.
   - In the *Pages* area (*Slides* area in PowerPoint), you can select a page or range of pages (slides) to print.
   - By default all pages (slides) are printed when you print a file.
7. Click the **Print** button to print your file.

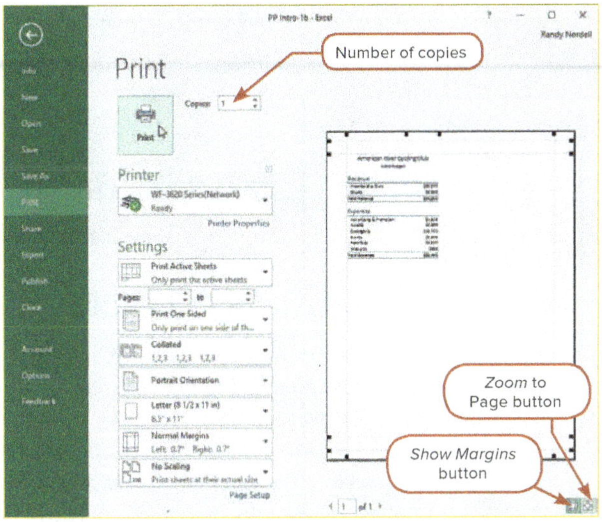

Intro-60 *Print* area on the *Backstage* view

> **ANOTHER WAY**
>
> Press **Ctrl+P** to open the *Print* area on the *Backstage* view.

Export as a PDF File

Portable document format, or ***PDF***, is a specific file format that is often used to share files that are not to be changed or to post files on a web site. When you create a PDF file from an Office application file, you are actually exporting a static image of the original file, similar to taking a picture of the file.

The advantage of working with a PDF file is that the format of the file is retained no matter who opens the file. PDF files open in the Windows Reader app or Adobe Reader, which is free software that is installed on most computers. Because a PDF file is a static image of a file, it is not easy for other people to edit your files. When you want people to be able to view a file but not change it, PDF files are a good choice.

▸HOW TO: Export a File as a PDF File

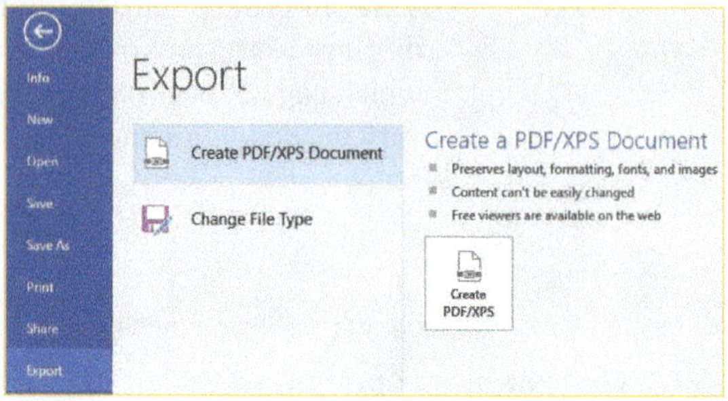

Intro-61 ***Export*** **a file as a PDF file**

1. Open the file you want to export as a PDF file.
2. Click the **File** tab and click **Export** to display the *Export* area on the Backstage view (Figure Intro-61).
3. Select **Create PDF/XPS Document** and click the **Create PDF/XPS**. The *Publish as PDF or XPS* dialog box opens.
   - XPS (XML Paper Specification) format is an alternative to a PDF file. XPS is a Microsoft format and is not widely used.
4. Select a location to save the file.
5. Type a name for the file in the *File name* area.
6. Click **Publish** to close the dialog box and save the PDF file.
   - A PDF version of your file may open. You can view the file and then close it.

MORE INFO

Microsoft Word can open PDF files, and you can edit and save the file as a Word document.

Document Properties

Document properties are hidden codes in a file that store identifying information about that file. Each piece of document property information is called a ***field***. You can view and modify document properties in the *Info* area of the *Backstage* view.

Some document properties fields are automatically generated when you work on a file, such as *Size*, *Total Editing Time*, *Created*, and *Last Modified*. Other document properties fields, such as *Title*, *Comments*, *Subject*, *Company*, and *Author*, can be modified. You can use document property fields in different ways such as inserting the *Company* field in a document footer.

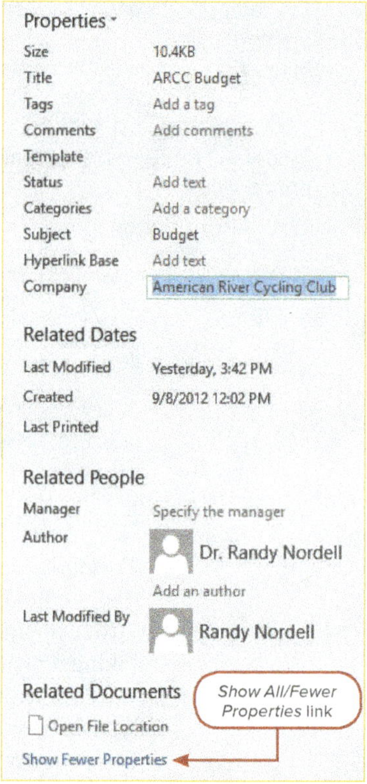

Intro-62 **Document properties**

▸HOW TO: View and Modify Document Properties

1. Click the **File** tab and click **Info**. The document properties display on the right (Figure Intro-62).
2. Click the text box area of a field that can be edited and type your custom document property information.
3. Click the **Show All Properties** link at the bottom to display additional document properties.
   - Click **Show Fewer Properties** to collapse the list and display fewer properties.
   - This link toggles between *Show All Properties* and *Show Fewer Properties*.
4. Click the **Back** arrow to return to the file.

Share a File

Windows 10 and Office 2016 have been enhanced to help you share files and collaborate with others. The *Share* area on the *Backstage* view lists different options for sharing files from within an Office application. When you save a file to your *OneDrive*, Office provides a variety of options to share your file (Figure Intro-63). The two main sharing options are ***Share with People*** and ***Email***. Within these two categories, you have a variety of ways to share a file with others. Your sharing options vary depending on the Office application you are using. The following list describes the sharing options available in the Office applications:

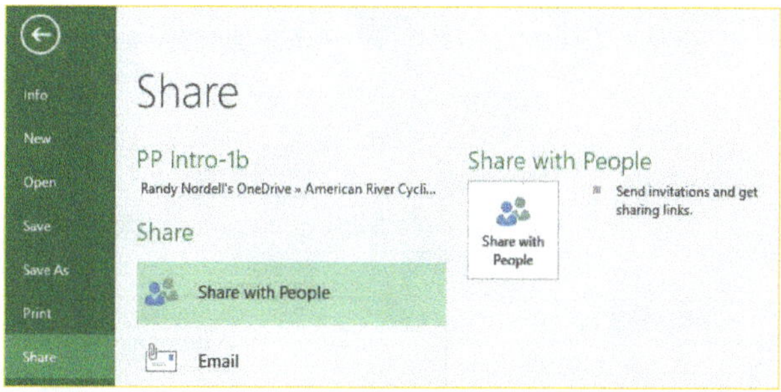

Intro-63 *Share* options on the *Backstage* view

- ***Word***: *Share with People*, *Email*, *Present Online*, and *Post to Blog*
- ***Excel***: *Share with People* and *Email*
- ***Access***: No *Sharing* option on the *Backstage* view
- ***PowerPoint***: *Share with People*, *Email*, *Present Online*, and *Publish Slides*

HOW TO: Share a File

1. Click the **File** tab to open the *Backstage* view and select **Share** on the left.
   - If your file is not saved in *OneDrive*, you are directed to first save the file to the cloud (*OneDrive*). Click the **Save to Cloud** button and save your file in *OneDrive*.
   - If your file is not saved to *OneDrive*, you will not have all available sharing options.
2. Share a *OneDrive* file with others by clicking **Share with People** on the left and then clicking the **Share with People** button on the right (see Figure Intro-63).
   - The *Backstage* view closes and the *Share* pane opens on the right side of the file (Figure Intro-64).
   - Alternatively, click the **Share** button in the upper right corner of the Office application window to open the *Share* pane (Figure Intro-65).
   - Type an email address in the *Invite people* text box. If you want to share the file with more than one person, separate email addresses with a semicolon.
   - Select **Can edit** or **Can view** from the permission drop-down list, which controls what others can do with your file.
   - You can include a message the recipients will receive.
   - Click the **Share** button below the message to send a sharing email to recipients.
   - Alternatively, click the **Get a sharing link** option at the bottom of the *Share* pane to create an *edit link* or *view-only link* (Figure Intro-66). You can then copy the sharing link and email it to others or post it in an online location.

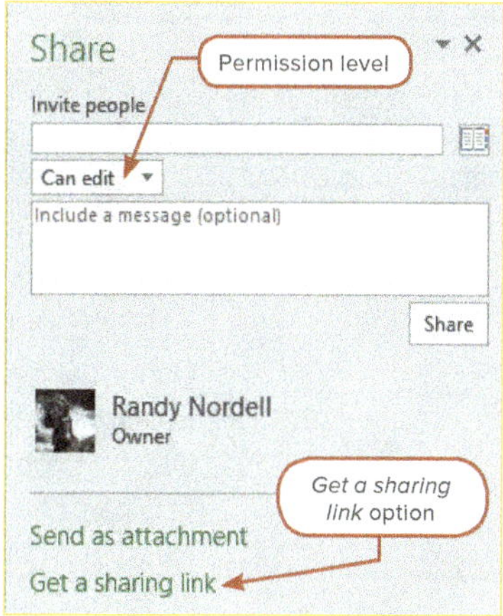

Intro-64 *Share* pane

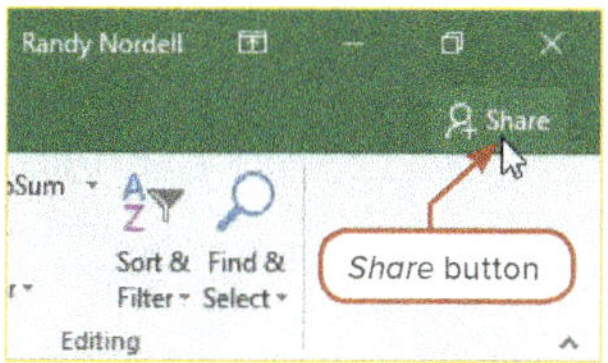

Intro-65 *The Share button opens the Share pane*

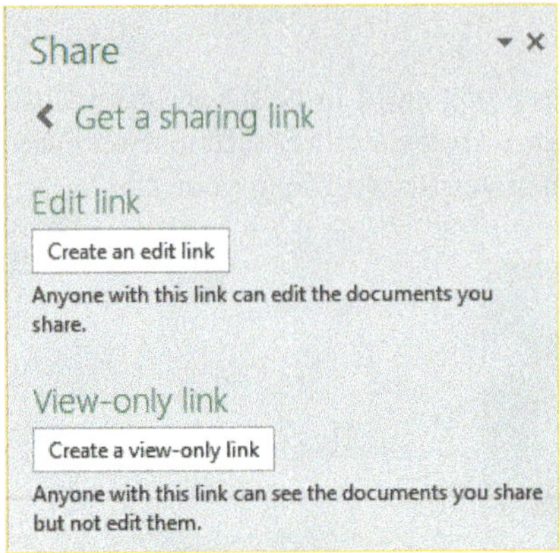

Intro-66 ***Get a sharing link*** **options in the** ***Share*** **pane**

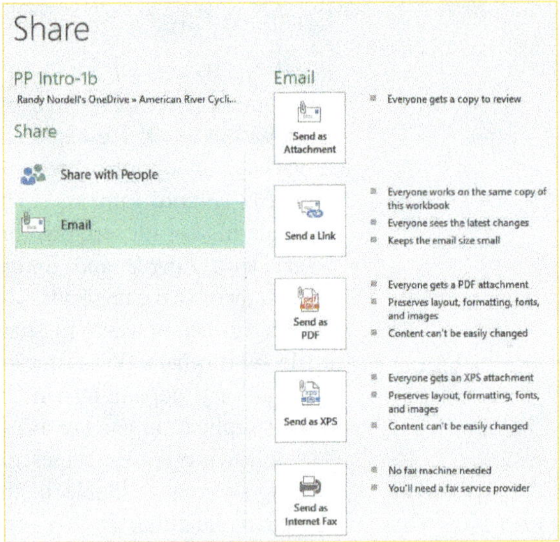

Intro-67 ***Email*** **share options in the** ***Share*** **area on the** ***Backstage*** **view**

3. Share a file through email by clicking the **Email** button on the left side of the *Share* area on the *Backstage* view and selecting an option (Figure Intro-67).
   - These *Email* share options use Microsoft Outlook (email and personal management Office application) to share the selected file through email.
   - The *Email* share options include *Send as Attachment*, *Send a Link*, *Send as PDF*, *Send as XPS*, and *Send as Internet Fax*.
   - A description of each of these *Email* share options are provided to the right of each option.

MORE INFO

Sharing options are also available if you save files to other online storage locations such as Dropbox and Box.

Program Options

Using the program options, you can apply global changes to the Office program. For example, you can change the default save location to your *OneDrive* folder or you can turn off the *Start* page that opens when you open an Office application.

Click the **File** tab and select **Options** on the left to open the **[Program] Options** dialog box (Word Options, Excel Options, etc.) (Figure Intro-68). Click one of the categories on the left to display the category options on the right. The categories and options vary depending on the Office application you are using.

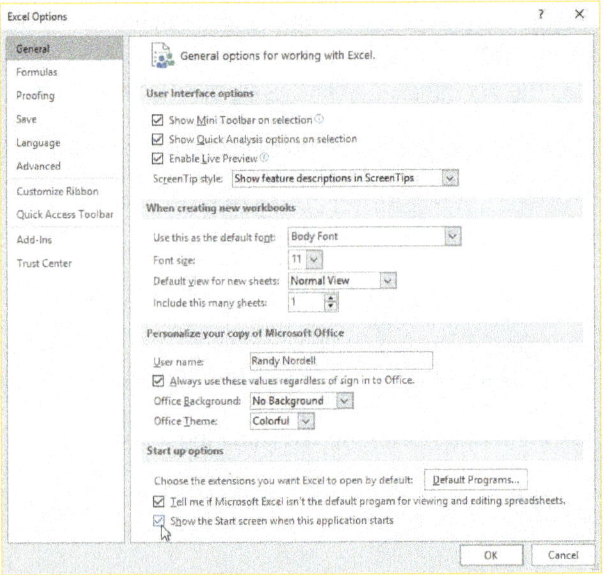

Intro-68 ***Excel Options*** **dialog box**

SLO INTRO. 6

Using the Ribbon, Tabs, and Quick Access Toolbar

You can use the *Ribbon*, tabs, groups, buttons, drop-down lists, dialog boxes, task panes, galleries, and the *Quick Access* toolbar to modify your Office files. This section describes different tools you can use to customize your files.

The Ribbon, Tabs, and Groups

The ***Ribbon***, which appears at the top of an Office file window, displays the many features available to use on your files. The *Ribbon* is a collection of ***tabs***. On each tab are ***groups*** of features. The tabs and groups that are available on each Office application vary. Click a tab to display the groups and features available on that tab.

Some tabs always display on the *Ribbon* (for example the *File* tab and *Home* tabs). Other tabs are ***context-sensitive***, which means that they only appear on the *Ribbon* when you select a specific object. Figure Intro-69 displays the context-sensitive *Table Tools Field* tab that displays in Access when you open a table.

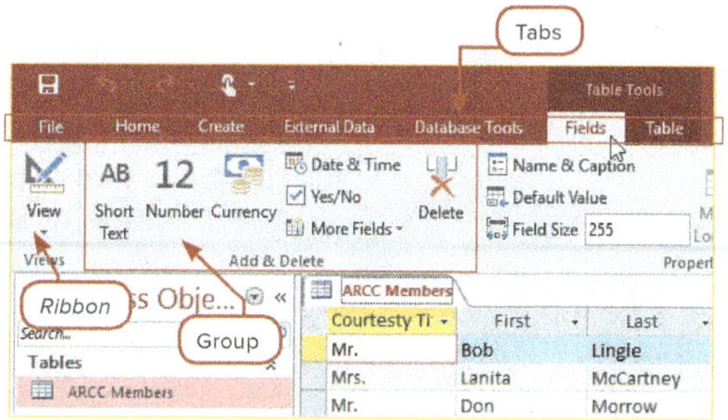

Intro-69 Context-sensitive *Table Tools Fields* tab displayed

Ribbon Display Options

The *Ribbon* displays by default in Office applications, but you can customize how the *Ribbon* displays. The ***Ribbon Display Options*** button is in the upper right corner of an Office application window (Figure Intro-70). Click the **Ribbon Display Options** button to select one of the three options:

- ***Auto-Hide Ribbon***: Hides the *Ribbon*. Click at the top of the application to display the *Ribbon*.
- ***Show Tabs***: *Ribbon* tabs display. Click a tab to open the *Ribbon* and display the tab.
- ***Show Tabs and Commands***: Displays the *Ribbon* and tabs, which is the default setting in Office applications.

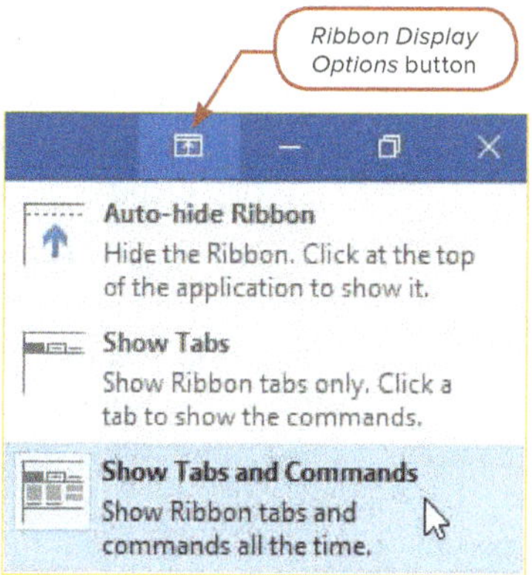

Intro-70 *Ribbon Display Options*

MORE INFO

Ctrl+F1 collapses or expands the *Ribbon*.

Buttons, Drop-Down Lists, and Galleries

Groups on each of the tabs contain a variety of ***buttons***, ***drop-down lists***, and ***galleries***. The following list describes each of these features and how they are used:

- ***Button***: Applies a feature to selected text or object. Click a button to apply the feature (Figure Intro-71).

- ***Drop-down list***: Displays the various options available for a feature. Some buttons are drop-down lists only, so when you click one of these buttons the drop-down list of options appears (Figure Intro-72). Other buttons are ***split buttons***, which have both a button you click to apply a feature and an arrow you click to display a drop-down list of options (Figure Intro-73).
- ***Gallery***: Displays a collection of option buttons. Click an option in a gallery to apply the feature. Figure Intro-74 is the *Styles* gallery. You can click the **More** button to display the entire gallery of options or click the **Up** or **Down** arrow to display a different row of options.

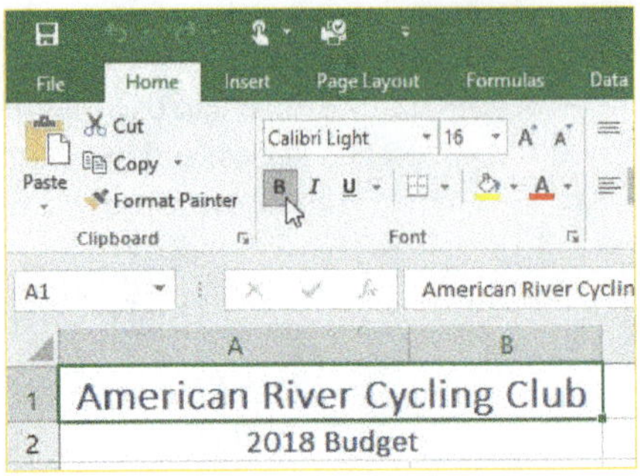

Intro-71 *Bold* button in the *Font* group on the *Home* tab

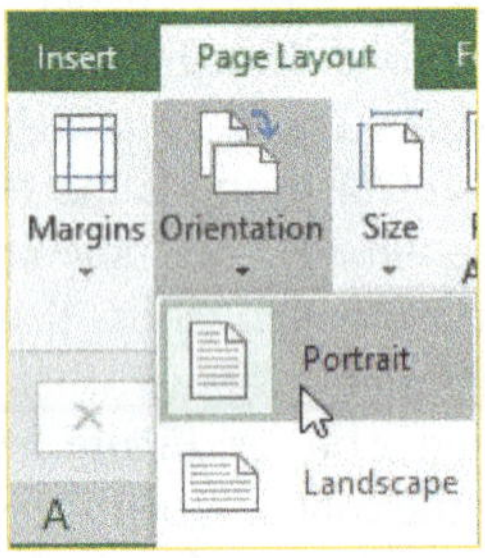

Intro-72 *Orientation* drop-down list

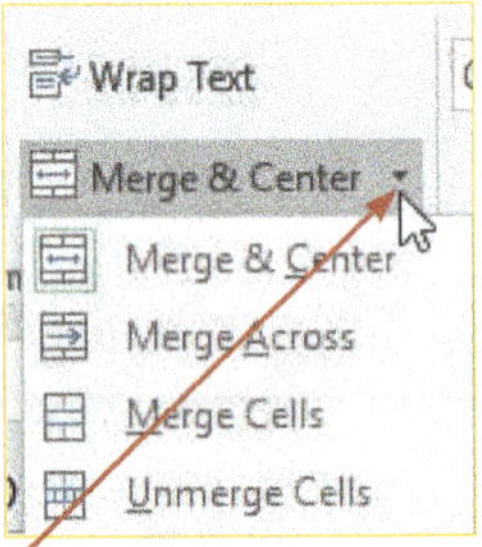

Intro-73 *Merge & Center* split button—button and drop-down list

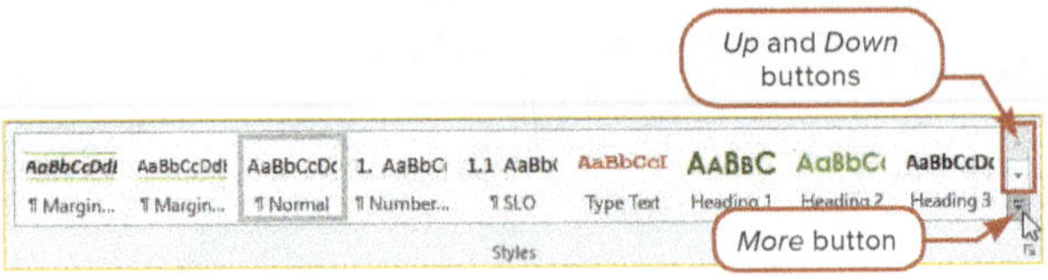

Intro-74 *Styles* gallery in Word

Dialog Boxes, Task Panes, and Launchers

Not all of the features that are available in an Office application are displayed in the groups on the tabs. Additional options for some groups display in a ***dialog box*** or ***task pane***. A ***launcher***, which is a small square in the bottom right of some groups, opens a dialog box or displays a task pane when you click it (see Figure Intro-76).

- ***Dialog box***: A new window that opens to display additional features. You can move a dialog box by clicking and dragging the title bar, which is the top of the dialog box where the title is displayed. Figure Intro-75 shows the *Format Cells* dialog box that opens when you click the *Alignment* launcher in Excel.

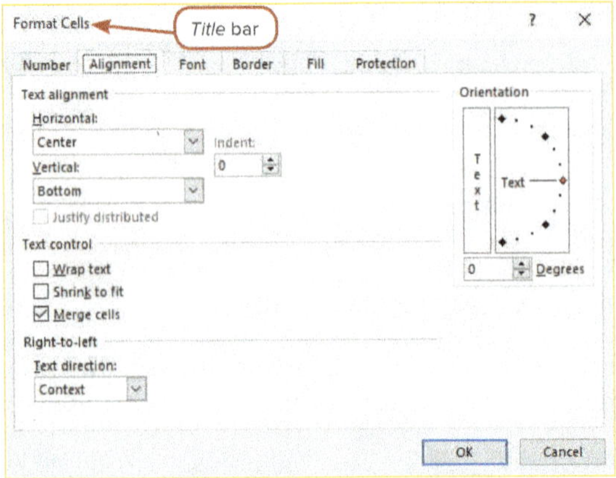

Intro-75 *Format Cells* dialog box

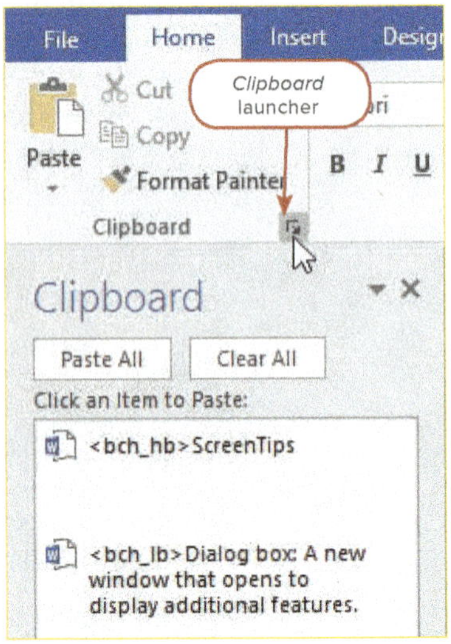

Intro-76 *Clipboard* pane

- ***Task pane***: Opens on the left or right of the Office application window. Figure Intro-76 shows the *Clipboard* pane, which is available in all Office applications. Task panes are named according to their feature (for example *Clipboard* pane or *Navigation* pane). You can resize a task pane by clicking and dragging its left or right border. Click the **X** in the upper right corner to close a task pane.

ScreenTips

ScreenTips display descriptive information about a button, drop-down list, launcher, or gallery selection. When you place your pointer on an item on the *Ribbon*, a *ScreenTip* displays information about the selection (Figure Intro-77). The *ScreenTip* appears temporarily and displays the command name, keyboard shortcut (if available), and a description of the command.

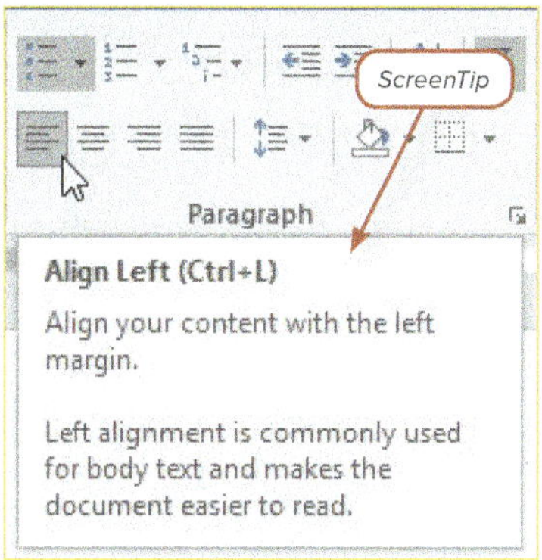

Intro-77 *Align Left ScreenTip*

Radio Buttons, Check Boxes, and Text Boxes

Dialog boxes and task panes contain a variety of features you can apply using ***radio buttons***, ***check boxes***, ***text boxes***, ***drop-down lists***, and other buttons (Figure Intro-78).

- ***Radio button***: A round button you click to select one option from a list of options. A selected radio button has a solid dot inside the round button.
- ***Check box***: A square button you click to select one or more options. A check appears in a check box you have selected.
- ***Text box***: An area where you can type text.

A task pane or dialog box may also include drop-down lists or other buttons that open additional dialog boxes. Figure Intro-78 shows the *Page Setup* dialog box in Excel, which includes a variety of radio buttons, check boxes, text boxes, drop-down lists, and other buttons that open additional dialog boxes (for example the *Print* and *Options* buttons).

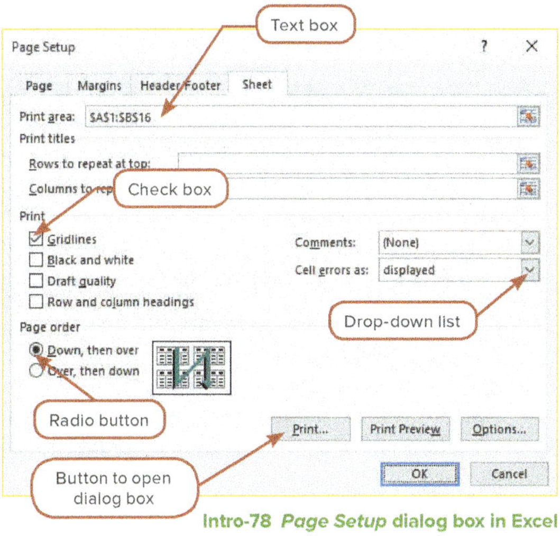

Intro-78 *Page Setup* dialog box in Excel

Quick Access Toolbar

The ***Quick Access toolbar*** is located above the *Ribbon* on the upper left of each Office application window. It contains buttons to apply commonly used commands such as *Save*, *Undo*, *Redo*, and *Open* (Figure Intro-79). The *Undo* button is a split button. You can click the

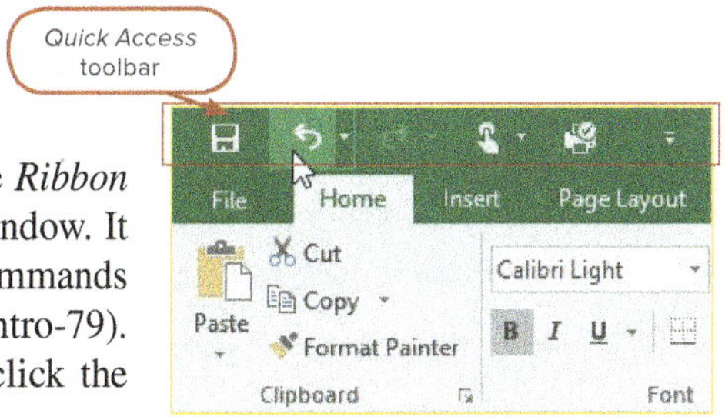

Intro-79 *Quick Access* toolbar

button to undo the last action performed or you can click the drop-down arrow to display and undo multiple previous actions.

Customize the Quick Access Toolbar

You can customize the *Quick Access* toolbar to include features you regularly use, such as *Quick Print*, *New*, and *Spelling & Grammar*. The following steps show how to customize the *Quick Access* toolbar in Word. The customization process is similar for the *Quick Access* toolbar in the other Office applications.

HOW TO: Customize the Quick Access Toolbar

1. Click the **Customize Quick Access Toolbar** drop-down list on the right edge of the *Quick Access* toolbar (Figure Intro-80).
2. Select a command to add to the *Quick Access* toolbar. The command displays on the *Quick Access* toolbar.
    - Items on the *Customize Quick Access Toolbar* drop-down list with a check mark are commands that are displayed on the *Quick Access* toolbar.
    - Deselect a checked item to remove it from the *Quick Access* toolbar.
3. Add a command that is not listed on the *Customize Quick Access Toolbar* by clicking the **Customize Quick Access Toolbar** drop-down list and selecting **More Commands**. The *Word Options* dialog box opens with the *Quick Access Toolbar* area displayed (Figure Intro-81).
4. Click the **Customize Quick Access Toolbar** drop-down list on the right and select **For all documents** or the current document.
    - If you select *For all documents*, the change is made to the *Quick Access* toolbar for all documents you open in Word.
    - If you select the current document, the change is made to the *Quick Access* toolbar in that document only.
5. Select the command to add from the alphabetic list of commands on the left and click the **Add** button.
    - If you can't find the command you're looking for, click the **Choose commands from** drop-down list and select **All Commands**.
    - The list on the right contains the commands that display on the *Quick Access* toolbar.
6. Rearrange commands on the *Quick Access* toolbar by selecting a command in the list on the right and clicking the **Move Up** or **Move Down** button.
7. Click **OK** to close the *Word Options* dialog box.

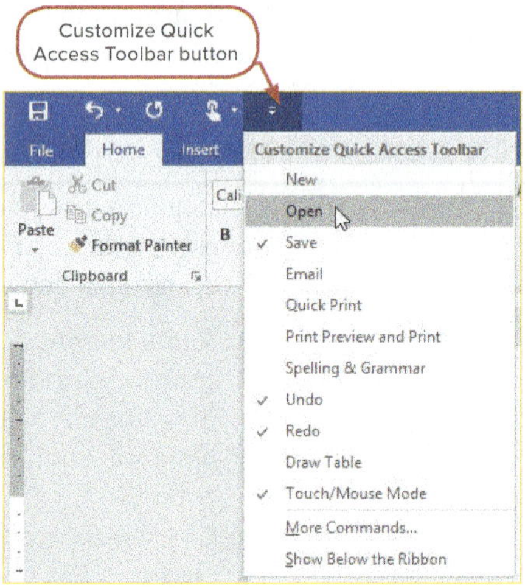

Intro-80 Add a command to the *Quick Access* toolbar

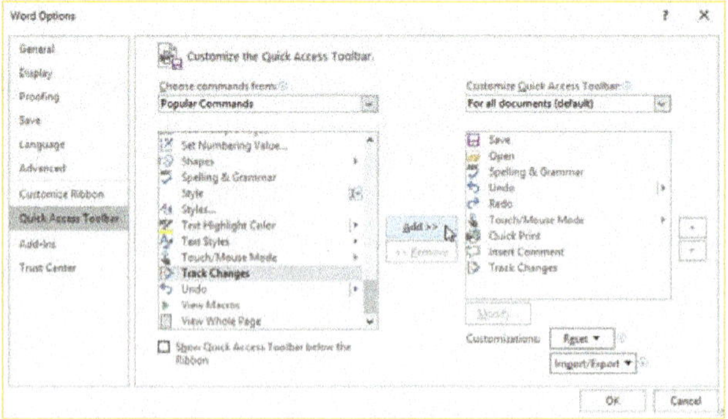

Intro-81 Customize the *Quick Access* toolbar in the *Word Options* dialog box

> **ANOTHER WAY**
>
> To remove an item from the *Quick Access* toolbar, right-click an item and select **Remove from Quick Access Toolbar**.

SLO INTRO. 7

Using Context Menus, the Mini Toolbars, and Keyboard Shortcuts

Most of the commands you use for formatting and editing your files display in groups on the tabs. But many of these features are also available using content menus, mini toolbars, and keyboard shortcuts. You can use these tools to quickly apply formatting or other options to text or objects.

Context Menu

A ***context menu*** displays when you right-click text, a cell, or an object such as a picture, drawing object, chart, or *SmartArt* (Figure Intro-82). The context menu is a vertical list of options, and the options are context-sensitive, which means they vary depending on what you right-click.

Context menus include options that perform an action (*Cut* or *Copy*), open a dialog box or task pane (*Format Cells* or *Hyperlink*), or display a drop-down list of selections (*Filter* or *Sort*).

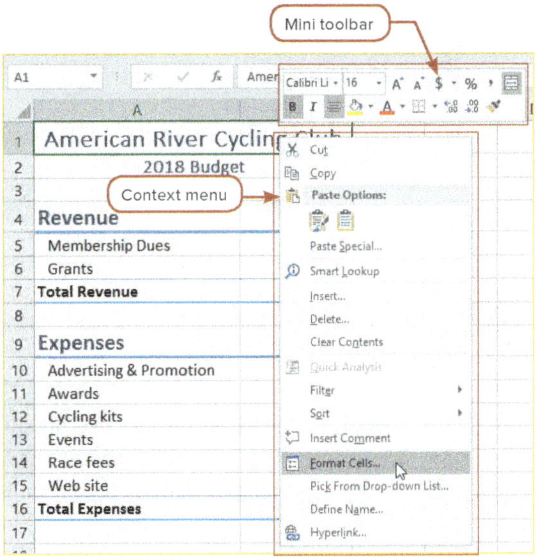

Intro-82 Context menu and mini toolbar

Mini Toolbar

The ***mini toolbar*** is another context menu that displays when you right-click or select text, a cell, or an object in your file (see Figure Intro-82). The mini toolbar is a horizontal rectangular menu that lists a variety of formatting options. These options vary depending on what you select or right-click. The mini toolbar contains a variety of buttons and drop-down lists. The mini toolbar typically displays above the context menu. The mini toolbar automatically displays when you select text or an object, such as when you select a row of a table in Word or PowerPoint.

Keyboard Shortcuts

You can also use a ***keyboard shortcut*** to quickly apply formatting or perform commands. A keyboard shortcut is a combination of keyboard keys that you press at the same time. These can include the **Ctrl**, **Shift**, **Alt**, letter, number, and function keys (for example **F1** or **F7**). The following table lists common Office keyboard shortcuts.

Common Office Keyboard Shortcuts

Keyboard Shortcut	Action or Displays	Keyboard Shortcut	Action or Displays
Ctrl+S	Save	**Ctrl+Z**	Undo
F12	*Save As* dialog *box*	**Ctrl+Y**	Redo or Repeat
Ctrl+O	*Open* area on the *Backstage* view	**Ctrl+1**	Single space
Shift+F12	*Open* dialog box	**Ctrl+2**	Double space
Ctrl+N	New blank file	**Ctrl+L**	Align left
Ctrl+P	*Print* area on the *Backstage view*	**Ctrl+E**	Align center
Ctrl+C	Copy	**Ctrl+R**	Align right
Ctrl+X	Cut	**F1**	*Help* dialog box
Ctrl+V	Paste	**F7**	*Spelling* pane
Ctrl+B	Bold	**Ctrl+A**	Select All
Ctrl+I	Italic	**Ctrl+Home**	Move to the beginning
Ctrl+U	Underline	**Ctrl+End**	Move to the end

MORE INFO

See Appendix A for additional Office 2016 keyboard shortcuts.

Function Keys on a Laptop

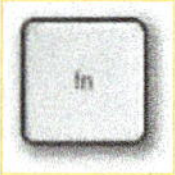

Intro-83 Function key

When using a laptop computer, function keys perform specific Windows actions on your laptop, such as increase or decrease speaker volume, open Windows *Settings*, or adjust the screen brightness. So when using a numbered function key, such as **F12** as a shortcut to open the *Save As* dialog box in an Office application, you may need to press the ***function key*** (**Fn** or **fn**) on your keyboard in conjunction with a numbered function key to activate the command (Figure Intro-83). The *function key* is typically located near the bottom left of your laptop keyboard next to the *Ctrl* key.

PAUSE & PRACTICE: INTRO-2

For this project, you work with a document for the American River Cycling Club. You modify the existing document, add document properties, customize the *Quick Access* toolbar, export the document as a PDF file, and share the document.

File Needed: ***ARCCTraining-Intro.docx*** *(Student data files are available in the* Library *of your SIMnet account)*
Completed Project File Names: ***[your initials] PP Intro-2a.docx*** and ***[your initials] PP Intro-2b.pdf***

1. Open Word 2016 and open the ***ARCCTraining-Intro*** file from your student data files. If the file opens in *Protected View*, click the **Enable Editing** button.
2. Save this document as [your initials] PP Intro-2a in the *American River Cycling Club* folder in your *OneDrive* folder.
   a. In *Pause & Practice Intro-1*, you created the *American River Cycling Club* folder in *OneDrive* or other storage area. Save this file in the same location.
   b. If you don't save this file in *OneDrive*, you will not be able to complete steps 7 and 9 in this project.

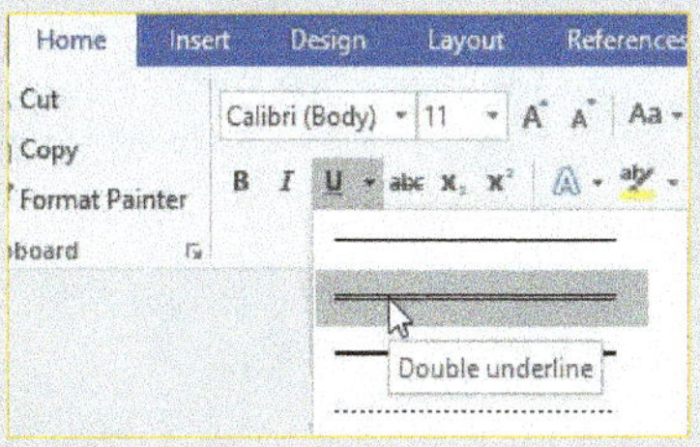

Intro-84 Apply *Double underline* to selected text.

3. Use a button, drop-down list, and dialog box to modify the document.
   a. Select the first heading, "**What is Maximum Heart Rate?**"
   b. Click the **Bold** button [*Home* tab, *Font* group].
   c. Click the **Underline** drop-down arrow and select **Double underline** (Figure Intro-84).
   d. Click the **launcher** in the *Font* group [*Home* tab] to open the *Font* dialog box (Figure Intro-85).
   e. In the *Size* area, select **12** from the list or type 12 in the text box.
   f. In the *Effects* area, click the **Small caps** check box to select it.
   g. Click **OK** to close the dialog box and apply the formatting changes.
   h. Select the next heading, "**What is Target Heart Rate?**"
   i. Repeat steps 3b–g to apply formatting to selected text.

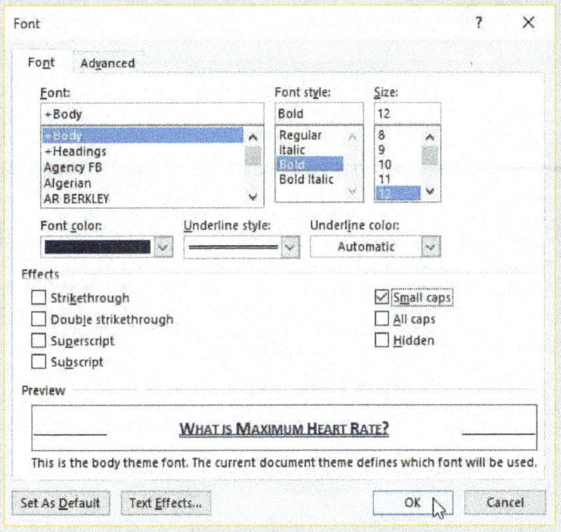

Intro-85 *Font* dialog box

4. Add document properties.
   a. Click the **File** tab to display the *Backstage* view.
   b. Select **Info** on the left. The document properties display on the right.
   c. Click the **Add a title** text box and type ARCC Training.
   d. Click the **Show All Properties** link near the bottom to display additional document properties.
   e. Click the **Specify the subject** text box and type Heart rate training.
   f. Click the **Specify the company** text box and type American River Cycling Club.
   g. Click the **Back** arrow on the upper left to close the *Backstage* view and return to the document.
5. Customize the *Quick Access* toolbar.
   a. Click the **Customize Quick Access Toolbar** drop-down arrow and select **Open** (Figure Intro-86).
   b. Click the **Customize Quick Access Toolbar** drop-down arrow again and select **Spelling & Grammar**.

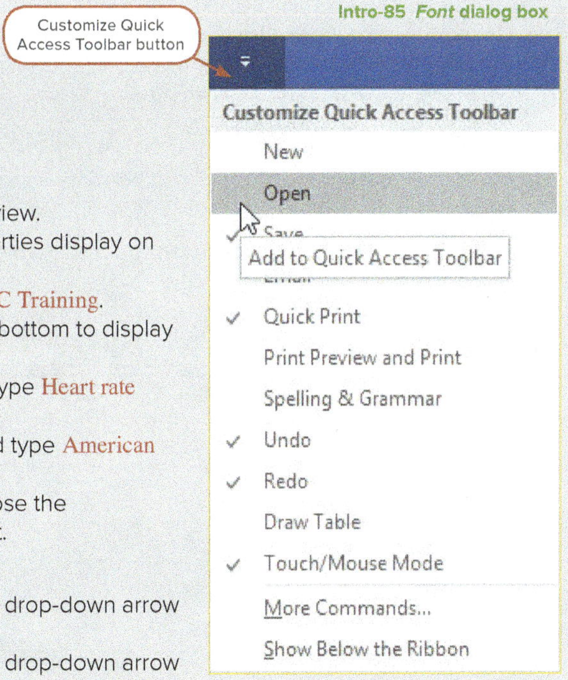

Intro-86 *Customize Quick Access Toolbar* drop-down list

   c. Click the **Customize Quick Access Toolbar** drop-down arrow again and select **More Commands**. The *Word Options* dialog box opens (Figure Intro-87).
   d. Select **Insert Comment** in the list of commands on the left.
   e. Click the **Add** button to add it to your *Quick Access* toolbar list on the right.
   f. Click **OK** to close the *Word Options* dialog box.
   g. Click the **Save** button on the *Quick Access* toolbar to save the document.

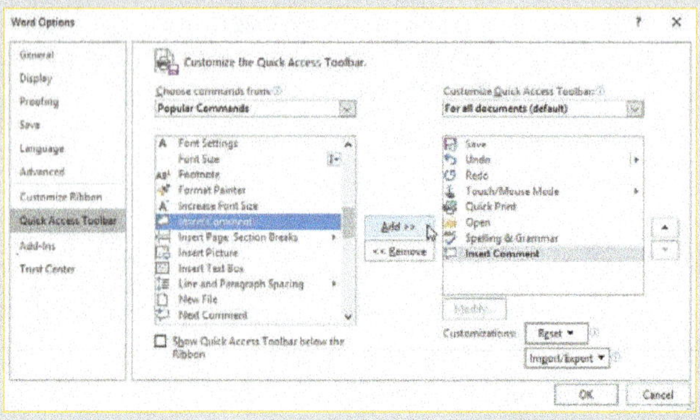

Intro-87 Customize the *Quick Access* toolbar in the *Word Options* dialog box

6. Export the file as a PDF file.
   a. Click the **File** tab to go to the *Backstage* view.
   b. Select **Export** on the left.
   c. Select **Create PDF/XPS Document** and click the **Create PDF/XPS** button. The *Publish as PDF or XPS* dialog box opens (Figure Intro-88).
   d. Select the **American River Cycling Club** folder in your *OneDrive* folder as the location to save the file.
   e. Type [your initials] PP Intro-2b in the *File name* area.
   f. Deselect the **Open file after publishing** check box if it is checked.
   g. Select the **Standard (publishing online and printing)** radio button in the *Optimize for* area.
   h. Click **Publish** to close the dialog box and create a PDF version of your file.

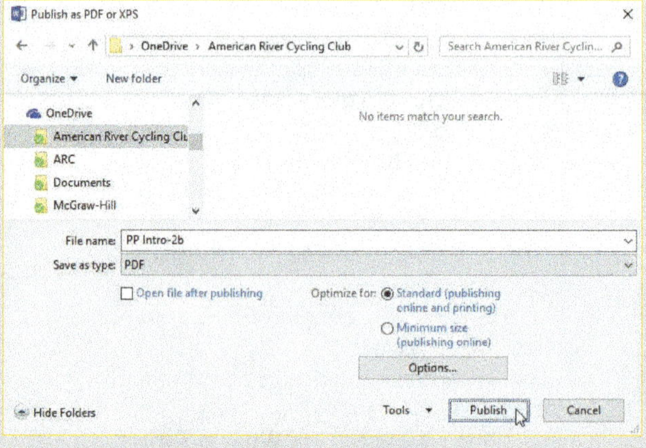

Intro-88 *Publish as PDF or XPS* dialog box

7. Get a link to share a document with your instructor. If your file is not saved in *OneDrive*, skip steps 7 and 9.
   a. Click the **Share** button in the upper right of the Word window. The *Share* pane opens on the right side of your document.
   b. Click **Get a sharing link** at the bottom of the *Share* pane.
   c. Click the **Create an edit link** button.
   d. Click **Copy** to copy the edit link (Figure Intro-89).

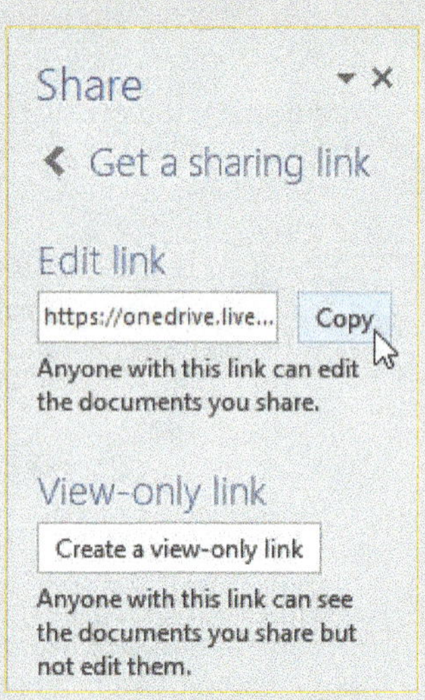

Intro-89 Copy a sharing link

8. Save and close the document (Figure Intro-90).

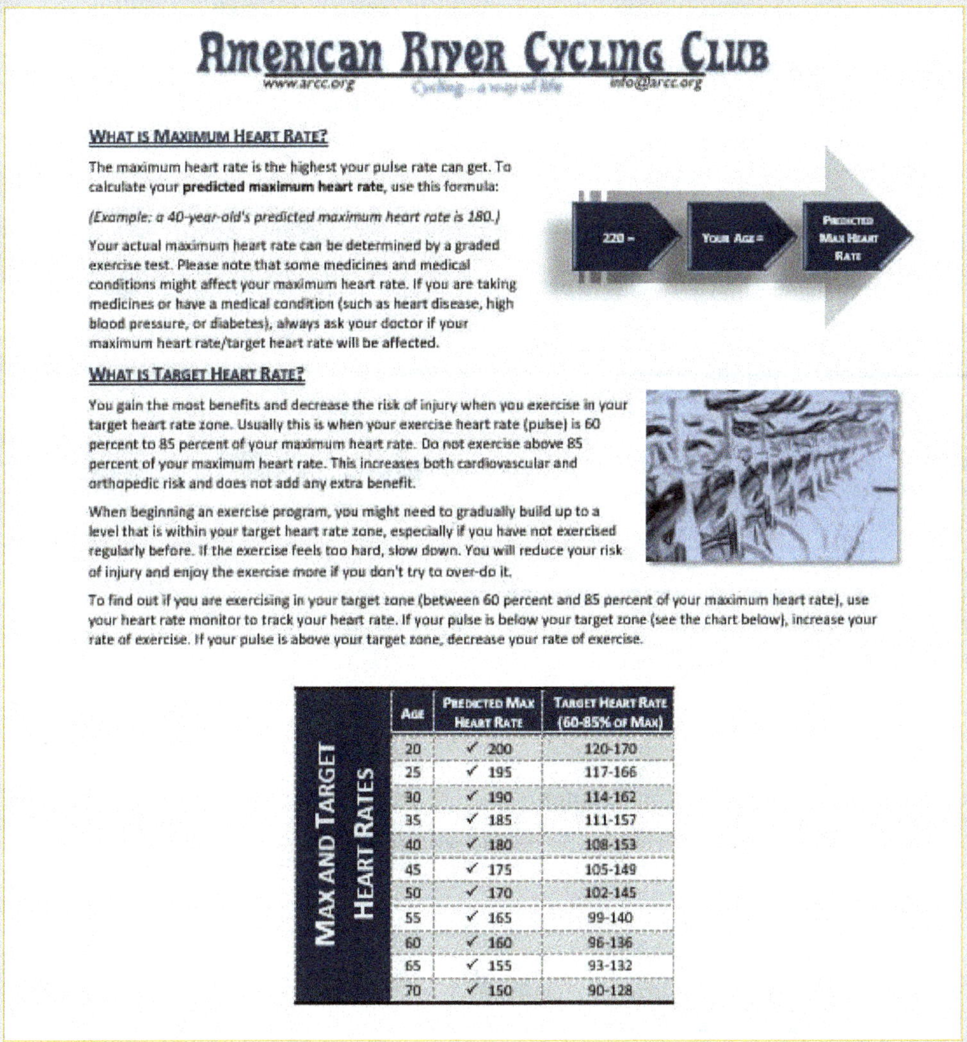

American River Cycling Club

www.arcc.org Cycling – a way of life info@arcc.org

What is Maximum Heart Rate?

The maximum heart rate is the highest your pulse rate can get. To calculate your **predicted maximum heart rate**, use this formula:

(Example: a 40-year-old's predicted maximum heart rate is 180.)

Your actual maximum heart rate can be determined by a graded exercise test. Please note that some medicines and medical conditions might affect your maximum heart rate. If you are taking medicines or have a medical condition (such as heart disease, high blood pressure, or diabetes), always ask your doctor if your maximum heart rate/target heart rate will be affected.

What is Target Heart Rate?

You gain the most benefits and decrease the risk of injury when you exercise in your target heart rate zone. Usually this is when your exercise heart rate (pulse) is 60 percent to 85 percent of your maximum heart rate. Do not exercise above 85 percent of your maximum heart rate. This increases both cardiovascular and orthopedic risk and does not add any extra benefit.

When beginning an exercise program, you might need to gradually build up to a level that is within your target heart rate zone, especially if you have not exercised regularly before. If the exercise feels too hard, slow down. You will reduce your risk of injury and enjoy the exercise more if you don't try to over-do it.

To find out if you are exercising in your target zone (between 60 percent and 85 percent of your maximum heart rate), use your heart rate monitor to track your heart rate. If your pulse is below your target zone (see the chart below), increase your rate of exercise. If your pulse is above your target zone, decrease your rate of exercise.

Max and Target Heart Rates

Age	Predicted Max Heart Rate	Target Heart Rate (60-85% of Max)
20	✓ 200	120-170
25	✓ 195	117-166
30	✓ 190	114-162
35	✓ 185	111-157
40	✓ 180	108-153
45	✓ 175	105-149
50	✓ 170	102-145
55	✓ 165	99-140
60	✓ 160	96-136
65	✓ 155	93-132
70	✓ 150	90-128

Intro-90 PP Intro-2a completed

9. Email the sharing link to your instructor.
   a. Using your email account, create a new email to send to your instructor.
   b. Include an appropriate subject line and a brief message in the body.
   c. Press **Ctrl+V** to paste the link to your document in the body of the email.
   d. Send the email message.

SLO INTRO. 8

Organizing and Customizing Folders and Files

The more you use your computer to create and use files, the more important it is to stay organized. You can use ***folders*** to store related files, which makes it easier for you to find, edit, and share your files. For example, you can create a folder for the college you attend. Inside the college folder, you can create a folder for each of your courses. Inside each of the course folders you might create a folder for student data files, solution files, and group projects. Folders can store any type of files; you are not limited to Office files.

Create a Folder

In *SLO Intro.3: Creating, Saving, Closing, and Opening Files*, you learned how to create a new folder when saving an Office file in the *Save As* dialog box. You can also create a Windows folder using *File Explorer*. You can create folders inside other folders.

HOW TO: Create a Windows Folder

1. Click the **Start** button and select **File Explorer** to open a *File Explorer* window.
    - Your folders and computer locations are listed on the left.
2. Select the location in the *Navigation* pane on the left where you want to create a new folder.
3. Click **Home** tab, and click the **New folder** button [*New* group]. A new folder is created (Figure Intro-91).
    - The *New Folder* button is also on the *Quick Access* toolbar in the *File Explorer* window.
4. Type the name of the new folder and press **Enter**.

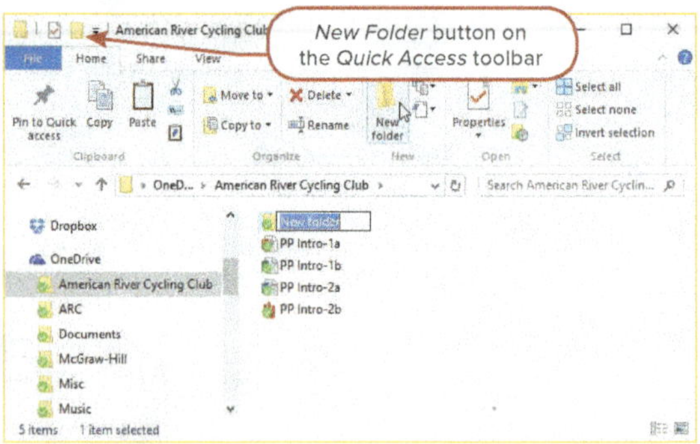

Intro-91 Create a new Windows folder

> **ANOTHER WAY**
>
> **Ctrl+Shift+N** creates a new folder in a Windows folder.

Move and Copy Files and Folders

Moving a file or folder is cutting it from one location and pasting it in another location. Copying a file or folder creates a copy of it, and you can paste in another location so the file or folder is in two or more locations. If you move or copy a folder, the files in the folder are moved or copied with the folder. Move or copy files and folders using the *Move to* or *Copy to* buttons on the *Home* tab of *File Explorer*, keyboard shortcuts (**Ctrl+X**, **Ctrl+C**, **Ctrl+V**), or the drag-and-drop method.

To move or copy multiple folders or files at the same time, press the **Ctrl** key and select multiple items to move or copy. Use the **Ctrl** key to select or deselect multiple non-adjacent files or folders. Use the **Shift** key to select a range of files or folders. Click the first file or folder in a range, press the **Shift** key, and select the last file or folder in the range to select all of the items in the range.

▶HOW TO: Move or Copy a File or Folder

1. Click the **Start** button and select **File Explorer** to open a *File Explorer* window.
2. Select a file or folder to move or copy.
   - Press the **Ctrl** key to select multiple files or folders.
3. Click the **Home** tab in the *File Explorer* window.
4. Click the **Move to** or **Copy to** button [*Organize* group] and select the location where you want to move or copy the file or folder (Figure Intro-92).
   - If the folder you want is not available, select **Choose location** to open the *Move Items* or *Copy Items* dialog box.
   - To use the keyboard shortcuts, press **Ctrl+X** to cut the file or folder or **Ctrl+C** to copy the file or folder from its original location, go to the desired new location, and press **Ctrl+V** to paste it.
   - To use the drag-and-drop method to move a file or folder, select the file or folder and drag and drop to the new location.
   - To use the drag-and-drop method to copy a file or folder, press the **Ctrl** key, select the file or folder, and drag and drop to the new location.

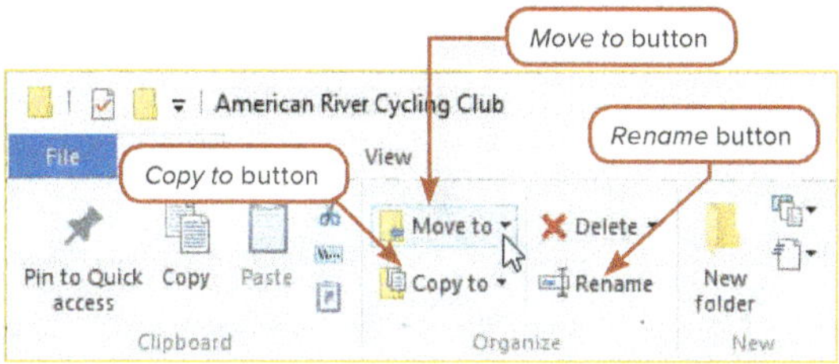

Intro-92 Move or copy a selected file or folder

ANOTHER WAY

Right-click a file or folder to display the context menu where you can select **Cut**, **Copy**, or **Paste**.

Rename Files and Folders

You can rename a file or folder in a *File Explorer* window. When you rename a file or folder, only the file or folder name changes, and the contents of the file or folder do not change.

▶HOW TO: Rename a File or Folder

1. Click the **Start** button and select **File Explorer** to open a *File Explorer* window.
2. Select the file or folder you want to rename.
3. Click the **Rename** button [*Home* tab, *Organize* group] (see Figure Intro-92).
4. Type the new name of the file or folder and press **Enter**.

ANOTHER WAY

Select a file or folder to rename, press **F2**, type the new name, and press **Enter**. You can also right-click a file or folder and select **Rename** from the context menu.

Delete Files and Folders

You can also easily delete files and folders. When you delete a file or folder, it is moved from its current location to the ***Recycle Bin*** on your computer where deleted items are stored. If a file or folder is in the *Recycle Bin*, you can restore this item to its original location or move it to a different location. You also have the option to permanently delete a file or folder; the item is deleted and not moved to the *Recycle Bin*. If an item is permanently deleted, you do not have the restore option.

HOW TO: Delete Files and Folders

1. Open a *File Explorer* window and select the file or folder you want to delete.
    - You can select multiple files and folders to delete at the same time.
2. Click the **Delete** drop-down arrow [*Home* tab, *Organize* group] to display the list of delete options (Figure Intro-93).
    - The default action when you click the *Delete* button (not the drop-down arrow) is *Recycle*.
3. Delete a file by selecting **Recycle**, which moves it to the *Recycle Bin*.
    - *Recycle* deletes the item(s) and moves it to the *Recycle Bin*.
    - When you *Recycle* an item, you are not by default prompted to confirm the deletion. Select **Show recycle confirmation** from the *Delete* drop-down list to receive a confirmation dialog box each time you delete or recycle an item.
4. Permanently delete a file by selecting **Permanently delete**. A confirmation dialog box opens. Click **Yes** to confirm the deletion.
    - *Permanently delete* deletes the item(s) from your computer.

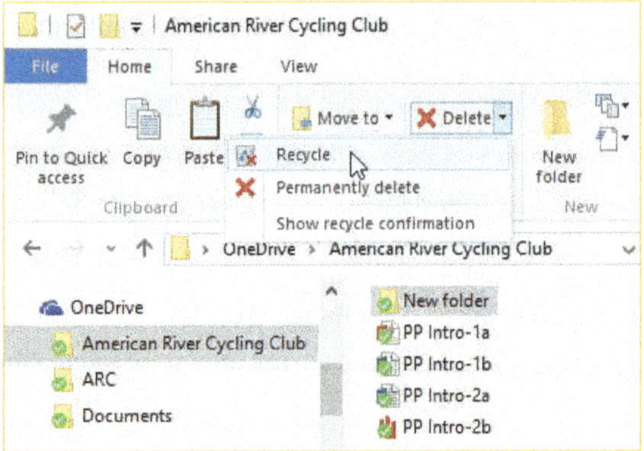

Intro-93 Delete selected folder

ANOTHER WAY

Press **Ctrl+D** or the **Delete** key on your keyboard to recycle selected item(s).
Press **Shift+Delete** to permanently delete selected item(s).

Create a Zipped (Compressed) Folder

If you want to share multiple files or a folder of files with classmates, coworkers, friends, or family, you can ***zip*** the files into a ***zipped folder*** (also called a ***compressed folder***). For example, you can't attach an entire folder to an email message, but you can attach a zipped folder to an email message. Compressing files and folders decreases their size. You can zip a group of selected files, a folder, or a combination of files and folders, and then share the zipped folder with others through email or in a cloud storage location such as *OneDrive*.

HOW TO: Create a Zipped (Compressed) Folder

1. Open a *File Explorer* window.
2. Select the file(s) and/or folder(s) you want to zip (compress).
3. Click the **Zip** button [*Share* tab, *Send* group] (Figure Intro-94). A zipped folder is created.
    - The name of the zipped folder is the name of the first item you selected to zip. You can rename this folder.
    - The icon for a zipped folder looks similar to the icon for a folder except it has a vertical zipper down the middle of the folder.

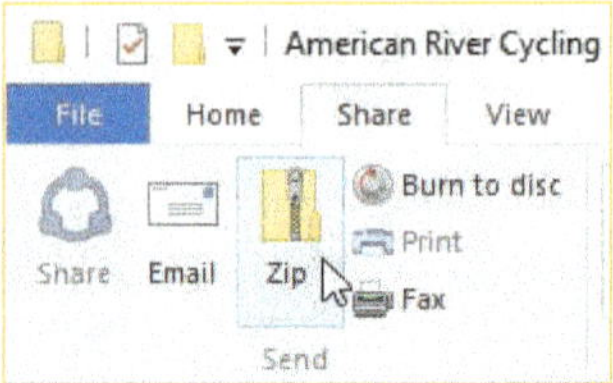

Intro-94 Create a zipped folder

ANOTHER WAY

Right-click a selected file(s) and/or folder(s), click **Send to**, and select **Compressed (zipped) folder**.

Extract a Zipped (Compressed) Folder

If you receive a zipped folder via email or download a zipped folder, save the zipped folder to your computer and then you can ***extract*** its contents. Extracting a zipped folder creates a regular Windows folder from the zipped folder.

HOW TO: Extract a Zipped (Compressed) Folder

1. Select the zipped folder to extract.
2. Click the **Compressed Folder Tools** tab.
3. Click the **Extract all** button (Figure Intro-95). The *Extract Compressed (Zipped) Folders* dialog box opens (Figure Intro-96).
4. Click **Extract** to extract the folder.
   - Both the extracted folder and the zipped folder display in the folder where they are located.
   - If you check the **Show extracted files when complete** check box, the extracted folder will open after extracting.

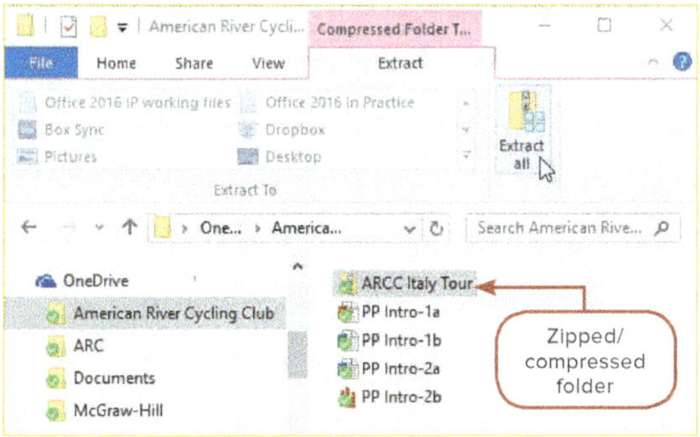

Intro-95 Extract files from a zipped folder

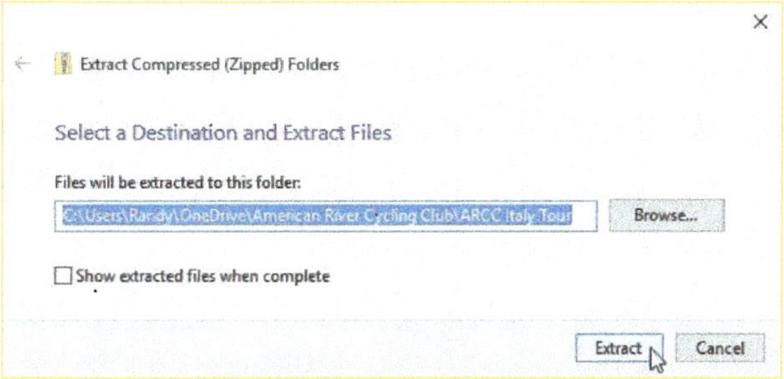

Intro-96 *Extract Compressed (Zipped) Folders* dialog box

ANOTHER WAY

Right-click a zipped folder and select **Extract All** from the context menu.

PAUSE & PRACTICE: INTRO-3

For this project, you copy and rename files in your *OneDrive* folder on your computer, create a folder, move files, create a zipped folder, and rename a zipped folder.

Files Needed: ***[your initials] PP Intro-1a.pptx***, ***[your initials] PP Intro-1b.xlsx***, ***[your initials] PP Intro-2a.docx***, ***[your initials] PP Intro-2b.docx***, and ***ARCC_Membership-Intro.accdb*** *(Student data files are available in the* Library *of your SIMnet account)*
Completed Project File Names: ***[your initials] PP Intro-1a.pptx***, ***[your initials] PP Intro-1b.xlsx***, ***[your initials] PP Intro-2a.docx***, ***[your initials] PP Intro-2b.docx***, ***[your initials]PP Intro-3.accdb***, and ***ARCC Italy Tour-2018*** (zipped folder)

1. Copy and rename a file.
   a. Click the Windows **Start** button and click **File Explorer** to open a *File Explorer* window. If *File Explorer* is not available on the *Start* menu, use *Cortana* to find and open a *File Explorer* window.
   b. Browse the *File Explorer* window to locate your student data files.
   c. Select the ***ARCC_Membership-Intro*** file.
   d. Click the **Copy to** button [*Home* tab, *Organize* group] and select **Choose location** from the drop-down list to open the *Copy Items* dialog box.
   e. Browse to locate the *American River Cycling Club* folder you created in *Pause & Practice: Intro-1*.
   f. Select the **American River Cycling Club** folder and click the **Copy** button to copy the ***ARCC_Membership-Intro*** file to the *American River Cycling Club* folder (Figure Intro-97). The *Copy Items* dialog box closes and the file is copied.
   g. In the open *File Explorer* window, browse to locate the *American River Cycling Club* folder and double-click the folder to open it.
   h. Click the ***ARCC_Membership-Intro*** file in the *American River Cycling Club* folder to select it.
   i. Click the **Rename** button [*Home* tab, *Organize* group], type [your initials] PP Intro-3 as the new file name, and press **Enter** (Figure Intro-98).

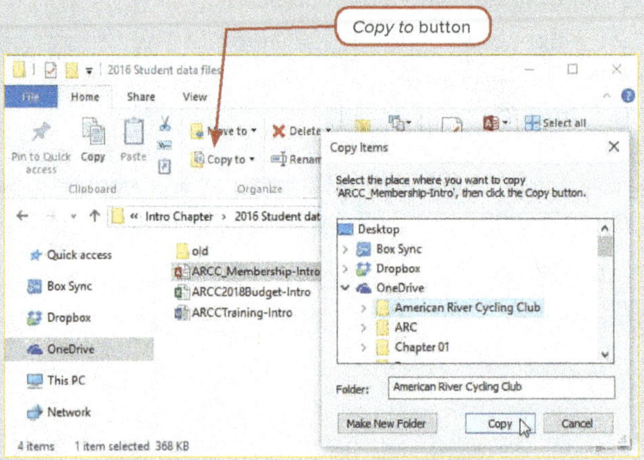

Intro-97 *Copy Items* dialog box

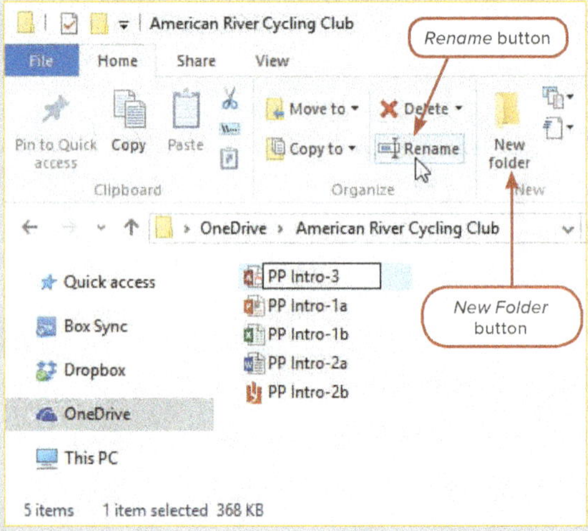

Intro-98 Rename a file

2. Create a new folder and move files.
   a. With the *American River Cycling Club* folder still open, click the **New folder** button [*Home* tab, *New* group] (see Figure Intro-98).
   b. Type ARCC Italy Tour as the name of the new folder and press **Enter**.

c. Select the ***[your initials] PP Intro-1a*** file.
d. Press the **Ctrl** key, select the ***[your initials] PP Intro-1b***, ***[your initials] PP Intro-2a***, ***[your initials] PP Intro-2b***, and ***[your initials] PP Intro-3*** files, and release the **Ctrl** key. All five files should be selected.
e. Click the **Move to** button [*Home* tab, *Organize* group] and select **Choose location** to open the *Move Items* dialog box (Figure Intro-99).
f. Browse to locate the *ARCC Italy Tour* folder in the *Move Items* dialog box.
g. Select the ***ARCC Italy Tour*** folder and click the **Move** button to move the selected files to the *ARCC Italy Tour* folder.
h. Double-click the ***ARCC Italy Tour*** folder to open it and confirm the five files are moved.
i. Click the **Up** or **Back** arrow above the *Navigation* pane to return to the *American River Cycling Club* folder (see Figure Intro-99).

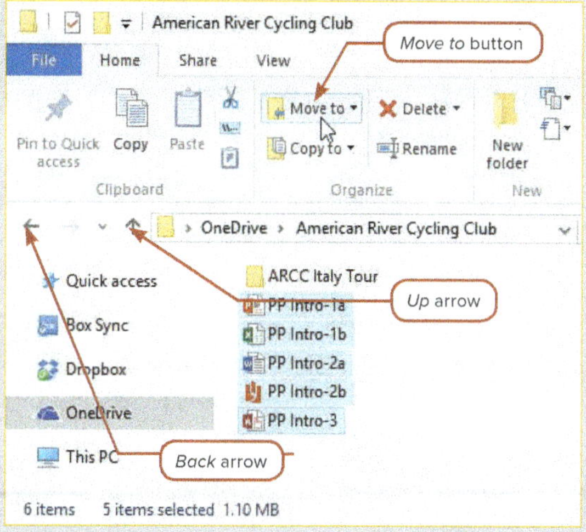

Intro-99 Move selected files to a different folder

3. Create a zipped folder.
   a. Select the ***ARCC Italy Tour*** folder.
   b. Click the **Zip** button [*Share* tab, *Send* group]. A zipped (compressed) folder is created.
   c. Place the insertion point at the end of the zipped folder name, type –2018, and press **Enter** (Figure Intro-100).

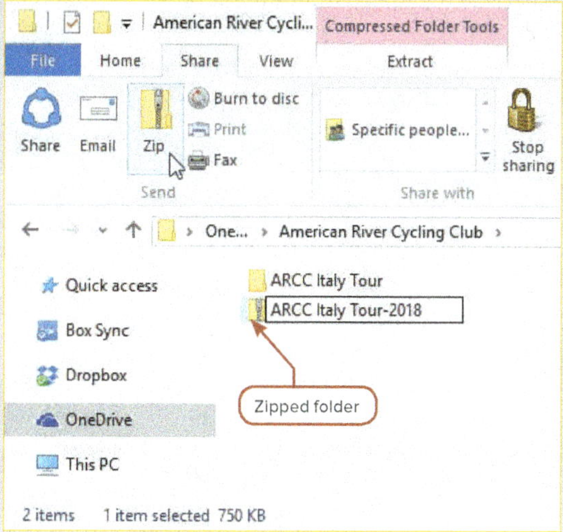

Intro-100 Create a zipped folder

4. Email the zipped folder to your instructor.
   a. Use your email account to create a new email to send to your instructor.
   b. Include an appropriate subject line and a brief message in the body.
   c. Attach the ***ARCC Italy Tour-2018*** zipped folder to the email message and send the email message.

Chapter Summary

Intro.1 Explore the features of Windows 10 (p. OI-2).

- ***Windows 10*** is a computer operating system.
- A ***Microsoft account*** is a free account you create. When you create a Microsoft account, you are given an email address, a ***OneDrive*** account, and access to ***Office Online***.
- The ***Windows desktop*** is the working area of Windows 10 and the ***Taskbar*** displays at the bottom of the desktop. You can rearrange icons on and pin applications to the *Taskbar.*
- Use ***Start menu*** in Windows 10 to select a task. You can pin applications to the *Start* menu and customize the arrangement of apps.
- ***Most Used*** items, ***File Explorer***, ***Settings***, the ***Power*** button, and ***All apps*** options display to the left of the *Start* menu.
- ***Apps*** are the applications or programs installed on your computer. App buttons are arranged in tiles on the Windows 10 *Start* menu.
- The ***Microsoft Store*** is a Windows 10 app you use to search for and install apps on your computer.
- You can install both ***traditional apps*** and ***modern apps*** in Windows 10.
- You can customize the *Start* menu and *Taskbar* to add, remove, or arrange apps.
- The *File Explorer* is a window that displays files and folders on your computer.
- *OneDrive* is the cloud storage area where you can store files in a private and secure online location.
- In Windows 10, the ***OneDrive folder*** is one of your file storage location options.
- You can access your *OneDrive* folders and files using an Internet browser window.
- ***Cortana*** is a search tool in Windows 10 used to locate information on your computer and the Internet.
- ***Task View*** displays all open apps and windows as tiles on your desktop where you can select an app or window to display or close.
- ***Settings*** is the redesigned *Control Panel* where you change many Windows settings.
- The ***Action Center*** displays notifications and buttons to open many common Windows settings and features.

Intro.2 Use the basic features of Office 2016 and navigate the Office 2016 working environment (p. OI-10).

- ***Office 2016*** is application software that includes ***Word***, ***Excel***, ***Access***, ***PowerPoint***, ***Outlook***, ***OneNote***, and ***Publisher***.
- *Office 2016* and ***Office 365*** include the same application products, but they differ in how you purchase them.
- ***Office desktop apps*** are the full-function Office 2016 or 365 products you install on your laptop or desktop computer.
- ***Office universal apps*** are a scaled-down version of Office applications you install on a tablet or mobile device.
- ***Office Online*** is free online software that works in conjunction with your online *Microsoft* account.
- When you open each of the Office applications, a ***Start page*** displays where you can open an existing file or create a new file.
- In the ***Backstage view*** in each of the Office applications, you can perform many common tasks such as saving, opening an existing file, creating a new file, printing, and sharing.
- ***Tell Me*** is the Office help feature that displays Office commands related to specific topics.
- Use the mouse (or touch pad) on your computer to navigate the pointer on your computer screen. Use the pointer or click buttons to select text or objects.
- When using Office 2016 on a touch-screen computer, use the touch screen to perform actions. You can choose between ***Touch Mode*** and ***Mouse Mode*** in Office applications.

Intro.3 Create, save, close, and open Office files (p. OI-17).

- You can create a new Office file from the *Start* page or *Backstage* view of the Office application you are using.
- When you save a file for the first time, assign the file a file name.

- You can create folders to organize saved files, and you can save a file as a different file name.
- A variety of different file types are used in each of the Office applications.
- You can close an Office file when you are finished working on it. If the file has not been saved or changes have been made to the file, you are prompted to save the file before closing.
- In each of the Office applications, you can open an existing file from the *Start* page or from the *Open* area on *Backstage* view.

Intro.4 Customize the view and display size in Office applications and work with multiple Office files (p. OI-25).

- Each Office application has a variety of display views.
- You can select an application view from the options on the ***View tab*** or the view buttons on the ***Status bar***.
- The ***Zoom*** feature changes the display size of your file.
- You can ***minimize***, ***restore down***, or ***maximize*** an open Office application window.
- You can work with multiple Office files at the same time and switch between open files.
- ***Snap Assist*** enables you to arrange an open window on one side of your computer screen and select another window to fill the other side of the screen.

Intro.5 Print, share, and customize Office files (p. OI-28).

- You can print a file in a variety of formats. The *Print* area on the *Backstage* view lists your print options and displays a preview of your file.
- You can export a file as a ***PDF (portable document format)*** file and save the PDF file to post to a web site or share with others.
- ***Document properties*** store information about a file.
- You can share Office files in a variety of ways and allow others to view or edit shared files. To share a file with others, save the file in *OneDrive*.
- Program options are available on the *Backstage* view. You can use the program options to apply global changes to an Office application.

Intro.6 Use the *Ribbon*, tabs, groups, dialog boxes, task panes, galleries, and the *Quick Access* toolbar (p. OI-33).

- The ***Ribbon*** appears at the top of an Office window. It contains ***tabs*** and ***groups*** with commands to format and edit files.
- The ***Ribbon Display Options*** provides different ways the *Ribbon* displays in Office applications.
- Within groups on each tab are a variety of ***buttons***, ***drop-down lists***, and ***galleries***.
- ***Dialog boxes*** contain additional features not always displayed on the *Ribbon*.
- Click the ***launcher*** in the bottom right corner of some groups to open a dialog box for that group.
- A ***ScreenTip*** displays information about commands on the *Ribbon*.
- Dialog boxes contain ***radio buttons***, ***check boxes***, ***drop-down lists***, and ***text boxes*** you can use to apply features.
- The ***Quick Access toolbar***, which contains buttons that allow you to perform commands, displays in all Office applications in the upper left.
- You can add or remove commands on the *Quick Access* toolbar.

Intro.7 Use context menus, mini toolbars, keyboard shortcuts, and function keys in Office applications (p. OI-37).

- A ***context menu*** displays when you right-click text or an object. The context menu contains different features depending on what you right-click.
- The ***mini toolbar*** is another context menu that displays formatting options.
- You can use ***keyboard shortcuts*** to apply features or commands.
- Some of the numbered ***function keys*** perform commands in Office applications. On laptops, you may have to press the function key (**Fn** or **fn**) to activate the numbered function keys.

Intro.8 Organize and customize Windows folders and Office files (p. OI-42).

- ***Folders*** store and organize your files.
- You can create, move, or copy files and folders. Files stored in a folder are moved or copied with that folder.
- You can rename a file to change the file name.
- When you delete a file or folder, it is moved to the ***Recycle Bin*** on your computer by default. Alternatively, you can permanently delete files and folders.
- You can ***zip*** files and/or folders into a ***zipped (compressed) folder*** to email or share multiple files as a single file.
- When you receive a zipped folder, you can ***extract*** the zipped folder to create a regular Windows folder and access its contents.

Check for Understanding

The SIMbook for this text (within your SIMnet account) provides the following resources for concept review:

- Multiple choice questions
- Short answer questions
- Matching exercises

USING MICROSOFT WINDOWS 10 AND OFFICE 2016

For these projects, you use your *OneDrive* to store files. If you don't already have a Microsoft account, see *SLO Intro.1: Using Windows 10* for information about creating a free personal Microsoft account.

Guided Project Intro-1

For this project, you organize and edit files for Emma Cavalli at Placer Hills Real Estate. You extract a zipped folder, rename files, manage multiple documents, apply formatting, and export as a PDF file. [Student Learning Outcomes Intro.1, Intro.2, Intro.3, Intro.4, Intro.5, Intro.6, Intro.7, Intro.8]

Files Needed: ***CavalliFiles-Intro*** (zipped folder) *(Student data files are available in the* Library *of your SIMnet account)*

Completed Project File Names: ***PHRE*** folder containing the following files: ***BuyerEscrowChecklist-Intro***, ***CavalliProspectingLetter-Intro***, ***[your initials] Intro-1a.accdb***, ***[your initials] Intro-1b.xlsx***, ***[your initials] Intro-1c.docx***, and ***[your initials] Intro-1d.docx***

Skills Covered in This Project

- Copy and paste a zipped folder.
- Create a new folder in your *OneDrive* folder.
- Extract a zipped folder.
- Move a file.
- Rename a file.
- Open a Word document.
- Use *Task View* to switch between two open Word documents.
- Save a Word document with a different file name.
- Change display size.
- Use a mini toolbar, keyboard shortcut, context menu, and dialog box to apply formatting to selected text.
- Export a document as a PDF file.

1. Copy a zipped folder and create a new *OneDrive* folder.
   a. Click the Windows **Start** button and click **File Explorer** to open the *File Explorer* window. If *File Explorer* is not available on the *Start* menu, use *Cortana* to find and open the *File Explorer* window.
   b. Browse in the *File Explorer* window to locate your student data files.
   c. Select the ***CavalliFiles-Intro*** zipped folder from your student data files and press **Ctrl+C** or click the **Copy** button [*Home* tab, *Clipboard* group] to copy the folder.
   d. Select your **OneDrive** folder on the left of the *File Explorer* window, and click the **New folder** button [*Home* tab, *New* group] to create a new folder. If you don't have *OneDrive* available, create the new folder in a location where you store your files.
   e. Type PHRE and press **Enter**.
   f. Press **Enter** again to open the *PHRE* folder or double-click the folder to open it.
   g. Press **Ctrl+V** or click the **Paste** button [*Home* tab, *Clipboard* group] to paste the copied ***CavalliFiles-Intro*** zipped folder in the *PHRE* folder.
2. Extract a zipped folder.
   a. Select the ***CavalliFiles-Intro*** zipped folder.
   b. Click the **Compressed Folder Tools Extract** tab and click the **Extract all** button. The *Extract Compressed (Zipped) Folders* dialog box opens.
   c. Uncheck the **Show extracted files when complete** box if it is checked.
   d. Click the **Extract** button (Figure Intro-101). The zipped folder is extracted, and the *PHRE* folder now contains two *CavalliFiles-Intro* folders. One folder is zipped and the other is a regular folder.

e. Select the zipped ***CavalliFiles-Intro*** folder and click the **Delete** button [*Home* tab, *Organize* group] to delete the zipped folder.

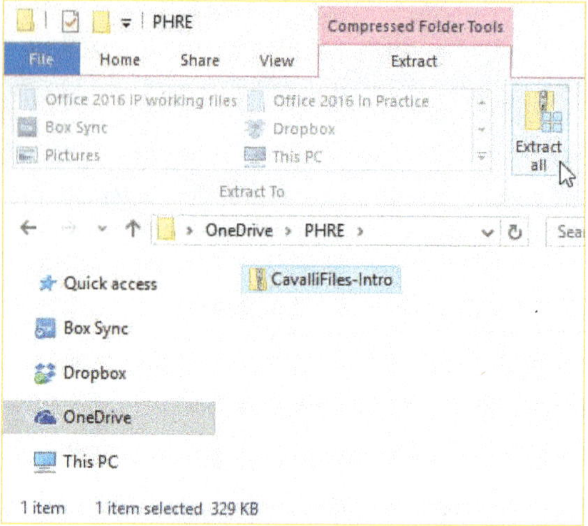

Intro-101 Extract a zipped folder

3. Move and rename files.
   a. With the *PHRE* folder still open, double-click the **CavalliFiles-Intro** folder to open it.
   b. Click the first file, press and hold the **Shift** key, and click the last file to select all four files.
   c. Press **Ctrl+X** or click the **Cut** button [*Home* tab, *Clipboard* group] to cut the files from the current location (Figure Intro-102).
   d. Click the **Up** arrow to move up to the *PHRE* folder.
   e. Press **Ctrl+V** or click the **Paste** button [*Home* tab, *Clipboard* group] to paste and move the files.
   f. Select the ***Cavalli files-Intro*** folder and press **Delete** to delete the folder.
   g. Select the ***CavalliPHRE-Intro*** file and click the **Rename** button [*Home* tab, *Organize* group].
   h. Type [your initials] Intro-1a and press **Enter**.
   i. Right-click the ***FixedMortgageRates-Intro*** file and select **Rename** from the context menu.
   j. Type [your initials] Intro-1b and press **Enter**.

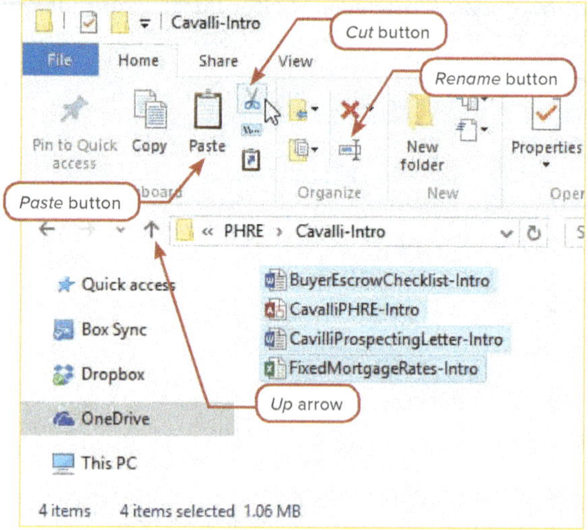

Intro-102 *Cut* files to move from a folder

4. Open two Word documents and rename a Word document.
   a. Press the **Ctrl** key and click the ***BuyerEscrowChecklist-Intro*** and ***CavalliProspectingLetter-Intro*** files to select both files.
   b. Press the **Enter** key to open both files in Word. If the files open in *Protected View*, click the **Enable Editing** button.
   c. Press the **Task View** button on your *Taskbar* (Figure Intro-103). All open windows display as tiles on your desktop.
   d. Select the ***BuyerEscrowChecklist-Intro*** document.
   e. Click the **File** tab to open the *Backstage* view and select **Save As** on the left.
   f. Click the **Browse** button to open the *Save As* dialog box.
   g. Type [your initials] Intro-1c in the *File name* text box and click **Save**. The file is saved in the *PHRE* folder.
   h. Click the **X** in the upper right corner of the Word window to close the document. The *CavalliProspectingLetter-Intro* document remains open.

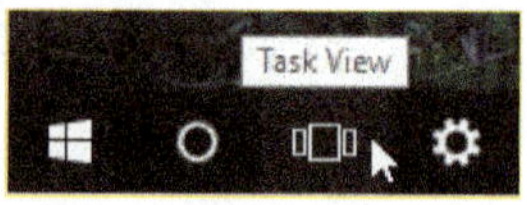

Intro-103 *Task View* button on the *Taskbar*

5. Change display size and edit and rename a Word document.
   a. Press the **Task View** button on your *Taskbar* and select the ***CavalliProspectingLetter-Intro*** document.

b. Click the **Zoom In** or **Zoom Out** button in the bottom right of the document window to change the display size to **120%** (Figure Intro-104).

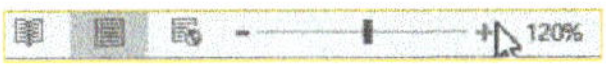

Intro-104 Use *Zoom* to change the display size to 120%

c. Select "**Placer Hills Real Estate**" in the first body paragraph of the letter and the mini toolbar displays (Figure Intro-105).

d. Click the **Bold** button on the mini toolbar to apply bold formatting to the selected text.

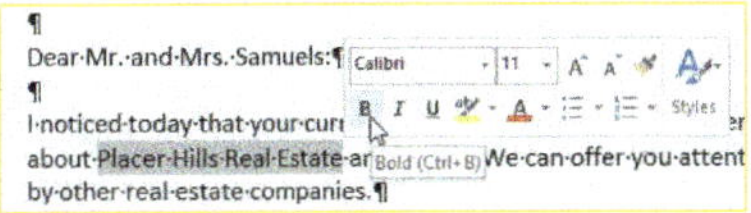

Intro-105 Use the mini toolbar to apply formatting

e. Select "**Whitney Hills resident**" in the first sentence in the second body paragraph and press **Ctrl+I** to apply italic formatting to the selected text.

f. Select the text that reads "**Emma Cavalli**," below "Best regards,".

g. Right-click the selected text and select **Font** from the context menu to open the *Font* dialog box.

h. Check the **Small Caps** box in the *Effects* area and click **OK** to close the *Font* dialog box.

i. With "**Emma Cavalli**" still selected, click the **Bold** button [*Home* tab, *Font* group].

j. Click the **File** tab, select **Save As** on the left, and click the **Browse** button to open the *Save As* dialog box.

k. Type [your initials] Intro-1d in the *File name* text box and click **Save**.

6. Export a Word document as a PDF file.

a. With the ***[your initials] Intro-1d*** still open, click the **File** tab to open the *Backstage* view.

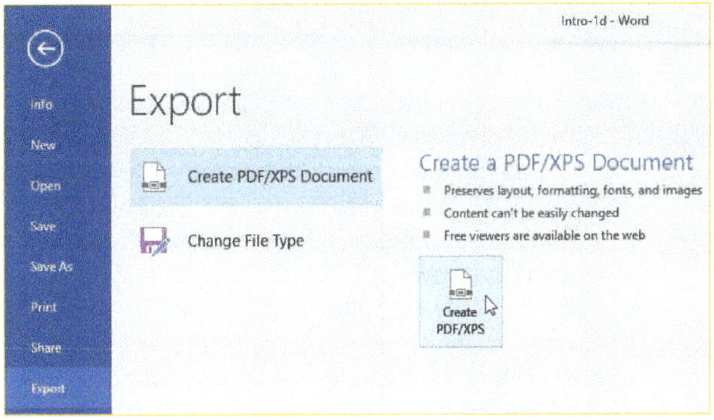

Intro-106 Export as a PDF file

b. Select **Export** on the left, select **Create PDF/XPS Document** in the *Export* area, and click the **Create PDF/XPS** button (Figure Intro-106). The *Publish as PDF or XPS* dialog box opens.

c. Deselect the **Open file after publishing** check box if it is checked.

d. Select the **Standard (publishing online and printing)** radio button in the *Optimize for* area.

e. Type [your initials] Intro-1e in the *File name* text box and click **Publish**.

f. Click the **File** tab to open the *Backstage* view and select **Save** on the left.

g. Click the **X** in the upper right corner of the Word window to close the document and Word.

7. Your *PHRE* folder should contain the files shown in Figure Intro-107.

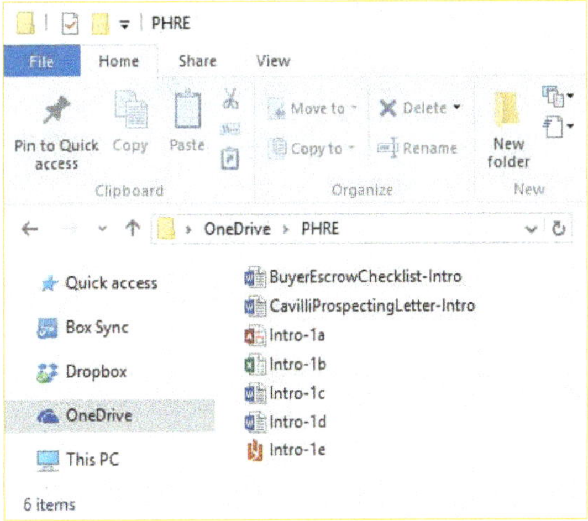

Intro-107 Intro-1 completed

Guided Project Intro-2

For this project, you modify an Excel file for Hamilton Civic Center. You create a folder, rename a file, add document properties, use *Tell Me* to search for a topic, share the file, and export a file as a PDF file. [Student Learning Outcomes Intro.1, Intro.2, Intro.3, Intro.5, Intro.6, Intro.7, Intro.8]

File Needed: ***HCCYoga-Intro.xlsx*** *(Student data files are available in the* Library *of your SIMnet account)*
Completed Project File Names: ***[your initials] Intro-2a.xlsx*** and ***[your initials] Intro-2b.pdf***

Skills Covered in This Project

- Open Excel and an Excel workbook.
- Create a new folder.
- Save an Excel workbook with a different file name.
- Add document properties to a file.
- Use *Tell Me* to search for a topic.
- Open a Word document.
- Share a file.
- Export a file as a PDF file.

1. Open Excel 2016 and open an Excel workbook.
   a. Click the Windows **Start** button and click **Excel 2016** to open this application. If Excel 2016 is not available on the *Start* menu, click the **Cortana** button on the *Taskbar*, type Excel, and then click **Excel 2016** in the search results to open it.
   b. From the Excel *Start* page, click **Open Other Workbooks** to display the *Open* area of the *Backstage* view.
   c. Click the **Browse** button to open the *Open* dialog box.
   d. Browse to the location where your student data files are stored, select the ***HCCYoga-Intro*** file, and click **Open** to open the Excel workbook. If the file opens in *Protected View*, click the **Enable Editing** button.
2. Save a file as a different file name in your *OneDrive* folder.
   a. Click the **File** tab to open the *Backstage* view and select **Save As** on the left.
   b. Click the **Browse** button to open the *Save As* dialog box.
   c. Select the **OneDrive** folder on the left and click the **New folder** button to create a new folder (Figure Intro-108). If *OneDrive* is not a storage option, select another location to create the new folder.
   d. Type HCC and press **Enter**.
   e. Double-click the **HCC** folder to open it.
   f. Type [your initials] Intro-2a in the *File name* area and click **Save** to close the dialog box and save the file.

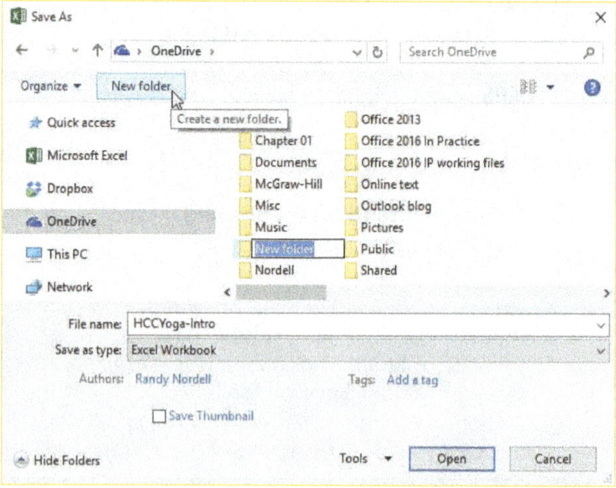

Intro-108 Create a new folder from the *Save As* dialog box

3. Add document properties to the Excel workbook.
   a. Click the **File** button to open the *Backstage* view and select **Info** on the left if it is not already selected. The document properties displays on the right.
   b. Place your insertion point in the *Title* text box ("Add a title") and type Yoga Classes as the worksheet title.

c. Click the **Show All Properties** link at the bottom of the list of properties to display more properties (Figure Intro-109).

d. Place your insertion point in the *Company* text box and type Hamilton Civic Center as the company name.

e. Click the **Back** arrow in the upper left of the *Backstage* window to return to the Excel workbook.

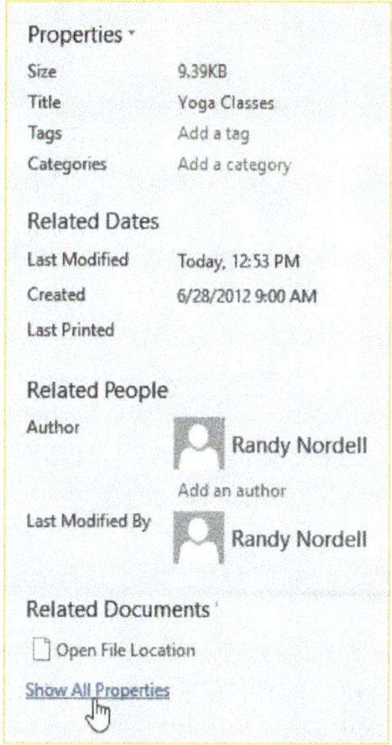

Intro-109 Add document properties

4. Use *Tell Me* to search for a topic.
   a. Click the **Tell Me** search box at the top of the *Ribbon* and type Cell formatting (Figure Intro-110).
   b. Select **Get Help on "Cell formatting"** to open the *Excel 2016 Help* dialog box.
   c. Click the first result link to display information about the topic.
   d. Click the **Back** arrow to return to the search list.
   e. Click the **X** in the upper right corner to close the *Excel 2016 Help* dialog box.

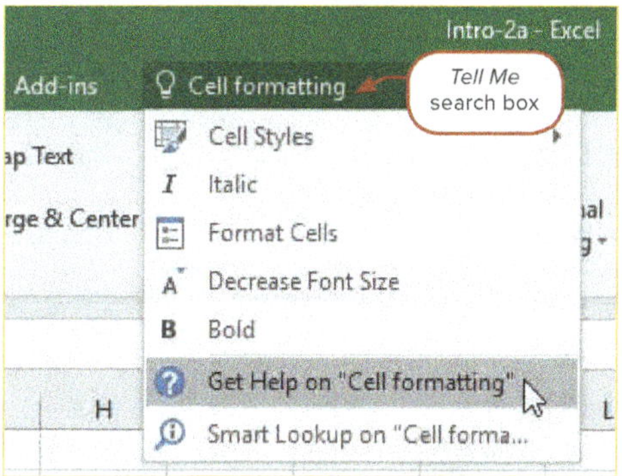

Intro-110 Use *Tell Me* to search for a topic

5. Share an Excel workbook with your instructor. If your file is not saved in *OneDrive*, skip step 5.
   a. Click the **Share** button in the upper right of the Excel worksheet. The *Share* pane opens on the right side of the worksheet (Figure Intro-111).
   b. Type your instructor's email address in the *Invite people* area.
   c. Select **Can edit** from the drop-down list below the email address if it is not already selected.
   d. Type a brief message in the body text box.
   e. Click the **Share** button.
   f. Click the **X** in the upper right corner of the *Share* pane to close the pane.
   g. Press **Ctrl+S** to save the worksheet.

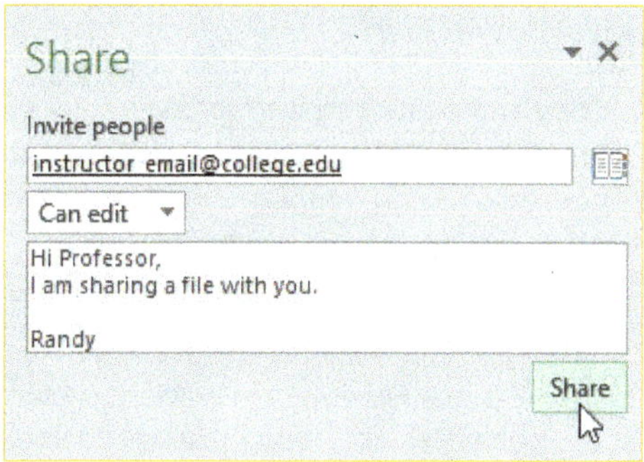

Intro-111 *Share* pane

6. Export an Excel file as a PDF file.
   a. Click the **File** tab to open the *Backstage* view.
   b. Select **Export** on the left, select **Create PDF/XPS Document** in the *Export* area, and click the **Create PDF/XPS** button (Figure Intro-112). The *Publish as PDF or XPS* dialog box opens.
   c. Deselect the **Open file after publishing** check box if it is checked.

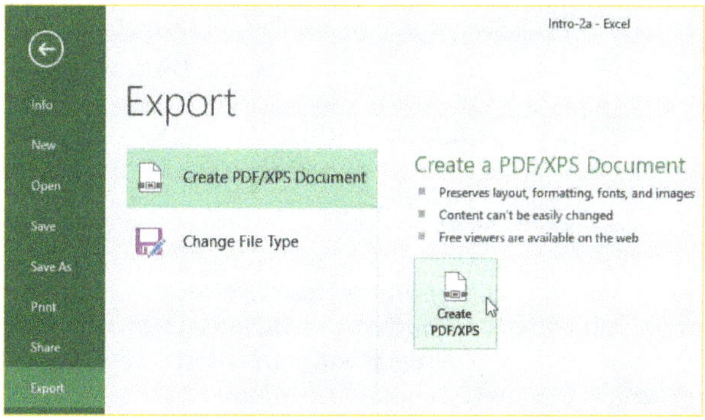

Intro-112 Export as a PDF file

d. Select the **Standard (publishing online and printing)** radio button in the *Optimize for* area.
e. Type [your initials] Intro-2b in the *File name* text box and click **Publish**.

7. Save and close the Excel file.
   a. Click the **File** tab to open the *Backstage* view and select **Save** on the left.
   b. Click the **X** in the upper right corner of the Excel window to close the file and Excel.

Independent Project Intro-3

For this project, you organize and edit files for Courtyard Medical Plaza. You extract a zipped folder, delete a folder, move files, rename files, export a file as a PDF file, and share a file.
[Student Learning Outcomes Intro.1, Intro.2, Intro.3, Intro.5, Intro.8]

File Needed: ***CMPFiles-Intro*** (zipped folder) *(Student data files are available in the* Library *of your SIMnet account)*
Completed Project File Names: ***[your initials] Intro-3a.pptx***, ***[your initials] Intro-3a-pdf.pdf***, ***[your initials] Intro-3b.accdb***, ***[your initials] Intro-3c.xlsx***, and ***[your initials] Intro-3d.docx***

Skills Covered in This Project

- Copy and paste a zipped folder.
- Create a new folder in your *OneDrive* folder.
- Extract a zipped folder.
- Delete a folder.
- Move a file.
- Rename a file.
- Open a PowerPoint presentation.
- Export a file as a PDF file.
- Open a Word document.
- Share a file.

1. Copy a zipped folder and create a new *OneDrive* folder.
   a. Open a *File Explorer* window, browse to locate the ***CMPFiles-Intro*** zipped folder in your student data files and copy the zipped folder.
   b. Go to your *OneDrive* folder and create a new folder named Courtyard Medical Plaza within the *OneDrive* folder. If *OneDrive* is not a storage option, select another location to create the new folder.
2. Paste a copied folder, extract the zipped folder, and move files.
   a. Paste the zipped folder in the *Courtyard Medical Plaza* folder.
   b. Extract the zipped folder and then delete the zipped folder.
   c. Open the ***CMPFiles-Intro*** folder and move all of the files to the *Courtyard Medical Plaza* folder.
   d. Return to the *Courtyard Medical Plaza* folder to confirm the four files were moved.
   e. Delete the ***CMPFiles-Intro*** folder.
3. Rename files in the *Courtyard Medical Plaza* folder.
   a. Rename the ***CMPStayingActive-Intro*** PowerPoint file to [your initials] Intro-3a.
   b. Rename the ***CourtyardMedicalPlaza-Intro*** Access file to [your initials] Intro-3b.
   c. Rename the ***EstimatedCalories-Intro*** Excel file to [your initials] Intro-3c.
   d. Rename the ***StayingActive-Intro*** Word file to [your initials] Intro-3d.
4. Export a PowerPoint file as a PDF file.
   a. From the *Courtyard Medical Plaza* folder, open the ***[your initials] Intro-3a*** file. The file opens in PowerPoint. If the file opens in *Protected View*, click the **Enable Editing** button.

b. Export this file as a PDF file. Don't have the PDF file open after publishing and optimize for **Standard** format.
c. Save the file as [your initials] Intro-3a-pdf and save in the *Courtyard Medical Plaza* folder.
d. Close the PowerPoint file and exit PowerPoint.

5. Share a file with your instructor. If your files are not saved in *OneDrive*, skip step 5.
   a. Return to your *Courtyard Medical Plaza* folder and open the ***Intro-3d*** file. The file opens in Word. If the file opens in *Protected View*, click the **Enable Editing** button.
   b. Open the *Share* pane.
   c. Type your instructor's email address and select **Can edit** from the permission drop-down list.
   d. Type a brief message and **Share** the file.
   e. Close the *Share* pane.
   f. Save and close the document and exit Word.
6. Close the *File Explorer* window containing the files for this project (Figure Intro-113).

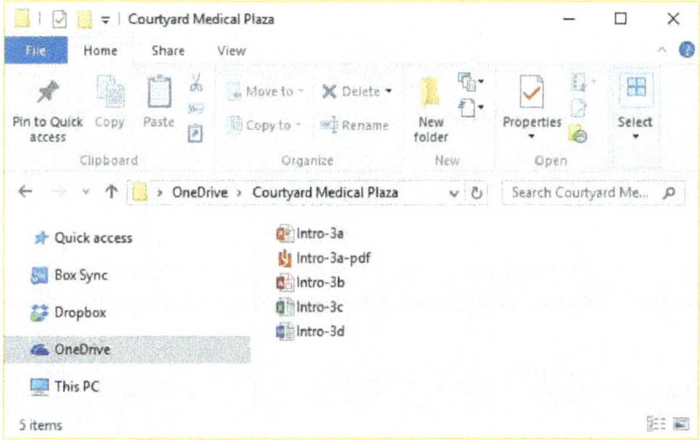

Intro-113 Intro-3 completed

Independent Project Intro-4

For this project, you modify a Word file for Life's Animal Shelter. You create a folder, rename a document, add document properties, modify a document, create a sharing link, export a document as a PDF file, and create a zipped folder.
[Student Learning Outcomes Intro.1, Intro.2, Intro.3, Intro.5, Intro.6, Intro.7, Intro.8]

File Needed: ***LASSupportLetter-Intro.docx*** *(Student data files are available in the* Library *of your SIMnet account)*
Completed Project File Names: ***[your initials] Intro-4a.docx***, ***[your initials] Intro-4b.pdf***, and ***LAS files*** (zipped folder)

Skills Covered in This Project

- Open a Word document.
- Create a new folder.
- Save a file with a different file name.
- Apply formatting to selected text.
- Add document properties to the file.
- Create a sharing link.
- Export a file as a PDF file.
- Create a zipped folder.

1. Open a Word document, create a new folder, and save the document with a different file name.
   a. Open Word 2016.
   b. From the Word *Start* page, open the ***LASSupportLetter-Intro*** document from your student data files. If the file opens in *Protected View*, click the **Enable Editing** button.
   c. Open the **Save As** dialog box and create a new folder named LAS in your *OneDrive* folder. If *OneDrive* is not a storage option, select another location to create the new folder.

d. Save this document in the *LAS* folder and use [your initials] Intro-4a as the file name.

2. Apply formatting changes to the document using a dialog box, keyboard shortcut, and mini toolbar.
   a. Select "**To**:" in the memo heading and use the launcher to open the *Font* dialog box.
   b. Apply **Bold** and **All caps** to the selected text.
   c. Repeat the formatting on the other three memo guide words "**From**:," "**Date**:," and "**Subject**:".
   d. Select "**Life's Animal Shelter**" in the first sentence of the first body paragraph and press **Ctrl+B** to apply bold formatting.
   e. Select the first sentence in the second body paragraph ("**Would you again consider** . . .") and use the mini toolbar to apply **italic** formatting.
3. Add the following document properties to the document:
   Title: Support Letter
   Company: Life's Animal Shelter
4. Get a link to share this document with your instructor and email your instructor the sharing link.
   a. Open the *Share* pane and click **Get a sharing link** at the bottom of the *Share* pane.
   b. Create an edit link to send to your instructor.
   c. Copy the edit link.
   d. Open the email you use for this course and create a new email message to send to your instructor.
   e. Type your instructor's email address, include an appropriate subject line, and type a brief message in the body of the email message.
   f. Paste (**Ctrl+V**) the sharing link in the body of the email message and send the message.
   g. Click the **Task View** button on the Windows *Taskbar* and select the ***Intro-4a*** document to display this document.
   h. Close the *Share* pane.
   i. Use the **Save** command on the *Quick Access* toolbar to save the file before continuing.
7. Export this document as a PDF file.
   a. Export this file as a PDF file. Don't have the PDF file open after publishing and optimize for **Standard** format.
   b. Save the file as [your initials] Intro-4b and save in the *LAS* folder.
   c. Save and close the document and exit Word.
8. Create a zipped folder.
   a. Using *File Explorer*, open the ***LAS*** folder in your *OneDrive* folder.
   b. Select the two files and create a zipped folder.
   c. Rename the zipped folder LAS files.
9. Close the open *File Explorer* window (Figure Intro-114).

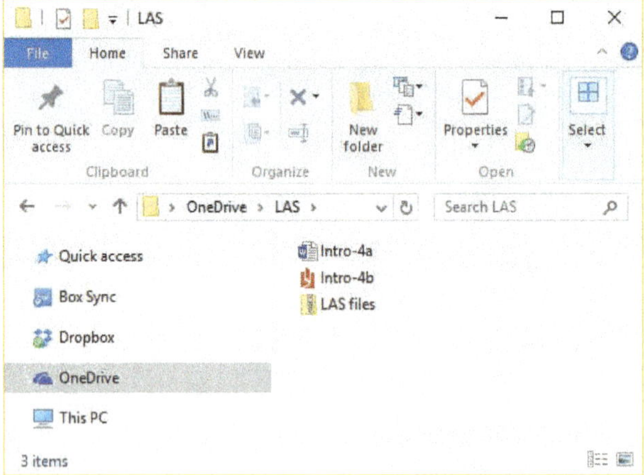

Intro-114 Intro-4 completed

Challenge Project Intro-5

For this project, you create folders to organize your files for this class and share a file with your instructor. [Student Learning Outcomes Intro.1, Intro.5, Intro.8]

Files Needed: Student data files for this course
Completed Project File Name: Share a file with your instructor

Using *File Explorer*, create *OneDrive* folders to contain all of the student data files for this class. Organize your files and folders according to the following guidelines:

- Create a *OneDrive* folder for this class.
- Create a *Student data files* folder inside the class folder.
- Copy and paste the student data files in the *Student data files* folder.
- Extract student data files and delete the zipped folder.
- Create a *Solution files* folder inside the class folder.
- Inside the *Solution files* folder, create a folder for each chapter.
- Create a folder to store miscellaneous class files such as the syllabus and other course handouts.
- Open one of the student data files and share the file with your instructor.

Challenge Project Intro-6

For this project, you save a file as a different file name, customize the *Quick Access* toolbar, share a file with your instructor, export a file as a PDF file, and create a zipped folder.
[Student Learning Outcomes Intro.1, Intro.2, Intro.3, Intro.5, Intro.6, Intro.8]

File Needed: Use an existing Office file
Completed Project File Names: ***[your initials] Intro-6a*** and ***[your initials] Intro-6b***

Open an existing Word, Excel, or PowerPoint file. Save this file in a *OneDrive* folder and name it [your initials] Intro-6a. If you don't have any of these files, use one from your Pause & Practice projects or select a file from your student data files.

With your file open, perform the following actions:

- Create a new folder on OneDrive and save the file to this folder using a different file name.
- Customize the *Quick Access* toolbar to add command buttons. Add commands such as *New*, *Open*, *Quick Print*, and *Spelling* that you use regularly in the Office application.
- Share your file with your instructor. Allow your instructor to edit the file.
- Export the document as a PDF file. Save the file as [your initials] Intro-6b and save it in the same *OneDrive* folder as your open file.
- Zip the files in the folder.

Microsoft® Office

IN PRACTICE

outlook

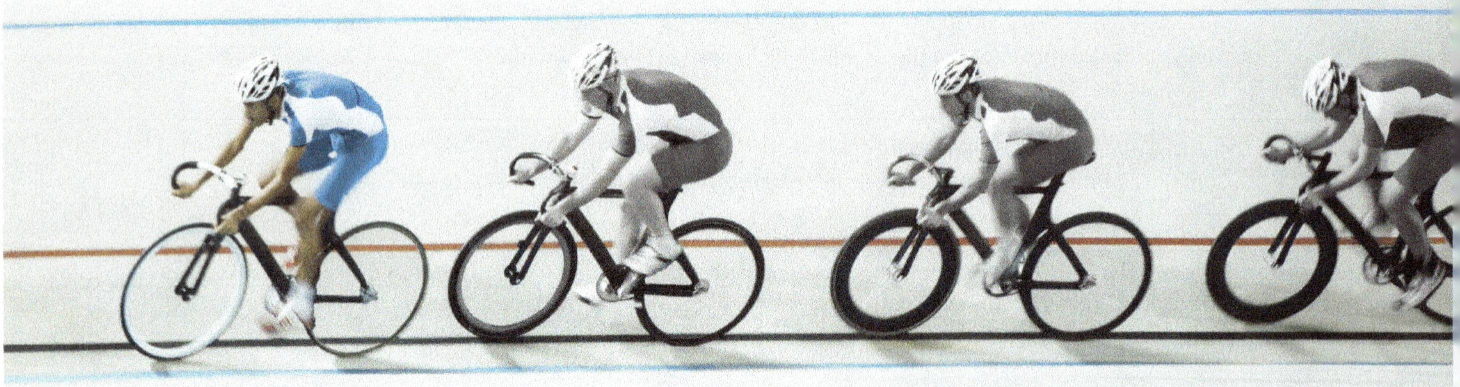

CHAPTER 1

Outlook Overview and Email Basics

OUTLOOK

CHAPTER OVERVIEW

Microsoft Outlook (usually referred to as ***Outlook***) is the most widely used email and personal management software today. It is used in both the business environment and as well as the personal and home environment. Outlook 2016 is part of the Microsoft Office 2016 suite of application software. This book covers the different aspects of Outlook and how this software is used to help manage your electronic communication, schedule your appointments and meetings, organize your personal and business contacts, and arrange your list of to-do items.

This first half of this book (Chapters 1–5) introduces you to the main features of Outlook. Once you complete the first half of the book, you will be proficient using the main features in Outlook. The remaining chapters cover each of these areas in depth and introduce you to the advanced aspects of Outlook. As you read each chapter and complete the projects, you will become an Outlook expert at home and at work.

Today, most people equate Microsoft Outlook with email, and these two terms have become almost synonymous in their use. Email is an integral part of Outlook, but Outlook is much more than just email which you will discover as you study each chapter. Almost everyone uses email on a daily basis, and Outlook is widely used in both the business and home environment to manage email accounts. It is important to remember that Outlook is not email but rather a computer software program that handles email accounts. Just as your mail carrier is not the mail itself but rather the person who delivers your mail to your home mailbox, Outlook delivers email received through your existing email account(s). Outlook requires you to create an email account to send and receive email.

Outlook enables you to create and send email, reply to received email, forward email to other recipients, save and manage email, and flag and categorize email. Email is one method of sending pictures and other types of computer files to others. Email is an integral part of personal and business activities, and it is hard to imagine a day without the use of an email program.

STUDENT LEARNING OUTCOMES (SLOs)

After completing this chapter, you will be able to:

- **SLO 1.1** Identify the basic components of Microsoft Outlook 2016 (p. O1- 3).
- **SLO 1.2** Navigate throughout the Outlook environment and identify the different panes in the Outlook window (p. O1-7).
- **SLO 1.3** Distinguish between Outlook being used as a stand-alone program and in a Microsoft Exchange environment (p. O1-14).
- **SLO 1.4** Distinguish between the different types of email accounts and set up an email account in Outlook (p. O1-14).
- **SLO 1.5** Use Outlook to create, send, and receive email (p. O1-17).
- **SLO 1.6** Use attachments in email (p. O1-29).
- **SLO 1.7** Differentiate email arrangements and icons (p. O1-34).
- **SLO 1.8** Explain the importance and process of cleaning up an Inbox (p. O1-37).

CASE STUDY

Throughout this book you have the opportunity to put into practice the application features that you are learning. Each chapter begins with a case study that introduces you to the Pause & Practice projects in the chapter. These Pause & Practice projects give you a chance to apply and practice key skills. Each chapter contains three to five Pause & Practice projects.

Central Sierra Insurance (CSI) is a multi-office insurance company that handles all lines of commercial and personal insurance policies. As a thriving and growing insurance agency, Central Sierra regularly hires qualified personnel to enhance their sales and support staff. CSI encourages its employees to be active in community organizations and events.

Pause & Practice 1-1: You set up an email account using Microsoft Outlook. You will need an email account that is provided by your school or a free email service such as gmail.com or outlook.com.

Pause & Practice 1-2: You send an email message to your instructor and use the *Cc* function to send a copy to yourself. You also read the message, reply to it, and print it for your records.

Pause & Practice 1-3: You reply to a message with an email attachment. You also forward the message to your instructor as an attachment and delete a message.

SLO 1.1

Working with Outlook

One of the main features in Outlook is handling email, but Outlook is so much more! It is personal management software that contains the following features:

- *Email*
- *Calendar*
- *Contacts*
- *Tasks*
- *Notes*
- *Journal*

Microsoft Outlook 2016 combines the email, calendar, contacts, tasks, notes, and journal features into personal management software (Figure 1-1). Each of the Outlook features operate independently; yet they integrate seamlessly. Outlook also integrates with Microsoft Word, Excel, Access, and other Microsoft products.

Email

Email is the commonly used term for ***electronic mail*** (Figure 1-2). Outlook provides users the capability of creating, sending, and receiving email. Outlook manages a single email account or multiple email accounts. In Outlook, email is activated by clicking the **Mail** button.

MORE INFO

Chapter 2 covers the special email features available in Outlook. Chapter 6 discusses the use of rules for handling both incoming and outgoing email, and Chapter 7 provides the reader with information about setting up the different types of email accounts.

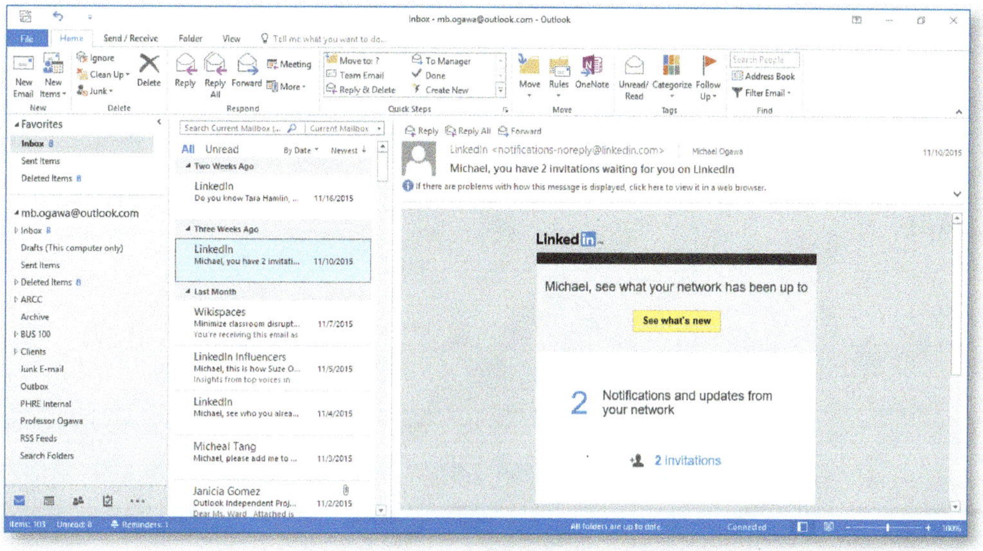

1-1 Outlook interface

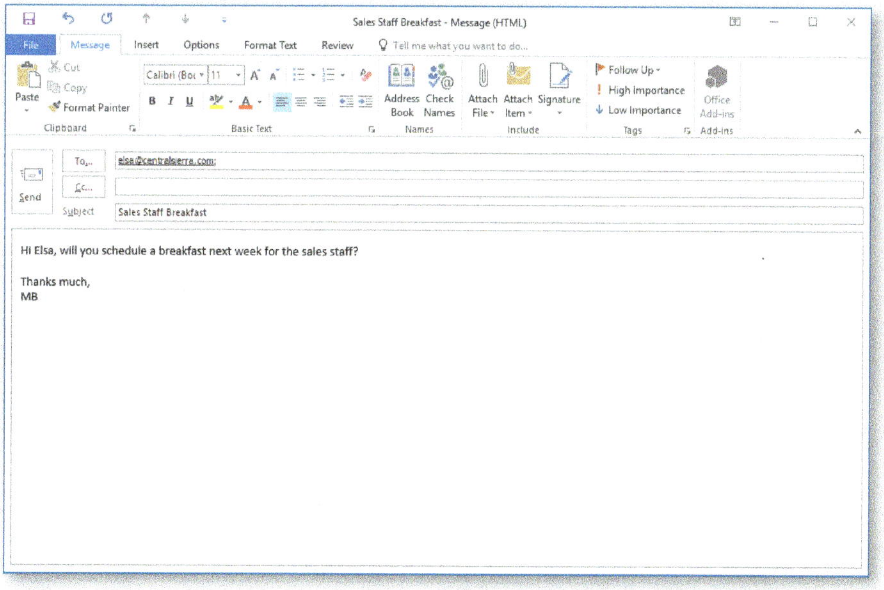

1-2 Email message

Calendar

Calendars organize daily, weekly, and monthly schedules. You may use a daily planner, a calendar that hangs on your wall at home or at work, or a smart phone to manage your daily activities. Outlook Calendar (Figure 1-3) is an electronic calendar for scheduling appointments or events. Outlook Calendar also replicates calendar entries, records electronic reminders, sends meeting requests, and shares calendar entries with other Outlook users or other devices.

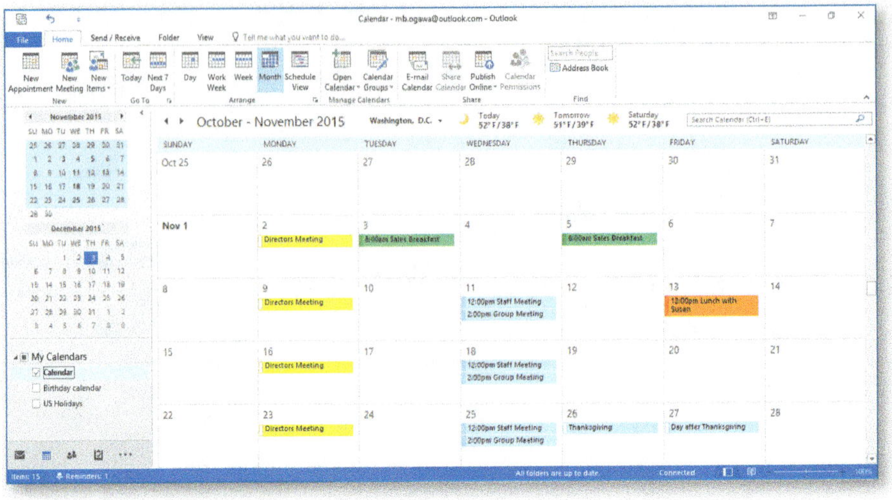

1-3 Outlook calendar

Another advantage of an Outlook calendar is that you can synchronize your work and home calendars. As the popularity of multifunction (smart) cell phones increases, the potential to have your Outlook calendar synchronized between your work, home, and cell phone is not only a reality but also commonplace for working professionals.

> **MORE INFO**
>
> Outlook Calendar is covered in Chapters 4 and 9 of this text.

Contacts

Outlook also provides an area to manage names, email addresses, phone numbers, and other information about business contacts, coworkers, friends, and family. Similar to the way the Outlook calendar replaces the old paper calendar, Outlook ***Contacts*** (Figure 1-4) allows you to electronically store personal information. It functions as a database, which is a collection of information. One of the many benefits of Outlook Contacts is creating, deleting, and managing contacts without being required to understand the structure and components of the database.

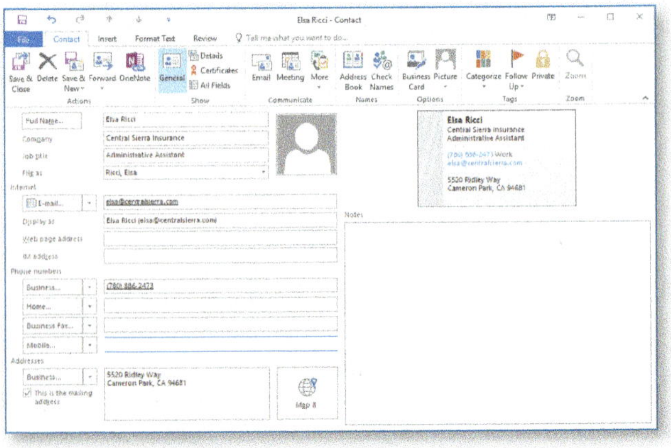

1-4 Outlook contact

Use Contacts to save personal and company information

in Outlook and also when populating a recipient list in an email, meeting request, or tasks request.

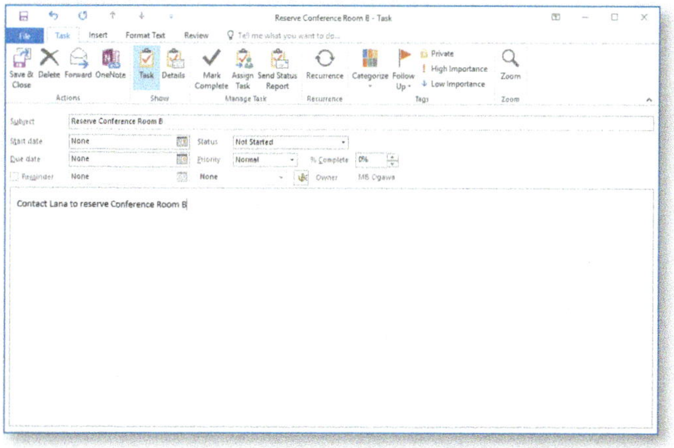

1-5 Outlook task

Tasks

Are you a list person? Do you constantly have a list of things to complete today or this week? Outlook provides a method of tracking tasks and projects that need to be completed through the use of Outlook Tasks. The ***Tasks*** (Figure 1-5) function is very similar to a notepad that you use to write down your to-do items and then cross them off as they are completed. Tasks are included in the Outlook ***To-Do List***, which lists both tasks and emails that have been flagged for action.

Four advantages of using Outlook Tasks are listed here:

- Tasks are electronic and are shared between computers and cell phones.
- Many details, which are not typically written down on a piece of paper, can be added to a task.
- Create reminders to alert you to an upcoming due date and time for a task.
- Assign Tasks to another Outlook user.

> **MORE INFO**
>
> Outlook tasks and to-do items are covered in Chapter 5.

Notes

Outlook ***Notes*** (Figure 1-6) are used to keep track of information that does not necessarily or neatly fall into the category of a calendar item, contact, or task. Do you ever end the day with a pocket full of scraps of paper with notes and reminders? Do you have sticky notes stuck to your computer monitor or refrigerator? Outlook Notes functions like electronic sticky notes—actually, they look just like them. Notes are an excellent way of storing information such as a username and password to log into a web site, gift ideas for family and friends, or a list of books you'd like to read.

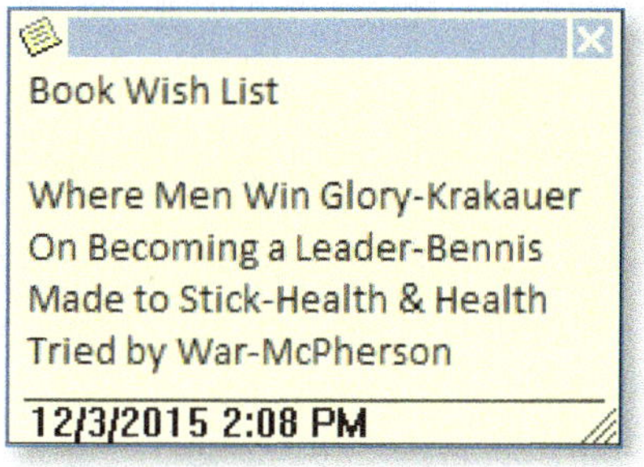

1-6 Outlook note

> **MORE INFO**
>
> Outlook Notes is covered in Chapter 10.

Journal

Outlook ***Journal*** (Figure 1-7) tracks the amount of time spent working on a particular document or project. The journal is primarily used in the business environment and enables you to associate specific Microsoft Office documents with a journal entry.

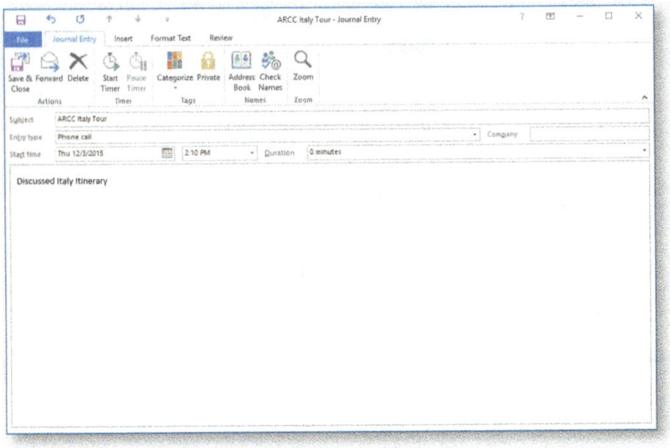

1-7 Outlook journal

> **MORE INFO**
>
> Chapter 10 introduces you to using Outlook Journal and provides you with ideas of how this feature might be used in the business setting.

SLO 1.2

Navigating Outlook

The Outlook working environment (Figure 1-8) has a much different look and feel than that of Microsoft Word, Excel, PowerPoint, and Access. The Outlook user interface is divided into multiple sections, called ***panes***. When working with different items such as email messages in Outlook, you select them by clicking each item. Selected items are typically highlighted in blue.

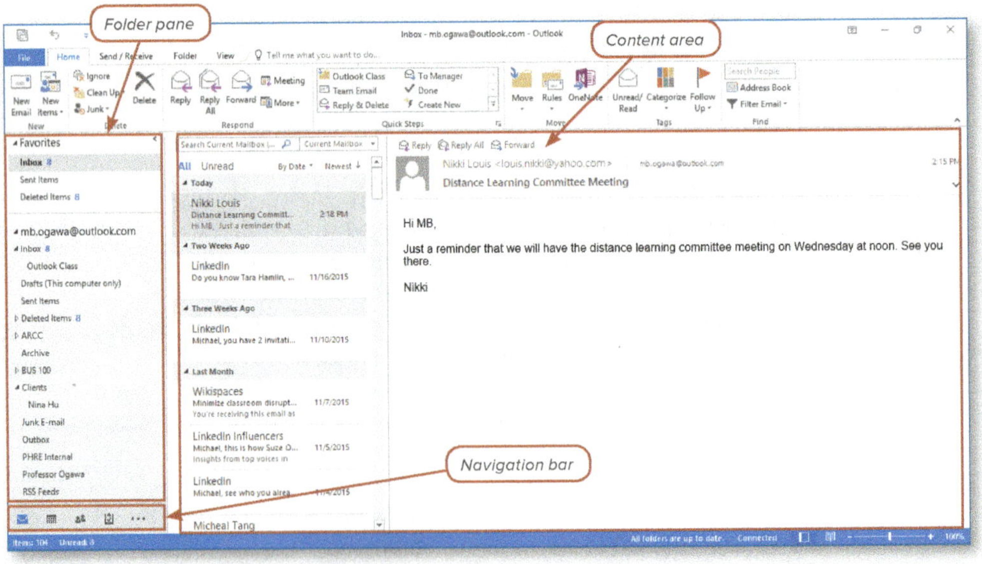

1-8 Outlook environment

As you work through this book and use Outlook, you will become familiar with the Outlook user interface and the different panes available. Outlook provides consistency throughout this program to allow you to quickly become comfortable navigating through its working environment.

Outlook Today

Outlook Today (Figure 1-9) is an introductory screen that provides you with information about your Inbox and other email folders, current calendar items, and upcoming tasks. *Outlook Today* displays in the *Folder* pane and is the default view when you open Outlook. *Outlook Today* can be customized to meet your personal needs.

MORE INFO

By default the Navigation Bar displays four icons and a Navigation Options button (. . .). To switch the display from icons to text, follow these steps: Click the **Navigation Options** button, and select **Navigation Options** to display the Navigation Options dialog box. Deselect the Compact Navigation check box and click **OK.** The Navigation Bar changes to a text display. Chapter 5 provides more information about customizing *Outlook Today*.

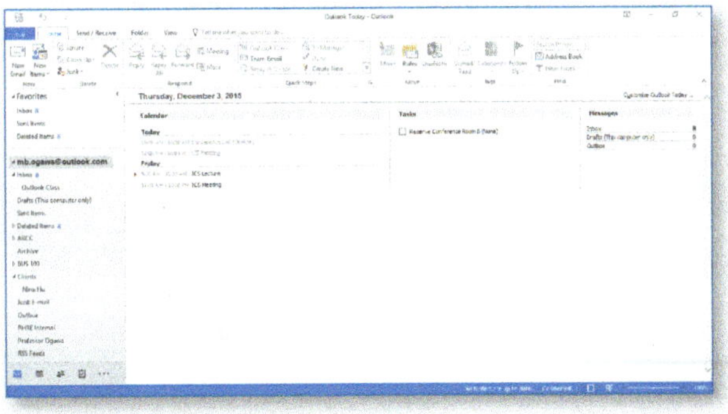

1-9 *Outlook Today*

Outlook Panes

The Outlook program window is divided into panes. The number and type of panes displayed varies for each Outlook view.

The ***Folder pane*** (Figure 1-10) is located on the left side of the Outlook window, and it contains folders for organizing your Outlook items. The contents of the *Folder* pane change based on the selected view. The main features of Outlook–Mail, Calendar, People, and Tasks are represented by icons in the Navigation Bar located at the bottom of the *Folder* pane. Click an icon to change views quickly and easily. Click the **Navigation Options** button (. . .) to display a list of Navigation options including Notes and Folders. You can use the keyboard shortcuts listed in Another Way to quickly navigate the Outlook window.

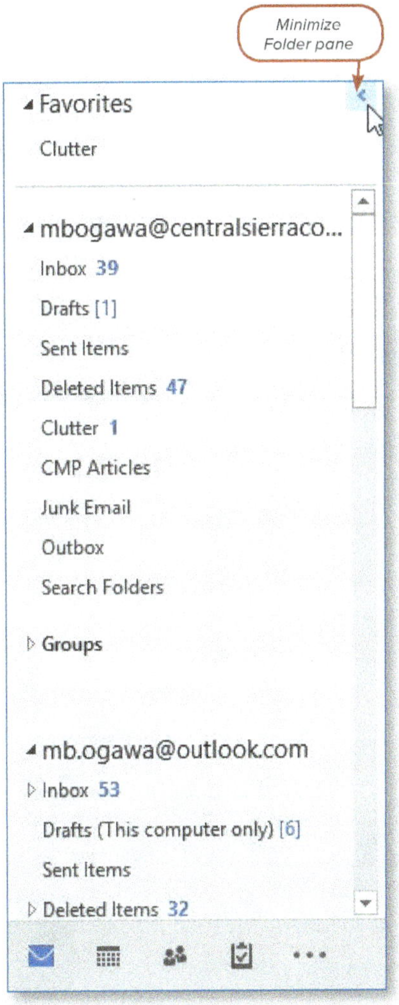

1-10 *Folder* pane

ANOTHER WAY

Mail: **Ctrl+1**
Calendar: **Ctrl+2**
Contacts: **Ctrl+3**
Tasks: **Ctrl+4**
Notes: **Ctrl+5**
Folder list: **Ctrl+6**
Shortcuts: **Ctrl+7**
Journal: **Ctrl+8**

You control the appearance of the Outlook window by selecting a view to display in the *Folder* pane. Click an icon in the Navigation Bar to change the Outlook view. Adjust the width of the *Folder* pane to increase or decrease the size of the selected view. Click the Minimize the Folder Pane button to increase the working area of the Outlook window.

HOW TO: Adjust the Width of the Folder Pane

1. Click and hold the right border of the *Navigation* pane (Figure 1-11).
2. Drag the border to the left or right as desired.

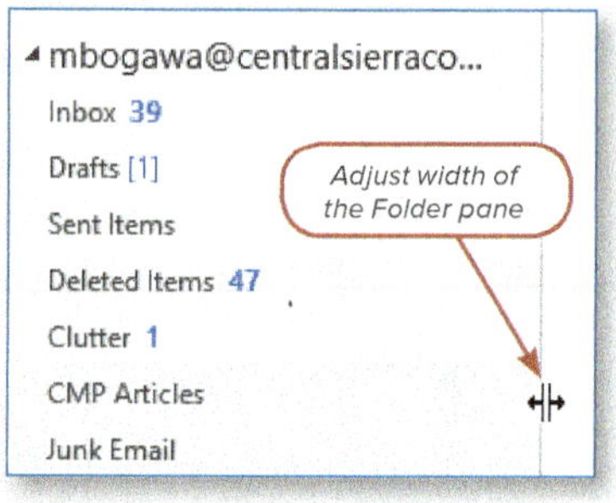

1-11 Resize the *Folder* pane

The ***Reading pane*** (Figure 1-12) is an optional pane that is available in most of the main features in Outlook, although it is primarily used with the *Mail* feature. The *Reading* pane displays the contents of the item selected in the *Folder* pane or content area. The *Reading* pane can be set to appear below or to the right of the *Folder* pane, or it can be turned off from the *View* tab. The *Reading* pane will vary depending on the task (e.g., Mail, Calendar, or Contacts) selected in the *Folder* pane.

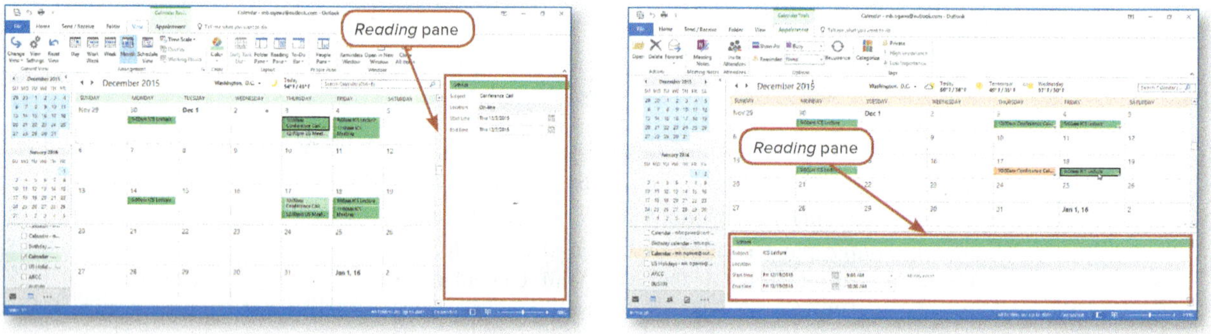

1-12 *Reading* pane displayed in the Calendar

HOW TO: Change the Location of the Reading Pane

1. Click the **Mail** button in the *Navigation* bar.
2. Click the **View** tab.
3. Click the **Reading Pane** button in the *Layout* group.
4. Choose the desired location: *Right*, *Bottom*, or *Off* (see Figure 1-13).

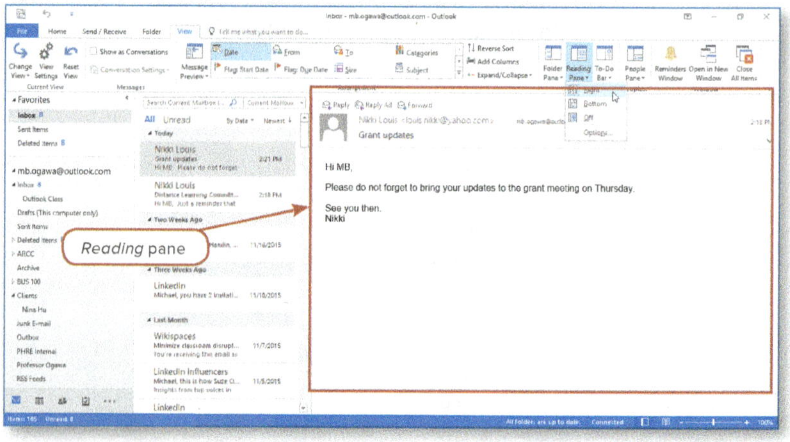

1-13 *Reading* pane

The *Reading* pane can also be resized in the same manner as the *Folder* pane. Move the boundary to the desired height or width by clicking and holding the top edge (when the *Reading* Pane displays at the bottom) or the left edge (when the *Reading* pane displays at the right).

The ***People pane*** (Figure 1-14) provides a collection of information associated with the sender including communication history, meeting requests, and attachments. Expand or collapse the *People* pane by clicking the Minimize the Folder button in the upper right corner of the *Folder* pane.

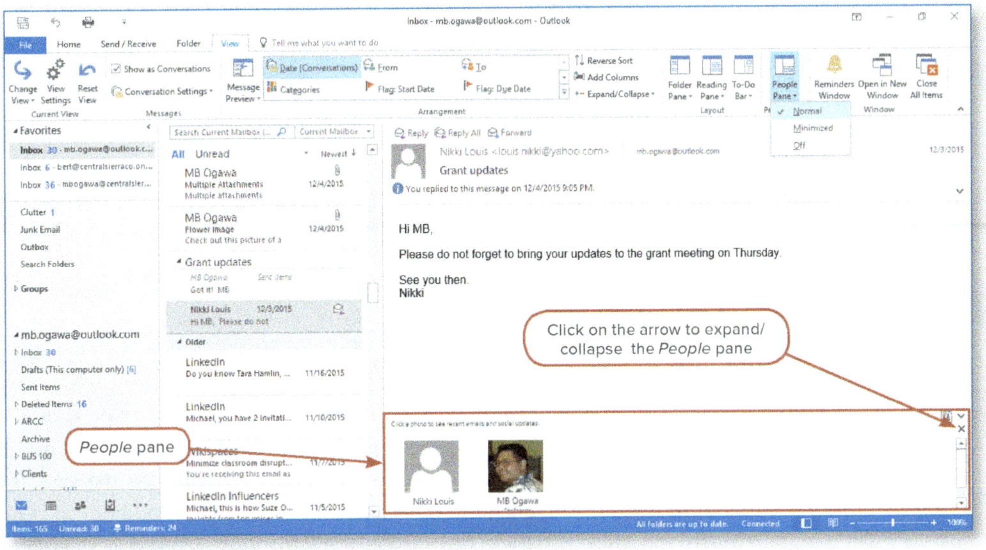

1-14 *People* pane

The *People* pane is not only available on the main interface of Outlook but also on email messages, meetings, contacts, and task requests. The *People* pane consolidates all activities associated with an individual into one area. The links in the *People* pane open an associated Outlook item.

> **MORE INFO**
>
> The *People* pane is covered in Chapters 2 and 3.

The Ribbon, Tabs, and Dialog Boxes

The main working environment in Outlook 2016 has a ***Ribbon*** (Figure 1-15), which includes a variety of ***tabs.*** The *Ribbon* appears at the top of the Outlook window and at the top of any open Outlook item (e.g., email, calendar item, contact, or task). Each tab has a variety of groups, and groups contain buttons, drop-down lists, and galleries.

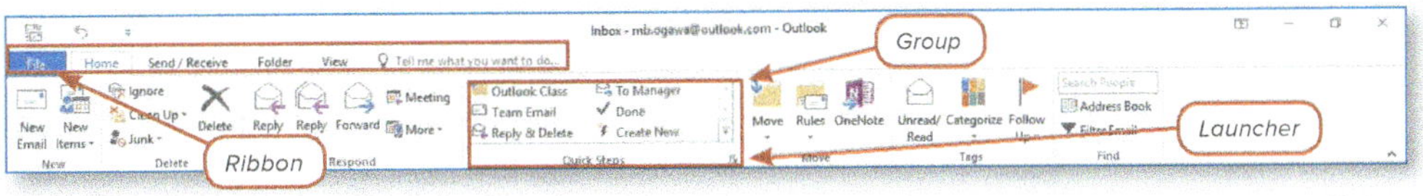

1-15 Outlook *Ribbon*

MORE INFO

Collapse the *Ribbon* by pressing **Ctrl+F1** or click the small up arrow in the upper right corner of the Outlook window. When the *Ribbon* is minimized, you can restore it by pressing **Ctrl+F1** or by clicking the small up arrow in the upper right corner of the Outlook window and selecting **Show Tabs and Commands**.

As you move your pointer over a button on the *Ribbon*, ***ScreenTips*** (Figure 1-16) appear that tell you what that button represents and provide a shortcut key combination if available.

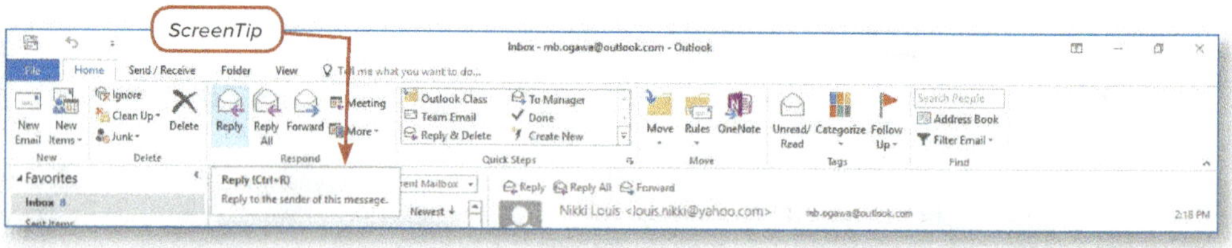

1-16 *ScreenTip*

Tabs are ***context sensitive***, which means that the choices of tabs and the content of the tabs change based on the Outlook item or Folder you select. Each tab is divided into ***groups*** where the size of the buttons in each group will vary depending on the size of the open window.

A few groups on each tab have a ***launcher*** button at the bottom right corner of the group. When you click the *launcher* button, a ***dialog box*** (Figure 1-17) opens. The opened dialog box contains additional options for the selected group.

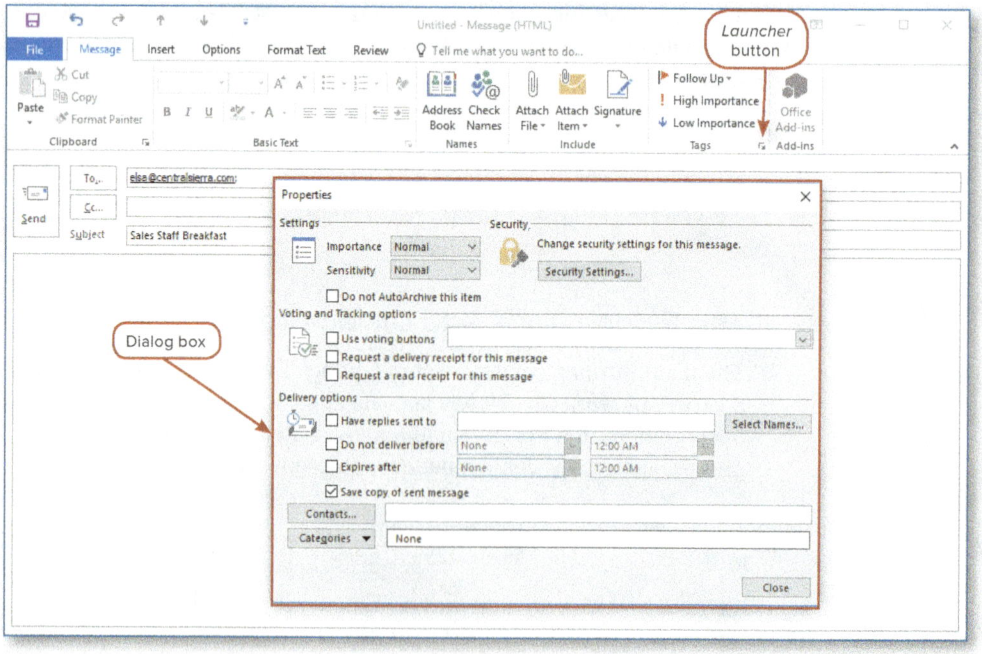

1-17 Dialog box

> **MORE INFO**
>
> The name of the dialog box is not always the same as the name of the group that was expanded. Some dialog boxes contain features that are distributed between a few groups.

> **MORE INFO**
>
> Many of the dialog boxes that you will use in Outlook 2016 are the same as or very similar to the dialog boxes used in previous versions of Outlook.

Views

Each of the features in Outlook (Mail, Calendar, Contacts, Tasks, Notes, and Journal) has preset views. The selected view controls how the folder selected in the *Folder* pane displays in the Outlook window. You can also create custom views.

HOW TO: Change to a Different View

1. Click the **View** tab.
2. Click the **Change View** button [*Current View* group] (Figure 1-18).

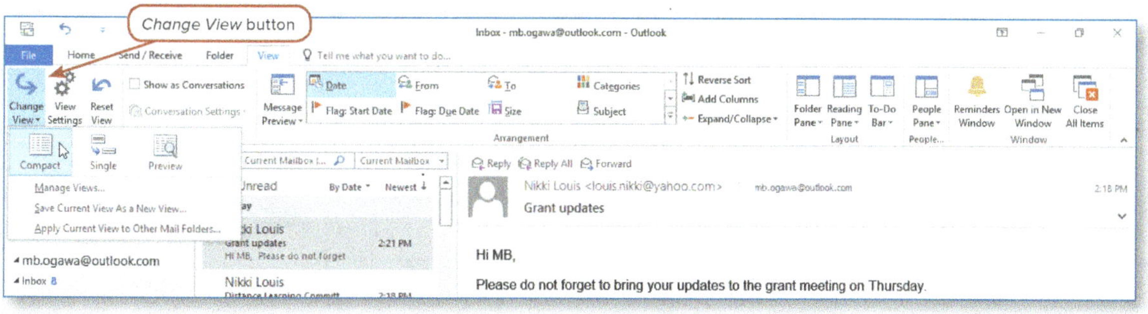

1-18 ***Change View*** **button**

3. Select the view you want. Notice the different views available; the different views are context sensitive.

Folder List

The ***Folder list*** (Figure 1-19) displays all the folders available in Outlook in the *Folder* pane. To display the Folder list, click the Navigation Options button [. . .] in the Navigation bar, and click Folders. The benefit of viewing the *Folder* list is that you can see all folders available in the folder hierarchy in which they reside, rather than viewing just one set of folders at a time. Use this view to move folders up or down a level or to drag specific items into a folder.

> **ANOTHER WAY**
>
> **Ctrl+6** displays the *Folder* list in the *Folder* pane. Additionally, you can press **Ctrl+Y** to select any folder.

> **MORE INFO**
>
> The *Folder* list is covered more thoroughly in Chapter 6 where we start using multiple folders for email, contacts, and tasks.

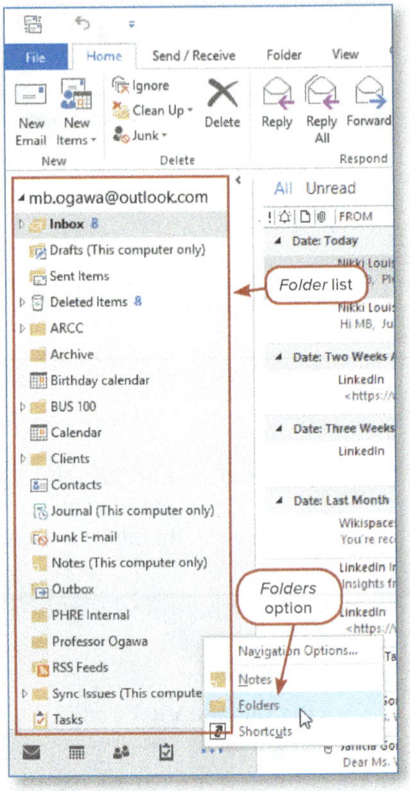

1-19 *Folder list*

Tell Me What You Want to Do. . .

New to Outlook 2016 is the ***Tell me what you want to do . . .*** feature (Figure 1-20). This feature is an alternative to the ***Outlook Help*** in previous versions of the software. As you type keywords related to your search, results display immediately and you can choose options available in Outlook, Outlook Help, or Smart Search. Each character you type further refines your search. The options in Outlook perform functions. Outlook Help provides additional information about your search. Smart Search performs an Internet search for your query, which can include background information, an image search, and a web search.

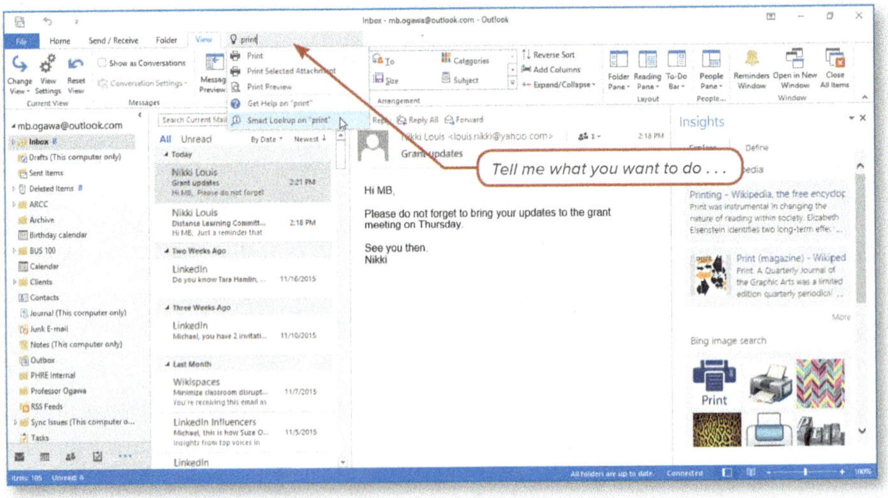

1-20 *Tell me what you want to do . . .* feature

> **MORE INFO**
>
> The **F1** function key on your computer keyboard opens the *Outlook Help* dialog box, which may be familiar if you used a previous version of Outlook.

SLO 1.3

Understanding Outlook Environments

Microsoft Outlook can be configured as either a ***stand-alone program*** or in conjunction with a Microsoft Exchange Server (also referred to as an ***Exchange server*** or Exchange). Many individuals use Outlook on their home computer without connecting to an *Exchange server;* this is what is meant by a stand-alone program. Outlook is still part of the Microsoft Office 2016 suite of software and is capable of performing all the main functions of this personal management software.

Outlook as a Stand-Alone Program

When using Outlook in the home or personal environment, Outlook connects directly with your ***Internet service provider*** (***ISP***) and manages your email through the accounts you set up. Outlook can handle a single email account or multiple email accounts. Advanced and specialty features in Outlook are only available when Outlook is used in conjunction with Exchange.

> **MORE INFO**
>
> Chapter 1 shows you how to set up an email account in Outlook. Managing multiple email accounts is covered in Chapter 7.

Outlook in an Exchange Environment

In the business environment, Microsoft Outlook is typically connected to a ***Microsoft Exchange Server***. Exchange on a business network handles all the incoming and outgoing mail. Each individual user of Exchange is actually a client of the Exchange network, and the network administrator sets up an account for each individual user. In addition to handling email, Exchange also stores all the data associated with calendars, contacts, tasks, notes, and journals.

Outlook in an Exchange environment has the same user interface as in a stand-alone environment, but Outlook with an Exchange server does allow you more functionality. An Exchange server will enable you to perform enhanced features such as:

- Using voting buttons and tracking responses
- Sending meeting requests and tracking responses
- Recalling messages
- Sharing your calendar, contacts, tasks, and email with others
- Using *MailTips*
- Using a common global contact list

> **MORE INFO**
>
> As you progress through this book, you will be informed when Outlook performs functions differently when using Outlook as a stand-alone program or with Exchange. Also, Appendix D provides a summary of Outlook features unique to an Exchange environment.

SLO 1.4

Adding an Email Account in Outlook

Multiple email accounts can be configured in Outlook. In previous versions of Outlook, only one Exchange account could be connected, but Outlook 2016 enables you to set up multiple Exchange accounts. Four types of email accounts can be configured in Outlook, and Outlook provides you with an ***Auto Account Setup Wizard*** to walk you through the process of adding an email account to Outlook.

Types of Email Accounts

Microsoft Exchange accounts are used primarily in medium to large business settings. These email accounts are set up through the company network or email administrator. An Exchange account has an individual mailbox assigned to each user and resides on an Exchange file server. Outlook connects to the Exchange server to retrieve your email. Exchange accounts use Messaging Application Programming Interface (MAPI) and provide enhanced functionality when used with Outlook. Recalling messages, tracking voting responses, and sharing Outlook with others on your Exchange system are features that are associated with Exchange accounts and Outlook.

POP3 accounts are Internet email accounts that are associated with your Internet service provider (ISP). If you have an ISP such as Comcast or AT&T, you have an email account (or multiple email accounts) through your provider. This POP3 account can be configured in Outlook to send and receive email. When using Outlook with this type of account, your email messages are downloaded to Outlook.

IMAP accounts are also Internet accounts but are not always associated with an ISP. IMAP accounts create folders on a server to store and organize messages for retrieval by other computers and give you the options to read message headers only and to select which messages to download. These types of accounts are becoming increasingly popular as personal email accounts. Gmail is an example of an IMAP email account.

HTTP accounts use the hypertext transfer protocol used on the web to create, view, send, and receive messages.

Add an Email Account

To create, send, and receive email, Outlook must be set up to recognize your email account. In the past, it has been a challenge to get all the specific information needed to set up an email account, but beginning with Outlook 2007, an ***Auto Account Setup*** (Figure 1-21) feature was added to automatically detect the incoming and outgoing server.

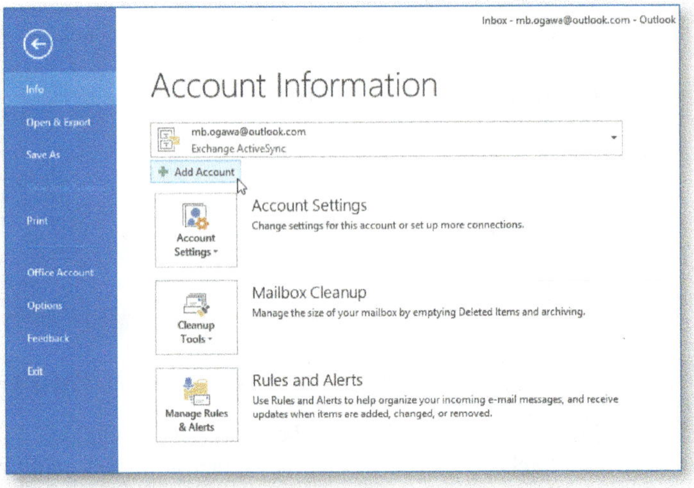

1-21 Account set up

To set up your account, you will need to supply your email address and password to access the account. This gives Outlook the location of your Exchange or Internet mailbox, and your password provides access to the account. An account only needs to be set up once, and it will be stored in Outlook for future use.

MORE INFO

The first time you open Outlook, you will be prompted to set up an account. The *Add New Account* dialog box automatically opens for you.
Outlook will automatically detect the type of email account being configured.

HOW TO: Set Up an Email Account

1. Click the **File** tab. The *Backstage* view opens.
2. Click the **Add Account** button. The *Add Account* dialog box opens (Figure 1-22).
3. Enter the following account settings in the text boxes:
   - *Your Name* (as you want it to appear in email)
   - *E-mail Address*
   - *Password*
   - *Retype Password*
4. Click **Next**. Outlook will automatically detect your email account and validate it with your password. Three green check marks display when your account has been configured properly (Figure 1-23).
5. Click **Finish** and you're ready to use Outlook.

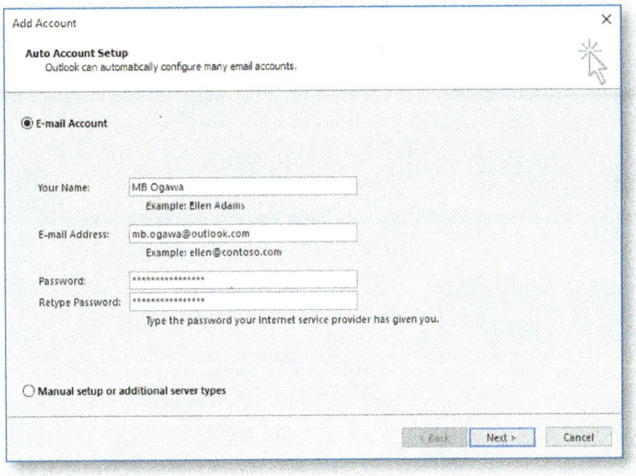

1-22 *Add Account* dialog box

MORE INFO

You may need to speak with your instructor or system administrator for details when adding your account.

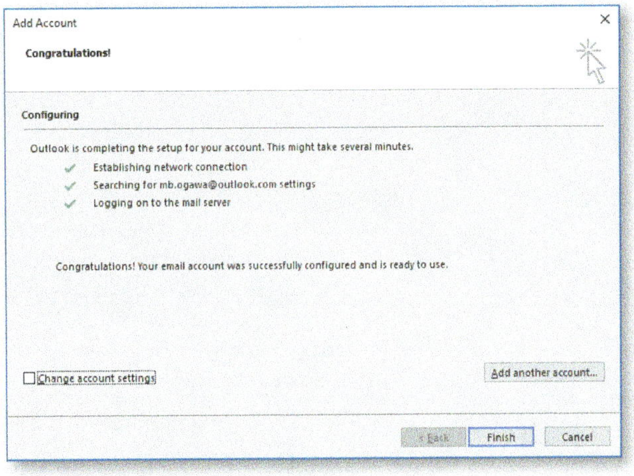

1-23 Successful configuration of an account

MORE INFO

Chapter 7 provides additional information on setting up multiple email accounts.

ANOTHER WAY

An email account can be added to Outlook when Outlook is closed by clicking **Mail** and then on **Email Accounts** on your computer's *Control Panel.*

PAUSE & PRACTICE: OUTLOOK 1-1

For this Pause and Practice project, you set up an email account using Microsoft Outlook. If you do not have an email account, you can set one up using a free service, such as Outlook (outlook.com) or Gmail (gmail.com).

Files Needed: None

1. Launch Outlook 2016.
2. Open the *Add Account* dialog box. If you are opening Outlook for the first time, a *Welcome to Microsoft Outlook 2016* dialog box displays. Click **Next** to begin the *Microsoft Outlook Account Setup.*
   a. Click the **File** tab to open the *Backstage* view and select **Info**.
   b. Click the **Add Account** button.
3. Input your account information.
   a. Type your name, email address, and password in the appropriate fields.
   b. Click **Next**. If you are using a school email account, you may need to contact your system administrator for the manual setup information.

SLO 1.5

Creating, Sending, and Receiving Email

Creating and sending an email message is very similar to sending a letter—just much easier and quicker! You select recipients, type the subject of the message, type the message, and send—no stamp or going to the post office.

ANOTHER WAY

Ctrl+N opens a new email message when you are in Outlook *Mail.*

MORE INFO

When you click the **New** button or press **Ctrl+N**, Outlook creates a new item of the task selected in Outlook. For example, if you select *Calendar* in the *Navigation* bar and click **New**, you get a new calendar appointment.

Create New Email

To create a new email message, make sure the *Mail* button (Figure 1-24) is selected in the *Navigation* bar and then click the **New Email** button in the *New* group on the *Home* tab. Outlook opens a new email message (Figure 1-25).

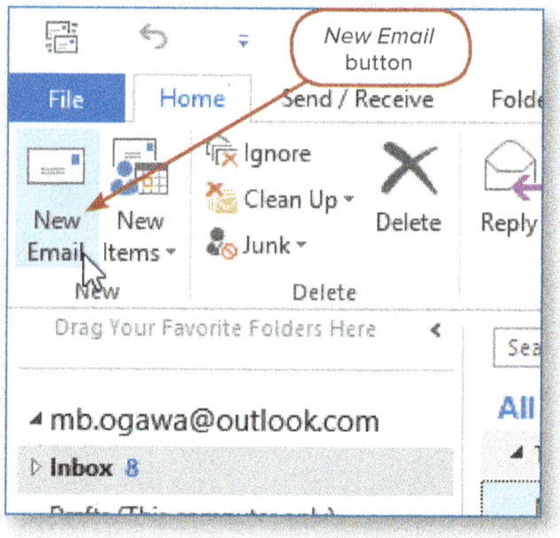

1-24 *New Email* button

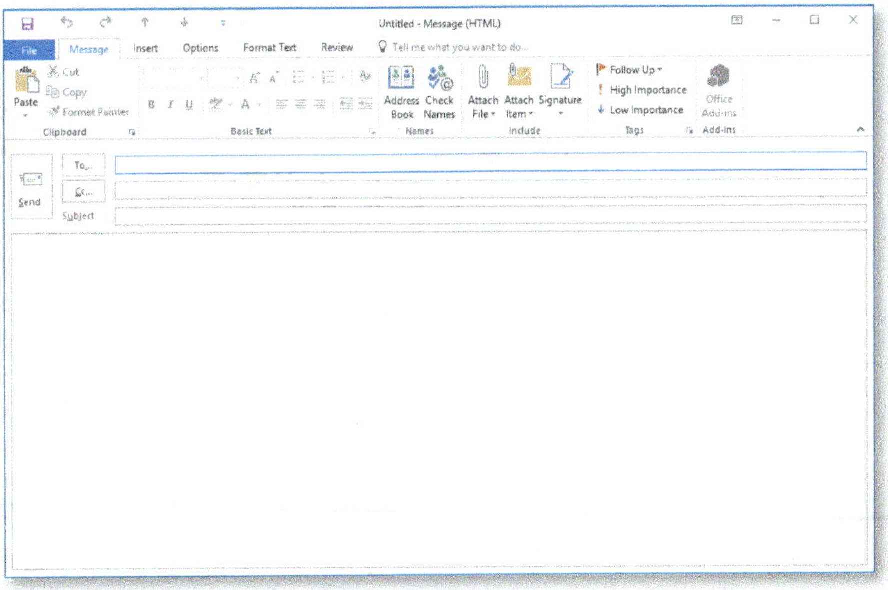

1-25 New email message

Select Recipients

An email message can be addressed to one recipient or multiple recipients. Type the email address into the ***To*** field or click the **To** button and select from your *Contact* list. If you are typing the email addresses, separate each email address with a semicolon (**;**).

When you click the *To* button (Figure 1-26), Outlook opens your *Contacts*. Choose a single recipient or select multiple recipients

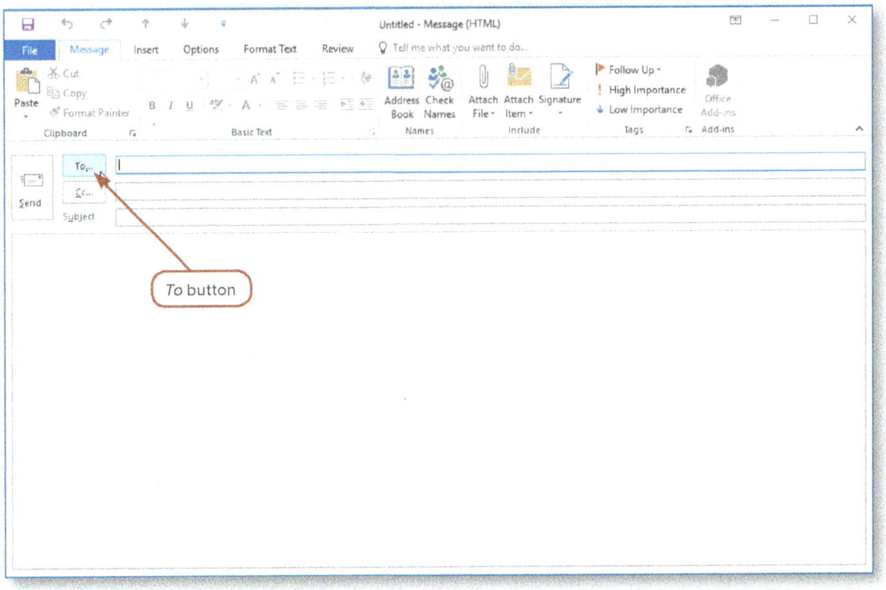

1-26 Select the *To* button

HOW TO: Select Recipients

1. Click the **Mail** button in the *Navigation* bar.
2. Click the **New Email** button to open a new email message.
3. Click the **To** button on the new email message. The *Select Names* dialog box opens.
   - You can also type an email address in the *To* field.
4. Select recipient(s) (Figure 1-27).
5. Click the **To** button below the names.
6. Click **OK** to close the *Select Names* dialog box.

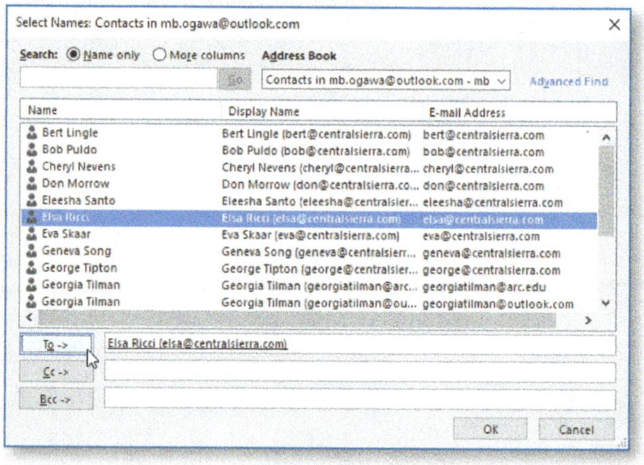

1-27 Select recipients from contacts list

ANOTHER WAY

When selecting multiple recipients from the contact list, Pressing the **Ctrl** key while clicking selects nonadjacent entries. Pressing the **Shift** key selects a range of recipients. To select an adjacent range of recipients, click the first item in the range, press the **Shift** key, and select the last item in the range. These shortcuts are common throughout many of the Microsoft Office applications.

Cc and Bcc

Two other options that are available when selecting recipients for your email message: ***Carbon Copy (Cc)*** and ***Blind carbon copy (Bcc)*** (Figure 1-28). *Cc* is used when someone is not the main recipient of the message, but they need to be kept informed of the contents of the message or ongoing email discussion.

Bcc is used when you do not want those receiving the email message to see other recipients' email addresses or names. When a recipient receives an email, he or she will be able to see other recipients' names and email addresses in both the *To* and *Cc* fields, but the *Bcc* field is hidden.

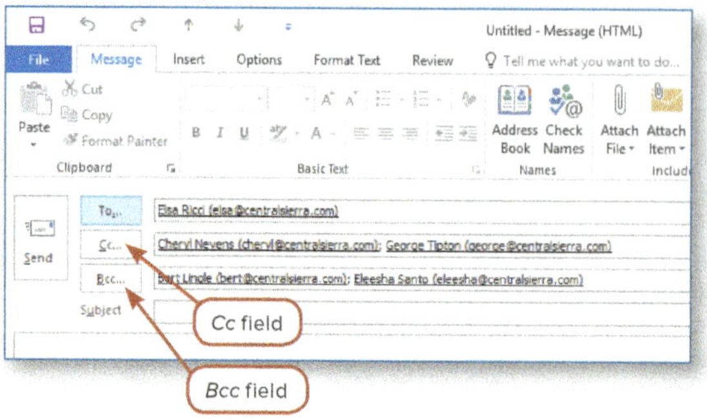

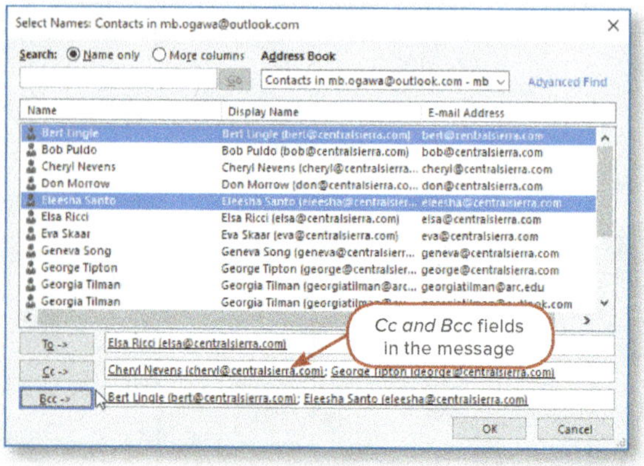

1-28 Select recipients in the *Cc* and *Bcc* fields

MORE INFO

Be careful about sharing email addresses with those outside your organization. *Bcc* is a great feature to provide confidentiality in email by hiding others' email addresses. To send an email, there must be at least one recipient in one of the recipient fields.

The *Cc* button appears on a new message and can be used like the *To* button to select recipients. By default, the *Bcc* button or field is not available when you open a new email message. Click either the *To* or *Cc* button to open the *Select Names* dialog box. Once this dialog box is open, the *Bcc* field is available.

ANOTHER WAY

In a new email message, click the **Options** tab and then click the **Bcc** button in the *Show Fields* group. *Bcc* recipients can now be selected by clicking the **Bcc** button (Figure 1-29).

Subject Line and Body

The ***Subject line*** alerts recipients to the subject of the email, and the ***body*** contains the contents of the email (Figure 1-29). When a new email message is created, the email is untitled (top center), but once a subject is typed, it becomes the message title.

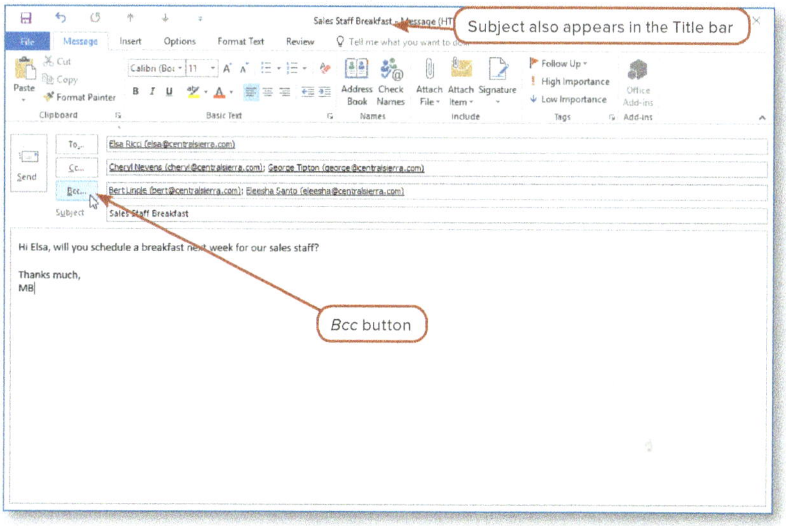

1-29 Select the *Bcc* button

MORE INFO

Use a subject line on every email, and keep it short and descriptive. Your subject line might determine whether or not your message gets read.

Format Text

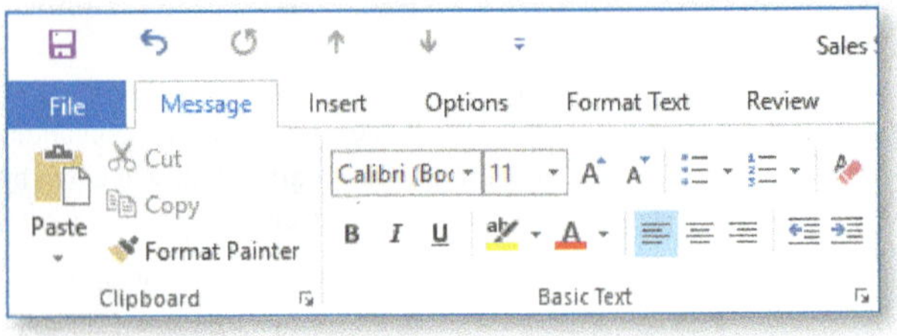

1-30 Formatting options

Outlook provides users with many of the same formatting features that are available in Microsoft Word. These text formatting features can be used in the body of the email message. Many of the commonly used formatting features are available on the *Message* tab in the *Basic Text* group (Figure 1-30). Expand the *Basic Text* group by clicking the *launcher* in the bottom right corner of the group. The Font dialog box opens.

More formatting options are available by clicking the **Format Text** tab, which opens this tab for additional formatting features (Figure 1-31).

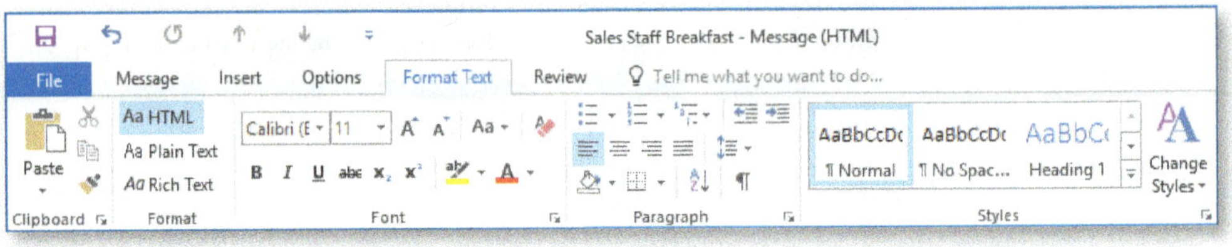

1-31 Additional formatting options

MORE INFO

Be careful to not overdo it with text formatting in the body of an email message. Depending on the type of email account the recipient has, text formatting might not be visible to the recipient.

Send an Email

Once you select your recipients and type the subject and body of the email, you are ready to send the email message. Click the **Send** button to the left of the *To* and *Cc* buttons and your email message will be sent. A copy of it will be automatically saved in the ***Sent Items*** folder in your *Folder* list.

▸HOW TO: Send an Email Message

1. Click the **New Email** button [*Home* tab, *New* group]. A new email message opens in a new window.
2. Click the **To** button and select the names or email addresses from the *Select Names* dialog box.
   - You can also add recipients to the *Cc* and *Bcc* fields.
3. Click **OK**. The email addresses will appear in the *To, Cc,* and/or *Bcc* fields.
4. Type a brief subject in the *Subject* field.

5. Type a brief message in the body of the message. Remember to always include your name in the body of the email.
6. Click **Send** (Figure 1-32).

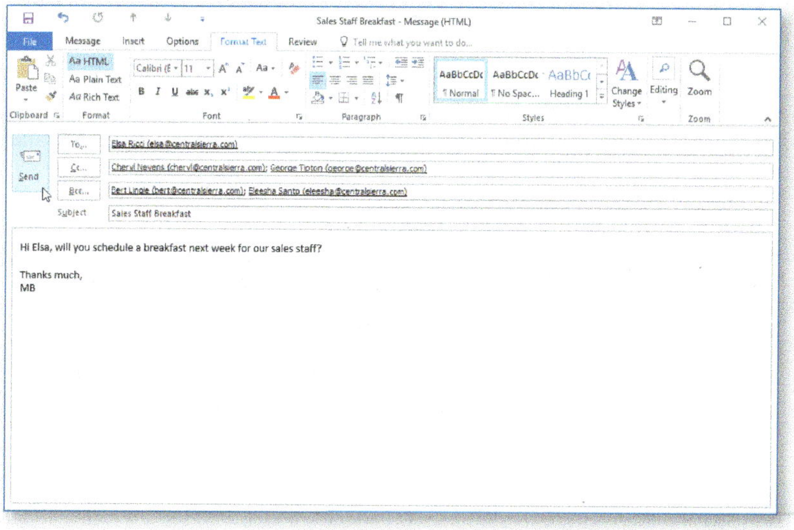

1-32 Sample email message

MORE INFO

Be careful about the information you include in an email message. An email can easily be forwarded to others, which can have ethical and confidentiality implications.

Save an Email Draft

If you are working on an email and do not have time to finish it or would like to look it over later before sending it, you can save and close the message. When you save a message in Outlook, it is stored in the ***Drafts*** folder in the *Folder* list.

To save an unfinished message, click the **Save** button on the ***Quick Access*** toolbar or press **Ctrl+S**. Microsoft Office Outlook automatically saves all unfinished messages for you. By default, unfinished messages are saved to your *Drafts* folder every three minutes (Figure 1-33). You can, however, change this time interval or location.

MORE INFO

Changing the default time interval for saving drafts is covered in Chapter 8.

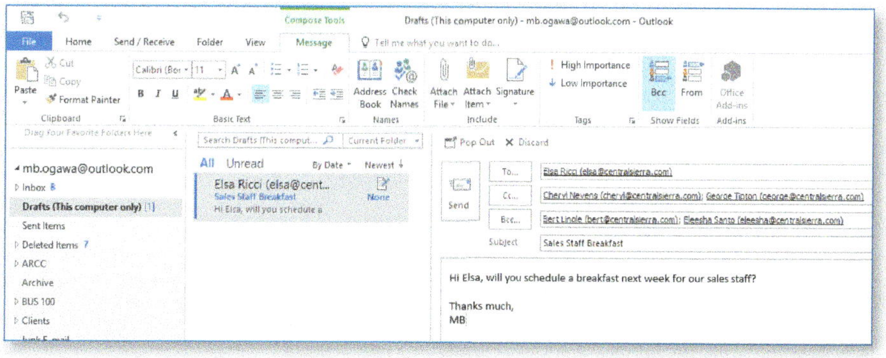

1-33 Saved draft message

Open an Email

To open an email in your Inbox, double-click the message. The message opens in a new window. Outlook provides users with a *Reading* pane, which allows the message to be read without opening it in a new window. To view the message in the *Reading* pane, click once on the message in the *Folder* pane and the contents of the message displays in the *Reading* pane (either to the right or at the bottom).

> **ANOTHER WAY**
>
> **Ctrl+O** opens a selected email from the *Folder* or *Reading* pane in a new window.

> **MORE INFO**
>
> Throughout this text when you are asked to open an email, use a new window; do not just view it in the *Reading* pane. Double-click an email in the *Folder* pane to open it.

Reply, Reply All, and Forward

When responding to an email, you have three main options: *Reply, Reply All,* and *Forward.* Use ***Reply*** to send a message to the original sender (Figure 1-34). ***Reply All*** sends a response to the sender and the other email recipients (those in the *To* and *Cc* lines). ***Forward*** enables you to send the email message you received to recipients of your choice.

Unlike previous versions, Outlook 2016 creates replies and forwarded messages within the Outlook window. If you prefer to write replies in a new window, click the **Pop Out** button in the reply message.

Both *Reply* and *Reply All* keep the same body and subject line. The body text moves down to make room for your message, and the subject is preceded by "RE:" to indicate this email is a reply. Either the original sender (*Reply*) or the sender and other recipients (*Reply All*) will automatically be in the *To* or *Cc* lines. When using *Reply All, Bcc* recipients are not included. The difference when using *Forward* is the *To* field will be empty and the subject includes "FW:" in front of the subject (Figure 1-35).

To use any of the response options, open the email and choose either *Reply*, *Reply All*, or *Forward. Another Way* includes keyboard shortcuts to help you quickly manage email.

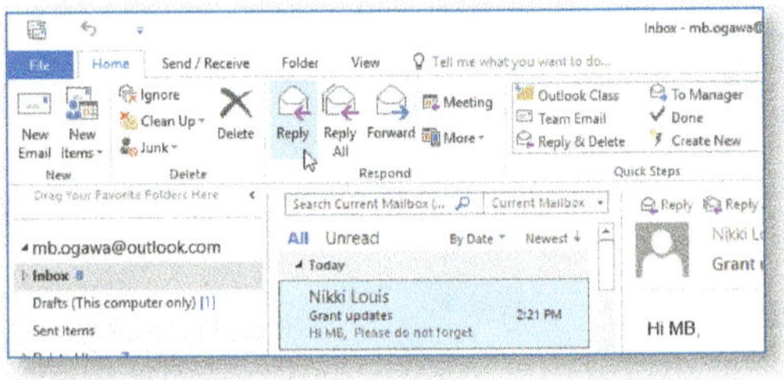

1-34 Reply to a message

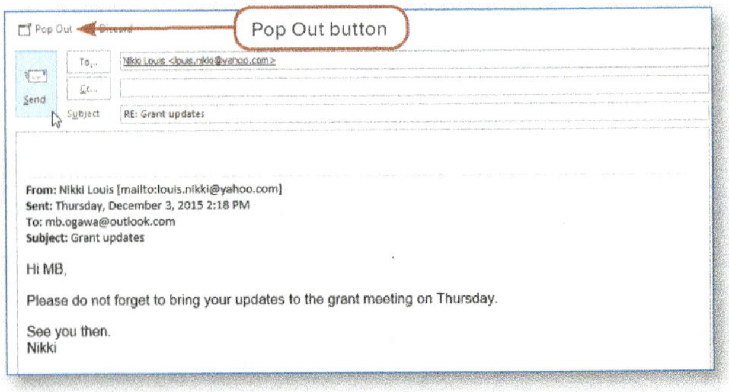

1-35 Sample reply message

ANOTHER WAY

Reply: **Ctrl+R**
Reply All: **Ctrl+Shift+R**
Forward: **Ctrl+F**

MORE INFO

When viewing a message in the *Folder* or *Reading* pane, the *Reply, Reply All,* and *Forward* buttons are located in the *Respond* group on the *Home* tab. Clicking any of these buttons opens the message.

MORE INFO

Use *Reply All* sparingly and only when it is absolutely necessary. Don't unnecessarily clutter up others' email Inboxes.

Save an Email in a Windows Folder

When an email message is sent, the original message remains in your Inbox and a copy of the message is automatically saved in the *Sent Items* folder. There are times when you want to save an important or sensitive email message outside Outlook. You can save email messages to a different folder on your computer.

HOW TO: Save an Email in a Windows Folder

1. Click the message to be saved in the *Folder* pane or open the message in a new window.
2. Click the **File** tab. The *Backstage* view opens.
3. Click the **Save As** button to open the *Save As* dialog box (Figure 1-36).
4. Browse to the desired location to save the file.
   - By default, the *File name* will be the subject line of the email. You can change this as desired.
5. Click the **Save** button.

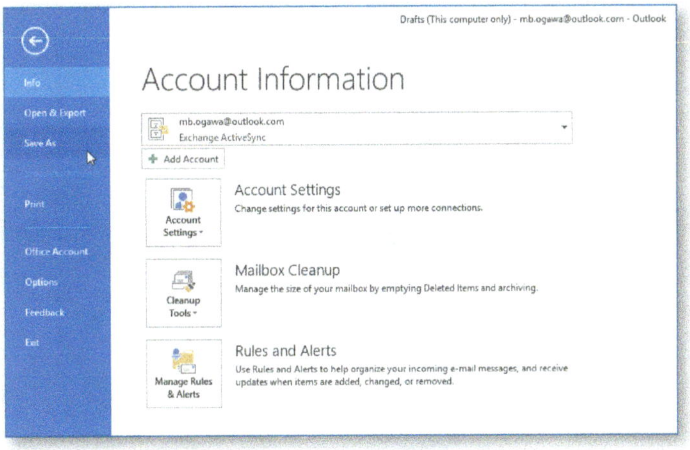

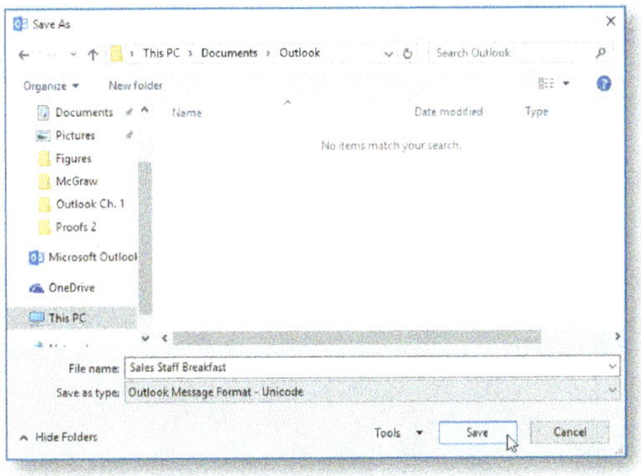

1-36 Save a message dialog box

ANOTHER WAY

F12 opens the *Save As* dialog box.

Print an Email

If you are on your way to a meeting and need additional information from an email in your Inbox, you might want to print the email to take with you. Also, you might want to print the contents of one of your Inbox folders. The *Print* option in Outlook prints either an individual email in ***Memo Style*** or the contents of a folder in ***Table Style***.

HOW TO: Print an Email

1. Select the email or folder to be printed.
2. Click the **File** tab to open the *Backstage* view.
3. Click the **Print** button (Figure 1-37).

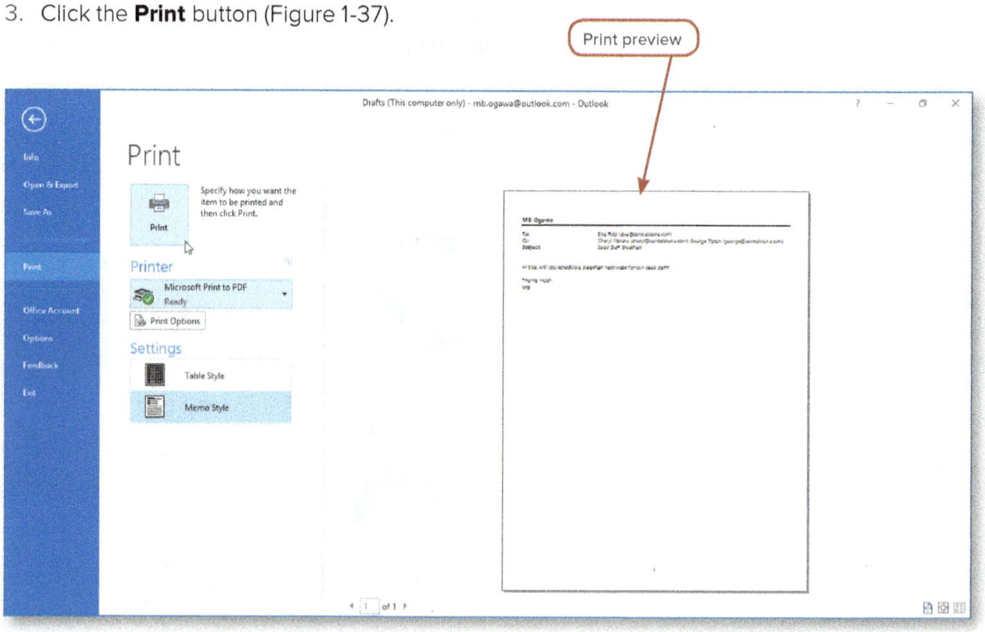

1-37 Print a message

4. Select the type of printout you would like in the *Print What* area.
5. Click the **Print** button.

ANOTHER WAY

Ctrl+P opens the *Print* area on the *Backstage* view.

Recall an Email Message

Have you ever sent a message and realized, after you pressed the *Send* button, that you omitted information, included incorrect information, or forgot to include an attachment? Outlook provides us with a ***Recall*** feature (Figure 1-38) that allows you to recall a message and gives you the option of replacing it with a new message.

The *Recall* feature only works in conjunction with an Exchange server. Assuming the original message has not been read, the original message is deleted, and the recipient is informed that you, the sender, deleted the message from his or her mailbox. If you are replacing the original message with a new one, the original message will be deleted when the *Recall* message is opened. The recall will fail if the recipient opens the original message before it is deleted or opened before the recall message. If you have selected the *Tell me if recall succeeds or fails for each recipient* check box, you will receive an email notification in your Inbox informing you of the recall status.

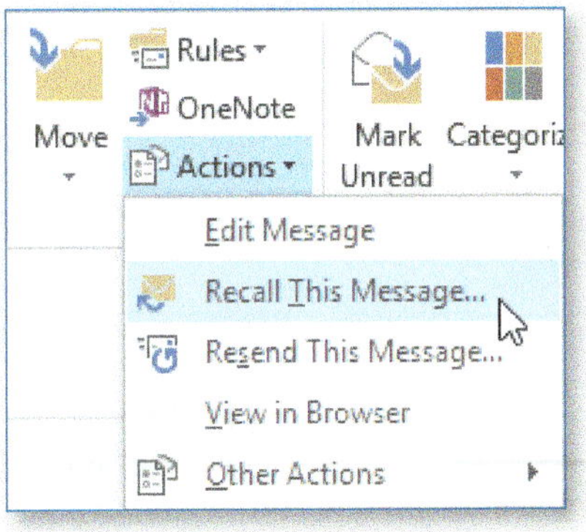

1-38 ***Recall This Message***

HOW TO: Recall an Email Message

1. Locate and open the message to be recalled in your *Sent Items* folder.
2. Click the **Actions** button [*Message* tab, *Move* group].
3. Choose **Recall This Message**. The *Recall This Message* dialog box opens (Figure 1-39).
4. Select *Delete unread copies of this message* or *Delete unread copies and replace with a new message.* Outlook tracks this action to let you know if the recall was successful.
5. Click **OK**.
   - If you are just deleting unread copies, Outlook performs the recall.
   - If you are replacing the email message with a new one, the original message opens so you can modify it. Press **Send** after editing the message to perform the recall and replace the original message with the new one.

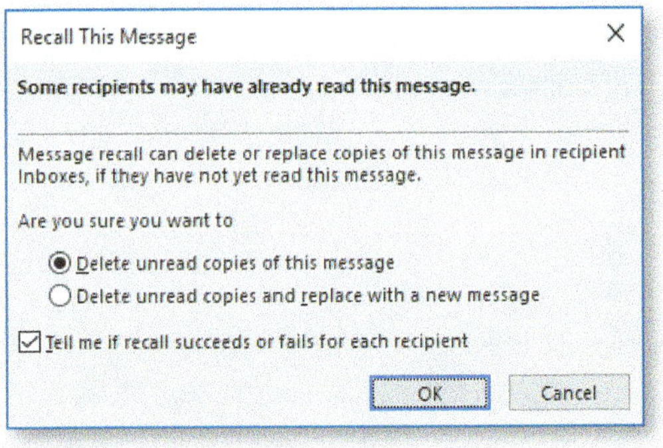

1-39 ***Recall This Message*** **dialog box**

MORE INFO

If you are recalling a message that was sent to a large number of recipients, you will not want to select the *Tell me if recall succeeds or fails for each recipient* check box. If you do select it, your Inbox will be filled with recall success/failure notifications.

Resend an Email Message

Resending a message is useful if you want to resend a previously sent message. If someone did not receive your original message or if you want to send the same message to new recipients, you can resend a previously sent message rather than creating and sending a new message. The process to resend a message is similar to recalling a message.

HOW TO: Resend an Email Message

1. Locate and open the message to be resent in your *Sent Items* folder.
2. Click the **Actions** button [*Message* tab, *Move* group].
3. Choose **Resend This Message**. (Figure 1-40).
4. Select recipients to receive the message.
5. Click **OK**.

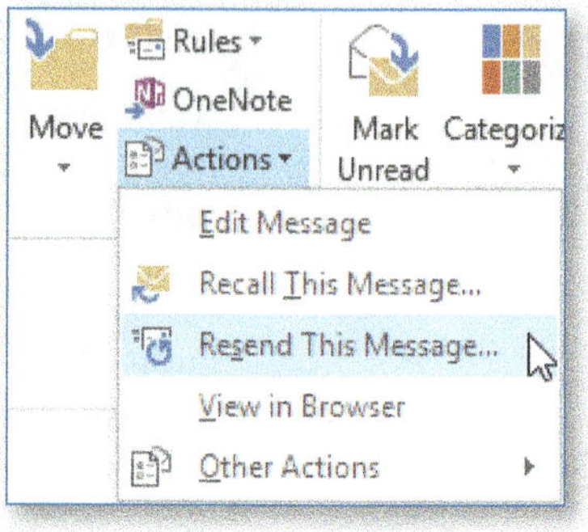

1-40 *Resend This Message*

ANOTHER WAY

Recall or resend an email message by opening the message and clicking the **File** tab where both the recall and resend options are available on the *Backstage* view.

PAUSE & PRACTICE: OUTLOOK 1-2

For this Pause and Practice project, you send an email message to your instructor and use the *Cc* function to send a copy to yourself. You also read the message, reply to it, and print it for your records.

Files Needed: None

1. Click the **Mail** button in the *Navigation* bar.
2. Create a new email message by clicking the **New Email** button [*Home* tab, *New* group].
3. Enter the following information in the email message fields:

   To: [your instructor's email address]
   Cc: [your email address]
   Subject: Central Sierra Information Request
   Body: Hi Don, could you please email me the latest employee information sheet when you have a chance?
   Thank you,
   [your name]
4. Click the **Send** button to send the message.
5. View the message you sent in your *Sent Items* folder using the *Reading* pane.
   a. Click the *Sent Items* folder.
   b. Select the message.
   c. Select the *Right* or *Bottom Reading* pane option based on your preference [*View* tab, *Layout* group, *Reading Pane* button].
6. Reply to the message.
   a. Click the **Reply** button [*Home* tab, *Respond* group].

b. Click the body section of the message and type the following:
I will look it up and send it to you as soon as I retrieve it.
[your name]
c. Click the **Send** button.

7. Print the reply message.
   a. Select the reply message in your Inbox.
   b. Click the **Print** button [*File* tab, *Backstage* view].
8. Print the reply message.
   a. Select the reply message in *Sent Items* folder.
   b. Click the **Print** button [*File* tab, *Backstage* view].
9. Submit the printed copy to your instructor (Figure 1-41).

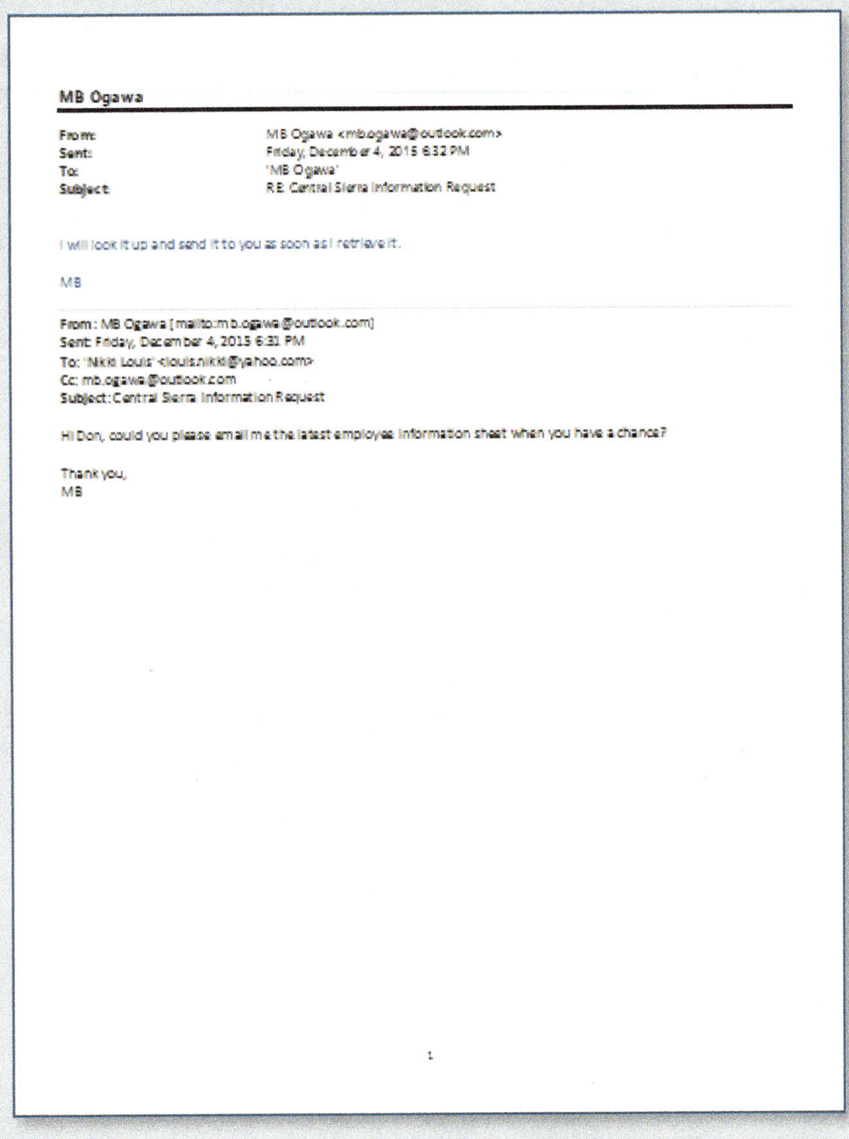

MB Ogawa

From: MB Ogawa <mb.ogawa@outlook.com>
Sent: Friday, December 4, 2015 6:32 PM
To: 'MB Ogawa'
Subject: RE: Central Sierra Information Request

I will look it up and send it to you as soon as I retrieve it.

MB

From: MB Ogawa [mailto:mb.ogawa@outlook.com]
Sent: Friday, December 4, 2015 6:31 PM
To: 'Nikki Louis' <louis.nikki@yahoo.com>
Cc: mb.ogawa@outlook.com
Subject: Central Sierra Information Request

Hi Don, could you please email me the latest employee information sheet when you have a chance?

Thank you,
MB

1

1-41 Pause & Practice 1-2 completed

SLO 1.6

Handling Attachments

One of the many benefits of email is that a file or multiple files can easily be attached to and sent with an email. Pictures, Word documents, and Excel spreadsheets are examples of files to attach to an email.

Attach a File

Outlook 2016 integrates with *OneDrive,* Microsoft's cloud storage system. You can attach a file from *OneDrive* or your local computer to an email message by clicking the **Attach File** button (Figure 1-42) on the *Message* tab in the *Include* group. Options include selecting a *Recent Item, Browse Web Locations,* or *Browse This PC.*

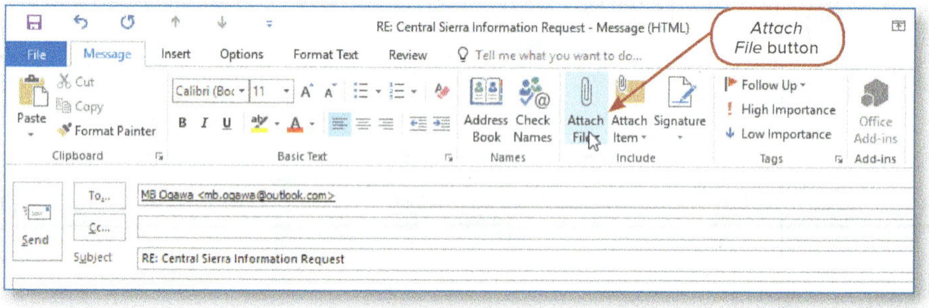

1-42 *Attach File* button

Certain file types and objects cannot be attached to email. Microsoft Access database files and entire folders cannot be attached to an email message. One way to get around this limitation is to ***compress*** or ***zip*** the files or folders and then attach the compressed (zipped) file.

You might have sent email messages asking your recipients to refer to an attachment, but you might not have always remembered to attach the referenced document to your message. New in 2016 is the ***Attachment Reminder*** feature. If you forget to attach a file and reference an attachment in your email message, Outlook warns you. An *Attachment Reminder* warning displays with two options *Don't Send* and *Send Anyway.* This ensures you attach files to email messages. Selecting *Don't Send* will return you to your message, while selecting *Send Anyway* will send your message as is (Figure 1-43).

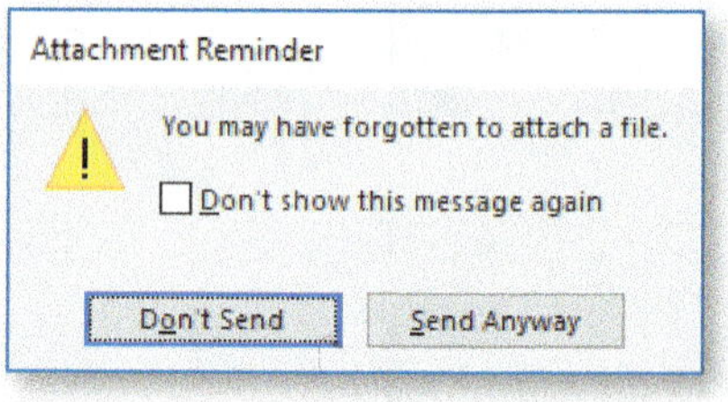

1-43 *Attachment Reminder*

HOW TO: Attach a File

1. Click the **Attach File** button [*Message* tab, *Include* group]. A list of recently used files is displayed.
2. Click **Browse this PC**. . .
3. Browse through the files on your computer (Figure 1-44).
4. Select the files. Use the **Ctrl** and **Shift** keys to select multiple files.

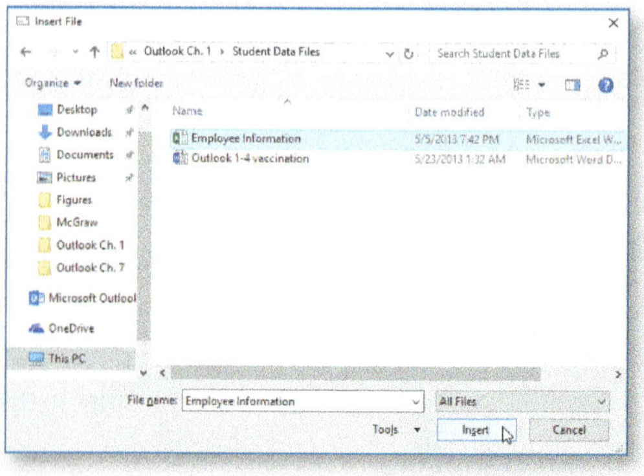

1-44 *Insert File* dialog box

5. Click **Insert**.
    - The attached files will appear below the subject line (Figure 1-45).

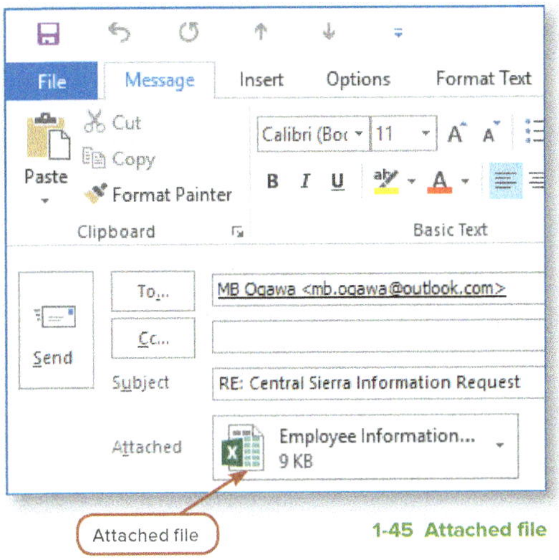

1-45 Attached file

MORE INFO

If you are attaching more than three or four files, consider grouping them in one compressed (zipped) folder and attach that folder to the message.

To compress or zip multiple files into one folder, select the files and then right-click **Send To, Compressed (zipped) Folder**. The compressed folder displays a zipper on it to distinguish it from other folders.

You can also attach files located in your *OneDrive* storage by selecting **Browse Web Locations** and clicking your *OneDrive* account. If you do not see your *OneDrive* account, you may need to log in to your Microsoft account.

Preview an Attachment

Outlook enables you to preview most types of attachments received in email messages without opening them. When you click the attachment as shown in Figure 1-45, the attachment displays in the body of the message (Figure 1-46). Return to the email message by clicking the **Show Message** button in the *Message* group on the *Attachments* tab.

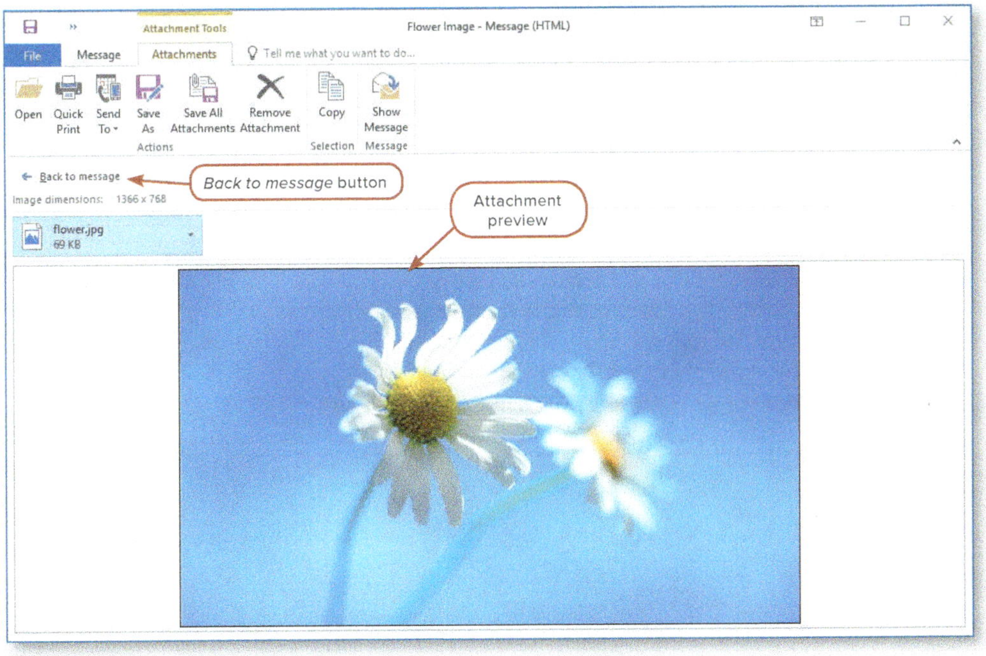

1-46 Preview an attachment

> **MORE INFO**
>
> When an attachment is being previewed, the area above the attachment displays the file name and the size of the attachment.

> **ANOTHER WAY**
>
> Click the **Back to message** text above the attachment to return to the message.

Open and Save Attachments

Usually when an attachment is received via email, you will want to open and/or save the attachment. The attachment displays below the subject line in the email.

Outlook 2016 made attachment handling much easier with the new drop-down arrow next to attachments. The drop-down list includes open, save, print, copy, or remove.

> **MORE INFO**
>
> Attachments are usually associated with specific software. For example, if you receive a compressed Excel worksheet, you need Excel on your computer to be able to open the file.

HOW TO: Open an Attachment

1. Open an email message. Click the drop-down arrow on the right of the attachment to display attachment handling options.
2. Click **Open**. It opens in a new window (Figure 1-47).

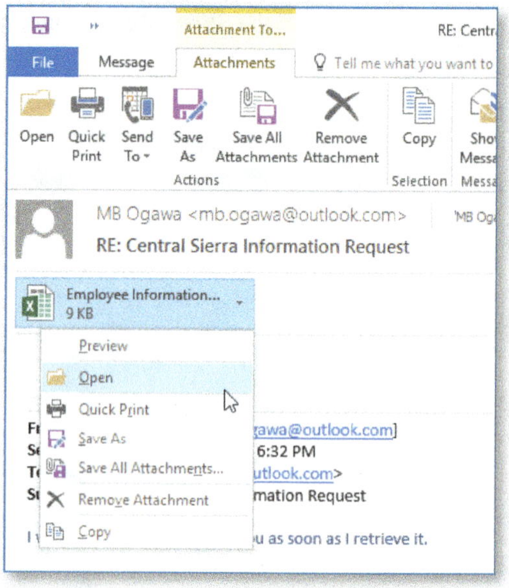

1-47 Opened attachment

> **MORE INFO**
>
> It is important to have virus protection software installed and up to date on your computer. Attachments and links in email messages are main ways viruses are spread between computers. Virus protection software could be the best investment you make each year.

> **ANOTHER WAY**
>
> Open an attachment by double-clicking the attachment, right-clicking the attachment and choosing **Open**, or clicking the **Open** button in the *Actions* group of the *Attachments* tab.

If an attachment is opened, it can be saved the same way you save any other open document. Typically, you can save an open document by pressing **Ctrl+S** or clicking the **Save** icon located on the *File* tab or *Quick Access* toolbar. Be sure to specify the location where you want the document saved.

> **ANOTHER WAY**
>
> **Ctrl+S** is the shortcut for save on most software.

An attachment can also be saved without opening it from the email.

HOW TO: Save an Attachment

1. Click the drop-down arrow next to the attachment.
2. Click **Save As**. The *Save As* dialog box opens.
3. Choose the desired location to save the file and specify a file name.
4. Click **Save**.

> **MORE INFO**
>
> If an email has multiple attachments, Outlook 2016 has a *Save All Attachments* option. Pressing it will allow you to save multiple attachments all at once rather than saving each one individually.

Forward an Email as an Attachment

When you forward an email with an attachment, the attachment is automatically included in the email to be forwarded. There might be times where you want to forward an entire email as an attachment rather than forwarding only the contents of the email.

HOW TO: Forward an Email as an Attachment

1. Open the message to be forwarded.
2. On the *Message* tab, click the **More** button in the *Respond* group.
3. Select **Forward as Attachment** (Figure 1-48). A new email opens with the selected email as an attachment. The subject line is the same as the original message with *FW:* in front indicating that the message is being forwarded (Figure 1-49).

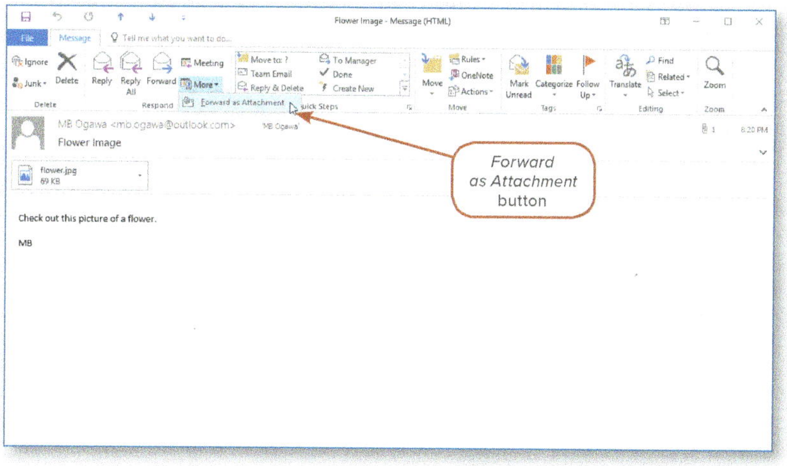

1-48 *Forward as Attachment button*

4. Select recipients and add any necessary information in the body of the message.
5. Press **Send**.

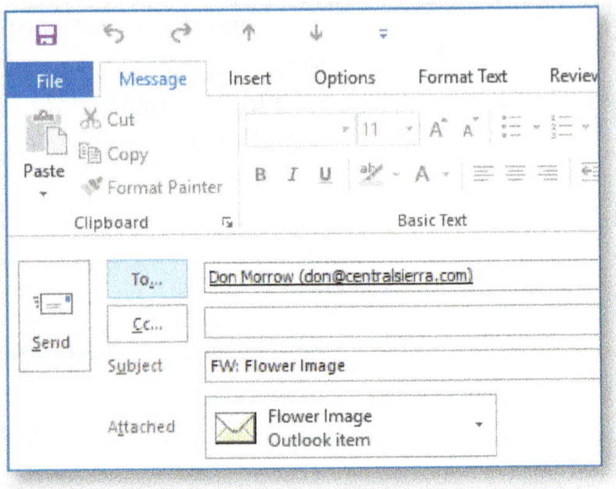

1-49 *Forward as Attachment* message

> **ANOTHER WAY**
>
> Press **Ctrl+Alt+F** to forward an open email or one selected in the *Folder* pane.

Attach Other Outlook Items

Other Outlook items such as contacts, tasks, calendar items, and Outlook business cards can be attached to an email and sent. These items can be sent either as an attachment or as text in the body of the email.

HOW TO: Attach Other Outlook Items

1. Start a **New** email message.
2. Click the **Insert** tab.
3. Click the **Attach Item** button (Figure 1-50) [*Message* tab, *Include* group].
4. Select the *Outlook Item*. The *Insert Item* dialog box opens.
5. Select a *Business Card, Calendar,* or *Outlook Item* from the drop-down list.
6. Select the items to be attached. Use the **Ctrl** key to select nonadjacent items or the **Shift** key to select a range of items.
7. Choose whether to insert the items as *Text only* or as an *Attachment* (Figure 1-51).
8. Click **OK**. The Outlook item will be attached to the email message.

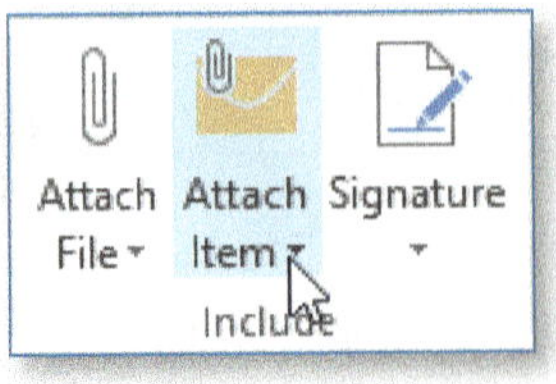

1-50 *Attach Item* button

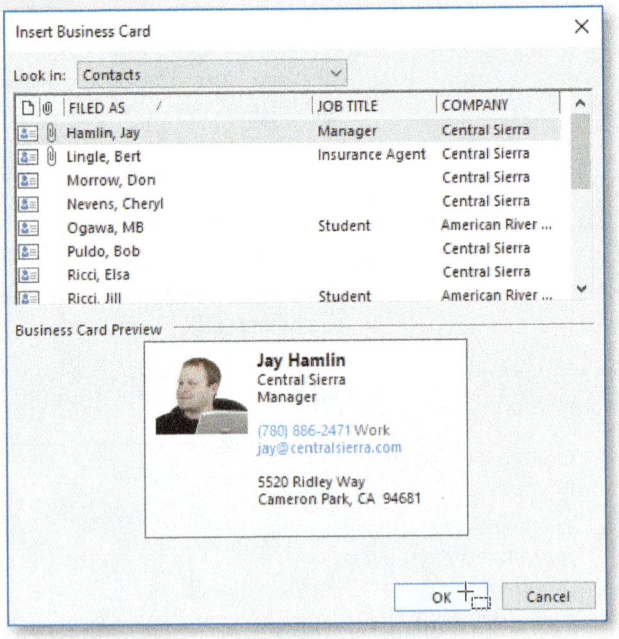

1-51 Insert an Outlook item as an attachment

> **MORE INFO**
>
> The *Attach Item* button is available in the *Include* group on *Message* tab, and the *Outlook Item* button is available in the *Include* group on the *Insert* tab. Both of these buttons open the *Insert Items* dialog box.

SLO 1.7

Understanding Arrangement and Icons

As mentioned in *SLO 1.2: Navigating Outlook,* the working environment in Outlook is divided into panes. There are typically three panes in Outlook: ***Folder, Reading****, and* ***People***. There is also the ***To-Do bar*** that can be open or collapsed.

In the *Folder* pane, you arrange emails in numerous different ways to meet your needs and preferences. Outlook also provides users with many ***icons*** to help easily and quickly identify different aspects of an email displayed in the *Folder* pane. The icons on each email in the *Folder* pane can tell you if a message has been read, if it has been replied to or forwarded, if there is an attachment, if it is marked ***important,*** if it is ***flagged*** for action, or if it is assigned to a ***category***.

The *Reading* pane includes additional details about a selected Outlook item such as the content of an email message. The *People* pane displays Outlook content related to a person including email, attachments, and meetings.

> **MORE INFO**
>
> ***Message options*** are covered in Chapter 3, which describes how to use the different features associated with Inbox icons. Chapter 5 covers how to customize the user interface.

Email Arrangement

Arrangement controls the order in which email messages display in the *Folder* pane. Typically email messages are arranged or sorted with the most recently received email at the top of the list (arranged by date and time in descending order). The *View* tab provides different *View* and *Arrangement* options. Outlook 2016 has upgraded the arrangement options so it is easier to quickly change the arrangement of emails.

Conversation arrangement (Figure 1-52) groups all emails related to a particular email conversation (by subject), which is intended to greatly reduce the number of redundant emails displayed in the *Folder* list (Figure 1-53). The *Conversation* arrangement groups emails together to occupy less space in your list of emails and gives you the ability to expand the conversation to see all related messages, including those in the *Sent Items* folder.

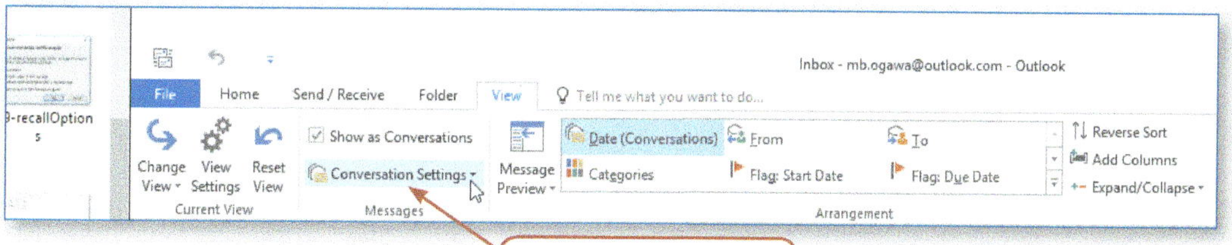

1-52 ***Conversation Settings*** **button**

When multiple emails exist within a conversation, clicking the small triangle to the left of an email will expand the conversation. Collapse the conversation by clicking the small triangle to the left of the conversation subject in the *Folder* pane.

Outlook includes many preset arrangement options. These options appear in the *Arrangement* group on the *View* tab.

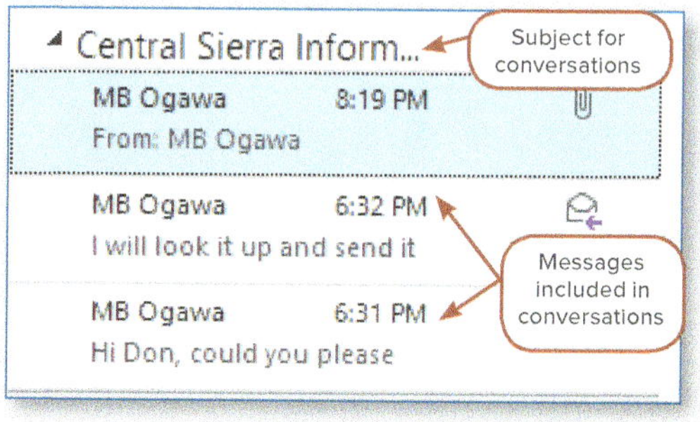

1-53 ***Conversation*** **arrangement**

> **MORE INFO**
>
> When you click the small triangle next to a conversation, the message expands to show the related messages in the current folder. When you click the triangle again, the conversation expands to include related messages in other folders.

Unread/Read Email

When the Inbox (or any other folder) is selected in the *Folder* pane, the contents of that folder display in the *Folder* pane. The vertical blue line to the left of the email shows whether or not the email has been read. When an email has not been read, the email is bold. Once the email has been opened and read, the email will no longer appear bold (Figure 1-54).

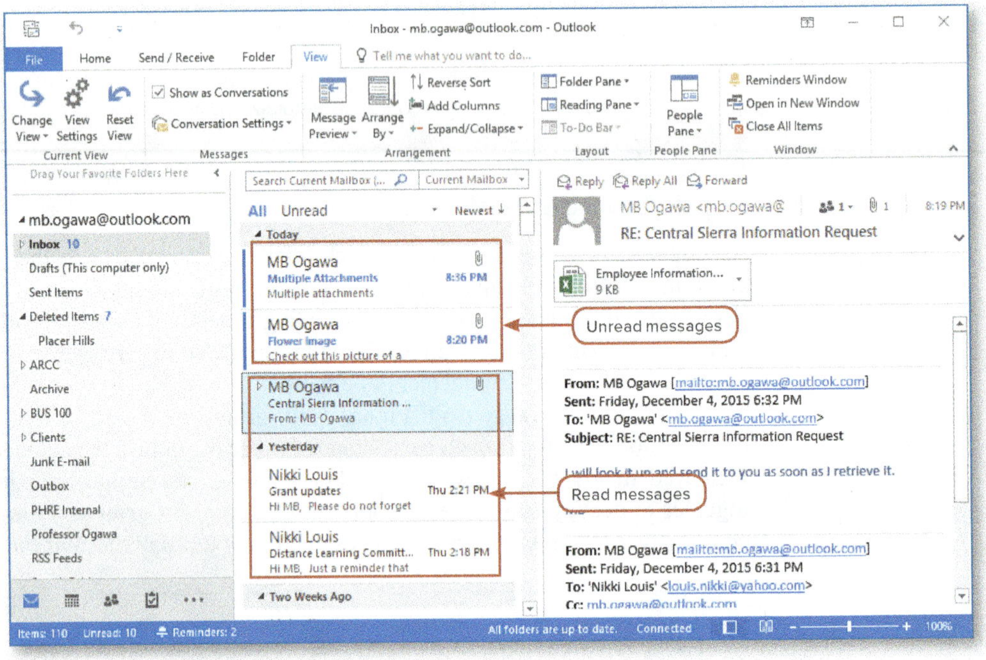

1-54 Read and unread messages

Mark as Unread/Read

When an email is opened, Outlook marks it as read. You might want to mark a message as unread to draw attention to it in the folder or *Folder* pane. Use the *Home* tab, *Tags* group to mark an email as ***unread*** or ***read***.

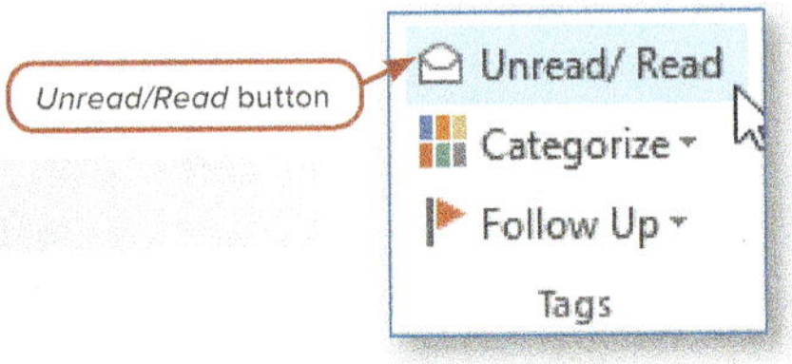

1-55 ***Unread/Read*** **button**

▶ HOW TO: Mark as Unread/Read

1. Select the email in the message list to be marked as read or unread.
2. In the *Home* tab *on Tags* group on the, click the **Unread/Read** button (Figure 1-55).

ANOTHER WAY

Right-click the email and choose *Mark as Unread* or *Mark as Read*.

MORE INFO

The entire contents of a folder can be marked as read by either right-clicking the folder and choosing **Mark All as Read** or by clicking the **Mark All as Read** button in the *Clean Up* group on the *Folder* tab.

Replied to and Forwarded

By scanning your email in the message list, you easily see the response action for each email. Messages that have been replied to have an envelope icon with an arrow pointing to the left, and those that have been forwarded have an envelope icon with an arrow pointing to the right (Figure 1-56).

Attachment

Outlook uses a ***paper clip*** icon to indicate that an email has an attachment (see Figure 1-56).

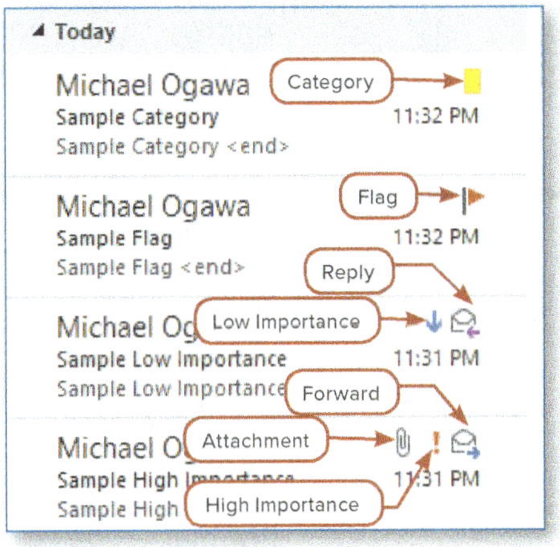

1-56 Sample Inbox

Flag

When a message is flagged for follow up or has a flag for recipients, the ***flag*** icon is used. This flag appears in different shades of red depending on the action of the flag (*Today, Tomorrow, This Week*) (see Figure 1-56).

Importance

Importance can be set for each email to one of three levels: ***high***, ***low***, and ***normal***. High importance is indicated by a red exclamation point, low importance uses a blue arrow pointed down, and normal importance uses no special icon (see Figure 1-56). (Normal importance is the default on all new email messages.)

Reminder

When an email is received that includes a reminder, it is marked with a small ***bell*** icon. An electronic reminder displays on your computer on the reminder day and time (Figure 1-57). You have the options of opening the email, dismissing the reminder, or choosing snooze to be reminded again later.

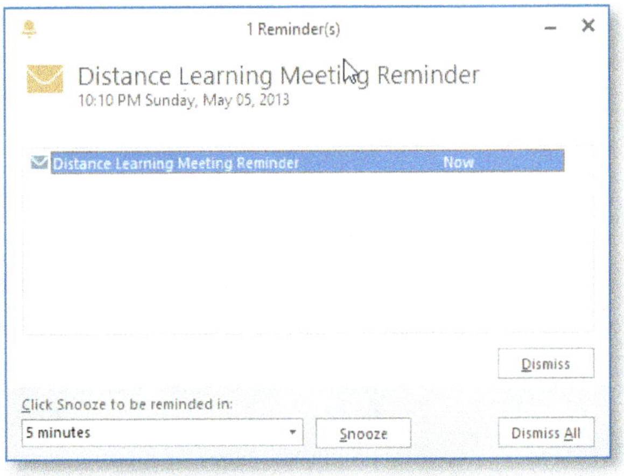

1-57 *Reminder(s)* window

Category

Categories are used to group Inbox items. Colors are used to distinguish categories, and the category names can be customized to meet your individual needs. Categories are not limited to email messages; they can also be advantageous for grouping contacts, tasks, and calendar items (see Figure 1-56).

SLO 1.8

Cleaning up your Inbox

It is important to manage your Inbox effectively. When you receive mail (postal mail) at home or work, you read it and then determine what action needs to be taken. Bills need to be paid, information needs to be filed and saved, junk mail discarded, and other mail is thrown away after you've responded to it. Your email Inbox is very similar. Throughout this text, you will learn about many different tools to help you effectively manage your Inbox. For now, it is important to learn how to delete an email you no longer need.

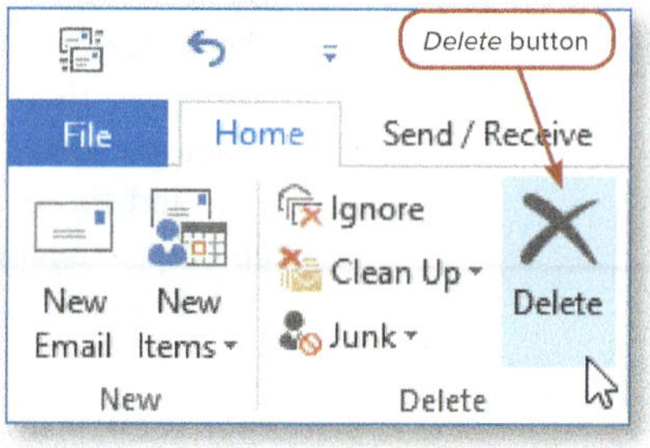

1-58 *Delete button*

Delete an Email

Select the emails to be deleted, and then either click the **Delete** button (Figure 1-58) in the *Delete* group on the *Home* tab or press the **Delete** key (not *Backspace*) on your computer keyboard. When an email is deleted, it is not gone forever. It has been moved from your *Inbox* (or the folder it is in) to your *Deleted Items* folder.

> **ANOTHER WAY**
>
> Outlook items can also be deleted by right-clicking the item and choosing **Delete**, or selecting an email message in the *Folder* pane and pressing **Ctrl+D**.

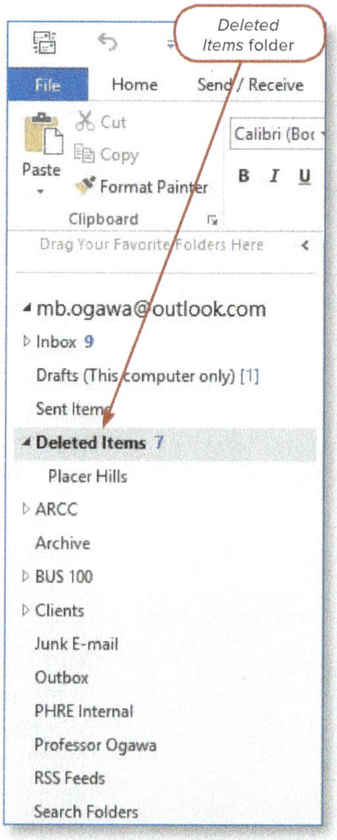

1-59 *Deleted Items folder*

Deleted Items Folder

Deleted Items is a folder (Figure 1-59) in your list of *Mail* folders. Deleted email, contacts, tasks, calendar items, and other Outlook items are stored in this folder when they are deleted from another location. By default, Outlook does not delete the items in the *Deleted Items* folder, but this is not a good location to store items you might need.

Clean Up and Ignore

By default, Outlook arranges emails displayed in the *Folder* pane by conversation. This helps to both group related items together and reduce the clutter and redundant emails in your Inbox. Two features added to further manage conversations in Outlook are ***Clean Up*** and ***Ignore***. *Clean Up* will remove redundant messages in an email conversation. *Clean Up* can also be used on an entire folder and subfolders (Figure 1-60).

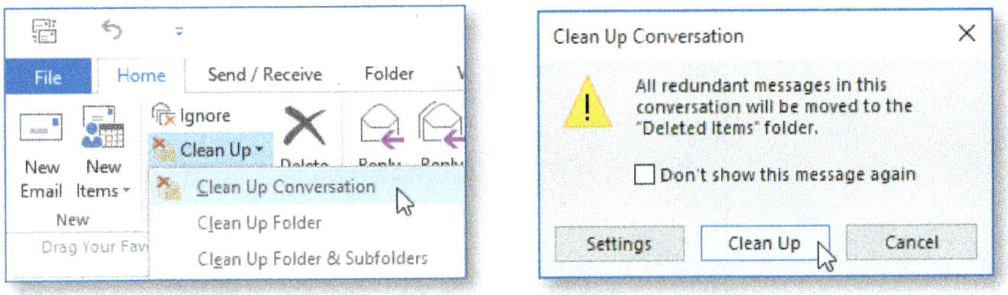

1-60 ***Clean Up Conversation*** **button and dialog box**

Ignore deletes all emails related to a specific conversation and deletes any new received email that is related to that conversation.

Both *Clean Up* and *Ignore* are handy features to help manage the volume of emails you receive. By default, when you *Clean Up* or *Ignore* a conversation, the deleted emails are moved to the *Deleted Items* folder.

Empty Deleted Items

It is a good idea to regularly empty your *Deleted Items* folder. The items in this folder can be manually deleted.

HOW TO: Empty Deleted Items

1. Click the **Deleted Items** folder in the *Folder* pane.
2. Click the **Folder** tab.
3. Click the **Empty Folder** button (Figure 1-61) in the *Clean Up* group. A dialog box opens confirming that you want to empty the *Deleted Items* folder.
4. Choose **Yes** to delete items in the *Deleted Items* folder.

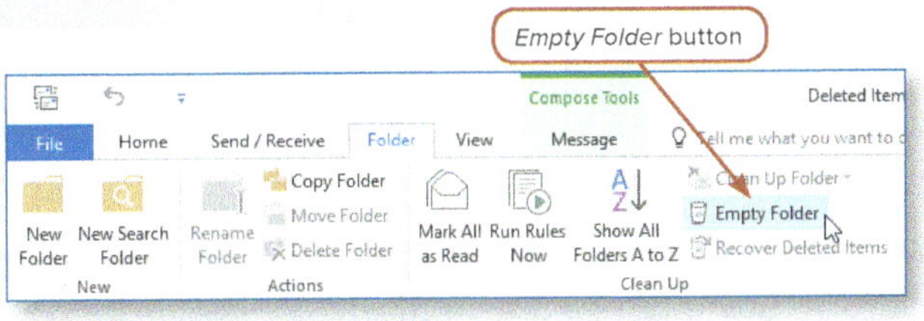

1-61 ***Empty Folder*** **button**

ANOTHER WAY

Right-click the **Deleted Items** folder and choose **Empty Folder**.

It is a good idea to have Outlook automatically empty the *Deleted Items* folder each time you exit Outlook. The default settings in Outlook can easily be changed to do this.

HOW TO: Change the Default Setting to Automatically Empty Deleted Items Each Time You Exit Outlook

1. Click the **File** tab to open the *Backstage* view.
2. Click the **Options** button on the left. The *Outlook Options* dialog box opens.
3. Click the **Advanced** button on the left.

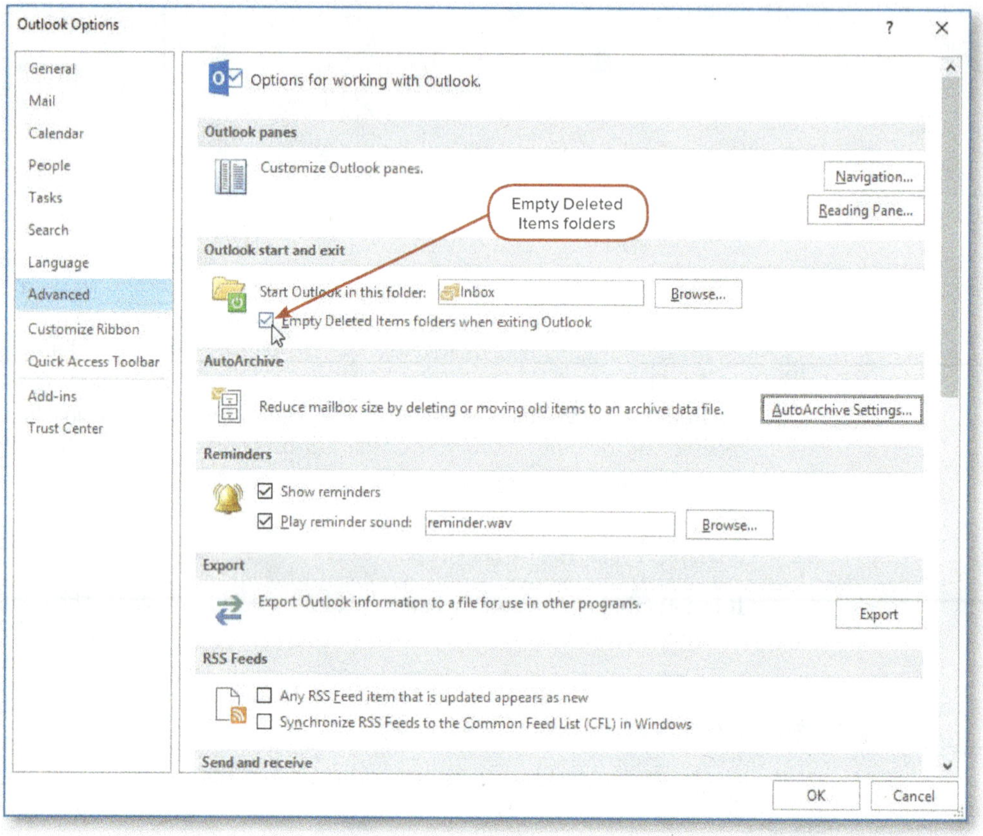

1-62 *Empty Deleted* Items *folder* when exiting Outlook option

4. Select the **Empty Deleted Items folder when exiting Outlook** check box (Figure 1-62).
5. Click **OK** to close the *Outlook Options* dialog box.

> **MORE INFO**
>
> The *Outlook Options* dialog box will be referenced throughout this text. This area allows you to customize settings in Outlook. *Outlook Options* and other Outlook features are located on the *Backstage* view, which is accessed by clicking the **File** tab. *Outlook Options* is covered in Chapter 7.

Even when Outlook items have been deleted and the *Deleted Items* folder has been emptied, Outlook still provides you with the ability to recover deleted items if you are using an Exchange server. The ***Recover Deleted Items*** button (Figure 1-63) in the *Clean Up* group on the *Folder* tab allows you to select previously deleted items to recover. These recovered items will be placed in your *Deleted Items* folder.

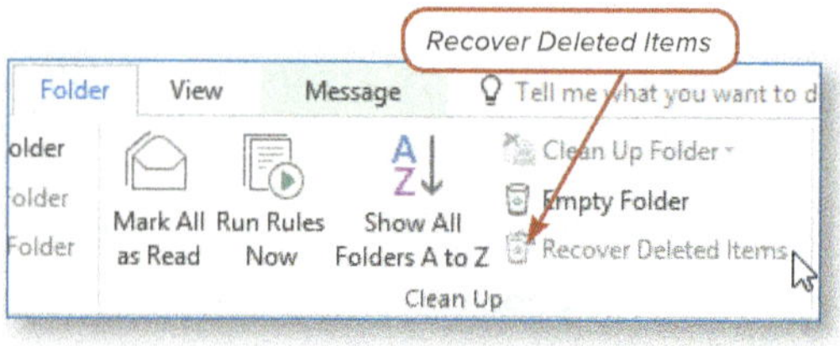

1-63 *Recover Deleted Items* button

PAUSE & PRACTICE: OUTLOOK 1-3

For this Pause and Practice project, you reply to a message with an email attachment. You also forward the message to your instructor as an attachment and delete a message.

File Needed: ***Employee Information.xlsx***

1. Reply to the message with the subject ***RE: Central Sierra Information Request***.
   a. Select the message in your Inbox.
   b. Click the **Reply** button in the message.
2. Add the following text to the body of the message:
   I just found the employee data sheet and attached it to this message.
   [your name]
3. Attach the file ***Employee Information.xlsx*** to the message.
   a. Click the *Attach File* button on the *Message* tab, *Include* group.
   b. Select **Browse This PC** from the drop-down list.
   c. Select the **Employee Information.xlsx** file.
   d. Click **Insert**.
4. Click the **Send** button to send the message. The message appears in your Inbox.
5. Select the message and forward it to your instructor as an attachment.
   a. Click the message to select it.
   b. Click the **Forward as Attachment** option [*Home* tab, *Respond* group, *More* button].
   c. Enter your instructor's email address in the *To* field.
   d. Enter the following text in the body of the message:
      Attached is the requested verification email for the employee data.
      [your name]
   e. Click the **Send** button.
6. Delete the initial reply message that indicated that you would send the message as soon as you retrieved it.
   a. Select the initial reply message in your Inbox.
   b. Click the **Delete** button [*Home* tab, *Delete* group].
7. Empty the *Deleted Items* folder.
   a. Click the **Deleted Items** folder.
   b. Click the **Empty Folder** button [*Folder* tab, *Clean Up* group].
   c. Click **No** unless you are certain you would like to permanently remove the the items in the *Deleted Items* folder. (Figure 1-64).

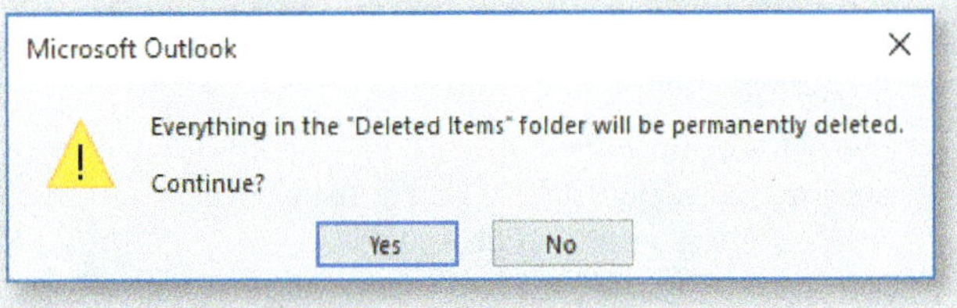

1-64 Confirmation for deleting items

Chapter Summary

1.1 Identify the basic components of Microsoft Outlook 2016 (p. O1-3).

- Outlook includes six major features: *Email, Calendar, Contacts, Tasks, Notes,* and *Journal.*
- ***Email:*** Users create, send, and receive email. It can manage a single email account or multiple email accounts.
- ***Calendar:*** An electronic calendar used to create appointments or events, edit these items, replicate calendar items, set electronic reminders, create meeting requests, and share calendar items with other Outlook users or other devices.
- ***Contacts:*** An area to record names, email, phone numbers, and other information about business contacts, coworkers, friends, and family.
- ***Tasks:*** An electronic notepad used to write down your to-do items and then cross them off as they are completed.
- ***Notes:*** Electronic sticky notes that are an excellent way of storing information such as a user name and password to log into a web site, gift ideas for family and friends, or a list of books you'd like to read.
- ***Journal:*** Primarily used in the business environment and enables you track time spent on a project or document.

1.2 Navigate throughout the Outlook environment and identify the different panes in the Outlook window (p. O1-7).

- ***Outlook Today*** is the welcome screen for Outlook which provides you with information about your mailbox, calendar items, and task list.
- The ***Navigation bar*** allows you to quickly switch between different features in Outlook.
- The ***Reading*** pane allows you to quickly read messages or see details in tasks. This can be shown on the bottom or right of the window.
- The ***Ribbon*** appears at the top of the Outlook window and includes a variety of ***tabs.*** Each tab displays a variety of ***groups***; groups contain buttons, drop-down lists, and galleries.
- You can choose from a variety of preset views to personalize your experience.
- The ***Folder list*** displays all of the folders in the *Folder* pane.
- ***Tell me what you want to do*** button allows you to quickly search for topics on which you might have a question or need additional information.

1.3 Distinguish between Outlook being used as a stand-alone program and in a Microsoft Exchange environment (p. O1-14).

- Outlook as a stand-alone program connects directly to your Internet service provider and can manage multiple email accounts.
- Outlook is typically connected to an ***Exchange server*** in business environments and has the following features:
  - Using voting buttons and tracking responses
  - Sending meeting requests and tracking responses
  - Recalling messages
  - Sharing your calendar, contacts, tasks, and email with others
  - Using *MailTips*
  - Using a common global contact list

1.4 Distinguish between the different types of email accounts and set up an email account in Outlook (p. O1-14).

- ***Microsoft Exchange*** accounts are used primarily in medium- to large-business settings. These email accounts are set up through the company network or email administrator. An Exchange account has an individual mailbox assigned to each user and resides on an Exchange file server.
- ***POP3*** accounts are Internet email accounts that are associated with your Internet service provider (ISP). When using this type of account, Outlook downloads the messages.
- ***IMAP*** accounts are also Internet accounts but are not always associated with an ISP. IMAP accounts create folders on a server to store and organize messages for retrieval by other computers and gives you the option to read message headers only and select which messages to download.
- ***HTTP*** accounts use the hypertext transfer protocol used on the web to create, view, send, and receive messages. This type of account is not automatically supported by Outlook but can be configured by installing an add-in.

- You can set up an email account by clicking the **Add Account** button [*File* tab].

1.5 Use Outlook to create, send, and receive email (p. O1-17).

- Select recipients, type the subject of the message, type the message, and send email messages.
- The ***To*** field indicates to whom a message is addressed, while the ***Cc*** field is used to send a carbon copy of a message to another person. The ***Bcc*** field is used to send a blind carbon copy of a message to a recipient. *Bcc* is used when you do not want those receiving the email message to see other recipients' email address or names.
- Sent messages that are sent are automatically copied to the ***Sent Items*** folder.
- If you are not ready to send an email message, save it as a draft to the ***Drafts*** folder.
- You can ***Reply, Reply All,*** or ***Forward*** a message.
- Save email messages as *.msg* files to a location on your computer.

1.6 Use attachments in email (p. O1-29).

- Attach files from your computer or OneDrive to email messages.
- You cannot attach a Microsoft Access file or a folder to an email message.
- Most common attachments, such as images, can be previewed by clicking them within a message.
- Attachments can be saved to your computer.
- Email messages can be forwarded to recipients as attachments.
- Attach Outlook items, such as business cards, to email messages.

1.7 Differentiate email arrangements and icons (p. O1-34).

- Email messages can be grouped in ***Conversation,*** which groups all emails related to a particular email conversation. This ensures your email is less cluttered, as only the newest message in a conversation displays.
- ***Unread*** messages are bolded, while ***read*** messages are not. Outlook allows you to mark messages that are read as unread or unread as read. Marking messages as unread ensures they maintain the bold appearance and are easy to identify.
- A ***paper clip*** icon is used to indicate that a message has an attachment.
- A ***flag*** is used to indicate that follow up on a message is needed.
- Set the importance of an email message as high, normal, or low to indicate the priority one should place on the message.
- Add reminders to email messages that require an action.
- Categories can be used to group emails by similar subjects.

1.8 Explain the importance and process of cleaning up an Inbox (p. O1-37).

- When you delete an email message, it is sent to the ***Deleted Items*** folder, as opposed to being deleted from your account.
- Emptying your *Deleted Items* folder will delete any messages that were moved to that location.
- ***Clean Up*** removes redundant messages in an email conversation. *Clean Up* can also be used on an entire folder and subfolders.
- ***Ignore*** deletes all emails related to a specific conversation and deletes any new received email that is related to that conversation.

Check for Understanding

The SIMbook for this text (within your SIMnet account), provides the following resources for concept review:

- Multiple-choice questions
- Matching exercises
- Short answer questions

Guided Project 1-1

For this project, you request a meeting with Jay Hamlin of Central Sierra Insurance to discuss ways of attracting new customers. You send an email message to request a meeting and include a *Cc* to yourself so that you can keep this message at the top of your message list.
[Student Learning Outcomes 1.1, 1.2, 1.5, 1.7]

Files Needed: None

Skills Covered in This Project

- Create a new message.
- Select *To* recipient.
- Select *Cc* recipient.
- Add a subject to a message.
- Add a body to a message.
- Mark a message as low importance.
- Flag a message for follow up.
- Send a message.

1. Create a new email message to Jay Hamlin.
   a. Click the **New Email** button [*Home* tab, *New* group].
   b. In the *To* field, type your instructor's email address.
   c. In the *Cc* field, type your email address.
   d. In the *Subject* field, type Attracting New Customers Meeting Request.
2. In the body of the message, type the following text:

   Hi Jay, I was wondering if you are available to meet next week to discuss our strategies to attract new customers. I am available on Monday from 2:00 P.M. to 3:00 P.M. or Tuesday from 3:00 P.M. to 4:00 P.M. Please let me know if either of these days work for your schedule. If not, please send me alternative times that you are available.

   Thanks,
   [your name]
3. Mark the message as *Low Importance* and flag the message for follow up.
   a. Click the **Low Importance** button [*Message* tab, *Tags* group].
   b. Click **Follow Up** [*Message* tab, *Tags* group] and select **Tomorrow**.
4. Click the **Send** button to send the message (Figure 1-65).

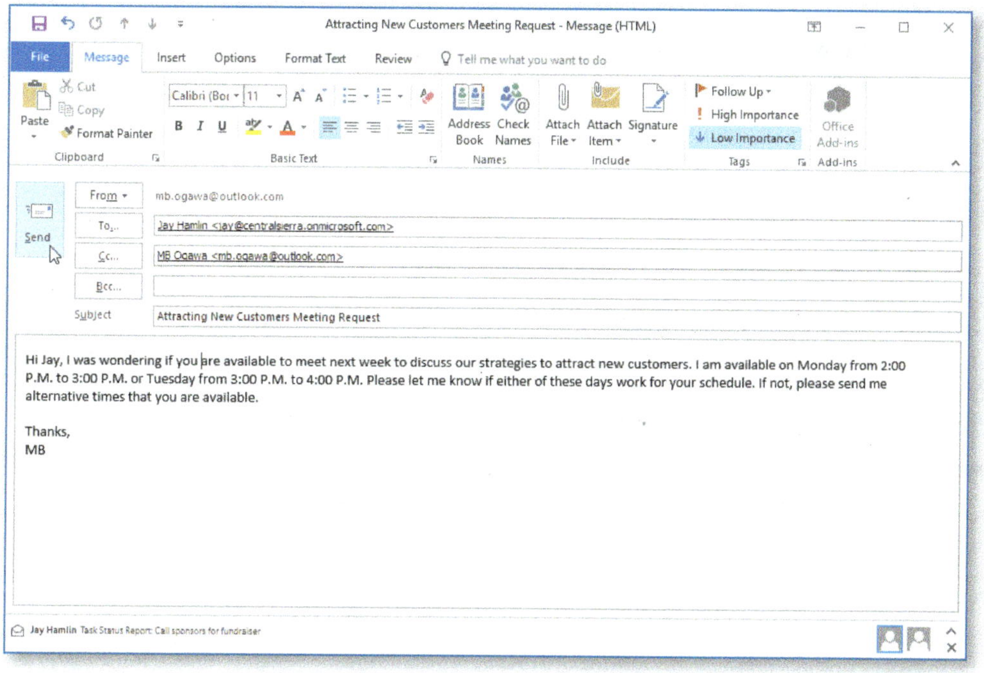

1-65 Guided Project 1-1 completed

Guided Project 1-2

For this project, you follow up with Jay since he was unable to respond to your first message. You forward your original message to him and ask if he is available to meet.
[Student Learning Outcomes 1.1, 1.2, 1.5, 1.7]

Files Needed: None

Skills Covered in This Project

- Identify an unread message.
- Open a message.
- Identify a message as low importance.
- Forward a message.
- Select *To* recipient.
- Add a *Bcc* to a message.
- Select *Bcc* recipient.
- Modify the body of a message.
- Remove *Low Importance* tag.
- Mark a message as high importance.
- Send a message.

1. Open the message sent in Guided Project 1-1.
   a. Click the **Mail** button to confirm you are in your Inbox.
   b. Double-click the message with the subject ***Attracting New Customers Meeting Request.*** The message should have the *Low Importance* tag (downward pointing arrow) on the message.

2. Forward the message to Jay Hamlin and modify the body of the message.
   a. Click the **Forward** button [*Home* tab, *Respond* group].
   b. In the *To* field, type jay@centralsierra.com.
   c. Click the **Bcc** button [*Message* tab, *Show Fields* group] to ensure the *Bcc* field is available.
   d. In the *Bcc* field, type your email address.
   e. In body of the message, type:
      Hi Jay, I just wanted to follow up with you regarding our meeting to attract new customers. Are you available next week to meet? Please let me know at your earliest convenience.
      Thank you,
      [your name]
3. Change the importance of the message from low importance to high importance.
   a. Click the **Low Importance** button [*Message* tab, *Tags* group] to remove *the Low Importance* tag.
   b. Click the **High Importance** button [*Message* tab, *Tags* group].
4. Click the **Send** button to send the message (Figure 1-66).

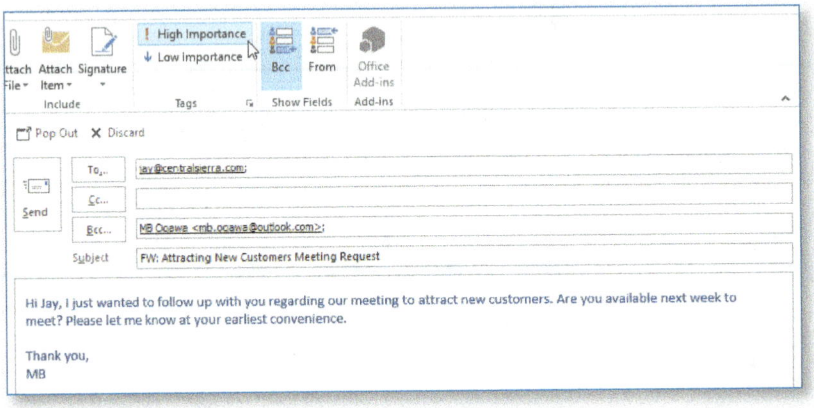

1-66 Guided Project 1-2 completed

Guided Project 1-3

For this project, you reply to the message as Jay Hamlin. You save a draft of your message, save a copy of your message as a *.msg* file, and print a copy of the message.
[Student Learning Outcomes 1.1, 1.2, 1.5, 1.7]

Files Needed: None
Completed Project File Name: ***[your initials] Outlook 1-3.msg***

Skills Covered in This Project

- Open a message.
- Identify a message as high importance.
- Reply to a message.
- Select a *Cc* recipient.
- Edit the body of a message.
- Save a message as a file.
- Send a message.
- Create a new message.
- Add an attachment to a message.

1. Open the message sent in Guided Project 1-2.
   a. Click the **Mail** button to confirm you are in your Inbox.
   b. Double-click the message with the subject ***FW: Attracting New Customers Meeting Request.*** The message should have the *High Importance* tag (red exclamation point) on the message.
2. Forward the message to Jay Hamlin and modify the body of the message.
   a. Click the **Forward** button [*Home* tab, *Respond* group].
   b. Ensure the *To* field has your email address.
   c. In the *Cc* field, type your instructor's email address.
   d. In the body of the message, type:
   Hi [your name], Thanks for checking in with me regarding the meeting about new customers. I accidentally missed your first message. I am available to meet on Tuesday at 2:00 P.M.
   Elsa, could you please schedule the conference room for us next week Tuesday from 2:00 P.M. to 3:00 P.M.
   Jay
3. Save the message to your computer.
   a. Click **Save As** [*File* tab].
   b. Locate the driver and folder where the file is to be stored.
   c. Change the file name to be ***[your initials] Outlook 1-3*** in the *File Name* area.
   d. Click the **Save** button.
4. Click the **Send** button to send the message.
5. Create a new email message to your instructor.
   a. Click the **New Email** button [*Home* tab, *New* group].
   b. In the *To* field, type your instructor's email address.
   c. In the *Cc* field, type your email address.
   d. In the *Subject* field, type [your initials] Outlook 1-3.
6. In the body of the message, type:

   Hi [instructor's name]. Attached are my three guided project assignments from Outlook Chapter 1.
   Thanks,
   [your name]
7. Attach the message you saved to your computer to the email message.
   a. Click the **Attach File** button. You will see a list of list of *Recent Items*. Click the **Browse this PC** button.
   b. Locate the message you saved in step 3.
   c. Select the message and click the **Insert** button (Figure 1-67).

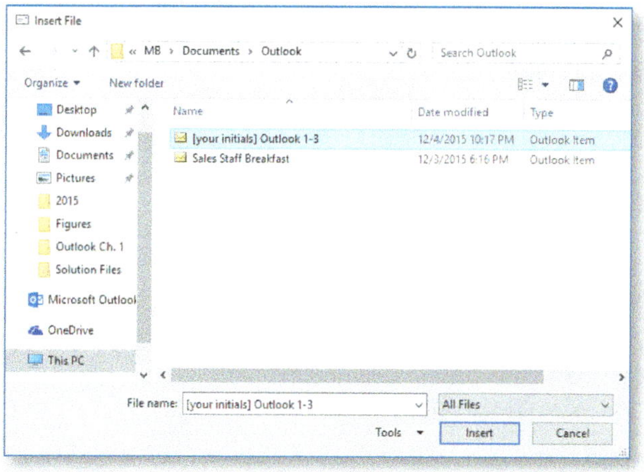

1-67 Attach a saved message

8. Click the **Send** button to send the message (Figure 1-68).

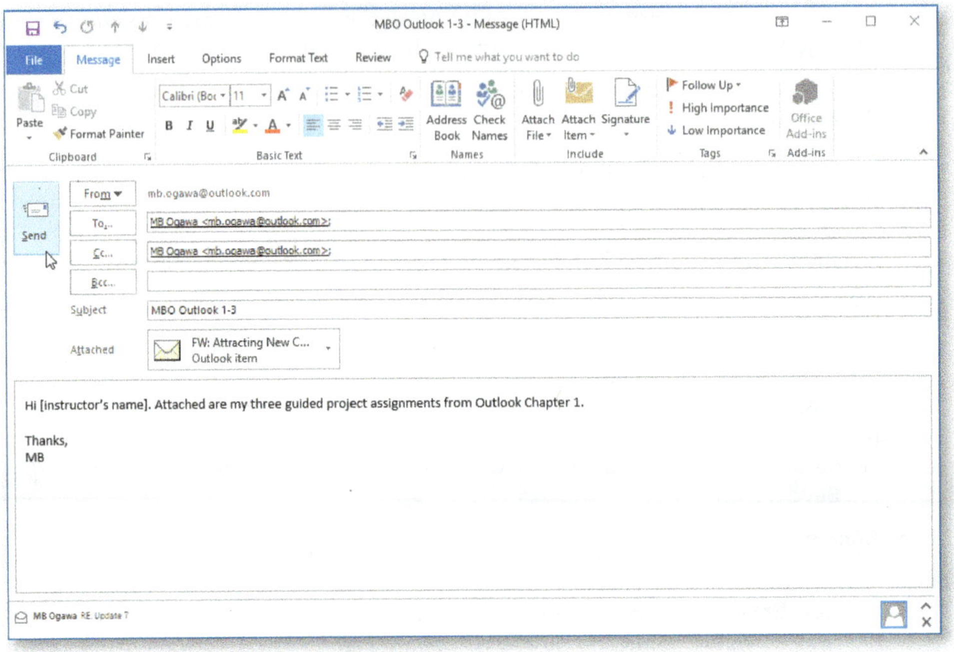

1-68 Guided Project 1-3 completed

Independent Project 1-4

You received a request from Mr. and Mrs. Dodge over the phone requesting a vaccination schedule for their newborn child. For this project, you send them an email message with a vaccination schedule. [Student Learning Outcomes 1.1, 1.2, 1.5, 1.6, 1.7]

File Needed: ***Outlook 1-4 vaccination.docx***

Skills Covered in This Project

- Create a new message.
- Select a *To* recipient.
- Select a *Cc* recipient.
- Add a subject.
- Add a message.
- Add an attachment to a message.
- Send a message.

1. Create a new email message to the Dodge family using the following information:
   a. In the *To* field, type your partner's email address.
   b. In the *Cc* field, type your email address.
2. In the *Subject* field, type Requested vaccination information for your newborn.

3. Type a short message to the Dodge family indicating that you attached the requested vaccination schedule.
4. Attach the file ***Outlook 1-4 vaccination.docx*** to the message.
5. Send the message (Figure 1-69).

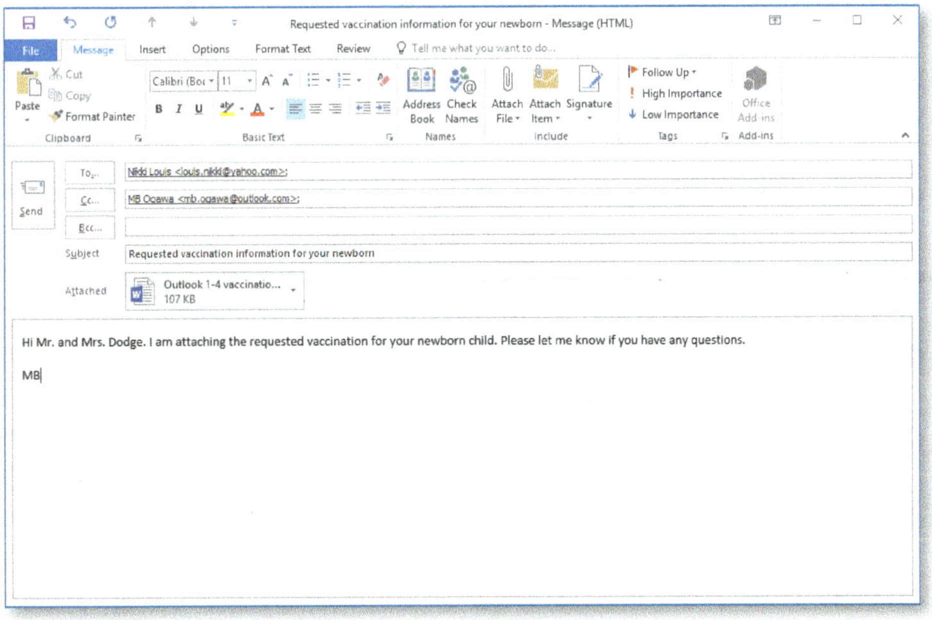

1-69 Independent Project 1-4 completed

Independent Project 1-5

You received a request from Dr. Lee at Courtyard Medical Plaza to verify the message to the Dodge family was sent. For this project, you send him the message that you sent and print a copy for the patient's records.
[Student Learning Outcomes 1.1, 1.2, 1.5, 1.6, 1.7, 1.8]

Files Needed: None

Skills Covered in This Project

- Open a message.
- Print a message.
- Forward a message as an attachment.
- Select a *To* recipient.
- Select a *Bcc* recipient.
- Add a message.
- Send a message.

1. Locate and open the message sent in Independent Project 1-4 with the subject ***Requested vaccination information for your newborn.*** The message has a paper clip icon next to it to indicate that it has an attachment.

2. Print the message in a memo format (Figure 1-70).
3. Forward the message as an attachment to the following recipients:
   a. In the *To* field, type your partner's email address.
   b. In the *Cc* field, type your email address.
4. Edit the body of the message to indicate to Dr. Lee that the attached message was sent to the Dodge family.
5. Send the message (Figure 1-71).

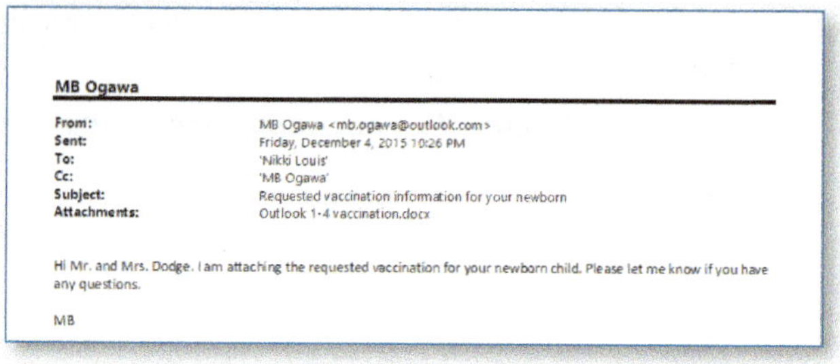
MB Ogawa

From:	MB Ogawa <mb.ogawa@outlook.com>
Sent:	Friday, December 4, 2015 10:26 PM
To:	'Nikki Louis'
Cc:	'MB Ogawa'
Subject:	Requested vaccination information for your newborn
Attachments:	Outlook 1-4 vaccination.docx

Hi Mr. and Mrs. Dodge. I am attaching the requested vaccination for your newborn child. Please let me know if you have any questions.

MB

1-70 Printed message in memo format

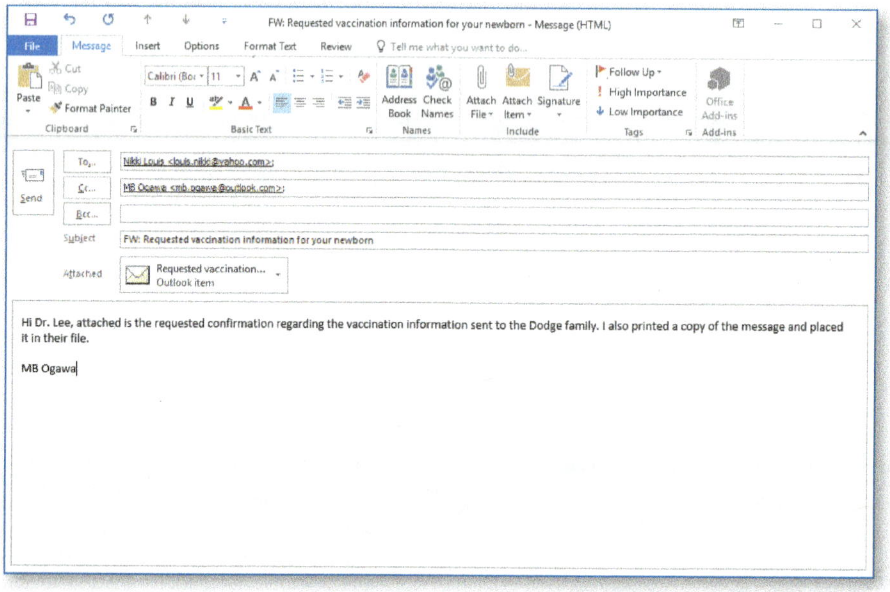

1-71 Independent Project 1-5 completed

Independent Project 1-6

You noticed that your Inbox is becoming cluttered because you included yourself as a *Cc* or *Bcc* on all of your previous messages to the Dodge family and Dr. Lee. For this project, you forward the messages as an attachment to yourself and your instructor to keep it as one message. Next, you clean your Inbox by deleting all previous messages regarding the Dodge family and Dr. Lee.
[Student Learning Outcomes 1.1, 1.2, 1.5, 1.6, 1.7, 1.8]

Files Needed: None

Skills Covered in This Project

- Open a message.
- Forward a message as an attachment.
- Select a *To* recipient.
- Select a *Bcc* recipient.
- Edit the subject.
- Edit the message.
- Send a message.
- Delete messages.

1. Locate and open the message sent in Independent Project 1-5 with the subject ***FW: Requested vaccination information for your newborn.*** The message has a paper clip icon next to it to indicate that it has an attachment.
2. Forward the message as an attachment to the following recipients:
   a. In the *To* field, type your email address.
   b. In the *Bcc* field, type your instructor's email address.
3. Edit the subject of the message to indicate that the message contains all of the Dodge family messages.
4. Edit the body of the message to indicate that the message is a summary of all messages related to the Dodge family.
5. Send the message (Figure 1-72).

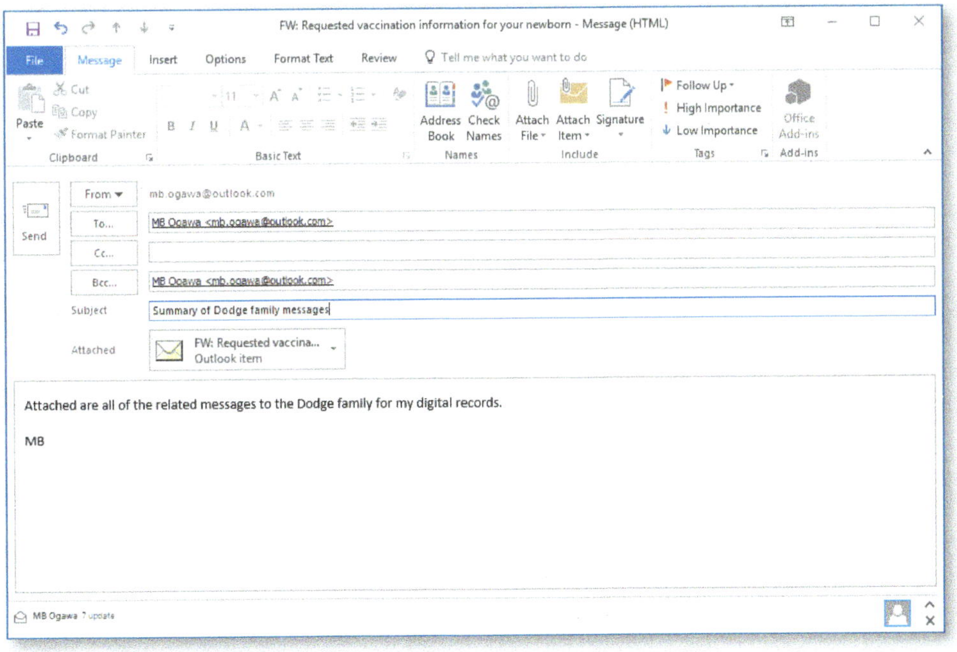

1-72 Message sent for Independent Project 1-6

6. Locate the following messages sent regarding the Dodge family:
   Requested vaccination information for your newborn
   FW: Requested vaccination information for your newborn
7. Delete the two messages listed in step 6 (Figure 1-73).

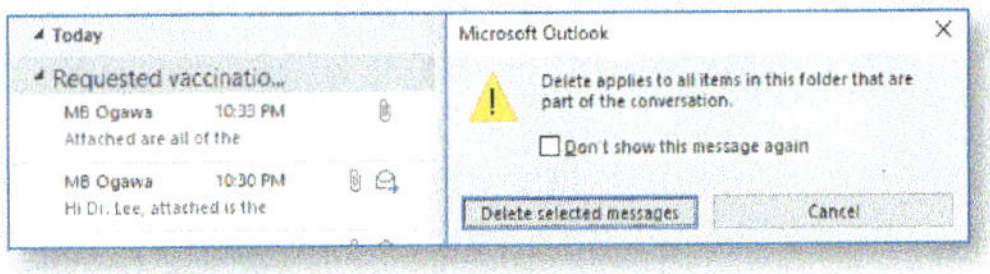

1-73 Deleting messages for Independent Project 1-6

Challenge Project 1-7

Search for an image online that is representative of you. Compose a message to your instructor with the image as an attachment that explains briefly why and how the image represents you.

Note: Use images that are legal under copyright. You many need to use a search engine such as http://search.creativecommons.org/ to find licensed content.
[Student Learning Outcomes 1.1, 1.2, 1.5, 1.6, 1.8]

Files Needed: None

- Send the message to your instructor.
- Add your email address to the *Cc* field.
- The subject of the message should be Challenge 1-7: Visually Representing [your name].
- Include the image as an attachment.
- Explain how the image represents you in three to five sentences.
- Add a citation for the image at the bottom of your message.

Challenge Project 1-8

Compose a message that includes a list of five activities you would like to try in the next five years. For each of the activities you list, compose a short paragraph about that activity and why you find it interesting. Research each of the activities you choose on the Internet. Use your own words when composing the paragraphs about each activity.
[Student Learning Outcomes 1.1, 1.2, 1.5, 1.8]

Files Needed: None

- Send the message to your instructor.
- Add your email address to the *Cc* field.
- The subject of the message should be Challenge 1-8: [your name]'s Activities.
- Use formatting to differentiate the activity names from their description and explanation for wanting to participate in each.

Challenge Project 1-9

Search for a job online that you would like to have. Compose an application letter to the employer highlighting a few reasons why you would be qualified for the position. The application letter should be short and concise. Attach your resume to the email message.
[Student Learning Outcomes 1.1, 1.2, 1.5, 1.6, 1.8]

Files Needed: None

- Send the message to your instructor.
- Add your email address to the *Cc* field.
- The subject of the message should be Challenge 1-9: [your name]'s application for [job name].
- Include your resume as an attachment.
- Address the body of the email message to your instructor.
- Include a few reasons why you would be qualified for the position in the body of the message.

CHAPTER 6

Folders, Rules, Quick Steps, and Search Folders

OUTLOOK

CHAPTER OVERVIEW

After completing the first half of this book, you now have a good understanding of the main components of Outlook—Email, Contacts, Calendar, and Tasks. Building on this essential foundation, we will delve into the numerous ways you can customize Outlook to best meet your needs. Outlook provides you with a range of features to help organize, categorize, and prioritize items within Outlook. Using folders, *Quick Steps*, rules, and search folders will help you to become a more efficient and effective Outlook user.

STUDENT LEARNING OUTCOMES (SLOs)

After completing this chapter, you will be able to:

SLO 6.1 Create, arrange, and modify Outlook folders (p. O6-211).

SLO 6.2 Create, apply, and change Outlook rules (p. O6-215).

SLO 6.3 Customize and use *Quick Steps* (p O6-225).

SLO 6.4 Utilize search folders to find email messages (p. O6-230).

CASE STUDY

For the Pause & Practice projects, you prepare for a group project and class by using folders, rules, Quick Steps, and search folders to help you more effectively and efficiently manage your email.

Pause & Practice 6-1: You create folders to organize your email messages. You begin by creating folders for your class, instructor, group project partners, and best friend. You delete the folder for your best friend.

Pause & Practice 6-2: You create two rules. The first rule is to move email from a specific instructor to the folder you created in the first Pause & Practice. The second rule moves all of your email messages from both of your group members into the folder you created in the first Pause & Practice.

Pause & Practice 6-3: You create two *Quick Steps* to help you be more efficient when working with email. For the first *Quick Step*, your instructor indicated that he or she wants you to email with a specific subject line. Rather than ensuring you type the right subject line for each message, you create a *Quick Step* for those messages. For the second *Quick Step*, you create tasks out of email messages for your group project to ensure you can view your work to complete in your tasks instead of searching through many email messages.

Pause & Practice 6-4: You utilize search folders to find information quickly. You create a search folder for email messages from your partners with attachments to allow you to easily locate files. You also want to use a search folder to quickly locate email messages from your instructor with the word *due* to quickly find messages with due dates or changes to due dates.

SLO 6.1

Using Folders

Most of you have a filing system in your home. You might have a filing cabinet with separate folders for monthly bills, insurance, income taxes, investments, and so forth. Can you imagine having just one drawer in your filing cabinet and throwing everything in that drawer? What a mess it would be and how hard it would it be to find an important paper.

In File Explorer, the Documents folder stores and organizes folders and files. Various types of files such as Word, Excel, PDF and picture files are stored in folders within the Documents folder. For example, you can create a folder named Travel within the Documents folder. Within the Travel folder, you can create subfolders to store pictures and itineraries of recent trips.

In Outlook, use ***folders*** to organize and group your emails, contacts, calendar, tasks, notes, and journals. In contrast to the generic type of folders used in Windows, Outlook folders are specific to the type of Outlook items stored. For example, a *Mail* folder is used to store email and a *Task* folder is used to store tasks.

Create a Folder

Creating folders in Outlook is actually very simple. The most important aspect to remember is that each Outlook folder is created to store a specific type of Outlook item. When the ***Create New Folder*** dialog box opens, it is important to confirm the type of folder you are creating and the location of the file.

In Outlook the following types of folders can be created:

- *Calendar Items*
- *Contact Items*
- *InfoPath Form Items*
- *Journal Items*
- *Mail and Post Items*
- *Note Items*
- *Task Items*

Follow these steps to create a new *Mail* folder. The steps are the same for creating any type of Outlook folder.

▶ HOW TO: Create a Folder

1. Click the **Mail** button in the *Navigation* bar.
2. Click the **Folder** tab.
3. Click the **New Folder** button in the *New* group (Figure 6-1). The *Create New Folder* dialog box opens (Figure 6-2).
4. Type the name of the new folder to be created.
5. Confirm that the *Folder* contains drop-down list displays **Mail and Post Items**.

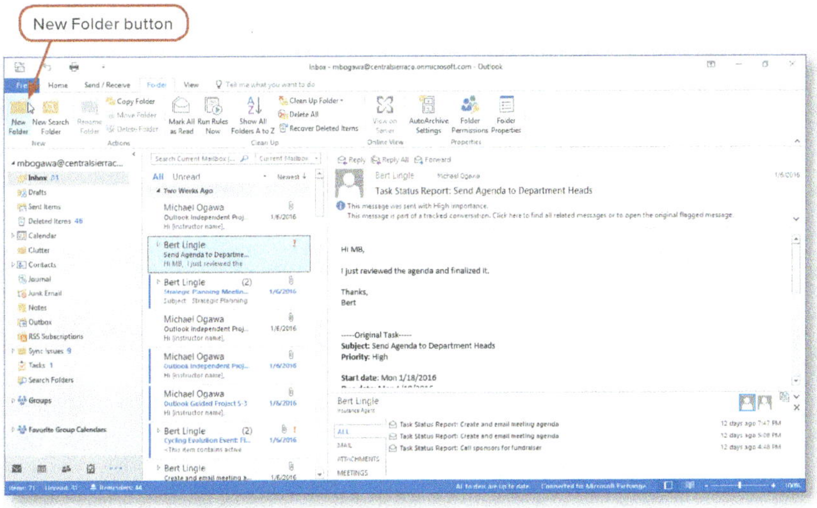

6-1 *New Folder* button

6. Specify the location of the new folder in the *Select where to place the folder* list.
7. Click **OK**.

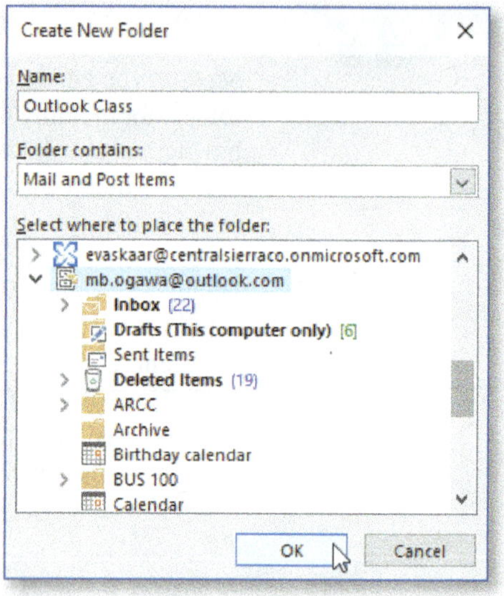

6-2 *Create New Folder* dialog box

> **ANOTHER WAY**
>
> You can create a new folder by right-clicking the folder inside which you would like to create a new folder and then selecting *New Folder*.

> **ANOTHER WAY**
>
> **Ctrl+Shift+E** opens the *Create New Folder* dialog box throughout Outlook.

Move a Folder

When you create a new folder in the wrong location or if you want to move a folder, you can use the Ribbon or the drag-and-drop method. The easiest way to move a folder to a new location is to click the folder to be moved in the *Folder* pane and drag and drop it to the new location. The folder and all its contents move to the new location.

Another way to move a folder is to use the ***Move*** feature.

HOW TO: Move a Folder

1. Select the folder to be moved in the *Folder* pane.
2. Click the **Folder** tab.
3. Click the **Move Folder** button in the *Actions* group (Figure 6-3). The *Move Folder* dialog box opens (Figure 6-4).
4. Click the desired location to move the folder in the *Move the selected folder to the folder list* dialog box.
5. Click **OK**. The folder and all its contents will be moved to the new location.

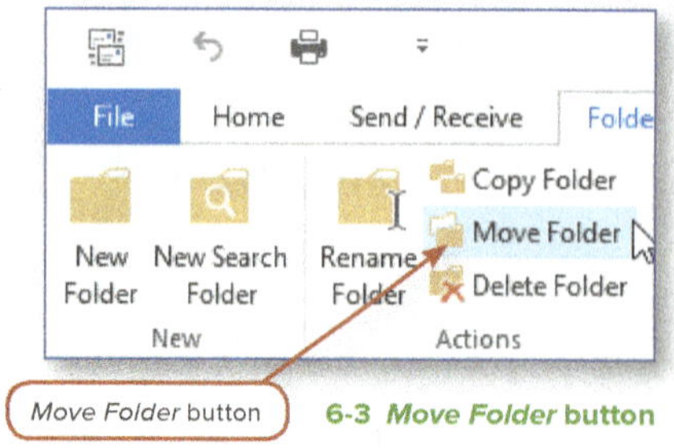

6-3 *Move Folder* button

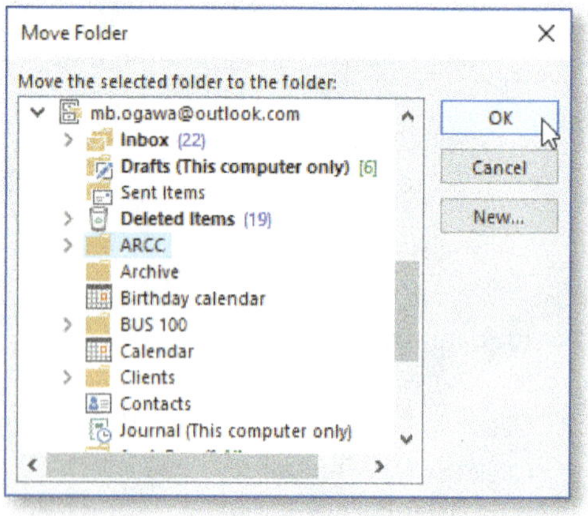

6-4 *Move Folder* dialog box

> **ANOTHER WAY**
>
> You can right-click the folder to be moved and choose **Move Folder**, or simply drag and drop the folder to a new location in the *Folder* pane.

Delete a Folder

Folders are sometimes created to store information temporarily. Folders can be deleted when they are no longer needed. When you delete a folder, all the items in the folder are deleted as well. The deleted folder is moved to the *Deleted Items* folder.

HOW TO: Delete a Folder

1. Select the folder to be deleted in the *Folder* pane.
2. Click the **Delete Folder** button in the *Actions* group on the *Folder* tab (Figure 6-5).
   - A warning dialog box opens asking you if you are sure you want to delete the folder and its contents.
3. Click **Yes** to delete the folder and all its contents.

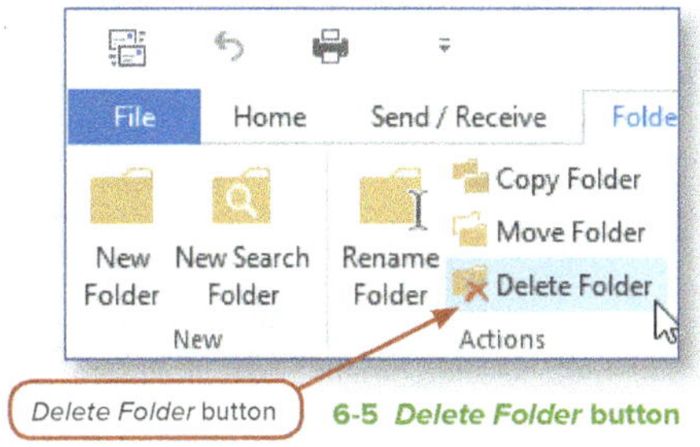

6-5 *Delete Folder* button

ANOTHER WAY

Right-click the folder to be deleted and choose **Delete Folder**.

ANOTHER WAY

Ctrl+D deletes the selected item. This shortcut will delete a folder or other selected Outlook items.

Use the Folders List

When you are in the Mail, Calendar, Contacts, Tasks, Notes, or Journal areas, only those folders associated with that part of Outlook display in the *Folder* pane. The ***Folders list*** (Figure 6-6) is a useful view to show all your Outlook folders in the *Folder* pane. This is also a good view to use when you are moving folders from one location to another.

MORE INFO

In all the areas of Outlook except Mail and the *Folders* list, your folders are not displayed in hierarchical structure. In other words, in these other areas it is hard to know whether or not a folder is located inside of another folder.

Display the Folders list by clicking the (. . .) button in the *Navigation* bar, and then clicking *Folders*.

ANOTHER WAY

Ctrl+6 displays the *Folders* list in the *Folder* pane.

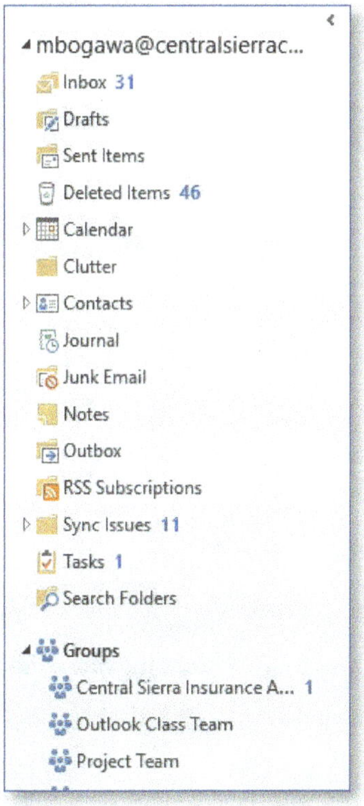

6-6 *Folders* list

PAUSE & PRACTICE: OUTLOOK 6-1

For this Pause and Practice project, you create folders to help organize email messages. You begin by creating folders for your class, instructor, group project partners, and best friend. You delete the folder for your best friend.

Files Needed: None

1. Create a folder for your class.
   a. Click the **Mail** button in the *Navigation* bar.
   b. Click the **Folder** tab.
   c. Click the **New Folder** button in the *New* group. The *Create New Folder* dialog box opens.
   d. Type BUS 100 in the *Name* text area.
   e. Confirm that the folder type in the Folder *contains* menu is **Mail and Post Items**.
   f. Specify your main email account folder in the *Select where to place the folder section*.
   g. Click **OK**.

2. Create a folder for your instructor.
   a. Click the **Mail** button in the *Navigation* bar.
   b. Click the **Folder** tab.
   c. Click the **New Folder** button in the *New* group. The *Create New Folder* dialog box opens.
   d. Type your instructor's name in the *Name* text area.
   e. Confirm that the folder type in the Folder *contains* menu is **Mail and Post Items**.
   f. Specify your main email account folder in the *Select where to place the folder* section.
   g. Click **OK**.

3. Create a folder for your group project.
   a. Click the **Mail** button in the *Navigation* bar.
   b. Click the **Folder** tab.
   c. Click the **New Folder** button in the *New* group. The *Create New Folder* dialog box opens.
   d. Type Group Project in the *Name* text area.
   e. Confirm that the folder type in the Folder *contains* menu is **Mail and Post Items**.
   f. Specify your main email account folder in the *Select where to place the folder* section.
   g. Click **OK**.

4. Create a folder for your best friend.
   a. Click the **Mail** button in the *Navigation* bar.
   b. Click the **Folder** tab.
   c. Click the **New Folder** button in the *New* group. The *Create New Folder* dialog box opens.
   d. Type Nicole in the *Name* text area.
   e. Confirm that the folder type in the Folder *contains* menu is **Mail and Post Items**.
   f. Specify your main email account folder in the *Select where to place the folder* section.
   g. Click **OK**.

5. Move the *[instructor name]* folder into the *[class name]* folder.
   a. Select **[instructor name]** folder in the *Folder* pane.
   b. Click the **Folder** tab.
   c. Click the **Move Folder** button in the *Actions* group. The *Move Folder* dialog box opens.
   d. Click the **BUS 100** folder in the *Move the selected folder to the folder* section.
   e. Click **OK**.

6. Move the *Group Project* folder into the *BUS 100* folder.
   a. Select **Group Project folder** in the *Folder* pane.
   b. Click the **Folder** tab.
   c. Click the **Move Folder** button in the *Actions* group. The *Move Folder* dialog box opens.
   d. Click the **[class name]** folder in the *Move the selected folder to the folder* section.
   e. Click **OK**.
7. Delete the *Nicole* folder.
   a. Select the **Nicole folder** in the *Folder* pane.
   b. Click the **Delete Folder** button in the *Actions* group on the *Folder* tab. A warning dialog box opens asking if you are sure you want to move the folder to the *Deleted Items* folder.
8. Click **Yes** to delete the folder and all its contents. Figure 6-7 is a sample of your folder list at the end of Pause & Practice 6-1.

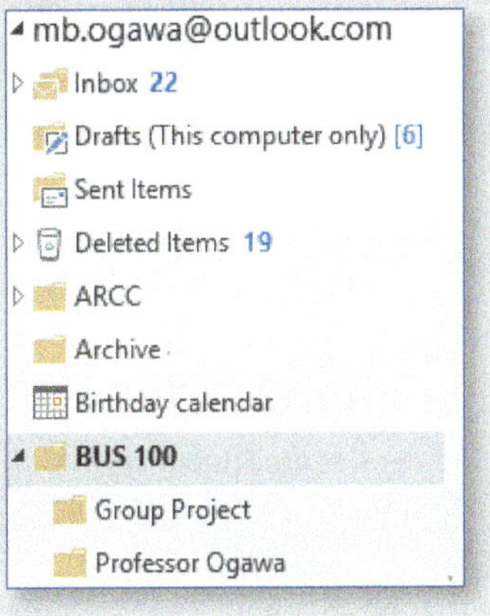

6-7 Pause & Practice 6-1 completed

SLO 6.2

Creating and Using Rules

You may receive email messages from each of your instructors, family members, or co-workers. When all of these emails appear in your Inbox, it is difficult to distinguish routine email messages from messages with a higher priority. To help organize your email messages, create folders and rules to automatically move email messages to an appropriate folder.

Rules might be one of the most useful features in Outlook. Rules can be used to check incoming or outgoing emails and apply an action. If you have ever used the *IF* function in Microsoft Excel, rules operate similar to this if/then logical principle. Most rules have two basic parts: a ***condition*** and an ***action***. An ***exception*** can also be added to the rule.

- ***Condition***: The condition is what Outlook looks for when an email is received or sent. This could be an email that includes a specific word or words in the subject or body, sent from a specific person, received through a specific email account, or marked as high importance.
- ***Action***: The action is what is done with the email when the condition is met. This could include moving the email to another folder, marking the email as high importance, categorizing the email with a specific category, deleting the email, or forwarding the email.
- ***Exception***: An exception can be used to nullify an action. For example, a rule can be set up to look for the word "BUS 310" in the subject line and move it to the *BUS 310* folder, except if it comes from the *Dean of the CSIT* area. Exceptions are not commonly used in rules.

Quick Steps are similar to rules, but they do not include a condition. So rather than automatically applying an action to an email when it meets a condition, *Quick Steps* can be applied to email on an individual basis. For example, a *Quick Step* can be used to create a meeting request from a received email message.

Create a Rule

A rule can be created quickly based on an email in your Inbox. When you create a rule based on an email message, you have a limited number of options for the condition and action, and you cannot include an exception.

If you receive several email messages with the subject "Outlook," create a rule to manage the emails. The rule would automatically move all emails with the word "Outlook" in the subject line to an *Outlook* folder.

HOW TO: Create a Rule Based on an Email in Your Inbox

1. Click the **Mail** button on the *Navigation* bar.
2. Open the email for which you would like to create a new rule.
3. Click the **Rules** button in the *Move* group on the *Message* tab.
4. Choose **Create Rule** (Figure 6-8). The *Create Rule* dialog box opens. Three conditions appear at the top of the dialog box, and three actions appear at the bottom of the dialog box (Figure 6-9).

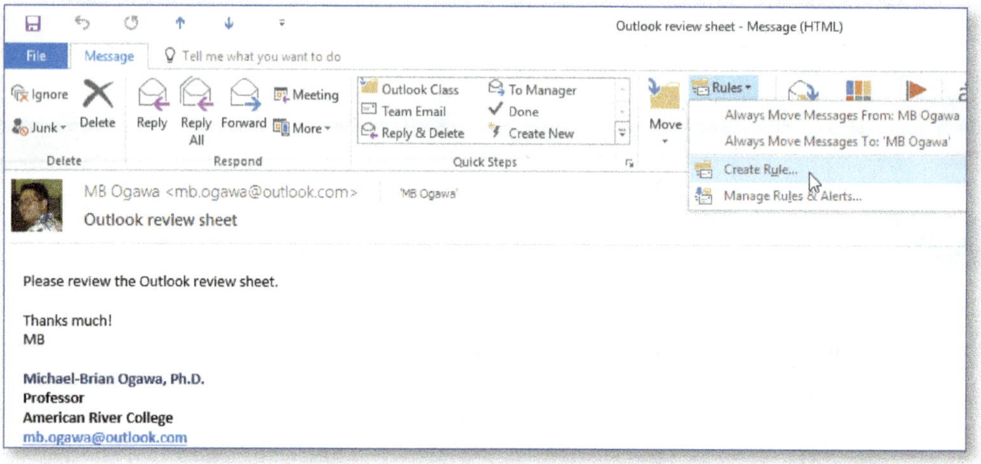

6-8 *Create Rule*

5. In the conditions area (the top half of the dialog box), select the **Subject contains** check box and make sure the word in the subject is correct. If not, correct it.
6. In the actions area (the bottom half of the dialog box), select the **Move the item to folder** check box and click the **Select Folder** button.
7. Select the desired folder from the folder list and press **OK** (Figure 6-10). The *Create Rule* dialog box will still be open. Confirm that the correct folder was selected (see Figure 6-10). If not, click the **Select Folder** button and select the correct folder.

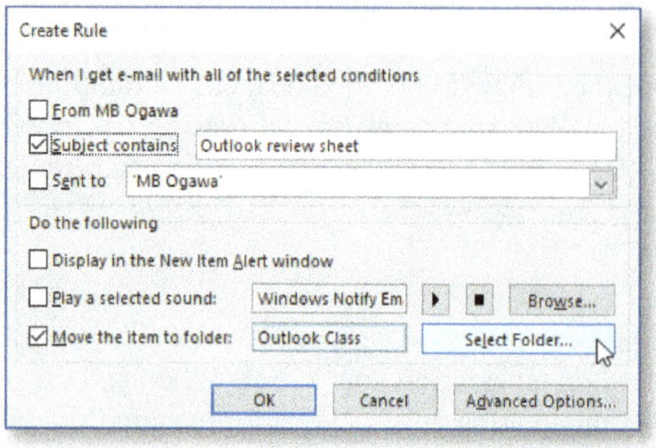

6-9 *Create Rule* dialog box

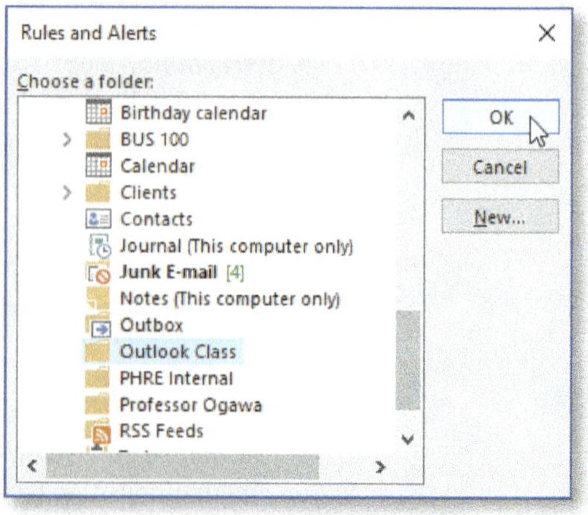

6-10 Select a folder for the rule

8. Click **OK**. A *Success* dialog box opens (Figure 6-11).
9. Select the **Run this rule now on messages already in the current folder** check box.
10. Click **OK**.
11. All the emails in your Inbox with a subject that matches the condition will be moved to the specified folder.

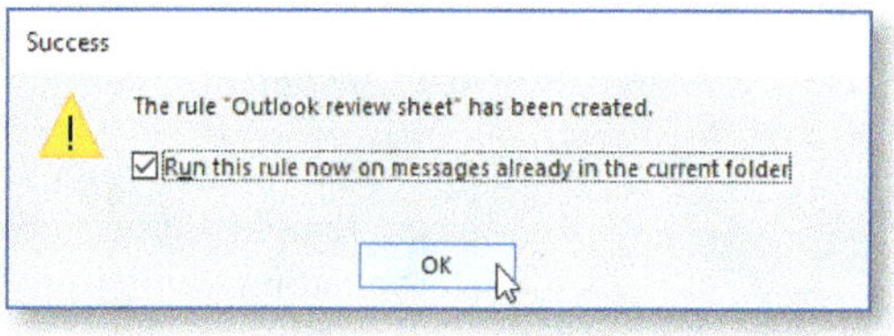

6-11 ***Success* dialog box**

> **MORE INFO**
>
> If you forget to create a folder before creating a rule, you can create a new folder in the *Rules and Alerts* dialog box by clicking the *New* button.

> **MORE INFO**
>
> When creating a rule that looks for a word in the subject, Outlook looks for *exactly* what you type. Common errors include misspellings and a space after the word. The word you type is not case sensitive.

> **ANOTHER WAY**
>
> *Right-click* an email message and choose *Rules* and then select *Create Rule*.

Create an Advanced Rule

Creating a *Rule* based on an email in your Inbox is effective and efficient, but you are limited by the number of conditions and actions from which to select.

To have additional customization options for the rules you create, open the ***Rules and Alerts*** dialog box (click the **Home** tab, click the **Rules** button in the *Move* group, and then select **Manage Rules & Alerts** as shown in Figure 6-12). This dialog box lists the rules existing on your computer and is used to create, modify, delete, and order the existing rules.

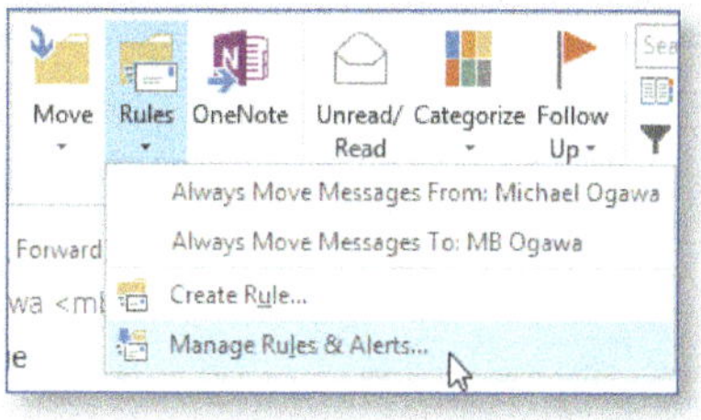

6-12 ***Manage Rules & Alerts***

When you click the *New Rule* button (Figure 6-13), the *Rules Wizard* dialog box opens. The *Rules Wizard* steps you through the creation of your rule and includes five steps.

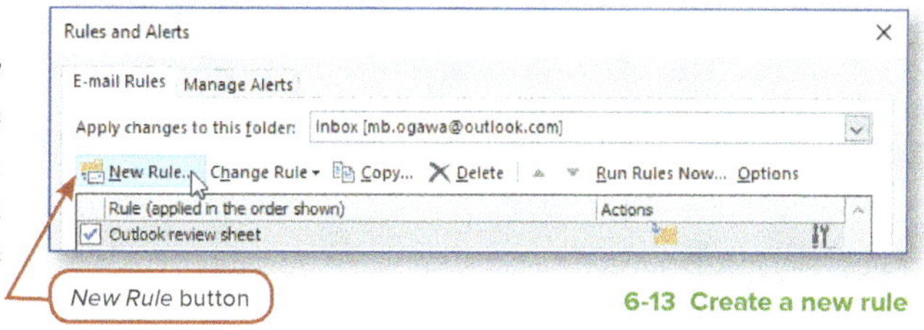

6-13 Create a new rule

- *Step 1*: Choose to use a rule template or create a blank rule. This step also determines whether this rule is applied to incoming or outgoing emails.
- *Step 2*: Select the condition of the rule.
- *Step 3*: Set the action Outlook is to perform if the condition is met.

- *Step 4*: Specify any exceptions to the rule.
- *Step 5*: Name and run the rule.

You can choose rule templates to create the most common types of rules. When you select a rule template, you move to the next step to specify the condition. You can also choose to start creating a rule from a blank rule.

▸HOW TO: Create a New Rule

1. Click the **Mail** button in the *Navigation* bar.
2. Click the **Rules** button in the *Move* group on the *Home* tab and choose **Manage Rules & Alerts**. The *Rules and Alerts* dialog box opens.
3. Click the **New Rule** button. The *Rules Wizard* dialog box opens.
4. Select **Apply rule on messages I receive** in the *Start from a blank rule* section (Figure 6-14).
5. Click **Next**. You move to the next step to select a condition for the rule.
6. Select the **from people or public group** check box. The condition displays in the bottom section of the dialog box.
7. Click the **people or public group** link in the bottom section (Figure 6-15). The *Rule Address* dialog box opens.
8. Select the name of the individual for the condition of the rule (Figure 6-16).
9. Click **From** and **OK**.
   - The *Rule Address* dialog box closes and you return to the *Rules Wizard* dialog box.
   - Notice the person's name appears in the bottom section as the condition for which Outlook is looking.

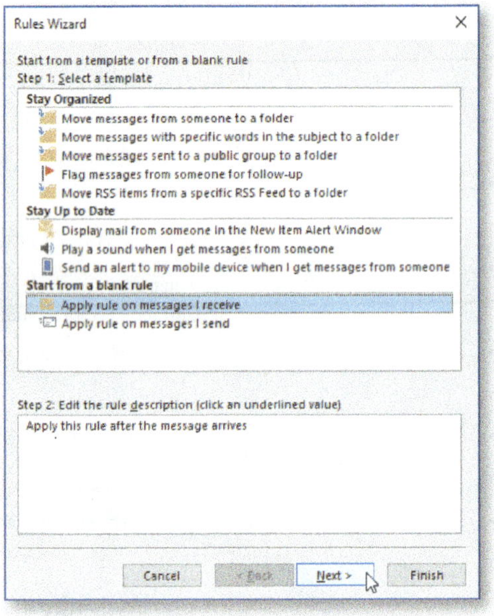

6-14 Create a new blank rule

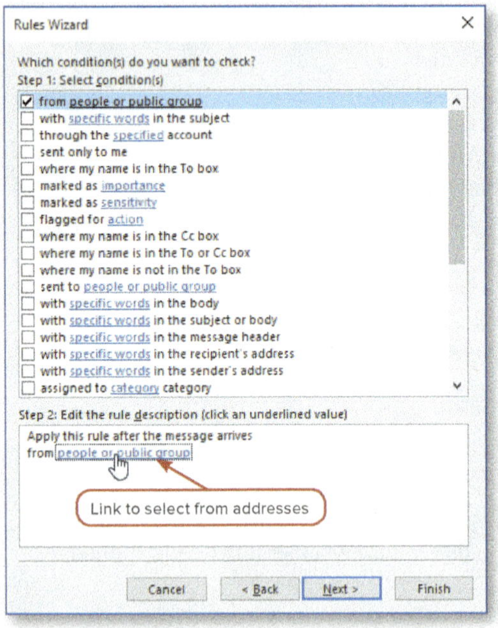

6-15 Click the people or public group link

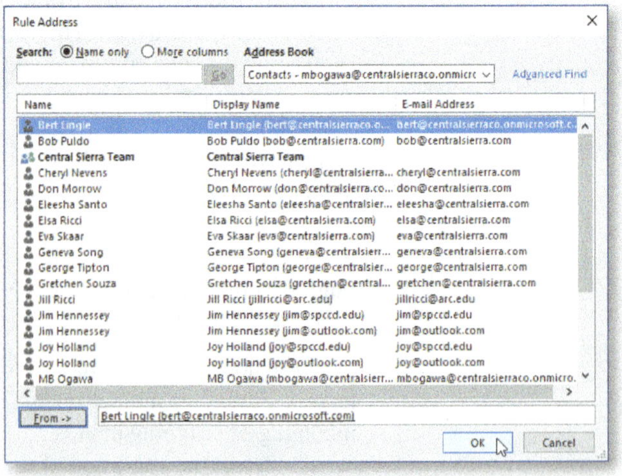

6-16 Select addresses

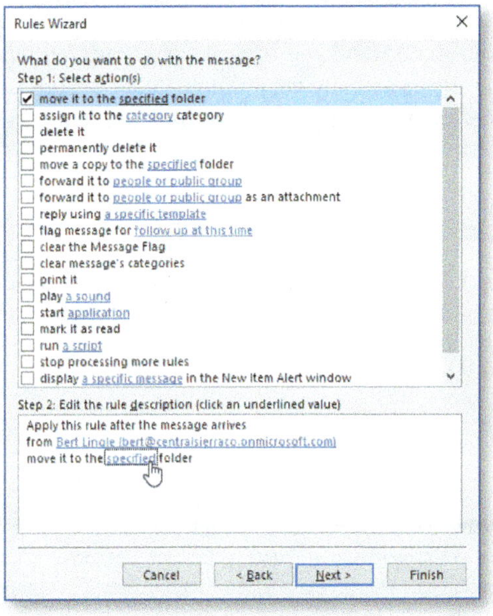

6-17 Select an action

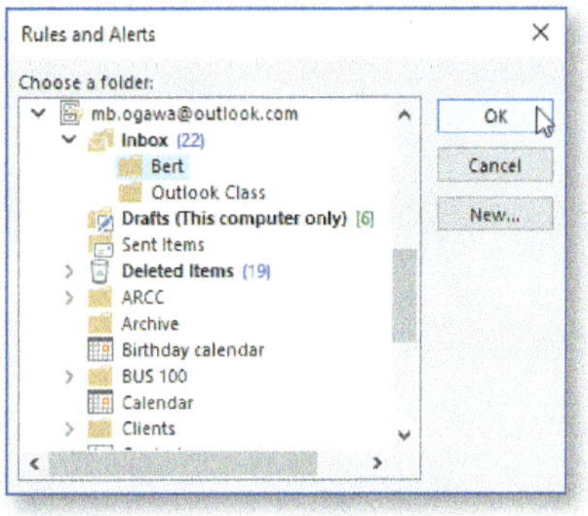

6-18 Select a location

10. Click **Next**. You move to the *action* step in the *Rules Wizard* dialog box.
11. Select the **move it to the specified folder** check box (Figure 6-17).
12. Click the **specified** folder link in the bottom section. The *Rules and Alerts* dialog box opens.
13. Click the desired folder and press **OK** (Figure 6-18). You return to the *Rules Wizard* dialog box. Always read the rule in the bottom section to make sure the condition and action are correct.
14. Click **Next**. You move to the *exceptions* step.
15. Click **Next**. No exceptions will be added to this rule. The *Finish rule setup* step appears.
16. Customize the name of the rule in the *Step 1* area.
17. Select the **Run this rule now on messages already in "Inbox"** check box (Figure 6-19).
18. Confirm that the **Turn on this rule** box is selected.
19. Read the rule one last time to confirm that the condition and action are correct.
20. Click **Finish**.
    - The rule checks the condition on all the emails in your Inbox.
    - If the condition is met, Outlook moves all emails matching the condition to the folder you created (see Figure 6-19). You return to the *Rules and Alerts* dialog box. Notice the new rule is in the list of rules.
21. Click **Apply** and then **OK**. (Figure 6-20).

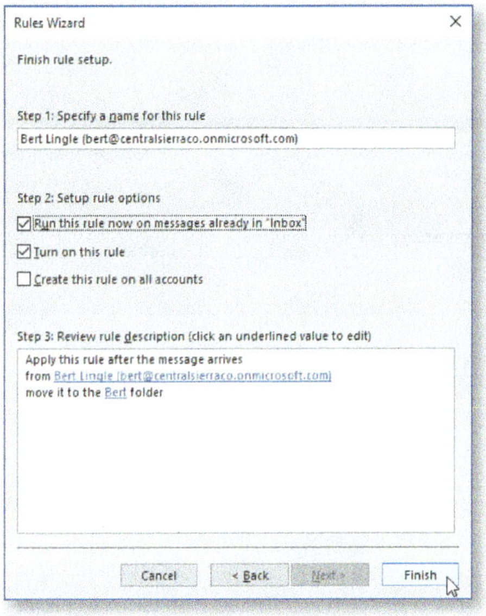

6-19 Setup rule options

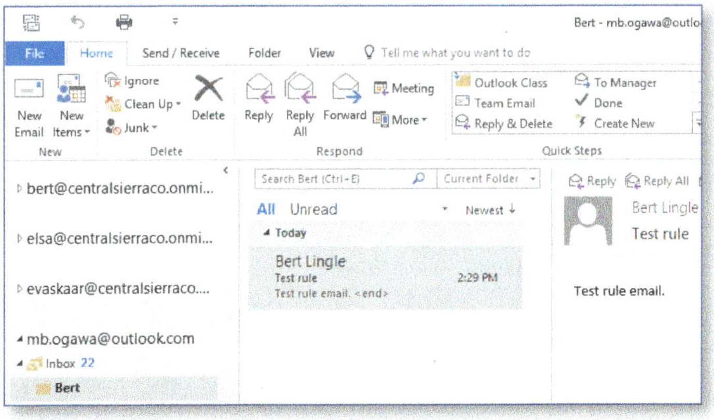

6-20 Email message automatically moved

Creating rules might seem like a daunting process, but once you have gone through the steps of creating a rule and understand the logical *condition*, *action*, *exception* sequence, you'll realize that creating rules is actually very simple. Not only are rules easy to create and use, but they are also very effective in helping you to organize and customize your Inbox.

MORE INFO

It is best to keep rules simple: a condition and one action (and an exception if necessary). The more conditions and actions you have in one rule, the greater the chance of either diluting the effectiveness of the rule or causing the rule to not function as intended.

MORE INFO

When using Outlook in a stand-alone environment, your rules are stored on your computer. If you are using Outlook in an Exchange environment, your rules are stored on the Exchange server. This means that most rules will run wherever you access Outlook, including Outlook Web Access. Some rules are client-only rules, which means they will only run on the computer on which they were created.

Modify a Rule

Once a rule is created, it is very easy to modify the condition, action, or exception. Rules can also be modified to run on different folders within your mailbox.

HOW TO: Modify a Rule

1. Click the **Mail** button on the *Navigation* bar.
2. Click the **Rules** button and select the **Manage Rules & Alerts** option.
3. Select the rule to be modified, click the **Change Rule** button, and then choose **Edit Rule Settings** (Figure 6-21). The *Rules Wizard* dialog box opens. Alternatively, double-click the rule to open the *Rules Wizard* dialog box.
4. Change the condition, action, exception, name, or folder on which the rule is to run.
5. Select the **Run this rule now on messages already in "Inbox"** check box after you modify a rule.
6. Click **Finish** to apply the changes and run the rule.

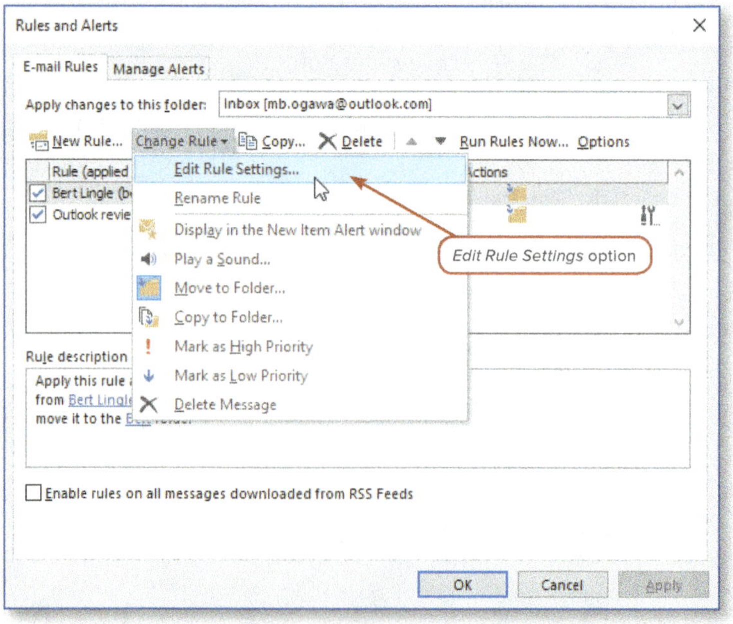

6-21 *Edit Rule Settings*

ANOTHER WAY

Another way to manage rules is to display the *Backstage* view, select Info on the left pane, and click **Manage Rules & Alerts**. The *Rules and Alerts* dialog box opens.

Delete or Turn On/Off a Rule

A rule can easily be deleted by selecting the rule in the *Rules and Alerts* dialog box and either pressing the *Delete* button or right-clicking the rule and choosing *Delete*.

One way to manage rules is to turn off a rule but not delete it. The rule can be turned on if you need to use it again.

HOW TO: Turn Off a Rule

1. Open the *Rules and Alerts* dialog box.
2. Deselect the check box to the left of the rule to turn it off (Figure 6-22).

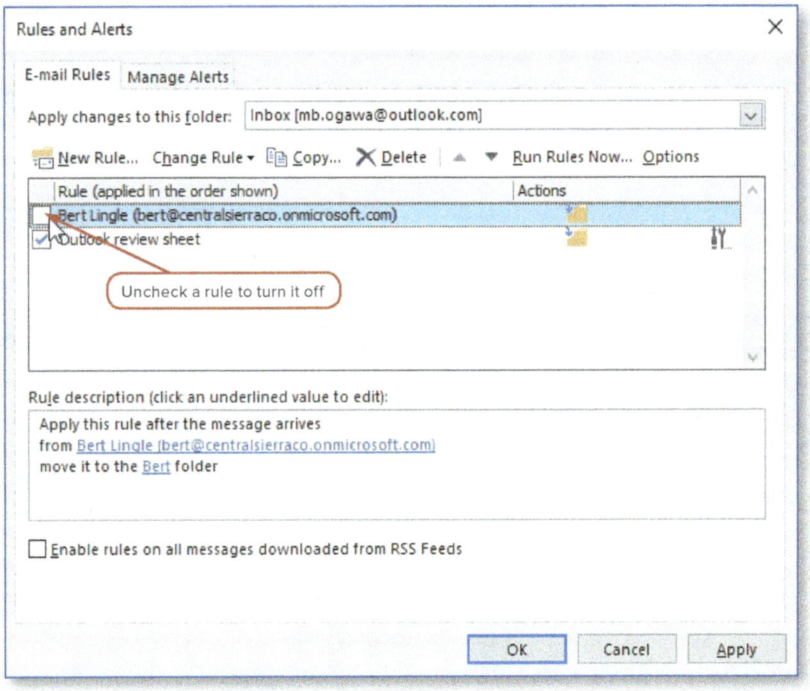

6-22 Turn off a rule

3. Click **Apply** and then **OK**. The rule is now turned off.

Turn on a rule by checking the box to the left of the rule in the *Rules and Alerts* dialog box. It is easy to view which rules are on or off by looking at your list of rules in the *Rules and Alerts* dialog box. A check in the check box indicates that a rule is turned on, and no check in the check box indicates that a rule is turned off.

> **MORE INFO**
>
> Outlook has a default rule (*Clear categories on mail*) that has been created for you. This rule clears any categories on incoming messages. It is important to keep this rule because you do not want others' categories conflicting with your categories.

Run a Rule

When a rule that was turned off is turned back on, it is important to run this rule on messages currently in the Inbox. Outlook provides you with a feature to run specific rules without having to step through the *Rules Wizard*.

Options include selecting the rules to be run, the folder on which to run each rule, and what type of messages on which to apply each rule (*All Messages*, *Unread Messages*, or *Read Messages*). A ***Rule Description*** displays in the middle of the dialog box for the selected rule.

HOW TO: Run a Rule

1. Click the **Rules** button [*Home* tab, *Move* group] and select **Manage Rules & Alerts**.
2. Select the *Rule* you want to run and click the **Run Rules Now** button. The *Run Rules Now* dialog box opens (Figure 6-23).
3. Check the rule to run. The *Rule Description* area displays the condition and action (and exception if applicable).
4. Specify the folder on which the rule is to run.
5. Specify the types of messages on which to apply the rule.
6. Click **Run Now**.
7. Click **Close** to close the *Run Rules Now* dialog box.

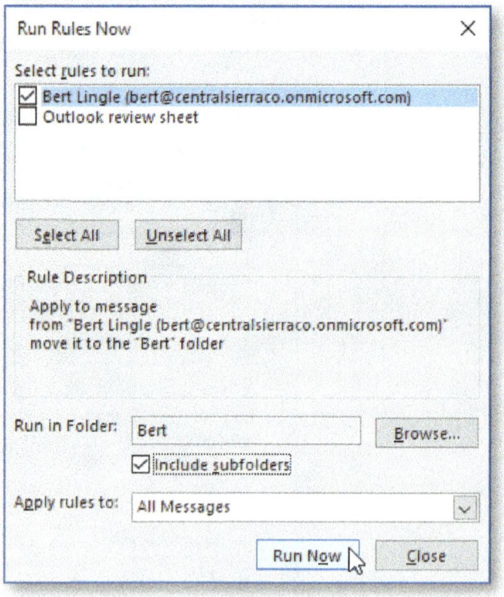

6-23 *Run Rules Now* dialog box

Rearrange Rules

As you begin using rules, you will find more and more uses for them. It will not be long before you have a long list of rules running in Outlook. The rules in Outlook are ***hierarchical***, which means that those at the top of the list are run before those at the bottom. It is important to order rules properly to prioritize the order in which the rules are run and minimize the potential for conflict. For example, if you have a rule to mark an email as important if it comes from a particular person and a rule to move all emails with attachments to an *Attachments* folder, you might have a conflict if you receive an email from that particular person and it has an attachment. If the attachment rule is above the mark it as important rule, the email message will be moved to the *Attachments* folder but not marked as important.

You will need to determine which action is the most important and make sure the rule is above the other rules in the *Rules and Alerts* dialog box. Use the up and down buttons in the dialog box to move rules up or down in the rule hierarchy.

▶ HOW TO: Reorder Rules

1. Open the *Rules and Alerts* dialog box.
2. Select the rule to be moved up or down in priority.
3. Click the *Move Up* or *Move Down* button (Figure 6-24).
4. Click **Apply** and **OK**.

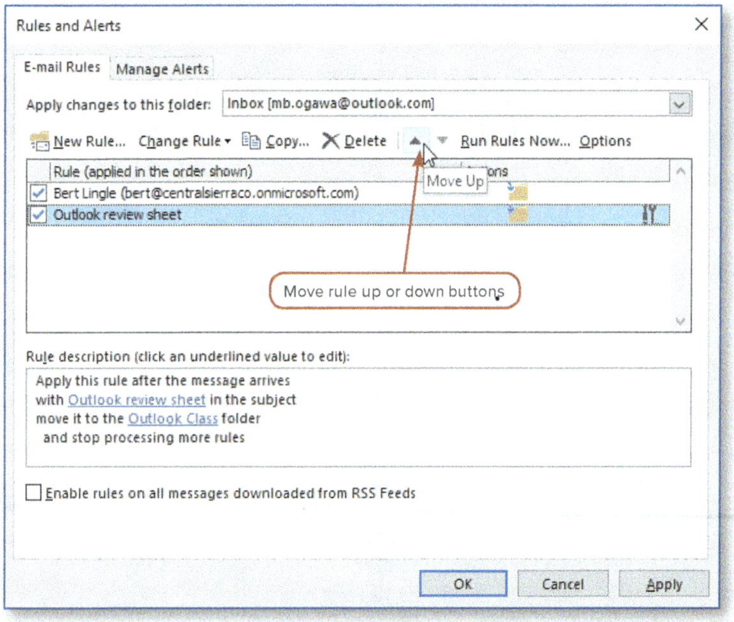

6-24 Move rules up or down

PAUSE & PRACTICE: OUTLOOK 6-2

For this Pause and Practice project, you create two rules. The first rule is to move email from a specific instructor to the folder you created in *Pause & Practice 6-1*. The second rule moves all of your email messages from both of your group members into the folder you created in *Pause & Practice 6-1*.

Files Needed: None

1. Create a *Rule* to move email messages from your instructor into the *[instructor name]* folder you created in *Pause & Practice 6-1*.
   a. Locate and open a message from your instructor.
   b. Click the **Rules** button in the *Move* group on the *Message* tab.
   c. Choose **Create Rule**. The *Create Rule* dialog box opens.
   d. In the conditions area (the top half of the dialog box), check **From [instructor name]** (the name will vary based on your instructor's name).
   e. In the actions area (the bottom half of the dialog box), check **Move the item to folder** and click the **Select Folder** button.
   f. Select the **[instructor name]** folder from the folder list and press **OK**. The instructor folder will be in the class name folder. It was moved in PP 6-1. The *Create Rule* dialog box remains open.
   g. Click **OK**.
   h. Select the **Run this rule now on messages already in "the selected folder"** check box.
   i. Click **OK**.
2. Create an advanced rule to move emails from your two partners into the *Group Project* folder (Figure 6-25).
   a. Click the **Mail** button in the *Navigation* bar.
   b. Click the **Rules** button in the *Move* group on the *Home* tab and choose **Manage Rules & Alerts**. The *Rules and Alerts* dialog box opens.

c. Click the **New Rule** button. The *Rules Wizard* dialog box opens.
d. Select **Apply rule on messages I receive** in the *Start from a blank rule* section.
e. Click **Next**. You will move to the next step to select a condition for the rule.
f. Check the **from people or public group** box. The condition displays in the bottom section of the dialog box.
g. Click the **people or public group** link in the bottom section. The *Rule Address* dialog box opens.
h. Select the names of your group members if they are in your contacts list or type their email addresses with a semi colon (;) between their email addresses.
i. Click **From** and **OK**.
j. Click **Next**. You move to the *action* step in the *Rules Wizard* dialog box.
k. Check the **move it to the specified folder** box.
l. Click the **specified** folder link in the bottom section. The *Rules and Alerts* dialog box opens.
m. Click the **Group Project** folder and press **OK**. You return to the *Rules Wizard* dialog box.
n. Click **Next**. You return to the *exceptions* step.

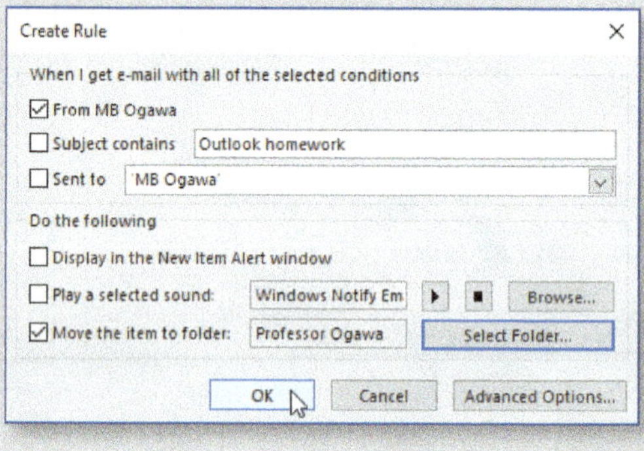

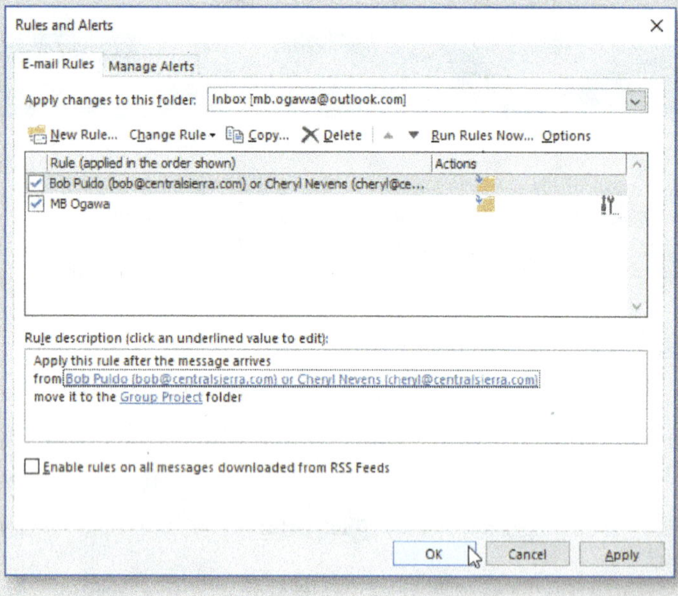

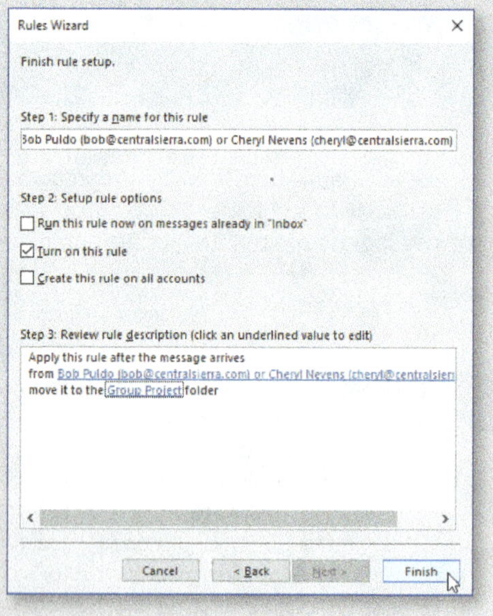

6-25 PP Outlook 6-2 completed

o. Click **Next**. No exceptions are required for this rule. The *Finish rule setup* step appears.
p. Type [Class Name] Group Project in the *Step 1* area.
q. Confirm that the **Turn on this rule** box is selected.
r. Read the rule one last time to confirm that the condition and action are correct.
s. Click **Finish**.
t. Click **Apply** and then **OK**.

SLO 6.3

Customize and Use Quick Steps

Quick Steps are powerful tools in Outlook. Similar to a rule, a *Quick Step* performs an action on a selected email. The main difference between a *Quick Step* and a rule is that *Quick Steps* are not based on a condition, but rather they are applied to the selected emails.

Modify an Existing Quick Step

Outlook has several preset *Quick Steps* created for you. When you select an email in your Inbox and click one of the *Quick Steps*, the *Quick Step* will automatically apply the action. For example, the *Reply & Delete Quick Step* (Figure 6-26) creates a reply message to the sender and deletes the original message.

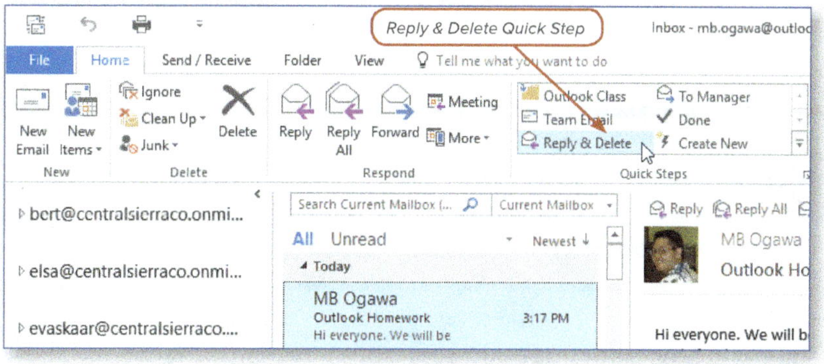

6-26 *Reply & Delete Quick Step*

You can customize *Quick Steps* to specify the action to be performed. For example, the *Team Email Quick Step* needs to have the recipients on your team selected to be able to perform the action.

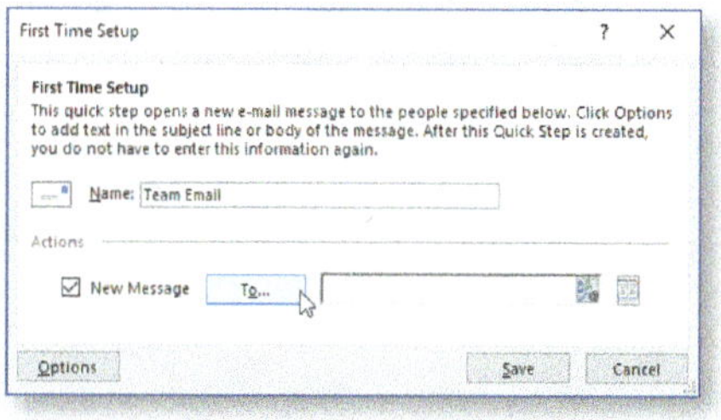

6-27 *First Time Setup* dialog box

▶ HOW TO: Modify an Existing Quick Step

1. Select the email in the *Content area* or open an email on which to apply the *Quick Step*.
2. Click a **Quick Step** [*Home* tab, *Quick Steps* group].
3. Click the **To** button (Figure 6-27) to select the team members to be included in this *Quick Step* and click **OK**. Or, enter the email addresses followed by a semicolon.
4. Change the **Name** of the *Quick Step* as desired.
5. Click the **Options** button to open the *Edit [Quick Step's name]* dialog box (Figure 6-28). You can add additional actions to the *Quick Step* in this dialog box.
6. Click the **Show Options** link to display additional options available for this action. The **Hide Options** link will hide these available options.
7. Click **Save** to close this dialog box and return to the *Customize Quick Step* dialog box.
8. Click **Save** to save this *Quick Step*.

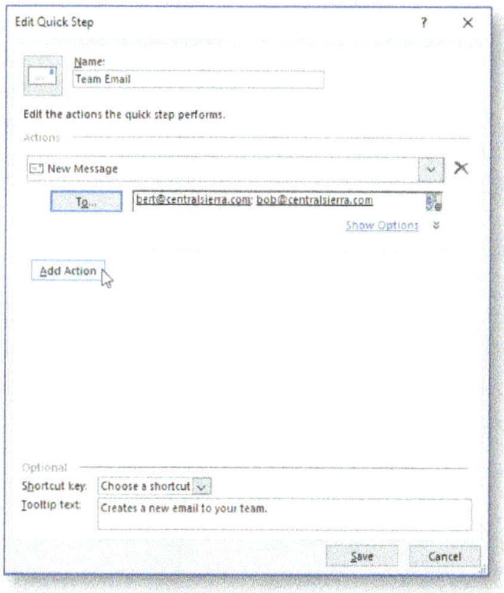

6-28 *Edit Quick Step* dialog box

ANOTHER WAY

A *Quick Step* can be applied to an email message by right-clicking the message in the *Content area*, choosing *Quick Steps*, and selecting the *Quick Step* to apply.

Create a New Quick Step

As you begin using *Quick Steps*, you will find the need to create your own custom *Quick Steps*. These new custom *Quick Steps* will appear in the *Quick Steps* group on the *Home* and *Message* tabs. *Quick Steps* are not limited to one action but can include multiple actions to be performed on a selected email message. For example, you can create a *Quick Step* to mark an email as high importance, mark it as read, and move it to a folder.

HOW TO: Create a New Quick Step

1. Click the **Create New** *Quick Step* button [*Home* tab, *Quick Steps* group] (Figure 6-29). The *Edit Quick Step* dialog box opens (Figure 6-30).
2. Type a name for the *Quick Step*.
3. Click the drop-down arrow to display a list of actions. *Note: The list of actions in Figure 6-30 is not a complete list.*
4. Select the action to be performed (see Figure 6-30). If additional criteria are available, the *Show Options* link appears below the action.
5. Click the **Add Action** button to add another action (Figure 6-31). An action can be deleted by clicking the **X** (delete) button to the right of the action (see Figure 6-31).

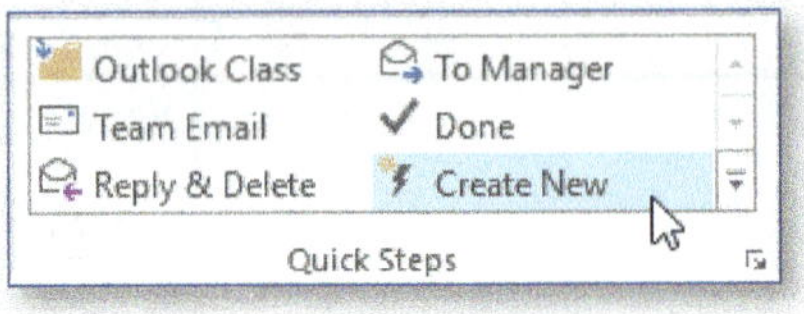

6-29 *Create New Quick Step* button

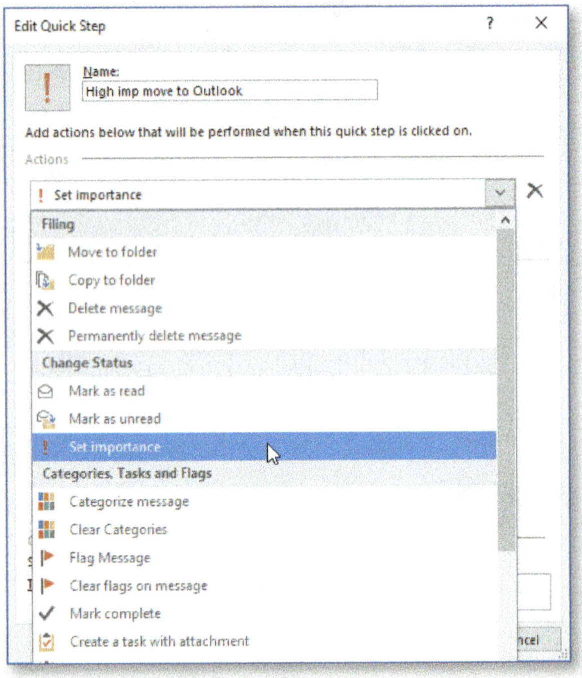

6-30 *Edit Quick Step* dialog box

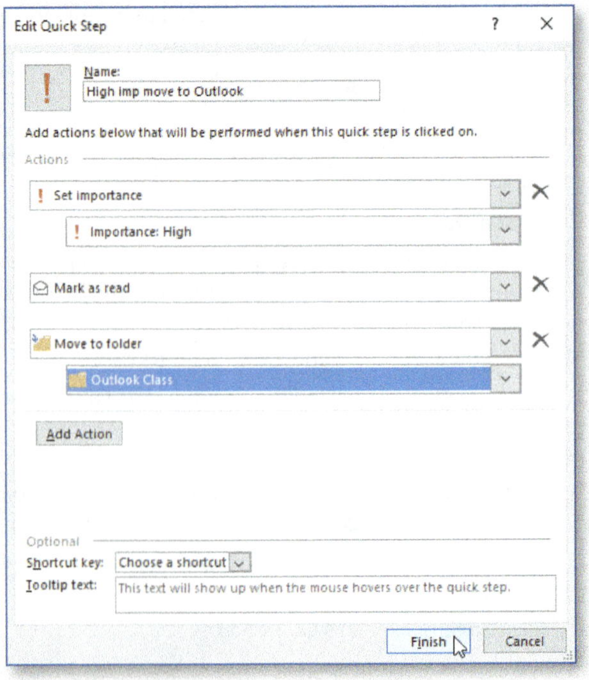

6-31 Completed *Quick Step*

6. In the *Tooltip text* area, type a description for this *Quick Step* (see Figure 6-31). This *Tooltip* appears when your pointer is placed over the *Quick Step*.
7. Click the **Finish** button when all the actions have been added (see Figure 6-31). The new *Quick Step* is included in the list of *Quick Steps*.

Manage Quick Steps

Like rules, *Quick Steps* can easily be managed. You can open the *Manage Quick Steps* dialog box by clicking the *Manage Quick Steps* option [*Home* tab, *Quick Steps* group, *More* button]. The *Manage Quick Steps* dialog box allows you to create new *Quick Steps* and modify, duplicate, or delete existing ones. Change the display order of *Quick Steps* by clicking the Up or Down arrows. You can also create groups to organize *Quick Steps* (Figure 6-32).

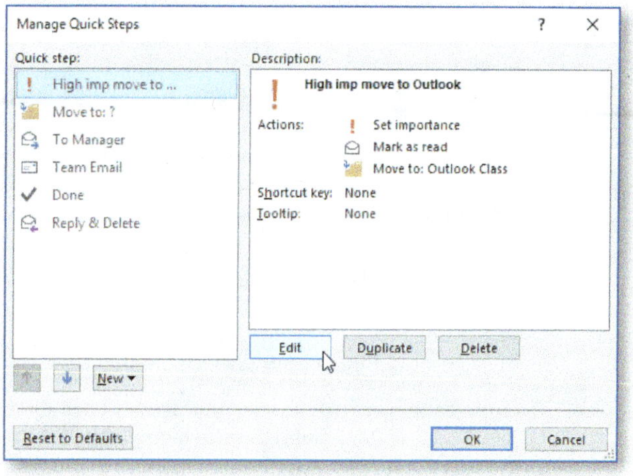

6-32 *Manage Quick Steps* dialog box

ANOTHER WAY

A shortcut can be added to a *Quick Step* by selecting a shortcut keystroke combination (Ctrl+Shift+number) when creating or editing a *Quick Step*.

MORE INFO

The *Restore Defaults* button in the *Manage Quick Steps* dialog box will restore the *Quick Steps* to their original settings.

PAUSE & PRACTICE: OUTLOOK 6-3

For this Pause and Practice project, you create two *Quick Steps* to help you be more efficient when working with email. For the first *Quick Step*, your instructor indicated that he or she wants you to send email with a specific subject line. Rather than checking that you typed the correct subject line for each message, you create a *Quick Step* for those messages. For the second *Quick Step*, you create tasks out of email messages for your group project to ensure you can view your work to complete in your tasks instead of searching through email messages.

Files Needed: None

1. Create a *Quick Step* to email your instructor with the subject *[class name]* (Figure 6-33).
   a. Click the **Create New** *Quick Step* button [*Home* tab, *Quick Steps* group]. The *Edit Quick Step* dialog box opens.
   b. In the *Name* text area type Email [instructor name].
   c. Click the drop-down list arrow to display a list of actions that can be performed.
   d. Select **New Message**.
   e. Click the **Show Options** link below the action.
   f. Click the **To** button. Select your instructor's email address and click the **To** button followed by **OK**. If your instructor's email address is not in your Contacts, type it into the *To* field in the *Edit Quick Step* dialog box.
   g. In the *Subject* field, type [class name].
   h. In the *Tooltip text* area, type Email to instructor for [class name].
   i. Click the **Finish** button to create the new *Quick Step*.
2. Create a *Quick Step* to create a task with an attachment (see Figure 6-33).
   a. Click the **Create New** *Quick Step* button [*Home* tab, *Quick Steps* group]. The *Edit Quick Step* dialog box opens.
   b. In the *Name* text area, type Group Project Task.
   c. Click the drop-down list arrow to display a list of actions that can be performed.
   d. Select **Create a task with attachment**.
   e. Click the **Add Action** button to add another action.
   f. Click the drop-down list arrow to display a list of actions that can be performed.
   g. Select **Delete message**.
   h. In the *Tooltip text* area, type Create task and delete message.
   i. Click the **Finish** button to create the new *Quick Step*.
3. Send an email message to one of your partners to request the draft of the executive summary.
   a. Click the **Mail** button in the *Navigation* bar.
   b. Click the **New Email** button [*Home* tab, *New* group].
   c. Enter the following information in your message:

      To: [partner's email address]
      Subject: Executive Summary Request
      Body: Hi [partner name],

      Please email me a draft of the executive summary when you finish it.

      Sincerely,
      [your name]
   d. Click **Send**.
4. Create a task from the message (see Figure 6-33).
   a. Locate the email your partner sent. It is in the *Group Project* folder.
   b. Click the **Group Project Task** *Quick Step* [*Home* tab, *Quick Steps* group].
   c. Click the **Save & Close** button.
5. Email the task to your instructor as an Outlook item.
   a. Click the **Mail** button in the *Navigation* bar.
   b. Click the **New Email** button [*Home* tab, *New* group].
   c. Enter the following information in your message:

      To: [instructor's email address]
      Cc: [your email address]
      Subject: Outlook Pause & Practice 6-3
      Body: Hi [instructor name],

Attached is the Outlook item for the Pause & Practice 6-3 exercise.

Sincerely,
[your name]

d. Click the **Attach Item** button [*Message* tab, *Include* group] and select **Outlook Item**.
e. Select the **Tasks** option and locate the task you created.
f. Click **OK**.
g. Click **Send**.

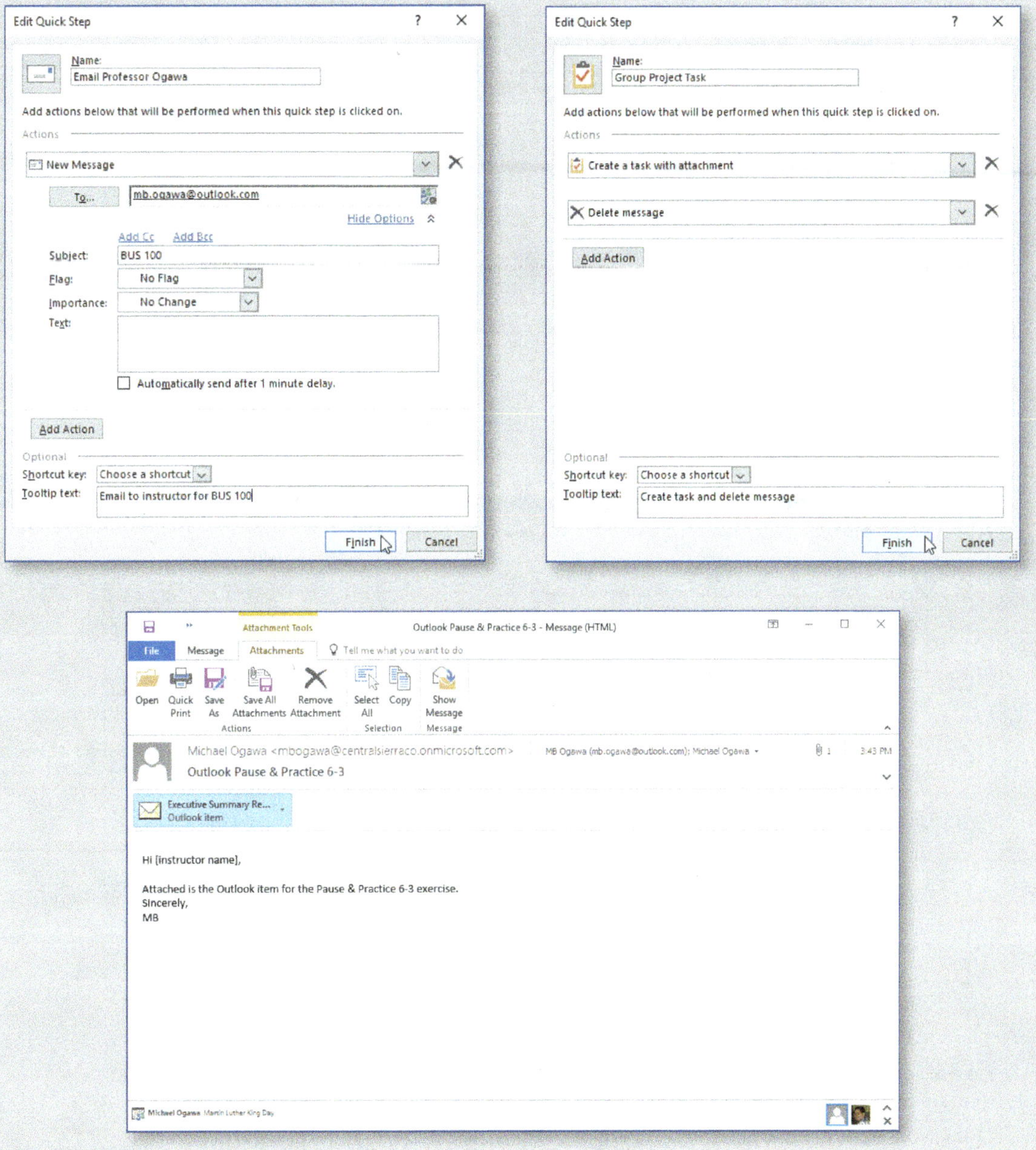

6-33 Pause & Practice 6-3 completed

SLO 6.4

Using Search Folders

Search folders are related to rules in that they look for a specific condition or criterion in email messages, and if the condition is met, the message displays in the search folder. Search folders differ from rules in that the message is not physically moved to a different location.

Search folders are virtual folders; they don't actually contain any messages, but rather they display email items that are located in other folders that meet a certain condition. For example, you can create a search folder for ***Unread Mail***. Any email message in your mailbox that is unread will be displayed in the *Content area* when you click the *Unread Mail* search folder in the *Folder* pane (Figure 6-34).

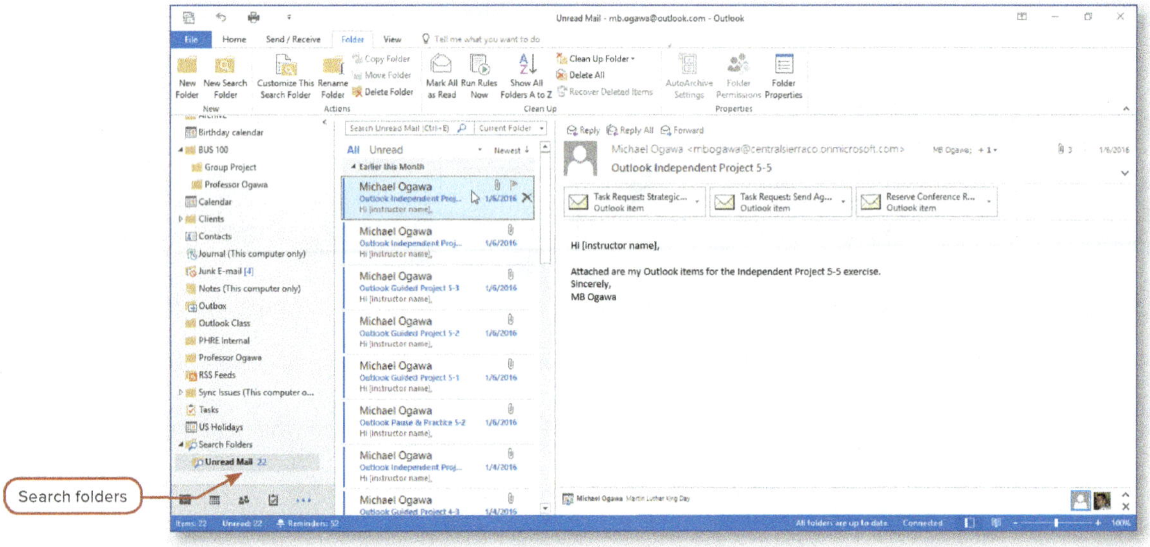

6-34 ***Unread Mail*** **search folder**

Create a New Search Folder

Suppose you want to create a search folder that looks for all the emails from your professor, but you do not want to create a rule to physically move these messages to a separate folder. A search folder can be created to find and display all the messages from your professor.

Search folders are very easy to create, customize, and delete.

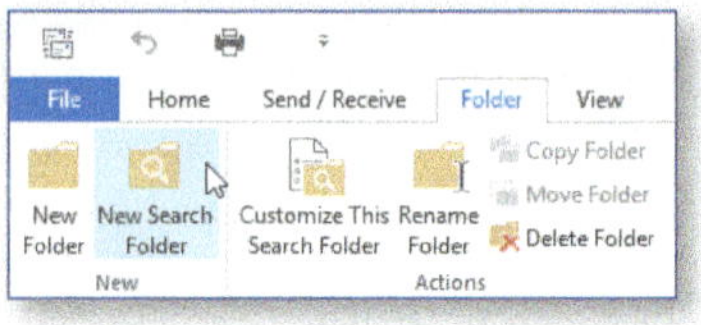

6-35 ***New Search Folder*** **button**

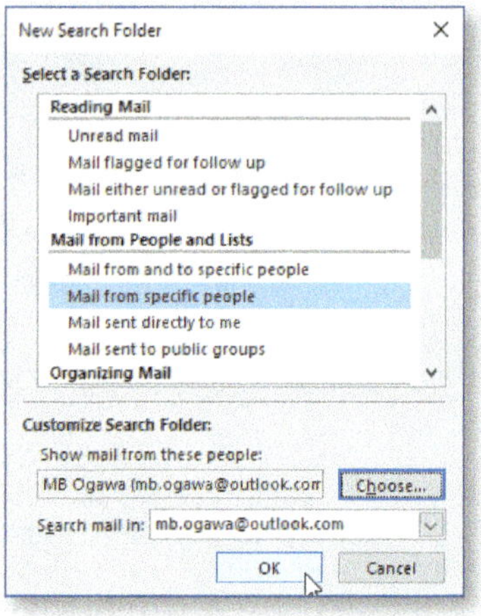

6-36 ***New Search Folder*** **dialog box**

▶ HOW TO: Create a New Search Folder

1. Click the **Mail** button in the *Navigation* bar.
2. Click the **Folder** tab and then the **New Search Folder** button in the *New* group (Figure 6-35). The *New Search Folder* dialog box opens.
3. Select **Mail from specific people** as the condition (Figure 6-36).
4. Click **Choose** to select a contact. The *Select Names* dialog box opens.
5. Select the name of the contact for the condition of the search folder.

6. Click the **From** button to add the contact or double-click the contact.
7. Click **OK** to close the *Select Names* dialog box.
8. Click **OK** to close the *New Search Folder* dialog box. The new search folder appears in your list of search folders in the *Folder* pane (Figure 6-37).

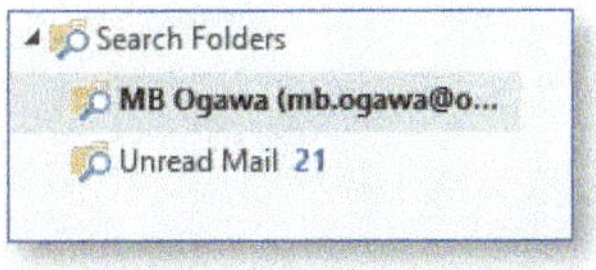

6-37 Search folder

ANOTHER WAY

A new search folder can also be created by pressing **Ctrl+Shift+P**.

When creating a new search folder, different criteria options are available from which to choose. You can also choose the *Create a custom Search Folder* option at the bottom of the *New Search Folder* dialog box for additional customization options.

Customize a Search Folder

You can customize search folders by changing the name of the folder, the criteria for the search, and/or the mailbox folders to be included in the search. When you create a new search folder, by default, all the mailbox folders (or personal folders) are included in the search for mail messages meeting the criterion.

HOW TO: Customize a Search Folder

1. Click the **Mail** button in the *Navigation* bar.
2. Select the search folder to be customized.
3. Click the **Folder** tab and then the **Customize This Search Folder** button in the *Actions* group (Figure 6-38). The *Customize* dialog box opens (Figure 6-39).
4. Select the criteria, or indicate which folders to include in the *Mail from these folders will be included in the Search Folder* selection box.
5. Click the **Browse** button to change the folders to be included in the search. The *Select Folder(s)* dialog box opens.
6. Select the folders to be included in the search for this search folder. Notice the *Search subfolders* option at the bottom of the dialog box (Figure 6-40).
7. Click **OK** to close the *Select Folder(s)* dialog box.
8. Click **OK** to close the *Customize* dialog box.

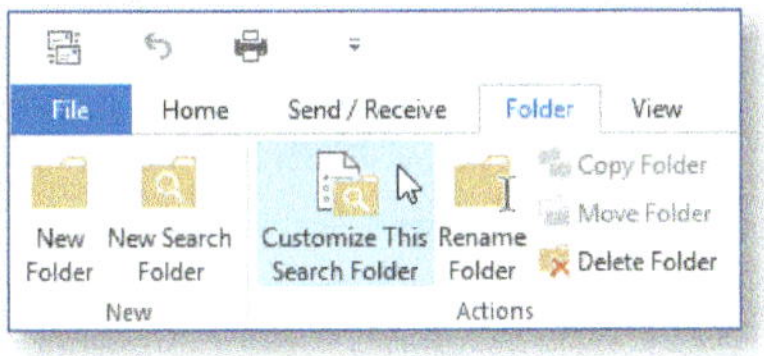

6-38 *Customize This Search Folder* button

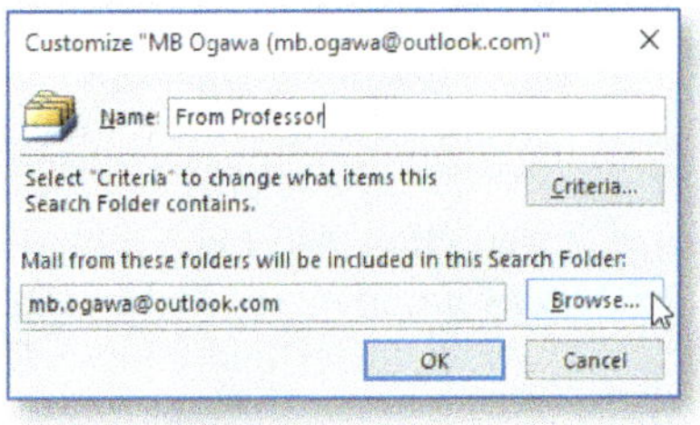

6-39 *Customize Search Folder* dialog box

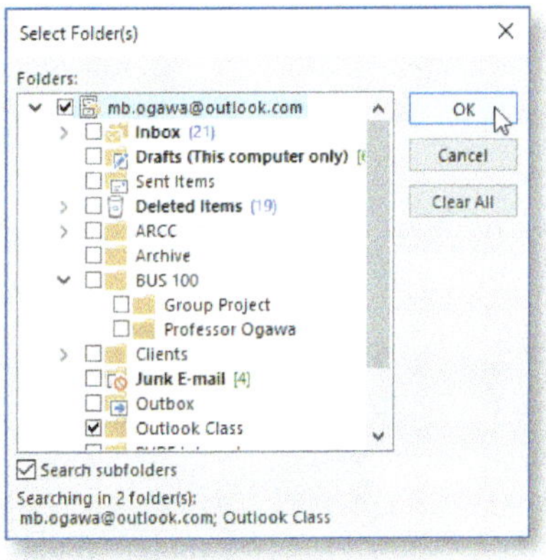

6-40 *Select Folder(s)* dialog box

> **MORE INFO**
>
> There is also a *Rename Folder* button in the *Actions* group on the *Folder* tab, which can be used to rename a search folder.

> **ANOTHER WAY**
>
> Right-click the search folder and choose **Customize This Search Folder**.

Search folders can also be customized to show either the total number of items in the folder or the number of unread items in the folder.

HOW TO: Customize the Number of Items Displayed in the Folder

1. Click a search folder.
2. Click the **Folder** tab.
3. Click the **Folder Properties** button in the *Properties* group. The *[Folder's Name] Properties* dialog box opens (Figure 6-41).
4. Click either *Show number of unread items* or *Show total number of items*.
5. Click **Apply** and then **OK**.

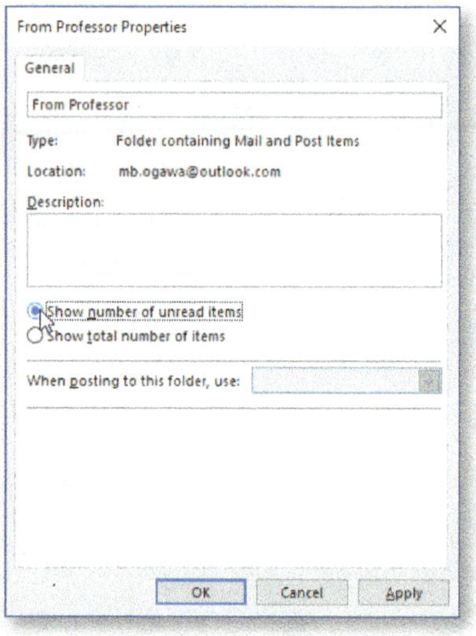

6-41 Search folder properties

> **ANOTHER WAY**
>
> Right-click the search folder and choose **Properties**.

> **MORE INFO**
>
> When a new search folder is created, the default setting is *Show number of unread items*. The number of unread items displays in blue parentheses. When *Show total number of items* is selected, the total number of items displays in green brackets.

Delete a Search Folder

Because search folders are virtual folders, they don't physically contain any email messages. When a search folder is deleted, none of the messages displayed in the search folder are deleted.

To delete a search folder, click the search folder in the *Folder* pane and click the **Delete Folder** button in the *Actions* group on the *Folder* tab or press **Delete** on your keyboard. You can also right-click the search folder and choose **Delete Folder**. When deleting a search folder, a dialog box opens asking if you want to delete the search folder and informing you that the items contained in the search folder will not be deleted (Figure 6-42). Press **Yes** to delete the search folder.

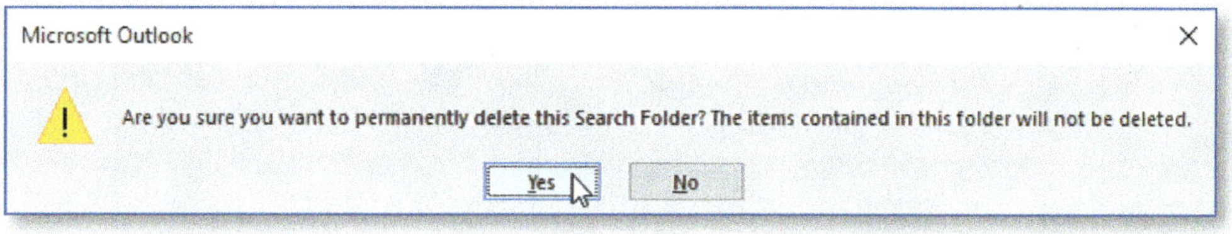

6-42 Delete search folder confirmation

ANOTHER WAY

Ctrl+D deletes a selected search folder throughout Outlook.

MORE INFO

Even though deleting a search folder will not delete the items contained in the search folder, email messages displayed in a search folder can be deleted by selecting the messages in the *Content area* and pressing **Delete**.

PAUSE & PRACTICE: OUTLOOK 6-4

For this Pause and Practice project, you utilize search folders to help you find information quickly. You create a search folder for email messages from your partners with attachments to allow you to easily locate files. You also want to use a search folder to quickly locate email messages from your instructor that contain the word *due* to quickly find messages with due dates or changes to due dates.

Files Needed: None

1. Create a new search folder to find messages from your partners with attachments.
   a. Click the **Mail** button in the *Navigation* bar.
   b. Click the **Folder** tab and then the **New Search Folder** button in the *New* group. The *New Search Folder* dialog box opens.
   c. Select **Create a custom Search Folder**.
   d. Click **Choose**. The *Custom Search Folder* dialog box opens.
   e. In the *Name* text area, type Group Project Attachments.
   f. Click the **Criteria** button. The *Search Folder Criteria* dialog box opens.
   g. In the *Messages* tab, type your partners' email addresses in the *From* text area or click the **From** button and select their contacts.
   h. Click the **More Choices** tab.
   i. Click the **Only items with** check box and ensure the option is set to **one or more attachments**.
   j. Click **OK** to close the *Search Folder Criteria* dialog box.
   k. Click **OK** to close the *Custom Search Folder* dialog box.
   l. Click **OK** to close the *New Search* Folder dialog box. The new search folder appears in your list of search folders in the *Folder* pane.
2. Customize the *Group Project Attachments* search folder to show the total number of items.
   a. Right-click the ***Group Project Attachments*** search folder and select **Properties**.
   b. Click the **Show total number of items** radio button.
   c. Click **OK**.

3. Create a new search folder to find messages from your instructor that contain the word *due* in the subject or body of the message.
   a. Click the **Mail** button in the *Navigation* bar.
   b. Click the **Folder** tab and then the **New Search Folder** button in the *New* group. The *New Search Folder* dialog box opens.
   c. Select **Create a custom Search Folder**.
   d. Click **Choose**. The *Custom Search Folder* dialog box opens.
   e. In the *Name* text area, type Class Due Dates.
   f. Click the **Criteria** button. The *Search Folder Criteria* dialog box opens.
   g. In the *Messages* tab, type your instructor's email address in the *From* text area or click the **From** button and select his or her contact.
   h. In the *Search for word(s)* text area, type Due. The search term is not case sensitive.
   i. Click the **In** drop-down arrow and select **subject field and message body**.
   j. Click **OK** to close the *Search Folder Criteria* dialog box.
   k. Click **OK** to close the *Custom Search Folder* dialog box.
   l. Click **OK** to close the *New Search Folder* dialog box. The new search folder will appear in your list of search folders in the *Folder* pane. See Figure 6-43 for completed Pause & Practice 6-4.

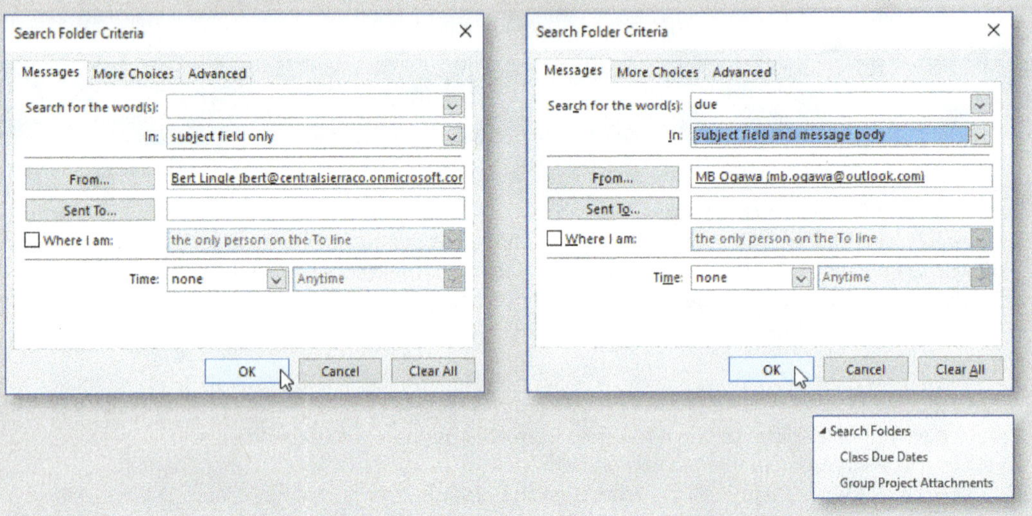

6-43 Pause & Practice 6-4 completed

Chapter Summary

6.1 Create, arrange, and modify Outlook folders (p. O6-211).

- ***Folders*** in Outlook are similar to a physical filing cabinet with folders to organize email and other Outlook items.
- Outlook folders are specific to each type of Outlook item, such as a folder for tasks.
- Once folders are created, they can be moved.
- Deleting a folder also deletes its contents.

6.2 Create, apply, and change Outlook rules (p. O6-215).

- ***Rules*** check incoming or outgoing emails and apply an action.
- Rules have three main parts: a condition, an action, and an exception.
- A ***condition*** checks if an email message meets a specific criteria.
- An ***action*** is what is done with the email when the condition is met.
- An ***exception*** nullifies an action if specific criteria are met.
- A *Rule* can be created from an email message.
- The *Rules Wizard* guides you through the process of creating a rule from scratch.
- Rules can be edited after they created.
- Rules run ***hierarchically***, therefore rules listed at the top run before those listed at the bottom.

6.3 Customize and use *Quick Steps* (p. O6-225).

- ***Quick Steps*** are similar to rules and can be applied to specific email messages.
- Outlook includes default *Quick Steps*, which are editable.
- New *Quick Steps* can be created for common tasks.

6.4 Utilize search folders to find email messages (p. O6-230).

- ***Search folders*** use virtual folders to display messages that meet specific criteria.
- You can create search folders for a variety of criteria including displaying only *Unread Mail*.
- Search folders display either the number of items in the virtual folder or the number of unread items.
- Deleting a search folder does not delete its contents because it is a virtual folder.

Check for Understanding

The SIMbook for this text (within your SIMnet account) provides the following resources for concept review:

- Multiple choice questions
- Matching exercises
- Short answer questions

USING MICROSOFT OUTLOOK 2016

Guided Project 6-1

For this project, you are a real estate agent for Placer Hills Real Estate (PHRE). You just started working with two new clients, Nina Hu and Jim Cross, who are both looking for new homes. You use folders and rules to manage client and company email.
[Student Learning Outcomes 6.1, 6.2]

Files Needed: None

Skills Covered in This Project

- Create folders.
- Move folders.
- Delete a folder.
- Create a *Rule*.
- Create an advanced rule.
- Run a rule.

1. Create a folder for clients.
   a. Click the **Mail** button in the *Navigation* bar.
   b. Click the **Folder** tab.
   c. Click the **New Folder** button in the *New* group. The *Create New Folder* dialog box opens.
   d. Type Clients in the *Name* text area.
   e. Confirm that the folder type is **Mail and Post Items** in the *Folder contains* menu.
   f. In the *Select where to place the folder* section, specify your main email account folder.
   g. Click **OK**.
2. Create a folder for Nina.
   a. Click the **Mail** button in the *Navigation* bar.
   b. Click the **Folder** tab.
   c. Click the **New Folder** button in the *New* group. The *Create New Folder* dialog box opens.
   d. Type Nina Hu in the *Name* text area.
   e. Confirm that the folder type is **Mail and Post Items** in the *Folder contains* menu.
   f. In the *Select where to place the folder* section, specify your main email account folder.
   g. Click **OK**.
3. Create a folder for PHRE Internal Messages.
   a. Click the **Mail** button in the *Navigation* bar.
   b. Click the **Folder** tab.
   c. Click the **New Folder** button in the *New* group. The *Create New Folder* dialog box opens.
   d. Type PHRE Internal in the *Name* text area.
   e. Confirm that the folder type is **Mail and Post Items** in the *Folder contains* menu.
   f. In the *Select where to place the folder* section, specify your main email account folder.
   g. Click **OK**.
4. Create a folder for Jim Cross.
   a. Click the **Mail** button in the *Navigation* bar.
   b. Click the **Folder** tab.
   c. Click the **New Folder** button in the *New* group. The *Create New Folder* dialog box opens.
   d. Type Jim Cross in the *Name* text area.
   e. Confirm that the folder type is **Mail and Post Items** in the *Folder contains* menu.

f. In the *Select where to place the folder* section, specify your main email account folder.
g. Click **OK**.

5. Move the *Nina Hu* folder into the *Clients* folder.
   a. In the *Folder* pane, select the **Nina Hu** folder.
   b. Click the **Folder** tab.
   c. Click the **Move Folder** button in the *Actions* group. The *Move Folder* dialog box opens.
   d. In the *Move the selected folder to the folder* section, click the **Clients** folder.
   e. Click **OK**.

6. Delete the *Jim Cross* folder since he decided move to another state and will not need your services.
   a. Select the **Jim Cross** folder in the *Folder* pane.
   b. Click the **Delete Folder** button in the *Actions* group on the *Folder* tab. A warning dialog box opens asking you if you want to move the Jim Cross folder to the Deleted Items folder.
   c. Click **Yes** to delete the folder and all its contents.

7. Send an email message to a partner as Nina Hu.
   a. Click the **Mail** button in the *Navigation* bar.
   b. Click the **New Email** button [*Home* tab, *New* group].
   c. Enter the following information in your message:

      To: [partner's email address]
      Subject: Pre-approval from bank
      Body: Hi [partner's name]

      I just received my pre-approval letter from the bank. I am approved for a purchase up to $375,000 ($75,000 down payment and $300,000 loan).

      Sincerely,
      Nina

   d. Click **Send**.

8. Create a *Rule* to move email messages from Nina into the *Nina Hu* folder.
   a. Locate and open a message from Nina.
   b. Click the **Rules** button in the *Move* group on the *Message* tab.
   c. Choose **Create Rule**. The *Create Rule* dialog box opens.
   d. In the conditions area (the top half of the dialog box), check **From Nina Hu** (the name may vary based on who sent you the message).
   e. In the actions area (the bottom half of the dialog box), check **Move the item to folder** and click the **Select Folder** button.
   f. Select the **Nina Hu** folder from the folder list and press **OK**. The *Create Rule* dialog box remains open.
   g. Click **OK**.
   h. Select the **Run this rule now on messages already in "Inbox"** check box.
   i. Click **OK**.

9. Create an advanced rule to move emails from your manager with attachments into the *PHRE Internal* folder.
   a. Click the **Mail** button in the *Navigation* bar.
   b. Click the **Rules** button in the *Move* group on the *Home* tab and choose **Manage Rules & Alerts**. The *Rules and Alerts* dialog box opens.
   c. Click the **New Rule** button. The *Rules Wizard* dialog box opens.
   d. Select **Apply rule on messages I receive** in the *Start from a blank rule* section.
   e. Click **Next**. You move to the next step to select a condition for the rule.
   f. Select the **with specific words in the recipient's address** check box. In the bottom section of this dialog box, the condition displays.
   g. Click the **specific words** link in the bottom section. The *Search Text* dialog box opens.
   h. Type phre.com in the top text area and click **Add**.

i. Click the **OK** button.
j. Click **Next**. You move to the *action* step in the *Rules Wizard* dialog box.
k. Select the **move it to the specified folder** check box.
l. In the bottom section, click the **specified** folder link. The *Rules and Alerts* dialog box opens.
m. Click the **PHRE Internal** folder and press **OK**. You will return to the *Rules Wizard* dialog box.
n. Click **Next**. You move to the *exceptions* step.
o. Click **Next**. No exceptions will be added to the rule. The *Finish rule setup* step appears.
p. Type PHRE Internal in the *Step 1* area.
q. Confirm that the **Turn on this rule** box is selected.
r. Read the rule one last time to confirm that the condition and action are correct.
s. Click **Finish**.
t. Click **Apply** and then **OK** (Figure 6-44).

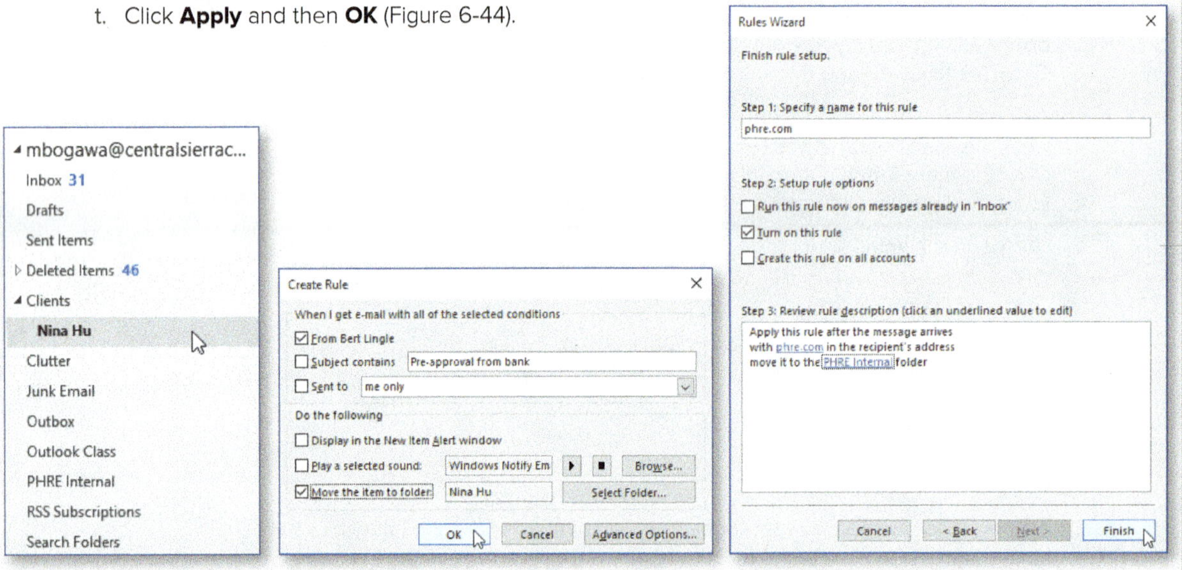

6-44 Guided Project 6-1 completed

Guided Project 6-2

As a real estate agent for PHRE, you send several emails on a regular basis. To improve your work efficiency, you create *Quick Steps*. You create a *Quick Step* to forward messages to your manager when you need approval and create an appointment when you meet with your clients.
[**Student Learning Outcome 6.3**]

Files Needed: None

Skills Covered in This Project

- Create a *Quick Step*.
- Use the *Forward* feature.
- Use options within actions.
- Add *Tooltips* to *Quick Steps*.
- Create an advanced *Quick Step*.
- Create appointments with a *Quick Step*.

1. Create a *Quick Step* to email your instructor with the subject *class name*.
   a. Click the **Create New** *Quick Step* button [*Home* tab, *Quick Steps* group]. The *Edit Quick Step* dialog box opens.
   b. In the *Name* text area, type Manager Approval.
   c. Click the drop-down arrow to display a list of actions.
   d. Select **Forward**.
   e. Click the **Show Options** link below the action.
   f. Click the **To** button. Select your partner's email address and click the **To** button or type it in the *To* text area. If your partner's email address is not in your Contacts, type it into the *To* field in the *Edit Quick Step* dialog box. Click **OK**.
   g. In the *Subject* field, type FW: Contract Approval.
   h. In the *Tooltip text* area, type Email to manager for approval.
   i. Click the **Finish** button to create the new *Quick Step*.

2. Create a *Quick Step* to create a task with an attachment.
   a. Click the **Create New** *Quick Step* button [*Home* tab, *Quick Steps* group]. The *Edit Quick Step* dialog box opens.
   b. In the *Name* text area type Client Meeting.
   c. Click the drop-down arrow to display a list of actions.
   d. Select **Create a task with attachment**.
   e. In the *Tooltip text* area, type Set up client meetings.
   f. Click the **Finish** button to create the new *Quick Step*.

3. Send an email message to your partners to request a meeting about possible locations.
   a. Click the **Mail** button in the *Navigation* bar.
   b. Click the **New Email** button [*Home* tab, *New* group].
   c. Enter the following information in your message:

      To: [partner's email address]
      Subject: Possible locations?
      Body: Hi [partner name],

      Can we meet next week Monday at 10:00 AM to discuss possible locations for my new home?

      Thanks,
      [your name]

   d. Click **Send**.

4. Create a task from the message.
   a. Locate the email your partner sent. It is in the *Group Project* folder.
   b. Click the **Client Meeting** *Quick Step* [*Home* tab, *Quick Steps* group].
   c. Change the start date to be next week **Monday**.
   d. Change the due date to be next week **Tuesday**.
   e. Click the **Save & Close** button.

5. Email the task to your instructor as an Outlook item.
   a. Click the **Mail** button in the *Navigation* bar.
   b. Click the **New Email** button [*Home* tab, *New* group].
   c. Enter the following information in your message:

      To: [instructor's email address]
      Cc: [your email address]
      Subject: Outlook Guided Project 6-2
      Body: Hi [instructor name],

Attached is the Outlook item for the Guided Project 6-2 exercise.

Sincerely,
[student name]

d. Click the **Attach Item** button [*Message* tab, *Include* group] and select **Outlook Item**.
e. Select the **Task** option and locate the task you created.
f. Click **OK**.
g. Click **Send** (Figure 6-45).

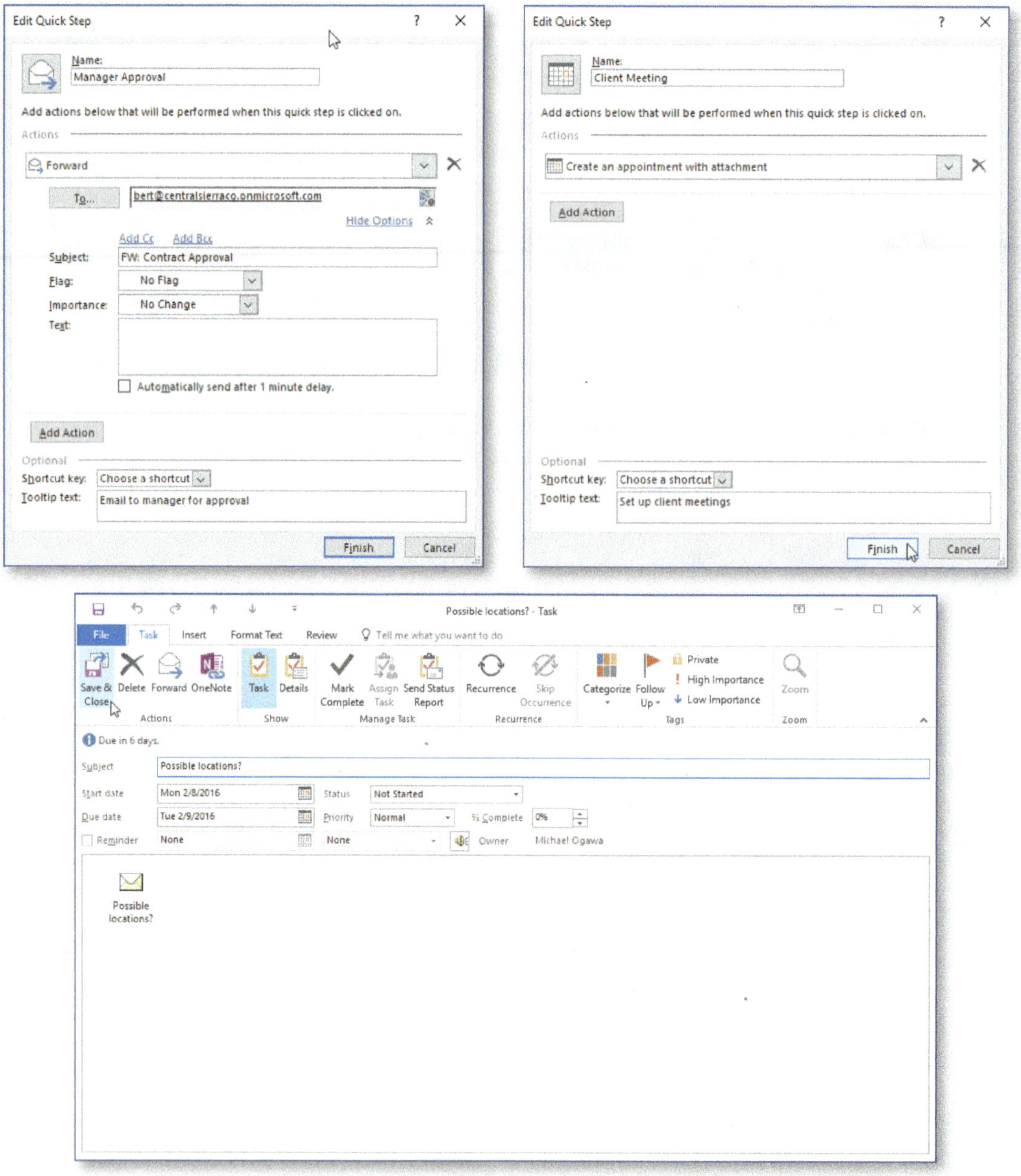

6-45 Guided Project 6-2 completed

Guided Project 6-3

While working with your coworkers and a variety of clients, you identified several email messages that you constantly reference. Therefore, you develop search folders to find messages that deal with executed contracts and messages from your manager with attachments.
[Student Learning Outcome 6.4]

Files Needed: None

Skills Covered in This Project

- Create a search folder.
- Search for specific words in search folders.
- Search for specific senders in search folders.
- Search for messages with attachments in search folders.
- Use multiple criteria for a search folder.
- Modify the messages shown in search folders
- Rename search folders.
- Modify a search folder.

1. Create a new search folder to find messages regarding executed contracts.
   a. Click the **Mail** button in the *Navigation* bar.
   b. Click the **Folder** tab and then click the **New Search Folder** button in the *New* group. The *New Search Folder* dialog box opens.
   c. Select **Mail with specific words**.
   d. Click **Choose**. The *Search Text* dialog box opens.
   e. In the first text area, type execute and click **Add**.
   f. In the first text area, type executed and click **Add**.
   g. In the first text area, type contract and click **Add**.
   h. In the first text area, type contracts and click **Add**.
   i. Click **OK** to close the *Search Text* dialog box.
   j. Click **OK** to close the *New Search Folder* dialog box.
   k. The new search folder appears in your list of search folders in the *Folder* pane.
2. Modify the search folder to be named *Executed Contracts* and show the total number of items in the search folder.
   a. Right-click the newly created search folder and select **Properties**.
   b. Replace the text in the first text area with Executed Contracts.
   c. Click the **Show total number of items** radio button.
   d. Click **OK**.
3. Create a new search folder to find messages from your manager with attachments.
   a. Click the **Mail** button in the *Navigation* bar.
   b. Click the **Folder** tab and then on the **New Search Folder** button in the *New* group. The *New Search Folder* dialog box opens.
   c. Select **Create a custom Search Folder**.
   d. Click **Choose**. The *Custom Search Folder* dialog box opens.
   e. In the *Name* text area, type Manager Attachments.
   f. Click the **Criteria** button. The *Search Folder Criteria* dialog box opens.
   g. Select the *Messages* tab and type your partners' email addresses into the *From* text area or click the **From** button and select their contacts.
   h. Click the *More Choices* tab.
   i. Click the **Only items with** check box and ensure the option is set to **one or more attachments**.
   j. Click **OK** to close the *Search Folder Criteria* dialog box.
   k. Click **OK** to close the *Custom Search Folder* dialog box.

l. Click **OK** to close the *New Search* Folder dialog box. The new search folder appears in your list of search folders in the *Folder* pane (Figure 6-46).

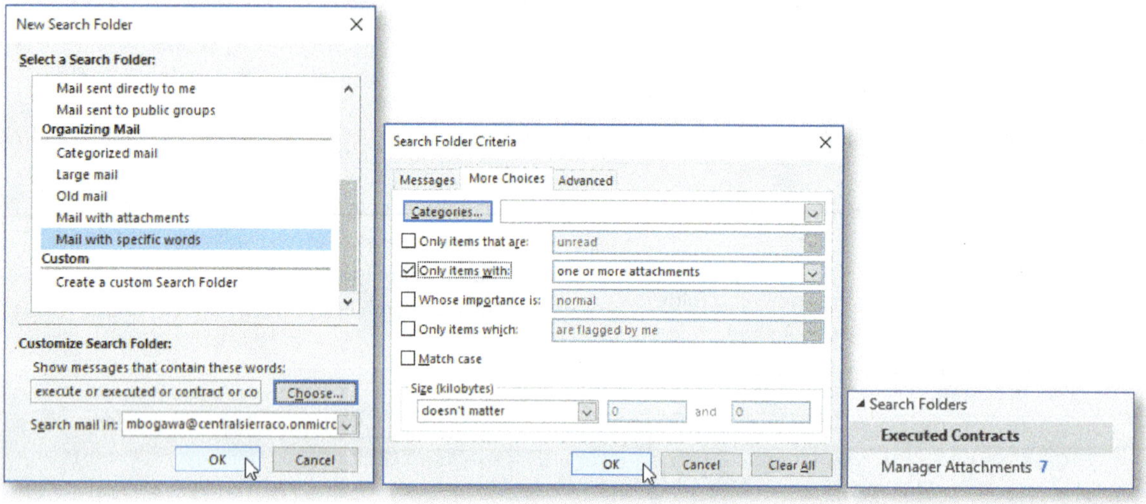

6-46 Guided Project 6-3 completed

Independent Project 6-4

For this project, you are coordinating the Cycling Evolution Event (CEE) for the American River Cycling Club (ARCC). This year, you take registrations via email. Therefore, you create folders and rules to automatically organize registration information. You also want to store email messages you send to the ARCC with updates in a specific folder to ensure you can quickly find the information.
[Student Learning Outcomes 6.1, 6.2]

Files Needed: None

Skills Covered in This Project

- Create folders.
- Move folders.
- Create a *Rule*.
- Create an advanced rule.
- Run a rule.

1. Create a folder to organize ARCC email.
   a. Create a folder named *ARCC*.
   b. Create a folder named *Registrations*.
   c. Create a folder named *Member updates*.
   d. Move the *Registrations* and *Member updates* folders into the *ARCC* folder.
2. Create a rule to organize registration email messages using the following criteria:

   Condition: Messages received with the term *Registration* in the subject.
   Action: Moved into the *Registrations* folder.
   Exception: Unless there is a question mark (**?**) in the message.

3. Create a rule to organize membership update messages you send based on the following criteria:

   Condition: Messages sent with the term *Membership update* in the subject.
   Action: Copy to the *Member updates* folder (Figure 6-47).

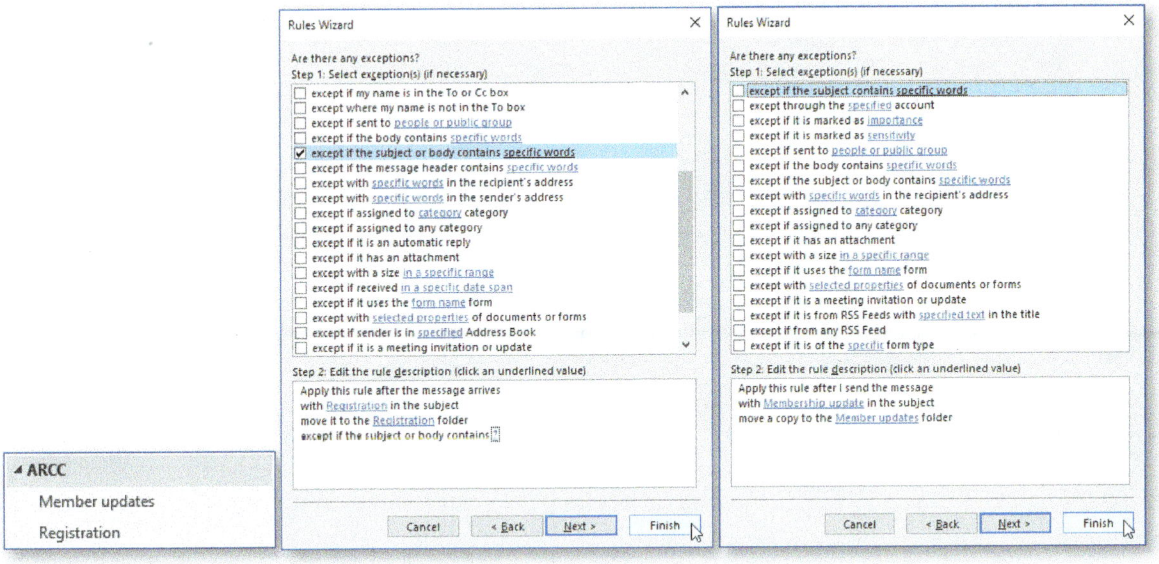

6-47 Independent Project 6-4 completed

Independent Project 6-5

After working on the registration last year, you remember that many of the ARCC members ask similar questions regarding the route. To make you work more efficient, you create a *Quick Step* to reply with the route information. You also create a *Quick Step* to quickly create messages to ARCC members. [Student Learning Outcome 6.3]

Files Needed: None

Skills Covered in This Project

- Create a *Quick Step*.
- Use the reply feature.
- Use new mail feature.
- Use options within actions.
- Add *Tooltips* to a *Quick Step*.
- Create an advanced *Quick Step*.
- Create appointments with a *Quick Step*.

1. Create a *Quick Step* to reply to ARCC members with the following information.

   Name: Route Reply
   Action: Reply
   Options text: Please see the following URL for the most updated route information: http://www.arcc.org/ceeroute/.
   Tooltip text: Reply with up-to-date route information.

2. Create a *Quick Step* to send email messages to ARCC members with the following information.

   Name: Membership update email
   Action: New Message
   To: members@arcc.org
   Options: [Leave blank]
   Subject: Membership update
   Tooltip text: Write membership update messages. (Figure 6-48).

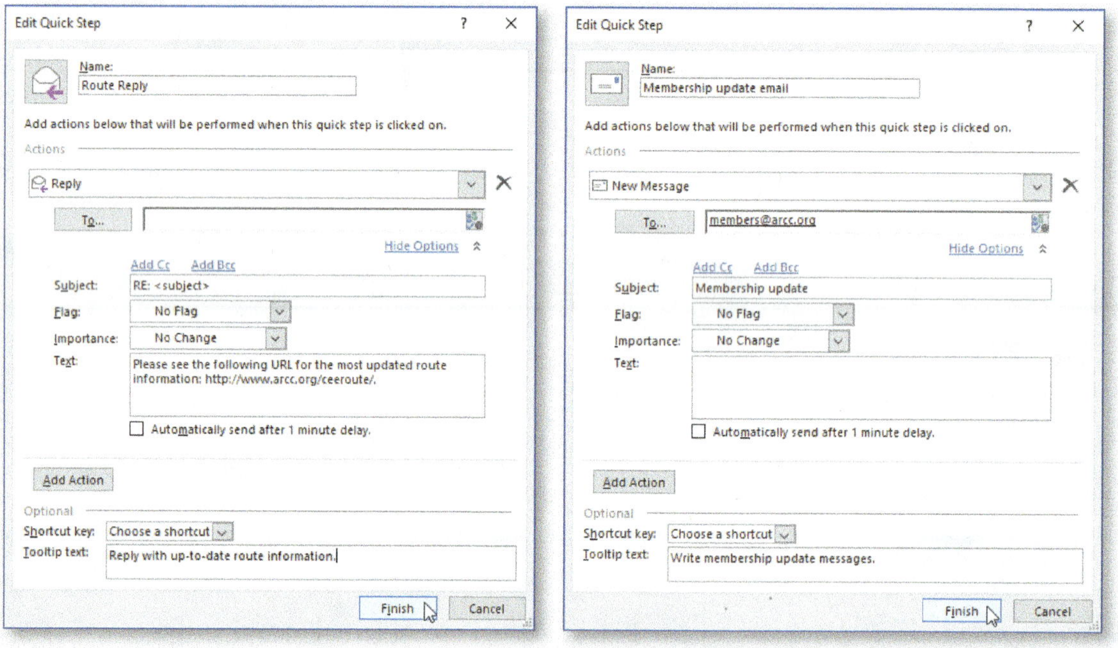

6-48 Independent Project 6-5 completed

Independent Project 6-6

As the CEE coordinator, you recall members asking about receipts for their payments. Since you started giving digital receipts via email, you create a search folder to quickly find receipts to send to participants who accidentally lost the initial message. You also remember participants asking about their T-shirt size to ensure they receive the correct shirt when they finish the event. Therefore, you create a new search folder to find T-shirt sizes for all participants, which allows you to search within the search folder for a particular member's registration.
[Student Learning Outcome 6.4]

Files Needed: None

Skills Covered in This Project

- Create a search folder.
- Search for specific words in search folders.
- Search for specific senders.
- Search for messages with attachments in search folders.
- Use multiple criteria for a search folder.
- Modify the messages shown in search folders.
- Rename search folders.
- Modify a search folder.

1. Create a new search folder to find messages regarding receipt messages using the following criteria:

   Search folder name: Receipts
   From: [your email address]
   Search for the term *Receipt* in the subject field only.
   Search for items with attachments.
   Show the total number of items for the search folder.

2. Create a new search folder to find T-shirt sizes using the following criteria:

   Search folder name: Shirt size
   To: [your email address]
   Search for the term *size* in the subject field and message body.
   All messages were received in the last month.
   Show the total number of items for the search folder (Figure 6-49).

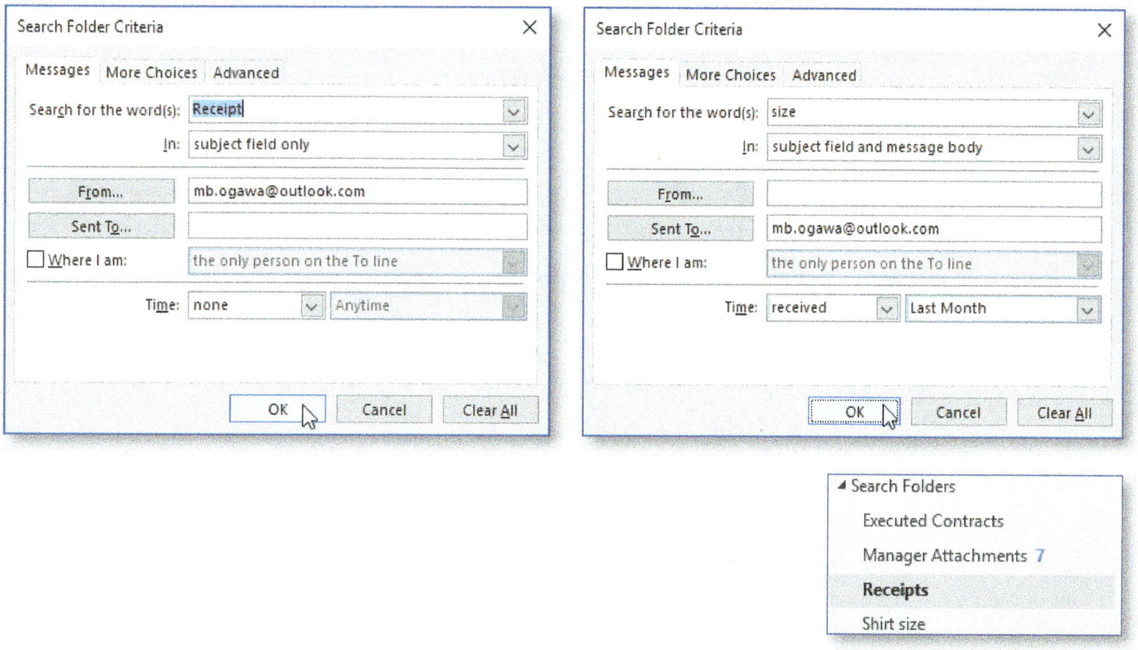

6-49 Independent Project 6-6 completed

Challenge Project 6-7

Consider the different types of email you send and receive for school, work, home, and other extracurricular activities. Identify at least two types of email you receive or send and how you can apply rules to manage your email. For example, you apply rules to emails received from specific people, words in the subject line, or flagged for action. After identifying the types of email you receive, create folders and rules to apply. Email a description of the folders created and rules applied to your instructor.
[Student Learning Outcomes 6.1, 6.2]

Files Needed: None

- Create at least two rules.
- Create folders for rules.
- Ensure you have a reason to justify each rule.
- Explain why the rule fits better than a *Quick Step* or search folder.
- Email your instructor using the following message format:

  Rule 1: [reason you are creating a rule for the type of message including why it works better than *Quick Steps* and search folders]
  Condition: [description of condition]
  Action: [description of action]
  Exception: [description of exceptions]
  Folder 1: [name and description of folder]

  Rule 2: [reason you are creating a rule for the type of message including why it works better than *Quick Steps* and search folders]
  Condition: [description of condition]
  Action: [description of action]
  Exception: [description of exceptions]
  Folder 2: [name and description of folder]

- Change the subject of your message to Outlook Challenge Project 6-7.

Challenge Project 6-8

Think about the different types of email messages you send and receive for school, work, home, and other extracurricular activities. Identify at least two types of email you receive and how you can apply *Quick Steps*. You can use *Quick Steps* for a variety of actions such as filing, changing status, creating categories, tasks, and flags, responding, creating new appointments, and managing conversations. After identifying possible *Quick Steps*, create folders for those that require a new folder. Email a description of the folders created and *Quick Steps* developed to your instructor.
[Student Learning Outcomes 6.1, 6.3]

Files Needed: None

- Create at least two *Quick Steps*.
- Create folders for *Quick Steps*.

- Ensure you have a reason to justify each *Quick Step*.
- Use at least two actions for each *Quick Step*.
- Explain why the *Quick Step* fits better than a rule or search folder.
- Email your instructor using the following message format:

  Quick Step 1: [reason you created a *Quick Step* for the type of message including why it works better than rules and search folders]
  Action: [description of action]
  Action: [description of action]
  Folder 1: [name and description of folder]

  Quick Step 2: [reason you created a *Quick Step* for the type of message including why it works better than rules and search folders]
  Action: [description of action]
  Action: [description of action]
  Folder 2: [name and description of folder]

- Change the subject of your message to be Outlook Challenge Project 6-8.

Challenge Project 6-9

You probably receive many email messages throughout the day for school, work, family, and extracurricular activities. Identify at least two types of email you send and receive and how you can apply search folders to help you find important messages. After identifying the types of email you send and receive, create search folders for those messages. Email a description of the search folders created to your instructor. [**Student Learning Outcome 6.4**]

Files Needed: None

- Create at least two search folders.
- Ensure you have a reason to justify each search folder.
- Identify criteria for the search folder.
- One of the search folders should contain more than one criterion.
- Email your instructor using the following message format:

  Search Folder 1: [reason you created the search folder including why it works better than rules and *Quick Steps*]
  Criteria: [description of criteria]

  Search Folder 2: [reason you created the search folder including why it works better than rules and *Quick Steps*]
  Criteria: [description of criteria]
  Criteria: [description of criteria]

- Change the subject of your message to be Outlook Challenge Project 6-9.

Word

Microsoft® Office IN PRACTICE word

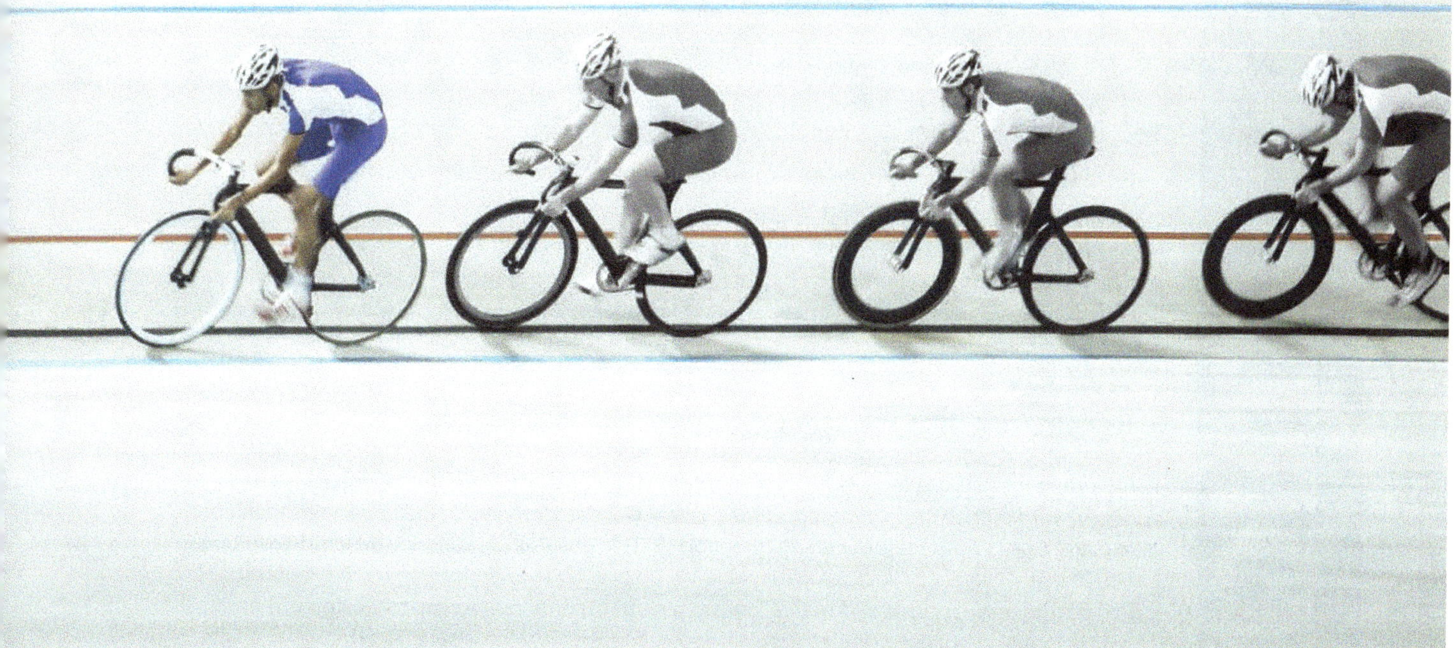

CHAPTER 1

Creating and Editing Documents

CHAPTER OVERVIEW

Microsoft Word (Word) has been and continues to be the leading word processing software in both the personal and business markets. Word improves with each new version and is used for creating and editing personal, business, and educational documents. Word allows you to create letters, memos, reports, flyers, brochures, and mailings without a vast amount of computer knowledge. This chapter covers the basics of creating and editing a Word document.

STUDENT LEARNING OUTCOMES (SLOs)

After completing this chapter, you will be able to:

SLO 1.1 Create, save, and open a Word document (p. W1-3).

SLO 1.2 Customize a document by entering and selecting text, using word wrap, and using *AutoComplete*, *AutoCorrect*, and *AutoFormat* features (p. W1-7).

SLO 1.3 Enhance a document using paragraph breaks, line breaks, spaces, and non-breaking spaces (p. W1-10).

SLO 1.4 Edit a document using cut, copy, paste, the *Clipboard*, and the undo, redo, and repeat features. (p. W1-15).

SLO 1.5 Customize a document using different fonts, font sizes, and attributes (p. W1-18).

SLO 1.6 Enhance a document using text alignment and line and paragraph spacing (p. W1-28).

SLO 1.7 Finalize a document using Word's research and proofing tools (p. W1-32).

SLO 1.8 Apply custom document properties to a document (p. W1-36).

CASE STUDY

Throughout this book you have the opportunity to put into practice the application features that you are learning. Each chapter begins with a case study that introduces you to the Pause & Practice projects in the chapter. These Pause & Practice projects give you a chance to apply and practice key skills realistic and practical context. Each chapter contains three to five Pause & Practice projects.

Placer Hills Real Estate (PHRE) is a real estate company with regional offices throughout central California. PHRE encourages agents to use standard formats for their business documents. This ensures consistency in document appearance while also allowing agents to personalize their correspondence to customers and colleagues. In the Pause & Practice projects in this chapter, you create a business document related to the real estate business.

WORD

Pause & Practice 1-1: Create a business letter in block format with mixed punctuation.

Pause & Practice 1-2: Edit the business letter using copy, paste, and *Format Painter*. Modify the font, font size, color, style, and effects of selected text.

Pause & Practice 1-3: Finalize the business letter by modifying line spacing and paragraph spacing, changing paragraph alignment, translating text, using research and proofing tools, and adding document properties.

MORE INFO

Appendix B (online resource) contains examples of business documents.

SLO 1.1

Creating, Saving, and Opening Documents

In Microsoft Word, you can create a variety of document types. Your creativity and knowledge of Word enables you to create, edit, and customize high-quality and professional-looking documents. You can create Word documents from a new blank document, from existing Word templates, or from existing documents. Word allows you to save documents in a variety of formats.

Create a New Document

All new documents are based on the ***Normal template*** (*Normal.dotm*). When you create a new Word document, a blank document displays in the Word window. This document has default fonts, font sizes, line and paragraph spacing, and margins, all of which are controlled by the *Normal* template.

HOW TO: Create a New Document

1. Click the **File** tab to open the *Backstage* view.
   - When you first open Word, the *Start* page is displayed. You can open a new blank document from the *Start* page.
2. Click the **New** button (Figure 1-1).
3. Select **Blank document**. A new blank document opens in Word.

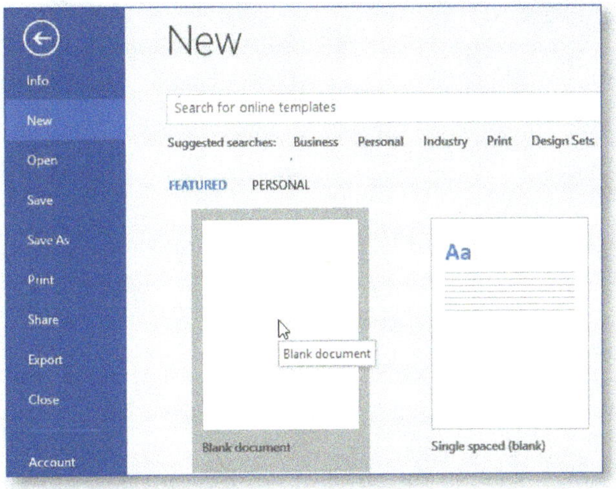

1-1 Open a new blank document

ANOTHER WAY

Ctrl+N opens a new blank document.

Save a Document

When you create a blank document, Word automatically assigns a generic file name to this document, such as *Document1*. Save all your new documents using the ***Save As dialog box***. You can save a Word document in a variety of file formats. By default, a Word document is saved as a ***.docx*** file. Other types of Word files are discussed throughout this text. The following table lists some of the more commonly used file formats.

Save Formats

Type of File	File Extension	Uses
Word Document	.docx	Standard Word 2016 document
Word Macro-Enabled Document	.docm	Word document with embedded macros
Word 97-2003 Document	.doc	Word document that is compatible with previous versions of Microsoft Word
Word Template	.dotx	Create a new document based upon a template
Word Macro-Enabled Template	.dotm	Create a new document based upon a template with embedded macros
Portable Document Format (PDF)	.pdf	Similar to a picture of a document that is used to preserve the formatting of a document
Rich Text Format (RTF)	.rtf	Generic file format that can be read by many different types of word processing programs while retaining the basic format of the document
Plain Text	.txt	Files contain only text with no special formatting and can be opened with most word processing programs
Open Document Text	.odt	Format used in the Open Office word processing program

HOW TO: Save a New Document

1. Click the **File** tab to open the *Backstage* view.
2. Click **Save** or **Save As** to display the *Save As* area on the *Backstage* view (Figure 1-2).
3. Select the location where you want to store your document.
   - You can save to your *OneDrive*, *This PC*, or other storage device.

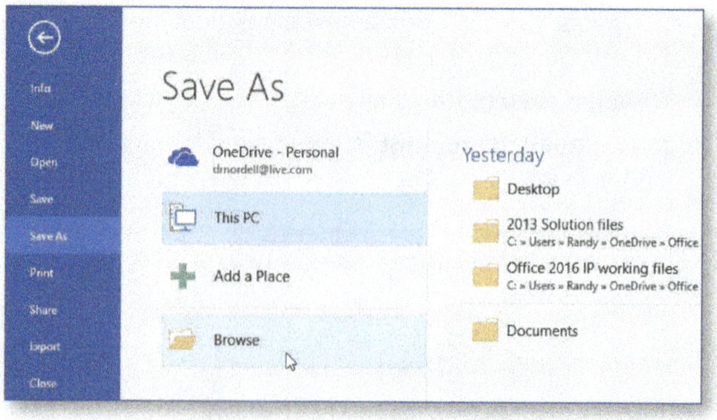

1-2 *Save As* area of the *Backstage* view

4. Click the **Browse** button or select a recently used folder in the *Folders* area on the right to open the *Save As* dialog box (Figure 1-3).
5. In the *Save As* dialog box, browse to the location on your *OneDrive*, computer, USB drive, or other storage device to save the file.
6. Type the file name in the *File name* area.
7. Click the **Save** button.

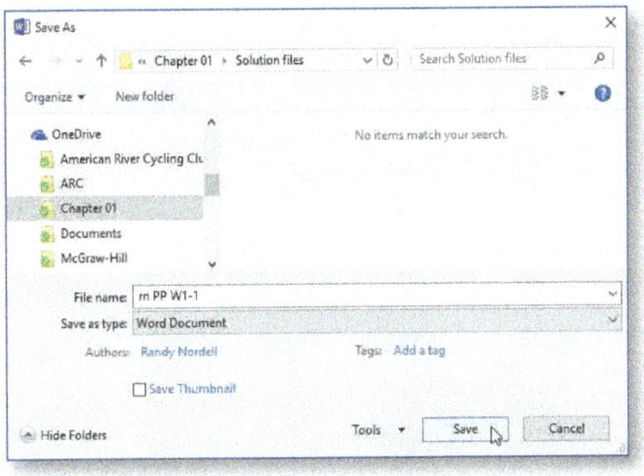

1-3 *Save As* dialog box

ANOTHER WAY

F12 opens the *Save As* dialog box. When using a laptop computer, you might have to press the **Fn** (Function) key and the **F12** key to open the *Save As* dialog box.

After you have named and saved a document, you can save changes to the document without opening the *Save As* dialog box in the following ways:

- Press **Ctrl+S**.
- Click the **Save** button on the *Quick Access* toolbar.
- Select **Save** from the *Backstage* view.

Save As a Different File Name

You can save a document as a different name by opening the *Save As* dialog box and typing a new file name. When you save a file with a different file name, the original document is not changed and is still available. Saving with a different file name creates a new version of the original document, but the new document has a different file name.

HOW TO: Save As a Different File Name

1. Click the **File** tab to open the *Backstage* view.
2. Click the **Save As** button to display the *Save As* area.
3. Click the **Browse** button or select a recent folder to open the *Save As* dialog box (see Figure 1-3).
   - From within Word (not the *Backstage* view), you can also press **F12** to open the *Save As* dialog box.
   - On some laptops, you might have to press the **Fn** (Function key) and the **F12** key to open the *Save As* dialog box.
4. In the *Save As* dialog box, browse to a location to save the file.
5. Type the file name in the *File name* area.
6. Click the **Save** button.

MORE INFO

Avoid saving too many different versions of the same document. Rename only when you have a good reason to have multiple versions of a document.

Open a Document

You can open an existing document from your computer, *OneDrive*, other storage location, or an attachment from an email. After you open a document, you can edit the content and save the changes to the document.

▶ HOW TO: Open a Document

1. Click the **File** tab to open the *Backstage* view.
2. Click the **Open** button to display the *Open* area on the *Backstage* view.
3. Select the location where the document is stored.
   - You can click **Recent** and select a document on the right to open it.
   - You can also open a document from *OneDrive* or *This PC*.
4. Select a file or folder to open it or click **Browse** to open the *Open* dialog box (Figure 1-4).
5. Select the file and click the **Open** button.
   - If the document opens in *Protected View*, click the **Enable Editing** button.

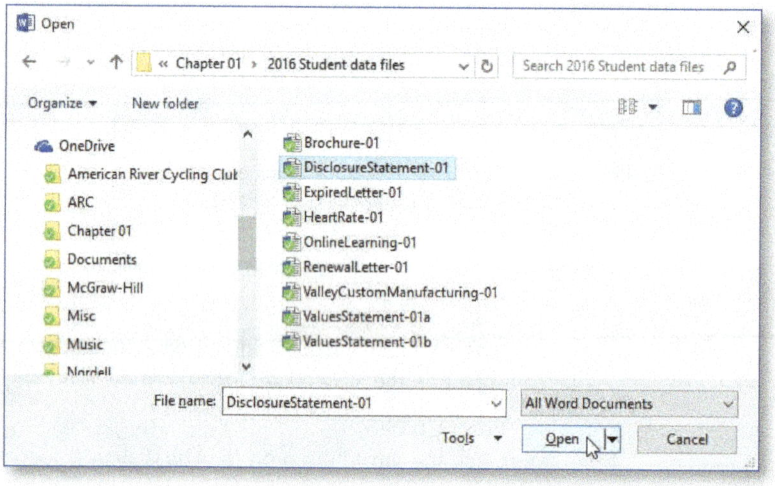

1-4 *Open* dialog box

> **ANOTHER WAY**
>
> **Ctrl+F12** opens the *Open* dialog box. Some laptops require **Fn+Ctrl+F12**.

Pin a Frequently Used Document

If you use a document frequently, you can pin it to the *Open* area on the *Backstage* view. Pinned documents appear at the top of the *Recent* documents list so you can quickly open the document. In the *Open* area on the *Backstage* view, click **Recent** and then click the **Pin** icon to the right of a file name to add the document to the *Pinned* area (Figure 1-5). Pinned files display in the *Pinned* area of the *Start* page and *Open* area of the *Backstage* view. Click the pinned file to open it.

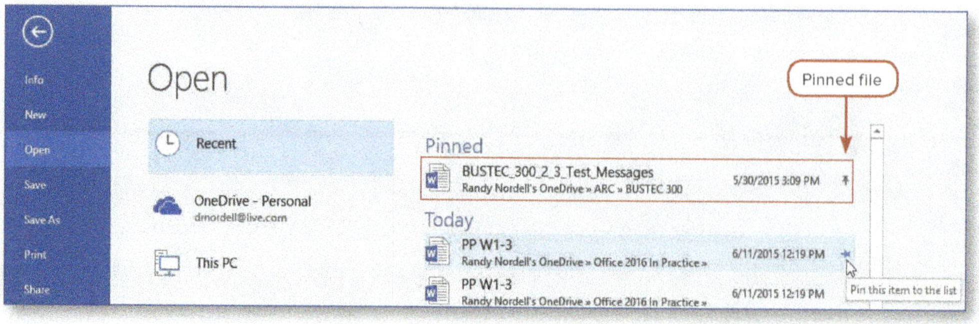

1-5 The *Pinned* area in the *Open* area on the *Backstage* view

Share and Export Options

Word 2016 provides you with sharing and export options. To share a document, you must first save the document to *OneDrive*. You can also export a Word document to PDF format. From the ***Share*** (Figure 1-6) and ***Export*** areas of the *Backstage* view, you have the following options:

- *Share with People* [*Share* area]
- *Email* [*Share* area]
- *Present Online* [*Share* area]
- *Post to Blog* [*Share* area]
- *Create PDF/XPS Document* [*Export* area]
- *Change File Type* [*Export* area]

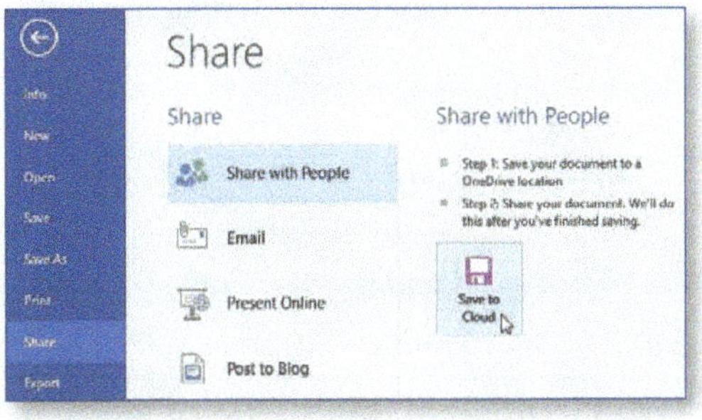

1-6 *Share* area of the *Backstage* view

SLO 1.2

Entering and Selecting Text

When creating or editing a document, you can type new text, insert text from another document, or copy text from a web page or another document. It is important to understand how to enter text, use word wrap, select text, show or hide formatting symbols, and use *AutoComplete* and *AutoCorrect* options to create professional-looking documents.

Type Text and Use Word Wrap

Word inserts text at the point in the document where the insertion point is flashing. By default, text is aligned at the left margin and the text wraps to the next line when it reaches the right margin, which is called ***word wrap***. Press **Enter** to begin a new paragraph or line of text.

Show/Hide Formatting Symbols

The ***Show/Hide*** feature allows you to display or hide the formatting symbols in your document. By default, *Show/Hide* is turned off and formatting symbols do not display in your document. When the *Show/Hide* feature is turned on, you can see paragraph breaks, line breaks, spaces, tabs, and other formatting symbols that help you create clean documents and edit existing documents (Figure 1-7).

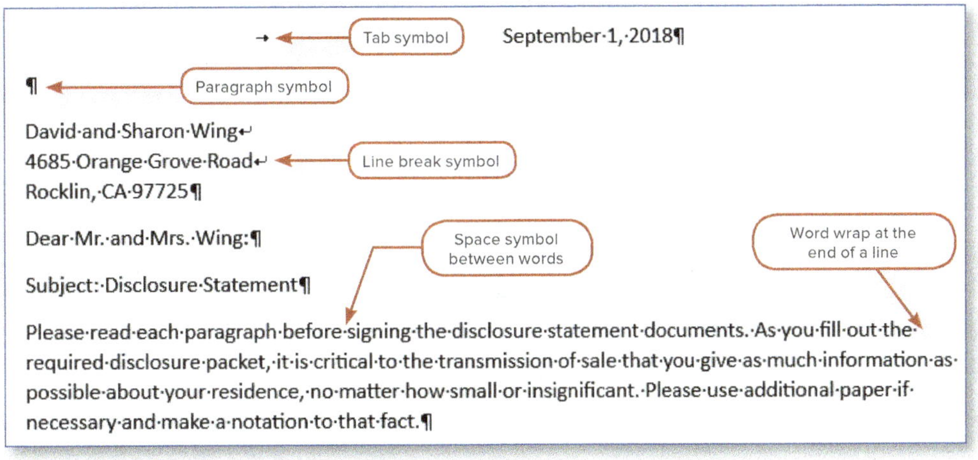

1-7 Document with *Show/Hide* turned on

Click the **Show/Hide** button in the *Paragraph* group on the *Home* tab to toggle on and off *Show/Hide* (Figure 1-8). These symbols do not print, but they allow you to see the formatting that is in the document when you view it on your screen.

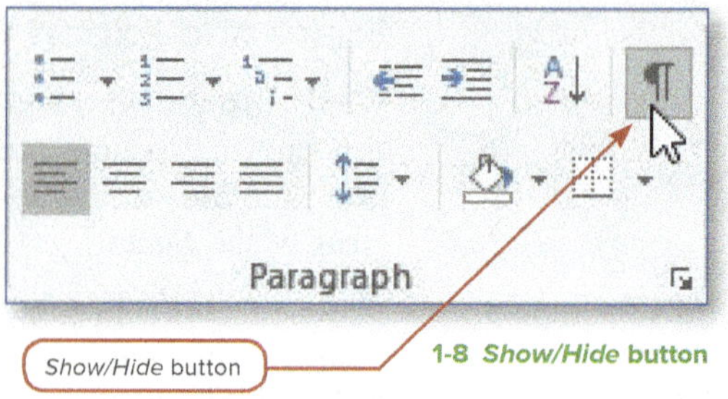

1-8 *Show/Hide* button

ANOTHER WAY

Ctrl+Shift+8 turns on and off *Show/Hide*.

MORE INFO

When editing a document that has inconsistent formatting, begin by turning on **Show/Hide**.

Select Text

Word allows you select words, lines, sentences, paragraphs, or the entire document so you can apply formatting, copy, move, or delete selected text. You do this by clicking and dragging the pointer over the desired text, but there are a variety of additional quick methods to select text. The following table lists ways to select text.

Selecting Text

Select	Method
Word	Double-click the word.
Line	Click in the *Selection* area, which is to the left of the left margin. Your pointer becomes a right-pointing arrow.
Multiple lines of text	Click in the *Selection* area and drag up or down.
Sentence	Press **Ctrl+Click**. Hold down the **Ctrl** key and click the sentence.
Paragraph	Double-click in the *Selection* area to the left of the paragraph.
Multiple paragraphs	Click in the *Selection* area to the left of the first line of the paragraph and drag down.
Entire document	Press **Ctrl+A** or **Ctrl+Click** in the *Selection* area. You can also click the **Select** button [*Home* tab, *Editing* group] and choose **Select All**.
Non-adjacent text	Select text, press and hold the **Ctrl** key, and select non-adjacent text.

ANOTHER WAY

F8 is the selection function key.

Press once: Use the arrow keys to select text.
Press twice: Select word.
Press three times: Select sentence.
Press four times: Select paragraph.
Press five times: Select entire document.

Press **Esc** to turn off **F8** selection.

AutoComplete

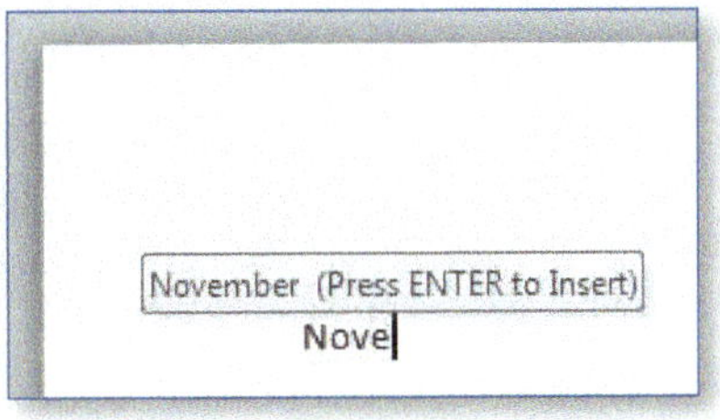

1-9 *AutoComplete* tag

When you type a day, month, or date, Word uses the ***AutoComplete*** feature to automatically complete typing the day, month, or date for you, which saves you a few key strokes and allows you to be more efficient and accurate when entering dates. As you begin to type the date, Word displays the information in an ***AutoComplete tag*** (Figure 1-9). Press **Enter** to accept the *AutoComplete* entry. If you do not want this *AutoComplete* entry, keep typing and the *AutoComplete* entry disappears.

AutoCorrect and AutoFormat

When you're typing, do you ever misspell a word by transposing letters or omitting a letter or adding a letter? Because we all regularly make typing mistakes, the ***AutoCorrect*** feature recognizes and corrects commonly misspelled words and some grammatical errors. Word automatically makes the following corrections:

- Eliminates two initial capitals in a word
- Capitalizes the first letter of a sentence
- Capitalizes the first letter of table cells
- Capitalizes the names of days
- Corrects accidental usage of the *Caps Lock* key
- Changes fractions such as 3/4 to ¾ and numbers such as 2nd to 2nd.

Word's ***AutoFormat*** controls the formatting of items such as numbered and bulleted lists, fractions, ordinal numbers, hyphens and dashes, quotes, indents, and hyperlinks. For example, when you type 3/4 followed by a space, *AutoFormat* automatically changes the format of the fraction to ¾.

AutoCorrect Smart Tag

When Word automatically makes a correction or formatting change, you have the option to accept the change, undo the change, stop Word from making the change, or control *AutoCorrect* using the *AutoCorrect Options* dialog box. If you keep typing, the change is accepted. Often when Word automatically corrects a word, you don't even recognize that a change has been made.

If you do not want to accept a change, you can click the ***AutoCorrect Options smart tag*** on the changed word to open the *AutoCorrect Options* menu (Figure 1-10). For example, when you type reference initials at the end of a business letter, Word automatically capitalizes the first letter. You can undo this automatic capitalization by clicking on the *AutoCorrect Options* smart tag and selecting **Undo Automatic Capitalization**.

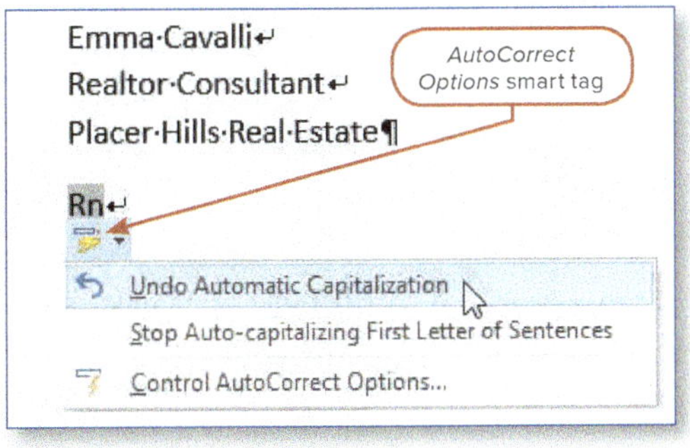

1-10 *AutoCorrect Options* smart tag

ANOTHER WAY

Press **Ctrl+Z** to reverse an automatic correction made by Word.

Add Custom AutoCorrect Entry

The *AutoCorrect* dialog box allows you to customize how Word automatically corrects and formats items in a document. In this dialog box, you can also add custom items to the *AutoCorrect* menu. For example, you can add a custom entry to the *AutoCorrect* menu to correct a misspelled word or type your name every time you type your initials.

▶ HOW TO: Add a Custom AutoCorrect Entry

1. Click the **File** tab to open the *Backstage* view.
2. Choose the **Options** button to open the *Word Options* dialog box.
3. Click the **Proofing** button on the left.
4. Select the **AutoCorrect Options** button. The *AutoCorrect* dialog box opens (Figure 1-11).
5. Type the text you want to replace in the *Replace* box.
6. Type the word(s) to replace the original text in the *With* box.
7. Choose **Add** to add this custom *AutoCorrect* entry.
   - You can delete *AutoCorrect* entries in the *AutoCorrect* dialog box by selecting the entry and clicking **Delete**.
   - You can also add exceptions to *AutoCorrect* by clicking the **Exceptions** button.
8. Click **OK** to close the *AutoCorrect* dialog box.
9. Click **OK** to close the *Word Options* dialog box.

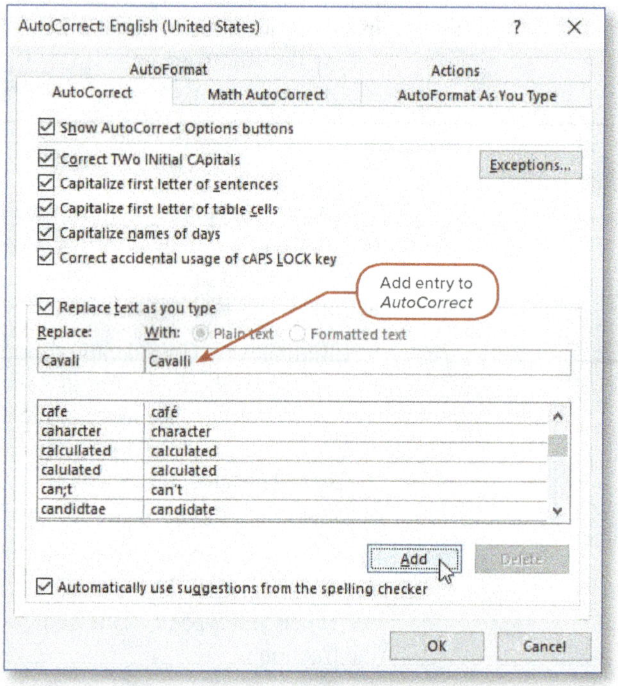

1-11 *AutoCorrect* dialog box

SLO 1.3 Using Paragraph Breaks, Line Breaks, and Non-Breaking Spaces

It is essential to create attractive and readable documents. Using paragraph and line breaks allows you to break up a document into more readable chunks of information. The different types of breaks can be used for different purposes when you are formatting documents.

Paragraph Breaks

The ***Enter*** key inserts a ***paragraph break*** and is marked by a ***paragraph symbol*** that displays at the end of each paragraph when *Show/Hide* is turned on (Figure 1-12). Use paragraph breaks to control the amount of white space between paragraphs of text within a document.

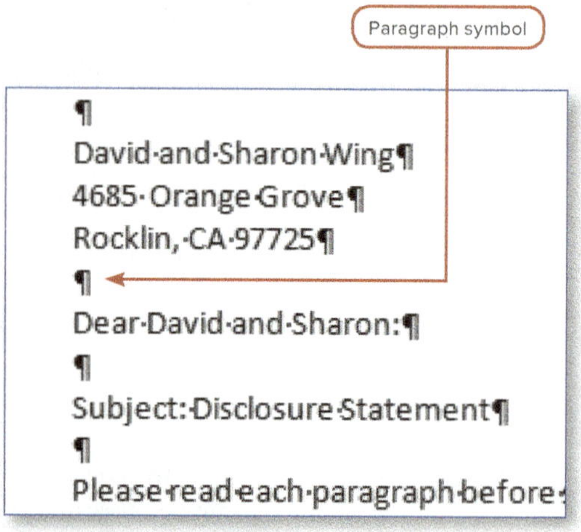

1-12 Paragraph breaks after and between lines

Many formatting features, such as indents, numbering, bullets, text alignment, line spacing, and paragraph spacing, are applied to an entire paragraph. For example, if your insertion point is within a paragraph and you change the line spacing to double space, double spacing is applied to that paragraph only. It is not applied to the entire document or just the line where the insertion point is located. For more on line and paragraph spacing, see *SLO 1.6: Changing Text Alignment, Line Spacing, and Paragraph Spacing*.

Line Breaks

*You can use **line breaks*** to control breaks between lines or sentences of text. The distinction between a paragraph break and a line break is that when line breaks are used, the text separated by line breaks is treated as one paragraph. Press **Shift+Enter** to insert a line break.

You can use line breaks within a numbered or bulleted list to allow for multiple lines of text on separate lines and blank lines between the text without creating a new number or bullet (Figure 1-13). When *Show/Hide* is turned on, the line break symbol is different from the paragraph symbol.

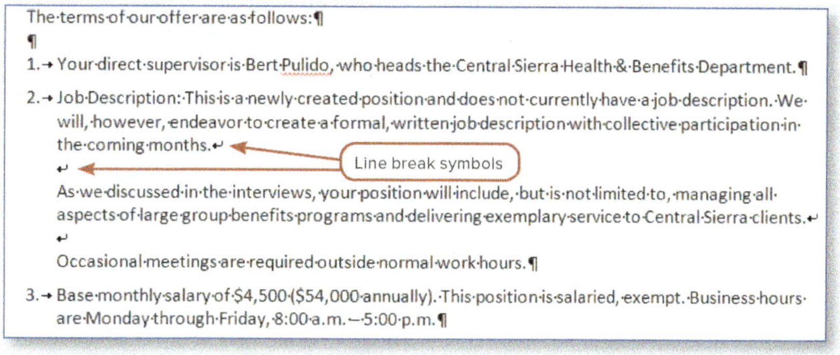

1-13 Line breaks used in a numbered list

Spaces and Non-Breaking Spaces

Spaces are included between words. Use the ***spacebar*** to insert a space. Current practice now dictates one space after most punctuation marks, including periods, commas, semi-colons, and ending quotation marks. Do not use spaces after a beginning quotation mark, before or after a hyphen in a hyphenated word, or when using a dash.

There might be times when you are typing a document and word wrap separates words that you want to keep together. For example, you might want to keep a person's first and last name or a date together on the same line. In this case, you can use a ***non-breaking space*** to keep these words together. To insert a non-breaking space, press **Ctrl+Shift+Spacebar** between words rather than inserting a regular space. In Figure 1-14, there is a non-breaking space between 8:00 and a.m., which keeps this information together.

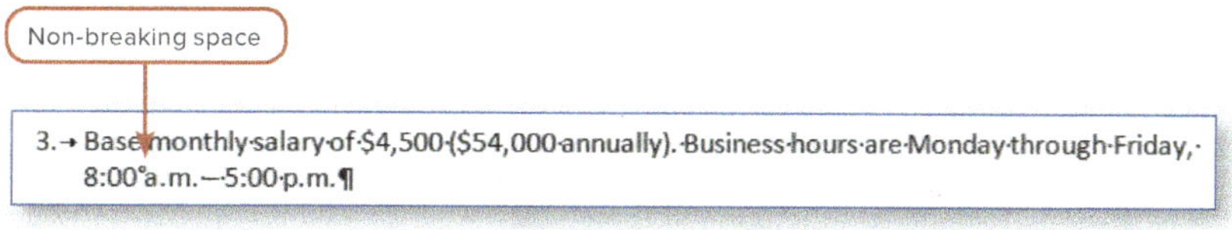

1-14 Non-breaking space used to keep text together

PAUSE & PRACTICE: WORD 1-1

In this project, you create a block format business letter for Emma Cavalli, a realtor consultant for Placer Hills Real Estate. In a block format business letter, all lines begin at the left margin. For more examples of business documents, see *Appendix B* (online resource).

File Needed: None
Completed Project File Name: ***[your initials] PP W1-1.docx***

1. Open a new document.
   a. Click the **File** tab, click **New**, and click **Blank document**. You can also click **Blank document** on the *Start* page when you open Word.
2. Save the document.
   a. Click the **File** tab to open the *Backstage* view.
   b. Click **Save** on the left and then click **Browse** to open the *Save As* dialog box (Figure 1-15).
   c. Browse to the location on your computer or storage device to save the document.
   d. Type [your initials] PP W1-1 in the *File name* area.
   e. Click **Save** to save the document.

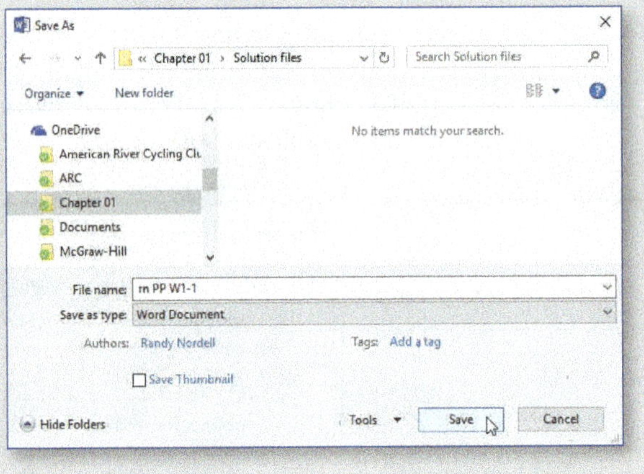

1-15 ***Save As* dialog box**

ANOTHER WAY

F12 opens the *Save As* dialog box. When using a laptop computer, you might have to press the **Fn** (Function) key and the **F12** key to open the *Save As* dialog box.

3. Create an *AutoCorrect* entry.
   a. Click the **File** tab to open the *Backstage* view and select **Options** on the left to open the *Word Options* dialog box.
   b. Click the **Proofing** button on the left and select **AutoCorrect Options** to open the *AutoCorrect* dialog box (Figure 1-16).
   c. Click the **AutoCorrect** tab if it is not already selected.
   d. Type Cavali in the *Replace* area.
   e. Type Cavalli in the *With* area.
   f. Click the **Add** button to add the *AutoCorrect* entry.
   g. Click **OK** to close the *AutoCorrect* dialog box.
   h. Click **OK** to close the *Word Options* dialog box.
4. Click the **Show/Hide** button [*Home* tab, *Paragraph* group] to turn on the *Show/Hide* feature.

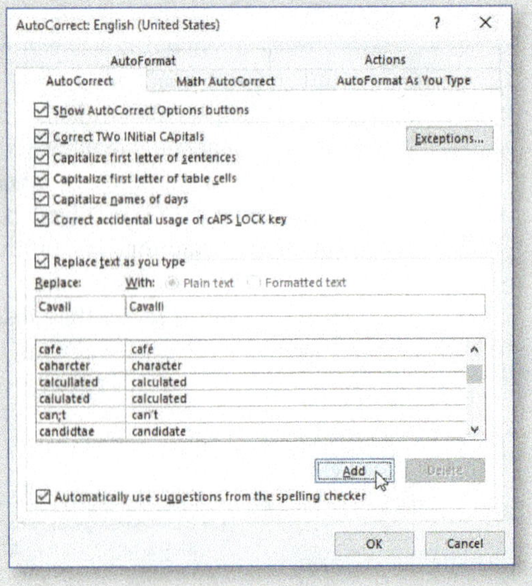

1-16 Add an *AutoCorrect* entry

5. Type the current date on the first line of the document. Type the date in month, day, year format (e.g., September 1, 2018).
   a. If the *AutoComplete* tag appears, press **Enter**, and the month is automatically inserted (Figure 1-17).
   b. Continue typing the rest of the date; press **Enter** if the *AutoCorrect* tag displays the current date.
   c. Press **Enter** two times after typing the date.

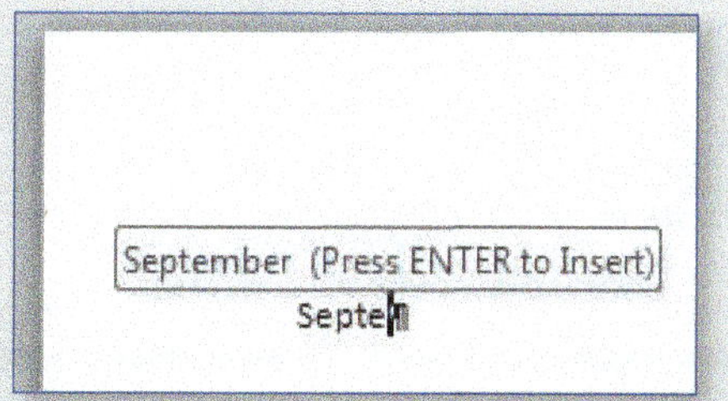

1-17 *AutoComplete* tag

6. Type the inside address, salutation, and subject line of the letter.
   a. Type David and Sharon Wing and press **Shift+Enter** to insert a line break.
   b. Type 4685 Orange Grove Road and press **Shift+Enter** to insert a line break.
   c. Type Rocklin, CA 97725 and press **Enter** to insert a paragraph break.
   d. Type Dear Mr. and Mrs. Wing: as the salutation and press **Enter**.
   e. Type Subject: Disclosure Statement as the subject and press **Enter**.

MORE INFO

In the salutation of a business letter, use "Dear" followed by a courtesy title (e.g., Mr., Mrs., Ms., Miss, or Dr.) and the person's last name.

7. Type the body paragraphs of the business letter and insert a non-breaking space.
   a. Type the following paragraph and press **Enter** once at the end of the paragraph. You will not need to press *Enter* at the end of each line since word wrap automatically moves text to the next line as you reach the right margin.

      Please read each paragraph before signing the disclosure statement documents. As you fill out the required disclosure packet, it is critical to the transmission of sale that you give as much information as possible about your residence, no matter how small or insignificant. Please use additional paper if necessary and make a notation to that fact.

   b. Type the following second paragraph and press **Enter** once at the end of the paragraph.

      If there is information about the neighborhood or neighbors that you as a buyer would want to know about, be sure to reveal that information. Be sure to address those types of questions on the Real Estate Transfer Disclosure Statement, item #11 on page 2.

   c. Delete the space between the words "Real" and "Estate" in the second paragraph and press **Ctrl+Shift+Spacebar** to insert a non-breaking space between.
8. Type the closing lines of the business letter.
   a. With your insertion point on the blank line below the second body paragraph, type Best regards, and then press **Enter** two times.

b. Type Emma Cavalli and press **Shift+Enter** to insert a line break.
c. Type Realtor Consultant and press **Shift+Enter** to insert a line break.
d. Type Placer Hills Real Estate and press **Enter** to insert a paragraph break.
e. Type your initials in lowercase letters and press **Shift+Enter** to insert a line break. Word automatically capitalizes the first letter because it is the first letter in a new paragraph.
f. Click the **AutoCorrect Options** smart tag and select **Undo Automatic Capitalization** (Figure 1-18) or press **Ctrl+Z** to undo automatic capitalization.

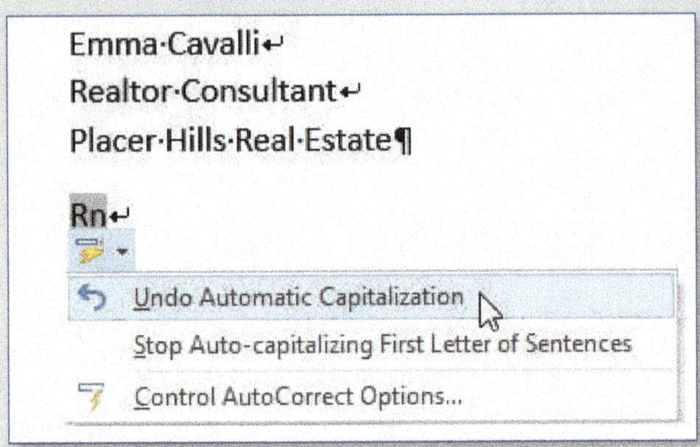

1-18 *AutoCorrect Options* smart tag

g. On the blank line below the reference initials, type Enclosure. An enclosure notation indicates to the reader that something is enclosed with the letter.

9. Press **Ctrl+S** to save the document (Figure 1-19). You can also save the document by clicking the **Save** button on the *Quick Access* toolbar or in the *Backstage* view.
10. Click the **File** tab and select **Close** (or press **Ctrl+W**) to close the document.

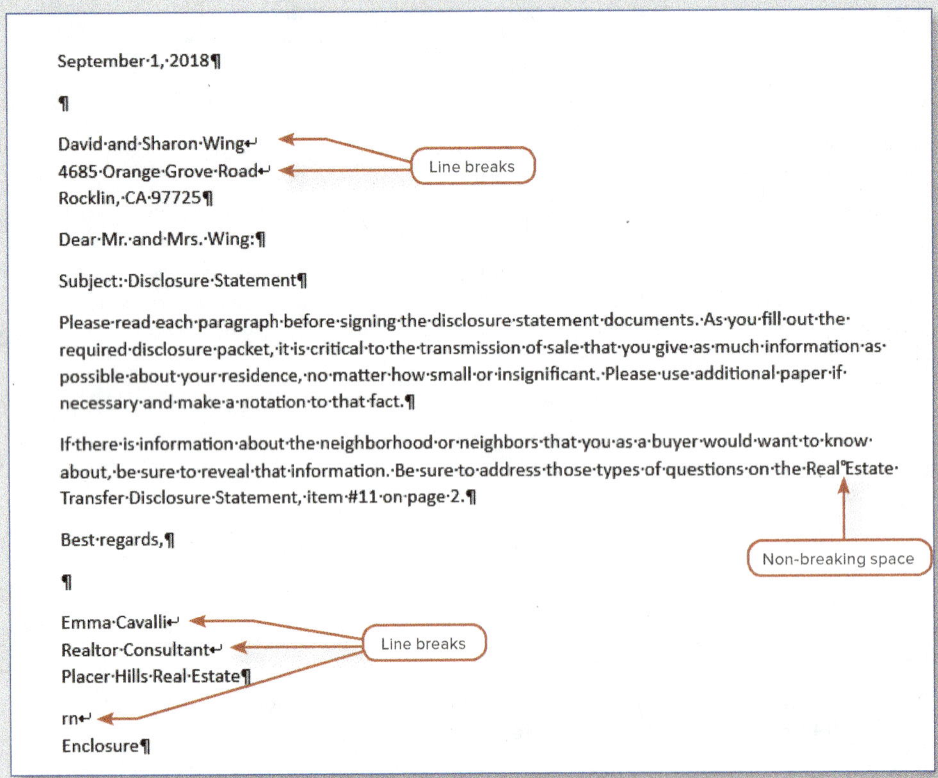
September·1,·2018¶

¶

David·and·Sharon·Wing↵
4685·Orange·Grove·Road↵
Rocklin,·CA·97725¶

Dear·Mr.·and·Mrs.·Wing:¶

Subject:·Disclosure·Statement¶

Please·read·each·paragraph·before·signing·the·disclosure·statement·documents.·As·you·fill·out·the· required·disclosure·packet,·it·is·critical·to·the·transmission·of·sale·that·you·give·as·much·information·as· possible·about·your·residence,·no·matter·how·small·or·insignificant.·Please·use·additional·paper·if· necessary·and·make·a·notation·to·that·fact.¶

If·there·is·information·about·the·neighborhood·or·neighbors·that·you·as·a·buyer·would·want·to·know· about,·be·sure·to·reveal·that·information.·Be·sure·to·address·those·types·of·questions·on·the·Real°Estate· Transfer·Disclosure·Statement,·item·#11·on·page·2.¶

Best·regards,¶

¶

Emma·Cavalli↵
Realtor·Consultant↵
Placer·Hills·Real·Estate¶

rn↵
Enclosure¶

1-19 PP W1-1 completed

SLO 1.4

Moving and Copying Text

Editing is an important phase in document creation. Editing involves not only proofreading and correcting grammar and spelling mistakes but also arranging text within a document, which can include cutting, copying, and pasting. Word makes it easy to move and copy information within a document or between multiple documents.

Move Text

Moving is actually removing text from one location (cutting) and placing it in another location (pasting). There are two methods you can use to move text: ***drag and drop*** or ***cut and paste***.

> **ANOTHER WAY**
>
> Press **Ctrl+C** to copy.
> Press **Ctrl+X** to cut.
> Press **Ctrl+V** to paste.

HOW TO: Move Text Using Drag and Drop

1. Select the text you want to move.
   - Refer to the *Select Text* section in *SLO 1.2: Entering and Selecting Text* for methods of selecting text.
2. Click and hold the selected text with your pointer.
3. Drag the text to the desired new location and release the pointer (Figure 1-20).

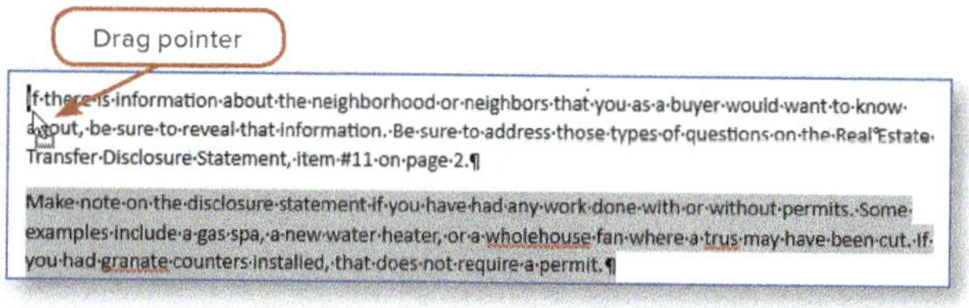

1-20 Move using drag and drop

There are a variety of ways to move text using cut and paste:

- ***Cut and Paste buttons***: Click the **Cut** and **Paste** buttons in the *Clipboard* group on the *Home* tab.
- ***Shortcut commands***: Press **Ctrl+X** to cut and **Ctrl+V** to paste.
- ***Context menu***: Right-click the selected text to display this menu.

HOW TO: Move Text Using Cut and Paste

1. Select the text you want to move.
2. Click the **Cut** button [*Home* tab, *Clipboard* group].
   - You can also press **Ctrl+X** or right-click the selected text and choose **Cut** from the context menu.
3. Place your insertion point in the desired location.
4. Click the **Paste** button [*Home* tab, *Clipboard* group].
   - You can also press **Ctrl+V** or right-click and choose from one of the *Paste Options* from the context menu. *Note: See the* Paste Text and Paste Options *section below for the different paste options available.*

Copy Text

An efficient method of inserting text into a document is to copy it from another location, such as a web page or a different document, and paste it into your document. Copying text leaves the text in its original location and places a copy of the text in a new location.

You can ***copy*** text by using the drag-and-drop method or the ***Copy*** and ***Paste*** buttons. Use the drag-and-drop method when copying text within the same document. The drag-and-drop method for copying is similar to the method for moving, except that you press the **Ctrl** key when dragging the text to be copied to an additional location.

▶ HOW TO: Copy Text Using Drag and Drop

1. Select the text you want to copy.
2. Press the **Ctrl** key and click and hold the selected text with your pointer.
   - A+ (plus sign) appears next to your pointer, indicating this text is being copied.
3. Drag to the desired new location and release the pointer (Figure 1-21). Release the **Ctrl** key after you have released the pointer.

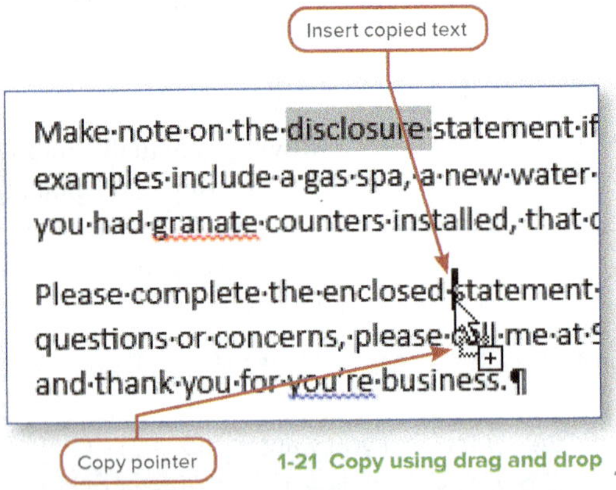

1-21 Copy using drag and drop

Copying text using the following copy and paste method is similar to moving text using the cut and paste method:

- ***Copy and Paste buttons***: Press the **Copy** and **Paste** buttons in the *Clipboard* group on the *Home* tab.
- ***Shortcut commands***: Press **Ctrl+C** to copy and **Ctrl+V** to paste.
- ***Context menu***: Right-click the selected text to display this menu.

Paste Text and Paste Options

You might want to paste plain text without formatting into a document, or you might want to merge the format from the source document into the new document. Word provides multiple paste options.

You have three primary paste options when you use the *Paste* button in the *Clipboard* group (Figure 1-22) or from the context menu:

- ***Keep Source Formatting***: Retains formatting from source document (the document where the text was copied)
- ***Merge Formatting***: Merges formatting from source document and current document
- ***Keep Text Only***: Pastes only unformatted text

The default paste option is *Keep Source Formatting*. In addition to these paste options, there are other context-specific paste options that are available when you paste information from lists, tables, or graphic objects.

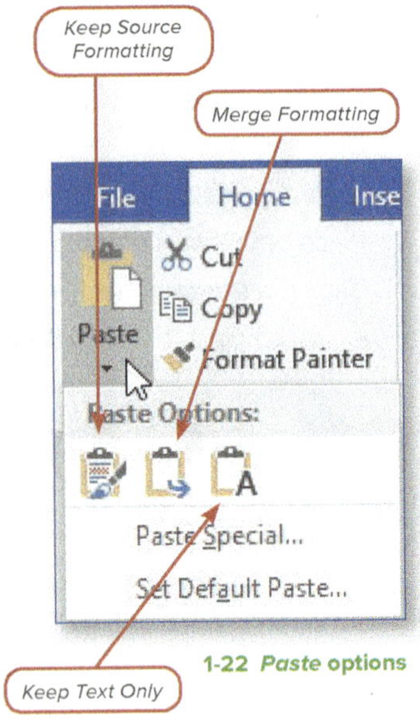

1-22 *Paste* options

MORE INFO

If you have trouble with the format of pasted text, try pasting the text as plain text and formatting the text *after* you have pasted it into the document.

Clipboard Pane

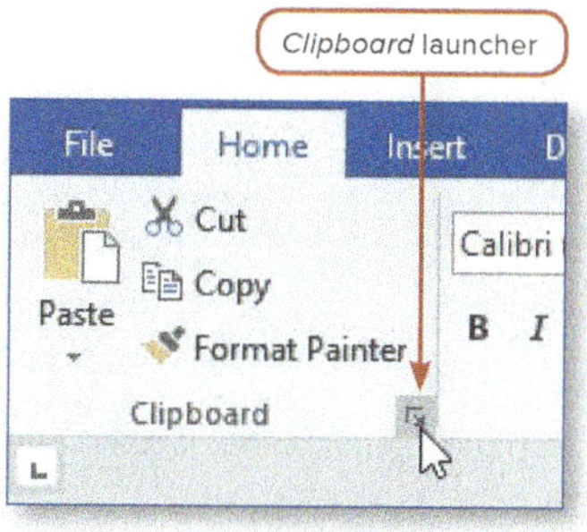

1-23 *Clipboard* launcher

When you copy or cut an item from a document, Word stores this information in the ***Clipboard***. From the *Clipboard*, you can select a previously copied item and paste it into a document. When Word is open, the *Clipboard* stores multiple items copied from Word documents and also items from web pages or other documents. The *Clipboard* stores text, pictures, tables, lists, and graphics.

The ***Clipboard pane*** displays all of the items stored in *Clipboard*. To display the *Clipboard* pane, click the **Clipboard** launcher in the bottom right corner of the *Clipboard* group on the *Home* tab (Figure 1-23). The *Clipboard* pane displays on the left side of the Word window and stores up to 24 copied items.

> **MORE INFO**
>
> The ***launcher*** (also referred to as the ***dialog box launcher***) is referred to throughout this text. Click the launcher in the bottom right corner of a group to open a dialog box or pane for additional options.

HOW TO: Use the Clipboard Pane to Paste Text

1. Select the text you want to copy or cut and click the **Copy** or **Cut** button [*Home* tab, *Clipboard* group].
   - You can also press **Ctrl+C** to copy or **Ctrl+X** to cut selected text.
2. Place your insertion point in the document where you want to paste the text.
3. Click the **Clipboard** launcher to open the *Clipboard* pane on the left side of the Word window (see Figure 1-23).
4. Click the item to paste or click the drop-down arrow to the right of the item and choose **Paste** (Figure 1-24). The selected content from the *Clipboard* is inserted in the document.
   - *Paste All* pastes all of the items in the *Clipboard* at the insertion point in the document.
   - *Clear All* empties the content of the *Clipboard*.
5. Click the **X** in the upper right corner of the *Clipboard* pane to close it.

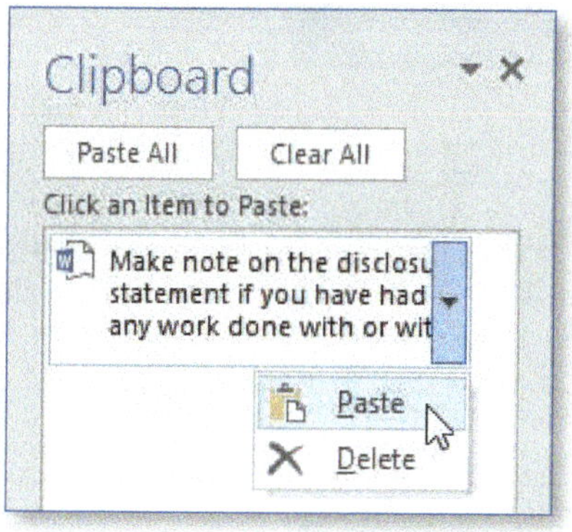

1-24 *Clipboard* pane

Undo Change

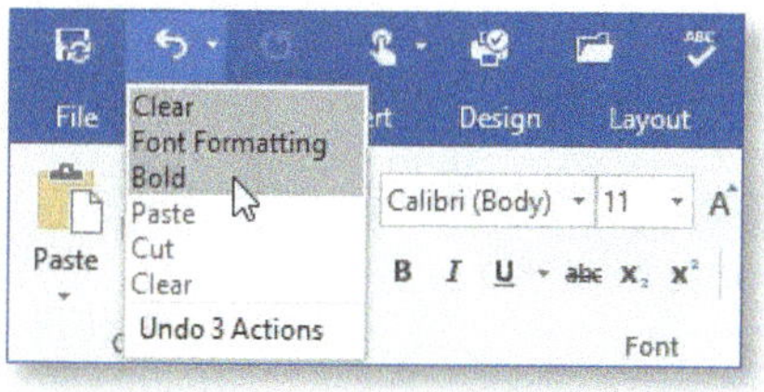

1-25 *Undo* button on the *Quick Access* toolbar

You can undo, redo, or repeat previous actions. All of these commands are available on the ***Quick Access toolbar***, which is above the *Ribbon* on the upper left.

When you click the ***Undo*** button, the last action you performed is reversed. You can undo multiple actions by clicking the **Undo** drop-down arrow to the right of the button and selecting the action to undo (Figure 1-25). For example if you select the third item in the list to undo, the previous two items will also undo.

Redo and Repeat Change

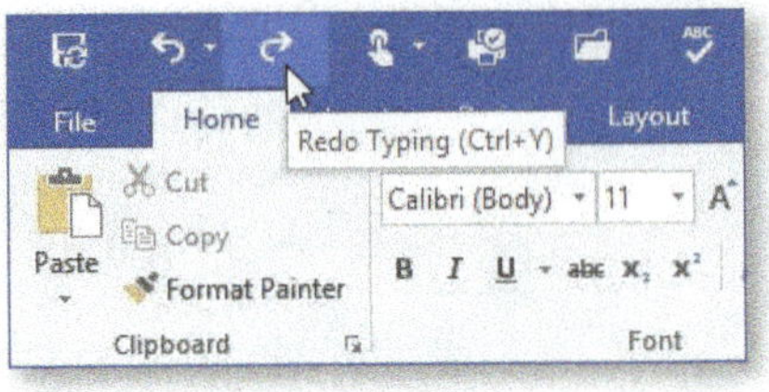

1-26 *Redo* button on the *Quick Access* toolbar

The ***Redo*** and ***Repeat*** features are similar to the undo feature. The same button is used for both of these commands, and it is context sensitive. Depending on the previous action performed, the button is either *Redo* or *Repeat*.

When you use the *Undo* button, the *Redo* button is activated so you can redo the previous change (Figure 1-26).

When you perform an action or apply formatting in a document, the *Repeat* button is activated (the icon changes) so you can repeat the previous action or formatting (Figure 1-27). For example, if you need to copy the date or a name into a document in multiple places, you can use the *Repeat* feature to accomplish this task quickly and accurately.

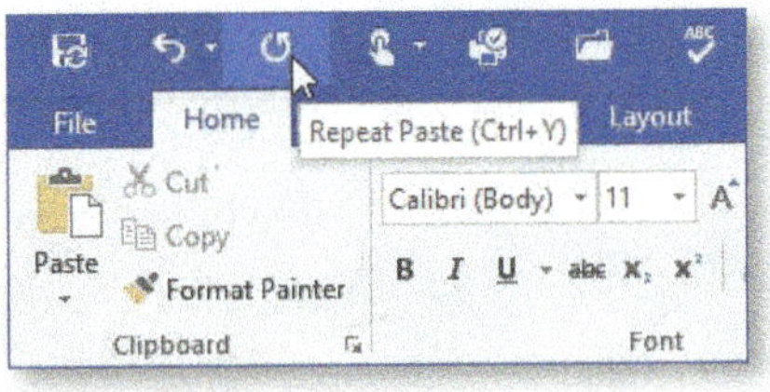

1-27 *Repeat* button on the *Quick Access* toolbar

ANOTHER WAY

Press **Ctrl+Z** to undo.
Press **Ctrl+Y** to redo or repeat.

SLO 1.5

Changing Fonts, Font Sizes, and Attributes

Word has many features that you can use to customize the appearance of the text within a document. You can change the font and font size; add styles such as bold, italics, and underlining; change the case of the text; add font and text effects; adjust the scale, spacing, and position of text; and change the default font settings. You can use buttons in the *Font* group on the *Home* tab, the *Font* dialog box, and the mini toolbar to apply formatting to text.

Font and Font Size

There are two main categories of fonts: serif and sans serif. ***Serif fonts*** have structural details (flair) at the top and bottom of most of the letters. Commonly used serif fonts include Cambria, Times New Roman, and Courier New. **Sans serif fonts** have no structural details on the letters. Commonly used sans serif fonts include Calibri, Arial, and Century Gothic.

Font size is measured in ***points*** (pt.); the larger the point, the larger the font. Most documents use between 10 and 12 pt. font sizes. Titles and headings generally are larger font sizes.

When creating a new document, you can choose a font and font size before you begin typing, and it applies to the entire document. If you want to change the font or font size of existing text, you must first select the text before applying the change.

MORE INFO

The default font and font size in Microsoft Word are *Calibri* and *11 pt.*, respectively.
Font size of 72 pt. is approximately 1" in height.

▶ HOW TO: Change Font and Font Size

1. Select the text you want to change.
2. Click the **Font** drop-down list to display the list of available fonts (Figure 1-28).
   - The *Font* drop-down list has three sections: *Theme Fonts*, *Recently Used Fonts*, and *All Fonts*.
3. Select the font you want to apply to the selected text.
4. Click the **Font Size** drop-down list to display the list of available font sizes (Figure 1-29).

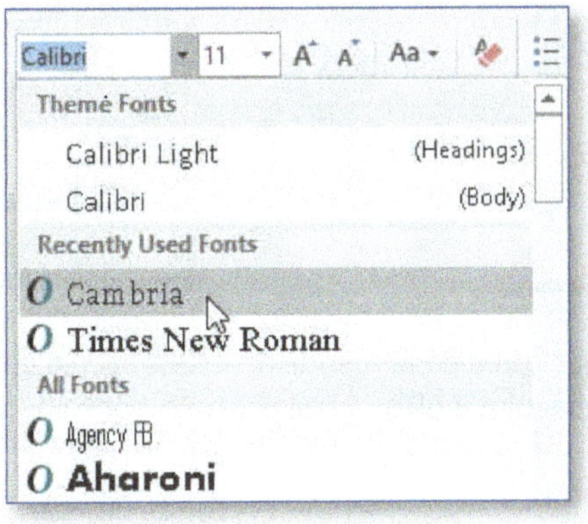

1-28 *Font* drop-down list

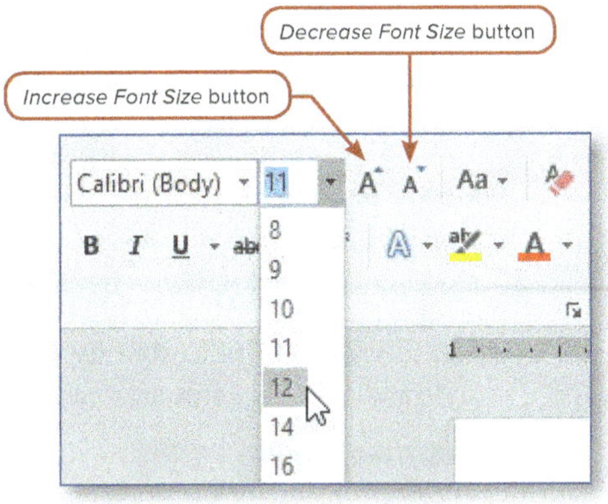

1-29 *Font Size* drop-down list

5. Select a font size to apply to selected text.
   - You can also click the **Font Size** area and type a size.
   - Click the **Increase Font Size** and **Decrease Font Size** buttons to increase or decrease the size of the font in small increments.

ANOTHER WAY

Press **Ctrl+>** (Ctrl+Shift+.) to *Increase Font Size*.
Press **Ctrl+<** (Ctrl+Shift+,) to *Decrease Font Size*.

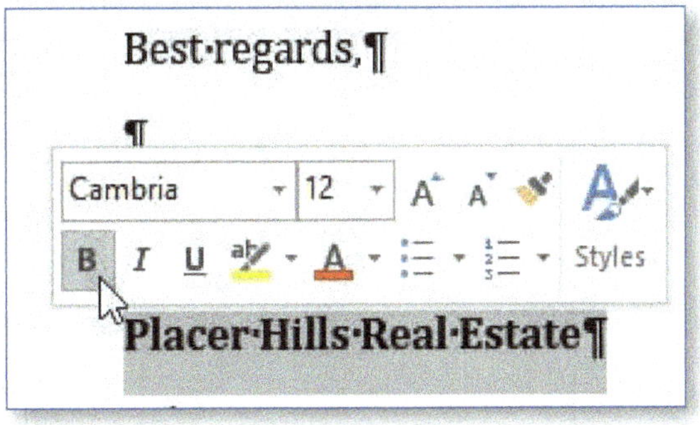

1-30 Select or right-click text to display the mini toolbar

The ***mini toolbar*** displays when you select or right-click text (Figure 1-30). You can use the mini toolbar to apply text formatting. Like the content menu, the mini toolbar is context-sensitive and displays different options depending on the selection you right-click.

Bold, Italic, and Underline Font Styles

You can add font styles such as ***Bold***, ***Italic***, and ***Underline*** to fonts to improve their appearance or call attention to specific text. The font style buttons for *Bold*, *Italic*, and *Underline* are available in the *Font* group on the *Home* tab.

To apply a font style, select the desired text and click the **Bold, Italic**, or **Underline** button in the *Font* group on the *Home* tab (Figure 1-31). You can also click a font style button to turn on a style, type the text, and click the font style button again to turn off the style.

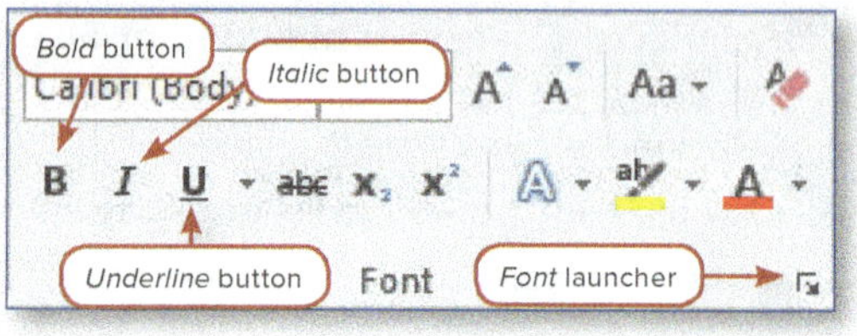

1-31 *Font* group on the *Home* tab

ANOTHER WAY

Ctrl+B applies *Bold* formatting.
Ctrl+I applies *Italic* formatting.
Ctrl+U applies *Underline* formatting.

Other Font Style Buttons

The following are other font styles and effects in the *Font* group on the *Home* tab. Some of these style and effect features are available on the mini toolbar when you select or right-click text:

- *Strikethrough*
- *Subscript*
- *Superscript*
- *Text Effects and Typography*, which includes *Outline, Shadow, Reflection, Glow, Number Styles, Ligatures*, and *Stylistic Sets*
- *Text Highlight Color*
- *Font Color*

Change Case

The ***Change Case*** feature provides a quick and easy way to change the case of a single word or group of words. The *Change Case* button is in the *Font* group on the *Home* tab (Figure 1-32). The different case options are:

- *Sentence case* (capitalizes the first letter of the sentence)
- *lowercase*
- *UPPERCASE*
- *Capitalize Each Word*
- *tOGGLE cASE* (changes letters that are uppercase to lowercase and lowercase letters to uppercase)

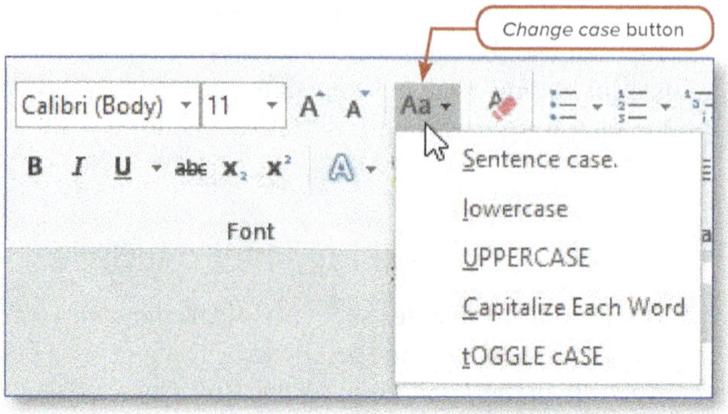

1-32 *Change Case* options

Font Dialog Box

The ***Font dialog box*** combines many of the font ***style*** and ***effect options*** in one location for easy access. You can open the *Font* dialog box (Figure 1-33) by clicking the **Font** launcher in the bottom right corner of the *Font* group.

In addition to the *Font*, *Font Style*, and *Size* commands on the *Font* tab, use the *Font* dialog box to change *Font Color*, *Underline Style*, *Underline Color*, and *Effects*. The *Preview* area displays a preview of selected changes, styles, and effects.

The *Advanced* tab lists *Character Spacing* options such as *Scale*, *Spacing*, *Position*, and *Kerning*. From this tab, you can also open the *Format Text Effects* dialog box.

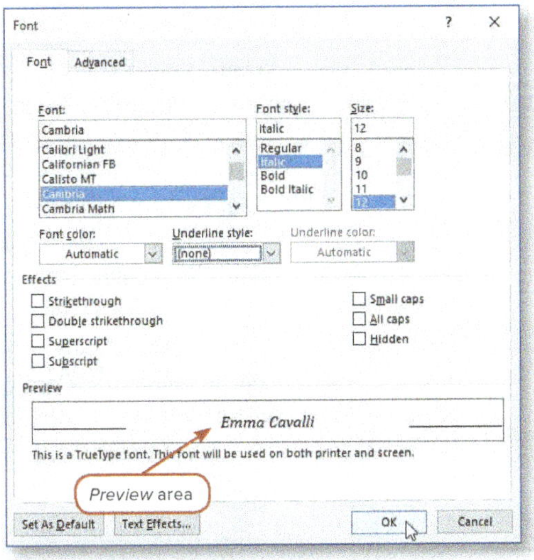

1-33 *Font* dialog box

> **ANOTHER WAY**
>
> **Ctrl+D** opens the *Font* dialog box.

Font Color

By default, the font color in a Word document is black. You can change the font color of selected text to add emphasis. The ***Font Color*** drop-down list in the *Font* dialog box displays a list of available font colors.

HOW TO: Change Font Color

1. Select the text you want to be a different color.
2. Click the **Font** launcher [*Home* tab, *Font* group]. The *Font* dialog box opens (Figure 1-34).
3. Click the **Font Color** drop-down arrow to display the list of font colors.
   - The drop-down list of font color options includes *Theme Colors*, *Standard Colors*, and *More Colors*. Theme colors are those colors associated with the theme of the document. For more on themes, see *SLO 2.7: Using Styles and Themes*.
4. Choose **OK** to close the *Font* dialog box.

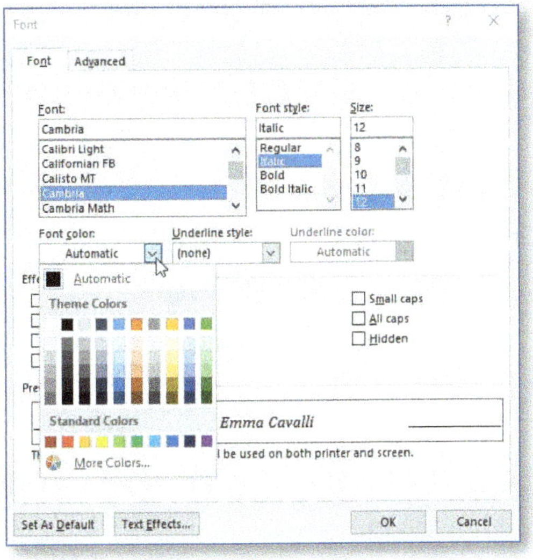

1-34 Change font color in the *Font* dialog box

> **ANOTHER WAY**
>
> Change the font color by clicking the **Font Color** button [*Home* tab, *Font* group].

Underline Style and Color

When you underline selected text, the default underline style is a solid black underline. Word provides a variety of additional underline styles. You can also change the color of the underline.

The ***Underline style*** and ***Underline color*** drop-down lists are available in the *Font* dialog box (Figure 1-35). A preview of how the formatted text will appear in your document is displayed in the *Preview* area of the *Font* dialog box.

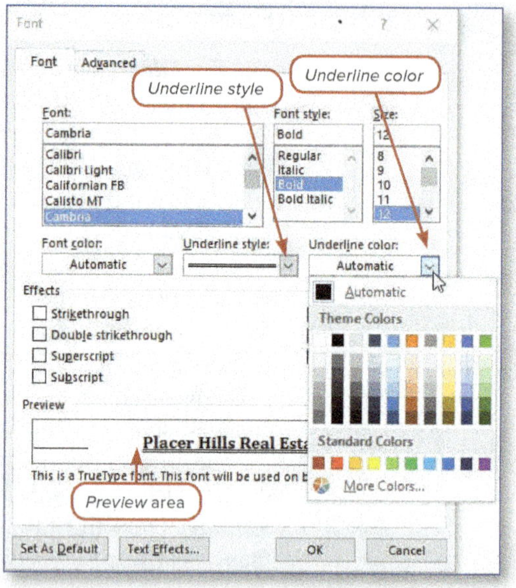

1-35 Change underline style and color

Font Effects

In the *Font* dialog box you can choose a variety of font effects from the ***Effects*** section. Some of these font effects are available in the *Font* group on the *Home* tab. The following table lists the different font styles and effects.

Font Styles and Effects

Style/Effect	Example
Bold	This **word** is in bold.
Italic	This *word* is in italic.
Bold and Italic	This ***word*** is in bold and italic.
Underline	This sentence is underlined.
Double underline	This word is double underlined.
Underline Words only	This sentence is words only underlined.
Thick underline with color	This word has a thick, colored underline.
Strikethrough	This ~~word~~ has a strikethrough.
Double strikethrough	~~This sentence has a double strikethrough.~~
Subscript	H_2O uses a subscript number.
Superscript	Footnotes and endnotes use superscript numbers or letters.[1]
Small caps	MICROSOFT WORD 2016 is in small caps.
All caps	THIS SENTENCE IS IN ALL CAPS.
Hidden	
Text Highlight Color	This word has a highlight color.
Font Color	This sentence has a font color applied.

MORE INFO

Hidden text appears in your on-screen document, but it does not print or display in print preview.

Character Spacing

The ***Character Spacing*** options allow you to add more or less space between letters and words. You can also vertically raise and lower letters and words (Figure 1-36).

The ***Scale*** option allows you to change the horizontal spacing of a word or group of words by a percentage. You can choose from preset percentages, or you can type a custom percentage for scaling.

Spacing has three options: *Normal*, *Expanded*, and *Condensed*. For *Expanded* and *Condensed*, you can choose the amount of points by which to expand the selected text.

The ***Position*** option vertically raises or lowers text by a selected number of points.

Kerning adjusts the space between letters in a proportional font.

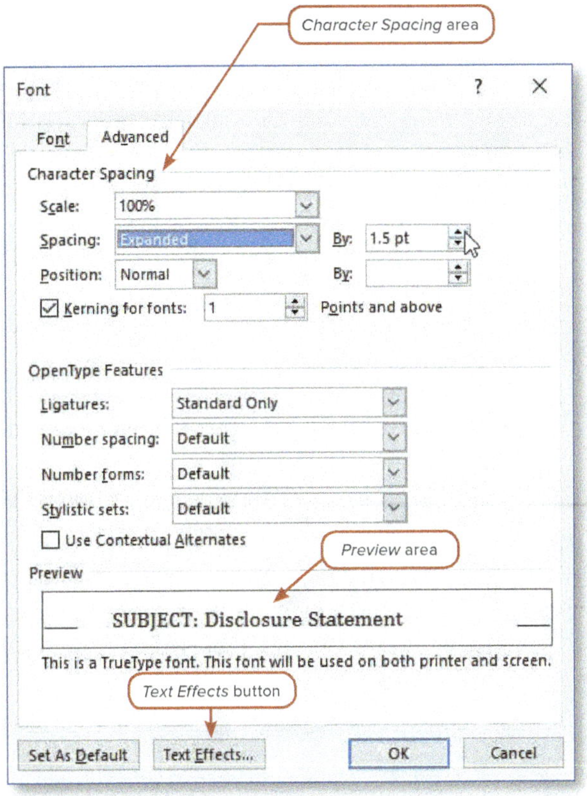

1-36 *Font* dialog box *Advanced* tab

Text Effects

Text Effects add special formatting features to selected text, such as *Outline*, *Shadow*, *Reflection*, and *Glow* (Figure 1-37). The *Text Effects* button is located in the *Font* group on the *Home* tab. There are many preset options for each of the different text effects, and there are more custom text effect options available in the *Format Text Effects* dialog box.

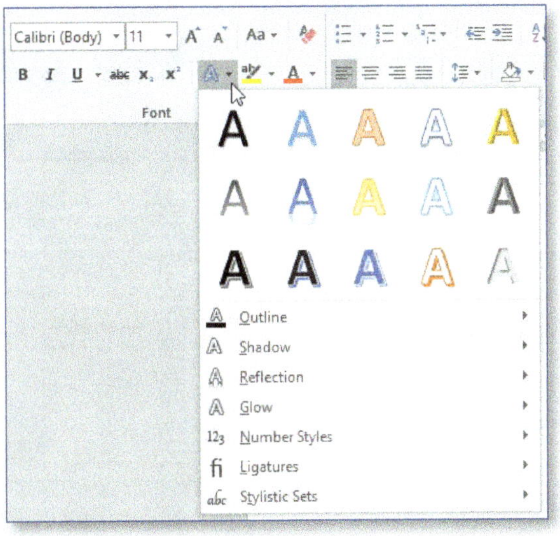

1-37 *Text Effects* button in the *Font* group

HOW TO: Use the Format Text Effects Dialog Box

1. Select the text you want to format.
2. Click the **Font** launcher [*Home* tab, *Font* group]. The *Font* dialog box opens.
3. Click the **Text Effects** button at the bottom. The *Format Text Effects* dialog box opens (Figure 1-38).
4. Click the **Text Fill & Outline** button to display fill and outline options.
   - Select **Text Fill** or **Text Outline** to expand and display options.
5. Click the **Text Effects** button to display text effect options.
   - Select **Shadow**, **Reflection**, **Glow**, **Soft Edges**, or **3-D Format** to expand and display options.
   - Each of these categories has *Presets* you can choose, or you can customize the effect.
6. Select the text effect of your choice. To the right of each option, you can choose a preset option from the drop-down list or customize the text effect as desired.
7. Click **OK** to close the *Format Text Effects* dialog box and click **OK** to close the *Font* dialog box.

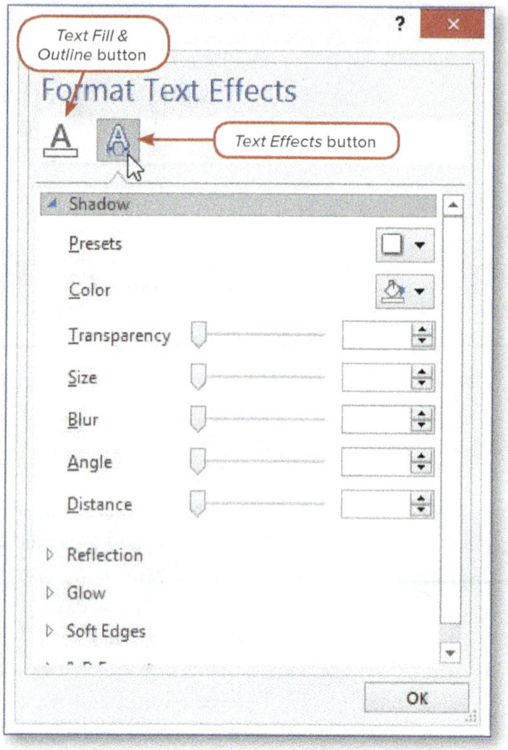

1-38 *Format Text Effects* dialog box

Format Painter

The ***Format Painter*** copies text formatting from selected text and applies the same formatting to other text in the same document or a different document. The *Format Painter* copies font, font size, line spacing, indents, bullets, numbering, styles, and other formatting features in Word. This feature saves time in applying formats and ensures consistency in document format.

HOW TO: Use the Format Painter

1. Select the text that has the formatting you want to copy.
2. Click the **Format Painter** button [*Home* tab, *Clipboard* group] (Figure 1-39). The *Format Painter* icon appears as your pointer (Figure 1-40).
3. Select the text you want to format, and Word applies the formatting to the selected text.
   - To apply formatting to multiple non-adjacent selections, double-click the **Format Painter** button and select the text you want to format. The *Format Painter* remains active until you turn off the feature.
   - Click the **Format Painter** button again or press the **Esc** key to turn off the *Format Painter*.

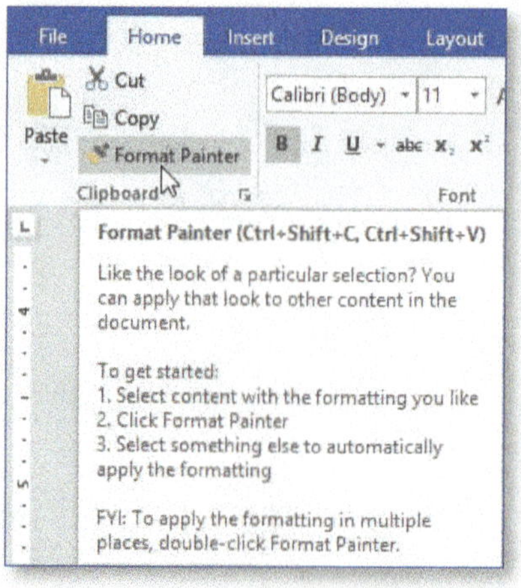

1-39 *Format Painter* button

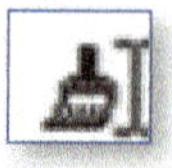
1-40 *Format Painter* icon

Clear All Formatting

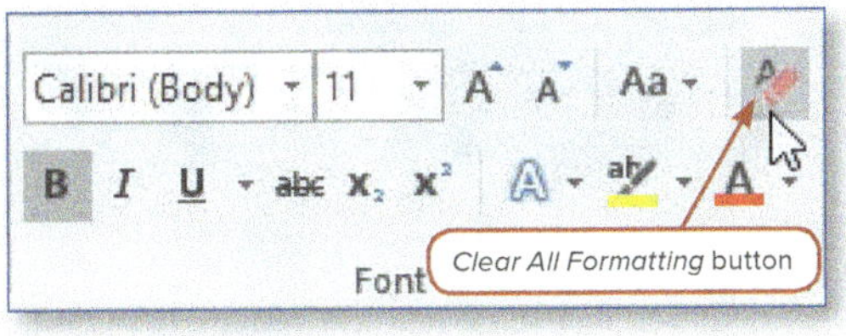

1-41 *Clear All Formatting* button in the *Font* group

The ***Clear All Formatting*** feature allows you to remove all formatting for the selected text and change it back to plain text (Figure 1-41). For example, if you have applied multiple formatting styles and effects to text, you can use the *Clear Formatting* feature rather than individually deselecting all of the formatting options previously selected.

> **MORE INFO**
>
> Be careful when using the *Clear Formatting* feature. It not only clears all text formatting but also clears line and paragraph spacing, numbering, bullets, and style formatting.

Change Default Font and Font Size

Recall that the default font in Microsoft Word is *Calibri* and the default font size is *11 pt*. This ***default*** setting is used on each new blank document you create. Each new document is based on the *Normal.dotm* template. This template stores the default settings for documents and controls document elements such as font, font size, line spacing, paragraph spacing, alignment, and styles.

You can change the default settings on the current document only or change the default settings in the *Normal* template. If you change the default settings for the *Normal* template, each new blank document you create uses this new default font and font size.

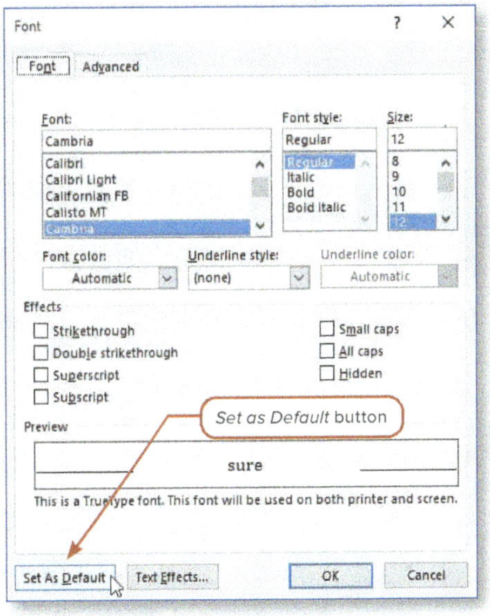

1-42 *Set As Default* button in the *Font* dialog box

HOW TO: Change the Default Font and Font Size

1. Select the text you want to format.
2. Click the **Font** launcher [*Home* tab, *Font* group]. The *Font* dialog box opens (Figure 1-42).
3. Click the **Font** tab if it is not already selected.
4. Select the font and font size to set as the default.
5. Click the **Set As Default** button on the bottom left. A confirmation dialog box opens giving you two options (Figure 1-43):
    - *This document only?*
    - *All documents based on the Normal template?*
6. Select an option and click **OK** to close the dialog box.
7. Click **OK** to close the *Font* dialog box.

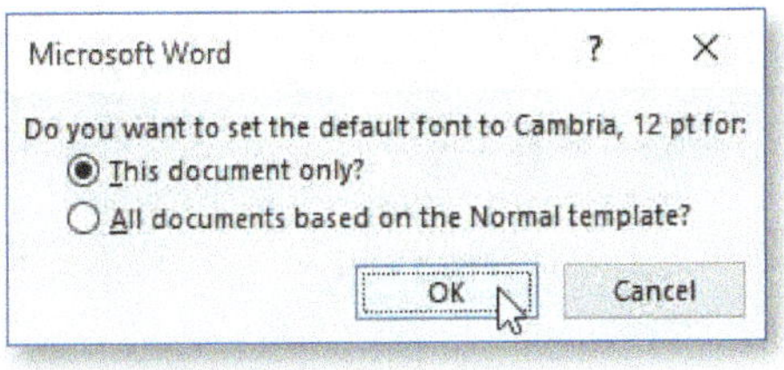

1-43 Change default setting confirmation options

> **MORE INFO**
>
> Be careful about changing the default settings in the *Normal* template. Do this only when you are sure you want to make this global default settings change.

PAUSE & PRACTICE: WORD 1-2

In this Pause & Practice project, you customize the content of the block format letter Emma created for Placer Hills Real Estate using cut, copy, paste, and the *Clipboard*. You also enhance your document by changing the font and applying font attributes.

Files Needed: ***[your initials] PP W1-1.docx*** and ***DisclosureStatement-01.docx*** *(Student data files are available in the* Library *of your SIMnet account)*
Completed Project File Name: ***[your initials] PP W1-2.docx***

1. Open the ***[your initials] PP W1-1*** document completed in *Pause & Practice 1-1*.
   a. Click the **File** tab to open the *Backstage* view and click **Open** on the left.
   b. Click **Browse** to open the *Open* dialog box.
   c. Browse to locate the ***[your initials] PP W1-1*** document, select the document, and click **Open**.
2. Save this document as ***[your initials] PP W1-2***.
   a. Click the **File** tab to open the *Backstage* view and select **Save As** on the left.
   b. Click **Browse** to open the *Save As* dialog box and select the desired location to save the file.
   c. Change the file name to [your initials] PP W1-2.
   d. Click **Save** to rename the document and close the *Save As* dialog box.
3. Open the ***DisclosureStatement-01*** document from your student date files. Ignore any spelling and grammar errors in this document; you will fix these in *Pause & Practice 1-3*. If the document opens in *Protected View*, click the **Enable Editing** button.
4. In the ***DisclosureStatement_01*** document, copy both paragraphs of text to the *Clipboard*.
   a. Press **Ctrl+A** to select the text.
   b. Press **Ctrl+C** or click the **Copy** button [*Home* tab, *Clipboard* group].
   c. Close the document without saving.
5. Paste the contents of the *Clipboard* into the document.
   a. In the ***[your initials] PP W1-2*** document, place your insertion point to the left of "Best regards,".
   b. Click the **Clipboard** launcher [*Home* tab, *Clipboard* group] to display the *Clipboard* pane.
   c. Click the **drop-down arrow** to the right of the copied text in the *Clipboard*.
   d. Select **Paste** (Figure 1-44). The paragraphs of text are pasted in the document at the insertion point.
   e. Close the *Clipboard* pane by clicking the **X** in the upper right corner.

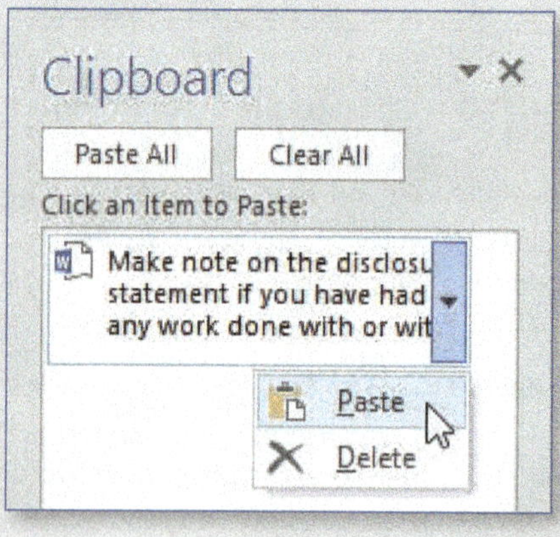

1-44 Paste text from the *Clipboard*

6. Copy the formatting of the first paragraph to the two new paragraphs.
   a. Place your insertion point in the first body paragraph of the letter.
   b. Click the **Format Painter** button [*Home* tab, *Clipboard* group].
   c. Select the last two paragraphs in the body of the letter. Be sure to include the paragraph mark at the end of the last body paragraph (Figure 1-45).

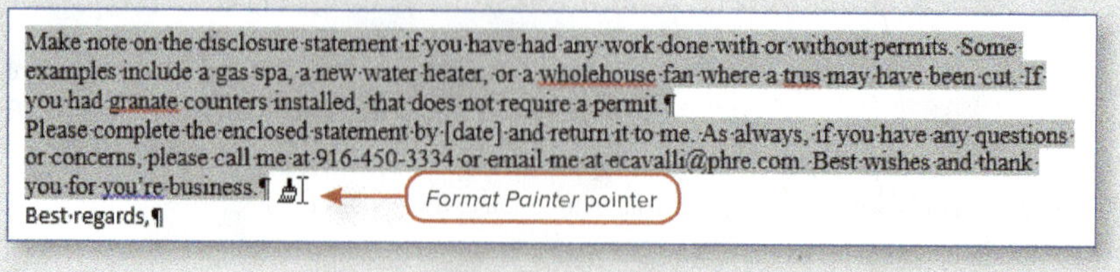

1-45 Use the *Format Painter* to apply formatting to selected text

7. Copy text using the drag-and-drop method.
   a. Click the **Show/Hide** button [*Home* tab, *Paragraph* group] to display formatting symbols.
   b. Select the word **"disclosure"** in the first sentence of the third body paragraph. Double-click a word to select it.
   c. Press the **Ctrl** key and click and hold the selected text with your pointer.
   d. Drag and drop the text between the words "enclosed" and "statement" in the last body paragraph (Figure 1-46). Make sure there is one space before and after the copied word.

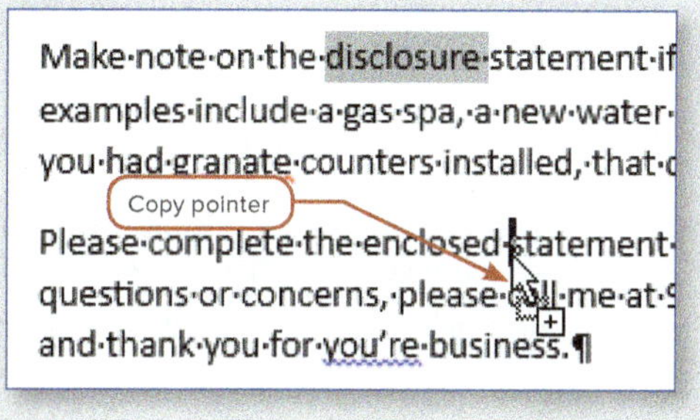

1-46 Copy text using drag and drop

8. Move a paragraph in the body of the letter.
   a. Select the entire third paragraph in the body of the letter (**"Make note . . ."**), including the paragraph mark at the end of the paragraph.
   b. Click the **Cut** button [*Home* tab, *Clipboard* group] or press **Ctrl+X**. The selected paragraph is cut from the document and stored in the *Clipboard*.
   c. Place your insertion point at the beginning of the second body paragraph.
   d. Click the top half of the **Paste** button [*Home* tab, *Clipboard* group] or press **Ctrl+V**.

9. Insert and format a date.
   a. Delete the placeholder "[date]" (including the brackets) in the last paragraph and type the date that is one week from today.
   b. Use month, day, year format (e.g., September 8, 2018).
   c. Select the date you just typed.
   d. Click the **Text Highlight Color** drop-down list button [*Home* tab, *Font* group] and choose the **Yellow** text highlight color (Figure 1-47).

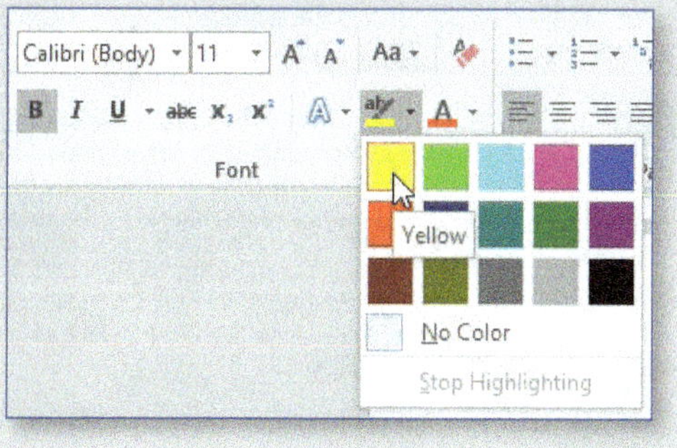

1-47 Apply text highlight color

10. Change the font and font size of the entire document.
    a. Press **Ctrl+A** to select all of the text in the document.
    b. Click the **Font** drop-down list button [*Home* tab, *Font* group] and select **Cambria**.
    c. Click the **Font Size** drop-down list button [*Home* tab, *Font* group] and select **12**.

11. Change the case and spacing of selected text.
    a. Select the word **"Subject"** in the subject line of the document.
    b. Click the **Change Case** button [*Home* tab, *Font* group] and select **UPPERCASE**. Do not use the *Font* dialog box to change the case.
    c. Select the entire subject line.
    d. Click the **Font** launcher [*Home* tab, *Font* group] to open the *Font* dialog box. **Ctrl+D** also opens the *Font* dialog box.
    e. Click the **Advanced** tab.
    f. In the *Character Spacing* area, click the **Spacing** drop-down list and select **Expanded**.
    g. In the *By* area to the right of *Spacing*, click the up arrow to change the character spacing to expanded by **1.5 pt** (Figure 1-48).
    h. Click **OK** to close the *Font* dialog box.

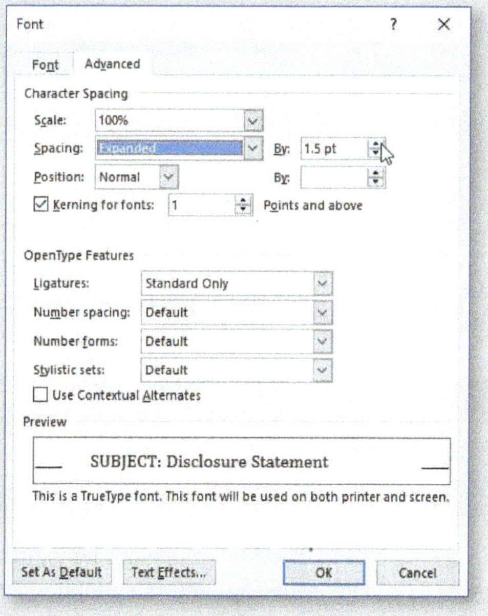

1-48 Change character spacing

12. Apply font styles to selected text.
    a. Select the email address **"ecavalli@phre.com"** in the last body paragraph.
    b. Click the **Font Color** drop-down list button [*Home* tab, *Font* group] and select **Dark Blue** in the *Standard Colors* area.
    c. Click the **Underline** button or press **Ctrl+U** to apply an underline to the selected email address.
    d. Select the writer's name **"Emma Cavalli"** (below "Best regards,").
    e. Click the **Font** launcher in the bottom right corner of the *Font* group to open the *Font* dialog box.
    f. Click the **Font** tab and check the **Small caps** box in the *Effects* area.
    g. Click **OK** to close the *Font* dialog box.
    h. Select the writer's title **"Realtor Consultant"** and click the **Italic** button or press **Ctrl+I**.
    i. Select the company name **"Placer Hills Real Estate"** and click the **Bold** button or press **Ctrl+B**.
13. Save and close the document (Figure 1-49).

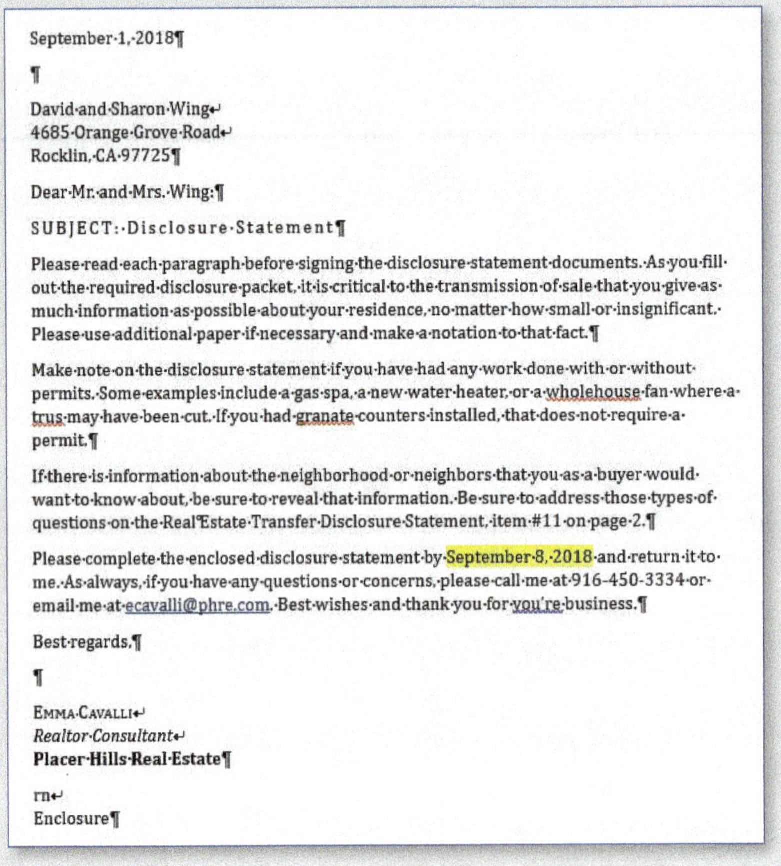
September 1, 2018¶

¶

David and Sharon Wing↵
4685 Orange Grove Road↵
Rockln, CA 97725¶

Dear Mr. and Mrs. Wing:¶

SUBJECT: Disclosure Statement¶

Please read each paragraph before signing the disclosure statement documents. As you fill out the required disclosure packet, it is critical to the transmission of sale that you give as much information as possible about your residence, no matter how small or insignificant. Please use additional paper if necessary and make a notation to that fact.¶

Make note on the disclosure statement if you have had any work done with or without permits. Some examples include a gas spa, a new water heater, or a wholehouse fan where a trus may have been cut. If you had granate counters installed, that does not require a permit.¶

If there is information about the neighborhood or neighbors that you as a buyer would want to know about, be sure to reveal that information. Be sure to address those types of questions on the Real Estate Transfer Disclosure Statement, item #11 on page 2.¶

Please complete the enclosed disclosure statement by September 8, 2018 and return it to me. As always, if you have any questions or concerns, please call me at 916-450-3334 or email me at ecavalli@phre.com. Best wishes and thank you for you're business.¶

Best regards,¶

¶

EMMA CAVALLI↵
Realtor Consultant↵
Placer Hills Real Estate¶

rn↵
Enclosure¶

1-49 PP W1-2 completed

SLO 1.6 Changing Text Alignment, Line Spacing, and Paragraph Spacing

In addition to word wrap, line breaks, and paragraphs breaks, you can use text alignment, line spacing, and paragraph spacing to control the layout and the white space between parts of your document.

Default Settings

Just as there are default settings for font and font size, there are default settings for paragraph alignment, line spacing, and paragraph spacing. These default settings are stored in the *Normal* template on which all new blank documents are based. The following table summarizes font, line spacing, and paragraph default settings:

Normal Template Default Settings

Setting	Default Setting
Font	Calibri
Font Size	11 pt.
Horizontal Paragraph Alignment	Left
Line Spacing	1.08 lines
Paragraph Spacing—Before	0 pt.
Paragraph Spacing—After	8 pt.

Paragraph Alignment

Paragraph alignment controls how a paragraph is aligned horizontally on the page. A paragraph can be a single word, a group of words, a sentence, or multiple sentences. Paragraphs are separated by paragraph breaks. A group of words using word wrap and line breaks is considered one paragraph.

The four different paragraph alignment options are:

- ***Left*** (default): The paragraph is aligned on the left margin.
- ***Center***: The paragraph is centered between the left and right margins.
- ***Right***: The paragraph begins and is aligned on the right margin.
- ***Justify***: The paragraph is aligned flush with both the left and right margins.

> **ANOTHER WAY**
>
> Press **Ctrl+L** to *Align Text Left*.
> Press **Ctrl+E** to *Center* text.
> Press **Ctrl+R** to *Align Text Right*.
> Press **Ctrl+J** to *Justify* text.

Change the alignment of a paragraph by clicking a paragraph alignment button in the *Paragraph* group on the *Home* tab (Figure 1-50). When changing the alignment of a single paragraph, the entire paragraph need not be selected; the insertion point only needs to be within the paragraph for the alignment to be applied. Text alignment can also be changed in the *Paragraph* dialog box, which we discuss later.

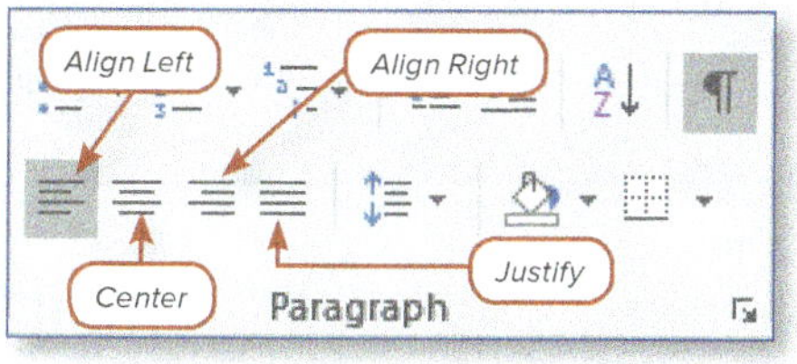

1-50 Paragraph alignment options in the *Paragraph* group

Line Spacing

Line spacing refers to the amount of blank space between lines of text within a paragraph. The default setting in Word is 1.08 lines, which is slightly more than single spacing. Most documents you type are single-spaced or 1.08 line spacing, but there are times you may want to use double-spacing (two lines), such as when typing an academic report.

As with paragraph alignment, you can apply line spacing to an individual paragraph, multiple paragraphs, or an entire document.

You change line spacing using the *Line and Paragraph Spacing* button in the *Paragraph* group on the *Home* tab (Figure 1-51). You can choose from the preset line spacing options, or you can select *Line Spacing Options* and set custom line spacing in the *Paragraph* dialog box.

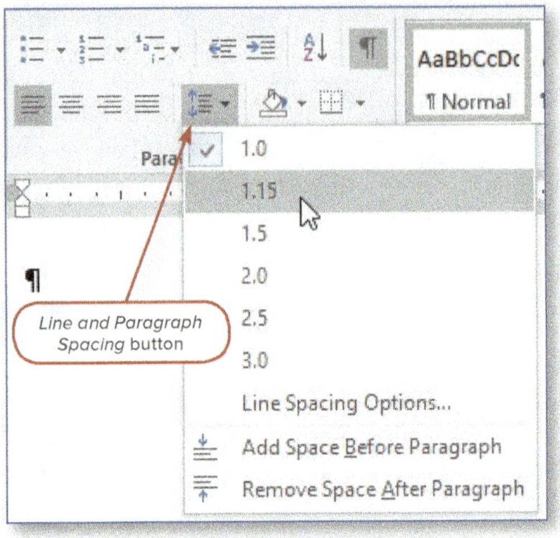

1-51 ***Line and Paragraph Spacing*** **button in the** ***Paragraph*** **group**

> **ANOTHER WAY**
>
> **Ctrl+1** applies single-space (1 line).
> **Ctrl+5** applies 1.5 line spacing.
> **Ctrl+2** applies double-space (2 lines).

In the *Paragraph* dialog box, you see different line spacing options (Figure 1-52). The *At Least* and *Exactly* options allow you to specify points of spacing, rather than lines of spacing, between lines of text. The *Multiple* option allows you to set a line spacing option that is not a whole number, such as 1.3 or 2.25 line spacing.

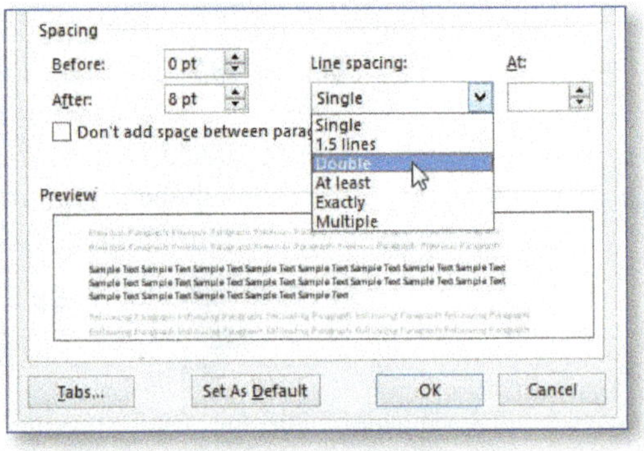

1-52 ***Line spacing*** **options in the** ***Paragraph*** **dialog box**

> **MORE INFO**
>
> If a document has inconsistent line spacing, it looks unprofessional. Select the entire document and set the line spacing to enhance consistency and improve readability.

Paragraph Spacing

While line spacing controls the amount of space between lines of text in a paragraph, ***paragraph spacing*** controls the amount of spacing before and after paragraphs. For example, you might want the text of a document to be single-spaced, but you prefer to have more blank space before and after paragraphs. You can use paragraph spacing to accomplish this task.

Before and ***After*** paragraph spacing is set in points. The default *After* paragraph spacing is 8 pt., which is a little less than one blank line. The default *Before* paragraph spacing is 0 pt.

Change *Before* and *After* paragraph spacing from the *Paragraph* group on the *Layout* tab (Figure 1-53). You can also change *Before* and *After* paragraph spacing in the *Paragraph* dialog box and from the *Line and Paragraph Spacing* button in the *Paragraph* group on the *Home* tab.

From the *Line and Paragraph Spacing* button in the *Paragraph* group on the *Home* tab, you can ***Add/Remove Space Before Paragraph*** or ***Add/Remove Space After Paragraph*** (Figure 1-54). These options are context sensitive, depending on whether there is already *Before* or *After* paragraph spacing.

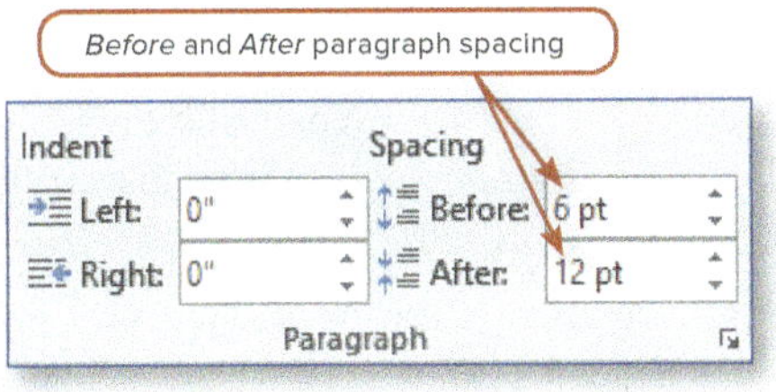

1-53 *Paragraph* group on the *Layout* tab

MORE INFO

Use line breaks to keep lines of text as a single paragraph. *Before* and *After* paragraph spacing is not applied to lines of text where line breaks are used.

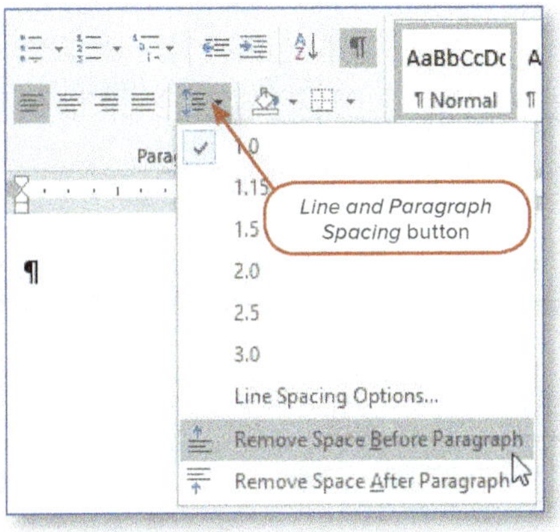

1-54 *Add/Remove* paragraph spacing options

Paragraph Dialog Box

The ***Paragraph dialog box*** combines many of the alignment and spacing options included in the *Paragraph* groups on the *Home* and *Layout* tabs.

HOW TO: Change Alignment and Spacing in the Paragraph Dialog Box

1. Select the text you want to format.
2. Click the **Paragraph** launcher [*Home* or *Layout* tab, *Paragraph* group] to open the *Paragraph* dialog box (Figure 1-55).
3. Click the **Alignment** drop-down list in the *General* area and select **Left**, **Centered**, **Right**, or **Justified**.
   - The *Indentation* section of this dialog box lets you control indents. Indents are covered in *SLO 2.3: Using Indents*.
4. In the *Spacing* section, you can change paragraph spacing and line spacing.
   - Type the number of points of spacing or use the up and down arrows.
   - The *Don't add space between paragraphs of the same style* check box controls paragraph spacing between paragraphs of the same style, which is primarily used with numbered and bulleted lists and outlines.
5. Click the **Line spacing** drop-down list to select a line spacing option.
   - You can select **Multiple** and type in a specific line spacing in the *At* area.
6. Notice the *Preview* area displays how your document will look with changes.
7. Click **OK** to close the *Paragraph* dialog box.

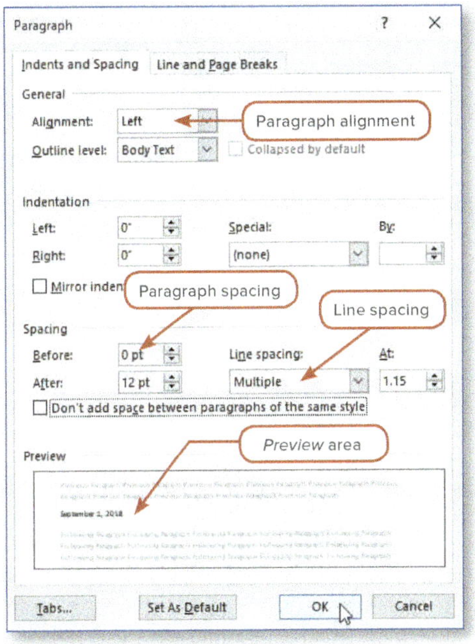

1-55 *Paragraph* dialog box

Change Default Line and Paragraph Spacing

You can set default paragraph alignment and spacing in the *Paragraph* dialog box. This process is similar to changing the font and font size default settings.

HOW TO: Change the Default Paragraph Alignment and Spacing

1. Click the **Paragraph** launcher [*Home* or *Layout* tab, *Paragraph* group] to open the *Paragraph* dialog box.
2. Click the **Indents and Spacing** tab if it is not already selected.
3. Make the desired changes to paragraph and line spacing.
4. Click the **Set As Default** button on the bottom left of the dialog box. Select one of the two options in the confirmation dialog box that opens (Figure 1-56):
   - *This document only?*
   - *All documents based on the Normal template?*
5. Click **OK**.

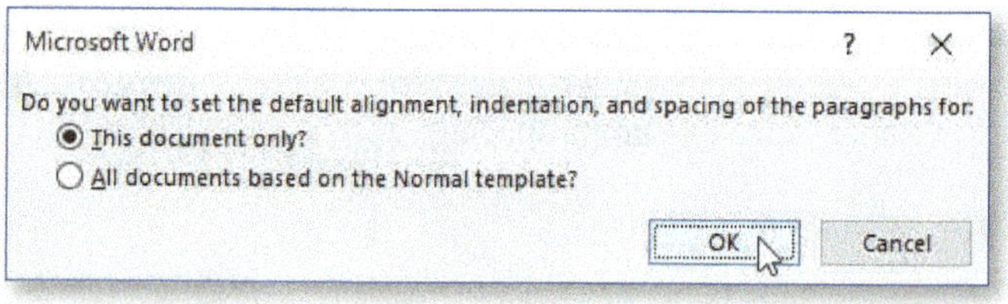

1-56 Change default setting confirmation options

SLO 1.7

Using Smart Lookup and Proofreading Tools

The words and grammar you use in a document reflect your professionalism and the reputation of your organization. Word provides you with many proofing and editing tools to improve the quality of the documents you produce. The *Smart Lookup* feature allows you to search for information on the Internet without leaving Word. The spelling, grammar, and thesaurus features help you to produce high-quality and professional-looking documents.

Smart Lookup and the Smart Lookup Pane

Smart Lookup is a new research feature in Word 2016. This feature uses Bing, an Internet search engine, to find information about a selected word or words in a Word document without leaving the application. The ***Smart Lookup pane*** displays information from the Internet about the words you select. You have the option to find additional information by clicking a hyperlink in the *Smart Lookup* pane, which opens an Internet browser displaying additional Internet content.

HOW TO: Use Smart Lookup and the Smart Lookup Pane

1. Select the word or words to research.
2. Click the **Smart Lookup** button [*Review* tab, *Insights* group] (Figure 1-57) to open the *Smart Lookup* pane on the right side of the Word window (Figure 1-58).
   - By default, the *Explore* area is displayed in the *Smart Lookup* pane.
   - Click the **Define** button at the top of the *Smart Lookup* pane to display a definition of the selected word(s).
   - A privacy notice appears in the Smart Lookup pane upon first use.

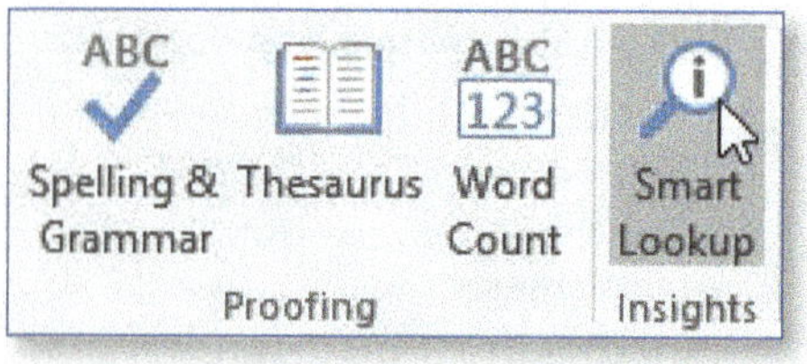

1-57 *Smart Lookup* button

3. View the research results in the *Smart Lookup* pane.
   - To view additional information about a research result, click the result title, which is a hyperlink that will open an Internet browser window displaying additional information about the topic.
   - To perform additional research on a different word, select the word in the document and click the **Smart Lookup** button again. The new results appear in the *Smart Lookup* pane.
4. Click the **X** in the upper right corner of the *Smart Lookup* pane to close the pane.

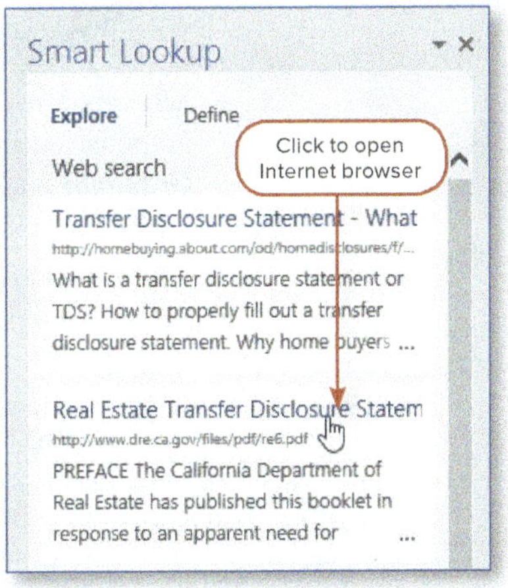

1-58 *Smart Lookup* pane

ANOTHER WAY

Right-click a word or selected word and select **Smart Lookup** from the context menu.

Automatic Spelling and Grammar Notifications

Recall that Word uses *AutoCorrect* to automatically correct many commonly misspelled words. But there are many ***spelling errors*** that Word does not automatically correct. When you are typing a document, Word is constantly checking the words you type against the words in its dictionary. When Word doesn't recognize a word, it marks it with a -Dot-dash ***red wavy underline***.

Word also checks the grammar of your document and marks potential word choice or ***grammatical errors*** with a ***blue wavy underline***.

MORE INFO

When Word marks a word as a possible spelling or grammatical error, it does not necessarily mean that the word is misspelled. Many proper nouns are not included in the dictionary.

HOW TO: Correct Spelling and Grammatical Errors

1. Right-click a word that has a red or blue wavy underline. A context menu opens that provides different editing options (Figure 1-59).
2. Select the correct word from the list to replace the misspelled word. You can also choose from the following editing options:
   - Select **Ignore All** to ignore all instances of this spelling throughout the document.
   - Select **Ignore Once** to ignore a potential grammar error.
   - Select **Add to Dictionary** to add the word to the Word dictionary.
3. Right-click the next item with a wavy red or blue underline to repeat the editing process.

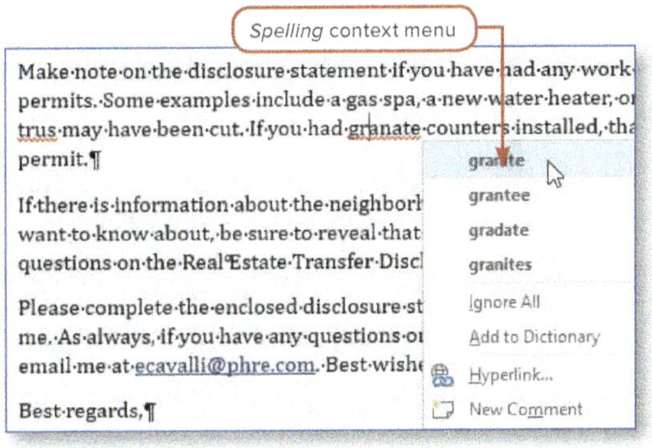

1-59 Correct a spelling error

Spelling and Grammar Panes

When finalizing a document, it is important to proofread it one last time and use the spelling and grammar check. This is especially true with longer documents. You can use the ***Spelling and Grammar panes*** to check your entire document for potential spelling and grammatical errors.

The *Spelling* and *Grammar* panes are context sensitive. The name of the pane (*Spelling* or *Grammar*) and the available options change depending on whether a potential spelling or grammatical error is detected.

HOW TO: Use the Spelling and Grammar Panes

1. Click the **Spelling & Grammar** button [*Review* tab, *Proofing* group] to open the *Spelling* pane (Figure 1-60).
   - The first potential spelling or grammatical error is displayed in the *Spelling* or *Grammar* pane.
2. If the word does not need to be changed, select **Ignore**, **Ignore All**, or **Add**.
   - If you select *Add*, the selected word is added to the dictionary so it is not detected as a potential error in the future.
3. If the word needs to be changed, select the correct word and select **Change** or **Change All**.
   - *Change* changes the word and *Change All* changes all instances of the misspelled word.
   - A definition of the selected word is displayed below the list of word options.
   - If no word options are available, retype the word in the body of the document.
4. Click **OK** to finish when the dialog box opens indicating the spell and grammar check is complete.

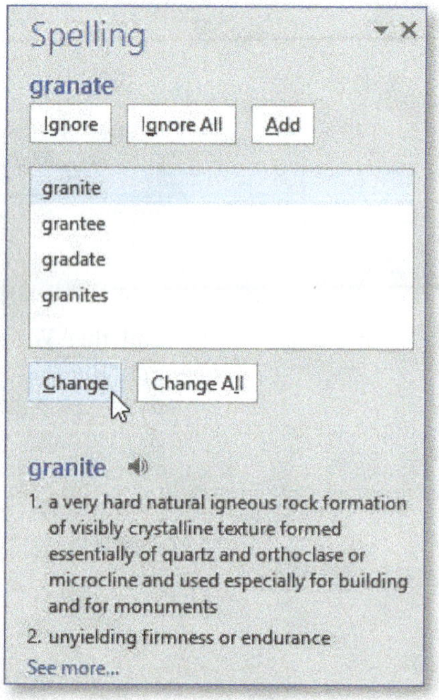

1-60 ***Spelling*** **pane**

> **ANOTHER WAY**
>
> **F7** opens the *Spelling and Grammar* pane.

Customize the Dictionary

When you spell check a document, you can easily add a word to the ***Word Dictionary***. When you add a word to the dictionary, Word actually creates a custom dictionary for you. You can manually add or delete words from the custom dictionary. Many proper nouns are marked as a misspelled word. You can add proper nouns you commonly use to the dictionary so they won't be marked as a misspelled word.

HOW TO: Add Words to the Custom Dictionary

1. Click the **File** tab to open the *Backstage* view.
2. Click the **Options** button to open the *Word Options* dialog box.

3. Click the **Proofing** button.
4. Click the **Custom Dictionaries** button. The *Custom Dictionaries* dialog box opens (Figure 1-61).
5. Select the dictionary to edit in the *Dictionary List*.
    - The *RoamingCustom.dic* is typically the default custom dictionary.
6. Click the **Edit Word List** button. Your custom dictionary dialog box opens (Figure 1-62). The words that have been previously added to your dictionary are displayed in the *Dictionary* area.
7. Click in the **Word(s)** area, type a word to add to your dictionary, and click the **Add** button to add the word to your dictionary.
    - To delete a word from the dictionary, select the word and click the **Delete** button.
8. Click **OK** when finished to close the *RoamingCustom.dic* dialog box.
9. Click **OK** to close the *Custom Dictionaries* dialog box.
10. Click **OK** to close the *Word Options* dialog box.

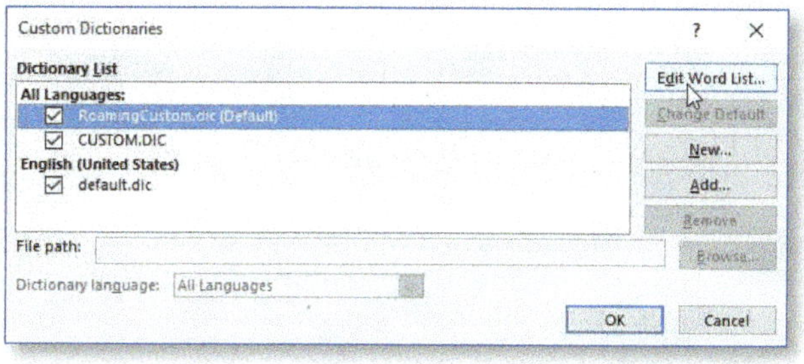

1-61 *Custom Dictionaries* dialog box

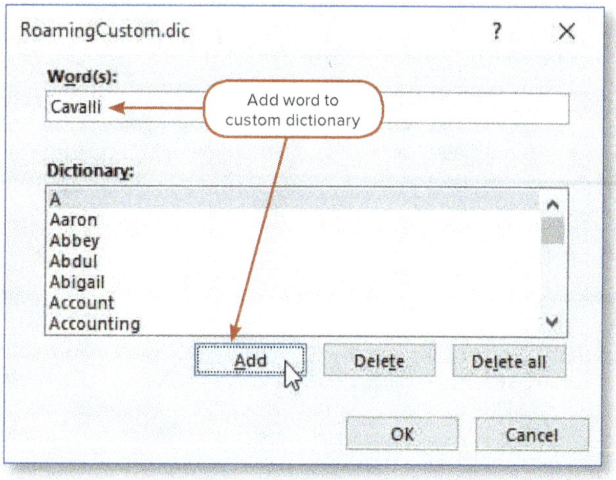

1-62 Add word to custom dictionary

The Thesaurus

Word provides a ***Thesaurus*** feature that you can use to find ***synonyms*** of words to add variety to your writing. A varied vocabulary indicates a more educated and professional writer.

There are two ways to use the *Thesaurus* to find synonyms. The first and quickest way is to select a word in the document and use the context menu (right-click) to replace a selected word with an appropriate synonym.

HOW TO: Find Synonyms Using the Context Menu

1. Right-click the word you want to replace with an appropriate synonym. The context menu displays.
2. Place your pointer on **Synonyms**. Another context menu appears with a list of synonym choices.
3. Select the synonym you prefer (Figure 1-63). The selected synonym replaces the selected word in the text and the menus close.

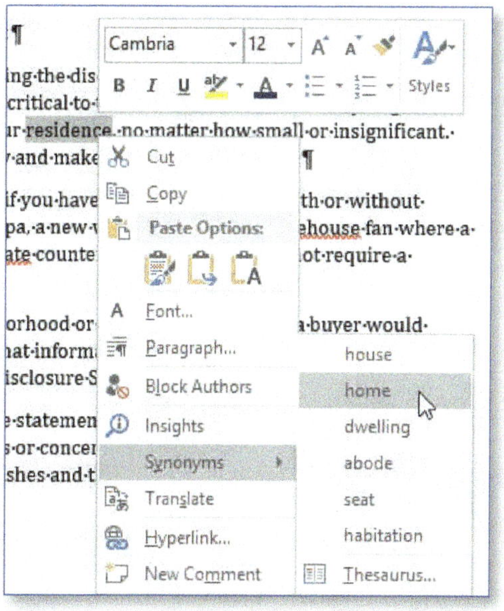

1-63 Use *Thesaurus* to find synonyms

You can also use the *Thesaurus* feature in the *Thesaurus* pane. This method allows you to search for synonyms of any word, not just a selected word in your document.

▶HOW TO: Use the Thesaurus

1. Click the **Thesaurus** button [*Review* tab, *Proofing* group]. The *Thesaurus* pane opens on the right side of the Word window (Figure 1-64).
2. Type a word in the *Search* text box and press **Enter** or click the **Search** button (magnifying glass icon). A list of synonyms appears in the *Thesaurus* area.
3. Choose from the synonyms listed.
   - Click the **arrow** to the right of the word to display the drop-down list. You have options to *Insert* or *Copy* the synonym.
   - You can also click a synonym in the list to look up synonyms for that word. Click the **Back** arrow to return to the previous synonym list.
4. Click the **X** in the upper right corner of the *Thesaurus* pane to close this pane.

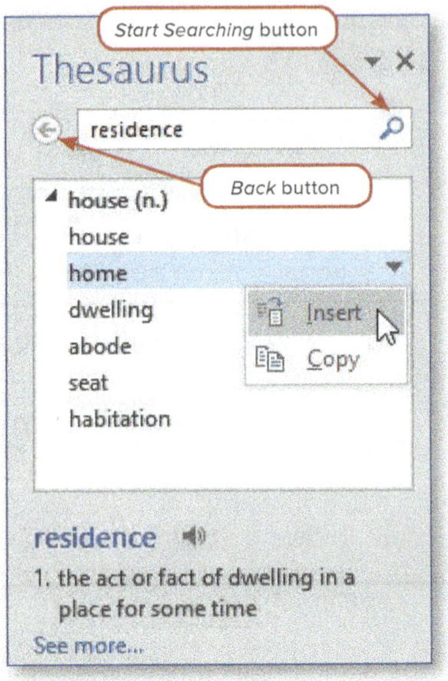

1-64 *Thesaurus* pane

> **ANOTHER WAY**
>
> **Shift+F7** opens the *Thesaurus* pane.

Word Count

Word provides a running ***word count*** in each document, which is displayed on the *Status* bar in the bottom left corner of the Word window (Figure 1-65). Click the **Word Count** area to open the *Word Count* dialog box to display more detailed information: number of pages, words, characters (no spaces), characters (with spaces), paragraphs, and lines (Figure 1-66). You can also choose whether or not to have Word count words in textboxes, footnotes, and endnotes.

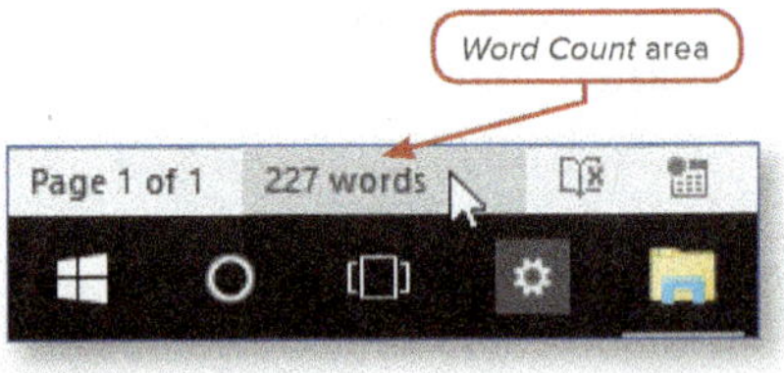

1-65 *Word Count* area on the *Status* bar

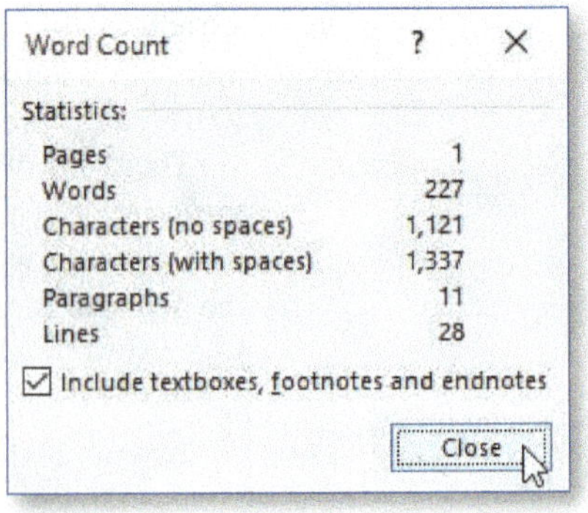

1-66 *Word Count* dialog box

> **ANOTHER WAY**
>
> Click the **Word Count** button in the *Proofing* group *on the Review* tab to open the *Word Count* dialog box.

SLO 1.8

Customizing Document Properties

Word allows you to include details about a document, which are called ***document properties***. These details are not visible in the text of the document but are included as hidden information within the document. These include fields such as *Title*, *Author*, *Comments*, *Subject*, *Company*, *Created*, and *Last Modified*. Some of the document properties are automatically generated, such as *Words*, *Total Editing Time*, and *Last Modified*, whereas other document property details can be edited individually.

Document Properties

The document properties can be viewed and edited in the *Info* area on the *Backstage* view. Document properties are saved within the document and can be viewed by others who view or use the document.

HOW TO: Add Document Properties

1. Click the **File** tab to display the *Backstage* view.
2. Click the **Info** button if it is not already selected.
3. Review the document properties on the right side of the window (Figure 1-67).
   - Document property field names are listed on the left, and the information in these fields is listed on the right.
4. Click in a field and type information to edit the document property.
   - Some properties cannot be changed. These properties are automatically generated by Word.
5. Click the **Show All/Fewer Properties** link at the bottom to display more or fewer document property fields.
6. After entering and reviewing document properties, click the **Back** arrow in the upper left corner of the *Backstage* view to return to the document.

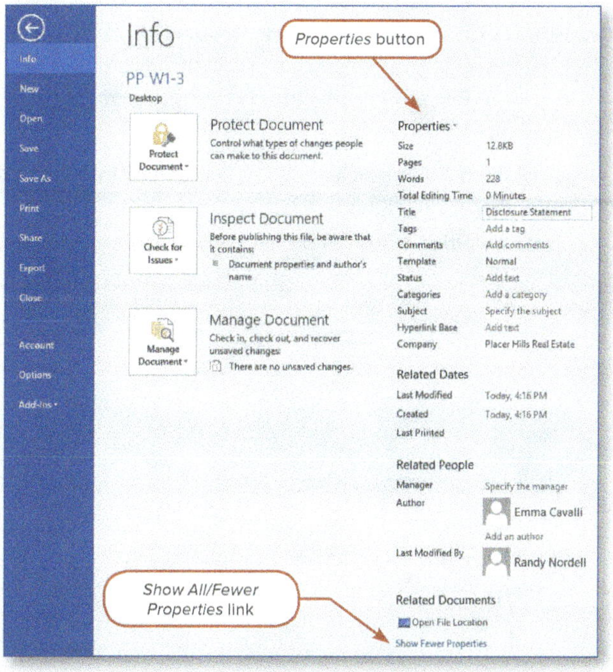

1-67 Document properties on the *Backstage* view

Advanced Properties

In addition to viewing and editing the document properties on the *Backstage* view, you can also display document properties in the ***Properties* dialog box** (Figure 1-68). In the *Info* area on the *Backstage* view, click the **Properties** button and select **Advanced Properties** to open the *Properties* dialog box.

You can modify the document properties on the *Summary* tab. The title of the *Properties* dialog box is context sensitive. The file name is displayed before *Properties* in the title bar of the dialog box.

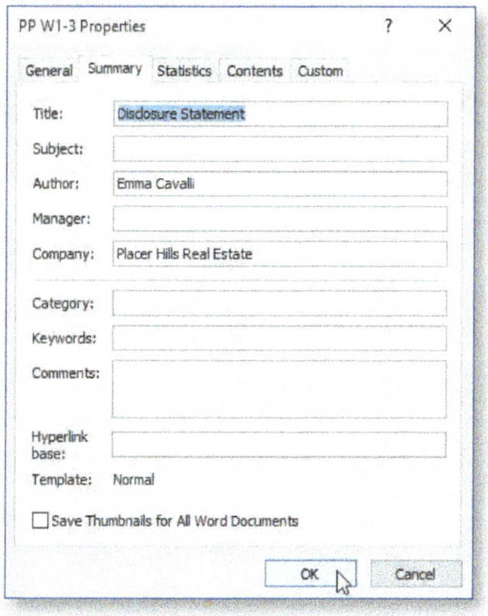

1-68 *Properties* dialog box

Print Document Properties

After customizing document properties, you can print the document properties included in a document. When you print document properties, only a page listing the document properties prints, not the document itself.

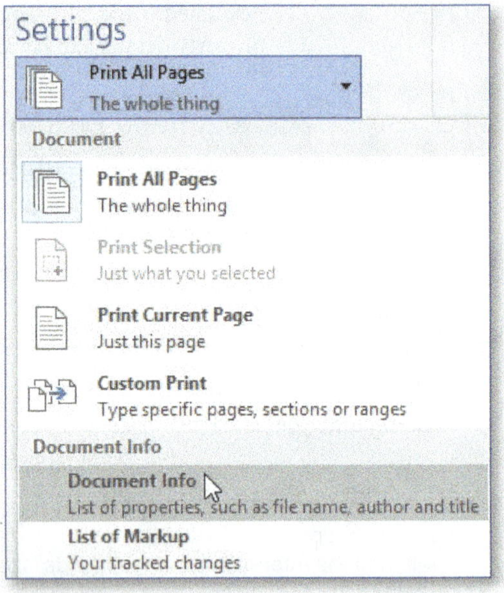

1-69 Print document properties

HOW TO: Print Document Properties

1. Click the **File** tab to open the *Backstage* view.
2. Select **Print** on the left.
3. Click **Print All Pages** and select **Document Info** from the drop-down list (Figure 1-69).
4. Click the **Print** button to print the document properties.

PAUSE & PRACTICE: WORD 1-3

In the final Pause & Practice project in this chapter, you add the finishing touches on a document for Placer Hills Real Estate. You customize paragraph and line spacing, change paragraph alignment, and use spelling and grammar checkers to produce an error-free document. You also modify the document properties.

File Needed: ***[your initials] PP W1-2.docx***
Completed Project File Name: ***[your initials] PP W1-3.docx***

1. Open the ***[your initials] PP W1-2*** document completed in *Pause & Practice 1-2*.
   a. Click the **File** tab to open the *Backstage* view and click **Open** on the left.
   b. Click **Browse** to open the *Open* dialog box.
   c. Browse to locate the ***[your initials] PP W1-2*** document, select the document, and click **Open**.
2. Save this document with a different file name.
   a. Click the **File** tab to open the *Backstage* view and select **Save As** on the left.
   b. Click **Browse** to open the *Save As* dialog box and select the desired location to save the file.
   c. Change the file name to [your initials] PP W1-3.
   d. Click **Save** to save the document with a different file name and close the *Save As* dialog box.
3. Change the line and paragraph spacing on the entire document.
   a. Press **Ctrl+A** to select the entire document.
   b. Click the **Paragraph** launcher [*Home* or *Layout* tab, *Paragraph* group] to open the *Paragraph* dialog box (Figure 1-70).

c. Change the *Line spacing* to **Single**.
d. Change the *After* spacing to **12 pt**. Use the up arrow or type in the amount of spacing.
e. Click **OK** to close the dialog box.

> **ANOTHER WAY**
>
> Change line spacing in the *Paragraph* group on the *Home* tab. Change *Before* and *After* paragraph spacing in the *Paragraph* group on the *Layout* tab.

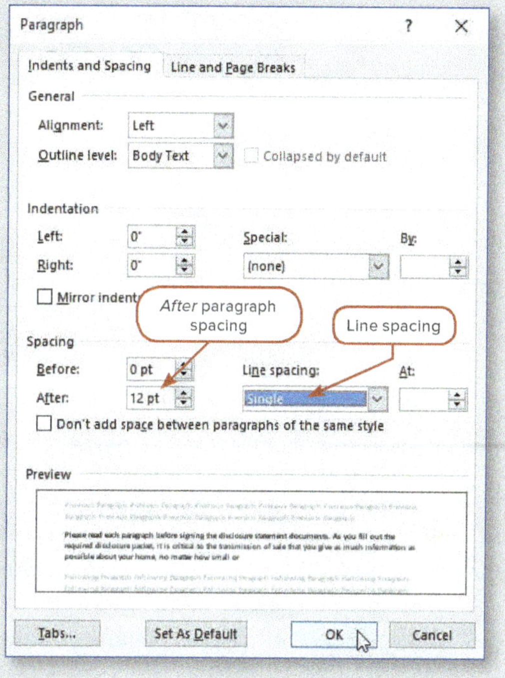

1-70 Change *Line spacing* and *After* paragraph spacing in the *Paragraph* dialog box

4. Add paragraph spacing before the date line of the business letter.
   a. Select or place your insertion point in the first line (date line) of the business letter.
   b. Click the **Layout** tab.
   c. Change the *Before* spacing to **72 pt**. (Figure 1-71). *Note: 72 pt. is approximately 1", which is commonly used as the spacing before the date line on business letters.*

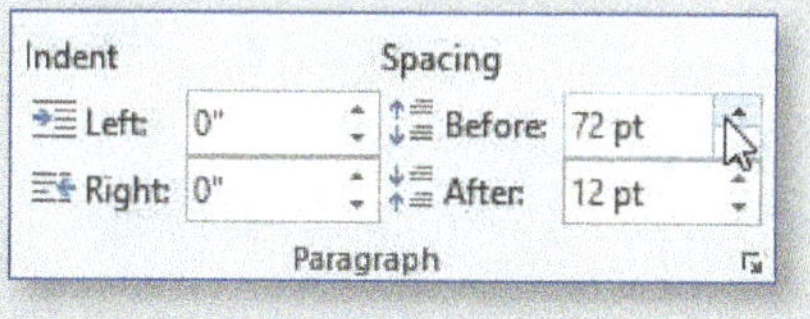

1-71 Change *Before* paragraph spacing in the *Paragraph* group

5. Change the paragraph alignment of selected text.
   a. Select or place your insertion point in the subject line of the business letter.
   b. Click the **Center** button [*Home* tab, *Paragraph* group] or press **Ctrl+E**.
6. Use the *Thesaurus* to find synonyms for selected words.
   a. Select the word **"reveal"** in the third body paragraph.
   b. Click the **Thesaurus** button [*Review* tab, *Proofing* group]. The *Thesaurus* pane opens on the right with a list of synonyms for the selected word (Figure 1-72).
   c. Click the **drop-down arrow** to the right of the word "divulge" and choose **Insert**. The word "reveal" is replaced with "divulge."
   d. Click the **X** in the upper right corner of the *Thesaurus* pane to close the pane.
   e. Right-click the word **"residence"** in the first body paragraph. A context menu opens.
   f. Point to **Synonyms** and a list of synonyms appears.
   g. Select **"home"** from the list of synonyms. The word "residence" is replaced with "home."

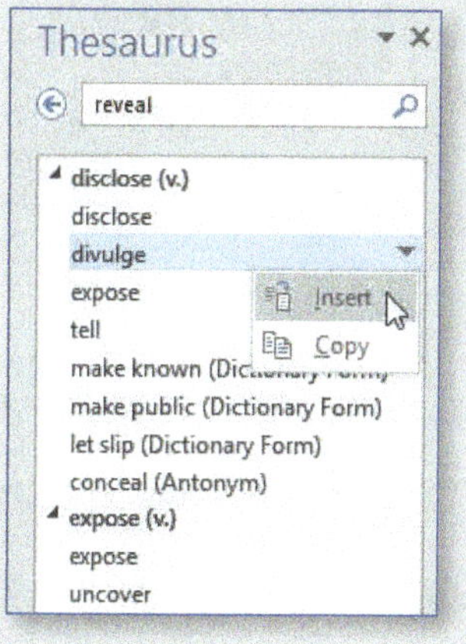

1-72 Insert a synonym from the *Thesaurus* pane

7. Add a word to the custom dictionary.
   a. Click the **File** tab to open the *Backstage* view.
   b. Click the **Options** button to open the *Word Options* dialog box.
   c. Click **Proofing** on the left.
   d. Click the **Custom Dictionaries** button in the *When correcting spelling in Microsoft Office programs* area. The *Custom Dictionaries* dialog box opens.

e. Select **RoamingCustom.dic** in the *Dictionary List*. If this dictionary is not available, select the available custom dictionary.
f. Click the **Edit Word List** button. The *RoamingCustom.dic* dialog box opens (Figure 1-73)
g. Type your last name in the *Word(s)* area and click the **Add** button. If your last name is already in the dictionary, the *Add* button is shaded gray.
h. Click **OK** to close the *RoamingCustom.dic* dialog box.
i. Click **OK** to close the *Custom Dictionaries* dialog box.
j. Click **OK** to close the *Word Options* dialog box.

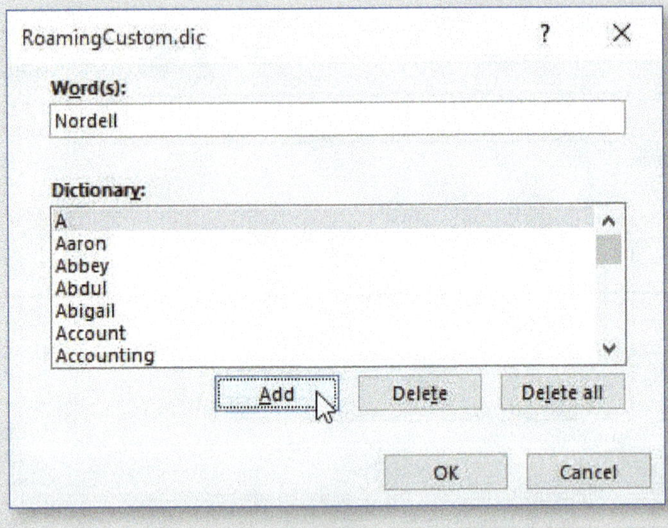

1-73 Add a word to the custom dictionary

8. Spell and grammar check the document.
   a. Right-click the word **"wholehouse"** in the second paragraph. A context list of words appears (Figure 1-74).
   b. Select **"whole house."** The correctly spelled word replaces the incorrectly spelled word.
   c. Click the **Spelling & Grammar** button [*Review* tab, *Proofing* group] or press **F7** to open the *Spelling* pane on the right (Figure 1-75).
   d. Select **"truss"** in the *Spelling* pane and click the **Change** button.
   e. Continue spell checking the remainder of the document. Change "granate" to **"granite"** and "you're" to **"your."**
   f. Click **Add** for "Cavalli" if it is marked as incorrect.
   g. Click **Ignore** for your reference initials if it is marked as incorrect.
   h. Click **Ignore** for the capitalization grammar error (lowercase reference initials).
   i. Click **OK** to close the dialog box that opens and informs you that the spelling and grammar check is complete. The *Spelling* pane closes.

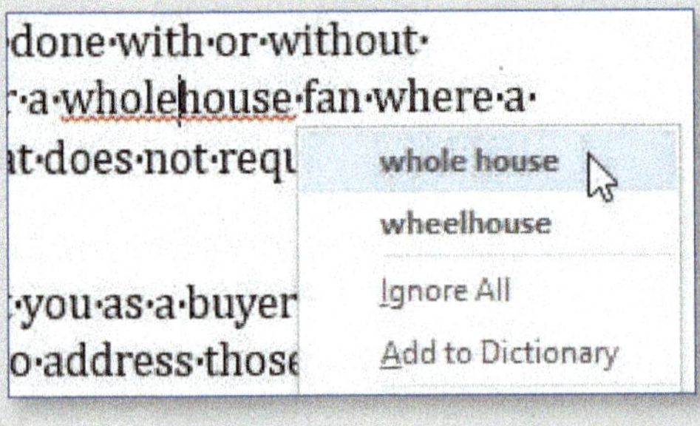

1-74 Correct spelling using the context menu

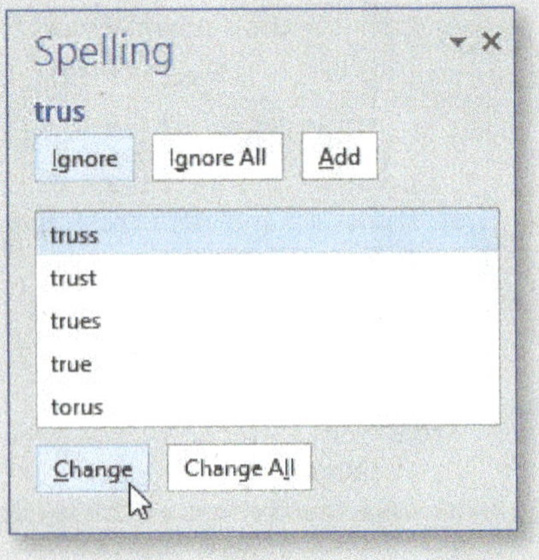

1-75 *Spelling* pane

9. Use *Smart Lookup* to research selected words.
   a. Select **"Transfer Disclosure Statement"** in the third body paragraph.
   b. Click the **Smart Lookup** button [*Review* tab, *Insights* group]. The *Smart Lookup* pane opens on the right. If you are using this feature for the first time, you might receive a message about privacy and have to click the **Got it** button before data is displayed.
   c. Review the research results on the *Smart Lookup* pane.
   d. Click the **X** in the upper right of the *Smart Lookup* pane to close the pane.

10. Add document properties to your letter.
    a. Click the **File** tab to open the *Backstage* view.
    b. Click **Info** on the left if it is not already selected. The document properties are displayed on the right side of the *Backstage* view (Figure 1-76).
    c. Click in the *Title* field and type Disclosure Statement.
    d. In the *Author* area, right-click the existing author and select **Remove Person**.
    e. In the *Author* area, click **Add an author**, type Emma Cavalli, and press **Tab**.
    f. Click the **Show All Properties** link at the bottom. More document properties are displayed.
    g. Click in the *Company* area and type Placer Hills Real Estate.
    h. Click the **Properties** drop-down list at the top of the *Properties* area and choose **Advanced Properties**. The document properties display in the *Summary* tab of the *Properties* dialog box.
    i. Click **OK** to close the *Properties* dialog box and click the **Back** arrow to return to the document.

11. Save and close the document (Figure 1-77).

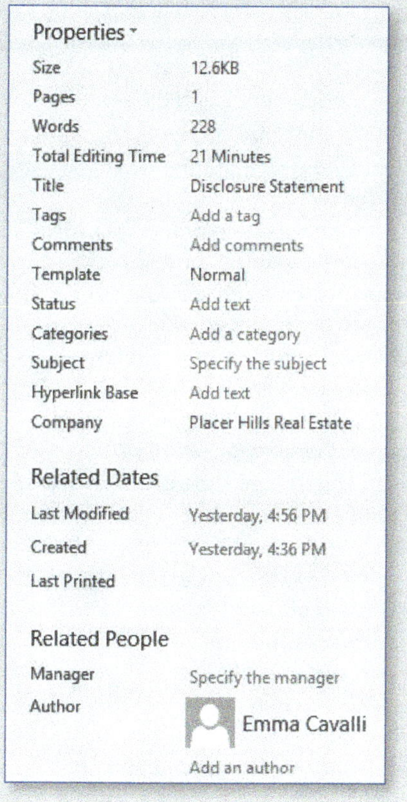

1-76 Document properties on the *Backstage* view

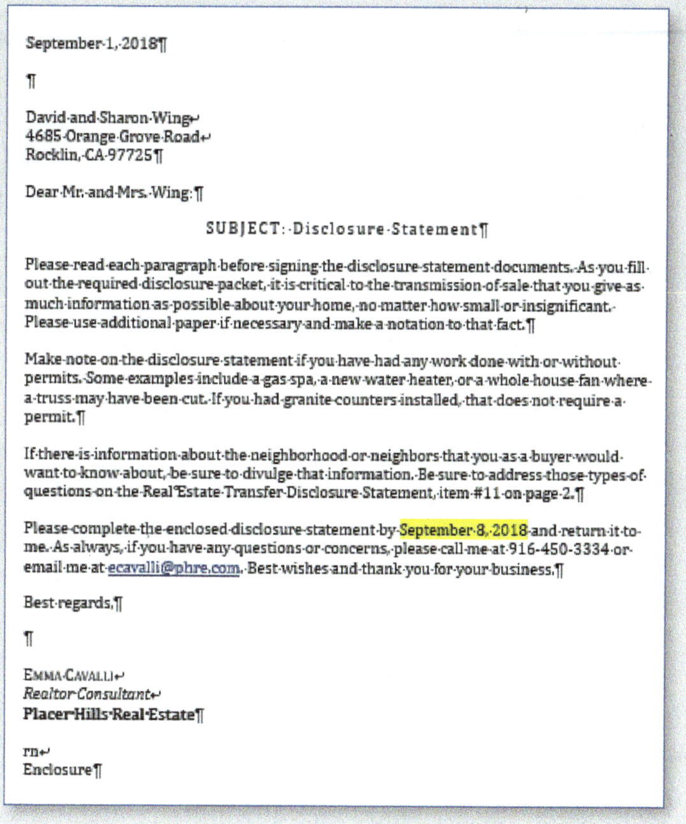
September·1,·2018¶

¶

David·and·Sharon·Wing↵
4685·Orange·Grove·Road↵
Rocklin,·CA·97725¶

Dear·Mr.·and·Mrs.·Wing:¶

SUBJECT:·Disclosure·Statement¶

Please·read·each·paragraph·before·signing·the·disclosure·statement·documents.·As·you·fill·out·the·required·disclosure·packet,·it·is·critical·to·the·transmission·of·sale·that·you·give·as·much·information·as·possible·about·your·home,·no·matter·how·small·or·insignificant.·Please·use·additional·paper·if·necessary·and·make·a·notation·to·that·fact.¶

Make·note·on·the·disclosure·statement·if·you·have·had·any·work·done·with·or·without·permits.·Some·examples·include·a·gas·spa,·a·new·water·heater,·or·a·whole-house·fan·where·a·truss·may·have·been·cut.·If·you·had·granite·counters·installed,·that·does·not·require·a·permit.¶

If·there·is·information·about·the·neighborhood·or·neighbors·that·you·as·a·buyer·would·want·to·know·about,·be·sure·to·divulge·that·information.·Be·sure·to·address·those·types·of·questions·on·the·Real·Estate·Transfer·Disclosure·Statement,·item·#11·on·page·2.¶

Please·complete·the·enclosed·disclosure·statement·by·September·8,·2018·and·return·it·to·me.·As·always,·if·you·have·any·questions·or·concerns,·please·call·me·at·916-450-3334·or·email·me·at·ecavalli@phre.com.·Best·wishes·and·thank·you·for·your·business.¶

Best·regards,¶

¶

EMMA·CAVALLI↵
Realtor·Consultant↵
Placer·Hills·Real·Estate¶

rn↵
Enclosure¶

1-77 PP W1-3 completed

Chapter Summary

1.1 Create, save, and open a Word document (p. W1-3).

- New Word documents are based on the ***Normal template*** (*Normal.dotx*).
- You can save documents with the existing file name or with a different file name.
- A ***Word document*** (***.docx***) is the standard file format. There are a variety of Word file formats in which to save a document.
- You can open, edit, and save existing Word documents.

1.2 Customize a document by entering and selecting text, using word wrap, and using *AutoComplete*, *AutoCorrect*, and *AutoFormat* features (p. W1-7).

- ***Word wrap*** automatically wraps text to the next line as you reach the right margin of the document.
- The ***Show/Hide*** button displays formatting symbols in the document to properly and consistently format documents.
- You can select text in a variety of ways, and you can select individual words, an entire line, multiple lines of text, a sentence, a paragraph, multiple paragraphs, or the entire document.
- ***AutoComplete*** automatically completes a day, month, or date for you.
- ***AutoCorrect*** automatically corrects commonly misspelled words and capitalization errors.
- ***AutoFormat*** automatically controls the formatting of items such as numbered and bulleted lists.
- You can add, delete, and edit *AutoCorrect* entries and customize *AutoCorrect* options in Word.

1.3 Enhance a document using paragraph breaks, line breaks, spaces, and non-breaking spaces (p. W1-10).

- The ***Enter*** key on the keyboard inserts a ***paragraph break***. The ***paragraph symbol*** is visible when *Show/Hide* is turned on.
- ***Line breaks*** control breaks between lines or sentences to retain paragraph formatting between lines.
- ***Non-breaking spaces*** keep related words together.

1.4 Edit a document using cut, copy, paste, the *Clipboard*, and the undo, redo, and repeat features (p. W1-15).

- You can move or copy selected text within a document. There are a variety of methods to ***cut***, ***copy***, and ***paste*** text in a document.
- The ***Clipboard*** stores text that you have cut or copied. You can use the *Clipboard* to paste text into your document.
- You can ***Undo***, ***Redo***, and ***Repeat*** previous actions when working on a document. These features are available on the ***Quick Access toolbar***.

1.5 Customize a document using different fonts, font sizes, and attributes (p. W1-18).

- ***Serif*** and ***sans serif*** are the two main categories of ***fonts***.
- Fonts are measured in ***points*** (pt.). Most documents use between 10 and 12 pt. font size.
- You can change fonts and font size for specific text or the entire document.
- ***Bold***, ***Italic***, and ***Underline*** are font styles that you can apply quickly to text.
- Other font effects include ***Strikethrough***, ***Subscript***, ***Superscript***, ***Small caps***, and ***All caps***.
- You can change the case of text in Word.
- The ***Font dialog box*** provides many ***font***, ***size***, ***style***, and ***effect options***.
- You can modify the ***scale***, ***spacing***, ***position***, and ***kerning*** of selected text.
- The ***Format Painter*** applies formatting from selected text to other text.
- The ***Clear Formatting*** feature removes all formatting applied to selected text.
- You can change the ***default*** font and font size in Word.

1.6 Enhance a document using text alignment and line and paragraph spacing (p. W1-28).

- ***Paragraph alignment*** describes how text is aligned horizontally between the margins of a document: ***Left***, ***Center***, ***Right***, or ***Justified***.
- ***Line spacing*** refers to the amount of blank space between lines of text in a paragraph.
- ***Paragraph spacing*** is the amount of space between paragraphs. Paragraph spacing is measured in points.

- You can modify alignment, line spacing, and paragraph spacing on the *Home* or *Layout* tab or in the ***Paragraph dialog box***.
- You can change the default line and paragraph spacing in Word.

1.7 Finalize a document using Word's research and proofing tools (p. W1-32).

- ***Smart Lookup*** is used to research selected word(s) without leaving Word. Research results display in the ***Smart Lookup pane***.
- By default, Word automatically checks documents for ***spelling*** and ***grammatical errors***.
- Word marks potential spelling, incorrect word, or grammatical errors with a colored wavy line under the words. You can correct errors by selecting from options in the context menu.
- You can manually spell and grammar check a document using the *Spelling and Grammar* pane.
- You can customize the ***Word dictionary*** by adding, deleting, or modifying words in the word list.
- The ***Thesaurus*** finds synonyms for words in your document.
- Word also provides you with a ***Word Count***.

1.8 Apply custom document properties to a document (p. W1-36).

- You can add ***document properties***, such as *Title, Author, Company, Subject, Created*, and *Last Modified*, into a document.
- You can add document properties on the *Backstage* view or in the *Properties* dialog box.

Check for Understanding

The SIMbook for this text (within your SIMnet account) provides the following resources for concept review:

- Multiple choice questions
- Matching exercises
- Short answer questions

USING MICROSOFT WORD 2016

Guided Project 1-1

In this project, Jennie Owings at Central Sierra Insurance is writing a business letter to Hartford Specialty regarding the renewal of the insurance policy for Valley Custom Manufacturing. This business letter is typed in block format and uses open punctuation. See *Appendix B* (online resource) for examples of business document formats and mixed and open punctuation.
[Student Learning Outcomes 1.1, 1.2, 1.3, 1.4, 1.5, 1.6, 1.7, 1.8]

File Needed: ***ValleyCustomManufacturing-01.docx*** *(Student data files are available in the* Library *of your SIMnet account)*
Completed Project File Name: ***[your initials] Word 1-1.docx***

Skills Covered in This Project

- Add document properties.
- Use block business letter format using open punctuation.
- Change line spacing.
- Change paragraph spacing.
- Use *AutoComplete*.
- Use paragraph breaks for proper spacing between the parts of a business letter.
- Copy and paste text from another document using the *Clipboard*.
- Use *Show/Hide*.
- Undo automatic capitalization.
- Change font size.
- Apply font styles.
- Use *Smart Lookup*.
- Use spelling and grammar checker.
- Add words to the dictionary.

---

1. Open a new Word document.
   a. Click the **File** tab to open the *Backstage* view.
   b. Click **New** on the left and click **Blank document**. You can also click **Blank document** from the *Start* page when you first open Word.
2. Save the document as ***[your initials] Word 1-1***.
   a. Click the **File** tab to open the *Backstage* view and select **Save As** on the left.
   b. Click **Browse** to open the *Save As* dialog box and select the desired location to save the file.
   c. Change the file name to [your initials] Word 1-1.
   d. Click **Save** to rename the document and close the *Save As* dialog box.
3. Add document properties.
   a. Click the **File** tab to open the *Info* area on the *Backstage* view and click the **Show All Properties** link.
   b. Type Valley Custom Manufacturing in the *Title* field.
   c. Type Central Sierra Insurance in the *Company* field.
   d. Click the **Back** arrow in the upper left of the *Backstage* view to return to the document.
4. Change the line and paragraph spacing of the document.
   a. Click the **Paragraph** launcher [*Home* or *Layout* tab, *Paragraph* group] to open the *Paragraph* dialog box (Figure 1-78).
   b. Change the *Line spacing* to **Single**.

c. Change the *After* paragraph spacing to **0 pt**.
d. Choose **OK** to close the *Paragraph* dialog box.

5. Use *AutoComplete* to type a date.
   a. Turn on **Show/Hide** [*Home* tab, *Paragraph* group] if it is not already turned on.
   b. Type the current date using month, day, year format (e.g., September 1, 2018). As you begin typing the date, *AutoComplete* completes the month and current date. Press **Enter** to accept the *AutoComplete* date.
   c. Press **Enter** four times (quadruple space) after the date.

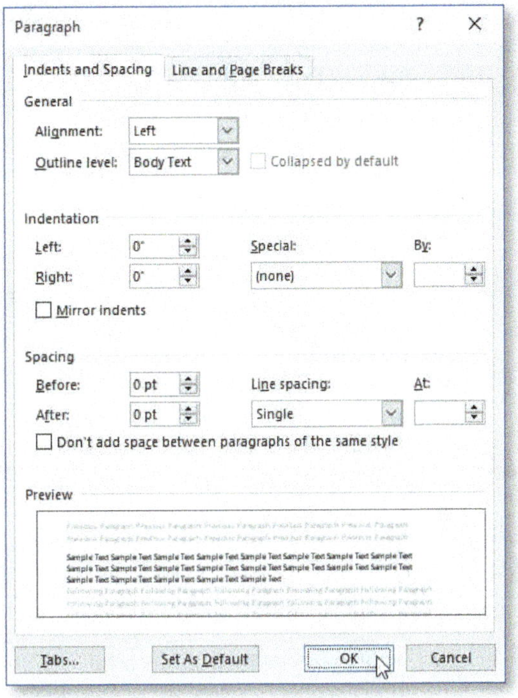

1-78 *Paragraph* dialog box

6. Type the inside address, salutation, and subject line.
   a. Type Mrs. Cammie Speckler and press **Enter** once at the end of the line.
   b. Type Hartford Specialty and press **Enter** once.
   c. Type 4788 Market Street, Suite A205 and press **Enter** once.
   d. Type San Francisco, CA 95644 and press **Enter** two times.
   e. Type Dear Mrs. Speckler as the salutation and press **Enter** two times. No colon is used after the salutation when using open punctuation.
   f. Type RE: Valley Custom Manufacturing as the subject line and press **Enter** two times.

7. Copy text from another document and paste it into the current document.
   a. Open the ***ValleyCustomManufacturing-01*** document from your student data files. If the document opens in *Protected View*, click the **Enable Editing** button.
   b. Press **Ctrl+A** to select the entire document.
   c. Click the **Copy** button [*Home* tab, *Clipboard* group] or press **Ctrl+C**.
   d. Close ***ValleyCustomManufacturing-01*** without saving the document.
   e. In the ***[your initials] Word 1-1*** document, place your insertion point on the last blank line of the document.
   f. Click the **Clipboard** launcher [*Home* tab, *Clipboard* group] to open the *Clipboard* pane (Figure 1-79).
   g. Click the **drop-down arrow** to the right of the copied text in the *Clipboard* and click **Paste**. The paragraphs of text are pasted in the body of the document.
   h. Click the **X** in the upper right corner of the *Clipboard* pane to close it.

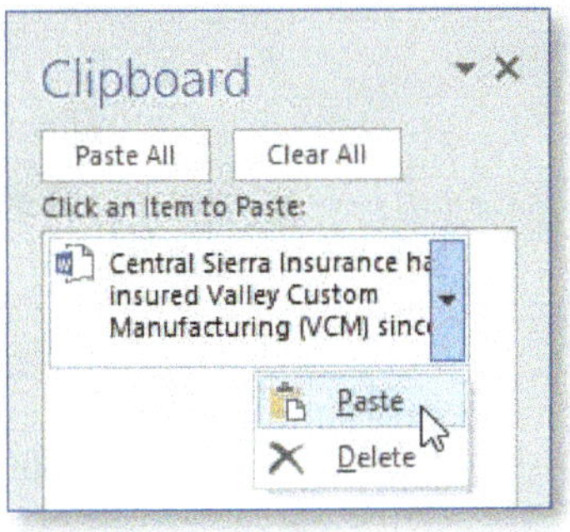

1-79 Paste from the *Clipboard*

8. Use the *Format Painter* to format the inserted paragraphs.
   a. Place your insertion point on the first line of the document (date line).
   b. Click the **Format Painter** button [*Home* tab, *Clipboard* group] to turn on the *Format Painter*.

c. Select the five body paragraphs of the letter to apply the formatting (Figure 1-80).

9. Insert a blank line between each of the body paragraphs so there is a double space after each body paragraph (one blank line between paragraphs).
   a. Place your insertion point at the end of the first body paragraph and press **Enter**. A paragraph symbol marks the end of each paragraph.
   b. Repeat for each of the remaining body paragraphs including the last body paragraph.

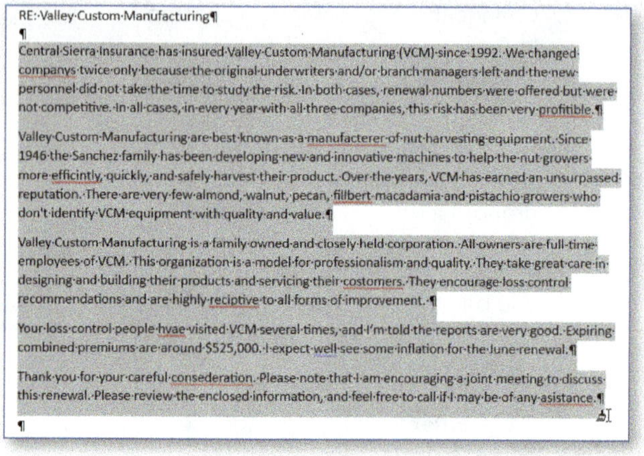
RE:·Valley·Custom·Manufacturing¶
¶
Central·Sierra·Insurance·has·insured·Valley·Custom·Manufacturing·(VCM)·since·1992.·We·changed·companys·twice·only·because·the·original·underwriters·and/or·branch·managers·left·and·the·new·personnel·did·not·take·the·time·to·study·the·risk.·In·both·cases,·renewal·numbers·were·offered·but·were·not·competitive.·In·all·cases,·in·every·year·with·all·three·companies,·this·risk·has·been·very·profitible.¶

Valley·Custom·Manufacturing·are·best·known·as·a·manufacterer·of·nut·harvesting·equipment.·Since·1946·the·Sanchez·family·has·been·developing·new·and·innovative·machines·to·help·the·nut·growers·more·efficintly,·quickly,·and·safely·harvest·their·product.·Over·the·years,·VCM·has·earned·an·unsurpassed·reputation.·There·are·very·few·almond,·walnut,·pecan,·fillbert·macadamia·and·pistachio·growers·who·don't·identify·VCM·equipment·with·quality·and·value.¶

Valley·Custom·Manufacturing·is·a·family·owned·and·closely·held·corporation.·All·owners·are·full-time·employees·of·VCM.·This·organization·is·a·model·for·professionalism·and·quality.·They·take·great·care·in·designing·and·building·their·products·and·servicing·their·costomers.·They·encourage·loss·control·recommendations·and·are·highly·reciptive·to·all·forms·of·improvement.·¶

Your·loss·control·people·hvae·visited·VCM·several·times,·and·I'm·told·the·reports·are·very·good.·Expiring·combined·premiums·are·around·$525,000.·I·expect·well·see·some·inflation·for·the·June·renewal.¶

Thank·you·for·your·careful·consederation.·Please·note·that·I·am·encouraging·a·joint·meeting·to·discuss·this·renewal.·Please·review·the·enclosed·information,·and·feel·free·to·call·if·I·may·be·of·any·asistance.¶
¶

1-80 Use the *Format Painter* to copy formatting

10. Enter the closing lines of the document.
    a. Place your insertion point on the last blank line below the body of the letter.
    b. Type Sincerely and press **Enter** four times.
    c. Type Jennie Owings, Vice President and press **Enter**.
    d. Type Central Sierra Insurance and press **Enter** two times.
    e. Type your reference initials (your first and last initials in lowercase letters with no punctuation).
    f. Press **Enter**. *AutoCorrect* automatically capitalizes the first letter of your reference initials.
    g. Click the **AutoCorrect Options** smart tag (Figure 1-81). The *AutoCorrect Options* smart tag appears when you place your pointer below your reference initials.
    h. Select **Undo Automatic Capitalization** to undo the automatic capitalization of your reference initials.
    i. Place your insertion point on the blank line below your reference initials and type Enclosure as an enclosure notation.

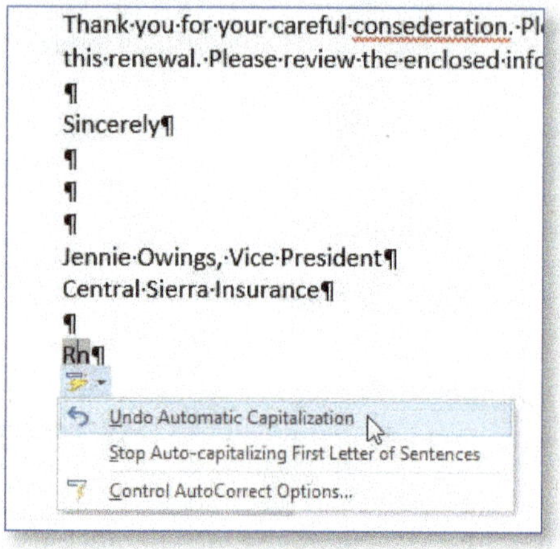

1-81 *AutoCorrect Options* smart tag

11. Select the entire document (**Ctrl+A**) and change the font size to **10 pt**. [*Home* tab, *Font* group].

12. Add *Before* paragraph spacing to the date line.
    a. Select or place your insertion point in the date line.
    b. Change the *Before* spacing to **72 pt**. [*Layout* tab, *Paragraph* group] (Figure 1-82).

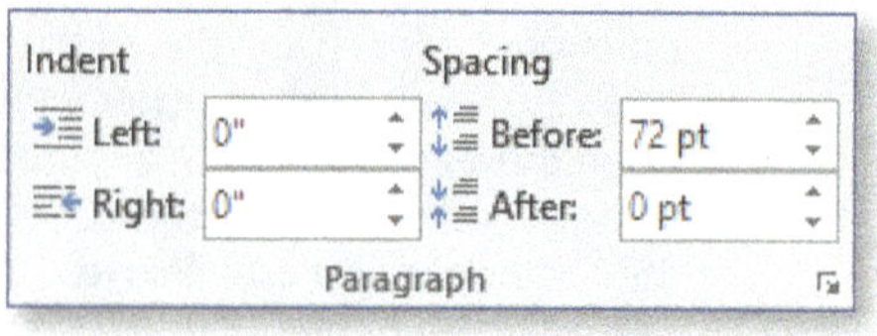

1-82 Change *Before* paragraph spacing on the date line

13. Apply a font style to selected text.
    a. Select the words **"Central Sierra Insurance"** in the first paragraph.
    b. Click the **Underline** button [*Home* tab, *Font* group] or press **Ctrl+U**.
    c. Select the words **"Valley Custom Manufacturing (VCM)"** in the first paragraph.
    d. Click the **Bold** button [*Home* tab, *Font* group] or press **Ctrl+B**.

14. Use *Smart Lookup* to research selected words.
    a. Select **"harvesting equipment"** in the second body paragraph.
    b. Click the **Smart Lookup** button [*Review* tab, *Insights* group]. The *Smart Lookup* pane opens on the right.

c. Review the research results on the *Smart Lookup* pane.

d. Click the **X** in the upper right of the *Smart Lookup* pane to close the pane.

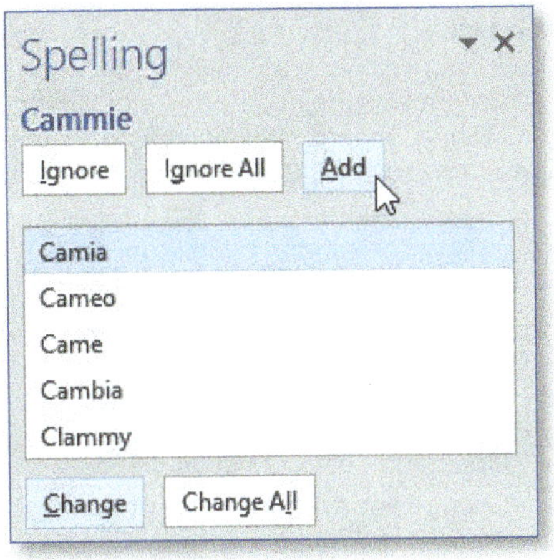

1-83 Add word to the dictionary

15. Spell and grammar check the entire document.
    a. Press **Ctrl+Home** to move to the top of the document.
    b. Click the **Spelling & Grammar** button [*Review* tab, *Proofing* group]. The *Spelling* pane opens (Figure 1-83).
    c. If "Cammie" and "Speckler" are marked as potential spelling errors, click **Add** to add each of these names to the dictionary.
    d. For the remaining spelling and grammatical errors, select the correct word in the *Spelling* (or *Grammar*) pane and click **Change**.
    e. If prompted to continue checking the document from the beginning, choose **Yes**.
    f. Click **Ignore** if your reference initials are marked as a potential spelling or grammatical error.
    g. Click **OK** to close the dialog box that informs you the spelling and grammar check is complete.

16. Save and close the document (Figure 1-84).

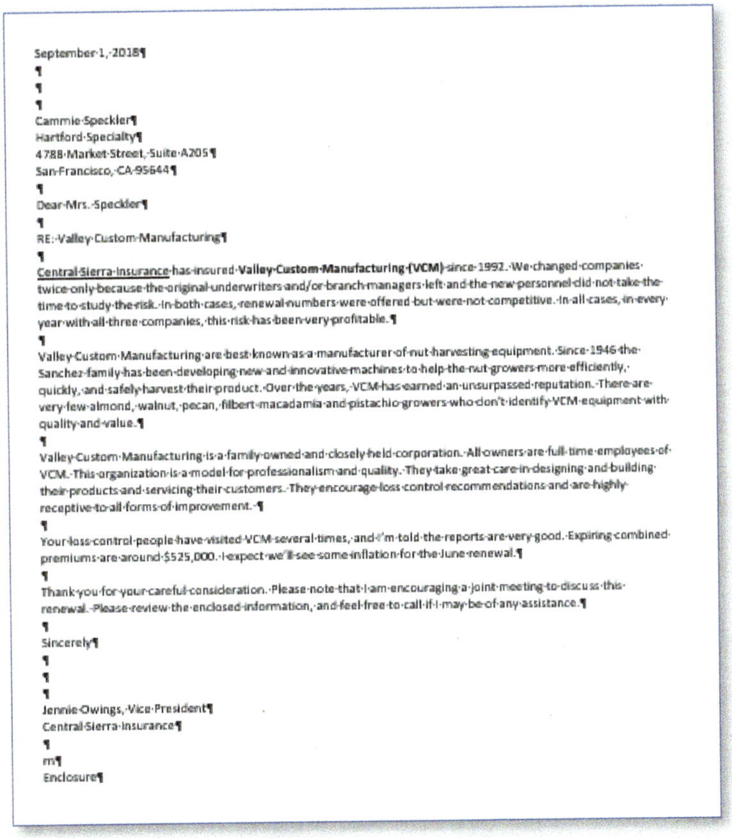

September 1, 2018

Cammie Speckler
Hartford Specialty
4788 Market Street, Suite A205
San Francisco, CA 95644

Dear Mrs. Speckler

RE: Valley Custom Manufacturing

Central Sierra Insurance has insured **Valley Custom Manufacturing (VCM)** since 1992. We changed companies twice only because the original underwriters and/or branch managers left and the new personnel did not take the time to study the risk. In both cases, renewal numbers were offered but were not competitive. In all cases, in every year with all three companies, this risk has been very profitable.

Valley Custom Manufacturing are best known as a manufacturer of nut harvesting equipment. Since 1946 the Sanchez family has been developing new and innovative machines to help the nut growers more efficiently, quickly, and safely harvest their product. Over the years, VCM has earned an unsurpassed reputation. There are very few almond, walnut, pecan, filbert macadamia and pistachio growers who don't identify VCM equipment with quality and value.

Valley Custom Manufacturing is a family owned and closely held corporation. All owners are full time employees of VCM. This organization is a model for professionalism and quality. They take great care in designing and building their products and servicing their customers. They encourage loss control recommendations and are highly receptive to all forms of improvement.

Your loss control people have visited VCM several times, and I'm told the reports are very good. Expiring combined premiums are around $525,000. I expect we'll see some inflation for the June renewal.

Thank you for your careful consideration. Please note that I am encouraging a joint meeting to discuss this renewal. Please review the enclosed information, and feel free to call if I may be of any assistance.

Sincerely

Jennie Owings, Vice President
Central Sierra Insurance

rn
Enclosure

1-84 Word 1-1 completed

Guided Project 1-2

Sierra Pacific Community College District is a multi-campus community college district. In this project, you format an informational handout regarding online learning.
[Student Learning Outcomes 1.1, 1.2, 1.3, 1.4, 1.5, 1.6, 1.7, 1.8]

File Needed: ***OnlineLearning-01.docx*** *(Student data files are available in the* Library *of your SIMnet account)*
Completed Project File Name: ***[your initials] Word 1-2.docx***

Skills Covered in This Project

- Open and edit an existing document.
- Change line spacing.
- Change paragraph spacing.
- Use *Show/Hide*.
- Change font size and apply color, styles, and effects.
- Cut and paste to move a paragraph.
- Use drag and drop to move a paragraph.
- Apply a shadow text effect.
- Use the *Format Painter*.
- Use spelling and grammar checker.
- Add document properties.

1. Open the ***OnlineLearning-01*** document from your student data files.
   a. Click the **File** tab to open the *Backstage* view and click **Open** at the left.
   b. Click **Browse** to open the *Open* dialog box.
   c. Browse to locate the ***OnlineLearning-01*** document, select the document, and click **Open**. If the document opens in *Protected View*, click the **Enable Editing** button.
2. Save the document as ***[your initials] Word 1-2***.
   a. Click the **File** tab to open the *Backstage* view and select **Save As** on the left.
   b. Click **Browse** to open the *Save As* dialog box and select the desired location to save the file.
   c. Change the file name to [your initials] Word 1-2.
   d. Click **Save** to rename the document and close the *Save As* dialog box.
3. Change the line and paragraph spacing of the entire document.
   a. Press **Ctrl+A** to select the entire document.
   b. Click the **Paragraph** launcher [*Home* or *Layout* tab, *Paragraph* group] to open the *Paragraph* dialog box (Figure 1-85).
   c. In the *Line spacing* area, select **Multiple** from the drop-down list.
   d. In the *At* area, type 1.2.
   e. Change the *After* paragraph spacing to **12 pt**.
   f. Click **OK** to close the *Paragraph* dialog box.
4. Turn on **Show/Hide** [*Home* tab, *Paragraph* group] and delete the one extra blank line between each paragraph including after the title.
5. Change the font and font size of the entire document.
   a. Select the entire document (**Ctrl+A**).
   b. Change the font to **Cambria** [*Home* tab, *Font* group].

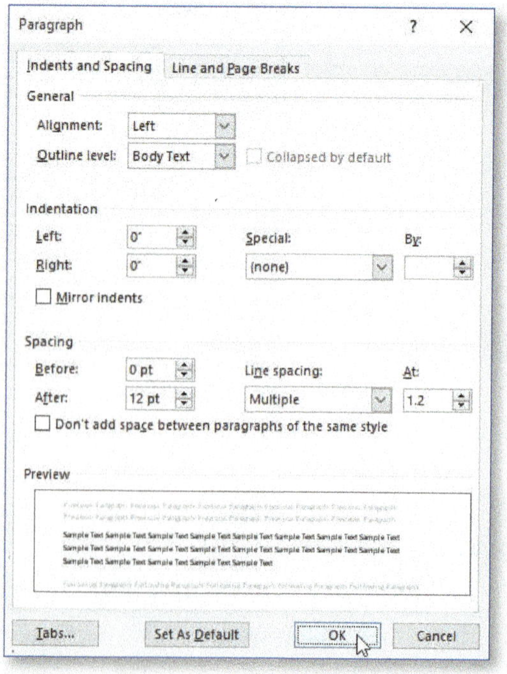

1-85 Change *Line spacing* and *After* paragraph spacing

6. Change the paragraph spacing, alignment, font size, styles, effects, and color of the title.
   a. Select the title of the document (**Online Learning Information**).
   b. Click the **Layout** tab.
   c. Change the *Before* spacing to **36 pt**. and the *After* spacing to **18 pt**. [*Paragraph* group].
   d. Click the **Center** button [*Home* tab, *Paragraph* group].
   e. Click the **Font** launcher [*Home* tab, *Font* group]. The *Font* dialog box opens (Figure 1-86).
   f. Change the *Font* style to **Bold** and change the *Font Size* to **24**.
   g. In the *Effects* area, click the **Small caps** check box.
   h. Click the **Font color** drop-down list and choose **Blue-Gray, Text 2** from the *Theme Colors*.
   i. Click the **Advanced** tab.
   j. Click the **Spacing** drop-down list and select **Expanded**. Change the *By* to **1.2 pt**.
   k. Click **OK** to close the *Font* dialog box.

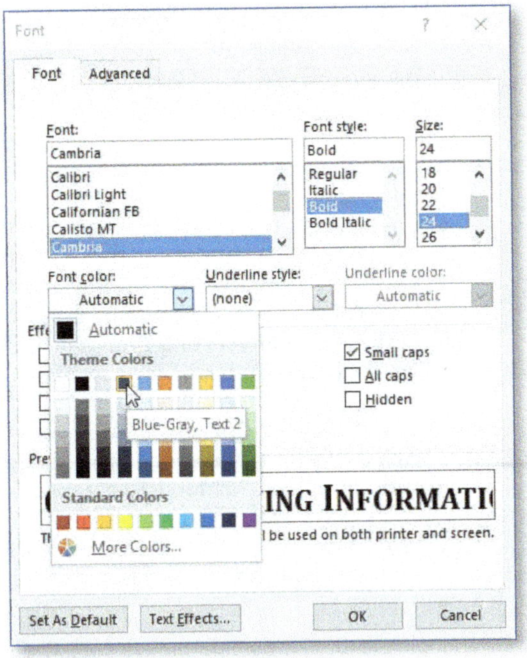

1-86 Change font style, size, effects, and color

7. Move paragraphs in the document and insert a heading.
   a. Select the last paragraph in the document, including the paragraph mark at the end of the document.
   b. Click the **Cut** button [*Home* tab, *Clipboard* group] or press **Ctrl+X**.
   c. Place your insertion point before the second line of the document ("Definition of Online Learning Modalities").
   d. Click the top half of the **Paste** button [*Home* tab, *Clipboard* group] or press **Ctrl+V**.
   e. Click at the beginning of the pasted paragraph and type Where are we now with Online Learning? and press **Enter**.
   f. Select the paragraph that begins "Hybrid Course:," including the paragraph mark at the end of the paragraph.
   g. Move this paragraph using the drag-and-drop method (click, hold, and drag) so it appears before the paragraph that begins with "Television or Tele-Web Course:" (Figure 1-87).

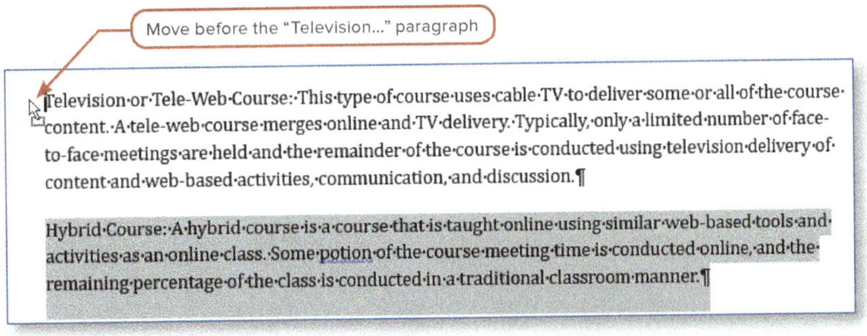

1-87 Move paragraph using drag and drop

8. Format section headings in the document and use the *Format Painter*.
   a. Select the first section heading ("**Where are we now with Online Learning?**").

b. Click the **Font** launcher [*Home* tab, *Font* group] to open the *Font* dialog box and click the **Font** tab (Figure 1-88).
c. Change the font *Size* to **12 pt**.
d. Change the *Font color* to **Blue-Gray, Text 2**.
e. Change the *Underline style* to **Double underline**.
f. Change the *Underline color* to **Blue-Gray, Text 2**.
g. In the *Effects* area, click the **All caps** check box.
h. Click **OK** to close the *Font* dialog box.
i. Click the **Text Effects and Typography** button [*Home* tab, *Font* group].
j. Place your pointer on **Shadow** and select **Offset Diagonal Bottom Right** (Figure 1-89).
k. With the formatted heading still selected, click the **Format Painter** button [*Home* tab, *Clipboard* group].
l. Select the next heading (**"Definition of Online Learning Modalities"**) to apply formatting.

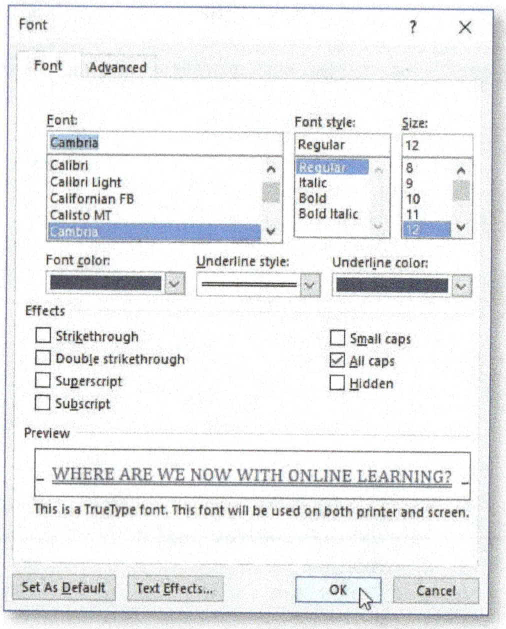

1-88 Format heading using the *Font* dialog box

9. Format paragraph headings in the document.
   a. Select the first paragraph heading (**"Online Course:"**), including the colon.
   b. Click the **Font** launcher [*Home* tab, *Font* group] to open the *Font* dialog box.
   c. Change the *Font style* to **Bold**.
   d. Change the *Font color* to **Blue-Gray, Text 2**.
   e. In the *Effects* area, click the **Small caps** check box.
   f. Click **OK** to close the *Font* dialog box.
10. Use the *Format Painter* to copy formatting to the other paragraph headings.
   a. With the **"Online Course:"** heading still selected, double click the **Format Painter** button.
   b. Select the other paragraph headings (**"Hybrid Course:", "Television or Tele-Web Course:",** and **"Web-Enhanced Course:"**) to apply the formatting.
   c. Click the **Format Painter** button again to turn off the *Format Painter*.

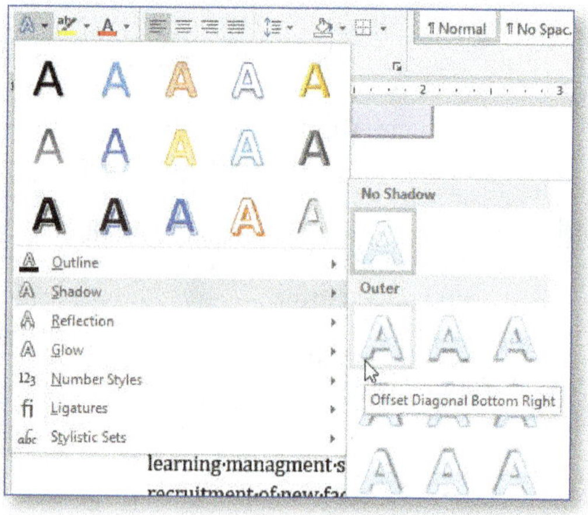

1-89 Apply *Shadow* text effect

11. Correct spelling and grammar in the document using the context menu.
   a. Right-click the first misspelled word (**"managment"**) and choose the correct spelling from the list of options.
   b. Repeat this process for **"potion."**
   c. Click **Ignore All** or **Ignore Once** if there are other words that are marked as potentially incorrect.
12. Select the sentence in parentheses at the end of the document, including the parentheses, and click the **Italic** button [*Home* tab, *Font* group] or press **Ctrl+I**.
13. Add document properties using the *Properties* dialog box.
   a. Click the **File** tab to open the *Backstage* view and click the **Info** button if it is not already selected.
   b. Click the **Properties** button on the right and choose **Advanced Properties**. The *Properties* dialog box opens.

c. In the *Title* area, type Online Learning Information.
d. In the *Subject* area, type Online Learning.
e. In the *Author* area, delete the existing author name and type Tanesha Morris as the author.
f. Click **OK** to accept changes and close the *Properties* dialog box.
g. Click the **Back** arrow in the upper left of the *Backstage* view to return to the document.

14. Save and close the document (Figure 1-90).

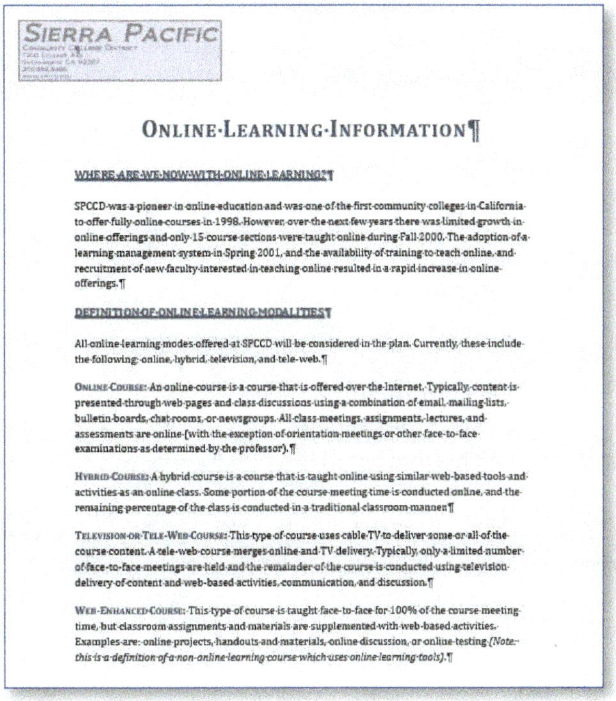

SIERRA PACIFIC

ONLINE LEARNING INFORMATION¶

WHERE ARE WE NOW WITH ONLINE LEARNING?¶

SPCCD was a pioneer in online education and was one of the first community colleges in California to offer fully online courses in 1998. However, over the next few years there was limited growth in online offerings and only 15 course sections were taught online during Fall 2000. The adoption of a learning management system in Spring 2001, and the availability of training to teach online, and recruitment of new faculty interested in teaching online resulted in a rapid increase in online offerings.¶

DEFINITION OF ONLINE LEARNING MODALITIES¶

All online learning modes offered at SPCCD will be considered in the plan. Currently, these include the following: online, hybrid, television, and tele-web.¶

ONLINE COURSE: An online course is a course that is offered over the Internet. Typically, content is presented through web pages and class discussions using a combination of email, mailing lists, bulletin boards, chat rooms, or newsgroups. All class meetings, assignments, lectures, and assessments are online (with the exception of orientation meetings or other face-to-face examinations as determined by the professor).¶

HYBRID COURSE: A hybrid course is a course that is taught online using similar web-based tools and activities as an online class. Some portion of the course meeting time is conducted online, and the remaining percentage of the class is conducted in a traditional classroom manner.¶

TELEVISION OR TELE-WEB COURSE: This type of course uses cable TV to deliver some or all of the course content. A tele-web course merges online and TV delivery. Typically, only a limited number of face-to-face meetings are held and the remainder of the course is conducted using television delivery of content and web-based activities, communication, and discussion.¶

WEB-ENHANCED COURSE: This type of course is taught face-to-face for 100% of the course meeting time, but classroom assignments and materials are supplemented with web-based activities. Examples are: online projects, handouts and materials, online discussion, or online testing *(Note: this is a definition of a non-online learning course which uses online learning tools).*¶

1-90 Word 1-2 completed

Guided Project 1-3

In this project, you create a memo for American River Cycling Club about using heart rate to increase the effectiveness of training. See *Appendix B* (online resource) for examples of business document formats. [Student Learning Outcomes 1.1, 1.2, 1.3, 1.5, 1.6, 1.7, 1.8]

File Needed: ***HeartRate-01.docx*** *(Student data files are available in the* Library *of your SIMnet account)*
Completed Project File Name: ***[your initials] Word 1-3.docx***

Skills Covered in This Project

- Open and edit an existing document.
- Change line spacing.
- Change paragraph spacing.
- Use *Show/Hide*.
- Add a memo heading to a document.
- Change paragraph alignment.
- Change font size and apply styles and effects.
- Use the *Format Painter*.
- Add text highlight color.
- Use non-breaking space.
- Use *Thesaurus*.
- Add words to the dictionary.
- Add document properties.

1. Open the ***HeartRate-01*** document from your student data files.
   a. Click the **File** tab to open the *Backstage* view and click **Open** on the left.
   b. Click **Browse** to open the *Open* dialog box.
   c. Browse to locate the ***HeartRate-01*** document, select the document, and click **Open**. If the document opens in *Protected View*, click the **Enable Editing** button.

2. Save the document as ***[your initials] Word 1-3***.
   a. Click the **File** tab to open the *Backstage* view and select **Save As** on the left.
   b. Click **Browse** to open the *Save As* dialog box and select the desired location to save the file.
   c. Change the file name to [your initials] Word 1-3.
   d. Click **Save** to rename the document and close the *Save As* dialog box.

3. Change the line and paragraph spacing of the entire document and insert a paragraph break between each paragraph.
   a. Press **Ctrl+A** to select the entire document.
   b. Click the **Paragraph** launcher [*Home* or *Layout* tab, *Paragraph* group]. The *Paragraph* dialog box opens.
   c. In the *Line spacing* area, select **Single** from the drop-down list.
   d. Change the *After* paragraph spacing to **0 pt**.
   e. Click **OK** to close the *Paragraph* dialog box.
   f. Turn on **Show/Hide** [*Home* tab, *Paragraph* group] if it is not already on.
   g. Click at the end of each paragraph and press **Enter** once to add a blank line between each of the paragraphs. Don't press *Enter* after the last body paragraph. A paragraph symbol marks the end of each paragraph.

4. Add a memo heading to the document.
   a. Place your insertion point at the beginning of the first paragraph and press **Enter**.
   b. Place the insertion point on the blank line above the first paragraph.
   c. Type TO: and press **Tab** two times.
   d. Type All ARCC Club Members and press **Enter** two times.
   e. Type FROM: and press **Tab** two times.
   f. Type Taylor Mathos, ARCC Coach and press **Enter** two times.
   g. Type DATE: and press **Tab** two times.
   h. Type the current date in month, day, year format (e.g., October 1, 2018) and press **Enter** two times.
   i. Type SUBJECT: and press **Tab** once.
   j. Type Heart Rate Training and press **Enter** two times.

5. Change the paragraph alignment and font styles of selected text.
   a. Select the second and third paragraphs in the body of the memo (beginning with **"220 – Your Age . . ."** and ending with **". . . heart rate is 180.)"**), including the paragraph mark at the end of the third paragraph.
   b. Click the **Center** button [*Home* tab, *Paragraph* group] or press **Ctrl+E**.
   c. Select the paragraph beginning **"220 – Your Age . . ."** and click the **Bold** button [*Home* tab, *Font* group] or press **Ctrl+B**.
   d. Select the next paragraph and click the **Italic** button [*Home* tab, *Font* group] or press **Ctrl+I**.
   e. Delete the blank line between the second and third paragraphs (Figure 1-91).

6. Change the font and style of selected text.
   a. Press **Ctrl+A** to select the entire document.

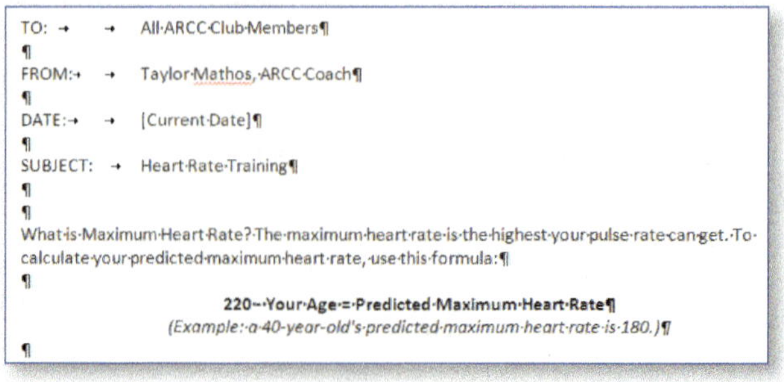
TO: → → All·ARCC·Club·Members¶
¶
FROM:→ → Taylor·Mathos,·ARCC·Coach¶
¶
DATE:→ → [Current·Date]¶
¶
SUBJECT: → Heart·Rate·Training¶
¶
¶
What·is·Maximum·Heart·Rate?·The·maximum·heart·rate·is·the·highest·your·pulse·rate·can·get.·To·calculate·your·predicted·maximum·heart·rate,·use·this·formula:¶
¶
220·–·Your·Age·=·Predicted·Maximum·Heart·Rate¶
(Example:·a·40-year-old's·predicted·maximum·heart·rate·is·180.)¶
¶

1-91 Memo heading added and paragraphs formatted

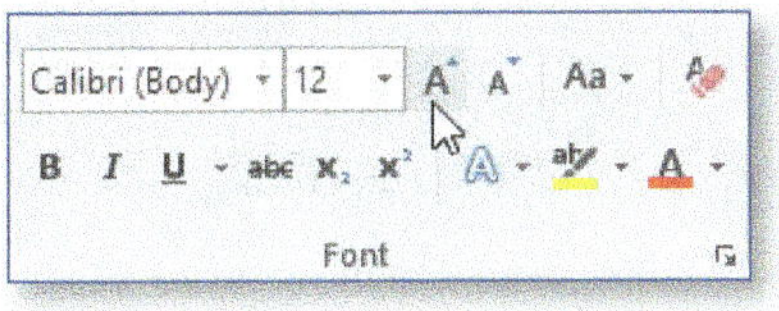

1-92 *Increase Font Size* button

b. Click the **Increase Font Size** button [*Home* tab, *Font* group] to increase the font size to 12 pt. (Figure 1-92).
c. Select the words **"Maximum Heart Rate?"** in the first sentence of the first body paragraph.
d. Click the **Font** launcher [*Home* tab, *Font* group] to open the *Font* dialog box (Figure 1-93).

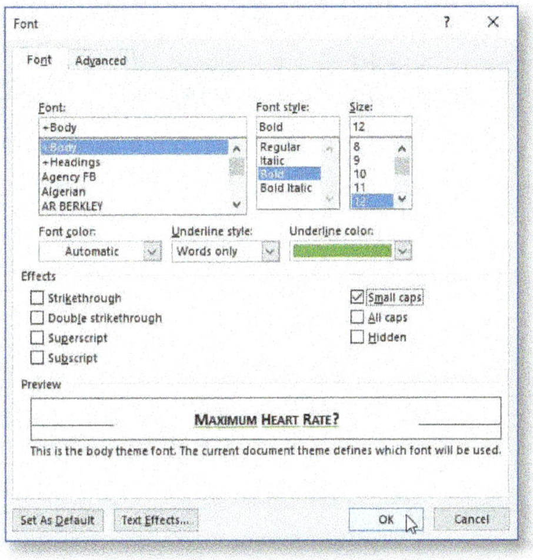

1-93 Change font style and effects

e. Change the *Font style* to **Bold**.
f. Change the *Underline style* to **Words only** and change the *Underline color* to **Green, Accent 6**.
g. In the *Effects* area, select the **Small caps** check box.
h. Click **OK** to close the *Font* dialog box.
i. With the words still selected, click the **Format Painter** button [*Home* tab, *Clipboard* group].
j. Select the words **"Target Heart Rate Zone"** in the first sentence of the fifth paragraph in the body ("You gain the most benefits . . ."). The *Format Painter* applies the formatting to the selected words.
k. Select the last two sentences of the fifth body paragraph (**"Do not exercise above 85 percent . . ."**) including the period at the end of the second sentence.
l. Click the **Text Highlight Color** drop-down arrow [*Home* tab, *Font* group] (Figure 1-94) and select **Gray-25%** text highlighting.

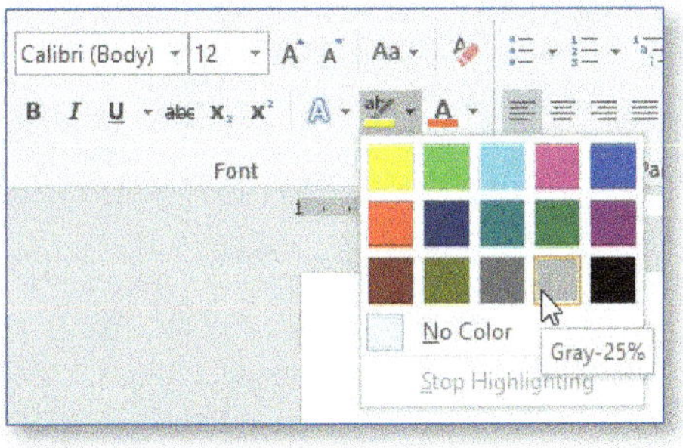

1-94 *Text Highlight Color* drop-down list

7. Use a non-breaking space to keep words together.
   a. In the first sentence of the fifth paragraph in the body ("You gain the most benefits . . ."), delete the space between the words "Target" and "Heart."
   b. Place your insertion point between these two words and press **Ctrl+Shift+Spacebar** to insert a non-breaking space. "Target" is wrapped to the next line so the words do not break between lines.
8. Add *Before* paragraph spacing to the first line of the memo heading.
   a. Place the insertion point in the first line of the memo heading (**"TO: . . ."**).
   b. Change the *Before* spacing to **72 pt**. [*Layout* tab, *Paragraph* group].
9. Use the *Thesaurus* to find synonyms for selected words.
   a. Right-click the word **"medicines"** in the third sentence of the fourth body paragraph ("Your actual maximum . . .").
   b. Point to **Synonyms** to display a list of synonyms.
   c. Select **"medications"** as the synonym (Figure 1-95).

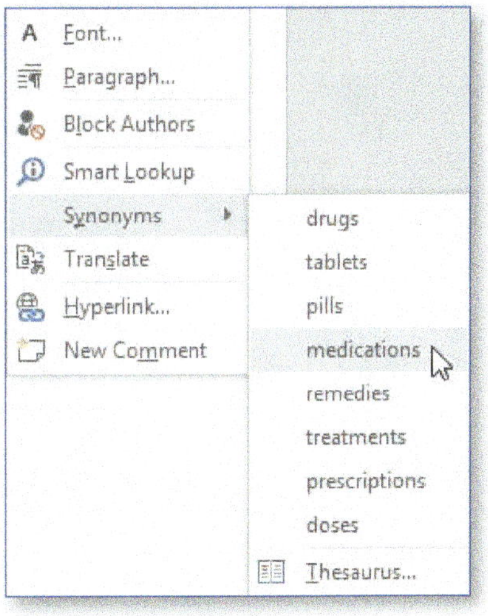

1-95 Select synonym from context menu

   d. In the last sentence of the fifth paragraph ("You gain the most benefits . . ."), right-click the word **"added."**
   e. Point to **Synonyms** and select **"additional."**

10. Add reference initials to the document.
    a. Click at the end of the last paragraph and press **Enter** two times.
    b. Type your reference initials in lowercase letters.

11. Add document properties.
    a. Click the **File** tab to open the *Backstage* view.
    b. Click the **Info** button, if it is not already selected, to display the document properties on the right.
    c. In the *Title* area, type Heart Rate Training.
    d. In the *Author* area, right-click the existing author and select **Remove Person**.
    e. In the *Author* area, type Taylor Mathos.
    f. Click the **Show All Properties** link at the bottom of the document properties.
    g. In the *Company* area, type ARCC.
    h. Click the **Back** arrow in the upper left of the *Backstage* view to return to the document.

12. Add words to the dictionary.
    a. Right-click the word **"Mathos"** in the second line of the memo heading.
    b. Choose **Add to Dictionary** from the context menu.
    c. If your reference initials are marked as incorrectly spelled (red wavy underline), right-click them and choose **Add to Dictionary**.

13. Save and close the document (Figure 1-96).

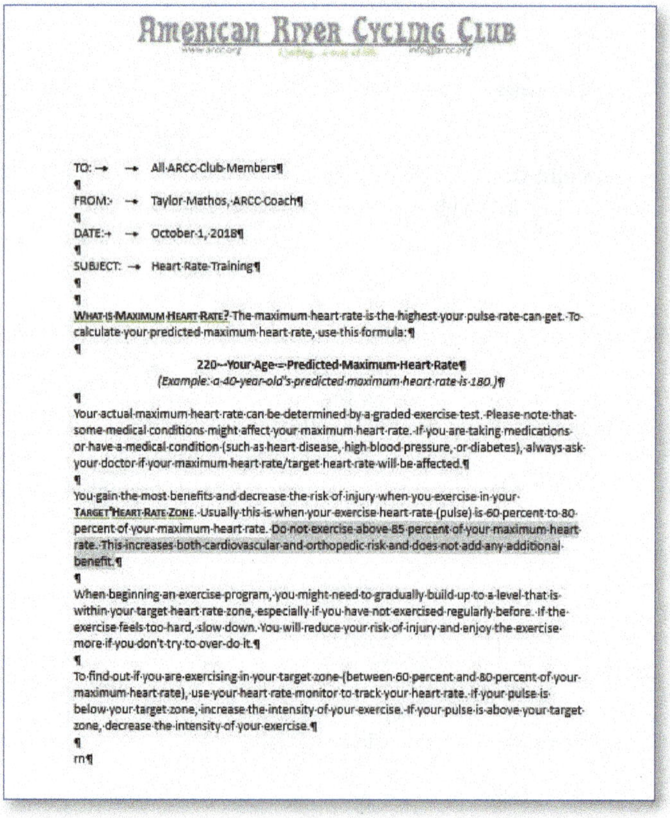

American River Cycling Club

TO: All ARCC Club Members

FROM: Taylor Mathos, ARCC Coach

DATE: October 1, 2018

SUBJECT: Heart Rate Training

WHAT IS MAXIMUM HEART RATE? The maximum heart rate is the highest your pulse rate can get. To calculate your predicted maximum heart rate, use this formula:

220 – Your Age = Predicted Maximum Heart Rate

(Example: a 40-year-old's predicted maximum heart rate is 180.)

Your actual maximum heart rate can be determined by a graded exercise test. Please note that some medical conditions might affect your maximum heart rate. If you are taking medications or have a medical condition (such as heart disease, high blood pressure, or diabetes), always ask your doctor if your maximum heart rate/target heart rate will be affected.

You gain the most benefits and decrease the risk of injury when you exercise in your TARGET HEART RATE ZONE. Usually this is when your exercise heart rate (pulse) is 60 percent to 80 percent of your maximum heart rate. Do not exercise above 85 percent of your maximum heart rate. This increases both cardiovascular and orthopedic risk and does not add any additional benefit.

When beginning an exercise program, you might need to gradually build up to a level that is within your target heart rate zone, especially if you have not exercised regularly before. If the exercise feels too hard, slow down. You will reduce your risk of injury and enjoy the exercise more if you don't try to over-do it.

To find out if you are exercising in your target zone (between 60 percent and 80 percent of your maximum heart rate), use your heart rate monitor to track your heart rate. If your pulse is below your target zone, increase the intensity of your exercise. If your pulse is above your target zone, decrease the intensity of your exercise.

rn

1-96 Word 1-3 completed

Independent Project 1-4

In this project, you format a business letter for Emma Cavalli to send to clients whose current home listings are expiring. See *Appendix B* (online resource) for examples of business document formats and mixed and open punctuation.
[Student Learning Outcomes 1.1, 1.2, 1.3, 1.4, 1.5, 1.6, 1.7, 1.8]

File Needed: ***ExpiredLetter-01.docx*** *(Student data files are available in the* Library *of your SIMnet account)*
Completed Project File Name: ***[your initials] Word 1-4.docx***

Skills Covered in This Project

- Open and edit an existing document.
- Change line spacing.
- Change paragraph alignment and spacing.
- Change font and font size.
- Use *Show/Hide*.
- Format document as a block format business letter with mixed punctuation.
- Move text.
- Change font styles and effects.
- Use *Smart Lookup*.
- Add document properties.
- Use spelling and grammar checker.

1. Open the ***ExpiredLetter-01*** document from your student data files.
2. Save this document as ***[your initials] Word 1-4***.
3. Apply the following formatting changes to the entire document:
   a. Select the entire document.
   b. Change the *Before* and *After* paragraph spacing to **0 pt**.
   c. Change the line spacing to **Single**.
   d. Change the paragraph alignment to **Left**.
   e. Change the font and font size to **Calibri** and **11 pt**.
4. Turn on **Show/Hide** and press **Enter** at the end of each paragraph to add a blank line after each paragraph (including the last paragraph).
5. Type and format the opening lines of the business letter.
   a. Press **Ctrl+Home** to move your insertion point to the top of the document.
   b. Type the current date (use August 15, 2018 format) and press **Enter** four times.
   c. Type the following inside address and press **Enter** two times after the last line:

      Mr. Rick Hermann
      9035 Masi Drive
      Fair Oaks, CA 95528

   d. Type Dear Mr. Hermann: as the salutation and press **Enter** two times after the salutation. There should be one blank line between the salutation and the body of the letter.
   e. Add **72 pt**. *Before* paragraph spacing to the date line.
6. Type the closing lines of the business letter.
   a. Place your insertion point on the blank line below the last body paragraph and press **Enter**.
   b. Type Best regards, and press **Enter** four times.
   c. Type the following closing lines:

      Emma Cavalli
      Realtor Consultant
      Placer Hills Real Estate

   d. Press **Enter** two times after the company name and type your reference initials in lowercase letters.

7. Move a paragraph and sentence.
   a. Move the third body paragraph so it appears before the second body paragraph. Make sure there is one blank line between each of the body paragraphs. If there is a blank space in front of the first word in the third paragraph, delete it.
   b. In the new second body paragraph ("There was a lot of detail . . ."), move the last two sentences to the beginning of the paragraph. Make sure there is proper spacing between sentences.
8. Apply formatting to text in the business letter.
   a. Select **"Placer Hills Real Estate"** in the first body paragraph and make the company name **Bold, Underline** (single line), and **Small caps**.
   b. Select the first sentence in the third paragraph including the period ("The service and experience . . .") and apply **Italic** formatting.
   c. Select the writer's name at the bottom and apply **Small caps** formatting.
   d. Select the writer's title and apply **Italic** formatting.
   e. Select the company name below the writer's title and apply **Bold** formatting.
9. Use *Smart Lookup* to research selected words.
   a. Select **"Placer Hills Real Estate"** in the first body paragraph.
   b. Click the **Smart Lookup** button [*Review* tab, *Insights* group]. The *Smart Lookup* pane opens on the right.
   c. Review the research results in the *Smart Lookup* pane.
   d. Click the **X** in the upper right of the *Smart Lookup* pane to close the pane.
10. Add the following document properties:
   a. *Title*: Expired Letter
   b. *Company*: Placer Hills Real Estate
   c. *Manager*: Kelsey Kroll
   d. *Author*: Emma Cavalli (right-click and choose **Remove Person** to remove existing author)
11. Spell and grammar check the entire document, make changes where necessary, and ignore proper nouns.
12. Save and close the document (Figure 1-97).

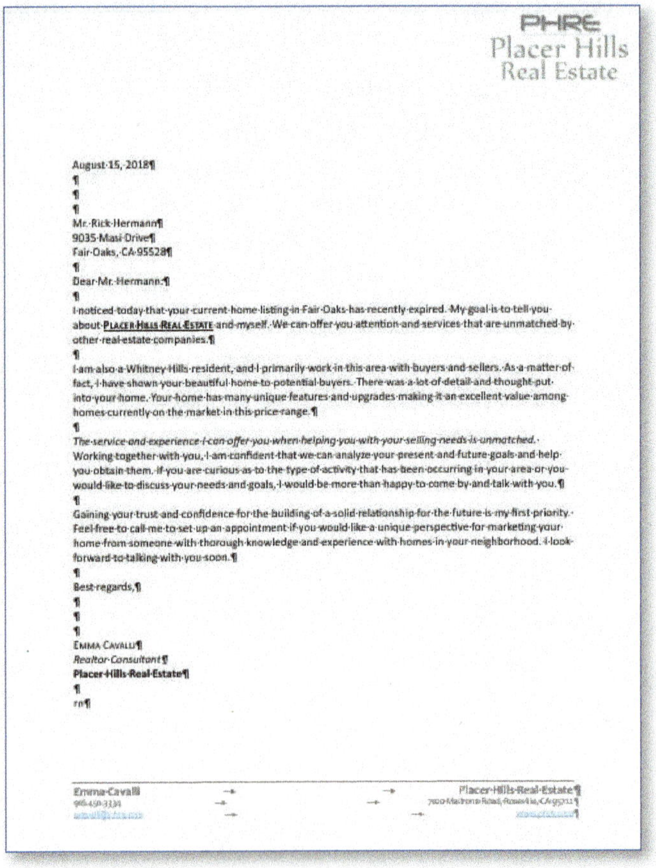
PHRE
Placer Hills
Real Estate

August 15, 2018

Mr. Rick Hermann
9035 Masi Drive
Fair Oaks, CA 95528

Dear Mr. Hermann:

I noticed today that your current home listing in Fair Oaks has recently expired. My goal is to tell you about PLACER HILLS REAL ESTATE and myself. We can offer you attention and services that are unmatched by other real estate companies.

I am also a Whitney Hills resident, and I primarily work in this area with buyers and sellers. As a matter of fact, I have shown your beautiful home to potential buyers. There was a lot of detail and thought put into your home. Your home has many unique features and upgrades making it an excellent value among homes currently on the market in this price range.

The service and experience I can offer you when helping you with your selling needs is unmatched. Working together with you, I am confident that we can analyze your present and future goals and help you obtain them. If you are curious as to the type of activity that has been occurring in your area or you would like to discuss your needs and goals, I would be more than happy to come by and talk with you.

Gaining your trust and confidence for the building of a solid relationship for the future is my first priority. Feel free to call me to set up an appointment if you would like a unique perspective for marketing your home from someone with thorough knowledge and experience with homes in your neighborhood. I look forward to talking with you soon.

Best regards,

EMMA CAVALLI
Realtor Consultant
Placer Hills Real Estate

rn

Emma Cavalli — Placer Hills Real Estate

1-97 Word 1-4 completed

Independent Project 1-5

In this project, you combine information from different documents to create a memo for Sierra Pacific Community College District. This memo is a draft of the values statement for the district. See *Appendix B* (online resource) for examples of business document formats.
[Student Learning Outcomes 1.1, 1.2, 1.3, 1.4, 1.5, 1.6, 1.7, 1.8]

File Needed: ***ValuesStatement-01a.docx*** and ***ValuesStatement-01b.docx*** *(Student data files are available in the* Library *of your SIMnet account)*
Completed Project File Name: ***[your initials] Word 1-5.docx***

Skills Covered in This Project

- Open and edit an existing document.
- Change line spacing.
- Change paragraph spacing.
- Change font and font size.
- Use *Show/Hide*.
- Format document as a memo.
- Use spelling and grammar checker.
- Change font styles and effects.
- Use the *Format Painter*.
- Move text.
- Add document properties.

---

1. Open the ***ValuesStatement-01a*** document from your student data files.
2. Save this document as ***[your initials] Word 1-5***.
3. Copy text from another document and paste it into the current document.
   a. Open the ***ValuesStatement-01b*** document from your student data files.
   b. Select all of the text in this document and copy to the *Clipboard*.
   c. Close the ***ValuesStatement-01b*** document without saving.
   d. In the ***[your initials] Word 1-5*** document, press **Enter** at the end of the document and paste the copied text from the *Clipboard*.
   e. **Delete** the extra paragraph breaks between the first four paragraphs and at the end of the document.
4. Select the entire document and apply the following formatting changes:
   a. Change *After* paragraph spacing to **12 pt**.
   b. Change the line spacing to **1.15**.
   c. Change the font and font size to **Calibri** and **10 pt**.
5. Type and format the heading lines in the memorandum.
   a. Turn on **Show/Hide**.
   b. Place your insertion point at the beginning of the document and press **Enter**.
   c. Place your insertion point on the blank line at the beginning of the document and type the following memo information. Press **Tab** (once or twice) after the guidewords to line up information at 1" and press **Enter** once at the end of the first three lines of the memo heading.

      TO: All SPCCD Faculty, Staff, and Managers
      FROM: Lanita Morrow, Chancellor
      DATE: type current date (use November 1, 2018 format)
      SUBJECT: Draft of SPCCD Values Statement

   d. On the first line of the memo heading, change the *Before* paragraph spacing to **24 pt**.
   e. On the "SUBJECT" line of the memo heading, change the *After* paragraph spacing to **18 pt**.
6. Spell and grammar check the entire document.
   a. Add the chancellor's first and last names to the dictionary if they are marked as potential spelling errors.
   b. Correct other spelling and grammar errors as necessary.

7. Apply formatting to a paragraph heading and use the *Format Painter* to copy formatting.
   a. Select the first paragraph heading (**"Access"**) in the body of the memo and apply the following formatting:

      Font style: **Bold**
      Font color: **Blue-Gray, Text 2**
      Underline: **Double Underline**
      Underline color: **Blue-Gray, Text 2**
      Effects: **Small caps**

   b. Use the *Format Painter* to apply these styles to each of the other paragraph headings in the body of the memo.
8. Move body paragraphs.
   a. Use cut and paste or drag and drop to move the body paragraphs so they are ordered alphabetically by paragraph heading. Exclude the first body paragraph. Be sure to include the paragraph symbol at the end of each paragraph when cutting or dragging.
   b. Verify there are not extra *Enters* (paragraph marks) between paragraphs at the end of the document. This document will fit on one page.
   c. Verify there are not extra spaces before the first word in each of the paragraphs.
9. Delete any extra blank lines at the end of the document so this document fits on one page.
10. Add the following document properties:
    a. *Title*: SPCCD Values Statement
    b. *Company*: Sierra Pacific Community College District
    c. *Author*: Yoon Soo Park (right-click and choose **Remove Person** to remove existing author)
11. Save and close the document (Figure 1-98).

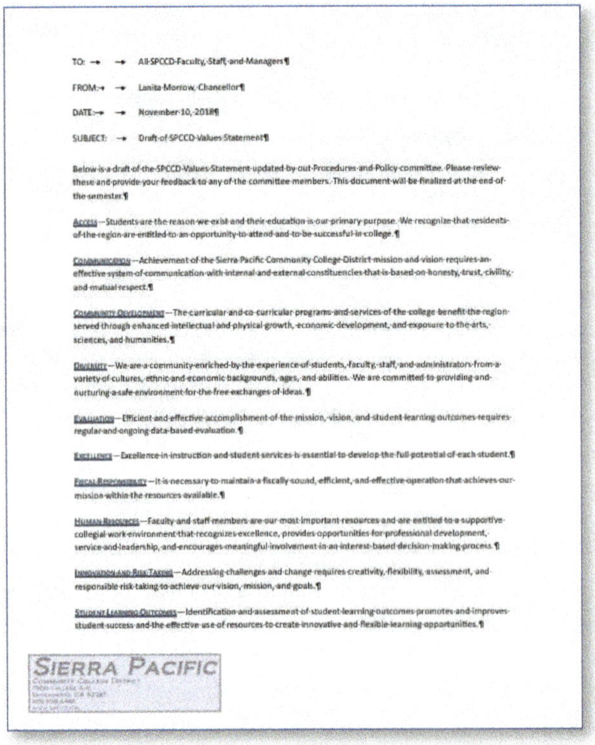

TO: All SPCCD Faculty, Staff, and Managers

FROM: Lanita Morrow, Chancellor

DATE: November 10, 2018

SUBJECT: Draft of SPCCD Values Statement

Below is a draft of the SPCCD Values Statement updated by out Procedures and Policy committee. Please review these and provide your feedback to any of the committee members. This document will be finalized at the end of the semester.

ACCESS—Students are the reason we exist and their education is our primary purpose. We recognize that residents of the region are entitled to an opportunity to attend and to be successful in college.

COMMUNICATION—Achievement of the Sierra Pacific Community College District mission and vision requires an effective system of communication with internal and external constituencies that is based on honesty, trust, civility, and mutual respect.

COMMUNITY DEVELOPMENT—The curricular and co-curricular programs and services of the college benefit the region served through enhanced intellectual and physical growth, economic development, and exposure to the arts, sciences, and humanities.

DIVERSITY—We are a community enriched by the experience of students, faculty, staff, and administrators from a variety of cultures, ethnic and economic backgrounds, ages, and abilities. We are committed to providing and nurturing a safe environment for the free exchanges of ideas.

EVALUATION—Efficient and effective accomplishment of the mission, vision, and student learning outcomes requires regular and ongoing data-based evaluation.

EXCELLENCE—Excellence in instruction and student services is essential to develop the full potential of each student.

FISCAL RESPONSIBILITY—It is necessary to maintain a fiscally sound, efficient, and effective operation that achieves our mission within the resources available.

HUMAN RESOURCES—Faculty and staff members are our most important resources and are entitled to a supportive collegial work environment that recognizes excellence, provides opportunities for professional development, service and leadership, and encourages meaningful involvement in an interest-based decision-making process.

INNOVATION AND RISK TAKING—Addressing challenges and change requires creativity, flexibility, assessment, and responsible risk taking to achieve our vision, mission, and goals.

STUDENT LEARNING OUTCOMES—Identification and assessment of student learning outcomes promotes and improves student success and the effective use of resources to create innovative and flexible learning opportunities.

SIERRA PACIFIC

1-98 Word 1-5 completed

Independent Project 1-6

In this project, you use formatting features in Word to create a professional and appealing brochure for Emma Cavalli at Placer Hills Real Estate.
[Student Learning Outcomes 1.1, 1.2, 1.3, 1.4, 1.5, 1.6, 1.7, 1.8]

File Needed: ***Brochure-01.docx*** *(Student data files are available in the* Library *of your SIMnet account)*
Completed Project File Name: ***[your initials] Word 1-6.docx***

Skills Covered in This Project

- Open and edit an existing document.
- Change font and font size.
- Change paragraph spacing.
- Change line spacing.
- Use *Show/Hide*.
- Change paragraph alignment.
- Change font styles and effects.
- Use the *Format Painter*.
- Move text.
- Use the thesaurus to find synonyms.
- Use *Smart Lookup*.
- Add document properties.

1. Open the ***Brochure-01*** document from your student data files.
2. Save this document as ***[your initials] Word 1-6***.
3. Select the entire document and apply the following formatting changes:
   a. Change the font and font size to **Cambria** and **10 pt**.
   b. Change the *After* paragraph spacing to **6 pt**.
   c. Change the line spacing to **Single**.
4. Apply formatting to the opening lines of the document.
   a. Select the first five lines of the document (**"Emma Cavalli"** to **"Email: ecavalli@phre.com"**) and change the *After* paragraph spacing to **2 pt**.
   b. Select the first six lines of the document (**"Emma Cavalli"** to **"Web: www.phre.com/ecavalli"**) and **Center** these lines.
   c. Select the first line of the document (**"Emma Cavalli"**) and apply the following changes:
      Font size: **12 pt**.
      Font style: **Bold**
      Font color: **Green, Accent 6, Darker 50%**
   d. Select the second line of the document ("**Realtor Consultant**") and apply **Bold** formatting.
   e. Select the third line of the document (**"Putting Your Needs First"**) and apply **Italic** formatting.
5. Apply formatting to a section heading and use the *Format Painter*.
   a. Select the first section heading, **"Personal Statement,"** and apply **Bold**, **Underline**, and **Small Caps** formatting.
   b. On the first section heading, change the *Before* paragraph spacing to **12 pt**. and the *After* paragraph spacing to **3 pt**.
   c. Use the *Format Painter* to copy this formatting to the other section headings:

      "Real Estate Experience"
      "Why I am a Real Estate Agent"
      "What Clients are Saying"
      "Professional Credentials"
      "Education & Training"

6. In the "Why I Am a Real Estate Agent" section, combine the four sentences into one paragraph, deleting paragraph marks and inserting spaces as needed. Turn on **Show/Hide**.
7. In the "What Clients are Saying" section, make the following changes:
   a. Select the second paragraph ("It was a pleasure . . ."), make it **Italic**, and change the *After* spacing to **0 pt**.
   b. Select the source of the quote (**"-Rod & Luisa Ellisor, Rocklin, CA"**) and right-align this text.
   c. Repeat the above two steps for the second quote ("Emma is conscientious . . .") and the source of the quote ("-Jon & Robin Anderson . . .").
8. Move the third section heading and the paragraph below it ("Why I Am a Real Estate Agent") so it appears before the second section ("Real Estate Experience").
9. Select the lines of text in the "Professional Credentials" section (don't include the heading) and change the *After* paragraph spacing to **3 pt**.
10. Use the *Format Painter* to repeat the above formatting to the lines of text (excluding the heading) in the "Education & Training" section.
11. Use the thesaurus to find an appropriate synonym for the following words:
    a. Replace "surpass" (in the "Personal Statement" section) with **"exceed."**
    b. Replace "emotions" (in the "Why I Am a Real Estate Agent" section) with **"sentiments."**
12. Use *Smart Lookup* to research selected words.
    a. Select **"University Nevada, Reno"** in the "Education & Training" section.
    b. Click the **Smart Lookup** button [*Review* tab, *Insights* group]. The *Smart Lookup* pane opens on the right.
    c. Review the research results in the *Smart Lookup* pane.
    d. Click the **X** in the upper right of the *Smart Lookup* pane to close the pane.
13. Add the following document properties:
    a. *Title*: Brochure
    b. *Company*: Placer Hills Real Estate
    c. *Author*: Emma Cavalli (right-click and choose **Remove Person** to remove existing author)
14. Save and close the document (Figure 1-99).

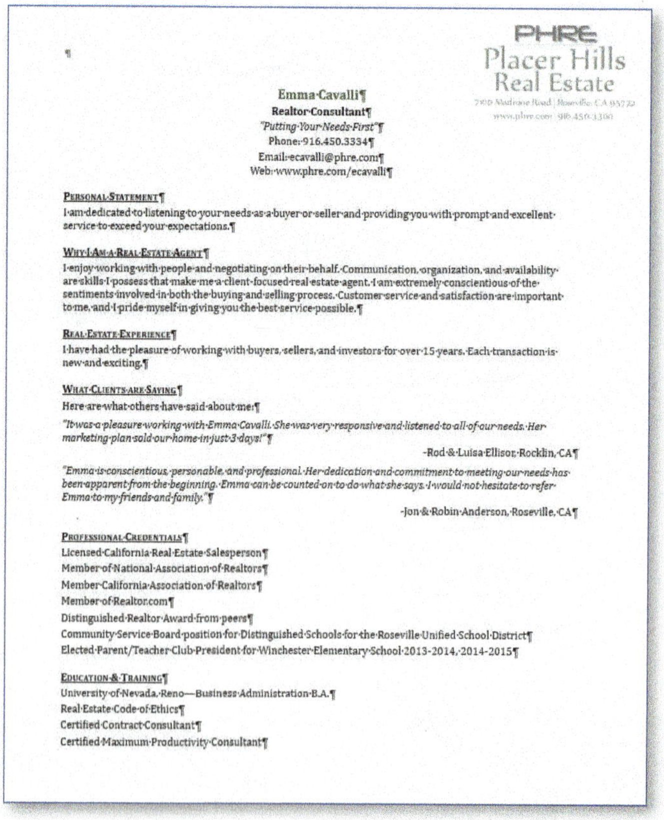

PHRE Placer Hills Real Estate

Emma Cavalli
Realtor Consultant
"Putting Your Needs First"
Phone: 916.450.3334
Email: ecavalli@phre.com
Web: www.phre.com/ecavalli

PERSONAL STATEMENT
I am dedicated to listening to your needs as a buyer or seller and providing you with prompt and excellent service to exceed your expectations.

WHY I AM A REAL ESTATE AGENT
I enjoy working with people and negotiating on their behalf. Communication, organization, and availability are skills I possess that make me a client-focused real estate agent. I am extremely conscientious of the sentiments involved in both the buying and selling process. Customer service and satisfaction are important to me, and I pride myself in giving you the best service possible.

REAL ESTATE EXPERIENCE
I have had the pleasure of working with buyers, sellers, and investors for over 15 years. Each transaction is new and exciting.

WHAT CLIENTS ARE SAYING
Here are what others have said about me:

"It was a pleasure working with Emma Cavalli. She was very responsive and listened to all of our needs. Her marketing plan sold our home in just 3 days!"

-Rod & Luisa Ellisor, Rocklin, CA

"Emma is conscientious, personable, and professional. Her dedication and commitment to meeting our needs has been apparent from the beginning. Emma can be counted on to do what she says. I would not hesitate to refer Emma to my friends and family."

-Jon & Robin Anderson, Roseville, CA

PROFESSIONAL CREDENTIALS
Licensed California Real Estate Salesperson
Member of National Association of Realtors
Member California Association of Realtors
Member of Realtor.com
Distinguished Realtor Award from peers
Community Service Board position for Distinguished Schools for the Roseville Unified School District
Elected Parent/Teacher Club President for Winchester Elementary School 2013-2014, 2014-2015

EDUCATION & TRAINING
University of Nevada, Reno—Business Administration B.A.
Real Estate Code of Ethics
Certified Contract Consultant
Certified Maximum Productivity Consultant

1-99 Word 1-6 completed

Improve It Project 1-7

In this project, you create a block format business letter for Margaret Jepson, an insurance agent at Central Sierra Insurance. You improve the formatting and text in this document and add opening and closing lines to create a properly formatted business letter. For more information on creating a correctly formatted block format business letter, see *Appendix B*.
[Student Learning Outcomes 1.1, 1.2, 1.3, 1.5, 1.6, 1.7, 1.8]

File Needed: ***RenewalLetter-01.docx*** *(Student data files are available in the* Library *of your SIMnet account)*
Completed Project File Name: ***[your initials] Word 1-7.docx***

Skills Covered in This Project

- Open and edit an existing document.
- Change font and font size.
- Change paragraph spacing.
- Change line spacing.
- Use spelling and grammar checker.
- Format a business letter.
- Change paragraph alignment.
- Change font styles and effects.
- Use the *Format Painter.*
- Add document properties.

1. Open the ***RenewalLetter-01*** document from your student data files.
2. Save this document as ***[your initials] Word 1-7***.
3. Select the entire document and apply the following formatting:
   a. *Line spacing*: **Single**
   b. *Before* and *After paragraph spacing*: **0 pt**.
   c. *Font*: **Calibri**
   d. *Font size*: **11 pt**.
4. Correct spelling and grammar as needed.
5. Type the opening lines of the business letter.
   a. Turn on **Show/Hide** if it is not already on.
   b. Place your insertion point at the top of the document and press **Enter**.
   c. On the blank line at the beginning of the document, type the current date (e.g., September 1, 2018) and press **Enter** four times.
   d. Type the following inside address and press **Enter** two times after the last line:

      Mr. Rick DePonte
      8364 Marshall Street
      Granite Bay, CA 95863

   e. Type Dear Mr. DePonte: as the salutation press **Enter** two times.
   f. Type Subject: Policy HO-2887-5546-B as the subject line and press **Enter** once.
   g. Apply **72 pt**. *Before* paragraph spacing on the date line.
6. Type the closing lines of the business letter.
   a. On the last blank line of the document, type Best regards, as the complimentary close and press **Enter** four times.
   b. Type the following information below as the writer's name, title, and company and press **Enter** two times after the last line:

Margaret Jepson, ARM, CIC, CRM
Insurance Agent
Central Sierra Insurance

c. Type your initials in lowercase letters as the reference initials and press **Enter** once. Undo the automatic capitalization of your reference initials.
d. Type Enclosure as the enclosure notation at the end of the business letter.

7. Apply formatting to the renewal premium information.
   a. **Center** the four lines of renewal premium information in the body of the letter.
   b. Apply **Bold** and **Small caps** formatting to the headings (not including the colons) for each of these four lines of renewal premium information.
   c. Format the "Total Premium" dollar amount as **Bold**, **Italic**, and **Double Underline**.
8. In the second body paragraph, type Hartford Specialty to replace the "*[Company Name]*" placeholder.
9. In the last body paragraph, type Rick to replace the "*[First Name]*" placeholder.
10. Add the following document properties:
    a. *Title*: Renewal Letter
    b. *Company*: Central Sierra Insurance
    c. *Author*: Margaret Jepson (right-click and choose **Remove Person** to remove existing author)
11. Save and close the letter (Figure 1-100).

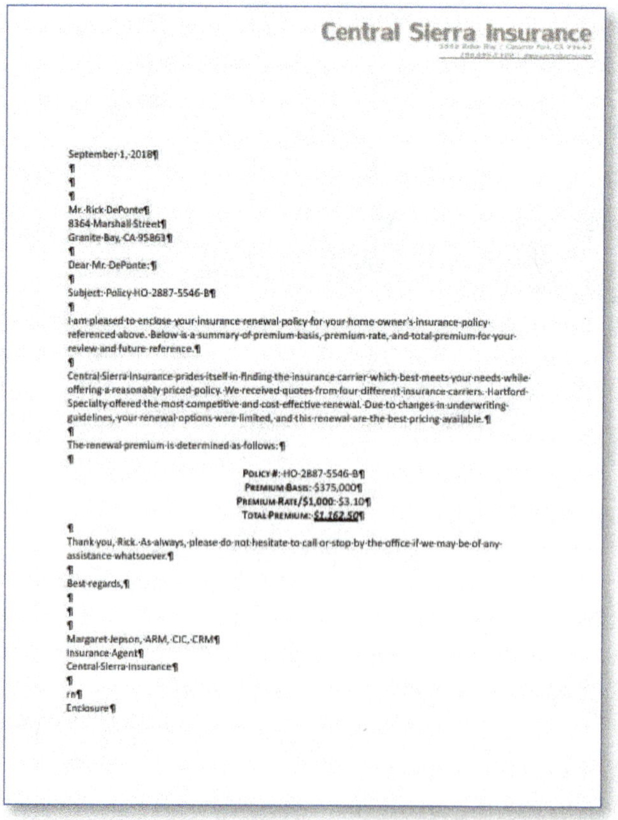

Central Sierra Insurance

September 1, 2018

Mr. Rick DePonte
8364 Marshall Street
Granite Bay, CA 95863

Dear Mr. DePonte:

Subject: Policy HO-2887-5546-B

I am pleased to enclose your insurance renewal policy for your home owner's insurance policy referenced above. Below is a summary of premium basis, premium rate, and total premium for your review and future reference.

Central Sierra Insurance prides itself in finding the insurance carrier which best meets your needs while offering a reasonably priced policy. We received quotes from four different insurance carriers. Hartford Specialty offered the most competitive and cost-effective renewal. Due to changes in underwriting guidelines, your renewal options were limited, and this renewal are the best pricing available.

The renewal premium is determined as follows:

Policy #: HO-2887-5546-B
Premium Basis: $375,000
Premium Rate/$1,000: $3.10
Total Premium: ***$1,162.50***

Thank you, Rick. As always, please do not hesitate to call or stop by the office if we may be of any assistance whatsoever.

Best regards,

Margaret Jepson, ARM, CIC, CRM
Insurance Agent
Central Sierra Insurance

rn
Enclosure

1-100 Word 1-7 completed

Challenge Project 1-8

Create a cover letter for a job application. A cover letter typically accompanies a resume to introduce an applicant to a prospective employer. You can use and modify an existing cover letter, or you can create a new one. It is important to customize each cover letter for each job for which you are applying.

There are many online resources available to help you with both content and format. One of the best online resources for writing is the Online Writing Lab (OWL) from Purdue University (http://owl.english.purdue.edu/owl/). You can search this site for helpful information about cover letters.
[Student Learning Outcomes 1.1, 1.2, 1.3, 1.4, 1.5, 1.6, 1.7, 1.8]

File Needed: None
Completed Project File Name: ***[your initials] Word 1-8.docx***

Open a new document and save this document as ***[your initials] Word 1-8***.

Type this document as a personal business letter in block format. For more information on formatting a personal business letter, see *Appendix B*. Modify your document according to the following guidelines:

- Move sentences and paragraphs as needed to produce a well-organized cover letter.
- Add words to the dictionary as needed.
- Use the *Thesaurus* to find synonyms as needed.
- Include document properties, and spell and grammar check the document.

Challenge Project 1-9

Create a list of five places you would like to visit in the next five years. For each of the places you list, compose a short paragraph about that place and why it is interesting to you. Research each of the places you choose on the Internet. Use your own words when composing the paragraphs about each place.
[Student Learning Outcomes 1.1, 1.2, 1.3, 1.4, 1.5, 1.6, 1.7, 1.8]

File Needed: None
Completed Project File Name: ***[your initials] Word 1-9.docx***

Open a new document and save it as ***[your initials] Word 1-9***. Modify your document according to the following guidelines:

- Create and format a title for the document.
- Format each of the headings by modifying the font, style, and attributes.
- Change line and paragraph spacing as needed to create an attractive and readable document.
- Use consistent line and paragraph spacing throughout the document.
- Use the *Format Painter* to keep formatting consistent throughout the document.
- Move the paragraphs so the places are listed in order of your preference.
- Include document properties, and spell and grammar check the document.

Challenge Project 1-10

Create a flyer for an upcoming event for an organization to which you belong. Be sure to include all the relevant information for this event and arrange it attractively and professionally on the page. [Student Learning Outcomes 1.1, 1.2, 1.3, 1.5, 1.6, 1.7, 1.8]

File Needed: None
Completed Project File Name: ***[your initials] Word 1-10.docx***

Open a new document and save it as ***[your initials] Word 1-10***. Modify your document according to the following guidelines:

- Create and format a title for the document.
- Format the information by modifying the fonts, styles, and attributes.
- Change line and paragraph spacing as needed to create an attractive and readable document.
- Change the text alignment as desired.
- Use the *Format Painter* to keep formatting consistent throughout the document.
- Include document properties, and spell and grammar check the document.

CHAPTER 2

Formatting and Customizing Documents

WORD

CHAPTER OVERVIEW

In addition to giving you the ability to create common business documents, Microsoft Word 2016 provides formatting and editing tools you can use to customize a variety of documents. Formatting features such as custom margins, tab stops, indents, page numbering, headers, footers, breaks, lists, styles, themes, borders, and shading help you to produce readable and attractive professional and personal documents.

STUDENT LEARNING OUTCOMES (SLOs)

After completing this chapter, you will be able to:

SLO 2.1 Format a document by customizing margins, page orientation, paper size, and vertical alignment (p.W2-66).

SLO 2.2 Improve alignment and page layout by setting, using, and editing tab stops in a document (p. W2-69).

SLO 2.3 Apply indents to control text alignment (p. W2-74).

SLO 2.4 Enhance document layout by inserting page numbers, headers, and footers (p. W2-79).

SLO 2.5 Control pagination with page and section breaks (p. W2-86).

SLO 2.6 Use customized bulleted and numbered lists to effectively present information (p. W2-88).

SLO 2.7 Apply styles and themes to improve consistency in document format (p. W2-92).

SLO 2.8 Use find and replace to edit a document (p. W2-97).

SLO 2.9 Improve overall document design and format with borders, shading, horizontal lines, and hyperlinks (p. W2-100).

CASE STUDY

Courtyard Medical Plaza has a preschool for its employees' children. The preschool is currently looking for qualified applicants to fill a vacant teacher position. In the Pause & Practice projects, you modify a résumé for Richelle Wilkinson. You apply features covered in this chapter to create an attractive and informative résumé.

Pause & Practice 2-1: Edit the résumé to change margins and set tab stops and indents.

Pause & Practice 2-2: Modify the résumé to include a header with text and a page number.

Pause & Practice 2-3: Enhance the résumé by using bulleted lists, a page break, and a theme.

Pause & Practice 2-4: Finalize the résumé by using find and replace, borders, shading, horizontal line, and hyperlinks.

SLO 2.1

Customizing Margins and Page Layout

You can use margins to create ***white space*** around the edges of a document. White space improves the readability of a document and prevents the document from appearing cluttered. The document type and content influence the margins you use. You can also customize a document by changing the page orientation, page size, or vertical alignment.

Page Layout Settings

When you open a new Word document, the default settings control margins, page orientation, paper size, and vertical alignment. The following table lists the default page layout settings for a new document:

Default Page Layout Settings

Page Layout Option	Default Setting
Margins	1" top, bottom, left, and right
Page Orientation	Portrait
Paper Size	8.5" × 11" (Letter)
Vertical Alignment	Top

These settings are applied to the entire Word document, and you can easily change all of these settings in Word.

Margin Settings

Margin settings are measured in inches; the default margin settings for a new Word document are 1". Word provides you with a variety of ***preset margin settings***. You can choose and change margins from the ***Margins*** drop-down list.

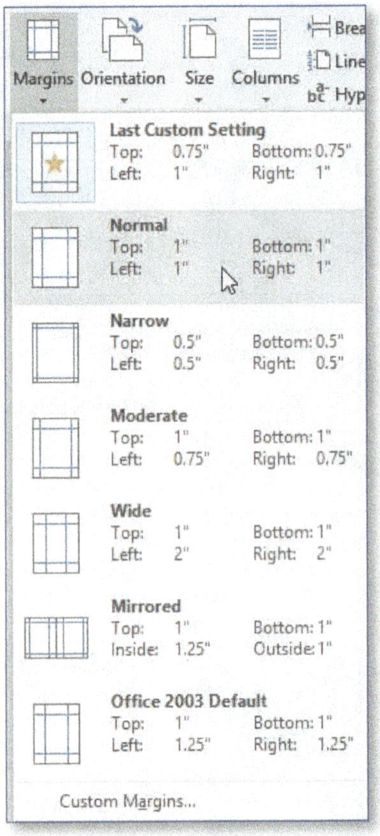

2-1 *Margins* drop-down list

▸ HOW TO: Change Margin Settings

1. With a document open in Word, click the **Layout** tab.
2. Click the **Margins** button [*Page Setup* group]. Preset margin options appear in the *Margins* drop-down list (Figure 2-1).
3. Select the desired margin settings from the drop-down list of options.

The *Margins* drop-down list provides preset margin options. You are not limited to these preset options; you can also create your own custom margin settings in the *Page Setup* dialog box.

> **MORE INFO**
>
> At the top of this *Margins* list, the ***Last Custom Setting*** option displays the most recent custom margin settings you have used.

Page Setup Dialog Box

If you want margin settings that are not listed in the preset margin settings in the *Margins* drop-down list, use the ***Page Setup dialog box*** (Figure 2-2) to change one or more of the margin settings and to create custom margins.

HOW TO: Set Custom Margins

1. Click the **Layout** tab.
2. Click the **Margins** button [*Page Setup* group] and select **Custom Margins**. The *Page Setup* dialog box opens (see Figure 2-2).
3. Click the **Margins** tab if it is not already selected.
4. Change the *Top*, *Bottom*, *Left*, and *Right* margin settings as desired. You can do this the following ways:
   - Click the **Top**, **Bottom**, **Left**, or **Right** margin box and type your desired margin setting.
   - Click the **up** or **down arrow** to increase or decrease the margin size. Each click of the up or down arrow increases or decreases the margins by 0.1".
   - Press **Tab** to move from one box to another in the *Margins* area.
5. View the *Preview* area to see how the margin settings appear when applied to the document.
6. Click the **Apply to** drop-down list and select the area to apply margin settings: **Whole document**, **This point forward**, or **This section**.
7. Click **OK** to apply the custom margin settings.

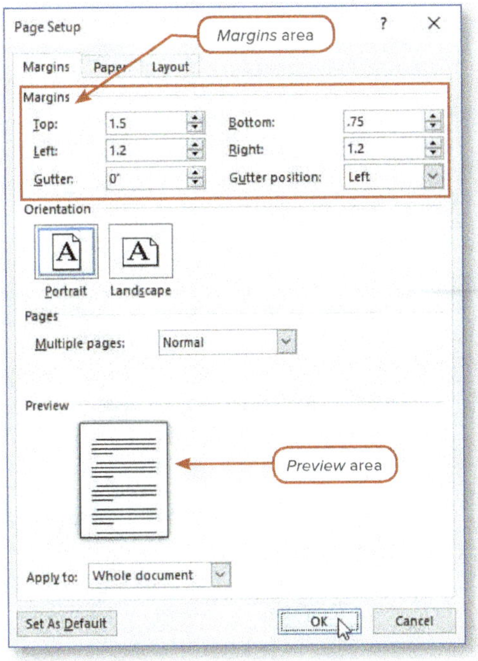

2-2 *Page Setup* dialog box

MORE INFO

Margin settings apply to the entire document by default. However, you can apply different margin settings to different sections of a document. Sections and section breaks are covered later in this chapter.

Page Orientation

Page orientation refers to the direction of the page. The two different orientation options in Word are ***Portrait*** and ***Landscape***. Portrait is the tall orientation (8.5" × 11"), which is the default page orientation in Word. Landscape is the wide orientation (11" × 8.5"). You can change page orientation by clicking the **Orientation** button in the *Page Setup* group on the *Layout* tab (Figure 2-3).

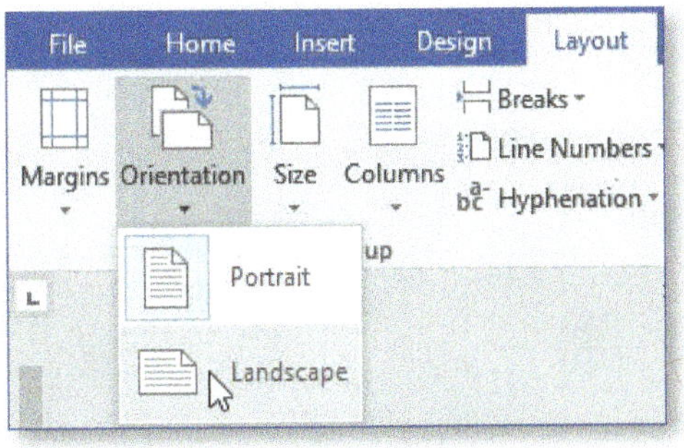

2-3 Page orientation settings

ANOTHER WAY

You can also change page orientation in the *Page Setup* dialog box.

Paper Size

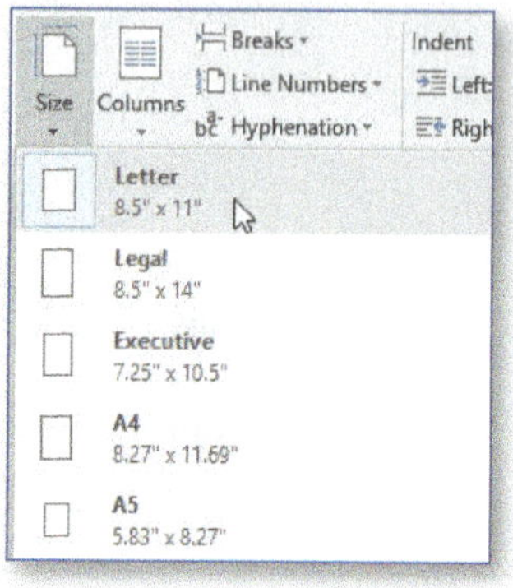

2-4 Paper size preset options

Paper size refers to the actual size of the paper of your final printed document. A new document in Word is standard letter size, which is 8.5" × 11" by default. Word also provides other preset paper size settings, some of which are displayed in Figure 2-4.

You can change paper size by clicking the **Size** button in the *Page Setup* group on the *Layout* tab. When a different paper size is set, the margins of the document do not change. You may need to adjust the margin setting when you change the paper size. You can also set a custom paper size in the *Page Setup* dialog box.

Vertical Alignment

If you are creating a flyer or a title page for a report, you might want to vertically center the information on the page. ***Vertical alignment*** controls the position of text between the top and bottom margins. Changing the vertical alignment of a page, section, or document is a much more effective method than using paragraph breaks (pressing *Enter* multiple times) to align information vertically. Word has four different vertical alignment options.

- *Top*: Text begins at the top margin of the document.
- *Center*: Text is centered vertically between the top and bottom margins.
- *Justified*: Space is automatically added between lines to fill the entire vertical space between the top and bottom margins.
- *Bottom*: Text begins at the bottom margin of the document.

HOW TO: Change Vertical Alignment

1. Click the **Layout** tab.
2. Click the **Page Setup** launcher [*Page Setup* group]. The *Page Setup* dialog box opens.
3. Click the **Layout** tab.
4. In the *Page* area, click the **Vertical alignment** drop-down list (Figure 2-5).
5. Select the vertical alignment option of your choice.

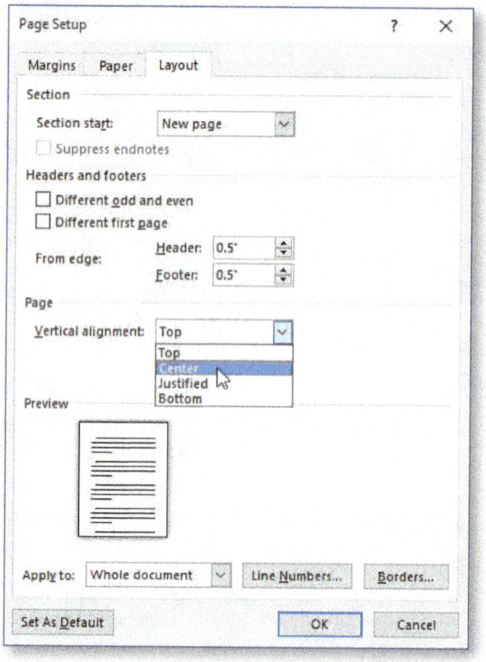

2-5 Change vertical alignment

Use the Ruler

Microsoft Word provides horizontal and vertical ***rulers*** that display both the typing line length and the vertical typing space available in a document. The rulers are broken into 1/8" increments. Half-inch markers are longer vertical or horizontal lines (depending on the ruler) and inch markers are numerical. On the rulers, the typing area is displayed in white, while the margin area is shaded (Figure 2-6). To display the rulers, check the **Ruler** box on the *View* tab in the *Show* group. This check box toggles on and off the display of the rulers.

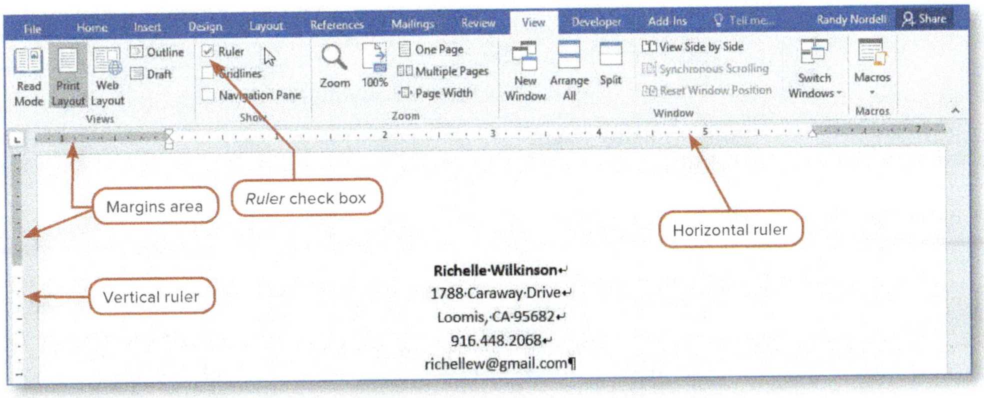

2-6 Horizontal and vertical rulers displayed

> **MORE INFO**
>
> The rulers are increasingly important and useful as you begin using tab stops, indents, columns, tables, and section breaks.

SLO 2.2

Setting, Using, and Editing Tab Stops

Tabs are useful tools to control the alignment of text. A tab is often used to indent the first line of a paragraph. A ***tab stop*** is where your insertion point stops when you press the *Tab* key. Tabs can also be used, for example, to align text in columns, or to begin the date at the horizontal midpoint on a modified block business letter.

The five different types of tabs stops that you can set and use in your documents are described in the following table:

Types of Tab Stops

Type of Tab Stop	Description	Tab Stop Indicator	Tab Stop in Use
Left	Text is left aligned at the tab stop		Left tab
Center	Text is centered on the tab stop		Center tab
Right	Text is right aligned at the tab stop		Right tab
Decimal	Decimal point is aligned at the tab stop		Decimal tab 620.50 8.375
Bar	A vertical bar (line) is inserted at the tab stop		There is a bar | tab between these words

Set a Tab Stop

Tabs are different from margins because tab stops apply to a paragraph or selected paragraphs rather than an entire document or sections of a document. This is important to keep in mind when setting, using, and editing tab stops.

By default in a Word document, there is left tab stop every 0.5". You can set tab custom stops in a new document before text is typed, or you can set tab stops in existing text. If you open a new blank document and set a left tab stop at 3.25", that tab stop applies to the entire document. On the other hand, if you open an existing document and set a tab stop on the first line, the tab stop is only set for that paragraph. When setting a tab stop in existing documents or text, remember to select all the text or paragraphs where you want the tab settings to apply.

There are two ways to set a tab stop in Word.

- *Tabs* dialog box
- Ruler

Set a Tab Stop Using the Tabs Dialog Box

The ***Tabs dialog box*** is an effective and easy method to set single or multiple tab stops. The *Tabs* dialog box is available from the *Paragraph* dialog box, which you can open from the *Paragraph* group on either the *Home* or *Layout* tabs.

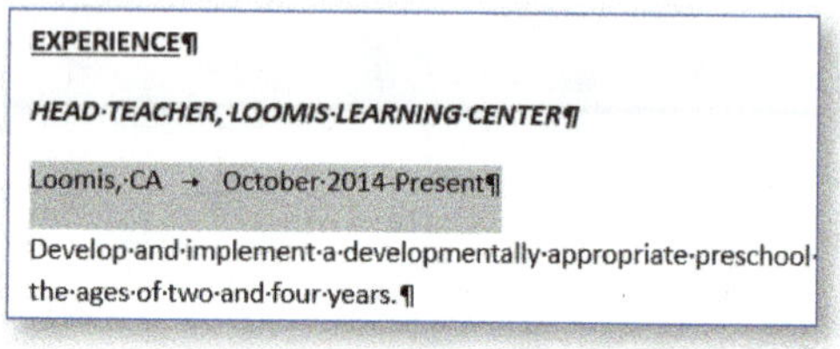

2-7 Select text before setting tab stops

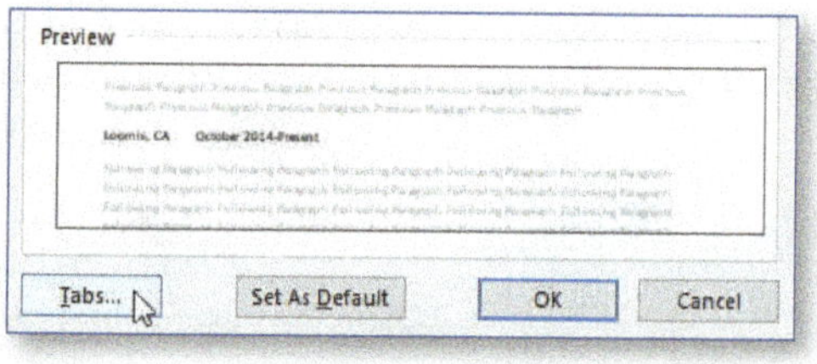

2-8 *Tabs* button in the *Paragraph* dialog box

▶HOW TO: Set a Tab Stop Using the Tabs Dialog Box

1. Select the text where you want to set a tab stop (Figure 2-7).
2. Click the **Home** tab.
3. Click the **Paragraph** launcher to open the *Paragraph* dialog box.
4. Click the **Tabs** button (Figure 2-8) to open the *Tabs* dialog box.
5. Click in the **Tab stop position** area and type the desired tab stop position.
6. In the *Alignment* area, select the type of tab stop radio button you want to set.
7. Click the **Set** button (Figure 2-9). The tab stop appears in the list of tab stops below the *Tab stop position* area.
8. Click **OK** to close the *Tabs* dialog box.
    - The tab stop is applied to the selected text.
    - The tab stop is visible on the ruler.

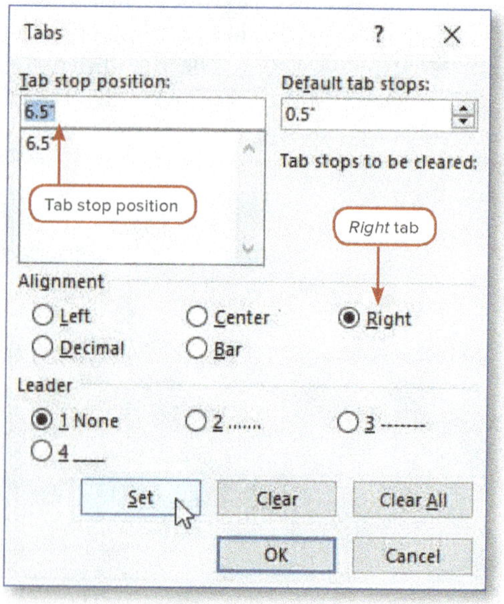

2-9 Set a right tab stop in the *Tabs* dialog box

MORE INFO

Set and use tab stops to align and balance columns of text rather than pressing *Tab* multiple times between columns.

Set a Tab Stop Using the Ruler

Using the ruler to set tab stops is a quick way to add them to a document. You can also easily move or remove tab stops using the ruler. Use the ***Tab selector*** to select the type of tab stop you want to insert. The *Tab* selector is located at the top of the vertical ruler on the left side of the Word window. When setting tab stops in an existing document, it is very important to select the text or paragraphs where you want the tab stop to apply before setting the tab stop.

▶ HOW TO: Set a Tab Stop Using the Ruler

1. Select the text where you want to set the new tab stop(s).
   - If the rulers are not displayed, check the **Ruler** box [*View* tab, *Show* group].
2. Click the **Tab** selector to select the type of tab stop to set (Figure 2-10).
3. Click the ruler to set a tab stop.
   - When setting tab stops using the ruler, click the bottom edge of the ruler to set a tab stop (Figure 2-11).

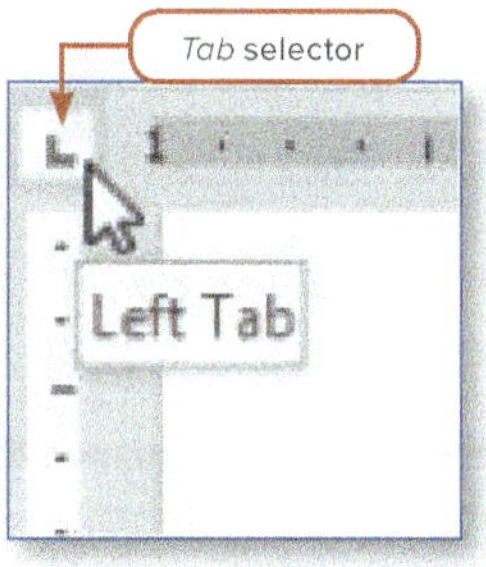

2-10 *Tab* selector

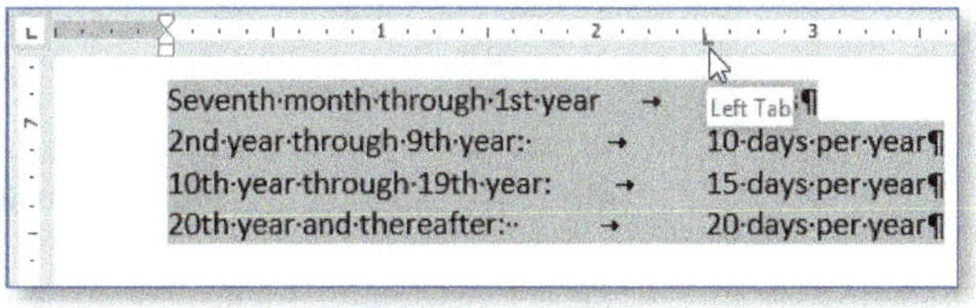

2-11 Set a left tab stop at 2.5" on the ruler

MORE INFO

Use the ***Format Painter*** to copy tab stops from one area of your document to another area.

Move a Tab Stop

It can be challenging to align text correctly and balance space between columns. But as you set and use tab stops more regularly, you become more comfortable selecting the correct type of tab stop to use, adjusting the settings of existing tab stops, and removing tab stops. When using multiple columns, adjust tab stops so you have about the same amount of white space between columns.

The easiest way to move tab stops is by using the ruler. When using the ruler to adjust a tab stop, be sure to select the appropriate text before moving a tab stop.

▶ HOW TO: Move a Tab Stop

1. Select the text or paragraphs where the tab stops you want to edit are set.
2. Left-click the **tab stop** on the ruler and drag it to the new location (Figure 2-12).
   - As you click the tab stop to be moved, a vertical alignment guide appears on your document. This alignment guide displays where your text aligns.

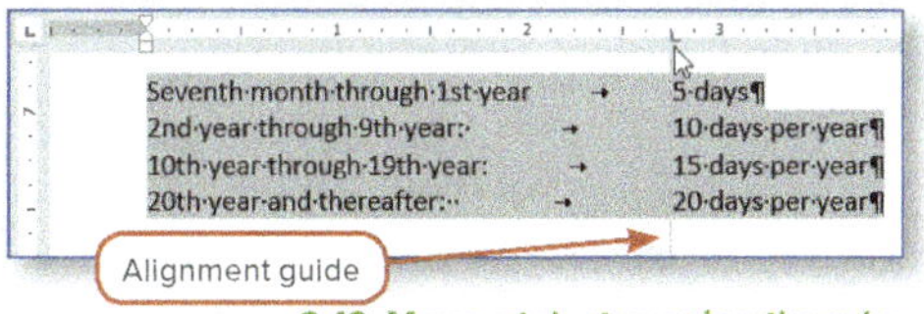

2-12 Move a tab stop using the ruler

- Press the **Alt** key when you are moving a tab stop to display a vertical guide that allows you to place the tab stop at a specific measurement (Figure 2-13).

3. Release the pointer to set the tab stop in the new location.
4. Repeat this process until you are satisfied with the placement of your tab stops.

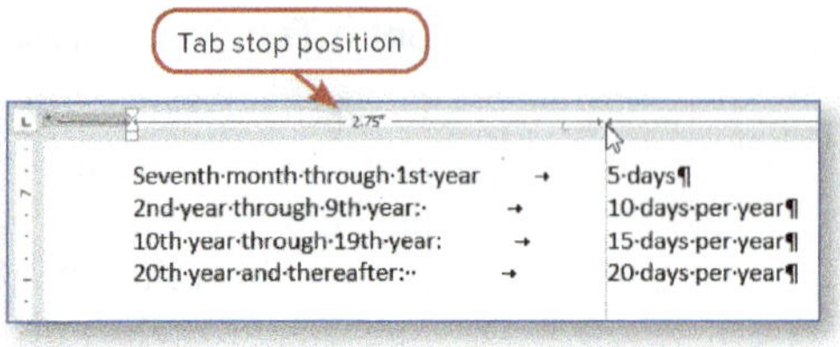

2-13 Use the *Alt* key to adjust a tab stop

ANOTHER WAY

Adjust tab stops in the *Tabs* dialog box by clearing an existing tab stop and setting a new tab stop.

Remove a Tab Stop

Occasionally, when setting tab stops using the ruler, you unintentionally add an unwanted tab stop. Or sometimes you might just want to remove unwanted tab stops. To remove tab stops from existing text, it is very important to select the text or paragraphs before deleting the tabs. When you remove or clear a tab stop, the tabbed text realigns to the default 0.5" tab stop or nearest remaining custom tab stop. Following are three different ways to remove tab stops:

- Drag a tab stop off (below) the ruler.
- Clear a single tab stop in the *Tabs* dialog box.
- Clear all tab stops in the *Tabs* dialog box.

To clear a single tab stop using the ruler, select the text or paragraphs, select the tab stop you want to remove, drag the tab stop down below the ruler, and release the pointer.

When using the *Tabs* dialog box to remove tab stops, you can clear a single tab stop or clear all existing tab stops on the selected text or paragraphs.

HOW TO: Clear a Tab Stop Using the Tabs Dialog Box

1. Select the text or paragraphs that contain the tab stops you want to remove.
2. Click the **Paragraph** launcher [*Home* or *Layout* tab] to open the *Paragraph* dialog box.
3. Click the **Tabs** button to open the *Tabs* dialog box.
4. To remove a single tab stop, select the tab stop to remove in the list of existing tab stops and click the **Clear** button (Figure 2-14). Repeat on any other tab stops you want to remove.
5. To clear all tab stops, click the **Clear All** button.
6. Click **OK** to close the *Tabs* dialog box.

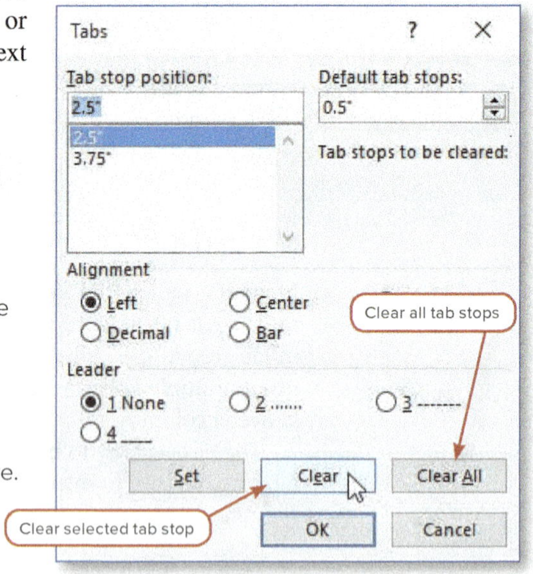

2-14 Clear a tab stop in the *Tabs* dialog box

Add a Tab Leader

You can use ***leaders*** to insert dots or a line between text when using tab stops. The most common type of leader is the dot leader, which is regularly used in a table of contents. In a table of contents, a dot leader is inserted between the text and the right aligned page number. You can also use leaders to insert a dashed line in the blank space between columns or to create a solid underline when creating a printed form.

Word has three different types of leaders. Examples of each of these are in the following table:

Types of Leaders

Leader	Example of Use
Dot	Chapter 1 4
Dash	Vacation Days -------- 10 days per year
Solid underline	Name_________________________

You can add leaders to existing or new tab stops, but they can only be added in the *Tabs* dialog box.

▶HOW TO: Add a Tab Leader

1. Select the text or paragraphs where you want to add a tab leader.
2. Click the **Paragraph** launcher [*Home* or *Layout* tab] to open the *Paragraph* dialog box.
3. Click the **Tabs** button to open the *Tabs* dialog box.
4. Select an existing tab stop or type a number in the *Tab stop position* text box to set a new tab stop.
5. Select the type of leader to apply in the *Leader* area.
6. Click **Set**. Figure 2-15 is an example of a dash leader.
7. Click **OK** to close the *Tabs* dialog box.

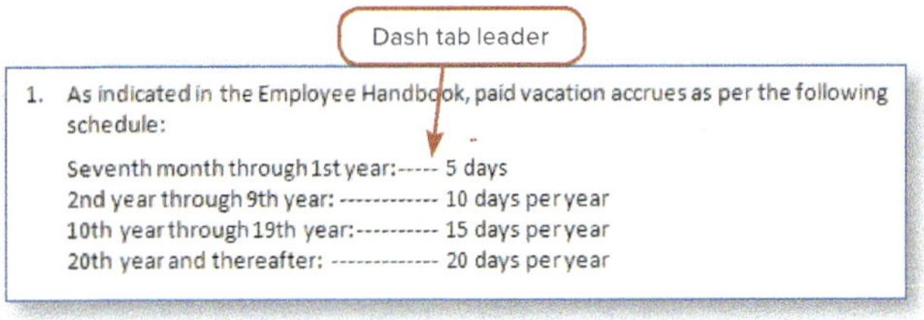

2-15 Tab stop with a dash leader

Change Default Tab Stops

By default, Word has a left tab stop every 0.5". When you set a tab stop in Word, this custom tab stop overrides all preceding default tab stops. The default tab stops after your custom tab stop still remain. For example, if you set a left tab stop at the horizontal midpoint (typically 3.25") and press **Tab** to move to the horizontal midpoint, your insertion point will move to the midpoint, not 0.5". But if you press **Tab** again, your insertion point will stop at the next default tab stop, which would be 3.5".

You can customize the interval for default tab stops. If you change the default tab stop setting, this change affects only the current document, not all new documents.

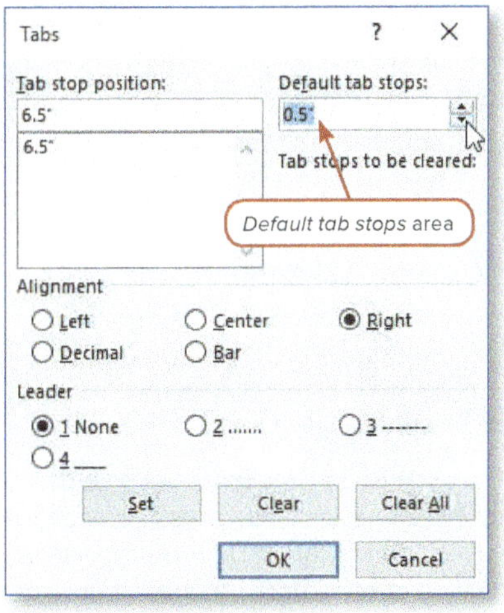

2-16 Change default tab stops

▶HOW TO: Change Default Tab Stops

1. Click the **Paragraph** launcher [*Home* or *Layout* tab] to open the *Paragraph* dialog box.
2. Click the **Tabs** button to open the *Tabs* dialog box.
3. In the *Default tab stops* area, use the up or down arrow to change the default tab stops (Figure 2-16).
4. Click **OK** to close the *Tabs* dialog box.

SLO 2.3

Using Indents

Indents are another powerful tool to help you control how text aligns between the left and right margins. Indents can be thought of as temporary margins, which apply to selected paragraphs. You can use indents to indent the first line of each paragraph, set off a long quote in a report, or indent the carry-over lines when creating bulleted or numbered lists.

Similar to setting tab stops, it is important to select the text where you want to apply indent settings. You can set indents using the ruler, the *Paragraph* group on the *Layout* tab, or the *Paragraph* dialog box. The four different types of indents that you can set and use in your document are described in the following table:

Types of Indents

Indent	Example of Use	Ruler Indent Marker
Left Indent	This line has a left indent.	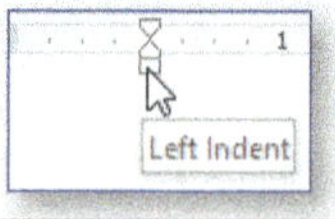
Right Indent	This line has a right indent.	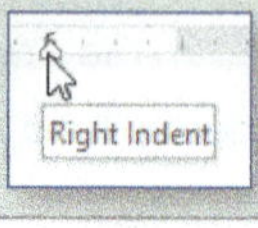
First Line Indent	This line has a first line indent.	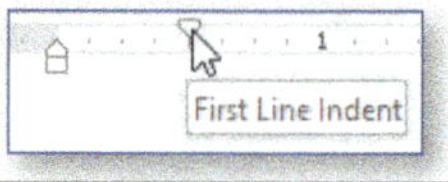
Hanging Indent	This line has a hanging indent.	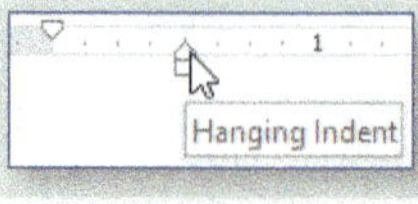

Left and Right Indents

Indents apply to an entire paragraph or multiple paragraphs, not just lines of text within a paragraph. When setting an indent, select the paragraph(s) on which to apply the indent. If your insertion point is in a paragraph, the indent you set applies to that paragraph only.

HOW TO: Set a Left and Right Indent Using the Ribbon

1. Select the text or paragraph where you want to apply the indent. If it is just one paragraph, place your insertion point in that paragraph.
2. Click the **Layout** tab.
3. Change the *Left* and *Right* indent settings [*Paragraph* group]. This change is applied to the selected text (Figure 2-17).
   - When an indent is set on a paragraph and you press *Enter* at the end of the paragraph, the indent carries over to the next paragraph.

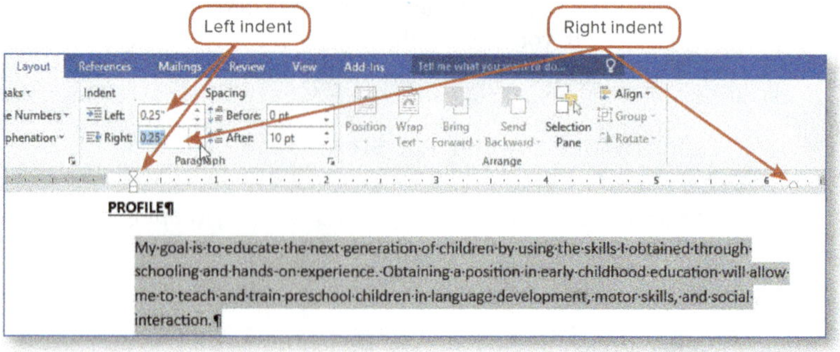

2-17 Change left and right indents

Indents can also be set using the ruler by dragging the indent marker to the desired location after you select the text you want to indent. As you drag the indent marker, an alignment guide displays the location where your text aligns.

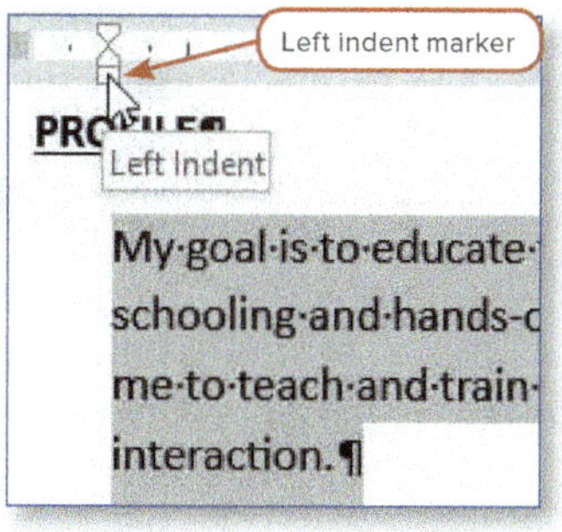

2-18 Change left indent using the ruler

▸HOW TO: Set Indents Using the Ruler

1. Select the text or paragraph you want to indent. If it is just one paragraph, place your insertion point in that paragraph.
2. Left click the **left indent marker** (bottom square), drag to the desired location, and release the pointer. The left indent is applied to the text (Figure 2-18).
3. Left click the **right indent marker**, drag to the desired location, and release the pointer. The right indent is applied to the text (Figure 2-19).

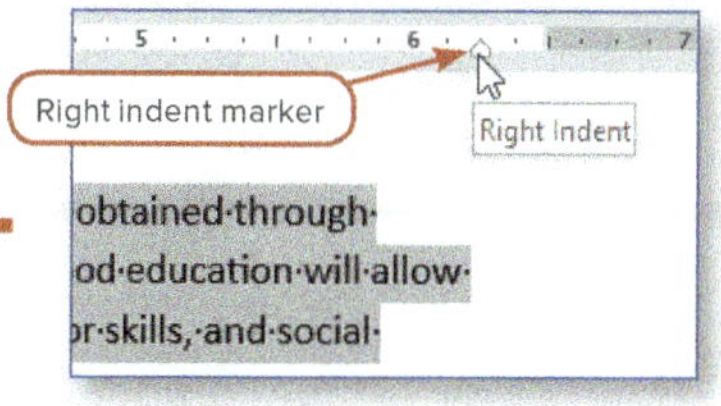

2-19 Change right indent using the ruler

> **ANOTHER WAY**
>
> Set left and right indents using the *Paragraph* dialog box. Click the **Paragraph** launcher to open the *Paragraph* dialog box.

The ***Decrease Indent*** and ***Increase Indent*** buttons in the *Paragraph* group on the *Home* tab increase or decrease the left indent in increments of 0.5" (Figure 2-20). Remove a left indent by clicking at the beginning of the paragraph and pressing **Backspace** or clicking the **Decrease Indent** button.

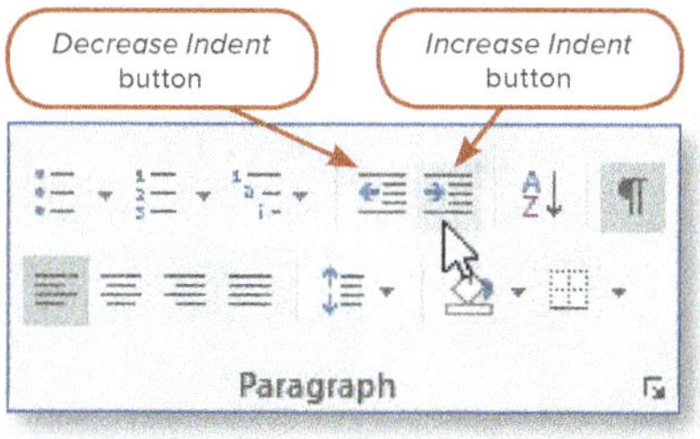

2-20 *Decrease Indent* and *Increase Indent* buttons

First Line and Hanging Indents

You can use a ***First line indent*** to indent the first line of a paragraph instead of using a tab. A ***Hanging indent*** is typically used with bulleted and numbered lists but can be used effectively to indent text that wraps to a second or more lines, such as a references page. You can use the *Paragraph* dialog box to set first line and hanging indents.

▸HOW TO: Set a First Line or a Hanging Indent Using the Paragraph Dialog box

1. Select the paragraph(s) you want to indent.
2. Click the **Paragraph** launcher [*Home* or *Layout* tab] to open the *Paragraph* dialog box.
3. Click the **Special** drop-down list in the *Indentation* area and choose the type of indent: **First line** or **Hanging** (Figure 2-21).
4. In the *By* area, type the indent amount or use the up or down buttons to increase or decrease the amount of the indent.
   - The *Preview* area displays the text with the indent applied.
5. Click **OK** to close the *Paragraph* dialog box.

You can also use the ruler to set a first line indent. Select the paragraph(s) you want to indent and drag the first line indent marker (top triangle) to the desired location (Figure 2-22). The alignment guide displays where the first line of each paragraph align.

To set a hanging indent using the ruler, select the paragraph(s) you want to indent and drag the hanging indent marker (bottom triangle) to the desired location (Figure 2-23). The alignment guide displays where the carryover lines of the paragraph align.

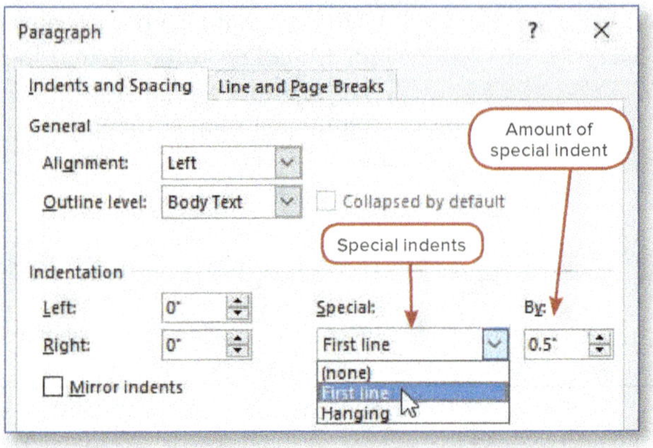

2-21 Set first line or hanging indent using the *Paragraph* dialog box

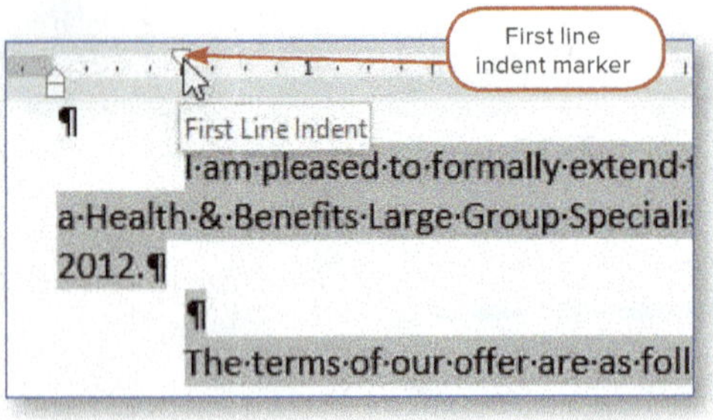

2-22 Set a first line indent using the ruler

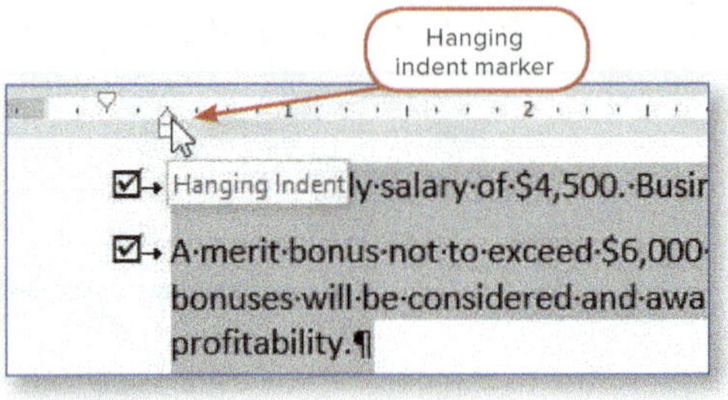

2-23 Set a hanging indent using the ruler

An ***outdent*** aligns text outside the left or right margins. Outdents are sometimes used to emphasize section headings so they are slightly to the left of the left margin. To apply an outdent, set a ***negative value*** (−0.25") in the indents area in the *Paragraph* dialog box or *Paragraph* group on the *Layout* tab or by dragging the indent marker outside of the left or right margins.

Remove Indents

Removing indents moves the indent markers back to either the left or right margin, so the margins control the alignment of text rather than the indents. Remember to select the paragraph or paragraphs before removing the indents. You can remove indents using the *Paragraph* dialog box or the *Paragraph* group on the *Layout* tab. When using either of these methods, set the indent value to 0" (Figure 2-24).

The ruler can also be used to remove indents. When using this method, select the text or paragraphs on which to remove the indents, and drag the indent marker(s) to the margin.

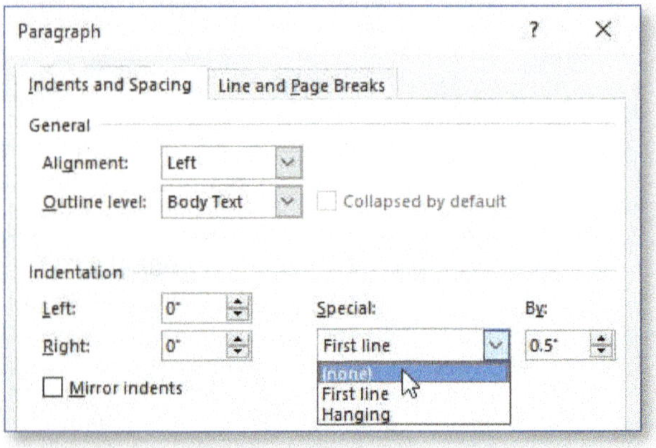

2-24 Remove indents using the *Paragraph* dialog box

PAUSE & PRACTICE: WORD 2-1

In this Pause & Practice project, you format a résumé for Richelle Wilkinson. This résumé is a two-page document, and you change the margins, set tab stops and leaders, and use indents.

File Needed: ***Resume-02.docx*** *(Student data files are available in the* Library *of your SIMnet account)*
Completed Project File Name: ***[your initials] PP W2-1.docx***

1. Open the ***Resume-02*** document from your student data files.
2. Save this document as [your initials] PP W2-1.
3. Change the margins of the résumé.
   a. Click the **Layout** tab.
   b. Click the **Margins** button [*Page Setup* group] and select **Custom Margins** from the drop-down list. The *Page Setup* dialog box opens.
   c. In the *Margins* area (Figure 2-25), click in the **Top** box, delete the existing margin, and type .75.
   d. Click in the **Bottom** box, delete the existing margin, and type .75.
   e. Click the **down arrow** to the right of the *Left* box to change the left margin to **1"**.
   f. Click the **down arrow** to the right of the *Right* box to change the right margin to **1"**.
   g. Click the **Apply to** drop-down list at the bottom of the dialog box and select **Whole document** if it is not already selected.
   h. Click **OK** to apply the new margin settings and close the dialog box.
4. Set a right tab stop with a dash leader.
   a. Select the **"Loomis, CA October 2014 Present"** text below "*HEAD TEACHER, LOOMIS LEARNING CENTER*."
   b. Click the **Paragraph** launcher [*Layout* or *Home* tab] to open the *Paragraph* dialog box.
   c. Click the **Tabs** button in the bottom left of the *Paragraph* dialog box to open the *Tabs* dialog box (Figure 2-26).
   d. Type 6.5 in the *Tab stop position* area.
   e. Select the **Right** radio button in the *Alignment* area.
   f. Select the **3** (dash leader) radio button in the *Leader* area.
   g. Click the **Set** button to set this tab stop and leader.
   h. Click the **OK** button to close the dialog box.
5. Use the *Format Painter* to apply the tab setting to multiple areas of the résumé.
   a. Place the insertion point in the line you just formatted.
   b. Double-click the **Format Painter** button [*Home* tab, *Clipboard* group].

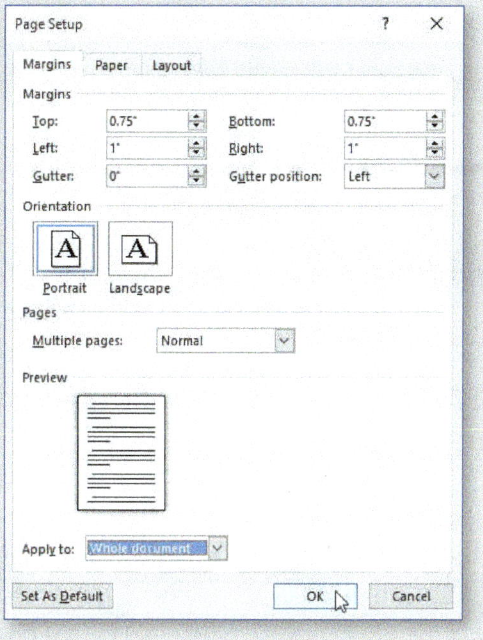

2-25 Change margins in the *Page Setup* dialog box

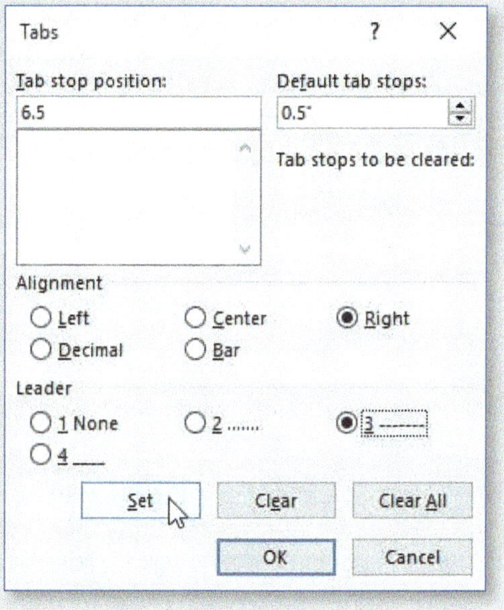

2-26 Set a right tab stop with a dash leader

c. Click each of the city, state, and date lines in the “EXPERIENCE” and “EDUCATION” sections to apply the tab settings as shown in Figure 2-27.
d. Click the **Format Painter** button to turn off copy format.

6. Remove an existing tab stop and set a left tab stop.
   a. On the second page, select the lines of text below the “REFERENCES” heading.
   b. Click the **Paragraph** launcher [*Layout* or *Home* tab] to open the *Paragraph* dialog box.
   c. Click the **Tabs** button in the bottom left of the *Paragraph* dialog box to open the *Tabs* dialog box.
   d. In the *Tab stop position* area, select the existing tab stop (**2.5"**) and click the **Clear** button to remove the existing tab.
   e. Type 3.75 in the *Tab stop position* area.
   f. Select the **Left** radio button in the *Alignment* area if it is not already selected.
   g. Select the **1 None** radio button in the *Leader* area if it is not already selected.
   h. Click the **Set** button to set this left tab stop (Figure 2-28).
   i. Click the **OK** button to close the dialog box.

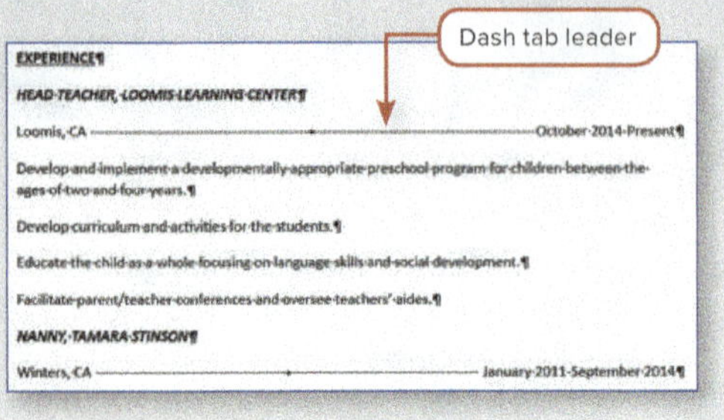

2-27 Use the *Format Painter* to apply tab settings

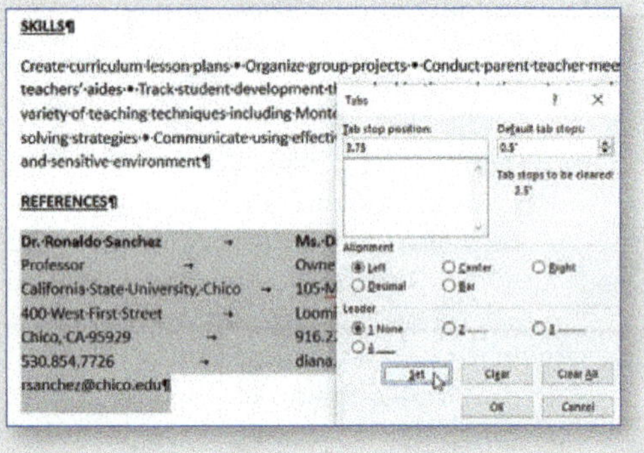

2-28 Set a left tab stop on selected text

7. Apply a left and right indent to selected text.
   a. Place the insertion point in the paragraph below the “PROFILE” heading on the first page.
   b. Click the **Layout** tab.
   c. Click the **Left** indent area [*Paragraph* group], type .25 to replace the existing setting, and press **Enter**.
   d. Click the **Right** indent area, type .25 to replace the existing setting, and press **Enter**.
8. Save and close this document (Figure 2-29).

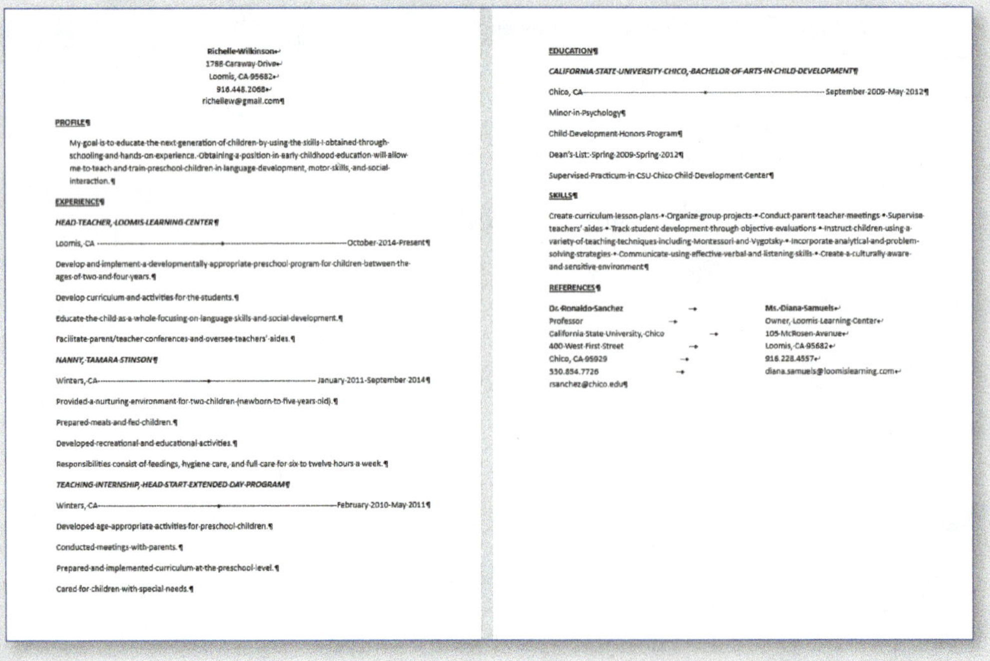

2-29 PP W2-1 completed

SLO 2.4

Inserting Page Numbers, Headers, and Footers

Page numbering, ***headers***, and ***footers*** are regularly used in multiple-page documents. You can set the header, footer, or page number to appear on each page of the document, which means you only have to type the information once, and Word repeats that information on each subsequent page. The header area of a document is above the top margin, and the footer area is below the bottom margin.

Page Numbering

When you use Word to insert page numbers, a ***page number field*** is inserted in the header or footer of the document. This page number field automatically displays the current page number. You can control the page number location and the page number format.

Insert Page Number

Word gives you a variety of page number locations, horizontal alignment options, and number format options. The following is a list of the basic page number placement options:

- *Top of Page*
- *Bottom of Page*
- *Page Margins*
- *Current Position*

HOW TO: Insert a Page Number

1. Click the **Insert** tab.
2. Click the **Page Number** button [*Header & Footer* group]. A drop-down list of options appears (Figure 2-30).
3. Click either **Top of Page** or **Bottom of Page**. Another drop-down list of page number options appears.
    - The top three options in this list are simple page numbers aligned at the left, center, or right.
    - Further down this list there are custom page number options.
4. Click one of the page number options to insert the current page number. The header or footer area opens with the page number inserted, and the *Header & Footer Tools Design* tab opens (Figure 2-31).
5. Click the **Close Header and Footer** button [*Close* group].

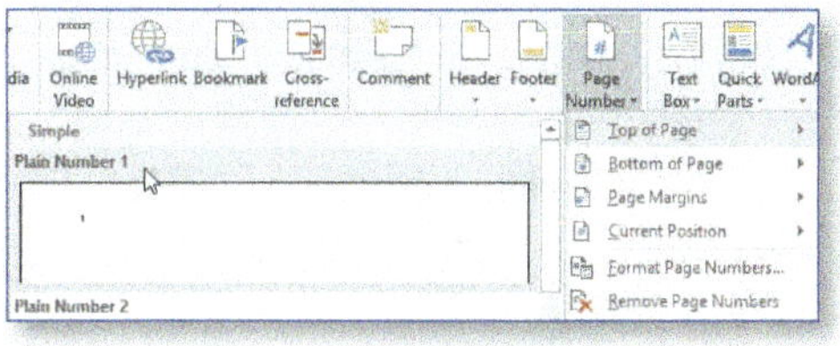

2-30 Insert page number

ANOTHER WAY

Close the header and footer by pressing the **Esc** key or double-clicking in the body of the document.

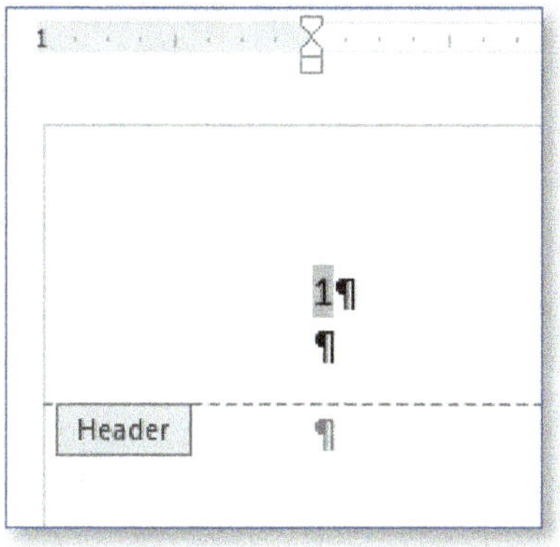

2-31 Page number inserted in the header on the left

Edit Page Number in Header or Footer

When you close the header or footer, the page number appears in gray rather than black like the text of the document. The header and footer areas are outside the boundaries of the margins. If you want to edit the page number or contents of the header or footer, you have to open the header or footer. There are three ways to do this:

- Right-click the header or footer and select **Edit Header** or **Edit Footer**.
- Click the **Insert** tab, click the **Header** or **Footer** button in the *Header & Footer* group, and choose **Edit Header** or **Edit Footer**.
- Double-click the header or footer area of the document.

Different First Page

There are times when you might not want the page number and header or footer to print on the first page, but you want it to appear on the second and continuing pages. For example, on both multiple-page business letters and reports, the page number is typically not on the first page but is on the second and subsequent pages. Word gives you the option to set a ***different first page***.

HOW TO: Set a Different First Page Header and Footer

1. Go to the first page of the document.
2. Open the header or footer if it is not already open. Use one of the following methods to open the header or footer if it is not already open:
   - Right-click the header or footer and select **Edit Header** or **Edit Footer**.
   - Click the **Insert** tab, click the **Header** or **Footer** button in the *Header & Footer* group, and choose **Edit Header** or **Edit Footer**.
   - Double-click in the header or footer area of the document.
3. Click the **Different First Page** check box [*Header & Footer Tools Design* tab, *Options* group] (Figure 2-32).
4. Click the **Close Header and Footer** button [*Close* group]. The page number, header, and footer no longer appear on the first page but do appear on the second and continuing pages.

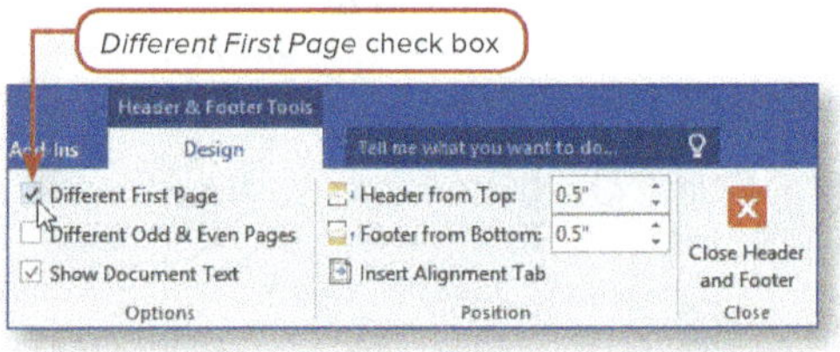

2-32 *Different First Page* check box

MORE INFO

When inserting a page number, header, or footer, it is best to insert it on the first page of the document. This becomes increasingly important as you add section breaks to a document.

Page Number Format

When using page numbering, you might want a different type of page number format, numbering to begin with a different page number, or a chapter number before the page number. The *Page Number Format* dialog box provides you with page numbering options (Figure 2-33).

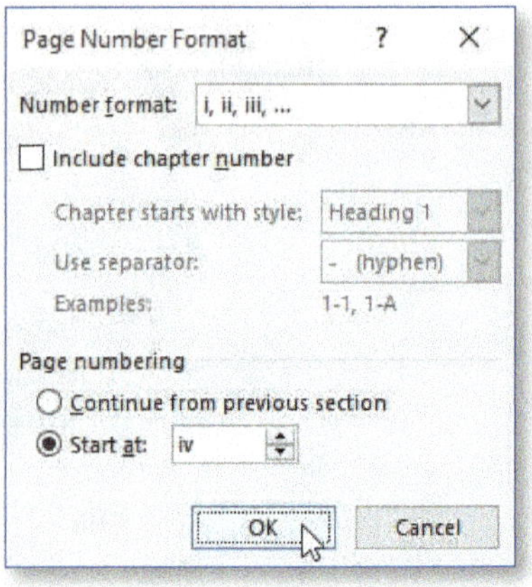

2-33 *Page Number Format* dialog box

▸HOW TO: Format Page Numbers

1. After inserting a page number, click the **Page Number** button [*Header & Footer Tools Design* or *Insert* tab, *Header & Footer* group] and select **Format Page Numbers**. The *Page Number Format* dialog box opens (see Figure 2-33).
2. Click the *Number format* **drop-down list** and select a page number format. There are six preset page numbering options from which to choose.
3. Select an option in the *Page numbering* section to *Continue from previous section* (default setting) or *Start at* a different page number.
   - Click the **Start at** radio button to set a different starting page number.
   - Type in the starting page number or use the up or down arrow to set the starting page number.
4. Click **OK** to close the *Page Number Format* dialog box.
5. Click·the **Close Header and Footer** button [*Close* group].

Remove Page Number

If you want to remove the page numbering from a document, there are two different ways to do this.

- Select **Remove Page Numbers** from the *Page Number* drop-down list (Figure 2-34).
- Open the header or footer and manually delete the page number.

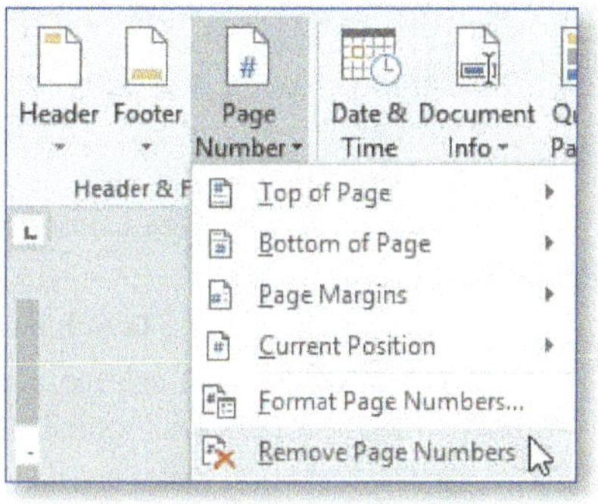

2-34 Remove page numbers

Insert Header and Footer Content

In addition to inserting page numbers into the header or footer of a document, you might want to include the number of pages in the document, date or time, title of the document, company name, or other custom content. You can enter information manually into the header or footer, or you can have Word insert document property fields.

▸HOW TO: Insert Custom Header and Footer Content

1. Click the **Insert** tab.
2. Click the **Header** button and choose **Edit Header** in the drop-down list, or double-click in the *Header* area of the document (above the top margin). The header of the document opens and the *Header & Footer Tools Design* tab displays.
   - When you edit a header or footer, both the header and footer open and the *Header & Footer Tools Design* tab displays.
   - On this tab, there is a *Navigation* group to help you move between the header and footer and move through the different headers and footers in the document (Figure 2-35).
3. Type your information in the *Header* area (Figure 2-36).
   - You can change the formatting and alignment as desired.
   - You can insert a page number with the header or footer open.
4. Click the **Close Header and Footer** button [*Close* group].

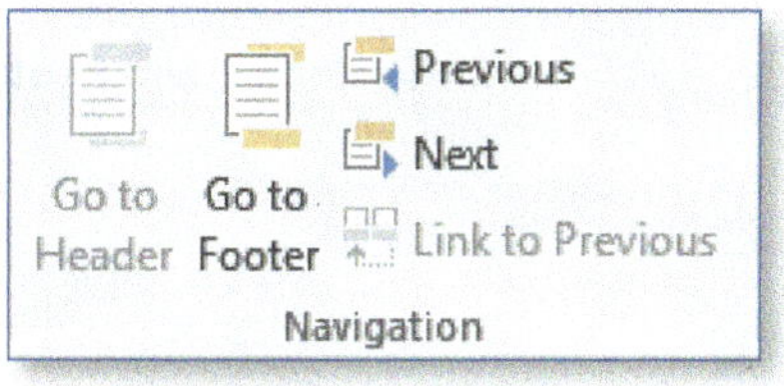

2-35 *Navigation* group on the *Header & Footer Tools Design* tab

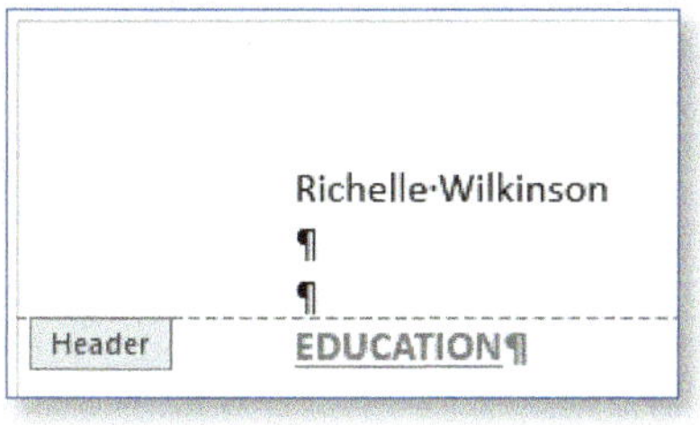

2-36 Enter custom information in the header

> **MORE INFO**
>
> There is a center tab stop at the horizontal midpoint and a right tab stop at the right margin in the header and footer areas. You can move these tab stops, remove them, or add additional tab stops.

Number of Pages Field

In addition to inserting the current page number in a document, you can add a field code to automatically insert the total number of pages in a document (*NumPages* field).

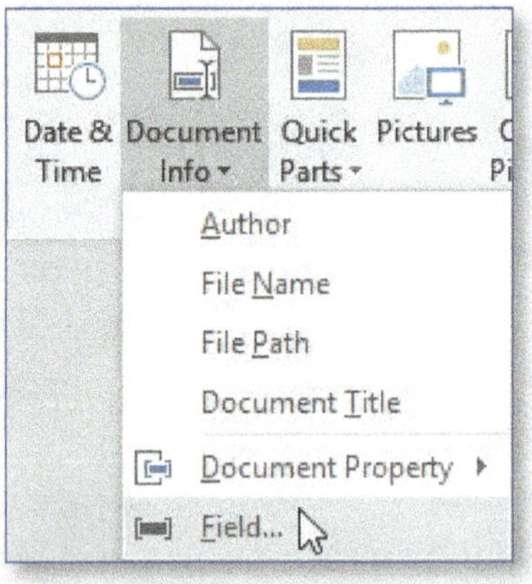

2-37 Insert field code

HOW TO: Insert the Number of Pages Field

1. Open the header or footer. The page number should already be inserted in the document.
2. Click before the page number, type Page, and press the **spacebar**.
3. Click after the page number and press the **spacebar**, type of, and press the **spacebar**.
4. Click the **Document Info** button [*Header & Footer Tools Design* tab, *Insert* group] (Figure 2-37).
   - You can also click the **Quick Parts** button.
5. Select **Field** from the drop-down list. The *Field* dialog box opens (Figure 2-38).
6. In the *Field names* area, scroll down and select **NumPages**. The description of the field is displayed in the *Description* area.
7. In the *Format* area, select a page number format.
8. Click **OK** to close the *Field* dialog box. The number of pages in the document displays (Figure 2-39).
9. Click the **Close Header and Footer** button [*Close* group].

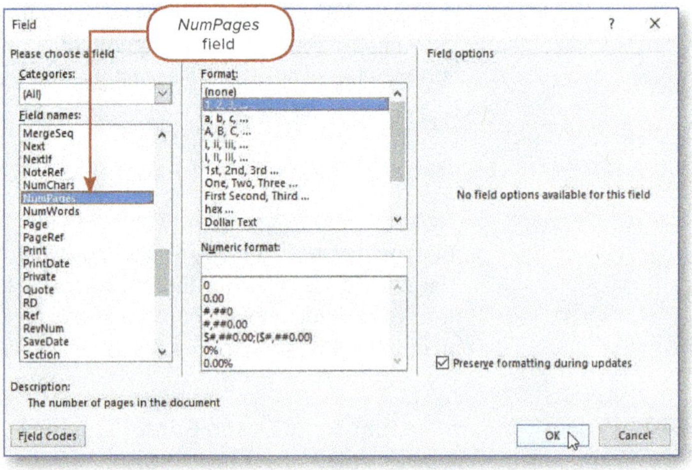

2-38 Insert *NumPages* field from the *Field* dialog box

> **MORE INFO**
>
> When inserting text before or after a page number, be sure to include a space between the word and the page number. Word does not automatically do this for you.

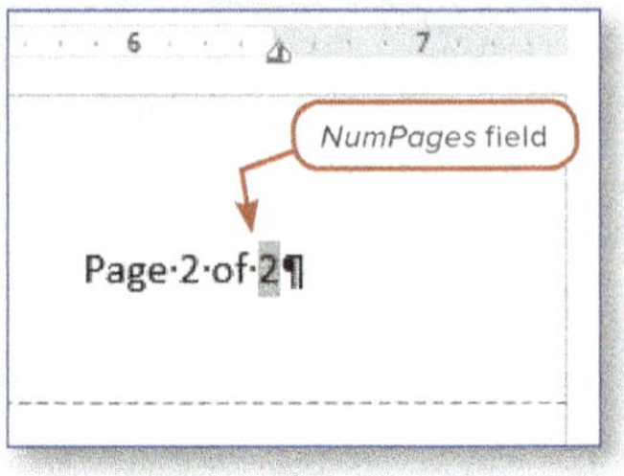

2-39 Page number and number of pages field inserted into the header

Date and Time

You can type a date or the time in the header or footer of a document, or you can have Word insert this information. The advantages of inserting the date and time are that you have a variety of date and time formats from which to choose, and you can choose to have the date and time update automatically each time you open the document.

▸HOW TO: Insert the Date and Time

1. Open the header or footer area and position the insertion point at the position where you want the date inserted.
2. Click the **Date & Time** button [*Header & Footer Tools Design* tab, *Insert* group]. The *Date and Time* dialog box opens (Figure 2-40).
3. Select the date or time format to use in the *Available formats* area.
4. Check the **Update automatically** check box if you want the date to update automatically.
   - Do not check *Update automatically* on time-sensitive documents where the date should remain constant.
5. Click **OK** to close the *Date and Time* dialog box. The date displays the header.
6. Click the **Close Header and Footer** button [*Close* group].

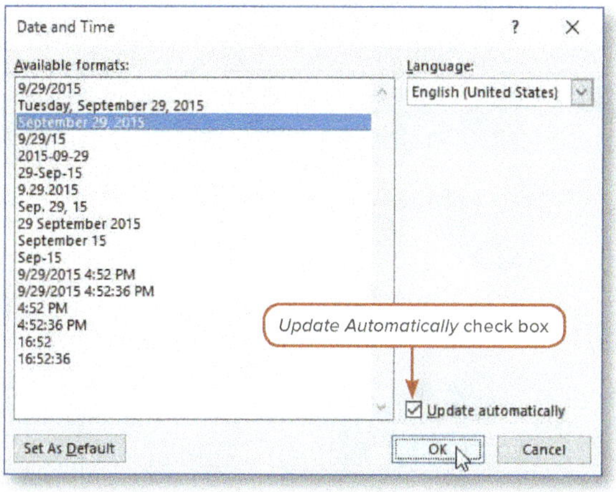

2-40 *Date and Time* dialog box

> **MORE INFO**
>
> Inserting a date or time is not limited to headers and footers. You can insert the date or time in the body of a document by clicking **Date & Time** [*Insert* tab, *Text* group].

Document Properties

When you have entered document properties in a Word document, you can automatically insert this information in the header or footer. For example, you might want to include the title of the document, name of the author, or date last modified. One of the advantages of inserting document properties rather than typing this information is that when you update the document properties, these fields automatically update in the header or footer and throughout the document.

▸HOW TO: Insert Document Properties

1. Open the header or footer and place the insertion point at the location where you want the document property inserted.
2. Click the **Document Info** button [*Header & Footer Tools Design* tab, *Insert* group] (Figure 2-41).
3. Select the document property field or click **Document Property** and select the document property of your choice from the drop-down list. The document property displays in the document (Figure 2-42).
   - You can also click the **Quick Parts** button [*Header & Footer Tools Design* tab, *Insert* group] and select **Document Property**.
   - Press the **right arrow** key on your keyboard to deselect a document property field.
4. Click the **Close Header and Footer** button [*Close* group].

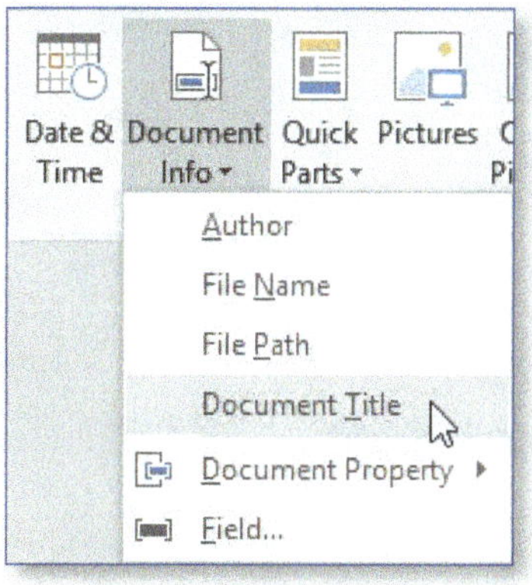

2-41 Insert document property field

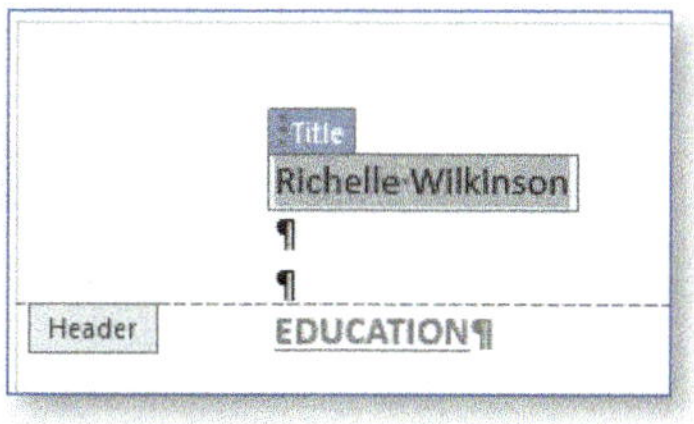

2-42 *Title* document property field inserted in the header

MORE INFO

Inserting document properties is not limited to headers and footers. Click the **Quick Parts** button [*Insert* tab, *Text* group] to insert this information in the body of a document.

Built-In Headers, Footers, and Page Numbers

In addition to inserting basic page numbers, manually adding header or footer content, and inserting date and time, Word provides you with a variety of built-in custom header, footer, and page number format options. Many of the header and footer options include document properties that are automatically inserted and updated.

HOW TO: Insert a Built-In Header, Footer, or Page Number

1. Click the **Insert** tab.
2. Click the **Header**, **Footer**, or **Page Number** button [*Header & Footer* group] and select a built-in header, footer, or page number from the choices in the drop-down list (Figure 2-43). The selected content displays into the document.
   - Document property fields update automatically with document property information.
   - Some fields, such as *Pick the date*, require you to input or select information.
3. Click the **Close Header and Footer** button [*Close* group].

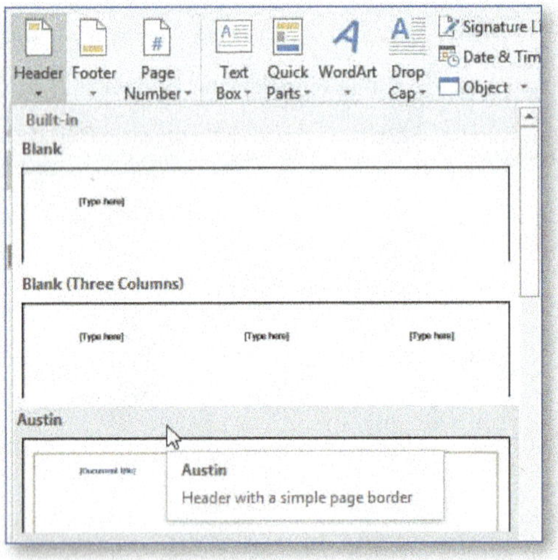

2-43 List of built-in headers

Keep in mind when you are using built-in headers, footers, and page numbers that many of these use tables, graphics, and advanced formatting, which makes editing more challenging without a thorough understanding of this type of content.

PAUSE & PRACTICE: WORD 2-2

In this Pause & Practice project, you modify the résumé from *Pause & Practice 2-1*. You add a header that appears only on the second page of this document and insert a document property field, page number, and Word field into the header.

File Needed: ***[your initials] PP W2-1.docx***
Completed Project File Name: ***[your initials] PP W2-2.docx***

1. Open the ***[your initials] PP W2-1*** document completed in *Pause & Practice 2-1*.
2. Save this document as [your initials] PP W2-2.

3. Edit the document properties.
   a. Click the **File** tab to open the *Backstage* view.
   b. In the *Info* area, click in the **Title** document property text box and type Richelle Wilkinson.
   c. Click the **Back** arrow to return to the résumé.
4. Insert a document property field in the header of the résumé.
   a. Place the insertion point at the beginning of the first page.
   b. Click the **Insert** tab.
   c. Click the **Header** button [*Header & Footer* group] and select **Edit Header** from the drop-down list. The header on the first page opens.
   d. Click the **Document Info** button [*Header & Footer Tools Design* tab, *Insert* group] and select **Document Title** from the drop-down list. The *Title* document property displays in the header.
   e. Leave the header open for the next instructions.
5. Insert a page number and number of pages field in the header and set it to display only on the second page.
   a. With the header still open, press the **right arrow** key once to deselect the document property field you just inserted.
   b. Press **Tab** two times to move to the right margin, type Page and **space** once.
   c. Click the **Page Number** button [*Header & Footer* group], select **Current Position** from the drop-down list, and select **Plain Number**. The page number displays in the header.
   d. **Space** once, type of, and **space** once.
   e. Click the **Document Info** (or **Quick Parts**) button [*Header & Footer Tools Design* tab, *Insert* group] and select **Field** from the drop-down list. The *Field* dialog box opens.
   f. Select **NumPages** in the *Field names* area (this is the field code to insert the total number of pages in the document) (Figure 2-44).

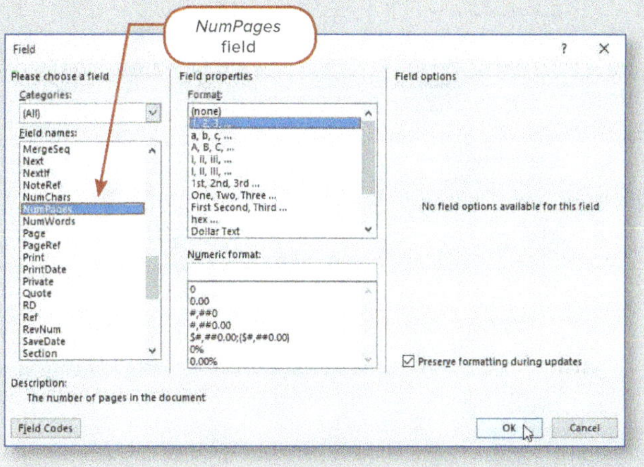

2-44 Insert *NumPages* field

   g. Select **1, 2, 3** in the *Format* area and click **OK** to insert the number of pages in the header.
   h. Press **Enter** two times to insert two blank lines after the header.
   i. Check to ensure that there are spaces between each of the words and page numbers.
   j. Check the **Different First Page** check box [*Header & Footer Tools Design* tab, *Options* group]. This removes the header content from the first page, but the header content displays on the second page (Figure 2-45).

2-45 Header with document property field, page number, and number of pages field

   k. Click the **Close Header and Footer** button [*Close* group] to close the header and return to the document.

6. Save and close the document (Figure 2-46).

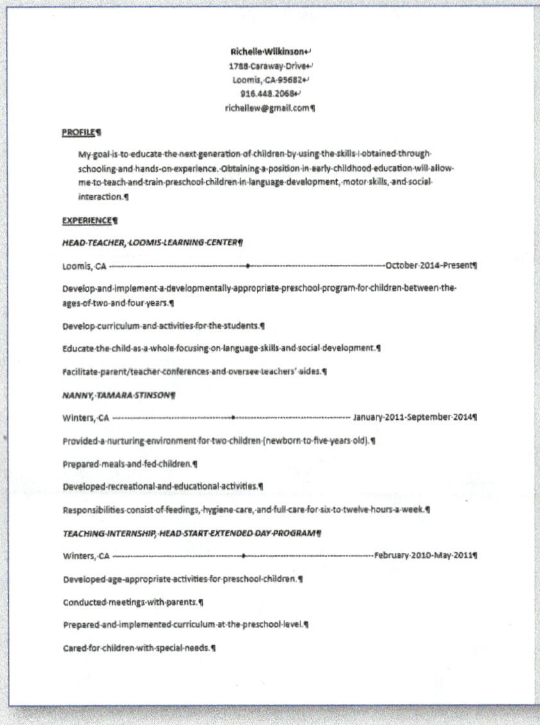
Richelle Wilkinson
1788 Caraway Drive
Loomis, CA 95682
916.448.2068
richellew@gmail.com

PROFILE

My goal is to educate the next generation of children by using the skills I obtained through schooling and hands-on experience. Obtaining a position in early childhood education will allow me to teach and train preschool children in language development, motor skills, and social interaction.

EXPERIENCE

HEAD TEACHER, LOOMIS LEARNING CENTER

Loomis, CA .... October 2014-Present

Develop and implement a developmentally appropriate preschool program for children between the ages of two and four years.

Develop curriculum and activities for the students.

Educate the child as a whole focusing on language skills and social development.

Facilitate parent/teacher conferences and oversee teachers' aides.

NANNY, TAMARA STINSON

Winters, CA .... January 2011-September 2014

Provided a nurturing environment for two children (newborn to five years old).

Prepared meals and fed children.

Developed recreational and educational activities.

Responsibilities consist of feedings, hygiene care, and full care for six to twelve hours a week.

TEACHING INTERNSHIP, HEAD START EXTENDED DAY PROGRAM

Winters, CA .... February 2010-May 2011

Developed age-appropriate activities for preschool children.

Conducted meetings with parents.

Prepared and implemented curriculum at the preschool level.

Cared for children with special needs.

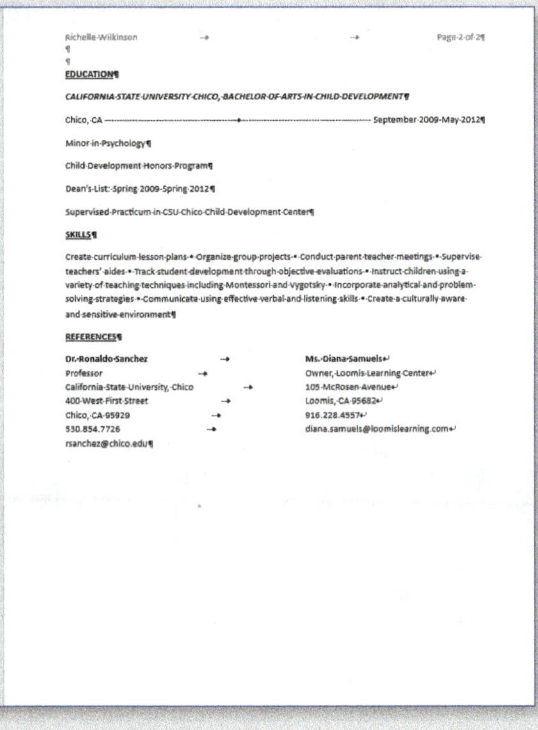
Richelle Wilkinson Page 2 of 2

EDUCATION

CALIFORNIA STATE UNIVERSITY CHICO, BACHELOR OF ARTS IN CHILD DEVELOPMENT

Chico, CA .... September 2009-May 2012

Minor in Psychology

Child Development Honors Program

Dean's List: Spring 2009-Spring 2012

Supervised Practicum in CSU Chico Child Development Center

SKILLS

Create curriculum lesson plans • Organize group projects • Conduct parent teacher meetings • Supervise teachers' aides • Track student development through objective evaluations • Instruct children using a variety of teaching techniques including Montessori and Vygotsky • Incorporate analytical and problem-solving strategies • Communicate using effective verbal and listening skills • Create a culturally aware and sensitive environment

REFERENCES

Dr. Ronaldo Sanchez
Professor
California State University, Chico
400 West First Street
Chico, CA 95929
530.854.7726
rsanchez@chico.edu

Ms. Diana Samuels
Owner, Loomis Learning Center
105 McRosen Avenue
Loomis, CA 95682
916.228.4557
diana.samuels@loomislearning.com

2-46 PP W2-2 completed

SLO 2.5

Using Page and Section Breaks

As you're typing a document and you get to the bottom of the page, Word automatically moves to the top of the next page so you can continue typing; this is referred to as a ***soft page break***. The document's content and margins determine how much information fits on a page and what information flows to a new page.

There may be times when you want to start a new page before you get to the bottom margin or you might want different margins or page orientation in a different section of your document. Word provides options for page and section breaks to control page endings and formatting (Figure 2-47).

> **MORE INFO**
>
> Turn **Show/Hide** [*Home* tab, *Paragraph* group] on when working with page and section breaks, so you can view the placement of these breaks.

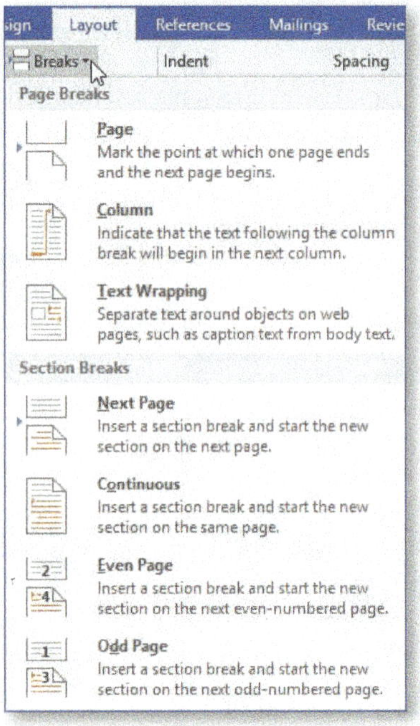

2-47 Page and section breaks

Page Breaks

Page breaks end one page and begin a new page. When you insert a *Page* break, you control where one page ends and a new page begins. There are three different types of page breaks: *Page*, *Column*, and *Text Wrapping*.

HOW TO: Insert a Page Break

1. Position the insertion point at the point in your document where you want to end one page and begin a new page.
2. Click the **Layout** tab.
3. Click the **Breaks** button [*Page Setup* group]. A drop-down list appears.
4. Select **Page** from the drop-down list. A page break displays in the document (Figure 2-48).
   - Turn on **Show/Hide** [*Home* tab, *Paragraph* group].
   - The *Page Break* indicator is visible and displays where the page breaks (Figure 2-49).

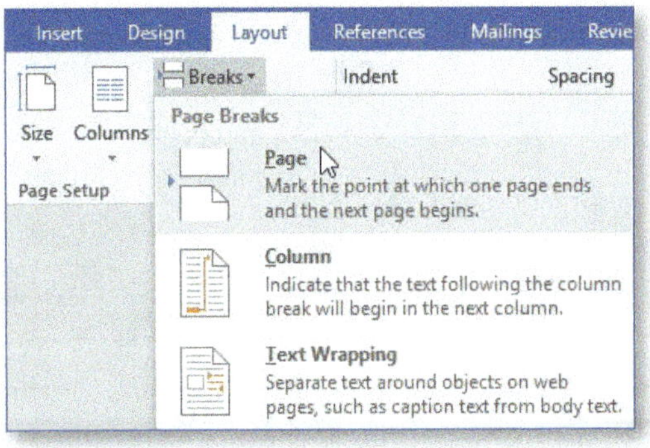

2-48 Insert *Page* break

ANOTHER WAY

Press **Ctrl+Enter** to insert a page break at the insertion point.

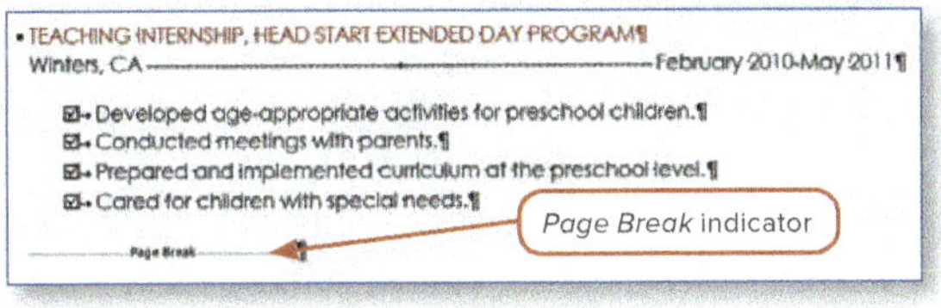

2-49 *Page* break inserted in a document

Section Breaks

Section breaks allow you even more formatting control over your document than page breaks. Section breaks can be used to format different headers, footers, and page numbering in different sections of your document. For example, if you want one page in your document to be landscape orientation, you can use a section break to control the format of an individual section. There are four different types of section breaks:

- ***Next Page***: Insert a section break and start the new section on the next page.
- ***Continuous***: Insert a section break and start the new section on the same page.
- ***Even Page***: Insert a section break and start the new section on the next even-numbered page.
- ***Odd Page***: Insert a section break and start the new section on the next odd-numbered page.

HOW TO: Insert a Next Page Section Break

1. Position the insertion point at the point in your document where you want to end one page and begin new section on a new page.
2. Click the **Layout** tab.
3. Click the **Breaks** button [*Page Setup* group]. A drop-down list appears.
4. Select **Next Page** from the drop-down list. A next page section break displays in the document.
   - Turn on **Show/Hide** [*Home* tab, *Paragraph* group].
   - The *Section Break (Next Page)* indicator is visible and displays where the next page section break occurs (Figure 2-50).

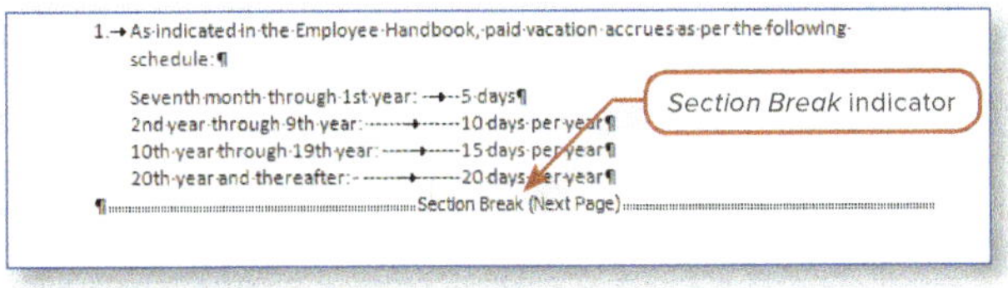

2-50 *Next Page* section break inserted in a document

Edit Page and Section Breaks

When finalizing a document, you might need to change the placement of a page or section break or remove a page or section break from the document. You can delete and move breaks in the same way you delete and move text from a document.

To delete a page or section break, select the break and press **Delete**.

There are two different ways to move a section or page break to a new location. First select the **Page Break** or **Section Break**, and then use one of the move options below:

- Cut and paste
- Drag and drop (Figure 2-51)

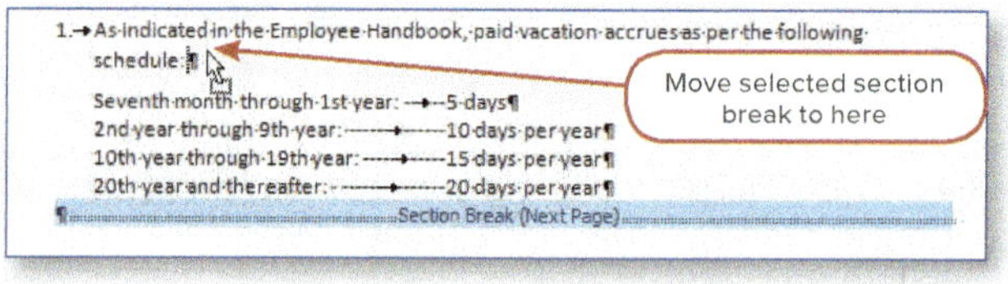

2-51 Move section break using drag and drop

SLO 2.6

Using Bulleted, Numbered, and Multilevel Lists

Bulleted and ***numbered lists*** highlight important information. Generally, use bulleted lists when the order of information is not important, and use numbered lists for sequential information. A ***Multilevel list*** can combine a variety of numbers, letters, and bullets. Word provides you with built-in bulleted, numbered, and multilevel lists, but you can also customize how the information in the list displays and aligns.

> **MORE INFO**
>
> When using bulleted and numbered lists, do not use a period at the end of lists containing only words or short phrases. If you are using complete sentences in your list, use a period at the end of each sentence.

Create a Bulleted List

You can create a bulleted list from existing text or you can create a new bulleted list. You choose the type of bullet to use from the *Bullet Library* in the *Bullets* drop-down list.

HOW TO: Create a Bulleted List

1. Select the text to be converted to a bulleted list, or, if you are beginning a new bulleted list, place the insertion point at the location where you want to begin the list.
2. Click the **Bullets** drop-down arrow [*Home* tab, *Paragraph* group] to open the library of bullet options (Figure 2-52).
   - If you click the *Bullets* button (not the *Bullets* drop-down arrow), the most recently used bullet is used for the bulleted list.
3. Select a bullet from the list of options.
4. Type your information after the bullet if you are typing a new bulleted list.
5. Press **Enter** after a bulleted item to add another bullet.
6. Press **Enter** two times after the last bullet, or click the **Bullets** button to turn off bullets.

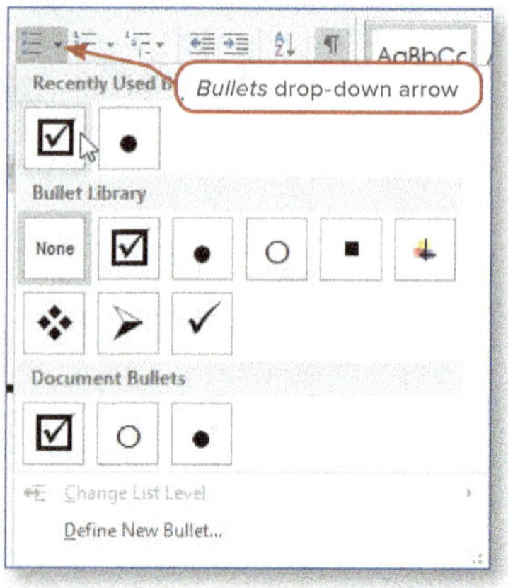

2-52 *Bullets* drop-down list

By default, bulleted lists are formatted using a hanging indent. The first line is indented 0.25" and the hanging indent is set at 0.5". You can adjust the indent using the *Decrease Indent* or *Increase Indent* buttons, ruler, or *Paragraph* dialog box.

You can add new bulleted items in the middle or at the end of the list by pressing **Enter** in front of or at the end of an existing bulleted item. To add a bulleted item before the first item in the list, click at the beginning of the first item and press **Enter**.

MORE INFO

You can use a line break (**Shift+Enter**) at the end of a bulleted sentence to add a blank line between bulleted items.

Customize a Bulleted List

In addition to using the bullets listed in the *Bullets Library*, you can select and use a custom bullet. You have the option of using a symbol from one of the font groups, or you can use a picture. If you use a picture, you can select one from the Bing Image Search or import a graphic of your own to use as a bullet.

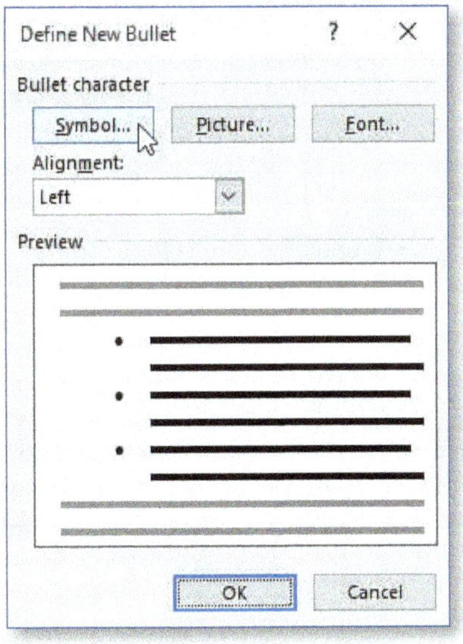

2-53 *Define New Bullet* dialog box

HOW TO: Customize a Bulleted List

1. Select the bulleted list.
2. Click the **Bullets** drop-down arrow [*Home* tab, *Paragraph* group] and select **Define New Bullet**. The *Define New Bullet* dialog box opens (Figure 2-53).
3. Click the **Symbol** or **Picture** button to open the *Symbol* or *Picture* dialog box.
   - If you click the **Symbol** button, the *Symbol* dialog box opens (Figure 2-54). From the *Font* drop-down list, you can select a symbol from any of the font sets (the most common are *Symbol*, *Wingdings*, and *Webdings*) or from *Recently used symbols*.
   - Each symbol has a character code to identify the symbol (see Figure 2-54).
   - If you click the **Picture** button, the *Insert Pictures* dialog box opens. You can import your own picture bullet from a file or use Bing Image Search to locate a picture to use as a bullet.
4. Select the bullet to use and click **OK** (or **Insert** or **Open** depending on the open dialog box) to close the dialog box.
5. Click **OK** to close the *Define New Bullet* dialog box.

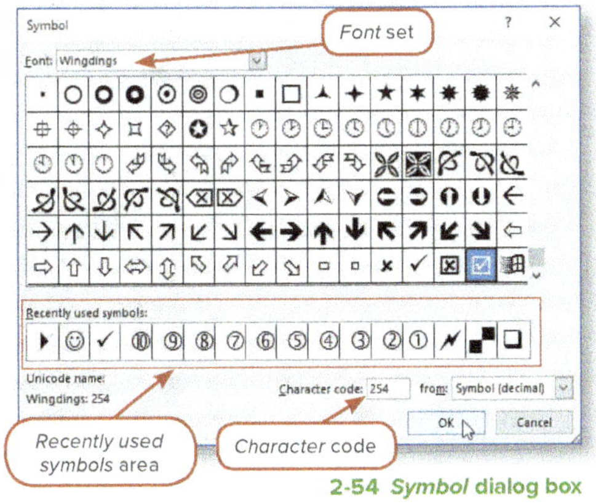

2-54 *Symbol* dialog box

You also have the option of having multiple levels of bullets with a different bullet for each level. Each subsequent bullet level is indented to distinguish it from the previous level. There are a few ways to increase or decrease the bullet level.

- Click the **Bullets** drop-down arrow [*Home* tab, *Paragraph* group] and select a bullet list level from the **Change List Level** drop-down list (Figure 2-55).
- Select or click at the beginning of a bulleted item and press **Tab** to increase bullet level.
- Select or click at the beginning of a bulleted item and click the **Increase Indent** button [*Home* tab, *Paragraph* group] to increase bullet level.
- Press **Shift+Tab** or click the **Decrease Indent** button to decrease the bullet level.

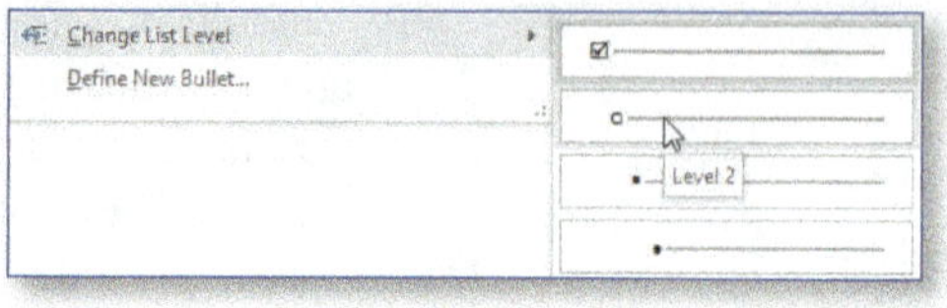

2-55 Change bulleted list level

Create a Numbered List

Creating a numbered list is similar to creating a bulleted list. The ***Numbering Library*** in the *Numbering* drop-down list contains number format options.

HOW TO: Create a Numbered List

1. Select the text you want to convert to a numbered list, or, if you are beginning a new numbered list, place the insertion point at the location where you want to begin the list.
2. Click the **Numbering** drop-down arrow [*Home* tab, *Paragraph* group] to open the *Numbering Library* of number format options (Figure 2-56).
   - If you click the *Numbering* button, the most recently used number format is used for the numbered list.
3. Select a number style from the list of options.
4. Type your information after the number if you are typing a new numbered list.
5. Press **Enter** after a numbered item to add another numbered item.
6. Press **Enter** two times after the last numbered item, or click the **Numbering** button to turn off numbering.

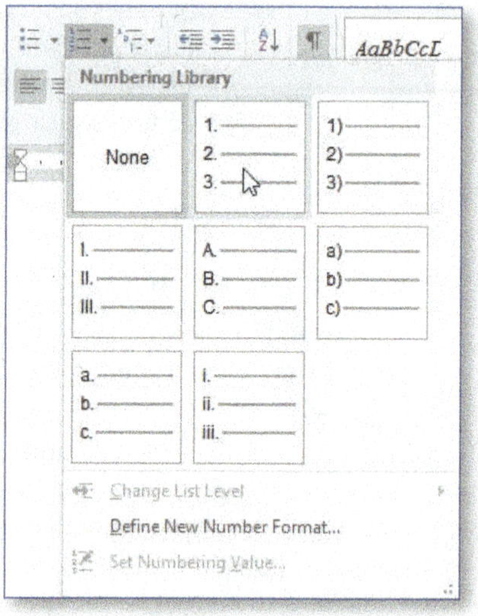

2-56 Numbering format options

ANOTHER WAY

Both the *Numbering* and *Bullets* drop-down lists are available from the mini toolbar when you select or right-click text.

Customize a Numbered List

In addition to being able to select a format from the *Numbering Library*, you also have the options to *Change List Level*, *Define New Number Format*, and *Set Numbering Value*.

The ***Change List Level*** option in the *Numbering* drop-down list allows you to select the level of the list. The numbering of each subsequent level of the list is dependent upon the number format you select.

You are not limited to the numbering formats available in the *Numbering* drop-down list. The ***Define New Number Format*** option allows you to customize how the numbered list displays.

▶ HOW TO: Customize a Numbered List

1. Select the text where you want to change the number format, or, if you are beginning a new numbered list, place the insertion point at the location where you want to begin the list.
2. Click the **Numbering** drop-down arrow [*Home* tab, *Paragraph* group], and select **Define New Number Format**. The *Define New Number Format* dialog box opens (Figure 2-57).
3. Click the **Number style** drop-down arrow to select a number format from the list of options.
   - You can also change the numbering font by clicking the **Font** button and selecting a font, size, and style to apply to the numbered list.
4. In the *Number format* area, customize how the numbers display.
   - Typically, a period follows the numbers, but you can change this to an ending parenthesis, hyphen, other character, or no punctuation.
5. Click the **Alignment** drop-down arrow to change number alignment.
   - Numbers align on the left by default, but you can change the number alignment to center or right.
6. The *Preview* area displays how your number format will appear in your document.
7. Click **OK** to apply the number format and close the dialog box.

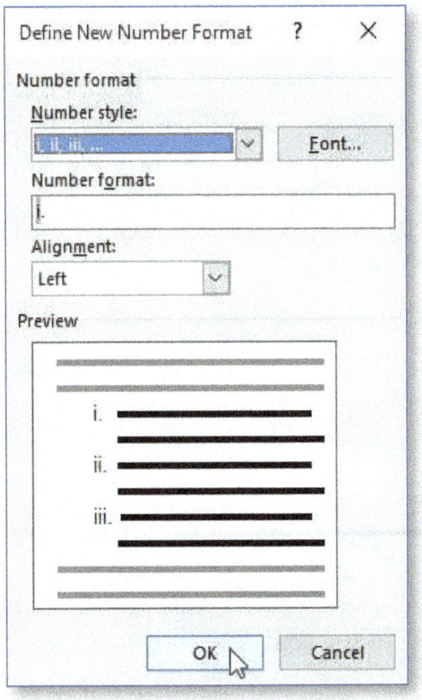

2-57 ***Define New Number Format* dialog box**

The ***Set Numbering Value*** dialog box includes options to *Start new list* or *Continue from previous list*. You can also set the number value to begin a new list. Open the *Set Numbering Value* dialog box from the *Numbering* drop-down list or right-click a numbered list and select *Set Numbering Value* from the context menu (Figure 2-58).

When using numbering, the context menu lists options to *Adjust List Indents*, *Restart at 1*, *Continue Numbering*, and *Set Numbering Value* (Figure 2-59).

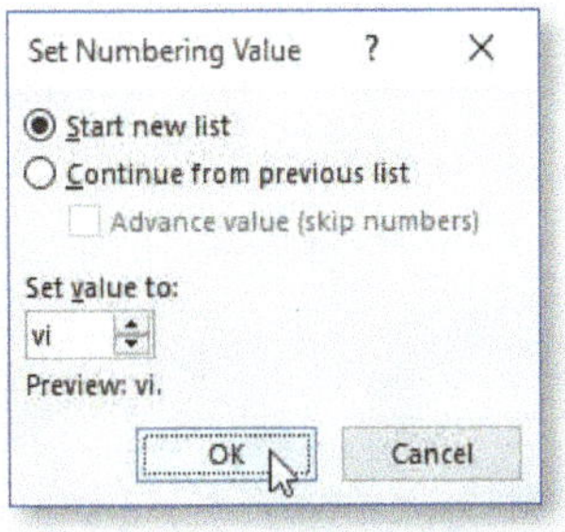

2-58 ***Set Numbering Value* dialog box**

> **MORE INFO**
>
> Use the *Format Painter* to copy numbered or bulleted list formatting to other areas in a document.

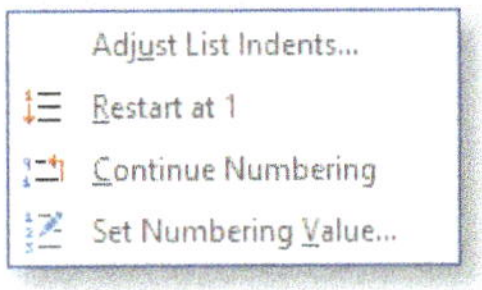

2-59 Context menu numbering options

Multilevel Lists

Multilevel lists allow you to customize a list using a combination of numbers, letters, or bullets. Word provides you with a *List Library* from which to select a multilevel list. You can customize an existing multilevel list or define your own list.

As you define a new multilevel list, you have the following options to customize each level of the list:

- Number format including font and starting number
- Number style, which can be a number, letter, Roman numeral, or bullet
- Position of the number and the text that follows

▸ HOW TO: Define a New Multilevel List

1. Select the text or the beginning point on which to apply a multilevel list.
2. Click the **Multilevel List** drop-down arrow [*Home* tab, *Paragraph* group].
3. Select **Define New Multilevel list** from the drop-down list. The *Define new Multilevel list* dialog box opens (Figure 2-60).
4. Click the **More** button in the bottom left of the dialog box to display all formatting options.
5. In the *Click level to modify* area, select the level you want to modify.
6. In the *Number format* area, select the number format, starting number, and number style for the selected level.
7. In the *Position* area, set the *Number alignment*, the *Aligned at* measurement (which is the first line indent), *Text indent at* measurement (which is the hanging indent).
8. Click the **Set for All Levels** button to open the *Set for All Levels* dialog box where you to set the indents for all levels (Figure 2-61).
9. Click **OK** to apply the multilevel list settings.

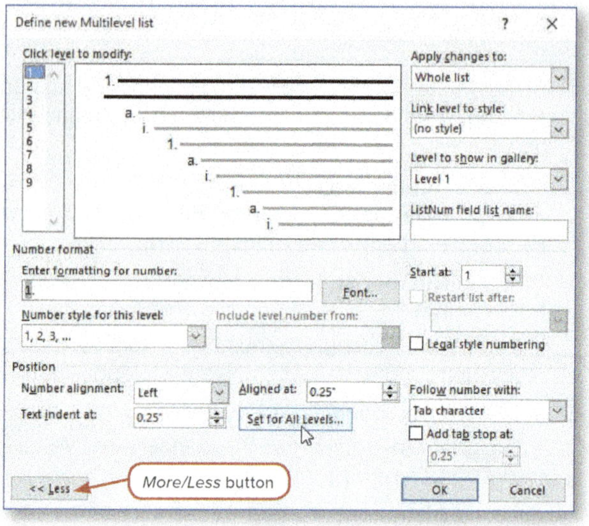

2-60 ***Define new Multilevel list*** **dialog box**

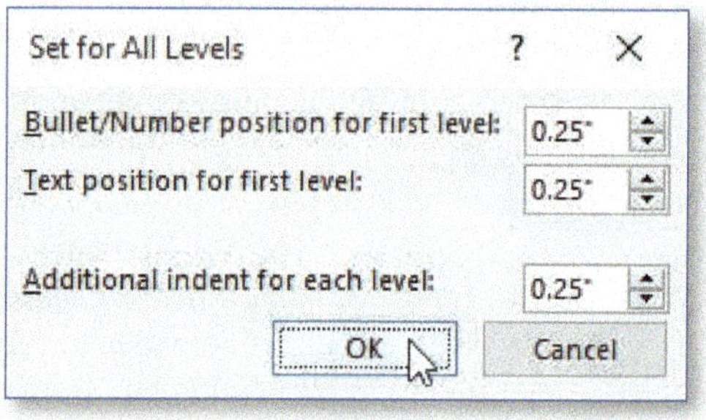

2-61 ***Set for All Levels*** **dialog box**

SLO 2.7

Using Styles and Themes

Styles are a collection of preset formatting that you can apply to a paragraph or selected text. A style can control the font, font size, style, color, effects, indents, line spacing, paragraph spacing, and borders applied to text. You can use styles to apply this preset formatting to titles, section headings, paragraph headings, text, lists, and tables. ***Themes*** are a collection of fonts, colors, and effects that you can apply to an entire document. Both styles and themes keep the formatting consistent throughout a single document or multiple documents.

Style Gallery

The ***Style gallery*** in the *Styles* group on the *Home* tab provides you with numerous built-in styles to apply to selected text in a document (Figure 2-62). The *Style* gallery does not display all of the available styles but rather displays the more commonly used styles.

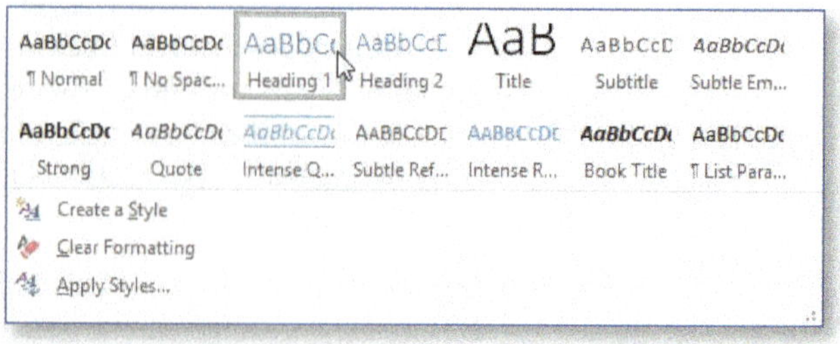

2-62 ***Style*** **gallery**

Apply a Built-In Style

You can quickly preview or apply styles to selected text or paragraphs. To preview a style, place the pointer on a style in the *Style* gallery. A live preview of the style displays on the selected text or paragraph. You can apply a style to the text by clicking a style in the *Style* gallery.

HOW TO: Apply a Built-In Style from the Style Gallery

1. Select the text or paragraph where you want to apply the style.
2. Select a style from the *Style* gallery [*Home* tab, *Styles* group].
   - To see all of the styles in the *Style* gallery, click the **More** button (Figure 2-63).
   - To see the next row of styles available in the *Style* gallery, click the **down arrow** at the right side of the gallery.

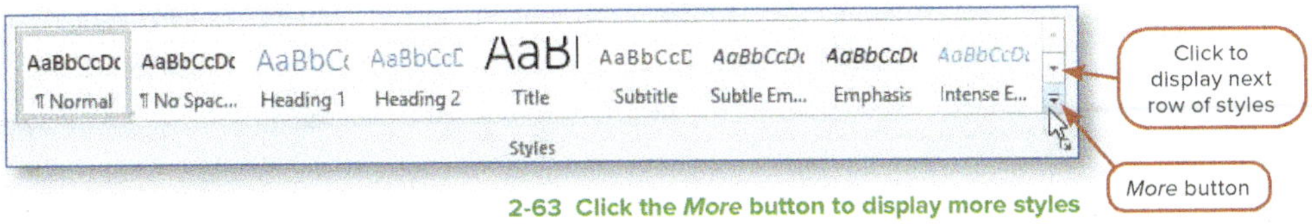

2-63 Click the *More* button to display more styles

ANOTHER WAY

Apply a style to selected text by selecting or right-clicking text, choosing **Styles** from the mini toolbar, and selecting the style to apply.

Modify a Style

Once a style has been applied to the text, you can change the formatting of this text. One way to do this is to make changes to font, font size, color, style, effects, etc., to the selected text without actually changing the style.

The other option is to modify the style. The advantage of modifying a style when you make a change is that the style will be consistent when applied to other text in a document. When you modify a style, text formatted with the modified style automatically updates to match the modified style. There are two ways to modify a style:

- ***Update [style name] to Match Selection***
- ***Modify*** style

HOW TO: Update Style to Match Selection

1. Apply a style to selected text.
2. Make formatting changes on the text where the style was applied.
3. Select the text you changed.
4. Right-click the style in the *Style* gallery and choose **Update *[style name]* to Match Selection** (Figure 2-64).
   - The style updates to match the selected text.
   - All other text with this style applied updates automatically.

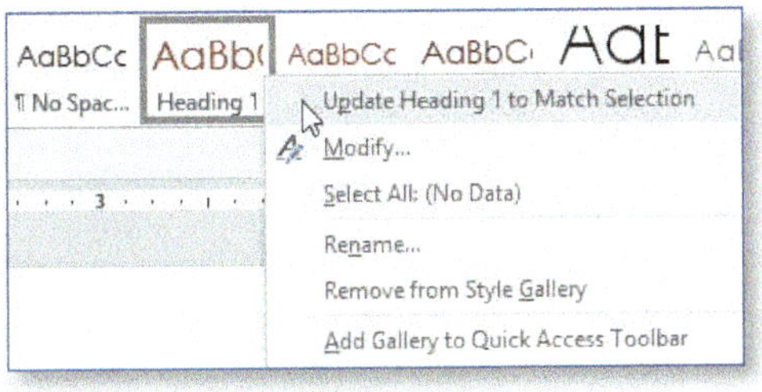

2-64 Update style to match selected text

You can also modify a style using the *Modify Style* dialog box.

HOW TO: Modify an Existing Style

1. Right-click the style to modify in the *Style* gallery and select **Modify**. The *Modify Style* dialog box opens (Figure 2-65).
2. Make desired changes to the style. You can make basic formatting changes in the *Formatting* area of this dialog box.
3. Click the **Format** button at the bottom left to open other dialog boxes, such as *Font, Paragraph, Tabs, Borders*, etc.
   - Make desired formatting changes to the style and click **OK** to apply changes.
   - The formatting changes display in the *Preview* area.
4. Click **OK** to apply the style change and to close the *Modify Style* dialog box.

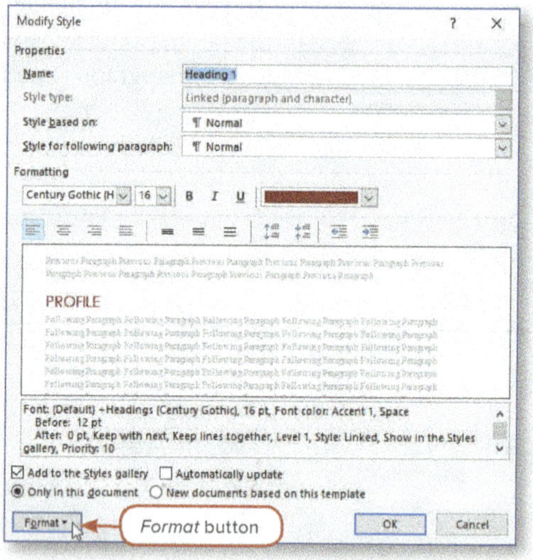

2-65 *Modify Style* dialog box

Apply a Theme

A theme is a collection of fonts, colors, and effects. Themes are similar to styles, but instead of just applying format to selected text, themes apply to an entire document. All documents have a theme; the default theme for a new document is *Office*. You can change the theme of a document or you can individually change the *Theme Colors, Theme Fonts*, or *Theme Effects* set in a document.

HOW TO: Apply a Document Theme

1. Click the **Design** tab.
2. Click the **Themes** button [*Document Formatting* group].
3. Select the theme to apply from the *Themes* gallery (Figure 2-66).
4. Click the **Colors, Fonts**, or **Effects** buttons [*Design* tab, *Document Formatting* group] to change each of these individually within the existing theme.

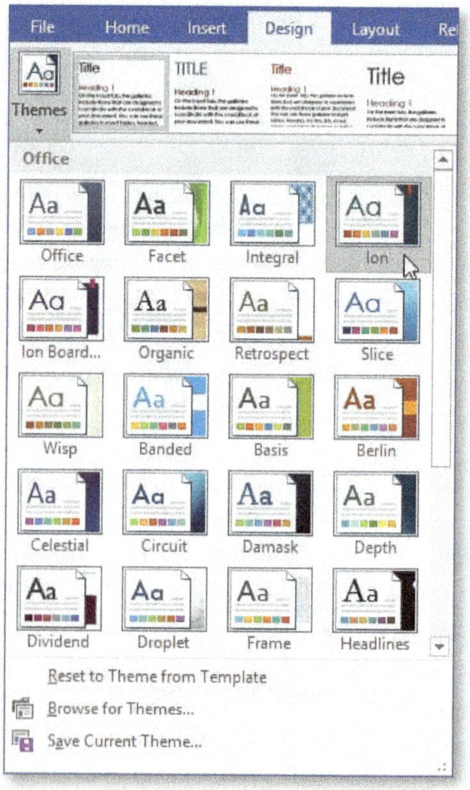

2-66 Change the *Theme* of a document

PAUSE & PRACTICE: WORD 2-3

In this Pause & Practice project, you modify the résumé you edited in *Pause & Practice 2-2*. You add a bulleted list, customize the bulleted list, insert a page break, apply and modify styles, and apply a document theme.

File Needed: ***[your initials] PP W2-2.docx***
Completed Project File Name: ***[your initials] PP W2-3.docx***

1. Open the ***[your initials] PP W2-2*** document completed in *Pause & Practice 2-2*.
2. Save this document as [your initials] PP W2-3.
3. Convert text to a bulleted list and customize the bullet.
   a. Select the four paragraphs of text below the "EXPERIENCE" heading and the city, state, and date line.
   b. Click the **Bullets** button [*Home* tab, *Paragraph* group]. The selected text converts to a bulleted list (Figure 2-67).
   c. With the bulleted paragraphs still selected, click the **Bullets** drop-down arrow and select **Define New Bullet**. The *Define New Bullet* dialog box opens.
   d. Click the **Symbol** button. The *Symbol* dialog box opens (Figure 2-68).
   e. Click the **Font** drop-down list and scroll down to select **Wingdings**.
   f. Scroll down the list of symbols and select the **check box** symbol (*Character code* 254).
   g. Click **OK** to close the *Symbol* dialog box.
   h. Click **OK** to close the *Define New Bullet* dialog box.

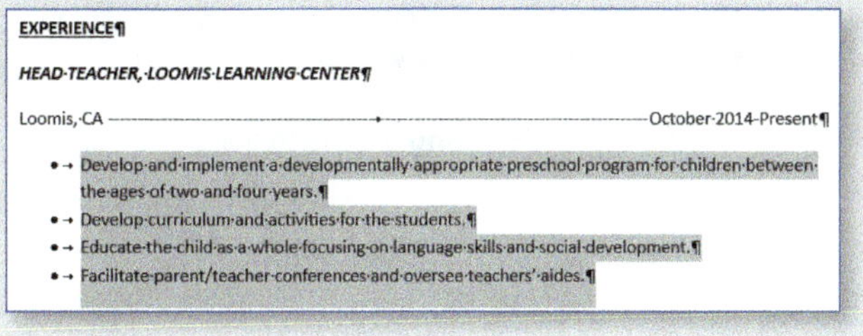

2-67 Apply bullets to selected text

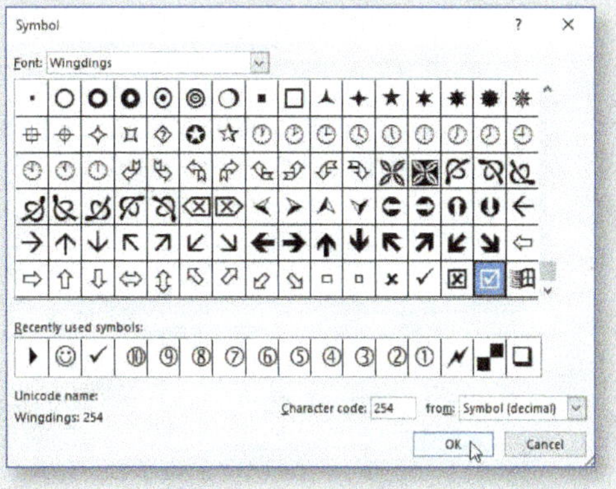

2-68 *Symbol* dialog box

4. Use the *Format Painter* to apply this bullet format to lines of text in the other "EXPERIENCE" sections and the "EDUCATION" section. Don't apply bullet formatting to the city, state, and date lines where the tab stops and leaders are applied.
5. Insert a page break in the document.
   a. Turn on **Show/Hide** [*Home* tab, *Paragraph* group].
   b. Place the insertion point in front of the "EDUCATION" heading.
   c. Select the **Layout** tab and click the **Breaks** button [*Page Setup* group].
   d. Select **Page** from the drop-down list. A page break displays at the bottom of the first page, and the "EDUCATION" section moves to the next page.
6. Change the theme and theme color of the document.
   a. Click the **Design** tab.
   b. Click the **Themes** button [*Document Formatting* group] and select **Ion** from the *Themes* gallery.
   c. Click the **Colors** button [*Document Formatting* group] and select **Red** from the *Theme Colors* drop-down list.

7. Apply styles from the *Style* gallery to selected text.
   a. On the first page of the résumé, select **"Richelle Wilkinson"** and click the **Title** style from the *Style* gallery [*Home* tab].
   b. With this text still selected, change the font size to **20 pt**.
   c. Apply the **Heading 1** style to each of the main headings ("PROFILE," "EXPERIENCE," "EDUCATION," "SKILLS," and "REFERENCES").
   d. Apply the **Heading 2** style to each of the bold and italicized subheadings in the "EXPERIENCE" and "EDUCATION" sections.
8. Modify a style.
   a. Select the **"PROFILE"** heading.
   b. Change the *Before* paragraph spacing to **16 pt**.
   c. Right-click the **Heading 1** style in the *Style* gallery and select **Update Heading 1 to Match Selection** (Figure 2-69). This style change is applied to all text with *Heading 1* style.
   d. On the second page, select **"CALIFORNIA STATE UNIVERSITY CHICO, BACHELOR OF ARTS IN CHILD DEVELOPMENT"** in the "EDUCATION" section and change the font size to **11 pt**.
   e. Right-click the **Heading 2** style in the *Style* gallery and select **Update Heading 2 to Match Selection**.
9. Save and close the document (Figure 2-70).

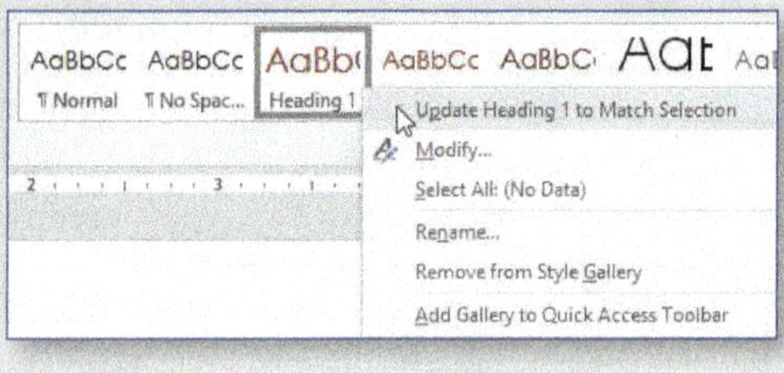

2-69 Update style to match selection

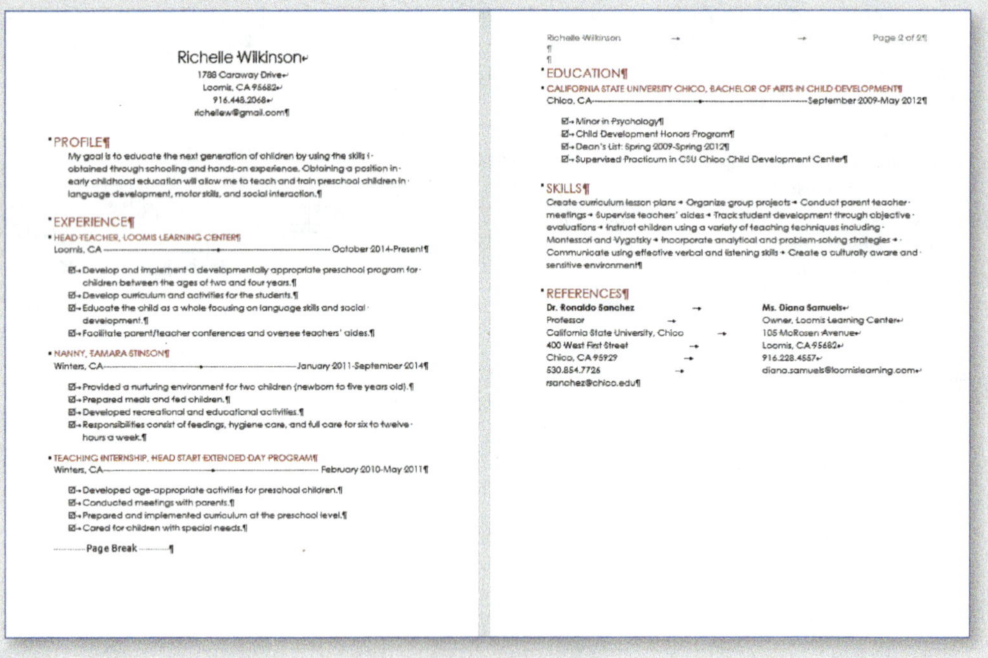

2-70 PP W2-3 completed

SLO 2.8

Using Find and Replace

Find and ***Replace*** are two extremely useful and powerful tools in Word. The *Find* feature allows you to search for and locate words and phrases in a document. The *Replace* feature allows you to search for a word or phrase and replace it with other text. You can also use *Find* and *Replace* to search for a specific type of formatting in a document and replace it with different formatting. These features are particularly useful in longer documents. When using *Find* or *Replace*, it is best to position your insertion point at the top of the document so Word searches from the beginning of your document.

Find

You can use the ***Navigation pane*** in Word to search for text and display all instances of the matching text. Word also highlights in yellow each instance of the matching text in the document. You are able to navigate through the document, see each instance, and edit as desired.

▸ HOW TO: Use Find in the Navigation Pane

1. Place your insertion point at the beginning of the document.
2. Click the **Find** button [*Home* tab, *Editing* group]. The *Navigation* pane opens on the left side of the Word window.
3. Click the **Search document** text box at the top of the *Navigation* pane and type the text you want to search.
   - The matching results display below the text box.
   - Word highlights the matching text in the document.
4. Click the **Next** or **Previous** search result buttons to move through each matching instance in the document (Figure 2-71).
   - You can also click the matching instances below the *Search document* text box to go to a specific occurrence of the matching text.

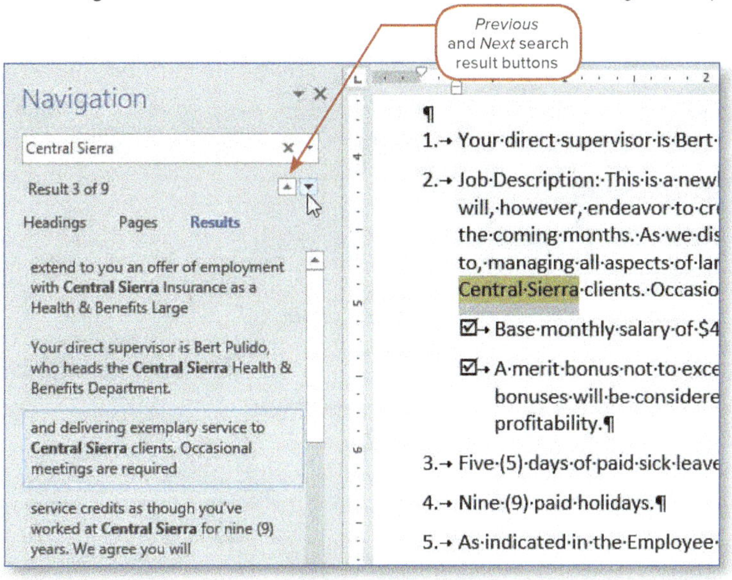

2-71 Use *Find* in the *Navigation* pane

5. Edit the highlighted text in the document if you want to make changes.
6. Click the **X** to the right of the *Search Document* text box to clear the current search.
7. Click the **X** in the upper right of the *Navigation* pane to close the pane.

> **ANOTHER WAY**
>
> **Ctrl+F** opens the *Find* feature in the *Navigation* pane.

Find and Replace

The ***Find and Replace*** dialog box provides you three different advanced options for searching your document:

- *Find*
- *Replace*
- *Go To*

The *Find* tab of the *Find and Replace* dialog box not only searches for text in your document but also searches for specific formatting (such as font styles, line spacing, or paragraph spacing). For example, you can search for all text that is bold or italic, or that has 6 pt. *After* paragraph spacing.

Use the *Replace* feature to search for text, formatting, or a combination of text and formatting and to replace the matching text with other text, formatting, or formatted text. This feature is a quick and efficient way to find and replace text in a document.

HOW TO: Use Replace

1. Place your insertion point at the beginning of the document.
2. Click the **Replace** button [*Home* tab, *Editing* group] or press **Ctrl+H**. The *Find and Replace* dialog box opens with the *Replace* tab displayed (Figure 2-72).
3. Click the **Find what** text box and type the text for which you are searching.
4. Click the **Replace with** text box and type the text you want to replace the found text.
5. Click the **More** button to display advanced find options. The *Less* button hides the advanced find options.
6. Click the **Format** or **Special** button to add formatting options or special characters to either the text for which you are searching or the replacement text.
   - Put the insertion point in the **Find what** or **Replace with** text box before selecting a format or special character.

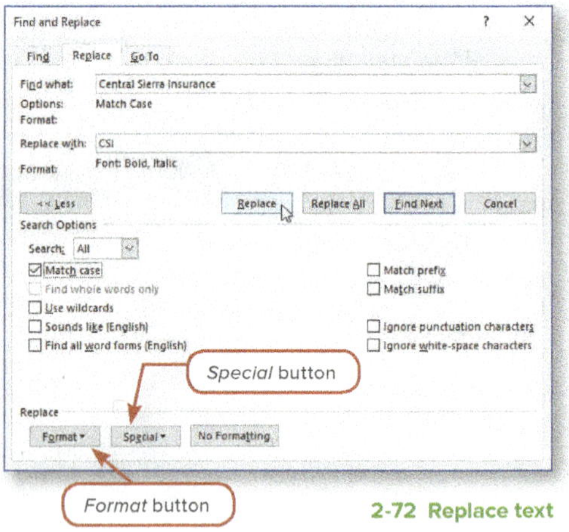

2-72 Replace text

7. Click the **Find Next** button to locate the first occurrence of the text (and formatting) for which you are searching.
   - It is best to click the **Less** button to collapse this dialog box when finding and replacing content in your document.
8. When the first occurrence is found, select **Replace** (this occurrence), **Replace All** (all occurrences), or **Find Next** (skip this occurrence without replacing and move to the next).
9. Click the **Find Next** button to move to the next occurrence of the matching text and formatting.
10. When you finish finding and replacing text in the document, a dialog box opens informing you that Word has finished searching the document. Click **OK** to close this dialog box.
11. Click the **X** in the upper right corner to close the *Find and Replace* dialog box.

When using *Find* or *Replace*, wildcards can be used to help find information. You can use wildcards before, after, or between words.

- ***Question mark (?)***: A wildcard for a single character. For example, ***w???*** finds any words that begins with "w" and contains four letters (e.g., when, with, warm, or wish).
- ***Asterisk (*)***: A wildcard for a string of characters. For example, **search*** finds any form of the word "search" (e.g., searches, searching, or searched).

ANOTHER WAY

Ctrl+H opens the *Find and Replace* dialog box with the *Replace* tab selected.

MORE INFO

It is a good idea to use *Match Case* when replacing acronyms (capital letters) with words so the replaced words will not be all upper case. Also, use *Find whole words only* to refine your search.

Go To

The ***Go To*** feature allows you to go quickly to specific items or locations in your document. This feature is different from *Find* in that *Go To* moves you to specific objects or locations in your document such as a page, section, or bookmark. This feature is available in the *Find and Replace* dialog box.

HOW TO: Use the Go To Feature

1. Click the **Find** drop-down arrow [*Home* tab, *Editing* group].
2. Select **Go To**. The *Find and Replace* dialog box opens with the *Go To* tab displayed (Figure 2-73).
3. In the *Go to what* area, select the item to go to from the list of options: *Page*, *Section*, *Line*, *Bookmark*, *Comment*, *Footnote*, etc.
   - The text box to the right is context sensitive and changes depending on the item chosen.
4. In the text box to the right, type in a page number, section, line, bookmark, etc.
5. Click the **Go To** button.
6. Click **Close** to close this dialog box.

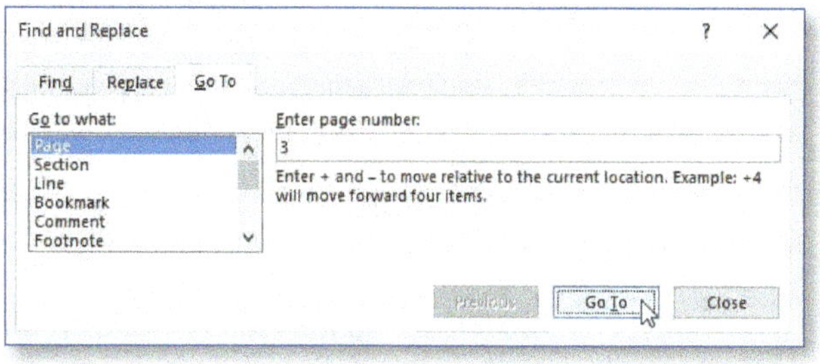

2-73 *Go To* in the *Find and Replace* dialog box

ANOTHER WAY

Ctrl+G or **F5** opens the *Find and Replace* dialog box with the *Go To* tab selected.

SLO 2.9

Using Borders, Shading, and Hyperlinks

Borders and ***shading*** are excellent ways to highlight or emphasize important information in a document. In Word, there are many different border and shading options including preset border options. You also have the option of applying custom borders and shading to selected text or paragraphs of your document.

A ***hyperlink*** functions like a button and is used to take a reader to a web page, open an existing or new document, open an email message, or move to another location in the current document. You can add a hyperlink to text or a graphic in a document.

Apply Built-In Borders

You can use the ***Borders drop-down list*** in the *Paragraph* group on the *Home* tab to quickly apply borders to selected text. Borders are typically applied to paragraphs, but they can also be applied to other selected text. Borders, by default, apply to the paragraph where your insertion point is unless you select specific text. Figure 2-74 shows the different types of built-in borders.

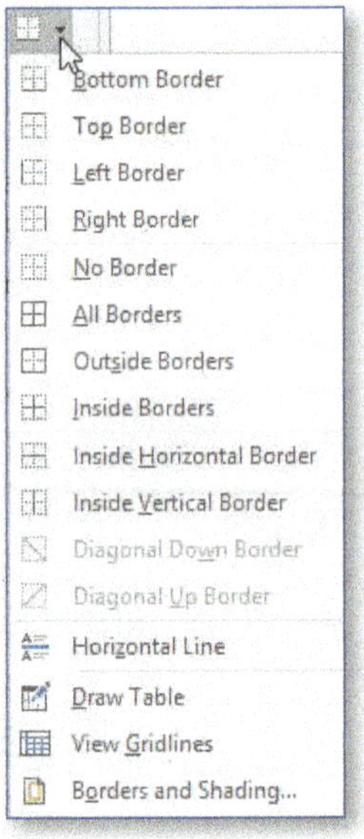

2-74 *Borders* drop-down list

HOW TO: Apply Built-In Borders

1. Select the paragraph or place the insertion point in the paragraph where you want to apply the border.
2. Click the **Home** tab.
3. Click the **Borders** drop-down arrow [*Paragraph* group] (see Figure 2-74).
4. Click the border option to apply to the selected paragraph.

MORE INFO

You can remove borders by selecting the paragraph or text on which the borders are applied and clicking the **No Border** option in the *Borders* drop-down list.

Customize Borders

The ***Borders and Shading dialog box*** provides many more options to customize the type of borders you use. Not only can you customize the style, width, and color of border line, but also you can customize where the border is placed in relation to the selected text. The *Borders and Shading* dialog box is available from the *Borders* drop-down list in the *Paragraph* group on the *Home* tab.

HOW TO: Apply Custom Borders

1. Select the paragraph(s) where you want to apply a border.
2. Click the **Borders** drop-down arrow [*Home* tab, *Paragraph* group] and choose the **Borders and Shading** option at the bottom of the list. The *Borders and Shading* dialog box opens (Figure 2-75).
   - In the *Apply to* area, select where you want to apply the borders. Your options are *Text* and *Paragraph*.

3. In the *Setting* area, select the type of border to use. Your options are *None*, *Box*, *Shadow*, *3-D*, and *Custom*.
4. In the *Style* area, select a style of the line from the list of options.
5. Click the **Color** drop-down arrow and select line color.
6. Click the **Width** drop-down arrow and select the width of the border line. The width of the line is measured in points.
7. View the *Preview* area to see how the border will appear in your document.
   - In the *Preview* area, you can customize how the borders appear by clicking the *Top*, *Bottom*, *Left*, or *Right* border buttons to turn on or off a border (see Figure 2-75).
8. Click the **Options** button to open the *Border and Shading Options* dialog box (Figure 2-76).
   - This dialog box includes the option to add in additional space (padding) between the border and the text at the *Top*, *Bottom*, *Left*, and *Right*.
   - The spacing is measured in points.
   - Click **OK** to close the *Border and Shading Options* dialog box.
9. Click **OK** to close the *Borders and Shading* dialog box.

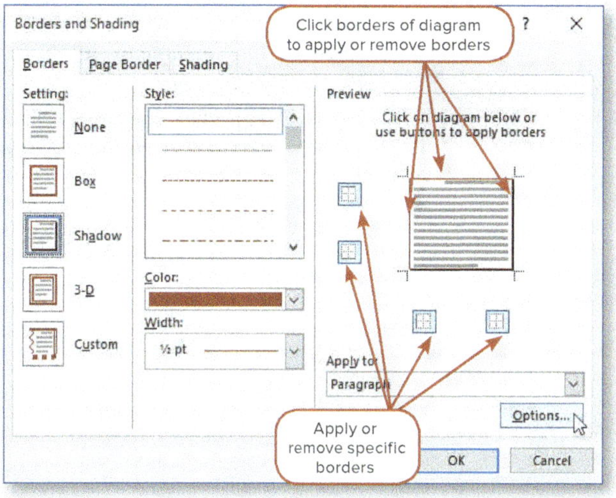

2-75 *Borders and Shading* dialog box

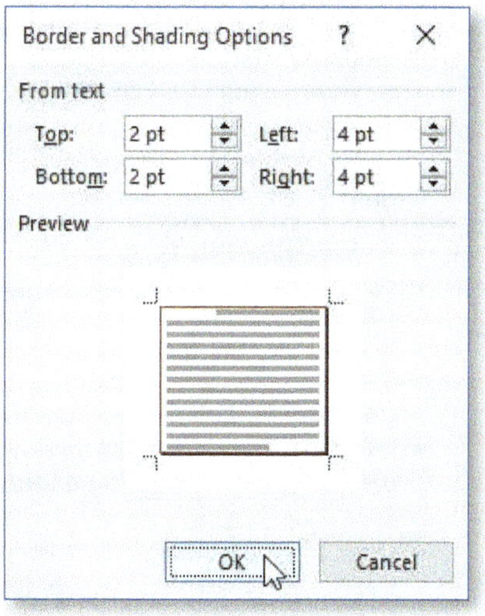

2-76 *Border and Shading Options* dialog box

MORE INFO

When you use the *Borders* button [*Paragraph* group], the last border selected becomes the function of the *Borders* button. For example, if you last applied a bottom border, you can apply a bottom border again by clicking the **Borders** button.

Apply Shading

Applying shading to a paragraph or text is very similar to applying borders. ***Shading*** applies a background color to selected text. *Shading* color options are available from the *Shading* drop-down list in the *Paragraph* group on the *Home* tab or in the *Borders and Shading* dialog box on the *Shading* tab.

The shading colors available are dependent upon the theme of the document. In the *Shading* drop-down list, you can select from *Theme Colors* or *Standard Colors* (Figure 2-77). If you want a color that is not available in the menu, you can click *More Colors* to select from a color palette.

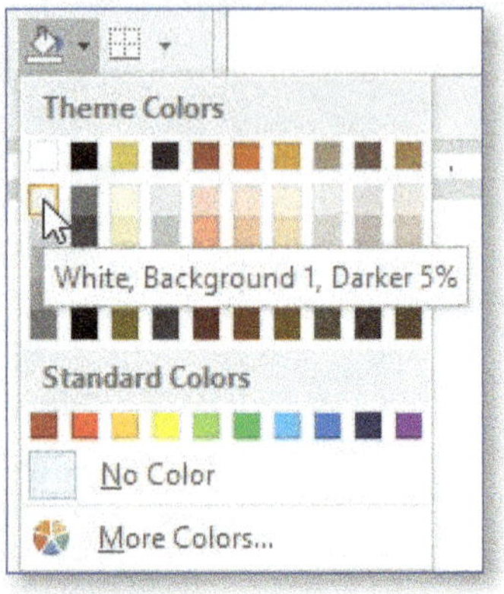

2-77 Shading color options from the *Shading* drop-down list

▶HOW TO: Apply Shading from the Borders and Shading Dialog Box

1. Select the paragraph(s) you want to shade.
2. Click the **Borders** drop-down arrow [*Home* tab, *Paragraph* group] and choose the **Borders and Shading** option at the bottom of the list. The *Borders and Shading* dialog box opens (Figure 2-78).
3. Click the **Shading** tab.
4. Click the **Fill** drop-down arrow and select a shading fill color.
   - Alternatively, select a shading *Style* and *Color* in the *Patterns* area.
   - From the *Style* drop-down list, you can select a gradient percent or a fill pattern as the shading style.
   - From the *Color* drop-down list, you can select a fill color for the gradient or pattern you selected.
   - You do not have to use a pattern style or color for shading. Usually just a fill color is sufficient.
5. Click **OK** to close the *Borders and Shading* dialog box.

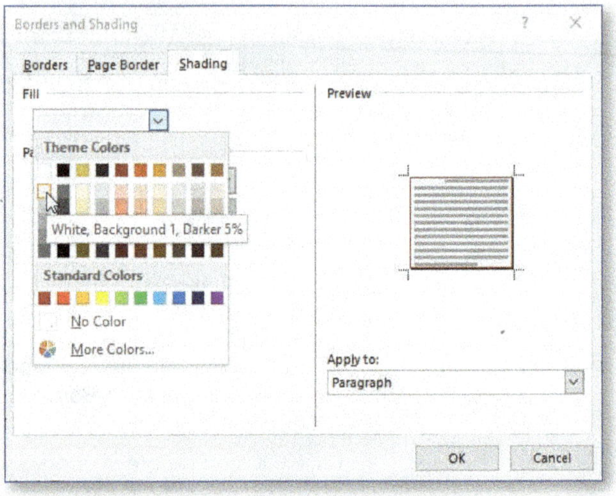

2-78 Shading options in the *Borders and Shading* dialog box

Apply a Page Border

Page borders are different from paragraph or text borders. A page border is around the entire page rather than selected paragraphs or text. Page borders are useful and attractive when creating flyers or handouts. A page border can be a line with varying styles, widths, and colors, or you can use art graphics as a page border.

▶HOW TO: Apply a Page Border

1. Click the **Design** tab.
2. Click the **Page Borders** button [*Page Background* group]. The *Borders and Shading* dialog box opens with the *Page Border* tab displayed (Figure 2-79).

3. In the *Setting* area, select the type of page border you want to apply.
4. From the *Style* list, select a border style.
    - Alternatively, you can select an art to apply as the border from the **Art** drop-down list.
5. Select a border color and width from the **Color** and **Width** drop-down lists.
6. In the *Preview* area, customize how the page border appears by clicking the **Top**, **Bottom**, **Left**, or **Right** border buttons to turn on or off borders.
7. In the *Apply to* area, select the page(s) where you want to apply the page border. Your options are:
    - *Whole document*
    - *This section*
    - *This section–First page only*
    - *This section–All except first page*
8. Click **OK** to close the *Borders and Shading* dialog box.

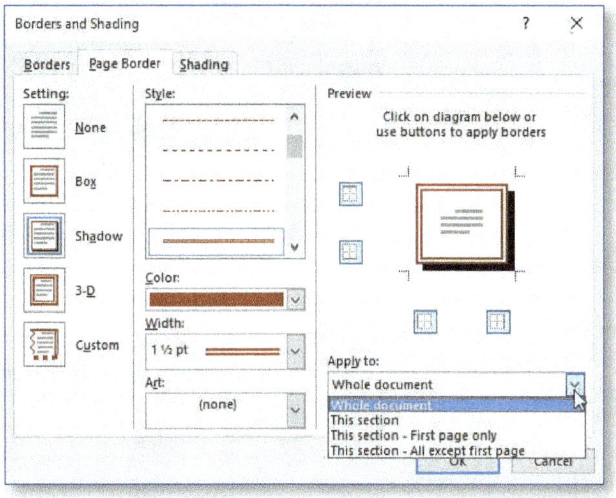

2-79 Apply a page border

MORE INFO

When you apply a page border, the text in the document is not affected because the page border is placed outside the margin boundaries.

Insert a Horizontal Line

In addition to being able to insert top and bottom borders on selected text, you can also insert a ***horizontal line*** to use as a border to separate information on a page. A horizontal line is actually a graphic object that is inserted into the document. When you insert a horizontal line, the line is the width of the page. More information about using and customizing graphics is covered in *SLO 4.5: Working with Graphics*.

HOW TO: Insert a Horizontal Line

1. Place your insertion point in the document where you want a horizontal line.
2. Click the **Borders** drop-down arrow [*Home* tab, *Paragraph* group].
3. Select **Horizontal Line** from the drop-down list (Figure 2-80).
    - The horizontal line is treated as a separate paragraph and has a paragraph mark to the right.

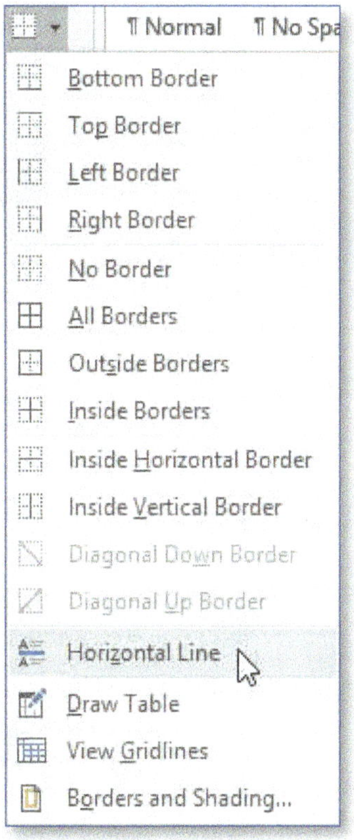

2-80 Insert a horizontal line

Create a Hyperlink

A hyperlink is an excellent way to direct users to information on a web site, another document, or a location in the same document. You can also create a hyperlink for an email address, which automatically opens a new Microsoft Outlook email message addressed to the recipient. You can create a hyperlink by selecting the text or figure you want to turn into a hyperlink and then providing the information about the location where the user will be directed. You can also customize the *ScreenTip* and the target frame.

> **MORE INFO**
>
> Typically, hyperlinks are underlined and a different color to distinguish them from regular text in a document. In a Word document, Press **Ctrl+Click** to follow a hyperlink.

The ***ScreenTip*** is the text that displays when you place your pointer over the hyperlink in the document. The ***target frame*** is the window where the hyperlink document or web site opens. There are many different target frame options from which to choose. Usually it is best to choose **New window** if the link is to a different document or a web page. An email hyperlink always opens in a new window.

HOW TO: Create a Hyperlink

1. Select the text or graphic where you want to create a hyperlink.
2. Click the **Insert** tab.
3. Click the **Hyperlink** button [*Links* group]. The *Insert Hyperlink* dialog box opens (Figure 2-81).
   - The text you selected in the document as the hyperlink is displayed in the *Text to display* area. If you type other text in this text box, it will replace the text you selected in the document.

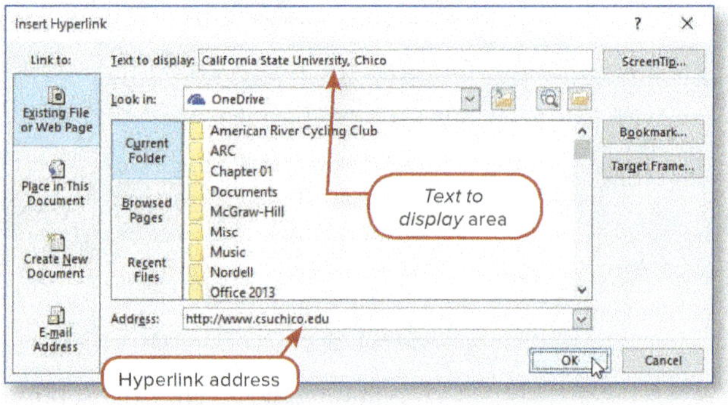

2-81 *Insert Hyperlink* dialog box

4. In the *Link to* area, select the type of hyperlink you want to create. Your options are *Existing File or Web Page*, *Place in This Document*, *Create New Document*, or *E-mail Address*.
   - If you are linking to a file, browse your computer in the *Look in* area to locate and select the file.
   - If you are linking to a web page, or type or paste (**Ctrl+V**) a web address in the *Address* area
   - If you are linking to a place in the document, a list of headings from which to choose displays.
   - If you are inserting a link to create a new document, options for the new document display.
   - If you are linking to an email address, you type in the email address and have the option to create a subject line for the email.

5. Click the **ScreenTip** button to insert text that displays when you place pointer over the hyperlink (Figure 2-82).
6. Type the *ScreenTip* text and click **OK** to close the *Set Hyperlink ScreenTip* dialog box.
7. Click the **Target Frame** button to open the *Set Target Frame* dialog box (Figure 2-83).
   - From the drop-down list of options, select where the hyperlink destination will be opened.
   - The *Set as default for all hyperlinks* check box allows you to make your target frame selection the default for all hyperlinks in your document.
8. Click **OK** to close the *Set Target Frame* dialog box.
9. Click **OK** to insert the hyperlink and close the *Insert Hyperlink* dialog box.

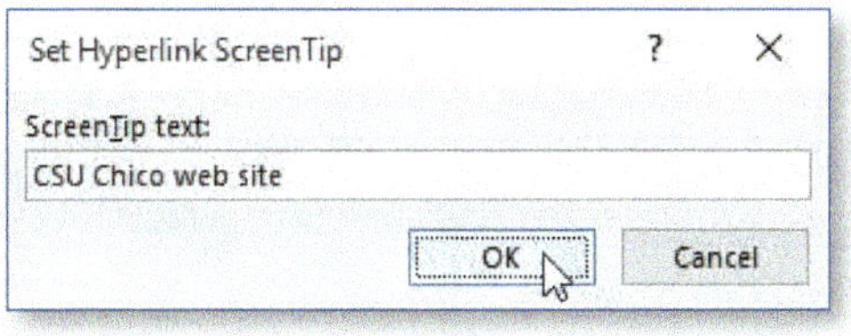

2-82 *Set Hyperlink ScreenTip* dialog box

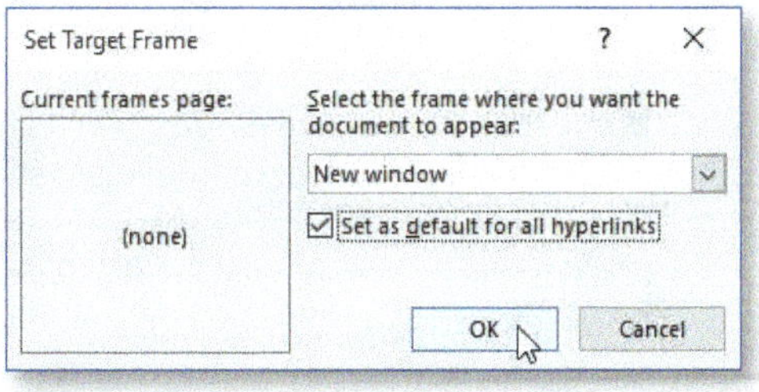

2-83 *Set Target Frame* dialog box

ANOTHER WAY

Ctrl+K opens the *Insert Hyperlink* dialog box.

Edit or Remove a Hyperlink

There might be times when you have incorporated text from a web site or another document that includes hyperlinks to a document, or you might want to edit a hyperlink in an existing document. Word allows you to quickly edit hyperlinks to change hyperlink information, add a *ScreenTip*, or change the target frame.

You can quickly remove a hyperlink from a document without deleting the text in the document. When you remove a hyperlink from existing text, the text in your document is not deleted. Only the hyperlink attached to the text is removed.

HOW TO: Edit or Remove a Hyperlink

1. Select or click the hyperlink to edit.
2. Click the **Hyperlink** button [*Insert* tab, *Links* group]. The *Edit Hyperlink* dialog box opens.
   - You can also press **Ctrl+K** or right-click the selected hyperlink and select **Edit Hyperlink**.
3. Change hyperlink information or options as needed.
4. Click the **Remove Link** button to remove an existing hyperlink (Figure 2-84).
   - When you remove a hyperlink, the *Edit Hyperlink* dialog box closes automatically.
5. Click **OK** to close the *Edit Hyperlink* dialog box if necessary.

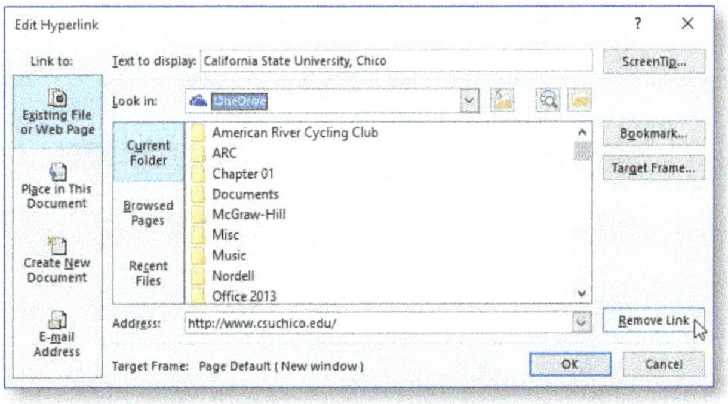

2-84 Edit or remove a hyperlink

ANOTHER WAY

Right-click a hyperlink and select **Edit Hyperlink** or **Remove Hyperlink**.

PAUSE & PRACTICE: WORD 2-4

In this Pause & Practice project, you finalize the résumé you worked on in *Pause & Practice 2-3*. You use *Find and Replace*, apply borders and shading to selected text, and add hyperlinks to the document.

File Needed: ***[your initials] PP W2-3.docx***
Completed Project File Name: ***[your initials] PP W2-4.docx***

1. Open the ***[your initials] PP W2-3*** document completed in *Pause & Practice 2-3*.
2. Save this document as [your initials] PP W2-4.
3. Use *Find and Replace* to replace the hyphen between dates with an en dash.
   a. Press **Ctrl+Home** to move to the top of the document.
   b. Click the **Replace** button [*Home* tab, *Editing* group] or press **Ctrl+H** to open the *Find and Replace* dialog box.
   c. In the *Find what* text box, type - (hyphen).
   d. Place the insertion point in the *Replace with* text box.
   e. Click the **More** button if the *Search Options* are not already displayed.
   f. Click the **Special** button and select **En Dash** (Figure 2-85).
   g. Click the **Less** button to collapse the **Find and Replace** dialog box (Figure 2-86).
   h. Click the **Find Next** button to locate the first instance of a hyphen.
   i. Choose **Find Next** to skip the hyphenated word in the first paragraph.
   j. Click the **Replace** button to replace each occurrence of a hyphen between the dates with an en dash; choose **Find Next** to skip and not replace each occurrence of a hyphenated word.
   k. Click **OK** when Word has finished searching the document.
   l. Click **Close** to close the *Find and Replace* dialog box.
4. Add borders and shading to a paragraph.
   a. Select the paragraph after the "PROFILE" heading on the first page. Be sure to include the paragraph mark at the end of the paragraph.

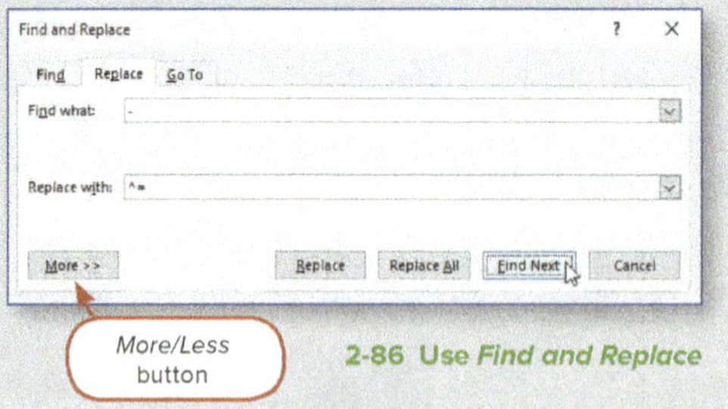

2-86 Use *Find and Replace*

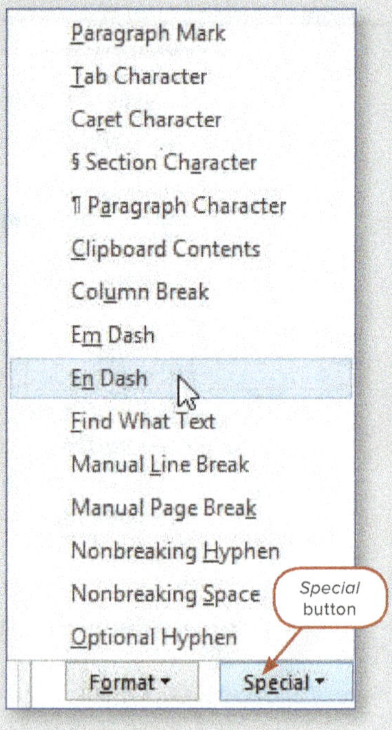

2-85 Select *En Dash* as the special character to replace a hyphen

MORE INFO

Word highlights each found occurrence. If you need to, you can move the *Find and Replace* dialog box to view highlighted text.

b. Click the **Borders** drop-down arrow [*Home* tab, *Paragraph* group] and select **Borders and Shading** to open the *Borders and Shading* dialog box.
c. Select **Shadow** in the *Setting* area.
d. Select the **solid line** in the *Style* area.
e. Click the **Color** drop-down list and select **Dark Red, Accent 1** (Figure 2-87).
f. Select **½ pt** in the *Width* area.
g. Select **Paragraph** in the *Apply to* area.
h. Click the **Options** button to open the *Border and Shading Options* dialog box and change *Top* and *Bottom* to **2 pt**.
i. Click **OK** to close the *Border and Shading Options* dialog box.
j. Click the **Shading** tab.
k. Click the **Fill** drop-down list and select **White, Background 1, Darker 5%** (Figure 2-88).
l. Click **OK** to close the *Borders and Shading* dialog box.

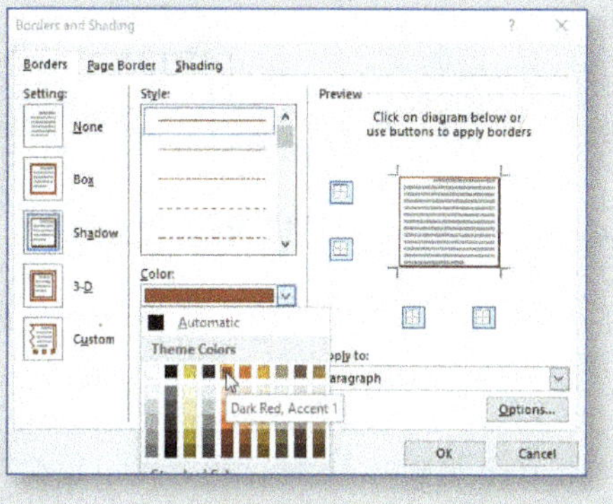

2-87 Select border color in the *Borders and Shading* dialog box

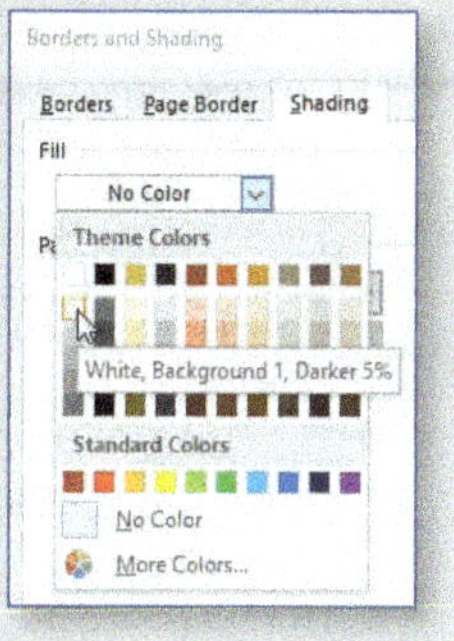

2-88 Apply shading to selected text

5. Add a bottom border to the header.
   a. Right-click the header on the second page and select **Edit Header** to open the header area on the second page.
   b. Place the insertion point in the first line of the header.
   c. Click the **Borders** drop-down arrow [*Home* tab, *Paragraph* group].
   d. Select **Bottom Border**. A bottom border displays below the header text.
   e. Click the **Close Header and Footer** button [*Header & Footer Tools Design* tab, *Close* group].
6. Insert a hyperlink to an email address.
   a. Select the email address in the heading information on the first page.
   b. Click the **Hyperlink** button [*Insert* tab, *Links* group] or press **Ctrl+K** to open the *Insert Hyperlink* dialog box (Figure 2-89).
   c. Click the **E-mail Address** button in the *Link to* area.
   d. Type richellew@gmail.com in the *Text to display* area.
   e. Type richellew@gmail.com in the *E-mail address* area. Word automatically inserts "mailto:" before the email address.
   f. Click the **ScreenTip** button. The *Set Hyperlink ScreenTip* dialog box opens (Figure 2-90).
   g. Type Email Richelle in the *ScreenTip text* area and click **OK** to close the *Set Hyperlink ScreenTip* dialog box.
   h. Click **OK** to close the *Insert Hyperlink* dialog box.

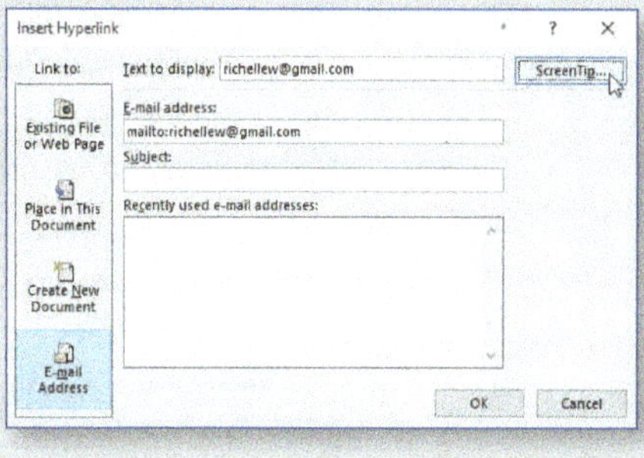

2-89 Insert hyperlink to an email address

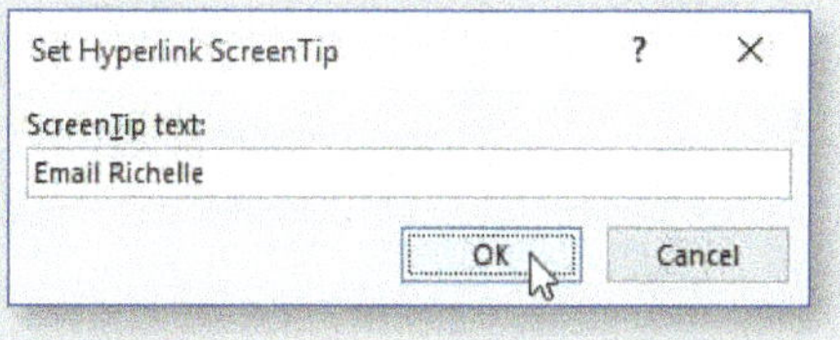

2-90 *Set Hyperlink ScreenTip* dialog box

7. Insert a hyperlink to a web site.
   a. In the "REFERENCES" section on the second page, select **"California State University, Chico."** Don't select this text in the "EDUCATION" section.
   b. Click the **Hyperlink** button or press **Ctrl+K** to open the *Insert Hyperlink* dialog box (Figure 2-91).
   c. Select **Existing File or Web Page** in the *Link to* area. The *Text to display* area has *California State University, Chico* already filled in.

d. In the *Address* area, type www.csuchico.edu. Word automatically inserts "http://" before the web address.

e. Click the **ScreenTip** button. The *Set Hyperlink ScreenTip* dialog box opens.

f. Type CSU Chico web site in the *ScreenTip text* area and click **OK** to close the *Set Hyperlink ScreenTip* dialog box.

g. Click the **Target Frame** button in the *Insert Hyperlink* dialog box to open the *Set Target Frame* dialog box.

h. Select **New window** from the drop-down list and check the **Set as default for all hyperlinks** check box (Figure 2-92).

i. Click **OK** to close the *Set Target Frame* dialog box and click **OK** to close the *Insert Hyperlink* dialog box.

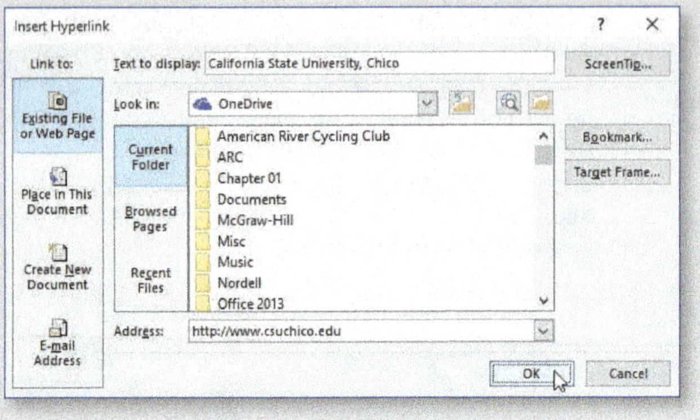

2-91 Insert hyperlink to a web page

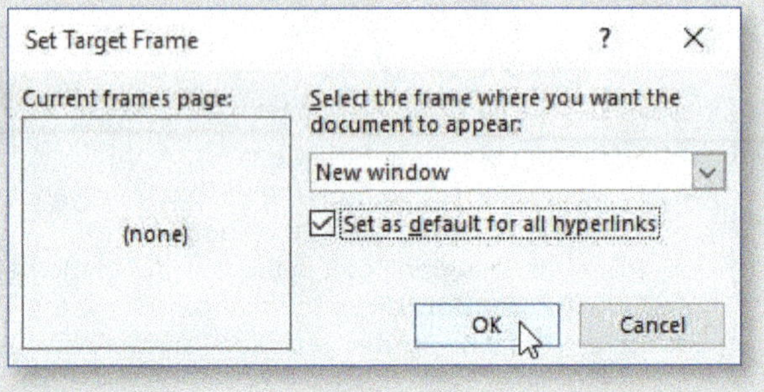

2-92 *Set Target Frame* dialog box

8. Automatically add hyperlinks to email addresses.
   a. Place the insertion point after "rsanchez @chico. edu" in the "REFERENCES" section on the second page.
   b. Press the **spacebar** once to automatically add a hyperlink to the email address.
   c. Place the insertion point after "diana.samuels@loomislearning.com" in the "REFERENCES" section on the second page and press the **spacebar** once to automatically add a hyperlink to the email address.
9. Save and close the document (Figure 2-93).

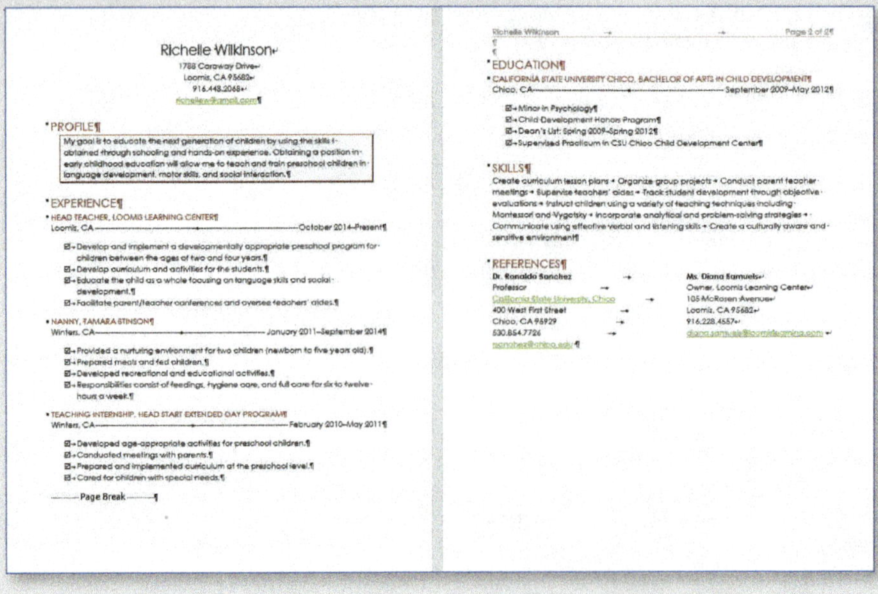

2-93 PP W2-4 completed

Chapter Summary

2.1 Format a document by customizing margins, page orientation, paper size, and vertical alignment (p. W2-66).

- Adjust the ***margins*** of a document to increase or decrease the ***white space*** surrounding the text. You can adjust the top, bottom, left, and right margins of a document.
- ***Landscape*** and ***Portrait*** are the two ***page orientation*** options.
- A standard sheet of paper is 8½" × 11". Select other paper sizes or create a custom paper size.
- ***Vertical alignment*** controls how text aligns between the top and bottom margins. By default, text aligns vertically at the top of the document. You can also use center, justified, or bottom vertical alignment.
- Use horizontal and vertical ***rulers*** to display the typing area on a document.
- You can change default page settings in the ***Page Setup dialog box***.

2.2 Improve alignment and page layout by setting, using, and editing tab stops in a document (p. W2-69).

- There are five different types of ***tab stops: Left, Center, Right, Decimal,*** and ***Bar***.
- Set, modify, or remove tab stops using the ruler or the ***Tabs dialog box***.
- Use the ***Tab selector*** on the left side of the ruler to select a type of tab stop to set.
- ***Leaders*** can be used with tab stops. There are three different types of leaders: ***Dot, Dash,*** and ***Solid underline***.
- In a Word document, default tab stops are set every 0.5". You can change the default tab stops.

2.3 Apply indents to control text alignment (p. W2-74).

- ***Indents*** can function as temporary margins and allow you to arrange paragraphs horizontally between the margins.
- There are four different types of indents: ***left, right, first line,*** and ***hanging***.
- You can apply, modify, and remove indents with the ruler, *Layout* tab, or *Paragraph* dialog box.

2.4 Enhance document layout by inserting page numbers, headers, and footers (p. W2-79).

- You can insert a ***page number*** into the header or footer in various locations.
- ***Headers*** and ***footers*** are areas above and below a document's top and bottom margins.
- The ***Different First Page*** option allows you to remove or have different first page content in the header or footer.
- You type header and footer content once and it appears on subsequent pages.
- You can customize headers and footers with text, page numbers, the date, and other document property fields.
- You have a variety of built-in header, footer, and page numbering options.

2.5 Control pagination with page and section breaks (p. W2-86).

- Use ***page breaks*** to control the ending and beginning of pages in a document.
- Use ***section breaks*** to allow for different page setup formatting on different sections of a document.
- There are four different options for section breaks: ***Next Page, Continuous, Even Page,*** and ***Odd Page***.
- Section breaks are visible in a document when the *Show/Hide* feature is turned on.

2.6 Use customized bulleted and numbered lists to effectively present information (p. W2-88).

- Use ***bulleted*** and ***numbered lists*** to emphasize important information.
- You can customize lists by using different symbols or pictures as bullets.
- Use numbering to display an ordered list.
- You can customize number format and levels.
- ***Multilevel lists*** allow you to customize a list using a combination of numbers, letters, or bullets.

2.7 Apply styles and themes to improve consistency in document format (p. W2-92).

- A ***style*** is a collection of preset formatting that you can apply to selected text.
- The ***Style gallery*** is a collection of built-in styles available in a document.
- You can modify existing styles.
- A ***theme*** is a collection of fonts, colors, and effects that you can apply to a document.

2.8 Use find and replace to edit a document (p. W2-97).

- The ***Find*** feature in Word allows you to search for specific text or format in a document.

- The ***Navigation pane*** displays all occurrences of the text for which you are searching.
- The ***Replace*** feature allows you to search for specific text in a document and replace it with other text.
- Both *Find* and *Replace* allow you to search for and replace formatting in a document.
- Use the ***Go To*** feature to go directly to a page, section, line, or other area in your document.

2.9 Improve overall document design and format by using borders, shading, horizontal lines, and hyperlinks (p.W2-100).

- *You can apply* ***borders*** and ***shading*** to text and paragraphs in a document.
- Word provides a variety of built-in border and shading options that you can apply to text, or you can customize borders and shading using the ***Borders and Shading dialog box***.
- You can apply ***page borders*** to an individual page or all pages in a document.
- A ***horizontal line*** is a graphic that you can insert into a document.
- A ***hyperlink*** takes readers to a web page, a different document, a different location in a document, or an email address. An email hyperlink opens Microsoft Outlook and places the recipient's email address in the email message.

Check for Understanding

The SIMbook for this text (within your SIMnet account) provides the following resources for concept review:

- Multiple choice questions
- Matching exercises
- Short answer questions

USING MICROSOFT WORD 2016

Guided Project 2-1

In this project, you create a form for contractors seeking insurance coverage at Central Sierra Insurance. You apply a theme, styles, a multilevel list, tab stops, leaders, indents, borders and shading, a page break, and page numbering.
[Student Learning Outcomes 2.1, 2.2, 2.3, 2.4, 2.5, 2.6, 2.7, 2.9]

File Needed: ***InsuranceQuestionnaire-02.docx*** *(Student data files are available in the* Library *of your SIMnet account)*
Completed Project File Name: ***[your initials] Word 2-1.docx***

Skills Covered in this Project

- Modify an existing document.
- Change margins.
- Apply a document theme and theme color.
- Change font size, line spacing, and paragraph spacing.
- Apply a style to selected text.
- Modify an existing style.
- Apply borders and shading to selected text.
- Set and use a tab stop with an underline leader.
- Apply and modify a multilevel list.
- Insert a page break.
- Insert a built-in page number in the footer.

1. Open the ***InsuranceQuestionnaire-02*** document from your student data files.
2. Save this document as [your initials] Word 2-1.
3. Change the margins of the document.
   a. Click the **Margins** button [*Layout* tab, *Page Setup* group] and select **Custom Margins**. The *Page Setup* dialog box opens.
   b. Change the *Left* and *Right* margins to **0.75"**.
   c. Click **OK** to close the *Page Setup* dialog box.
4. Change the theme and theme color of the document.
   a. Click the **Themes** button [*Design* tab, *Document Formatting* group].
   b. Select **Integral** from the drop-down list.
   c. Click the **Colors** button [*Document Formatting* group] (Figure 2-94).
   d. Select **Aspect** from the drop-down list.
5. Change the font size, paragraph spacing, and line spacing of the entire document.
   a. Press **Ctrl+A** to select the entire document.
   b. Change the font size to **11 pt**.
   c. Change the line spacing to **Single (1.0)**.
   d. Change the *After* paragraph spacing to **6 pt**.
6. Apply styles to selected text.
   a. Place the insertion point in the first line of text ("Contractor's Insurance Questionnaire").

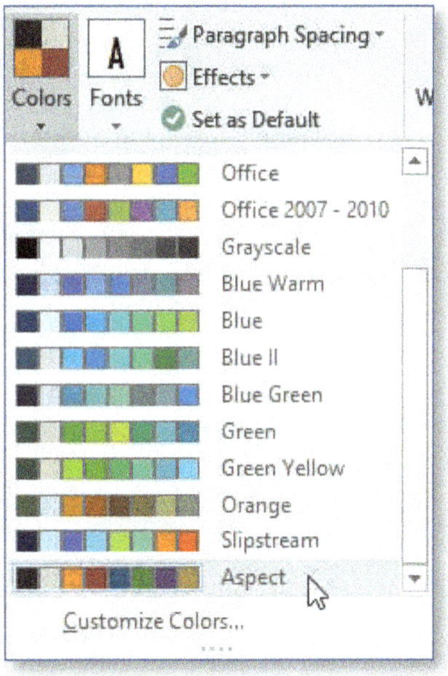

2-94 ***Theme Colors* drop-down list**

b. Click the **Title** style [*Home* tab, *Styles* group] in the *Style* gallery.
c. Select the second line of the document (**"Please carefully** . . . **"**).
d. Right-click the selected text, click **Styles** on the mini toolbar, and select **Book Title** from the *Style* gallery.
e. With this text still selected, click the **Change Case** button [*Home* tab, *Font* group] and select **UPPERCASE**.
f. Select **"Applicant's Instructions"** and apply the **Intense Quote** style from the *Style* gallery.
g. In the next paragraph ("Please answer ALL questions . . ."), apply the **Strong** style to the three words in all caps (**"ALL," "NONE,"** and **"NONE"**).
h. On the second page of the document, select **"Insurance Application Disclaimer"** and apply the **Intense Quote** style.

7. Modify an existing style.
   a. Click the **More** button [*Home* tab, *Styles* group] to display all of the styles in the *Style* gallery.
   b. Right-click the **Intense Quote** style in the *Style* gallery and select **Modify** (Figure 2-95). The *Modify Style* dialog box opens.
   c. In the *Formatting* area, change the font size to **12 pt**.
   d. Click the **Format** button on the bottom left and select **Paragraph**. The *Paragraph* dialog box opens.
   e. Change the *Left* and *Right* indent to **0**.
   f. Click **OK** to close the *Paragraph* dialog box.
   g. Click the **Only in this document** radio button if it is not already selected to apply the style changes to only this document.
   h. Click **OK** to close the *Modify Style* dialog box. The style changes apply to all text formatted with the *Intense Quote* style on both the first and second pages.

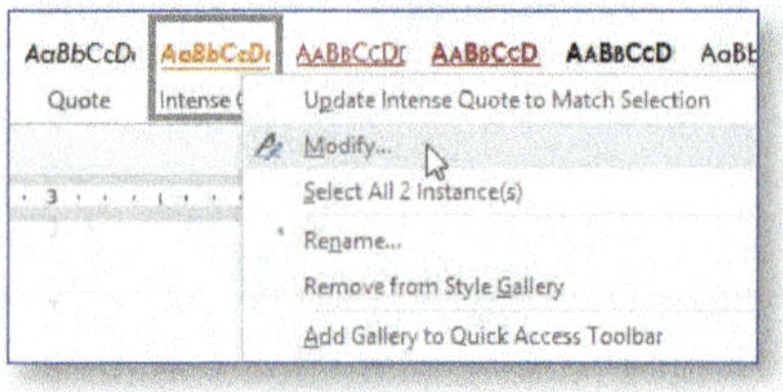

2-95 Modify an existing style

8. Add borders and shading to selected text.
   a. On the second page, select the first three paragraphs below "Insurance Application Disclaimer."
   b. Click the **Borders** drop-down arrow [*Home* tab, *Paragraph* group] and select **Borders and Shading** to open the *Borders and Shading* dialog box (Figure 2-96).
   c. In the *Setting* area, select **Custom**.
   d. In the *Style* area, select the **solid line** border.
   e. In the *Color* area, select **Orange**, **Accent 1**.
   f. In the *Width* area, select **1 pt**.
   g. In the *Preview* area, click the **Left** and **Right** border buttons (see Figure 2-96).
   h. In the *Apply to* area, select **Paragraph**.
   i. Click the **Options** button to open the *Border and Shading Options* dialog box.
   j. Change the *Left* and *Right* settings to **5 pt.** and click **OK** to close the *Border and Shading Options* dialog box.
   k. Click the **Shading** tab (Figure 2-97), and from the *Fill* drop-down list, select **Orange**, **Accent 1**, **Lighter 80%**.
   l. Click **OK** to close the *Borders and Shading* dialog box.

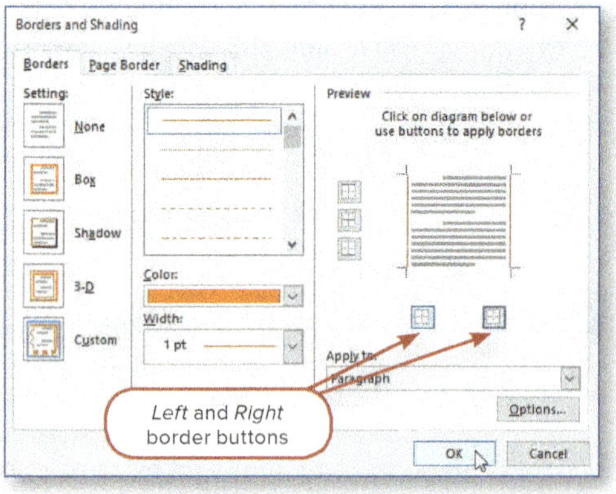

2-96 Apply a left and right border

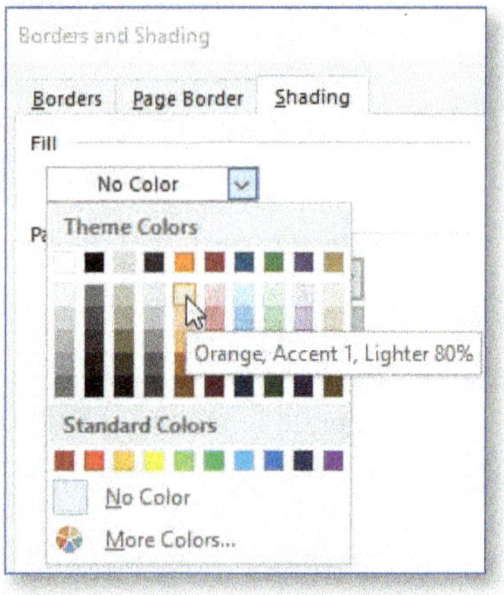

2-97 Select shading *Fill* color

9. Change the paragraph spacing and add a tab stop with an underline leader to selected text.
   a. On the second page, select the last three lines of text.
   b. Click the **Paragraph** launcher [*Home* or *Layout* tab] to open the *Paragraph* dialog box.
   c. Change the *Before* paragraph spacing to **12 pt**.
   d. Click the **Tabs** button to open the *Tabs* dialog box (Figure 2-98).
   e. Type 7 in the *Tab stop position* area.
   f. Click the **Right** radio button in the *Alignment* area.
   g. Click the **4** (solid underline) radio button in the *Leader* area.
   h. Click the **Set** button to set this tab stop and click **OK** to close the *Tabs* dialog box.
   i. Click at the end of the "Name and Title of the Insured" line and press **Tab**. A solid underline displays across the page to the right margin.
   j. Repeat step i on the next two lines.

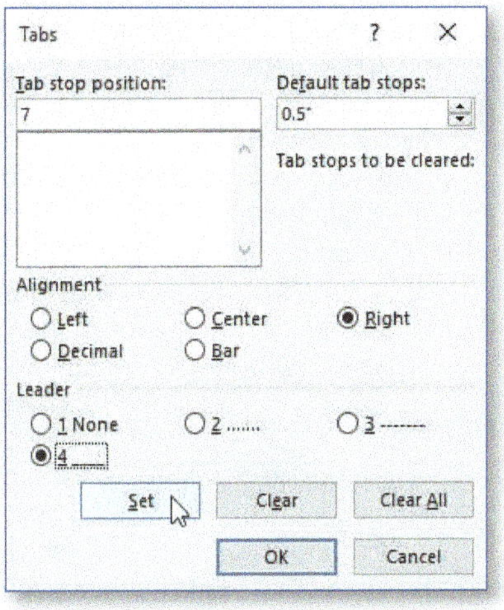

2-98 Set a right tab stop with an underline leader

10. Add a multilevel list to selected text and modify lists settings.
   a. Select the lines of text beginning with **"Applicant"** on the first page and ending with the last **"If yes, please explain:"** on the second page.
   b. Click the **Multilevel List** button [*Home* tab, *Paragraph* group] and select the **1), a), i)** option.
   c. With the text still selected, click the **Multilevel List** button again and select **Define New Multilevel List**. The *Define new Multilevel list* dialog box opens.
   d. Click the **Set for All Levels** button to open the *Set for All Levels* dialog box (Figure 2-99).
   e. Set the *Bullet/Number position for first level* to **0"**.
   f. Set the *Text position for first level* to **0.3"**.
   g. Set the *Additional indent for each level* to **0.3"**.
   h. Click **OK** to close the *Set for All Levels* dialog box and click **OK** to close the *Define new Multilevel list* dialog box.

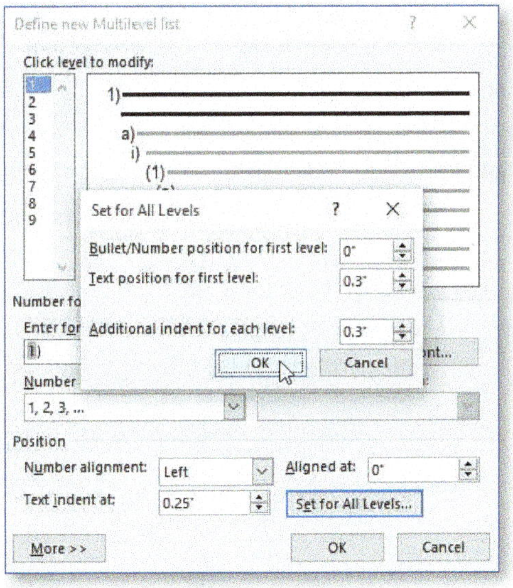

2-99 Change settings for a multilevel list

11. Increase indent on selected lines.
   a. Click anywhere on the list to deselect it.
   b. Place your insertion point in 13 in the numbered list ("If yes, . . .") and click **Increase Indent** [*Home* tab, *Paragraph* group]. This line is now letter *a)*.
   c. Repeat step b on each of the lines in the list that begin with "If yes, . . ." There should be 28 numbered items in the list when you finish this process.

12. Change paragraph spacing on the multilevel list and add a right tab stop with an underline leader.
   a. Select the entire multilevel list.
   b. Click the **Paragraph** launcher [*Home* or *Layout* tab] to open the *Paragraph* dialog box.
   c. Deselect the **Don't add space between paragraphs of the same style** check box (Figure 2-100).
   d. Click the **Tabs** button to open the *Tabs* dialog box.
   e. In the *Tab stop position* area, type 7.

f. Click the **Right** radio button in the *Alignment* area.
g. Click the **4** (solid underline) radio button in the *Leader* area.
h. Click the **Set** button to set this tab stop and click **OK** to close the *Tabs* dialog box.
i. Click at the end of the first numbered item ("Applicant:") and press **Tab**. A solid underline displays across the page to the right margin.
j. Repeat step i on each of the numbered and lettered paragraphs.

13. Save the document.
14. Insert a page break in the document.
    a. Place the insertion point before the text in number 22 in the multilevel list.
    b. Press **Ctrl+Enter** to insert a page break.

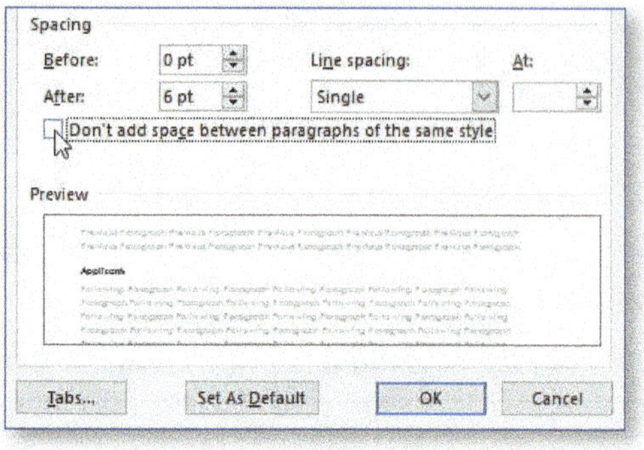

2-100 Add spacing between lines of text with the same style

15. Add a page number in the footer of the document.
    a. Press **Ctrl+Home** to move to the top of the document.
    b. Click the **Page Number** button [*Insert* tab, *Header & Footer* group].
    c. Place your pointer on **Bottom of Page** to display the drop-down list.
    d. Scroll down and choose **Bold Numbers 3** in the *Page X of Y* section. The page numbers display at the right of the footer.
    e. Click the blank line below the page numbers in the footer and press **Backspace** to delete the blank line.
    f. Click the **Close Header and Footer** button [*Header & Footer Tools Design* tab, *Close* group].
16. Save and close the document (Figure 2-101).

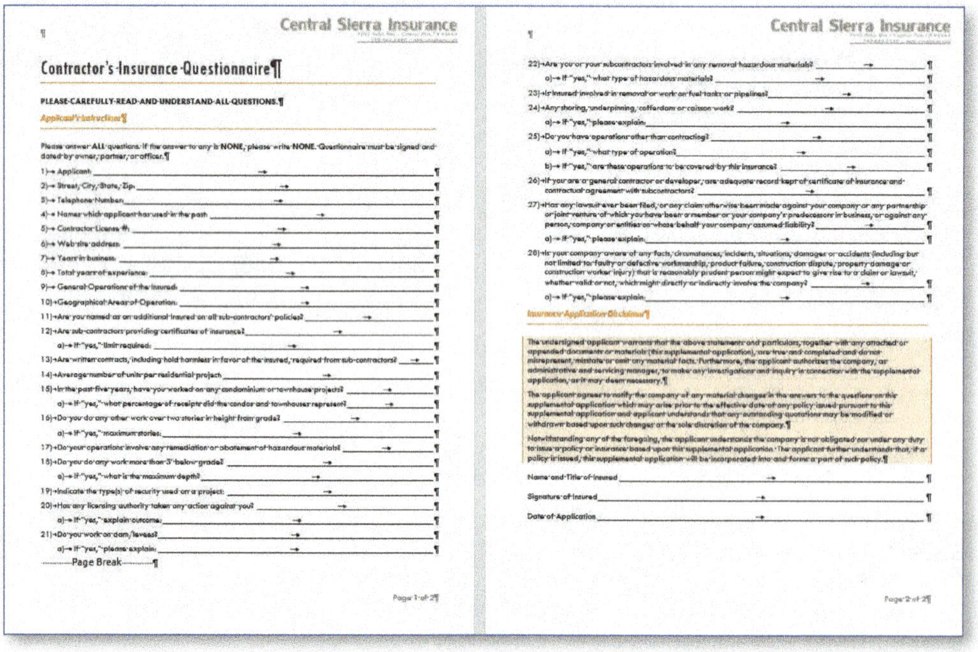

2-101 Word 2-1 completed

Guided Project 2-2

In this project, you create a checklist for employees at Placer Hills Real Estate to track the tasks they need to complete when a house enters escrow. You create a bulleted list, modify a bullet in a list, set and modify tab stops, apply and modify styles, and insert document properties in the footer.
[Student Learning Outcomes 2.1, 2.2, 2.3, 2.4, 2.6, 2.7, 2.9]

File Needed: ***SellerEscrowChecklist-02.docx*** *(Student data files are available in the* Library *of your SIMnet account)*
Completed Project File Name: ***[your initials] Word 2-2.docx***

Skills Covered in this Project

- Modify an existing document.
- Change margins, line spacing, font, and font size.
- Set a tab stop using the ruler.
- Set a tab stop with leader.
- Apply a style to selected text.
- Modify an existing style.
- Apply and customize a bulleted list.
- Use the *Format Painter*.
- Insert a document property field and date in the footer.
- Apply a border in the footer.

1. Open the ***SellerEscrowChecklist-02*** document from your student data files.
2. Save this document as [your initials] Word 2-2.
3. Change margins, vertical alignment, line spacing, and font and font size, and delete blank lines.
   a. Click the **Margins** button [*Layout* tab, *Page Setup* group] and select **Normal** from the drop-down list.
   b. Click the **Page Setup** launcher to open the *Page Setup* dialog box and click the **Layout** tab.
   c. In the *Page* area, change *Vertical alignment* to **Center** and click **OK** to close the *Page Setup* dialog box.
   d. Press **Ctrl+A** to select the entire document.
   e. Change the font to **Calibri** and change the font size to **12 pt**.
   f. Change the line spacing to **2.0** (Double).
   g. Turn on **Show/Hide**.
   h. Delete all of the blank lines between the lines of text.
4. Add text to the document.
   a. In the second line of the document, place the insertion point after "Seller" and press **Tab** once.
   b. Type Property Address.
   c. Place the insertion point after "Escrow Company" and press **Tab** once.
   d. Type Escrow #.
   e. Place the insertion point after "Tasks to be Completed" and press **Tab** once.
   f. Type Date Completed.
5. Set tab stops using the ruler to align information. If the ruler is not displayed, check the **Ruler** box [*View* tab, *Show* group].
   a. Select the second and third lines of text (beginning with **"Seller"** and ending with **"Escrow #"**).
   b. Verify that the **Left Tab** is selected in the *Tab* selector area to the left of the horizontal ruler.
   c. Click the ruler at **3.5"** to set a left tab stop. If you click the wrong location on the ruler, drag the tab stop to the correct location (Figure 2-102).

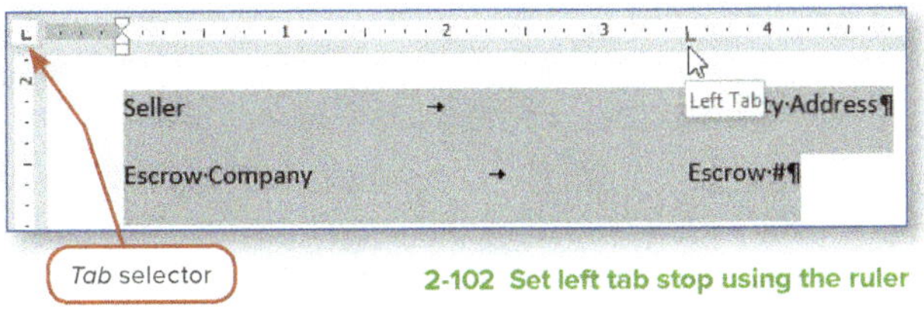

2-102 Set left tab stop using the ruler

d. Select the fourth line of text (beginning with "Tasks").
e. Click the **Tab** selector to change to a **Center Tab** stop (Figure 2-103).
f. Click the ruler at **5.5"** to set a center tab stop.

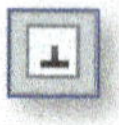

2-103 Center tab stop

6. Set tab stops and add leaders to create lines for users to fill in information.
   a. Select the second and third lines of text (beginning with "Seller").
   b. Click the **Paragraph** launcher to open the *Paragraph* dialog box.
   c. Click the **Tabs** button to open the *Tabs* dialog box.
   d. Type 3 in the *Tab stop position* area.
   e. Click the **Right** radio button in the *Alignment* area.
   f. Click the **4** (solid underline) radio button in the *Leader* area.
   g. Click the **Set** button to set this tab stop.
   h. Type 6.5 in the *Tab stop position* area.
   i. Click the **Right** radio button in the *Alignment* area.
   j. Click the **4** (solid underline) radio button in the *Leader* area.
   k. Click the **Set** button to set this tab stop and click **OK** to close the *Tabs* dialog box.
7. Use tab stops to align text and insert underline leader.
   a. Place the insertion point before "Property Address" and press **Tab** once.
   b. Place the insertion point to the right of "Property Address" and press **Tab** once.
   c. Place the insertion point before "Escrow #" and press **Tab** once.
   d. Place the insertion point to the right of "Escrow #" and press **Tab** once.
8. Apply styles to selected text and update a style.
   a. Place the insertion point in the first line of text ("Seller Escrow Checklist").
   b. Select **Title** style in the *Style* gallery [*Home* tab, *Styles* group].
   c. Change the *After* paragraph spacing to **24 pt**. [*Layout* tab, *Paragraph* group].
   d. Click the **Center** alignment button [*Home* tab, *Paragraph* group] to center the title.
   e. Select **"Tasks to be Completed"** and apply the **Book Title** style from the *Style* gallery.
   f. Change the font size of the selected text to **14 pt**. and apply a **Double underline**.
   g. Right-click the **Book Title** style in the *Style* gallery and select **Update Book Title to Match Selection**. The *Book Title* style is updated.
   h. Select "**Date Completed**" and apply the **Book Title** style.
9. Create a bulleted list to selected text and apply a custom bullet.
   a. Select the lines of text beginning with **"Open Escrow . . . "** and ending with **"Disclosures Sent to Agent."**
   b. Click the **Bullets** drop-down arrow [*Home* tab, *Paragraph* group] and select **Define New Bullet**. The *Define New Bullet* dialog box opens.
   c. Click the **Symbol** button to open the *Symbol* dialog box (Figure 2-104).
   d. Click the **Font** drop-down arrow and select **Wingdings**.
   e. Scroll down the list and select the **open square** bullet (Character code 113).
   f. Click **OK** to close the *Symbol* dialog box.
   g. Click the **Font** button in the *Define New Bullet* dialog box. The *Font* dialog box opens.
   h. Change the *Size* to **14 pt**.
   i. Click **OK** to close the *Font* dialog box and click **OK** to close the *Define New Bullet* dialog box.
   j. With the bulleted list still selected, click the **Decrease Indent** button to align the bulleted list at the left margin.

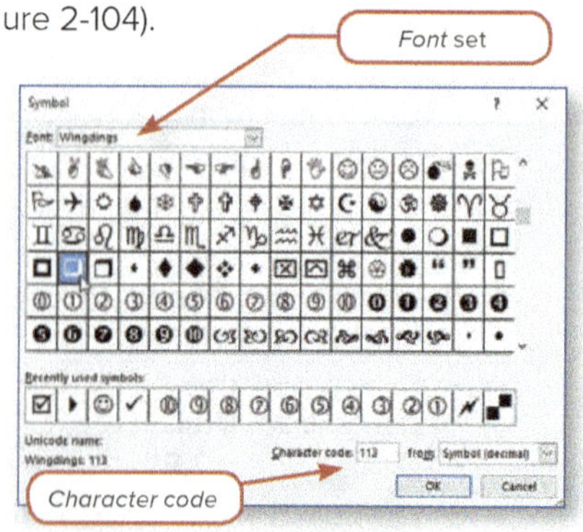

2-104 Select a symbol for a custom bullet

10. Change the hanging indent and add tab stops.
    a. Select the bulleted list.
    b. Click the **Paragraph** launcher to open the *Paragraph* dialog box.

c. Change the *Hanging* indent to **0.3"**.
d. Click the **Tabs** button to open the *Tabs* dialog box (Figure 2-105).
e. Type 4.5 in the *Tab stop position* area.
f. Click the **Left** radio button in the *Alignment* area, click the **1 None** radio button in the *Leader* area, and click the **Set** button to set this tab stop.
g. Type 6.5 in the *Tab stop position* area.
h. Click the **Right** radio button in the *Alignment* area, click the **4** (solid underline) radio button in the *Leader* area, and click the **Set** button to set this tab stop, and click **OK** to close the *Tabs* dialog box.
i. Place the insertion point after "Open Escrow with Escrow Company" and press **Tab** two times. A solid underline displays between 4.5" and 6.5".
j. Repeat step i on the remaining lines in the bulleted list.

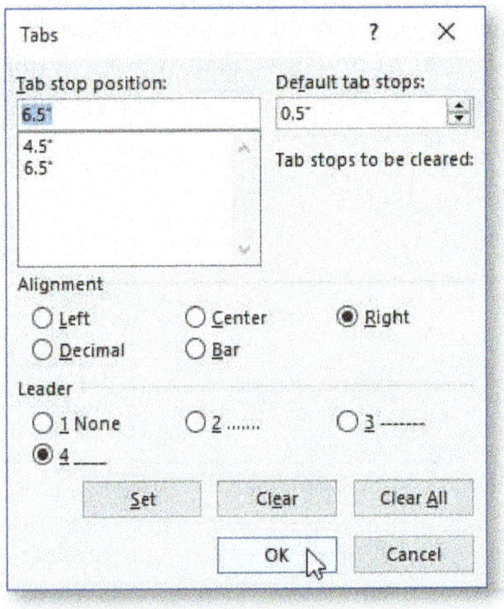

2-105 *Tabs* dialog box

11. Add text to the document.
   a. Press **Enter** after the solid underline in the last line of text in the document.
   b. Click the **Bullets** button [*Home* tab, *Paragraph* group] to turn off the bullet on this line.
   c. Type Fax/Email Clear Pest Report and press **Enter**.
   d. Type Title and press **Enter**.
   e. Type Lender and press **Enter**.
   f. Type Buyer's Agent.

12. Apply a style to selected text and use the *Format Painter*.
   a. Select **"Fax/Email Clear Pest Report"** and apply the **Subtle Reference** style.
   b. Place the insertion point in one of the bulleted items.
   c. Click the **Format Painter** button [*Home* tab, *Clipboard* group] to copy the formatting of this bulleted item.
   d. Select the last three lines of text (beginning with **"Title . . ."**). The *Format Painter* copies the bullet formatting and tab settings to these lines of text.
   e. Press **Tab** two times after each of these last three lines to insert the tabs and leaders.

13. Insert a document property field, the date, and a border in the footer of the document.
   a. Click the **Footer** button [*Insert* tab, *Header & Footer* group] and select **Edit Footer** from the drop-down list to open the footer.
   b. Click the **Document Info** button [*Header & Footer Tools Design* tab, *Insert* group], click **Document Property**, and select **Company**. The *Company* document property field displays in the footer.
   c. Press the **right arrow** key once to deselect the *Company* field.
   d. Press **Tab** two times, type Last updated:, and **space** once. The text aligns at the right side of the footer.
   e. Click the **Date & Time** button [*Header & Footer Tools Design* tab, *Insert* group] to open the *Date and Time* dialog box.
   f. Select the spelled out month, day, year option (e.g., January 1, 2018), check the **Update automatically** box, and click **OK** to insert the date and close the dialog box.
   g. Select all of the text in the footer and change the font to **Calibri** and the font size to **10 pt**.
   h. Click the **Borders** drop-down arrow [*Home* tab, *Paragraph* group] and select **Borders and Shading** to open the *Borders and Shading* dialog box.
   i. Click the **Color** drop-down list and select **Black, Text 1**.
   j. Click the **Width** drop-down list and select **1 pt**.
   k. In the *Preview* area, click the **Top** border button to apply a top border to the footer.

l. Click **OK** to close the *Borders and Shading* dialog box.
m. Click the **Close Header and Footer** button [*Header & Footer Tools Design* tab, *Close* group].

14. Save and close the document (Figure 2-106).

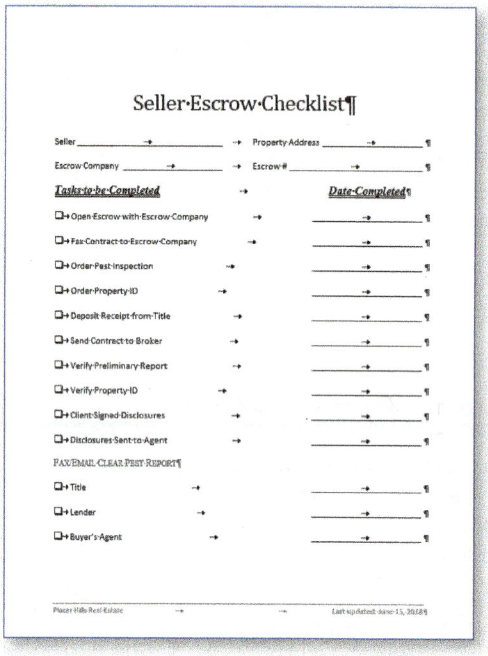

Seller Escrow Checklist

Seller ____________ Property Address ____________
Escrow Company ____________ Escrow # ____________

Tasks to be Completed	***Date Completed***
☐ Open Escrow with Escrow Company	____________
☐ Fax Contract to Escrow Company	____________
☐ Order Pest Inspection	____________
☐ Order Property ID	____________
☐ Deposit Receipt from Title	____________
☐ Send Contract to Broker	____________
☐ Verify Preliminary Report	____________
☐ Verify Property ID	____________
☐ Client Signed Disclosures	____________
☐ Disclosures Sent to Agent	____________
FAX/EMAIL CLEAR PEST REPORT	
☐ Title	____________
☐ Lender	____________
☐ Buyer's Agent	____________

Placer Hills Real Estate Last updated: June 15, 2018

2-106 Word 2-2 completed

Guided Project 2-3

In this project, you edit and format the personal training guide for the American River Cycling Club to improve readability and effectiveness. You use find and replace, apply a document theme, modify styles, customize numbered and bulleted lists, apply borders and shading, and insert headers, footers, and document properties.
[Student Learning Outcomes 2.1, 2.3, 2.4, 2.6, 2.7, 2.8, 2.9]

File Needed: ***PersonalTrainingProgram-02.docx*** *(Student data files are available in the* Library *of your SIMnet account)*
Completed Project File Name: ***[your initials] Word 2-3.docx***

Skills Covered in this Project

- Modify an existing document.
- Apply a document theme.
- Change margins.
- Change line spacing and paragraph spacing.
- Apply a style to selected text.
- Apply borders and shading to selected text.
- Update an existing style.
- Customize a multilevel bulleted list.
- Use *Find*.
- Use *Find* and *Replace*.
- Insert a hyperlink.
- Insert header, footer, page number, and document properties.

1. Open the ***PersonalTrainingProgram-02*** document from your student data files.
2. Save this document as [your initials] Word 2-3.
3. Apply a document theme and change the line and paragraph spacing.
   a. Click the **Themes** button [*Design* tab, *Document Formatting* group] and select **Slice** from the drop-down list of theme options.
   b. Click the **Margins** button [*Layout* tab, *Page Setup* group] and select **Custom Margins** to open the *Page Setup* dialog box.
   c. Change the *Left* and *Right* margins to **1"** and click **OK** to close the *Page Setup* dialog box.
   d. Press **Ctrl+A** to select the entire document.
   e. Change the line spacing to **1.15** and change the *After* paragraph spacing to **10 pt**.
   f. Turn on **Show/Hide**.
4. Apply styles to the title, subtitle, and section headings.
   a. Select the title (first line) of the document.
   b. Apply the **Title** style from the *Style* gallery [*Home* tab, *Styles* group].
   c. Change the font size to **20 pt**. and apply **bold** and **center** alignment.
   d. Select the subtitle (second line) of the document.
   e. Apply the **Subtitle** style from the *Style* gallery.
   f. Change the font size to **16 pt**. and **center** it.
   g. Select the first section heading (**"General Guidelines"**).
   h. Apply the **Heading 1** style from the *Style* gallery.
   i. Apply the **Heading 1** style to the remaining section headings in the document (**"Personal Training Program Guidelines," "More About Long Rides," "Training Intensity and Heart Rate," "Tracking Training Miles versus Hours," and "Using a Training Log"**).
5. Update a style in the document.
   a. Select the first section heading (**"General Guidelines"**) including the paragraph mark at the end of the line.
   b. Change the *Before* paragraph spacing to **12 pt**. and the *After* paragraph spacing to **6 pt**.
   c. Click the **Borders** drop-down arrow [*Home* tab, *Paragraph* group] and select **Borders and Shading**. The *Borders and Shading* dialog box opens.
   d. In the *Setting* area, select **Shadow**.
   e. In the *Style* area, select the **solid line**.
   f. In the *Color* area, select **Dark Blue**, **Accent 1**, **Darker 50%** (Figure 2-107).
   g. In the *Width* area, select **1 pt**.
   h. In the *Apply to* area, select **Paragraph**.
   i. Click the **Shading** tab, and in the *Fill* area, select **Dark Blue**, **Accent 1**, **Lighter 80%**.
   j. In the *Apply to* area, select **Paragraph**, and click **OK** to close the *Borders and Shading* dialog box.
   k. With the heading still selected, right-click the **Heading 1** style in the *Style gallery* and select **Update Heading 1 to Match Selection**. All of the headings in the document with the *Heading 1* style applied update automatically.

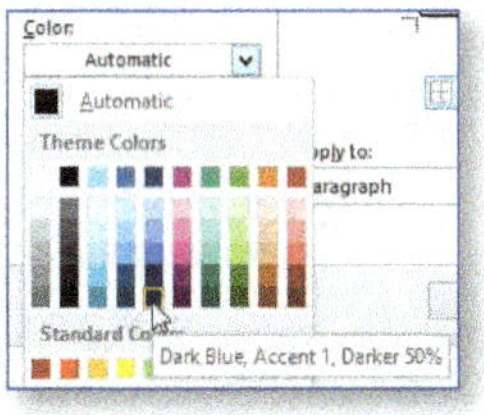

2-107 Select border line color

6. Customize the bullets and indents for the bulleted list.
   a. Right-click the first bulleted item on the first page and select **Adjust List Indents**. The *Define new Multilevel list* dialog box opens.
   b. Click **1** in the *Click level to modify* area.
   c. In the *Number style for this level* area, select **New Bullet** from the drop-down list (Figure 2-108). The *Symbol* dialog box opens.

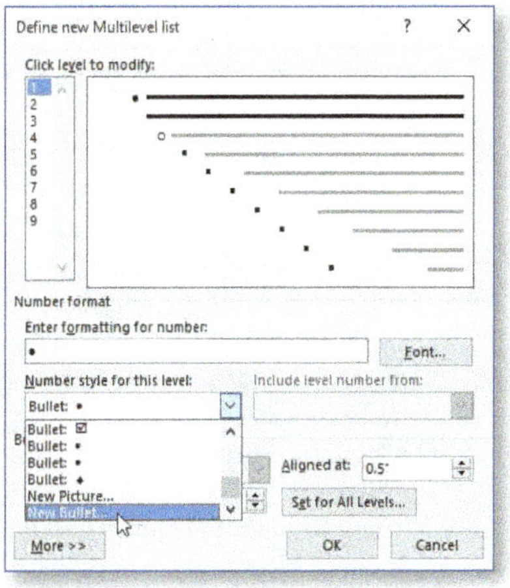

2-108 Customize bulleted list

d. In the *Font* area, select **Webdings** from the drop-down list, click the **right pointing triangle** (Character code 52), and click **OK** to close the *Symbol* dialog box (Figure 2-109).

e. Click **2** in the *Click level to modify* area in the *Define new Multilevel list* dialog box.

f. In the *Number style for this level* area, select **New Bullet** from the drop-down list. The *Symbol* dialog box opens.

g. In the *Font* area, select **Webdings** from the drop-down list, click the **double right pointing triangle** (Character code 56), and click **OK** to close the *Symbol* dialog box.

h. Click the **Set for All Levels** button in the *Define new Multilevel list* dialog box. The *Set for All Levels* dialog box opens (Figure 2-110).

i. Change the *Bullet/Number position for first level* to **0.25"**, change the *Text position for first level* to **0.5"**, and change *Additional indent for each level* to **0.25"**.

j. Click **OK** to close the *Set for All Levels* dialog box and click **OK** to close the *Define new Multilevel list* dialog box. All of the first and second level bullets and indents in the entire document are changed.

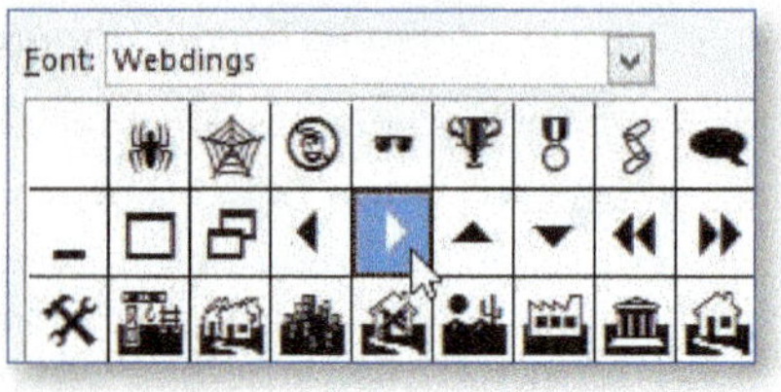

2-109 Select bullet from *Webdings* font set

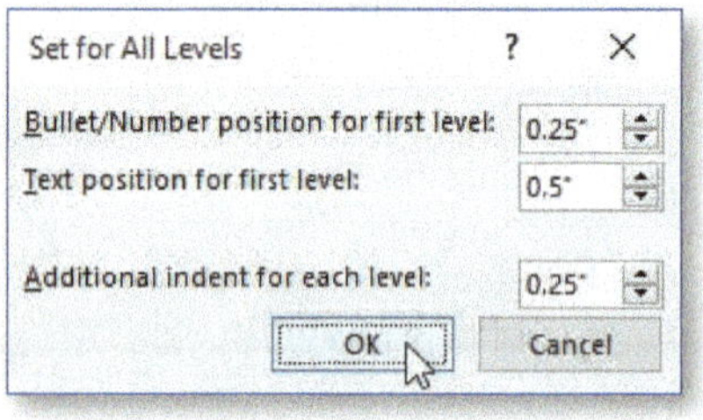

2-110 Set indents for all levels

7. Use the *Find* feature to find text in the document.
   a. Press **Ctrl+Home** to go to the beginning of the document.
   b. Click the **Find** button [*Home* tab, *Editing* group] or press **Ctrl+F** to open *Find* in the *Navigation* pane.
   c. Type personal training program in the *Search Document* area. All instances of this text appear in the *Navigation* pane.
   d. Click after "personal training program" in the first body paragraph on the first page and type (PTP). Make sure there is one space before and after "(PTP)".
   e. Select **"PTP"** (not the parentheses) and apply **italic** format.
   f. Click the **X** in the upper right of the *Navigation* pane to close this pane.

8. Use the replace feature to find and replace text in the document.
   a. Press **Ctrl+Home** to go to the beginning of the document.
   b. Click the **Replace** button [*Home* tab, *Editing* group] to open the *Find and Replace* dialog box with the *Replace* tab selected (Figure 2-111).
   c. In the *Find what* area, type personal training program.
   d. In the *Replace with* area, type PTP.
   e. Click the **More** button to display more search options.
   f. Click the **Format** button and select **Font** to open the *Replace Font* dialog box.
   g. Click **Italic** in the *Font style* area and click **OK** to close the *Replace Font* dialog box.

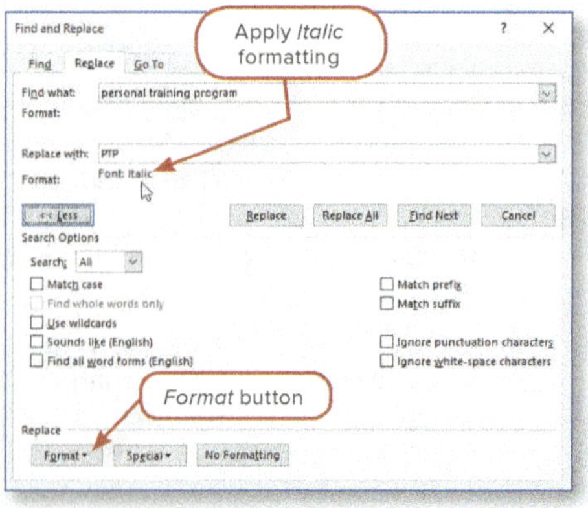

2-111 Replace text with text and formatting

h. Click the **Less** button to collapse the *Find and Replace* dialog box.
i. Click the **Find Next** button to find the first occurrence of "personal training program" in the document.
j. Do not replace this text in the title, first body paragraph, or section heading. Replace all other occurrences of "personal training program" with "*PTP*". Click the **Replace** button to replace the highlighted occurrence or click the **Find Next** button to skip and not replace an occurrence.
k. Click **OK** when you are finished searching the document and click **Close** to close the *Find and Replace* dialog box.

9. Add a hyperlink to the document.
   a. Select the subtitle of the document (**"American River Cycling Club"**).
   b. Click the **Hyperlink** button [*Insert* tab, *Links* group] or press **Ctrl+K** to open the *Insert Hyperlink* dialog box.
   c. Click the **Existing File or Web Page** button in the *Link to* area.
   d. Type www.arcc.org in the *Address* area. Word automatically inserts "http://" before the web address.
   e. Click the **ScreenTip** button to open the *Set Hyperlink ScreenTip* dialog box.
   f. Type American River Cycling Club in the *ScreenTip text* area and click **OK** to close the *Set Hyperlink ScreenTip* dialog box.
   g. Click the **Target Frame** button to open the *Set Target Frame* dialog box.
   h. Select **New window** from the drop-down list.
   i. Click **OK** to close the *Set Target Frame* dialog box and click **OK** to close the *Insert Hyperlink* dialog box.

10. Insert header and footer on the second and continuing pages.
   a. Press **Ctrl+Home** to move to the beginning of the document.
   b. Click the **Page Number** button [*Insert* tab, *Header & Footer* group].
   c. Click **Top of Page** and select **Accent Bar 2** from the drop-down list. The page number displays in the header area.
   d. Check the **Different First Page** check box [*Header & Footer Tools Design* tab, *Options* group] to remove the header from the first page so it only displays on the second and continuing pages.

11. Insert document property fields in the footer.
   a. With the header still open, click the **Go to Footer** button [*Navigation* group].
   b. Click the **Next** button [*Navigation* group] to move to the footer on the second page.
   c. Click the **Document Info** button [*Insert* group], click **Document Property**, and select **Company** to insert the company document property field.
   d. Press the **right arrow** key once to deselect the property field.
   e. Press **Tab** two times to move the insertion point to the right margin in the footer.
   f. Click the **Document Info** button [*Insert* group] and select **Document Title** to insert the title document property field.
   g. Press **Ctrl+A** to select all of the text in the footer.
   h. Apply **bold** and **italic** formatting and change the font size to **10 pt**.
   i. Click the **Go to Header** button [*Header & Footer Tools Design* tab, *Navigation* group] to move to the header on the second page.
   j. Press **Ctrl+A** to select all of the text in the header and change the font size to **10 pt**.
   k. Click the **Close Header and Footer** button [*Header & Footer Tools Design* tab, *Close* group]. The header and footer information should appear on the second and continuing pages in the document.

12. Save and close the document (Figure 2-112).

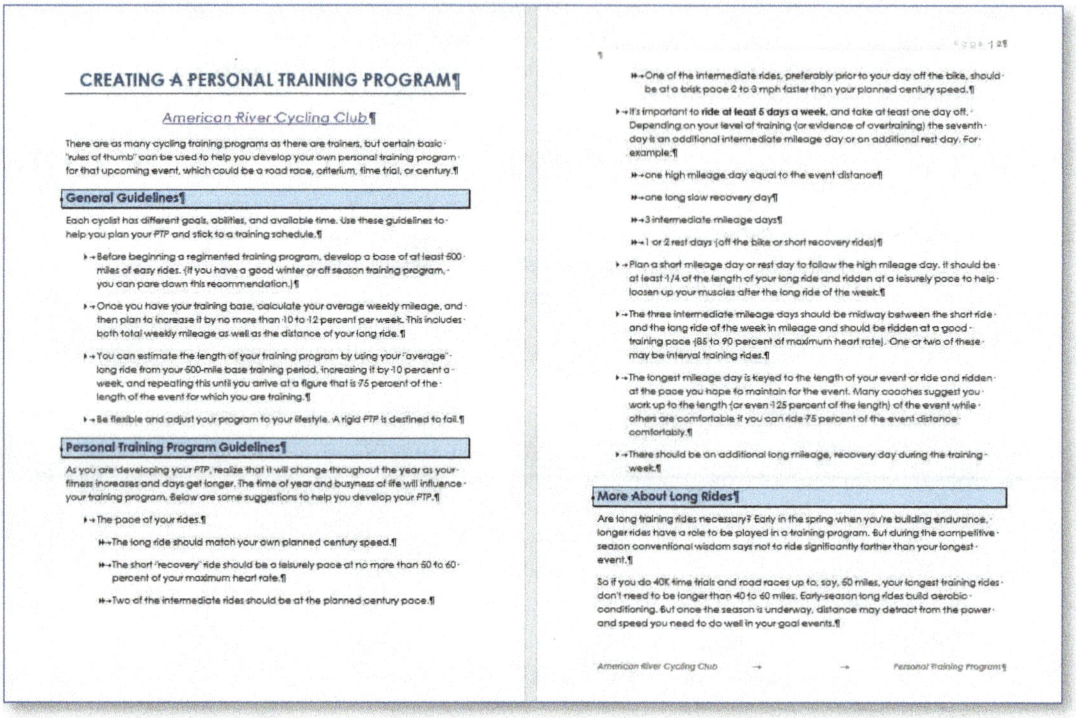

CREATING A PERSONAL TRAINING PROGRAM

American River Cycling Club

There are as many cycling training programs as there are trainers, but certain basic "rules of thumb" can be used to help you develop your own personal training program for that upcoming event, which could be a road race, criterium, time trial, or century.

General Guidelines

Each cyclist has different goals, abilities, and available time. Use these guidelines to help you plan your *PTP* and stick to a training schedule.

- Before beginning a regimented training program, develop a base of at least 500 miles of easy rides. (If you have a good winter or off season training program, you can pare down this recommendation.)
- Once you have your training base, calculate your average weekly mileage, and then plan to increase it by no more than 10 to 12 percent per week. This includes both total weekly mileage as well as the distance of your long ride.
- You can estimate the length of your training program by using your "average" long ride from your 500-mile base training period, increasing it by 10 percent a week, and repeating this until you arrive at a figure that is 75 percent of the length of the event for which you are training.
- Be flexible and adjust your program to your lifestyle. A rigid *PTP* is destined to fail.

Personal Training Program Guidelines

As you are developing your *PTP*, realize that it will change throughout the year as your fitness increases and days get longer. The time of year and busyness of life will influence your training program. Below are some suggestions to help you develop your *PTP*.

- The pace of your rides.
  - The long ride should match your own planned century speed.
  - The short "recovery" ride should be a leisurely pace at no more than 50 to 60 percent of your maximum heart rate.
  - Two of the intermediate rides should be at the planned century pace.
  - One of the intermediate rides, preferably prior to your day off the bike, should be at a brisk pace 2 to 3 mph faster than your planned century speed.
- It's important to **ride at least 5 days a week**, and take at least one day off. Depending on your level of training (or evidence of overtraining) the seventh day is an additional intermediate mileage day or an additional rest day. For example:
  - one high mileage day equal to the event distance
  - one long slow recovery day
  - 3 intermediate mileage days
  - 1 or 2 rest days (off the bike or short recovery rides)
- Plan a short mileage day or rest day to follow the high mileage day. It should be at least 1/4 of the length of your long ride and ridden at a leisurely pace to help loosen up your muscles after the long ride of the week.
- The three intermediate mileage days should be midway between the short ride and the long ride of the week in mileage and should be ridden at a good training pace (85 to 90 percent of maximum heart rate). One or two of these may be interval training rides.
- The longest mileage day is keyed to the length of your event or ride and ridden at the pace you hope to maintain for the event. Many coaches suggest you work up to the length (or even 125 percent of the length) of the event while others are comfortable if you can ride 75 percent of the event distance comfortably.
- There should be an additional long mileage, recovery day during the training week.

More About Long Rides

Are long training rides necessary? Early in the spring when you're building endurance, longer rides have a role to be played in a training program. But during the competitive season conventional wisdom says not to ride significantly farther than your longest event.

So if you do 40K time trials and road races up to, say, 50 miles, your longest training rides don't need to be longer than 40 to 60 miles. Early-season long rides build aerobic conditioning. But once the season is underway, distance may detract from the power and speed you need to do well in your goal events.

American River Cycling Club *Personal Training Program*

2-112 Word 2-3 completed (pages 1 and 2 of 5)

Independent Project 2-4

In this project, you use styles, indents, lists, tab stops, the replace feature, footers, and document properties to customize the Emergency Procedures document for Sierra Pacific Community College District. [Student Learning Outcomes 2.1, 2.2, 2.3, 2.4, 2.6, 2.7, 2.8, 2.9]

File Needed: ***EmergencyProcedures-02.docx*** *(Student data files are available in the* Library *of your SIMnet account)*
Completed Project File Name: ***[your initials] Word 2-4.docx***

Skills Covered in this Project

- Modify an existing document.
- Apply a document theme and theme color.
- Change margins and font size.
- Apply and modify a style.
- Apply a border to selected text.
- Apply and customize a numbered and bulleted list.
- Use the *Format Painter.*
- Set and modify tab stops.
- Use *Replace.*
- Insert a footer with document properties and current date.
- Insert a page border.
- Center text vertically.

1. Open the ***EmergencyProcedures-02*** document from your student data files.
2. Save this document as [your initials] Word 2-4.
3. Change the theme to **Integral** and the theme color to **Red**.
4. Change the top, bottom, left, and right margins to **0.75"**.
5. Select the entire document and change the font size to **12 pt**.
6. Format the title of the document.
   a. Select the title of the document and apply **Heading 1** style.
   b. Open the *Font* dialog box, apply **All caps** effect, and change the font size to **16 pt**.
   c. Change the *Before* paragraph spacing to **0 pt**.
   d. Add a **bottom border** to the title using the **Borders** drop-down list.
7. Select each of the bold section headings and apply the **Heading 2** style.
8. Modify the *Heading 2* style.
   a. Select the first section heading (**"Emergency Telephones [Blue Phones]"**).
   b. Change *Before* paragraph spacing to **12 pt**. and *After* paragraph spacing to **3 pt**.
   c. Apply **small caps** effect and **underline**.
   d. Update **Heading 2** style to match this heading. All of the section headings are updated.
9. Turn on **Show/Hide** and delete all of the blank lines in the document.
10. Select the bulleted list in the first section and change it to a numbered list.
11. Apply numbering format, make formatting changes, and use the *Format Painter*.
    a. Apply numbering to the text in the following sections: "*Assaults, Fights, or Emotional Disturbances*"; "*Power Failure*"; "*Fire*"; "*Earthquake*"; and "*Bomb Threat*."
    b. Select the numbered list in the "Bomb Threat" section.
    c. Open the *Paragraph* dialog box, set before and after paragraph spacing to **2 pt**., and deselect the **Don't add space between paragraphs of the same style** check box.
    d. Use the *Format Painter* to copy this numbering format to each of the other numbered lists.
    e. Reset each numbered list so it begins with **1** (right-click the first item in each numbered list and select **Restart at 1** from the context menu).
12. Customize a bulleted list and use the *Format Painter*.
    a. Select the text in the "Accident or Medical Emergency" section.
    b. Use a **solid square bullet** (*Wingdings*, Character code 110).
    c. Confirm the left indent is **0.25"** and hanging indent is **0.25"**. If they are not, make these changes.
    d. Set *Before* and *After* paragraph spacing to **2 pt**.
    e. Deselect the **Don't add space between paragraphs of the same style** check box (*Paragraph* dialog box).
    f. Use the *Format Painter* to apply this bulleted list format to the following text in the following sections: "*Tips to Professors and Staff*" and "*Response to Students*."
13. Change indent and paragraph spacing and apply a style.
    a. Select the text below the "Emergency Telephone Locations" heading.
    b. Set a **0.25"** left indent.
    c. Set *Before* and *After* paragraph spacing to **2 pt**.
    d. Confirm the **Don't add space between paragraphs of the same style** box is unchecked.
    e. In the "Emergency Telephone Locations" section, apply **Book Title** style to each of the telephone locations. Select only the location, not the text in parentheses or following text.
14. Change left indent and paragraph spacing and set a tab stop with a dot leader.
    a. Select the text below the "Emergency Phone Numbers" heading.
    b. Set a **0.25"** left indent for this text.
    c. Set *Before* and *After* paragraph spacing to **2 pt**.

d. Confirm the **Don't add space between paragraphs of the same style** box is unchecked.
e. With the text still selected, set a right tab stop at **7"** and use a **dot leader (2)**.
f. Press **Tab** before the phone number on each of these lines. The phone numbers align at the right margin with a dot leader between the text and phone number.

15. Apply the **Intense Reference** style to the paragraph headings in the "Accident or Medical Emergency" section (*"Life-Threating Emergencies"* and *"Minor Emergencies"*). Don't include the colon when selecting the paragraph headings.

16. Use the *Replace* feature to replace all instances of "Phone 911" with "PHONE 911" with **bold** font style.

17. Insert a footer with document property fields and the current date that appears on every page.
    a. Edit the footer and use the ruler to move the center tab stop to **3.5"** and the right tab stop to **7"**.
    b. Insert the **Title** document property field on the left. Use the **right arrow** key to deselect the document property field.
    c. Insert the **Company** document property field at center. Use the center tab stop for alignment. Use the **right arrow** key to deselect the document property field.
    d. Insert a date (use January 1, 2018 format) that updates automatically on the right. Use the right tab stop for alignment.
    e. Change the font size of all the text in the footer to **10 pt**.
    f. Add a **top border** to the text in the footer using the **Borders** drop-down list.

18. Insert a page border on the entire document. Use **Shadow** setting, **solid line** style, **Dark Red**, **Accent 1** color, and **1 pt**. line width.

19. Center the entire document vertically.

20. Save and close the document (Figure 2-113).

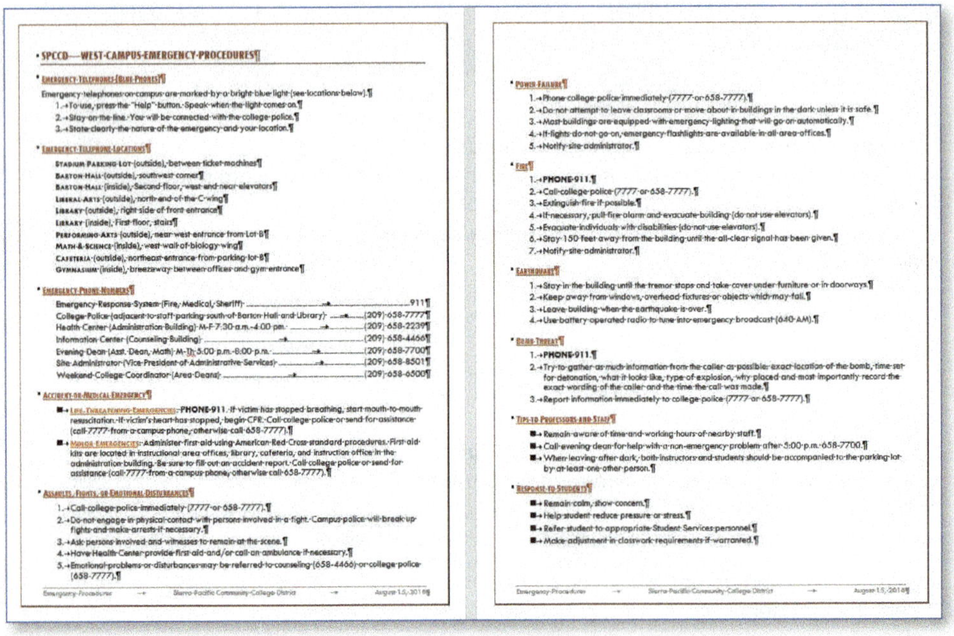
SPCCD—WEST CAMPUS EMERGENCY PROCEDURES

EMERGENCY TELEPHONES (BLUE PHONES)

Emergency telephones on campus are marked by a bright blue light (see locations below).
1. To use, press the "Help" button. Speak when the light comes on.
2. Stay on the line. You will be connected with the college police.
3. State clearly the nature of the emergency and your location.

EMERGENCY TELEPHONE LOCATIONS

STADIUM PARKING LOT (outside), between ticket machines
BARTON HALL (outside), southwest corner
BARTON HALL (inside), Second floor, west end near elevators
LIBERAL ARTS (outside), north end of the C wing
LIBRARY (outside), right side of front entrance
LIBRARY (inside), First floor, stairs
PERFORMING ARTS (outside), near west entrance from Lot B
MATH & SCIENCE (inside), west wall of biology wing
CAFETERIA (outside), northeast entrance from parking lot B
GYMNASIUM (inside), breezeway between offices and gym entrance

EMERGENCY PHONE NUMBERS

Emergency Response System (Fire, Medical, Sheriff) 911
College Police (adjacent to staff parking south of Barton Hall and Library) .... (209) 658-7777
Health Center (Administration Building) M-F 7:30 a.m.-4:00 pm. .... (209) 658-2239
Information Center (Counseling Building) .... (209) 658-4466
Evening Dean (Asst. Dean, Math) M-Th 5:00 p.m.-8:00 p.m. .... (209) 658-7700
Site Administrator (Vice President of Administrative Services) .... (209) 658-8501
Weekend College Coordinator (Area Deans) .... (209) 658-6500

ACCIDENT OR MEDICAL EMERGENCY

- LIFE-THREATENING EMERGENCIES: **PHONE 911**. If victim has stopped breathing, start mouth-to-mouth resuscitation. If victim's heart has stopped, begin CPR. Call college police or send for assistance (call 7777 from a campus phone, otherwise call 658-7777).
- MINOR EMERGENCIES: Administer first aid using American Red Cross standard procedures. First aid kits are located in instructional area offices, library, cafeteria, and instruction office in the administration building. Be sure to fill out an accident report. Call college police or send for assistance (call 7777 from a campus phone, otherwise call 658-7777).

ASSAULTS, FIGHTS, OR EMOTIONAL DISTURBANCES

1. Call college police immediately (7777 or 658-7777).
2. Do not engage in physical contact with persons involved in a fight. Campus police will break up fights and make arrests if necessary.
3. Ask persons involved and witnesses to remain at the scene.
4. Have Health Center provide first aid and/or call an ambulance if necessary.
5. Emotional problems or disturbances may be referred to counseling (658-4466) or college police (658-7777).

Emergency Procedures Sierra Pacific Community College District August 15, 2016

POWER FAILURE

1. Phone college police immediately (7777 or 658-7777).
2. Do not attempt to leave classrooms or move about in buildings in the dark unless it is safe.
3. Most buildings are equipped with emergency lighting that will go on automatically.
4. If lights do not go on, emergency flashlights are available in all area offices.
5. Notify site administrator.

FIRE

1. **PHONE 911.**
2. Call college police (7777 or 658-7777).
3. Extinguish fire if possible.
4. If necessary, pull fire alarm and evacuate building (do not use elevators).
5. Evacuate individuals with disabilities (do not use elevators).
6. Stay 150 feet away from the building until the all-clear signal has been given.
7. Notify site administrator.

EARTHQUAKE

1. Stay in the building until the tremor stops and take cover under furniture or in doorways.
2. Keep away from windows, overhead fixtures or objects which may fall.
3. Leave building when the earthquake is over.
4. Use battery operated radio to tune into emergency broadcast (640 AM).

BOMB THREAT

1. **PHONE 911.**
2. Try to gather as much information from the caller as possible: exact location of the bomb, time set for detonation, what it looks like, type of explosion, why placed and most importantly record the exact wording of the caller and the time the call was made.
3. Report information immediately to college police (7777 or 658-7777).

TIPS TO PROFESSORS AND STAFF

- Remain aware of time and working hours of nearby staff.
- Call evening dean for help with a non-emergency problem after 5:00 p.m. 658-7700.
- When leaving after dark, both instructors and students should be accompanied to the parking lot by at least one other person.

RESPONSE TO STUDENTS

- Remain calm, show concern.
- Help student reduce pressure or stress.
- Refer student to appropriate Student Services personnel.
- Make adjustment in classwork requirements if warranted.

Emergency Procedures Sierra Pacific Community College District August 15, 2016

2-113 Word 2-4 completed

Independent Project 2-5

In this project, you format a bank authorization letter for Placer Hills Real Estate. You modify the formatting of an existing document, apply a theme, apply and modify styles, set tab stops, apply borders, and insert and edit hyperlinks.
[Student Learning Outcomes 2.1, 2.2, 2.7, 2.9]

File Needed: ***BankAuthorization-02.docx*** *(Student data files are available in the* Library *of your SIMnet account)*
Completed Project File Name: ***[your initials] Word 2-5.docx***

Skills Covered in this Project

- Modify an existing document.
- Apply a document theme.
- Change margins.
- Insert an automatically updated date.
- Apply and modify a style.
- Expand font spacing.
- Change paragraph spacing.
- Use the *Format Painter.*
- Set and use tab stops.
- Apply borders and shading to selected text.
- Insert a hyperlink.
- Edit a hyperlink.

1. Open the ***BankAuthorization-02*** document from your student data files.
2. Save this document as [your initials] Word 2-5.
3. Change the theme to **Wisp**.
4. Change the margins to **Normal**.
5. Select the entire document and change the *After* paragraph spacing to **18 pt**.
6. Press **Enter** after the first line of the document, insert (don't type) the current date (use January 1, 2018 format), and set it to update automatically.
7. Click at the end of the document, press **Enter**, and type the following information. Use line breaks (**Shift+Enter**) after the first three lines. (*Note: The email address is automatically converted to a hyperlink; you will edit this later.*)

   Emma Cavalli
   Placer Hills Real Estate
   ecavalli@phre.com
   916-450-3334
8. Select the date line and change the *After* paragraph spacing to **30 pt**.
9. Use the *Format Painter* to copy the date line format to the **"Sincerely,"** line.
10. Apply styles and use the *Format Painter*.
    a. Apply the **Title** style to the first line of the document and change the *Before* paragraph spacing to **36 pt**.
    b. Select **"Authorization Letter to Lender,"** apply the **Intense Reference** style, and expand the font *Spacing* to **1 pt**.
    c. Select the five lines of text beginning with **"Bank/Financial Institution:"** and ending with **"Borrower Name(s):"** and apply the **Book Title** style.
    d. Use the *Format Painter* to copy the "Bank/Financial Institution" format to **"Seller/Borrower Signature(s)"**.
11. Set a tab stop with a leader.
    a. Select the five lines of text beginning with **"Bank/Financial Institution:"** and ending with **"Borrower Name(s):."**

b. Set a right tab stop at **6.5"** with a **solid underline leader**.
c. Press **Tab** after each of these five lines to insert the solid underline leader to the right margin.

12. Apply a border and shading to the paragraph.
    a. Select the paragraph beginning **"Please consider . . . "**.
    b. Apply a border with **Shadow** setting, **solid line** style, **Black**, **Text 1**, **Lighter 50%** color, and **1½ pt**. line width.
    c. Change the border options so there is **4 pt**. from text on the top, bottom, left, and right.
    d. Set the shading fill color to **White**, **Background 1**, **Darker 5%**.
13. Select the "**Seller/Borrower Signature(s)**" line and apply a custom border that is **solid line**, **Black**, **Text 1**, and **2¼ pt**. width, and apply it to the **top** of the selected paragraph.
14. Insert and customize a hyperlink.
    a. Select "**Placer Hills Real Estate**" in the closing lines and insert a hyperlink.
    b. Type www.phre.com as the web page address.
    c. Type Placer Hills Real Estate as the *ScreenTip*.
    d. Set the target frame to **New window** and make this the default for all hyperlinks.
15. Edit the "ecavalli@phre.com" email hyperlink and type Email Emma Cavalli as the *ScreenTip*.
16. Save and close the document (Figure 2-114).

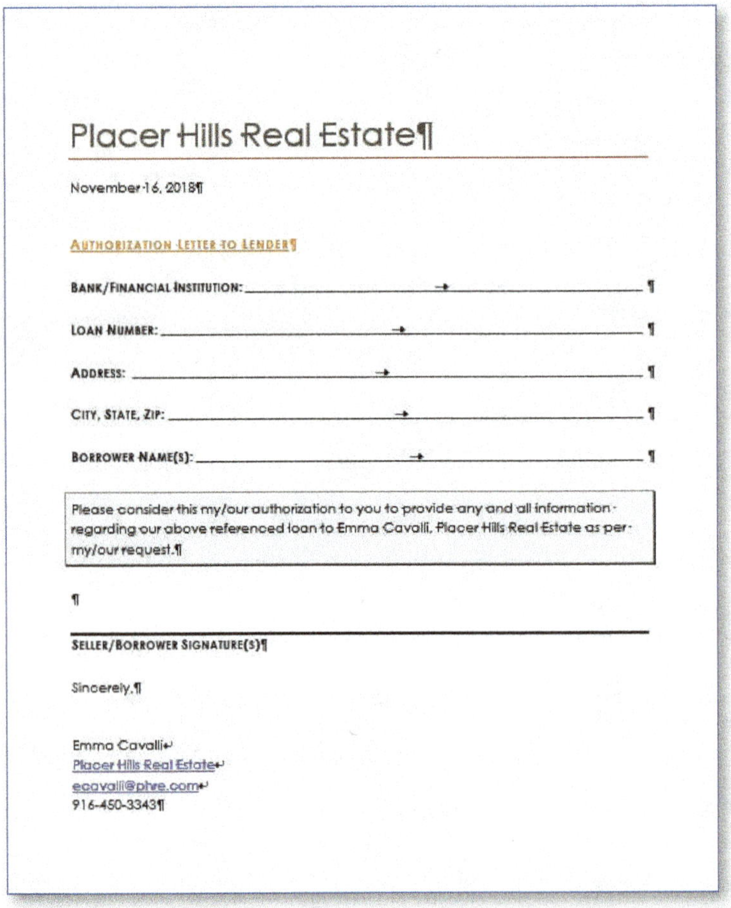
Placer Hills Real Estate¶

November 16, 2018¶

AUTHORIZATION LETTER TO LENDER¶

BANK/FINANCIAL INSTITUTION: ¶

LOAN NUMBER: ¶

ADDRESS: ¶

CITY, STATE, ZIP: ¶

BORROWER NAME(S): ¶

Please consider this my/our authorization to you to provide any and all information regarding our above referenced loan to Emma Cavalli, Placer Hills Real Estate as per my/our request.¶

¶

SELLER/BORROWER SIGNATURE(S)¶

Sincerely,¶

Emma Cavalli
Placer Hills Real Estate
ecavalli@phre.com
916-450-3343¶

2-114 Word 2-5 completed

Independent Project 2-6

In this project, you edit, format, and customize the conference registration form for Central Sierra Insurance's Agriculture Insurance Conference. You use a continuous section break, find and replace, tab stops and leaders, styles, bullets, indents, borders, shading, and hyperlinks.
[Student Learning Outcomes 2.1, 2.2, 2.3, 2.4, 2.5, 2.6, 2.7, 2.8, 2.9]

File Needed: ***ConferenceRegistrationForm-02.docx*** *(Student data files are available in the* Library *of your SIMnet account)*
Completed Project File Name: ***[your initials] Word 2-6.docx***

Skills Covered in this Project

- Modify an existing document.
- Change margins, font, font size, line spacing, and paragraph spacing.
- Insert a header.
- Apply a style.
- Use *Find and Replace*.
- Insert a continuous section break.
- Insert a horizontal line.
- Set different margins for different sections.
- Customize a bulleted list and indents.
- Set and use tab stops and leaders.
- Apply borders and shading to selected text.
- Insert hyperlinks.

1. Open the ***ConferenceRegistrationForm-02*** document from your student data files.
2. Save this document as [your initials] Word 2-6.
3. Change the top and bottom margins to **0.5"**.
4. Select all of the text in the document and change the font size to **10 pt**., line spacing to **1** (Single), and *After* paragraph spacing to **6 pt**.
5. Apply styles to title and subtitle.
   a. Select and cut the first line of the document and paste it in the header.
   b. Delete the blank line below the text in the header.
   c. Select the text in the header, apply **Title** style, align **center**, change the *After* paragraph spacing to **6 pt**., and close the header.
   d. In the body of the document, select the first two lines beginning with "Central Sierra Insurance," apply **Subtitle** style, align **center**, and change the *After* paragraph spacing to **6 pt**.
6. Use *Find* and *Replace*.
   a. Use *Find* to locate all occurrences of "Agriculture Insurance Conference."
   b. Apply **italic** formatting to each occurrence except in the header.
   c. Use *Replace* to find all occurrences of "Oct." (include the period) and replace with **"May"**.
   d. Use *Replace* to find all occurrences of "Westfield Hotel & Spa" and replace with **"Northgate Resort"** with **Bold Italic** font style.
7. Click at the end of the second body paragraph ("Please help us to determine . . .") and insert a **continuous** section break.
8. On the blank line below the section break, insert a **Horizontal Line** from the **Borders** drop-down list (see "Insert a Horizontal Line" in *SLO 2.9: Using Borders, Shading, and Hyperlinks*).
9. Click in the document below the section break and change the left and right margins to **1.25"** and apply to **This section**.
10. Set a tab stop with a leader.
    a. Select the first two lines of text below the horizontal line.
    b. Set a right tab stop at **6"** with a **solid underline leader**.
    c. Press **Tab** after each of these lines to insert the solid underline leader to the right margin.

11. Define a new multilevel list and customize bullets and indents.
    a. Press the **Ctrl** key and select the four different bulleted lists in the document. The *Ctrl* key allows you to select non-adjacent text in the document. Don't select the text between each of the bulleted lists, and make sure all bulleted items are selected.
    b. Open the *Define new Multilevel list* dialog box (in the *Multilevel List* drop-down list).
    c. On the first, second, and third levels, change the bullet to a shaded open square bullet (*Wingdings*, Character code 113).
    d. Change the font size of the bullets on each of the first three levels to **12 pt**.
    e. Set the indents for all levels so that the first level begins at **0"**, the text for the first level begins at **0.25"**, and additional indent for each level is **0.25"**.

12. Set tab stops with a leader.
    a. Select the **"Flying—Arrival time:"** line.
    b. Set a **right** tab stop at **3"** with a **solid underline leader**.
    c. Press **Tab** after this line to insert the leader.
    d. Select the **"I need directions to *Northgate Resort* from:"** line.
    e. Set a **right** tab stop at **5"** with a **solid underline leader**.
    f. Press **Tab** after this line to insert the leader.

13. Change indents and apply custom borders and shading to selected text.
    a. Select the last two lines of the document, align **center**, and change the left and right indents to **1"**.
    b. With these two lines selected, apply a top and bottom **double line** border, **¾ pt**. width, and **Dark Blue**, **Text 2** color.
    c. Apply **Dark Blue**, **Text 2**, **Lighter 80%** shading to the selected text.

14. Insert and customize hyperlinks to email addresses.
    a. Use *Find* to locate the first occurrence of "apelandale@centralsierra.com."
    b. Select this email address and insert a hyperlink.
    c. Type apelandale@centralsierra.com as the *Text to display* and *E-mail address*. In the *E-mail address* text box, "mailto:" is automatically inserted in front of the email address.
    d. Type Email Asia Pelandale as the *ScreenTip*.
    e. Repeat steps b–d above on the second occurrence of this email address.

15. Save and close the document (Figure 2-115).

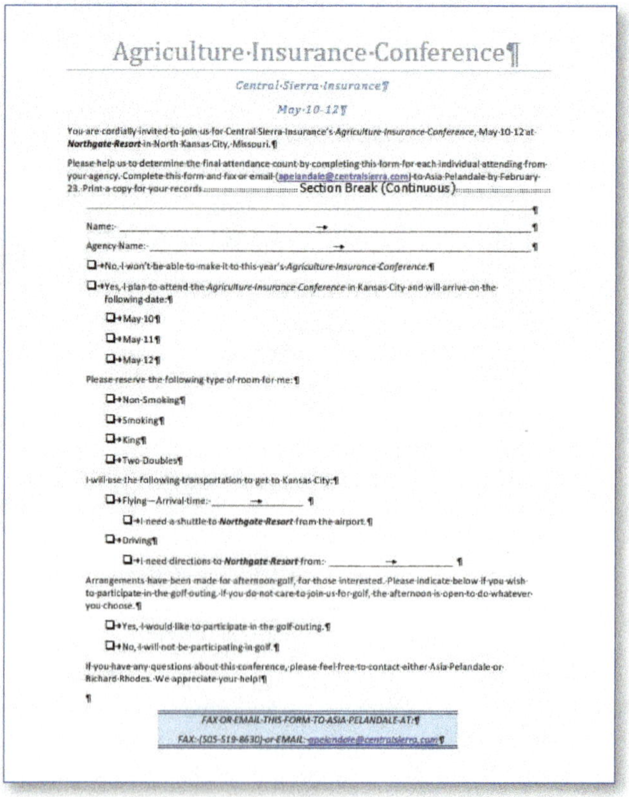

Agriculture Insurance Conference

Central Sierra Insurance

May 10-12

You are cordially invited to join us for Central Sierra Insurance's *Agriculture Insurance Conference*, May 10-12 at ***Northgate Resort*** in North Kansas City, Missouri.

Please help us to determine the final attendance count by completing this form for each individual attending from your agency. Complete this form and fax or email (apelandale@centralsierra.com) to Asia Pelandale by February 23. Print a copy for your records. Section Break (Continuous)

Name: ____________________

Agency Name: ____________________

- No, I won't be able to make it to this year's *Agriculture Insurance Conference*.
- Yes, I plan to attend the *Agriculture Insurance Conference* in Kansas City and will arrive on the following date:
  - May 10
  - May 11
  - May 12

Please reserve the following type of room for me:

- Non-Smoking
- Smoking
- King
- Two Doubles

I will use the following transportation to get to Kansas City:

- Flying—Arrival time: __________
  - I need a shuttle to ***Northgate Resort*** from the airport.
- Driving
  - I need directions to ***Northgate Resort*** from: __________

Arrangements have been made for afternoon golf, for those interested. Please indicate below if you wish to participate in the golf outing. If you do not care to join us for golf, the afternoon is open to do whatever you choose.

- Yes, I would like to participate in the golf outing.
- No, I will not be participating in golf.

If you have any questions about this conference, please feel free to contact either Asia Pelandale or Richard Rhodes. We appreciate your help!

FAX OR EMAIL THIS FORM TO ASIA PELANDALE AT:

FAX: (505-519-8630) or EMAIL: apelandale@centralsierra.com

2-115 Word 2-6 completed

Improve It Project 2-7

In this project, you clean up a document that contains shortcuts for Microsoft Outlook. Courtyard Medical Plaza wants to make this document available to all of its employees. You use tab stops, styles, and many other page layout features that you have learned in this chapter to create a professional and attractive reference document.
[Student Learning Outcomes 2.1, 2.2, 2.4, 2.5, 2.7, 2.9]

File Needed: ***OutlookShortcuts-02.docx*** *(Student data files are available in the* Library *of your SIMnet account)*
Completed Project File Name: ***[your initials] Word 2-7.docx***

Skills Covered in this Project

- Modify an existing document.
- Change margins, line spacing, and paragraph spacing.
- Apply and modify a style.
- Apply borders and shading to selected text.
- Set and modify tab stops and leaders.
- Use the *Format Painter.*
- Insert a page break.
- Edit footer content and tab stops.

1. Open the ***OutlookShortcuts-02*** document from your student data files.
2. Save this document as [your initials] Word 2-7.
3. Change the page orientation to **Landscape**.
4. Change the top margin to **0.5**" and the bottom, left, and right margins to **0.75**".
5. Select the entire document and change the line spacing to **1.0** (or **Single**) and the *After* paragraph spacing to **4 pt**.
6. Remove the bottom border from the title and change the *After* paragraph spacing to **0 pt**.
7. Apply custom borders and shading, change paragraph spacing, and modify the *Heading 1* style.
   a. Select "**Global Outlook Commands**."
   b. Apply a custom **single line** top and bottom border with **1 pt**. width and **Dark Blue**, **Text 2** color, and apply **White**, **Background 1**, **Darker 5%** shading.
   c. Change the *Before* paragraph spacing to **12 pt**. and the *After* spacing to **0 pt**.
   d. Update **Heading 1** to match selected text.
   e. Apply the **Heading 1** style to each of the remaining section headings ("*Mail*," "*Calendar*," "*Contacts*," "*Tasks*," "*Notes*," "*Journal*," and "*Formatting*").
8. Change paragraph spacing, set tab stops, and modify the *Heading 2* style.
   a. Select the third line of text on the first page ("Activity Shortcut . . .") and change the *Before* paragraph spacing to **6 pt**. and the *After* spacing to **3 pt**.
   b. Apply **Small caps** formatting to the selected text.
   c. Set **left** tab stops on the selected text at **3"**, **5"**, and **8.25"**.
   d. Update **Heading 2** to match selected text.
   e. Apply the **Heading 2** style to the first line of text ("Activity Shortcut . . .") after each section heading to create column headings.
9. Set tab stops and leaders to align text under the column headings and use the *Format Painter* to copy formatting.
   a. In the first section ("Global Outlook Commands") below the column headings ("ACTIVITY SHORTCUT . . ."), select all of the tabbed text beginning with "**Go to Mail**" and ending with "**Delete selected item**."

b. Set the following tabs stops:
   3" left tab stop with **dot leader (2)**
   5" left tab stop with **no leader (1)**
   8.25" left tab stop with **dot leader (2)**
c. Use the *Format Painter* to apply the tab settings to the remaining text below the column headings ("ACTIVITY SHORTCUT . . .") in the other sections.
d. Turn on **Show/Hide** and delete any blank lines in the document.

10. Remove the existing footer and insert a custom footer.
    a. Place your insertion point at the beginning of the document.
    b. Edit the footer and remove all content.
    c. Open the *Tabs* dialog box and **Clear All** existing tab stops.
    d. Set a center tab stop at **4.75"** and the right tab stop at **9.5"**.
    e. Insert the **Company** document property field on the left side of the footer.
    f. Press the **right arrow** key to deselect the document property field, **tab** to the center tab stop, and insert the **Title** (or **Document Title**) document property field.
    g. Press the **right arrow** key to deselect the document property field, **tab** to the right tab stop.
    h. Type Page, **space** once, insert a plain page number in the current position.
    i. **Space** once, type of, **space** once, and insert the *NumPages* field (use **1,2,3**. . . format).
    j. Apply a **single line** top border in the footer with **1 pt**. width, **Dark Blue**, **Text 2** color.
    k. Change the font size of all of the text in the footer to **10 pt**.
    l. Set the footer so it does not appear on the first page.

11. On the third page, insert a **page break** before the "Formatting" heading. This document fits on four pages.

12. Save and close the document (Figure 2-116).

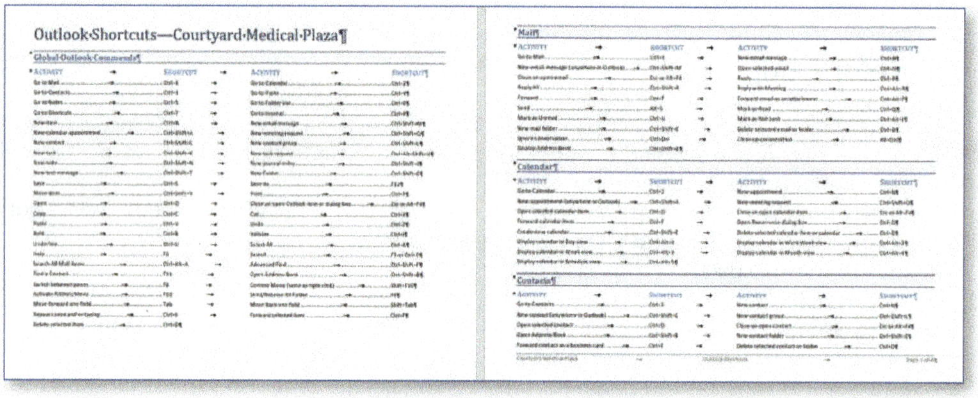

2-116 Word 2-7 completed (pages 1 and 2 of 4)

Challenge Project 2-8

Create an agenda for an upcoming meeting for an organization you are a member of, such as a club, church, volunteer organization, student group, or neighborhood association. Research online to find the common components of agendas. Robert's Rules of Order is a good source of information about meetings and guidelines for meeting protocol.
[Student Learning Outcomes 2.1, 2.2, 2.3, 2.6, 2.7, 2.9]

File Needed: None
Completed Project File Name: ***[your initials] Word 2-8.docx***

Create a new document and save it as [your initials] Word 2-8. An agenda can include, but is not limited to, the following items:

- Organization name as the title
- Meeting date, start time, and end time
- Meeting location
- Meeting attendees
- Topic headings
- Topic subheadings (include details for each topic heading)
- The time each topic is expected to last

Modify your document according to the following guidelines:

- Apply styles.
- Use a multilevel list for the agenda items and subheadings.
- Customize number or bullet format and indents as needed.
- Use a right tab stop with a leader to line up the amount of time allocated for each main topic heading.
- Apply borders, shading, and/or a horizontal line to create an attractive agenda.
- Adjust margins as needed.
- Include an appropriate header and/or footer.

Challenge Project 2-9

Update your résumé using some of the document formatting features learned in this chapter. Edit your résumé so it is consistently formatted, easy to read, and professional looking. Research résumés online to get ideas about formatting and content.
[Student Learning Outcomes 2.1, 2.2, 2.3, 2.4, 2.5, 2.6, 2.7, 2.8, 2.9]

File Needed: None
Completed Project File Name: ***[your initials] Word 2-9.docx***

Open your existing résumé or create a new document and save it as [your initials] Word 2-9. Modify your document according to the following guidelines:

- Apply a document theme.
- Apply styles to headings and subheadings to improve consistency in format.
- Adjust margins as needed.
- Use bulleted lists with customized bullets and indents to attractively arrange information.
- Set and use tab stops and indents as necessary to align information.
- Apply borders, shading, and/or a horizontal line to emphasize information in your résumé.
- Use page or section breaks as needed.
- Use *Find and Replace* as needed.
- Insert hyperlinks for appropriate information (e.g., email address and company names).
- If your résumé is more than one page, include a header and/or footer on the second and continuing pages.

Challenge Project 2-10

Format your favorite recipe using some of the formatting features learned in this chapter. You can look up recipes online on the Food Network, Epicurious, Simply Recipes, or other food web sites. [**Student Learning Outcomes 2.1, 2.2, 2.3, 2.6, 2.7, 2.9**]

File Needed: None
Completed Project File Name: ***[your initials] Word 2-10.docx***

Create a new document and save it as [your initials] Word 2-10. Your recipe should include, but is not limited to, the following:

- Recipe title
- Descriptive paragraph about the recipe
- Tab stops to arrange quantity and ingredients (and special instructions if needed)
- Numbered, step-by-step instructions
- Recipe source and/or additional information

Modify your document according to the following guidelines:

- Apply a document theme.
- Apply styles.
- Adjust margins as needed.
- Set and use a combination of tab stops (e.g., left, right, center, decimal, bar, and leaders) as necessary to attractively line up information.
- Use a numbered list for instructions.
- Use left, right, first line, and/or hanging indents as necessary.
- Apply borders, shading, page border, and/or a horizontal line to set off information in your recipe.
- Insert hyperlinks to appropriate information (e.g., link to online recipe).

CHAPTER 3

Collaborating with Others and Working with Reports

WORD

CHAPTER OVERVIEW

Creating a long report with a table of contents, citations, footnotes or endnotes, a reference page, and headers and footers can be a challenging task. Word 2016 has numerous tools that automatically create these components in a report or a multipage document. Using these tools not only saves you time when you are working on this type of document but also improves consistency within your documents. Word also provides you with a variety of collaboration tools to help you more efficiently and effectively work with others on documents.

STUDENT LEARNING OUTCOMES (SLOs)

After completing this chapter, you will be able to:

SLO 3.1 Insert, review, edit, and customize comments (p. W3-134).

SLO 3.2 Modify and review a document using *Track Changes* and share an online document (p. W3-137).

SLO 3.3 Insert and edit footnotes and endnotes in a document (p. W3-144).

SLO 3.4 Create a bibliography with properly formatted sources and insert citations into a document (p. W3-149).

SLO 3.5 Create and edit a table of contents based on headings (p. W3-161).

SLO 3.6 Insert a cover page and modify content and content control fields (p. W3-164).

SLO 3.7 Apply and customize headers and footers in a multipage document (p. W3-167).

CASE STUDY

American River Cycling Club (ARCC) is a community cycling club that promotes fitness for the entire region. ARCC members include recreational cyclists who enjoy the exercise and camaraderie and competitive cyclists who compete in road, mountain, and cyclocross races throughout the cycling season.

For the Pause & Practice projects, you create a report for club members about how to develop a personal training program. In this report, you incorporate many of the report features covered in the chapter to produce a professional-looking and useful report.

Pause & Practice 3-1: Review a report that includes comments and edits marked with tracked changes.

Pause & Practice 3-2: Insert endnotes into the report, convert endnotes to footnotes, add reference sources, insert citations, and create a bibliography page.

Pause & Practice 3-3: Apply styles to headings, create a table of contents based on the headings in the document, modify the table of contents, insert a cover page, customize headers and footers in the report, and share an online file.

SLO 3.1

Using Comments

When you are collaborating with other people on a report or document, you can use ***comments*** to provide feedback in the document without making changes to the text of the document. For example, you might use comments to ask a question, make a suggestion, or provide additional information. You can also use comments when working alone on a document to make notes to yourself. You can customize how comments appear in a document, review comments in a document, edit comments, and delete comments.

Insert a Comment

When you insert a comment, the comment appears in a ***balloon*** in the ***Markup area***, which is the area to the right of a document. The *Markup* area opens when a document has comments or tracked changes (we discuss tracking changes in *SLO 3.2: Using Track Changes and Sharing*). Comments in a document are marked with the name of the author of the comment and time or date the comment was created. The text of the comment appears below the author's name in the balloon. You can insert a comment on a single word or a group of words.

HOW TO: Insert a Comment

1. Select the text where you want to insert a comment.
   - When you place your insertion point at the beginning of a word or within a word, the comment is attached to the entire word.
2. Click the **New Comment** button [*Review* tab, *Comments* group] (Figure 3-1).
   - The comment balloon appears in the *Markup* area to the right of the Word window.
   - The comment time or date displays as either minutes or hours ago (e.g., 4 minutes ago), or, if it was created more than 24 hours ago, the date displays.
   - The word or words in the document with the comment attached are highlighted.
3. Type comment text in the balloon (Figure 3-2).

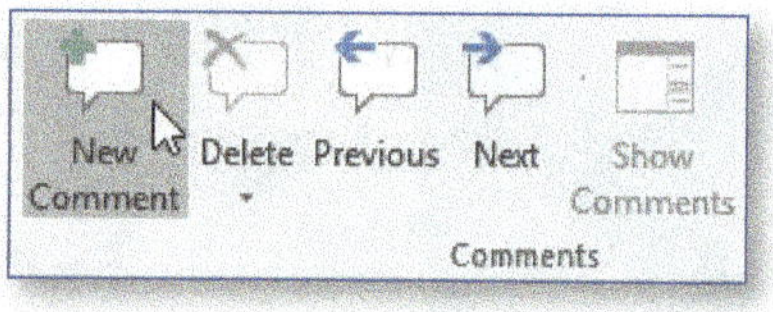

3-1 *New Comment* button

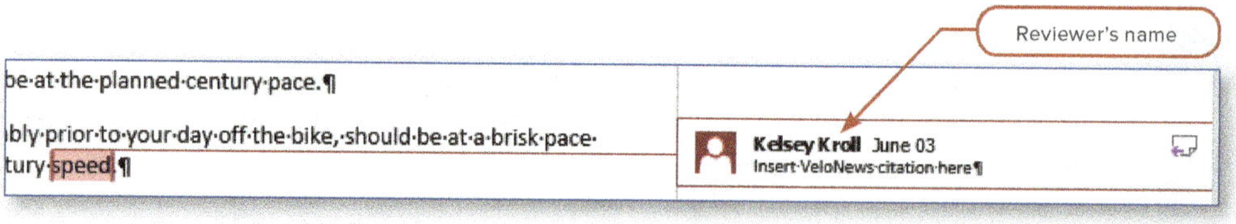

3-2 Comment in a balloon in the *Markup* area

4. Click the document to return to the document.

MORE INFO

The *Display for Review* view [*Review* tab, *Tracking* group] determines how comments display in the document. *Display for Review* views are covered in the next section, *SLO 3.2: Using Track Changes and Sharing*.

Change User Name

Each comment made in Word is attributed to the user name stored in Office. When you are signed in to Word with your Microsoft Account, Word uses this information as the ***user name***. Word uses your user name as the ***author*** of each new document you create. Each person editing a document is referred to as a ***reviewer***.

If you are using a public computer, such as in a computer lab on your college campus, the user name is a generic name given to Office on that computer. To make sure comments you make in a document are attributed to you, you can change your user name and initials in Office.

HOW TO: Change User Name

1. Click the **Tracking** launcher [*Review* tab, *Tracking* group] to open the *Track Changes Options* dialog box.
2. Click the **Change User Name** button to open the *Word Options* dialog box (Figure 3-3).
3. Type your name in the *User name* text box.
4. Type your initials in the *Initials* text box.
5. Check the **Always use these values regardless of sign in to Office** box.
6. Click **OK** to close the *Word Options* dialog box.
7. Click **OK** to close the *Track Changes Options* dialog box.

ANOTHER WAY

Click the **File** tab to open the *Backstage* view and click **Options** to open the *Word Options* dialog box where you can change user name and initials.

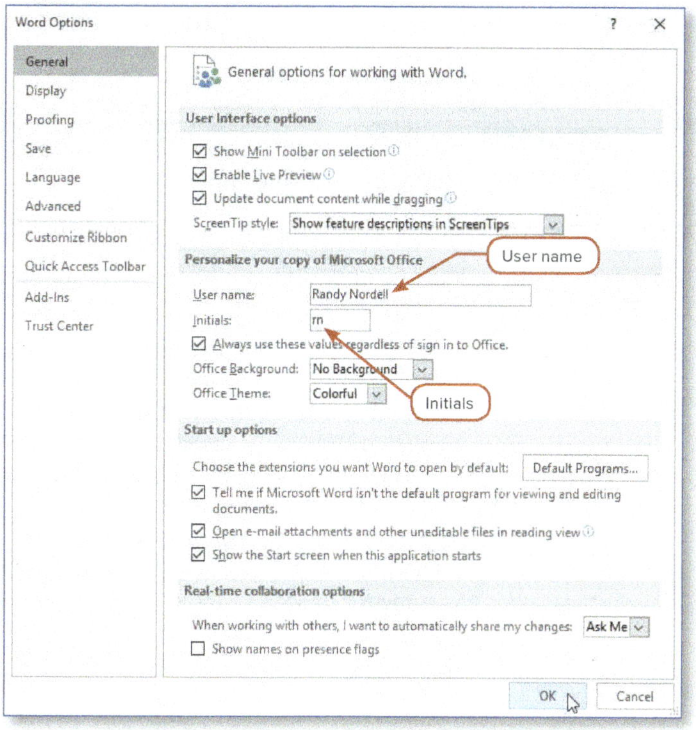

3-3 Change user name and initials in the *Word Options* dialog box

Review Comments

Each comment in a document is attributed to the reviewer who made the comment. When you place your pointer on text in a document where a comment is attached, a tag displays with the reviewer's name, the date and time of the comment, and the comment text (Figure 3-4).

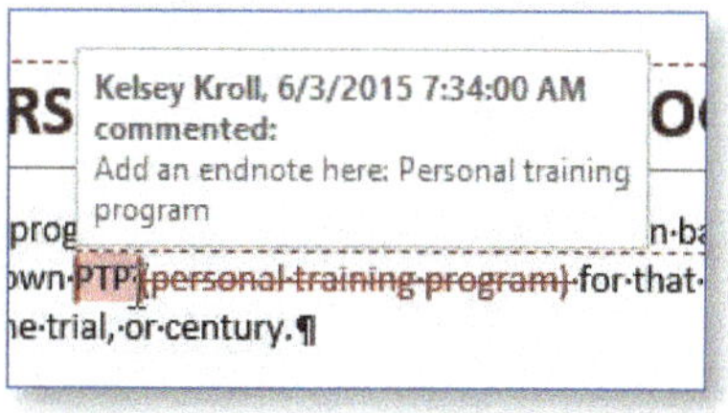

3-4 Comment details displayed in a tag

If you are working on a long document with multiple comments, Word provides navigation tools to move to the next or previous comment in the document. Click the **Next** or **Previous** button in the *Comments* group on the *Review* tab

(Figure 3-5) to move to the next or previous comment in your document.

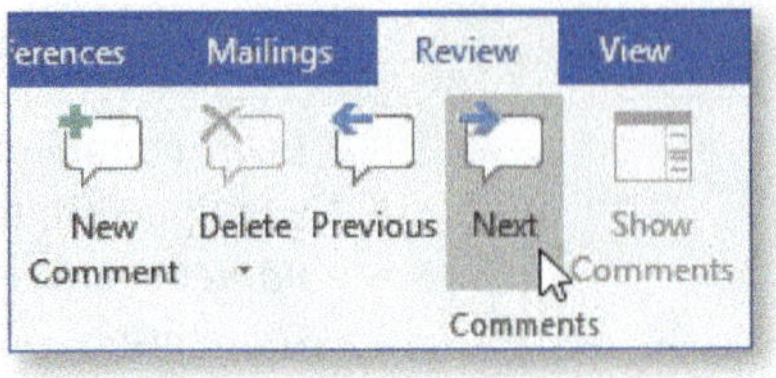

3-5 Move to the next comment

Reply to a Comment

To reply to a comment, click the **Reply** button on the right side of the comment in the *Markup* area (Figure 3-6). A reply area opens within the existing comment where you can type a reply below the original comment.

> **ANOTHER WAY**
>
> Right-click an existing comment in the *Markup* area or the highlighted text in a document with a comment attached and select **Reply To Comment** from the context menu.

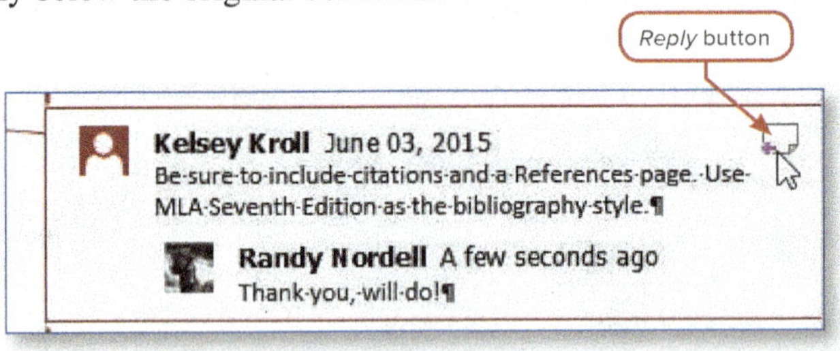

3-6 Reply to a comment

Mark Comment Done

You can also mark a comment as done when you have taken action on a comment but don't want to delete the comment. When a comment is marked as done, the text of the comment changes to a light gray color, and the highlighted text in the document where the comment is attached is a lighter shade of the comment color.

To mark a comment as done, right-click an existing comment in the *Markup* area or the highlighted text in a document with a comment attached and select **Mark Comment Done** from the context menu (Figure 3-7). You can toggle off *Mark Comment Done* from the context menu to make the comment active.

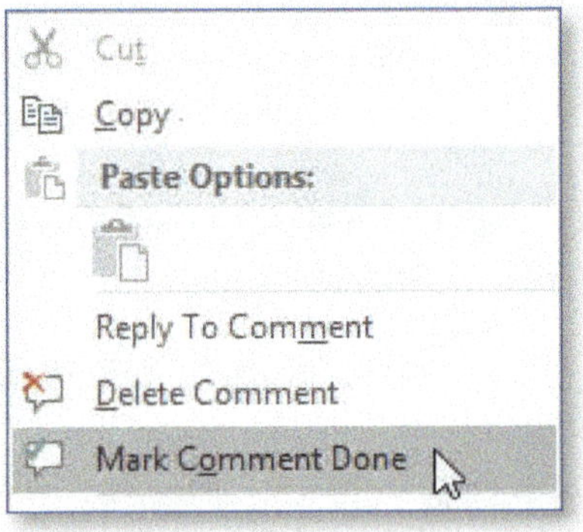

3-7 *Mark Comment Done*

Edit and Delete Comments

You can edit comments by clicking the comment balloon and editing existing text or typing new text. You can also right-click highlighted text in your document that has a comment attached and select **Edit Comment** from the context menu.

Once you have finished reviewing comments, you can delete them. You can delete comments individually or delete all the comments in the document.

HOW TO: Delete Comments

1. Click the comment balloon or the highlighted comment text in the document.
   - You can also click **Next** or **Previous** [*Review* tab, *Comments* group] to select a comment (see Figure 3-5).
2. Click the top half of the **Delete** button [*Review* tab, *Comments* group] to delete the selected comment.
   - You can also right-click a comment and select **Delete Comment** from the context menu.

3. Click the bottom half of the **Delete** button for more delete options.
   - Click the **Delete All Comments in Document** button to delete all the comments in the document (Figure 3-8).

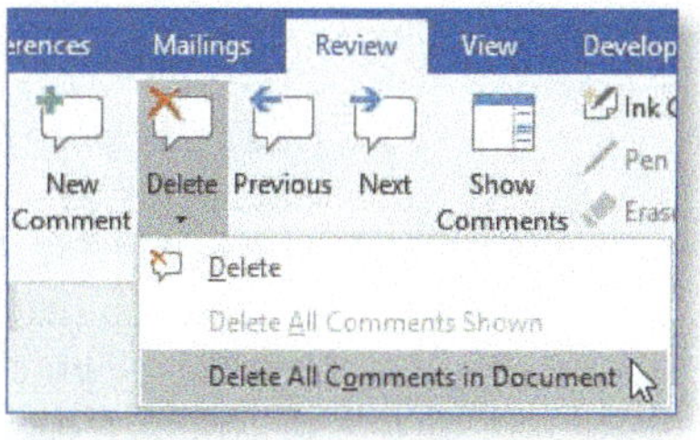

3-8 Delete all comments in the document

SLO 3.2

Using Track Changes and Sharing

Track Changes is a valuable editing tool in Word that marks changes you and others insert in a document so all reviewers can see these changes. This feature is very useful when working with a group on a report or project. As you review tracked changes in a document, you can accept, reject, or skip the marked changes. You have different options for viewing how tracked changes display in the document. Word also gives you the ability to share online documents with others and use real-time collaboration.

Track Changes

To mark editing changes in a document, you must first turn on *Track Changes*. Once you have turned on *Track Changes*, you can add, delete, and change text and formatting in the document. These changes are tracked in the body of the document and in balloons in the *Markup* area. Each line in the document that has a change is marked with a vertical gray or red line (depending on *Display for Review* view, which is covered in the next section) to the left of the line so reviewers can easily tell where changes have been made.

HOW TO: Use Track Changes

1. Click the **Track Changes** button [*Review* tab, *Tracking* group] (Figure 3-9).
   - When *Track Changes* is turned on, this button is highlighted.
   - You can also click the bottom half of the **Track Changes** button and select **Track Changes** to turn on *Track Changes*.
2. Edit, delete, insert, or format text in the document.
   - The *Display for Review* view determines how editing changes appear in the document. The *Display for Review* views are covered in the next section.
3. Click the **Track Changes** button to turn off *Track Changes*.

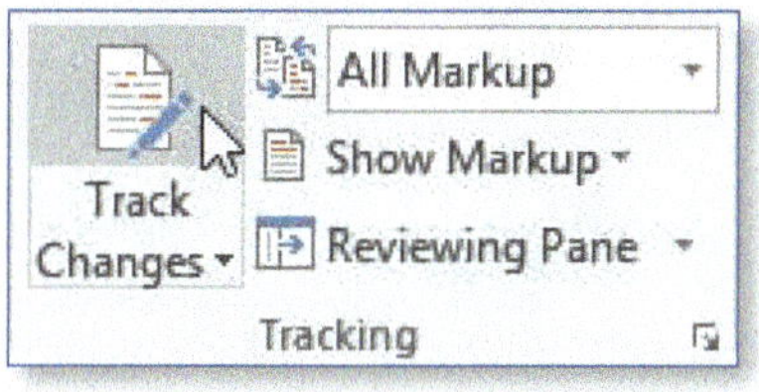

3-9 Turn on *Track Changes*

ANOTHER WAY

Ctrl+Shift+E toggles *Track Changes* on and off.

Display for Review Views

The ***Display for Review*** view determines how editing changes appear when using *Track Changes*. Click the **Display for Review** drop-down list in the *Tracking* group on the *Review* tab to select a *Display for Review* view (Figure 3-10). The following table lists and describes each of these different views:

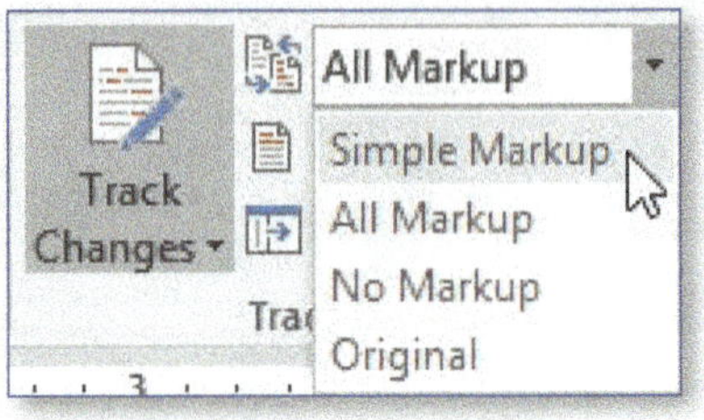

3-10 *Display for Review* views

Display for Review Views

Display for Review View	Description
Simple Markup	Displays a final version of the document with the proposed changes incorporated. A red line to the left of a line marks changed lines in the document. Click the **Show Comments** button [*Review* tab, *Comments* group] to display or hide comments in the document.
All Markup	Displays added, deleted, and edited text in the body of the document. Formatting changes and comments display in balloons on the right. A gray line to the left of a line marks changed lines in the document.
No Markup	Displays a final version of the document with the proposed changes incorporated. All editing changes and comments are hidden.
Original	Displays the original document with proposed changes not incorporated. All editing changes and comments are hidden.

All Markup is the view people typically use when reviewing a document with changes tracked (Figure 3-11). If you view your document in ***Simple Markup***, ***No Markup***, or ***Original*** view, the tracked changes are still in the document, but they are hidden so you can view a clean (without markup) final or original version of the document. It is important to understand and use these different views when using *Track Changes* to edit a document.

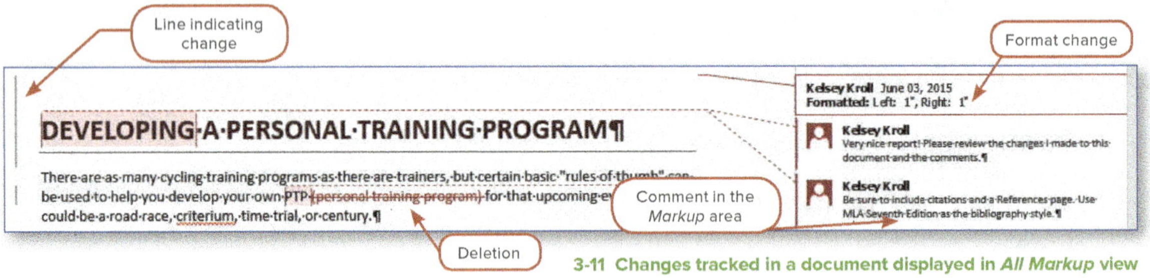

3-11 Changes tracked in a document displayed in *All Markup* view

> **MORE INFO**
>
> The **Show Comments** button [*Review* tab, *Comments* group] is only active in *Simple Markup* view where you choose how comments display. In *All Markup* view, comments always display. In *No Markup* and *Original* views, comments do not display.

Accept and Reject Changes

After a document has been marked up with editing changes, you can review each proposed change and either accept or reject the change. It's best to work in *All Markup* view when reviewing a document with changes tracked. When you accept an editing or formatting change,

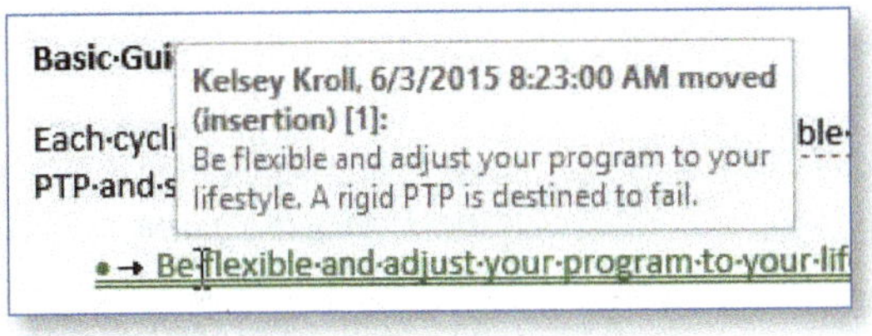

3-12 Tracked changes details displayed in a tag

the change is applied to the document, and the inline markup and/or balloon is removed. When you reject an editing or formatting change, the text and formatting revert back to their original form.

Similar to comments, each editing change is attributed to a reviewer. When you place your pointer on a change in the body of the text or on a balloon, a tag displays the reviewer's name, the date and time of the change, and a description of the change (Figure 3-12).

HOW TO: Accept and Reject Changes

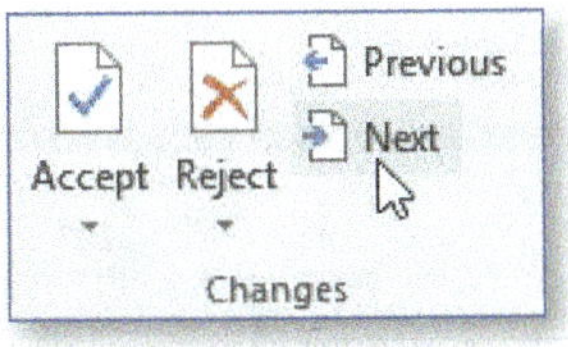

3-13 Move to the next revision in the document

1. Place the insertion point at the beginning of the document (**Ctrl+Home**).
2. Click the **Display for Review** drop-down list [*Review* tab, *Tracking* group] and select **All Markup** if this is not the current view.
3. Click the **Next** button [*Review* tab, *Changes* group] to select the next change made to the document (Figure 3-13).
   - Click the **Previous** button to select the previous revision.
   - If you are in *No Markup* or *Original* view and press the *Next* or *Previous* button, the view automatically changes to *All Markup*.
4. Click the **Accept** or **Reject** button [*Review* tab, *Changes* group] to accept or reject the change and move to the next revision.
   - If you click the bottom half of the **Accept** button, there are additional options: *Accept and Move to Next*, *Accept This Change*, *Accept All Changes Shown*, *Accept All Changes*, and *Accept All Changes and Stop Tracking* (Figure 3-14).
   - If you click the bottom half of the **Reject** button, there are additional options: *Reject and Move to Next*, *Reject Change*, *Reject All Changes Shown*, *Reject All Changes*, and *Reject All Changes and Stop Tracking*.
   - When accepting and rejecting changes, Word also stops on comments. Click **Accept** to leave the comment in the document or **Reject** to delete the comment.
   - You can also click **Next** to skip a comment or revision in the document.

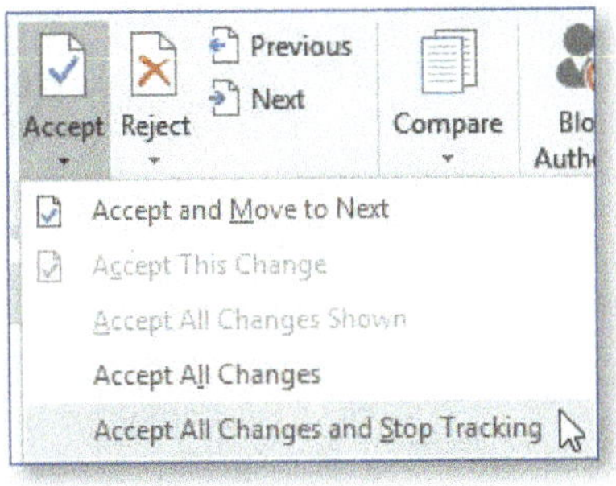

3-14 *Accept All Changes and Stop Tracking* option

5. Continue accepting or rejecting changes in the document.
6. After you reach the last change in the document, a dialog box opens confirming there are no more comments or tracked changes in the document. Click **OK** (Figure 3-15).
   - When all changes have been accepted or rejected, there will be no vertical lines to the left of the text in the body of the document.

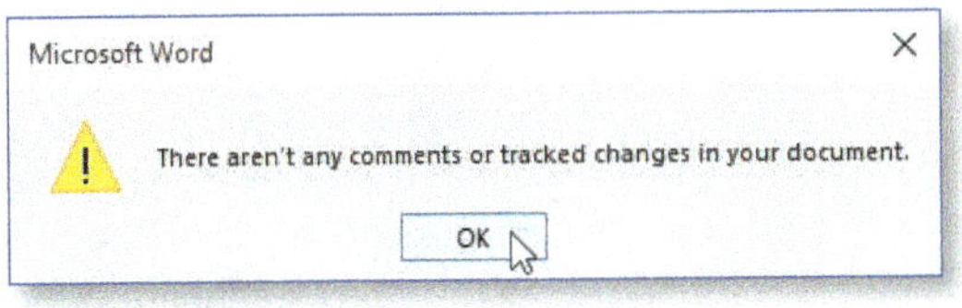

3-15 Dialog box that appears after reviewing the document

ANOTHER WAY

Right-click a change and select **Accept "description of change"** or **Reject "description of change"** from the context menu.

Reviewing Pane

If you are working with a document that has many editing changes marked with tracked changes or comments, the ***Reviewing pane*** is a useful tool. The *Reviewing* pane is a separate pane that includes all tracked changes and comments, and it can be displayed vertically on the left side of the Word window or horizontally at the bottom of the Word window (Figure 3-16). If there are a lot of changes and comments in a document and all of the balloons cannot fit in the *Markup* area, the *Reviewing* pane automatically opens.

To open the *Reviewing* pane, click the **Reviewing Pane** button in the *Tracking* group on the *Review* tab and select either **Reviewing Pane Vertical** or **Reviewing Pane Horizontal**.

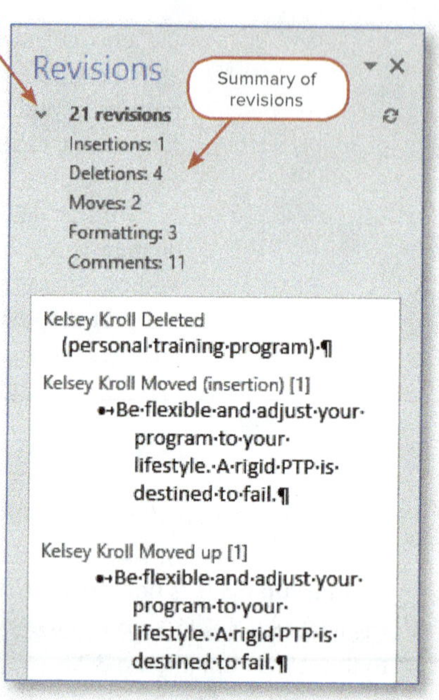

3-16 *Reviewing* pane displayed vertically

> **MORE INFO**
>
> When the *Reviewing* pane is open, the title of the pane is *Revisions*. This book refers to this pane as the *Reviewing* pane.

At the top of the *Reviewing* pane, a summary displays the number of revisions in the document. Click the arrow to the left of the revision summary to display a breakdown of the number of insertions, deletions, moves, formatting changes, and comments in the document. You can right-click any of the revisions in the *Reviewing* pane and accept or reject changes from the context menu.

Share an Online File

In addition to collaborating with others on a document using *Comments* and *Track Changes*, Word also provides you with the option of sharing an online file with others. Sharing an online file gives you the ability to work with others on the same file at the same time, which is called ***real-time collaboration***.

You can share any files you have saved in your *OneDrive*. If you try to share a file that is not saved in *OneDrive*, you are prompted to save your document to *OneDrive* before sharing it. In the ***Share*** pane, you can type or select the recipients, set the permission level of the shared file, type a message recipients receive through email, or get a sharing link.

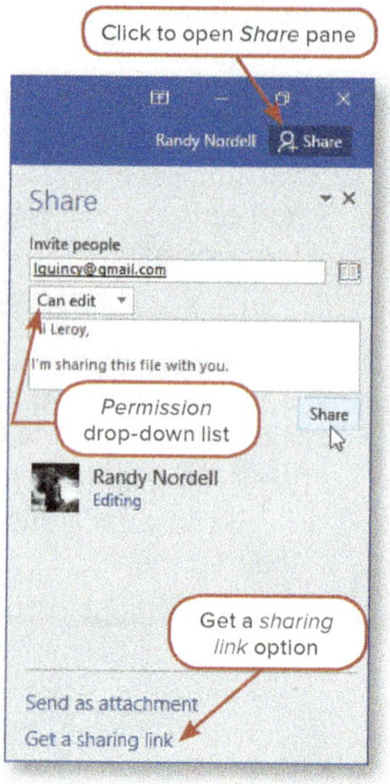

3-17 Share a *OneDrive* file

HOW TO: Share an Online File

1. Open the file you want to share.
   - If the file is not saved in *OneDrive*, save the file to *OneDrive*.
2. Click the **Share** button in the upper right of the Word window to open the *Share* pane to the right of the Word window (Figure 3-17).

- You can also open the *Share* pane from the *Backstage* view. Click the **File** button to open the *Backstage* view, click **Share** on the left, select **Share with People**, and click the **Share with People** button. The *Backstage* view closes and the *Share* pane opens in the Word document.

3. Type or select the email address of the person with whom you are sharing the file in the *Invite people* area.
    - If you are using Outlook as your email program, you can select recipients from your *Outlook Contacts*. Click the **Address Book** button to the right of the *Invite people* text box, select recipients, and click **OK** to close the *Address Book* dialog box.
    - If typing multiple email addresses, separate each with a semi-colon.
4. Select **Can edit** or **Can view** from the *Permission* drop-down list.
5. Type a message to recipient(s) in the *Message* area.
6. Click the **Share** button. An email is sent to people you invited.
7. Click the **X** to close the *Share* pane.

Create a Sharing Link

You can also choose to create a sharing link (hyperlink) to share a file with others rather than sending an email through Word. You can get a sharing link, copy it, and email it to others as another way of sharing. You have the option of generating an ***Edit link*** or a ***View-only link***.

HOW TO: Create a Sharing Link

1. Open the file you want to share.
    - If the file is not saved in *OneDrive*, save the file to *OneDrive*.
2. Click the **Share** button in the upper right of the Word window to open the *Share* pane to the right of the Word window.
3. Click **Get a sharing link** at the bottom of the *Share* pane (see Figure 3-17).
    - Alternatively, you can click **Send as attachment**, and email the file as a Word document or PDF file.
4. Click the **Create an edit link** or **Create a view-only link** button (Figure 3-18). A link is created that you can copy and give to others.
5. Click the **Copy** button to copy the sharing link (Figure 3-19).
    - You can paste the copied sharing link in an email, Word document, or other online location.
6. Click the **Back** arrow to the left of *Get a sharing link* at the top of the *Share* pane to return to the main *Share* pane, or click the **X** to close the *Share* pane.

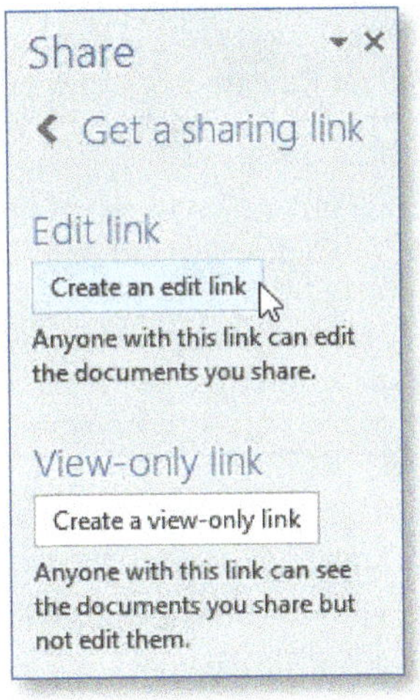

3-18 Create a sharing link

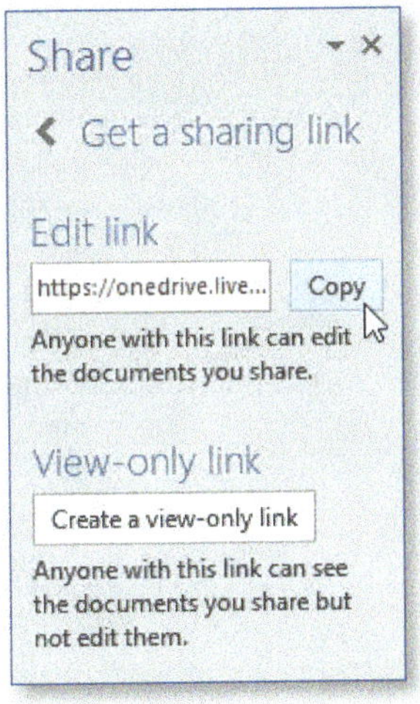

3-19 Copy a sharing link

PAUSE & PRACTICE: WORD 3-1

For this Pause & Practice project, you modify the *Developing a Personal Training Program* report for American River Cycling Club using comments and *Track Changes.*

Files Needed: ***PersonalTrainingProgram-03.docx*** *(Student data files are available in the* Library *of your SIMnet account)*
Completed Project File Names: ***[your initials] PP W3-1.docx***

1. Open the ***PersonalTrainingProgram-03*** document from your student data files.
2. Save the document as [your initials] PP W3-1.
3. Change user name and initials.
   a. Click the **Tracking** launcher [*Review* tab, *Tracking* group] to open the *Track Changes Options* dialog box.
   b. Click the **Change User Name** button to open the *Word Options* dialog box.
   c. In the *Personalize your copy of Microsoft Office* area, type your first and last name in the *User name* text box.
   d. Type your first and last initials in lowercase letters in the *Initials* text box.
   e. Check the **Always use these values regardless of sign in to Office** box.
   f. Click **OK** to close the *Word Options* dialog box.
   g. Click **OK** to close the *Track Changes Options* dialog box.
4. Change *Display for Review* view.
   a. Click the **Display for Review** drop-down list [*Review* tab, *Tracking* group] and select **Original** to view the original document without changes (Figure 3-20).
   b. Click the **Display for Review** drop-down list again and select **No Markup** to view the final document with proposed changes applied.
   c. Click the **Display for Review** drop-down list again and select **Simple Markup** to view the document with proposed changes applied. A red line on the left indicates changes in the document.
   d. If the comment text displays in the balloons, click the **Show Comments** button [*Review* tab, *Comments* group] to hide comment text and display only comment balloons.
   e. Click the **Display for Review** drop-down list again and select **All Markup** to view the final document with proposed changes visible inline and comments in balloons in the *Markup* area.

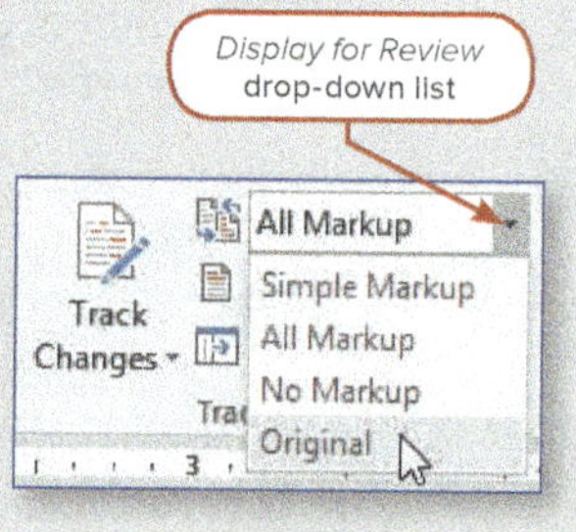

3-20 Change *Display for Review* view

5. Turn on the *Reviewing* pane and reject changes.
   a. Click the **Reviewing Pane** drop-down arrow [*Review* tab, *Tracking* group] and select **Reviewing Pane Vertical**. The *Reviewing* pane displays on the left side of the Word window.
   b. In the *Reviewing* pane, find where a bulleted item was moved ("Kelsey Kroll Moved (insertion) [1]").
   c. Right-click **"Kelsey Kroll Moved (insertion) [1]"** and select **Reject Move** from the context menu (Figure 3-21).
   d. Click the **X** in the upper right corner of the *Reviewing* pane to close it.

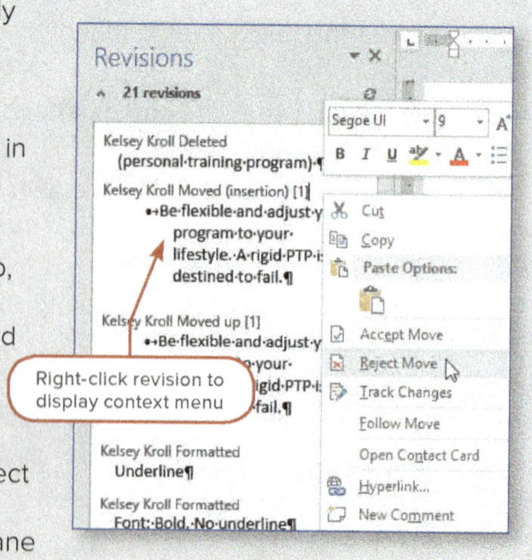

3-21 Reject moved text in the *Reviewing* pane

6. Accept changes in the document.
   a. Move to the top of the document (**Ctrl+Home**).
   b. Click the **Next** button [*Review* tab, *Changes* group] to select the first change.
   c. Click the top half of the **Accept** button [*Review* tab, *Changes* group] to accept the change and move to the next change.
   d. Click the **Next** button [*Review* tab, *Changes* group] three times to move through the first three comments and to locate the next tracked change ("personal training program" deleted).
   e. Click the top half of the **Accept** button to accept the change and move to the next change.
   f. Click the bottom half of the **Accept** button and select **Accept All Changes** from the drop-down list (Figure 3-22). All of the remaining changes in the document are accepted. Only comments are remaining in the *Markup* area.

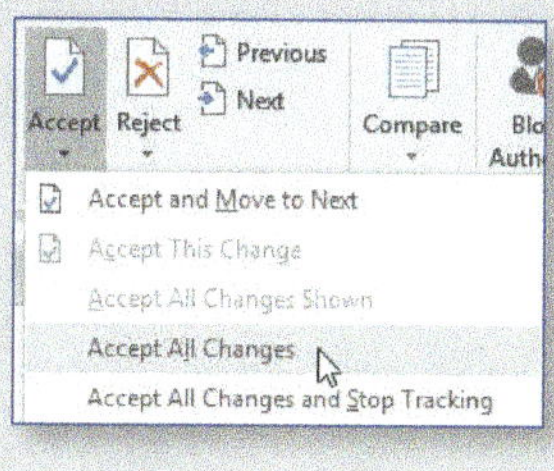

3-22 Accept all changes in the document

7. Mark a comment as done and reply to a comment.
   a. Move to the top of the document and click the **Next** button [*Review* tab, *Comments* group] to move to the first comment.
   b. Right-click the comment in the *Markup* area and select **Mark Comment Done**. A comment marked as done becomes grayed out.
   c. Click the **Next** button to move to the next comment.
   d. Click the **Reply** button in the upper right corner of the comment in the *Markup* area (Figure 3-23).
   e. Type Thank you, will do!

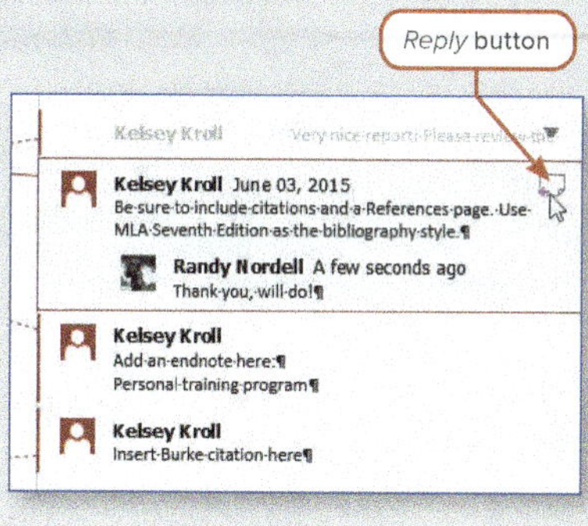

3-23 Reply to a comment

8. Delete selected comments in the document.
   a. Click the **Next** button [*Review* tab, *Comments* group] to move to the next (third) comment.
   b. Click the top half of the **Delete** button [*Review* tab, *Comments* group] to delete the comment.
   c. Continue clicking **Next** and **Delete** to delete the remaining comments. Don't delete the first two comments on the first page.
9. Add comments to the document.
   a. Place the insertion point at the top of the document (**Ctrl+Home**).
   b. Click the **New Comment** button [*Review* tab, *Comments* group] to insert a new comment.
   c. Type Also insert a cover page and table of contents in the new comment.
   d. Select the first word in the first body paragraph ("**There**").
   e. Click the **New Comment** button and type Proofread this report one more time in the new comment.
10. Use *Track Changes* to revise the document.
    a. Click the top half of the **Track Changes** button [*Review* tab, *Tracking* group] to turn on track changes (or press **Ctrl+Shift+E**).
    b. Select the word **"Basic"** in the first section heading below the first body paragraph.
    c. Type General to replace the selected word. Make sure there is one space after the word (turn on **Show/Hide**, if necessary).
    d. Place your insertion point after "Training" in the second section heading on the first page ("Personal Training Guidelines").
    e. **Space** once and type Program to insert the word between "Training" and "Guidelines." Make sure there is one space between the words.
    f. Click the **Track Changes** button to turn off *Track Changes*.
11. Save and close the document (Figure 3-24).

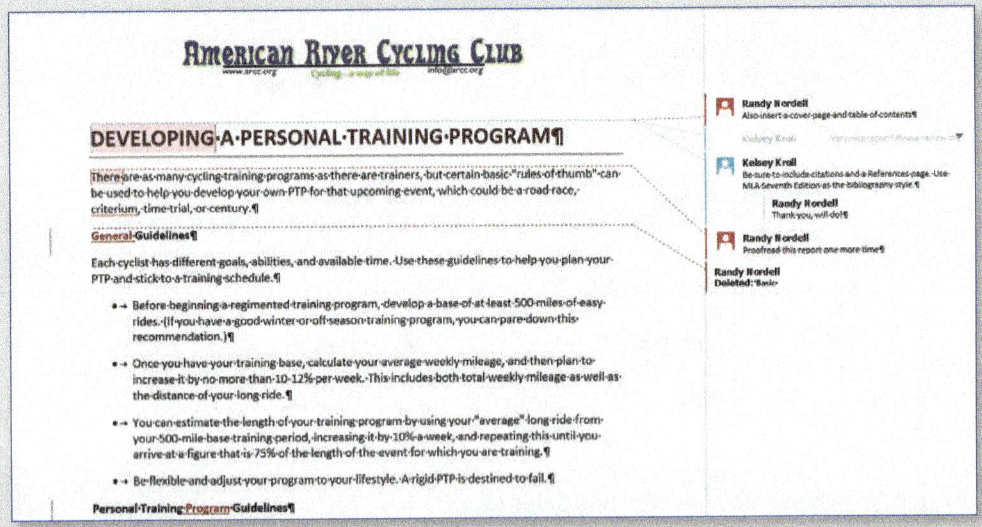

3-24 PP W3-1 completed

SLO 3.3

Using Footnotes and Endnotes

Footnotes and ***endnotes*** cite reference sources used in a document. You can also use them to include additional notational information. Footnotes display at the bottom of each page, while endnotes display at the end of the document.

As you insert footnotes and endnotes into your document, Word numbers them consecutively. If you insert a footnote or endnote before or between existing notes, Word automatically reorders notes. You can also customize number format and convert footnotes to endnotes or endnotes to footnotes.

Insert a Footnote

When a footnote is inserted into a document, a ***reference marker***, which is a number or letter in superscript format (smaller font size and slightly raised above the typed line), displays directly after the word. Word then places the insertion point at the bottom of the page to insert the text of the footnote. A thin top border above the note separates the note from the text in the body of the document.

Footnotes display in the body of the document at the bottom of the page, not in the footer, and the text on a page with a footnote adjusts to allow space for the footnote.

HOW TO: Insert a Footnote

1. Position the insertion point directly after the word where the footnote is to be inserted.
2. Click the **References** tab.
3. Click the **Insert Footnote** button [*Footnotes* group] (Figure 3-25).
   A reference marker is inserted in the body of the document (Figure 3-26),

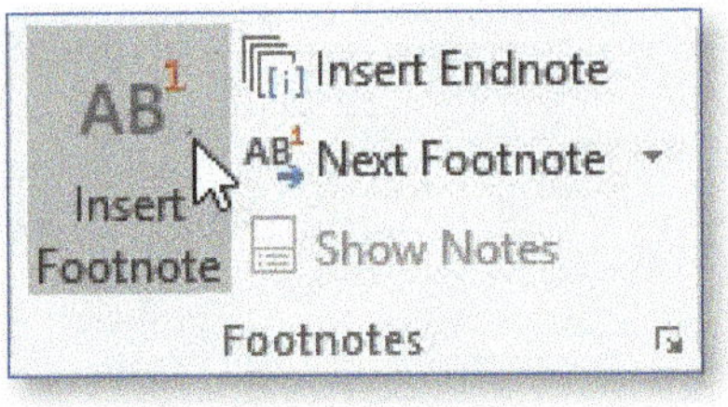

3-25 *Insert Footnote* button

and the insertion point is positioned after the corresponding reference marker in the footnote area of the page.

4. Type the footnote text in the footnote area of the page (Figure 3-27).

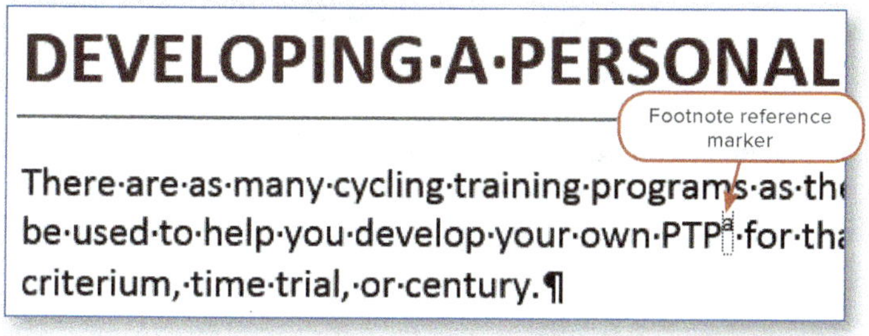

3-26 Footnote reference marker in the body of the document

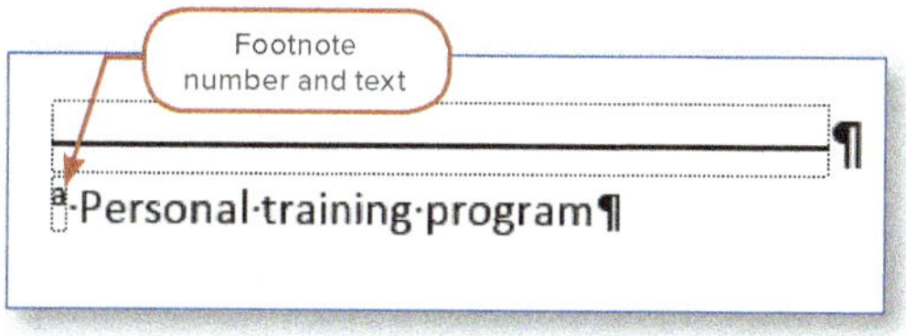

3-27 Footnote text at the bottom of the page

5. Click in the body of the document to leave the footnote area and to return to the document.

Insert an Endnote

Inserting endnotes is similar to inserting footnotes. The main difference is the text for the endnote displays after the text at the end of the document rather than at the bottom of the page where the note appears.

HOW TO: Insert an Endnote

1. Position the insertion point directly after the word where the endnote is to be inserted.
2. Click the **References** tab.
3. Click the **Insert Endnote** button [*Footnotes* group] (Figure 3-28). The reference marker displays in the body of the document and the insertion point is positioned after the corresponding reference marker at the end of the document.
4. Type the endnote text.
5. Click in the body of the document to leave the endnote area and to return to the document.

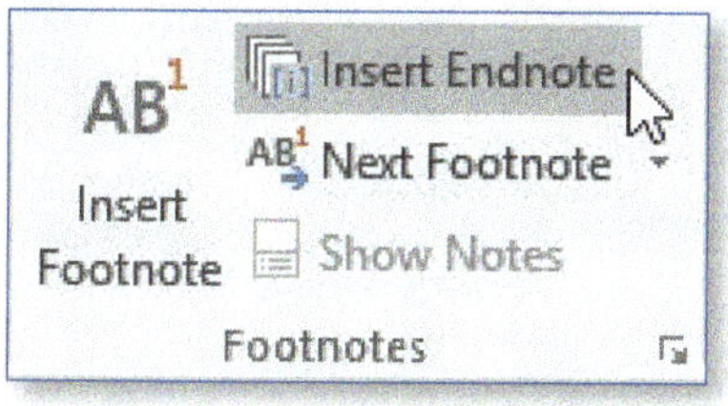

3-28 *Insert Endnote* button

ANOTHER WAY

Alt+Ctrl+F inserts a footnote. **Alt+Ctrl+D** inserts an endnote.

View Footnotes and Endnotes

Once you have inserted footnotes or endnotes in your document, it is easy to see the footnote or endnote text at the bottom of a page or at the end of the document, but you might have a difficult time locating the reference markers in the body of the document. Word provides you with a tool to easily locate footnote reference markers in your document.

Click the **Next Footnote** button in the *Footnotes* group on the *References* tab to move to the next footnote (Figure 3-29). Click the **Next Footnote** drop-down arrow to display a list of options to move to the next or previous footnote or endnote. Click the **Show Notes** button in the *Footnotes* group to toggle between the note reference markers (in the body of the document) and the note text (in the footnote or endnote area).

Word also displays the text of the footnote or endnote when you put your pointer over a reference marker (Figure 3-30).

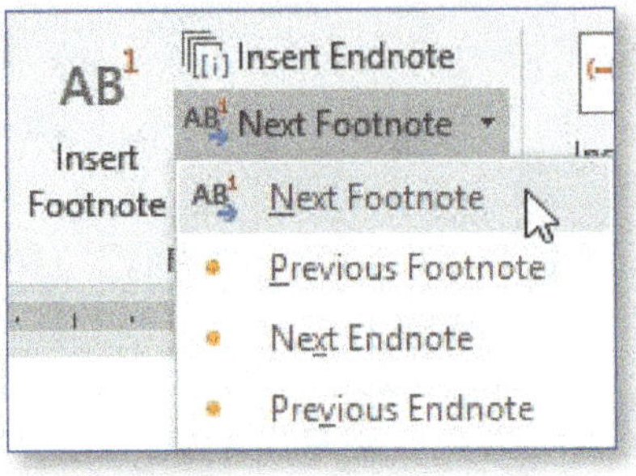

3-29 *Next Footnote* drop-down list

> **ANOTHER WAY**
>
> Use the *Go To* feature in the *Find and Replace* dialog box to go to a specific note. Press **Ctrl+G** to open the *Find and Replace* dialog box with the *Go To* tab displayed.

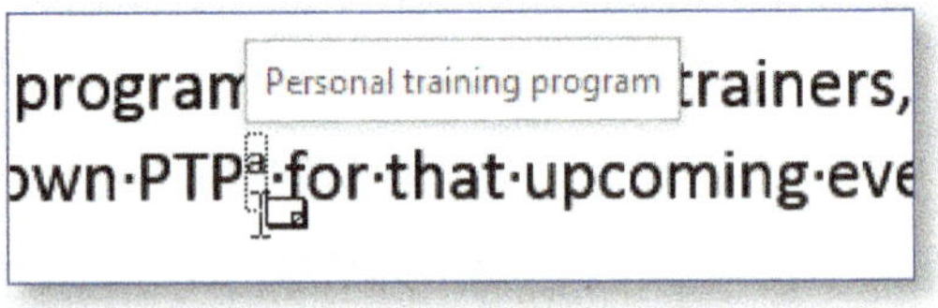

3-30 Footnote text displayed as a tag

Customize Footnotes and Endnotes

By default, footnotes are numbered consecutively with numbers (1, 2, 3) and endnotes are numbered with lowercase roman numerals (i, ii, iii). Letters or symbols such as an asterisk (*), section mark (§), or number symbol (#) are other reference marker options. You can customize how notes are numbered and where they display in a document.

▸HOW TO: Customize Footnotes and Endnotes

1. Click the **Footnotes** launcher [*Reference* tab, *Footnotes* group] to open the *Footnote and Endnote* dialog box (Figure 3-31).
2. Select the **Footnotes** or **Endnotes** radio button in the *Location* area.
   - In the drop-down list for *Footnotes*, you have the option to position the footnote text at the *Bottom of page* (default) or *Below text*.
   - In the drop-down list for *Endnotes*, you have the option to position the endnote text at the *End of document* (default) or *End of section*.
3. In the *Format* area, you can change any of the following: *Number format, Custom mark, Start at,* or *Numbering*.
4. In the *Apply changes* area, you can apply changes to the *Whole document* or *This section* (if there are sections in your document).
5. Click **Apply** to close the dialog box and apply the changes. Do not press *Insert*, which inserts a footnote or endnote in the document.

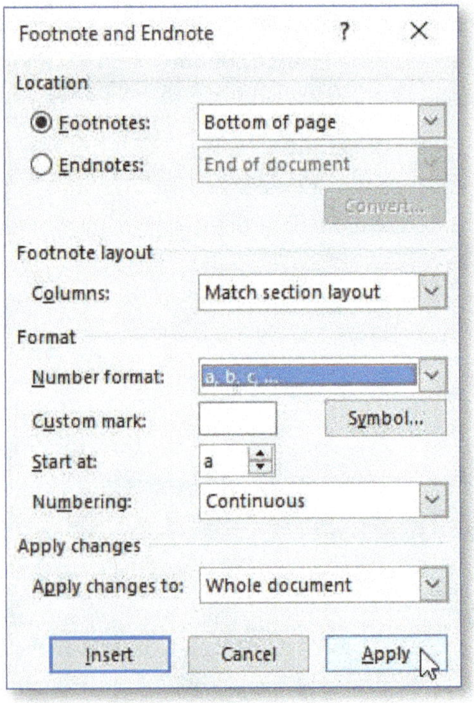

3-31 *Footnote and Endnote* dialog box

MORE INFO

You can also use the *Footnote and Endnote* dialog box to insert a footnote or endnote.

Modify Footnote and Endnote Format

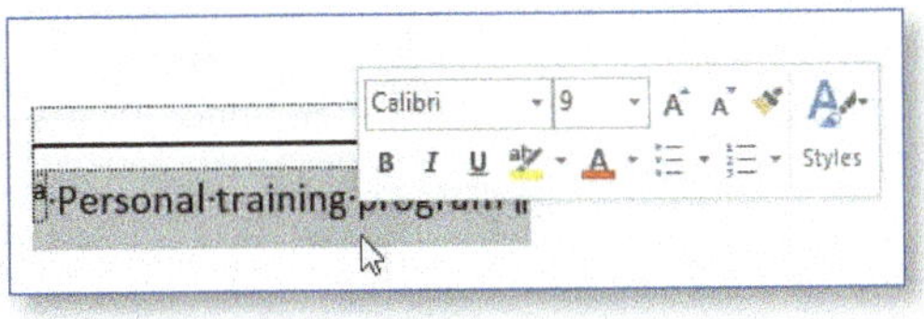

3-32 Apply formatting to footnote text

In addition to customizing note placement and format, you can also change the format of footnote and endnote text. You do this the same way you format regular text in the document.

Select the footnote or endnote text and apply any formatting changes such as font, font size, style, line or paragraph spacing, or text effects (Figure 3-32). You can apply changes using the buttons on the *Home* or *Layout* tab, the context menu (right-click selected text), the mini toolbar, or keyboard shortcuts.

Modify Footnote and Endnote Styles

The appearance of the footnotes and endnotes in your document is determined by styles. Styles control the font, font size, text styles and effects, and paragraph formatting. When you insert a footnote in your document, Word applies the *Footnote Text* style.

You can modify the *Footnote Text* or *Endnote Text* style, which automatically updates all of your footnote or endnote text to reflect the changes you made to the style.

HOW TO: Modify the Footnote or Endnote Style

1. Right-click the footnote or endnote text and select **Style** from the context menu. The *Style* dialog box opens and the name of the style displays in the *Styles* area (Figure 3-33).
2. Click the **Modify** button to open the *Modify Style* dialog box.
3. Change the basic font formatting in the *Formatting* area.
4. Click the **Format** button to display a list of other formatting options (Figure 3-34).
   - When you select a format option, another dialog box opens.
   - Make any desired formatting changes and click **OK** to close the dialog box.
5. Click **OK** to close the *Modify Style* dialog box.
6. Click **Apply** to apply changes to the style and close the *Style* dialog box.

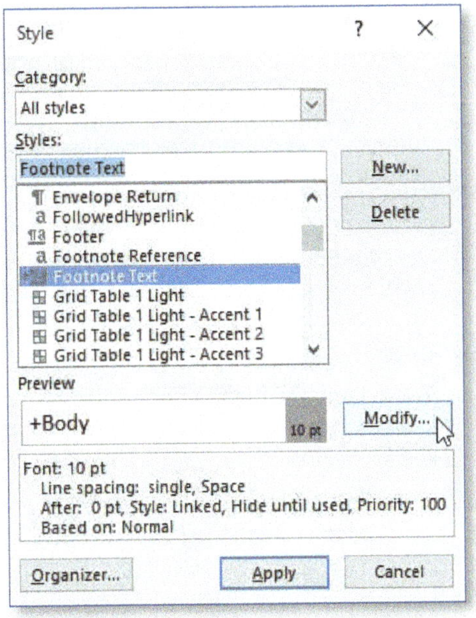

3-33 *Style* dialog box

Convert Footnotes and Endnotes

There might be times when you want to convert footnotes to endnotes or endnotes to footnotes. Rather than deleting and recreating the notes, you can use the ***Convert Notes*** feature. When you convert notes, Word automatically renumbers the reference markers and moves the note text to the correct location in the document.

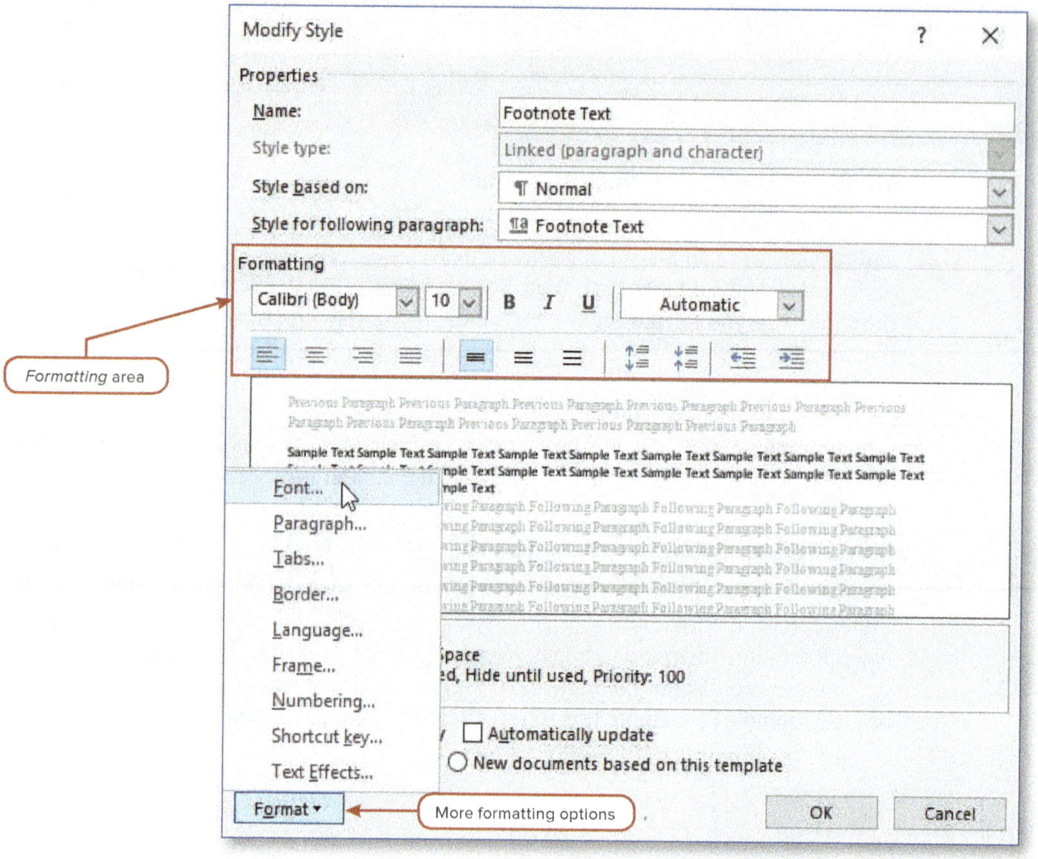

3-34 *Modify Style* dialog box

▸ HOW TO: Convert Footnotes and Endnotes

1. Click the **Footnotes** launcher [*References* tab, *Footnotes* group] to open the *Footnote and Endnote* dialog box.
2. Cick the **Convert** button in the *Location* area. The *Convert Notes* dialog box opens (Figure 3-35).
3. Select from one of the three convert options: **Convert all footnotes to endnotes**, **Convert all endnotes to footnotes**, or **Swap footnotes and endnotes**.
4. Click **OK** to close the *Convert Notes* dialog box.
5. Click **Close** to close the *Footnote and Endnote* dialog box.
   - Do not click *Insert* or Word will insert a footnote or endnote.

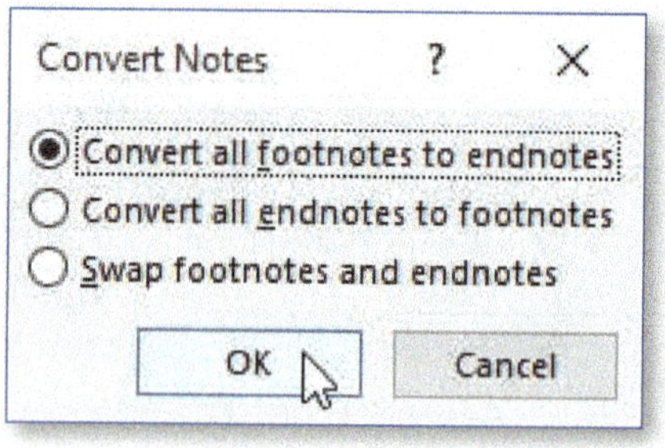

3-35 *Convert Notes* dialog box

MORE INFO

All three of the convert options are active *only* if you have both footnotes and endnotes in your document. Otherwise, only one option is active.

You can convert individual notes using the context menu. Right-click a footnote or endnote (*not* the reference marker in the text of the document) and select **Convert to Endnote** or **Convert to Footnote** (Figure 3-36).

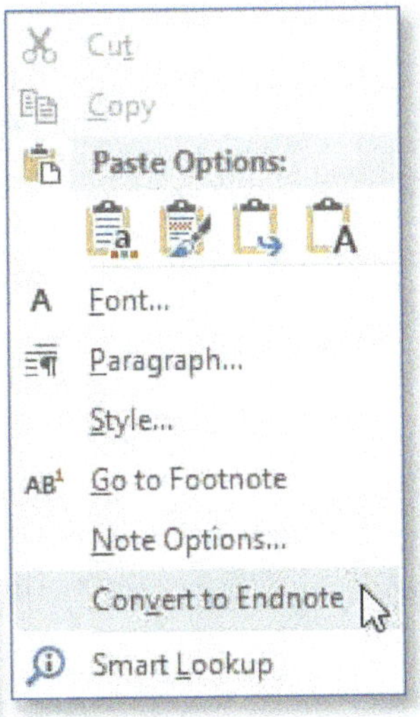

3-36 Convert individual note

Move Footnotes and Endnotes

You can move footnotes and endnotes in the same way you move text in a document. To move a note, select the **reference marker** in the body of the document (Figure 3-37) and use one of the following methods:

- Drag and drop
- **Ctrl+X** to cut and **Ctrl+V** to paste
- **Cut** and **Paste** buttons [*Home* tab, *Clipboard* group]
- **Cut** and **Paste** options in the context menu

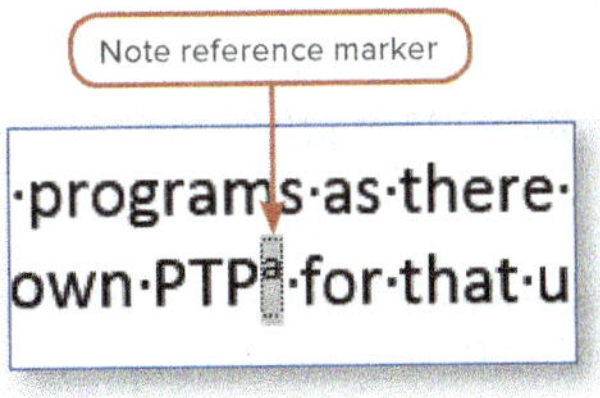

3-37 Select note reference marker to move

MORE INFO

When moving a note, select the note carefully to ensure that you are only moving the note and not any spaces, text, or paragraph marks.

Delete Footnotes and Endnotes

When you delete a note, Word removes the reference marker and the text of the note. Your remaining notes renumber and remain in consecutive order. To delete a note, always delete the note reference marker in the body of the document, which also deletes the note text in the footnote or endnote area.

HOW TO: Delete a Note

1. Select the **reference marker** in the body of the document (*not* the text of the footnote or endnote at the bottom of the page or end of the document).
2. Press **Delete** on the keyboard.
   - Deleting footnote or endnote text in the footnote or endnote area will not delete the note reference marker in the body of the document.
3. Check to ensure proper spacing around text where the note was deleted.

SLO 3.4

Creating a Bibliography and Inserting Citations

Typically, the most tedious and time-consuming aspect of writing a research paper is compiling sources, creating a bibliography page, and citing sources in the body of the report. A ***source*** is the complete bibliographic reference for a book, journal article, or web page. A ***citation*** is the abbreviated source information that you place in the body of the report to credit the source of the information you use. A ***bibliography*** or ***works cited*** page lists the sources used in the report. Word includes tools to create sources, insert citations, and create a bibliography or works cited page at the end of your report.

Report Styles

There are a variety of report styles, and each differs not only in the overall format of the report but also in the format for sources and citations. The most common report styles are the following:

- ***APA*** (American Psychological Association)
- ***Chicago*** (*The Chicago Manual of Style)*
- ***MLA*** (Modern Language Association)
- ***Turabian*** (*Manual for Writers of Research Papers, Theses, and Dissertations*)

MLA and APA are the two most common report formats. The following table lists some of the general characteristics of each of these two report styles. Within each of these report formats, there can be much variance depending on the preference of your college or instructor. Always follow the formatting instructions your instructor provides.

Common Report Styles

Report Features	APA	MLA
Font	11 or 12 pt.	11 or 12 pt.
Line Spacing	Academic APA is double-spaced and business APA is single spaced.	Double-space.
Margins	For an unbound report, use 1" for all margins. For a left bound report, use 1.5" left margin and 1"top, bottom, and right margins.	Use 1" margins.
Heading Information	Heading information is typically typed on a title page.	Left align at the top of the first page and include author's name, instructor's name, class, and date on separate lines.
Title	The title is either on the title page or horizontally centered on the first page of the report.	Center on the first page of the report.
Header	Include report title and page number on the right.	Include author's last name and page number on the right.
Uses	Typically use in social and behavioral sciences, business, and nursing.	Typically use in humanities.

Bibliography Styles

As you begin compiling the sources for your report, the first thing you need to do is select the ***bibliography style*** of the report. The bibliography style determines how citations display in the body of the report and how references appear on a references, bibliography, or works cited page.

▶ HOW TO: Select the Bibliography Style of the Report

1. Click the **Reference** tab.
2. Click the **Style** drop-down arrow [*Citations & Bibliography* group].
3. Select the style of the report from the drop-down list of report styles (Figure 3-38).

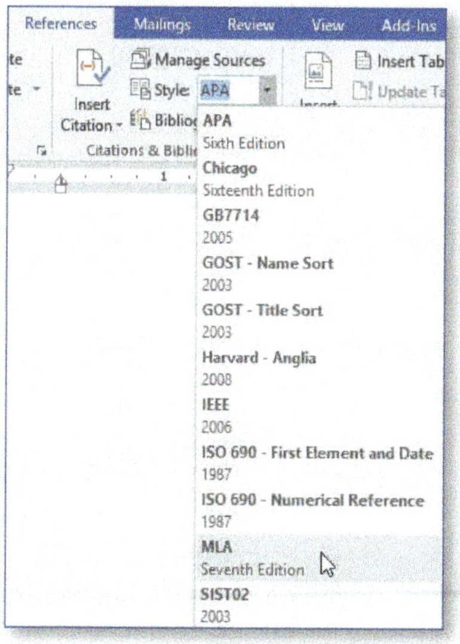

3-38 Select bibliography style

MORE INFO

The report style you select controls the formatting of sources and citations; it does not control the overall formatting of your report. To do that, you must apply the correct formatting to the body of your report.

Add a New Source

As you are writing a report, you should gather bibliographic information about sources used in your report (author; title of book, journal, or article; publication date and edition; publisher or online location). When you use the ***Add New Source*** feature, Word inserts a citation in your report at the insertion point and stores this source information. You then can access stored sources to insert additional citations and to create a bibliography page.

▶ HOW TO: Add a New Source

1. Position the insertion point in your document at the point where you want to insert a citation.
2. Click the **Insert Citation** button [*References* tab, *Citations & Bibliography* group].
3. Select **Add New Source**. The *Create Source* dialog box opens (Figure 3-39).

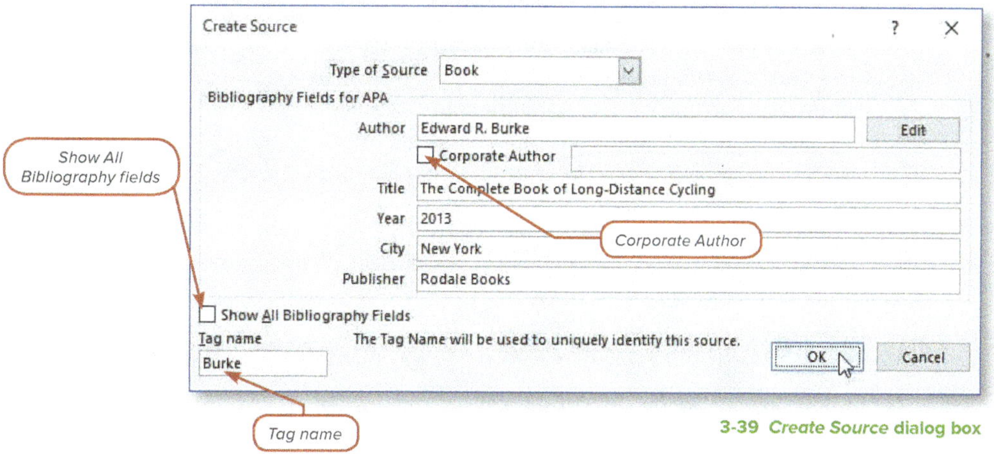

3-39 *Create Source* dialog box

4. Click the **Type of Source** drop-down list and select the type of source.
   - The fields for the source change depending on the type of source you choose.

5. Type the author information in the *Author area*. You will enter this information differently depending on the author(s) of the source.
   - *Individual Author*: In the *Author* field, type first name, middle initial, and last name (with no commas).
   - *Multiple Authors*: Click the **Edit** button to the right of the *Author* area to open the *Edit Name* dialog box. Type the author information in the *Add name* fields. Click the **Add** button to add additional authors. You can also reorder multiple authors by selecting an author in the *Names* area and clicking the **Up** or **Down** button. Click **OK** to close the *Edit Name* dialog box (Figure 3-40).
   - *Corporate Author* (e.g., USA Cycling or Velo News): Click the **Corporate Author** check box in the *Create Source* dialog box and type the corporate author.

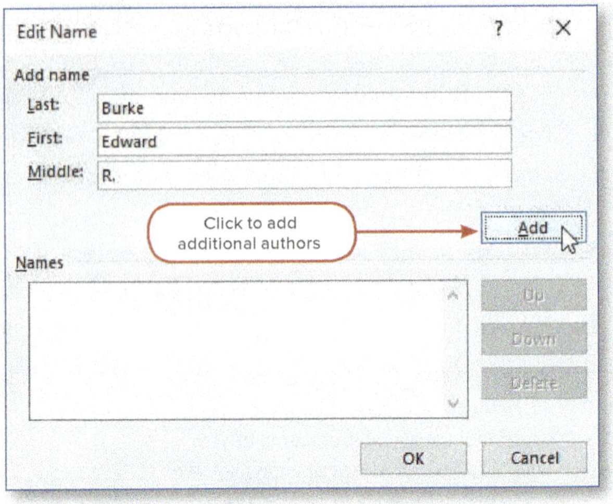

3-40 *Edit Name* dialog box

6. Type other source information as needed (see Figure 3-39).
   - As you type in other source information, Word automatically creates a *Tag name* for your source.
   - You can edit the *Tag name* if desired.
7. Click the **Show All Bibliography Fields** check box to display more fields. For example, you might need to type the edition of the book.
8. Click **OK** to close the *Create Source* dialog box.
   - The citation displays in the document in the report style you selected (Figure 3-41).

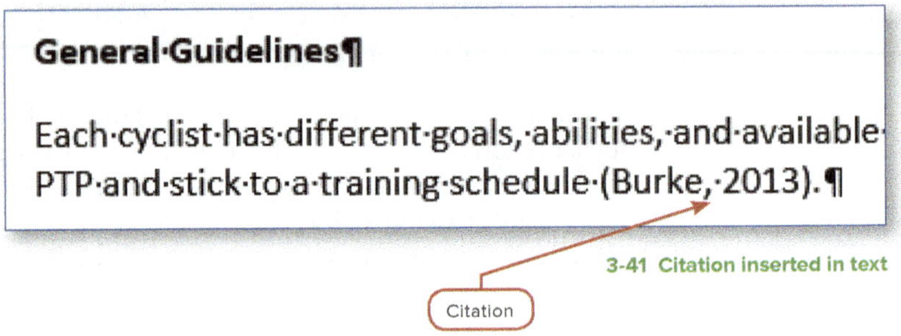

3-41 Citation inserted in text

Insert a Citation

Often you cite a source more than once in a report. Once you have added a source to your document, you can insert this same citation again in your document without entering the source information again. When inserting a citation, you can choose from citations you have previously created.

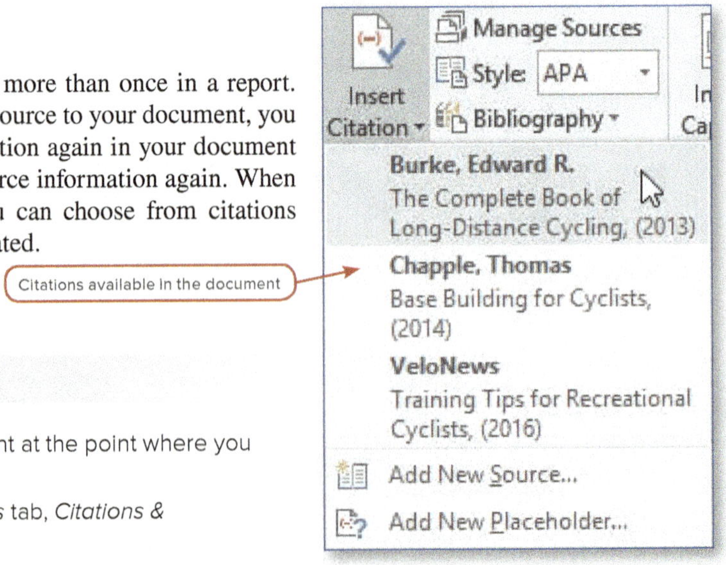

3-42 Insert citation from a previously created source

▶HOW TO: Insert a Citation

1. Position the insertion point in your document at the point where you want a citation inserted.
2. Click the **Insert Citation** button [*References* tab, *Citations & Bibliography* group].
   - A list of previously used or created sources is displayed in the drop-down list (Figure 3-42).

3. Select from your list of sources.
   - The citation is inserted in the document.
   - When you insert a citation, Word automatically inserts a space between the citation and the preceding word.

MORE INFO

When inserting citations, the citation typically is placed one space after the preceding word and directly before the punctuation mark. Always check your document to ensure proper spacing.

Insert a Placeholder

There might be times when you need to insert a citation but do not have all of the bibliographic information to create the source. You can insert a ***placeholder*** in the report to temporarily mark a spot where a citation needs to be completed. Later, you can add bibliographic source information for any placeholders inserted in the document.

HOW TO: Insert a Placeholder

1. Position the insertion point in your document at the point where you want a placeholder inserted.
2. Click the **Insert Citation** button [*References* tab, *Citations & Bibliography* group].
3. Select **Add New Placeholder**. The *Placeholder Name* dialog box opens (Figure 3-43).
4. Type the name of the placeholder.
   - You can't use spaces between words in the placeholder text because the placeholder name is the tag name of the source.
   - Use can use an underscore between words when naming a placeholder.
5. Click **OK**. The placeholder displays in the document and looks similar to a citation (Figure 3-44).

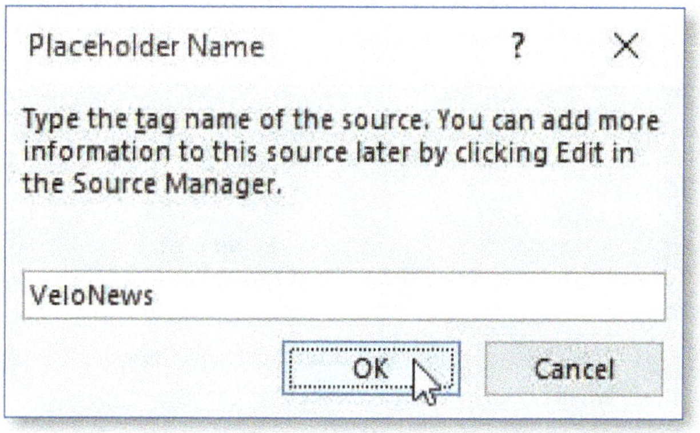

3-43 Insert a placeholder

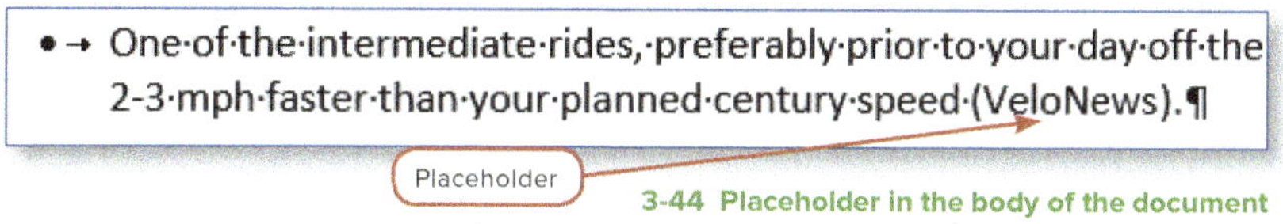

3-44 Placeholder in the body of the document

Manage Sources

The ***Source Manager*** dialog box allows you to edit existing sources, add bibliographic information to placeholders, create new sources, and copy sources that were created and used in other documents. The *Source Manager* dialog box displays the sources used in your report, the placeholders that need bibliographic information, and a master list of all sources you have previously used.

▸HOW TO: Manage Sources

1. Click the **Manage Sources** button [*References* tab, *Citations & Bibliography* group]. The *Source Manager* dialog box opens (Figure 3-45).

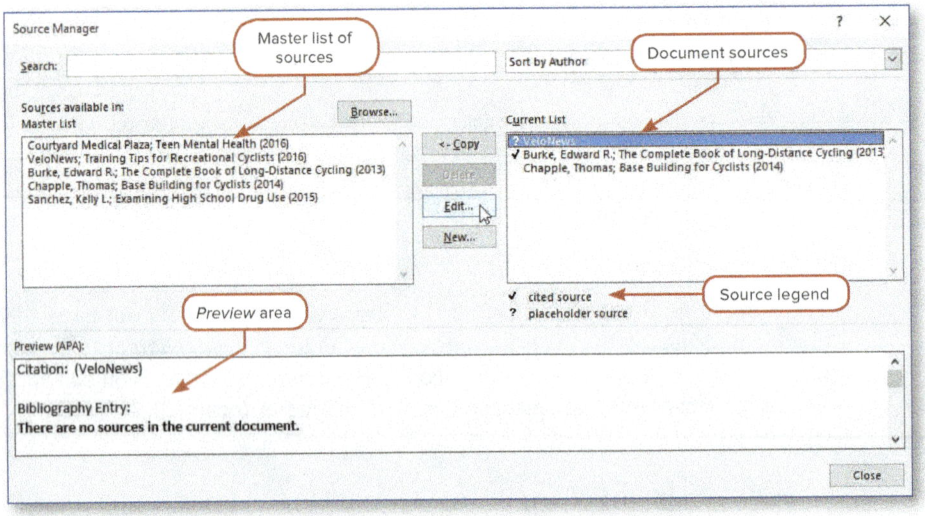

3-45 *Source Manager* dialog box

- The *Master List* of sources on the left displays *all* available sources. Some of these may have been created in other Word documents.
- The *Current List* displays the sources available in your current document.
- Sources that are cited in the document have a check mark next to them.
- Sources that are placeholders have a question mark next to them and require additional information.
- The *Preview* area displays the contents of your source.

2. To copy a source from the *Master List* to the *Current List*, select the source and press the **Copy** button. The copied source remains on the *Master List*.
3. To edit a source from either list, select the source and click the **Edit** button (see Figure 3-45). The *Edit Source* dialog box opens.
   - Make changes to the source and press **OK**.
   - Word automatically updates any citations in your document if you make changes to the source.
4. To add bibliographic information to a placeholder, select the placeholder and click the **Edit** button. The *Edit Source* dialog box opens.
   - Add bibliographic information to the placeholder and press **OK**.
   - When bibliographic information is added to a placeholder, it becomes a complete source and the question mark next to it changes to a check.
   - Word automatically replaces the placeholder with a citation in your document when you add bibliographic information to a placeholder.
5. To create a new source, click the **New** button. The *Create Source* dialog box opens.
   - Type in the bibliographic information and press **OK**.
   - This source is now available as a citation to insert in your document.
   - This source is also added to the *Master List*.
6. To delete a source from either list, select the source and click the **Delete** button.
   - You cannot delete a source from the *Current List* if it is cited in the document. You must first delete the citation in the document before deleting a source in the *Source Manager* dialog box.
   - If a source is in both lists and you delete it from one list, it is not deleted from the other list.
7. Click **Close** to close the *Source Manager* dialog box and apply any changes made.

Edit Citations and Sources

After citations and placeholders are inserted into the document, you can edit the citation or source without using the *Source Manager* dialog box. When you click a citation or placeholder in your document, you see a drop-down list of editing options (Figure 3-46):

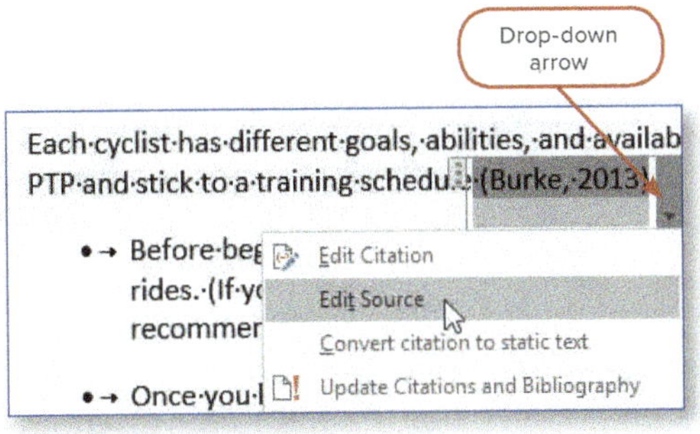

3-46 Edit citation and source options

- ***Edit Citation***: This option opens the *Edit Citation* dialog box and allows you to add a page number to the citation or suppress any currently displayed information.
- ***Edit Source***: This option opens the *Edit Source* dialog box and allows you to update source bibliographic information.
- ***Convert citation to static text***: This option changes the citation from a Word field that is automatically generated and updated to static text that is not updated.
- ***Update Citations and Bibliography***: This option updates your bibliography page to reflect any changes you have made to citations or sources.

MORE INFO

You can edit citations and placeholders using either the drop-down list or the context menu.

You can move or delete a citation or placeholder in the body of the text by clicking the citation or placeholder handle on the left and dragging it to a new location (to move) or by pressing **Delete** (to delete) on your keyboard (Figure 3-47).

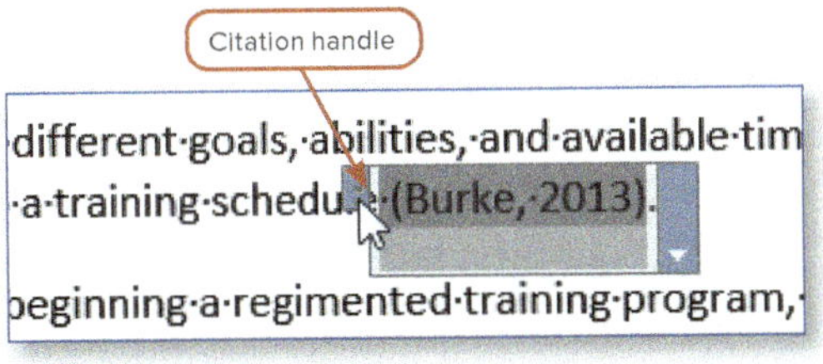

3-47 Select a citation to move or delete

Insert a Bibliography

Once you have created your sources and inserted citations in the body of the report, you are ready to create a bibliography page. The bibliography page is automatically generated from the sources in your document and is formatted according to the *Bibliography Style* you selected. Word provides you with a few bibliography options.

The *Bibliography*, *References*, and *Works Cited* built-in options insert a title before the sources. The *Insert Bibliography* option just inserts the sources; you can add a title of your choice. If you plan to include a table of contents in your report, it is best to use one of the built-in options because Word applies a style for the bibliography title, which allows the bibliography page to automatically be included in the table contents.

HOW TO: Insert a Bibliography

1. Position the insertion point in your document at the point where you want the bibliography to begin.
    - It is usually best to insert a page break (**Ctrl+Enter**) at the end of the document and begin the bibliography on a new page.

2. Click the **Bibliography** button [*References* tab, *Citations & Bibliography* group] to display the list of options (Figure 3-48).
3. Select your bibliography option. The bibliography is inserted in the document.

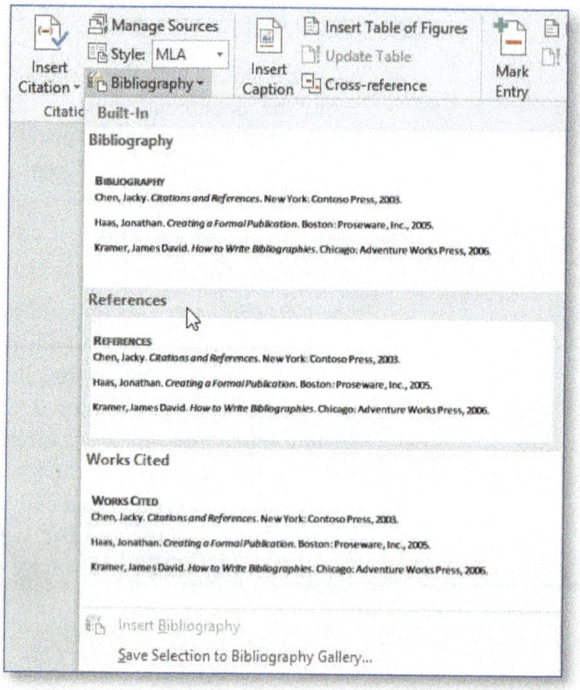

3-48 Insert *References* page

If changes are made to sources after the bibliography page has been inserted, you have to update the bibliography. Click one of the references on the bibliography page to select the entire bibliography and click **Update Citations and Bibliography** (Figure 3-49).

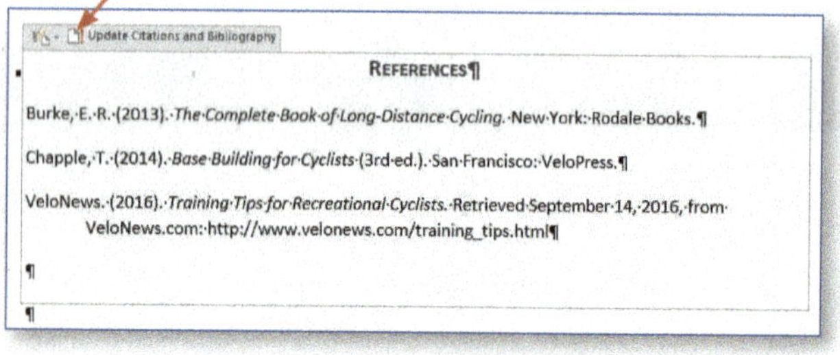

3-49 *References* page inserted into the document

ANOTHER WAY

Right-click the bibliography and choose **Update Field** or press **F9** to update the bibliography.

PAUSE & PRACTICE: WORD 3-2

For this Pause & Practice project, you modify the *Developing a Personal Training Program* report for American River Cycling Club. You accept tracked changes, delete comments, add and modify notes, select the report style, add sources and citations, and insert a bibliography page.

File Needed: ***[your initials] PP W3-1.docx***
Completed Project File Name: ***[your initials] PP W3-2.docx***

1. Open the ***[your initials] PP W3-1*** document completed in *Pause & Practice 3-1*.
2. Save this document as [your initials] PP W3-2.
3. Accept tracked changes and delete all comments in the document.
    a. Click the bottom half of the **Accept** button [*Review* tab, *Changes* group] and select **Accept All Changes**.
    b. Click the bottom half of the **Delete** button [*Review* tab, *Comments* group] and select **Delete All Comments in Document**.

4. Insert endnotes into the report.
   a. Position the insertion point after "PTP" and before the space (first page, first body paragraph). Turn on **Show/Hide**, if necessary.
   b. Click **Insert Endnote** [*References* tab, *Footnotes* group]. Word moves the insertion point to the endnote area on the last page.
   c. Type Personal training program in the endnote area.
   d. Position the insertion point after the first instance of "Max VO2" and before the space (third page, second sentence in the "Training Intensity and Heart Rate" section).

MORE INFO

Use the *Find* feature in the *Navigation* pane to locate specific words.

   e. Click **Insert Endnote** [*References* tab, *Footnotes* group] and type The highest rate of oxygen consumption attainable during maximal or exhaustive exercise in the endnote area.
   f. Position the insertion point after "RPM" and before the period (third page, "Sample Session" section).
   g. Click **Insert Endnote** [*References* tab, *Footnotes* group] and type Revolutions per minute in the endnote area.
   h. Apply **bold** and **italic** formatting to the words "maximal" and "exhaustive" in the second endnote (Figure 3-50).

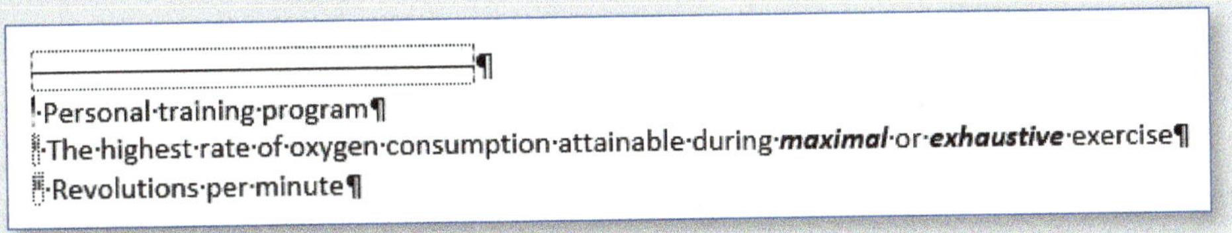

3-50 Endnotes added to report

5. Convert endnotes to footnotes and change numbering.
   a. Click the **Footnotes** launcher [*References* tab, *Footnotes* group]. The *Footnote and Endnote* dialog box opens.
   b. Click the **Convert** button to open the *Convert Notes* dialog box (Figure 3-51).
   c. Select **Convert all endnotes to footnotes** if it is not already selected and click **OK**.
   d. Click **Close** to the close the *Footnote and Endnote* dialog box.
   e. Click the **Footnotes** launcher again to open the *Footnote and Endnote* dialog box.
   f. Click the **Footnotes** radio button if it is not already selected.
   g. Click the **Number format** drop-down arrow and select **a, b, c . . .** (Figure 3-52). Don't change any of the other *Format* settings.
   h. Choose **Apply** to close the *Footnote and Endnote* dialog box and apply the changes.
   i. Check your document to confirm that endnotes have been converted to footnotes and that the number format has been changed.

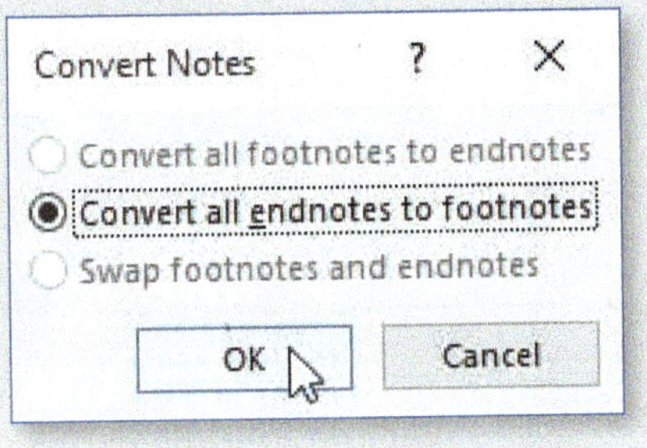

3-51 Convert endnotes to footnotes

6. Change the style of the footnotes.
   a. Right-click the footnote text at the bottom of the first page.
   b. Select **Style** from the context menu (not mini toolbar). The *Style* dialog box opens.
   c. Click the **Modify** button to open the *Modify Style* dialog box (Figure 3-53).
   d. Change the font size to **9 pt**.
   e. Change line spacing to **1.5** (see Figure 3-53).
   f. Click **OK** to close the *Modify Style* dialog box.
   g. Choose **Apply** to close the *Style* dialog box.
7. Select the report style for sources and citations.
   a. Click the **Style** drop-down list [*References* tab, *Citations & Bibliography* group].
   b. Select **MLA Seventh Edition**.
8. Add a new source and insert a citation.
   a. On the first page, position the insertion point after the word "schedule" and before the period (end of first paragraph, "General Guidelines" section).
   b. Click the **Insert Citation** button [*References* tab, *Citations & Bibliography* group].

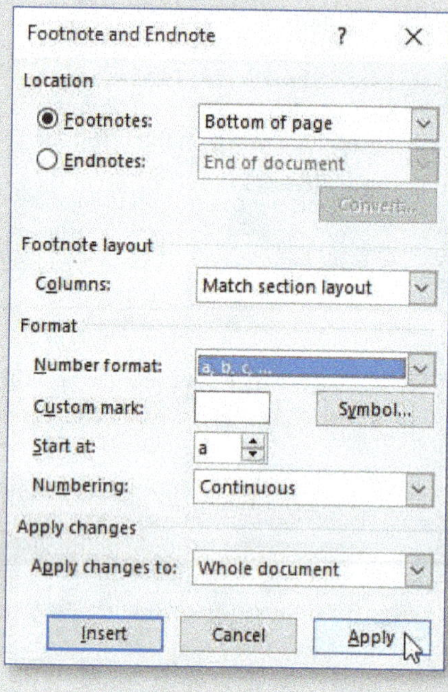

3-52 Change number format of footnotes

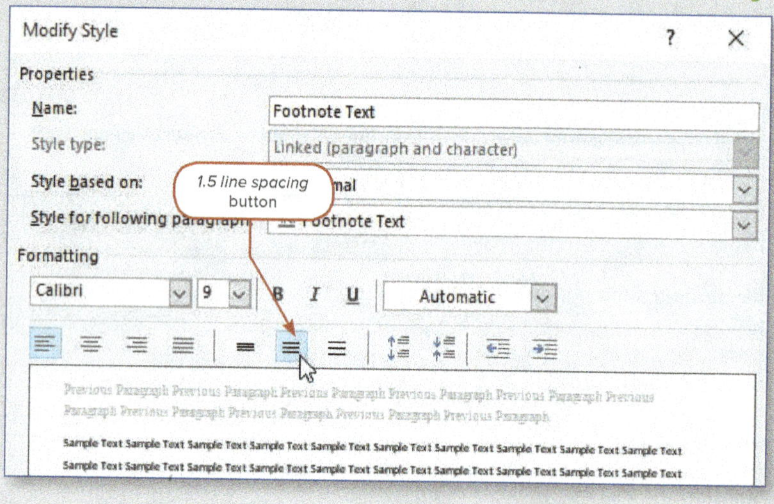

3-53 Modify *Footnote Text* style

   c. Select **Add New Source**. The *Create Source* dialog box opens (Figure 3-54).
   d. Select **Book** as the type of source.
   e. Type Edward R. Burke in the *Author* field.
   f. Type the following source information in the *Create Source* dialog box:

      Title: The Complete Book of Long-Distance Cycling
      Year: 2013
      City: New York
      Publisher: Rodale Books
      Tag name: Burke

   g. Click **OK** to add the source, insert the citation, and close the dialog box.

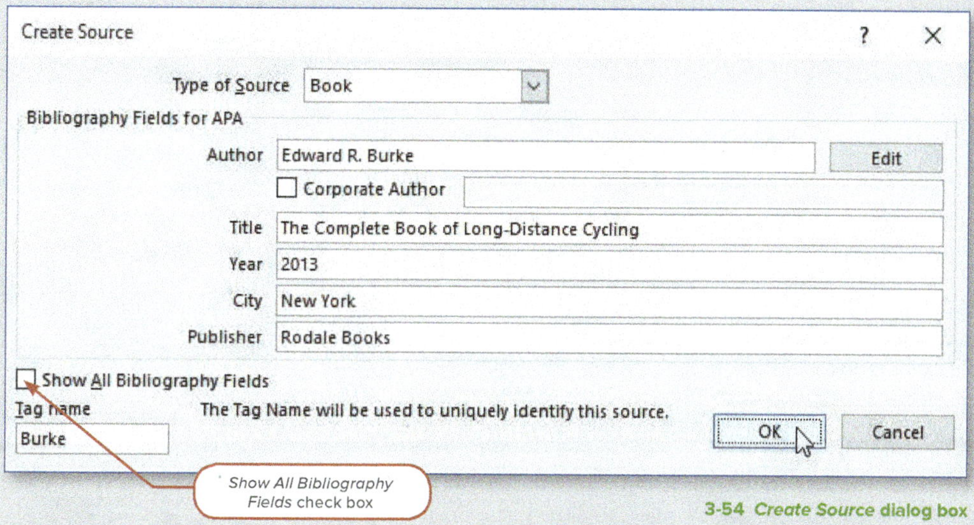

3-54 ***Create Source* dialog box**

9. Add a placeholder to the report.
   a. Go the first page and position the insertion point after the word "speed" and before the period (last bulleted item, "Pace of Rides" section). You can also press **Ctrl+G** to open the *Go To* tab in the *Find and Replace* dialog box where you can quickly go to a specific page.
   b. Click the **Insert Citation** button [*References* tab, *Citations & Bibliography* group].
   c. Select **Add New Placeholder**. The *Placeholder Name* dialog box opens.
   d. Type VeloNews (no space between words) as the placeholder text.
   e. Press **OK** to insert the placeholder and close the dialog box.
10. Manage sources to add a new source and complete bibliographic information for the placeholder.
   a. Click the **Manage Sources** button [*References* tab, *Citations & Bibliography* group]. The *Source Manager* dialog box opens.
   b. Select **VeloNews** in the *Current List* area and click the **Edit** button to open the *Edit Source* dialog box.
   c. Check the **Show All Bibliography Fields** box and type the following source information:

      Type of Source: **Document from Web site**
      Corporate Author (check **Corporate Author** check box): VeloNews
      Name of Web Page: Training Tips for Recreational Cyclists
      Name of Web Site: VeloNews.com
      Year: 2016
      Year Accessed: 2016
      Month Accessed: September
      Day Accessed: 14
      URL: http://www.velonews.com/training_tips.html

   d. Click **OK** to close the *Edit Source* dialog box. The placeholder is updated as a complete source.
   e. Click the **New** button to create a new source.
   f. Check the **Show All Bibliography Fields** box and type the following source information:

      Type of Source: **Book**
      Author: Thomas Chapple
      Title: Base Building for Cyclists
      Year: 2014

City: San Francisco
Publisher: VeloPress
Edition: 3rd
Tag name: Chapple

g. Click **OK** to close the *Create Source* dialog box.
h. Click **Close** to close the *Source Manager* dialog box.

11. Insert citations into the report.
    a. Go to the second page and position the insertion point after "rest day" and before the period (second sentence of first paragraph, "Number of Rides per Week" section).
    b. Click the **Insert Citation** button [*References* tab, *Citations & Bibliography* group] (Figure 3-55).
    c. Select the **Chapple, Thomas** source. The citation displays in the report.
    d. Use the **Insert Citation** button to insert the following citations:

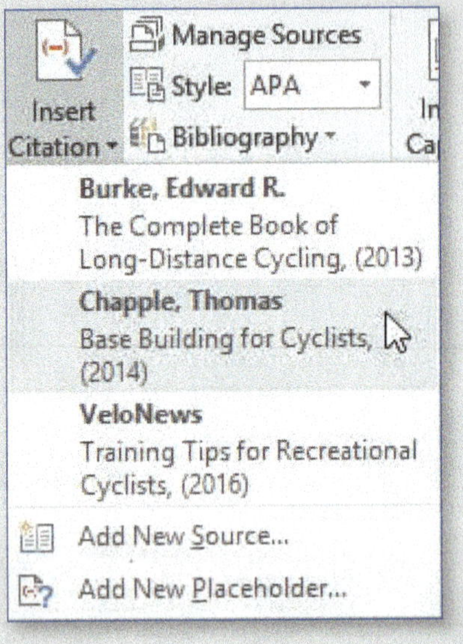

3-55 Insert a citation

Burke, Edward, R.: after "training week" and before the period (page 2, last bulleted item in the "Duration of Rides" section).
Chapple, Thomas: after "maximum heart rate" and before the period (page 3, first paragraph in "Training Intensity and Heart Rate" section).
VeloNews: after "overtraining" and before the period (page 3, at the end of "Other Heart Rate Factors" section).

12. Insert a bibliography and change report style.
    a. Position the insertion point on the blank line at the end of the document and press **Ctrl+Enter** to insert a page break.
    b. Click the **Bibliography** button [*References* tab, *Citations & Bibliography* group] and select **References** from the drop-down list. The *Reference* page is inserted on the blank page at the end of the document.
    c. **Center** the *References* title and apply **10 pt**. after paragraph spacing.
    d. Click the **Style** drop-down list [*References* tab, *Citations & Bibliography* group] and select **APA Sixth Edition**.

13. Save and close the document (Figure 3-56).

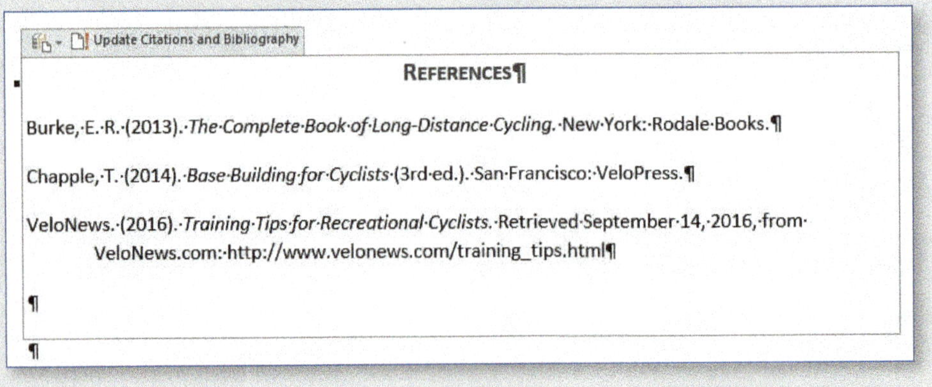
Update Citations and Bibliography

REFERENCES¶

Burke,·E.·R.·(2013).·*The·Complete·Book·of·Long-Distance·Cycling.*·New·York:·Rodale·Books.¶

Chapple,·T.·(2014).·*Base·Building·for·Cyclists*·(3rd·ed.).·San·Francisco:·VeloPress.¶

VeloNews.·(2016).·*Training·Tips·for·Recreational·Cyclists.*·Retrieved·September·14,·2016,·from·VeloNews.com:·http://www.velonews.com/training_tips.html¶

¶

¶

3-56 PP W3-2 References page

SLO 3.5

Inserting a Table of Contents

Most long reports have a ***table of contents*** to provide readers with an overview of the material covered in the report. The table of contents reflects the headings in the report; some tables of contents list only the main headings while others might list second- and third-level headings. Typically, a table of contents lists headings on the left and page numbers on the right with a dot leader separating them.

You can create a table of contents manually by typing headings, using a tab with a dot leader, and then typing the page number. But with Word, you can automatically generate a table of contents based upon the headings in your report, which saves you time. If you generate your table of contents this way, it automatically updates if topics are changed or moved or if page numbering changes in the report.

Use Heading Styles for a Table of Contents

Word can automatically generate a table of contents listing the headings in your report if you apply ***heading styles*** to each heading. Styles control the appearance of text by applying a specific font, font size, color, font styles and effects, and spacing to the text on which a style is applied. The document ***theme*** determines the appearance of the styles. The *Styles* gallery displays many of the commonly used styles.

> **MORE INFO**
>
> Styles and themes were introduced in Chapter 2 (see *SLO 2.7: Using Styles and Themes*).

The first step in automatically generating a table of contents in a report is to apply a heading style to each heading in the document. Word provides you with multiple levels of heading styles (e.g., Heading 1, Heading 2, etc.).

HOW TO: Apply Heading Styles

1. Select the heading where you want to apply a style.
2. Click the heading style to apply [*Home* tab, *Styles* group] (Figure 3-57). The style is applied to the heading.

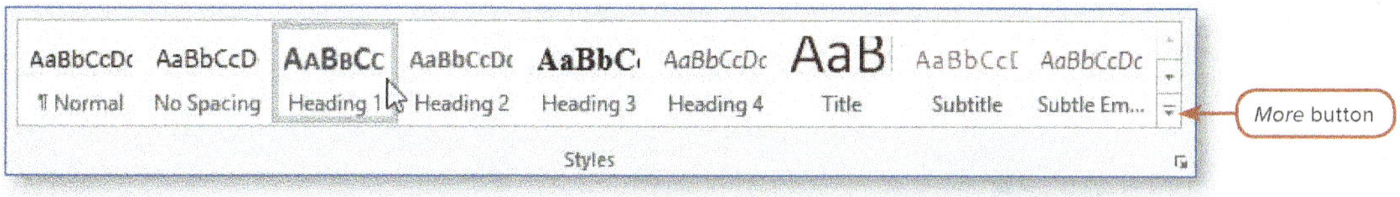

3-57 Document styles displayed in the *Style* gallery

- Apply *Heading 1* to main headings, *Heading 2* to second level headings, and other heading styles as needed.
- When you place the insertion point on a style, Word displays a live preview of the style and temporarily applies the style to the selected text.
- Click the **More** button to expand the *Style* gallery to display additional styles.

3. Continue to select headings and apply styles. Every heading you want in your table of contents must have a style.
   - When a heading style has been applied to text, there is an *Expand/Collapse* button to the left of the heading (Figure 3-58). Click the **Expand/Collapse** button to expand or collapse the text below the heading.

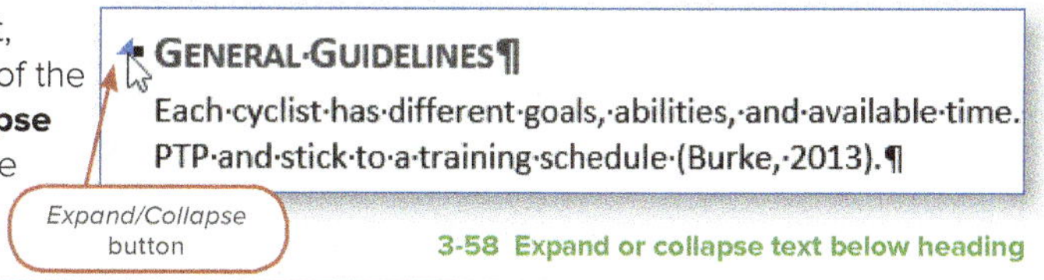

3-58 Expand or collapse text below heading

Insert a Built-In Table of Contents

You can insert a built-in table of contents that includes the headings in your document. Word inserts the table of contents at the point in your report where the insertion point is located. It is a good idea to insert a blank page before the first page of your report for your table of contents.

HOW TO: Insert a Built-In Table of Contents

1. Place the insertion point before the first line of the report and press **Ctrl+Enter** to insert a page break.
2. Position the insertion point at the top of the new first page.
3. Click the **References** tab.
4. Click the **Table of Contents** button [*Table of Contents* group] (Figure 3-59).
5. Select a built-in table of contents to insert. The table of contents displays in your report (Figure 3-60).

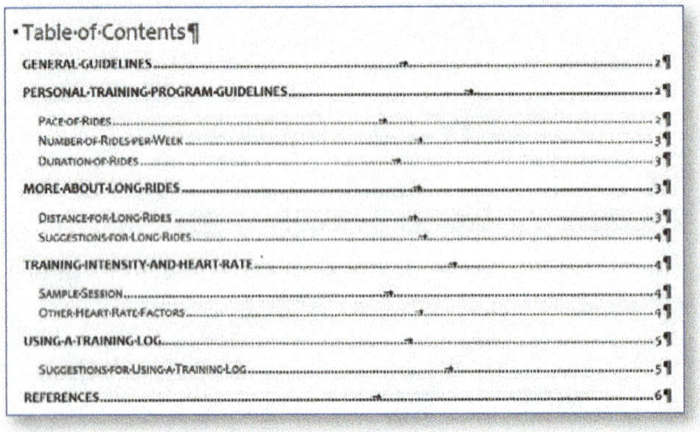

3-60 Table of contents inserted into the report

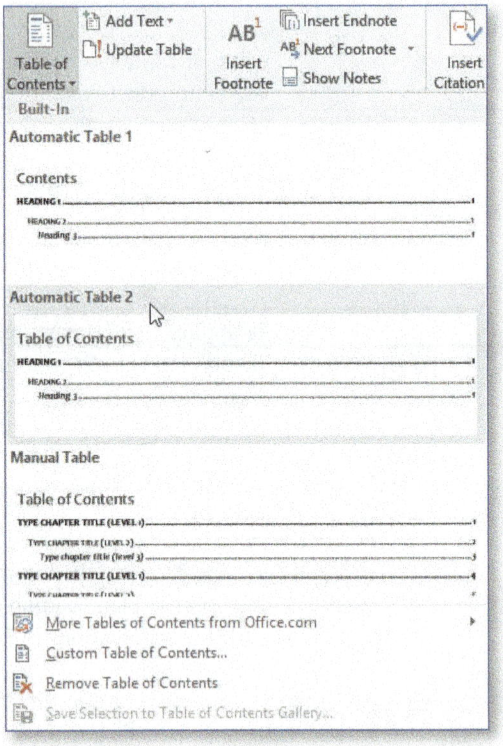

3-59 Insert built-in table of contents

- Each heading in the table of contents is a hyperlink. Press the **Ctrl** key and click a heading in the table of content to move you to the heading in the body of the document.

Insert a Custom Table of Contents

You can insert a custom table of contents and modify the format and appearance of the table. When you insert a custom table of contents, the "Table of Contents" title is not automatically inserted as it is when you insert a built-in table of contents. If you want a title on your custom table of contents page, you should type it before inserting your table of contents.

MORE INFO

It is usually best to just apply font formatting (not a heading style) to the table of contents title. If you apply a heading style to the table of contents title, the table of contents title is included as an item in the table of contents when it is updated.

▶ HOW TO: Insert a Custom Table of Contents

1. Place the insertion point before the first line of your report and press **Ctrl+Enter** to insert a page break.
2. Position the insertion point at the top of the new first page.
   - If desired, type a title for the table of contents and press **Enter**.
   - Do not apply a heading style to the title.
3. Click the **Table of Contents** button [*References* tab, *Table of Contents* group].
4. Select **Custom Table of Contents**. The *Table of Contents* dialog box opens (Figure 3-61).
   - A preview of the table of contents appears in the *Print Preview* area.
5. Click the **Formats** drop-down list in the *General* area and select a table of contents format.
6. Select the number of heading levels to display in the *Show levels* area.
7. Below the *Print Preview* area, you can choose to not show page numbers, choose to not right align page numbers, and select the type of tab leader to use with right-aligned page numbers.
8. Click **OK** to insert the table of contents.

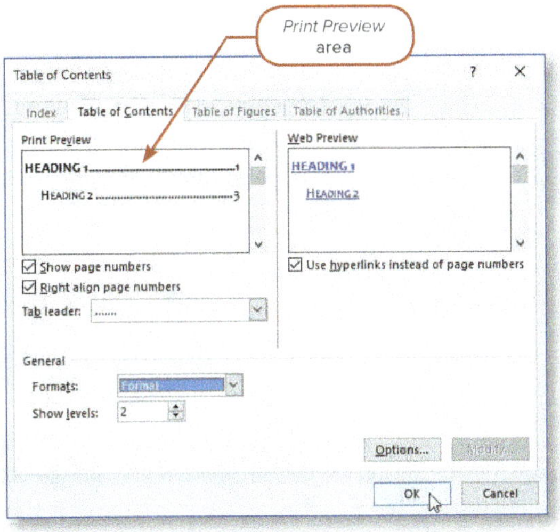

3-61 *Table of Contents* dialog box

Modify a Table of Contents

After inserting a table of contents, you might decide that you want a different format or to change the levels of headings that are displayed. When you update a table of contents, you are actually replacing the old table of contents with a new one.

▶ HOW TO: Modify a Table of Contents

1. Click anywhere in the table of contents.
2. Click the **Table of Contents** button [*References* tab, *Table of Contents* group].
3. Select **Custom Table of Contents**. The *Table of Contents* dialog box opens.
4. Make changes to the table of contents.
5. Click **OK**. A dialog box opens, confirming you want to replace the existing table of contents (Figure 3-62).
6. Click **Yes** to replace the table of contents.

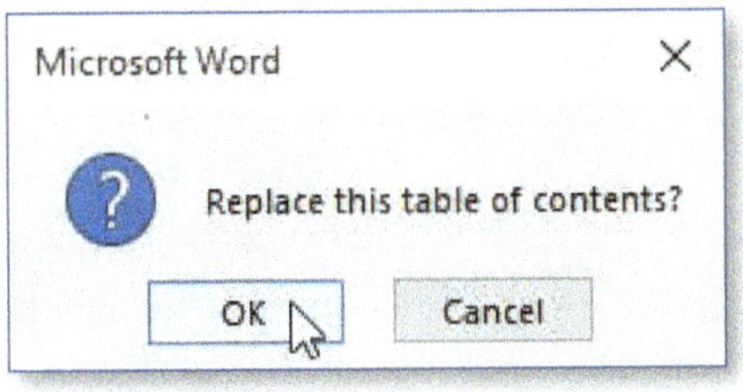

3-62 Replace existing table of contents

Update a Table of Contents

When you make changes to your report such as adding or modifying headings, content, or page breaks, the content and page numbers in the table of contents may no longer be accurate. You need to update the table of contents to reflect these changes. You have the option of updating only page numbers or updating the entire table of contents, which includes both headings and page numbers.

HOW TO: Update a Table of Contents

1. Click anywhere in the table of contents.
2. Click the **Update Table** button [*References* tab, *Table of Contents* group]. The *Update Table of Contents* dialog box opens (Figure 3-63).
3. Select either **Update page numbers only** or **Update entire table**.
4. Click **OK** to update the table of contents.

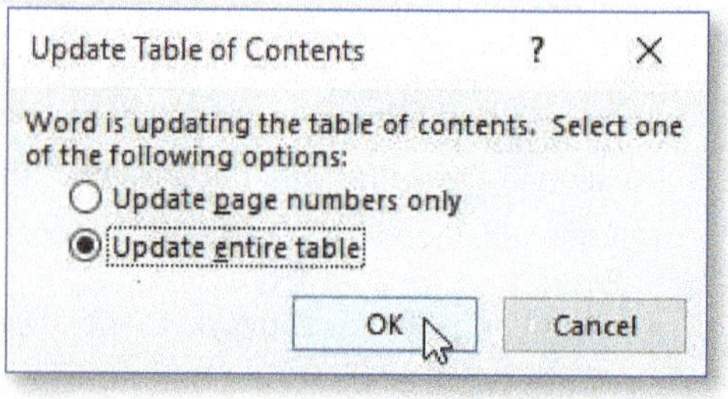

3-63 Update table of contents

ANOTHER WAY

Press **F9** or right-click the table of contents and select **Update Field** to update the table of contents.

Remove a Table of Contents

If you no longer want a table of contents in your report, you can easily remove it. Click the **Table of Contents** button in the *Table of Contents* group on the *References* tab and select **Remove Table of Contents**. The table of contents is removed from your document (Figure 3-64).

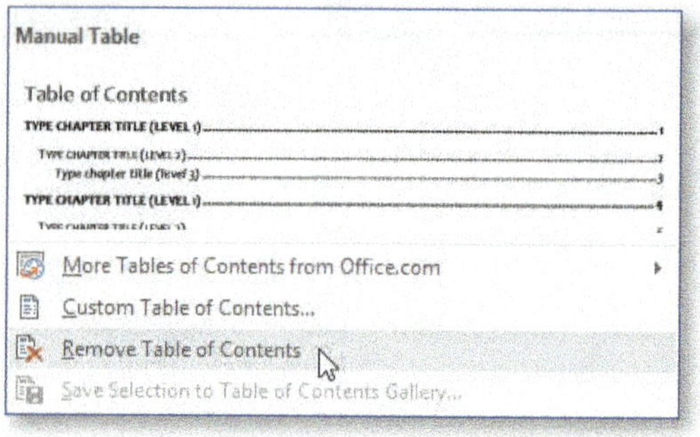

3-64 Remove table of contents

SLO 3.6

Inserting a Cover Page

Some reports have a title page as the cover or introduction. If you're writing a formal report in APA style, there is a specific way you must organize the title page. But if you're presenting a market analysis or product feasibility report at work, you might want a ***cover page*** to introduce the report with professional appeal. Word provides you with a variety of cover page options.

Insert a Built-In Cover Page

When you insert a cover page into a document, Word automatically inserts it at the beginning of the document and inserts a page break to move the existing first page content to the second page.

To insert a cover page, click the **Cover Page** button in the *Pages* group on the *Insert* tab and select one of the built-in cover pages from the drop-down list (Figure 3-65). More custom cover pages are available on Office.com. Select **More Cover Pages from Office.com** to display a list of additional cover pages.

Customize Cover Page Content

The built-in cover pages in Word are arrangements of graphics, text boxes, and Word fields. Some of the fields are ***document property fields*** and some are ***content control fields***, fields where you can type custom information. You can customize the content of the fields, delete

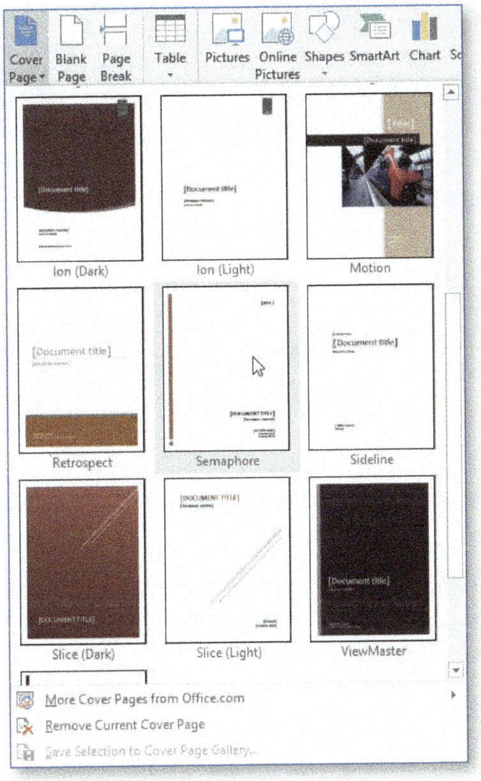

3-65 Insert built-in cover page

unwanted fields, and modify the graphics and text boxes on the cover page. The theme of your document controls the format of cover pages. Colors and fonts in a cover page change based on the selected theme.

Customize Document Property Content

If you have added information to the document properties of your document, Word automatically populates the document properties fields in the cover page. When you type information into a document property field on the cover page, Word adds this information to your document properties.

▸ HOW TO: Customize Document Properties

1. Click the **File** tab to open the *Backstage* view and select **Info** to display document properties (Figure 3-66).
2. Click the **Show All Properties** link at the bottom.
   - This link toggles between *Show All Properties* and *Show Fewer Properties*.
3. Add or modify document property content.
   - Some fields, such as *Last Modified* and *Created*, cannot be modified.
   - To remove the *Author*, right-click the author and select **Remove Person**.
4. Click the **Back** arrow to return to the document. Word updates the document property fields on the cover page.

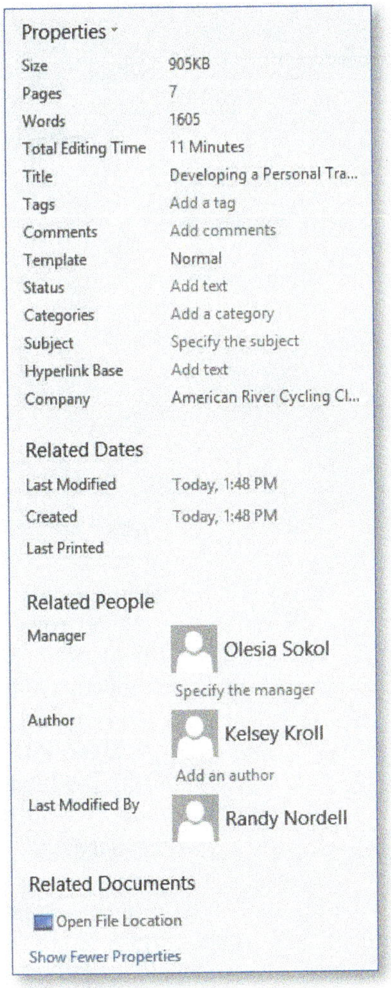

3-66 Document properties on the *Backstage* view

Add or Remove Document Property Fields

You can also add document property fields to the cover page or remove them. When you add a document property field to a cover page, the content of this field is automatically populated with the information from your document properties.

▸ HOW TO: Add Document Property Fields

1. Position the insertion point at the place where you want to insert the document property field.
2. Click the **Insert** tab.
3. Click the **Quick Parts** button [*Text* group] (Figure 3-67).
4. Choose **Document Property**.
5. Select a document property field from the drop-down list. The document property field is inserted into the document.

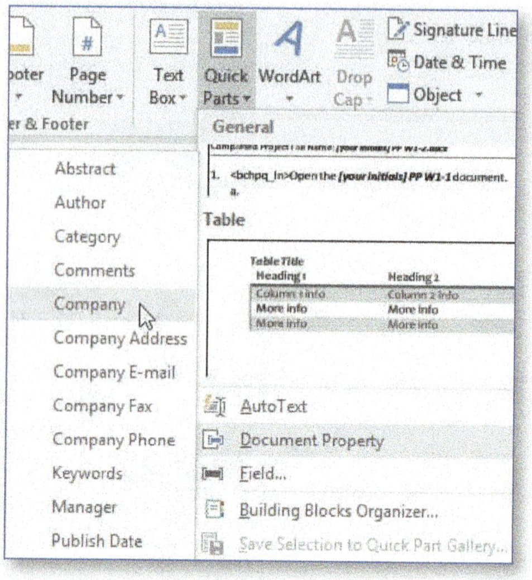

3-67 Insert document property field

MORE INFO

You can insert document property fields anywhere in a document.

To remove a document property field, click the **field handle** to select the field and press **Delete** (Figure 3-68). Make sure to check for proper spacing and paragraph breaks when you delete a document property field.

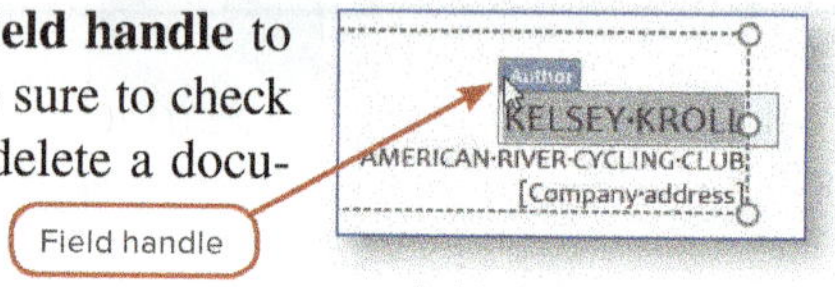

3-68 Select and delete document property field

MORE INFO

Deleting the contents of a document property or content control field does not delete the field. To remove a field, click the **field handle** to select the field and press **Delete**.

Customize Content Control Fields

When you insert a cover page into a document, many of the fields are content control fields, which are fields where you type or select custom content (Figure 3-69). You may want to add content to some of these fields and remove others. You can remove Word content control fields the same way you remove a document property field (see Figure 3-68).

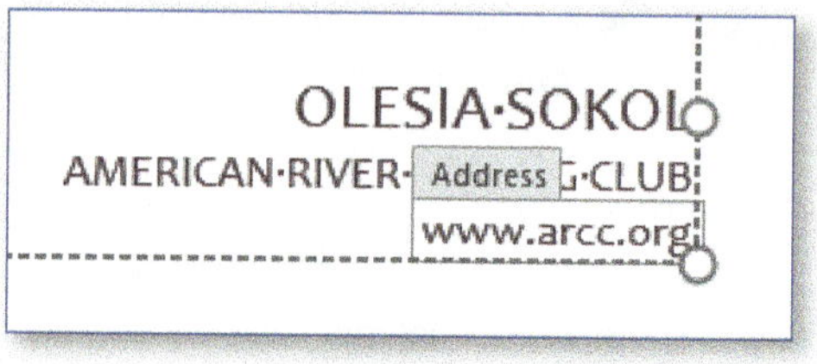

3-69 Type text into a content control field

To insert custom content into a content control field, click in the field and type the information. You can type whatever information you want into a content control field. For example, you can type a web address into the *Address* field (see Figure 3-69).

Remove a Cover Page

You might decide that you no longer want a cover page or that you want to insert a different one. Removing a cover page is similar to removing a table of contents. Click the **Cover Page** button on the *Insert* tab and select **Remove Current Cover Page** (Figure 3-70).

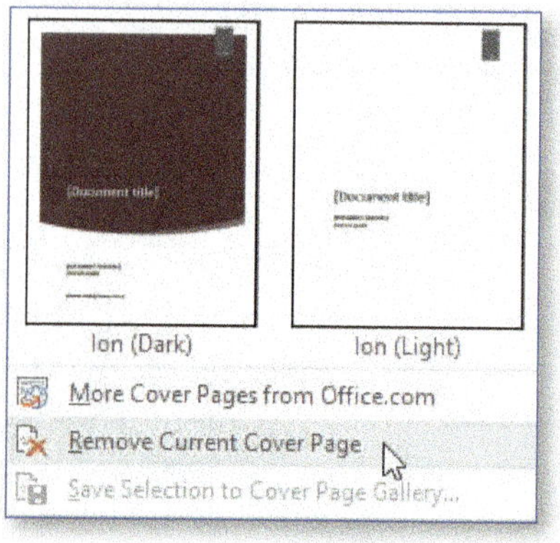

3-70 Remove cover page

When you remove a cover page, Word deletes the entire contents of the cover page and removes the page break.

SLO 3.7

Using Advanced Headers and Footers

You can use headers and footers to include page numbers and document information at the top or bottom of each page in a report or multipage document. Headers appear at the top of the page and footers appear at the bottom. You type headers and footers just once, and they automatically display on subsequent pages. You can automatically insert page numbers in the header or footer. You can also add custom content such as text, document property fields, the date, or borders.

Page and Section Breaks

For multipage documents, it is a good idea to insert page or section breaks to control page endings or special formatting in different sections. A *Page* break controls where one page ends and another begins. Use a *Next Page* section break when special document layout formatting is applied to a whole page or multiple pages of a document, such as landscape orientation to one page of the document. Use a *Continuous* section break when you apply special formatting to a section of the document, such as two-column format to specific text on one page.

MORE INFO

Don't use a section break to control page endings where a page break will suffice.

HOW TO: Insert a Page or Section Break

1. Place the insertion point in the document at the point where you want the page or section break.
   - If you are inserting a continuous section break, it is best to select the text on which to apply the section break.
   - When you insert a continuous break on selected text, Word inserts a continuous section break before and after the selected text.
2. Click the **Breaks** button [*Layout* tab, *Page Setup* group] (Figure 3-71).
3. Select the type of break from the drop-down list.

ANOTHER WAY

Ctrl+Enter inserts a page break.

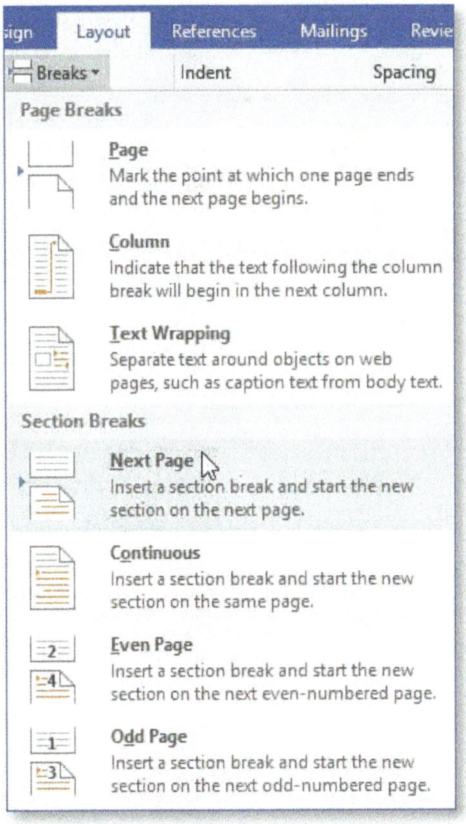

3-71 Insert page or section break

When working with page and section breaks, it is best to have the *Show/Hide* feature turned on so you can see where these breaks are located in a document. To delete a page or section break, select the break and press **Delete**.

Built-In Headers, Footers, and Page Numbers

Word provides you with a variety of built-in headers, footers, and page numbering options that you can insert into a document. You can also customize this built-in content. You can insert this content with the header or footer open or while you are in the main document.

HOW TO: Insert a Built-In Header, Footer, or Page Number

1. Click the **Insert** tab.
2. Click the **Header**, **Footer**, or **Page Number** button [*Header & Footer* group].
3. Select the built-in header, footer, or page number from the drop-down list (Figure 3-72). The content displays and the header or footer area opens.
   - If you're inserting a page number, select the position (*Top of Page*, *Bottom of Page*, *Page Margins*, or *Current Position*) to insert the page number.
   - Additional built-in headers, footers, and page numbers display when you place your pointer on *More Headers (Footer or Page Numbers) from* Office.com.

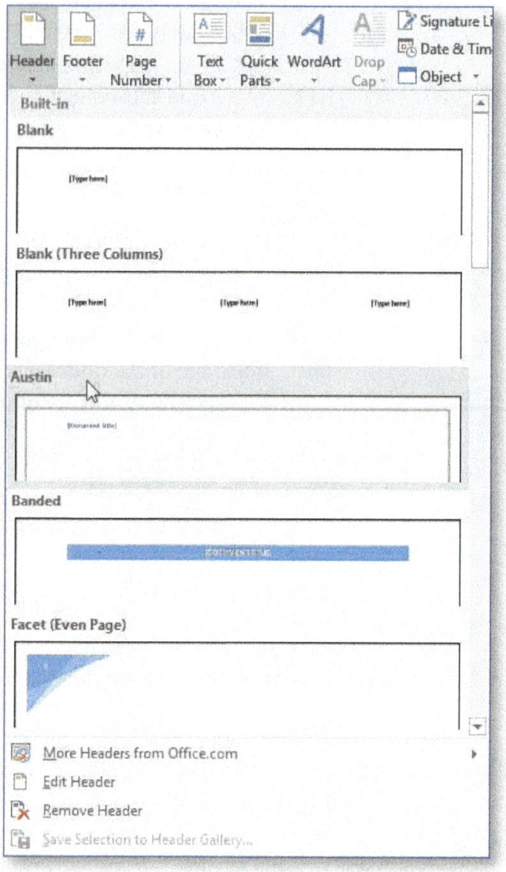

3-72 Insert built-in header

Many of the built-in headers and footers in Word contain document property fields or content control fields. You can enter information in the document property area and these fields are automatically populated. For content control fields such as *Date* or *Address*, you can select or type the content to display in these fields (see Figure 3-69).

Customize Header and Footer Content

You are not limited to built-in content in the header and footer of your document. You can type text or insert or delete content control fields. You can format header and footer text as you would other text in your document; you can apply font formatting and borders, insert graphics, and modify or set tabs for alignment.

You can edit a header or footer in the following ways:

- Double-click the header or footer area of the document.
- Right-click the header or footer area and select **Edit Header** or **Edit Footer**.
- Click the **Header** or **Footer** button [*Insert* tab, *Header & Footer* group] and select **Edit Header** or **Edit Footer**.

HOW TO: Insert Custom Content in the Header or Footer

1. Edit the header or footer. See above for different ways to edit the header or footer. The *Header & Footer Tools Design* tab opens (Figure 3-73).

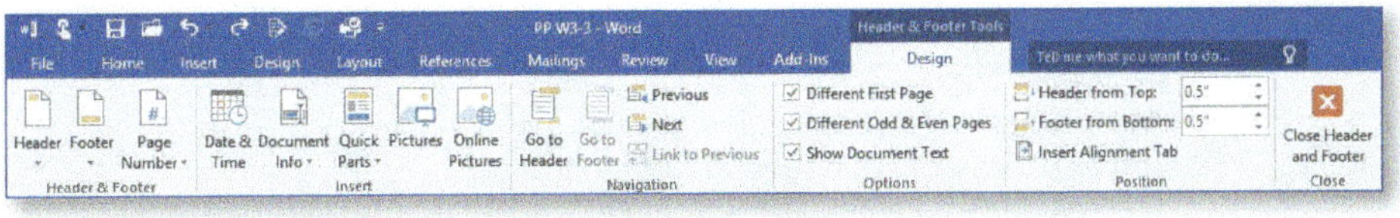

3-73 *Header & Footer Tools Design* tab

2. Insert content from the *Header & Footer Tools Design* tab.
3. Type content or select a document property field to display in the header or footer.
4. Align information in the header or footer (Figure 3-74).

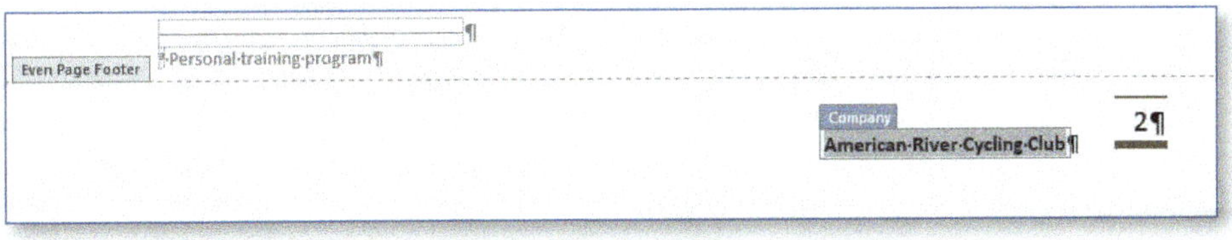

3-74 Built-in footer and document property field inserted in the footer

- By default, a center tab stop is set at the midpoint between the left and right margins and a right tab stop is set at the right margin.
- You can insert a tab by clicking the **Insert Alignment Tab** button [*Position* group].
- You can modify, add, or remove tabs on the ruler or in the *Tabs* dialog box [*Paragraph* dialog box, *Tabs* button].

5. Change the position of the header and footer in the *Position* group.
   - By default, the header and footer are positioned 0.5" from the top and bottom of the page.
   - You can change these settings in the *Page Setup* dialog box on the *Layout* tab.
6. Click **Close Header and Footer** to return to the main document.

Different First Page Header and Footer

On many reports, you don't include a page number or header and footer content on the first page, but this information is included on subsequent pages. When you select the ***Different First Page*** option, Word removes existing content from the header and footer on the first page. You can choose to leave the first page header and footer blank, or you can insert content that is different from the header and footer on second and subsequent pages.

HOW TO: Insert a Different First Page Header and Footer

1. Edit the header or footer on the first page of the document.
2. Check the **Different First Page** check box [*Header & Footer Tools Design* tab, *Options* group] (Figure 3-75).
   - When the *Different First Page* check box is checked, the header (or footer) tab displays *First Page Header* (or *First Page Footer*) to distinguish it from other headers and footers in the

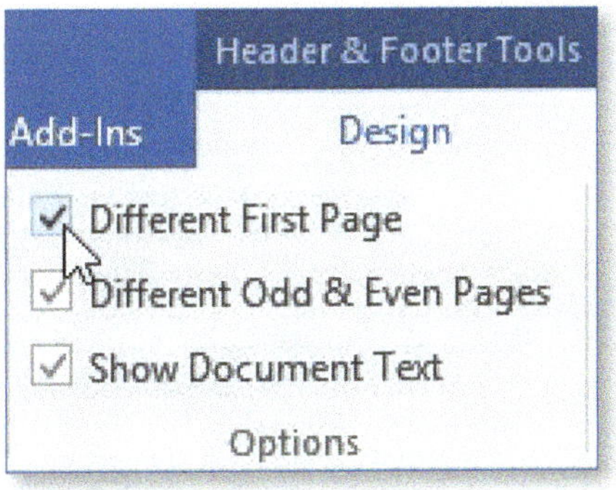

3-75 Apply *Different First Page* header and footer

document, which are labeled *Header* (or *Footer)* (Figure 3-76).
- The header (or footer) tab label changes when you apply other header and footer formatting such as odd and even pages or have different headers for different sections of your document.

3. Click **Close Header and Footer**.

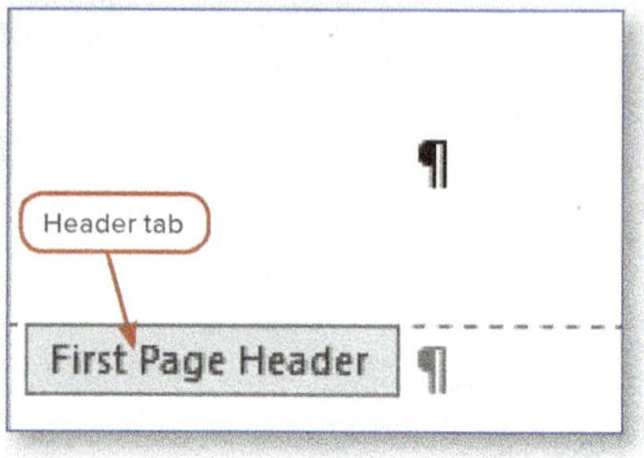

3-76 First page header

Different Odd and Even Pages

Just as you can have different header and footer content on the first page, Word provides you with the option of having ***different odd and even pages*** header and footer content on a multipage document. For example, you might want the title of the report to appear on all even pages in the footer and the page number and a company name to appear on odd pages.

MORE INFO

It is best to insert header and footer content on the first page of your document and then make any desired header and footer option changes.

HOW TO: Insert Different Odd and Even Headers and Footers

1. Edit the header or footer on the first page of the document.
2. Check the **Different Odd & Even Pages** check box [*Header & Footer Tools Design* tab, *Options* group] (see Figure 3-75).
   - When the *Different Odd & Even Pages* check box is checked, the header (or footer) tab displays *Odd* (or *Even*) *Page Header* (or *Footer*) to distinguish it from other headers and footers in the document (Figure 3-77).
3. Click **Close Header and Footer**.

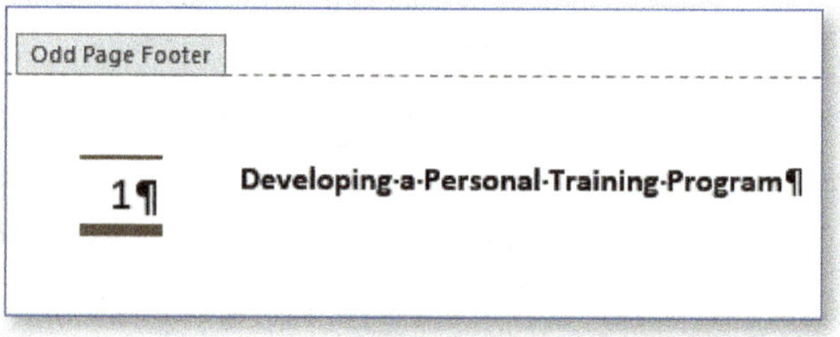

3-77 Odd page footer

Link to Previous Header or Footer

Section breaks separate your document into different sections. When you have different sections in your document, the headers and footers are by default linked to previous headers and footers. For example, a page number that appears in the footer of the first section of a document will also appear in the same position in the next section footer because it is linked to the previous footer. You can break this link to format header and footer content in one section independently of the header or footer in another section.

HOW TO: Link or Unlink a Header or Footer

1. Edit the header or footer to be unlinked from the previous section.
   - By default the *Link to Previous* button is on (shaded).
   - The *Same as Previous* label displays on the right of the header or footer.

2. Click the **Link to Previous** button [*Header & Footer Tools Design* tab, *Navigation* group] to unlink it from the previous section (Figure 3-78).

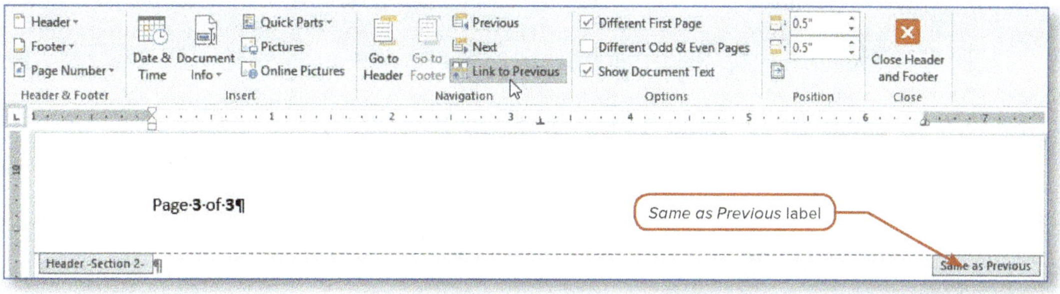

3-78 ***Link to Previous* button**

- The *Same as Previous* label is no longer displayed.
- The header or footer content still displays, but you can now change it without it changing the header or footer content in the previous section.

3. Click the **Link to Previous** button if you want to link header or footer content to a previous section after it has been unlinked.
    - Click **Yes** in the dialog box that opens asking if you want to link the header or footer to the previous section (Figure 3-79).

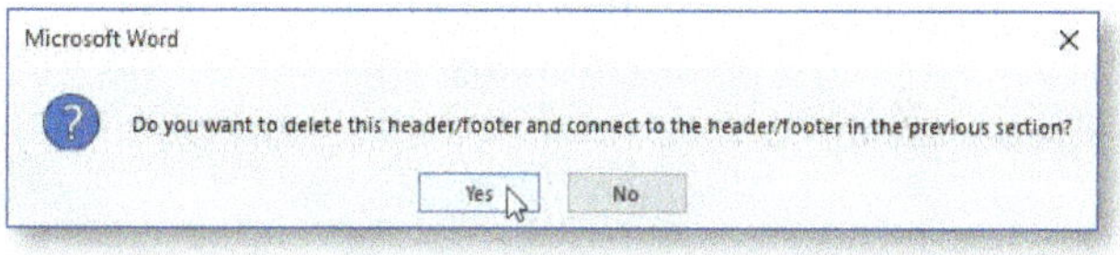

3-79 Link header or footer to previous section

4. Click the **Close Header and Footer** button.

Format Page Numbers

When you number the pages in your document, you can change the page number format and starting page number. For example, on a report you might want to number the front matter pages (title page, table of contents, executive summary) with roman numerals and number the body pages with regular numbers. If you are using different numbering for different sections of a document, you need to insert a next page section break between sections. This allows you to format the page numbering of each section differently.

HOW TO: Format Page Numbers

1. Select the page number to format in the header or footer.
2. Click the **Page Number** button [*Header & Footer Tools Design* tab, *Header & Footer* group].
3. Select **Format Page Numbers** from the drop-down list. The *Page Number Format* dialog box opens (Figure 3-80).
4. Click the **Number format** drop-down list and select the number format.
5. Select either the **Continue from previous section** or **Start at** radio button in the *Page numbering* area.
    - If you select *Continue from previous section*, the numbering continues consecutively from the previous section.
    - If you select *Start at*, you select the starting page number for the section.
6. Click **OK** to close the *Page Number Format* dialog box.

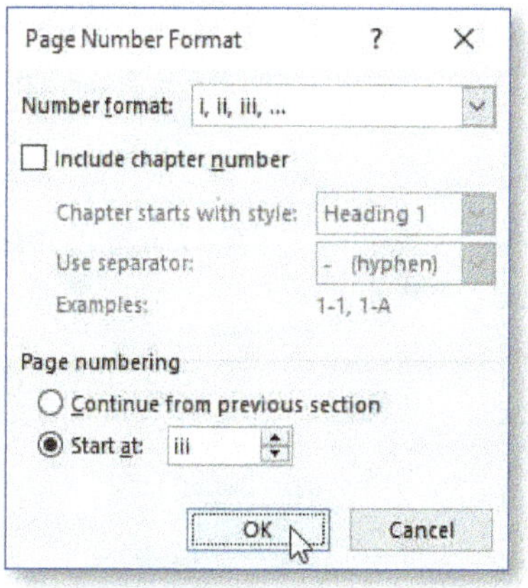

3-80 ***Page Number Format* dialog box**

When you include a Word cover page in a multipage document, the cover page is *not* considered the first page. Word considers the cover page as "page 0" when inserting page numbers in the header or footer, table of contents, or cross-reference links. For this reason, the page numbering in your document might be different from the page number displayed in the *Status* bar (bottom left of the Word window) of the document.

Navigate between Headers and Footers

When you are in a header or footer of a document, there are a variety of buttons you can use to navigate the header or footer areas: ***Go to Header***, ***Go to Footer***, ***Previous***, and ***Next***. These navigation buttons are in the *Navigation* group on the *Header & Footer Tools Design* tab (Figure 3-81).

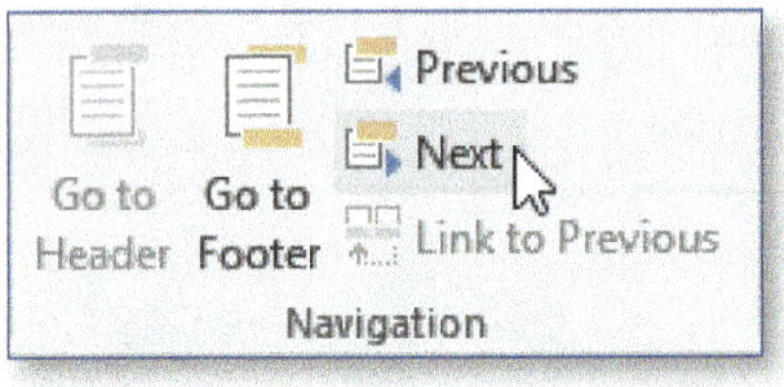

3-81 Header and footer navigation buttons

Remove a Header or Footer

To remove all header or footer content from a document, you can open the header or footer and manually delete the content. All linked header or footer content is also removed when you do this. Word can also automatically remove the header or footer from a document.

HOW TO: Remove a Header or Footer

1. Click the **Insert** button.
2. Click the **Header or Footer** button [*Header & Footer* group].
3. Select **Remove Header** or **Remove Footer** from the drop-down list (Figure 3-82). The header or footer content is removed.

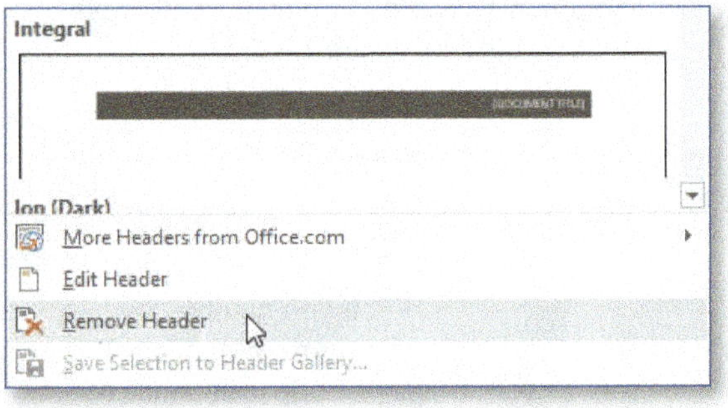

3-82 Remove header

PAUSE & PRACTICE: WORD 3-3

For this Pause & Practice project, you continue to modify the *Personal Training Program* report for the American River Cycling Club. You apply styles to headings in the report, insert and modify a table of contents, insert and modify a cover page, and insert customized footers.

File Needed: ***[your initials] PP W3-2.docx***
Completed Project File Name: ***[your initials] PP W3-3.docx***

1. Open the ***[your initials] PP W3-2*** document completed in *Pause & Practice 3-2*.
2. Save this document as [your initials] PP W3-3.
3. Apply styles to the headings in the report.
   a. Select the **"General Guidelines"** heading on the first page.
   b. Click the **Heading 1** style [*Home* tab, *Styles* group] to apply this style to the selected heading (Figure 3-83). If the *Heading 1* style is not visible, click the **More** button to display the entire *Styles* gallery.

c. Apply the **Heading 1** style to the following headings (bolded headings in the document):

Personal Training Program Guidelines
More about Long Rides
Training Intensity and Heart Rate
Using a Training Log

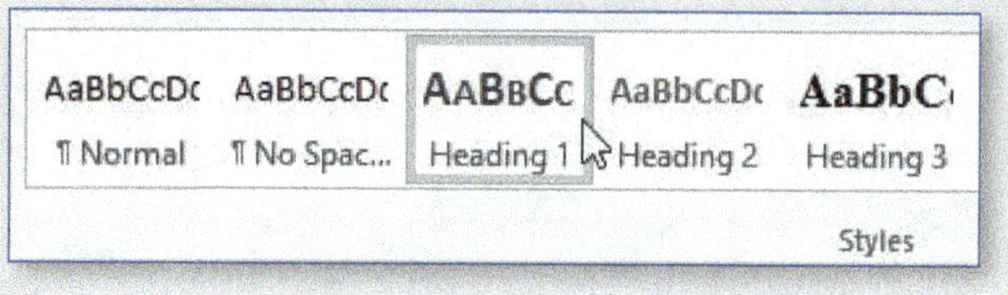

3-83 Apply *Heading 1* style

d. Apply the **Heading 2** style to the following subheadings (underlined headings in the document):

Pace of Rides
Number of Rides per Week
Duration of Rides
Distance for Long Rides
Suggestions for Long Rides
Sample Session
Other Heart Rate Factors
Suggestions for Using a Training Log

4. Add a table of contents at the beginning of the report.
   a. Turn on **Show/Hide** [*Home* tab, *Paragraph* group].
   b. Position the insertion point at the beginning of the document before the title ("Developing a Personal Training Program") and press **Ctrl+Enter** to insert a page break.
   c. Position the insertion point before the page break on the new first page.
   d. Click the **Table of Contents** button [*References* tab, *Table of Contents* group] (Figure 3-84).
   e. Select **Automatic Table 2** from the drop-down list. The table of contents displays on the first page of the report.

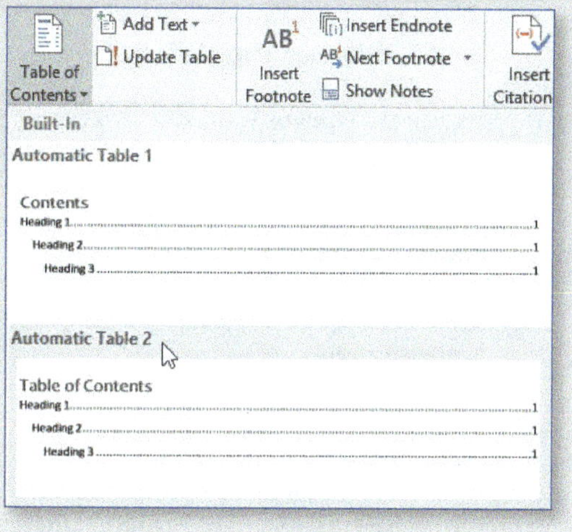

3-84 Insert table of contents

5. Customize the table of contents.
   a. Position the insertion point anywhere in the body of the table of contents.
   b. Click the **Table of Contents** button [*References* tab, *Table of Contents* group].
   c. Select **Custom Table of Contents** to open the *Table of Contents* dialog box (Figure 3-85).
   d. Click the **Formats** drop-down list and select **Formal**.
   e. Set the number of levels to **2** in the *Show levels* area.
   f. Check the **Show page numbers** and **Right align page numbers** boxes if they are not already checked.

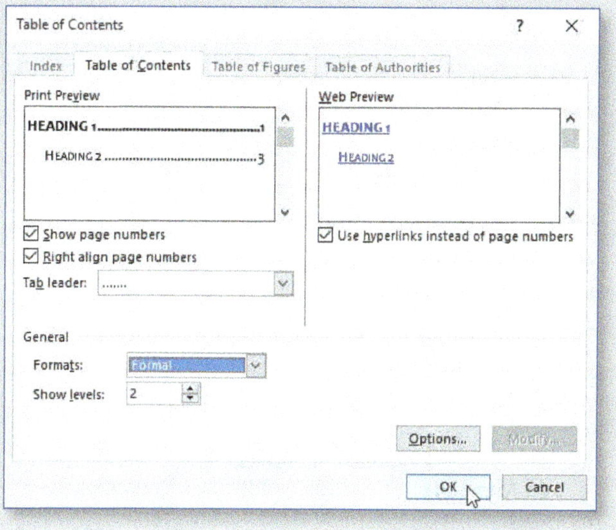

3-85 Customize table of contents

   g. Select the dot leader option from the *Tab leader* drop-down list if it is not already selected.
   h. Click **OK** to close the dialog box. A dialog box opens, confirming you want to replace the existing table of contents (Figure 3-86).
   i. Click **OK** to replace the existing table of contents.

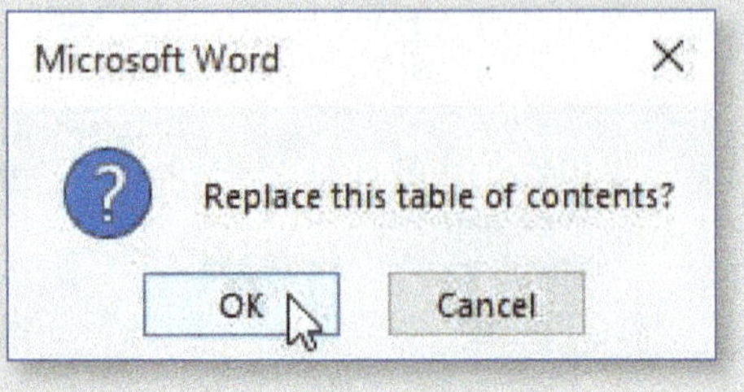

3-86 Replace existing table of contents

6. Insert page breaks and update table of contents.
   a. On the second page, position the insertion point in front of the "Number of Rides per Week" heading and press **Ctrl+Enter** to insert a page break and move this heading to the next page.
   b. Repeat this process on the following headings:
      Suggestions for Long Rides
      Using a Training Log
   c. Press **Ctrl+Home** to move to the beginning of the document.
   d. Click the **Update Table** button [*References* tab, *Table of Contents* group]. The *Update Table of Contents* dialog box opens.
   e. Select the **Update entire table** radio button and click **OK** (Figure 3-87).
   f. If there is a blank line above the table of contents, select the **paragraph mark** and press **Delete**.
   g. Select the entire table of contents (including the heading) and change the font to **Calibri**.

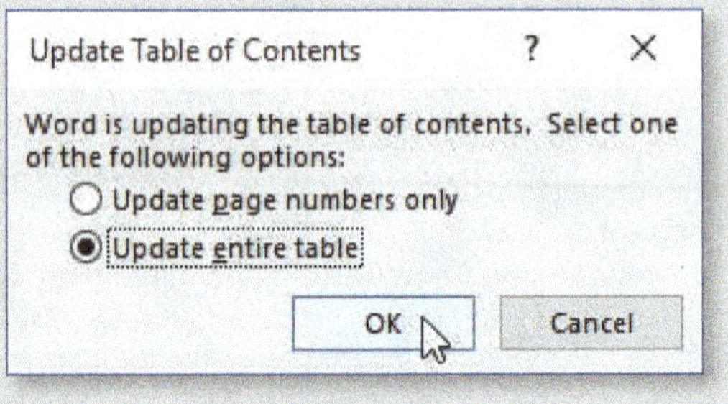

3-87 Update entire table of contents

7. Customize document properties.
   a. Click the **File** tab to open the *Backstage* view and select **Info** to display document properties.
   b. Click the **Show All Properties** link in the document properties area.
   c. Add the following document properties:
      Title: Developing a Personal Training Program
      Company: American River Cycling Club
      Manager: Olesia Sokol
   d. In the *Author* area, right-click the author's name and select **Remove Person**.
   e. Click the **Back** arrow to return to the report.
8. Add a cover page and customize fields.
   a. Click the **Cover Page** button [*Insert* tab, *Pages* group] and select **Semaphore**. The cover page displays on the page before the table of contents.
   b. Click the **Date** field drop-down arrow to display the calendar and select the current date.
   c. Click the **Author** document property field, select the field handle (Figure 3-88), and press **Delete** to delete the field. The insertion point is on the blank line where the *Author* field was removed.
   d. Click the **Quick Parts** button [*Insert* tab, *Text* group].
   e. Choose **Document Property** and select **Manager** from the drop-down list. The cover page includes the *Manager* document property field.

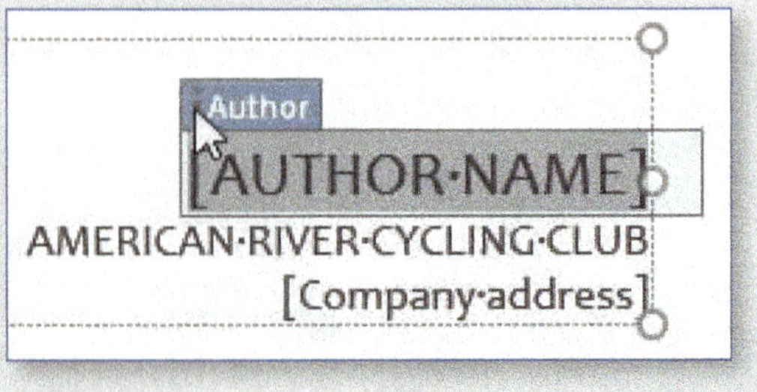

3-88 Select and delete document property field

f. Click the **Company Address** field and type www.arcc.org in the field.
g. Right-click the **Subtitle** field ("[Document Subtitle]") and select **Remove Content Control** from the context menu.
h. Click the **Title** field and apply **bold** format. Bold formatting applies to the entire *Title* field.
i. Save the document.

9. Insert odd page and even page footers.
   a. Press **Ctrl+Home** to move to the top of the document.
   b. Click the **Footer** button [*Insert* tab, *Header & Footer* group] and select **Edit Footer** to open the footer area.
   c. Check the **Different First Page** (if it is not already checked) and the **Different Odd & Even Pages** boxes [*Header & Footer Tools Design* tab, *Options* group].
   d. Click the **Next** button [*Navigation* group] to move to the odd page footer on the second page (Figure 3-89).

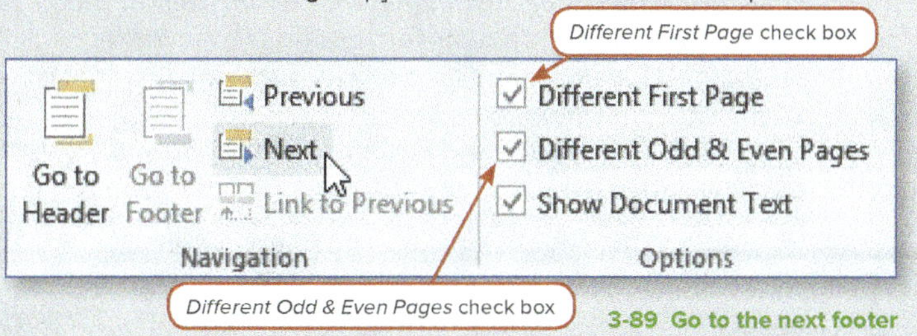

3-89 Go to the next footer

   e. Click the **Page Number** button [*Header & Footer* group].
   f. Select **Bottom of Page** and select **Two Bars 1** from the drop-down list (Figure 3-90). The page number "1" displays on the second page.

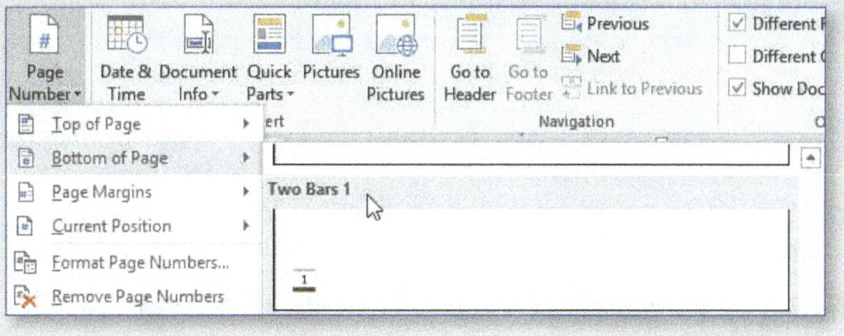

3-90 Select built-in page number

> **MORE INFO**
>
> Word considers the cover page as page 0. The table of contents page is page 1.

   g. Click the **Next** button [*Navigation* group] to move to the even page footer on the next page.
   h. Click the **Page Number** button [*Header & Footer* group], select **Bottom of Page**, and select **Two Bars 2** from the drop-down list. The page number "2" displays on the right.
   i. Leave the footer open to add custom content in the next step.

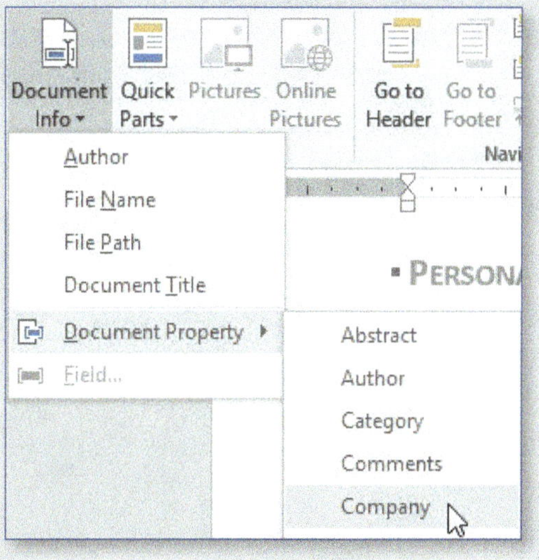

3-91 Insert document property field

10. Add custom content to the odd and even footers.
   a. Place the insertion point in the even page footer.
   b. Press **Ctrl+R** or click the **Align Right** button to position the insertion point on the right.
   c. Click the **Document Info** button [*Header & Footer Tools Design* tab, *Insert* group] (Figure 3-91).

d. Select **Document Property** and choose **Company** from the drop-down list. The *Company* document property field displays on the right side of the footer area.
e. Select the **Company** document property field, change the font size to **10 pt.**, and apply **bold** formatting.
f. Click the **Previous** button [*Header & Footer Tools Design* tab, *Navigation* group] to move to the odd page footer on the previous page. The insertion point should be on the left after the page number "1."
g. Click the **Document Info** button [*Header & Footer Tools Design* tab, *Insert* group] and select **Document Title** from the drop-down list. The *Title* document property field displays in the footer.
h. Select the **Title** document property field, change the font size to **10 pt.**, and apply **bold** formatting.
i. Click the **Close Header and Footer** button [*Header & Footer Tools Design* tab, *Close* group].

11. Review the document to ensure correct page numbering.
    a. There should be no header or footer on the cover page of the document.
    b. The table of contents page should be numbered "1" in the footer on the left with the title of the report following the page number.
    c. The first body page of the report should be numbered "2" in the footer on the right with the company name preceding the page number.
    d. Each subsequent page should be numbered consecutively with odd and even footers.
12. Create a sharing link to share this file with your instructor.
    a. Save this document on *OneDrive* if you haven't already. If you don't have the ability to save to *OneDrive*, skip all of step 12.
    b. Click the **Share** button in the upper right of the Word window. The *Share* pane opens on the right (Figure 3-92).
    c. Click **Get a sharing link** at the bottom of the *Share* pane.
    d. Click the **Create an edit link** button (Figure 3-93).
    e. Click **Copy** to copy the edit link.
    f. Use your email account to create a new email to your instructor.
    g. Include an appropriate subject line and a brief message in the body.
    h. Press **Ctrl+V** to paste the link to your document in the body of the email and send the email message.
13. Return to the Word document and click the **X** in the upper right corner of the *Share* pane to close it.

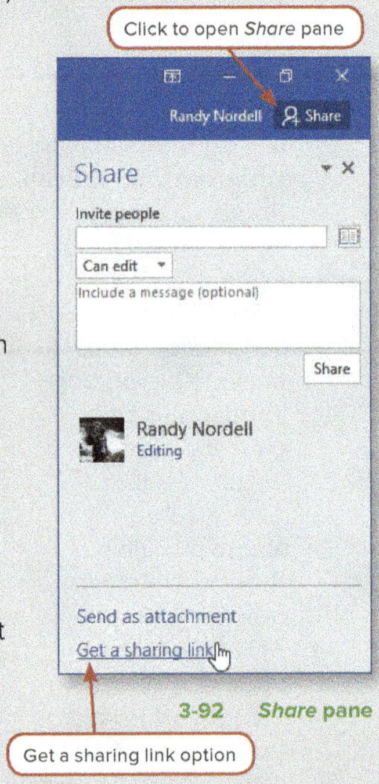

3-92 *Share* pane

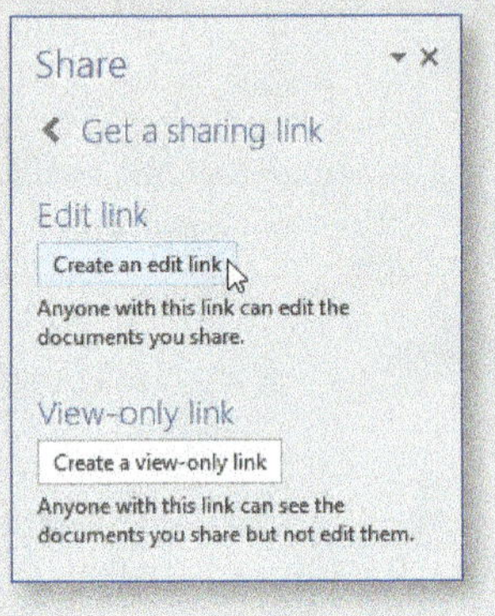

3-93 Create an edit link

14. Save and close the document (Figure 3-94).

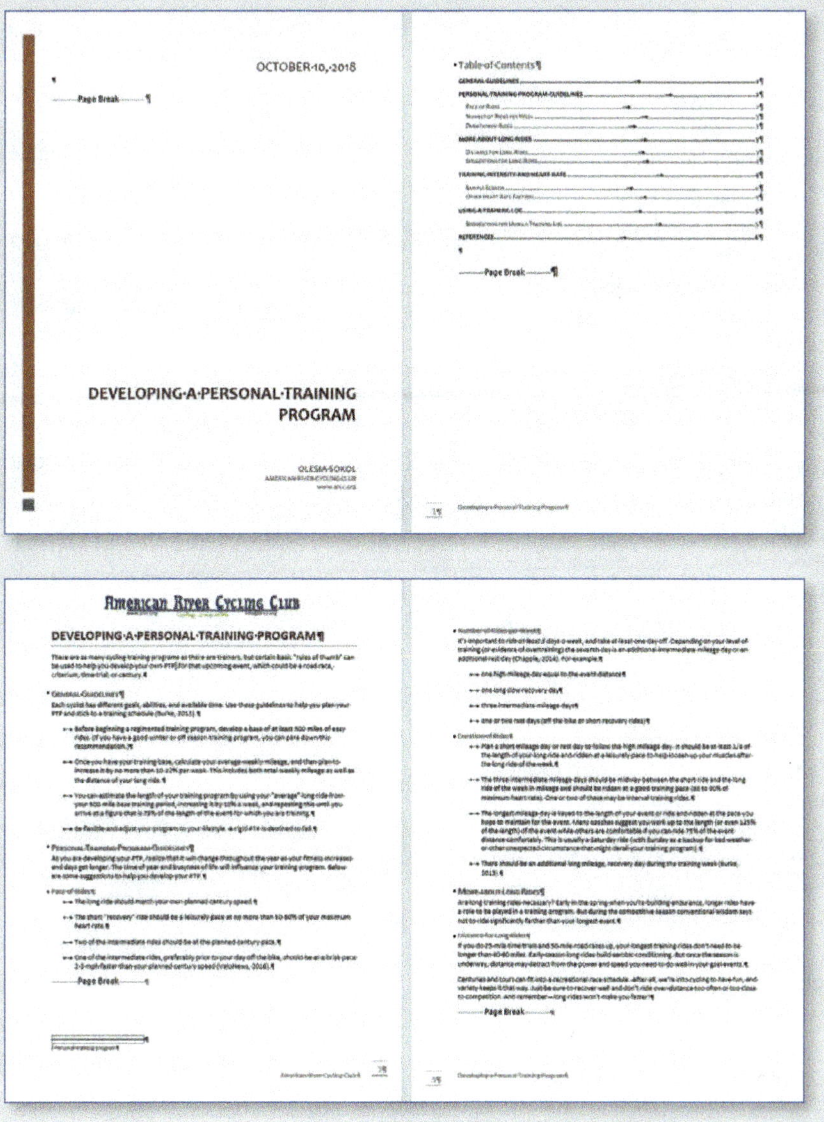

3-94 PP W3-3 completed (pages 1-4 of 7)

Chapter Summary

3.1 Insert, review, edit, and customize comments (p. W3-134).

- You can use ***comments*** to insert a note or provide feedback in a document without changing the content or format of the document.
- Users can add, edit, or delete comments. Comments appear to the right of the document in the ***Markup area***.
- Comments are numbered sequentially in a document and are associated with a Microsoft Office ***user name*** and ***initials***, which you can customize in the *Word Options* dialog box.
- Multiple reviewers can add comments to a document.
- Use the ***Next*** and ***Previous*** buttons to review the comments in the document.
- When you place your pointer on a comment, a tag provides details about the user name and date and time of the comment.
- You can delete comments individually or delete all comments in the document.

3.2 Modify and review a document using *Track Changes* and share an online document (p. W3-137).

- ***Track Changes*** is a collaboration tool that allows reviewers to make and track changes made in a document.
- There are four different ***Display for Review views*** to display changes in a document: ***All Markup***, ***Simple Markup***, ***No Markup***, and ***Original***.
- When *Track Changes* is on, each change is attributed to a reviewer and his or her user name.
- You can review changes using the ***Previous*** and ***Next*** buttons.
- You can accept or reject individual changes in the document, or you can accept or reject all of the changes in the document.
- The ***Reviewing pane***, which can be displayed vertically on the left side of the document or horizontally at the bottom of the document, displays all of the changes in the document.
- You can customize which markups display in the document.
- Use the *Track Changes Options* dialog box to customize how tracked changes appear in your document.
- You can share online files with others, and more than one user can edit an online file at the same time, which allows ***real-time collaboration*** on documents.
- The ***Share pane*** provides different options for sharing an online document.

3.3 Insert and edit footnotes and endnotes in a document (p. W3-144).

- Use ***footnotes*** and ***endnotes*** to include additional information or reference sources.
- Footnotes appear at the bottom of the page and endnotes appear at the end of the document.
- A ***reference marker*** is a number, letter, or symbol that indicates a footnote or endnote in the body of the document.
- Change the location, number format, and starting number for footnotes and endnotes in the *Footnote and Endnote* dialog box.
- Word styles control the format of footnotes and endnotes. Change these styles to modify how your footnote and endnote text appears in the document.
- Convert footnotes to endnotes or endnotes to footnotes using the ***Convert Notes*** dialog box.
- Move footnotes and endnotes using the drag and drop method or using cut and paste.
- When you delete a footnote or endnote reference marker in the body of the document, the associated footnote and endnote text is also deleted. Footnotes and endnotes automatically renumber if one is deleted or inserted.

3.4 Create a bibliography with properly formatted sources and insert citations in a document (p. W3-149).

- A ***source*** is the complete bibliographic information for a reference (e.g., book, web page, journal article) used in a report.
- A ***citation*** is the abbreviated source information used in the body of a report.
- The ***bibliography style*** controls the format of the sources on the bibliography page and citations in the body of the document.
- Add a ***placeholder*** to temporarily mark a citation in the body of a report.
- Use the ***Source Manager*** dialog box to create and edit sources, edit placeholders, and view available sources.

- Insert a ***bibliography*** or ***works cited*** page to list the sources in your document.

3.5 Create and edit a table of contents based on headings in a document (p. W3-161).

- Word can automatically generate a ***table of contents*** for a document.
- ***Heading styles*** (e.g., Heading 1, Heading 2) determine the content for a table of contents.
- You can use built-in table of contents formats or customize the format of the table of contents.
- Use the *Table of Contents* dialog box to customize the format and the number of levels displayed in the table of contents.
- When document headings or pagination change, you can automatically update the table of contents to reflect these changes.

3.6 Insert a cover page and modify content and content control fields (p. W3-164).

- There are a variety of built-in ***cover pages*** available to add to your documents.
- A cover page has graphics, colors, text boxes, and Word fields that you can customize. The document theme controls the colors and fonts on the cover page.
- Use ***document property*** and ***content control fields*** to display information on the cover page. You can customize or delete this content.

3.7 Apply and customize headers and footers in a multipage document (p. W3-167).

- ***Headers*** and ***footers*** provide information and page numbers in a document. Headers are located at the top and footers are located at the bottom of a document.
- ***Page*** and ***section breaks*** control pagination and page numbering in a document.
- You can insert a variety of built-in headers, footers, and page numbers into a document.
- You can customize content and page numbering in headers and footers.
- ***Different first page*** headers and footers allow you to include different information on the first page of a document.
- *Use **odd and even page*** headers and footers to display different information on odd and even pages in a document.
- Change the page number format and starting page number in the *Page Number Format* dialog box.

Check for Understanding

The SIMbook for this text (within your SIMnet account) provides the following resources for concept review:

- Multiple choice questions
- Matching exercises
- Short answer questions

USING MICROSOFT WORD 2016

Guided Project 3-1

For this project, you customize the *Online Learning Plan* for Sierra Pacific Community College District. You review comments and tracked changes, add document properties, apply styles, create a table of contents, insert and modify footnotes, insert headers and footers, and add a customized cover page. [Student Learning Outcomes 3.1, 3.2, 3.3, 3.5, 3.6, 3.7]

File Needed: ***OnlineLearningPlan-03.docx*** *(Student data files are available in the* Library *of your SIMnet account)*
Completed Project File Name: ***[your initials] Word 3-1.docx***

Skills Covered in this Project

- Modify user name and initials.
- Reject and accept tracked changes.
- Reply to a comment and mark a comment as done.
- Customize document properties.
- Apply styles to selected text.
- Insert page breaks.
- Insert a table of contents.
- Insert footnotes.
- Modify footnote number format.
- Insert built-in page numbers and document property fields in the footer.
- Insert a cover page and remove and add document property fields.
- Update a table of contents.

1. Open the ***OnlineLearningPlan-03*** document from your student data files.
2. Save this document as [your initials] Word 3-1.
3. Change user name and initials.
   a. Click the **Tracking** launcher [*Review* tab, *Tracking* group] to open the *Track Changes Options* dialog box.
   b. Click the **Change User Name** button to open the *Word Options* dialog box.
   c. In the *Personalize your copy of Microsoft Office* area, type your first and last name in the *User name* text box.
   d. Type your first and last initials in lowercase letters in the *Initials* text box.
   e. Check the **Always use these values regardless of sign in to Office** box.
   f. Click **OK** to close the *Word Options* dialog box and click **OK** to close the *Track Changes Options* dialog box.
4. Display the *Reviewing* pane and reject changes.
   a. Click the **Display for Review** drop-down list [*Review* tab, *Tracking* group] and select **All Markup** to view the document with comments and proposed changes visible.
   b. Click the **Reviewing Pane** drop-down arrow [*Review* tab, *Tracking* group] and select **Reviewing Pane Vertical**. The *Reviewing* pane displays on the left side of the Word window.
   c. In the *Reviewing* pane, find where "Hasmik Kumar Deleted **Television or Tele-Web Course—**."
   d. Right-click this deletion and select **Reject Deletion** from the context menu (Figure 3-95).
   e. Click the **X** in the upper right corner of the *Reviewing* pane to close it.

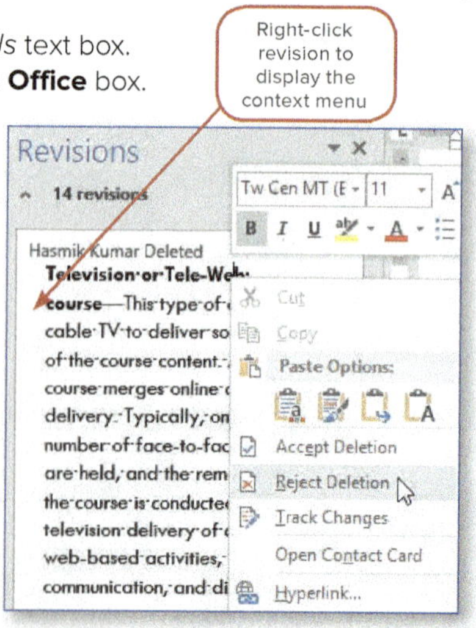

3-95 Reject a deletion in the *Reviewing* pane

5. Accept changes in the document.
    a. Move to the top of the document (**Ctrl+Home**).
    b. Click the **Next** button [*Review* tab, *Changes* group] to select the first change.
    c. Click the top half of the **Accept** button [*Review* tab, *Changes* group] to accept the change and move to the next change.
    d. Click the top half of the **Accept** button again to accept the next change.
    e. Click the bottom half of the **Accept** button and select **Accept All Changes** from the drop-down list (Figure 3-96). All of the remaining changes in the document are accepted. Only comments are remaining in the *Markup* area.

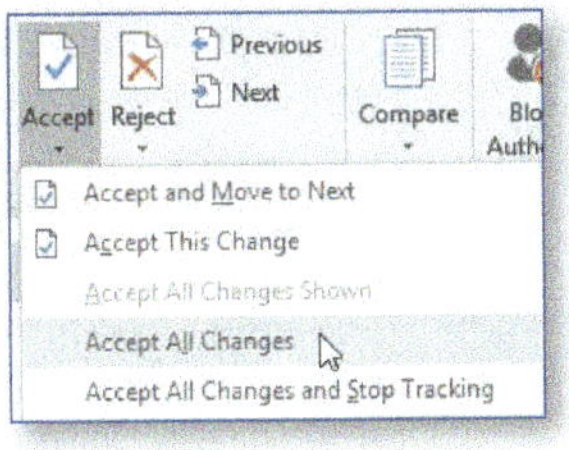

3-96 Accept all changes in the document

6. Reply to a comment, mark a comment as done, and delete a comment.
    a. Move to the top of the document and click the **Next** button [*Review* tab, *Comments* group] to move to the first comment.
    b. Click the **Reply** button in the upper right corner of the comment in the *Markup* area.
    c. Type Done!
    d. Right-click the top part of the comment in the *Markup* area and select **Mark Comment Done** (Figure 3-97). The comment and reply becomes grayed out.
    e. Click the **Next** button [*Review* tab, *Comments* group] to move to the second comment (not the reply to the first comment).
    f. Click the top half of the **Delete** button [*Review* tab, *Comments* group] to delete the comment.
    g. Click the **Display for Review** drop-down list [*Review* tab, *Tracking* group] and select **No Markup** so comments are not visible.

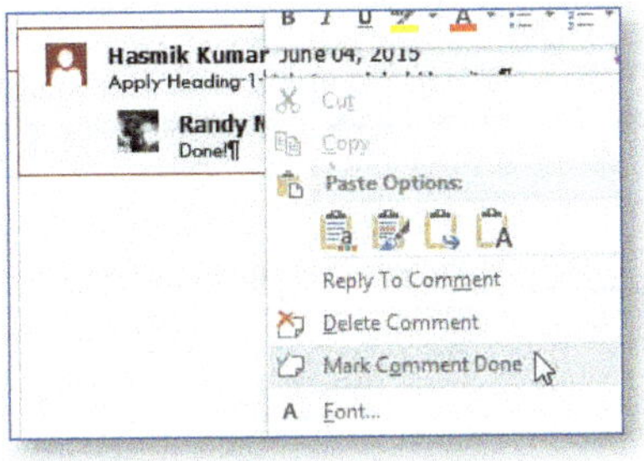

3-97 *Mark Comment Done* option from the context menu

7. Add document properties.
    a. Click the **File** tab to open the *Backstage* view.
    b. Click **Show All Properties** in the *Properties* area.
    c. Add the following document properties:

        Title: Online Learning Plan
        Company: Sierra Pacific Community College District
        Manager: Hasmik Kumar

    d. Click the **Back** arrow to return to the document.

8. Apply styles to the document.
    a. Go to the first page of the document, select the title (**"Online Learning Plan"**), and apply the **Title** style.
    b. Select the subtitle (**"Sierra Pacific Community College District"**) and apply the **Subtitle** style.
    c. Apply the **Heading 1** style to all of the main headings (those in all caps and bold) in the document.
    d. Apply the **Heading 2** style to all subheadings (those underlined) in the document.

9. Insert a table of contents into the report.
    a. Click in front of the first main heading in the document ("Purpose of this Plan") and press **Ctrl+Enter** to insert a page break.
    b. On the new first page of the document, place the insertion point directly after the subtitle and press **Enter**.
    c. Click the **Table of Contents** button [*References* tab, *Table of Contents* group] (Figure 3-98).

d. Select **Automatic Table 2**. The table of contents displays below the subtitle.
e. Select the words **"Table of Contents"** in the table of contents and apply **Black, Text 1** font color.
f. If there is a blank line between the subtitle and "Table of Contents," delete it.

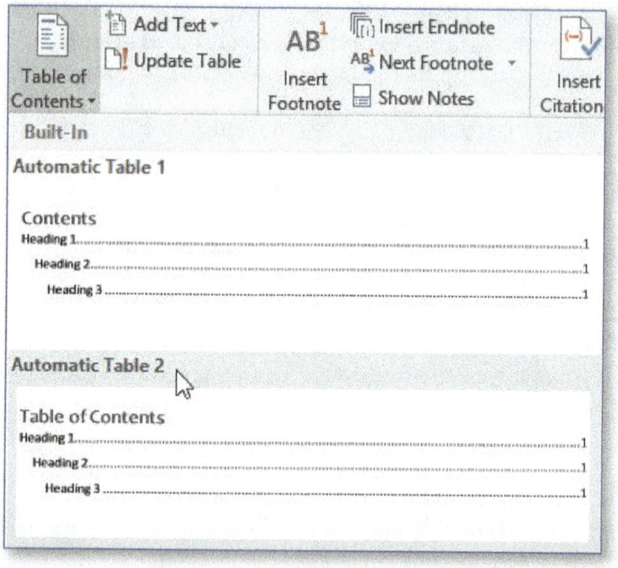

3-98 Insert table of contents

10. Insert footnotes into the document.
    a. Go to the second page of the document and position the insertion point after "Web-Enhanced course" and before the dash.
    b. Click the **Insert Footnote** button [*References* tab, *Footnotes* group]. A footnote reference marker is inserted after the text and the insertion point is positioned at the bottom of the page in the *Footnotes* area.
    c. Type This is a non-OL course that uses OL tools. in the footnote area.
    d. On the second page of the document, position the insertion point after "(OL)" and before the space (first body paragraph, second sentence).
    e. Click the **Insert Footnote** button and type Online learning is referred to as OL throughout this report. in the footnote area. This footnote becomes footnote 1 and the other footnote automatically becomes number 2.
11. Modify footnote number format.
    a. Click the **Footnotes** launcher to open the *Footnote and Endnote* dialog box (Figure 3-99).
    b. Select **i, ii, iii**, . . . from the *Number format* drop-down list.
    c. Click **Apply** to close the dialog box and apply the number format change.
12. Insert and modify content in the footer.
    a. Press **Ctrl+Home** to move to the top of the document.
    b. Click the **Footer** button [*Insert* tab, *Header & Footer* group] and select **Edit Footer**.
    c. Click the **Document Info** button [*Header & Footer Tools Design* tab, *Insert* group] and select **Document Title** from the drop-down list to insert the *Title* document property field.
    d. Press the **right arrow** once to deselect the document property field and press **Tab** to move to the center preset tab stop.
    e. Click the **Document Info** button, select **Document Property**, and select **Company** from the drop-down list.
    f. Press the **right arrow** once to deselect the document property field and press **Tab** to move to the right preset tab stop.

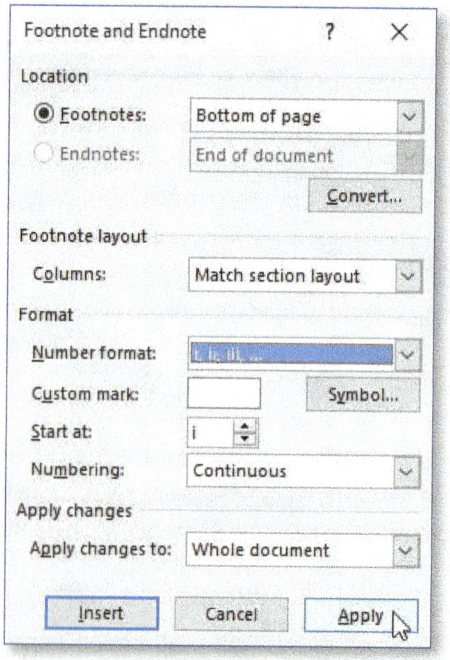

3-99 Modify footnote number format

g. Click the **Page Number** button [*Insert* tab, *Header & Footer* group], select **Current Position**, and select **Bold Numbers** from the drop-down list.
h. Select all of the text in the footer and change the font size to **10 pt**. (Figure 3-100).

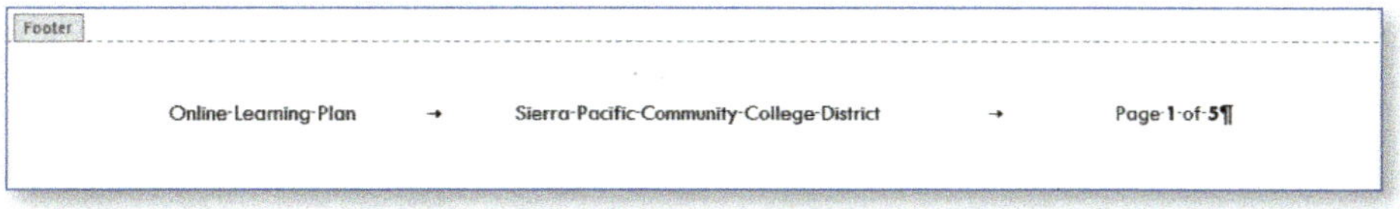

3-100 Document properties and built-in page number inserted into the footer

i. Click the **Close Header and Footer** button [*Header & Footer Tools Design* tab, *Close* group].

13. Insert a page break.
    a. Position the insertion point before the last subheading ("How are Courses and Programs Selected for Online Learning Delivery?") on page 2 of the report.
    b. Press **Ctrl+Enter** to insert a page break.

14. Insert a cover page and modify content control fields.
    a. Press **Ctrl+Home** to move to the top of the document.
    b. Click the **Cover Page** button [*Insert* tab, *Pages* group].
    c. Select the **Retrospect** built-in cover page from the drop-down list. The cover page is inserted before the first page of the document.
    d. Click the **Subtitle** ("Document Subtitle") content control field handle and press **Delete** (Figure 3-101).
    e. Click the **Author** content control field handle and press **Delete**.
    f. With the insertion point on the blank line where the *Author* field was deleted, click the **Quick Parts** button [*Insert* tab, *Text* group].
    g. Select **Document Property** and select **Manager** from the drop-down list.
    h. Apply **bold** formatting to the *Company* document property field.
    i. Type www.spccd.edu in the *Address* ("Company Address") field. The web address displays in all caps; you will fix this in the next step.
    j. Select the **Address** document property field, open the *Font* dialog box, deselect the **All caps** check box, and click **OK**. The web address changes to lowercase (Figure 3-102).

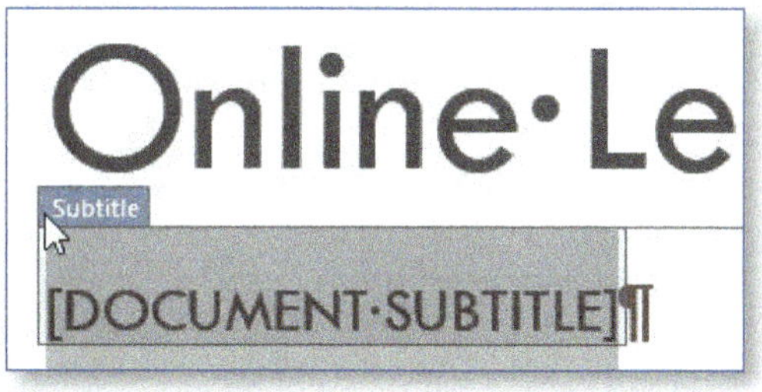

3-101 Select and delete content control field

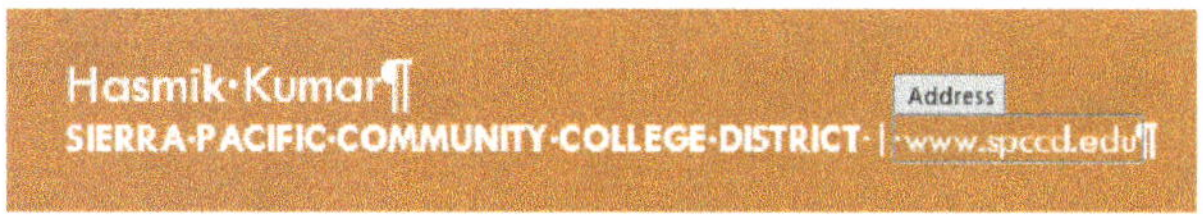

3-102 Document property fields modified on the cover page

15. Update the table of contents.
    a. Click in the table of contents.
    b. Click the **Update Table** button [*References* tab, *Table of Contents* group]. The *Update Table of Contents* dialog box opens (Figure 3-103).
    c. Select the **Update entire table** radio button.
    d. Click **OK** to close the dialog box and update the table.
16. Save and close the document (Figure 3-104).

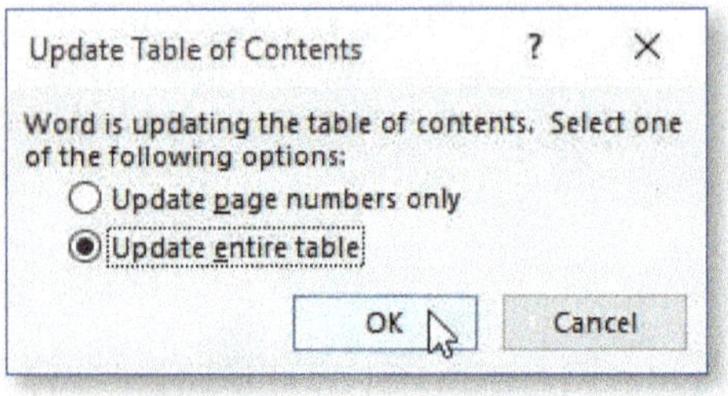

3-103 *Update Table of Contents* dialog box

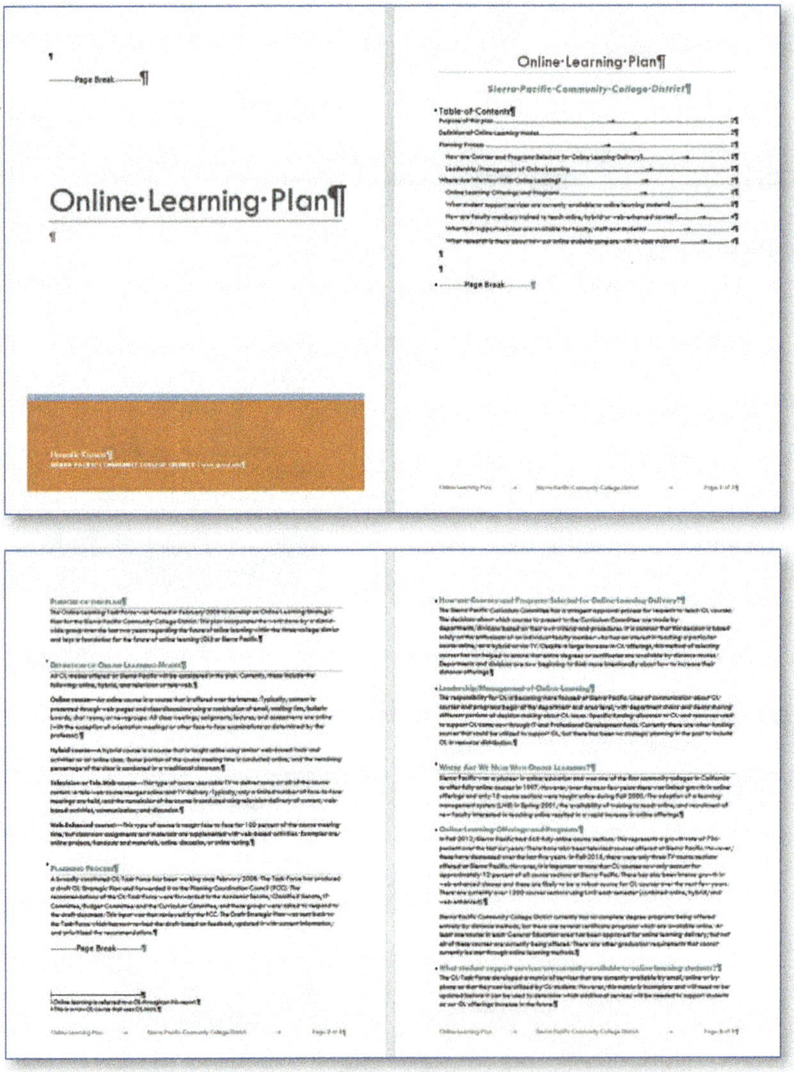

3-104 Word 3-1 completed (pages 1-4 of 6)

Guided Project 3-2

For this project, you create a multipage insurance renewal letter that Central Sierra Insurance will send on behalf of Valley Custom Manufacturing. You review comments and tracked changes, use *Track Changes*, format this document as a business letter, insert a document property field, insert and customize header content, use footnotes and endnotes, and insert a page and section break.
[Student Learning Outcomes 3.1, 3.2, 3.3, 3.7]

File Needed: ***ValleyCustomManufacturing-03.docx*** *(Student data files are available in the* Library *of your SIMnet account)*
Completed Project File Name: ***[your initials] Word 3-2.docx***

Skills Covered in this Project

- Review tracked changes and comments.
- Use *Track Changes*.
- Change *Display for Review* view.
- Format the document as a block format business letter.
- Insert a next page section break.
- Change margins and header location on a section of a document.
- Use a different first page header.
- Insert a document property, date, and page number in the header.
- Format the page number in the header.
- Apply a bottom border.
- Insert footnotes.
- Convert footnotes to endnotes and change number format.
- Insert a page break to control pagination.
- Accept tracked changes.
- Share a document.

1. Open the ***ValleyCustomManufacturing-03*** document from your student data files.
2. Save this document as [your initials] Word 3-2.
3. Review a comment, accept tracked changes, and delete a comment.
   a. Click the **Display for Review** drop-down list [*Review* tab, *Tracking* group] and select **All Markup**.
   b. Read the comment in the *Markup* area at the top of the document and review the tracked changes in the document.
   c. Click the **Next** button [*Review* tab, *Changes* group] to move to the first tracked change (not comment).
   d. Click the bottom half of the **Accept** button [*Review* tab, *Changes* group] and select **Accept and Move to Next**.
   e. Click the bottom half of the **Accept** button and select **Accept All Changes**.
   f. Click the bottom half of the **Delete** button [*Review* tab, *Comments* group] and select **Delete All Comments in Document**.
4. Change user name and initials.
   a. Click the **Tracking** launcher [*Review* tab, *Tracking* group] to open the *Track Changes Options* dialog box.
   b. Click the **Change User Name** button to open the *Word Options* dialog box.
   c. In the *Personalize your copy of Microsoft Office* area, type your first and last name in the *User name* text box.
   d. Type your first and last initials in lowercase letters in the *Initials* text box.
   e. Check the **Always use these values regardless of sign in to Office** box.
   f. Click **OK** to close the *Word Options* dialog box and click **OK** to close the *Track Changes Options* dialog box.

5. Turn on *Track Changes* and format the first page of the document as a block format business letter.
   a. Click the **Track Changes** button [*Review* tab, *Tracking* group] to turn on *Track Changes* and turn on **Show/Hide**. All of the changes you make will be tracked.
   b. Place your insertion point in front of "LIABILITY" on the first page.
   c. Click the **Breaks** button [*Layout* tab, *Page Setup* group] and select **Next Page** section break from the drop-down list.
   d. Move to the last blank line on the first page (in front of the section break), type Sincerely, and press **Enter** four times.
   e. Type Jennie Owings, Vice President and press **Enter** once.
   f. Type Central Sierra Insurance and press **Enter** two times.
   g. Type your initials in lowercase letters with no spaces or punctuation and press **Enter**. Word automatically capitalizes the first letter of your initials. Use the **smart tag** to undo automatic capitalization (Figure 3-105).
   h. Type Enclosure on the line after your reference initials.
   i. Press **Ctrl+Home** to go to the top of the document and press **Enter** four times.
   j. Place the insertion point on the first blank line at the top and click the **Date & Time** button [*Insert* tab, *Text* group]. The *Date and Time* dialog box opens.
   k. Select the date in proper business letter format (e.g., January 1, 2018), check the **Update automatically** box, and click **OK** to close the dialog box and insert the date.
   l. Select the dateline and apply **24 pt**. *Before* paragraph spacing.

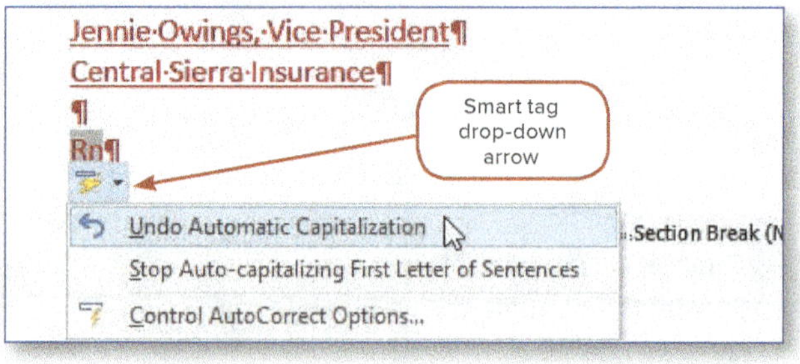

3-105 Use the smart tag to undo automatic capitalization

6. Modify the margins and header position in the second section of the document.
   a. Place your insertion point in the second section of the document (page 2 or 3).
   b. Click the **Margins** button [*Layout* tab, *Page Setup* group] and select **Custom Margins** from the drop-down list. The *Page Setup* dialog box opens.
   c. Change the *Top* margin to **1.5"** and the *Left* and *Right* margins to **1.25"**.
   d. Click the **Layout** tab (Figure 3-106).
   e. In the *Headers and footers* area, change the *From edge Header* setting to **1"**.
   f. Click the **Apply to** drop-down list and select **This section**.
   g. Click **OK** to close the dialog box and apply the settings.
7. Insert header content on the second and continuing pages.
   a. Press **Ctrl+Home** to move to the top of the document.

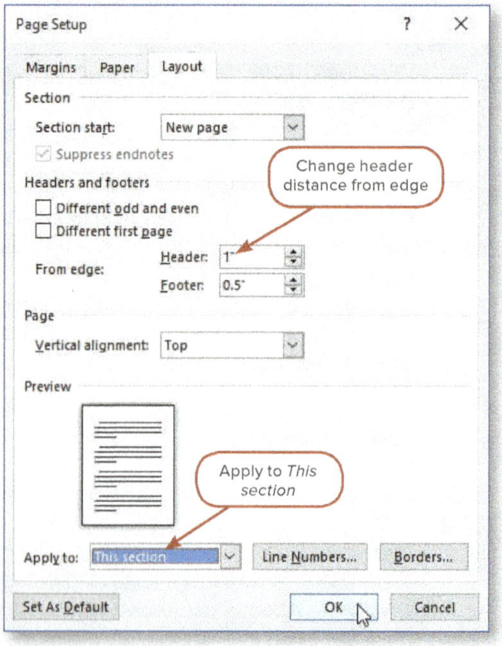

3-106 Change header position in this section of the document

b. Click the **Header** button [*Insert* tab, *Header & Footer* group] and select **Edit Header** from the drop-down list.
c. Check the **Different First Page** box [*Header & Footer Tools Design* tab, *Options* group].
d. Click the **Next** button [*Header & Footer Tools Design* tab, *Navigation* group] to move to the header in section 2.
e. Click the **Document Info** button [*Header & Footer Tools Design* tab, *Insert* group] and select **Document Title**.
f. Press the **right arrow** on the keyboard to deselect the document property field and press **Enter**.
g. Click the **Date & Time** button [*Header & Footer Tools Design* tab, *Insert* group]. The *Date and Time* dialog box opens.
h. Select the date in proper business letter format (e.g., January 1, 2018), check the **Update automatically** check box, and click **OK** to close the dialog box and insert the date.
i. Leave the header open for the next instructions.

8. Insert page number in the header and format page number.
 a. With the header still open, press **Enter** after the date.
 b. Type Page and **space** once.
 c. Click the **Page Number** button [*Header & Footer Tools Design* tab, *Header & Footer* group], click **Current Position**, and select **Plain Number** from the drop-down list of page number options.
 d. Click the **Page Number** button and select **Format Page Numbers** to open the *Page Number Format* dialog box (Figure 3-107).
 e. Click the **Start at** radio button in the *Page numbering* area and change the page number to **2**.
 f. Click **OK** to close the dialog box.
 g. Place the insertion point after the page number and press **Enter** two times.
 h. Select the page number line, click the **Borders** drop-down list [*Home* tab, *Paragraph* group], and select **Bottom Border**.
 i. Click the **Close Header and Footer** button [*Header & Footer Tools Design* tab, *Close* group]. The header appears on the second and continuing pages.

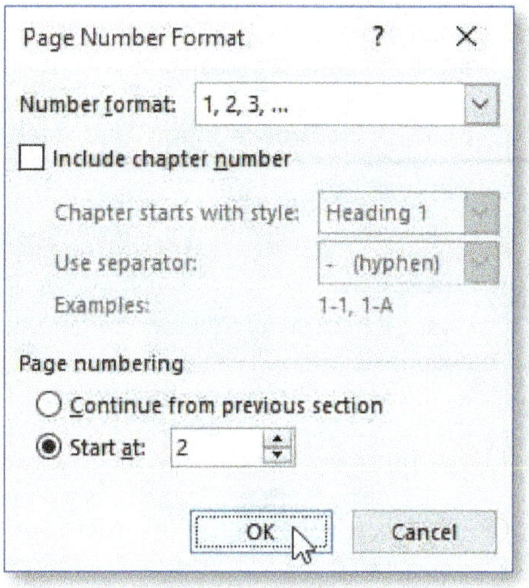

3-107 Change *Start at* page number

9. Insert footnotes.
 a. Go to page 4 and place the insertion point after the period at the end of the last line of text (after "reports are included.").
 b. Click the **Insert Footnote** button [*References* tab, *Footnotes* group].
 c. Type A list of drivers was faxed as a separate attachment. in the footnotes area.
 d. Go to the first page and place the insertion point after the period at the end of the fourth body paragraph (after "2018 renewal.").
 e. Click the **Insert Footnote** button and type Inflation is anticipated to be 2 percent. in the footnotes area.

10. Convert footnotes to endnotes and change number format.
 a. Click the **Footnotes** launcher to open the *Footnote and Endnote* dialog box.
 b. Click the **Convert** button. The *Convert Notes* dialog box opens (Figure 3-108).
 c. Select the **Convert all footnotes to endnotes** radio button and click **OK** to close the *Convert Notes* dialog box.

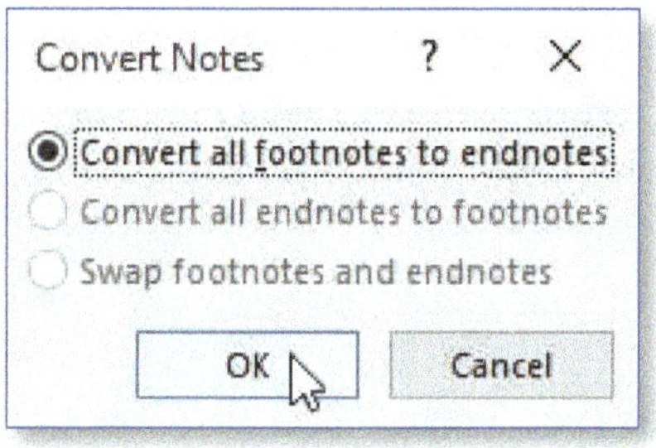

3-108 Convert footnotes to endnotes

d. Click **Close** to close the *Footnote and Endnote* dialog box.
e. Click the **Footnotes** launcher again to open the *Footnote and Endnote* dialog box (Figure 3-109).
f. Select the **Endnotes** radio button if it is not selected.
g. Click the **Number format** drop-down list and select **a, b, c, ...**
h. Click the **Apply changes to** drop-down list and select **Whole document**.
i. Click **Apply** to close the dialog box and apply the changes.

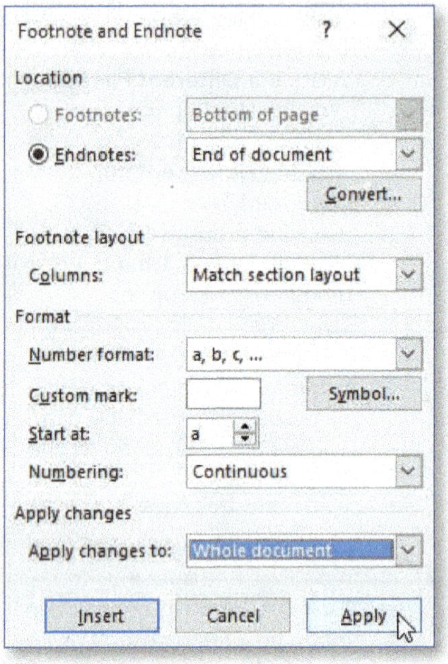

3-109 Change endnote number format

11. Insert a page break.
    a. Go to page 2 and place the insertion point in front of the "PROPERTY" heading.
    b. Click the **Breaks** button [*Layout* tab, *Page Setup* group].
    c. Select **Page** in the *Page Breaks* area. A page break is inserted, and the "PROPERTY" heading and following text are moved to page 3.
12. Change *Display for Review* view and accept all tracked changes.
    a. Click the **Display for Review** drop-down list [*Review* tab, *Tracking* group] and select **Simple Markup**. A red line on the left indicates where changes were made.
    b. Scroll through the four pages to review the document.
    c. Click the bottom half of the **Accept** button [*Review* tab, *Tracking* group] and select **Accept All Changes and Stop Tracking**.
13. Share the document with your instructor.
    a. Save this document on *OneDrive* if you haven't already. If you don't have the ability to save to *OneDrive*, skip all of step 13.
    b. Click the **Share** button in the upper right of the Word window to open the *Share* pane (Figure 3-110).
    c. Type your instructor's email address in the *Invite people* text box.
    d. Select **Can edit** in the drop-down list below the email address.
    e. Type a brief message to your instructor and click the **Share** button.
    f. Click the **X** in the upper right corner of the *Share* pane to close it.

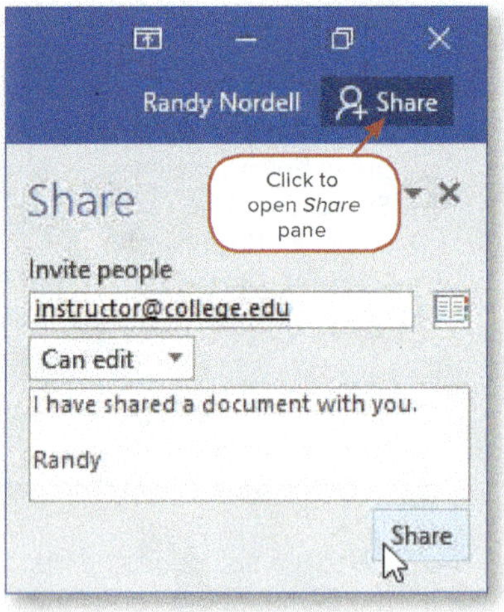

3-110 Share a document

14. Save and close the document (Figure 3-111).

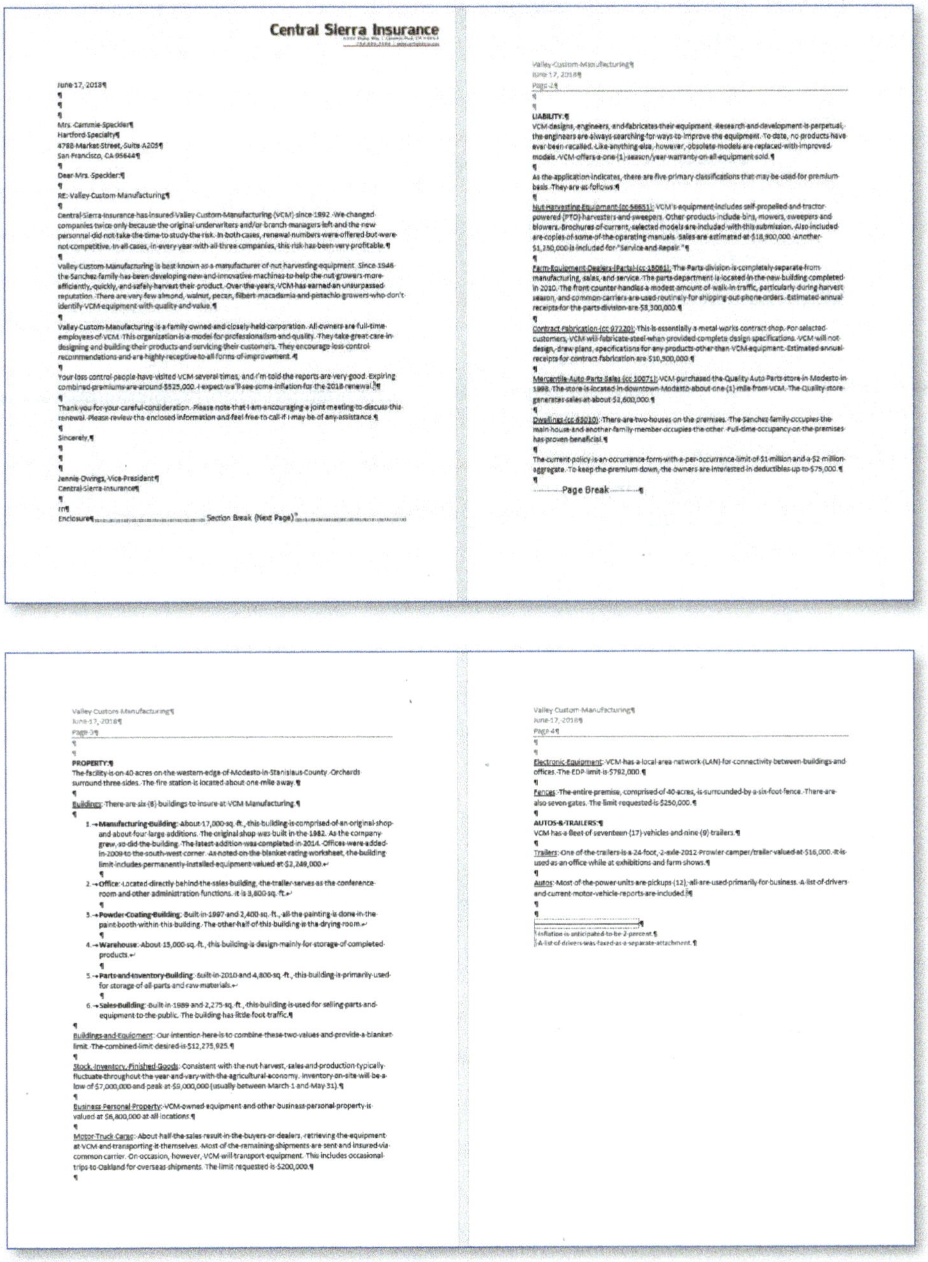

3-111 Word 3-2 completed

Guided Project 3-3

For this project, you customize the *Teen Substance Abuse* report for Courtyard Medical Plaza. You use *Comments* and *Track Changes*, and you add citations, a bibliography page, table of contents, headers and footers, and a cover page.
[Student Learning Outcomes 3.1, 3.2, 3.4, 3.5, 3.6, 3.7]

File Needed: ***TeenSubstanceAbuse-03.docx*** *(Student data files are available in the* Library *of your SIMnet account)*
Completed Project File Name: ***[your initials] Word 3-3.docx***

Skills Covered in this Project

- Turn on *Track Changes* and change *Display for Review* view.
- Set bibliography style.
- Insert a placeholder for a citation.
- Create a source and insert a citation.
- Use the *Source Manager* to edit a placeholder and create a new source.
- Insert a bibliography page.
- Use styles to format title and headings.
- Create a table of contents.
- Insert built-in odd and even headers and footers.
- Insert a document property field into a header.
- Update a table of contents.
- Insert and customize a cover page.
- Accept all tracked changes.
- Share a document.

1. Open the ***TeenSubstanceAbuse-03*** document from your student data files.
2. Save this document as [your initials] Word 3-3.
3. Change user name and initials.
   a. Click the **Tracking** launcher [*Review* tab, *Tracking* group] to open the *Track Changes Options* dialog box.
   b. Click the **Change User Name** button to open the *Word Options* dialog box.
   c. In the *Personalize your copy of Microsoft Office* area, type your first and last name in the *User name* text box.
   d. Type your first and last initials in lowercase letters in the *Initials* text box.
   e. Check the **Always use these values regardless of sign in to Office** box.
   f. Click **OK** to close the *Word Options* dialog box and click **OK** to close the *Track Changes Options* dialog box.
4. Turn on *Track Changes* and change the *Display for Review* view.
   a. Click the **Track Changes** button [*Review* tab, *Tracking* group] to turn on *Track Changes* and turn on **Show/Hide**. All of the changes you make will be tracked.
   b. Click the **Display for Review** drop-down list [*Review* tab, *Tracking* group] and select **Simple Markup**. Tracked changes are indicated by a red line on the left.
5. Select the report style and insert placeholders for a citation.
   a. Click the **Style** drop-down list [*References* tab, *Citations & Bibliography* group].
   b. Select **Chicago Sixteenth Edition**.
   c. On the first page in the "What Problems Can Teen Substance Abuse Cause?" section, place the insertion point at the end of the last sentence in the second paragraph ("unsafe substances") and before the period.
   d. Click the **Insert Citation** button [*References* tab, *Citations & Bibliography* group] and select **Add New Placeholder**. The *Placeholder Name* dialog box opens.
   e. Type Foundation and click **OK**. The placeholder for the citation displays in the report.
   f. On the second page in the "Can Teen Substance Use And Abuse Be Prevented?" section, place the insertion point at the end of the last sentence in the first paragraph ("and drugs") and before the period.

g. Click the **Insert Citation** button and select the **Foundation** placeholder from the drop-down list (Figure 3-112).

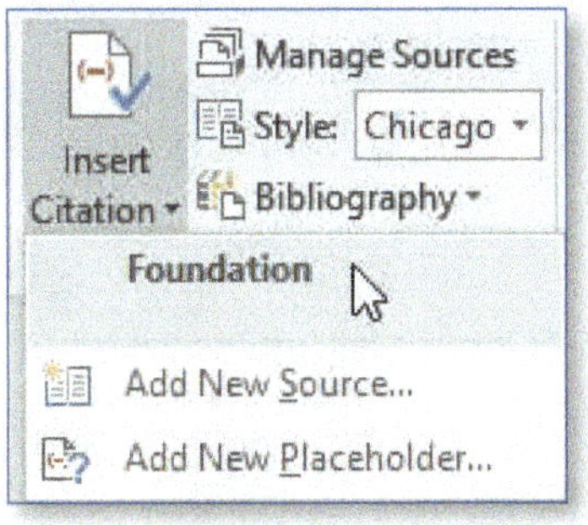

3-112 Insert placeholder for a citation

6. Insert a citation into the report.
   a. On the first page in the "What Is Teen Substance Abuse?" section, place the insertion point at the end of the last sentence in the second paragraph ("most often") and before the period.
   b. Click the **Insert Citation** button and select **Add New Source**. The *Create Source* dialog box opens (Figure 3-113).
   c. Check the **Show All Bibliography Fields** box and create a new source with the following information:

      Type of Source: **Journal Article**
      Author: Kelly L. Sanchez
      Title: Examining High School Drug Use
      Journal Name: Journal of Secondary Education
      Year: 2015
      Pages: 22-26
      Volume: XXI
      Issue: 2
      Tag Name: Sanchez

   d. Click **OK** to close the dialog box and insert the citation. The citation is inserted into the report.

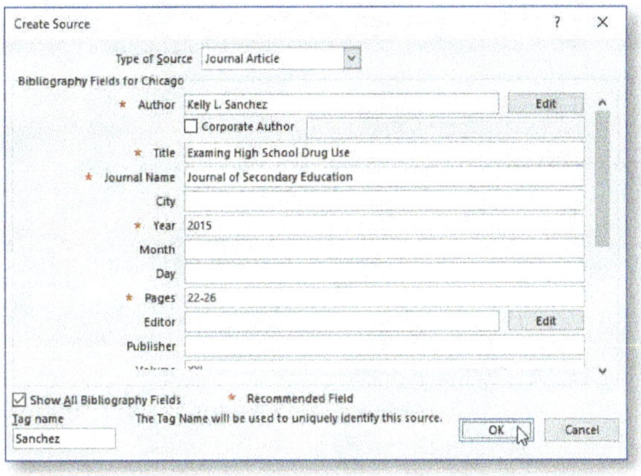

3-113 *Create Source* dialog box

7. Use the *Source Manager* to create a new source and provide source information for a placeholder.
   a. Click the **Manage Sources** button [*References* tab, *Citations & Bibliography* group] to open the *Source Manager* dialog box.
   b. In the *Current List* area, select the **Foundation** placeholder and click **Edit**. The *Edit Source* dialog box opens.
   c. Use the following information to edit the placeholder source:

      Type of Source: **Web site**
      Corporate Author: Foundation for Teen Health
      Name of Web Page: Making Good Choices
      Year: 2014
      Year Accessed: 2016
      Month Accessed: June
      Day Accessed: 25
      URL: http://www.foundationforteenhealth.org/choices.htm

   d. Click **OK** to close the dialog box and update the placeholders. The placeholders in the report are updated with the proper citation from the source information.
   e. With the *Source Manager* dialog box still open, click the **New** button. The *Create Source* dialog box opens.
   f. Create a new source with the following information:

      Type of Source: **Document From Web site**
      Corporate Author: Courtyard Medical Plaza
      Name of Web Page: Teen Mental Health
      Name of Web Site: Courtyard Medical Plaza

Year: 2016
Month: March
Day: 6
URL: http://www.cmp.com/Teen_Mental_Health.pdf
Tag Name: CMP

g. Click **OK** to close the dialog box and click **Close** to close the *Source Manager* dialog box.

8. Insert citations into the report.
   a. On the first page in the "Why Do Teens Abuse Drugs And Alcohol?" section, place the insertion point at the end of the last sentence in the second paragraph ("increased risk") and before the period.
   b. Click the **Insert Citation** button and select the **Courtyard Medical Plaza** citation from the drop-down list.
   c. On the second page in the "What Should You Do If You Find Out That Your Teen Is Using?" section, place the insertion point at the end of the last sentence in the second paragraph ("or both") and before the period.
   d. Click the **Insert Citation** button and select the **Sanchez, Kelly L**. citation from the drop-down list.
9. Insert a bibliography page at the end of the document.
   a. Press **Ctrl+End** to move to the end of the document.
   b. Press **Ctrl+Enter** to insert a page break.
   c. With the insertion point on the blank last page, click the **Bibliography** button [*References* tab, *Citations & Bibliography* group].
   d. Select **Bibliography** to insert the built-in bibliography into the document.
10. Apply styles to the title and section headings and insert a table of contents.
   a. Apply the **Title** style to the title of the report on the first page.
   b. Apply the **Heading 1** style to each of the bold section headings in the report.
   c. Press **Ctrl+Home** to move the insertion point to the beginning of the report.
   d. Click the **Blank Page** button [*Insert* tab, *Pages* group] to insert a blank page before the first page of the report.
   e. Place your insertion point at the top of the new first page, type Teen Substance Abuse, and press **Enter**. The text should be formatted as *Title* style. If it's not, apply the **Title** style.
   f. Click the **Table of Contents** button [*References* tab, *Table of Contents* group] and select **Automatic Table 1** from the drop-down list. The table of contents is inserted below the title.
11. Insert odd and even page headers and customize content.
   a. With the insertion point still on the first page, click the **Header** button [*Insert* tab, *Header & Footer* group].
   b. Select **Motion (Odd Page)** from the drop-down list of built-in headers.
   c. Delete the existing text to the left of the page number.
   d. Click the **Document Info** button, click **Document Property**, and select **Company** from the drop-down list.
   e. Delete the page number in the colored bar in the header and place the insertion point on the blank line below the text in the header.
   f. Check the **Different Odd & Even Pages** check box [*Header & Footer Tools Design* tab, *Options* group] (Figure 3-114).

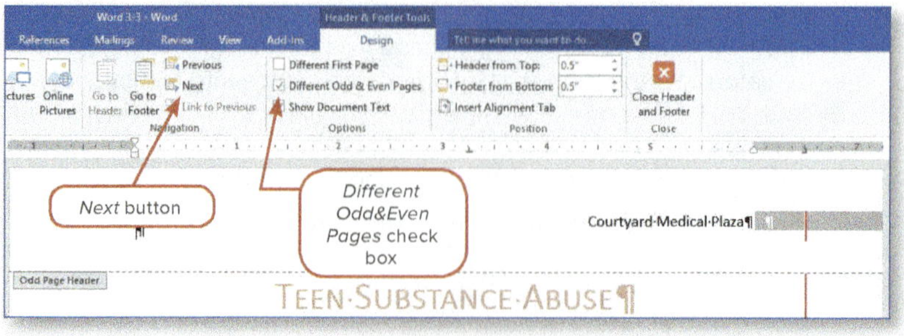

3-114 Odd page header inserted and content customized

g. Click the **Next** button to move to the *Even Page Header*.
h. Click the **Header** button [*Header & Footer Tools Design* tab, *Header & Footer* group] and select **Motion (Even Page)** from the drop-down list.
i. Delete the page number in the colored bar in the header and leave the header open.

12. Insert odd and even page footers.
a. With the *Even Page Header* still open, click the **Go to Footer** button [*Header & Footer Tools Design* tab, *Navigation* group] to move to the *Even Page Footer*.
b. Click the **Page Number** button [*Header & Footer* group], click **Bottom of Page**, and select **Brackets 2**.
c. Click the **Previous** button [*Navigation* group] to move to the *Odd Page Footer*.
d. Click the **Page Number** button [*Header & Footer* group], click **Bottom of Page**, and select **Brackets 2**.
e. Click the **Close Header and Footer** button [*Close* group].

13. Insert page breaks to control page endings.
a. Go to page 2, click in front of the last section heading ("What Are The Signs Of Substance Abuse"), and insert a **page break**.
b. Go to page 3, click in front of the last section heading ("Can Teen Substance Use And Abuse Be Prevented"), and insert a **page break**.

14. Update the table of contents.
a. Click the table of contents on the first page.
b. Click the **Update Table** button at the top of the content control field. The *Update Table of Contents* dialog box opens (Figure 3-115).
c. Select the **Update entire table** radio button and click **OK**.

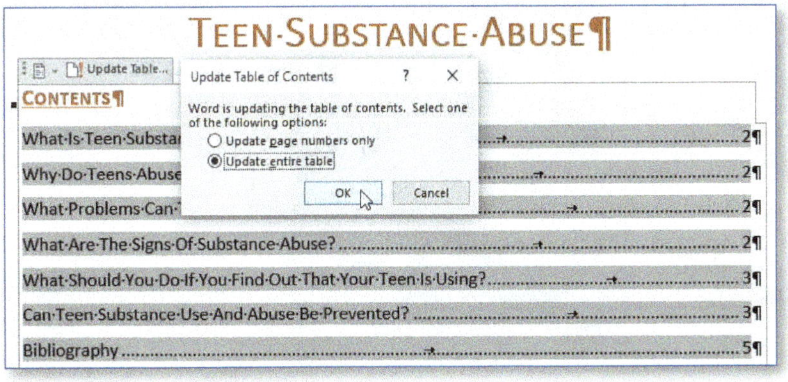

3-115 Update table of contents

15. Insert and customize a cover page.
a. Press **Ctrl+Home** to move to the top of the document.
b. Click the **Cover Page** button [*Insert* tab, *Pages* group].
c. Select the **Slice (Dark)** built-in cover page from the drop-down list. The cover page is inserted before the first page of the document.
d. Select the **Title** document property field, apply **Bold** formatting, and change the font size to **40 pt**.
e. Click the **Subtitle** content control field handle and press **Delete**.
f. Press **Ctrl+Home** to move the insertion point to the top of the cover page.
g. Click the **Quick Parts** button [*Insert* tab, *Text* group], select **Document Property**, and select **Company** from the drop-down list.
h. Select the **Company** document property field, apply **Bold** and **Small Caps** formatting, and change the font size to **24 pt**.

16. Review comments and track changes.
a. Click the **Display for Review** drop-down list [*Review* tab, *Tracking* group] and select **All Markup**.
b. Right-click the comment in the *Markup* area at the top of the third page and select **Mark Comment Done**.
c. Click the bottom half of the **Accept** button and select **Accept All Changes and Stop Tracking**.

d. Click the **Display for Review** drop-down list [*Review* tab, *Tracking* group] and select **No Markup**.

17. Share the document with your instructor.
   a. Save this document on *OneDrive* if you haven't already. If you don't have the ability to save to *OneDrive*, skip all of step 17.
   b. Click the **Share** button in the upper right of the Word window to open the *Share* pane (Figure 3-116).
   c. Type your instructor's email address in the *Invite people* text box.
   d. Select **Can edit** in the drop-down list below the email address.
   e. Type a brief message to your instructor and click the **Share** button.
   f. Click the **X** in the upper right corner of the *Share* pane to close it.
18. Save and close the document (Figure 3-117).

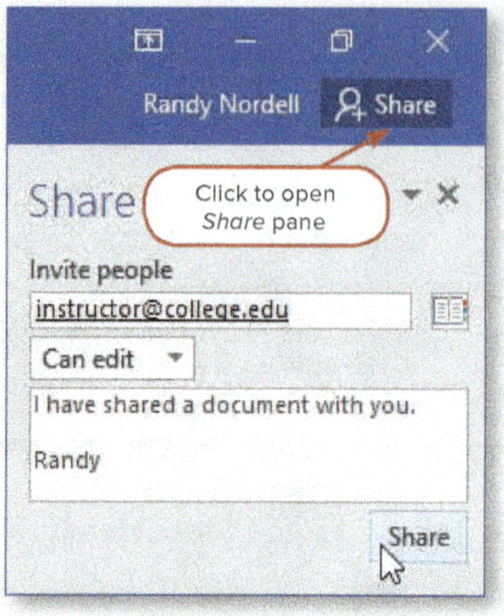

3-116 Share a document

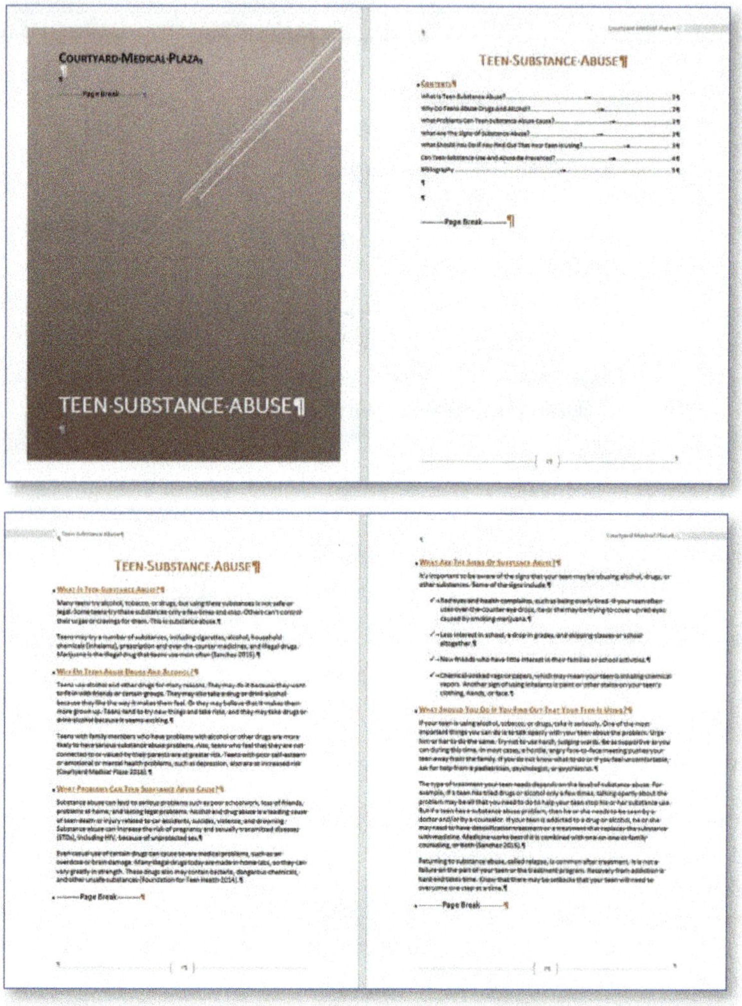

3-117 Word 3-3 completed (pages 1-4 of 6)

Independent Project 3-4

For this project, you modify the *Tips for Better Heart Rate Monitor Training* document from the American River Cycling Club. You use *Track Changes* and comments, insert and modify endnotes, insert placeholders, create sources, insert a bibliography page, insert a table of contents and cover page, and use custom headers and footers.
[Student Learning Outcomes 3.1, 3.2, 3.3, 3.4, 3.5, 3.6, 3.7]

File Needed: ***HeartRateMonitorTraining-03.docx*** *(Student data files are available in the* Library *of your SIMnet account)*
Completed Project File Name: ***[your initials] Word 3-4.docx***

Skills Covered in this Project

- Use comments and *Track Changes*.
- Insert endnotes.
- Insert a placeholder for a citation.
- Use the *Source Manager* to edit placeholders and create a new source.
- Change the bibliography style.
- Insert a bibliography page.
- Convert endnotes to footnotes.
- Insert a table of contents.
- Insert and modify a cover page.
- Insert custom headers and footers.
- Insert page breaks.
- Change footnote number format.
- Mark a comment as done.
- Accept tracked changes.

1. Open the ***HeartRateMonitorTraining-03*** document from your student data files.
2. Save this document as [your initials] Word 3-4.
3. Change user name and initials.
   a. Open the *Track Changes Options* dialog box (**Tracking** launcher) and click the **Change User Name** button to open the *Word Options* dialog box.
   b. In the *Personalize your copy of Microsoft Office* area, type your first and last name in the *User name* text box and your first and last initials in lowercase letters in the *Initials* text box.
   c. Check the **Always use these values regardless of sign in to Office** box, click **OK** to close the *Word Options* dialog box, and click **OK** to close the *Track Changes Options* dialog box.
4. Turn on *Track Changes* and insert a comment.
   a. Turn on **Track Changes** and change the *Display for Review* view to **Simple Markup** if it is not already selected.
   b. Select the title, insert a **New Comment**, and type Insert endnotes, citations, a references page, a table of contents, and a cover page in the new comment.
   c. Click the **Show Comments** button to close the *Markup* area on the right and display only the comment balloon and not the comment text.
5. Insert endnotes.
   a. Insert an endnote at the end of the first body paragraph on the first page (after the period).
   b. Type See the References page for related book and articles. in the endnote area.
   c. Insert an endnote at the end of the paragraph (after the period) in the "Analyze Your Heart Rate Data" section on the first page.
   d. Type See the ARCC web site (www.arcc.org) for information about specific heart rate monitors. in the endnote area.
   e. Insert an endnote at the end of the second paragraph (after the period) in the "Comparing Heart Rate Values with Others" section on the second page.
   f. Type 220-age is an estimate of maximum heart rate. in the endnote area.
6. Insert placeholders for citations.
   a. Place the insertion point at the end of the second paragraph and before the period in the "Know Your Resting Heart Rate" section and insert a placeholder named **RoadCycling**.

   b. Place the insertion point at the end of the second paragraph and before the period in the "Perform a Threshold Test" section and insert a placeholder named **Segura**.
   c. Place the insertion point at the end of the body paragraph and before the period in the "Not Analyzing Heart Rate Data" section and insert a placeholder named **Wallace**.

7. Use the *Source Manager* dialog box to provide source information for the three placeholders. Check the **Show All Bibliography Fields** box, if necessary.
   a. Edit the *RoadCycling* placeholder to include the following information.
      Type of Source: **Document from Web site**
      Corporate Author: Road Cycling
      Name of Web Page: Training with a Heart Rate Monitor
      Name of Web Site: RoadCycling.com
      Year: 2015
      Year Accessed: 2016
      Month Accessed: August
      Day Accessed: 25
      URL: http://www.roadcycling.com/heart_rate.html
   b. Edit the *Segura* placeholder to include the following information.
      Type of Source: **Article in a Periodical**
      Author: Manuel A. Segura
      Title: Maximizing Threshold Training
      Periodical Title: Cycling Weekly
      Year: 2016
      Month: March
      Day: 1
      Pages: 35-41
   c. Edit the *Wallace* placeholder to include the following information.
      Type of Source: **Book**
      Author: Ingrid L. Wallace
      Title: Understanding Heart Rate
      Year: 2014
      City: Chicago
      Publisher: Penguin Books

8. Convert all endnotes to footnotes.

9. Change the bibliography style and insert a references page at the end of the document.
   a. Change the bibliography style of the report to **APA**.
   b. Place your insertion point on the blank line at the end of the document and insert a **page break**.
   c. Insert the built-in **References** page on the last page.
   d. **Center** the *References* heading and apply **10 pt**. *After* paragraph spacing.

10. Insert a table of contents.
   a. Place the insertion point at the top of the document and insert a **page break**.
   b. Place the insertion point at the top of the new first page and type Table of Contents.
   c. Change the font size to **14 pt**., apply **bold** and **small caps** formatting, and press **Enter**.
   d. Insert a **Custom Table of Contents** and use **Simple** format, show 2 levels of headings, show page numbers, right align page numbers, and use a dot tab leader.

11. Insert a cover page.
   a. Insert the **Ion (Dark)** built-in cover page.
   b. Select the **Year** field and choose the current date.
   c. Select the **Title** field, change the font size to **44 pt**., apply **bold** formatting, and align **center**.
   d. Delete the **Subtitle** and **Author** fields. Be sure to delete the entire fields, not just the text.
   e. Select the **Company** field, change the font size to **12 pt**., and apply **bold** formatting.
   f. Select the **Company Address** field and type www.arcc.org.

12. Insert a header and footer.
    a. Place the insertion point in the table of contents on the second page of the document.
    b. Edit the header, type Page, **space** once, and insert a plain page number in the current position.
    c. **Align Right** the header information (use **Align Right**, not a tab).
    d. Go to the footer on the second page, type American River Cycling Club on the left and www.arcc.org on the right (use tabs to align the text on the right).
    e. Apply a **solid line**, **Black, Text 1** color, **¾ pt**. width, **top** and **bottom border** to the information in the footer.
    f. Change the font size of the information in the header and footer to **10 pt**.
    g. Close the header and footer. No header or footer should appear on the cover page.
13. Insert a **page break** before the "Analyze Your Heart Rate Data" and "Not Being Aware of Factors Affecting Heart Rate" headings.
14. Change the footnote number format to **A, B, C**.
15. Mark a comment as done and accept all tracked changes.
    a. Click the **Show Comments** button to display comments.
    b. Right-click the comment near the top of the third page and **Mark Comment Done**.
    c. Accept all changes in the document and stop tracking changes.
    d. Click the **Show Comments** button again so the text of the comment does not display.
16. **Update** the entire table of contents.
17. Save and close the document (Figure 3-118).

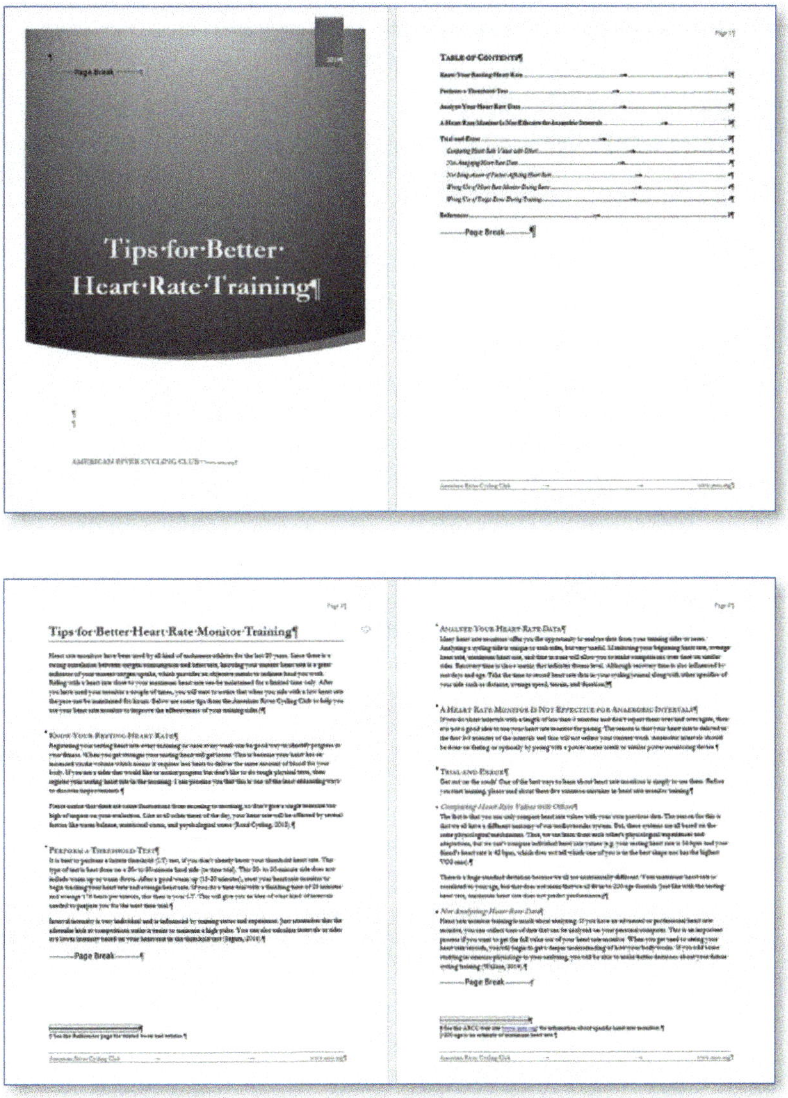

3-118 Word 3-4 completed (pages 1-4 of 6)

Independent Project 3-5

Sierra Pacific Community College District gives incoming college students a *Student Success Tips* document. For this project, you review comments and tracked changes, apply heading styles, and insert footnotes, placeholders, and a works cited page, table of contents, and cover page.
[Student Learning Outcomes 3.1, 3.2, 3.3, 3.4, 3.5, 3.6, 3.7]

File Needed: ***StudentSuccess-03.docx*** *(Student data files are available in the* Library *of your SIMnet account)*
Completed Project File Name: ***[your initials] Word 3-5.docx***

Skills Covered in this Project

- Review and delete a comment.
- Reject and accept tracked changes.
- Apply title and heading styles.
- Insert and modify footnotes.
- Insert a placeholder.
- Use the *Source Manager* to update a reference.
- Change the bibliography style.
- Insert a works cited page.
- Insert a table of contents.
- Use different odd and even page footers.
- Insert page numbers and a document property field into the footer.
- Insert and customize a cover page.
- Insert a page break.
- Update a table of contents.
- Share a document.

1. Open the ***StudentSuccess-03*** document from your student data files.
2. Save this document as [your initials] Word 3-5.
3. Review and delete selected comments and tracked changes.
   a. Change the *Display for Review* view to **All Markup**.
   b. Read the comment at top of the document and then **delete** the comment.
   c. Find the first tracked change in the document (left, right, and top margin changed) and **Reject Format Change**.
   d. Review the changes in the document and then **Accept All Changes** in the document.
4. Apply styles to the title and headings.
   a. Apply the **Title** style to the title on the first page.
   b. Apply the **Heading 1** style to all the bold headings
   c. Apply the **Heading 2** style to all the underlined headings.
5. Insert footnotes and apply text formatting.
   a. On the first page, insert a footnote after "Weekly Schedules" in the "Schedule Your Time" section.
   b. Type Weekly Schedules are available from your counselor or in the college bookstore. as the footnote text.
   c. Insert a footnote at the end of "Be sure to schedule your time for all these in your 119 hours." (after the period) in the "Schedule Your Time" section.
   d. Type Be sure to schedule recreational time in your 119 hours. as the footnote text.
6. Move a footnote and modify footnote number format.
   a. Select the first footnote reference marker (in the body) and move it so it appears after "Weekly Schedule" in the "Track Your Time" section (use drag and drop or cut and paste).
   b. Deselect the moved footnote and change the footnote number format to **a, b, c**.
7. Insert placeholders in the body of the document.
   a. In the "Introduction" section on the first page, insert a new placeholder named Navarro at the end of the body paragraph (and before the period).

b. In the "Test Anxiety" section on the second page, insert a new placeholder named Sierra at the end of the body paragraph (and before the period).
c. In the "Goal Setting" section on the fourth page, insert the Navarro placeholder (not a new placeholder) at the end of the intro paragraph (and before the period).

8. Use the *Source Manager* to update placeholder reference information.
   a. Open the *Source Manager* and edit the *Navarro* placeholder to include the following information. Check the **Show All Bibliography Fields** box, if necessary.

      Type of Source: **Book**
      Author: Tessa C. Navarro
      Title: Study Skills for College Students
      Year: 2017
      City: Chicago
      Publisher: McGraw-Hill

   b. Edit the *Sierra* placeholder to include the following information.

      Type of Source: **Document from Web site**
      Corporate Author: Sierra Pacific Community College District
      Name of Web Page: Tips for Student Success
      Name of Web Site: spccd.edu
      Year: 2016
      Year Accessed: 2016
      Month Accessed: September
      Day Accessed: 2
      URL: http://www.spccd.edu/tips4success.pdf

9. Change bibliography style and insert a works cited page.
   a. Change the bibliography style to **MLA**.
   b. Place your insertion point on the blank line at the end of the document and insert a **page break**.
   c. Insert a **Works Cited** page.

10. Insert a table of contents.
   a. Place your insertion point at the beginning of the document and insert a **page break**.
   b. Type Student Success Tips on the first line on the new first page (before the page break) and press **Enter**.
   c. On the blank line below "Student Success Tips," insert the **Automatic Table 1** table of contents.
   d. Apply the **Title** style to "Student Success Tips" on the new first page.

11. Insert a footer and add custom content.
   a. Edit the footer on the first page of the document (table of contents).
   b. Check the **Different Odd & Even Pages** box.
   c. Insert the **Accent Bar 2** from the *Page Number, Current Position* drop-down list.
   d. Press **Tab** two times and insert the **Document Title** (or **Title**) document property field.
   e. Go to the even page footer and insert the **Accent Bar 2** from the *Page Number, Current Position* drop-down list.
   f. Press **Tab** two times and insert the **Company** document property field.
   g. Change the font size to **10 pt**. and apply **bold** formatting to the footer content in both the even and odd page footers.
   h. Close the footer.

12. Insert and customize a cover page.
   a. Insert the **Slice (Light)** cover page.
   b. Delete the **Subtitle** ("Document subtitle") and **Course** ("Course title") document property fields.
   c. Change the font size of the title on the cover page to **40 pt**. and apply **bold** formatting.

13. Insert a **page break** before the "Physical Signs of Test Anxiety" heading.

14. Update the entire table of contents.

15. Share the document with your instructor.
    a. Save this document on *OneDrive* if you haven't already. If you don't have the ability to save to *OneDrive*, skip all of step 15.
    b. Click the **Share** button in the upper right of the Word window to open the *Share* pane.
    c. Type your instructor's email address in the *Invite people* text box.
    d. Select **Can edit** in the drop-down list below the email address.
    e. Type a brief message to your instructor and click the **Share** button.
    f. Click the **X** in the upper right corner of the *Share* pane to close it.
16. Save and close the document (Figure 3-119).

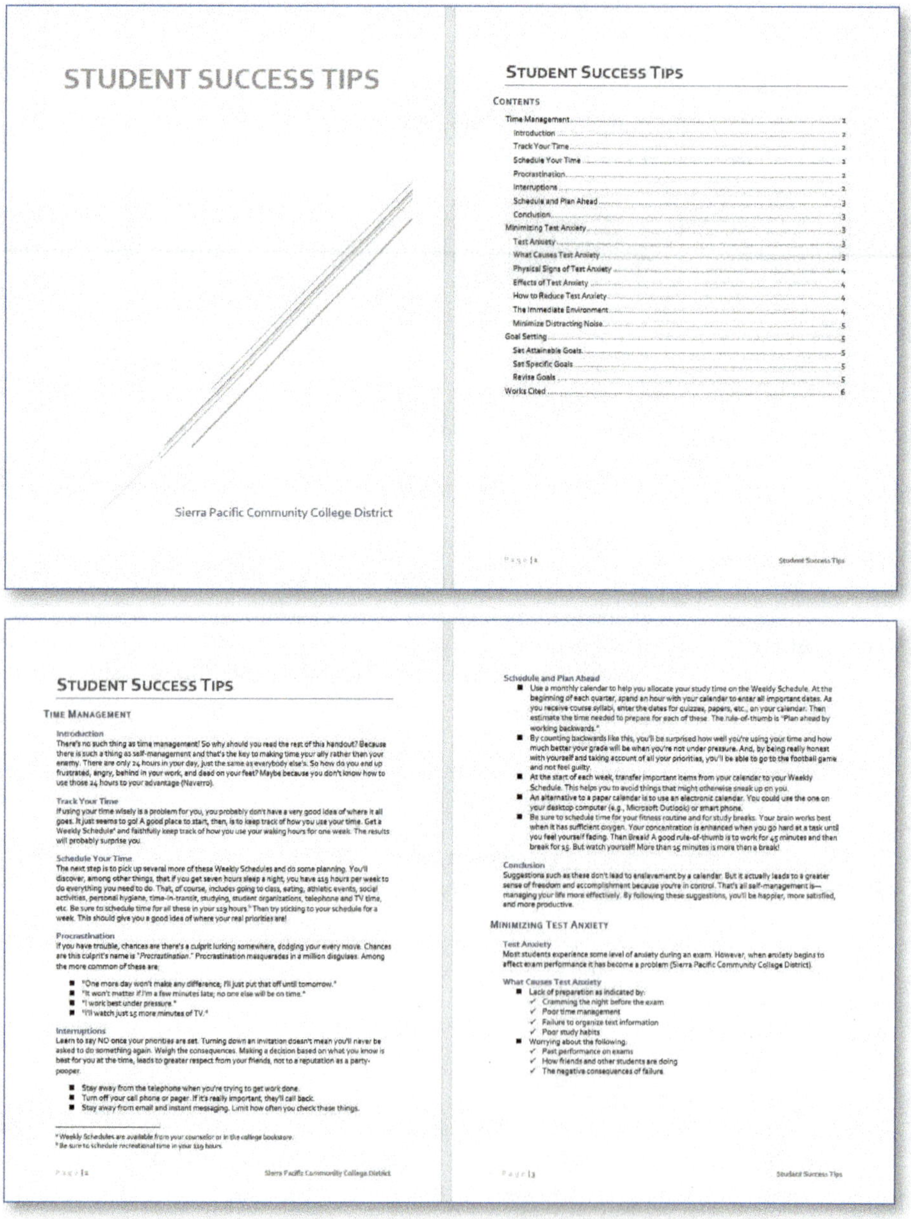

3-119 Word 3-5 completed (pages 1-4 of 7)

Independent Project 3-6

Courtyard Medical Plaza works closely with the Skiing Unlimited winter ski program. For this project, you modify the *Skiing Unlimited Training Guide* using *Track Changes* to include footnotes, a table of contents, cover page, and headers and footers.
[Student Learning Outcomes 3.1, 3.2, 3.3, 3.5, 3.6, 3.7]

File Needed: ***SkiingUnlimitedTrainingGuide-03.docx*** *(Student data files are available in the* Library *of your SIMnet account)*
Completed Project File Name: ***[your initials] Word 3-6.docx***

Skills Covered in this Project

- Review and delete a comment.
- Change the *Display for Review* view.
- Modify a document using *Track Changes.*
- Change margins.
- Apply title and heading styles.
- Insert a custom table of contents.
- Insert a page number in the header.
- Insert a document property field into the footer.
- Insert page breaks.
- Insert a cover page.
- Customize cover page content and insert a document property field.
- Review and accept tracked changes.
- Update a table of contents.

1. Open the ***SkiingUnlimitedTrainingGuide-03*** document from your student data files.
2. Save this document as [your initials] Word 3-6.
3. Change user name and initials.
   a. Open the *Track Changes Options* dialog box (**Tracking** launcher) and click the **Change User Name** button to open the *Word Options* dialog box.
   b. In the *Personalize your copy of Microsoft Office* area, type your first and last name in the *User name* text box and your first and last initials in lowercase letters in the *Initials* text box.
   c. Check the **Always use these values regardless of sign in to Office** box, click **OK** to close the *Word Options* dialog box, and click **OK** to close the *Track Changes Options* dialog box.
4. Change *Display for Review* view, review and delete a comment, and turn on *Track Changes.*
   a. Change the *Display for Review* view to **All Markup** and review tracked changes in the document.
   b. Read the comment on the first page and then **delete** the comment.
   c. Turn on **Track Changes** and change the *Display for Review* view to **Simple Markup**.
5. Change the left and right margins to **1"**.
6. Apply styles to the title and headings.
   a. Apply the **Title** style to the title on the first page.
   b. Apply the **Heading 1** style to all the bold headings.
   c. Apply the **Heading 2** style to all the underlined headings.
   d. Apply the **Heading 3** style to all the italicized headings.
7. Insert and customize footnotes.
   a. Insert a footnote after the "Skiing Procedures" heading on the first page.
   b. Type Skiing procedures vary depending on the clients' needs. as the footnote text.
   c. Insert a footnote after the "Guiding Techniques" heading on the second page.
   d. Type A minimum of two guides is required for all clients. as the footnote text.
   e. Change the footnote *Number format* to **A, B, C** and change *Numbering* to **Continuous**.

8. Insert a custom table of contents.
   a. Place your insertion point at the beginning of the document and insert a **page break**.
   b. Type Table of Contents on the first line on the new first page and press **Enter**.
   c. Apply the **Title** style to "Table of Contents" on the new first page.
   d. Place the insertion point on the blank line below the "Table of Contents" heading and before the page break.
   e. Insert a **Custom Table of Contents**, use **Fancy** format, show 2 levels of headings, show page numbers, right align page numbers, and do not include a tab leader.
9. Insert header and footer.
   a. On the first page (table of contents), insert the **Bold Numbers 3** built-in page number at the top of the page.
   b. Remove the extra line in the header.
   c. In the footer on the same page, insert the **Title** document property field on the left. Use the right arrow key to deselect the document property field.
   d. Insert the **Company** field on the right. Use tabs to align the field on the right.
   e. **Bold** the text in the footer and close the footer.
10. Insert page breaks to keep headings with the text below.
    a. Insert a **page break** before the "Beginning Wedge Christie Turns" heading (page 4).
    b. Insert a **page break** before the "Introduction to Equipment" heading (page 5).
11. Insert and modify a cover page.
    a. Insert the **Grid** cover page.
    b. Delete the **Subtitle** field.
    c. On the blank line between the *Title* and *Abstract* fields, insert the **Company** document property field.
    d. Delete the **Abstract** field.
    e. Select the **Company** document property field, change the font size to **20 pt.**, apply **bold** formatting, and change the text color to **Blue-Gray, Text 2**.
12. Change *Display for Review* view, accept tracked changes, and turn off **Track Changes**.
    a. Change the *Display for Review* view to **All Markup** and review the changes in the document.
    b. Turn off **Track Changes** and accept all tracked changes in the document.
13. Update the entire table of contents.
14. Save and close the document (Figure 3-120).

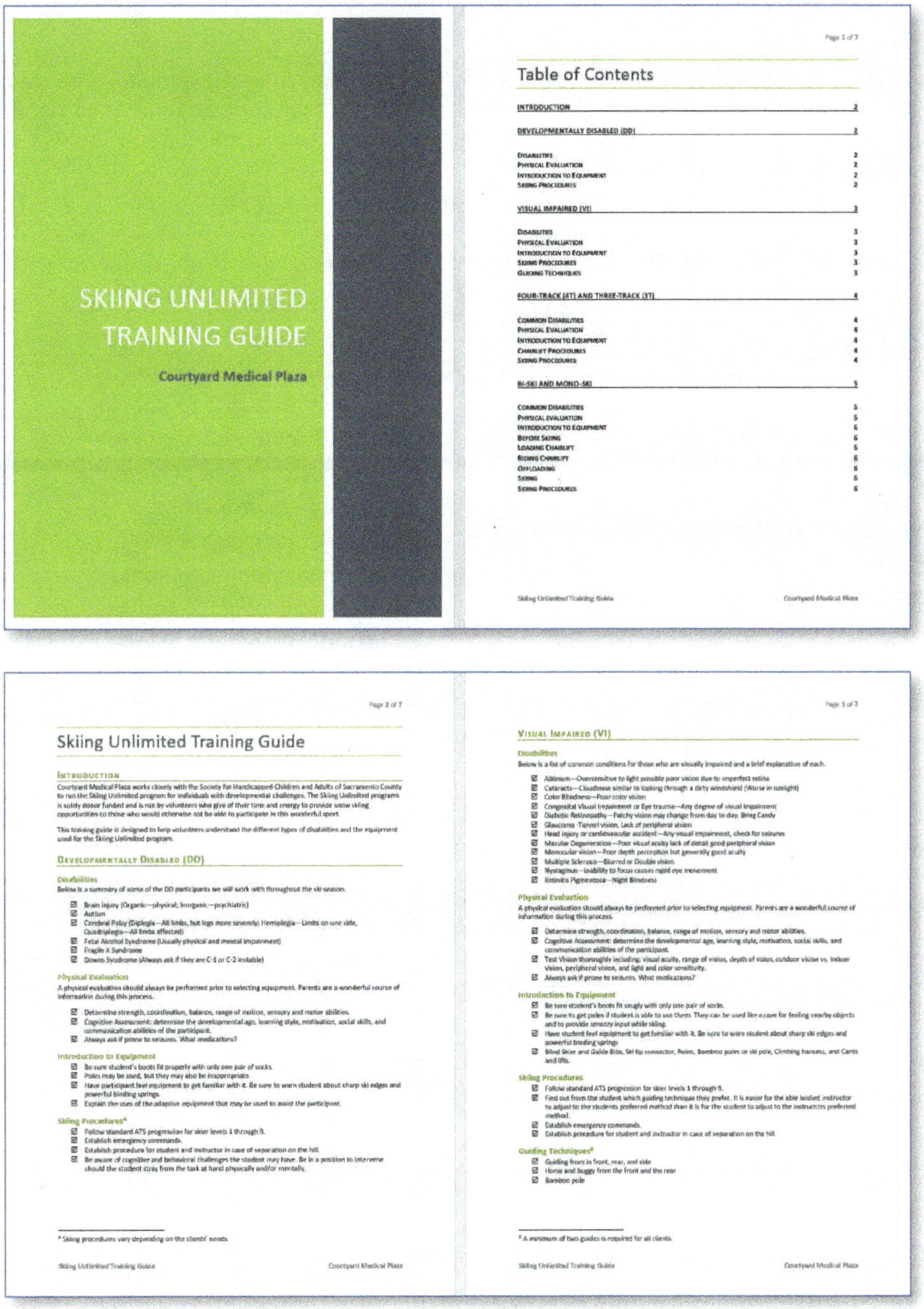

3-120 Word 3-6 completed (pages 1-4 of 8)

Improve It Project 3-7

American River Cycling Club is working with a cycling tour company to set up a trip to cycle through the Tuscany region of Italy. The original document from the cycling tour company needs to be improved. Modify this document to remove some of the existing content and add a cover page, table of contents, footnotes, and a footer.
[Student Learning Outcomes 3.1, 3.2, 3.3, 3.5, 3.6, 3.7]

File Needed: ***ItalyTourItinerary-03.docx*** *(Student data files are available in the* Library *of your SIMnet account)*
Completed Project File Name: ***[your initials] Word 3-7.docx***

Skills Covered in this Project

- Delete a comment and review tracked changes.
- Change the *Display for Review* view.
- Make edits using *Track Changes*.
- Remove existing cover page, table of contents, and header and footer.
- Apply a style and update a style.
- Insert page breaks.
- Move and delete an endnote.
- Convert endnotes to footnotes.
- Insert and customize footnotes.
- Insert a custom table of contents.
- Edit document properties.
- Insert and modify a cover page.
- Insert custom footer content.
- Review and accept tracked changes.
- Share a document.

1. Open the ***ItalyTourItinerary-03*** document from your student data files.
2. Save this document as [your initials] Word 3-7.
3. Change user name and initials.
   a. Open the *Track Changes Options* dialog box (**Tracking** launcher) and click the **Change User Name** button to open the *Word Options* dialog box.
   b. In the *Personalize your copy of Microsoft Office* area, type your first and last name in the *User name* text box and your first and last initials in lowercase letters in the *Initials* text box.
   c. Check the **Always use these values regardless of sign in to Office** box, click **OK** to close the *Word Options* dialog box, and click **OK** to close the *Track Changes Options* dialog box.
4. Change *Display for Review* view, review and delete a comment, and turn on *Track Changes*.
   a. Change the *Display for Review* view to **All Markup** and review the changes in the document.
   b. Read the comment on the first page and then delete the comment.
   c. Turn on **Track Changes** and change the *Display for Review* view to **Simple Markup**.
5. Remove existing content.
   a. Click the **Cover Page** button (*Insert* tab, *Pages* group] and select **Remove Current Cover Page**.
   b. Click the **Table of Contents** button (*References* tab, *Table of Contents* group] and select **Remove Table of Contents**.
   c. Remove the existing headers and footers on all pages of the itinerary.
6. Change the page orientation to **Landscape**.
7. Apply a heading style and update a style.
   a. Apply the **Day** style to the "Day 1: . . ." heading on the first page.
   b. Select the "Day 1" heading and **Update Heading 1 to Match Selection**. The new *Heading 1* style applies to all day headings in the document.
8. Insert page breaks.
   a. Click in front of "Day 3" and insert a **page break**.
   b. Repeat this on each of the odd numbered days so only two days appear on each page.

9. Add text and apply style.
   a. Place your insertion point on the blank line after the distance in the "Day 2" section.
   b. Press **Enter** and type Notes and Questions at the insertion point.
   c. Apply **Day** style to the text you just typed.
   d. Repeat steps b and c to insert this information at the end of the "Day 4" and "Day 6" sections.
   e. In the "Day 8" section, place your insertion point on the blank line below the "Kilometers to Miles Conversion" information and above the endnotes.
   f. Press **Enter**, type Notes and Questions, and apply **Day** style to the text you just typed.
10. Move and delete endnotes and convert endnotes to footnotes.
    a. Move the first endnote marker (after the distance on "Day 3") to appear in the "Day 2" section after the distance ("83 km").
    b. Change the text to Day 2 is the longest day of the tour. in the endnote text area.
    c. Delete the second endnote reference marker after "Day 4." The endnote text is removed when you delete the reference marker.
    d. Convert all endnotes to footnotes.
11. Insert and customize footnotes.
    a. After the "Day 4" distance ("0-26 km"), insert a footnote and type Day 4 is an optional riding day. in the footnote text area. *Note: The footnote number may not be consecutive until you accept tracked changes.*
    b. After the "Day 5" distance ("42-58 km"), insert a footnote and type Day 5 has two routes from which to choose. in the footnote text area.
    c. After the "Day 6" distance ("52-68 km"), insert a footnote and type Day 6 has three routes from which to choose. in the footnote text area.
    d. Change the footnote *Number format* to **a, b, c** and change *Numbering* to **Continuous** if it is not already selected.
12. Insert a custom table of contents.
    a. Place your insertion point at the beginning of the document and insert a **page break**.
    b. Type Contents on the first line on the new first page (before the page break) and press **Enter**.
    c. Insert a **Custom Table of Contents**, use **Distinctive** format, show 1 level of headings, show page numbers, right align page numbers, and include a solid line tab leader.
    d. Select the "Day 1" through "Day 8" lines of text in the table of contents and apply **12 pt**. *After* paragraph spacing.
13. Edit the following document properties.
    Title: Cycling Classic Tuscany: Tour Itinerary
    Company: American River Cycling Club
14. Insert and modify a cover page.
    a. Insert the **Semaphore** cover page.
    b. Select the current date as the date.
    c. Change the font size of the *Title* field to **48 pt**. and apply **bold** format.
    d. Delete the **Subtitle** (*Document Subtitle*) and **Author** fields.
    e. Change the font size of the *Company* field to **14 pt**. and apply **bold** format.
    f. Select the *Address* field and type www.arcc.org in the field.
15. Insert footers on the second and continuing pages.
    a. On the second page of the document (table of contents), edit the footer.
    b. Change the alignment to **right**, insert the **Company** document property field, deselect the field (right arrow key), and **space** once.
    c. Type | (press **Shift+** to type a vertical line) and **space** once.
    d. Type Page and **space** once.
    e. Insert a plain page number in the current position.
    f. **Bold** all of the text in the footer and close the footer.

16. Change *Display for Review* view, accept tracked changes, and turn off *Track Changes*.
    a. Change the *Display for Review* view to **All Markup**.
    b. Review the tracked changes in the document.
    c. Turn off **Track Changes** and accept all tracked changes in the document.
17. Share the document with your instructor.
    a. Save this document on *OneDrive* if you haven't already. If you don't have the ability to save to *OneDrive*, skip all of step 17.
    b. Click the **Share** button in the upper right of the Word window to open the *Share* pane.
    c. Type your instructor's email address in the *Invite* people text box.
    d. Select **Can edit** in the drop-down list below the email address.
    e. Type a brief message to your instructor and click the **Share** button.
    f. Click the **X** in the upper right corner of the *Share* pane to close it.
18. Save and close the document (Figure 3-121).

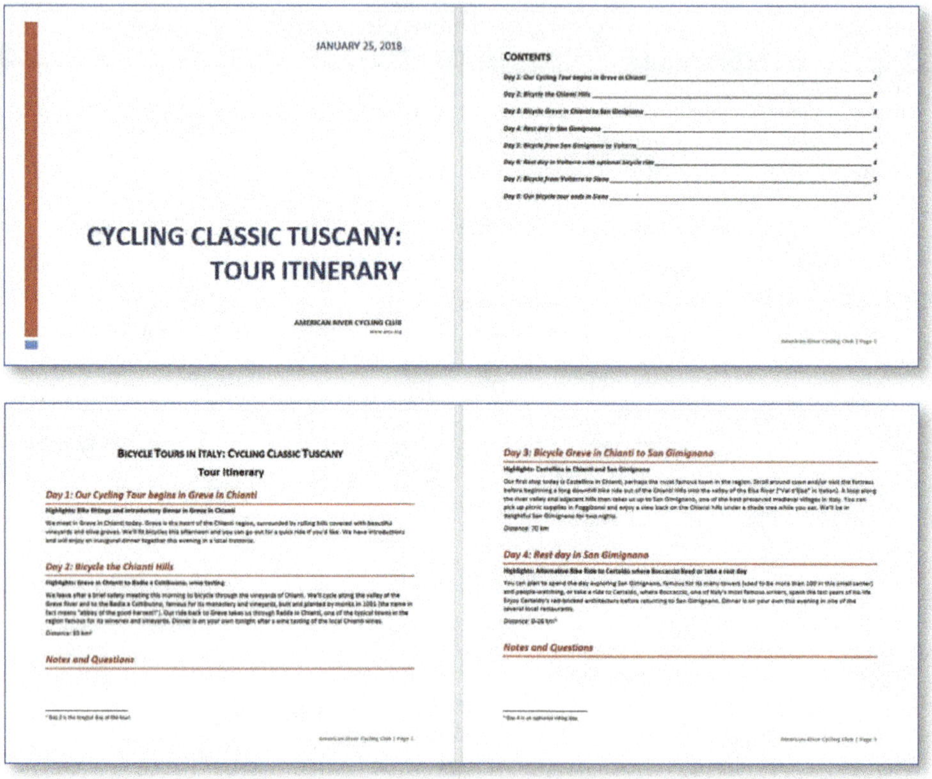

3-121 Word 3-7 completed (pages 1-4 of 6)

Challenge Project 3-8

Modify a report you have written for another class to include citations, a bibliography or works cited page, table of contents, cover page, and headers and footers. Use comments and *Track Changes*.
[Student Learning Outcomes 3.1, 3.2, 3.4, 3.5, 3.6, 3.7]

File Needed: None
Completed Project File Name: ***[your initials] Word 3-8.docx***

Open an existing report you have created and save it as [your initials] Word 3-8.

Modify your document according to the following guidelines:

- Turn on *Track Changes* and insert comments where necessary.
- Select the citation style to use for your report (e.g., APA, MLA, Chicago).
- Add citations to the body of your report and create sources.
- Add placeholders for citations in the body of your report.
- Insert a bibliography or works cited page at the end of your report.
- Use the *Source Manager* to edit placeholders and sources and add new sources, if necessary.
- Insert other citations in the body as necessary.
- Update the bibliography page.
- Apply headings styles and insert a table of contents.
- Insert a cover page and customize content.
- Insert a header, footer, and page number from the built-in list of options.
- Use different first page headers and footers.
- Insert page breaks to control pagination as necessary.

Challenge Project 3-9

Add footnotes and endnotes, heading styles, a table of contents, a cover page, and headers and footers to a multipage document that you have written. Use comments and *Track Changes*.
[Student Learning Outcomes 3.1, 3.2, 3.3, 3.5, 3.6, 3.7]

File Needed: None
Completed Project File Name: ***[your initials] Word 3-9.docx***

Open an existing report you have written for another class and save it as [your initials] Word 3-9.

Modify your document according to the following guidelines:

- Turn on *Track Changes* and insert comments where necessary.
- Add endnotes to the document.
- Convert endnotes to footnotes.
- Change the number format for footnotes.
- Move a footnote to a new location and delete a footnote.

- Insert a custom header or footer in your document.
- Add a page number in the header or footer of the document.
- Insert page breaks to control pagination as necessary.
- Apply headings styles and insert a table of contents.
- Insert a cover page and customize content.
- Insert custom header and footer content.
- Use different first page or odd and even page headers and footers.
- Insert page breaks to control pagination as necessary.

Challenge Project 3-10

Modify a report or multipage document you have written for another class to include a table of contents, a cover page, and headers and footers. Use comments and *Track Changes*.
[Student Learning Outcomes 3.1, 3.2, 3.5, 3.6, 3.7]

File Needed: None
Completed Project File Name: ***[your initials] Word 3-10.docx***

Open an existing report or multipage document and save it as [your initials] Word 3-10.

Modify your document according to the following guidelines:

- Turn on *Track Changes* and insert comments where necessary.
- Apply *Heading 1* and *Heading 2* styles to the headings of your document. If the document does not have headings, add two levels of headings to the document.
- Insert a built-in or custom table of contents as the first page of your document.
- Include two levels of headings in the table of contents.
- Customize the *Title*, *Company*, and *Author* document property fields.
- Insert a cover page of your choice.
- Customize the cover page by adding or removing a document property or content control fields.
- Add custom information to content control fields.
- Insert a header, footer, and page number from the built-in list of options.
- Use different first page or odd and even page headers and footers.
- Insert page breaks to control pagination as necessary.
- Update the table of contents.

CHAPTER 4

Using Tables, Columns, and Graphics

CHAPTER OVERVIEW

Tables, columns, and graphics enhance the appearance and readability of your Word documents. For example, you can use tables to attractively arrange and align information in column and row format, and columns improve readability and provide additional white space in a document. You can also insert and manipulate graphics to add attention-grabbing visual elements to your documents. This chapter introduces you to the Word tools that allow you to add and customize tables, columns, and graphics.

STUDENT LEARNING OUTCOMES (SLOs)

After completing this chapter, you will be able to:

SLO 4.1 Improve the design and readability of a document by using tables to present and arrange information (p. W4-210).

SLO 4.2 Modify a table by changing column and row size, aligning text, using the *Table Properties* dialog box, sorting data, and using *AutoFit* (p. W4-214).

SLO 4.3 Enhance the appearance and function of a table by applying borders and shading, using table styles, inserting formulas, and converting text into a table (p. W4-220).

SLO 4.4 Modify the layout and design of a document using columns to present information (p. W4-227).

SLO 4.5 Enrich a document by adding and modifying graphic elements such as pictures, shapes, *SmartArt*, and *WordArt* (p. W4-231).

CASE STUDY

For the Pause & Practice projects in this chapter, you modify a brochure for Emma Cavalli, a realtor consultant with Placer Hills Real Estate (PHRE). In the past, Emma distributed brochures that were poorly designed and negatively impacted the effectiveness of her message. You modify one of Emma's brochures to include tables, columns, and graphics to improve the overall layout and effectiveness of the document.

Pause & Practice 4-1: Modify an existing brochure to include a table that presents information attractively.

Pause & Practice 4-2: Enhance the table in the brochure by using borders, shading, and table styles.

Pause & Practice 4-3: Improve the readability of the brochure by arranging text in columns.

Pause & Practice 4-4: Add visual elements to the brochure to improve the overall design of the document.

WORD

SLO 4.1

Creating and Editing Tables

In Chapter 2, you learned about aligning information into column and row format using tab stops. ***Tables*** are another tool that you can use to organize information into column and row format. In addition to lining up information, tables allow you more formatting options than tabs.

> **MORE INFO**
>
> On web pages, most of the information is organized into table and row format even though you might not see table borders or structure.

Tables

You can insert tables almost anywhere in a Word document. A table consists of individual ***cells*** where you enter information. Cells are grouped into ***columns*** and ***rows***. When using tables, it is important to distinguish between cells, columns, and rows (Figure 4-1).

- ***Cell***: The area where a column and row intersect
- ***Column***: A vertical grouping of cells (think of vertical columns that support a building)
- ***Row***: A horizontal grouping of cells (think of horizontal rows of seating in a stadium or auditorium)

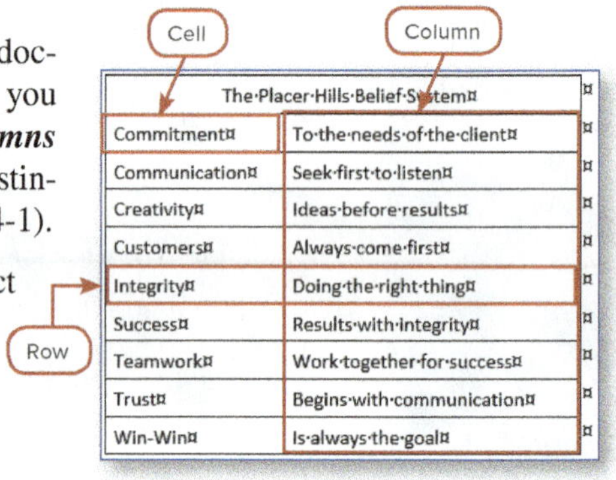

4-1 Table

HOW TO: Insert a Table

1. Place your insertion point in your document where you want to insert a table.
2. Click the **Insert** tab.
3. Click the **Table** button [*Tables* group] to open the drop-down list.
4. Click and drag across the *Insert Table* grid to select the number of columns and rows you want in the table (Figure 4-2). The table is inserted into your document.
   - As you drag across the grid, the *Insert Table* label changes to display the size of the table (e.g., *3×7 Table*).

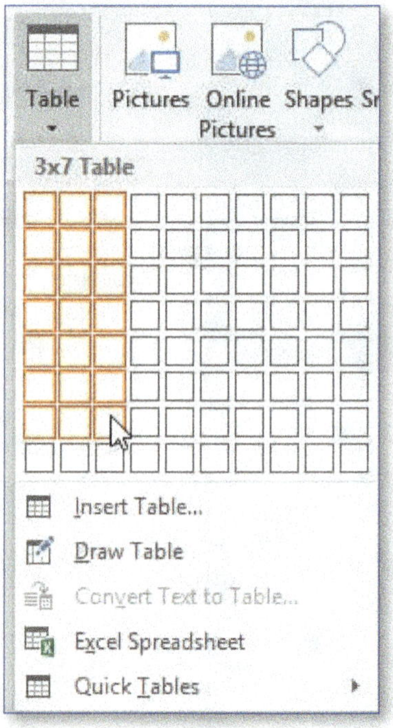

4-2 *Insert Table* drop-down list

> **MORE INFO**
>
> Word lists table dimensions in column and row format. For example, a three-column and seven-row table is a 3×7 table.

When you insert a table using the *Insert Table* grid, the table size is limited depending on the size and resolution of your computer screen. You can also insert a table using the ***Insert Table*** dialog box.

▸ HOW TO: Insert a Table Using the Insert Table Dialog Box

1. Click the **Insert** tab.
2. Click the **Table** button [*Tables* group] to open the drop-down list.
3. Select **Insert Table**. The *Insert Table* dialog box opens (Figure 4-3).
4. Select the desired number of columns and rows in the *Table size* area.
5. Select how the table is distributed horizontally between the left and right margins in the *AutoFit behavior* area.
6. Choose **OK** to insert the table.

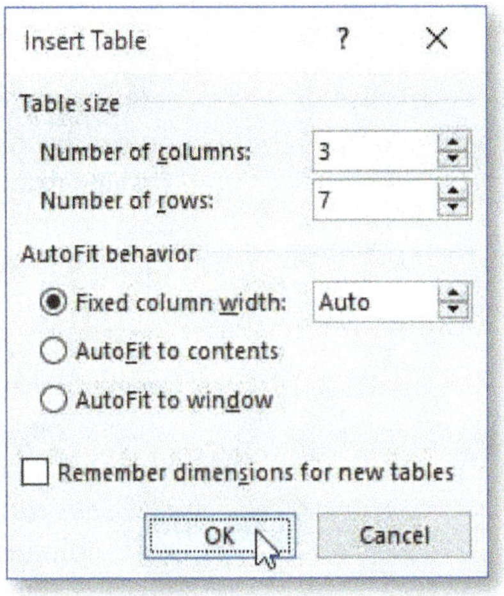

4-3 *Insert Table* dialog box

Navigate within a Table

To move the insertion point within a table, press **Tab** (or the **right arrow** key on your keyboard) to move forward one cell in the current row. When you get to the end of a row and press *Tab*, the insertion point moves to the first cell in the next row. **Shift+Tab** (or the **left arrow** key) moves you back one cell at a time. You can also use your pointer and click in a cell to insert the insertion point.

Table Tools Layout Tab

When you insert a table into a document, the ***Table Tools tabs*** display on the *Ribbon*. There are two *Table Tools* tabs: ***Design*** and ***Layout***. These context-sensitive toolbars display whenever you place the insertion point in the table or select a region of the table. The *Table Tools Layout* tab provides a variety of formatting options (Figure 4-4). For more on the *Table Tools Design* tab, see *SLO 4.3: Formatting and Editing Tables*.

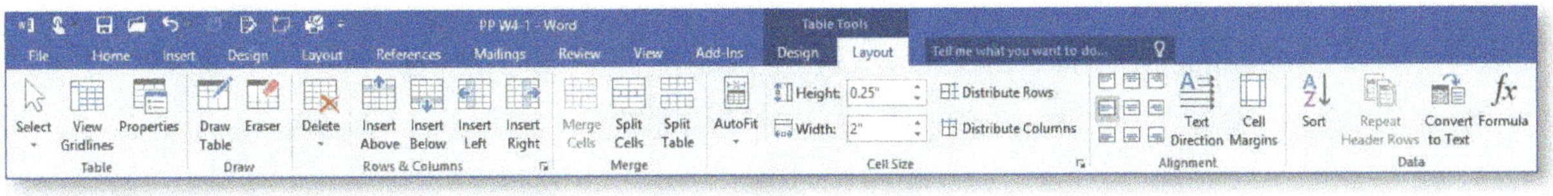

4-4 *Table Tools Layout* tab

Select Table and Text

When working with tables, you can select the entire table, a cell, column, or row, or multiple cells, columns, or rows to apply formatting changes. Word provides a variety of table selection tools.

- ***Table selector handle***: This handle appears in the upper left of the table when the pointer is on the table (Figure 4-5). Click the **table selector** to select the entire table.

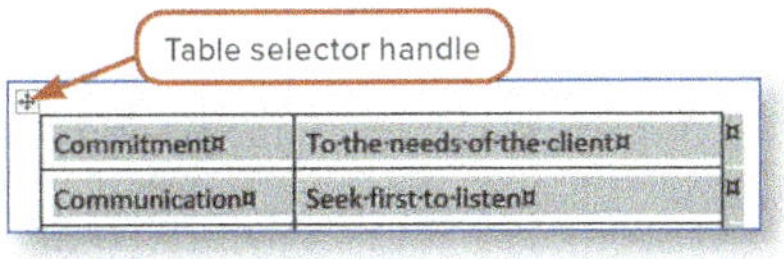

4-5 Table selector handle

- ***Row selector***: The row selector is the right-pointing arrow when your pointer is just to the left of the table row (Figure 4-6). When the pointer becomes the row selector, click to select a single row. To select multiple rows, click and drag up or down.
- ***Column selector***: The column selector is the thick, black down arrow when your pointer is on the top of a column (Figure 4-7). When the pointer becomes the column selector, click to select a single column. To select multiple columns, click and drag left or right.
- ***Cell selector***: The cell selector is the thick, black right-pointing arrow when your pointer is just inside the left border of a cell (Figure 4-8). When the pointer becomes the cell selector, click to select a single cell. To select multiple cells, click and drag left, right, up, or down. When the cell selector displays, double-click to select the entire row.
- ***Select button***: The select button is on the *Table Tools Layout* tab in the *Table* group. Click the **Select** button to access a drop-down list of table selection options (Figure 4-9).

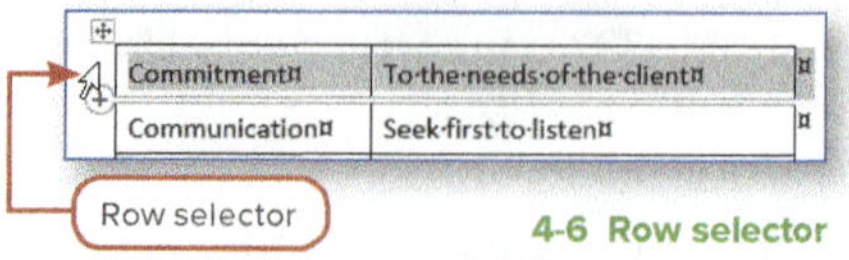

4-6 Row selector

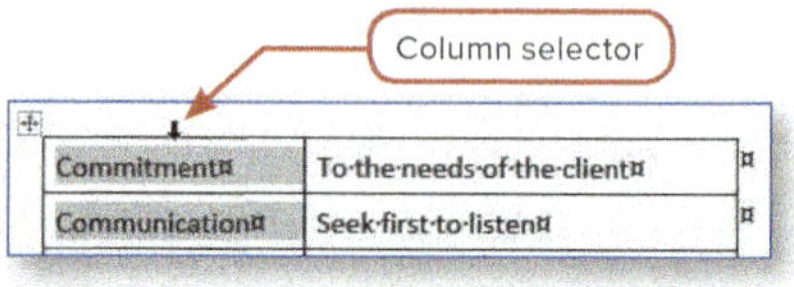

4-7 Column selector

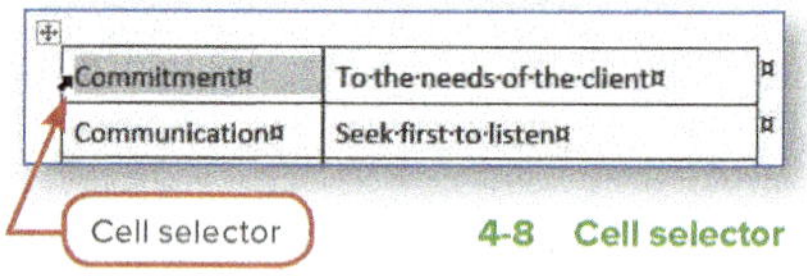

4-8 Cell selector

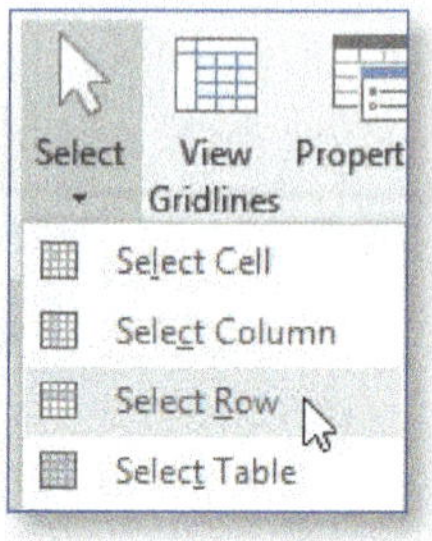

4-9 *Select* drop-down list

Add Rows and Columns

When you insert a table into a document, you are not locked into your original table dimensions; you can always add columns and rows to the table in a variety of ways.

- ***Insert Control***: Place your pointer on the left outside edge of a row or top outside edge of a column to display the insert row or column control (plus sign). Click the **insert control** to add a row or column (Figure 4-10). Select multiple rows or columns and click the insert control to add the number or rows or columns selected.
- ***Table Tools Layout tab***: In the *Rows & Columns* group, you can insert a row above or below the current row or a column to the left or right of the current column (see Figure 4-4).
- ***Mini toolbar***: Select a cell, row, column, or table to display the mini toolbar. You can also right-click the table to display the mini toolbar. Click the **Insert** button to display a list of insert options (Figure 4-11).
- ***Insert Cells dialog box***: Open this dialog box by clicking the **Rows & Columns** launcher on the *Table Tools Layout* tab (Figure 4-12).
- ***Tab***: When your insertion point is in the last cell in the last row, you can press **Tab** to insert a new row below the last row.

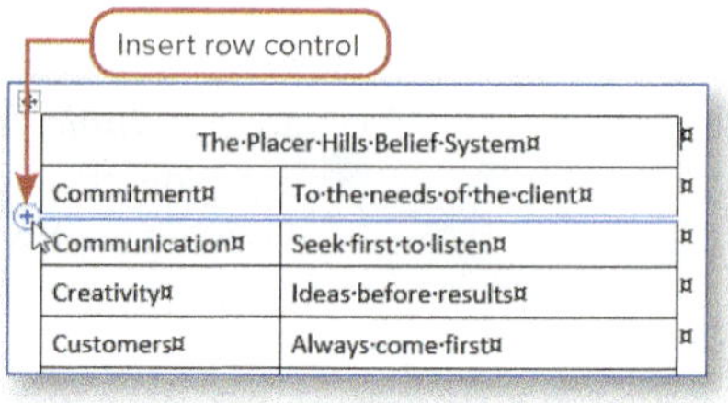

4-10 Insert row control

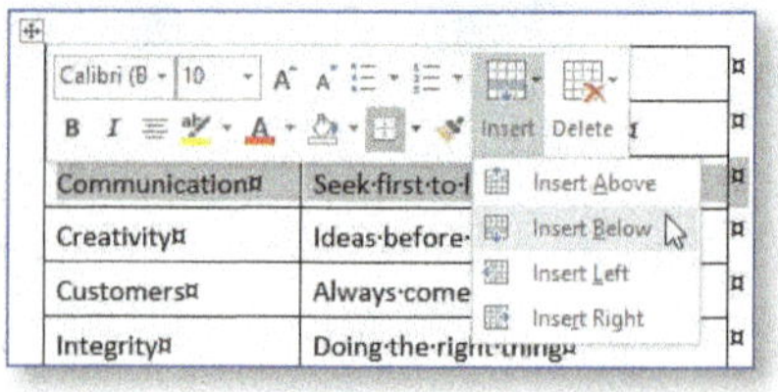

4-11 Use the mini toolbar to insert a row

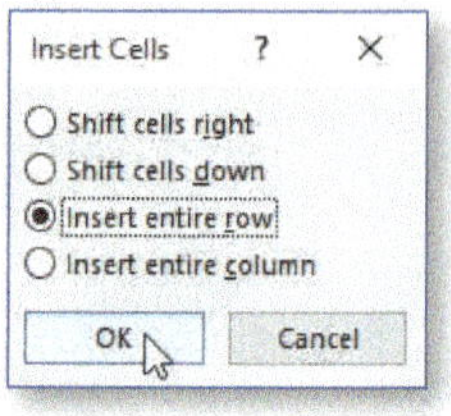

4-12 *Insert Cells* dialog box

> **MORE INFO**
>
> Be careful when using *Shift cells right* from the *Insert Cells* dialog box. Selecting this option moves cells to the right creating a new column in that one row, not the entire table.

Merge and Split Cells

Many times when you use tables you want to span information across multiple columns, such as when you are inserting a title or subtitle in a table. You can do this by merging columns, rows, and cells.

HOW TO: Merge Cells

1. Select the cells to merge.
2. Click the **Table Tools Layout** tab.
3. Click the **Merge Cells** button [*Merge* group] (Figure 4-13). The cells merge into one cell.

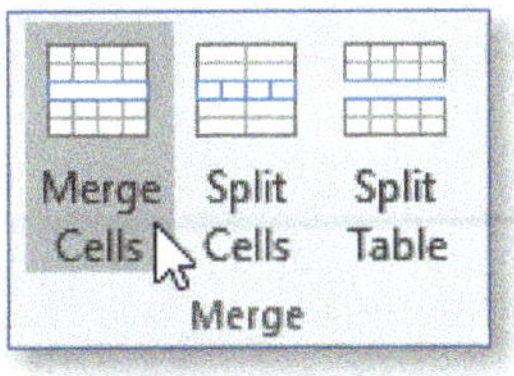

4-13 *Merge Cells* button

Word also allows you to split a cell into multiple cells. You can split cells that were previously merged or split a single cell into multiple columns and rows. When you are splitting cells, the *Split Cells* dialog box prompts you to specify the number of columns and rows.

HOW TO: Split Cells

1. Select the cell(s) to split.
2. Click the **Table Tools Layout** tab.
3. Click the **Split Cells** button [*Merge* group]. The *Split Cells* dialog box opens (Figure 4-14).
4. Select the number of columns and rows that you want in the split cell.
   - By default, the *Merge cells before split* check box is selected. When you select this check box, Word merges the selected cells before splitting them into the desired number of columns and rows.
5. Click **OK** to split the cells.

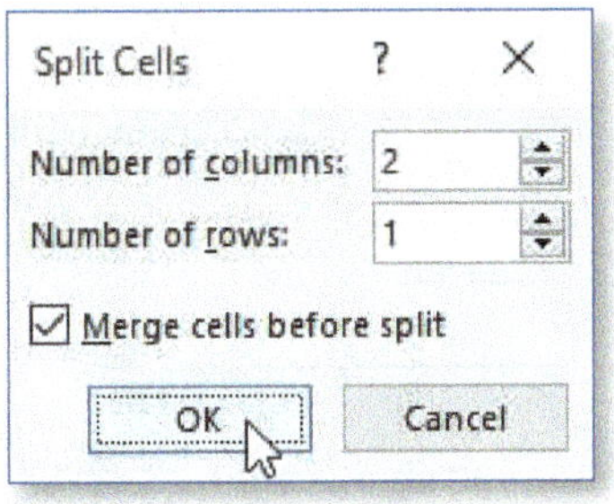

4-14 *Split Cells* dialog box

> **ANOTHER WAY**
>
> Both *Merge Cells* and *Split Cells* are available from the context menu.

Copy or Move Columns and Rows

You can copy or move columns and rows in a table similar to how you copy or move text in a document. Select the column or row to copy or move, and use one of the following methods:

- ***Keyboard Shortcuts***: **Ctrl+C** (copy), **Ctrl+X** (cut), and **Ctrl+V** (paste).
- ***Context menu***: Right-click the selected column or row and select **Cut, Copy**, or **Paste**.

- ***Drag and drop***: Drag and drop the column or row in the new location to move it. Hold the **Ctrl** key while dragging and dropping to copy a column or row.
- ***Clipboard group on the Home tab***: Use the **Cut, Copy**, and **Paste** buttons in this group.

Delete Columns and Rows

At some point, you may need to remove columns or rows from your table. Removing columns and rows is very similar to inserting columns and rows. Click the **Delete** button in the *Rows & Columns* group on the *Table Tools Layout* tab or the mini toolbar to remove cells, columns, rows, or an entire table. You have the following options (Figure 4-15):

- *Delete Cells . . .* : Opens the *Delete Cells* dialog box.
- *Delete Columns*
- *Delete Rows*
- *Delete Table*

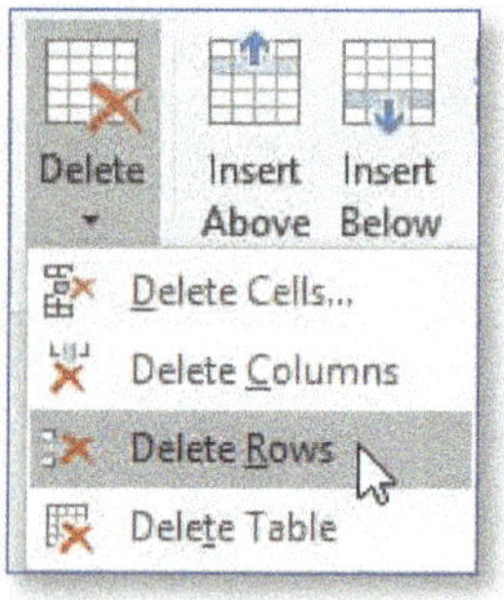

4-15 *Delete* options

Delete a Table

If you select an entire table and press *Delete* on your keyboard, only the information in the table is deleted; the blank table remains in your document. To delete a table, you select the **Delete Table** option from the *Delete* drop-down on the *Table Tool Layout* tab or mini toolbar (see Figure 4-15). The **Delete Table** option is also available on the context menu when you select and right-click a table.

SLO 4.2

Arranging Text in Tables

You can adjust the width of columns and the height of rows and control how text is aligned within the cells of a table. Word provides you with a variety of table resizing and text alignment options. You also can sort information automatically within a table.

Resize Columns and Rows

Many times you need to adjust columns and rows to better fit the information in the table. When you insert a table into a document, the default size for the table is the width of the document. You can manually adjust the width of columns and the height of rows in a couple of ways.

Drag the column or row borders to increase or decrease the size of a column or row. When you place your pointer on the vertical border of a column, the pointer changes to a ***resizing pointer*** (Figure 4-16). Drag the column border to the left or right to adjust the size of the column. You can use the same method to adjust the height of a row by dragging the top or bottom border of a row up or down.

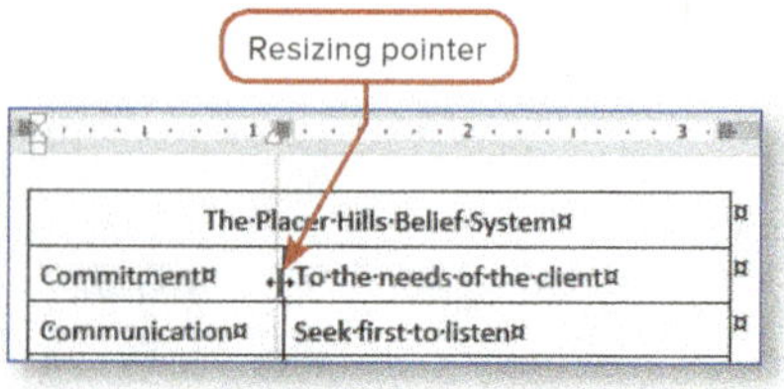

4-16 Manually adjust column width

> **MORE INFO**
>
> When you manually adjust the height of a row, it adjusts the height of the selected row only. Usually, you want to keep the height of rows consistent.

Word also allows you to type a specific size for columns and rows. It is best to adjust the size of columns and rows before merging cells. After cells are merged, it is difficult to adjust column and row sizes of a table. If you're adjusting the size of columns or rows after merging cells, be very specific about the cells you select.

HOW TO: Resize Columns and Rows

1. Select the cells, columns, or rows you want to resize.
2. Click the **Table Tools Layout** tab.
3. Change the height or width to the desired size [*Cell Size* group] (Figure 4-17).
   - Manually type the specific size or use the up or down arrows (spinner box) to resize.

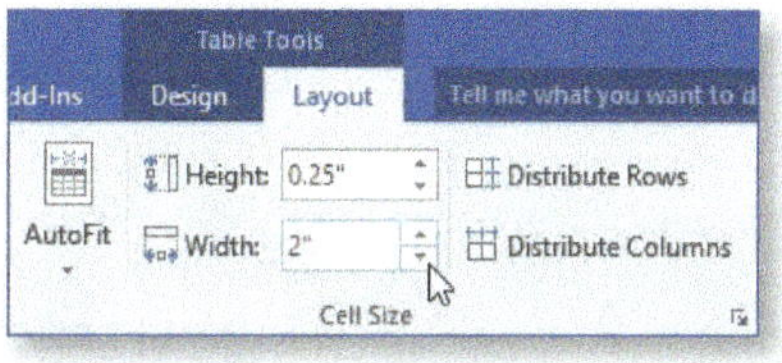

4-17 Set cell *Height* and *Width*

AutoFit a Table

When you insert a table into a document, the table is automatically set to the width of the document (inside the left and right margins). Word has three different ***AutoFit*** options to adjust the column width of the table. Click the **AutoFit** button in the *Cell Size* group on the *Table Tools Layout* tab to display the *AutoFit* options (Figure 4-18).

- ***AutoFit Contents***: Adjusts column widths to fit the contents of the table
- ***AutoFit Window***: Distributes the column widths so the table fits across the width of the page (this is the default setting when you insert a table into a document)
- ***Fixed Column Width***: Adjusts columns to a fixed column width

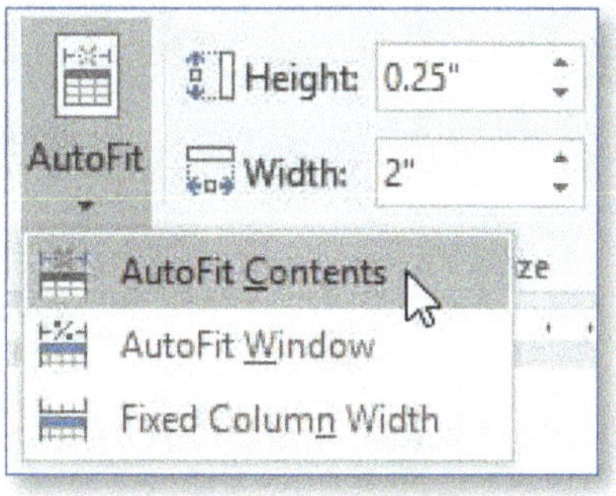

4-18 *AutoFit* options

MORE INFO

When you insert a table, the table has the same formatting as the text in the document. If your rows seem too high, it might be because your document contains *Before* or *After* paragraph spacing that is controlling the height of the rows in your table.

Distribute Rows and Columns

Word provides you with features to evenly distribute rows and columns, which is useful when the sizes of columns and rows in a table are uneven. ***Distribute Rows*** and ***Distribute Columns*** are on the *Table Tools Layout* tab in the *Cell Size* group (Figure 4-19).

- ***Distribute Rows***: This feature evenly distributes the rows based on the height of the existing table, making all rows a consistent height.
- ***Distribute Columns***: This feature evenly distributes the columns based on the width of the existing table, making all columns the same width.

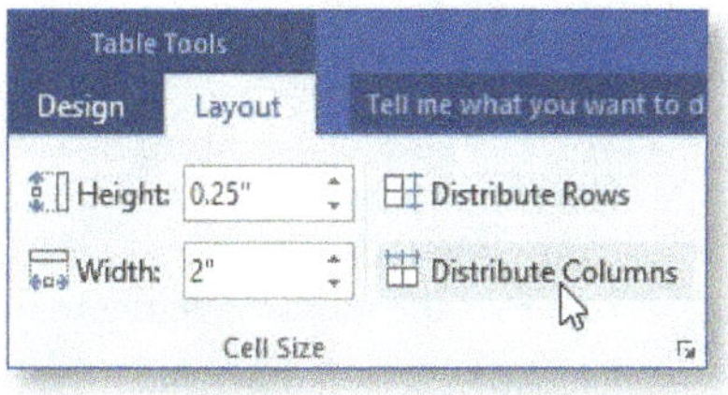

4-19 Distribute rows and columns

ANOTHER WAY

AutoFit and *Distribute* options are available from the context menu when a table is selected.

Text Alignment

In Chapter 1, you learned about paragraph alignment and how to left align, right align, center, or justify text. In Chapter 2, you learned how to change the vertical alignment of a page or section. Similarly, when using tables, you have both horizontal and vertical alignment options. Text can be aligned vertically and horizontally within a cell and can be aligned independently of other cells. There are nine alignment options within the cell of a table. The following alignment options are in the *Alignment* group on the *Table Tools Layout* tab (Figure 4-20):

- *Align Top Left*
- *Align Top Center*
- *Align Top Right*
- *Align Center Left*
- *Align Center*
- *Align Center Right*
- *Align Bottom Left*
- *Align Bottom Center*
- *Align Bottom Right*

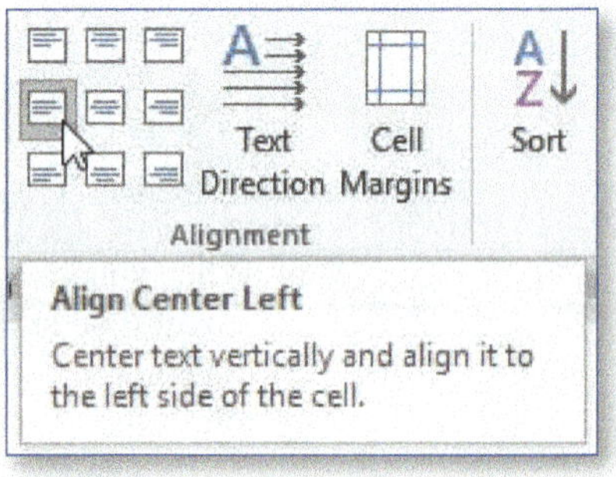

4-20 Text alignment options within a table

MORE INFO

For horizontal alignment, text in the table is usually aligned on the left and numbers are aligned on the right. If you increase row height, it's generally best to vertically center text within a cell.

Cell Margins

In addition to being able to change alignment in cells, you can also adjust ***cell margins***. Just like the margins on a Word document, the cells of a table have top, bottom, left, and right margins. Cell margins add space around text within a cell. The default cell margins are 0" top and bottom, and 0.08" left and right.

HOW TO: Change Cell Margins

1. Select the entire table to change the cell margins for all cells in the table.
   - You can also change cell margins on individual cells.
2. Click the **Table Tools Layout** tab.
3. Click the **Cell Margins** button [*Alignment* group]. The *Table Options* dialog box opens (Figure 4-21).
4. Enter the desired changes to the *Top*, *Bottom*, *Left*, and *Right* cell margins.
   - You can also add spacing between cells in the *Default cell spacing* area. This puts padding (space) around the outside of the cells.
   - If you don't want the size of your table to be automatically adjusted, deselect the **Automatically resize to fit contents** check box.
5. Click **OK** to apply the cell margin settings.

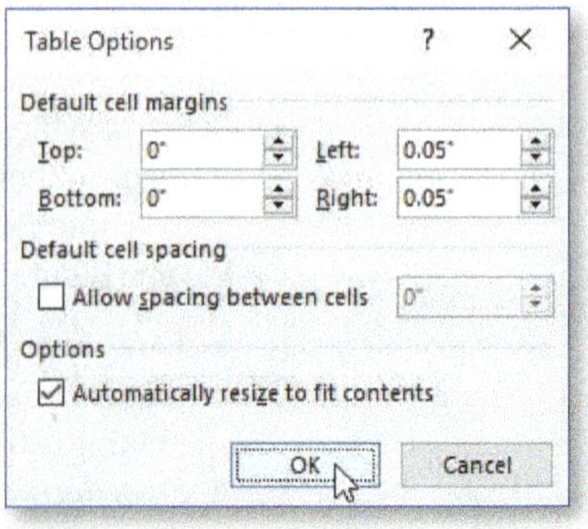

4-21 *Table Options* dialog box

Table Properties Dialog Box

The ***Table Properties*** dialog box consolidates many table sizing and alignment options in one location. In the dialog box, there are separate tabs for *Table*, *Row*, *Column*, *Cell*, and *Alt Text*. To open the *Table Properties* dialog box, click the **Properties** button in the *Table* group on the *Table Tools Layout* tab (Figure 4-22). You can also open the *Table Properties* dialog box from the context menu.

- ***Table tab***: Adjusts the size of the table, alignment, text wrapping, positioning, borders and shading, and cell margins
- ***Row tab***: Adjusts the height of rows and controls how rows break between pages
- ***Column tab***: Adjusts the width of columns
- ***Cell tab***: Adjusts the width of cells, vertical alignment of information in cells, and cell margins
- ***Alt Text tab***: Alternative text (Alt text) is an information tag that displays when place your pointer on the table. Screen readers use Alt text in tables to accommodate those with visual impairments. Alt text is very common on web pages.

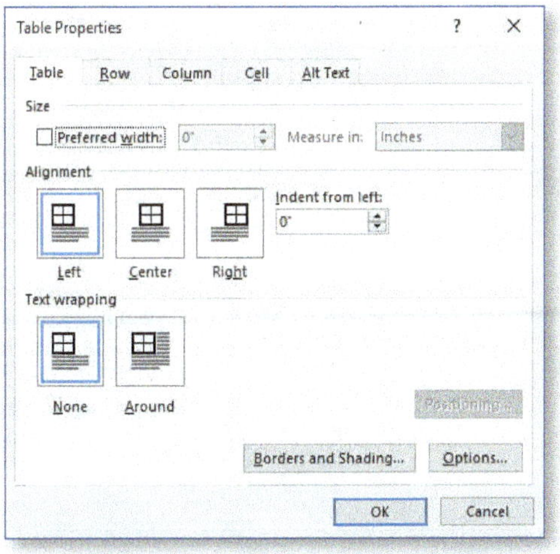

4-22 *Table Properties* dialog box

Sort Data in Tables

A very useful feature in Word is the ability to sort information within a table. You might want to arrange the text in the first column of a table alphabetically or sort numbers in descending order. When you use the ***Sort*** feature on a table, rows of information rearrange according to how you specify the sort.

▶HOW TO: Sort Data in a Table

1. Place your insertion point in the table.
2. Select the **Table Tools Layout** tab.
3. Click the **Sort** button [*Data* group]. The entire table is selected and the *Sort* dialog box opens (Figure 4-23).
4. Click the **Sort by** drop-down list and select the column to use to sort the table.
   - You can sort by any of the columns in the table.
5. Click the **Type** drop-down list and select the type of sort to perform.
   - You can sort by *Text*, *Number*, or *Date*.
6. Click the **Using** drop-down list and select the cell information to use in the sort.
   - *Paragraphs* is the default option and usually this is the only option available.

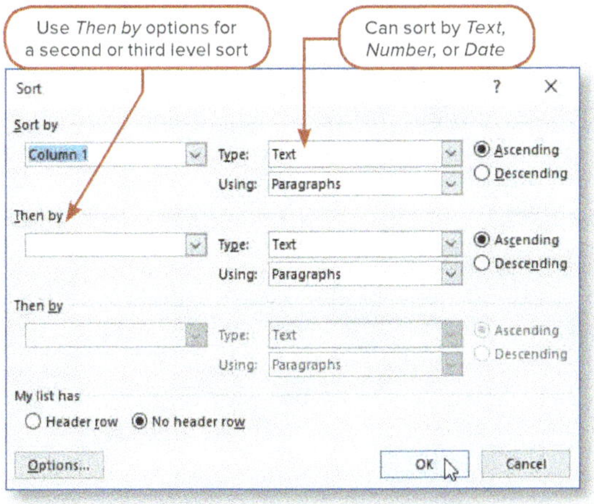

4-23 *Sort* dialog box

7. Select **Ascending** (A to Z or 1 to 10) or **Descending** (Z to A or 10 to 1) for the sort order.
   - Add a second or third sort on different columns if desired. Click the **Then by** drop-down list to add additional sorts.
   - If your table has a header row (title or column headings), click the **Header row** radio button to omit this row from the sort.
8. Click **OK** to perform the sort. Your table is sorted according to your settings.

MORE INFO

If your table has both a title and column headings, select the rows of the table to be sorted before clicking the **Sort** button so that only the data in the table is sorted.

ANOTHER WAY

Manually sort rows using copy (**Ctrl+C**), cut (**Ctrl+X**), and paste (**Ctrl+V**), or the drag and drop method.

PAUSE & PRACTICE: WORD 4-1

For this Pause & Practice project, you begin modifying Emma Cavalli's brochure. You add a table to the end of this document and then modify the table.

File Needed: ***Brochure-04.docx*** *(Student data files are available in the* Library *of your SIMnet account)*
Completed Project File Name: ***[your initials] PP W4-1.docx***

1. Open the ***Brochure-04*** document from your student data files.
2. Save this document as [your initials] PP W4-1.
3. Move to the end of the document and insert a table.
   a. Press **Ctrl+End** to move to the end of the document.
   b. Click the **Insert** tab.
   c. Click the **Table** button [*Tables* group] and select a **3×7** table using the table grid. The table displays in the document.
4. Type the information in the following table. Press **Tab** to move from one cell to the next cell in the row. Leave the third column blank.

Commitment	To the needs of the client	
Communication	Seek first to listen	
Integrity	Doing the right thing	
Customers	Always come first	
Teamwork	Work together for success	
Success	Results with integrity	
Creativity	Ideas before results	

5. Delete a column and insert rows.
   a. Place the insertion point in any cell in the last column.
   b. Click the **Delete** button [*Table Tools Layout* tab, *Rows & Columns* group] and select **Delete Columns**.
   c. Place the insertion point in the second row and click the **Insert Below** button [*Table Tools Layout* tab, *Rows & Columns* group]. A blank row is inserted below the second row.
   d. Type the following information in the new third row:

Trust	Begins with communication

   e. Click the last cell of the table (bottom right cell) and press **Tab** to insert a new row at the bottom of the table.
   f. Type the following information in the new last row:

Win-Win	Is always the goal

6. *AutoFit* the table and adjust column and row size.
   a. Place your insertion point in the table.
   b. Click the **AutoFit** button [*Table Tools Layout* tab, *Cell Size* group] and select **AutoFit Contents**. The column widths adjust to fit the contents of the table.
   c. Place the insertion point in the first column.
   d. Change the *Width* to **1.2"** [*Table Tool Layout* tab, *Cell Size* group]
   e. Place the insertion point in the second column.
   f. Change the *Width* to **2"**.
   g. Use the table selector handle to select the entire table.
   h. Click the **Properties** button [*Table Tool Layout* tab, *Table* group] to open the *Table Properties* dialog box (Figure 4-24).
   i. Click the **Row** tab and check the **Specify height** box.
   j. Type .25 in the *Specify height* field and select **Exactly** in the *Row height is* drop-down list.
   k. Click **OK** to close the *Tables Properties* dialog box and apply these settings.

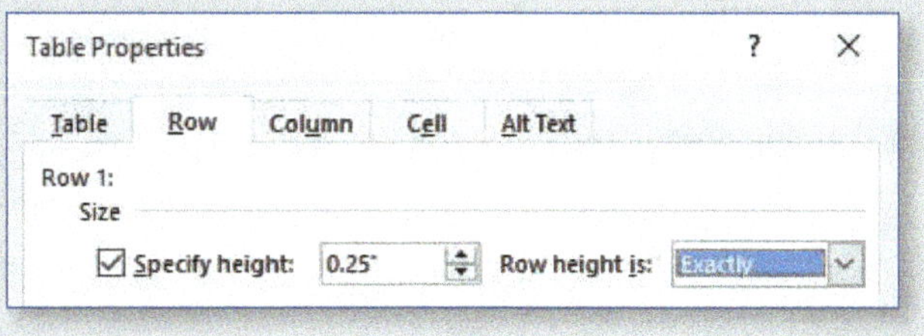

4-24 Change row height on the selected table

7. Insert a row and merge cells.
   a. Click anywhere in the table so the entire table is no longer selected.
   b. Select the first row of the table.
   c. Click the **Insert** button on the mini toolbar and select **Insert Above** to insert a new row at the top of the table.
   d. Select the new first row (if it is not already selected) and click the **Merge Cells** button [*Table Tools Layout* tab, *Merge* group]. The cells in the first row merge into one cell.
   e. Type The Placer Hills Belief System in the merged first row.
8. Sort the table by text in the first column.
   a. Select the **second through tenth (last) rows** of the table. Don't select the first merged row.
   b. Click the **Sort** button [*Table Tools Layout* tab, *Data* group]. The *Sort* dialog box opens (Figure 4-25).

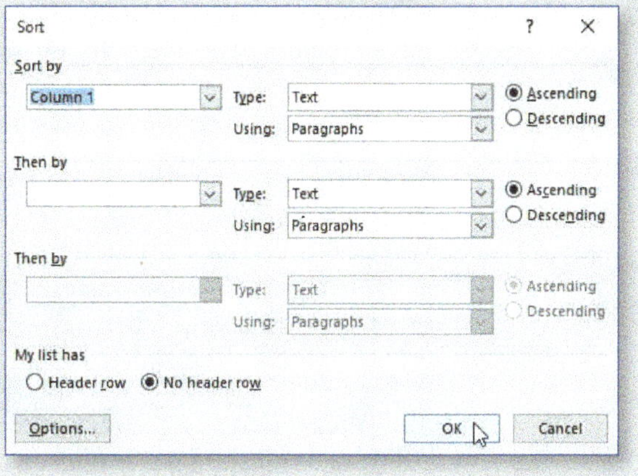

4-25 Sort table by first column in ascending order

c. Sort by **Column 1** in **Ascending** order. Leave *Type* as **Text** and *Using* as **Paragraphs**.
d. Click **OK** to sort the rows below the title in alphabetical order.

9. Change cell margins and text alignment.
   a. Select the entire table.

> **MORE INFO**
>
> Click the **table selector** handle in the upper left of the table or click the **Select** button in the *Table* group on the *Table Tool Layout* tab and choose **Select Table**.

   b. Click the **Cell Margins** button [*Table Tools Layout* tab, *Alignment* group]. The *Table Options* dialog box opens (Figure 4-26).
   c. Change the *Left* and *Right* cell margins **0.05"**.
   d. Check the **Automatically resize to fit contents** box (if it is not already checked) and click **OK**.
   e. With the table still selected, click the **Align Center Left** button (first alignment button in the second row) [*Table Tools Layout* tab, *Alignment* group].
   f. Place the insertion point in the first row of the table to deselect the table.
   g. Right-click the first row of the table and click the **Center** button on the mini toolbar. The title centers horizontally.
10. Save and close this document (Figure 4-27).

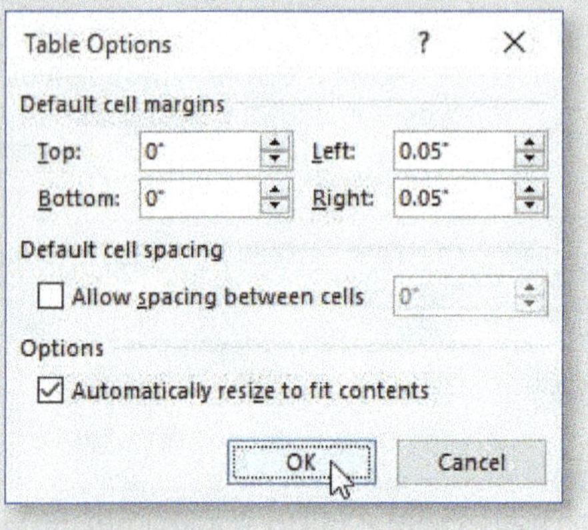

4-26 Change cell margins

The·Placer·Hills·Belief·System¤	
Commitment¤	To·the·needs·of·the·client¤
Communication¤	Seek·first·to·listen¤
Creativity¤	Ideas·before·results¤
Customers¤	Always·come·first¤
Integrity¤	Doing·the·right·thing¤
Success¤	Results·with·integrity¤
Teamwork¤	Work·together·for·success¤
Trust¤	Begins·with·communication¤
Win-Win¤	Is·always·the·goal¤

4-27 PP W4-1 completed (table only displayed)

SLO 4.3

Formatting and Editing Tables

In addition to the ability to adjust the structure of tables, Word provides you with many tools to enhance the overall appearance of tables. For example, you can add custom borders and shading and table styles to tables. You can also add formulas to tables and convert text into tables.

Table Tools Design Tab

Word provides you with two *Table Tools* tabs when you work with tables: *Design* and *Layout*. Both tabs are context-sensitive and are only displayed when the table or portion of the table is selected or when the insertion point is in the table. The ***Table Tools Design tab*** allows you to apply table style options, table styles, and borders (Figure 4-28). You can also draw tables using the tools on this tab.

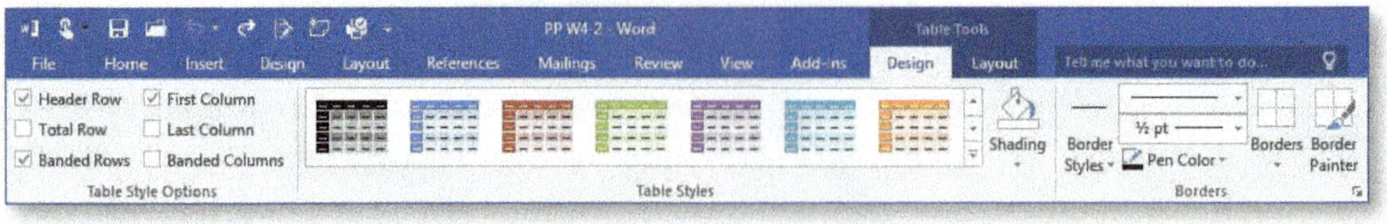

4-28 Table Tools Design tab

Table Borders

By default, when you insert a table, Word formats the table with borders. You can apply borders to an individual cell, a group of cells, or an entire table. When applying borders, it is important to be very specific when selecting the area of the table on which to apply the borders.

The *Borders* button is in the *Borders* group on the *Table Tools Design* tab, in the *Paragraph* group on the *Home* tab or on the mini toolbar. The *Borders* drop-down list displays a variety of border options (Figure 4-29). You can also apply borders using the *Borders and Shading* dialog box.

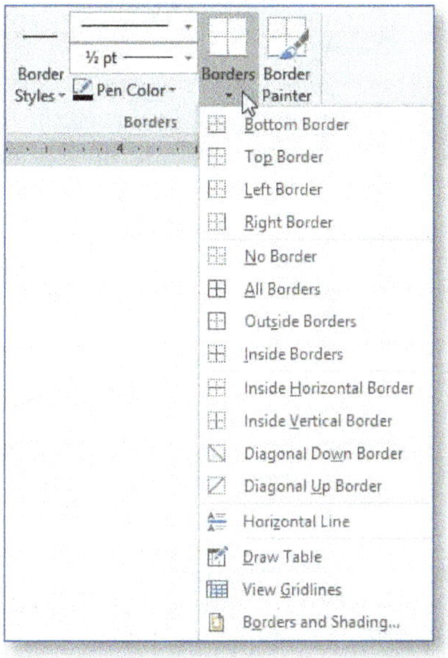

4-29 *Borders* drop-down list

▸ HOW TO: Apply Borders to a Table Using the Borders and Shading Dialog Box

1. Select the entire table or the desired area of the table where you want borders.
2. Click the **Borders** button [*Table Tools Design* tab, *Borders* group] and select **Borders and Shading** to open the *Borders and Shading* dialog box (Figure 4-30).
   - Alternatively, click the **Borders** button [*Home* tab, *Paragraph* group] or the **Borders** button on the mini toolbar.
   - The selection in the *Apply to* area depends on whether you are applying borders to the entire table or selected cells or rows.
3. In the *Setting* area, select the type of border from the list of options.
   - You can remove all borders by selecting **None**.
4. Select the *Style* of the border from the list of options.
5. Click the **Color** drop-down list and select the color of the border.
6. Click the **Width** drop-down list and select the width of the border.
7. In the *Preview* area, you can see how your borders will be applied to your table.
   - In the *Preview* area, you can also apply or deselect borders on specific areas of your table.
   - Click the border buttons in the *Preview* area or click the diagram borders to turn borders on or off.
8. Click **OK** to apply the border settings and close the *Borders and Shading* dialog box.

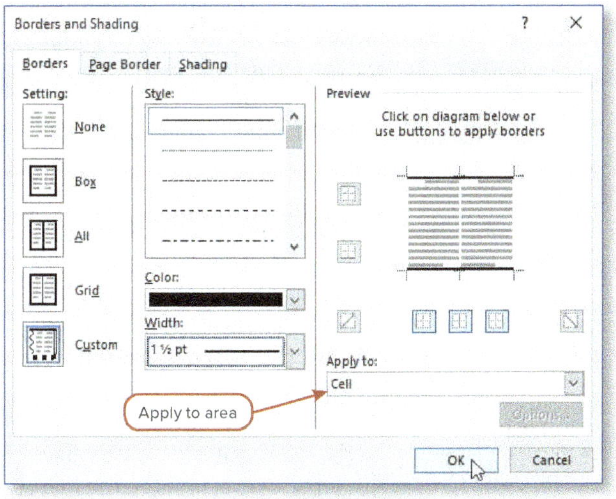

4-30 *Borders and Shading* dialog box

View Gridlines

When borders are removed from a table, it is difficult to see the column and row structure of your table. If you don't have table borders, click **View Gridlines** [*Table Tools Layout* tab, *Table* group]. Gridlines display in the document only; they do not print (Figure 4-31).

THE·PLACER·HILLS·BELIEF·SYSTEM¤	
COMMITMENT¤	To·the·needs·of·the·client¤
COMMUNICATION¤	Seek·first·to·listen¤
CREATIVITY¤	Ideas·before·results¤
CUSTOMERS¤	Always·come·first¤
INTEGRITY¤	Doing·the·right·thing¤
SUCCESS¤	Results·with·integrity¤
TEAMWORK¤	Work·together·for·success¤
TRUST¤	Begins·with·communication¤
WIN-WIN¤	Is·always·the·goal¤

4-31 Table displayed with *View Gridlines* and no borders

Table Shading

Like table borders, you can apply shading to specific cells or to an entire table. In the *Shading* drop-down list in the *Table Styles* group on the *Table Tools Design* tab, you can choose from *Theme Colors* or *Standard Colors* (Figure 4-32). Theme colors change depending on the theme of your document. You can choose a custom color by selecting **More Colors**, which opens the *Colors* dialog box. You can remove shading by selecting **No Color**.

You can also apply, change, or remove shading from the *Shading* tab in the *Borders and Shading* dialog box.

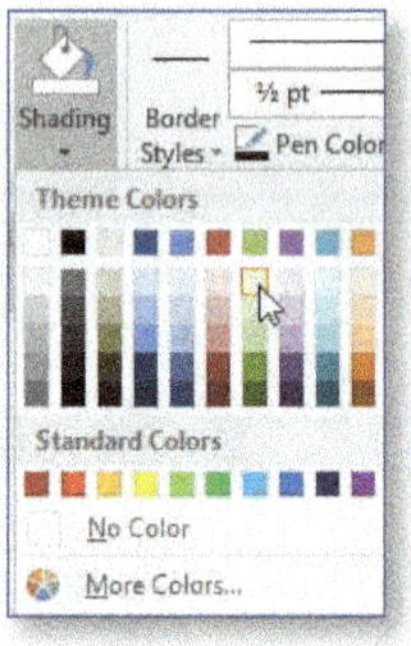

4-32 Table *Shading* options

ANOTHER WAY

Apply borders and shading from the mini toolbar by right-clicking the table or a portion of the table.

Table Styles

Table Styles are built-in styles that you can apply to your tables, which are similar to text styles (see *SLO 2.7: Using Styles and Themes*). Table styles include a variety of borders, shading, alignment, and formatting options. Word provides a wide variety of built-in table styles in the *Table Styles* group on the *Table Tools Design* tab. Click the **More** button on the bottom right to display the *Table Styles* gallery (Figure 4-33).

After you apply a table style, you can still customize all aspects of the table. You can also remove all formatting of a table by selecting the **Clear** option at the bottom of the *Table Styles* gallery.

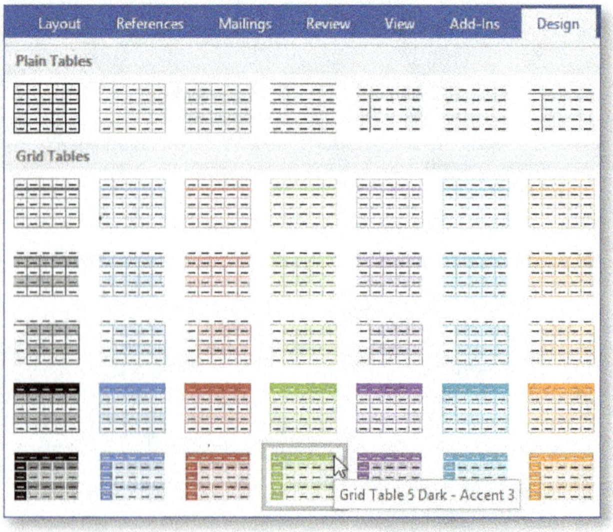

4-33 *Table Styles* gallery

Table Style Options

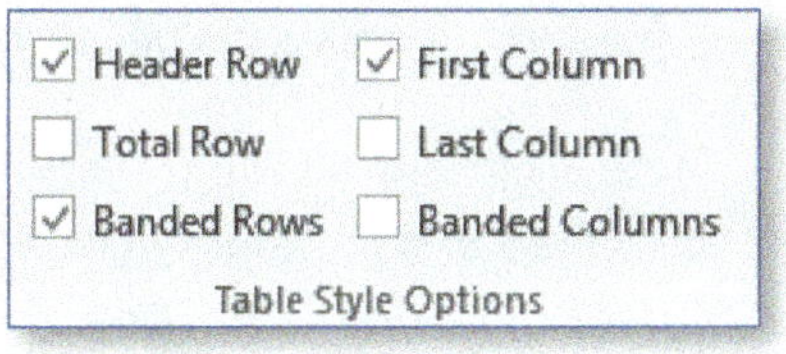

4-34 *Table Style Options* group

Word offers a variety of ***Table Style Options*** to customize tables (Figure 4-34). For example, many tables have a header row or column, or a total or last row, where you might want to apply special formatting for emphasis. When you select any of these *Table Style Options*, Word applies special formatting to the table style you select. Select your table style options before applying a table style.

MORE INFO

Banded Rows apply shading to every other row. You can also apply ***Banded Columns*** in the *Table Style Options* group.

HOW TO: Apply a Table Style and Table Style Options

1. Select the table on which to apply a table style.
2. Click the **Table Tools Design** tab.
3. Select the *Table Style Options* you want to apply to the table [*Table Style Options* group] (see Figure 4-34).
   - Consider the content of your table when deciding which table style options to choose.
   - When you select or deselect table style options, the thumbnails of the table styles in the *Table Styles* gallery change to reflect the options you have chosen.
4. Click the **More** button to display the *Table Styles* gallery (see Figure 4-33).
   - You can scroll down in the *Table Styles* gallery to view more table styles.
5. Choose a table style. Word applies the style and options to your table.
   - When you point to a table style in the *Table Styles* gallery, Word provides a live preview of the table style so you can preview the style on your table.

Insert a Formula in a Table

In addition to making your tables more attractive and easier to read with formatting and style options, you can add ***formulas*** to tables to automatically calculate amounts. For example, you can add a formula in a total row of the table to total the numbers in the rows above (Figure 4-35).

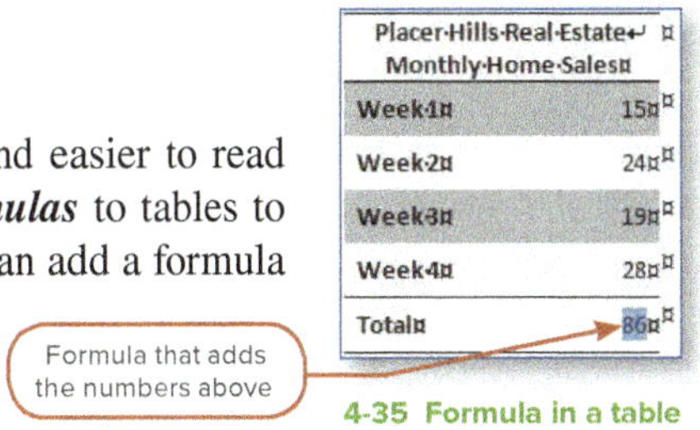

4-35 Formula in a table

MORE INFO

Remember, it's best to align amount figures on the right in a table.

Most formulas used in tables in Word are simple formulas that calculate numbers in a column or row. When you insert a formula, Word, by default, inserts the ***SUM*** formula and adds the range of numbers in the column or row. Word also allows you to insert formulas that are more complex.

▸ HOW TO: Insert a Formula in a Table

1. Place the insertion point in the cell where you want to insert the formula.
2. Click the **Table Tools Layout** tab.
3. Click the **Formula** button [*Data* group]. The *Formula* dialog box opens (Figure 4-36).
4. The formula appears in the *Formula* box.
   - You can select different formula functions from the *Paste function* drop-down list.
5. Click the **Number format** drop-down list and select a number format.
6. Click **OK** to insert the formula.

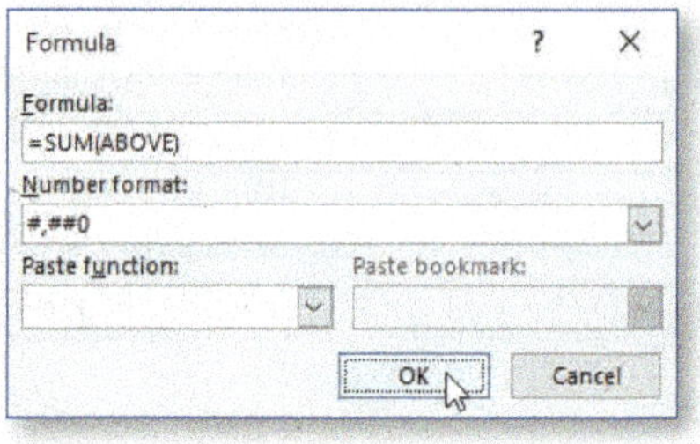

4-36 *Formula* dialog box

Update a Formula

A formula automatically adds values in a table, and you can automatically update a formula if values in the table change. The following are two ways to update a formula:

- Right-click the formula and select **Update Field**.
- Select the formula and press the **F9** function key (you might have to press **Fn+F9** if using a laptop).

Convert Text to a Table

You will not always create a table from scratch. You may want to create a table from existing text. For example, you might want to convert text that is arranged using tabs into a table, or you might want to convert a table into text. Word provides you with options to ***convert text to a table*** or ***convert a table to text***.

When converting text into a table, the selected text must be separated by tabs, commas, paragraph breaks, or other characters. Word uses these characters to separate text into individual cells in the table.

▸ HOW TO: Convert Text to a Table

1. Select the text to be converted to a table.
2. Click the **Insert** tab.
3. Click **Tables** [*Tables* group] and select **Convert Text to Table**. The *Convert Text to Table* dialog box opens (Figure 4-37).
4. In the *Table size* area, select the number of columns or rows.
   - Word automatically detects the size of the table you need.
   - You might not be able to change one or both of the values, depending on the text you selected.
5. In the *AutoFit behavior* area, select an *AutoFit* option.
   - The default setting is *Fixed column width*.
6. In the *Separate text at* area, select how you want Word to separate columns and rows.
   - Word automatically picks an option based on the text you have selected.
7. Click **OK** to convert the text to a table.

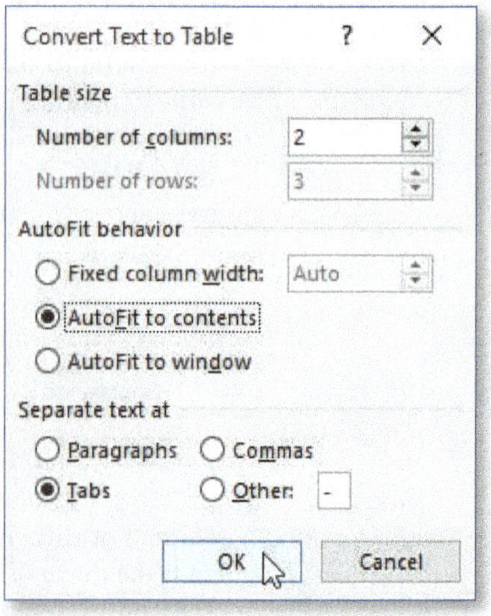

4-37 *Convert Text to Table* dialog box

> **MORE INFO**
>
> To convert a table to text, click the **Convert to Text** button [*Table Tool Layout* tab, *Data* group] to open the *Convert Table to Text* dialog box.

PAUSE & PRACTICE: WORD 4-2

For this Pause & Practice project, you continue to modify Emma's brochure. You apply a table style and table style options to the table you created in the previous Pause & Practice project. You also convert text to a table and apply borders and shading.

File Needed: ***[your initials] PP W4-1.docx***
Completed Project File Name: ***[your initials] PP W4-2.docx***

1. Open the ***[your initials] PP W4-1*** document completed in *Pause & Practice 4-1*.
2. Save this document as [your initials] PP W4-2.
3. Apply table style options and a table style.
   a. Select the table at the end of the document.
   b. Click the **Table Tools Design** tab.
   c. Select **Header Row, Banded Rows**, and **First Column** [*Table Style Options* group] if they are not already selected. The other check boxes should not be selected.
   d. Click the **More** button in the *Table Styles* group to open the *Table Styles* gallery.
   e. Select the **Grid Table 5 Dark – Accent 3** style (Figure 4-38) to apply the style to the table.

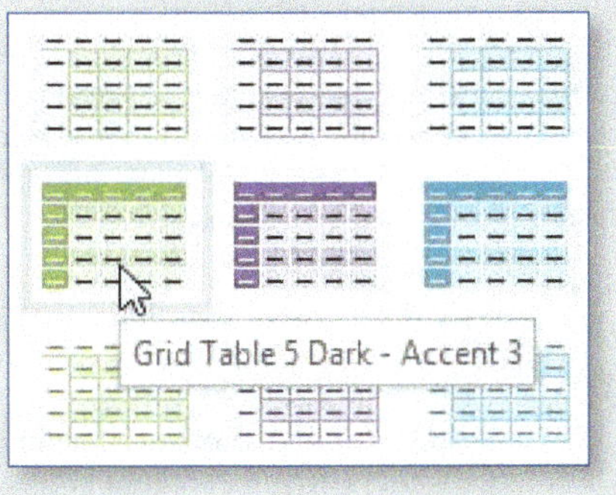

4-38 Select table style

4. Apply a custom top and bottom border to the table.
   a. Select the **first row** (title) of the table.
   b. Click the **Borders** button [*Table Tools Design* tab, *Borders* group or on the mini toolbar] and select **Borders and Shading**. The *Borders and Shading* dialog box opens.
   c. In the *Setting* area, select **Custom**.
   d. Click the **Color** drop-down list and select **Black, Text 1**.
   e. Click the **Width** drop-down list and select **1½ pt**
   f. In the *Style* area, select the **solid line** (first line style in the list) if it is not already selected.
   g. In the *Preview* area, click the **top boundary** of the cell to add a top border (Figure 4-39).
   h. Click **OK** to close the dialog box and add the border.

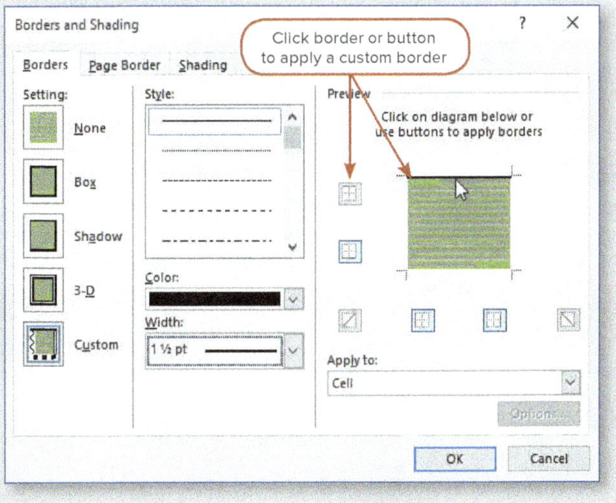

4-39 Apply custom borders

i. Select the entire **bottom row** of the table.
j. Open the *Borders and Shading* dialog box and apply the same custom border to the bottom of the selected row (**Black, Text 1; 1½ pt.; solid line**).
k. Click **OK** to add the border and close the dialog box.

5. Vertically align text in cells.
   a. Select the entire table and click the **Properties** button [*Table Tools Layout* tab, *Table* group] to open the *Table Properties* dialog box.
   b. Click the **Cell** tab and select **Center** in the *Vertical alignment* area.
   c. Click **OK** to close the dialog box.

6. Apply formatting changes to the text in the table.
   a. Select the first row.
   b. Open the *Font* dialog box, change *Size* to **12** and *Font color* to **Black, Text 1**, and check **All caps** in the *Effects* area.
   c. Click **OK** to close the *Font* dialog box.
   d. Select the first column, not including the title.
   e. Open the *Font* dialog box and check **Small caps** in the *Effects* area.
   f. Click **OK** to close the *Font* dialog box.

7. Convert text to a table.
   a. On the first page, select the three lines of text after "Realtor Consultant" ("**Phone**" through "**www.phre.com/ecavalli**"). Be sure to include the paragraph mark at the end of the third line, but don't select the blank line below the three lines of text.
   b. Click the **Insert** tab.
   c. Click the **Table** button [*Tables* group] and select **Convert Text to Table**. The *Convert Text to Table* dialog box opens (Figure 4-40).
   d. Change the *AutoFit behavior* to **AutoFit to contents**.
   e. Click **OK** to convert selected text to a table.

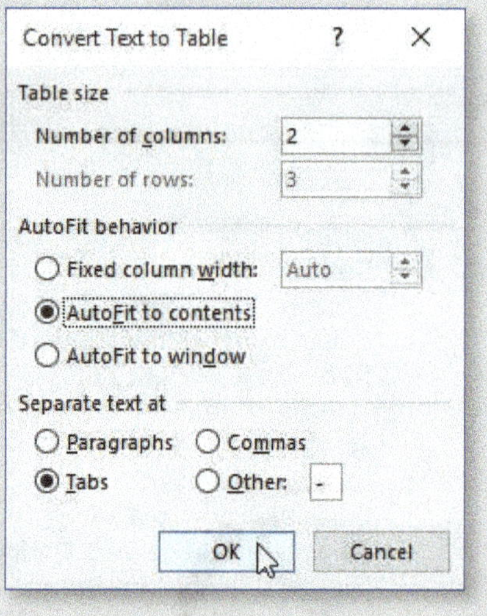

4-40 *Convert Text to Table* dialog box

8. Remove all borders and add custom borders and shading.
   a. With the table selected, click the **Borders** drop-down arrow [*Table Tools Design* tab, *Borders* group].
   b. Select **No Border** to remove all borders.
   c. With the table still selected, click the **Borders** drop-down arrow and select **Top Border**.
   d. With the table still selected, click the **Borders** drop-down arrow and select **Bottom Border**.
   e. With the table still selected, click the **Shading** drop-down arrow [*Table Tools Design* tab, *Table Styles* group] and select **Olive Green, Accent 3, Lighter 80%** (Figure 4-41).

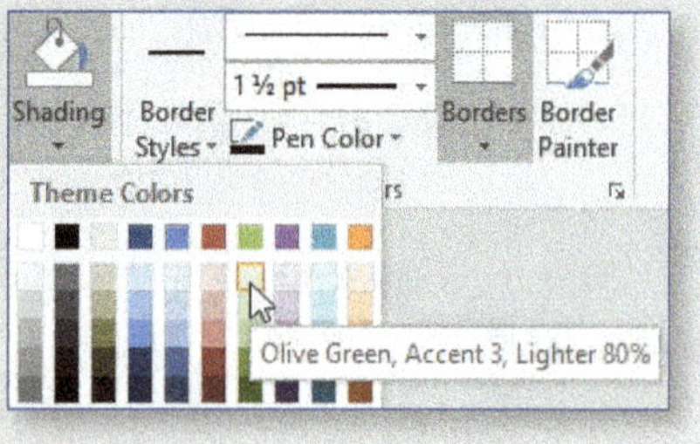

4-41 Select *Shading* color

9. Save and close the document (Figure 4-42).

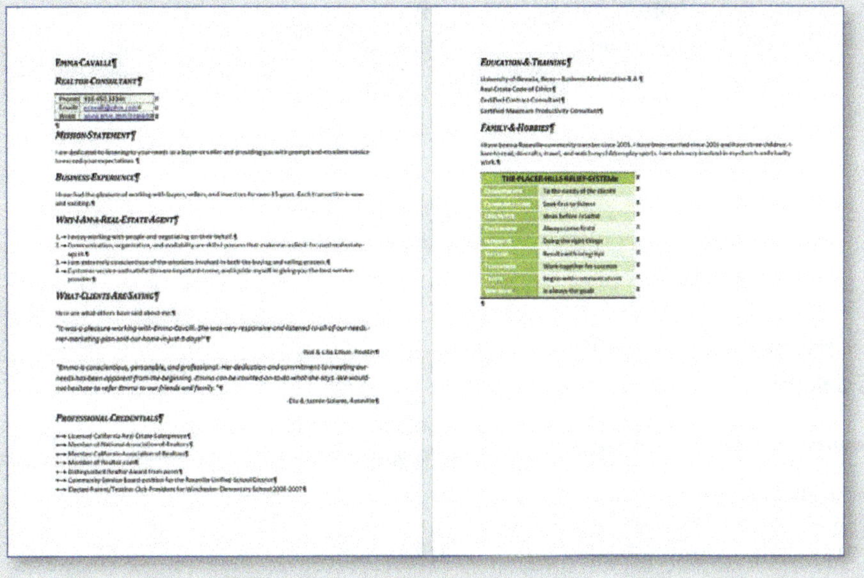

4-42 PP W4-2 completed

SLO 4.4

Using Columns

You can use columns to arrange text and tables into narrower widths and improve the readability, layout, and design of a document. In a normal Word document, text is arranged in a single column. You can apply columns to an entire document or to selected sections of a document. Word has preset column setting options, or you can customize column settings to meet your needs. You can use column and section breaks to control column endings and balance columns.

Preset Column Settings

You can apply column settings to a new document or to a document with existing text. To apply preset column settings, click the **Columns** button on the *Layout* tab in the *Page Setup* group (Figure 4-43). The *Two* and *Three* column options set columns with equal width, while the *Left* and *Right* column options arrange your document in two columns of unequal width.

When you apply columns to a document, the column settings apply only to that section of the document. If there are no section breaks, columns apply to the entire document.

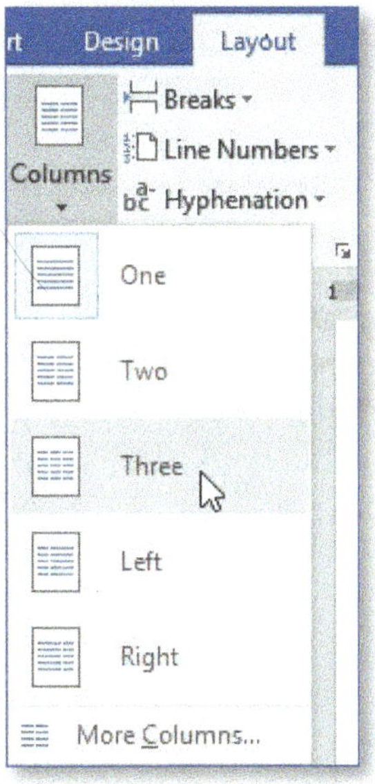

4-43 Preset column options

Customize Columns

Use the ***Columns dialog box*** to apply column settings or customize current column settings. In the *Columns* dialog box, you can select the number of columns, adjust the column width and space between columns, insert a line between columns, and select the portion of the document to apply the column settings.

HOW TO: Customize Columns Using the Columns Dialog Box

1. Click the **Layout** tab.
2. Click the **Columns** button [*Page Setup* group].
3. Select **More Columns**. The *Columns* dialog box opens (Figure 4-44).
4. Select column settings from the *Presets* options or *Number of columns* box.
   - Based on the number of columns you choose, Word automatically sets the column width and spacing.
   - The default spacing between columns is 0.5".
   - You can choose to have more than three columns in the *Number of columns* area.
5. In the *Width and spacing* area, adjust the column widths and spacing as desired.
6. Deselect the **Equal column widths** check box to apply unequal column widths.
   - When *Equal column width* is deselected, you can adjust the width and spacing of each column individually.
   - When *Equal column width* is selected, you can adjust the width and spacing to apply to all columns.
7. Click the **Apply to** drop-down list and select the portion of the document where you want to apply column settings.
   - You can apply column settings to the *Whole document* or from *This point forward*.
   - When *This point forward* is selected, Word inserts a continuous section break at the insertion point in the document and applies column settings to the text after the continuous section break.
   - If you select text, you will be given the option to apply column settings to *Selected text* in the *Apply to* area.
8. Check the **Line between** check box to insert a vertical line between columns.
9. View the *Preview* area to see a diagram of how your columns will appear.
10. Click **OK** to apply column settings.

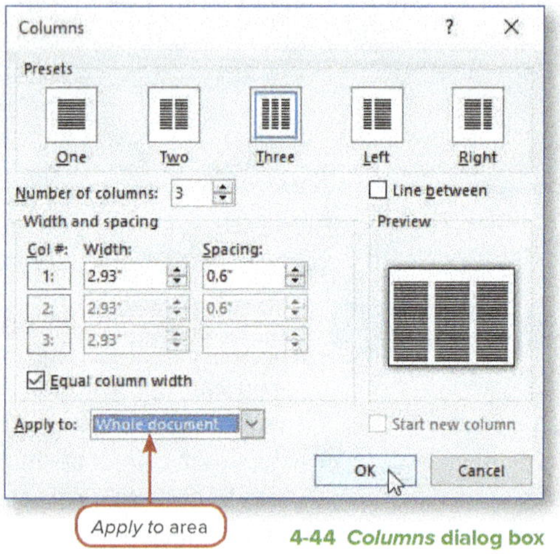

4-44 *Columns* dialog box

Convert Text to Columns

You can apply column settings to the *Whole document*, from *This point forward*, or to *Selected text*. Depending on the portion of the document where you are applying column settings, Word applies the column settings and inserts any needed section breaks. The *Apply to* drop-down list in the *Columns* dialog box displays these options (see Figure 4-44). The following table describes how Word handles each of the options:

Apply to Column Options

Columns Applied to	Actions
Whole Document	Word applies column settings to the entire document. No section breaks are added.
This point forward	Word inserts a continuous section break before the insertion point in the document and applies the column setting beginning at the insertion point, which becomes a new section of the document.
Selected text	When text is selected and column settings are applied, Word inserts a continuous section break before and after the selected text. The column settings apply only to that section.

Insert a Column Break

Column widths control the horizontal text wrapping, while the top and bottom margins or section breaks control where a column ends and wraps to the next column. You can insert ***column breaks*** to end a column and move subsequent text to the next column.

HOW TO: Insert a Column Break

1. Place the insertion point where you want the column to end or the next column to begin.
2. Click the **Layout** tab.
3. Click the **Breaks** button [*Page Setup* group].
4. Select **Column** in the *Page Breaks* options (Figure 4-45).
   - You see a column break indicator when *Show/Hide* is turned on (Figure 4-46).

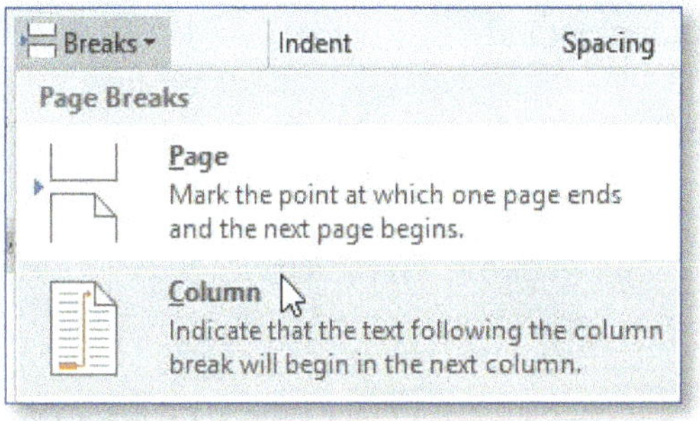

4-45 Insert *Column* break

ANOTHER WAY

Ctrl+Shift+Enter inserts a column break.

MORE INFO

Always turn on **Show/Hide** (**Ctrl+Shift+8**) when using page, section, or column breaks to help you see these elements in your document.

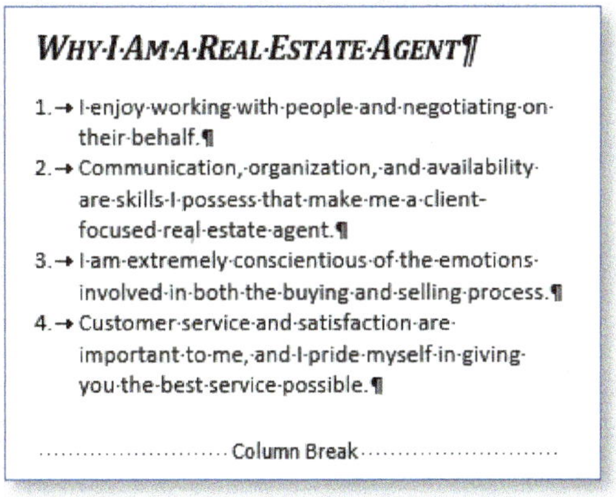

4-46 *Column* break inserted

Balance Columns

Column breaks are one way to balance columns on a page. Another way is to use a ***continuous section break***. To make columns approximately equal in length on a page, insert a continuous section break at the end of the last column on the page. Word automatically adjusts your columns so they are about the same length.

▶ HOW TO: Balance Columns Using a Continuous Section Break

1. Place the insertion point at the end of the last column in your document.
2. Click the **Layout** tab.
3. Click the **Breaks** button [*Page Setup* group].
4. Select **Continuous** in the *Section Breaks* options.
   - You see a continuous section break indicator when *Show/Hide* is turned on.

MORE INFO

Balancing columns using a continuous section break works only if there are no other column breaks controlling column endings on that page.

PAUSE & PRACTICE: WORD 4-3

For this Pause & Practice project, you apply columns to Emma's brochure. With the use of columns and column breaks, you arrange the columns and make the document fit on one page.

File Needed: ***[your initials] PP W4-2.docx***
Completed Project File Name: ***[your initials] PP W4-3.docx***

1. Open the ***[your initials] PP W4-2*** document completed in *Pause & Practice 4-2*.
2. Save this document as [your initials] PP W4-3.
3. Change the page orientation and margins.
   a. Click the **Orientation** button [*Layout* tab, *Page Setup* group] and select **Landscape**.
   b. Click the **Margins** button and choose **Custom Margins**.
   c. Change the *Top* margin to **1.2"**, and the *Bottom, Left,* and *Right* margins to **0.5"**.
   d. Click **OK** to close the dialog box and apply the margin settings. If a dialog box opens informing you that the margins are outside the printable area, click **Ignore**.
4. Arrange the text in columns and customize columns.
   a. Move to the top of the document.
   b. Click the **Columns** button [*Layout* tab, *Page Setup* group] and choose **Two**. The text displays in two columns.
   c. Click the **Columns** button again [*Layout* tab, *Page Setup* group] and choose **More Columns**. The *Columns* dialog box opens (Figure 4-47).
   d. Select **Three** in the *Presets* area.
   e. In the *Width and spacing* area, change the *Spacing* to **0.6"**.
   f. Click the **Apply to** drop-down list and select **Whole document**.
   g. Click **OK** to apply custom column settings.
5. Use column breaks to control column endings.
   a. Place the insertion point in front of "What Clients Are Saying."

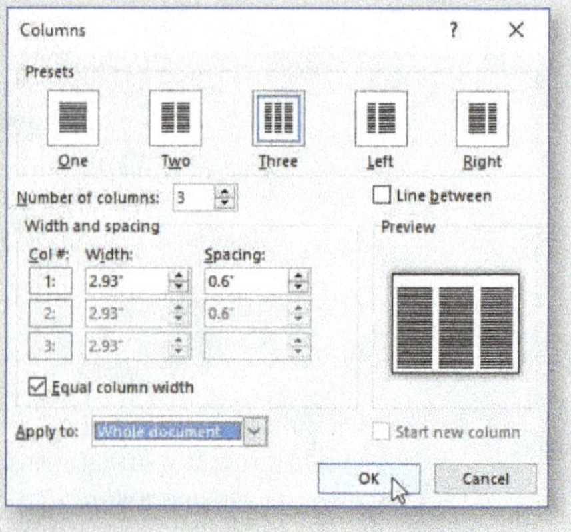

4-47 Customize column settings

b. Click the **Breaks** button [*Layout* tab, *Page Setup* group] and select **Column** to insert a column break.
c. Place the insertion point in front of "Education & Training."
d. Press **Ctrl+Shift+Enter** to insert a column break.

6. Save and close the document (Figure 4-48).

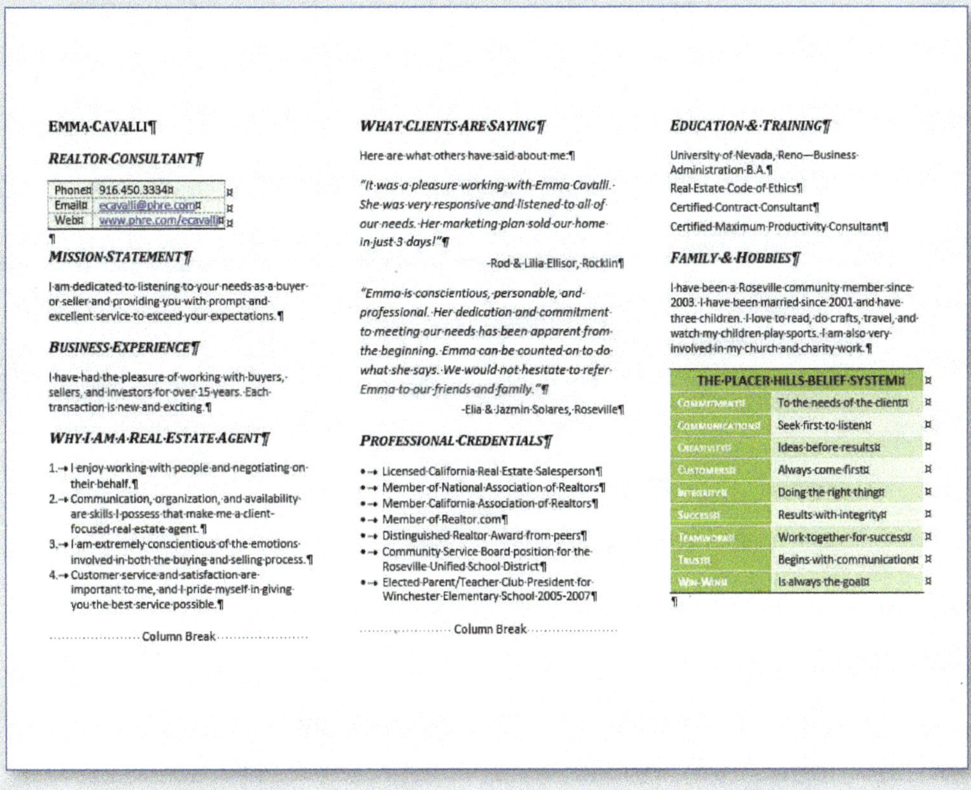
EMMA CAVALLI

REALTOR CONSULTANT

Phone	916.450.3334
Email	ecavalli@phre.com
Web	www.phre.com/ecavalli

MISSION STATEMENT

I am dedicated to listening to your needs as a buyer or seller and providing you with prompt and excellent service to exceed your expectations.

BUSINESS EXPERIENCE

I have had the pleasure of working with buyers, sellers, and investors for over 15 years. Each transaction is new and exciting.

WHY I AM A REAL ESTATE AGENT

1. I enjoy working with people and negotiating on their behalf.
2. Communication, organization, and availability are skills I possess that make me a client-focused real estate agent.
3. I am extremely conscientious of the emotions involved in both the buying and selling process.
4. Customer service and satisfaction are important to me, and I pride myself in giving you the best service possible.

Column Break

WHAT CLIENTS ARE SAYING

Here are what others have said about me:

"It was a pleasure working with Emma Cavalli. She was very responsive and listened to all of our needs. Her marketing plan sold our home in just 3 days!"

-Rod & Lilia Ellisor, Rocklin

"Emma is conscientious, personable, and professional. Her dedication and commitment to meeting our needs has been apparent from the beginning. Emma can be counted on to do what she says. We would not hesitate to refer Emma to our friends and family."

-Elia & Jazmin Solares, Roseville

PROFESSIONAL CREDENTIALS

- Licensed California Real Estate Salesperson
- Member of National Association of Realtors
- Member California Association of Realtors
- Member of Realtor.com
- Distinguished Realtor Award from peers
- Community Service Board position for the Roseville Unified School District
- Elected Parent/Teacher Club President for Winchester Elementary School 2005-2007

Column Break

EDUCATION & TRAINING

University of Nevada, Reno—Business Administration B.A.
Real Estate Code of Ethics
Certified Contract Consultant
Certified Maximum Productivity Consultant

FAMILY & HOBBIES

I have been a Roseville community member since 2003. I have been married since 2001 and have three children. I love to read, do crafts, travel, and watch my children play sports. I am also very involved in my church and charity work.

THE PLACER HILLS BELIEF SYSTEM	
Commitment	To the needs of the client
Communication	Seek first to listen
Creativity	Ideas before results
Customers	Always come first
Integrity	Doing the right thing
Success	Results with integrity
Teamwork	Work together for success
Trust	Begins with communication
Win-Win	Is always the goal

4-48 PP W4-3 completed

Working with Graphics

SLO 4.5

You can use graphics to visually present information and enhance a document. Graphics can be pictures stored on your computer, online pictures, shapes, *SmartArt*, and *WordArt*. You can insert and customize graphic images to meet your specific needs and effectively present information visually.

Pictures and Online Pictures

You can use pictures and graphics to enhance your documents with a visual element. You can add your own pictures and graphics to Word documents. In addition to using your own pictures and graphics, Word uses Bing images to find a wide variety of online pictures to add to your documents. Word uses the term *picture* generically to refer to any type of visual image that is saved as a graphic file. Below is a table of common types of graphic formats:

Types of Graphics

Format	Full Name	Extension	Details
PNG	Portable Network Graphics	.png	Used with pictures and editing pictures; high-quality resolution
JPEG	Joint Photographic Experts Group	.jpeg or .jpg	Relatively small file size; many pictures are saved and distributed in JPEG format
TIFF	Tagged Image File Format	.tiff	Used with high-quality digital photos and has a larger file size than JPEG or PNG
GIF	Graphics Interchange Format	.gif	Used with graphics with fewer colors
WMF	Windows Metafile	.wmf	Windows format used with many graphic images
BMP	Windows Bitmap	.bmp	Proprietary Windows format used with many Microsoft graphic images

Insert a Picture

To enhance a document, insert your own picture or a picture you have saved. See the steps below to insert a picture into a document.

▸HOW TO: Insert a Picture

1. Place the insertion point in the document at the approximate area where you want the picture inserted.
2. Click the **Insert** tab.
3. Click the **Pictures** button [*Illustrations* group]. The *Insert Picture* dialog box opens (Figure 4-49).

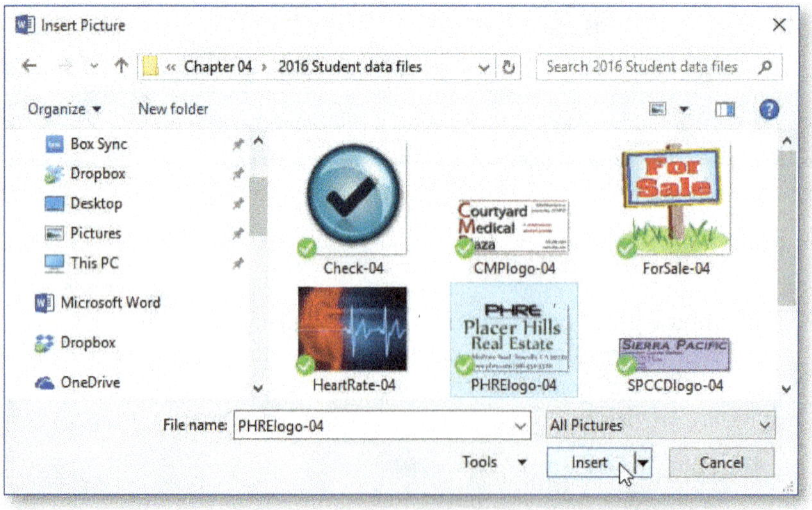

4-49 *Insert Picture* dialog box

4. Browse to the location on your computer and select a picture.
5. Click the **Insert** button to insert the picture and close the *Insert Picture* dialog box.

You might find a picture on the Internet and want to include it in a document. You can either save the picture and insert it as explained above or copy the picture and paste it into your document. Press **Ctrl+C** to copy the picture and **Ctrl+V** to paste the picture.

Include pictures obtained from the web only if you have permission from the image owner to avoid copyright infringement. For academic purposes, you may include images if you reference their sources as you would any other research citation.

ANOTHER WAY

Use the context menu (right-click) to both copy the picture and paste it into a document.

Insert an Online Picture

Word provides a variety of online picture choices using ***Bing Image Search***. When using an image from *Bing Image Search*, make sure you have the permission of the image owner to avoid copyright infringement.

▸ HOW TO: Search for and Insert an Online Picture

1. Place the insertion point in the document where you want the picture inserted.
2. Click the **Insert** tab.
3. Click the **Online Pictures** button [*Illustrations* group] to open the *Insert Pictures* dialog box.
4. Click the *Bing Image Search* text box, type the keywords for the image you want to find, and press **Enter**.
   - Thumbnails of the pictures appear in the list below (Figure 4-50).
   - The light yellow information bar explains that some images require a license or fee to use.
   - Click **X** in the upper right of this information bar to display only those images requiring no license or fee. Click **Show all web results** to display all images, some of which require a license or fee.
5. Select the picture to insert into your document.
   - Click the **View Larger** button in the bottom right corner of a graphic to view a larger picture.
   - Click the **X** in the upper right corner to close the larger image.
6. Click the **Insert** button to insert the picture into your document.

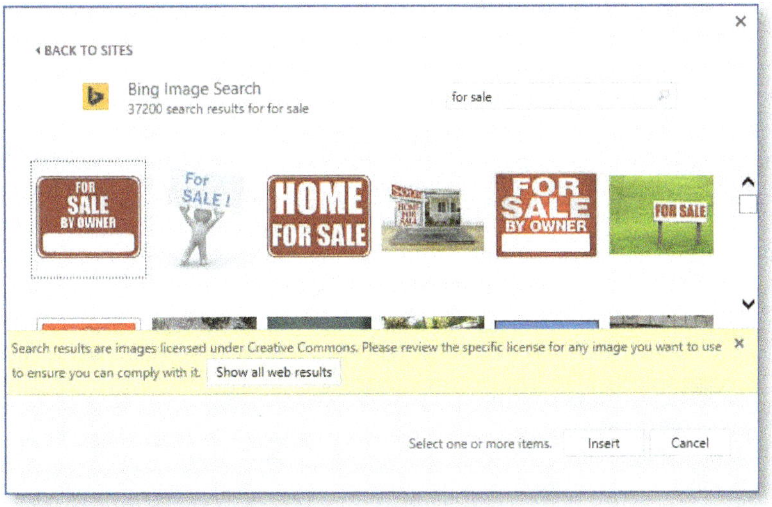

4-50 Insert an online picture

Arrange a Graphic in a Document

Once you have inserted an image into a document, you can adjust its size and position in the document. Word provides you with a number of options to resize, align, wrap text around, insert a caption, and group graphics in your document.

Resize a Graphic

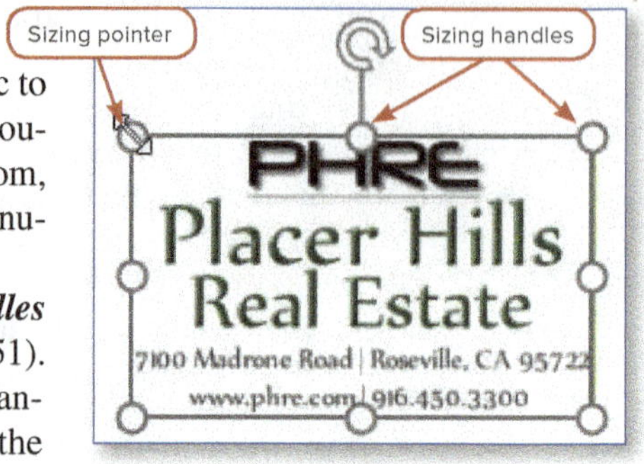

4-51 Resize graphic using the sizing handles

In most cases, you will need to resize your graphic to fit properly in your document. You can do this a couple of different ways. You can drag the top, bottom, side, or corner handles to resize the graphic manually, or you can set a specific size for the graphic.

When you select (click) a graphic, ***sizing handles*** appear on each side and in each corner (Figure 4-51). To resize the graphic, click and hold one of the handles and drag in or out to decrease or increase the size of the graphic. Use the corner handles to keep the resized image proportional. If you use the side, top, or bottom handles to resize, the proportions of the image may become distorted.

You can also resize the image to a specific size or to a percentage of its original size.

HOW TO: Resize an Image

1. Click the image to select it. The *Picture Tools Format* tab displays on the *Ribbon*.
2. Click the **up** or **down** arrows in the *Height* or *Width* area [*Size* group] to increase or decrease the size (Figure 4-52).
   - Resizing in this manner keeps the graphic proportional.
3. Alternatively, click the **Size** launcher to open the *Layout* dialog box with the *Size* tab displayed (Figure 4-53).
4. Change the size of the graphic to a specific size in the *Height* and *Width* areas.
   - You can also scale the graphic to make it a percentage of its original size in the *Scale* area.
   - Check the **Lock aspect ratio** box selected to prevent the graphic from becoming distorted in size.
   - The *Original size* area displays the original size of the graphic. Click the **Reset** button to reset the graphic to its original.
5. Click **OK** to resize the graphic and close the dialog box.

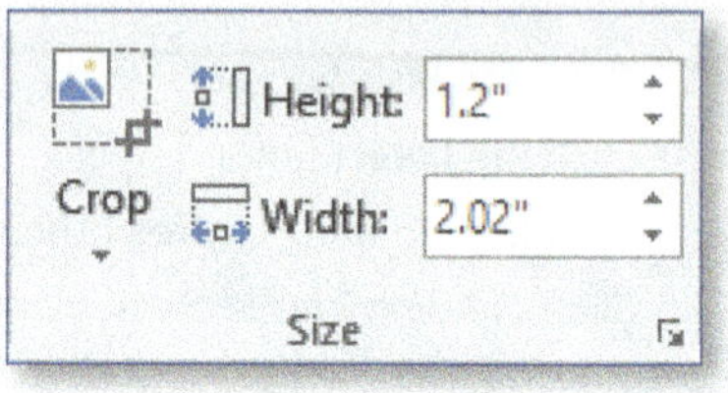

4-52 *Size* group on the *Picture Tools Format* tab

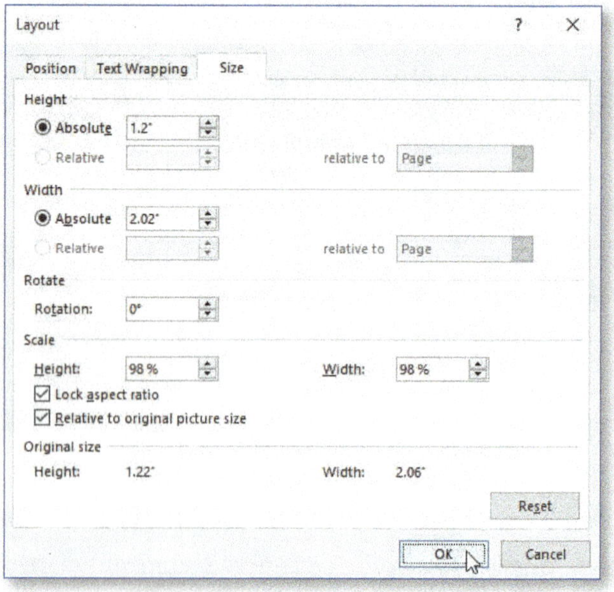

4-53 *Size* options in the *Layout* dialog box

ANOTHER WAY

Open the *Layout* dialog box by right-clicking the graphic and selecting **Size and Position**.

Wrap Text around a Graphic

You can select how the text aligns or wraps around your graphic with a variety of ***text wrapping*** options. You can control how the text wraps around the graphic and choose to position the graphic in front of or behind the text.

▸ HOW TO: Wrap Text around a Graphic

1. Click the graphic to select it.
2. Click the **Wrap Text** button [*Picture Tools Format* tab, *Arrange* group] (Figure 4-54).
3. Select a text wrapping option.
4. Select **More Layout Options** to open the *Layout* dialog box with the *Text Wrapping* tab displayed (Figure 4-55).
   - Use the *Layout* dialog box to customize text wrapping [*Text Wrapping* tab], specify the position of the graphic [*Position* tab], and resize the graphic [*Size* tab].
5. In the *Wrap text* area, you can choose *Both sides*, *Left only*, *Right only*, or *Largest only*.
6. In the *Distance from text* area, set a specific distance from the graphic to wrap text.
7. Click **OK** to close the *Layout* dialog box.

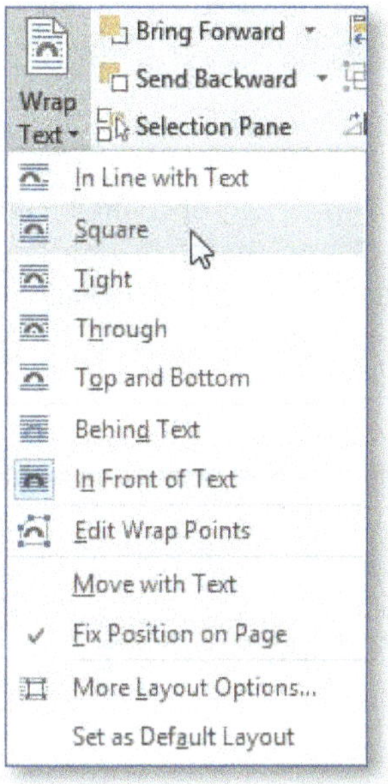

4-54 *Wrap Text* options

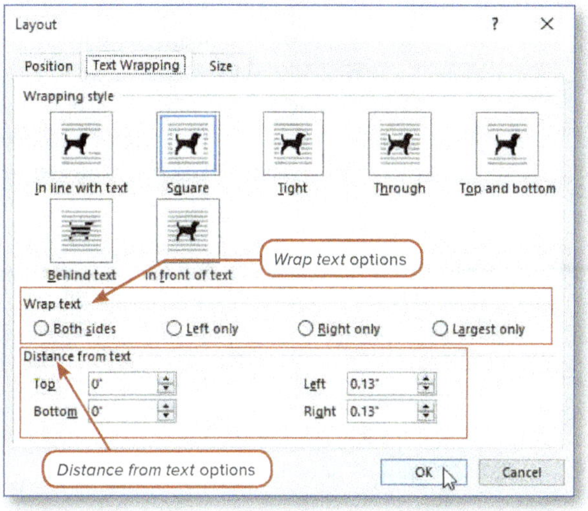

4-55 *Text Wrapping* tab in the *Layout* dialog box

You can also click the **Layout Options** button to the right of a selected graphic and select a text wrapping option (Figure 4-56). Click the **See more** link to open the *Layout* dialog box.

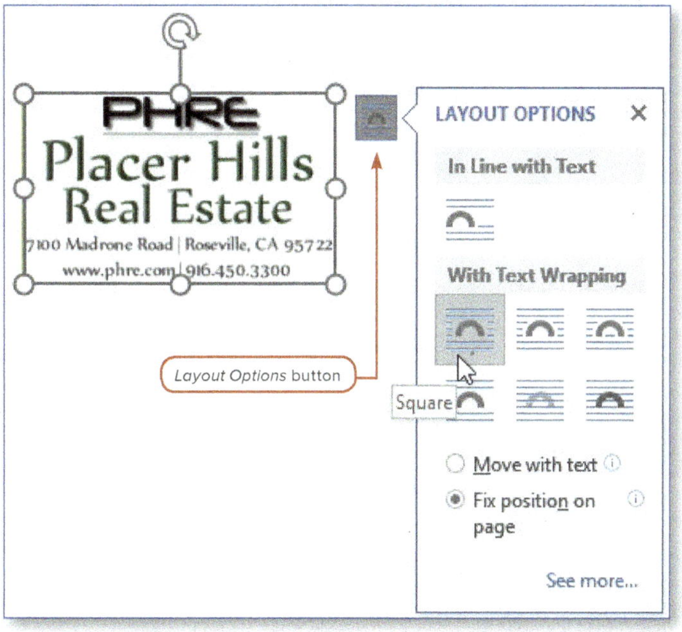

4-56 *Layout Options* menu

> **MORE INFO**
>
> *In Line with Text* is the default option when you insert a graphic into a document.

Position a Graphic

In addition to adjusting the size of a graphic and specifying how text wraps around a graphic, you can also specify the position of the graphic in your document. You can align a graphic left, right, or center by selecting the graphic and clicking the **Align** button in the *Arrange* group on the *Picture Tools Format* tab (Figure 4-57).

You can position a graphic in a document in a specific location by dragging the graphic to the desired location. You can also specify the location relative to the margins, page, or column. For example, you can position a graphic 5" from the left margin and 6" from the top margin of the document. The *Position* tab in the *Layout* dialog box offers customization options (Figure 4-58).

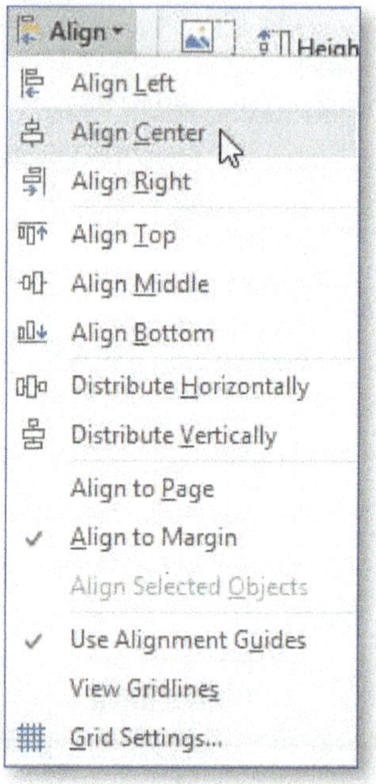

4-57 *Align* options

HOW TO: Position a Graphic

1. Click the graphic to select it.
2. Click the **Picture Tools Format** tab.
3. Click the **Position** button [*Arrange* group] and select **More Layout Options**. The *Layout* dialog box opens with the *Position* tab selected (see Figure 4-58).
4. Set both the horizontal and vertical alignment of the graphic.
   - In the *Horizontal* area, you have the following positioning options: *Alignment*, *Book layout*, *Absolute position*, and *Relative position*.
   - In the *Vertical* area, you have the following positioning options: *Alignment*, *Absolute position*, and *Relative position*.
5. Use the radio buttons, text boxes, and drop-down lists in the *Horizontal* and *Vertical* areas to align the graphic at a specific location in the document.
6. Click **OK** to close the dialog box.

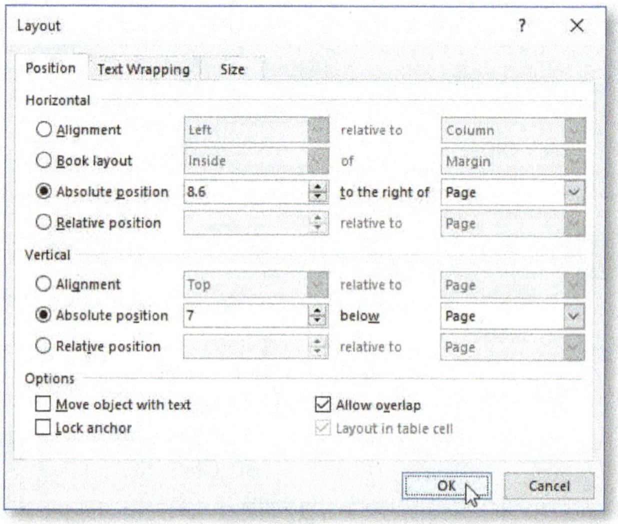

4-58 *Position* tab in the *Layout* dialog box

> **ANOTHER WAY**
>
> Open the *Layout* dialog box by clicking the **Size** launcher [*Picture Tools Format* tab].

Insert a Caption

You might want to add a caption to a picture or chart that you insert into a document. The *Insert Caption* option creates a text box below the graphic where you can enter a caption (Figure 4-59).

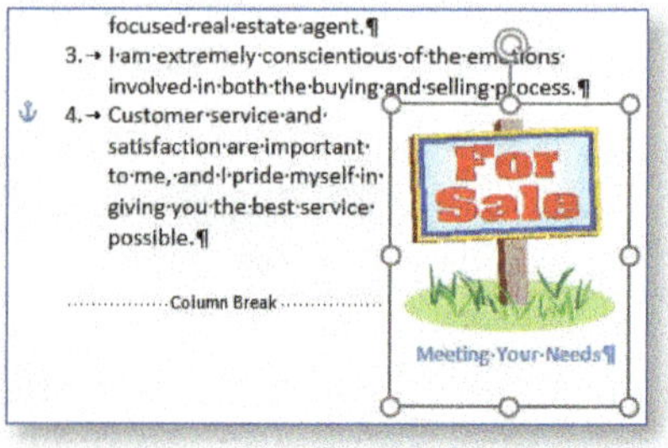

4-59 Graphic with caption below

HOW TO: Insert a Caption

1. Select the graphic that needs a caption.
2. Right-click the graphic and select **Insert Caption** from the context menu. The *Caption* dialog box opens (Figure 4-60).
   - Word automatically creates a caption for the object you have selected.
   - In the *Caption* text box, you can add a description after the label, but you cannot delete the label.
   - After you add a caption to a graphic, you can delete the label and number and customize the caption text.
3. Click the **Label** drop-down list and choose **Equation, Figure**, or **Table**.
   - You can add a custom label by clicking the **New Label** button and typing a custom label.
   - You can remove the label (but not the number) by checking the **Exclude label from caption** option.
4. Click the **Position** drop-down list and select the location of the caption.
5. Click **OK** to insert the caption.
6. You can edit the caption in the text box after it is added to the graphic (Figure 4-61). You can also customize the size and color of the caption text and adjust the size and positioning of the text box.

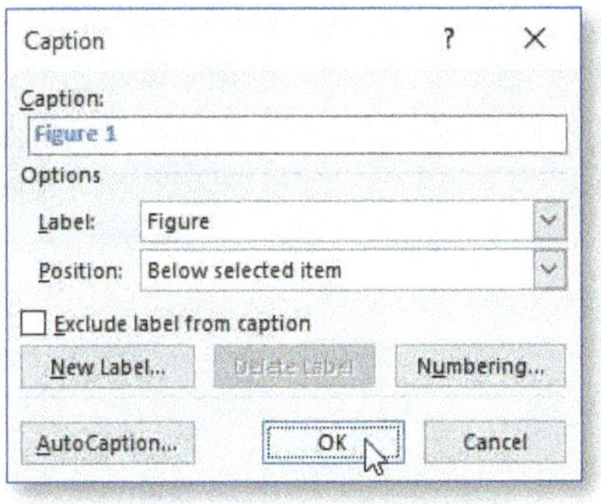

4-60 *Caption* dialog box

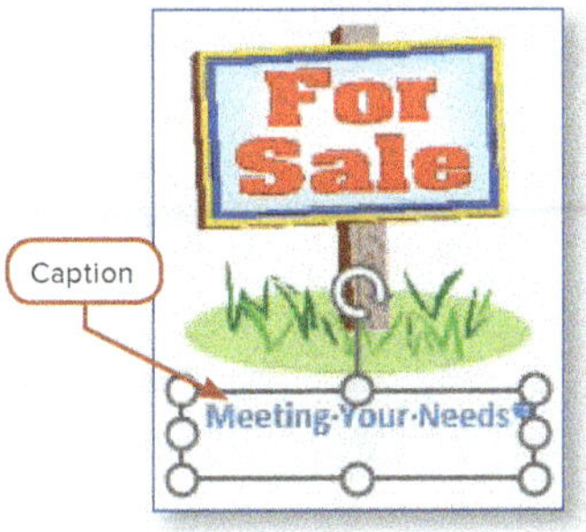

4-61 Caption added to graphic

ANOTHER WAY

Insert a caption by clicking the **Insert Caption** button [*References* tab, *Captions* group].

Group Graphic Objects

When you work with graphics, you may want to ***group*** together related graphics and objects. For example, you might want to group a picture and caption. The advantage of doing this is that the grouped graphics become one object that you can be resize and position together.

HOW TO: Group and Ungroup Graphics

1. Press the **Ctrl** key and click the graphics to be grouped (Figure 4-62).
2. Click the **Group** button [*Picture Tools Format* tab, *Arrange* group].
3. Select **Group**. The selected objects become one grouped object (Figure 4-63).
4. To ungroup grouped items, select the grouped object, click the **Group** button in the *Arrange* group on the *Picture Tools Format* tab, and select **Ungroup**.

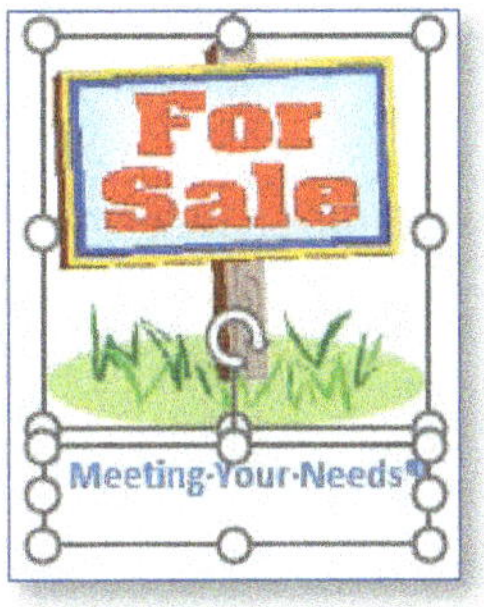

4-62 Multiple objects selected to be grouped together

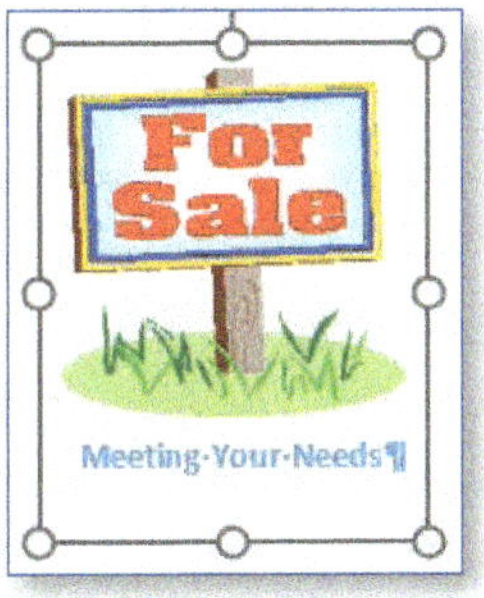

4-63 Grouped objects

ANOTHER WAY

Group and *Ungroup* options are available in the context menu by right-clicking selected graphics or a grouped object.

Insert and Customize a Shape

In addition to pictures, you can insert other types of graphic items into your Word documents. For example, Word provides a variety of ***shapes*** that you can insert into your document.

When you insert a shape or line into your document, you are actually drawing the object in your document. Word's *Shapes* gallery groups shapes into categories (Figure 4-64). Once you draw a shape in your document, you can edit the size, position, alignment, and text wrapping of the object.

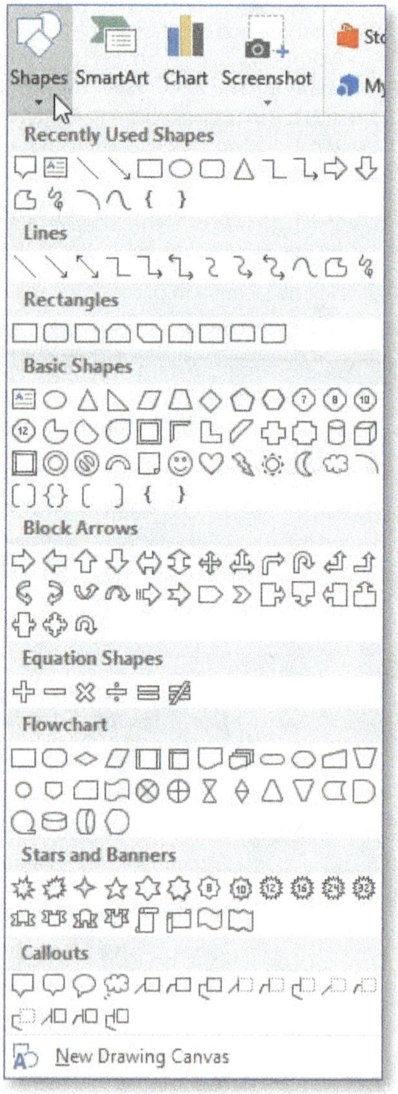

4-64 ***Shapes*** **drop-down list**

HOW TO: Insert a Shape

1. Click the **Insert** tab.
2. Click the **Shapes** button [*Illustrations* group] to display the gallery of shape options.
3. Select the shape you want to use. Your pointer becomes a drawing crosshair (large, dark plus sign) when you position the pointer in the document.
4. Click and drag to create the shape (Figure 4-65). When you release the pointer, the shape is inserted into the document.
   - You don't have to be perfectly accurate when you create the shape because you can easily resize the shape after you draw it.
   - You can change the text wrapping on a shape so the shape appears on top of or behind the text, or you can have text wrap around a shape.

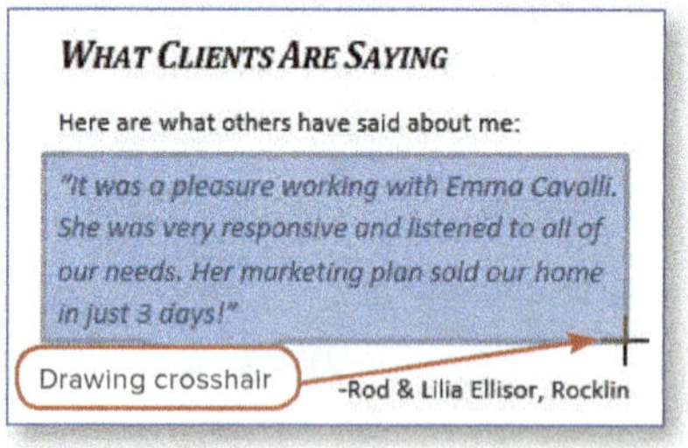

4-65 Draw a shape

MORE INFO

If you want to create a perfect square or circle or to draw a straight line, press the **Shift** key while drawing.

Once a shape has been inserted into a document, you can move or resize it. Also, you can change the line size, color, and fill of the shapes. See Figure 4-66 and its callouts for examples of the available selection and sizing handles. The following is a list of those options:

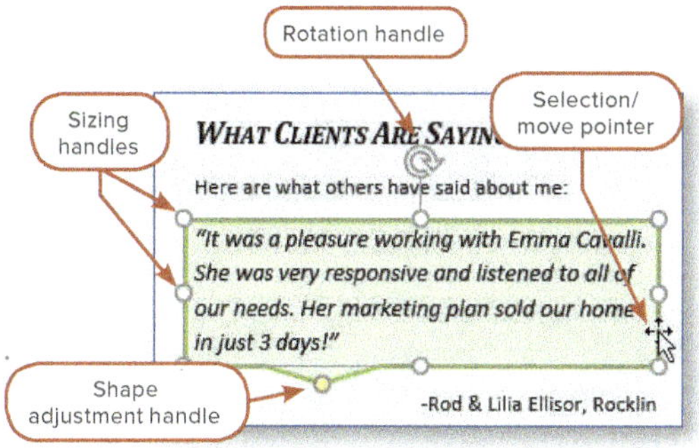

4-66 Shape selected with handles displayed

- ***Selection/move pointer***: This pointer (four-pointed arrow) allows you to select and move objects. Select multiple objects by pressing the **Ctrl** key and selecting the objects.
- ***Sizing handles***: Eight sizing handles are located on corners and sides of the shape. When you select one of these, the pointer becomes a sizing pointer (two-pointed arrow).
- ***Rotation handle***: The rotation handle is the circular arrow at the top of the selected shape. Rotate a shape by clicking and dragging this handle to the left or right.
- ***Shape Adjustment handle***: This handle is the yellow circle. You can use this handle to change the shape of an object (not all shapes have this handle available). You can also use this handle to change the size or location of a callout, corner roundness, and other shape elements.

You can change the ***Shape Fill, Shape Outline***, and ***Shape Effects*** of a shape. Each of these areas includes many customization options to enhance shapes. When you select a shape, the *Drawing Tools Format* tab displays on the *Ribbon* (Figure 4-67).

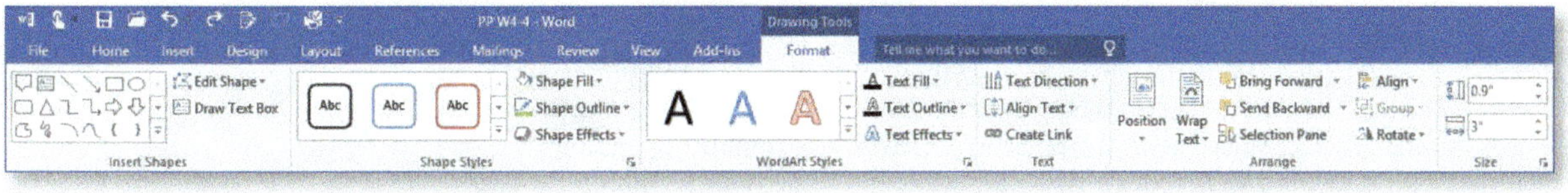

4-67 Drawing Tools Format tab

Insert and Customize SmartArt

SmartArt allows you to graphically present information in your document in a visually attractive way. *SmartArt* includes a variety of categories, and within each category, numerous options are available (see Figure 4-68).

SmartArt graphics are a combination of shapes and text boxes. Once you insert a *SmartArt* graphic into a document, you can use ***SmartArt Tools Design*** and ***SmartArt Tools Format*** tabs to customize the text content and the graphic's structure.

HOW TO: Insert and Customize SmartArt

1. Position your insertion point in your document where you want to insert the *SmartArt*.
2. Click the **Insert** tab.
3. Click the **SmartArt** button [*Illustrations* group]. The *Choose a SmartArt Graphic* dialog box opens (Figure 4-68).
4. Select a *SmartArt* graphic. A preview and description of the *SmartArt* displays on the right of the dialog box.
5. Click **OK** to insert the *SmartArt* into the document.

6. Add text to the graphic objects in the *SmartArt* graphic (Figure 4-69).
   - Alternatively, click the arrow on the left side of the *SmartArt* graphic to display the *Text* pane where you can type text in the *SmartArt* graphic.
   - You can format the text in the *SmartArt* as you would regular text in a document.
   - You can also format text in the *SmartArt* using *Text Fill*, *Text Outline*, and *Text Effects* on the *SmartArt Tools Format* tab.

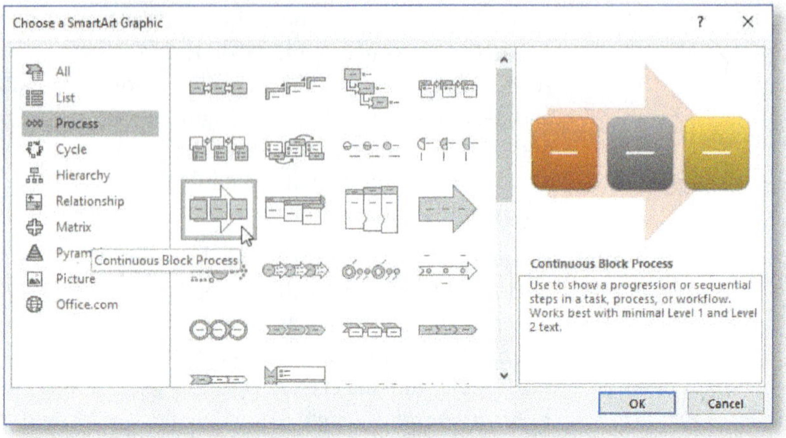

4-68 *Choose a SmartArt Graphic* dialog box

7. Customize the graphic objects in a *SmartArt* graphic using the *SmartArt Tools Design* and *Format* tabs.
   - The *SmartArt Tools Design* tab controls the overall design and colors of the *SmartArt* objects.
   - The *SmartArt Tools Format* tab allows you to customize the shape of objects, colors, borders, fill, and effects.

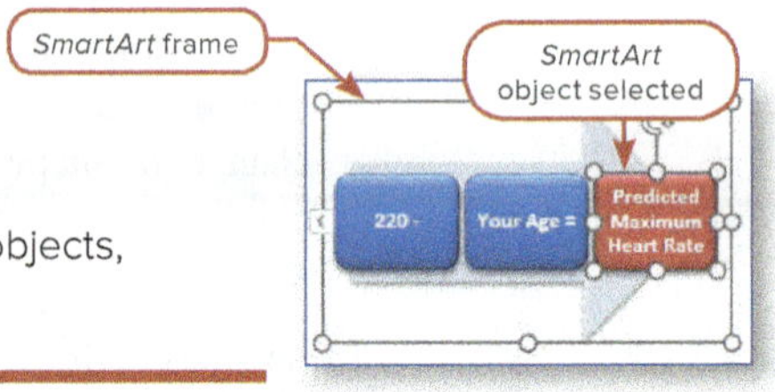

4-69 *SmartArt* with text inserted

Insert and Customize WordArt

WordArt can visually enhance a title of a document or add emphasis to certain text within a document. When you insert *WordArt*, you are actually inserting a text box in the document that can then be manipulated as a graphic. Once you insert *WordArt* in a document, you can resize and move it, and you can change the color, fill, and effects of this object.

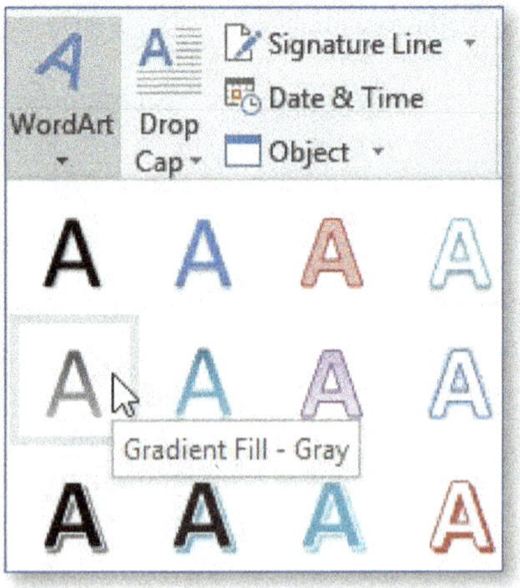

4-70 *WordArt* gallery

▸HOW TO: Insert WordArt

1. Position your insertion point in your document where you want to insert the *WordArt*.
   - Alternatively, select text in the document to convert to a *WordArt* object.
2. Click the **Insert** tab.
3. Click the **WordArt** button [*Text* group] and select a *WordArt* style from the gallery of options (Figure 4-70). The *WordArt* text box displays in your document.
4. Type the text you want to format as *WordArt*.
   - The placeholder text (*Your text here*) is selected when you insert the *WordArt* (Figure 4-71). Type to replace the placeholder text. If the placeholder text is deselected, select it before typing your text.
5. Click anywhere in your document away from the text box to deselect the *WordArt* graphic.

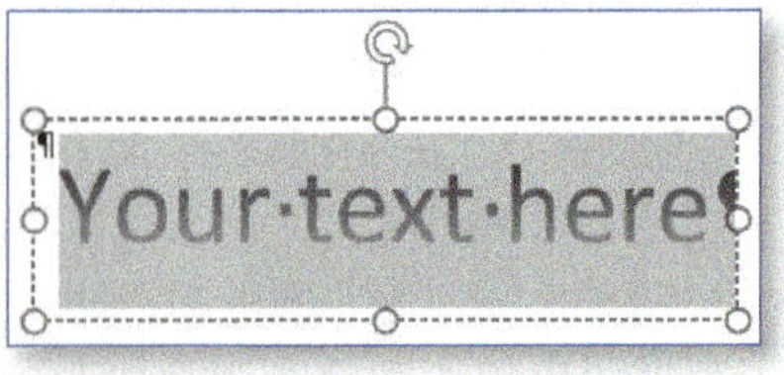

4-71 *WordArt* inserted into a document

Customizing *WordArt* is similar to customizing other graphic objects in Word. When you select the *WordArt* text box, the ***Drawing Tools Format*** tab displays (Figure 4-72). From this tab, you can change the style of the *WordArt*, add a border to the text box, and change the fill, outline, and effects of the *WordArt* text.

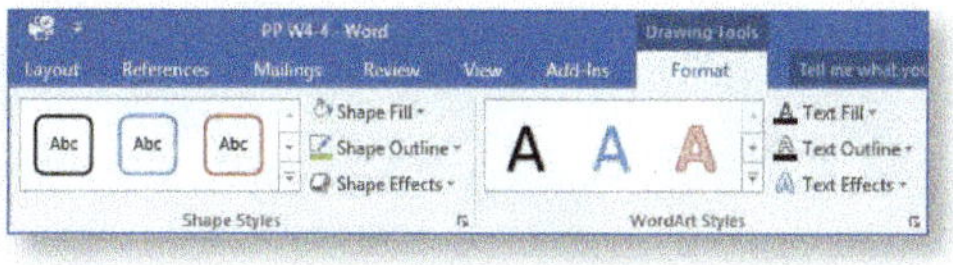

4-72 ***Drawing Tools Format*** **tab**

Resize *WordArt* by using the sizing handles on the corners and sides. Rotate the *WordArt* text box with the rotation handle. You can change the position and text wrapping of the *WordArt* in the same way you manipulate other graphics.

Enhance Graphics with Styles

Each of the different types of graphics has a variety of styles, fills, outlines, and effects that you can apply. Context-sensitive tabs appear when you select a graphic object. These context-sensitive tabs contain a variety of ***style galleries*** (Figure 4-73).

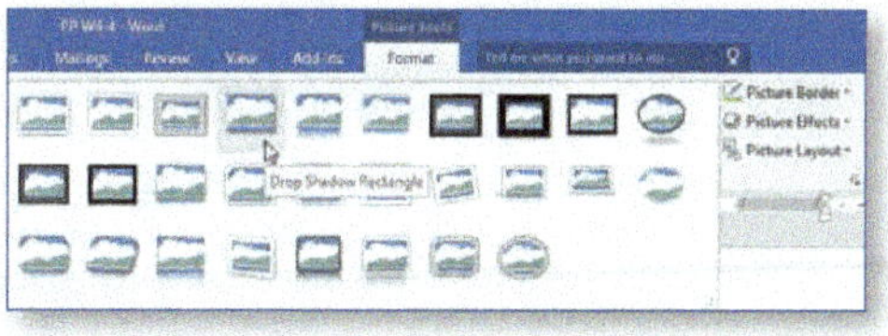

4-73 ***Picture Styles*** **gallery**

When applying styles to graphics, Word provides you with a ***live preview***. When you place your pointer on a style from one of the style galleries, Word temporarily applies the style to the selected graphic to preview how it will appear in the document.

Insert Symbols and Special Characters

In addition to pictures, *WordArt*, shapes, *SmartArt*, and other types of graphic objects, Word has a variety of symbols and other special characters that you can insert into a document (Figure 4-74). The *Symbols*, *Wingdings*, and *Webdings* font sets have an assortment of characters and symbols you can insert into a document. Additional special characters available, such as the em dash, en dash, and copyright and trademark symbols.

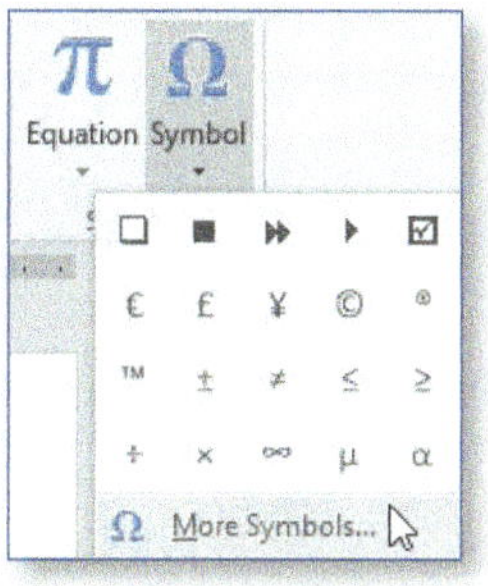

4-74 ***Symbol*** **button on the** ***Insert*** **tab**

HOW TO: Insert a Symbol

1. Click the **Insert** tab.
2. Click the **Symbol** button [*Symbols* group] to display a drop-down list of recently used symbols.
3. Select **More Symbols** (see Figure 4-74). The *Symbol* dialog box opens (Figure 4-75).
4. Click the **Font** drop-down list on the *Symbols* tab to select the font set.
   - Or, click the **Special Character** tab to display the list of available special characters.
5. Click a symbol or special character to insert.
   - Each character has a numerical code that identifies it. The *Character code* area displays this code.
6. Click **Insert** to insert the symbol in the document.
7. Click **Close** to close the dialog box.

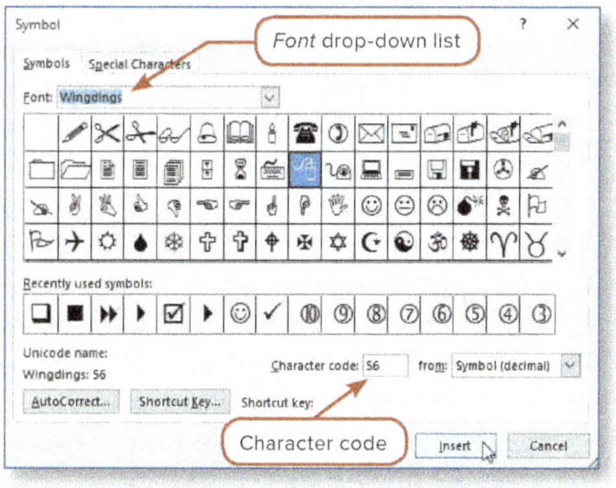

4-75 ***Symbol*** **dialog box**

PAUSE & PRACTICE: WORD 4-4

For this Pause & Practice project, you finalize Emma's brochure by inserting a picture, shapes, and *WordArt*. You format and arrange these graphic objects attractively in the document.

Files Needed: ***[your initials] PP W4-3.docx, PHRElogo-04.png***, and ***ForSale-04*** *(Student data files are available in the* Library *of your SIMnet account)*
Completed Project File Name: ***[your initials] PP W4-4.docx***

1. Open the ***[your initials] PP W4-3*** document completed in *Pause & Practice 4-3*.
2. Save this document as [your initials] PP W4-4.
3. Insert the Placer Hills Real Estate logo at the bottom right corner of the document.
   a. Position the insertion point below the table in the third column.
   b. Click the **Pictures** button [*Insert* tab, *Illustrations* group]. The *Insert Picture* dialog box opens.
   c. Select the ***PHRElogo-04*** file from the student data files and click **Insert**.
4. Arrange and format the logo.
   a. With the logo selected, click the **Wrap Text** button [*Picture Tools Format* tab, *Arrange* group] and choose **In Front of Text**.
   b. In the *Height* box [*Size* group], type 1.2 and press **Enter** (Figure 4-76). The width automatically adjusts to keep the picture proportional.
   c. Click the middle of the picture and drag the graphic near the bottom right corner of the document.
   d. Click the **Picture Border** button [*Picture Styles* group] and select **Olive Green, Accent 3** (Figure 4-77).
   e. Click the **Picture Border** again, click **Weight**, and select **1½ pt**.
   f. Click the **Position** button [*Arrange* group] and select **More Layout Options**. The *Layout* dialog box opens with the *Position* tab displayed (Figure 4-78).
   g. In the *Horizontal* area, select the **Absolute position** radio button, type 8.6, click the **to the right of** drop-down list, and select **Page**.
   h. In the *Vertical* area, select the **Absolute position** radio button, type 7, click the **below** drop-down list, and select **Page**.
   i. Click **OK** to close the dialog box.

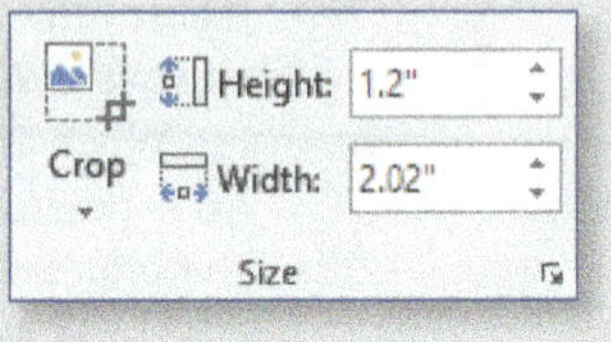

4-76 Adjust the size of a graphic

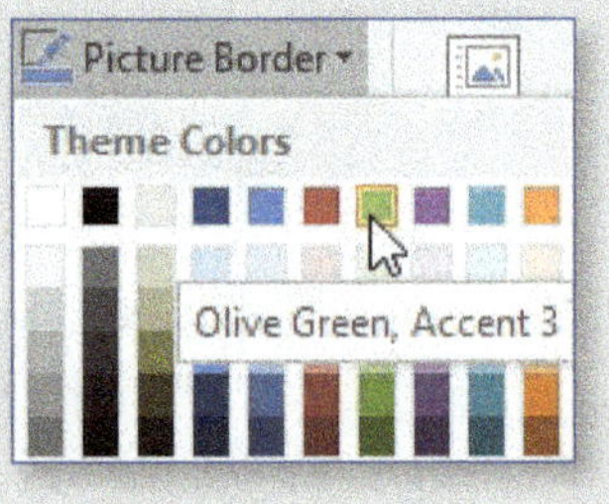

4-77 Select *Picture Border* color

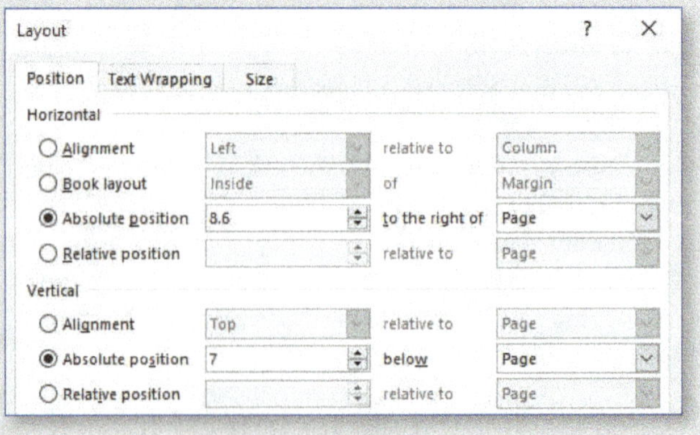

4-78 Customize position of the logo

5. Add a picture near the bottom of the first column.
   a. Click at the end of the fourth numbered item in the first column.
   b. Click the **Pictures** button [*Insert* tab, *Illustrations* group]. The *Insert Picture* dialog box opens.
   c. Select the ***ForSale-04*** picture from the student data files and click **Insert**.
   d. With the picture selected, change the *Height* [*Picture Tools Format* tab, *Size* group] to **1.2"** and press **Enter**.

e. Right-click the picture, choose **Wrap Text**, and select **Square**.
f. Click the middle of the picture and drag it so it is to the right of the fourth numbered item in the first column (see Figure 4-79).

6. Insert a caption for the picture.
   a. Right-click the picture and choose **Insert Caption**. The *Caption* dialog box opens.
   b. Click **OK** to close the *Caption* dialog box and insert the caption.
   c. Delete the placeholder text in the caption text box and type Meeting Your Needs as the caption. If the caption covers the bottom of the graphic, select the border of the caption and use the down keyboard arrow to move it down slightly.
   d. Press **Ctrl+E** or click the **Center** button [*Home* tab, *Paragraph* group] to center the text in the caption.
   e. With the caption still selected, press the **Ctrl** key and click the picture to select it also. Both the picture and the caption should be selected.
   f. Click the **Group** button [*Picture Format Tools* tab, *Arrange* group] and choose **Group**. The two objects group into one object (Figure 4-79).

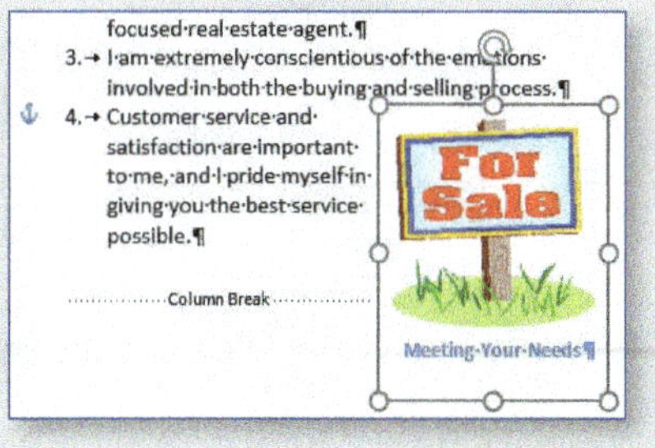

4-79 Picture and caption grouped

7. Change the paragraph spacing on the two quotes in the second column.
   a. Place your insertion point in the first quoted paragraph in the second column (beginning with "It was a pleasure . . .").
   b. Change the *After* paragraph spacing to **12 pt**.
   c. Place your insertion point in the second quoted paragraph in the second column (beginning with "Emma is conscientious . . .").
   d. Change the *After* paragraph spacing to **12 pt**.

8. Add and format a shape to the quoted text.
   a. Click the **Shapes** button [*Insert* tab, *Illustration* group] and select **Rectangular Callout** (Figure 4-80). Your pointer changes to a crosshair (dark plus sign).
   b. On the first quote in the second column, drag from the upper left to the lower right to draw the shape over the quoted text (Figure 4-81).
   c. With the shape still selected, click the **Send Backward** drop-down arrow [*Drawing Tools Format* tab, *Arrange* group] and select **Send Behind Text** (Figure 4-82). The text displays on top of the shape.
   d. Click the *Shape Styles* **More** button [*Drawing Tools Format* tab, *Shape Styles* group] to display the gallery of shape styles.
   e. Select **Colored Outline – Olive Green, Accent 3** (Figure 4-83).
   f. Click the **Shape Fill** button [*Drawing Tools Format* tab, *Shape Styles* group] and select **Olive Green, Accent 3, Lighter 80%**.

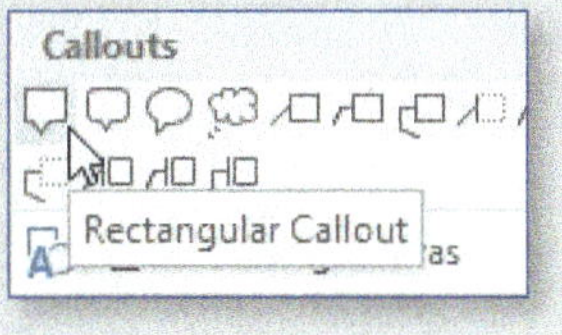

4-80 Select shape

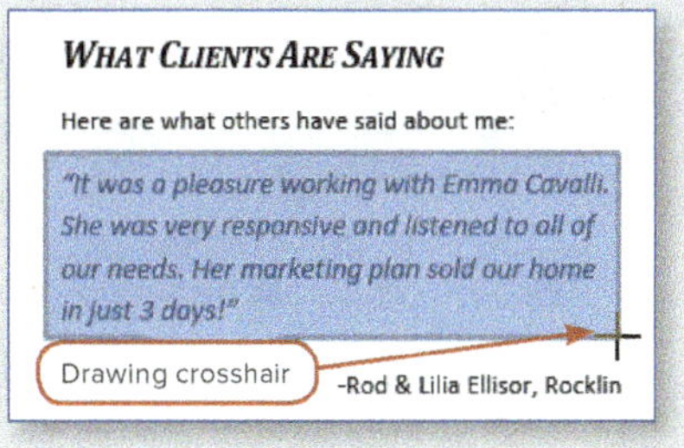

4-81 Draw rectangular shape

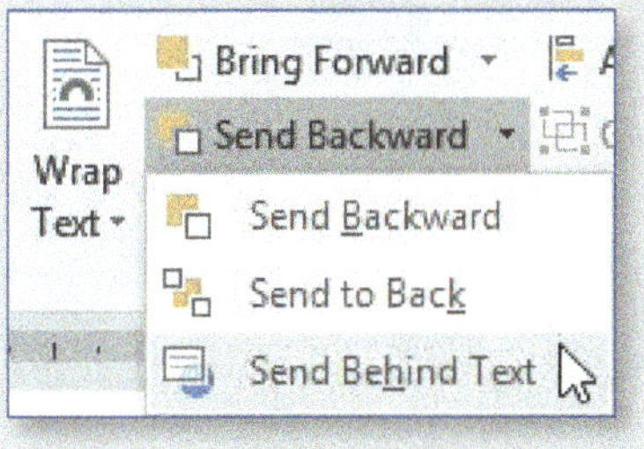

4-82 *Send Behind Text*

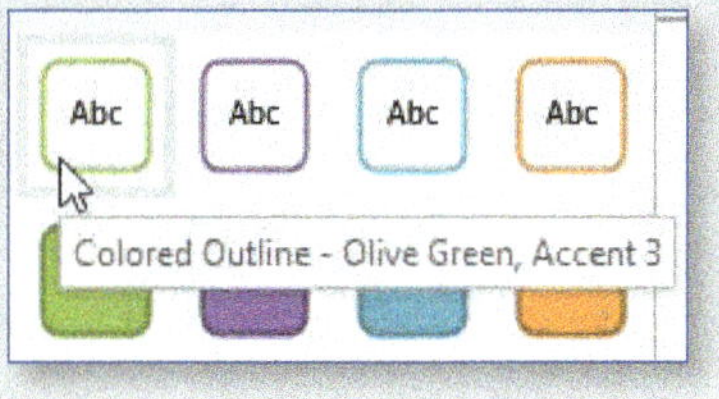

4-83 Apply a shape style

g. Click the **Shape Effects** button [*Drawing Tools Format* tab, *Shape Styles* group], select **Shadow**, and choose **Offset Diagonal Bottom Right** (Figure 4-84).
h. Change the *Shape Height* to **0.9"** and the *Shape Width* to **3"** [*Drawing Tools Format* tab, *Size* group].
i. Drag the shape to position it evenly behind the text. You can also use the keyboard arrow keys to position a selected shape.

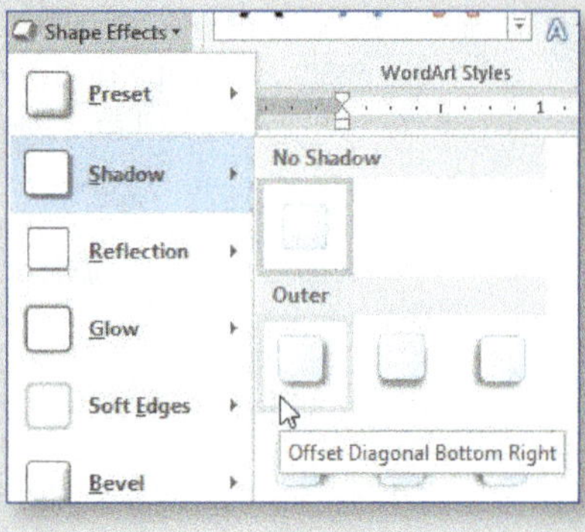

4-84 Select a shape *Shadow* option

9. Replicate and align the callout shape.
   a. With the shape still selected, press **Ctrl+C** to copy it and **Ctrl+V** to paste the copy of the shape into the document.
   b. Drag the new shape over the second quote.
   c. With the second shape still selected, change the *Shape Height* to **1.4"** [*Drawing Tools Format* tab, *Size* group].
   d. Drag the shape to position it evenly behind the text (Figure 4-85).
   e. With the second shape selected, press the **Shift** key and click the right edge of the first shape to select both shapes.
   f. Click the **Align** button [*Drawing Tools Format* tab, *Arrange* group] and select **Align Center**.
   g. Use the up or down arrow keys to adjust the vertical position of the selected shape.

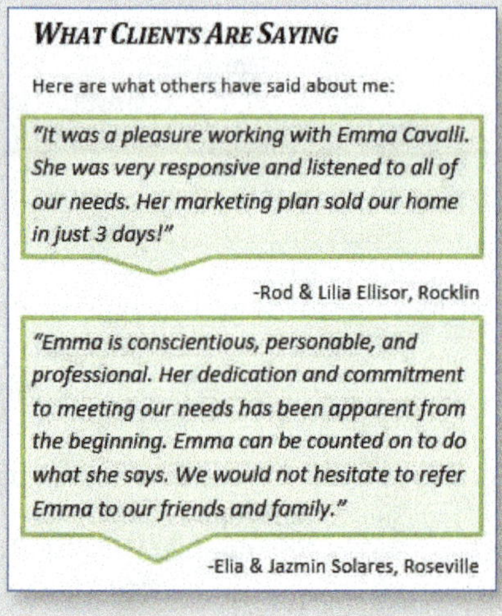

4-85 Shapes positioned behind text

10. Add *WordArt* to the brochure and customize it.
   a. At the top of the first column, select the text "**Emma Cavalli**" (including the paragraph mark).
   b. Click the **WordArt** button [*Insert* tab, *Text* group].
   c. Select **Gradient Fill – Gray** to convert the selected text to *WordArt* (Figure 4-86).
   d. With the *WordArt* selected, change the *Shape Height* to **0.8"** and the *Shape Width* to **3.6"** [*Drawing Tools Format* tab, *Size* group].
   e. Click the **Text Effects** button [*Drawing Tools Format* tab, *WordArt Styles* group], click **Reflection**, and select **Tight Reflection, touching** (Figure 4-87).

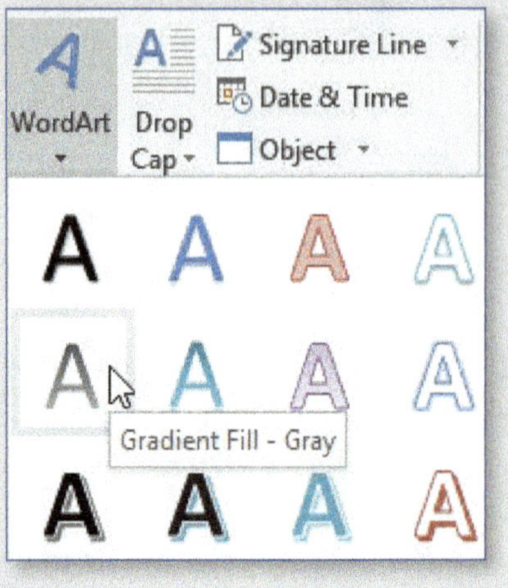

4-86 Select *WordArt* style

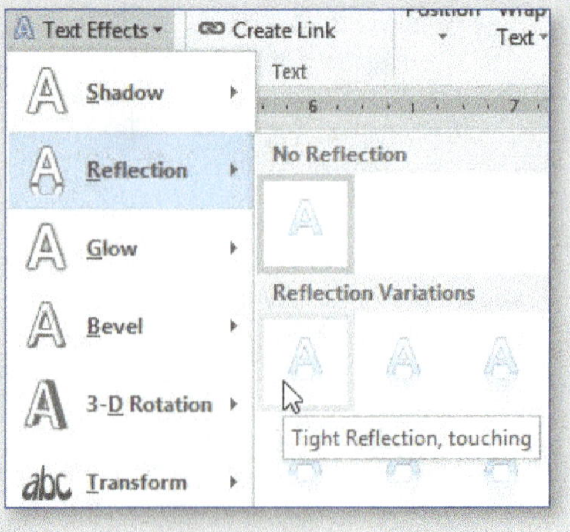

4-87 Apply a *Reflection* text effect

f. Click the **Position** button [*Drawing Tools Format* tab, *Arrange* group] and select **More Layout Options**. The *Layout* dialog box opens.
g. In the *Horizontal* area, change the *Absolute position* to **0.2" to the right of Page**.
h. In the *Vertical* area, change the *Absolute position* to **0.2" below Page**.
i. Click **OK** to close the *Layout* dialog box.

11. Save and close the document (Figure 4-88).

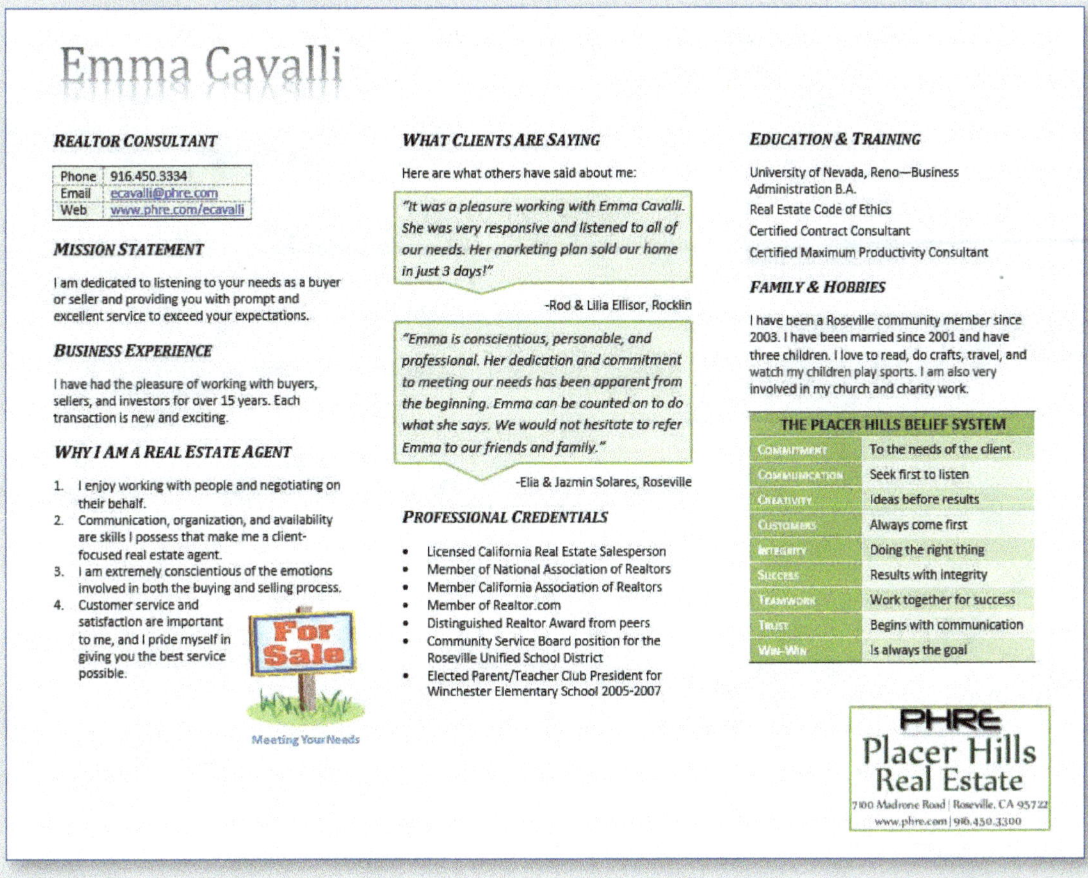

Emma Cavalli

REALTOR CONSULTANT

Phone	916.450.3334
Email	ecavalli@phre.com
Web	www.phre.com/ecavalli

MISSION STATEMENT

I am dedicated to listening to your needs as a buyer or seller and providing you with prompt and excellent service to exceed your expectations.

BUSINESS EXPERIENCE

I have had the pleasure of working with buyers, sellers, and investors for over 15 years. Each transaction is new and exciting.

WHY I AM A REAL ESTATE AGENT

1. I enjoy working with people and negotiating on their behalf.
2. Communication, organization, and availability are skills I possess that make me a client-focused real estate agent.
3. I am extremely conscientious of the emotions involved in both the buying and selling process.
4. Customer service and satisfaction are important to me, and I pride myself in giving you the best service possible.

For Sale

Meeting Your Needs

WHAT CLIENTS ARE SAYING

Here are what others have said about me:

"It was a pleasure working with Emma Cavalli. She was very responsive and listened to all of our needs. Her marketing plan sold our home in just 3 days!"

-Rod & Lilia Ellisor, Rocklin

"Emma is conscientious, personable, and professional. Her dedication and commitment to meeting our needs has been apparent from the beginning. Emma can be counted on to do what she says. We would not hesitate to refer Emma to our friends and family."

-Elia & Jazmin Solares, Roseville

PROFESSIONAL CREDENTIALS

- Licensed California Real Estate Salesperson
- Member of National Association of Realtors
- Member California Association of Realtors
- Member of Realtor.com
- Distinguished Realtor Award from peers
- Community Service Board position for the Roseville Unified School District
- Elected Parent/Teacher Club President for Winchester Elementary School 2005-2007

EDUCATION & TRAINING

University of Nevada, Reno—Business Administration B.A.
Real Estate Code of Ethics
Certified Contract Consultant
Certified Maximum Productivity Consultant

FAMILY & HOBBIES

I have been a Roseville community member since 2003. I have been married since 2001 and have three children. I love to read, do crafts, travel, and watch my children play sports. I am also very involved in my church and charity work.

THE PLACER HILLS BELIEF SYSTEM	
Commitment	To the needs of the client
Communication	Seek first to listen
Creativity	Ideas before results
Customers	Always come first
Integrity	Doing the right thing
Success	Results with integrity
Teamwork	Work together for success
Trust	Begins with communication
Win-Win	Is always the goal

PHRE
Placer Hills Real Estate
7100 Madrone Road | Roseville, CA 95722
www.phre.com | 916.450.3300

4-88 PP W4-4 completed

Chapter Summary

4.1 Improve the design and readability of a document by using tables to present and arrange information (p. W4-210).

- ***Tables*** organize information in column and row format. A ***column*** is a vertical grouping of cells, and a ***row*** is a horizontal grouping of cells.
- A ***cell*** is where a column and row intersect.
- Use ***Tab*** to move forward to the next cell and ***Shift+Tab*** to move to the previous cell.
- ***Table Tools Layout*** and ***Table Tools Design*** tabs provide you with many table formatting features.
- You can copy or move columns or rows in a table.
- You can add or delete columns and rows from existing tables.
- When working with tables, you can select individual cells, a range of cells, rows, columns, or an entire table.
- A group of cells can be merged to create one cell. Cells can also be split into multiple cells.

4.2 Modify a table by changing the column and row size, aligning text, using the *Table Properties* dialog box, sorting data in tables, and using *AutoFit* (p. W4-214).

- You can resize columns and rows in a table.
- Use the ***AutoFit*** feature to automatically resize the table to fit the contents of the table, the window, or a fixed width.
- Text in a cell can be aligned both horizontally and vertically.
- ***Cell margins*** control the amount of spacing around the text within a cell.
- The ***Table Properties*** dialog box provides size and alignment options for cells, rows, columns, or an entire table.
- You can sort table information in ascending or descending order.

4.3 Enhance the appearance and function of a table by applying borders and shading, using table styles, inserting formulas, and converting text into a table (p. W4-220).

- You can apply borders and shading to parts of a table or to the entire table.
- ***Table Styles*** are collections of borders, shading, and formatting that you can apply to a table. Word provides a gallery of table styles.
- You can apply ***Table Style Options*** to a header row, total row, banded rows, first column, last column, or banded columns.
- ***Formulas*** in a table perform mathematical calculations.
- You can convert existing text into a table or convert an existing table to text.

4.4 Modify the layout and design of a document by using columns to present information (p. W4-227).

- You can arrange text in a document in columns.
- You can choose from preset column settings or you can customize column settings and space between columns using the ***Columns dialog box***.
- ***Column breaks*** control column endings.
- Balance columns with column breaks or a ***continuous section break***.

4.5 Enrich a document by adding and modifying graphic elements such as pictures, shapes, *SmartArt*, and *WordArt* (p. W4-231).

- Pictures and graphics add visual appeal to a document. Word can insert a variety of graphic file types.
- You can resize a graphic and position it at a specific location in a document.
- ***Text wrapping*** controls how text wraps around graphics.
- The Layout dialog box has options to change the position, text wrapping, and size of graphic objects.
- You can insert customized captions for graphics.
- Graphic objects can be ***grouped*** together to create one graphic object, which makes resizing and positioning easier.
- ***Shapes*** can be inserted into a document and resized and customized. You can change fill color, outline color and width, and shape effects.
- ***SmartArt*** graphically presents information in a document.

- ***WordArt*** is special text formatting that you can insert into a document.
- Word provides a variety of formatting options and styles for *SmartArt*, *WordArt*, and other graphic objects.
- You can insert a variety of symbols and special characters into documents. Use the *Symbols* dialog box to select different symbols and characters.

Check for Understanding

The SIMbook for this text (within your SIMnet account) provides the following resources for concept review:

- Multiple choice questions
- Matching exercises
- Short answer questions

USING MICROSOFT WORD 2016

Guided Project 4-1

For this project, you modify the values statement document for Sierra Pacific Community College District to arrange text in columns, insert the company logo, and use shapes.
[**Student Learning Outcomes 4.4, 4.5**]

Files Needed: ***ValuesStatement-04.docx*** and ***SPCCDlogo-04.png*** *(Student data files are available in the Library of your SIMnet account)*
Completed Project File Name: ***[your initials] Word 4-1.docx***

Skills Covered in This Project

- Change page orientation.
- Change margins.
- Apply columns to text.
- Modify column settings.
- Insert a column break.
- Insert a picture.
- Change picture color.
- Modify picture size and position.
- Insert a shape.
- Modify shape size and position.
- Modify shape fill and outline.

---

1. Open the ***ValuesStatement-04*** document from your student data files.
2. Save this document as [your initials] Word 4-1.
3. Change the orientation and margins of the document.
   a. Change the orientation of the document to **Landscape**.
   b. Change the top and bottom margins to **0.5"**.
   c. Change the left and right margins to **0.75"**.
4. Apply column formatting to the text in the body of the document.
   a. Place the insertion point in front of the first paragraph heading ("Access").
   b. Click the **Columns** button [*Layout* tab, *Page Setup* group] and select **More Columns**. The *Columns* dialog box opens (Figure 4-89).
   c. Select **Three** in the *Presets* area.
   d. Change the *Spacing* to **0.4"** in the *Width and spacing* area.
   e. Click the **Apply to** drop-down list and select **This point forward**.
   f. Click **OK** to close the *Columns* dialog box.
5. Insert a column break to balance the columns on the page.
   a. Place the insertion point in front of the "Student Learning Outcomes" paragraph heading.
   b. Click the **Breaks** button [*Layout* tab, *Page Setup* group] and select **Column**.

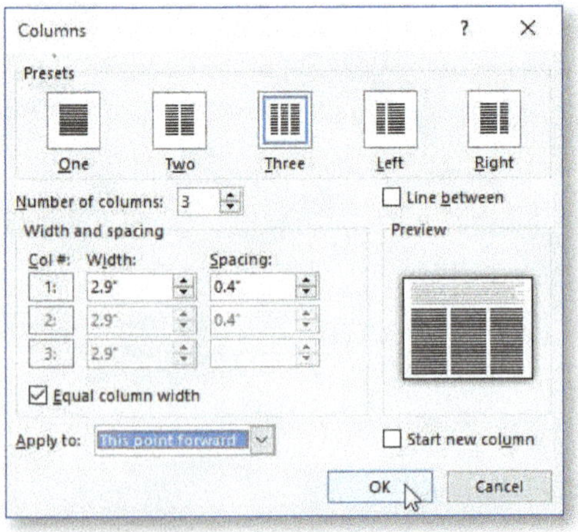

4-89 *Columns* dialog box

6. Insert, resize, and position the company logo on the bottom left of the document.
   a. Click at the end last paragraph in the first column.
   b. Click the **Pictures** button [*Insert* tab, *Illustrations* group].
   c. Select the ***SPCCDlogo-04*** file from the student data files and click **Insert**.
   d. Click the **Wrap Text** button [*Picture Tools Format* tab, *Arrange* group] and select **Behind Text**.
   e. Right-click the logo and choose **Size and Position**. The *Layout* dialog box opens (Figure 4-90).
   f. In the *Scale* area on the *Size* tab, change the *Height* to **120%** and press **Tab**. The width automatically adjusts to keep the logo proportional.
   g. Click the **Position** tab.
   h. In the *Horizontal* area, change the *Absolute position* to **0.3"** *to the right of* **Page**.
   i. In the *Vertical* area, change the *Absolute position* to **7.2"** *below* **Page**.
   j. Click **OK** to close the *Layout* dialog box.

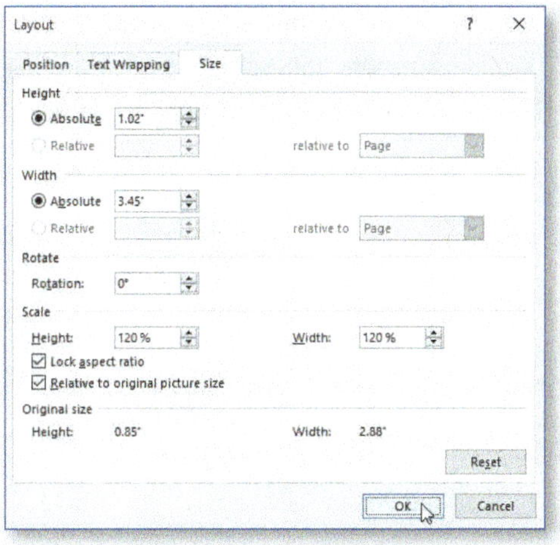

4-90 Resize logo as a percentage of its original size

7. Change the color of the logo.
   a. With the logo selected, click the **Color** button [*Picture Tools Format* tab, *Adjust* group].
   b. Select **Saturation: 0%** in the *Color Saturation* area (Figure 4-91).

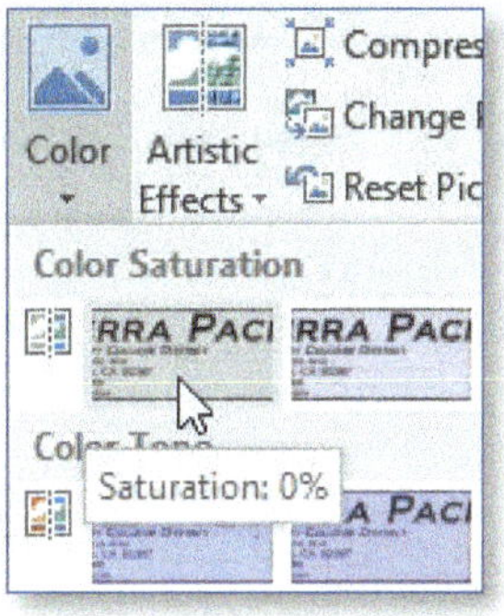

4-91 Change *Color Saturation*

8. Add a shape around the title, resize the shape, and modify the outline and fill.
   a. Click the **Shapes** button [*Insert* tab, *Illustrations* group].
   b. Select **Snip Single Corner Rectangle** from the *Shapes* gallery (*Rectangles* area). Your pointer becomes a crosshair (dark plus sign) (Figure 4-92).
   c. Click and drag the crosshair over the title and then release the pointer (Figure 4-93).

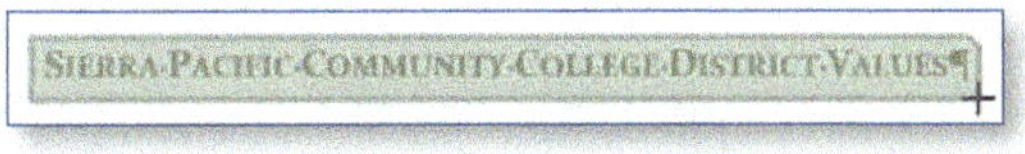

4-93 Draw shape around the title

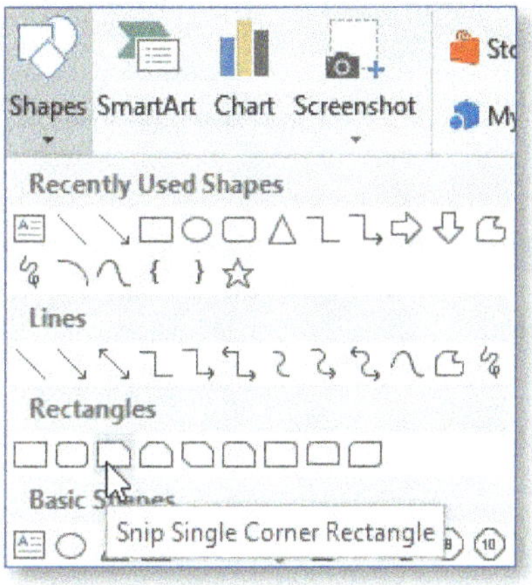

4-92 Select shape

   d. Click the **Shape Fill** button [*Drawing Tools Format* tab, *Shape Styles* group] and select **White, Background 1, Darker 15%**.
   e. Click the **Shape Outline** button [*Drawing Tools Format* tab, *Shape Styles* group] and select **White, Background 1, Darker 50%**.
   f. Click the **Shape Outline** button again, select **Weight**, and select **1½ pt**.
   g. Click the **Send Backward** drop-down arrow [*Drawing Tools Format* tab, *Arrange* group] and select **Send Behind Text** from the drop-down list.
   h. Change the *Shape Height* [*Drawing Tools Format* tab, *Size* group] to **0.4"** and the *Shape Width* to **6.3"**.

i. Click the **Align** button [*Drawing Tools Format* tab, *Arrange* group] and select **Align Center**.
j. Use the up and down keyboard arrow keys to vertically center the shape behind the title.

9. Save and close the document (Figure 4-94).

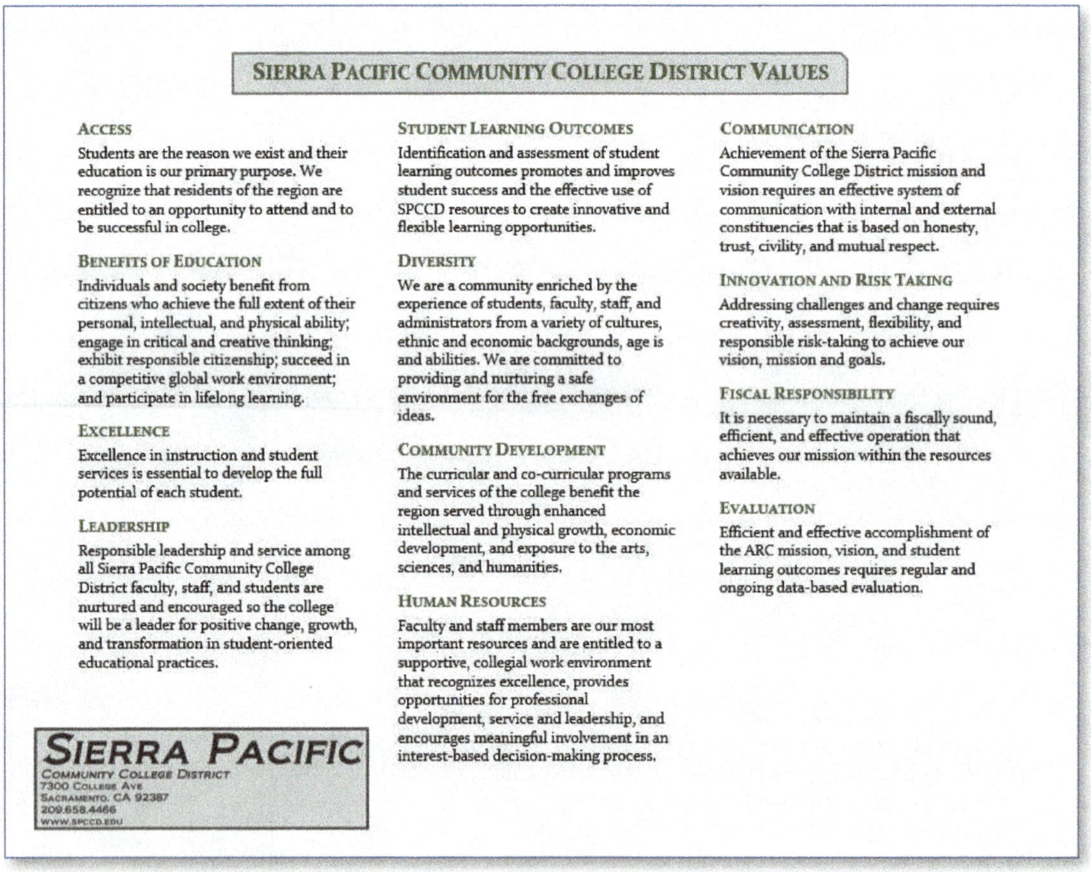

SIERRA PACIFIC COMMUNITY COLLEGE DISTRICT VALUES

ACCESS
Students are the reason we exist and their education is our primary purpose. We recognize that residents of the region are entitled to an opportunity to attend and to be successful in college.

BENEFITS OF EDUCATION
Individuals and society benefit from citizens who achieve the full extent of their personal, intellectual, and physical ability; engage in critical and creative thinking; exhibit responsible citizenship; succeed in a competitive global work environment; and participate in lifelong learning.

EXCELLENCE
Excellence in instruction and student services is essential to develop the full potential of each student.

LEADERSHIP
Responsible leadership and service among all Sierra Pacific Community College District faculty, staff, and students are nurtured and encouraged so the college will be a leader for positive change, growth, and transformation in student-oriented educational practices.

SIERRA PACIFIC
COMMUNITY COLLEGE DISTRICT
7300 COLLEGE AVE
SACRAMENTO, CA 92387
209.658.4466
WWW.SPCCD.EDU

STUDENT LEARNING OUTCOMES
Identification and assessment of student learning outcomes promotes and improves student success and the effective use of SPCCD resources to create innovative and flexible learning opportunities.

DIVERSITY
We are a community enriched by the experience of students, faculty, staff, and administrators from a variety of cultures, ethnic and economic backgrounds, age is and abilities. We are committed to providing and nurturing a safe environment for the free exchanges of ideas.

COMMUNITY DEVELOPMENT
The curricular and co-curricular programs and services of the college benefit the region served through enhanced intellectual and physical growth, economic development, and exposure to the arts, sciences, and humanities.

HUMAN RESOURCES
Faculty and staff members are our most important resources and are entitled to a supportive, collegial work environment that recognizes excellence, provides opportunities for professional development, service and leadership, and encourages meaningful involvement in an interest-based decision-making process.

COMMUNICATION
Achievement of the Sierra Pacific Community College District mission and vision requires an effective system of communication with internal and external constituencies that is based on honesty, trust, civility, and mutual respect.

INNOVATION AND RISK TAKING
Addressing challenges and change requires creativity, assessment, flexibility, and responsible risk-taking to achieve our vision, mission and goals.

FISCAL RESPONSIBILITY
It is necessary to maintain a fiscally sound, efficient, and effective operation that achieves our mission within the resources available.

EVALUATION
Efficient and effective accomplishment of the ARC mission, vision, and student learning outcomes requires regular and ongoing data-based evaluation.

4-94 Word 4-1 completed

Guided Project 4-2

For this project, you modify a document about maximum and target heart rate for the American River Cycling Club. You arrange text in a table and insert and modify *SmartArt* and a picture.
[**Student Learning Outcomes 4.1, 4.2, 4.3, 4.5**]

File Needed: ***MaximumHeartRate-04.docx*** and ***HeartRate-04.png*** *(Student data files are available in the* Library *of your SIMnet account)*
Completed Project File Name: ***[your initials] Word 4-2.docx***

Skills Covered in This Project

- Insert and resize *WordArt*.
- Position and modify *WordArt*.
- Convert text to a table.
- Apply a table style.
- Modify table and text alignment.
- Change cell margins in a table.
- Insert and add text to a *SmartArt* graphic.
- Resize, position, and format *SmartArt*.
- Insert, resize, and position a picture.
- Insert a caption.
- Align and group graphic objects.

1. Open the ***MaximumHeartRate-04*** document from your student data files.
2. Save this document as [your initials] Word 4-2.
3. Insert *WordArt* as the title of the document and modify the *WordArt* object.
   a. Select the title of the document, **"American River Cycling Club"** (including the paragraph mark).
   b. Click the **WordArt** button [*Insert* tab, *Text* group].
   c. Select **Fill – Red, Accent 2, Outline – Accent 2** from the *WordArt* gallery (Figure 4-95).
   d. Change the *Shape Width* [*Drawing Tools Format* tab, *Size* group] to **6.5"**.
   e. Click the **Position** button [*Drawing Tools Format* tab, *Arrange* group] and select **More Layout Options**. The *Layout* dialog box opens (Figure 4-96).
   f. In the *Horizontal* area, select **Alignment** and **Centered** *relative to* **Margin**.
   g. In the *Vertical* area, select **Absolute position** and enter **0.2"** *below* **Page**.
   h. Click **OK** to close the *Layout* dialog box.
   i. Click the **Text Effects** button [*Drawing Tools Format* tab, *WordArt Styles* group] and select **Reflection**.
   j. Select **Tight Reflection, touching** (Figure 4-97).

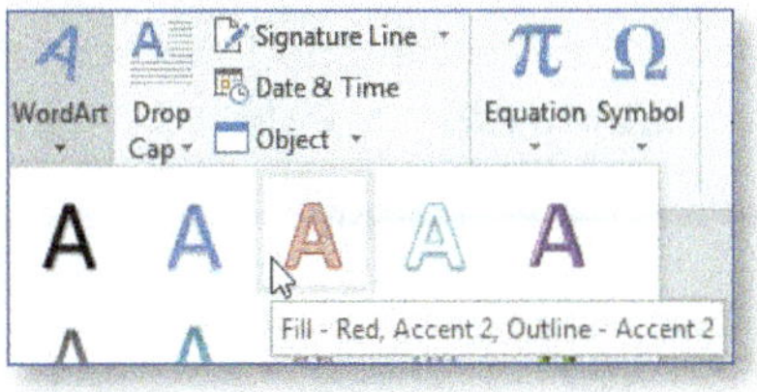

4-95 Insert *WordArt*

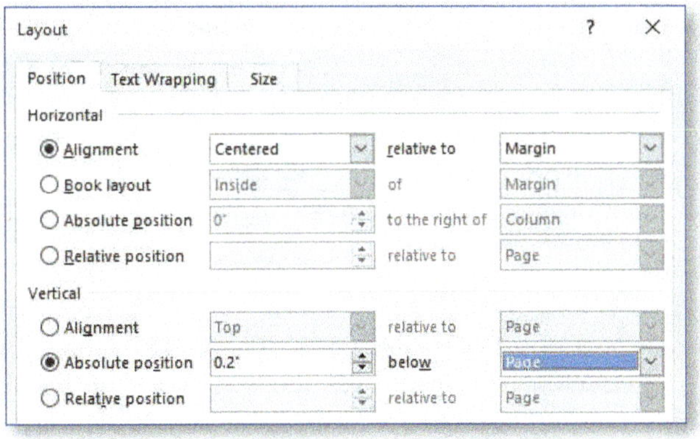

4-96 Adjust position of *WordArt*

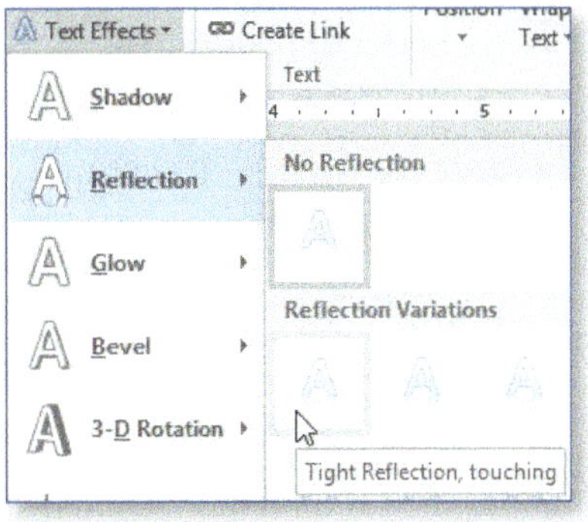

4-97 Apply *Reflection* option

4. Convert text into a table and format the table.
   a. Select all of the tabbed text at the bottom of the document.
   b. Click the **Table** button [*Insert* tab, *Tables* group] and select **Convert Text to Table**. The *Convert Text to Table* dialog box opens.
   c. Click the **AutoFit to contents** radio button in the *AutoFit behavior* area.
   d. Click **OK** to close the dialog box.
   e. Click the **Table Tools Design** tab.
   f. Check the **Header Row** and **Banded Rows** boxes [*Table Style Options* group] and deselect the other check boxes.
   g. In the *Table Styles* group, click the **More** button to display the *Table Styles* gallery.

h. Select **Grid Table 4 – Accent 2** (Figure 4-98).
i. In the second column of the first row, place the insertion point before "Zone," press **Backspace** to delete the space between words, and press **Enter**.
j. In the third column of the first row, place the insertion point before "Heart," press **Backspace** to delete the space between words, and press **Enter**.

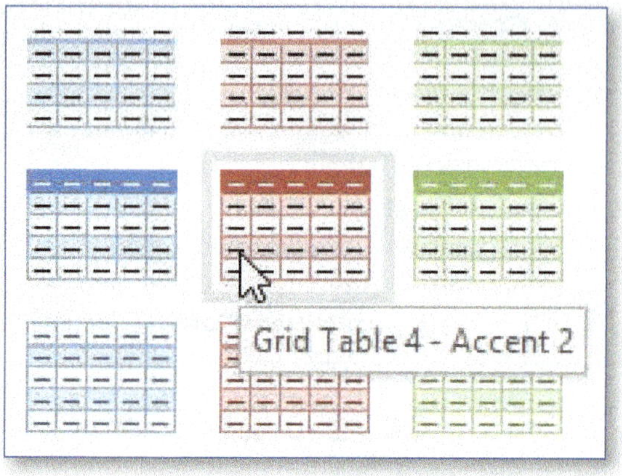

4-98 *Table Styles* gallery

5. Adjust the size and alignment of the table.
   a. Use the table selector handle to select the entire table.
   b. Click the **Align Center** button [*Table Tool Layout* tab, *Alignment* group] (Figure 4-99).
   c. With the table still selected, click the **Properties** button [*Table Tools Layout* tab, *Table* group].
   d. Click the **Table** tab, select **Center** in the *Alignment* area, and click **OK** to close the dialog box.
   e. Click the **Cell Margins** button [*Table Tools Layout* tab, *Alignment* group]. The *Table Options* dialog box opens.
   f. Change the *Top* and *Bottom* cell margins to **0.03"** and the *Left* and *Right* cell margins to **0.1"**.
   g. Click **OK** to close the *Table Options* dialog box.

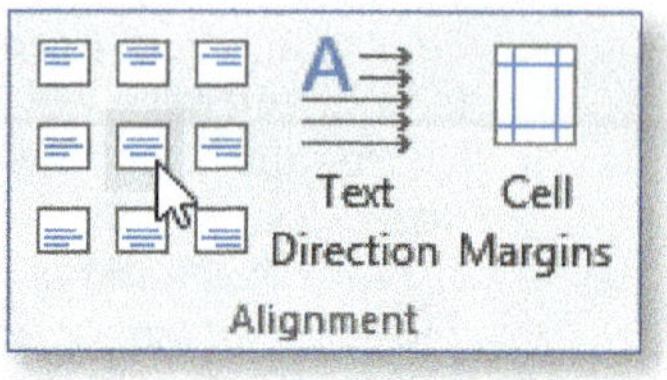

4-99 *Align Center* the text in the table

6. Insert and modify a *SmartArt* graphic.
   a. Place the insertion point at the end of the second body paragraph, "(*Example*: . . .)," in the first section.
   b. Click the **SmartArt** button [*Insert* tab, *Illustrations* group]. The *Choose a SmartArt Graphic* dialog box opens (Figure 4-100).
   c. Click **Process** in the list of *SmartArt* types.
   d. Select **Continuous Block Process** and click **OK** to insert the *SmartArt*.
   e. Click the first placeholder text (*[Text]*) and type 220, **space** once, and type – (hyphen or minus).
   f. Click the next placeholder text and type Your Age, **space** once, and type =.
   g. Click the last placeholder text and type Predicted Maximum Heart Rate.

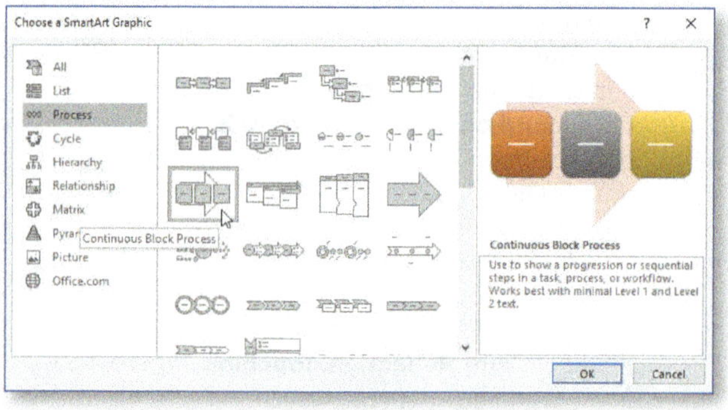

4-100 *Choose a SmartArt Graphic* dialog box

7. Format, resize, and position the *SmartArt*.
   a. Click the outside frame of the *SmartArt* graphic. *Note: Make sure the entire* SmartArt *is selected and not an object within the graphic.*
   b. In the *Size* group [*SmartArt Tools Format* tab], change the *Shape Height* to **1.5"** and the *Shape Width* to **2.6"**.
   c. Click the **Wrap Text** button [*SmartArt Tools Format* tab, *Arrange* group] and select **Square**.
   d. Click the **Position** button [*SmartArt Tools Format* tab, *Arrange* group] and select **More Layout Options**. The *Layout* dialog box opens (Figure 4-101).

e. In the *Horizontal* area, change the *Absolute position* to **4.5"** *to the right of* **Margin**.
f. In the *Vertical* area, change *Absolute position* to **0.4"** *below* **Margin**.
g. Click **OK** to close the *Layout* dialog box.
h. With the *SmartArt* still selected, select **Intense Effect** as the *SmartArt* style [*SmartArt Tools Design* tab, *SmartArt Styles* group] (Figure 4-102).
i. Click the edge of the first text box to select it, and press **Ctrl+B** to apply bold format. Repeat this format on the other two text boxes.
j. Select the last text box (if it is not already selected) and click the **SmartArt Tools Format** tab.
k. Click the **Shape Fill** button and select **Red, Accent 2** as the fill color (Figure 4-103).

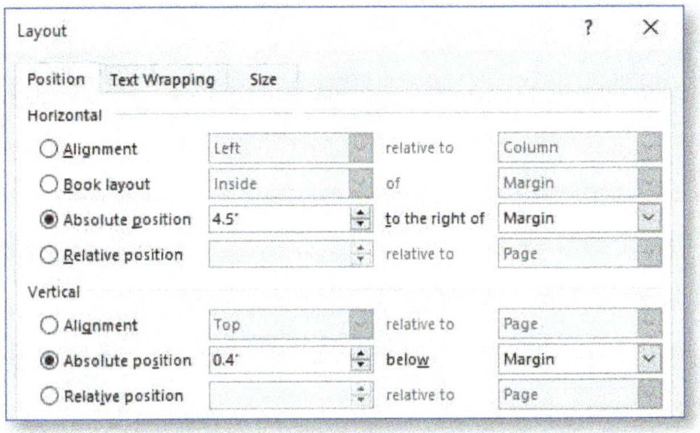

4-101 Adjust *SmartArt* position

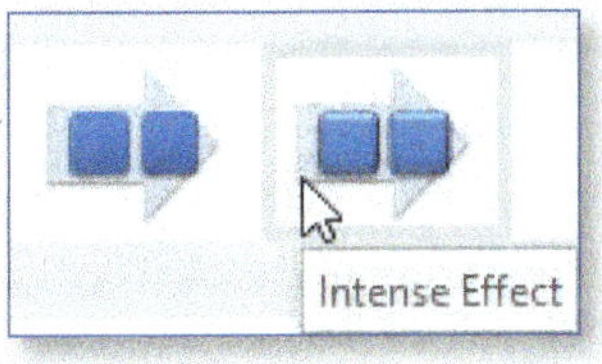

4-102 Apply *SmartArt* style

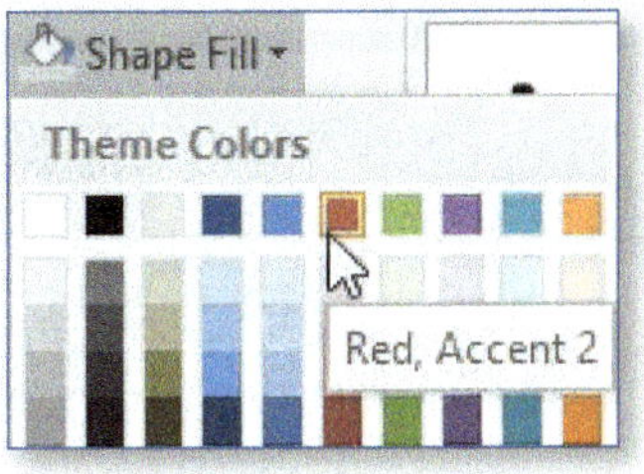

4-103 Change *Shape Fill* color

8. Insert a picture and resize and position the graphic.
   a. Place the insertion point at the end of the second section heading ("Target Heart Rate").
   b. Click the **Pictures** button [*Insert* tab, *Illustrations* group] to open the *Insert Picture* dialog box.
   c. Locate the ***HeartRate-04*** picture from your student data files and click **Insert**.
   d. Change the *Height* [*Picture Tools Format* tab, *Size* group] to **1"** (the width adjusts automatically).
   e. Click the **Wrap Text** button [*Picture Tools Format* tab, *Arrange* group] and select **Tight**.
   f. Click the **Align** button [*Picture Tools Format* tab, *Arrange* group] and select **Align Right**.

9. Format the picture and insert a caption.
   a. With the picture selected, click the **More** button in the *Pictures Styles* group [*Picture Tools Format* tab] to display the gallery of styles.
   b. Select the **Bevel Rectangle** picture style (Figure 4-104).
   c. Right-click the picture and select **Insert Caption** from the context menu. The *Insert Caption* dialog box opens.
   d. Click **OK** to insert the caption.
   e. Select the caption text, click the **Text Fill** button [*Drawing Tools Format* tab, *WordArt Styles* group], and select **Red, Accent 2** as the text color.
   f. With the caption text still selected, type Know your target heart rate to replace the caption placeholder text.
   g. In the *Size* group [*Drawing Tools Format* tab], change the caption *Height* to **0.2"** and the *Width* to **1.5"**.
   h. Press the **Ctrl** key and click the picture. Both the caption and picture should be selected.
   i. Click the **Align** button [*Drawing Tools Format* tab, *Arrange* group] and select **Align Center**.
   j. Click the **Group** button [*Arrange* group] and select **Group**. The picture and caption are grouped into one object.

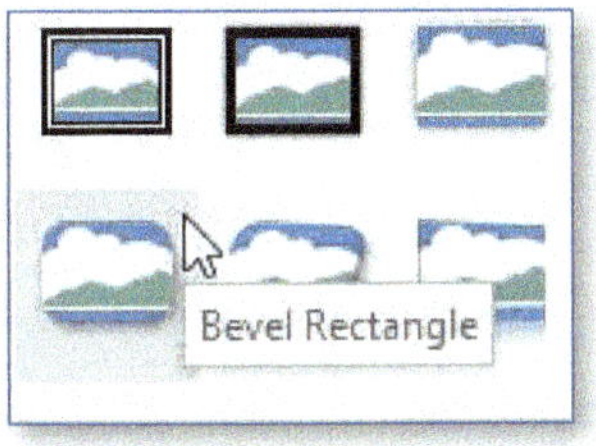

4-104 Apply *Picture Style*

10. Save and close the document (Figure 4-105).

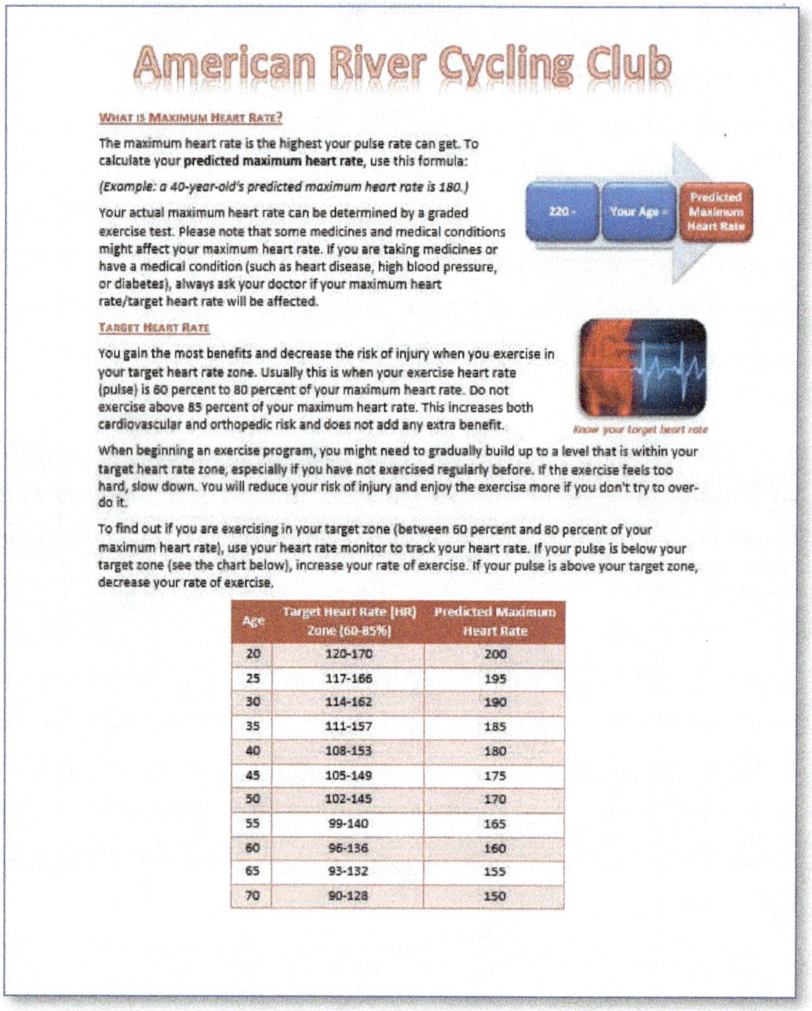

American River Cycling Club

WHAT IS MAXIMUM HEART RATE?

The maximum heart rate is the highest your pulse rate can get. To calculate your **predicted maximum heart rate**, use this formula:

(Example: a 40-year-old's predicted maximum heart rate is 180.)

Your actual maximum heart rate can be determined by a graded exercise test. Please note that some medicines and medical conditions might affect your maximum heart rate. If you are taking medicines or have a medical condition (such as heart disease, high blood pressure, or diabetes), always ask your doctor if your maximum heart rate/target heart rate will be affected.

TARGET HEART RATE

You gain the most benefits and decrease the risk of injury when you exercise in your target heart rate zone. Usually this is when your exercise heart rate (pulse) is 60 percent to 80 percent of your maximum heart rate. Do not exercise above 85 percent of your maximum heart rate. This increases both cardiovascular and orthopedic risk and does not add any extra benefit.

Know your target heart rate

When beginning an exercise program, you might need to gradually build up to a level that is within your target heart rate zone, especially if you have not exercised regularly before. If the exercise feels too hard, slow down. You will reduce your risk of injury and enjoy the exercise more if you don't try to over-do it.

To find out if you are exercising in your target zone (between 60 percent and 80 percent of your maximum heart rate), use your heart rate monitor to track your heart rate. If your pulse is below your target zone (see the chart below), increase your rate of exercise. If your pulse is above your target zone, decrease your rate of exercise.

Age	Target Heart Rate (HR) Zone (60-85%)	Predicted Maximum Heart Rate
20	120-170	200
25	117-166	195
30	114-162	190
35	111-157	185
40	108-153	180
45	105-149	175
50	102-145	170
55	99-140	165
60	96-136	160
65	93-132	155
70	90-128	150

4-105 Word 4-2 completed

Guided Project 4-3

For this project, you format a buyer escrow checklist for Placer Hills Real Estate. You convert text to a table, format the table, and insert a picture.
[Student Learning Outcomes 4.1, 4.2, 4.3, 4.5]

Files Needed: ***BuyerEscrowChecklist-04.docx***, ***Check-04.png***, and ***PHRElogo-04.png*** *(Student data files are available in the* Library *of your SIMnet account)*
Completed Project File Name: ***[your initials] Word 4-3.docx***

Skills Covered in This Project

- Convert text to a table.
- Add columns to a table.
- Apply bullets and modify alignment.
- *AutoFit* a table.
- Apply table styles and borders.
- Modify row width and column height.
- Center text vertically in a table.
- Insert, resize, and position a picture.
- Change picture color.
- Use absolute position and text wrapping.
- Apply border and effects to a picture.

1. Open the ***BuyerEscrowChecklist-04*** document from your student data files.
2. Save this document as [your initials] Word 4-3.
3. Convert text to a table.
   a. Select the text beginning with **"Task"** through **"Verify Preliminary Report with Lender."**
   b. Click the **Table** button [*Insert* tab, *Tables* group].
   c. Click the **Convert Text to Table** button. The *Convert Text to Table* dialog box opens.
   d. Click **OK** to accept the default settings. The text converts to a table with 1 column and 14 rows.
4. Add columns and column headings to the table.
   a. With the table selected, click the **Table Tools Layout** tab.
   b. Click the **Insert Right** button [*Rows & Columns* group] to insert a blank column to the right of the existing column.
   c. Click the **Insert Right** button two more times to insert two more columns. Your table should now have four columns.
   d. Type the following column headings in the first row:
      Column 2: Date Completed
      Column 3: Initials
      Column 4: Notes
5. Add bullets to selected text.
   a. Select all of the text in the first column below "Task."
   b. Apply an **open square bullet** to these items (*Wingdings*, Character code 111).
   c. Click the **Decrease Indent** button once so the first line indent is at 0" and the hanging indent is at 0.25".
6. Apply table style and apply formatting.
   a. Place your insertion point in the first cell in the first column.
   b. Click the **AutoFit** button [*Table Tools Layout* tab, *Cell Size* group] and select **AutoFit Contents**.
   c. Click the **Table Tools Design** tab.
   d. In the *Table Style Options* group, select **Header Row** and **Banded Rows**. The other options should be unchecked.
   e. Click the **More** button in the *Table Styles* group to open the gallery of table styles.
   f. Select **Grid Table 5 Dark** style (Figure 4-106).
   g. Select the column headings (first row of the table).
   h. **Bold** and **center** the column headings. You might have to click the **Bold** button more than once to bold all column headings.

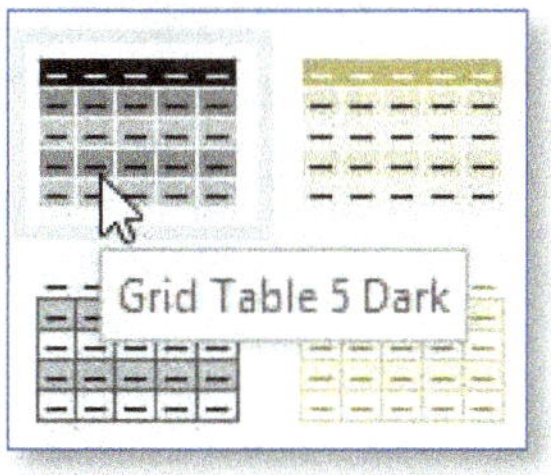

4-106 Apply table style

7. Modify cell size and alignment.
   a. Use the table selector handle to select the entire table, or use the **Select** button [*Table Tools Layout* tab, *Table* group] and click **Select Table**.
   b. Change the *Height* [*Table Tools Layout* tab, *Cell Size* group] to **0.35"**. The row height changes on the entire table.
   c. With the table still selected, click the **Properties** button [*Table Tools Layout* tab, *Table* group]. The *Table Properties* dialog box opens.

d. Click the **Cell** tab, select **Center** in the *Vertical alignment* area, and click **OK** to close the *Table Properties* dialog box.
e. Place your insertion point in the fourth column and change the *Width* [*Table Tools Layout* tab, *Cell Size* group] to **1.5"**.

8. Insert a picture and position it in the document.
   a. Place your insertion point at the end of the "Buyer(s):" line after the solid underline tab leader.
   b. Click the **Pictures** button [*Insert* tab, *Illustrations* group]. The *Insert Pictures* dialog box opens.
   c. Locate the ***Check-04*** file from your student data files and click **Insert**.
   d. In the *Size* group [*Picture Tools Format* tab], change the *Height* to **1.5"** (the width adjusts automatically).
   e. Click the **Wrap Text** button [*Picture Tools Format* tab, *Arrange* group] and select **Tight**.
   f. Click the **Color** button [*Picture Tools Format* tab, *Adjust* group] and select **Olive Green, Accent color 2 Dark** in the *Recolor* area (Figure 4-107).
   g. Click the **Position** button [*Picture Tools Format* tab, *Arrange* group] and select **More Layout Options** to open the *Layout* dialog box (Figure 4-108).
   h. In the *Horizontal* area, change the *Absolute position* to **5.5"** *to the right of* **Margin**.
   i. In the *Vertical* area, change the *Absolute position* to **0.7"** *below* **Margin**.
   j. Click **OK** to close the *Layout* dialog box.

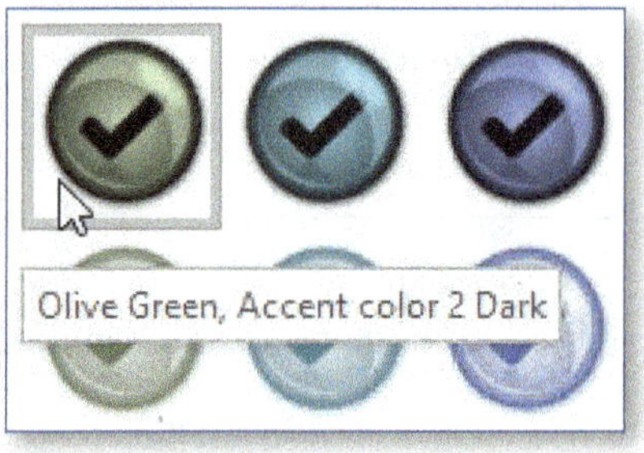

4-107 Change picture color

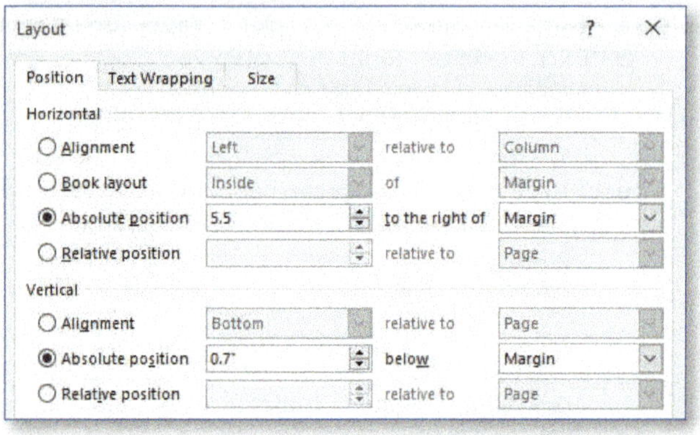

4-108 Position picture

9. Insert a picture in the upper right of the document.
   a. Place your insertion point at the end of the title.
   b. Click the **Pictures** button [*Insert* tab, *Illustrations* group]. The *Insert Picture* dialog box opens.
   c. Select the ***PHRElogo-04*** file from the student data files and click **Insert**.
   d. Right-click the picture, select **Wrap Text**, and choose **In Front of Text**.
   e. Click the **Position** button [*Picture Tools Format* tab, *Arrange* group] and select **More Layout Options** to open the *Layout* dialog box.
   f. In the *Horizontal* area, change the *Absolute position* to **6.2"** *to the right of* **Page**.
   g. In the *Vertical* area, change the *Absolute position* to **0.2"** *below* **Page**.
   h. Click **OK** to close the *Layout* dialog box.
   i. Click the **Picture Border** button [*Picture Tools Format* tab, *Picture Styles* group] and select **Olive Green, Accent 2** (Figure 4-109).
   j. Click the **Picture Border** button, click **Weight**, and select **1 ½ pt**.
   k. Click the **Picture Effects** button [*Picture Tools Format* tab, *Picture Styles* group], select **Shadow**, and select **Offset Bottom** (middle option in first row).

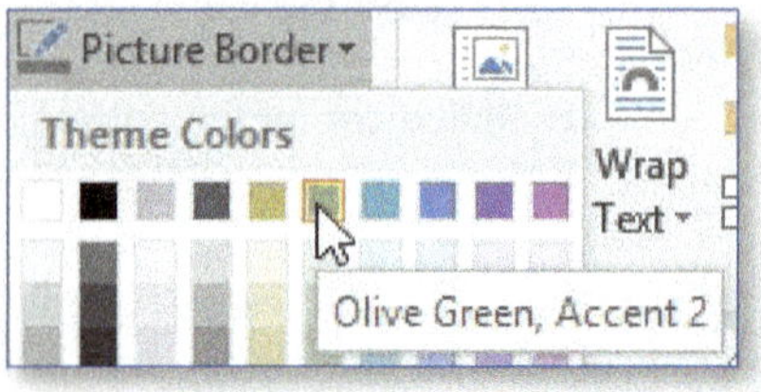

4-109 Apply *Picture Border* color

10. Save and close the document (Figure 4-110).

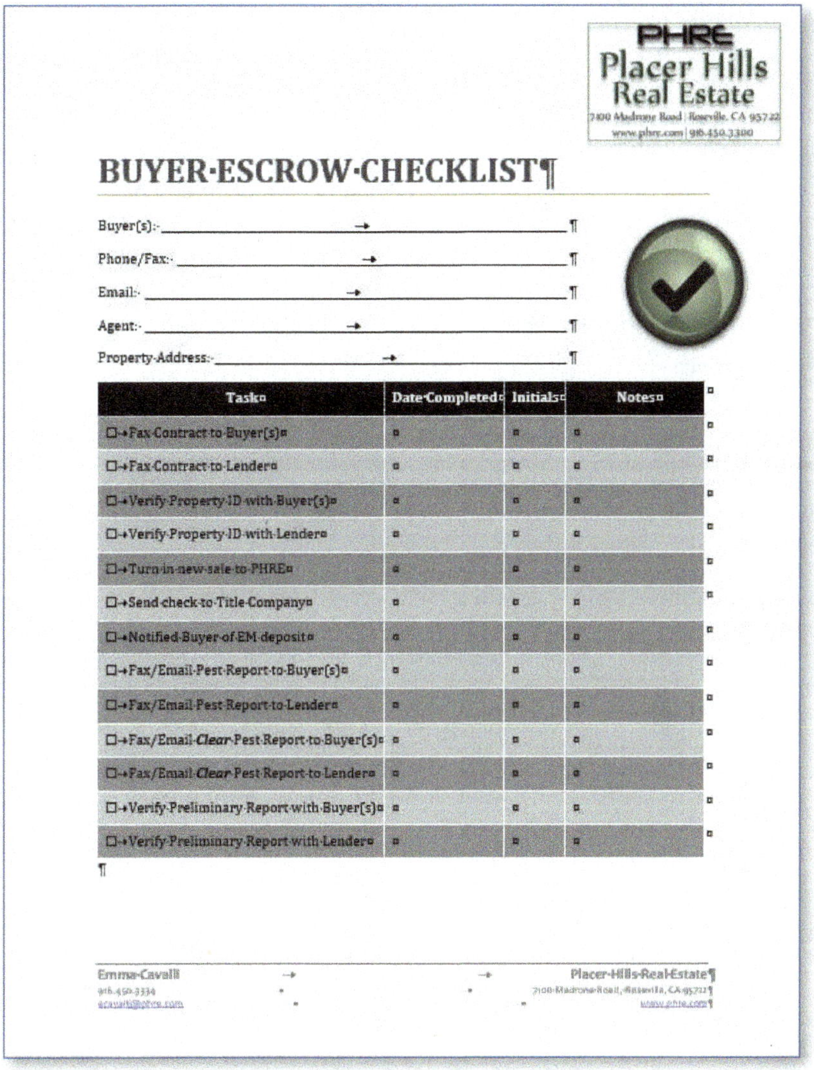
PHRE
Placer Hills Real Estate
7100 Madrone Road | Roseville, CA 95722
www.phre.com | 916.450.3300

BUYER ESCROW CHECKLIST

Buyer(s): ______________________________

Phone/Fax: ______________________________

Email: ______________________________

Agent: ______________________________

Property Address: ______________________________

Tasks	Date Completed	Initials	Notes
☐ Fax Contract to Buyer(s)			
☐ Fax Contract to Lender			
☐ Verify Property ID with Buyer(s)			
☐ Verify Property ID with Lender			
☐ Turn in new sale to PHRE			
☐ Send check to Title Company			
☐ Notified Buyer of EM deposit			
☐ Fax/Email Pest Report to Buyer(s)			
☐ Fax/Email Pest Report to Lender			
☐ Fax/Email *Clear* Pest Report to Buyer(s)			
☐ Fax/Email *Clear* Pest Report to Lender			
☐ Verify Preliminary Report with Buyer(s)			
☐ Verify Preliminary Report with Lender			

Emma Cavalli
916.450.3334
ecavalli@phre.com

Placer Hills Real Estate
7100 Madrone Road, Roseville, CA 95722
www.phre.com

4-110 Word 4-3 completed

Independent Project 4-4

For this project, you format a vaccination schedule for Courtyard Medical Plaza by converting text to a table, formatting the table, and inserting a picture.
[Student Learning Outcomes 4.1, 4.2, 4.3, 4.5]

Files Needed: ***VaccinationSchedule-04.docx, CMPLogo-04.png***, and ***Vaccination-04.png*** *(Student data files are available in the* Library *of your SIMnet account)*
Completed Project File Name: ***[your initials] Word 4-4.docx***

Skills Covered in This Project

- Convert text to a table.
- Apply a table style.
- *AutoFit* table and change row height.
- Center text vertically.
- Sort text in a table.
- Insert rows and add information.
- Merge cells.
- Apply custom borders.
- Apply a style to text.
- Insert and position a picture.
- Adjust size and position of a picture.
- Apply a picture effect.
- Add and format a caption.
- Group a caption and picture.

1. Open the ***VaccinationSchedule-04*** document from your student data files.
2. Save this document as [your initials] Word 4-4.
3. Select the tabbed text in the middle of the document and convert it to a table (accept default settings). Don't include the blank line below the tabbed text.
4. Select the entire table and apply the following changes:
   a. Select **Banded Rows** in the *Table Style Options* group [*Table Tools Design* tab] and deselect all other check boxes.
   b. Apply the **List Table 1 Light – Accent 2** table style (Figure 4-111).
   c. Change the font size on all of the text in the table to **10 pt**.
   d. Choose **AutoFit Window**.
   e. Change row height to **0.25"**.
   f. Center all text vertically within each cell. *(Hint: Use the* Cell *tab in the* Table Properties *dialog box.)*
   g. Sort the table in **Ascending** order by **Name of Vaccine**. Be sure to select **Header row** in the *My list has* area of the *Sort* dialog box.

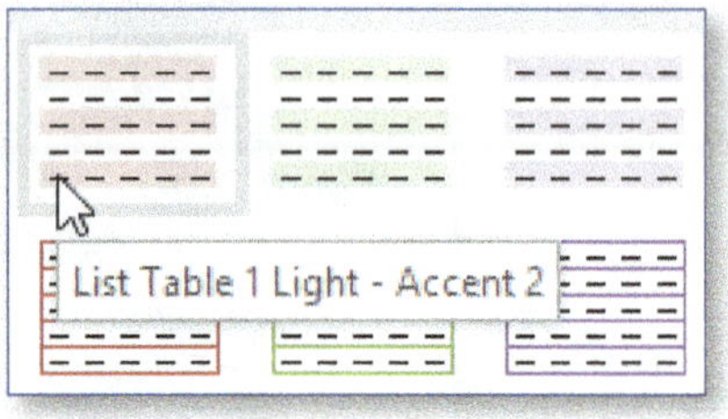

4-111 Apply table style

5. Make the following changes to the table:
   a. Insert a row above the first row.
   b. Merge the three cells in the new first row and type the following: RECOMMENDED VACCINATION SCHEDULE
   c. **Bold** and **center** the first row and change the font size to **11 pt**.
   d. **Bold** and **italicize** the second row.
   e. Select the first row, apply a **solid line, Black, Text 1** color, **1½ pt**. width **top** and **bottom** border.
   f. Select the second row, apply a **solid line, Black, Text 1** color, **1½ pt**. width **bottom** border.
   g. Select the last row, apply a **solid line, Black, Text 1** color, **1½ pt**. width **bottom** border.
   h. **Align Center** [*Table Tools Layout* tab, *Alignment* group] the column headings and the text in the third column.
6. Insert the following information alphabetically into the table. Insert rows where needed.

Meningococcal conjugate (MCV)	At 11-12 years	1
Hepatitis B (HepB)	At birth, 1-2 months, and 6 months	3

7. Modify the title of the document ("Vaccination Schedule").
   a. Apply **Title** style to the title of the document.
   b. Change the *After* paragraph spacing to **8 pt**.
   c. **Center** the title horizontally.
   d. Apply **small caps** and **bold** formatting to the title.

8. Insert and modify a picture.
   a. Place the insertion point after the title and insert the ***CMPLogo-04*** picture from you student data files.
   b. Change text wrapping to **Top and Bottom**.
   c. Change the height of the logo to **1"**. Verify the logo remains proportional.
   d. Apply the **Offset Diagonal Bottom Right** shadow picture effect.
   e. Set the horizontal and vertical absolute position at **0.2"** to the right of and below page.
9. Insert a picture and add a caption.
   a. Place the insertion point after the first body paragraph and insert the ***Vaccination-04*** picture from your student data files.
   b. Change the text wrapping to **Square**.
   c. Change the height of the picture to **1.3"**. Verify the graphic remains proportional.
   d. Drag the picture so it is to the right of the first and second paragraphs.
   e. Insert a caption and type Don't neglect your vaccinations! as the caption text.
   f. **Center** the caption text, change the font color to **Red, Accent 2**, and turn off italics if it is applied to the text.
   g. Select the caption and the picture and **Align Center**.
   h. **Group** the caption and the picture.
   i. Set the horizontal absolute position at **6"** to the right of margin.
   j. Set the vertical absolute position at **0.8"** below margin.
10. Save and close the document (Figure 4-112).

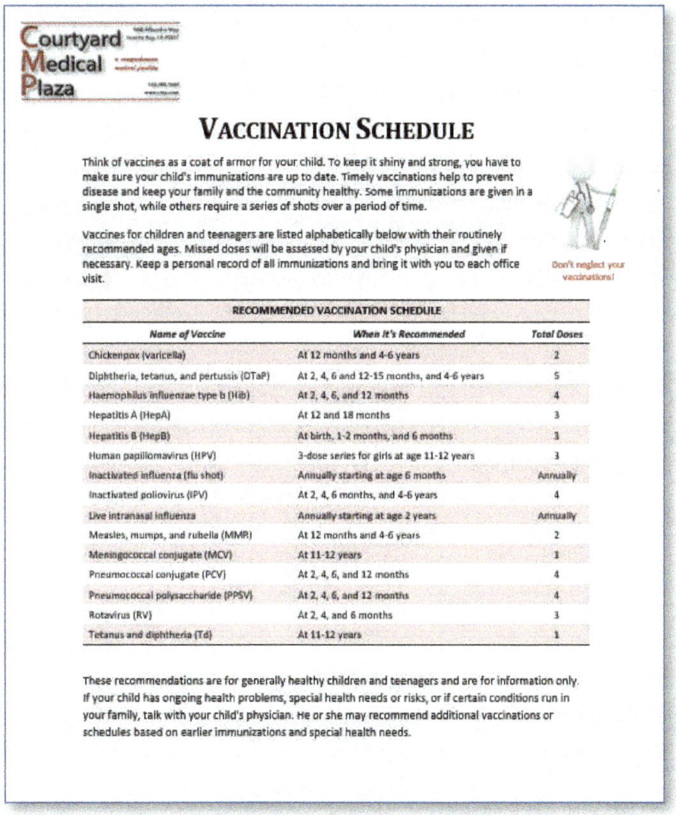

Courtyard Medical Plaza

VACCINATION SCHEDULE

Think of vaccines as a coat of armor for your child. To keep it shiny and strong, you have to make sure your child's immunizations are up to date. Timely vaccinations help to prevent disease and keep your family and the community healthy. Some immunizations are given in a single shot, while others require a series of shots over a period of time.

Vaccines for children and teenagers are listed alphabetically below with their routinely recommended ages. Missed doses will be assessed by your child's physician and given if necessary. Keep a personal record of all immunizations and bring it with you to each office visit.

Don't neglect your vaccinations!

RECOMMENDED VACCINATION SCHEDULE		
Name of Vaccine	*When It's Recommended*	*Total Doses*
Chickenpox (varicella)	At 12 months and 4-6 years	2
Diphtheria, tetanus, and pertussis (DTaP)	At 2, 4, 6 and 12-15 months, and 4-6 years	5
Haemophilus influenzae type b (Hib)	At 2, 4, 6, and 12 months	4
Hepatitis A (HepA)	At 12 and 18 months	3
Hepatitis B (HepB)	At birth, 1-2 months, and 6 months	3
Human papillomavirus (HPV)	3-dose series for girls at age 11-12 years	3
Inactivated influenza (flu shot)	Annually starting at age 6 months	Annually
Inactivated poliovirus (IPV)	At 2, 4, 6 months, and 4-6 years	4
Live intranasal influenza	Annually starting at age 2 years	Annually
Measles, mumps, and rubella (MMR)	At 12 months and 4-6 years	2
Meningococcal conjugate (MCV)	At 11-12 years	1
Pneumococcal conjugate (PCV)	At 2, 4, 6, and 12 months	4
Pneumococcal polysaccharide (PPSV)	At 2, 4, 6, and 12 months	4
Rotavirus (RV)	At 2, 4, and 6 months	3
Tetanus and diphtheria (Td)	At 11-12 years	1

These recommendations are for generally healthy children and teenagers and are for information only. If your child has ongoing health problems, special health needs or risks, or if certain conditions run in your family, talk with your child's physician. He or she may recommend additional vaccinations or schedules based on earlier immunizations and special health needs.

4-112 Word 4-4 completed

Independent Project 4-5

For this project, you create an emergency telephone information sheet for Sierra Pacific Community College District (SPCCD). You add and modify a *SmartArt* graphic, convert text to a table, insert a new table, format the tables, and insert the company logo.
[Student Learning Outcomes 4.1, 4.2, 4.3, 4.5]

Files Needed: ***EmergencyTelephones-04.docx*** and ***SPCCDlogo.png*** *(Student data files are available in the* Library *of your SIMnet account)*
Completed Project File Name: ***[your initials] Word 4-5.docx***

Skills Covered in This Project

- Modify an existing document.
- Insert a *SmartArt* graphic.
- Add text to a *SmartArt* graphic.
- Resize, change color of, and apply a style to *SmartArt*.
- Convert text to a table and *AutoFit*.
- Sort text in a table.
- Insert a row, merge cells, and add information.
- Apply a table style.
- Change cell margins and alignment.
- Apply a style to text.
- Insert a table and type text.
- Insert a picture.
- Adjust a picture size and position.
- Insert a symbol and the current date.

1. Open the ***EmergencyTelephones-04*** document from your student data files.
2. Save this document as [your initials] Word 4-5.
3. Insert a *SmartArt* graphic and add text.
   a. Place your insertion point in front of the second section heading ("Emergency Telephone Locations").
   b. Insert the **Vertical Chevron List** *SmartArt* graphic from the *List* category (Figure 4-113).
   c. Type 1 in the graphic text box in the upper left of the *SmartArt* graphic.
   d. Type 2 in the graphic text box below.
   e. Type 3 in the third graphic text box in the first column of the graphic.

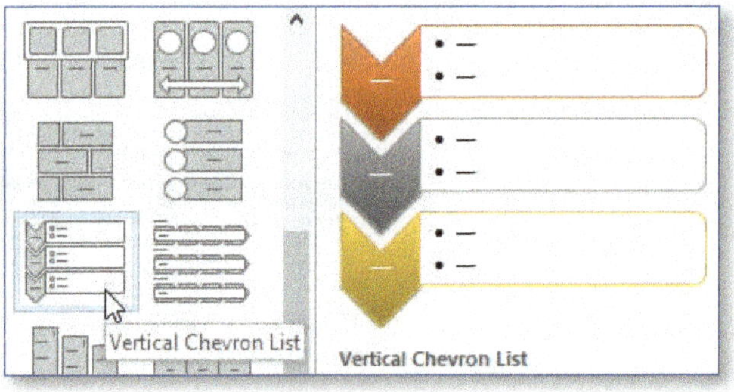

4-113 Insert *SmartArt* graphic

   f. Type the following text in the bulleted text boxes in the second column. You do not need to add bullets because bullets are already included in the *SmartArt*.

      - Press the "Help" button
      - Speak when the light comes on

      - Stay on the line
      - You will be connected with the college police

      - State clearly the nature of the emergency and your location

   g. Delete the extra bullet in the last graphic in the second column.
4. Resize and format the *SmartArt* graphic.
   a. Select the frame of the graphic to select the entire graphic.
   b. Change the height to **2.5"** and the width to **4.2"**.
   c. Change the text wrapping to **Top and Bottom**.

d. Change the color of the entire *SmartArt* graphic to **Dark 2 Fill** (Figure 4-114).
e. Apply the **Intense Effect** *SmartArt* style.

5. Convert text to a table.
   a. Select the tabbed text below the second section heading ("Emergency Telephone Locations"). Do not select the paragraph mark below the last row.
   b. Convert this text to a table and select **AutoFit to contents**.

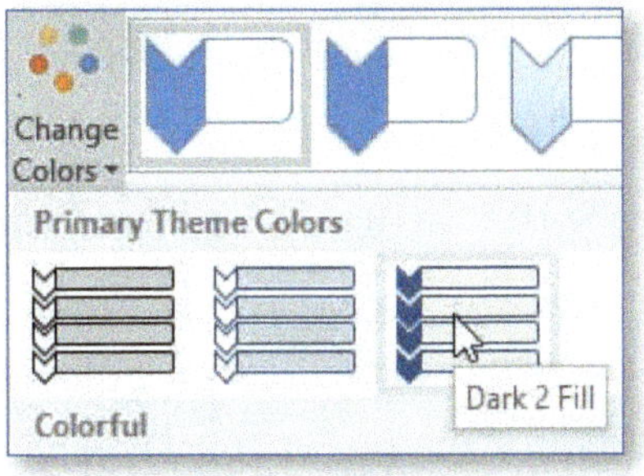

4-114 Change *SmartArt* colors

6. Sort the table text in ascending order by the first column.
7. Add a title row and insert text.
   a. Add a row above the first row.
   b. Merge the cells in this row.
   c. Type Blue Emergency Telephones in the merged first row.
8. Format the table.
   a. Select **Header Row, First Column**, and **Banded Rows** in the *Table Style Options* group. Deselect all other options.
   b. Apply the **List Table 2** table style.
   c. Select the entire table and change the top and bottom cell margins to **0.04"** and the left and right cell margins to **0.1"**.
   d. Vertically **center** all text in the table. *(Hint: Use the* Cell *tab in the* Table Properties *dialog box.)*
   e. Horizontally **center** the text in the first row. This text should be centered vertically and horizontally.
9. Insert, resize, and position the SPCCD logo.
   a. Insert the ***SPCCDlogo_04*** picture (from your student data files) at the top of the document.
   b. Change the width to **3"** and keep the size proportional.
   c. Change the text wrapping to **Top and Bottom** and drag the logo above the title.
   d. Set the horizontal and vertical absolute position at **0.3"** to the right of the page and below the page.
   e. Change the *Color* [*Picture Tools Format* tab, *Adjust* group] to **Saturation: 0%**.
10. Modify the footer to include a symbol and the current date.
   a. Edit the footer and **space** once at the end of the text on the right side of the footer.
   b. Insert a **solid circle** symbol from the *Symbol* font set (Character code 183) and **space** once after it.
   c. Type Revised: and **space** once.
   d. Insert the current date in MM/DD/YY format and set it so that it does not update automatically.
11. Save and close the document (Figure 4-115).

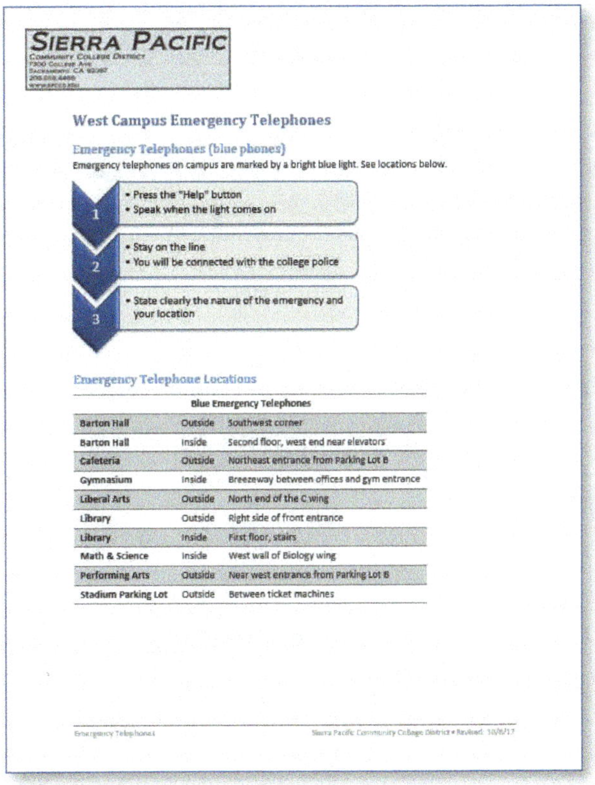
SIERRA PACIFIC

West Campus Emergency Telephones

Emergency Telephones (blue phones)

Emergency telephones on campus are marked by a bright blue light. See locations below.

1 • Press the "Help" button • Speak when the light comes on

2 • Stay on the line • You will be connected with the college police

3 • State clearly the nature of the emergency and your location

Emergency Telephone Locations

Blue Emergency Telephones		
Barton Hall	Outside	Southwest corner
Barton Hall	Inside	Second floor, west end near elevators
Cafeteria	Outside	Northeast entrance from Parking Lot B
Gymnasium	Inside	Breezeway between offices and gym entrance
Liberal Arts	Outside	North end of the C wing
Library	Outside	Right side of front entrance
Library	Inside	First floor, stairs
Math & Science	Inside	West wall of Biology wing
Performing Arts	Outside	Near west entrance from Parking Lot B
Stadium Parking Lot	Outside	Between ticket machines

4-115 Word 4-5 completed

Independent Project 4-6

For this project, you modify a memo for Life's Animal Shelter. You edit an existing table, add rows and a column, format the table, insert formulas into the table, and insert and modify *WordArt*.
[Student Learning Outcomes 4.1, 4.2, 4.3]

File Needed: ***WeeklyExpenses-04.docx*** *(Student data files are available in the* Library *of your SIMnet account)*
Completed Project File Name: ***[your initials] Word 4-6.docx***

Skills Covered in This Project

- Modify an existing document.
- Modify a table row height.
- Change cell alignment.
- Add rows and a column to a table.
- Merge table rows.
- Modify borders and shading of the table.
- Insert formulas into a table.
- Set formula number format.
- Update formulas.
- Format selected text.
- Insert *WordArt*.
- Modify and position *WordArt*.
- Change paragraph spacing.
- Insert a date.

1. Open the ***WeeklyExpenses-04*** document from your student data files.
2. Save this document as [your initials] Word 4-6.
3. Sort the table in ascending order by the "Expenses" column (the table has a header row).
4. Add rows, a column, and text to the table.
   a. Insert two rows above the first row.
   b. Insert one row below the last row.
   c. Insert one column to the right of the last column.
   d. Merge the cells in the first row and type Life's Animal Shelter.
   e. Merge the cells in the second row and type Weekly Expenses.
   f. If there is a paragraph symbol at the end of the title and subtitle text, delete the paragraph symbol in these two rows.
   g. Type Totals in the last column in the third row.
   h. Type Totals in the first column in the last row.
5. Modify row height and text alignment.
   a. Change the row height on the entire table to **0.3"**.
   b. **Align Center** (vertical and horizontal) the first two rows.
   c. **Align Center Left** the first column below the two merged rows.
   d. **Align Center Right** columns 2–9 (including blank cells) below the two merged rows.
6. Remove table borders and apply custom borders and shading.
   a. Select the table, remove all borders, and turn on **View Gridlines** [*Table Tools Layout* tab, *Table* group].
   b. Apply a **double line, Black, Text 1** color, **1½ pt**. width **top** border to the first row.
   c. Apply a **double line, Black, Text 1** color, **1½ pt**. width **bottom** border to the last row.
   d. Apply a **single line, Black, Text 1** color, **½ pt**. width **top** and **bottom** border to the third row.
   e. Apply a **single line, Black, Text 1** color, **½ pt**. width **top** border to the last row.
   f. Select the cells in the first column below the two merged rows and add a **single line**, **Black, Text 1** color, **½ pt**. width **right** border. Don't include the first two rows (title and subtitle).
   g. Select the cells in the last column below the two merged rows, and add a **single line**, **Black, Text 1** color, **½ pt**. width **left** border to the last column. Don't include the first two rows (title and subtitle).

h. Apply **Orange, Accent 6, Lighter 60%** shading fill to the first two rows.
i. Apply **Orange, Accent 6, Lighter 60%** shading fill to the last row.
j. Apply **Orange, Accent 6, Lighter 60%** shading fill to the last column.
k. Turn off **View Gridlines**.

7. Insert formulas into the table.
   a. In the last row of the second column, insert a formula [*Table Tools Layout* tab, *Data* group] to add the figures above. The formula should be **=SUM(ABOVE)**. Use the **$#,##0.00;($#,##0.00)** number format (Figure 4-116).
   b. Insert the same formula and number format in remaining cells in the last row, except for the last column.
   c. In the last column of the fourth row, insert a formula to add the figures to the left. The formula should be **=SUM(LEFT)**. Use the **$#,##0.00;($#,##0.00)** number format.
   d. Insert the same formula and number format in remaining rows in the last column. Make sure to insert the correct formula in each of these cells **=SUM(LEFT)**. Replace "ABOVE" with "LEFT" in the formula, if needed.

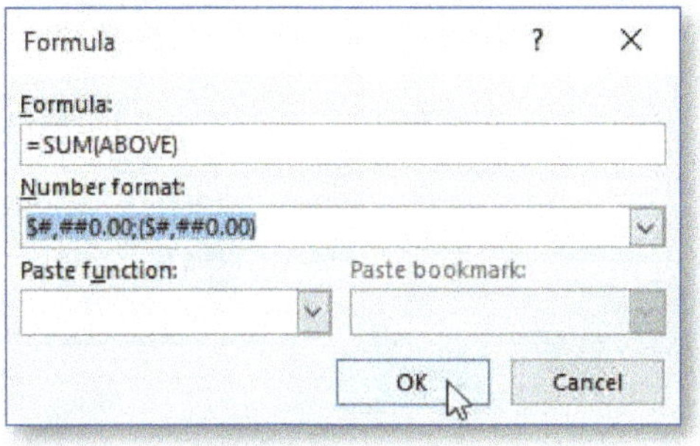

4-116 Insert a formula into the table

8. Change expense data and update formulas.
   a. Change the wages for Wednesday to 592.75.
   b. Right-click the total amounts in this column and row and select **Update Field** from the context menu to update the totals.
   c. Update the formula for grand total (bottom right cell).

9. Format text in the table.
   a. Apply **bold**, **small caps**, and **12 pt**. font size to the text in the first two rows.
   b. **Bold** and **italicize** text in the third row.
   c. **Bold** and **italicize** text and totals in the last row.
   d. **Bold** and **italicize** totals in the last column.
   e. **Italicize** the expense categories in the first column.
   f. Select the table and **AutoFit Contents**.

10. Insert and customize *WordArt* for the company logo.
   a. At the top of the document, insert **WordArt** and use **Fill – Red, Accent 2, Outline – Accent 2** (Figure 4-117).
   b. Type Life's Animal Shelter as the text for the *WordArt*.
   c. Change the text to **small caps** and **40 pt**.
   d. Change the text fill to **Orange, Accent 6**.
   e. Change the **Shadow** text effect to **Offset Right**.
   f. Use the *Layout* dialog box to change the horizontal **Alignment** to **Centered** relative to **Margin** and change vertical **Absolute position** to **0.2"** below **Page**.

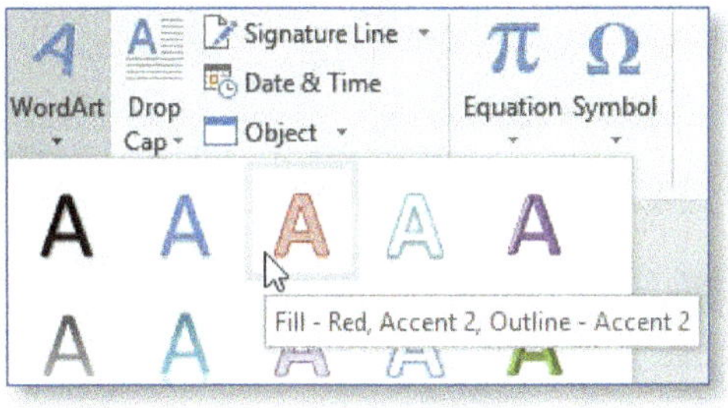

4-117 Insert *WordArt*

11. Modify the heading lines of the memo.
   a. Add **36 pt**. before paragraph spacing on the first line of the memo heading ("TO: . . .").
   b. Insert the current date on the date line in the memo heading to replace the placeholder text and set it to update automatically (use January 1, 2018 format).

12. Save and close the document (Figure 4-118).

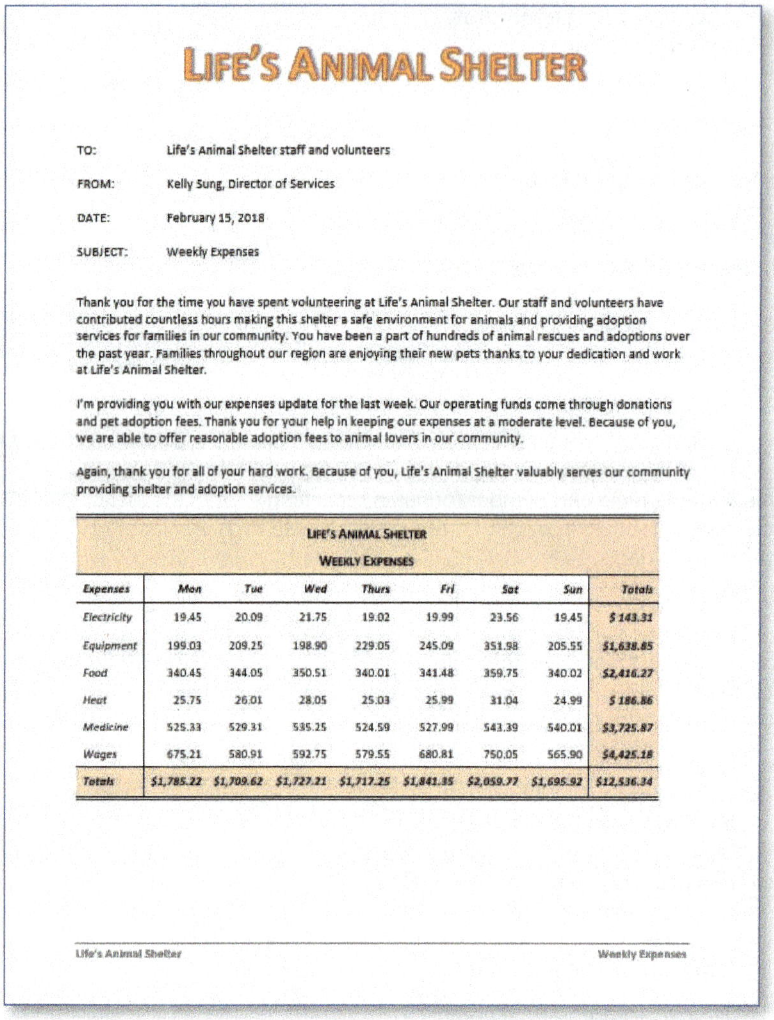

LIFE'S ANIMAL SHELTER

TO: Life's Animal Shelter staff and volunteers

FROM: Kelly Sung, Director of Services

DATE: February 15, 2018

SUBJECT: Weekly Expenses

Thank you for the time you have spent volunteering at Life's Animal Shelter. Our staff and volunteers have contributed countless hours making this shelter a safe environment for animals and providing adoption services for families in our community. You have been a part of hundreds of animal rescues and adoptions over the past year. Families throughout our region are enjoying their new pets thanks to your dedication and work at Life's Animal Shelter.

I'm providing you with our expenses update for the last week. Our operating funds come through donations and pet adoption fees. Thank you for your help in keeping our expenses at a moderate level. Because of you, we are able to offer reasonable adoption fees to animal lovers in our community.

Again, thank you for all of your hard work. Because of you, Life's Animal Shelter valuably serves our community providing shelter and adoption services.

LIFE'S ANIMAL SHELTER WEEKLY EXPENSES								
Expenses	*Mon*	*Tue*	*Wed*	*Thurs*	*Fri*	*Sat*	*Sun*	*Totals*
Electricity	19.45	20.09	21.75	19.02	19.99	23.56	19.45	***$ 143.31***
Equipment	199.03	209.25	198.90	229.05	245.09	351.98	205.55	***$1,638.85***
Food	340.45	344.05	350.51	340.01	341.48	359.75	340.02	***$2,416.27***
Heat	25.75	26.01	28.05	25.03	25.99	31.04	24.99	***$ 186.86***
Medicine	525.33	529.31	535.25	524.59	527.99	543.39	540.01	***$3,725.87***
Wages	675.21	580.91	592.75	579.55	680.81	750.05	565.90	***$4,425.18***
Totals	***$1,785.22***	***$1,709.62***	***$1,727.21***	***$1,717.25***	***$1,841.35***	***$2,059.77***	***$1,695.92***	***$12,536.34***

Life's Animal Shelter Weekly Expenses

4-118 Word 4-6 completed

Improve It Project 4-7

For this project, you edit a document for Courtyard Medical Plaza. You arrange text in columns, position the company logo, and apply formatting to improve the overall layout of the document. [Student Learning Outcomes 4.4, 4.5]

Files Needed: ***StayingActive-04.docx*** and ***CMPlogo.png*** *(Student data files are available in the* Library *of your SIMnet account)*
Completed Project File Name: ***[your initials] Word 4-7.docx***

Skills Covered in This Project

- Modify an existing document.
- Apply style formatting to the title and headings.
- Change font size and alignment.
- Change paragraph spacing.
- Arrange text in columns.
- Change spacing between columns.
- Use a column break to balance columns.
- Insert a picture.
- Update formulas.
- Format selected text.
- Insert *WordArt*.
- Modify and position *WordArt*.
- Change paragraph spacing.
- Insert a date.

1. Open the ***StayingActive-04*** document from your student data files.
2. Save this document as [your initials] Word 4-7.
3. Modify the title of the document.
   a. Apply **Intense Reference** style to the title ("Tips for Staying Active").
   b. Change to **18 pt**. font size.
   c. Align **center**.
   d. Change the *Before* paragraph spacing to **36 pt**. and *After* paragraph spacing to **12 pt**.
4. Modify section headings of the document.
   a. Apply **Subtle Reference** style to the section headings ("Try Some of the Following Suggestions" and "To Keep Exercise Fun and Interesting").
   b. Format both section headings to **14 pt**. font size and align **center**.
   c. Format both section headings to change *Before* paragraph spacing to **12 pt**. and *After* paragraph spacing to **6 pt**.
5. Format the last line of the document to make it part of the bulleted list that precedes it and format it consistently with the other bulleted items.
6. Apply column format to the multilevel list following the first section heading.
   a. Select the multilevel list in the first section and apply two-column format. Do not include the section heading. If the section break above the list has a number, turn off numbering on this line.
   b. Use **0.75"** space between columns.
7. Apply column format to the bulleted list following the second section heading.
   a. Select the bulleted list in the second section and apply two-column format. Do not include the section heading. If the section break above the list has a bullet, turn off bullets on this line.
   b. Modify the columns to use **0.75"** space between columns.
   c. Insert a **column break** before the third bulleted item to balance the columns.
8. Place the insertion point at the end of the first section heading ("Try Some of the Following Suggestions") and **delete** the paragraph mark.
9. Place the insertion point at the end of the second section heading ("To Keep Exercise Fun and Interesting") and **delete** the paragraph mark.
10. Insert, resize, and position a picture.
    a. Insert the ***CMPlogo-04*** picture at the top of the document.
    b. Change the width to **2.5"** and keep the size proportional.
    c. Change the text wrapping to **In Front of Text**.
    d. Change the horizontal and vertical absolute position to **0.2"** to the right of and below page.

11. Save and close the document (Figure 4-119).

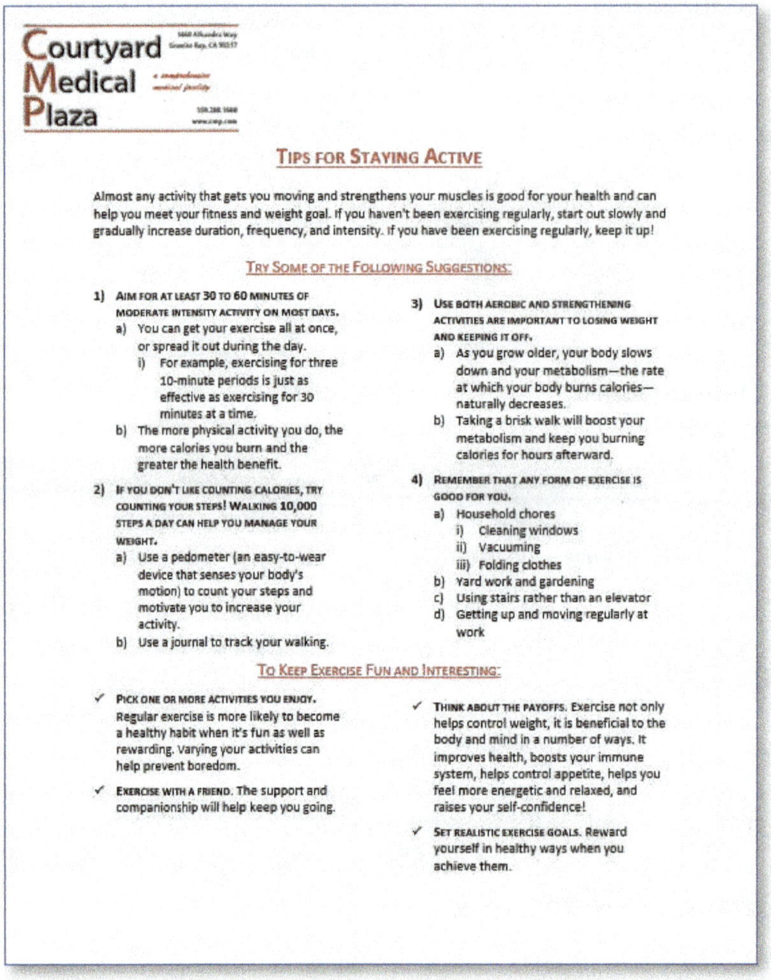
Courtyard
Medical
Plaza

TIPS FOR STAYING ACTIVE

Almost any activity that gets you moving and strengthens your muscles is good for your health and can help you meet your fitness and weight goal. If you haven't been exercising regularly, start out slowly and gradually increase duration, frequency, and intensity. If you have been exercising regularly, keep it up!

TRY SOME OF THE FOLLOWING SUGGESTIONS:

1) AIM FOR AT LEAST 30 TO 60 MINUTES OF MODERATE INTENSITY ACTIVITY ON MOST DAYS.
   a) You can get your exercise all at once, or spread it out during the day.
      i) For example, exercising for three 10-minute periods is just as effective as exercising for 30 minutes at a time.
   b) The more physical activity you do, the more calories you burn and the greater the health benefit.
2) IF YOU DON'T LIKE COUNTING CALORIES, TRY COUNTING YOUR STEPS! WALKING 10,000 STEPS A DAY CAN HELP YOU MANAGE YOUR WEIGHT.
   a) Use a pedometer (an easy-to-wear device that senses your body's motion) to count your steps and motivate you to increase your activity.
   b) Use a journal to track your walking.
3) USE BOTH AEROBIC AND STRENGTHENING ACTIVITIES ARE IMPORTANT TO LOSING WEIGHT AND KEEPING IT OFF.
   a) As you grow older, your body slows down and your metabolism—the rate at which your body burns calories—naturally decreases.
   b) Taking a brisk walk will boost your metabolism and keep you burning calories for hours afterward.
4) REMEMBER THAT ANY FORM OF EXERCISE IS GOOD FOR YOU.
   a) Household chores
      i) Cleaning windows
      ii) Vacuuming
      iii) Folding clothes
   b) Yard work and gardening
   c) Using stairs rather than an elevator
   d) Getting up and moving regularly at work

TO KEEP EXERCISE FUN AND INTERESTING:

✓ PICK ONE OR MORE ACTIVITIES YOU ENJOY. Regular exercise is more likely to become a healthy habit when it's fun as well as rewarding. Varying your activities can help prevent boredom.

✓ EXERCISE WITH A FRIEND. The support and companionship will help keep you going.

✓ THINK ABOUT THE PAYOFFS. Exercise not only helps control weight, it is beneficial to the body and mind in a number of ways. It improves health, boosts your immune system, helps control appetite, helps you feel more energetic and relaxed, and raises your self-confidence!

✓ SET REALISTIC EXERCISE GOALS. Reward yourself in healthy ways when you achieve them.

4-119 Word 4-7 completed

Challenge Project 4-8

A budget can help you track actual or anticipated spending and compare the amount you spend with your earnings. For this project, you use skills you learned in this chapter to create a weekly or monthly budget. [**Student Learning Outcomes 4.1, 4.2, 4.3, 4.5**]

File Needed: None
Completed Project File Name: ***[your initials] Word 4-8.docx***

Create a new document and save it as [your initials] Word 4-8.

A budget can include, but is not limited to, the following elements:

- Document title
- Time frame of the budget
- Expenditure categories
- Days in the week or weeks in the month
- Row and column totals

Modify your document according to the following guidelines:

- Format your budget in a table.
- Use column headings for days or weeks.
- Use row headings for expense categories.
- Use formulas to total rows and columns.
- Sort table by expenditure amounts.
- Apply table style formatting.
- Adjust shading and borders as needed.
- Adjust column width and row height.
- Modify cell margins.
- Format row and column totals.
- Insert a picture.
- Format, resize, and position a picture.
- Adjust document margins as needed.
- Include an appropriate header and/or footer.

Challenge Project 4-9

Most newspapers and magazines arrange text in column format to improve readability and overall attractiveness of the document. For this project, you arrange an existing document you have written (e.g., an essay, blog entry, article for a newspaper, or posting for Craigslist) in column format.
[Student Learning Outcomes 4.4, 4.5]

File Needed: None
Completed Project File Name: ***[your initials] Word 4-9.docx***

Open an existing document you have created and save it as [your initials] Word 4-9.

A document in column format can include, but is not limited to, the following elements:

- Document title
- Byline
- Section headings
- Graphics

Modify your document according to the following guidelines:

- Format your article in column format. Don't include the title as part of the columns.
- Change space and/or add a line between columns.
- Use a column or continuous section break to balance the columns.
- Insert a graphic.
- Adjust size, wrapping, and position of the graphic.
- Add a caption to the graphic.
- Adjust margins as needed.
- Include an appropriate header and/or footer.

Challenge Project 4-10

A weekly schedule can help you organize and manage work, school, family, and personal time more effectively. For this project, use a table to create a weekly schedule and calculate the time you spend on each daily activity.
[**Student Learning Outcomes 4.1, 4.2, 4.3, 4.5**]

File Needed: None
Completed Project File Name: ***[your initials] Word 4-10.docx***

Create a new document and save it as [your initials] Word 4-10.

A weekly schedule can include, but is not limited to, the following elements:

- Document title
- Days of the week
- Time commitment categories
- Row and column totals

Modify your document according to the following guidelines:

- Format your weekly schedule in table.
- Use column headings for days of the week.
- Use row headings for time commitment categories.
- Use formulas to total rows and columns.
- Apply table style formatting.
- Adjust shading and borders as needed.
- Adjust column width and row height.
- Adjust cell margins as needed.
- Format row and column totals.
- Insert a picture.
- Format, resize, and position a picture.
- Adjust document margins as needed.
- Include an appropriate header and/or footer.

Excel

Microsoft® Office

IN PRACTICE

excel

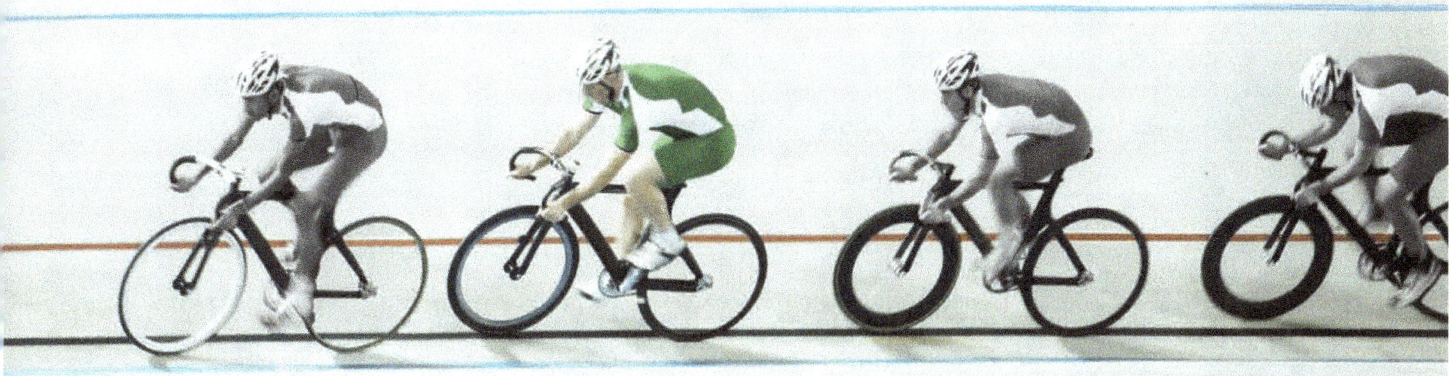

CHAPTER 1

Creating and Editing Workbooks

CHAPTER OVERVIEW

Microsoft Excel (Excel) is spreadsheet software for creating an electronic workbook. A workbook consists of rows and columns used to organize data, perform calculations, print reports, and build charts. With Excel, you can create simple to complex personal or business workbooks. This chapter presents basic procedures for creating and editing an Excel workbook.

STUDENT LEARNING OUTCOMES (SLOs)

After completing this chapter, you will be able to:

SLO 1.1 Create, save, and open an Excel workbook (p. E1-3).

SLO 1.2 Enter and edit labels and values in a worksheet (p. E1-6).

SLO 1.3 Use the *SUM* function to build a simple formula (p. E1-19).

SLO 1.4 Format a worksheet with font attributes, borders, fill, cell styles, and themes (p. E1-21).

SLO 1.5 Modify columns and rows in a worksheet (p. E1-31).

SLO 1.6 Insert, delete, and move worksheets in a workbook (p. E1-37).

SLO 1.7 Modify the appearance of a workbook by adjusting zoom size, changing views, and freezing panes (p. E1-42).

SLO 1.8 Review and prepare a workbook for final distribution by spell checking, setting properties, and adjusting page setup options (p. E1-47).

CASE STUDY

Throughout this book you have the opportunity to put into practice the application features that you are learning. Each chapter begins with a case study that introduces you to the Pause & Practice projects in the chapter. These Pause & Practice projects give you a chance to apply and practice key skills in a realistic and practical context. Each chapter contains three to five Pause & Practice projects.

Paradise Lakes Resort (PLR) is a vacation company with properties located throughout northern Minnesota. PLR staff use Excel to track revenue, to monitor expenses, to maintain employee records, and similar tasks. In the Pause & Practice projects for Chapter 1, you create, edit, and format a workbook that displays categories of revenue for one week.

Pause & Practice 1-1: Open, edit, and save a workbook.

Pause & Practice 1-2: Use *SUM* and format data in a worksheet.

Pause & Practice 1-3: Edit columns, rows, and sheets in a workbook.

Pause & Practice 1-4: Finalize a workbook for distribution.

EXCEL

SLO 1.1

Creating, Saving, and Opening a Workbook

In Microsoft Excel, the file that you open, edit, and save is a ***workbook***. Each workbook contains ***worksheets***, which are comparable to individual pages in a Word document. A worksheet is also referred to as a ***spreadsheet*** or a ***sheet***, and you can use these terms interchangeably. This text also uses the terms "workbook" and "file" interchangeably.

Create a New Workbook

By default, a new workbook includes one worksheet, but a workbook can include multiple sheets. The worksheet ***tab*** is located near the bottom left of the workbook window and is labeled *Sheet1*.

When you first open Excel, the ***Excel Start page*** displays. From the *Start* page, you can create a new blank workbook, open a recently saved workbook, or create a workbook from an Excel template (a model workbook). Click **Blank workbook** to start a new blank workbook. You can also select *Blank workbook* from the *New* area in the *Backstage* view.

ANOTHER WAY

Press **Esc** to leave the Excel *Start* page and open a blank workbook.

HOW TO: Create a New Workbook

1. Click the **File** tab to display the *Backstage* view.
2. Select **New** on the left to display the *New* area in the *Backstage* view (Figure 1-1).

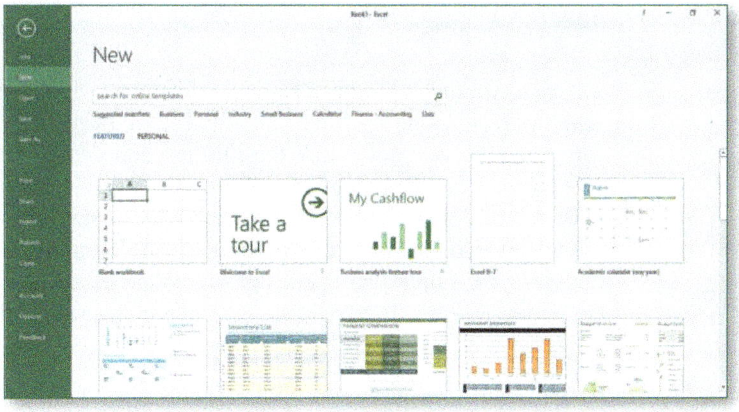

1-1 *Backstage* view for creating new workbooks

3. Click **Blank workbook** to create a new blank workbook.

ANOTHER WAY

Press **Ctrl+N** to open a new workbook.

Save and Close a Workbook

When you open a blank workbook, Excel automatically assigns a file name, such as *Book1*. The first time you save a workbook, you should type a descriptive file name for the workbook in the *Save As* dialog box. You can save a workbook on your computer, in a *OneDrive* folder, or on external media.

HOW TO: Save a New Workbook

1. Click the **File** tab to display the *Backstage* view.
2. Select **Save As** on the left to display the *Save As* area.
   - You can press **Ctrl+S** to open the *Save As* area in the *Backstage* view for a workbook that has not yet been saved.
3. Select the location to save your workbook.
   - Click **This PC** to see recently used folders.
   - Click **Browse** to open the *Save As* dialog box for further navigation.
   - Click **OneDrive** to see your cloud folder names.
4. Click the folder name to open the *Save As* dialog box (Figure 1-2).
5. Type the file name in the *File name* area.
6. Click **Save** to close the *Save As* dialog box.

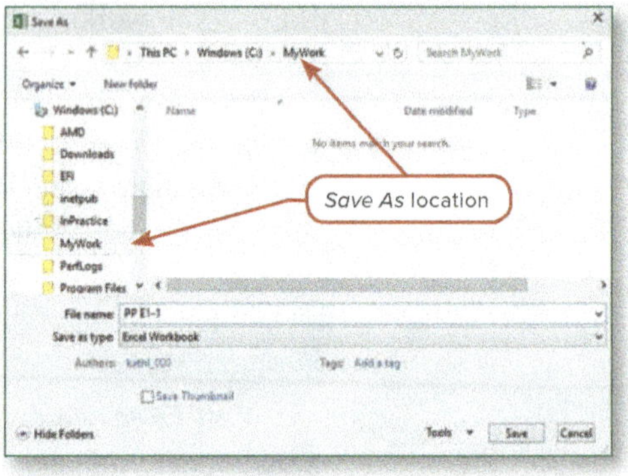

1-2 *Save As* dialog box

ANOTHER WAY

Press **F12** (**FN+F12**) to open the *Save As* dialog box.

Once a workbook has been saved, you can re-save it with the same file name by pressing **Ctrl+S** or by clicking the **Save** button in the *Quick Access toolbar*.

To close a workbook, click the **File** tab and choose **Close**. You can press **Ctrl+W** or **Ctrl+F4** to close a workbook, too. These commands leave Excel running with a blank screen so that you can open another file or start a new workbook.

You can also click the **X** (**Close** button) in the upper right corner of the window. If the workbook is the only one open, this command closes the file and exits Excel. If multiple workbooks are open, clicking the *Close* button closes only the active workbook.

Open a Workbook

A workbook can be opened from the *Start* page, the *Open* area in the *Backstage* view, or the *Open* dialog box. When a workbook is opened from an Internet or unrecognized source, it opens in ***Protected View***. Click **Enable Editing** when you know that it is safe to work with the file.

HOW TO: Open a Workbook

1. Click the **File** tab to open the *Backstage* view.
2. Click **Open** to display the *Open* area.

3. Select the location where the workbook is stored.
   - The *Recent* list displays workbook file names on the right.
   - The *This PC* option lists recently used folder names.
   - Click **Browse** to locate a folder.
4. Click the folder name that stores the file.
5. Select the workbook name and click **Open** (Figure 1-3).

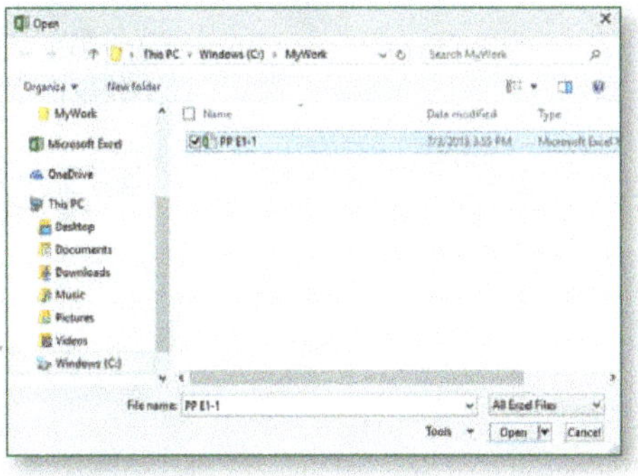

1-3 *Open* dialog box

ANOTHER WAY

Ctrl+O displays the *Open* area in the *Backstage* view. **Ctrl+F12** displays the *Open* dialog box.

MORE INFO

From an Explorer window, you can double-click a workbook file name to launch Excel and open the workbook.

Save a Workbook with a Different File Name

To preserve an existing workbook, you can open and save it with a different file name, creating a copy of the original file with a new name. Follow the same steps that you would when saving a new workbook.

HOW TO: Save a Workbook with a Different File Name

1. Click the **File** tab to open the *Backstage* view.
2. Click **Save As** to display the *Save As* area.
3. Navigate to and select the folder name to open the *Save As* dialog box.
   - You can press **F12** (**FN+F12**) to open the *Save As* dialog box.
4. Type the name in the *File name* area.
5. Click **Save** to close the *Save As* dialog box and save the file.

Workbook File Formats

Excel workbooks are saved as ***.xlsx*** files, indicated as *Excel Workbook* in the *Save As* dialog box. You can save a workbook in other formats for ease in sharing data. For example, you can save a workbook in *Excel 97-2003* format so that a coworker with an earlier version of Excel can use the data. Or you can create a PDF file of a workbook to provide data to users who do not have Excel.

The *Save as type* area of the *Save As* dialog box lists available formats (Figure 1-4). The following table lists common formats for saving an Excel workbook.

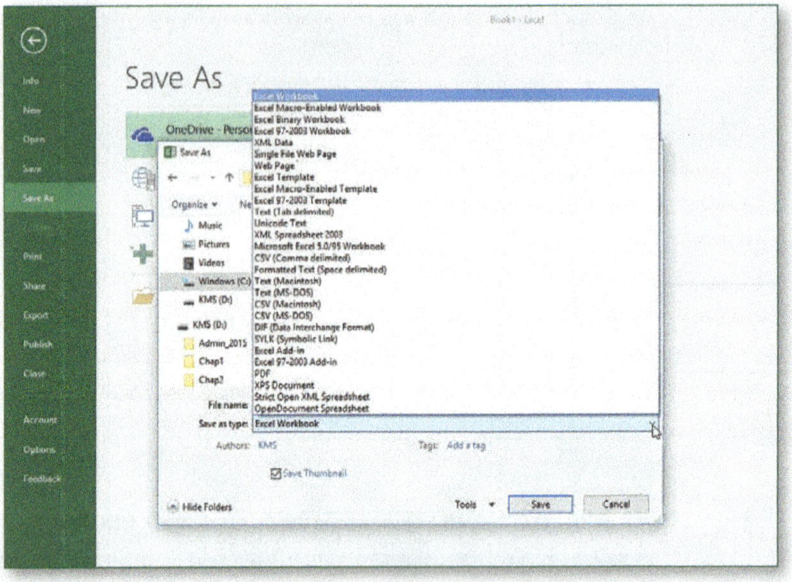

1-4 Workbook file formats

Save Formats

Type of Document	File Name Extension	Uses of This Format
Excel Workbook	.xlsx	Excel workbook compatible with versions 2010 and later
Excel Macro-Enabled Workbook	.xlsm	Excel workbook with embedded macros
Excel 97-2003 Workbook	.xls	Excel workbook compatible with older versions of Microsoft Excel
Excel Template	.xltx	Model or sample Excel workbook stored in the Custom Office Templates folder
Excel Macro-Enabled Template	.xltm	Model or sample Excel workbook with embedded macros stored in the Custom Office Templates folder
Portable Document Format (PDF)	.pdf	An uneditable image of the workbook for viewing that can be opened with free software
Text (tab-delimited)	.txt	Data only with columns separated by a tab character. File can be opened by many applications.
Comma Separated Values (CSV)	.csv	Data only with columns separated by a comma. File can be opened by many applications.
OpenDocument Spreadsheet	.ods	Workbook for the Open Office suite as well as Google Docs
Web Page	.htm, .html	Excel workbook formatted for posting on a web site that includes data, graphics, and linked objects

SLO 1.2

Entering and Editing Data

A worksheet consists of columns and rows. Columns are labeled with letters and rows are labeled with numbers. You enter data in a ***cell***, which is the intersection of a column and a row. Each cell is identified with a ***cell reference*** (or ***cell address***), the column letter and row number that represents the location of the cell. Cell A1 is the intersection of column A and row 1. A rectangular group of cells is a ***range***. The range address **A1:B3** identifies six cells in two columns and three rows.

You see column and row headings as well as gridlines on the worksheet to help you identify the location of data. You can change these options from the *View* tab if you prefer to see a cleaner background for your work. The *Gridlines* and *Headings* settings in the *Show* group are toggles that display or hide these features.

MORE INFO

From the *View* tab, you can also display or hide the formula bar and the ruler.

Enter Labels and Values

Data in a worksheet cell is text, a number, or a formula. A ***label*** is text that displays a name, a main title, row or column titles, and similar descriptive information. Labels are not included in calculations. A ***value*** is a number that can be used in a calculation or is the result of a calculation. A ***formula*** is a calculation or expression that displays a result.

When you type data that includes alphabetic characters and numbers, Excel treats that data as a label. Examples include a street address or an ID such as ABC123. When you type data with numbers that are not used in calculations, enter the data as a label by typing an apostrophe (') before the data. Examples of this type of data include a telephone or Social Security number without hyphens.

MORE INFO

If you type a Social Security number *with* hyphens, Excel will identify it as a label.

When a label in a cell is longer or wider than the cell, the label spills into an empty adjacent cell. If adjacent cells are not empty, the label is truncated or cut off in the cell, but the entire entry is visible in the ***Formula bar***. The *Formula* bar appears below the *Ribbon* and displays the contents of the selected cell. When a value is too large for the width of the cell, the cell displays a series of # symbols or shows the value in exponential notation (part of the number with E+n as in 1235E+4). You can simply widen the column to see all cell contents.

To enter data, click the cell with the pointer to select and activate the cell. The pointer appears as a solid, white cross (a thick plus sign) when selecting data in the worksheet. The ***active cell*** displays a solid border, and its address appears in the ***Name box*** (Figure 1-5).

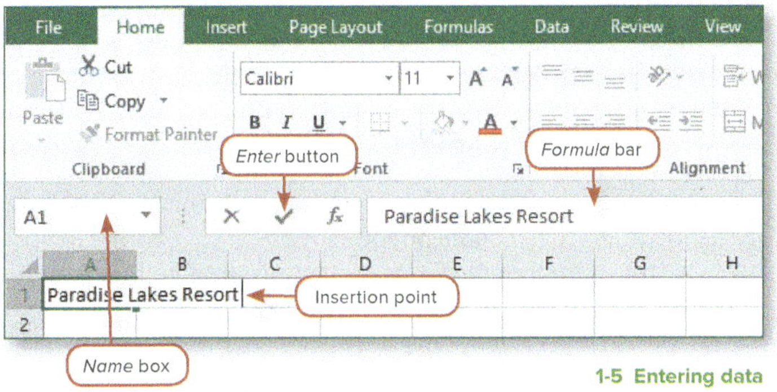

1-5 Entering data

▶ HOW TO: Enter Data into a Workbook

1. Select the cell and type the data.
   - The label or value appears in the cell with an insertion point and in the *Formula* bar.
2. Press **Enter** to complete the entry and activate the cell below.
   - Press **Tab** to complete the entry and activate the cell to the right.
   - Press any keyboard directional arrow key to complete the entry and activate the cell in the direction of the arrow.
   - Press **Ctrl+Enter** to complete the entry and keep the current cell active.
   - Click the **Enter** button in the *Formula* bar to complete the entry and keep the cell active.

Edit Cell Contents

You can edit cell data as you type or after the entry is complete. To edit as you type, press the **Backspace** key to delete characters to the left of the insertion point. Or use arrow keys to move the insertion point and press the **Delete** key to erase characters to the right of the insertion point. To edit a completed entry, start *Edit* mode by double-clicking the cell or by pressing **F2 (FN+F2)**. The word "Edit" appears in the *Status* bar to alert you that data entry is in progress. Position the insertion point either in the cell or in the *Formula* bar, make the change, and press any completion key.

When using some keyboard function keys, you may need to press the **FN** key with the function key to access the command. This depends on the type of computer as well as the keyboard. This text will show a shortcut like this **F2 (FN+F2)** as a reminder to note your keyboard layout.

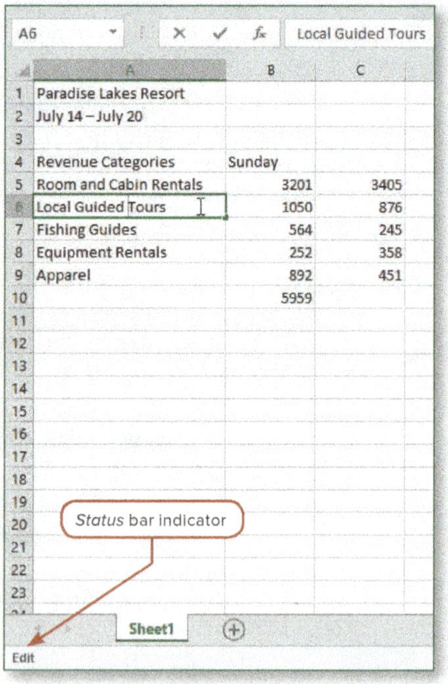

1-6 *Edit* mode

▶ HOW TO: Edit Cell Contents

1. Double-click the cell to be edited.
   - You can also click the cell and press **F2 (FN+F2)** to start *Edit* mode.
2. Position the insertion point in the cell or the *Formula* bar (Figure 1-6).
3. Edit the data.
4. Press **Enter**.

Replace or Clear Cell Contents

To replace data in a cell, select the cell and type the new data. Then press **Enter**, click the **Enter** button in the *Formula* bar, or press any completion key. The new data displays in the cell. To delete data from a cell, select the cell and press **Delete** or click the **Clear** button [*Home* tab, *Editing* group]. From the **Clear** button options, you can choose *Clear All*, *Clear Formats*, or *Clear Contents* (Figure 1-7). Pressing the **Delete** key removes the contents and preserves formatting.

▸ HOW TO: Clear Cell Contents

1. Select the cell or cells.
2. Press **Delete** on the keyboard.
   - Click the **Clear** button [*Home* tab, *Editing* group] and choose an option.
   - *Clear All* removes formatting and content.
   - *Clear Formats* only clears formatting and keeps data.
   - *Clear Contents* deletes content but keeps formatting.

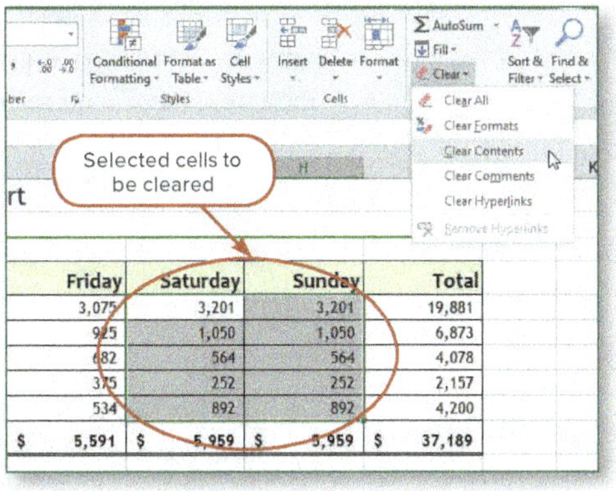

1-7 *Clear* button options

Align and Indent Cell Contents

Excel recognizes a combination of letters, numbers, spaces, and other characters as a label. Labels are aligned on the left and bottom of the cell. When you type only numbers into a cell, Excel identifies the entry as a value. Values are aligned on the right and bottom of the cell.

You can change the vertical and horizontal ***alignment*** of data in a cell from the *Alignment* group on the *Home* tab (Figure 1-8). Horizontal alignment choices are *Align Left*, *Center*, and *Align Right*. Vertical alignment options are *Top Align*, *Middle Align*, and *Bottom Align*.

An ***indent*** moves cell contents away from the left edge of the cell. In Figure 1-8, labels in rows 5:9 are offset from the label in row 4. The **Increase Indent** button [*Home* tab, *Alignment* group] moves cell contents one space to the right if the data is left-aligned. You can remove an indent by clicking the **Decrease Indent** button [*Home* tab, *Alignment* group].

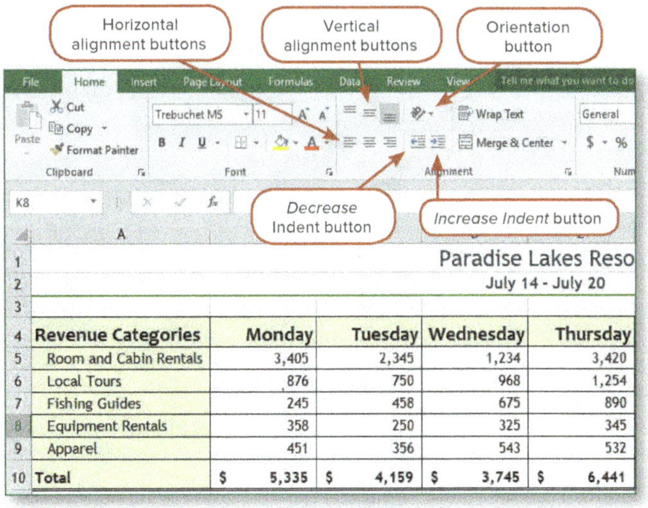

1-8 Alignment and indent options

▸ HOW TO: Align and Indent Text

1. Select the cell.
2. Click a horizontal text alignment button [*Home* tab, *Alignment* group].
   - *Center* positions a label midway between the left and right boundaries of the cell.
   - *Align Left* starts a label at the left boundary of the cell.
   - *Right Align* sets a label to end at the right cell boundary.
3. Click a vertical text alignment button [*Home* tab, *Alignment* group].
   - *Middle Align* positions data midway between the top and bottom cell boundaries.
   - *Top Align* places data at the top cell boundary.
   - *Bottom Align* aligns data at the bottom boundary of the cell.
4. Click an indent button [*Home* tab, *Alignment* group].
   - The *Increase Indent* button moves data toward the right cell boundary.
   - The *Decrease Indent* button moves data toward the left cell boundary.

In addition to horizontal and vertical settings, the *Alignment* group on the *Home* tab includes the *Orientation* button to display data vertically or at an angle. These settings are also available in the *Format Cells* dialog box on the *Alignment* tab (Figure 1-9).

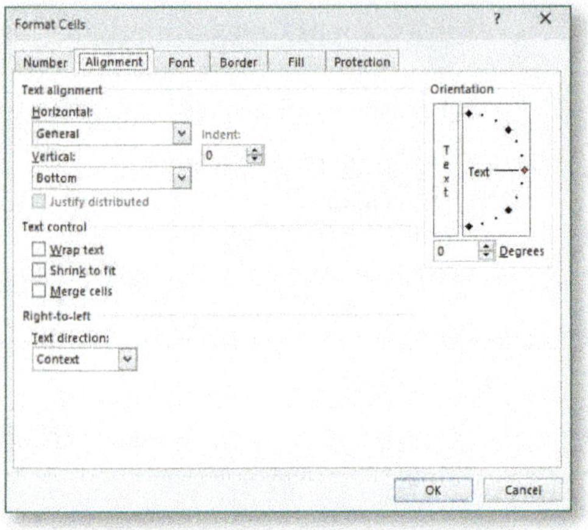

1-9 *Alignment* tab, *Format Cells* dialog box

MORE INFO

Click the **Alignment** launcher [*Home* tab, *Alignment* group] or press **Ctrl+1** to open the *Format Cells* dialog box.

Select Cells

As you format or edit a worksheet, the first step is to select the cell or cells to be edited. Select a single cell by clicking it. Select a range by clicking the first cell and dragging the pointer in any direction to select adjacent cells. The following table outlines basic selection methods.

Selection Methods

Selection	Instructions
Entire Column or Row	Point to and click the column heading. Point to and click the row heading.
All Worksheet Cells	Press **Ctrl+A** or click the **Select All** button (above the row 1 heading and to the left of the column A heading). 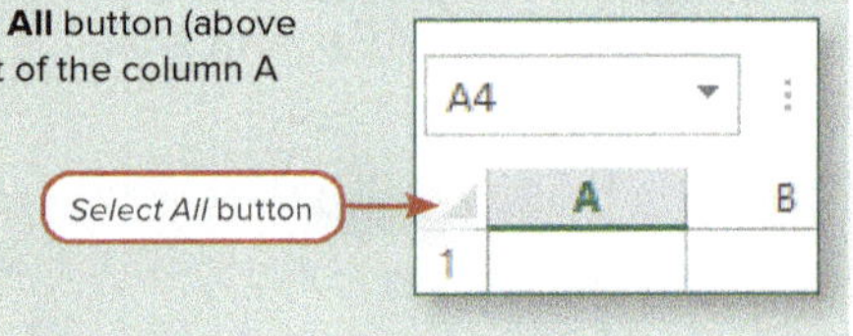
Adjacent Cells by Dragging the Pointer	Click the first cell and drag the selection pointer over the cells to be included. Release the pointer button.
Adjacent Cells Using the Shift Key and the Pointer	Click the first cell, press **Shift**, and click the last cell in the range.
Adjacent Cells Using the Shift and Arrow Keys	Click the first cell, press **Shift**, and press any **Arrow** key.
Nonadjacent Cells	Click a cell or select the first range, press **Ctrl**, and select the next cell or range. Release the pointer button first; then release the **Ctrl** key.
Single Cell or Range Using the *Name Box*	Type a cell or range address in the *Name* box and press **Enter**. 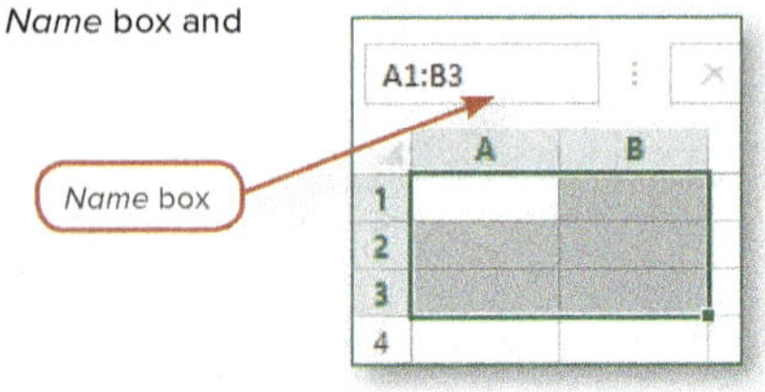

You can see selected cell ranges in Figure 1-10.

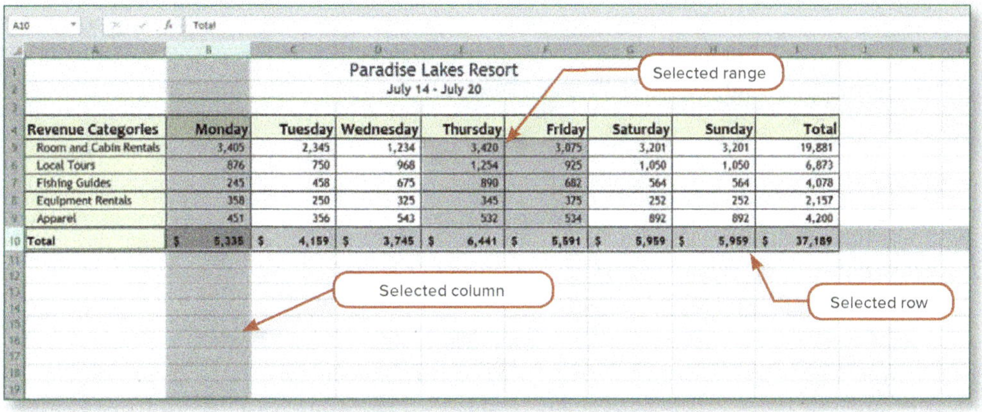

1-10 Selected cells in a worksheet

> **MORE INFO**
>
> To enter data column by column, select the entire cell range, type the first entry, and press **Enter**. Continue to type each entry and press **Enter**. The insertion point moves down each column and to the top of the next column based on the selected range.

The pointer changes shape depending on the current task or mode. The following table describes the shapes and indicates when they appear.

Pointer Shapes

Pointer Icon	Pointer Use
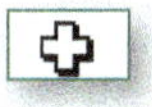	***Selection pointer*** (thick, white cross or plus sign) selects a cell or range; the selection pointer appears when you move the pointer over a cell.
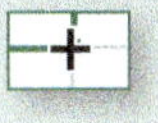	***Fill pointer*** (crosshair or thin, black plus sign) copies cell contents or completes a series; it appears when you place the pointer on the *Fill Handle*, the tiny, black square in the bottom right corner of a selected cell or range.
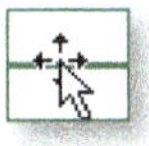	***Move pointer*** (solid, white arrow with a black four-pointed arrow) moves data; it appears when you place the pointer on the border of a selected cell or range.
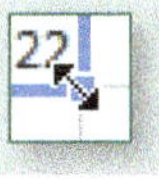	***Resize pointer*** (two-pointed arrow) adjusts a formula cell range or an object; it appears when you place the pointer on a selection handle in a formula range or on a sizing handle for a selected object.

The Fill Handle

A ***series*** is a list of labels or values that follows a pattern. An example of a label series is the days of the week or the months of the year. A series of values is 1, 3, 5, 7, 9. Excel recognizes patterns and can complete most series with the ***Fill Handle***. If there is no recognizable series, the *Fill Handle* copies the data.

The *Fill Handle* is a small, black square in the lower right corner of the cell or selected range. You drag this handle across the cell range for the series or to copy data. When you release the pointer button, the data is completed, and the *Auto Fill Options* button displays near the end of the series. This button provides choices for how to complete the series, but you usually need not make any changes.

For series such as the days of the week and the months, you only need enter the first item in the series. For other series, such as 2, 4, 6, 8, you need to enter at least two items for Excel to recognize the pattern.

▸HOW TO: Use the Fill Handle to Create a Series

1. Type the first item in the series and press **Enter**.
   - Press **Ctrl+Enter** to keep the cell active.
   - Type two or three entries to identify a custom series.
2. Select the cell with the entry.
   - Select all cells with data that identify the series.
3. Point to the *Fill Handle* to display the *Fill* pointer (thin, black plus sign) (Figure 1-11).
4. Click and drag the *Fill* pointer through the last cell for the series.
   - A series can be horizontal or vertical.
   - You can double-click the *Fill* pointer to complete data down a column if other columns are already completed to the last row.
5. Release the pointer button.
   - The series is complete and the *Auto Fill Options* button appears.
6. Click the **Auto Fill Options** button.
   - Choose an option as desired (Figure 1-12).
7. Press **Esc** to remove the *Auto Fill Options* button or continue to the next task.

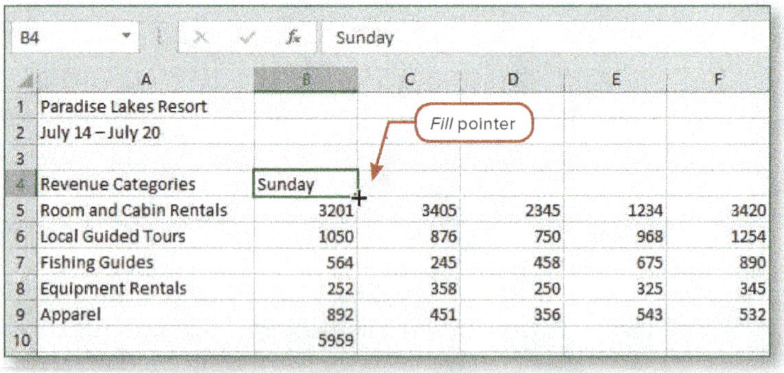

1-11 Use the *Fill Handle* to complete a series

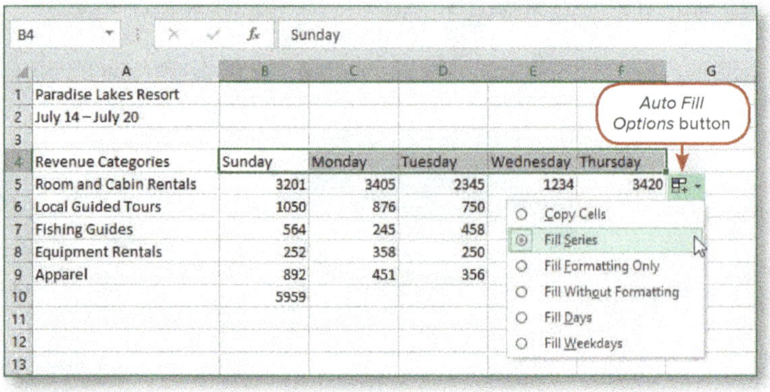

1-12 Completed series with *Auto Fill Options* button

AutoComplete

AutoComplete is an Excel feature that displays a suggested label in a column when the first character or two that you type matches a label already in the column. *AutoComplete* enables you to quickly and accurately complete repetitive data. It works only for data that is alphanumeric, not for a column of values.

In a column that lists city names, for example, a particular city name might be repeated many times. The first time it appears, you type it as usual. On the second and succeeding occurrences of the name, as soon as you type the first character, Excel completes the label but waits for you to accept it. If the *AutoComplete* suggestion is correct, press **Enter**. If the suggestion is not correct, continue typing the label as needed.

Excel usually makes a suggestion after you type a single character in a cell in the column. If the column has more than one entry that begins with that character, type a second character and *AutoComplete* makes another or a better suggestion.

> **MORE INFO**
>
> In a column of data, right-click a cell and choose **Pick From Drop-down List** to display a list of all labels already used in the column.

HOW TO: Use AutoComplete

1. Type the first character in a label.
   - A suggested label appears in the cell.
   - Type a second and third character when there are many labels that begin with the same letter.
   - You can type uppercase or lowercase characters to display an *AutoComplete* suggestion.
2. Press **Enter** to accept the *AutoComplete* suggestion (Figure 1-13).
   - Continue typing to ignore an *AutoComplete* suggestion.
   - Press **Enter** to complete a new label.

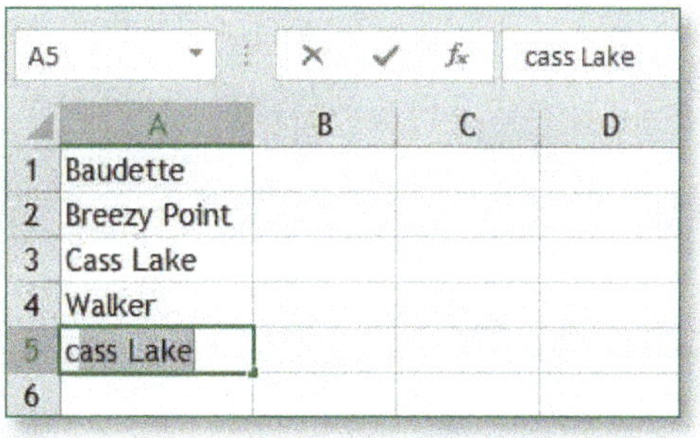

1-13 *AutoComplete* suggestion

Cut, Copy, and Paste Cell Contents

Excel has the same *Cut*, *Copy*, and *Paste* commands as other Windows applications. Use the ***Cut*** command to move data from one location to another. The ***Copy*** command duplicates cell contents to a different location. The ***Paste*** command places cut or copied data in the selected location. Data is cut or copied from a ***source cell*** or range and is pasted in a ***destination cell*** or range. When you cut or copy data, it is usually stored on the Windows *Clipboard* as well as the *Office Clipboard*.

Move or Cut Cell Contents

You can move data using drag and drop, keyboard shortcuts, or *Cut* and *Paste* in the *Clipboard* group on the *Home* tab. Drag and drop is quick when you want to move or copy cells within a visible range on the worksheet. When you use the drag-and-drop method, the source data is not stored on either clipboard.

HOW TO: Move Data Using Drag and Drop

1. Select the cell(s) to be moved.
2. Point to a border of the selection to display a move pointer (white arrow with four-pointed arrow).
3. Click and drag the selection to the new location (Figure 1-14).
   - A preview selection shows the destination address.
4. Release the pointer button.

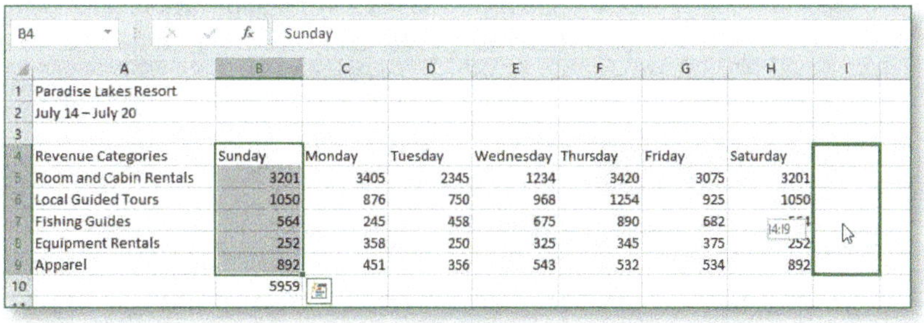

1-14 Drag and drop to move data

> **MORE INFO**
>
> Add an external mouse to a computer with a touchpad for ease in selecting cells and dragging and dropping data.

When you use the *Cut* command from the *Ribbon* or the keyboard, the selected data is placed on both clipboards. You can paste once from the Windows *Clipboard*. You can paste multiple times from the *Office Clipboard*. There are three methods to cut data:

- *Ribbon* buttons: **Cut** and **Paste** buttons [*Home* tab, *Clipboard* group]
- Shortcut commands: **Ctrl+X** to cut and **Ctrl+V** to paste
- Context menu: Right-click and select **Cut**; right-click and select **Paste**

HOW TO: Move Data Using Cut and Paste

1. Select the cell or range to be moved.
2. Click the **Cut** button [*Home* tab, *Clipboard* group].
   - A moving border surrounds the source cell(s) (Figure 1-15).
3. Select the destination cell.
   - Select the top-left cell in a destination range.
4. Click the **Paste** button [*Home* tab, *Clipboard* group].
   - If the destination cell(s) are not empty, pasted data overwrites existing data.

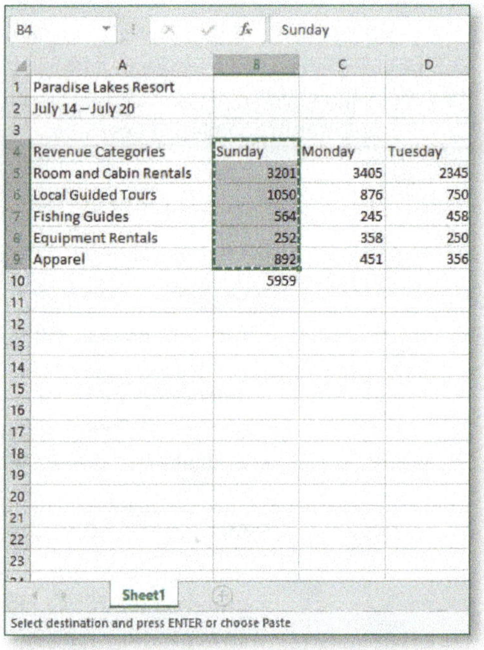

1-15 Cut data has moving border

> **MORE INFO**
>
> After cutting data, right-click the destination cell and select **Insert Cut Cells** to avoid overwriting existing data.

The Office Clipboard

The ***Office Clipboard*** stores cut or copied data from Office applications and makes the data available for pasting in any application. The *Office Clipboard* can hold up to 24 items with each cut or copied item appearing, in turn, at the top of the pane. Click the **Clipboard** launcher to open the *Clipboard* task pane.

HOW TO: Use the Office Clipboard

1. Click the **Home** tab.
2. Click the **Clipboard** launcher to open the *Clipboard* pane (Figure 1-16).
3. Click **Clear All** to empty the *Clipboard*.
   - The button is grayed out if there is no data on the clipboard.

4. Select data to be cut or copied.
5. Click the **Copy** button [*Home* tab, *Clipboard* group].
   - Use any *Cut* or *Copy* command from the *Ribbon* or keyboard.
   - Each item rotates into the first position in the *Clipboard* pane.
6. Select a destination cell.
7. Click the item icon in the *Clipboard* to paste it.
   - You can paste an item multiple times in different locations.
8. Click the **Close** button (X) to hide the *Clipboard*.

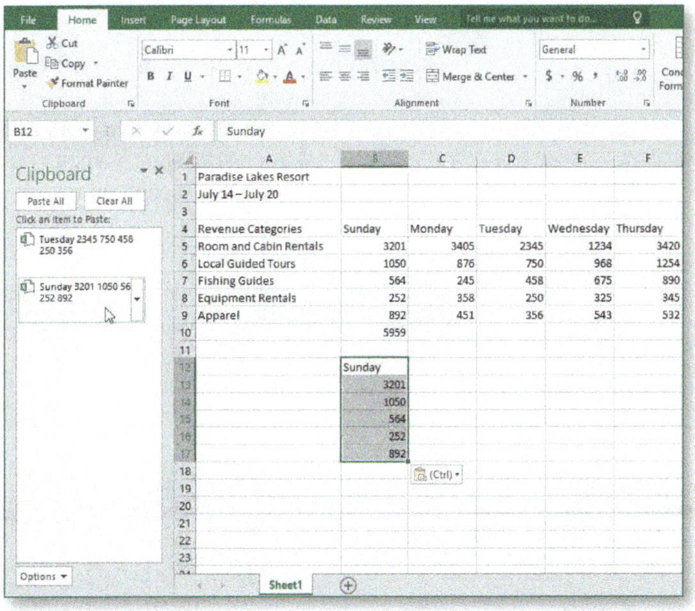

1-16 *Clipboard* pane

> **MORE INFO**
>
> To remove an item from the *Clipboard* task pane, click its drop-down arrow and choose **Delete**.

Copy Cell Contents

Copying data places a duplicate on the *Clipboard* so that it can be pasted in another location. When you use a *Ribbon*, keyboard, or context menu command, you can paste the data multiple times. You can copy data using the drag-and-drop method and paste it multiple times, even though the copied data is not placed on the *Clipboard*.

The *Copy* command stores data on the *Clipboard*, and the *Paste* command duplicates *Clipboard* contents in the worksheet.

- *Ribbon* buttons: **Copy** and **Paste** buttons [*Home* tab, *Clipboard* group]
- Shortcut commands: **Ctrl+C** to copy and **Ctrl+V** to paste
- Context menu: Right-click and choose **Copy**; right-click and choose **Paste**

▸ HOW TO: Copy Data Using Drag and Drop

1. Select the cell(s) to be copied.
2. Point to a border of the selection to display the move pointer.
3. Press **Ctrl** to display the copy pointer.
   - The copy pointer is a white arrow with a tiny plus sign.
4. Drag the selection to the desired location (Figure 1-17).
   - A preview selection shows where the copy will be pasted.
5. Continue to press **Ctrl** and drag to the next location for another copy.
6. Release the pointer button first and then release **Ctrl**.

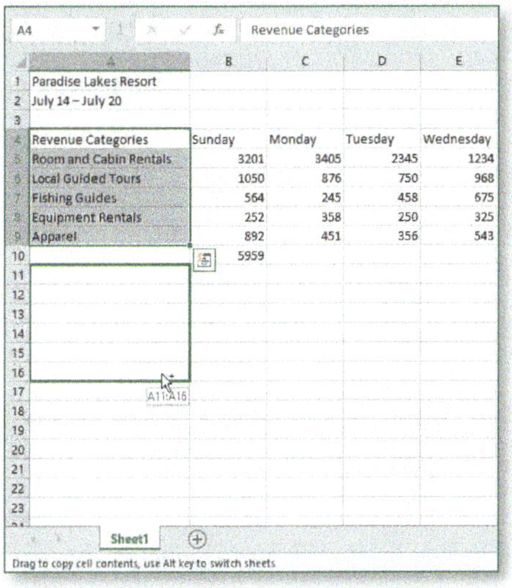

1-17 Copy data using drag and drop

Paste Options

When you paste data, you can choose how it is copied in the new location. You can paste data and formatting, only the data, only the formatting, and so on. To see the options, click the lower half of the **Paste** button [*Home* tab, *Clipboard* group] to open the ***Paste Options*** gallery. The gallery also displays when you right-click a destination cell.

The table describes the icons in the *Paste Options* gallery:

Paste Options

Group	Paste Icon	Paste Option	Description
Paste		*Paste*	Copies all data and formatting; this is the default option.
		Formulas	Copies all data and formulas, but no formatting
		Formulas & Number Formatting	Copies all data and formulas with formatting
		Keep Source Formatting	Copies all data and formatting; same as *Paste*
		Match Destination Formatting	Copies data and applies formatting used in the destination
		No Borders	Copies all data, formulas, and formatting except for borders
		Keep Source Column Widths	Copies all data, formulas, and formatting and sets destination column widths to the same width as the source columns
		Transpose	Copies data and formatting and reverses data orientation so that rows are pasted as columns and columns are pasted as rows
		Merge Conditional Formatting	Copies data and *Conditional Formatting* rules. This option is available only if the copied data has conditional formatting.
Paste Values		*Values*	Copies only formula results (not the formulas) without formatting
		Values & Number Formatting	Copies only formula results (not the formulas) with formatting
		Values & Source Formatting	Copies only formula results (not the formulas) with all source formatting
Other Paste Options		*Formatting*	Copies only formatting, no data
		Paste Link	Pastes a 3-D reference to data or a formula
		Picture	Pastes a selectable picture object of the data. Data is static, but the object can be formatted like any object.
		Linked Picture	Pastes a selectable picture object of the data. The copied data is dynamic and reflects edits made in the source data. The picture can be formatted like any object.

> **MORE INFO**
>
> The *Paste Special* command opens a dialog box with additional options to paste comments, data validation, themes, and arithmetic operations.

PAUSE & PRACTICE: EXCEL 1-1

In this project, you open an Excel workbook that tracks revenue for one week at Paradise Lakes Resort. You add labels and values to complete the report; align labels; and edit, cut, and paste data. Your worksheet will have deliberate spelling errors for checking in a later Pause & Practice exercise.

File Needed: ***ParadiseLakes-01.xlsx***
Completed Project File Name: ***[your initials] PP E1-1.xlsx***

1. Open a workbook.
   a. Click the **File** tab and click **Open**.
   b. Navigate to the folder where your data files are stored.
   c. Double-click the name of the folder to open it.
   d. Locate the file name ***ParadiseLakes-01*** and click to select it.
   e. Click **Open**.
   f. Click **Enable Editing** if the workbook has opened in *Protected View* (Figure 1-18).

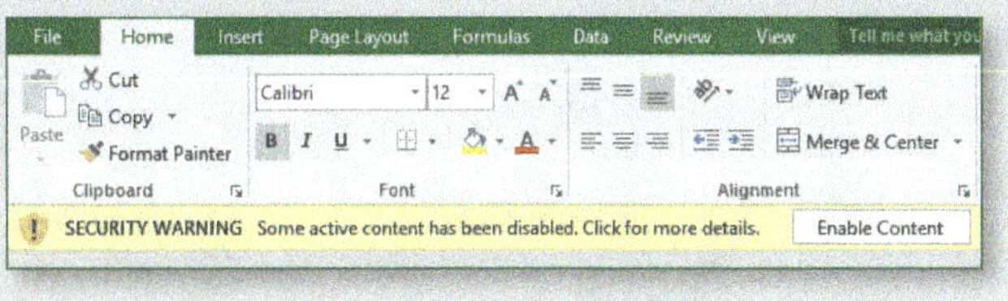

1-18 Worksheet opened in *Protected View*

2. Save the workbook with a different name.
   a. Press **F12** (**FN+F12**) to open the *Save As* dialog box.
   b. Select a location to save the workbook.
   c. Change the file name to [your initials] PP E1-1 in the *File name* area.
   d. Click **Save** to save the file and close the *Save As* dialog box.

3. Enter data.
   a. Click cell **A1** and type Paradise Lakes Resort.
   b. Press **Enter**.
   c. Click cell **A10**, type Total, and press **Enter**.
   d. Type the values shown below in cells **G5:H9**.

	G	H
5	3075	3201
6	925	1050
7	682	564
8	375	252
9	534	892

4. Use the *Fill Handle* to complete a series.
   a. Click **B4**.
   b. Point to the *Fill Handle* (small, black square in the lower right corner) until the *Fill* pointer (thin, black plus sign) appears.
   c. Click and drag the *Fill* pointer to reach cell **H4**.
   d. Release the pointer button.

5. Edit worksheet data.
   a. Click cell **B10**.
   b. Press **Delete** to remove the contents.
   c. Double-click cell **A4** to start *Edit* mode.
   d. Click to position the insertion point and delete the "i" in "Categories" to create a deliberate spelling error.
   e. Press **Enter** to accept the edit.
   f. Click cell **A9** and type Aparel with the error. You will correct errors in Pause & Practice 1-4.
   g. Press **Enter** to replace the entry.

6. Indent and align text.
   a. Select cells **A5:A9**.
   b. Click the **Increase Indent** button twice [*Home* tab, *Alignment* group].
   c. Select cells **B4:H4**.
   d. Click the **Center** button [*Home* tab, *Alignment* group].

7. Cut and paste data.
   a. Select cells **B4:B9**.
   b. Click the **Cut** button [*Home* tab, *Clipboard* group].
   c. Click cell **I4**.
   d. Click the **Paste** button [*Home* tab, *Clipboard* group].
   e. Select cells **C4:I9**.
   f. Point to any border of the selected range to display a four-pointed arrow with a white arrow.
   g. Drag the range to start in cell **B4** and release the pointer button.
   h. Click cell **A1**.

8. Save and close the workbook (Figure 1-19).
   a. Press **Ctrl+S** to save the workbook with the same file name.
   b. Click the **Close** button in the upper right corner to exit Excel.

	A	B	C	D	E	F	G	H
1	Paradise Lakes Resort							
2	July 14 – July 20							
3								
4	Revenue Categores	Monday	Tuesday	Wednesday	Thursday	Friday	Saturday	Sunday
5	Room and Cabin Rentals	3405	2345	1234	3420	3075	3201	3201
6	Local Tours	876	750	968	1254	925	1050	1050
7	Fishing Guides	245	458	675	890	682	564	564
8	Equipment Rentals	358	250	325	345	375	252	252
9	Aparel	451	356	543	532	534	892	892
10	Total							
11								

1-19 PP E1-1 completed

SLO 1.3

Using the SUM Function

A ***formula*** calculates a result for numeric data in a cell. A ***function*** is a built-in formula. ***SUM*** is a function that adds the values in a cell range. The terms "formula" and "function" are used interchangeably.

To use the *SUM* function, click the cell where you want to show a total. Then click the **AutoSum** button [*Home* tab, *Editing* group]. Excel inserts the function =SUM() with a suggested range of cells to be added between the parentheses. If that range is correct, press **Enter**, **Ctrl+Enter**, or click the **Enter** button in the *Formula* bar to complete the function. If the suggested range is not correct, you can select a different range or choose cells individually and then press a completion key. The sum is shown in the cell, and the function is visible in the *Formula* bar.

> **ANOTHER WAY**
>
> The *Function Library* group on the *Formulas* tab has an *AutoSum* button. You can also enter = SUM() in a cell by pressing **Alt** and the **+/=** key on the top keyboard row.

HOW TO: Use the SUM Function

1. Click the cell for the total.
2. Click the **AutoSum** button [*Home* tab, *Editing* group] (Figure 1-20).
3. Press **Enter** to accept the range and complete the function.
   - Drag the pointer to select a different range before pressing **Enter**.
   - If the row or column of values to be added is adjacent to the formula cell as shown in Figure 1-20, you can double-click the **AutoSum** button to insert and accept the function.

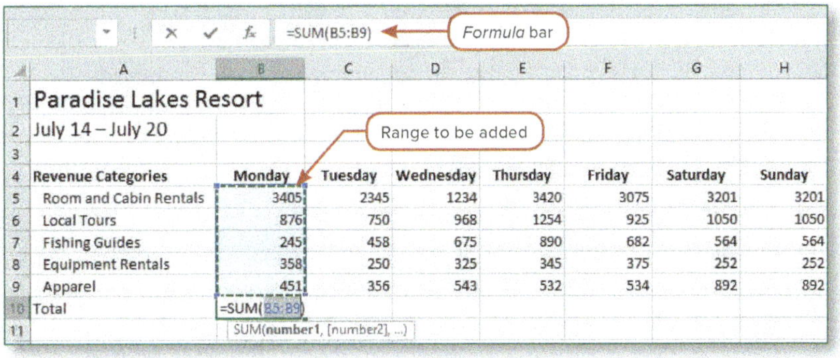

1-20 *SUM* function

> **MORE INFO**
>
> You can display formulas instead of results by clicking the **Show Formulas** button on the *Formulas* tab or by pressing **Ctrl+~**.

Function Syntax

An Excel function has ***syntax***, the required elements and the order of those elements for the function to work. Every function starts with the equals sign [=] followed by the name of the function and a set of parentheses. Within the parentheses, you enter the argument(s). An

argument is the cell reference or value required to complete the function. A function can have a single or multiple arguments. In = SUM(B5:B9), the argument is the range B5:B9. Multiple arguments in a function are separated by commas. There are three arguments in this function: =SUM(B5, B10, B15).

SUM(B5:B9)

SUM(B5, B10, B15)

Copy the SUM Function

The *SUM* function can be copied using regular copy and paste commands as well as the *Fill Handle*. When *SUM* is used to total data in rows or columns, you can enter the formula in the first column or row and copy it to the other locations. In Figure 1-21, for example, the same function is used in cells B10 through H10, each with its own argument. The formula in cell B10 is =SUM(B5:B9), the formula for cell C10 is =SUM(C5:C9) and so on. When a function is copied into adjacent cells, use the *Fill Handle*. Excel copies the formula and adjusts each argument based on the location in the worksheet.

HOW TO: Use the Fill Handle to Copy a Function

1. Click the cell with the function to be copied.
2. Point to the *Fill Handle* in the lower right corner.

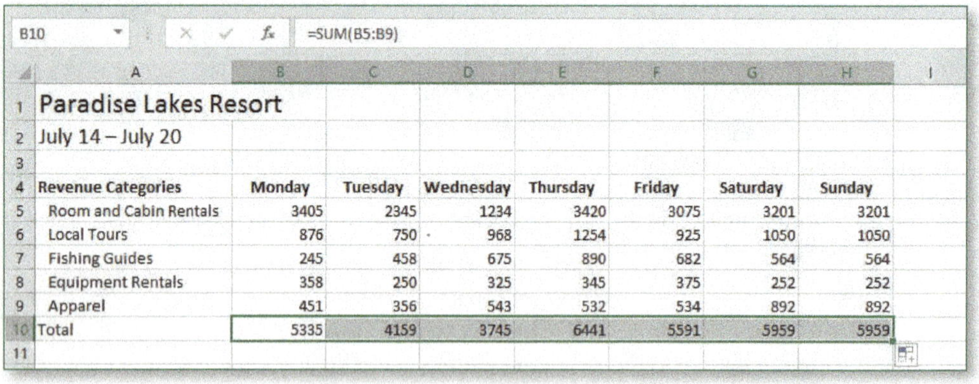
B10 =SUM(B5:B9)

	A	B	C	D	E	F	G	H
1	Paradise Lakes Resort							
2	July 14 – July 20							
3								
4	Revenue Categories	Monday	Tuesday	Wednesday	Thursday	Friday	Saturday	Sunday
5	Room and Cabin Rentals	3405	2345	1234	3420	3075	3201	3201
6	Local Tours	876	750	968	1254	925	1050	1050
7	Fishing Guides	245	458	675	890	682	564	564
8	Equipment Rentals	358	250	325	345	375	252	252
9	Apparel	451	356	543	532	534	892	892
10	Total	5335	4159	3745	6441	5591	5959	5959
11								

1-21 Use the *Fill Handle* to copy a function

3. Click and drag the *Fill* pointer across the cells where the function should be pasted (Figure 1-21).

ANOTHER WAY

You can use regular copy and paste commands to copy a function or formula to any location on the worksheet.

Edit the Function Argument

If you edit a value in a cell that is referenced in a formula or function, the results are automatically recalculated. If you must change a cell or range argument in a function, however, you use *Edit* mode to enter new references. In *Edit* mode, you can make a change in the *Formula* bar or in the cell. You can often use the ***Range Finder*** to drag or select a new range, too. The *Range Finder* is an Excel feature that highlights and color-codes formula cells as you enter or edit a formula or function.

HOW TO: Edit an Argument Range in the Formula Bar

1. Select the cell with the function.
2. Click the argument cell range in the *Formula* bar.
   - The *Range Finder* highlights the argument range in the worksheet.
   - The range is color-coded in the *Formula* bar to match the highlighted range (Figure 1-22)
3. Type the new cell references in the *Formula* bar.
4. Press **Enter**.
   - You can click the **Enter** button in the *Formula* bar to complete the edit.

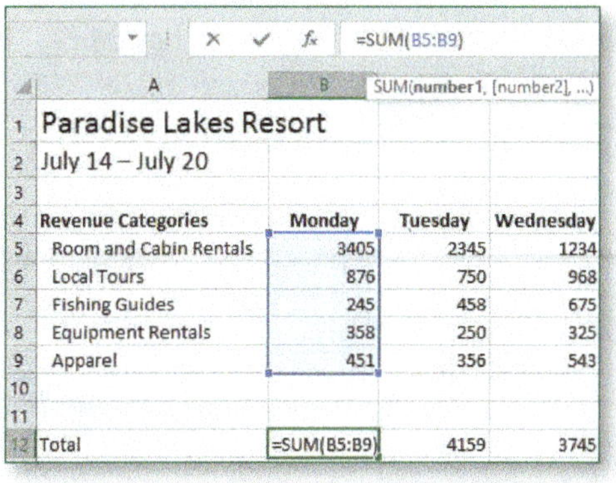

=SUM(B5:B9)

SUM(number1, [number2], ...)

	A	B	C	D
1	Paradise Lakes Resort			
2	July 14 – July 20			
3				
4	Revenue Categories	Monday	Tuesday	Wednesday
5	Room and Cabin Rentals	3405	2345	1234
6	Local Tours	876	750	968
7	Fishing Guides	245	458	675
8	Equipment Rentals	358	250	325
9	Apparel	451	356	543
10				
11				
12	Total	=SUM(B5:B9)	4159	3745

1-22 Argument range is color-coded

You can drag a *Range Finder* handle to select a different argument range, expanding or shrinking the number of included cells. This is easy to do when the formula cell is not adjacent to the range.

ANOTHER WAY

Double-click the cell with the function and edit the argument in the cell.

HOW TO: Edit an Argument Range by Dragging

1. Double-click the cell with the function.
   - *Edit* mode starts (Figure 1-23).
2. Drag the selection handle down to expand the argument range.
   - Drag the selection handle up to shrink the argument range.
3. Press **Enter** to complete the change.
   - Click the **Enter** button in the *Formula* bar.

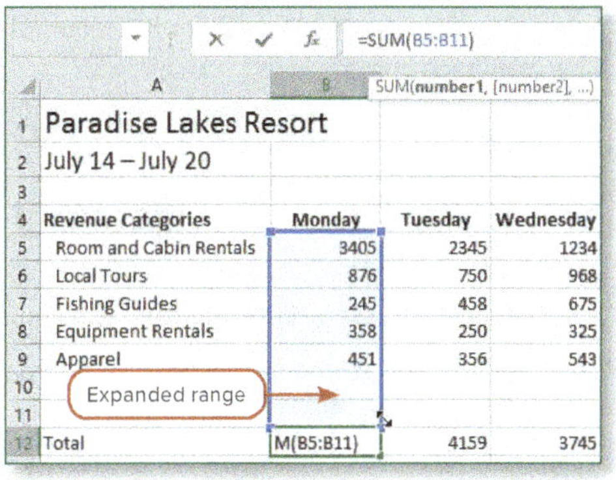

=SUM(B5:B11)

SUM(number1, [number2], ...)

	A	B	C	D
1	Paradise Lakes Resort			
2	July 14 – July 20			
3				
4	Revenue Categories	Monday	Tuesday	Wednesday
5	Room and Cabin Rentals	3405	2345	1234
6	Local Tours	876	750	968
7	Fishing Guides	245	458	675
8	Equipment Rentals	358	250	325
9	Apparel	451	356	543
10				
11				
12	Total	M(B5:B11)	4159	3745

1-23 Edit a cell reference range by dragging

SLO 1.4

Formatting a Worksheet

A new workbook uses a default ***theme*** named *Office* which is a collection of fonts, colors, and special effects. The default theme applies the 11 point Calibri font and the *General* number format to all cells. You can change the theme as well as individual font attributes, or you can add fill and borders to highlight or emphasize data.

Font Face, Size, Style, and Color

A ***font*** is a type design for alphanumeric characters, punctuation, and keyboard symbols. ***Font size*** specifies the size of the character, measured in ***points*** (pt.). A point is equal to 1/72 of an inch. The ***font style*** refers to the thickness or angle of the characters and includes settings such as **bold**, underline or *italic*. ***Font color*** is the hue of the characters in the cell. You can apply any of these font attributes to a single cell or a range of cells.

Default font attributes for Excel 2016 workbooks are:

- Font: Calibri
- Font size: 11 point
- Font color: Black, Text 1

> **MORE INFO**
>
> The font list displayed on your computer depends on your Windows installation and other applications that are installed.

HOW TO: Customize Font, Style, Font Size, and Font Color

1. Select the cell or range to be formatted.
   - You can format cells before any data is entered if you prefer.
2. Click the **Font** drop-down list [*Home* tab, *Font* group].
   - A list of available fonts is displayed.
3. Point to a font name.
   - *Live Preview* shows the selected data with the new font applied (Figure 1-24).
4. Click the **Font Size** drop-down list [*Home* tab, *Font* group] and select a size.
   - *Live Preview* shows the selected data in the new size.
   - You can type a custom size in the *Font Size* area.
   - You can also click the **Increase Font Size** or **Decrease Font Size** button [*Home* tab, *Font* group] to adjust the font size in 1-point increments.
5. Click the **Bold**, **Italic**, or **Underline** button [*Home* tab, *Font* group] to apply a style.
   - You can apply multiple styles.
6. Click the **Font Color** drop-down list [*Home* tab, *Font* group] and select a color.
   - Click the **Font Color** button (not the arrow) to apply the most recent font color shown on the button.

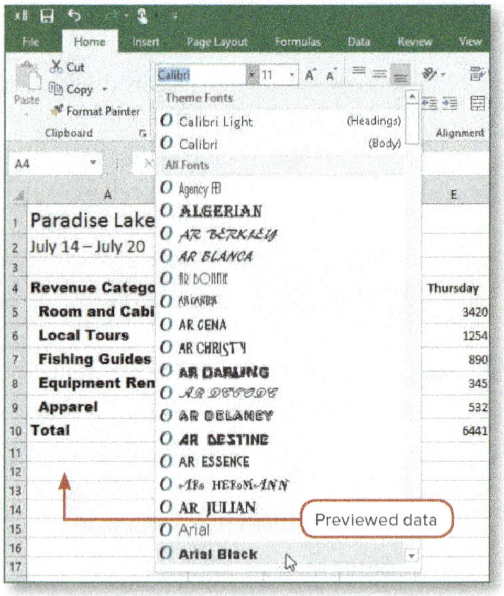

1-24 ***Live Preview*** **when selecting a font name**

The ***mini toolbar*** includes common commands from the *Font*, *Alignment*, and *Number* groups. It appears when you right-click a cell or selected range (Figure 1-25).

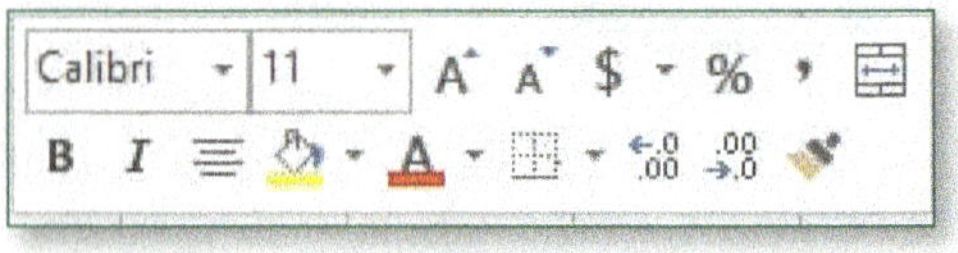

1-25 Mini toolbar

The *Format Cells* dialog box includes basic format settings and more. It has six tabs: *Number*, *Alignment*, *Font*, *Border*, *Fill*, and *Protection*.

- Mini toolbar: Right-click a cell or selected range.
- *Format Cells* dialog box: Click the **Font** launcher in the *Font* group, press **Ctrl+1** or right-click a selected cell and choose **Format Cells** (Figure 1-26).

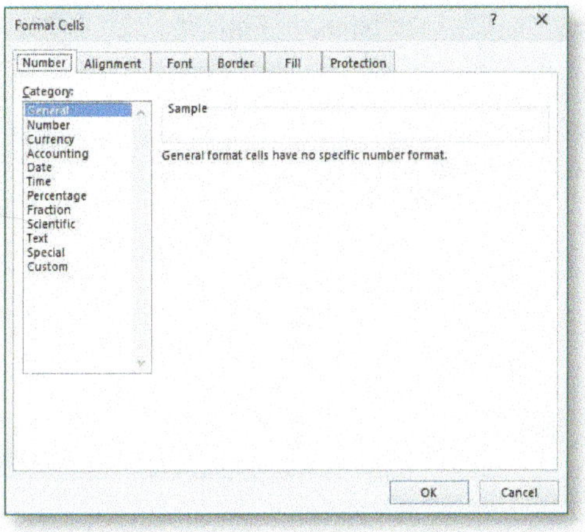

1-26 *Format Cells* dialog box

The Format Painter

The ***Format Painter*** copies formatting attributes and styles from one cell to another cell or range. You can apply your custom formats without having to redefine each attribute, saving time and ensuring an exact duplicate.

▸HOW TO: Use the Format Painter

1. Select a cell that contains the formatting you want to copy.
2. Click the **Format Painter** button [*Home* tab, *Clipboard* group].
   - The pointer changes to a thick, white cross with a tiny paint brush.
   - Double-click the **Format Painter** button to lock it for painting formats to multiple areas in the worksheet.
3. Click the cell or drag across the range to be formatted (Figure 1-27).
4. Release the pointer button.
   - The *Format Painter* is canceled.
   - If the *Format Painter* command is locked, click the **Format Painter** button or press **Esc** to turn it off.

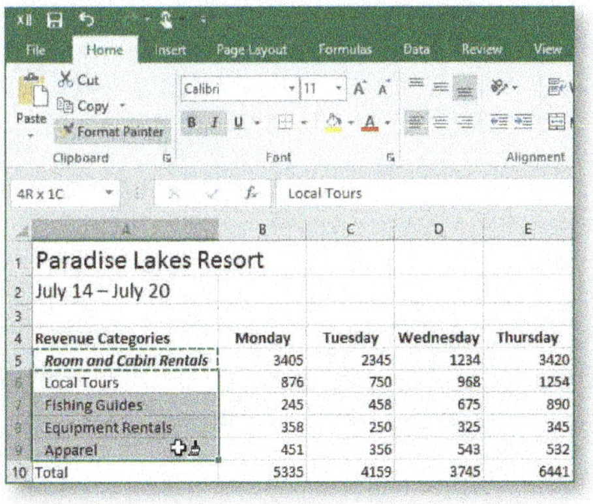

1-27 Copy formats to a range using *Format Painter*

Number Formats

You can format values with currency symbols, decimal points, commas, percent signs, and more so that data is quickly recognized and understood. The *Number* group on the *Home* tab includes command buttons for *Accounting*, *Percent*, and *Comma* styles as well as command buttons to *Increase Decimal* or *Decrease Decimal*. Dates and times are values, and *Date* and *Time* formats are included in the *Number* group. From the *Format Cells* dialog box, you can apply and customize these number formats or create your own format.

▸HOW TO: Format Numbers

1. Select the cell or range of values.
2. Click a command button [*Home* tab, *Number* group] (Figure 1-28).

- Click the **Number Format** drop-down list to choose a format.
- Press **Ctrl+1** to open the *Format Cells* dialog box and click the **Number** tab to select a format.

3. Click the **Increase Decimal** or **Decrease Decimal** button to control the number of decimal places.
    - When a cell displays a series of pound or number symbols (#####), you can widen the column to see the value.

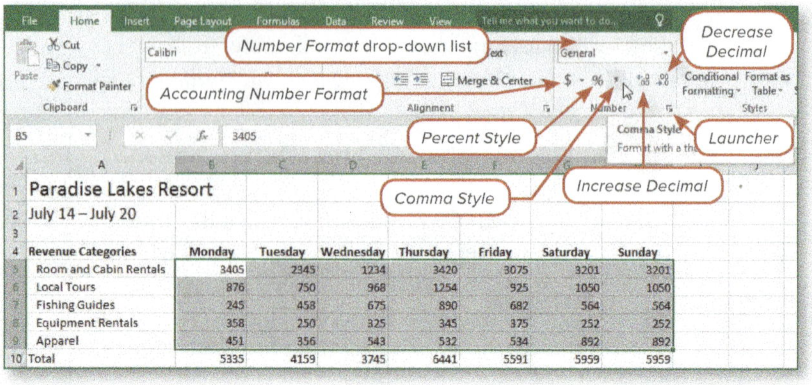

1-28 ***Number*** **group on the *Home* tab**

ANOTHER WAY

Click the **Number** launcher [*Home* tab] to open the *Format Cells* dialog box.

Borders and Fill

A ***border*** is an outline for a cell or a range. You can design a border to separate main or column headings, to emphasize totals, or to group data. ***Fill*** is a background color or pattern and is used to highlight or draw attention to data. You can use the *Ribbon* or the *Format Cells* dialog box to apply borders and fill color.

HOW TO: Add Borders and Fill Using the Ribbon

1. Select the cell or range.
2. Click the arrow next to the **Borders** button [*Home* tab, *Font* group].
    - The **Borders** button shows the most recently used border style.
3. Select a border option from the list (Figure 1-29).
    - To remove a border, choose **No Border**.
4. Click the arrow for the **Fill Color** button [*Home* tab, *Font* group].
    - Click the **Fill Color** button to apply the most recently selected color.
    - To remove a fill, choose **No Fill**.

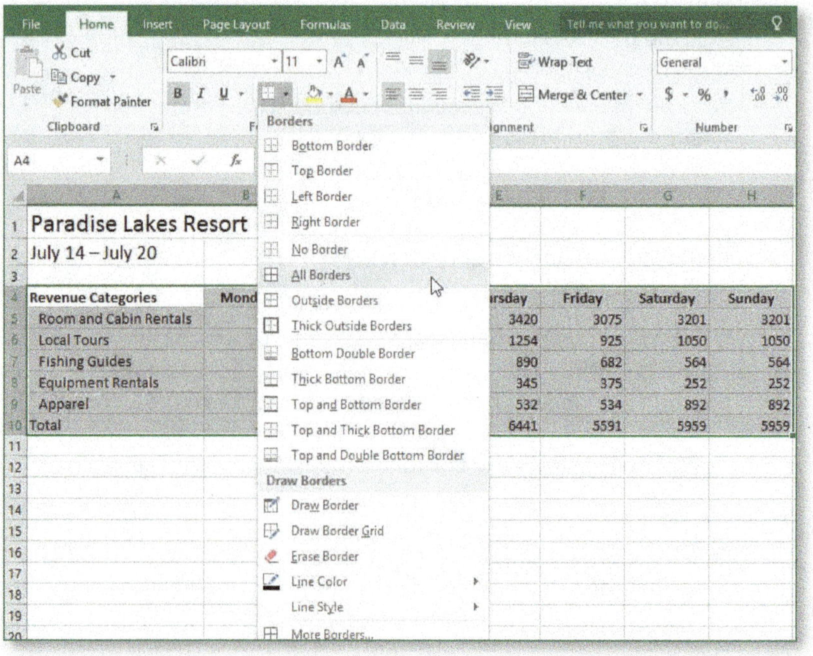

1-29 ***Borders*** **drop-down list**

5. Select a color tile in the palette (Figure 1-30).
   - *Live Preview* displays the cell or range with the color applied.
   - Click **More Colors** to build a custom color.

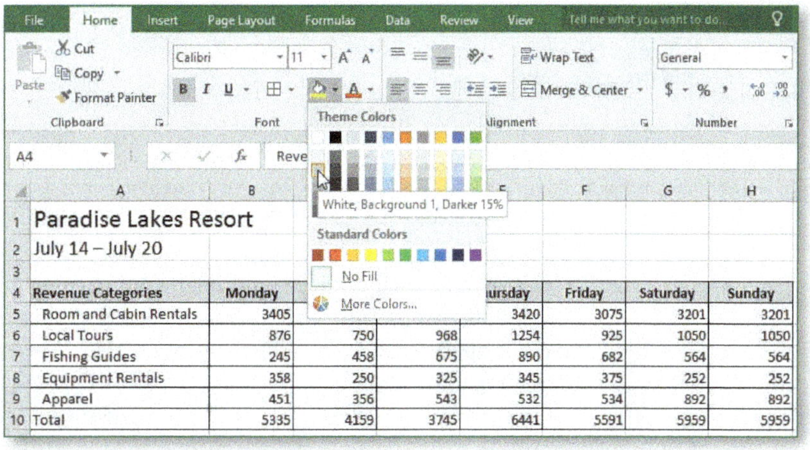

1-30 *Fill Color* palette

The *Format Cells* dialog box has a *Border* tab and a *Fill* tab. From the *Border* tab, you can choose a different line style, a different color, or different positions for the border. From the *Fill* tab, you can design patterned or gradient fills. A ***pattern*** fill uses crosshatches, dots, or stripes. A ***gradient*** is a blend of two or more colors. Use fill choices carefully, because they affect the readability of your data.

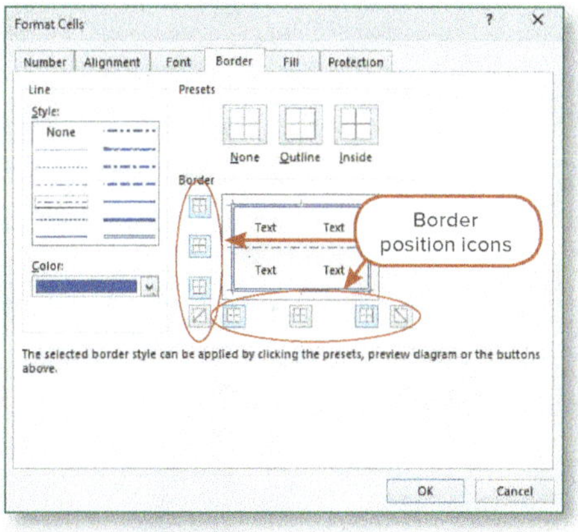

1-31 Build a custom border in the *Format Cells* dialog box

HOW TO: Add Borders and Fill Using the Format Cells Dialog Box

1. Select the cell or range.
2. Click the **Font** launcher [*Home* tab, *Font* group] to open the *Format Cells* dialog box.
   - Press **Ctrl+1** to open the *Format Cells* dialog box.
   - Right-click a cell in the range and select **Format Cells**.
3. Click the **Border** tab (Figure 1-31).
   - Click **None** to remove all borders.
4. Choose a color from the *Color* drop-down list.
   - Select the color before choosing a line style or location.
5. Select a line style in the *Style* area.
6. Click **Outline** in the *Presets* area to apply an outside border.
   - The *Preview* area shows the border.
   - Build a custom border by clicking the desired icons in the *Border* area or by clicking the desired position in the *Preview* area.
7. Click the **Fill** tab (Figure 1-32).

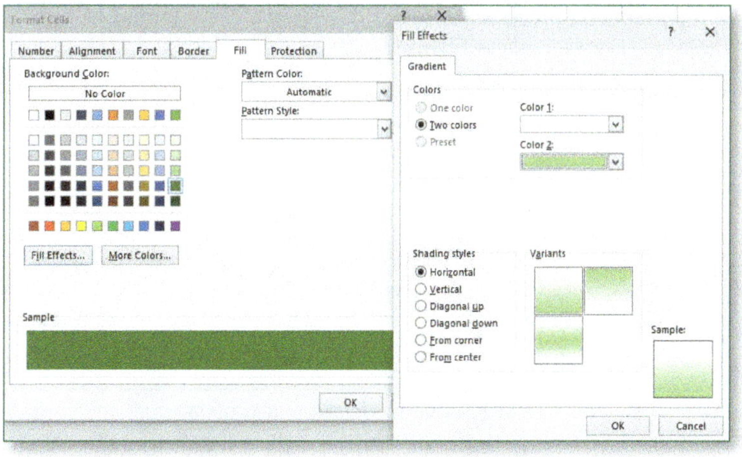

1-32 *Fill* tab in the *Format Cells* dialog box and *Fill Effects* dialog box

8. Select a color tile in the *Background Color* area.
   - Select a color from the *Pattern Color* list and select a pattern from the *Pattern Style* list.
   - Click **Fill Effects** to apply a gradient. Choose two colors, a shading style, and a variant.
9. Click **OK** to close the *Format Cells* dialog box.

Cell Styles

A ***cell style*** is a set of formatting elements that includes font style, size, color, alignment, borders, and fill as well as number formats. Like other formatting, you select the cell or range and then apply a cell style. When you apply a cell style, the style format overwrites individual formatting already applied. After a cell style is applied, however, you can individually change any of the attributes. The *Cell Styles* gallery is located in the *Styles* group on the *Home* tab.

MORE INFO

Your screen size and settings determine if you see part of the *Cell Styles* gallery in the *Ribbon* or only the *Cell Styles* button.

HOW TO: Apply Cell Styles

1. Select the cell or range.
2. Click the **More** button in the *Cell Styles* gallery.
   - Click the **Cell Styles** button [*Home* tab, *Styles* group] to open the gallery (Figure 1-33).

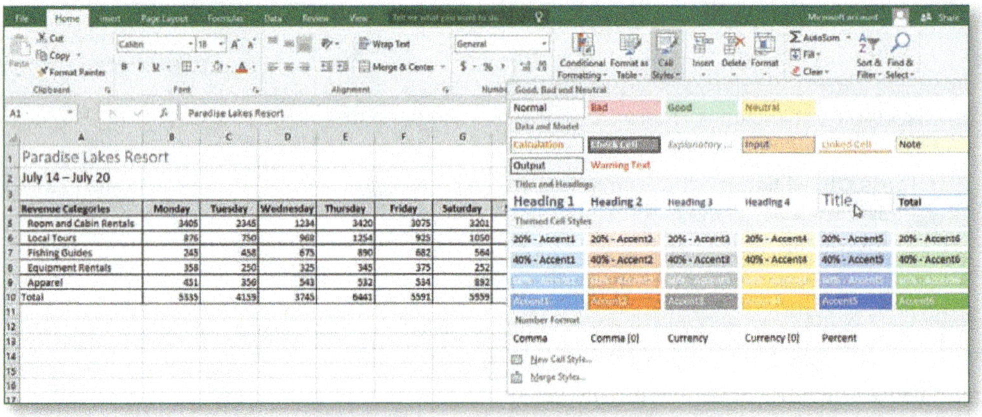

1-33 *Cell Styles* gallery and *Live Preview* for selected cell

3. Point to a style name to see a *Live Preview* in the worksheet.
4. Click a style name to apply it.

Workbook Themes

A workbook ***theme*** is a professionally designed set of fonts, colors, and effects. When you change the workbook theme, data formatted with theme settings are reformatted with the new theme fonts, colors, and effects. You can change the theme to quickly restyle a worksheet without having to individually edit cell formats throughout the sheet.

A theme includes a font name for headings and one for body text, and some themes use the same font for both. You can see the names of *Theme Fonts* at the top of the *Font* list. *Theme Colors* are identified in the color palettes for the **Fill** and **Font Color** buttons [*Home* tab, *Font* group]. Cell styles use font and color settings from the theme.

The *Themes* gallery lists built-in themes, and there are additional themes available online. You can also create and save your own theme.

HOW TO: Change the Workbook Theme

1. Click the **Theme** button [*Page Layout* tab, *Themes* group]
   - The *Themes* gallery opens.
2. Point to a theme name.
   - *Live Preview* displays the worksheet with new format settings (Figure 1-34).

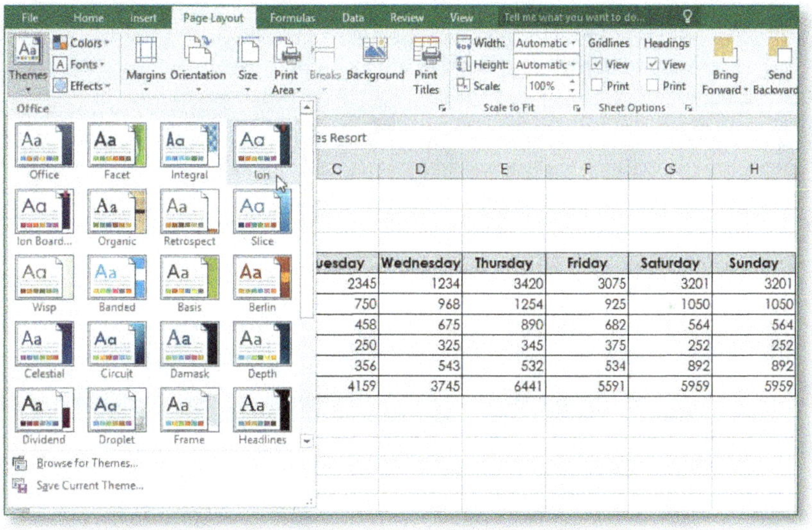

1-34 *Themes* gallery and a *Live Preview* in the worksheet

3. Click a theme icon to apply a different theme.
   - Display the **Font** button list [*Home* tab, *Font* group] to see the new theme font names at the top of the list.
   - Display the **Font Color** and **Fill Color** button galleries [*Home* tab, *Font* group] to see new theme colors.

MORE INFO

Rest the pointer on the **Themes** button [*Page Layout* tab, *Themes* group] to see the name of the current theme.

PAUSE & PRACTICE: EXCEL 1-2

In this project, you open the workbook you created in *Pause & Practice Excel 1-1*. You add totals using *SUM* and copy the function using *AutoFill*. Your format changes result in truncated or cutoff data; you learn how to adjust column widths in the next learning objective and will fix this problem in the next Pause & Practice project.

File Needed: ***[your initials] PP E1-1**.xlsx*
Completed Project File Name: ***[your initials] PP E1-2**.xlsx*

---

1. Open a workbook and save it as a different name.
   a. Click the **File** tab and choose **Open**. If you have just started Excel and the file name appears in the *Recent* list in the Excel *Start* page, click the name to open it. Otherwise, click **Open Other Workbooks** at the bottom of the *Start* page.
   b. Locate the folder where your file is stored.
   c. Open ***[your initials] PP E1-1***. (Click **Enable Editing** if the workbook has opened in *Protected View*).
   c. Press **F12** (**FN+F12**) to open the *Save As* dialog box.
   d. Locate the folder where your files are saved.
   e. Edit the file name to [your initials] PP E1-2 and click **Save**.
2. Calculate daily totals using *SUM*.
   a. Click cell **B10**.
   b. Click the **AutoSum** button [*Home* tab, *Editing* group].
   c. Press **Enter** to accept the suggested range and to complete the formula.
3. Copy a function using the *Fill Handle*.
   a. Click cell **B10**.
   b. Point to the *Fill Handle* in the lower right corner of the cell.
   c. Click and drag the *Fill* pointer to cell **H10** (Figure 1-35). Release the pointer button.

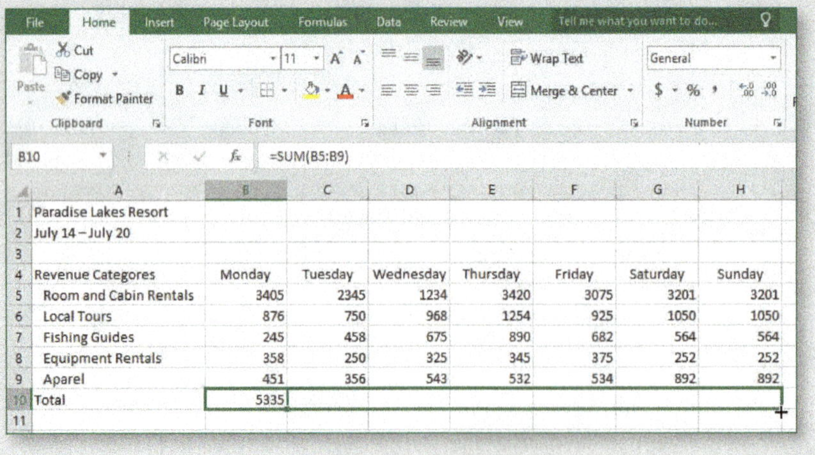

1-35 Copy a function with the *Fill* pointer

4. Calculate sales category totals.
   a. Click cell **J5**.
   b. Double-click the **AutoSum** button [*Home* tab, *Editing* group] to accept and complete the formula.

5. Edit the argument cell range.
   a. Click cell **J5**.
   b. Click the *Formula* bar within the range **B5:I5**.
   c. Position the insertion point and edit the range to **B5:h5**. When you type the "h," you will see a *Formula AutoComplete* list which you can ignore (Figure 1-36).
   d. Press **Enter** to accept the new range.

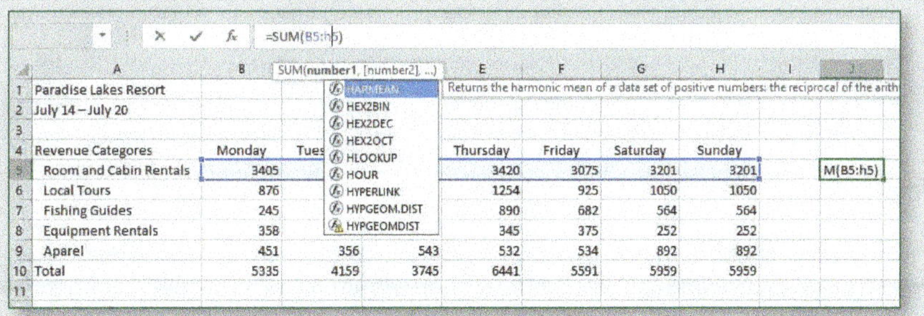

1-36 Edit the cell reference in the *Formula* bar

6. Copy a function using the *Fill Handle*.
   a. Select cell **J5** and point to the *Fill Handle*.
   b. Click and drag the *Fill* pointer to cell **J10**. Release the pointer button.
7. Drag and drop to move a cell range.
   a. Select cells **J5:J10**.
   b. Point to any border of the selected range to display the move pointer.
   c. Drag the range to cells **I5:I10**.
   d. In cell **I4**, type Total.
8. Apply cell styles.
   a. Select cell **A1** and click the **Cell Styles** button or the **More** button [*Home* tab, *Styles* group] to open the *Cell Styles* gallery.
   b. Click **Title** in the *Titles and Headings* group.
   c. Select cell **A2** and click the **Cell Styles** button or the **More** button [*Home* tab, *Styles* group].
   d. Select **Heading 2** in the *Titles and Headings* group.
   e. Select cells **A10:I10** and open the *Cell Styles* gallery [*Home* tab, *Styles* group].
   f. Select **Total** in the *Titles and Headings* group.
   g. Select cells **A4:A10**, press **Ctrl**, and select cells **B4:I4** to add them to the selection.
   h. Open the *Cells Style* gallery and select **20%, Accent1** in the *Themed Cell Styles* category.
   i. Click cell **F1** to deselect cells and view the styles.
9. Change the theme and apply font attributes.
   a. Click the **Themes** button [*Page Layout* tab, *Themes* group] and choose **Facet** from the gallery.
   b. Select cell **A4** and click the **Home** tab.
   c. Click the **Font** drop-down list [*Font* group] and select **Candara** in the *All Fonts* section.
   d. Click the **Font Size** drop-down list and select **16 pt**.
   e. Click the **Bold** button [*Font* group].
   f. Select cells **A5:I10**.
   g. Click the **Font Size** drop-down list and choose **12 pt**.
10. Use the *Format Painter*.
   a. Click cell **A4**.
   b. Click the **Format Painter** button [*Home* tab, *Clipboard* group].
   c. Drag to paint cells **B4:I4** and release the pointer button (Figure 1-37).

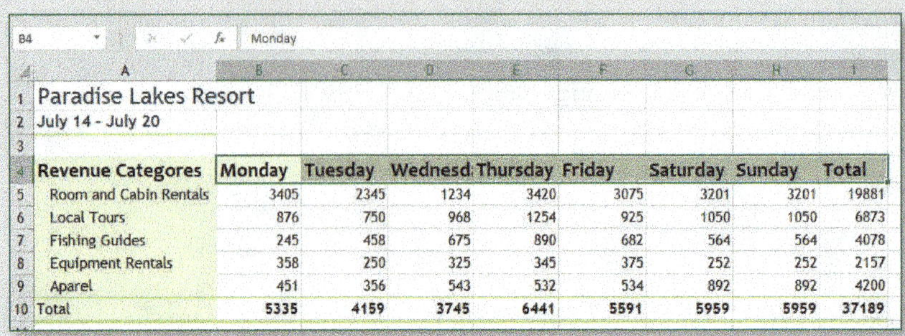

1-37 Paint the format from cell A4

11. Apply number formats and align text.
    a. Select cells **B5:I9**.
    b. Click the **Comma Style** button [*Home* tab, *Number* group] and leave cells B5:I9 selected.
    c. Click the **Decrease Decimal** button [*Home* tab, *Number* group] two times while cells B5:I9 are selected.
    d. Select cells **B10:I10**.
    e. Click the **Accounting Number Format** button [*Home* tab, *Number* group]. You may see a series of # symbols in the cells.
    f. Click the **Decrease Decimal** button [*Home* tab, *Number* group] two times.
    g. Select cells **B4:I4**.
    h. Click the **Align Right** button [*Home* tab, *Alignment* group]. Not all labels are visible with this alignment setting.
    i. Apply **Bold** to cell **A10**.

12. Add borders.
    a. Select cells **A4:I10** and click the **Border** button arrow [*Home* tab, *Font* group].
    b. Select **All Borders**. The border format from the *Total* cell style in row 10 is overwritten with the *All Borders* format.
    c. Select cells **A10:I10** and press **Ctrl+1** to open the *Format Cells* dialog box.
    d. Click the **Border** tab.
    e. Click the bottom border icon In the *Border* preview area to remove the border (Figure 1-38).
    f. Click the double solid line style (second column, seventh style).
    g. In the preview area, click the bottom border position to reset the border (Figure 1-39).
    h. Click **OK** to close the *Format Cells* dialog box and to apply the new border.
    i. Select cells **A2:I2** and open the *Format Cells* dialog box.
    j. Click the **Border** tab and click the bottom border position two times to remove the bottom border.
    k. Click the **Color** drop-down list, and select **Dark Green, Accent 2, Darker 25%**.

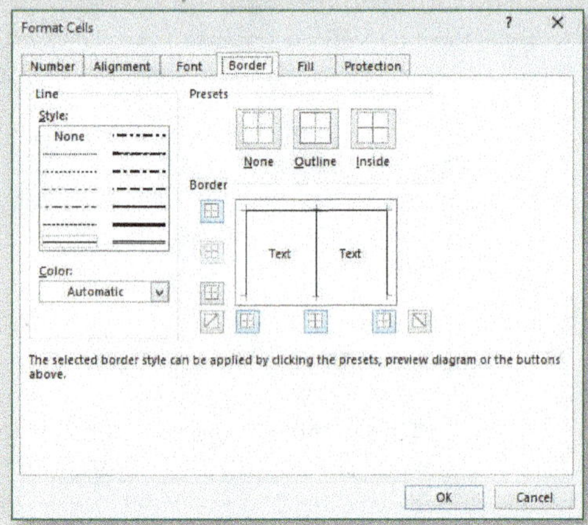

1-38 Remove the bottom border

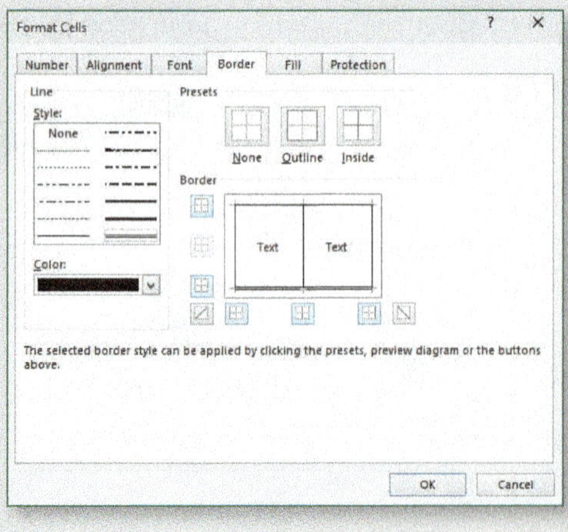

1-39 Reset the bottom border

l. Select the thick, solid line style (second column, fifth style).
m. In the preview area, click the bottom border location to reset the border.
n. Click **OK** and then click cell **A1**.

13. Click the **Save** button in the *Quick Access* toolbar.
14. Click the **File** tab and click **Close**, or press **Ctrl+W** to close the workbook (Figure 1-40).

	A	B	C	D	E	F	G	H	I
1	Paradise Lakes Resort								
2	July 14 - July 20								
3									
4	Revenue Categores	Monday	Tuesday	ednesday	Thursday	Friday	Saturday	Sunday	Total
5	Room and Cabin Rentals	3,405	2,345	1,234	3,420	3,075	3,201	3,201	19,881
6	Local Tours	876	750	968	1,254	925	1,050	1,050	6,873
7	Fishing Guides	245	458	675	890	682	564	564	4,078
8	Equipment Rentals	358	250	325	345	375	252	252	2,157
9	Aparel	451	356	543	532	534	892	892	4,200
10	Total	$ 5,335	$ 4,159	$ 3,745	$ 6,441	$ 5,591	$ 5,959	$ 5,959	$ 37,189
11									

1-40 PP E1-2 completed

SLO 1.5

Modifying Columns and Rows

A worksheet has a default number of rows and columns, each in the default width and height for the workbook theme. There are over 1 million rows and more than 16,000 columns available for use. You can modify the width of a column, insert columns, change the height of a row, delete a column, and more.

MORE INFO

Unused rows and columns are ignored when you print a worksheet with default print settings.

Adjust Column Width and Row Height

The default width for a column in a worksheet using the Office theme is 8.43 characters (64 pixels) in the default font. Column width can be set to any value between 0 and 255 characters. The default height of each row is 15 points (20 pixels). A ***pixel*** measures one screen dot. You can change ***column width*** or ***row height*** by dragging the border between column or row headings, by using the context menu, or by selecting a command from the **Format** button list [*Home* tab, *Cells* group]. You can adjust one or more columns or rows at the same time.

HOW TO: Change Column Width or Row Height

1. Select one or more cells in the same column.
   - The cells need not be in adjacent rows.
2. Click the **Format** button [*Home* tab, *Cells* group].
3. Select **Row Height**.
   - The *Row Height* dialog box opens.

4. Enter a height in points and click **OK**.
   - The row height is adjusted for the rows in which you selected cells.
5. Select one or more cells in the same row.
   - The cells need not be in adjacent columns.
6. Click the **Format** button [*Home* tab, *Cells* group].
7. Select **Column Width**.
   - The *Column Width* dialog box opens.
8. Enter a new width in characters and click **OK** (Figure 1-41).

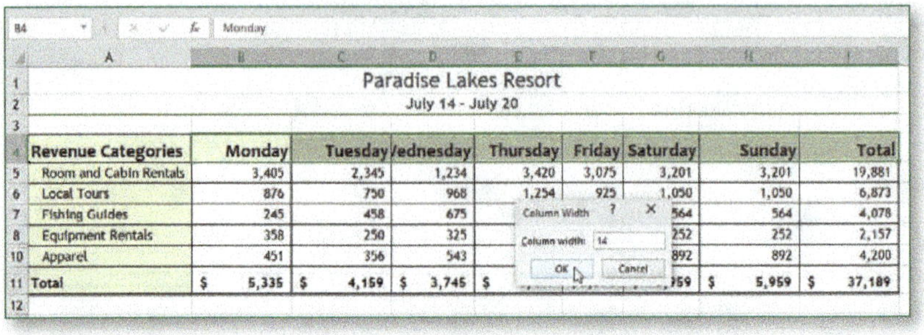

1-41 Change the column width for several columns

> **MORE INFO**
>
> Click the **Format** button [*Home* tab, *Cells* group] and select **Default Width** to change the default column width for the entire worksheet.

You can quickly change column widths and row heights using the worksheet headings. Point to the border between two column or row headings and click and drag to set a new width or height. When you point to a border, the pointer changes to a resize arrow, and you will see a *ScreenTip* with the setting as you drag. You can use this method with multiple columns or rows, too. Drag across the headings to select the number of columns or rows to be adjusted, and then click and drag any border in the selected group.

AutoFit Columns and Rows

The ***AutoFit*** feature resizes column width or row height to fit the width or height of the longest or tallest entry. The quickest way to *AutoFit* a column is to double-click the right border of the column heading (Figure 1-42). To *AutoFit* a row, double-click the bottom border of the row heading. You can *AutoFit* multiple columns or rows by first selecting them and double-clicking any border within the selection. You can also use the *AutoFit Column Width* or the *AutoFit Row Height* commands on the **Format** button in the *Cells* group on the *Home* tab.

HOW TO: AutoFit Column Width or Row Height

1. Point to the border to the right of the column heading or below the row heading.
   - Drag to select more than one column or row.
2. Double-click the resize arrow.
   - All selected columns and rows are set to fit the longest or tallest entry.

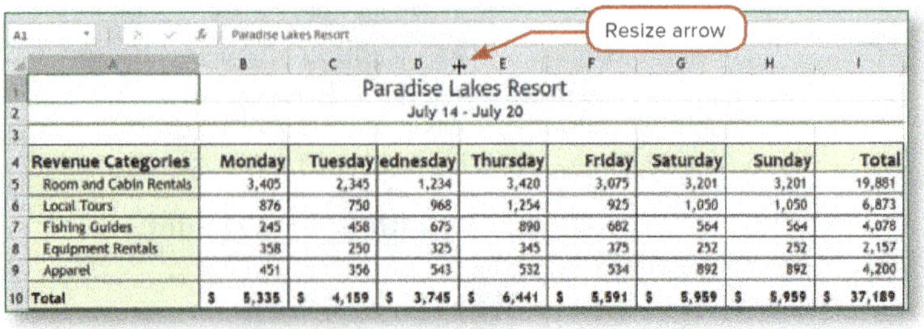

1-42 Double-click a column border to *AutoFit* its width to the longest item

Wrap Text, Merge Cells, and Center Across Selection

When a label is too long for the column width, it spills into an empty adjacent cell. If that adjacent cell is not empty, a long label may be cut off within the cell. You can widen the column, or you can wrap text. Wrapped text is often used to show lengthy column titles on more than one line (Figure 1-43).

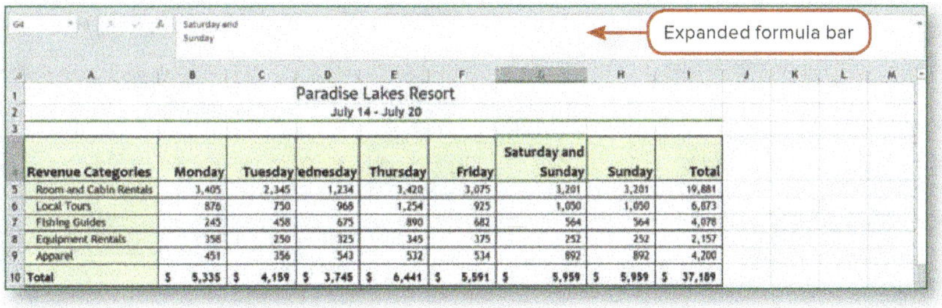

1-43 Label in cell G4 is wrapped to two lines; *Formula* bar is expanded

The ***Wrap Text*** command displays a label on multiple lines within the cell, splitting the label between words to fit the width of the column. You can control where the label splits by inserting a manual ***line break***. Press **Alt+Enter** after the word where you want a new line to start. When using multi-line labels, you can expand the *Formula* bar by clicking the **Formula Bar** expand or collapse button at the right edge of the *Formula* bar.

MORE INFO

After using the *Wrap Text* command, you may need to adjust the column width or row height to better display the label.

HOW TO: Wrap Text in a Cell

1. Select the cell with the label.
2. Click the **Home** tab.
3. Click the **Wrap Text** button in the *Alignment* group.
    - To control the split, edit the cell and click at the desired location. Press **Alt+Enter** to insert a manual line break and then press **Enter** to finish.
4. Adjust the column width and row height as desired.

ANOTHER WAY

As you type a label, press **Alt+Enter** at the point where a new line should start, finish the label, and press **Enter**. The *Wrap Text* command is automatically enabled.

The ***Merge & Center*** command combines two or more cells into one cell and centers the data within the combined cell. This command is a quick way to center a main label over multiple columns. Because the result is one large cell, you can format the area with special fill effects. When you use *Merge & Center*, the data must be in the upper left cell of the selection.

The *Merge & Center* button [*Home* tab, *Alignment* group] includes options to merge cells without centering and to unmerge cells.

▸ HOW TO: Merge and Center

1. Select the cells to be merged and centered.
   - You can merge and center the cells first and then enter the data.
2. Click the **Home** tab.
3. Click the **Merge & Center** button [*Alignment* group] (Figure 1-44).

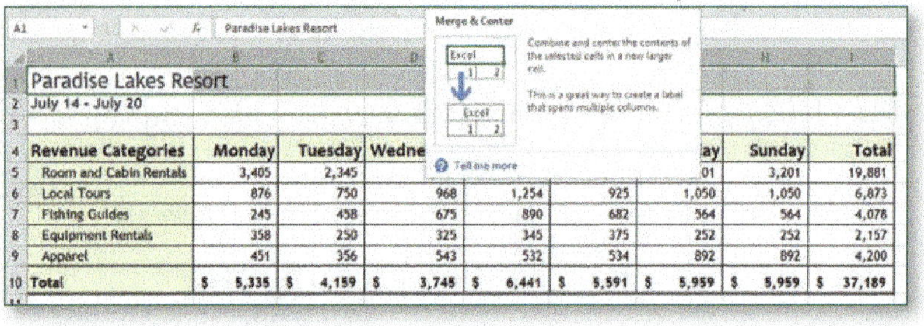

1-44 Select cells to merge and center

The ***Center Across Selection*** command horizontally centers multiple rows across multiple columns. When you have two or three rows of labels to center, you can select the entire range and center them with one command. This command does not merge cells, and you can still insert and delete rows and columns in the centered area.

The *Center Across Selection* command is on the *Alignment* tab in the *Format Cells* dialog box.

▸ HOW TO: Center Across a Selection

1. Select the cell range that includes the data to be centered.
   - Select all rows with data to be centered.
   - Select columns to identify the range over which the labels should be centered.
2. Click the **Alignment** launcher [*Home* tab, *Alignment* group].
3. Click the **Horizontal** drop-down arrow and choose **Center Across Selection** (Figure 1-45).
4. Click **OK**.

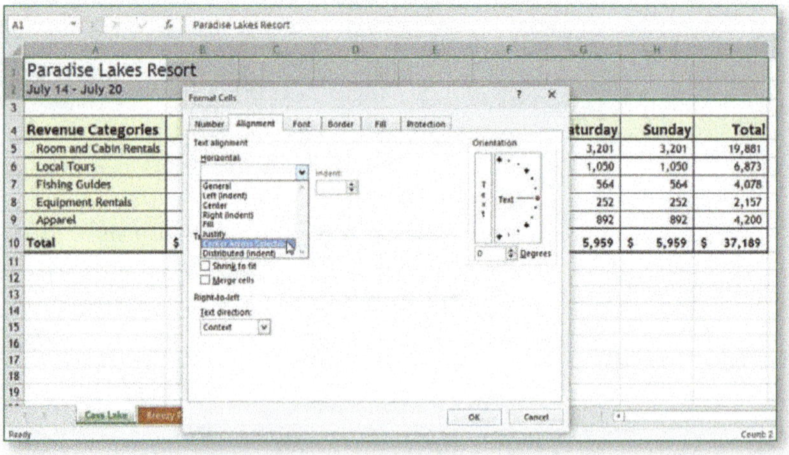

1-45 Selection identifies area for centering

Insert and Delete Columns and Rows

You can insert or delete rows or columns in a worksheet. When you do, Excel moves existing data to make room for new data or to fill the gap left by deleted data. Functions or formulas are automatically updated to include an inserted row or column, and they reflect deleted rows or columns in the argument or range.

You can insert rows and columns from options on the **Insert** button [*Home* tab, *Cells* group]. You can also right-click a column or row heading and choose **Insert** from the context menu. To insert multiple columns or rows, first select the number of columns or rows that you want to insert. For example, if you want to insert two columns to the left of column A, select columns A:B. Then use any **Insert** command to insert two new columns.

HOW TO: Insert a Column or a Row

1. Select a cell in the column to the right of where a new column is to be inserted.
2. Click the arrow on the **Insert** button [*Home* tab, *Cells* group].
3. Select **Insert Sheet Columns**.
   - A column is inserted to the left of the current column.
4. Right-click the row heading below the row where a new row should appear.
5. Choose **Insert** from the context menu (Figure 1-46).
   - A row is inserted above the selected row.

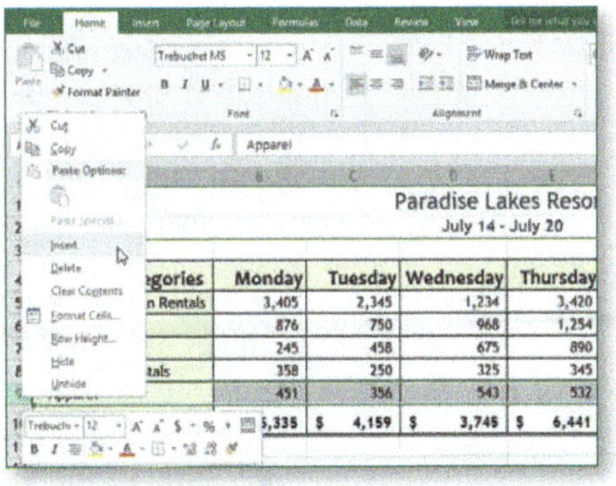

1-46 Insert a row above row 9

When you delete a column or row, data is deleted and remaining columns and rows shift to the left or up. Most functions or formulas are updated if you delete a row or column that is within the argument range.

You can delete rows and columns from the **Delete** button [*Home* tab, *Cells* group] or from the context menu. To delete multiple columns or rows, select them and use the **Delete** command.

ANOTHER WAY

Select a cell and press **Ctrl+plus sign (+)** in the numeric keypad. Choose **Entire Column** or **Entire Row** and press **Enter**. Press **Ctrl+minus sign (−)** in the numeric keypad to delete a column or row.

HOW TO: Delete Columns or Rows

1. Select a cell in the column to be deleted.
2. Click the arrow on the **Delete** button [*Home* tab, *Cells* group].
3. Select **Delete Sheet Columns**.
   - The entire column is deleted.
   - Remaining columns shift to the left.
4. Right-click the row heading for the row to be deleted.
   - The context menu opens.
5. Choose **Delete**.
   - The entire row is deleted.
   - Remaining rows shift up.

MORE INFO

You can delete or insert cells with the **Insert Cells** or **Delete Cells** commands [*Home* tab, *Cells* group]. Be careful with these commands, because they delete only cells, move adjacent data, and can have unexpected results in a worksheet.

Hide and Unhide Columns and Rows

If a worksheet has more data than necessary for your current task, you can hide data to optimize screen space. In a checkbook register with data for several years, you might want to hide rows from two years ago so that you only see the current year's data. You should not delete the old data because it is necessary for record-keeping.

Hidden rows and columns are available and included in calculations and can be shown whenever necessary. The ***Hide*** and ***Unhide*** commands apply to columns or rows; you cannot hide cells. When a column or row is hidden, there is a tiny gap between the column or row headings. In addition, column or row headings are not consecutive, so you can quickly identify what is hidden.

HOW TO: Hide and Unhide Columns or Rows

1. Click the row or column heading of the row or column to be hidden.
   - Select multiple row or column headings as desired.
   - Rows or columns need not be adjacent.
2. Right-click one of the selected row or column headings.
   - The context menu opens.
3. Select **Hide** (Figure 1-47).
   - The entire row or column is hidden.
   - Formula references to hidden cells are maintained.
4. Drag across the column or row headings where there are hidden columns or rows.
   - Drag from the column to the left of a hidden column to one column to the right of a hidden column.
   - Drag from the row above hidden rows to one row below hidden rows.
5. Right-click one of the selected row or column headings.
   - The context menu opens.
6. Select **Unhide**.

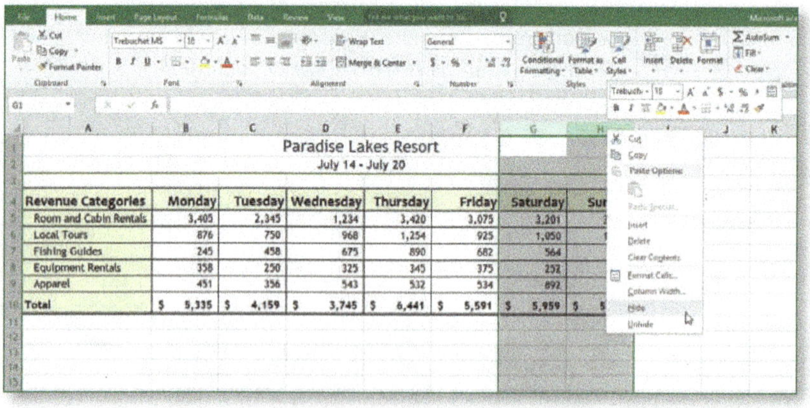

1-47 Hide two columns

ANOTHER WAY

To hide or unhide columns or rows, select the column or row headings, click the **Format** button [*Home* tab, *Cells* group], choose **Hide & Unhide**, and select the desired command.

SLO 1.6

Modifying Worksheets

Each worksheet in an Excel workbook has a worksheet tab near the bottom left of the Excel window that displays the name of the sheet. A new workbook starts with one sheet, but the number of worksheets is limited only by the size of memory on the computer. You can insert and delete sheets, rename them, and change the tab color. You can also hide, copy, or move sheets.

Insert and Delete Worksheets

You can keep related worksheets in a single workbook for ease in managing your files and tasks. For example, a monthly workbook could include revenue and expense, payroll, and customer data sheets. When there are multiple worksheets in a workbook, activate a sheet by clicking its tab name.

You can insert worksheets from the **Insert** button [*Home* tab, *Cells* group] or by simply clicking the **New Sheet** button to the right of the tab names. You can also right-click an existing sheet tab and choose **Insert** to open an *Insert* dialog box. Inserted worksheets are named *SheetN*, where *N* is the next available number.

To delete the active worksheet, right-click the sheet tab and select **Delete**. You can also click the arrow on the **Delete** button [*Home* tab, *Cells* group] and select **Delete Sheet**.

> **MORE INFO**
>
> Press **Ctrl+Page Down** to move to the next worksheet in the tab order. Press **Ctrl+Page Up** to move to the previous sheet.

HOW TO: Insert and Delete Worksheets

1. Click the **New Sheet** button (plus sign) to the right of the worksheet tabs (Figure 1-48).
   - A new sheet is inserted to the right of the active sheet.
2. Click the arrow on the **Insert** button [*Home* tab, *Cells* group].
3. Select **Insert Sheet**.
   - A new sheet is inserted to the left of the active sheet.
4. Right-click a tab and select **Insert**.
   - The *Insert* dialog box opens.
5. Select **Worksheet** and click **OK**.
   - The new sheet is inserted to the left of the active sheet.
6. Right-click a sheet tab and choose **Delete**.
   - The sheet is deleted.
7. Click the arrow on the **Delete** button [*Home* tab, *Cells* group] and select **Delete Sheet**.
   - The sheet is deleted.

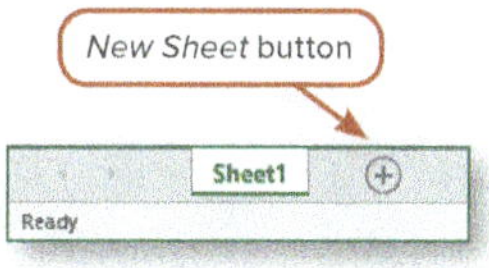

1-48 *New Sheet* button

> **ANOTHER WAY**
>
> Press **Shift+F11** to insert a worksheet to the left of the active sheet.

> **MORE INFO**
>
> To delete or insert multiple sheets, select multiple tabs. Then right-click one of the selected tabs and choose **Delete** or **Insert**.

Rename Worksheets and Change Tab Color

New worksheets are named *Sheet1*, *Sheet2*, and so on, but you can rename a worksheet to identify its contents and purpose. The tab width adjusts to display the name, so if you use lengthy names, you limit the number of tabs visible at the same time. When you cannot see all the tabs, use the ***tab scrolling buttons*** located to the left of the leftmost tab name. Move forward and backward through the tabs, or you can right-click a tab scrolling button to display the *Activate* dialog box with a list of existing worksheet names (Figure 1-49). The tab scrolling buttons are enabled when needed.

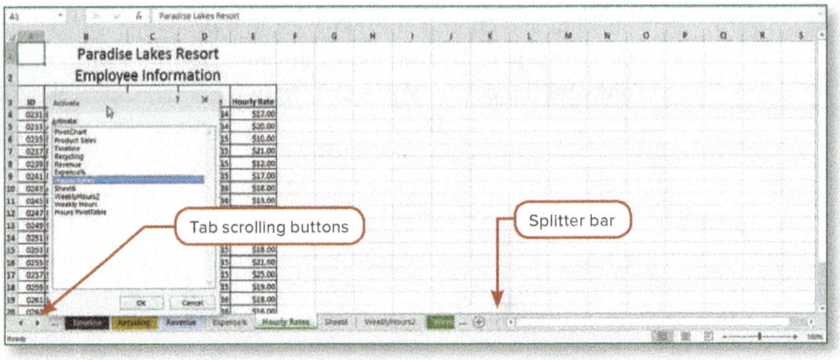

1-49 Activate dialog box and tab scrolling buttons

> **MORE INFO**
>
> The number of tab names visible at one time depends on the width of the horizontal scroll bar. Use the tab splitter to resize the horizontal scroll bar.

You can apply a ***tab color*** to further distinguish a particular sheet. The color palette includes tiles for theme and standard colors as well as an option to build a custom color.

HOW TO: Rename a Worksheet and Apply a Tab Color

1. Double-click the worksheet tab.
   - You can right-click the tab and select **Rename**.
2. Type the new name on the tab and press **Enter**.
   - You can click the **Format** button [*Home* tab, *Cells* group] and select **Rename Sheet**.
3. Right-click the worksheet tab.
4. Choose **Tab Color** from the context menu to open the palette (Figure 1-50).
   - You can click the **Format** button [*Home* tab, *Cells* group] and select **Tab Color**.

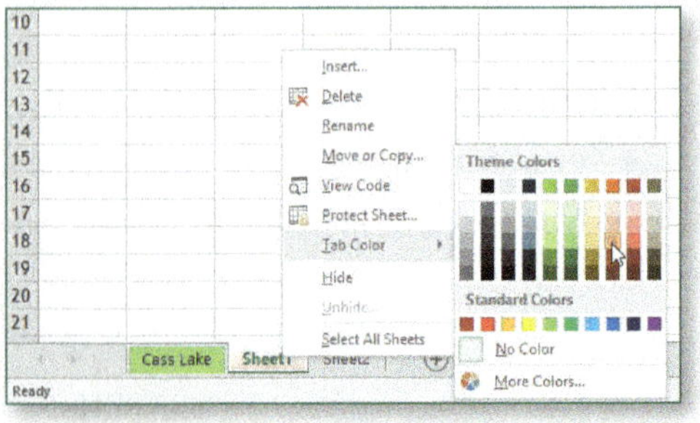

1-50 Change the tab color

5. Select a color.
6. Click another tab to better see the tab color.

Move and Copy Worksheets

You can rearrange (move) tabs to display the worksheets in your preferred left-to-right order. You can also move worksheets to another workbook.

You can copy a worksheet to make an exact duplicate of the data and formatting. When you copy a worksheet, the copy is named with the same name as the original followed by a number in parentheses (i.e., *January (2)*).

When moving sheets within a workbook, you simply drag the tab to the desired location. When moving or copying to another workbook, however, use the ***Move or Copy*** dialog box.

You can move or copy multiple sheets, too. Select sheet names using **Ctrl** or **Shift**. The word *[Group]* displays in the title bar. After you complete the move or copy command, right-click any tab in the group and choose **Ungroup**.

HOW TO: Move and Copy Worksheets

1. Point to the worksheet tab to be moved.
2. Drag the pointer to the desired location in the tab names.
   - A triangle and a worksheet icon preview where the worksheet will be moved (Figure 1-51).
3. Release the pointer button.
4. Right-click the worksheet tab to be copied.
5. Select **Move or Copy**.
   - The *Move or Copy* dialog box opens.
   - You can also click the **Format** button [*Home* tab, *Cells* group] to select **Move or Copy Sheet**.
6. Click the **To book** drop-down arrow and choose a workbook name.
   - To copy the sheet in the same workbook, choose its name.
   - To copy the worksheet into a different workbook, choose its name; the workbook must be open.
7. In the *Before sheet* list, choose a sheet name as desired.
   - Choose **(move to end)** to place the copied sheet as the last tab.
8. Select the **Create a copy** box (Figure 1-52).
9. Click **OK** to close the dialog box.
   - The copied worksheet has the same name as the original followed by *(2)*.
10. Rename the copied sheet as desired.

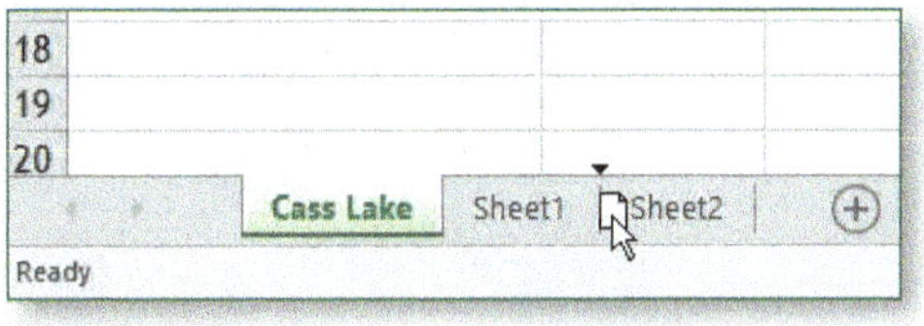

1-51 Drag a sheet tab to a position

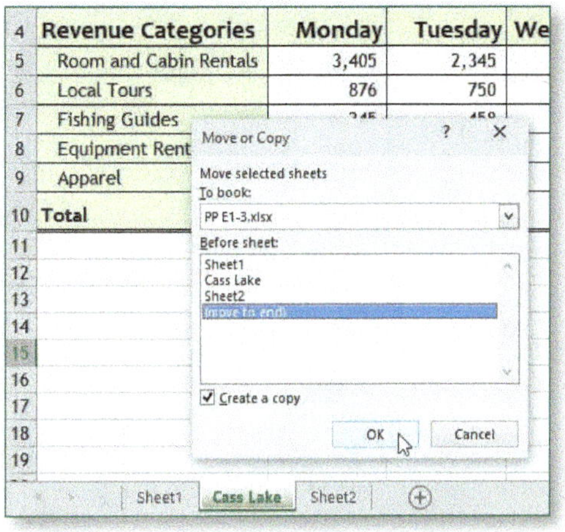

1-52 *Move or Copy* dialog box

ANOTHER WAY

To copy a worksheet by dragging, press **Ctrl** and drag the tab to the desired location for the copy.

PAUSE & PRACTICE: EXCEL 1-3

In this project, you open ***[your initials] PP E1-2*** and adjust column heights and row widths, insert a row, merge and center cells, and add borders. You also copy and rename sheets, apply tab colors, and delete worksheets.

File Needed: ***[your initials] PP E1-2**.xlsx*
Completed Project File Name: ***[your initials] PP E1-3**.xlsx*

1. Open the ***[your initials] PP E1-2*** workbook completed in *Pause & Practice 1-2*.
2. Save the file as [your initials] PP E1-3.
3. Change the width of columns B through I.
   a. Point to the column **B** heading to display a down-pointing arrow.
   b. Click and drag to reach column **I**.
   c. Click the **Format** button [*Home* tab, *Cells* group].
   d. Select **Column Width** from the menu.
   e. Enter 14 in the *Column Width* dialog box.
   f. Click **OK** to set the new width for the selected columns.
4. Change the row height for rows 4 and 10.
   a. Click the row **4** heading.
   b. Press **Ctrl** and click the row **10** heading. Two rows are selected.
   c. Right-click the row **4** heading.
   d. Choose **Row Height** from the menu.
   e. Enter 24 as the new height.
   f. Click **OK** to set the row height for both rows.
5. Insert a row.
   a. Right-click row heading **9**.
   b. Choose **Insert**. The inserted row is row 9, and the remaining rows have shifted down.
   c. In cell **A9**, type Food & Beverage. The new row uses the same format as the other rows (Figure 1-53).
   d. Press **Enter**.

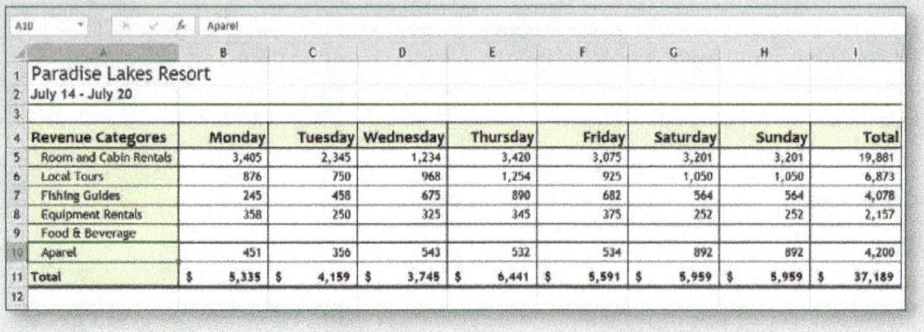
A10 Aparel

Paradise Lakes Resort
July 14 - July 20

Revenue Categores	Monday	Tuesday	Wednesday	Thursday	Friday	Saturday	Sunday	Total
Room and Cabin Rentals	3,405	2,345	1,234	3,420	3,075	3,201	3,201	19,881
Local Tours	876	750	968	1,254	925	1,050	1,050	6,873
Fishing Guides	245	458	675	890	682	564	564	4,078
Equipment Rentals	358	250	325	345	375	252	252	2,157
Food & Beverage								
Aparel	451	356	543	532	534	892	892	4,200
Total	$ 5,335	$ 4,159	$ 3,745	$ 6,441	$ 5,591	$ 5,959	$ 5,959	$ 37,189

1-53 New row and label inserted

6. Hide a row.
   a. Select cell **A9**.
   b. Click the **Format** button [*Home* tab, *Cells* group].
   c. Select **Hide & Unhide** in the *Visibility* category.
   d. Select **Hide Rows**. The selected row is hidden.
7. Center titles across a selection.
   a. Select cells **A1:I2**.
   b. Click the **Alignment** launcher [*Home* tab, *Alignment* group].

c. Click the **Horizontal** drop-down arrow and choose **Center Across Selection**.
d. Click **OK**.

8. Rename a worksheet and change the tab color.
   a. Double-click the **Sheet1** tab name.
   b. Type Cass Lake.
   c. Press **Enter**.
   d. Right-click the **Cass Lake** tab name and select **Tab Color**.
   e. Select **Green Accent 1, Darker 50%** (fifth column).
9. Copy and rename a worksheet.
   a. Right-click the **Cass Lake** tab.
   b. Choose **Move or Copy**. The *Move or Copy* dialog box opens.
   c. Choose **(move to end)** in the *Before Sheet* list.
   d. Select the **Create a copy** box.
   e. Click **OK**. The copied sheet is named *Cass Lake (2)*.
   f. Double-click the **Cass Lake (2)** tab, type Breezy Point, and press **Enter**.
   g. Right-click the **Breezy Point** tab and choose **Tab Color**.
   h. Format the tab color to **Orange, Accent 4, Darker 25%**.
   i. Select cells **B5:H10** and press **Delete** (Figure 1-54).
   j. Press **Ctrl+Home**.

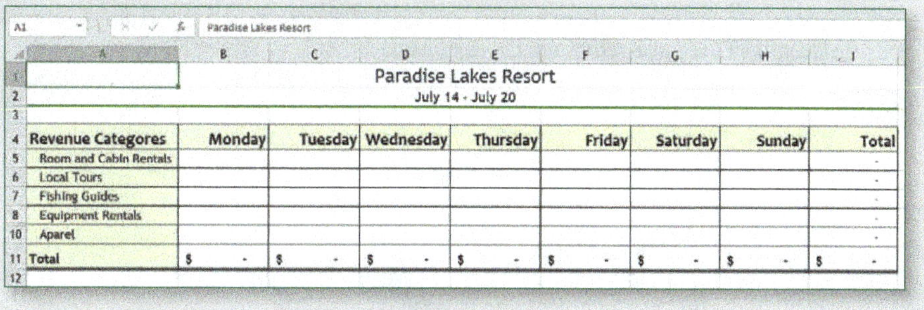

Revenue Categores	Monday	Tuesday	Wednesday	Thursday	Friday	Saturday	Sunday	Total
Room and Cabin Rentals								-
Local Tours								-
Fishing Guides								-
Equipment Rentals								-
Aparel								-
Total	$ -	$ -	$ -	$ -	$ -	$ -	$ -	$ -

1-54 Data deleted on copied sheet

10. Click the **Cass Lake** tab and press **Ctrl+Home**.
11. Press **Ctrl+S** to save the workbook.
12. Click the **File** tab and click **Close** to close the workbook (Figure 1-55).

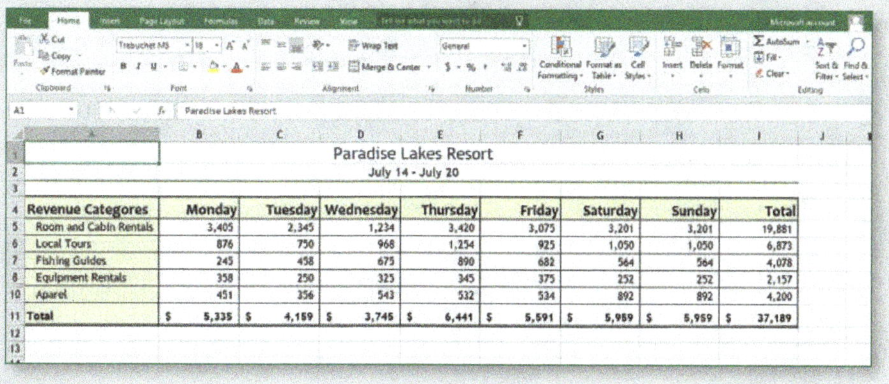

Revenue Categores	Monday	Tuesday	Wednesday	Thursday	Friday	Saturday	Sunday	Total
Room and Cabin Rentals	3,405	2,345	1,234	3,420	3,075	3,201	3,201	19,881
Local Tours	876	750	968	1,254	925	1,050	1,050	6,873
Fishing Guides	245	458	675	890	682	564	564	4,078
Equipment Rentals	358	250	325	345	375	252	252	2,157
Aparel	451	356	543	532	534	892	892	4,200
Total	$ 5,335	$ 4,159	$ 3,745	$ 6,441	$ 5,591	$ 5,959	$ 5,959	$ 37,189

1-55 PP E1-3 completed worksheet

SLO 1.7

Modifying the Appearance of the Workbook

You can adjust how you see data in a worksheet to make your work as easy as possible. You can select a view, zoom in or out on the data, freeze parts of the screen, split the worksheet into two panes, and switch between multiple open windows.

Workbook Views

The *View* tab has a *Workbook Views* group with three main views or layouts for working in an Excel worksheet. The views are ***Normal***, ***Page Layout***, and ***Page Break Preview***.

- *Normal* view is the default and is used to create and modify a worksheet.
- *Page Layout* view opens the header and footer areas, indicates margin areas, and shows rulers.
- *Page Break Preview* displays printed pages with dashed or dotted lines to mark where new pages start.

There are buttons for *Normal* view, *Page Layout* view, and *Page Break Preview* on the right side of the *Status* bar.

> **MORE INFO**
>
> The **Ribbon Display Options** button (on the right of the workbook title bar) can be used to hide the *Ribbon* for maximum screen space in any workbook view.

HOW TO: Switch Workbook Views Using the Status Bar

1. Click the **View** tab.
   - The *Normal* button is activated in the *Workbook Views* group.
2. Click the **Page Layout** button in the *Status* bar.
   - This view displays the header, the footer, and margin areas (Figure 1-56).

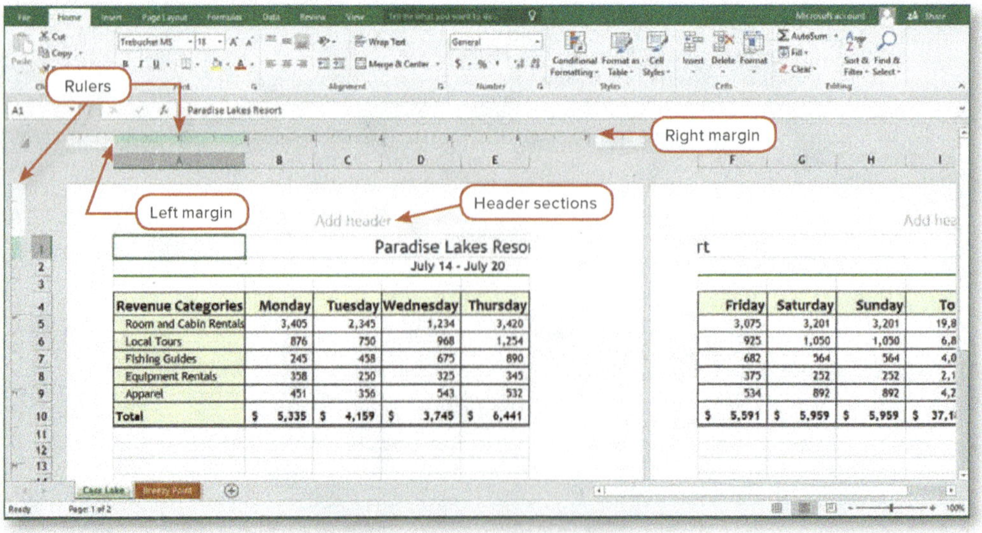

1-56 ***Page Layout* view**

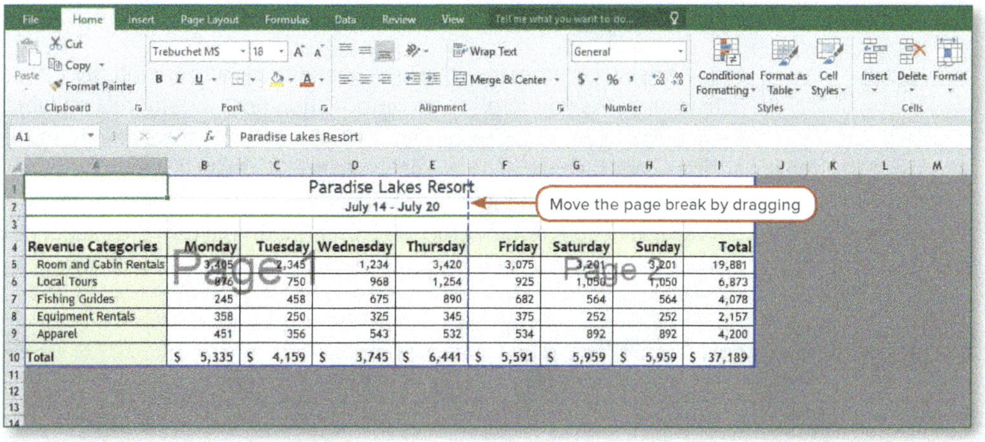

1-57 *Page Break Preview*

3. Click the **Page Break Preview** button in the *Status* bar.
   - If the data does not fit on a single page, a dashed line indicates where the second page will start (Figure 1-57).
4. Click the **Normal** button in the *Status* bar.

Zoom Options

You can change a sheet's magnification to see more of the data at once (zoom out) or to scrutinize content more carefully (zoom in). There is a *Zoom* group on the *View* tab as well as *Zoom* controls in the *Status* bar.

The *Status* bar controls include a **Zoom In** button, a **Zoom Out** button, and the **Zoom** slider. The slider is the vertical bar in the middle of the horizontal line which you can drag to change the magnification level.

HOW TO: Change Zoom Levels

1. Click the **Zoom In** button in the *Status* bar.
   - The magnification is increased in 10% increments with each click.
2. Click the **Zoom Out** button in the *Status* bar.
   - The magnification is decreased in 10% increments with each click.
3. Drag the **Zoom** slider in the middle of the horizontal line to the left or right to set a value (Figure 1-58).
   - The magnification percentage is displayed to the right of the line.
4. Click the **Zoom** button [*View* tab, *Zoom* group].
   - The *Zoom* dialog box includes preset values.
5. Click a radio button to choose a *Magnification* level.
   - Select **Fit selection** for a selected range to fill the screen.
   - Choose **Custom** to enter any magnification value.
6. Click **OK**.

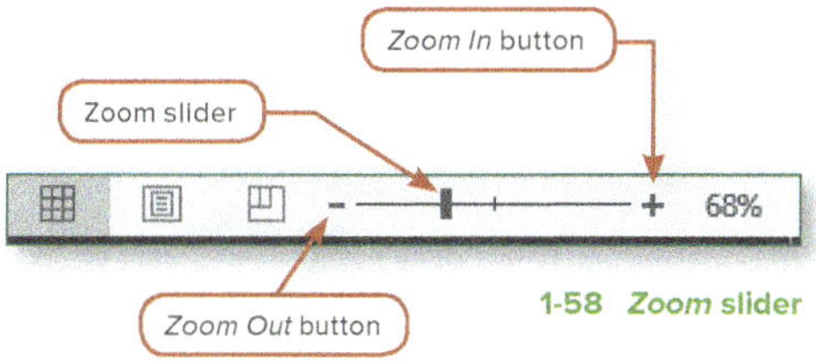

1-58 *Zoom slider*

ANOTHER WAY

The *Zoom* group [*View* tab] has ***100%*** and ***Zoom to Selection*** buttons.

Freeze Panes

In a worksheet with many rows and columns of information, it is not possible to see all the data at once. As you scroll to see information on the right, related labels or values on the left scroll out of view. The ***Freeze Panes*** command locks rows or columns in view so that you can position data for easy review. The worksheet is divided into two or four panes (sections) with a thin, black border to indicate the divisions.

The active cell becomes the top left corner of the moving pane. For example, if you select cell B5 and select the *Freeze Panes* command, column A and rows 1:4 are stationary.

HOW TO: Freeze and Unfreeze Panes

1. Select a cell in the worksheet.
   - Click a cell one row below the last row to be frozen.
   - Click a cell one column to the right of the last column to be locked.
2. Click the **Freeze Panes** button [*View* tab, *Window* group].
   - Select **Freeze Top Row** to lock row 1 in view, regardless of the active cell.
   - Choose **Freeze First Column** to keep the first column in view, regardless of the active cell.
3. Select **Freeze Panes**.
   - All rows above and all columns to the left of the active cell are locked in position.
   - A thin, black border identifies frozen rows and columns.
4. Scroll the data in any direction (Figure 1-59).
5. Click the **Freeze Panes** button [*View* tab, *Window* group].
6. Select **Unfreeze Panes**.
   - The black border is removed.

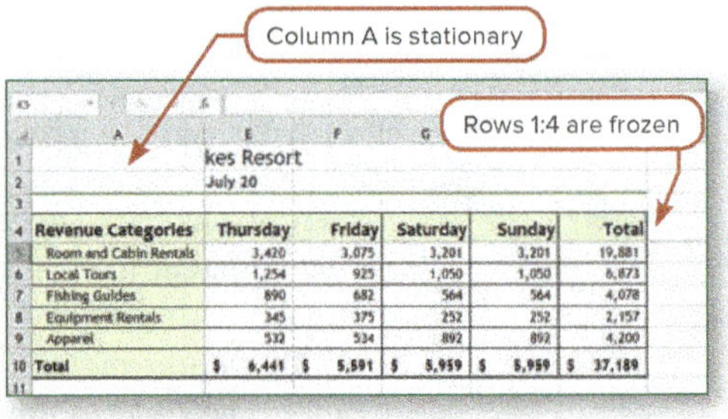

1-59 ***Freeze Panes*** **results when cell B5 is selected and columns B:D are scrolled left**

Split a Worksheet into Panes

The ***Split*** command divides a worksheet into two or four display panes. Each pane shows the same sheet, but you can arrange each pane to show different or the same rows and columns. There is only one active cell, and you may not see it in all the panes. Because it is one worksheet, an edit can be made in any pane.

The panes are split based on the position of the active cell when you give the command. A ***splitter bar*** is a light gray bar that spans the window, either horizontally, vertically, or both. You can drag a splitter bar to resize the panes.

HOW TO: Split a Worksheet

1. Select the cell for the location of a split.
   - Click a cell in column A (except cell A1) to split the worksheet into two horizontal panes.
   - Click a cell in row 1 (but not cell A1) to split the worksheet into two vertical panes.
   - Click a cell to split the worksheet into four panes.
2. Click the **Split** button [*View* tab, *Window* group].

3. Drag a splitter bar to resize a pane (Figure 1-60).
4. Click the **Split** button [*View* tab, *Window* group] to remove the split.

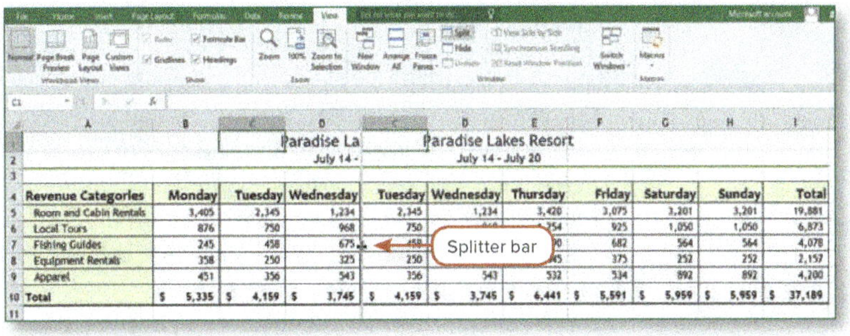

1-60 Split worksheet

> **ANOTHER WAY**
>
> You can remove a window split by double-clicking the splitter bar.

Hide or Unhide Worksheets

A ***hidden worksheet*** is a worksheet whose tab is not displayed. It is part of the workbook and can be referenced in calculations. A worksheet might be hidden to prevent accidental changes to it, or it might hold data that should not be easily visible. You can hide a worksheet using the **Format** button [*Home* tab] or by right-clicking the sheet tab. You cannot hide a worksheet if it is the only sheet in the workbook.

> **MORE INFO**
>
> The command to print an *Entire Workbook* does not print a hidden worksheet.

HOW TO: Hide and Unhide Worksheets

1. Right-click the sheet tab to hide.
   - Press **Ctrl** to select multiple sheets, then right-click any one of the selected tabs.
2. Select **Hide**.
   - The worksheet tab is hidden.
3. Right-click any worksheet tab.
4. Select **Unhide**.
   - The *Unhide sheet* dialog box opens.
5. Select the tab name to unhide (Figure 1-61).
6. Click **OK**.

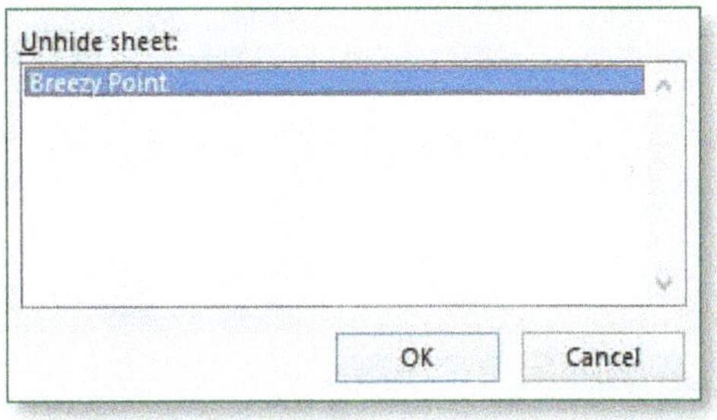

1-61 *Unhide sheet* dialog box

> **MORE INFO**
>
> The *Hide* command on the *View* tab hides a workbook. A hidden workbook can be used to store programming routines such as macros or external reference data that should be protected from viewing or accidental editing.

Switch Windows Command

When more than one workbook is open, the ***Switch Windows*** command changes or cycles through open workbooks. You can switch windows from the *Ribbon*, from the Windows taskbar, or with the keyboard shortcut **Ctrl+F6**. When you click the **Switch Windows** button [*View* tab, *Window* group], a menu lists the names of open workbooks so that you can select one. To use the Windows taskbar, point to the Excel icon to see a thumbnail with the file name of each open workbook and click the one to be edited. The keyboard shortcut toggles between the last two viewed workbooks.

When only two workbooks are open, you can view them side by side. The *View Side by Side* button is grayed out when only one workbook is open. For side-by-side viewing, you can scroll the windows together or separately. *Synchronous Scrolling* moves both workbooks in the same direction at the same time. This is especially helpful when worksheets have the same types of data in the same locations. Synchronous scrolling is automatically enabled when you choose the *View Side by Side* command.

HOW TO: Switch Windows Using the Ribbon

1. Open two or more workbooks.
2. Click the **Switch Windows** button [*View* tab, *Window* group].
   - The names of open workbooks are listed.
3. Click the name of the workbook to view.

MORE INFO

If three or more workbooks are open when you select the *View Side by Side* command, the *Compare Side by Side* dialog box opens with the names of open workbooks. The one you select is displayed side by side with the active workbook.

View Multiple Worksheets

The ***New Window*** command opens a new separate window with the same workbook. The new window displays the workbook name in the title bar followed by a colon and number. Combined with the ***Arrange All*** command, you can position different parts of the workbook to make comparisons or monitor changes as you work. Figure 1-62 shows different sheets in the same workbook.

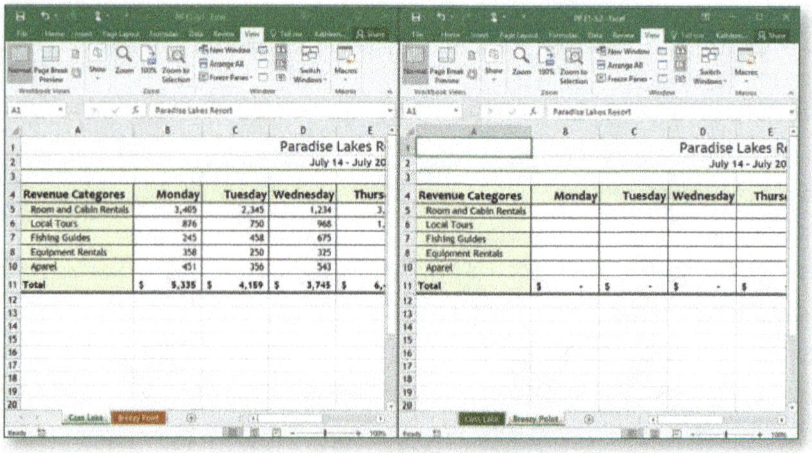

1-62 Two windows for a workbook

MORE INFO

You can open as many windows as needed and arrange them all.

▶ HOW TO: View Multiple Worksheets at the Same Time

1. Click the **View** tab and click the **New Window** button [*Window* group].
   - A second window opens for the same workbook and is active.
   - Both windows are maximized.
2. Click the **Arrange All** button [*View* tab, *Window* group].
   - The *Arrange Windows* dialog box opens.
3. Choose an option for arranging the windows.
   - The active window is arranged on the left (vertically tiled) or at the top (horizontally tiled).
   - If several workbooks are open but only the active workbook has multiple windows, choose **Windows of active workbook** so that only those windows are arranged.
4. Click **OK**.
   - The active window is arranged on the left or at the top.
5. Click the **Maximize** button in either title bar.
   - The window is full size.
6. Click the **Close** button (**X**) in the title bar to close the window.
   - The other window is displayed at its tiled size.
7. Click the **Maximize** button.

SLO 1.8

Finalizing a Workbook

Before you distribute your work to others, make sure that it is ready for sharing. A quick spell check can help locate and correct misspelled labels. You can enter document properties or insert headers and footers to help identify your work. You can control how your worksheet prints by setting margins, changing the orientation, or adjusting page breaks.

Check Spelling

The ***Spelling*** command scans a worksheet and locates words that do not match entries in the main Office dictionary; it also finds duplicate words. The dictionary is shared among all Office applications, and you can add labels to it, such as unusual or technical words. You can spell check the entire worksheet or a selected range.

The *Spelling* dialog box includes options for handling an error as shown in the following table:

Spelling Dialog Box Options

Option	Action
Ignore Once	Skips the occurrence of the label
Ignore All	Skips all occurrences of the same spelling of the label
Add to Dictionary	Adds the label to the default dictionary
Change	Changes the label to the highlighted entry in the *Suggestions* box
Change All	Same as *Change*, but changes the same label throughout the worksheet
Delete	Appears for *Repeated Word*. Click to delete one occurrence of the label.
AutoCorrect	Adds the label to the *AutoCorrect* list
Options	Opens the *Excel Options* dialog box to the *Proofing* tab for changing default settings
Undo Last	Reverses the most recent correction
Cancel	Discontinues spell checking

▶ HOW TO: Spell Check a Worksheet

1. Press **Ctrl+Home** to move to cell **A1**.
   - Start at the beginning of the worksheet.
   - Select a range to limit spell checking to that group of cells.
2. Click the **Review** tab and click the **Spelling** button [*Proofing* group].
   - The first error is located.
   - A list of suggested corrections is displayed.
3. Select the correct spelling in the list.
   - If there is no acceptable suggestion, click the **Not in Dictionary** box and type the correct spelling of the label.
4. Click **Change** to replace the misspelled label (Figure 1-63).
5. Click **Close** when spelling is complete.

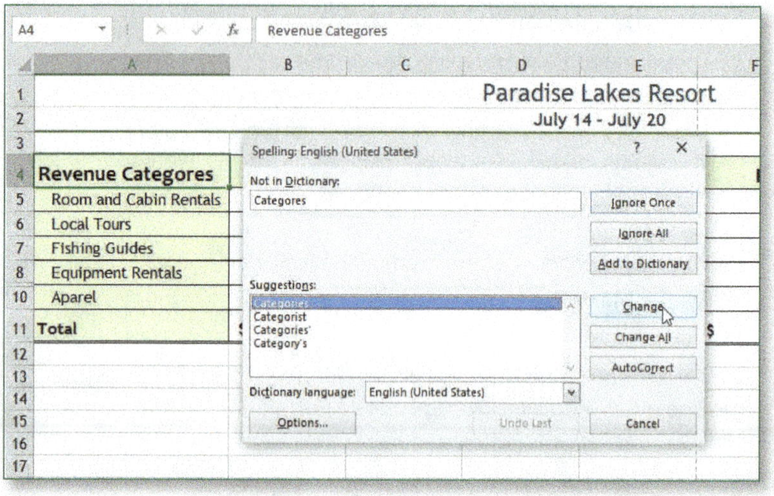

1-63 ***Spelling* dialog box**

Document Properties

A ***document property*** or ***metadata*** is a field of information. Metadata are settings and content including the author name, the date the file was created, the type and size of file, and more. Some properties are uneditable such as dates and file size; these settings are automatically updated. You can edit other document properties, including *Title*, *Author*, and *Subject*. A partial list of properties is available in the *Backstage* view on the right in the *Info* pane.

▶ HOW TO: Add Document Properties in Backstage View

1. Click the **File** tab to display the *Backstage* view.
2. Select **Info** if it is not already selected.
   - Property field names are listed.
   - An editable property has an entry box.
3. Click an entry box to enter or edit an item (Figure 1-64).
4. Return to the workbook and save the file.

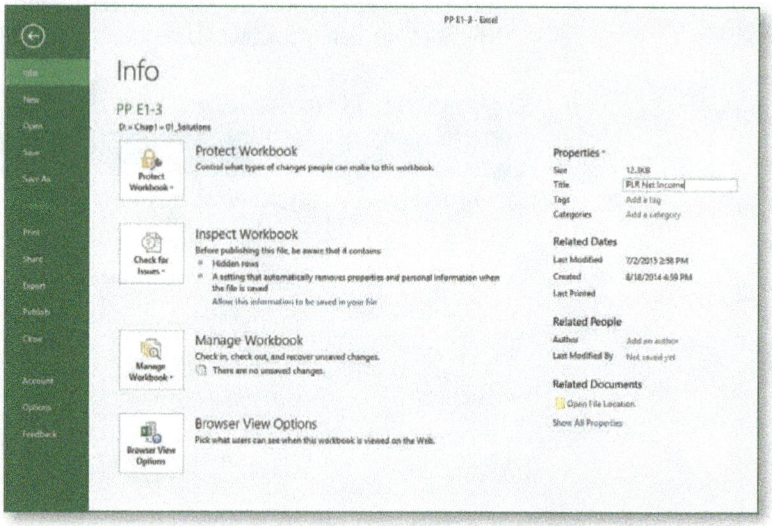

1-64 Workbook properties

The Properties Dialog Box

You can review all properties in the *Properties* dialog box. The *General*, *Statistics*, and *Contents* tabs list uneditable metadata. The *Summary* tab has properties such as the title, subject, and keywords. Keywords are used in file search commands. On the *Custom* tab, you can choose an additional property and type a default value.

HOW TO: Open the Properties Dialog Box

1. Display the *Backstage* view and click **Info**.
2. Click the **Properties** button.
3. Select **Advanced Properties**.
   - The *Properties* dialog box opens (Figure 1-65).
4. Click a tab to view or edit a property.
5. Click **OK** to close the dialog box.

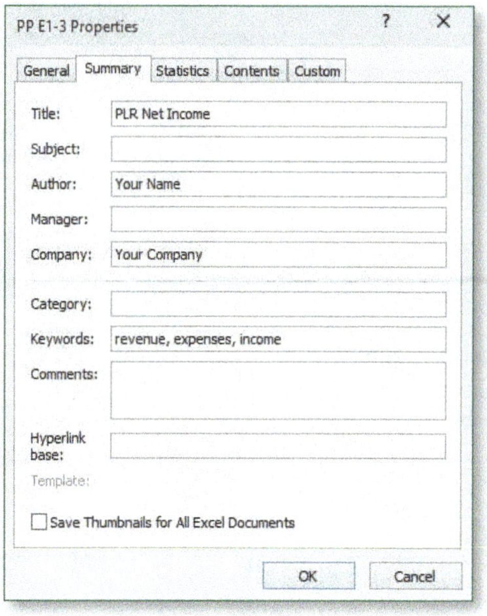

1-65 *Properties* dialog box

The Page Setup Dialog Box

The *Page Setup* dialog box offers several command groups for controlling how a worksheet prints. The commands are from the *Sheet Options*, *Scale to Fit*, and *Page Setup* groups on the *Page Layout* tab as well as commands for setting headers and footers. The ***Page Setup*** launcher [*Page Layout* tab, *Page Setup* group] opens the dialog box.

ANOTHER WAY

Open the *Page Setup* dialog box by clicking the launcher in the *Scale to Fit* or the *Sheet Options* group on the *Page Layout* tab.

Each tab in the *Page Setup* dialog box has a *Print*, a *Print Preview*, and an *Options* button (Figure 1-66). The *Options* button opens the *Printer Properties* dialog box. The following table summarizes commands on each tab in the *Page Setup* dialog box:

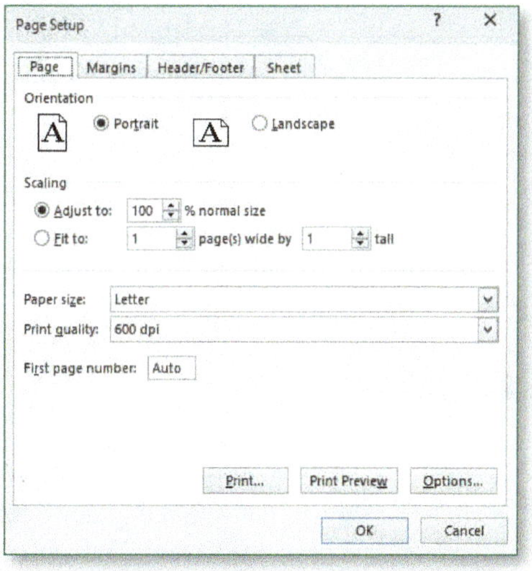

1-66 *Page* tab in the *Page Setup* dialog box

Page Setup Dialog Box Options

Tab	Available Settings
Page	Set the *Orientation* to *Portrait* or *Landscape*. Use *Scaling* to shrink or enlarge the printed worksheet to the paper size. Choose a *Paper size* or set *Print quality*. Define the *First page number*.
Margins	Adjust *Top*, *Bottom*, *Left*, and *Right* worksheet margins. Set *Header* and *Footer* top and bottom margins. *Center on page* horizontally and/or vertically.
Header/Footer	Choose a preset header or footer layout. Create a custom header or footer. Specify first and other page headers. Set header and footers to scale with worksheet and to align with margins.
Sheet	Identify a *Print area* other than the entire worksheet. Identify *Print titles* to repeat on each page. Print *Gridlines*, *Row and column headings*, *Comments*, and *Error messages*.

MORE INFO

You can make changes to multiple worksheets at the same time from the *Page Setup* dialog box. Select the tabs first to group the worksheets.

ANOTHER WAY

Open the *Page Setup* dialog box by clicking the *Page Setup* link in the *Print* area on the *Backstage* view.

Margins, Page Orientation, and Paper Size

A new Excel workbook uses the following default settings:

- Top and bottom margins: 0.75"
- Left and right margins: 0.7"
- Header and footer margins: 0.3"
- Portrait orientation
- Letter size paper

The *Margins* button [*Page Layout* tab, *Page Setup* group] lists *Normal*, *Wide*, and *Narrow* for margin settings as well as *Custom Margins*. When you select **Custom Margins**, the *Page Setup* dialog box opens to the *Margins* tab. Here you can set any value for any margin area, including the header and the footer. You can also center the page horizontally or vertically from this tab.

The *Orientation* button [*Page Setup* group, *Page Layout* tab] has two choices, *Portrait* or *Landscape*. A portrait page is taller than it is wide. A landscape page is wider than it is tall. The *Size* button lists paper sizes, but your printer must be able to accommodate the size.

You can modify settings for one worksheet or for several worksheets at a time. To format multiple worksheets, you need to group the worksheet tabs. Do this by clicking the first tab name, holding down **Shift**, and clicking the last tab name to select all sheets between those two names. You can also click the first tab name, press **Ctrl**, and click nonadjacent sheet names to create a group.

ANOTHER WAY

Right-click any sheet tab and choose **Select All Sheets** to group all sheets in the workbook for formatting.

HOW TO: Set Margins, Page Orientation, and Paper Size

1. Click the **Margins** button [*Page Layout* tab, *Page Setup* group].
2. Select **Custom Margins** to open the *Page Setup* dialog box (Figure 1-67).
   - The dialog box opens to the *Margins* tab.
3. Type each margin setting as desired.
   - You can use the spinner buttons to change the margin value.
4. Select the **Horizontally** box in the *Center on page* area.
   - This command centers the data between the left and right margins.
   - You can also vertically center the data on the page.
5. Click the **Page** tab in the *Page Layout* dialog box.
6. Select the radio button for **Portrait** or **Landscape**.
7. Click the **Paper size** arrow and select a paper size.
   - The default paper size is 8½ × 11", which is called *Letter*.
8. Click **OK** to close the dialog box.

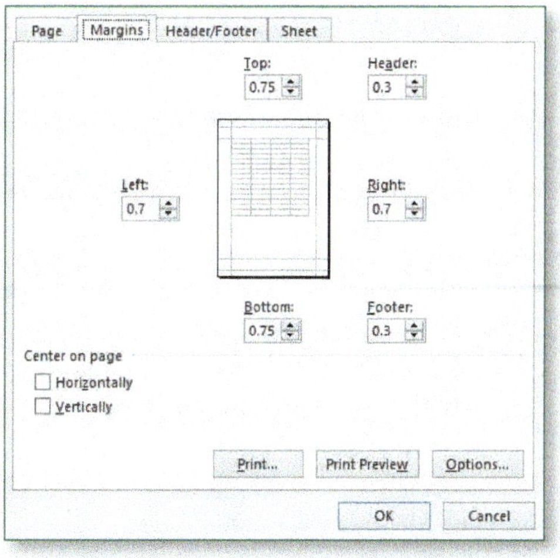

1-67 *Margins* tab in the *Page Setup* dialog box

MORE INFO

Top and bottom margins must be greater than header and footer margins. If they are not, worksheet data prints over header and footer text.

ANOTHER WAY

In *Page Layout* view, you can set margins using the ruler. Display the rulers by clicking the *View* tab and selecting the *Ruler* box [*Show* group]. Point to a margin boundary to display a two-pointed arrow and drag the pointer to a new setting.

Headers and Footers

A ***header*** is information that prints at the top of each page. A ***footer*** is data that prints at the bottom of each page. You can use a header or a footer to display identifying information such as a company name or logo, page numbers, the date, or the file name.

Each header or footer has left, middle, and right sections. Information in the left section is left aligned, data in the middle section is centered, and material in the right section is right aligned. You can select a predefined header and footer, or you can create your own.

MORE INFO

Predefined headers and footers include one, two, or three elements, separated by commas. One element prints in the center section. Two elements print in the center and right sections. Three elements use all three sections.

Headers and footers are not visible in *Normal* view, but you can see them in *Page Layout* view or *Print Preview*. Headers and footers are inserted and edited in *Page Layout* view at the top or bottom of the worksheet.

HOW TO: Insert a Header and Footer Using the Ribbon

1. Select the worksheet.
   - You can select more than one worksheet to apply the same header or footer.
2. Click the **Insert** tab.
3. Click the **Header & Footer** button [*Text* group].
   - The view changes to *Page Layout* view.
   - Three header sections are visible at the top of the worksheet.
   - The *Header & Footer Tools Design* tab is active.
4. Click a header section.
5. Click an element name in the *Header & Footer Elements* group [*Header & Footer Tools Design* tab].
   - A code is inserted with an ampersand (&) and the element name enclosed in square brackets (Figure 1-68).
   - You can type your own label in a section.
   - You can select and delete codes and text in a section.
6. Click the **Go To Footer** button [*Header & Footer Tools Design* tab, *Navigation* group].
7. Click a footer section.
8. Click an element name in the *Header & Footer Elements* group [*Header & Footer Tools Design* tab].
   - The related code is inserted.
   - You can type your own label in a footer section.
   - You can select and delete codes and text in a section.
9. Click any worksheet cell.
   - The header and footer appear as they will print.
   - The *Header & Footer Tools Design* tab is hidden.
10. Click the **Normal** button in the *Status* bar.
    - The header and footer are not visible in *Normal* view.

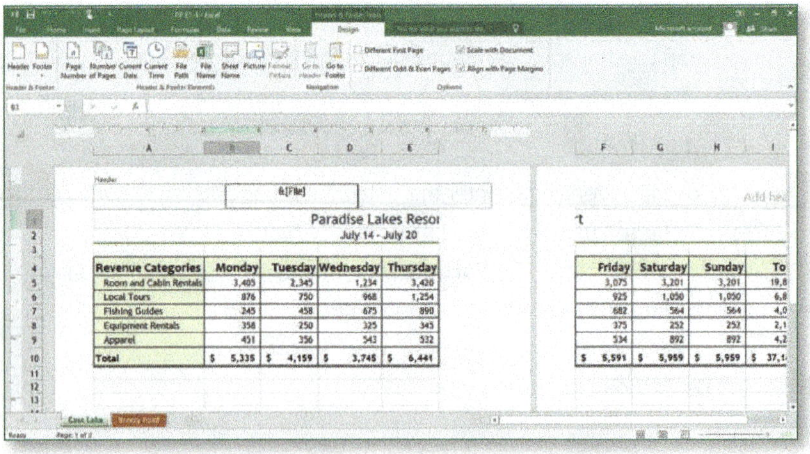

1-68 Header section in *Page Layout* view

ANOTHER WAY

To insert a built-in header or footer, click the **Header or Footer** button [*Header & Footer Tools Design* tab, *Header & Footer* group] and make a selection.

MORE INFO

In a typed header or footer label such as "Research & Development," type two ampersands in the section like this: *Research && Development*. This distinguishes the required ampersand from the one used in an element code such as &[Date].

You can also use the *Page Setup* dialog box to insert a header or a footer. There is a *Header & Footer* tab which includes the preset headers and footers as well as a *Custom Header* or *Custom Footer* option.

HOW TO: Insert Headers or Footers on Multiple Sheets

1. Select a single or multiple worksheet tabs.
   - Click the first worksheet tab for the group, press **Shift**, and click the last tab.
   - Click a worksheet tab, press **Ctrl**, and click a nonadjacent tab.
   - Right-click any tab and click **Select All Sheets**.
2. Click the **Page Setup** launcher [*Page Layout* tab, *Page Setup* group.
   - The *Page Setup* dialog box opens.
3. Click the **Header/Footer** tab.
4. Click the arrow for the *Header* or the *Footer* text box (Figure 1-69).
   - A list of built-in header or footer layouts opens.
   - Choose **(none)** to remove a header or footer.
5. Choose a predefined header or footer.
   - The header or footer is displayed in the preview area.
6. Click **Custom Header** or **Custom Footer** to open the *Header* or *Footer* dialog box (Figure 1-70).
7. Click a section.
8. Click a button to insert an element.
   - Point to a button to see its *ScreenTip*.
   - The text or code appears in the section.
9. Click **OK** to close the *Header* or *Footer* dialog box.
   - The custom header or footer is displayed in the preview area.
10. Click **OK** to close the *Page Setup* dialog box.
11. Right-click a sheet tab and choose **Ungroup Sheets**.

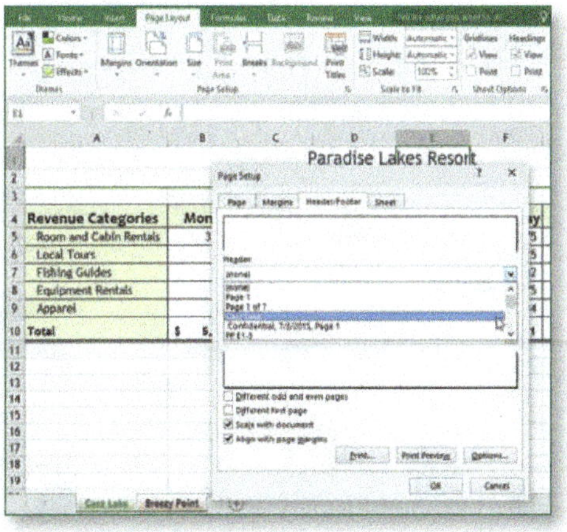

1-69 Select a built-in header or footer in the *Page Setup* dialog box

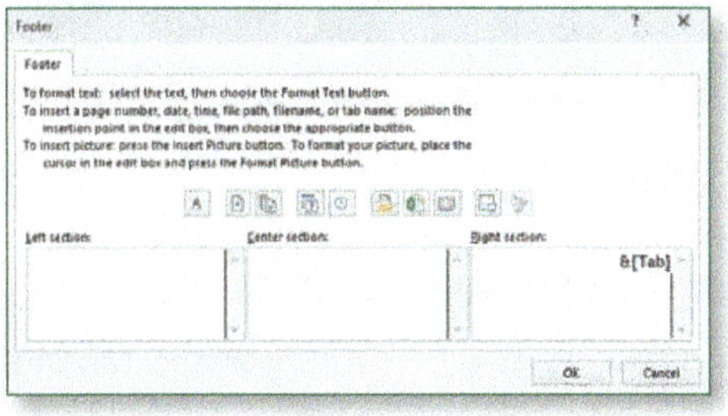

1-70 *Footer* dialog box

You can remove a header or footer in *Page Layout* view or from the *Page Setup* dialog box. To remove headers and footers from multiple worksheets, select the sheet tabs so that they are grouped. In *Page Layout* view, click the header or footer section and delete labels and codes. From the *Page Setup* dialog box, you can simply select **(none)** from the *Header* or *Footer* drop-down list.

HOW TO: Remove Headers and Footers

1. Select the worksheet(s).
2. Click the **Page Setup** launcher [*Page Layout* tab, *Page Setup* group].
3. Click the **Header/Footer** tab.
4. Click the **Header** or **Footer** drop-down list and select **(none)**.
5. Click **OK** to close the *Page Setup* dialog box.
6. Ungroup sheets if needed.

Page Breaks

A ***page break*** is a printer code that starts a new page. When worksheet data spans more than one printed page, automatic page breaks are inserted based on the paper size, the margins, and scaling. Automatic page breaks readjust as you add or delete data. You can insert manual page breaks, too. Manual page breaks do not adjust as you make edits.

In *Page Break Preview*, an automatic page break displays as a dotted or dashed blue line. A manual page break appears as a solid, blue line.

HOW TO: Insert a Page Break

1. Select the cell for the location of a page break.
   - Select a cell in column A below the row where you want to start a new page.
   - Select a cell in row 1 to the right of the column where you want to start a new page.
   - Select a cell below and to the right of where new pages should start.
2. Click the **Page Layout** tab.
3. Click the **Breaks** button.
4. Select **Insert Page Break** (Figure 1-71).
   - A manual page break is shown as a thin, solid line in the worksheet in *Normal* view.

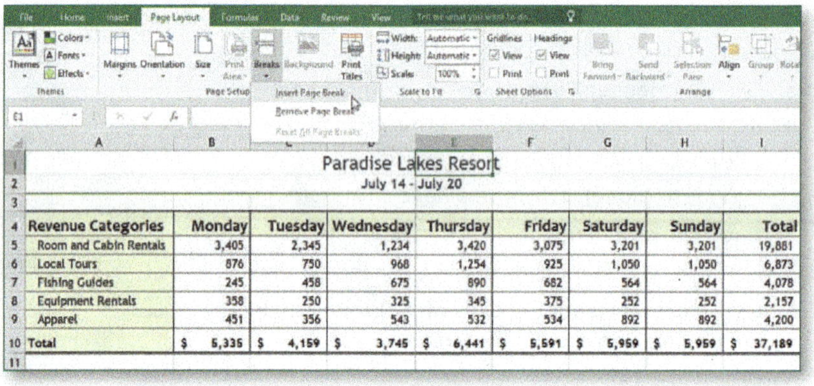

1-71 Page break inserted after column D

Preview and Move a Page Break

In *Page Break Preview*, you can move an automatic or a manual page break by dragging its blue line. You can see how the data is affected and evaluate the new printed pages. Depending on the amount of data, as you move one page break, another automatic break may be inserted. When you move an automatic page break, it becomes a manual page break.

MORE INFO

To move a page break in *Normal* view, you must delete the existing break and insert a new one; you cannot drag the line.

HOW TO: Preview and Move a Page Break

1. Click the **Page Break Preview** button in the *Status* bar.
   - You can adjust the zoom size in *Page Break Preview*.
2. Point to the page break (dashed or solid, blue line) to display a two-pointed arrow.
3. Drag the pointer to a new location (Figure 1-72).
   - You cannot drag an automatic page break to the right of its current location.

4. Release the pointer button.
   - A manual page break appears as a solid, blue line.
   - Another automatic page break may be inserted if the data requires it.
5. Click the **Normal** button in the *Status* bar.

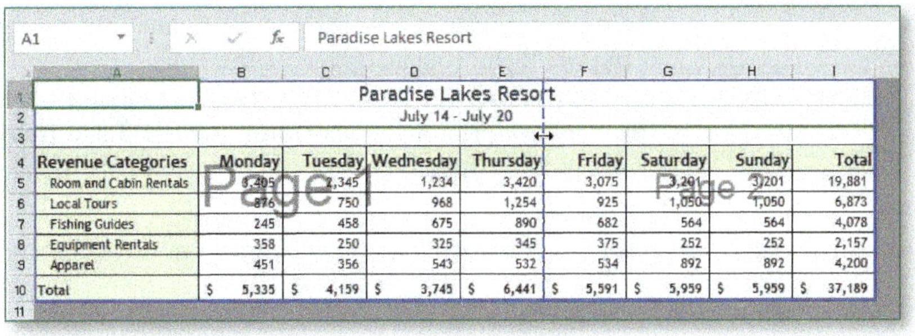

1-72 Drag a page break line to a new position

Remove a Manual Page Break

You can remove a manual page break in *Normal* view or *Page Break Preview*. Click a cell immediately to the right of or below the break and then click the **Remove Page Break** button [*Page Layout* tab, *Page Setup* group]. When you delete a manual page break, Excel may insert a new automatic page break.

> **MORE INFO**
>
> An automatic page break can be "deleted" by inserting a manual page break before it.

HOW TO: Remove a Manual Page Break

1. Click the **Page Break Preview** button in the *Status* bar.
2. Click a cell immediately to the right of or below the page break to be removed.
3. Click the **Breaks** button [*Page Layout* tab, *Page Setup* group].
   - You can select **Reset All Page Breaks** to remove all manual page breaks.
4. Click **Remove Page Break** (Figure 1-73).
   - An automatic page break is inserted if required.

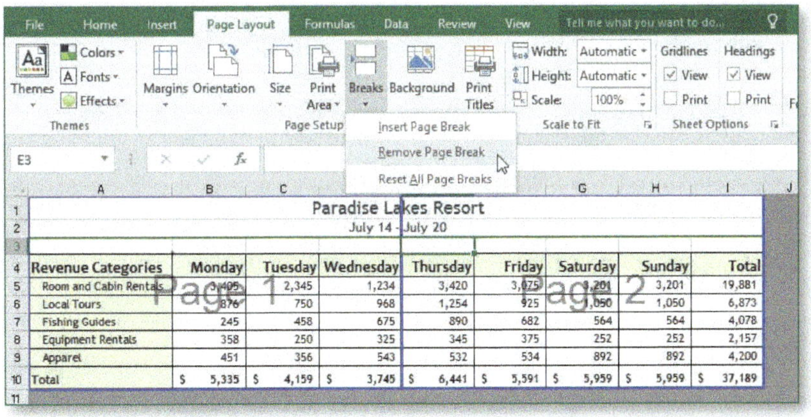

1-73 Remove a manual page break

> **ANOTHER WAY**
>
> In *Page Break Preview*, you can drag a manual page break off the page to the right. Excel will insert an automatic page break if required by the margins and other settings.

Customize Print Settings

You can print the entire workbook, the current worksheet, or a selected cell range by making a choice in the *Settings* area in the *Backstage view* for the *Print* command. The *Sheet Options* and *Page Setup* groups on the *Page Layout* command tab include additional options for repeating titles, displaying a background image, and printing gridlines, column letters, and row numbers.

Gridlines, the vertical and horizontal lines that form the columns and rows, are a visual guide to your working on the sheet. Row and column headings serve a similar purpose—to help you navigate in a worksheet. By default, the gridlines and headings do not print but you can print them from an option on the *Page Layout* tab.

A ***print title*** is a row or column of data that is repeated on each printed page. For example, you can print main labels from rows 1:3 and from column A on each printed page of a 20-page worksheet.

HOW TO: Print Gridlines, Print Titles, and Column and Row Headings

1. Click the **Page Layout** tab.
2. Select the **Print** box under *Gridlines* in the *Sheet Options* group.
3. Select the **Print** box under *Headings* in the *Sheet Options* group.
4. Click the **Print Titles** button [*Page Layout* tab, *Page Setup* group].
   - The *Page Setup* dialog box opens to the *Sheet* tab.
5. Select the **Rows to repeat at top** box.
6. Drag to select the heading(s) for the row(s) to print on each page.
   - The dialog box collapses as you select row headings.
   - The dialog box expands when you release the pointer button.
   - You can type a reference such as $1:$3 to repeat data in the first three rows.
7. Select the **Columns to repeat at left** box (Figure 1-74).
8. Drag to select the heading(s) for the column(s) to print on each page.
   - The dialog box collapses as you select column headings.
   - You can type a reference such as $A:$A to repeat data in column A.
9. Click **OK**.

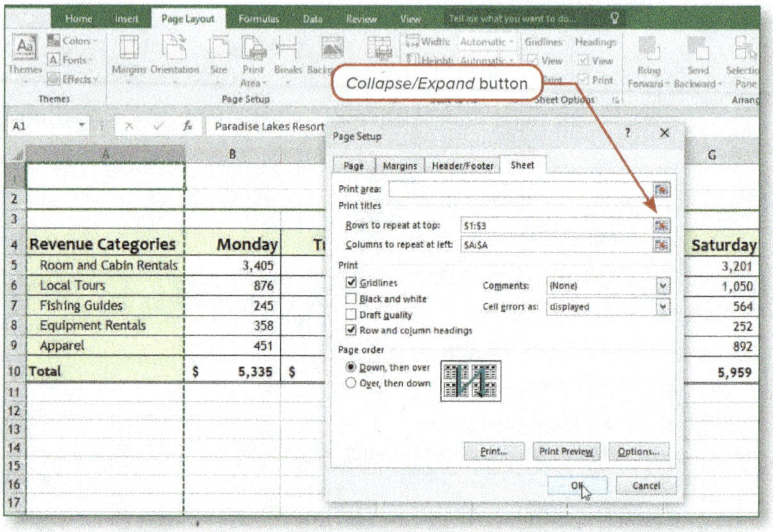

1-74 ***Sheet* tab in the *Page Setup* dialog box**

> **ANOTHER WAY**
>
> You can print *Gridlines* and *Row and column headings* from an option in the *Page Setup* dialog box.

Scale to Fit

The ***Scale to Fit*** command enlarges or shrinks printed data to fit a specific number of pages or a particular paper size. You can scale printed data as a percentage of normal size or by setting the number of pages. Normal size is how the data would print in the current font size and is shown as *Automatic* in the *Scale to Fit* group [*Page Layout* tab].

HOW TO: Scale to Fit

1. Click the **Page Layout** tab.
2. Click the **Width** drop-down list [*Scale to Fit* group] and select an option.

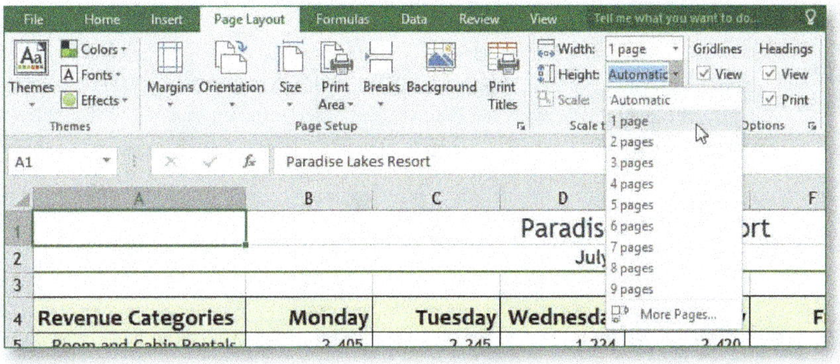

1-75 *Scale to Fit* options

3. Click the **Height** drop-down list [*Scale to Fit* group] and select an option (Figure 1-75).
   - You can click the **Scale** button spinner arrows to set a percentage of the normal size.

ANOTHER WAY

Click the **Scale to Fit** launcher [*Page Layout* tab, *Scale to Fit group*] to open the *Page Setup* dialog box and set options in the *Scaling* area.

Print Area

A ***print area*** is the data that prints when you give a *Print* command. The default is the entire worksheet, but you can identify any range of cells as a print area. You can add adjacent data to a print area, and you can clear a print area to return to the default.

HOW TO: Set and Clear a Print Area

1. Select the cells to print.
   - You can select nonadjacent ranges but they print on separate pages.
2. Click the **Page Layout** tab.
3. Click the **Print Area** button [*Page Setup* group] (Figure 1-76).
4. Select **Set Print Area**.
   - You can see the print area in the *Backstage view* for the *Print* command and in *Page Break Preview*.
   - A print area is saved with the workbook.
5. Click the **Print Area** button [*Page Layout* tab, *Page Setup* group].
6. Select **Clear Print Area**.
   - All print areas are cleared.
   - The default print area of the entire sheet is reset.

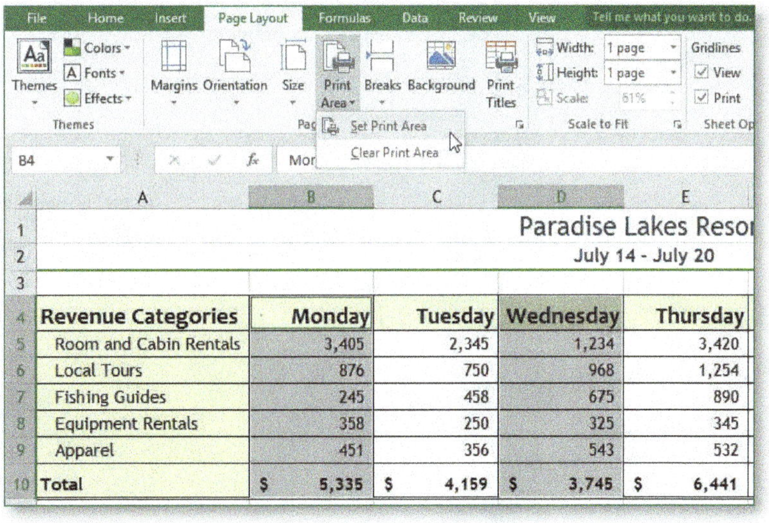

1-76 Nonadjacent print areas

> **MORE INFO**
>
> You can select one or more ranges and choose **Print Selection** in the *Settings* area for the *Print* command in the *Backstage* view. Nonadjacent ranges print on separate pages. These selections are not saved with the workbook.

> **ANOTHER WAY**
>
> You can define a print area from the *Sheet* tab in the *Page Setup* dialog box.

Print a Worksheet or Workbook

The *Print* command in the *Backstage view* provides a preview so that you can make changes before actual printing. The *Show Margins* button toggles the display of margin and column markers which can be dragged to new settings. The *Zoom to Page* button toggles between two zoom settings for the preview.

HOW TO: Preview and Print a Worksheet

1. Click the **File** tab and select **Print**.
   - You can also click **Print Preview** in the *Page Setup* dialog box to open the *Print* command in the *Backstage* view.
2. Click **Show Margins** to display margin and column markers (Figure 1-77).
3. Click **Zoom to Page** to toggle between zoom sizes.
4. Set the number of *Copies*.
   - Type a number or use the spinner arrows.
5. Click the **Printer** arrow.
   - Choose the printer name.
   - Make sure the printer is ready.

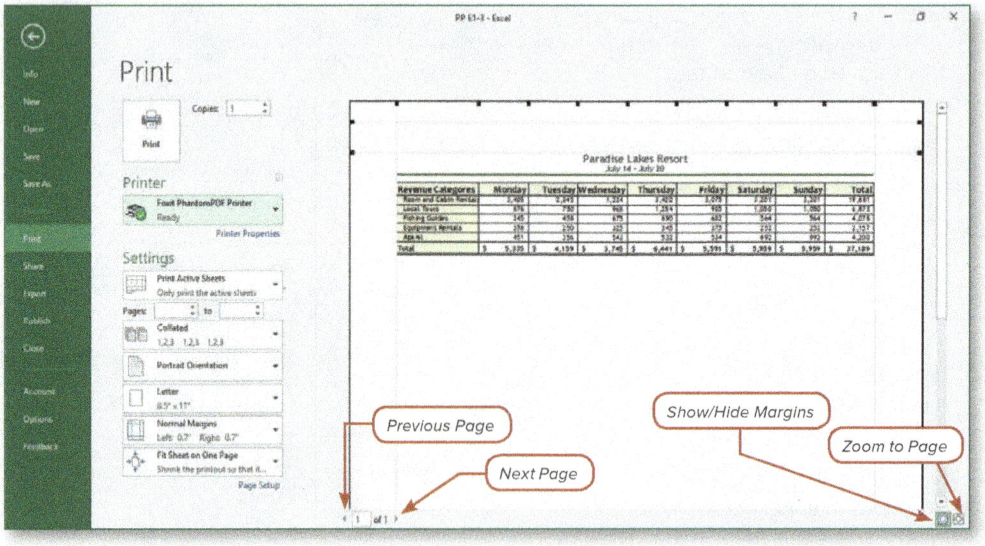

1-77 *Backstage* view for *Print*

6. Click the **Settings** arrow.
   - The active sheets are the default.
   - Cell ranges must be selected in order to print a selection.
   - The workbook setting prints all worksheets.
7. Specify which pages to print.
   - The default is all pages of the worksheet.
   - Click the **Next Page** or **Previous Page** arrow to navigate through multiple pages.
8. Verify orientation, paper size, margin settings, and scaling.
   - You can make changes from the *Page Setup* dialog box by clicking the **Page Setup** link at the bottom of the *Settings* area.
9. Click **Print**.
   - The data is sent to the printer.
   - The *Backstage view* closes.

ANOTHER WAY

Press **Ctrl+P** to open the *Print* command in the *Backstage view*.

PAUSE & PRACTICE: EXCEL 1-4

In this project, you open ***[your initials] PP E1-3.xlsx*** to unhide a row, add data, and hide a sheet. You also spell check a worksheet, set document properties, and finalize the workbook for distribution.

File Needed: ***[your initials] PP E1-3.xlsx***
Completed Project File Name: ***[your initials] PP E1-4.xlsx***

1. Open ***[your initials] PP E1-3*** completed in *Pause & Practice 1-3*.
2. Save the workbook as [your initials] PP E1-4.
3. Select the **Cass Lake** worksheet.
4. Unhide row 9.
   a. Click and drag to select row headings **8:10**.
   b. Right-click either of the selected row headings.
   c. Choose **Unhide** from the context menu.
5. Enter the following data in cells **B9:H9**. The data is formatted the same as row 8.

	B	C	D	E	F	G	H
Food & Beverage	254	209	198	402	519	677	399

6. Hide a worksheet.
   a. Right-click the **Breezy Point** tab.
   b. Choose **Hide**.

7. Check spelling.
   a. Press **Ctrl+Home**.
   b. Click the **Spelling** button [*Review* tab, *Proofing* group].
   c. Click **Change** to accept the suggested correction for "Categores."
   d. Click **Change** to accept the suggested correction for "Aparel."
   e. Click **OK** when spell checking is finished.
   f. Press **Ctrl+Home**.
8. Enter document properties.
   a. Click the **File** tab to display the *Backstage* view.
   b. Click the **Show All Properties** link at the bottom of the properties list.
   c. Click the *Title* text box and type PP Excel 1-4.
   d. Click the *Subject* text box and type Weekly Revenue.
   e. In the *Status* text box, type Draft (Figure 1-78).

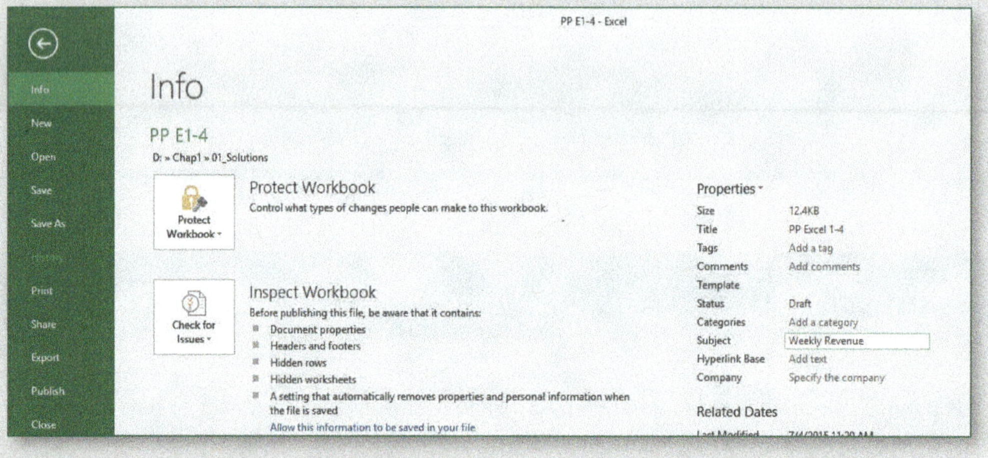

1-78 Properties in *Backstage* view

   f. Click the **Show Fewer Properties** link at the bottom of the properties list.
   g. Return to the worksheet.
9. Change page setup options.
   a. Click the **Page Layout** tab.
   b. Click the **Orientation** button and select **Landscape**.
   c. Click the **Page Setup** launcher to open the *Page Setup* dialog box.
   d. On the **Page** tab, click the **Fit to** button.
   e. Set **1** page wide and **1** page tall.
   f. Click the **Margins** tab.
   g. Select the **Horizontally** box in the *Center on page* area.
   h. Do not close the dialog box.
10. Add a header and footer.
   a. Click the **Header/Footer** tab.
   b. Click the **Header** drop-down list and select ***[your initials] PP E1-4***. The file name displays in the preview center section.
   c. Click the **Footer** drop-down list and select **Cass Lake** to insert the sheet name in the center section of the footer.
   d. Click **OK** to close the *Page Setup* dialog box.

11. Preview and print the worksheet.
    a. Click the **File** tab and select **Print**. *Print Preview* displays how the worksheet will print.
    b. Select the printer.
    c. Click **Print** to print the worksheet.
12. Save and close the workbook (Figure 1-79).

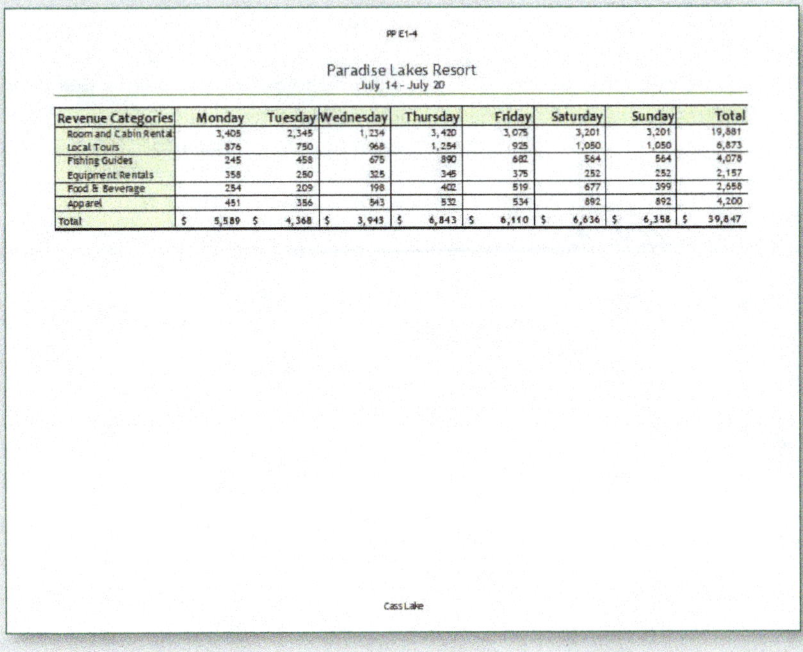

PP E1-4

Paradise Lakes Resort
July 14 - July 20

Revenue Categories	Monday	Tuesday	Wednesday	Thursday	Friday	Saturday	Sunday	Total
Room and Cabin Rental	3,405	2,345	1,234	3,420	3,075	3,201	3,201	19,881
Local Tours	876	750	968	1,254	925	1,050	1,050	6,873
Fishing Guides	245	458	675	890	682	564	564	4,078
Equipment Rentals	358	250	325	345	375	252	252	2,157
Food & Beverage	254	209	198	402	519	677	399	2,658
Apparel	451	356	543	532	534	892	892	4,200
Total	$ 5,589	$ 4,368	$ 3,943	$ 6,843	$ 6,110	$ 6,636	$ 6,358	$ 39,847

Cass Lake

1-79 PP E1-4 completed

Chapter Summary

1.1 Create, save, and open an Excel workbook (p. E1-3).

- A new Excel workbook has one worksheet and is named *BookN*, with numbers assigned in order throughout a work session.
- Save a workbook with a descriptive name that identifies the contents and purpose.
- Create a new workbook from the *Excel Start* page or from the *New* command on the *File* tab.
- A workbook that is opened or copied from an online source will open in ***Protected View***.
- An Excel workbook is an *.xlsx* file, but it can be saved in other formats for easy sharing of data.

1.2 Enter and edit labels and values in a worksheet (p. E1-6).

- Data is entered in a cell which is the intersection of a column and a row. Each cell has an address or reference.
- Data is recognized as a label or a value. Labels are not used in calculations. A label is left-aligned in the cell; a value is right-aligned.
- A ***formula*** is a calculation that displays a value as its result in the worksheet.
- Press **F2** (**FN+F2**) or double-click a cell to start *Edit* mode. After making the change, press **Enter** to complete the edit.
- Horizontal alignment options for cell data include *Align Left*, *Center*, and *Align Right*. Data can also be indented from the cell border. Vertical alignment choices are *Top Align*, *Middle Align*, and *Bottom Align*.
- A group or selection of cells is a ***range***. You can use the pointer and keyboard shortcuts to select a range.
- Use the ***Fill Handle*** to create a series that follows a pattern. The *Fill Handle* copies data when there is no pattern.
- ***AutoComplete*** supplies a suggestion for a column entry that begins with the same character as a label already in the column.
- Cut, copy, and paste commands include drag and drop as well as regular Windows ***Cut***, ***Copy***, and ***Paste*** buttons on the *Home* tab, context menus, and keyboard shortcuts.

1.3 Use the *SUM* function to build a simple formula (p. E1-19).

- A ***function*** is a built-in formula. Results appear in the worksheet cell, but the function is displayed in the *Formula* bar.
- The *AutoSum* button [*Home* tab, *Editing* group] inserts the *SUM* function in a cell to add the values in a selected range.
- Each function has ***syntax*** which is its required parts in the required order. A function begins with an equals sign (=), followed by the name of the function. After the name, the function ***argument*** is shown in parentheses.
- You can change a function argument by entering new cell references in the *Formula* bar or by dragging the range border in the worksheet.
- When you copy a function, Excel adjusts cell references to match their locations in the worksheet.

1.4 Format a worksheet with font attributes, borders, fill, cell styles, and themes (p. E1-21).

- Apply font attributes from the *Font* group on the *Ribbon* or from the *Format Cells* dialog box.
- Font attributes include the ***font*** name or face, the ***font size***, font styles such as bold, italic, and underline, and the ***font color***.
- Number formats include decimals, commas, currency symbols, and percent signs. They also determine how negative values appear in the worksheet.
- Number formats are applied from the *Ribbon* or the *Format Cells* dialog box.
- The ***Format Painter*** copies formatting from one cell to another.
- Add borders or fill color to cells for easy identification, clarification, and emphasis.
- A ***cell style*** is a preset collection of font, font size, alignment, color, borders, and fill color and is based on the theme.
- A ***theme*** is a collection of fonts, colors, and special effects for a workbook.
- You can use themes and cell styles to quickly format a worksheet with consistent, professionally designed elements.

1.5 Modify columns and rows in a worksheet (p. E1-31).

- The default column width and row height depend on the font size defined by the workbook theme.
- You can change the width of a column or the height of a row by dragging the border between the headings.
- ***AutoFit*** a column or row by double-clicking the border between the headings.
- The ***Format*** button [*Home* tab, *Cells* group] includes commands to change ***row height*** and ***column width***.
- Insert or delete a column or a row by right-clicking the column or row heading and choosing *Insert* or *Delete*.
- The *Insert* and *Delete* buttons include commands for inserting and deleting rows and columns.
- Display a label on multiple lines in a cell using the ***Wrap Text*** command to split the label.
- The ***Merge & Center*** command combines two or more cells into one and centers the data within that new cell.
- The ***Center Across Selection*** command can be used to center multiple rows of data across the same range.
- One or multiple rows or columns can be hidden, but they are still available for use in a formula.

1.6 Insert, delete, and move worksheets in a workbook (p. E1-37).

- The number of worksheets in a workbook is limited only by the amount of computer memory.
- You can click the *New Sheet* button next to the worksheet tabs to insert a new sheet in a workbook.
- The *Insert* and *Delete* buttons include options to insert and delete worksheets.
- You can double-click a worksheet tab, type a name, and press **Enter** to rename a sheet.
- You can apply a ***tab color*** to distinguish a particular sheet by changing the background color.
- Move a worksheet tab to another location in the list of tabs by dragging it to that location.
- You can create an exact duplicate of a worksheet in the same or another workbook with the ***Move or Copy*** command or the context menu.

1.7 Modify the appearance of a workbook by adjusting zoom size, changing views, and freezing panes (p. E1-42).

- A workbook can be viewed in three ways: ***Normal***, ***Page Layout***, and ***Page Break Preview***.
- Switch views from the *Status* bar buttons or from the *Workbook Views* group on the *View* tab.
- Adjust the zoom size to display more or less data on screen. Zoom controls are available in the *Status* bar and from the *View* tab.
- Use the ***Freeze Panes*** command to lock selected rows or columns on screen so that you can scroll data while keeping important data in view.
- The ***Split*** command divides the screen into multiple sections so that you can see different areas of a large worksheet at once.
- You can hide a worksheet from view and unintended editing.
- When multiple workbooks are open, the ***Switch Windows*** command lists the open workbook names.
- You can switch among open workbooks from the Windows taskbar.
- The ***New Window*** command displays the same workbook in a second window. Use this command with the ***Arrange All*** command to view different areas or sheets of a workbook at the same time.

1.8 Review and prepare a workbook for final distribution by spell checking, setting properties, and adjusting page setup options (p. E1-47).

- Spell checking a workbook follows the same steps as other Office applications.
- A ***document property*** is ***metadata*** stored with the file.

- Some properties are supplied by Excel and cannot be edited. Other document properties are added or edited by the user.
- Several properties are visible and can be edited in the *Info* area in the *Backstage* view.
- You can open the *Properties* dialog box to build or edit properties.
- The *Page Layout* tab includes commands to set page margins and orientation.
- ***Headers*** and ***footers*** can be added to print at the top and bottom of each page.
- When a worksheet fills more than one printed page, Excel inserts automatic page breaks.
- You can insert manual ***page breaks*** to change where a new page starts.
- From commands on the *Page Layout* tab or in the *Page Setup* dialog box, you can print ***gridlines*** as well as row and column headings.
- You can make additional changes to the printed worksheet from the ***Print*** area in the *Backstage* view. These include choosing to print only a selection or the entire workbook.

Check for Understanding

The SIMbook for this text (within your SIMnet account) provides the following resources for concept review:

- Multiple choice questions
- Matching exercises
- Short answer questions

USING MICROSOFT EXCEL 2016

Guided Project 1-1

Life's Animal Shelter (LAS) maintains data in an Excel workbook that tracks daily expenses for categories that include supplies, animal food, and wages. You will create a new workbook for the current week, enter and format the data, and prepare the workbook for distribution.
[Student Learning Outcomes 1.1, 1.2, 1.3, 1.4, 1.5, 1.6, 1.7, 1.8]

File Needed: None
Completed Project File Name: ***[your initials] Excel 1-1.xlsx***

Skills Covered in This Project

- Create and save a workbook.
- Enter labels and values.
- Use the *Fill Handle*.
- Set column widths and row heights.
- Merge and center labels.
- Apply a workbook theme and cell styles.
- Apply font attributes and insert borders.
- Use *SUM* and set number formatting.
- Copy and rename worksheets.
- Set worksheet tab color.
- Change page setup options.
- Use spell check.
- Adjust zoom size and freeze panes.

1. Create and save a workbook.
   a. Click the **File** tab to open the *Backstage* view.
   b. Select **New** and then click **Blank workbook**.
   c. Click the **Save** button on the *Quick Access* toolbar to open the *Save As* dialog box.
   d. Select the folder to save the workbook, or **Browse** to a location on *OneDrive*, your computer, or external media.
   e. Name the workbook [your initials] Excel 1-1 in the *File name* area.
   f. Click **Save**.
2. Enter data with deliberate errors.
   a. In cell **A1**, type Life's Aminal Shelter with the spelling error and press **Enter**.
   b. In cell **A2**, type Setember 1 through 7 with the spelling error and press **Enter**.
   c. In cell **A4**, type Expens Categories and press **Enter**.
3. Adjust column width.
   a. Point to the border between the column **A** and column **B** headings to display a two-pointed arrow.
   b. Double-click to *AutoFit* column **A**.
4. Enter labels and values as shown in Figure 1-80.

	A	B	C	D	E	F	G	H
1	Life's Aminal Shelter							
2	Setember 1 through 7							
3								
4	Expens Categories	Monday						
5	Pet nutrition	55.25	47.5	38.55	27.45	42.5	35.25	51.75
6	Veterinary supplies	27.85	32.35	35	25	28.5	38.75	44.85
7	Shelter supplies	78	56.45	65.35	55	70	60.25	45.35
8	Salaries and wages	475						
9	Utilities (prorated)	45						
10								

1-80 Labels and values to be entered with errors in cells A1:A2 and A4

5. Use the *Fill Handle* to fill a series and copy data.
   a. Select cell **B4**.
   b. Click and drag the *Fill* pointer to cell **H4**.
   c. Select cells **B8:B9**. There is one *Fill Handle* shown in cell B9.
   d. Click and drag the *Fill* pointer to cell **H9**. When there is no discernible pattern, the *Fill Handle* copies data.
   e. Point to the border between the column **D** and column **E** headings to display a two-pointed arrow.
   f. Double-click to *AutoFit* column **D**.

6. Merge and center labels.
   a. Select cells **A1:H1** and click the **Merge & Center** button [*Home* tab, *Alignment* group].
   b. Select cells **A2:H2** and click the **Merge & Center** button [*Home* tab, *Alignment* group].
   c. Select cells **B4:H4**.
   d. Click the **Center** button [*Home* tab, *Alignment* group].

7. Choose a workbook theme.
   a. Click the **Themes** button [*Page Layout* tab, *Themes* group].
   b. Choose **Integral** from the gallery.
   c. Click the **Home** tab. All labels and values are set in the **Tw Cen MT** font.

8. Apply cell styles.
   a. Select cell **A1** and click the **Cells Styles** button or the **More** button [*Home* tab, *Styles* group].
   b. Select **Title** in the *Titles and Headings* category. For the *Integral* theme, a title is format in the *Tw Cen MT Condensed* font, 18 points.
   c. Select cell **A2** and click the **Cells Styles** or the **More** button [*Home* tab, *Styles* group].
   d. Select **Heading 2** in the *Titles and Headings* category. The second level heading uses *Tw Cen MT* bold, 13 points. Both styles use a dark blue color.
   e. Select cells **A4:A9**.
   f. Press **Ctrl** and select cells **B4:H4**. Two ranges are selected.
   g. Click the **Cells Styles** or the **More** button [*Home* tab, *Styles* group].
   h. Select **40%, Accent 1** in the *Themed Cell Styles* category.
   i. Click the **Bold** button [*Home* tab, *Font* group].
   j. Select cell **A10**.
   k. Type Total and press **Enter**. The format from the column is automatically applied.

9. Apply font attributes.
   a. Select cells **A4:H10**.
   b. Click the **Font size** drop-down list [*Home* tab, *Font* group] and select **12**.
   c. Change the font size for cell **A2** to **14**.
   d. Select cells **A5:A9**.
   e. Click the **Increase Indent** button [*Home* tab, *Alignment* group] two times.
   f. Select cell **A10** and click the **Align Right** button [*Home* tab, *Alignment* group].

10. Use the *SUM* function and copy a formula.
    a. Select cell **B10**.
    b. Click the **AutoSum** button [*Home* tab, *Editing* group] and press **Enter** to accept the suggested range.
    c. Select cell **B10** and drag the *Fill* pointer to cell **H10**.

11. Apply number formatting.
    a. Select cells **B5:H10**.
    b. Click the **Accounting Number Format** button [*Home* tab, *Number* group]. Column widths are adjusted to accommodate the values.
    c. Click the **Decrease Decimal** button [*Home* tab, *Number* group] two times. Column widths do not adjust.

12. Change row heights.
   a. Click the heading for row **4**.
   b. Press **Ctrl** and click the row **10** heading. Two rows are selected.
   c. Right-click the row **4** heading.
   d. Choose **Row Height** and type 25 as the new height.
   e. Click **OK**.
   f. Click the heading for row **5** and drag down to select rows **5:9**.
   g. Point to the bottom border of the row **9** heading to display the resize arrow.
   h. Drag the pointer down to reach a height of **21.00** (**28 pixels**) and release the pointer button (Figure 1-81).

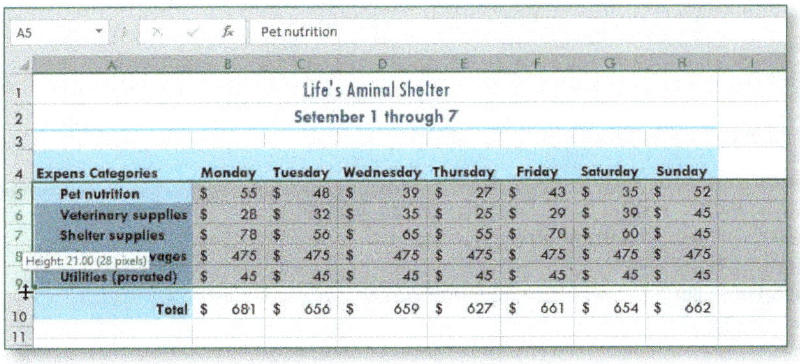

1-81 Change row heights for rows 5:9

13. Insert a row and change column width.
   a. Select cell **A9** and then right-click row heading **9**.
   b. Choose **Insert** from the context menu. The new row is located above the selected row; other rows shift down.
   c. In cell **A9**, type Cages and equipment.
   d. Point to the border between columns **A** and **B** to display the resize arrow.
   e. Drag the pointer to a width of **22.50** (**185 pixels**) and release the pointer button.

14. Enter the following data in row **9**. A zero (0) is displayed as a small dash.

	B	C	D	E	F	G	H
Cages and equipment	35	35	25	0	0	35	40

15. Insert borders and change the font size.
   a. Select cells **A4:H11**.
   b. Click the **Borders** button drop-down list and choose **All Borders**.
   c. Select cell **A2** and press **Ctrl+1** to open the *Format Cells* dialog box.
   d. Click the **Border** tab.
   e. Click the blue bottom border in the preview area to remove it.
   f. Click the **Color** drop-down arrow and select **Black, Text 1**.
   g. Click to select the solid, thick line (second column, sixth style) in the *Style* group,
   h. Click the bottom border In the preview area (Figure 1-82).
   i. Click **OK**.
   j. Select cell **A1** and change the font size to **24**.

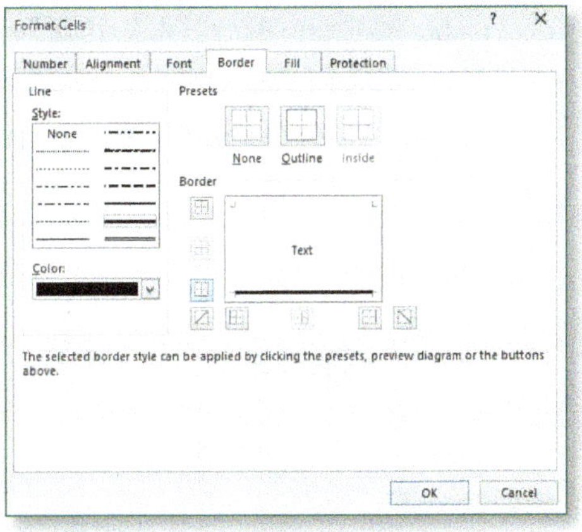

1-82 Create a custom border

16. Rename the sheet and set the tab color.
    a. Double-click the **Sheet1** tab name.
    b. Type Week 1 and press **Enter**.
    c. Click the **Format** button [*Home* tab, *Cells* group].
    d. Select **Tab Color** in the *Organize Sheets* category.
    e. Select **Blue Accent 2, Darker 50%**.
17. Spell check a worksheet.
    a. Press **Ctrl+Home** to go to cell **A1**.
    b. Click the **Spelling** button [*Review* tab, *Proofing* group].
    c. Type Animal in the *Not in Dictionary* box and click **Change**.
    d. Choose "September" in the *Suggestions* list and click **Change**.
    e. Correct "Expens" when the error is located.
    f. Click **OK**.
    g. Press **Ctrl+Home**.
18. Change page setup options.
    a. Click the **Page Layout** tab and click the **Page Setup** launcher.
    b. On the **Page** tab, select the **Landscape** radio button.
    c. Click the **Margins** tab.
    d. Select the **Horizontally** box under *Center on page*.
    e. Click the **Header/Footer** tab.
    f. Click the **Header** drop-down list and choose ***[your initials] Excel 1-1*** to insert the file name in the center section.
    g. Click **OK**.
    h. Press **Ctrl+F2** to preview the worksheet.
    i. Press **Esc** to close the *Backstage* view.
19. Copy and edit a worksheet.
    a. Right-click the **Week 1** tab name.
    b. Select **Move or Copy** from the menu.
    c. Select **(move to end)** in the *Before sheet* list.
    d. Select the **Create a copy** box and click **OK**.
    e. On the copied worksheet, select cells **B5:H10** and delete the data.
    f. Double-click cell **A2** to start *Edit* mode.
    g. Change "September 1 through 7" to September 8 through 14.
    h. Double-click the **Week 1 (2)** tab name.
    i. Type Week 2 and press **Enter**.
    j. Right-click the **Week 2** tab name and choose **Tab Color**.
    k. Select **Green Accent 4, Darker 50%**.
20. Click the **Week 1** sheet tab.
21. Click the **File** tab and select **Print** to preview the **Week 1** worksheet.
22. Change the zoom size and freeze panes.
    a. Select cell **B5**.
    b. Click the **Zoom In** button in the *Status* bar five times.
    c. Click the **Freeze Panes** button [*View* tab, *Window* group].
    d. Choose **Freeze Panes**.
    e. Scroll the window on the right so that column **F** is immediately to the right of column **A** (Figure 1-83).
    f. Select cell **A1**.

	A	F	G	H	I
1					
2					
3					
4	Expense Categories	Friday	Saturday	Sunday	
5	Pet nutrition	$ 43	$ 35	$ 52	
6	Veterinary supplies	$ 29	$ 39	$ 45	
7	Shelter supplies	$ 70	$ 60	$ 45	
8	Salaries and wages	$ 475	$ 475	$ 475	
9	Cages and equipment	$ -	$ 35	$ 40	
10	Utilities (prorated)	$ 45	$ 45	$ 45	
11	Total	$ 661	$ 689	$ 702	
12					

1-83 Panes frozen and positioned

23. Save and close the workbook (Figure 1-84).

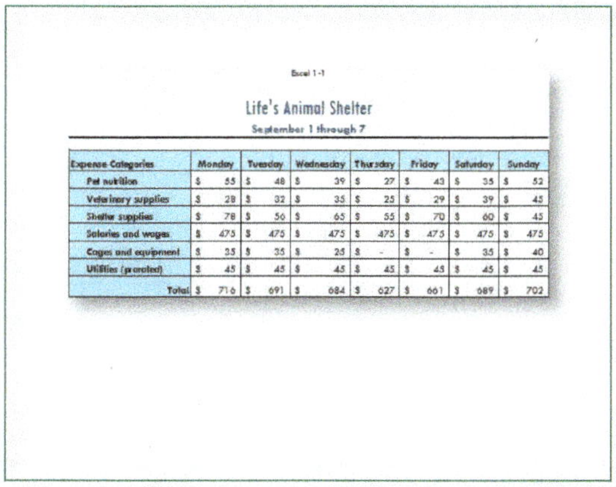

Excel 1-1

Life's Animal Shelter

September 1 through 7

Expense Categories	Monday	Tuesday	Wednesday	Thursday	Friday	Saturday	Sunday
Pet nutrition	$ 55	$ 48	$ 39	$ 27	$ 43	$ 35	$ 52
Veterinary supplies	$ 28	$ 32	$ 35	$ 25	$ 29	$ 39	$ 45
Shelter supplies	$ 78	$ 56	$ 65	$ 55	$ 70	$ 60	$ 45
Salaries and wages	$ 475	$ 475	$ 475	$ 475	$ 475	$ 475	$ 475
Cages and equipment	$ 35	$ 35	$ 25	$ -	$ -	$ 35	$ 40
Utilities (prorated)	$ 45	$ 45	$ 45	$ 45	$ 45	$ 45	$ 45
Total	$ 716	$ 691	$ 684	$ 627	$ 661	$ 689	$ 702

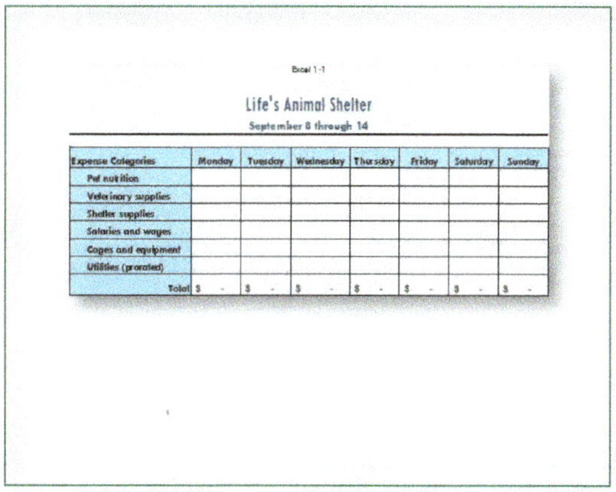

Excel 1-1

Life's Animal Shelter

September 8 through 14

Expense Categories	Monday	Tuesday	Wednesday	Thursday	Friday	Saturday	Sunday
Pet nutrition							
Veterinary supplies							
Shelter supplies							
Salaries and wages							
Cages and equipment							
Utilities (prorated)							
Total	$ -	$ -	$ -	$ -	$ -	$ -	$ -

1-84 Excel 1-1 completed

Guided Project 1-2

In this project, you edit a worksheet for Eller Software Services representative Adam White. He maintains client data with sales revenue and specific products or services. You plan to format the data, complete the calculation, and prepare the worksheet for sharing with management.
[Student Learning Outcomes 1.1, 1.2, 1.3, 1.4, 1.5, 1.6, 1.8]

File Needed: ***EllerSoftwareServices-01.xlsx*** [*Student data files are available in the Library of your SIMnet account.*]
Completed Project File Name: ***[your initials] Excel 1-2.xlsx***

Skills Covered in This Project

- Open and save a workbook.
- Choose a workbook theme.
- Enter and copy labels using the *Fill Handle*.
- Set font attributes and number formats.
- Use *SUM*.
- Center labels across a selection.
- Change page orientation and scale a worksheet for printing.
- Design borders.
- Insert a row and hide a column.
- Rename and apply color to sheet tabs.
- Adjust page setup options.

1. Open the workbook ***EllerSoftwareServices-01.xlsx*** from your student data files. If the workbook has opened in *Protected View*, click **Enable Editing** in the security bar.
2. Save the workbook with a new file name.
   a. Press **F12** (**FN+F12**) to open the *Save As* dialog box.
   b. Navigate to the folder where your files are stored.
   c. Rename the file [your initials] Excel 1-2.
   d. Click **Save**.

3. Choose a workbook theme.
   a. Click the **Themes** button [*Page Layout* tab, *Themes* group].
   b. Choose **Ion** from the gallery. A different font, *Century Gothic*, is used for all data in the worksheet.
   c. Double-click the border between the column **C** and column **D** headings to *AutoFit* column **C**.

4. Enter and copy data.
   a. Select cell **F5**, type **MN**, and press **Enter**.
   b. Select cell **F5** and point to the *Fill Handle*.
   c. Click and drag the *Fill* pointer to cell **E13**.

5. Format data.
   a. Select cells **D5:D13**.
   b. Press **Ctrl+1** to open the *Format Cells* dialog box.
   c. Click the **Number** tab.
   d. In the *Category* list, click **Special**.
   e. Select **Phone Number** in the *Type* list and click **OK** (Figure 1-85).
   f. Select cells **I6:I13**.
   g. Click the **Comma Style** button [*Home* tab, *Number* group].
   h. Select cell **I5**.
   i. Click the **Accounting Number Format** button [*Home* tab, *Number* group]. A series of # symbols means the column is not wide enough to display the data (Figure 1-86).

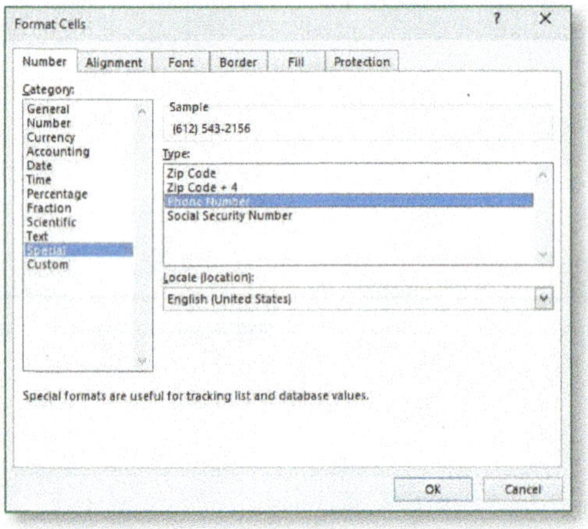

1-85 Special number format

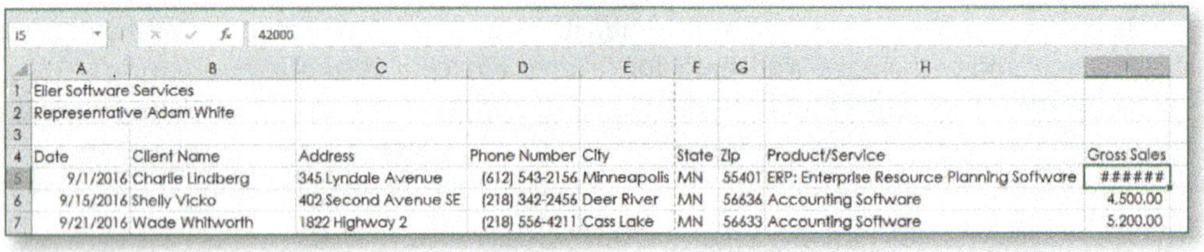

1-86 Column I is not wide enough

   j. Double-click the border between the column **I** and column **J** headings to *AutoFit* column **I**.

6. Enter and edit the reference range for the *SUM* function.
   a. Click cell **A15**, type Total, and press **Enter**.
   b. Select cell **I15**.
   c. Click the **AutoSum** button [*Home* tab, *Editing* group]. The suggested range includes an empty row.
   d. Click cell **I5** and drag to select cells **I5:I13**. Your selected range is highlighted and shown in the *Formula* bar and in the cell (Figure 1-87).
   e. Press **Enter** to accept the range. The *Accounting Number* format is applied.

7. Center labels across a selection.
   a. Select cells **A1:I2** and click the **Alignment** launcher [*Home* tab, *Alignment* group].
   b. Click the **Horizontal** arrow and select **Center Across Selection**.
   c. Click **OK**.

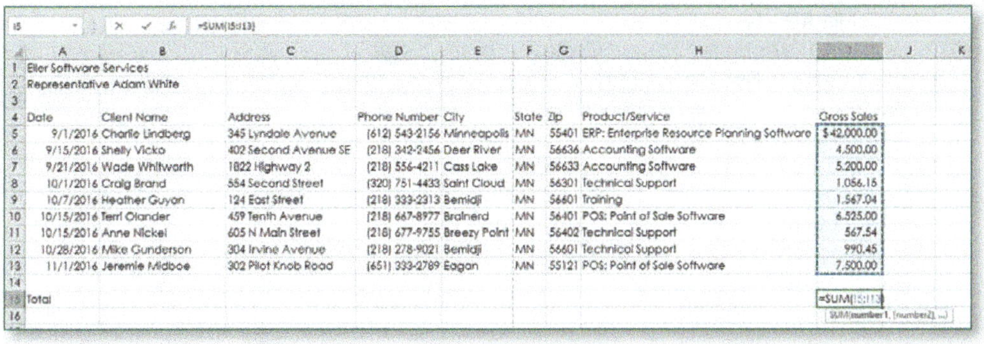

1-87 New range selected for *SUM*

8. Apply font attributes and cell styles.
   a. Select cell **A1**, click the **Font Size** drop-down list [*Home* tab, *Font* group], and select **24**.
   b. Select cell **A2** and change the font size to **18**.
   c. Select cells **A4:A15**, press **Ctrl**, and then select cells **B4:I4**.
   d. Click the **Cell Styles** button or the **More** button and select **40% - Accent3** in the *Themed Cell Styles* category.
   e. While the cells are selected, click the **Bold** button [*Home* tab, *Font* group].
   f. Select cell **I15** and apply the **Total** cell style.
   g. Select cells **A4:I4**.
   h. Click the **Font Size** drop-down list [*Home* tab, *Font* group] and select **12**.
   i. Click the **Center** button [*Home* tab, *Alignment* group].
   j. *AutoFit* column **D**.
   k. Select cell **A15** and click the **Align Right** button [*Home* tab, *Alignment* group].

9. Edit a label.
   a. Double-click cell **H9** to start *Edit* mode.
   b. Press **Home** to position the insertion point before the word "Training".
   c. Type ERP and press **Spacebar**.
   d. Press **Enter**.

10. Insert a row.
    a. Right-click row heading **10**.
    b. Choose **Insert** from the context menu.
    c. In cell **A10**, type 10/10/16 and press **Tab**.
    d. Complete the data as shown here. For the phone number, do not type any spaces; it is automatically formatted when you press **Tab** to move to the next cell.

       B10 Hillary Marschke
       C10 245 West Third Avenue
       D10 3203555443(press **Tab**)
       E10 sa (press **Tab**)
       F10 m (press **Tab**)
       G10 56301
       H10 t (press **Tab**)
       I10 750

11. Apply borders.
    a. Select cells **A4:I14**.
    b. Click the **Border** drop-down arrow [*Home* tab, *Font* group] and choose **All Borders**.

c. Select cells **A16:I16**.
d. Press **Ctrl+1** to open the *Format Cells* dialog box and click the **Border** tab.
e. Select the solid, single line (first column, sixth option) in the *Style* list.
f. Click the top border In the *Border* preview area.
g. Select the solid, double line (second column, seventh option) in the *Style* list.
h. Click the bottom border In the *Border* preview area (Figure 1-88).
i. Click **OK**.
j. Select cells **A15:I16**.
k. Click the **Border** arrow [*Home* tab, *Font* group] and choose **Left Border**.
l. Click the **Border** arrow [*Home* tab, *Font* group] and choose **Right Border**.

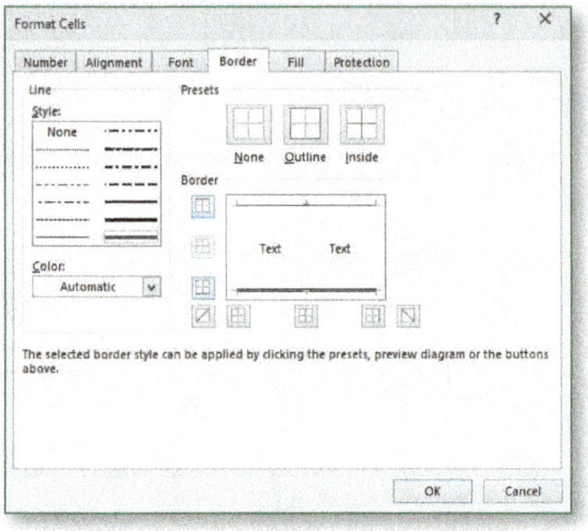

1-88 Design a double border

12. Hide a column.
    a. Right-click the column **F** heading.
    b. Select **Hide**.
    c. Press **Ctrl+Home**.
13. Rename and color a sheet tab.
    a. Double-click the **Sheet1** tab.
    b. Type MN Clients and press **Enter**.
    c. Right-click the **MN Clients** tab.
    d. Select **Tab Color** and choose **Gold, Accent 3**.
14. Change page setup options.
    a. Click the **Page Layout** tab.
    b. Click the **Orientation** button [*Page Setup* group] and choose **Landscape**.
    c. In the *Scale to Fit* group, click the **Width** arrow and choose **1 page**.
    d. Click the **Insert** tab.
    e. Click the **Header & Footer** button In the *Text* group. The view switches to *Page Layout* with the insertion point in the center header section. The *Header & Footer Tools Design* toolbar displays.
    f. Click the **Go to Footer** button in the *Navigation* group.
    g. Click the **Footer** button in the *Header & Footer* group (Figure 1-89).

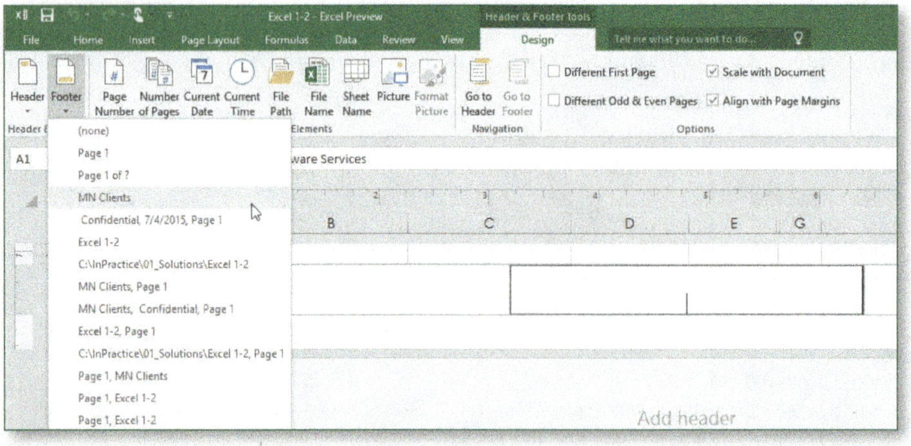

1-89 Select a built-in footer

h. Choose **MN Clients** to insert the sheet name in the footer. The *Header & Footer Tools Design* toolbar closes.
i. Click the **Normal** button in the *Status* bar. The footer is not visible in this view.

15. Preview and print the worksheet.
    a. Select **Print** from the *File* tab.
    b. Review the worksheet layout.
    c. Click **Print** or press **Esc** to return to the workbook.
16. Save and close the workbook (Figure 1-90).

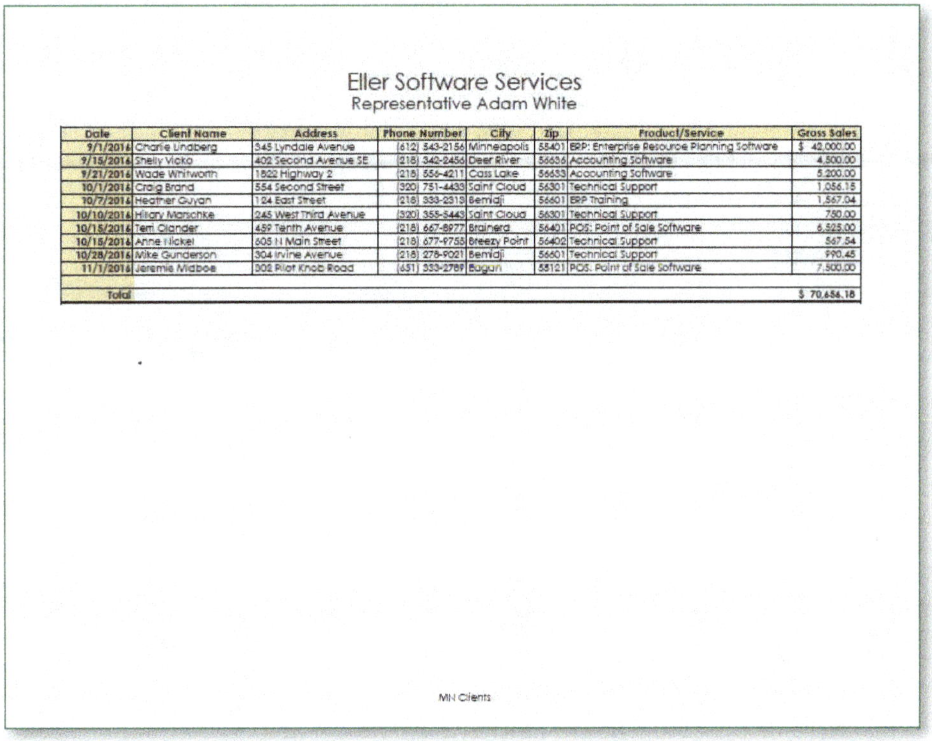

Eller Software Services
Representative Adam White

Date	Client Name	Address	Phone Number	City	Zip	Product/Service	Gross Sales
9/1/2016	Charlie Lindberg	345 Lyndale Avenue	(612) 543-2156	Minneapolis	55401	ERP: Enterprise Resource Planning Software	$ 42,000.00
9/15/2016	Shelly Vicko	402 Second Avenue SE	(218) 342-2456	Deer River	56636	Accounting Software	4,500.00
9/21/2016	Wade Whitworth	1822 Highway 2	(218) 556-4211	Cass Lake	56633	Accounting Software	5,200.00
10/1/2016	Craig Brand	554 Second Street	(320) 751-4433	Saint Cloud	56301	Technical Support	1,056.15
10/7/2016	Heather Guyan	124 East Street	(218) 333-2313	Bemidji	56601	ERP Training	1,567.04
10/10/2016	Hilary Marschke	245 West Third Avenue	(320) 355-5443	Saint Cloud	56301	Technical Support	750.00
10/15/2016	Terri Olander	459 Tenth Avenue	(218) 667-8977	Brainerd	56401	POS: Point of Sale Software	6,525.00
10/15/2016	Anne Nickel	605 N Main Street	(218) 677-9755	Breezy Point	56402	Technical Support	567.54
10/28/2016	Mike Gunderson	304 Irvine Avenue	(218) 278-9021	Bemidji	56601	Technical Support	990.45
11/1/2016	Jeremie Midboe	302 Pilot Knob Road	(651) 333-2789	Eagan	55121	POS: Point of Sale Software	7,500.00
Total							$ 70,656.18

MN Clients

1-90 Excel 1-2 completed

Guided Project 1-3

In this project, you edit a worksheet for Wear-Ever Shoes that tracks their product inventory. You change the zoom size, reset the panes, and format data. You copy an existing formula to calculate the value of the current stock and insert a column for new data. After adjusting print options, you set a print area for a specific product line.
[Student Learning Outcomes 1.1, 1.2, 1.4, 1.5, 1.6, 1.7, 1.8]

File Needed: ***WearEverShoes-01.xlsx*** [*Student data files are available in the Library of your SIMnet account.*]
Completed Project File Name: ***[your initials] Excel 1-3.xlsx***

Skills Covered in This Project

- Open and save a workbook.
- Change zoom size and remove a split.
- Freeze panes.
- Format labels and values.
- Use the *Fill Handle* to copy a formula and fill a series.
- Check spelling.
- Apply a workbook theme, cell styles, and font attributes.
- Merge and center labels.
- Insert a column and adjust column widths and row heights.
- Adjust alignment, indents, and borders.
- Rename the sheet tab.
- Use *Page Layout* view to insert a footer.

1. Open and rename a workbook.
   a. Open the workbook ***WearEverShoes-01.xlsx*** from your student data files. If the workbook has opened in *Protected View*, click **Enable Editing** in the security bar.
   b. Press **F12** (**FN+F12**) and locate the folder where your files are saved.
   c. Save the workbook as [your initials] Excel 1-3.
2. Remove a split and freeze panes.
   a. Click the **Split** button [*View* tab, *Window* group]. The split is removed.
   b. Click cell **A4** to freeze the column titles at this position.
   c. Click the **Freeze Panes** button [*View* tab, *Window* group].
   d. Choose **Freeze Panes**. There is a solid border between rows 3 and 4 to mark the pane.
   e. Scroll to row **31** and click cell **E31**. The column titles are frozen.
   f. Type 3 and press **Enter** (Figure 1-91).
   g. Press **Ctrl+Home**. The insertion point returns to cell **A4**.

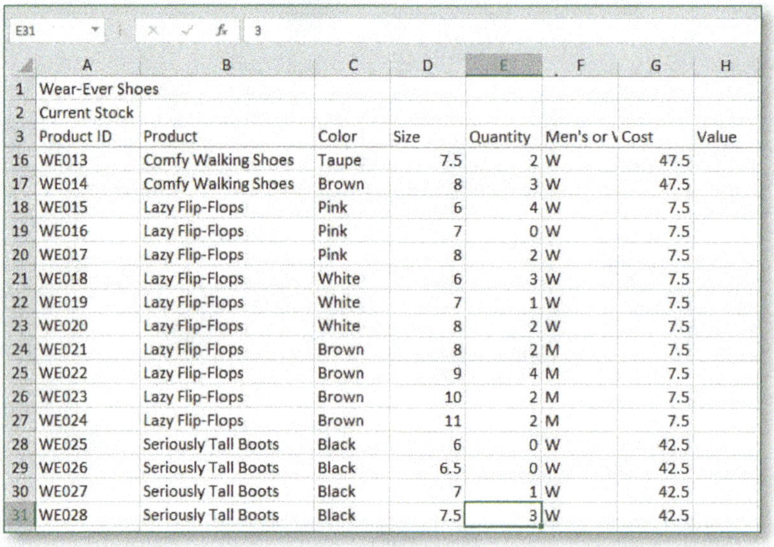

E31 | 3

	A	B	C	D	E	F	G	H
1	Wear-Ever Shoes							
2	Current Stock							
3	Product ID	Product	Color	Size	Quantity	Men's or \	Cost	Value
16	WE013	Comfy Walking Shoes	Taupe	7.5	2	W	47.5	
17	WE014	Comfy Walking Shoes	Brown	8	3	W	47.5	
18	WE015	Lazy Flip-Flops	Pink	6	4	W	7.5	
19	WE016	Lazy Flip-Flops	Pink	7	0	W	7.5	
20	WE017	Lazy Flip-Flops	Pink	8	2	W	7.5	
21	WE018	Lazy Flip-Flops	White	6	3	W	7.5	
22	WE019	Lazy Flip-Flops	White	7	1	W	7.5	
23	WE020	Lazy Flip-Flops	White	8	2	W	7.5	
24	WE021	Lazy Flip-Flops	Brown	8	2	M	7.5	
25	WE022	Lazy Flip-Flops	Brown	9	4	M	7.5	
26	WE023	Lazy Flip-Flops	Brown	10	2	M	7.5	
27	WE024	Lazy Flip-Flops	Brown	11	2	M	7.5	
28	WE025	Seriously Tall Boots	Black	6	0	W	42.5	
29	WE026	Seriously Tall Boots	Black	6.5	0	W	42.5	
30	WE027	Seriously Tall Boots	Black	7	1	W	42.5	
31	WE028	Seriously Tall Boots	Black	7.5	3	W	42.5	

1-91 Panes frozen at cell A4

3. Change zoom size and unfreeze the pane.
   a. Click the **100%** button [*View* tab, *Window* group].
   b. Click the **Freeze Panes** button [*View* tab, *Window* group].
   c. Choose **Unfreeze Panes**.
   d. Click cell **A1**.
4. Check spelling in the worksheet.
   a. Click the **Spelling** button [*Review* tab, *Proofing* group]. The first occurrence of "Hikin" is found as misspelled.
   b. Select **Hiking** in the *Suggestions* list.
   c. Click **Change All** to correct all occurrences of the misspelled word (Figure 1-92).
   d. Click **OK**.

5. Use the *Fill Handle* to copy a formula.
   a. Click **H4**. The formula is visible in the *Formula* bar. The formula multiples the quantity by the cost to calculate the value of the current stock (Figure 1-93).
   b. Point to the *Fill Handle* for cell **H4**.
   c. Double-click the *Fill* pointer. The formula is copied down the entire column.
   d. Press **Ctrl+Home**.

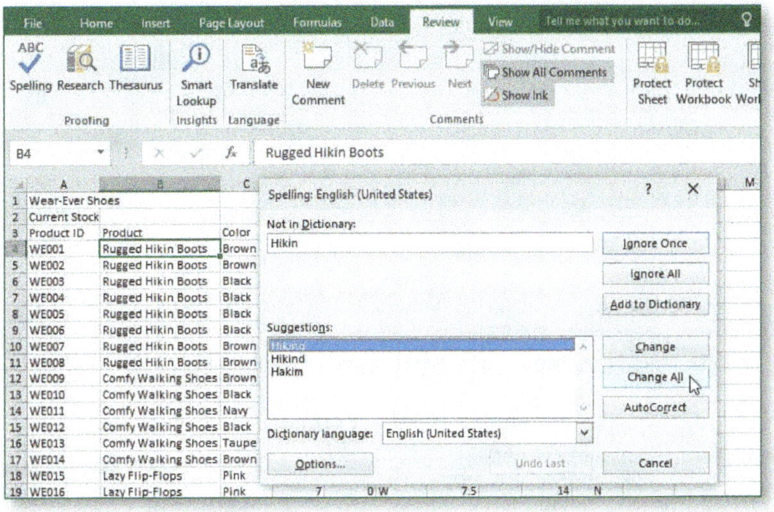

1-92 Change all occurrences of a misspelled word

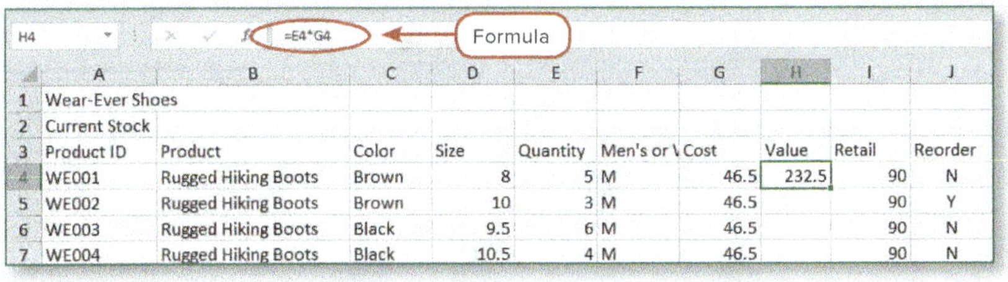

1-93 Formula to be copied

6. Click the **Themes** button [*Page Layout* tab, *Themes* group] and choose **Ion** from the gallery.

7. Merge and center the titles.
   a. Select cells **A1:J1** and click the **Merge & Center** button [*Home* tab, *Alignment* group].
   b. Merge and center cells **A2:J2**.

8. Apply cell styles and adjust row height.
   a. Select cell **A1**, click the **Cell Styles** button or the **More** button [*Home* tab, *Styles* group], and select **Title** in the *Titles and Headings* category.
   b. Select cell **A2** and apply the **Heading 4** style.
   c. Click the **Font Size** arrow [*Home* tab, *Font* group] and select **14 pt**. Your font size change overwrites the font size of the cell style.
   d. Point to the row **1** heading and drag to select row headings **1:2**.
   e. Click the **Format** button [*Home* tab, *Cells* group] and choose **Row Height**.
   f. Type 22 as the new row height and press **Enter**.
   g. Select cells **A3:J3**.
   h. From the *Cell Styles* gallery [*Home* tab], select **40% - Accent3**.
   i. Apply **bold** to the selected cells.
   j. Click the row **3** heading.
   k. Point to the bottom border of the row heading to display the resize arrow.
   l. Drag the resize arrow to **21.00** (**28 pixels**) as the new row height and release the pointer button (Figure 1-94).
   m. Click the **Zoom Out** button in the *Status* bar if necessary so that you can see all rows (1:39).

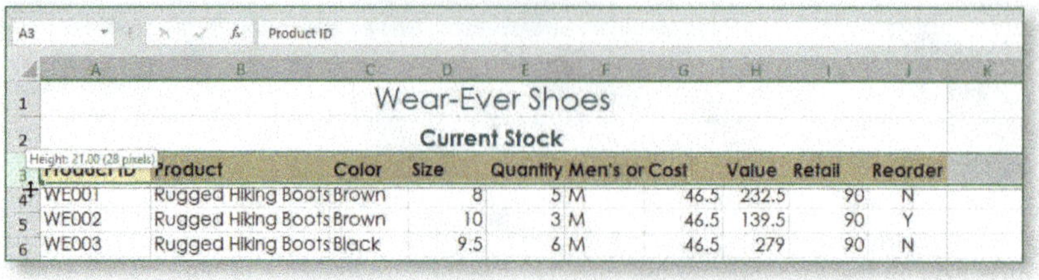

1-94 Adjust row height from the row heading

9. Change alignment, format values, apply borders, and increase the indent.
   a. Select cells **D4:F39**.
   b. Click the **Center** button [*Home* tab, *Alignment* group].
   c. Select cells **G4:H39**.
   d. Click the **Accounting Number Format** button [*Home* tab, *Alignment* group].
   e. Click cells **A3:J39**.
   f. Click the **Borders** drop-down arrow [*Home* tab, *Font* group] and select **All Borders**.
   g. While the cells are selected, click the **Font size** drop-down arrow [*Home* tab, *Font* group] and choose **12**.
   h. Select cells **B4:C39** and click the **Increase Indent** button [*Home* tab, *Alignment* group] one time. This moves the label away from the border for easier reading.
   i. Click and drag to select columns **A:J**.
   j. Double-click the border between columns J and K to *AutoFit* the selected columns (Figure 1-95).
   k. Select and **center** align the labels in row **3**.

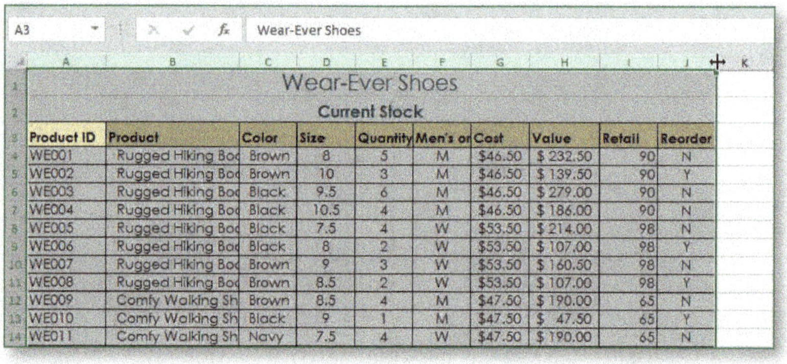

1-95 Select column headings to *AutoFit*

10. Insert a column and fill data.
    a. Right-click column heading **B**.
    b. Choose **Insert** from the context menu.
    c. In cell **B3**, type Disc? and press **Enter**.
    d. In cell **B4**, type No and press **Enter**.
    e. In cell **B5**, type No and press **Enter**.
    f. In cell **B6**, type Yes and press **Enter**.
    g. Select cells **B4:B6** and increase the indent twice.
    h. Select cells **B4:B6** and double-click the *Fill* pointer (Figure 1-96).
    i. Select cells **A4:A39** and increase the indent one time.
    j. Press **Ctrl+Home**.

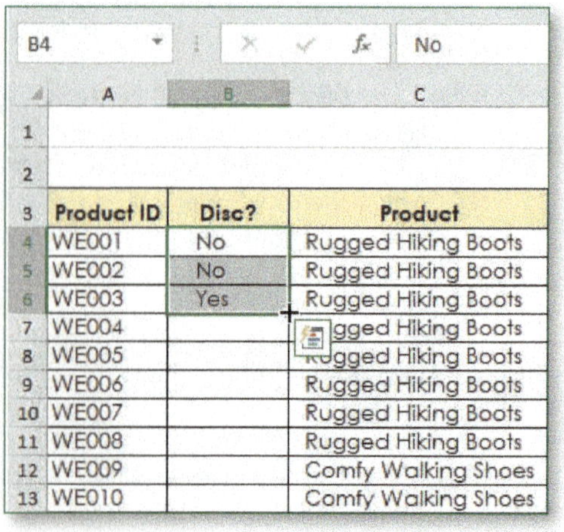

1-96 Double-click the *Fill* pointer to complete a series

11. Rename the sheet tab.
    a. Double-click the **Sheet1** tab.
    b. Type Inventory and press **Enter**.

12. Use *Page Layout* view to insert a footer.
    a. Click the **Page Layout** button in the *Status* bar.
    b. Click the center header section. The *Header & Footer Tools Design* tab is active.
    c. Click the **Header & Footer Tools Design** tab.
    d. Click the **Go to Footer** button [*Header & Footer Tools Design* tab, *Navigation* group].
    e. Click the middle section if necessary.
    f. Click the **File Name** button in the *Header & Footer Elements* group. The code is *&[File]*.
    g. Click a worksheet cell to see the file name.
    h. Switch to *Normal* view and press **Ctrl+Home**.
13. Change page setup options.
    a. Click the **Page Layout** tab and click the **Page Setup** launcher.
    b. Display the *Page* tab and select the **Landscape** radio button under *Orientation*.
    c. Select the **Fit to** radio button and enter 1 page wide by 1 tall.
    d. Click **OK**.
14. Set a print area.
    a. Select cells **A1:K11**.
    b. Click the **Page Layout** tab.
    c. Click the **Print Area** button [*Page Setup* group] and select **Set Print Area**.
    d. Press **Ctrl+Home**.
    e. Click the **File** tab and select **Print** to preview the worksheet print area.
    f. Print the area and return to *Normal* view.
15. Click the **Save** button in the *Quick Access* toolbar to save the workbook changes. The print area is saved.
16. Close the workbook (Figure 1-97).

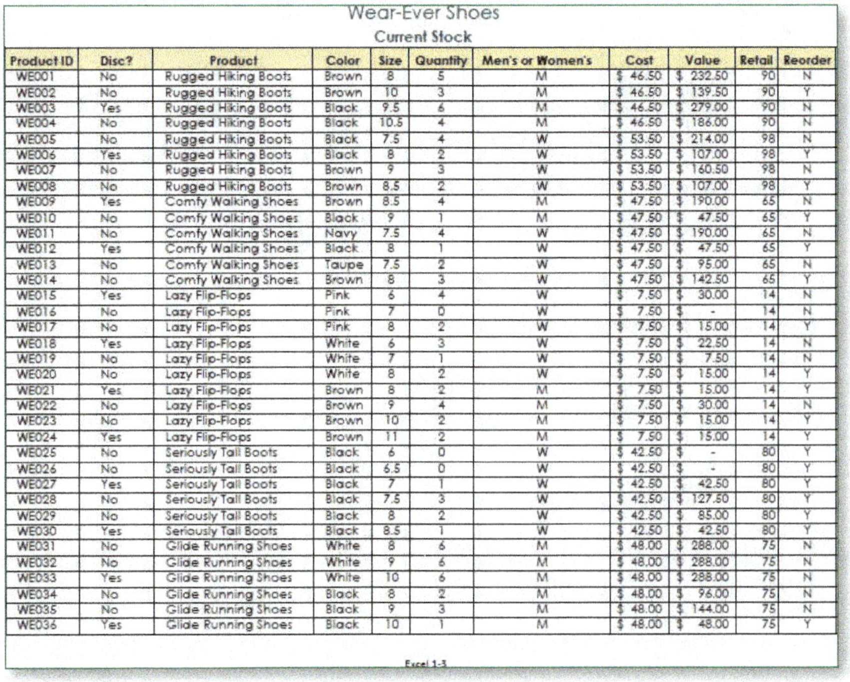

Wear-Ever Shoes
Current Stock

Product ID	Disc?	Product	Color	Size	Quantity	Men's or Women's	Cost	Value	Retail	Reorder
WE001	No	Rugged Hiking Boots	Brown	8	5	M	$ 46.50	$ 232.50	90	N
WE002	No	Rugged Hiking Boots	Brown	10	3	M	$ 46.50	$ 139.50	90	Y
WE003	Yes	Rugged Hiking Boots	Black	9.5	6	M	$ 46.50	$ 279.00	90	N
WE004	No	Rugged Hiking Boots	Black	10.5	4	M	$ 46.50	$ 186.00	90	N
WE005	No	Rugged Hiking Boots	Black	7.5	4	W	$ 53.50	$ 214.00	98	N
WE006	Yes	Rugged Hiking Boots	Black	8	2	W	$ 53.50	$ 107.00	98	Y
WE007	No	Rugged Hiking Boots	Brown	9	3	W	$ 53.50	$ 160.50	98	N
WE008	No	Rugged Hiking Boots	Brown	8.5	2	W	$ 53.50	$ 107.00	98	Y
WE009	Yes	Comfy Walking Shoes	Brown	8.5	4	M	$ 47.50	$ 190.00	65	N
WE010	No	Comfy Walking Shoes	Black	9	1	M	$ 47.50	$ 47.50	65	Y
WE011	No	Comfy Walking Shoes	Navy	7.5	4	W	$ 47.50	$ 190.00	65	N
WE012	Yes	Comfy Walking Shoes	Black	8	1	W	$ 47.50	$ 47.50	65	Y
WE013	No	Comfy Walking Shoes	Taupe	7.5	2	W	$ 47.50	$ 95.00	65	N
WE014	No	Comfy Walking Shoes	Brown	8	3	W	$ 47.50	$ 142.50	65	Y
WE015	Yes	Lazy Flip-Flops	Pink	6	4	W	$ 7.50	$ 30.00	14	N
WE016	No	Lazy Flip-Flops	Pink	7	0	W	$ 7.50	$ -	14	N
WE017	No	Lazy Flip-Flops	Pink	8	2	W	$ 7.50	$ 15.00	14	Y
WE018	Yes	Lazy Flip-Flops	White	6	3	W	$ 7.50	$ 22.50	14	N
WE019	No	Lazy Flip-Flops	White	7	1	W	$ 7.50	$ 7.50	14	N
WE020	No	Lazy Flip-Flops	White	8	2	W	$ 7.50	$ 15.00	14	Y
WE021	Yes	Lazy Flip-Flops	Brown	8	2	M	$ 7.50	$ 15.00	14	Y
WE022	No	Lazy Flip-Flops	Brown	9	4	M	$ 7.50	$ 30.00	14	N
WE023	No	Lazy Flip-Flops	Brown	10	2	M	$ 7.50	$ 15.00	14	Y
WE024	Yes	Lazy Flip-Flops	Brown	11	2	M	$ 7.50	$ 15.00	14	Y
WE025	No	Seriously Tall Boots	Black	6	0	W	$ 42.50	$ -	80	Y
WE026	No	Seriously Tall Boots	Black	6.5	0	W	$ 42.50	$ -	80	Y
WE027	Yes	Seriously Tall Boots	Black	7	1	W	$ 42.50	$ 42.50	80	Y
WE028	No	Seriously Tall Boots	Black	7.5	3	W	$ 42.50	$ 127.50	80	Y
WE029	No	Seriously Tall Boots	Black	8	2	W	$ 42.50	$ 85.00	80	Y
WE030	Yes	Seriously Tall Boots	Black	8.5	1	W	$ 42.50	$ 42.50	80	Y
WE031	No	Glide Running Shoes	White	8	6	M	$ 48.00	$ 288.00	75	N
WE032	No	Glide Running Shoes	White	9	6	M	$ 48.00	$ 288.00	75	N
WE033	Yes	Glide Running Shoes	White	10	6	M	$ 48.00	$ 288.00	75	N
WE034	No	Glide Running Shoes	Black	8	2	M	$ 48.00	$ 96.00	75	N
WE035	No	Glide Running Shoes	Black	9	3	M	$ 48.00	$ 144.00	75	N
WE036	Yes	Glide Running Shoes	Black	10	1	M	$ 48.00	$ 48.00	75	Y

Excel 1-3

1-97 Excel 1-3 completed

Independent Project 1-4

As staff at Blue Lake Sports Company, you are expected to prepare the monthly sales worksheet. You edit and format data, complete calculations, and prepare the workbook for distribution. You also copy the sheet for next month's data.
[Student Learning Outcomes 1.1, 1.2, 1.3, 1.4, 1.5, 1.6, 1.8]

File Needed: ***BlueLakeSports-01.xlsx*** [*Student data files are available in the Library of your SIMnet account.*]
Completed Project File Name: ***[your initials] Excel 1-4.xlsx***

Skills Covered in This Project

- Open and save a workbook.
- Choose a workbook theme.
- Edit and format data.
- Center labels across a selection.
- Use *SUM* and the *Fill Handle*.
- Adjust column width and row height.
- Insert a header and a footer.
- Adjust page layout options.
- Copy and rename a worksheet.

1. Open ***BlueLakeSports-01.xlsx*** from your student data files. If the workbook has opened in *Protected View*, click **Enable Editing** in the security bar.
2. Save the workbook as [your initials] Excel 1-4 in your usual location.
3. Apply the **Slice** theme to the worksheet.
4. Edit worksheet data.
   a. Edit the title in cell **A2** to display Monthly Sales by Department.
   b. Edit cell **D6** to 1950.
5. Select cells **A1:F2** and apply the *Center Across Selection* command.
6. Select and delete row **8**.
7. Use the *Fill Handle* to complete a series.
   a. Select cell **B3**.
   b. Use the *Fill Handle* to complete the series to **Week 4** in column **E**.
   c. *AutoFit* the columns to display the complete label.
8. Use *SUM* and the *Fill Handle* to calculate totals.
   a. Use the **AutoSum** button to build a *SUM* function in cell **F4**.
   b. Use the *Fill Handle* to copy the formula in cell **F4** to cells **F5:F16**.
   c. Delete the contents of cell **F17** if you copied the formula to that cell.
   d. Select cells **B17:F17** and click the **AutoSum** button. The *SUM* formula is inserted, and a **Quick Analysis** options button appears (Figure 1-98).
   e. Press **Esc** to ignore the *Quick Analysis* options.

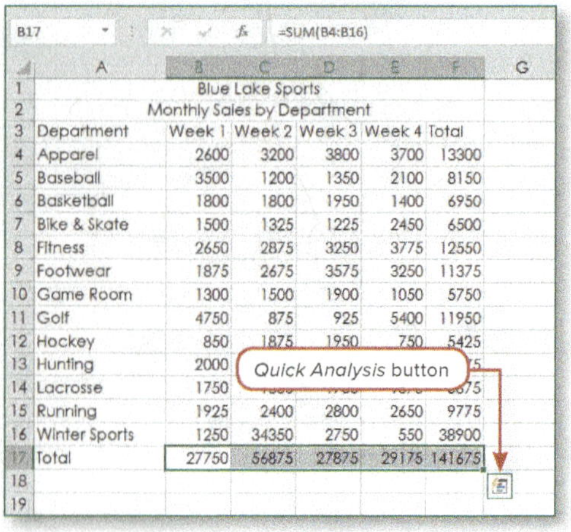

1-98 *AutoSum* complete with *Quick Analysis* button

9. Format labels and values.
   a. Select cells **A1:A2** and increase the font size to **18**.
   b. Increase the row height of rows **1:2** to **24 (32 pixels)**.
   c. Format cells **A3:F3** as **Bold** and increase the row height to **18 (24 pixels)**.
   d. Center the data in cells **B3:F3**.
   e. Format all values with **Comma Style** and decrease the decimal two times.
   f. Apply the **All Borders** format to cells **A3:F17**.
   g. Select cells **B17:F17** and apply the **Accounting Number Format** with no decimal places.
   h. *AutoFit* each column that does not display all data.

10. Finalize the worksheet.
   a. Click the **Insert** tab and click the **Header & Footer** button.
   b. In the right header section, insert the **Sheet Name** field.
   c. Go to the footer and click the right section.
   d. Type [your first and last name] (Figure 1-99).

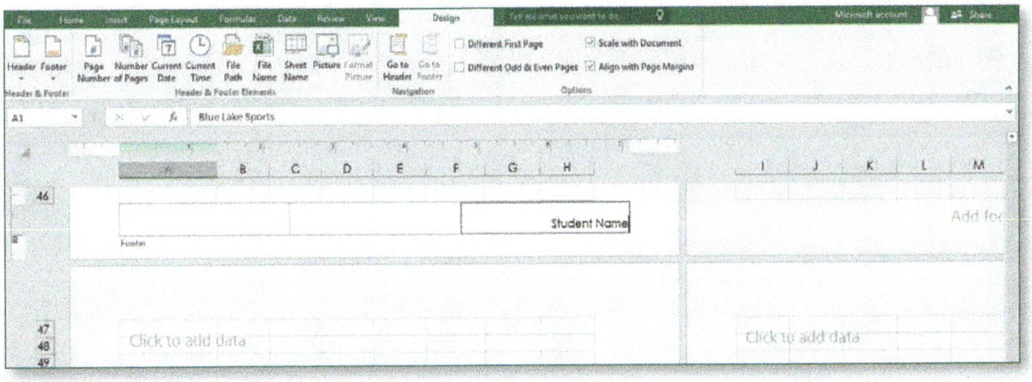

1-99 Add a footer in *Page Layout* view

   e. Click a cell in the worksheet and return to *Normal* view.
   f. Center the worksheet horizontally on the page.

11. Copy and rename a worksheet.
   a. Right-click the *January* sheet tab and choose **Move or Copy**.
   b. Make a copy of the sheet at the end.
   c. Rename the copied sheet February.
   d. Format the *February* sheet tab color to **Dark Blue, Accent 1**.
   e. Delete the values in cells **B4:E16** and press **Ctrl+Home**.
   f. Return to the *January* sheet.

12. Preview the *January* sheet.

13. Save and close the workbook (Figure 1-100).

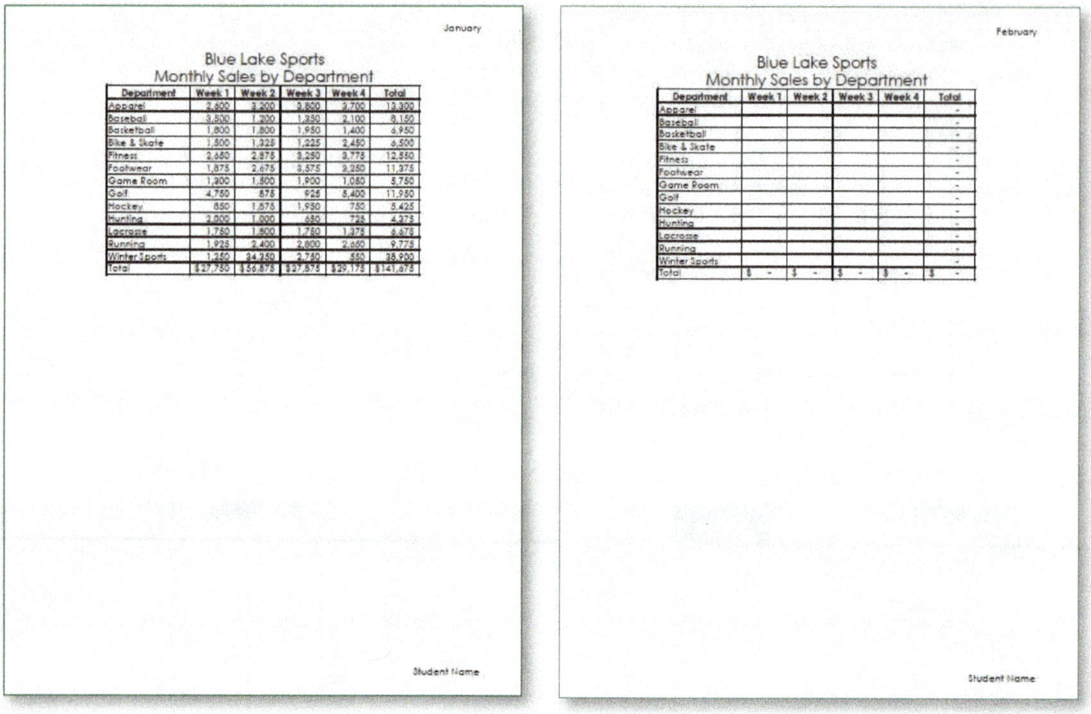

Blue Lake Sports
Monthly Sales by Department

Department	Week 1	Week 2	Week 3	Week 4	Total
Apparel	2,600	3,200	3,800	3,700	13,300
Baseball	3,500	1,200	1,350	2,100	8,150
Basketball	1,800	1,800	1,950	1,400	6,950
Bike & Skate	1,500	1,325	1,225	2,450	6,500
Fitness	2,650	2,875	3,250	3,775	12,550
Footwear	1,875	2,675	3,575	3,250	11,375
Game Room	1,300	1,500	1,900	1,050	5,750
Golf	4,750	875	925	5,400	11,950
Hockey	850	1,875	1,950	750	5,425
Hunting	2,000	1,000	650	725	4,375
Lacrosse	1,750	1,800	1,750	1,375	6,675
Running	1,925	2,400	2,800	2,650	9,775
Winter Sports	1,250	34,350	2,750	550	38,900
Total	$27,750	$56,875	$27,875	$29,175	$141,675

Blue Lake Sports
Monthly Sales by Department

Department	Week 1	Week 2	Week 3	Week 4	Total
Apparel					-
Baseball					-
Basketball					-
Bike & Skate					-
Fitness					-
Footwear					-
Game Room					-
Golf					-
Hockey					-
Hunting					-
Lacrosse					-
Running					-
Winter Sports					-
Total	$ -	$ -	$ -	$ -	$ -

1-100 Excel 1-4 completed

Independent Project 1-5

Clemenson Imaging employs certified staff to perform mobile medical imaging at several hospitals statewide. Your worksheet maintains a log of which hospitals were visited and what images were made. You need to format the data and finalize the worksheet.
[Student Learning Outcomes 1.1, 1.2, 1.3, 1.4, 1.5, 1.6, 1.7, 1.8]

File Needed: ***ClemensonImaging-01.xlsx*** *[Student data files are available in the Library of your SIMnet account.]*
Completed Project File Name: ***[your initials] Excel 1-5.xlsx***

Skills Covered in This Project

- Open and save a workbook.
- Use *SUM*.
- Unfreeze panes and change the zoom size.
- Format data.
- Merge and center labels.
- Adjust column width and row height.
- Design borders.
- Copy a sheet and rename a tab.
- Add document properties.
- Change page layout options.

1. Open ***ClemensonImaging-01.xlsx*** from your student data files and save it as [your initials] Excel 1-5. If the workbook has opened in *Protected View*, click **Enable Editing** in the security bar.
2. Edit the label in cell **A1** to insert LLC after "Clemenson Imaging." Edit the label in cell **A2** to show "Second Quarter . . ." instead of "First Quarter."
3. Merge and center the label in cell **A1** across the worksheet data and then do the same for the label in cell **A2**.
4. Scroll to and select cell **A41**. Type Total. Right-align this label and apply bold format.
5. Use *SUM* in cell **F41** to add the values in cells **F5:F40**.
6. Unfreeze the panes and set a zoom size to display rows 1:30.
7. *AutoFit* columns **D** and **G**.
8. Format data.
   a. Click cell **A1** and set the font size to **18**.
   b. Change the label in cell **A2** to a font size of **14**.
   c. Select cells **A4:H4** and apply bold and center.
   d. Format cells **A4:H4** to use the **White, Background 1, Darker 15%** fill color.
   e. Format the row height for row **4** to **21.00 (28 pixels)**.
   f. Select cells **A4:H41** and apply **All Borders**.
   g. Select cells **A41:H41** and apply the fill color **White, Background 1, Darker 15%**.
   h. Make the value in cell **F41** bold.
9. Set page layout options.
   a. Change the page orientation to **Landscape**.
   b. Center the worksheet horizontally.
   c. Scale the sheet to fit on a single page.
   d. Add a footer that displays the current date in the left section and your first and last name in the right section.
   e. *Autofit* columns that do not display all the data.
10. Add document properties.
    a. Click the **File** tab and select **Info**.
    b. Click the **Properties** drop-down arrow and select **Advanced Properties**.
    c. Click the **Title** box and type Procedures.
    d. Click the **Author** box and type your first and last name (Figure 1-101).
    e. Return to the worksheet.

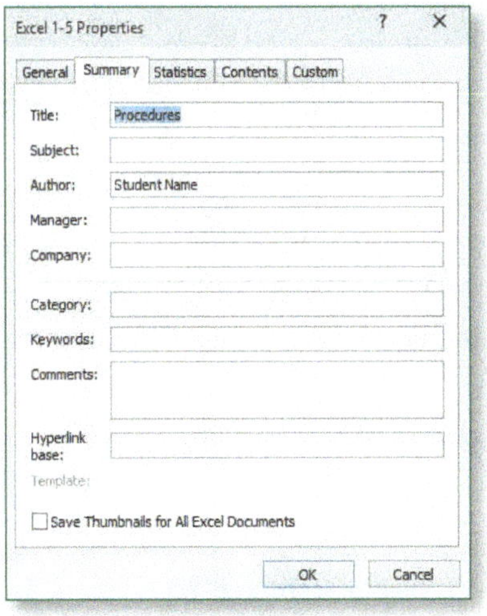

1-101 *Properties* dialog box

11. Rename *Sheet1* as Qtr 2.
12. Copy the *Qtr 2* sheet and place it at the end. Name the copy Qtr 3. Set this tab color to **Blue, Accent 1, Darker 50%**.
13. On the *Qtr 3* sheet, edit the label in cell **A2** to show "Third Quarter . . .".
14. Delete the contents of cells **A5:H40** on the *Qtr 3* sheet.
15. Select cell **A5** and return to the *Qtr 2* sheet.
16. Press **Ctrl+Home** and preview the entire workbook (Figure 1-102).
17. Save and close the workbook (Figure 1-103).

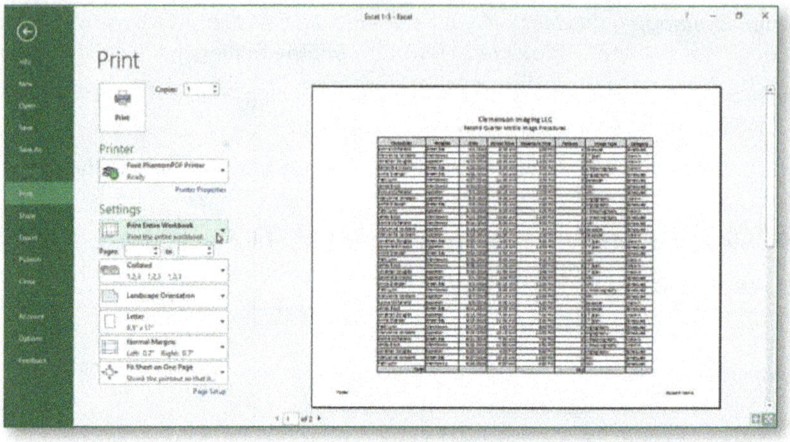

1-102 Entire workbook selected for preview and print

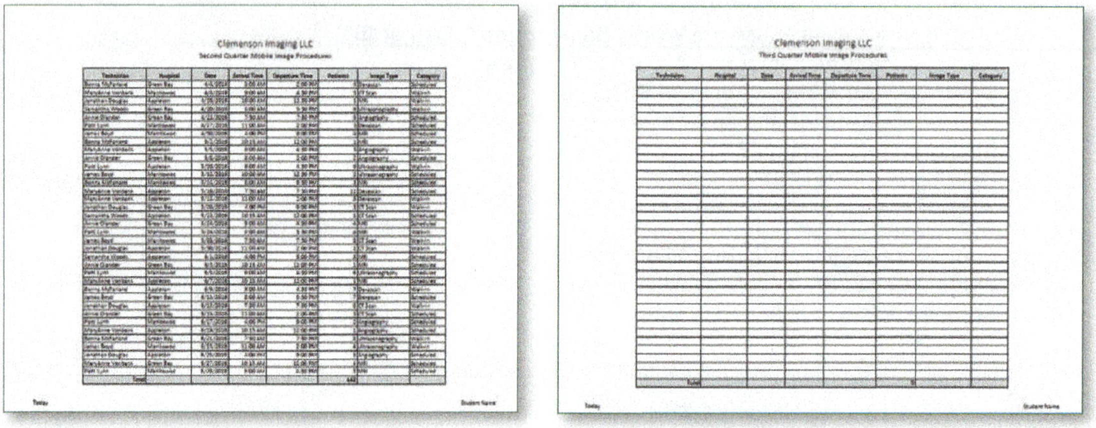

1-103 Excel 1-5 completed

Independent Project 1-6

As accounts receivable clerk for Livingood Income Tax & Accounting, you track daily payments from clients in an Excel worksheet. After entering the data, you format the worksheet and prepare it for distribution to coworkers.
[**Student Learning Outcomes 1.1, 1.2, 1.3, 1.4, 1.5, 1.6, 1.8**]

File Needed: None
Completed Project File Name: ***[your initials] Excel 1-6.xlsx***

Skills Covered in This Project

- Create and save a workbook.
- Enter labels, dates, and values.
- Use the *Fill Handle* to build series.
- Use *SUM*.
- Change font size and attributes.
- Adjust column width and row height.
- Choose a theme and cell styles.
- Choose page layout options.
- Rename and apply color to sheet tabs.

1. Create a new workbook and save it as [your initials] Excel 1-6. If the workbook has opened in *Protected View*, click **Enable Editing** in the security bar.
2. Apply the **Organic** theme for the workbook.
3. In cell **A1**, type Livingood Income Tax and Accounting and press **Enter**.
4. In cell **A2**, type Accounts Receivable and press **Enter**.
5. In row **4**, type the labels as shown here in Figure 1-104:

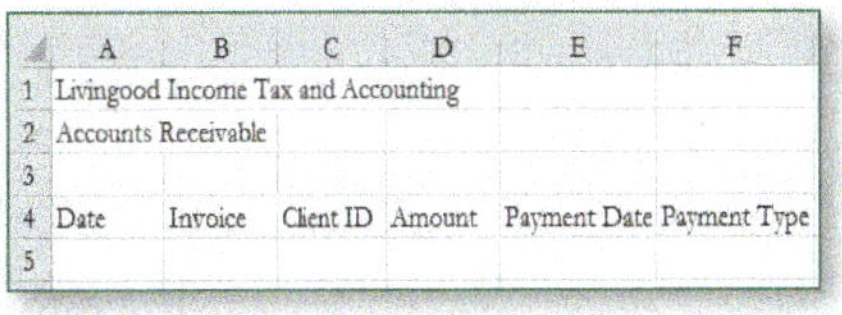

	A	B	C	D	E	F
1	Livingood Income Tax and Accounting					
2	Accounts Receivable					
3						
4	Date	Invoice	Client ID	Amount	Payment Date	Payment Type
5						

1-104 Data to be entered

6. *AutoFit* or widen the columns to display each label in row 4 in its cell.
7. In cell **A5**, type 8/18/17 to enter the date. In cell **A6**, type 8/20/17 to set a pattern for the dates.
8. Select cells **A5:A6** and use the *Fill Handle* to fill in dates to cell A15.
9. In cell **B5**, type 1001 for the first invoice number. In cell **B6**, type 1002 to set a pattern for the invoice numbers.
10. Select cells **B5:B6** and use the *Fill Handle* to fill in invoice numbers to reach cell B15.
11. In cell **C5**, type LITA001 as the first client ID. In cell **C6**, type LITA002 to set a pattern.
12. Use the *Fill Handle* to complete the client ID numbers.
13. Type 425 in cell **D5**. In cell **D6**, type 450 to set the pattern and fill in the amounts.

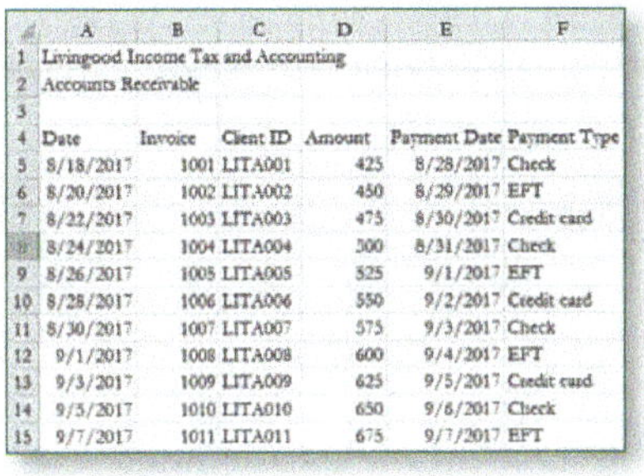

	A	B	C	D	E	F
1	Livingood Income Tax and Accounting					
2	Accounts Receivable					
3						
4	Date	Invoice	Client ID	Amount	Payment Date	Payment Type
5	8/18/2017	1001	LITA001	425	8/28/2017	Check
6	8/20/2017	1002	LITA002	450	8/29/2017	EFT
7	8/22/2017	1003	LITA003	475	8/30/2017	Credit card
8	8/24/2017	1004	LITA004	500	8/31/2017	Check
9	8/26/2017	1005	LITA005	525	9/1/2017	EFT
10	8/28/2017	1006	LITA006	550	9/2/2017	Credit card
11	8/30/2017	1007	LITA007	575	9/3/2017	Check
12	9/1/2017	1008	LITA008	600	9/4/2017	EFT
13	9/3/2017	1009	LITA009	625	9/5/2017	Credit card
14	9/5/2017	1010	LITA010	650	9/6/2017	Check
15	9/7/2017	1011	LITA011	675	9/7/2017	EFT

1-105 All columns filled

14. Type the first two payment dates in column **E** and fill the cells (Figure 1-105).
15. Type the first three payment types in cells **F5:F7** and then use the *Fill Handle* to complete the cells in column F.
16. Format data.
    a. Select cells **C5:C15**, increase the indent one time, and *AutoFit* the column. Do the same for the payment type data.
    b. Format the values in column **D** as **Accounting Number Format**.
    c. Select cells **A1:A2** and change the font size to **18**. Center the labels across cells **A1:F2**.
    d. Select the labels in row **4** and apply bold format center alignment.
    e. *AutoFit* columns that do not show all the data.
    f. Apply **All Borders** to cells **A4:F15**. Apply an **Outside Border** for cells **A1:F2**.
    g. Apply the **Green, Accent 1, Lighter 60%** fill color to cells **A1:F2** and **A4:F4**.
    h. Apply the **Green, Accent 1, Lighter 60%** fill color to cells **A6:F6**.
    i. Use the **Ctrl** key to select the data in rows **8**, **10**, **12**, and **14** and apply the same fill color.
17. Rename *Sheet1* as AR and set the tab color to **Green, Accent 1**.
18. Define page layout and add document properties.
    a. Center the worksheet horizontally on the page.
    b. Create a header with the sheet name in the left section and your name in the right section.
    c. Delete an existing author name and key your first and last name as *Author* in the *Properties* dialog box.
    d. Type Receivables in the *Title* box (Figure 1-106).
    e. Preview your worksheet.

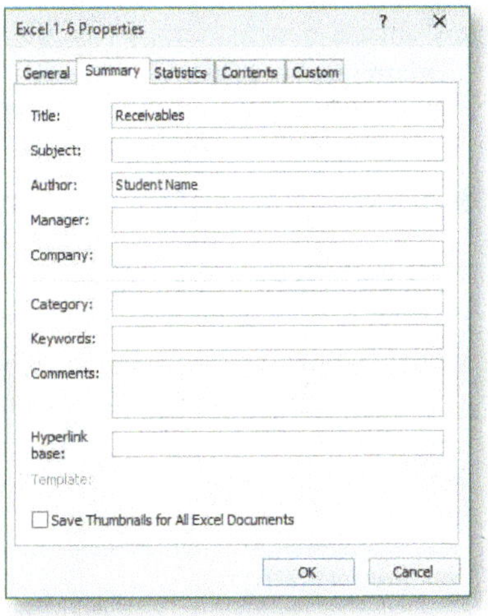

1-106 Properties entered in dialog box

19. Save and close the workbook (Figure 1-107).

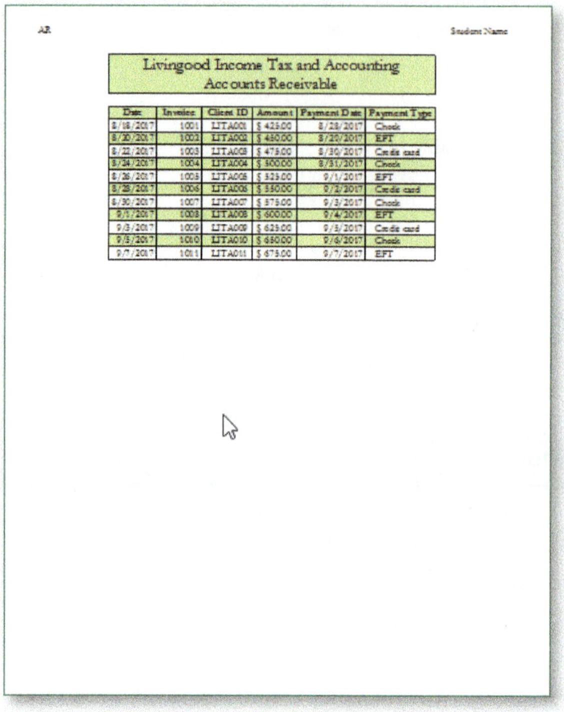
AR Student Name

Livingood Income Tax and Accounting
Accounts Receivable

Date	Invoice	Client ID	Amount	Payment Date	Payment Type
8/18/2017	1001	LITA001	$ 425.00	8/28/2017	Check
8/20/2017	1002	LITA002	$ 450.00	8/29/2017	EFT
8/22/2017	1003	LITA003	$ 475.00	8/30/2017	Credit card
8/24/2017	1004	LITA004	$ 500.00	8/31/2017	Check
8/26/2017	1005	LITA005	$ 525.00	9/1/2017	EFT
8/28/2017	1006	LITA006	$ 550.00	9/2/2017	Credit card
8/30/2017	1007	LITA007	$ 575.00	9/3/2017	Check
9/1/2017	1008	LITA008	$ 600.00	9/4/2017	EFT
9/3/2017	1009	LITA009	$ 625.00	9/5/2017	Credit card
9/5/2017	1010	LITA010	$ 650.00	9/6/2017	Check
9/7/2017	1011	LITA011	$ 675.00	9/7/2017	EFT

1-107 Excel 1-6 completed

Improve It Project 1-7

In this project, you complete a worksheet that maintains flight statistics for Boyd Air. The data has been imported from the reservation system, and you now need to add finishing touches.
[Student Learning Outcomes 1.1, 1.2, 1.3, 1.4, 1.5, 1.6, 1.7, 1.8]

File Needed: ***BoydAir-01.xlsx*** [*Student data files are available in the Library of your SIMnet account.*]
Completed Project File Name: ***[your initials] Excel 1-7.xlsx***

Skills Covered in This Project

- Open and save a workbook.
- Change the zoom level and remove a split.
- Enter and merge and center labels.
- Insert a row and set column width.
- Format data.
- Use *SUM*.
- Apply cell styles.
- Rename and color the sheet tab.
- Adjust page layout options.
- Add document properties.

1. Open the workbook ***BoydAir-01.xlsx*** from your student data files. If the workbook has opened in *Protected View*, click **Enable Editing** in the security bar.
2. Save the workbook as [your initials] Excel 1-7.

3. Remove the split from the window.
4. Type Boyd Air in cell **A1** and Flight Statistics in cell **A2**.
5. Merge and center the labels in cells **A1** and **A2**. Change the font size for both labels to **16**.
6. Insert a row at row **3**.
7. Select the labels in row **4** and make them bold and centered. *AutoFit* columns to show each label in row 4.
8. Change the zoom size to **100%**.
9. Select cells **B5:D18**, press **Ctrl**, and select cells **G5:G18**. Increase the indent one time.
10. Apply **All Borders** for cells **A4:H19**.
11. Calculate the total number of passengers in cell **H19**.
12. Apply the **Accent2** cell style to cells **A3:H3** and cells **A20:H20**.
13. Select cells **A3:H3** and **A20:H20**and apply an **Outside Border**.
14. Modify page layout options.
    a. Change the orientation to **Landscape**.
    b. Center the worksheet horizontally on the page.
    c. Show the file name in the left header section.
    d. Type your first and last name in the right header section.
15. Name the sheet tab Feb-Mar and format the tab color as **Orange, Accent 2**.
16. Set the document properties to show your first and last name as the *Author*. In the *Title* field, type Flight Stats.
17. Preview your worksheet.
18. Save and close the workbook (Figure 1-108).

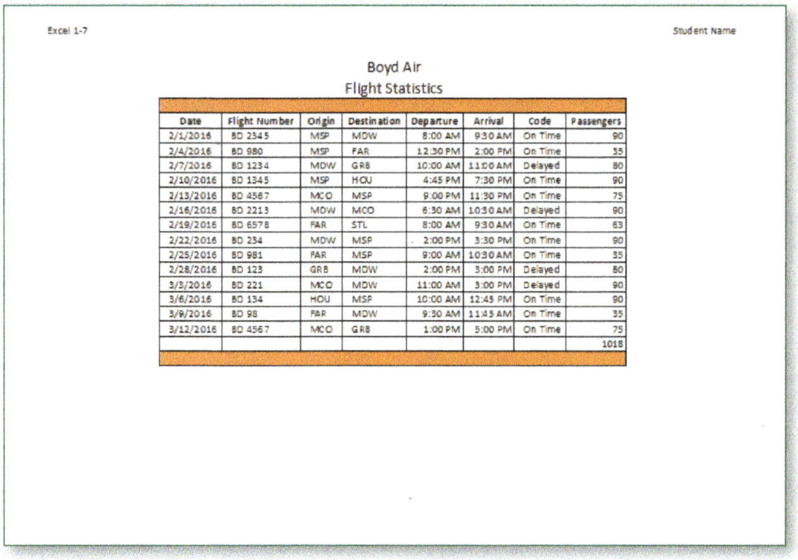
Excel 1-7 Student Name

Boyd Air
Flight Statistics

Date	Flight Number	Origin	Destination	Departure	Arrival	Code	Passengers
2/1/2016	BD 2345	MSP	MDW	8:00 AM	9:30 AM	On Time	90
2/4/2016	BD 980	MSP	FAR	12:30 PM	2:00 PM	On Time	35
2/7/2016	BD 1234	MDW	GRB	10:00 AM	11:00 AM	Delayed	80
2/10/2016	BD 1345	MSP	HOU	4:45 PM	7:30 PM	On Time	90
2/13/2016	BD 4567	MCO	MSP	9:00 PM	11:30 PM	On Time	75
2/16/2016	BD 2213	MDW	MCO	6:30 AM	10:30 AM	Delayed	90
2/19/2016	BD 6578	FAR	STL	8:00 AM	9:30 AM	On Time	63
2/22/2016	BD 234	MDW	MSP	2:00 PM	3:30 PM	On Time	90
2/25/2016	BD 981	FAR	MSP	9:00 AM	10:30 AM	On Time	35
2/28/2016	BD 123	GRB	MDW	2:00 PM	3:00 PM	Delayed	80
3/3/2016	BD 221	MCO	MDW	11:00 AM	3:00 PM	Delayed	90
3/6/2016	BD 134	HOU	MSP	10:00 AM	12:45 PM	On Time	90
3/9/2016	BD 98	FAR	MDW	9:30 AM	11:45 AM	On Time	35
3/12/2016	BD 4567	MCO	GRB	1:00 PM	5:00 PM	On Time	75
							1018

1-108 Excel 1-7 completed

Challenge Project 1-8

In this project, you create a workbook that lists and tracks candy and beverage sales at a gourmet chocolate store for selected holidays or special events. You enter and format the data and then finalize the workbook for distribution.
[**Student Learning Outcomes 1.1, 1.2, 1.3, 1.4, 1.5, 1.6, 1.8**]

File Needed: None
Completed Project File Name: ***[your initials] Excel 1-8.xlsx***

Create a new workbook and save it as [your initials] Excel 1-8. Modify your workbook according to the following guidelines:

- Choose a workbook theme.
- Determine and type a name for the store in cell **A1**. In cell **A2**, type Sales by Holiday.
- Starting in cell **B3**, type names of four chocolate candies and one chocolate beverage (cells B3:F3).
- Type the names of five holidays, celebrations, or special events in cells **A4:A8**.
- Fill in values to reflect dollar or unit sales, and format these values appropriately.
- Calculate a total for each holiday and a total for each candy or beverage. Add labels for these values.
- Use cell styles, borders, fill color, or other formatting to design your worksheet.
- *AutoFit* columns and adjust row heights as needed.
- Insert a footer that includes your name in one section and the date in another section.
- Use portrait orientation and fit the worksheet to a single page. Center it horizontally.
- Name the sheet tab and set a tab color.
- Enter the company name in the *Title* field in the document properties.

Challenge Project 1-9

In this project, you create a worksheet for a photography club that rents retail space for selling used equipment. The equipment includes camera bodies, lenses, tripods, cases, accessories, books, and more. You are building the worksheet so that expected selling prices can be entered each month for each item.
[**Student Learning Outcomes 1.1, 1.2, 1.4, 1.5, 1.6, 1.7, 1.8**]

File Needed: None
Completed Project File Name: ***[your initials] Excel 1-9.xlsx***

Create a new workbook and save it as [your initials] Excel 1-9. Modify your workbook according to the following guidelines:

- Create and type a name for the photography club as a main label. As a second label, type a label that specifies the purpose of the worksheet.
- In cell **B3**, type Jan. Fill the months to **Dec** in column **M**.
- Starting in cell **A4**, type the names of ten items related to any type of photography equipment in column **A**. Research a web site that sells similar items.

- As the January price for the first item, type a value that makes sense as a resale price. For the February price, type a value that is a few dollars more than the January price. Select these two cells and fill prices for the remaining months.
- Repeat the tasks in the previous step for each of the ten items to fill in values for all the items.
- Use cell styles, borders, fill color, or other formatting to design the worksheet.
- Adjust column widths and row heights.
- Insert a header that includes your name in the right section.
- Use landscape orientation and fit the worksheet to a single page.
- In the document properties, enter the club's name in the *Author* field.
- Name the worksheet tab and choose a tab color.
- Split the sheet at cell **G1**. Arrange the data so that you see cell **A1** in each window.

Challenge Project 1-10

In this project, you create a spreadsheet that details your expected monthly income and expenses. [**Student Learning Outcomes 1.1, 1.2, 1.3, 1.4, 1.5, 1.6, 1.8**]

File Needed: None
Completed Project File Name: ***[your initials] Excel 1-10.xlsx***

Create a new workbook and save it as [your initials] Excel 1-10. Modify your workbook according to the following guidelines:

- Type the main label Expected Monthly Income and Estimated Expenses. Type your name as a second label.
- Type Income in cell **A3**. In cells **A4:A7**, enter labels for four categories of income. For example, you may have regular wages from one or more jobs, interest from a certificate of deposit, rent from property that you own, income from Internet sales, etc. Include descriptive labels, enter values in column **B**, and include a total income calculation using *SUM*.
- In cell **D3**, type Expenses. In cells **D4:D9**, enter labels for six categories of expenses. These include rent, a mortgage payment, insurance, loan payments, food, clothing, entertainment, transportation, and so on. Complete labels, enter values in column **E**, and use *SUM* to calculate total expenses.
- Format the data with borders, fill color, font styles, and number formats. Adjust page layout options so that the sheet fits on a single portrait page.
- Spell check the sheet.
- Name the sheet Jan and choose a tab color.
- Copy the sheet and name the copy Feb. Choose a different tab color.
- Delete the expense amounts on the *Feb* sheet.
- Make a copy of the *Feb* sheet to create a worksheet for March.
- Add document properties to identify the workbook.

CHAPTER 2

Working with Formulas and Functions

CHAPTER OVERVIEW

With its capabilities in mathematical, scientific, engineering, and other calculations, Excel is a valuable tool for business, government, education, and you. You can use Excel to create a simple addition formula or a sophisticated calculation with layers of arithmetic. In this chapter, you learn how to build a basic formula and how to use mathematical rules. You also explore Excel function categories.

STUDENT LEARNING OUTCOMES (SLOs)

After completing this chapter, you will be able to:

SLO2.1 Build and edit basic formulas (p. E2-89).

SLO2.2 Set mathematical order of operations in a formula (p. E2-91).

SLO2.3 Use absolute, mixed, relative, and 3D references in a formula (p. E2-93).

SLO2.4 Use formula auditing tools in a worksheet (p. E2-99).

SLO2.5 Work with *Statistical* and *Date & Time* functions (p. E2-106).

SLO2.6 Work with functions from the *Financial*, *Logical*, and *Lookup & Reference* categories (p. E2-114).

SLO2.7 Build functions from the *Math & Trig* category (p. E2-122).

CASE STUDY

In the Pause & Practice projects in this chapter, you work with a multi-sheet workbook for Paradise Lakes Resort (PLR), the northern Minnesota chain of resorts. You build formulas to complete a simple income statement, to calculate data for the boutique division, and to track information about the youth camp.

Pause & Practice 2-1: Build and audit formulas in a worksheet.

Pause & Practice 2-2: Insert *Statistical* and *Date & Time* functions in a workbook.

Pause & Practice 2-3: Use *Financial*, *Logical*, *Lookup*, and *Math & Trig* functions in a workbook.

EXCEL

SLO 2.1

Building and Editing a Formula

An Excel ***formula*** is an expression or statement that uses common arithmetic operations to carry out a calculation. Basic arithmetic operations are addition, subtraction, multiplication, and division. The formula is entered in a cell and refers to other cells or ranges in the worksheet or workbook. The formula appears in the *Formula* bar, but the results appear in the cell.

You learned in Chapter 1 that a function is a built-in formula. Like a function, a formula begins with an equals sign (=). After the equals sign, you enter the address of the first cell, followed by the arithmetic operator, followed by the next cell in the calculation. An example of a simple addition formula is **=B5+B6** which adds the values in cells B5 and B6.

Basic arithmetic operators are listed in the table. Enter arithmetic operators using the numeric keypad or the symbols on the number keys at the top of the keyboard.

Character	Arithmetic Operator
+	Addition
–	Subtraction
*	Multiplication
/	Division

In the multiplication formula **=C5*C6**, the value in cell C5 is multiplied by the value in cell C6. You can use cell references in a formula or a value known as a ***constant***. In the formula **=D5*85%**, the constant is 85%.

Type a Formula

For a simple formula, you can easily type it. Click the cell, type the equals sign, type the first cell address, type the operator, type the next cell address, and so on. Press any completion key when the formula is finished. Formulas are not case sensitive, so you can type cell addresses in lowercase letters. Excel automatically converts cell references to uppercase when the formula is completed. If you press **Esc** before completing a formula, it is canceled and nothing is entered in the cell.

As you type a cell address after the equals sign, ***Formula AutoComplete*** displays a list of functions and range names that match the character that you typed. You can ignore the list and continue typing. In addition, the ***Range Finder*** highlights and color codes each cell as you type its address.

HOW TO: Type a Formula

1. Click the cell for the formula.
2. Type an equals sign (=) to begin the formula.
3. Type the column letter for the first cell reference (Figure 2-1).
   - *Formula AutoComplete* displays a list of functions and range names.
   - You can type a lowercase or uppercase character.
4. Type the row number for the cell reference.
   - The *Range Finder* color codes the cell and its reference.
5. Type the arithmetic operator.
6. Type the cell address for the next reference.

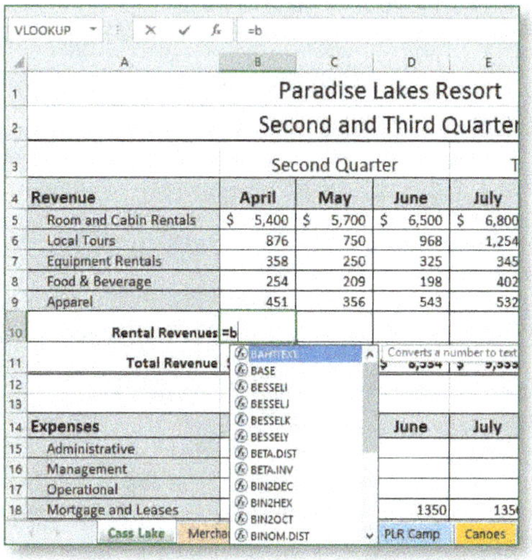

2-1 *Formula AutoComplete* while typing a formula

7. Press **Enter**.
    - The result displays in the cell where the formula is located (Figure 2-2).
    - The *Formula* bar displays the formula.
    - You can click the **Enter** button (the check mark) on the *Formula* bar to complete a formula.
    - You can press **Ctrl+Enter** to complete a formula.

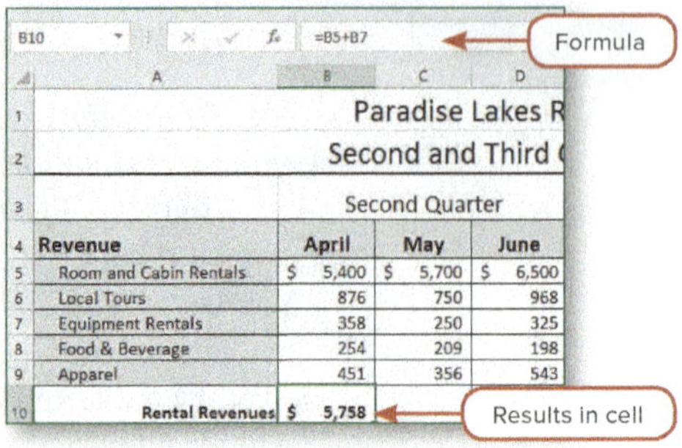

2-2 Formula and result

Point and Click to Build a Formula

Instead of typing a cell address, you point to and click the cell to enter its address in a formula. This method guards against your typing the wrong address. You will not see a *Formula AutoComplete* list, but the *Range Finder* will highlight and color code the cells.

HOW TO: Point and Click to Build a Formula

1. Click the cell for the formula.
2. Type an equals sign (=) to start the formula.
3. Point to and click the first cell for the formula.
    - The reference is entered in the cell and in the *Formula* bar.
    - The *Range Finder* highlights and color codes the reference.
    - If you click the wrong cell, click the correct cell to replace the address.
4. Type the arithmetic operator.
5. Point to and click the next cell for the formula (Figure 2-3).
    - The reference is entered in the cell and in the *Formula* bar.
    - The *Range Finder* highlights and color codes the reference.
6. Press **Enter**.
    - The result displays in the cell.
    - The *Formula* bar displays the formula.
    - Click the **Enter** button on the *Formula* bar or press **Ctrl+Enter** to complete a formula.

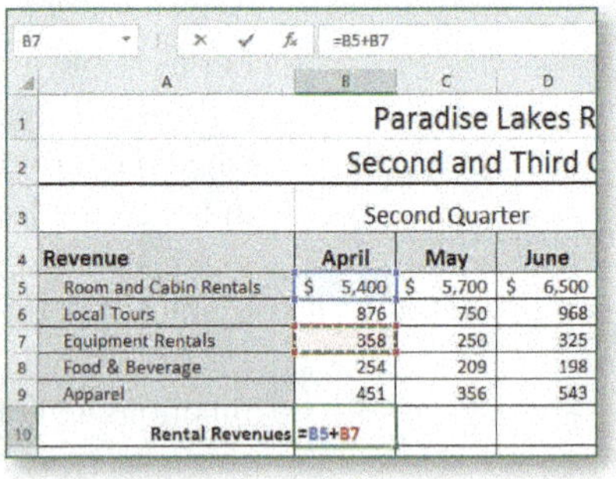

2-3 Point and click to build a formula

Edit a Formula

You edit a formula in *Edit* mode by double-clicking its cell or by clicking the *Formula* bar while the cell is active. The *Range Finder* highlights and color codes the formula cell as well as the cells used in the formula. You can add or remove cells and operators to build a new formula in the cell or in the *Formula* bar.

> **ANOTHER WAY**
>
> Click the cell and press **F2 (FN+F2)** to start *Edit* mode.

▸ HOW TO: Edit a Formula

1. Double-click the formula cell.
   - The *Range Finder* highlights and color codes the cells.
2. Edit the formula in the cell (Figure 2-4).
   - Edit the cell address or type a different operator.
   - Select a cell address and click a different cell to replace the reference.
   - You can make the same edits in the *Formula* bar.
3. Press **Enter**.
   - Click the **Enter** button on the *Formula* bar or press **Ctrl+Enter** to complete a formula.

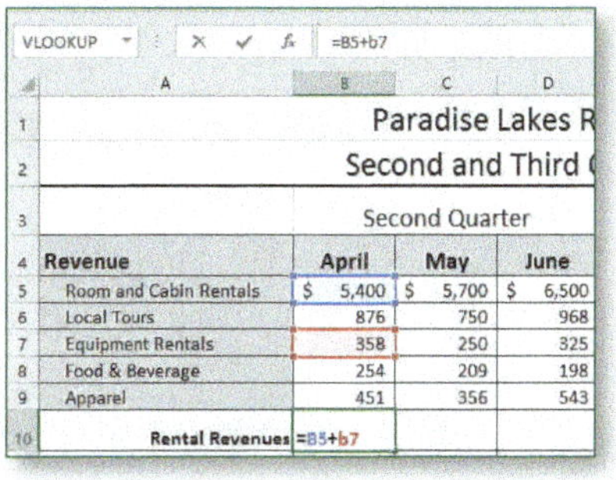

2-4 Edit a formula in the cell

SLO 2.2

Setting Mathematical Order of Operations

A formula can have more than one operator, such as a combination of addition and multiplication. Figure 2-5 illustrates two formulas a restaurant might use to calculate a bill for a couple who ordered the same items. The formula in cell B6 lists the additions first and multiplies by 2; the total of $24 is incorrect. The formula in cell B8 is the same except for the parentheses; the correct amount is $42.

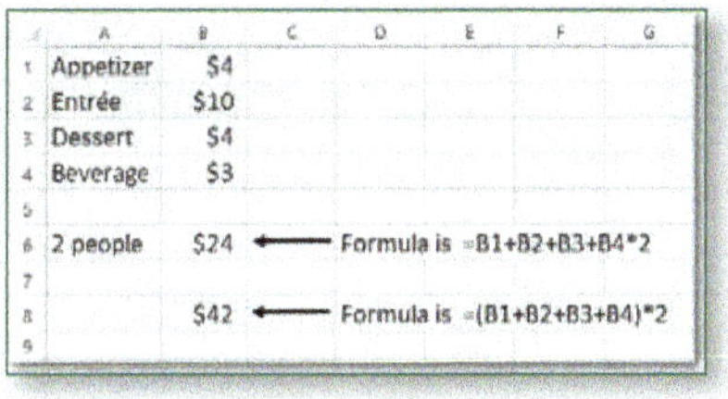

2-5 Formulas with multiple operators

Excel follows ***mathematical order of operations***, which is the sequence of arithmetic calculations. The order in which the mathematics in a formula is carried out depends on the operator as well as left-to-right order. The basic sequence is left to right, but multiplication and division are done before addition and subtraction. This concept is also known as ***order of precedence*** or ***math hierarchy***.

You control the order of operations with parentheses. The formula in cell B8 (Figure 2-5) uses parentheses to reorder the calculation. The parentheses group the addition ($4+$10+$4+$3 = 21) and then multiplies by 2 ($21*2 = 42).

In a formula with multiple operators, references enclosed in parentheses are calculated first. If a value with an exponent exists, it is calculated next. Multiplication and division follow and finally addition and subtraction. When two operators have the same precedence, Excel calculates them from left to right.

Mathematical Order of Precedence

Operator	Operation	Order or Precedence
()	Parentheses	First
^	Exponent	Second
*	Multiplication	Third
/	Division	Third
+	Addition	Fourth
–	Subtraction	Fourth

> **MORE INFO**
>
> Use a popular acronym to recall arithmetic order of the operations: **P**lease **E**xcuse **M**y **D**ear **A**unt **S**ally (**P**arentheses, **E**xponentiation, **M**ultiplication, **D**ivision, **A**ddition, **S**ubtraction).

Exponents raise a number to a power. The formula **3^3** multiplies 3 * 3 * 3, 27. Use the caret symbol (^) to build a formula with an exponent.

Multiple Operators in a Formula

When different operators are used in a formula, you must determine how the calculation should be completed and if parentheses are necessary to set the proper order. Here are formulas with two operators. Since addition and subtraction are equal in priority, Excel calculates from left to right.

$$\mathbf{2+5-3=4} \qquad \mathbf{5+1-3=3}$$

Below are formulas with two operators with different priority. Excel calculates the multiplication first and then follows left to right order.

$$\mathbf{2+5*3=17} \qquad \mathbf{2*5+3=13}$$

Consider this formula with three different operators. Since multiplication and division are equal priority but higher than addition, the multiplication is first, followed by the division (left to right). The result of those calculations is added to 5.

$$\mathbf{=2*5/2+5=10}$$

▶ HOW TO: Use Multiple Operators in a formula

1. Type = to start the formula.
2. Type ((left parenthesis) to start the calculation that should have priority.
   - The calculation in parentheses can occur anywhere in the formula.
3. Click the first cell for the calculation to be enclosed in parentheses.
4. Type the arithmetic operator.
5. Click the next cell for the calculation to be enclosed in parentheses.
6. Type) (right parenthesis) to end the calculation with priority (Figure 2-6).
   - You must have matching parentheses.
7. Complete the formula.
8. Press **Enter**.

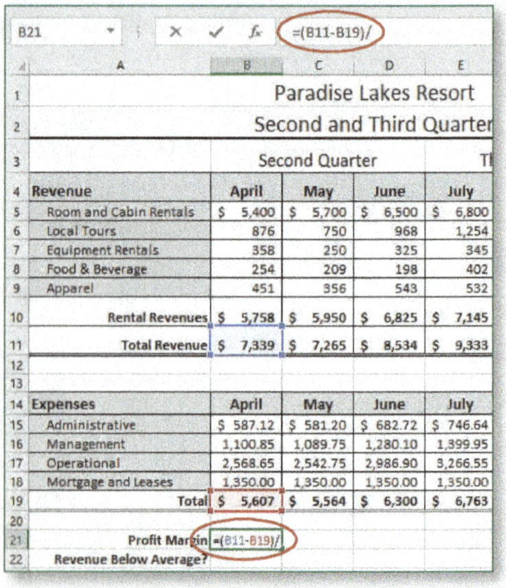

2-6 Set the order of operation with parentheses

SLO 2.3

Using Absolute, Mixed, Relative, and 3D References

Cell references in a formula are identified in different ways. How a cell reference is identified affects how the formula is adjusted when it is copied.

- A ***relative cell reference*** is the location of a cell, such as cell **B2**. In column B, the formula is **=B5+B7**, but when copied to column C, it is **=C5+C7**. When you copy a formula with relative references, copied references are updated to the new locations.
- An ***absolute cell reference*** is indicated with dollar signs as in cell **$B$2**. When an absolute reference is copied, it does not change. In the formula **=$B$6−C7**, $B$6 would not change when copied anywhere in the workbook. C7, on the other hand, would reflect where the copy is located. You can type the dollar signs in an absolute reference, but it is easier to use the **F4 (FN+F4)** function key. When building a formula, enter the cell address and then press **F4 (FN+F4)**.
- A ***mixed cell reference*** has one relative and one absolute reference. Cell **$B2** is a mixed reference. When it is copied, it always refers to column B, but the row number updates relative to where the copy is located. The formula **=$B5+C$6** has two mixed references. When copied, this formula will always show column B for the first address and row 6 for the second address.
- A ***3D cell reference*** is a cell located in another worksheet in the same workbook. It can be absolute, mixed, or relative. A 3D reference includes the name of the sheet as in **Sheet2!B2** or **Inventory!$B2**. The sheet name is followed by an exclamation point. When you point and click to build a 3D reference, the sheet name and exclamation point are automatically entered. When the sheet name includes special characters (@, #, &, etc.), the name is enclosed in single quotes as in **'Inventory#'!$B2**. When you type a 3D reference, you must spell the sheet name correctly and include the exclamation point and single quotes.

The following table illustrates each cell reference type:

Cell Reference Types

Cell Reference	Reference Type	Behavior When Copied
B2	Relative	Cell address updates to new location(s).
$B$2	Absolute	Cell address does not change.
$B2	Mixed	Column does not change; row updates to new location(s).
B$2	Mixed	Row does not change; column updates to new location(s).
Sheet2!B2	3D Relative	Cell address updates to new location(s).

MORE INFO

When used in a reference, the dollar sign ($) and the exclamation point (!) are identifiers. The dollar sign is not treated as a currency symbol, and the exclamation point is not considered punctuation.

Copy a Formula with a Relative Reference

When a formula with relative references is copied, the copied formulas use cell addresses that reflect their locations in the worksheet. In the Paradise Lakes worksheet shown in Figure 2-7, the formula to calculate rental revenue in cell B10 is **=B5+B7**. The formula for cell C10 is **=C5+C7**. The formula in cell B10 can be copied to cells C10:G10 and will automatically adjust for each column.

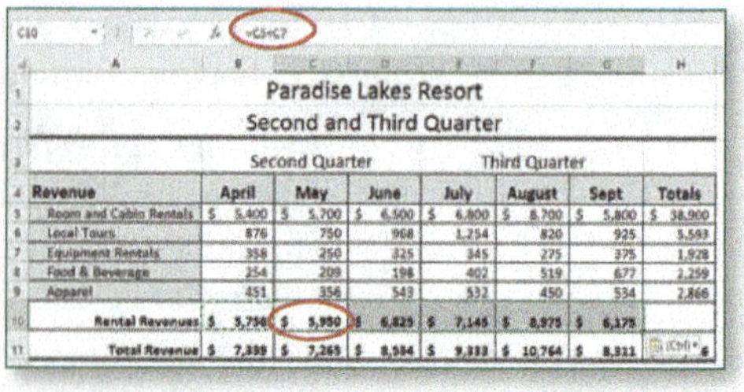

2-7 Copy a formula with a relative reference

HOW TO: Copy a Formula with a Relative Reference

1. Select the cell with the formula.
   - You can select multiple adjacent cells.
2. Press **Ctrl+C** to copy the formula(s).
   - Click and drag the *Fill* pointer if the copies are adjacent to the original formula(s).
   - Use the **Copy** button on the *Home* tab if you prefer.
3. Select the destination cell or range.
   - Click the first cell in a destination range when pasting multiple cells.
4. Press **Ctrl+V** to paste the formula (see Figure 2-7).
   - The pasted formula reflects its location on the worksheet.
   - Ignore the **Paste Options** button.
   - Use the **Paste** button on the *Home* tab if you prefer.

Build and Copy a Formula with an Absolute Reference

An absolute reference in a formula maintains that address when copied. An example is a worksheet in which expenses are calculated as a percentage of revenue. You type the percentage once in a worksheet cell, use an absolute reference to that cell in the first formula, and copy the formula.

To change a cell address to an absolute reference, press the **F4 (FN+F4)** function key while keying or editing the formula. The first press of the key inserts dollar signs for the row and column reference. Another press of the **F4 (FN+F4)** key makes it a mixed reference, and each press of the key cycles through the next option.

HOW TO: Build and Copy a Formula with an Absolute Reference

1. Click the cell for the formula.
2. Type an equals sign (=) to begin the formula.
3. Click the cell to be referenced in the formula.
4. Press **F4 (FN+F4)**.
   - The reference becomes absolute (Figure 2-8).
5. Complete the formula and press **Enter**.

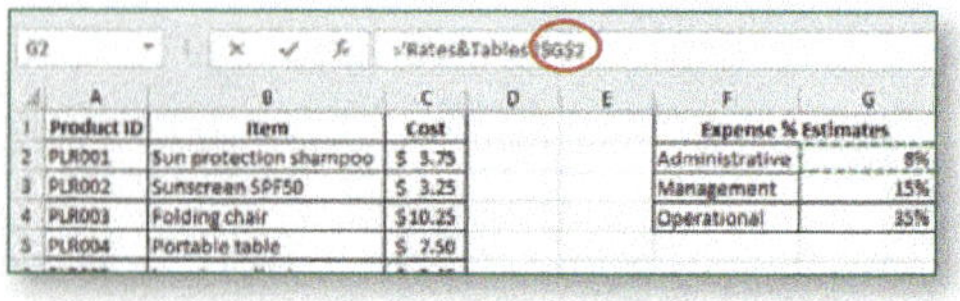

2-8 Make a reference absolute

6. Select the cell with the formula.
7. Press **Ctrl+C** to copy the formula(s).
   - Click and drag the *Fill* pointer if the copies are adjacent to the original formula.
   - Use the **Copy** button on the *Home* tab if you prefer.
8. Select the destination cell or range.
9. Press **Ctrl+V** to paste the formula.
   - The pasted formula uses the same cell reference as the original.
   - Use the **Paste** button on the *Home* tab if you prefer.
   - Ignore the **Paste Options** button.

MORE INFO

When you type a constant in a formula, such as **=B7*12**, the constant (12) is treated as an absolute value.

Build and Copy a Formula with a Mixed Reference

A mixed cell reference has one relative and one absolute reference in the cell address. Part of the copied formula is unchanged and part is updated. A mixed reference has one dollar sign. You still use the **F4 (FN+F4)** function key, because each press of the key cycles through displaying the dollar signs in different combinations.

HOW TO: Build and Copy a Formula with a Mixed Reference

1. Click the cell for the formula.
2. Type an equals sign (=) to begin the formula.
3. Click the cell to be referenced in the formula.
4. Press **F4 (FN+F4)**.
   - The reference is absolute.
5. Press **F4 (FN+F4)** again.
   - The column reference is relative and the row reference is absolute.
6. Press **F4 (FN+F4)** again (Figure 2-9).
   - The row reference is relative and the column reference is absolute.
7. Complete the formula and press **Enter**.
8. Select the formula cell.
9. Press **Ctrl+C** to copy the formula(s).
   - Drag the *Fill* pointer if copies are adjacent to the original formula.
   - You can use the **Copy** button on the *Home* tab.
10. Click the destination cell or range.
11. Press **Ctrl+V** to paste the formula.
    - The pasted formula keeps the absolute part of the reference but updates the relative part.
    - Use the **Paste** button on the *Home* tab if you prefer.

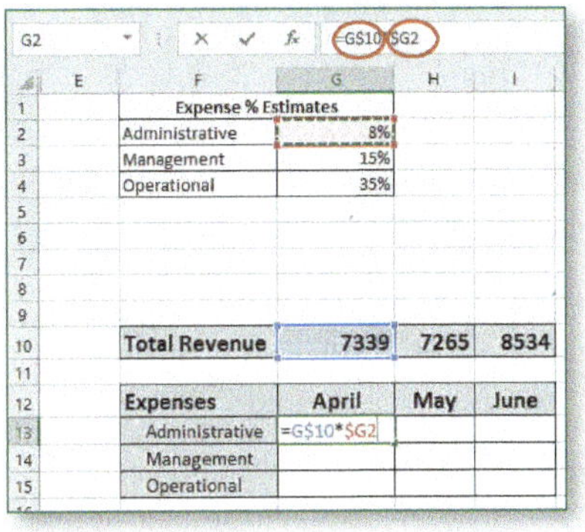

2-9 Formula with a mixed reference

Create a Formula with a 3D Reference

An important feature of an Excel workbook is that you can refer to data on any sheet in a formula. This type of formula is called a ***3D reference***, because it uses more than one sheet or surface to calculate a result.

A 3D reference includes the name of the worksheet and can be absolute, mixed, or relative.

Sample 3D References

Cell on Sheet1	Formula on Sheet1	Results
B4	=B3+Sheet2!B3+Sheet3!B3	Adds the values in cell B3 on Sheet1, Sheet2, and Sheet3
B7	=SUM(B4:B6)+Sheet2!A12	Adds the values in cells B4:B6 on Sheet1 to the value in cell A12 on Sheet2
C8	=C7*Sheet2!$D$4	Multiplies the value in cell C7 by the value in cell D4 on Sheet2
D10	=Sheet2!$B$2/Sheet3!B2	Divides the value in cell B2 on Sheet2 by the value in cell B2 on Sheet3

MORE INFO

An external reference formula refers to a cell in another workbook. It can be absolute, mixed, or relative. An external reference includes the name of the workbook in square brackets as in **[PLRSales]Sheet!B$2.**

HOW TO: Create a Formula with a 3D Reference

1. Click the cell for the formula.
2. Type =.
3. Select the sheet tab with the cell to be used in the formula.
4. Click the required cell.
   - Press **F4 (FN+F4)** to make the reference absolute or mixed as needed.
5. Type the operator (Figure 2-10).
6. Click the next cell for the formula.
   - The next cell can be on the same or another sheet.
7. Type the next operator and complete the formula as needed.
8. Press **Enter** or any completion key.

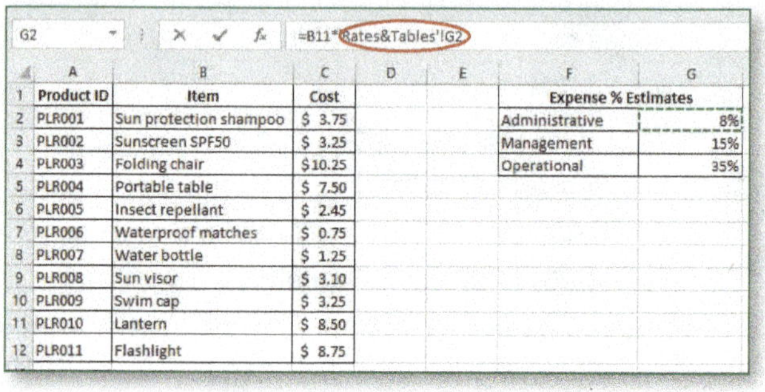

2-10 3D cell reference

Range Names and Formula AutoComplete

A ***range name*** is a label assigned to a single cell or a group of cells. You can use range names instead of cell references in a formula. Instead of **=B11*10%**, you can name cell B11 as "Revenue" to build the formula **=Revenue*10%**. Descriptive range names help you interpret a formula. In addition, named cell ranges appear in the *Formula AutoComplete* list for ease in building formulas. A named cell range is an absolute reference in a formula.

You create a range name from the *Name* box or from the *Defined Names* group on the *Formulas* tab. The *Name Manager* command in this group enables you to create, edit, and delete range names. If you alter a range name, Excel automatically updates formulas that use that range name. There is also a command that enables you to name a range and apply it to existing formulas that refer to those cells.

Follow these basic rules for naming a cell range:

- Begin a range name with a letter.
- Use a short, descriptive name.
- Do not use spaces or special characters in a range name.
- Separate words in a range name with an underscore as in "First_Qtr," or use initial caps for each word such as "FirstQtr."
- Do not name a range with a single character such as "N."
- Do not name a range with a cell reference such as "B2."

To use the name in a formula, type the first character of the name when it is required to display the *Formula AutoComplete* list. You may need to type a second character to see the name in a workbook that has many range names. Select the range name in the list and press **Tab**, or double-click the name to enter it in the formula. Range names are automatically substituted in formulas when you select the named cell range in the worksheet while building a formula.

HOW TO: Name a Range and Use Formula AutoComplete

1. Select the cell or range to be named.
2. Click the **Name** box at the left of the *Formula* bar.
3. Type the name and press **Enter** (Figure 2-11).
4. Click the cell for the formula.
5. Type = to start the formula
6. Type the first one or two letters of the range name.
   - The *Formula AutoComplete* list shows range and function names.
   - The list is alphabetical, and function names are uppercase.
7. Find the range name and double-click it (Figure 2-12).
   - The name is inserted in the formula.
   - You can also click the name in the list to highlight it and press **Tab**.
8. Complete the formula.
9. Press **Enter** when the formula is complete.

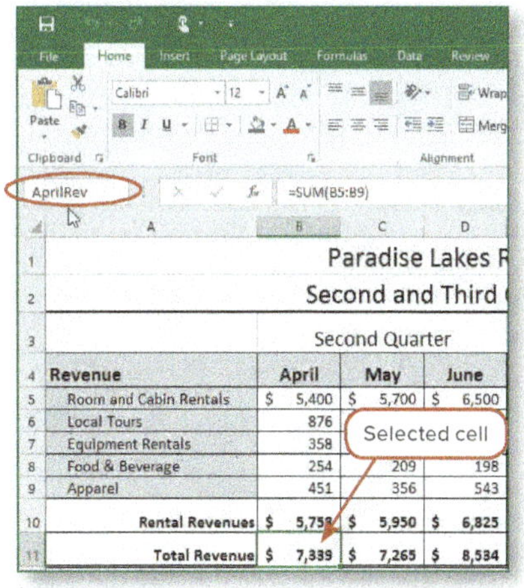

2-11 Name a range in the *Name* box

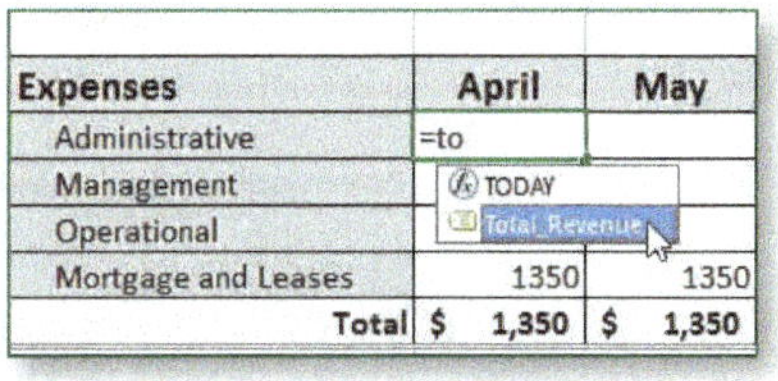

2-12 Use *Formula AutoComplete* with a range name

In addition to selecting cell ranges to name them, you can use row and column labels to create range names. The *Create from Selection* button on the *Formulas* tab automatically assigns range names based on labels in the top row, the left column, or both.

▸HOW TO: Create Names from a Selection

1. Select the range including row or column labels (or both) (Figure 2-13).
   - Values and related labels must be adjacent.
2. Click the **Create from Selection** button [*Formulas* tab, *Defined Names* group].
   - The *Create Names from Selection* dialog box opens.
3. Select the **Top row** or **Left column** box.
   - You can choose both options if appropriate for the data.
   - There are options for the bottom row and right column.
4. Click **OK**.
5. Click the **Name box** arrow on the *Formula* bar.
   - All range names are listed.

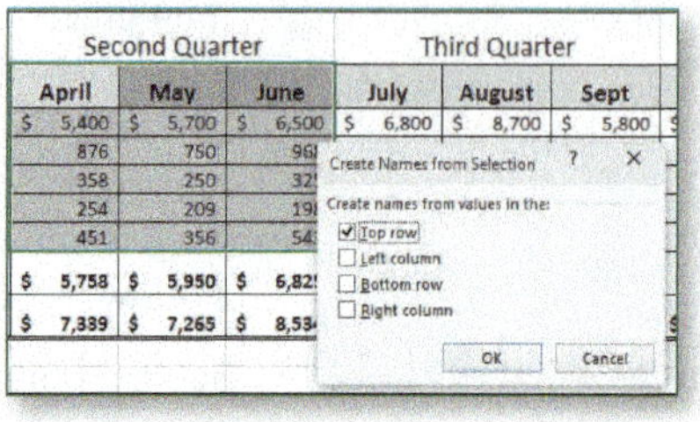

2-13 *Create Names from Selection* dialog box

The **Define Name** button [*Formulas* tab, *Defined Names* group] opens the *New Name* dialog box. Here you can type the name, enter a comment, select the cells, and specify a ***scope***. The scope determines if the range applies to a particular sheet or to the entire workbook. By default, a range name applies to the workbook. If you use the name "JanSales" on Sheet1, you cannot use it again on Sheet2, unless you scope each name to a particular sheet. When you scope names to a worksheet, you can use the name multiple times in the workbook.

▸HOW TO: Define and Scope a Range Name

1. Select the cell range to be named.
2. Click the **Define Name** button [*Formulas* tab, *Defined Names* group].
   - The *New Name* dialog box opens.
3. Type the range name in the *Name* box.
4. Click the **Scope** drop-down list (Figure 2-14).
   - Choose the name of a worksheet as desired.
5. Select or edit the *Refers to* entry.
   - The selected cell range address displays.
   - If no cells are selected, you can type or select the range address.
6. Click **OK**.

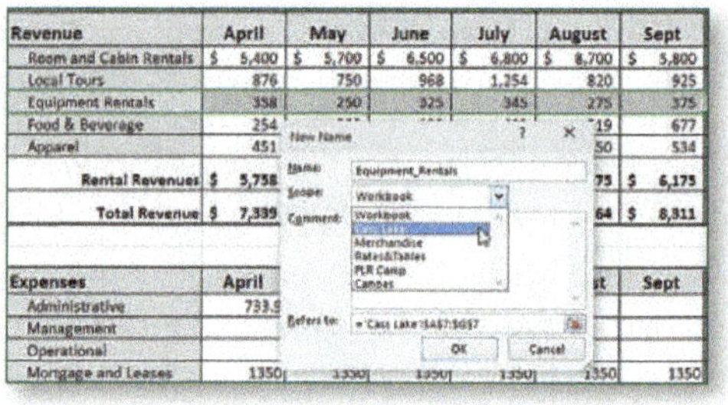

2-14 *New Name* dialog box

The *Use in Formula* button [*Formulas* tab, *Defined Names* group] displays a list of range names for insertion in a formula. You can do the same from the *Paste Name* dialog box, opened when you press the **F3 (FN+F3)** function key.

▸HOW TO: Paste a Range Name in a Formula and Paste a List

1. Click the formula cell and type =.
2. Press **F3 (FN+F3)** to open the *Paste Name* dialog box.
   - Range names are listed in alphabetical order.

3. Find the range name and double-click it (Figure 2-15).
    - You can also highlight the range name and press **Enter** or click **OK**.
    - The range name displays in the formula.
    - The worksheet displays the highlighted range.
4. Complete the formula and press **Enter**.
5. Click a blank cell in an unused area of the worksheet.
    - You can select a cell on another worksheet.
6. Click the **Use in Formula** button [*Formulas* tab, *Defined Names* group].
7. Select **Paste Names**.
    - The *Paste Name* dialog box opens.
8. Click **Paste List**.
    - A list of range names and cell references is pasted.
    - You can edit and format these cells.

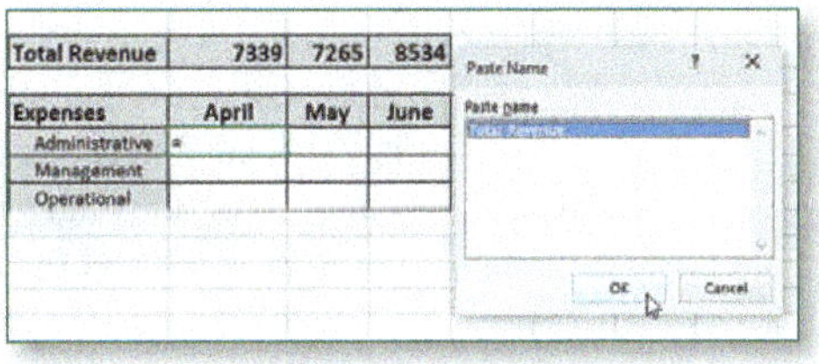

2-15 Choose a range name for the formula

SLO 2.4

Using Formula Auditing Tools

Formula auditing is the process of reviewing formulas for accuracy. Excel automatically audits formulas as you enter them and when you open a workbook based on its error checking rules [*File* tab, *Options*, *Formulas* pane]. Excel recognizes many errors, but not all of them. For example, if you type a formula that multiplies the values in two cells when it should add the values, you must find that error on your own. There are also circumstances when Excel identifies an error, but the formula is correct.

> **MORE INFO**
>
> You can set whether automatic error checking is enabled and you can select which rules are used in the *Excel Options* dialog box.

When Excel finds an error in a formula, it displays a small green error triangle in the top left corner of the cell. Click the cell to see the *Trace Error* button and point to the button to see a *ScreenTip* about the error. The *Trace Error* button has a drop-down list with options for dealing with the error.

HOW TO: Trace an Error

1. Click the cell with the triangle error.
    - The *Trace Error* button appears.
2. Point to the **Trace Error** button to display a *ScreenTip*.
3. Click the **Trace Error** drop-down list (Figure 2-16).
    - Options for handling the error are listed.
4. Choose an option for the error.
    - The options depend on the type of error.
    - Select **Ignore Error** if the formula is correct.

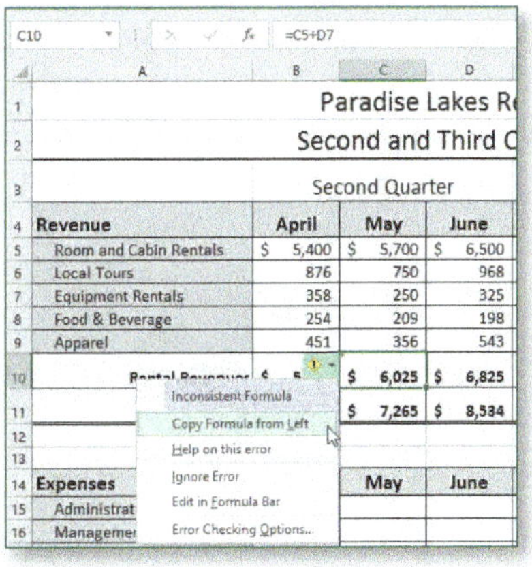

2-16 *Trace Error* button and its drop-down list

In addition to the green triangle error, Excel functions can result in a standard error message in the cell. For example, if you create a division formula that divides by a blank cell, the result is *#DIV/0!* When you click the **Trace Error** button, it is identified as a division by zero error. Excel error messages occur for a syntax error, such as spelling a function name incorrectly, using an incorrect operator or symbol, having the wrong number of arguments, and so on. A standard error message starts with the number sign (#) and ends with an exclamation point (!).

MORE INFO

From the *Go to Special* dialog box [**Find & Select** button, *Home* tab, *Editing* group], you can highlight cells with formula errors, blank cells, and cells with precedents and dependents. This command helps identify potential problems in a workbook.

The Formula Auditing Group

The *Formula Auditing* group on the *Formulas* tab has tools to check formulas for logic, consistency, and accuracy. These commands enable you to examine what contributes to a formula and analyze if the formula is correct. The tools are helpful but they do require that you correct the problem.

Button	Description
Trace Precedents	Displays lines with arrows to identify all cells referenced in the formula in the active cell
Trace Dependents	Displays lines with arrows to all cells that use the active cell directly or indirectly in a formula
Remove Arrows	Removes all lines and arrows from the *Trace Precedents* or *Trace Dependents* buttons
Show Formulas	Displays formulas in the cells
Error Checking	Checks data against the error rules in Excel Options
Evaluate Formula	Steps through each part of a formula and displays an outcome for each part so that an error can be isolated
Watch Window	Opens a floating window that displays selected cells and values for monitoring

Trace Precedents and Dependents

A ***precedent*** is a cell that contributes to the formula results. Excel displays lines from the formula cell to each precedent cell for an easy way to audit your formula. A ***dependent*** is a cell that is affected by the active cell. Excel displays lines from the active cell to each cell that depends on the value in that cell. When the lines and arrows are blue, the precedents or dependents do not have an error. If the lines and arrows are red, the precedents or dependents have some type of recognized error. If a precedent or dependent cell is located on a different worksheet, a black line and arrow point to a small worksheet icon, but this does not identify the actual error cell address.

HOW TO: Use Formula Auditing Tools

1. Click the **Show Formulas** button [*Formulas* tab, *Formula Auditing* group].
    - Each formula displays in its cell.
    - Show or hide formulas by pressing **Ctrl+~**.
2. Select the formula cell.

3. Click the **Trace Precedents** button [*Formulas* tab, *Formula Auditing* group].
   - Lines and arrows identify cells that contribute to the formula results (Figure 2-17).
   - You can trace precedents and dependents with formulas shown or hidden.
4. Click the **Remove Arrows** button [*Formulas* tab, *Formula Auditing* group].
   - Clicking the button removes all arrows.
   - Click the **Remove Arrows** drop-down list to specify the type of arrow to remove.
5. Click a cell that is referenced in a formula.
   - The cell need not have a formula.

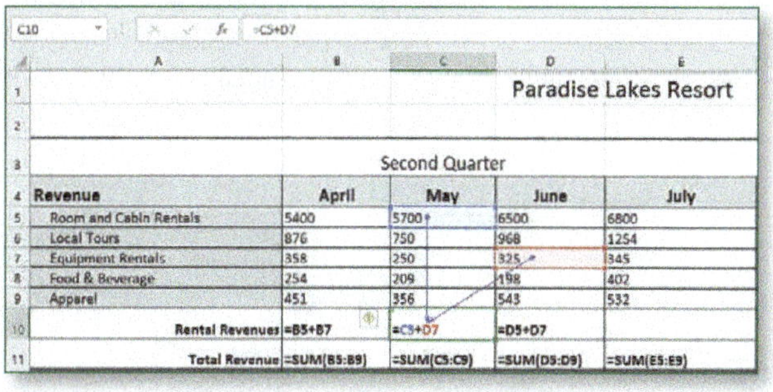

2-17 *Trace Precedents* arrows with formulas shown

6. Click the **Trace Dependents** button [*Formulas* tab, *Formula Auditing* group].
   - Lines and arrows trace to cells that are affected by the active cell.
7. Click the **Remove Arrows** button [*Formulas* tab, *Formula Auditing* group].
8. Click the **Show Formulas** button [*Formulas* tab, *Formula Auditing* group].
   - Formulas are hidden.
   - Show or hide formulas by pressing **Ctrl+~**.

MORE INFO

In a complex worksheet with sophisticated formulas, click the **Trace Precedents** button [*Formulas* tab, *Formula Auditing* group] once to trace the first layer of precedents. Then click the button again to trace the precedents of the precedents.

The Formula Correction Message Window

As you complete a formula with a minor error (e.g. typing "5c" as a cell address), Excel displays a message box with information about the error (Figure 2-18). For many of these types of errors, review the suggested correction and select **Yes**. For an error that Excel finds but cannot offer a solution, a message box opens with suggestions but you need to solve the problem on your own.

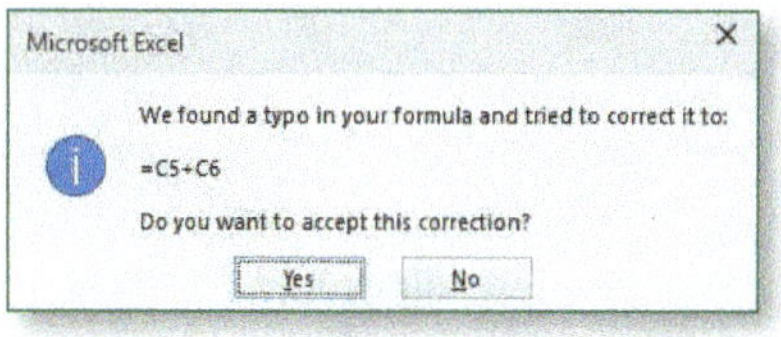

2-18 Formula correction message window

Circular Reference

A ***circular reference*** is an error that occurs when a formula includes the cell address of the formula. For example, if the formula in cell **B10** is **=B5+B10**, the reference is circular. When you try to complete such a formula, a message box opens as shown in Figure 2-19. The *Status* bar displays the location of circular references, but Excel does not correct this type of error. You can keep a circular reference in a worksheet, but the formula results are inaccurate.

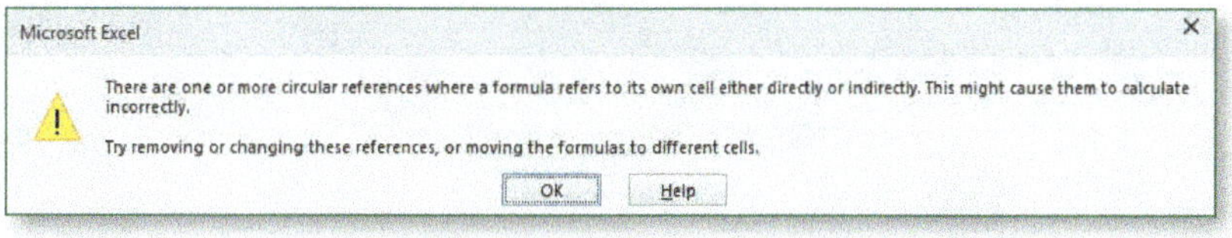

2-19 Circular reference and its message window

MORE INFO

A workbook can be saved with a circular reference. When you open it, you will see the message box, and the reference is noted in the *Status* bar.

PAUSE & PRACTICE: EXCEL 2-1

For this project, you build formulas in a Paradise Lakes Resort worksheet. You use mixed and absolute references, a 3D reference, and set order of precedence. You also name cell ranges and use auditing tools.

File Needed: ***ParadiseLakes-02.xlsx*** *[Student data files are available in the* Library *of your SIMnet account.]*
Completed Project File Name: ***[your initials] PP E2-1.xlsx***

1. Open the ***ParadiseLakes-02.xlsx*** workbook from your student data files.
2. Save the workbook as [your initials] PP E2-1. (If the workbook opens in *Protected View*, click **Enable Editing**.)
3. Enter and copy an addition formula.
   a. Click cell **B10** on the **Cass Lake** sheet.
   b. Type = to start a formula.
   c. Click cell **B5** to insert the first rental item in the formula.
   d. Type + as the mathematical operator.
   e. Click cell **B7** to add the second rental item. The formula is **=B5+B7** (Figure 2-20).
   f. Press **Enter** or click the **Enter** button on the *Formula* bar. The result is $5,758.
   g. Select cell **B10** and point to the *Fill* handle.
   h. Drag the *Fill* pointer to copy the formula to cells **C10:H10**. Ignore the *Auto Fill Options* button.

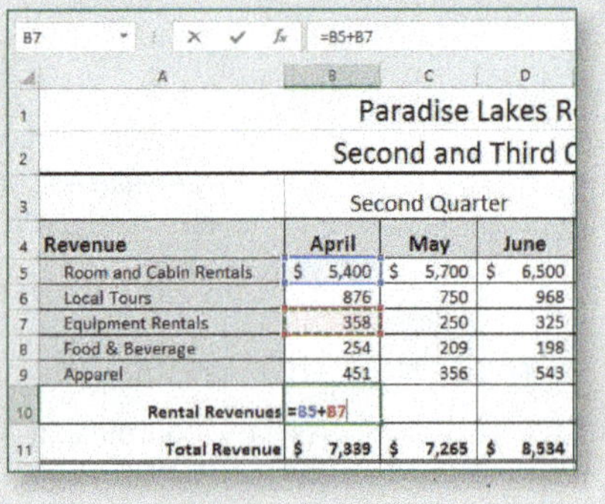

2-20 Point and click to build a formula

4. Create and copy a 3D formula with absolute cell references.
   a. Select cell **B15**. Administrative expense is calculated by multiplying the total revenue for the month by a set percentage.
   b. Type = to start the formula.
   c. Click cell **B11**, the total revenue for April.
   d. Type * to indicate multiplication.
   e. Click the **Rates&Tables** sheet tab. The sheet name is inserted in the *Formula* bar with single quotes and an exclamation point.
   f. Click cell **G2**, the percentage for administrative expenses. The cell address is added to the formula.
   g. Press **F4 (FN+F4)** to make the reference absolute (Figure 2-21).
   h. Press **Enter**. The formula is complete and the *Cass Lake* sheet is active.
   i. Select cell **B15** and drag the *Fill* pointer to copy the formula to cells **C15:G15**. The reference to cell G2 does not change, but the reference to cell B11 does (Figure 2-22).

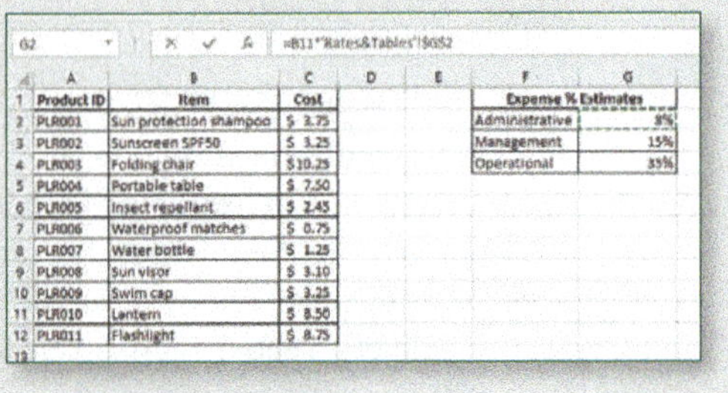

2-21 Absolute 3D reference in the formula

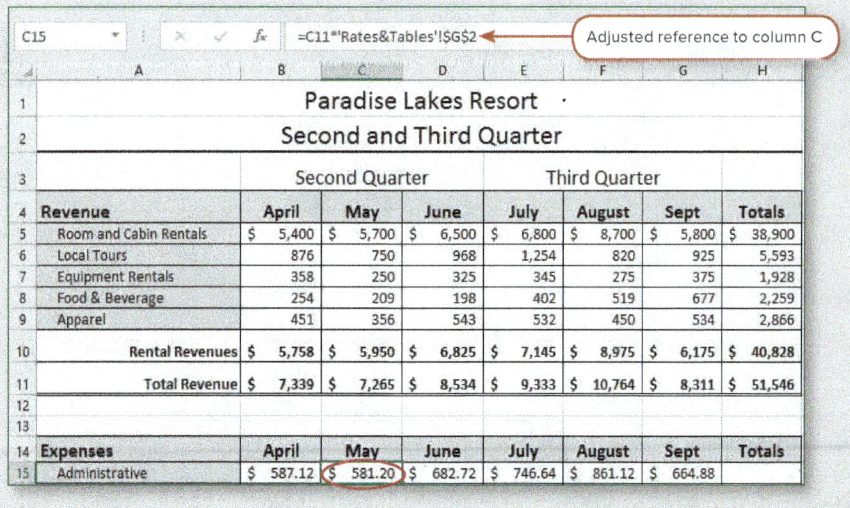

	A	B	C	D	E	F	G	H
1	Paradise Lakes Resort							
2	Second and Third Quarter							
3		Second Quarter			Third Quarter			
4	Revenue	April	May	June	July	August	Sept	Totals
5	Room and Cabin Rentals	$ 5,400	$ 5,700	$ 6,500	$ 6,800	$ 8,700	$ 5,800	$ 38,900
6	Local Tours	876	750	968	1,254	820	925	5,593
7	Equipment Rentals	358	250	325	345	275	375	1,928
8	Food & Beverage	254	209	198	402	519	677	2,259
9	Apparel	451	356	543	532	450	534	2,866
10	Rental Revenues	$ 5,758	$ 5,950	$ 6,825	$ 7,145	$ 8,975	$ 6,175	$ 40,828
11	Total Revenue	$ 7,339	$ 7,265	$ 8,534	$ 9,333	$ 10,764	$ 8,311	$ 51,546
12								
13								
14	Expenses	April	May	June	July	August	Sept	Totals
15	Administrative	$ 587.12	$ 581.20	$ 682.72	$ 746.64	$ 861.12	$ 664.88	

2-22 Copied formula with absolute reference

5. Create and copy a 3D formula with mixed references.
   a. Select cell **B16**. Management expense is calculated by multiplying the total revenue for the month by the set percentage.
   b. Type = to start the formula.
   c. Click cell **B11**, the total revenue for April.
   d. Press **F4 (FN+F4)** to make the reference absolute ($B$11).
   e. Press **F4 (FN+F4)** to make the reference mixed with the row reference absolute (B$11). When the formula is copied, the row will not change but the column reference will (Figure 2-23).
   f. Type * for multiplication.
   g. Click the **Rates&Tables** sheet tab. The sheet name is inserted in the *Formula* bar.
   h. Click cell **G3**, the percentage for management expenses.
   i. Press **F4 (FN+F4)** to make the reference absolute ($G$3).
   j. Press **F4 (FN+F4)** to make the reference mixed with the row reference absolute (G$3).
   k. Press **F4 (FN+F4)** to make the reference mixed with the column reference absolute ($G3) (Figure 2-24). When the formula is copied, the column will not change but the row will.

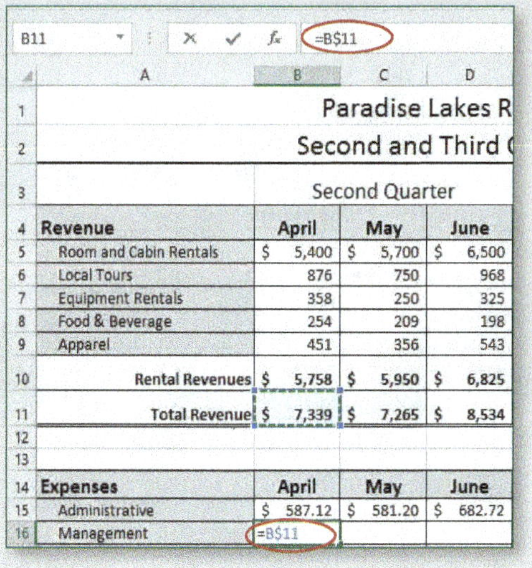

	A	B	C	D
1	Paradise Lakes R			
2	Second and Third (			
3		Second Quarter		
4	Revenue	April	May	June
5	Room and Cabin Rentals	$ 5,400	$ 5,700	$ 6,500
6	Local Tours	876	750	968
7	Equipment Rentals	358	250	325
8	Food & Beverage	254	209	198
9	Apparel	451	356	543
10	Rental Revenues	$ 5,758	$ 5,950	$ 6,825
11	Total Revenue	$ 7,339	$ 7,265	$ 8,534
12				
13				
14	Expenses	April	May	June
15	Administrative	$ 587.12	$ 581.20	$ 682.72
16	Management	=B$11		

2-23 Mixed cell reference

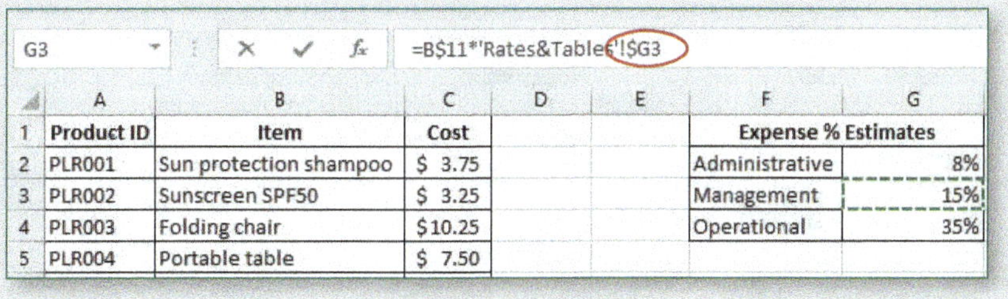

	A	B	C	D	E	F	G
1	Product ID	Item	Cost			Expense % Estimates	
2	PLR001	Sun protection shampoo	$ 3.75			Administrative	8%
3	PLR002	Sunscreen SPF50	$ 3.25			Management	15%
4	PLR003	Folding chair	$10.25			Operational	35%
5	PLR004	Portable table	$ 7.50				

2-24 Absolute reference to column G

l. Press **Enter**. The formula is complete and the *Cass Lake* sheet is active.
m. Select cell **B16** and drag its *Fill* pointer to cell **B17**.
n. Keep cells **B16:B17** selected and drag the *Fill* pointer for cell B17 to copy the formulas to cells **C16:G17**.

6. Use *Formula Auditing* tools.
   a. Click cell **D17** to view how the mixed reference formula has been copied.
   b. Click the **Trace Precedents** button [*Formulas* tab, *Formula Auditing* group]. The formula refers to cell D11 on the **Cass Lake** sheet and to the **Tables&Rates** sheet.
   c. Click cell **E16** and click the **Trace Precedents** button. The formula refers to cell E11 on the **Cass Lake** sheet and to the **Tables&Rates** sheet (Figure 2-25).
   d. Click the **Remove Arrows** button [*Formulas* tab, *Formula Auditing* group].
   e. Click the **Show Formulas** [*Formulas* tab, *Formula Auditing* group] to see all formulas. This view does not display number formatting (Figure 2-26).

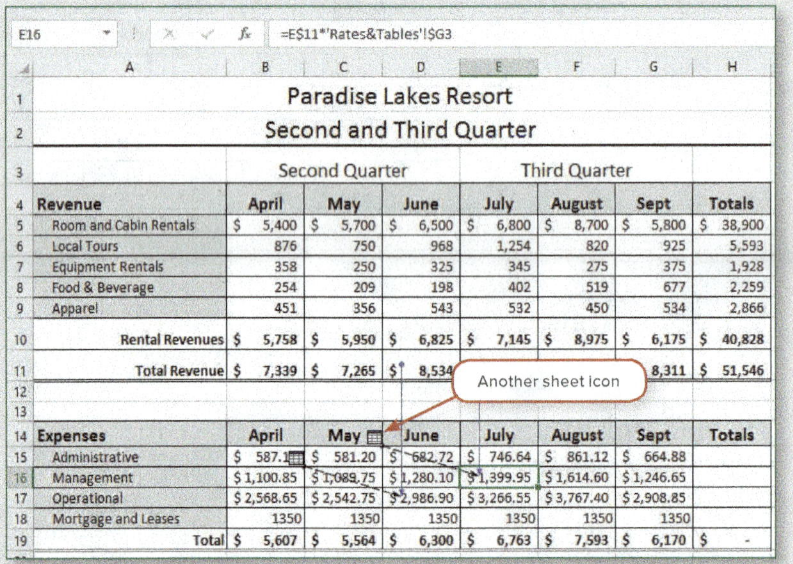

2-25 Formula precedents

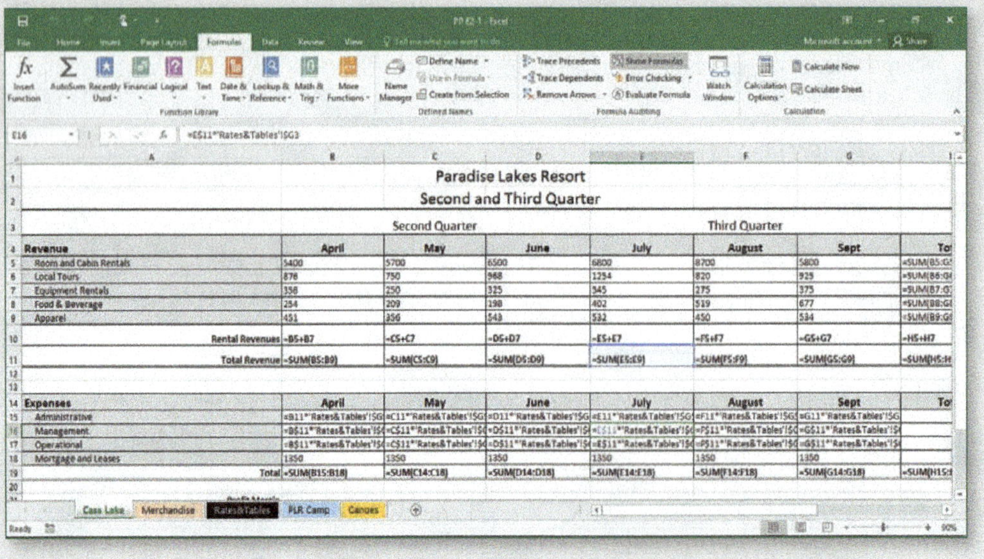

2-26 Formulas displayed in worksheet

   f. Click the **Show Formulas** [*Formulas* tab, *Formula Auditing* group] to hide the formulas.

7. Edit a formula and correct an error.
   a. Select cells **H15:H18** and click the **AutoSum** button [*Home* tab, *Editing* group]. The *SUM* function displays in each cell.
   b. Widen column **H** to display all data.
   c. Double-click cell **H16** to start *Edit* mode.
   d. Edit the cell range to **B15:G16** and press **Enter** to create a deliberate error. The green error triangle appears in the upper right corner of the cell.
   e. Click cell **H16** to display the **Trace Error** button and then click the button. This formula is now inconsistent with others in the column (Figure 2-27).

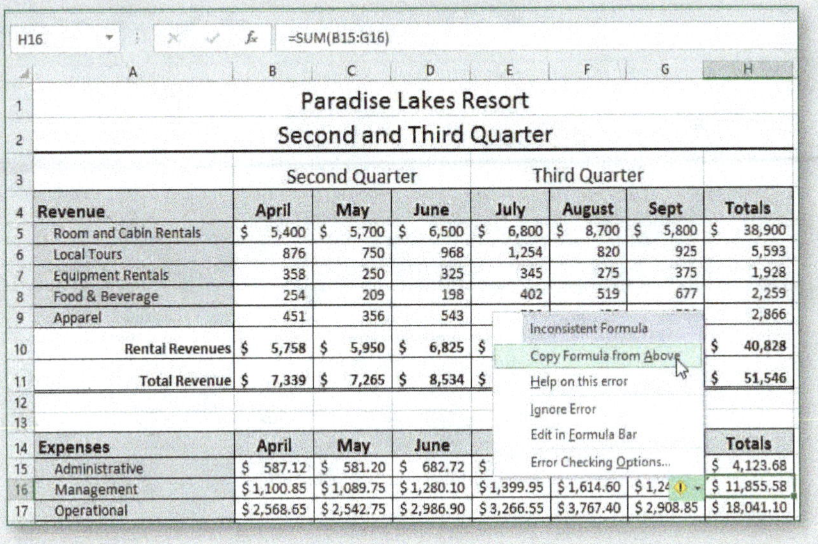

2-27 *Trace Error* button and options

   f. Select **Copy Formula from Above** to correct the error.
   g. Click cell **H16** and click the **Trace Precedents** button [*Formulas* tab, *Formula Auditing* group]. The formula refers to the correct cells in row 16.
   h. Click the **Remove Arrows** button [*Formulas* tab, *Formula Auditing* group].

8. Set mathematical order of operations.
   a. Select cell **B21**. Profit margin, as a percentage, is revenue minus expenses divided by revenue. The formula is **=(B11–B19)/B11**; the parentheses are necessary so that the subtraction is done before the division.
   b. Type =(to start the formula and insert the opening parenthesis.
   c. Click cell **B11**, the total revenue for April.
   d. Type – for subtraction.
   e. Click cell **B19**, total expenses for April.
   f. Type) to set the precedence with the closing parenthesis.
   g. Type / for division and click cell **B11** (Figure 2-28).
   h. Press **Enter**. The result is formatted as *Accounting Number* format to match the source cells and displays a zero due to rounding.

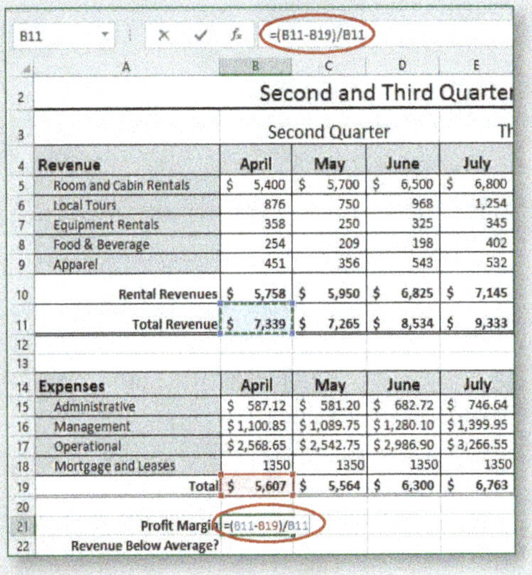

2-28 Set arithmetic order

i. Click cell **B21** and click the **Percent Style** button [*Home* tab, *Number* group].
j. Copy the formula in cell **B21** to cells **C21:G21**.

9. Name a cell range.
   a. Select cell **H11** and click the **Name** box.
   b. Type TotalRevenue in the *Name* box and press **Enter**.
   c. Select cells **B11:G11**.
   d. Click the **Define Name** button [*Formulas* tab, *Defined Names* group].
   e. Type Monthly_Rev in the *Name* box and click **OK** (Figure 2-29).
   f. Click cell **A1**.
   g. Click the **Name box** arrow and choose **TotalRevenue**. Cell H11 is selected.
   h. Click the **Name box** arrow and choose **Monthly_Rev**. Cells B11:G11 are selected.
10. Format cells **B16:H18** as **Comma Style**. Decrease the decimal two times.
11. Select cells **B15:H15** and decrease the decimal two times.
12. Press **Ctrl+Home**. Save and close the workbook (Figure 2-30).

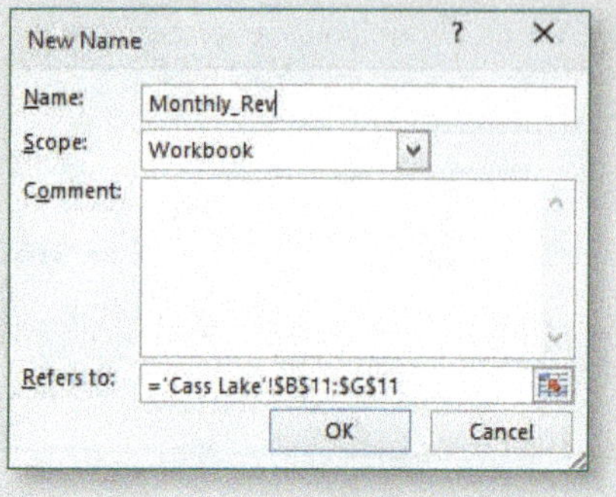

2-29 Use the *New Name* dialog box to name a range

	Paradise Lakes Resort						
	Second and Third Quarter						
	Second Quarter			Third Quarter			
Revenue	**April**	**May**	**June**	**July**	**August**	**Sept**	**Totals**
Room and Cabin Rentals	$ 5,400	$ 5,700	$ 6,500	$ 6,800	$ 8,700	$ 5,800	$ 38,900
Local Tours	876	750	968	1,254	820	925	5,593
Equipment Rentals	358	250	325	345	275	375	1,928
Food & Beverage	254	209	198	402	519	677	2,259
Apparel	451	356	543	532	450	534	2,866
Rental Revenues	$ 5,758	$ 5,950	$ 6,825	$ 7,145	$ 8,975	$ 6,175	$ 40,828
Total Revenue	$ 7,339	$ 7,265	$ 8,534	$ 9,333	$ 10,764	$ 8,311	$ 51,546
Expenses	**April**	**May**	**June**	**July**	**August**	**Sept**	**Totals**
Administrative	$ 587	$ 581	$ 683	$ 747	$ 861	$ 665	$ 4,124
Management	1,101	1,090	1,280	1,400	1,615	1,247	$ 7,732
Operational	2,569	2,543	2,987	3,267	3,767	2,909	$ 18,041
Mortgage and Leases	1350	1350	1350	1350	1350	1350	$ 8,100
Total	$ 5,607	$ 5,564	$ 6,300	$ 6,763	$ 7,593	$ 6,170	$ 37,997
Profit Margin	24%	23%	26%	28%	29%	26%	
Revenue Below Average?							

2-30 PP E2-1 completed

SLO 2.5

Working with Statistical and Date & Time Functions

A function is a built-in formula. Like a formula, a function starts with an equals sign (=) followed by the name of the function. Each function has its own syntax, its set of rules for correct execution. The syntax includes arguments, which are cell references and other elements necessary for the function to work properly.

> **MORE INFO**
>
> A formula such as **=B2+B3−B6** is usually not called a function since it has no function name.

Excel functions are grouped into categories on the *Formulas* command tab in the *Function Library* group. This group also has an *Insert Function* button which opens the *Insert Function* dialog box. From this dialog box, you can display an alphabetical list of all functions, a list by category, or a recently used list. You can also search for a function by name in this dialog box.

The *Statistical* function category includes calculations that determine an average, a maximum, a minimum, and a count. These common functions are options on the *AutoSum* button on the *Home* tab. The *Formulas* tab also has an *AutoSum* button with the same options.

AVERAGE Function

The *AVERAGE* function calculates the arithmetic ***mean*** of a range of cells. The mean is determined by adding all the values and dividing the result by the number of values. The *AVERAGE* function ignores empty cells or cells that include labels. When calculating an average, do not include total values in the range to be averaged.

The *AVERAGE* function has one argument, *numberN*. A number argument can be a range such as B11:G11. You can average up to 255 numbers (or ranges). The proper syntax for an *AVERAGE* function is:

=AVERAGE(number1, [number2], [number3], . . .)

The *Number1* argument is required and others are optional.

When you choose a function from the *AutoSum* button, you will see the function name, an assumed range within parentheses, and an ***Argument ScreenTip*** below the cell that displays the syntax. When you choose to type a function, the *ScreenTip* shows the next argument in bold type as a guideline.

▶ HOW TO: Use the AVERAGE Function

1. Click the cell for the function.
2. Click the **AutoSum** button arrow [*Formulas* tab, *Function Library* group].
3. Select **Average**.
   - The function and an assumed argument range display in the *Formula* bar and in the cell.
4. Select the correct cell range (Figure 2-31).
   - You can type cell addresses rather than selecting cells.
   - When the selected cells have been named, the range name is substituted in the formula.

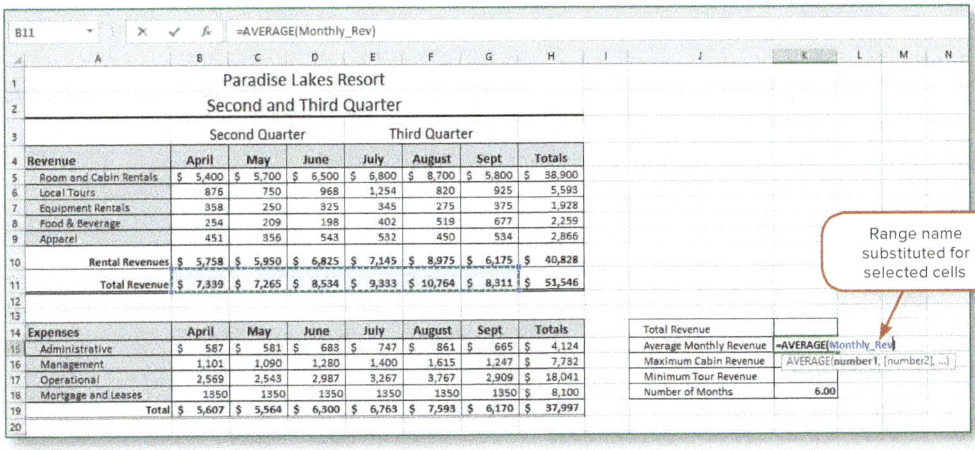

2-31 *AVERAGE* function

5. Press **Enter**.
   - You can use any completion key.

MORE INFO

The *MEDIAN* function in the *Statistical* category determines the precise middle value in the range.

COUNT Functions

There are five functions in the *Statistical* category that are *COUNT* functions which tally the number of items in a range. The basic *COUNT* function is an option on the *AutoSum* button, but it appears in the list as *Count Numbers*. The *COUNT* function includes only cells with values in its result.

From the *Statistical* group, you can choose *COUNTA* which includes cells with values and labels. There is a *COUNTBLANK* function that counts cells that are empty. The following table describes the *Statistical COUNT* functions.

MORE INFO

In the *Database* function category, there are *DCOUNT* and *DCOUNTA* functions. This category is available from the *Insert Function* dialog box.

Statistical COUNT Functions

Count Functions	Description	Example Syntax
COUNT (Count Numbers)	Counts the cells in a range that contain values	=COUNT(A1:A15)
COUNTA	Counts the cells in a range that contain any data type	=COUNTA(A1:A15)
COUNTBLANK	Counts empty cells in a range	=COUNTBLANK(A1:A15)
COUNTIF	Counts the cells in a range that meet the criteria argument	=COUNTIF(A1:A15, "Services")
COUNTIFS	Counts the cells in one or more criteria ranges that meet respective criteria arguments	=COUNTIFS(B2:B5, "=A", C2:C5, "=21")

The *COUNT* function has one argument, *valueN*. You can count up to 255 cells or ranges. The proper syntax for a *COUNT* function is:

=COUNT(value1, [value2], [value3], . . .)

The *Value1* argument is required.

HOW TO: Use the COUNT Function

1. Click the cell for the function.
2. Click the **AutoSum** button arrow [*Formulas* tab, *Function Library* group].
3. Select **Count Numbers**.
   - The *COUNT* function is inserted with an assumed range.
   - The function appears in the cell and in the *Formula* bar (Figure 2-32).

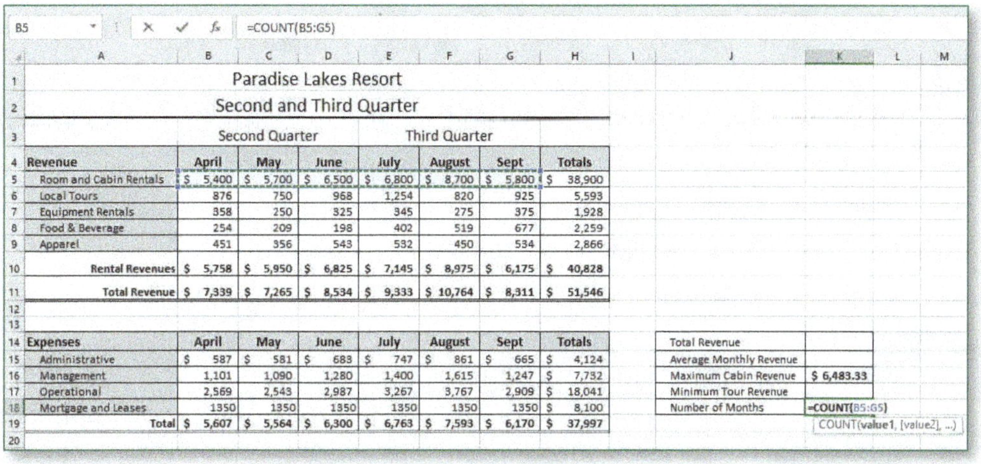

	Paradise Lakes Resort						
	Second and Third Quarter						
	Second Quarter			Third Quarter			
Revenue	April	May	June	July	August	Sept	Totals
Room and Cabin Rentals	$ 5,400	$ 5,700	$ 6,500	$ 6,800	$ 8,700	$ 5,800	$ 38,900
Local Tours	876	750	968	1,254	820	925	5,593
Equipment Rentals	358	250	325	345	275	375	1,928
Food & Beverage	254	209	198	402	519	677	2,259
Apparel	451	356	543	532	450	534	2,866
Rental Revenues	$ 5,758	$ 5,950	$ 6,825	$ 7,145	$ 8,975	$ 6,175	$ 40,828
Total Revenue	$ 7,339	$ 7,265	$ 8,534	$ 9,333	$ 10,764	$ 8,311	$ 51,546

Expenses	April	May	June	July	August	Sept	Totals
Administrative	$ 587	$ 581	$ 683	$ 747	$ 861	$ 665	$ 4,124
Management	1,101	1,090	1,280	1,400	1,615	1,247	$ 7,732
Operational	2,569	2,543	2,987	3,267	3,767	2,909	$ 18,041
Mortgage and Leases	1350	1350	1350	1350	1350	1350	$ 8,100
Total	$ 5,607	$ 5,564	$ 6,300	$ 6,763	$ 7,593	$ 6,170	$ 37,997

Total Revenue	
Average Monthly Revenue	
Maximum Cabin Revenue	$ 6,483.33
Minimum Tour Revenue	
Number of Months	=COUNT(B5:G5)

2-32 *COUNT* function

4. Select the correct cell range.
   - You can type cell addresses rather than selecting cells.
5. Press **Enter** or any completion key.

MORE INFO

If you use *COUNT* with a range of labels, the result is zero (0).

MAX and MIN Functions

The *MAX* function finds the largest value in a range, and the *MIN* function finds the smallest value. Both functions are options on the *AutoSum* button. Each has one argument, the cells to be evaluated.

The proper syntax for *MAX* and *MIN* functions is:

=MAX(number1, [number2], [number3], . . .)
=MIN(number1, [number2], [number3], . . .)

In many worksheets, an argument range is a group of adjacent cells such as B11:G11, but the cells need not be next to each other. You can select individual cells anywhere in the worksheet for an argument, and they are separated by commas as in =MAX(B11, B15, B18).

HOW TO: Use the MAX Function with Nonadjacent Cells

1. Click the cell for the function.
2. Click the **AutoSum** button arrow [*Formulas* tab, *Function Library* group].

3. Select **Max** (Figure 2-33).
   - The function displays in the cell and in the *Formula* bar.
   - The *Argument ScreenTip* shows the next argument in bold **number1**.

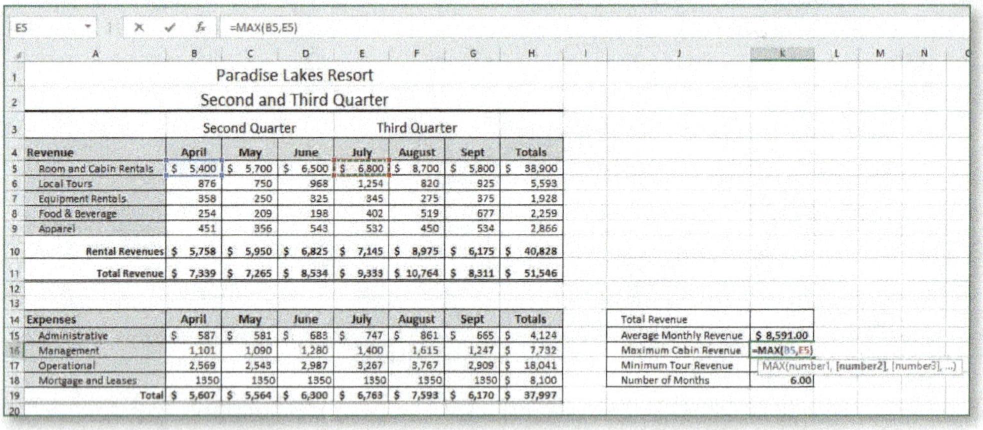

2-33 Use nonadjacent cells for *MAX*

4. Click the first cell to be evaluated.
5. Type , (a comma) to separate the arguments.
   - The *Argument ScreenTip* shows the next argument in bold **number2**.
6. Click the next cell to be evaluated.
7. Type a comma , to add additional cells to the argument.
8. Press **Enter** when all the cells are listed.

AutoCalculate

The ***AutoCalculate*** feature is located on the right side of the *Status* bar where statistical and mathematical results are displayed for selected cells. The calculations are *Average*, *Count*, *Numerical Count*, *Maximum*, *Minimum*, and *Sum*. The *Count* calculation is the equivalent of *COUNTA*, and *Numerical Count* is the same as *COUNT*. *AutoCalculate* allows you to see results without inserting a function in the worksheet. You can see and change which calculations are visible by right-clicking that area of the *Status* bar to open the *Customize Status Bar* menu.

HOW TO: Use AutoCalculate

1. Select the cell range or individual cells in the worksheet.
2. View the results on the *Status* bar (Figure 2-34).
   - Selected options appear on the *Status* bar when appropriate; there is no *SUM* when you select labels.
3. Right-click the right side of the *Status* bar.
   - The *Customize Status Bar* menu opens.
   - If a function has a check mark to the left, it is active.

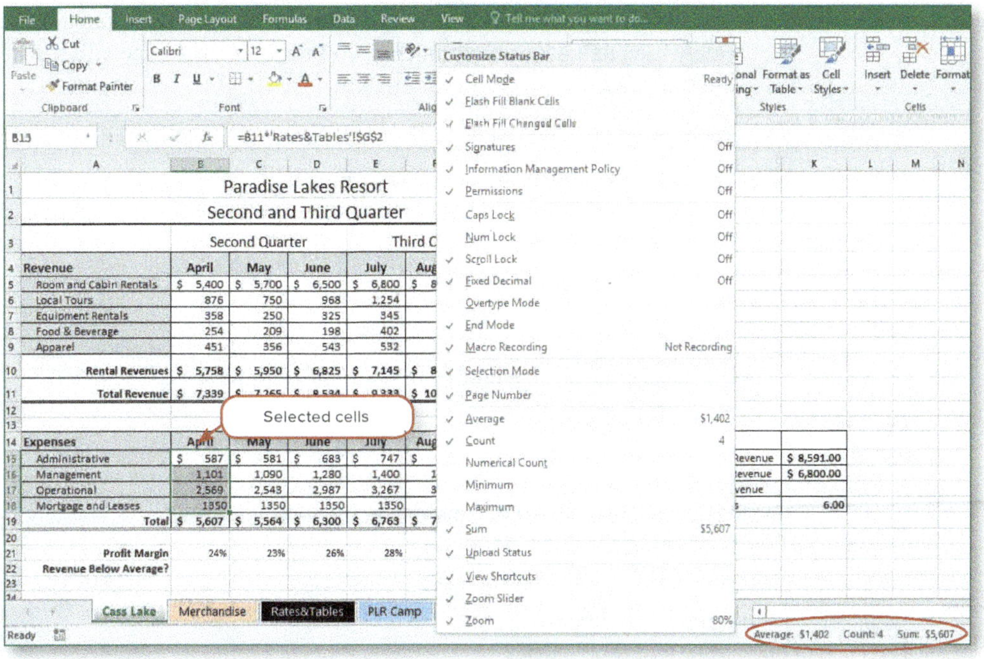

2-34 *AutoCalculate* results and other *Status* bar options

4. Select a calculation name to activate it and show it on the *Status* bar.
5. Select a calculation name with a check mark to hide it from the *Status* bar.

TODAY and NOW Functions

The *Date & Time* category has many functions for date and time arithmetic, for converting dates and times to values, and for controlling how dates and times are displayed.

The *TODAY* function inserts the current date in the cell and updates each time the workbook is opened. It uses the computer's clock, and the syntax is =TODAY(). The parentheses are necessary, but there are no arguments. The *NOW* function uses the syntax =NOW() and has no arguments. These two functions are ***volatile*** which means that the result depends on the current date, time, and computer.

After either function is inserted, you can format results to show both the date and the time. The *Format Cells* dialog box has a *Date* category and a *Time* category with many preset styles. There are also two date formats available from the *Number Format* list [*Home* tab, *Number* group], *Short Date* and *Long Date*.

In its handling of dates, Excel treats each date as a ***serial number***, a unique value assigned to each date. Excel starts by setting January 1, 1900, as number 1; January 2, 1900 is number 2, and so on. January 1, 2018, is number 43101. You can see the serial number for any date by applying the *General* format to the cell.

MORE INFO

On the *Advanced* pane in the *Excel Options* dialog box [*File* tab], you can set a 1904 date system which matches the date system in the Macintosh operating system.

You can select **TODAY** or **NOW** from the *Date & Time* function category. Since they are widely used and have no arguments, you may prefer to type either with the help of *Formula AutoComplete*.

HOW TO: Insert TODAY with Formula AutoComplete

1. Click the cell.
2. Type =to to display a filtered *Formula AutoComplete* list (Figure 2-35).
   - The list appears as soon as you type a character.
   - Each additional character further limits the list of names.

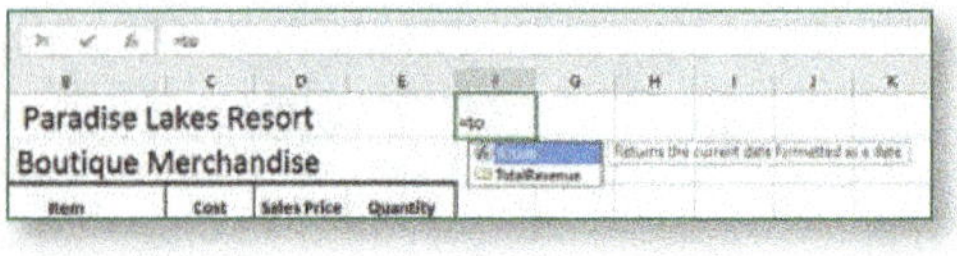

2-35 *Formula AutoComplete* list

3. Point to the function name and double-click.
   - Instead of double-clicking the name, point and click once to select it and press **Tab**.
   - The name and parentheses are inserted.
   - If you accidentally press **Enter** to select a name and see an error in the cell, delete the cell contents and try again.
4. Press **Enter** to complete the function (Figure 2-36).
   - Excel supplies the closing parenthesis.
   - The current date is shown in the cell.
   - The *TODAY* function has no arguments.

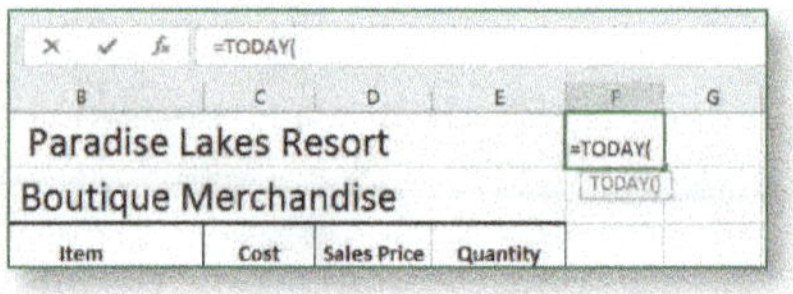

2-36 TODAY inserted in cell

PAUSE & PRACTICE: EXCEL 2-2

For this project, you open your Pause & Practice file and insert Excel functions to complete more of the worksheet. You insert functions from the *AutoSum* button and by typing. You also use *AutoCalculate* to check results.

File Needed: ***[your initials] PP E2-1.xlsx***
Completed Project File Name: ***[your initials] PP E2-2.xlsx***

1. Open the ***[your initials] PP E2-1.xlsx*** workbook completed in *Pause & Practice 2-1* and save it as [your initials] PP E2-2.
2. Enter functions using the *AutoSum* button.
   a. Click the **Cass Lake** worksheet tab and select cell **K14**.
   b. Click the **AutoSum** arrow button [*Formulas* tab, *Function Library* group].
   c. Choose **Sum**. The function name and parentheses are inserted, and a *Function ScreenTip* is visible.
   d. Select cells **B11:G11**. The range is highlighted on screen, and Excel has substituted the defined name that you set in *Pause & Practice 2-1* (Figure 2-37).
   e. Press **Enter**.
   f. Select cell **K15** and click the **AutoSum** arrow button [*Formulas* tab, *Function Library* group].
   g. Choose **Average**. The name and parentheses are inserted.
   h. Select cells **B11:G11**. The range is highlighted, but the range name is substituted.
   i. Press **Enter**. Average sales are $8,591.

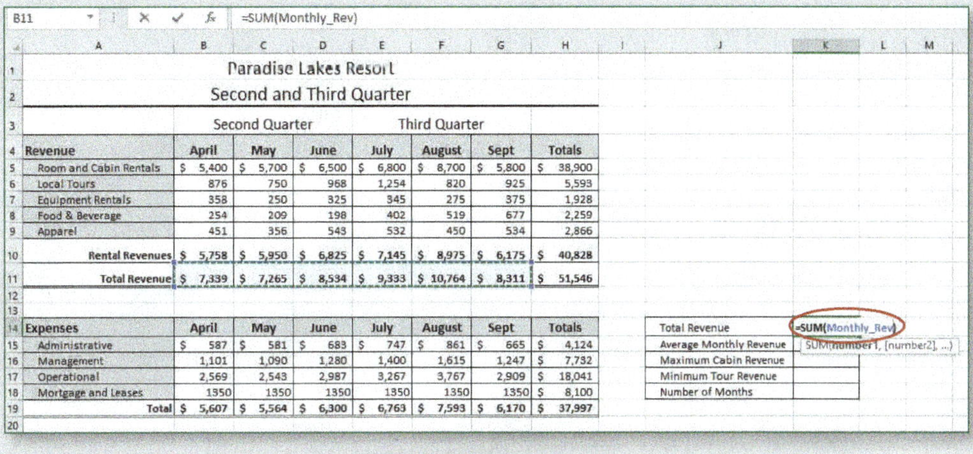

2-37 Range name substituted in formula

3. Enter the *MAX* function by typing.
   a. Select cell **K16**.
   b. Type =ma to display the *Formula AutoComplete* list. You only need type as many characters as necessary to see the function name.
   c. Point to **MAX** in the list, click to select it, and press **Tab** (Figure 2-38).
   d. Select cells **B5:G5** for the *number1* argument. This range is not named.
   e. Press **Enter**. Excel supplies the closing parenthesis.

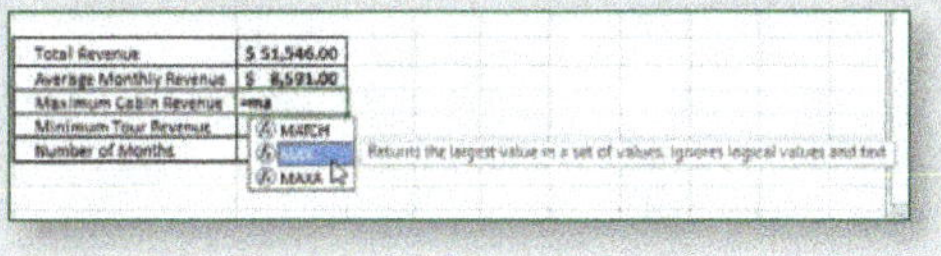

2-38 Choose *MAX* from *Formula AutoComplete* list

4. Copy and edit a function.
   a. Select cell **K16** and use the *Fill* pointer to copy the formula to cell **K17**.
   b. Double-click cell **K17**. Note that the argument cell range was updated because it was a relative reference.
   c. Replace the function name *MAX* in the cell with **min** (Figure 2-39).
   d. Press **Enter**. The minimum value is $750.

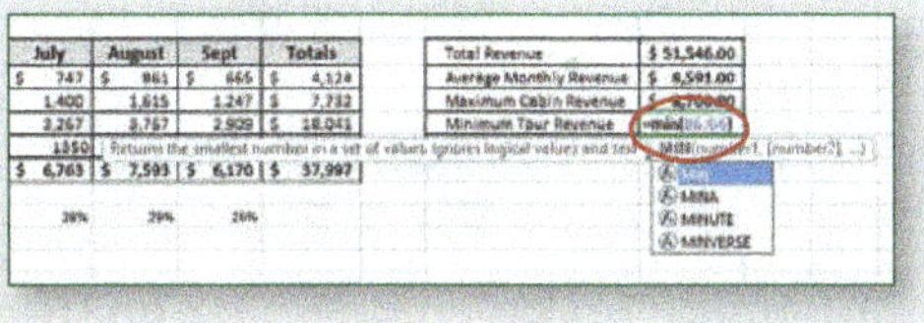

2-39 Edit a function name

5. Type the *COUNT* function.
   a. Select cell **K18**.
   b. Type =cou to display the *Formula AutoComplete* list.
   c. Double-click **COUNTA** in the list. This function counts cells with labels and values. The *ScreenTip* shows the first argument as *value1*.
   d. Select cells **B4:G4** to count the months. The formula is =COUNTA(B4:G4).
   e. Press **Enter**. The final parenthesis is supplied, and the result is 6.00.
   f. Select cells **K14:K18** and decrease the decimal two times.
   g. Apply the **General** format to cell **K18** [*Home* tab, *Number* group, *Number Format* drop-down list].

6. Check results with *AutoCalculate*.
   a. Select cells **B11:G11**.
   b. Right-click near the middle of the *Status* bar to display the options.
   c. Verify that **Average, Count,** and **Sum** are checked.
   d. Left-click anywhere in the *Status* bar to close the menu.
   e. Compare the values shown in the *Status* bar with the results in column K.

7. Insert the *TODAY* function.
   a. Select cell **A25**.
   b. Click the **Formulas** tab.
   c. Click the **Date & Time** button [*Function Library* group].
   d. Find and select **TODAY**. A *Function Arguments* dialog box notes that this function does not have any arguments and that it is volatile (Figure 2-40).
   e. Click **OK**. The current date is inserted.
   f. Press **Ctrl+Home**.
9. Save and close the workbook (Figure 2-41).

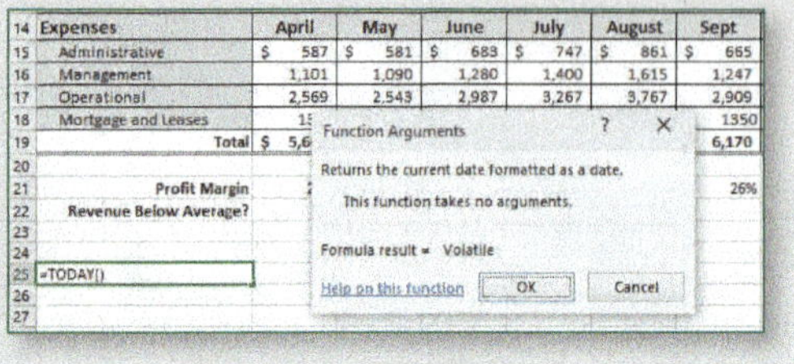

2-40 *Function Arguments* dialog box for *TODAY*

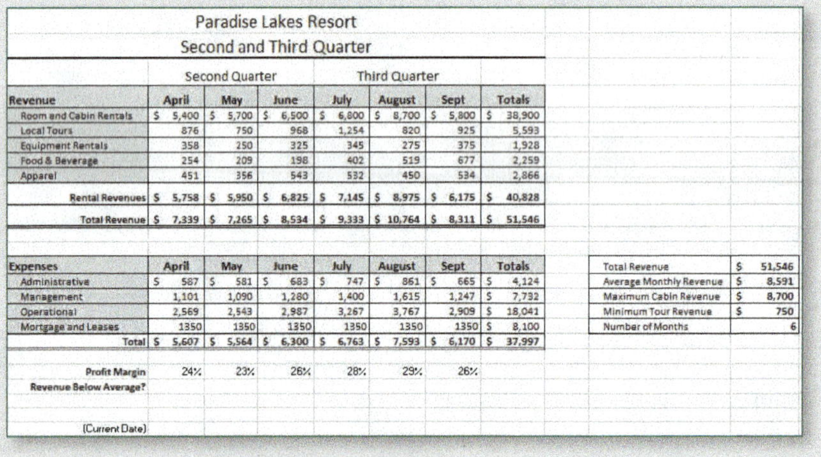

Paradise Lakes Resort
Second and Third Quarter

	Second Quarter			Third Quarter			
Revenue	**April**	**May**	**June**	**July**	**August**	**Sept**	**Totals**
Room and Cabin Rentals	$ 5,400	$ 5,700	$ 6,500	$ 6,800	$ 8,700	$ 5,800	$ 38,900
Local Tours	876	750	968	1,254	820	925	5,593
Equipment Rentals	358	250	325	345	275	375	1,928
Food & Beverage	254	209	198	402	519	677	2,259
Apparel	451	356	543	532	450	534	2,866
Rental Revenues	$ 5,758	$ 5,950	$ 6,825	$ 7,145	$ 8,975	$ 6,175	$ 40,828
Total Revenue	$ 7,339	$ 7,265	$ 8,534	$ 9,333	$ 10,764	$ 8,311	$ 51,546

Expenses	**April**	**May**	**June**	**July**	**August**	**Sept**	**Totals**
Administrative	$ 587	$ 581	$ 683	$ 747	$ 861	$ 665	$ 4,124
Management	1,101	1,090	1,280	1,400	1,615	1,247	$ 7,732
Operational	2,569	2,543	2,987	3,267	3,767	2,909	$ 18,041
Mortgage and Leases	1350	1350	1350	1350	1350	1350	$ 8,100
Total	$ 5,607	$ 5,564	$ 6,300	$ 6,763	$ 7,593	$ 6,170	$ 37,997
Profit Margin	24%	23%	26%	28%	29%	26%	
Revenue Below Average?							
(Current Date)							

Total Revenue	$ 51,546
Average Monthly Revenue	$ 8,591
Maximum Cabin Revenue	$ 8,700
Minimum Tour Revenue	$ 750
Number of Months	6

2-41 PP E2-2 completed

SLO 2.6

Working with Financial, Logical, and Lookup Functions

The *Financial* category includes functions that determine loan payments, the amount of interest earned, the rate of return on an investment, and more. Most of the functions in the *Logical* category display TRUE or FALSE as the result, but the *IF* function is in this group. An *IF* function can test if monthly revenue is above or below average and display "Yes" or "No" in the cell. The *Lookup & Reference* category is used to find and display information from a list in the workbook. For example, you might use a *Lookup* function to insert a price from a price list.

The Function Arguments Dialog Box

Functions require arguments in a particular order. They are easy to learn and build when you use the *Function Arguments* dialog box. This dialog box opens when you choose a function name from a category on the *Formulas* tab or when you use the *Insert Function* dialog box.

The *Function Arguments* dialog box shows each argument with an entry box and an explanation (Figure 2-42). You can select cells to enter an address, or you can type directly in the entry box. In addition to doing the work for you, the *Function Arguments* dialog box helps you learn the proper syntax for a function.

Function arguments may be required or optional. Optional arguments generally add some level of refinement to the calculation. In the *Function Arguments* dialog box and the

ScreenTip, a required argument name is shown in bold. When you use *Formula AutoComplete* to build a function, the *ScreenTip* shows optional arguments in square brackets (e.g., [type]).

When you are not sure about a function's name or category, you can search for it in the *Insert Function* dialog box. Open this dialog box by clicking the **Insert Function** button on the *Formulas* tab [*Function Library* group] or the same button to the left of the *Formula* bar. In the search area, type the name of the function or a brief description of what you want the function to do. For example, you can type "rate of return" to list *Financial* functions that calculate a rate of return for an investment.

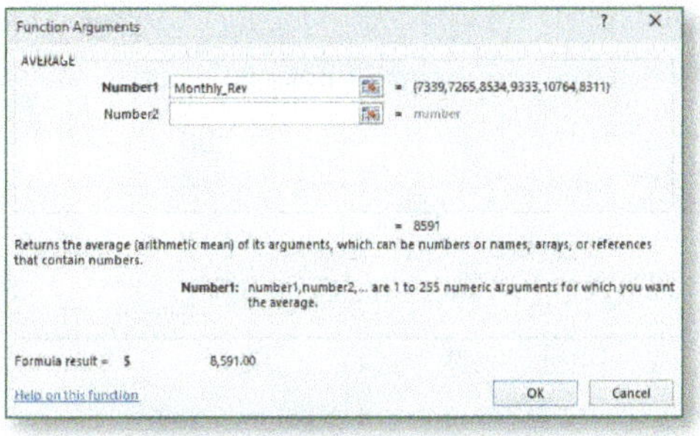

2-42 *Function Arguments* dialog box for *AVERAGE*

ANOTHER WAY

Shift+F3 opens the *Insert Function* dialog box.

PMT Function

The *PMT* function is in the *Financial* category. It calculates a constant loan payment amount for a period of time at a stated interest rate. When you borrow money for tuition or to buy a car, you can use the *PMT* function to determine your monthly payment for a selected payback time.

The *PMT* function has five arguments. Three of them are required: *rate*, *nper*, and *pv*. The other arguments are optional, *fv* and *type*. The proper syntax for a *PMT* formula is:

=PMT(rate, nper, pv, [fv], [type])

- ***Rate*** is the interest rate, a percentage of the amount borrowed. Most rates are set at a yearly rate. To determine monthly payments, you must divide the rate by 12.
- ***Nper*** is the total number of periods for repayment. If you make monthly payments for five years, the *nper* argument is 60.
- ***Pv*** is the present value, the amount borrowed.
- ***Fv*** is any future value after the last payment, an amount still owed at the end of the loan. When the *fv* argument is omitted, it means zero or that you have paid back the entire amount.
- ***Type*** indicates if payments are made at the beginning or the end of the period. Most loan payments are at the beginning of the period, because the interest amount is less. The number *1* is used to set payment at the beginning of the period.

Figure 2-43 shows a PMT function in cell B7 **=PMT(B6/12,B5*12,B4,,1)**. In the *Formula* bar, arguments are separated by commas. Where there are two commas with nothing between them, an argument has been omitted. In this case, it is the *fv* argument.

B6/12 is the interest *rate* divided by 12 to determine a monthly payment.
B5*12 is the *nper* argument, the number of years times 12, to determine the total number of payments.
B4 is the *pv* argument, the amount of money borrowed.
1 is the *type* argument and indicates that payment occurs at the beginning of the period.

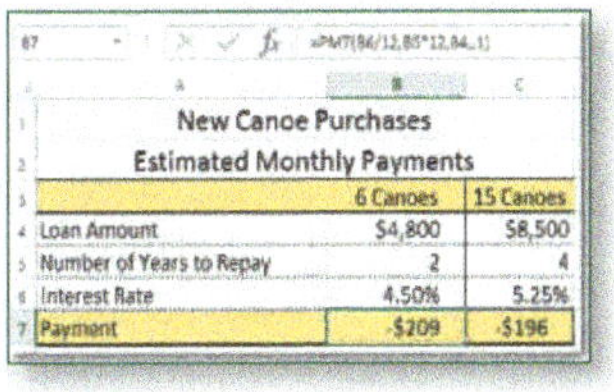

2-43 *PMT* function is in cell B7

The *PMT* result is a negative number, because the function is calculated from the borrower's point of view. It is money paid out.

▸ HOW TO: Use the PMT Function

1. Click the cell where the function results should display.
2. Click the **Insert Function** button to the left of the *Formula* bar.
   - The *Insert Function* dialog box opens.
3. Type payment in the *Search for a function* box.
4. Click **Go** (Figure 2-44).
   - A list of functions that include some type of payment displays.
5. Select **PMT** and click **OK**.
   - The *Function Arguments* dialog box opens.
   - The dialog box includes a description of the function.
6. Click the **Rate** box and click the cell with the interest rate.
   - You can type the rate in the entry box with the percent sign.
   - An explanation of the argument is displayed.
7. Type /12 immediately after the address in the *Rate* box.
   - Divide by 12 for monthly payments.
   - If payments are quarterly, divide by 4.
8. Click the **Nper** box and click the cell that contains the loan term.
9. Type *12 immediately after the address in the *Nper* box.
   - If the loan term is years and payments are quarterly, multiply by 4.
   - If the cell already displays the total number of payments, just click to enter the address.
10. Click the **Pv** box and click the cell that contains the amount of the loan.
11. Click the **Type** box.
    - The *Fv* argument is usually omitted, because loans require a zero balance at the end.
12. Type 1 in the *Type* box to set a payment at the beginning of the period (Figure 2-45).
    - Most loan payments are at the beginning, because the payment is less than if it were at the end of the period.
13. Click **OK**.

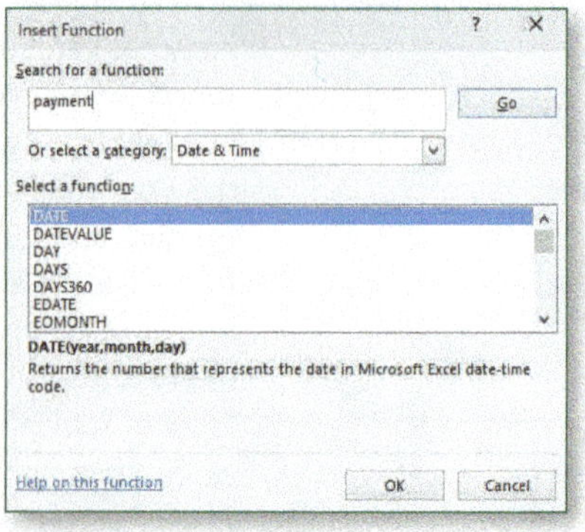

2-44 *Insert Function* dialog box

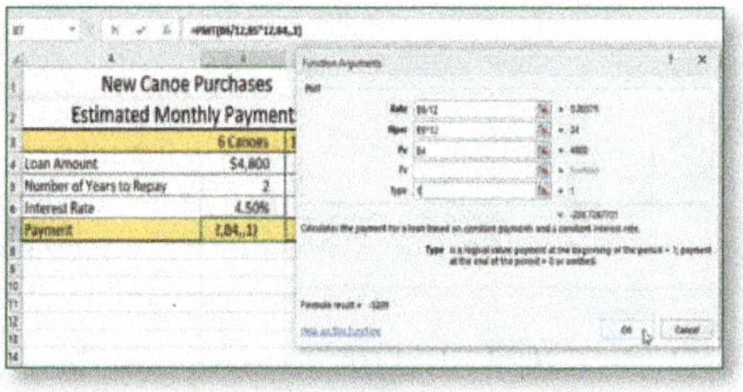

2-45 *Function Arguments* dialog box for *PMT*

MORE INFO

To show the payment as a positive value, type a minus sign (−) before the loan amount in the worksheet or before its cell address in the *Function Arguments* dialog box.

ANOTHER WAY

Choose the *PMT* function from the **Financial** button [*Formulas* tab, *Function Library* group].

IF Function

The *IF* function tests a condition or statement; if it is true, there is a specified result; if it is false, there is an alternative result. In the Paradise Lakes revenue worksheet, you can use an

IF formula to determine if each month's revenue is above average. If it is, you can display "Yes," in the cell, and if it is not, you can display "No."

> **MORE INFO**
>
> An *IF* function is similar to an *IF* statement in many programming languages.

An *IF* function has three arguments, and its syntax is:

=IF(logical_test, value_if_true, value_if_false)

- The ***logical_test*** is the value or statement to be evaluated.
- The ***value_if_true*** is the result displayed in the cell when the *logical_test* is true. You can select a cell, enter text, or use a formula for this argument.
- The ***value_if_false*** is the result displayed in the cell when the *logical_test* is false. You can select a cell, enter text, or use a formula for this argument.

An *IF* function can use comparison or logical operators in its arguments. The following table describes the comparison operators:

Comparison Operators

Operator	Description
=	Equal to
<>	Not equal to
>	Greater than
>=	Greater than or equal to
<	Less than
<=	Less than or equal to

Figure 2-46 has an *IF* function in cell D5 **=IF(B5>=4,18,20)**. When you use the *Function Arguments* dialog box to build a function, the commas to separate arguments are entered automatically.

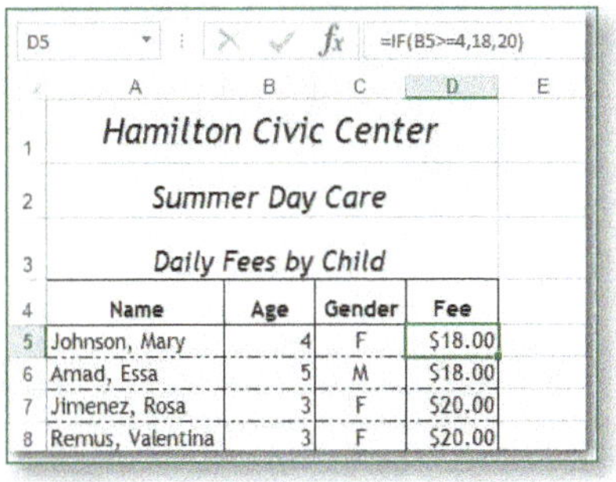

2-46 ***IF*** **function in cell D5**

B5>=4 is the *logical_test*. It determines if the value in cell B5 is equal to or greater than 4. Cell B5 is a relative reference so when the formula is copied, it will update to show the new row. The *value_if_true* argument is **18**. If the age is 4 or higher, the fee is $18. This value is a constant. It does not change when the formula is copied. The *value_if_false* argument is **20**, another constant. If the age is not 4 or higher, it must be lower and the fee is $20. The constant does not change when the formula is copied.

You can insert the *IF* function from the *Logical* category on the *Formulas* tab, from the *Insert Function* button, or by typing it. When you type an *IF* function, you must type the commas to separate arguments, and you must enclose text arguments within quotation marks.

▶ HOW TO: Build an IF Function

1. Click the cell for the function.
2. Click the **Logical** button [*Formulas* tab, *Function Library* group].
   - The list of *Logical* functions opens.
3. Select **IF** in the list.
   - The *Function Arguments* dialog box for *IF* opens.
4. Click the **Logical_test** box.
5. Click the cell that will be evaluated.
   - Make the reference absolute if you know that the formula will be copied and that the reference should not change.
6. Type a comparison operator immediately after the cell address.
7. Type a value or click a cell to complete the expression to be tested.
   - You can build a statement such as B11=K15 or B11<10000.
   - Make a cell reference absolute or mixed if necessary.
8. Click the **Value_if_true** box.
9. Type the label or click a cell that contains data that should be displayed if the *logical_test* is true.
   - You can type a value in the text box.
10. Click the **Value_if_false** box.
11. Type the label or click a cell that contains data that should be displayed if the *logical_test* is false (Figure 2-47).
    - Results for the current cell are displayed in the *Function Arguments* dialog box.

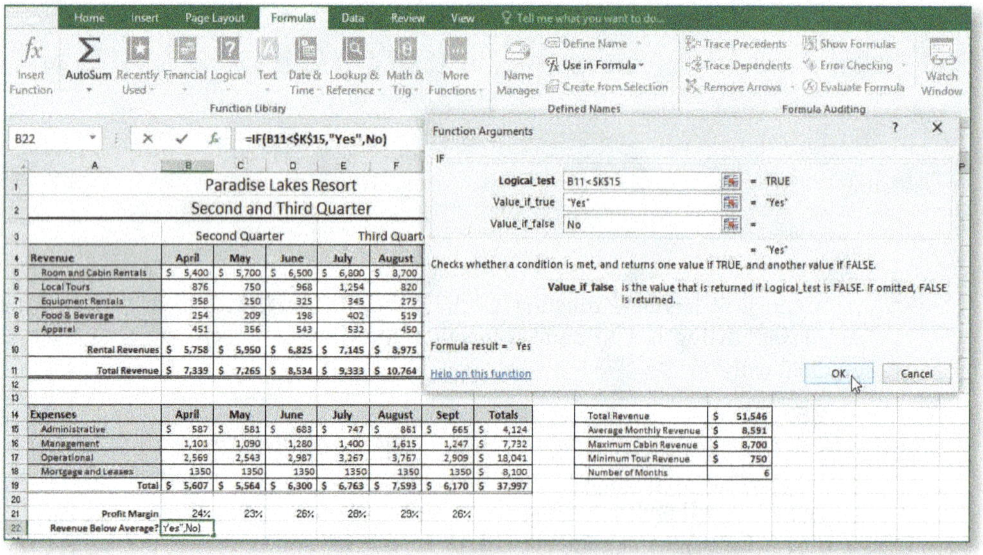

2-47 *Function Arguments* dialog box for *IF*

12. Click **OK**.

MORE INFO

The *value_if_false* argument for the *logical_test* can be another *IF* function which allows you to test for more than one possibility.

Lookup Functions

A *Lookup* function displays a piece of data from a range of cells in another part of the workbook. There are two *Lookup* functions: *VLOOKUP* (vertical) and *HLOOKUP* (horizontal). These two functions have the same syntax and similar arguments. *VLOOKUP* uses a lookup table that is organized in columns, and *HLOOKUP* uses a lookup range that is laid out in rows.

A *VLOOKUP* function has four arguments, and the syntax is:

=VLOOKUP (lookup_value, table_array, col_index_num, [range_lookup])

- The ***lookup_value*** is the data to be found or looked up. It is usually a cell address, but you can type a value or a text string. The function locates this *lookup_value* in the first column of the table array. It then displays data from the designated column in the same row as the *lookup_value*.
- The ***table_array*** is a range of cells, sorted in ascending order by the first column. The range can be located on a different worksheet or in a different workbook. It is good practice to name the range so that its reference is absolute.
- The ***col_index_num*** sets which column in the *table_array* contains the data to be displayed in the result. The columns are counted from left to right.
- The ***[range lookup]*** is optional and is often omitted. This argument is either TRUE or FALSE. TRUE means that Excel finds the closest match to the *lookup_value*, not always a good choice. If the data in the table array is sorted, TRUE will generally return the correct match. When you set this argument to FALSE, the data can be in any order.

Figure 2-48 shows a *VLOOKUP* function in cell D3 in the worksheet on the left. The result (250) is from the third column in row 6 in the table array in the worksheet on the right. These are two sheets in the same workbook.

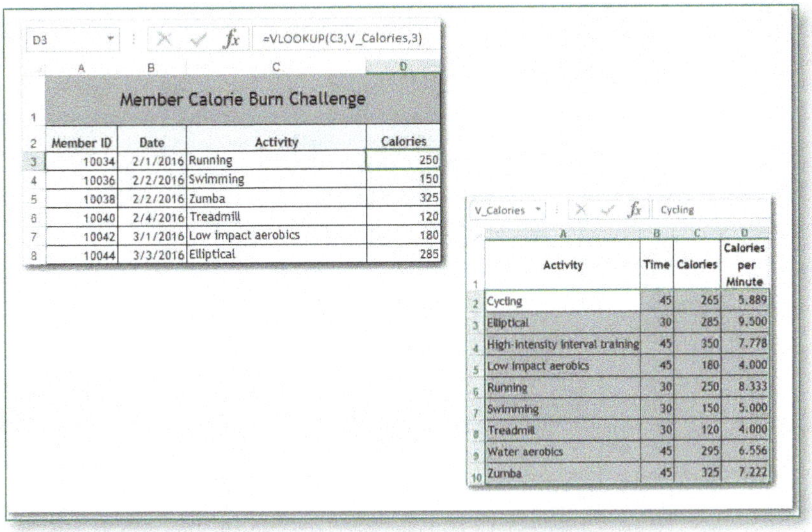

2-48 *VLOOKUP* function in cell D3 on the left

=VLOOKUP(C3,V_Calories,3)

The *lookup_value* argument is cell C3 ("Running").
The *table_array* argument is a named cell range, *V_Calories*. The "V" is a reminder that this range is a vertical lookup table. The *V_Calories* range is cells A2:D10 in the sheet on the right.
The *col_index_num* argument is *3* so that the result is from the third column, the "Calories" column, in the *V_Calories* range.
The *range_lookup* argument is omitted or TRUE. The data in the table array (on the right) is sorted so TRUE is acceptable for this argument.

You can insert the *VLOOKUP* function from the *Lookup & Reference* category on the *Formulas* tab or by searching for it in the *Insert Function* dialog box. When you are experienced using the function, you can type it in the cell and use *Formula AutoComplete*.

▸ HOW TO: Enter the VLOOKUP Function

1. Click the cell for the function.
2. Click the **Lookup & Reference** button [*Formulas* tab].
3. Select **VLOOKUP**.
   - The *Function Arguments* dialog box opens.
   - Move the dialog box if it covers data that you need to see or select.
4. Click the **Lookup_value** box.
5. Click the cell to be matched.
   - The *lookup_value* is typically a cell in the same row as the function.
   - This reference is usually relative.
6. Click the **Table_array** box.
7. Select the cell range with the lookup data.
   - When the lookup table is named, the range name is substituted.
   - The *Function Arguments* dialog box collapses while you select cells.
8. Press **F4 (FN+F4)** to make the reference absolute if cell addresses are used.
   - When a range name has been substituted, you need not do this.
9. Click the **Col_index_num** box.
10. Type the column number, counting from the left, that contains the data to be displayed (Figure 2-49).
    - The result for the current cell is displayed in the dialog box.

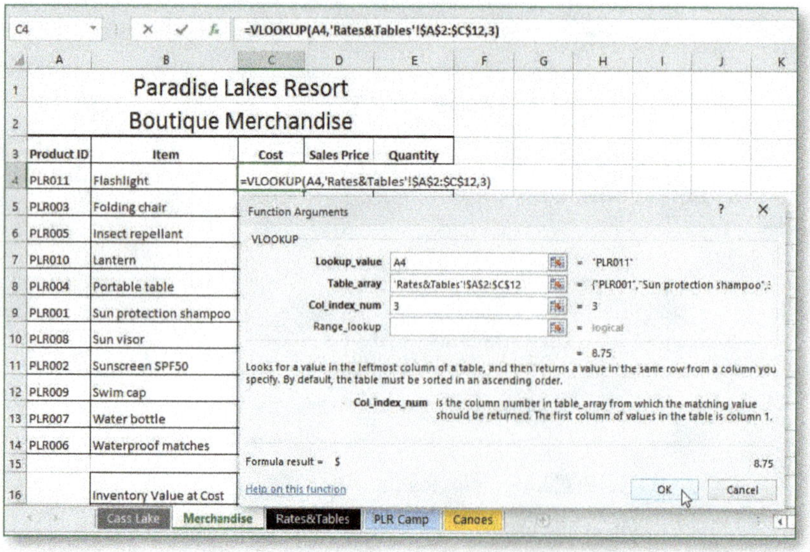

2-49 *Function Arguments dialog box for VLOOKUP*

11. Leave the *Range_lookup* argument box empty if the data in the table array is sorted.
12. Click **OK**.

The *HLOOKUP* function has a *row_index_num* argument instead of the *col_index_num* argument. *The table_array* is set up horizontally as seen in Figure 2-50, and the first row is arranged in alphabetical order from left to right. The *HLOOKUP* function is in cell C6 in the sheet on the left. The lookup table is named *H_Fees*, shown in the sheet on the right.

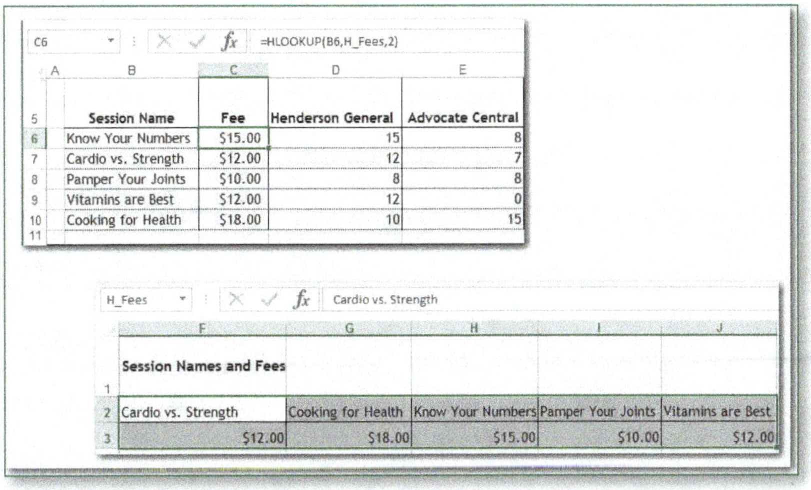

2-50 *HLOOKUP* in cell C6

=HLOOKUP(B6,H_Fees,2)

The *lookup_value* argument is cell B6 ("Know Your Numbers").
The *table_array* argument is a named cell range, *H_Fees*. The "H" is a visual cue for a horizontal lookup table. The *H_Fees* range is cells F2:J3 on the right.
The *row_index_num* argument is *2* so that the data shown in cell C6 is from the second row of the *H_Fees* range.
The *range_lookup* argument is omitted, because the data range is sorted alphabetically from left to right.

> **MORE INFO**
>
> The *range_lookup* argument TRUE (or omitted) finds the largest value that is less than or equal to the *lookup_value*.

▶ HOW TO: Use The HLOOKUP Function

1. Click the cell for the function.
2. Click the **Lookup & Reference** button [*Formulas* tab].
3. Select **HLOOKUP**.
   - The *Function Arguments* dialog box opens.
4. Click the **Lookup_value** box.
5. Click the cell to be matched.
   - The *lookup_value* is typically a cell in the same row as the function.
   - This reference is usually relative.
6. Click the **Table_array** box.

7. Select the cell range with the lookup data.
   - When the lookup table is named, the range name is substituted.
   - The *Function Arguments* dialog box collapses while you select cells.
8. Press **F4 (FN+F4)** to make the reference absolute when cell addresses are used.
9. Click the **Row_index_num** box.
10. Type the row number, counting the first row of the *table_array* as 1 (Figure 2-51).
    - The result for the current cell is displayed in the dialog box.

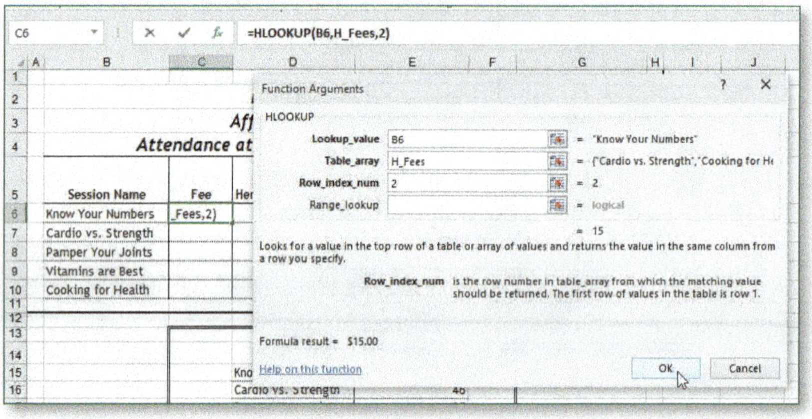

2-51 *HLOOKUP Function Arguments* dialog box

11. Leave the *Range_lookup* argument box empty if the data in the table array is sorted.
12. Click **OK**.

SLO 2.7

Using Math & Trig Functions

You have already used *SUM* from the *Math & Trig* function category. There are functions in this category to display the absolute value of data, one to calculate the cosine of an angle, or one that returns the power of a number. You might recognize the function *PI* or π from a math class. Three *Math & Trig* functions that are often used in business or personal calculations are *ROUND*, *SUMIF*, and *SUMPRODUCT*.

ROUND Function

Rounding means that a value is adjusted to display a specified number of decimal places or a whole number. You can round the numbers on your tax return in the United States which means that you need not show any cents, just dollars.

The *ROUND* function has two arguments, *number* and *num_digits*.

=ROUND(number, num_digits)

- The ***number*** is the cell or the value to be adjusted.
- The ***num_digits*** sets the number of decimal places for rounding. When this argument is zero (0), the value is displayed as the nearest whole number. When the *num_digits* argument is greater than zero, the value is rounded to that number of decimal places. You can use a negative number for the *num_digits* argument which rounds the value to the left of the decimal point. Make sure you understand the results when you round to the left of the decimal point.

When a value used in rounding is 5 or greater, results round up to the next digit. If you round 5.523 to show zero (0) decimal places, it rounds up to display as 6 because the value after the decimal point is 5. If you round 5.423 to two places, it rounds to 5.42 because the value used for rounding is 3. The *Increase Decimal* and *Decrease Decimal* buttons follow these rounding principles for displaying values in the cell as do the *Accounting Number* and *Currency* formats. These formats, however, keep the full unrounded value in the cell and use that value in calculations.

> **MORE INFO**
>
> When a value is rounded, the rounded value is used in calculations, not the full unrounded number.

HOW TO: Use the ROUND Function

1. Click the cell for the function.
2. Type =rou and press **Tab**.
   - *Formula AutoComplete* inserts the function in the cell.
   - The *number* argument is bold in the *ScreenTip*.
3. Select the cell to be rounded.
   - The cell address appears in the cell and in the *Formula* bar.
   - You can type a value if there is no cell reference.
4. Type , (a comma) to separate the arguments.
   - The *num_digits* argument is bold in the *ScreenTip*.
5. Type a number to set the number of decimal places (Figure 2-52).
6. Press **Enter**.

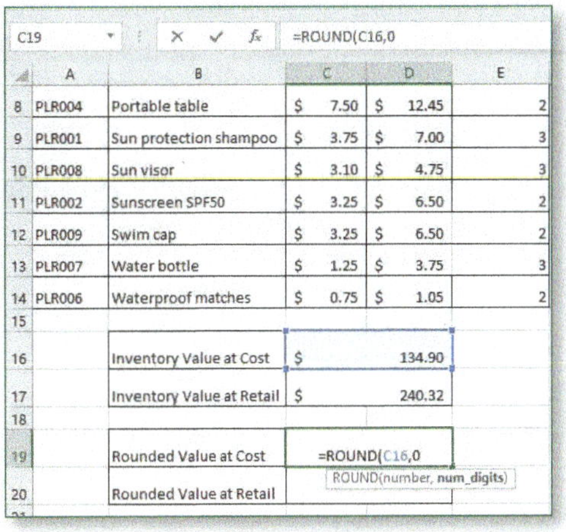

2-52 Type the *ROUND* function

> **MORE INFO**
>
> Excel has a *ROUNDDOWN* function that always rounds a number down. The *ROUNDUP* function rounds a value up.

SUMIF Function

The *SUMIF* function controls which data in a range is included in the total. It allows you to eliminate cells from the calculation by criteria that you set. ***Criteria*** are restrictions, conditions, or rules that must be met. In a *SUMIF* function, cell values are included in the sum only if they match the criteria.

The *SUMIF* function has three arguments.

=SUMIF (range, criteria, [sum_range])

- The ***range*** is the range of cells to be evaluated or searched, the values that are compared to the criteria.
- The ***criteria*** argument defines which cells from the range should be included in the sum. You can use comparison operators, cell references, a value, or text. When you use text or a comparison operator, the criteria must be enclosed in quotation marks.

- The *[sum_range]* is the cell range to be summed. This argument is optional, because it is omitted when the range to be summed is the same as the *range* argument.

Figure 2-53 illustrates a *SUMIF* function in cell I5 that totals sales for products that have a price greater than $10.

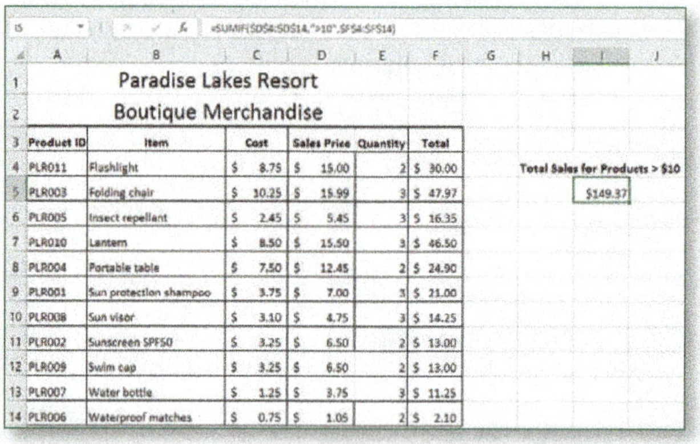

=SUMIF($D$4:$D$14,">10",$F$4:$F$14)

Paradise Lakes Resort

Boutique Merchandise

Product ID	Item	Cost	Sales Price	Quantity	Total
PLR011	Flashlight	$ 8.75	$ 15.00	2	$ 30.00
PLR003	Folding chair	$ 10.25	$ 15.99	3	$ 47.97
PLR005	Insect repellant	$ 2.45	$ 5.45	3	$ 16.35
PLR010	Lantern	$ 8.50	$ 15.50	3	$ 46.50
PLR004	Portable table	$ 7.50	$ 12.45	2	$ 24.90
PLR001	Sun protection shampoo	$ 3.75	$ 7.00	3	$ 21.00
PLR008	Sun visor	$ 3.10	$ 4.75	3	$ 14.25
PLR002	Sunscreen SPF50	$ 3.25	$ 6.50	2	$ 13.00
PLR009	Swim cap	$ 3.25	$ 6.50	2	$ 13.00
PLR007	Water bottle	$ 1.25	$ 3.75	3	$ 11.25
PLR006	Waterproof matches	$ 0.75	$ 1.05	2	$ 2.10

Total Sales for Products > $10

$149.37

2-53 *SUMIF* function in cell I5

=SUMIF($D$4:$D$14,">=10",$F4:$F14)

The *range* argument is the sales price column, cells $D$4:$D$14. It is an absolute reference so that the formula can be copied.

The *criteria* argument is >=10, shown in quotation marks. The quotation marks are added automatically when you use the *Function Arguments* dialog box.

The *sum_range* argument is cells $F$4:$F$14, the cells to be added if the price is greater than 10.

> **MORE INFO**
>
> You can use wildcards (* or ?) in a criteria argument. For example, to sum sales for all items that begin with the letter S, use **s*** as the criteria. Criteria are not case-sensitive.

HOW TO: Build a SUMIF Function

1. Click the cell for the function.
2. Click the **Math & Trig** button [*Formulas* tab, *Function Library* group].
3. Select **SUMIF**.
4. Click the **Range** box.
5. Select the cell range to be compared against the criteria.
   - Make the reference absolute if the formula might be copied.
   - Press **F3 (FN+F3)** to paste a range name rather than selecting the range.
6. Click the **Criteria** box.
   - Type text to be compared or a value to be matched.
   - Type an expression with operators to be evaluated.
   - Quotation marks are automatically supplied.

7. Click the **Sum_range** box (Figure 2-54).
    - Select the cells to be added.
    - If the cells to be added are the same as those in the *range* argument, leave the entry blank.

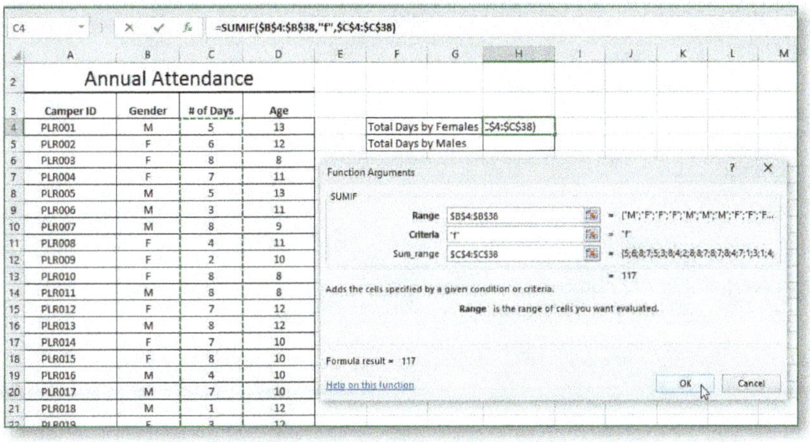

2-54 ***Function Arguments*** **dialog box for *Sumif***

8. Click **OK**.

SUMPRODUCT Function

The *SUMPRODUCT* function calculates the sum of the product of several ranges. It multiplies the cells identified in its *array* arguments and then it totals those individual products. A ***product*** is the result of a multiplication problem; 4 is the product of 2 times 2. An ***array*** is a range of cells in a row or a column. An array has a ***dimension***, which is the number of columns or rows. The arrays A1:A5 and C1:C5 have the same dimension, five rows and one column.

The *SUMPRODUCT* function has the following syntax.

=SUMPRODUCT(array1, array2, [arrayN])

- The ***array1*** argument is the first range of cells for the multiplication.
- The ***array2*** argument is the range that is multiplied by the corresponding cells in the *array1* range. These two ranges must have the same number of cells, the same dimension.

It is possible to use more than two arrays so that you could have an *array3* argument or even more.

In Figure 2-55, the *SUMPRODUCT* function in cell C22 multiplies the first array C6:C20 by the corresponding values in cells F6:F20 and totals those products.

=SUMPRODUCT(C6:C20,F6:F20)

The value in cell C6 is multiplied by cell F6, cell C7 is multiplied by cell F7, and so on. Those individual products are summed, and the result is $249.15.

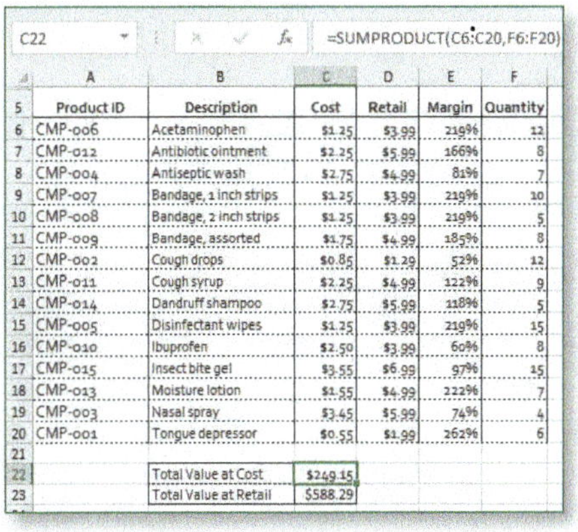

2-55 ***SUMPRODUCT*** **in cell C22**

HOW TO: Build a SUMPRODUCT Function

1. Click the cell for the function.
2. Click the **Math & Trig** button [*Formulas* tab, *Function Library* group].
3. Select **SUMPRODUCT**.
   - The *Function Arguments* dialog box opens.
4. Click the **Array1** box.
5. Select the first cell range to be multiplied.
6. Click the **Array2** box.
7. Select the next cell range to be multiplied (Figure 2-56).
   - Both arrays must have the same number of cells and rows.
   - Use as many arrays as required for the calculation.

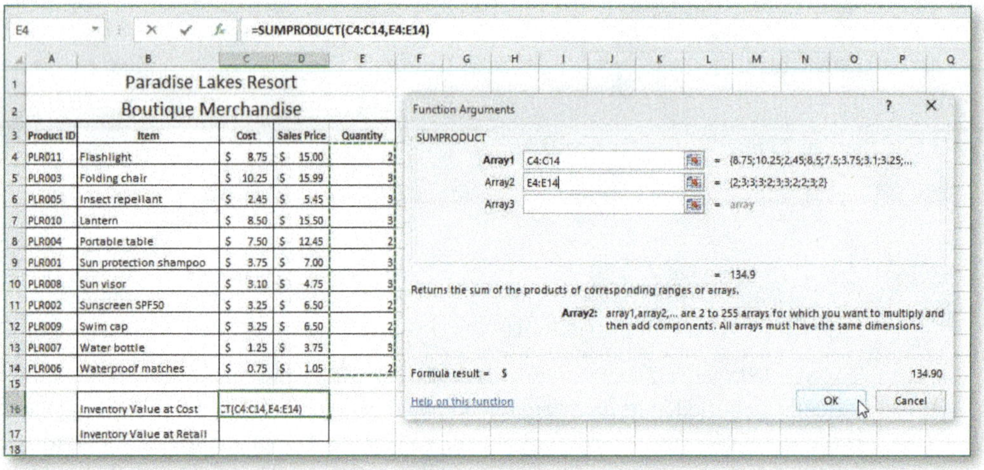

2-56 ***Function Arguments*** **dialog box for *SUMPRODUCT***

8. Click **OK**.

MORE INFO

If an array in a *SUMPRODUCT* formula includes an empty cell, Excel treats that value as 0, but the multiplication by zero does not affect the sum.

PAUSE & PRACTICE: EXCEL 2-3

For this project, you continue working on the workbook for Paradise Lakes. You calculate totals related to camp attendance and merchandise inventory using functions from the *Math & Trig*, *Financial*, *Logical*, *Lookup & Reference*, and *Date & Time* categories.

File Needed: ***[your initials] PP E2-2.xlsx***
Completed Project File Name: ***[your initials] PP E2-3.xlsx***

1. Open the ***[your initials] PP E2-2.xlsx*** workbook completed in *Pause & Practice 2-2* and save it as [your initials] PP E2-3.
2. Click the **Cass Lake** worksheet tab.
3. Enter an *IF* function to determine if a month's revenue was below average.
   a. Click cell **B22** and click the **Formulas** tab.
   b. Click the **Logical** button In the *Function Library* group and select **IF**. The *Function Arguments* dialog box opens.
   c. Click the **Logical_test** text box and click cell **B11**.
   d. After "B11" in the *Logical_test* box, type < for a less than operator.
   e. Click cell **K15** and press **F4 (FN+F4)** to make this an absolute reference.
   f. Click the **Value_if_true** box and type Yes. You need not type quotation marks when you use the *Function Arguments* dialog box.
   g. Press **Tab** to move to the *Value_if_false* box. Excel supplies the quotation marks for "Yes."
   h. Type No (Figure 2-57).
   i. Click **OK**. For April, the result is *Yes*.
   j. Click cell **B22** and click the **Center** button [*Home* tab, *Font* group].
   k. Use the *Fill* pointer to copy the formula in cell **B22** to cells **C22:G22**.
   l. Press **Ctrl+Home**.

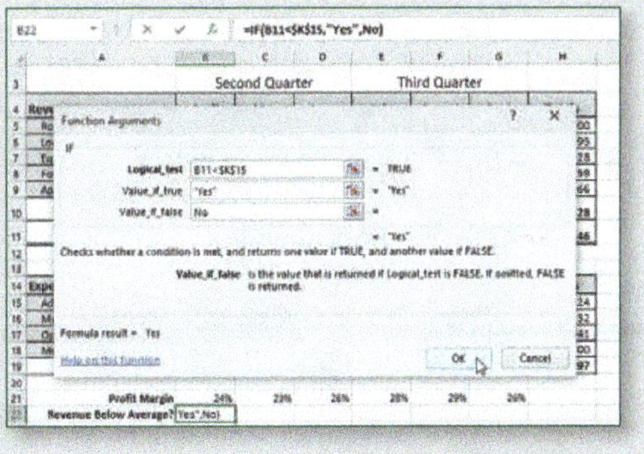

2-57 Build an *IF* function

4. Use *SUMIF* to calculate results.
   a. Click the **PLR Camp** worksheet tab. The number of attendees is tracked with the camper's ID, gender, and age.
   b. Select cell **H4**, and click the **Formulas** tab.
   c. Click the **Math & Trig** button in the *Function Library* group and select **SUMIF**.
   d. Click the **Range** text box and select cells **B4:B38**.
   e. Press **F4 (FN+F4)** to make the reference absolute.
   f. Press **Tab** and type f in the *Criteria* box. Criteria are not case-sensitive. The cells in column B will be checked to determine if they show "F."
   g. Click the **Sum_range** box, select cells **C4:C38**, and press **F4 (FN+F4)**. The values in this range will be summed for those rows in which the gender is F (Figure 2-58).
   h. Click **OK**. Female camp days are 117.
   i. Click cell **H4** and use the *Fill* pointer to copy the formula to cell **H5**.
   j. Edit the formula in cell **H5** to show m instead of "f."

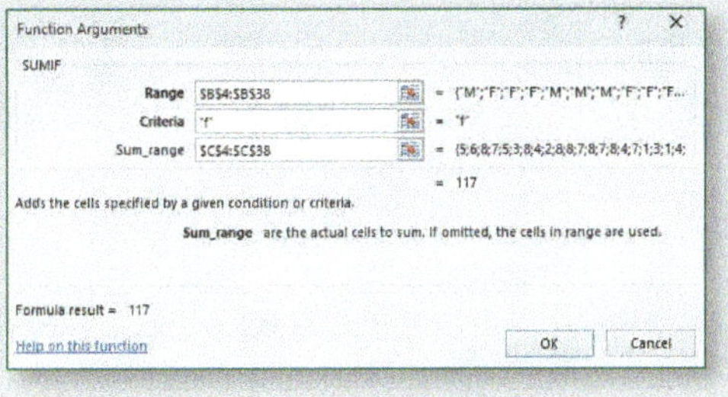

2-58 Build a *SUMIF* function

5. Use *VLOOKUP* to display costs.
   a. Click the **Merchandise** sheet tab and select cell **C4**. Individual costs are missing, but they are listed on the **Rates&Tables** sheet.
   b. Click the **Lookup & Reference** button [*Formulas* tab, *Function Library* group].
   c. Select **VLOOKUP**.
   d. Click the **Lookup_value** box and select cell **A4**.
   e. Click the **Table_array** box. The table with the costs is on the **Rates&Tables** sheet.
   f. Click the **Rates&Tables** worksheet tab and select cells **A2:C12**. This array or range includes the ID, the name, and the cost. The costs are in column C, the third column from the left.

g. Press **F4 (FN+F4)** to make the array an absolute reference.
h. Click the **Col_index_num** box and type 3. The ID in cell A4 will be located in cells A2:C12 on the **Rates&Tables** sheet, and the cost in the third column will be displayed.
i. Click the **Range_lookup** box and type false (Figure 2-59).
j. Click **OK**. The cost for the first item is $8.75.
k. Copy the formula in cell **C4** to cells **C5:C14**.

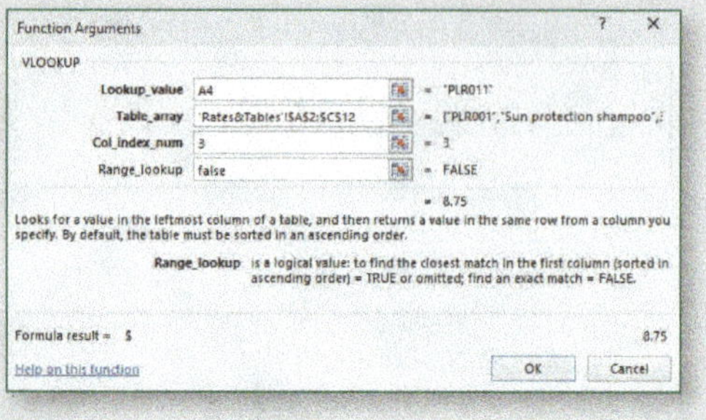

2-59 Build a *VLOOKUP* function

6. Use *SUMPRODUCT* to calculate inventory values.
   a. Click cell **C16**. This is a merged and centered cell.
   b. Click the **Formulas** tab.
   c. Click the **Math & Trig** button in the *Function Library* group and select **SUMPRODUCT**.
   d. Click the **Array1** box and select cells **C4:C14**. There are 11 values in this range.
   e. Click the **Array2** box and select cells **E4:E14**. There are 11 values in this range, and each one will be multiplied by the corresponding value in the same row in column C.
   f. Click **OK**. The value of the inventory at cost is 134.9.
   g. Click cell **C17**, type =sump, and press **Tab**. The function is inserted and the *ScreenTip* shows the next argument, *array1*.
   h. Select cells **D4:D14** and type , (a comma) to separate the first argument from the second.
   i. Select cells **E4:E14** (Figure 2-60). You need not type the closing parenthesis.
   j. Press **Enter**. The value is 240.32.
   k. Select cells **C16:C17** and apply the **Accounting Number** format.

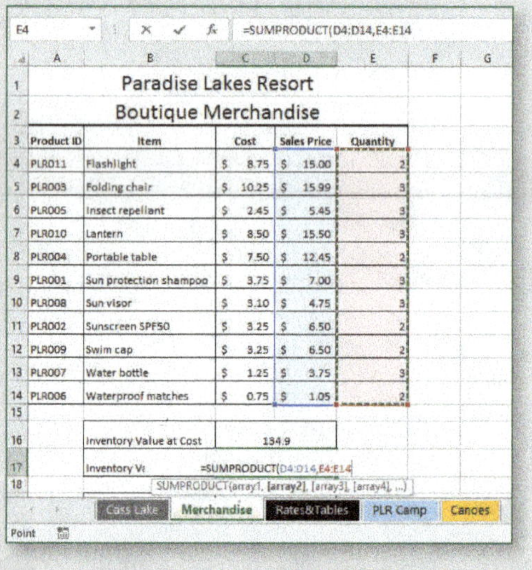

2-60 Type a *SUMPRODUCT* function

7. Use the *ROUND* function.
   a. Select cell **C19**.
   b. Click the **Math & Trig** button [*Formulas* tab, *Function Library* group].
   c. Select **ROUND**.
   d. In the *Number* text box, click cell **C16**.
   e. Type 0 in the *Num_digits* text box.
   f. Press **Enter**. The value is rounded up to $135.00.
   g. Copy the formula in cell **C19** to cell **C20**. The value from cell C17 is rounded down to $240.00.

8. Use the PMT function to determine payments for new canoe purchases.
   a. Click the **Canoes** sheet tab and click cell **B7**.
   b. Click the **Formulas** tab and the **Financial** button [*Function Library* group].
   c. Select **PMT**.
   d. Click the **Rate** box and click cell **B6**.
   e. Immediately after "B6," type /12 to divide the rate by 12 for monthly payments.

f. Click the **Nper** box and click cell **B5**. Type *12 to multiply by 12 for 12 months per year.
g. Click the **Pv** box and click cell **B4**. This is the amount of the loan.
h. Click the **Fv** box. Leave this blank to indicate no balance due at the end of the loan term.

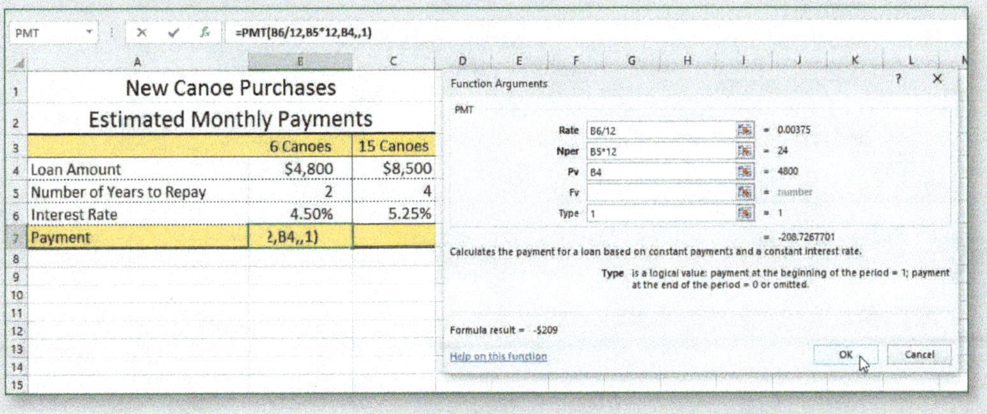

2-61 PMT function for payment at the beginning of the period

i. Click the **Type** box and type 1. The payment will made at the beginning of the month (Figure 2-61).
j. Click **OK**. The payment is –$209, a negative value because it is money paid out. This cell was formatted to show no decimal places.

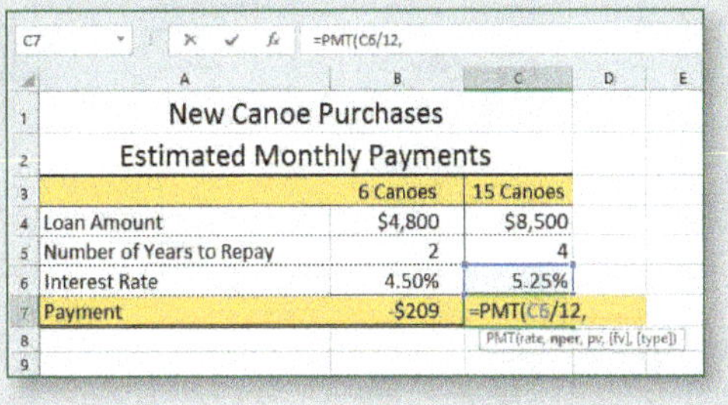

2-62 Type a PMT function

9. Type the PMT function.
   a. Click cell **C7**.
   b. Type =pm, and press **Tab**. The *ScreenTip* shows the first argument, *rate*.
   c. Click cell **C6** and type /12,. This divides the rate by 12 and enters a comma to separate the arguments (Figure 2-62).
   d. Click cell **C5** for the *nper* argument, type *12, to multiply by 12 and enter a comma to separate the arguments.
   e. Click cell **C4** for the *pv* argument, the amount of the loan.
   f. Type , (a comma) to move to the *fv* argument.
   g. Type , (another comma) to move to the *type* argument. *Formula AutoComplete* lists two options for the argument (Figure 2-63).
   h. Double-click **1-beginning of the period** in the *ScreenTip*.
   i. Press **Enter**. The payment is –$196.
   j. Press **Ctrl+Home**.

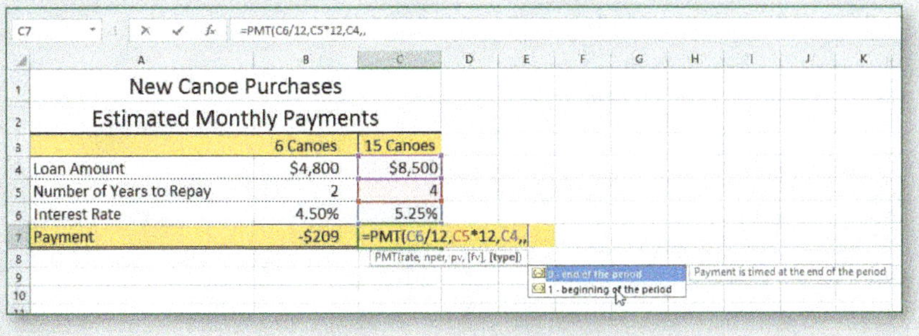

2-63 *Formula AutoComplete* for argument choices

10. Save and close the workbook (Figure 2-64).

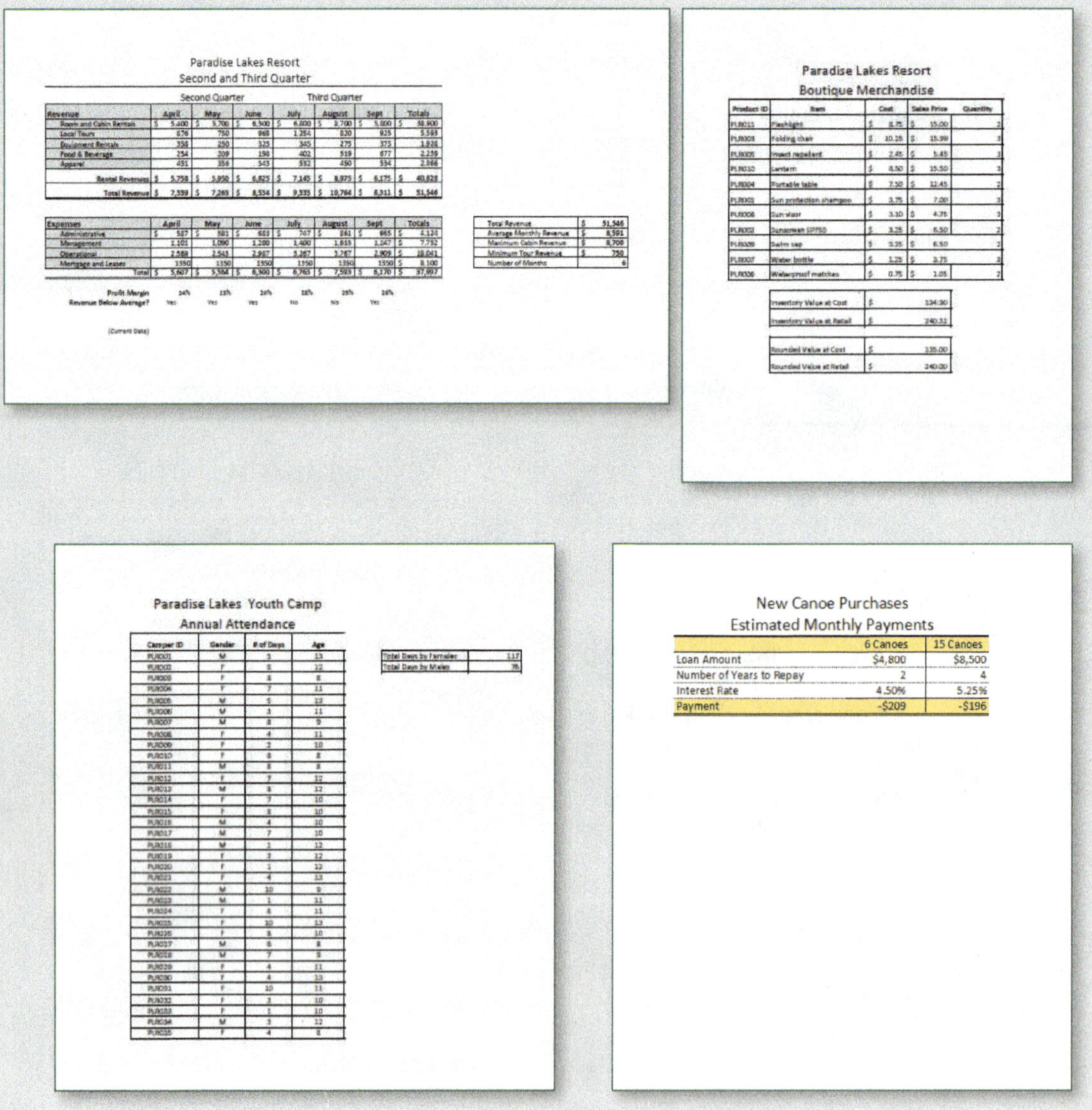

2-64 PP 2-3 completed

Chapter Summary

2.1 Build and edit basic formulas (p. E2-89).

- A ***formula*** is a calculation that uses arithmetic operators, worksheet cells, and constant values. Basic arithmetic operations are addition, subtraction, multiplication, and division.
- You can type a formula in the cell or you can point and click to select cells.
- When you type a formula, ***Formula AutoComplete*** displays suggestions for completing the formula.
- Formulas are edited in the *Formula* bar or in the cell to change cell addresses, use a different operator, or add cells to the calculation.

2.2 Set mathematical order of operations (p. E2-91).

- Excel follows mathematics rules for the order in which operations are carried out when a formula has more than one operator.
- You can control the sequence of calculations by placing operations that should be done first within parentheses.
- Use the following acronym to help remember the order of arithmetic operations: **P**lease **E**xcuse **M**y **D**ear **A**unt **S**ally (**P**arentheses, **E**xponentiation, **M**ultiplication, **D**ivision, **A**ddition, **S**ubtraction).

2.3 Use absolute, mixed, relative, and 3D references in a formula (p. E2-93).

- A ***relative cell reference*** in a formula is the cell address which, when copied, updates to the address of the copy.
- An ***absolute cell reference*** is the cell address with dollar signs as in $A$5. This reference does not change when the formula is copied.
- A ***mixed cell reference*** contains one relative and one absolute address as in $B5 or B$5. When copied, the absolute part of the reference does not change.
- A ***3D cell reference*** is a cell in another worksheet in the same workbook. It includes the name of the worksheet followed by an exclamation point as in *Inventory!B2*.
- You can name a single cell or a group of cells with a defined ***range name***.
- You can use range names in formulas instead of cell addresses.
- *Formula AutoComplete* displays range names so that you can paste them in a formula.
- A named range is an absolute reference.

2.4 Use formula auditing tools in a worksheet (p. E2-99).

- Excel highlights several types of formula errors as you work, but you still need to review errors and make corrections.
- Excel automatically error-checks formulas based on its internal rules. A potential error is marked in the upper left corner of the cell with a small triangle.
- ***Formula auditing*** tools include several commands to aid your review of workbook formulas and functions.
- The *Formula Auditing* group on the *Formulas* tab includes the *Trace Precedents* and *Trace Dependents* buttons.
- A ***circular reference*** is an error that occurs when a formula includes the address of the formula.
- Some errors are noted as you press a completion key and can be quickly corrected by accepting the suggested correction in the message window.

2.5 Use *Statistical* and *Date & Time* functions (p. E2-106).

- The *AVERAGE* function calculates the arithmetic mean by adding values and dividing by the number of values.
- The *COUNT* function tallies the number of cells in a range. There are different *COUNT* functions based on whether cell contents are labels, values, or blank.
- *MAX* and *MIN* functions find the largest and the smallest values, respectively, in a range.
- Commonly used statistical functions are options on the *AutoSum* button.
- The ***AutoCalculate*** feature displays numerical results such as *Sum*, *Average*, and *Count* on the *Status* bar for selected cells.
- The *Date & Time* category includes a *TODAY* function and a *NOW* function that display the current date and time.

2.6 Work with functions from the *Financial*, *Logical*, and *Lookup & Reference* categories. (p. E2-114).

- Use the *Function Arguments* dialog box for help in completing an Excel function.

- The *Function Arguments* dialog box includes a description of the function and an explanation of each argument.
- The *PMT* function from the *Financial* category calculates a constant payment amount for a loan.
- The *Logical* function *IF* evaluates a statement or condition and displays a particular result when the statement is true and another result when the condition is false.
- A *Lookup* function displays data from a cell located in another part of the workbook.
- Two widely used *Lookup* functions are *VLOOKUP* (vertical) and *HLOOKUP* (horizontal).

2.7 Build functions from the *Math & Trig* category (p. E2-122).

- The *ROUND* function adjusts a value up or down based on the number of decimal places.
- The *SUMIF* function includes cells in a total only if they meet a set criteria or condition.
- The *SUMPRODUCT* function multiplies corresponding cells from an ***array*** and then totals the results of each multiplication.

Check for Understanding

The SIMbook for this text (within your SIMnet account) provides the following resources for concept review:

- Multiple choice questions
- Matching exercises
- Short answer questions

USING MICROSOFT EXCEL 2016

Guided Project 2-1

Courtyard Medical Plaza (CMP) has doctor offices, a pharmacy, x-ray and lab services, insurance and billing support, optometry and dental facilities, and onsite dining. You will complete an inventory worksheet for the pharmacy as well as insurance and payment data for the optometry group.
[**Student Learning Outcomes 2.1, 2.2, 2.3, 2.4, 2.5, 2.6, 2.7**]

File Needed: ***CourtyardMedical-02.xlsx*** *[Student data files are available in the* Library *of your SIMnet account.]*
Completed Project File Name: ***[your initials] Excel 2-1.xlsx***

Skills Covered in This Project

- Build and copy formulas.
- Name cell ranges.
- Use *AVERAGE*, *MAX*, and *MIN*.
- Use relative, mixed, absolute, and 3D cell references in formulas.
- Use *SUMIF*.
- Check results with *AutoCalculate*.
- Use the *VLOOKUP* function.
- Set mathematical order of operations.
- Use formula auditing tools.
- Use the *PMT* and *SUMPRODUCT* functions.
- Insert the *TODAY* function.

1. Open the ***CourtyardMedical-02.xlsx*** workbook from your student data files and save it as [your initials] Excel 2-1.
2. Enter and copy subtraction formulas.
   a. Click cell **E2** on the **Lookup_Data** worksheet. To calculate the dollar amount of the margin, subtract the cost from the retail price.
   b. Type an equals sign (=) to start the formula.
   c. Click cell **D2**, the retail price.
   d. Type a minus sign, or hyphen (–) to subtract, and click cell **C2**, the cost.
   e. Click the **Enter** button (check mark) on the *Formula* bar. The pointer stays in the formula cell. The margin for acetaminophen is $1.49.
   f. Drag the *Fill* pointer to copy the formula in cell **E2** to cells **E3:E16**. The *Auto Fill Options* button appears near cell E16.
   g. Click the **Auto Fill Options** button and choose **Fill Without Formatting** (Figure 2-65). This option copies the formula without the top border from cell E2.
   h. Format cells **E3:E16** as **Currency**.
   i. Click the **Optometry** sheet tab and select cell **G5**.
   j. Type = to start the formula to subtract the deductible amount from the billed amount.
   k. Click cell **E5**, the billed amount.
   l. Type –, click cell **F5**, the deductible amount, and press **Enter**.
   m. Copy the formula in cell **G5** to cells **G6:G24** without formatting to maintain the fill color.

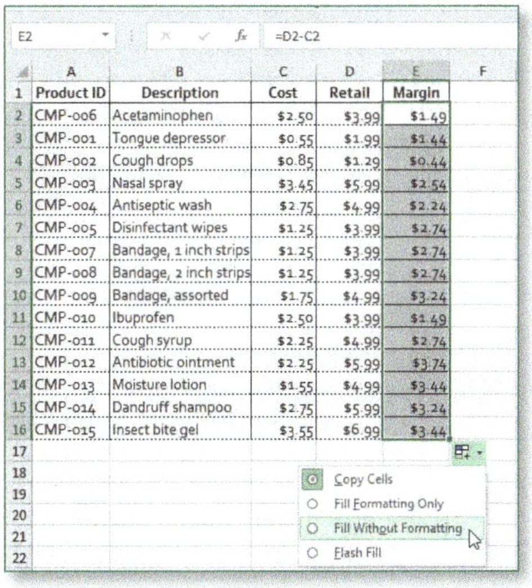

2-65 Copy without formatting to preserve borders

3. Name cell ranges.
   a. Select cells **E5:E24**. This named range will refer to the billable amounts.
   b. Click the **Name** box.
   c. Type Billables in the *Name* box and press **Enter**.
   d. Click the **Lookup_Data** worksheet tab.
   e. Select cells **A2:D16**. This named range will not include the calculated margin.
   f. Click the **Name** box.
   g. Type Costs in the *Name* box and press **Enter**.
   h. Select cells **H2:I5** and click the **Formulas** tab.
   i. Click the **Create from Selection** button [*Defined Names* group]. Excel will create range names based on the labels in the column on the left.
   j. Select the **Left column** box and click **OK**.
   k. Click cell **A1** and click the **Name** box arrow to see the range names in the worksheet (Figure 2-66).

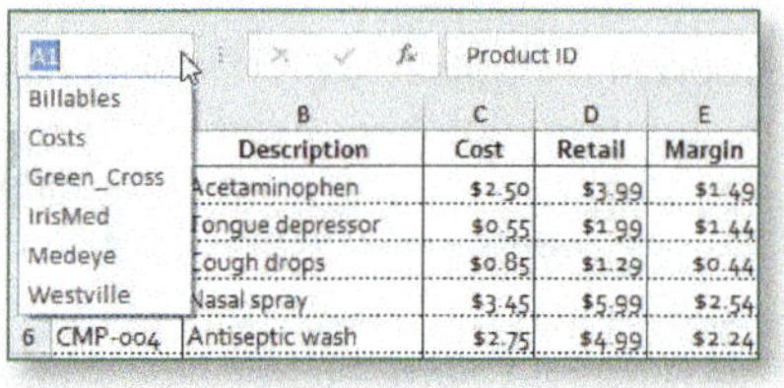

2-66 Range names in the worksheet

4. Use range names with *AVERAGE*, *MIN*, and *MAX*.
   a. Click the **Optometry** sheet tab and select cell **D27**.
   b. Type =aver and press **Tab**.
   c. Select cells **E5:E24** and press **Enter**. The range name is substituted in the formula when you select the cells in the worksheet.
   d. Select cell **D28**, click the **AutoSum** button arrow [*Home* tab, *Editing* group], and select **Max**.
   e. Select cells **E5:E24** and press **Enter**.
   f. Use *MIN* in cell **D29** with the same cell range.

5. Set the order of operations in a 3D formula.
   a. Click the **Insurance** sheet tab and select cell **D5**. The total with service charge is calculated by multiplying 1 plus the percentage times the billed amount. The percentages are on the **Lookup_Data** sheet in named ranges.
   b. Type = and click cell **C5**.
   c. Type *(immediately after **C5**. The next part of the formula will be calculated first.
   d. Type 1+ immediately after the left parenthesis. The calculation is (1+ the percentage).
   e. Click the **Lookup_Data** sheet tab. The sheet name is displayed in the *Formula* bar.
   f. Click cell **I2**. The range name is substituted. Because it is an absolute reference, the sheet name is removed (Figure 2-67).
   g. Press **Enter**. Because the formula refers to another sheet and a range name, the missing parenthesis is not automatically supplied (Figure 2-68).
   h. Click **Yes** to accept the suggested correction.
   i. Copy the formula to cells **D5:D9** for the Green Cross patients.

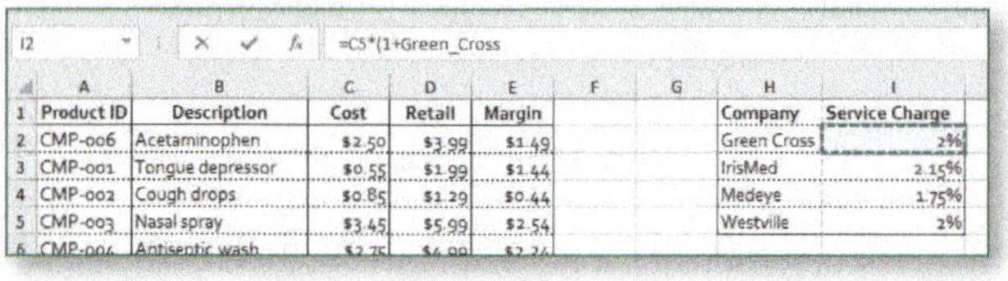

2-67 3D formula with a range name

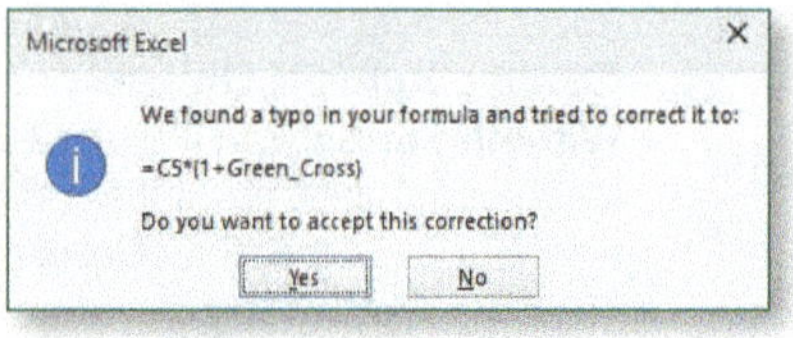

2-68 Formula correction message window

6. Edit and copy a formula.
   a. Click cell **D9** and copy the formula to cell **D10**.
   b. Double-click cell **D10** to start *Edit* mode.
   c. Select the range name **Green_Cross** in the cell or *Formula* bar (Figure 2-69).
   d. Click the **Lookup_Data** sheet tab and select cell **I3**. The *IrisMed* range name replaces *Green_Cross*, and the parenthesis is maintained.

e. Press **Enter**. Four decimal places are shown for some results.
f. Copy the formula in cell **D10** to cells **D11:D16**.
g. Double-click cell **D16** and select **IrisMed** in the cell or in the *Formula* bar.
h. Press **F3 (FN+F3)** to open the *Paste Name* dialog box.
i. Select **Medeye** in the list and click **OK**.
j. Press **Enter**.
k. Copy the formula in cell **D16** to cells **D17:D20**.
l. Complete the formulas for Westville insurance.

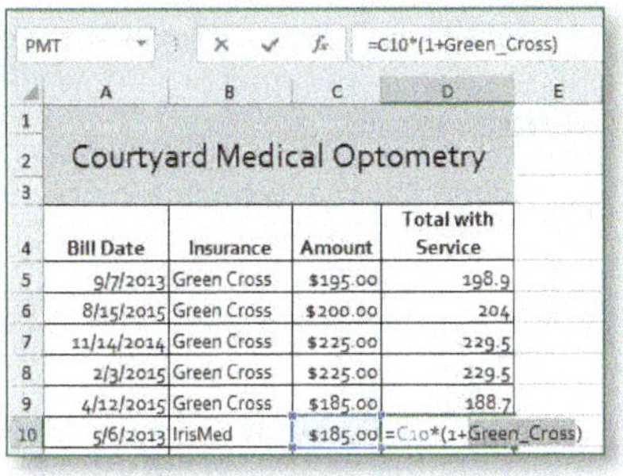

2-69 Edit the range name in a formula

7. Format cells **D5:D24** as **Currency** from the *Number Format* drop-down list. The values are rounded to two decimals places.
8. Use the *SUMIF* function to calculate billable amounts by insurance company.
   a. Click the **Optometry** worksheet tab and select cell **D31**.
   b. Click the **Math & Trig** button [*Formulas* tab, *Function Library* group].
   c. Select **SUMIF**.
   d. Click the **Range** box and select cells **C5:C24**.
   e. Click the **Criteria** box and select cell **C31** to use a relative reference to the company name.
   f. Click the **Sum_range** text box and select cells **E5:E24**. The range name is substituted (Figure 2-70).
   g. Click **OK**. The result is 1030, the total amount billed to Green Cross.

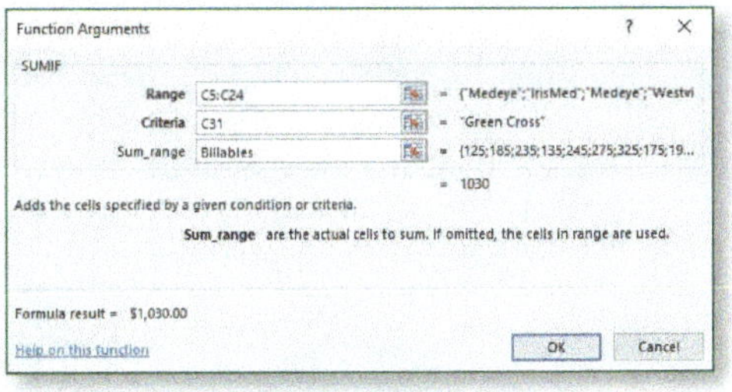

2-70 Different *range* and *sum_range* arguments for *SUMIF*

9. Verify results with *AutoCalculate*.
   a. Select cells **E13:E15**.
   b. Press **Ctrl** and select cells **E20:E21**. These are the billable amounts for the Green Cross insurance company.
   c. Compare the *SUM* in the *Status* bar with the result in cell **D31** (Figure 2-71).
10. Copy the *SUMIF* function with a relative reference.
    a. Select cell **D31**.
    b. Drag the *Fill* pointer to copy the formula in cell **D31** to cells **D32:D34**. The *Auto Fill Options* button appears near cell D34.
    c. Select cell **D32**. The reference to cell C31 in the original formula is updated to cell C32 in the copied formula (Figure 2-72).

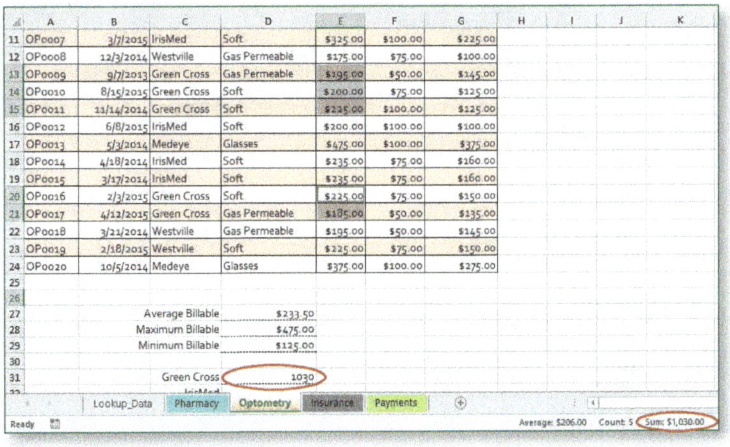

2-71 *AutoCalculate* results in Status bar

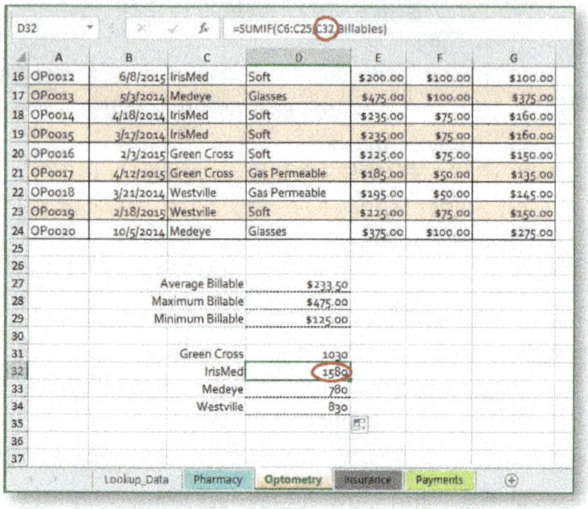

2-72 Relative reference is adjusted after copying

11. Format cells **D31:D34** as **Currency** from the *Number Format* drop-down list. Press **Ctrl+Home**.
12. Use *VLOOKUP* with a range name to display costs.
    a. Click the **Pharmacy** worksheet tab and select cell **C6**. Cost and retail prices are missing.
    b. Click the **Lookup & Reference** button [*Formulas* tab, *Function Library* group] and select **VLOOKUP**.
    c. Click the **Lookup_value** box and click cell **A6**. The ID in column A will be located in the table array.
    d. Click the **Table_array** box. All prices are in the *Lookup_Data* sheet.
    e. Click the **Lookup_Data** sheet tab and select cells **A2:D16**. This range *Costs* is substituted when you select the cells; the range name is not substituted if you type the range address. Notice that the cost is in the third column.
    f. Click the **Col_index_num** box and type 3 (Figure 2-73).

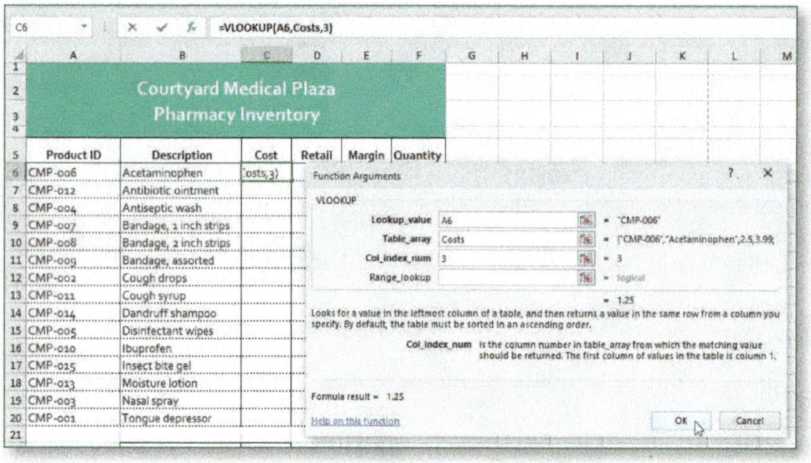

2-73 *VLOOKUP* and its arguments

    g. Click **OK**. The acetaminophen cost is 1.25.
    h. Copy the formula in cell **C6** to cells **C7:C20** without formatting. Format cells **C6:C20** as **Currency**.
13. Type the *VLOOKUP* function.
    a. Click cell **D6**.
    b. Type =vl and press **Tab**. The first argument is *lookup_value*.
    c. Select cell **A6** and type a comma (,) to separate the arguments. The next argument is *table_array*.
    d. Type costs,. You can type the name or select it in the *Formula AutoComplete* list (Figure 2-74).

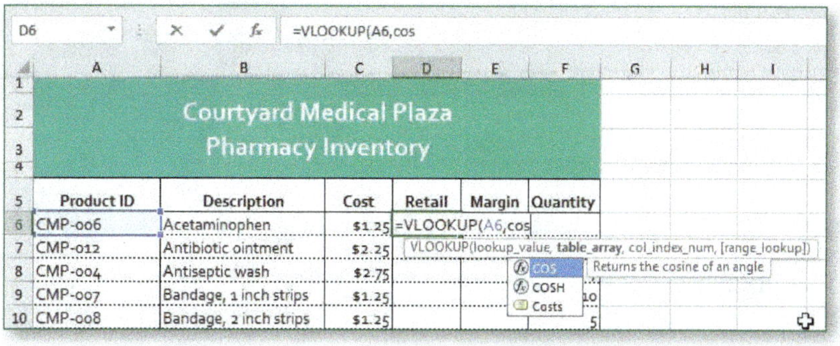

2-74 ***Formula AutoComplete*** **shows range names**

e. Type 4 for the *Col_index_num* argument, because the retail price is in the fourth column of the *Costs* range.
f. Press **Enter**. The closing parenthesis is supplied, and the retail price for acetaminophen is 3.99.
g. Copy the formula in cell **D6** to cells **D7:D20** without formatting and then format the cells as **Currency**.

14. Set order of precedence in a formula.
    a. Click cell **E6**. The formula to calculate the margin subtracts the cost from the retail price and then divides by the cost. The margin is shown as a markup percentage.
    b. Type =(to start the formula and enter the opening parenthesis.
    c. Click cell **D6** for the retail price.
    d. Type – and click cell **C6** to subtract the cost from the retail price.
    e. Type) for the closing parenthesis. This forces the subtraction to be carried out first.
    f. Type / for division and click cell **C6** to divide the results by the cost (Figure 2-75).
    g. Press **Enter**. The results are formatted as currency.
    h. Apply **Percent Style** to cell **E6**. A margin of 219% means that the retail price is more than two times the cost.
    i. Copy the formula in cell **E6** to cells **E7:E20** without formatting; then apply **Percent Style** to cells **E7:E20**.

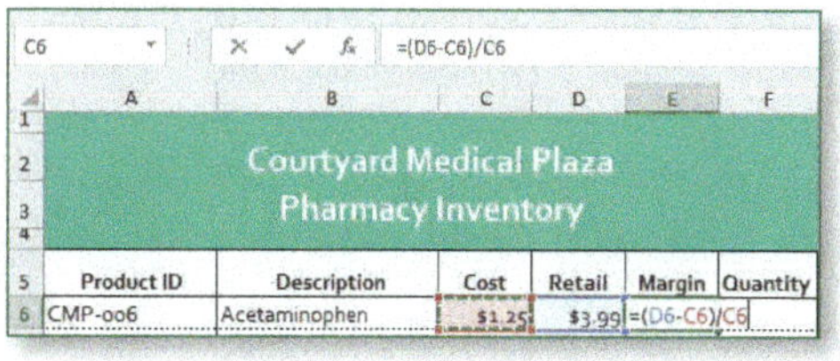

2-75 Formula with multiple operators

15. Trace precedents and dependents for formulas.
    a. Select cell **C6**.
    b. Click the **Trace Precedents** button [*Formulas* tab, *Formula Auditing* group]. The formula uses data from another worksheet and from cell **A6**.
    c. Select cell **E6** and click the **Trace Precedents** button.
    d. Select cell **D7** and click the **Trace Dependents** button. The arrow points to cell **E7**.
    e. Click the **Remove Arrows** button [*Formulas* tab, *Formula Auditing* group].

16. Enter a *SUMPRODUCT* function to calculate inventory values.
    a. Click cell **C22**.
    b. Click the **Math & Trig** button [*Formulas* tab, *Function Library* group] and select **SUMPRODUCT**.
    c. Click the *Array1* box and select cells **C6:C20**.
    d. Click the *Array2* box and select cells **F6:F20**. Both arrays have the same dimension (Figure 2-76).
    e. Click **OK**. The result in E22 is 249.15. Each value in column C is multiplied by its corresponding value in column E, and those results are summed.

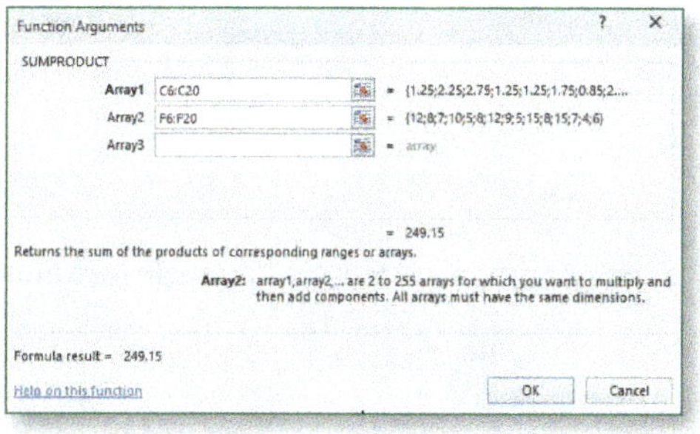

2-76 Two arrays for SUMPRODUCT

17. Type the *SUMPRODUCT* function.
    a. Click cell **D23**.
    b. Type =sump and press **Tab**. The first argument is *array1*.
    c. Select cells **D6:D20** and type a comma (,) to separate the arguments. The next argument is *array2*.
    d. Select cells **F6:F20** and press **Enter** (Figure 2-77). The result is 588.29.
    e. Format cells **D22:D23** as **Currency**. Press **Ctrl+Home**.

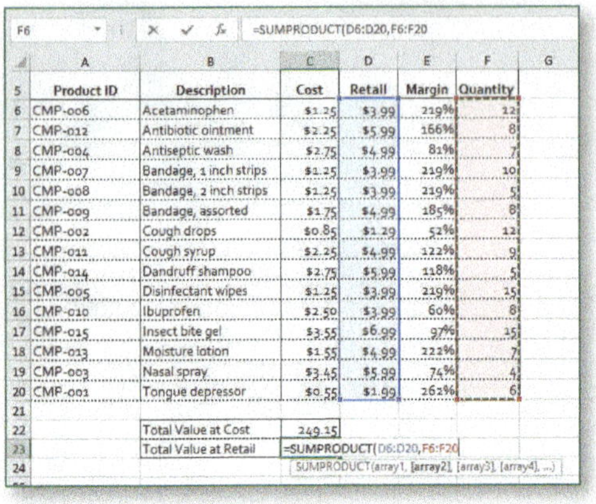

2-77 Both arrays have the same dimension

18. Use *PMT* to calculate patient payments.
    a. Click the **Payments** sheet tab and select cell **B6**.
    b. Click the **Financial** button [*Formulas* tab, *Function Library* group] and select **PMT**.
    c. Click the **Rate** box and type 2.75%/12. You can type the rate when it is not shown in a cell. Yearly rates are divided by 12 for monthly payments.
    d. Click the **Nper** box and type 24. The length of the loan is indicated in the label in cell A4. Two-year financing means 24 monthly payments.
    e. Click the **Pv** box and click cell **A6**, the amount of a loan.
    f. Press **F4 (FN+F4)** to make the reference absolute ($A$6). Press **F4 (FN+F4)** again to make a mixed reference A$6.
    g. Press **F4 (FN+F4)** once more to make the reference mixed $A6.
    h. Click the **Type** box and type 1 for payment at the beginning of the month. The *Fv* argument is blank (Figure 2-78).
    i. Click **OK**. The payment for financing $500 is ($21.39).
    j. Copy the formula to cells **B7:B11**. The reference to cell $A6 is mixed, and the *rate* and *nper* values that you typed are absolute.

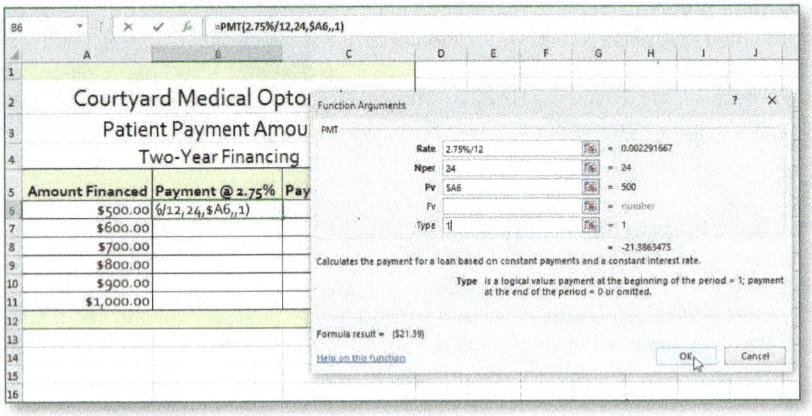

2-78 PMT arguments

19. Copy and edit a *PMT* function with a mixed reference.
    a. Copy the formula in cell **B6** to cell **C6**. The reference to cell $A6 is correct, but you need to edit the *Rate* argument.
    b. Select cell **C6** and click the **Insert Function** button in the *Formula* bar. The *Function Arguments* dialog box opens with the formula.
    c. Click the **Rate** text box and edit the calculation to 3.25%/12.
    d. Click **OK**. The payment for financing $500 at 3.25% is ($21.49).
    e. Copy the formula to cells **C7:C11**.

20. Enter the TODAY function.
    a. Select cell **A14**.
    b. Type =to, press **Tab**, and press **Enter**.
    c. Press **Ctrl+Home**.
21. Save and close the workbook (Figure 2-79).

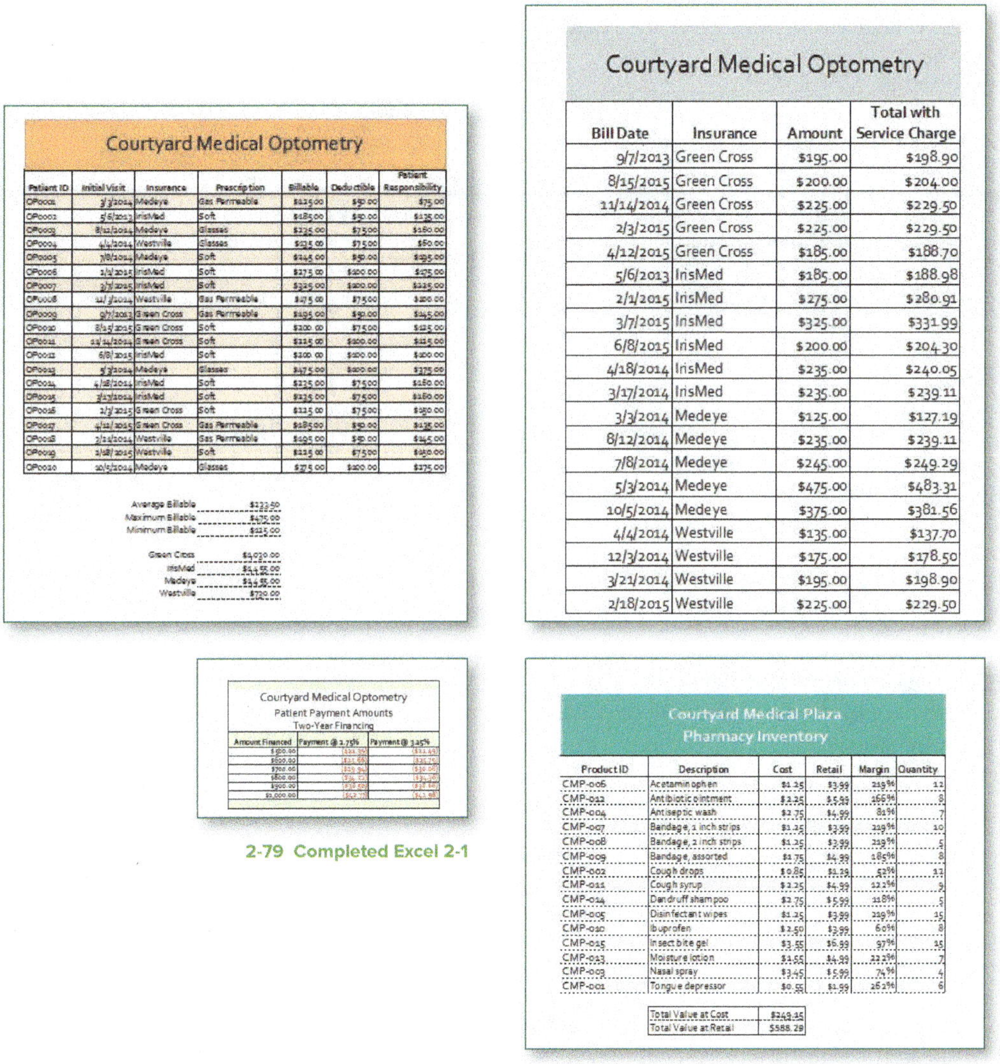

Courtyard Medical Optometry

Bill Date	Insurance	Amount	Total with Service Charge
9/7/2013	Green Cross	$195.00	$198.90
8/15/2015	Green Cross	$200.00	$204.00
11/14/2014	Green Cross	$225.00	$229.50
2/3/2015	Green Cross	$225.00	$229.50
4/12/2015	Green Cross	$185.00	$188.70
5/6/2013	IrisMed	$185.00	$188.98
2/1/2015	IrisMed	$275.00	$280.91
3/7/2015	IrisMed	$325.00	$331.99
6/8/2015	IrisMed	$200.00	$204.30
4/18/2014	IrisMed	$235.00	$240.05
3/17/2014	IrisMed	$235.00	$239.11
3/3/2014	Medeye	$125.00	$127.19
8/12/2014	Medeye	$235.00	$239.11
7/8/2014	Medeye	$245.00	$249.29
5/3/2014	Medeye	$475.00	$483.31
10/5/2014	Medeye	$375.00	$381.56
4/4/2014	Westville	$135.00	$137.70
12/3/2014	Westville	$175.00	$178.50
3/21/2014	Westville	$195.00	$198.90
2/18/2015	Westville	$225.00	$229.50

2-79 Completed Excel 2-1

E2-139

Guided Project 2-2

Hamilton Civic Center (HCC) is a nonprofit community fitness center with an indoor pool, sauna, indoor track, project room, racquetball courts, meeting rooms, and a boutique. In this workbook, you complete tasks related to health seminars, a member challenge, and the daycare program.
[Student Learning Outcomes 2.1, 2.2, 2.3, 2.4, 2.5, 2.6, 2.7]

File Needed: ***HamiltonCivic-02.xlsx*** *[Student data files are available in the* Library *of your SIMnet account.]*
Completed Project File Name: ***[your initials] Excel 2-2.xlsx***

Skills Covered in This Project

- Create and copy formulas.
- Name cell ranges.
- Use relative and absolute references.
- Set mathematical order of operations.
- Use *AutoCalculate* and formula auditing tools.
- Use *VLOOKUP* and *HLOOKUP*.
- Create an *IF* function.
- Create a *SUMIF* function.
- Use the *TODAY* function.

1. Open the ***HamiltonCivic-02.xlsx*** workbook from your student data files and save it as [your initials] Excel 2-2.
2. Name cell ranges.
   a. On the *Seminars* sheet, select cells **B6:B10**, and click the **Name** box.
   b. Type Seminars in the *Name* box and press **Enter**.
   c. Click the **Data** sheet tab. You will name the cell ranges used in the *Lookup* functions.
   d. Select cells **A2:D10** and click the **Name** box.
   e. Type V_Calories in the *Name* box and press **Enter**. This will remind you that this range is a vertical table array.
   f. Select cells **F2:J3** and click the **Name** box.
   g. Type H_Fees and press **Enter**. This range is a horizontal table array.
3. Enter and copy a division formula.
   a. Select cell **D2** on the **Data** worksheet. To calculate calories per minute, divide the total calories by the number of minutes.
   b. Type an equals sign (=) to start the formula.
   c. Click cell **C2**, the total number of calories. This formula uses relative references.
   d. Type / for division.
   e. Click cell **B2**, the number of minutes, and press **Enter**. As many decimal places as fit in the cell are displayed (Figure 2-80).

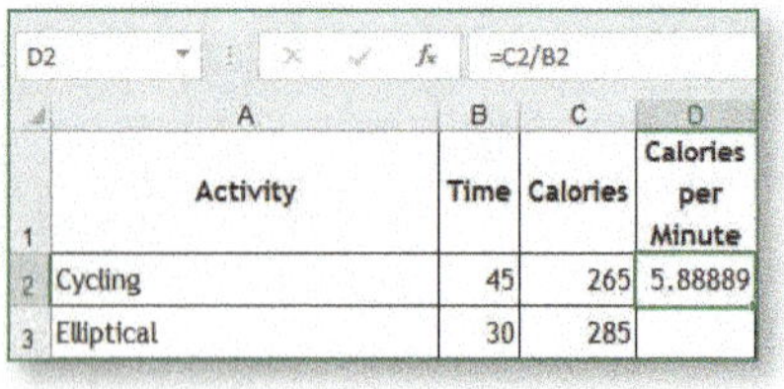

2-80 Decimal positions fill the cell

   f. Drag the *Fill* pointer to copy the formula in cell **D2** to cells **D3:D10**. Ignore the *Auto Fill Options* button.
   g. While cells **D2:D10** are selected, click the **Decrease Decimal** button [*Home* tab, *Number* group] two times. The sets the same number of decimal positions for all results.
4. Use *HLOOKUP* with a range name to display fees.
   a. Click the **Seminars** worksheet tab and select cell **C6**. Fees are in the *H_Fees* range.
   b. Click the **Lookup & Reference** button [*Formulas* tab, *Function Library* group] and select **HLOOKUP**.
   c. Click the **Lookup_value** box and click cell **B6**.
   d. Click the **Table_array** box.

e. Type h_fees the name of the range. It is not case sensitive, and quotation marks are not necessary.
f. Click the **Row_index_num** box and type 2 because the fees are in the second row of the *H_Fees* range (Figure 2-81).
g. Click **OK**. The fee is $15.00.
h. Copy the formula in cell **C6** to cells **C7:C10**.

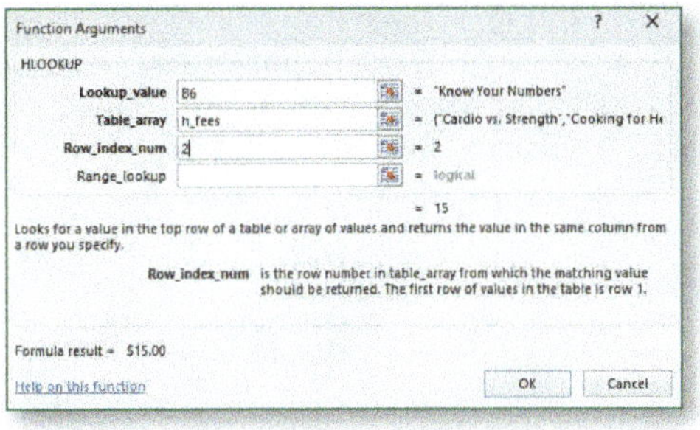

2-81 Arguments for *HLOOKUP*

5. Enter and copy an addition formula.
   a. Click cell **E15** and type an equals sign (=) to start the formula.
   b. Click cell **D6**, the number of attendees for the seminar in Hendersonville.
   c. Type + for addition.
   d. Click cell **E6** to add the number of attendees for Advocate Central.
   e. Type +, click cell **F6**, type +, and click cell **G6** (Figure 2-82).
   f. Press **Enter**.
   g. Drag the *Fill* pointer to copy the formula in cell **E15** to cells **E16:E19**. Ignore the *Auto Fill Options* button.
   h. Click cell **E20**, click the **AutoSum** button [*Home* tab, *Editing* group], and press **Enter**. The total is 209 attendees.

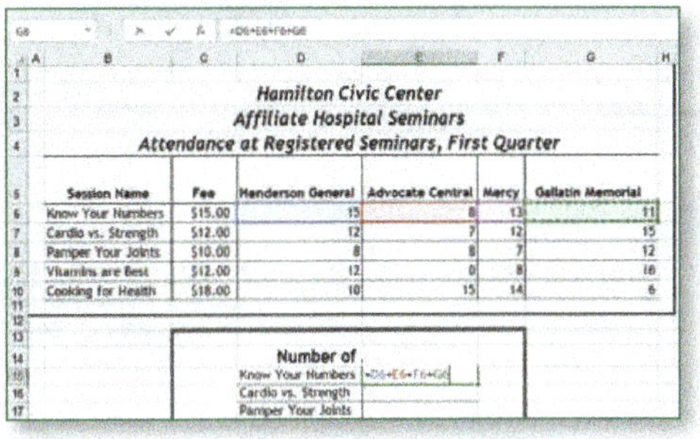

2-82 Simple addition formula

6. Set order of operations in a formula.
   a. Select cell **E24**. The fee is multiplied by the sum of the attendees at each hospital. Cells D6:G6 must be added first and that result is multiplied by cell C6.
   b. Type = to start the formula and click cell **C6**.
   c. Type * to multiply.
   d. Type (for the opening parenthesis. This forces the addition to be carried out first.
   e. Click cell **D6**, type +, click cell **E6**, type +, click cell **F6**, type +, and click cell **G6**.
   f. Type) for the closing parenthesis (Figure2-83).
   g. Press **Enter**. The result is 705.
   h. Format cell **E24** as **Currency** and copy the formula to cells **E25:E28**.
   i. Click cell **E29**, click the **AutoSum** button [*Home* tab, *Editing* group], and press **Enter**.

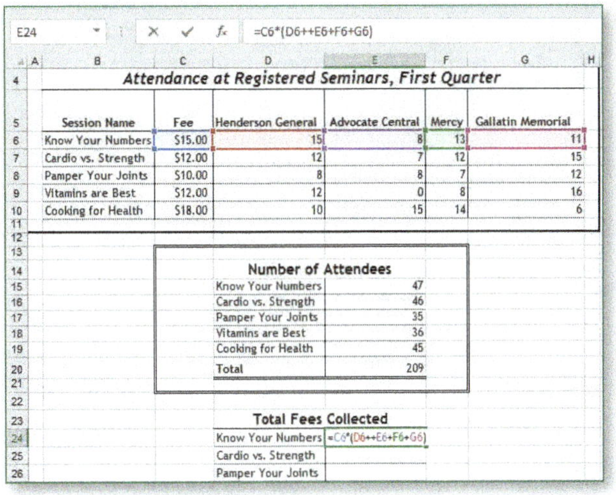

2-83 Addition done before multiplication

7. Use *AutoCalculate* and formula auditing tools.
   a. Select cells **E24:E28**.
   b. Compare the *SUM* in the *Status* bar with the result in cell E29.
   c. Select cell **E15**.

d. Click the **Trace Precedents** button [*Formulas* tab, *Formula Auditing* group].
e. Click the **Trace Dependents** button. The formula in cell E15 has both precedent and dependent cells (Figure 2-84).
f. Click the **Remove Arrows** button [*Formulas* tab, *Formula Auditing* group].

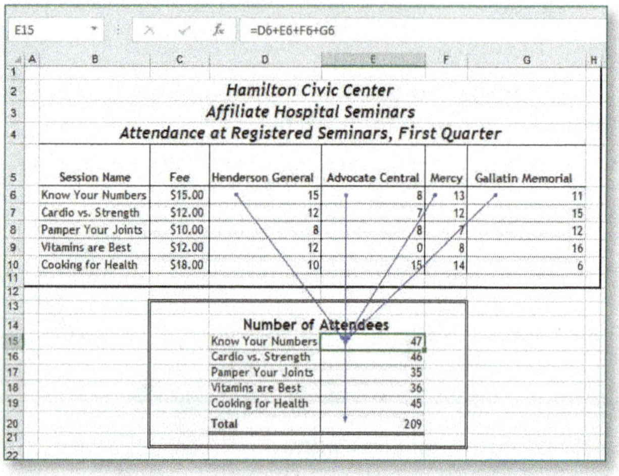
E15 =D6+E6+F6+G6

Hamilton Civic Center
Affiliate Hospital Seminars
Attendance at Registered Seminars, First Quarter

Session Name	Fee	Henderson General	Advocate Central	Mercy	Gallatin Memorial
Know Your Numbers	$15.00	15	8	13	11
Cardio vs. Strength	$12.00	12	7	12	15
Pamper Your Joints	$10.00	8	8	7	12
Vitamins are Best	$12.00	12	0	8	16
Cooking for Health	$18.00	10	15	14	6

Number of Attendees

Know Your Numbers	47
Cardio vs. Strength	46
Pamper Your Joints	35
Vitamins are Best	36
Cooking for Health	45
Total	209

2-84 Precedent and dependent cells

8. Use *VLOOKUP* with a range name to display calories expended.
   a. Click the **Data** sheet tab.
   b. Click the **Name** box arrow and select **V_Calories**. Notice that total calories are in the third column.
   c. Click the **Calorie Tracking** sheet tab and select cell **D3**. Calories by activity are within the range *V_Calories*.
   d. Click the **Lookup & Reference** button [*Formulas* tab, *Formula Auditing* group] and select **VLOOKUP**.
   e. Click the **Lookup_value** box and click cell **C3**. The activity name in column C will be located in the table array.
   f. Click the **Table_array** box and press **F3 (FN+F3)** to open the *Paste Name* dialog box.
   g. Double-click **V_Calories** to insert it.
   h. Click the **Col_index_num** box and type 3 (Figure 2-85).
   i. Click **OK**. Calories for the first activity are 250.
   j. Copy the formula in cell **D3** to cells **D4:D23**.

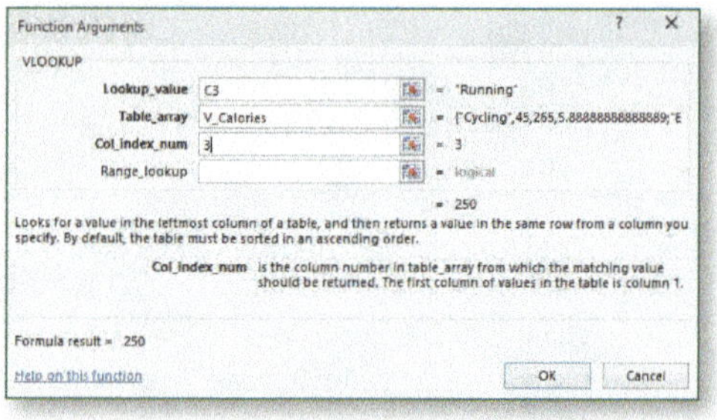

2-85 Arguments for the *VLOOKUP* function

9. Build a *SUMIF* formula with absolute and relative references.
   a. Select cell **D28** on the **Calorie Tracking** sheet.
   b. Click the **Recently Used** button [*Formulas* tab, *Function Library* group].
   c. Look for and choose **SUMIF**. (If you do not see *SUMIF* in the list, click the **Math & Trig** button to find and select **SUMIF**.)
   d. Click the **Range** box and select cells **C3:C23**, the range that will be evaluated.
   e. Press **F4 (FN+F4)** to make the cell references absolute.
   f. Click the **Criteria** box and select cell **C28** to find rows with "cycling" as the activity.
   g. Click the **Sum_range** box and select cells **D3:D23**, the values to be summed if the activity is cycling.

h. Press **F4 (FN+F4)** to make the references absolute (Figure 2-86).

i. Click **OK**. The result is 795 calories.

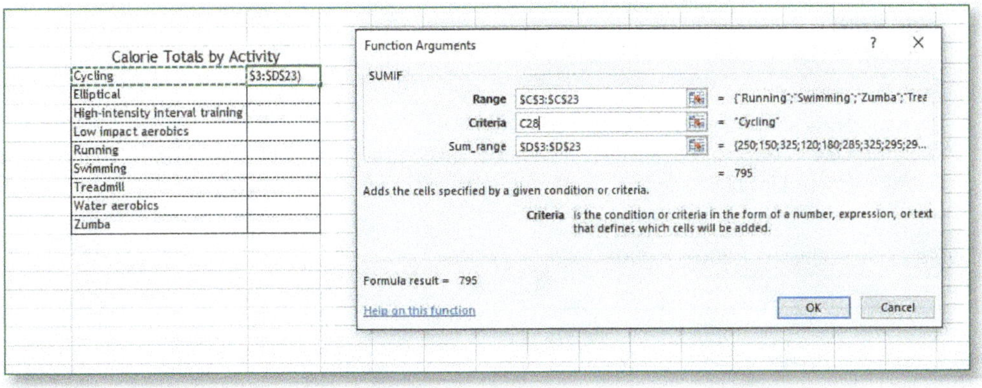

2-86 *SUMIF* function for cycling

10. Copy the formula in cell **D28** to cells **D29:D36** without formatting (Figure 2-87).

11. Create an *IF* function to calculate a fee based on age.
    a. Click the **Day Care** sheet tab and select cell **D5**.
    b. Click the **Logical** button [*Formulas* tab, *Function Library* group] and select **IF**.
    c. Click the **Logical_test** box and click cell **B5**.
    d. Type >=4 to test if the child is 4 years old or greater.
    e. Click the **Value_if_true** box and click cell **I9**. The fee for a child 4 years old or greater is $18.
    f. Press **F4 (FN+F4)** to make the reference absolute.
    g. Click the **Value_if_false** box and click cell **I8**. If the child is not 4 years old or greater, the child is between 1 and 3 years old.
    h. Press **F4 (FN+F4)** to make the reference absolute (Figure 2-88).
    i. Click **OK**. The fee for Mary is $18.
    j. Format the result as **Currency**.
    k. Copy the formula in cell **D5** to cells **D6:D14**.

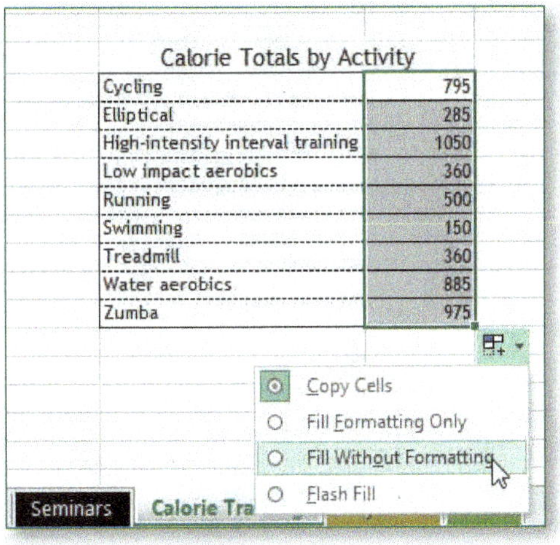

2-87 Copy the formula without formatting

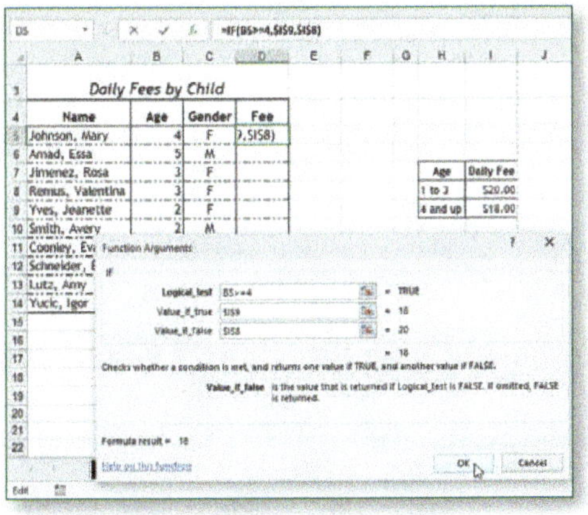

2-88 *IF* function to determine the fee

12. Insert the current date as a function.
    a. Click the **Data** sheet tab and click cell **A12**.
    b. Type =to and press **Tab** to select the function.
    c. Press **Enter**.
    d. Press **Ctrl+Home**.
13. Paste range names.
    a. Click the **New sheet** button in the sheet tab area.
    b. Click the **Use in Formula** button [*Formulas* tab, *Defined Names* group] and select **Paste Names**.
    c. Click the **Paste List** button in the *Paste Name* dialog box.
    d. *AutoFit* each column and name the tab Range Names.
14. Save and close the workbook (Figure 2-89).

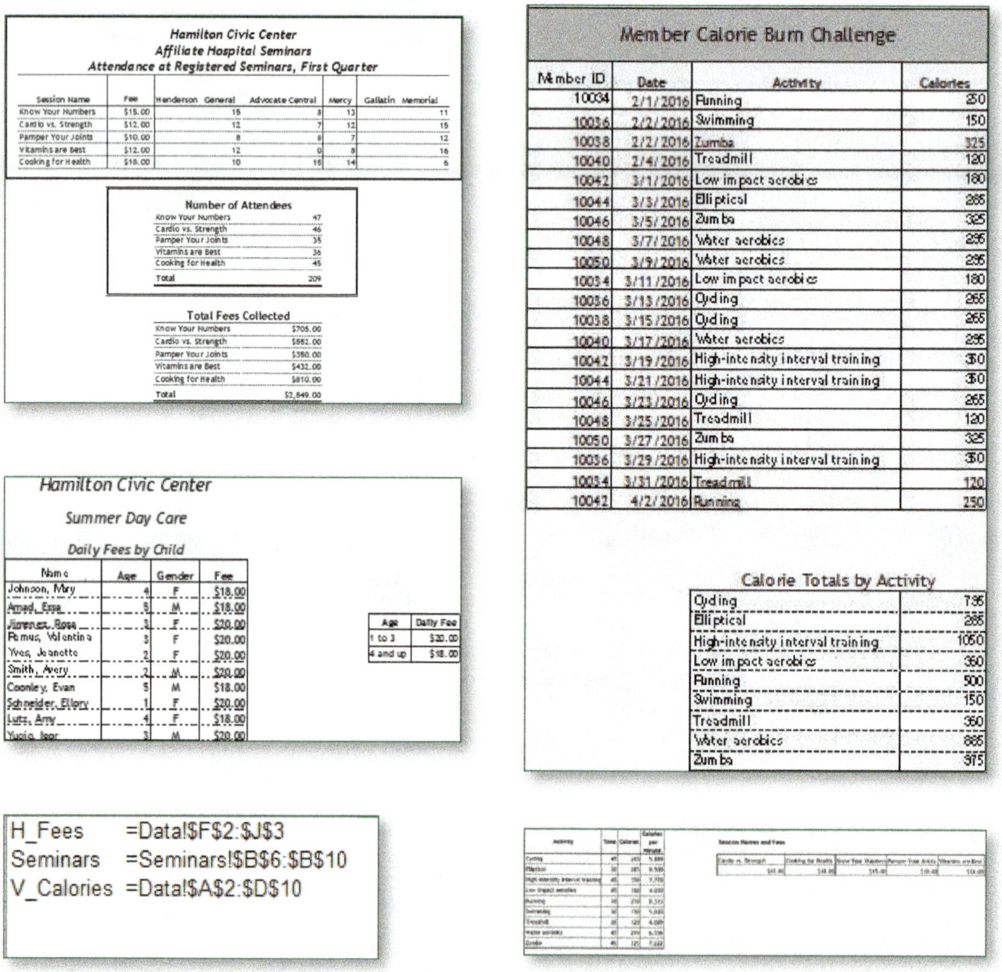

2-89 Excel 2-2 completed

Guided Project 2-3

Sierra Pacific Community College District (SPCCD) consists of four individual community colleges. The workbook for this project includes an amortization schedule for student loans and a fee and credit hour summary for several departments.
[Student Learning Outcomes 2.1, 2.2, 2.3, 2.4, 2.5, 2.6, 2.7]

File Needed: ***SierraPacific-02.xlsx*** *[Student data files are available in the* Library *of your SIMnet account.]*
Completed Project File Name: ***[your initials] Excel 2-3.xlsx***

Skills Covered in This Project

- Name cell ranges.
- Create and copy formulas.
- Set mathematical order of operations.
- Use absolute references in formulas.
- Insert the current date as a function.
- Use the *PMT* function.
- Audit formulas.
- Use *SUMIF* and *SUMPRODUCT*.

1. Open the ***SierraPacific-02.xlsx*** workbook from your student data files and save it as [your initials] Excel 2-3.
2. Set range names for the workbook.
   a. On the **Student Loan** sheet, select cells **B5:C8**.
   b. Click the **Create from Selection** button [*Formulas* tab, *Defined Names* group].
   c. Verify that the **Left column** box in the *Create Names from Selection* dialog box is selected.
   d. Deselect the **Top row** box if it is checked and click **OK**.
   e. Select cells **E5:F7**. Repeat steps a–d to create range names.
   f. Click the **Name Manager** button [*Formulas* tab, *Defined Names* group] to view the names in the *Name Manager* dialog box (Figure 2-90).
   g. Click **Close**.

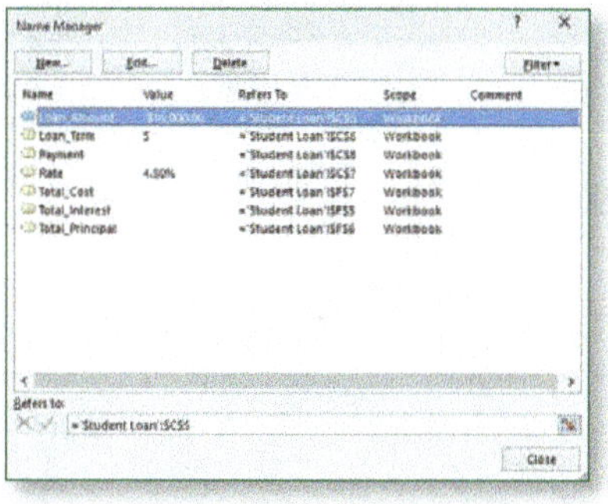

2-90 *Name Manager* dialog box

3. Enter a *PMT* function.
   a. Select **C8**.
   b. Click the **Financial** button [*Formulas* tab, *Function Library* group] and select **PMT**.
   c. Click the **Rate** box and click cell **C7**. The range name *Rate* is substituted.
   d. Type /12 immediately after **Rate** to divide by 12 for monthly payments.
   e. Click the **Nper** box and click cell **C6**. The substituted range name is *Loan_Term*.
   f. Type *12 after **Loan_Term** to multiply by 12.
   g. Click the **Pv** box and type a minus sign (–) to set the argument as a negative amount.
   h. Click cell **C5** (*Loan_Amount*) for the *pv* argument. A negative loan amount reflects the lender's perspective, since the money is paid out now (Figure 2-91).

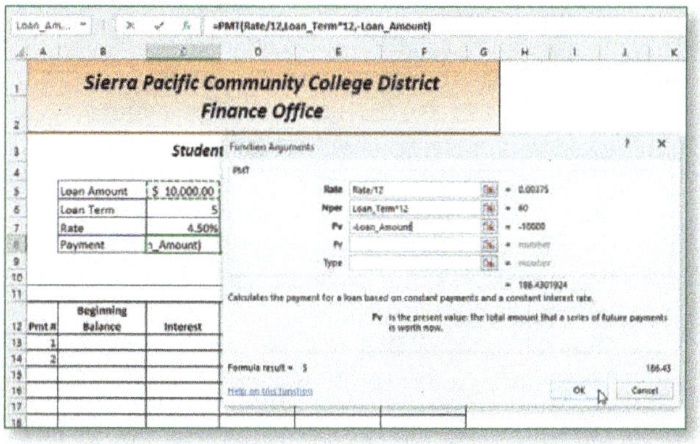

2-91 *Pv* argument is negative in the *PMT* function

i. Leave the *Fv* and *Type* boxes empty.
j. Click **OK**. The payment for a loan at this rate is $186.43, shown as a positive value.

4. Create a total interest formula.
   a. Click cell **F5** (*Total_Interest*). This value is calculated by multiplying the monthly payment by the total number of payments to determine total outlay. From this amount, you subtract the loan amount.
   b. Type = and click cell **C8** (the *Payment*).
   c. Type * to multiply and click cell **C6** (*Loan_Term*).
   d. Type *12 to multiply by 12 for monthly payments.
   e. Type – immediately after ***12** to subtract.
   f. Click cell **C5** (the *Loan_Amount*). The formula is *Payment*Loan_Term*12–Loan_Amount*. Parentheses are not required, because the multiplications are done from left to right, followed by the subtraction (Figure 2-92).
   g. Press **Enter**. The result is $1,185.81.

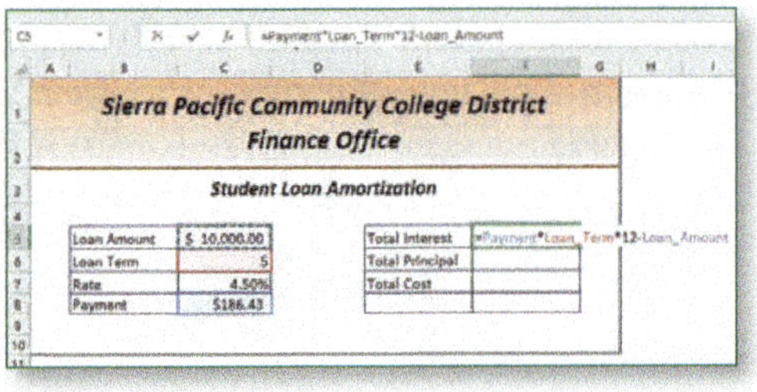

2-92 Left-to-right operations

5. Create the total principal formula and the total loan cost.
   a. Select cell **F6** (*Total_Principal*). This value is calculated by multiplying the monthly payment by the total number of payments. From this amount, subtract the total interest.
   b. Type = and click cell **C8** (the *Payment*).
   c. Type * to multiply and click cell **C6** (*Loan_Term*).
   d. Type *12 to multiply by 12 for monthly payments.
   e. Type – immediately after ***12** to subtract.
   f. Click cell **F5** (the *Total_Interest*). The formula is *Payment*Loan_Term*12–Total_Interest*.
   g. Press **Enter**. Total principal is the amount of the loan.
   h. Click cell **F7**, the *Total_Cost* of the loan. This is the total principal plus the total interest.
   i. Type =, click cell **F5**, type +, click cell **F6**, and then press **Enter**.

6. Build an amortization schedule.
   a. Click cell **B13**. The beginning balance is the total cost of the loan.
   b. Type =, click cell **F7**, and press **Enter**.
   c. Format the value as **Accounting Number Format**.
   d. Select cell **C13**. The interest for each payment is calculated by multiplying the balance in column B by the rate divided by 12.
   e. Type = and click cell **B13**.
   f. Type *(and click cell **C7**.
   g. Type /12). Parentheses are necessary so that the division is done first (Figure 2-93).
   h. Press **Enter** and format the results as **Accounting Number Format**.
   i. Select cell **D13**. The portion of the payment that is applied to the principal is calculated by subtracting the interest portion from the payment.
   j. Type =, click cell **C8** (the *Payment*).
   k. Type –, click cell **C13**, and press **Enter**.
   l. Click cell **E13**. The total payment is the interest portion plus the principal portion.
   m. Type =, click cell **C13**, type +, click cell **D13**, and then press **Enter**. The value matches the amount in cell **C8**.
   n. Select cell **F13**. The ending balance is the beginning balance minus the payment.
   o. Type =, click cell **B13**, type –, click cell **E13**, and then press **Enter**. The ending balance is $10,999.38.

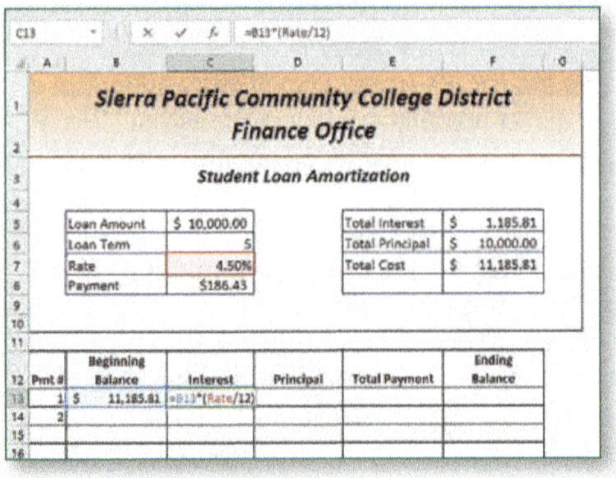

2-93 The interest formula

B13	=Total_Cost
C13	=B13*(Rate/12)
D13	=Payment−C13
E13	=C13+D13
F13	=B13−E13

7. Fill data and copy formulas.
   a. Select cells **A13:A14**. This is a series with an increment of 1.
   b. Drag the *Fill* pointer to reach cell **A72**. This sets 60 payments for a five-year loan term.
   c. Select cell **B14**. The beginning balance for the second payment is the ending balance for the first payment.
   d. Type =, click cell **F13**, and press **Enter**.
   e. Double-click the *Fill* pointer for cell **B14** to fill the formula down to row **72**. The results are zero until the rest of the schedule is complete.
   f. Select cells **C13:F13**.
   g. Double-click the *Fill* pointer at cell **F13**. All of the formulas are filled (copied) to row **72** (Figure2-94).
   h. Scroll to see the values in row **72**. The loan balance reaches 0.
   i. Press **Ctrl+Home**.

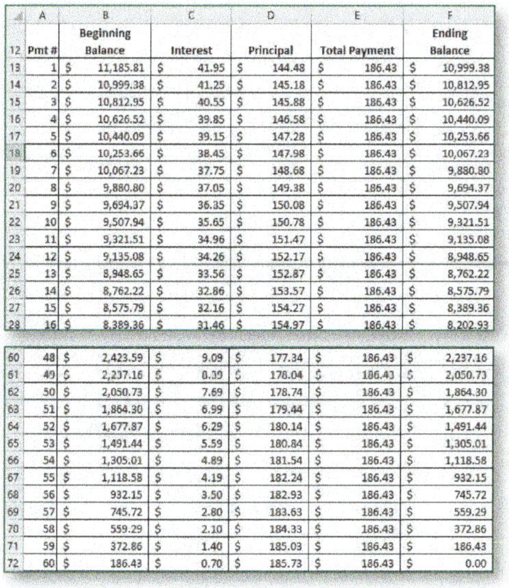

	A	B	C	D	E	F
12	Pmt #	Beginning Balance	Interest	Principal	Total Payment	Ending Balance
13	1	$ 11,185.81	$ 41.95	$ 144.48	$ 186.43	$ 10,999.38
14	2	$ 10,999.38	$ 41.25	$ 145.18	$ 186.43	$ 10,812.95
15	3	$ 10,812.95	$ 40.55	$ 145.88	$ 186.43	$ 10,626.52
16	4	$ 10,626.52	$ 39.85	$ 146.58	$ 186.43	$ 10,440.09
17	5	$ 10,440.09	$ 39.15	$ 147.28	$ 186.43	$ 10,253.66
18	6	$ 10,253.66	$ 38.45	$ 147.98	$ 186.43	$ 10,067.23
19	7	$ 10,067.23	$ 37.75	$ 148.68	$ 186.43	$ 9,880.80
20	8	$ 9,880.80	$ 37.05	$ 149.38	$ 186.43	$ 9,694.37
21	9	$ 9,694.37	$ 36.35	$ 150.08	$ 186.43	$ 9,507.94
22	10	$ 9,507.94	$ 35.65	$ 150.78	$ 186.43	$ 9,321.51
23	11	$ 9,321.51	$ 34.96	$ 151.47	$ 186.43	$ 9,135.08
24	12	$ 9,135.08	$ 34.26	$ 152.17	$ 186.43	$ 8,948.65
25	13	$ 8,948.65	$ 33.56	$ 152.87	$ 186.43	$ 8,762.22
26	14	$ 8,762.22	$ 32.86	$ 153.57	$ 186.43	$ 8,575.79
27	15	$ 8,575.79	$ 32.16	$ 154.27	$ 186.43	$ 8,389.36
28	16	$ 8,389.36	$ 31.46	$ 154.97	$ 186.43	$ 8,202.93
60	48	$ 2,423.59	$ 9.09	$ 177.34	$ 186.43	$ 2,237.16
61	49	$ 2,237.16	$ 8.39	$ 178.04	$ 186.43	$ 2,050.73
62	50	$ 2,050.73	$ 7.69	$ 178.74	$ 186.43	$ 1,864.30
63	51	$ 1,864.30	$ 6.99	$ 179.44	$ 186.43	$ 1,677.87
64	52	$ 1,677.87	$ 6.29	$ 180.14	$ 186.43	$ 1,491.44
65	53	$ 1,491.44	$ 5.59	$ 180.84	$ 186.43	$ 1,305.01
66	54	$ 1,305.01	$ 4.89	$ 181.54	$ 186.43	$ 1,118.58
67	55	$ 1,118.58	$ 4.19	$ 182.24	$ 186.43	$ 932.15
68	56	$ 932.15	$ 3.50	$ 182.93	$ 186.43	$ 745.72
69	57	$ 745.72	$ 2.80	$ 183.63	$ 186.43	$ 559.29
70	58	$ 559.29	$ 2.10	$ 184.33	$ 186.43	$ 372.86
71	59	$ 372.86	$ 1.40	$ 185.03	$ 186.43	$ 186.43
72	60	$ 186.43	$ 0.70	$ 185.73	$ 186.43	$ 0.00

2-94 Formulas copied down columns

8. Build a multiplication formula and set order of mathematical operations.
   a. Click the **Fees & Credit** sheet tab and select cell **F7**. Credit hours times number of sections times the fee calculates the total fees from a course.
   b. Type =, click cell **C7**, type *, click cell **D7**, type *, click cell **E7**, and then press **Enter**. No parentheses are necessary because multiplication is done in left to right order.
   c. Select cell **G7**. Fee collected per credit hour is determined by dividing the value in cell F7 by the number of sections times credit hours times average enrollment.
   d. Type =, click cell **F7**, and type / (. Parentheses are necessary so that left to right order is overridden.
   e. Click cell **C7**, type *, and click cell **D7**.
   f. Type *, click cell **C20**, and press **F4 (FN+F4)** to make the reference absolute (Figure 2-95).
   g. Press **Enter**. A message box notes that the closing parenthesis is missing.
   h. Click **Yes** in the message box.
   i. Select cells **F7:G7** and double-click the *Fill* pointer to copy the formulas.
   j. Format cells **G7:G18** as **Currency** and set a bottom border for cells **F18:G18**.

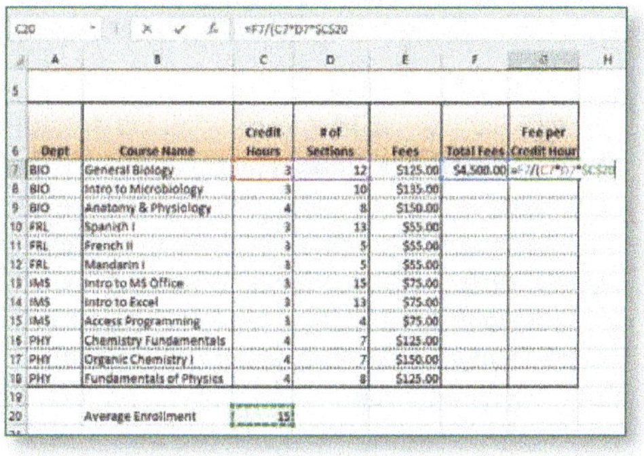

C20 =F7/(C7*D7*$C$20

	A	B	C	D	E	F	G	H
5								
6	Dept	Course Name	Credit Hours	# of Sections	Fees	Total Fees	Fee per Credit Hour	
7	BIO	General Biology	3	12	$125.00	$4,500.00	=F7/(C7*D7*$C$20	
8	BIO	Intro to Microbiology	3	10	$135.00			
9	BIO	Anatomy & Physiology	4	8	$150.00			
10	FRL	Spanish I	3	13	$55.00			
11	FRL	French II	3	5	$55.00			
12	FRL	Mandarin I	3	5	$55.00			
13	IMS	Intro to MS Office	3	15	$75.00			
14	IMS	Intro to Excel	3	13	$75.00			
15	IMS	Access Programming	3	4	$75.00			
16	PHY	Chemistry Fundamentals	4	7	$125.00			
17	PHY	Organic Chemistry I	4	7	$150.00			
18	PHY	Fundamentals of Physics	4	8	$125.00			
19								
20		Average Enrollment	15					

2-95 Formula to calculate fee per credit hour

9. Use *SUMIF*.
   a. Select cell **D26**. Fees by department can be calculated.
   b. Click the **Math & Trig** button [*Formulas* tab, *Function Library* group] and select **SUMIF**.
   c. Click the **Range** box and select cells **A7:A18**. This range will be matched against the criteria.
   d. Press **F4 (FN+F4)** to make the reference absolute.
   e. Click the **Criteria** box and type bio.
   f. Click the **Sum_range** box, select cells **F7:F18**, and press **F4 (FN+F4)**.

g. Click **OK**. Total fees for the Biology department are 13350.
h. Format the results as **Currency**.

10. Copy a *SUMIF* function and check formula errors.
   a. Click cell **D26** and drag its *Fill* pointer to copy the formula to cells **D27:D29** without formatting.
   b. Double-click cell **D27**. You need to change the criteria.
   c. Edit the criteria argument in the *Formula* bar or in the cell to display frl. Do not change the quotation marks or any other punctuation (Figure 2-96).
   d. Press **Enter** or click the **Enter** button in the *Formula* bar. An error triangle appears in the top left corner of cell **D27**.
   e. Click cell **D27** and point to its **Trace Error** button to see the *ScreenTip* (Figure 2-97). The formula has different criteria than the immediately preceding formula, but this is correct.
   f. Click the **Trace Error** button and choose **Ignore Error**.
   g. Double-click cell **D28** and edit the criteria argument to display ims.
   h. Edit the argument in cell **D29** to show the department initials.
   i. Format cells **D27:D29** as **Currency**.

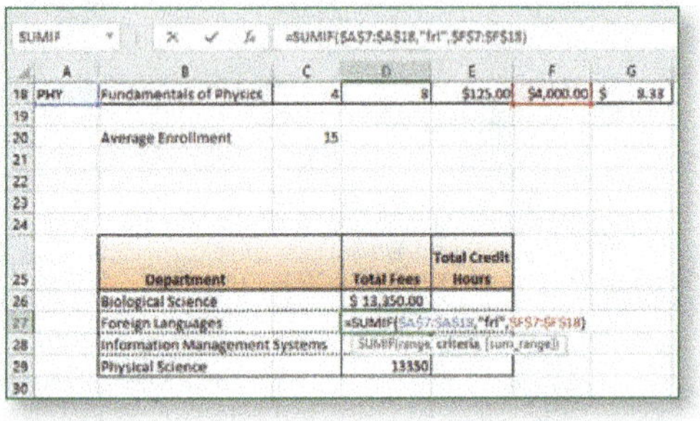

2-96 Edit the SUMIF criteria in the cell or in the *Formula* bar

11. Use *SUMPRODUCT* and trace an error.
   a. Select cell **E26** and click the **Formulas** tab.
   b. Click the **Math & Trig** button in the *Function Library* group and select **SUMPRODUCT**.
   c. Click the **Array1** box and select cells **C7:C9**, credit hours for courses in the Biology Department.
   d. Click the **Array2** box and select cells **D7:D9**, the number of sections for the Biology Department.
   e. Click **OK**. The Biology Department has 98 total credit hour offerings.
   f. Click cell **E26** and point to its **Trace Error** button. The formula omits adjacent cells in columns C and D, which is correct.
   g. Click the **Trace Error** button and select **Ignore Error**.

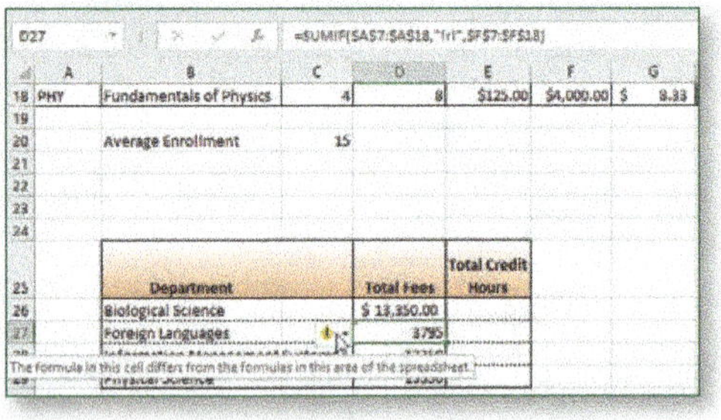

2-97 *Trace Error* button and its *ScreenTip*

12. Copy and edit *SUMPRODUCT*.
   a. Click cell **E26** and drag its *Fill* pointer to copy the formula to cells **E27:E29** without formatting.
   b. Click cell **E27** and click the **Insert Function** button in the *Formula* bar.
   c. Select and highlight the range in the *Array1* box and select cells **C10:C12**. The range you select replaces the range in the dialog box (Figure 2-98).

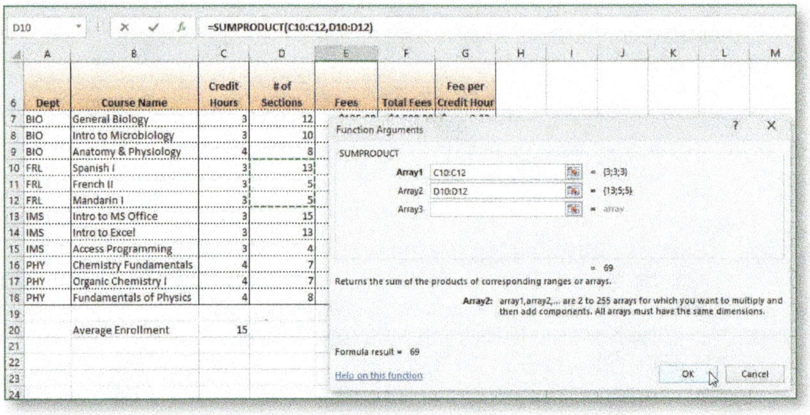

2-98 Replace the *ArrayN* arguments

d. Select the range in the *Array2* box and select cells **D10:D12**.
e. Click **OK**.
f. Edit and complete the formulas in cells **E28:E29** and ignore errors.

13. Insert the current date as a function.
    a. Select cell **G30**.
    b. Type =to and press **Tab** to select the function.
    c. Press **Enter**.
    d. Press **Ctrl+Home**.
14. Paste range names.
    a. Click the **New sheet** button in the sheet tab area.
    b. Name the new sheet **Range Names**.
    c. Press **F3 (FN+F3)** to open the *Paste Name* dialog box.
    d. Click the **Paste List** button.
    e. *AutoFit* each column.
15. Save and close the workbook (Figure 2-99).

Sierra Pacific Community College District
Credit Hours and Fees by Department

Dept	Course Name	Credit Hours	# of Sections	Fees	Total Fees	Fee per Credit Hour
BIO	General Biology	3	12	$125.00	$4,500.00	$ 8.33
BIO	Intro to Microbiology	3	10	$135.00	$4,050.00	$ 9.00
BIO	Anatomy & Physiology	4	8	$150.00	$4,800.00	$ 10.00
FRL	Spanish I	3	13	$55.00	$2,145.00	$ 3.67
FRL	French II	3	5	$55.00	$825.00	$ 3.67
FRL	Mandarin I	3	5	$55.00	$825.00	$ 3.67
IMS	Intro to MS Office	3	15	$75.00	$3,375.00	$ 5.00
IMS	Intro to Excel	3	13	$75.00	$2,925.00	$ 5.00
IMS	Access Programming	3	4	$75.00	$900.00	$ 5.00
PHY	Chemistry Fundamentals	4	7	$125.00	$3,500.00	$ 8.33
PHY	Organic Chemistry I	4	7	$150.00	$4,200.00	$ 10.00
PHY	Fundamentals of Physics	4	8	$125.00	$4,000.00	$ 8.33

Average Enrollment 15

Department	Total Fees	Total Credit Hours
Biological Science	$ 13,350.00	98
Foreign Languages	$ 3,795.00	69
Information Management Systems	$ 7,200.00	96
Physical Science	$ 11,700.00	88

Loan_Amount	='Student Loan'!$C$5
Loan_Term	='Student Loan'!$C$6
Payment	='Student Loan'!$C$8
Rate	='Student Loan'!$C$7
Total_Cost	='Student Loan'!$F$7
Total_Interest	='Student Loan'!$F$5
Total_Principal	='Student Loan'!$F$6

Sierra Pacific Community College District
Finance Office

Student Loan Amortization

Loan Amount	$ 10,000.00		Total Interest	$ 1,183.81
Loan Term	5		Total Principal	$ 10,000.00
Rate	4.50%		Total Cost	$ 11,183.81
Payment	$186.43			

Pmt #	Beginning Balance	Interest	Principal	Total Payment	Ending Balance
1	$ 11,183.81	$ 41.93	$ 144.48	$ 186.43	$ 10,999.38
2	$ 10,999.38	$ 41.25	$ 145.18	$ 186.43	$ 10,812.95
3	$ 10,812.95	$ 40.55	$ 145.88	$ 186.43	$ 10,626.52
4	$ 10,626.52	$ 39.85	$ 146.58	$ 186.43	$ 10,440.09
5	$ 10,440.09	$ 39.15	$ 147.28	$ 186.43	$ 10,253.66
6	$ 10,253.66	$ 38.45	$ 147.98	$ 186.43	$ 10,067.23
7	$ 10,067.23	$ 37.75	$ 148.68	$ 186.43	$ 9,880.80
8	$ 9,880.80	$ 37.05	$ 149.38	$ 186.43	$ 9,694.37
9	$ 9,694.37	$ 36.35	$ 150.08	$ 186.43	$ 9,507.94
10	$ 9,507.94	$ 35.65	$ 150.78	$ 186.43	$ 9,321.51
11	$ 9,321.51	$ 34.96	$ 151.47	$ 186.43	$ 9,135.08
12	$ 9,135.08	$ 34.26	$ 152.17	$ 186.43	$ 8,948.65
13	$ 8,948.65	$ 33.56	$ 152.87	$ 186.43	$ 8,762.22
14	$ 8,762.22	$ 32.86	$ 153.57	$ 186.43	$ 8,575.79
15	$ 8,575.79	$ 32.16	$ 154.27	$ 186.43	$ 8,389.36
16	$ 8,389.36	$ 31.46	$ 154.97	$ 186.43	$ 8,202.93
17	$ 8,202.93	$ 30.76	$ 155.67	$ 186.43	$ 8,016.50
18	$ 8,016.50	$ 30.06	$ 156.37	$ 186.43	$ 7,830.07
19	$ 7,830.07	$ 29.36	$ 157.07	$ 186.43	$ 7,643.64
20	$ 7,643.64	$ 28.66	$ 157.77	$ 186.43	$ 7,457.21
21	$ 7,457.21	$ 27.96	$ 158.47	$ 186.43	$ 7,270.78
22	$ 7,270.78	$ 27.27	$ 159.16	$ 186.43	$ 7,084.35
23	$ 7,084.35	$ 26.57	$ 159.86	$ 186.43	$ 6,897.92
24	$ 6,897.92	$ 25.87	$ 160.56	$ 186.43	$ 6,711.49
25	$ 6,711.49	$ 25.17	$ 161.26	$ 186.43	$ 6,525.06
26	$ 6,525.06	$ 24.47	$ 161.96	$ 186.43	$ 6,338.63
27	$ 6,338.63	$ 23.77	$ 162.66	$ 186.43	$ 6,152.20
28	$ 6,152.20	$ 23.07	$ 163.36	$ 186.43	$ 5,965.77
29	$ 5,965.77	$ 22.37	$ 164.06	$ 186.43	$ 5,779.34
30	$ 5,779.34	$ 21.67	$ 164.76	$ 186.43	$ 5,592.91
31	$ 5,592.91	$ 20.97	$ 165.46	$ 186.43	$ 5,406.48
32	$ 5,406.48	$ 20.27	$ 166.16	$ 186.43	$ 5,220.05
33	$ 5,220.05	$ 19.58	$ 166.86	$ 186.43	$ 5,033.62
34	$ 5,033.62	$ 18.88	$ 167.55	$ 186.43	$ 4,847.19
35	$ 4,847.19	$ 18.18	$ 168.25	$ 186.43	$ 4,660.75
36	$ 4,660.75	$ 17.48	$ 168.95	$ 186.43	$ 4,474.32
37	$ 4,474.32	$ 16.78	$ 169.65	$ 186.43	$ 4,287.89
38	$ 4,287.89	$ 16.08	$ 170.35	$ 186.43	$ 4,101.46
39	$ 4,101.46	$ 15.38	$ 171.05	$ 186.43	$ 3,915.03
40	$ 3,915.03	$ 14.68	$ 171.75	$ 186.43	$ 3,728.60
41	$ 3,728.60	$ 13.98	$ 172.45	$ 186.43	$ 3,542.17
42	$ 3,542.17	$ 13.28	$ 173.15	$ 186.43	$ 3,355.74
43	$ 3,355.74	$ 12.58	$ 173.85	$ 186.43	$ 3,169.31
44	$ 3,169.31	$ 11.88	$ 174.55	$ 186.43	$ 2,982.88
45	$ 2,982.88	$ 11.19	$ 175.24	$ 186.43	$ 2,796.45
46	$ 2,796.45	$ 10.49	$ 175.94	$ 186.43	$ 2,610.02
47	$ 2,610.02	$ 9.79	$ 176.64	$ 186.43	$ 2,423.59
48	$ 2,423.59	$ 9.09	$ 177.34	$ 186.43	$ 2,237.16
49	$ 2,237.16	$ 8.39	$ 178.04	$ 186.43	$ 2,050.73
50	$ 2,050.73	$ 7.69	$ 178.74	$ 186.43	$ 1,864.30
51	$ 1,864.30	$ 6.99	$ 179.44	$ 186.43	$ 1,677.87
52	$ 1,677.87	$ 6.29	$ 180.14	$ 186.43	$ 1,491.44
53	$ 1,491.44	$ 5.59	$ 180.84	$ 186.43	$ 1,305.01
54	$ 1,305.01	$ 4.89	$ 181.54	$ 186.43	$ 1,118.58
55	$ 1,118.58	$ 4.19	$ 182.24	$ 186.43	$ 932.15
56	$ 932.15	$ 3.50	$ 182.93	$ 186.43	$ 745.72
57	$ 745.72	$ 2.80	$ 183.63	$ 186.43	$ 559.29
58	$ 559.29	$ 2.10	$ 184.33	$ 186.43	$ 372.86
59	$ 372.86	$ 1.40	$ 185.03	$ 186.43	$ 186.43
60	$ 186.43	$ 0.70	$ 185.73	$ 186.43	$ 0.00

2-99 Completed Excel 2-3

Independent Project 2-4

Central Sierra Insurance (CSI) sets bonus percentages based on commissions earned by each agent and calculates totals by branch office. This workbook also tracks fundraising efforts of employees for a community event.
[Student Learning Outcomes 2.1, 2.2, 2.3, 2.5, 2.6, 2.7]

File Needed: ***CentralSierra-02.xlsx*** *[Student data files are available in the* Library *of your SIMnet account.]*
Completed Project File Name: ***[your initials] Excel 2-4.xlsx***

Skills Covered in This Project

- Create, copy, and edit formulas.
- Name cell ranges.
- Set mathematical order of operations.
- Set cell references to be absolute.
- Use the *NOW* function.
- Use *HLOOKUP* and *VLOOKUP* functions.
- Use the *SUMIF* function.
- Build an *IF* function.

1. Open the ***CentralSierra-02.xlsx*** workbook from your student data files and save it as [your initials] Excel 2-4. Review the data on each sheet.
2. On the **Tables** sheet, select cells **A6:B10** and create range names from this selection.
3. Select cells **B1:F2** and click the **Name** box. Name this as H_Rates.
4. Create an *HLOOKUP* function to display the bonus rate.
   a. Click the **Commissions** sheet tab and select cell **F5**.
   b. Start the *HLOOKUP* function and use cell **E5** as the *lookup_value*.
   c. For the *table_array* argument, use the **H_Rates** range.
   d. Use the second row for the *row_index_num* argument (Figure 2-100).

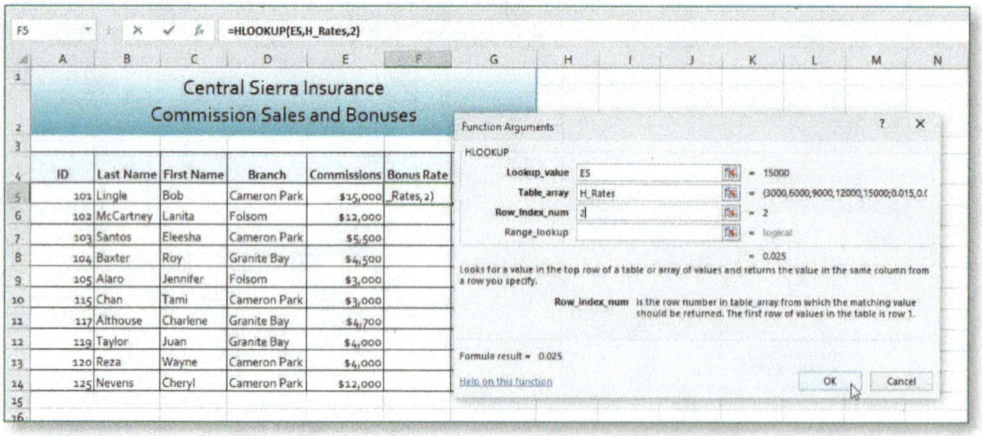

2-100 ***HLOOKUP*** **function to display bonus rate**

5. Format the results as **Percent Style** with two decimal places.
6. Copy the formula in cell **F5** to cells **F6:F14**.
7. Set order of operations to calculate total earnings.
   a. Select cell **G5**.
   b. Build a formula to add the commissions amount (E5) to the commissions amount times the rate (F5*E5). Use parentheses to set the multiplication as the first calculation.
   c. Copy the formula in cell **G5** to cells **G6:G14**.

8. Create and copy a *SUMIF* function to calculate total earnings by branch office.
   a. Select cell **E18**.
   b. Start the *SUMIF* function with cells **$D$5:$D$14** as the *Range* argument.
   c. The *Criteria* argument is a relative reference to cell **C18**.
   d. Select cells **G5:G14** for the *Sum_range* argument and make the references absolute.
   e. Copy the formula in cell **E18** to cells **E19:E20** without formatting.
   f. Format cells **E18:E20** as **Currency**.
9. Total the earnings in cell **E21**.
10. Create and format the current date.
    a. Select cell **G23** and insert the *NOW* function.
    b. Select cell **G23** and click the **Number** group launcher [*Home* tab]. On the *Number* tab, select the **Date** category.
    c. Scroll the *Type* list to find the date that displays the month spelled out, the date, a comma, and a four-digit year (Figure 2-101).
    d. Click **OK**. Press **Ctrl+Home**.

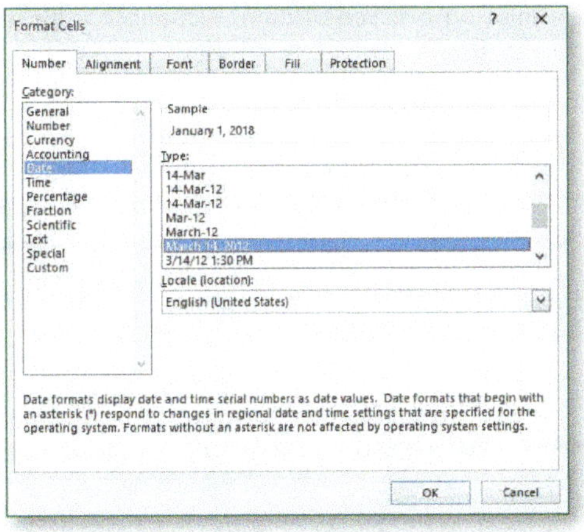

2-101 Date format selected

11. Create and copy a *VLOOKUP* function to display goals for each funding source.
    a. Click the **Family Day** sheet tab and select cell **F6**.
    b. Start the *VLOOKUP* function and use cell **E6** as the *lookup_value*.
    c. Click the **Tables** sheet tab for the *table_array* argument and use cells **$A$6:$B$10**.
    d. Use the second column as the *col_index_num* argument.
    e. Copy the formula in cell **F6** to cells **F7:F20** without formatting to preserve the fill color.
    f. Format cells **F7:F20** as **Currency** with no decimal places.
12. Create and copy an *IF* function.
    a. Select cell **H6** and start an *IF* function.
    b. Type a *logical_argument* to determine if cell **G6** is greater than or equal to (>=) cell **F6**.
    c. Type **Yes** as the *Value_if_true* argument and **No** as the *Value_if_false* argument.
    d. Copy the formula in cell **H6** to cells **H7:H20** without formatting to maintain the fill color.
    e. Center align cells **H6:H20**.
    f. Press **Ctrl+Home**.
13. Insert a new sheet at the end of the tab names and paste the range names starting in cell A1. Name the worksheet as Range Names.
14. Save and close the workbook (Figure 2-102).

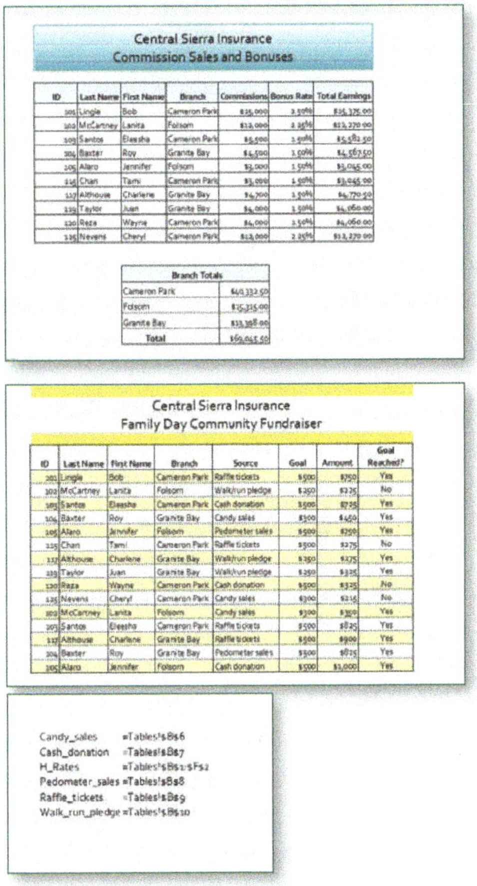

2-102 Excel 2-4 completed

Independent Project 2-5

San Diego Sailing keeps data about its fleet of rental and charter boats in a workbook. One of the sheets is missing a piece of data and another sheet has circular reference errors. You will complete work on these sheets, calculate projected rates for each boat, and build basic statistics about past rentals. [Student Learning Outcomes 2.1, 2.2, 2.3, 2.4, 2.5, 2.6, 2.7]

File Needed: ***SanDiegoSailing-02.xlsx*** *[Student data files are available in the* Library *of your SIMnet account.]*
Completed Project File Name: ***[your initials] Excel 2-5.xlsx***

Skills Covered in This Project

- Create and copy formulas.
- Use formula auditing tools.
- Set mathematical order of operations.
- Use relative, mixed, and 3D cell references.
- Use *COUNTIF* and *SUMIF* functions.
- Build an *IF* formula.
- Insert the *TODAY* function.

1. Open the ***SanDiegoSailing-02.xlsx*** workbook from your student data files. When a workbook has a circular reference, a message box appears immediately as you open it (Figure 2-103).

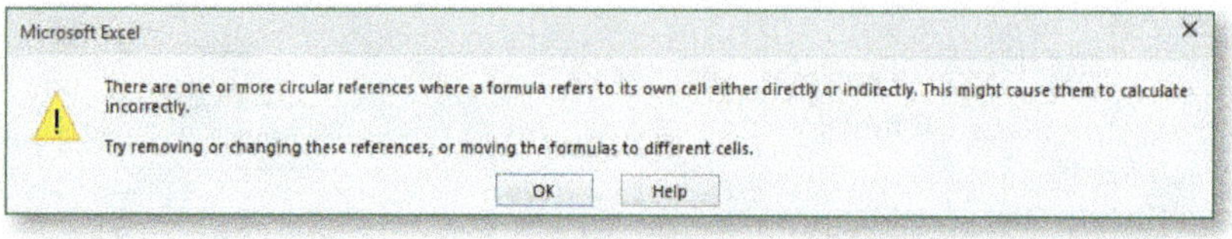

2-103 Circular reference message

2. Click **OK** in the message box. There is a message in the *Status* bar that there are *Circular References*.
3. Save the workbook as [your initials] Excel 2-5. Review the data on each sheet.
4. Use formula auditing tools.
   a. Click the **New Prices** sheet tab and review the *Status* bar.
   b. Click cell **D5**. The formula should be 1 plus the value in cell D4.
   c. Click the **Formulas** tab and click the **Trace Precedents** button in the *Formula Auditing* group. The worksheet icon means that the formula has a 3D reference to another sheet.
   d. Click the **Evaluate Formula** button [*Formula Auditing* group]. The circular reference is identified (Figure 2-104).
   e. Click **Close** and click the **Remove Arrows** button [*Formula Auditing* group].

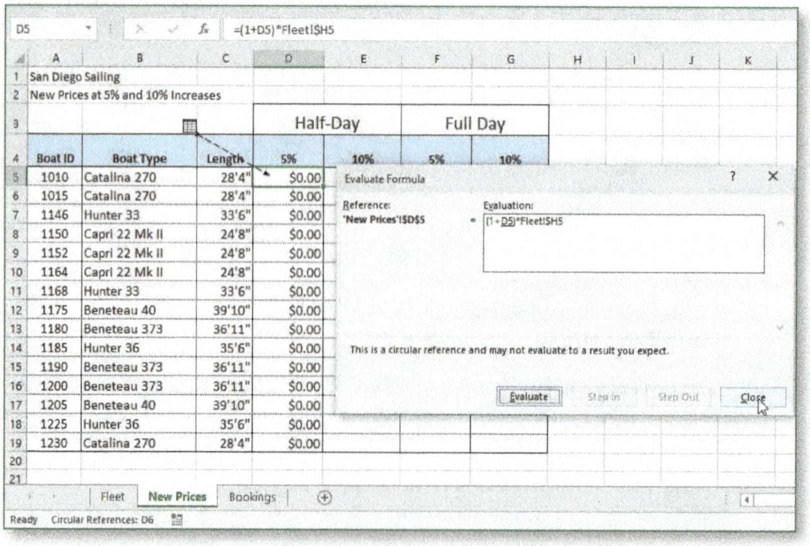

2-104 *Evaluate Formula* dialog box

5. Edit and copy a formula with mixed references.
   a. Edit the formula in cell D5 to show D$4 instead of "D5." The formula multiplies one plus the percentage value in cell D4 by the current rate on the **Fleet** sheet ($H5). With an absolute reference to row 4 and column H on the **Fleet** sheet, you can copy the formula down the column (Figure 2-105).
   b. Copy the formula in cell **D5** to cells **D6:D19** without formatting to preserve the border. When the circular reference message box opens, click **OK**.
   c. Select cells **D5:D19** and drag the *Fill* pointer to copy the formulas to cells **E5:E19**.
   d. Click cell **E6**. The formula is adjusted to use the percentage value in cell E4. Note also that the reference on the **Fleet** sheet ($H6) is adjusted to show the correct row.

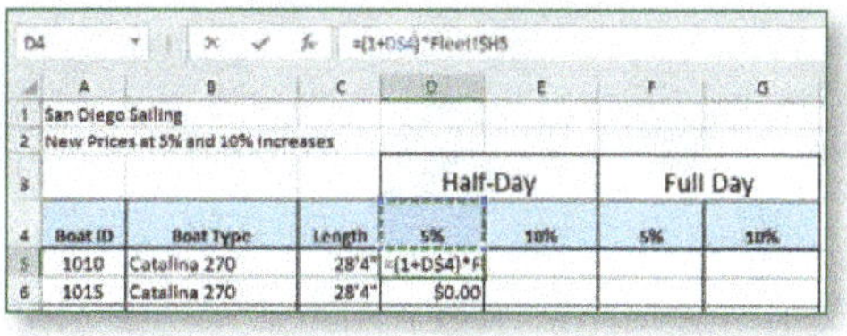

2-105 Mixed reference in the edited formula

6. Build a formula with mixed references.
   a. Click cell **F5** and type =(1+ to start the formula.
   b. Select cell **F4** and make it an absolute reference to the row but not the column.
   c. Type)* for the closing parenthesis and multiplication.
   d. Click cell **I5** on the **Fleet** sheet, and make the reference absolute for the column but not the row (Figure 2-106).
   e. Copy the formula down column F without formatting to preserve the border.
   f. Format cells **F5:F19** as **Currency** and then copy cells **F5:F19** to cells **G5:G19**.

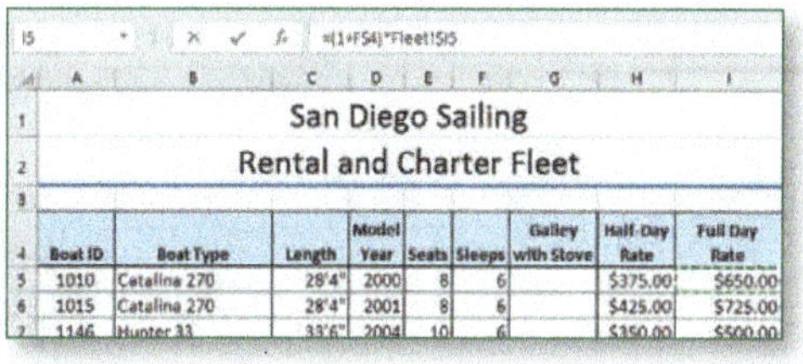

2-106 Mixed references in the new formula

7. Build an *IF* function formula.
   a. Click the **Fleet** sheet tab and select cell **G5**. Rental boats must be able to seat 8 or more people to have a stove in the galley.
   b. Create an *IF* function in which the *logical_test* argument determines if there are 8 or more seats.
   c. Use **Yes** for the *value_if_true* argument. Use **No** for the *value_if_false* argument.
   d. Copy the formula to cells **G6:G19** without formatting and then center the data in column G.
8. Insert the *TODAY* function in cell **B21**. Format the date to show the month spelled out, the date, and four digits for the year.
9. Create a division formula.
   a. Click the **Bookings** sheet tab and select cell **F5**. Average revenue per passenger can be determined by dividing the fee by the number of passengers.
   b. Build the division formula.
   c. Copy the formula in cell **F5** to cells **F6:F19**.
10. Create and copy a *COUNTIF* function to count bookings by boat type.
    a. Select cell **D27**.
    b. Start the *COUNTIF* function from the *Statistical* category by clicking the **More Functions** button in the *Function Library* group.
    c. Use cells **$C$5:$C$19** as the *Range* argument.
    d. To set a *Criteria* argument that will select all boats in the "Beneteau" group, the criteria is **ben***. If you type the formula, include quotation marks.
    e. Copy the formula in cell **D27** to cells **D28:D30**.
    f. Edit the criteria in each copied formula in cells **D28:D30** to reflect the boat type.
11. Create and copy a *SUMIF* function to calculate total revenue by boat type.
    a. Select cell **E27**.
    b. Start the *SUMIF* function with cells **$C$5:$C$19** as the *Range*.

c. The *Criteria* is ben*.
d. The *Sum_range* is cells **$E$5:$E$19**.
e. Copy the formula in cell **E27** to cells **E28:E30**.
f. Edit the criteria in each copied formula in cells **E28:E30** as needed.

12. Complete formatting.
    a. Apply the **Currency** format to all values that represent money.
    b. Format the labels in cells **A1:A2** as **18** point.
    c. Select cells **A1:F2** and center them across the selection.
    d. Merge and center the label in cell **C25** over cells C25:E25 and format it at **16** points.
    e. Bold and center the labels in rows **4** and **26**.
    f. Select cells **A4:F19** and apply **All Borders**. Do the same for cells **C25:E30**.
    g. Center the page horizontally.
13. Save and close the workbook (Figure 2-107).

San Diego Sailing Bookings
Revenue per Passenger

Date	Boat ID	Boat Type	# of Passengers	Total Fees	Revenue per Passenger
4/5/2016	1010	Catalina 270	4	$525.00	$131.25
4/8/2016	1015	Catalina 270	6	$850.00	$141.67
4/11/2016	1146	Hunter 33	6	$500.00	$83.33
4/14/2016	1150	Capri 22 Mk II	6	$525.00	$87.50
4/17/2016	1152	Capri 22 Mk II	4	$325.00	$81.25
4/20/2016	1164	Capri 22 Mk II	3	$475.00	$158.33
4/23/2016	1168	Hunter 33	6	$725.00	$120.83
4/26/2016	1175	Beneteau 40	10	$850.00	$85.00
4/29/2016	1180	Beneteau 373	8	$350.00	$43.75
5/2/2016	1185	Hunter 36	8	$650.00	$81.25
5/5/2016	1190	Beneteau 373	10	$625.00	$62.50
5/8/2016	1200	Beneteau 373	8	$725.00	$90.63
5/11/2016	1205	Beneteau 40	12	$850.00	$70.83
5/14/2016	1225	Hunter 36	8	$725.00	$90.63
5/17/2016	1230	Catalina 270	6	$675.00	$112.50

Bookings by Type

	Count	Total Revenue
Beneteau	5	$3,400.00
Capri 22 Mk II	3	$1,325.00
Catalina 270	3	$2,050.00
Hunter	4	$2,600.00

San Diego Sailing
Rental and Charter Fleet

Boat ID	Boat Type	Length	Model Year	Seats	Sleeps	Galley with Stove	Half-Day Rate	Full Day Rate
1010	Catalina 270	28'4"	2000	8	6	Yes	$375.00	$650.00
1015	Catalina 270	28'4"	2001	8	6	Yes	$425.00	$725.00
1146	Hunter 33	33'6"	2004	10	6	Yes	$350.00	$500.00
1150	Capri 22 Mk II	24'8"	2005	6	4	No	$325.00	$500.00
1152	Capri 22 Mk II	24'8"	2005	6	4	No	$325.00	$500.00
1164	Capri 22 Mk II	24'8"	2006	6	4	No	$325.00	$500.00
1168	Hunter 33	33'6"	2007	10	6	Yes	$425.00	$725.00
1175	Beneteau 40	39'10"	2008	12	6	Yes	$489.00	$750.00
1180	Beneteau 373	36'11"	2009	10	6	Yes	$369.00	$725.00
1185	Hunter 36	35'6"	2009	10	6	Yes	$349.00	$550.00
1190	Beneteau 373	36'11"	2010	10	6	Yes	$369.00	$625.00
1200	Beneteau 373	36'11"	2010	10	6	Yes	$369.00	$625.00
1205	Beneteau 40	39'10"	2012	12	6	Yes	$489.00	$750.00
1225	Hunter 36	35'6"	2012	10	6	Yes	$349.00	$725.00
1230	Catalina 270	28'4"	2012	8	6	Yes	$439.00	$675.00

San Diego Sailing
New Prices at 5% and 10% increases

			Half-Day		Full Day	
Boat ID	Boat Type	Length	5%	10%	5%	10%
1010	Catalina 270	28'4"	$393.75	$412.50	$682.50	$715.00
1015	Catalina 270	28'4"	$446.25	$467.50	$761.25	$797.50
1146	Hunter 33	33'6"	$367.50	$385.00	$525.00	$550.00
1150	Capri 22 Mk II	24'8"	$341.25	$357.50	$525.00	$550.00
1152	Capri 22 Mk II	24'8"	$341.25	$357.50	$525.00	$550.00
1164	Capri 22 Mk II	24'8"	$341.25	$357.50	$525.00	$550.00
1168	Hunter 33	33'6"	$446.25	$467.50	$761.25	$797.50
1175	Beneteau 40	39'10"	$513.45	$537.90	$787.50	$825.00
1180	Beneteau 373	36'11"	$387.45	$405.90	$761.25	$797.50
1185	Hunter 36	35'6"	$366.45	$383.90	$577.50	$605.00
1190	Beneteau 373	36'11"	$387.45	$405.90	$656.25	$687.50
1200	Beneteau 373	36'11"	$387.45	$405.90	$656.25	$687.50
1205	Beneteau 40	39'10"	$513.45	$537.90	$787.50	$825.00
1225	Hunter 36	35'6"	$366.45	$383.90	$761.25	$797.50
1230	Catalina 270	28'4"	$460.95	$482.90	$708.75	$742.50

2-107 Excel 2-5 completed

Independent Project 2-6

Placer Hills Real Estate has regional offices throughout central California, and each office tracks its listings and sales data. In the workbook, you need to insert agent names, calculate market days, and determine sale price as a percentage of list price. You also calculate summary statistics.
[Student Learning Outcomes 2.1, 2.3, 2.5, 2.6, 2.7]

File Needed: ***PlacerHills-02.xlsx*** *[Student data files are available in the* Library *of your SIMnet account.]*
Completed Project File Name: ***[your initials] Excel 2-6.xlsx***

Skills Covered in This Project

- Create and copy formulas.
- Use dates in a subtraction formula.
- Name cell ranges.
- Use relative and 3D cell references in formulas.
- Use the *VLOOKUP* function.
- Use *AVERAGE*, *MAX*, *MIN*, and *COUNT*.
- Use *COUNTIF*.

1. Open the ***PlacerHills-02.xlsx*** workbook from your student data files and save it as [your initials] Excel 2-6. Review the data on each sheet.
2. Build a subtraction formula with dates.
   a. Select cell **N4** on the **Listings** sheet. You can subtract the older date from the later date to determine the number of days on the market.
   b. Type = and click cell **M4**, the sold date.
   c. Type – for subtraction and click cell **B4**, the listing date.
   d. Press **Enter**. The result is formatted as a date (Figure 2-108).

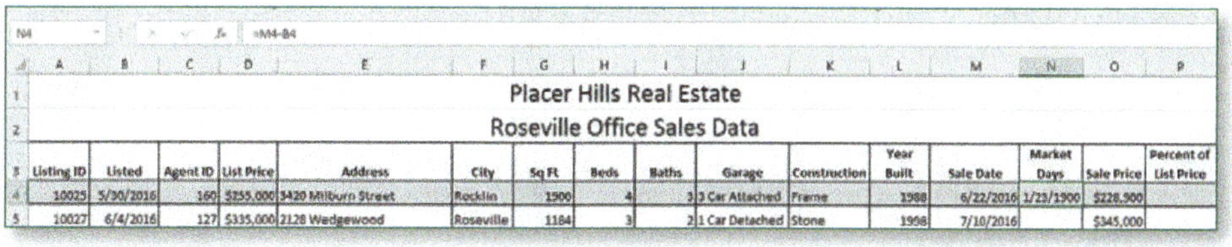

2-108 Result is formatted as a date

   e. Copy the formula in cell **N4** to cells **N5:N12** without formatting to preserve the fill color.
   f. Format cells **N4:N12** as **General**.
3. Calculate the sold price as a percentage of the list price.
   a. Select cell **P4** and type =.
   b. Build a formula to divide the selling price by the list price.
   c. Copy the formula without formatting and format the column as **Percent Style** with **two** decimal places.
4. Use the *VLOOKUP* function to insert the agent's last name in a new column.
   a. Insert a column at column **D**.
   b. Type Name in cell **D3** and click cell **D4**.
   c. Start a *VLOOKUP* function and set the agent ID (C4) as the *lookup_value* argument.
   d. Use an absolute reference to cells **A2:B7** on the **Agents** sheet for the *table_array* argument. Do not include column titles in a table array.
   e. Enter the appropriate number for the *col_index_num* argument to display the agent's last name.
   f. Copy the formula without formatting to display each agent's name and *AutoFit* the column width.
5. Name cell ranges.
   a. Select cells **E3:E12**.
   b. Press **Ctrl** and select cells **G3:G12, L3:L12**, and **P3:P12**.
   c. Click the **Create from Selection** button [*Formulas* tab, *Defined Names* group] and use the **Top row** to create range names.

d. Press **Ctrl+Home**.
e. Set this sheet to fit one page, landscape orientation.
f. Insert a footer that displays your name in the right section.

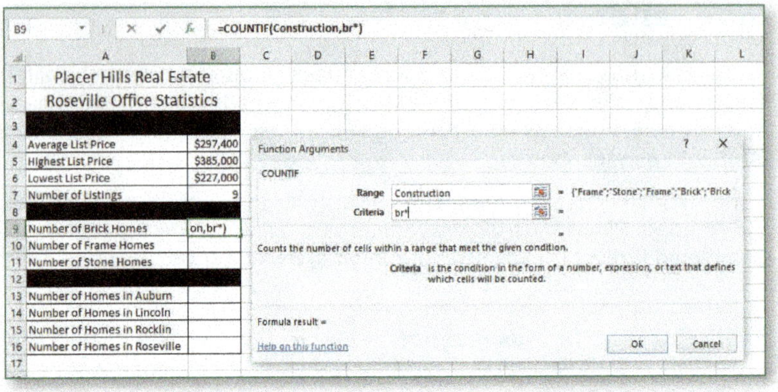

2-109 Arguments for COUNTIF

6. Calculate statistics for the agency.
   a. Click the **Statistics** sheet tab and select cell **B4**.
   b. Click the **AutoSum** button arrow and choose *Average*. There is no assumed range.
   c. Press **F3 (FN+F3)** to open the *Paste Name* dialog box.
   d. Choose **List_Price** and click **OK**. Press **Enter**.
   e. Continue on this sheet to calculate the highest and lowest list prices as well as the number of listings. Be careful to select the correct range name.
7. Use *COUNTIF* to calculate statistics.
   a. Select cell **B9**.
   b. Click the **More Functions** button in the *Function Library* group, choose **Statistical**, and select **COUNTIF**.
   c. For the *Range* argument, use the range name **Construction** (Figure 2-109).
   d. Type br* for the *Criteria* and click **OK**.
   e. Copy the formula and edit the criteria for cells **B10:B11**.
   f. Start a new *COUNTIF* function in cell **B13** with the appropriate range name. Then copy and edit the formula for cells **B14:B16**. Be sure to use criteria that will distinguish between the two city names that begin with "ro."
8. Center the sheet horizontally. Add a footer with your name in the center section.
9. Save and close the workbook (Figure 2-110).

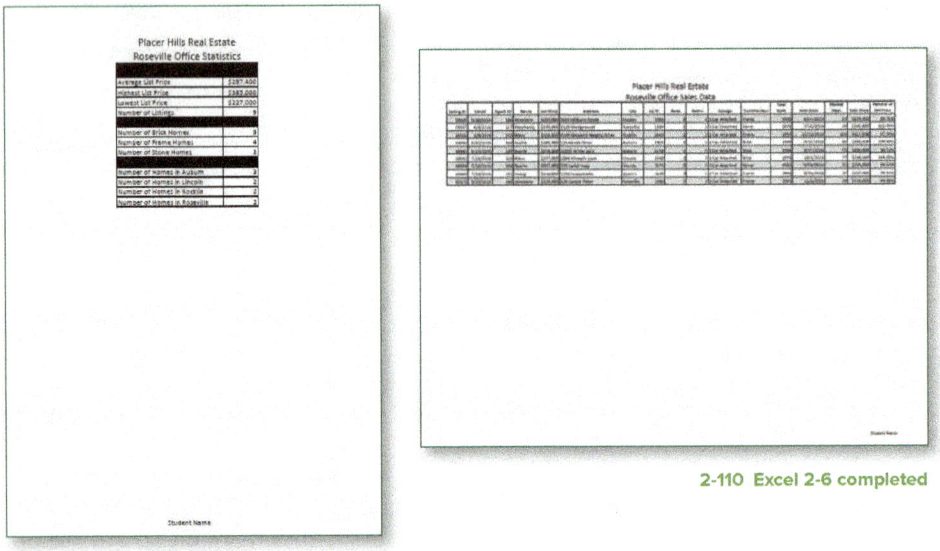

2-110 Excel 2-6 completed

Improve It Project 2-7

Mary's Rentals serves light-to-heavy equipment rental needs of contractors as well as the general public. Data has been imported from an Access database and needs to be handled for better management in Excel. Once that is done, you can calculate several statistics for the company.
[Student Learning Outcomes 2.1, 2.3, 2.4, 2.5, 2.7]

File Needed: ***MarysRentals-02.xlsx*** *[Student data files are available in the* Library *of your SIMnet account.]*
Completed Project File Name: ***[your initials] Excel 2-7.xlsx***

Skills Covered in This Project

- Use formula auditing tools.
- Name cell ranges.
- Create, copy, and edit formulas.
- Use relative references and range names in formulas.
- Use *Statistical* functions.
- Use functions from the *Math & Trig* category.

1. Open the ***MarysRentals-02.xlsx*** workbook from your student data files and save it as [your initials] Excel 2-7. The *Equipment* sheet is an inventory of equipment available for rental.
2. Correct errors on the *Rentals* sheet.
   a. Click the **Rentals** tab. This data was imported from an Access database, and there are error triangles in many cells.
   b. Select cells **A2:A47** and click the **Trace Error** button near cell A2 (Figure 2-111). This data was imported as text (labels) but should be set as values.
   c. Select **Convert to Number**. The data is formatted as a value and is right-aligned.
   d. Repeat for cells **B2:C47**.
   e. Center align cells **E2:E47**. This column specifies whether the rental was daily, weekly, or monthly.
   f. Press **Ctrl+Home**.

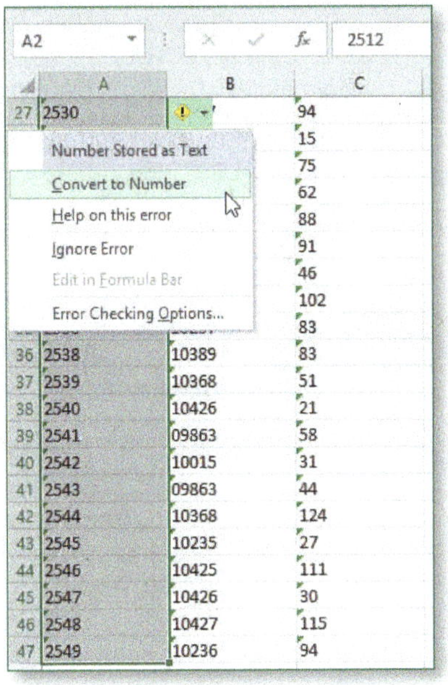

2-111 *Trace Error* button for a selected range

3. Name cell ranges.
   a. Select cells **B1:B47**, press **Ctrl**, and select cells **E1:E47** and cells **I1:I47**.
   b. Create names from the selection.
   c. Press **Ctrl+Home**.
4. Create and copy a *SUMIF* function with a relative reference.
   a. Click the **Generators** sheet tab and select cell **C5**.
   b. Start the *SUMIF* function with *Equipment_ID* as the *Range* argument.
   c. The *Criteria* argument is cell **A5**.
   d. The *Sum_range* argument is the *Total_Cost* range.
   e. Copy the formula in cell **C5** to cells **C6:C7**. The relative cell reference to cell A5 is adjusted.
   f. Format cells **C5:C7** as **Currency** with no decimal places.
5. Build a custom border.
   a. Select cells **A4:C7**.
   b. Press **Ctrl+1** to open the *Format Cells* dialog box and click the **Border** tab.
   c. In the *Presets* section, click the **Outline** button.
   d. In the *Style* section, click the dotted line style (second option, first column, just below *None*).

e. Click the middle horizontal position in the *Border* preview area.
f. In the *Style* section, click the single solid line style (last option, first column).
g. Click the middle vertical position in the *Border* preview area (Figure 2-112).
h. Click **OK**.

6. Complete formatting.
   a. Apply bold and centering to cells **A4:C4**.
   b. Format cells **A1:A2** to **16** points.
   c. Select cells **A1:C2** and use **Center Across Selection**.
   d. Center the sheet horizontally.
   e. Insert a header with your name in the right section.

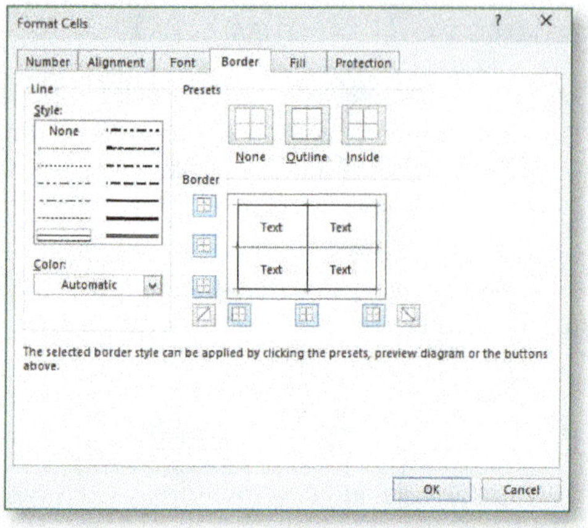

2-112 Build a custom border in the *Format Cells* dialog box

7. Use *SUMIF* to calculate daily, weekly, and monthly income rentals.
   a. Click the **Income Data** sheet tab and select cell **B4**.
   b. Start the *SUMIF* function with **Type** as the *Range* argument.
   c. Type d for daily income as the *Criteria* argument.
   d. The *Total_Cost* range is the *Sum_range* argument.
   e. In cells **B5:B6**, enter *SUMIF* formulas or copy and edit the formula in cell B4.
   f. Use *SUM* in cell **B7**.
   g. Format cells **B4:B7** as **Currency** with no decimal places.

8. Use *COUNTIF* to count rentals by type.
   a. Select cell **B9** and start the *COUNTIF* function from the *Statistical* category.
   b. Use the range name **Type** as the *Range* argument. The *Criteria* is d.
   c. Create a separate formula in cells **B10:B11**, or copy and edit the formula in cell B9.

9. Add a border and fill.
   a. Select cells **A3:B12**.
   b. Click the **Font** group launcher [*Home* tab] and click the **Border** tab.
   c. Click the **Outline** button in the *Presets* section.
   d. In the *Style* section, click the single solid line style (last option, first column).
   e. Click the middle vertical position in the *Border* preview area.
   f. In the *Style* section, click the dotted line style (second option, first column).
   g. Click the middle horizontal position in the *Border* preview area.
   h. Click **OK**.
   i. Select cells **A3:B3, A8:B8**, and **A12:B12**.
   j. Click the arrow with the **Fill Color** button and choose **Black, Text 1, Lighter 50%**.
   k. Select cells **A1:B2** and use **Center Across Selection**.
   l. Increase the font size for cells **A1:B2** to **16**.
   m. Center the sheet horizontally.
   n. Insert a footer with your name in the right section.

10. Save and close the workbook (Figure 2-113).

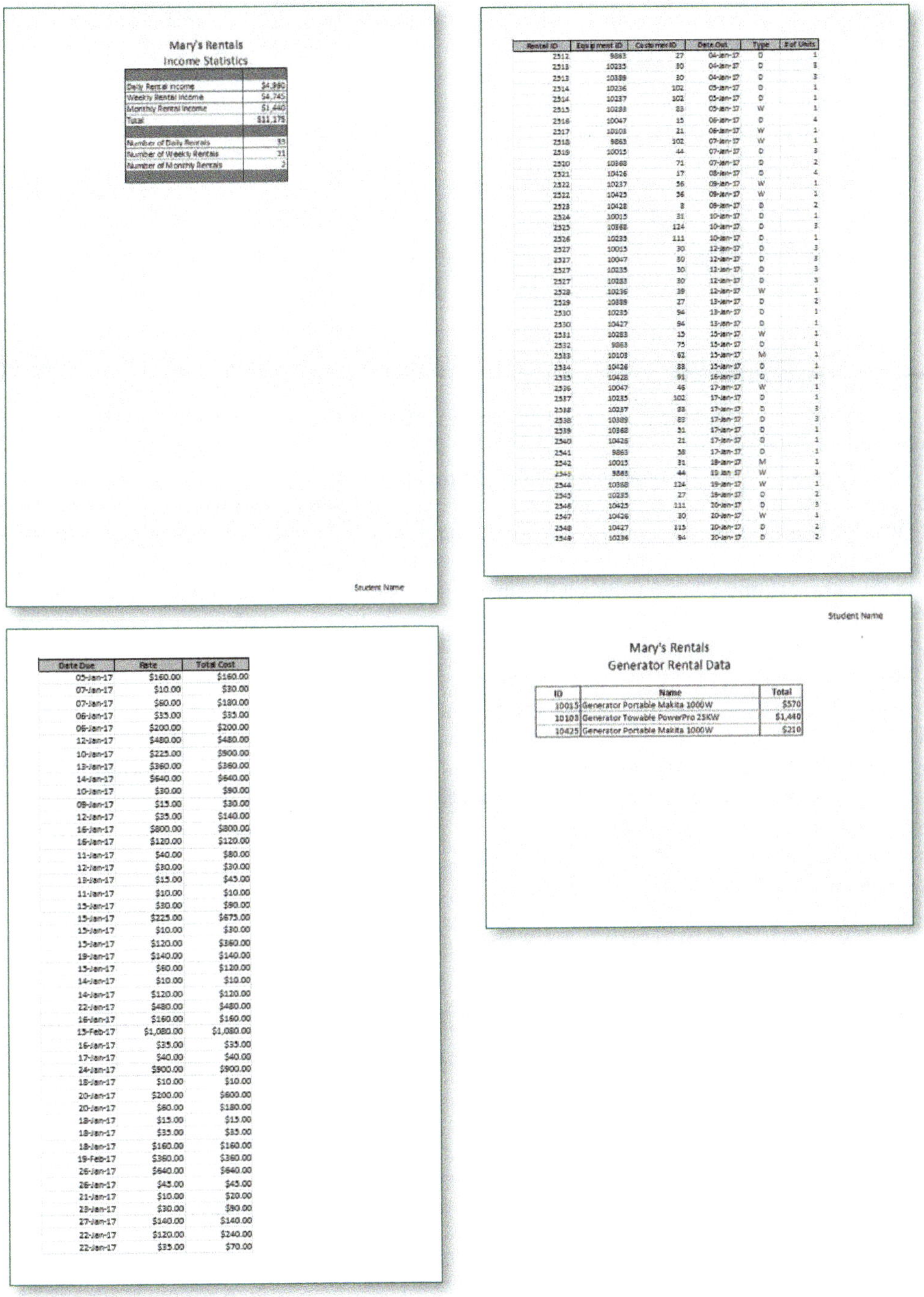

Mary's Rentals
Income Statistics

Daily Rental Income	$4,990
Weekly Rental Income	$4,745
Monthly Rental Income	$1,440
Total	$11,175
Number of Daily Rentals	33
Number of Weekly Rentals	11
Number of Monthly Rentals	2

Student Name

Rental ID	Equipment ID	Customer ID	Date Out	Type	# of Units
2512	9863	27	04-Jan-17	D	1
2513	10235	30	04-Jan-17	D	3
2513	10389	30	04-Jan-17	D	3
2514	10236	102	05-Jan-17	D	1
2514	10237	102	05-Jan-17	D	1
2515	10283	83	05-Jan-17	W	1
2516	10047	15	06-Jan-17	D	4
2517	10103	21	06-Jan-17	W	1
2518	9863	102	07-Jan-17	W	1
2519	10015	44	07-Jan-17	D	3
2520	10368	71	07-Jan-17	D	2
2521	10426	17	08-Jan-17	D	4
2522	10237	56	09-Jan-17	W	1
2522	10425	56	09-Jan-17	W	1
2523	10428	8	09-Jan-17	D	2
2524	10015	31	10-Jan-17	D	1
2525	10368	124	10-Jan-17	D	3
2526	10235	111	10-Jan-17	D	1
2527	10015	30	12-Jan-17	D	3
2527	10047	30	12-Jan-17	D	3
2527	10235	30	12-Jan-17	D	3
2527	10283	30	12-Jan-17	D	3
2528	10236	39	12-Jan-17	W	1
2529	10389	27	13-Jan-17	D	2
2530	10235	94	13-Jan-17	D	1
2530	10427	94	13-Jan-17	D	1
2531	10283	15	15-Jan-17	W	1
2532	9863	75	15-Jan-17	D	1
2533	10103	62	15-Jan-17	M	1
2534	10426	88	15-Jan-17	D	1
2535	10428	91	16-Jan-17	D	3
2536	10047	46	17-Jan-17	W	1
2537	10235	102	17-Jan-17	D	1
2538	10237	88	17-Jan-17	D	3
2538	10389	83	17-Jan-17	D	3
2539	10368	31	17-Jan-17	D	1
2540	10426	21	17-Jan-17	D	1
2541	9863	38	17-Jan-17	D	1
2542	10015	31	18-Jan-17	M	1
2543	9863	44	19-Jan-17	W	1
2544	10368	124	19-Jan-17	W	1
2545	10235	27	19-Jan-17	D	1
2546	10425	111	20-Jan-17	D	3
2547	10426	30	20-Jan-17	W	1
2548	10427	115	20-Jan-17	D	2
2549	10236	94	20-Jan-17	D	2

Date Due	Rate	Total Cost
05-Jan-17	$160.00	$160.00
07-Jan-17	$10.00	$30.00
07-Jan-17	$60.00	$180.00
06-Jan-17	$35.00	$35.00
06-Jan-17	$200.00	$200.00
12-Jan-17	$480.00	$480.00
10-Jan-17	$225.00	$900.00
13-Jan-17	$360.00	$360.00
14-Jan-17	$640.00	$640.00
10-Jan-17	$30.00	$90.00
09-Jan-17	$15.00	$30.00
12-Jan-17	$35.00	$140.00
16-Jan-17	$800.00	$800.00
16-Jan-17	$120.00	$120.00
11-Jan-17	$40.00	$80.00
12-Jan-17	$30.00	$30.00
13-Jan-17	$15.00	$45.00
11-Jan-17	$10.00	$10.00
13-Jan-17	$30.00	$90.00
15-Jan-17	$225.00	$675.00
15-Jan-17	$10.00	$30.00
15-Jan-17	$120.00	$360.00
19-Jan-17	$140.00	$140.00
15-Jan-17	$60.00	$120.00
14-Jan-17	$10.00	$10.00
14-Jan-17	$120.00	$120.00
22-Jan-17	$480.00	$480.00
16-Jan-17	$160.00	$160.00
15-Feb-17	$1,080.00	$1,080.00
16-Jan-17	$35.00	$35.00
17-Jan-17	$40.00	$40.00
24-Jan-17	$900.00	$900.00
18-Jan-17	$10.00	$10.00
20-Jan-17	$200.00	$600.00
20-Jan-17	$60.00	$180.00
18-Jan-17	$15.00	$15.00
18-Jan-17	$35.00	$35.00
18-Jan-17	$160.00	$160.00
19-Feb-17	$360.00	$360.00
26-Jan-17	$640.00	$640.00
26-Jan-17	$45.00	$45.00
21-Jan-17	$10.00	$20.00
23-Jan-17	$30.00	$90.00
27-Jan-17	$140.00	$140.00
22-Jan-17	$120.00	$240.00
22-Jan-17	$35.00	$70.00

Student Name

Mary's Rentals
Generator Rental Data

ID	Name	Total
10015	Generator Portable Makita 1000W	$570
10103	Generator Towable PowerPro 25KW	$1,440
10425	Generator Portable Makita 1000W	$210

2-113 Excel 2-7 completed

Challenge Project 2-8

For this project, you create a workbook for a hair products company that includes an inventory list and an invoice form. You use *VLOOKUP* to enter the cost of the product on the invoice and then calculate a total with taxes for each product.
[**Student Learning Outcomes 2.1, 2.2, 2.3, 2.5, 2.6**]

File Needed: None
Completed Project File Name: ***[your initials] Excel 2-8.xlsx***

Create and save a workbook as [your initials] Excel 2-8. Modify your workbook according to the following guidelines:

- In cell **A1**, type a name for the hair products company. In cell **A2**, type Customer Invoice. In cells **A4:D4**, enter these labels: Product ID, Cost, Quantity, and Total with Tax. Do not include a comma or a period. Name this sheet tab Invoice.
- Insert a new sheet and name it Stock. In cells **A1:C1**, enter labels for Product ID, Name, and Cost with no punctuation.
- In cells **A2:C11**, enter data for ten products that can be purchased from your company. Use *AutoFill* to create a series for the *Product ID*. Since this range will be used as the table array in a *VLOOKUP* function, the product IDs must be in ascending order, either A to Z or low value to high value. Name the cell range Stock (without the labels in row 1).
- Below the *Stock* range, enter Tax Rate as a label. In a cell either to the right or below the label, enter 3.75% as the rate.
- On the *Invoice* sheet, type any three of the product IDs in cells **A5:A7**. Use *VLOOKUP* in column B to display the cost. In the *Quantity* column, type three values to indicate the number ordered.
- In the *Total with Tax* column, build a formula to multiply the cost by the quantity ordered. This result should be multiplied by one plus the tax rate on the *Stock* sheet. Show a grand total in row 8.
- Use the *TODAY* function in cell **A10** on the *Invoice* sheet and format the date to show the date, the month with a three-letter abbreviation, and the year as two-digits.
- Complete formatting on the *Invoice* sheet. Select a workbook theme if desired, use cell styles, or build your own designs.
- Add a header that shows your name in the right section.
- Set document properties to show your name as the author and the company name as the title. Spell check the workbook if necessary.

Challenge Project 2-9

For this project, you create a workbook for a mobile services provider to calculate revenue from purchased mobile apps. You enter and format data and use *SUMPRODUCT* to determine revenue by category.
[**Student Learning Outcomes 2.1, 2.3, 2.5, 2.7**]

File Needed: None
Completed Project File Name: ***[your initials] Excel 2-9.xlsx***

Create and save a workbook as [your initials] Excel 2-9. Modify your workbook according to the following guidelines:

- In cell **A1**, enter a name for your mobile services company.
- In cell **A2**, type Last Month's Activity.
- In cells **B3**:**D3**, enter the labels App Name, Times Downloaded, and Cost.
- In cell **A4**, type Books as the first category. In cells **A7, A10,** and **A13**, type the names of three other categories of mobile applications. Examples might be Travel, Entertainment, Games, Health, Sports, and so on.
- In cells **B5:D6**, complete data for two apps in the *Books* category. Then do the same for the other categories.
- Starting in row **18**, create a section that calculates revenue from each app category using the *SUMPRODUCT* function.
- In a cell below the data, use the *TODAY* function and format the date to show a short date.
- Select a workbook theme if desired, use cell styles, or set your own formatting.
- Add a footer that shows the current date in the left section and your name in the right section.
- Set document properties to show your name as the author and a title of your choice. Spell check the workbook if necessary.

Challenge Project 2-10

In this project, you create a workbook that calculates monthly payments for a major purchase at four possible interest rates and different payback times.
[Student Learning Outcomes 2.1, 2.3, 2.4, 2.5, 2.6]

File Needed: None
Completed Project File Name: ***[your initials] Excel 2-10.xlsx***

Create and save a workbook as [your initials] Excel 2-10. Modify your workbook according to the following guidelines:

- Enter main labels that identify the worksheet and your proposed purchase.
- Build the first section for a *PMT* formula with the labels Loan, Rate, Term, and Payment. Since you plan to copy the section to show other possibilities, do not use range names.
- Fill in values for the loan amount, an interest rate, and the term. Include the percent sign when you type the interest rate. For the term, you can use the number of years or the number of months.
- Use *PMT* to calculate the payment made at the beginning of the month (*Type* argument). If you set months for the term, do not multiply the *Nper* argument by 12.
- Copy the entire section once below the current location with a blank row or two between. Then copy these two groupings one or two columns to the right. You should have four possible payment scenarios on the sheet.
- Edit the interest rate and term for each of the copied sections. Be consistent in how you indicate the term of the loan (years or months). Assume that the loan amount is the same.
- In a row below the data, use the *TODAY* function and format the date to show a short date.
- Make formatting choices to building an easy-to-read report for your possibilities.
- Add a footer with your name in the right section.
- Set document properties to show your name as the author, and spell check the workbook if necessary.

CHAPTER 3

Creating and Editing Charts

CHAPTER OVERVIEW

In addition to building formulas and functions in a worksheet, you can use Excel to graph or chart data. After selecting values and labels, you can quickly create a professional looking chart with a few clicks of the mouse. This chapter introduces you to the basics of creating, editing, and formatting Excel charts.

STUDENT LEARNING OUTCOMES (SLOs)

After completing this chapter, you will be able to:

- **SLO 3.1** Create Excel chart objects and chart sheets (p. E3-163).
- **SLO 3.2** Use quick layouts and chart styles to design a chart (p. E3-167).
- **SLO 3.3** Edit chart elements including titles, data labels, and source data (p. E3-172).
- **SLO 3.4** Format chart elements with shape styles, fill, outlines, and special effects (p. E3-179).
- **SLO 3.5** Use pictures, shapes, and *WordArt* in a chart (p. E3-183).
- **SLO 3.6** Build pie charts and combination charts (p. E3-188).
- **SLO 3.7** Create sunburst and waterfall charts (p. E3-191).
- **SLO 3.8** Insert and format sparklines in a worksheet (p. E3-194).

CASE STUDY

In the Pause & Practice projects in this chapter, you use data in a Paradise Lakes Resort workbook to build charts that compare revenue categories for two quarters. You build column and pie charts as objects and separate sheets. You also add trendlines and sparklines to further illustrate aspects of the data.

Pause & Practice 3-1: Create and edit column and bar charts.

Pause & Practice 3-2: Edit and format charts and chart elements.

Pause & Practice 3-3: Create and format pie, combo, and sunburst charts and insert sparklines.

EXCEL

SLO 3.1

Creating a Chart Object and a Chart Sheet

An Excel ***chart*** is a visual representation of numeric data in a worksheet. A chart helps you identify trends, make comparisons, and recognize patterns in the numbers. Charts are dynamic and linked to the data, so when values in the worksheet change, the chart is automatically redrawn. You can display a chart in the worksheet with its data, or you can place a chart on its own sheet.

There are different kinds of charts, and Excel can recommend the best chart type based on your selected data. It is essential, however, that you select appropriate data for a chart, because it is possible to build charts that illustrate nothing of any consequence. With experience and practice, you will learn how to create charts that have meaning to your work.

Create a Chart Object

A ***chart object*** is a selectable item surrounded by a square border that is separate from worksheet data. A chart object contains chart elements such as titles, axes, and gridlines, and each element is selectable, too. You can size and position a chart object in a worksheet, and you can size and position each chart element on the chart.

Source data are the cells that contain values and labels to be graphed in a chart. When you select data for a chart, you usually do not include sums, averages, or similar calculations. In Figure 3-1, the source data includes the series names in column A, the category names in row 4,

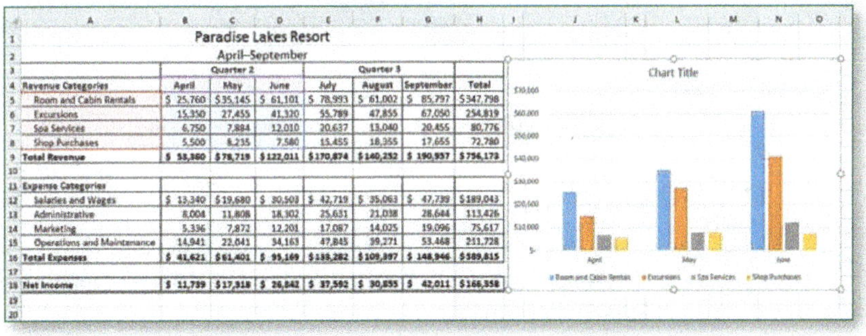

3-1 Chart object and its source data

and four values for each of three months. Each of the values is a ***data point***, a cell containing a value. Each group of data points or values is a ***data series***. In this example, there are four data series, one for each revenue category. Each data series has a name or label.

The text label that describes a data series is a ***category label***. In Figure 3.1, the category labels are the month names.

> **ANOTHER WAY**
>
> You can create a default chart object by selecting the data and pressing **Alt+F1**.

Data for a chart is best arranged with labels and values in adjacent cells and no empty rows. If you do not include labels for the source data, there are no labels in the chart to describe the data. An empty row within the source data is graphed as a data point with a value of zero (0) and will distort the chart's ability to illustrate a comparison or trend.

When you select contiguous source data (all cells are next to each other), the **Quick Analysis** button appears in the lower right corner of the selection. The *Quick Analysis* tool lists command groups you would be likely to use for the selected data, such as *Formatting, Charts,* or *Totals.* When you select the *Charts* command, Excel shows recommended chart types. As you point to each type, you see a preview of the chart. Click the preferred type to create the chart object in the worksheet.

HOW TO: Create a Chart Object from the Quick Analysis Tool

1. Select the source data range with labels and values.
   - The *Quick Analysis* button appears at the lower right corner of the range.
2. Click the **Quick Analysis** button.
   - A dialog box with command categories opens.
3. Select **Charts**.
   - Possible chart types are listed (Figure 3-2).
4. Point to a chart type.
   - A preview of the chart object is displayed.
5. Click to select the chart type.
   - The chart object displays in the worksheet.

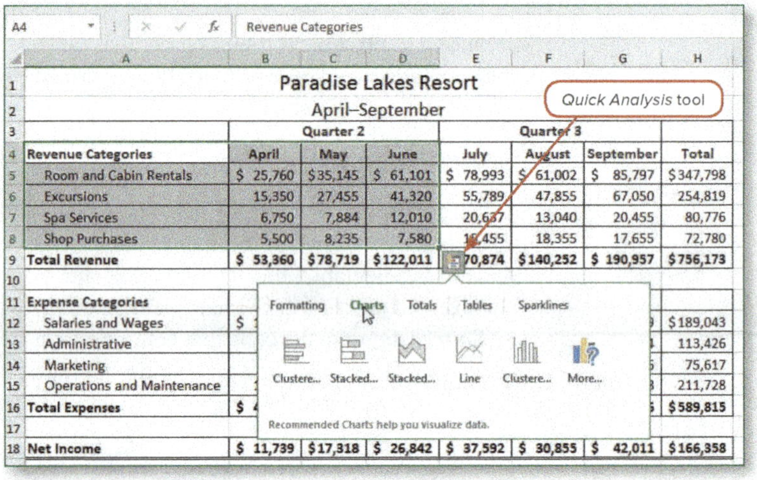

3-2 Chart options for selected data

Excel Chart Types

Excel has many chart types and most types have subtypes or variations. The most common chart types are column or bar, line, and pie, but Excel can build powerful scientific and statistical charts. The following table describes Excel chart types:

Excel Chart Types

Chart Type	Purpose	Data Example	Categories (Labels)	Values (Numbers)
Column	Illustrates data changes over a period of time or shows comparisons among items	Monthly sales data for three automobile models	Horizontal axis	Vertical axis
Bar	Displays comparisons among individual items or values at a specific period of time	Number of pairs sold for eight shoe styles	Vertical axis	Horizontal axis
Pie	Uses one data series to display each value as a percentage of the whole	Expenses or revenue by department for one quarter		One data series shown by slice size
Line	Displays trends in data over time, emphasizing the rate of change	Number of weekly web site views over a ten-week period	Horizontal axis	Vertical axis
Area	Displays the magnitude of change over time and shows the rate of change	Yearly consumption of apples, bananas, and pears over a ten-year period	Horizontal axis	Vertical axis

Continued

Chart Type	Purpose	Data Example	Categories (Labels)	Values (Numbers)
XY (Scatter) or *Bubble*	Displays relationships among numeric values in two or more data series; these charts do not have a category.	Number of times a patient visits a doctor, amount billed to insurance, and cost billed to patient	Horizontal axis (value 1-x)	Vertical axis (value 2-y)
Stock	Displays three series of data to show fluctuations in stock prices from high to low to close	Opening, closing, and high price for Microsoft stock each day for 30 days	Horizontal axis	Vertical axis
Surface	Displays optimum combinations of two sets of data on a surface	Perceived outside temperature at ten temperature and ten humidity levels	Horizontal axis (value 1-x)	Horizontal axis (value 1-x)
Radar	Displays the frequency of multiple data series relative to a center point. There is an axis for each category.	Style, comfort, and value ratings for three snow boot styles	NA	NA
TreeMap	Displays a hierarchical view of data with different sized and colored rectangles and sub-rectangles to compare the sizes of groups	Soda sales by product name, continent, country, and city	NA	NA
Sunburst	Displays a hierarchical view of data with concentric rings. The top hierarchy is the inner ring and each outer ring is related to its adjacent inner ring.	Tablet sales by screen size, continent, country, and city	NA	NA
Histogram	Column-style chart that shows frequencies within a distribution	Number of students in each of five grade categories for an exam	Horizontal axis	Vertical axis
Box & Whisker	Displays the distribution of data with minimum, mean, maximum, and outlier values	Sales prices of home in five suburbs during a three-week period	Horizontal axis	Vertical axis
Waterfall	Plots each element in a running total and displays negative and positive effects of each on the total	Banking or savings account register	Horizontal axis	Vertical axis
Funnel	Plots values that progressively decrease from one stage or process to the next	Job applications received, applications selected, initial interviews, team interviews, HR interview, job offer	Vertical axis	Horizontal axis
Combo Chart	Uses two types of charts to graph values that are widely different	Line chart for number of monthly web site visits and a column chart for monthly sales of online golf gloves	Either	Either

Size and Position a Chart Object

When you select a chart object, it is active and surrounded by eight selection handles. A ***selection handle*** is a small circle shape on each corner and in the middle of each side. To select the chart object, point to its border and click. When the chart object is selected, the *Range Finder* highlights the source data in the worksheet. When you point to a selection handle, you will see a two-pointed resize arrow. Drag a corner handle to size the height and width proportionally.

To move a chart object, point to the chart border to display a four-pointed move pointer. Then drag the chart object to the desired location.

When a chart is active or selected, the *Chart Tools Design* and *Format* tabs are available in the *Ribbon* and three *Quick Chart Tools* are available in the top right corner of the object: *Chart Elements, Chart Styles,* and *Chart Filters.*

MORE INFO

You can select individual elements or parts of the chart, and each element has its own selection handles.

HOW TO: Move and Size a Chart Object

1. Select the chart object.
   - Point to the border of the chart and click.
2. Point to the outside border of the chart to display a move pointer.
   - Point anywhere along the border.
3. Drag the chart object to a new location and release the pointer button (Figure 3-3).
4. Point to a corner selection handle to display a resize arrow.
5. Drag the pointer to resize the chart proportionally.

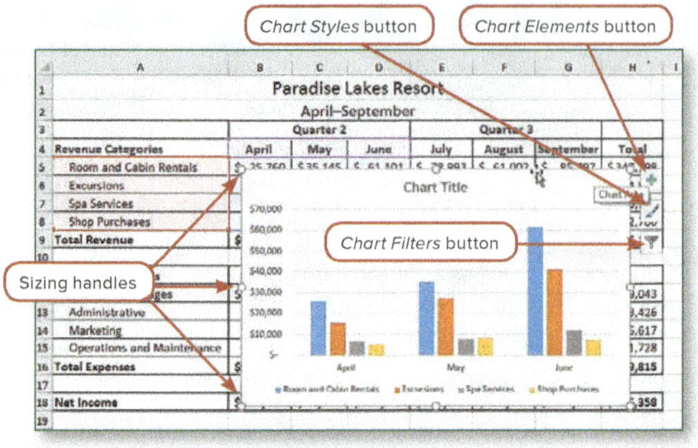

3-3 Selected chart object and move pointer

Create a Chart Sheet

A ***chart sheet*** is an Excel chart that is displayed on its own sheet in the workbook. A chart sheet does not have rows, columns, and cells, but the chart is linked to its data on the source worksheet.

From the *Quick Analysis* tool or the *Insert* tab, Excel creates a chart object. You must move the chart object to its own sheet with the *Move Chart* button on the *Chart Tools Design* tab. Excel uses default sheet names *Chart1, Chart2,* and so on, but you can type a descriptive name in the *Move Chart* dialog box, or you can rename the sheet at any time.

You can create an automatic column chart sheet by selecting the data and pressing the **F11** (**FN+F11**) function key.

> **MORE INFO**
>
> When the *Recommended Charts* button does not recommend a chart type, select the source data again in a left-to-right order. If there are still no suggestions, click the **All Charts** tab and choose a type.

Source data for a chart need not be contiguous. The *Quick Analysis* tool does not appear for noncontiguous data, but you can click the **Recommended Charts** button in the *Charts* group on the *Insert* tab. The *Insert Chart* dialog box opens and recommends chart types.

HOW TO: Create a Chart Sheet for Noncontiguous Cells

1. Select the values and labels for the chart.
   - Select the first range, press the **Ctrl** key, and select each range (Figure 3-4).
2. Click the **Recommended Charts** button [*Insert* tab, *Charts* group].
   - The *Insert Chart* dialog box opens.
   - You can click the **All Charts** tab to select any chart type.
3. Click the thumbnail for a chart type to preview the results.

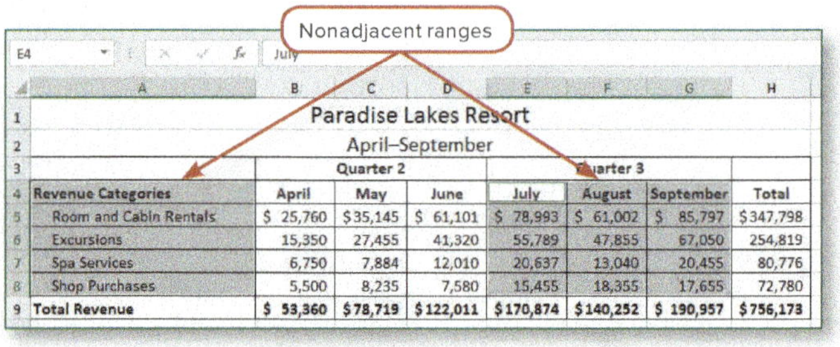

3-4 Source data ranges that are not next to each other

4. Click the preferred chart type and click **OK**.
   - The chart object is active.
   - The *Chart Tools* tabs are available.
5. Click the **Move Chart** button [*Chart Tools Design* tab, *Location* group].
6. Click the **New sheet** radio button (Figure 3-5).
7. Type a descriptive name for the chart sheet.
8. Click **OK**.

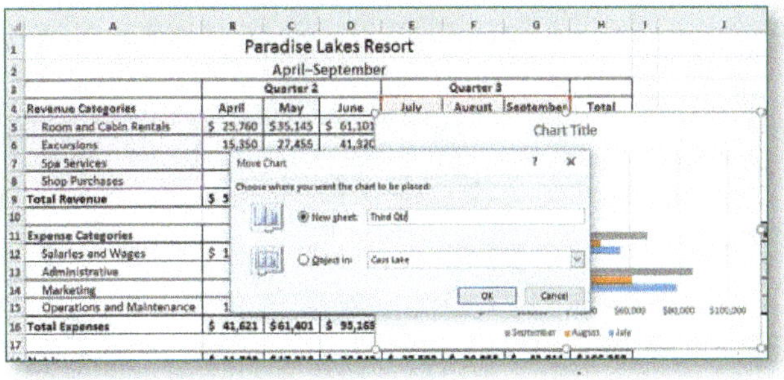

3-5 *Move Chart* dialog box

SLO 3.2

Using Quick Layouts and Chart Styles

A newly created chart has a default layout, color, and style. Excel has various tools to help you enhance the appearance of your chart for originality, readability, and appeal. The *Chart Tools Design* tab includes commands for selecting a chart layout, choosing a chart style, or changing the color scheme.

Apply a Quick Layout

A ***chart layout*** is a set of elements and the location of those elements. Elements are individual parts of a chart such as a main title, a legend, and axis titles. The *Quick Layout* button [*Chart Tools Design* tab, *Chart Layouts* group] opens a gallery of predefined layouts (Figure 3-6). As you point to an option in the gallery, *Live Preview* redraws the chart. When a chart layout adds an element such as a title, the element displays a generic label like "Chart Title." You can add or remove individual elements, as well as edit placeholder text.

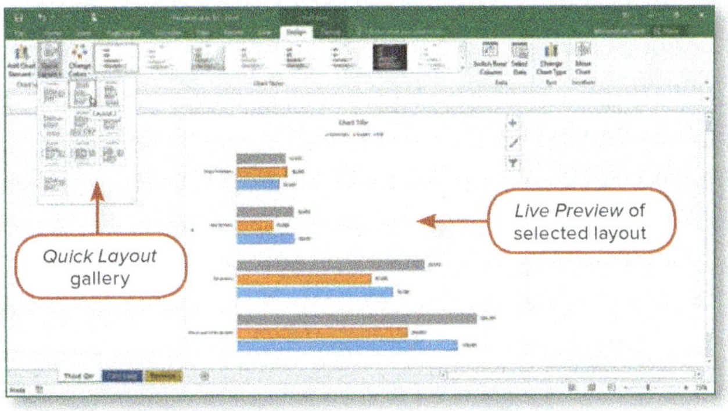

3-6 *Quick Layout* gallery

▸ HOW TO: Apply a Quick Layout to a Chart

1. Select the chart object or the chart sheet tab.
2. Click the **Quick Layout** button [*Chart Tools Design* tab, *Chart Layouts* group].
   - The gallery displays thumbnail images of each layout.
   - Quick layouts are named *Layout 1* through the last number.
3. Point to a layout to preview it in the chart.
4. Click a thumbnail to select it.
   - The chart is reformatted with the *Quick Layout* elements.

> **MORE INFO**
>
> The number of *Quick Layout* options depends on the chart type. For example, there are more layouts for a column chart than for a pie chart.

Apply a Chart Style

A ***chart style*** is a preset combination of colors and effects for a chart, its background, and its elements. The chart styles that are available for a chart are based on the current workbook theme. If you change the theme, the chart style colors are updated, and your chart reflects the new color palette. You can find chart styles in the *Chart Styles* group on the *Chart Tools Design* tab. Like a chart layout, you can preview the effects of a chart style as you point to each style in the gallery.

HOW TO: Apply a Chart Style

1. Select the chart object or the chart sheet tab.
2. Click the *Chart Styles* **More** button to open the gallery or point to a *Style* thumbnail [*Chart Tools Design* tab, *Chart Styles* group].
   - The number of styles depends on the chart type (Figure 3-7).
   - Chart styles are named *Style 1* through the last number.
3. Point to a style thumbnail to see a *Live Preview* in the chart.
4. Click to select a style.
   - The chart is redrawn with the selected style.

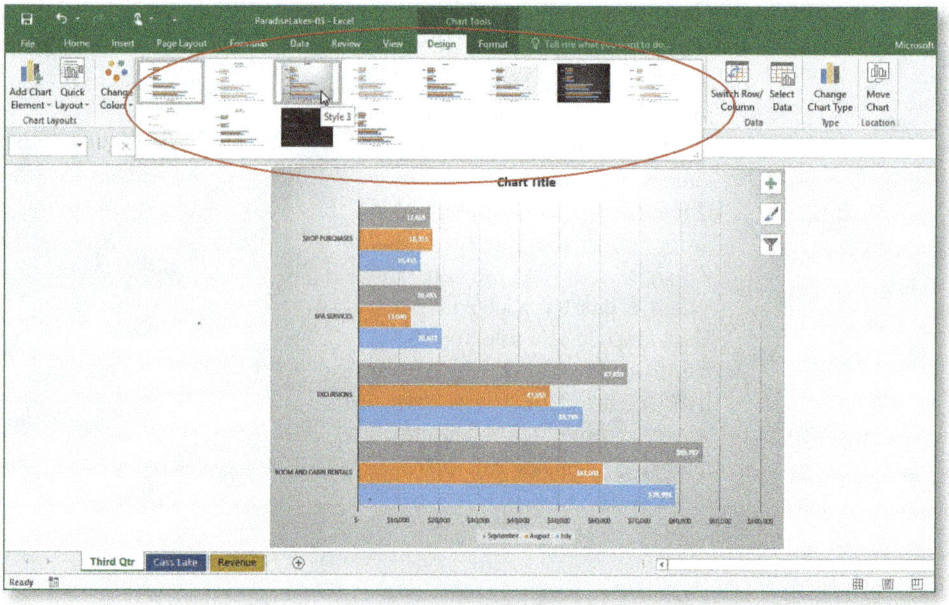

3-7 *Chart Styles* gallery and preview of selected style

> **MORE INFO**
>
> Some chart styles affect the chart layout. For example, a style may reposition the legend or a main title when it adds a 3D effect.

Change Chart Colors

The workbook theme and the chart style form the basis for a chart's color scheme. The *Chart Styles* group [*Chart Tools Design* tab] includes a *Change Colors* button with optional color palettes. These palettes are divided into *Colorful* and *Monochromatic* groups.

HOW TO: Change Chart Colors

1. Select the chart object or the chart sheet tab.
2. Click the **Change Colors** button [*Chart Tools Design* tab, *Chart Styles* group].
   - A gallery of color palettes opens (Figure 3-8).
   - Color schemes are named *Color 1* through the last number.
3. Point to a palette to see a *Live Preview* in the chart.
4. Click to select a palette.
   - The chart is formatted with new colors.

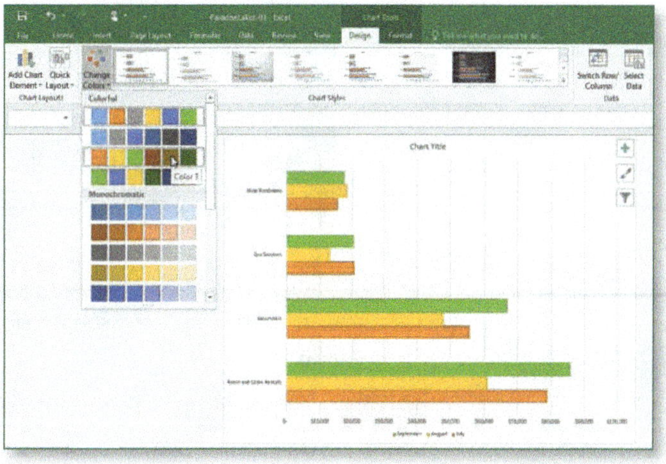

3-8 *Change Colors* gallery

Print a Chart

A chart object can be printed on the page with worksheet data, or it can be printed separately. To print a chart with the data, deselect the chart object by clicking a worksheet cell. Size and position the chart and scale the sheet to fit a printed page. Then use regular *Page Setup* commands to complete the print task, such as choosing the orientation or inserting headers or footers.

MORE INFO

When you insert a header or footer in a selected chart object, that header or footer is not inserted on the worksheet.

To print only the chart object on its own sheet, select it and use regular *Print* and *Page Setup* options. A selected chart object, by default, prints scaled to fit a landscape page. A chart sheet also prints in landscape orientation fit to the page.

HOW TO: Print a Chart with Its Source Data

1. Click any cell in the worksheet.
   - Size and position the chart object as needed.
2. Click the **File** tab to open the *Backstage* view (Figure 3-9).
3. Select **Print**.

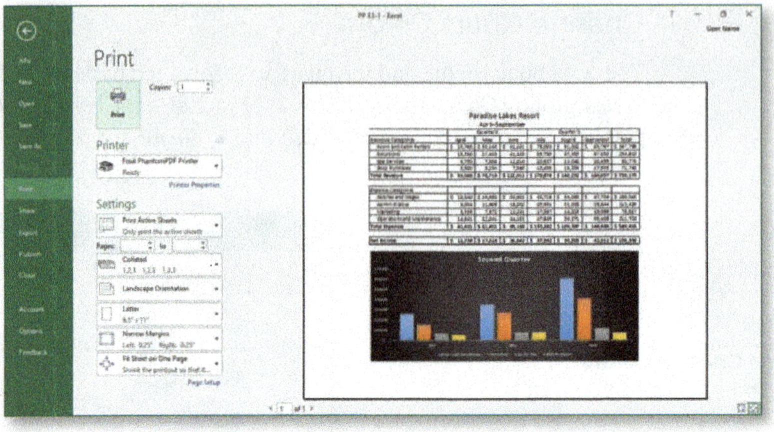

3-9 Print a chart with the data

4. Choose print settings as needed.
   - Set margins and scale the sheet to fit.
5. Click **Print**.

PAUSE & PRACTICE: EXCEL 3-1

In this project, you insert a clustered column chart object in a worksheet that tracks revenue and expenses for Paradise Lakes Resort. You also insert a clustered bar chart sheet to highlight second quarter results.

File Needed: ***ParadiseLakes-03.xlsx*** *[Student data files are available in the* Library *of your SIMnet account.]*
Completed Project File Name: ***[your initials] PP E3-1.xlsx***

1. Open the ***ParadiseLakes-03*** workbook from your student data files and save it as [your initials] PP E3-1.
2. Create a chart object.
   a. Select cells **A4:D8** on the **Cass Lake** sheet. These are labels and values for the chart.
   b. Click the **Quick Analysis** button and select **Charts**.
   c. Click **Clustered Column**.
3. Position and size the chart object.
   a. Click the chart object if it is not selected.
   b. Point to the chart border to display a move pointer.
   c. Drag the chart object so that its top left corner is at cell **A20**.
   d. Point to the lower right selection handle to display a resize arrow.
   e. Drag the pointer to reach cell **H35**.
4. Choose a quick layout.
   a. Select the chart object if necessary.
   b. Click the **Quick Layout** button [*Chart Tools Design* tab, *Chart Layouts* group].
   c. Click **Layout 3** (Figure 3-10).

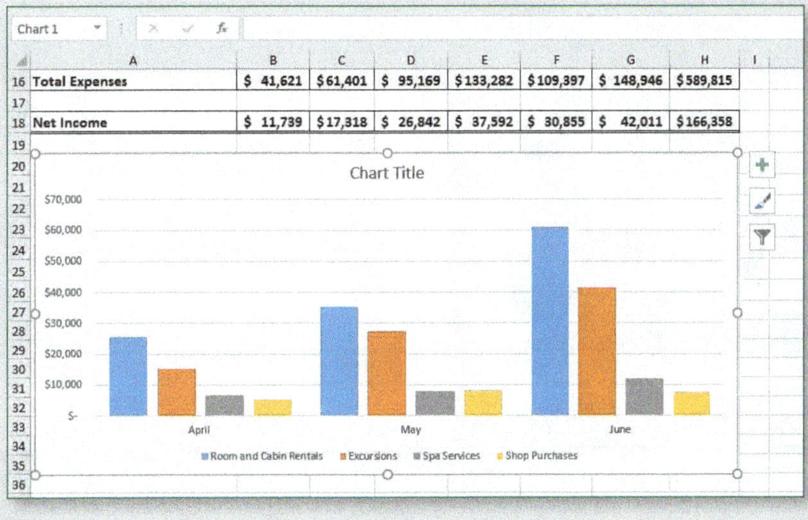

3-10 Chart object sized and positioned

5. Create a chart sheet.
   a. Select cells **A4:A8**.
   b. Press **Ctrl** and select cells **E4:G8**.
   c. Click the **Recommended Charts** button [*Insert* tab, *Charts* group].
   d. Select **Clustered Bar**.
   e. Click **OK**. The chart object is inserted and selected.
   f. Click the **Move Chart** button [*Chart Tools Design* tab, *Location* group].
   g. Click the **New sheet** radio button.
   h. Type Qtr 3 as the sheet name.
   i. Click **OK**. The chart sheet tab is active.
6. Choose a chart style.
   a. Click the **More** button to open the *Chart Styles* gallery [*Chart Tools Design* tab, *Chart Styles* group].
   b. Select **Style 7**.
7. Preview the charts.
   a. Select the **Qtr 3** sheet if necessary.
   b. Click the **File** tab to open the *Backstage* view.
   c. Choose **Print** to preview the chart sheet (Figure 3-11).
   d. Click the **Back** button to return to the worksheet.
   e. Click the **Cass Lake** worksheet tab and select cell **A1**.
   f. Click the **File** tab and select **Print**. The worksheet and chart are previewed on a single page.
   g. Click the **Back** button to return to the worksheet.

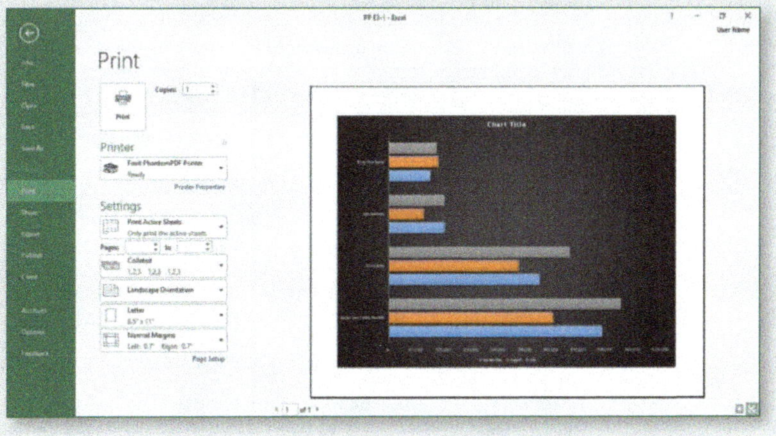

3-11 Print preview for chart sheet

8. Save and close the workbook (Figure 3-12).

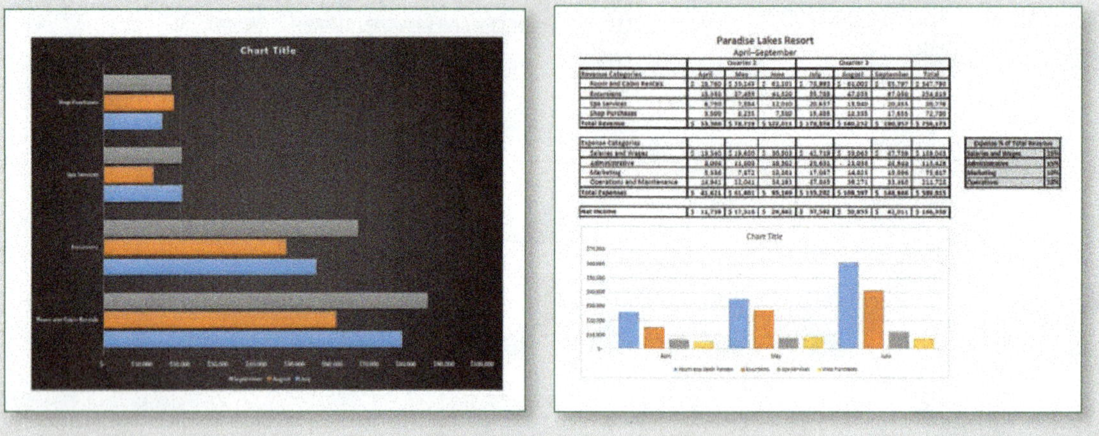

3-12 PP E3-1 completed chart object and chart sheet

SLO 3.3

Editing Chart Elements and Data

A ***chart element*** is a separate, clickable, editable object. The chart layout and style affects which elements are initially displayed, but you can add, remove, format, size, and position elements as you design a chart. The following table describes common chart elements:

Excel Chart Elements

Element	Description
Axis	Horizontal or vertical boundary that identifies what is plotted
Axis title	Optional description for the categories or values
Chart area	Background for the chart; can be filled with a color, gradient, or pattern
Chart floor	Base or bottom for a 3D chart
Chart title	Optional description or name for the chart
Chart wall	Vertical background for a 3D chart
Data label	Optional element that displays values with the marker for each data series
Data marker	Element that represents individual values. The marker is a bar, a column, a slice, or a point on a line.
Data point	A single value or piece of data from a data series
Data series	Group of related values that are in the same column or row and translate into the columns, lines, pie slices, and other markers
Gridline	Horizontal or vertical line that extends across the plot area to help in identifying values
Horizontal (category) axis	Describes what is shown in the chart and is created from row or column headings. In a bar chart, the category axis is the vertical axis; the category axis is the horizontal axis in a column chart.

Continued

Element	Description
Legend	Element that explains symbols, textures, or colors used to differentiate data series
Plot area	Rectangular area bounded by the horizontal and vertical axes
Tick mark	Small line or marker on an axis to guide in reading values
Trendline	Line or curve that displays averages in the data and can be used to forecast future averages
Vertical (value) axis	Shows the numbers on the chart. In a bar chart, the vertical axis is along the bottom; in a column chart, the vertical axis is along the side.

MORE INFO

Not all charts have all elements. For example, a pie chart does not have any axes or axes titles.

Add and Remove Chart Elements

When you point to a chart element, a *ScreenTip* describes it. When you click the element, it is active and surrounded by selection handles, as shown for the legend in Figure 3-13. In addition to clicking, you can select an element from the *Chart Elements* drop-down list on the *Chart Tools Format* tab. The name of the selected element appears in the *Chart Elements* box.

You show or hide chart elements from the *Chart Elements* button in the top right corner of a chart. When you click the button, the *Chart Elements* pane opens with a list of available elements for the chart type. In this pane, select or deselect the box to show or remove an element. To hide the pane, click the **Chart Elements** button again.

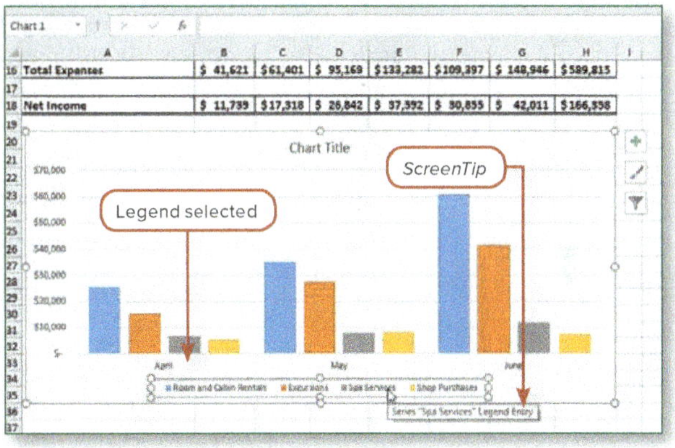

3-13 Selected legend and ScreenTip for a data series

ANOTHER WAY

Click the **Add Chart Element** button [*Chart Tools Design* tab, *Chart Layouts* group] to show a chart element.

Chart and Axes Titles

Chart layouts may include placeholders, which are text box objects, for a main chart title and for axes titles. If the quick layout does not include titles, you can add them. In either case, you must edit the placeholder text.

A main chart title is usually positioned above the chart, but within the chart area. Once you insert the text box, you can select it and move it anywhere on the chart. You might use an axis title to clarify what is represented by the categories or the values. If the chart represents the data well, axes titles are often not necessary.

HOW TO: Insert a Chart Title

1. Click the chart object or the chart sheet tab.
2. Click the **Chart Elements** button in the top right corner of the chart.
3. Select the **Chart Title** box.
   - The *Chart Title* placeholder displays above the chart.
4. Click the **Chart Title** arrow in the *Chart Elements* pane to select a position for the title.
5. Triple-click the *Chart Title* placeholder text to select it (Figure 3-14).
   - The mini toolbar opens.
6. Type a title to replace the placeholder text.
7. Click the chart border.
   - The title object is deselected.
   - If you press **Enter** while typing in the text box, you insert a new line in the title. Press **Backspace** to remove it and then click the chart border.

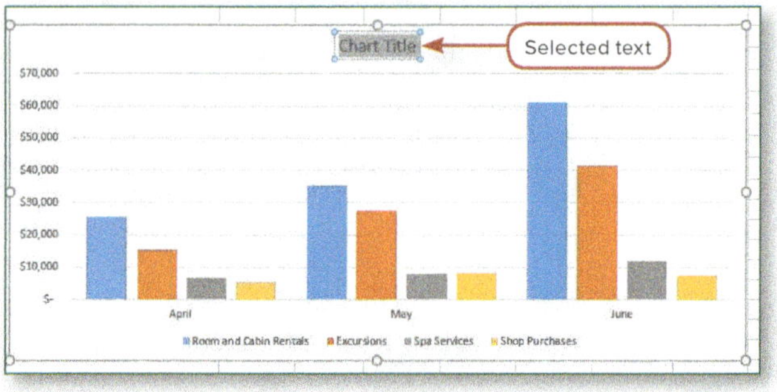

3-14 Placeholder text to be edited

To edit placeholder text, you can also select the object and type text in the *Formula* bar. Then press **Enter**, or click the **Enter** button in the *Formula* bar to complete it. The label appears in the *Formula* bar as you type, and you will not see it on the chart until you press **Enter**.

All text within an object can be formatted with font attributes from the *Font* and *Alignment* groups [*Home* tab] when the element is selected. When you want to apply a format to a portion of the text, click to place an insertion point inside the element and select the characters to be changed.

> **MORE INFO**
>
> When you double-click a chart element, its *Format* pane opens with format and design choices for that element.

Removing a chart element makes more room for the actual chart. In Figure 3-15, for example, the vertical axis title "Dollars" is probably not necessary. By removing it, the chart resizes to fit the chart area. You can always show the element again if you change your mind.

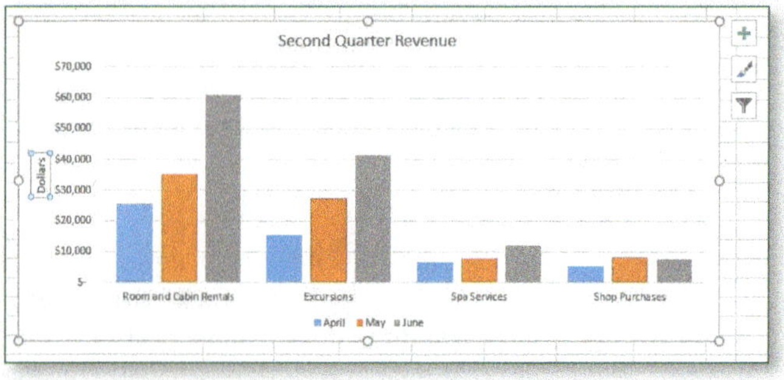

3-15 Delete an axis title to make more room for the chart

To delete a chart element, select it and press **Delete**. You can confirm which element is selected in the *Chart Elements* box on the *Chart Tools Format* tab [*Current Selection* group].

HOW TO: Delete a Chart Element

1. Click the chart element.
   - The element displays selection handles.
   - Confirm which element is selected in the *Chart Elements* list box [*Chart Tools Format* tab, *Current Selection* group].
2. Press **Delete**.
   - The chart resizes to fit the area.
   - You can also right-click the chart element and choose **Delete**.

> **ANOTHER WAY**
>
> To remove an element, click the **Chart Elements** button in the top right corner of the chart and deselect the box for that element.

Data Labels

Data labels display the number represented by a column, bar, pie slice, or other marker on the chart. Because the value axis uses a scale, it cannot show a precise value, but a data label can display that number. Data labels should be used when there are not too many data series because they can clutter a chart. Or you can select just one or two of the data points (the individual bars or columns) and show labels for only that data.

Data labels are displayed from the *Chart Elements* button on the chart or from the same button on the *Chart Tools Design* tab [*Chart Layouts* group].

HOW TO: Add Data Labels

1. Select the chart object or the chart sheet tab.
2. Click the **Chart Elements** button in the top right corner of the chart.
3. Select the **Data Labels** box.
   - *Live Preview* shows data labels for each data point in the data series
4. Point to **Data Labels** in the pane and point to its arrow (Figure 3-16).
   - Position choices for the labels are listed.
   - *Live Preview* updates as you point to each option.
5. Choose a location for the data labels.

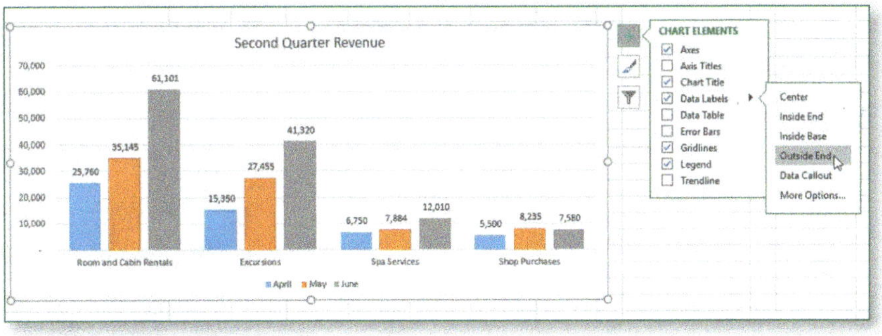

3-16 Data labels shown outside bar markers

Data Table

A chart ***data table*** is a columnar display of the values for each data series in a chart, located just below the chart. When your readers do not have access to the source data for a chart, a data table can supply valuable information.

To include a data table below your chart, you can use the *Add Chart Element* button on the *Chart Tools Design* tab in the *Chart Layouts* group or the *Chart Elements* button on the chart. You can show a data table with or without legend markers, a mini legend to the left of the table (Figure 3-17).

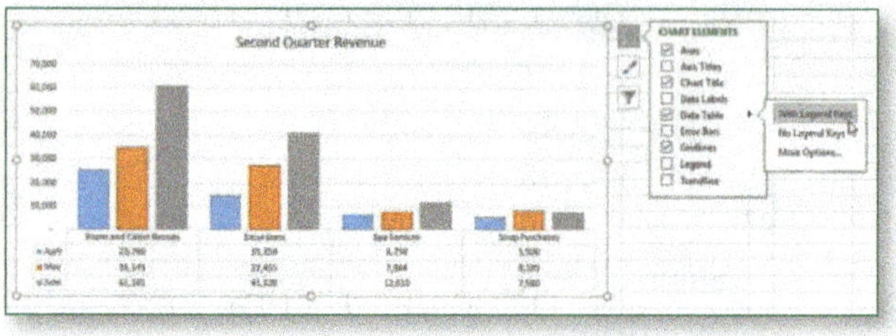

3-17 Data table element for a chart

Trendlines

A ***trendline*** is a chart element that plots patterns using a moving average of the current data. It uses a straight or curved line and can extend past the data to predict future averages. Some charts cannot display a trendline, such as a stacked chart, a pie chart, or a 3D chart. A basic linear trendline is appropriate for values that tend to increase or decrease as time passes. A trendline traces data for one data series as seen in Figure 3-18. If you have multiple data series, as in a typical column chart, you can add a trendline for each series.

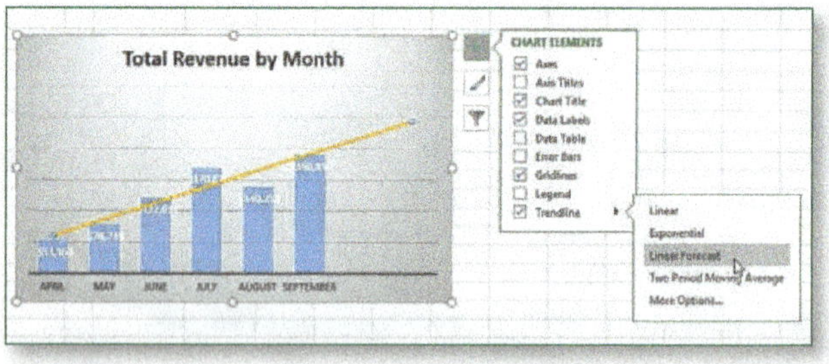

3-18 Column chart with "Total Revenue" linear trendline

> **ANOTHER WAY**
>
> Right-click a data series marker (its column) and choose **Add Trendline** to open the *Format Trendline* task pane and build a trendline.

HOW TO: Add a Trendline to a Chart

1. Click the chart object or the chart sheet tab.
2. Click the **Chart Elements** button in the top right corner of the chart.
3. Select the **Trendline** box in the *Chart Elements* pane.
   - The *Add Trendline* dialog box lists the names of the data series.
   - When there is only one data series, the trendline is added to the chart.
4. Choose a data series for the trendline and click **OK** (Figure 3-19).
5. Point to the **Trendline** arrow in the *Chart Elements* pane.
   - Choose **Linear** to show a line for existing data.
   - Choose **Linear Forecast** to build a line for current and future data.

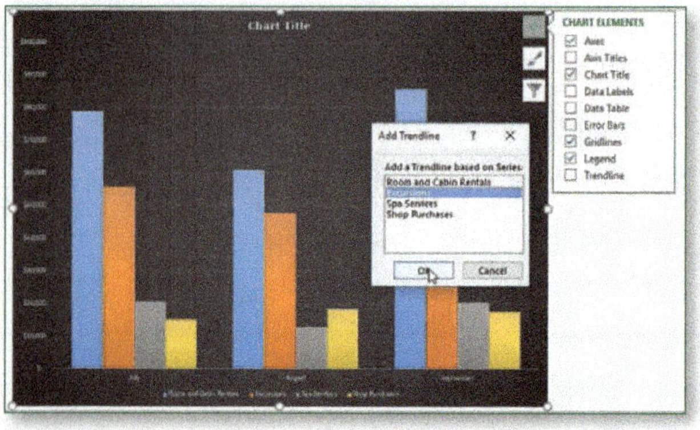

3-19 *Add Trendline* dialog box for chart with multiple data series

MORE INFO

Excel uses logarithmic and other statistical concepts as it builds a trendline. Explore these options in the *Trendline Format* task pane if your work often requires trendlines.

Switch Row and Column Data

Excel plots the data series based on the number of rows and columns selected in the worksheet and the chart type. Based on your choices, Excel determines if the labels are along the bottom or the side of the chart. When necessary, you can change which data series is plotted on the x-axis and which is plotted on the y-axis. In a column chart, the x-axis is along the bottom of the chart; the y-axis is along the left.

HOW TO: Switch Row and Column Data

1. Click the chart object or the chart sheet tab.
2. Click the **Switch Row/Column** button [*Chart Tools Design* tab, *Data* group] (Figure 3-20).
   - The data series become the categories.
   - You can toggle between how columns and rows are plotted.

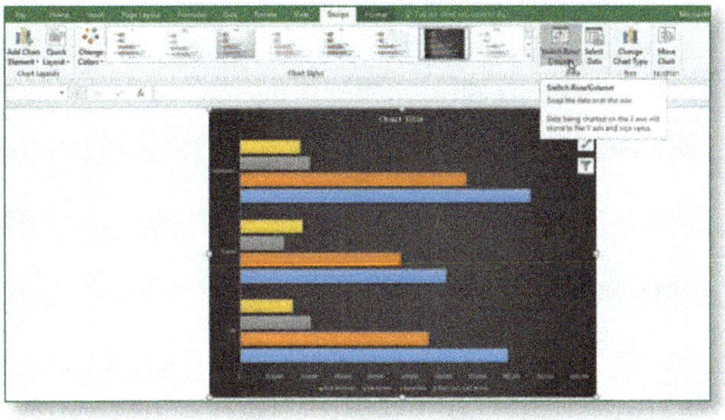

3-20 Column and row data switched

ANOTHER WAY

Click the **Chart Filters** button in the top right corner of the chart and choose **Select Data** at the bottom of the pane to open the *Select Data Source* dialog box and switch row and column data.

Change the Chart Type

When a chart does not depict what you intended, you need a variety of chart types for a project, or you simply prefer a different chart, you can easily change the chart type. Changing the type assumes that the source data is the same and that it can be graphed in the new chart. You should not, for example, change a column chart with three data series into a pie chart, because a pie chart has only one series. The resulting chart would not represent the data as expected.

The *Change Chart Type* button is on the *Chart Tools Design* tab in the *Type* group. For a selected chart object or sheet, you can also right-click and choose **Change Chart Type** from the context menu. The *Change Chart Type* dialog box has *Recommended Charts* and *All Charts* tabs like the *Insert Chart* dialog box.

HOW TO: Change the Chart Type

1. Click the chart object or chart sheet.
2. Click the **Change Chart Type** button [*Chart Tools Design* tab, *Type* group].
   - The *Change Chart Type* dialog box opens.

3. Click the **Recommended Charts** tab.
   - Click **All Charts** tab if the recommended charts are not adequate.
4. Click a thumbnail image to preview the chart in the dialog box.
5. Select a chart type and click **OK**.

Filter Source Data

A chart displays all the categories and all the data series. You can, however, filter or refine which data is displayed by hiding categories or series. A ***filter*** is a requirement or condition that identifies which data is shown and which is hidden. Chart filters do not change the underlying cell range for a chart, but they enable you to focus on particular data.

You filter chart data from the *Chart Filters* button in the top right corner of the chart or in the *Select Data Source* dialog box.

HOW TO: Filter Source Data

1. Select the chart object or chart sheet tab.
2. Click the **Chart Filters** button in the top right corner.
   - The *Chart Filters* pane shows a check mark for series and categories that are shown.
3. Deselect the box for a series or category to be hidden.
4. Click **Apply** (Figure 3-21).
   - The chart is redrawn.
5. Click the **Chart Filters** button to close the pane.
   - You can show the hidden data when desired.

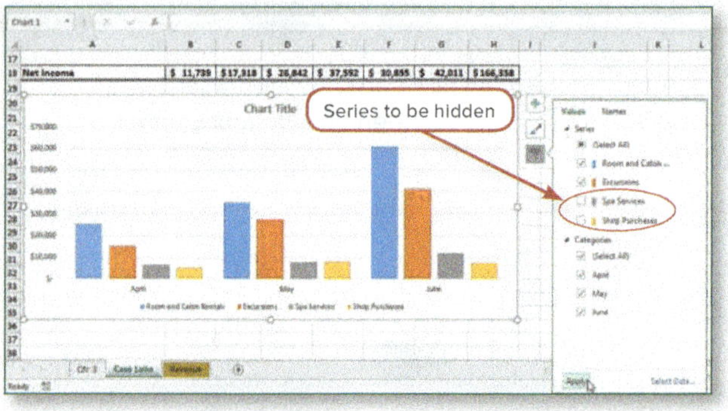

3-21 *Chart Filters* pane

Edit Source Data

The cells used to build a chart are its source data. This data can be edited to change, add, or remove cells. In a column chart, for example, you can add a data series, or another column. To add or delete a data series in a chart object, select the chart and drag the sizing arrow in the lower right corner of the highlighted cell range to expand or shrink the data range, as shown in Figure 3-22. Removing cells from the data range deletes that data series from the chart.

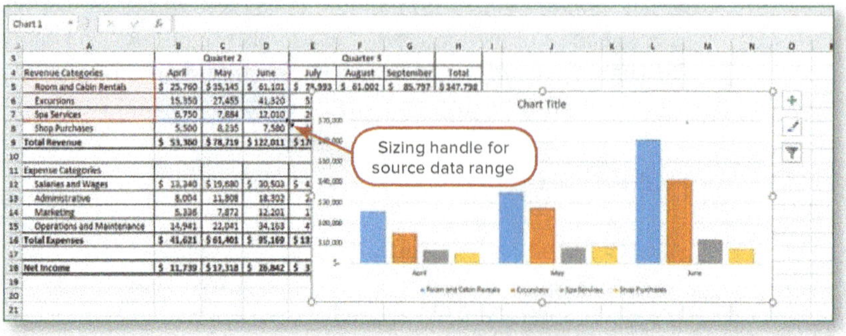

3-22 The "Shop Purchases" column will be removed from chart

To edit the source data for a chart sheet, click the **Select Data** button on the *Chart Tools Design* tab [*Data* group] to open the *Select Data Source* dialog box.

▸ HOW TO: Add a Data Series in a Chart Sheet

1. Click the chart sheet tab.
2. Click the **Select Data** button [*Chart Tools Design* tab, *Data* group].
   - The *Select Data Source* dialog box opens.
   - The worksheet is active, and the source cells are highlighted.
3. Select the new cell range in the worksheet (Figure 3-23).
   - If the cell ranges are not adjacent, select the first one, type a comma, and select the next range.
   - You can type cell addresses in the *Chart data range* box rather than selecting cells.
4. Click **OK**.
   - The chart sheet is active and redrawn with the edited source data range.

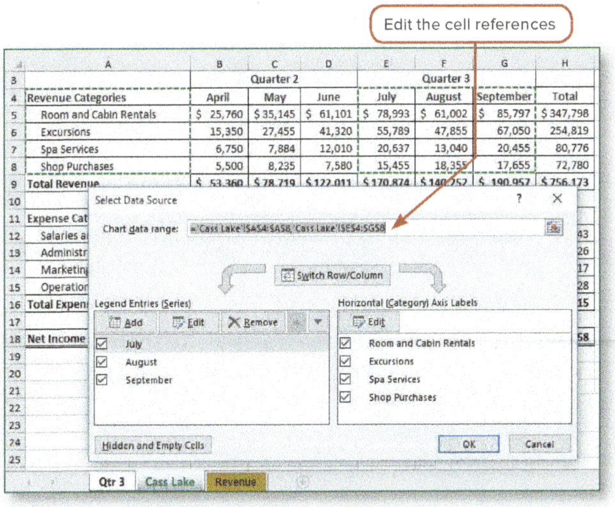

3-23 *Select Data Source* dialog box for a chart sheet

ANOTHER WAY

You can open the *Select Data Source* dialog box by clicking **Select Data** at the bottom of the *Chart Filters* pane. You can define filters from this dialog box by selecting or deselecting a series or category name box.

SLO 3.4

Formatting Chart Elements

Quick Layout and *Chart Styles* apply formatting, but you can change most attributes to personalize your work. Making your own format choices enables you to distinguish your charts from those of other Excel users. You can also use company, association, or school colors and images to further differentiate your charts.

Some chart elements consist of a group of related elements. A data series, for example, is the group of values for a particular item. Within each data series, there are data points. You can format the entire data series or an individual data point.

When you select a chart element, certain options on the *Chart Tools Design* tab apply to only that element. When the chart area (background) is selected, for example, you can change only its fill or border color.

Apply a Shape Style

A ***shape style*** is a predesigned set of borders, fill colors, and effects for a chart element. ***Shape fill*** is the background color, and ***shape outline*** is the border around the element. ***Shape effects*** include shadows, glows, bevels, or soft edges. All of these commands are available in the *Shape Styles* group on the *Chart Tools Format* tab.

> **MORE INFO**
>
> You can click the **Undo** button to remove a format choice in a chart.

Shape styles are shown in a gallery and are grouped as *Theme Styles* or *Presets*. Point to an icon to see a *ScreenTip* with a descriptive name and click an icon to apply it to the selected element. *Live Preview* is available for a chart object but not for a chart sheet.

HOW TO: Apply a Shape Style

1. Select the chart element.
    - Confirm or select a chart element by clicking the **Chart Elements** drop-down arrow [*Chart Tools Format* tab, *Current Selection* group] and choosing the name.
    - If you accidentally open the *Format* task pane for a chart element, close it.
2. Click the **More** button [*Chart Tools Format* tab, *Shape Styles* group].
    - Each icon in the *Shape Styles* gallery displays fill, outline, and effects (Figure 3-24).
    - Point to an icon to see its name and *Live Preview* in a chart object.
3. Click a shape style icon.
    - The chart element is reformatted.

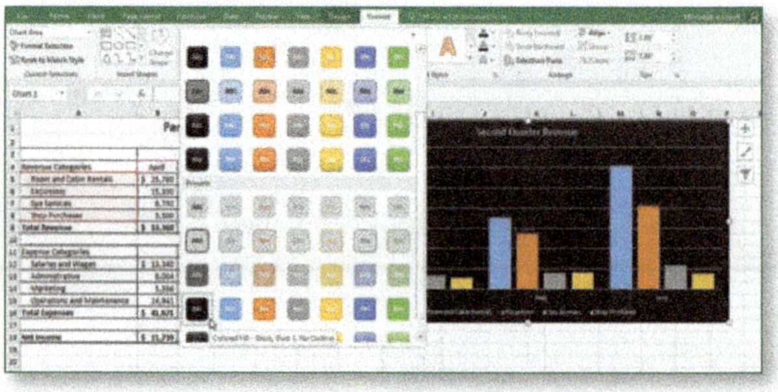

3-24 *Shape Style* gallery for the chart area

Apply Shape Fill, Outline, and Effects

Fill color, outline width and color, and special effects are available separately, and your choices override shape style settings already applied.

For fill color, you choose from the gallery, standard colors, or a custom color. After you choose a color, you can refine it to use a gradient, a variegated blend of the color.

HOW TO: Apply Gradient Fill to a Chart Element

1. Select the chart element.
    - Confirm or select a chart element from the **Chart Elements** list [*Chart Tools Format* tab, *Current Selection* group].
2. Click the **Shape Fill** button [*Chart Tools Format* tab, *Shape Styles* group].
    - The gallery and menu options are listed.
3. Point to a color tile to see its name in a *ScreenTip*.
    - *Live Preview* applies the color to an element in a chart object.
4. Select a color tile to apply the color.
5. Click the **Shape Fill** [*Chart Tools Format* tab, *Shape Styles* group].
6. Choose **Gradient** to open the gallery (Figure 3-25).
7. Point to a tile to see its description.
8. Click the preferred gradient.

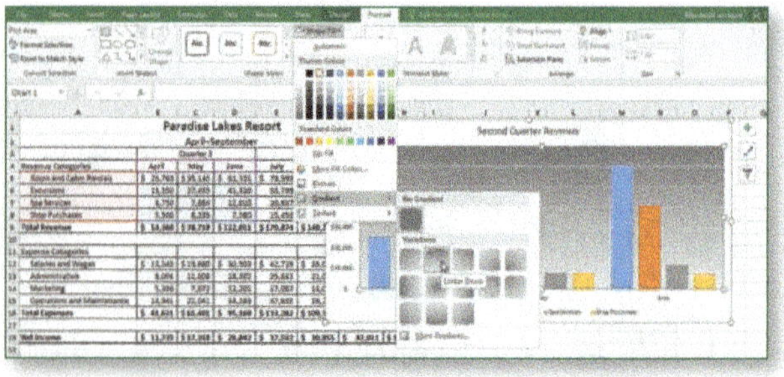

3-25 *Shape Fill* and *Gradient* galleries

> **ANOTHER WAY**
>
> You can apply most formats from the *Home* tab for a selected chart element.

The outline for a shape is a border that surrounds or encircles the element. Not all chart elements are suited to an outline, but elements such as the chart or plot area often benefit from the use of an outline. When you add an outline to a chart element, you can select a weight or thickness for the line as well as a color. The thickness of an outline is measured in points, like fonts. Excel provides a gallery of weights to help you visualize the width. After you apply an outline, it is easier to see the effect if you deselect the chart object.

HOW TO: Apply an Outline to a Chart Element

1. Select the chart element.
2. Click the **Shape Outline** button [*Chart Tools Format* tab, *Shape Styles* group].
   - The gallery and menu options are listed.
3. Choose a color.
4. Click the **Shape Outline** button [*Chart Tools Format* tab, *Shape Styles* group].
5. Click **Weight** to open its gallery.
6. Choose a width for the outline (Figure 3-26).
7. Click a worksheet cell or another chart element to see the outline.

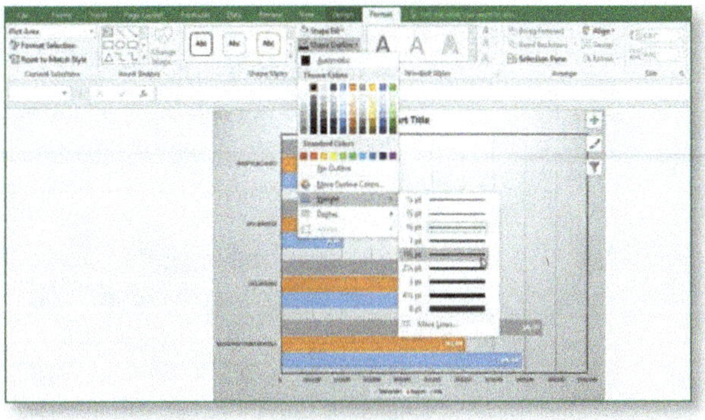

3-26 *Outline color* and *Weight* galleries

> **MORE INFO**
>
> To remove shape fill or outline, select the object, click the command button, and choose **No Fill** or **No Outline**.

Special effects that are commonly used are bevels and shadows, because they give an element a realistic, three-dimensional look. These effects are best used on larger elements, such as the chart area, because they can overwhelm smaller elements.

To remove an effect, select the element and click the **Shape Effects** button. Choose the effect group to select the first option such as **No Shadow** or **No Bevel**.

HOW TO: Apply an Effect to a Chart Element

1. Select the chart element.
2. Click the **Shape Effects** button [*Chart Tools Format* tab, *Shape Styles* group].
   - The gallery lists effect groups and then variations for each group.
3. Select a group for the effect (Figure 3-27).
   - If a group name is grayed out, it is not available for the selected element.
4. Point to an icon to see its name.
5. Click to choose an effect.
6. Click a worksheet cell or another chart element to see the outline.

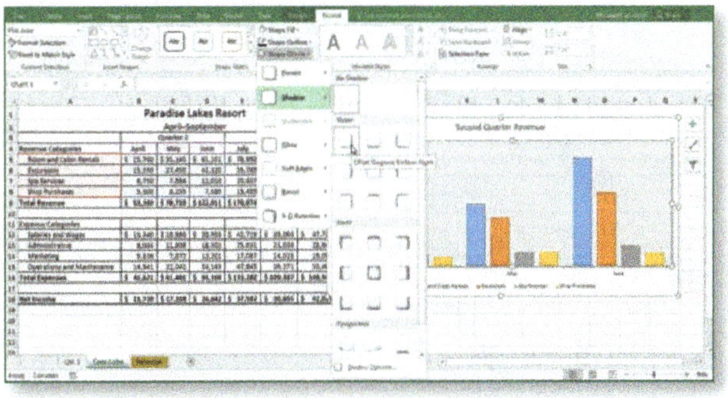

3-27 *Shape Effects* gallery for the plot area

The Format Task Pane

Every chart element has a *Format* task pane that consolidates shape, fill, and color options and provides custom commands for the element. To open the *Format* pane for a chart element, double-click the element or right-click it and choose **Format** [*Element Name*] from the menu. The *Format* pane opens to the right of the workbook window and automatically updates to reflect the selected element.

> **ANOTHER WAY**
>
> Open a *Format* task pane for a selected object by clicking the **Format Selection** button [*Chart Tools Format* tab, *Selection* group].

A task pane lists command options at the top of the pane. In Figure 3-28, *Title Options* and *Text Options* are available because the selected element is a chart title. The small triangle next to the first *Options* name enables you to choose a different chart element.

For each options group, most *Format* task panes have at least two buttons. The *Fill & Line*, *Effects*, and *Options* buttons are common, but there are other buttons for selected elements. Point to a button to see its *ScreenTip*. When you click a button, the pane displays relevant commands.

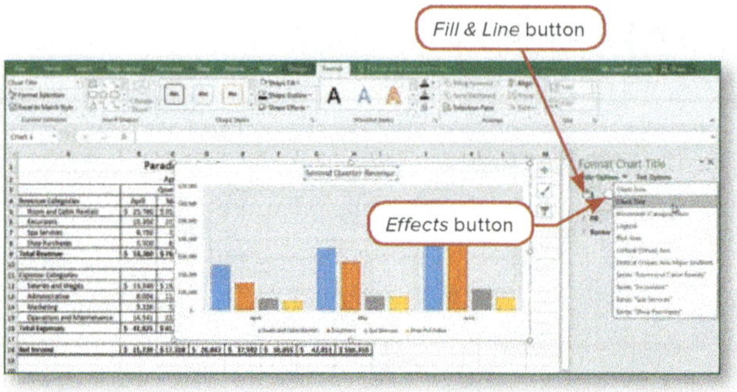

3-28 *Format Chart Title* pane

> **MORE INFO**
>
> Expand or collapse a command group in the *Format* task pane by clicking the command name.

HOW TO: Use the Format Task Pane to Change Shape Fill

1. Double-click the chart element.
   - The *Format* task pane for the element opens on the right.
   - Select another element in the chart to see its task pane.
   - You can also select an element and click the **Format Selection** button [*Chart Tools Format* tab, *Current Selection* group] to open the task pane.
2. Click the name of the *Options* group at the top of task pane.
   - For some chart elements, there is only one group.
3. Click the **Fill & Line** button in the *Format* task pane.
4. Click **Fill** to expand the group.
5. Click the **Fill Color** button to open the gallery (Figure 3-29).
6. Choose the desired color.

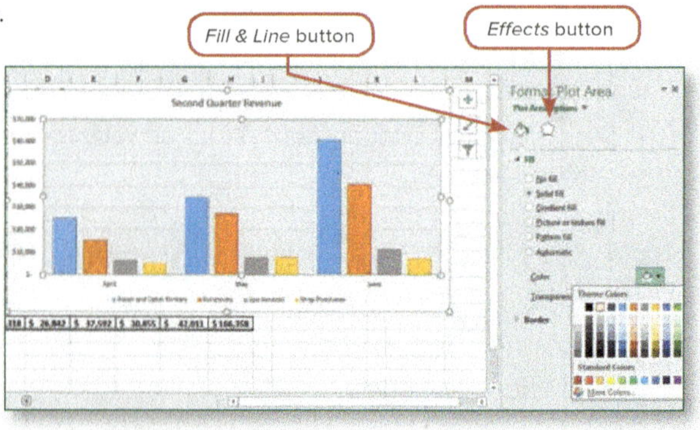

3-29 *Fill & Line* command in the *Format Plot Area* task pane

While the *Fill & Line* and *Effects* buttons offer similar commands for all elements, the *Options* button in a *Format* task pane is specific to the element. For a data series in a column chart, for example, these commands determine whether numbers are shown to the right or left of the chart (secondary or primary axis), or whether the columns overlap. A pie chart, on the other hand, has options that allow you to rotate the pie or explode slices.

HOW TO: Use the Format Task Pane to Format Data Labels

1. Double-click a data label element in the chart.
   - Right-click an element and choose **Format Data Labels**.
   - All data labels for one series are selected.
2. Choose **Label Options** at the top of the task pane.
   - Point to a button to see a *ScreenTip*.
   - *Text Options* are also available.
3. Click the **Label Options** button.
4. Click **Label Options** or **Number** to expand the command group.
5. Select format options for the labels (Figure 3-30).
   - Formats are applied as you select them.
6. Close the task pane.

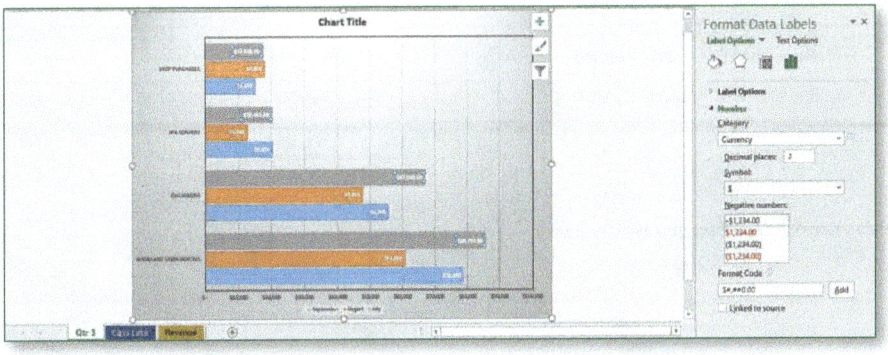

3-30 *Format Data Labels* pane

SLO 3.5 Using Pictures, Shapes, and WordArt in a Chart

A chart can be enhanced with pictures, shapes, or *WordArt.* Pictures can be inserted as separate design objects on the chart, or they can be used as fill for a chart element. You can draw a shape such as an arrow or a lightning bolt to highlight a particular data point on a chart. *WordArt* is often applied to a chart title for a distinctive look.

Use a Picture as Shape Fill

An image can be used to fill the chart area, the plot area, or a marker, especially bars, columns, or pie slices. You have probably seen bar charts with stick figures to illustrate population numbers or column charts with tiny automobile images to show auto sales. You can use an image file from your computer, from external media, or from an online source. And always verify that you have permission to use an image in your work.

The size and design of the picture is important, and you should guard against making the chart appear busy. You can edit some attributes of a picture in Excel, but this depends on the picture format.

A picture is inserted from the **Fill** command on the *Format* task pane for the element. After you have inserted a picture, the task pane displays ***Stretch*** and ***Stack*** options. *Stretch* enlarges and elongates a single copy of a picture to fill the element. The *Stack* choice sizes and repeats the image to fill the area. There is also a ***Stack and Scale*** setting for precise matching of the number of images used per unit of value.

> **MORE INFO**
>
> When you select the *Picture or texture fill* command for a chart element, it displays the most recently used image, if any, in the element.

HOW TO: Use a Picture as Fill

1. Double-click the chart element for the fill.
   - The *Format* task pane opens.
   - You can also right-click the element and choose **Format [*Element Name*]**.
2. Click the **Fill & Line** button in the *Format* task pane.
3. Click **Fill** to expand the group.
4. Select the **Picture or texture fill** radio button.
   - If the last-used picture or texture displays in the chart element, ignore it. It will be replaced.

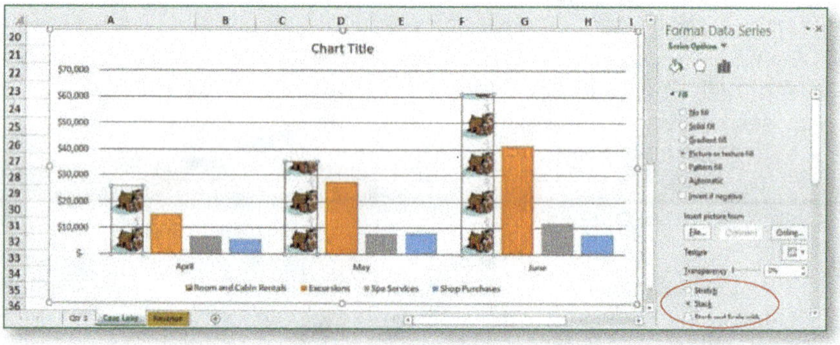

3-31 Image used as fill for data series

5. Click **Online** to search for an image or click **File** to choose a stored image.
6. Find and insert the image.
   - The picture is placed in the chart element.
7. Click the **Stack** button in the task pane (Figure 3-31).
   - Copies of the picture fill the element.

> **MORE INFO**
>
> Insert an image as a separate design element on a chart from the *Insert* tab and edit it from the *Picture Format* tab.

Insert Shapes

The *Shapes* gallery is located in the *Insert Shapes* group on the *Chart Tools Format* tab. These predefined shapes include arrows, lines, circles, and other basic figures. Shapes can be used to highlight or emphasize a point in the chart. They can be drawn anywhere on the chart, but are usually placed on the background or the plot area so they do not obscure any data. A shape, once drawn, is a clickable, selectable object. When it is selected, the *Picture Tools Format* tab is available with commands for altering the appearance of the shape and there is also the *Format Shape* task pane.

HOW TO: Insert a Shape in a Chart

1. Select the chart object or the chart sheet tab.
2. Click the **More** button [*Chart Tools Format* tab, *Insert Shapes* group].

3. Select the shape.
4. Click and drag to draw the shape on the chart (Figure 3-32).
    - The shape is selected.
5. Type text for the shape.
    - Text is optional.
    - Some shapes cannot display text.
6. Click the **Drawing Tools Format** tab to format the shape.
    - You can also apply formatting from the *Format Shape* task pane.
7. Click a worksheet cell or another chart element to deselect the shape.

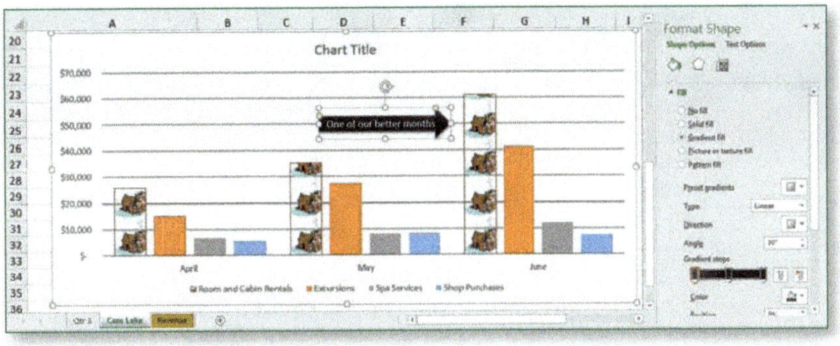

3-32 Shape inserted in chart

ANOTHER WAY

Insert a shape from the *Shapes* button on the *Insert* tab [*Illustrations* group].

Use WordArt in a Chart

WordArt is a text box with preset font style, fill, and effects. *WordArt* is best used for main titles, because it can make smaller elements unreadable. You apply a *WordArt* style from the *Chart Tools Format* tab, *WordArt Styles* group. You can further design a *WordArt* style by individually changing its fill, outline, and effects.

MORE INFO

You can insert a *WordArt* text box from the *Insert* tab [*Text* group] and position it on the chart.

HOW TO: Use WordArt in a Chart

1. Select the chart title object.
    - You can also apply *WordArt* to an axis title, a data label, or the legend.
2. Click the **More** button to open the *WordArt Styles* gallery [*Chart Tools Format* tab, *WordArt Styles* group].
3. Point to a style icon to see a *ScreenTip* with a description.
    - The styles use colors and effects from the workbook theme.
    - *Live Preview* works in a chart object but not on a chart sheet.
4. Click the preferred style (Figure 3-33).

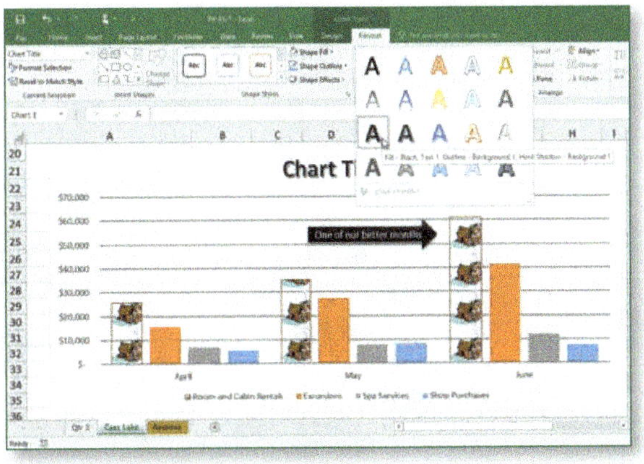

3-33 *WordArt Style* gallery for selected chart title

PAUSE & PRACTICE: EXCEL 3-2

For this project, you open your Pause & Practice file to edit and format the Paradise Lakes Resort charts. You switch row and column data, remove chart elements, and change the chart type. Finally, you format the charts for increased visual appeal.

File Needed: ***[your initials] PP E3-1.xlsx***
Completed Project File Name: ***[your initials] PP E3-2.xlsx***

1. Open the ***[your initials] PP E3-1*** workbook completed in *Pause & Practice 3-1* and save it as [your initials] PP E3-2.
2. Switch the row and column data in the chart object.
   a. Click the **Cass Lake** worksheet tab.
   b. Point to the border or edge of the chart object and click to select it.
   c. Click the **Switch/Row Column** button [*Chart Tools Design* tab, *Data* group].
3. Edit, add, and remove chart elements.
   a. Click to select the chart title box.
   b. Point to the placeholder text and triple-click to select all of it.
   c. Type Second Quarter Activity.
   d. Click the chart border to deselect the title.
   e. Click the **Chart Elements** button in the top right corner of the chart.
   f. Select the **Axis Titles** box.
   g. Select the horizontal *Axis Title* placeholder below the columns and press **Delete**.
   h. Select the vertical *Axis Title* placeholder.
   i. Click the *Formula* bar, type Revenue, and press **Enter** (Figure 3-34).
   j. Click a worksheet cell to deselect the chart object.

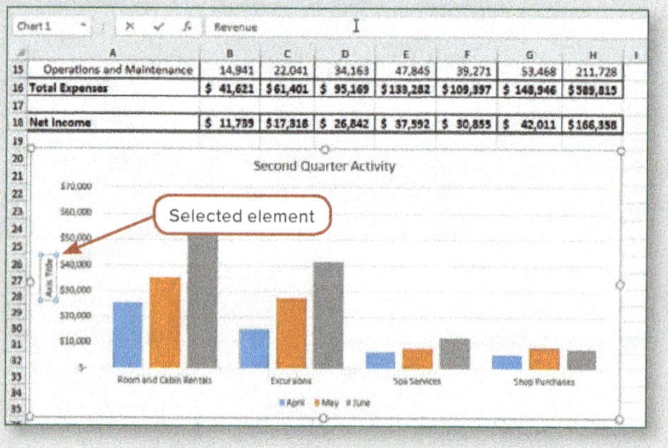

3-34 Edit the text in the *Formula* bar

4. Change the chart type.
   a. Click the **Qtr 3** sheet tab.
   b. Click the **Change Chart Type** button [*Chart Tools Design* tab, *Type* group].
   c. Click the **Recommended Charts** tab.
   d. Find and select the first **Clustered Column** in the pane on the left.
   e. Click **OK**.
5. Filter the source data.
   a. Click the **Chart Filters** button at the top right corner of the chart.
   b. Deselect the **Excursions** box in the *Series* area.
   c. Click **Apply**.
   d. Click the **Chart Filters** button to close the pane (Figure 3-35).

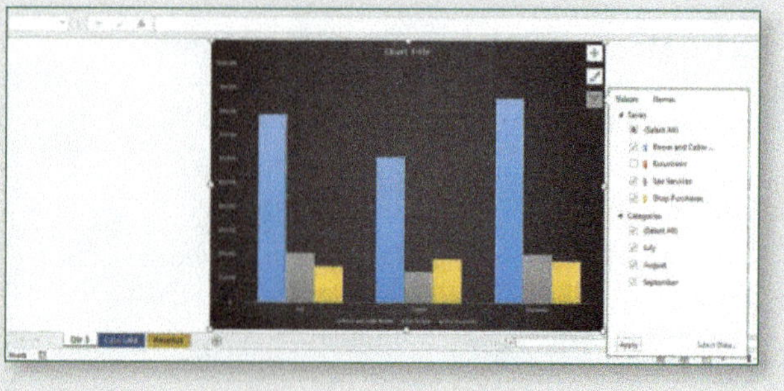

3-35 Filtered data in chart

6. Apply shape styles and outlines to chart elements.
   a. Click the **Cass Lake** tab and select the chart object.
   b. Click the **Chart Elements** drop-down arrow [*Chart Tools Format* tab, *Current Selection* group].
   c. Choose **Plot Area** to select the plot area of the chart.
   d. Click the **More** button [*Chart Tools Format* tab, *Shape Styles* group].
   e. Click **Subtle Effect – Gold, Accent 4** in the fourth row in the *Theme Styles* group.
   f. Click the drop-down arrow for the **Shape Outline** button [*Chart Tools Format* tab, *Shape Styles* group].
   g. Choose **Black, Text 1** in the top row of the *Theme Colors*.
   h. Click the **Chart Elements** drop-down arrow [*Chart Tools Format* tab, *Current Selection* group].
   i. Choose **Vertical (Value) Axis Major Gridlines** to select the major gridlines in the plot area.
   j. Click the icon with the **Shape Outline** button [*Chart Tools Format* tab, *Shape Styles* group] to apply the last-used color (**Black, Text 1**).
   k. Click the **Chart Elements** drop-down arrow [*Chart Tools Format* tab, *Current Selection* group] and choose **Chart Area**.
   l. Apply **Black, Text 1** for the outline (Figure 3-36).
   m. Click a worksheet cell.

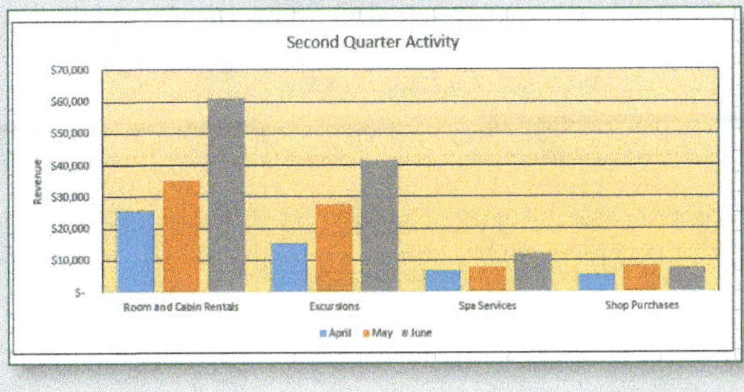

3-36 Plot area formatted

7. Use a picture as fill.
   a. Click the **Qtr 3** tab.
   b. Double-click one of the "Room and Cabin Rentals" columns to open the *Format Data Series* task pane.
   c. Click the **Fill & Line** button.
   d. Click **Fill** to expand the command group.
   e. Select the **Picture or texture fill** button.
   f. Click **Online**, type log cabin in the *Bing Image Search* box, and press **Enter**.
   g. Choose an image and insert it (Figure 3-37). If you choose an image that cannot be used as fill, a message appears in the columns; just select a different picture.
   h. Select the **Stack** radio button in the *Format Data Series* task pane.
   i. Click **Fill** to collapse the command group and click **Border** to expand its group.
   j. Select the **Solid line** button.
   k. Click the **Color** button and choose **Black, Text 1**.
   l. Close the task pane.

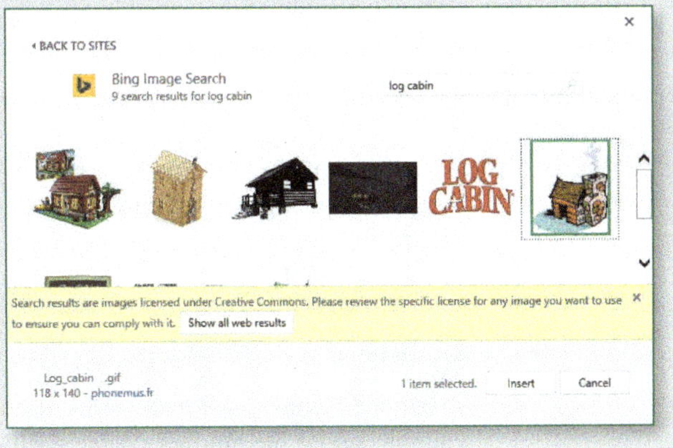

3-37 Online search for a picture as fill

8. Use *WordArt* in a chart.
   a. Triple-click the **Chart Title** placeholder text to select the text.
   b. Type Third Quarter Activity.
   c. Triple-click the new label and change the font size to **32 pt**.
   d. Click the border area of the chart title to display the selection handles.
   e. Click the **More** button [*Chart Tools Format* tab, *WordArt Styles* group].
   f. Choose **Fill – Gray-25%, Background 2, Inner Shadow** (third row).

9. Format the legend.
   a. Click to select the legend.
   b. Click the **Home** tab and change the font size to **12 pt**.
   c. Click the chart border to deselect the legend.
   d. Click a worksheet cell and press **Ctrl+Home**.
10. Save and close the workbook (Figure 3-38).

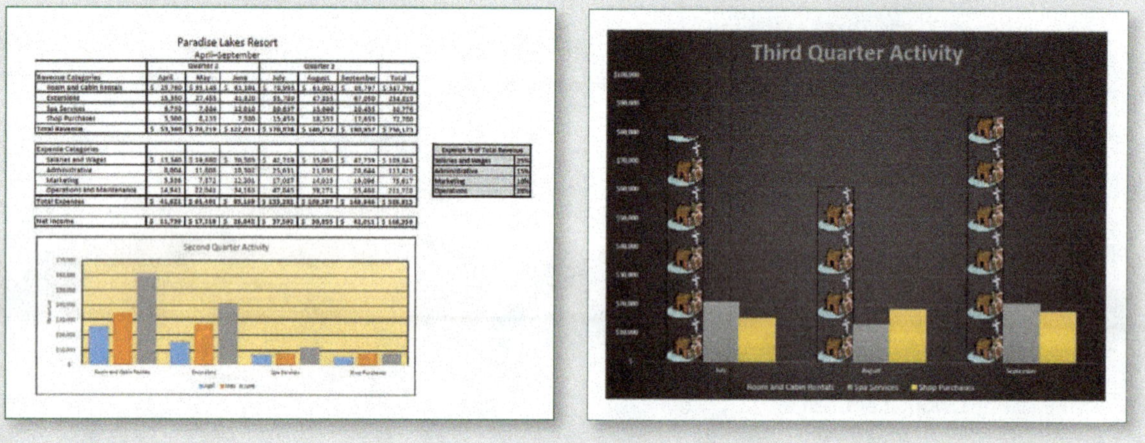

3-38 PP E3-2 completed worksheet and chart sheet

SLO 3.6

Building Pie and Combination Charts

A pie chart represents one set of related values and shows the proportion of each value to the total. A combination chart uses at least two sets of values and plots each data series with a different chart type. A combination chart can also have two value axes, one on the left and one on the right.

Create a 3-D Pie Chart

A pie chart graphs one data series and illustrates how each number relates to the whole. Be cautious about the number of categories, because a pie chart with hundreds of slices is difficult to interpret and does not depict the relationship among the values.

As you develop chart-building skills, you can choose a type from the *Charts* group on the *Insert* tab. When you select a chart type button, you see a gallery with available subtypes. As you point to each subtype, *Live Preview* previews the chart.

From the *Insert Pie or Doughnut Chart* button on the *Insert* tab, you can select from a gallery of 2-D or 3-D pie types as well as a doughnut shape (Figure 3-39). A doughnut chart is a pie chart with a hollow center. There are also options for a pie chart with a bar or another pie chart.

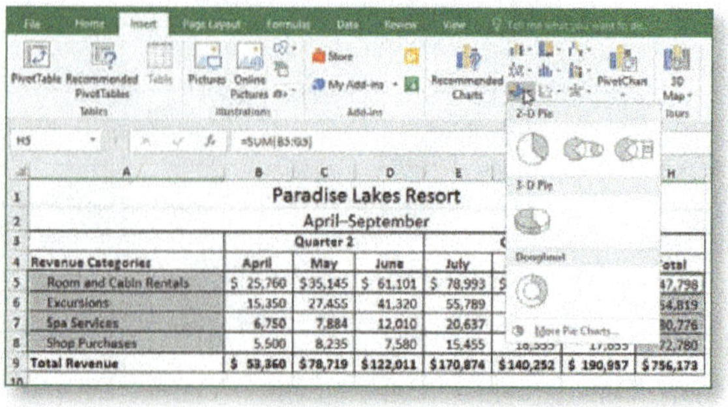

3-39 Selected data series and categories for a pie chart

HOW TO: Create a 3-D Pie Chart Sheet

1. Select the cells that include the values and the category labels.
   - The labels and values need not be adjacent.
2. Click the **Insert Pie or Doughnut Chart** button [*Insert* tab, *Charts* group].
3. Choose **3-D Pie**.
   - A pie chart object is placed in the worksheet.
4. Click the **Move Chart** button [*Chart Tools Design* tab, *Location* group].
5. Click the **New sheet** button.
6. Type a name for the chart sheet.
7. Click **OK**.

Pie Chart Elements and Options

In a pie chart, the data series is represented by the whole pie. A data point is a slice of the pie. You can format the data series as a whole, or you can format individual slices.

A pie chart can display a legend and a title. It does not, however, have axes and does not use axes titles. Data labels can be used in place of a legend, because they show the same information.

Custom commands for a pie chart are the angle of the first slice and the percent of explosion. These commands are available on the *Format* task pane for the data series (the whole pie) or for a selected data point (one slice). The angle of the first slice allows you to rotate the pie. The first slice starts at the top of the chart at 0° (zero degrees). As you increase that value, the slice arcs to the right. *Live Preview* displays the results, too.

Exploding a pie slice emphasizes that slice, because it moves the slice away from the rest of the pie. This uses more white space in the chart, and the pie gets smaller. You set explosion as a percentage.

HOW TO: Rotate a Pie Chart and Explode a Slice

1. Double-click the pie shape.
   - The *Format Data Series* task pane opens.
   - You can also right-click the pie shape and choose **Format Data Series**.
2. Click the **Series Options** button.
3. Drag the vertical slider to set the *Angle of first slice.*
   - The percentage is shown in the entry box.
   - You can also type a percentage or use the spinner arrows to set a value.
4. Click the data point (slice) to explode.
   - The *Format Data Point* task pane opens.
5. Drag the vertical slider to set the *Pie Explosion* (Figure 3-40).
   - The percentage is shown in the entry box.
   - The larger the percentage, the farther the slice is from the rest of the pie.
   - You can type a percentage or use the spinner arrows to set a value.

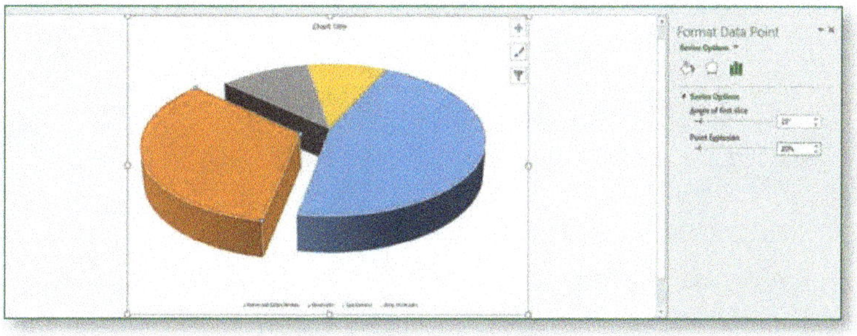

3-40 Exploded pie slice with angle of first slice changed

MORE INFO

You can explode all the slices in a pie chart by selecting the data series, not a data point.

Create a Combination Chart

A combination chart includes at least two chart types such as a line chart and a column chart. Paradise Lakes Resort can use a combination chart to compare revenue from cabin and room rentals to total revenue. These two values reflect a different scale of numbers, so showing one series as a line and the other as a column focuses the comparison (Figure 3-41).

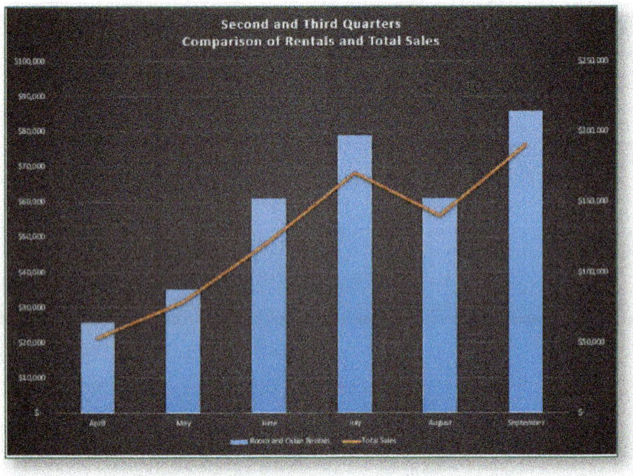

3-41 Line-Column combination chart

MORE INFO

A line and column combination chart resembles a column chart with a trendline, but the combination chart uses actual values. The trendline predicts values.

The most common combination of chart types is line and column, but you can also use a line and area combination. Excel offers an option to create a custom combination, but it is best to use this only after you have experience charting your data.

MORE INFO

Not all chart types can be combined. If you try to do so, Excel opens a message box to inform you.

Create a combination chart from the *Insert Combo Chart* button in the *Charts* group on the *Insert* tab as well as from the *All Charts* tab in the *Insert Chart* dialog box.

HOW TO: Create a Combination Chart

1. Select the cell ranges for the chart.
   - The cell ranges need not be contiguous.
2. Click the **Insert Combo Chart** button [*Insert* tab, *Charts* group].
   - Suggested combinations are displayed.
   - Point to a subtype to see a description and a *Live Preview* (Figure 3-42).
3. Select the chart subtype.
   - A combo chart object displays in the worksheet.
   - You can move the chart to its own sheet if desired.

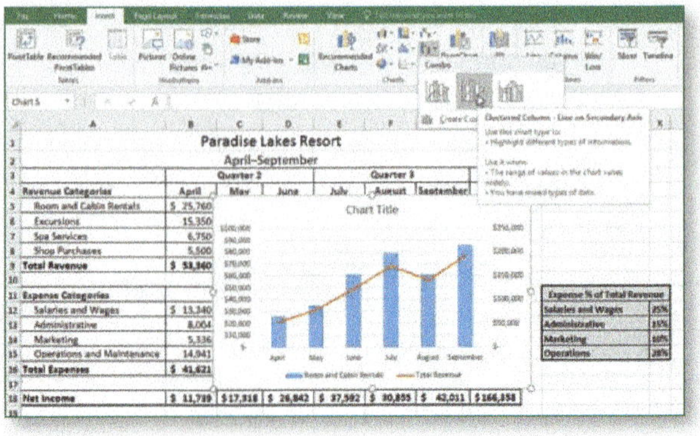

3-42 Insert Combo Chart button options

Combination Chart Elements and Options

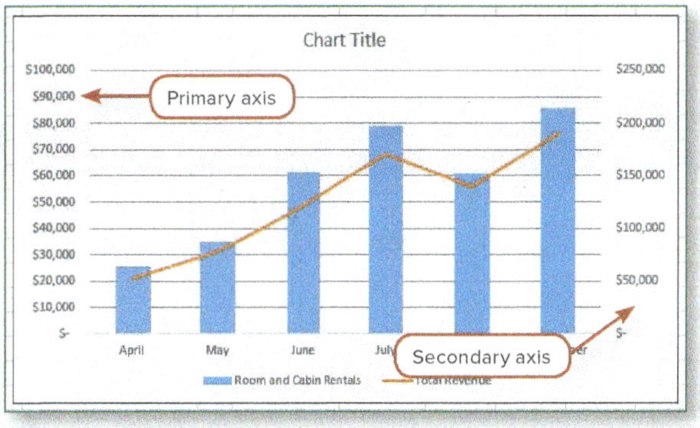

3-43 Secondary axis for a combo chart

A combination chart has at least two data series, each graphed in its own chart type. Keep this type of chart relatively simple, because its purpose is to compare unlike items and too many data series complicate what viewers see.

In a combination chart, you can display values on two vertical axes. The axis on the left is the primary axis; the one on the right is secondary (Figure 3-43). This option is best when the values are very different or use a different scale.

For the secondary axis, Excel builds the number scale based on the data. Select the data series to be plotted on the secondary axis and choose the option from the *Series Options* command group in the *Format* task pane. You can also define a secondary axis in the *Insert Chart* or the *Change Chart Type* dialog boxes.

A combination chart has the same elements and commands as a regular column or line chart. You can apply chart styles and layouts, as well as shape fill, outline, effects, pictures, shapes, and *WordArt.*

▸HOW TO: Display a Secondary Axis on a Combination Chart

1. Select the chart object or the chart sheet tab.
2. Select the data series to be shown on the secondary axis.
   - Select the line or any column in a line-column combo chart.
   - You can also choose the data series from the *Chart Elements* box [*Chart Tools Format* tab, *Current Selection* group].
3. Click the **Format Selection** button [*Chart Tools Format* tab, *Current Selection* group].
4. Click the **Series Options** button in the task pane (Figure 3-44).
5. Click the **Secondary Axis** radio button.
   - Additional options for the axis depend on the chart type.
6. Close the *Format Data Series* task pane.

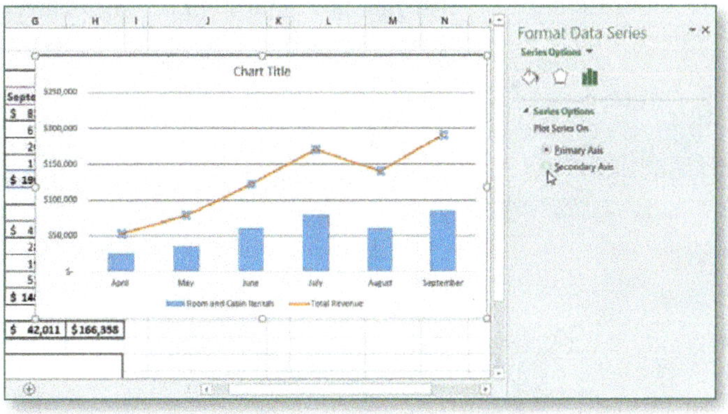

3-44 *Format Data Series* task pane to define a secondary axis

SLO 3.7

Creating Sunburst and Waterfall Charts

New chart types in Excel 2016 visualize data in ways that previously required engineering or similar specialized software. With a sunburst chart, you can show relationships between multiple categories of data. A waterfall chart depicts a running total for financial data so that you can assess the impact of negative and positive cash flows. These charts have many characteristics of standard Excel charts, but they have a few limitations related to requirements for the data they plot.

Create a Sunburst Chart

A ***sunburst chart*** is a hierarchy chart that illustrates the relationship among categories and subcategories of data. It resembles a doughnut chart with concentric rings for each layer of data as shown in Figure 3-45. A ***hierarchy*** is a division of data that identifies a top group followed by lesser groups. The student population at your college can be illustrated in a hierarchy with gender at the top, followed by age group, then home city, followed by area of study, and so on.

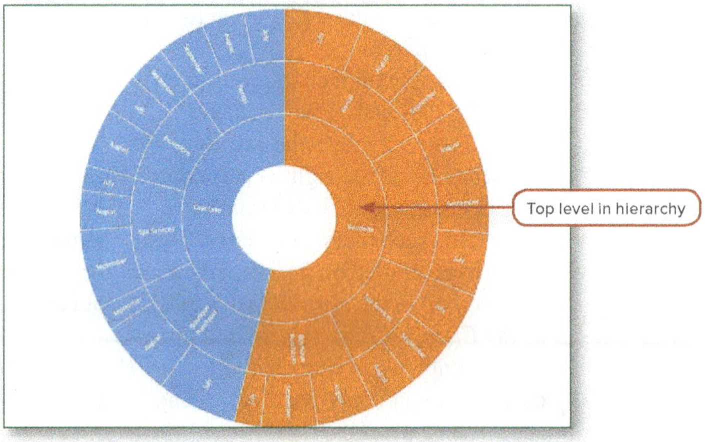

3-45 Sunburst chart for third quarter revenue for two locations

Paradise Lakes Resort keeps a record of revenue by location, category, and month. The inner ring in Figure 3-45 is the top level of the hierarchy, the location. The second level is the revenue category (Rentals, Excursions, etc.), and the outside ring is the month's revenue. From the chart, you can see that Baudette contributed slightly more than half of the total revenue and that the boutique purchases at Cass Lake were high.

A sunburst chart has one data series and no axes. It can display a title, data labels, and a legend. The *Chart Tools Design* and *Format* tabs provide basic options for fine-tuning the appearance of the chart.

The *Insert Hierarchy Chart* button [*Insert* tab, *Charts* group] has two subtypes, *Sunburst* and *TreeMap*. These subtypes can handle large amounts of data, but be careful not to build charts that are difficult to interpret due to their size.

> **MORE INFO**
>
> A *TreeMap* chart illustrates hierarchical data using rectangles of various sizes and colors to represent the divisions and subdivisions.

HOW TO: Create a Sunburst Chart

1. Select the source data with labels and values.
   - The **Quick Analysis** button appears, but the *Charts* group does not include the *Sunburst* chart type.
2. Click the **Insert Hierarchy Chart** button [*Insert* tab, *Charts* group].
   - A menu lists the subtypes.
3. Point to **Sunburst** to see a *Live Preview*.

4. Click **Sunburst** to select it.
    - A chart object is placed in the worksheet.
5. Click the **Move Chart** button [*Chart Tools Design* tab, *Location* group].
6. Select **New sheet**.
7. Type a name for the chart sheet and click **OK**.
    - The *Chart Tools Design* and *Format* tabs are available.
8. Click the sunburst shape to select the circle.
9. Point to a category name in the inner ring and click to select the data point.
    - The category and its related items are selected (Figure 3-46).

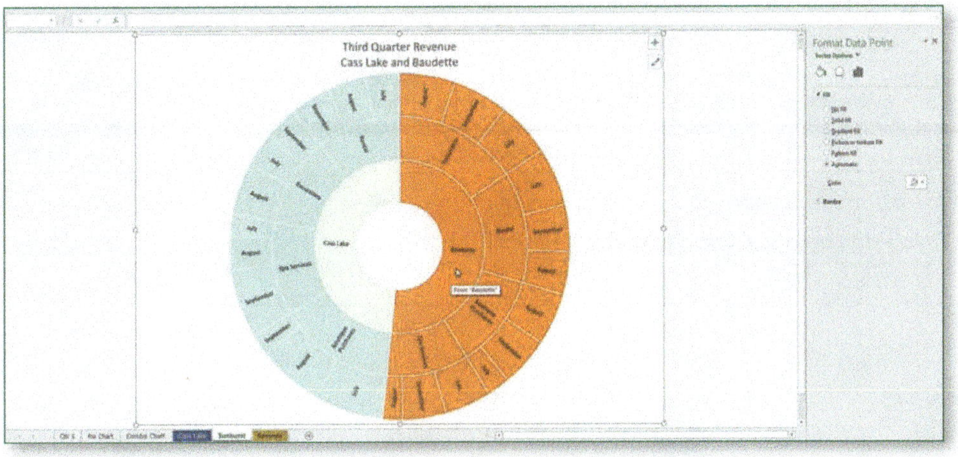

3-46 Sunburst chart sheet with selected data point

10. Format the data point as desired.
    - If the *Format Data Point* task pane is not open, click the **Format Selection** button [*Chart Tools Format* tab, *Current Selection* group].
11. Click outside the chart background to deselect the chart.

MORE INFO

The *Hierarchy* charts do not appear in any *Recommended Charts* list, but they are listed on the *All Charts* tab.

Create a Waterfall Chart

A ***waterfall chart*** is a financial chart that displays a moving total for positive and negative values. A waterfall chart graphs how each expense or outlay affects the account. You might, for example, build a waterfall chart to visualize your monthly income sources (inflows) and expenditures (outlays) to watch how you spend your resources.

In Figure 3-47, it is obvious that payroll consumes most of the cash account for Paradise Lakes Resort. In a waterfall chart, the depth or height of the marker indicates the value. In the figure, the beginning balance and ending total markers rest on the bottom axis. The other amounts are described as floating.

A waterfall chart plots one data series and has a legend that clarifies the increase, decrease, and total colors. A waterfall chart can also include axes, titles, gridlines, and data labels.

The *Insert Waterfall or Stock Chart* button is in the *Charts* group on the *Insert* tab. These charts do not appear in the *Recommended Charts* list, but they are available on the *All Charts* tab.

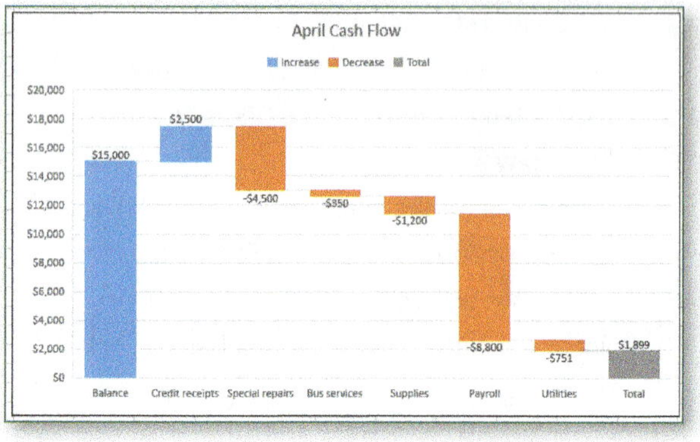

3-47 Waterfall chart for cash flow

▸ HOW TO: Create a Waterfall Chart Sheet

1. Select the source data with labels and values.
   - The *Quick Analysis* button appears but does not have an option for a waterfall chart.
2. Click the **Insert Waterfall or Stock Chart** button [*Insert* tab, *Charts* group].
   - A menu lists the subtypes.
3. Click **Waterfall**.
   - A chart object is placed in the worksheet.
4. Click the **Move Chart** button [*Chart Tools Design* tab, *Location* group].
5. Select **New sheet**.
6. Type a name for the chart sheet and click **OK**.
   - The *Chart Tools Design* and *Format* tabs are available.
7. Click a column marker to select the data series.
8. Click the ending marker to select only it.
9. Click the **Format Selection** button [*Chart Tools Format* tab, *Current Selection* group].
10. Click the **Series Options** button in the task pane.
11. Expand the *Series Options* group.
12. Select the **Set as total** box (Figure 3-48).
    - The marker rests on the bottom axis and is no longer floating.
13. Close the task pane and click outside the chart to deselect it.

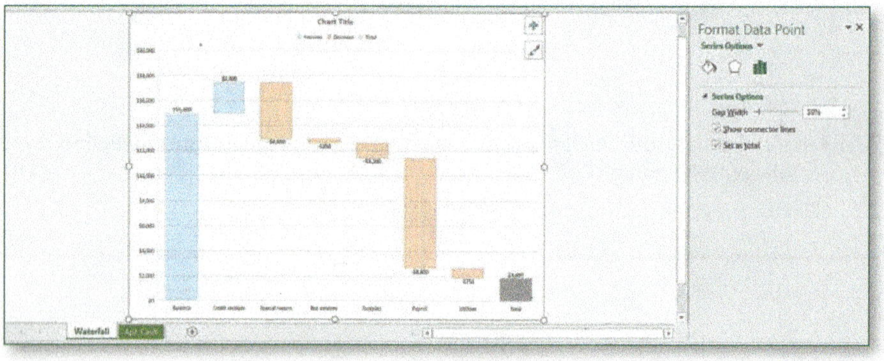

3-48 Set a marker as a total

SLO 3.8

Inserting and Formatting Sparklines

Sparklines are miniature charts in a cell or cell range. They can be used to illustrate trends and patterns without adding a separate chart object or sheet. They do not have the same characteristics as an Excel chart.

Sparklines are created from a selected data range and placed in a location range, usually next to the data (Figure 3-49). They are embedded in the cell, almost like a background. If you enter a label or value in a cell with a sparkline, that data appears on top of the sparkline.

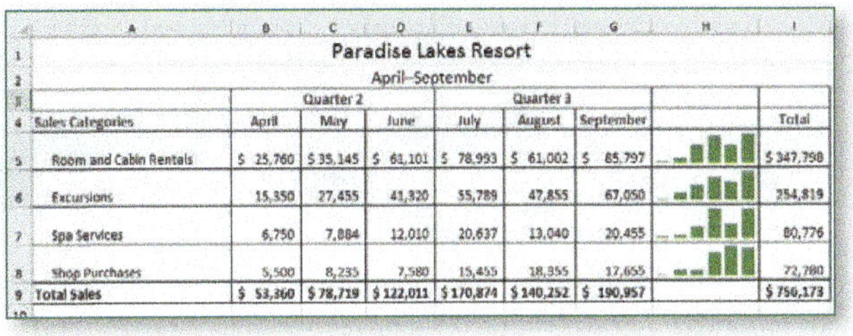

3-49 Column sparklines in a worksheet

Insert Sparklines

There are three sparkline types: ***Line***, ***Column***, and ***Win/Loss***. The *Sparklines* commands are located on the *Insert* tab of the worksheet. The *Data Range* is the range of cells to be graphed, and the *Location Range* is the cell or range for the sparklines. The ***Sparkline Tools Design*** tab opens when you select the sparkline group.

HOW TO: Insert Column Sparklines in a Worksheet

1. Select the cell range of data to be graphed.
2. Click the **Column Sparkline** button [*Insert* tab, *Sparklines* group].
   - The selected range address is shown in the *Data Range* entry box.
   - You can select or edit the data range here.
3. Click the *Location Range* box.
4. Select the cell or range for the sparklines (Figure 3-50).
5. Click **OK**.

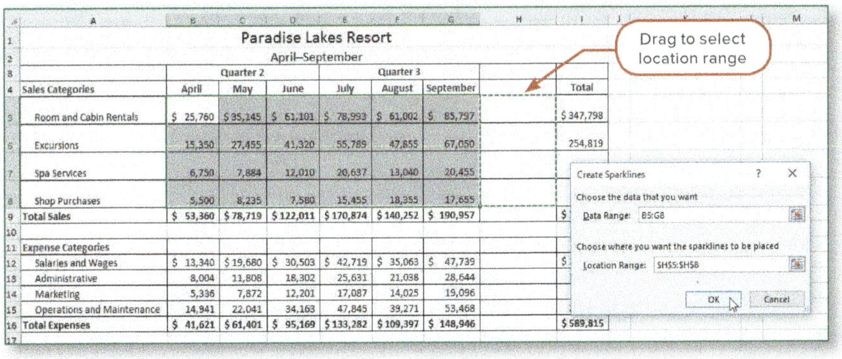

3-50 *Create Sparklines* dialog box

Sparkline Design Tools

When sparklines are selected, the *Sparkline Tools Design* tab opens. This context-sensitive tab includes several options for changing the appearance of the sparklines. There is a *Sparkline Style* option that changes the color scheme for the sparkline group, but you can also change colors with the *Sparkline Color* command. The *Marker Color* command enables you to choose a different color for identified values. A ***marker*** for a sparkline is the data point value. You can use different colors to highlight the high, low, first, or last value as well as negative values.

When you define a location range for sparklines, they are embedded as a group. If you select any cell in the sparkline range, the entire group is selected. Subsequent commands affect all sparklines in the group. From the *Group* section on the *Sparkline Tools Design* tab, you can ungroup the sparklines so that you can format them individually.

From the *Sparkline Tools Design* tab, you can also change the type of sparkline, such as making a column sparkline into a line sparkline. The *Show* group lists the marker values that can be highlighted. When you select one of these options, that marker in the sparkline is formatted with a different color.

HOW TO: Format Sparklines

1. Click a cell with a sparkline.
   - The sparkline group is selected.
2. Click the *Sparkline Line Tools Design* tab.
3. Click the **More** button [*Sparkline Tools Design* tab, *Style* group].
4. Choose a sparkline style.
   - The sparkline group is recolored.
5. Select the **High Point** box in the *Show* group (Figure 3-51).
   - A default color based on the sparkline style is applied to the highest value in the sparkline for each row.

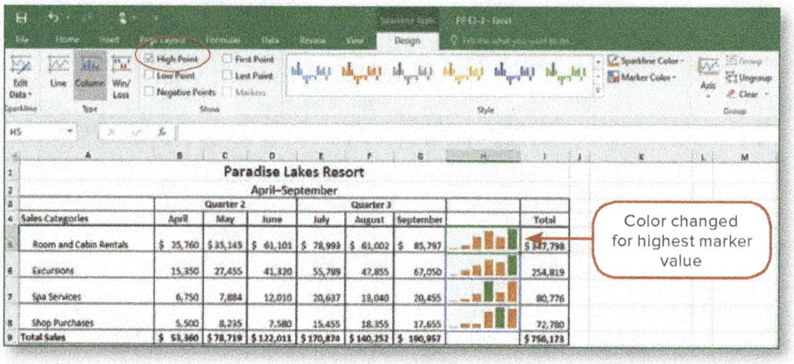

3-51 *High Point* marker selected for sparklines

6. Click the **Sparkline Color** button [*Sparkline Tools Design* tab, *Style* group].
7. Choose a color for the sparkline group.
   - The sparkline group is recolored, and the color from the *Sparkline Style* is overridden.
8. Click the **Marker Color** button [*Sparkline Tools Design* tab, *Style* group].
9. Choose **High Point** and select a color.
   - The color for the highest value is reset.

Clear Sparklines

You can remove sparklines from a worksheet with the *Clear* command in the *Group* group on the *Sparkline Tools Design* tab. After sparklines are cleared, you may also need to delete the column where they were located or reset row heights and column widths.

HOW TO: Clear Sparklines

1. Select any cell in the sparklines range.
2. Click the arrow with **Clear Selected Sparklines** button [*Sparkline Tools Design* tab, *Group* group].
3. Choose **Clear Selected Sparklines Groups**.

MORE INFO

When you ungroup sparklines, you can select a single sparkline cell and clear it.

PAUSE & PRACTICE: EXCEL 3-3

For this project, you complete Paradise Lakes' revenue report by inserting a pie chart that shows the proportion of each revenue category. You also insert a combination chart sheet to compare rentals with total revenue and a sunburst chart to analyze third quarter revenue. Finally, you insert sparklines in the worksheet.

File Needed: ***[your initials] PP E3-2.xlsx***
Completed Project File Name: ***[your initials] PP E3-3.xlsx***

1. Open the ***[your initials] PP E3-2*** workbook completed in *Pause & Practice 3-2* and save it as [your initials] PP E3-3.
2. Create a pie chart for total sales revenue.
   a. Select the **Cass Lake** tab.
   b. Select cells **A5:A8** as the category.
   c. Press **Ctrl** and select cells **H5:H8** as the data series.
   d. Click the **Insert Pie or Doughnut Chart** button [*Insert* tab, *Charts* group].
   e. Choose **3-D Pie**.
   f. Click the **Move Chart** button [*Chart Tools Design* tab, *Location* group].
   g. Click the **New sheet** button and type Pie Chart as the sheet name.
   h. Click **OK**.
3. Format a pie chart.
   a. Select the **Pie Chart** tab.
   b. Click the **Chart Title** placeholder to select it and then triple-click the **Chart Title** placeholder text.
   c. Type Second and Third Quarters and press **Enter**.
   d. Type Sources of Revenue on the second line.
   e. Drag to select the first line of the title.
   f. Use the mini toolbar to change the font size to **24 pt**.
   g. Drag to select the second line of the title.
   h. Use the mini toolbar to change the font size to **18 pt**. (Figure 3-52).
   i. Click the chart border to deselect the title.
   j. Double-click the pie to open the *Format Data Series* task pane.
   k. Click the **Series Options** button in the *Format Data Series* task pane.
   l. Click the **Room and Cabin Rentals** slice to change to the *Format Data Point* task pane.
   m. Set the pie explosion percentage at **10%**.
   n. Close the task pane.
   o. Select the legend at the bottom of the chart to display selection handles.
   p. Click the **Home** tab and change the font size to **14 pt** (Figure 3-53).

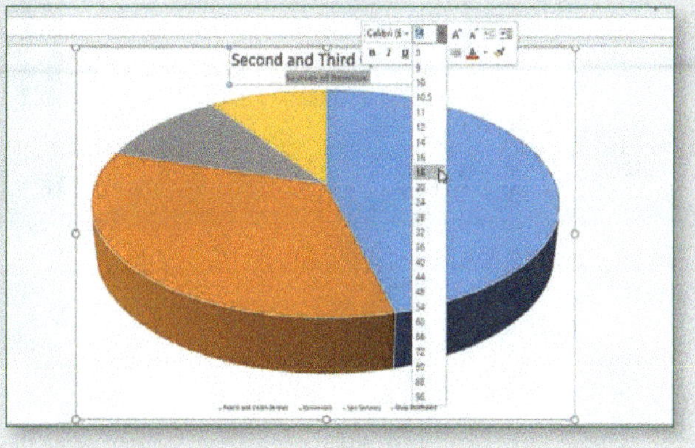

3-52 Chart titles typed and font size changed

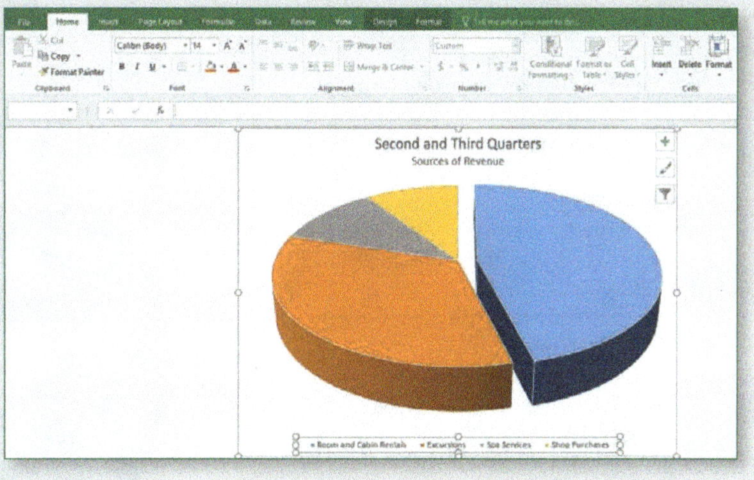

3-53 Selected legend with new font size

4. Create a combination chart for total sales revenue and room and cabin rentals.
   a. Select the **Cass Lake** tab.
   b. Select cells **A4:G5** as one data series and category.

c. Press **Ctrl** and select cells **A9:G9** as another data series and category.
d. Click the **Insert Combo Chart** button [*Insert* tab, *Charts* group].
e. Choose **Clustered Column – Line on Secondary Axis**.
f. Click the **Move Chart** button [*Chart Tools Design* tab, *Location* group].
g. Click the **New sheet** button and type Combo Chart as the sheet name.
h. Click **OK**.

5. Format a combination chart.
   a. Select the **Combo Chart** tab, select the **Chart Title** placeholder, and then triple-click the placeholder text.
   b. Type Second and Third Quarters and press **Enter**.
   c. Type Comparison of Rentals and Total Revenue on the second line.
   d. Click the chart border to deselect the chart title.
   e. Choose **Style 6** [*Chart Tools Design* tab, *Chart Styles* group] (Figure 3-54).
   f. Click the background to deselect the chart.

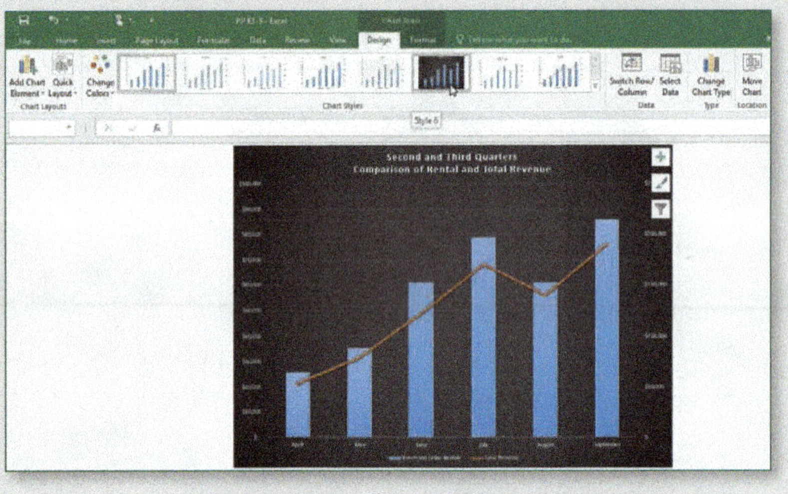

3-54 Combo chart with Style 6

6. Create a sunburst chart for third quarter revenue analysis.
   a. Select the **Revenue** tab.
   b. Select cells **A5:D28** as the data series and categories. This chart will illustrate revenue for Cass Lake and Baudette.
   c. Click the **Insert Hierarchy Chart** button [*Insert* tab, *Charts* group].
   d. Choose **Sunburst**.
   e. Click the **Move Chart** button [*Chart Tools Design* tab, *Location* group].
   f. Click the **New sheet** button and type Sunburst as the sheet name.
   g. Click **OK**.
   h. Select the **Chart Title** placeholder and type Third Quarter Revenue.
   i. Press **Enter** and type Cass Lake and Baudette on the second line (Figure 3-55).
   j. Click the chart border to deselect the title object.
   k. Click to select the title object and change its font size to **16 pt**.
   l. Click the background to deselect the chart.

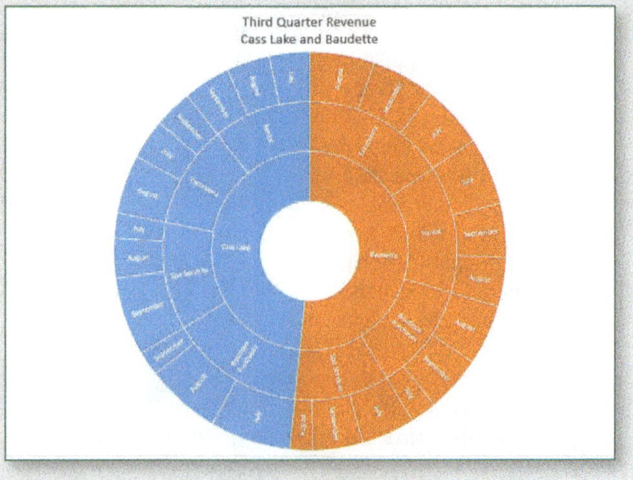

3-55 Sunburst chart with edited title

7. Insert sparklines in a worksheet.
   a. Select the **Cass Lake** tab.
   b. Right-click the column **H** heading and choose **Insert** to insert a new column.
   c. Select the cell range **B5:G8** as the data to be charted with sparklines.
   d. Click the **Column Sparkline** button [*Insert* tab, *Sparklines* group].
   e. Click the **Location Range** box, and select cells **H5:H8**.
   f. Click **OK**.
8. Format sparklines.
   a. Click the **Sparkline Color** button [*Sparkline Tools Design* tab, *Style* group] and select **Green, Accent 6, Darker 25%**.
   b. Select the sparkline group if necessary, click the **Format** button [*Home* tab, *Cells* group], and change the **Row Height** to **30 (40 pixels)**.
   c. Format column **H** to a width of **16.00 (117 pixels)**.
   d. Press **Ctrl+Home**.
9. Save and close the workbook (Figure 3-56).

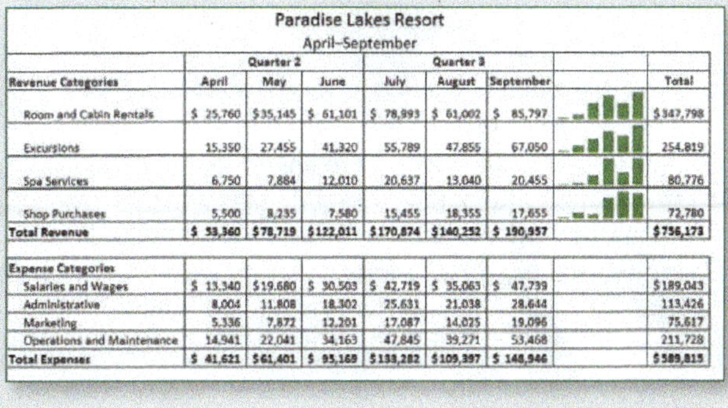
Paradise Lakes Resort
April–September

	Quarter 2			Quarter 3				
Revenue Categories	April	May	June	July	August	September		Total
Room and Cabin Rentals	$ 25,760	$35,145	$ 61,101	$ 78,993	$ 61,002	$ 85,797		$347,798
Excursions	15,350	27,455	41,320	55,789	47,855	67,050		254,819
Spa Services	6,750	7,884	12,010	20,637	13,040	20,455		80,776
Shop Purchases	5,500	8,235	7,580	15,455	18,355	17,655		72,780
Total Revenue	$ 53,360	$78,719	$122,011	$170,874	$140,252	$ 190,957		$756,173
Expense Categories								
Salaries and Wages	$ 13,340	$19,680	$ 30,503	$ 42,719	$ 35,063	$ 47,739		$189,043
Administrative	8,004	11,808	18,302	25,631	21,038	28,644		113,426
Marketing	5,336	7,872	12,201	17,087	14,025	19,096		75,617
Operations and Maintenance	14,941	22,041	34,163	47,845	39,271	53,468		211,728
Total Expenses	$ 41,621	$61,401	$ 93,169	$133,282	$109,397	$ 148,946		$589,815

3-56 PP E3-3 completed worksheet

Chapter Summary

3.1 Create Excel chart objects and chart sheets (p. E3-163).

- A ***chart*** is a visual representation of worksheet data.
- A ***chart object*** is a selectable item or element in a worksheet.
- A ***chart sheet*** is an Excel chart on its own tab in the workbook.
- The cells with values and labels used to build a chart are its ***source data***.
- Chart objects and sheets are linked to their source data and contain editable chart elements such as data labels or a chart title.
- Commonly used chart types are *Column, Line, Pie,* and *Bar,* and Excel can build sophisticated statistical, financial, and scientific charts.
- You can size and position a chart object in a worksheet, or move it to its own sheet using the *Move Chart* button in the *Location* group on the *Chart Tools Design* tab.
- The *Quick Analysis* tool includes a command group for charts, and it appears when the selected source data is contiguous.

3.2 Use Quick layouts and chart styles to design a chart (p. E3-167).

- A ***chart layout*** is a set of elements and their locations in a chart.
- The *Quick Layout* button [*Chart Tools Design* tab, *Chart Layouts* group] includes predefined layouts for the current chart type.
- A ***chart style*** is a predefined combination of colors and effects for chart elements.
- Chart styles are based on the current workbook theme.
- The *Change Colors* command [*Chart Tools Design* tab, *Chart Styles* group] provides quick color palettes for customizing a chart.
- A chart object can be printed with its worksheet data or on its own sheet.
- A chart sheet prints on its own page in landscape orientation.

3.3 Edit chart elements including titles, data labels, and source data (p. E3-172).

- A ***chart element*** is a selectable and editable part or item in the chart.
- Chart elements include chart and axes titles, data labels, legends, gridlines, and more, depending on the type of chart.
- Excel plots data based on the number of rows and columns selected and the chart type, but you can switch the row and column data.
- You can change some chart types into another type using the *Change Chart Type* button on the *Chart Tools Design* tab.
- Chart data can be filtered to hide and display values or categories without changing the source data.
- Source data for a chart can be edited to use a different cell range or to add or remove a data series.

3.4 Format chart elements with shape styles, fill, outlines, and special effects (p. E3-179).

- A ***shape style*** is a predesigned set of fill colors, borders, and effects.
- ***Shape fill***, ***outline***, and ***effects*** can also be applied to a chart element from the *Chart Tools Format* tab.
- A chart element has a *Format* task pane that includes fill, outline, and effects commands as well as specific options for the element.
- Most formats can also be applied to a selected chart element from the *Home* tab.

3.5 Use pictures, shapes, and *WordArt* in a chart (p. E3-183).

- For chart shapes that have a fill color, you can use a picture as fill.
- Images used as fill can be from your own or online sources, but not all pictures work well as fill.
- Shapes are predefined outline drawings available from the *Insert Shapes* group on the *Chart Tools Format* tab or from the *Illustrations* group on the *Insert* tab.
- Shapes can be placed on a chart to highlight or draw attention to a particular element.
- ***WordArt*** is a text box with a preset design, often used to format a chart title.

3.6 Build pie charts and combination charts (p. E3-188).

- A pie chart has one data series and shows each data point as a slice of the pie.

- A pie chart does not have axes, but it does have options to rotate or explode slices.
- A combination chart uses at least two chart types to highlight, compare, or contrast differences in data or values.
- You can format a combination chart to show a secondary axis when values are widely different or use different scales.

3.7 Create sunburst and waterfall charts (p. E3-191).

- A ***sunburst chart*** has one data series that is grouped in a ***hierarchy***.
- A sunburst chart illustrates the relationship among the hierarchies in a pie-like chart with concentric rings.
- A ***waterfall chart*** depicts a running total for positive and negative values.
- A waterfall chart is used for financial or other data that shows inflows and outlays of resources.
- A waterfall chart resembles a column chart and has category and value axes.
- You can place a sunburst chart or a waterfall chart as an object or on a separate sheet.

3.8 Insert and format sparklines in a worksheet (p. E3-194).

- A ***sparkline*** is a miniature chart in a cell or range of cells in the worksheet.
- Three sparkline types are available: ***Line***, ***Column***, and ***Win/Loss***.
- When inserted in a range of cells, sparklines are grouped and can be ungrouped.
- The *Sparkline Tools Design* tab is visible when a sparkline is selected and includes formatting options such as setting the color or identifying high and low values.

Check for Understanding

The SIMbook for this text (within your SIMnet account) provides the following resources for concept review:

- Multiple choice questions
- Matching exercises
- Short answer questions

USING MICROSOFT EXCEL 2016

Guided Project 3-1

Life's Animal Shelter (LAS) is an animal care and adoption agency that accepts unwanted and abandoned domestic animals. For this project, you create expense charts and insert sparklines to help the agency track expenses for the first six months of the year. You also build a waterfall chart to graph cash flow for a month.
[Student Learning Outcomes 3.1, 3.2, 3.3, 3.4, 3.5, 3.6, 3.7, 3.8]

File Needed: ***LAS-03.xlsx*** *[Student data files are available in the* Library *of your SIMnet account.]*
Completed Project File Name: ***[your initials] Excel 3-1.xlsx***

Skills Covered in This Project

- Create a chart object.
- Create a chart sheet.
- Apply *Quick Layout* and chart styles.
- Add and format chart elements.
- Change the chart type.
- Filter the data series.
- Insert a shape in a chart.
- Create and format a combination chart.
- Insert and format sparklines in a worksheet.
- Create and format a waterfall chart.

1. Open the ***LAS-03*** workbook from your student data files and save it as [your initials] Excel 3-1.
2. Create a pie chart object.
   a. Select the **Jan-June** sheet and select cells **A5:A10**. Press **Ctrl** and select cells **I5:I10**.
   b. Click the **Insert Pie or Doughnut Chart** button [*Insert* tab, *Charts* group].
   c. Select the **2D-Pie** chart subtype.
3. Create a chart sheet.
   a. Select the pie chart object.
   b. Click the **Move Chart** button [*Chart Tools Design* tab, *Location* group].
   c. Click the **New sheet** button.
   d. Type Pie Chart in the text box.
   e. Click **OK**.
4. Apply a chart style.
   a. Click the **More** button [*Chart Tools Design* tab, *Chart Styles* group].
   b. Select **Style 12**.
5. Edit and format chart elements.
   a. Click the chart title element.
   b. Click the *Formula* bar, type January through June Expenses, and press **Enter**.
   c. Triple-click the new label in the chart and change the font size to **28 pt**.
   d. Click the legend element to select it and to deselect the title element.
   e. Click the **Font Size** arrow [*Home* tab, *Font* group] and change the legend size to **12 pt**.
   f. Select the *Chart Area* element, the chart background.
   g. Click the **Shape Outline** button [*Chart Tools Format* tab, *Shape Styles* group].
   h. Choose **Black**, **Text 1** as the color.
   i. Click the **Shape Outline** button again.

j. Choose **Weight** and select **1 pt**.
k. Click outside the chart background to see the outline (Figure 3-57).

6. Create a bar chart object.
   a. Click the **Jan-June** sheet tab.
   b. Select cells **A4:G9** as source data, omitting the *Rent* expense.
   c. Click the **Quick Analysis** button and select **Charts**.
   d. Select **Clustered Bar**.
   e. Point to the chart border to display a move pointer.
   f. Drag the chart object so that its top left corner is at cell **A13**.
   g. Point to the bottom right selection handle to display a resize arrow.
   h. Drag the pointer to reach cell **I30** (Figure 3-58).

7. Change the chart type.
   a. Click the bar chart object.
   b. Click the **Change Chart Type** button [*Chart Tools Design* tab, *Type* group].
   c. Click the **Recommended Charts** tab.
   d. Choose **Clustered Column** in the left pane.
   e. Click **OK**.

8. Filter the source data.
   a. Click the column chart object.
   b. Click the **Chart Filters** button in the top right corner of the chart.
   c. Deselect the **January**, **February**, and **March** boxes.
   d. Click **Apply** in the *Chart Filters* pane (Figure 3-59).
   e. Click the **Chart Filters** button to close the pane.

9. Edit, format, and add chart elements.
   a. Click the chart title object.
   b. Click the *Formula* bar.
   c. Type Second Quarter Variable Expenses and press **Enter**.
   d. Click the **Chart Elements** arrow [*Chart Tools Format* tab, *Current Selection* group] and choose **Chart Area**.
   e. Click the **Shape Outline** button [*Chart Tools Format* tab, *Shape Styles* group].
   f. Choose **Black**, **Text 1** as the color.
   g. Click the **Shape Outline** button again and choose **Weight** and **1 pt**.

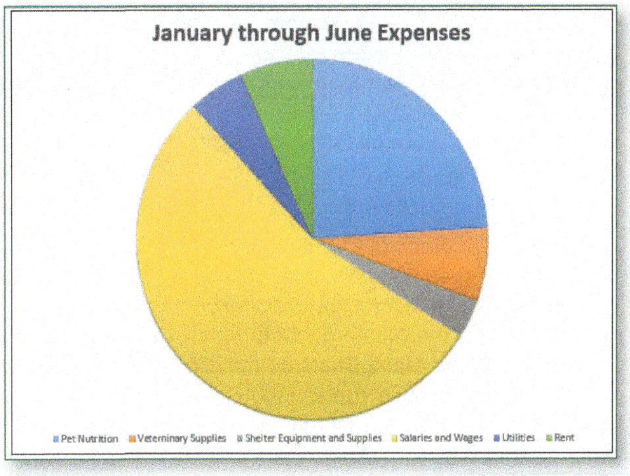

3-57 Pie Chart sheet with format changes

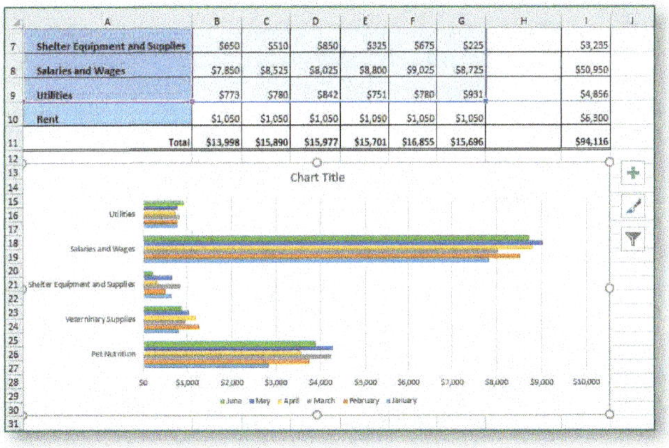

3-58 Bar chart object sized and positioned

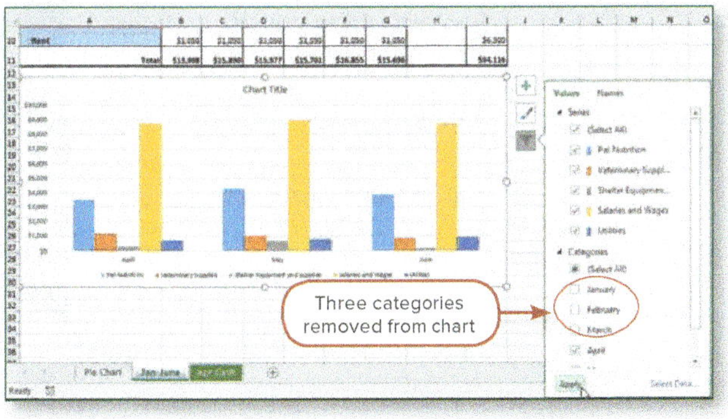

3-59 Chart filters applied

h. Click the **Change Colors** button [*Chart Tools Design* tab, *Chart Styles* group].
i. Choose **Color 3** in the *Colorful* group.
j. Click the **Chart Elements** arrow [*Chart Tools Format* tab, *Current Selection* group] and choose **Plot Area**.
k. Click the **Shape Fill** button [*Chart Tools Format* tab, *Shape Styles* group].
l. Choose **Gold**, **Accent 4**, **Lighter 80%** as the color.
m. Click a worksheet cell.

10. Create a combination chart sheet.
   a. Select cells **A9:G9**. Press **Ctrl** and select cells **A11:G11**.
   b. Click the **Insert Combo Chart** button [*Insert* tab, *Charts* group].
   c. Select the **Clustered Column-Line** chart subtype.
   d. Click the **Move Chart** button [*Chart Tools Design* tab, *Location* group].
   e. Click the **New sheet** button, type Combo Chart as the name, and click **OK**.
   f. Double-click the line marker in the chart.
   g. Click the **Series Options** button in the *Format Data Series* task pane.
   h. Select the **Secondary Axis** box in the task pane (Figure 3-60).
   i. Close the task pane.

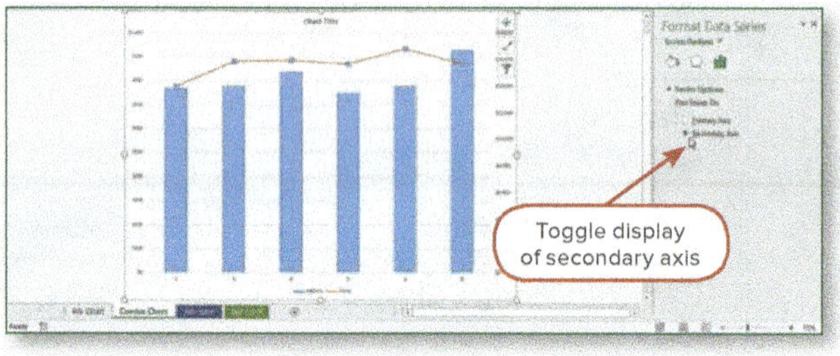

3-60 Combo chart and a secondary axis

11. Edit and format chart elements.
   a. Edit the chart title placeholder to Utilities Expense and Total Expenses.
   b. Select the chart area.
   c. Apply a **1 pt**. **Black, Text 1** outline to the chart area.
   d. Click one of the column markers to select the data series.
   e. Click the **More** button [*Chart Tools Format* tab, *Shape Styles* group].
   f. Select **Moderate Effect – Black, Dark 1** in the *Theme Styles* group.
   g. Click the line marker.
   h. Click the **Shape Outline** button [*Chart Tools Format* tab, *Shape Styles* group].
   i. Choose **Gold**, **Accent 4** as the color.
   j. Click the **Shape Outline** button again and choose **Weight** and **3 pt** (Figure 3-61).

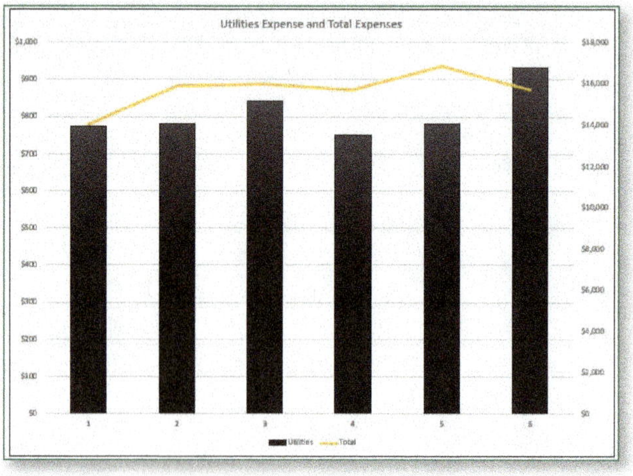

3-61 Line and column formatted in combo chart

12. Insert sparklines in the worksheet.
   a. Click the **Jan-June** sheet tab.
   b. Select cells **B5:G9** as the data range.
   c. Click the **Column Sparkline** button [*Insert* tab, *Sparklines* group].
   d. Select cells **H5:H9** for the *Location Range* and click **OK**.
   e. Click the **Sparkline Color** button [*Sparkline Tools Design* tab, *Style* group].
   f. Choose **White, Background 1**, **Darker 50%**.

13. Insert a shape in a chart.
    a. Select the column chart object.
    b. Click the **More** button [*Chart Tools Format* tab, *Insert Shapes* group].
    c. Select the **Text Box** shape [*Basic Shapes* group].
    d. Draw a text box like the one shown in Figure 3-62.
    e. Type Utilities are to be removed from an updated chart per management request.
    f. Drag a selection handle to size the text box shape if necessary.
    g. Point to a border of the *Text Box* shape to display a four-pointed arrow and position it if needed.

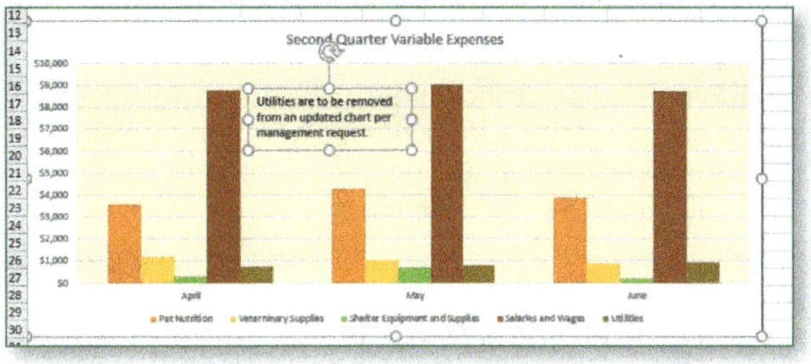

3-62 Text box shape inserted in chart

14. Click a worksheet cell and press **Ctrl+Home**.

15. Create a waterfall chart object.
    a. Select the **Apr Cash** sheet tab.
    b. Select cells **A5:B14**. This data represents cash coming in and going out for April.
    c. Click the **Insert Waterfall or Stock Chart** button [*Insert* tab, *Charts* group].
    d. Select **Waterfall**.

16. Size and position a chart object.
    a. Point to the chart border to display the move pointer.
    b. Drag the chart object so that its top left corner is at cell **C1**.
    c. Point to the bottom right selection handle to display the resize arrow.
    d. Drag the pointer to cell **L20**.

17. Format chart elements.
    a. Double-click the Net Cash column marker and then click the marker again to open the *Format Data Point* pane.
    b. Click the **Series Options** button in the task pane and expand the *Series Options* group.
    c. Select the **Set as total** box.
    d. Triple-click the chart title placeholder text and type April Cash Flow.
    e. Select the chart area and apply a **1 pt. black** outline.
    f. Click a worksheet cell and press **Ctrl+Home**.

18. Save and close the workbook (Figure 3-63).

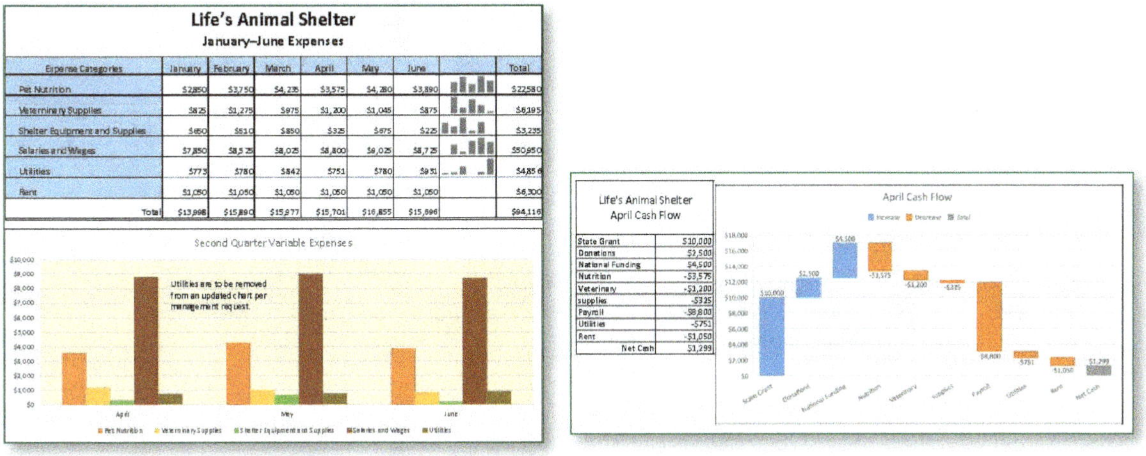

3-63 Excel 3-1 completed worksheets and charts

Guided Project 3-2

Wear-Ever Shoes is a shoe outlet with several locations. In a worksheet that tracks sales of popular items for the past six months, you create a bar chart to compare the number of pairs sold by style. You also create a combination chart to compare number of pairs sold and unit cost for each style. For another set of data, you create a sunburst chart to illustrate sales by shoe style, gender, and color.
[Student Learning Outcomes 3.1, 3.2, 3.3, 3.4, 3.5, 3.6, 3.7]

File Needed: ***WearEverShoes-03.xlsx*** *[Student data files are available in the* Library *of your SIMnet account.]*
Completed Project File Name: ***[your initials] Excel 3-2.xlsx***

Skills Covered in This Project

- Create a chart sheet.
- Change the chart type.
- Apply a chart style.
- Add and format chart elements.
- Use a picture as fill.
- Create and format a combination chart.
- Use *WordArt* in a chart.
- Create and format a sunburst chart.

1. Open the ***WearEverShoes-03*** workbook from your student data files and save it as [your initials] Excel 3-2.
2. Create a column chart sheet.
   a. Select cells **A5:B16** on the **Unit Sales** sheet.
   b. Click the **Quick Analysis** button and choose **Charts**.
   c. Select **Clustered Column**.
   d. Click the **Move Chart** button [*Chart Tools Design* tab, *Location* group].
   e. Click the **New sheet** button.
   f. Type Sales Chart and click **OK**.
3. Change the chart type.
   a. Click the **Sales Chart** sheet tab if necessary.
   b. Click the **Change Chart Type** button [*Chart Tools Design* tab, *Type* group].
   c. Click the **Recommended Charts** tab.
   d. Choose **Clustered Bar** in the left pane and click **OK**.
4. Apply a chart style.
   a. Click the **Chart Styles** button in the top right corner of the chart.
   b. Select **Style 7**.
   c. Click the **Chart Styles** button to close the pane.
5. Add fill color to a data series.
   a. Double-click one of the bars to open the *Format Data Series* task pane.
   b. Click the **Fill & Line** button in the task pane.
   c. Click **Fill** to expand the command group.
   d. Select the **Vary colors by point** box.
6. Use a picture as fill for a data point.
   a. Click the "Classy Pumps" bar to display its *Format Data Point* task pane.
   b. Click the **Fill & Line** button in the task pane.
   c. Click **Fill** to expand the command group.
   d. Click the **Picture or texture fill** button.
   e. Click **Online** to open the *Insert Pictures* dialog box.
   f. Type heels in the *Bing Image Search* box and press **Enter** (Figure 3-64).

g. Select an image and click **Insert**.
h. Click the **Stack** radio button in the task pane.
i. Close the task pane and click the chart border.

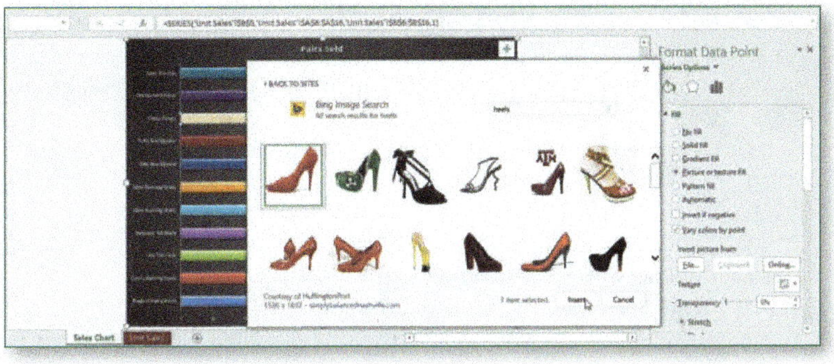

3-64 Online image search for fill in a data point

7. Create a combination chart sheet.
   a. Click the **Unit Sales** sheet tab.
   b. Select cells **A5:A16**. Press **Ctrl** and select cells **E5:F16**.
   c. Click the **Insert Combo Chart** button [*Insert* tab, *Charts* group].
   d. Select the **Clustered Column-Line on Secondary Axis** chart subtype.
   e. Click the **Move Chart** button [*Chart Tools Design* tab, *Location* group].
   f. Click the **New sheet** button.
   g. Type Cost&Retail and click **OK**.

8. Edit chart elements.
   a. Click the chart title placeholder.
   b. Type Cost and Selling Price Comparison in the *Formula* bar and press **Enter**.
   c. Select the chart title box.
   d. Click the **Home** tab and change the font size to **20 pt**.
   e. Select the chart area and apply a **¾ pt**. **black** outline.
   f. Select one of the column shapes.
   g. Click the **More** button [*Chart Tools Format* tab, *Shapes Styles* group].
   h. Choose **Intense Effect - Blue**, **Accent 1** in the bottom row of the *Theme Styles* gallery.
   i. Select the line marker.
   j. Click the **Shape Outline** button [*Chart Tools Format* tab, *Shape Styles* group] and choose **Black, Text 1** as the color.
   k. Change the weight of the line to **3 pt**.

9. Use *WordArt* in a chart.
   a. Click the chart title.
   b. Click the **More** button [*Chart Tools Format* tab, *WordArt Styles* group].
   c. Choose **Fill - Black**, **Text 1**, **Shadow** in the first row of the gallery.
   d. Click the chart border to deselect the title.

10. Create a sunburst chart.
    a. Click the **Grouped Sales** sheet tab.
    b. Select cells **A5:D24**.
    c. Click the **Insert Hierarchy Chart** button [*Insert* tab, *Charts* group].
    d. Click **Sunburst** to select it.
    e. Click the **Move Chart** button [*Chart Tools Design* tab, *Location* group].
    f. Select **New sheet**, type Sunburst, and click **OK**.

11. Format a sunburst chart.
    a. Click the chart title element.
    b. Triple-click the placeholder text to select it.
    c. Type Sales by Style, Color, and Gender.
    d. Click the sunburst shape to select the circle.

e. Point to the **Comfy Walking Shoes** arc in the inner ring and click twice to select the data point. The data point is the wedge that represents two colors of the style. You can confirm your selection on the *Chart Tools Format* tab in the *Current Selection* group. It should display "Branch Comfy Walking."

f. Click the **Format Selection** button [*Chart Tools Format* tab, *Current Selection* group].

g. Click the **Fill & Line** button.

h. Click **Fill** to expand the command group.

i. Choose **Solid fill** and click the **Color** button.

j. Choose **Orange**, **Accent 6**, **Lighter 40%**.

k. Close the task pane.

l. Click outside the chart background to deselect the chart.

12. Save and close the workbook (Figure 3-65).

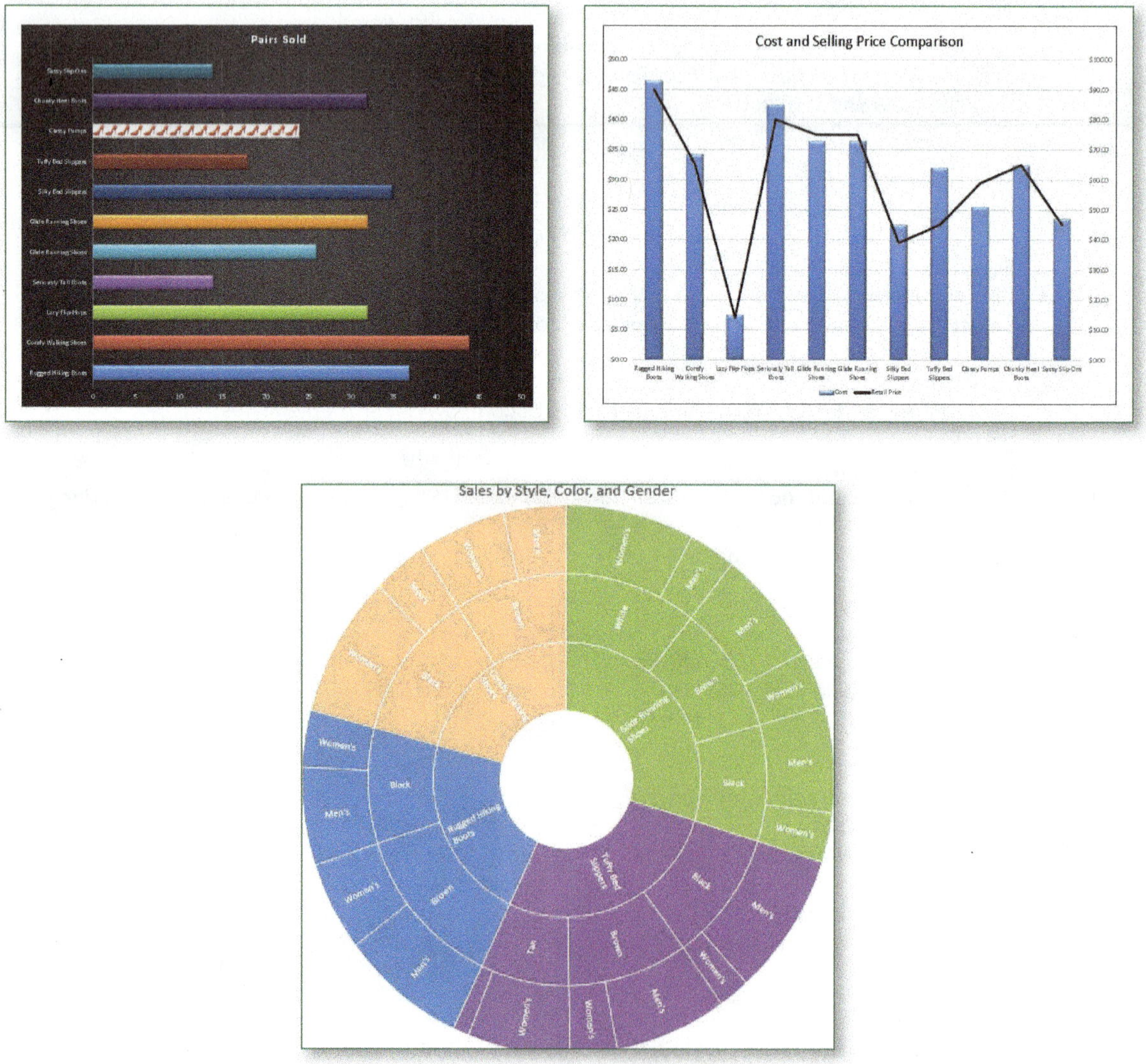

3-65 Excel 3-2 completed chart sheets

Guided Project 3-3

Blue Lake Sports has locations in several major cities and tracks sales by department in each store. For this project, you create a pie chart that shows each store's share of golf-related sales for the first quarter. You also create a line chart to illustrate week-to-week sales for specific departments in one of the stores and insert sparklines in the data.
[Student Learning Outcomes 3.1, 3.2, 3.3, 3.4, 3.6, 3.8]

File Needed: ***BlueLakeSports-03.xlsx*** *[Student data files are available in the* Library *of your SIMnet account.]*
Completed Project File Name: ***[your initials] Excel 3-3.xlsx***

Skills Covered in This Project

- Create, size, and position a pie chart object.
- Apply a chart style.
- Change the chart type.
- Add and format chart elements.
- Create a line chart sheet.
- Apply a chart layout.
- Insert and format sparklines in a worksheet.

1. Open the ***BlueLakeSports-03*** workbook from your student data files and save it as [your initials] Excel 3-3.
2. Create a pie chart object.
   a. Select the **Revenue by Department** sheet, select cells **A4:F4**, press **Ctrl**, and select cells **A13:F13**.
   b. Click the **Recommended Charts** button [*Insert* tab, *Charts* group].
   c. Choose **Pie** and click **OK**.
3. Apply a chart style.
   a. Select the chart object.
   b. Click the **More** button [*Chart Tools Design* tab, *Chart Styles* group].
   c. Select **Style 12**.
4. Size and position a chart object.
   a. Point to the chart object border to display the move pointer.
   b. Drag the chart object so its top left corner is at cell **A21**.
   c. Point to the bottom right selection handle to display the resize arrow.
   d. Drag the pointer to cell **G36**.
5. Change the chart type.
   a. Select the pie chart object and click the **Change Chart Type** button [*Chart Tools Design* tab, *Type* group].
   b. Select the **All Charts** tab and choose **Pie** in the left pane.
   c. Choose **3-D Pie** and click **OK**.
6. Format pie chart elements.
   a. Double-click the pie to open its *Format Data Series* task pane.
   b. Click the **Atlanta** slice to update the pane to the *Format Data Point* task pane. (Rest the pointer on a slice to see its identifying *ScreenTip*.)
   c. Click the **Series Options** button in the *Format Data Series* task pane.
   d. Set the pie explosion percentage at **10%**.
   e. Close the task pane.
   f. Click the chart object border to deselect the **Atlanta** slice.
7. Add and format chart elements in a pie chart.
   a. Click the **Chart Elements** button in the top right corner of the chart.
   b. Select the **Data Labels** box.

c. Click the **Data Labels** arrow to open its submenu and choose **More Options**.
d. Click the **Label Options** button In the *Format Data Labels* pane.
e. Click **Label Options** to expand the group.
f. Select the **Percentage** box.

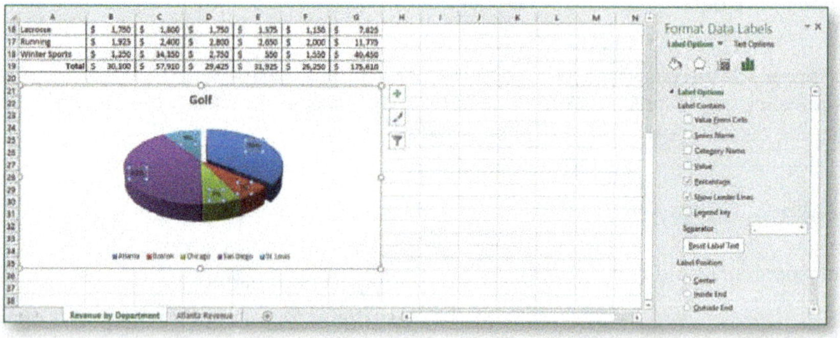

3-66 *Format Data Point* task pane for data labels

g. Deselect the **Value** box (Figure 3-66).
h. Press **Ctrl+B** to apply bold.
i. Change the font size to **12 pt** [*Home* tab, *Font* group].
j. Click the chart object border to select it.
k. Click the **Shape Outline** button [*Chart Tools Format* tab, *Shape Styles* group] and choose **Purple, Accent 4, Darker 50%**.
l. Click the **Shape Outline** button and choose **Weight** and **1 pt**.
m. Click a worksheet cell.

8. Create a line chart sheet.
   a. Select the **Atlanta Revenue** sheet tab.
   b. Select cells **A4:E7**.
   c. Click the **Quick Analysis** button and choose **Charts**.
   d. Select **Line**.
   e. Click the **Move Chart** button [*Chart Tools Design* tab, *Location* group].
   f. Click the **New sheet** button.
   g. Type Promo Depts and click **OK**.
9. Apply a chart layout.
   a. Click the **Quick Layout** button [*Chart Tools Design* tab, *Chart Layouts* group].
   b. Select **Layout 5** to add a data table to the chart sheet (Figure 3-67).

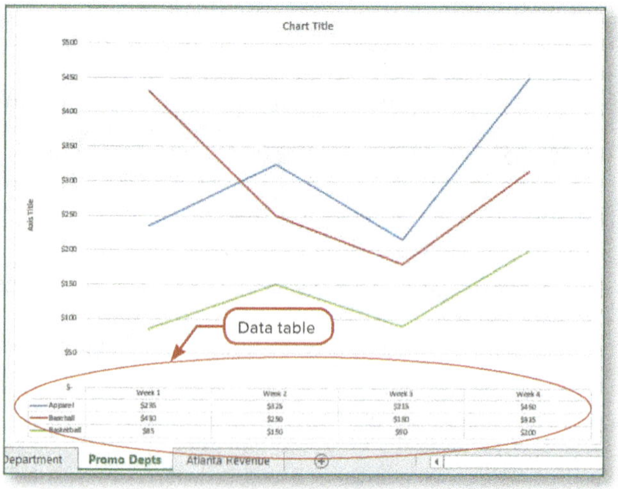

3-67 Data table added by *Quick Layout*

10. Change the chart type.
    a. Click the **Change Chart Type** button [*Chart Tools Design* tab, *Type* group].
    b. Select the **All Charts** tab and choose **Line with Markers** in the *Line* category.
    c. Click **OK**.

11. Edit chart elements in a line chart.
    a. Click the chart title placeholder.
    b. Type Special Promotion Departments in the formula bar and press **Enter**.
    c. Click the vertical axis title placeholder.
    d. Type Dollar Sales in the formula bar and press **Enter**.
    e. Click the **Chart Elements** drop-down arrow [*Chart Tools Format* tab, *Current Selection* group].
    f. Choose **Series "Apparel"** to select the line in the chart.
    g. Click the **Format Selection** button [*Chart Tools Format* tab, *Current Selection* group].
    h. Click the **Fill & Line** button in the *Format Data Series* task pane.
    i. Click **Marker** and then click **Marker Options** to expand the group (Figure 3-68).
    j. Choose **Built-in** and select **10 pt**.
    k. Click the *Series Options* triangle at the top of the task pane and choose **Series "Baseball"** (Figure 3-69).
    l. Apply the same marker changes for the baseball series.
    m. Select the basketball series and make the same marker changes.
    n. Close the task pane and click outside the chart.

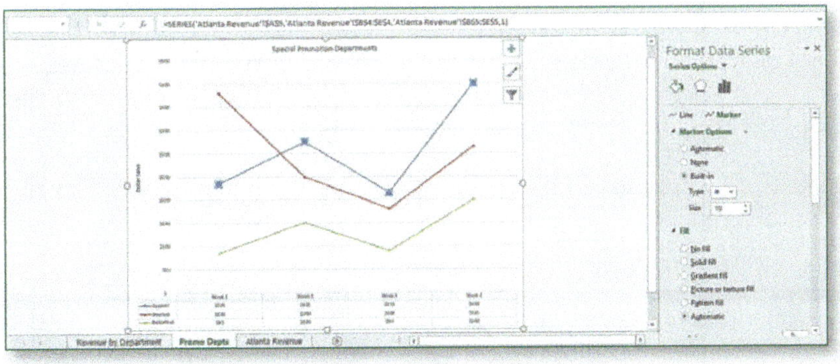

3-68 Marker options for the data series

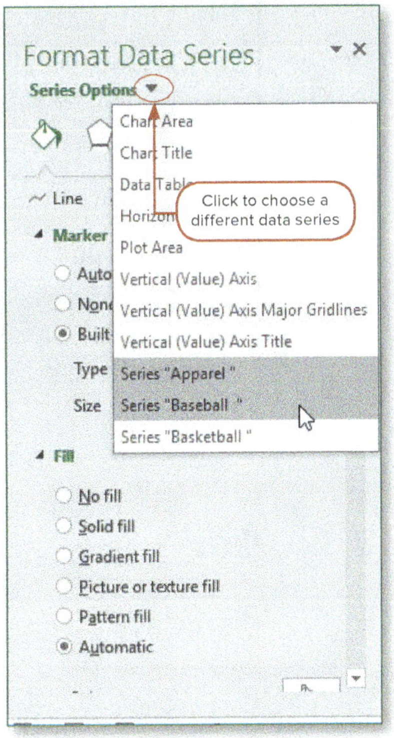

3-69 New data series selected

12. Insert sparklines in the worksheet.
    a. Click the **Atlanta Revenue** tab.
    b. Right-click the column **F** heading and choose **Insert**.
    c. Select cells **B5:E18** as the data range.
    d. Click the **Line Sparkline** button [*Insert* tab, *Sparklines* group].
    e. Select cells **F5:F18** in the *Location Range* box.
    f. Click **OK**.

13. Format sparklines in worksheet.
    a. Click the **Format** button [*Home* tab, *Cells* group] and change the **Row Height** to **24**.
    b. Click the **Format** button [*Home* tab, *Cells* group] and set the **Column Width** to **35**.
    c. Select the **Markers** box in the *Show* group in the *Sparkline Tools Design* tab.
    d. Click the **Sparkline Color** button [*Sparkline Tools Design* tab, *Style* group].
    e. Choose **Black**, **Text 1** for the line color.
    f. Click cell **A1**.

14. Change the page orientation to landscape.
15. Save and close the workbook (Figure 3-70).

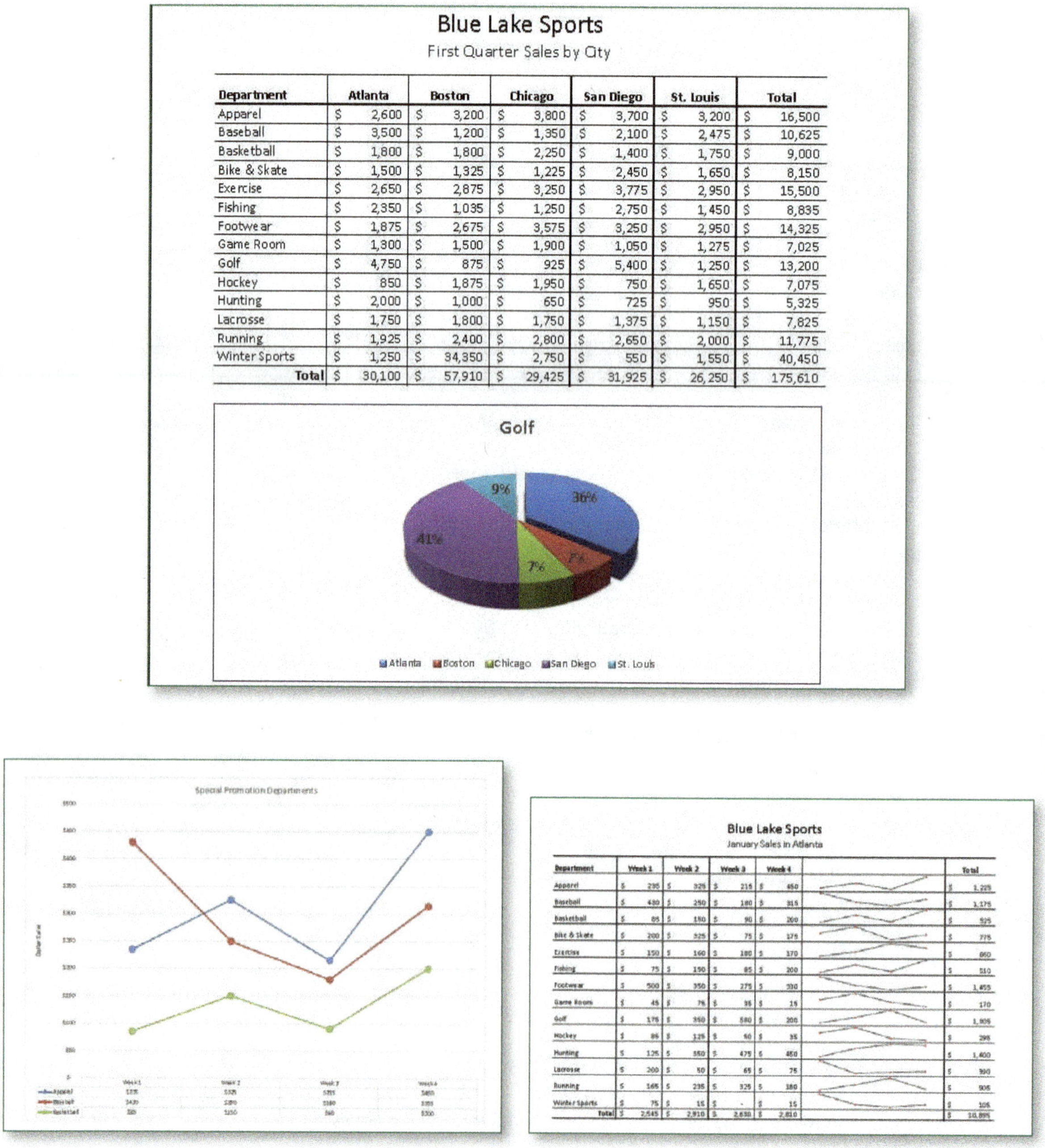

Blue Lake Sports

First Quarter Sales by City

Department	Atlanta	Boston	Chicago	San Diego	St. Louis	Total
Apparel	$ 2,600	$ 3,200	$ 3,800	$ 3,700	$ 3,200	$ 16,500
Baseball	$ 3,500	$ 1,200	$ 1,350	$ 2,100	$ 2,475	$ 10,625
Basketball	$ 1,800	$ 1,800	$ 2,250	$ 1,400	$ 1,750	$ 9,000
Bike & Skate	$ 1,500	$ 1,325	$ 1,225	$ 2,450	$ 1,650	$ 8,150
Exercise	$ 2,650	$ 2,875	$ 3,250	$ 3,775	$ 2,950	$ 15,500
Fishing	$ 2,350	$ 1,035	$ 1,250	$ 2,750	$ 1,450	$ 8,835
Footwear	$ 1,875	$ 2,675	$ 3,575	$ 3,250	$ 2,950	$ 14,325
Game Room	$ 1,300	$ 1,500	$ 1,900	$ 1,050	$ 1,275	$ 7,025
Golf	$ 4,750	$ 875	$ 925	$ 5,400	$ 1,250	$ 13,200
Hockey	$ 850	$ 1,875	$ 1,950	$ 750	$ 1,650	$ 7,075
Hunting	$ 2,000	$ 1,000	$ 650	$ 725	$ 950	$ 5,325
Lacrosse	$ 1,750	$ 1,800	$ 1,750	$ 1,375	$ 1,150	$ 7,825
Running	$ 1,925	$ 2,400	$ 2,800	$ 2,650	$ 2,000	$ 11,775
Winter Sports	$ 1,250	$ 34,350	$ 2,750	$ 550	$ 1,550	$ 40,450
Total	$ 30,100	$ 57,910	$ 29,425	$ 31,925	$ 26,250	$ 175,610

3-70 Excel 3-3 completed worksheet and charts

Independent Project 3-4

For this project, you create a column chart to illustrate April–September revenue for Classic Gardens and Landscapes. You also build a pie chart sheet to graph the proportion that each category contributes to total revenue.
[Student Learning Outcomes 3.1, 3.2, 3.3, 3.4, 3.5, 3.6]

File Needed: ***ClassicGardens-03.xlsx*** *[Student data files are available in the* Library *of your SIMnet account.]*
Completed Project File Name: ***[your initials] Excel 3-4.xlsx***

Skills Covered in This Project

- Create a chart object.
- Size and position a chart object.
- Edit and format chart elements.
- Edit the source data for a chart.
- Build a pie chart sheet.
- Use texture as fill.
- Add and format data labels in a chart.

1. Open the ***ClassicGardens-03*** workbook from your student data files and save it as [your initials] Excel 3-4.
2. Create a **Clustered Column** chart object for cells **A4:G9**.
3. Move the chart object so that its top left corner is at cell **A12**. Size the bottom of the chart to reach cell **H30**.
4. Edit the chart title to display CGL Major Sales Revenue on one line and Second and Third Quarters on the second line.
5. Apply chart **Style 14** to the chart.
6. Format the first line of the chart title to a font size of **20 pt**. Format the second title line as **16 pt**.
7. Apply a **½ point Black, Text 1** outline to the chart area.
8. Verify that the chart is still selected. In the highlighted range in the worksheet, drag the resize pointer to remove the *Design Consulting* data series from the chart (Figure 3-71).

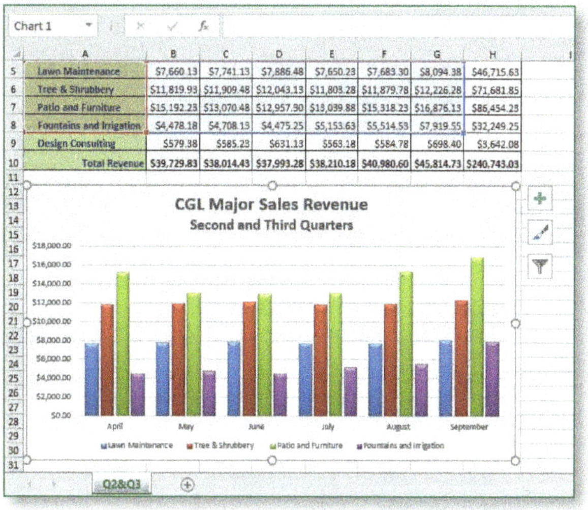

3-71 Resize the chart by dragging the resize pointer

9. Create a *3-D Pie* chart for cells **A4:A9** and cells **H4:H9**. Move the chart to its own sheet named Revenue Breakdown.
10. Edit the chart title to display Revenue by Category. Change the font size to **32**.
11. Select the legend and change the font size to **12**.
12. Apply the **Woven mat** texture fill to the *Patio and Furniture* slice.
13. Add data labels to display in the center of each slice.
    a. Display the *Format Data Labels* task pane, choose the **Accounting** format, and set **0** decimal places.
    b. While the data labels are selected, change the font size to **14 pt** and apply **bold** [*Home* tab, *Font* group].

14. Deselect the chart.
15. Save and close the workbook (Figure 3-72).

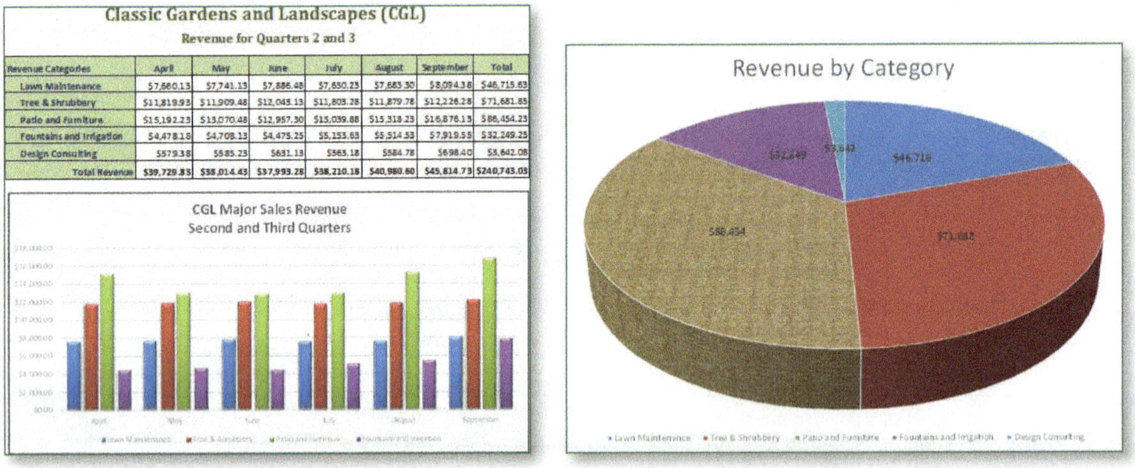

Classic Gardens and Landscapes (CGL)

Revenue for Quarters 2 and 3

Revenue Categories	April	May	June	July	August	September	Total
Lawn Maintenance	$7,660.13	$7,741.13	$7,886.48	$7,650.23	$7,683.30	$8,094.38	$46,715.63
Tree & Shrubbery	$11,819.93	$11,909.48	$12,043.13	$11,803.28	$11,879.78	$12,226.28	$71,681.85
Patio and Furniture	$15,192.23	$13,070.48	$12,957.30	$15,039.88	$15,318.23	$16,876.13	$88,454.23
Fountains and Irrigation	$4,478.18	$4,708.13	$4,475.25	$5,153.63	$5,514.53	$7,919.55	$32,249.25
Design Consulting	$579.38	$585.23	$631.13	$563.18	$584.78	$698.40	$3,642.08
Total Revenue	$39,729.83	$38,014.43	$37,993.28	$38,210.18	$40,980.60	$45,814.73	$240,743.03

3-72 Excel 3-4 completed chart sheets

Independent Project 3-5

For this project, you create a stacked bar chart to illustrate projected tuition and fee amounts for Sierra Pacific Community College District (SPCCD). You also create a pie chart to show total projected revenue for the time period and add sparklines to the worksheet.
[Student Learning Outcomes 3.1, 3.2, 3.3, 3.4, 3.6, 3.8]

File Needed: ***SierraPacific-03.xlsx*** *[Student data files are available in the* Library *of your SIMnet account.]*
Completed Project File Name: ***[your initials] Excel 3-5.xlsx***

Skills Covered in This Project

- Create a chart object.
- Size and position a chart object.
- Apply a chart style.
- Switch row and column data.
- Edit chart source data.
- Create a pie chart sheet.
- Edit and format chart elements.
- Insert and format sparklines in a sheet.

1. Open the ***SierraPacific-03*** workbook from your student data files and save it as [your initials] Excel 3-5.
2. Select cells **A3:E7** and use the *Quick Analysis* tool to create a stacked bar chart object.
3. Size and position the chart below the worksheet data in cells **A10:G28**.
4. Apply **Chart Style 6**.
5. Edit the chart title to display Tuition Revenue Projection.

6. Apply a ½ pt **Dark Blue**, **Text 2** outline to the chart object.
7. Edit the source data to remove the utilization and facilities fees from the chart.
8. Switch the row and column data for the chart so that semester names are shown on the vertical axis.
9. Create a 3-D pie chart sheet for cells **A4:A7** and cells **F4:F7**. Move the chart to a new sheet named Total Revenue.
10. Apply **Chart Style 3** and a **black ½ pt** outline.
11. Edit the chart title to Projected Revenue Sources.
12. Format the legend font size to **12 pt**.
13. Create a column sparkline with cell **G8** as the location range for cells **B8:E8**. Format cell **G8** with an **Outside Border** [*Home* tab, *Font* group].
14. Save and close the workbook (Figure 3-73).

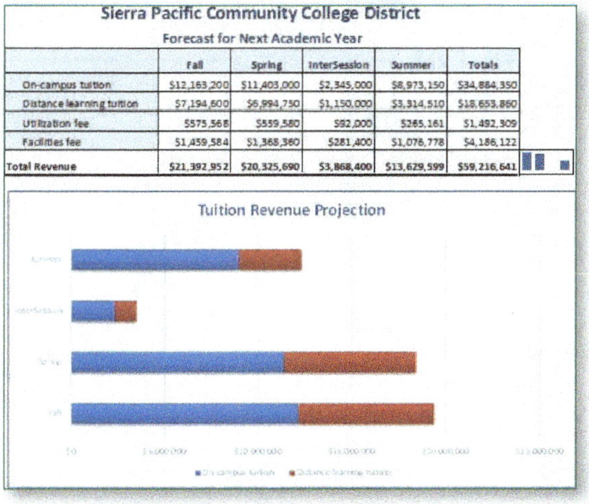
Sierra Pacific Community College District

Forecast for Next Academic Year

	Fall	Spring	InterSession	Summer	Totals
On-campus tuition	$12,163,200	$11,403,000	$2,345,000	$8,973,150	$34,884,350
Distance learning tuition	$7,194,600	$6,994,750	$1,150,000	$3,314,510	$18,653,860
Utilization fee	$575,568	$559,580	$92,000	$265,161	$1,492,309
Facilities fee	$1,459,584	$1,368,360	$281,400	$1,076,778	$4,186,122
Total Revenue	$21,392,952	$20,325,690	$3,868,400	$13,629,599	$59,216,641

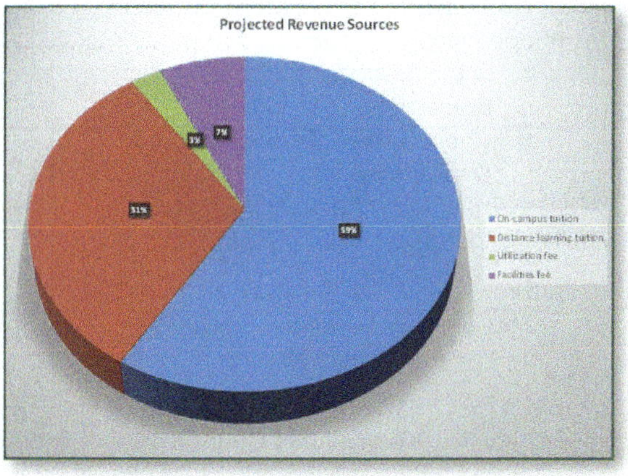

3-73 Excel 3-5 completed worksheet and chart

Independent Project 3-6

Courtyard Medical Plaza (CMP) is a full-service medical office complex providing customers with a variety of medical services in one location. For this project, you create charts to illustrate data about the number of procedures performed at CMP as well as how patients came to the facility. Your final task is to prepare a waterfall chart for the operations account.
[Student Learning Outcomes 3.1, 3.2, 3.3, 3.4, 3.5, 3.7]

File Needed: ***CourtyardMedical-03.xlsx*** *[Student data files are available in the* Library *of your SIMnet account.]*
Completed Project File Name: ***[your initials] Excel 3-6.xlsx***

Skills Covered in This Project

- Create a column chart sheet.
- Add and edit chart elements.
- Add and format a trendline in a chart.
- Insert a text box shape in a chart.
- Display gridlines in a chart.
- Use gradient fill for a chart object.
- Create a waterfall chart.

1. Open the ***CourtyardMedical-03*** workbook from your student data files and save it as [your initials] Excel 3-6.
2. Select the **Patient Arrivals** worksheet. Create a clustered column chart sheet for cells **A5:M5** and cells **A7:M7**. Move the chart to its own sheet named Immed Care.
3. Edit the chart title to display Immediate Care Patient Count.
4. Click the **Chart Elements** button and select **Trendline**.
5. Click the options arrow next to **Trendline** and select **More Options** to open the *Format Trendline* task pane.
   a. In the *Forecast* group, set the **Forward** value to **12**.
   b. Choose **Olive Green**, **Accent 3**, **Darker 50%** for the line color.
   c. Set the **Width** of the trendline to **4 pt**.
6. Draw a *Text Box* shape between the 300 and 400 gridlines and type The number of patients who come in for Immediate Care services will continue to grow. (Figure 3-74).

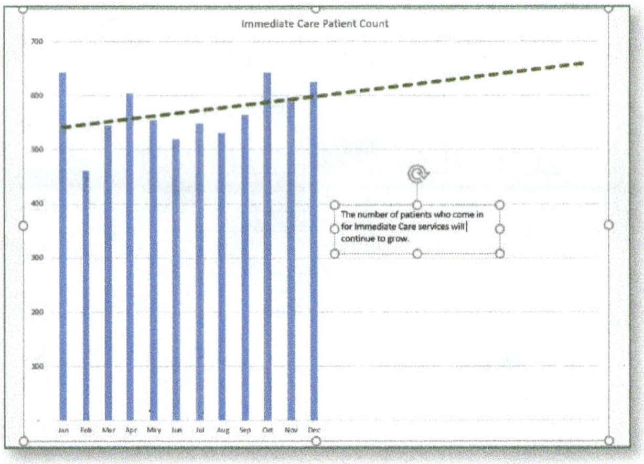

3-74 Text box shape in a chart

7. Select the **Procedures Count** worksheet and use the *Quick Analysis* tool to create a clustered column chart for cells **A5:D16** on its own sheet named Procedures Chart.
8. Edit the chart title to Number of Procedures on the first line and Three-Month Period on the second line.
9. Change the chart type to a clustered bar chart.
10. Click the **Chart Elements** button. Show **Primary Major Vertical**, **Primary Major Horizontal** and **Primary Minor Vertical** gridlines. Format each gridline element to use **Black**, **Text 1**, **Lighter 50%**.
11. Use the **Shape Fill** button to format the plot area to **Tan**, **Background 2**.
12. Select the **Operations** sheet tab and create a waterfall chart object for cells **A3:B9**.
13. Position the waterfall chart object so that its top left corner is at cell **A11**. Size the object to reach cell **I28**.
14. Select the ending balance marker and set it as a total.
15. Edit the chart title placeholder to CMP Operations Account.
16. Select the chart area and apply a **1 pt black** outline.
17. Click a worksheet cell and press **Ctrl+Home**.
18. Save and close the workbook (Figure 3-75).

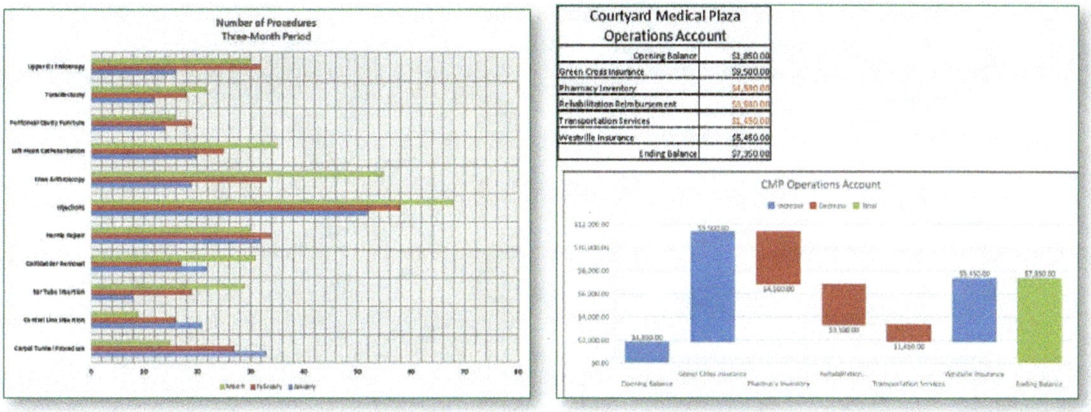

3-75 Excel 3-6 completed worksheet and charts

Improve It Project 3-7

Central Sierra Insurance is a multi-office insurance company that handles commercial and personal insurance products. In this project, you add missing data and verify that the charts are updated. [Student Learning Outcomes 3.2, 3.3, 3.4]

File Needed: ***CentralSierra-03.xlsx*** *[Student data files are available in the* Library *of your SIMnet account.]*
Completed Project File Name: ***[your initials] Excel 3-7.xlsx***

Skills Covered in This Project

- Edit source data.
- Switch row and column data.
- Change chart colors.
- Apply a chart style.
- Add and format elements in a chart.
- Change the chart type.

1. Open the ***CentralSierra-03*** workbook from your student data files and save it as [your initials] Excel 3-7. There are two chart objects on the worksheet.
2. Insert a new row at row 8.
3. Type Motorcycle in cell **A8**. In cells **B8:D8**, type these values: 15, 82, and 24.
4. Change the pie chart object to a **3-D Pie** and apply **Chart Style 3**. Notice that a data series for "Motorcycle" has been added.
5. Switch the row and column data for the column chart. The data series for "Motorcycle" is not included.
6. Click the **Select Data** button [*Chart Tools Design* tab, *Data* group] and reset the source data to show cells **A5:D10**.
7. Change the column chart color scheme to **Color 11** in the *Monochromatic* list.
8. Format chart elements.
   a. Use the **Shape Fill** button [*Chart Tools Format* tab, *Shape Styles* group] to apply **Olive Green, Accent 3** fill for the **Side Wall** of the column chart.
   b. Use the **Shape Fill** button to apply the **Linear Down** gradient in the *Light Variations* group to the side wall.

c. Apply the same fill and gradient to the **Walls** element.
d. Apply the **Olive Green**, **Accent 3**, **Lighter 60%** with no gradient to the **Floor** element.
e. Select the horizontal gridlines and use the **Shape Outline** button to format them with **Black**, **Text 1**, **Lighter 50%**.

9. Select the pie chart object and change the colors to **Color 11** in the *Monochromatic* group.
10. Use **Olive Green**, **Accent 3** as shape fill for the pie chart area with a **Linear Down** gradient from the light variations.
11. Apply a **½ pt Olive Green**, **Accent 3**, **Darker 25%** outline to both chart objects.
12. Save and close the workbook (Figure 3-76).

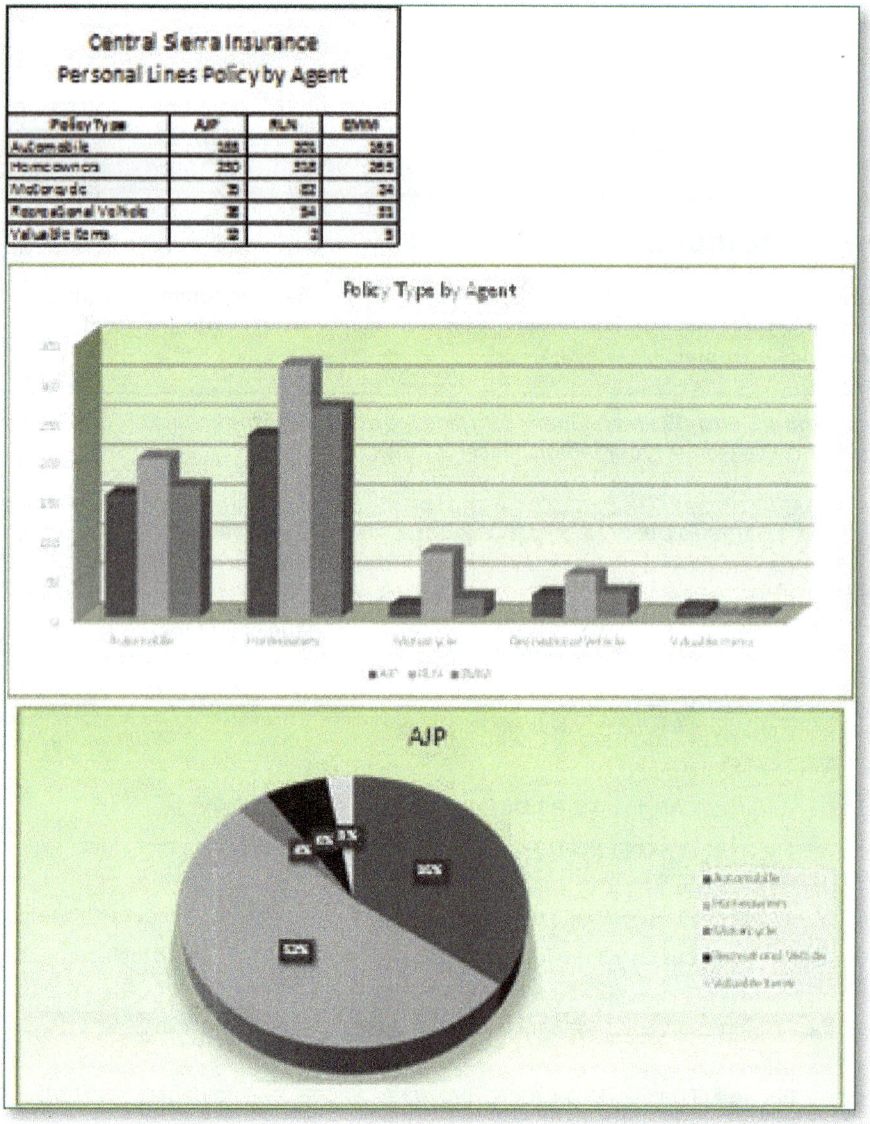

3-76 Excel 3-7 Completed worksheet with charts

Challenge Project 3-8

For this project, you build a worksheet by copying a worksheet from one of the student data files, editing data, and creating a TreeMap chart.
[Student Learning Outcomes 3.1, 3.2, 3.3, 3.7]

File Needed: ***WearEverShoes-03.xlsx*** *[Student data files are available in the* Library *of your SIMnet account.]*
Completed Project File Name: ***[your initials] Excel 3-8.xlsx***

Create a new workbook and save it as [your initials] Excel 3-8. Modify your workbook according to the following guidelines:

- Open the ***WearEverShoes-03*** workbook from your student data files.
- Copy the **Grouped Sales** sheet to ***[your initials] Excel 3-8***. Close ***WearEverShoes-03***.
- Rename the *Grouped Sales* sheet as My Groups.
- Delete column **C** to create two levels in the hierarchy, the style name and the color. Each item has a value.
- Select a topic of interest or relevance to you that can be placed in a two-level hierarchy like the worksheet. Examples are college department and course name; company name and functional area; state and city; music type and song title. Assign different values if appropriate to your data.
- Edit the data in the worksheet to reflect your groups and subgroups. Edit the title labels also.
- Type a main and secondary title for your data. Format your worksheet.
- Select the appropriate data and create a *TreeMap* hierarchy chart on its own sheet.
- Edit the chart title and apply a chart style.
- Edit the source data to increase or decrease values and see how the *TreeMap* is adjusted.

Challenge Project 3-9

For this project, you create a worksheet and accompanying charts to track daily usage of your smartphone, tablet, or smart watch.
[Student Learning Outcomes 3.1, 3.2, 3.3, 3.4, 3.5, 3.6]

File Needed: None
Completed Project File Name: ***[your initials] Excel 3-9.xlsx***

Create a new workbook and save it as [your initials] Excel 3-9. Modify your workbook according to the following guidelines:

- Enter the days of the week as column headings, starting in cell B2.
- As row headings starting in cell A3, type the names of five daily tasks or activities for your device. Examples are "Send text," "Receive phone call," "Use GPS," "View video," or similar tasks.
- Enter a value for the number of times you perform each task on each day.
- Type a main title for your data in row 1. Format your data.
- Create a column chart object that compares the number of times for each task on Monday.

- Size and position the chart object below the worksheet data.
- Change the layout or apply a chart style.
- Edit the chart title placeholder to display an appropriate title.
- Format chart elements to create an attractive, easy-to-understand chart of your data.
- For the task with the greatest Monday value, create another column chart that displays daily numbers for that one task.
- Size and position this chart object below the first chart.
- Format the second chart to complement the first chart.

Challenge Project 3-10

For this project, you create a worksheet with a column/line combo chart that compares air temperature and humidity level in your city or town for 10 days. You also insert a single sparkline in the data. [Student Learning Outcomes 3.1, 3.2, 3.3, 3.4, 3.6, 3.8]

File Needed: None
Completed Project File Name: ***[your initials] Excel 3-10.xlsx***

Create a new workbook and save it as [your initials] Excel 3-10. Modify your workbook according to the following guidelines:

- In a worksheet, enter dates in cells **A4:A13** for each of the last 10 days or each of the next 10 days.
- In column B, enter a recorded or predicted temperature in degrees for each date at 12 noon. Use an online weather reference or a weather app.
- In column C, enter corresponding humidity levels as percentages. Use the same weather reference or make an estimate.
- Type a main title for the data as well as column labels.
- Create a clustered column/line combo chart with a secondary axis for the percentages. Move the chart to its own sheet.
- Change the layout or apply a chart style.
- Edit and format the chart elements as needed.
- In the worksheet, select the range of temperature values as the data range for a line sparkline. As the location range, select cell **D14**. Format column D as **32.00 (229 pixels)** wide.
- Format the sparkline and adjust row heights to better display the data and the sparkline.

CHAPTER 4

Formatting, Organizing, and Getting Data

EXCEL

CHAPTER OVERVIEW

Excel can use data from many sources as well as provide data to other programs. When data is shared among applications, the data is usually in a list or table layout like a database. This chapter covers how to format data as an Excel table, how to sort and filter data, how to get data from other sources, and how to build a *PivotTable*.

STUDENT LEARNING OUTCOMES (SLOs)

After completing this chapter, you will be able to:

SLO 4.1 Create and format a list as an Excel table (p. E4-222).

SLO 4.2 Apply *Conditional Formatting* rules as well as *Color Scales, Icon Sets,* and *Data Bars* (p. E4-228).

SLO 4.3 Sort data by one or more columns or by attribute (p. E4-234).

SLO 4.4 Filter data by using *AutoFilters* and by creating an *Advanced Filter* (p. E4-238).

SLO 4.5 Use subtotals, groups, and outlines for tabular data in a worksheet (p. E4-242).

SLO 4.6 Import data into an Excel worksheet from a text file, a database file, and other sources (p. E4-248).

SLO 4.7 Export Excel data as a text file and into a Word document (p. E4-254).

SLO 4.8 Build and format a *PivotTable* (p. E4-258).

CASE STUDY

For the Pause & Practice projects in this chapter, you create worksheets for Paradise Lakes Resort. To complete the work, you format a list as an Excel table, sort and filter data, import and clean data, and create a *PivotTable*.

Pause & Practice 4-1: Format data as an Excel table and set conditional formatting.

Pause & Practice 4-2: Sort, filter, and subtotal data.

Pause & Practice 4-3: Import and *Flash Fill* data in a workbook.

Pause & Practice 4-4: Create and format a *PivotTable* and a *PivotChart.*

SLO 4.1

Creating and Formatting an Excel Table

An Excel ***table*** is a list of related pieces of information that is formatted with a title row followed by rows of data (Figure 4-1). When data is in table format, you can organize, sort, filter, and calculate data easily and quickly, much like a database.

The ***header row*** is the first row of a table with descriptive titles or labels. Each row of data is a ***record*** and each column is a ***field.*** The label in the header row is sometimes referred to as the ***field name.*** When you format Excel data as a table, follow these guidelines to optimize your tables for use of Excel commands:

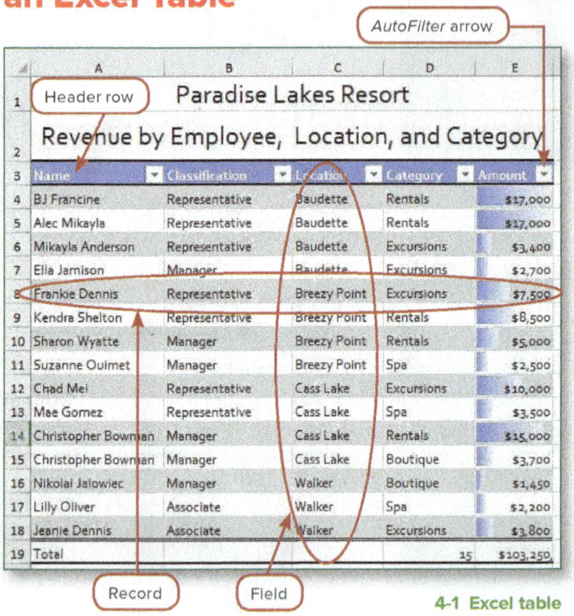

4-1 Excel table

- Type descriptive labels in the first row and begin each label with a letter, not a number.
- Assign each header a unique label; do not repeat any of the descriptive labels.
- Keep the same type of data within each column (e.g., text or values).
- Do not leave blank rows within the data.
- Keep the table separate from other data on the worksheet.

Create an Excel Table

When data is arranged as a list and conforms to the guidelines just described, a simple format command creates an Excel table. Select the data and click the **Format as Table** button in the *Styles* group on the *Home* tab to open the *Table Styles* gallery. Choose a style and click **OK** in the *Format as Table* dialog box. When the data is selected, you can also click the **Table** button in the *Tables* group on the *Insert* tab to open the *Format as Table* dialog box and create the table with a default style.

After your data is formatted as a table, each label in the header row displays an ***AutoFilter*** arrow, and the *Table Tools Design* tab opens with command groups for modifying the table. Recall from Chapter 3 that a filter is criteria that determines which data is shown and which is hidden. From *AutoFilter* arrows, you can show records for employees in a particular location or for revenue from certain months.

> **MORE INFO**
>
> *AutoFilter* arrows replace the worksheet column headings when you scroll down in a table with many records. *AutoFilter* arrows do not print.

HOW TO: Create an Excel Table

1. Select the cells to be formatted as a table.
   - Include the header row with column titles.
2. Click the **Format as Table** button [*Home* tab, *Styles* group] to open the table gallery.
3. Choose a table style from the *Table Styles* gallery (Figure 4-2).

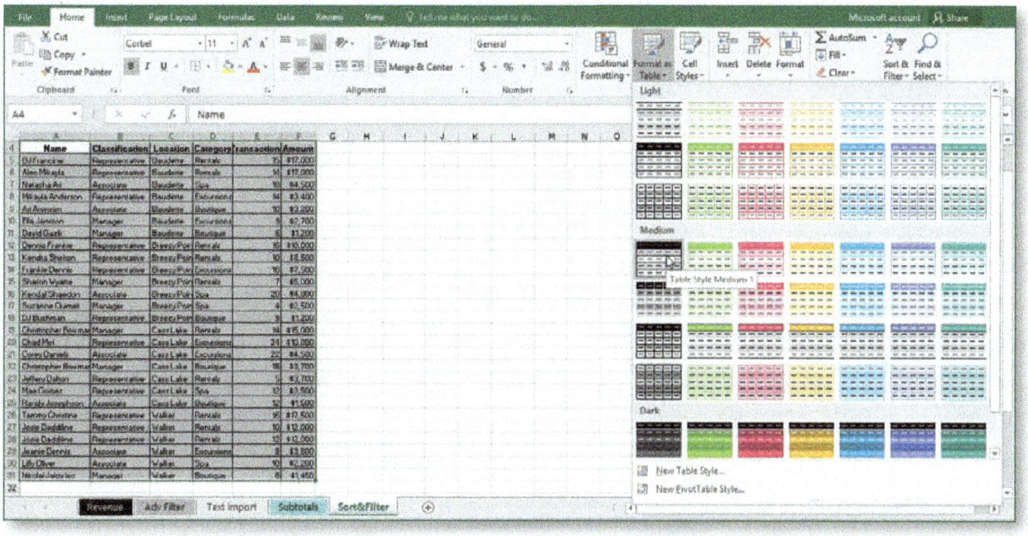

4-2 ***Table Styles*** **gallery and selected data**

- Table styles are organized in light, medium, and dark categories.

4. Confirm the cell range in the *Format As Table* dialog box.
   - You can drag to select a different range, if necessary.
5. Select the **My table has headers** box in the *Format As Table* dialog box.
   - When the selected range does not have column titles, Excel inserts a row above the data with the labels *Column1, Column2,* and so on. You can edit these names.
6. Click **OK**.
   - When the selected range includes data from an outside source, you will see a message box asking to remove the data connection. Click **Yes** to create the table (Figure 4-3).

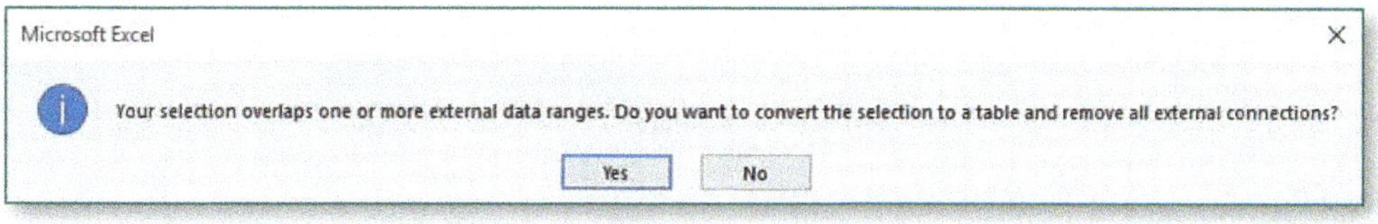

4-3 Message box for data from an outside source

ANOTHER WAY

Select the header and data rows, click the **Quick Analysis** tool, and choose **Tables**. Then click the **Table** button to format the data in a default table style. This method is not available for data from an outside source.

Table Styles and Options

A ***table style*** is a predesigned set of format settings with a color scheme, alternating fill for rows and columns, vertical and horizontal borders, and more. You select a style when you create a table from the **Format as Table** button, but you can apply a different style at any time. Predefined table styles are classified as *Light, Medium,* and *Dark* and use colors based on the workbook theme. You can remove a style by selecting *None* in the *Light* group.

HOW TO: Apply a Table Style

1. Click any cell within the table.
   - The *Table Tools Design* tab opens.
2. Click the **More** button [*Table Tools Design* tab, *Table Styles* group].
   - The *Table Styles* gallery opens.
   - Styles are named *Table Style Light 1, Table Style Medium 4, Table Style Dark 8,* and so on.
   - The *None* style is the first icon in the *Light* group.
3. Point to a style icon to see a *Live Preview* in the table.
4. Click to select and apply a style.

MORE INFO

You can create and save a custom table style by clicking the **More** button in the *Table Styles* group [*Table Tools Design* tab] and choosing **New Table Style**.

The *Table Style Options* group on the *Table Tools Design* tab includes commands for showing or hiding various parts of the table such as the header row or a total row. When you show a total row, a blank row inserts as the last row, and you can choose which calculation displays in each column. Other options are banded columns or rows, which alternate fill or borders. There is also a command to apply bold to data in the first or last column, or both. You can also hide the *AutoFilter* arrows.

HOW TO: Display a Total Row in a Table

1. Click any cell within the table.
   - The *Table Tools Design* tab opens.
2. Select the **Total Row** box [*Table Tools Design* tab, *Table Style Options* group].
   - The total row displays as the last row in the table.
3. Click a cell in the total row and click its arrow to open the calculation list.
   - The default calculation is *Sum* for numeric data.
4. Choose the calculation for the column (Figure 4-4).
   - You can use *Count* for alphanumeric columns.

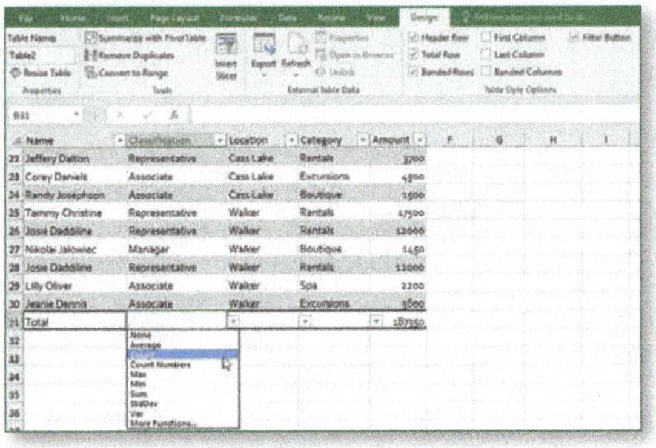

4-4 Table with total row

The Table Tools and Properties Groups

The *Tools* group on the *Table Tools Design* tab includes commands to remove duplicate records and to convert the table to a regular cell range. The *Insert Slicer* command opens a filter window for hiding or showing records in the table. The *Properties* group includes the table name and a command to resize the table.

A ***duplicate row*** is a record in a table that has exactly the same information in one or more columns. The *Remove Duplicates* command scans a table to locate and delete rows with repeated data in the specified columns. In the *Remove Duplicates* dialog box, you set which columns might have duplicate data. If you check all the columns, a row must have the same data in every column as another row.

HOW TO: Remove Duplicates

1. Click any cell within the table.
2. Click the **Remove Duplicates** button [*Table Tools Design* tab, *Tools* group] (Figure 4-5).
3. Select the box for each column that might have duplicate data.
   - Click **Unselect All** to remove all check marks and select a single label.
   - Excel recognizes headers and does not scan them for duplicate content.
4. Click **OK**.
   - A message box indicates how many duplicate values were removed and how many unique values remain.
5. Click **OK**.
   - The rows are removed from the table.
   - The command does not preview which rows are deleted.
   - You can **Undo** this command if needed.

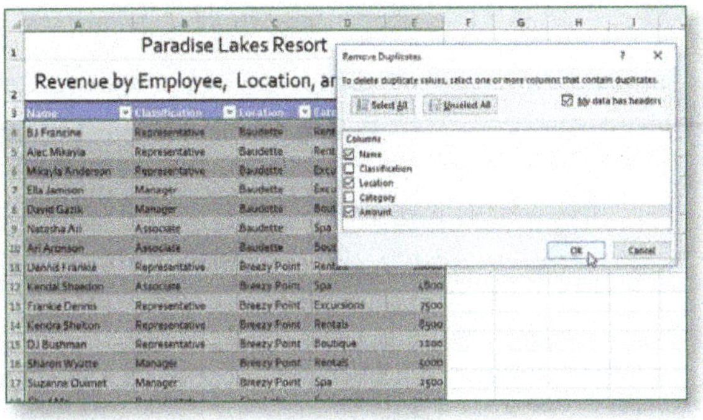

4-5 *Remove Duplicates* dialog box

The *Insert Slicer* command opens a floating window that is used as a visual filter, allowing you to work with smaller pieces of large datasets. If a table has 10,000 records but you are concerned with one location or category, you can insert a slicer to control which records display in the table. A *Slicer* window is an object that can be sized and positioned, and it displays selection handles like other objects. The *Slicer Tools Options* tab is available when a slicer object is active with settings to customize the floating window.

HOW TO: Insert a Slicer

1. Click any cell within the table.
2. Click the **Insert Slicer** button [*Table Tools Design* tab, *Tools* group] (Figure 4-6).
   - The *Insert Slicers* dialog box lists all field names in the table.
3. Select the box for the field to be used for filtering.
   - You can select more than one field to open multiple slicers.
4. Click **OK**.
   - The *Slicer* window is a selectable object.
   - All records display in the table.
5. Click an item name to filter the data.
   - The records are filtered.
   - You can press **Ctrl** and click another item to use more than one filter.
   - You can also toggle the **Multi-Select** button in the *Slicer* title bar so that you can click or tap to select multiple items for filtering.

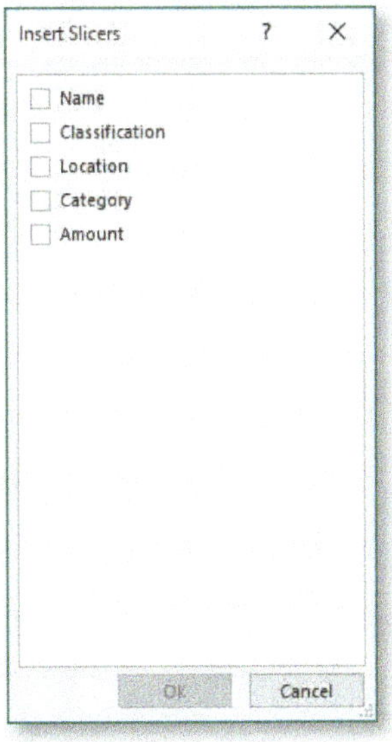

4-6 *Insert Slicers* dialog box

6. Click the **Clear Filter** button in the *Slicer* title bar.
   - All the records display.
7. Click the **More** button [*Slicer Tools Options* tab, *Slicer Styles* group].
8. Select a style for the *Slicer.*
9. Click the **Columns** spinner button [*Slicer Tools Options* tab, *Buttons* group] to set the number of columns in the *Slicer* (Figure 4-7).

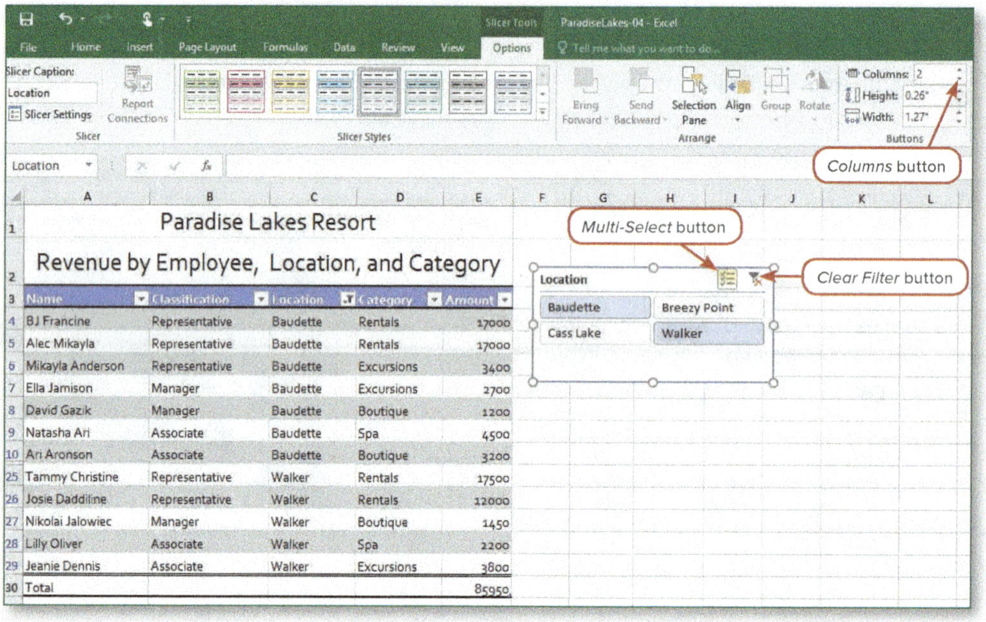

4-7 *Slicer* window for a table

10. Click and drag a corner selection handle to resize the *Slicer.*
    - You can set a specific size in the *Size* group [*Slicer Tools Options* tab].
11. Press **Delete** to remove the *Slicer* window.
    - The *Slicer* window must be selected to be deleted.

The *Convert to Range* command removes table formatting and options, but it does keep font style and fill colors. You may need to convert a table to a range when combining data from different sources or when sharing data with applications that require unformatted data.

HOW TO: Convert a Table to a Range

1. Click any cell within the table.
2. Click the **Convert to Range** button [*Table Tools Design* tab, *Tools* group] (Figure 4-8).
3. Click **Yes** in the message box.
   - The data is shown as a regular range of cells.
   - Font size, font style, and colors remain.
   - You can format the data as needed.

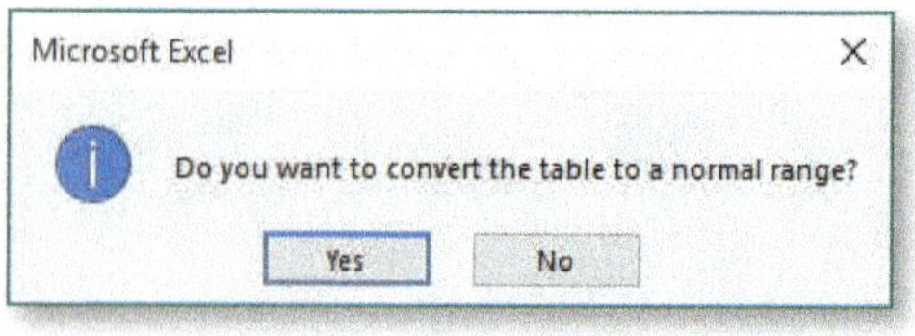

4-8 *Convert to Normal Range* message box

> **MORE INFO**
>
> If a normal data range has a header row, you can show *AutoFilter* arrows by clicking the **Filter** button on the *Data* tab.

Tables are named automatically as *TableN* where *N* is a number. To change the name to a more descriptive label, click the **Table Name** box in the *Properties* group on the *Table Tools Design* tab and type the name. You cannot use spaces in a table name, and table names in a workbook must be unique. From the *Properties* group, you can also open the *Resize Table* dialog box to select an expanded or reduced cell range for the table. A table also has a resize arrow in its bottom right cell that you can drag to grow or shrink the table. Tables grow automatically when you press **Tab** after the last item in the last row to start a new record.

Structured References and Table Formulas

In addition to the table name, each column is assigned a name using the label in its header row. The column name with its table name is known as a ***structured reference.*** An example is *Table1[Category]* as the reference for the category column in *Table1.* Column names are enclosed in square brackets. In addition to column names, there are specific item names. They are *#All, #Data, #Headers, #This Row,* and *#Totals,* each preceded by the # symbol as an identifier.

Structured references are supplied automatically in formulas making it easy to identify what is being calculated. When you point to build a formula, you will see [@*ColumnName*] as the reference with @ inserted as an identifier (Figure 4-9). The table name and structured reference names appear in *Formula AutoComplete* lists, and you can refer to those ranges in formulas outside the table. As you work with structured references, you can expand the *Formula* bar to better see a lengthy formula. The **Expand/Collapse Formula Bar** button is on the right edge of the *Formula* bar.

> **MORE INFO**
>
> To enter cell references in a table formula instead of structured references, disable **Use table names in formulas** in Excel *Options* [*File* tab, *Options, Formulas* pane].

Tables are automatically expanded to include a new column when you type a label adjacent to the last row heading. As part of its *Table AutoExpansion* feature, Excel copies a formula to complete a column with a calculation.

HOW TO: Add a Calculation Column in a Table

1. Select the cell to the right of the last column heading in the table.
2. Type the new column label and press **Enter**.
   - A column is added to the table.
3. Select the cell below the new label.
4. Type = to start a formula.
5. Click the table cell with the value to be used in the formula.
   - The column name in square brackets preceded an **@** symbol is inserted.
6. Complete the formula (Figure 4-9).

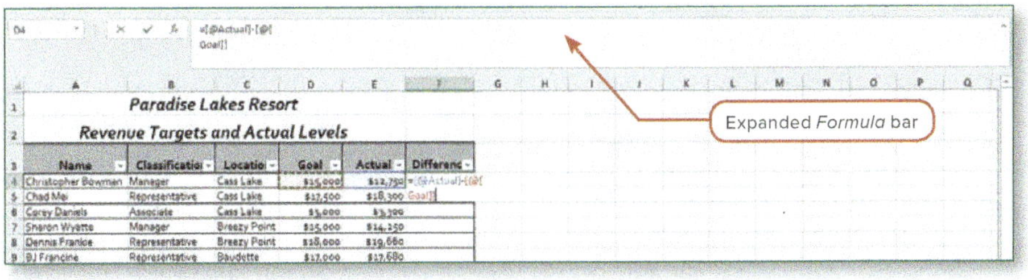

4-9 Structured references in a table

- You can refer to other cells in the table or the worksheet or type a constant.

7. Press **Enter**.
   - The formula is copied down the entire column.
   - You can enter the formula in any row in the column for it to be copied.

MORE INFO

You can disable automatic copying of table formulas in the *AutoCorrectOptions, AutoFormat As You Type* tab [*File* tab, *Options, Proofing* pane].

SLO 4.2

Applying Conditional Formatting

Conditional formatting commands apply formats to cells only when the cells meet the criteria. For example, you can use conditional formatting to display revenue amounts below a certain level in a bold red font. Conditional formatting is dynamic; the formatting adapts if the data changes.

Basic conditional formatting commands are *Highlight Cells Rules* and *Top/Bottom Rules.* For these commands, you set the rule or criteria in a dialog box and choose the format. Another type of conditional formatting is ***data visualization***, in which the cell displays a fill color, a horizontal bar, or an icon.

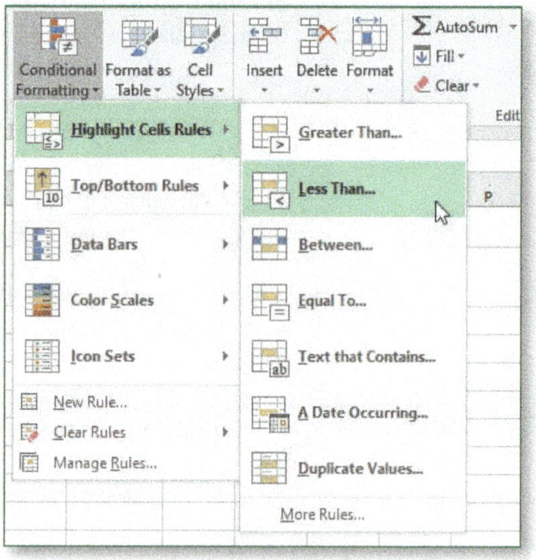

4-10 *Highlight Cells Rules* menu

Highlight Cells Rules

Highlight Cells Rules use relational or comparison operators to determine if the value or label should be formatted. *Highlight Cells Rules* include common operators such as *Equal To* and *Greater Than.* You can also create your own rule using other operators or a formula.

You can access all of the conditional formatting options from the *Conditional Formatting* button in the *Styles* group on the *Home* tab (Figure 4-10). You can also choose a default conditional formatting rule from the *Quick Analysis* tool options.

HOW TO: Create a "Less Than" Highlight Cells Rule

1. Select the cell range.
2. Click the **Conditional Formatting** button [*Home* tab, *Styles* group].
3. Select **Highlight Cells Rules** and select **Less Than**.
   - The *Less Than* dialog box opens.
4. Type a value in the *Format cells that are LESS THAN* box.
   - *Live Preview* applies the default format to cells that meet the criteria.

5. Click the arrow for the *with* box.
   - A list of preset formats is available.
6. Choose a format (Figure 4-11).
   - You can choose *Custom Format* to open the *Format Cells* dialog box and build a format.
7. Click **OK**.
   - Formatting is applied to cells that meet the criteria.
   - Click a cell away from the range to better see the formatting.

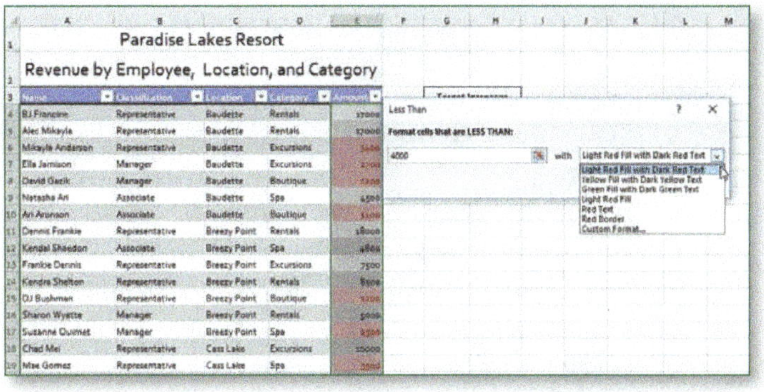

4-11 *Less Than* dialog box

Top/Bottom Rules

Top/Bottom Rules use ranking to format the highest (top) or lowest (bottom) items, either by number or percentage. You set the number or percentage in the dialog box as well as the format. You can also set a rule to format values that are above or below average (Figure 4-12).

For a selected range, the *Formatting* group in the *Quick Analysis* tool provides the most likely conditional formatting choices.

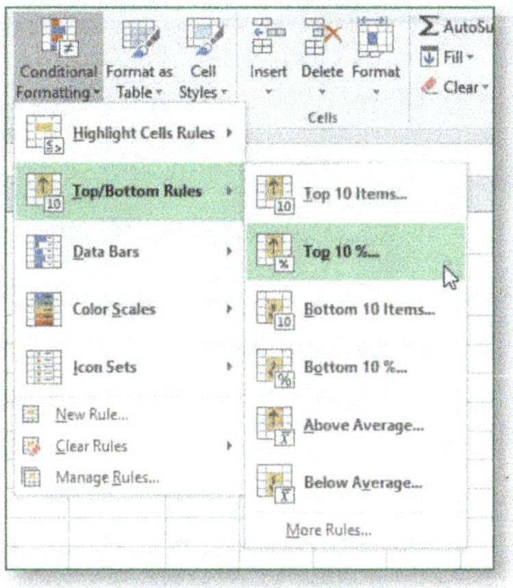

4-12 *Top/Bottom Rules*

HOW TO: Create a Top 10% Rule

1. Select the cell range.
   - The *Quick Analysis* button appears in the bottom right cell of the range.
2. Click the **Quick Analysis** button.
3. Choose **Formatting**.
   - Commonly used conditional format choices are listed.
4. Choose **Top 10%** (Figure 4-13).
   - The number of cells equal to the *Top 10%* of the number of cells in the column are formatted with a default format.
   - You can edit the format to use different attributes.

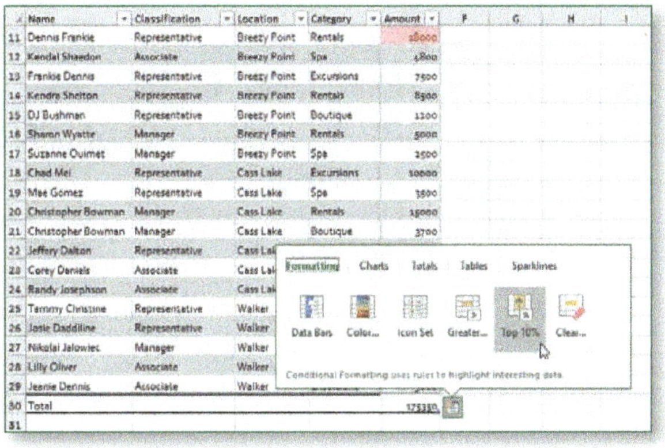

4-13 *Quick Analysis* options for conditional formatting

Use a Formula for a Rule

In addition to the *Highlight Cells* or *Top/Bottom* rules, you can create a conditional formatting formula using operators, criteria, and settings in the *New Formatting Rule* dialog box. You can, for example, build a rule to format cells in the amount column if the location is Baudette. A formula must result in either TRUE or FALSE (a Yes or No question) to be used as criteria.

▸HOW TO: Use a Formula in a Conditional Formatting Rule

1. Select the cell range.
2. Click the **Conditional Formatting** button [*Home* tab, *Styles* group].
3. Select **New Rule**.
   - The *New Formatting Rule* dialog box opens.
   - The choices in the dialog box update based on the rule type.
4. Choose **Use a formula to determine which cells to format** in the *Select a Rule Type* list.
5. In the *Edit the Rule Description* area, type = in the *Format values where this formula is true* box.
   - You must start the formula with an equals sign (=).
   - The formula must be built so that the result is either TRUE or FALSE.
6. Type the formula.
   - Use relative cell references to the first row of data (Figure 4-14).
   - When you click to enter the cell reference, it is absolute; press **F4 (FN+F4)** to make it relative.
   - Text in the formula must be enclosed in quotation marks.
7. Click **Format** to open the *Format Cells* dialog box.
8. Build the format and click **OK**.
9. Click **OK** to close the *New Formatting Rule* dialog box.
   - Cells that meet the formula condition are formatted.

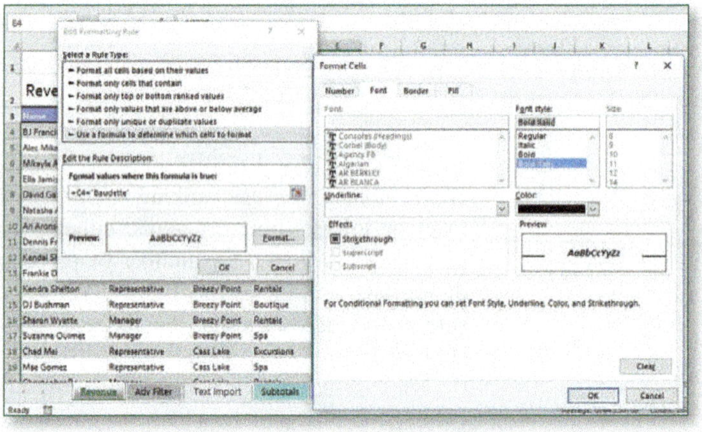

4-14 *New Formatting Rule* and *Format Cells* dialog boxes

Data Bars, Color Scales, and Icon Sets

Data visualization formats cells with icons, fill color, or shaded bars to distinguish values. Visualization formats highlight low, middle, or top values or compare the values to each other. Data visualization commands are *Data Bars, Color Scales,* and *Icon Sets.*

These three commands are part of the conditional formatting group, because they apply a rule for determining what is shown in the cell. You can choose which colors or icons are applied from the *Conditional Formatting* button [*Home* tab, *Styles* group]. When you select an option from the *Quick Analysis* button, however, a default choice is applied.

▸HOW TO: Format Data with Data Bars

1. Select the cell range.
2. Click the **Quick Analysis** button.
3. Choose **Formatting**.
   - *Data Bars* compare the value in each cell to the other values in the range by the length of the bar.
   - *Color Scales* use a variation of two or three colors to indicate low, middle, and high values.

- *Icon Sets* inserts icons that represent the upper, middle, or lower values of the cell range.

4. Choose **Data Bars** (Figure 4-15).
   - A default data bar style and color is applied.

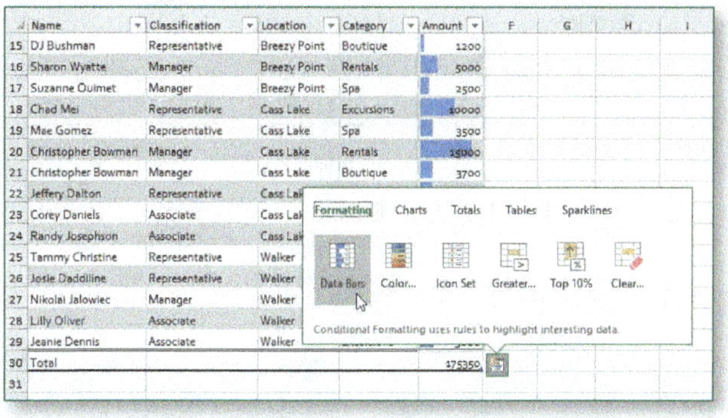

4-15 Setting *Data Bars* from the *Quick Analysis* button

Manage Conditional Formatting Rules

You can edit any conditional formatting rule, including data visualization commands, from the *Conditional Formatting Rules Manager* dialog box. From this dialog box, you can reset the range to be formatted, change the actual format, change the rule, or delete the rule.

If you select the formatted range before you start the *Manage Rules* command, the rule for that selection is shown in the *Conditional Formatting Rules Manager* dialog box. You can also show all the rules in the current or another sheet (Figure 4-16).

When you click **Edit Rule**, the *Edit Formatting Rule* dialog box opens. This dialog box is similar to the *New Formatting Rule* dialog box, and you set options the same way.

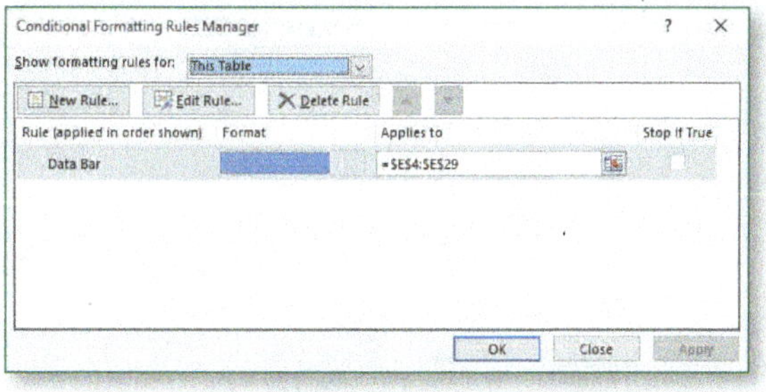

4-16 *Conditional Formatting Rules Manager* dialog box

HOW TO: Manage Conditional Formatting Rules

1. Select the formatted cell range.
2. Click the **Conditional Formatting** button [*Home* tab, *Styles* group].
3. Choose **Manage Rules**.
   - *Current Selection* is listed in the *Show formatting rules for* box.
   - Choose **This Worksheet** to list all rules in the worksheet.
4. Select the rule name to be modified.
5. Select **Edit Rule**.
   - The *Edit Formatting Rule* dialog box opens.
   - The current *Rule Description* displays.
   - You can select another rule type in the top half of the dialog box.
6. Make choices to change the rule in the *Edit the Rule Description* area.
   - The options depend on the rule type (Figure 4-17).
   - Click **Format** when available to open the *Format Cells* dialog box.

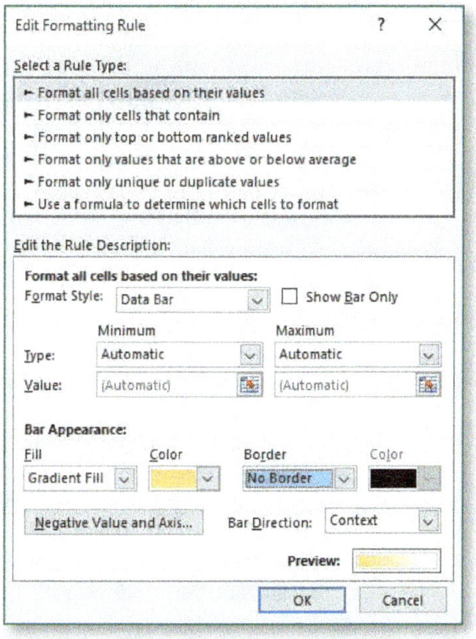

4-17 *Edit Formatting Rule* dialog box for data bars

7. Click **OK** to close the *Edit Formatting Rule* dialog box.
8. Click **OK** to close the *Conditional Formatting Rules Manger* dialog box.

You can clear conditional formatting from a selected range or from the entire sheet. For a selected range, click the **Quick Analysis** button and choose **Clear...** You can also choose **Clear Rules** from the *Conditional Formatting* button menu.

PAUSE & PRACTICE: EXCEL 4-1

For this project, you format data as a table, add a total row, and remove duplicate records. As you complete formulas on the sheet, you see structured references. You also set conditional formatting with data bars.

File Needed: ***ParadiseLakes-04.xlsx*** *[Student data files are available in the* Library *of your SIMnet account.]*
Completed Project File Name: ***[your initials] PP E4-1.xlsx***

1. Open the ***ParadiseLakes-04*** workbook from your student data files and save it as [your initials] PP E4-1.
2. Click the **Revenue** sheet tab.
3. Format data as an Excel table.
   a. Select cells **A3:E30**.
   b. Click the **Format as Table** button [*Home* tab, *Styles* group].
   c. Select **Table Style Medium 20** from the gallery.
   d. Verify that the **My table has headers** box is selected in the *Format As Table* dialog box.
   e. Click **OK**.
4. Add a total row to a table.
   a. Click a cell within the table.
   b. Select the **Total Row** box [*Table Tools Design* tab, *Table Style Options* group].
   c. Click cell **D31** and choose **Count** from the drop-down list.
   d. Select cells **E4:E31** and format them as **Currency**. Decrease the decimal two times to show zero decimal places (Figure 4-18).

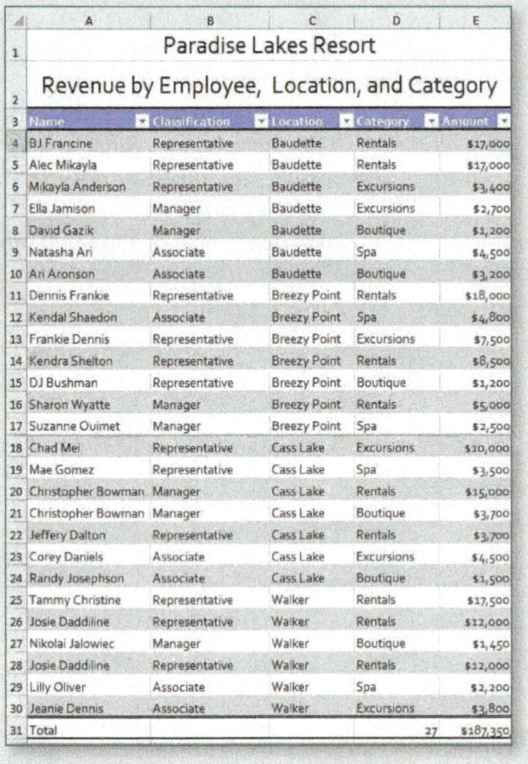

	A	B	C	D	E
1	Paradise Lakes Resort				
2	Revenue by Employee, Location, and Category				
3	Name	Classification	Location	Category	Amount
4	BJ Francine	Representative	Baudette	Rentals	$17,000
5	Alec Mikayla	Representative	Baudette	Rentals	$17,000
6	Mikayla Anderson	Representative	Baudette	Excursions	$3,400
7	Ella Jamison	Manager	Baudette	Excursions	$2,700
8	David Gazik	Manager	Baudette	Boutique	$1,200
9	Natasha Ari	Associate	Baudette	Spa	$4,500
10	Ari Aronson	Associate	Baudette	Boutique	$3,200
11	Dennis Frankie	Representative	Breezy Point	Rentals	$18,000
12	Kendal Shaedon	Associate	Breezy Point	Spa	$4,800
13	Frankie Dennis	Representative	Breezy Point	Excursions	$7,500
14	Kendra Shelton	Representative	Breezy Point	Rentals	$8,500
15	DJ Bushman	Representative	Breezy Point	Boutique	$1,200
16	Sharon Wyatte	Manager	Breezy Point	Rentals	$5,000
17	Suzanne Ouimet	Manager	Breezy Point	Spa	$2,500
18	Chad Mei	Representative	Cass Lake	Excursions	$10,000
19	Mae Gomez	Representative	Cass Lake	Spa	$3,500
20	Christopher Bowman	Manager	Cass Lake	Rentals	$15,000
21	Christopher Bowman	Manager	Cass Lake	Boutique	$3,700
22	Jeffery Dalton	Representative	Cass Lake	Rentals	$3,700
23	Corey Daniels	Associate	Cass Lake	Excursions	$4,500
24	Randy Josephson	Associate	Cass Lake	Boutique	$1,500
25	Tammy Christine	Representative	Walker	Rentals	$17,500
26	Josie Daddiline	Representative	Walker	Rentals	$12,000
27	Nikolai Jalowiec	Manager	Walker	Boutique	$1,450
28	Josie Daddiline	Representative	Walker	Rentals	$12,000
29	Lilly Oliver	Associate	Walker	Spa	$2,200
30	Jeanie Dennis	Associate	Walker	Excursions	$3,800
31	Total			27	$187,350

4-18 Data formatted as a table

5. Remove duplicate rows in a table.
   a. Click a cell within table.
   b. Click the **Remove Duplicates** button [*Table Tools Design* tab, *Tools* group].
   c. Click **Unselect All** to deselect all the boxes.
   d. Select the **Name** box and the **Amount** box. When you can look for duplicate data in specific columns, you can speed up search activities.
   e. Click **OK** in the *Remove Duplicates* dialog box. There is one record that will be removed, the one for Josie Daddiline. The records for Christopher Bowman are not duplicated in the selected columns.
   f. Click **OK** in the message box.

6. Apply conditional formatting using data bars.
   a. Select cells **E4:E29**.
   b. Click the **Conditional Formatting** button [*Home* tab, *Styles* group].
   c. Point to **Data Bars** to see its menu.
   d. Select **Blue Data Bar** in the *Gradient Fill* group (Figure 4-19).

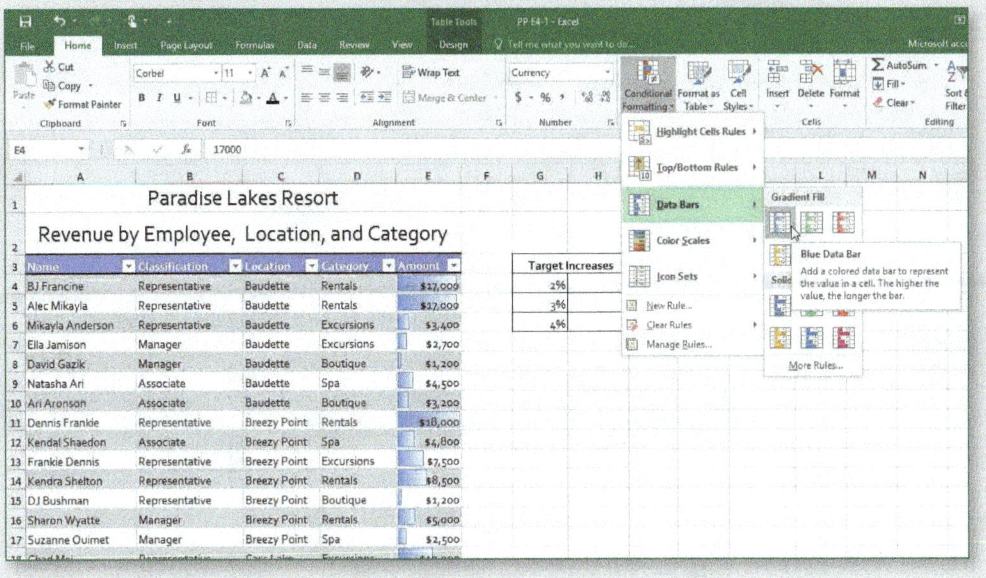

4-19 Choose a gradient fill for data bars

7. Manage conditional formatting rules.
   a. Select cells **E3:E29**.
   b. Click the **Conditional Formatting** button [*Home* tab, *Styles* group].
   c. Choose **Manage Rules**.
   d. Click **Edit Rule**.
   e. Click the **Color** arrow for **Fill** in the *Bar Appearance* area.
   f. Choose **Gold, Accent 3**.
   g. Click the arrow for **Border** in the *Bar Appearance* area.
   h. Choose **No Border** (Figure 4-20).
   i. Click **OK** to close the *Edit Formatting Rule* dialog box.
   j. Click **OK** to close the *Conditional Formatting Rules Manager* dialog box.
8. Refer to a structured reference in a formula.
   a. Select cell **H4** and type = to start a formula.
   b. Click cell **E30** to insert a structured reference to the total in the Amount column.
   c. Type * (1+, click cell **G4**, and type) to calculate a new total that reflects a 2% increase (Figure 4-21).

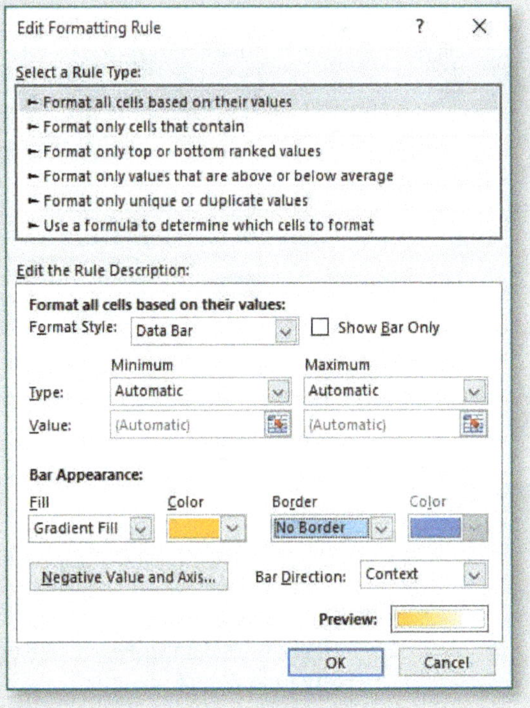

4-20 Edit the rule for data bars

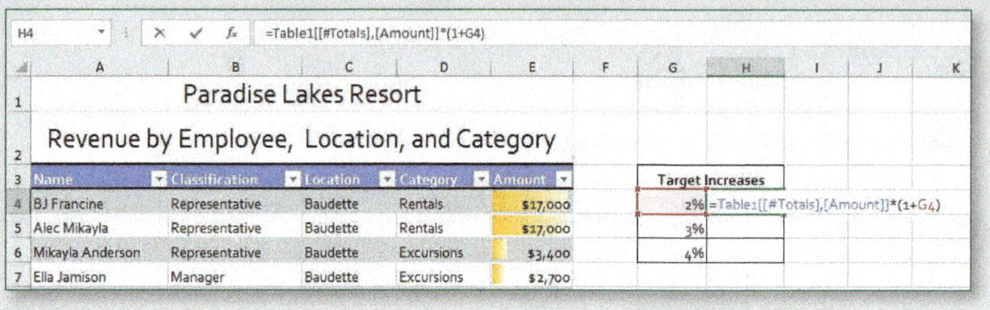

4-21 Structured reference in a formula

d. Press **Enter**. The target total is $178,857.

e. Copy the formula to cells **H5:H6**.

9. Save and close the workbook (Figure 4-22).

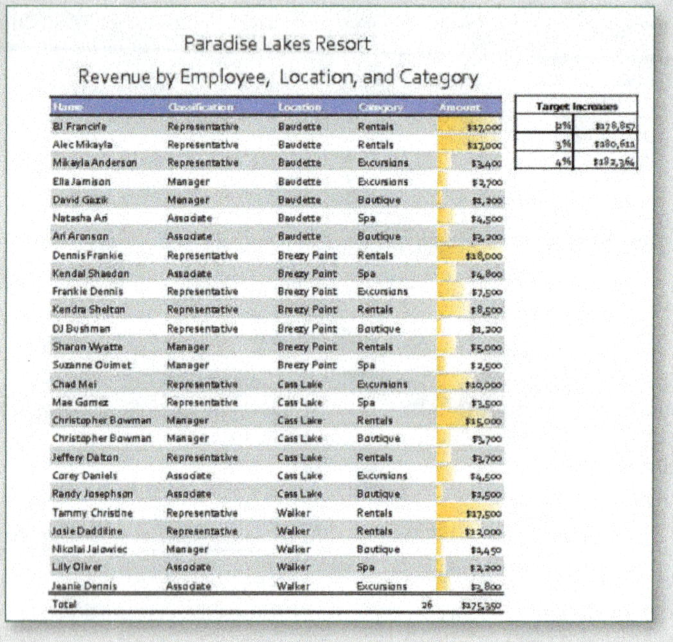

4-22 Completed PP E 4-1

SLO 4.3

Sorting Data

Sorting is the process of arranging rows of data in an identified order. For Paradise Lakes Resort, you can arrange the revenue table by employee classification to compare results for a particular job title. Or you may want to order the rows from highest amount to lowest.

You sort data in ascending or descending order. ***Ascending*** order sorts data alphabetically from A to Z or numerically from smallest to largest value. In a ***descending*** sort, data are arranged alphabetically Z to A or numerically from largest to smallest value.

Sort Options

To be sorted, data must be organized in rows and columns like an Excel table, but it need not be formatted as a table. In addition to text or number sorting, you can sort data by fill color, font color, or cell icon from *Conditional Formatting*.

The *Sort & Filter* button on the *Home* tab in the *Editing* group lists *A to Z* sort, *Z to A* sort, and *Custom Sort* (multiple columns) commands. The same commands are available in the *Sort & Filter* group on the *Data* tab as separate buttons.

Sort Data by One Column

When data has a header row followed by rows of data with at least one empty row above and below the data, you can click any cell in the column you want to sort and choose a sort command. Excel recognizes and sorts the entire dataset.

Data to be sorted can be text, numbers, or dates. Dates are treated as values. An ascending sort (smallest to largest) arranges dates so that the earliest date is first. A descending date sort organizes the data so that the most current date is first.

You can undo a sort task by clicking the **Undo** button [*Quick Access* toolbar]. You can also sort data many times to arrange it in your preferred order.

▶ HOW TO: Sort Data by a Single Column

1. Select a cell in the column to be used for sorting.
   - Click a cell with data, not the column header.
2. Click the **Sort A to Z** button [*Data* tab, *Sort & Filter* group] (Figure 4-23).
   - The records are arranged in alphabetical or smallest-to-largest order based on the first character in each cell in the column.
   - If the first character in an alphanumeric column is a value or special character, that record is sorted at the top.
3. Click the **Sort Z to A** button [*Data* tab, *Sort & Filter* group].
   - The records are arranged in reverse alphabetical or largest-to-smallest order based on the first character.
   - If the first character in an alphanumeric column is a value or special character, that record is sorted at the bottom.

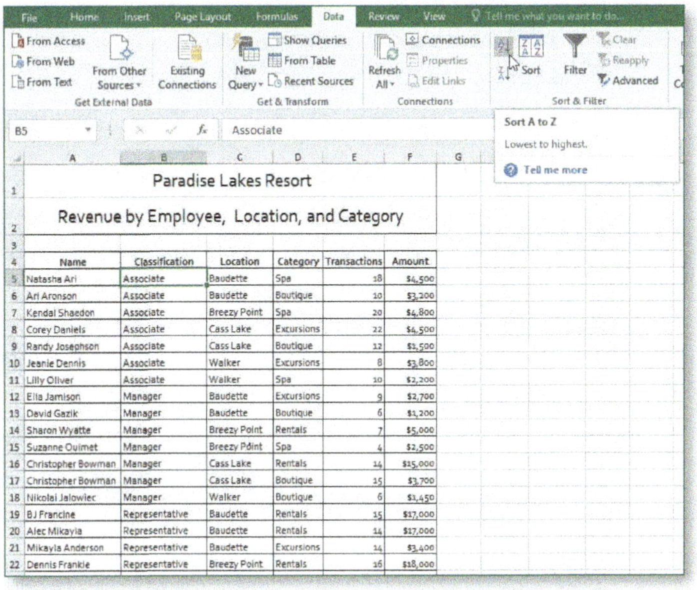

4-23 "Classification" column sorted A to Z

ANOTHER WAY

To sort by a single column, right-click a cell in the column, choose **Sort**, and then choose the type of sort.

Sort Data by Multiple Columns

You can sort data by more than one column. An example of data that is often sorted by two columns is a list with cities in one column and states or provinces in another. Such data is sorted by state so that Alabama is before Arizona, and within a particular state, the cities are also sorted alphabetically. When you use the *Sort & Filter* button [*Home* tab, *Editing* group] or a sort button on the *Data* tab, you sort first by the least important field. You can also use the *Sort* dialog box which opens when you click the **Sort** button [*Data* tab, *Sort & Filter* group] or when you choose **Custom Sort** from the *Sort & Filter* button options.

The data in Figure 4-24 are sorted by two columns, classification and amount. When you use the *Sort* dialog box, you set the *Classification* field first and then the *Amount*. When you use the *Sort & Filter* button, you sort first by the *Amount* and then by the *Classification*.

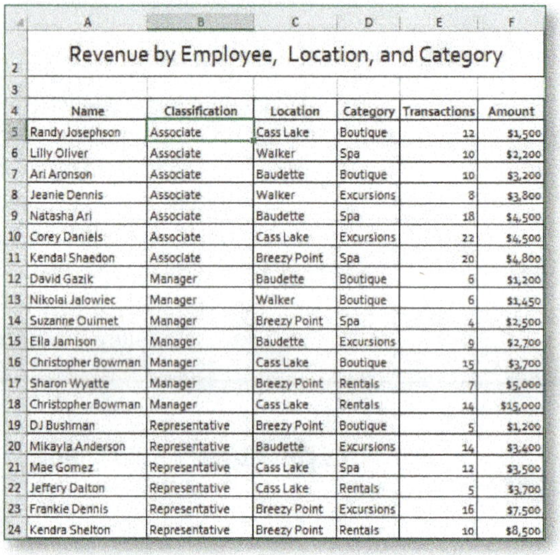

	A	B	C	D	E	F
2	Revenue by Employee, Location, and Category					
3						
4	Name	Classification	Location	Category	Transactions	Amount
5	Randy Josephson	Associate	Cass Lake	Boutique	12	$1,500
6	Lilly Oliver	Associate	Walker	Spa	10	$2,200
7	Ari Aronson	Associate	Baudette	Boutique	10	$3,200
8	Jeanie Dennis	Associate	Walker	Excursions	8	$3,800
9	Natasha Ari	Associate	Baudette	Spa	18	$4,500
10	Corey Daniels	Associate	Cass Lake	Excursions	22	$4,500
11	Kendal Shaedon	Associate	Breezy Point	Spa	20	$4,800
12	David Gazik	Manager	Baudette	Boutique	6	$1,200
13	Nikolai Jalowiec	Manager	Walker	Boutique	6	$1,450
14	Suzanne Ouimet	Manager	Breezy Point	Spa	4	$2,500
15	Ella Jamison	Manager	Baudette	Excursions	9	$2,700
16	Christopher Bowman	Manager	Cass Lake	Boutique	15	$3,700
17	Sharon Wyatte	Manager	Breezy Point	Rentals	7	$5,000
18	Christopher Bowman	Manager	Cass Lake	Rentals	14	$15,000
19	DJ Bushman	Representative	Breezy Point	Boutique	5	$1,200
20	Mikayla Anderson	Representative	Baudette	Excursions	14	$3,400
21	Mae Gomez	Representative	Cass Lake	Spa	12	$3,500
22	Jeffery Dalton	Representative	Cass Lake	Rentals	5	$3,700
23	Frankie Dennis	Representative	Breezy Point	Excursions	16	$7,500
24	Kendra Shelton	Representative	Breezy Point	Rentals	10	$8,500

4-24 Data sorted by "Classification" and "Amount"

▸ HOW TO: Sort Data by Multiple Columns

1. Select a cell in the range to be sorted.
   - Click a cell with data, not the column header.
2. Click the **Sort** button [*Data* tab, *Sort & Filter* group].
   - The *Sort* dialog box opens.
   - The range is highlighted in the worksheet.
   - You can click the **Sort & Filter** button [*Home* tab, *Editing* group] and select **Custom Sort**.
3. Select the **My data has headers** box if your data has a header row.
4. Click the **Sort by** arrow and select the column heading for the first sort level.
5. Click the **Sort On** arrow.
   - Use *Values* for text or numbers.
   - If the data has a cell attribute such as a font color, select the name of the attribute.
6. Click the **Order** arrow and choose a sort option.
   - For columns with numbers or dates, the options are *Smallest to Largest* and *Largest to Smallest.*
   - The *Custom List* option provides special sorting orders for days of the week and months of the year so that data is sorted chronologically.
7. Click **Add Level** to add a second sort column.
8. Click the **Then by** arrow and select the second column heading.
9. Click the **Sort On** arrow and choose **Values** or an attribute.
10. Click the **Order** arrow and choose a sort order (Figure 4-25).
    - Click the **Options** button in the *Sort* dialog box to specify case-sensitive sorting or to change the orientation of ascending and descending sorts.
11. Click **OK**.

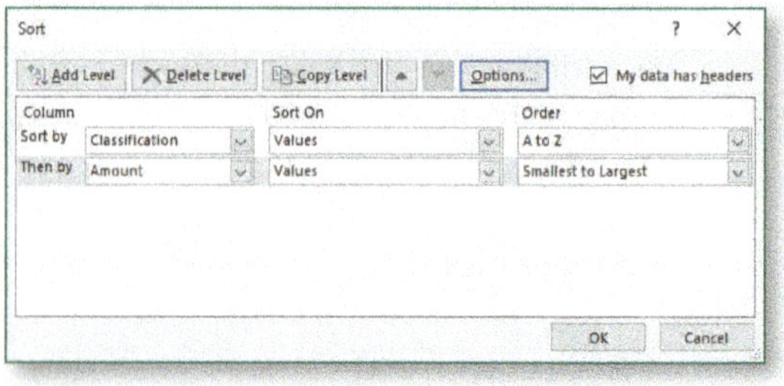

4-25 *Sort* dialog box

Sort Data by Cell Attribute

An ***attribute*** is a setting or property. Cell attributes that can be used for sorting are font color, fill color, and cell icon. These choices are options for the *Sort On* choice in the *Sort* dialog box, and they are listed when you choose **Sort** from a cell's context menu.

When you sort by font or cell color, the *Order* choices are the colors used in the column. You choose a color and set its position in the sorted column.

A cell icon is the symbol placed in a cell by conditional formatting. Column E in Figure 4-26 has an icon set sorted with hollow icons on the top.

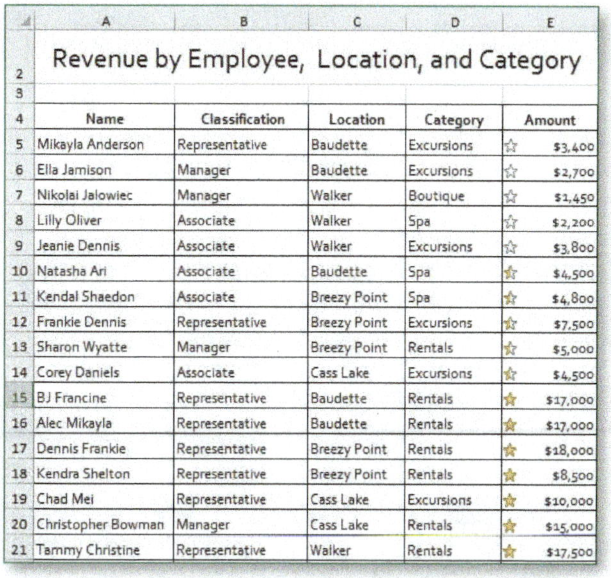

	A	B	C	D	E
2	Revenue by Employee, Location, and Category				
3					
4	Name	Classification	Location	Category	Amount
5	Mikayla Anderson	Representative	Baudette	Excursions	$3,400
6	Ella Jamison	Manager	Baudette	Excursions	$2,700
7	Nikolai Jalowiec	Manager	Walker	Boutique	$1,450
8	Lilly Oliver	Associate	Walker	Spa	$2,200
9	Jeanie Dennis	Associate	Walker	Excursions	$3,800
10	Natasha Ari	Associate	Baudette	Spa	$4,500
11	Kendal Shaedon	Associate	Breezy Point	Spa	$4,800
12	Frankie Dennis	Representative	Breezy Point	Excursions	$7,500
13	Sharon Wyatte	Manager	Breezy Point	Rentals	$5,000
14	Corey Daniels	Associate	Cass Lake	Excursions	$4,500
15	BJ Francine	Representative	Baudette	Rentals	$17,000
16	Alec Mikayla	Representative	Baudette	Rentals	$17,000
17	Dennis Frankie	Representative	Breezy Point	Rentals	$18,000
18	Kendra Shelton	Representative	Breezy Point	Rentals	$8,500
19	Chad Mei	Representative	Cass Lake	Excursions	$10,000
20	Christopher Bowman	Manager	Cass Lake	Rentals	$15,000
21	Tammy Christine	Representative	Walker	Rentals	$17,500

4-26 Data sorted by the cell icon in "Amount" column

▸ HOW TO: Sort Data by Cell Attribute

1. Select a cell in the column to sort.
2. Click the **Sort** button [*Data* tab, *Sort & Filter* group].
   - The *Sort* dialog box opens.
   - You can also click the **Sort & Filter** button [*Home* tab, *Editing* group] and select **Custom Sort**.
3. Select the for **My data has headers** box if the data has a header row.
4. Click the **Sort by** arrow and select the column heading.
5. Click the **Sort On** arrow and choose the attribute.
   - The column must have data with different font colors, cells with different fill colors, or cell icons.
6. Click the leftmost **Order** arrow and choose a color or icon.
7. Click the rightmost **Order** arrow and choose **On Top** or **On Bottom**.
8. Click **Add Level**.
9. Click the **Then by** arrow and select the same column heading.
10. Click the **Sort On** arrow and choose the attribute.
11. Click the leftmost **Order** arrow and choose a color or icon.
12. Click the rightmost **Order** arrow and choose **On Top** or **On Bottom** (Figure 4-27).
    - Add and define as many sort levels as there are colors or icons to be sorted.
13. Click **OK**.

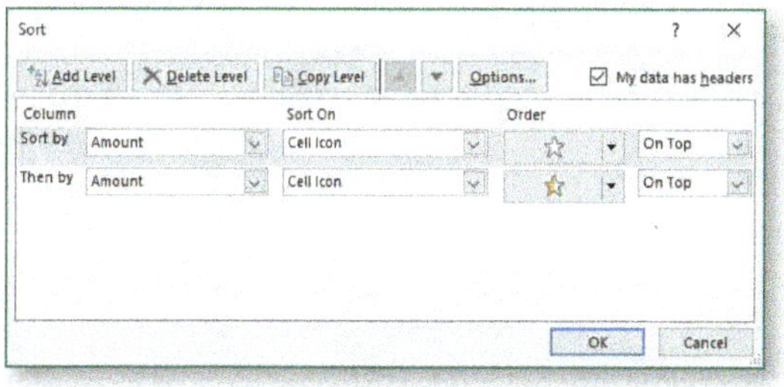

4-27 Cell icon order in the *Sort* dialog box

MORE INFO

To sort by icon sets, you can right-click a cell with the icon that you want first and select **Sort** and then **Put Selected Cell Icon on Top**.

Sort Data in an Excel Table

When data is formatted as a table, you can sort from the *AutoFilter* arrows with each label in the header row. Sort choices are listed at the top of the pane that opens when you click an *AutoFilter* arrow.

HOW TO: Sort Data in an Excel Table

1. Click the **AutoFilter** arrow for the column heading that represents the lowest sort level.
   - The *AutoFilter* pane lists sort choices at the top.
2. Choose **Sort A to Z** or **Sort Smallest to Largest** (Figure 4-28).
   - *Sort Smallest to Largest* appears for numeric data.
   - The table is sorted by the column.
3. Click the **AutoFilter** arrow for the column heading that represents the top sort level.
4. Choose **Sort A to Z** or **Sort Smallest to Largest**.
   - The table maintains the sort order from the first selected column within the sorted data for the top-level column.

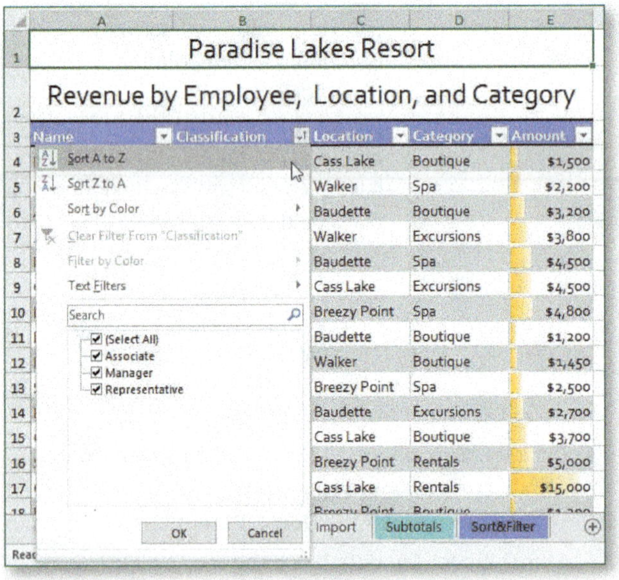

4-28 ***AutoFilter* arrow sort choices**

SLO 4.4

Filtering Data

You can usually work more efficiently when you filter large amounts of data to show rows of importance to your task. You can, for example, filter data to show records for the year, the month, the individual, the product, or similar grouping. When you filter data, information that does not meet the requirements is temporarily hidden. A filter specifies which data are shown and which are hidden.

AutoFilters

In list-type data or an Excel table, the *Filter* button [*Data* tab, *Sort & Filter* group] displays or hides the *AutoFilter* arrow for each label in the header row. When you click an *AutoFilter* arrow, a pane displays sort options, filter types based on the data type, and check boxes for every piece of data. You can select boxes to mark which records display, or you can build a filter.

▸ HOW TO: Display and Use AutoFilters

1. Select a cell in the list.
2. Click the **Filter** button [*Data* tab, *Sort & Filter* group].
   - *AutoFilter* arrows appear in the header row with each label.
   - *AutoFilter* arrows display by default in an Excel table.
3. Click the **AutoFilter** arrow for the column used for filtering.
   - All items are selected and displayed in the data.
   - Filter options depend on the type of data in the column.
4. Click the **(Select All)** box to remove all check marks.
5. Select the box for each item to be shown (Figure 4-29).
6. Click **OK**.
   - Records that meet the criteria display with row headings in blue.
   - Records that do not meet the criteria and their row numbers are hidden.
   - A filter symbol appears with the column *AutoFilter* arrow.

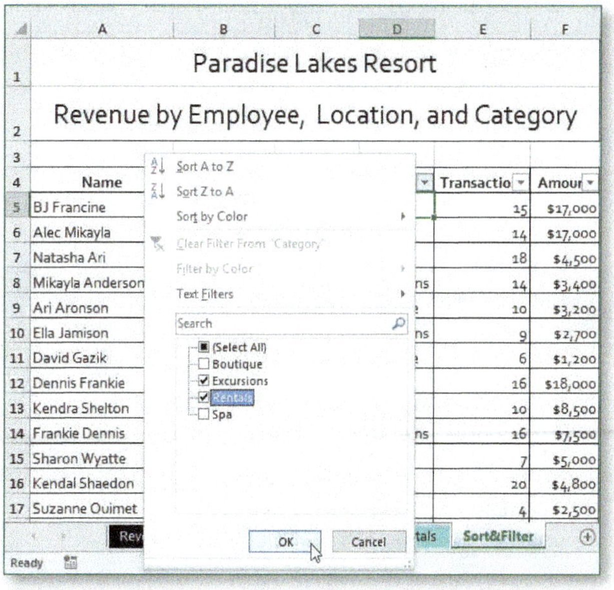

4-29 ***AutoFilter*** **for "Category" column**

ANOTHER WAY

An *AutoFilter* arrow and a *Slicer* window display the same results.

To remove a filter and display the complete list, click the **AutoFilter** arrow for the column and choose **Clear Filter From (ColumnName)**. You can also click the **Clear** button in the *Sort & Filter* group on the *Data* tab.

Custom AutoFilter

A ***custom AutoFilter*** is criteria that you build in a dialog box. A custom *AutoFilter* gives you more options for how rows display, because you can use multiple criteria with *AND* and *OR*. For a column with alphanumeric data, *Text Filters* are available, and there are *Number Filters* and *Date Filters* for columns with those types of data. Operators use common words such as *Equals, Begins With,* or *Contains* (Figure 4-30).

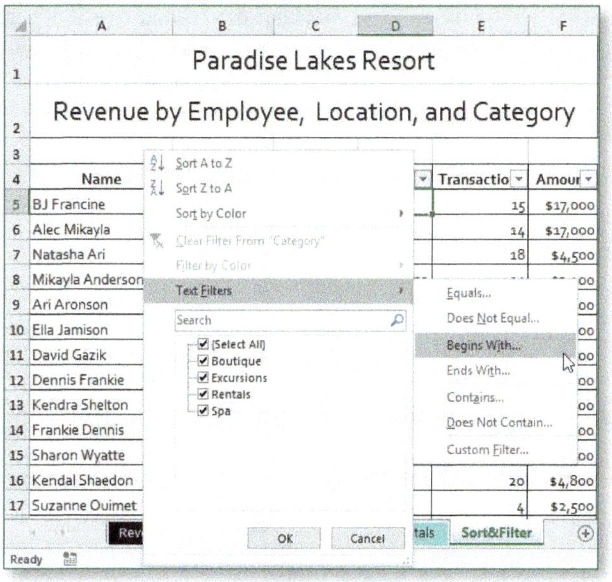

4-30 Text filters for a custom ***AutoFilter***

▸ HOW TO: Create a Custom Text AutoFilter

1. Select a cell in the data to filter.
2. Click the **Filter** button [*Data* tab, *Sort & Filter* group] to display *AutoFilter* arrows for the header row.
3. Click the **AutoFilter** arrow for the column used for filtering.
4. Select **Text Filters** and choose an operator.
   - The *Custom AutoFilter* dialog box opens.
5. Type criteria for the first operator in the box on the right.
   - You can also select a value from the drop-down list.
   - You can use wildcard characters.
6. Click the **And** or **Or** radio button.
   - *Or* conditions include rows that match either criteria.
   - *And* conditions are more restrictive and require that both criteria be met.
7. Click the arrow to choose a second operator.
   - A second operator is optional.
8. Type or select criteria for the second operator (Figure 4-31).
9. Click **OK**.
   - Rows in the data are filtered.

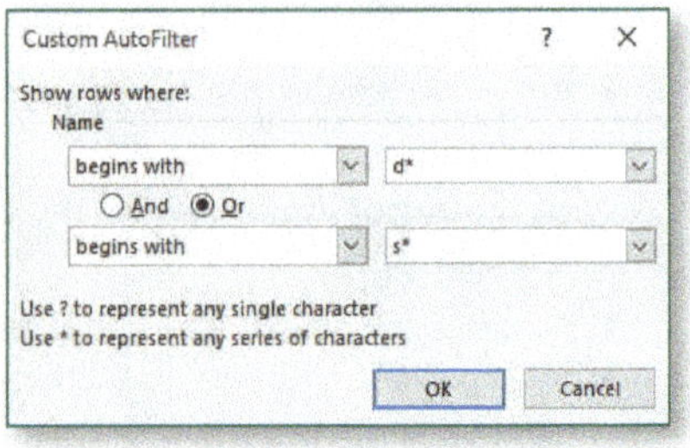

4-31 *Custom AutoFilter* dialog box

Advanced Filter

For an *Advanced Filter,* you build a criteria range separate from the data and type the conditions within that range. You can show the results in the data range, or you can display filtered data in another location on the sheet. Using another location for results allows you to create separate reports with filtered rows while the main list displays all data. An *Advanced Filter* requires more set-up work but allows you to apply more complex filters. You can even use a formula in the criteria.

A ***criteria range*** is at least two rows in which the first row must use the same column names as the data; the second row is where criteria is entered. You need not use all column names, and you can use more than one row for criteria. You can create a criteria range in empty rows anywhere on the worksheet or on another sheet. In Figure 4-32, the criteria range is cells G5:K6.

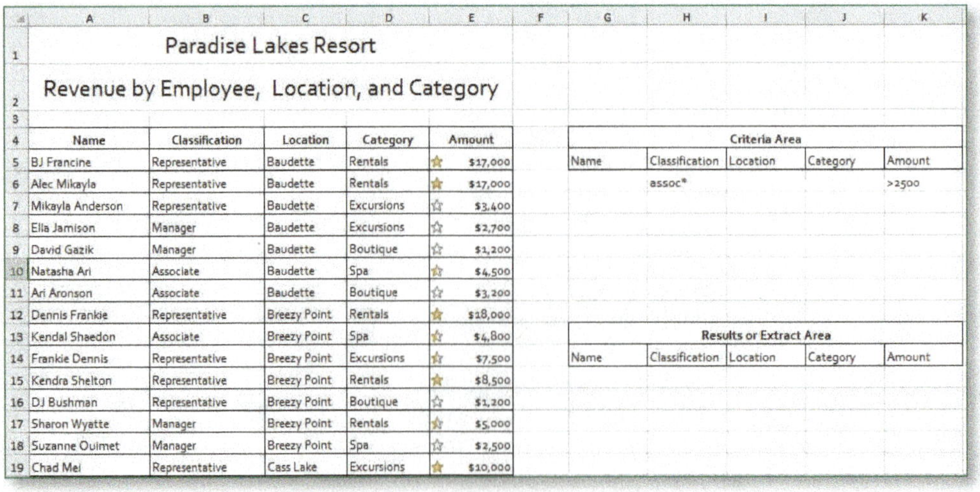

	A	B	C	D	E	F	G	H	I	J	K
1	Paradise Lakes Resort										
2	Revenue by Employee, Location, and Category										
3											
4	Name	Classification	Location	Category	Amount		Criteria Area				
5	BJ Francine	Representative	Baudette	Rentals	$17,000		Name	Classification	Location	Category	Amount
6	Alec Mikayla	Representative	Baudette	Rentals	$17,000			assoc*			>2500
7	Mikayla Anderson	Representative	Baudette	Excursions	$3,400						
8	Ella Jamison	Manager	Baudette	Excursions	$2,700						
9	David Gazik	Manager	Baudette	Boutique	$1,200						
10	Natasha Ari	Associate	Baudette	Spa	$4,500						
11	Ari Aronson	Associate	Baudette	Boutique	$3,200						
12	Dennis Frankie	Representative	Breezy Point	Rentals	$18,000						
13	Kendal Shaedon	Associate	Breezy Point	Spa	$4,800		Results or Extract Area				
14	Frankie Dennis	Representative	Breezy Point	Excursions	$7,500		Name	Classification	Location	Category	Amount
15	Kendra Shelton	Representative	Breezy Point	Rentals	$8,500						
16	DJ Bushman	Representative	Breezy Point	Boutique	$1,200						
17	Sharon Wyatte	Manager	Breezy Point	Rentals	$5,000						
18	Suzanne Ouimet	Manager	Breezy Point	Spa	$2,500						
19	Chad Mei	Representative	Cass Lake	Excursions	$10,000						

4-32 *Advanced Filter* set up

Multiple rows below the header row in the criteria range set *AND* or *OR* conditions. If you enter criteria on the same row, they are treated as *AND* conditions. In Figure 4-32, "assoc*" in cell H6 and ">2500" in cell K6 are criteria. Both criteria must be met for a record to be displayed. For an *OR* condition, use a second (or third) row in the criteria range. An *OR* filter displays a record if any one of the requirements is met.

To show filtered results in another location, you also create an ***output*** or ***extract range***. You specify one row for this range, and it should include the same column headings as the data. In Figure 4-32, the extract range is cells G14:K14. Filtered rows are copied below these headings and take up as many rows as necessary. The output range must be on the same worksheet as the data, but you can copy the results to another sheet or another workbook.

HOW TO: Create an Advanced Filter

1. Select labels in the header row for fields that will be used for filtering.
   - You can copy all the labels in the header row if preferred.
2. Copy the labels to a *Criteria* area.
   - The criteria area can be on the same or another sheet in the workbook.
   - If the criteria range is above the data, leave at least one blank row between it and the data.
3. Copy the labels again to an *Extract* area.
   - The output or extract area must be on the same sheet as the data.
   - Leave blank rows below the labels for the filtered results.
4. Type criteria in the criteria range.
   - Criteria is not case sensitive.
   - You can use wildcard characters in the criteria.
5. Click a cell in the data range.
6. Click the **Advanced** button [*Data* tab, *Sort & Filter* group].
   - The *Advanced Filter* dialog box opens.
7. Select **Copy to another location** In the *Action* group.
8. Verify or select the range (including the header row) in the *List range* box.
   - If the data range is named, press **F3 (FN+F3)** and select the name.
9. Select the criteria cell range with its header row in the *Criteria range* box.
   - If the criteria range is named, press **F3 (FN+F3)** and select the name.
   - You can type cell references to identify the criteria range.
10. Select the extract range in the *Copy to* box.
    - This range is the row of labels.
11. Click **OK** (Figure 4-33).

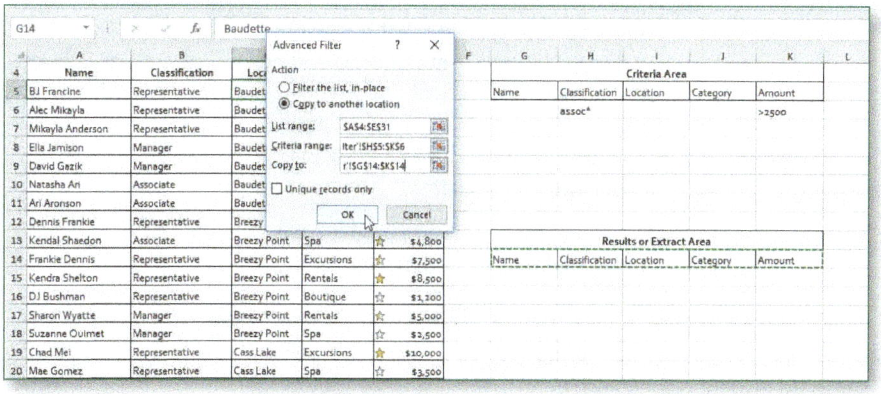

4-33 *Advanced Filter* dialog box

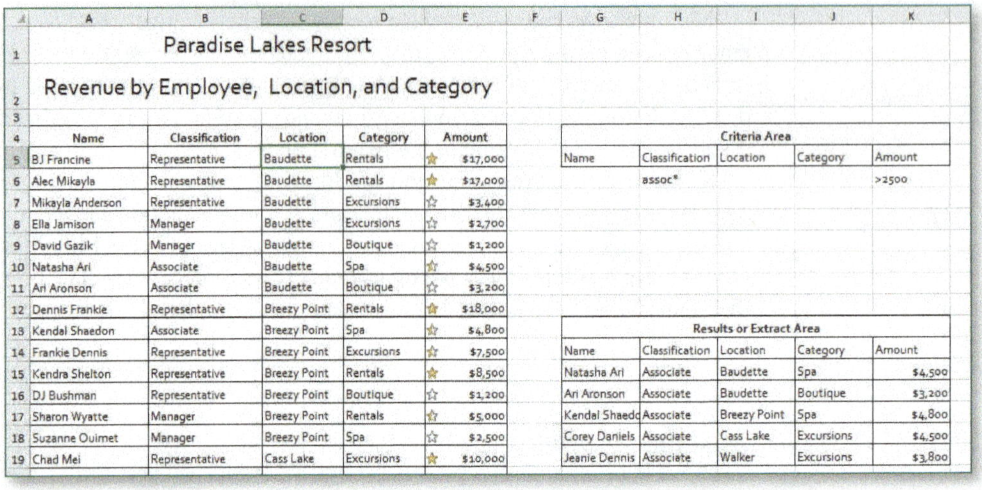

	A	B	C	D	E	F	G	H	I	J	K
1	Paradise Lakes Resort										
2	Revenue by Employee, Location, and Category										
3											
4	Name	Classification	Location	Category	Amount		Criteria Area				
5	BJ Francine	Representative	Baudette	Rentals	$17,000		Name	Classification	Location	Category	Amount
6	Alec Mikayla	Representative	Baudette	Rentals	$17,000			assoc*			>2500
7	Mikayla Anderson	Representative	Baudette	Excursions	$3,400						
8	Ella Jamison	Manager	Baudette	Excursions	$2,700						
9	David Gazik	Manager	Baudette	Boutique	$1,200						
10	Natasha Ari	Associate	Baudette	Spa	$4,500						
11	Ari Aronson	Associate	Baudette	Boutique	$3,200						
12	Dennis Frankie	Representative	Breezy Point	Rentals	$18,000						
13	Kendal Shaedon	Associate	Breezy Point	Spa	$4,800		Results or Extract Area				
14	Frankie Dennis	Representative	Breezy Point	Excursions	$7,500		Name	Classification	Location	Category	Amount
15	Kendra Shelton	Representative	Breezy Point	Rentals	$8,500		Natasha Ari	Associate	Baudette	Spa	$4,500
16	DJ Bushman	Representative	Breezy Point	Boutique	$1,200		Ari Aronson	Associate	Baudette	Boutique	$3,200
17	Sharon Wyatte	Manager	Breezy Point	Rentals	$5,000		Kendal Shaedo	Associate	Breezy Point	Spa	$4,800
18	Suzanne Ouimet	Manager	Breezy Point	Spa	$2,500		Corey Daniels	Associate	Cass Lake	Excursions	$4,500
19	Chad Mei	Representative	Cass Lake	Excursions	$10,000		Jeanie Dennis	Associate	Walker	Excursions	$3,800

4-34 ***Advanced Filter*** **results copied to another location**

- Filtered rows are copied to the output range below the copied labels (Figure 4-34).

> **MORE INFO**
>
> Enter < > as criteria to display records that have any entry in the column. Enter = as criteria to show rows that have no entry in the column.

SLO 4.5

Using Subtotals, Groups, and Outlines

A ***subtotal*** is a summary row for data that is grouped. A ***group*** is a set of data that has the same entry in one or more columns. You can see groups by "Location" with a subtotal in the "Amount" column in Figure 4-35. An ***outline*** is a summary that groups records so that individual groups can be displayed or hidden from view. These three features are Excel commands that make it easy to organize and calculate results for worksheets with large sets of data.

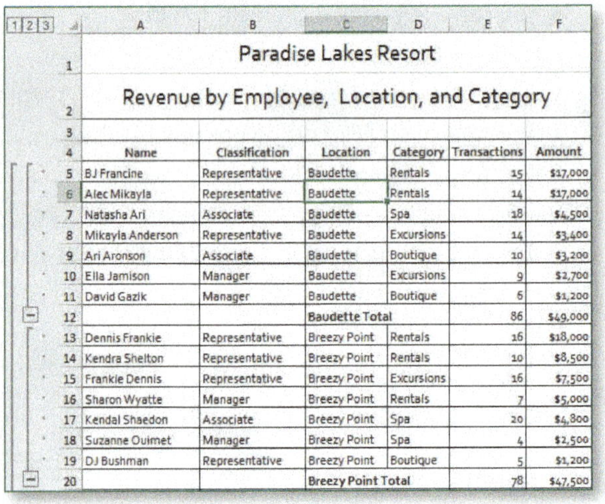

	A	B	C	D	E	F
1	Paradise Lakes Resort					
2	Revenue by Employee, Location, and Category					
3						
4	Name	Classification	Location	Category	Transactions	Amount
5	BJ Francine	Representative	Baudette	Rentals	15	$17,000
6	Alec Mikayla	Representative	Baudette	Rentals	14	$17,000
7	Natasha Ari	Associate	Baudette	Spa	18	$4,500
8	Mikayla Anderson	Representative	Baudette	Excursions	14	$3,400
9	Ari Aronson	Associate	Baudette	Boutique	10	$3,200
10	Ella Jamison	Manager	Baudette	Excursions	9	$2,700
11	David Gazik	Manager	Baudette	Boutique	6	$1,200
12			Baudette Total		86	$49,000
13	Dennis Frankie	Representative	Breezy Point	Rentals	16	$18,000
14	Kendra Shelton	Representative	Breezy Point	Rentals	10	$8,500
15	Frankie Dennis	Representative	Breezy Point	Excursions	16	$7,500
16	Sharon Wyatte	Manager	Breezy Point	Rentals	7	$5,000
17	Kendal Shaedon	Associate	Breezy Point	Spa	20	$4,800
18	Suzanne Ouimet	Manager	Breezy Point	Spa	4	$2,500
19	DJ Bushman	Representative	Breezy Point	Boutique	5	$1,200
20			Breezy Point Total		78	$47,500

4-35 Grouped rows with a subtotal in "Amount" column

The Subtotal Command

The ***Subtotal*** command in the *Outline* group on the *Data* tab inserts summary rows for a sorted list and formats the data as an *outline.* The *Subtotal* command is available for a normal range of cells, not an Excel table. The *Subtotal* command includes *SUM, AVERAGE, MAX,* or *MIN* as well as other *Statistical* functions.

To use the *Subtotal* command, the data should have a header row with data rows following, and you must sort the rows by the main field (column) to be summarized or totaled. To display revenue numbers by location, for example, sort the data by location. The *Subtotal* command groups the rows by this field but can show subtotals for any column.

> **MORE INFO**
>
> If data is formatted as an Excel table, convert it to a normal cell range [*Table Tools Design* tab, *Tools* group] to use the *Subtotal* command.

HOW TO: Display Subtotals

1. Sort the data by the column by which subtotals will be calculated.
2. Click a cell in the data range.
3. Click the **Subtotal** button [*Data* tab, *Outline* group].
   - When data has a header row followed by data rows, the range is selected.
4. Click the **At each change in** arrow.
5. Choose the column heading name that was used for sorting.
   - Subtotals need not be shown for this column.
6. Click the **Use function** arrow and select the function.
7. In the **Add subtotal to** list, select each field that should display a subtotal.
   - Make sure the function applies to the column data type; for example, do not use *Sum* for a text column.
8. Choose **Replace current subtotals**.
   - If the range already has subtotals, they are replaced.
9. Choose **Summary below data** (Figure 4-36).
   - The "Summary" row can be placed above the data if you prefer.
   - You can also allow a group to split across pages.
   - You can remove subtotals from this dialog box.
10. Click **OK** (Figure 4-37).
    - A subtotal row appears below each group.
    - A grand total appears after the last row of data.
    - Outline buttons appear to the left of the column and row headings.
    - The outline is expanded, showing all details.

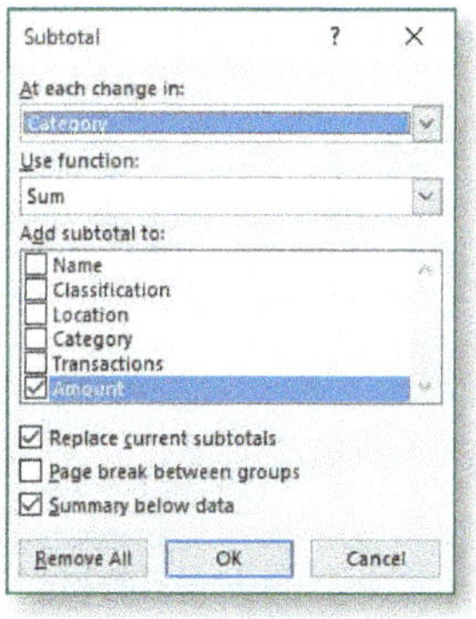

4-36 *Subtotal* dialog box

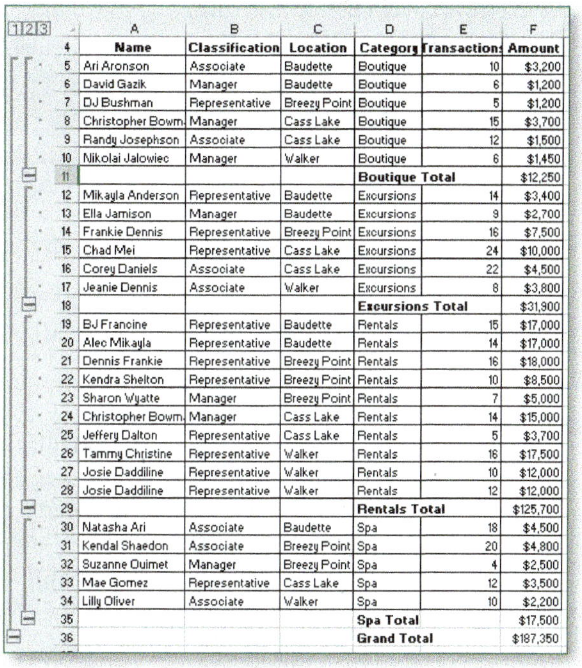

	A	B	C	D	E	F
4	Name	Classification	Location	Category	Transactions	Amount
5	Ari Aronson	Associate	Baudette	Boutique	10	$3,200
6	David Gazik	Manager	Baudette	Boutique	6	$1,200
7	DJ Bushman	Representative	Breezy Point	Boutique	5	$1,200
8	Christopher Bowm	Manager	Cass Lake	Boutique	15	$3,700
9	Randy Josephson	Associate	Cass Lake	Boutique	12	$1,500
10	Nikolai Jalowiec	Manager	Walker	Boutique	6	$1,450
11				Boutique Total		$12,250
12	Mikayla Anderson	Representative	Baudette	Excursions	14	$3,400
13	Ella Jamison	Manager	Baudette	Excursions	9	$2,700
14	Frankie Dennis	Representative	Breezy Point	Excursions	16	$7,500
15	Chad Mei	Representative	Cass Lake	Excursions	24	$10,000
16	Corey Daniels	Associate	Cass Lake	Excursions	22	$4,500
17	Jeanie Dennis	Associate	Walker	Excursions	8	$3,800
18				Excursions Total		$31,900
19	BJ Francine	Representative	Baudette	Rentals	15	$17,000
20	Alec Mikayla	Representative	Baudette	Rentals	14	$17,000
21	Dennis Frankie	Representative	Breezy Point	Rentals	16	$18,000
22	Kendra Shelton	Representative	Breezy Point	Rentals	10	$8,500
23	Sharon Wyatte	Manager	Breezy Point	Rentals	7	$5,000
24	Christopher Bowm	Manager	Cass Lake	Rentals	14	$15,000
25	Jeffery Dalton	Representative	Cass Lake	Rentals	5	$3,700
26	Tammy Christine	Representative	Walker	Rentals	16	$17,500
27	Josie Daddiline	Representative	Walker	Rentals	10	$12,000
28	Josie Daddiline	Representative	Walker	Rentals	12	$12,000
29				Rentals Total		$125,700
30	Natasha Ari	Associate	Baudette	Spa	18	$4,500
31	Kendal Shaedon	Associate	Breezy Point	Spa	20	$4,800
32	Suzanne Ouimet	Manager	Breezy Point	Spa	4	$2,500
33	Mae Gomez	Representative	Cass Lake	Spa	12	$3,500
34	Lilly Oliver	Associate	Walker	Spa	10	$2,200
35				Spa Total		$17,500
36				Grand Total		$187,350

4-37 "Amount" subtotals for each category

The *Subtotal* command inserts the *SUBTOTAL* function in each cell with a result. Its arguments are *Function_num* and *RefN. Function_num* is a number from 1 through 11 that specifies which calculation was selected in the *Subtotal* dialog box. If you chose *Sum,* for example, the function is =SUBTOTAL(9,F5:F11). *Ref1* is the range to be summed.

> **MORE INFO**
>
> The *Function_num* arguments are in alphabetical order, so that *AVERAGE* is 1, *COUNT* is 2, and so on. You can see the argument list in Excel *Help* for the function.

Outline Buttons

An outline groups and summarizes data. A worksheet can have only one outline; the outline can include all of the worksheet data or a portion of the data. Outlines have levels, indicated by the numbered buttons to the left of the column headings. Each *Outline Level* button shows an increasing level of detail. An outline can have up to eight levels. The worksheet in Figure 4-37 has three levels: a grand total (1), a category total for each group (2), and all the rows (3).

Each group has an *Expand/Collapse* button, shown to the left of the row headings. This button is a toggle and shows a minus sign (−) or a plus sign (+). When an individual group is collapsed, you do not see details for that group, only the subtotal.

HOW TO: Use Outline Buttons

1. Click a collapse button (−) to hide details for a group.
   - Only the subtotal row displays.
2. Click an expand button (+) to display details for a group.
3. Click the **Level 1** button (1) to reveal the grand total.
4. Click the **Level 2** button (2) to see the second outline level details (Figure 4-38).
5. Click the **Level 3** button (3) to display all details.

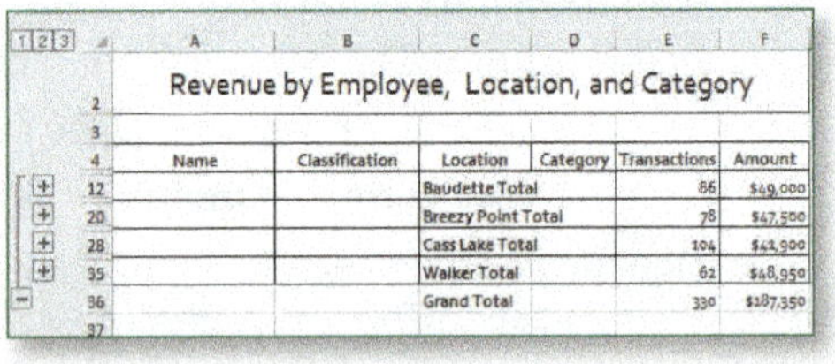

	A	B	C	D	E	F
2	Revenue by Employee, Location, and Category					
3						
4	Name	Classification	Location	Category	Transactions	Amount
12			Baudette Total		86	$49,000
20			Breezy Point Total		78	$47,500
28			Cass Lake Total		104	$41,900
35			Walker Total		62	$48,950
36			Grand Total		330	$187,350
37						

4-38 Level 2 outline results

Create an Auto Outline

An ***Auto Outline*** inserts groups based on where formulas are located. Consistent data and formulas that follow a pattern are necessary, and the formulas can be in specific rows or columns. The data in Figure 4-39 is grouped by location, and there is a *SUM* formula after each group in column E and F.

When data is not properly formatted, Excel displays a message that an *Auto Outline* cannot be created.

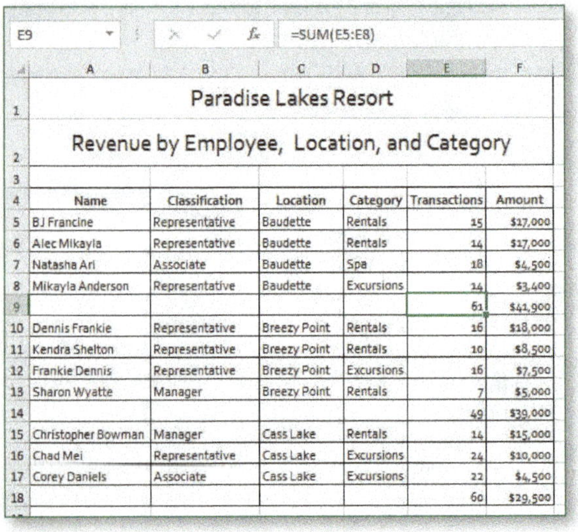

E9 =SUM(E5:E8)

	A	B	C	D	E	F
1	Paradise Lakes Resort					
2	Revenue by Employee, Location, and Category					
3						
4	Name	Classification	Location	Category	Transactions	Amount
5	BJ Francine	Representative	Baudette	Rentals	15	$17,000
6	Alec Mikayla	Representative	Baudette	Rentals	14	$17,000
7	Natasha Ari	Associate	Baudette	Spa	18	$4,500
8	Mikayla Anderson	Representative	Baudette	Excursions	14	$3,400
9					61	$41,900
10	Dennis Frankie	Representative	Breezy Point	Rentals	16	$18,000
11	Kendra Shelton	Representative	Breezy Point	Rentals	10	$8,500
12	Frankie Dennis	Representative	Breezy Point	Excursions	16	$7,500
13	Sharon Wyatte	Manager	Breezy Point	Rentals	7	$5,000
14					49	$39,000
15	Christopher Bowman	Manager	Cass Lake	Rentals	14	$15,000
16	Chad Mei	Representative	Cass Lake	Excursions	24	$10,000
17	Corey Daniels	Associate	Cass Lake	Excursions	22	$4,500
18					60	$29,500

4-39 Data sorted by location with formulas for each group

▶ HOW TO: Create an Auto Outline

1. Click a cell within the data range.
2. Click the **Group** button arrow [*Data* tab, *Outline* group].
3. Select **Auto Outline**.
   - Outline level buttons are inserted.
   - The outline is expanded.
4. Click each collapse button to hide details (Figure 4-40).

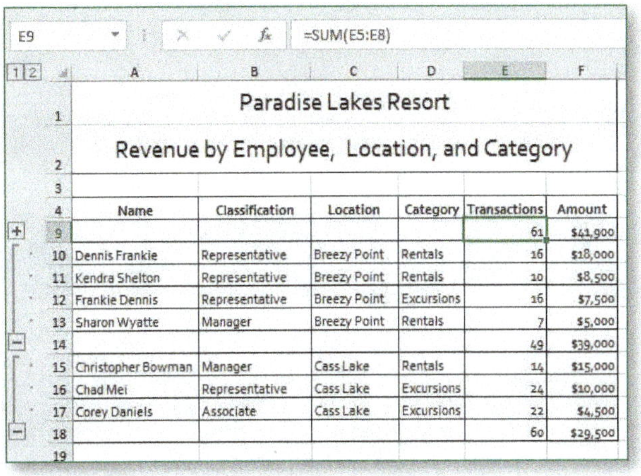
E9 =SUM(E5:E8)

	A	B	C	D	E	F
1	Paradise Lakes Resort					
2	Revenue by Employee, Location, and Category					
3						
4	Name	Classification	Location	Category	Transactions	Amount
9					61	$41,900
10	Dennis Frankie	Representative	Breezy Point	Rentals	16	$18,000
11	Kendra Shelton	Representative	Breezy Point	Rentals	10	$8,500
12	Frankie Dennis	Representative	Breezy Point	Excursions	16	$7,500
13	Sharon Wyatte	Manager	Breezy Point	Rentals	7	$5,000
14					49	$39,000
15	Christopher Bowman	Manager	Cass Lake	Rentals	14	$15,000
16	Chad Mei	Representative	Cass Lake	Excursions	24	$10,000
17	Corey Daniels	Associate	Cass Lake	Excursions	22	$4,500
18					60	$29,500
19						

4-40 ***Auto Outline*** **with two levels**

Define Groups

You can create a group, by rows or columns, for data that does not have totals or formulas. This can be a time-consuming task for a large set of records, but you can use groups to hide irrelevant records and concentrate on groups that require editing.

To define groups, data must be sorted or arranged so that you can select a range of cells to indicate the group. In addition, you must insert a blank summary row either above or below the group (or a blank column to the left or right of the group). You can use blank rows to enter subtitles for the data before or after grouping.

The data in Figure 4-41 is sorted by the "Classification" column, so that groups can be created for each job title. Note that a blank row has been inserted after each group.

▶ HOW TO: Define a Group

1. Sort the data (or arrange columns) based on the preferred grouping.
2. Insert a blank row at the end of each sort group (or at the start of each group).
   - Insert the blank row above the group if you want to label each group.
   - For column data, the summary column is usually to the right of the group.
3. Select the row or column headings for the first group.
   - Do not include the blank row or column.
   - You can select a range of cells that spans the rows or columns for the group.
4. Click the **Group** button [*Data* tab, *Outline* group].
   - The rows or columns are grouped.
   - Outline level buttons are inserted.
   - The data is expanded.
   - When you select a range of cells, not the row or column headings, the *Group* dialog box opens. Choose **Rows** or **Columns** if the dialog box opens and click **OK**.
5. Repeat steps 1–4 for each group (see Figure 4-41).

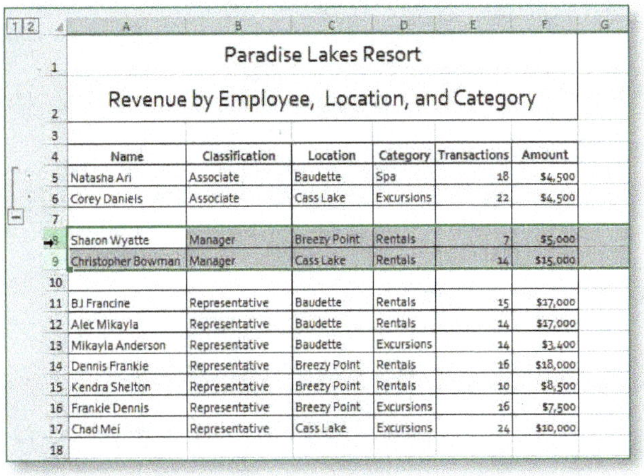

	A	B	C	D	E	F	G
1	Paradise Lakes Resort						
2	Revenue by Employee, Location, and Category						
3							
4	Name	Classification	Location	Category	Transactions	Amount	
5	Natasha Ari	Associate	Baudette	Spa	18	$4,500	
6	Corey Daniels	Associate	Cass Lake	Excursions	22	$4,500	
7							
8	Sharon Wyatte	Manager	Breezy Point	Rentals	7	$5,000	
9	Christopher Bowman	Manager	Cass Lake	Rentals	14	$15,000	
10							
11	BJ Francine	Representative	Baudette	Rentals	15	$17,000	
12	Alec Mikayla	Representative	Baudette	Rentals	14	$17,000	
13	Mikayla Anderson	Representative	Baudette	Excursions	14	$3,400	
14	Dennis Frankie	Representative	Breezy Point	Rentals	16	$18,000	
15	Kendra Shelton	Representative	Breezy Point	Rentals	10	$8,500	
16	Frankie Dennis	Representative	Breezy Point	Excursions	16	$7,500	
17	Chad Mei	Representative	Cass Lake	Excursions	24	$10,000	
18							

4-41 Data sorted by "Classification"; blank rows inserted after each title

> **MORE INFO**
>
> To clear an *Auto Outline* or remove all groups, click a cell within the group. Then click the **Ungroup** button arrow [*Data* tab, *Outline* group] and select **Clear Outline**.

PAUSE & PRACTICE: EXCEL 4-2

For this project, you sort and filter data for Paradise Lakes Resort based on location. You use a *Number Filter* to displays records within a range of values, build an advanced filter, and include subtotals in the workbook.

File Needed: ***[your initials] PP E4-1.xlsx***
Completed Project File Name: ***[your initials] PP E4-2.xlsx***

1. Open the***[your initials]PP E4-1*** workbook completed in *Pause & Practice 4-1* and save it as [your initials] PP E4-2.
2. Click the **Sort&Filter** sheet tab.
3. Sort data in a worksheet.
    a. Click cell **A5**.
    b. Click the **Sort** button [*Data* tab, *Sort & Filter* group].
    c. Select the **My data has headers** box, if necessary.
    d. Click the **Sort by** arrow and select **Location**.
    e. Choose **Values** for *Sort On* and **A to Z** for *Order*.
    f. Click **Add Level**.
    g. Click the **Then by** arrow and select **Amount**.
    h. Choose **Values** for *Sort On* and **Largest to Smallest** for *Order* (Figure 4-42).
    i. Click **OK**. The data in is sorted alphabetically by location and then by amount in descending order.

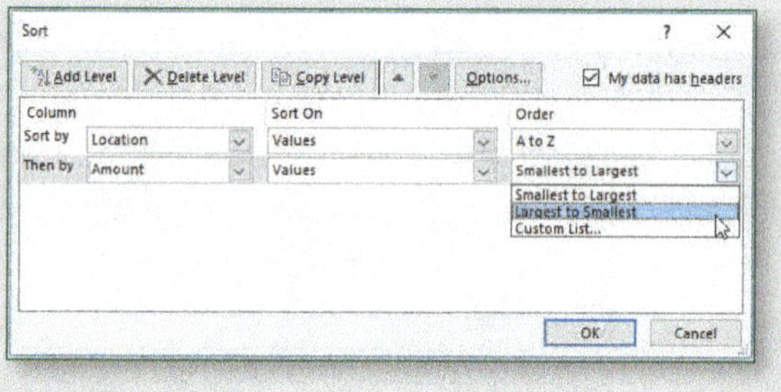

4-42 Multiple column sort with text and numeric data

4. Use a *Number AutoFilter*.
    a. Click cell **A5**.
    b. Click the **Filter** button [*Data* tab, *Sort & Filter* group] to display *AutoFilter* arrows.
    c. Click the *AutoFilter* arrow for "Amount."
    d. Point to **Number Filters** and select **Between**.
    e. Type 5000 in the **is greater than or equal to** box.
    f. Type 10000 in the **is less than or equal to** box (Figure 4-43).
    g. Click **OK**.
5. Click the **Adv Filter** sheet tab.
6. Set a criteria range.
    a. In cell **H6**, type assoc*.
    b. Type >1500 in cell **K6**.
7. Run an *Advanced Filter*.
    a. Click cell **A5**.
    b. Click the **Advanced** button [*Data* tab, *Sort & Filter* group].
    c. Select the **Copy to another location** radio button.
    d. Verify that cells **A4:E31** are identified in the **List range** box.

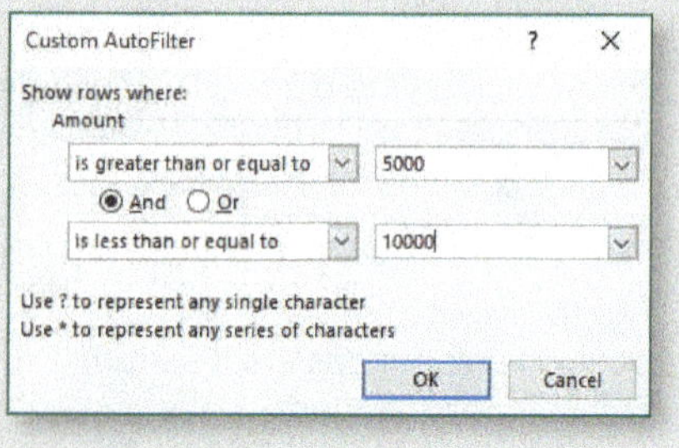

4-43 *Custom AutoFilter* dialog box for "Amount" between $5,000 and $10,000

e. Click the **Criteria range** box and select cells **G5:K6**.
f. Click the **Copy to** box and select cells **G14:K14** (Figure 4-44).
g. Click **OK**. Six records are extracted and displayed.

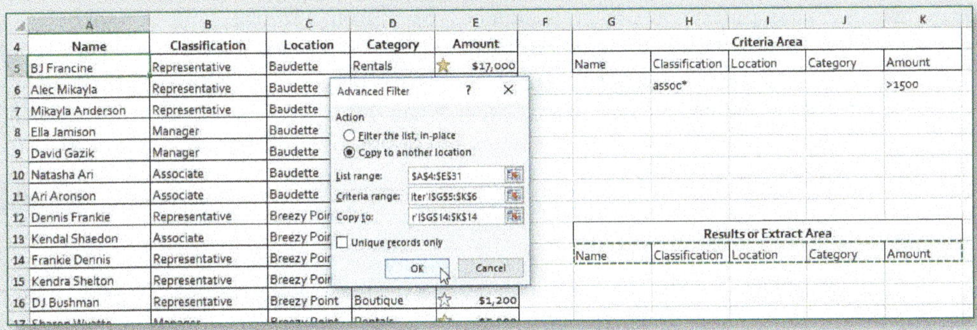

4-44 Criteria and extract ranges; *Advanced Filter* dialog box

8. Click the **Subtotals** sheet tab.

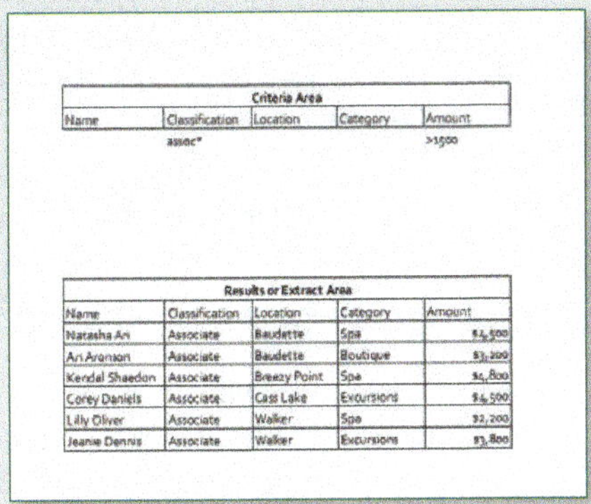

9. Show subtotals in a list.
   a. Click a cell in the **Location** column. The records are sorted by this column.
   b. Click the **Subtotal** button [*Data* tab, *Outline* group].
   c. Click the **At each change in** arrow and choose **Location**.
   d. Click the **Use function** arrow and choose **Sum**.
   e. Select **Transactions** and **Amount** in the **Add subtotal to list** box.
   f. Click **OK** (Figure 4-45).

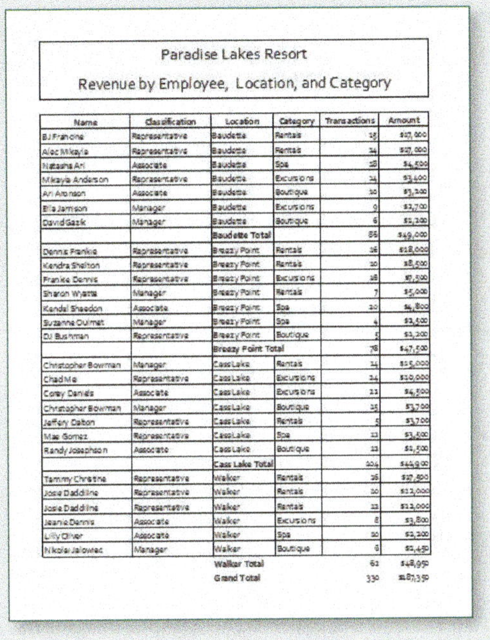

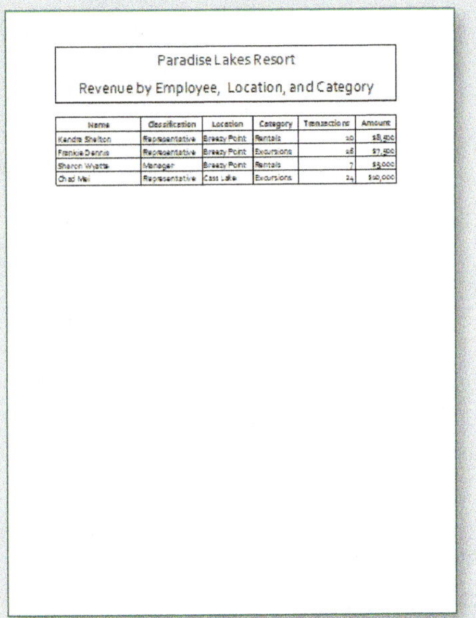

4-45 Completed PP E4-2 worksheets

10. Save and close the workbook.

SLO 4.6

Importing Data

Importing is the process of getting data from an outside source into an Excel worksheet. For example, you can probably import data from your bank into a worksheet so that you can analyze your transactions. ***External data*** is data that originated in another program or format. You import or copy external data into Excel from a ***source,*** which might be a text file, a database, or a web location. Imported data in a worksheet is almost always in list or table format.

The *Get External Data* command group on the *Data* tab establishes a connection to the source so that data can be refreshed. When you copy data into a worksheet using a *Copy and Paste* command, there is no connection to the source. Data connections are discussed later in this section.

Text Files

A ***text file*** is a document that includes raw data with no formatting. Text files are *.txt* (text) documents such as those created in NotePad or WordPad. Another widely used text format is *.csv* (comma separated values); you might see this type of file when you download a bank statement.

Text files separate data into ***fields.*** In one method, a character such as a comma or a tab separates the fields, and the file is described as ***delimited*** (e.g., tab-delimited file). A ***delimiter*** is the character used to separate the data. Common delimiters are the tab, space, and comma characters.

A second way to separate fields in a text file is by ***fixed width***. Each field is a specified number of characters followed by a space. If the first name field is set at 25 characters, the name "Tom," is imported as 3 characters plus 22 spaces. The second field always starts at position 26.

When you click the **From Text** button in the *Get External Data* group on the *Data* tab, the ***Text Import Wizard*** guides you through the importing steps.(Figure 4-46).

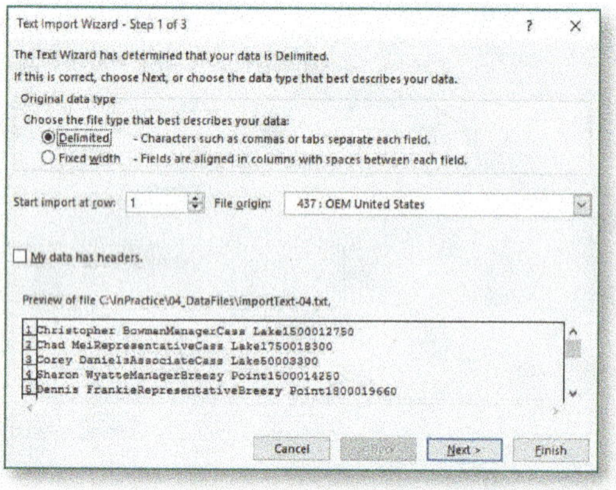

4-46 *Text Import Wizard – Step 1*

MORE INFO

Many legacy or mainframe computer systems use fixed width files for data.

HOW TO: Import a Tab-Delimited Text File into a Worksheet

1. Select the cell in which imported data should begin.
2. Click the **From Text** button [*Data* tab, *Get External Data* group].
3. Navigate to and select the text file name in the *Import Text File* dialog box.
4. Click **Import** (Figure 4-47).
5. Select the **Delimited** radio button in the *Text Import Wizard – Step 1 of 3* window.
   - A preview of the data displays.

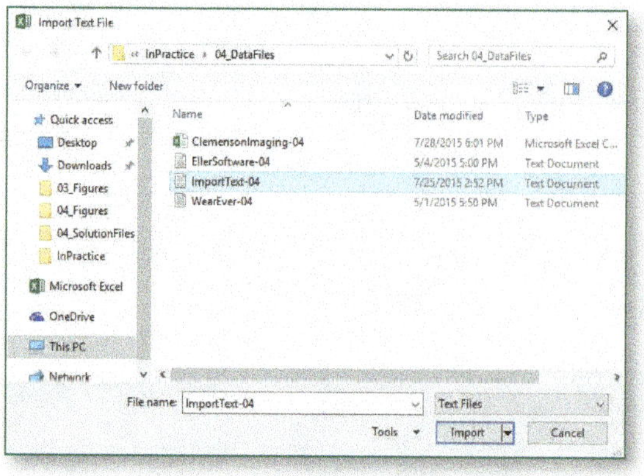

4-47 *Import Text File* dialog box

6. Click the spinner arrow for **Start import at row** to set the first row of imported text.
7. Click **Next**.
8. Select the **Tab** box in the *Text Import Wizard – Step 2 of 3* window.
    - The *Data preview* shows how the data will be separated into columns.
9. Click **Next**.
    - The *Step 3 of 3* window allows you to set formats as the data is imported.
    - This is optional; you can format data after it is imported.
10. Click **Finish**.
11. Select the radio button for **Existing worksheet** in the *Import Data* dialog box.
    - You can change or select the beginning cell location.
    - When you choose **New worksheet**, imported data starts at cell A1.
12. Click **OK**.
    - The data is available in the worksheet.
13. Right-click a cell within the imported data and select **Data Range Properties**.
    - The *External Data Range Properties* dialog box opens (Figure 4-48).
    - The *Name* is the name for the data connection.
    - You can specify when and how data is refreshed or updated.
14. Click **OK** to close the *External Data Range Properties* dialog box.

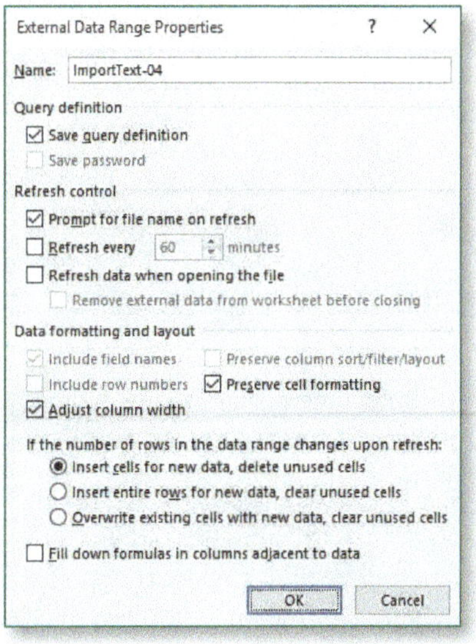

4-48 ***External Data Range Properties* dialog box**

Word Documents

You cannot "import"a Word document into Excel, but you can copy and paste data from Word into a worksheet. You can keep the Word formatting, or you can choose the current worksheet format.

HOW TO: Copy Data from a Word Document

1. Select the cell in which imported data should begin.
2. Start Word and open the document.
3. Select the data to be copied.
4. Click the **Copy** button [*Home* tab, *Clipboard* group].
5. Switch to the Excel worksheet.
6. Click the arrow with the **Paste** button [*Home* tab, *Clipboard* group].
7. Choose **Match Destination Formatting** from the *Paste* gallery.
    - The data is pasted in the worksheet.
    - If you click the **Paste** button, data is pasted with the Word format.

ANOTHER WAY

Save a Word document as a text file (*.txt*) and import the text file into Excel.

Access Database Files

Most organizations and enterprises maintain large amounts of data in a database. A ***database*** is a collection of related tables, queries, forms, and reports. ***Microsoft Access*** is a relational database management system that is part of the Office suite. You can import a table or a query from an Access database into an Excel worksheet. In Access, a table is a data list, and a query is a subset of the list.

When a database includes many tables and queries, the *Select Table* dialog box opens so that you can choose the table or query to import. Access data is imported as an Excel table, a *PivotTable,* or a *PivotChart.*

> **MORE INFO**
>
> If a database has a single table or query, it is automatically imported into Excel; the *Select Table* dialog box does not open.

HOW TO: Import an Access Table into a Worksheet

1. Select the cell in which imported data should begin.
2. Click the **From Access** button [*Data* tab, *Get External Data* group].
3. Navigate to and select the database name in the *Select Data Source* dialog box.
4. Click **Open**.
   - If only one table or query exists in the database, it is imported.
5. Select the name of the table or query in the *Select Table* dialog box (Figure 4-49).

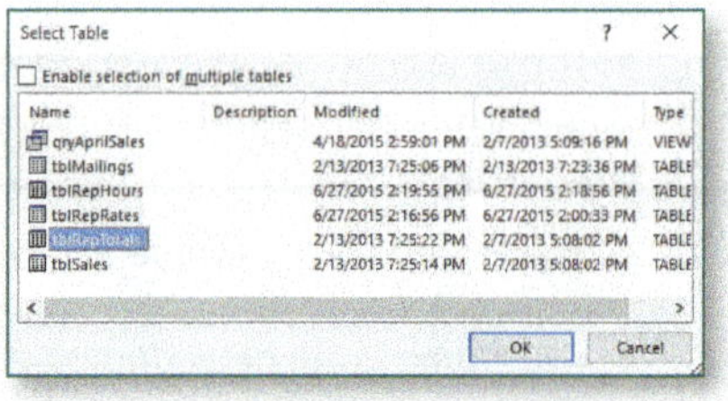

4-49 *Select Table* dialog box

6. Click **OK**.
7. Select **Table** and **Existing worksheet** in the *Import Data* dialog box.
   - You can choose a new worksheet for imported data or select a different cell.
   - You can also import data as a *PivotTable,* a *PivotChart,* or as a connection for later use.
8. Click **OK**.
   - The data is imported in an Excel table.
   - Field names from the Access table or query are column headings in the Excel table.
9. Click the *Table Tools Design* tab.
10. Click the **Properties** button [*External Table Data* group].
    - The *External Data Properties* dialog box opens (Figure 4-50).
    - You can adjust formatting and refresh options.
11. Click the **Connection Properties** button (to the right of the *Name* box).
    - The *Connection Properties* dialog box opens.
    - You can type a description for the data connection.
    - You can set how the data is refreshed or updated.
    - The *Definition* tab identifies the source of the imported data.
12. Click **OK** to close the *Connection Properties* dialog box.
13. Click **OK** to close the *External Data Properties* dialog box.

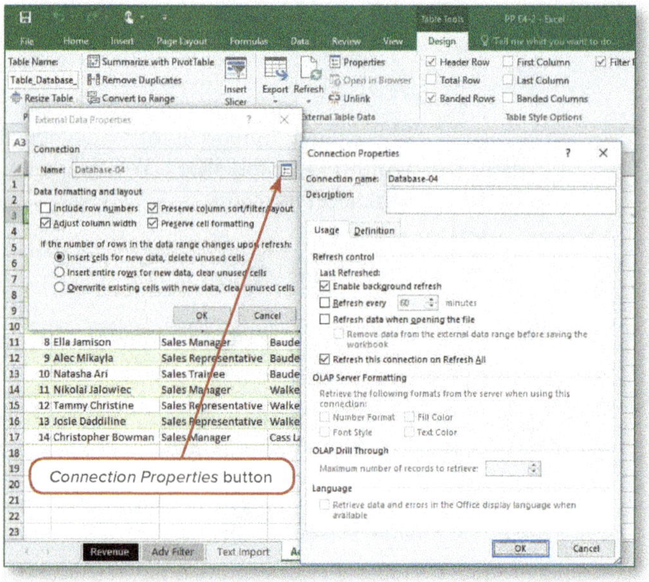

4-50 *External Data Properties* and *Connection Properties* dialog boxes

> **MORE INFO**
>
> You can import tables and queries from relational data bases such as SQL Server with the *From Other Sources* button [*Data* tab, *Get External Data* group].

Web Site Data

Web sites that deal with research, statistics, demographics, and similar public data often have downloadable text or Excel files for importing. Most web sites, however, have protected multimedia content with images, video, and audio, not list-type data for importing into Excel.

When you use the *From Web* command, data are identified by a small red arrow in a yellow-orange box. When you click the arrow, the importable data is selected, and the arrow changes to a blue check mark. Data from a web page establishes a connection to the URL that you can refresh. If the URL changes, you must edit the query to find the new address.

> **MORE INFO**
>
> You can copy web page data and paste it in Excel. This data includes links, images, and other elements. There is no data connection.

HOW TO: Create a Web Query to Import Data

1. Navigate to the web site and select the URL in the *Address* bar.
2. Press **Ctrl+C** to copy the URL to the Windows *Clipboard*.
3. Select the cell in which imported data should begin.
4. Click the **From Web** button [*Data* tab, *Get External Data* group].
   - The *New Web Query* dialog box opens.
   - Use the resize arrow at the bottom right corner to resize the dialog box.
5. Select the default URL in the *Address* bar in the *New Web Query* dialog box.
6. Press **Ctrl+V** to paste the copied URL in the *Address* bar.
7. Click **Go** or press **Enter**.
   - If an error message box opens about scripts that cannot be run, click **Yes**.
8. Navigate to the data to be imported.
9. Click the **Click to select this table** arrow (yellow-orange arrow) next to data to import (Figure 4-51).
   - The arrow changes to a blue check mark, the **Click to deselect this table** arrow.
10. Click **Import**.
    - The *Import Data* dialog box opens.

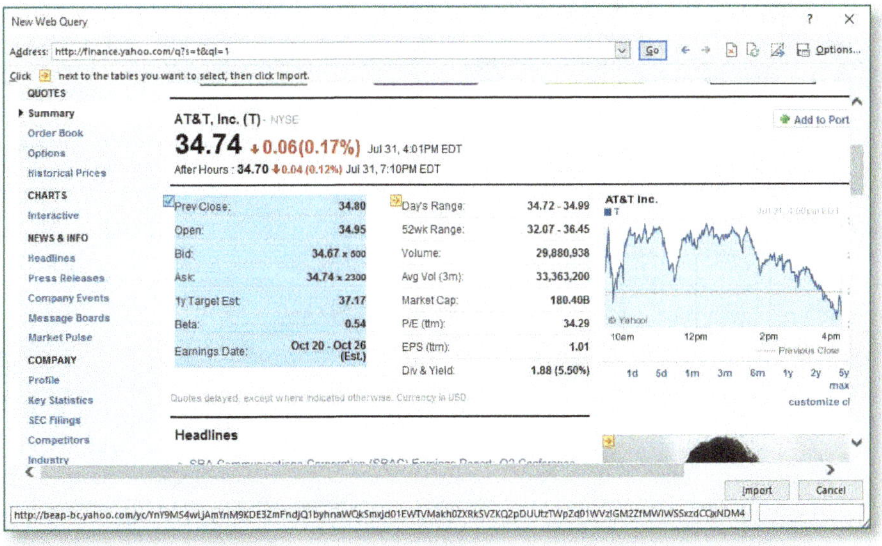

4-51 *New Web Query* dialog box

11. Click **OK**.
    - You may see a brief screen message as data is imported.
    - The imported data is unformatted.

Workbook Connections

When you use the *Get External Data* group on the *Data* tab, Excel establishes a connection that you can edit, refresh, name, or remove. A ***connection*** is an identifier and a link for data that originated outside the workbook. All connections are listed in the *Workbook Connections* dialog box. In this dialog box, you can select the connection name and open its *Properties* dialog box to edit various settings.

A data connection to an Internet location is named *Connection*. A data connection to a text or database file is named the same as the original file. You can change the name of a data connection to a descriptive name in the *Properties* dialog box.

When you open a workbook that has data connections, you will usually see a security warning bar at the top of the worksheet. When you are sure that the connection is safe, click **Enable Content** to work with the data.

HOW TO: Manage Data Connections

1. Click the **Connections** button [*Data* tab, *Connections* group].
    - The *Workbook Connections* dialog box lists current connections.
2. Select the name of the connection.
3. Click the link **Click here to see where the selected connections are used** in the lower pane.
    - This identifies where the data is located in the workbook (Figure 4-52).

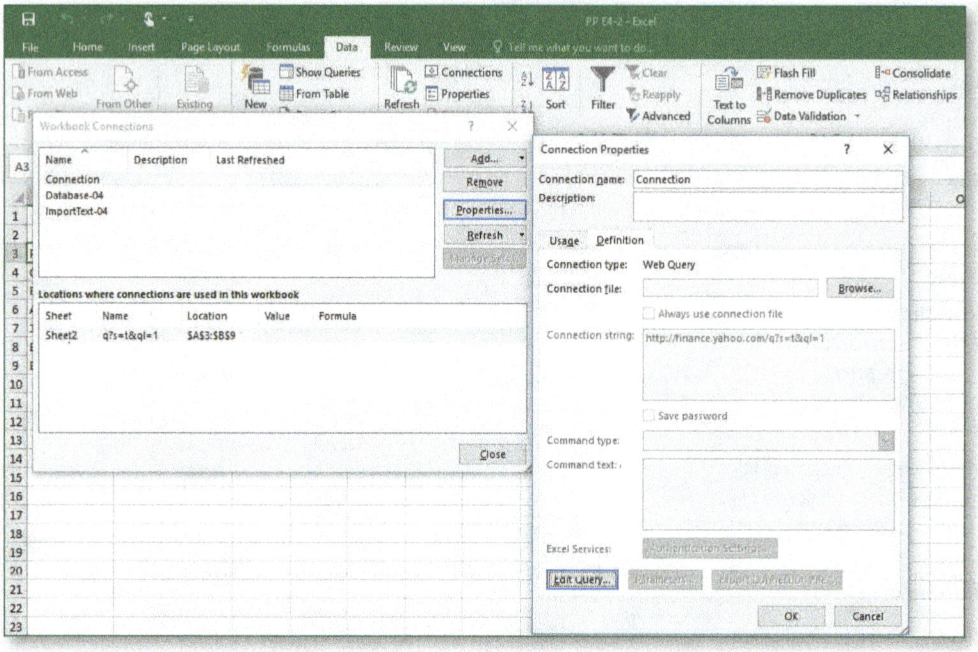

4-52 *Workbook Connections* and *Connection Properties* dialog boxes

4. Click **Refresh** to update the selected connection.
   - The *Import Text File* dialog box opens for a text file so that you can import it again.
   - A database source is automatically refreshed if the file is accessible.
   - An Internet source updates if the URL is accessible.
5. Click **Properties** to open the *Connection Properties* dialog box.
   - You can set how the data are refreshed, change the connection name, or add a description.
   - Click the *Definition* tab to edit a web query to update a URL.
6. Click **OK** to close the *Connection Properties* dialog box.
7. Click **Close** to save changes.

Flash Fill

Imported data often needs to be "cleaned" because it may not be in the correct sort order, it may have missing or incorrect data, and so on. ***Flash Fill*** is a feature that recognizes a pattern in the first cell and suggests data for the remaining rows in a column. It can be used to quickly complete new, missing, or incorrect data. For example, imagine that imported data lists first and last names in a single column, but you want first and last names in separate columns. Type the first person's name in an empty column next to the original column. As you start to type a second name below the first one, *Flash Fill* previews the completed column. Just press **Enter** to complete the column. Then do the same for the person's last name in the next column to the right. The *Flash Fill Options* button appears after you press **Enter** so that you can undo the fill if necessary or accept all the suggestions.

HOW TO: Flash Fill Data in a Worksheet

1. Click the first cell in an empty column next to the original data.
   - The first *Flash Fill* column must be adjacent to the original data.
   - Use an empty column or insert a column.
2. Type the data as you want it to appear.
3. Press **Enter** and type data in the cell below the first cell.
   - The suggested list is previewed.
   - If the suggested list does not appear, try typing a third item in the column (Figure 4-53).
   - The data must be consistent and follow a recognizable pattern.
4. Press **Enter** to complete the *Flash Fill*.
   - If there is no *Flash Fill* suggestion list, click the **Flash Fill** button [*Data* tab, *Data Tools* group] with the insertion point in the column.

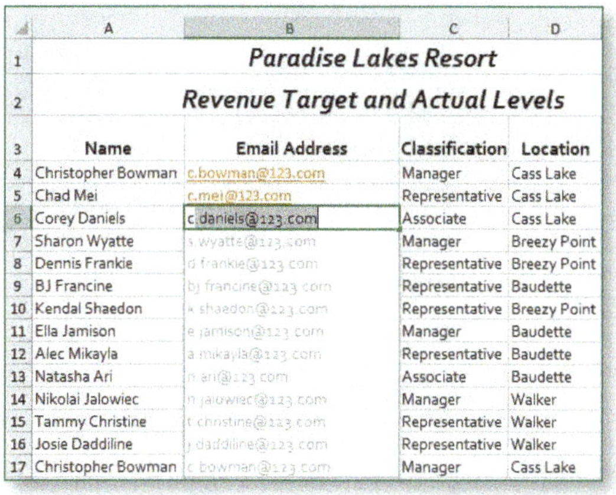

4-53 *Flash Fill* suggestion list

ANOTHER WAY

To split data into separate columns, insert blank columns to the right. Select the column to be split and click the **Text to Columns** button [*Data* tab, *Data Tools* group]. Complete the *Convert Text to Columns Wizard*.

SLO 4.7

Exporting Data

Exporting is the process of saving data in a format that can be used by another program or application. This can be as simple as providing a PDF file for viewing, copying data into Word, or saving worksheet data as a text file.

Export Data as a Text File

Most software applications can read a text file, a common way to transfer or share data. You can save Excel data as a tab-delimited, space-delimited, or comma-delimited file. When you save worksheet data as a text file, Excel renames the sheet with the same file name that you type for the text file. You can save only one worksheet in a text file. If a workbook has multiple sheets, a message box will alert you that only the current sheet will be saved.

HOW TO: Save Excel Data as a Tab-Delimited File

1. Click the worksheet tab with data to export.
   - The insertion point can be in any cell.
2. Click the **File** tab and select **Export**.
3. Select **Change File Type**.
4. Select **Text (Tab delimited)** as the file type (Figure 4-54).

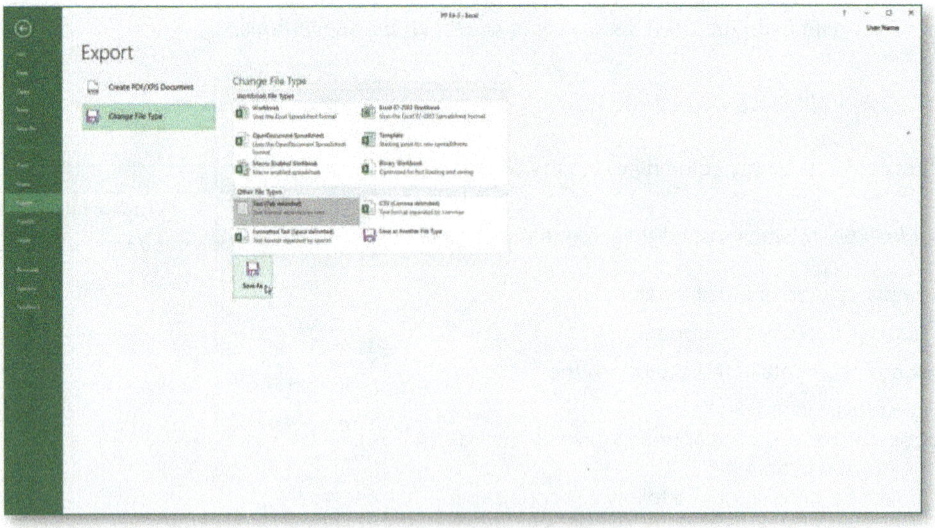

4-54 *Export* command in *Backstage* view

5. Click **Save As**.
   - The *Save As* dialog box opens with *Text (tab-delimited)* as the *Save as type*.
6. Navigate to the location for the exported data.
7. Type a file name for the text file in the *File name* box.
8. Click **Save**.
   - If a workbook has more than one sheet, a message box reminds you that only one sheet can be exported. Click **OK** in this message box.
9. Click **Yes** to acknowledge that Excel features may be lost.
   - The worksheet tab has the same name as the exported file.
10. Rename the sheet tab as desired.

11. Click the **File** tab and choose **Save As**.
12. Select **Excel Workbook** as the *Save as type* in the *Save As* dialog box.
13. Navigate to the folder for saved work.
14. Select or type the original workbook file name and click **Save**.
15. Click **Yes** to replace the file.
16. Close the workbook.
    - The exported text file is available in the folder selected for saving.
    - The original workbook is unchanged and resaved.

MORE INFO

To use Excel data in an Access table, export the data as a text file. You can then import the text file into an Access table.

Export Data via the Clipboard

Excel data can be copied and pasted into a Word document as well as other applications. The *Paste* button gallery in Word has options to paste a table, to paste text separated by tabs or spaces, and to paste a picture object. The *Paste Special* command in the gallery has an option to paste a *Microsoft Excel Worksheet Object*. With this option, you can paste a link to the Excel data in Word to launch Excel, edit the worksheet, and resave the Excel file. You can also paste without a link which opens an Excel window in Word that has most Excel commands but does not affect the original Excel file.

HOW TO: Create a Microsoft Excel Worksheet Object

1. Open the Word document and position the insertion point at the location for the Excel data.
2. Switch to the Excel worksheet.
3. Select the cells to be copied.
4. Click the **Copy** button [*Home* tab, *Clipboard* group].
    - The data can be formatted as a table or a normal range.
    - You can also press **Ctrl+C** to copy.
5. Switch to the Word document.
6. Click the arrow with the **Paste** button [*Home* tab, *Clipboard* group] and choose **Paste Special**.
7. Select **Microsoft Excel Worksheet Object** in the *Paste Special* dialog box.
8. Select **Paste link** in the *Paste Special* dialog box (Figure 4-55).
9. Click **OK**.
    - The data is pasted as a worksheet object.
10. Complete work in the Word document.
    - Use horizontal alignment commands to position the object, if necessary.
    - You can double-click anywhere in the object to launch Excel and open the source workbook.

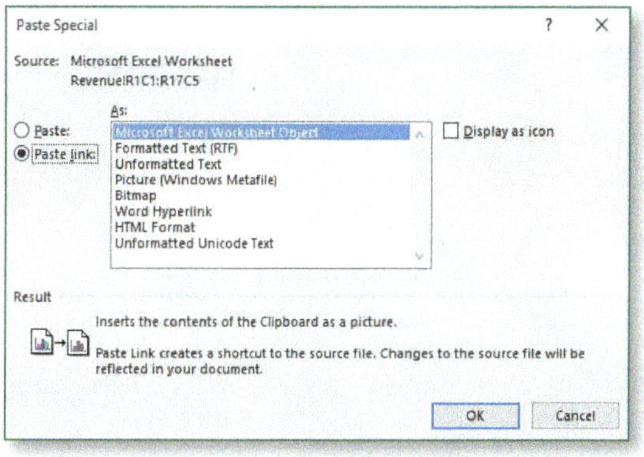

4-55 *Paste Special* dialog box

SharePoint Lists

A ***SharePoint server*** is a web platform that runs *Microsoft SharePoint,* a family of products that allows for collaboration and simultaneous work by groups of people via the Internet. You can export data in an Excel table to a SharePoint list so that others in your work circle have access to the data. The *Export* button is in the *External Table Data* group on the *Table Tools Design* tab, and it launches the *Export Table to SharePoint List Wizard.* To work with a SharePoint server, you must have an Internet connection and permission from the network administrator.

PAUSE & PRACTICE: EXCEL 4-3

For this project, you import data from a text file into an Excel worksheet, format the data as an Excel table, copy data from a Word document, and use *Flash Fill* to complete the worksheet for Paradise Lakes Resort.

Files Needed: ***[your initials] PP E4-2.xlsx,ImportText-04.txt***, and **CopyWord-04.docx** *[Student data files are available in the* Library *of your SIMnet account.]*
Completed Project File Name: ***[your initials] PP E4-3.xlsx***

1. Open the ***[your initials] PP E4-2*** workbook completed in *Pause & Practice 4-2* and save it as [your initials] PP E4-3.
2. Import data from a text file.
   a. Select cell **A4** on the **Text Import** tab.
   b. Click the **From Text** button [*Data* tab, *Get External Data* group].
   c. Navigate to and select ***ImportText-04.txt*** from your student data files in the *Import Text File* dialog box.
   d. Click **Import**.
   e. Select **Delimited** in the *Text Import Wizard – Step 1 of 3* dialog box and click **Next**.
   f. Select the **Tab** box in the *Text Import Wizard – Step 2 of 3* dialog box and click **Next**.
   g. Click **Finish** to accept the *General* format.
   h. Click **OK** in the *Import Data* dialog box.
3. Copy data from a Word document.
   a. Select cell **A18**.
   b. Open Microsoft Word and open the ***CopyWord-04*** document from your student data files.
   c. Select all the data and click the **Copy** button [*Home* tab, *Clipboard* group].
   d. Switch to the Excel window.
   e. Click the arrow with the **Paste** button [*Home* tab, *Clipboard* group] and choose **Match Destination Formatting** (Figure 4-56).

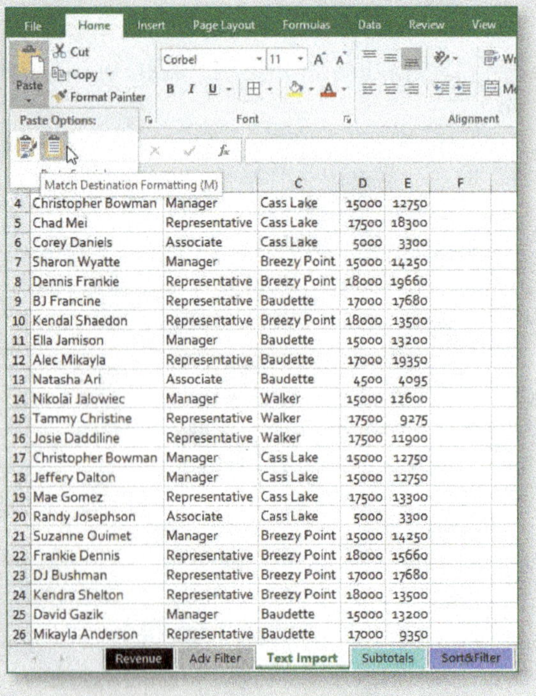

4-56 ***Paste Options*** **for copied data**

f. Select cells **D4:E27** and apply the **Currency** number format with zero decimals.
g. Adjust the widths of columns **C:E** to **11.43 (85 pixels)**.

4. Use *Flash Fill* to create an email address column.
   a. Insert a column between columns **A** and **B**.
   b. Type Email Address in cell **B3**.
   c. Increase the width of the "Email Address" column to **31.00 (222 pixels)**.
   d. In cell **B4** type c.bowman@somewhere.com and press **Enter**.
   e. Select cell **B5** and type c.m to start the second address and display the *Flash Fill* suggested list.
   f. Press **Enter**. If the *Flash Fill* suggestion list did not appear, click the **Flash Fill** button [*Data* tab, *Data Tools* group].

5. Format data as an Excel table.
   a. Select cells **A3:F27**. Since the data was imported from different sources, you must select the range.
   b. Click the **Format as Table** button [*Home* tab, *Styles* group].
   c. Choose **Table Style Light 1** and click **OK**. The data connections must be removed to create an Excel table.
   d. Choose **Yes** in the message box (Figure 4-57).

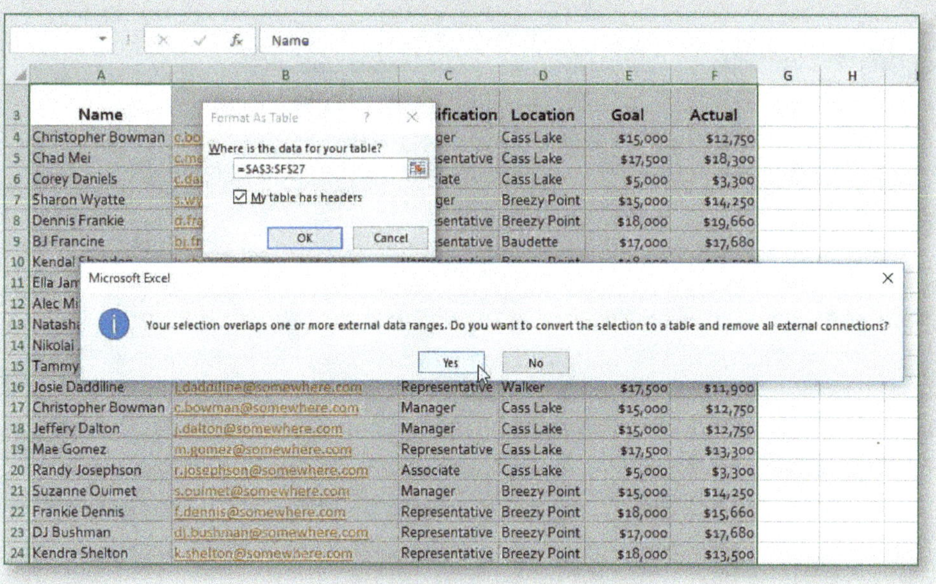

4-57 Message box to remove data connections

6. Add a column with a calculation to a table.
   a. Type Difference in cell **G3** and press **Enter**.
   b. Change the column width to **10.70 (80 pixels)** and use a black bottom border for the cell.
   c. Type = in cell **G4** to start the formula and click cell **F4**.
   d. Type – for subtraction and click cell **E4** (Figure 4-58).
   e. Press **Enter** to copy the formula in the column.
   f. Select cells **G4:G27** and press **Ctrl+1** to open the *Format Cells* dialog box.
   g. On the *Number* tab, choose **Currency** with zero decimal places and negative numbers in red, and close the dialog box.
   h. Select cells **A1:G1** and click the **Merge & Center** button [*Home* tab, *Alignment* group] to remove the centering. Then click the **Merge & Center** button again to re-center the cells over the new range.
   i. Repeat the steps to re-center cells **A2:G2**.
   j. Change the orientation to **Landscape**.

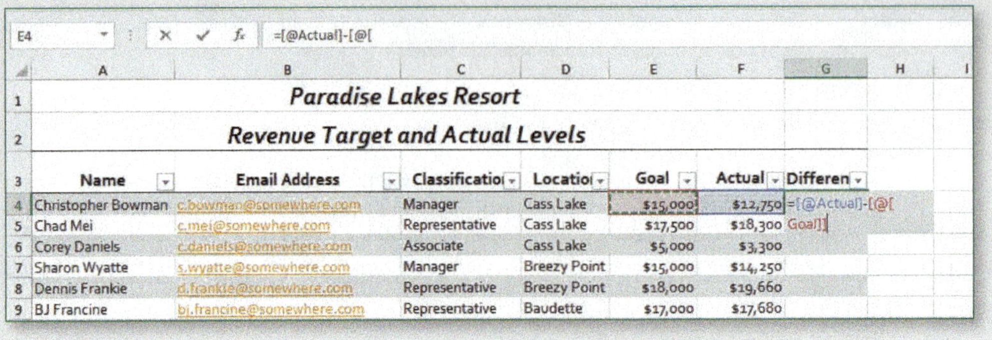

E4 =[@Actual]-[@[

	A	B	C	D	E	F	G
1	Paradise Lakes Resort						
2	Revenue Target and Actual Levels						
3	Name	Email Address	Classification	Location	Goal	Actual	Difference
4	Christopher Bowman	c.bowman@somewhere.com	Manager	Cass Lake	$15,000	$12,750	=[@Actual]-[@[
5	Chad Mei	c.mei@somewhere.com	Representative	Cass Lake	$17,500	$18,300	Goal]]
6	Corey Daniels	c.daniels@somewhere.com	Associate	Cass Lake	$5,000	$3,300	
7	Sharon Wyatte	s.wyatte@somewhere.com	Manager	Breezy Point	$15,000	$14,250	
8	Dennis Frankie	d.frankie@somewhere.com	Representative	Breezy Point	$18,000	$19,660	
9	BJ Francine	bj.francine@somewhere.com	Representative	Baudette	$17,000	$17,680	

4-58 Structured references in a table formula

7. Save and close the workbook. Close the Word document (Figure 4-59).

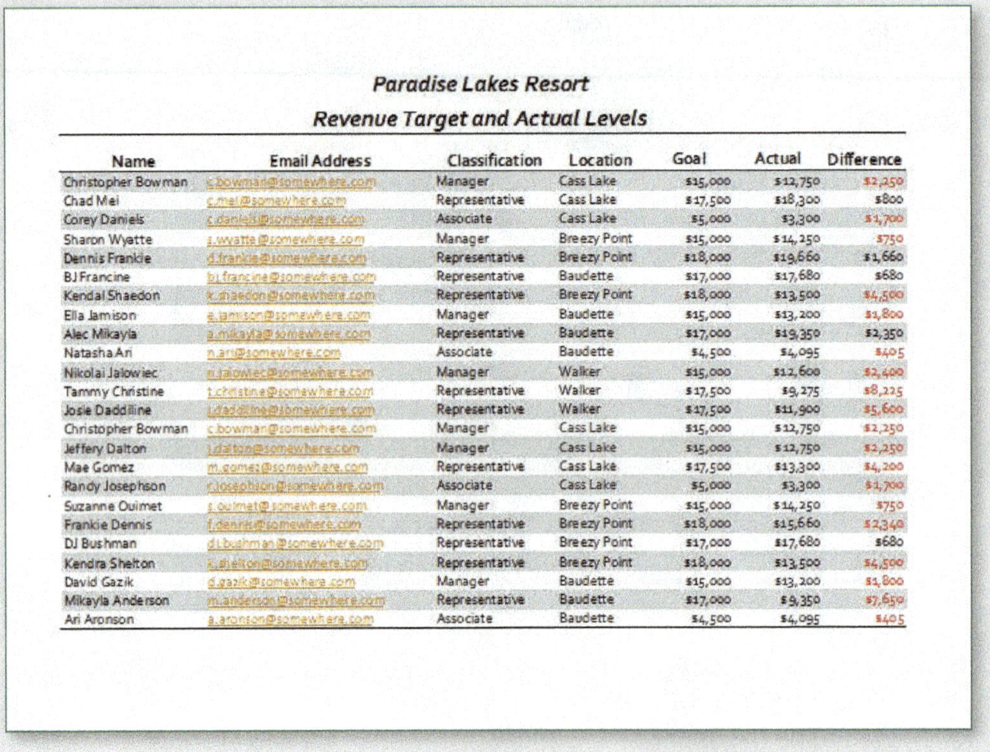

Paradise Lakes Resort

Revenue Target and Actual Levels

Name	Email Address	Classification	Location	Goal	Actual	Difference
Christopher Bowman	c.bowman@somewhere.com	Manager	Cass Lake	$15,000	$12,750	$2,250
Chad Mei	c.mei@somewhere.com	Representative	Cass Lake	$17,500	$18,300	$800
Corey Daniels	c.daniels@somewhere.com	Associate	Cass Lake	$5,000	$3,300	$1,700
Sharon Wyatte	s.wyatte@somewhere.com	Manager	Breezy Point	$15,000	$14,250	$750
Dennis Frankie	d.frankie@somewhere.com	Representative	Breezy Point	$18,000	$19,660	$1,660
BJ Francine	bj.francine@somewhere.com	Representative	Baudette	$17,000	$17,680	$680
Kendal Shaedon	k.shaedon@somewhere.com	Representative	Breezy Point	$18,000	$13,500	$4,500
Ella Jamison	e.jamison@somewhere.com	Manager	Baudette	$15,000	$13,200	$1,800
Alec Mikayla	a.mikayla@somewhere.com	Representative	Baudette	$17,000	$19,350	$2,350
Natasha Ari	n.ari@somewhere.com	Associate	Baudette	$4,500	$4,095	$405
Nikolai Jalowiec	n.jalowiec@somewhere.com	Manager	Walker	$15,000	$12,600	$2,400
Tammy Christine	t.christine@somewhere.com	Representative	Walker	$17,500	$9,275	$8,225
Josie Daddiline	j.daddiline@somewhere.com	Representative	Walker	$17,500	$11,900	$5,600
Christopher Bowman	c.bowman@somewhere.com	Manager	Cass Lake	$15,000	$12,750	$2,250
Jeffery Dalton	j.dalton@somewhere.com	Manager	Cass Lake	$15,000	$12,750	$2,250
Mae Gomez	m.gomez@somewhere.com	Representative	Cass Lake	$17,500	$13,300	$4,200
Randy Josephson	r.josephson@somewhere.com	Associate	Cass Lake	$5,000	$3,300	$1,700
Suzanne Ouimet	s.ouimet@somewhere.com	Manager	Breezy Point	$15,000	$14,250	$750
Frankie Dennis	f.dennis@somewhere.com	Representative	Breezy Point	$18,000	$15,660	$2,340
DJ Bushman	dj.bushman@somewhere.com	Representative	Breezy Point	$17,000	$17,680	$680
Kendra Shelton	k.shelton@somewhere.com	Representative	Breezy Point	$18,000	$13,500	$4,500
David Gazik	d.gazik@somewhere.com	Manager	Baudette	$15,000	$13,200	$1,800
Mikayla Anderson	m.anderson@somewhere.com	Representative	Baudette	$17,000	$9,350	$7,650
Ari Aronson	a.aronson@somewhere.com	Associate	Baudette	$4,500	$4,095	$405

4-59 PP E4-3 completed worksheet

SLO 4.8

Building and Formatting PivotTables

A ***PivotTable*** is a cross tabulation report based on list-type data. It is a separate worksheet in which you can sort, filter, and calculate large amounts of data. *PivotTables* are analysis tools, an important part of ***Business Intelligence (BI)***. Business intelligence is a combination of applications and processes that enable you to "drill-down" into data and assess various types of results or changes. In a table or list with thousands of records, you can build a *PivotTable* to quickly show average revenue by state, by city, or other criteria, and, just as quickly, return to the entire list (Figure 4-60).

PivotTables are interactive, because you rearrange the report for analysis by clicking or dragging. Rearranging data is *pivoting* the data so that you can look at it from a different perspective. It takes time and practice to create and understand all the features of a *PivotTable,* but it is easy to experiment placing fields, sorting data, or filtering results.

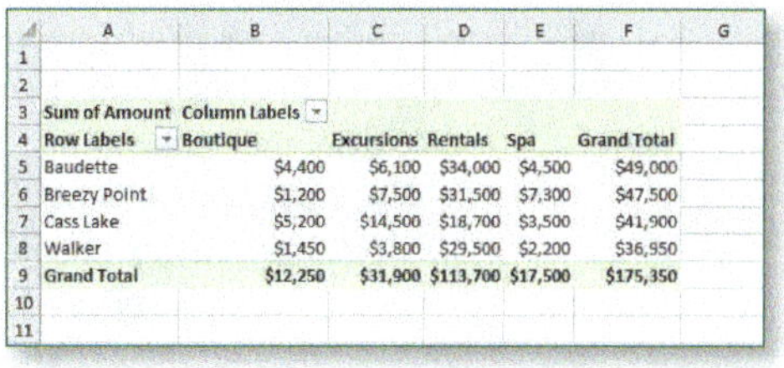

4-60 An Excel *PivotTable*

Create a PivotTable

Data for a *PivotTable* should follow the same guidelines as those recommended for an Excel table in the beginning of this chapter. Data can be formatted as a table but need not be. A *PivotTable* is placed on its own sheet in the workbook.

The *Tables* group on the *Insert* tab includes the *PivotTable* button as well as the *Recommended PivotTables* button. When you are first learning about *PivotTables,* the *Recommended PivotTables* button may help you gain experience building these reports.

After you create a *PivotTable,* the *PivotTable Tools Analyze* and *Design* tabs are available for additional format choices and data commands.

HOW TO: Create a PivotTable

1. Click a cell in the data range.
   - The data range must have a header row.
2. Click the **Recommended PivotTables** button [*Insert* tab, *Tables* group] (Figure 4-61).
   - A data range is assumed and highlighted in the worksheet.
3. Point to a preview tile on the left to see a *ScreenTip* for the proposed *PivotTable.*
4. Select the preferred *PivotTable* and click **OK**.
   - The *PivotTable* report is created on a separate sheet.

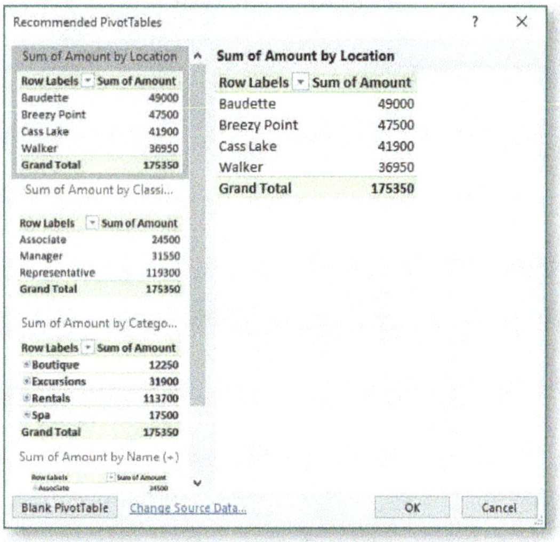

4-61 *RecommendedPivotTables* for a data range

The PivotTable Fields Pane

A *PivotTable* is created on a new sheet in the workbook, and the *PivotTable Fields* pane opens at the right. From this pane, you can add and remove fields from the report and drag field names into different areas in the pane to reset how the data are organized (Figure 4-62).

There are *Filters, Columns, Rows,* and *Values* areas in the pane. Each item from a field in the *Rows* area appears in its own row in the *PivotTable.* Each item in a field in the *Columns* area displays as a column. Columns and rows are usually the categories of data, not the actual values. Fields in the *Values* area are the ones that are summed, averaged, counted, or otherwise used in a calculation. *Filters* are fields placed as separate buttons above the *PivotTable* which act like *AutoFilter* arrows. Row and column labels include a filter arrow in the body of the *PivotTable,* and row data have collapse/expand buttons for certain field layouts. You can filter data from the filter arrows with a field, or you can insert a *Slicer* window.

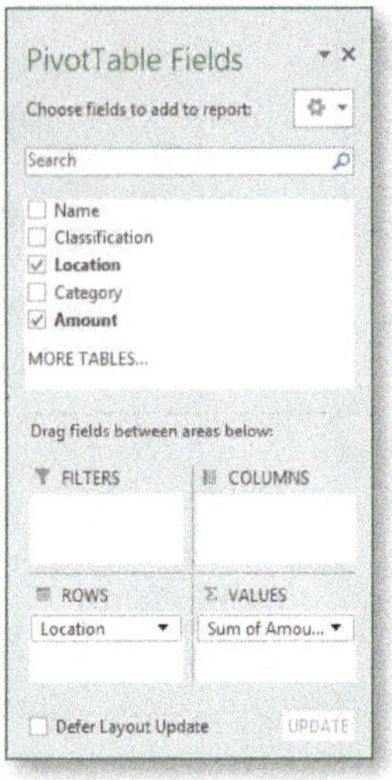

4-62 *PivotTable Fields* pane

HOW TO: Adjust Fields in a PivotTable

1. Click a cell in the body of the *PivotTable.*
2. Drag a field name from the *Choose fields to add to report* area into the *Columns* area in the *PivotTable Fields* pane and release the pointer button.
   - Columns for the field items are added to the report.
   - A grand total column is added.
3. Drag a field name into the *Filters* area and release the pointer button (Figure 4-63).

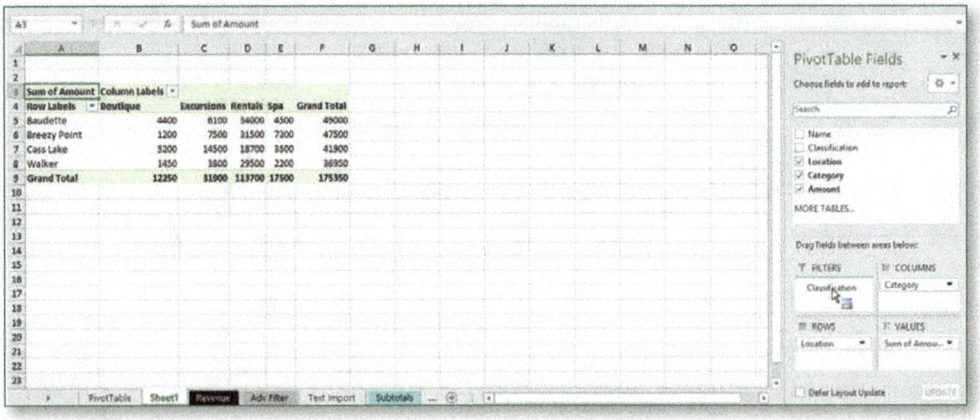

4-63 Drag fields in the *PivotTable Fields* pane

   - The field is added as a filter button in row 1 of the *PivotTable.*
   - No filter is applied.
4. Drag a field name from the *Rows* area to the left and into the worksheet area.
   - The field is removed from the *PivotTable.*
5. Drag a field name from one area in the *PivotTable Fields* pane to another area.
   - The *PivotTable* is updated after each change.

Field Settings

Fields in a *PivotTable* include various settings that depend on the type of data. ***Field Settings*** for a text field include layout and print options as well as subtotal and filter choices. The *Layout* group on the *PivotTable Tools Design* tab includes many of the same commands as the *Field Settings* dialog box.

The ***Value Field Settings*** for a *PivotTable Values* field determine how data is summarized. The default function is *SUM,* but you can change the function or select a custom percentage, difference, or ranking. From the *Value Field Settings* dialog box, you can edit the label that appears in the *PivotTable,* choose a function, and set how numbers are formatted. To select a field in a *PivotTable,* click the field name in the *Row Labels* row or any cell in the column.

ANOTHER WAY

You can right-click a field in the *PivotTable* and select **Field Settings** or **Value Field Settings** to open the dialog box.

MORE INFO

You can show a field more than once in a *PivotTable* and choose different settings for each occurrence.

HOW TO: Change Value Field Settings in a PivotTable

1. Click the arrow for *Sum of [Field Name]* in the *Values* area in the *PivotTable Fields* pane.
2. Select **Value Field Settings** from the menu.
   - The *Value Field Settings* dialog box opens.
   - You can also click one of the field values in the *PivotTable* and click the **Field Settings** button [*PivotTable Tools Analyze* tab, *Active Field* group] to open the dialog box.
3. Click the **Custom Name** box and type a new label as desired.
   - The label cannot be the same as the field name in the *PivotTable Fields* pane.
4. Select the **Summarize Values By** tab, if necessary.
5. Choose the function from the *Summarize value field by* list.
6. Click **Number Format**.
7. Select the preferred number format in the *Format Cells* dialog box (Figure 4-64).

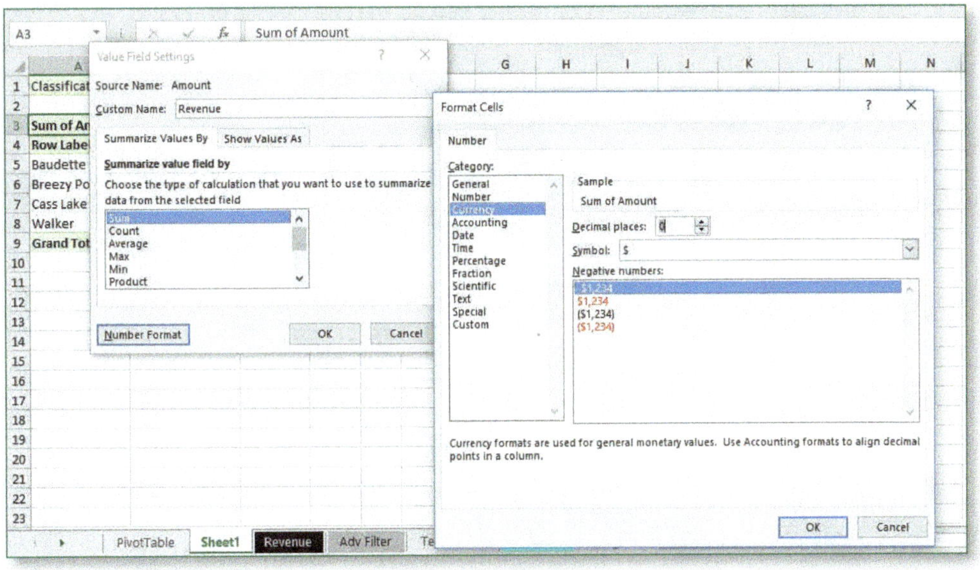

4-64 ***Value Field Settings*** **dialog box and** ***Number Format*** **options**

8. Click **OK** to close the *Format Cells* dialog box.
9. Click **OK** to close the *Value Field Settings* dialog box.
   - The new label displays in the *PivotTable* and in the task pane.
   - The entire field is reformatted.

Format a PivotTable

A *PivotTable* can be formatted from the *PivotTable Tools Design* tab or from the *Home* tab. The *PivotTable Tools Design* tab includes *PivotTable* styles and layout options. *PivotTable* styles are similar to Excel table styles. You can choose from a gallery to apply fill, border, and font color. Changes made from the *PivotTable Tools Design* tab affect the entire table.

The *Layout* group on the *PivotTable Tools Design* tab provides options for displaying subtotals and grand totals. The *Report Layout* command offers choices for the report design and selections for repeated labels. From the *PivotTable Style Options* group, you can choose whether row and column headings are bold and filled and whether columns and rows are banded with fill or borders. These style options are dependent on the *PivotTable* style.

From the *Home* tab, you can change the font size and style, set alignment, and more. When you apply changes from the *Home* tab, the format is applied to the selected cell or cells.

HOW TO: Format a PivotTable

1. Click a cell in the *PivotTable*.
2. Click the **More** button for the *PivotTable Styles* group [*PivotTable Tools Design* tab].
   - The style gallery is categorized by light, medium, and dark colors.
3. Point to a style icon to see a *Live Preview*.
   - The styles are named *Pivot Style Light 1, Pivot Style Light 2,* and so on.
   - You can design your own style.
4. Click to select a style.
5. Select the box for **Banded Rows** in the *PivotTable Styles Options* group [*PivotTable Tools Design* tab].
   - The rows are filled or a border is applied, based on the selected *PivotTable* style.
6. Select the box for **Banded Columns** in the *PivotTable Styles Options* group [*PivotTable Tools Design* tab].
   - The columns are filled or a border is applied.
7. Click the **Grand Totals** button [*PivotTable Tools Design* tab, *Layout* group] (Figure 4-65).

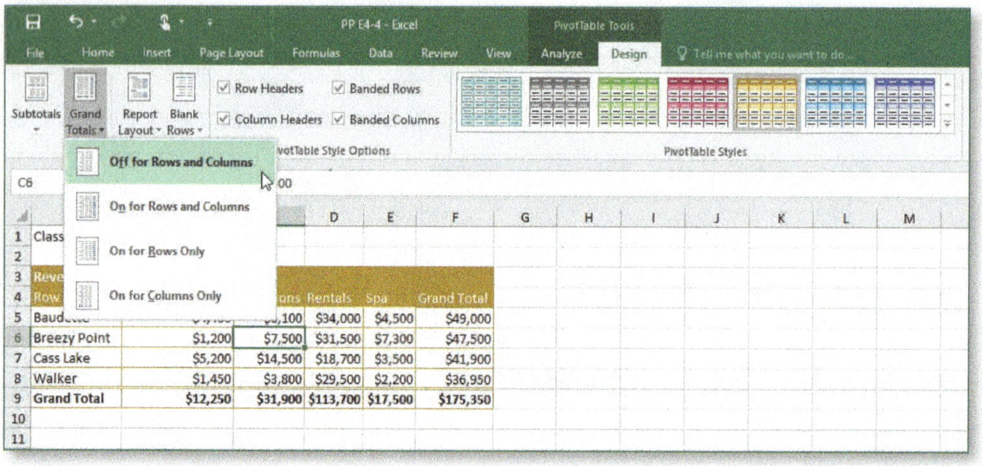

4-65 Display or hide total column and row

8. Choose **Off for Rows and Columns**.
   - The total column and row are removed.
   - You can show totals by selecting **On for Columns and Rows**.

Refresh a PivotTable

Although a *PivotTable* is based on worksheet data, the *PivotTable* is not automatically updated if the data are edited. This is a security measure because a *PivotTable* can be associated with data in a different workbook or an external source such as a database. You can use the context-sensitive menu for any cell in the *PivotTable* and choose **Refresh**, or you can click the **Refresh** button in the *Data* group on the *PivotTable Tools Analyze* tab.

> **MORE INFO**
>
> There is a *PivotTable* option to automatically refresh the data each time the workbook is opened. Click the **Options** button [*PivotTable Tools Analyze* tab, *PivotTable* group] and select the **Data** tab.

HOW TO: Refresh Data in a PivotTable

1. Click any cell in the *PivotTable*.
2. Click the **Refresh** button [*PivotTable Tools Analyze* tab, *Data* group].
   - The *PivotTable* data is updated.
   - You can refresh all data connections in the workbook by clicking the arrow for the **Refresh** button and selecting **Refresh All**.

Create a PivotChart

A ***PivotChart*** contains charted data that updates with the *PivotTable* and has the same field buttons and filter options. The *PivotChart* button is on the *PivotTable Tools Analyze* tab.

A *PivotChart* can be formatted like an Excel chart from its *PivotChart Tools Design* and *Format* tabs. You can select a style, switch row and column data, change the chart type, and so on. When the chart object is selected, you will also see the *PivotChart Tools Analyze* tab with the same commands as the *PivotTable Tools Analyze* tab, and the *PivotChart Fields* pane on the right. A *PivotChart* and its *PivotTable* are linked, and you can make changes from command tabs for the table or the chart.

> **MORE INFO**
>
> You can create a *PivotChart* directly from a list in the worksheet; its underlying *PivotTable* is automatically created.

HOW TO: Create a PivotChart

1. Click a cell in the *PivotTable*.
2. Click the **PivotChart** button [*PivotTable Tools Analyze* tab, *Tools* group].
   - The *Insert Chart* dialog box opens.
3. Select a chart type from the list on the left.
4. Select a subtype for the chart.
5. Click **OK** (Figure 4-66).

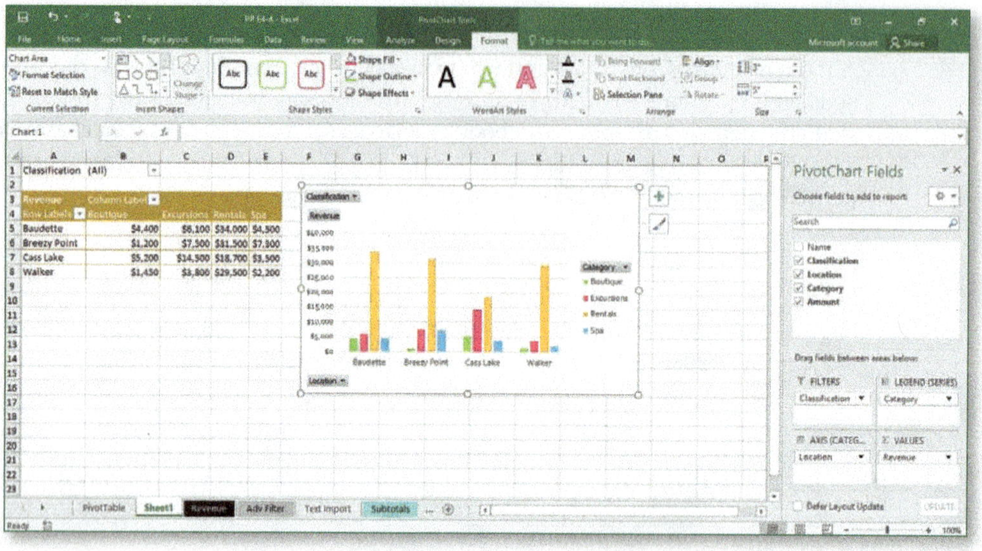

4-66 *PivotChart* inserted as chart object

- The chart displays as a chart object.
- The *PivotChart Tools Analyze, Design,* and *Format* tabs are available.
- The *PivotChart Fields* pane is similar to the *PivotTable Fields* pane.

PAUSE & PRACTICE: EXCEL 4-4

For this project, you create a *PivotTable* for Paradise Lakes Resort using the Excel table as its source. You also create a *PivotChart* and add a slicer to the worksheet. Your workbook now has data connections, so you may see a security warning when you open the file, depending on the settings of your computer.

File Needed: ***[your initials] PP E4-3.xlsx***
Completed Project File Name: ***[your initials] PP E4-4.xlsx***

1. Open the ***[your initials] PP E4-3*** workbook completed in *Pause & Practice 4-3*. The security bar informs you that the data connections have been disabled (Figure 4-67).
2. Click **Enable Content**. (If you did not see the security bar, continue to step 3.)
3. Save the workbook as [your initials] PP E4-4.
4. Create a *PivotTable*.
   a. Click cell **A4** on the **Revenue** sheet tab.
   b. Click the **Recommended PivotTables** button [*Insert* tab, *Tables* group].

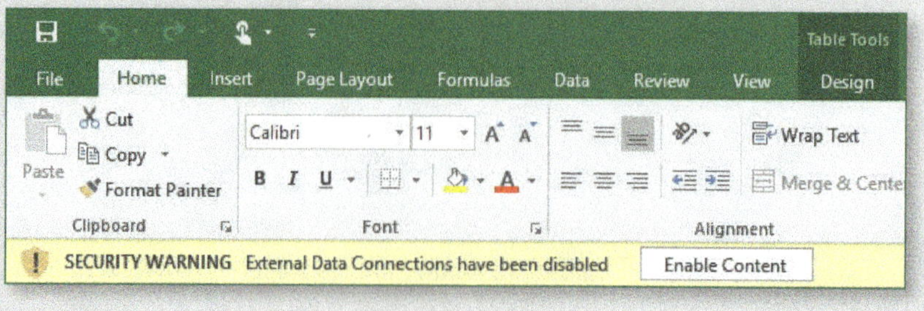

4-67 Security warning for a workbook with data connections

c. Locate and click the **Sum of Amount by Location** preview tile.
d. Click **OK**.
e. Name the worksheet tab PivotTable.

5. Add a field and a *Slicer* window in a *PivotTable.*
   a. Drag the **Category** field from the *Choose fields to add to report* group to the *Columns* area in the *PivotTable Fields* pane.
   b. Click the **Insert Slicer** button [*PivotTable Tools Analyze* tab, *Filter* group].
   c. Select the **Classification** box and click **OK** (Figure 4-68).
   d. Select and drag the *Slicer* window to position it below the *PivotTable.*

6. Format fields in a *PivotTable.*
   a. Right-click cell **B5**.
   b. Choose **Value Field Settings** from the menu.
   c. Click **Number Format** and set **Currency** format with zero decimal places.
   d. Click **OK** to close each dialog box.

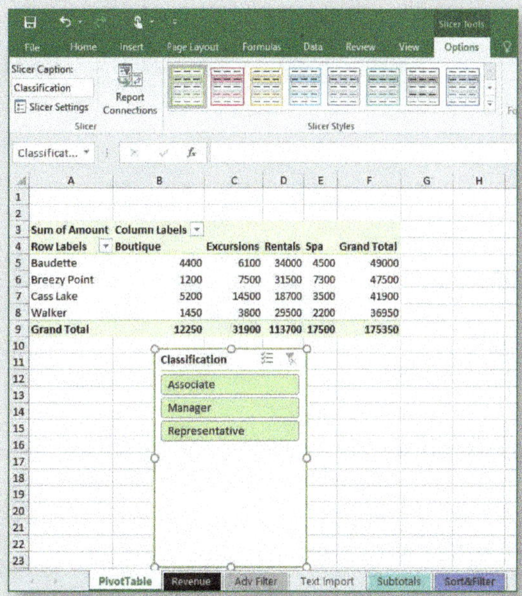

4-68 Field added to *Columns* area and *Slicer* window inserted

7. Create a *PivotChart.*
   a. Click the **PivotChart** button [*PivotTable Tools Analyze* tab, *Tools* group].
   b. Select **Clustered Column** from the *Column* group and click **OK**.
   c. Click the **Quick Layout** button [*PivotChart Tools Design* tab, *Chart Layouts* group].
   d. Select **Layout 3**.
   e. Click to select the **Chart Title** placeholder.
   f. Click the *Formula* bar, type Revenue by Category, and press **Enter**.
   g. Position the chart object so that its top left corner is at cell **H3**.

8. Adjust fields in a *PivotTable* and *PivotChart.*
   a. Click **Representative** in the *Slicer* window. The data is filtered in the *PivotTable* and in the *PivotChart.*
   b. Click the **Category** button in the chart.
   c. Deselect **(Select All)** to remove all the check marks (Figure 4-69).
   d. Select the **Excursions** and **Rentals** boxes and click **OK**.

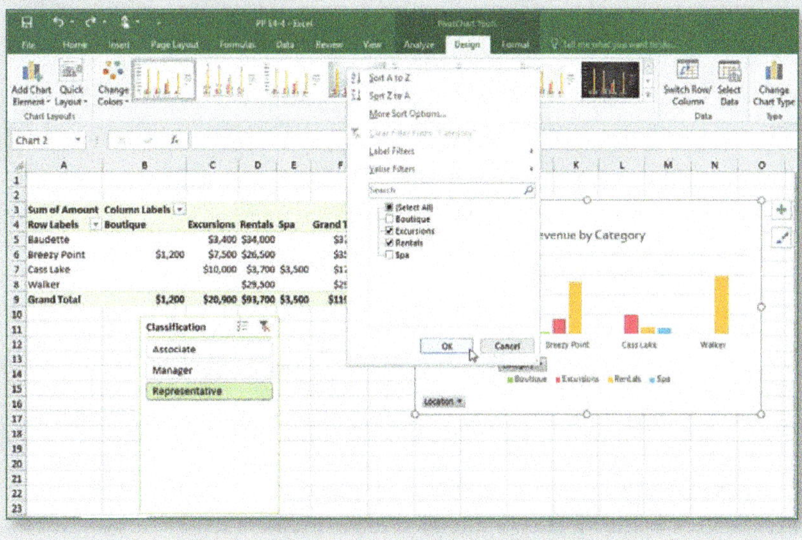

4-69 Data is filtered in the chart and the table

9. Click cell **A1**.

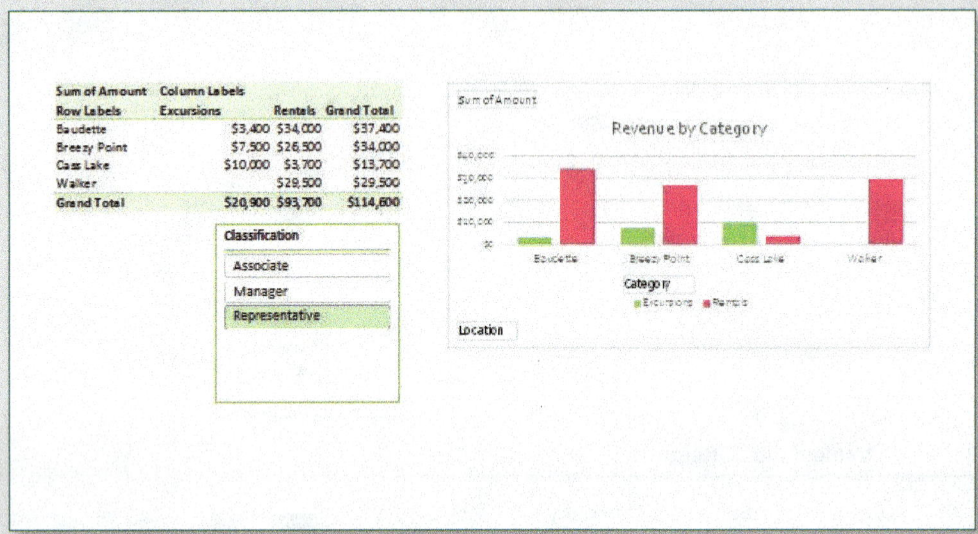

4-70 Completed worksheet for PP E4-4

10. Save and close the workbook (Figure 4-70).

Chapter Summary

4.1 Create and format a list as an Excel table (p. E4-222).

- An Excel ***table*** provides enhanced commands for sorting, filtering, and calculating data.
- A table is a list with a ***header row,*** *AutoFilter* arrows with the labels in the header row, and the same type of data in each column.
- When any cell in a table is selected, the *Table Tools Design* tab is available with commands for editing and formatting the table.
- A ***table style*** is a preset combination of colors and borders.
- Table style options enable you to display a total row, to emphasize the first or last column, and to add shading to rows or columns.
- The *Table Tools* group on the *Table Tools Design* tab has commands to remove duplicate rows, to convert a table to a normal cell range, or to insert a *slicer* window for filtering the data.
- The automatic name for a table and several of its parts are ***structured references.***
- Structured references appear in *Formula AutoComplete* lists and are substituted automatically in formulas that refer to certain cell ranges in the table.

4.2 Apply *Conditional Formatting* rules as well as *Color Scales, Icon Sets,* and *Data Bars* (p. E4-228).

- ***Conditional formatting*** formats only cells that meet specified criteria.
- *Highlight Cells Rules* use relational or comparison operators such as *Greater Than* or *Equals* to determine which cells are formatted.
- *Top/Bottom Rules* use ranking or averages to format cells.
- In the *New Rule* dialog box, you can create a rule that uses a formula to determine which cells are formatted.
- ***Data visualization*** uses rules to format cells with *Icon Sets, Color Scales,* or *Data Bars.*
- You can edit any conditional formatting rule with the *Manage Rules* command.
- Conditional formatting can be removed from a selected cell range or from the entire sheet with the *Clear Rules* command.

4.3 Sort data by one or more columns or by attribute (p. E4-234).

- ***Sorting*** is a process that arranges data in order, either ***ascending*** (A to Z) or ***descending*** (Z to A).
- Data can be sorted by one or by multiple columns.
- For a single column sort, use the *Sort A to Z* or *Sort Z to A* button in the *Sort & Filter* group on the *Data* tab.
- For a multiple column sort, use the *Sort* dialog box by clicking the *Sort* button on the *Data* tab.
- You can perform a multiple column sort within the data by sorting in lowest to highest sort priority.
- From the *Sort* dialog box, data can also be sorted by cell attribute including font color, cell color, or cell icon.
- Data in an Excel table can be sorted from the *AutoFilter* arrows with labels in the header row.

4.4 Filter data by using *AutoFilters* and by creating an *Advanced Filter* (p. E4-238).

- The *Filter* button [*Data* tab, *Sort & Filter* group] displays an *AutoFilter* arrow for each column heading in list-type data.
- From an *AutoFilter* arrow, you can select records to be shown or hidden or build a custom filter.
- A custom *AutoFilter* uses operators such as *Equals* or *Greater Than* as well as AND and OR conditions.
- An ***Advanced Filter*** provides filter options such as using a formula in the filter definition.
- An *Advanced Filter* requires a criteria range in the same workbook and can display filtered results separate from the data.

4.5 Use subtotals, groups, and outlines for tabular data in a worksheet (p. E4-242).

- The ***Subtotal*** command inserts summary rows for sorted data using *SUM* or a statistical function.
- The *Subtotal* command formats the data as an ***outline,*** which groups records so that they can be displayed or hidden.

- Outline buttons appear next to row and column headings and determine the level of detail shown in the data.
- An ***Auto Outline*** creates groups based on formulas that are located in a consistent pattern in a list.
- Groups can be defined by sorting data, inserting blank rows, and using the *Group* button in the *Outline* group on the *Data* tab.

4.6 Import data into an Excel worksheet from a text file, a database file, and other sources (p. E4-248).

- To save time and increase accuracy, you can ***import*** text files into a worksheet.
- Common text file formats include *.txt* (text) and *.csv* (comma separated values).
- Data in a text file is ***delimited*** or ***fixed width.***
- The ***Text Import Wizard*** guides you through the steps of importing data.
- You can copy data from a Word document into a worksheet.
- From a ***Microsoft Access database,*** you can import a table or a query into a worksheet.
- If a web site has table-formatted data, you can use the *From Web* command on the *Data* tab to import data into a worksheet.
- Data that has been imported from a command in the *Get External Data* group establishes a data connection so that the data can be refreshed.
- The ***Flash Fill*** command recognizes and copies typing actions from one or more cells and suggests data for the remaining rows in the same column.

4.7 Export Excel data as a text file and into a Word document (p. E4-254).

- Data in a worksheet can be exported for use in another program or application.
- Excel data can be exported as a text file.
- Text file formats can be tab-, space-, or comma-delimited.
- The Windows or Office *Clipboard* can be used to copy data from Excel into Word and other programs.

4.8 Build and format a *PivotTable* (p. E4-258).

- A ***PivotTable*** is a cross-tabulated summary report on its own worksheet.
- When a *PivotTable* is active, the *PivotTable Tools Analyze* and *Design* tabs are available.
- When any cell in a *PivotTable* is selected, the *PivotTable Fields* pane is open on the right side of the window.
- The *PivotTable Fields* pane includes a list of available fields and areas in the report in which the fields can be positioned.
- You can drag field names in the *PivotTable Fields* pane to reposition them and analyze data from a different perspective.
- Fields in a *PivotTable* can be modified and formatted from the *Field Settings* dialog box.
- *PivotTables* can be formatted from the *PivotTable Tools Design* tab, and selected cells can be formatted from the *Home* tab.
- A ***PivotChart*** is a chart based on a *PivotTable* with the same features as the *PivotTable.*

Check for Understanding

The SIMbook for this text (within your SIMnet account) provides the following resources for concept review:

- Multiple choice questions
- Matching exercises
- Short answer questions

USING MICROSOFT EXCEL 2016

Guided Project 4-1

For this project, you import a text file to complete the inventory worksheet for Wear-Ever Shoes. You use *Flash Fill* to enter product codes and sort the data by supplier and code. You use *AutoFilter* for several tasks, format data as an Excel table, prepare subtotals, build a *PivotTable,* and export data as a text file.
[Student Learning Outcomes 4.1, 4.2, 4.3, 4.4, 4.5, 4.6, 4.7, 4.8]

Files Needed: ***WearEver-04.xlsx*** and ***WearEver-04.txt*** *[Student data files are available in the* Library *of your SIMnet account.]*
Completed Project File Names: ***[your initials] Excel 4-1.xlsx*** and ***[your initials] Excel 4-1.txt***

Skills Covered in This Project

- Import a text file.
- Use *Flash Fill* to complete data.
- Sort data.
- Use an *AutoFilter.*
- Set conditional formatting.
- Create an Excel table.
- Use the *Subtotal* command.
- Create and format a *PivotTable.*
- Export data as a tab-delimited file.

1. Open the ***WearEver-04*** workbook from your student data files and save it as [your initials] Excel 4-1.
2. Import a text file.
   a. Select cell **I4**.
   b. Click the **From Text** button [*Data* tab, *Get External Data* group].
   c. Find and select the ***WearEver-04.txt*** file from your student data files in the *Import Text File* window.
   d. Click **Import**.
   e. Verify that the **Delimited** button is selected in the first *Wizard* window and click **Next**.
   f. Verify that the **Tab** box is selected and click **Next**.
   g. Do not change any formats and click **Finish**.
   h. Click **OK** in the *Import Data* dialog box. The supplier name and phone number are imported and added to the list.
3. Use the **Format Painter** button to copy formatting from cell **H4** to cells **I4:J4**.
4. *AutoFit* columns **I:J**.
5. Select cells **A1:J2** and click the **Launcher** in the *Alignment* group [*Home* tab]. From the *Horizontal* list, choose **Center Across Selection**.
6. Use *Flash Fill* to insert product codes.
   a. Insert a column between columns **B** and **C**.
   b. Type Code in cell **C4**.
   c. Type RHB in cell **C5**.
   d. Type r and press **Enter** in cell **C6**. Regular *AutoComplete* completes the entries based on what is already in the column.
   e. In cell **C7**, type r and press **Enter**.

f. Click the **Fill** button [*Home* tab, *Editing* group]. The *Flash Fill* suggestion list did not appear because there is no recognizable pattern.
g. Choose **Flash Fill**.
h. *AutoFit* column **C**.

7. Sort data in multiple columns.
   a. Click cell **A5**.
   b. Click the **Sort** button [*Data* tab, *Sort & Filter* group].
   c. Select the **My data has headers** box, if necessary.
   d. Click the **Sort by** arrow and choose **Supplier**.
   e. Verify that **Values** is selected for *Sort On*.
   f. Choose **A to Z** for *Order*.
   g. Click **Add Level**.
   h. Click the **Then by** arrow and choose **Code**.
   i. Verify that **Values** is selected for *Sort On* and that **A to Z** is selected for *Order*.
   j. Click **OK** (Figure 4-71).

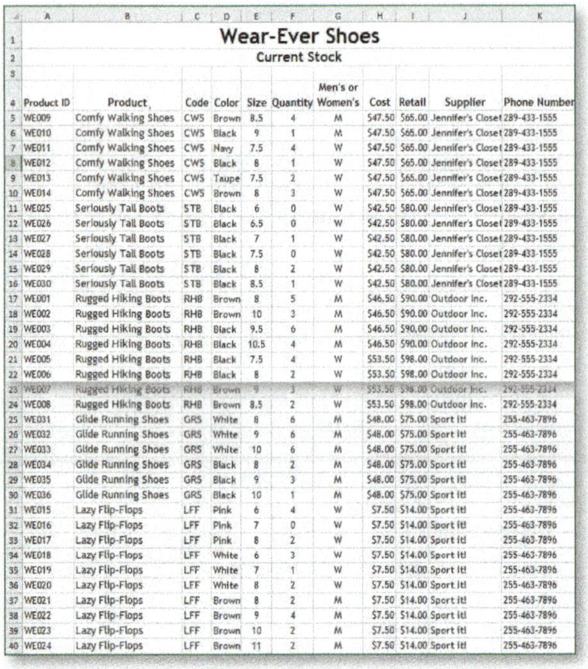

	A	B	C	D	E	F	G	H	I	J	K
1	Wear-Ever Shoes										
2	Current Stock										
3											
4	Product ID	Product	Code	Color	Size	Quantity	Men's or Women's	Cost	Retail	Supplier	Phone Number
5	WE009	Comfy Walking Shoes	CWS	Brown	8.5	4	M	$47.50	$65.00	Jennifer's Closet	289-433-1555
6	WE010	Comfy Walking Shoes	CWS	Black	9	1	M	$47.50	$65.00	Jennifer's Closet	289-433-1555
7	WE011	Comfy Walking Shoes	CWS	Navy	7.5	4	W	$47.50	$65.00	Jennifer's Closet	289-433-1555
8	WE012	Comfy Walking Shoes	CWS	Black	8	1	W	$47.50	$65.00	Jennifer's Closet	289-433-1555
9	WE013	Comfy Walking Shoes	CWS	Taupe	7.5	2	W	$47.50	$65.00	Jennifer's Closet	289-433-1555
10	WE014	Comfy Walking Shoes	CWS	Brown	8	3	W	$47.50	$65.00	Jennifer's Closet	289-433-1555
11	WE025	Seriously Tall Boots	STB	Black	6	0	W	$42.50	$80.00	Jennifer's Closet	289-433-1555
12	WE026	Seriously Tall Boots	STB	Black	6.5	0	W	$42.50	$80.00	Jennifer's Closet	289-433-1555
13	WE027	Seriously Tall Boots	STB	Black	7	1	W	$42.50	$80.00	Jennifer's Closet	289-433-1555
14	WE028	Seriously Tall Boots	STB	Black	7.5	0	W	$42.50	$80.00	Jennifer's Closet	289-433-1555
15	WE029	Seriously Tall Boots	STB	Black	8	2	W	$42.50	$80.00	Jennifer's Closet	289-433-1555
16	WE030	Seriously Tall Boots	STB	Black	8.5	1	W	$42.50	$80.00	Jennifer's Closet	289-433-1555
17	WE001	Rugged Hiking Boots	RHB	Brown	8	5	M	$46.50	$90.00	Outdoor Inc.	292-555-2334
18	WE002	Rugged Hiking Boots	RHB	Brown	10	3	M	$46.50	$90.00	Outdoor Inc.	292-555-2334
19	WE003	Rugged Hiking Boots	RHB	Black	9.5	6	M	$46.50	$90.00	Outdoor Inc.	292-555-2334
20	WE004	Rugged Hiking Boots	RHB	Black	10.5	4	M	$46.50	$90.00	Outdoor Inc.	292-555-2334
21	WE005	Rugged Hiking Boots	RHB	Black	7.5	4	W	$53.50	$98.00	Outdoor Inc.	292-555-2334
22	WE006	Rugged Hiking Boots	RHB	Black	8	2	W	$53.50	$98.00	Outdoor Inc.	292-555-2334
23	WE007	Rugged Hiking Boots	RHB	Brown	9	3	W	$53.50	$98.00	Outdoor Inc.	292-555-2334
24	WE008	Rugged Hiking Boots	RHB	Brown	8.5	2	W	$53.50	$98.00	Outdoor Inc.	292-555-2334
25	WE031	Glide Running Shoes	GRS	White	8	6	M	$48.00	$75.00	Sport it!	255-463-7896
26	WE032	Glide Running Shoes	GRS	White	9	6	M	$48.00	$75.00	Sport it!	255-463-7896
27	WE033	Glide Running Shoes	GRS	White	10	6	M	$48.00	$75.00	Sport it!	255-463-7896
28	WE034	Glide Running Shoes	GRS	Black	8	2	M	$48.00	$75.00	Sport it!	255-463-7896
29	WE035	Glide Running Shoes	GRS	Black	9	3	M	$48.00	$75.00	Sport it!	255-463-7896
30	WE036	Glide Running Shoes	GRS	Black	10	1	M	$48.00	$75.00	Sport it!	255-463-7896
31	WE015	Lazy Flip-Flops	LFF	Pink	6	4	W	$7.50	$14.00	Sport it!	255-463-7896
32	WE016	Lazy Flip-Flops	LFF	Pink	7	0	W	$7.50	$14.00	Sport it!	255-463-7896
33	WE017	Lazy Flip-Flops	LFF	Pink	8	2	W	$7.50	$14.00	Sport it!	255-463-7896
34	WE018	Lazy Flip-Flops	LFF	White	6	3	W	$7.50	$14.00	Sport it!	255-463-7896
35	WE019	Lazy Flip-Flops	LFF	White	7	1	W	$7.50	$14.00	Sport it!	255-463-7896
36	WE020	Lazy Flip-Flops	LFF	White	8	2	W	$7.50	$14.00	Sport it!	255-463-7896
37	WE021	Lazy Flip-Flops	LFF	Brown	8	2	M	$7.50	$14.00	Sport it!	255-463-7896
38	WE022	Lazy Flip-Flops	LFF	Brown	9	4	M	$7.50	$14.00	Sport it!	255-463-7896
39	WE023	Lazy Flip-Flops	LFF	Brown	10	2	M	$7.50	$14.00	Sport it!	255-463-7896
40	WE024	Lazy Flip-Flops	LFF	Brown	11	2	M	$7.50	$14.00	Sport it!	255-463-7896

4-71 Data sorted by "Supplier" and "Code"

8. Apply conditional formatting.
   a. Select cells **F5:F40**, the quantity in stock.
   b. Click the **Conditional Formatting** button [*Home* tab, *Style* group].
   c. Click **Highlight Cells Rules** and select **Less Than**.
   d. Type 2 in the *Format cells that are LESS THAN* box.
   e. Click **OK** to accept the *Light Red Fill with Dark Red Text* format.

9. Use an *AutoFilter*.
   a. Click cell **A5**.
   b. Click the **Filter** button [*Data* tab, *Sort & Filter* group].
   c. Click the *AutoFilter* arrow for the **Supplier** column.
   d. Deselect the **(Select All)** box to remove all the check marks.
   e. Select the **Jennifer's Closet** box.
   f. Click **OK**. The data is filtered to show only records from one supplier.

10. Copy the **Inventory** worksheet to the right and name the copy Women's. Set the tab color to **Gold, Accent 4**.

11. Clear a filter and conditional formatting.
    a. On the **Women's** sheet, click the *AutoFilter* arrow for the **Supplier** column.
    b. Select **Clear Filter from "Supplier."**
    c. Click the **Filter** button [*Data* tab, *Sort & Filter* group] to hide the *AutoFilter* arrows.
    d. Click the **Conditional Formatting** button [*Home* tab, *Style* group].
    e. Select **Clear Rules** and select **Clear Rules From Entire Sheet**.

12. Create an Excel table.
    a. Select cells **A4:K40** on the **Women's** sheet.
    b. Click the **Format as Table** button [*Home* tab, *Styles* group].

c. Choose **Table Style Medium 5** in the *Table Styles* gallery.
d. Confirm the range in the *Format as Table* dialog box and click **OK**.
e. Select **Yes** in the message box to remove the data connection (Figure 4-72).

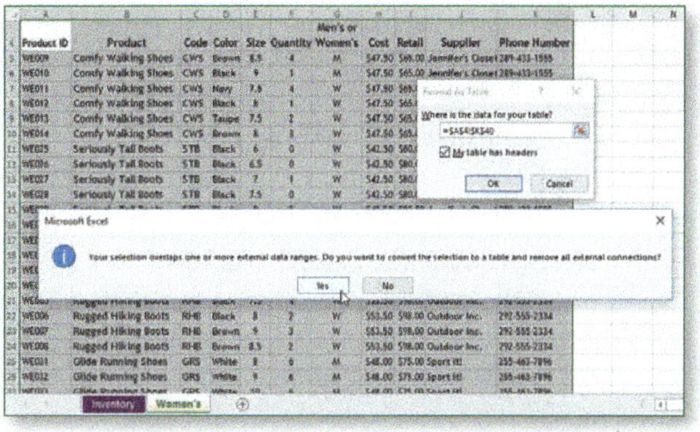

4-72 Data connection will be removed to create the table

13. Add a calculated column to a table.
    a. Insert a column at column **J**.
    b. Type Markup in cell **J4** and press **Enter**.
    c. Type = in cell **J5** to start the formula and click cell **I5**.
    d. Type – for subtraction and click cell **H5**.
    e. Press **Enter** to copy the formula.
14. Filter data in a table.
    a. Click the *AutoFilter* arrow for the **Men's or Women's** column.
    b. Deselect the **(Select All)** box to remove all the check marks.
    c. Select the **W** box and click **OK**.
    d. Press **Ctrl+Home** (Figure 4-73).

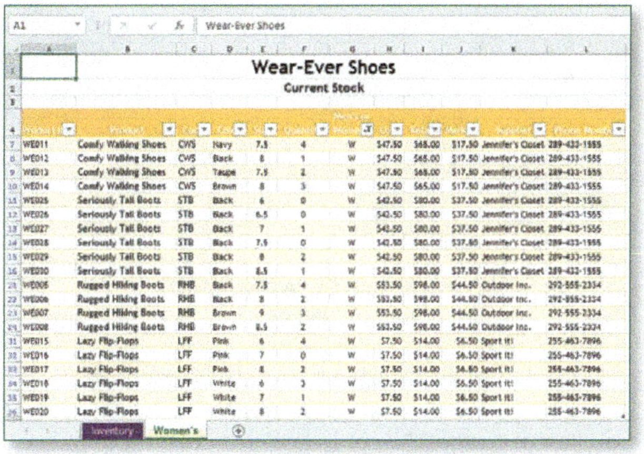

4-73 Table filtered to show women's products

15. Copy the **Inventory** worksheet to the end and name the copy Subtotals. Set the tab color to **Orange**, **Accent 6**.
16. Clear a filter and conditional formatting.
    a. On the **Subtotals** sheet, clear the filter for the **Supplier**.
    b. Click the **Filter** button [*Data* tab, *Sort & Filter* group] to hide the *AutoFilter* arrows.
    c. Click the **Conditional Formatting** button [*Home* tab, *Style* group] and clear rules from the sheet.
17. Use the *Subtotal* command.
    a. On the **Subtotals** sheet, select cell **J5**. The records are sorted by the "Supplier" column.
    b. Click the **Subtotal** button [*Data* tab, *Outline* group].
    c. Click the **At each change in** arrow and choose **Supplier**.
    d. Click the **Use function** arrow and choose **Count**.
    e. Check the **Supplier** box in the *Add subtotal to* area.
    f. Deselect any other selected fields in the *Add subtotal to* list (Figure 4-74).
    g. Click **OK**. A subtotal row displays at the bottom of each group and shows how many products are available from each supplier.
    h. Format the label in cell **I17** as **right-aligned**.

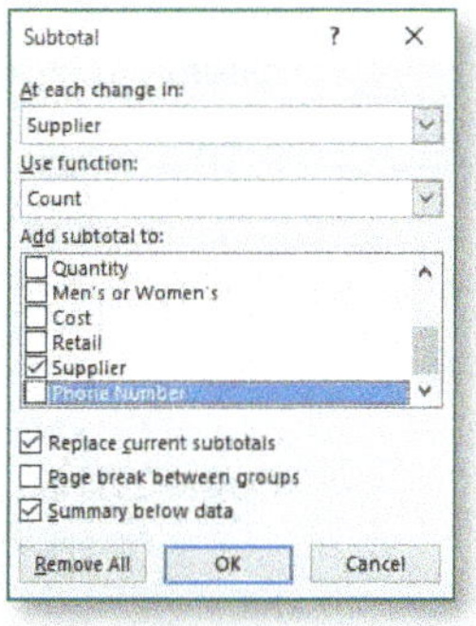

4-74 *Subtotal* dialog box to count number of products by supplier

i. **Right-align** the remaining subtotal labels in column **I** (Figure 4-75).

18. Create a *PivotTable.*
    a. Click the **Inventory** sheet tab and select cell **A5**.
    b. Click the **PivotTable** button [*Insert* tab, *Tables* group].
    c. Verify that the *Table/Range* is **$A$4:$K$40** in the *Create PivotTable* dialog box and that the *New Worksheet* button is selected (Figure 4-76).
    d. Click **OK**. A blank *PivotTable* layout displays on a new sheet.
19. Add fields in a *PivotTable.*
    a. Select the **Product** box in the *PivotTable Fields* pane to place it in the *Rows* area.
    b. Select the **Quantity** box to place it in the *Values* area.
    c. Drag the **Supplier** field name into the *Columns* area.
20. Format a *PivotTable.*
    a. Click the **More** button in the *PivotTable Styles* group [*PivotTable Tools Design* tab].
    b. Select **PivotTable Style Medium 7**.
    c. Select the **Banded Rows** box [*PivotTable Tools Design* tab, *PivotTable Style Options* group].
    d. Select the **Banded Columns** box [*PivotTable Tools Design* tab, *PivotTable Style Options* group] (Figure 4-77).
    e. Name the sheet PivotTable.
21. Copy the **Inventory** worksheet to the end and do not rename it.
22. On the copied sheet, clear the filter from the **Supplier** column and remove the *AutoFilter* arrows.
23. Export data as a tab-delimited file.
    a. Click cell **A1** in the copied sheet.
    b. Click the **File** tab and select **Export**.
    c. Select **Change File Type**.
    d. Select **Text (Tab delimited)** as the file type.
    e. Click **Save As**.
    f. Navigate to the save location for the exported data in the *Save as type* dialog box.
    g. Type Excel 4-1 as the file name.

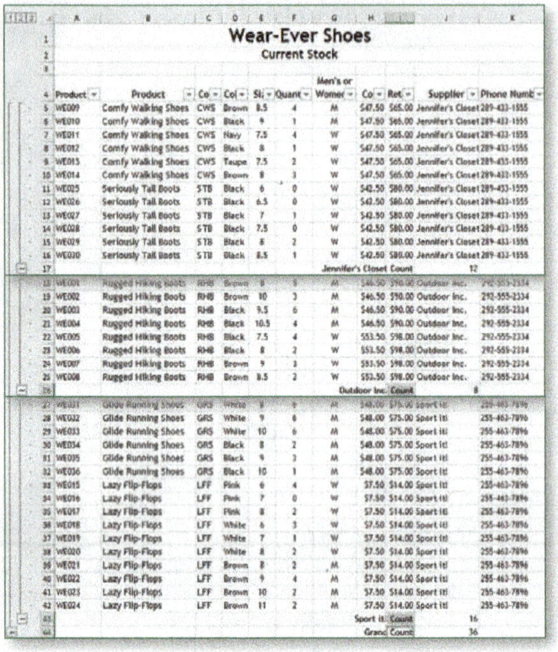

4-75 Subtotals inserted for each group

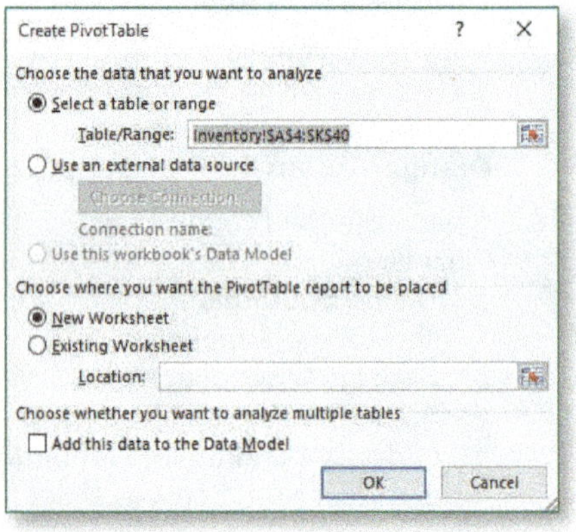

4-76 *Create PivotTable* dialog box

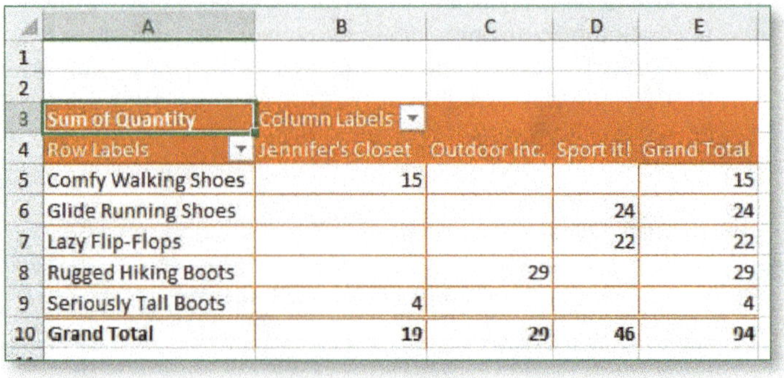

Sum of Quantity	Column Labels			
Row Labels	Jennifer's Closet	Outdoor Inc.	Sport it!	Grand Total
Comfy Walking Shoes	15			15
Glide Running Shoes			24	24
Lazy Flip-Flops			22	22
Rugged Hiking Boots		29		29
Seriously Tall Boots	4			4
Grand Total	19	29	46	94

4-77 Formatted *PivotTable*

h. Click **Save**.

i. Click **OK** in the message box to save only the current sheet (Figure 4-78).

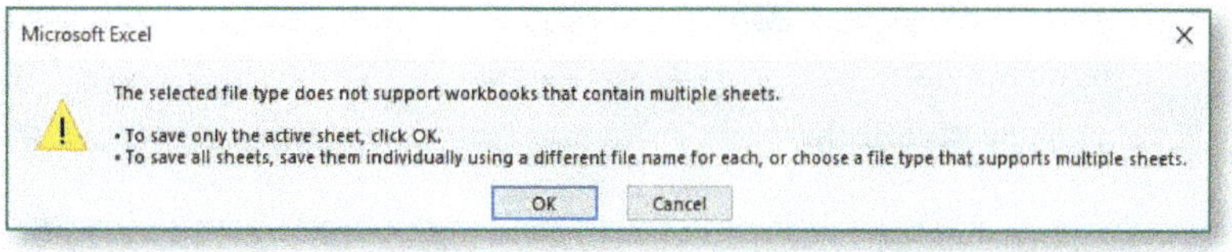

4-78 Only the current sheet is saved as a text file

j. Click **Yes** in the message box about features being lost. The sheet is renamed and the data is exported to a *.txt* file.

24. Save the workbook with the same file name.
    a. Click the **File** tab and choose **Save As**.
    b. Navigate to the folder for saved work.
    c. Select **Excel Workbook** as the *Save as type* in the *Save As* dialog box.
    d. Select ***[your initials] Excel 4-1*** from the list.
    e. Click **Save** and select **Yes** to replace the *.xlsx* file that you saved at the beginning of this project.
    f. Close the workbook (Figure 4-79).

Wear-Ever Shoes

Current Stock

Product	Product	Co	Col	Si	Quant	Men's or Womer	Co	Ret	Supplier	Phone Numb
WE009	Comfy Walking Shoes	CWS	Brown	8.5	4	M	$47.50	$65.00	Jennifer's Closet	289-433-1555
WE010	Comfy Walking Shoes	CWS	Black	9	1	M	$47.50	$65.00	Jennifer's Closet	289-433-1555
WE011	Comfy Walking Shoes	CWS	Navy	7.5	4	W	$47.50	$65.00	Jennifer's Closet	289-433-1555
WE012	Comfy Walking Shoes	CWS	Black	8	1	W	$47.50	$65.00	Jennifer's Closet	289-433-1555
WE013	Comfy Walking Shoes	CWS	Taupe	7.5	2	W	$47.50	$65.00	Jennifer's Closet	289-433-1555
WE014	Comfy Walking Shoes	CWS	Brown	8	3	W	$47.50	$65.00	Jennifer's Closet	289-433-1555
WE025	Seriously Tall Boots	STB	Black	6	0	W	$42.50	$80.00	Jennifer's Closet	289-433-1555
WE026	Seriously Tall Boots	STB	Black	6.5	0	W	$42.50	$80.00	Jennifer's Closet	289-433-1555
WE027	Seriously Tall Boots	STB	Black	7	1	W	$42.50	$80.00	Jennifer's Closet	289-433-1555
WE028	Seriously Tall Boots	STB	Black	7.5	0	W	$42.50	$80.00	Jennifer's Closet	289-433-1555
WE029	Seriously Tall Boots	STB	Black	8	2	W	$42.50	$80.00	Jennifer's Closet	289-433-1555
WE030	Seriously Tall Boots	STB	Black	8.5	1	W	$42.50	$80.00	Jennifer's Closet	289-433-1555

4-79 Excel 4-1 completed inventory worksheet

Guided Project 4-2

Classic Gardens and Landscapes is building a workbook with data about revenue and promotion campaigns. You copy data from Word and import data from an Access database. You set conditional formatting, format an Excel table, sort and filter data, and build a *PivotTable* and *PivotChart*.
[Student Learning Outcomes 4.1, 4.2, 4.3, 4.4, 4.5, 4.6, 4.7, 4.8]

Files Needed: ***ClassicGardens-04.xlsx, Database-04.accdb,*** and ***ClassicGardens-04.docx*** *[Student data files are available in the* Library *of your SIMnet account.]*
Completed Project File Names: ***[your initials] Excel 4-2.xlsx*** and ***[your initials] Excel 4-2.csv***

Skills Covered in This Project

- Copy data from Word.
- Use conditional formatting with an icon set.
- Prepare data for an *Auto Outline.*
- Import a table from a database file.
- Apply a table style and show a total row.
- Sort and filter data in a table.
- Build and format a *PivotTable.*
- Build a *PivotChart.*
- Filter data in a *PivotChart.*
- Export data as a comma-separated text file.

1. Open the ***ClassicGardens-04*** workbook from your student data files and save it as [your initials] Excel 4-2.
2. Select the **Quarterly** sheet; insert six columns between columns **G** and **H**.
3. Copy data from Word.
   a. Open the Word document ***ClassicGardens-04. docx*** from your student data files.
   b. Select all the data in Word and copy it.
   c. Select cell **H4** in the Excel workbook.
   d. Click the **Paste** button arrow [*Home* tab, *Clipboard* group] and choose **Match Destination Formatting**.
   e. Select cell **N5** and click the **AutoSum** button [*Home* tab, *Editing* group].
   f. Verify or select the range **B5:M5** and press **Enter**.
   g. Double-click the *Fill* handle for cell **N5** to copy the formula to cells **N6:N10**.
   h. Select cells **H10:M10** and click the **AutoSum** button [*Home* tab, *Editing* group].
4. Apply conditional formatting.
   a. Select cells **N5:N9**.
   b. Click the **Quick Analysis** button.
   c. Verify that **Formatting** is selected.
   d. Choose **Icon Set** (Figure 4-80).The cells display an icon to represent the upper, middle, or lower values of the range.
5. *AutoFit* the columns and make sure all data is visible.

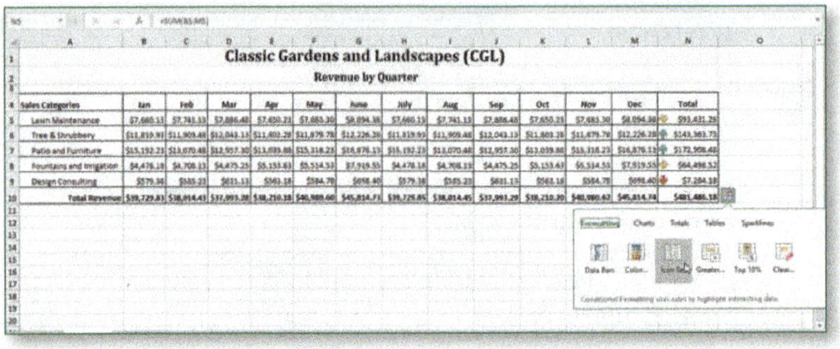

4-80 Icon set conditional formatting

6. Click the **AutoOutline** sheet tab.
7. Use *AutoSum* to calculate subtotals and totals.
   a. Select cells **E5:E18**, press **Ctrl** and select cells **I5:I18**, **M5:M18**, and **Q5:Q18** (Figure 4-81).
   b. Click the **AutoSum** button [*Home* tab, *Editing* group].
   c. Select cells **R5:R18** and click the **AutoSum** button [*Home* tab, *Editing* group]. Excel sums the *Qtr 1, Qtr 2, Qtr 3,* and *Qtr 4* columns.
   d. Select cells **B19:R19** and click the **AutoSum** button [*Home* tab, *Editing* group].
   e. *AutoFit* columns as needed.
   f. Select cells **E21:E25**, press **Ctrl** and select cells **I21:I25**, **M21:M25**, and **Q21:Q25**.
   g. Click the **AutoSum** button [*Home* tab, *Editing* group].

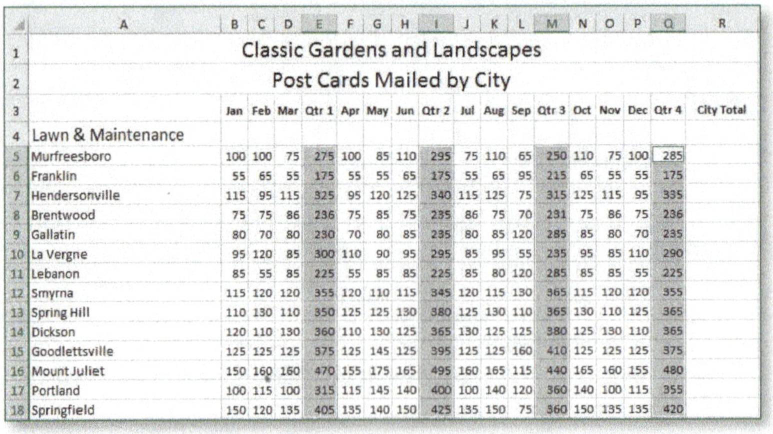

	A	B	C	D	E	F	G	H	I	J	K	L	M	N	O	P	Q	R
1	Classic Gardens and Landscapes																	
2	Post Cards Mailed by City																	
3		Jan	Feb	Mar	Qtr 1	Apr	May	Jun	Qtr 2	Jul	Aug	Sep	Qtr 3	Oct	Nov	Dec	Qtr 4	City Total
4	Lawn & Maintenance																	
5	Murfreesboro	100	100	75	275	100	85	110	295	75	110	65	250	110	75	100	285	
6	Franklin	55	65	55	175	55	55	65	175	55	65	95	215	65	55	55	175	
7	Hendersonville	115	95	115	325	95	120	125	340	115	125	75	315	125	115	95	335	
8	Brentwood	75	75	86	236	75	85	75	235	86	75	70	231	75	86	75	236	
9	Gallatin	80	70	80	230	70	80	85	235	80	85	120	285	85	80	70	235	
10	La Vergne	95	120	85	300	110	90	95	295	85	95	55	235	95	85	110	290	
11	Lebanon	85	55	85	225	55	85	85	225	85	80	120	285	85	85	55	225	
12	Smyrna	115	120	120	355	120	110	115	345	120	115	130	365	115	120	120	355	
13	Spring Hill	110	130	110	350	125	125	130	380	125	130	110	365	130	110	125	365	
14	Dickson	120	110	130	360	110	130	125	365	130	125	125	380	125	130	110	365	
15	Goodlettsville	125	125	125	375	125	145	125	395	125	125	160	410	125	125	125	375	
16	Mount Juliet	150	160	160	470	155	175	165	495	160	165	115	440	165	160	155	480	
17	Portland	100	115	100	315	115	145	140	400	100	140	120	360	140	100	115	355	
18	Springfield	150	120	135	405	135	140	150	425	135	150	75	360	150	135	135	420	

4-81 *SUM* function used in a consistent pattern

   h. Use *AutoSum* in cells **R21:R25**, in cells **E28:E33**, **I28:I33**, **M28:M33**, **Q28:Q33**, and in cells **R28:R33** to complete the worksheet.
   i. *AutoFit* the columns.

8. In cell **B35**, type = to start a formula.
9. Click cell **B19**, type +, click cell **B26**, type +, click cell **B34**, and press **Enter**. The formula is =**B19+B26+B34**.
10. Copy the formula in cell **B35** to cells **C35:R35**. *AutoFit* the columns, if necessary.
11. Create an *Auto Outline.*
   a. Click cell **B5**.
   b. Click the arrow for the **Group** button [*Data* tab, *Outline* group] and choose **Auto Outline** (Figure 4-82). The *Auto Outline* command uses column and row formulas to group the data.
   c. Click the **Level 2** column outline button (above the column headings).Only the quarter totals display (Figure 4-83).

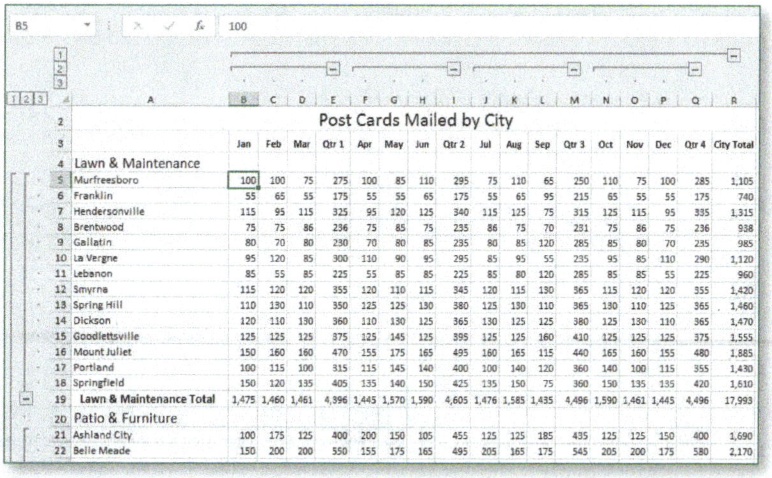

4-82 *AutoOutline* with three row levels and three column levels

12. Import a table from an Access database.
   a. Click the **Table** sheet tab.
   b. Select cell **A4**.
   c. Click the **From Access** button [*Data* tab, *Get External Data* group].
   d. Find and select ***Database-04.accdb*** from your student data files in the *Select Data Source* window.
   e. Click **Open**.
   f. Click **tblMailings** in the *Select Table* dialog box (Figure 4-84).
   g. Click **OK**.
   h. Select **Table** and **Existing worksheet** if necessary and click **OK**.

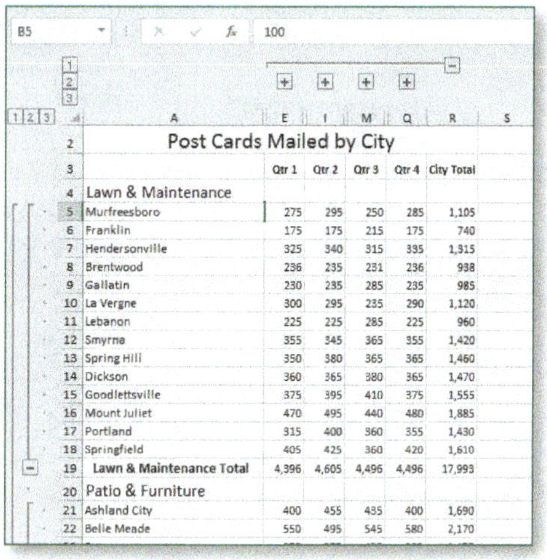

4-83 Outline collapsed at Level 2 column group

13. Apply a table style and show a total row.
   a. Click cell **B5** in the table.
   b. Click the **More** button [*Table Tools Design* tab, *Table Styles* group].
   c. Choose **Table Style Medium 15**.
   d. Select the **Total Row** box [*Table Tools Design* tab, *Table Style Options* group].
   e. Click cell **C30** and choose **Sum**. Then copy the formula to cells **D30:M30**.

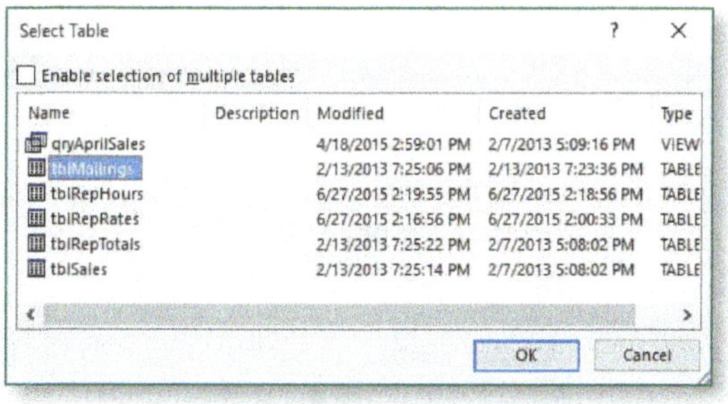

4-84 *Select Table* dialog box for an Access database

14. Sort and filter data in an Excel table.
    a. Click the *AutoFilter* arrow for **City**.
    b. Choose **Sort A to Z**.
    c. Click the *AutoFilter* arrow for **City**.
    d. Select **Text Filters** and **Equals**.
    e. Type c* in the first criteria box to select cities that begin with "C."
    f. Select the **Or** radio button.
    g. Verify that **equals** is selected as the second operator.
    h. Type m* in the second criteria box to select cities that begin with "M" (Figure 4-85).
    i. Click **OK**.

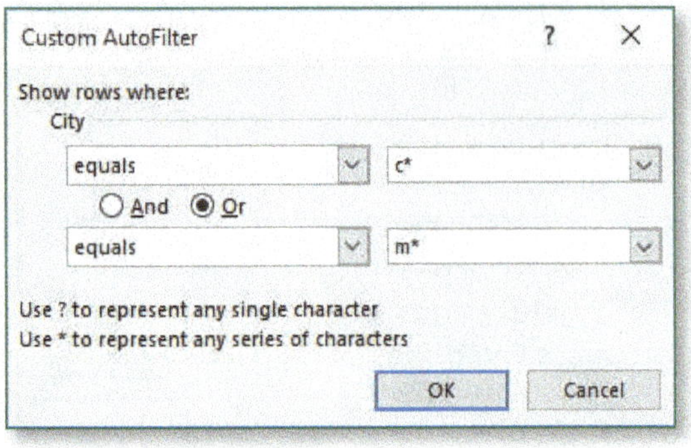

4-85 ***Custom AutoFilter*** **for cities that begin with "C" or "M"**

15. Merge and center the labels in rows **1:2** and set them to a font size of **18 pt**. (Figure 4-86).

16. Select the **Pivot Source** sheet tab.

17. Create a *PivotTable*.
    a. Select cell **A5**.
    b. Click the **Recommended PivotTables** button [*Insert* tab, *Tables* group].
    c. Select the **Sum of # of Responses by Department** thumbnail and click **OK**.
    d. Select the **City** and **# Mailed** boxes in the *Choose fields to add to report* area to add them to the report.
    e. Drag the **Department** field from the *Rows* area to the *Filters* area in the *PivotTable Fields* pane (Figure 4-87).

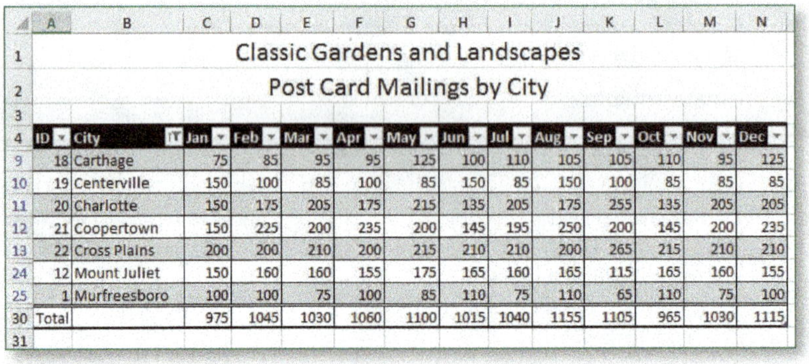

Classic Gardens and Landscapes

Post Card Mailings by City

	ID	City	Jan	Feb	Mar	Apr	May	Jun	Jul	Aug	Sep	Oct	Nov	Dec
9	18	Carthage	75	85	95	95	125	100	110	105	105	110	95	125
10	19	Centerville	150	100	85	100	85	150	85	150	100	85	85	85
11	20	Charlotte	150	175	205	175	215	135	205	175	255	135	205	205
12	21	Coopertown	150	225	200	235	200	145	195	250	200	145	200	235
13	22	Cross Plains	200	200	210	200	215	210	210	200	265	215	210	210
24	12	Mount Juliet	150	160	160	155	175	165	160	165	115	165	160	155
25	1	Murfreesboro	100	100	75	100	85	110	75	110	65	110	75	100
30	Total		975	1045	1030	1060	1100	1015	1040	1155	1105	965	1030	1115

4-86 Imported data sorted and filtered

18. Format a *PivotTable*.
    a. Right-click cell **B4** and select **Value Field Settings** from the context menu.
    b. Click **Number Format**.
    c. Choose **Number** as the *Category*.
    d. Select zero decimal places.
    e. Select the **Use 1000 Separator (,)** box.
    f. Click **OK** to close each dialog box.
    g. Apply the same number format for "Sum of # Mailed" field.
    h. Click the **More** button [*PivotTable Tools Design* tab, *PivotTable Styles* group].
    i. Select **PivotTable Style Medium 9** [*PivotTable Tools Design* tab, *PivotTable Styles* group].
    j. Select the **Banded Rows** box [*PivotTable Tools Design* tab, *PivotTable Styles Options* group].

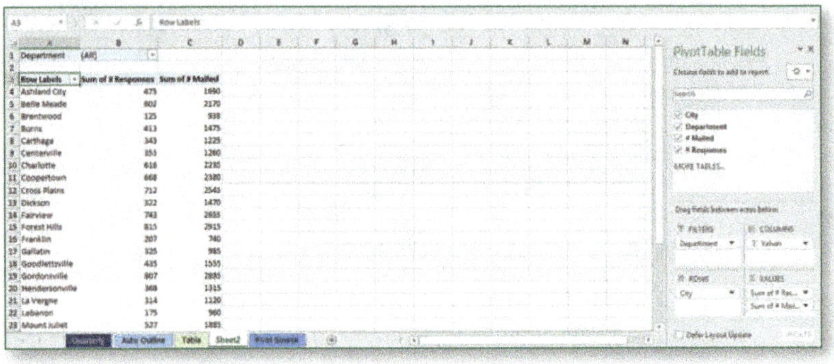

4-87 ***PivotTable*** **layout**

k. Select the **Banded Columns** box [*PivotTable Tools Design* tab, *PivotTable Styles Options* group] (Figure 4-88).

19. Create and format a *PivotChart*.
    a. Click the **PivotChart** button [*PivotTable Tools Analyze* tab, *Tools* group].
    b. Select **Bar** as the chart type and **Clustered Bar** as the subtype.
    c. Click **OK**.
    d. Position the chart object so that its top-left corner is at cell **E3**.
    e. Drag the bottom-right selection handle to reach cell **O24**.
    f. Click the **More** button [*PivotChart Tools Design* tab, *Chart Styles* group].
    g. Choose **Style 5**.
    h. Click the **Shape Outline** button [*PivotChart Tools Format* tab, *Shape Styles* group].
    i. Select **Blue, Accent 1**.

	A	B	C
1	Department	(All)	
2			
3	Row Labels	Sum of # Responses	Sum of # Mailed
4	Ashland City	473	1,690
5	Belle Meade	602	2,170
6	Brentwood	125	938
7	Burns	413	1,475
8	Carthage	343	1,225
9	Centerville	353	1,260
10	Charlotte	618	2,235
11	Coopertown	668	2,380
12	Cross Plains	712	2,545
13	Dickson	322	1,470
14	Fairview	743	2,655
15	Forest Hills	815	2,915
16	Franklin	207	740
17	Gallatin	325	985
18	Goodlettsville	435	1,555
19	Gordonsville	807	2,885
20	Hendersonville	368	1,315
21	La Vergne	314	1,120
22	Lebanon	175	960
23	Mount Juliet	527	1,885
24	Murfreesboro	309	1,105
25	Portland	389	1,430
26	Smyrna	300	1,420
27	Spring Hill	460	1,460
28	Springfield	450	1,610
29	Grand Total	11,253	41,428

4-88 Formatted *PivotTable*

20. Filter data in a *PivotChart*.
    a. Click the **Department** filter button in the chart.
    b. Select the **Select Multiple Items** box.
    c. Deselect the **(All)** box.
    d. Select the **Landscape Design** box and click **OK**.
    e. Select cell **A13** to deselect the *PivotTable* and *PivotChart* (Figure 4-89).
    f. Name the sheet PivotTable.

	A	B	C
1	Department	Landscape Design	
2			
3	Row Labels	Sum of # Responses	Sum of # Mailed
4	Centerville	353	1,260
5	Charlotte	618	2,235
6	Forest Hills	815	2,915
7	Gallatin	325	985
8	La Vergne	314	1,120
9	Portland	389	1,430
10	Springfield	450	1,610
11	Grand Total	3,264	11,555

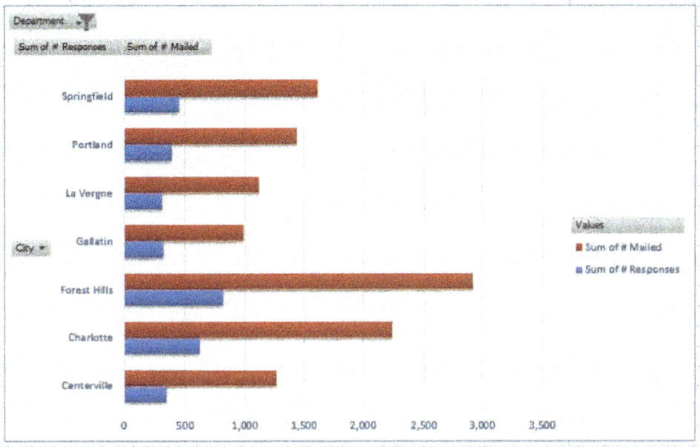

4-89 Filtered data in *PivotChart* and *PivotTable*

21. Export data as a comma-separated file.
    a. Click the **Quarterly** sheet tab.
    b. Click the **File** tab and select **Export**.
    c. Select **Change File Type**.
    d. Select **CSV (Comma delimited)** as the file type.
    e. Click **Save As**.
    f. Navigate to the save location for the exported data in the *Save as type* dialog box.

g. Type Excel 4-2 as the file name.
h. Click **Save**.
i. Click **OK** in the message box to save the current sheet.
j. Click **Yes** in the message box about lost features. The sheet is renamed and the data is exported to a *.csv* file.
k. Rename the sheet as Quarterly.

22. Save the workbook with the same file name.
    a. Click the **File** tab and choose **Save As**.
    b. Navigate to the folder for saved work.
    c. Select **Excel Workbook** as the *Save as type* in the *Save As* dialog box.
    d. Select ***[your initials] Excel 4-2*** from the list.
    e. Click **Save** and click **Yes** to replace the file.
23. Save and close the workbook. Close Word.

Guided Project 4-3

Clemenson Imaging analyzes expense reports from field representatives as well as patient and image data. To complete the worksheets, you format data as a table and build an advanced filter. You import a comma-separated text file (*.csv*) and use the *Subtotal* command. Finally, you display data in a *PivotTable*.
[Student Learning Outcomes 4.1, 4.2, 4.3, 4.4, 4.5, 4.6, 4.7, 4.8]

Files Needed: ***ClemensonImaging-04.xlsx, ClemensonImaging-04.csv,*** and ***ClemensonImaging.docx***
[Student data files are available in the Library *of your SIMnet account.]*
Completed Project File Names: ***[your initials] Excel 4-3.xlsx*** and ***[your initials] Excel 4-3.docx***

Skills Covered in This Project

- Format data as an Excel table.
- Build an *Advanced Filter.*
- Apply conditional formatting to filtered results.
- Sort data by multiple columns.
- Import a comma-separated text file.
- Use the *Subtotal* command.
- Export data via the *Clipboard.*
- Create a *PivotTable.*

1. Open the ***ClemensonImaging-04*** workbook from your student data files and save it as [your initials] Excel 4-3.
2. Copy the **Past&Projected** sheet before the **Criteria** sheet and name the copied sheet Adv Filter.
3. Create and format an Excel table.
    a. Select cells **A4:E60** on the **Adv Filter** sheet.
    b. Click the **Quick Analysis** tool and choose **Tables**.
    c. Click **Table**.
4. Apply a table style.
    a. Click cell **A5** in the table.
    b. Click the **More** button [*Table Tools Design* tab, *Table Styles* group].
    c. Select **Table Style Medium 15**.

5. Create an output range for an *Advanced Filter*.
   a. Select cells **A4:E4** and copy and paste them to cell **G4**.
   b. Type Extract Range in cell **G3** and set the font to **Cambria 16 pt**.
   c. Adjust column widths to show the labels.

6. Create an *Advanced Filter*.
   a. Click the **Criteria** sheet tab.
   b. Type >12/31/16 in cell **A3** to find records after 2016.
   c. Type mri in cell **B3**.
   d. Type >12/31/14 in cell **A4** to find records after 2014.
   e. Type ct scan in cell **B4**. This criteria will find records dated 2017 or later for MRIs *and* records for CT scans after 2014 (Figure 4-90).

	A	B	C	D	E
1	Criteria Range				
2	Month	Image	Patients	Total Hours	# of Employees
3	>12/31/16	mri			
4	>12/31/14	ct scan			

4-90 Criteria for *Advanced Filter*

   f. Click cell **A5** on the **Adv Filter** sheet.
   g. Click the **Advanced** button [*Data* tab, *Sort & Filter* group].
   h. Select the **Copy to another location** radio button.
   i. Verify that the **List range** is cells **A4:E60**. If the range is incorrect, click and drag to select the range including the header row.
   j. Click the **Criteria range** box and select cells **A2:B4** on the **Criteria** sheet.
   k. Click the **Copy to** box and select cells **G4:K4**.
   l. Click **OK** in the *Advanced Filter* dialog box.

7. Sort data in the output range.
   a. Right-click cell **H5**, choose **Sort**, and select **Sort A to Z**.
   b. Right-click cell **G5**, choose **Sort**, and select **Sort Oldest to Newest**. This sorts the results by date, earliest date first.

8. Apply conditional formatting and borders.
   a. Select cells **I5:I14**.
   b. Click the **Conditional Formatting** button [*Home* tab, *Styles* group].
   c. Choose **Highlight Cells Rules** and **Greater Than**.
   d. Type 750 and choose **Green Fill with Dark Green Text**.
   e. Click **OK**.
   f. Select cells **G5:K14** and apply **All Borders** (Figure 4-91).
   g. Press **Ctrl+Home**.

Extract Range

Month	Image	Patients	Total Hours	# of Employees
Apr 2015	CT Scan	1000	1800	5
Aug 2015	CT Scan	500	2400	3
Dec 2015	CT Scan	500	2400	2
Apr 2016	CT Scan	500	2400	3
Aug 2016	CT Scan	750	2400	3
Dec 2016	CT Scan	500	1800	4
Jan 2017	MRI	1000	1800	3
Apr 2017	CT Scan	750	2400	2
May 2017	MRI	750	3000	4
Aug 2017	CT Scan	500	2400	3

4-91 *Advanced Filter* results

9. Import a comma-separated values text file.
   a. Click the **Expense Info** sheet tab.
   b. Select cell **A5**.
   c. Click the **From Text** button [*Data* tab, *Get External Data* group].
   d. Find and select the ***ClemensonImaging-04.csv*** file from your student data files in the *Import Text File* window.
   e. Click **Import**.
   f. Select the **Delimited** button in the first *Wizard* window and click **Next**.
   g. Deselect the **Tab** box and select the **Comma** box.
   h. Click **Next**.
   i. Click the date column in the *Data preview* area in the third *Wizard* window.
   j. Click the **Date** radio button in the *Column data format* group (Figure 4-92).

k. Click **Finish**, deselect the **Add this data to the Data Model** box in the *Import Data* dialog box, and click **OK**.
l. Select columns **A:D** and size each column to **12.14 (90 pixels)** wide.
m. Deselect the columns.

10. Use the *Subtotal* command.
    a. Click cell **A5**.
    b. Click the **Sort A to Z** button [*Data* tab, *Sort & Filter* group] to sort by last name.
    c. Click the **Subtotal** button [*Data* tab, *Outline* group].
    d. Verify that **Last Name** is selected for **At each change in**.
    e. Click the **Use function** arrow and choose **Average**.
    f. Check the **Amount** box in the *Add subtotal to* area.
    g. Click **OK**.
    h. Format the values in column **D** as **Currency** with zero decimal places.

11. Collapse outline groups.
    a. Click the collapse symbol (–) for Allen in row **8**.
    b. Click the collapse symbol (–) for McAllister (Figure 4-93).

12. Create a *PivotTable*.
    a. Click the **Past&Projected** sheet tab.
    b. Select cells **A4:E60**.
    c. Click the **Quick Analysis** tool and choose **Tables**.
    d. Point to each *PivotTable* option to see the *Live Preview*.
    e. Choose the option that shows a sum of the employees, the total hours, and the patients (Figure 4-94).
    f. Rename the sheet PivotTable.
    g. Drag the **Month** field in the *Rows* area in the *PivotTable Fields* pane out of the pane and into the worksheet.

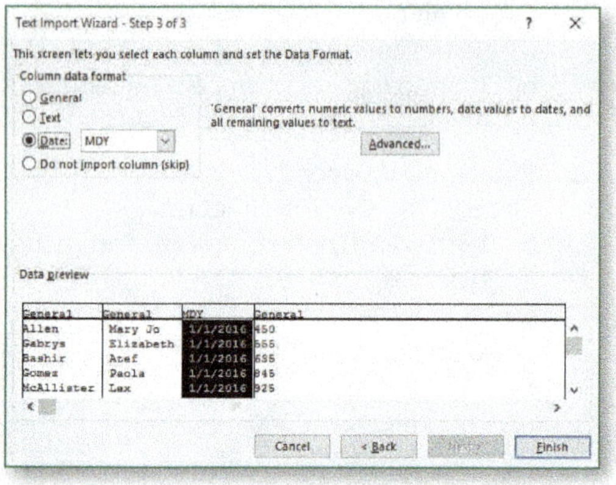

4-92 *Text Import Wizard* to set format

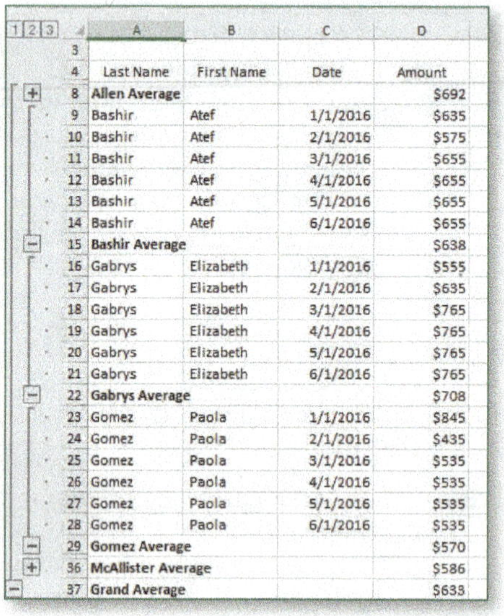

4-93 Subtotals added and outline collapsed for two groups

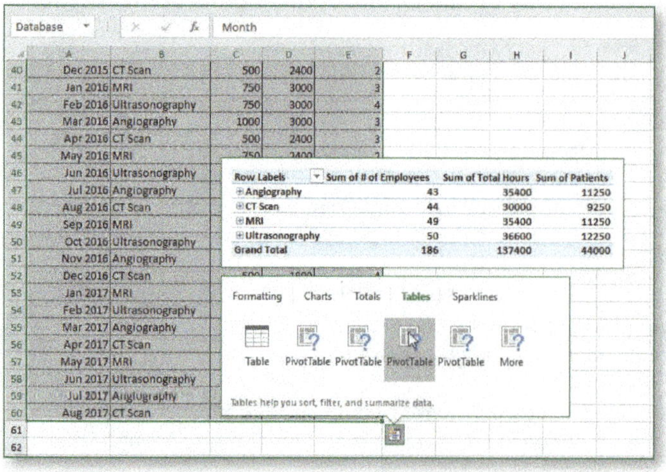

4-94 Suggested *PivotTable* choices from the *Quick Analysis* tool

13. Format a *PivotTable*.
    a. Click cell **C4**.
    b. Click the **Field Settings** button [*PivotTable Tools Analyze* tab, *Active Field* group].
    c. Click **Number Format**.
    d. Choose **Number** as the *Category*.
    e. Select the **Use 1000 Separator (,)** box and set zero decimal places.
    f. Click **OK** to close each dialog box.
    g. Apply the same number format for the "Sum of Patients" field.
    h. Click the **More** button [*PivotTable Tools Design* tab, *PivotTable Styles* group].
    i. Select **PivotTable Style Dark 9** [*PivotTable Tools Design* tab, *PivotTable Styles* group].
    j. Select the **Banded Rows** box [*PivotTable Tools Design* tab, *PivotTable Styles Options* group].
    k. Select the **Banded Columns** box [*PivotTable Tools Design* tab, *PivotTable Styles Options* group] (Figure 4-95).

14. Create and format a *PivotChart*.
    a. Click the **PivotChart** button [*PivotTable Tools Analyze* tab, *Tools* group].
    b. Select **Bar** as the chart type and **Stacked Bar** as the subtype.
    c. Click **OK**.
    d. Position the chart object so that its top-left corner is at cell **A12**.
    e. Drag the bottom-right selection handle to reach cell **J30**.
    f. Click the **More** button [*PivotChart Tools Design* tab, *Chart Styles* group] and choose **Style 8**.
    g. Click the **Change Colors** button [*PivotChart Tools Design* tab, *Chart Styles* group].
    h. Select **Color 5** in the *Monochromatic* group.
    i. Deselect the **# of Employees** box in the *PivotChart Fields* pane (Figure 4-96).
    j. Click cell **A1**.

	A	B	C	D
1				
2				
3	Row Labels	Sum of # of	Sum of Total Hours	Sum of Patients
4	Angiography	43	35,400	11,250
5	CT Scan	44	30,000	9,250
6	MRI	49	35,400	11,250
7	Ultrasonography	50	36,600	12,250
8	Grand Total	186	137,400	44,000

4-95 *PivotTable* with new settings

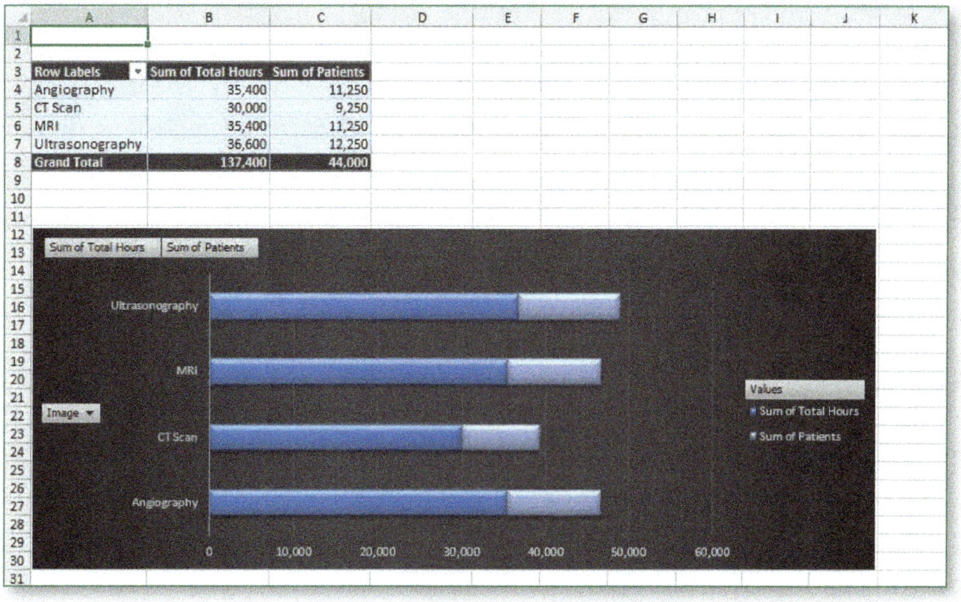

4-96 *PivotChart* object

15. Export data using the *Clipboard*.
    a. Click the **Adv Filter** sheet tab.
    b. Select cells **G4:K14** and click the **Copy** button [*Home* tab, *Clipboard* group].
    c. Open the **ClemensonImaging-04** Word document from your student data files.
    d. Press **Ctrl+End** to position the insertion point.
    e. Click the arrow with the **Paste** button [*Home* tab, *Clipboard* group] and choose **Paste Special**.
    f. Select **Microsoft Excel Worksheet Object** in the *Paste Special* dialog box.
    g. Select the **Paste link** radio button in the *Paste Special* dialog box and click **OK**.
    h. Click the **Center** button [*Home* tab, *Paragraph* group].
    i. Save the Word document as ***[your initials] Excel 4-3*** in your usual folder (Figure 4-97).
    j. Close Word.
16. Save and close the Excel workbook.

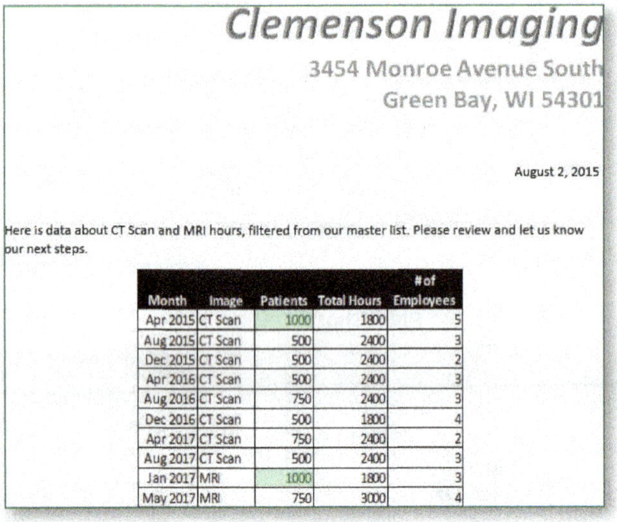
Clemenson Imaging
3454 Monroe Avenue South
Green Bay, WI 54301

August 2, 2015

Here is data about CT Scan and MRI hours, filtered from our master list. Please review and let us know our next steps.

Month	Image	Patients	Total Hours	# of Employees
Apr 2015	CT Scan	1000	1800	5
Aug 2015	CT Scan	500	2400	3
Dec 2015	CT Scan	500	2400	2
Apr 2016	CT Scan	500	2400	3
Aug 2016	CT Scan	750	2400	3
Dec 2016	CT Scan	500	1800	4
Apr 2017	CT Scan	750	2400	2
Aug 2017	CT Scan	500	2400	3
Jan 2017	MRI	1000	1800	3
May 2017	MRI	750	3000	4

4-97 Word document with pasted Excel object

Independent Project 4-4

Eller Software Services has received contract revenue information in a text file. You import, sort, and filter the data. You also create a *PivotTable*, prepare a worksheet with subtotals, and format related data as an Excel table.
[Student Learning Outcomes 4.1, 4.3, 4.4, 4.5, 4.6, 4.8]

Files Needed: ***EllerSoftware-04.xlsx*** and ***EllerSoftware-04.txt*** *[Student data files are available in the Library of your SIMnet account.]*
Completed Project File Name: ***[your initials] Excel 4-4.xlsx***

Skills Covered in This Project

- Import a text file.
- Use *AutoFilters*.
- Sort data by multiple columns.
- Create a *PivotTable*.
- Format fields in a *PivotTable*.
- Use the *Subtotal* command.
- Format data in an Excel table.
- Sort data in an Excel table.

1. Open the ***EllerSoftware-04*** workbook from your student data files and save it as [your initials] Excel 4-4.
2. Import the ***EllerSoftware-04.txt*** file from your student data files beginning in cell **A4**. The text file has a header row and is tab-delimited.

3. Format the values in column **H** as **Currency** with zero decimal places.
4. Click cell **G4** and show *AutoFilter* arrows.
5. Use the *AutoFilter* arrow to sort by date with the earliest date first. Then use the *AutoFilter* arrow to sort by product/service name in ascending order.
6. Filter the *Date* column to show only contracts for **September** using the **All Dates in the Period** option.
7. Select cells **A1:H2** and press **Ctrl+1** to open the *Format Cells* dialog box. On the *Alignment* tab, choose **Center Across Selection**.
8. Change the font size for cells **A1:H2** to **20 pt** (Figure 4-98).

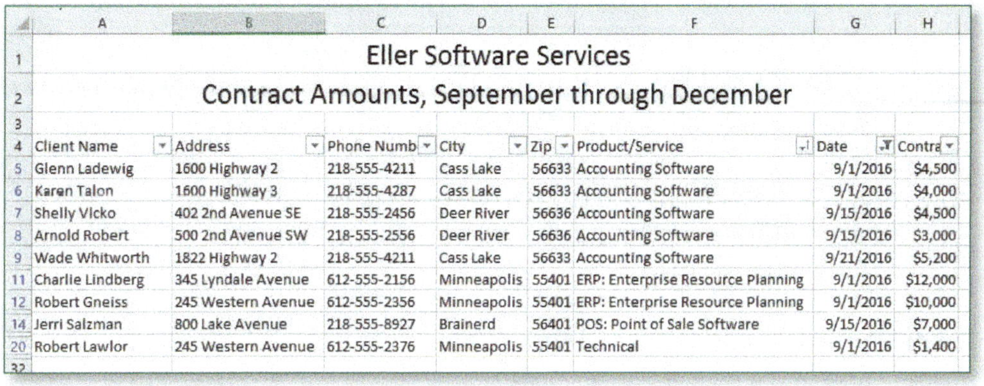

Eller Software Services

Contract Amounts, September through December

	Client Name	Address	Phone Numb	City	Zip	Product/Service	Date	Contra
5	Glenn Ladewig	1600 Highway 2	218-555-4211	Cass Lake	56633	Accounting Software	9/1/2016	$4,500
6	Karen Talon	1600 Highway 3	218-555-4287	Cass Lake	56633	Accounting Software	9/1/2016	$4,000
7	Shelly Vicko	402 2nd Avenue SE	218-555-2456	Deer River	56636	Accounting Software	9/15/2016	$4,500
8	Arnold Robert	500 2nd Avenue SW	218-555-2556	Deer River	56636	Accounting Software	9/15/2016	$3,000
9	Wade Whitworth	1822 Highway 2	218-555-4211	Cass Lake	56633	Accounting Software	9/21/2016	$5,200
11	Charlie Lindberg	345 Lyndale Avenue	612-555-2156	Minneapolis	55401	ERP: Enterprise Resource Planning	9/1/2016	$12,000
12	Robert Gneiss	245 Western Avenue	612-555-2356	Minneapolis	55401	ERP: Enterprise Resource Planning	9/1/2016	$10,000
14	Jerri Salzman	800 Lake Avenue	218-555-8927	Brainerd	56401	POS: Point of Sale Software	9/15/2016	$7,000
20	Robert Lawlor	245 Western Avenue	612-555-2376	Minneapolis	55401	Technical	9/1/2016	$1,400

4-98 Imported data sorted and filtered

9. Copy the **Contracts** sheet to the end and name the copy Data.
10. Clear the date filter and hide the *AutoFilter* arrows.
11. Select cell **A5** and click the **PivotTable** button [*Insert* tab] to create a blank *PivotTable* layout on its own sheet named PivotTable.
12. Show the **Product/Service** and **Contract** fields in the *PivotTable*.
13. Drag the **Contract** field from the *Choose fields to add to report* area below the **Sum of Contract** field in the *Values* area so that it appears twice in the report layout and the pane (Figure 4-99).

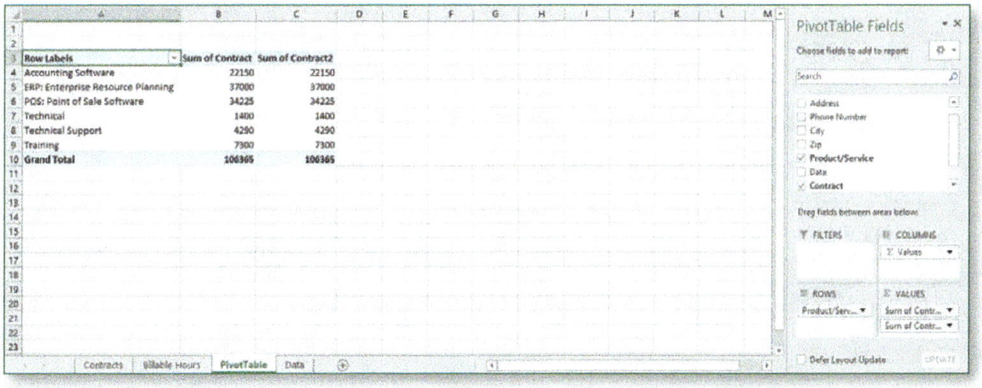

4-99 "Contract" field appears twice in the report

14. Select cell **C4** and click the **Field Settings** button [*PivotTable Tools Analyze* tab, *Active Fields* group]. Type Average Contract as the *Custom Name*, choose **Average** as the calculation, and set the *Number Format* to **Currency** with zero decimal places.

15. Select cell **B4** and set its *Custom Name* to Total Contracts and the number format to **Currency** with zero decimal places.

16. Apply **PivotTable Style Dark 3**.

17. Select the **Data** sheet tab and copy cells **A1:A2**. Paste them in cell **A1** on the **PivotTable** sheet. Set **Align Left** for both cells and **16 pt** as the font size (Figure 4-100).

18. Copy the **Data** sheet to the end and name the copy Subtotals.

19. Select cell **D5** and sort by **City** in **A to Z** order.

20. Use the *Subtotal* command to show a **SUM** for the contract amounts for each city.

21. Click the **Billable Hours** sheet tab and select cell **A4**.

22. Click the **Format as Table** button [*Home* tab, *Styles* group], use **Table Style Medium 10**, and remove the data connections.

23. Type 5% Add On in cell **E4** and press **Enter**.

24. Build a formula in cell **E5** to multiply cell **D5** by **105%**.

25. Select cells **A1:E2** and center them across the selection.

26. Use the *AutoFilter* arrows to sort first by date in oldest to newest order and then by client name in ascending order.

27. Save and close the workbook (Figure 4-101).

	A	B	C
1	Eller Software Services		
2	Contract Amounts, September through December		
3	Row Labels	Total Contracts	Average Contract
4	Accounting Software	$22,150	$3,692
5	ERP: Enterprise Resource Planning	$37,000	$12,333
6	POS: Point of Sale Software	$34,225	$5,704
7	Technical	$1,400	$1,400
8	Technical Support	$4,290	$858
9	Training	$7,300	$1,217
10	Grand Total	$106,365	$3,939
11			

4-100 Completed *PivotTable*

Eller Software Services

Contract Amounts, September through December

Client Name	Address	Phone Number	City	Zip	Product/Service	Date	Contract
Martin Green	127 Oak Street	218-555-2353	Bemidji	56601	Accounting Software	12/15/2016	$950
Mike Gunderson	304 Irvine Avenue	218-555-9021	Bemidji	56601	Technical Support	10/28/2016	$990
Heather Guyan	124 East Street	218-555-2313	Bemidji	56601	Training	10/7/2016	$1,500
Paula Valentine	127 Oak Street	218-555-2313	Bemidji	56601	Training	10/15/2016	$950
			Bemidji Total				$4,390
Jerri Salsman	800 Lake Avenue	218-555-8927	Brainerd	56401	POS: Point of Sale Software	9/15/2016	$7,000
Terri Olander	439 10th Avenue	218-555-8977	Brainerd	56401	POS: Point of Sale Software	10/15/2016	$6,525
Christine Barton	902 Clinton Street	218-555-8977	Brainerd	56401	POS: Point of Sale Software	11/15/2016	$5,500
Michelle Cronin	800 Lake Avenue	218-555-8977	Brainerd	56401	POS: Point of Sale Software	12/15/2016	$4,500
Patricia Glunz	902 Gunter Street	218-555-8900	Brainerd	56401	POS: Point of Sale Software	12/15/2016	$3,200
			Brainerd Total				$26,725
Glenn Ladewig	1600 Highway 2	218-555-4211	Cass Lake	56633	Accounting Software	9/1/2016	$4,500
Karen Talon	1600 Highway 3	218-555-4287	Cass Lake	56633	Accounting Software	9/1/2016	$4,000
Wade Whitworth	1822 Highway 2	218-555-4211	Cass Lake	56633	Accounting Software	9/21/2016	$5,200
Thomas Larson	1044 Highway 2	218-555-1234	Cass Lake	56633	Training	10/15/2016	$2,500
			Cass Lake Total				$16,200
Shelly Vicko	402 2nd Avenue SE	218-555-2456	Deer River	56636	Accounting Software	9/15/2016	$4,500
Arnold Robert	500 2nd Avenue SW	218-555-2556	Deer River	56636	Accounting Software	9/15/2016	$3,000
			Deer River Total				$7,500
Jeremie Midboe	Pilot Knob Road	651-555-2789	Eagan	55121	POS: Point of Sale Software	11/1/2016	$7,500
			Eagan Total				$7,500
Charlie Lindberg	345 Lyndale Avenue	612-555-2156	Minneapolis	55401	ERP: Enterprise Resource Planning	9/1/2016	$12,000
Robert Gneiss	245 Western Avenue	612-555-2356	Minneapolis	55401	ERP: Enterprise Resource Planning	9/1/2016	$10,000
Susan Charlotte	507 Lyndale Avenue	612-555-2177	Minneapolis	55401	ERP: Enterprise Resource Planning	11/1/2016	$15,000
Robert Lawlor	245 Western Avenue	612-555-2376	Minneapolis	55401	Technical	9/1/2016	$1,400
			Minneapolis Total				$38,400
Craig Brand	554 2nd Street	320-555-4433	Saint Cloud	56301	Technical Support	10/1/2016	$1,050
Arthur Weston	554 3rd Street	320-555-4433	Saint Cloud	56301	Technical Support	10/1/2016	$750
Richard Malinowski	309 Fifth Street	320-555-4433	Saint Cloud	56301	Technical Support	10/1/2016	$750
Elizabeth Jones	450 Fifth Street	320-555-4422	Saint Cloud	56301	Technical Support	10/1/2016	$750
Hilary Marschke	245 West 3rd Avenue	320-555-5443	Saint Cloud	56301	Training	11/15/2016	$750
Juan Garcia	400 South Avenue	320-555-5448	Saint Cloud	56301	Training	11/15/2016	$800
Amir Atef	300 South Avenue	320-555-5443	Saint Cloud	56301	Training	12/15/2016	$800
			Saint Cloud Total				$5,650
			Grand Total				$106,365

Eller Software Services

Billable Hours

Client Name	Product/Service	Date	Billable	5% Add On
Amir Atef	Training	12/15/2016	4.00	4.2
Arnold Robert	Accounting Software	9/15/2016	5.00	5.25
Arthur Weston	Technical Support	10/1/2016	3.00	3.15
Arthur Weston	Technical Support	3/3/2017	6.00	6.3
Charlie Lindberg	ERP: Enterprise Resource Planning	9/1/2016	4.00	4.2
Charlie Lindberg	ERP: Enterprise Resource Planning	4/3/2017	6.00	6.3
Christine Barton	POS: Point of Sale Software	11/15/2016	4.00	4.2
Christine Barton	POS: Point of Sale Software	11/15/2016	2.00	2.1
Craig Brand	Technical Support	10/1/2016	8.00	8.4
Elizabeth Jones	Technical Support	10/1/2016	3.50	3.675
Glenn Ladewig	Accounting Software	9/1/2016	5.00	5.25
Heather Guyan	Training	10/7/2016	3.25	3.4125
Heather Guyan	Training	2/3/2017	4.50	4.725
Hilary Marschke	Training	11/15/2016	5.00	5.25
Hilary Marschke	Training	11/15/2016	5.00	5.25
Hilary Marschke	Training	3/6/2017	5.00	5.25
Jeremie Midboe	POS: Point of Sale Software	11/1/2016	3.50	3.675
Jerri Salsman	POS: Point of Sale Software	3/9/2017	4.50	4.725
Juan Garcia	Training	11/15/2016	4.00	4.2
Karen Talon	Accounting Software	9/1/2016	3.50	3.675
Karen Talon	Accounting Software	10/1/2016	5.50	5.775
Martin Green	Accounting Software	12/15/2016	5.00	5.25
Martin Green	Accounting Software	3/7/2017	4.00	4.2
Michelle Cronin	POS: Point of Sale Software	12/15/2016	4.00	4.2
Michelle Cronin	POS: Point of Sale Software	12/15/2016	4.00	4.2
Mike Gunderson	Technical Support	10/28/2016	4.75	4.9875
Mike Gunderson	Technical Support	12/28/2016	4.50	4.725
Patricia Glunz	POS: Point of Sale Software	12/15/2016	3.25	3.4125
Paula Valentine	Training	10/15/2016	4.00	4.2
Paula Valentine	Training	10/15/2016	4.00	4.2
Paula Valentine	Training	11/15/2016	4.00	4.2
Paula Valentine	Training	4/5/2017	4.00	4.2
Richard Malinowski	Technical Support	10/1/2016	4.50	4.725
Richard Malinowski	Technical Support	1/3/2017	3.00	3.15
Robert Gneiss	ERP: Enterprise Resource Planning	9/1/2016	6.00	6.3
Robert Gneiss	ERP: Enterprise Resource Planning	2/5/2017	7.00	7.35
Robert Lawlor	Technical Support	1/6/2017	2.75	2.8875
Shelly Vicko	Accounting Software	9/15/2016	5.00	5.25
Shelly Vicko	Accounting Software	11/16/2016	5.00	5.25
Susan Charlotte	ERP: Enterprise Resource Planning	11/1/2016	6.00	6.3
Susan Charlotte	ERP: Enterprise Resource Planning	3/3/2017	8.00	8.4
Terri Olander	POS: Point of Sale Software	10/15/2016	6.50	6.825
Thomas Larson	Training	12/5/2016	5.00	5.25
Thomas Larson	Training	3/16/2017	4.00	4.2
Wade Whitworth	Accounting Software	11/14/2016	5.00	5.25
Wade Whitworth	Accounting Software	2/3/2017	6.00	6.3
Wade Whitworth	Accounting Software	3/17/2017	5.00	5.25

4-101 Completed Excel table and *Subtotals* sheet

Independent Project 4-5

Boyd Air is monitoring flight arrival status as well as capacities. Before formatting the data as an Excel table, you will export it as a text file for use in the reservation software. You will filter the data in the table, build a *PivotTable,* and create a *PivotChart.*
[Student Learning Outcomes 4.1, 4.2, 4.3, 4.4, 4.7, 4.8]

File Needed: ***BoydAir-04.xlsx*** *[Student data files are available in the* Library *of your SIMnet account.]*
Completed Project File Names: ***[your initials] Excel 4-5.xlsx*** and ***[your initials] Excel 4-5.txt***

Skills Covered in This Project

- Export data as a text file.
- Format data as an Excel table.
- Use a number filter in a table.
- Set conditional formatting with an icon set.
- Filter data by cell icon.
- Create and format a *PivotTable.*
- Create and format a *PivotChart.*

1. Open ***BoydAir-04*** workbook from your student data files and save it as [your initials] Excel 4-5.
2. Export the data to a tab-delimited text file named ***[your initials] Excel 4-5*** in your usual location for saving work.
3. Rename the sheet tab Stats after the data is exported.
4. Use the *Save As* command to save and replace ***[your initials] Excel 4-5*** as an **Excel Workbook**.
5. Select cell **A4** and format the data as an Excel table using **Table Style Medium 21**.
6. Copy the **Stats** sheet to the end and name the copy PM Flights.
7. Select the **PM Flights** sheet and use a *Greater Than* filter to display flights with a departure time after 12:00 PM (Figure 4-102).
8. Select the **Stats** worksheet, select cells **I5:I32**, and set conditional formatting to use **3 Stars** from the *Icon Sets*.
9. Build a two-level *Custom Sort* for the *Capacity* column to sort by icon. Show the solid gold star at the top, followed by the half-gold star. The silver star will default to the bottom (Figure 4-103).

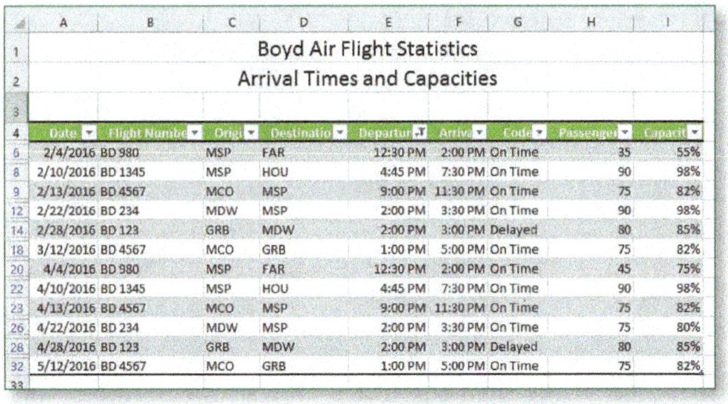

4-102 Filter results for *Departure Time* field

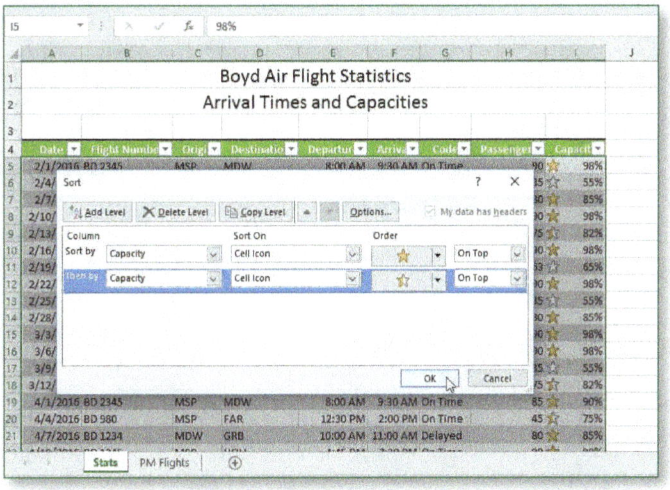

4-103 Custom sort for the *3 Stars* icon set

10. Select the **Stats** worksheet, select cells **A4:I32**, and use the *Quick Analysis* tool to create a *PivotTable* to display average of capacity by origin (Figure 4-104).

11. Select cell **B3** in the *PivotTable* and use **Field Settings** to set a **Number Format** of **Percentage** with two decimal places. Edit the *Custom Name* to display **Average Capacity**.

12. Add the **Passengers** field to the *PivotTable VALUES* area with a sum calculation. Edit the field settings to display **# of Passengers** as the custom name. Set the number format to **Number** with zero decimals and a thousand's separator.

13. Use **PivotTable Style Light 8** for the *PivotTable* and show banded columns and rows.

14. Add a **3-D Pie PivotChart** to the sheet and position the chart object to start in cell **E3**. Size the chart to reach cell **N22**.

15. Select the legend in the chart and set its font size to **11** from the *Home* tab.

16. Show **Data Labels** on the chart positioned at the **Inside End**. Select a data label and format all labels from the *Home* tab as **bold** and **10 pt**.

17. Select cell **A1** and rename the sheet PivotTable&Chart (Figure 4-105).

18. Save and close the workbook.

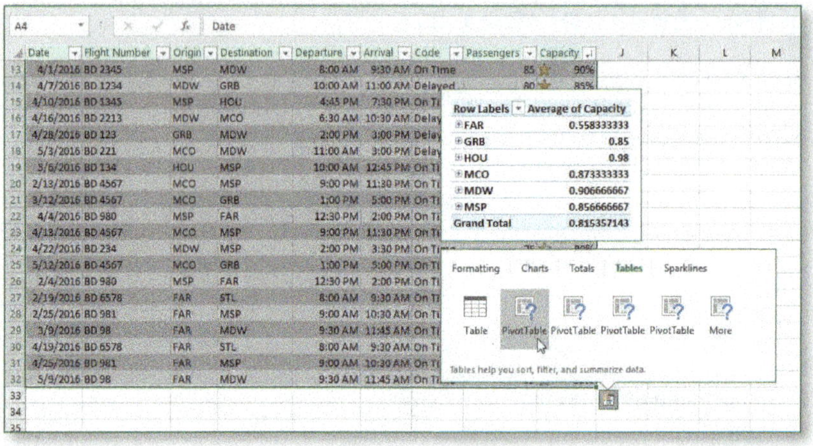

4-104 *PivotTable* suggestions from the *Quick Analysis* tool

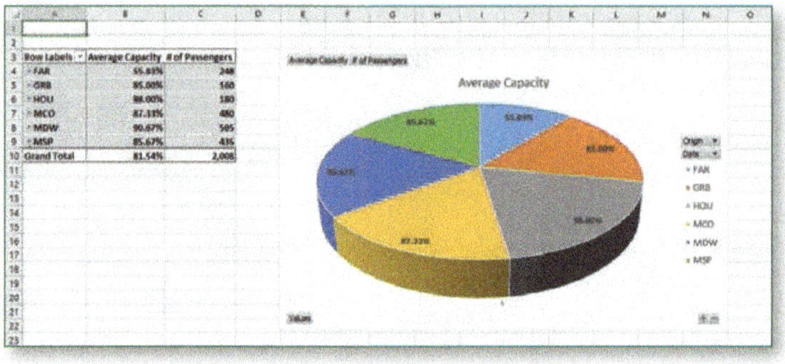

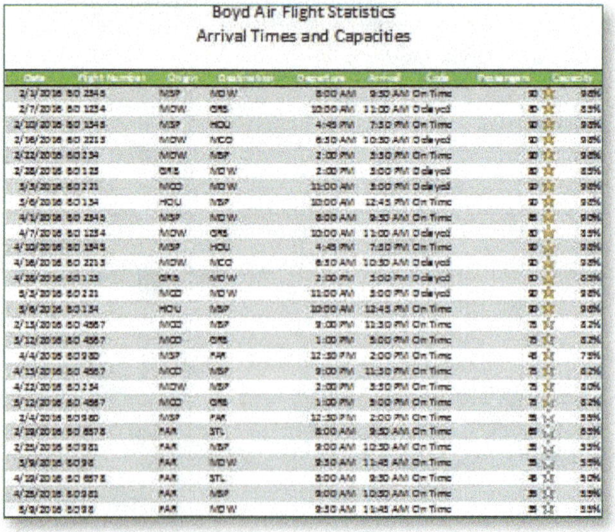

4-105 Excel 4-5 completed sheets

Independent Project 4-6

Life's Animal Shelter has a list of suppliers in a worksheet which must be copied to Word for use by another staff member. You will build an advanced filter to show suppliers for specific product categories and define groups based on supplier name. Your final task is to create an Excel table for sorting and filtering.
[Student Learning Outcomes 4.1, 4.3, 4.4, 4.5, 4.7]

File Needed: ***LAShelter-04.xlsx*** *[Student data files are available in the* Library *of your SIMnet account.]*
Completed Project File Names: ***[your initials] Excel 4-6.xlsx*** and ***[your initials] Excel 4-6.docx***

Skills Covered in This Project

- Copy Excel data to Word.
- Create an advanced filter.
- Use *Flash Fill* to complete a column.
- Format data as a table.
- Filter data.
- Define groups in a worksheet.

1. Open the ***LAShelter-04*** workbook from your student data files and save it as [your initials] Excel 4-6.
2. Select the **LAS Suppliers** sheet, select cells **A4:D32**, and copy them to the Windows *Clipboard.*
3. Open Word and create a new document.
4. Paste the data into Word with the **Use Destination Styles** option (Figure 4-106).
5. Save the Word document as [your initials] Excel 4-6.docx.
6. Close the Word document and exit Word.
7. Click the **Criteria** sheet tab.
8. Type *cage* in cell **A2** and type *carrier* in cell **A3**. This is *OR* criteria that will find products that include either the word "cage" or the word "carrier."
9. Select the **LAS Suppliers** sheet and format the labels in row **4** as **bold** and **centered** to distinguish the header row from other data.

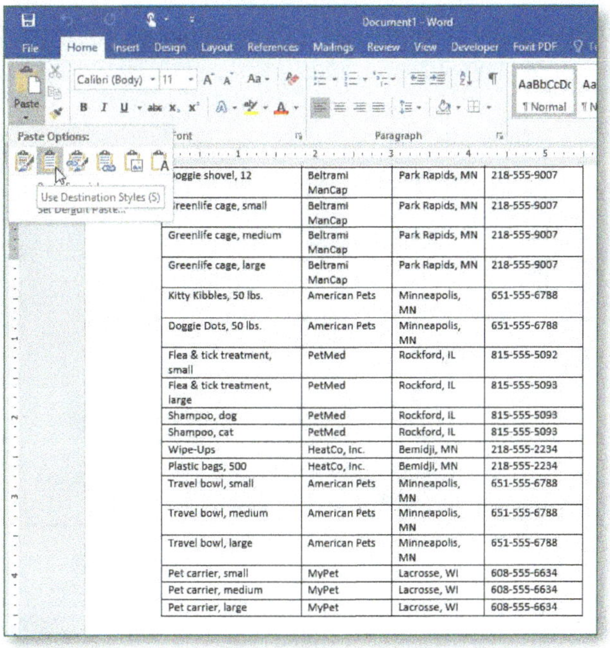

4-106 Word *Paste Options* for Excel data

10. Click cell **A5** on the **LAS Suppliers** sheet.
11. Build an advanced filter that uses the data on the **LAS Suppliers** sheet, the criteria range on the **Criteria** sheet, and cells **F6:G6** as the output range. In the *Advanced Filter* dialog box, select the **Unique records only** box (Figure 4-107).

12. Replace the criteria with *bowl* and *collar* to build a second advanced filter and show the filtered results as indicated on the worksheet.

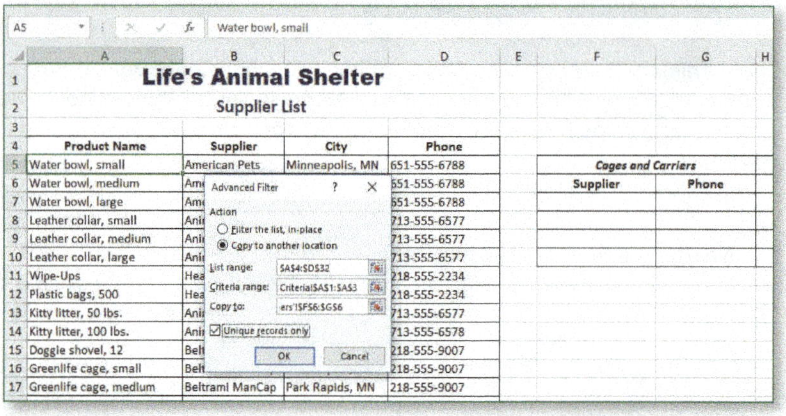

4-107 Advanced filter to select unique records

13. Select cells **A4:D32** and copy them to cell **A4** on the **Table** sheet. Remove all borders.
14. Select cells **A5:A32** and sort the data by product name in ascending order.
15. Type (651) 555-6788 in cell **E5**.
16. Type (2 in cell **E6** and press **Enter** when the *Flash Fill* suggestion appears.
17. Type Phone in cell **E4** and delete column **D**. Set column **D** to a width of **15.71 (115 pixels)**.
18. Format the data as a table using **Table Style Medium 2**.
19. Filter the data to show the suppliers located in Minnesota.
20. Select cells **A1:A2** and remove the **Merge & Center** command. Set both cells to **Align Left**. Then select cells **A1:D2** and use the **Center Across Selection** command (Figure 4-108).

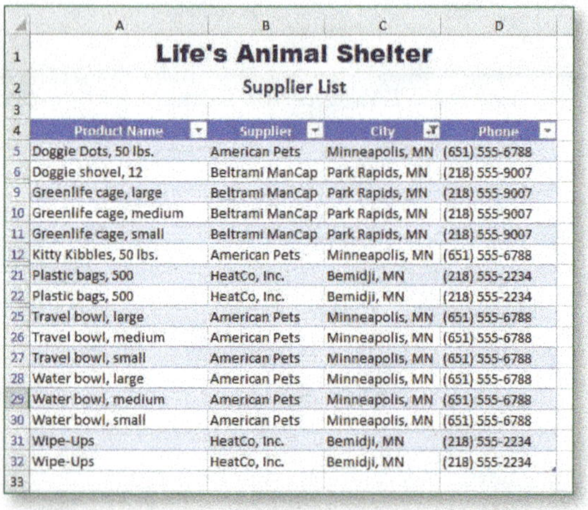

4-108 Completed table

21. Select the **By City** worksheet tab.
22. Sort by **City** in **A to Z** order.
23. Insert a row at row **5** and type Bemidji in cell **A5**. Left-align the label.
24. Insert a row at row **10** and type Houston in cell **A10**. **Bold** the label.
25. Insert blank rows and type labels for the remaining cities.
26. Select the row headings for rows **6:9** and click the **Group** button [*Data* tab, *Outline* group]. Do not include the row with the city name in the group.
27. Repeat the command to group the rows for each city (Figure 4-109).

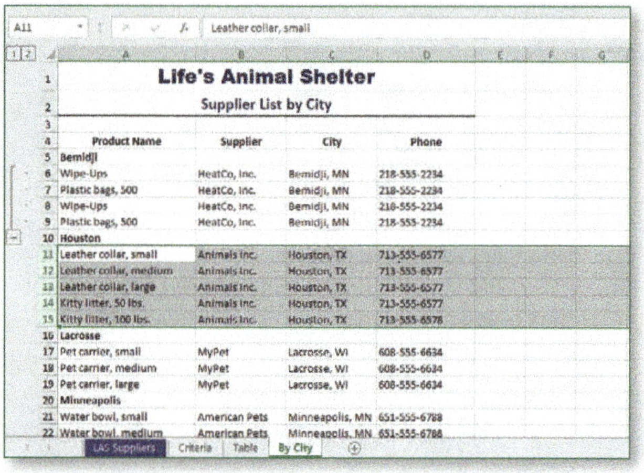

4-109 Data manually defined in groups

28. Select and delete column **C**.
29. Collapse the *Houston* and *Minneapolis* groups (Figure 4-110).

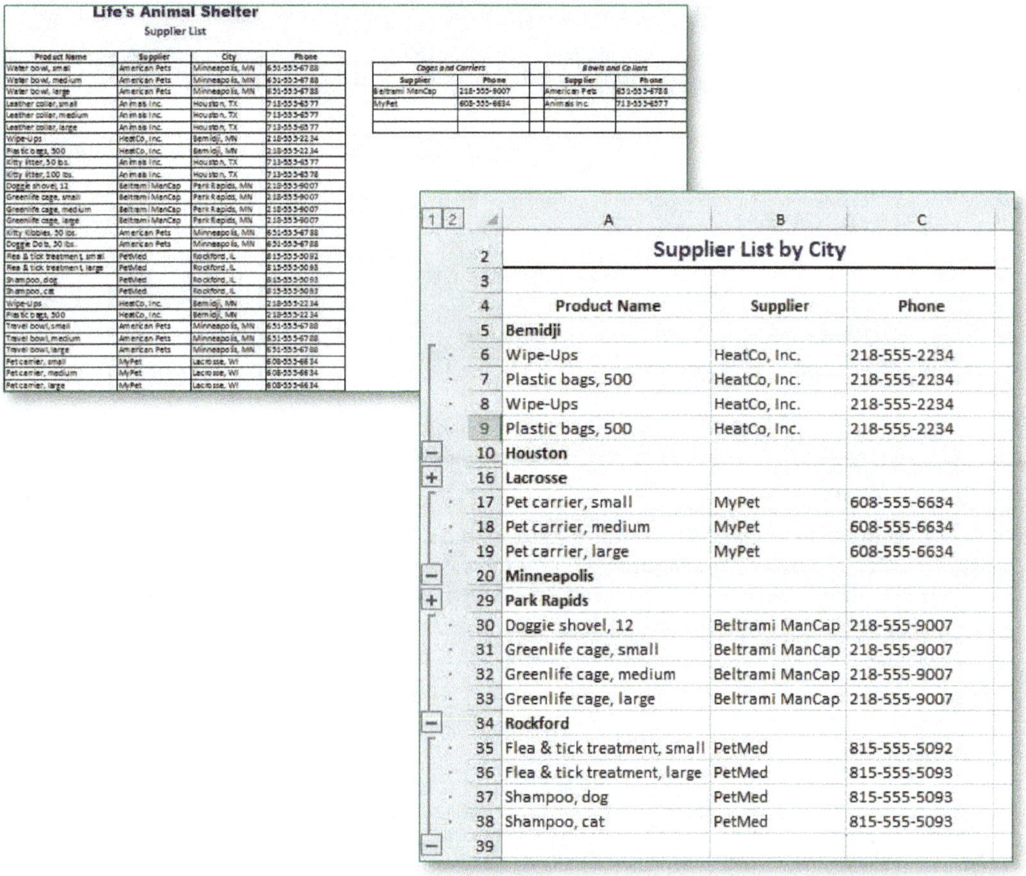

Life's Animal Shelter

Supplier List

Product Name	Supplier	City	Phone
Water bowl, small	American Pets	Minneapolis, MN	651-555-6788
Water bowl, medium	American Pets	Minneapolis, MN	651-555-6788
Water bowl, large	American Pets	Minneapolis, MN	651-555-6788
Leather collar, small	Animals Inc.	Houston, TX	713-555-6377
Leather collar, medium	Animals Inc.	Houston, TX	713-555-6377
Leather collar, large	Animals Inc.	Houston, TX	713-555-6377
Wipe-Ups	HeatCo, Inc.	Bemidji, MN	218-555-2234
Plastic bags, 500	HeatCo, Inc.	Bemidji, MN	218-555-2234
Kitty litter, 50 lbs.	Animals Inc.	Houston, TX	713-555-6377
Kitty litter, 100 lbs.	Animals Inc.	Houston, TX	713-555-6378
Doggie shovel, 12	Beltrami ManCap	Park Rapids, MN	218-555-9007
Greenlife cage, small	Beltrami ManCap	Park Rapids, MN	218-555-9007
Greenlife cage, medium	Beltrami ManCap	Park Rapids, MN	218-555-9007
Greenlife cage, large	Beltrami ManCap	Park Rapids, MN	218-555-9007
Kitty Kibbles, 50 lbs.	American Pets	Minneapolis, MN	651-555-6788
Doggie Dots, 50 lbs.	American Pets	Minneapolis, MN	651-555-6788
Flea & tick treatment, small	PetMed	Rockford, IL	815-555-5092
Flea & tick treatment, large	PetMed	Rockford, IL	815-555-5093
Shampoo, dog	PetMed	Rockford, IL	815-555-5093
Shampoo, cat	PetMed	Rockford, IL	815-555-5093
Wipe-Ups	HeatCo, Inc.	Bemidji, MN	218-555-2234
Plastic bags, 500	HeatCo, Inc.	Bemidji, MN	218-555-2234
Travel bowl, small	American Pets	Minneapolis, MN	651-555-6788
Travel bowl, medium	American Pets	Minneapolis, MN	651-555-6788
Travel bowl, large	American Pets	Minneapolis, MN	651-555-6788
Pet carrier, small	MyPet	Lacrosse, WI	608-555-6634
Pet carrier, medium	MyPet	Lacrosse, WI	608-555-6634
Pet carrier, large	MyPet	Lacrosse, WI	608-555-6634

Cages and Carriers			*Bowls and Collars*	
Supplier	Phone		Supplier	Phone
Beltrami ManCap	218-555-9007		American Pets	651-555-6788
MyPet	608-555-6634		Animals Inc.	713-555-6377

	A	B	C
2	**Supplier List by City**		
3			
4	**Product Name**	**Supplier**	**Phone**
5	**Bemidji**		
6	Wipe-Ups	HeatCo, Inc.	218-555-2234
7	Plastic bags, 500	HeatCo, Inc.	218-555-2234
8	Wipe-Ups	HeatCo, Inc.	218-555-2234
9	Plastic bags, 500	HeatCo, Inc.	218-555-2234
10	**Houston**		
16	**Lacrosse**		
17	Pet carrier, small	MyPet	608-555-6634
18	Pet carrier, medium	MyPet	608-555-6634
19	Pet carrier, large	MyPet	608-555-6634
20	**Minneapolis**		
29	**Park Rapids**		
30	Doggie shovel, 12	Beltrami ManCap	218-555-9007
31	Greenlife cage, small	Beltrami ManCap	218-555-9007
32	Greenlife cage, medium	Beltrami ManCap	218-555-9007
33	Greenlife cage, large	Beltrami ManCap	218-555-9007
34	**Rockford**		
35	Flea & tick treatment, small	PetMed	815-555-5092
36	Flea & tick treatment, large	PetMed	815-555-5093
37	Shampoo, dog	PetMed	815-555-5093
38	Shampoo, cat	PetMed	815-555-5093
39			

4-110 Excel 4-6 completed worksheets

30. Save and close the workbook.

Improve It Project 4-7

Placer Hills Real Estate wants its latest *PivotTable* to show sales by agent listing, but the table needs additional work. In the source data, you also need to highlight certain listings for insurance purposes. In a separate table, you plan to create a calculation column to show the number of market days.
[Student Learning Outcomes 4.1, 4.2, 4.8]

File Needed: ***PlacerHills-04.xlsx*** *[Student data files are available in the* Library *of your SIMnet account.]*
Completed Project File Name: ***[your initials] Excel 4-7.xlsx***

Skills Covered in This Project

- Pivot fields in a *PivotTable*.
- Format fields in a *PivotTable*.
- Add a field to a table.
- Set conditional formatting with a formula.

1. Open the ***PlacerHills-04*** workbook from your student data files and save it as [your initials] Excel 4-7.
2. Select the **Listings** sheet and use a formula to set conditional formatting for cells **A5:A26**. The formula is **=k5="frame"** to determine if the construction is frame. Set the format to use light blue fill.
3. Select the **PivotTable** sheet, drag the **City** field out of the *Rows* area, and drag the **Agent ID** field to the *Rows* area.
4. Drag the **Sale Price** field into the *Values* area so that it is shown twice in the *PivotTable.*
5. Format the first occurrence of the **Sales Price** field to show a sum with **Currency** format, zero decimals, and a custom name of Total Sales. Format the second occurrence to show an average with the same **Currency** format and the name Average Sale.
6. Apply **PivotTable Style Light 15**.
7. Select cells **A3:C9** in the *PivotTable.* Click the **Border** button [*Home* tab, *Font* group] and apply **All Borders**. Select cell **A1**.
8. Select the **Table** sheet tab.
9. Type Days in cell **O4**. In cell **O5**, build an *IF* formula to display the number of days on the market. The *logical_test* determines if the sale date is greater than the list date. The *value_if_true* argument is the sale date minus the list date. For the *value_if_false* argument, press **Spacebar** once to leave the cell blank when there is no sale date.
10. Save and close the workbook (Figure 4-111).

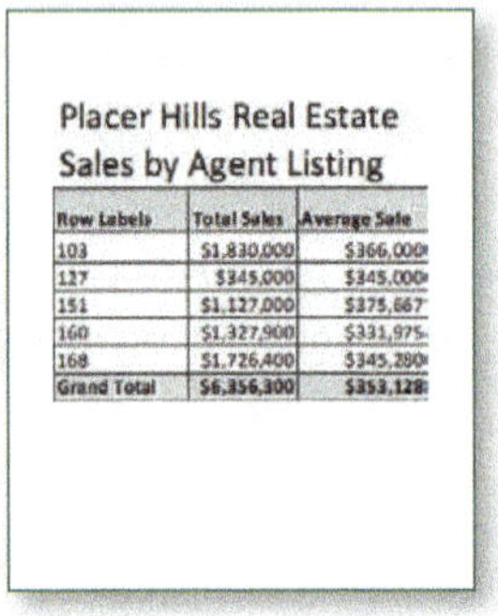

Placer Hills Real Estate
Sales by Agent Listing

Row Labels	Total Sales	Average Sale
103	$1,830,000	$366,000
127	$345,000	$345,000
151	$1,127,000	$375,667
160	$1,327,900	$331,975
168	$1,726,400	$345,280
Grand Total	$6,356,300	$353,128

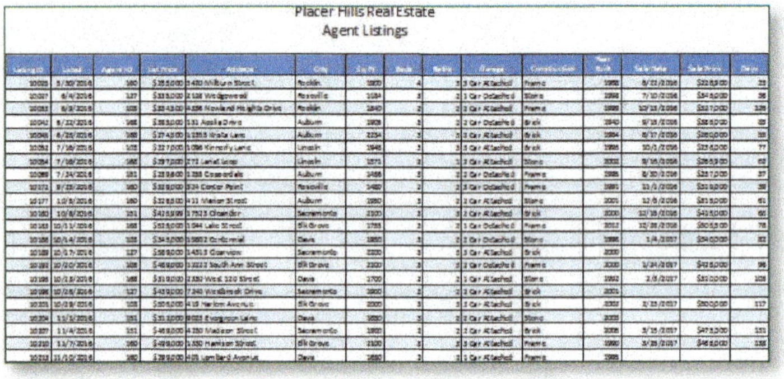

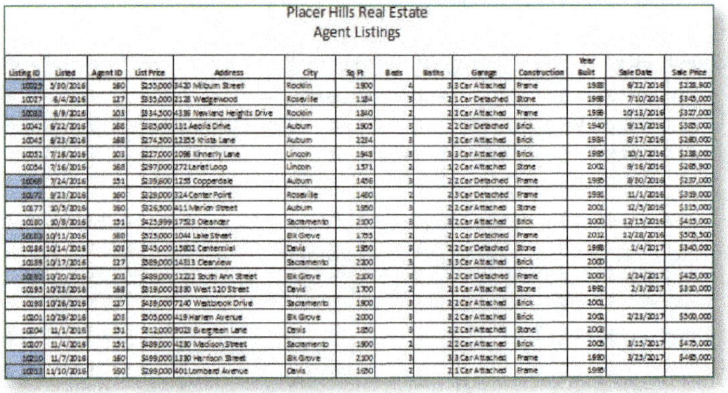

4-111 Excel 4-7 completed worksheets

Challenge Project 4-8

For this project, you build a worksheet for a company that sells four varieties of socks in four eastern states. When the data is complete, you will format the data as an Excel table.
[Student Learning Outcomes 4.1, 4.2, 4.3]

File Needed: None
Completed Project File Name: ***[your initials] Excel 4-8.xlsx***

Create a new workbook and save it as [your initials] Excel 4-8. Modify your workbook according to the following guidelines:

- Type the labels State, Model, Month, Pairs, and Price in cells **A4:E4**.
- In cells **A5:A8**, type Connecticut, Maine, New Hampshire, and Vermont.
- In cell **B5**, type the style name for one type of sock sold by the company. Copy the name to cells **B6:B8**.
- In cells **C5**, type January and copy the month to cells **C6:C8**.
- In cells **D5:D8**, enter values for how many pairs were sold in each state in January. In column E, enter and copy a price for this sock style.
- Copy cells **A5:E8** and paste the range in cell **A9** to create a February group. Edit the month and the number of pairs sold.
- Copy cells **A5:E12** and paste the range in cell **A13** to create the data for another sock style. In this range, edit the style name, the number of pairs sold, and the price. The price is the same for all rows in this group.
- Copy and paste to complete two more ranges for two sock styles, so that you have January and February data for four sock styles for each state.
- Set conditional formatting to show one of the state names in a format different from the other states.
- Name the sheet Data and make a copy named Table.
- On the **Table** sheet, format the data as an Excel table with a light table style.
- Type Total in cell **F4** and create a formula to calculate the dollar amount of sales in the column.
- Show a total row for the table with results for the number of pairs and sales dollars.
- Add additional formatting to the table as needed.
- Use the *AutoFilter* arrows to sort by style and then by state.
- Enter a name for the company in cell **A1**. Enter a label in cell **A2** that describes the data.

Challenge Project 4-9

For this project, you explore the Bureau of Labor Statistics web site to download data for use in a worksheet. After you have arranged and formatted the data, you copy it to a Word document.
[Student Learning Outcomes 4.1, 4.2, 4.6, 4.7]

File Needed: None
Completed Project File Names: ***[your initials] Excel 4-9.xlsx*** and ***[your initials] Excel 4-9.docx***

Create a new workbook and save it as [your initials] Excel 4-9. Modify your workbook according to the following guidelines:

- Go to www.bls.gov/data.
- Review the subject areas and choose one to explore. Find a topic and subtopic which provides an *.xlsx* file for download.
- Download or copy the data into your worksheet.
- Format the data as an Excel table if it is not already formatted, or apply a different table style.
- Determine and apply conditional formatting for some aspect of the data.
- Determine and set a different sort order.
- Add a main title to your worksheet and set other format attributes to effectively display your information.
- Copy the data to a new Word document and save the Word document as [your initials] Excel 4-9.docx.

Challenge Project 4-10

For this project, you create a worksheet that lists names, birth dates, and hair color for 20 people. You format the list as a table for sorting and filtering. You convert the table to a range and use the *Subtotal* command.
[Student Learning Outcomes 4.1, 4.3, 4.4, 4.5]

File Needed: None
Completed Project File Name: ***[your initials] Excel 4-10.xlsx***

Create a new workbook and save it as [your initials] Excel 4-10. Modify your workbook according to the following guidelines:

- Type your first name, your last name, your birthdate, and your hair color in a row using one column for each item.
- Type data for 19 more people, using fictitious or real data. Use birthdates that are the same year as yours as well as four other years, so that your list has only five different years. Use at least three hair colors in your list, such as brown, blond, red.
- Format the data as a table and apply a table style.
- Sort the date by birthdate with the youngest people listed first. Then filter the data to show only those records from the first year listed in the data.
- Make a copy of the sheet and convert the table to a normal range. Use the *Subtotal* command to count the number of persons with each hair color.

PowerPoint

Microsoft® Office

IN PRACTICE

powerpoint

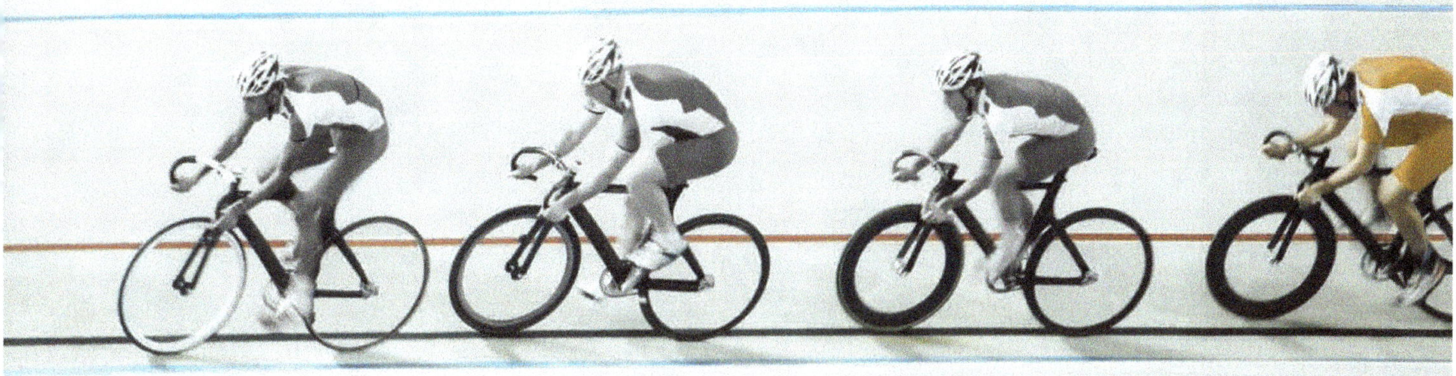

CHAPTER 1

Creating and Editing Presentations

POWERPOINT

CHAPTER OVERVIEW

Microsoft PowerPoint is the leading presentation software. Whether you need to create a quick display or a very polished presentation with dazzling graphics, creative animation effects, and video, PowerPoint has all the tools you need. You can use PowerPoint for slide shows with computer projection equipment in meeting rooms, for self-running presentations viewed by individuals, or for presentations shown on the web. This chapter covers the basics of starting and editing a PowerPoint presentation.

STUDENT LEARNING OUTCOMES (SLOs)

After completing this chapter, you will be able to:

SLO 1.1 Create, open, and save a presentation (p. P1-3).

SLO 1.2 Work with slides, layouts, placeholders, and text (p. P1-14).

SLO 1.3 Navigate between slides and organize content by reproducing and rearranging slides (p. P1-23).

SLO 1.4 Change theme colors and fonts (p. P1-29).

SLO 1.5 Insert headers and footers to add identifying information (p. P1-33).

SLO 1.6 Insert, resize, and align a picture from a file (p. P1-37).

SLO 1.7 Apply and modify transition effects to add visual interest (p. P1-40).

SLO 1.8 Preview a presentation and print slides, handouts, and outlines (p. P1-42).

SLO 1.9 Apply presentation properties (p. P1-45).

CASE STUDY

Throughout this book you have the opportunity to put into practice the application features that you are learning. Each chapter begins with a case study that introduces you to the Pause & Practice projects in the chapter. These Pause & Practice projects give you a chance to apply and practice key skills. Each chapter contains three to five Pause & Practice projects.

Hamilton Civic Center (HCC) is a nonprofit community fitness center that partners with the local hospital for educational events. Doctors and nurses provide classes on a variety of health and wellness issues for adults. HCC also works with local schools to support their academic programs and sponsors events for children.

In this chapter, you develop a presentation about training for an upcoming marathon that is being promoted to HCC members.

Pause & Practice 1-1: Create a presentation and develop text content.

Pause & Practice 1-2: Apply a presentation theme, change theme colors and fonts, and edit content.

Pause & Practice 1-3: Add interest with pictures and apply transitions, and print supplements.

SLO 1.1

Creating, Opening, and Saving Presentations

PowerPoint provides several ways to start, view, and save a presentation. Always save your presentation if you will need to access it again. If you close the presentation before saving it, your content is lost.

Create a Presentation

When PowerPoint first opens, you can start a new presentation or open an existing presentation that is listed on the left. Clickable images called ***thumbnails*** have a name below each one. If you prefer to work on text content only, click the **Blank Presentation** thumbnail to go directly to your first slide so you can begin developing content.

Other thumbnails represent built-in ***Themes*** that provide a unified look for all the slides in a presentation. Most themes have color or graphic treatments that create a background design. When you click a theme, a dialog box opens where you can choose from four or more ***Variants*** showing different color combinations. Variants may have different graphics, too. Once these choices are made, you can start developing content.

The following three How-to Boxes explain several different ways to start a presentation.

HOW TO: Create a Presentation When First Opening PowerPoint

1. Open PowerPoint and you will see the *Backstage* view (Figure 1-1).
2. Click **Blank Presentation** to go directly to your first slide.

Or

3. Click a **Theme** to open a dialog box (Figure 1-2).
4. Click the arrow buttons below the slide example to see how colors are applied to different layouts.

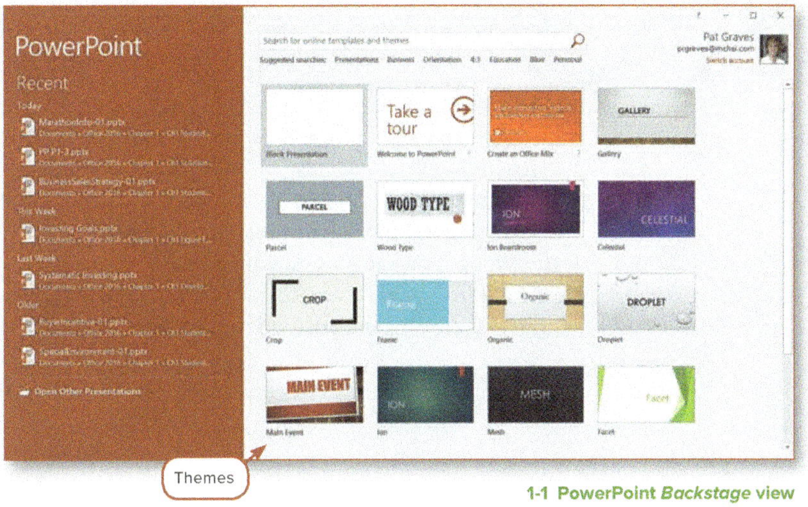

1-1 PowerPoint *Backstage* view

5. Select one of four *Variants* on the right that provide different color combinations.
6. Click **Create**.

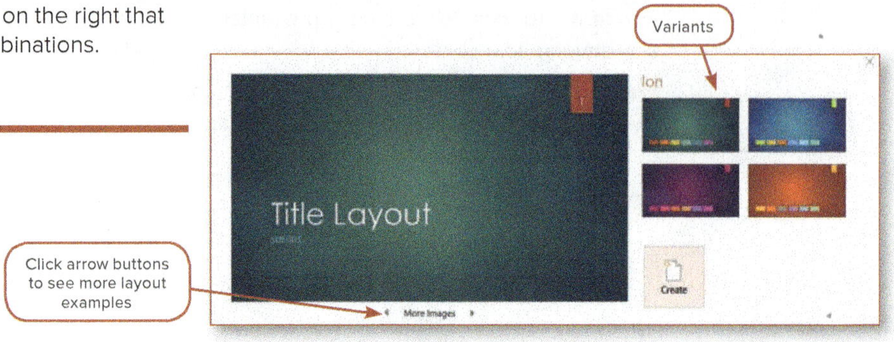

1-2 Theme *Variants*

When you create a new presentation, PowerPoint assigns a generic name, such as *Presentation1*, that appears in the title bar. Additional new presentations are named in the same way. When you save the presentation with a new name, that name appears in the title bar.

> **MORE INFO**
>
> When your content is complete, save your presentation (discussed on pages P1-10 – P1-12) and then close it by clicking the **File** tab and then clicking **Close**. To close PowerPoint, click the **Close** button (an **X**) in the upper right corner of the title bar. If you click the **Close** button before saving, your presentation will automatically close or you will be asked if you want to save your presentation if changes have been made.

HOW TO: Create a New Presentation When PowerPoint Is Open

1. Click the **File** tab to open the *Backstage* view.
2. Click **New** and use one of these methods to start a presentation:
   - Select a *Theme*, select a *Variant*, and click **Create** to open the presentation with the selected theme and colors.
   - Double-click a *Theme* to open the presentation with that theme and the default *Variant* colors.
   - Double-click **Blank Presentation** to go directly to your first slide.

Or

3. Press **Ctrl+N** to open a new blank presentation.

A theme simplifies the process of creating professional looking presentations by providing consistent background graphics, colors, and font settings. A ***template*** contains the characteristics of a theme and usually provides sample content you can edit or delete if you want only the background a template provides. Many themes and templates are available in PowerPoint by searching online when you start a new presentation, or they can be downloaded at Office.com. You can save downloaded themes and templates so they are available for future use. *SLO 1.4: Changing Theme Colors and Fonts* provides information about searching within PowerPoint and customizing theme settings.

> **MORE INFO**
>
> Your computer must be connected to the Internet to download themes and templates.

▶ HOW TO: Create a New Presentation from Online Templates and Themes

1. Click the **File** tab to open the *Backstage* view.
2. Click **New**. In the search box, type a word, such as small business, and click the **Start searching** button (Figure 1-3). Available templates and themes appear.
   - Filter your results by typing the word and and then typing a second search word such as travel.
   - Click the **Start searching** button to search again.

Or

3. Click one of the *Suggested searches* for general topics and available templates and themes will appear.
   - Filter your results by clicking one of the terms in the *Category* list on the right (Figure 1-4).
   - Filter your results by typing the word or before another search word and searching again.
4. Click a thumbnail to open a dialog box to review other slides in addition to the title slide. Some templates include a description (Figure 1-5).
5. Click **Create** and the presentation opens.
   - The presentation may contain sample content that you need to delete before adding your content.

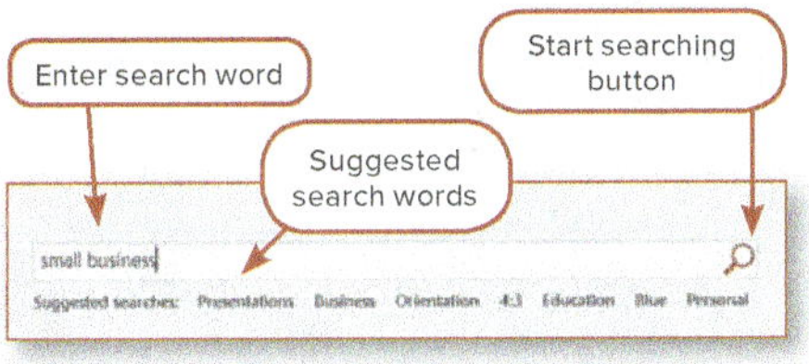

1-3 Search for online themes and templates

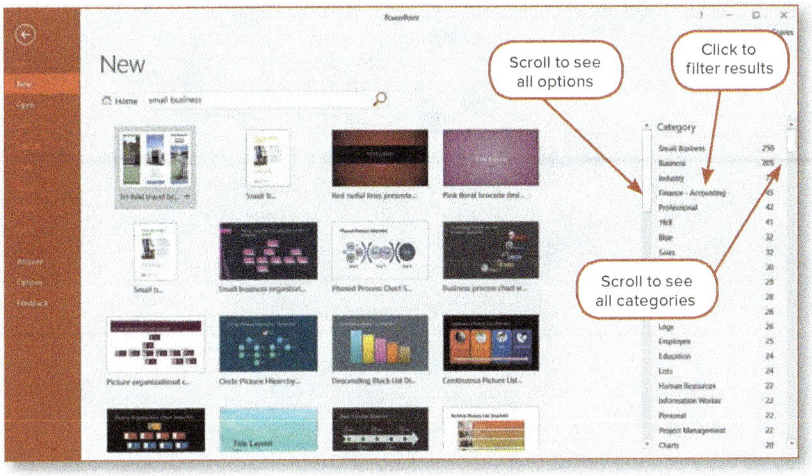

1-4 Search results for online themes and templates

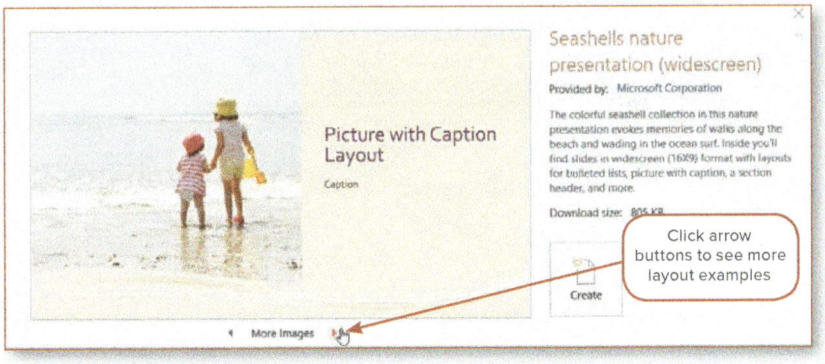

1-5 Template with description and sample content

You can use an existing presentation to start a new presentation. To do this, open a presentation file from a source such as your computer, USB drive, local network, cloud space such as *OneDrive*, or an email attachment.

▶ HOW TO: Open a Recent Presentation

1. Start PowerPoint and click the **File** tab to open the *Backstage* view.
2. Click **Open** to display the *Open* area on the *Backstage* view.

3. Select **Recent** and click a presentation name on the right to open it.
   - If you open a presentation frequently, you can pin it.
   - Click the **Pin** icon to the right of the presentation name (Figure 1-6) and the presentation name moves to the top in a *Pinned* area.

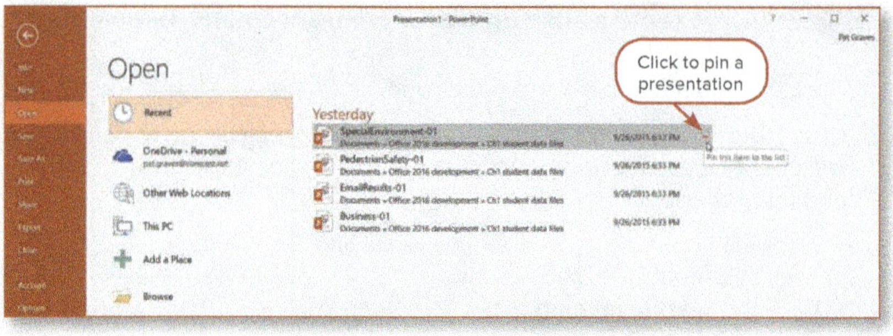

1-6 Pin a presentation in the *Open* area on the *Backstage* view

Or

4. Select **OneDrive** or **This PC** to open folders and files from these locations (Figure 1-7). Click the presentation name to open it.

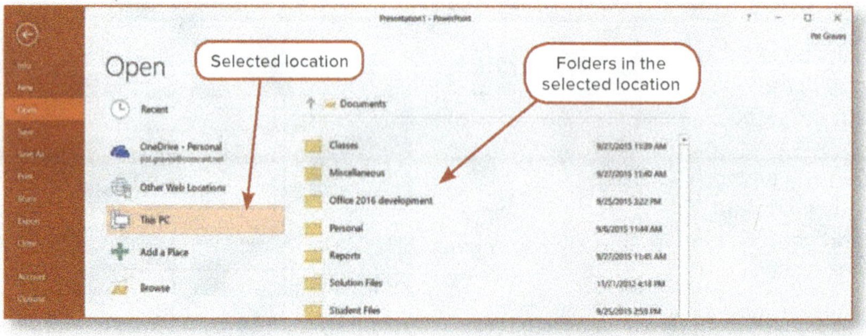

1-7 Folders in *This PC*

Or

5. Click **Browse** and the *Open* dialog box appears where you can find folders and files from other locations (Figure 1-8). Select the file and click **Open** to display the presentation and close the dialog box.

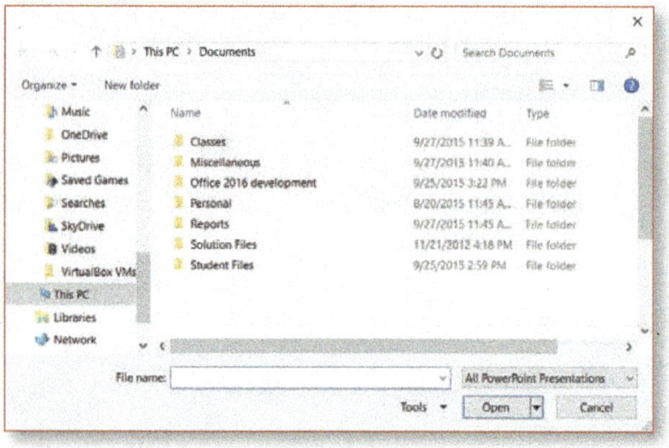

1-8 *Open* dialog box

MORE INFO

For instructions to set up a *OneDrive* account, refer to *SLO Intro.1: Using Windows 10* in *Intro Chapter 1: Windows 10, Office 2016, and File Management*.

ANOTHER WAY

Ctrl+O opens the *Backstage* view where you can open a presentation. **Ctrl+F12** opens the *Open* dialog box. Some laptops require **Fn+Ctrl+F12**.

Views

PowerPoint provides different views to help you create slides, organize them, and display them in a slide show. When you start a new presentation, it opens in ***Normal*** view. The *Ribbon* displays across the top of the window and has nine tabs with commands organized in groups (Figure 1-9). Additional tabs, such as the *Drawing Tools Format* tab, open depending on what you are doing. Several tabs contain commands similar to those in Word, whereas other tabs display features that are unique to PowerPoint.

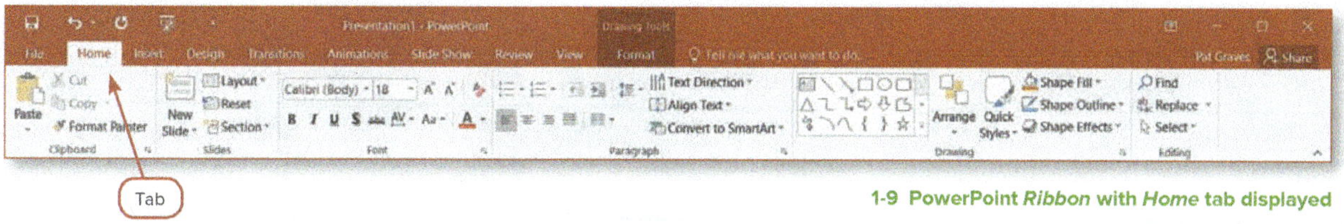

1-9 PowerPoint *Ribbon* with *Home* tab displayed

The area below the *Ribbon* is divided into panes where you create and work on slides: A *Thumbnail* pane is on the left and a *Slide* pane is on the right. A *Notes* pane may display below the slide. You can change views using commands on the *View* tab [*Presentation Views* group] (Figure 1-10) or the *View* buttons on the *Status* bar at the bottom of the window.

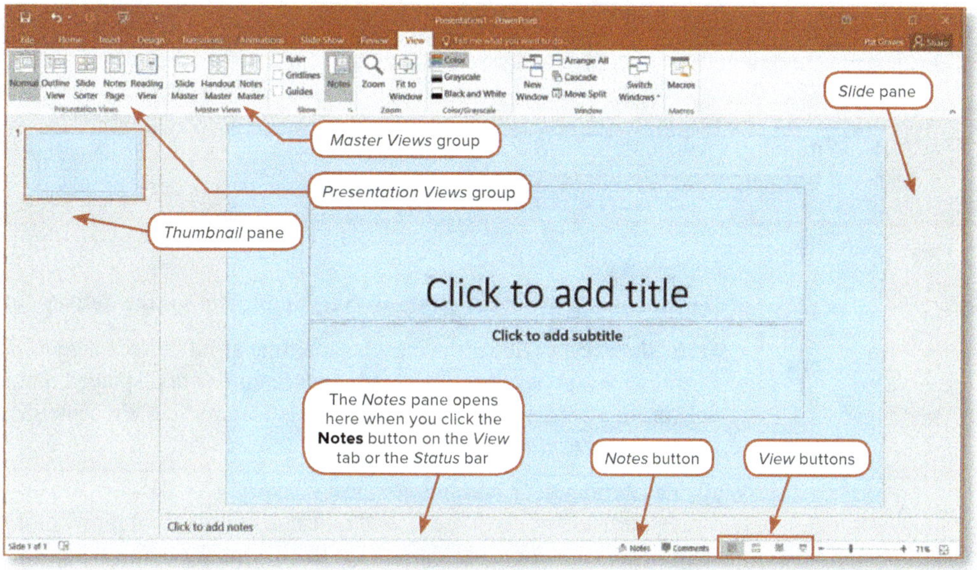

1-10 *Normal* view with *View* tab and *Notes* pane displayed

The *View* tab has five *Presentation Views* that include the following:

- ***Normal View***: The default view where you enter content and move between slides as you develop them. Click the *Normal* button or the *Notes* button to open a *Notes* pane below the slide to add speaker notes for individual slides.
- ***Outline View***: The left pane displays slide titles and bulleted text instead of slide thumbnails.

- ***Slide Sorter View***: Slides appear as thumbnails so it is easy to reorganize slides and apply transition effects to control how the slides advance.
- ***Notes Page View***: Each slide appears at the top of a page with space below the slide where you can type speaker notes.
- ***Reading View***: The slide show displays at full-screen or another window size controlled by the viewer. Navigation controls are in the *Status* bar at the bottom of the window.

The *Master Views* group includes the following: ***Slide Master***, ***Handout Master***, and ***Notes Master***. These views are used to change formatting that affects the whole presentation.

The *View* buttons located on the *Status* bar provide easy access to different PowerPoint views regardless of which *Ribbon* tab is currently open (Figure 1-11).

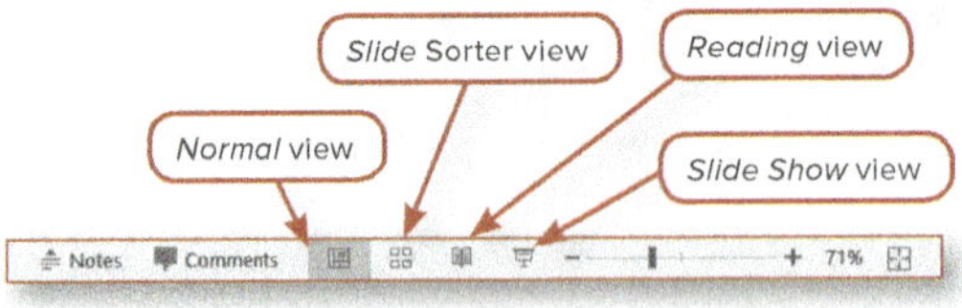

1-11 *View* buttons

▸ HOW TO: Change Views

1. Click the **View** tab. Note that *Normal* is selected in the *Presentation Views* group and you can see the *Slide* and *Thumbnail* panes.
2. Observe the changes as you access each different view using buttons on the *View* tab or *Status* bar:
   - Click the **Outline** button and text appears on the left instead of slide thumbnails.
   - Click the **Slide Sorter** button to display all slide thumbnails in your presentation.
   - Click the **Notes Page** button and your current slide appears at the top of a page.
   - Click the **Reading View** button to see your slides in a window.
   - Click the **Normal** button to return to *Normal* view.

The following two more views are very important for the delivery of your presentation:

- ***Slide Show View***: Slides appear one at a time at full-screen size for audience viewing.
- ***Presenter View***: Speaker notes and other features are displayed that are helpful for delivering a presentation. For more on this feature, see "Presenter View" in *SLO 3.5: Controlling Display Options*.

While developing your presentation, test it in *Slide Show* view so you can see the content in the way your audience will see it, and rehearse your presentation before using it.

Start a presentation slide show from the beginning by pressing **F5**; start with the current slide by clicking the **Slide Show** button on the *Status* bar. You may also use buttons on the *Slide Show* tab (Figure 1-12).

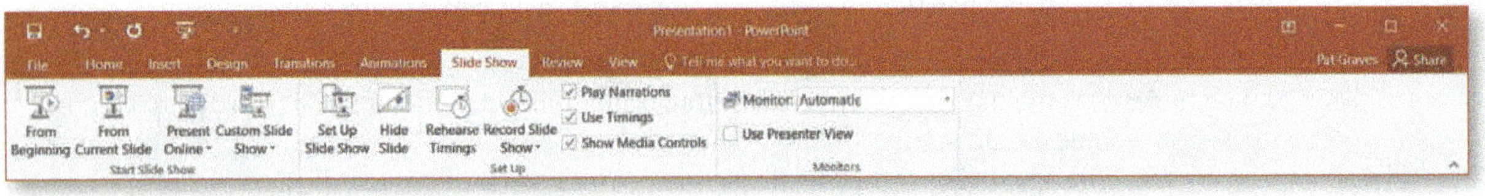

1-12 *Slide Show* tab

▸ HOW TO: Start a Presentation from the Slide Show Tab

1. Click the **Slide Show** tab.
2. Click the **From Beginning** button [*Start Slide Show* group] to display slides from the beginning, regardless of which slide is the current slide.
3. Click the **From Current Slide** button to display slides starting with the current slide.
4. Move through the slides by clicking the screen or pressing one of several keys on the keyboard: **spacebar**, **Enter**, **Page Down**, **Down** arrow, or **N**.

Adjusting pane sizes can help you better focus on one aspect of your presentation. For example, thumbnails become larger when you increase the size of the thumbnail pane and you have more room to write when you increase the size of the notes pane. In each case, the slide becomes a little smaller.

▸ HOW TO: Adjust Pane Sizes

1. Point to the pane border separating the *Thumbnail* pane and the *Slide* pane until your pointer turns into a sizing pointer with two arrows (Figure 1-13).
2. Click and drag the pane border to the right to increase thumbnail size and to the left to decrease thumbnail size.
3. If the *Notes* pane is not open, click the **Notes** button [*View* tab, *Show* group or *Status* bar].
4. Point to the pane border separating the *Slide* pane and the *Notes* pane.

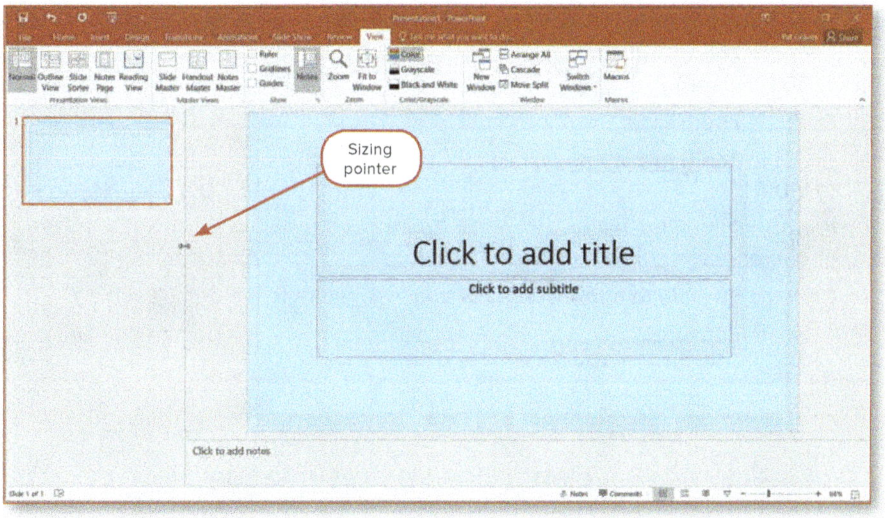

1-13 *Thumbnail* pane and *Notes* pane size is increased

5. Click and drag the *Notes* pane border up or down to increase or decrease the *Notes* pane size.
6. Click and drag the *Notes* pane border down to the bottom of the window or click the **Notes** button on the *Status* bar to remove this pane.

Use ***Zoom*** to increase the current slide size in *Normal* view when you need to see more detail. Use the *Zoom* dialog box to set a specific magnification level or adjust the magnification by using the *Zoom* slider. You can use *Zoom* on the *Slide Sorter* view also.

▶ HOW TO: Use the Zoom Dialog Box

1. Click the **Zoom** button [*View* tab, *Zoom* group] and the *Zoom* dialog box opens.
2. Select a preset zoom percentage such as 200% (Figure 1-14) or enter a percentage number, such as 150%.
3. Click **OK**. The slide size is increased and you can see only a portion of the slide.
4. Click the **Zoom** button again, select **Fit**, and click **OK** to return to the default setting so the entire slide displays.

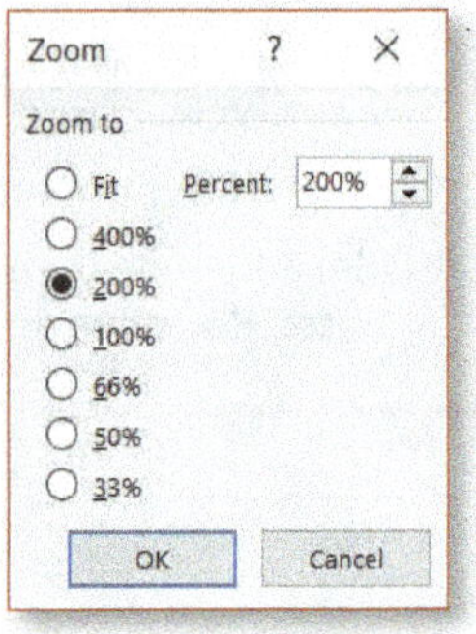

1-14 *Zoom* dialog box

The *Zoom* controls are located on the right side of the *Status* bar and the current slide size percentage is shown. At 100%, the slider is in the center. Drag the slider or click the **Zoom** buttons to adjust the slide size.

▶ HOW TO: Use the Zoom Controls

1. Click the **Zoom Out** button several times to decrease the view to 50% (Figure 1-15).
2. Drag the **Zoom** slider to the center.
3. Click the **Zoom In** button several times to increase the view to 150%.
4. Click the line on the left or right of the **Zoom** slider to increase or decrease the percentage.
5. Click the **Fit slide to current window** button to return to the default setting.
6. Click the percentage to open the *Zoom* dialog box. Select a percentage and click **OK** to close the dialog box.

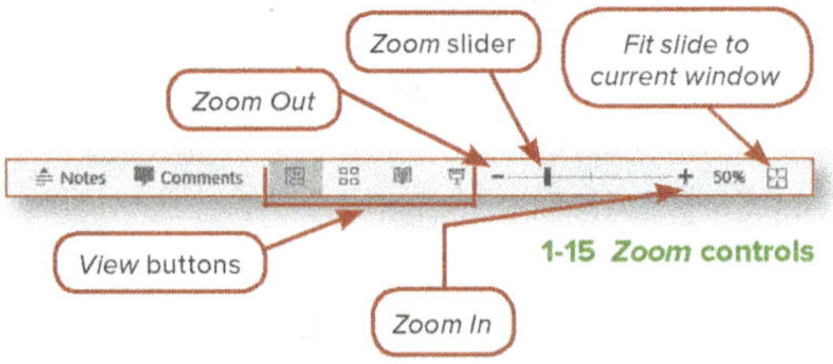

1-15 *Zoom* controls

Save and Close a Presentation

PowerPoint assigns each new presentation a generic name such as *Presentation1*. When you save the presentation for the first time, change the generic name to a more meaningful name.

▶ HOW TO: Save a Presentation

1. Click the **File** tab to open the *Backstage* view.
2. Click **Save** or **Save As** to display the *Save As* area (Figure 1-16).
3. Select the location where you want to save your presentation: *OneDrive, Other Web Locations,* or *This PC*.
   - Select an appropriate folder. If you select the wrong folder, click the blue **Up** arrow and select again.
   - Type a file name in the box that appears at the top and click the **Save** button

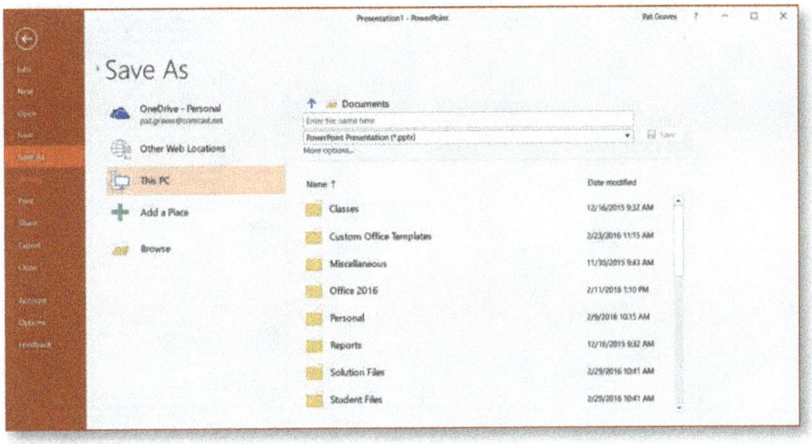

1-16 *Save As* area on the *Backstage* view

4. Click the **Browse** button to open the *Save As* dialog box (Figure 1-17).
   - Browse to the appropriate folder to save the file.
   - Type the presentation name in the *File name* area and click the **Save** button.

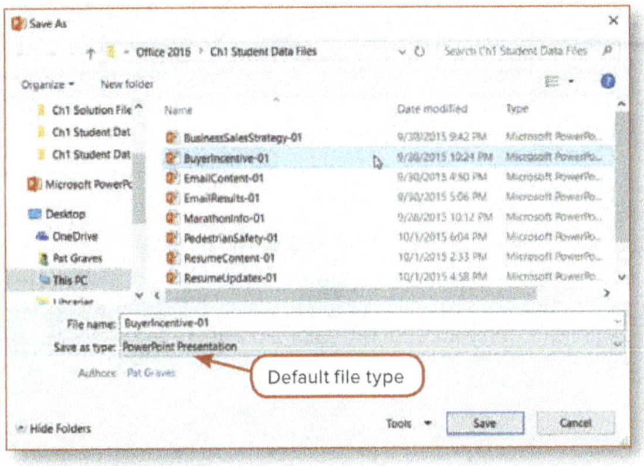

1-17 *Save As* dialog box

When saving for the first time, you can also click the **Save** button on the *Quick Access* toolbar, or press **Ctrl+S**, to open the *Save As* area on the *Backstage* view. As you revise your presentation, simply clicking the **Save** button on the *Quick Access* toolbar will resave it with the same name in the same location.

If you want to create a second version of that file, then click the **File** tab and then click **Save As** to resave it with a different name in the same or different location. The original presentation is not affected by any changes you make to the second presentation.

ANOTHER WAY

Press **F12** to open the *Save As* dialog box.

You can save PowerPoint presentations in a variety of formats. By default, PowerPoint 2016 presentations are saved with the .pptx file extension. To change the type of presentation format, select the format of your choice from the *Save as type* area in the *Save As* dialog box (Figure 1-18).

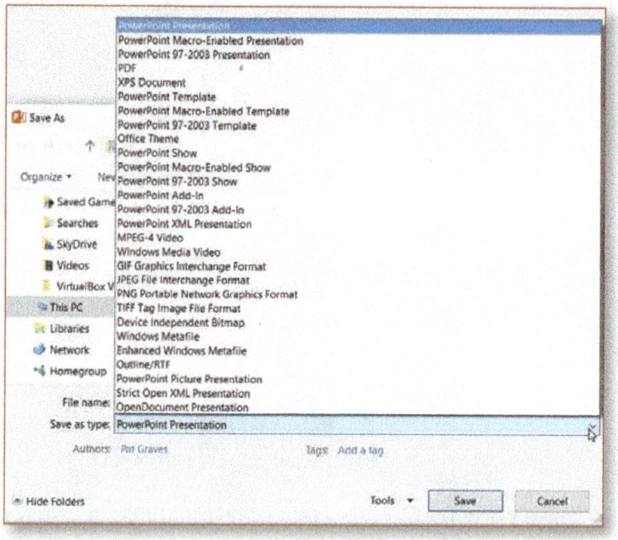

1-18 ***Save As* file types**

The following table lists available formats that are most commonly used for PowerPoint:

Save Formats

Type of Presentation	File Extension	Uses of This Format
PowerPoint Presentation	.pptx	PowerPoint presentation compatible with 2007–2016 software versions that use an XML-enabled file format. This is the default file format.
PowerPoint 97-2003 Presentation	.ppt	PowerPoint presentation compatible with 1997–2003 software versions. Newer software features are not supported.
PDF (Portable Document Format)	.pdf	Similar to pictures of slides, with each slide shown as a separate page. The file size may be smaller than the original presentation, so this format often works well for presentations distributed electronically.
PowerPoint Template	.potx	PowerPoint template that can be used to format presentations.
Windows Media Video or Mpeg-P4 Video	.wmv or .mp4	PowerPoint presentation saved as a video that will play on many media players. Three resolution sizes are available, and all create large file sizes.
Outline/RTF	.rtf	A presentation text-only outline with a small file size for easy sharing.
PowerPoint Picture Presentation	.pptx	PowerPoint presentation that converts each slide into an image. It helps to reduce file size or create images for inclusion in other documents.
Open Document Presentation	.odp	PowerPoint presentation that can be opened in applications that use the Open Document Presentation format, such as Google.Docs or OpenOffice.org.

MORE INFO

Other file formats are used to save individual slides or images on slides. These graphic file formats include .jpg, .png, .tif, .bmp, .wmf, or .emf. These formats are explained on page P1-38.

When you are finished with a presentation, save your final version and then close the presentation by clicking the **File** tab, and then clicking **Close** or clicking the **Close** button [**X**] in the upper right corner of the title bar.

Share and Export Options

From the *Backstage* view you have options for ***sharing*** (Figure 1-19) or ***exporting*** (Figure 1-20) your presentation using different file formats. Not all classroom computer lab configurations permit access to shared online sites or network locations.

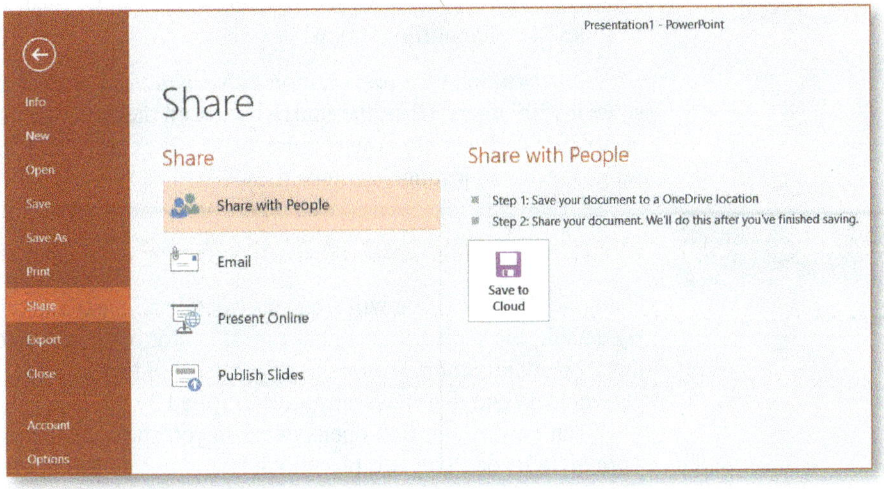

1-19 *Share* options

Share

- ***Share with People***: Saves your presentation to a *OneDrive* location so you can share it with others.
- ***Email***: Sends your presentation as an attachment in the file type you choose.
- ***Present Online***: Requires a Microsoft Account so people can link to your slide show through a web browser.
- ***Publish Slides***: Sends presentation files to a shared library or SharePoint site.

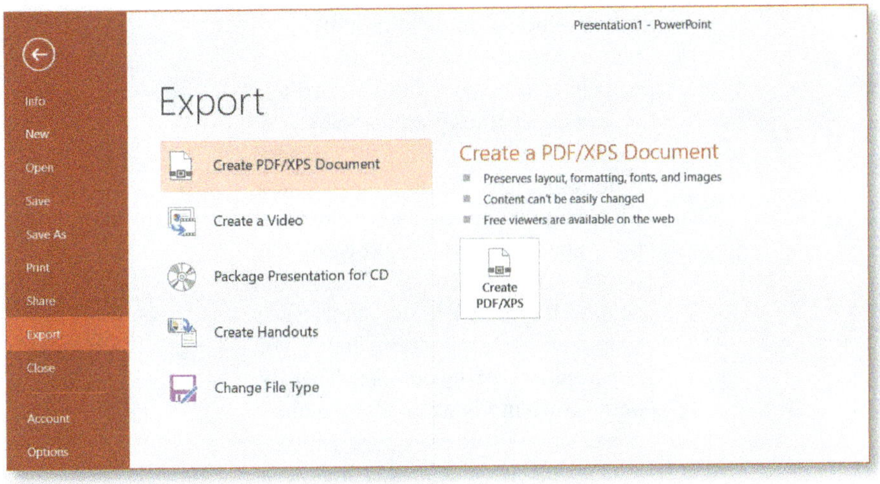

1-20 *Export* options

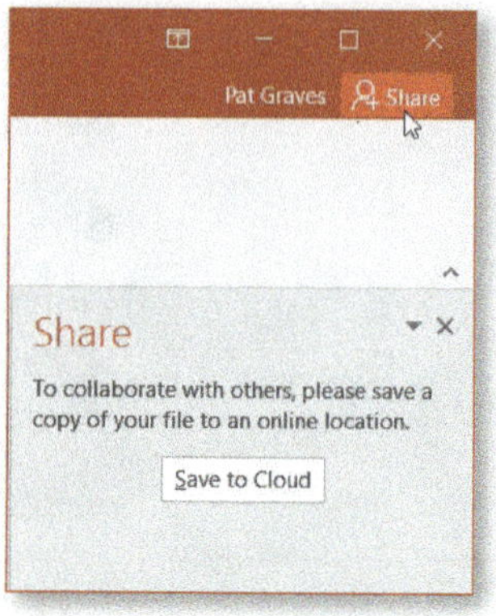

1-21 *Share* button

Export

- ***Create PDF/XPS Document***: Preserves formatting and reduces file size for easier distribution.
- ***Create a Video***: Saves your presentation as a video.
- ***Package Presentation for CD***: Saves your presentation and all linked or embedded files.
- ***Create Handouts***: Transfers slides and notes to a Word document that you can re-format.
- ***Change File Type***: Saves your presentation or individual slides in different file formats.

While working on a presentation in *Normal* view, you can share it with others. Click the **Share** button on the upper right of your PowerPoint window (Figure 1-21). Click **Save to Cloud** and then select the online location for your files.

SLO 1.2

Working with Slides, Layouts, Placeholders, and Text

Using *Normal* view, you will frequently enter slide text and other objects using ***placeholders***. By default, these placeholders have no fill color or border, but you may choose to emphasize them by adding color. You can resize placeholders as needed to fit content. The available placeholders and their positions are controlled by the particular ***layout*** that you choose.

When PowerPoint first opens or when you start a blank presentation, the first slide has a ***Title Slide*** layout with two placeholders: a presentation title and a subtitle. You can add text directly into these placeholders or you can type slide titles and bulleted text in *Outline* view. The font, font size, and alignment are preset, but you can change them as you develop your presentation. Keep in mind that text should be brief, straight to the point, and easy to read.

Add Slides and Choose Layouts

To insert additional slides, you click the **New Slide** button on the *Home* tab. After a title slide, PowerPoint automatically inserts a ***Title and Content*** layout. This layout is used for developing most slides; it has a placeholder for the slide title and a placeholder for inserting bulleted text or content such as pictures, tables, or charts. From that point forward, each time you click the top of the **New Slide** button, you add a new slide with the same layout as the previous one (unless you use the *Title Slide* layout again). If you click the **New Slide** drop-down arrow (bottom half), you see a gallery of layouts, such as the ones shown in Figure 1-22, for a blank presentation using the *Office Theme*.

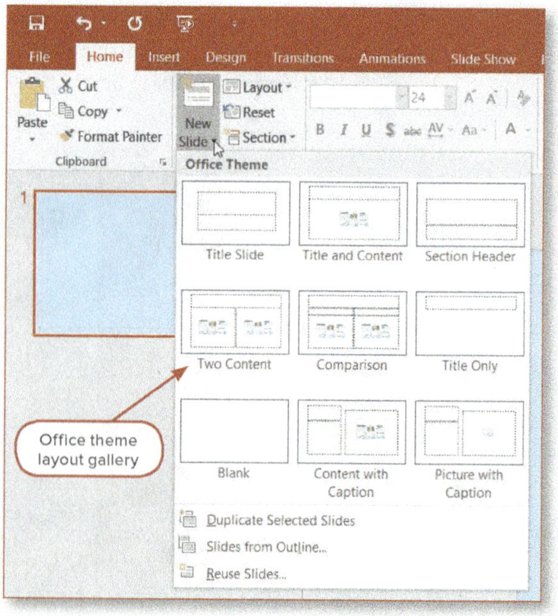

1-22 Slide layouts

Layouts provide a starting point for your slide designs. You can change layouts or customize each slide for the content you are developing. The available layouts vary based on the current theme. The most common layouts are described in the following table:

Slide Layouts

Layout Name	Layout Description
Title Slide	A layout used for a presentation's opening slide. It contains a title and a subtitle placeholder.
Title and Content	A layout used for the body of a presentation. It contains a placeholder for the slide title and a larger placeholder for many different kinds of content.
Section Header	This layout is similar to a Title Slide layout and usually has a slightly different appearance. It can divide a lengthy presentation or introduce different topics or speakers.
Two Content	This layout has a slide title placeholder and two smaller content placeholders to display either two brief lists or a list and a graphic object, such as a picture or chart.
Comparison	A layout that is similar to the Two Content layout, but it works better for comparing two lists because it provides a heading area above each content placeholder.
Title Only	A layout with only one placeholder for the title (usually at the top) of the slide.
Blank	This layout has no placeholders.
Content with Caption	A layout that is similar to the Two Content layout, but one area is designated for content, such as a table or chart, while the other area is meant for descriptive text.
Picture with Caption	This layout has a large area for a picture and another area for descriptive text.

HOW TO: Choose and Change Slide Layouts

1. Choose a layout for a new slide using one of these methods:
   - Click the **New Slide** button [*Home* tab, *Slides* group] to insert a slide with the default layout.
   - Click the **New Slide** drop-down arrow [*Home* tab, *Slides* group] and select a layout from the layout gallery. The current theme name will appear at the top.
2. Change the layout of a selected slide by following these steps:
   - Click the **Layout** button [*Home* tab, *Slides* group].
   - From the layout gallery, select a different layout.
   - Repeat this process to try another layout.
3. Click the **Undo** button [*Quick Access* toolbar] to remove the layout change.

Enter Text in Placeholders

When you first see placeholders on slides, they appear as boxes with a thin, dotted border. When you click inside the placeholder, it becomes active with a blinking insertion point where you can type or edit text (Figure 1-23). Click the border to select the placeholder and the line becomes solid (Figure 1-24). In both cases, ***sizing handles*** that are small white circles appear on the corners and sides. A ***rotation handle*** that is a circular arrow appears at the top.

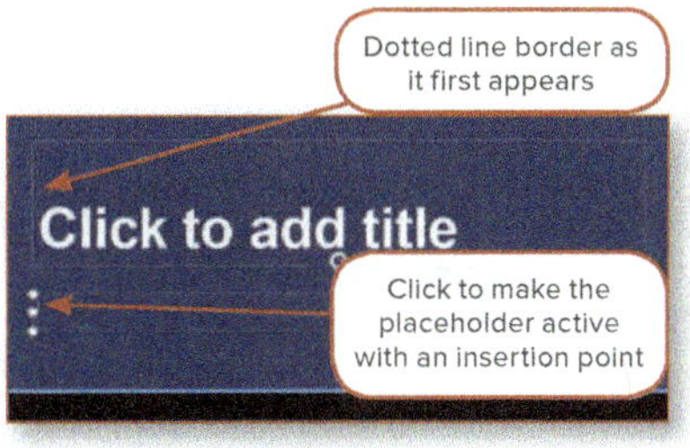

1-23 Placeholders for text

By default, PowerPoint automatically fits text in a placeholder. Therefore, keep the wording of titles concise so the text does not become too small. Depending on the font that is used, title text for individual slides is usually 36–44 points. When using the *Title Slide* layout, the title text is usually 54–72 points.

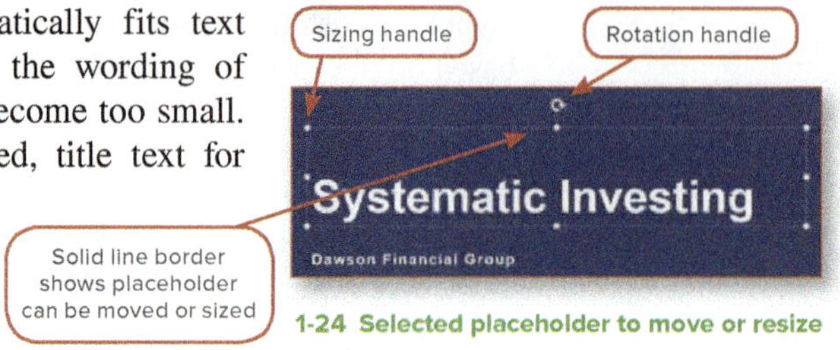

1-24 Selected placeholder to move or resize

> **MORE INFO**
>
> A point is a unit of measurement in typography used to represent the height of text characters and the space between lines. The number of points in one inch is 72. The widescreen slide size is 13.33" × 7.5" (*Width* × *Height*).

In body placeholders, a bullet (a small symbol such as a circle or square) automatically appears when you type text and press **Enter**. Bullets help mark the beginning of a line, so people recognize items as separate. You can also add subpoints that are indented below a bulleted item. Be sure your list is very concise, usually no more than six items, and the text size is 20–28 points. Larger font sizes are very important if you are presenting in a large room so your audience can read slide text from a distance. However, if you are preparing a presentation to be viewed on a computer or online, you can use smaller font sizes.

Bulleted lists are appropriate when items require no particular order. If you need to show items in order, use a numbered list instead.

HOW TO: Work with Lists

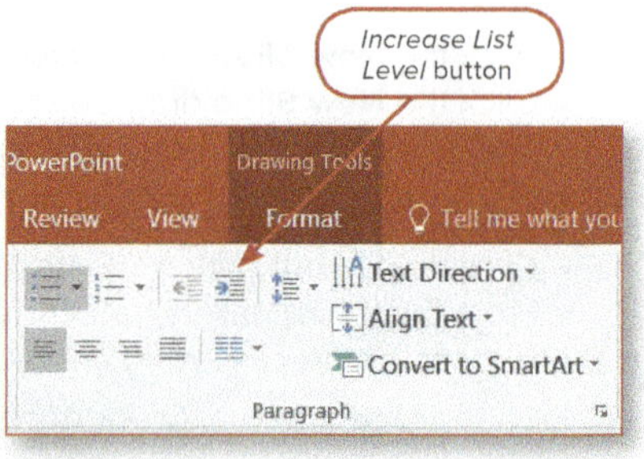

1-25 Paragraph group on the *Home* tab

1. Click after the first bullet in the body placeholder and type text.
2. Press **Enter** to type another bulleted item using the same list level.
3. Press **Tab** or click the **Increase List Level** button [*Home* tab, *Paragraph* group] (Figure 1-25) to indent a bulleted item to the right (Figure 1-26).
4. Use *Outline View* to enter several text slides. *Outline View* displays all slide titles and bulleted text in the left pane.
   - Click the **Outline View** button [*View* tab, *Presentation Views* group].
   - Position your insertion point at the beginning of a bulleted item and press **Shift+Tab** or click the **Decrease List Level** button [*Home* tab, *Paragraph* group] (Figure 1-27) to move a bulleted item to the left to create a slide title.
   - Change text capitalization as needed for a title (Figure 1-28).

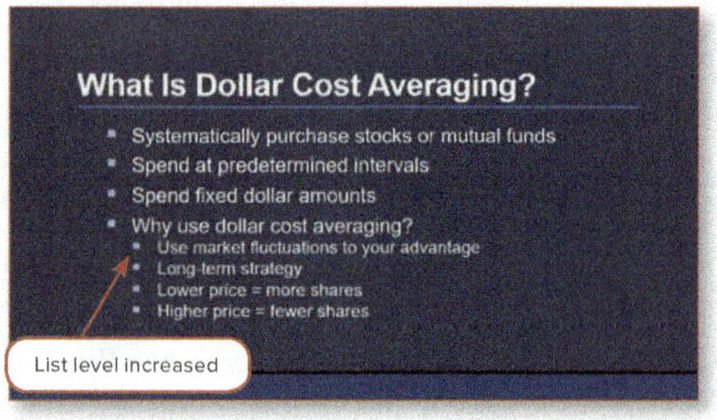

1-26 Bulleted list slide

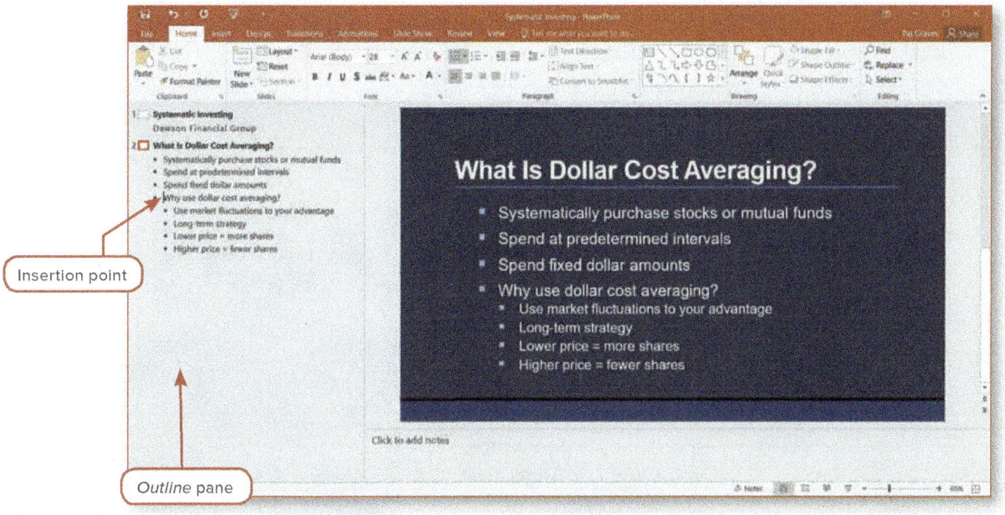

1-27 Slide with bulleted text before list level changes

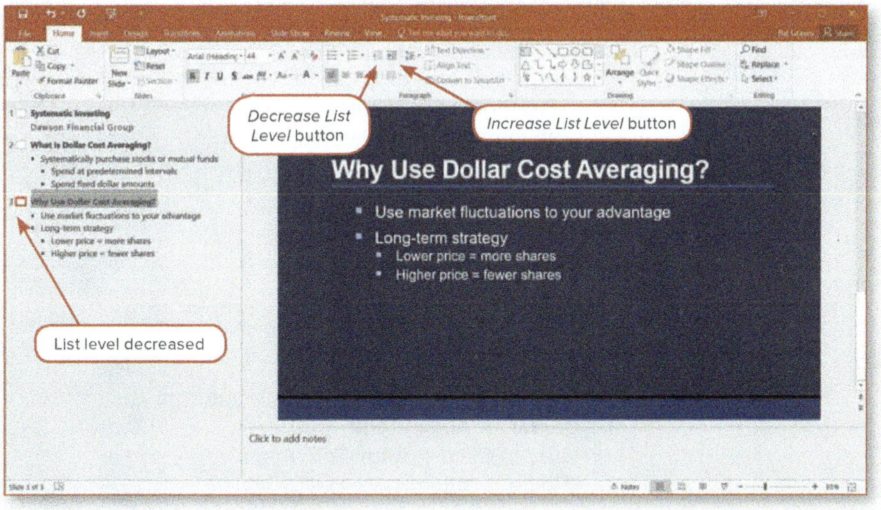

1-28 New slide created by decreasing the list level

5. Convert a bulleted list to a numbered list by selecting the text to be changed and then clicking the **Numbering** button [*Home* tab, *Paragraph* group].

> **MORE INFO**
>
> To move from the title to the body placeholder, press **Ctrl+Enter**. If you are in the last placeholder, press **Ctrl+Enter** to create a new slide.

Align, Move, and Resize Placeholders

How text is positioned within placeholders is controlled by ***horizontal alignment*** and ***vertical alignment***. A small margin automatically appears in placeholders so the text within them does not touch the border.

▸HOW TO: Align Text and Placeholders

1. Align selected text within placeholders horizontally or vertically using these options:
   - *Horizontal*: Choose **Align Left**, **Center**, **Align Right**, or **Justify** (aligns text on both the left and right) [*Home* tab, *Paragraph* group]. *Justify* is rarely used on slides because it can cause irregular spacing between words.
   - *Vertical*: Click **Align Text** [*Home* tab, *Paragraph* group] and then choose **Top**, **Middle**, or **Bottom** (See Figure 1-29).

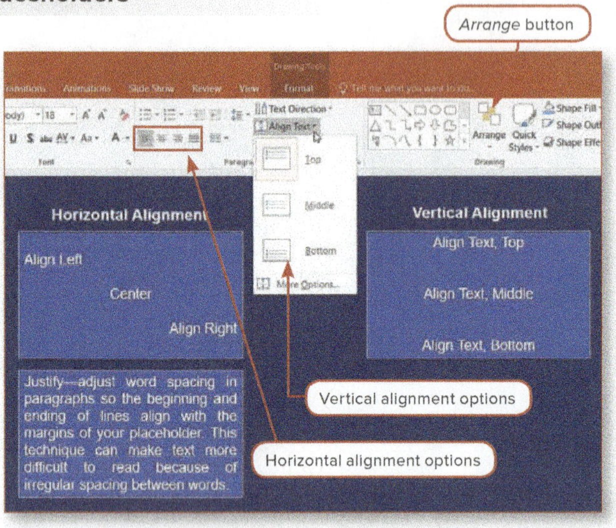

1-29 ***Align Text* within placeholders**

2. Align selected placeholders with one another. The same drop-down list of options appears on two tabs, so use the tab that is most convenient to you.
   - Click the **Arrange** button [*Home* tab, *Drawing* group] and then choose **Align**.
   - Click the **Align** button [*Drawing Tools Format* tab, *Arrange* group].
3. Choose an alignment option from the drop-down list (Figure 1-30):
   - *Horizontal*: Choose **Align Left**, **Align Center**, or **Align Right**.
   - *Vertical*: Choose **Align Top**, **Align Middle**, or **Align Bottom**.

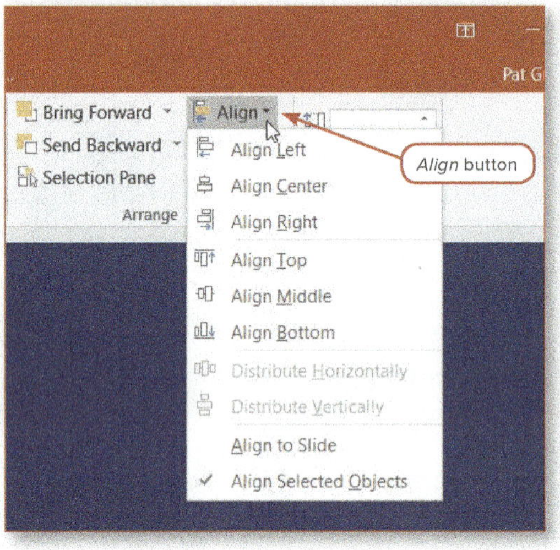

1-30 ***Align* options**

Move a placeholder by pointing to its border so your pointer changes to a move arrow (with four points) (Figure 1-31). Click to select the placeholder and drag it to a new position. Use the same technique for moving other objects such as shapes and pictures.

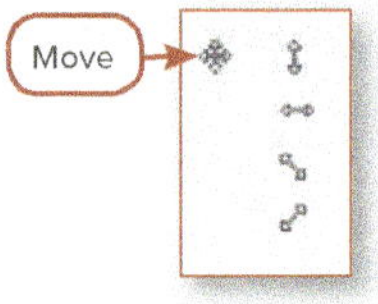

1-31 Move and resize pointers

To increase or decrease placeholder size, point to a corner or side ***sizing handle*** until your pointer changes to a ***resize pointer*** (with two points) (see Figure 1-31). As you drag to resize, your pointer changes to a crosshair and the area you will keep is grayed out (Figure 1-32). When you release the pointer, the circle handles appear again. Drag a corner sizing handle (with a diagonal resize pointer) to change both the horizontal and vertical dimensions at the same time.

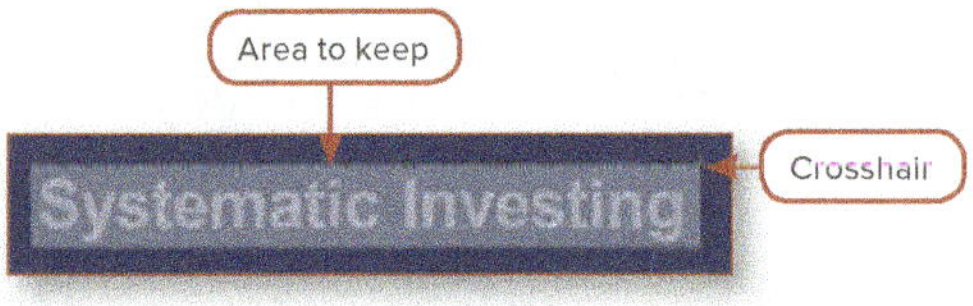

1-32 Resize a placeholder

You can control the way placeholders and other objects are resized by pressing one of three keys as you drag:

- *Ctrl*: The placeholder size changes from a fixed center point.
- *Shift*: The height and width proportions are maintained as the size changes.
- *Ctrl+Shift*: The placeholder resizes from the center and remains in proportion.

Another way to precisely resize a placeholder is to enter the exact dimensions in the *Size* group on the *Drawing Tools Format* tab (Figure 1-33).

All of these techniques for moving, aligning, and resizing also apply to pictures and other objects. If you don't like a change that you made, click the **Reset** button in the *Slides* group on the *Home* tab.

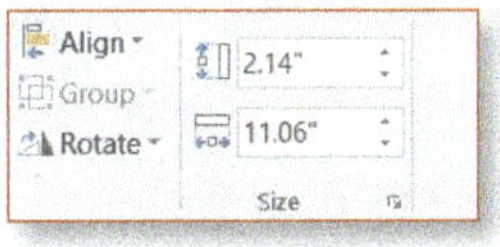

1-33 *Size* group

Edit Text

Notice that your pointer changes when you are working with text. When you see a blinking insertion point, PowerPoint is waiting for you to type text. When you point to text, your pointer changes to a text selection tool so you can click and drag to select text.

Much like Word, commands for editing text are on the *Home* tab in the following groups (from left to right) (Figure 1-34):

- *Clipboard group*: **Cut**, **Copy**, **Paste**, and **Format Painter**.
- *Font group*: Character formatting commands such as **Bold**, **Italic**, **Underline**, **Case**, **Font**, and **Font Size**.
- *Paragraph group*: Paragraph formatting commands such as **Align**, **Bullets**, **Numbering**, and **Increase List Level**.

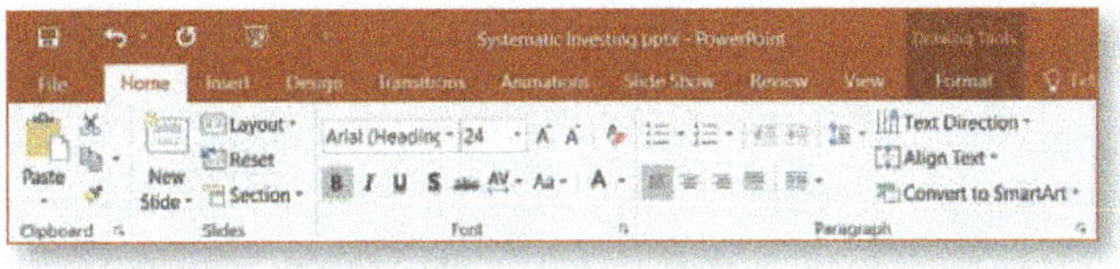

1-34 *Clipboard, Font,* and *Paragraph* groups on the *Home* tab

Also, many text formatting options are available on the mini toolbar (Figure 1-35), which appears when text is selected. You can undo or redo actions using commands on the *Quick Access* toolbar.

ANOTHER WAY

Ctrl+X	Cut
Ctrl+C	Copy
Ctrl+V	Paste
Ctrl+Z	Undo
Ctrl+Y	Redo

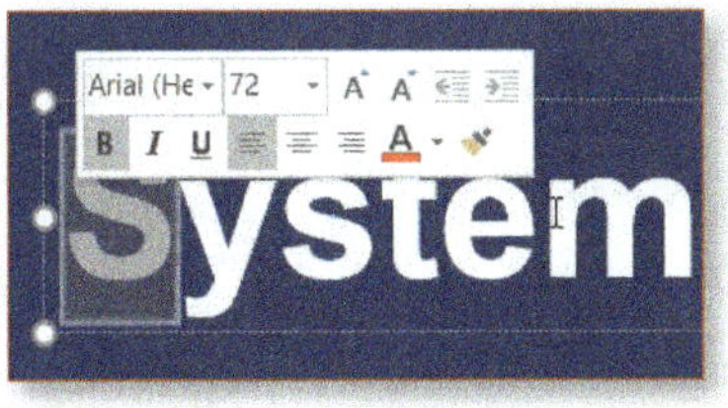

1-35 Mini toolbar

HOW TO: Delete Text

1. Press **Delete** to remove text to the right of the insertion point.
2. Press **Backspace** to remove text to the left of the insertion point.
3. Select text and press **Delete** to remove several words at one time.

Click outside a text placeholder to deselect it. Handles no longer appear.

Change Text Case

Text ***case*** refers to how text is capitalized. In several themes, text appears in a placeholder in uppercase (all capital) letters. Be careful when using uppercase letters, because they may not be as easy to read as text with initial caps (the first letter only is capitalized). People can generally read lowercase text faster than uppercase text. Also, uppercase words in email are thought to represent shouting, and this negative connotation might carry over to your presentation if you overuse capital letters. Use uppercase letters when you really want to emphasize selected words or brief phrases.

HOW TO: Change Case

1. Select the text to be changed.
2. Click the **Change Case** button [*Home* tab, *Font* group].
3. Choose from the options **Sentence case.**, **lowercase**, **UPPERCASE**, **Capitalize Each Word**, or **tOGGLE cASE** (Figure 1-36).

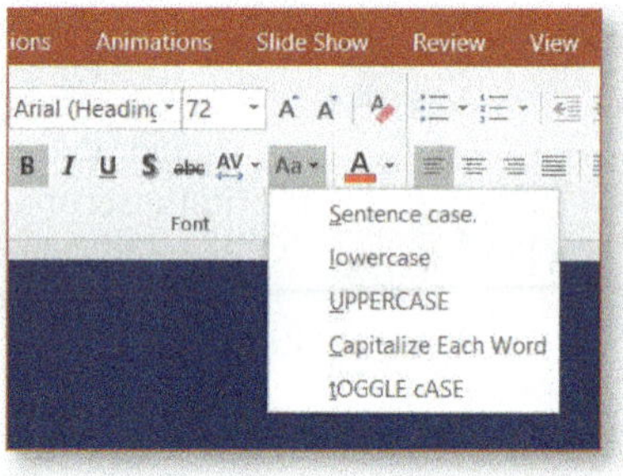

1-36 ***Change Case* options**

Change List Bullet Symbols

You can change the bullet symbol in a placeholder if it seems inappropriate or if its color blends too much with the slide background.

HOW TO: Change Bullet Symbols

1. Select the text or placeholder where you want to change the bullet.
   - Select text in the placeholder to change the bullet for one or more bulleted items.
   - Select the bulleted placeholder to change all bullets in the placeholder.
2. Click the **Bullets** drop-down arrow [*Home* tab, *Paragraph* group] and then select **Bullets and Numbering** to open the *Bullets and Numbering* dialog box (Figure 1-37).
3. Select one of the pre-defined bullets.
4. Enter a different number in the *Size* box to increase or decrease the bullet size.
5. Click the **Color** button to select a different bullet color.
6. Click the **Customize** button to open the *Symbol* dialog box (Figure 1-38), where you can select from many symbols displayed in several fonts.

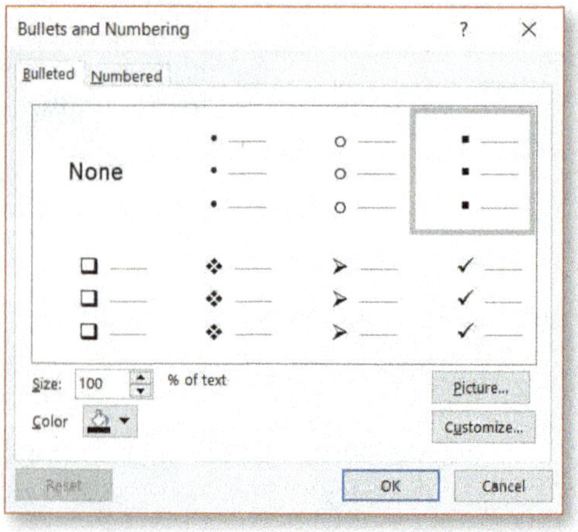

1-37 ***Bullets and Numbering* dialog box**

7. Select a symbol and a *Character code* appears. This is a unique number that your computer uses to identify the symbol you have chosen.
8. Click **OK** to add that symbol to the *Bullets and Numbering* dialog box.
9. Select the bullet and click **OK** to change the bullets on selected text.

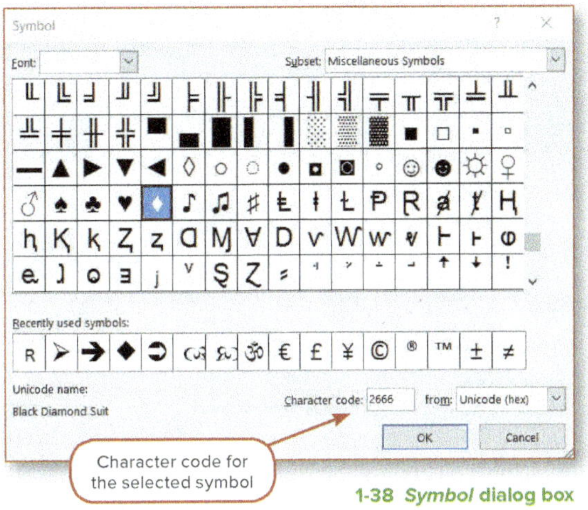

1-38 *Symbol* dialog box

The three ***Wingdings*** fonts have most of the available character bullets from the *Symbols* dialog box. You can also select picture bullets that are more decorative from the *Bullets and Numbering* dialog box.

The Format Painter

To copy formatting from text, shapes, or pictures and apply these settings to another selection, use the ***Format Painter***. You can apply the changes on the same slide or on different slides.

HOW TO: Use the Format Painter

1. Select the text or other object with the format that you want to copy.
2. Click **Format Painter** [*Home* tab, *Clipboard* group] (see Figure 1-34). Your pointer changes to a paintbrush.
3. Move the paintbrush over the text or other object that you want to change and click to apply the formatting.
4. Apply the change to multiple selections by double-clicking the **Format Painter** button.
5. Press **Esc** to stop formatting.

Reuse Slides from Another Presentation

You can add slides from another presentation without opening it as long as you can access the location where it is stored.

HOW TO: Reuse Slides

1. Click between two slides in the thumbnail area where you want one or more new slides inserted. A red line between the slides indicates your insertion point.
2. Click the **New Slide** drop-down arrow [*Home* tab, *Slides* group] and select **Reuse Slides** from the bottom of the layout gallery. The *Reuse Slides* pane automatically opens.
3. Click the **Browse** button in the *Reuse Slides* pane and then click **Browse File** (Figure 1-39).

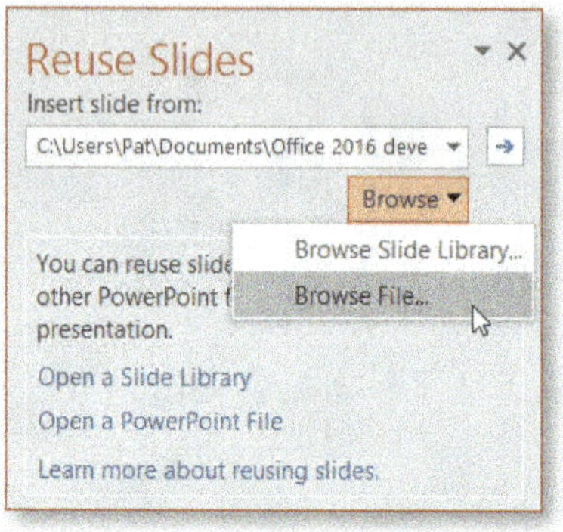

1-39 *Reuse Slides* pane

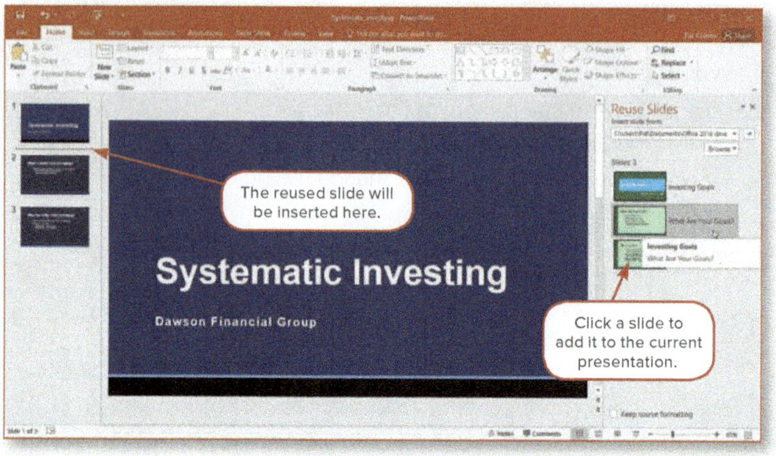

1-40 Reuse slides

4. Find the location where your presentation with the slides you need is saved and select the file name.
5. Click **Open**. The slides in this second presentation appear in the *Reuse Slides* pane with text showing their titles (Figure 1-40).
6. Click the slides you want to insert in your current presentation.
   - By default, the reused slides will appear with the formatting of your current presentation.
   - If you want the inserted slides to retain their design from the original presentation, select the **Keep source formatting** checkbox at the bottom of the *Reuse Slides* pane before inserting them.
7. Click the **Close** button at the top of the *Reuse Slides* pane.

MORE INFO

When task panes open, they are docked on the right side of the PowerPoint window. If you have a wide computer screen and you are using PowerPoint in a window size that does not fill the screen, you can drag a pane away from the window so your slide size becomes larger. Double-click the pane to dock it on the right of the window again.

Check Spelling and Word Usage

PowerPoint's ***AutoCorrect*** feature repairs many simple errors such as changing "teh" to "the" or "recieve" to "receive" as you enter text on your slides. You can customize *AutoCorrect* options to include words that you frequently misspell or abbreviate when the word should be spelled.

PowerPoint will automatically add a red, wavy line below words it does not recognize. Use the ***Spelling*** feature to correct errors at any time during a presentation but always when you are making your final adjustments. You still need to carefully read the content to find any words that may have been missed, such as names or words that might not be in the spelling dictionary. If your audience sees mistakes when viewing your slide show, your credibility is undermined.

▸ HOW TO: Check Spelling

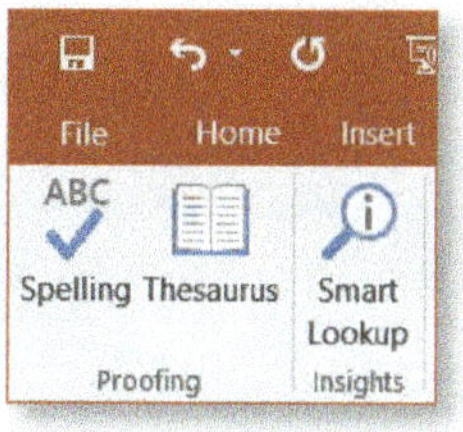

1-41 ***Spelling*** **button on the** ***Review*** **tab**

1. Click the **Spelling** button [*Review* tab, *Proofing* group] (Figure 1-41). The *Spelling* pane opens on the right (Figure 1-42).
2. Consider each word that is identified and whether or not the suggested spelling is correct.
3. Click the **Audio** button on the *Spelling* pane to hear the word pronounced.
4. Click the **Change** button to insert a suggested spelling; click the **Ignore** button if you want to skip the suggestion.
5. Click **OK** when the spell check is complete. The *Spelling* pane automatically closes.

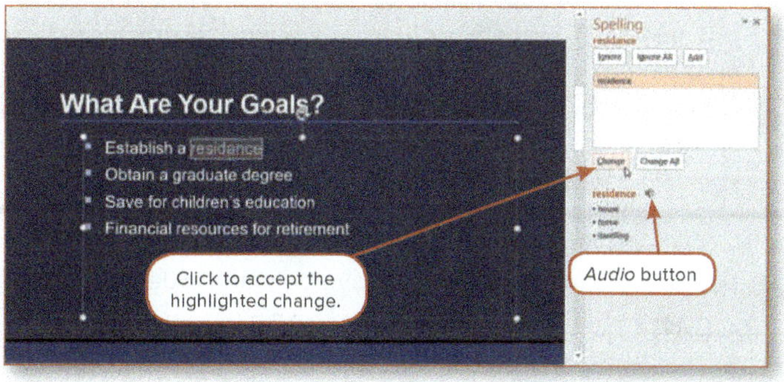

1-42 ***Spelling*** **pane**

If you want to replace an awkward word or one that is used too frequently, use PowerPoint's ***Thesaurus*** to find a more appropriate word.

▸ HOW TO: Use the Thesaurus

1. Click the word you want to change.
2. Click the **Thesaurus** button [*Review* tab, *Proofing* group]. The *Thesaurus* pane opens and the selected word appears in the search box (Figure 1-43). Words with similar meanings appear below it.
3. Click a word in this list to see more options; click the **Back** arrow to return to the original list.
4. Click the **Down** arrow on the right of a word in this list and choose **Insert**. The selected word on your slide is replaced with the new word.
5. Click the **Close** button at the top of the *Thesaurus* pane.

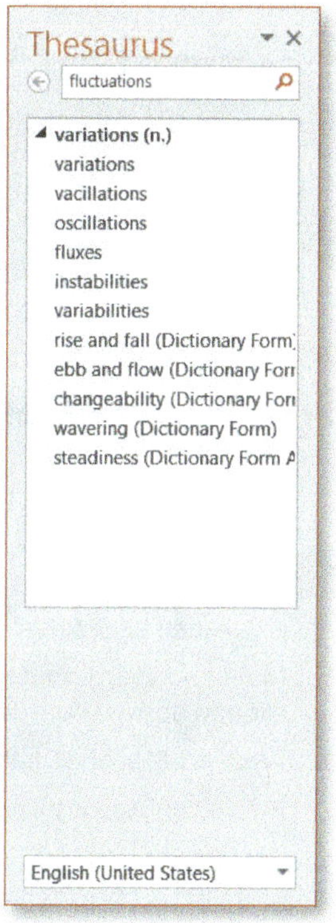

1-43 ***Thesaurus*** **word choices**

SLO 1.3

Navigating between Slides and Organizing Content

When developing a presentation, you might need to move between slides as ideas occur to you or when you have new information to add. You can rearrange slides at any time. Always examine your sequence carefully when all slides are complete. The final order must be logical to you and to your audience.

Navigate between Slides

In *Normal* view, you can move between slides by clicking the **Next Slide** and **Previous Slide** buttons, clicking scroll arrows, or dragging the scroll box to the right of the window. You can also click thumbnails or use keyboard shortcuts.

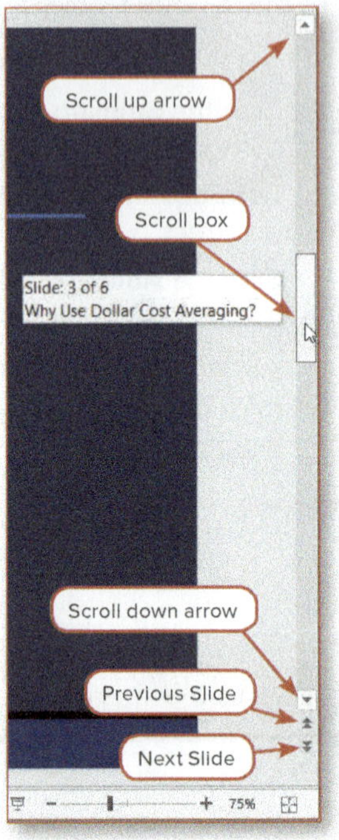

1-44 Navigate between slides

▸HOW TO: Navigate between Slides

1. Use one of these methods to move between slides using the scroll bar and buttons on the right:
   - Click the **Next Slide** button or the **Scroll Down** arrow to go to the next slide.
   - Click the **Previous Slide** button or **Scroll Up** arrow to go to the previous slide.
   - Click above or below the scroll box to move between slides one at a time.
   - Drag the *Scroll* box up or down to move to a specific slide, using the slide indicator (Figure 1-44).
2. Use one of these methods to move between slides using the *Thumbnail* pane.
   - Click a slide thumbnail to make that slide active.
   - Click between slide thumbnails to select a position for a new slide. A red line indicates your insertion point.
3. Press the following shortcut keys:

First slide	**Home**
Last slide	**End**
Next slide	**Page Down** or **Down** arrow
Previous slide	**Page Up** or **Up** arrow

Copy, Paste, and Duplicate Slides

To reuse a slide's content or format, copy the thumbnail. It is stored in your computer's temporary storage area called the ***Clipboard***. The original slide remains in its position. Paste the copied slide where you need it and edit the text.

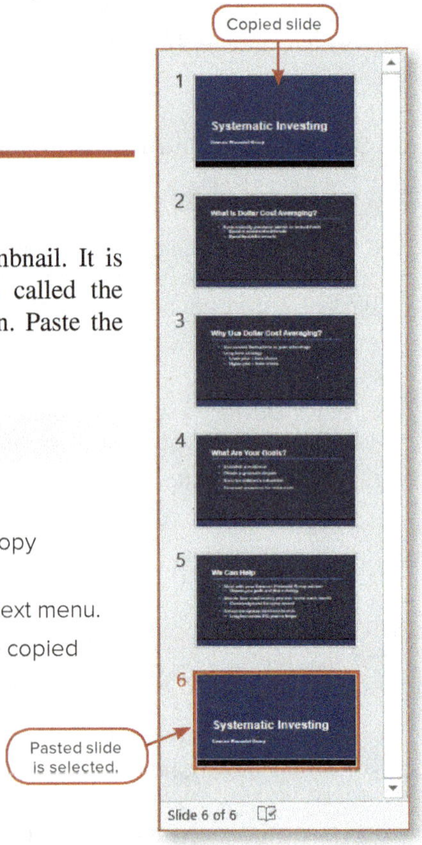

1-45 Copy and paste a selected slide

▸HOW TO: Copy and Paste Slides

1. Select the thumbnail of the slide to be copied (Figure 1-45).
2. Press **Ctrl+C** or click the **Copy** button [*Home* tab, *Clipboard* group] to copy the slide.
   - You can also right-click a slide thumbnail and select **Copy** from the context menu.
3. Move the insertion point to the place between slides where you want the copied slide to appear. A red line indicates your insertion point.
4. Press **Ctrl+V** or click the **Paste** button [*Home* tab, *Clipboard* group].
   - You can also right-click a slide thumbnail and select **Paste** from the context menu.
5. Edit the text on the new slide as needed.

Duplicating also creates a second copy of a slide. You can drag the second slide to a different position.

▸ HOW TO: Duplicate Slides

1. Select the thumbnail of the slide to be duplicated.
2. Press **Ctrl+D** to duplicate the slide. The second slide appears immediately after the original slide and the new slide is selected.
   - You can also right-click a slide thumbnail and select **Duplicate Slide** from the context menu.

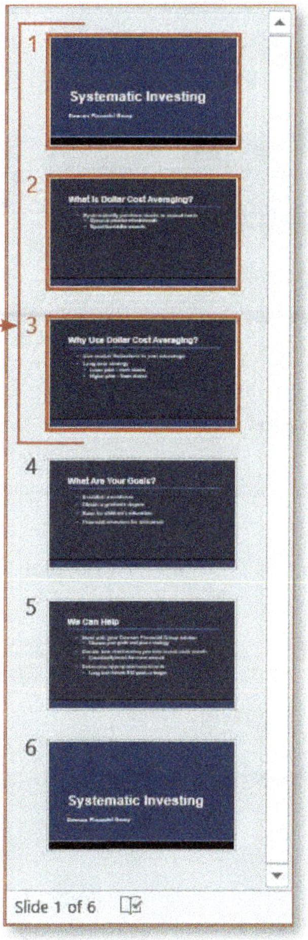

1-46 Adjacent slides selected

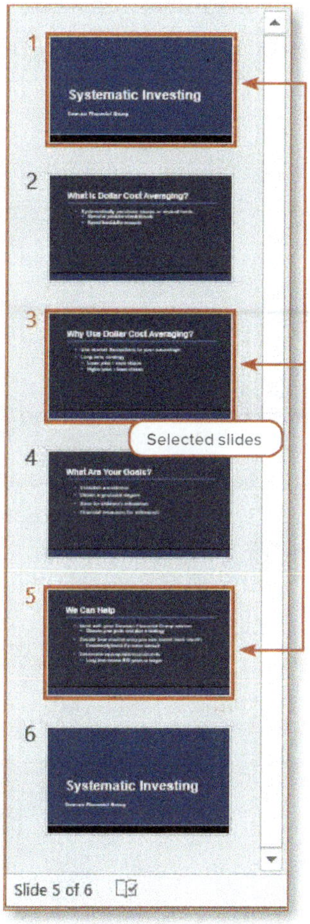

1-47 Nonadjacent slides selected

Select Multiple Slides

If you need to make the same changes to more than one slide, you can select more than one slide thumbnail.

▸ HOW TO: Select Multiple Slides

1. Select multiple adjacent slides (in order) by selecting the first slide and then pressing **Shift** while you click the last slide (Figure 1-46).
2. Select multiple nonadjacent slides (not in order) by selecting the first slide and then pressing **Ctrl** while you click each of the slides you need to select (Figure 1-47).

Rearrange Slide Order

You can rearrange slides at any time while developing a presentation. In the *Thumbnail* pane you can drag slide thumbnails up or down. On the *Outline* view, you can drag the slide icons. You can also cut slides and paste them into different positions. However, when your presentation has more slides than can be seen in the *Thumbnail* pane, it is best to rearrange slides using *Slide Sorter* view (Figure 1-48).

The *Slide Sorter* view enables you to see your presentation as a whole. The thumbnails are arranged from left to right in rows. By default, they are shown at a 100% size. Click buttons on the *Status* bar to change this percentage. The **Zoom In** button will increase the slide thumbnail size if you need to see the slide content better; the **Zoom Out** button will decrease the slide thumbnail size and you see more slides at one time.

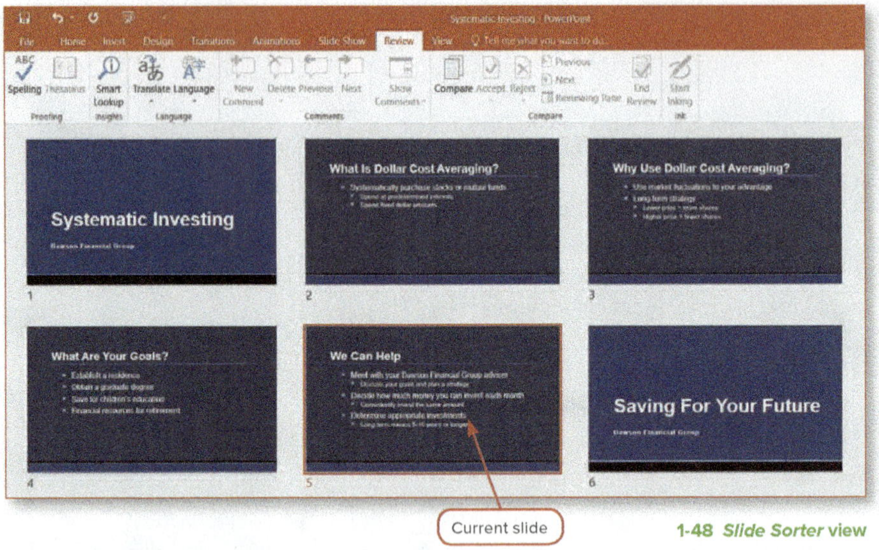

1-48 *Slide Sorter* view

▶ HOW TO: Rearrange Slides in Slide Sorter View

1. Click the **Slide Sorter** button on the *Status* bar.
2. Click the **Zoom In** or **Zoom Out** buttons to adjust the size of the thumbnails.
3. Click and drag the slide thumbnails into their new positions (Figure 1-49).

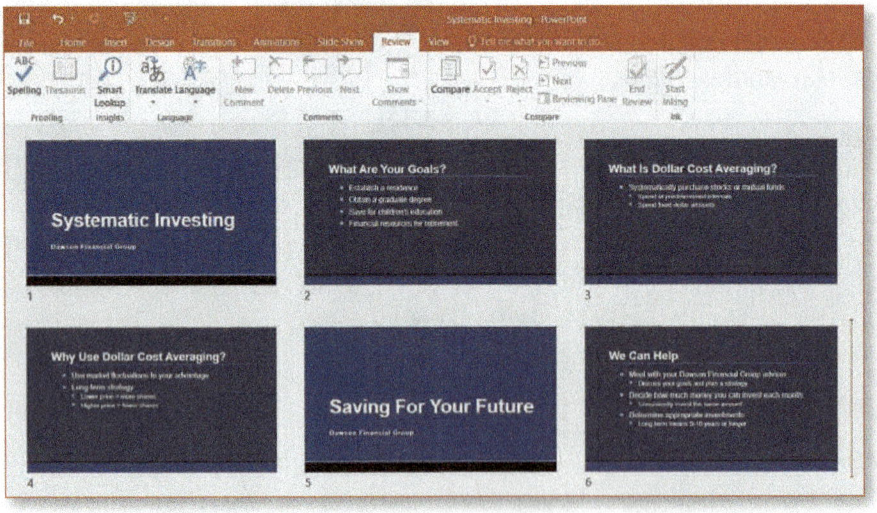

1-49 Slides rearranged

Delete Slides

Remove slides by deleting slide thumbnails in *Normal* view and *Slide Sorter* view or by deleting the slide icon in *Outline* view. You can also use the **Cut** button on the *Home* tab in the *Clipboard* group. This method is helpful because if you change your mind about the deletion later, you can paste the deleted slides back into the presentation from the *Clipboard*.

HOW TO: Delete Slides

1. Right-click the slide thumbnail (or the *Slide* icon in *Outline* view). Click **Delete Slide** from the context menu.

Or

2. Select the slide thumbnail (or the *Slide* icon in *Outline* view). Press **Delete** or click **Cut** [*Home* tab, *Clipboard* group].

PAUSE & PRACTICE: POWERPOINT 1-1

For this project, you develop the text for a presentation about upcoming marathon events at the Hamilton Civic Center. This presentation promotes event preparation for participants. You start with a blank presentation, add slides, reuse slides from another presentation, and change formatting.

File Needed: ***Marathon Info-01.pptx*** *(Student data files are available in the* Library *of your SIMnet account.)*
Completed Project File Name: ***[your initials] PP P1-1.pptx***

1. Open PowerPoint and click **Blank Presentation** to start a new presentation.
   a. If PowerPoint is already open, press **Ctrl+N** or click the **File** tab, click **New**, and then click **Blank Presentation**.
2. Name and save the presentation.
   a. Press **F12** to open the *Save As* dialog box.
   b. Browse to the location where you want to save your files and double-click to open the appropriate folder (Figure 1-50). If necessary, click the **New Folder** button, type a name for the new folder, and then double-click to open it.
   c. Type [your initials] PP P1-1 in the *File name* area.
   d. Verify that the *Save as type* area says "PowerPoint Presentation."
   e. Click **Save**. The *Save As* dialog box closes.

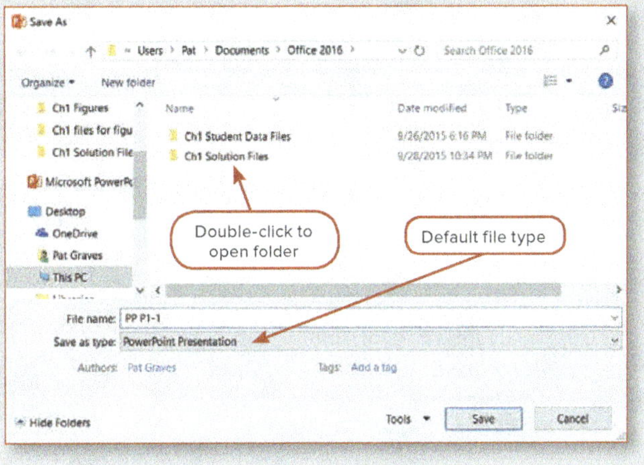

1-50 *Save As* dialog box

3. Display slide 1. Type the following text in the placeholders:

   Title: Take the Right Steps

   Subtitle: Train for a Marathon

4. Click the **New Slide** button [*Home* tab, *Slides* group] twice to add two new slides. The slide thumbnails will appear blank, but the slides have the *Title and Content* layout with two placeholders. Type the following text on slides 2 and 3:

Slide 2 Title: What Is Your Goal?

Bulleted items:
- Run the second half faster
- Beat a time you've run before
- Or
- Finish the marathon

Slide 3 Title: Start Early to Be Ready

Bulleted items:
- Begin 5-16 weeks in advance
- Get a physical check up
- Prepare gear for running
- Join a training group
- Enjoy camaraderie
- Be accountable
- Run 3-4 times a week

5. Change a slide layout and adjust the text.
   a. Display slide 3 and click the **Layout** button [*Home* tab, *Slides* group]. Next, select the **Two Content** layout.
   b. Select the last four bulleted items on the left placeholder and press **Ctrl+X** to cut them.
   c. Click the right placeholder and press **Ctrl+V** to paste them.
   d. Delete any extra bullets by placing your insertion point on that line and pressing **Backspace**.
   e. Select the middle two bulleted items on the right placeholder and press **Tab** or click the **Increase List Level** button [*Home* tab, *Paragraph* group] to format them as indented subpoints under the first-level item (Figure 1-51).

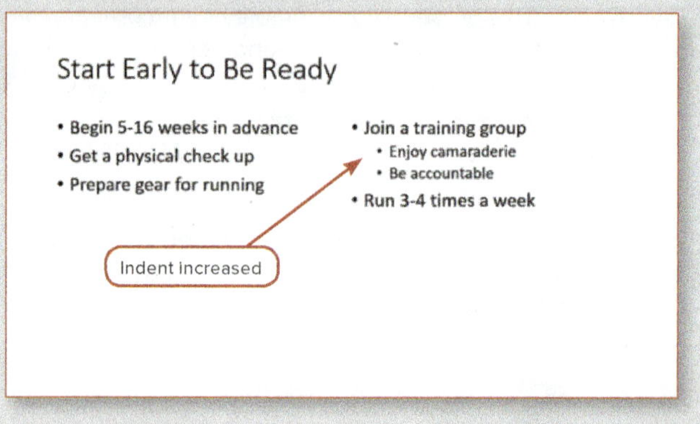

1-51 *Two Content* layout

6. Insert three slides from another presentation.
   a. Display slide 3. Click the **New Slide** drop-down arrow and select **Reuse Slides**.
   b. On the *Reuse Slides* pane, click the **Browse** button; then select **Browse File** and locate your student data files.
   c. Select the presentation ***MarathonInfo-01*** and click **Open**. (This presentation has spelling errors that you will fix later.)
   d. Click three slides (Figure 1-52) to insert them: "Practice Runs," "Eat Energy Foods," and "Get Running Apparel."
   e. Close the *Reuse Slides* pane.

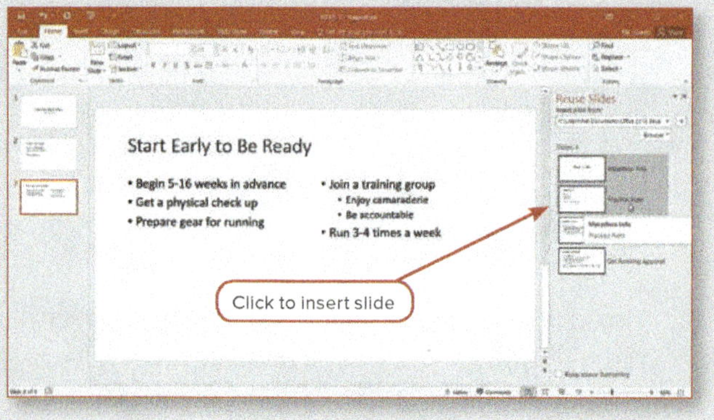

1-52 Reuse slides

7. Rearrange slides.
   a. Click the thumbnails and drag them up or down so the six slides are in this order: "Take the Right Steps," "What is Your Goal?," "Start Early to Be Ready," "Get Running Apparel," "Eat Energy Foods,"and "Practice Runs."

8. Insert and duplicate a new slide.
   a. Display slide 6. Click the **New Slide** drop-down arrow and select the **Title Only** layout.
   b. Type Look It UP! in the title placeholder on slide 7. (Figure 1-53).
   c. Select the title text and change the font size to **72 pt**.
   d. Select this slide thumbnail and press **Ctrl+D** to duplicate it to create slide 8.

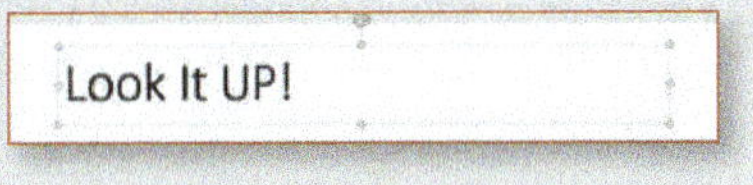

1-53 Placeholder text resized

9. Edit and duplicate a slide.
   a. Display slide 8. Replace the title with the text Mark It DOWN!.
   b. Select this slide thumbnail and press **Ctrl+D** to duplicate it to create slide 9.
10. Display slide 9. Change the title text to See You THERE!
11. Click the **Spelling** button [*Review* tab, *Proofing* group] and correct each of the spelling errors ("performance," "soreness," "banana," and "yogurt").
12. Save and close the presentation (Figure 1-54). You will continue to work on this presentation for *Pause & Practice 1-2* and *Pause & Practice 1-3*.

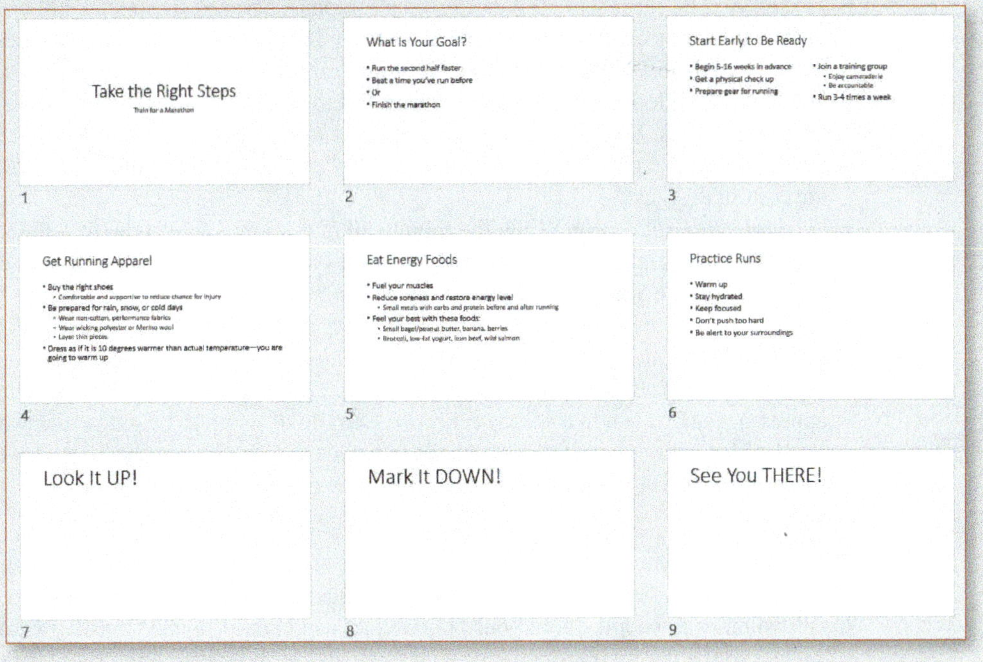

1-54 PP P1-1 completed

SLO 1.4

Changing Theme Colors and Fonts

In PowerPoint, you can quickly change theme colors and fonts using the *Design* tab. If you want to make additional theme changes, use the *Slide Master* tab. The ***Slide Master*** stores information about slide backgrounds, layouts, colors, and fonts for each theme. In this section, you change theme colors and fonts using both of these tabs so you can learn to choose the method that is most efficient for what you need to change.

When you start a new presentation and search online for templates and themes, you may find backgrounds with artwork or pictures that match your topic perfectly. The file names you see below each thumbnail do not distinguish between themes and templates. Many of the presentations that appear in a search will have the PowerPoint default file extension (*.pptx*). Those saved as template files will have a different file extension (*.potx*). Depending on how your software is set up, you may not see these file extensions when you open files.

> **MORE INFO**
>
> To display file extensions, open your *File Explorer* window. Click the **View** tab and select **File name extensions.** You can also make this change on your computer's *Control Panel.* Right click the **Start** button and select **Control Panel**. Select **Appearance and Personalization** and select **File Explorer Options** to open the *File Explorer Options* dialog box. Select the **View** tab and remove the check for *Hide extensions for known file types*. Click **OK**.

You can search through general categories or enter a specific search word to get more targeted results. Themes and templates are provided by Microsoft and other companies.

Your searches will provide results that include the following:

- *Theme*: A slide show with only background graphics and text treatments but no content. Different layouts control where slide objects are positioned. You can control design elements with the *Slide Master* to create custom designs.
- *Template*: A slide show with the characteristics of a theme but also with sample content on several slides. You can edit the content or remove individual slides that you do not need for your presentation. You can control design elements with the *Slide Master* to create custom designs.
- *Template, title slide only*: While the thumbnail may show a title slide, that slide might be the only content in the presentation. Other slides may be blank or have no related graphic background. The *Slide Master* has not been used.
- *Template, individual slide only*: Thumbnails may show only a diagram or chart that can be revised for a new presentation. Usually, the *Slide Master* has not been used.
- *Different slide sizes*: Two slide sizes will appear. The thumbnails that have an almost square appearance are shown in a 4:3 ***aspect ratio***, the ratio of width to height, which was the standard for many years. The thumbnails in a wide-screen size are shown in PowerPoint's default 16:9 aspect ratio, which reflects the shape of current computer screens.

People who frequently see presentations become very familiar with the slide show designs that appear in common software. So seeing a slide show with a contemporary looking design that truly matches the topic is refreshing. Caring enough to match your theme to your topic speaks volumes to people about your preparedness and competence. Consider carefully what you select so the design is suitable for your topic and for how your slide show is used.

HOW TO: Apply a Theme to an Existing Presentation

1. Click the **Design** tab.
2. Click the **More** button in the *Themes* gallery to see additional themes.
3. Point to a thumbnail to see a live preview of that theme on the current slide (Figure 1-55).
4. Click the thumbnail to apply the theme.

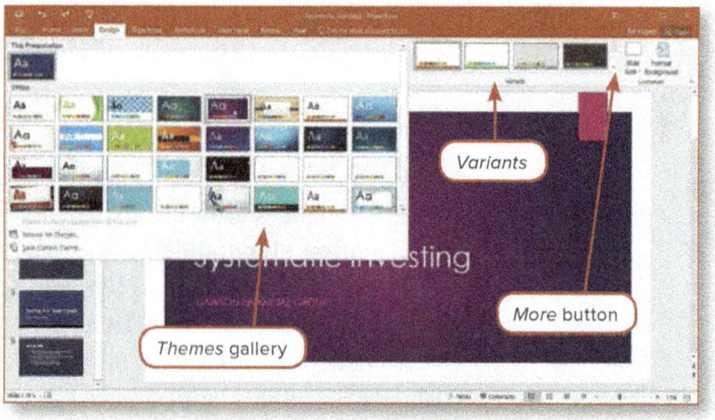

1-55 ***Design*** **tab and** ***Themes*** **gallery**

ANOTHER WAY

To apply two themes in one presentation, apply your first theme to all slides then select the slides that should be different. Right-click another theme and select **Apply to Selected Slides**. Be careful when using this option so that your content does not seem disjointed.

Change Theme Colors

When changing theme colors, select colors that are appropriate for your topic. Also consider where you will present. Because of room lighting, colors for a slide show projected on a large screen are not as clear or vibrant as what you see on a computer screen directly in front of you. These differences can influence your color choices. Be sure your text is easy to read with a high contrast between the text and background colors (dark on light or light on dark).

Every presentation, even a blank one, begins with a set of colors that have been chosen to work well together. With each built-in theme, PowerPoint provides ***Variants*** on the *Design* tab that show different theme colors and some variants have different graphics. Many more theme colors are available.

HOW TO: Change Theme Colors Using the Design Tab

1. Click the **Design** tab.
2. Click the **More** button [*Variants* group].
3. Select **Colors** and a drop-down list appears showing theme colors (Figure 1-56).
4. Point to a set of theme colors and you see a live preview of those colors on your current slide. The blank, Office theme will show a live preview only if the background colors have changed.
5. Click the colors or a theme name to apply it to all slides.

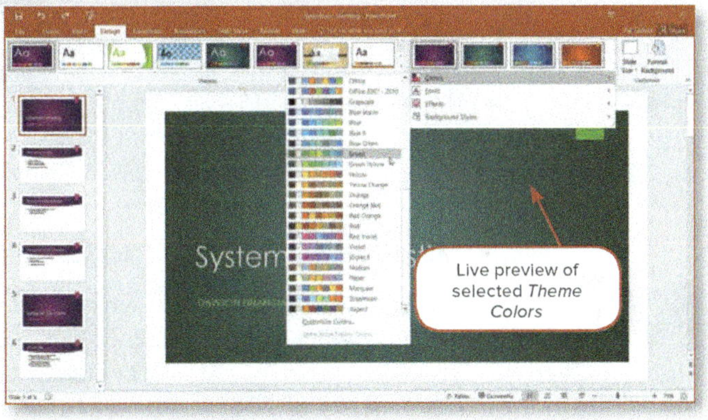

1-56 *Design* tab and *Theme Colors*

The first two colors in each color theme represent the background and text colors; the remaining six show accent colors. Once you select theme colors, you can apply a ***Background Style*** to change to a light or dark variation of background and text colors. Click the **More** button [*Design* tab, *Variants* group] and select **Background Styles**. Point to a color in the gallery to see a live preview; click a color to apply it.

Not all of the themes you find online permit color changes in the same way. It depends on how the background design was created. For more on customizing theme colors, see *SLO 3.1: Creating Custom Theme and Background Colors*.

Change Theme Fonts

Select your fonts carefully. Some fonts seem very traditional and serious; others appear more playful and flamboyant. Use fonts that are appropriate for your presentation topic.

Consider how legible the font is with the background color you are using. Letters can appear very thin and are not easy to read unless you apply bold. Also consider issues related to where you present. The lighting and room size affect how readable the text is on a large screen and you must use large font sizes. If you are designing a presentation to be displayed for a single person on your notebook or tablet computer, you can use smaller font sizes.

Every presentation, even a blank one, begins with a pair of ***Theme Fonts***. The heading font is used for slide titles and the body font is used for all other text. Sometimes the same font is used for both. You can view or change *Theme Fonts* from the *Design* tab or from the *Slide Master* tab.

▸ HOW TO: Change Theme Fonts Using the Design Tab

1. Click the **Design** tab.
2. Click the **More** button [*Variants* group].
3. Select **Fonts** and a drop-down list appears showing theme fonts (Figure 1-57).
4. Point to a pair of theme fonts and you see a live preview of those fonts applied to the current slide.
5. Click a theme font pair to apply it to all slides.

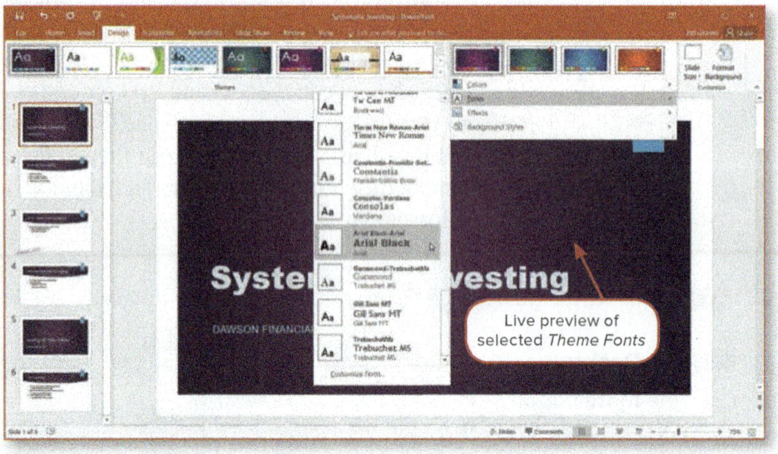

1-57 *Design* tab and *Theme Fonts*

Use the Slide Master to Change Theme Colors and Fonts

It is best to use the *Slide Master* tab to change theme colors or theme fonts when you are also changing other design elements. For example, you could customize slide layouts or background graphics by adding a company logo to all slides in a presentation. Each *Slide Master* has a variety of layouts, shown in the pane at the left, that control positioning of different types of content. If you are adding graphics or changing only specific layout colors, then select only the layout you want to change. Changes made on the first layout at the top of this pane generally apply to all other layouts.

▸ HOW TO: Change Theme Colors and Fonts Using the Slide Master

1. Click the **View** tab.
2. Click the Slide Master button [*Master Views* group] (Figure 1-58) to open the *Slide Master* tab.
3. Scroll up to select the first layout, the *Slide Master* layout, at the top of the *Thumbnails* pane so your changes will affect all layouts.
4. Click the **Colors** button [*Background* group] and a drop-down list appears showing theme colors (Figure 1-59).
5. Point to a set of theme colors and you see a live preview of those colors on your current *Slide Master* layout.
6. Click the colors or a theme color name to apply it to all *Slide Master* layouts.

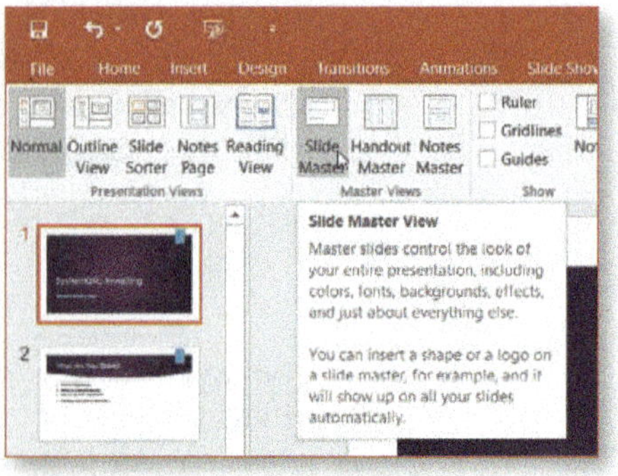

1-58 *Slide Master* button on the *View* tab

7. Click the **Background Styles** button [*Slide Master* tab, *Background* group] to change the background to light or dark variations (Figure 1-60).
   - You can apply different *Background Styles* to various *Slide Master* layouts.
   - This feature is available on the *Design* tab, also.
8. Click the **Fonts** button [*Slide Master* tab, *Background* group] and a drop-down list appears showing theme fonts.
9. Point to a pair of theme fonts and you see a live preview of those fonts applied to the current layout.
10. Click a theme font pair to apply it to all layouts.
11. Click the **Close Master View** button [*Slide Master* tab, *Close* group].

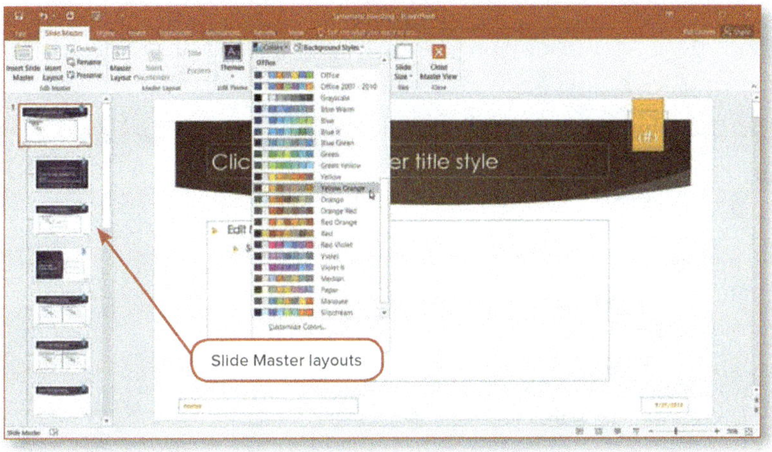

1-59 *Slide Master* tab and *Theme Colors*

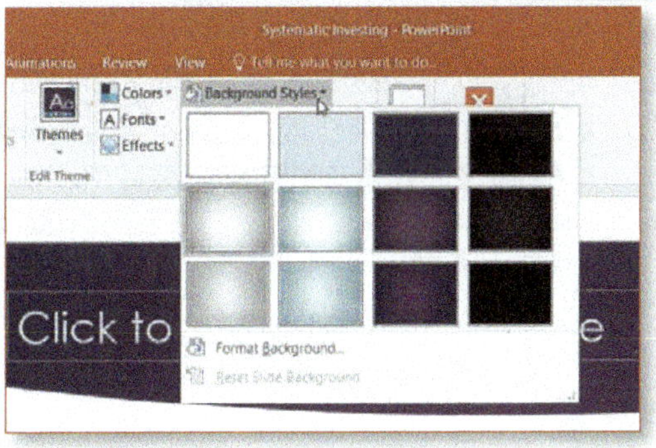

1-60 *Background Styles*

SLO 1.5

Inserting Headers and Footers

If you want to include identifying information on all slides of a presentation, use the *Header & Footer* command on the *Insert* tab (Figure 1-61). ***Footers*** are displayed on every slide with placeholders for the date and time, slide number, and footer text. These placeholders often appear across the bottom of the slide, but they may appear in different places depending on the theme. You can choose to show footers on all slides or only on selected slides.

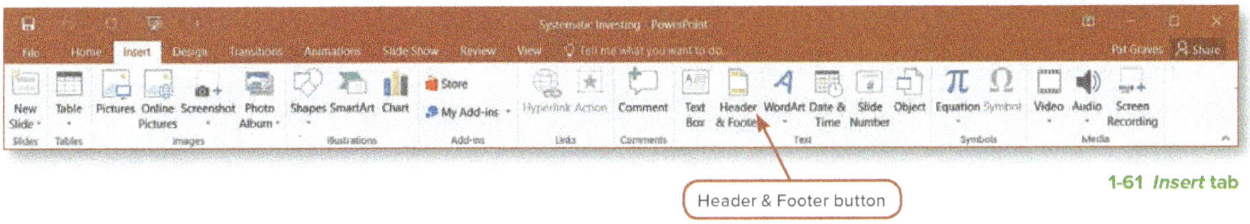

1-61 *Insert* tab

Create a Slide Footer

When you enter information using the *Header and Footer* dialog box, placeholders appear on the slides. You can move these placeholders if you wish.

▶ HOW TO: Create a Slide Footer

1. Click the **Insert** tab.
2. Click the **Header & Footer** button [*Text* group]. The *Header and Footer* dialog box displays.
3. Click the **Slide** tab (Figure 1-62).
4. Click the check boxes to select the following as needed:
   - **Date and time**: Choose between **Update automatically** to show the current date or **Fixed** to enter a specific date.
   - **Slide number**: Each slide is numbered.
   - **Footer**: Type text you want to appear on each slide.
5. Check the box for **Don't show on title slide** if you do not want footer information to appear on any slide created with the *Title Slide* layout.
6. Apply your choices by clicking one of these buttons:
   - **Apply:** the settings are applied to the current slide only.
   - **Apply to All:** the settings are applied to all slides.

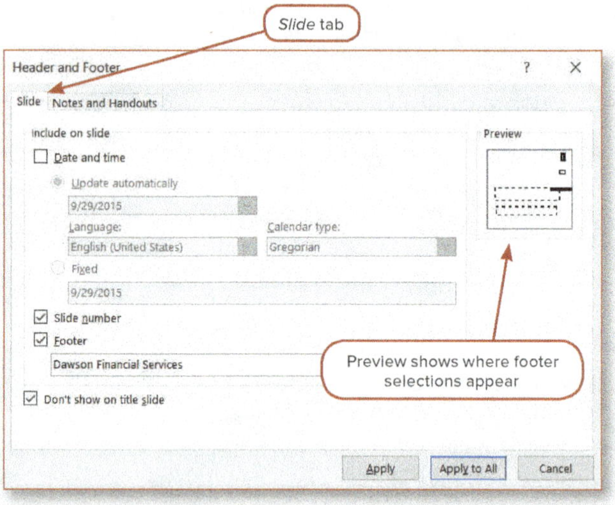

1-62 *Slide* tab in the *Header and Footer* dialog box

Create a Notes and Handouts Header

Because notes and handouts are usually printed documents, they can include ***header*** information that appears at the top of each page. Control all settings for notes and handouts in the same way you control slide footers.

▶ HOW TO: Create a Notes and Handouts Header

1. Click the **Insert** tab.
2. Click the **Header & Footer** button [*Text* group]. The *Header and Footer* dialog box displays.
3. Click the **Notes and Handouts** tab (Figure 1-63).
4. Click the check boxes to select the following as needed:
   - **Date and time**: Choose between **Update automatically** to show the current date or **Fixed** to enter a specific date.
   - **Page number**: Each page is numbered.
   - **Header**: Type text you want to appear on each page.
   - **Footer**: Type text you want to appear on each page.
5. Click the **Apply to All** button to apply your settings to all pages.

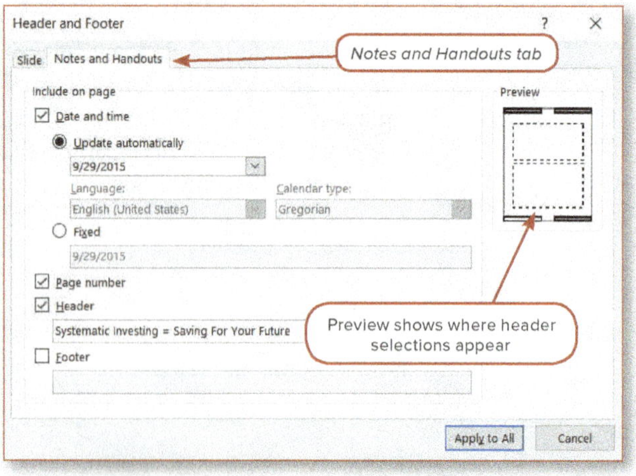

1-63 *Notes and Handouts* tab in the *Header and Footer* dialog box

If you leave items blank in the *Header and Footer* dialog box, empty placeholders show on your slide, but no information appears in *Slide Show* view.

PAUSE & PRACTICE: POWERPOINT 1-2

For this project, you continue working on the presentation about training for a marathon. You add a theme then change theme colors and fonts to revise two individual slides. Finally, you add a footer to your slides and add page numbering to the notes and handout pages.

File Needed: ***[your initials] PP P1-1.pptx***
Completed Project File Name: ***[your initials] PP P1-2.pptx***

1. Open the presentation you completed in *Pause & Practice 1-1*.
   a. Click the **File** tab to open the *Backstage* view and click **Open** on the left.
   b. Click **Browse** to open the *Open* dialog box.
   c. Locate the folder where you want to save this file.
   d. Select the **[your initials] PP P1-1** presentation and click **Open**.
2. Rename and save the presentation.
   a. Click the **File** tab to open the *Backstage* view and select **Save As** on the left.
   b. Click **Browse** to open the *Save As* dialog box.
   c. Locate the folder where your files are saved.
   d. Change the file name to [your initials] PP P1-2.
   e. Click **Save** to save the presentation and close the *Save As* dialog box.
3. Apply a theme.
   a. Click the **Design** tab.
   b. Click the **More** button [*Themes* group] to open the *Themes* gallery (Figure 1-64).
   c. Click the **Facet** theme so it is applied to all slides.

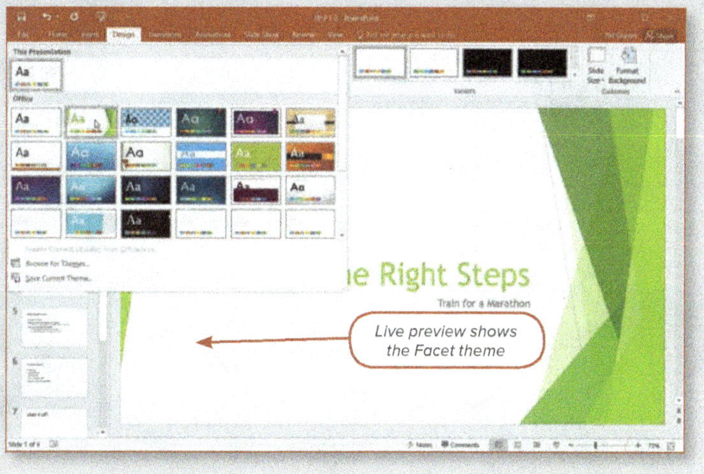

1-64 *Themes gallery*

4. Change theme colors and the background style.
   a. Click the **More** button [*Design* tab, *Variants* group] and select **Colors**.
   b. Scroll down the list and select the **Aspect** theme.
   c. Click the **More** button again and select **Background Styles**.
   d. Select **Style 4**, which applies a solid black background (Figure 1-65).

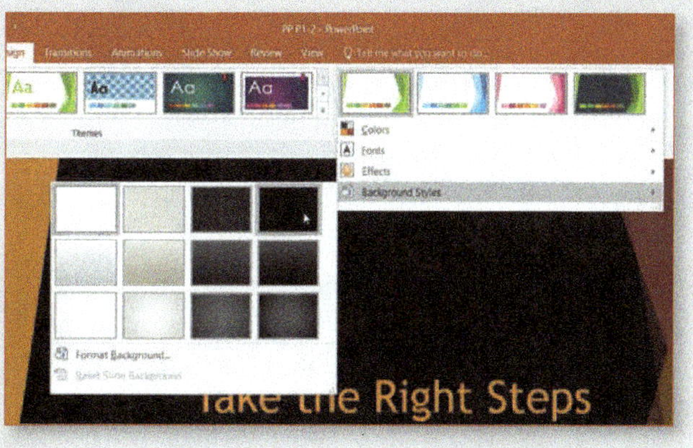

1-65 *Background Styles*

5. Change theme fonts.
   a. Click the **More** button [*Design* tab, *Variants* group] and select **Fonts**.
   b. Scroll down the list and click the **TrebuchetMS** font pair (Figure 1-66).

6. Modify and move the title.
   a. Display slide 1. Select the title placeholder and apply these font changes: **60 pt.**, **Bold** [*Home* tab, *Font* group], and **Align Left** [*Home* tab, *Paragraph* group].
   b. Click the **Arrange** button [*Home* tab, *Drawing* group], select **Align**, and select **Align Top**.
   c. Select the word **Right**. Click the **Change Case** button [*Home* tab, *Font* group] and select **UPPERCASE**.
   d. Resize the placeholder by dragging the right horizontal sizing handle so the text fits on one line.
7. Modify and move the subtitle.
   a. Select the subtitle placeholder on slide 1 and apply these font changes: **36 pt.**, **Bold** [*Home* tab, *Font* group], and **Align Left** [*Home* tab, *Paragraph* group].
   b. Move the subtitle placeholder below the title and select both placeholders.
   c. Click the **Arrange** button [*Home* tab, *Drawing* group], select **Align**, and then select **Align Left**.
8. Change the bullet.
   a. Display slide 2. Select the bulleted text and click the **Bullets** drop-down arrow [*Home* tab, *Font* group].
   b. Select **Bullets and Numbering**.
   c. Change the *Size* to **100%** of text.
   d. Click the **Color** button and select **Red, Accent 2** (Figure 1-67).
   e. Click the **Customize** button to open the *Symbol* dialog box.
   f. Change the *Subset* to **Geometric Shapes** (Figure 1-68). Select the **Black Square** (Character code 25A0).
      - If the **Wingdings** font is available, select a similar symbol (Character code 110).
   g. Click **OK** to insert the symbol and close the *Symbol* dialog box. Click **OK** again to close the *Bullets and Numbering* dialog box.
   h. Click to position your insertion point before the word "**Or**" on the third bulleted item.
   i. Press **Backspace** to remove the bullet from this item only. Apply **bold**.
9. Add a slide footer.
   a. Display slide 2 and click the **Header & Footer** button [*Insert* tab, *Text* group].
   b. On the *Slide* tab, select **Slide number** and **Footer** (Figure 1-69).

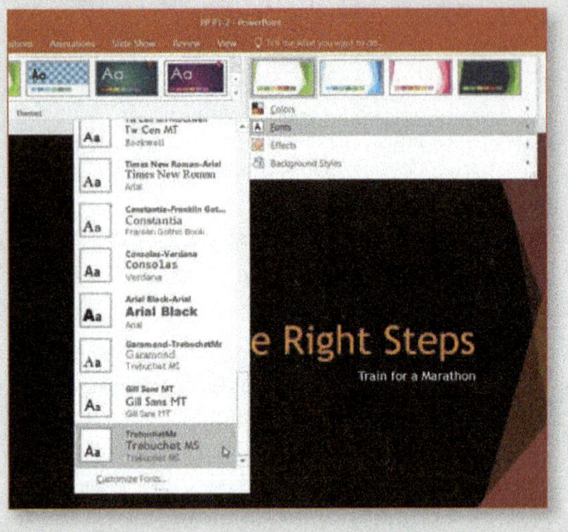

1-66 Change *Theme* font

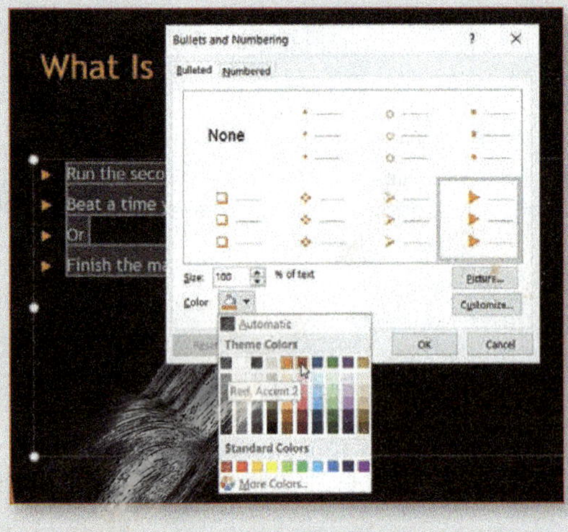

1-67 Change bullet size and color

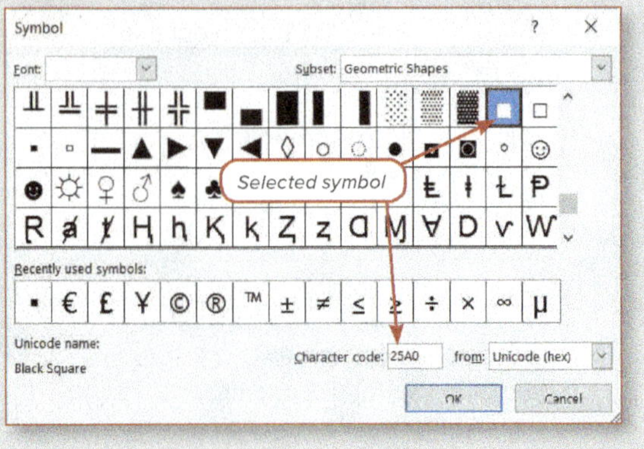

1-68 *Symbol* dialog box

c. In the *Footer* text box, type Take the Right Steps, Train for a Marathon.
d. Select **Don't show on title slide**.
e. Click the **Apply** button. The dialog box closes and the footer appears only on this slide.
f. Press **Shift** and click the footer and the page number placeholders to select them both. Increase the font size to **18 pt**. [*Home* tab, *Font* group].

10. Save and close the presentation (Figure 1-70).

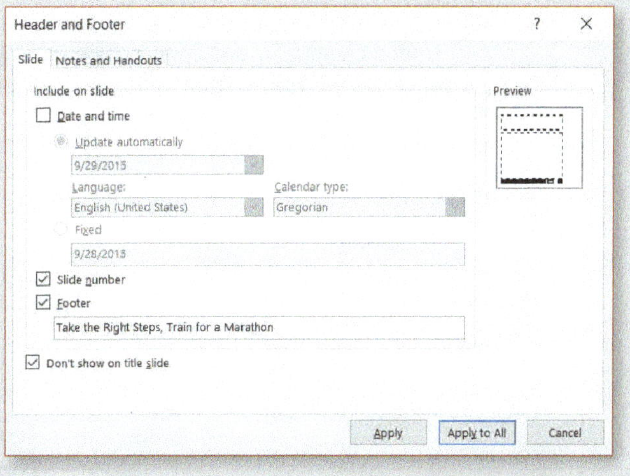

1-69 *Header and Footer* dialog box with changes

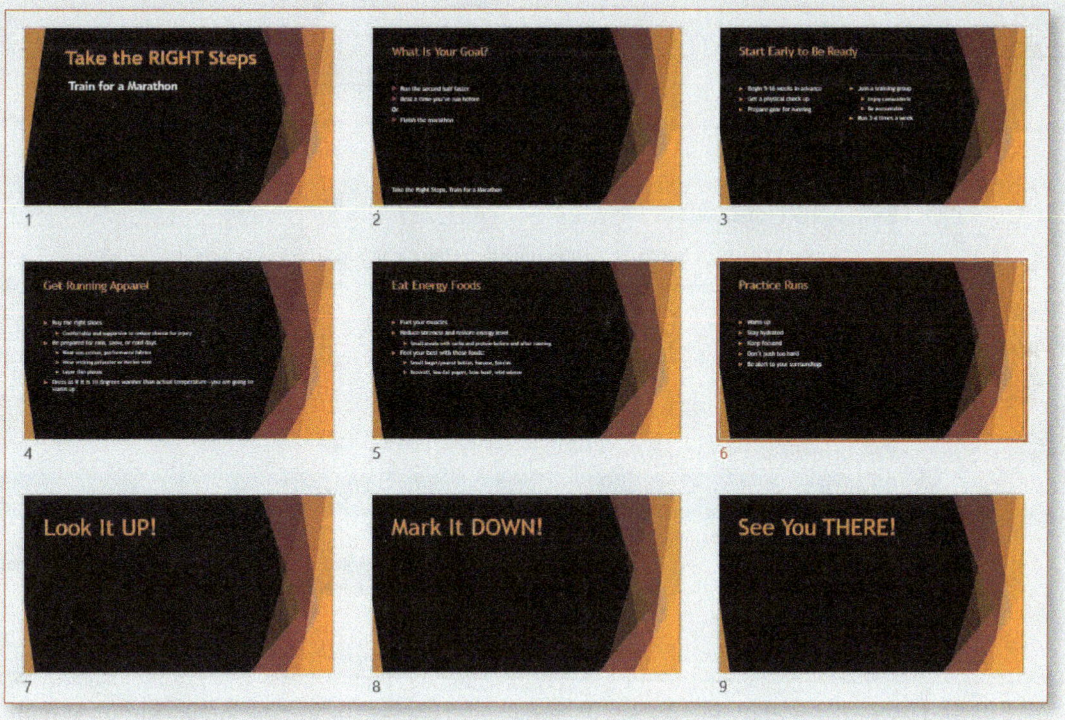

1-70 PP P1-2 completed

SLO 1.6

Working with a Picture from a File

An old adage says "A picture is worth a thousand words." That saying is still true today, because pictures bring a sense of realism to a presentation. Select pictures appropriate for your topic. Include pictures obtained from web sites only if you have the permission of the image owner to avoid copyright infringement. For academic purposes, you may include images if you reference their sources as you would any other research citation.

Insert a Picture

PowerPoint supports different graphic file types, so you can insert almost any digital image from a camera, or one created by scanning a document, into a slide show. To insert a picture, click the **Picture** button in the *Images* group on the *Insert* tab. Be aware that pictures can increase the file size of your presentation dramatically.

HOW TO: Insert a Picture

1. Click the **Insert** tab.
2. Click the **Pictures** button.
3. Select the drive and folder where your picture is saved.
4. Select the file you want to insert (Figure 1-71).
5. Click **Insert**.

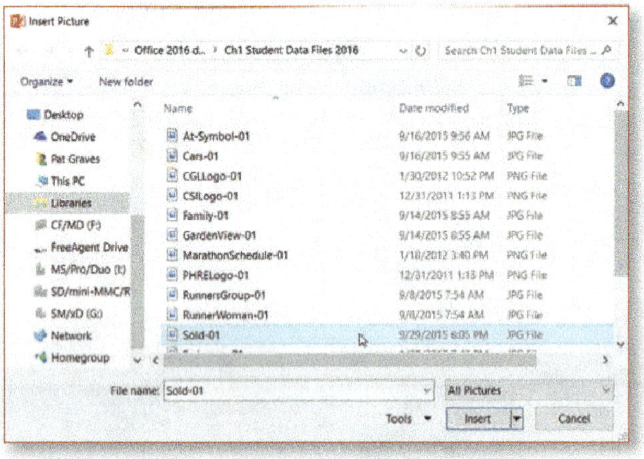

1-71 *Insert Picture* dialog box

ANOTHER WAY

Once you have located your picture file, insert the picture by double-clicking the file name.

The following table lists the more commonly used graphic file formats for pictures and illustrations.

Graphic File Formats

Picture File Type	Extension	Uses of This Format
JPEG (Joint Photographic Experts Group)	.jpg	Used for photographs and complex graphics. Handles gradual color blending well. Produces a smaller file size than most other formats. Transparency is not supported.
PNG (Portable Network Graphics)	.png	Used for photographs and complex graphics. Supports transparency so areas removed from the image appear blank on the slide.
GIF (Graphics Interchange Format)	.gif	Suited for line art and simple drawings because it is limited to 256 colors. Used for simple animated graphics. Does not handle gradual color blending well. Supports transparency.
Windows Metafile and Enhanced Windows Metafile	.wmf and .emf	Used for simple 16-bit or 32-bit graphics.
Device Independent Bitmap	.bmp	Images usually display well in their original size, but if you increase size, the image will be distorted.
TIFF (Tagged Image File Format)	.tiff	Designed for print publications. Produces high-quality images with large file sizes. Supports transparency.

Resize a Picture

To resize a picture, point to a sizing handle (white circle on the border) and drag it. Dragging the corner sizing handles will maintain correct proportions because they move diagonally to change both horizontal and vertical dimensions at the same time. Dragging the side handles can cause distortion because the height or width is changed independently.

You can precisely resize a picture by entering dimensions in the *Size* group on the *Picture Tools Format* tab (Figure 1-72) that appears when a picture is selected. When you change the *Height* or *Width* measurement [*Size* group], the other measurement will automatically adjust.

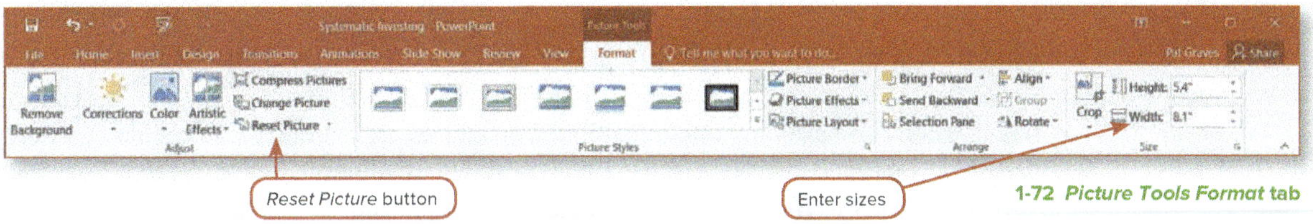

1-72 *Picture Tools Format* tab

Maintain the correct ratio between height and width to avoid distorting the image. You can make a picture smaller and still retain its clarity, but some pictures cannot be made larger without becoming blurred or distorted. If you change the size incorrectly, restore the picture's original dimensions by clicking the **Reset Picture** button [*Picture Tools Format* tab, *Adjust* group] and selecting **Reset Picture & Size**. Depending on the picture's resolution, you may need to resize it again to fit your slide.

Align a Picture

As you place pictures and other graphic objects on slides, consider how they are aligned. Everything on the slide should align in some way. You can align selected pictures and other objects with each other or on the slide in the same way you align placeholders (see *Align, Move, and Resize Placeholders* in *SLO 1:2 Working with Slides, Layouts, Placeholders, and Text*.) Click the **Align** button [*Picture Tools Format* tab, *Arrange* group] and select the alignment from the drop-down list (Figure 1-73):

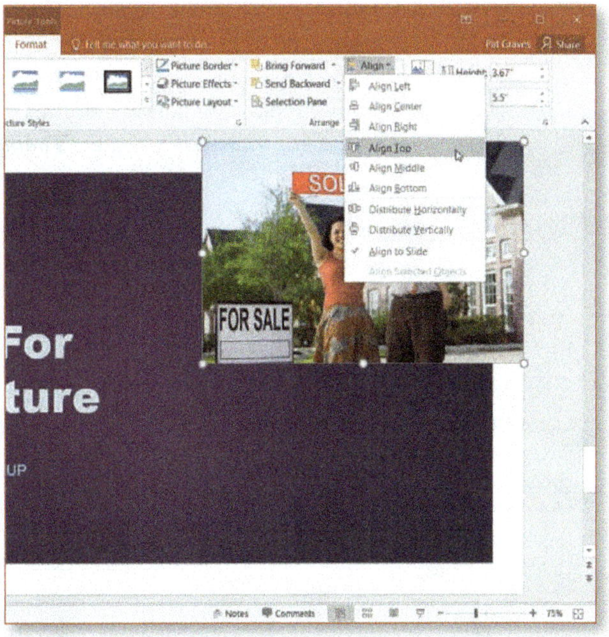

1-73 *Align Top* and *Align Right*

- *Horizontal alignment*: **Align Left**, **Align Center**, or **Align Right**
- *Vertical alignment*: **Align Top**, **Align Middle**, or **Align Bottom**

The picture shown in Figure 1-73 displays the following alignment: **Align Right**, **Align Top**, and **Align to Slide**.

SLO 1.7

Applying and Modifying Transitions

A ***transition*** is the visual effect of movement that occurs when one slide changes to the next slide. Each transition effect in PowerPoint provides a different type of movement. You can find these in the *Transition to This Slide* gallery on the *Transitions* tab (Figure 1-74).

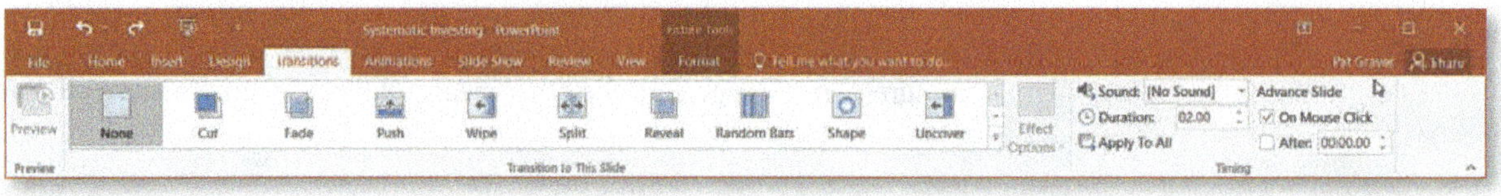

1-74 *Transitions* tab

Each slide can have only one transition. You can set transitions for one slide at a time in *Normal* view or apply the same transition to all slides. If you want to use different transitions, select thumbnails in *Normal* view or *Slide Sorter* view and click a transition to apply it to those slides. Once a transition has been applied, an icon symbolizing movement appears with the slide thumbnail.

Although it is possible to apply different transitions on every slide in a presentation, it is neither practical nor advisable. People are very accustomed to PowerPoint use today and know that slides are going to change. Random movements using many different transitions do not entertain an audience and may be distracting or even annoying. Control movement skillfully to reinforce your message. For example, you could apply a "quiet" transition for most of your presentation (sort of like turning pages in a book or an e-reader) and then apply a more "energetic" transition to key slides to grab attention or signal the beginning of a new topic. Use the *Slide Sorter* view to see more slides at once and decide which slides might benefit from a different movement.

In the *Timing* group, the **Advance Slide** options control whether slides advance **On Mouse Click** (the default) or after the number of seconds that you specify. You can also add sound to a transition using the *Timing* group.

HOW TO: Apply Transitions

1. Select the slide thumbnail where you want a transition to appear.
2. Click the **Transitions** tab.
3. Click the **More** button [*Transition to This Slide* group] to see additional transitions (Figure 1-75) organized by the following categories:
   - *Subtle*
   - *Exciting*
   - *Dynamic Content*
4. Apply one transition to all slides in the presentation.
   - Select a transition effect.

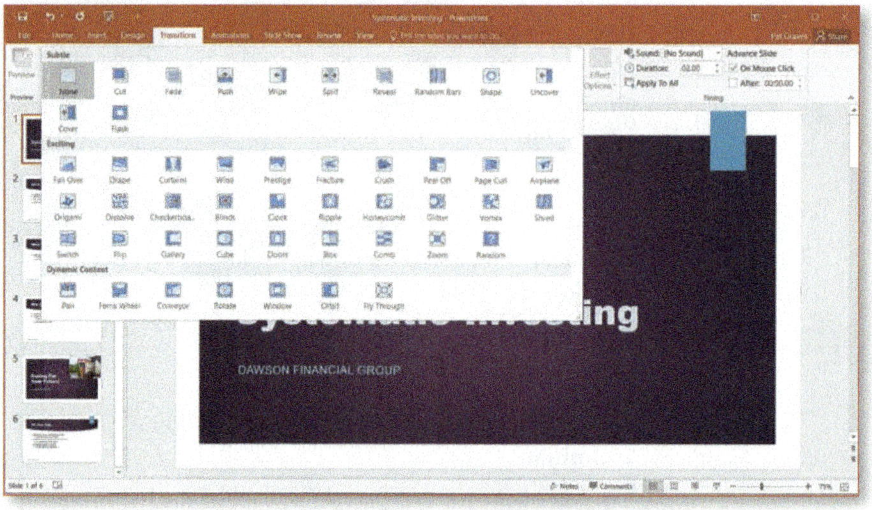

1-75 *Transitions* gallery

- Select **On Mouse Click** [*Timing* group] if it is not already selected.
- Click the **Apply to All** button [*Timing* group].

5. Apply a different transition to selected slides.
   - Click the **Slide Sorter** button on the *Status* bar.
   - Press **Ctrl** as you click to select one or more slides that should have a different transition.
   - Click to apply a different transition effect and the movement is displayed on the selected slides.
   - Select **On Mouse Click** [*Timing* group] if it is not already selected. (Figure 1-76).

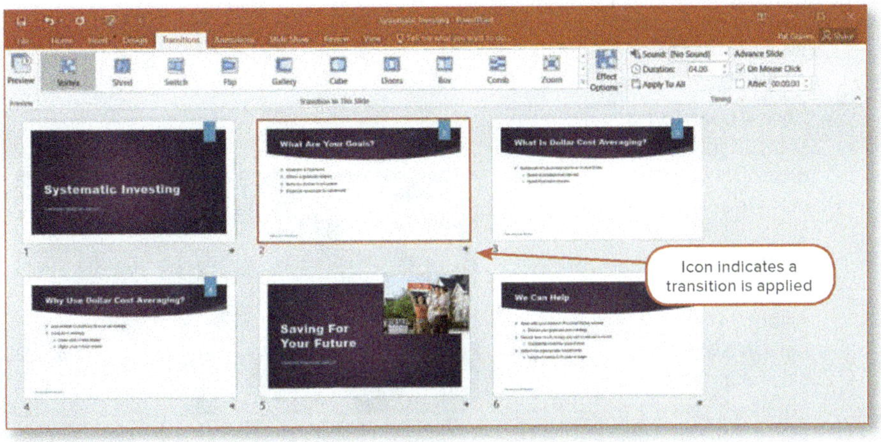

1-76 Change transitions on selected slides in *Slide Sorter* view

6. Preview slides in different views to test the movement.
   - *Slide Sorter* view: Click the **Slide Sorter** button on the *Status* bar. Select a slide thumbnail and click **Preview** [*Transitions* tab, *Preview* group]. Repeat for other slides.
   - *Normal* view: Click the **Normal View** button on the *Status* bar. Select a slide and click **Preview**. Click the **Next Slide** button to advance from slide to slide.
   - *Slide Show* view: Click the **Slide Show** tab and press **N** to advance from slide to slide.
   - Click the **From Beginning** button [*Start Slide Show* group] to view the slide show from the first slide. Click to advance from slide to slide.

Duration, shown in seconds, controls how fast the slides change. Duration seconds vary based on the selected transition effect. Movement might be barely visible if the duration is fast; a slower duration of five or more seconds will cause the movement to be much more noticeable. Enter a different number to change the duration and experiment to see what works best for your content.

Select Effect Options

Effect Options control the direction of transition movement. Each transition can have only one effect option, but most transitions provide two or more options from which you can choose. You can apply these options as you are setting up your transitions or later when you are editing your presentation.

HOW TO: Select Effect Options

1. Select a slide with a transition.
2. Click the **Effect Options** button [*Transition* tab, *Transition to This Slide* group] to see a drop-down list showing directional movements (Figure 1-77).
3. Select an effect option to apply it.

4. Apply the effect option to multiple transitions if appropriate:
   - Click **Apply To All** [*Transition* tab, *Timing* group] if this movement is appropriate for all slides.
   - If different transitions have been applied, select the slide thumbnails in *Slide Sorter* view with the same transition and then apply the appropriate effect option.

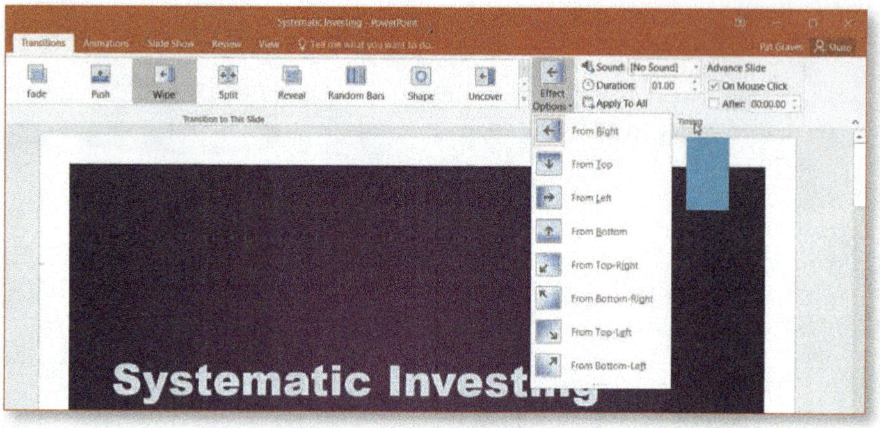

1-77 Transition *Effect Options*

5. Preview the slides in *Slide Show* view to test all transitions and effect options.

SLO 1.8

Exploring Print Options

You may want to proofread your presentation content on paper or review the slides with a colleague. Or you may want to prepare audience handouts or your own printed materials to use while you are giving the presentation. PowerPoint 2016 provides convenient ways to preview and print presentation slides, handouts, notes pages, or outlines.

Preview a Presentation

Before printing, check your slides to ensure everything looks as you intended. The *Backstage* view [*File* tab, *Print* button] displays each slide or handout page in your presentation as it will look when printed. Use the navigation controls at the bottom of the window to go through the slides or pages one at a time. You can also use the scroll bar on the right. Adjust slide or page size using the *Zoom* controls on the lower right.

The look of your slides in *Backstage* view is influenced by the selected printer. The preview image shows in color if you are printing with a color printer or in ***grayscale*** (shades of black) if you are printing with a printer that prints only black. In a work setting, you may have a small desktop printer for printing rough draft copies with black print and a network printer for printing more expensive, high-quality color pages.

If you design slides in color and plan to print slides or handouts in grayscale, preview your slides in grayscale to confirm that all text is readable. You may need to adjust a few colors to get good results.

In *Backstage* view, select a printer from the available list of local and network printers. ***Print Settings*** are shown as buttons with the current setting displayed. Click the list arrow for a list of the following options:

- *Which Slides to Print*: Choose *Print All Slides*, *Print Selection*, *Print Current Slide*, or *Custom Range* using slide numbers entered in the *Slides* box (slides 1–3 or slides 1–3, 5, 8)
- *What to Print*: Choose *Full Page Slides*, *Notes Pages*, *Outline*, or *Handouts*. You can print handouts with 1, 2, 3, 4, 6, or 9 slides on a page with the sequence of slides arranged horizontally or vertically. You can also specify *Frame Slides*, *Scale to Fit Paper* (increases slide size), or *High Quality*.

- *Print Side*: Choose between *Print One Sided* or *Print on Both Sides*. You can choose to *Flip pages on long edge* or *Flip pages on short edge* to control how pages will turn if they are bound together at the top or side like a book. However, not all printers can print on both sides, so you may not see these options.
- *Print Order*: Choose between *Collated* and *Uncollated*. Usually slides print in order (collated), but you may want to print multiple copies page by page (uncollated).
- *Orientation*: Choose between *Landscape* and *Portrait*. By default, slides print in landscape orientation; notes and handouts print in portrait orientation. This option is not available if you are printing full-size slides.
- *Color Range*: Choose among *Color*, *Grayscale*, or *Pure Black and White*.

Below the print *Settings* in *Backstage* view, you can click the **Edit Header & Footer** link to open the *Header and Footer* dialog box and then enter or revise information on the *Notes and Handouts* tab.

Print a Slide

The default print settings print each slide on letter-size paper. Adjust print settings as needed to print the current or selected slides.

HOW TO: Print a Slide in Grayscale

1. Click the **File** tab.
2. Click **Print** on the left.
3. Select an appropriate printer.
4. Locate the *Settings* area. Click the list arrow for each box and choose options from the drop-down list, such as the following:
   - *Which Slides to Print*: **Print Current Slide**
   - *What to Print*: **Full Page Slides**
   - *Print Order*: **Collated**
   - *Color Range*: **Grayscale** (Figure 1-78)
5. Enter the number of copies, if you need more than one.
6. Click the **Print** button at the top.

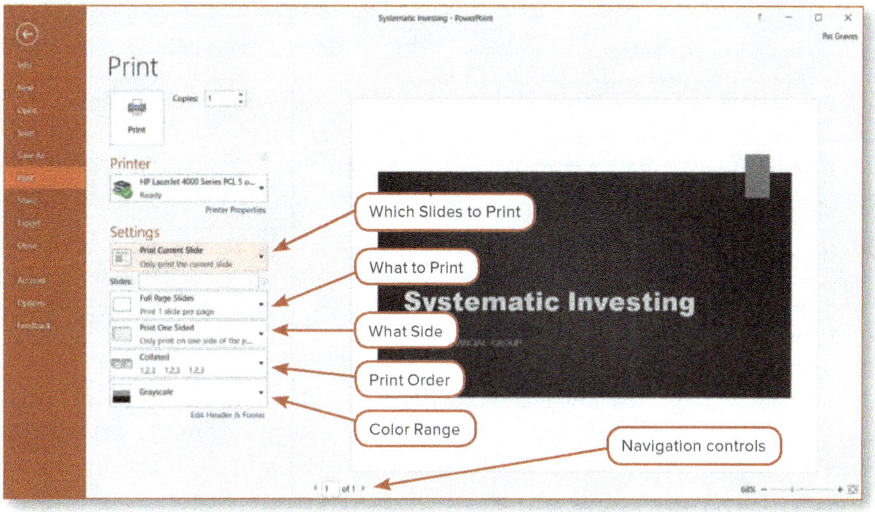

1-78 Print settings for a full-size slide

Print a Handout

Handouts print one to nine slides on a page. You can use these pages as audience handouts or for your own reference during a presentation. Selecting *Scale to Fit Paper* increases the slide size. *Framing* shows the shape of slides, which is helpful when printing slides with a white background on white paper. Depending on the number of slides, changing the page orientation to landscape may increase slide size.

When preparing handouts for an audience, consider which slides will be important for the audience to have. You can specify which slides to include and perhaps reduce the number of pages required for printing.

▶ HOW TO: Print a Handout for Selected Slides in Color

1. Click the **File** tab.
2. Click **Print** on the left.
3. Select a color printer.
4. Locate the *Settings* area. Click the list arrow for each box and choose options from the drop-down list, such as the following:
    - *Which Slides to Print*: Type the specific slides needed (1, 3–4, 6) in the *Slides* box to print a *Custom Range*.
    - *What to Print*: **6 Slides Horizontal**
    - *Print Order*: **Collated**
    - *Orientation*: **Portrait Orientation**
    - *Color Range*: **Color** (Figure 1-79)
5. Type the number of copies, if you need more than one.
6. Click the **Print** button at the top.

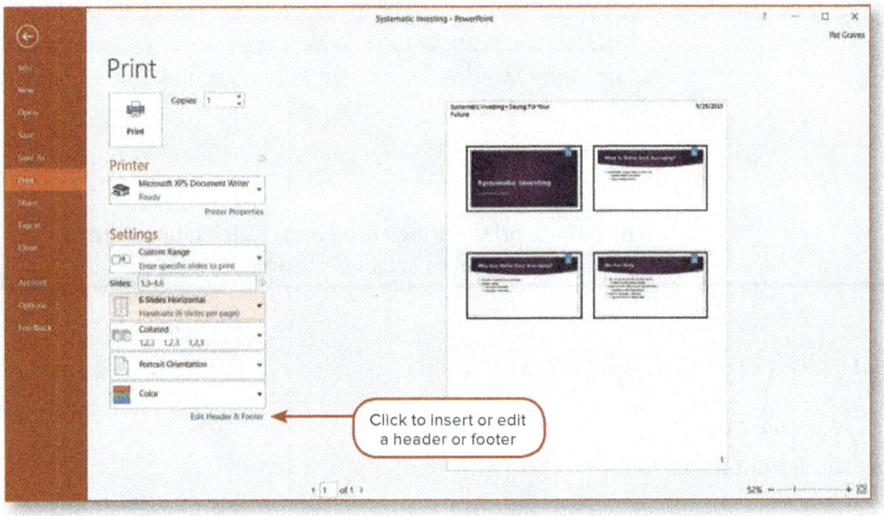

1-79 Print settings for a handout

Print an Outline

If a presentation consists of mostly slides with titles and bulleted lists, printing an outline is a very concise way to display the content. Only the text is shown.

▶ HOW TO: Print an Outline in Pure Black and White

1. Click the **File** tab.
2. Click the **Print** button on the left.
3. Select an appropriate printer.
4. Locate the *Settings* area. Click the list arrow and choose options from the drop-down list, such as the following:
    - *Which Slides to Print*: **Print All Slides**
    - *What to Print*: **Outline**
    - *What Side*: **Print One Sided**
    - *Print Order*: **Collated**

- *Orientation*: **Portrait Orientation**
- *Color Range*: **Pure Black and White** (Figure 1-80)

5. Enter the number of copies, if you need more than one.
6. Click the **Print** button at the top.

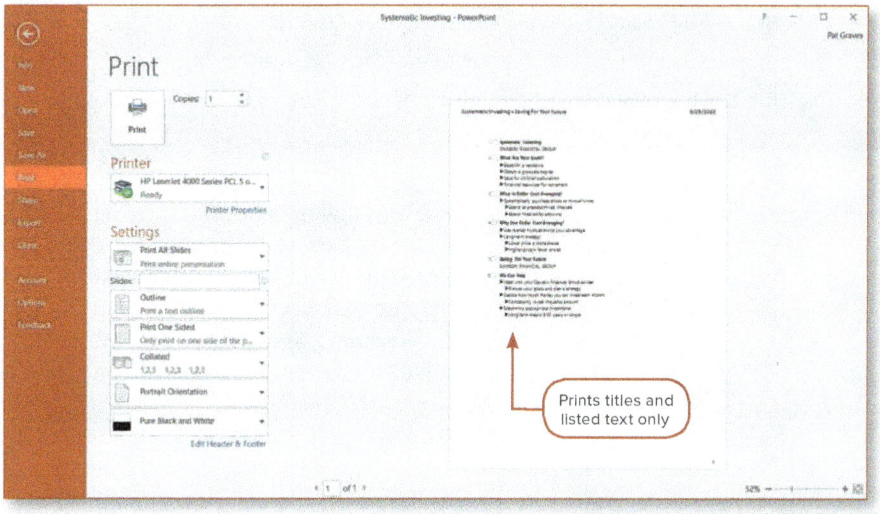

1-80 Print settings for an outline

SLO 1.9

Applying Properties

PowerPoint automatically records information called ***properties***, or ***metadata***, that identify details of your presentation to help you manage and track files. Some information is generated automatically such as the file size, creation date, and number of slides. These details are not visible in the presentation; they appear on the *Backstage* view or the *Properties* dialog box. Items shown with fields can be edited by inserting your own content such as title and author. Properties can be viewed by others who use the presentation.

HOW TO: Add Properties Using Backstage View

1. Click the **File** tab to display the *Backstage* view.
2. Click **Info** if it is not already selected.
3. Point to the properties listed on the right. The property field names are followed by the information for the current presentation.
   - Some properties cannot be changed because they are automatically generated.
   - A text box with a red border indicates a property field where the information can be edited (Figure 1-81). Click the box to add your content.

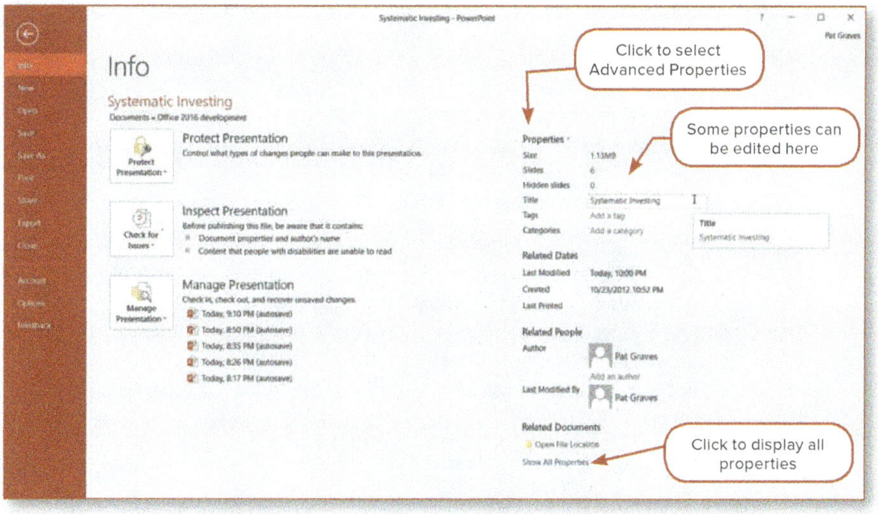

1-81 Document properties on the *Backstage* view

4. Click **Show All Properties** to access additional information.
5. Click a text box and type information to edit the document property.
6. Click the **Back** arrow in the upper left corner of the *Backstage* view to return to your presentation.

To open the *Properties* dialog box, click the **File** tab to display the *Backstage* view and then click **Info**. Click the **Properties** button and select **Advanced Properties**. Properties are organized in the following five tabs: *General*, *Summary*, *Statistics*, *Contents*, and *Custom* (Figure 1-82). You can edit properties on the *Summary* tab.

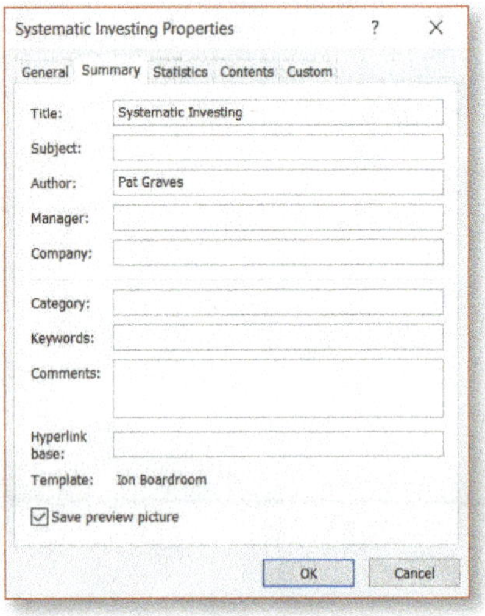

1-82 *Properties* dialog box

PAUSE & PRACTICE: POWERPOINT 1-3

For this final Pause & Practice project, you finish the presentation about training for a marathon. You insert, resize, and align several pictures, apply transitions, change the presentation properties, and print a handout.

Files Needed: ***[your initials] PP P1-2.pptx, RunnersGroup-01.jpg, RunnerWoman-01.jpg***, and ***MarathonSchedule-01.jpg*** *(Student data files are available in the* Library *of your SIMnet account.)*
Completed Project File Name: ***[your initials] PP P1-3.pptx***

1. Open the presentation you completed in *Pause & Practice 1-2*.
   a. Click the **File** tab to open the *Backstage* view and click **Open** on the left.
   b. Click **Browse** to open the *Open* dialog box.
   c. Locate the folder where your files are saved.
   d. Select the ***[your initials] PP P1-2*** presentation and click **Open**.
2. Rename and save the presentation.
   a. Click the **File** tab to open the *Backstage* view and select **Save As** on the left.
   b. Click **Browse** to open the **Save As** dialog box.
   c. Locate the folder where you want to save this file.
   d. Change the file name to [your initials] PP P1-3.
   e. Click **Save** to save the presentation and close the *Save As* dialog box.
3. Insert, resize, and align a picture on the slide.
   a. Display slide 1. Click the **Insert** tab, and then click the **Pictures** button [*Images* group].
   b. Locate your student data files.

c. Select ***RunnersGroup-01*** and click **Insert** (or double-click the file name) to insert the picture (Figure 1-83).

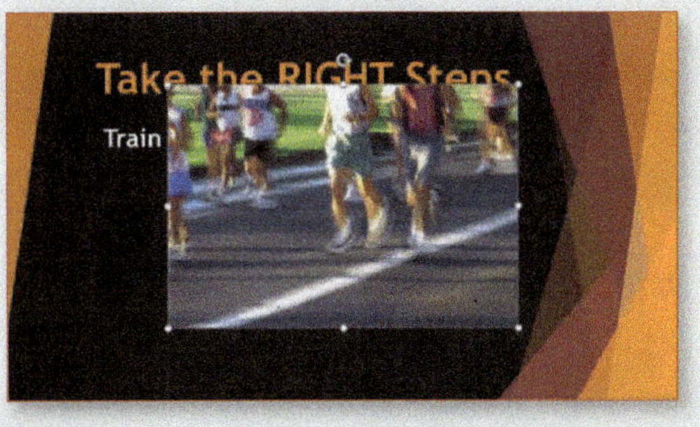

1-83 Picture of runners inserted

d. With the picture selected, click the **Align** button [*Picture Tools Format* tab, *Arrange* group].
   - Select **Align Bottom**.
   - Repeat to select **Align Right**.

e. Drag the picture's left horizontal sizing arrow to resize the picture so the *Width* is **8.5"** (Figure 1-84).
   - Because the picture is already blurred to reflect the speed of running, it looks fine when you stretch the picture.
   - If necessary, move the subtitle so it is between the title and picture.

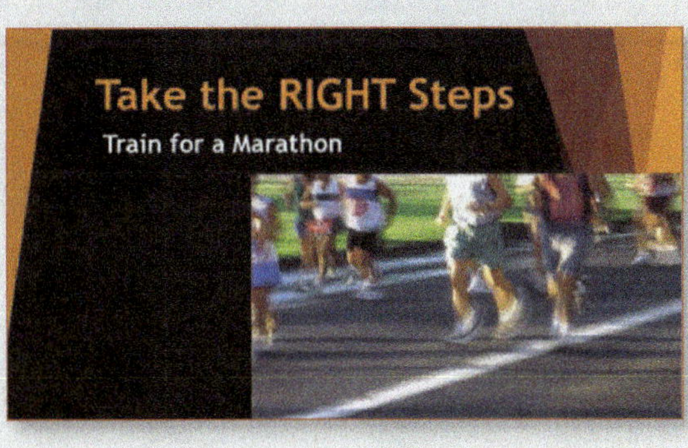

1-84 Picture resized and aligned

4. Insert and align a picture.
   a. Display slide 6. Click the **Insert** tab and click the **Pictures** button.
   b. Locate your student data files.
   c. Select ***RunnerWoman-01*** and click **Insert** (or double-click the file name) to insert the picture.
      - No resizing is required for this picture.
   d. Select the picture and click the **Align** button [*Picture Tools Format* tab, *Arrange* group] and select **Align Right**.

5. Add a new slide and insert a picture of a table.
   a. With slide 6 displayed. Click the **New Slide** drop-down arrow [*Home* tab, *Slides* group].
   b. Select the **Title Only** layout.
   c. Type the title Upcoming Marathons.
   d. Click the **Insert** tab, and then click the **Pictures** button [*Images* group].
   e. Locate your student data files.
   f. Select ***MarathonSchedule-01*** and click **Insert** (or double-click the file name) to insert the picture.
   g. Increase the picture *Width* to **8.5"** (*Picture Tools Format* tab, *Size* group).
   h. Move the table so it is approximately centered in the black area (Figure 1-85).

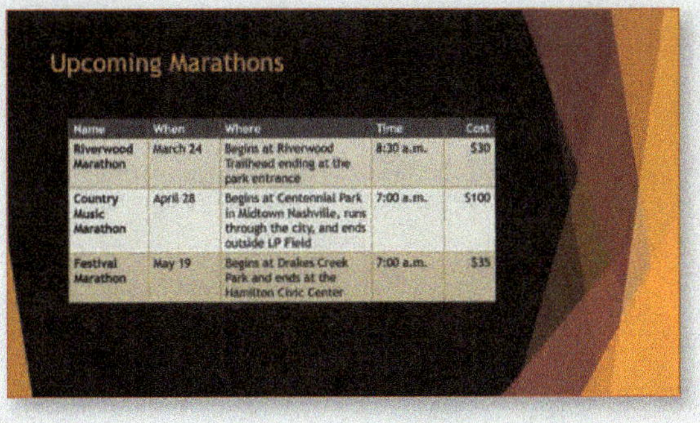

1-85 Picture of a table inserted and positioned

6. Adjust placeholder size and alignment.
   a. Display slide 8. Select the title placeholder and resize it horizontally on the right side so the text fits in the placeholder without extra horizontal space or word wrapping.
   b. Click the **Align** button [*Drawing Tools Format* tab, *Arrange* group] and select **Align Left**. Repeat to select **Align Top** (Figure 1-86).
   c. Display slide 9. Repeat steps 6a and 6b using **Align Center** and **Align Bottom**.

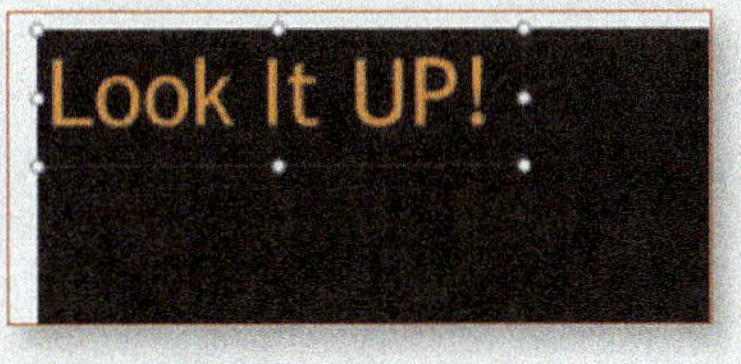

1-86 Title placeholder aligned top and left

d. Display slide 10. Repeat steps 6a and 6b using **Align Right** and **Align Middle**.
e. Change the font color for the word "THERE!" on slide 10 to **Tan, Text 2** [*Home* tab, *Font* group].

7. Apply one transition to all slides.
   a. Click the **Slide Sorter** button [*Status* bar].
   b. Click the **Transitions** tab.
   c. Click the **Wipe** transition from the gallery.
   d. Click **Effect Options** [*Transition* tab, *Transition to This Slide* group].
   e. Select **From Left** (Figure 1-87).

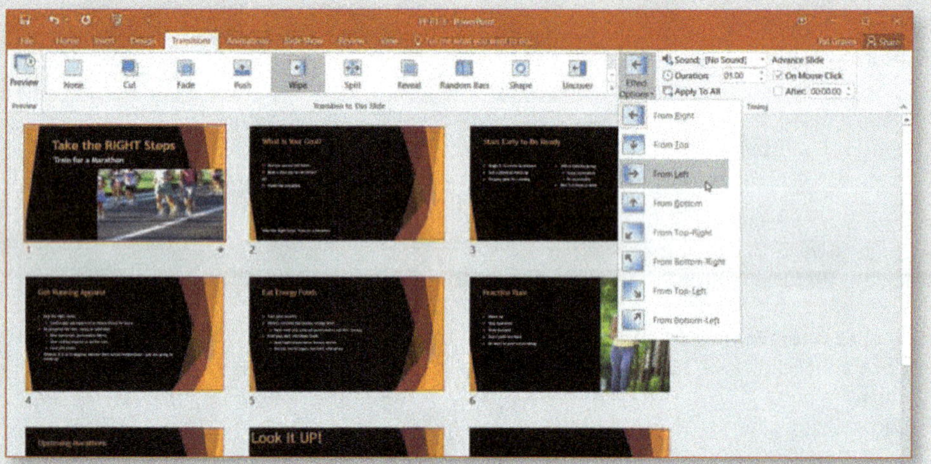

1-87 Transition *Effect Options*

   f. Click **Apply To All** [*Transition* tab, *Timing* group].

8. Select each of the following slides and apply different transitions (listed first) and effect options to emphasize the content.
   Slide 2: **Zoom**, **In**
   Slide 7: **Doors**, **Vertical**
   Slide 8: **Pan**, **From Bottom**
   Slide 9: **Pan**, **From Top**
   Slide 10: **Pan**, **From Left**

9. Test transition movements.
   a. In *Slide Sorter* view, press **Ctrl+A** to select all slides.
   b. Click **Preview** [*Transitions* tab] to see the movements.
   c. Select the first slide and click the **Slide Show** button [*Status* bar].
   d. Click to advance each slide so you can see the movements in *Slide Show* view. At the end, click or press **Esc** to exit *Slide Show* view.

10. Change presentation properties.
   a. Click the **File** tab to open the *Backstage* view.
   b. Click **Info** on the left if it is not already selected. The properties display on the right.
   c. Click the *Title* field and type Train for a Marathon.
   d. Click the **Properties** button, then select **Advanced Properties** to open the *Properties* dialog box (Figure 1-88).

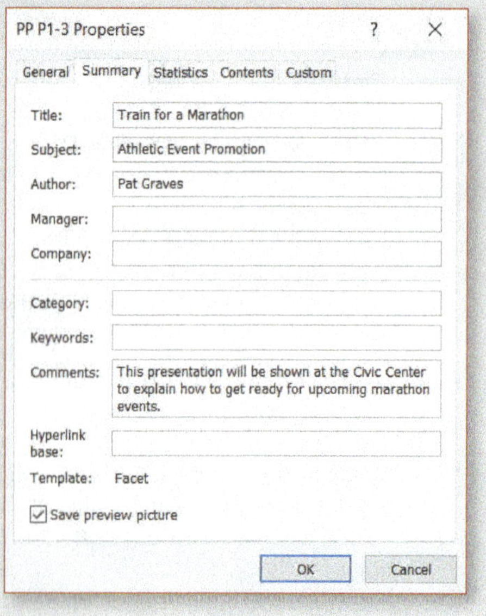

1-88 *Properties* dialog box

e. Click the **Summary** tab and type the following information in the respective fields:

Title: Train for a Marathon (already entered)
Subject: Athletic Event Promotion
Author: Your Name *(unless it already appears)*
Comments: This presentation will be shown at the Civic Center to explain how to get ready for upcoming marathon events.

f. Click **OK** to close the *Properties* dialog box and return to *Backstage* view.

11. Print slides as a handout. If your computer is not connected to a printer, skip step e.
    a. Click the **Print** button on the left.
    b. Select the appropriate printer.
    c. Change the following *Settings* by clicking the list arrow for each option (repeat as necessary for more than one change) (Figure 1-89):
       Which Slides to Print: **Print All Slides**
       What to Print: **Handouts, 6 Slides Horizontal, Frame Slides, Scale to Fit Paper**
       Print Order: **Collated**
       Orientation: **Portrait**
       Color Range: **Grayscale** (or **Color** if you prefer)

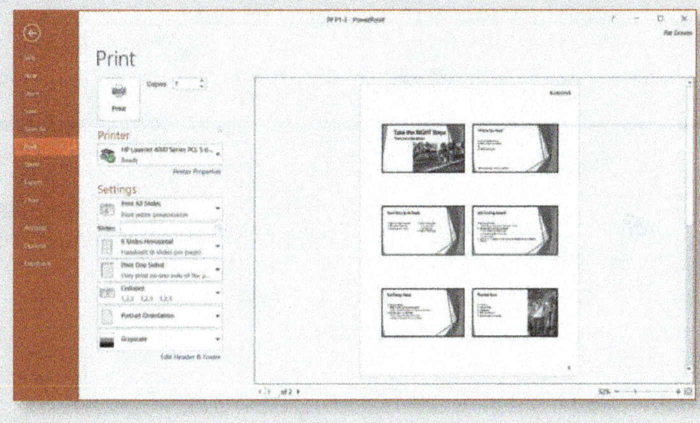

1-89 *Print* settings

    d. Preview the handout by clicking the navigation buttons to see both pages.
    e. Click the **Print** button at the top of the *Backstage* view.
    f. If necessary, click the **Back** button to close *Backstage* view.

12. Press **Ctrl+S** to save the presentation (or click **Save** on the *File* tab or the *Quick Access* toolbar). Close the presentation (Figure 1-90).

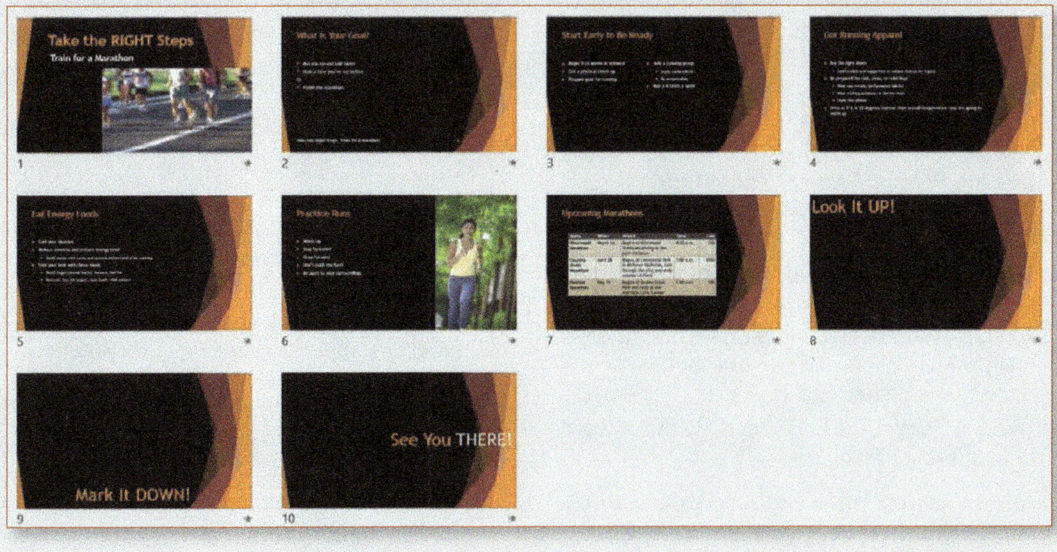

1-90 PP P1-3 completed

Chapter Summary

1.1 Create, open, and save a presentation (p. P1-3).

- You can start developing presentation content with a blank presentation, a ***Theme***, an existing presentation, or a ***Template***.
- PowerPoint views enable you to look at your content in different ways.
- The ***Zoom*** feature allows you to adjust the size of the current slide.
- The standard file format for presentation files has an extension of *.pptx*.
- In *Backstage* view, PowerPoint provides a variety of save and send options. For example, you can save a presentation as a PDF file or email a presentation file as an attachment.
- Additional themes and templates are available by searching online through PowerPoint or downloading them at Office.com.

1.2 Work with slides, layouts, placeholders, and text (p. P1-14).

- Use ***placeholders*** for presentation text and objects such as pictures, tables, and charts. You can resize, reposition, and align text placeholders on slides.
- The *New Slide* button displays a gallery of slide layouts with placeholders arranged for different content.
- You can change fonts using commands on the *Home* tab or the mini toolbar.
- *Change Case* changes the way words are capitalized.
- In bulleted lists, you can change the bullet symbol, size, and color.
- Use the ***Format Painter*** to copy formatting from one object and apply it to another object.
- The *Reuse Slides* feature enables you to insert slides from another presentation.
- Although potential spelling errors are automatically marked, you also can use the *Spelling* dialog box to check for errors.
- Use the ***Thesaurus*** to find synonyms for words in your presentation.

1.3 Navigate between slides and organize content by reproducing and rearranging slides (p. P1-23).

- You can move selected slides using a variety of methods to rearrange their sequence.
- Copy, paste, duplicate, and delete slides using the *Slides* pane or *Slide Sorter* view.

1.4 Change theme colors and fonts (p. P1-29).

- Presentation themes provide a cohesive look through the consistent use of background designs, colors, and font treatments.
- Consider the topic and tone of your presentation when choosing theme colors and fonts.

1.5 Insert headers and footers to add identifying information (p. P1-33)

- Both headers and footers are used for notes pages and handouts. They are applied to all pages or to individual pages.
- Footers usually appear at the bottom of slides but can appear in other locations. They are applied to all slides, all slides except the title slide, or to individual slides.

1.6 Insert, resize, and align a picture from a file (p. P1-37).

- PowerPoint supports different graphic file types; you can insert almost any digital image into slide shows.
- Use ***sizing handles*** or enter exact dimensions to increase or decrease a picture's size.
- Avoid distortion when resizing pictures by maintaining accurate height and width ratios.
- You can align pictures with one another or with the slide.

1.7 Apply and modify transition effects to add visual interest (p. P1-40).

- A ***transition*** is the visual effect that appears when one slide changes into another slide.
- The ***Effect Options*** command enables you to control the direction of transition movement.
- You can apply transitions to one slide, multiple slides, or to all slides in a presentation.

1.8 Preview a presentation and print slides, handouts, and outlines (p. P1-42).

- *Backstage* view allows you to examine each slide in your presentation before printing.
- The printer you select influences how slides appear in *Backstage* view.
- ***Grayscale*** shows shades of black.

- ***Print Settings*** control which slides to print, what to print, and the print order, orientation, and color range.

1.9 Apply presentation properties (p. P1-45).

- ***Properties*** are automatically recorded in your presentation file.
- You can add properties such as subject, keywords, or category to help manage and track files.
- Edit properties in *Backstage* view under *Info* or by opening the *Properties* dialog box.

Check for Understanding

The SIMbook for this text (within your SIMnet account) provides the following resources for concept review:

- Multiple choice questions
- Matching exercises
- Short answer questions

USING MICROSOFT POWERPOINT 2016

Guided Project 1-1

Jason Andrews is a sales associate for Classic Gardens and Landscaping (CGL) and frequently talks to customers when they visit the CGL showroom. For this project, you prepare a presentation he can use when introducing customers to CGL services.
[Student Learning Outcomes 1.1, 1.2, 1.3, 1.4, 1.5, 1.6]

Files Needed: ***GardenView-01.jpg*** and ***CGLLogo-01.png*** *(Student data files are available in the* Library *of your SIMnet account.)*
Completed Project File Name: ***[your initials] PowerPoint 1-1.pptx***

Skills Covered in This Project

- Create a new presentation using a theme.
- Change theme colors and background style.
- Change theme fonts.
- Add slides.
- Change font size.
- Rearrange slides.
- Use the *Format Painter*.
- Insert a footer.
- Check spelling.
- Adjust placeholder position.
- Insert, align, and resize a picture.
- Save a presentation.

1. Create a new presentation using a theme.
   a. Click the **File** tab, and then click **New**.
   b. Double-click the **Ion** theme (Figure 1-91).

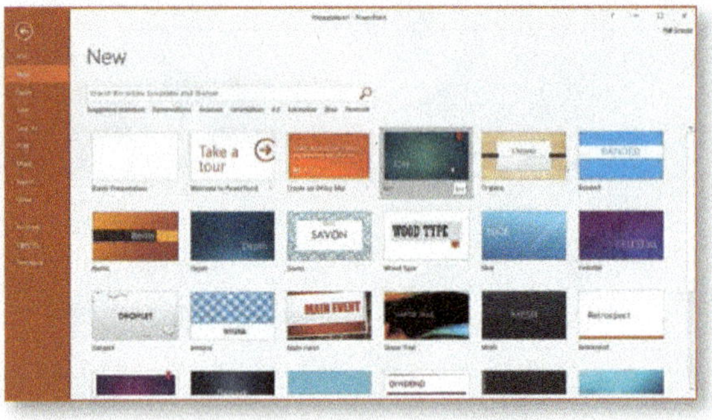

1-91 *Ion* theme selected

2. Save the presentation as [your initials] PowerPoint 1-1.
3. Change the theme colors.
   a. Click the **Design** tab.
   b. Click the **More** button [*Variants* group] to select each of the following options:
      Colors: Scroll down the list and select the **Paper** theme.
      Background Styles: Select **Style 3** from the gallery (Figure 1-92).
      Fonts: Select the **Candara** font group.
4. Type the following text in the placeholders on slide 1. Press **Ctrl+Enter** to move between placeholders.
   Title: Creating Beautiful Outdoor Spaces
   Subtitle: Jason Andrews, Sales Associate
5. Format the title and subtitle.
   a. Apply **bold** and **shadow** [*Home* tab, *Font* group] format to both the title and subtitle.
   b. Change the title font size to **66 pt**. and resize the title placeholder to remove extra space at the top.
   c. Change the subtitle font size to **28 pt**.
6. Add slides.
   a. Click the **New Slide** button [*Home* tab, *Slides* group] to add a new slide that automatically has the **Title and Content** layout. Type the following text for slide 2:

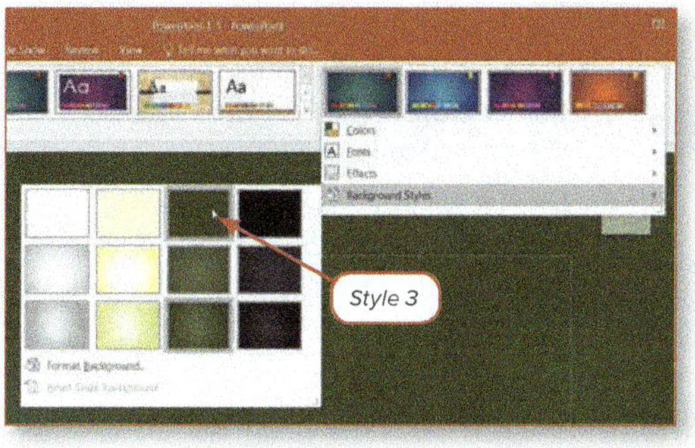

1-92 *Background Styles*

Title	Our Services
Bulleted items	• Garden center • Tree nursery • Gift shop • Delivery and installation • Patios and irrigation systems

b. Repeat this process to create three new slides with the following text:

Slide 3 title	Available Products
Bulleted items	• Shrubs, perennials, annuals • Soils and mulches • Garden décor including fountains • Shade trees and evergreen screening trees • Flowering or ornamental trees • Trees and plants for Christmas
Slide 4 title	Why Sustainable Design?
Bulleted items	• Energy efficiency increased • Water efficiency increased • Dependency on chemicals decreased • Vigor assured through native and hardy plants
Slide 5 title	We Make It Easy

Bulleted items	• We can do the entire project or we can assist
	  • You can do as much, or as little, as you like
	• We will provide:
	  • Landscape design planning or just advice
	  • Soil testing
	  • Low-cost delivery
	  • Fountain set up

c. Click the **New Slide** drop-down arrow [*Home* tab, *Slides* group] and click the **Title Slide** layout. Type this text in the placeholders:

Title	Call for a Consultation
Subtitle	615-792-8833

d. Increase the font size for the subtitle phone number to **32 pt**.

7. Move the slide 5 thumbnail before slide 4.
8. Apply **bold** and use the *Format Painter*.
   a. Display slide 2, select the title text, and apply **bold** [*Home* tab, *Font* group].
   b. Double-click the **Format Painter** button [*Home* tab, *Clipboard* group] so you can apply this change more than one time.
   c. Press **Page Down** and click the title text on slide 3 to apply the same change.
   d. Repeat for slides 4 and 5.
   e. Click the **Format Painter** button or press **Esc** to stop applying formatting.
9. Create a footer with the company name in the footer text.
   a. Click the **Header & Footer** button [*Insert* tab, *Text* group] to open the *Header and Footer* dialog box.
   b. On the *Slide* tab, check the following options: **Date and time** with **Update automatically**, **Slide number**, and **Footer** (Figure 1-93).

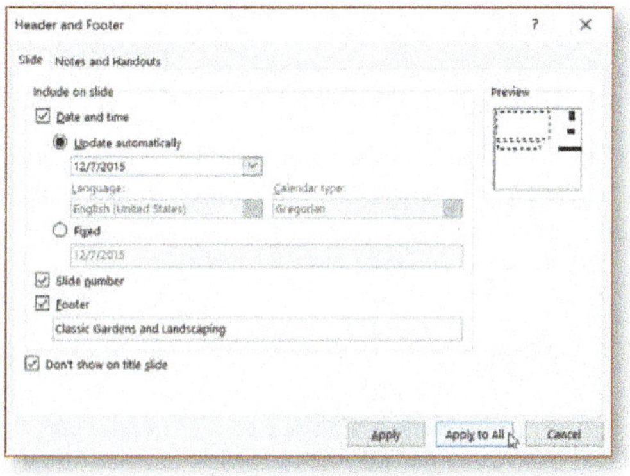

1-93 *Header and Footer* **dialog box**

c. In the *Footer* text box, type Classic Gardens and Landscaping.
d. Select **Don't show on title slide**.
e. Click the **Apply to All** button.

10. Click the **Spelling** button [*Review* tab, *Proofing* group] and correct any spelling errors you find.
11. Format the title slide so it is more distinctive.
    a. Display slide 1.
    b. Select the subtitle and click the **Change Case** button [*Home* tab, *Font* group]. Select **Capitalize Each Word**.
    c. Resize the title and subtitle placeholders to fit the text.
    d. Click the **Insert** tab, and then click the **Pictures** button to open the *Insert Pictures* dialog box.
    e. Locate your student data files.
    f. Select ***GardenView-01*** and ***CGL Logo-01***. Click **Insert**.
    g. Resize the logo *Width* to **5.5"** [*Picture Tools Format* tab, *Size* group] and the *Height* will automatically adjust.
    h. Align the text and pictures as shown in Figure 1-94.

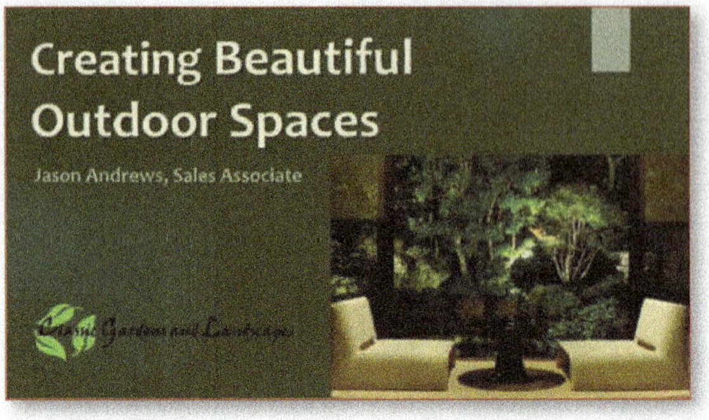

1-94 Completed title slide

12. Save and close the presentation (Figure 1-95).

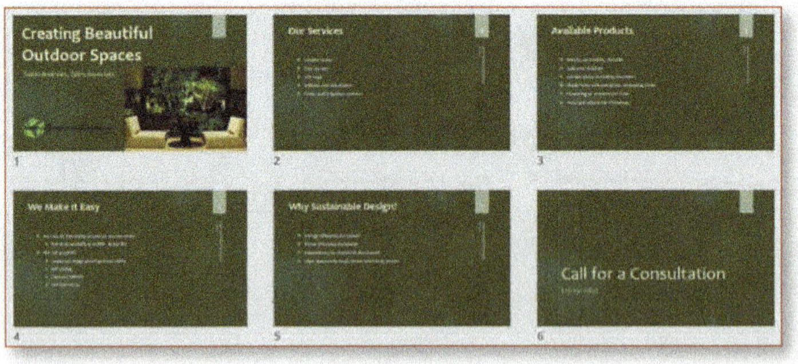

1-95 PowerPoint 1-1 completed

Guided Project 1-2

Solution Seekers, Inc., a management consulting firm, is preparing a series of brief presentations to be used in a training program for new hires. For this project, you develop a presentation about how to get better results when writing email messages.
[Student Learning Outcomes 1.1, 1.2, 1.3, 1.6, 1.7, 1.8, 1.9]

Files Needed: ***EmailResults-01.pptx***, ***EmailContent-01.pptx***, and ***AtSymbol-01.jpg*** *(Student data files are available in the* Library *of your SIMnet account.)*
Completed Project File Name: ***[your initials] PowerPoint 1-2.pptx***

Skills Covered in This Project

- Open a presentation.
- Change bullets.
- Reuse slides from another presentation.
- Rearrange slides.
- Check spelling.
- Adjust placeholder position.
- Insert a picture.
- Apply transitions.
- Preview a presentation.
- Change presentation properties.
- Print a handout.
- Save a presentation.

1. Open and resave a presentation.
   a. Click the **File** tab, select **Open**, and click **Browse**.
   b. Locate your student data files and double-click ***EmailResults-01*** to open the presentation.
   c. Press **F12** to open the *Save As* dialog box and save this presentation as [your initials] PowerPoint 1-2 in the appropriate location.

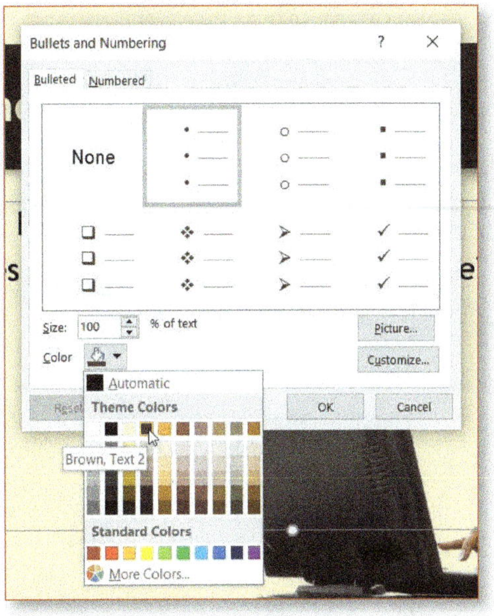

1-96 Change bullet color

2. Change the bullets for additional emphasis.
   a. Display slide 2 and select the bulleted text.
   b. Click the **Bullets** drop-down arrow [*Home* tab, *Paragraph* group].
   c. Select **Bullets and Numbering**.
   d. Click the **Color** button and select **Orange, Accent 6** (Figure 1-96).
   e. Change the size to **90%** of text.
   f. Click the **Customize** button to open the *Symbol* dialog box.
   g. Change the *Subset* to **Geometric Shapes** (Figure 1-97). Select the **Black Right-Pointing Pointer** (Character code 25BA)
      - If the font **Wingdings 3** is available, select a similar symbol (Character code 117).
   h. Click **OK** to close the *Symbol* dialog box. Click **OK** again to close the *Bullets and Numbering* dialog box.
3. Reuse slides from another presentation.
   a. Display slide 2. Click the **New Slide** drop-down arrow and select **Reuse Slides**.
   b. Click **Browse** on the *Reuse Slides* pane and then select **Browse file**. Locate your student data files.
   c. Select the presentation ***EmailContent-01*** and click **Open**. (This presentation has spelling errors that you will correct later.)
   d. Click all four slides on the *Reuse* Slides pane to insert them (Figure 1-98).
   e. Close the *Reuse Slides* pane.

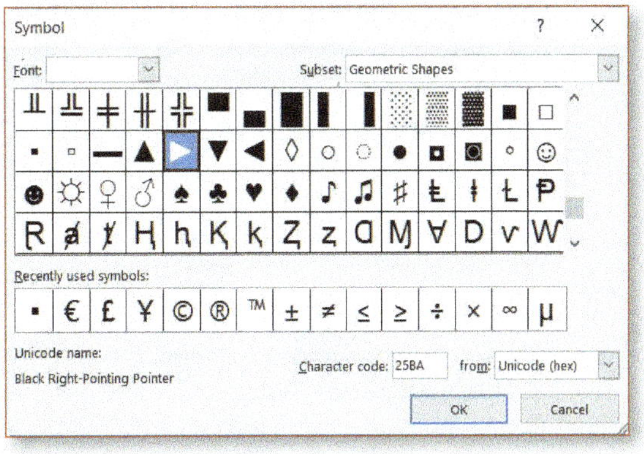

1-97 Change bullet symbol

4. Use the *Slides* pane to rearrange the six slides in this order: "Getting Results with Email," "Ask These Questions," "Why?," "Write a Meaningful Subject Line," "Organize It!," and "Keep It Short."
5. Click the **Spelling** button [*Review* tab, *Proofing* group] and correct all of the spelling errors: receive, Careless, organized, capture, response, and separate. The spelling of Email on slide 1 is correct and can be ignored.

6. Use the *Format Painter* to change bullets.
   a. Display slide 2 and select the body placeholder with the bulleted text.
   b. Double-click the **Format Painter** button [*Home* tab, *Clipboard* group] so you can apply what you have copied more than one time.
   c. Press **Page Down** and click the list on slide 3 to apply the change for the first-level bullets.
   d. Repeat for slides 4 and 5.
   e. Press **Esc** to end formatting.

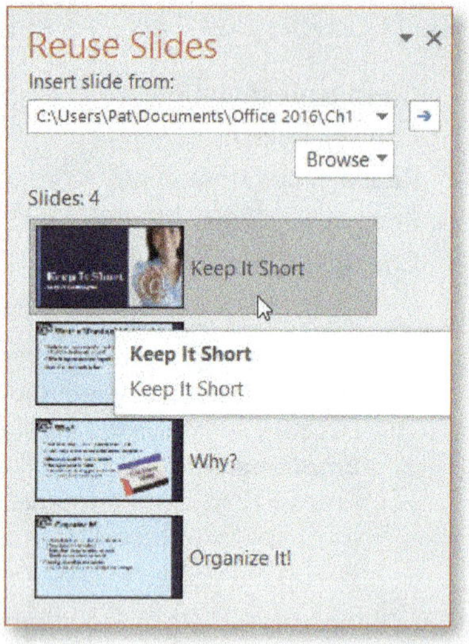

1-98 ***Reuse Slides* pane**

7. Change and position text.
   a. Display slide 6 and delete the picture on the right.
   b. Select the subtitle text, "Keep It Meaningful," and resize the placeholder to fit the text.
   c. Select the title text, "Keep It Short," change the font size to **24 pt**., and resize the placeholder to fit the text.
   d. Position the title text above the subtitle text on the orange shape at the right. Change the font color to **Black**, **Text 1**.
   e. Select both placeholders and click **Arrange** [*Home* tab, *Drawing* group], select **Align**, and select **Align Right** (Figure 1-99).
8. Insert and align a picture.
   a. Click the **Insert** tab, and then click the **Pictures** button.
   b. Locate your student data files.
   c. Select ***AtSymbol-01*** and click **Insert**.
   d. Click **Align** [*Picture Tools Format* tab, *Arrange* group] and select **Align Left**.
9. Apply one transition and effect option to all slides.

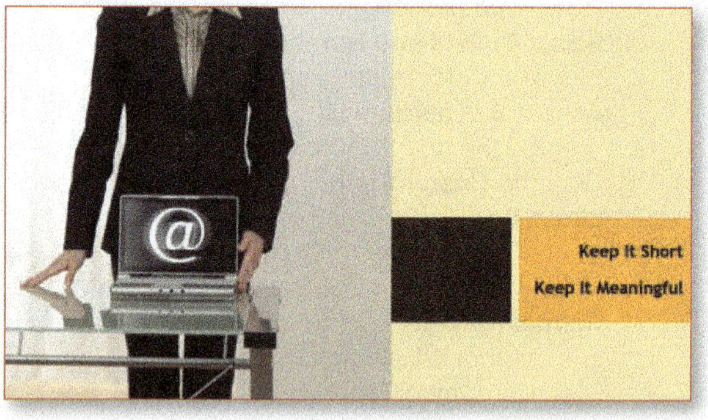

1-99 Completed ending slide

   a. Click the **Transitions** tab.
   b. Click the **Switch** transition from the gallery.
   c. Click **Effect Options** [*Transition to This Slide* group] and select **Left**.
   d. Click **Apply To All** [*Timing* group].
10. Preview the presentation.
    a. Click the **Slide Sorter** button [*Status* bar].
    b. Press **Ctrl+A** to select all slides. Click **Preview** [*Transitions* tab] to examine the movements in *Slide Sorter* view.
    c. Click the first slide and click the **Slide Show** button [*Status* bar]. Advance through the slides to see the movements in *Slide Show* view.
11. Change presentation properties.
    a. Click the **File** tab to open *Backstage* view, and then click **Info**.
    b. Click the **Properties** button and select **Advanced Properties**. Click the **Summary** tab and type this information as needed in the respective fields:

    Title: Getting Results with Email
    Subject: Writing
    Author: Your Name (unless it already appears)
    Comments: This presentation is for the new hire seminar.

    c. Click **OK** to close the *Properties* dialog box.

12. Print slides as a handout.
    a. Click the **Print** button on the left of the *Backstage* view.
    b. Select the appropriate printer.
    c. Change the following *Settings* by clicking the button list arrow for each option:

Which Slides to Print:	**Print All Slides**
What to Print:	**Handouts**, **6 Slides Horizontal**, **Frame Slides**, **Scale to Fit Paper**
Print Order:	**Collated**
Orientation:	**Portrait**
Color Range:	**Grayscale** (or **Color** if you prefer)

    d. Click the **Print** button at the top of the *Backstage* view.
13. Save and close the presentation (Figure 1-100).

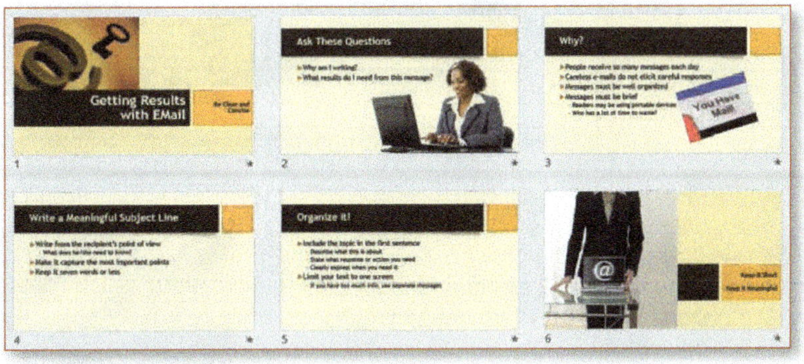

1-100 PowerPoint 1-2 completed

Guided Project 1-3

At Placer Hills Real Estate, realtors are always thinking of ways to help sellers make their homes more marketable and help buyers find the right home. For this project, you prepare a presentation for realtors to use when they speak with individual clients to explain how sellers can provide an added-value benefit by offering a home warranty.
[Student Learning Outcomes 1.1, 1.2, 1.5, 1.6, 1.7, 1.9]

Files Needed: ***PHRELogo-01.png*** and ***BuyerIncentive-01.pptx*** *(Student data files are available in the* Library *of your SIMnet account.)*
Completed Project File Name: ***[your initials] PowerPoint 1-3.pptx***

Skills Covered in This Project

- Create a new presentation using an online template.
- Change font size.
- Adjust picture position.
- Insert a picture.
- Reuse slides from another presentation.
- Check spelling.
- Insert a footer.
- Apply transitions.
- Change presentation properties.
- Save a presentation.

1. Create a new presentation using an online template.
    a. Click the **File** tab, and then click **New**.
    b. Type the word marketing in the search box and click the **Start Searching** button or press **Enter**.

c. Select the **Business sales strategy proposal presentation** (Figure 1-101) and click **Create** to download the presentation. (If you are unable to download the file, it is available as the presentation ***BusinessSalesStrategy-01*** in your student data files.)

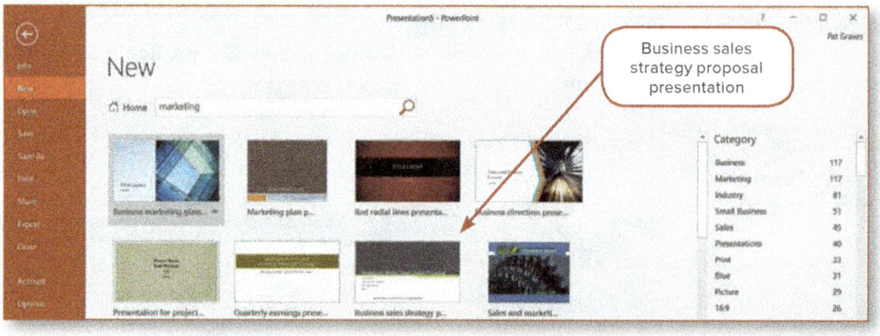

1-101 Online marketing themes and templates

d. Remove the presentation content. Select slide 1 in the *Thumbnail* pane, press **Ctrl+A** to select all slides, and press **Delete**. The slides are deleted from the presentation.

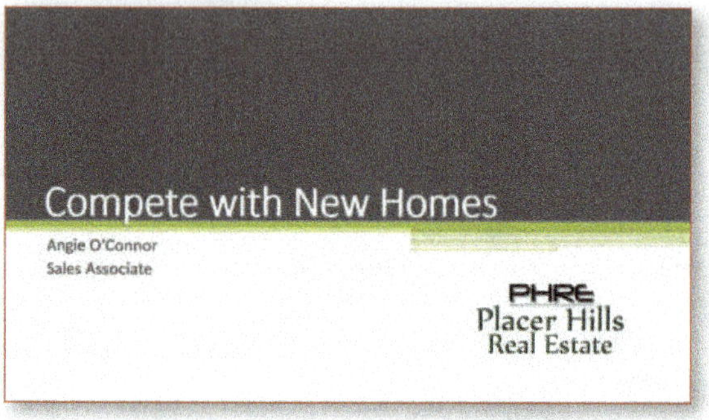

1-102 Completed title slide

2. Click the **New Slide** button [*Home* tab, *Slides* group] and the slide that appears automatically has a *Title Slide* layout. Type the following text in the placeholders:
   Title: Compete with New Homes
   Subtitle: Angie O'Connor Sales Associate
3. Save the presentation as [your initials] PowerPoint 1-3 in the appropriate location.
4. Increase the title font size to **60 pt**. and apply **bold** [*Home* tab, *Font* group].
5. Insert the PHRE company logo.
   a. Click the **Pictures** button [*Insert* tab, *Images* group] and locate your student data files.
   b. Select ***PHRELogo-01*** and click **Insert** (or double-click the file name) to insert the picture.
   c. Increase the logo size (*Width* **3"** and the *Height* automatically adjusts).
   d. Position this logo in the lower right as shown in Figure 1-102.
6. Reuse slides from another presentation.
   a. Click the **New Slide** drop-down arrow and select **Reuse Slides**.
   b. Click **Browse** on the *Reuse Slides* pane. Select **Browse file** and locate your student data files.
   c. Select the presentation ***BuyerIncentive-01*** and click **Open**.
   d. Click slides **2–6** (starting with the "Seller Needs" slide) on the *Reuse Slides* pane to insert them (Figure 1-103).
   e. Close the *Reuse Slides* pane.
7. Click the **Spelling** button [*Review* tab, *Proofing* group] and correct the following spelling errors: Competitive, maintained, replacement, and deductible.

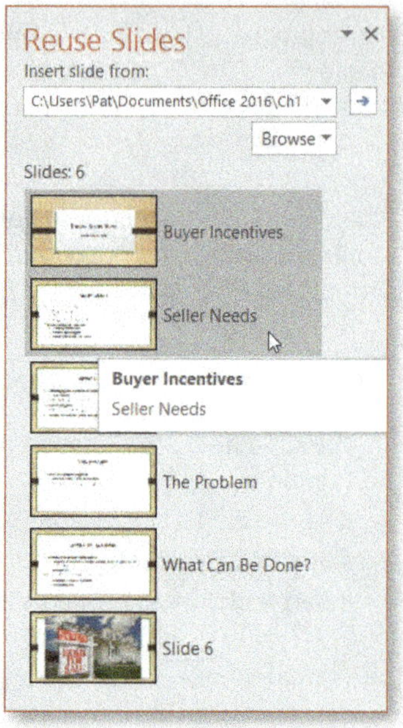

1-103 *Reuse Slides* pane

8. Display slide 6. Resize the picture using the center sizing handle to stretch it to the bottom of the slide.
9. Add a footer.
    a. Click the **Header & Footer** button [*Insert* tab, *Text* group].
    b. On the *Slide* tab, select **Slide number** and **Footer**.
    c. In the *Footer* text box, type Placer Hills Real Estate.
    d. Select **Don't show on title slide**.
    e. Click the **Apply to All** button. The footer appears in small text on the upper right.
    f. Delete the footer that is over the picture on slide 6.

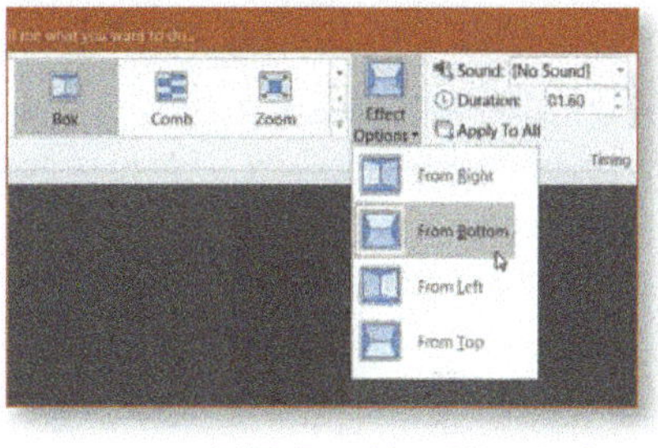

1-104 Transition *Effect Options*

10. Apply one transition to all slides.
    a. Click the **More** button [*Transitions* tab, *Transition to This Slide* group] to open the gallery. Click the **Box** effect.
    b. Click **Effect Options** [*Transitions* tab, *Transition to This Slide* group]. Select **From Bottom** (Figure 1-104).
    c. Click **Apply To All** [*Transitions* tab, *Timing* group].
    d. Select slide 1. Click the **Slide Show** button [*Status* bar] and advance through the slides to see the movements in *Slide Show* view.
11. Change presentation properties.
    a. Click the **File** tab, then click **Info**.
    b. Click the **Properties** button and select **Advanced Properties** to open the *Properties* dialog box. Type the following information as needed in the respective fields:
    Title: Compete with New Homes
    Subject: Sales Strategies
    Author: Angie O'Connor
    Comments: Seller can offer a home warranty to encourage buyer purchase.
    c. Click the **OK** to close the *Properties* dialog box.
12. Save and close the presentation (Figure 1-105).

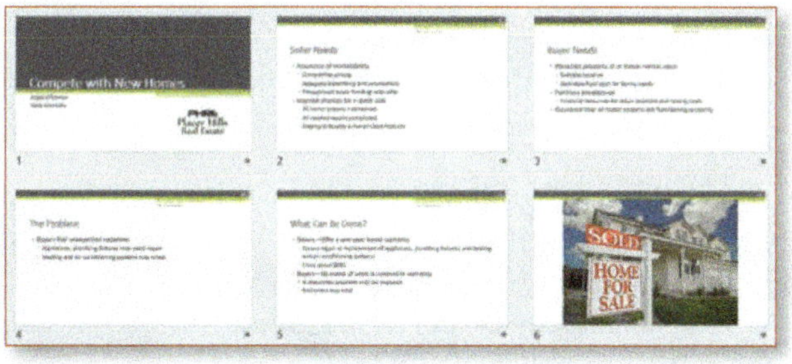

1-105 PowerPoint 1-3 completed

Independent Project 1-4

Wilson Home Entertainment Systems (WHES) assists customers with everything from a single television purchase to a home network installation to the design and construction of an elaborate home theater. For this project, you work on a presentation that sales representatives can use to describe the capabilities of WHES to potential customers.
[Student Learning Outcomes 1.1, 1.2, 1.4, 1.6, 1.7, 1.9]

Files Needed: ***SpecialEnvironment-01.pptx***, ***WHESLogo-01.png***, ***Family-01.jpg***, and ***Theater1-01.jpg*** *(Student data files are available in the* Library *of your SIMnet account.)*
Completed Project File Name: ***[your initials] PowerPoint 1-4.pptx***

Skills Covered in This Project

- Open a presentation.
- Add slides.
- Apply a theme.
- Change theme colors.
- Insert a picture.
- Adjust placeholders.
- Check spelling.
- Apply transitions.
- Change presentation properties.
- Save a presentation.

1. Open the presentation ***SpecialEnvironment-01***.
2. Save the presentation as [your initials] PowerPoint 1-4.
3. After slide 1, insert two new slides with the *Title and Content* slide layout. Type the following text for slides 2 and 3:

   Slide 2 title: Our Residential Services
   Bulleted items:
   - Design
   - Sales
   - Installation
   - Maintenance

   Slide 3 title: Sales
   Bulleted items:
   - Authorized dealer for the highest-quality home theater technology in the industry
   - Televisions
   - Projectors
   - Blu-Ray Players
   - Cables

4. Apply a theme and change theme colors.
   a. Select the **Integral** theme and the third **Variant** (Figure 1-106).
   b. Select the **Orange Red** theme colors.

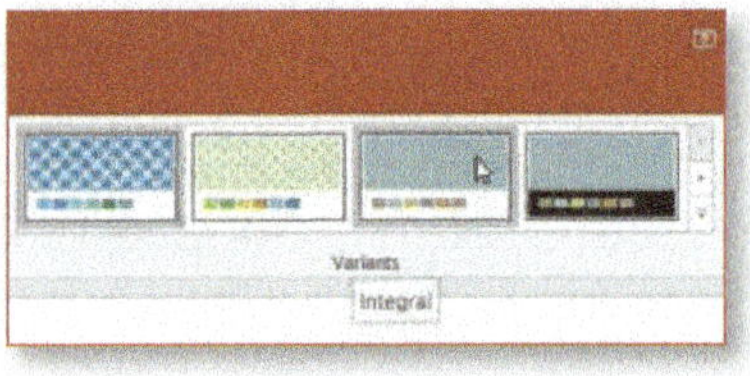

1-106 Change variant

5. Insert different pictures.
   a. Display slide 1 and delete the popcorn picture.
   b. Delete the subtitle placeholder.
   c. Insert ***Family-01*** and ***WHESLogo-01*** from your student data files.
   d. Increase the family picture size (*Height* **5"** and *Width* **7.52"**) and align it on the top right (Figure 1-107).
   e. Align the logo on the bottom right.
   f. Change the title placeholder font color to **White, Background 1**, apply **bold**, increase the font size to **66 pt**., and apply a **Shadow**.
   g. Resize the title placeholder so it word wraps as shown. Move it to the red area on the left.

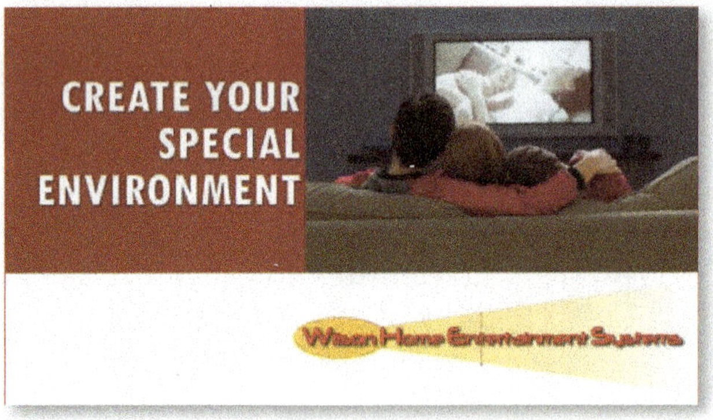

1-107 Completed title slide

6. Click the **Spelling** button and correct the following spelling errors: cabling, television, and calibration.
7. Increase the text size and insert a picture.
   a. Display slide 2. Select the bulleted text placeholder and change the font size to **40 pt**.
   b. Insert ***Theater1-01*** from your student data files.
   c. Increase the picture size (*Height* **5"** and *Width* **7.52"**) and align it on the bottom right.
8. Display slide 6. Increase the picture size (*Height* **2.18"** and *Width* **9"**) and center it horizontally in the space below the text.

9. Apply one transition to all slides.
   a. Select the **Cube** transition.
   b. Apply the **From Bottom** effect option.
   c. Click **Apply To All**.
10. Open the *Properties* dialog box and insert the following presentation properties as needed on the *Summary* tab:

    Title: Create Your Special Environment
    Subject: Residential Services
    Author: Liam Martin

11. Close the *Properties* dialog box.
12. Save and close the presentation (Figure 1-108).

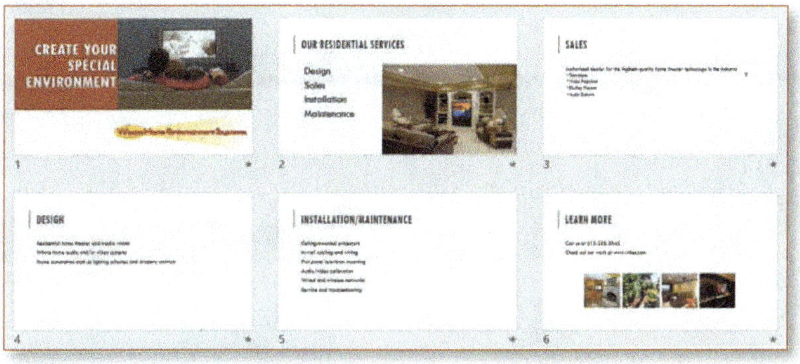

1-108 PowerPoint 1-4 completed

Independent Project 1-5

The Advising Offices in the Sierra Pacific Community College (SPCC) District work to assist students throughout the completion of their academic programs. Because SPCC has a large population of students who are retraining themselves for different types of employment, job-related information is especially important. For this project, you prepare a presentation about writing resumes.
[Student Learning Outcomes 1.1, 1.2, 1.3, 1.4, 1.7, 1.8]

Files Needed: ***ResumeUpdates-01*** and ***ResumeContent-01.pptx*** *(Student data files are available in the* Library *of your SIMnet account.)*
Completed Project File Name: ***[your initials] PowerPoint 1-5.pptx***

Skills Covered in This Project

- Open a presentation.
- Change theme background style and fonts.
- Change case.
- Adjust sizing and alignment.
- Add slides.
- Reuse slides from another presentation.
- Check spelling.
- Apply transitions.
- Print a handout.
- Save a presentation.

1. Open the **ResumeUpdates-01** presentation from your student data files.
2. Save the presentation as [your initials] PowerPoint 1-5.
3. Change theme style and font.
   a. Change the *Background Style* to **Style 4** (Figure 1-109).
   b. Change the *Theme Fonts* to **Georgia**.
4. Adjust placeholder sizing and text.
   a. Display slide 1 and select the title placeholder. Change text alignment to **Align Left**.
   b. Resize the placeholder so the text word wraps on two lines.
   c. Select the subtitle placeholder and change text alignment to **Align Left** (Figure 1-110).

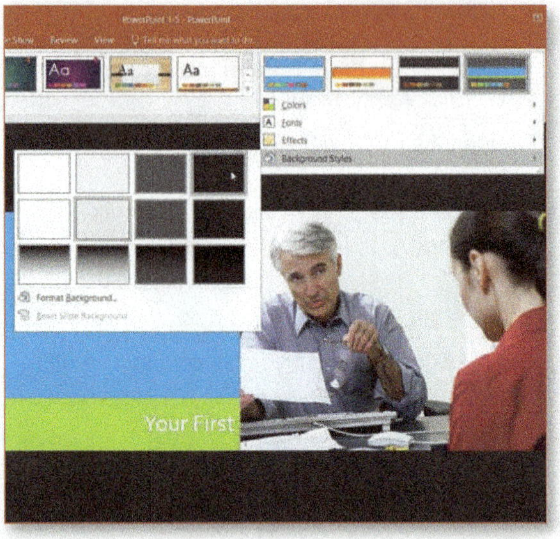

1-109 *Background Styles*

5. Insert two new slides after slide 2 with the *Title and Content* layout. Type the following text for slides 3 and 4:

Slide 3 title: Accomplishments, Not Duties
Bulleted items:
- Include only the most impressive details about your career
- Quantify your day-to-day tasks
- How many times?
- What was the result?
- How much money was saved?

Slide 4 title: Proofread
Bulleted items:
- Employers take spelling and grammar errors as signs of carelessness
- Ask a trusted friend or colleague to look at your resume

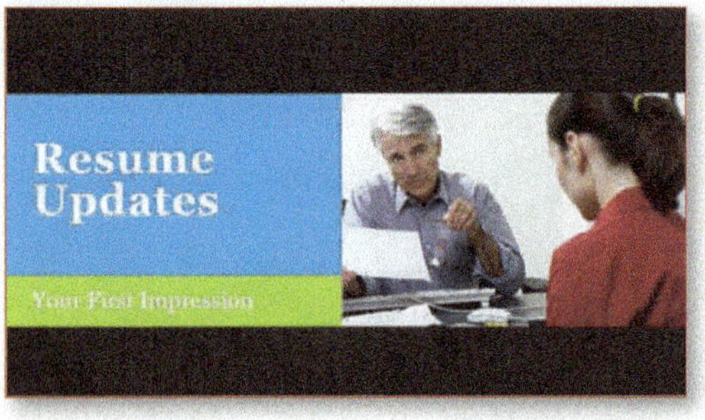

1-110 Completed title slide

6. Reuse slides from another presentation.
   a. Move your insertion point after slide 3.
   b. Open the *Reuse Slides* pane and browse to find ***ResumeContent-01*** from your student data files.
   c. Insert all three slides and close the *Reuse Slides* pane.
7. Display slide 8.
   a. Select the title placeholder and change text alignment to **Align Left**. Type Success!.
   b. Resize the title placeholder to fit the text.
   c. Delete the subtitle placeholder.
8. Correct the following spelling errors: Improve, redundant, achievements, and any other errors you find.
9. Apply the **Reveal** transition with the **Through Black from Right** effect option to all slides.
10. Print slides as an outline (Figure 1-111).
11. Save and close the presentation (Figure 1-112).

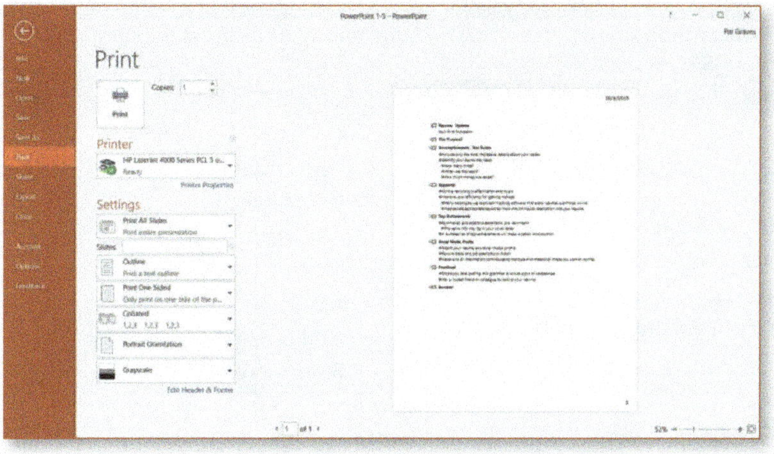

1-111 Outline

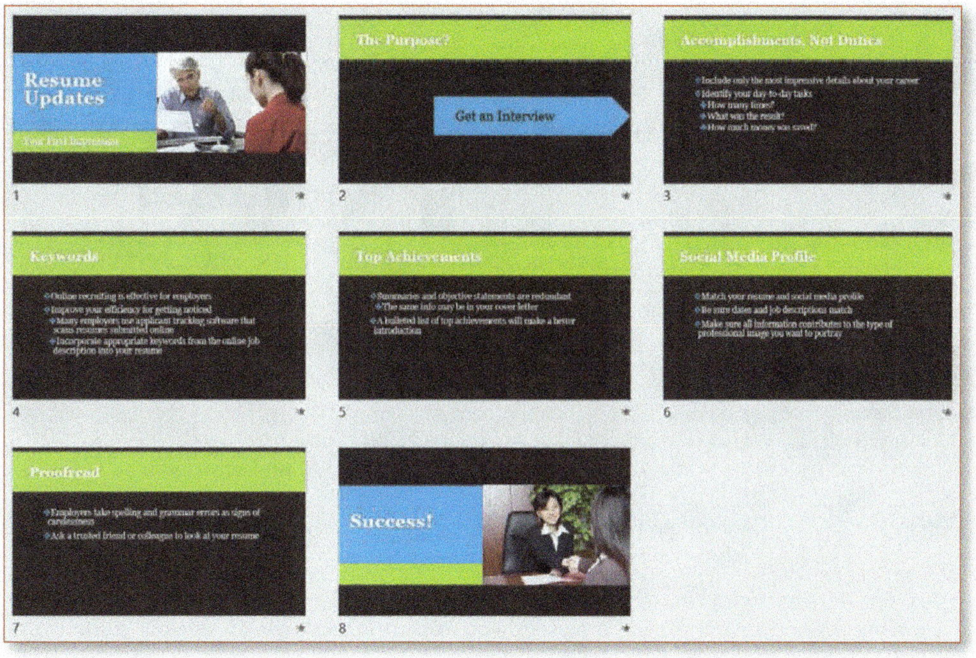

1-112 PowerPoint 1-5 completed

Independent Project 1-6

At the Hamilton Civic Center, workshops are offered to the community to address fitness, health, and wellness issues. For this project, you develop a presentation for an upcoming series about helping families become more active.
[Student Learning Outcomes 1.1, 1.2, 1.3, 1.4, 1.5, 1.6, 1.7, 1.9]

Files Needed: ***PedestrianSafety-01.pptx***, ***Walk1-01.jpg***, and ***Walk2-01.jpg*** *(Student data files are available in the* Library *of your SIMnet account.)*
Completed Project File Name: ***[your initials] PowerPoint 1-6.pptx***

Skills Covered in This Project

- Create a new presentation using a theme.
- Change theme colors and fonts.
- Change case.
- Reuse slides from another presentation.
- Check spelling.
- Rearrange slides.
- Insert a picture.
- Adjust placeholders.
- Insert a footer.
- Apply transitions.
- Add presentation properties.
- Save a presentation.

1. Create a new presentation and select the **Retrospect** theme.
2. Save the presentation as [your initials] PowerPoint 1-6.
3. Change the following theme options:

   Theme Colors: **Yellow Orange**
   Background Styles: **Style 6**
   Theme Fonts: **Arial Black-Arial**
4. Display slide 1 and type the following text:

   Title: Pedestrian Safety Matters
   Subtitle: Keeping That New Year's Resolution To Be More Active
5. Select the subtitle text and change the case to **Capitalize Each Word**.

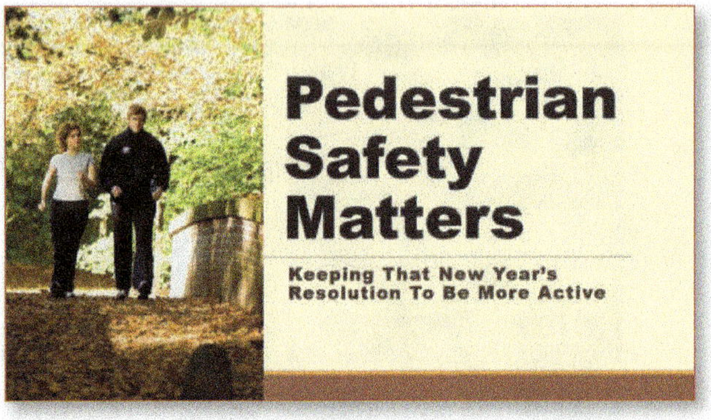

1-113 Completed title slide

6. Insert a picture and resize the placeholders.
   a. Insert the picture ***Walk1-01*** from your student data files on slide 1.
   b. Change the picture *Height* to **7.5"** and choose **Align Top** and **Align Left** so you have room for text on the right.
   c. Change text alignment for the title and subtitle placeholders to **Align Left**. Resize the placeholders so the text wraps as shown in Figure 1-113.
7. Reuse slides from another presentation.
   a. Open the *Reuse Slides* pane and browse to find ***PedestrianSafety-01*** from your student data files.
   b. Insert all five slides and close the *Reuse Slides* pane.
8. Display slide 2. Put your insertion point in front of the word "Guard" and press **Enter** to show this text as the last item in the list.
9. Correct the following spelling errors: pedestrians, aggressive, Remember, traffic, Regardless, and cloudy.
10. Adjust slide order to match the sequence shown in Figure 1-114.
11. Add a footer with the text Pedestrian Safety Matters. Apply it to all slides except the title slide.
12. Insert and position a picture.
    a. Display slide 6. From your student data files, insert the picture ***Walk2-01***.
    b. Change the picture *Height* to **7.5"**.
    c. Position the picture with **Align Top** and **Align Right**.

13. Apply the **Push** transition with the **From Right** effect option to all slides.
14. Preview the transitions in *Slide Show* view.
15. Open the *Properties* dialog box and insert the following presentation properties on the *Summary* tab:

    Title: Pedestrian Safety Matters
    Subject: Active Lifestyle
    Author: Anna Lorenzo
16. Close the *Properties* dialog box.
17. Save and close the presentation (Figure 1-115).

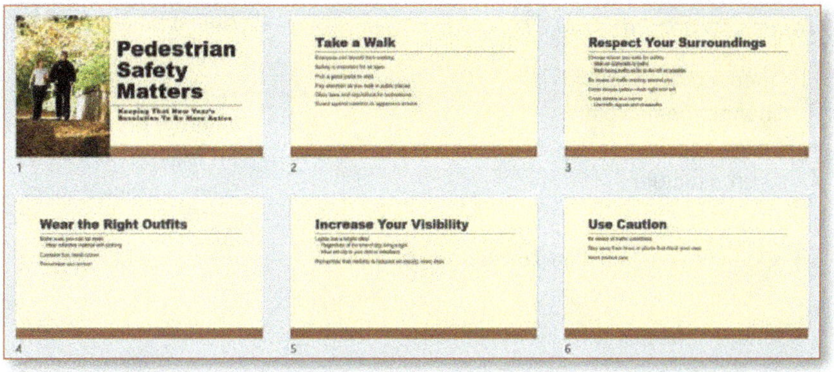

1-114 Slide order

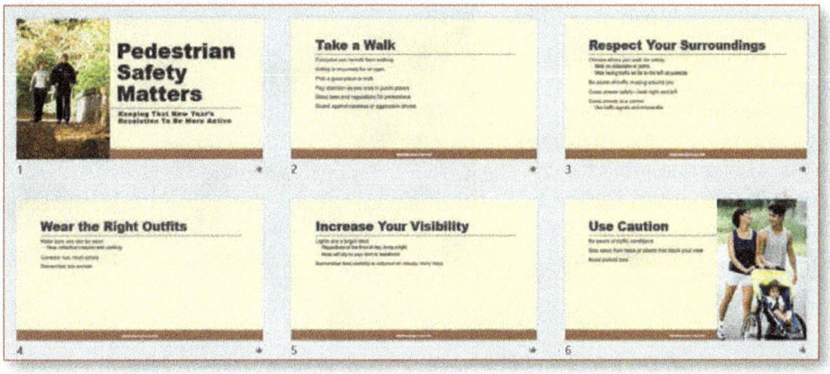

1-115 PowerPoint 1-6 completed

Improve It Project 1-7

For this project, you revise a presentation for Margaret Jepson, insurance agent at Central Sierra Insurance. You adjust theme colors and fonts, and add other information to the slide show, including a picture. [Student Learning Outcomes 1.1, 1.2, 1.3, 1.4, 1.5, 1.6, 1.7, 1.8, 1.9]

Files Needed: ***TotaledCar-01.pptx***, ***Travel-01.jpg***, and ***CSILogo-01.png*** *(Student data files are available in the* Library *of your SIMnet account.)*
Completed Project File Name: ***[your initials] PowerPoint 1-7.pptx***

Skills Covered in This Project

- Open a presentation.
- Change theme colors.
- Check spelling.
- Insert a picture.
- Adjust placeholders.
- Insert a footer.
- Apply transitions.
- Change presentation properties.
- Print a handout.
- Save a presentation.

1. Open the presentation ***TotaledCar-01*** from your student data files.
2. Save the presentation as [your initials] PowerPoint 1-7.
3. Change the following theme options:

   Theme Colors: **Blue Green**
   Background Style: **Style 3**
   Theme Font: **Trebuchet MS**
4. Format text and insert a picture logo.
   a. Display slide 1 and change the title font size to **66 pt**.
   b. Delete the subtitle placeholder.
   c. Insert the picture ***CSILogo-01*** from your student data files, change the *Width* to **5"**. Position the logo below the title on the shape across the bottom of the slide (Figure 1-116).

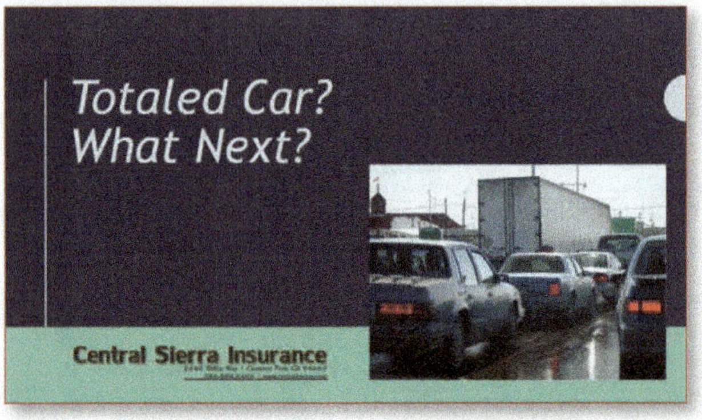

1-116 Completed title slide

5. Change a layout and insert a picture.
   a. Display slide 5. Change the slide layout to **Section Header**.
   b. Type the following text on two lines in the placeholder near the top of the slide. The text is right aligned and this placeholder right aligns with the title placeholder below.

      780-886-2400
      Margaret Jepson
   c. Insert the picture ***Travel-01***, and change the *Width* to **7"**. Position it on the left as shown in Figure 1-117.
6. Add footer text and slide numbering to all slides except the title slide.

   Slide footer text: The Totaled Car
7. Add header text and page numbering.

   Handout header text: Central Sierra Insurance
8. Apply and preview transitions.
   a. Select the **Clock** transition with the **Counterclockwise** effect option.
   b. Apply this transition to all slides.
   c. Preview the transitions.
9. Open the *Properties* dialog box and insert the following presentation properties as needed on the *Summary* tab.

   Title: Totaled Car? What Next?
   Subject: Accident Insurance
   Author: Margaret Jepson

10. Print a handout with the following options: **6 Slides Horizontal**, **Frame Slides**, and **Scale to Fit Paper** (Figure 1-117).
11. Save and close the presentation.

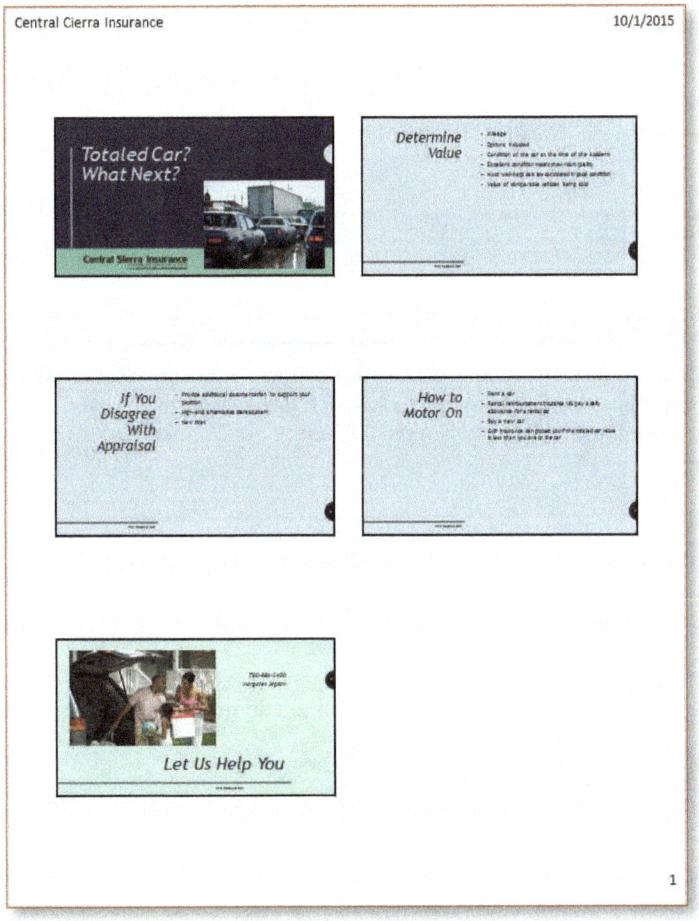

1-117 PowerPoint 1-7 completed, printed as a handout

Challenge Project 1-8

For this project, tell the story of your favorite vacation. Create six slides that introduce the topic and describe your main points with bulleted lists. Insert photographs to illustrate locations and resize them to fit with related text.
[Student Learning Outcomes 1.1, 1.2, 1.4, 1.5, 1.6, 1.7, 1.8, 1.9]

File Needed: None
Completed Project File Name: ***[your initials] PowerPoint 1-8.pptx***

Create a new presentation and save it as [your initials] PowerPoint 1-8. Modify your presentation according to the following guidelines:

- Search for an online theme that is appropriate for your topic. Apply it to your presentation.
- Use different slide layouts for variety.
- Insert three or more pictures.
- Add a footer.
- Apply transitions.
- Check spelling and include presentation properties.
- Print a handout.

Challenge Project 1-9

Think about different jobs for which you are qualified. On the Internet, research four different jobs and identify several characteristics and requirements for each job. Many online resources provide job-related information, such as www.careerbuilder.com or the *Occupational Outlook Handbook* at www.bls.gov/ooh/.
[Student Learning Outcomes 1.1, 1.2, 1.3, 1.4, 1.5, 1.6, 1.7, 1.8, 1.9]

File Needed: None
Completed Project File Name: ***[your initials] PowerPoint 1-9.pptx***

Create a new presentation and save it as [your initials] PowerPoint 1-9. Modify your presentation according to the following guidelines:

- Select an appropriate theme and use the *Design* tab to change colors and fonts as needed for your topic.
- Create a distinctive title slide.
- Write bulleted lists describing the characteristics and requirements of each different job with no more than six lines of bulleted text on each slide.
- Apply transitions.
- Check spelling and include presentation properties.
- Print handouts with six slides on a page.

Challenge Project 1-10

For this project, develop a presentation about how a presenter can manage nervous tendencies when presenting in front of an audience. Include information from your own experiences and refer to online resources, such as www.presentationmagazine.com.
[Student Learning Outcomes 1.1, 1.2, 1.3, 1.4, 1.5, 1.6, 1.7, 1.8, 1.9]

File Needed: None
Completed Project File Name: ***[your initials] PowerPoint 1-10.pptx***

Create a new presentation and save it as [your initials] PowerPoint 1-10. Modify your presentation according to the following guidelines:

- Select an appropriate theme and use the *Design* tab to change colors and fonts as needed for your topic.
- Create a distinctive title slide.
- Write bulleted lists describing typical causes of nervousness and suggest ways to control nervousness when presenting.
- Insert pictures to illustrate concepts.
- Apply transitions.
- Check spelling and include presentation properties.
- Print an outline of the presentation.

CHAPTER 2

Illustrating with Pictures and Information Graphics

POWERPOINT

CHAPTER OVERVIEW

In our world today, we are surrounded by information graphics. We see them in television programming, web sites, and published material of all kinds. We interpret signage that helps us get from place to place and readily recognize many iconic images that help us with everyday tasks. These graphics communicate visually and can be more effective than long passages of text.

PowerPoint gives you the ability to create information graphics—to visually display information in ways that help an audience quickly grasp the concepts you are presenting. You can choose from many options, such as adding shapes or color for emphasis, pictures to illustrate, diagrams to show processes, and charts to show data relationships.

STUDENT LEARNING OUTCOMES (SLOs)

After completing this chapter, you will be able to:

SLO 2.1 Work with shapes, select theme colors and standard colors, and apply styles (p. P2-71).

SLO 2.2 Create interesting and eye-catching text effects with *WordArt* styles and text effects (p. P2-80).

SLO 2.3 Search for pictures and illustrations, modify picture appearance, and compress picture file size (p. P2-82).

SLO 2.4 Organize information in a grid format using tables and customize the arrangement of columns and rows (p. P2-91).

SLO 2.5 Format portions of a table by applying styles, colors, and effects (p. P2-96).

SLO 2.6 Show processes and relationships with *SmartArt* graphics (p. P2-101).

SLO 2.7 Improve the appearance of *SmartArt* graphics by applying styles, colors, and effects (p. P2-104).

SLO 2.8 Create charts that show relationships between data values and emphasize data in different ways based on the chart type and chart elements (p. P2-108).

SLO 2.9 Format a chart by applying preset styles or manually customizing individual chart elements (p. P2-113).

CASE STUDY

Classic Gardens and Landscapes (CGL) is a landscape design company that creates beautiful and low-maintenance landscapes for outdoor living spaces. Frank and Sandra Hunter recently bought a new home from a builder. It has minimal landscaping, so they contacted Gerod Sunderland, a landscape designer for CGL, to discuss improvements.

Gerod visited the property and designed plans with several options for trees, shrubs, and plants. You have been asked to prepare a presentation illustrating his key points for his meeting with the Hunters.

Pause & Practice 2-1: Add visual interest with picture enhancements and creative text designs.

Pause & Practice 2-2: Prepare a table.

Pause & Practice 2-3: Create an organization chart and convert text to a *SmartArt* graphic.

Pause & Practice 2-4: Create column and pie charts with an enhanced appearance.

SLO 2.1

Working with Shapes, Colors, and Styles

Shapes can emphasize key points. For example, an arrow can point to an object, or a line can connect two related objects. You can draw a variety of shapes using drawing tools from PowerPoint's ***Shapes*** gallery; each shape has both an outline and fill color. The ***Shape Styles*** galleries make it easy to apply preset colors and shape effects or you can customize shape effects as you illustrate your slides.

Shapes and Text Boxes

The *Shapes* gallery (Figure 2-1) is on the *Home* tab [*Drawing* group], the *Insert* tab [*Illustrations* group], and the *Drawing Tools Format* tab [*Insert Shapes* group]. Shapes are grouped in the following categories:

- *Recently Used Shapes*
- *Lines*
- *Rectangles*
- *Basic Shapes*
- *Block Arrows*
- *Equation Shapes*
- *Flowchart*
- *Stars and Banners*
- *Callouts*
- *Action Buttons*

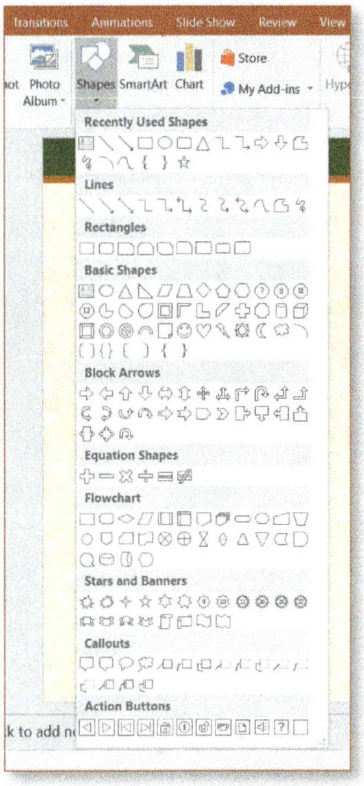

2-1 *Shapes* gallery

To insert a shape, select the shape you want from the *Shapes* gallery and use the following features to draw and adjust your shape:

- *Crosshair:* A large plus sign used to draw the shape
- *Sizing handles:* White circles on the corners and sides of the shapes used to change shape size
- *Rotation handle:* A circular arrow on the top used to make shapes angle
- *Adjustment handle:* Yellow circles used to change curves or points

You can add text to shapes and format the text as you do text in a placeholder or in a text box. However, the text in shapes or in text boxes does not appear in *Outline* view.

▸ HOW TO: Insert a Shape

1. Click the **Insert** tab.
2. Click the **Shapes** button [*Illustrations* group] to display the *Shapes* gallery.
3. Select the shape you want and your pointer becomes a crosshair (Figure 2-2).
4. Click and drag to draw the shape in the approximate size you need (Figure 2-3). The shape appears with sizing handles and a rotation handle. It may have adjustment handles.
5. Click and drag an adjustment handle to change areas within a shape such as the tip of an arrow or star, the corners of a rounded rectangle, or the line used with a callout.
6. Add text, if needed, by typing in the selected shape as you would type in a placeholder.
7. Resize the shape if necessary and move it to the appropriate position on the slide.

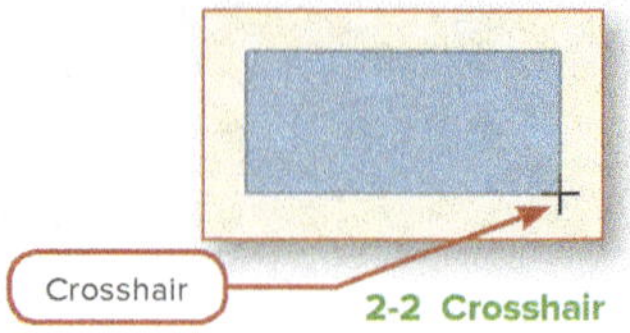

2-2 Crosshair drawing a shape

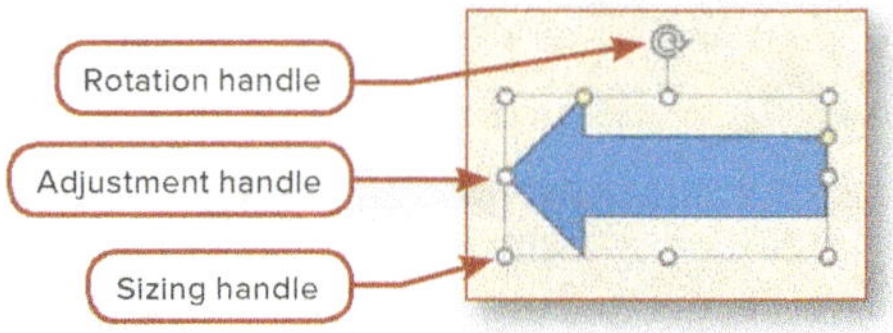

2-3 Shape with handles

When you need more than one of the same shape, you can efficiently draw them using ***Lock Drawing Mode***.

> **MORE INFO**
>
> Press the **Shift** key while you drag to constrain shapes. The oval becomes round, the rectangle becomes square, and lines are straight.

▸ HOW TO: Insert Multiple Shapes

1. Click the **Insert** tab.
2. Click the **Shapes** button [*Illustrations* group] to display the *Shapes* gallery.
3. Right-click the shape you want, and click **Lock Drawing Mode** (Figure 2-4).
4. Draw the first shape. Repeat to draw more of the same shape.
5. Press **Esc** to turn off *Lock Drawing Mode* when you are finished.

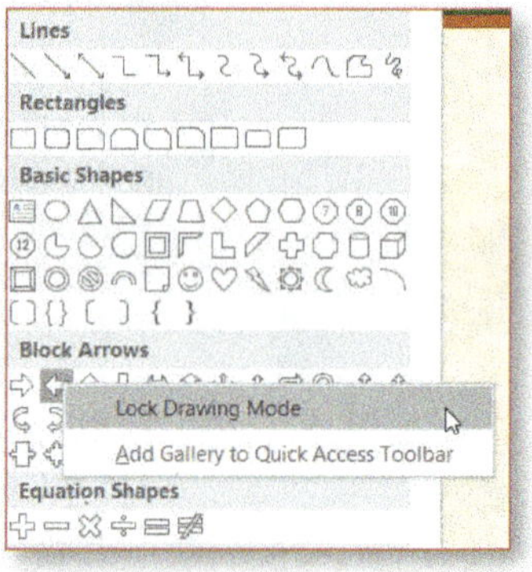

2-4 *Lock Drawing Mode*

When you select an existing shape, the *Drawing Tools Format* tab opens and the *Shapes* gallery displays on the left in the *Insert Shapes* group. If the existing shape does not fit your purpose, you can easily change the shape.

▸ HOW TO: Change a Shape

1. Select the shape to be changed.
2. Click the **Edit Shape** drop-down arrow [*Drawing Tools Format* tab, *Insert Shapes* group] (Figure 2-5).

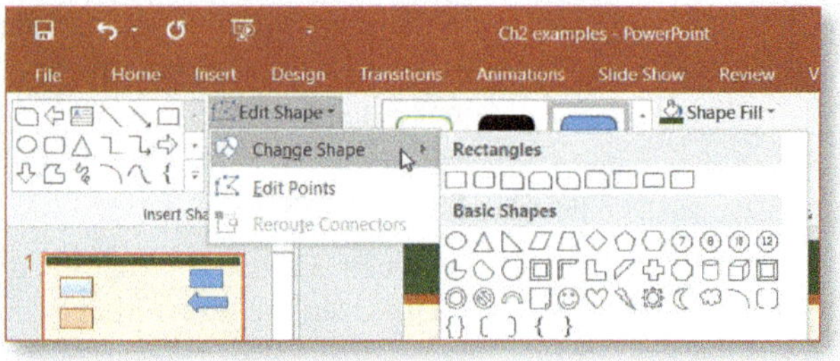

2-5 *Change Shape*

3. Select **Change Shape** and click a different shape from the *Shapes* gallery.
4. Click a blank area of the slide to deselect the shape.
5. Click **Undo** to return to your original shape.

Using ***text boxes***, you can add text anywhere on a slide without using placeholders. For example, you can add notations to identify slide objects or insert brief phrases you want to emphasize. Text boxes can be sized and moved around like any other shape.

HOW TO: Insert a Text Box

1. Click the **Insert** tab.
2. Click the **Text Box** button [*Text* group] and your pointer changes to an insertion point. Create a text box using one of the following methods:
   - Click the slide background to place your insertion point where you want the text to appear. Begin typing and the text box expands as you enter text. The *Home* tab opens.
   - Click and drag to change the pointer to a crosshair and draw a text box (Figure 2-6) in the approximate width you need. The *Home* tab opens. The text box height adjusts as you type text.
3. Resize if necessary by dragging sizing handles or entering *Height* and *Width* sizes [*Drawing Tools Format* tab, *Size* group] (Figure 2-7).
4. Click and drag the text box to move it to an appropriate position on the slide.

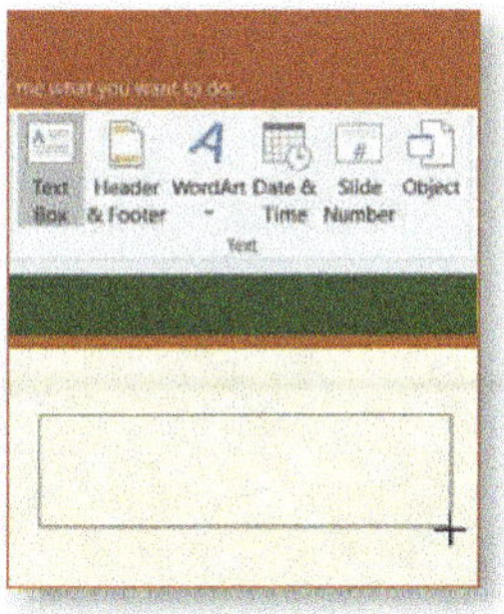

2-6 Draw a text box

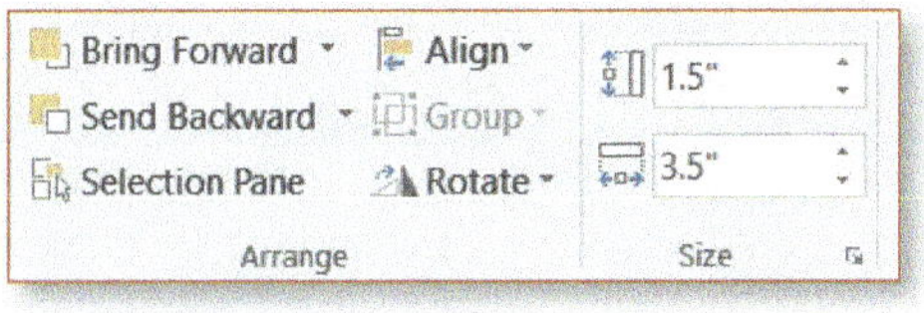

2-7 Size measurements

Style Galleries and Effect Options

Different *Style* galleries provide collections of preset effects for shapes, pictures, or other objects. You can customize all effects using the related button such as ***Shape Effects, Picture Effects***, or ***Text Effects*** to access drop-down galleries. You can choose from *Shadow*, *Reflection*, *Glow*, *Soft Edges*, *Bevel*, *3D Rotation*, or *Transform*. These options are described in the following table. You can also apply one or more effects without first using styles from a gallery.

Effect Options

Effect	Options
Shadow	***Shadow*** effects appear in three groupings. An ***Outer*** shadow shows behind an object from different directions. An ***Inner*** shadow makes part of the object looked raised. A ***Perspective*** shadow shows below so the object appears to float.
Reflection	A ***Reflection*** shows a mirror image below an object, like a reflection on a shiny surface or on water. You can control how close the reflection is to the object.
Glow	***Glow*** provides a colored area around an object that fades into the background color on your slide. Glow colors by default are based on the current theme colors, but you can use other colors. The size of the *Glow* is measured in points.

Continued

Effect	Options
Soft Edges	Shapes and other objects have either straight edges or well-defined curves. ***Soft Edges*** creates a feathered edge that gradually blends into the background color. The size of the blending area is measured in points from the edge of the object inward. The larger the point size, the less you see of the object.
Bevel	***Bevel*** effects add light and dark areas to create a dimensional appearance. Objects or text can look raised or inset.
3D Rotation	***3D Rotation*** effects include ***Parallel***, ***Perspective***, and ***Oblique*** options that create an illusion of depth by rotating an object from front to back.
Transform	***Transform*** is a *Text Effect* used to change the shape of words. It is not available for shapes or pictures.

The width of your PowerPoint window affects how galleries are displayed on the various tabs. If you have a narrow PowerPoint window, you need to click a **Quick Style** button to open a gallery. If your window is wide, part of a gallery displays, and you click the **More** button to open the complete gallery.

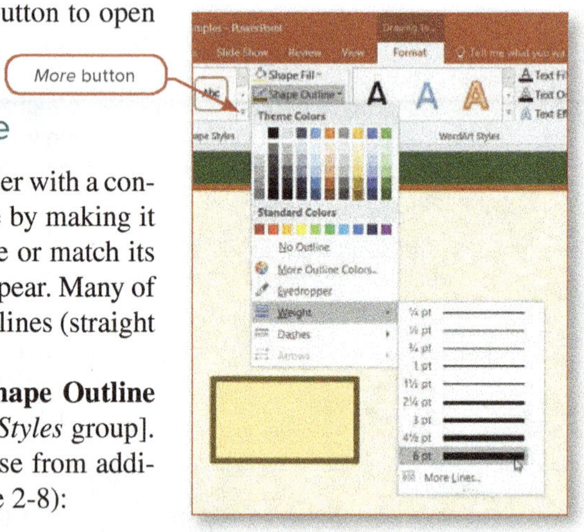

2-8 *Shape Outline Weight*

Adjust Outline Weight and Style

Emphasize a shape outline by making it wider with a contrasting color; deemphasize a shape outline by making it thinner. You can choose to show no outline or match its color to the shape to make the outline disappear. Many of the options for shape outlines also apply to lines (straight or curved) that you draw.

Select a shape or line and click the **Shape Outline** button [*Drawing Tools Format* tab, *Shape Styles* group]. Click one of the following options to choose from additional variations in a drop-down list (Figure 2-8):

- ***Weight:*** Displays line thickness measured in points
- ***Dashes:*** Displays lines made with various combinations of dots and dashes (Figure 2-9)
- ***Arrows:*** Displays arrowheads or other shapes for both ends of a line

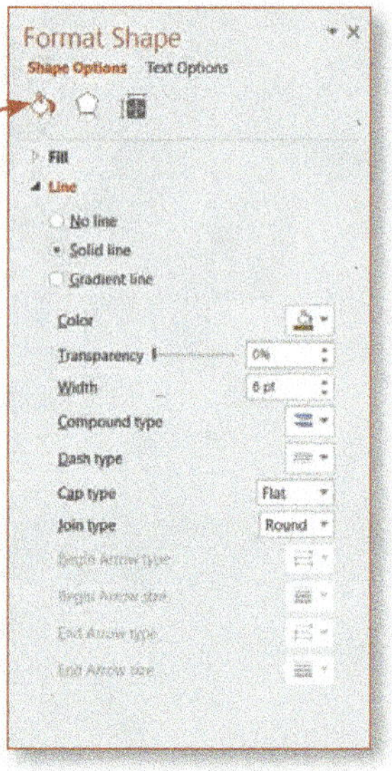

2-10 *Format Shape pane*

At the bottom of these three drop-down lists, select **More Lines** to open the *Format Shape* pane (Figure 2-10) where you can customize the following *Line* options:

- ***Color:*** Provides color choices
- ***Transparency:*** Adjusts transparency percentages
- ***Width:*** Controls the thickness of lines measured in points
- ***Compound type:*** Provides outlines with two or more lines in different thicknesses
- ***Dash type:*** Displays lines made with various combinations of dots and dashes

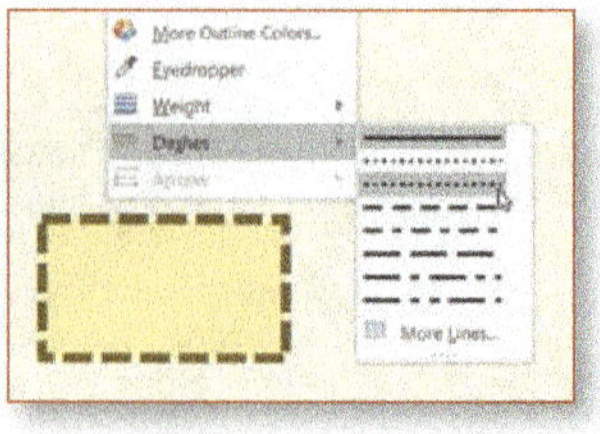

2-9 *Shape Outline Dashes*

- ***Cap type:*** Controls the look (*Square*, *Round*, or *Flat*) of the ends of lines; it is usually applied to single lines or arrows
- ***Join type:*** Controls the look (*Round*, *Bevel*, *Miter*) for the connection point where two lines meet (for example, at the corner of a rectangle or square)
- ***Begin and End Arrow type:*** Controls the shape for both ends of an arrow
- ***Begin and End Arrow size:*** Controls the size of the shape at both ends of an arrow

The *Format Shape* pane is a convenient place to change many options. Figure 2-10 shows the *Fill & Line* tab with *Line* options displayed because a line was selected when the pane opened. Different options appear if you have a shape selected or if you choose a *Gradient* line. Above *Line* you can select *Fill* to change shape colors. You can click the arrow in front of these options to expand or collapse each list.

Additional tabs under *Shape Options* on the *Format Shape* pane include *Effects* and *Size & Properties* with related options on each tab. Click the icons at the top of the pane to select different tabs.

ANOTHER WAY

Right-click a shape and then select **Format Shape** from the context menu to open the *Format Shape* pane.

Themes and Standard Colors

As you learned in Chapter 1, each PowerPoint *Theme* starts with a set of *Theme Colors* that provide background and accent colors. When you apply *Theme Colors* for shapes and text, these colors automatically change when you select a different set of *Theme Colors*.

Consider all of the colors used throughout your presentation when you select colors because some are more appropriate than others. This section explains how colors are arranged in PowerPoint and describes different ways to "mix" custom colors. The same techniques for choosing colors apply to color fills or outline colors.

Change Solid and Gradient Fill Colors

To change the color of a selected shape, click the **Shape Fill** button [*Drawing Tools Format* tab, *Shape Styles* group] to open the ***Theme Colors*** gallery (Figure 2-11). Notice the colors arranged in the first row. The first four colors represent background and text colors; however, you can use these colors for other slide objects as well. The remaining six colors represent accent colors. These colors appear when viewing gallery styles and some effect options such as *Glow*. Beneath each color on the first row is a column of lighter and darker shades (shown as percentages) of that color. When you point to any color, a *ScreenTip* shows its name.

Below the *Theme Colors* is a single row of ***Standard Colors*** arranged in the order of a rainbow. When standard colors are used, they remain in effect even if *Theme Colors* change.

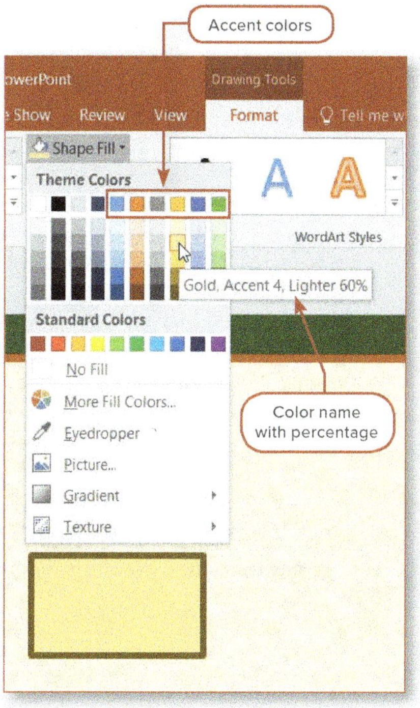

2-11 *Theme Colors* gallery

Gradient colors blend two or more colors together. Using the *Format Shape* pane, you can select from preset colors or customize your own gradient color by changing the colors and how they blend.

HOW TO: Change Gradient Colors Using the Format Shape Pane

1. Select a shape and click the **Shape Fill** button [*Drawing Tools Format* tab, *Shape Styles* group].
2. Select **Gradient** to select from a gallery of light and dark variations of the current fill color that blend the colors in different directions (Figure 2-12).
3. Click **More Gradients** at the bottom of the gallery to open the *Format Shape* pane to customize the colors.
4. Choose **Gradient fill** and make selections under *Fill* options from the following:
   - *Preset gradients:* Theme color variations (Figure 2-13)
   - *Type: Linear, Radial, Rectangular,* or *Path*
   - *Direction:* Options change based on the selected *Type*.
   - *Angle:* The percentage changes with each *Type* and *Direction*.
   - *Gradient stops:* Shapes on the gradient bar that you can move to control where colors change (Figure 2-14)
5. Select a *Gradient stop* and change its settings to control color blending:
   - *Delete a stop:* Click the **Remove Gradient Stop** button or drag the stop down to remove it from the gradient bar.
   - *Add a stop:* Click the **Add Gradient Stop** button or click the gradient bar where you want the stop to appear.
   - *Color:* Select the stop, and then change the color.
   - *Position:* Enter a different percentage or drag the stop on the gradient bar to change its position.
   - *Transparency:* Click the arrows to change the percentage. When *Transparency* is 0%, the color is opaque (solid). As the percentage increases, the color becomes increasingly transparent and more of the background color shows through.
   - *Brightness:* Click the arrows to change the percentage. As the percentage decreases from 100%, the color softens.
6. Check **Rotate with shape** to maintain the color settings when a shape or text is rotated so it angles on the slide.
7. Select **No line** or **Solid line** under *Line* options to control whether or not an outline shows around a shape or text.
8. Click the **X** at the top of the pane to close the *Format Shape* pane.

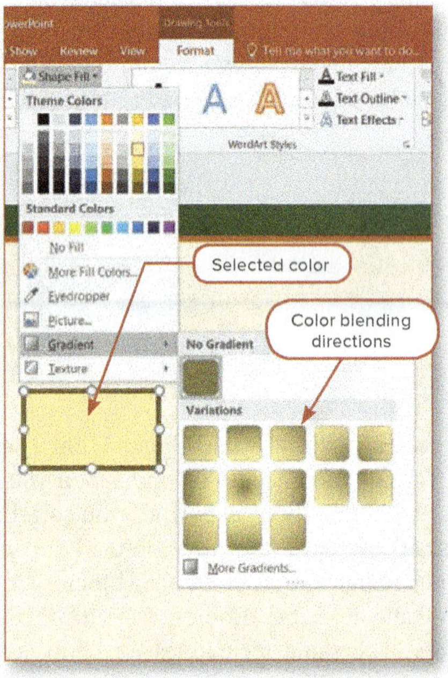

2-12 Gradient color variations for the selected color

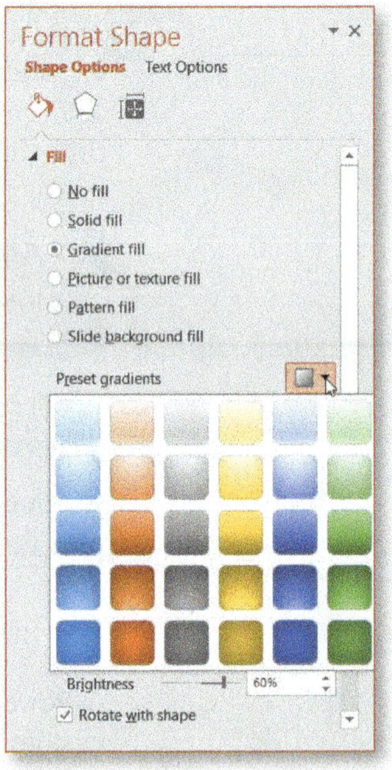

2-13 Preset gradients based on theme colors

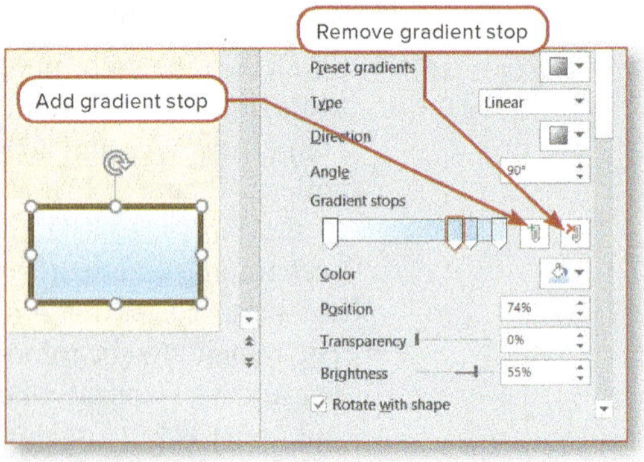

2-14 Gradient stops

MORE INFO

To apply gradient colors to *WordArt*, click the **Text Fill** button [*Drawing Tools Format* tab, *WordArt Styles* group] and select **Gradient** or select **Text Options**, then **Gradient fill** on the *Format Shape* pane.

Select Custom Colors

The *Colors* dialog box provides many solid color options on two tabs so you can either pick from displayed colors or mix a custom color. The new color appears in the lower right corner so you can compare it to the original color. Custom colors are not affected by any changes made to theme colors.

HOW TO: Use the Standard Tab to Select a Color

1. Select a shape and click the **Shape Fill** button [*Home* tab, *Drawing* group or *Drawing Tools Format* tab, *Shape Styles* group].
2. Click **More Fill Colors** to open the *Colors* dialog box.
   - Select the *Standard* tab (Figure 2-15).
   - Colors are arranged in a honeycomb shape with colors blending from white to black below.
3. Click a color to apply it and notice the *New* color that appears on the right above the *Current* color.
4. Adjust the *Transparency* as needed.
5. Click **OK** to apply the new color.

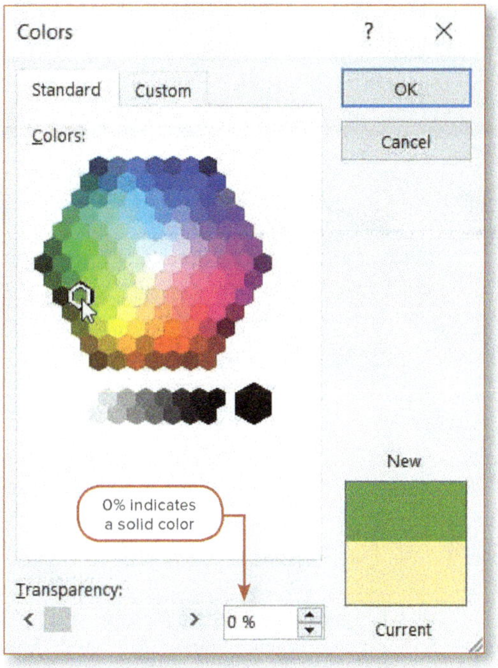

2-15 *Standard* tab in *Colors* dialog box

When you need more precision in selecting a color, use the *Custom* tab on the *Colors* dialog box. Colors are arranged like a rainbow, and you drag a crosshair to select a different color. You drag the crosshair up or down to change the color intensity and then move a slider to adjust how light or dark the color appears. Color model information is shown on the *Custom* tab also. The ***RGB model*** is typically used for computer displays and colors are formed by blending values of the three numbers for *Red*, *Green*, and *Blue*. Highly saturated colors at the top have higher number values (255 maximum). You can use these numbers to match colors in different shapes and in different presentations.

HOW TO: Use the Custom Tab to Mix a Color

1. Select a shape and click the **Shape Fill** button [*Home* tab, *Drawing* group or *Drawing Tools Format* tab, *Shape Styles* group].
2. Click **More Fill Colors** to open the *Colors* dialog box.

3. Click the *Custom* tab (Figure 2-16) and a crosshair is positioned for the *Current* color.
    - Drag the crosshair horizontally to select a different color. Notice the new color that appears on the right above the *Current* color.
    - When the crosshair is at the top, colors are highly ***saturated*** (intense and vibrant).
    - As you move the crosshair down, colors become less saturated (duller and less intense).
4. Drag the slider on the right to adjust the ***luminosity*** (lightness or brightness).
    - Drag up to add white and increase the luminosity.
    - Drag down to add black and decrease the luminosity.
5. Adjust the *Transparency* as needed.
6. Click **OK** to apply the new color.

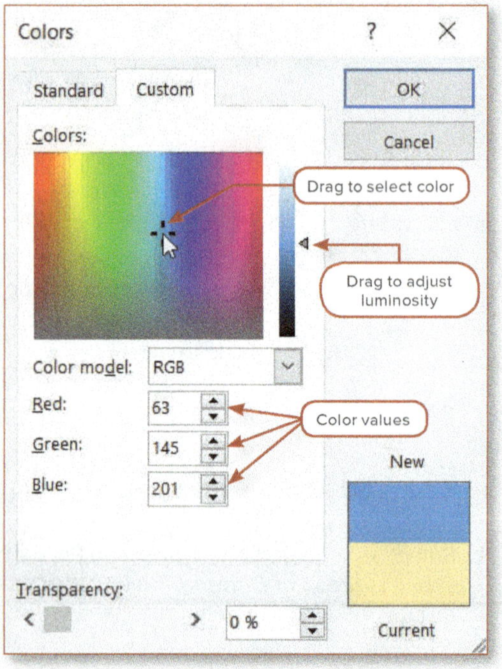

2-16 ***Custom* tab in *Colors* dialog box**

MORE INFO

Use the *Custom* tab in the *Colors* dialog box if you need to enter specific RGB values to match a color such as a color used for a business or college logo.

Use the Eyedropper for Color Matching

You can match the exact color of an object in PowerPoint with the ***Eyedropper*** and apply it to a shape.

HOW TO: Use the Eyedropper

1. Place the object, such as a picture, and the shape to be changed on the same slide. Select the shape.
2. Click the **Shape Fill** button [*Home* tab, *Drawing* group or *Drawing Tools Format* tab, *Shape Styles* group] and select **Eyedropper**.
3. Move your pointer (now an Eyedropper) around in the picture and a live preview of each color appears. Pause to see a *ScreenTip* showing the *RGB* (Red Green Blue) values (Figure 2-17).
4. Click to select a color and it is applied to your selected shape.

Or

5. Press **Esc** to cancel the *Eyedropper* without selecting a color.

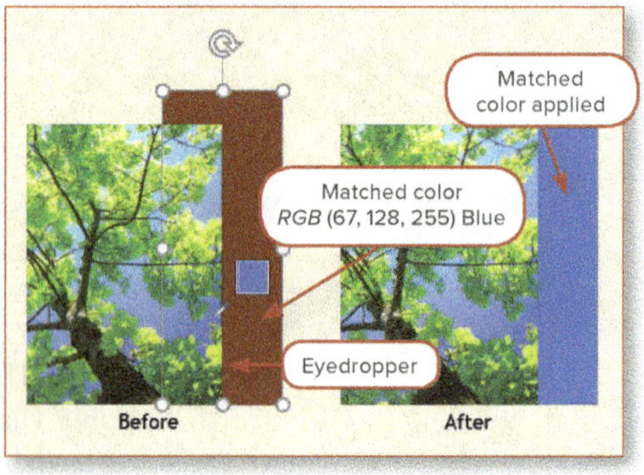

2-17 ***Eyedropper* live preview and *RGB* colors**

To match a color anywhere on your computer screen, left-click and hold as you drag the Eyedropper to other areas of the screen outside of PowerPoint.

Apply Picture, Texture, or Pattern Fills

You can fill shapes with more than colors. The following options are available by clicking the **Shape Fill** button [*Drawing Tools Format* tab, *Shape Styles* group] or from the *Format Shape* pane. With *WordArt*, the *Text Fill* button [*Drawing Tools Format* tab, *WordArt Styles* group] is used.

- ***Picture fill:*** Fills the shape with a picture from a file or from an online search
- ***Texture fill:*** Applies an image such as woven fabric or wood
- ***Pattern fill:*** Applies a mixture of two colors in various dotted or crosshatch designs

HOW TO: Apply Picture, Texture, or Pattern Fills

1. Select a shape and click the **Shape Fill** button [*Home* tab, *Drawing* group or *Drawing Tools Format* tab, *Shape Styles* group].
2. From the drop-down list, select **Picture** to open the *Insert Pictures* dialog box. Browse or search for a picture and click **Insert**. The picture fills the shape.

Or

3. From the drop-down list, select **Texture** to open the gallery (Figure 2-18). Click a texture to fill the shape or click **More Textures** to open the *Format Shape* pane.
   - Select **Picture or texture fill** and then click the **File** button or the **Online** button to search for textures that are saved as a picture.

Or

4. Select a shape and right-click. Select **Format Shape** from the callout menu to open the *Format Shape* pane.
   - Click **Fill**, if necessary, to display *Fill* options.
   - Select **Pattern fill** (Figure 2-19).
   - Click a pattern to fill the shape.
   - Change *Foreground* and *Background* colors as needed.
   - Click other patterns to see how different these colors look in different patterns.
5. Close the *Format Shape* pane.

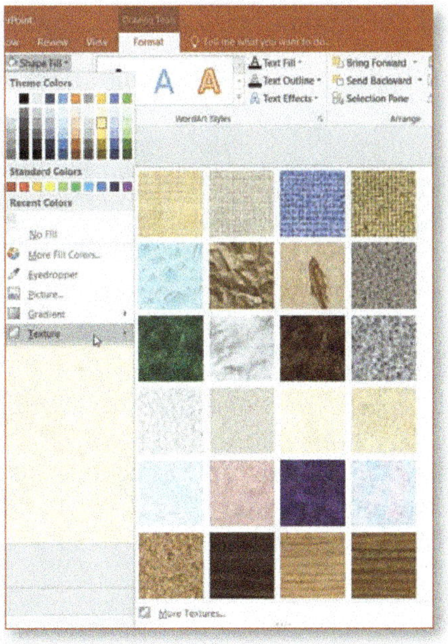

2-18 *Texture* fills

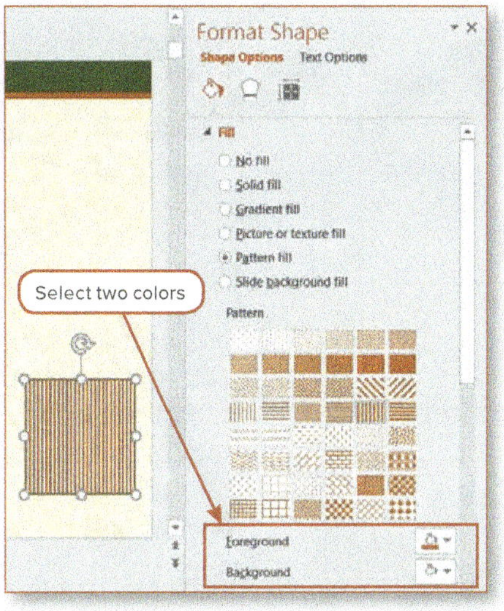

2-19 *Pattern* fills on the *Format Shape* pane

SLO 2.2

Applying WordArt Styles and Text Effects

You can apply interesting ***text effects*** for many purposes. For example, you can make slide titles more attractive and easier to read, or you can provide a bold focal point on a slide. One way is to start by inserting ***WordArt***.

▸ HOW TO: Apply WordArt Styles

1. Click the **WordArt** button [*Insert* tab, *Text* group] to open the *WordArt Styles* gallery (Figure 2-20).
   - The gallery has preset text effects showing a variety of solid, gradient, and pattern fill colors.
2. Click to select a *WordArt* style.
   - A text box displays on your slide with sample text that you edit to create a *WordArt* object (Figure 2-21).
3. Use the *Font* group [*Home* tab] to apply the following character formatting:
   - Select a different font or attribute such as bold or italic.
   - Change the font size by entering a point size or using the **Increase Font Size** and **Decrease Font Size** buttons.
   - Click the **Character Spacing** button to control the distance between letters. You can expand or condense the spacing.

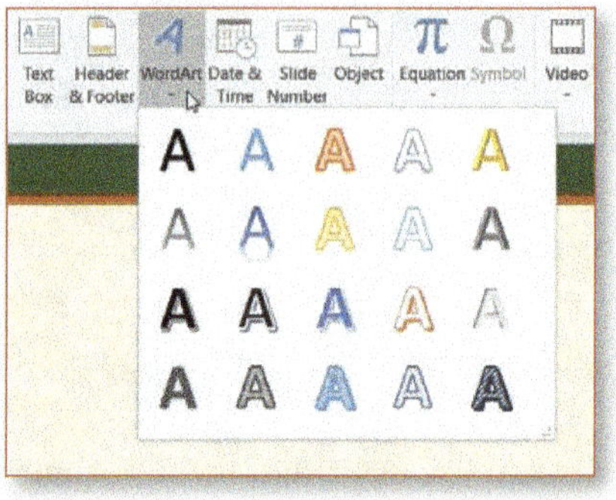

2-20 *WordArt Styles* gallery

2-21 *WordArt* as it first appears

MORE INFO

When using text in a large size, *Tight* character spacing conserves space yet keeps the text easy to read.

You can also start with text in a placeholder or text box and then apply text effects. With either method, you use commands on the *WordArt Styles* group [*Drawing Tools Format* tab] (Figure 2-22) to customize your text. These commands—*Text Fill, Text Outline, and Text Effects*—are similar to the *Shape* commands.

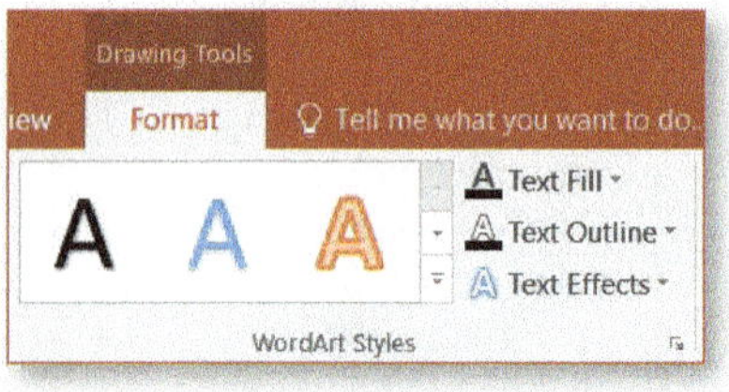

2-22 *WordArt Styles* group

▸ HOW TO: Apply Text Effects to Existing Text

1. Select a *WordArt* object or text in a placeholder or text box.
   - Click the **More** button [*Drawing Tools Format* tab, *WordArt Styles* group] to open the *Styles* gallery.
   - Point to a style to see a live preview applied to your text (Figure 2-23).
   - Click a style to apply it.

2. Use the *WordArt Styles* group [*Drawing Tools Format* tab] to change colors and add special effects:
   - Click the **Text Fill** button to select **Theme** or other color options.
   - Click the **Text Outline** button to select **Theme** or other color options as well as line weight and style.
   - Click the **Text Effects** button and select from *Shadow, Reflection, Glow, Bevel, 3D Rotation*, or *Transform* effects and then choose the option you prefer.

Or

3. Select a *WordArt* object or text box and right-click to open the context menu. Click **Format Shape** to open the *Format Shape* pane.
   - Select **Shape Options** to change *Fill* or *Line* options.
   - Select **Text Options** to change *Text Fill* or *Text Outline* options.

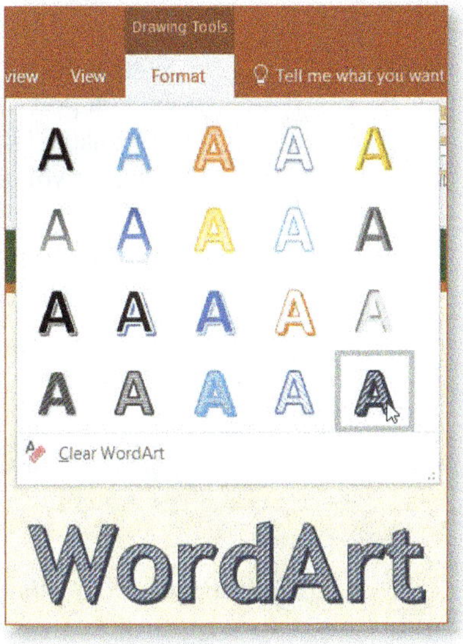

2-23 ***WordArt*** **object with a style applied**

> **MORE INFO**
>
> If the *WordArt Styles* gallery is not open on your *Drawing Tools Format* tab, click the **Quick Styles** button.

Changing the text outline color and increasing line weight emphasizes the outline just as it does on shapes. Different line styles can create interesting effects. Using pictures or patterns as fill colors can add a creative touch when text is shown in a large size. A variety of different colors and effects are shown in Figure 2-24.

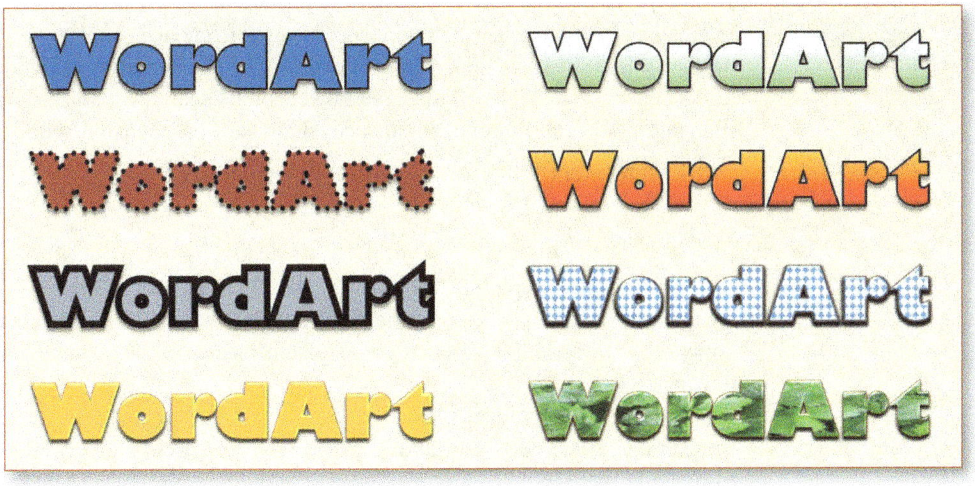

2-24 Sample fill and line effects

> **ANOTHER WAY**
>
> Select the text in a *WordArt* object and right-click. Click **Format Text Effects** from the context menu to open the *Format Shape* pane with *Text Options* listed.

Transform effects are unique to text and are used to warp a word or phrase to different shapes or to follow a path. For example, text can angle, flow in a circle, and arc up or down. As you point to different *Transform* effects, a live preview shows how your text will look in that shape. Once a *Transform* effect has been applied, text size is not limited to the font size because you can drag the *WordArt* sizing handles. *Transform* effects also provide one or more yellow adjustment handles that control the slant of letters or the curve of text.

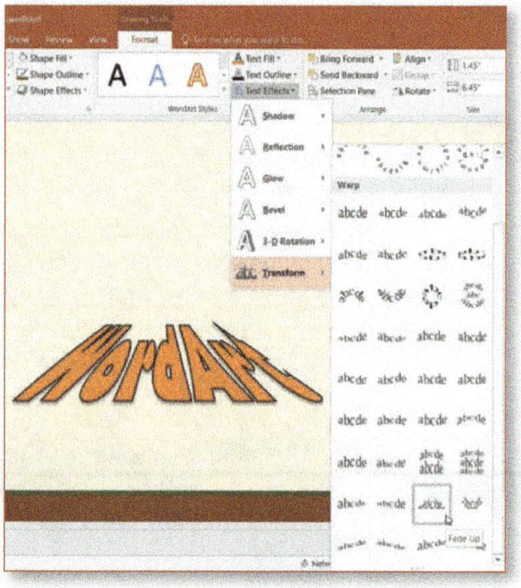

2-25 *Transform Fade Up* effect applied

HOW TO: Apply a Transform Effect

1. Select a *WordArt* object.
2. Click the **Text Effects** button [*Format* tab, *WordArt Styles* group].
3. Select **Transform** from the drop-down list (Figure 2-25) to open the *Transform* gallery.
4. Point to an effect to see a live preview applied to your text.
5. Click an effect to apply it.
6. Adjust as needed using sizing and adjustment handles.

SLO 2.3

Working with Pictures

In Chapter 1, you learned how to insert pictures from files, change their size, and align them on the slide. In this section, you use a variety of photo editing techniques to enhance a picture's appearance. You will also use PowerPoint's search capabilities to find images to help illustrate presentation concepts and consider various licensing requirements for the use of images available online.

Apply Picture Styles

When you select a picture on a slide, the *Picture Tools Format* tab becomes available. Different *Styles* allow you to frame pictures, give them a 3D appearance, add a reflection, or apply other treatments. You can choose from preset options using the *Picture Effects* drop-down galleries.

When you use multiple pictures in a presentation, try to maintain consistency and use the same or a similar style for each of them. If you use different styles, be sure you have a reason for making them look different so the effects do not appear random.

HOW TO: Apply a Picture Style

1. Select a picture and click the **Picture Tools Format** tab.
2. Click the **More** button on the gallery [*Picture Styles* group] to see the predefined effects (Figure 2-26).

3. Drag your pointer over the styles to see a live preview applied to your picture. A *ScreenTip* showing the style name appears.
4. Click a style to apply it to your picture.
5. Change to a different style by selecting a new style from the gallery.

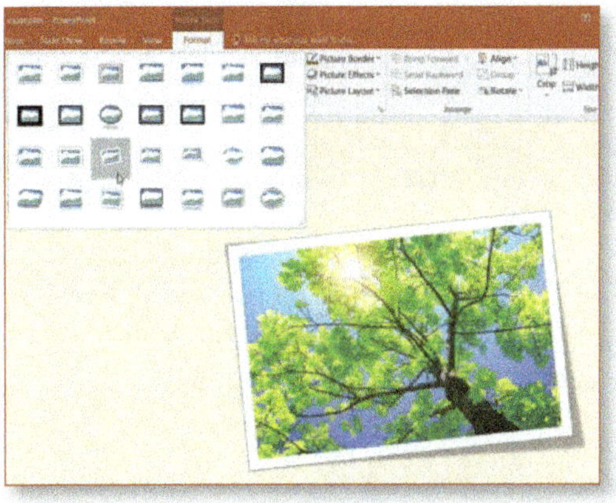

2-26 Picture style applied

Picture Effects are similar to *Shape Effects*. Each different effect has many options you can adjust.

▸HOW TO: Apply or Modify Picture Effects

1. Select a picture and click the **Picture Effects** button [*Picture Tools Format* tab, *Picture Styles* group].
2. Point to each effect in the drop-down list to see a gallery (Figure 2-27) that provides many different options.
3. Select **Options** at the bottom of each gallery to open the *Format Picture* pane where you can make changes to fine-tune a specific effect.
   - Right-click the picture and select **Format Picture** from the context menu to open the *Format Picture* pane.
4. Remove a picture style by selecting the picture and clicking the **Reset Picture** button [*Picture Tools Format* tab, *Adjust* group].

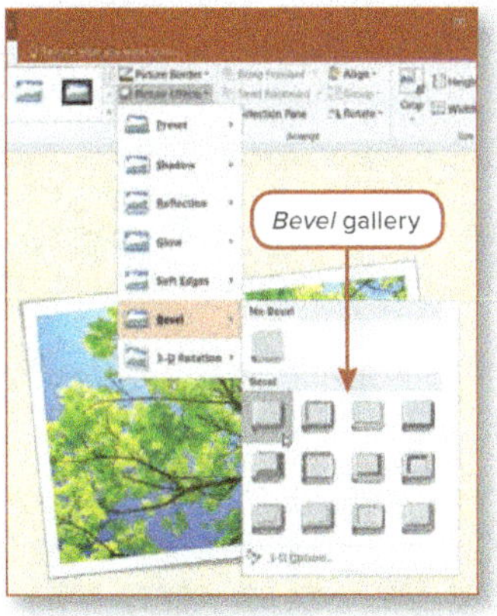

2-27 *Picture Effects*

Crop a Picture

You can ***crop*** (trim) unwanted areas of a selected picture by dragging black ***cropping handles*** on the corners and sides of the picture that appear when you click the **Crop** button. When you point to these handles, your pointer changes to a black shape that resembles the cropping handle. Be careful when dragging to be sure you are moving a cropping handle and not a sizing handle.

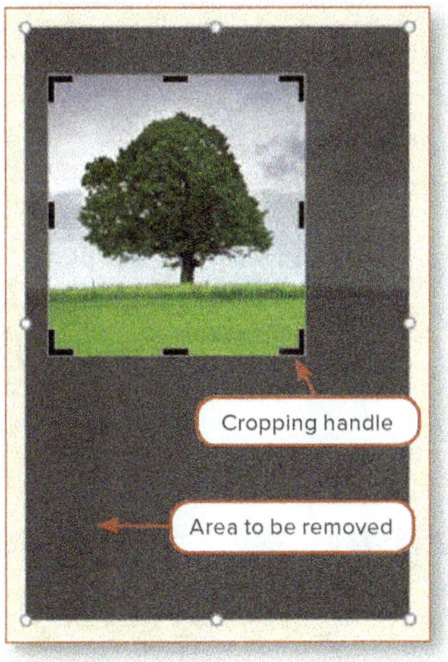

2-28 Cropped area of a picture

▸HOW TO: Crop a Picture

1. Select a picture and click the **Crop** button [*Picture Tools Format* tab, *Size* group].
2. Drag one or more cropping handles toward the center of the picture; the area to be removed from the edges is grayed out (Figure 2-28).
3. Click the **Crop** button again to accept this change.

Always check your pictures and crop them as needed to be sure they have a strong focal point. Excess detail clutters a picture and does not help your viewers quickly grasp what you want them to see.

Change Picture Colors

Pictures are digital photographs usually made up of many colors to achieve the realism that they portray. PowerPoint's *Color* feature allows you to vary picture colors. For example, you might want to make a picture look old, or fade the picture so text over the picture is easy to read.

HOW TO: Change Picture Colors

1. Select a picture you want to change.
2. Click the **Color** button [*Picture Tools Format* tab, *Adjust* group] to open a gallery showing different color options (Figure 2-29).
   - The current option within each group is highlighted.
3. Select one or more options to customize your picture colors:
   - ***Color Saturation:*** Colors are more muted as you move from the center to the left as saturation becomes lower; colors are more intense as you move from the center to the right as saturation increases.
   - ***Color Tone:*** Colors on the left have cool tones and lower temperature values; colors on the right have warm tones and higher values.
   - ***Recolor:*** Options on the first row include *Grayscale*, *Sepia*, *Washout*, and percentages of *Black and White*. The second and third rows display dark and light monotone variations of accent colors.

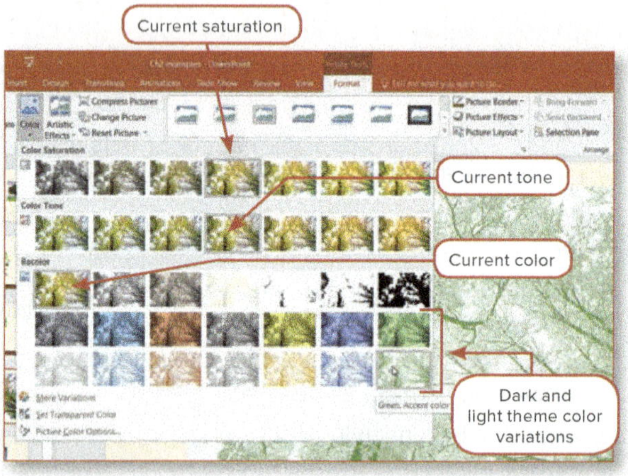

2-29 ***Color gallery***

4. Click **Picture Color Options** at the bottom of the gallery to open the *Format Picture* pane with the **Picture Color** options displayed.

Set a Transparent Color

An image with a white background works well on a slide with a white background (or on a typical Word document) because you see just the image. However, a white background can detract from an image if you place it on a slide background with a contrasting color.

Use the ***Set Transparent Color*** feature to remove a single-color background. Because this feature removes only one color, it does not work well for pictures that have a lot of detail and many colors.

HOW TO: Set a Transparent Color

1. Select a picture.
2. Click the **Color** button [*Picture Tools Format* tab, *Adjust* group].

3. Click **Set Transparent Color** and your pointer changes to a pen tool.
4. Point to the area of the picture you want to remove and click.
   - All of the pixels with that color value disappear, revealing what is behind the picture (Figure 2-30).

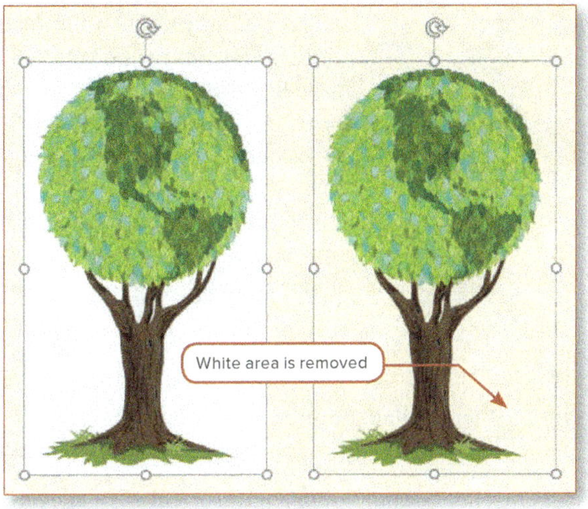

2-30 *Set Transparent Color* applied

Compress Pictures

Pictures can greatly increase your presentation file size. You can ***compress*** single pictures or all pictures at one time to reduce the picture resolution depending on the quality you need. For print you generally need a higher resolution, and for on-screen viewing a lower resolution is usually fine. Resolution options are expressed in *pixels per inch (ppi)* and are based on *Target output* such as *Print (220 ppi)* or *Web (150 ppi)*. The ppi measurement for viewing on screen is very different from the *dots per inch (dpi)* print measurement for printing on paper. An inexpensive printer can produce 1,200 or more dpi, which produces crisp, clear letterforms that are easy to read on paper.

Deleting cropped areas of pictures removes unused information and, therefore, reduces file size. Compression only affects how the pictures display in the presentation file and not the original picture files.

HOW TO: Compress Picture File Size

1. Select a picture.
2. Click the **Compress Picture** button [*Picture Tools Format* tab, *Adjust* group] to open the *Compress Pictures* dialog box (Figure 2-31).
3. Deselect **Apply only to this picture** if you want the compression to apply to all pictures in the presentation.
4. Select **Delete cropped areas of pictures** if you have cropped pictures.
5. Select the appropriate *Target output*. Some options will be grayed out if they are not available for your selected picture.
6. Click **OK** to close the dialog box.

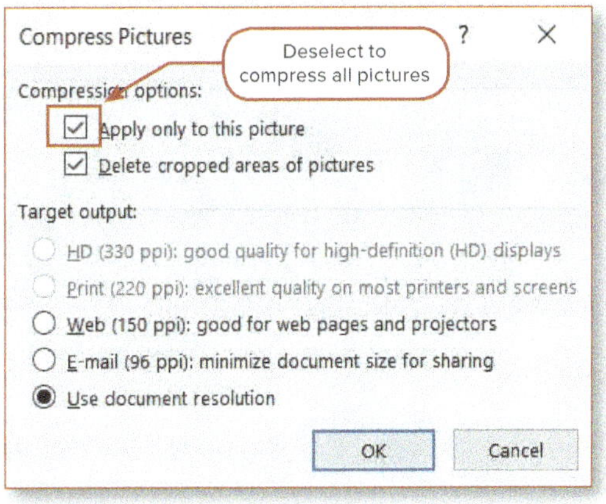

2-31 *Compress Pictures* dialog box

Insert Online Pictures and Illustrations

Click the **Picture** button [*Insert* tab, *Images* group] to open the *Insert Pictures* dialog box where you can search for pictures (digital photographs or illustrations) that you have saved in folders on your computer or any other location. Click the **Online Picture** button [*Insert* tab,

Images group] to open the *Insert Pictures* dialog box where you can search the web using *Bing Image Search* or search on your *OneDrive* location. Pictures you find on the web may have licensing restrictions or require fees to use them. The *Insert Pictures* dialog box does not provide a way to filter the results based on your intended use.

When the search results appear, each picture has a *ScreenTip* identifying its name and a magnifying button you can click to temporarily increase the thumbnail size.

In the lower left corner of the dialog box, the picture name, pixel size, and web source appears. A ***pixel*** is an abbreviated term for *picture element*, a single unit of information about color.

HOW TO: Search for and Insert a Picture or Illustration

1. Click the **Online Pictures** button [*Insert* tab, *Images* group] (Figure 2-32) to open the *Insert Pictures* dialog box.
2. Type the search word In the *Bing Image Search* box (Figure 2-33).
3. Click the **Search** button (or press **Enter**) to activate the search.
   - Thumbnails of all the pictures that match your search word appear that are licensed under Creative Commons (Figure 2-34). **CC Only** shows in the search box.
4. Click the drop-down arrow by **CC Only** and select **All Images** to expand your search.
5. Click to select the picture you want.
6. Press **Ctrl** while you click to select more than one picture.
7. Click the **Insert** button. The picture downloads and the *Insert Pictures* dialog box closes.

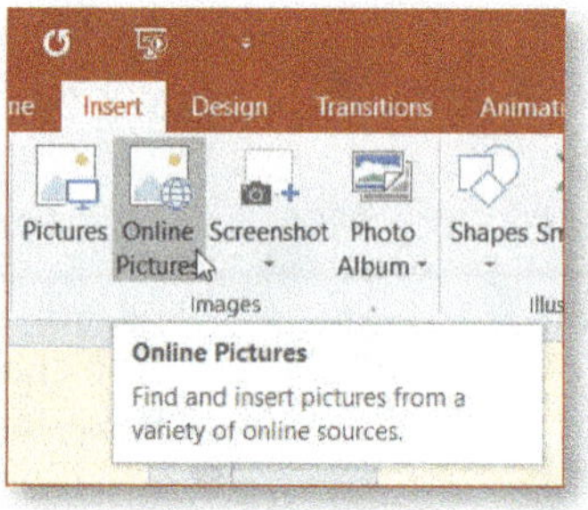

2-32 *Online Pictures* button

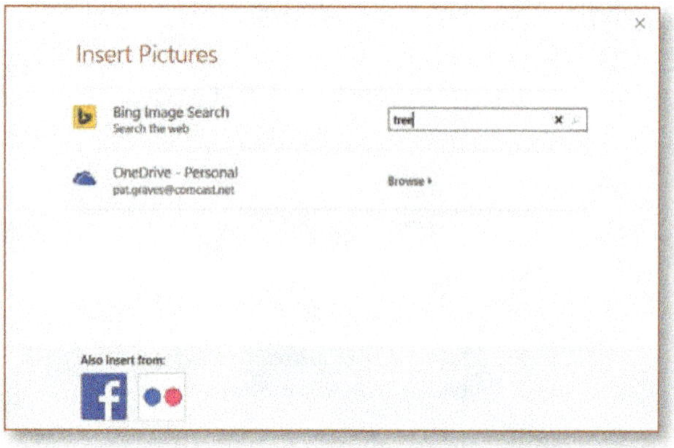

2-33 *Insert Pictures* dialog box

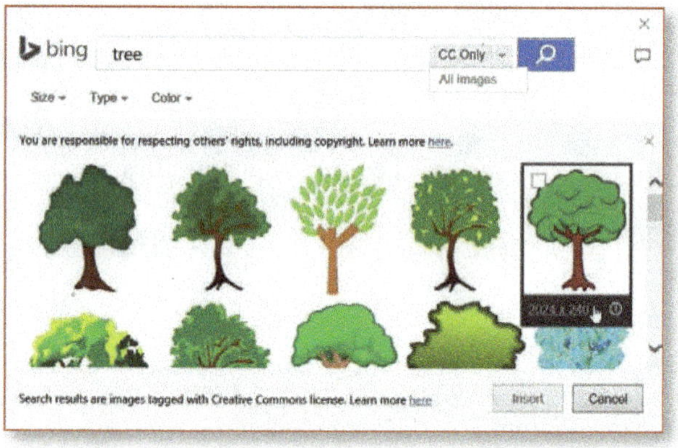

2-34 Pictures from search

MORE INFO

Open the *Insert Pictures* dialog box when creating a new slide by clicking the **Online Pictures** icon on the content placeholder.

MORE INFO

Be careful to select images that are appropriate for your topic. Some cartoon-like illustrations look amateurish and may not be appropriate for academic or business presentations.

Creative Commons Licensing

A Creative Commons (CC) license enables the free distribution of copyrighted work when the creator wants to give people the right to copy, use, or remix by building upon the work. This right is usually for non-commercial purposes. The creator can make requirements for attribution so the creator is credited for the work. You can read more about these requirements at https://creativecommons.org.

You can activate a search on the Creative Commons site for images, music, and video using Google, Google Images, or other search engines to locate work listed with the CC license. However, the results cannot be guaranteed because no registration is required to use a CC license. You still need to contact the creator (copyright holder) directly or contact the web site where you found the content.

Another way to find images that you can save for future use is through Microsoft's *Bing* search engine at www.bing.com. Select an **Images** search, type a word in the search box, press **Enter**, and the results display. Click the link for **License** (Figure 2-35) to filter your results to one of the following criteria:

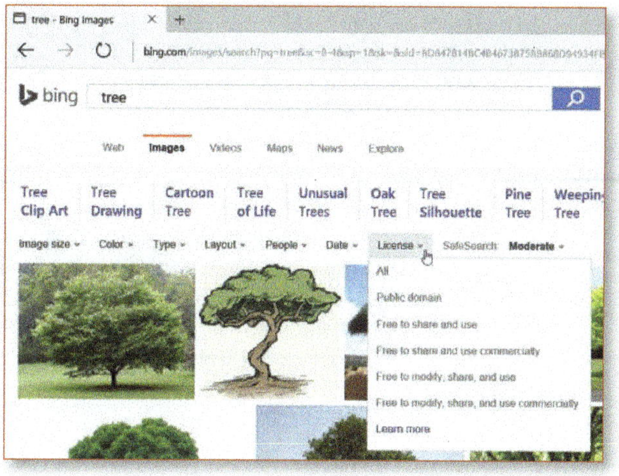

2-35 Image search at Bing.com

- Public Domain
- Free to share and use
- Free to share and use commercially
- Free to modify, share, and use
- Free to modify, share, and use commercially

Bing does not verify CC licensing; you still need to go to the image's web site to determine the actual licensing being used.

PAUSE & PRACTICE: POWERPOINT 2-1

When Gerod Sunderland shares his landscaping proposal with homeowners, he provides detailed printed information and uses a presentation to illustrate concepts. For this project, you add pictures and other objects to his presentation and apply a variety of styles and colors to enhance the content.

File Needed: ***LandscapingProposal-02.pptx*** *(Student data files are available in the* Library *of your SIMnet account.)*
Completed Project File Name: ***[your initials] PP P2-1.pptx***

1. Open the presentation ***LandscapingProposal-02***.
2. Save the presentation as [your initials] PP P2-1.

3. Add a rectangle.
   a. Display slide 1 and click the **Shapes** button [*Insert* tab, *Illustrations* group].
   b. Select the **Rectangle** shape.
   c. Click and drag to draw a rectangle across the top of the slide.
   d. Change the rectangle *Height* to **.4"** and *Width* to **13.33"** [*Drawing Tools Format* tab, *Size* group].
   e. Click the **Shape Fill** button [*Drawing Tools Format* tab, *Shape Styles* group] and select **Green, Accent 6** (Figure 2-36).
   f. Click the **Shape Outline** button [*Drawing Tools Format* tab, *Shape Styles* group] and select **No Outline**.
   g. Position the rectangle below the orange line.

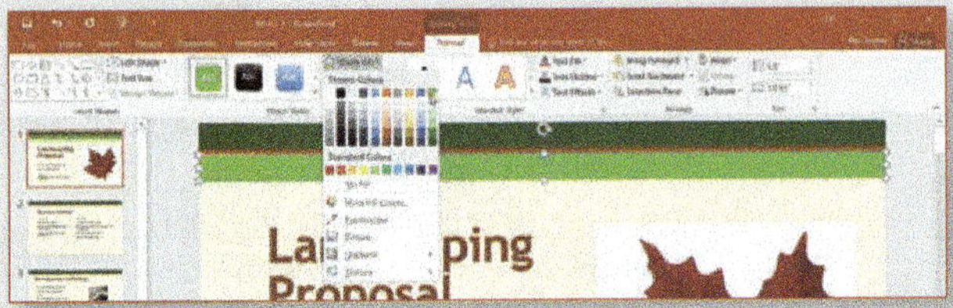

2-36 Change *Shape Fill* color

4. Add text effects.
   a. Select the title on slide 1 and click the **Text Effects** button [*Drawing Tools Format* tab, *WordArt Styles* group].
   b. Select **Bevel** and then **Circle** (Figure 2-37).
   c. Click the **Text Effects** button again, select **Shadow**, and then select **Offset Diagonal Bottom Right**.

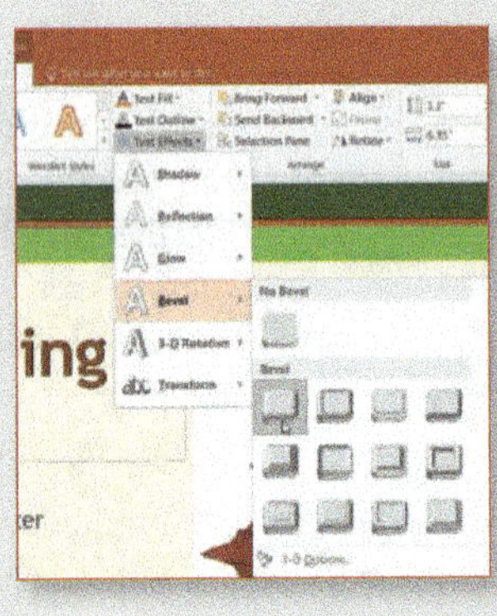

2-37 Apply *Text Effects*

5. Make a picture color transparent.
   a. Select the picture of a leaf on slide 1.
   b. Click **Color** [*Picture Tools Format* tab, *Adjust* group].
   c. Select **Set Transparent Color** and your pointer changes to a pen tool.
   d. Click the white area around the leaf so it becomes transparent (Figure 2-38).

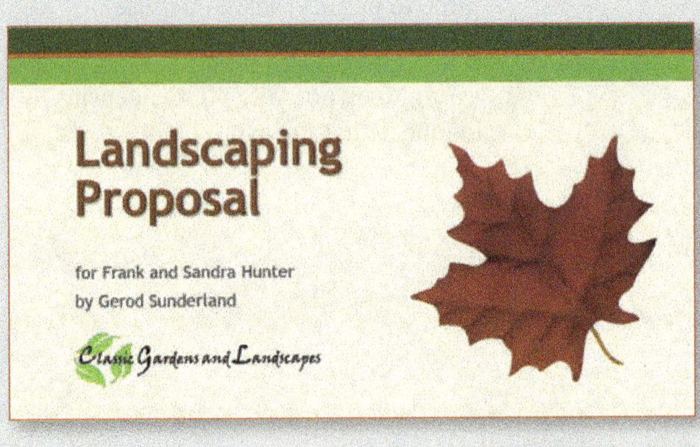

2-38 Completed slide 1

6. Apply effects and use the *Format Painter*.
   a. Display slide 2 and select the left list heading placeholder.
   b. Click the **Shape Fill** button [*Drawing Tools Format* tab, *Shape Styles* group] and select **Texture**.
   c. Click the **Papyrus** option (first row).
   d. Apply **Bold** [*Home* tab, *Font* group].
   e. With the placeholder still selected, click the **Format Painter** button [*Home* tab, *Clipboard* group]. Click the list heading placeholder on the right to apply the copied format.

7. Add a frame shape.
   a. Display slide 3. Click the **Shape** button [*Insert* tab, *Illustrations* group] and select the **Frame** shape under the *Basic Shapes* heading.
   b. Click and drag to draw a frame.
   c. Adjust the frame size (*Height* **1"** and *Width* **3.3"**) [*Drawing Tools Format* tab, *Size* group].
   d. With the frame selected, type Allow three days.
   e. Change the font size to **24 pt**.

8. Change to a different shape and color.
   a. Select the frame shape on slide 3. Click the **Edit Shape** button [*Drawing Tools Format* tab, *Insert Shapes* group] and select **Change Shape**.
   b. Click the **Bevel** shape under the *Basic Shapes* heading.
   c. Change the *Shape Fill* [*Drawing Tools Format* tab, *Shape Styles* group] to **Gold, Accent 4**.
   d. Position this shape below the bulleted text (Figure 2-39).

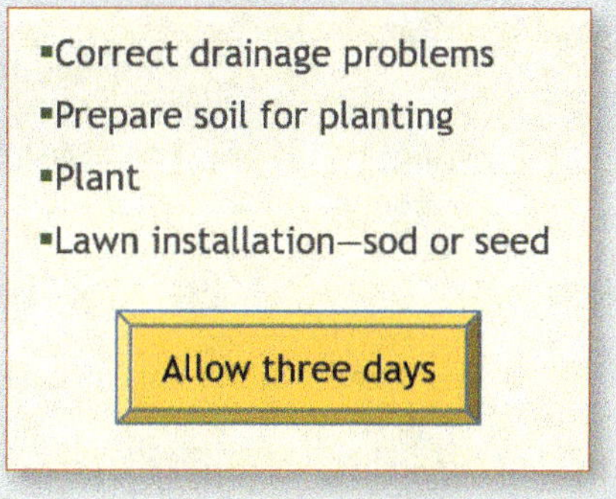

2-39 Text box positioned below list

9. Search for and insert an online picture on slide 3.
   a. Click the **Online Pictures** button [*Insert* tab, *Images* group] to open the *Insert Pictures* dialog box.
   b. Type the word soil in the *Bing Image Search* box.
   c. Click **Search** (or press **Enter**) to activate the search. Results will be similar to Figure 2-40.
   d. Locate a picture of a plant in soil similar to the one in Figure 2-41.
   e. Point to the picture and text appears at the bottom. Point to that area to see the picture's size information and its web address. Make a note of this web address for step 10. Click **Insert**.

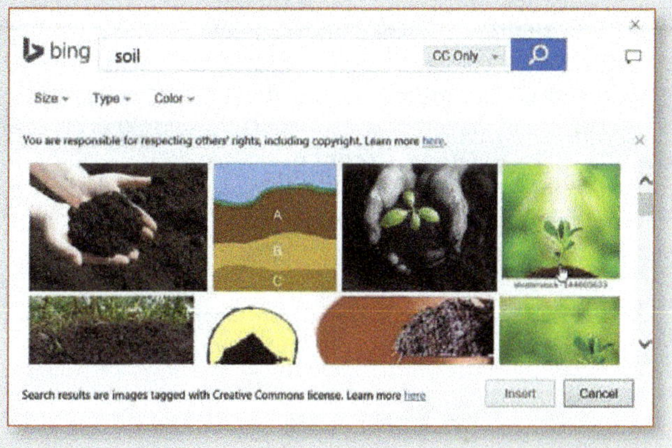

2-40 *Online Pictures* search results

10. Resize and crop a picture.
   a. Select the picture on slide 3 and change its size as needed to fit in the blank area on the right of the slide.
   b. Click the **Crop** button [*Picture Tools Format* tab, *Size* group] and crop a little space from all four edges to focus more on the plant.
   c. Click the **Crop** button again to accept the crop.
   d. Click the **More** button [*Picture Tools Format* tab, *Picture Styles* group] and select the **Rotated White** picture style.
   e. Insert a text box [*Insert tab, Text* group] and type the picture's source information.
   f. Position the text box below the picture (see Figure 2-41).

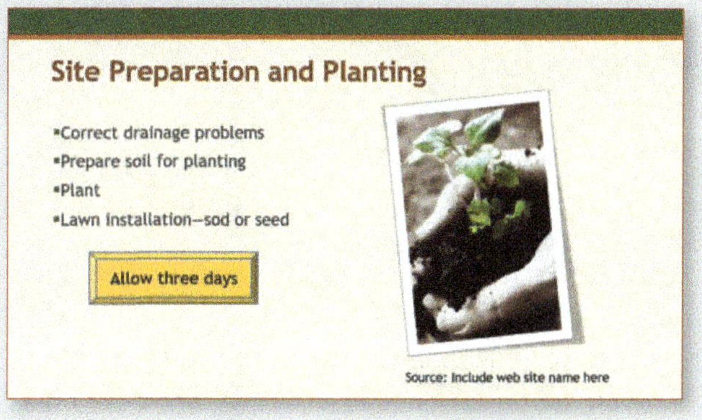

2-41 Completed slide 3

11. Compress a picture to reduce presentation file size.
   a. Select the picture on slide 3 and click **Compress Pictures** [*Picture Tools Format* tab, *Adjust* group].
   b. Deselect **Apply only to this picture**.
   c. Select **Use document resolution** for the *Target output*.
   d. Click **OK**.

12. Add *WordArt* text.
    a. Display slide 8. Click the **WordArt** button [*Insert* tab, *Text* group].
    b. Select the **Gradient Fill – Gold, Accent 4, Outline – Accent 4** style from the style gallery.
    c. Type Thank you for your business! in the *WordArt* text box.
    d. Move the *WordArt* object so it is at the top of the picture (Figure 2-42).
    e. Change the *Character Spacing* [*Home* tab, *Font* group] to **Tight**.

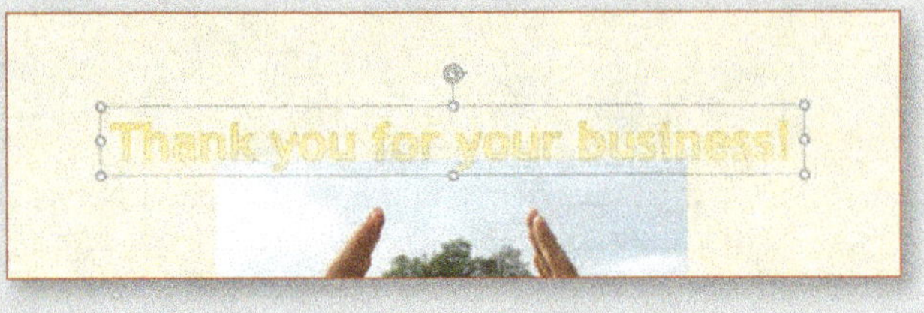

2-42 ***WordArt*** **with gradient fill applied**

13. Change the *WordArt* gradient fill and outline colors.
    a. Select the *WordArt* object, if necessary, and click the **Text Fill** button [*Drawing Tools Format* tab, *WordArt Styles* group]. Select **Gradient** and click **More Gradients** to open the *Format Shape* pane. All gradient options appear in the pane.
    b. Select the second gradient stop (at Position **4%**) and click the **Remove gradient stop** button.
    c. Select the left gradient stop (at Position **0%**) and change the color to **Green, Accent 6, Lighter 40%**.
    d. Select the right gradient stop and change the color to **Green, Accent 6, Darker 50%** (Figure 2-43).
    e. Close the *Format Shape* pane.
    f. Select the *WordArt* object, if necessary, and click the **Text Outline** button [*Drawing Tools Format* tab, *WordArt Styles* group]. Change the outline color to **Black, Text 1**.

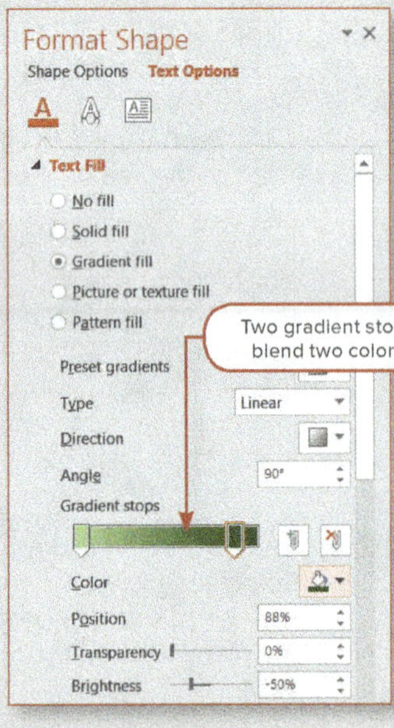

2-43 ***Format Shape*** **pane**

14. Apply a *Transform* effect to the *WordArt*.
    a. Click the **Text Effects** button [*Drawing Tools Format* tab, *WordArt Styles* group]. From the drop-down list, select **Transform**. On the *Transform* gallery, click the **Deflate Bottom** effect (Figure 2-44).
    b. Resize the *WordArt* (*Height* **2"** and *Width* **10"**). Click **Align** [*Drawing Tools Format* tab, *Arrange* group] and click **Align Center** so the *WordArt* fits across the top of the picture (Figure 2-45).

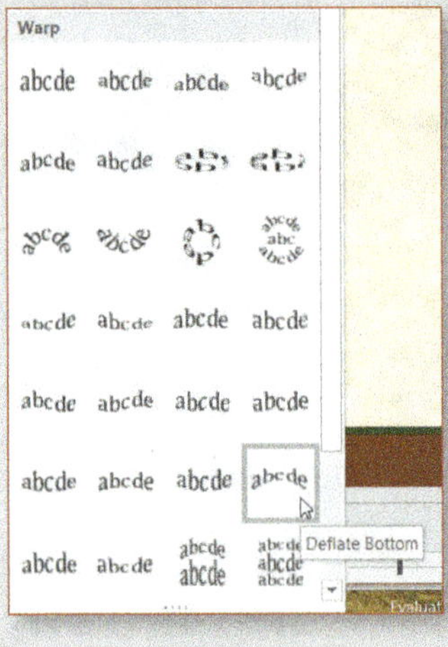

2-44 ***WordArt Transform*** **gallery**

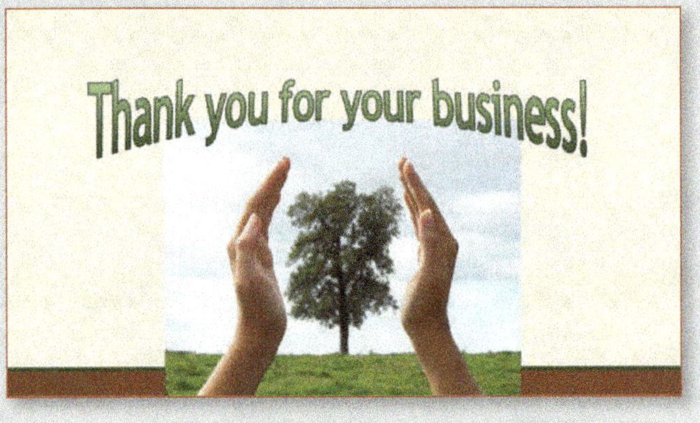

2-45 ***Deflate Bottom Transform*** **effect applied and adjusted**

15. Save and close your presentation (Figure 2-46).

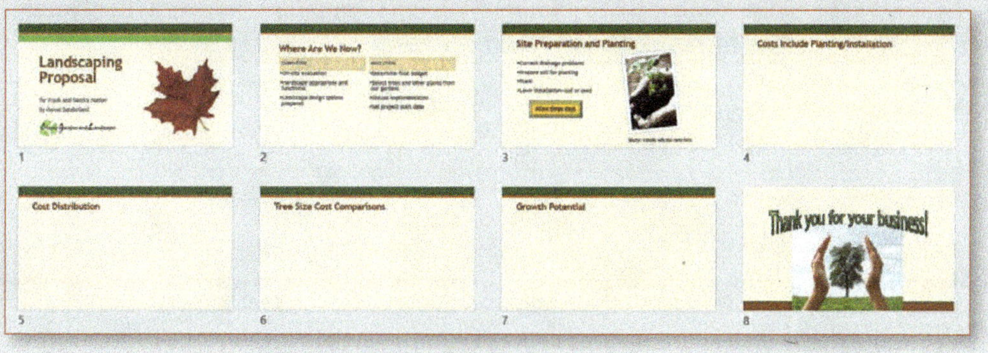

2-46 PP P2-1 completed

SLO 2.4

Creating a Table

Tables show data in an organized and easy-to-read format because information is arranged in ***columns*** (vertical) and ***rows*** (horizontal). The intersection of a column and row is a ***cell***. ***Border*** lines and ***shading*** show the table structure. Working with PowerPoint tables is much like working with tables in Word. You can create a table from a content placeholder when you create a new slide or by using options on the *Insert* tab.

Once you create a table, you can change its size as well as column width and row height. Use table formatting to emphasize the contents in different ways and help your audience interpret the data. If you plan to project your slides on a large screen, be sure your table information is concise so you can use a minimum font size of 20 points. If a table requires a lot of detailed information, then prepare the table as a full-page handout with body text at an 11–12 point size. You could prepare a PowerPoint slide to reference the handout as you explain the table, or perhaps show only a portion of the table on a slide.

Insert and Draw Methods

You can create the columns and rows of a table in different ways. Click the **Table** button [*Insert* tab, *Tables* group] to visually select columns and rows by dragging over them. The table dimensions (such as *3×4 Table* meaning three columns by four rows) are shown at the top of the drop-down list. By default, columns and rows appear on the slide with even sizing, but you can adjust column width and row height as you add information.

HOW TO: Insert a Table and Select Columns and Rows

1. Display the slide where you want the table.
2. Click the **Insert** tab.
3. Click the **Table** button [*Tables* group] to open the drop-down list.
4. Drag across and down to select the number of columns and rows you need (Figure 2-47).

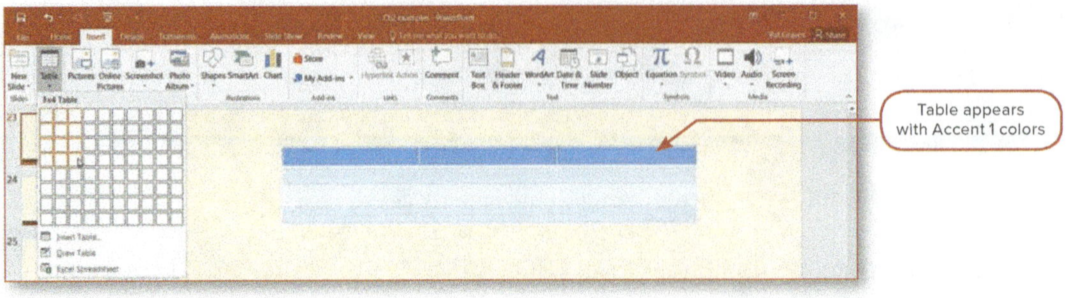

2-47 Table cells selected

5. Release the pointer to insert the table.

Use the **Insert Table** command [*Insert* tab, *Tables* group] to create a table by entering a specific number of columns and rows.

▶ HOW TO: Insert a Table and Enter the Number of Columns and Rows

1. Display the slide where you want to insert the table.
2. Click the **Insert** tab.
3. Click the **Table** button [*Tables* group] to open the drop-down list.
4. Click **Insert Table** and the *Insert Table* dialog box opens (Figure 2-48).
5. Specify the number of columns and rows you need.
6. Click **OK** to close the *Insert Table* dialog box and insert the table.

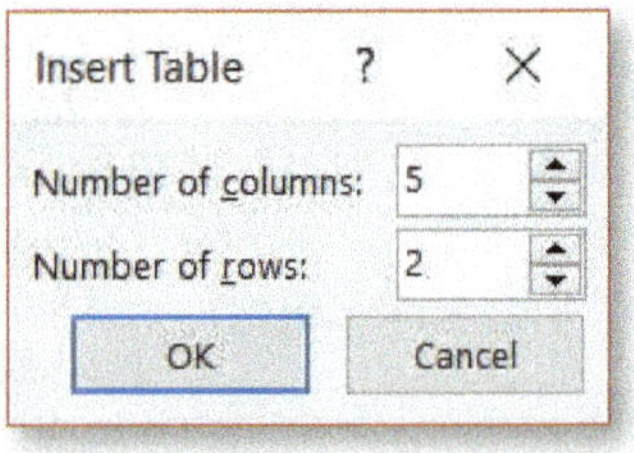

2-48 *Insert Table* dialog box

To insert a table on a new slide, click the **Table** icon in the empty content placeholder to open the *Insert Table* dialog box. Enter the number of columns and rows to create the table. Because of the placeholder size, the table width will be slightly wider than when you click the **Insert** button to create a table.

The final way to create a table is by drawing the table area and dividing it into columns and rows. This method works well when space is limited on the slide because of other content.

▶ HOW TO: Draw a Table

1. Display the slide where you want the table.
2. Click the **Insert** tab.
3. Click the **Table** button [*Tables* group] to open the drop-down list.
4. Click **Draw Table** and your pointer changes to a pen.
5. Drag the pen to draw the outside border of the table in the size you want.
6. Click the **Draw Table** button [*Table Tools Design* tab, *Draw Borders* group] to activate the pen again.

7. Drag the pen inside the table to insert horizontal and vertical lines that divide the table into rows and columns (Figure 2-49).
   - Start dragging near but not touching the outside border and the lines will expand on both ends to reach the borders.
8. Press **Esc** to turn off the pen tool.

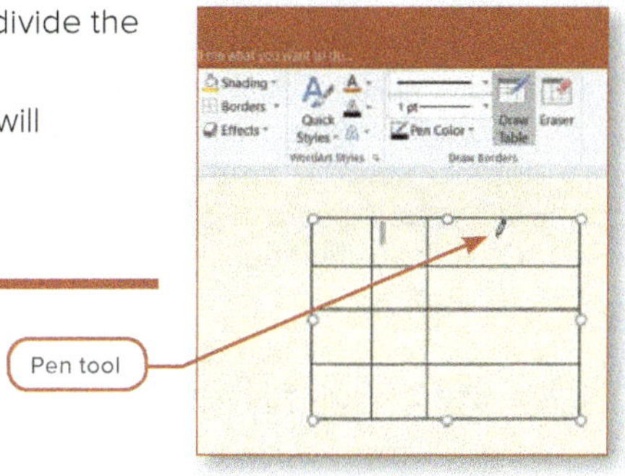

2-49 *Draw Table*

Regardless of the method you use to create a table, the *Table Tools Design* tab (Figure 2-50) and *Table Tools Layout* tab (Figure 2-51) are available when the table is active.

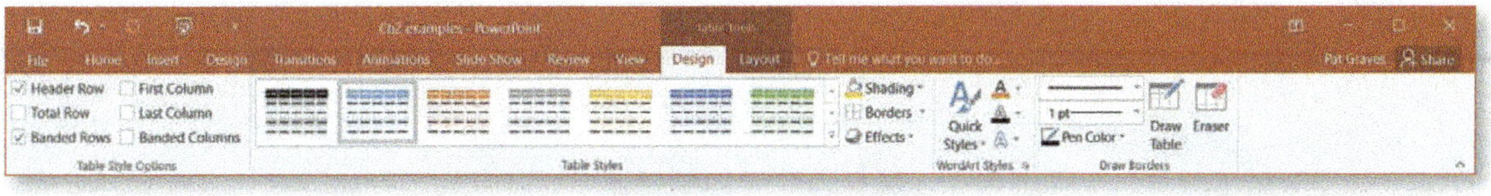

2-50 *Table Tools Design* tab

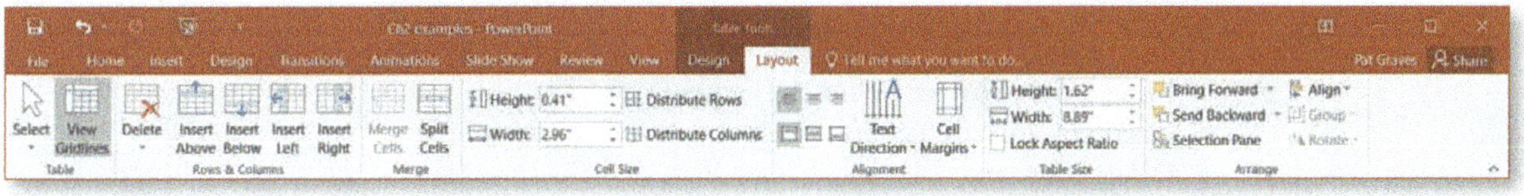

2-51 *Table Tools Layout* tab

Move and Select

Your insertion point indicates where you are within a table to add text. To move from cell to cell, use one of the following methods:

- Press **Tab** to move to the next cell on the right (or the first cell in the next row).
- Press **Shift+Tab** to move to the previous cell on the left.
- Press arrow keys to move in different directions from the current cell.
- Click a cell to move the insertion point to that cell.

Where you point within a table influences whether you select individual cells, columns, rows, or the entire table. Your pointer changes to a selection pointer (a black arrow that points in different directions based on what you are selecting).

HOW TO: Select Cells, Columns, Rows, and the Table

1. Select a cell by pointing inside the left border and clicking when your pointer turns into a black arrow that angles.
2. Select a column by using one of the following methods:
   - Point above the column's top border and click when your pointer turns into a downward-pointing black arrow (Figure 2-52).
   - Move your insertion point to any cell in the column. Click the **Select** button [*Table Tools Layout* tab, *Table* group] and click **Select Column.**

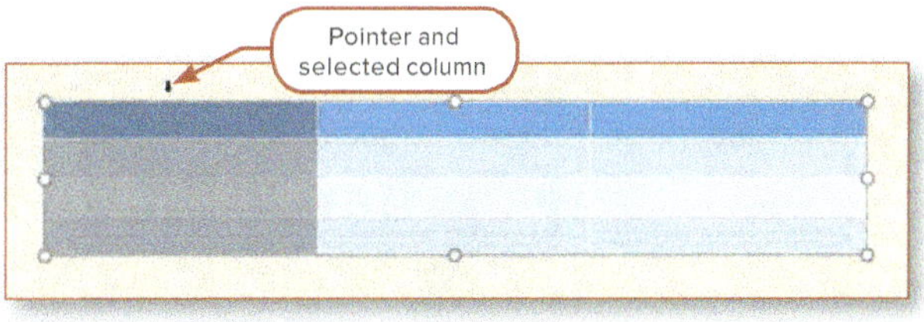

2-52 Select table column

3. Select a row by using one of the following methods:
   - Point outside the table to the left of a row and click when your pointer turns into a right-pointing black arrow (Figure 2-53).
   - Move your insertion point to any cell in the row. Click the **Select** button [*Table Tools Layout* tab, *Table* group] and click **Select Row**.

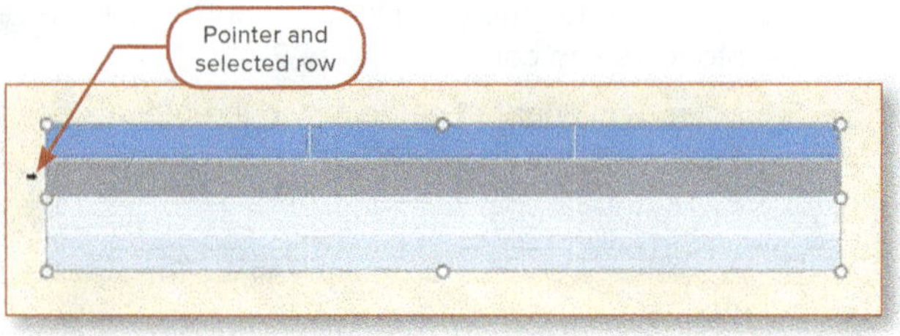

2-53 Select table row

4. Select multiple cells, columns, or rows by using one of the following methods:
   - Drag across adjacent cells.
   - Press **Shift** as you click additional adjacent cells.
5. Select an entire table by using one of the following methods:
   - Drag across all cells in the table.
   - Move your insertion point to any cell in the table. Click the **Select** button [*Table Tools Layout* tab, *Table* group] and click **Select Table**.

Insert and Delete Rows and Columns

After you begin entering table content, you may need to add rows or columns. You can change a table's structure in several ways:

- Insert rows above or below the current row.
- Insert columns to the left or right of the current column.
- Delete rows and columns.

HOW TO: Insert and Delete Rows and Columns

1. Click inside the table.
2. Click the **Table Tools Layout** tab.
3. Insert a row or column.
   - Click a table cell next to where you want to add a column or row.
   - Click the **Insert Above** or **Insert Below** buttons [*Rows & Columns* group] to add rows.
   - Click the **Insert Left** or **Insert Right** buttons [*Rows & Columns* group] to add columns.
4. Delete a row or column.
   - Click a table cell where you want to delete a column or row.
   - Click the **Delete** button and select **Delete Columns** or **Delete Rows** [*Rows & Columns* group] (Figure 2-54).

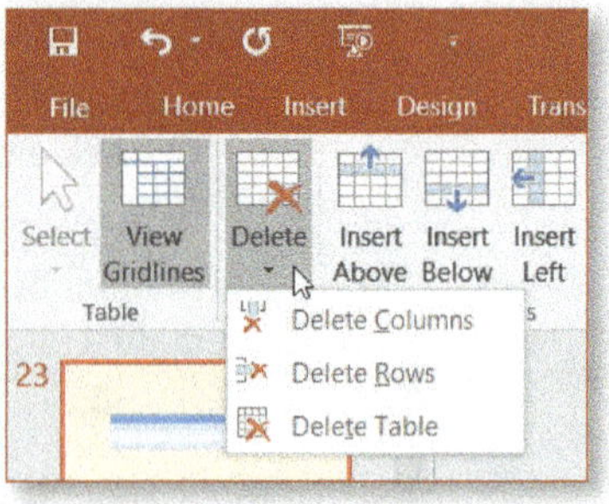

2-54 *Delete* button

ANOTHER WAY

Right-click a row or column and insert or delete rows and columns by selecting the appropriate option from the mini toolbar.

Merge and Split Cells

Use the ***Merge Cells*** command to combine two or more cells in a row or column. For example, you can merge all the cells in the top row of a table so a title will span all columns. Use the ***Split Cells*** command to divide any single cell into two or more cells.

HOW TO: Merge and Split Cells

1. Select the cells to be merged.
2. Click the *Table Tools Layout* tab.
3. Click the **Merge Cells** button [*Merge* group] to combine those cells into one cell.
4. Select the cell (or cells) to be split.
5. Click the *Table Tools Layout* tab.
6. Click the **Split Cells** button [*Merge* group] to open the *Split Cells* dialog box and enter the number of columns and rows that you need.
7. Click **OK** to close the dialog box.

ANOTHER WAY

Click the **Eraser** button [*Table Tools Design* tab, *Draw Borders* group] and your pointer turns into an eraser. Click a border within the table to remove it and merge cells. Press **Esc** to turn off the **Eraser**.

Adjust Sizing

You often need to resize tables to display information appropriately. Column widths will vary based on content, but row height should usually be consistent.

HOW TO: Resize a Table, Cells, Columns, and Rows

1. Resize a table.
   - Enter sizes in the *Height* and *Width* boxes [*Table Tools Layout* tab, *Table Size* group].
   - Click and drag table sizing handles as you would to resize a shape.
2. Resize a cell, column, or row.
   - Point to a cell, column, or row border. When your pointer changes to a splitter (Figure 2-55), click and drag to increase or decrease the size of the cell, column, or row.
   - Select the cell, column, or row to change; then enter the size you want in the *Height* and *Width* boxes [*Table Tools Layout* tab, *Cell Size* group].
3. Resize a column to fit the text within it.
   - Point to a column border and double-click when your pointer changes to a splitter.
4. Distribute column width or row height evenly.
   - Select the columns or rows to be changed.
   - Click the **Distribute Rows** or **Distribute Columns** buttons [*Table Tools Layout* tab, *Cell Size* group].

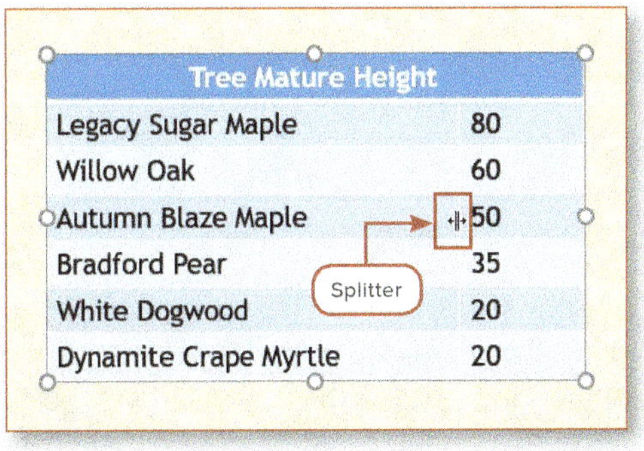

2-55 Change column width

> **MORE INFO**
>
> To maintain column width proportions, press **Shift** as you drag table sizing handles or select **Lock Aspect Ratio** [*Table Tools Layout* tab, *Table Size* group] before entering *Height* or *Width* sizes.

SLO 2.5

Formatting a Table

You can format text in a table as you can any other text such as changing fonts and text effects. You can also change cell margins and text direction. While shading and borders may appear decorative, these effects can make a table easier to interpret. For example, shading on rows can make the text easier to read across rows; shading on a column can draw attention to the text displayed there. PowerPoint provides many preset styles using color combinations derived from theme colors. You can customize effects to create a unique design.

Table Style Options and Effects

On the *Table Tools Design* tab, the ***Table Styles*** gallery provides options for a table's design. The first style on each row of options is shown in black and white while the other six styles are in theme accent colors. Table styles are arranged in the following categories:

- *Best Match for Document*
- *Light*
- *Medium*
- *Dark*

Each table style is influenced by the features checked for ***Table Style Options*** [*Table Tools Design* tab]. Fill colors that emphasize table cells vary depending on which of the following options you select:

- ***Header Row*** or ***Total Row:*** The first or last row has a darker color and has bold text in a contrasting color.
- ***First Column*** or ***Last Column:*** The first or last column has a darker color and has bold text in a contrasting color.
- ***Banded Rows*** or ***Banded Columns:*** The rows or columns have alternating colors. *Banded Rows* makes reading across the table easier. *Banded Columns* emphasizes the separate columns.

HOW TO: Apply a Table Style and Change Options

1. Click anywhere in the table you want to change.
2. Click the **Table Tools Design** tab.
3. Click the **More** button in the *Table Styles* group to see the complete gallery (Figure 2-56). The current style is highlighted.
4. Point to a style to see a live preview. *ScreenTips* identify each style name.

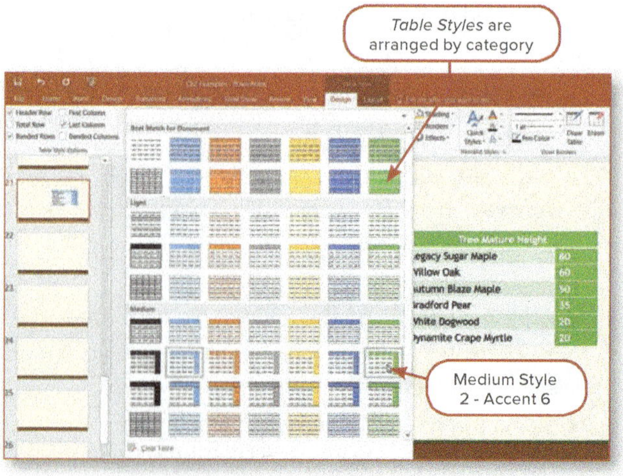

2-56 *Table Styles*

5. Click a style to apply it.
6. Adjust the *Table Style Options* as needed.
   - Check **Header Row** and **Banded Rows** [*Table Style Options* group].
   - Deselect **Banded Rows** and select **Banded Columns** [*Table Style Options* group].

If you want to remove table formatting, click the **More** button [*Table Tools Design* tab, *Table Styles* group] and click **Clear Table**. To emphasize the table or cells within the table, such as a heading row, you can apply effects to selected areas.

HOW TO: Apply Table Effects

1. Select the table, or the cells, to be changed.
2. Click the **Effects** button [*Table Tools Design* tab, *Table Styles* group (Figure 2-57).
3. Select one of the following effects:
   - **Cell Bevel**
   - **Shadow**
   - **Reflection**
4. Point to an option to see a live preview. *ScreenTips* identify each option name.
5. Click an option to apply it.

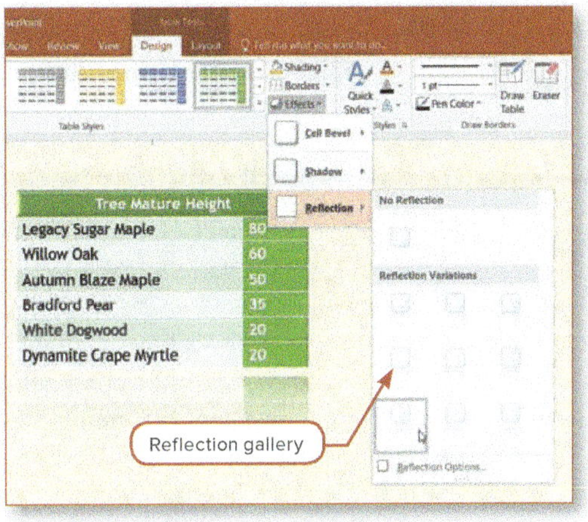

2-57 *Reflection Effects*

Shading and Border Colors

After you apply a built-in table style, you can change colors to emphasize your content or better match other aspects of your presentation. Select the cells you want to change and use the *Shading* button [*Table Tools Design* tab, *Table Styles* group] to select a different color (Figure 2-58). The icon for this button is the same as a *Shape Fill* button.

Border lines separate cells and outline the edge of the table, but not all table styles show border lines. To add lines, use the *Borders* button [*Table Tools Design* tab, *Table Styles* group] and each available option shows where the border line will be applied when that option is selected (Figure 2-59).

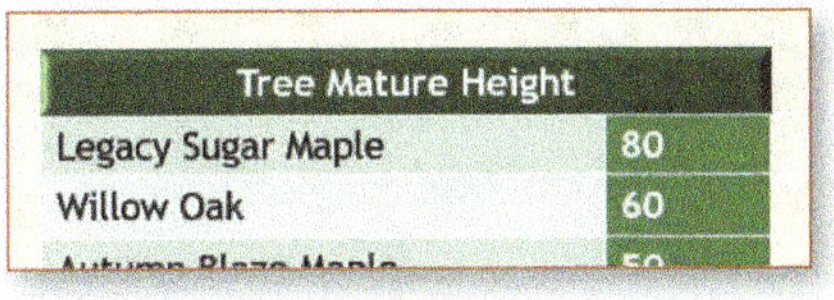

2-58 **Shading emphasizes content**

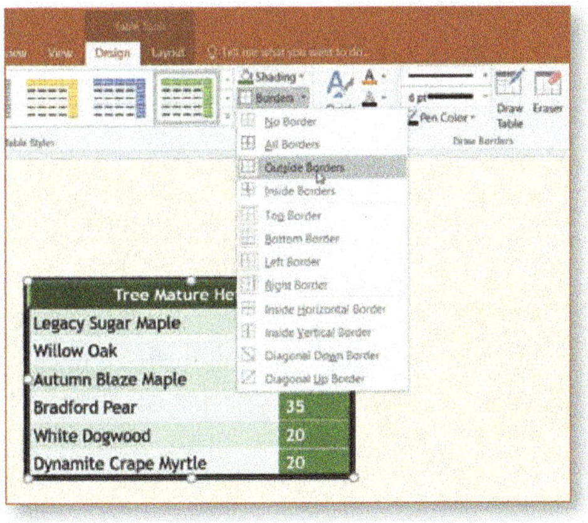

2-59 *Pen Weight* **changed and** *Outside Borders* **applied**

Select the appropriate area before you apply the border change. If you want the border lines thicker, increase the *Pen Weight* [*Table Tools Design* tab, *Draw Borders* group] before you apply the border change. You can remove borders from selected cells by clicking the **Borders** button and selecting **No Border**.

Also, you can apply, change, and remove borders using the ***Pen*** tools [*Table Tools Design* tab, *Draw Borders* group]:

- ***Pen Color:*** Change line color.
- ***Pen Style:*** Choose a different line style.
- ***Pen Weight:*** Change line thickness.
- ***Draw Table:*** Draw table area as well as column and row border lines.
- ***Eraser:*** Remove border lines.

It may take a little practice to use the pen to change table lines and not start a new table. Select the **Eraser** and click each border line you need to remove.

Cell Alignment

Within cells, text is aligned on the left by default, which is appropriate for words and phrases. However, numbers should usually be right-aligned so your audience can more easily interpret values.

If cells have a single line of text, center the text vertically in the cells. If some cells contain more text than other cells, top alignment generally works best because reading is easier with a consistent beginning position. Bottom alignment works well for column headings when they have more than one line of text.

Click the **Align** buttons [*Table Tools Layout* tab, *Alignment* group] and choose from the following horizontal and vertical alignment options:

- *Horizontal alignment:* ***Align Left, Center, Align Right***
- *Vertical alignment:* ***Align Top, Center Vertically, Align Bottom***

Cell Margins and Text Direction

Space is needed between the border lines of a cell and the text in the cell. The default internal margin spacing is *Normal.* You can change the spacing by clicking the **Cell Margins** button [*Table Tools Layout* tab, *Alignment* group] and choose from one of the following options (Figure 2-60):

- *Normal:* Top/Bottom **.05"** and Left/Right **.1"**
- *None:* All Sides **0"**
- *Narrow:* All Sides **0.05"**
- *Wide:* All Sides **0.15"**

Click **Custom Margins** to open the *Cell Text Layout* dialog box to enter other measurements.

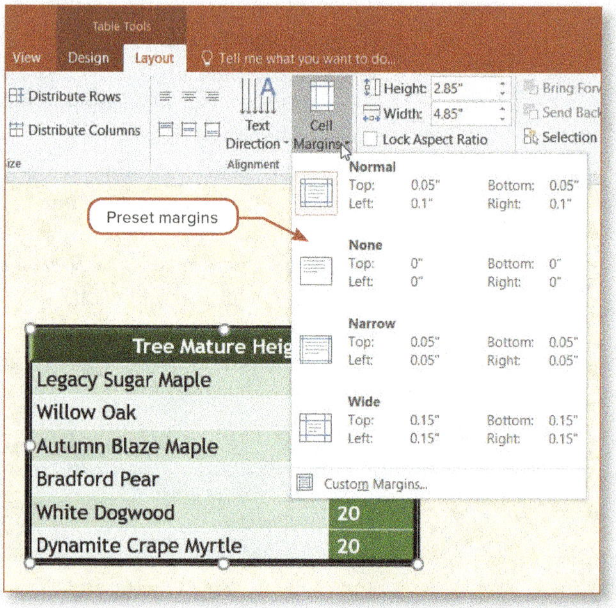

2-60 *Cell Margins* options

Text is, by default, arranged horizontally in each cell. Be careful when changing text direction because your text may not be as easy to read. Click **Text Direction** and choose one of the following four options (Figure 2-61):

- *Horizontal*
- *Rotate all text 90°*
- *Rotate all text 270°*
- *Stacked*

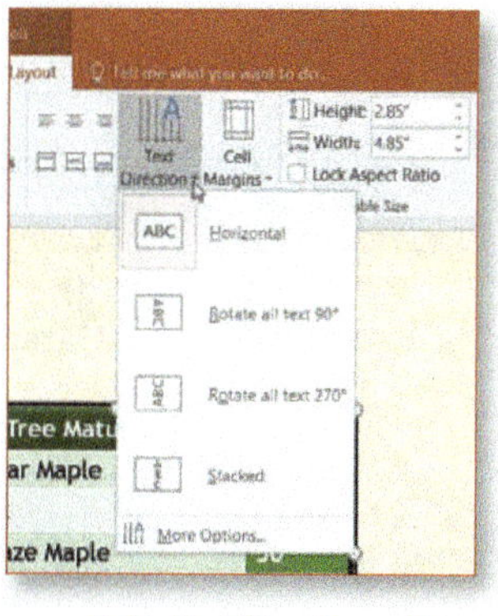

2-61 *Text Direction* options

PAUSE & PRACTICE: POWERPOINT 2-2

For this project you create a table of costs, insert a row of data, and format the table to blend with other colors used in the landscaping presentation. You also add a text box to show an alternative cost.

File Needed: ***[your initials] PP P2-1.pptx*** *(Student data files are available in the* Library *of your SIMnet account.)*
Completed Project File Name: ***[your initials] PP P2-2.pptx***

1. Open the presentation ***[your initials] PP P2-1*** and save it as [your initials] PP P2-2.
2. Create a table.
   a. Display slide 4 and click the **Insert Table** icon on the content placeholder to open the *Insert Table* dialog box.
   b. Enter 4 columns and 5 rows on the *Insert Table* dialog box. Click **OK** to close the dialog box and create the table.
   c. Type the following table text: (Note: PowerPoint does not recognize Hydroseeding, but this is the correct spelling.)

Item	Quantity	Cost Each	Totals
Trees–shade	3	500	1,500
Trees–ornamental	3	150	450
Perennials	30	12	360
Hydroseeding sq. ft.	8,000	.10	800

   d. Click and drag across the table to select all cells. Change the *Font Size* to **20 pt**. [*Home* tab, *Font* group] (Figure 2-62).
3. Adjust table sizing and alignment.
   a. Adjust column width by pointing to each border separating the columns and double-clicking when your pointer changes to a splitter.
      - For the right side of the "Totals" column, the pointer will change to a splitter if you deselect the table and then point just inside the right border. Drag to make the column fit the text.

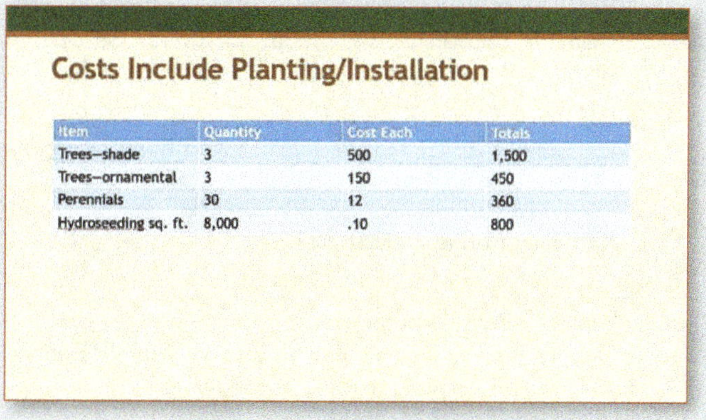

2-62 Table as it first appears with font size change

b. Point above the "**Quantity**" column and click when your pointer turns into a black arrow. Drag across the "**Cost Each**" and "**Totals**" columns to select all cells in those columns. Click the **Align Right** button [*Table Tools Layout* tab, *Alignment* group].

4. Insert rows and add text.
   a. Click the "**Perennials**" cell and click the **Insert Above** button [*Table Tools Layout* tab, *Rows & Columns* group].
   b. Add the following text to the newly inserted row:

      Shrubs 10 40 400

   c. Click in the "**Hydroseeding**" cell and click the **Insert Below** button [*Table Tools Layout* tab, *Rows & Columns* group].
   d. Select the last three cells on the new row and click the **Merge Cells** button [*Table Tools Layout* tab, *Merge* group].
   e. Add the following text:

      Total 3,510

5. Select table styles, options, and shading.
   a. Click the **More** button [*Tables Tools Design* tab, *Table Styles* group] and select the **Medium Style 3, Accent 6** style.
   b. Check **Header Row, Total Row,** and **Banded Rows** [*Tables Tools Design* tab, *Table Style Options* group] if they are not already checked.
   c. Select a row with gray shading. Click the **Shading** button [*Table Tools Design* tab, *Table Styles* group] and select **Green, Accent 6, Lighter 80%**. Repeat for the remaining two gray rows.
   d. Select the last row. Click the **Shading** button and select **Green, Accent 6, Lighter 60%**.
   e. Select the first row. Click the **Effects** button [*Table Tools Design* tab, *Table Styles* group], click **Cell Bevel**, and select **Cool Slant** (Figure 2-63).

Item	Quantity	Cost Each	Totals
Trees–shade	3	500	1,500
Trees–ornamental	3	150	450
Shrubs	10	40	400
Perennials	30	12	360
Hydroseeding sq. ft.	8,000	.10	800
Total			3,510

2-63 Style, row shading, and *Bevel* effect applied

6. Add borders and a shadow effect.
   a. Select the table.
   b. Click the **Pen Color** button [*Table Tools Design* tab, *Draw Borders* group] and select **Green, Accent 6, Darker 50%**.
   c. Click the **Pen Weight** button [*Table Tools Design* tab, *Draw Borders* group] and select **6 pt**.
   d. Click the **Borders** drop-down arrow [*Table Tools Design* tab, *Table Styles* group] and select **Outside Borders**.
   e. Select the table and click the **Effects** button [*Table Tools Design* tab, *Table Styles* group]. Click **Shadow** and select **Offset Diagonal Bottom Right** in the *Outer* category.

7. Center the table so it is centered on the slide.
   a. Click **Align** [*Table Tools Layout* tab, *Arrange* group] and select **Align Center**. Click **Align** again and select **Align Middle**.

8. Insert a text box.
   a. Click the **Text Box** button [*Insert* tab, *Text* group] and click the slide below the table to start a text box. Type the following text:

      Sod cost for 8,000 sq. ft. @ .60 = $4,800

b. Change the font size to **20 pt**. [*Home* tab, *Font* group].
c. Click the **Shape Fill** button [*Home* tab, *Drawing* group] and select **Green, Accent 6, Lighter 60%**.
d. Resize the text box as necessary so the text fits on one line. Move it to the lower right of the slide (Figure 2-64).

9. Save and close your presentation (Figure 2-65).

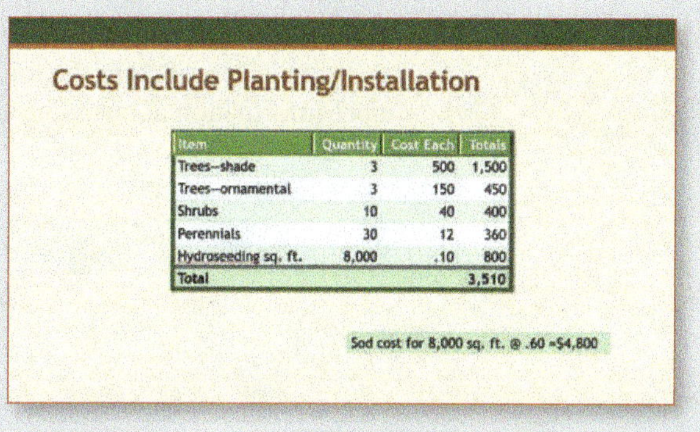

2-64 Completed table on slide 4

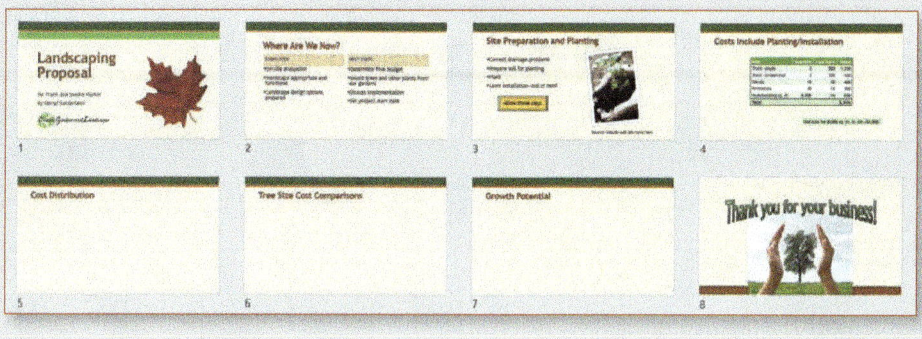

2-65 PP P2-2 completed

SLO 2.6

Creating a SmartArt Graphic

To clearly illustrate concepts such as processes, cycles, or relationships, you can create a diagram using ***SmartArt graphics*** to help your audience see connections or sequences. This is a very important communication strategy; the shapes of the diagram are concisely labeled for each concept and the shapes are connected in various ways. For example, you can show subtopics radiating from a central topic or sequential steps in a work flow.

The *SmartArt Tools Design* tab (Figure 2-66) provides options for the overall layout and styles of the *SmartArt* graphics. You can add shapes and rearrange the order of shapes.

The *SmartArt Tools Format* tab (Figure 2-67) provides options to customize shape and text styles, fill colors, outline colors, and effects.

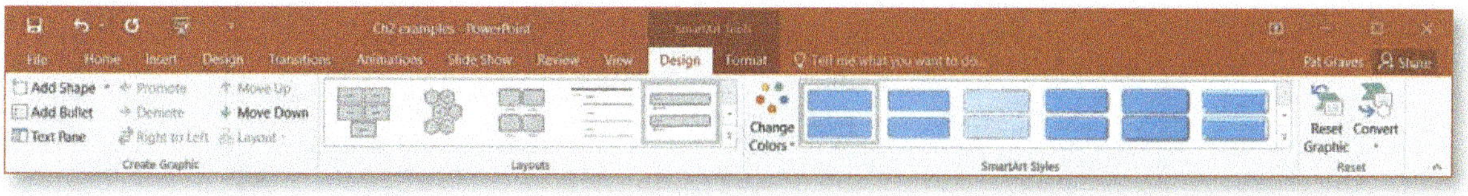

2-66 *SmartArt Tools Design* tab

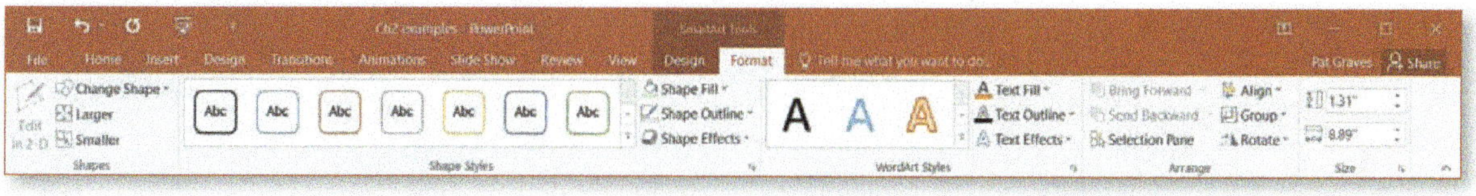

2-67 *SmartArt Tools Format* tab

SmartArt Layouts

SmartArt layouts (diagrams) are organized by type in the *Choose a SmartArt Graphic* dialog box; each type is described in the following table. When you select a layout, PowerPoint provides more information about using that specific layout.

SmartArt Graphic Layout Types and Purposes

Type	Purpose
List	Illustrates non-sequential or grouped information
Process	Illustrates sequential steps in a process or workflow
Cycle	Illustrates a continuing sequence or concepts related to a central idea
Hierarchy	Illustrates a decision tree or top-to-bottom relationship such as an organizational chart
Relationship	Illustrates concepts that are connected such as contrasting, opposing, or converging
Matrix	Illustrates the relationship of four parts to the whole
Pyramid	Illustrates proportional or interconnected relationships
Picture	Shows pictures as integral parts of many different diagrams
Office.com	Shows diagrams from layouts on Office.com

HOW TO: Create a SmartArt Graphic

1. Click the **Insert SmartArt Graphic** icon on the content placeholder to open the *Choose a SmartArt Graphic* dialog box.

Or

2. Display the slide where you want to insert the *SmartArt* graphic and click the **Insert** tab.
3. Click the **SmartArt** button [*Illustrations* group] to open the *Choose a SmartArt Graphic* dialog box.
4. Select a type from the list on the left (Figure 2-68).
5. Click a layout in the gallery to select it.
6. Click **OK** to close the dialog box. The *SmartArt* graphic appears on the slide with sample text.

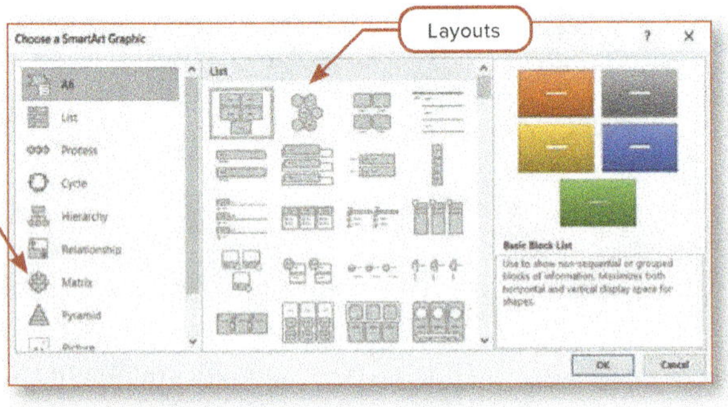

2-68 *Choose a SmartArt Graphic* dialog box

When you insert a *SmartArt* graphic using the *SmartArt* button on the *Insert* tab, the initial size of the *SmartArt* frame may be different than if you inserted the *SmartArt* graphic using the content placeholder on a new slide with a *Title and Content* layout. You may need to resize the frame for your content to fit appropriately on your slide.

If the layout you choose has picture placeholders on the shapes, such as the *Continuous Picture List* layout shown in Figure 2-69, click each picture icon to open the *Insert Pictures* dialog box. Locate the picture you want to use and click **Insert**. The picture is sized automatically and shaped to fit the current picture placeholder.

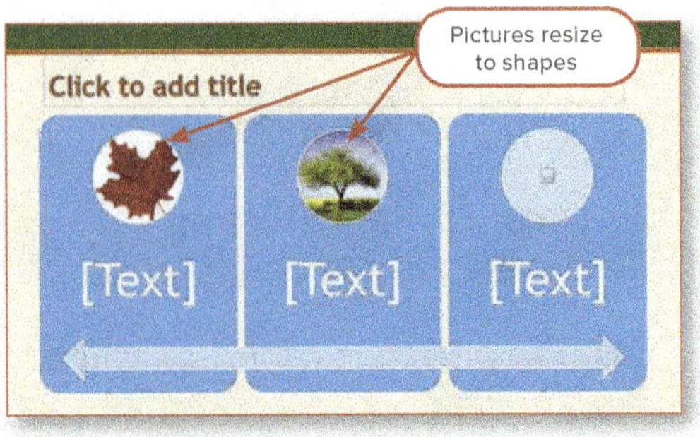

2-69 *SmartArt Continuous Picture List* layout

Add Text

Click the **Text Pane** button [*SmartArt Tools Design* tab, *Create Graphic* group] to open a pane beside your layout. As you type in the pane, *SmartArt* text appears as a bulleted list and also in the *SmartArt* shapes. Text becomes smaller in the shapes as you enter more text, so it is important to use only a few words. You can resize or move the *Text pane*.

List layouts often work well if you have two levels of bulleted text: Level 1 (the first line) and Level 2 (text indented to a sublevel). How text is arranged when using two levels of information varies based on the selected layout. Notice in Figure 2-70 that Level 1 text is in a shape and Level 2 text is in a bulleted list below the shape.

HOW TO: Type SmartArt Text Using the Text Pane

1. Open the *Text pane,* if necessary, by using one of the following methods:
   - Click the **Text Pane** button [*SmartArt Tools Design* tab, *Create Graphic* group].
   - Click the smaller **Text Pane** button on the left side of the *SmartArt* frame.
2. Type text after the first bullet to add Level 1 text.
3. Press **Enter** to add a new item. Another shape appears in your *SmartArt* layout, and shape sizes automatically adjust.
4. Press **Tab** to indent for Level 2 text (Figure 2-70).
5. Press **Shift** + **Tab** to go from Level 2 text to Level 1 text.
6. Use arrow keys to move through the listed items.
7. Remove a shape by deleting the related bulleted text in the *Text pane.*
   - The *Text pane* automatically closes when you click outside the *SmartArt* layout.
   - If you want to keep the current *SmartArt* layout active, click the pane's **Close** button or the **Text Pane** button to close the pane.

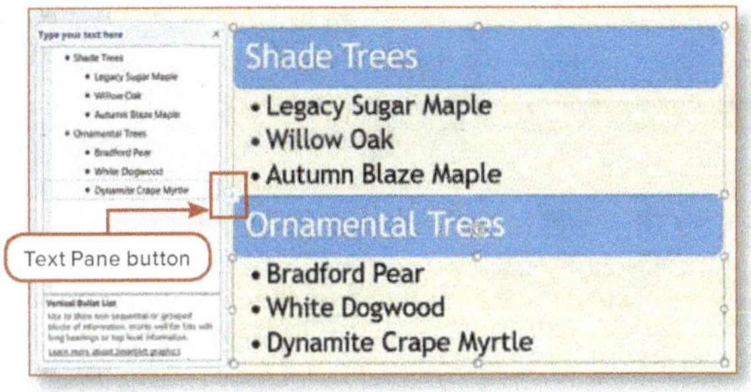

2-70 *SmartArt Text Pane*

Another way to add text is to type directly into each *SmartArt* shape so you can easily see how your text fits without becoming too small. Pressing **Tab** does not move your insertion point between shapes. You can paste copied text but you cannot drag text into a *SmartArt* shape.

HOW TO: Type Text in SmartArt Shapes

1. Close the *Text Pane,* if open, by clicking the **Close** button in the top-right corner of the pane.
2. Click each *SmartArt* shape to select it and type your text. A dashed border appears on the shape as you type or edit your text.
3. Click outside the *SmartArt* frame, or press **Esc**, when you are finished (Figure 2-71).

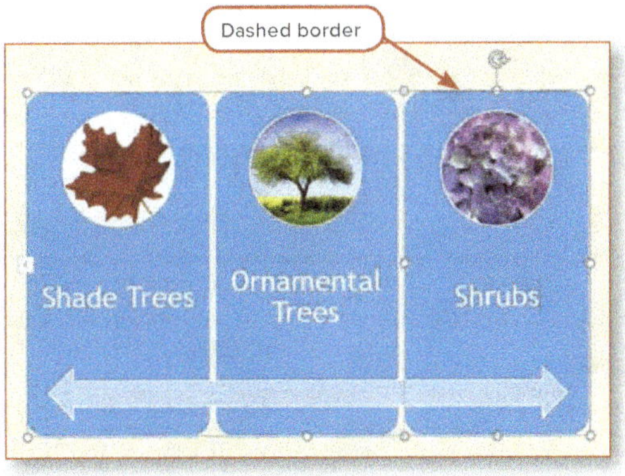

2-71 Add text in the *SmartArt Continuous Picture List* layout

If you already have listed information on your slide, you can quickly change bulleted text to a *SmartArt* graphic. The gallery layouts that first appear are designed for listed information, but you can access all of the other layouts, too.

HOW TO: Convert Text to a SmartArt Graphic

1. Select the bulleted text placeholder or the text within the placeholder that you want to convert to a *SmartArt* graphic.
2. Click the **Home** tab.
3. Click the **Convert to SmartArt Graphic** button [*Paragraph* group] (Figure 2-72). The gallery displays layouts that are designed to show listed information.
4. Click a layout to apply it.

Or

5. Click **More SmartArt Graphics** to open the *Choose a SmartArt Graphic* dialog box.
6. Select from all layouts and then click **OK** to close the dialog box and insert the *SmartArt* graphic.

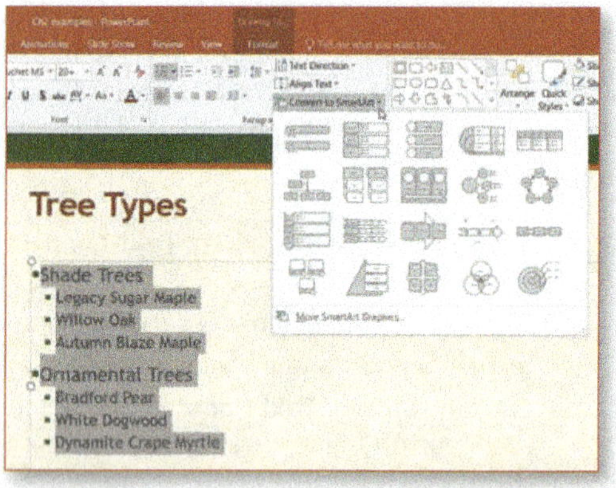

2-72 Convert to *SmartArt* graphic

SLO 2.7

Formatting a SmartArt Graphic

When you create a *SmartArt* graphic, by default it appears using the first accent color in the current color theme. You can customize many style options and colors using the *SmartArt Tools Design* tab as well as rearrange shape order, add shapes, or change layouts.

SmartArt Styles

The ***SmartArt Styles*** gallery provides different effects for emphasizing the diagram shapes. In the ***3-D*** category, the styles have a dimensional effect. When choosing these styles, be sure that your diagram is not distorted or difficult to interpret.

HOW TO: Apply SmartArt Styles

1. Select the *SmartArt* graphic.
2. Click the **SmartArt Tools Design** tab.
3. Click the **More** button [*SmartArt Styles* group] to open the *SmartArt Styles* gallery (Figure 2-73).
4. Point to a style to see a live preview.
5. Click a style to apply it.

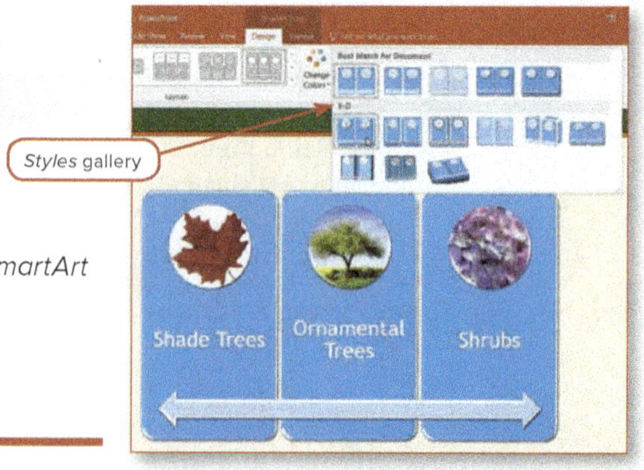

2-73 *SmartArt* graphic styles

Change Colors

The ***Change Colors*** gallery provides a quick way to change all the colors in a *SmartArt* graphic at the same time. Color options are arranged in categories using theme accent colors; some show variations of the same color while others have different colors.

Individual shape colors within a *SmartArt* graphic can be changed as you would any other shape.

▶ HOW TO: Change SmartArt Colors

1. Select the *SmartArt* graphic.
2. Change colors for the entire diagram by clicking the **Change Colors** button [*SmartArt Tools Design* tab, *SmartArt Styles* group] and selecting a gallery option (Figure 2-74).
3. Change the color of a selected shape within a diagram by clicking the **Shape Fill** button or the **Shape Outline** button [*SmartArt Tools Format* tab, *Shape Styles* group] and choosing an appropriate color.

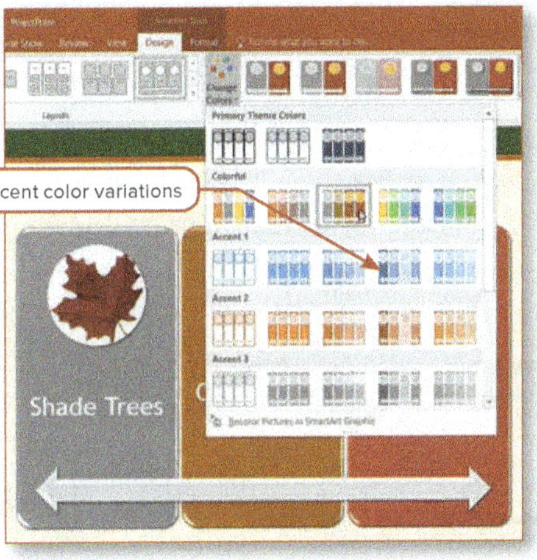

2-74 *SmartArt* graphic *Change Colors* options

Change Layouts

You may find that the *SmartArt* graphic layout you have chosen is not appropriate for the particular process or relationship you are trying to show. Or you might need a layout that displays two levels of information.

▶ HOW TO: Change Layouts

1. Select the *SmartArt* graphic.
2. Click the **SmartArt Tools Design** tab, and click the **More** button [*Layouts* group] to open the *Layouts* gallery (Figure 2-75).
3. Point to a layout to see a live preview of that layout.
4. Click a layout to apply it.

Or

5. Click **More Layouts** to open the *Choose a SmartArt Graphic* dialog box.
6. Select from all layouts and then click **OK** to close the dialog box and apply the new layout.

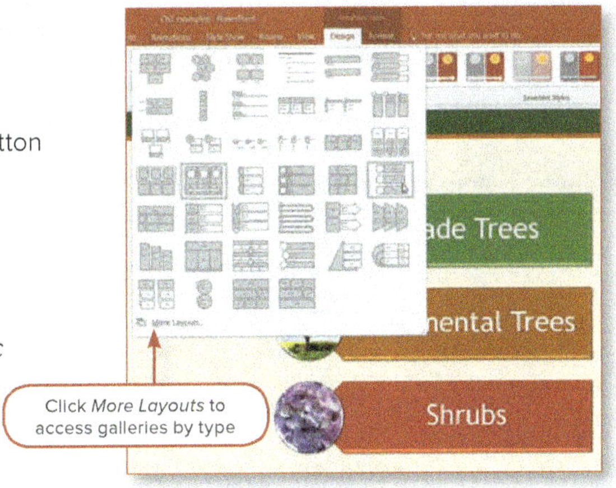

2-75 *SmartArt graphic* layouts

Add Shapes

The ***Add Shape*** button on the *SmartArt Tools Design* tab inserts shapes in relation to the selected shape. The available options include the following:

- *Add Shape After*
- *Add Shape Before*
- *Add Shape Above*
- *Add Shape Below*
- *Add Assistant*

Being able to control where a new shape appears is important. For example, you can add shapes to an organization chart as new employees are hired. An assistant shape is only available for organization charts.

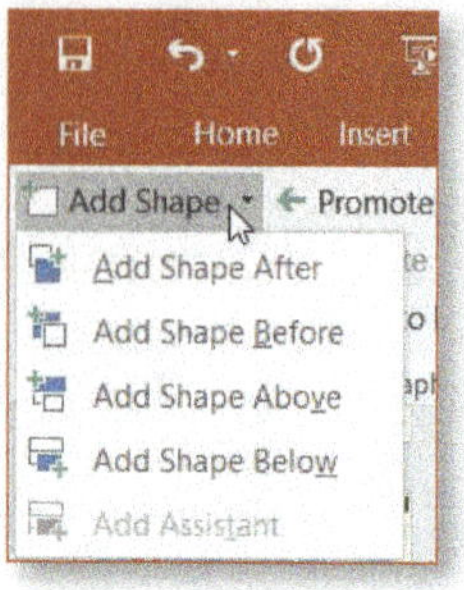

2-76 *Add Shape* options

HOW TO: Add Shapes

1. Select the shape closest to where you want to add a shape.
2. Click the **SmartArt Tools Design** tab.
3. Click the **Add Shape** drop-down arrow [*Create Graphic* group] (Figure 2-76) and select the position where you want to add the new shape.

To change the flow of a diagram, click the **Right to Left** button [*SmartArt Tools Design* tab, *Create Graphic* group].

PAUSE & PRACTICE: POWERPOINT 2-3

For this project you create an organization chart showing the CGL employees who will be managing various aspects of the landscaping for Frank and Sandra Hunter. You also convert one of the existing lists to a *SmartArt* graphic and rearrange slide objects for an interesting appearance. The *SmartArt* styles applied blend with other colors in the presentation.

File Needed: ***[your initials] PP P2-2.pptx*** *(Student data files are available in the* Library *of your SIMnet account.)*
Completed Project File Name: ***[your initials] PP P2-3.pptx***

1. Open the presentation ***[your initials] PP P2-2*** and save it as [your initials] PP P2-3.
2. Create a new slide and insert a *SmartArt* graphic.
   a. Display slide 1. Click the **New Slide** drop-down arrow and select the **Title and Content** layout.
   b. Type the slide title Your CGL Team.
   c. Click the **Insert a SmartArt Graphic** icon on the content placeholder to open the *Choose a SmartArt Graphic* dialog box.
   d. Select the *Hierarchy* type from the list on the left.
   e. Click the **Organization Chart** layout and click **OK** to close the dialog box and insert the *SmartArt* graphic.
3. Insert text.
   a. Select each *SmartArt* shape and type the text displayed in Figure 2-77.

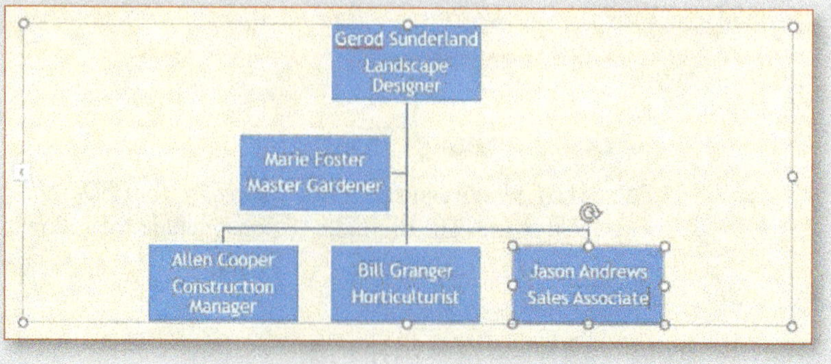

2-77 Organization chart

b. Press **Enter** after each name within a shape. Let the job titles word wrap as needed.

4. Change the organization chart using the *SmartArt Tools Design* tab.
   a. Change the flow by clicking the **Right to Left** button [*Create Graphic* group].
   b. Click the **More** button [*SmartArt Styles* group] and select the **Inset** effect (Figure 2-78).
   c. Click the **Change Colors** button [*SmartArt Styles* group] and scroll down to select **Gradient Loop, Accent 6** (Figure 2-79).

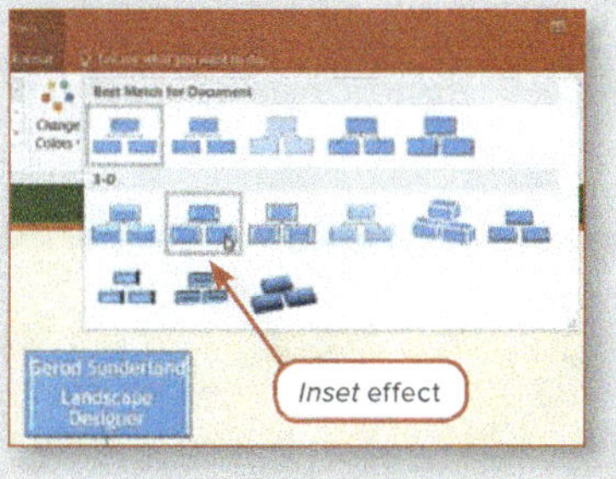

2-78 *SmartArt* graphic styles

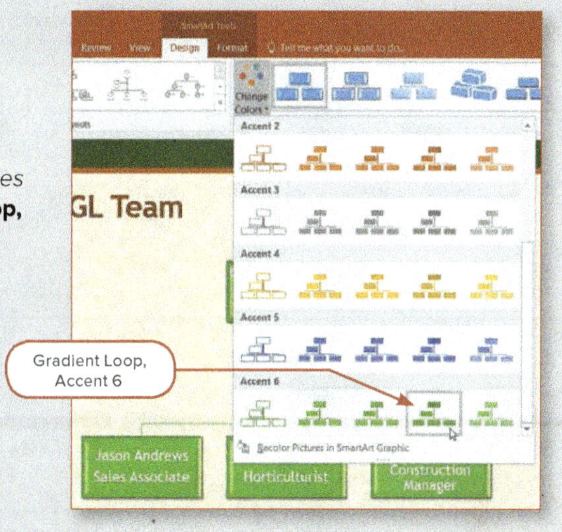

2-79 New colors applied

5. Change bulleted text to a *SmartArt* graphic.
   a. Display slide 4. Select the bulleted text and click the **Convert to SmartArt** button [*Home* tab, *Paragraph* group].
   b. Click the **Vertical Bullet List**. The *SmartArt* list fills the slide and is too large since other objects are already on the slide (Figure 2-80).

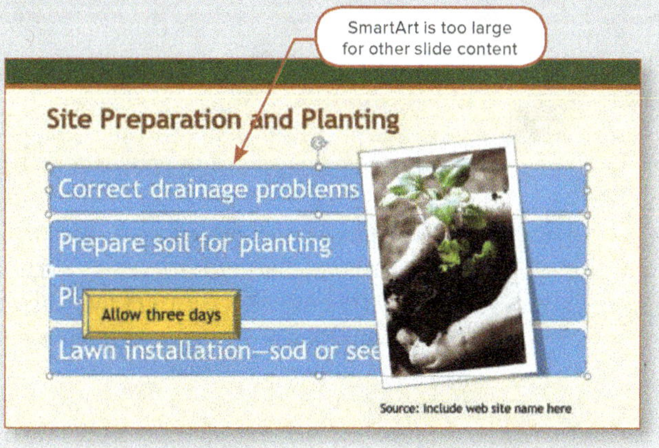

2-80 *SmartArt* graphic shapes as they originally appear

6. Change the *SmartArt* graphic so it fits on the slide with the other objects.
   a. Press **Ctrl** while you click each *SmartArt* shape to select them all. Change the font to **24 pt**.
   b. Select the *SmartArt* frame (not individual shapes) and resize it (*Height* **3"** and *Width* **5"**) [*SmartArt Tools Format* tab, *Size* group] to better fit the text and other objects on the slide.
   c. Change the style to **Inset** [*SmartArt Tools Design* tab, *SmartArt Styles* group].
   d. Click the **Change Colors** button [*SmartArt Tools Design* tab, *SmartArt Styles* group] and select **Gradient Range – Accent 6**.
   e. Rearrange slide objects as displayed in Figure 2-81. Be careful to point to the *SmartArt* frame when moving it so the whole diagram moves and not just an individual shape within the frame.

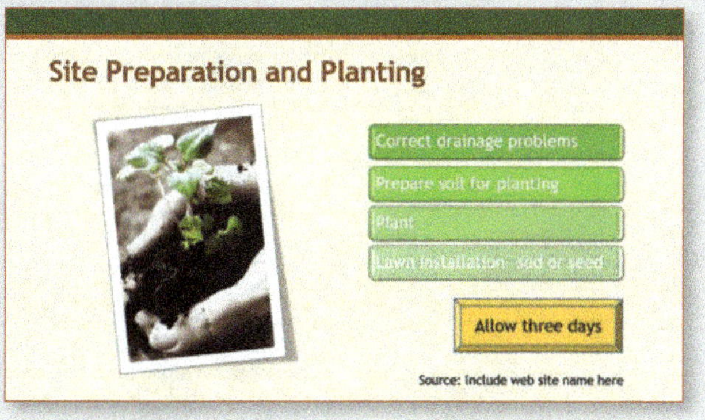

2-81 Completed slide 4

7. Save and close your presentation (Figure 2-82).

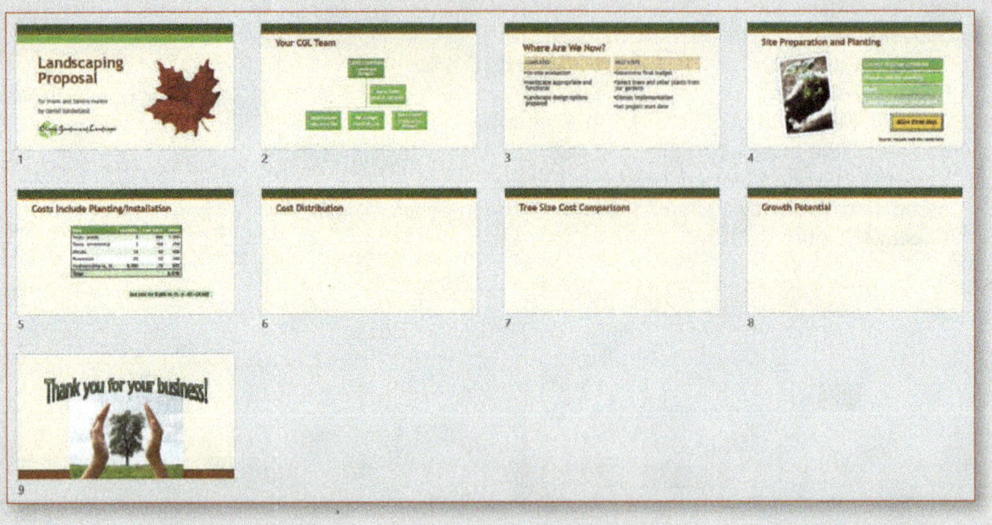

2-82 PP P-3 completed

SLO 2.8

Creating a Chart

Charts help viewers interpret data and make comparisons. If you have lots of data, then create your chart in Excel and copy it to a PowerPoint slide. However, for most situations, PowerPoint's *Chart* feature will provide all the options you need.

To insert a chart in PowerPoint 2016, click the **Insert Chart** icon on a new slide content placeholder or click the **Insert** tab and click the **Chart** button [*Illustrations* group] to add a chart to an existing slide. You can choose a chart type to control how data is represented such as with columns, bars, lines, or pie slices. The following table lists chart types and describes their purposes:

Chart Types and Purposes

Type	Purpose
Column	Shows a comparison of values or data changes over time. Categories are shown on the horizontal axis and values are shown on the vertical axis. Columns may be clustered to show a range of values or groupings. Columns in a category may be stacked to emphasize the total category value rather than the subsections that make up the category.
Line	Shows data changes over time; works well to show trends with multiple data series plotted at even intervals. Categories are shown on the horizontal axis and values are shown on the vertical axis. Markers can indicate individual values.
Pie	Shows the values in a data series in proportional sizes that make up a whole pie. Values cannot be negative or zero values. Percentages or actual values can be displayed near or on pie slices. This category also includes *Doughnut* charts that show parts of a whole but can contain more than one data series as rings.
Bar	Similar to column charts except bars are horizontal; works well for comparison of values. Categories are shown on the vertical axis and values are shown on the horizontal axis.

Continued

Type	Purpose
Area	Shows data changes over time; emphasizes the total values across a trend.
X Y (Scatter)	Shows the relationships between data using values on both the X and Y axes to plot data points; works well to emphasize where data sets have similar values. This category also includes *Bubble* charts.
Stock	Shows fluctuation of stock prices with high, low, and close values displayed over time.
Surface	Shows the differences between two sets of data. Instead of values, color bands represent the same range of values as in a topographic map showing land elevations.
Radar	Shows the combined values of several data series with values relative to a center point.
Treemap	Displays categories by color arranged in a structure that helps to compare proportions within a hierarchy.
Sunburst	Displays data in a circular pattern of rings that create a hierarchy with the highest level in the center. With multiple categories, this chart shows how the outer rings relate to the inner rings.
Histogram	Shows the distribution of data grouped by frequencies. Can include a cumulative total.
Box & Whisker	Shows multiple data sets organized by quartiles (ranked data divided into four equal groups) and shown as proportional boxes. Variability is shown as lines above or below the boxes. Outliers are plotted as individual points.
Waterfall	Shows how an initial value is affected by the addition of positive and negative values with columns that reflect a running total.
Combo	Combines two charts such as a column chart with a line chart displayed over it.

MORE INFO

Use *Help* to search for "chart types" to see examples and get tips on how to arrange data in a worksheet.

The *Chart Tools Design* tab (Figure 2-83) and the *Chart Tools Format* tab (Figure 2-84) are available when a chart is active.

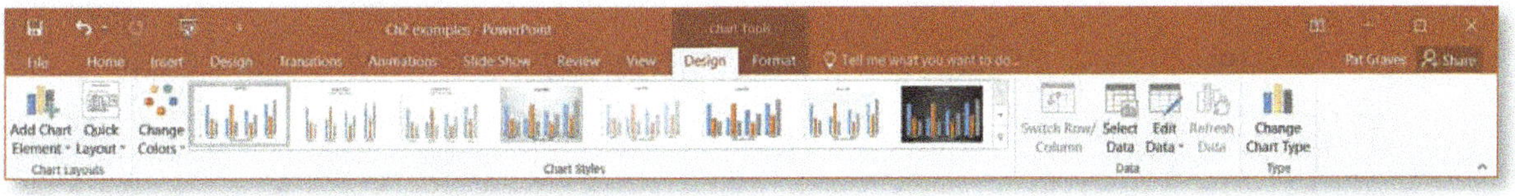

2-83 *Chart Tools Design tab*

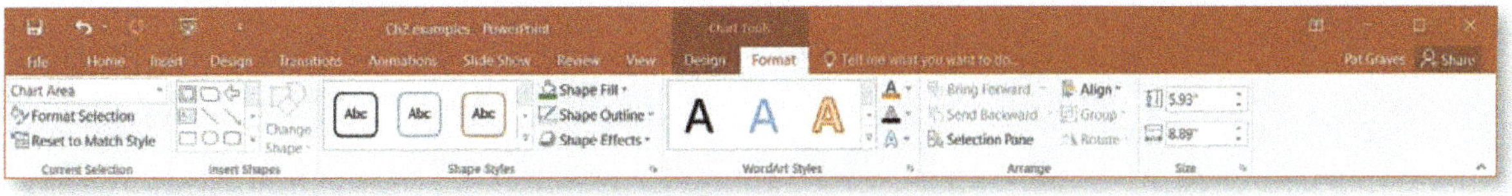

2-84 *Chart Tools Format tab*

When you insert a chart in PowerPoint, a ***spreadsheet*** opens with sample data in rows and columns. A group of data values from each column is a ***data series;*** a group of data values from each row is a ***category***. You can edit the sample data by entering your own information or you could copy and paste data from Excel, Word, or Access. If you need to revise the data in Excel, click the **Excel** button in the spreadsheet title bar.

Because the spreadsheet and PowerPoint chart are linked, the changes you make to the spreadsheet are automatically reflected in the chart.

HOW TO: Insert a Chart

1. Click the **Insert** tab; then click the **Chart** button [*Illustrations* group]. You can also click the **Insert Chart** icon on a new slide content placeholder.
   - In the *Insert Chart* dialog box (Figure 2-85), chart types are listed on the left and a variety of chart layouts for each type appear on the right.
   - A *ScreenTip* identifies chart names.
2. Click a layout to select a chart.
3. Click **OK** to close the dialog box and insert the chart.
   - A spreadsheet automatically opens showing sample data that you edit (Figure 2-86).

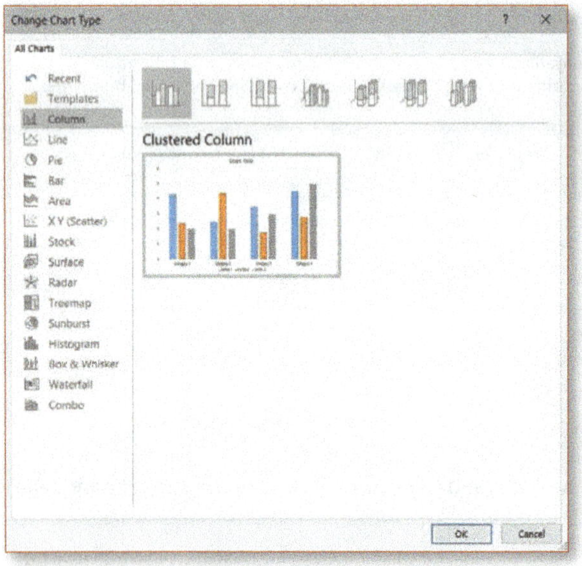

2-85 *Insert Chart* dialog box

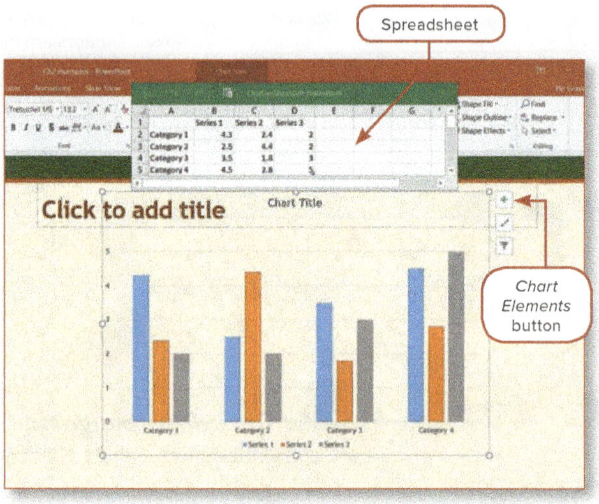

2-86 Spreadsheet linked to a chart

> **MORE INFO**
>
> When you insert a chart using the *Insert* tab, the size of the chart frame will be different than when you insert a chart from the *Title and Content* placeholder as you create a new slide. Resize the chart frames as needed.

The chart frame displays ***chart elements,*** the objects that make up the chart. Chart elements vary based on the type of chart used. You can see which chart elements are shown by clicking the **Chart Elements** button, the top button (with a green plus sign) on the right of the chart frame. You can add or remove elements by changing selections from the list. Other chart elements appear in the drop-down list box in the *Current Selection* group on the *Chart*

Tools Format tab and in the *Format* pane when you are working on the chart. The following table defines chart elements:

Chart Elements and Definitions

Element	Definition
Y-Axis (Vertical)	Also called the *Value Axis*; displayed vertically with numbers usually arranged on the left of a chart
X-Axis (Horizontal)	Also called the *Category Axis;* displayed horizontally with word or number labels across the bottom of the chart
Axis Titles	Both the Y-Axis and the X-Axis can include titles to name values or categories
Chart Area	The background area where the entire chart is displayed in a frame
Chart Title	A chart may include a title
Data Labels	Used to identify data series or its individual points; may include values
Data Markers	The graphical representation of values shown as columns, bars, slices, or data points
Data Table	The data that creates the chart is shown in table format below the chart
Error Bars	Used to show margins of error or standard deviation amounts
Floor	Area at the bottom of a 3-D chart that creates an illusion of depth
Gridlines	Lines that appear behind a chart to help the viewer judge values
Legend	The key that identifies each data series by color
Plot Area	The rectangle between the vertical and horizontal axes that appears behind the data markers
Tick Marks	Lines of measurement on an axis that help to interpret values on each axis
Trendline	Shows averages on 2-D charts that are not stacked and can extend beyond actual data to predict future values
Walls	Areas, including Back Walls and Side Walls, of a 3-D chart behind the data markers that help to create an illusion of depth

Enter Data and Edit

After you replace the spreadsheet sample data with your data, you can close the spreadsheet. If you need to revise the data as you work on the chart in PowerPoint, you can open the spreadsheet again.

HOW TO: Edit Data in the Spreadsheet

1. Select the chart you want to modify.
2. Click the top of the **Edit Data** button [*Chart Tools Design* tab, *Data* group] to display the spreadsheet (Figure 2-87).
   - If you need to modify the data in Excel, click the **Edit Data** drop-down arrow and choose **Edit Data in Excel** to display the Excel worksheet.
   - You can click and drag the Excel window to a different location or resize it if more or less space is needed.

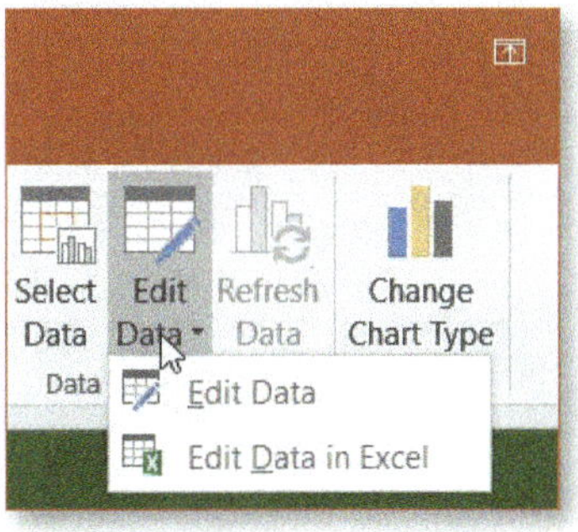

2-87 *Edit Data* button

3. Replace cell contents (Figure 2-88) by clicking in the **cell** and typing your data.
4. Move around in the spreadsheet by clicking your pointer or using keyboard shortcuts as follows:
   - Press **Enter** to move the insertion point down one row.
   - Press **Shift+Enter** to move the insertion point up one row.
   - Press **Tab** to move the insertion point to the next cell on the right.
   - Press **Shift+Tab** to move to the previous cell on the left.
   - Press arrow keys to move in any direction.
5. Click the spreadsheet **Close** button to return to the PowerPoint chart.

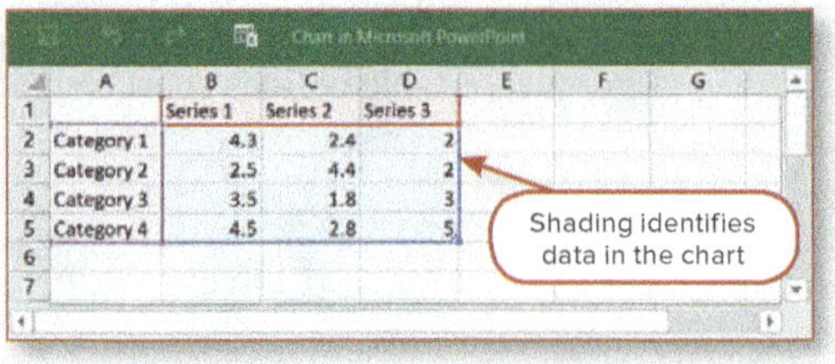

2-88 Default spreadsheet data

> **MORE INFO**
>
> Remove the sample data on the spreadsheet by clicking the **Select All** button (above the row 1 heading and to the left of the column A heading) and then pressing **Delete**.

Spreadsheet columns may need adjustments to show all data. If a cell displays number signs (#) rather than the data you entered, the cell is not wide enough to display cell contents.

- Change column width by pointing to the top of the column and dragging the splitter or double-click the line between columns to auto fit the contents.
- Be sure the shading of the selected rows and columns (see Figure 2-88) correctly identifies the category, series, and data cells. Drag a corner sizing handle to adjust.
- Columns in a spreadsheet with blank cells must be deleted so the related chart displays without a blank space.
- You can add new columns or rows in the spreadsheet or edit the spreadsheet in Excel.

HOW TO: Modify the Spreadsheet

1. Select the chart you want to modify.
2. Click the top of the **Edit Data** button [*Chart Tools Design* tab, *Data* group].
3. Adjust column width. Position your pointer on the vertical line to the right of the column heading (Figure 2-89); then use one of these methods:
   - Drag to the correct width.
   - Double-click and the column automatically adjusts to fit the widest data entered in that column.
   - Right-click to open the context menu and select **Column Width**, then type the width number on the *Column Width* dialog box. Click **OK** to close the dialog box.
4. Use Excel to modify data.
   - Click the **Edit Data** drop-down arrow [*Chart Tools Design* tab, *Data* group] and choose **Edit Data in Excel**. The Excel window displays.

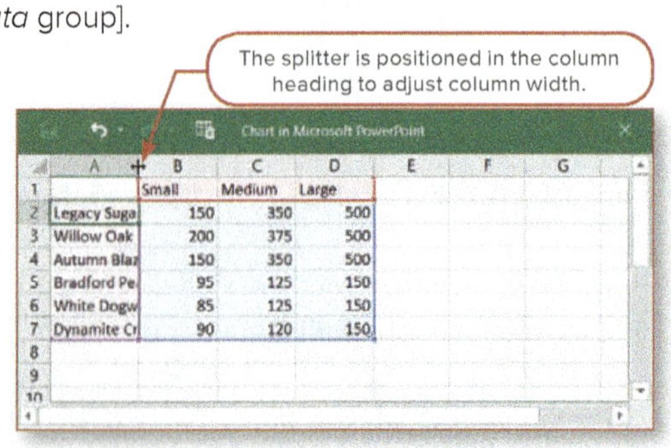

2-89 Adjust column width

- Click a cell where you need to add a cell, row, or column. Click the **Insert** drop-down arrow [*Home* tab, *Cells* group] and select the option you need.
- Adjust column width or edit titles and data values as you normally would within Excel.
- Close Excel to return to the chart on your slide.

In PowerPoint, switch the data series by clicking the **Switch Row/Column** button [*Chart Tools Design* tab, *Data* group]. In a column chart, for example, data displayed on the X-axis (bottom) and Y-axis (left) will be reversed.

Change Chart Type

Click the **Change Chart Type** button [*Chart Tools Design* tab, *Type* group] to open the *Change Chart Type* gallery where you can choose from the many different layouts. For example, Figure 2-90 shows data in a line chart and Figure 2-91 shows the same data in a clustered column chart.

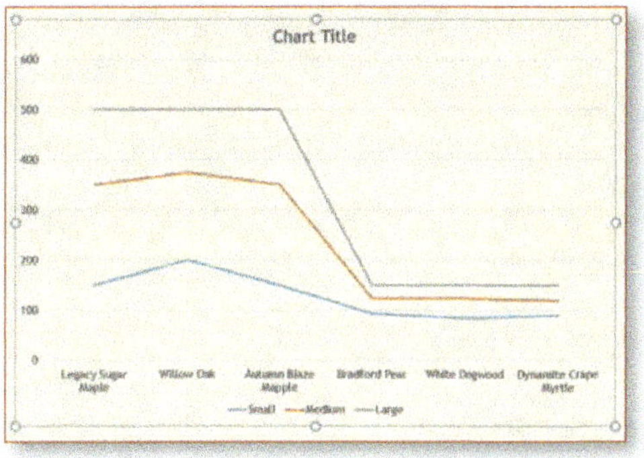

2-90 Line chart

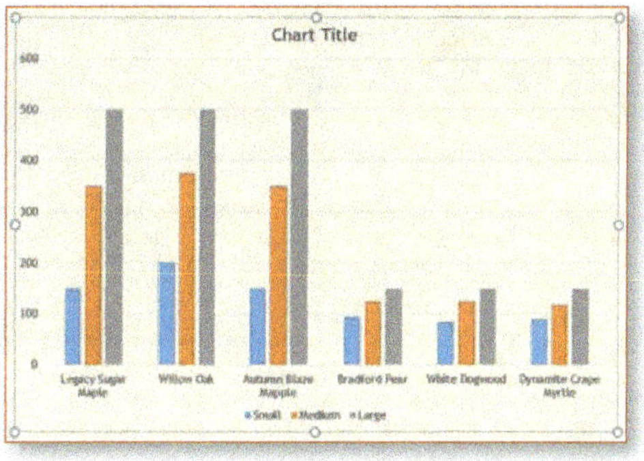

2-91 Clustered column chart

SLO 2.9

Formatting a Chart

You can change the look of a chart by applying preset styles or manually customizing individual chart elements.

Chart Styles and Colors

The ***Chart Styles*** gallery [*Chart Tools Design* tab] provides preset effects for chart elements including the chart background. Click the **More** button to see styles arranged by number. Click a style to apply it (Figure 2-92).

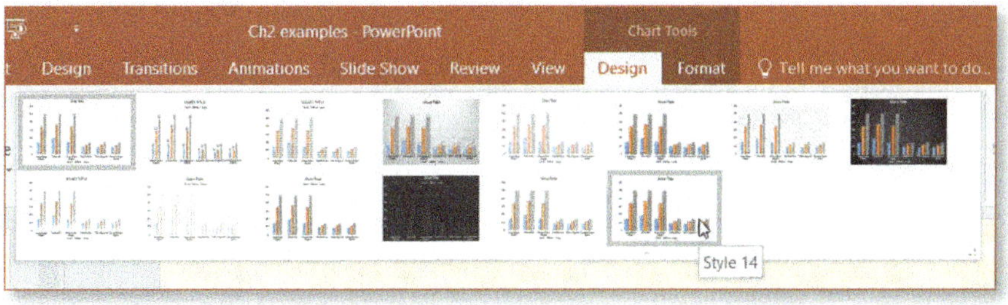

2-92 *Chart Styles* gallery

> **MORE INFO**
>
> If your PowerPoint window is narrow, you may need to click the **Quick Styles** button [*Chart Tools Design* tab] to open the *Chart Styles* gallery.

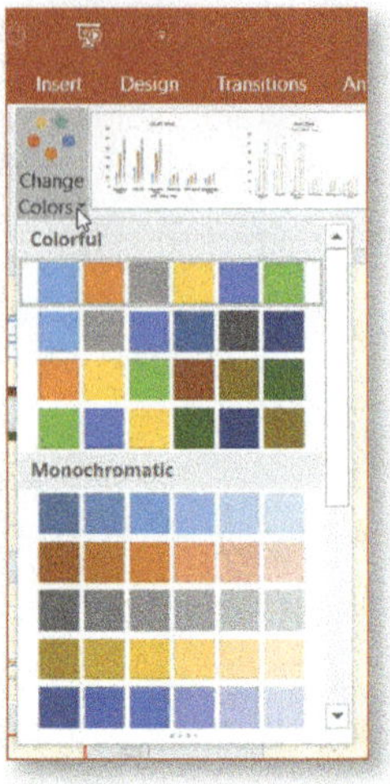

2-93 *Chart Colors* gallery

Click the **Change Colors** button [*Chart Tools Design* tab] to select ***Colorful*** or ***Monochromatic*** (shades of one color) combinations based on theme colors (Figure 2-93). The colors you choose then show in all the available chart styles. Be careful when selecting colors so the chart shapes (columns, bars, lines, or pie slices) are easy to distinguish for value comparisons. The colors also need to coordinate with your overall presentation (Figure 2-94).

If possible, avoid arranging red and green colors together. People who have difficulty recognizing different colors are most likely to have problems with red and green because they can look beige or gray.

> **ANOTHER WAY**
>
> You can also access *Chart Styles* and *Chart Colors* using the *Chart Styles* button (with a paintbrush icon) to the right of each chart.

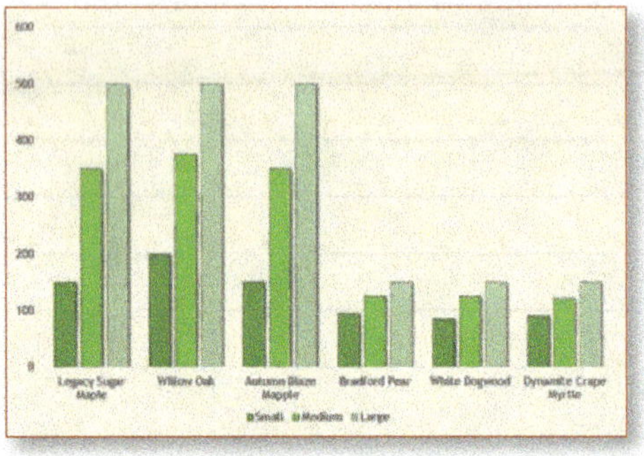

2-94 Chart style applied and colors changed

Format Chart Elements

You can select chart elements (objects) and apply formatting in several ways.

HOW TO: Format a Chart Element

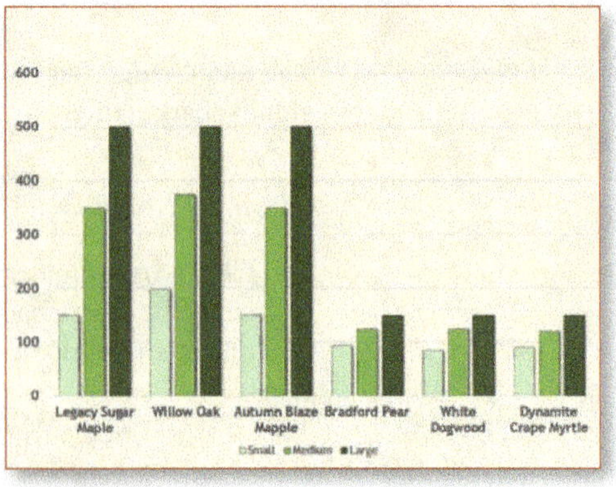

2-95 Colors changed on data series

1. Change colors and effects for a selected chart element using the Chart Tools Format tab:
   - Click the **Chart Tools Format** tab, click the **Shape Fill**, **Shape Outline**, or **Shape Effects** buttons [*Shape Styles* group] and choose appropriate colors and effects (Figure 2-95).
   - When text is selected, click the **Text Fill**, **Text Outline**, or **Text Effects** buttons [*WordArt Styles* group] and choose appropriate colors and effects.
2. Use one of these methods to open the *Format* pane (displayed on the right) and change options as needed:
   - Click the **Chart Tools Format** tab, select the element you need to change in the *Current Selection* drop-down list box. Click **Format Selection** [*Chart Tools Format* tab, *Current Selection* group] to open the *Format* pane for that element.
   - Double-click to open the appropriate *Format* pane or right-click and choose the **Format** option for that element to open the appropriate *Format* pane.
   - Click the **Chart Elements** button beside the chart and select a particular element. Click the triangle beside each element to select from different options. Click **More Options** to open the appropriate *Format* pane.

To change the chart area size, point to any sizing handle (the white circles on the chart frame) and resize by dragging. You can resize chart elements, but be careful not to distort size relationships.

You can fill elements of a chart with pictures. While a chart area picture might provide an interesting background, be careful when using pictures to avoid making the chart cluttered or the text difficult to read. The goal is always to create a chart that is easy to interpret.

In Figure 2-96, the chart area has a solid fill. The plot area has a gradient fill with the darkest color at the bottom which helps to emphasize the height of the columns. In Figure 2-97, the chart type is a *3-D Column Chart.* The column heights (especially for the shorter columns) are not as easy to compare in this chart as they are in Figure 2-96.

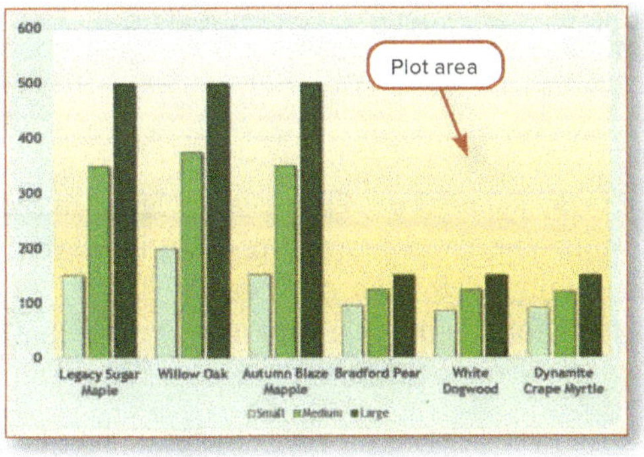

2-96 Chart plot area with gradient fill

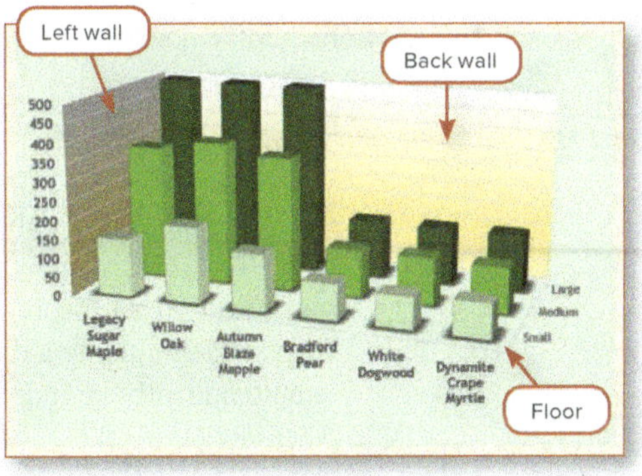

2-97 Chart with *3-D Rotation*

Legends and Labels

The ***legend*** identifies each data series by color. It is usually displayed on the right, but you can move it to other positions, display it horizontally above or below the plot area, or delete it.

▶ HOW TO: Change Legend Position and Colors

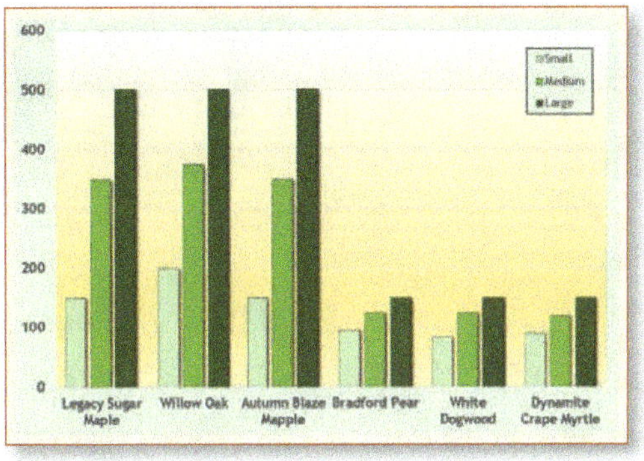

2-98 Legend moved and recolored

1. Change the selected legend's position by using one of the following methods:
   - Click the **Chart Tools Format** tab, select **Legend** in the *Current Selection* drop-down list box, and click **Format Selection** [*Chart Tools Format* tab, *Current Selection* group] to open the *Format Legend* pane. Select a position. Deselect **Show the legend without overlapping the chart** if you want the legend to appear over the plot area (Figure 2-98).
   - Double-click to open the *Format Legend* pane or right-click and choose **Format Legend** to open the *Format Legend* pane. Select a position.
   - Click the **Chart Elements** button beside the chart, click the **Legend** triangle, and then select a position or choose **More Options** to open the *Format Legend* pane.
   - Select the legend and drag it to another position within the chart area. Resize it as needed.
2. Change the selected legend's colors by using one of the following methods:
   - Click the **Chart Tools Format** tab, click the **Shape Fill** or **Shape Outline** buttons, and select different colors.
   - Right-click the legend and choose **Format Legend** to open the *Format Legend* pane. Click the **Fill & Line** tab and then select appropriate fill and border colors.
3. Remove a selected legend by using one of the following methods:
   - Click the **Chart Elements** button beside the chart and deselect the **Legend**.
   - Select the legend and press **Delete**.

Data labels display values for each data series. These labels appear in different places based on the chart style. Use the *Format Data Labels* pane to customize labels.

▸HOW TO: Display Data Labels

1. Select the chart and then click the **Chart Element** button beside the chart to open the list of *Chart Elements.*
2. Click **Data Labels** and select a position or click **More Options** to open the *Format Data Labels* pane.
   - Change *Label Options* to control the display and position of the value as well as *File & Line, Effects, Size & Properties* options.
   - Click **Text Options** and then select icons at the top of the pane to control *Text Fill & Outline* colors, apply *Text Effects,* and add a *Text Box.*

Using data labels above or inside columns enables the viewer to see the exact data value as well as the size relationships that the columns represent. However, the columns must be wide enough to display the numbers without overlapping. If the columns are too narrow (Figure 2-99), using a data table for this purpose is more effective. In a data table, the legend is automatically included, so it was removed from the plot area in Figure 2-100.

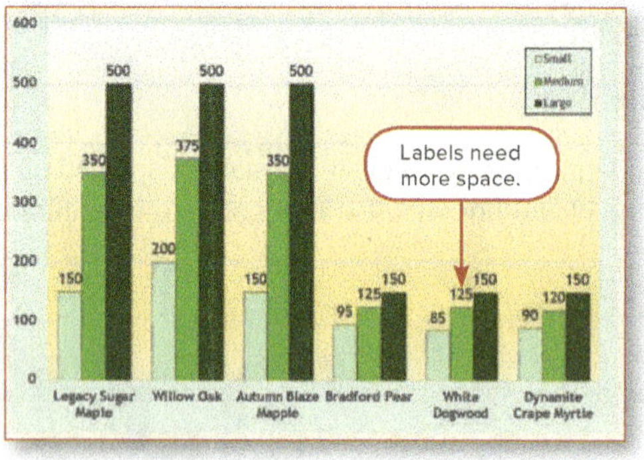

2-99 Data labels

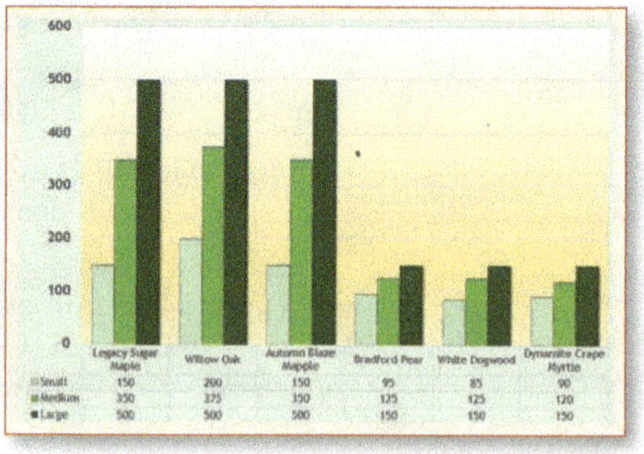

2-100 Data table

▸HOW TO: Display a Data Table

1. Select the chart and then click the **Chart Element** button beside the chart to open the list of *Chart Elements.*
2. Deselect **Data Labels** and **Legend** if these elements are selected. They will automatically display in the table.
3. Click **Data Table** and the table appears below the chart.
4. Point to any number in the data table, right-click to open the context menu, and select **Format Data Table** to open the *Format Data Table* pane. **Table Options** are displayed with three icons at the top of the pane.
   - Change *Data Table Options* (column icon) to control table borders and the legend key (the color that identifies each data series).
   - Click the *Fill & Line* icon (paint bucket) or the *Effects* icon (pentagon) to make color and effect changes.
   - Click **Text Options** and then select icons at the top of the pane to change *Text Fill & Outline Colors,* apply *Text Effects,* or add a *Text Box.*

A pie chart has one data series. Each slice represents a value and the size of the slice illustrates its relationship to the whole. The number of slices is best limited to six or seven slices; too many slices make a pie chart difficult to interpret.

Unlike a column or line chart, a pie chart does not have axes or axes titles. Data labels are often used instead of a legend because they are easier to interpret. You have several options for where data labels appear, either on the slices or outside the slices (Figure 2-101). Be sure to select an option that makes it easy for the viewer to match the number with the related slice. Usually the label font size must be increased. The *Format Data Labels* pane has many options you can explore (Figure 2-102).

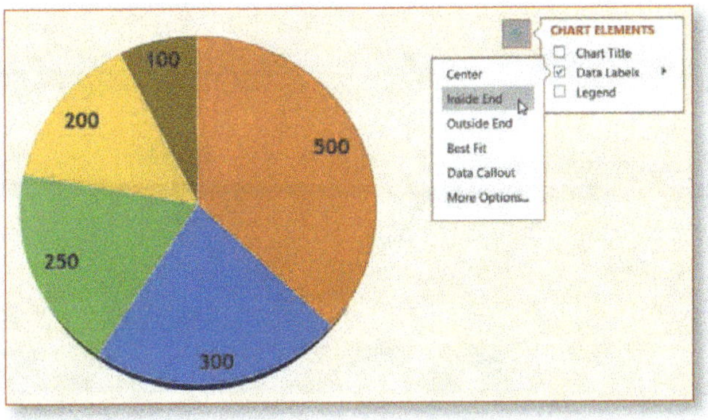

2-101 Pie chart data label positions

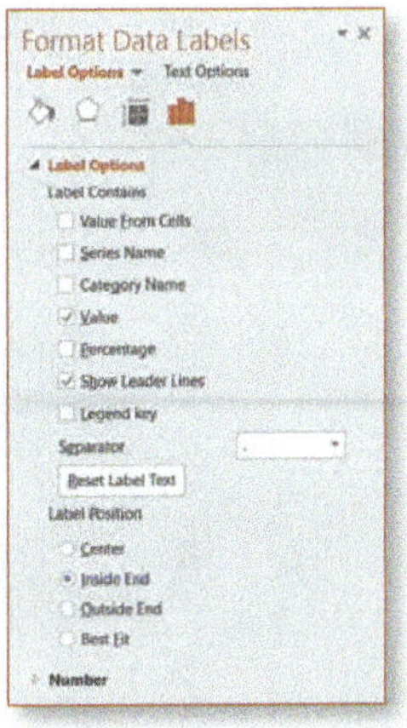

2-102 *Format Data Labels* pane

Explode a Pie Slice

You can ***explode*** (separate) pie chart slices by dragging the pie slices away from the center. However, when all slices are separated, no single slice is emphasized. To emphasize just one slice, it is best to first design a pie chart as you want it to look and then drag that one slice away from the pie. Consider, also, how your colors are applied so the most noticeable or brightest color is used for the slice that you want to emphasize (Figure 2-103).

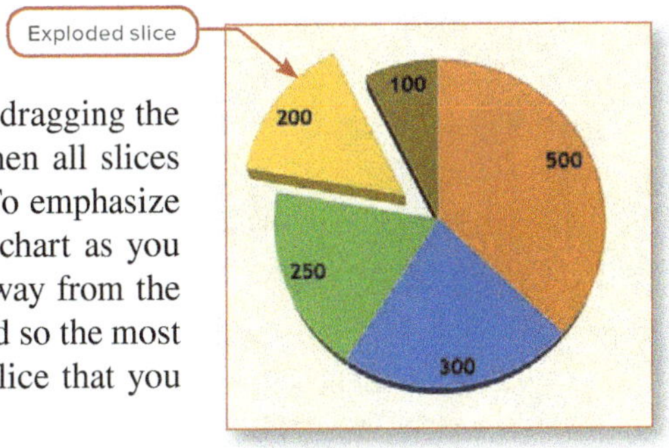

2-103 3-D pie chart with exploded slice

HOW TO: Explode a Pie Slice

1. Click a pie to select the pie object.
2. Click again to select just one pie slice. Check the handles to be sure you have selected the correct slice and not a label on the slice.
3. Click and drag slightly away from the center of the pie so the slice is emphasized.

As you drag a pie slice away from the center, the entire pie becomes smaller. You can make the whole pie larger by resizing the plot area. Removing the legend creates more space for the pie, too.

PAUSE & PRACTICE: POWERPOINT 2-4

For this project, you create a pie and two clustered column charts showing the cost distribution for CGL landscaping, cost comparisons for tree sizes, and the height of mature trees being considered for the new landscape.

Files Needed: ***[your initials] PP P2-3.pptx*** and ***Trees-02.jpg*** *(Student data files are available in the* Library *of your SIMnet account.)*
Completed Project File Name: ***[your initials] PP 2-4.pptx***

1. Open the presentation file ***[your initials] PP P2-3*** and save it as [your initials] PP P2-4.
2. Create a 3-D pie chart.
   a. Select slide 6, "**Cost Distribution**."
   b. Click the **Insert Chart** icon on the content placeholder.
   c. Select the **Pie** chart type then select the **3-D Pie** layout. Click **OK**.
   d. Replace the spreadsheet sample data with the data in the following list. Point to the top of the column and then click and drag the splitter to resize columns.

	Cost
Trees—Shade	1,500
Trees—Ornamental	450
Shrubs	400
Perennials	360
Hydroseeding sq. ft.	800

3. Resize the spreadsheet window so you can proof all entries. Be sure all chart data is selected (Figure 2-104).
4. Close the spreadsheet.

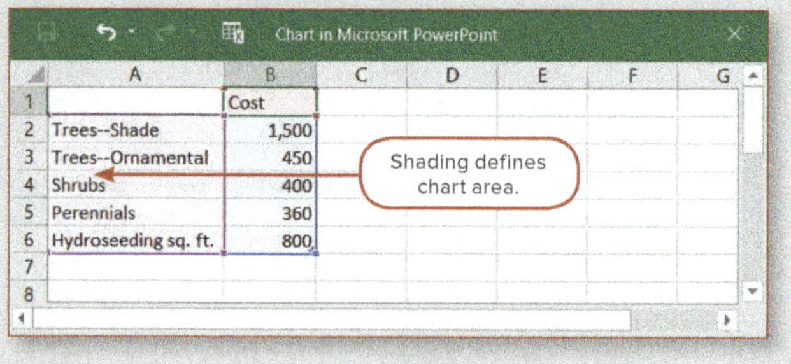

2-104 Spreadsheet linked to a chart

5. Format the 3-D pie chart.
   a. Delete the **Cost** chart title in the chart area because it duplicates the slide title.
   b. Click **Style 3** [*Chart Tools Design* tab, *Chart Styles* group].
   c. Verify that **Chart Area** [*Chart Tools Format* tab, *Current Selection* group] is selected. Click the **Shape Fill** button [*Chart Tools Format* tab, *Shape Styles* group]. Select **No Fill**.
   d. Click the **Shape Outline** button [*Chart Tools Format* tab, *Shape Styles* group] and select **No Outline**.
   e. From the drop-down list, select the **Series "Cost" Data Labels** [*Chart Tools Format* tab, *Current Selection* group]. Increase the font size to **20 pt**. [*Home* tab, *Font* group].
   f. Click the **Legend** and increase the font size to **20 pt**. [*Home* tab, *Font* group].
   g. Click and drag the legend to the upper right of the **Chart Area**.
   h. From the drop-down list, select the **Plot Area** [*Chart Tools Format* tab, *Current Selection* group]. Drag the center sizing handles to increase the plot area height so it matches the chart area height. The pie will be larger (Figure 2-105).
   i. Select the single slice for "**Trees—Ornamental**" and explode that slice by dragging it down slightly.

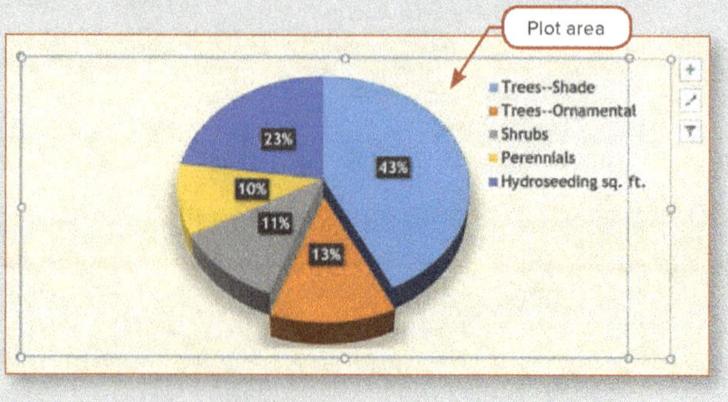

2-105 Slice exploded and legend repositioned

6. Create a clustered column chart.
   a. Select slide 7, "**Tree Size Cost Comparisons**." Click the **Insert Chart** icon on the content placeholder.
   b. Click the **Clustered Column** layout and click **OK**.
   c. Replace the spreadsheet data with the following data:

	Small	Medium	Large
Legacy Sugar Maple	150	350	500
Willow Oak	200	375	500
Autumn Blaze Maple	150	350	500
Bradford Pear	95	125	150
White Dogwood	85	115	150
Dynamite Crape Myrtle	90	120	150

   d. Close the spreadsheet. If you need to check the data, click the **Edit Data** button [*Chart Tools Design* tab, *Data* group].
   e. Delete the chart title in the chart area.
   f. Change the chart style to **Style 8** [*Chart Tools Design* tab, *Chart Styles* group] which has a dark fill for the chart area.

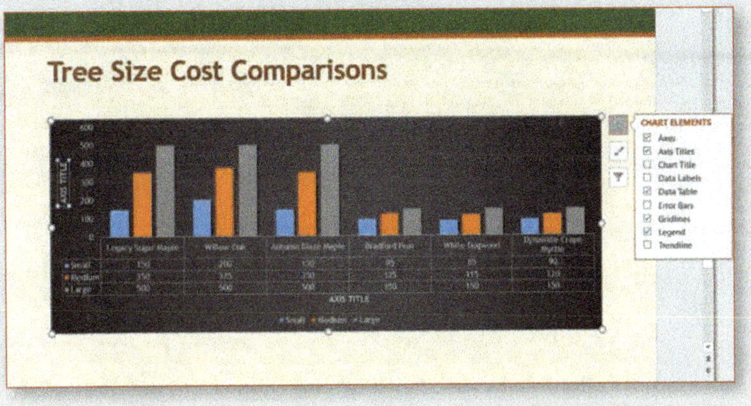

2-106 Clustered column chart with *Style 8* applied and chart elements listed on the right

7. Add chart elements.
   a. Click the **Chart Elements** button on the right side of the chart to display the list of elements (Figure 2-106).
   b. Select the following **Axes**, **Axis Titles**, **Data Table**, **Gridlines**, and **Legend** if they are not already selected.
      - The **Data Table** automatically appears below the columns.
8. Adjust chart formatting by selecting the following elements in the chart area. If necessary, confirm that you have the correct element selected [*Chart Tools Format* tab, *Current Selection* group].
   a. Select the *Vertical (Value) Axis Title* (rotated text on the Y-axis) and edit the text by typing Tree Cost.
   b. Select the *Horizontal (Category) Axis Title* (X-axis) below the data table and press **Delete**.
   c. Select the **Legend** and press **Delete**.
   d. Drag the chart area center sizing handle up to increase the height. Adjust the chart area size (*Height* **5"** and *Width* **11.5"**) [*Chart Tools Format* tab, *Size* group].
   e. Move the chart area up slightly so the blank space above and below the chart is even.
   f. Select each of the following chart elements and click **Shape Fill** [*Chart Tools Format* tab, *Shape Styles* group] to change the colors (Figure 2-107):
      - *Chart Area:* **Gold, Accent 4, Lighter 60%**

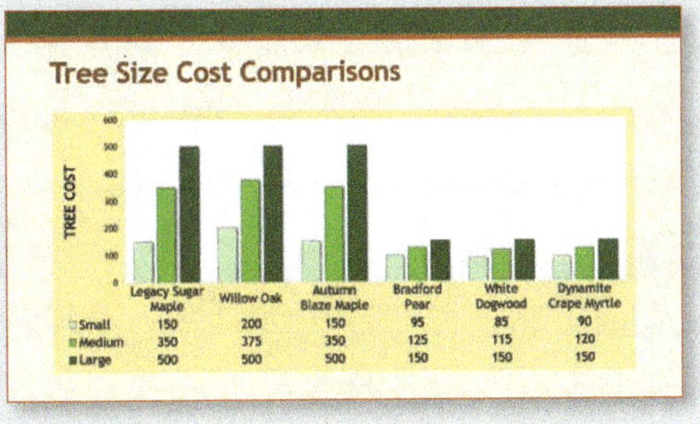

2-107 Completed chart

- *Plot Area:* **White, Background 1**
- *Large Series:* **Green, Accent 6, Darker 50%**
- *Medium Series:* **Green, Accent 6**
- *Small Series:* **Green, Accent 6, Lighter 60%**

g. Change text color and sizes.
- Select each text element and change the font color to **Black, Text 1**.
- Increase the font size on the axis title to **20 pt**.
- Increase the table text and axis numbers to **18 pt**.

9. Create another clustered column chart.

a. Select slide 8, "**Growth Potential**." Click **Chart** [*Insert* tab, *Illustrations* group] because this slide does not have a content placeholder.

b. Click the **Clustered Column** layout and click **OK** to close the dialog box.

c. Replace the spreadsheet data with the following data:

	Height
Legacy Sugar Maple	80
Willow Oak	60
Autumn Blaze Maple	50
Bradford Pear	35
White Dogwood	20
Dynamite Crape Myrtle	20

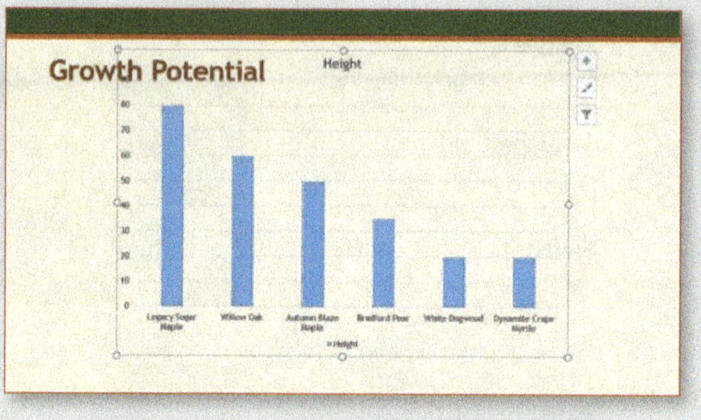

2-108 Column chart as it first appears

d. Delete the extra columns in the spreadsheet so the chart columns on the slide can expand in the available space (Figure 2-108).
- Select spreadsheet **Column C** and **Column D** headings and the entire columns are selected.
- Right-click, then select **Delete**. The columns are empty and the remaining columns fill the chart area.
- Verify that data is correctly selected and adjust spreadsheet borders if necessary.

e. Close the spreadsheet.
- The chart area is not as wide as in the previous chart because you inserted the chart directly on the slide rather than inserting it through a content placeholder that had different proportions.

10. Format the chart.

a. Delete the chart title and the legend.

b. Resize the chart area (*Height* of **5.5"** and *Width* **10"**) [*Chart Tools Format* tab, *Size* group].

c. Position the chart evenly on the slide.

d. Click the **More** button [*Chart Tools Design* tab, *Chart Styles* group] and change the chart style to **Style 14**.

e. Select the columns and change the color to **Green, Accent 6**.

f. Change font colors and sizes as follows:
- *Vertical (Value) Axis:* **Black, Text 1, Bold**, and **20 pt**.
- *Horizontal (Category) Axis:* **Black, Text 1, Bold**, and **18 pt**.

11. Select the *Chart Area* and apply a picture fill.

a. From the drop-down list, select **Chart Area** [*Chart Tools Format* tab, *Current Selection* group] and click **Format Selection** to open the *Format Chart Area* pane.

b. Select **Picture or texture fill**.

c. Click **File** and browse to your student data files. Select **Trees-02** and click **Insert**.

d. Change the *Transparency* percentage to **60%** (by dragging the slider or typing the percentage) to soften the picture's colors since it is behind the columns and text (Figure 2-109).
e. Close the Format Chart Area pane.

12. Click the **Transitions** tab and then select the **Wipe** transition with the **From Left** *Effect Options*. Click **Apply to All** [*Timing* group].
13. Save and close your presentation (Figure 2-110).

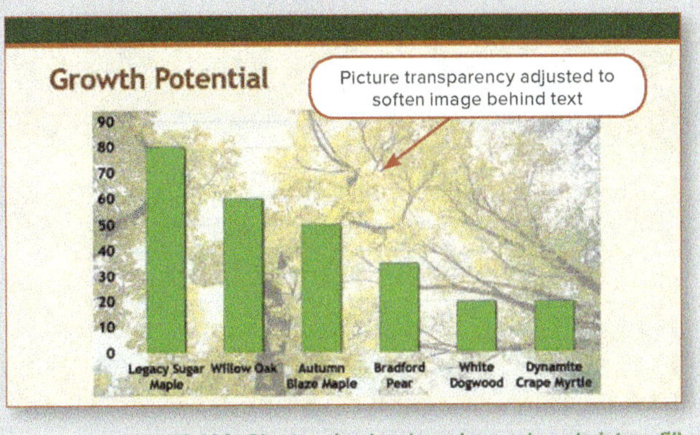

2-109 Chart resized, colors changed, and picture fill

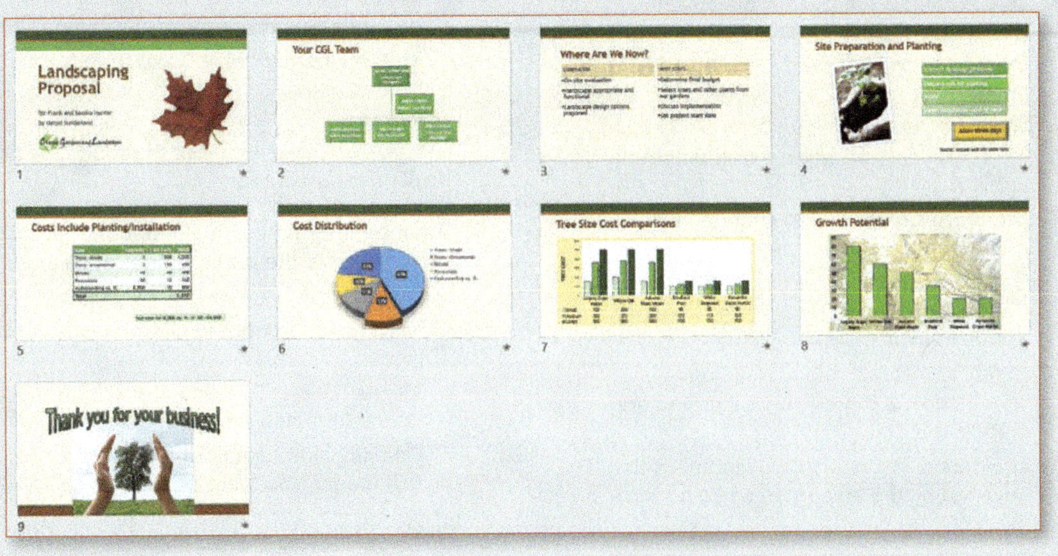

2-110 PP P2-4 completed

Chapter Summary

2.1 Work with shapes, select theme colors and standard colors, and apply styles (p. P2-71).

- Change shape size by entering exact height and width sizes or by dragging sizing handles.
- Use ***Lock Drawing Mode*** to draw the same shape multiple times.
- Use ***text boxes*** to position text anywhere on a slide.
- PowerPoint's various ***style*** galleries provide collections of preset effects for shapes, pictures, or other objects.
- Line ***Weight*** is the line thickness measured in points.
- ***Dashes*** show lines with a combination of dots and dashes.
- When you apply ***Theme Colors*** to shapes, the colors change when a different theme is applied.
- ***Standard Colors*** do not change when a different theme is applied.
- Computer screens use the ***RGB model*** that displays colors by blending values for *red, green,* and *blue.*
- Highly ***saturated*** colors are intense and vibrant; colors that are not saturated are muddy and dull.
- ***Luminosity*** is a measure of lightness that is adjusted by the amount of white or black in the color.
- The ***Eyedropper*** is used to match any color on your computer screen.

2.2 Create interesting and eye-catching text effects with *WordArt* styles and text effects (p. P2-80).

- The ***WordArt*** styles gallery shows a collection of preset text effects.
- The ***Transform*** effect warps text into different shapes or follows a path.
- You can fill *WordArt* with solid or gradient colors, textures, patterns, or pictures.
- Use the *Line Style* option in the *Format Shape* dialog box to customize line styles.

2.3 Search for pictures and illustrations, modify picture appearance, and compress picture file size (p. P2-82).

- Use the ***Insert Pictures*** dialog box to search for online pictures and illustrations.
- The *Picture Styles* gallery shows a collection of preset picture effects.
- To remove a picture style, click the *Reset Picture* button.
- Use ***Crop*** to trim unwanted areas of a selected picture.
- Increase ***Color Saturation*** to make picture colors more vibrant; decrease color saturation to make picture colors more muted.
- ***Color Tone*** changes a picture's cool or warm tones.
- Select *Color* and then ***Recolor*** to change a picture's color to a monotone color.
- The ***Set Transparent Color*** feature can make one color in a picture transparent. This feature works well to remove white backgrounds.
- Use ***Compress Pictures*** to reduce the file size of your presentation.

2.4 Organize information in a grid format using tables and customize the arrangement of columns and rows (p. P2-91).

- You can insert and delete table ***columns*** and ***rows.***
- ***Merge*** table cells to join them; ***split*** table cells to create multiple cells.
- Column width usually varies based on content; row height is usually a consistent size.

2.5 Format a table by applying styles, colors, and effects (p. P2-96).

- You can apply *WordArt Styles* to table text.
- ***Table Styles*** provide options for a table's design using theme accent colors.
- ***Table Style Options*** control how columns and rows are emphasized to feature areas of the table.
- Border lines can separate cells and shading can emphasize cells.
- Horizontal cell alignment options include *Align Left, Center,* or *Align Right;* vertical cell alignment options include *Align Top, Center Vertically,* or *Align Bottom.*

2.6 Show processes and relationships with *SmartArt* graphics (p. P2-101).

- Use ***SmartArt graphics*** to create diagrams that illustrate concepts such as processes, cycles, or relationships.

- ***SmartArt layouts*** are organized by categories.
- Each layout includes information about how you can use it or the meaning it conveys.
- Type text directly in each *SmartArt* shape or type text in the *Text Pane.*
- Change bulleted text to a *SmartArt* graphic by clicking the **Convert to SmartArt Graphic** button.

2.7 Improve the appearance of *SmartArt* graphics by applying styles, colors, and effects (p. P2-104).

- ***SmartArt Styles*** provide a gallery of *Effect Options.*
- The ***Change Colors*** button provides a gallery of color options arranged in categories.
- The ***Add Shape*** button inserts shapes in relation to the selected shape.
- You can format or individually resize shapes within a *SmartArt* graphic.

2.8 Create charts that show relationships between data values and emphasize data in different ways based on the chart type and chart elements (p. P2-108).

- Charts in PowerPoint are linked to spreadsheets where data is entered. Changes made to the data will automatically appear in the chart.
- Charts created in Excel can be edited in PowerPoint because they are linked.
- A group of data values is a ***data series.***
- *Chart Layouts* are arranged in categories including *Column, Line, Pie, Bar,* and *Area.*
- The ***Chart Area*** displays the entire chart including all ***chart elements.***
- The *Plot Area* provides a background for *Data Markers,* the columns, bars, or slices that represent data.

2.9 Format a chart by applying preset styles or manually customizing individual chart elements (p. P2-113).

- ***Chart Styles*** provide a gallery of preset effects for chart elements.
- The ***Legend*** is a key that identifies each data series by color.
- The *Change Colors* button provides a gallery of colorful or monochromatic colors for chart elements.
- You can customize chart elements individually to enhance their appearance.
- To emphasize a pie slice, you can **explode** it by separating the slice from the rest of the pie chart.

Check for Understanding

The SIMbook for this text (within your SIMnet account) provides the following resources for concept review:

- Multiple choice questions
- Matching exercises
- Short answer questions

USING MICROSOFT POWERPOINT 2016

Guided Project 2-1

Guest satisfaction has always been important to the success of Paradise Lakes Resort (PLR) in Minnesota. The general manager plans to use feedback from social media to identify problems and to guide improvements at the resort. In this project you illustrate a presentation the general manager will use to explain these concepts to employees at PLR.
[Student Learning Outcomes 2.1, 2.2, 2.3, 2.6, 2.7]

File Needed: ***SocialMedia-02.pptx*** *(Student data files are available in the* Library *of your SIMnet account.)*
Completed Project File Name: ***[your initials] PowerPoint 2-1.pptx***

Skills Covered in This Project

- Apply a picture style.
- Adjust size dimensions.
- Apply text effects.
- Insert a text box.
- Create a *SmartArt* graphic.
- Apply a *SmartArt* style and effects.

1. Open the presentation ***SocialMedia-02***. This design theme shows slide titles at the bottom of all slides except the title slide.
2. Save the presentation as [your initials] PowerPoint 2-1.
3. Resize a picture and apply a style.
   a. Select the lake picture on slide 1.
   b. Change the picture *Width* to **6"** [*Picture Tools Format* tab, *Size* group]. The *Height* automatically adjusts.
   c. Apply the **Metal Oval** picture style [*Picture Tools Format* tab, *Picture Styles* group].
   d. Position the picture on the left (Figure 2-111).

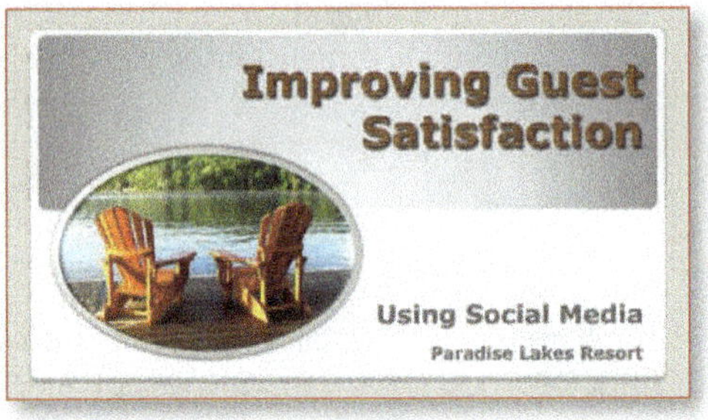

2-111 Title slide

4. Adjust the title text to complement the wood decking shown in the picture.
   a. Select the title text "Improving Guest Satisfaction" on slide 1 and increase the font size to **60 pt**.
   b. Adjust the placeholder so it fits the text and move it down slightly.
   c. Select the title text and click the **Text Fill** button [*Drawing Tools Format* tab, *WordArt Styles* group], select **Texture**, and select **Medium Wood**.
   d. With the title text selected, click the **Text Effects** button, select **Shadow**, and select **Shadow Options**. The *Format Shape* pane opens. Change the following settings:
      Transparency: **20%**
      Blur: **5 pt**.
      Angle: **50°**
      Distance: **5 pt**.
   f. Close the *Format Shape* pane.
5. Insert a new slide with a *Title and Content* layout after slide 1.

6. Add text and a shape.
   a. Display slide 2 and type the slide title Why Social Media? In this theme, the title placeholder is at the bottom of the slide.
   b. Type the following bulleted text:

      Revenue
      Market Share
      Guest Satisfaction
      Guest Loyalty

   c. Resize the bulleted list placeholder so it fits the text and move the text to the right (Figure 2-112).
   d. Click the **Shapes** button [*Insert* tab, *Illustrations* group] to open the gallery. Select the **Up Arrow** shape (*Block Arrow* category).
   e. Draw an arrow (*Height* **3.5"** and *Width* **2.5"**). Then position the arrow to the left of the text.
   f. With the arrow selected, click the **More** button [*Drawing Tools Format* tab, *Shape Styles* group] and apply the **Intense Effect, Orange, Accent 1**.

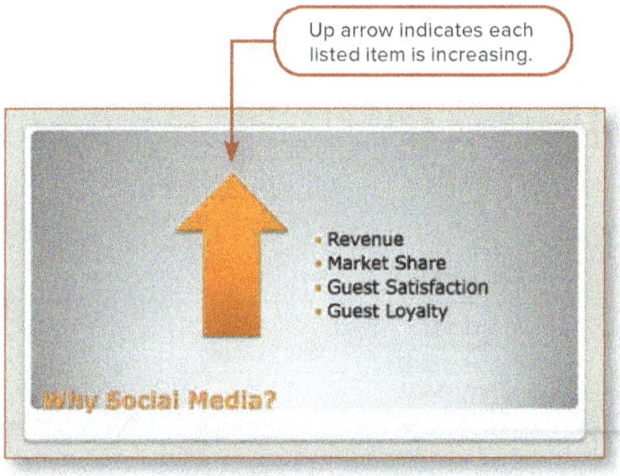

2-112 Slide 3 with a shape

7. Insert a new slide with a *Blank* layout after slide 4.
8. Create a *SmartArt* graphic and insert an additional shape on slide 5.
   a. Click the **Insert** tab.
   b. Click the **SmartArt** button and select the **Cycle** type.
   c. Select the **Continuous Cycle** layout and click **OK**.
   d. Add the following text to each shape starting with the top shape and continuing in a clockwise direction around the circle:

      More Rentals
      Rentals
      Social Media Comments
      Improvements
      Better Social Media Comments

   e. Select the "**Better Social Media Comments**" shape, click the **Add Shape** drop-down arrow [*SmartArt Tools Design* tab, *Create Graphic* group] and select **Add Shape After**.
   f. Type Higher Ratings in the new shape.
   g. Click the **Intense Effect** style [*SmartArt Tools Design* tab, *SmartArt Styles* group].
   h. Select all shapes with text by pressing **Ctrl** while you click each one. Change the font size to **20 pt**. and apply **bold** [*Home* tab, *Font* group].
   i. With all the shapes selected, resize the shapes horizontally (*Width* **2.75"**) so the word "Improvements" fits on one line (Figure 2-113).
9. Insert a text box.
   a. Click the **Text Box** button [*Insert* tab, *Text* group] and click inside the cycle layout.
   b. Type the following text and resize the text box so that the text wraps on two lines as shown in Figure 2-113:

      With the help of NewMediaMarketing.com

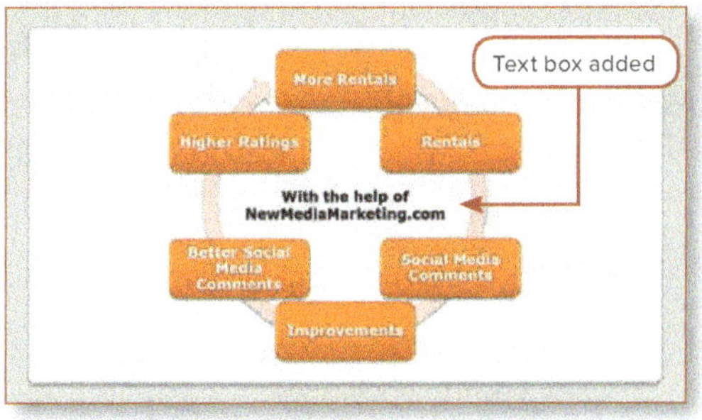

2-113 Slide 4 with *SmartArt* graphic and effects added

c. Change the font size to **20 pt**., apply **bold**, and center the text [*Home* tab, *Font* group].
d. Adjust the text box size, if necessary, and center it in the middle of the cycle layout as shown in Figure 2-113.

10. Apply a transition.
    a. Click the **Reveal** transition effect [*Transitions* tab, *Transition to This Slide* group].
    b. Click **Apply To All** [*Transitions* tab, *Timing* group].
11. Save and close the presentation (Figure 2-114).

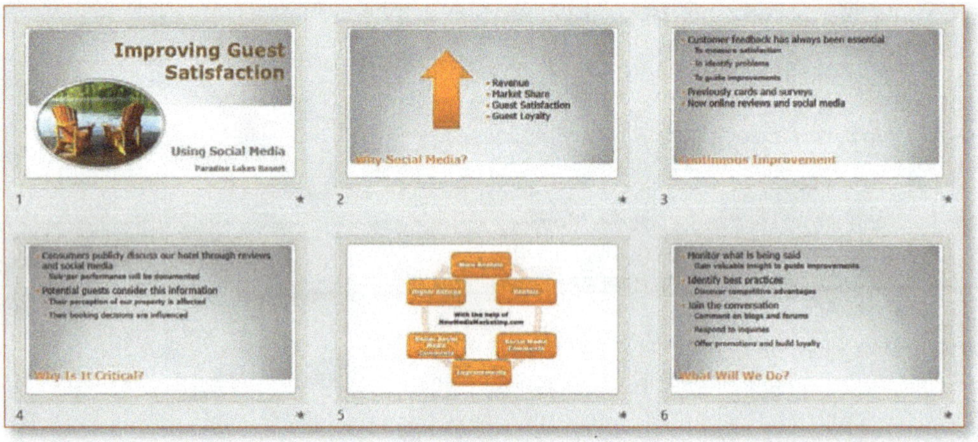

2-114 PowerPoint 2-1 completed

Guided Project 2-2

For this project, you prepare a presentation with key points essential to maintain a healthy lifestyle and show examples of weight loss calorie requirements for men and women at different ages. The doctors at Courtyard Medical Plaza will use this presentation to encourage clients to be more active.
[Student Learning Outcomes 2.1, 2.2, 2.3, 2.4, 2.5, 2.6, 2.7]

File Needed: ***StayingActive-02.pptx*** *(Student data files are available in the* Library *of your SIMnet account.)*
Completed Project File Name: ***[your initials] PowerPoint 2-2.pptx***

Skills Covered in This Project

- Apply text effects.
- Create a *SmartArt* graphic.
- Apply a *SmartArt* style and effects.
- Insert an online picture.
- Crop a picture.
- Apply a picture style.
- Adjust size dimensions.
- Insert a text box.
- Insert and format a table.

1. Open the presentation ***StayingActive-02***.
2. Save the presentation as [your initials] PowerPoint 2-2.

3. Format the presentation title.
   a. Select the title placeholder on slide 1.
   b. Click the **Text Effects** button [*Drawing Tools Format* tab, *WordArt Styles* group], click **Transform**, and select **Square** (*Square* is the first style under *Warp*). The text fills the title placeholder.
   c. Click the **Bring Forward** drop-down arrow [*Drawing Tools Format* tab, *Arrange* group], and select **Bring to Front** so the green triangle is behind the text.
   d. Click the **Text Fill** button [*Drawing Tools Format* tab, *WordArt Styles* group], select **Texture**, and click **More Textures** to open the *Format Shape* pane.
   e. Select **Pattern fill** and then choose the **Large checker board** pattern.
   f. Change the *Foreground Color* to **Aqua, Accent 1, Lighter 40%** and the *Background Color* to **White, Text 1**.
   g. Click **Text Fill** to close those options on the *Format Shape* pane. Click **Text Outline** to open outline options. Select **Solid line** and change the color to **Black, Background 1**.
   h. Click the **Text Effects** icon at the top of the pane. Select **Glow**.
   i. Change the *Color* to **Green, Accent 2, Lighter 60%** and the *Transparency* to **20%**. Verify the *Size* is **10 pt**. (Figure 2-115).
   j. Close the *Format Shape* pane.

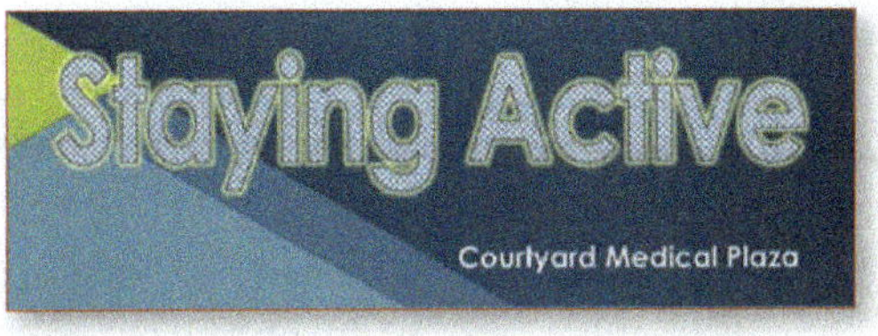

2-115 Text Effects for presentation title

4. Insert a *SmartArt* graphic, apply a style, and change colors using the *SmartArt Tools Design* tab.
   a. Display slide 2 and click the **SmartArt** icon on the content placeholder to open the *Choose a SmartArt Graphic* dialog box.
   b. Select the **Hierarchy** type and the **Horizontal Hierarchy** layout. Click **OK** to close the dialog box and insert the SmartArt graphic.
   c. Delete the three shapes on the right.
   d. Click the **Text Pane** button on the left of the *SmartArt* frame, if necessary, to open the *Text Pane*.
   e. Type Keep Moving after the first bullet. Type the following items after the indented bullets:

      Moderate Intensity Activity
      Count Steps (Press **Enter** to add another bullet.)
      Combine Aerobic and Strengthening

   f. Click the *Text Pane* **Close** button.
   g. Select the **Subtle Effect** *SmartArt* style [*SmartArt Tools Design* tab, *SmartArt Styles* group].
   h. Click the **Change Colors** button [*SmartArt Tools Design* tab, *SmartArt Styles* group] and select **Colorful Range, Accent Colors 4 to 5** (Figure 2-116).

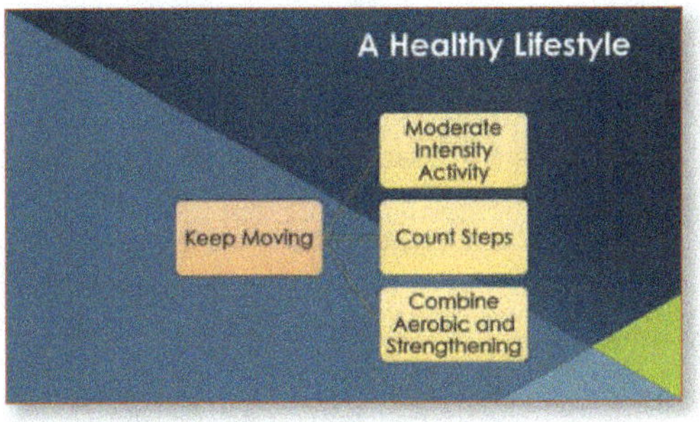

2-116 *SmartArt* graphic with style and colors changed

5. Search for a picture and apply a picture style.
   a. Display slide 3. Click the **Online Pictures** button [*Insert* tab, *Images* group] to open the *Insert Pictures* dialog box.
   b. Search for an online picture using the search word gardening.
   c. On the search results dialog box, click the list arrow by the *Search* button to select **All Images**. Select an appropriate picture and click **Insert**.
   d. Select the **Rotated White** picture style [*Picture Tools Format* tab, *Picture Styles* group].
   e. Resize the picture as needed so it fits on the right of the slide.

6. Crop a picture and apply a picture style.
   a. Display slide 5 and select the picture. Click the **Crop** button [*Picture Tools Format* tab, *Size* group] and crop the picture to focus only on the family. Click **Crop** again to accept your change.
   b. Select the **Rotated White** picture style [*Picture Tools Format* tab, *Picture Styles* group] to match the other picture.
   c. Move the picture to the right of the slide.
7. Insert a new slide after slide 6 with a *Title and Content* layout.
8. Add text.
   a. On slide 7, type the title text Calorie Examples.
   b. Click the **Text Box** button [*Insert* tab, *Text* group], click below the title, and type Gaining 5 pounds a year.
   c. Apply **Bold** and change the font size to **20 pt**. [*Home* tab, *Font* group].
   d. Resize the text box as needed. Right-align the text box and the slide title.
9. Insert a table, add text, and modify formatting.
   a. Click the **Table** icon on the content placeholder on slide 7.
   b. Enter **6** columns and **5** rows on the *Insert Table* dialog box. Click **OK** to close the dialog box.
   c. Type the text shown in Figure 2-117.

Shading reflects the same person at two ages.

Age	Height	Weight	Maintain	Fat Loss	Extreme Fat Loss
20	5 ft 10 in	200	2,647	2,118	1,600
25	5 ft 10 in	225	2,769	2,215	1,800
30	6 ft 2 in	240	2,916	2,333	1,920
35	6 ft 2 in	265	3,038	2,430	2,120

2-117 Table with formatting changes

   d. Select all cells and change the font size to **20 pt**. [*Home* tab, *Font* group]. Change to **Center** alignment [*Table Tools Layout* tab, *Alignment* group].
   e. Adjust column width by double-clicking the border line between columns. Deselect the table, if necessary, so your pointer changes to a splitter to adjust the right border of the last column so the text fits on one line. When you stop dragging, the table is selected again.
   f. Change the *Pen Color* to **Black, Background 1** and verify the *Pen Weight* is **1 pt**. [*Table Tools Design* tab, *Draw Borders* group].
   g. Click the **Borders** button, and select **All Borders** [*Table Tools Design* tab, *Table Styles* group].
   h. Select the second and third rows. Click the **Shading** button [*Table Tools Design* tab, *Table Styles* group] and select **Aqua, Accent 1, Lighter 80%**.
   i. Select the fourth and fifth rows. Click the **Shading** button [*Table Tools Design* tab, *Table Styles* group] and select **Aqua, Accent 1, Lighter 60%**.
   j. Center the table on the slide.
10. Duplicate the table and edit the text in the second table.
   a. Select the table on slide 7 and press **Ctrl+D** to duplicate it.
   b. Position the second table centered near the bottom of the slide.
   c. Edit the table content to match the text shown in Figure 2-118.

Age	Height	Weight	Maintain	Fat Loss	Extreme Fat Loss
20	5 ft 7 in	150	2,041	1,633	1,225
25	5 ft 7 in	175	2,163	1,730	1,400
30	5 ft 9 in	180	2,204	1,763	1,440
35	5 ft 9 in	205	2,325	1,860	1,640

2-118 Table with text edits

11. Insert and format a shape to identify table contents on slide 7.
   a. Click the **Shapes** button [*Insert* tab, *Illustrations* group] and select the **Oval**. Draw an oval shape and adjust its size (*Height* **0.9"** and *Width* **2"**) [*Drawing Tools Format* tab, *Size* group].
   b. Click the **Shape Fill** button [*Drawing Tools Format* tab, *Shape Styles* group] and change the color to **Gold, Accent 5, Lighter 40%**.
   c. Click the **Shape Outline** button [*Drawing Tools Format* tab, *Shape Styles* group] and change the color to **Green, Accent 2**. Repeat to change the *Weight* to **3 pt**.

d. Type the word Female. Change the font color to **Black, Background 1** and apply **Bold**.
e. Click the **Edit Shape** button [*Drawing Tools Format* tab, *Insert Shapes* group] and select **Change Shape**. Select **Explosion 1** in the *Stars and Banners* category.
f. Position this shape at the left corner of the bottom table (Figure 2-119).

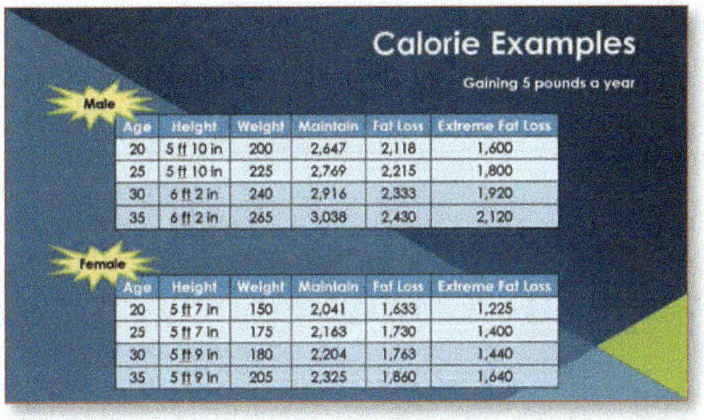

2-119 Slide 7 completed tables

12. Duplicate and edit a shape.
    a. Select the "**Female**" shape and press **Ctrl+D** to duplicate it.
    b. Position the second shape at the left corner of the top table.
    c. Change the text to Male.
13. Format the table:
    a. Display slide 8 and select the table. If necessary, change the *Pen Color* to **Black, Background 1** and the *Pen Weight* to **1 pt**. [*Table Tools Design* tab, *Draw Borders* group].
    b. Click **Borders** [*Table Tools Design* tab, *Table Styles* group] and select **All Borders**.
    c. Change the font size for all text to **20 pt**.
    d. Select all cells and click the **Center Vertically** button [*Table Tools Layout* tab, *Alignment* group].
    e. Change the table size (*Height* **4.5"** and *Width* **9"**) and click the **Center** button [*Table Tools Layout* tab, *Alignment* group] to center it horizontally on the slide.
14. Apply a transition.
    a. Click the **Cube** transition effect [*Transitions* tab, *Transition to This Slide* group].
    b. Click **Apply To All** [*Transitions* tab, *Timing* group].
15. Save and close the presentation (Figure 2-120).

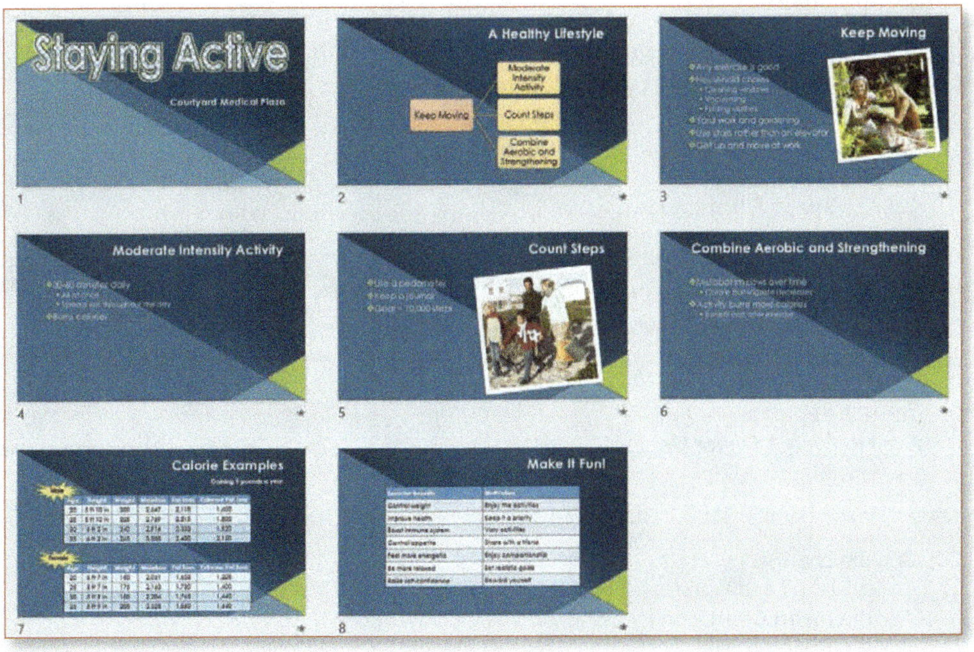

2-120 PowerPoint 2-2 completed

Guided Project 2-3

Solution Seekers, Inc., has been asked to develop a presentation for a meeting of personnel managers about salary trends for information technology workers. For this project, you modify tables and prepare charts showing average salaries and salaries for selected jobs.
[Student Learning Outcomes 2.1, 2.2, 2.3, 2.5, 2.6, 2.7, 2.8]

File Needed: ***InfoTechSalaries-02.pptx*** *(Student data files are available in the* Library *of your SIMnet account.)*
Completed Project File Name: ***[your initials] PowerPoint 2-3.pptx***

Skills Covered in This Project

- Convert text to a *SmartArt* graphic.
- Apply a *SmartArt* style and effects.
- Create a pie chart.
- Format a table.
- Create a column chart.
- Apply chart styles.
- Format chart elements.
- Insert *WordArt* and apply effects.
- Apply a picture style.
- Insert and align text boxes.

1. Open the presentation ***InfoTechSalaries-02***.
2. Save the presentation as [your initials] PowerPoint 2-3.
3. Convert bulleted text to a *SmartArt* graphic and modify the style and colors.
   a. Display slide 2. Select the bulleted text and click the **Convert to SmartArt** button [*Home* tab, *Paragraph* group].
   b. Select **More SmartArt Graphics** to open the *Choose a SmartArt Graphic* dialog box.
   c. Select the **Relationship** type and the **Counterbalance Arrows** layout. Click **OK** to close the dialog box.
   d. Apply the **Cartoon** style [*SmartArt Tools Design* tab, *SmartArt Styles* group].
   e. Select the down arrow shape pointing to "Fewer Layoffs" and click the **Shape Fill** drop-down arrow [*SmartArt Tools Format* tab, *Shape Styles* group].
   f. Select **Gradient** and under *Dark Variations,* click **Linear Down** to emphasize the downward movement.
   g. Select the up arrow and repeat step f to apply a **Linear Up** gradient (Figure 2-121).

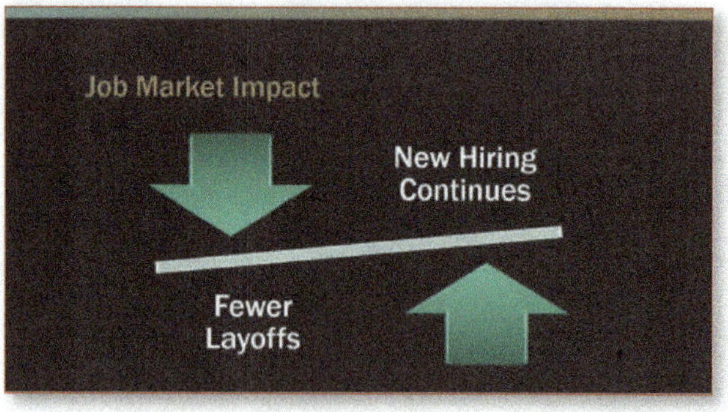

2-121 Slide 2 *SmartArt* graphic with color changes

4. Insert a new slide after slide 2 with a *Title and Content* layout.
5. Create a pie chart.
   a. Display slide 3 and type the slide title Employee Salary Satisfaction.
   b. Click the **Insert Chart** icon in the content placeholder.
   c. Click the **Pie** chart type. Then select the **3-D Pie**. Click **OK** to close the dialog box and insert the chart.

d. Replace the spreadsheet data with the data shown in Figure 2-122. Close the spreadsheet.

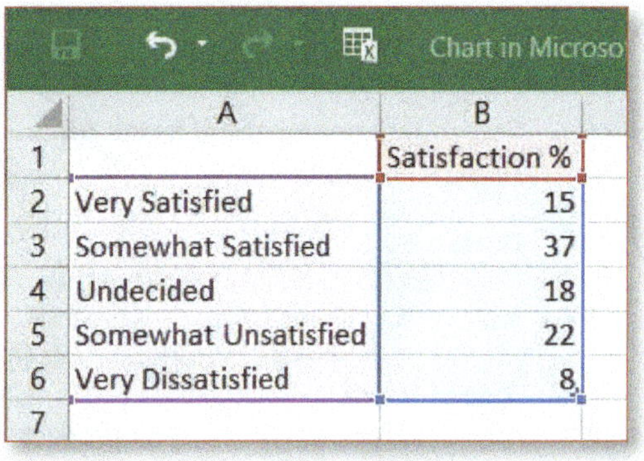

	A	B
1		Satisfaction %
2	Very Satisfied	15
3	Somewhat Satisfied	37
4	Undecided	18
5	Somewhat Unsatisfied	22
6	Very Dissatisfied	8
7		

2-122 Spreadsheet linked to a chart

6. Modify a pie chart.
   a. Drag the chart title "**Satisfaction%**," to the top left of the chart area. Increase the font size to **24 pt**. [*Home* tab, *Font* group].
   b. Click the **Chart Elements** button on the right side of the slide and select **Legend**. Select **Right**.
   c. Increase the font size to **20 pt**. [*Home* tab, *Font* group] and drag the legend to the bottom right of the chart area.
   d. Click the **Chart Elements** button again and select **Data Labels**. Select **Inside End**.
   e. Click the **Chart Elements** list box arrow [*Chart Tools Format* tab, *Current Selection* group] and select **Series "Satisfaction %" Data Labels**. Increase the font size to **24 pt**. and apply **Bold** [*Home* tab, *Font* group] (Figure 2-123).

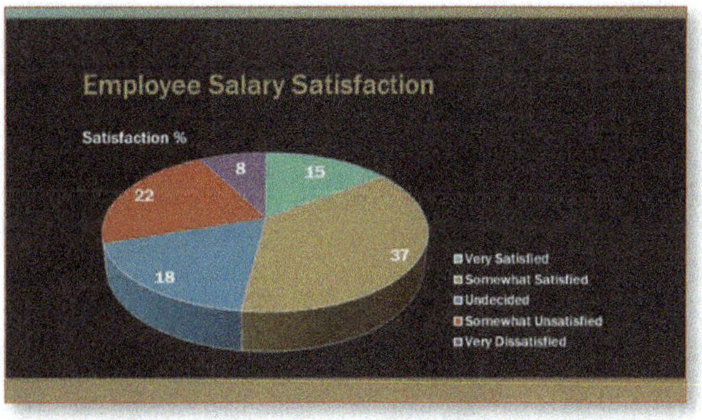

2-123 Slide 3 completed pie chart

7. Modify table formatting.
   a. Display slide 4 and select the table. Increase the font size to **20 pt**. [*Home* tab, *Font* group].
   b. Select **Header Row** and **Banded Rows** [*Table Tools Design* tab, *Table Style Options* group].
   c. Apply the **Themed Style 1, Accent 2** style [*Table Tools Design* tab, *Table Styles* group].
   d. Increase the table size (*Height* **4"**) [*Table Tools Layout* tab, *Table Size* group].
   e. Click the **Center Vertically** button [*Table Tools Layout* tab, *Alignment* group].
   f. Select columns 2–5 and click **Align Right** [*Table Tools Layout* tab, *Alignment* group].

8. After slide 4, insert a new slide with a *Title and Content* layout.

9. Create a column chart.
   a. Select slide 5 and type the slide title Salary Change, Selected Jobs.
   b. Click the **Insert Chart** button on the content placeholder.
   c. Select the **Clustered Column** chart and click **OK**.
   d. Replace the spreadsheet data with the data shown in Figure 2-124. Select **Column D**, right-click, and select **Delete**. By removing the blank column, the chart displays correctly with no blank space. Close the spreadsheet.

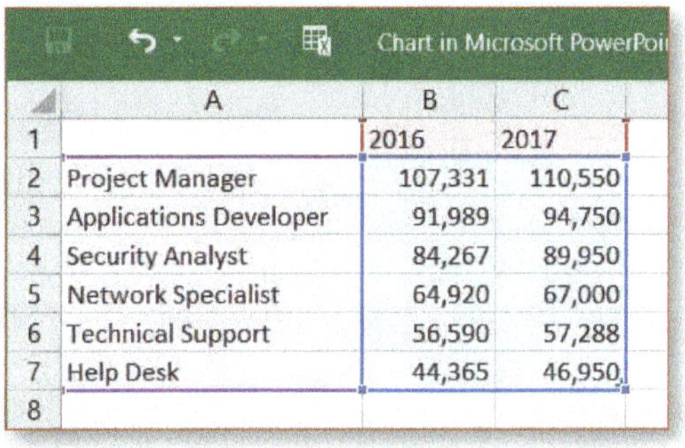

	A	B	C
1		2016	2017
2	Project Manager	107,331	110,550
3	Applications Developer	91,989	94,750
4	Security Analyst	84,267	89,950
5	Network Specialist	64,920	67,000
6	Technical Support	56,590	57,288
7	Help Desk	44,365	46,950
8			

2-124 Spreadsheet linked to a chart

10. Modify a column chart.
   a. Delete the "**Chart Title**" placeholder.
   b. Click the **Chart Elements** button on the right side of the chart, select **Legend**, and then click **More Options** to open the *Format Legend* pane.

c. Click the **Legend Options** heading, if necessary, to open the list of options. Select **Top Right** and deselect **Show the legend without overlapping the chart**.
d. Close the *Format Chart Area* pane.
e. Select the **Legend** and click the **Shape Fill** button [*Chart Tools Format* tab, *Shape Styles* group]. Change the legend color to **Brown, Accent 2, Darker 50%**.
f. Click the chart frame to select the **Chart Area** and change the **Shape Fill** color to **Teal, Accent 1, Darker 50%**.
g. Select the **Legend** and increase the font size to **18 pt**. [*Home* tab, *Font* group]. Repeat to increase the **Vertical (Value) Axis** font size to **18 pt**.
h. Select the **Horizontal (Category) Axis** and increase the font size to **20 pt**. (Figure 2-125).

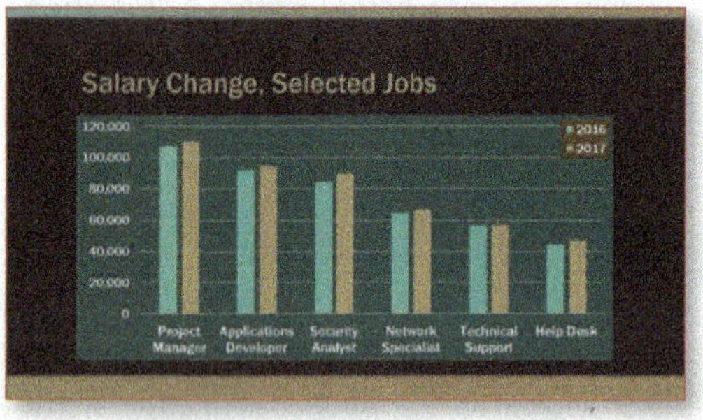

2-125 Slide 5 completed clustered column chart

11. Select the picture on slide 6 and apply the **Moderate Frame, Black** picture style [*Picture Tools Format* tab, *Picture Styles* group].
12. Insert *WordArt* text on slide 6.
    a. Click the **WordArt** button [*Insert* tab, *Text* group] and select the **Fill – White, Text 1, Outline – Background 1, Hard Shadow – Accent 1** style.
    b. Type Employees Are Valuable in the *WordArt* placeholder and move this text above the picture.
    c. With the *WordArt* placeholder selected, click the **Text Effects** button [*Drawing Tools Format* tab, *WordArt Styles* group], select **Shadow**, and click **Offset Diagonal Bottom Right**.
    d. Click the **Text Outline** button [*Drawing Tools Format* tab, *WordArt Styles* group] and select **Black, Background 2**.
    e. Deselect the *WordArt* text (Figure 2-126).

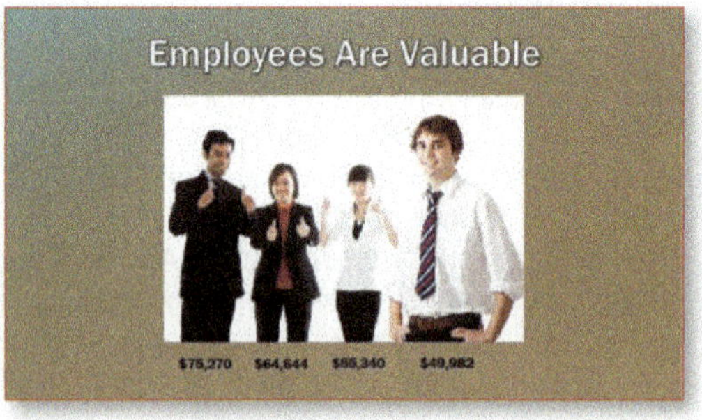

2-126 Slide 6 picture style, text effects, and text boxes

13. Insert text boxes on slide 6 for salary numbers.
    a. Click the **Text Box** button [*Insert* tab, *Text* group], click below the picture, and type $75,270. Change the font color to **Black, Background 2**, increase the font size to **20 pt**., and apply **Bold**.
    b. Position this salary below the first person on the left in the picture.
    c. With the salary text box selected, press **Ctrl+D** and position the duplicated text box below the second person in the picture. Repeat for the remaining two people in the picture.
    d. Edit the text boxes to change the three duplicated salaries to $64,644, $55,340, and $49,982.
    e. Select all of the salary text boxes and click the **Arrange** button [*Home* tab, *Drawing* group]. Select **Align** and click **Align Selected Objects** if necessary. Repeat to click **Align Bottom** (see Figure 2-126).

14. Apply transitions.
    a. Click the **Blinds** transition effect [*Transitions* tab, *Transition to This Slide* group].
    b. Click **Apply To All** [*Transitions* tab, *Timing* group].
    c. Apply the **Zoom** transition to slide 6.
15. Save and close the presentation (Figure 2-127).

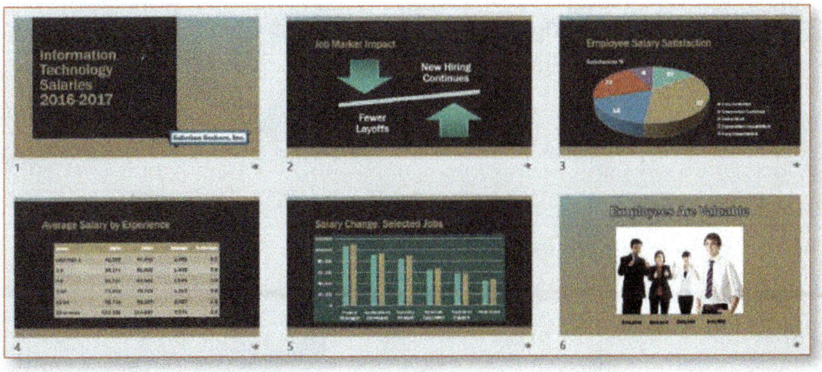

2-127 PowerPoint 2-3 completed

Independent Project 2-4

At Pool & Spa Oasis, sales associates must educate new spa owners about keeping spa water safe with proper maintenance. For this project, you prepare a presentation that emphasizes the routine to follow, explains pH level numbers, and lists available products that are typically used to balance water.
[Student Learning Outcomes 2.1, 2.2, 2.3, 2.4, 2.5, 2.6, 2.7]

File Needed: ***Balancing-02.pptx*** (*Student data files are available in the* Library *of your SIMnet account.*)
Completed Project File Name: ***[your initials] PowerPoint 2-4.pptx***

Skills Covered in This Project

- Insert *WordArt* and apply effects.
- Adjust size dimensions.
- Insert an online picture.
- Apply a picture style.
- Create a *SmartArt* graphic.
- Apply a *SmartArt* style and effects.
- Insert and format a table.
- Insert a text box.
- Change solid and gradient colors.

1. Open the presentation ***Balancing-02***.
2. Save the presentation as [your initials] PowerPoint 2-4.

3. Change the title text arrangement.
   a. Display slide 1. Delete the title text "**Balancing Act**," but leave the word "**The**" as shown.
   b. Insert *WordArt* with the style **Fill – White, Outline – Accent 1, Glow – Accent 1**.
   c. Type Balancing Act.
   d. Apply a **Shadow, Offset Right** *Text Effect*.
   e. Click the **Character Spacing** button [*Home* tab, *Font* group] and choose **Tight**.
   f. Apply the *Transform* text effect of **Cascade Up**.
   g. Increase the *WordArt* size (*Height* **3"** and *Width* **9"**) and position it as shown in Figure 2-128.

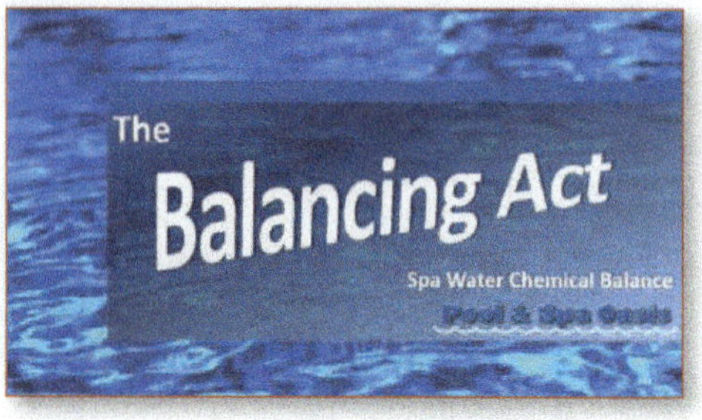

2-128 Slide 1 with *WordArt*

4. Insert a picture and adjust text spacing. The bulleted list placeholder on slide 2 has a gradient fill color so it cannot be resized without distorting the slide.
   a. Display slide 2. On the first indented line in the bulleted list, place your insertion point in front of the word "correct." Press **Shift+Enter** to insert a line break so the remaining text go to the next line without starting a new paragraph. Repeat to split the next line twice: before "microorganisms" and "Bromine."
   b. Search for an online picture using the words hot tub and insert a picture similar to the one shown in Figure 2-129.
   c. Resize the picture as needed to fit on the right side of the slide.
   d. Apply the **Bevel Rectangle** picture style.
   e. Position the picture as shown.

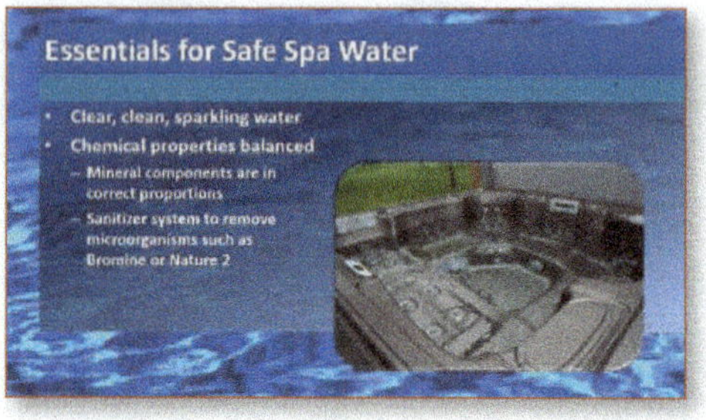

2-129 Slide 2 with inserted picture and picture style

5. Insert a *SmartArt* graphic, add text, and change formatting.
   a. Display slide 4. Insert a *SmartArt* graphic from the *Process* category with the **Continuous Block Process** layout.
   b. Type Test Water, Add Necessary Products, and Enjoy! in the three shapes.
   c. Resize the *SmartArt* graphic (*Height* **5"** and *Width* **9.5"**).
   d. Apply the **Polished** *SmartArt* style.
   e. Select the **arrow** and apply **Gradient** colors. Select **More Gradient** to open the *Format Shape* pane.
   f. Select a *Preset gradient* of **Light Gradient – Accent 2**. The *Type* is **Linear** and change the *Direction* to **Linear Left**.
   g. Modify the gradient stops:
      - *First stop:* Color **Light Blue, Background 2**; Position **0%**
      - *Second stop:* Color **Light Turquoise, Accent 2, Lighter 80%**; Position **40%**; Brightness **80%**
      - *Third stop:* Remove
      - *Fourth stop:* Color **Turquoise, Accent 2, Lighter 40%**; Position **100%**; Brightness **40%**

h. Close the *Format Shape* pane.
i. Apply **Bold** to all *SmartArt* text.
j. Position the *SmartArt* graphic as shown in Figure 2-130.

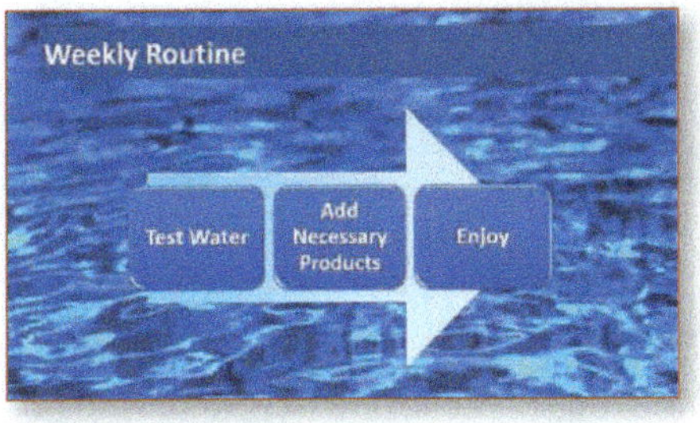

2-130 Slide 4 *SmartArt* graphic with style and color changes

6. Insert a table, add text, and change formatting.
   a. Display slide 5. Insert a table with **3** columns and **4** rows.
   b. Select **Header Row** and **Banded Rows**.
   c. Type the following text:

Level	Numbers	Results
High	8.0	Alkaline, Scale
Good	7.2 – 7.6	Ideal pH Range
Low	6.0	Acidic, Corrosion

   d. Change the font size to **20 pt**. for all table text.
   e. Apply the **Themed Style 1, Accent 1** table style.
   f. Select each column and adjust the *Cell Width* as follows: left column is **1.5"**, middle column is **2.8"**, and right column is **2.8"**.
   g. Change the alignment on the middle column to **Center**.
   h. Center the table on the slide.

7. Insert a text box.
   a. Insert a text box below the table on slide 5. Type Drain and replace spa water every 60-90 days.
   b. Change the font size to **20 pt**.
   c. Change the shape fill to **Turquoise, Accent 2, Lighter 80%**.
   d. Resize the text box, if necessary, so the text fits on one line. Position it below the table aligned with the right of the table.

8. Copy and format a table.
   a. Select the table on slide 5 and copy it.
   b. Display slide 6 and paste the table.
   c. Delete the middle column and size the table so it is **9"** wide.
   d. Delete the table text and add three rows.
   e. Type the following text:

Products	Purpose
Sanitizer	Type needed depends on sanitizer system
Test Strips	Measures chemical levels
Shock Treatment	Breaks down organic or unfiltered material
Total Alkalinity	Increases or decreases to balance pH levels
Calcium Increaser	Balances dissolved calcium
Stain and Scale Prevention	Removes metallic impurities

   f. Adjust the column width as needed to avoid word wrapping.
   g. Center the table on the slide.

9. Apply the **Ripple** transition with the **From Top-Left** effect option to all slides.

10. Save and close the presentation (Figure 2-131).

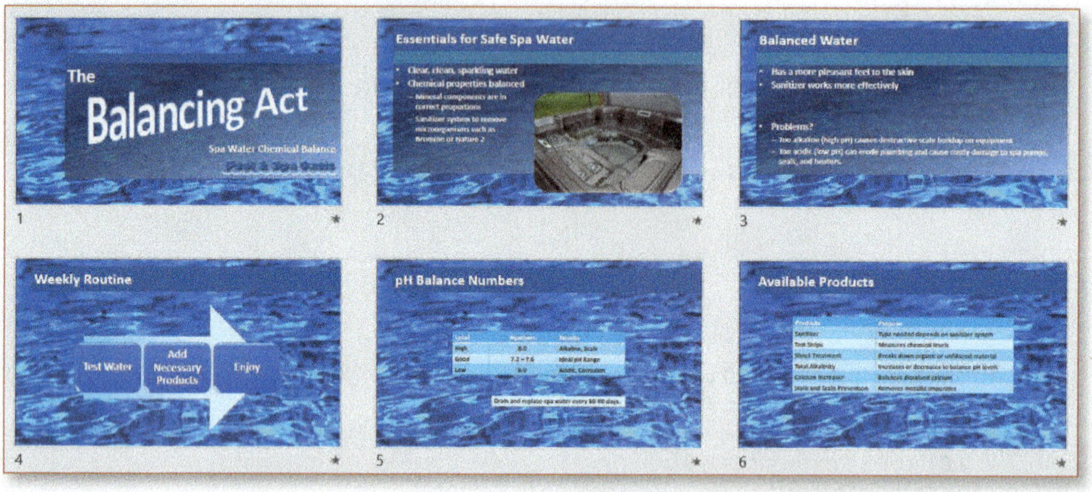

2-131 PowerPoint 2-4 completed

Independent Project 2-5

Prospective home buyers need to understand mortgage requirements and how to prepare to apply for a mortgage. Angie O'Connor at Placer Hills Real Estate wants to use a presentation on her notebook computer to help guide her discussions about these concepts with clients. For this project, you develop the presentation.
[Student Learning Outcomes 2.1, 2.3, 2.4, 2.5, 2.6, 2.7, 2.8]

Files Needed: ***PreparetoBuy-02.pptx*** and ***PlacerHillsSold-02.jpg*** (*Student data files are available in the* Library *of your SIMnet account.*)
Completed Project File Name: ***[your initials] PowerPoint 2-5.pptx***

Skills Covered in This Project

- Insert a picture.
- Crop a picture.
- Apply a picture style.
- Adjust size dimensions.
- Insert a chart and edit data.
- Apply chart styles.
- Format chart elements.
- Insert text boxes.
- Insert and format a table.
- Convert text to a *SmartArt* graphic.
- Apply a *SmartArt* style and effects.

1. Open the presentation ***PreparetoBuy-02***.
2. Save the presentation as [your initials] PowerPoint 2-5.

3. Insert and modify a picture.
   a. On slide 1, insert the **PlacerHillsSold-02** picture from your student data files.
   b. Crop the picture on the left and right as shown in Figure 2-132.
   c. Resize the picture (*Height* **5.5"** and the *Width* automatically adjusts).
   d. Apply the **Rounded Diagonal Corner, White** picture style.
   e. Position the picture on the right side of the slide as shown in Figure 2-132.

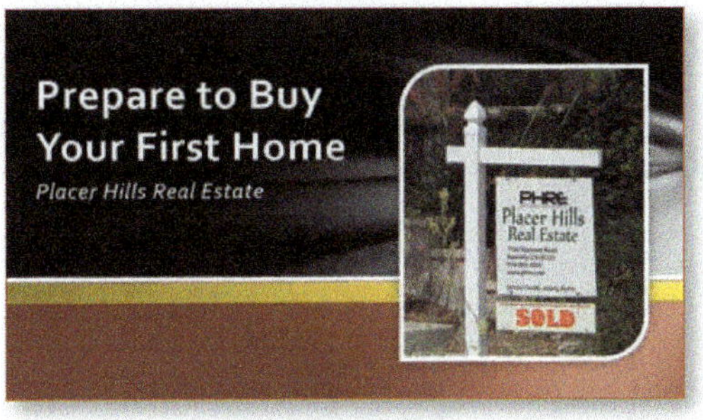

2-132 Slide 1 with inserted picture and picture style

4. Insert a chart showing how fixed mortgage rates have changed over time.
   a. Display slide 4. Click the **Insert Chart** button on the content placeholder.
   b. Select the **Line** chart type and then select the **Line with Markers** chart layout. Click **OK**.
   c. Replace the spreadsheet data with the data shown in Figure 2-133.
      - Be sure the selection area includes row 10 to avoid error messages.
      - Delete **Column D** so the corresponding chart area is correct with no blank space.
      - Close the spreadsheet.

Chart in M

	A	B	C
1		Rate	Points
2	1974	9.19	1.2
3	1979	11.2	1.6
4	1984	13.88	2.5
5	1989	10.32	2.1
6	1994	8.38	1.8
7	1999	7.44	1
8	2004	5.84	0.7
9	2009	5.04	0.7
10	2014	4.17	0.6
11			

2-133 Spreadsheet linked to a chart

5. Examine the line chart as it first appears (Figure 2-134).
   - It is accurate, but the data series lines are too thin and data markers too small.
   - The following changes (steps 6–13) will make the chart easier to interpret.

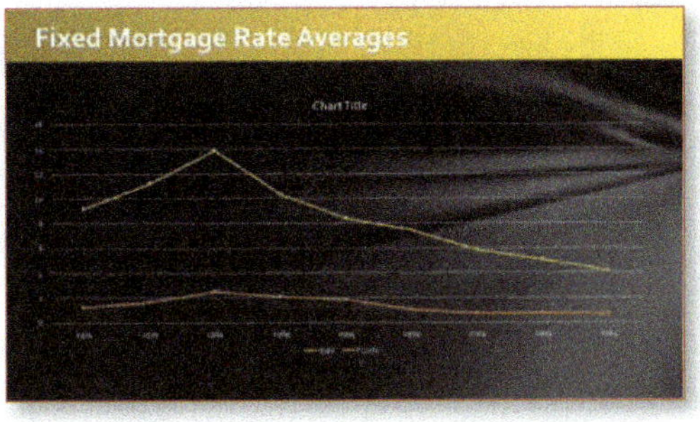

2-134 Line chart as it first appears

6. Delete the chart title.

7. Change the chart area *Shape Fill* to **Brown, Background 2**.

8. Format the line and markers on the "Rate" series.
   a. Select the "Rate" line and right-click. Select **Format Data Series** to open the *Format Data Series* pane (Figure 2-135).
   b. Click the **Fill & Line** icon at the top of the pane.
   c. Click **Line** options at the top of the pane below the icons and change the *Width* to **3 pt**.
   d. Click **Marker** options below the icons and select the following:
      - *Marker Options:* **Built-in**; *Type:* **Square**, and *Size:* **15** (Figure 2-136)
      - *Fill:* **Solid fill**; *Color:* **Orange, Accent 2**

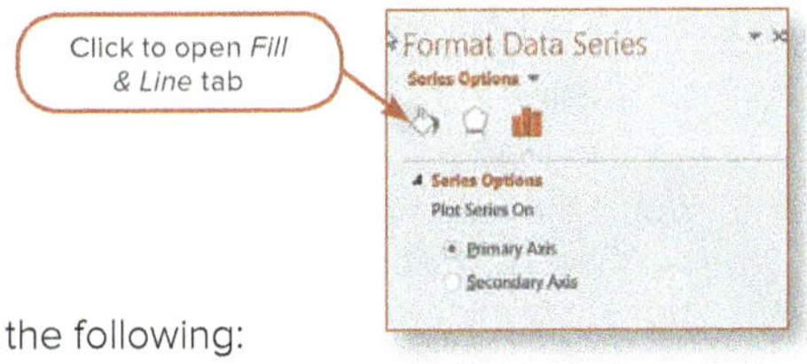

2-135 *Format Data Series* pane

9. Format the line and markers on the "Points" series.
   a. Select the "Points" line. Click **Line** options and select the following:
      - *Line:* **Solid line**; *Color:* **Orange, Accent 4**
      - *Width:* **3 pt**.

b. Select **Marker** options and select the following:
   - *Marker Options:* **Built-in**; *Type:* **Diamond**; *Size:* **20**
   - *Marker Fill:* **Solid fill**; Color: **Red, Accent 5**

10. Close the *Format Data Series* pane.
11. Select the *Horizontal (Category) axis* and increase the font size to **16 pt**. and apply **bold**. Repeat for the *Vertical (Value) axis.*
12. Select the **Chart Area**, change the *Width* to **11"**, and center the chart horizontally.
13. Move the chart up slightly to make room for a source notation at the bottom of the slide.
    a. Insert a text box and type the following:

       Information based on Freddie Mac survey data
       http://www.freddiemac.com/pmms/pmms30.htm

    b. Position the text box as displayed in Figure 2-137.

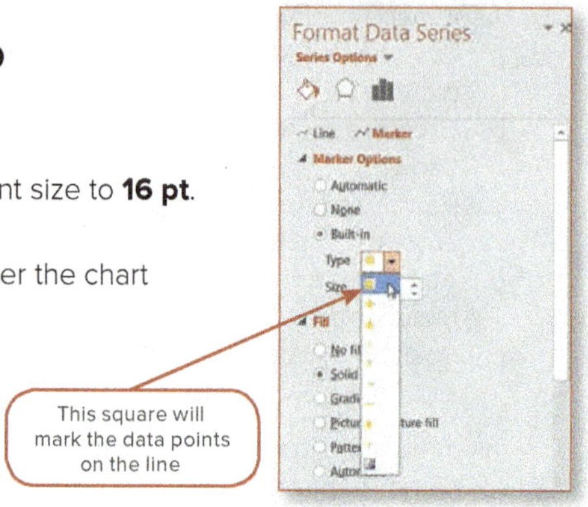

2-136 ***Format Data Series*** **pane with** ***Marker*** **options**

14. Insert and format a table:
    a. Display slide 5 and insert a table with **5** columns and **3** rows.
    b. Type the text shown in Figure 2-138.
    c. Select all text and change the font size to **24 pt**. Adjust column width as needed.
    d. Select columns **2–5** and change to **Center** alignment.
    e. Change to **Bottom** alignment in the first row and change the row *Shading* to **Gold, Accent 1, Darker 25%**.
    f. Align the table in the horizontal and vertical center on the slide.

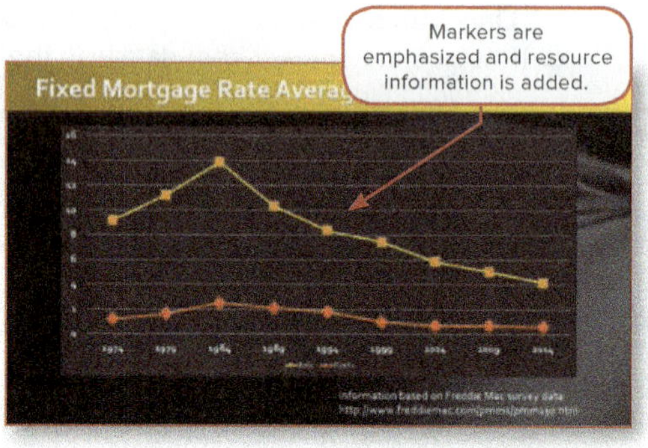

2-137 Slide 4 completed line chart

15. Insert a text box above the table on the left.
    a. Type $250,000.
    b. Change the font to **40 pt**. and **bold**.
16. Insert a text box below the table on the right.
    a. Type the following text on three lines:

       Lender rates are influenced by credit scores.
       Plan for a 20% down payment to avoid cost of points.
       Add taxes and insurance premiums.

Loan Product	Rate	Number of Payments	Monthly Payments	Total Paid
15 Year Fixed	3.11%	180	$1,739.71	$313,147.80
30 Year Fixed	3.88%	360	$1,176.31	$423,471.60

2-138 Table for slide 5

17. Convert a list to a *SmartArt* graphic.
    a. Display slide 6. Select the bulleted text and convert it to a *SmartArt* graphic with the **Vertical Curved List** layout.
    b. Resize the *SmartArt* frame on the right so it fits the longest line of text.
18. Apply the following changes to the *SmartArt* graphic:
    a. Change the colors to **Colorful Range, Accent Colors 2 to 3**.
    b. Apply the **Moderate Effect** *SmartArt* style.
    c. Select all of the white circles and change the *Shape Fill* to **Red, Accent 5, Darker 25%** and apply the *Bevel* effect of **Cool Slant**.
    d. Center the *SmartArt* graphic horizontally on the slide (Figure 2-139).

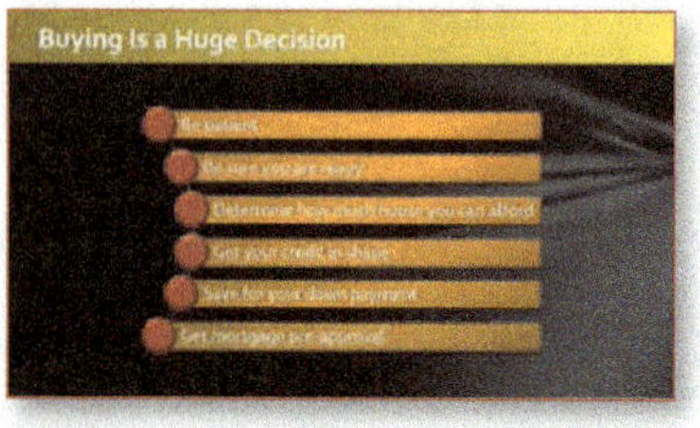

2-139 Slide 6 ***SmartArt*** **graphic with style and effects changed**

19. Apply the **Shape** transition with the **Out** effect option to all slides.
20. Save and close the presentation (Figure 2-140).

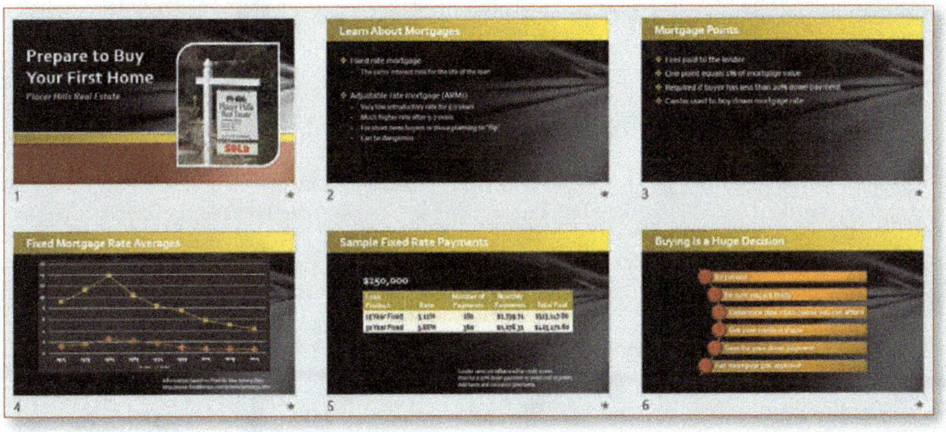

2-140 PowerPoint 2-5 completed

Independent Project 2-6

Kathy Sung, Director of Services at Life's Animal Shelter (LAS), will talk to a luncheon group of businesspeople. For this project, you develop the presentation she will use to explain the needs of LAS and describe ways people can contribute through donations or by volunteering their time.
[Student Learning Outcomes 2.1, 2.2, 2.3, 2.4, 2.5, 2.6, 2.7]

Files Needed: ***YouCanHelp-02.pptx, CountryStroll-02.jpg, DayCare-02.jpg, Food-02.jpg, Groom-02.jpg,*** and ***RoyalTreatment-02.jpg*** (*Student data files are available in the* Library *of your SIMnet account.*)
Completed Project File Name: ***[your initials] PowerPoint 2-6.pptx***

Skills Covered in This Project

- Apply text effects.
- Apply a picture style.
- Set transparent color.
- Recolor a picture.
- Adjust size dimensions.
- Insert a text box.
- Insert and format a table.
- Convert text to a *SmartArt* graphic.
- Create a *SmartArt* graphic with pictures.
- Apply a *SmartArt* style and effects.

1. Open the presentation ***YouCanHelp-02***.
2. Save the presentation as [your initials] PowerPoint 2-6.
3. Display slide 1. Change the title *Text Fill* color to **Dark Red, Accent 1, Darker 25%**. Apply the *Bevel* text effect of **Angle**.

4. Change the font size to **80 pt**. and resize the placeholder on the right so one word is on each line.
5. Resize a picture and remove a background color.
   a. Select the dog picture on slide 1.
   b. Increase the picture size (*Height* **5.9"** and *Width* **4.7"**).
   c. Use *Set Transparent Color* to remove the white area in the picture.
   d. Position the dog picture as shown in Figure 2-141.
6. Apply a picture style.
   a. Display slide 2 and increase the picture size (*Height* **5.84"** and *Width* **8"**).
   b. Apply the **Moderate Frame, Black** picture style.
   c. Center the picture horizontally and position it near the top of the slide.
7. Insert a text box and apply formatting:
   a. Insert a text box below the picture and type the following text:
      Our operating funds come through donations and pet adoption fees.
   b. Change the *Font Color* to **White, Background 1** and *Font Size* to **20 pt**.
   c. Resize the text box so the text wraps on two lines as shown in Figure 2-142.
   d. Change the *Shape Outline* to **White, Background 1** and the *Weight* to **3 pt**.
   e. Change the *Shape Fill* to **Black, Text 1**.
   f. Center the text box horizontally below the picture.
8. Copy and paste a slide.
   a. Select the slide 2 thumbnail and press **Ctrl+C**.
   b. Move your insertion point after slide 3 and press **Ctrl+V**.
9. Format the new slide 4.
   a. Replace the text in the text box below the picture with the words We Need Your Help!
   b. Resize the text box to fit the text and center it horizontally under the picture.
   c. Select the picture and change the *Color* to **Orange, Accent color 2 Dark** (Figure 2-143).
10. Convert a list to a *SmartArt* graphic.
    a. Display slide 5 and convert the list to a **Vertical Bullet List** *SmartArt* graphic.
    b. Increase the *SmartArt* frame height to **4.7"** so the text size increases.
    c. Reduce the width to **9"**.
    d. Apply the **Cartoon** *SmartArt* style.

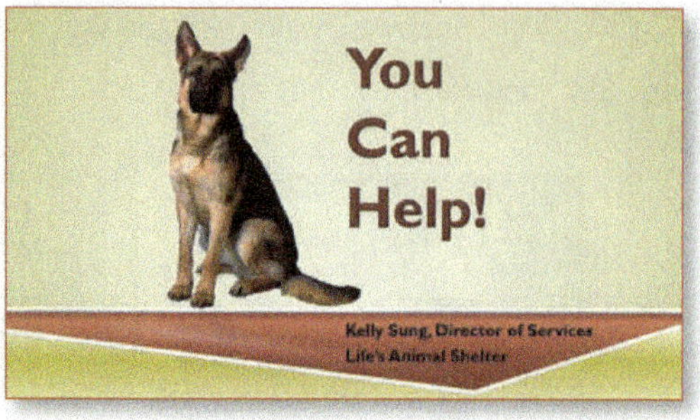

2-141 Slide 1 with picture added, white background removed

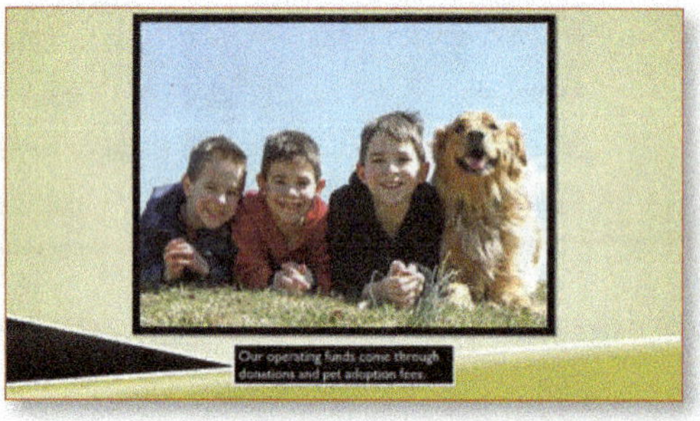

2-142 Slide 2 with picture and text box inserted

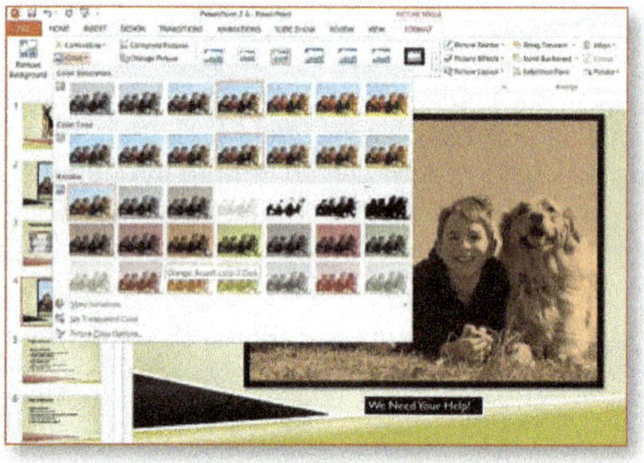

2-143 Slide 4 with picture recolored

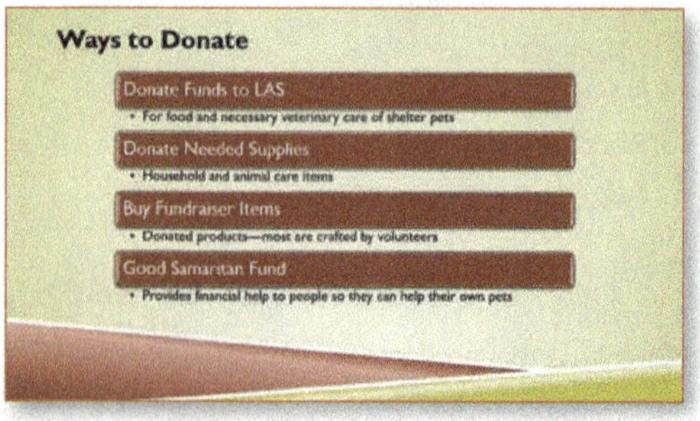

2-144 Slide 5 *SmartArt* graphic converted from bulleted text

e. Move the *SmartArt* up and center it horizontally as displayed in Figure 2-144.

11. Convert a list to a picture type *SmartArt* graphic.
    a. Display slide 6 and convert the list to a **Picture Lineup** *SmartArt* graphic.
    b. Click the **Picture** icon on each shape to open the *Insert Pictures* dialog box.
    c. Browse to locate your student data files and insert the following pictures going from left to right (Figure 2-145):

       1 ***DayCare-02***
       2 ***CountryStroll-02***
       3 ***RoyalTreatment-02***
       4 ***Food-02***
       5 ***Groom-02***

       Each picture is automatically resized.

12. Insert a new slide after slide 6 with a *Title and Content* layout.
    a. Type the title Items We Need
    b. Insert a table with **3** columns and **5** rows.
    c. Type the table text shown in Figure 2-146.
    d. Increase the font size to **20 pt**.
    e. Adjust column width so each column fits the longest line of text.
    f. Center the table on the slide.

13. Apply the *Gallery* transition to all slides.

14. Save and close the presentation (Figure 2-147).

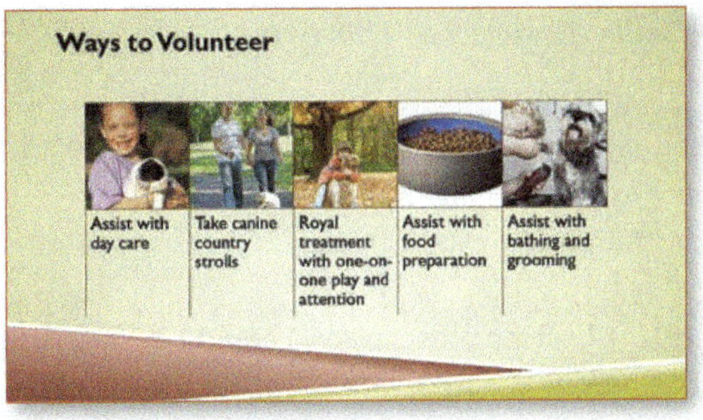

2-145 Slide 6 *SmartArt* graphic picture layout

Cleaning	Paper Products and Bedding	Dog and Cat Play
Bleach	Paper Towels	Dog and Cat Treats
Pine Sol	Paper Plates	Chewies
Mop Heads	Plastic Containers with Lids	Collars
Towels	Blankets	Leashes

2-146 Table text

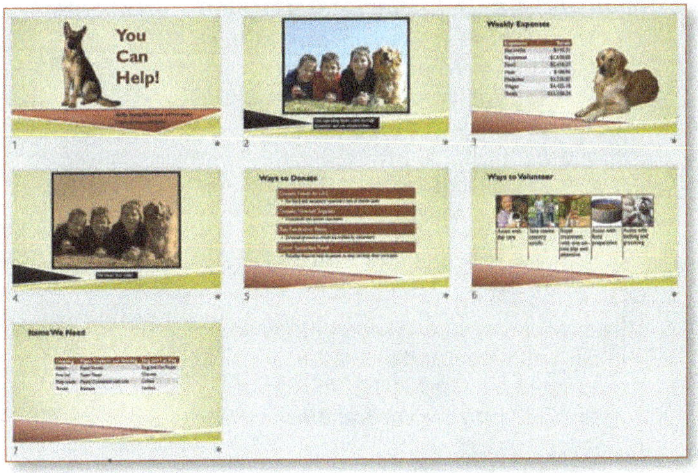

2-147 PowerPoint 2-6 completed

Improve It Project 2-7

The Hamilton Civic Center needs a presentation to explain benefits of yoga and encourage members to join yoga classes. For this project, you revise a presentation to add pictures, create a *SmartArt* graphic and apply various styles and effects for a contemporary appearance.
[Student Learning Outcomes 2.2, 2.3, 2.4, 2.5, 2.6, 2.7]

File Needed: ***Yoga-02.pptx*** (*Student data files are available in the* Library *of your SIMnet account.*)
Completed Project File Name: ***[your initials] PowerPoint 2-7.pptx***

Skills Covered in This Project

- Apply text effects.
- Insert an online picture.
- Apply a picture style.
- Reposition slide objects.
- Convert text to a *SmartArt* graphic.
- Apply a *SmartArt* style and effects.
- Format a table.
- Compress pictures.

1. Open the presentation ***Yoga-02*** that has a *Standard* size (4:3 aspect ratio). The slide size is 10"×7.5" compared to the slide size of 13.33"×7.5" for the default Widescreen size (16:9 aspect ratio).
2. Save the presentation as [your initials] PowerPoint 2-7.
3. Format the title slide for a more dynamic appearance.
   a. Search online and insert a yoga picture similar to the one shown in Figure 2-148.
   b. Resize the picture as needed.
   c. Apply a **Bevel Rectangle** picture style.
   d. Select the title placeholder and apply the **Wave 1** *Transform text effect.*
4. Recolor the logo picture.
   a. Select the logo and change the picture *Color* to **Blue, Accent color 5 Light**. This change replaces the black with a color that matches theme colors.
   b. Use *Set Transparent Color* to remove the white so your background color shows.
   c. Change the logo *Width* to **2.5"** and the *Height* will automatically adjust.
5. Arrange title slide objects as shown in Figure 2-148.
6. Change listed text to a *SmartArt* graphic.
   a. Display slide 3 and select the bulleted list. Convert it to a *SmartArt* graphic using the **Vertical Block List** layout.
   b. Apply the **White Outline** *SmartArt* style.
   c. Apply the **Colorful Range – Accent Colors 4 to 5** *SmartArt* colors (Figure 2-149).
7. Insert, position, and compress pictures.
   a. Display slide 4. Search online and insert an appropriate yoga picture.
   b. Resize the picture if needed and position it on the right.
   c. Apply a **Bevel Rectangle** picture style.
   d. Resize the bulleted text placeholder as needed to fit with the picture.

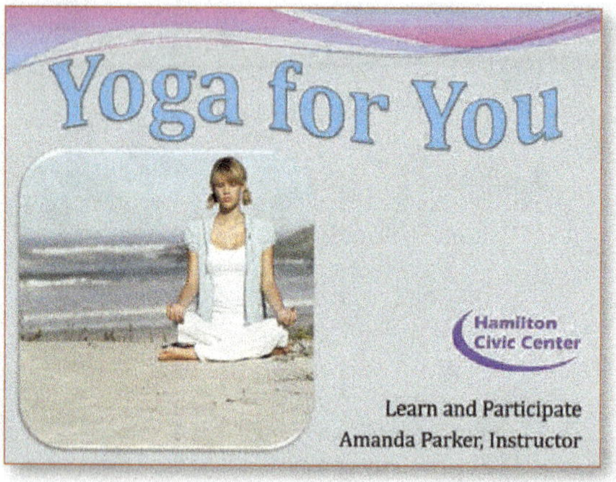

2-148 Title slide

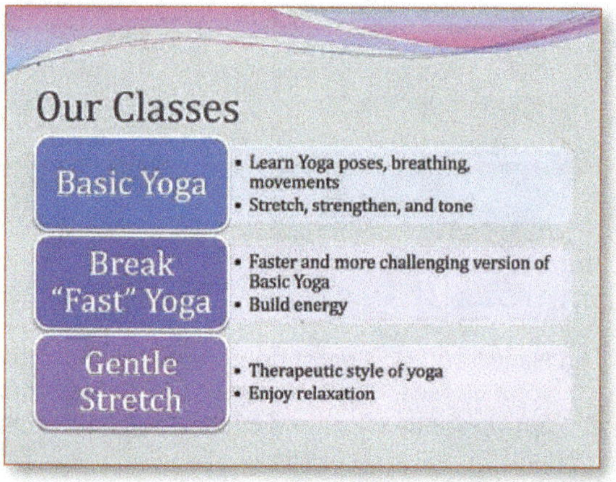

2-149 *SmartArt* graphic *Vertical Block List* layout

e. Display slide 5. Repeat steps 7a–d.
f. Select the picture, and click **Compress Pictures**. Use document resolution, delete cropped areas of pictures, and apply compression to all pictures.

8. Modify the table.
   a. Display slide 6. Select the table text and increase the font size to **20 pt**.
   b. Apply the **Medium Style 2 – Accent 4** table style.
   c. Select the title row and apply the **Riblet** *Bevel* effect.
   d. Increase the table *Height* to **2.5"**.
   e. Center the text vertically in all cells.
   f. Add a **1 pt**. border to all cells using the **Blue, Accent 4, Darker 50%** pen color (Figure 2-150).
   g. Align the table vertically in the middle of the slide.

Classes	Days	Hours
Basic Yoga	Mon/Wed	4:15 – 5:15 p.m.
Break "Fast" Yoga	Tues/Thurs	7:00 – 8:10 a.m.
Gentle Stretch	Fri	10:00 – 11:30 a.m.

2-150 Slide 6 table

9. Apply the **Dissolve** transition to all slides.
10. Save and close your presentation (Figure 2-151).

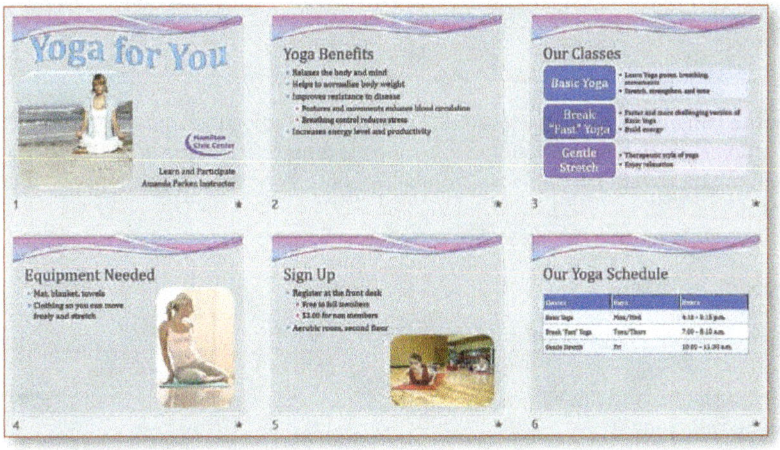

2-151 PowerPoint 2-7 completed

Challenge Project 2-8

For this project, do online comparison shopping for items you would be likely to buy such as clothing, household products, or automotive supplies. Prepare slides describing the products and apply text effects to the slide titles. Prepare a chart that shows costs either for the same product at several web sites or similar products at the same site.
[Student Learning Outcomes 2.1, 2.2, 2.3, 2.4, 2.5, 2.6, 2.7, 2.8, 2.9]

File Needed: None
Completed Project File Name: ***[your initials] PowerPoint 2-8.pptx***

Create a new presentation and save it as [your initials] PowerPoint 2-8. Modify your presentation according to the following guidelines:

- Select an appropriate theme and apply color and font changes as needed for your topic.
- Prepare a title slide and product description slides.
- Search online for a related image and insert it on the title slide.
- Add one or more shapes to emphasize a slide object.
- Insert a *SmartArt* graphic to illustrate a process or relationship.
- Create a table summarizing some of your findings.
- Create two charts to compare specific items.

Challenge Project 2-9

Using data from the United States Department of Labor published online by the Bureau of Labor Statistics (http://www.bls.gov), prepare a presentation explaining current trends in the labor force. For example, you could show unemployment rate comparisons from different regions or wage estimates for various occupations in different states.
Student Learning Outcomes 2.1, 2.2, 2.3, 2.4, 2.5, 2.6, 2.7, 2.8, 2.9]

File Needed: None
Completed Project File Name: ***[your initials] PowerPoint 2-9.pptx***

Create a new presentation and save it as [your initials] PowerPoint 2-9. Modify your presentation according to the following guidelines:

- Select an appropriate theme and apply color and font changes as needed for your topic.
- Create a title slide using a *Transform* text effect.
- Include several bulleted slides describing current trends.
- Search for appropriate pictures, resize as needed, and apply a picture style to each one.
- Add one or more shapes to emphasize a slide object.
- Insert a *SmartArt* graphic to illustrate a process or relationship.
- Prepare a table showing salaries for several jobs in different locations or for data changing over time.
- Prepare a chart comparing employment statistics from your state or region.

Challenge Project 2-10

Using information from one of your favorite coffee or soft drink manufacturers, such as the facts you can find at www.thecoca-colacompany.com or www.pepsico.com, prepare a presentation comparing different products. You could show the diversity of the product line or list promotional products with pricing. From financial information provided on the sites, you could feature total revenue, total profits, or other interesting performance data in your presentation.
[Student Learning Outcomes 2.1, 2.2, 2.3, 2.4, 2.5, 2.6, 2.7, 2.8, 2.9]

File Needed: None
Completed Project File Name: ***[your initials] PowerPoint 2-10.pptx***

Create a new presentation and save it as [your initials] PowerPoint 2-10. Modify your presentation according to the following guidelines:

- Select an appropriate theme and apply color and font changes as needed for your topic.
- Create a distinctive title slide using *WordArt* combined with a shape to create interest.
- Search online for appropriate pictures and insert three or more.
- Adjust picture sizes and apply picture styles.
- Prepare slides listing key factors contributing to the company's growth.
- Feature selected financial information in a table.
- Prepare a *SmartArt* graphic illustrating a specific process or relationship from historical or operational information.
- Create a chart showing comparisons for data such as net revenue, operating profit, or growth over a period of time.

CHAPTER 3

Preparing for Delivery and Using a Slide Presentation

POWERPOINT

CHAPTER OVERVIEW

This chapter shows you how to create new theme colors customized for your topic, apply animation so selected slide objects appear just at the right time in your presentation, and link to a video from a web site. You also explore PowerPoint's rehearsal features to help you perfect your delivery timing and techniques, project your presentation more effectively, and prepare a presentation to be self-running. Finally, you learn how to save a presentation so it can be distributed on a CD.

STUDENT LEARNING OUTCOMES (SLOs)

After completing this chapter, you will be able to:

- **SLO 3.1** Create custom theme and background colors (p. P3-147).
- **SLO 3.2** Apply animation to add interest and reinforce content (p. P3-155).
- **SLO 3.3** Link to an online video (p. P3-158).
- **SLO 3.4** Use rehearsal techniques to prepare for presentation delivery (p. P3-164).
- **SLO 3.5** Control display options for different screen sizes (p. P3-167).
- **SLO 3.6** Present effectively and professionally using projection equipment (p. P3-173).
- **SLO 3.7** Use annotation pens to highlight information and save presentation markings (p. P3-176).
- **SLO 3.8** Prepare a self-running presentation that loops (p. P3-179).
- **SLO 3.9** Use the *Package Presentation for CD* feature to prepare a slide show for display on other computers (p. P3-181).

CASE STUDY

Specialists at Solution Seekers, Inc., frequently present to both large and small groups as they work with clients to improve business performance. Davon Washington is creating a series of seminars for new hires to help them be more productive and professional. For this project, you work with Davon to finish the presentation he has developed for a seminar on presentation planning.

Pause & Practice 3-1: Create custom theme and background colors. Add interest with animation and video.

Pause & Practice 3-2: Rehearse a presentation and prepare for a widescreen display.

Pause & Practice 3-3: Practice slide show delivery features.

Pause & Practice 3-4: Prepare a self-running presentation and package a presentation to a folder.

SLO 3.1

Creating Custom Theme and Background Colors

Themes create a unified appearance for your presentation. When you use themes effectively, the information you present on a topic is seen by your viewers as one "package" and not a collection of random slides. You may need to match specific colors in a company logo or a school's colors, so in this section you will prepare custom theme colors that create a unique palette and help you work more efficiently. Then you will explore different ways to apply pattern, gradient, and picture fills and consider issues to keep in mind when applying these fills to slide backgrounds.

Custom Theme Colors

As you worked with shapes, colors, and styles in previous chapters, you saw how theme colors are arranged across the top of the *Theme Colors* gallery. Recall that various percentages of each color appear below the top row colors (Figure 3-1). This section takes a closer look at where PowerPoint automatically applies theme colors to various graphics you create.

Four sample slides are shown in Figure 3-2 with the *Facet* theme and *Blue* theme colors. The white background is the *Background 1* color with decorative shapes in *Accent 1* and *Accent 2* colors.

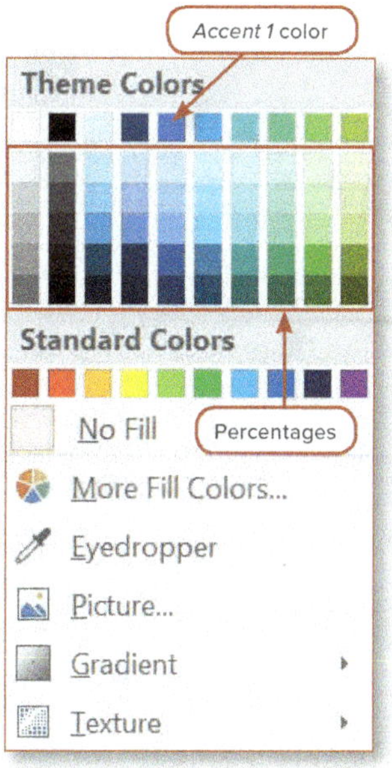

3-1 *Theme Colors* gallery

- ***Slide 1***: The photograph has a border of *Text 2* color.
- ***Slide 2***: The first color samples show the two sets of *Background* and *Text* colors. The second color samples show *Accent colors 1–6*.
- ***Slide 3***: The bullets and the *SmartArt* shapes are shown in the *Accent 1* color.
- ***Slide 4***: The table has *Accent 2* color variations. The chart shows all six *Accent* colors. They appear based on the order data is entered in the spreadsheet.

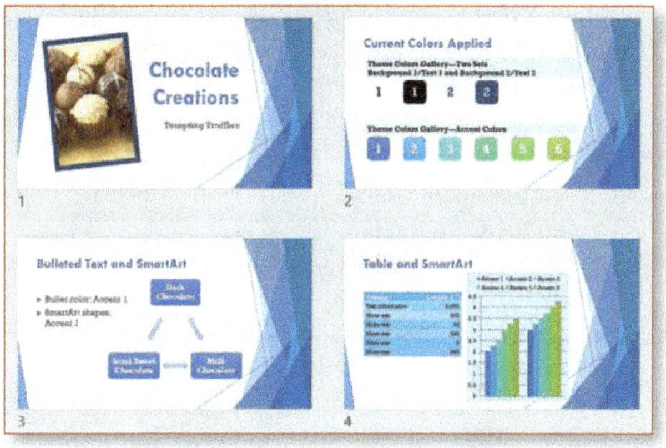

3-2 Sample slides showing graphics with *Blue* theme colors

Accent colors (Figure 3-3) appear from left to right in both the *Shape Styles* gallery and the *Table Styles* gallery (Figures 3-4 and 3-5). Other galleries show options in a similar way.

You can boost productivity by creating custom theme colors because the colors you choose are available to you in the galleries as you develop your slide show. When you save custom theme colors, the colors are also available to use again in another presentation. Keep the following guidelines in mind when you create custom theme colors:

3-3 *Blue* theme accent colors

- Select your background color first and then select other colors that work well on the background.

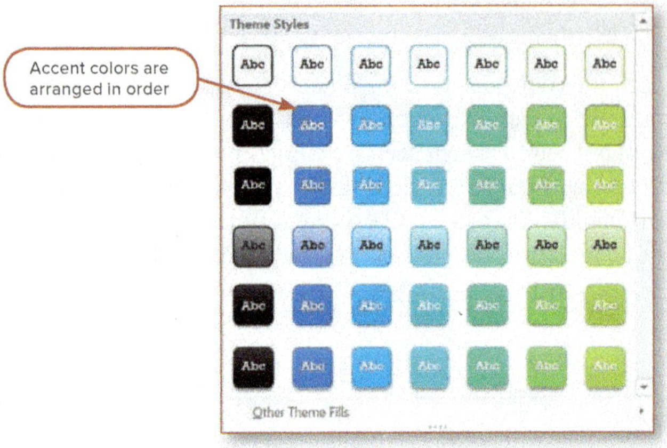

3-4 ***Shape Styles*** **gallery**

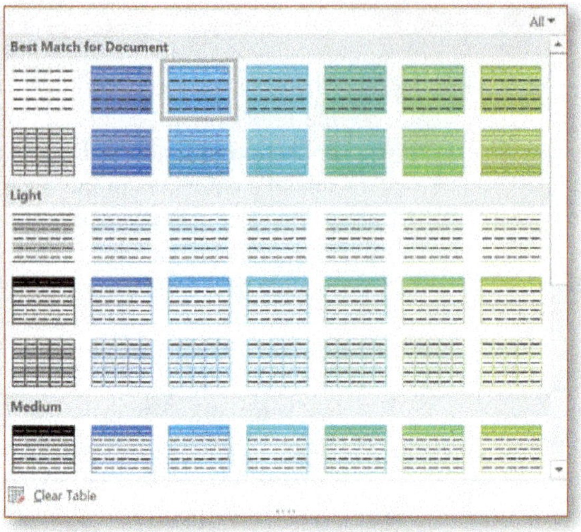

3-5 ***Table Styles*** **gallery**

- Pick a text color that has a high contrast with your background color so words are easy to read.
- Select the *Accent 1* color carefully because it will appear automatically as the fill color when you draw shapes. The *Accent 1* color is the first choice, also, in galleries that show color options.

Use the *Design* tab to quickly change theme colors. The following example illustrates changing to brown and yellow theme colors that are more appropriate for a presentation about chocolate.

HOW TO: Create New Theme Colors

1. Start a new presentation using a design theme or open an existing presentation.
2. Click the **More** button [*Design* tab, *Variants* group].
3. Select **Colors** to open the list of built-in theme colors. The current color theme is selected (Figure 3-6).
4. Select **Customize Colors** to open the *Create New Theme Colors* dialog box (Figure 3-7).
5. Change individual colors as needed to create your custom theme (Figure 3-8). For this example, the *Text/ Background – Dark 1* and *Light 1* colors do not require a change.
   - Click the **list arrow** on a color button to open the *Themes Colors* gallery.
   - Click **More Colors** to open the *Colors* dialog box.

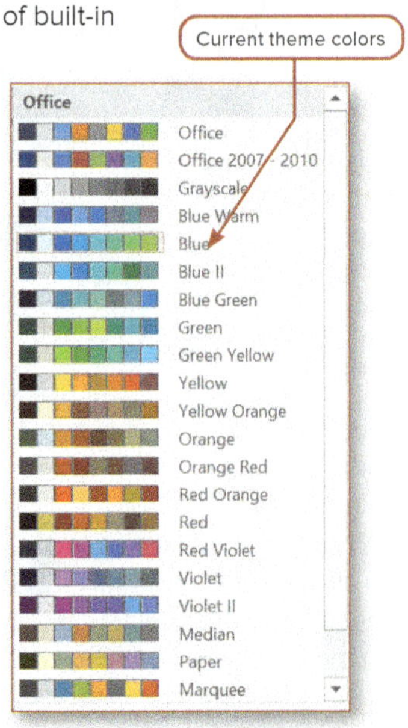

3-6 ***Theme Colors*** **gallery**

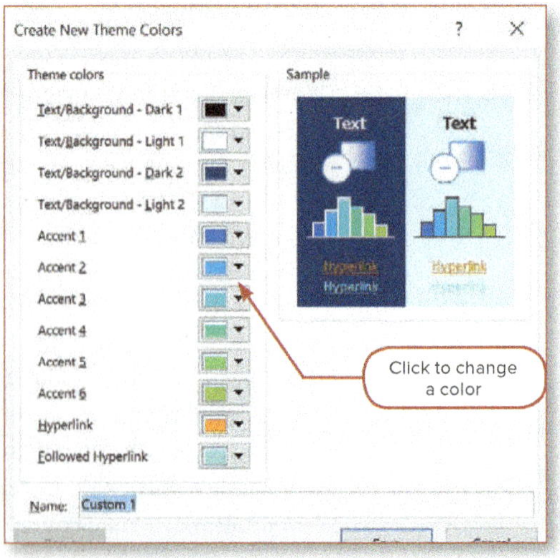

3-7 ***Create New Theme Colors*** **dialog box showing** ***Blue*** **theme colors**

- Click the **Standard** or **Custom** tab, choose a color, and click **OK**.
- Repeat for each of the colors you want to change.

6. Name the new custom theme.
7. Click the **Save** button. The new custom theme is automatically applied and the name will appear in the *Custom* section of your list of available theme colors so you can use it again.

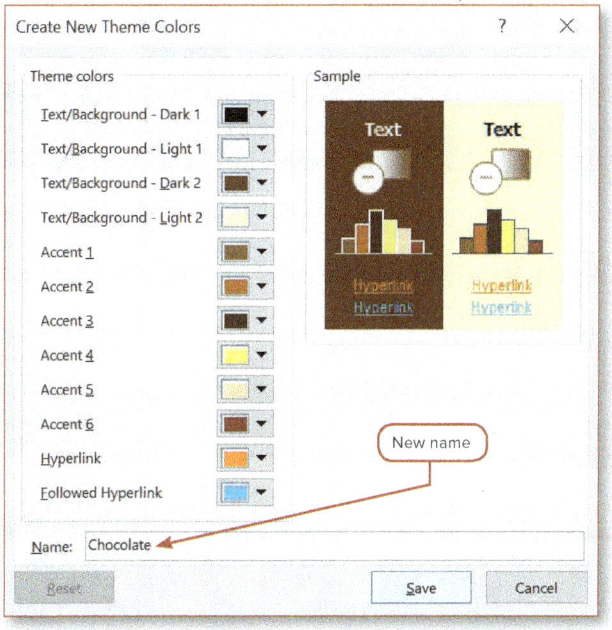

3-8 ***Create New Theme Colors*** **dialog box showing custom colors**

The same sample slides are shown in Figure 3-9 with the new colors. Controlling color this way is more efficient than using an existing theme and having to select a custom color each time you create various illustrations. If any slide text, such as a slide title, retains the original colors, click the **Reset** button [*Home* tab, *Slides* group] to update the colors.

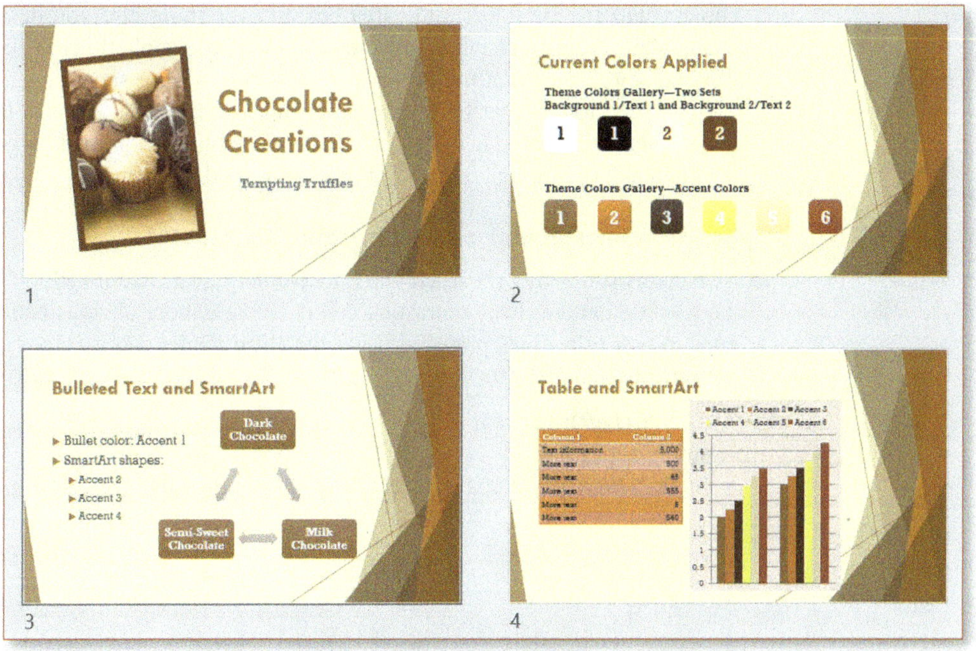

3-9 ***Chocolate*** **theme colors applied to sample slides**

Color combinations influence the tone of your presentation. Your options are endless, but you may want to consider a few of the following tonal effects:

- Varied and vibrant or similar with subtle differences
- Soothing and tranquil or lively and energetic

- Youthful or mature
- Historic or high tech

When you think about colors for your topic, consider your audience and be respectful of cultural differences. People tend to assign meaning to colors based on their cultural background and life experiences. A few examples of colors that have symbolic meaning include the following:

- ***White***: Purity and cleanliness in the American culture, death in some other cultures
- ***Red***: Health (red blood) in the medical field, loss (negative values) in the financial field
- ***Green***: Sickness (infection) in the medical field, wealth (money) in the financial field

> **MORE INFO**
>
> To examine this concept further, look online for information about color meaning, symbolism, or the psychology of color.

Custom Background Colors

The *Format Background* pane has options similar to those you have used on the *Format Shape* pane (*See SLO 2.1: Working with Shapes, Colors, and Styles*). When you change background colors, text colors do not change. Also, the position of placeholders or the graphic shapes that appear on design themes do not change.

When you choose colors and creative effects for backgrounds, remember that your color choices will fill the entire slide area behind everything else you design on a slide. These changes are visible throughout the presentation if you apply them to all slides, so you should examine your changes at full screen size to be sure you are satisfied with the results.

You need to consider how your background affects text, too. If a theme or template has graphic shapes included in its design, then a solid color background fill is a good choice. Select a color that has a strong contrast from the color used for text (light on dark or dark on light).

Format a Background with Pattern and Gradient Fills

Two colors (the *Foreground* and the *Background*) create pattern fills. Two similar colors create a subtle pattern; two contrasting colors create a more obvious pattern. Notice the difference in two title slides prepared using the *Wisp* theme and a *Dark Horizontal* background pattern fill (Figure 3-10).

- ***Slide 1 (Left)***: The text is difficult to read on a background with pattern colors that have a strong contrast.
- ***Slide 2 (Right)***: The text is easier to read on a background with pattern colors that are similar.

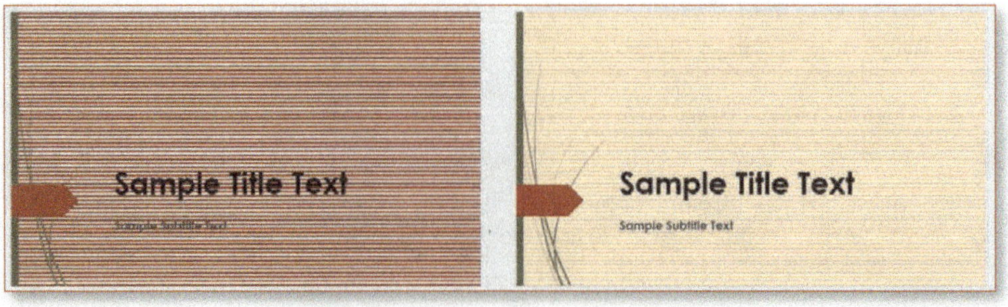

3-10 *Wisp* theme title slide with the same background pattern in different colors

HOW TO: Add a Background Pattern Fill

1. Point to the slide background and right-click to open the context menu.
2. Click **Format Background** to open the *Format Background* pane.
3. Select the **Pattern fill** option.
4. Choose an appropriate *Foreground Color* and *Background Color*.
5. Choose one of the patterns. By default, this change is applied to the current slide only.
6. Click **Apply to All** to apply this change to the entire presentation.
7. Click **Reset Background** if you want to restore the background's original design.
8. Close the *Format Background* pane.

ANOTHER WAY

Open the *Format Background* pane by clicking the **Format Background** button [*Design* tab, *Customize* group]. You can also click the **Slide Master** button [*View* tab, *Master views* group], click the **Background Styles** button [*Slide Master* tab, *Background* group], and then click **Format Background.**

Preset gradient colors are based on theme colors or you can select custom colors. You first choose the *Type* of gradient that controls how the colors blend, and then you choose the *Direction* of color change. Based on these choices, gradient stops appear on the color bar. Move, delete, or add gradient stops to modify how the colors blend. The color change is more gradual with more distance between the stops. Compare the title slides of the *Wisp* design theme shown in Figures 3-11 and 3-12. These two slides started with the same preset gradient fill of *Bottom Spotlight – Accent 4* with a type of *Linear;* however, the gradient stop settings were changed differently.

Figure 3-11

- *Linear Up* direction
- Three gradient stops are used.

Figure 3-12

- *Linear Diagonal – Top Left to Bottom Right* direction
- The three gradient stops on the left of the color bar are close together for a defined color change; the three right stops are spread apart for a more gradual color change.

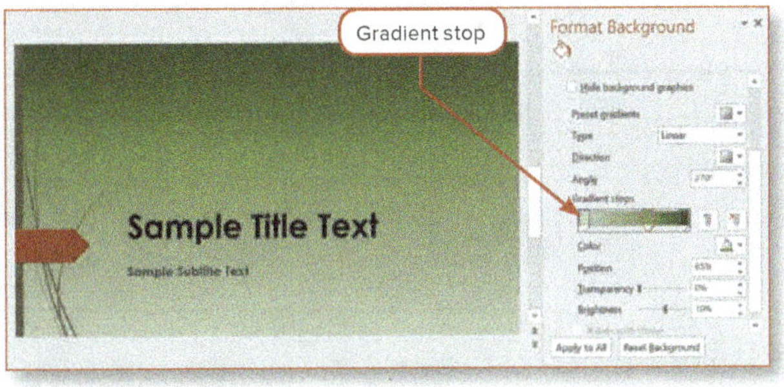

3-11 *Wisp* theme title slide with a custom background gradient fill

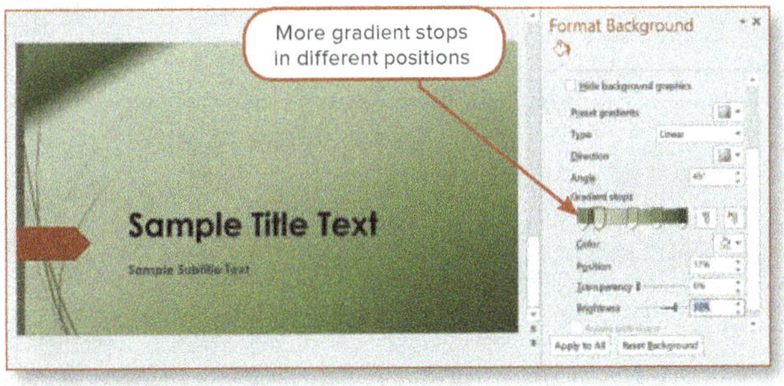

3-12 *Wisp* theme title slide with a custom background gradient fill showing different gradient stops

▶ HOW TO: Add a Background Gradient Fill

1. Point to the slide background that you want to change and right-click to open the context menu.
2. Click **Format Background** to open the *Format Background* pane.
3. Select the **Gradient fill** option. By default, changes are applied to the current slide only.
4. Click the **Preset gradients** button and select a color such as **Light Gradient – Accent 2** or **Top Spotlight – Accent 4** from the gallery of options.
5. Click the **Type** drop-down arrow and choose one of the options: **Linear**, **Radial**, **Rectangular**, **Path**, or **Shade from title**.
6. Click the **Direction** button and choose a direction for color blending if one is available.
   - The *Angle* degree is available only for the *Linear* type, and it automatically adjusts based on the direction you choose.
   - Type a different number in the *Angle* box or click the arrows to change the number in 10 degree increments.
7. Add or remove gradient stops.
   - Click the **Add gradient stop** button to add gradient stops.
   - Click the **Remove gradient stop** button or drag the gradient stop down to remove it from the color bar.
8. Change colors by selecting a gradient stop and clicking the **Color** button. Choose a different color.
9. Change color blending by selecting the gradient stop and dragging it to a different position on the color bar.
   - Drag the stops to rearrange them if you want to change the order.
   - Change percentages for each stop position to precisely adjust the positions.
10. Adjust *Brightness* and *Transparency* as needed.
11. Click **Apply to All** to apply this background to every slide in your presentation.
12. Click **Reset Background**, if necessary, to restore the settings before you made changes.
13. Close the *Format Background* pane.

ANOTHER WAY

You can access various *Background Styles* [*Design* tab, *Variants* group or *Slide Master* tab, *Background* group] that show light and dark color combinations based on theme colors.

Format a Background with Picture and Texture Fills

Pictures help you tell your story, communicate without words, and convey emotions that are difficult to express in words. Pictures can provide a dramatic background for your presentation. However, placing text over pictures is challenging because of the many colors that are used in pictures. Textures can use many colors, too, or show a lot of detail. Pictures in a small size can be used as textures to fill a slide with many small pictures. The examples in this section show you several ways to combine background pictures and text.

▶ HOW TO: Add a Background Picture Fill

1. Point to the slide background that you want to change and right-click to open the context menu.
2. Click **Format Background** to open the *Format Background* pane.
3. Select the **Picture or texture fill** option. By default, changes are applied to the current slide only.

4. Click the **File** button to insert a picture from your collection.
5. Click the **Online** button to search for a picture using the *Insert Picture* dialog box.
   - Type your search word and click the **Search** button or press **Enter**.
   - Select the picture you want to use and click **Insert**.
6. Use one of the following methods to soften the picture colors so text and other objects on the slide are easy to see:
   - Increase the *Transparency* percentage on the *Format Background* pane. This setting mutes the colors but the original colors are still evident.
   - Click the **Picture** icon at the top of the *Format Background* pane, and then click **Picture Color**. Click the **Presets** drop-down arrow to choose from different saturation levels or click the **Recolor** drop-down arrow to choose from dark and light accent colors for a monotone effect.
   - If you decide not to change the picture's colors, click the **Reset** button to restore the picture to its original state.
7. Click **Apply to All** to apply this background to every slide in your presentation.
8. Click **Reset Background** to restore the background to its original state.
9. Close the *Format Background* pane.

MORE INFO

You can change a slide background at any time while you are working on a presentation.

The following figures show options you can explore using the *Format Background* pane to soften background pictures or use placeholder fill colors so that text on pictures or textures is easy to read. A single flower that is almost a square image (Figure 3-13) is used differently in Figures 3-14 – 3-16. The first slide in each figure illustrates a problem while the second and third slides show possible solutions. Figure 3-17 illustrates several options for using textures as a background.

Notice the following characteristics for the three slides shown in Figure 3-14:

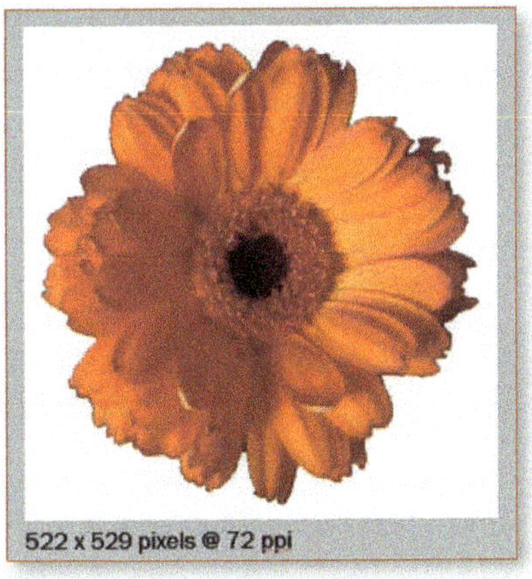

3-13 A flower picture used in background examples

- **Slide 1 (left)**: Because this picture is almost square (522×529 pixels) when it is stretched to fill the width of a widescreen display (*Height* 7.5" and *Width* 13.33"), part of the flower is cut off at the top and bottom. This is not necessarily a problem, just what happens if you use a square picture. The title text, however, is not easy to read over the dark colors of the flower. This is a problem as your slide text should be legible no matter what background designs you use.

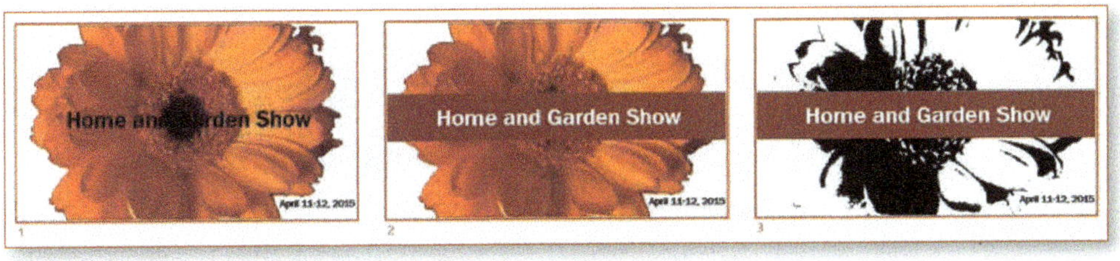

3-14 A large square picture used as a background fill with color changes

- **Slide 2 (center)**: The title placeholder is the same width as the slide. A dark red fill is applied and the white text has a shadow so now the text is easy to read.
- **Slide 3 (right)**: The title placeholder treatment is the same as slide 2. The picture was recolored using the preset *Black and White: 25%* color. This creates a more abstract image.

Notice the following characteristics for the three slides shown in Figure 3-15:

- **Slide 4 (left)**: The large flower does not fill the slide when inserted in its original size, so now the complete flower appears. The *Tile picture as texture* option was selected with *Alignment* changed to *Center*. *Tiling* causes the picture to be repeated to fill the slide area so parts of the flower are shown around the center flower. Like slide 1 in Figure 3-14, the text is difficult to read.
- **Slide 5 (center)**: The title placeholder resembles slide 2 in Figure 3-14, but this time the fill color transparency is 30%. More of the flower shows through, yet the text is still easy to read.
- **Slide 6 (right)**: The picture was recolored with preset *Gray – 25%, Background color 2 Light*. Black text is used with no shadow to avoid making the text appear blurred.

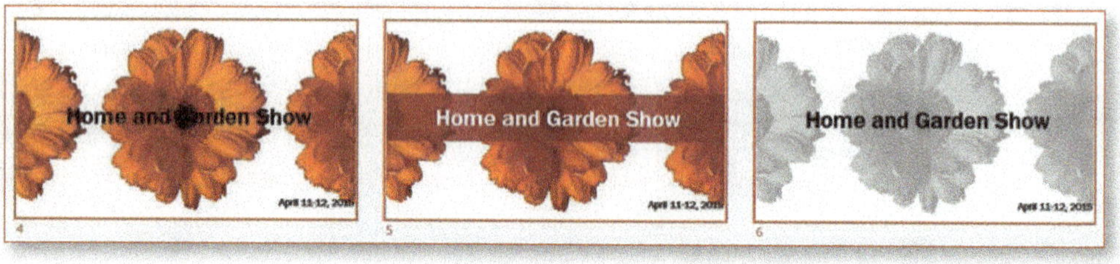

3-15 A large square picture used as a tiled background fill with color changes

If you tile a picture or texture that is small, many images fill the screen for an effect like wallpaper. If these images still seem too large, you can adjust the *Tiling Options* and reduce the *Scale* percentage to display each image in a smaller size. *Offset* points control how much the tiled images are indented from the left (*Offset X*) and top (*Offset Y*).

Notice the following characteristics for the three slides shown in Figure 3-16:

- **Slide 7 (left)**: The *Tile picture as texture* option was selected so many of these small flower images (200 × 203 pixels) fill the screen. For an appropriate fit on the slide, *Alignment* was changed to *Top left*, then *Offset* and *Scale* were adjusted. Like slide 4 in Figure 3-15, the text is difficult to read.
- **Slide 8 (center)**: The flower picture was recolored with preset *Grayscale*. The title placeholder colors were changed to a black fill with red text. The placeholder size was increased, too, for greater emphasis.
- **Slide 9 (right)**: The repeating picture for this slide is a small rectangle (40 by 77 pixels) with a bevel effect so it looks like a real tile. The title text is left aligned and the placeholder is filled with a gold color. A rectangle was added on the right so the date would be easy to read and to help create an asymmetrical focal point with the single large flower. This flower has a transparent background rather than white as in the previous examples.

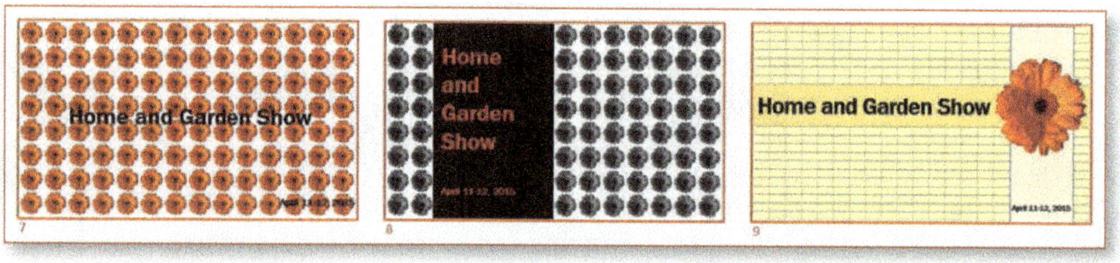

3-16 Small pictures tiled for a background fill with color changes

Textures available on the *Format Background* pane are small images, so it is generally best to tile them because the effect is more pleasing. When stretched to fill a slide, the textures may be too bold or blurred. Notice the following characteristics for the slides shown in Figure 3-17:

- **Slide 10 (left)**: The *Paper bag* texture was applied and its bold appearance dominates the slide.
- **Slide 11 (center)**: The same texture was tiled so multiple small images repeat and no other change was made.
- **Slide 12 (right)**: The same texture was tiled and the *Mirror type* changed to *Both*. This creates a pattern with horizontal and vertical mirror images.

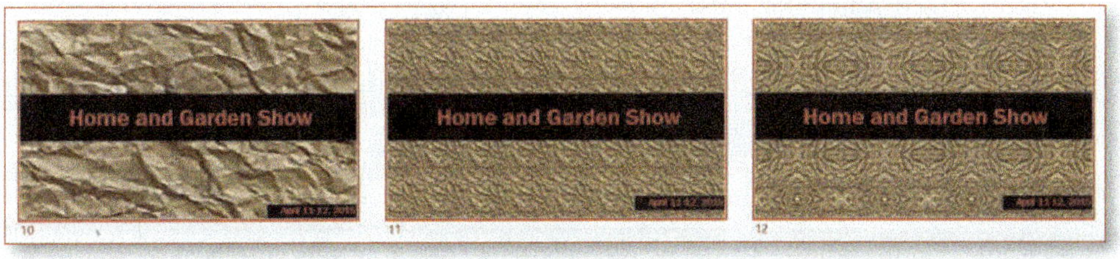

3-17 The same texture used as a background fill with different settings

SLO 3.2

Applying Animation

Animation is the movement of objects on a slide. Animation creates a more dynamic presentation and can keep your audience focused on concepts.

Observe creative animation techniques by noticing how objects and text move in movies or in television commercials. As you decide what effects to use, try to select movements that enhance your content and support your message. Animation can be overdone when it is not used skillfully. Be sure you apply animation for the right reasons and not just for entertainment value. Use animation sparingly because too much can be distracting.

When planning movement, also consider the transitions (the movement between slides). When a presentation is supporting a speaker, you want to keep the transitions calmer and apply animation effects to draw attention to information on selected slides only.

Add Entrance, Exit, and Emphasis Effects

Animation effects are arranged in the categories that are shown in different colors on the gallery (Figure 3-18):

- ***Entrance***: A movement that occurs when an object appears on the slide (green)
- ***Emphasis***: A movement that calls attention to an object that remains on the slide (yellow)
- ***Exit***: A movement that occurs when an object leaves the slide (red)

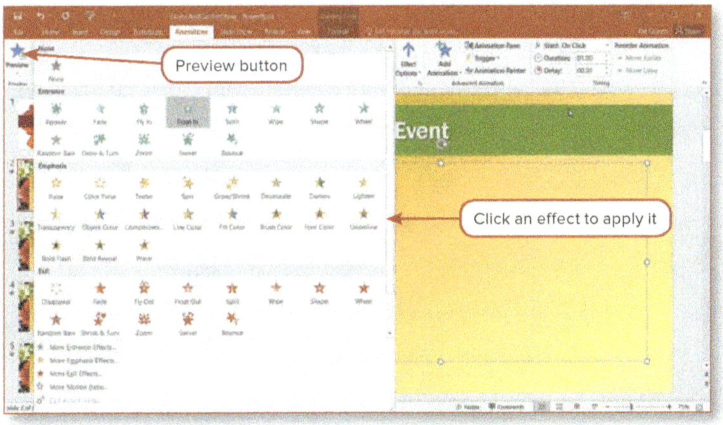

3-18 *Animations* gallery

Note that some effects are for text only. When animating objects, those effects are gray in the gallery and are not available.

▸ HOW TO: Apply an Animation Effect

1. Select the text or object to animate.
2. Click the **Animations** tab.
3. Open the *Animations* gallery using one of these methods:
   - Click the **More** button on the gallery [*Animation* group].
   - Click the **Add Animation** button [*Advanced Animation* group] if the *Animations* gallery is not open because your PowerPoint window is narrow.
4. Click an effect to apply it. A number appears on the slide beside the text or object showing that it is animated.
5. Click the **Preview** button to test the animation.
6. Repeat to animate additional objects as desired. Each animated object is numbered in sequence to show animation order.
7. Remove an animation by clicking the animation number and pressing **Delete**.

MORE INFO

Animation numbers display only when the *Animations* tab is open.

Effect Options, Timing, and Duration

Each different animation has ***Effect Options*** that control the direction of movement.

▸ HOW TO: Change Effect Options

1. Select the animated object.
2. Click the **Effect Options** button [*Animations* tab, *Animation* group].
3. Select an appropriate **Direction** and **Sequence** if it is available.

For the *Float In* effect shown in Figure 3-19, two directions are available. Other effects have many different options. You select only one direction for each animation.

The sequence shown in this figure is *By Paragraph* because the animated object is a list. Animation numbers display before each bulleted item so they appear individually. If you choose *As One Object*, only one animation number displays and the complete list appears at the same time. If you choose *All at Once*, the same animation number displays for each text item and the complete list appears at the same time.

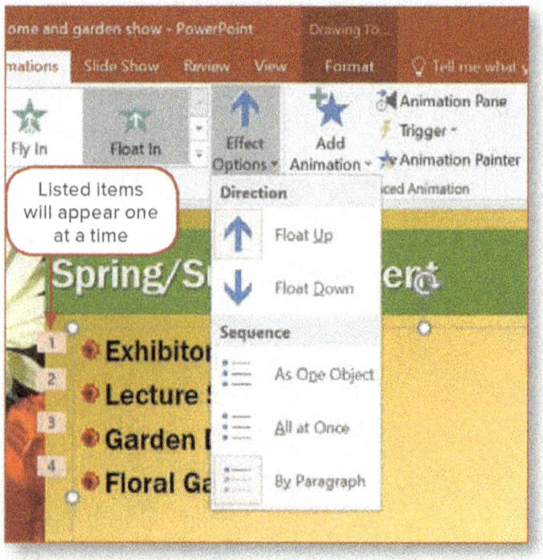

3-19 Animation and effect options applied

Some people are critical of animating text because viewers cannot read text until it stops moving. If you are going to spend significant time discussing each item in a list, adding each item as you start talking about it makes sense. However, animating a list has no value if your statements are brief or if you discuss the complete list in general terms.

You can adjust animation *Timing* using the following commands on the *Animations* tab in the *Timing* group:

- ***Start***: When the *On Click* option is selected, the speaker controls when animation begins by clicking at an appropriate time. The *With Previous* or *After Previous* options cause the animation to occur automatically.
- ***Duration***: By default, the time to complete each animation ranges from .50 to 2.00 seconds depending on the movement. Increasing the duration seconds extends the time an object is moving so the movement appears slower.
- ***Delay***: The default setting is no delay, but you can enter seconds so the animation begins after a specified time.
- ***Reorder Animation***: When multiple objects are animated, click **Move Earlier** or **Move Later** to adjust the sequence of animation.

HOW TO: Adjust Animation Timing and Duration

1. Select the animated object.
2. Click the *Start* drop-down arrow [*Animations* tab, *Timing* group] and select from **On Click**, **With Previous**, or **After Previous** (Figure 3-20).
3. Increase or decrease *Duration* by changing the seconds.
4. Enter seconds or click the *Delay* arrows to specify the time (in seconds) before the animation starts.
5. Click the **Preview** button [*Preview* group] to test the animation.
6. Reorder animation if necessary using the **Move Earlier** and **Move Later** buttons.

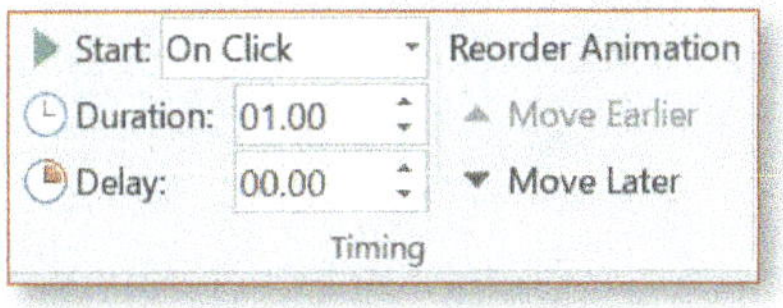

3-20 *Animations* tab, *Timing* group

When you animate several objects, check the animation numbers to be sure the sequencing is appropriate (Figure 3-21). Each number represents the mouse click on which the animation occurs. If a single object's *Start* is **With Previous** or **After Previous**, then the object's number will match the previous object's number. If either of these *Start* options is applied to all objects, then the number will display as "0".

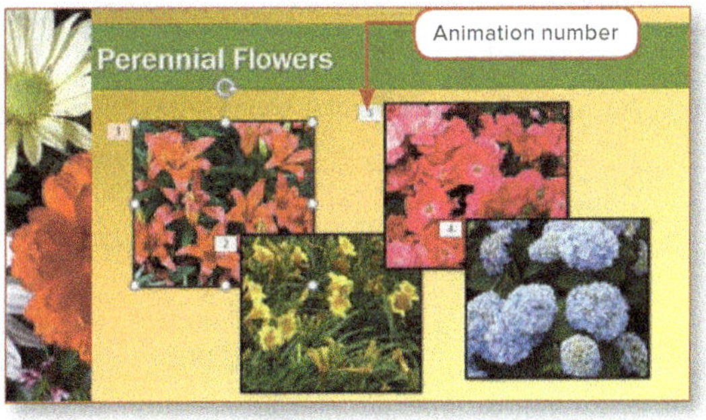

3-21 Numbers indicate animation order

If your presentation is designed to support you as a speaker, coordinate the animation timing with your speaking. This technique usually works best in small segments only because precise timing is almost impossible to predict when you are presenting in real time to an audience. If you are designing a self-running presentation for a trade show exhibit, for example, your animation can be much more dramatic and extensive because the slide show is not dependent on a speaker's pace.

SLO 3.3

Linking to an Online Video

Many videos are available online, but not all of them can be played within PowerPoint. When you search for a video using the *Insert Video* dialog box, the videos found from YouTube are most likely to play within PowerPoint as long as you have Internet access. You click **Insert** to put the video on your slide, but the actual video is not saved in your presentation. An image of the video appears and the necessary information to link to it is saved in your presentation.

When you search for videos, you may find a compelling interview or demonstration that will enliven your presentation, but be sure the video relates to your topic and adds value.

HOW TO: Link a Presentation to an Online Video

1. Select the PowerPoint slide where you want to show the video. Be sure your computer has Internet access.
2. Click the **Insert** tab.
3. Click the **Video** button [*Media* group] and select **Online Video** (Figure 3-22) to open the *Insert Video* dialog box (Figure 3-23).
4. Type a word in the *YouTube* search box and click the **Search** button.
5. Available videos appear with *ScreenTips* that identify names.
   - Source information appears in the lower left corner of the dialog box (Figure 3-24).

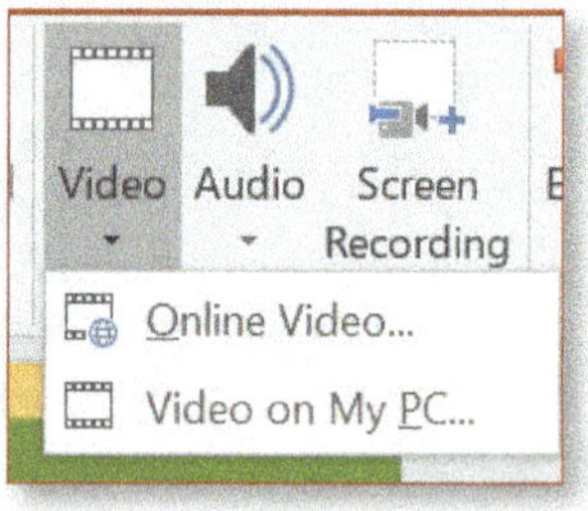

3-22 *Video* button on the *Insert* tab

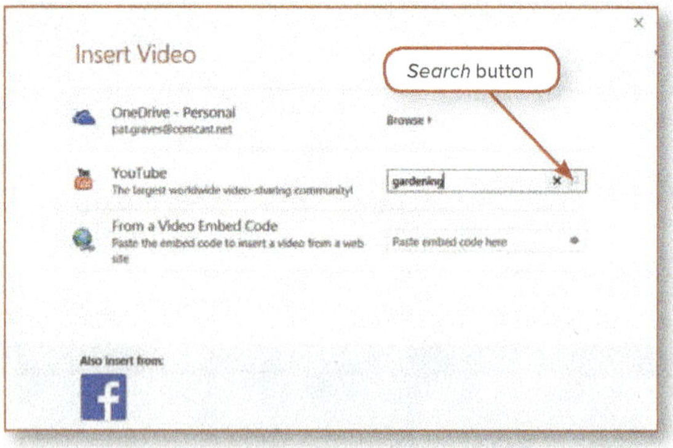

3-23 *Insert Video* dialog box showing search options

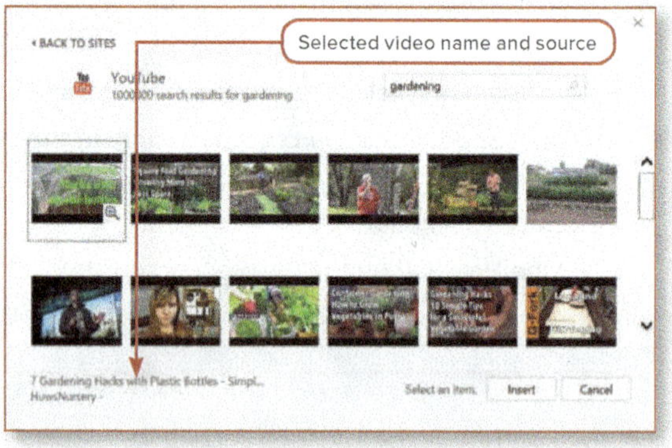

3-24 *Insert Video* dialog box showing search results

6. Click **Insert** and the video appears on your slide.
7. Add the appropriate source information as needed below the video.

> **MORE INFO**
>
> A linked video will not play in a presentation that you send by email or one that you prepare on your computer and later view on your phone through Office Online. The link that creates a path to the file is broken.

Play the Online Video

To play an online video in PowerPoint, the computer used to display your presentation must have Internet access.

The clarity you see in playback depends on the resolution of the original video and how it was compressed for online distribution. Resolution is expressed in pixel width and height. With more pixels, image clarity and detail improves.

As with all computer technology, video capabilities continue to improve and many videos can be played at full-screen size from their online source. However, video sharing sites often provide video in the standard definition size (640 × 480 pixels) or even smaller. Be careful when increasing the size of a video object on your slide to avoid reducing image quality. Test how the video plays before you use it in your presentation. You can drag the video object to reposition it on the slide just as you would a picture or shape.

▸ HOW TO: Resize and Play an Online Video

1. Select *Normal* view, if necessary, and select the video object.
2. Increase the size of the video by using one of the following methods:
   - Drag handles.
   - Enter specific *Height* and *Width* measurements [*Video Tools Format* tab, *Size* group].
   - Click the **Size** launcher to open the *Format Video* pane (Figure 3-25). Click the **Size & Properties** icon at the top of the pane. Adjust size by changing *Height* and *Width* measurements or changing the *Scale Height* and *Scale Width* percentages.
3. Maintain video dimensions as you resize. Right-click the video object and select **Format Video** to open the ***Format Video*** pane, if necessary.
   - Check **Lock aspect ratio** and **Relative to original picture size** to maintain dimensions as your resize.
   - Check **Best scale for slide show** to select a different resolution.
4. Reposition the video object as needed.
5. Play the video in *Normal* view.
   - Click the **Play** button [*Video Tools Playback* tab, *Preview* group] to start the video.
   - If the video can play within PowerPoint, a timeline will appear below the video with playback controls you can use to play, pause, mute, and access other options (Figure 3-26).
   - Click the **Play** button on the video to play it.
   - Notice the clarity of the video as you play it. If the image is degraded after resizing, click the **Reset Design** drop-down arrow [*Video Tools Format* tab, *Adjust* group] and click **Reset Design & Size** to restore the video to its original dimensions.

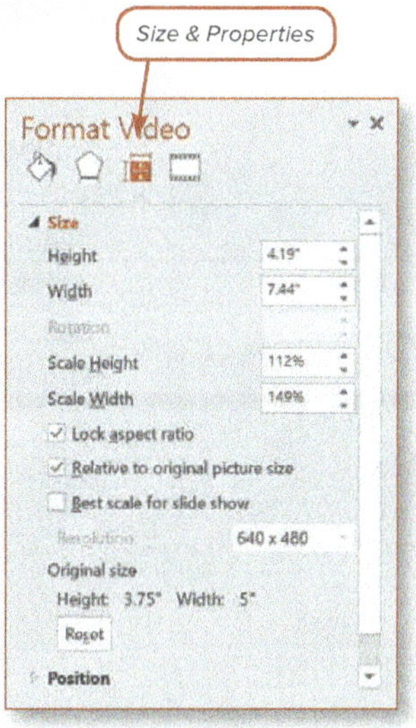

3-25 *Format Video* pane

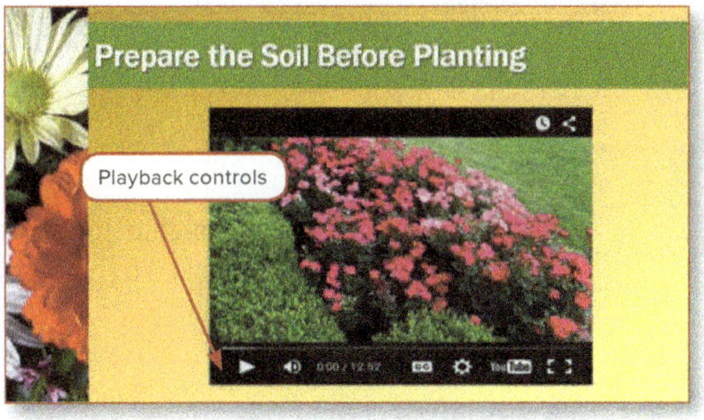

3-26 Video playing in *Normal* view

6. Play the video in *Slide Show* view.
   - Select **Play Full Screen** [*Video Tools Playback* tab, *Video Options* group] if the video can be played at full screen size.
   - Click the **Slide Show** button [*Status* bar] to start your slide show on the current slide.
   - Click the **Play** button in the middle of the video.
   - The same timeline described in step 7 appears at the bottom of the video as it plays.
   - Press **Esc** to stop the slide show and return to *Normal* view.
7. Make the video start automatically in *Slide Show* view.
   - Click the **Start** list box [*Video Tools Playback* tab, *Video Options* group] and select **Automatically**.
   - Click the **Slide Show** tab and the **From Beginning** button [*Start Slide Show* group]. Advance to the slide with the video to test that it begins playing automatically.
8. Move your pointer so it does not appear on the video while it is playing.
9. Advance to the next slide when the video playback ends.

MORE INFO

If you find an online video that you want to use in PowerPoint, you may be able to link to it without searching for it in PowerPoint. You can copy the video's embed codes (the host web address, name of the video, and playback size information) that are included with a video in a sharing section on the host page. Then open the *Insert Video* dialog box and paste the embed codes. Information to link to the video is saved in your presentation, so Internet access is required to play the video.

Obtain Permission

Linking to a video for classroom purposes falls under the guidelines of ***fair use*** for education and crediting the source may be sufficient. However, business use is different. Just like television programming or movies in a theater, videos are copyrighted by the creator. You need permission before you link to, display, or distribute video that is copyrighted. Obtaining permission is time consuming and can be expensive. If the creator does not give you permission, you must find another video and start the process again.

HOW TO: Obtain Permission to Use an Online Video

1. Go to the web site where the video is posted and identify the user name of the creator.
2. Click a link to go to more profile information or, in some cases, another web site.
3. Look for terms of use and find contact information.
4. Send an email message explaining the following:
   - How you want to use the video
   - What portion of the video you will use
   - When you will use the video
   - How you will show credits on the slide where the video is displayed.
   - Your contact information for the creator's response

With the dynamic nature of the web, a video you find may be available for only a limited time. You may need to request a high resolution copy of the video and the creator may charge you for this service.

MORE INFO

The **Copyright Act of 1976** is the primary basis of copyright law in the United States. It specifies fair use that permits limited use for such purposes as research, teaching, and scholarship. The **Digital Millennium Copyright Act of 1998** addresses issues of online copyright infringement.

PAUSE & PRACTICE: POWERPOINT 3-1

Davon Washington has almost finished the slide show for his seminar on presentation planning. For this project, you create custom theme colors that better match the Solution Seekers, Inc. logo, modify a background style, animate several slide objects, and link to a video on a web site.

File Needed: ***PresentationPlanning-03.pptx*** *(Student data files are available in the* Library *of your SIMnet account)*
Completed Project File Name: ***[your initials] PP P3-1.pptx***

1. Open the presentation ***PresentationPlanning-03***.
2. Save the presentation as [your initials] PP P3-1.
3. Create new theme colors.
   a. Click the **More** button [*Design* tab, *Variants* group].
   b. Click **Colors** and select **Customize Colors** to open the *Create New Theme Colors* dialog box (Figure 3-27).
   c. Change four colors. For each change, click the color drop-down arrow and select **More Colors** to open the *Colors* dialog box. Click the **Custom** tab and enter the numbers for *Red*, *Green*, and *Blue* from the following table:

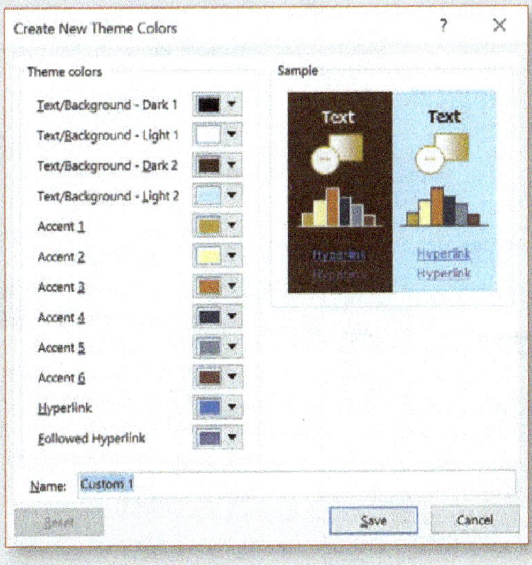

3-27 Original theme colors

	Text/Back-ground – Light 2	Accent 1	Accent 2	Accent 3
Red	234	3	102	181
Green	214	110	0	139
Blue	184	131	51	128

   d. Name the new custom theme Planning (Figure 3-28).
   e. Click the **Save** button. The new custom theme is saved in the ***Custom*** section of your list of available theme colors.
4. Apply a gradient fill as shown in Figure 3-29.
   a. Display slide 1.
   b. Point to the slide background and right-click. Select **Format Background** to open the *Format Background* pane.
   c. Select the **Gradient fill** option.
   d. Click the **Type** drop-down arrow and choose **Linear** if it is not selected.
   e. Click the **Direction** drop-down arrow and choose **Linear Diagonal – Top Right to Bottom Left**. The *Angle* percentage automatically adjusts to 135%.
   f. Click the **Add gradient stop** button, if necessary, so you have four gradient stops.
   g. Click each gradient stop from left to right (Figure 3-30) and adjust the *Color*, *Position*, *Brightness*, and *Transparency* values as needed to match values in the following table:

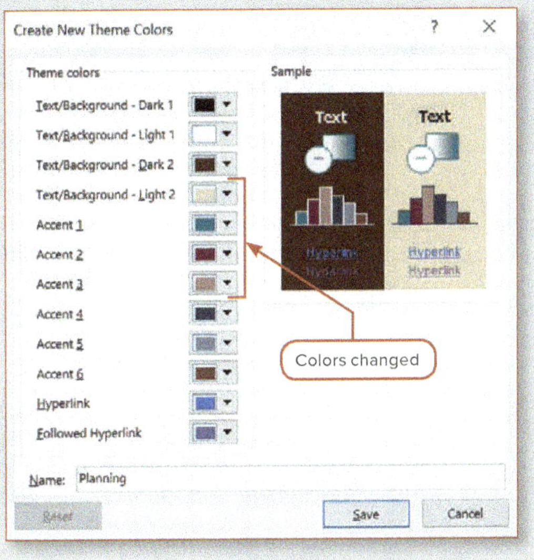

3-28 *Planning* theme colors

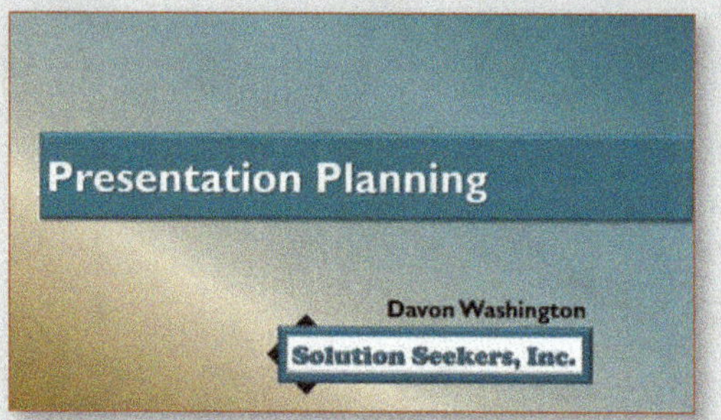

3-29 Title slide background gradient fill

Gradient Stops	Stop 1	Stop 2	Stop 3	Stop 4
Color	*Dark Teal, Accent 1*	*Dark Teal, Accent 1, Lighter 60%*	*Tan, Text 2*	*Tan, Text 2, Darker 50%*
Position	*0%*	*30%*	*70%*	*100%*
Transparency	*0%*	*50%*	*0%*	*0%*
Brightness	*0%*	*0%*	*0%*	*–50%*

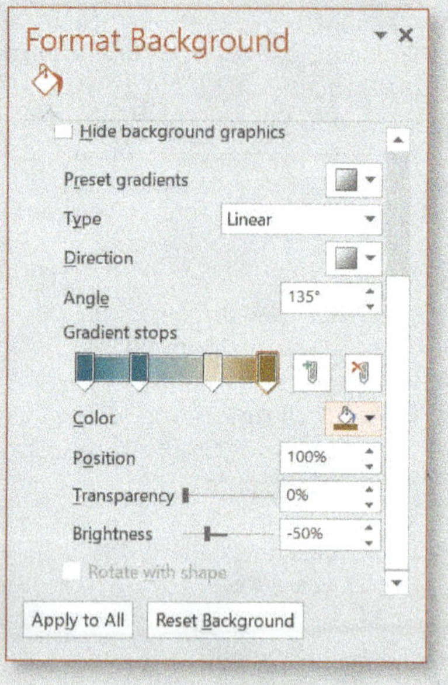

3-30 Gradient stops adjusted

5. Create a *Picture fill* background.
   a. Display slide 2. On the *Format Background* pane, select **Picture or texture fill** and click the **File** button to open the *Insert Picture* dialog box.
   b. Locate your student data files, select ***Presenter-03***, and click **Insert**.
   c. Click the **Picture** icon at the top of the *Format Background* pane and then click **Picture Color**.
   d. Click the **Recolor** drop-down arrow and choose **Tan, Background color 2 Light** (Figure 3-31).
   e. Close the *Format Background* pane.

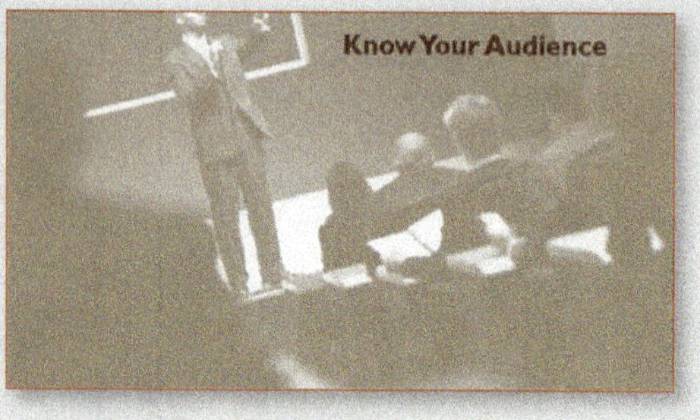

3-31 Background picture fill recolored

6. Apply a transition.
   a. Click the **Transitions** tab and apply the **Wipe** transition.
   b. Click the **Effect Options** button and select **From Left**.
   c. Click **Apply to All** [*Timing* group].
7. Apply animation.
   a. Click the **Animations** tab and repeat steps b–g for each object in the following table.
   b. Select the text or object to be animated.
   c. Click the **More** button on the *Animation* gallery or click the **Add Animation** button [*Advanced Animation* group] if the gallery is not open.
   d. Click an animation to apply it.
   e. Click the **Effect Options** button and select the **Direction** and **Sequence** or **Amount**.
   f. Adjust settings for *Start*, *Duration*, and *Delay*. Some of the settings will appear by default.
   g. Click the **Preview** button [*Preview* group] or **Slide Show** button [*Status* bar] to test the animation.

Slide	Object	Animation Effect	Effect Options	Start	Duration	Delay
4	Down arrow and possible body sequences text box	*Wipe* (Entrance)	*From Top*	*On Click*	*02.00*	None
5	First impression text	*Wave* (Emphasis)	*By Paragraph*	*After Previous*	*00.50*	None
7	Quoted text	*Bounce* (Entrance)	*As One Object*	*After Previous*	*02.00*	*01:00*
8	Road picture	*Grow & Turn* (Entrance)	None	*With Previous*	*02.00*	*01:00*
14	Heart	*Spin* (Emphasis)	*Clockwise, Two Spins*	*With Previous*	*02.00*	None

8. Insert a new blank slide after slide 14.
9. Insert an online video, adjust its size, and add source information.
   a. Display slide 15. Click the **Video** button [*Insert* tab, *Media* group] and select **Online Video** to open the *Insert Video* dialog box.
   b. Type the words presentation skills in the *YouTube Search* box and click **Search**.
   c. Select an appropriate video from the search results and click **Insert**.
   d. Increase the size so the width is approximately 7" wide.
   e. Center the video on the slide.
   f. Click the **Play** button [*Video Tools Playback* tab, *Preview* group] to activate the video.
   g. Click the **Play** button on the video to test it.
   h. Reduce the size of the video for a clear image if necessary.
   i. Add a text box below the video with source information.
10. Test all of your transitions and animations in your presentation.
11. Save and close the presentation (Figure 3-32).

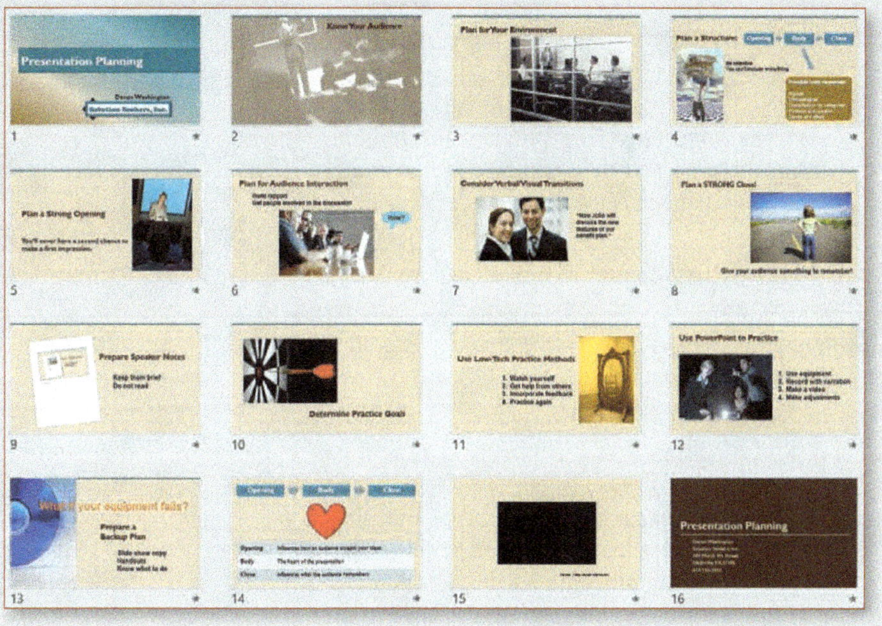

3-32 PP P3-1 completed

SLO 3.4

Using Rehearsal Techniques

Everyone, no matter how experienced, can benefit from rehearsing a presentation. Practicing your delivery ensures that each slide's information supports what you are saying. Practice builds confidence, too.

Speaker Notes

Speaker notes help you remember what you need to say in your presentation, but they should never include text that would tempt you to read to your audience. Notes should be your personal reminders, such as items to emphasize or terminology to define. Notes should not be a script for everything you are going to say. For example, you could include statistics you want to mention, a quote you want to say but not show on a slide, a list of upcoming events, or additional resources for your audience. Even if you don't use the speaker notes you prepare, having them available while you present can be comforting and help to reduce nervousness.

As you think about what to include in your notes, plan for smooth and logical transitions between the various topics of your presentation. You can compose your notes using the *Notes* pane in *Normal* view or you can change to *Notes Page* view.

HOW TO: Use the Notes Pane in Normal View

1. Click the **Notes** button [*View* tab, *Show* group] or the **Normal** button [*View* tab, *Presentation Views* group] to show the *Notes* pane.
2. Expand the *Notes* pane by dragging the border up (Figure 3-33).
3. Remove the ***Notes*** pane by dragging the border down. Click the **Notes** button or the **Normal** button to restore it.

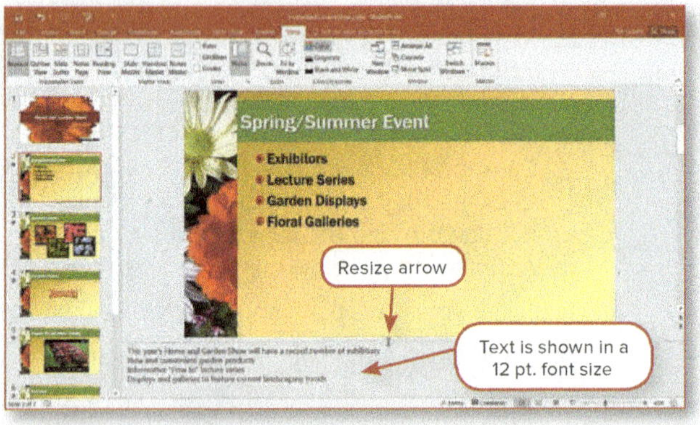

3-33 Increased *Notes* pane size

The *Notes Page* view provides much more space to type text than you have when using the *Notes* pane in *Normal* view.

HOW TO: Use Notes Page View

1. Click the **Notes Page** button [*View* tab, *Presentation Views* group] to show the slide at the top of a page with a large text box below.
2. Type your notes in the text box (Figure 3-34).

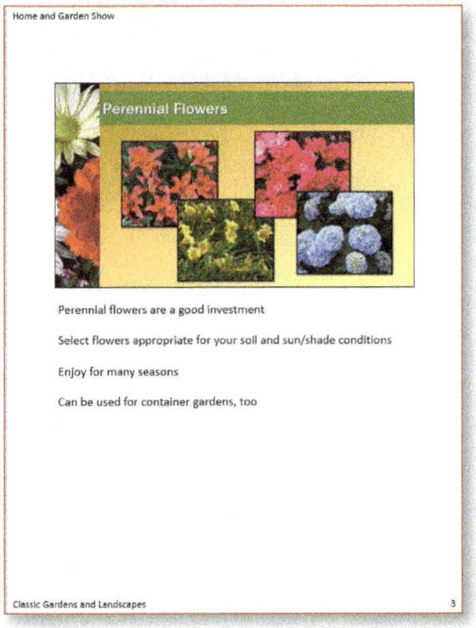

3-34 *Notes Page* view with slide and text

You may want to increase the font size before you print the pages because large text is easier for you to see on a lectern or podium while you are speaking. You will need your notes to be visible even if overhead lighting is dimmed so slide colors display better on the projection screen.

> **ANOTHER WAY**
>
> Printed handouts with a few handwritten reminders can work well for speaker notes.

HOW TO: Print Notes Pages

1. Click the **File** tab and click **Print**.
2. For *Print Layout*, choose **Notes Pages** and check **Scale to Fit Paper** to make the slide images larger (Figure 3-35).
3. Omit the **Frame Slide** option for *Notes Pages*. A single-line border around the entire page is unnecessary.
4. Click the **Print** button.

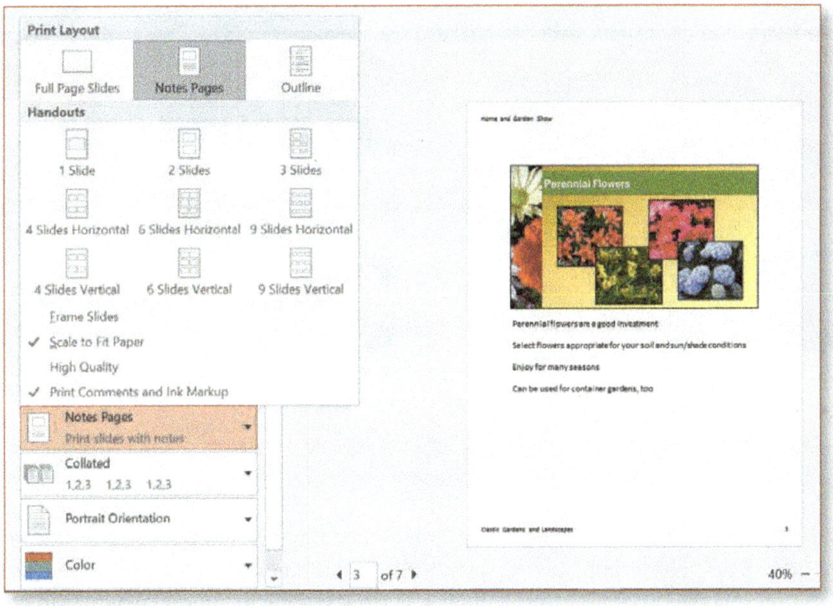

3-35 Print settings for *Notes Pages*

Rehearse Timings

PowerPoint's ***Rehearse Timings*** feature makes it easy to judge the pace of your presentation. When you use this feature to rehearse, the time you spend on each slide is recorded as you move through the presentation. The timings that you save from rehearsing appear below each slide in *Slide Sorter* view. This view enables you to see the "big picture" aspect of your presentation. You can compare the time spent on each slide and consider spending less time on certain slides and more time on other slides where the content takes longer to explain. You can save the timings to automate the presentation so it is self-running. If you are presenting to an audience, remove the timings so you can control when the slides advance.

HOW TO: Rehearse Timings

1. Click the **Rehearse Timings** button [*Slide Show* tab, *Set Up* group] and your slide show will start.
   - A *Recording* dialog box appears in the upper left corner (Figure 3-36). It shows the time each slide is displayed and the total elapsed time.
   - Click the **Next Slide** button (or press the **spacebar**) to advance.
   - Click the **Pause** or **Repeat** buttons as needed.
   - When you reach the end of your presentation, a message will ask if you want to save your timings.

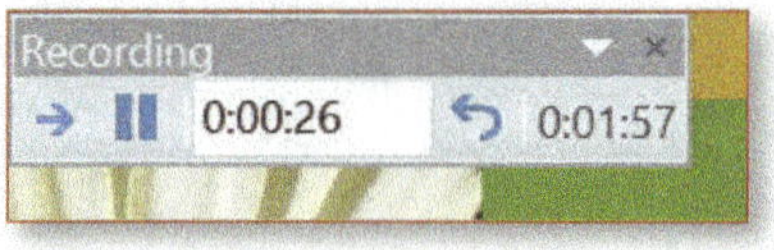

3-36 Current slide time and total elapsed time

2. Click **Yes** and the timings, in seconds, will display below each slide in *Slide Sorter* view (Figure 3-37). (The seconds shown in this example are brief because they were recorded when testing the presentation. The times may be much longer in an actual presentation.)

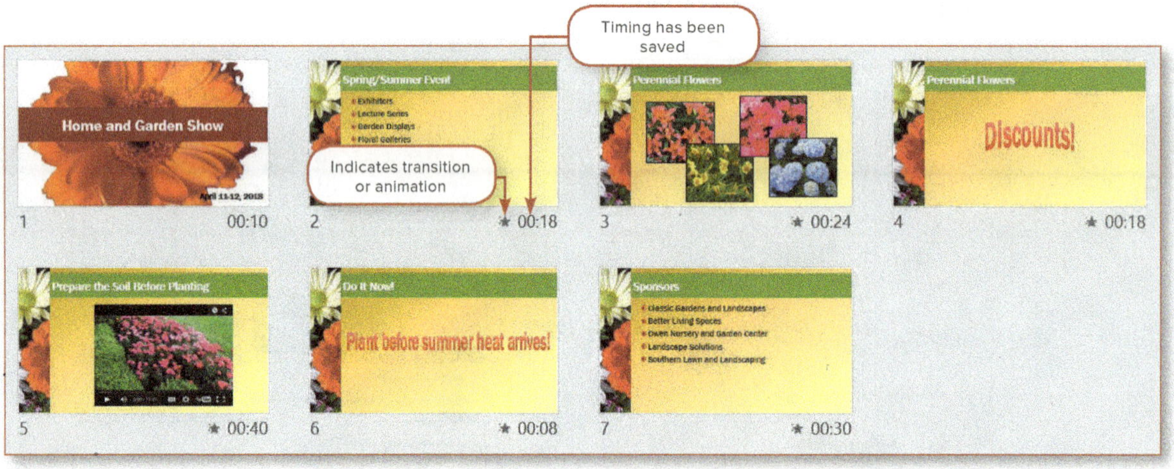

3-37 Slide timings appear below each slide thumbnail.

In rehearsal, go through your presentation and practice what you will say while each slide displays. Use printed notes pages while you are practicing. If possible, stand to replicate more closely the experience you will have when speaking to your audience. Knowing how and where to stand in relation to the keyboard and monitor you are using takes a little practice. Your body posture is important. Good posture makes you appear confident and it positively affects how your voice projects. If possible, rehearse with the equipment you will use to deliver the presentation.

Set Timings Manually

You can enter all timings manually, but it is quicker to rehearse your presentation, save the timings, and adjust the time as needed for individual slides.

HOW TO: Modify Timings

1. Click the **Transitions** tab and be sure the **After** option is selected [*Transitions* tab, *Timing* group] and second numbers are showing (Figure 3-38).
2. Change the number of seconds for each slide, as needed, to increase or decrease the amount of time the slide is displayed.

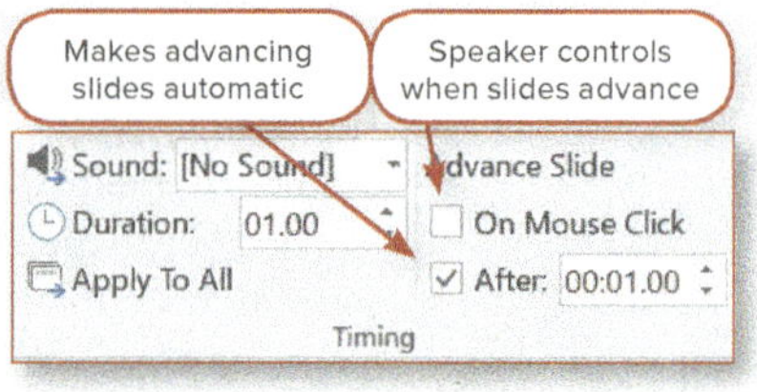

3-38 *Transitions* tab, *Timings* group

3. Deselect the **On Mouse Click** option if you want the slides to advance automatically.
4. Remove timings by clicking the **Record Slide Show** button [*Slide Show* tab, *Set Up* group], select **Clear**, and then select **Clear Timing on Current Slide** or **Clear Timings on All Slides** (Figure 3-39).

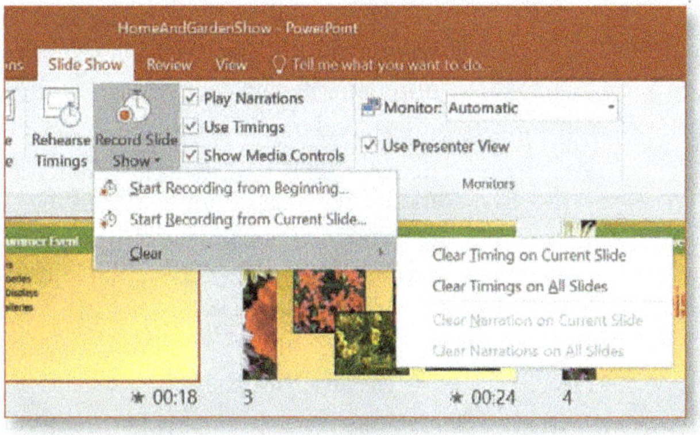

3-39 *Clear Timings* options

Prepare for Mishaps

Be sure you have backup copies of your presentation in case you experience equipment failure and you need to switch to a different computer. In a worst-case situation, where both your computer and projector have malfunctioned, you can present using your handouts to support what you say. All experienced presenters encounter such problems at some time during their careers.

SLO 3.5

Controlling Display Options

As you learned in Chapter 1, online themes and templates are available in different sizes called ***Standard*** and ***Widescreen***. The default size for PowerPoint 2016 is *Widescreen;* the default size before PowerPoint 2013 was *Standard.* Therefore, you may encounter files that require updating to fit your current screen size, or you may need to adjust the size of your presentation to fit an older projection screen in a room where you will deliver your presentation.

Adjust Slide Size

Today widescreen computers (like television screens) use a 16:9 or 16:10 aspect ratio (the ratio of width to height). A slide show designed in the 16:9 aspect ratio takes advantage of this wide horizontal space because it fills the screen. A slide show designed in the 4:3 aspect ratio (more square) and displayed on a widescreen will be positioned in the center of the screen with black areas on both sides. Both of these slide sizes are available on the *Design* tab in the *Customize* group and you can change from one to the other by clicking the **Slide Size** button and choosing **Standard (4:3)** or **Widescreen (16:9)**. Two other sizes are available on the *Slide Size* dialog box and you can create a custom size if necessary. These sizes are listed in the following table and illustrated as blue and green thumbnails in Figure 3-40:

Slide Sizes

Aspect Ratios	Width in Inches	Height in Inches
Standard 4:3	10	7.5
16:9	10	5.625
16:10	10	6.25
Widescreen 16:9	13.333	7.5

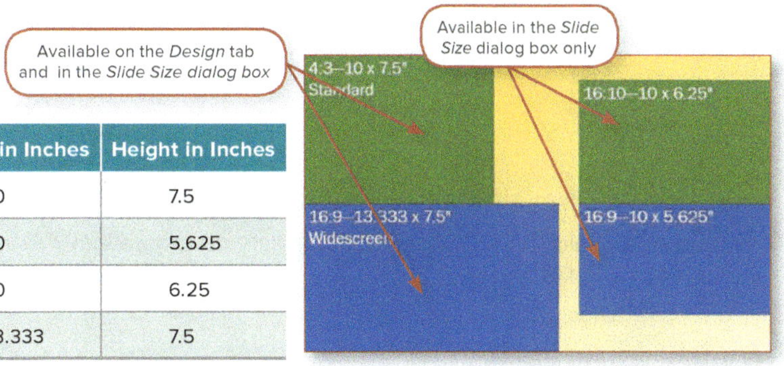

3-40 Slide sizes illustrated

The two wide sizes available in the *Slide Size* dialog box (illustrated in Figure 3-40 on the right) look smaller because their width is 10", the same as the Standard 4:3 width. On your computer screen they will look almost the same as the *Widescreen* size, but ruler measurements and object sizes will be different because of the difference in width and height.

Changing between slide show sizes is a simple process, but necessary adjustments after the change can be time consuming. You need to consider how the change affects the text and graphics on your slide. Both *Standard* and *Widescreen* sizes have the same vertical measurement, so the width is what changes. Adjustments are usually needed so slide objects fit on the slides.

If you change from 4:3 to 16:9 or 16:10, the vertical size is reduced which compresses the slide vertically. Pictures or text in placeholders may not fit appropriately.

Be aware of these height and width differences when changing slide sizes. If you think you may need to change back to your original size, save the original presentation as a separate file before you begin making changes for the new size. By doing this, you can avoid all the resizing changes that would be necessary to return to the original size.

HOW TO: Change the Aspect Ratio

1. Click the **Design** tab.
2. Click the **Slide Size** button [*Customize* group], and then click either **Standard (4:3)** or **Widescreen (16:9)** to select a different size.
3. From the dialog box that appears, select either **Maximize** or **Ensure Fit** for the best scaling option.
4. Click **Custom Slide Size** to open the *Slide Size* dialog box. Sizes for printing and four sizes for on-screen viewing are available. You can choose from the following:
   - *On-screen Show (4:3):* 10" × 7.5" (Standard)
   - *On-screen Show (16:9):* 10" × 5.625"
   - *On-screen Show (16:10):* 10" × 6.25"
   - *Widescreen (16:9):* 13.333" × 7.5"
5. Click **OK** (Figure 3-41). If necessary, select either **Maximize** or **Ensure Fit**.

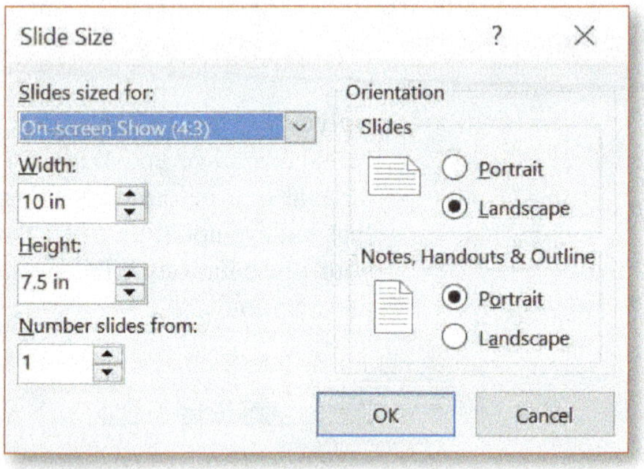

3-41 *Slide Size* dialog box

Presenter View

Presenter View allows you to display your presentation on the screens of two monitors. For example, you could use a tablet or laptop and a large screen television. Or in a presentation room with built-in equipment, you might use a desktop computer with a ceiling-mounted projector and a large screen. The computer you are using must support the use of multiple monitors.

Setting up your monitors depends on your equipment. For example, if you are using a tablet or laptop, you can choose an option in PowerPoint to automatically extend your display.

HOW TO: Modify Display Settings to Extend a Tablet or Laptop

1. Click the **File** tab and select **Options** to open the **PowerPoint Options** dialog box.
2. Select **Advanced**. In the *Display* category, select **Automatically extend display when presenting on a laptop or tablet**. Click **OK**.
3. Insert a wireless display adapter into a television HDMI port and then connect a laptop or tablet to the television through that adapter. Specific instructions will vary depending on your equipment.

If you have two monitors connected to one computer, you need to modify your computer's display settings to extend to the second monitor. This is a *Microsoft Windows* function.

HOW TO: Modify Display Settings for Two Monitors

1. Click the *Windows* **Start** button and select **Settings** to open the *Settings* dialog box.
2. Click **System** and then select **Display**. Under *Customize your display*, two monitors will appear (Figure 3-42).
3. Click **Identify** and numbers appear on each monitor.
   - The *Orientation* should automatically be set for **Landscape**.
4. Click the **Multiple Displays** list box arrow and select **Extend these displays**.
5. Select **Monitor 1** and choose **Make this my main display**.
6. Click **Apply**.
7. Select **Advanced display settings** to make additional changes such as resolution or color calibration for both monitors.
8. Close the *Settings* dialog box.

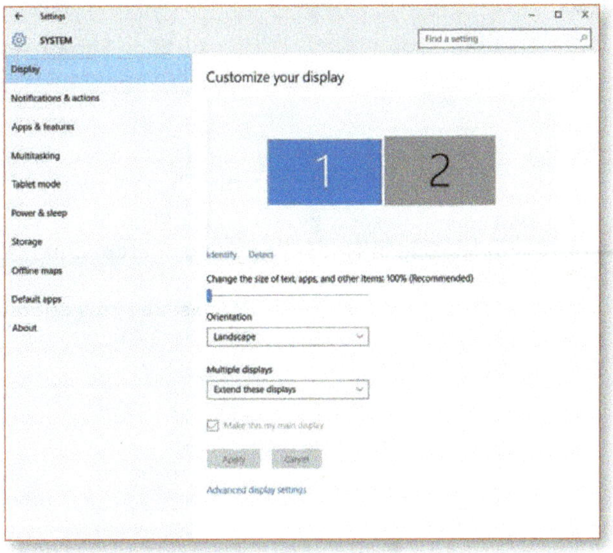

3-42 Customize display settings using Windows 10

These settings also can be made from the *Control Panel* [*Windows System* folder]. Select **Appearance and Personalization**, **Display**, and then **Change display settings**.

PowerPoint can automatically detect when two monitors are connected and will recognize one monitor as your primary monitor for *Presenter View* that shows your view of the presentation and includes the displayed slide, the navigation tools, the next slide, and an area for notes. The second monitor (or projector) displays the full-size slide show for your audience. Using *Presenter View* is helpful because while you are speaking you can:

- View the current slide and see the next slide in your presentation.
- Use convenient navigation tools.
- Have speaker notes available on the monitor for easy reading instead of needing printed notes.
- View thumbnails for all slides in the presentation and click thumbnails to display slides out of sequence.
- Zoom in to sections of a slide.
- Use pen tools without the audience seeing how you select pen options.
- Make the screen that's visible to your audience black yet still have speaker notes available to you.

To practice your presentation, it is possible to use *Presenter View* with only one monitor.

▶HOW TO: Use Presenter View

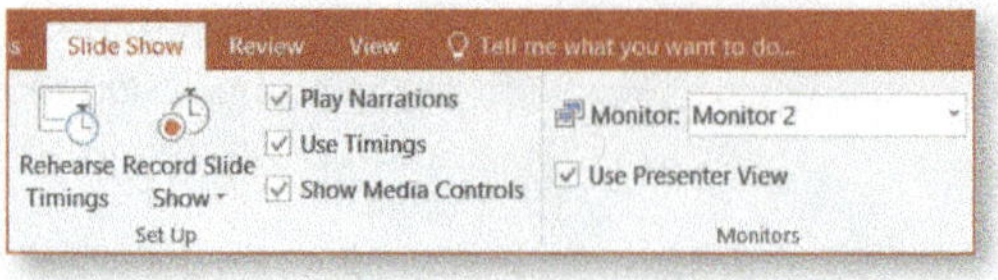

3-43 ***Use Presenter View*** **option on the** ***Slide Show*** **tab**

1. Click the **Slide Show** tab.
2. Select **Use Presenter View** [*Monitors* group] (Figure 3-43).
3. Follow these steps when using two monitors:
   - Click the **Monitor** drop-down arrow [*Monitors* group] to select the monitor used for audience viewing of your full-size slide show.
   - Choose the other monitor listed to swap between the monitors used for *Presenter View* and audience viewing.
   - Start your slide show by clicking the **Slide Show** button [*Status* bar] or clicking the **From Beginning** or **From Current Slide** buttons [*Start Slide Show* group].

Or

4. When using one monitor, press **Alt+F5** or follow these steps:
   - Start your slide show by clicking the **Slide Show** button on the *Status* bar or clicking the **From Beginning** or **From Current Slide** buttons [*Start Slide Show* group].
   - In *Slide Show* view, click the **More slide show options** button on the control bar on the bottom left (Figure 3-44).
   - Select **Show Presenter View**.

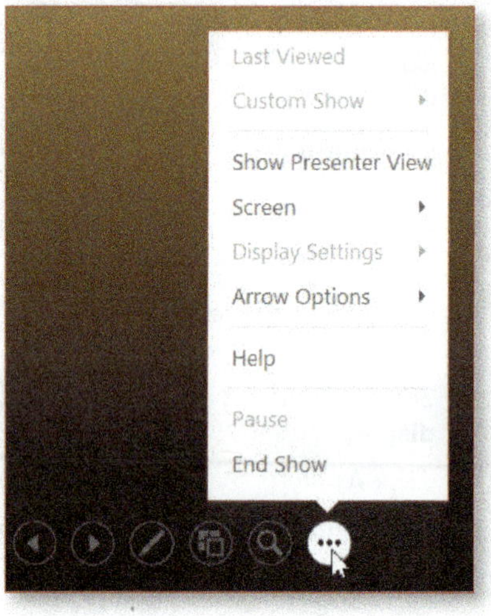

3-44 Control bar in ***Slide Show*** **view and** ***More slide show options***

5. Review features of *Presenter View* (Figure 3-45).
   - The current slide displays on the left. The current notes appear on the lower right; the next slide appears on the upper right.
   - Click buttons at the bottom of the notes pane to increase or decrease text size.
   - Notice the slide show time displayed above the slide. Click **Pause the timer** to stop the seconds from increasing, but this change does not affect automatic transitions. Click **Resume the timer** to continue the time.
   - Click **Restart the timer** to set the time back to **0:00:00**.
   - Options above the slide include **Show Taskbar** so you can easily switch to other applications, **Display Settings** to swap monitors or duplicate a slide show, or **End Slide Show**.
   - Click the **Advance to next slide** button in the navigation area below the slide to move forward through your slides or click the **Return to the previous slide** button to move back.

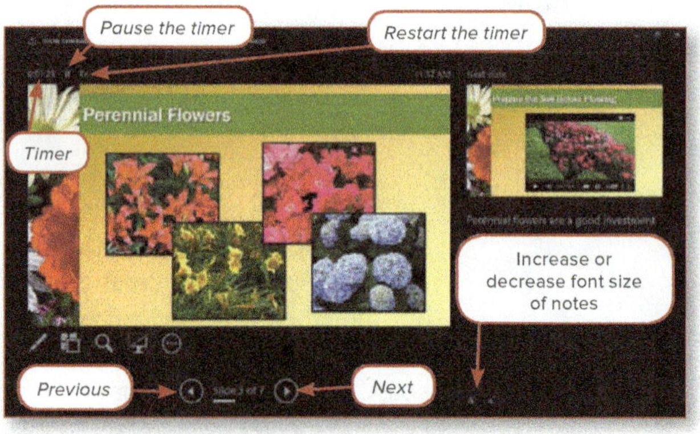

3-45 ***Presenter View*** **window**

6. Review the control bar options in *Presenter View* (Figure 3-46).
   - Click the **Pen and laser pointer tools** button to select options for marking on your slide.
   - Click the **See all slides** button to show slide thumbnails. Click a thumbnail to jump to a different slide out of sequence.
   - Click the **Zoom into the slide** button, drag the selection area over an object or text you want to magnify so you can show detail, and then click. That section of the screen is displayed for your audience. Click the same button again (now **Zoom out**) to return to normal screen size.

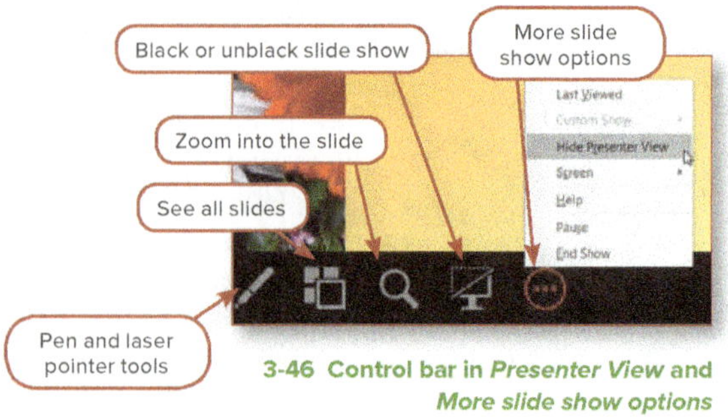

3-46 Control bar in ***Presenter View*** **and** ***More slide show options***

- Click the **Black or unblack** button to make your second monitor appear blank and temporarily hide your current slide.
- Click **More slide show options** to choose other options such as **Hide Presenter View** so PowerPoint displays on your primary monitor.
- Press **Esc** or click **End Slide Show** to exit the slide show.

PAUSE & PRACTICE: POWERPOINT 3-2

For this project, you add speaker notes, print notes pages, and rehearse a presentation. You will use *Presenter View* to display your slide show.

File Needed: ***[your initials] PP P3-1.pptx***
Completed Project File Name: ***[your initials] PP P3-2.pptx***

1. Open the ***[your initials] PP P3-1*** presentation completed in *Pause & Practice 3-1*.
2. Save the presentation as [your initials] PP P3-2.
3. Create a visual transition between topics.
   a. Insert a new slide with the *Section Header* layout after slides 3, 9, and 15.
   b. Delete the subtitle placeholder on each new slide and type the title text as follows:
      - Slide 4 title: Presentation Structure (Figure 3-47)
      - Slide 10 title: Presentation Practice
      - Slide 16 title: Summary

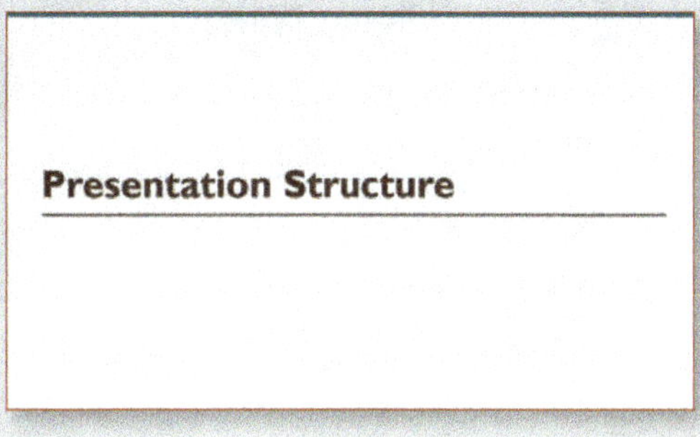

3-47 *Section Header* slide layout

4. Prepare speaker notes for two slides that do not have notes.
   a. Display slide 11, "Prepare Speaker Notes," and click the **Notes Page** button [*View* tab, *Presentation Views* group].
   b. Click the **Zoom In** button several times to increase the percentage to **120%** so you can easily see the text you will add.
   c. Type the following bulleted text [*Home* tab, *Paragraph* group] with a blank space between items for easy reading (Figure 3-48):
      - Print slide with discussion points below
         - Make notes brief (like cue cards)
         - Keep text large so it is easy to read
      - Can be a "safety net" (builds confidence)
      - Use to rehearse a presentation
      - Do not read during a presentation

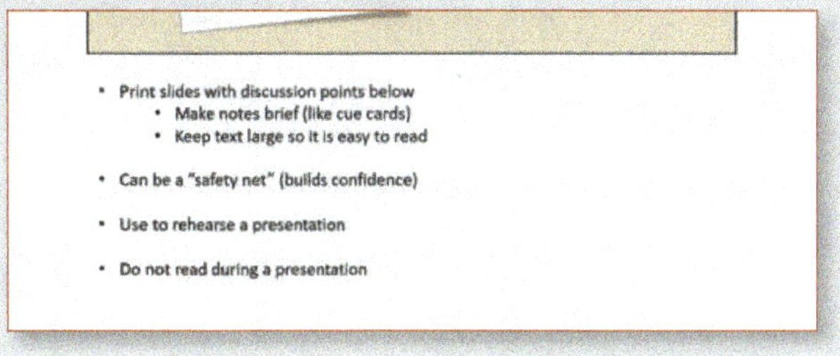

3-48 *Notes Page* view with text

   d. Click the **Next Slide** button [*Scroll* bar] or press **Page Down** to display the *Notes Page* for slide 12. Add the following text:
      - Experience is the best teacher
      - Identify strengths and develop them

- Identify weaknesses and work to overcome them
- Reduce tendency to be nervous

e. Click the **Normal** button [*View* tab, *Presentation Views* group].

5. Print notes pages for slides 11 and 12.
   a. Click the **File** tab and click **Print**.
   b. Select the appropriate printer and make sure that you are printing just one copy.
   c. For *Slides*, type 11-12 to print a *Custom Range*.
   d. For *Print Layout*, choose **Notes Pages** and select **Scale to Fit Paper** (Figure 3-49).
   e. Click the **Print** button.

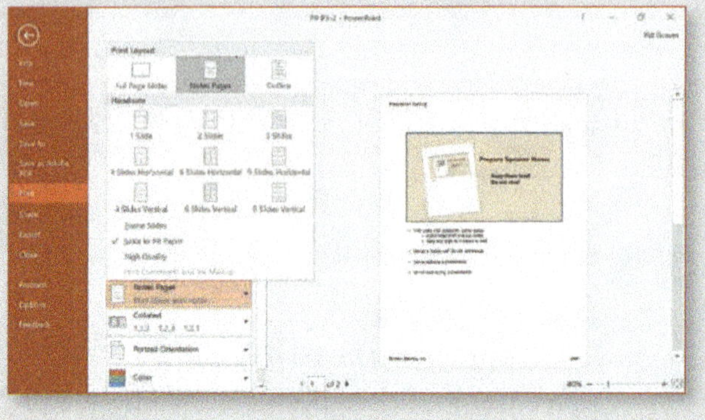

3-49 Print settings for *Notes Pages*

6. Rehearse your presentation and save timings.
   a. Click the **Slide Show** tab.
   b. Click the **Rehearse Timings** button [*Set Up* group]. The *Recording* dialog box opens and timing begins.
   c. Click the **Next Slide** button to advance each slide after approximately 3–5 seconds (for the purpose of practicing this feature).
   d. Click **Yes** at the end of your presentation to save your timings.
   e. Click the **Slide Sorter** button [*Status* bar] to see the timings displayed below each slide.

7. Change how slides advance and modify presentation timings.
   a. Click the **Transitions** tab.
   b. Deselect **On Mouse Click** [*Transitions* tab, *Timing* group].
   c. Change the *After* timing to **3** seconds.
   d. Click the **Apply To All** button.
   e. Change the *After* timing on the *Section Header* slides (slides 4, 10, and 16) to **1** second (shown as **00:01**) (Figure 3-50).

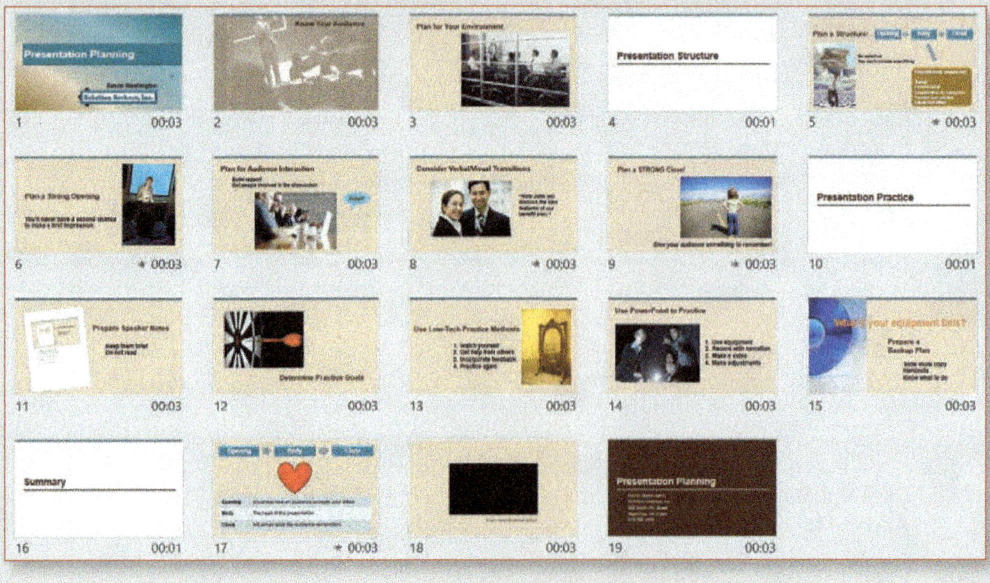

3-50 PP P3-2 completed

8. Review your presentation using *Presenter View*.
   a. Click the **Slide Show** tab.
   b. Click **Use Presenter View** [*Monitors* group].
   c. Review your slides.
      - If you have two monitors, click the **From Beginning** button [*Start Slide Show* group].
      - If you have one monitor, start your slide show. Click the **More slide show options** button on the control bar at the bottom left and select **Show Presenter View**.
9. Save and close the presentation.

SLO 3.6

Presenting Using Projection Equipment

When you look at the front of a presentation room from where people are seated, the ideal location for a speaker is to the left of the projection screen. People are conditioned to read from left to right, so it is natural for the audience to first look at the speaker and then at the projection screen. Many situations are less than ideal, however, so be flexible when you cannot control the speaker area. Keep the following guidelines in mind:

- Become familiar with your equipment so you won't feel awkward using it.
- Be sure the computer or other device you are using has an adequate battery charge if you are using a wireless system to project your slide show.
- If possible, load your slide show before the audience enters the room so you are not seen scrambling around with preliminary preparations. Arrive early and test your presentation to be sure all content works correctly.
- Allow time to relax before your presentation starts. Almost everyone feels nervous before a presentation begins. This reaction is normal and just shows you are respectful of the situation. Harness your nervous energy in a positive way.
- Have your title slide displayed as people enter the room.
- If possible, greet people to make them feel welcome. Let people know that you are glad to have the opportunity to share with them.

Position Equipment

Using a computer while you speak can create challenges. If you are using a desktop or notebook computer, you must see the computer screen when facing the audience and be able to access the computer to advance slides. Controlling your slide show using a tablet computer or even a smart phone makes it easy to advance slides using a touch screen, but these devices must work with your projector or a television if you are using a wireless display adapter.

In presentation rooms, you may need to place your computer on a table. A podium (or lectern) may be available to hold your computer or printed notes pages. Be careful, however, that the podium does not create a barrier between you and the audience. Move away from it when you can.

Even if your computer has a wireless Internet connection and is running on battery power, you may need to manage power cords for other equipment. Connections may not be convenient. Be sure to keep cables and cords away from the area where you and audience members will be walking or tape cords to the floor.

Navigate in a Slide Show

You have advanced through a slide show by pressing the spacebar or clicking a slide. You can use other methods to advance, to go to specific slides, or to end a slide show.

During a slide show, navigation buttons are on the lower left of each slide (Figure 3-51). They are barely noticeable unless you point to that area.

- *Previous* or *Next*: Move between slides.
- *Pen and laser pointer tools*: Shows the menu for pen options.
- *See all slides*: Displays slide thumbnails; click a thumbnail to jump to that slide. Click the **Back** button to return to your previous slide.
- *Zoom into the slide*: Provides a selection area you can drag over your slide to magnify a section of the screen so you can show detail. You can drag the magnified area to show other portions of the screen in the large size. Right-click or press **Esc** to return to the current slide.
- *More slide show options*: Shows the menu for presentation options. For example, you can make the screen go black, change to *Presenter View*, or end a slide show.

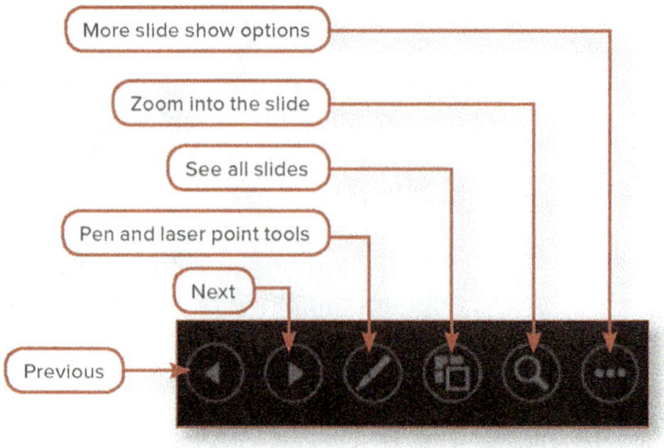

3-51 Control bar in *Slide Show* view

Control Slide Display

The audience needs to focus on you, the speaker. Slides support your message, but you may not want a slide displayed all the time. Also, going from a blank screen to your next slide can seem dramatic.

Blank Slides

If you know in advance that you need to discuss a topic unrelated to your slides, then plan ahead and place one or more slides with a black background in specific places in your slide show. During a presentation, you can blank the screen by pressing **B** on your keyboard to display an empty black screen or **W** to display an empty white screen. Be careful about using the white option, however, because an all-white screen can create glare that will be unpleasant for your audience. In the on-screen navigation, you can click a button to blank your screen to black then click it again to display your slide.

Hide and Reveal Slides

Hiding a slide is helpful when you have information that is not essential to your presentation, but you want to have that slide available if you need it depending on time and audience interest. For example, you could hide slides containing information such as:

- References
- Additional pictures
- Additional details about a topic
- Optional charts, diagrams, or tables

Select one or more slides and click the **Hide Slide** button [*Slide Show* tab, *Set Up* group] (Figure 3-52). In *Normal* and *Slide Sorter* views, the slide thumbnail for a hidden slide appears grayed out with a diagonal line through the slide number.

During a slide show, you can display a hidden slide by typing the slide number and pressing **Enter**.

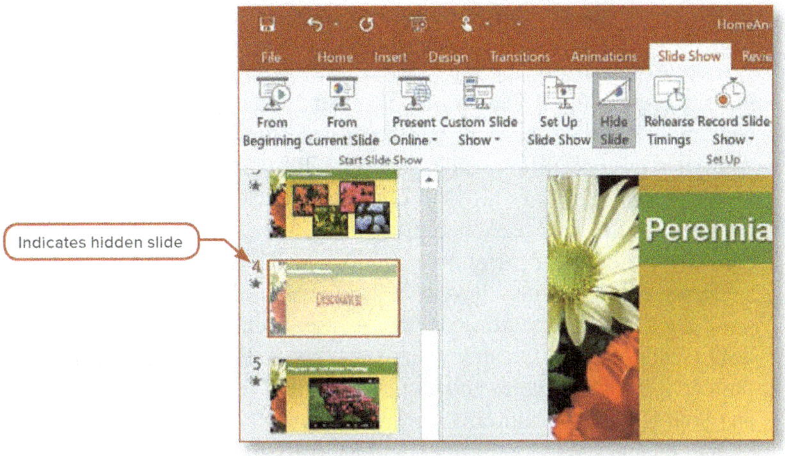

3-52 *Hide Slide* button and hidden slide 12

> **MORE INFO**
>
> You can print hidden slides. Click the **File** tab, then select **Print**. Click the **Print All Slides** option and select **Print Hidden Slides**.

Use Keyboard Shortcuts

Keyboard shortcuts are convenient if you have easy access to your keyboard while speaking.

Slide Show Navigation Shortcuts

Press	Action
N, spacebar, right arrow, down arrow, **Enter**, or **Page Down**	Advance to the next slide.
P, **Backspace**, left arrow, up arrow, or **Page Up**	Go to the previous slide.
Slide number, then **Enter**	Go to a particular slide.
Ctrl+S	Open *All slides* dialog box, select slide, and click **Go To**.
B or period	Blanks the screen to black.
W or comma	Blanks the screen to white.
S	Stop or restart an automatic show.
Plus sign	Zoom in.
Minus sign	Zoom out.
H or slide number, then **Enter**	Go to a hidden slide.

The presentation context menu is available during a slide show by right-clicking when you point anywhere on a slide (Figure 3-53).

Remote Control and Laser Pointer

A ***remote control*** enables you to move away from your computer as you are presenting. If you do this, you can interact with your audience more naturally because you don't need to stay close to your computer to control how slides advance. Remote control devices come in many styles from small clickers to clickers that resemble pens with USB storage. When presenting, be sure you have extra batteries available for the remote control.

Remote controls may have a built-in ***laser pointer***, or you can purchase a separate pointing device. A laser pointer shows a small dot (usually red) on the slide where you point. PowerPoint's laser pointer feature resembles this dot. To use this feature, press **Ctrl** and your left mouse button while you point on the screen and your pointer changes to a dot that can be red, green, or blue.

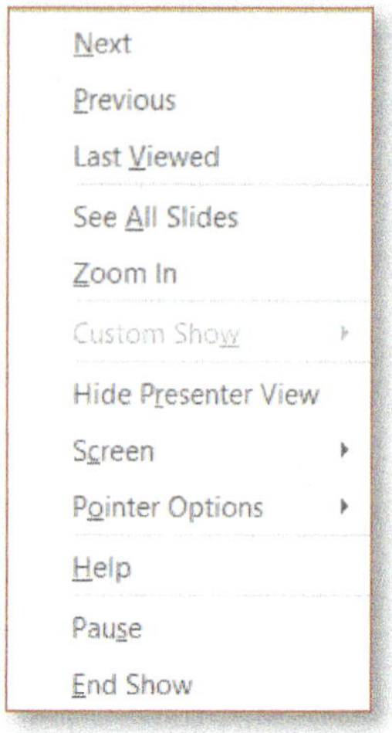

3-53 Presentation context menu

HOW TO: Change Laser Pointer Color

1. Click the *Set Up Slide Show* button [*Slide Show* tab, *Set Up* group] to open the *Set Up Show* dialog box (Figure 3-54).
2. Click the **Laser pointer color** list box arrow and select **green** or **blue**.
3. Click **OK**.

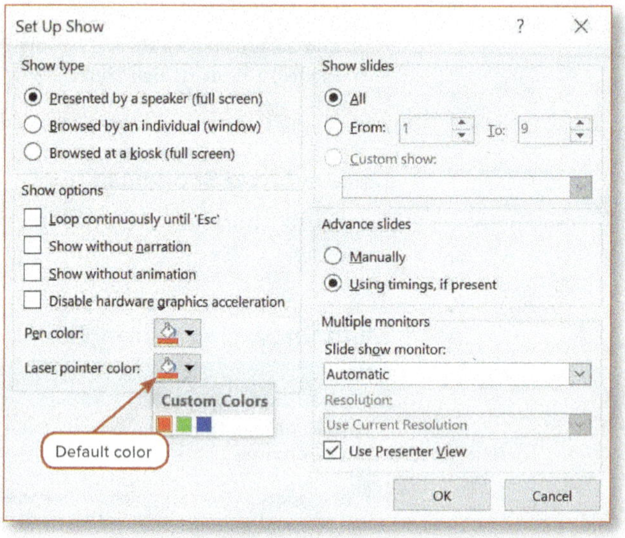

3-54 Change laser pointer color in the *Set Up Show* dialog box

A dot on the screen directs audience attention to a particular location. Be sure you show the dot long enough for your audience to find it and keep the dot steady. Do not bounce it around on the screen with random movements because this distracts viewers. A very small pointer movement on your computer screen creates a large movement on a projection screen.

SLO 3.7

Using Annotation Pens

You can call attention to information by writing or drawing on slides during a presentation. These markings are called ***ink annotations***. While controlling the pointer to write with a hand-held mouse is a little awkward, using a stylus or your finger to draw on a tablet is more natural. You can record audience feedback and make simple drawings on slides. When you reach the end of your presentation, you can save ink annotations. All markings, even if you draw a rectangle, are saved as lines and not as shapes.

To write or draw on a slide, use the ***Pen***. To add a color overlay on text, use the ***Highlighter*** just as you would mark text to highlight information on paper. When you change ***Ink Color***, be sure the color you select contrasts with the slide background so it is easy to see.

HOW TO: Use the Pen and Highlighter

1. Start a slide show and go to the slide you want to annotate.
2. Select the *Pen* or *Highlighter* using one of the following methods:
   - Click the **Pen** button in the navigation area (Figure 3-55) to open the context menu. Select an option as desired.
   - Right-click anywhere on the slide to open the context menu and select **Pointer Options**. Select an option as desired (Figure 3-56).
3. Begin writing or drawing on one or more slides.
4. Remove markings. Right-click, select **Pointer Options** from the context menu, and select **Eraser**. Click markings to delete each continuous pen stroke.
5. Change ink color. Right-click, select **Pointer Options** from the context menu, and select the **Ink Color** option. Select a different color (Figure 3-57).
6. Click **Keep** at the end of a presentation to save ink annotations. The markings are saved as lines that you can edit.

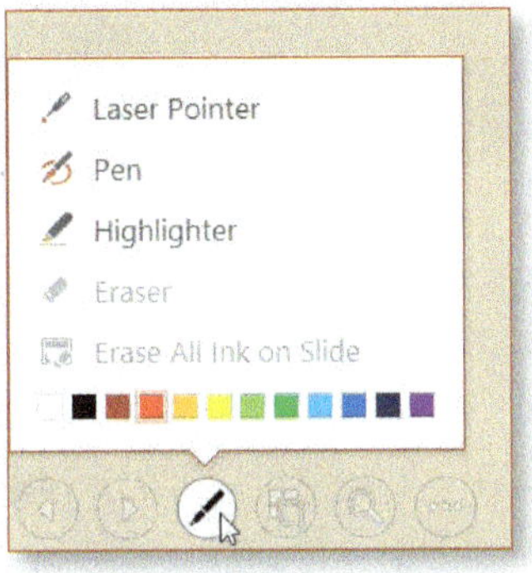

3-55 Pen and laser pointer tools

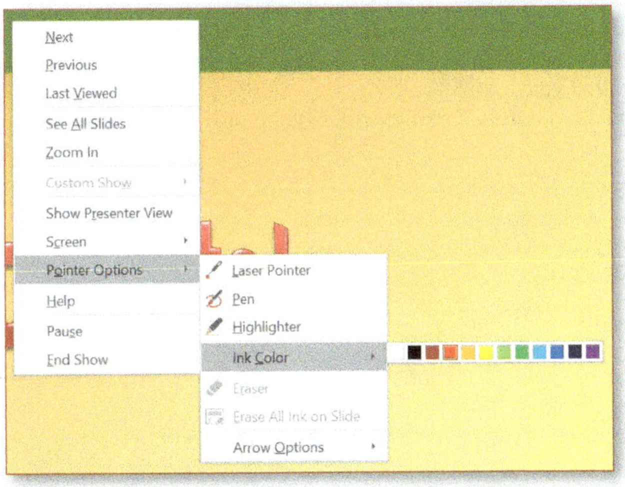

3-56 Change *Ink Color* for the *Pen* or *Highlighter*

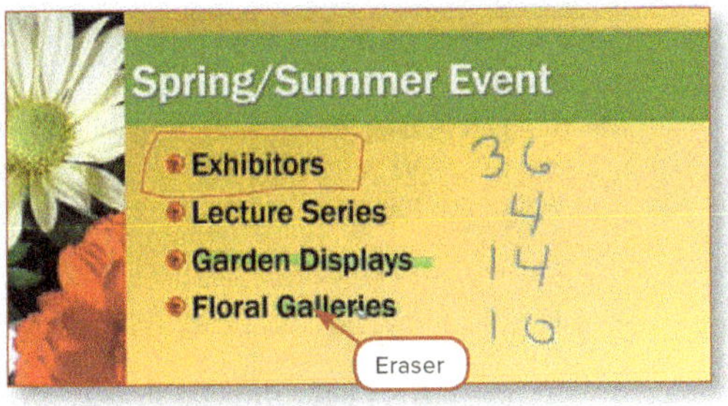

3-57 Ink annotations and the *Eraser* tool

Pen tools are available in *Presenter View*, also. You can also control many of these options using keyboard shortcuts summarized in the following table:

Ink Markup Shortcuts

Press	Action
Ctrl+P	Changes the pointer to a pen
Ctrl+A	Changes the pointer to an arrow
Ctrl+E	Changes the pointer to an eraser
Ctrl+M	Shows or hides ink markup
E	Erases markings on the screen

PAUSE & PRACTICE: POWERPOINT 3-3

For this project, you use PowerPoint features to present more effectively. You hide and reveal slides, blank slides, practice with the laser pointer, change pen colors, use the pen and highlighter, and save annotations.

File Needed: ***[your initials] PP P3-2.pptx***
Completed Project File Name: ***[your initials] PP P3-3.pptx***

1. Open the ***[your initials] PP P3-2*** presentation completed in *Pause & Practice 3-2*.
2. Save the presentation as [your initials] PP P3-3.
3. Click the **Transitions** tab and change the slide transitions.
   a. Select **On Mouse Click** and deselect **After** [*Timing* group].
   b. Click **Apply To All** [*Timing* group].
4. Select slide 4 and click the **Hide Slide** button [*Slide Show* tab, *Set Up* group].
   a. Click the **From Beginning** button [*Slide Show* tab, *Start Slide Show* group] to start a slide show and advance through slides to confirm that you automatically go from slide 3 to slide 5.
   b. Display slide 6 in *Slide Show* view, type 4, and press **Enter** to show the hidden slide.
5. Practice blanking slides in *Slide Show* view.
   a. Press **B** to blank a slide to black. Press **B** to return to the slide.
   b. Press **W** to blank a slide to white. Press **W** to return to the slide.
   c. Press **Esc** to exit *Slide Show* view.
6. Change the laser pointer color.
   a. Click the **Set Up Slide Show** button [*Slide Show* tab, *Set Up* group] to open the *Set Up Show* dialog box.
   b. Click the **Laser pointer color** list box arrow and select **Blue**.
   c. Click **OK**.
   d. Practice using the laser pointer in *Slide Show* view. Press **Ctrl** and the left mouse button as you move the pointer on your slide.
7. Use the pen and highlighter.
   a. Go to slide 7 in *Slide Show* view.
   b. Right-click to open the context menu, select **Pointer Options**, and then repeat for each of the following actions:
      - Select **Ink Color** and select the color **Blue**.
      - Select the **Pen**. Draw a circle around the shape with the word "How" (Figure 3-58).
      - Select the **Highlighter**.
      - Select **Ink Color** and select the color **Light Blue**.
      - Draw a line twice to highlight the word "involved."

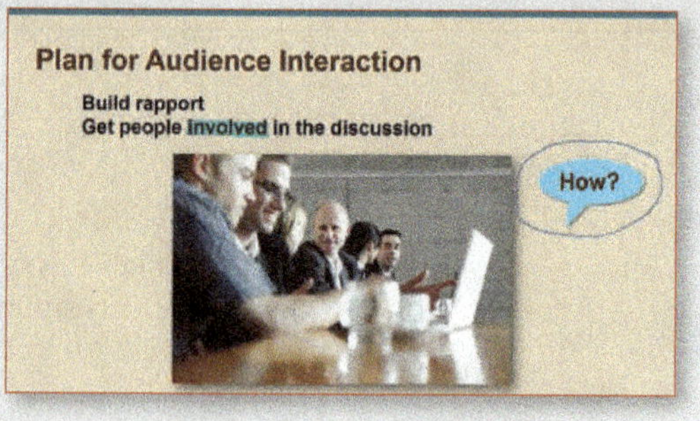

3-58 Pen color changed

   c. Type 13 and press **Enter** to go to slide 13. Use the **Highlighter** to highlight the words "Get help" and "feedback."
   d. Type 17 and press **Enter** to go to slide 17. Use the **Highlighter** to highlight the words "how an audience," "accepts," "heart," "what an audience," and "remembers."
   e. Right-click to open the context menu, select **Pointer Options**, and then select **Eraser**. Click to remove the highlights from the words "how an audience" and "what an audience."
   f. Advance to the end of the presentation and click **Keep** to save your annotations.

8. Save and close your presentation (Figure 3-59).

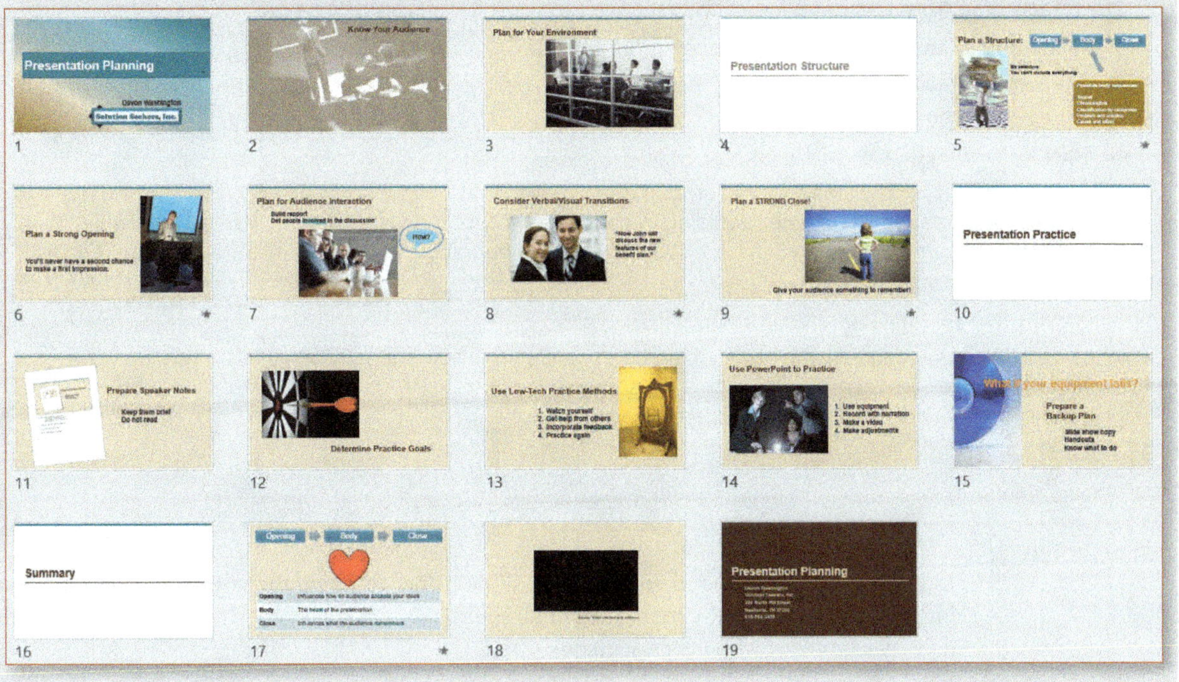

3-59 PP P3-3 completed

SLO 3.8

Preparing a Self-Running Presentation

A self-running slide show, also referred to as a ***kiosk presentation***, can be set up to run continuously without someone being present to advance the slides of the presentation. This type of presentation works well for trade shows or open house events where people walk up to a computer screen and watch the slide show. For example, self-running presentations can be used for marketing products to customers or to educate patients in medical office waiting rooms. You can record narration to accompany the slides. You can also set up the slide show to ***loop*** so it will automatically repeat and cycle continuously from beginning to end.

Record a Slide Show with Narration

To record voice narration for your presentation, your computer must have a microphone and sound card. Like rehearsal, you can use this feature to practice what you will say during a presentation and evaluate your vocal qualities. You can also make a narrated slide show available as a complete presentation to distribute on CDs or DVDs or to post online for viewers.

Prepare carefully to decide what you will say as each slide displays. Use notes pages or other resources as references.

▸ HOW TO: Record Narration

1. Click the **Slide Show** tab.
2. Click the **Record Slide Show** drop-down arrow [*Set Up* group] and then select **Start Recording from Beginning** or **Start Recording from Current Slide** to open the *Record Slide Show* dialog box.
3. Select **Slide and animation timings** if it is not already selected.
4. Select **Narrations, ink, and laser pointer**. (This option is available only if your computer has a microphone.)
5. Click **Start Recording** (Figure 3-60).
    - A *Recording* box appears in the top left corner of the screen.
    - You can advance, pause, or resume recording in the same way you do when you rehearse a presentation (see *SLO 3.4: Using Rehearsal Techniques*).

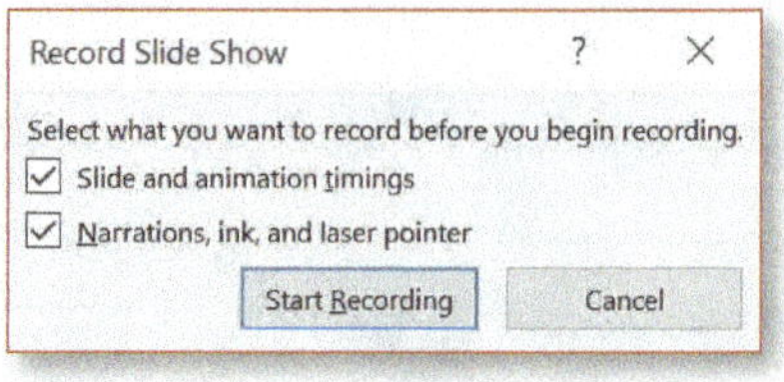

3-60 *Record Slide Show* dialog box

6. Speak clearly into your microphone as each slide displays.
    - At the end of the presentation, the narration and slide timings will automatically be saved.
    - Separate audio files are recorded on each slide and an audio icon appears in the lower right of each slide thumbnail. Review your slide show and listen to your narration.
7. Save your presentation.

Press **Esc** if you need to end the slide show before reaching the last slide. You can clear timing or narration on the current slide or all slides. When you play back a narration, the recording is synchronized with the presentation.

▸ HOW TO: Clear Timings or Narration

1. Click the **Slide Show** tab.
2. Click the **Record Slide Show** drop-down arrow [*Set Up* group] and then select **Clear**.
3. Select from these options:

    Clear Timing on Current Slide
    Clear Timing on All Slides
    Clear Narration on Current Slide
    Clear Narration on All Slides

If you need to display the slide show without narration, click the **Set Up Show** button [*Slide Show* tab, *Set Up* group]. Select **Show without narration** and click **OK**.

Set Up a Kiosk Presentation with Looping

Depending on how you plan to use it, a kiosk presentation may need different design guidelines than a slide show that is shown by a presenter. While other presentations provide minimal text because the slides support the speaker's message, a kiosk presentation may contain more information because it is a stand-alone product. If your kiosk presentation is displayed in a public place with a lot of distractions, then splashy graphics can be used to grab attention. On the other hand, if your kiosk presentation is for educational purposes in a quiet setting such as a doctor's office, the slides might be designed more like pages in a book with smaller text and more detailed information.

▶ HOW TO: Set Up a Kiosk Presentation

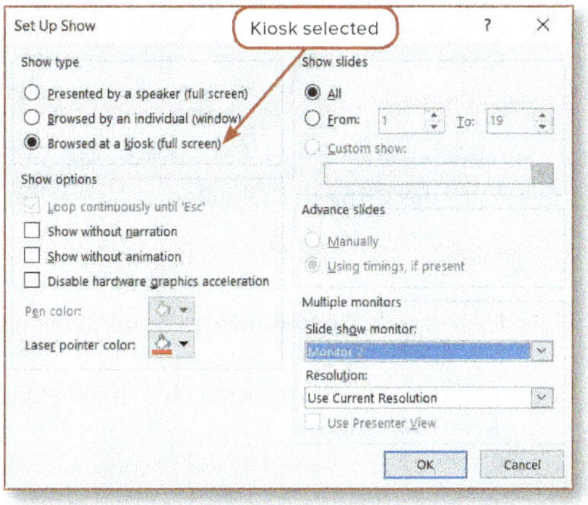

3-61 *Set Up Show* dialog box

1. Click the **Slide Show** tab.
2. Click the **Set Up Slide Show** button [*Set Up* group] to open the *Set Up Show* dialog box (Figure 3-61).
3. Choose the following settings:
   - *Show type*: **Browsed at a kiosk (full screen)**.
   - *Show options*: **Loop continuously until 'Esc'** is automatically selected and grayed out because you chose a kiosk.
   - *Show slides*: **All** or enter the first and last slide numbers you want to display.
   - *Advance slides*: **Use timings, if present** is automatically selected for a kiosk.
   - *Slide show monitor*: If you are using more than one monitor, select the appropriate monitor for the slide show.
   - *Resolution*: **Use Current Resolution** or the highest resolution possible for your equipment.
   - **Use Presenter View** is not available for a kiosk presentation.
4. Click **OK**.
5. Save the presentation with these changes.

SLO 3.9

Packaging a Presentation to a CD or Folder

The ***Package Presentation for CD*** feature allows you to easily transport one or more presentations for use on another computer. You can copy your presentation file and any linked files to a blank CD (CD-R, recordable or CD-RW, rewritable) or to a folder on your computer, network location, or removable drive.

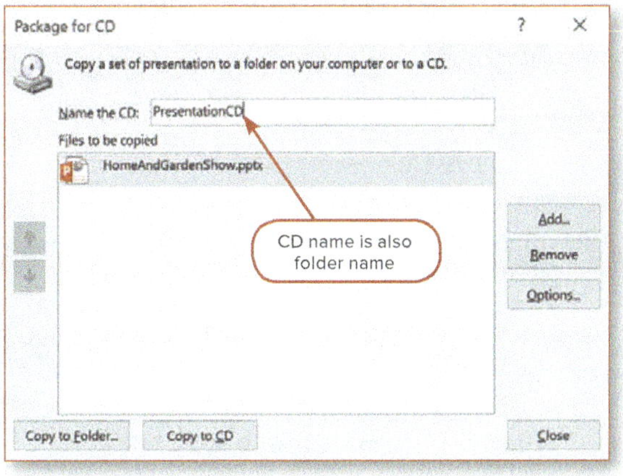

3-62 *Package for CD* dialog box

▶ HOW TO: Save a Presentation to a CD or Folder

1. Insert a CD in your CD/DVD drive if you are saving to that location.
2. Click the **File** tab and select **Export**.
3. Select **Package Presentation for CD**. Click the **Package for CD** button to open the *Package for CD* dialog box.
4. Type a name for the CD (Figure 3-62).
5. Click the **Options** button to open the ***Options*** dialog box (Figure 3-63) and choose from the following options:
   - **Linked Files:** Preserves links and copies any external files such as audio or video files.
   - **Embedded TrueType fonts**: Assures that the fonts used in your presentation are available on the playback computer.

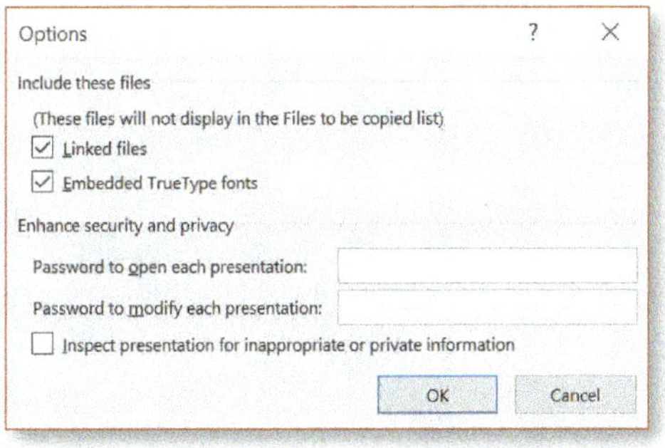

3-63 *Options* dialog box

- **Password**: Enhances security for opening or modifying a presentation.
- **Inspect**: Checks for inappropriate or private information.

6. Click **OK**.
7. Save the presentation using one of the following methods:
   - Click the **Copy to CD** button and click **Yes** to verify that you want to include linked files.

   Or

   - Click the **Copy to Folder** button to open the *Copy to Folder* dialog box (Figure 3-64). Type a name for the folder and browse for the location to save the presentation. Select the option to **Open folder when complete** if you want to see all the files that are copied. Click **OK**.

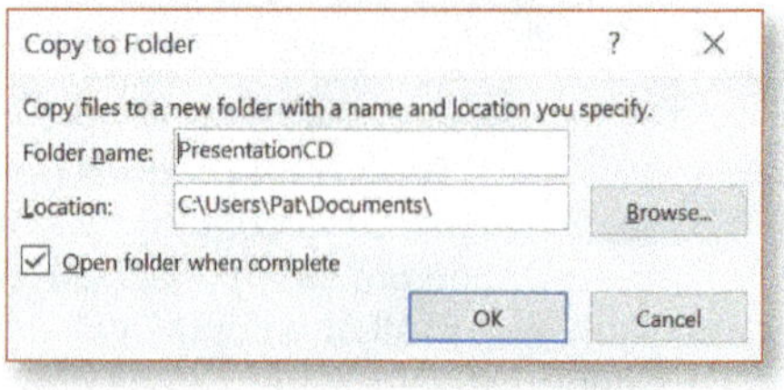

3-64 *Copy to Folder* dialog box

8. Click **No** when the packaging process is complete to indicate that you don't need to make another copy. Click **Close**.
9. Test the presentation by loading it from the folder or from the CD.

MORE INFO

If file size requirements exceed the storage capacity of a CD, you can convert your slide show to a video and then use DVD burning software to save the files to a DVD. PowerPoint does not support direct burning to DVDs.

PAUSE & PRACTICE: POWERPOINT 3-4

This project consists of two parts. You record a presentation with audio if you have a microphone connected to your computer in Part A. In Part B, you prepare a kiosk presentation, set it up to loop so it is self-running, and then use the *Package Presentation for CD* feature to save it to a folder.

File Needed: ***[your initials] PP P3-2.pptx***
Completed Project File Name: ***[your initials] PP P3-4a.pptx*** **and** ***[your initials] PP P3-4b.pptx***

Part A (Microphone Required)

1. Open the ***[your initials] PP P3-2*** presentation completed in *Pause & Practice 3-2*.
2. Save the presentation as [your initials] PP P3-4a and change to *Slide Sorter* view.
3. Delete slides 6–19. For this project, you need only slides 1–5.
4. Remove the timings.
   a. Click the **Record Slide Show** button [*Slide Show* tab, *Set Up* group] and select **Clear**.
   b. Select **Clear Timings on All Slides** (Figure 3-65).

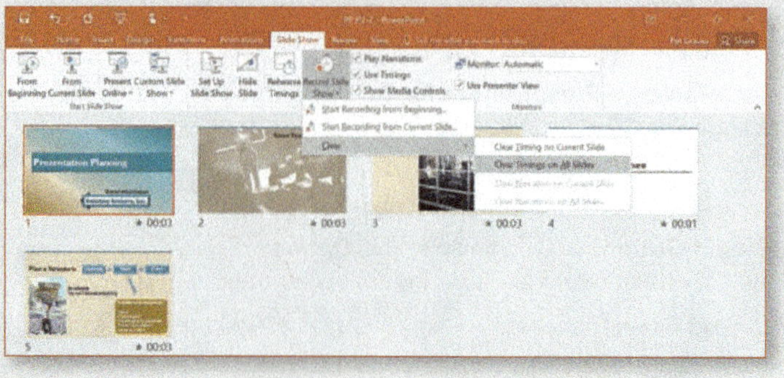

3-65 Clear timings on all slides

5. Click the **Notes Page** button [*View* tab, *Presentation Views* group] and add notes to two slides.
   a. Display the *Notes Page* for slide 2. Add four items after the first line of text and add bullets [*Home* tab, *Paragraph* group]:
      - What is their background?
      - What is their educational level?
      - How familiar are they with your topic?
      - Are they likely to be accepting of your ideas or resistant?
   b. Display the *Notes Page* for slide 3. Add two more bulleted items at the end of the bulleted text:
      - Overall cleanliness and organization of the room
      - Temperature level for comfort
   c. Print the notes pages for slides 1-3 and 5 to use as a reference when recording the slide show.
6. Click the **Record Slide Show** drop-down arrow [*Slide Show* tab, *Set Up* group] and select **Start Recording from Beginning**.
   a. Select **Slide and animation timings** and **Narrations, ink, and laser pointer** (Figure 3-66).
   b. Click **Start Recording**.
   c. Speak clearly into your microphone as you go through the slide show. If you don't have a microphone, go through the slide show to practice. Your timings will be saved and sound icons will appear even if no sound was recorded.

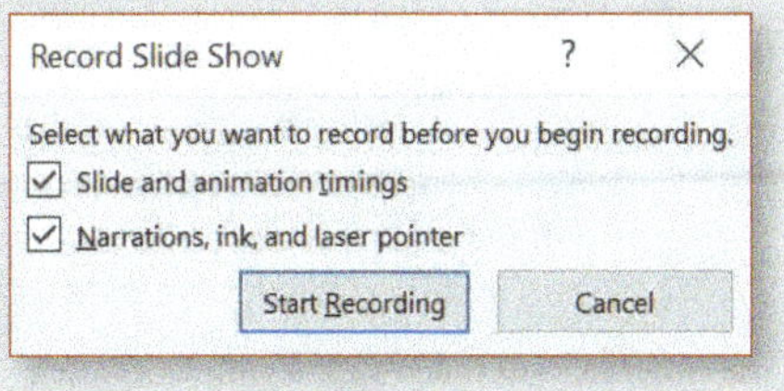

3-66 *Record Slide Show* dialog box

7. Review the presentation and listen to the narration.
8. Save and close the presentation.

Part B

1. Open the presentation ***[your initials] PP P3-2*** again.
2. Save the presentation as [your initials] PP P3-4b.
3. Apply timing so slides change rapidly.
   a. Confirm that **On Mouse Click** [*Transitions* tab, *Timing* group] is not selected.
   b. Change *Duration* to **01.00** and *After* to **00:02:00**.
   c. Click **Apply to All** (Figure 3-67).

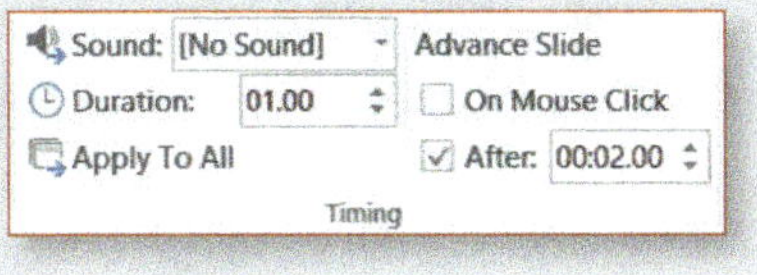

3-67 *Timing* group on the *Transitions* tab

4. Click the **Set Up Slide Show** button [*Slide Show* tab, *Set Up* group] to open the *Set Up Show* dialog box.
   a. Select the following settings (Figure 3-68):
      - *Show type*: **Browsed at a kiosk (full screen)**.
      - *Show options*: **Loop continuously until 'Esc'** is automatically checked for a kiosk.
      - *Show slides*: **All**.
      - *Advance slides*: **Use timings, if present** is automatically checked for a kiosk.
      - *Slide show monitor*: Select the appropriate monitor.
      - **Use Presenter View** is not available because you selected a kiosk presentation.
   b. Click **OK**.

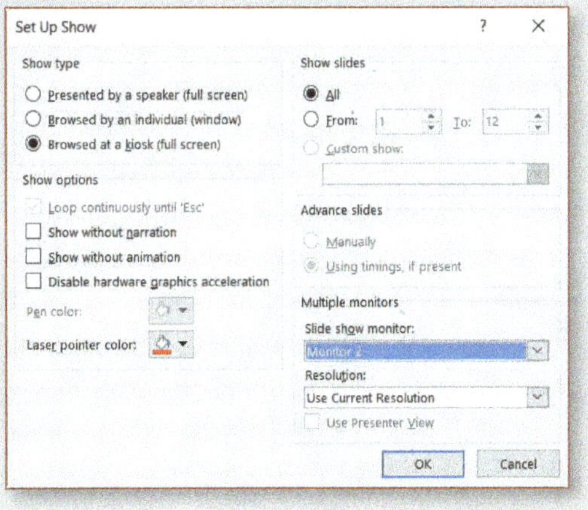

3-68 *Set Up Show* dialog box

5. Use the *Package Presentation for CD* feature to save a presentation to a folder.
   a. Click the **File** tab and select **Export**.
   b. Click **Package Presentation for CD** and click the **Package for CD** button to open the *Package for CD* dialog box.
   c. Type Planning for the name of the CD.
6. Click the **Options** button to open the *Options* dialog box and select the following:
   a. Choose **Linked Files** to preserve links and copy any external files such as audio or video files.
   b. Choose **Embedded TrueType fonts** to assure that the fonts you use in your presentation are available on the playback computer.
   c. Click **OK** and the dialog box closes.
7. Click the **Copy to Folder** button to open the *Copy to Folder* dialog box. The name you typed for the CD automatically appears.
   a. Click **Browse** to open the *Choose Location* dialog box and find the place where you want to save the presentation. Click **Select**.
   b. Select the option to **Open folder when complete**.
   c. Click **OK** and the dialog box closes.
   d. Click **Yes** if you receive a message about including linked files.
      - A *File Explorer* window opens showing the files in the open *Planning* folder (Figure 3-69).
8. Move the *File Explorer* window so you can close the *Package for CD* dialog box.

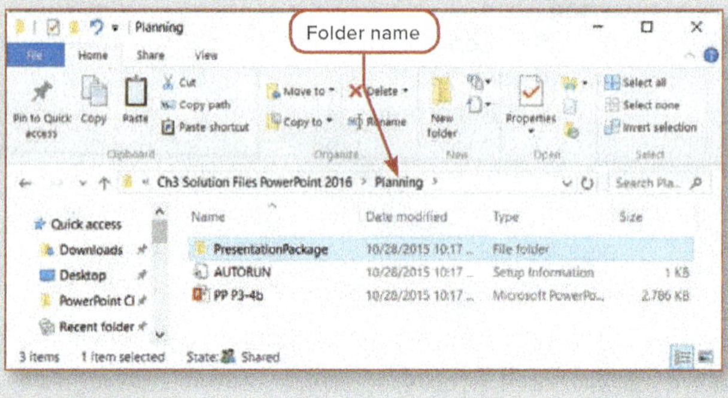

3-69 Folder for completed slide show

9. Close your original ***[your initials] PP P3-4b*** presentation.
10. Test the saved presentation by opening it from the *Planning* folder. Double click the ***[your initials] PP P3-4b*** file name.
11. Close the presentation and folder.

Chapter Summary

3.1 Create custom theme colors and background fills (p. P3-147).

- Design themes create a unified appearance for your presentation.
- The *Accent 1* theme color is the color that appears, by default, each time you draw a shape.
- Create custom theme colors by selecting different colors for background, text, and accent colors. Select the background color first and then select other colors that work well on that background.
- Modify backgrounds using the *Format Background* dialog box to apply a custom pattern, gradient, or picture fill.
- Carefully control how text is placed over background pictures and other fills so text is easy to read.

3.2 Apply animation to add interest and reinforce content (p. P3-155).

- ***Animation*** adds movement to slide objects and text.
- Animation is applied through ***Entrance***, ***Exit***, and ***Emphasis*** effects.
- If more than one animation is used, each animation is numbered in sequence.
- ***Effect Options*** control the direction and sequence of movement.
- Animation ***Start*** options include *On Click*, *With Previous*, or *After Previous*.
- ***Duration*** is the time that it takes to complete an animation.

3.3 Link to an online video (p. P3-158).

- Search for an online video using the *Insert Video* dialog box.
- You need Internet access and a video must currently be available online if you want to link to it during a PowerPoint presentation.
- Some videos cannot be played effectively at full screen size because the resolution is too low.
- Playback controls appear at the bottom of the video.

3.4 Use rehearsal techniques to prepare for presentation delivery (p. P3-164).

- Type ***speaker notes*** using the *Notes* pane or *Notes Page* view.
- Print speaker notes for reference during a presentation.
- Use ***Rehearse Timings*** to practice and judge the pace of your presentation.
- You can manually adjust timings to increase or decrease the time a slide is displayed.
- Prepare backup copies of your presentation and your notes.

3.5 Control display options for different screen sizes (p. P3-167).

- The dimensions of your slides vary based on the aspect ratio (the ratio of width to height) you use.
- PowerPoint's default aspect ratio is ***Widescreen*** *16:9;* the ***Standard*** *4:3* is available.
- *Presenter View* displays the current slide, next slide, notes, and navigation controls on one monitor, while the slide show displays on a second monitor or projection screen.
- *Presenter View* can be used with one monitor or multiple monitors/devices.

3.6 Present effectively and professionally using projection equipment (p. P3-173).

- Use the slide show toolbar, context menu, or keyboard shortcuts to navigate to different slides in a presentation.
- To blank a slide to black, press **B;** to blank a slide to white, press **W**.
- When you hide a slide, it is still in the presentation but will not display during a slide show unless you go to that specific slide by typing its number and pressing **Enter**.
- Use a ***remote control*** to advance slides so you can move away from your computer.
- Use PowerPoint's ***laser pointer*** to temporarily display a dot on the slide during a slide show.

3.7 Use annotation pens to highlight information and save presentation markings (p. P3-176).

- Use the ***Pen*** or ***Highlighter*** to mark or draw on a slide during a slide show.
- Use the ***Eraser*** to remove markings during a slide show.
- These markings, called ***ink annotations***, can be saved at the end of the presentation.

3.8 Prepare a self-running presentation that loops (p. P3-179).

- If your computer has a microphone, you can include narration in a presentation.
- A self-running presentation, a ***kiosk presentation***, is set to automatically ***loop*** so it runs continuously.
- Use the *Set Up Show* dialog box to choose options for a kiosk presentation.

3.9 Use the *Package Presentation for CD* feature to prepare a slide show for display on other computers (p. P3-181).

- The ***Package Presentation for CD*** feature saves linked files to a CD or other location.
- To assure that the fonts you used to create your presentation are available on the computer you will use to display your presentation, select ***Embedded TrueType Fonts***.

Check for Understanding

The SIMbook for this text (within your SIMnet account) provides the following resources for concept review:

- Multiple choice questions
- Matching exercises
- Short answer questions

USING MICROSOFT POWERPOINT 2016

Guided Project 3-1

One of the community colleges in the Sierra Pacific Community College District has finished construction of a new building for their business program. A dedication ceremony and open house is planned. For this project, you finalize the presentation for this special program.
[Student Learning Outcomes 3.1, 3.2, 3.4, 3.5, 3.6, 3.8]

Files Needed: ***Dedication-03.pptx*** and ***Building-03.jpg*** *(Student data files are available in the* Library *of your SIMnet account.)*
Completed Project File Names: ***[your initials] PowerPoint 3-1.pptx***

Skills Covered in This Project

- Apply a background picture fill.
- Apply animation and effect options.
- Create and print notes pages.
- Rehearse a presentation and save timings.
- Use *Presenter View*.
- Use slide show navigation tools, keyboard shortcuts, and insert blank slides.

1. Open the ***Dedication-03*** presentation from your student data files.
2. Save the presentation as [your initials] PowerPoint 3-1.
3. Apply a background picture fill with a softened effect to all slides.
   a. Display slide 1. Point to the slide background and right-click to open the context menu. Click **Format Background** to open the *Format Background* pane.
   b. Select the **Picture or texture fill** option.
   c. Click the **File** button to open the *Insert Pictures* dialog box.
   d. Locate your student data files, select the ***Building-03*** picture, and click the **Insert** button.
   e. Click the **Picture** button at the top of the pane and then click **Picture Color**. Click the **Recolor** drop-down list and select **Blue, Accent color 2 Dark** (Figure 3-70).

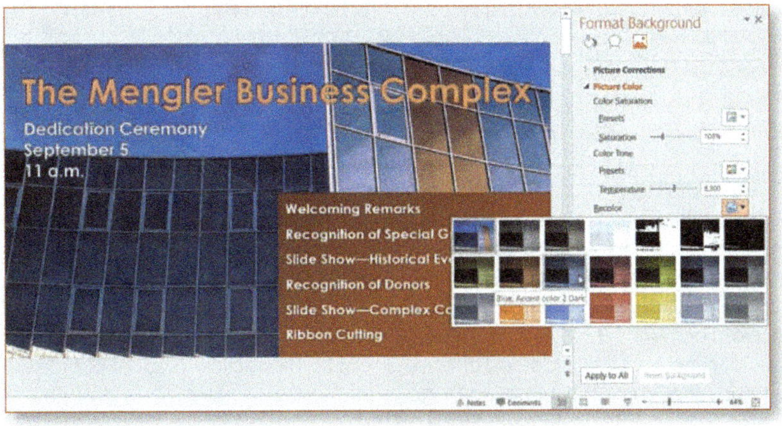

3-70 Picture background with *Recolor* options

   f. Click **Apply to All** so this picture is used as the background for all slides.

4. Restore the background picture to its original color on two slides.
   a. Display slide 1. On the *Format Background* pane under *Picture Color,* click the **Reset** button.
   b. Display slide 2 and click the **Reset** button again.
5. Prepare a black slide so the speaker can talk for a few moments with no slide displayed.
   a. Display slide 6. On the *Format Background* pane, click **Fill** at the top of the pane if it is not selected. Select the **Solid fill** option.
   b. Click the **Color** drop-down arrow and select **Black, Background 1**.
   c. Close the *Format Background* pane.
6. Apply a transition to all slides.
   a. Click the **Transitions** tab and apply the **Shape** transition.
   b. Click the **Effect Options** button [*Animation* group] and select **Diamond**.
   c. Click **Apply to All** [*Timing* group] (Figure 3-71).

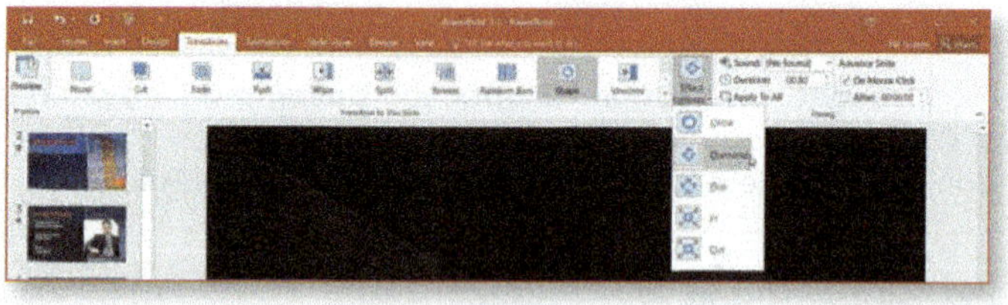
3-71 *Transition Effect Options*

7. Apply animation and effect options using the settings shown in the following table.
   a. Select the text or object to be animated.
   b. Click the **More** button on the gallery [*Animation* group] or click the **Add Animation** button [*Animations* tab, *Advanced Animation* group] if the *Animation* gallery is not displayed.
   c. Click an animation effect to apply it.
   d. Click the **Effects Options** button [*Animation* group] to apply *Direction, Sequence,* or *Amount* settings. Some settings will appear by default.
   e. Adjust settings for *Start* and *Duration* [*Timing* group] as needed.
   f. Click the **Preview** button [*Preview* group] or **Slide Show** button [*Status* bar] to test the animation.

Slide	Object	Animation Effect	Effect Options	Start	Duration
1	Text box for the agenda on the right	*Wipe* (Entrance)	*From Bottom, By Paragraph*	*On Click*	*00.50*
3	Picture	*Shape* (Entrance)	*Out, Diamond*	*After Previous*	*02:00*
7	Text box about space design	*Zoom* (Entrance)	*Object Center, As One Object*	*On Click*	*00:50*
7	Text box about wireless access	*Zoom* (Entrance)	*Object Center, As One Object*	*On Click*	*00:50*
8	Text box with donor names	*Wipe* (Entrance)	*From Bottom, All At Once*	*After Previous*	*01:00*

8. Use *Slide Show* view to practice use of navigation tools, keyboard shortcuts, and blanking slides.
   a. Display slide 1 and click the **Slide Show** button [*Status* bar].
   b. Click the **Next** button in the control bar to advance slides.
   c. Click the **See all slides** button in the control bar to see slide thumbnails; click a thumbnail to jump to a specific slide.
   d. Right-click anywhere on the slide and choose **Zoom In**. Right-click to zoom out to regular slide size.
   e. Press **N** to advance through animation or go to the next slide; press **P** to go to the previous animation or slide.
   f. Type 5 and press **Enter** to go to slide 5.
   g. Press **B** to blank a slide; press **B** to view the slide again.
   h. Press **Esc** to exit *Slide Show* view.

9. Prepare speaker notes on two slides.
   a. Select slide 1. Click the **Notes Page** button [*View* tab, *Presentation Views* group].
   b. Click the **Zoom** button on the *Notes Page* and increase the *Percent* to **150%** so you can more easily see the text. Click **OK**.
   c. Add the following text with a blank line between each item (Figure 3-72):

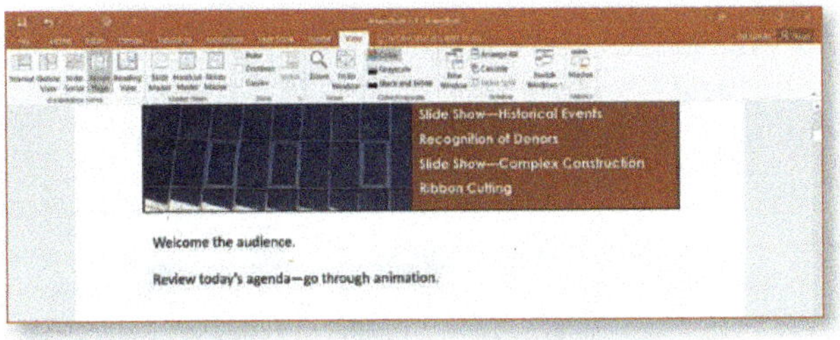

3-72 *Notes Page* view showing speaker notes

Slide 1: Welcome the audience

Review today's agenda—go through animation

Slide 5: Fostered business innovation and involvement

Developed the Business Development Institute

Expanded internship opportunities

   d. Click the **Normal** button [*View* tab, *Presentation Views* group] to return to *Normal* view.

10. Print notes pages for slides 4 and 5.
   a. Click the **File** tab and click **Print**.
   b. Select the appropriate printer and make sure that you are printing just one copy.
   c. For *Slides*, type 4–5 to print a *Custom Range*.
   d. For *Print Layout*, choose **Notes Pages** and check **Scale to Fit Paper** (Figure 3-73).
   e. Click the **Print** button.

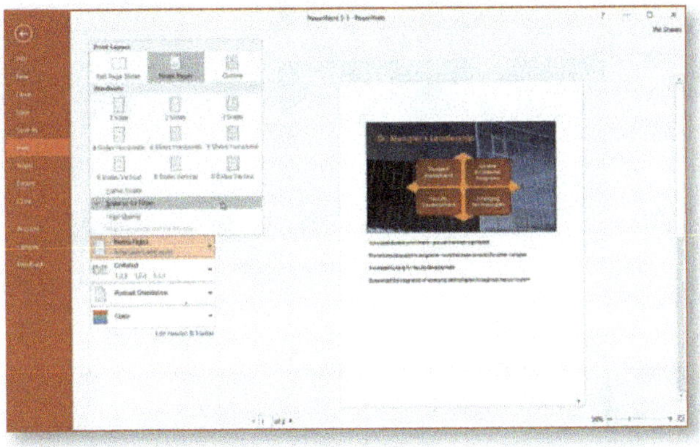

3-73 Print view of *Notes Page*

11. Rehearse and save timings.
   a. Click the **Rehearse Timings** button [*Slide Show* tab, *Set Up* group] to open the *Recording* dialog box and start timing.
   b. Click the **Next Slide** button to advance each slide and animation effect after approximately 3–5 seconds.
   c. Click **Yes** at the end of your presentation to save your timings. The timings are displayed below each slide in *Slide Sorter* view.

12. Use *Presenter View* to review your presentation.
   a. Click the **Slide Show** tab.
   b. Deselect **Use Timings** [*Set Up* group].
   c. Click **Use Presenter View** [*Monitors* group].
   d. Click the **From Beginning** button [*Start Slide Show* group].
      - If you have one monitor, right-click and select **Show Presenter View**.
   e. Click the **Advance to next slide** button to review your slides.
   f. Click the **Zoom into the slide** button to magnify a section of the slide. Click **Zoom Out** (the same button) to return to the normal slide size (Figure 3-74).

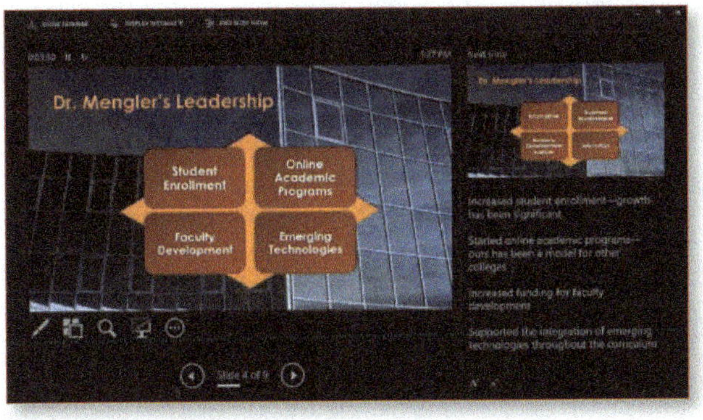

3-74 *Presenter View*

g. Click the **See all slides** button to view thumbnails of all slides. Click to display different slides.
h. Press **Esc** to exit *Presenter View.*

13. Save and close the presentation (Figure 3-75).

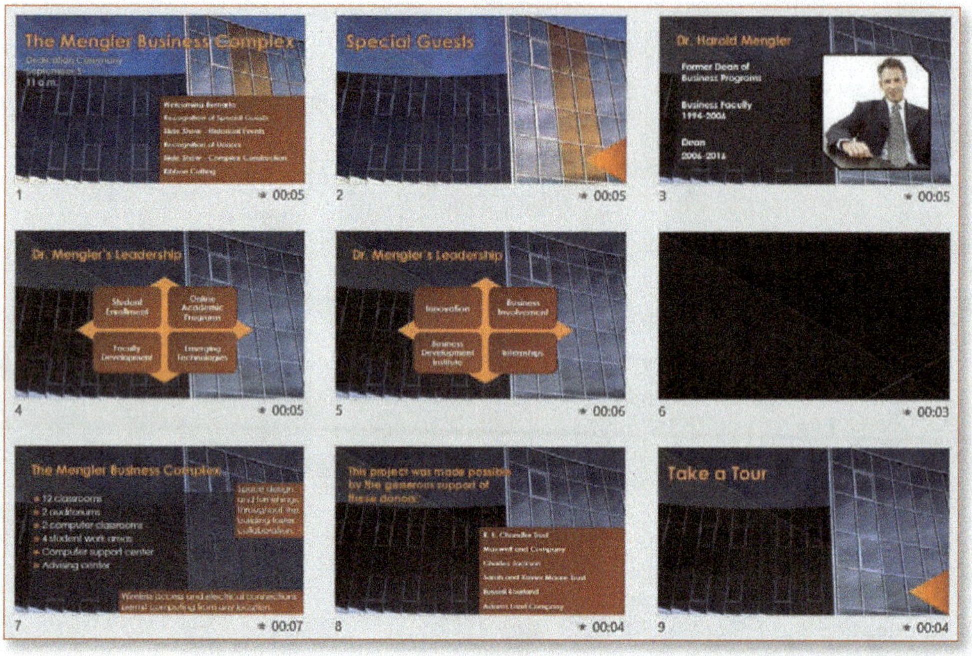

3-75 PowerPoint 3-1 completed

Guided Project 3-2

For the second training session for new hires on presenting effectively, Davon Washington, management consultant at Solution Seekers, Inc., is preparing guidelines for designing slides and developing content in a visual way. For this project, you finish the presentation that Davon has prepared and save it on a CD so participants can refer to it after the session.
[Student Learning Outcomes 3.1, 3.2, 3.3, 3.4, 3.7, 3.9]

Files Needed: ***SlideShowDevelopment-03.pptx***, ***Background-03.jpg***, and ***Applause-03.jpg*** *(Student data files are available in the* Library *of your SIMnet account.)*
Completed Project File Names: ***[your initials] PowerPoint 3-2.pptx*** and folder ***Develop Slides***

Skills Covered in This Project

- Apply a background picture fill.
- Create custom theme colors.
- Apply animation and effect options.
- Print notes pages.
- Add ink annotations.
- Use the *Package Presentation for CD* feature.

1. Open the ***SlideShowDevelopment-03*** presentation from your student data files.
2. Save the presentation as [your initials] PowerPoint 3-2.
3. Apply a background picture fill to all slides.
   a. Point to the background and right-click. Select **Format Background** to open the *Format Background* pane.
   b. Select the **Picture or texture fill** option.
   c. Click the **File** button to open the *Insert Pictures* dialog box.
   d. Locate your student data files, select ***Background-03,*** and click **Insert** (Figure 3-76).
   e. Click **Apply to All** so this picture is the background for all slides.

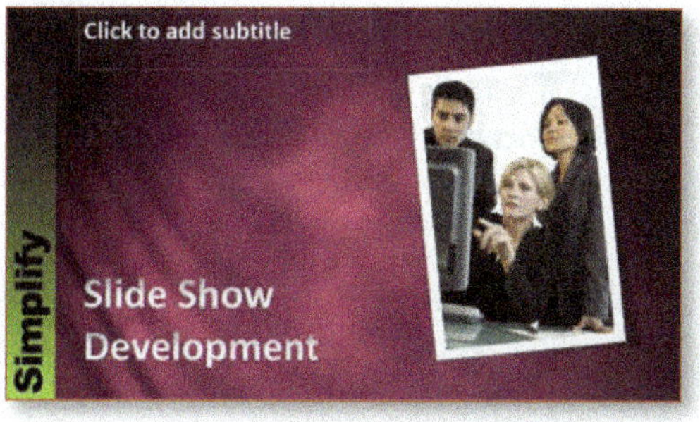

3-76 Title slide with new background picture fill

4. Display slide 12. Repeat step 3 to apply a different background picture, ***Applause-03,*** for this slide only.
   a. Change the *Offset left* to **−9%** and the *Offset top* to **−5%** for better picture positioning on the slide. (*Offset right* is 0% and *Offset bottom* is −9%.)
   b. Close the *Format Background* pane.
5. Prepare a new custom color theme to blend with the background picture.
   a. Click the **More** button [*Design* tab, *Variants* group].
   b. Click **Colors** and click **Customize Colors** to open the *Create New Theme Colors* dialog box.
   c. Change five accent colors according to the following table.
      - For each change, click the color drop-down arrow and select **More Colors** to open the *Colors* dialog box.
      - Click the **Custom** tab and enter the numbers for *Red, Green,* and *Blue.*

	Accent 1	Accent 2	Accent 3	Accent 4	Accent 5
Red	255	157	255	38	95
Green	247	175	217	203	30
Blue	220	210	82	236	60

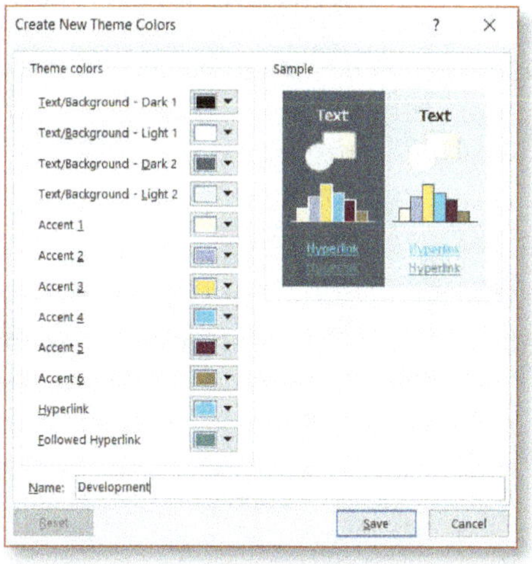

3-77 New theme colors

   d. Name the new custom theme Development (Figure 3-77).
   e. Click the **Save** button.
6. Select the following slides and adjust text and object colors:
   a. *Slide 7*: Select the *SmartArt* graphic. Click the **Change Colors** button [*SmartArt Tools Design* tab, *SmartArt Styles* group] and select the **Colored Fill – Accent 5** style in the *Accent 5* category (Figure 3-78).
   b. *Slide 12*: Select the text box. Click the **Shape Fill** button [*Home* tab, *Drawing* group] and select **Plum, Accent 5**.

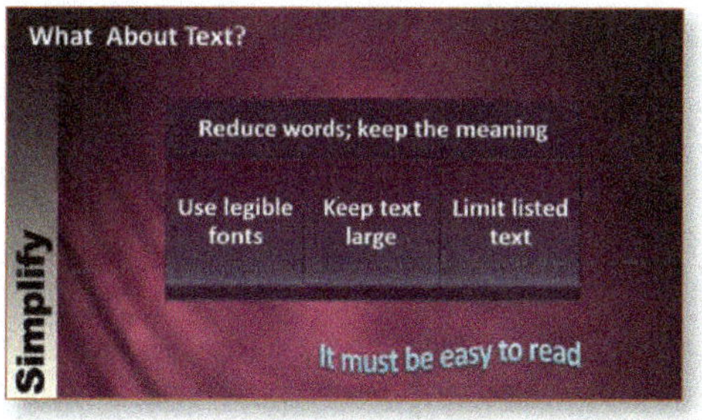

3-78 *SmartArt* recolored

7. Apply a transition to all slides.
   a. Click the **Transitions** tab and apply the **Reveal** transition.
   b. Click the **Effect Options** button [*Transition to this Slide* group] and select **Smoothly from Right**.
   c. Change the *Duration* to **02:00** [*Timing* group].
   d. Click **Apply to All**.
8. Apply animation on four slides and change effect options as shown in the following table.
   a. Select the text or object to be animated.
   b. Click the **Animations** tab and click the **More** button on the *Animation* gallery. (Click the **Add Animation** button [*Advanced Animation* group] if the gallery is not open.)
   c. Click an effect to apply it.
   d. Click the **Effects Options** button [*Animation* group] to apply *Direction, Sequence,* or *Amount* settings.
   e. Adjust settings for *Start and Duration* [*Timing* group] as needed to match the table. Some settings will appear by default.
   f. Click the **Preview** button [*Preview* group] or **Slide Show** button [*Status* bar] to test the animation.

Slide	Object	Animation Effect	Effect Options	Start	Duration
2	Ducks	*Fly In* (Entrance)	*From Left*	*On Click*	*02.00*
2	Slide Show Development text box	*Bounce* (Entrance)	None	*After Previous*	*02.00*
4 and 5	Grouped text box and up arrow	*Float In* (Entrance)	*Float Up*	*After Previous*	*01.00*
4 and 5	Grouped text box and down arrow	*Float In* (Entrance)	*Float Down*	*After Previous*	*01.00*
6	Color wheel	*Spin* (Emphasis)	*Clockwise, Two Spins*	*After Previous*	*03.00*

9. Display slide 1. Click the **Notes Page** button [*View* tab, *Presentation Views* group]. Advance through all slides and read the speaker notes to review tips for slide design.
10. Print notes pages for slides 7 and 11.
    a. Click the **File** tab and click **Print**.
    b. Select the appropriate printer and make sure that you are printing just one copy.
    c. Choose the following settings:
       - *Slides*: 7, 11 for a *Custom Range*.
       - *Print Layout*: **Notes Pages** and **Scale to Fit Paper** (Figure 3-79).
    d. Click the **Print** button.
11. Add ink annotations on slides 4, 5, and 7.
    a. Display slide 4. Click the **Slide Show** button [*Status* bar] to start your slide show on this slide.
    b. Right-click to open the context menu, select **Pointer Options** and **Highlighter**. Highlight the word "**organization**" in the text box.
    c. Display slide 5, repeat step 11b and highlight the words "**creative thinking**" in the text box.
    d. Display slide 7, right-click to open the context menu. Select **Pointer Options** and **Pen**. Circle the words "**Reduce words**" and "**keep the meaning**."
    e. Advance to the end of the presentation and click **Keep** to save your ink annotations.

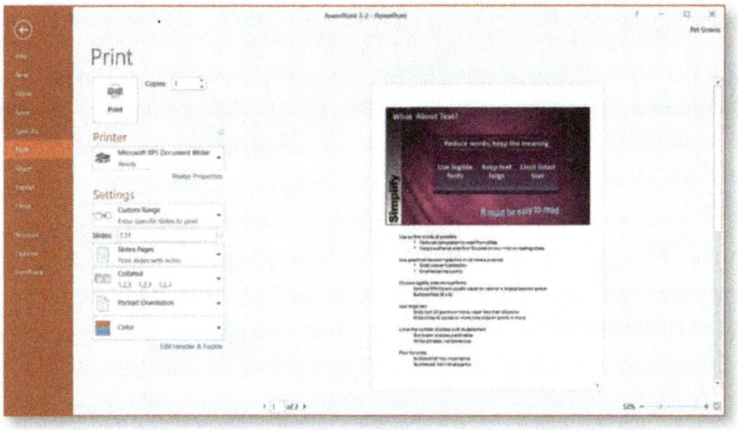

3-79 Print *Notes Pages*

12. Save the presentation (Figure 3-80).

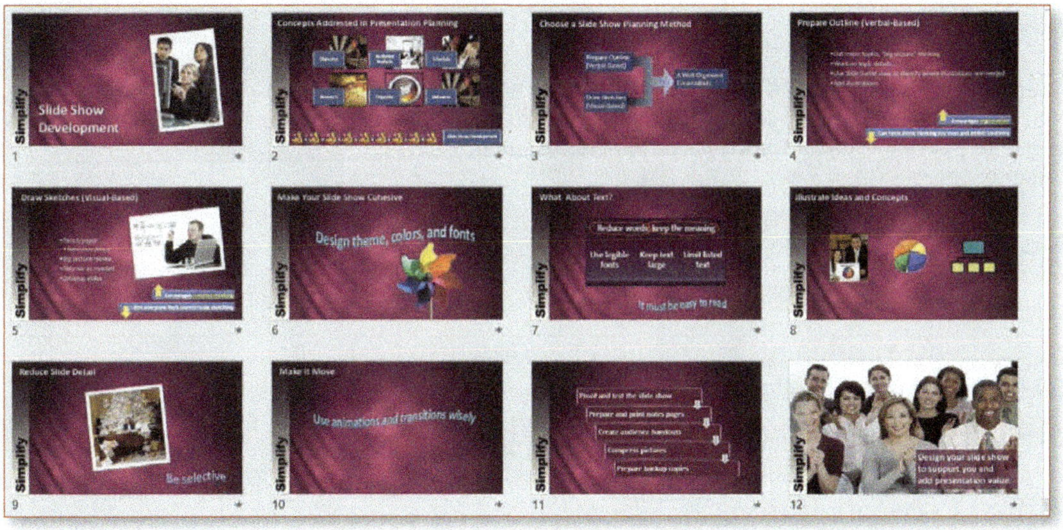

3-80 PowerPoint 3-2 completed

13. Use the *Package Presentation for CD* feature to save the presentation to a folder.
   a. Click the **File** tab and select **Export**.
   b. Click **Package Presentation for CD** and click the **Package for CD** button to open the *Package for CD* dialog box.
   c. Type Develop Slides to name the CD.
   d. Click the **Options** button to open the *Options* dialog box and select **Linked Files** and **Embedded TrueType fonts** (Figure 3-81).
   e. Click **OK**.
   f. Click the **Copy to Folder** button to open the *Copy to Folder* dialog box.
   The folder name appears and is the same name you typed for the CD. Deselect the **Open folder when complete** option.

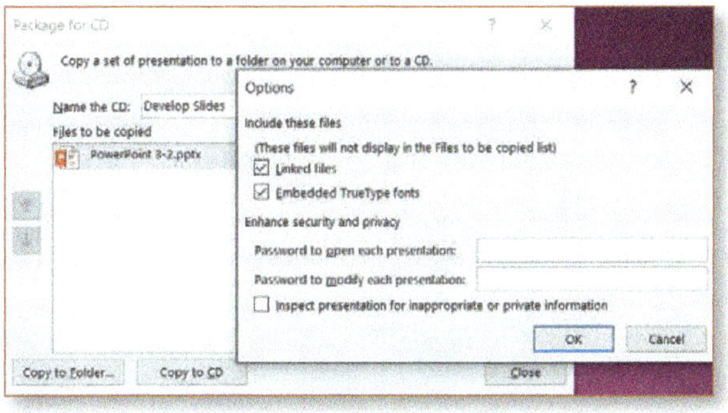

3-81 *Package for CD* and *Copy to Folder* dialog boxes

g. Browse for the location to save the presentation and click the **Select** button.
h. Click **OK** to close the *Copy to Folder* dialog box.
i. Click **Yes** when a message appears asking if you want to include linked files.
j. Click **Continue** when another message appears about comments and annotations.
k. Close the *Package for CD* dialog box.
l. Close the presentation.

14. Open the "packaged" presentation.
    a. Open the *Develop Slides* folder where you "packaged" the presentation. Notice that additional files have been saved in this folder.
    b. Double-click the file name in the folder to open the presentation. If you receive a security warning, click the **Enable** button.
15. Test the presentation and then close it.

Guided Project 3-3

At an upcoming meeting of the American River Cycling Club, Eric Salinas is giving a presentation about the importance of knowing your target heart rate and exercising with your heart rate at an appropriate target level. For this project, you finalize the presentation.
[Student Learning Outcomes 3.1, 3.3, 3.4, 3.5, 3.8]

Files Needed: ***HeartRateARCC-03.pptx*** and ***RiderAir.jpg*** *(Student data files are available in the* Library *of your SIMnet account.)*
Completed Project File Name: ***[your initials] PowerPoint 3-3.pptx***

Skills Covered in This Project

- Create custom theme colors.
- Apply a background picture fill.
- Link to a video on a web site.
- Use *Presenter View.*
- Create and print notes pages.
- Record a presentation with narration.
- Prepare a kiosk presentation.

1. Open the ***HeartRateARCC-03*** presentation from your student data files.
2. Save the presentation as [your initials] PowerPoint 3-3.
3. Prepare a new custom color theme to blend with the heart picture on slide 3.
    a. Click the **More** button [*Design* tab, *Variants* group].
    b. Select **Colors** and click **Customize Colors** to open the *Create New Theme Colors* dialog box.
    c. Click the **Color** drop-down arrow for each change, and select **More Colors** to open the *Colors* dialog box. Click the **Custom** tab and enter the *Red, Green,* and *Blue* numbers shown in the following table for four colors.

	Text/Background – Dark 2	Accent 1	Accent 2	Accent 3
Red	24	36	204	227
Green	66	99	0	108
Blue	77	116	0	9

d. Name the new custom theme ARCC (Figure 3-82).
e. Click the **Save** button and the new colors will automatically be applied to all slides.

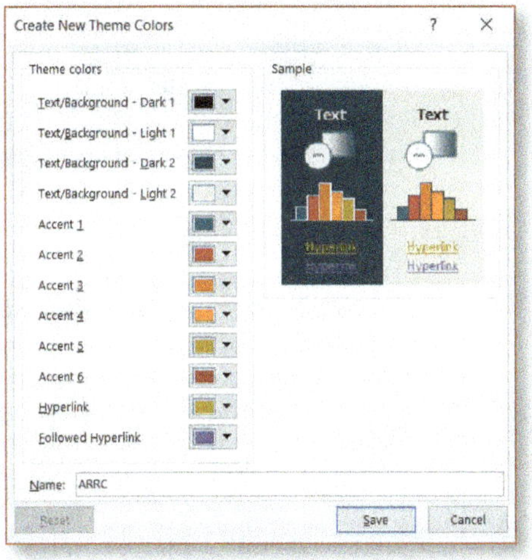

3-82 New ARCC color theme

4. Format the title slide by adding a background picture fill.
   a. Display slide 1. Point to the background, right-click, and select **Format Background** to open the *Format Background* pane.
   b. Select the **Picture or texture fill** option.
   c. Click the **File** button to open the *Insert Pictures* dialog box.
   d. Locate your student data files, select ***RiderAir-03***, and click **Insert**.
   e. Click **Picture** at the top of the pane and select **Picture Color**. Click the **Recolor** button and select **Black and White**: **25%** (Figure 3-83).
   f. Close the *Format Background* pane.
5. Increase the subtitle font size on the title slide to **36 pt**. and resize the placeholder so one word fits on each line.

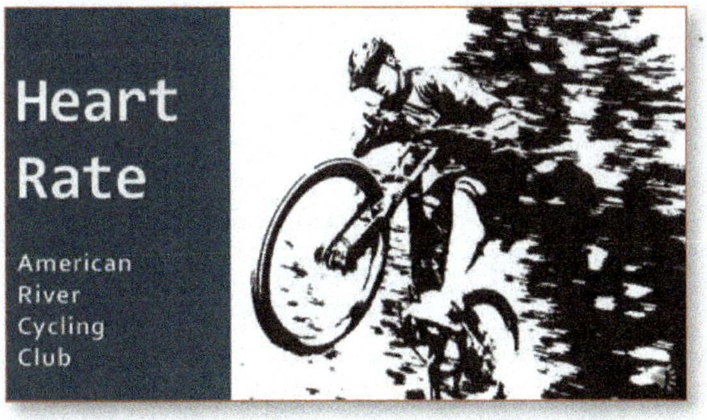

3-83 Completed title slide

6. Find and insert an online video.
   a. Display slide 5 and click the **Insert** tab.
   b. Click the **Video** button [*Media* group] and select **Online Video** to open the *Insert Video* dialog box.
   c. Type the words Col de la Madone in the *YouTube* search box and click the **Search** button. Select an appropriate video. Click **Insert**.
   d. Position the video to the left of the picture and resize it (*Width* **5.5"**), if necessary. Be sure the video quality remains acceptable.
   e. Below the video, add the appropriate source information in a text box.
   f. Play the video in *Slide Show* view by clicking the **Start** button in the middle of the video.
7. Apply a transition. Choose **Cube** [*Transitions* tab, *Transition to This Slide* group] with the **From Right** effect options. Click **Apply To All**.
8. Use *Presenter View* to review your presentation.
   a. Click the **Slide Show** tab.
   b. Click **Use Presenter View** [*Monitors* group].
   c. Click the **From Beginning** button [*Start Slide Show* group] to start your presentation.
      • If you have one monitor, right-click and select **Show Presenter View**.
   d. Click the **Advance to the next slide** button to advance slides as you review them.
   e. At the bottom of the Notes pane, click the **Make the text larger** button to increase the text size for notes on all slides. Scroll to read the text on slide 3 (Figure 3-84).
   f. Press **Esc** to end the slide show.

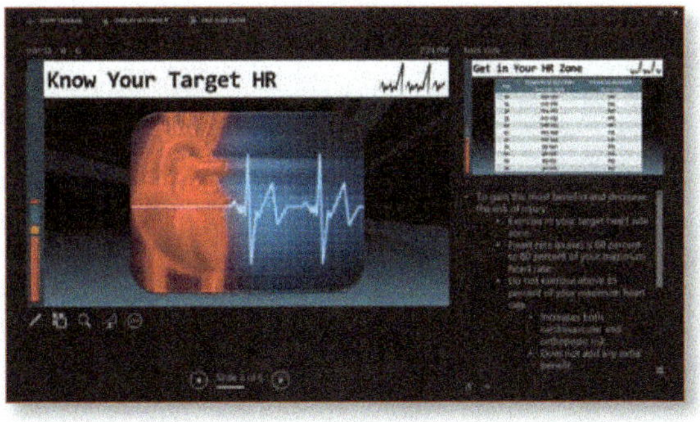

3-84 *Presenter View*

9. Print notes pages for slides 3 and 4.
   a. Click the **File** tab. Click **Print**.
   b. Select the appropriate printer and make sure that you are printing just one copy.
   c. For *Slides*, type 3-4 to choose a *Custom Range*.
   d. For *Print Layout*, choose **Notes Pages** and select **Scale to Fit Paper**.
   e. Click the **Print** button.

10. Record a slide show with narration.
    a. Click the **Record Slide Show** button [*Slide Show* tab, *Set Up* group] and select **Start Recording from Beginning** to open the *Record Slide Show* dialog box.
    b. Select both options and click **Start Recording** (Figure 3-85). The *Recording* dialog box appears.
    c. Speak clearly into your microphone as each slide is displayed.
    d. Click the **Next Slide** navigation button to advance each slide.

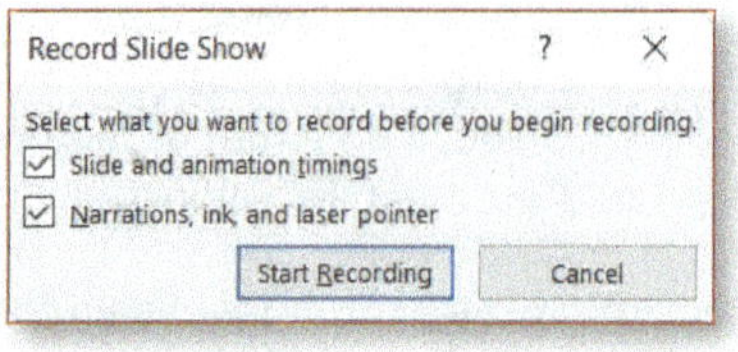

3-85 *Record Slide Show* dialog box

11. Prepare a kiosk presentation with looping.
    a. Click the **Set Up Slide Show** button [*Slide Show* tab, *Set Up* group] to open the *Set Up Show* dialog box.
    b. Select the *Show type* **Browsed at a kiosk (full screen)**.
    c. For *Show slides* select **All**.
    d. Select the **Primary Monitor**.
    e. Click **OK**.

12. Save and close your presentation (Figure 3-86).

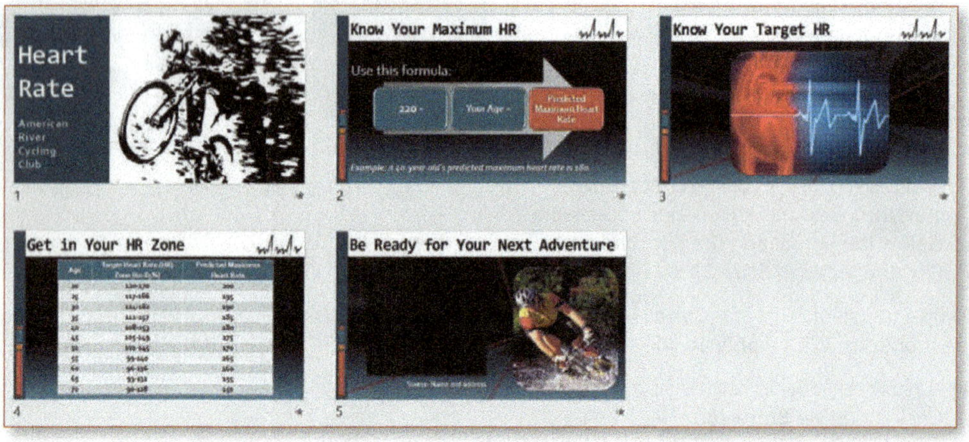

3-86 PowerPoint 3-3 completed

Independent Project 3-4

The sales representatives at Wilson Home Entertainment Systems review acceptable viewing distances when talking with clients who are in the early stages of planning a home theater or media room. They discuss options for televisions or projection systems for the spaces being planned. For this project, you complete a presentation to prepare clients for an in-home consultation.
[Student Learning Outcomes 3.1, 3.2, 3.4, 3.6, 3.7, 3.8]

Files Needed: ***ScreenSizes-03.pptx***, ***TVCabinet-03.jpg***, ***TVWallMount-03.jpg***, and ***Projector-03.jpg***
(Student data files are available in the Library of your SIMnet account.*)*
Completed Project File Name: ***[your initials] PowerPoint 3-4.pptx***

Skills Covered in This Project

- Change slide size.
- Apply a background picture fill.
- Apply animation and effect options.
- Rehearse a presentation and save timings.
- Use slide show navigation tools, keyboard shortcuts, and blank slides.
- Hide and reveal slides.
- Use the laser pointer feature.
- Use annotation pens.
- Prepare a kiosk presentation.

1. Open the ***ScreenSizes-03*** presentation from your student data files. This presentation is saved in the **Standard (4:3)** format.
2. Click the **Slide Size** button [*Design* tab, *Customize* group] and click **Widescreen (16:9)** (Figure 3-87). The slide size has changed from 10" to 13.33" wide.
3. Save the presentation in the widescreen size as [your initials] PowerPoint 3-4.
4. Open the *Format Background* pane and change the background to a picture fill on three slides. Locate your student data files and insert the following pictures:
   a. *Slide 5*: **TVCabinet-03**
   b. *Slide 6*: **TVWallMount-03**
   c. *Slide 7*: **Projector-03**

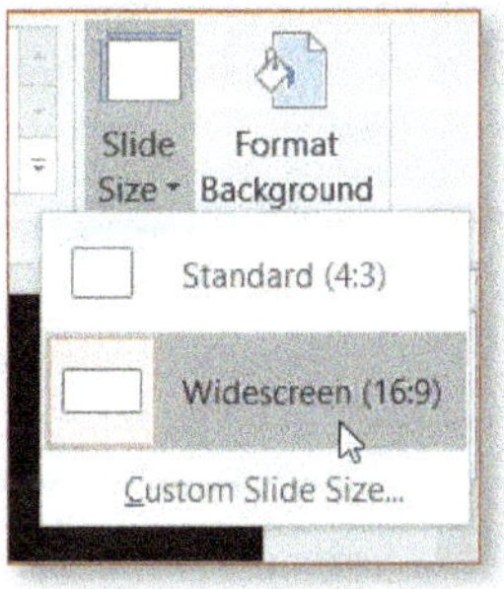

3-87 *Slide Size*

5. Close the *Format Background* pane.
6. Right-align the text boxes at the bottom of slides 5, 6, and 7 to better fit the widescreen size (Figure 3-88).
7. Right-align the WHES logo on slides 1 and 8.
8. Apply the **Vortex** transition with the **From Bottom** effect option. Change the *Duration* to **3.00**. Apply these settings to all slides (Figure 3-89).
9. Apply animation on four slides and change settings as needed to match the following table.

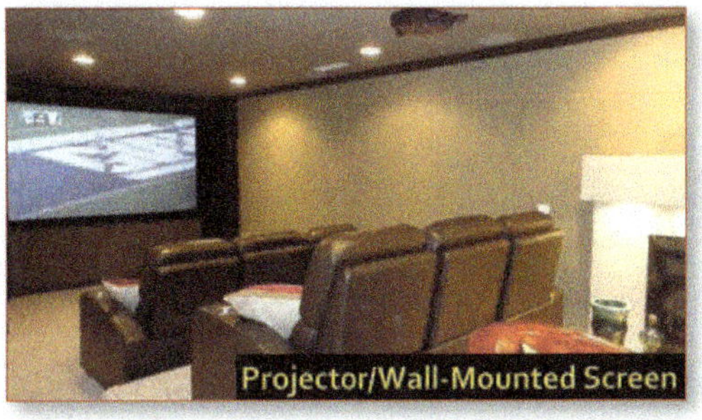

3-88 Background picture fill

Slide	Object	Animation Effect	Effect Options	Start	Duration
2	Question mark	*Spin* (Emphasis)	*Counterclockwise, Two Spins*	*After Previous*	*02.00*
5, 6, 7	Text box	*Fly In* (Entrance)	*From Top-Left, As One Object*	*After Previous*	*00.50*

10. Rehearse the presentation and save timings.
11. Modify the timings to advance each slide after 5 seconds.
12. Hide slide 4.

13. Use the *Set Up Show* dialog box to change *Advance Slides* to **Manually**. Click **OK**.
14. Practice the following slide show features in *Slide Show* view:
    a. Use the control bar buttons to move to the next slide.
    b. Press **B** to blank a slide. Press **B** to display the slide again.
    c. Right-click to open the context menu, select **Pointer Options,** and change the *Laser Pointer* color.
    d. Go to the hidden slide 4.
    e. Point to slide objects (Height, Lighting, and Viewing Angle) with the laser pointer.
    f. Use keyboard shortcuts. Type 2 and press **Enter** to go to slide 2.
15. Add annotations on slides 3 and 4 using the **Pen** with **Red** ink and keep annotations. Use *Presenter View* and practice making annotations on the presenter slide.
    a. *Slide 3*: Circle the "**55-60**" and "**100**" screen sizes.
    b. *Slide 4*: Go to this hidden slide and circle the following phrases in the bulleted items: "**level with the middle,**" "**reduce color clarity,**" and "**visibility at all seats.**"
    c. Keep ink annotations
16. Prepare a kiosk presentation with looping.
    a. Select **Use Timings** on the *Slide Show* tab.
    b. Click the **Set Up Slide Show** button to open the *Set Up Show* dialog box.
    c. For *Show Slides,* select **All**.
    d. For *Advance Slides,* select **Use timings, if present**.
    e. Select **Browsed at a kiosk (full screen)** (Figure 3-90).
    f. Select the appropriate monitor.
    g. Click **OK**.
17. Save and close the presentation (Figure 3-91).

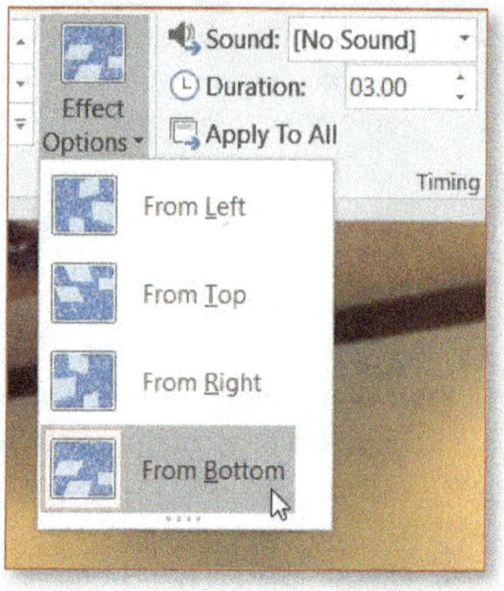

3-89 *Vortex* transition effect options

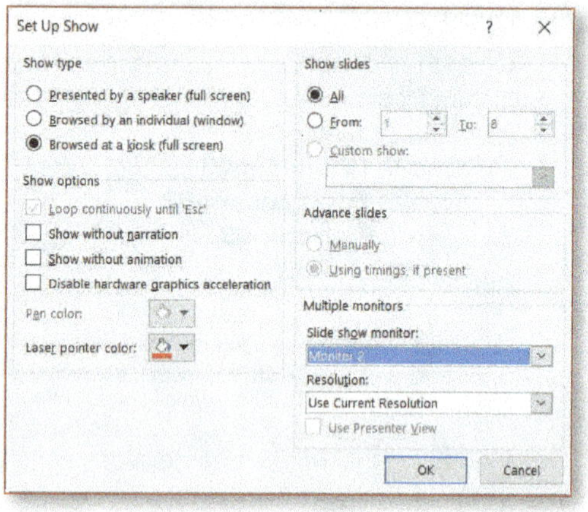

3-90 *Set Up Show* dialog box

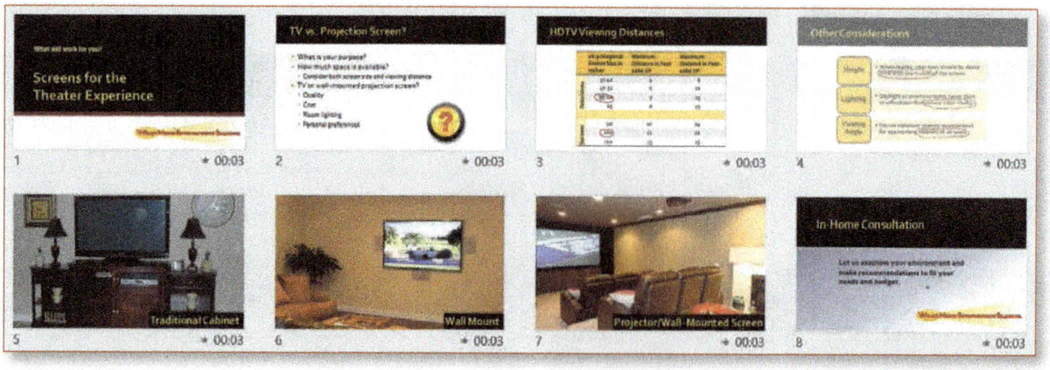

3-91 PowerPoint 3-4 completed

Independent Project 3-5

For the third training session for new hires on presenting effectively, Davon Washington, management consultant at Solution Seekers, Inc., is preparing guidelines for delivering a presentation with projection equipment. For this project, you finish the presentation that Davon has prepared.
[Student Learning Outcomes 3.1, 3.2, 3.4, 3.5, 3.7, 3.8]

File Needed: ***PresentationDelivery-03.pptx*** *(Student data files are available in the* Library *of your SIMnet account.)*
Completed Project File Name: ***[your initials] PowerPoint 3-5.pptx***

Skills Covered in This Project

- Apply a background picture fill.
- Apply animation and effect options.
- Create and print notes pages.
- Hide and reveal slides.
- Rehearse a presentation and save timings.
- Use *Presenter View.*
- Use ink annotation pens.
- Record a presentation with narration.

1. Open the ***PresentationDelivery-03*** presentation from your student data files.
2. Save the presentation as [your initials] PowerPoint 3-5.
3. Apply the **Fade** transition with the **Smoothly** effect option. Change the *Duration* to **01.00**. Click **Apply To All**.
4. Apply animation on five slides and change effect options, start, and duration settings as shown in the following table. Some of these settings will appear by default.

Slide	Object	Animation Effect	Effect Options	Start	Duration
2	Text "You get only one . . ."	*Bounce* (Entrance)	*As One Object*	*After Previous*	*02.00*
5	Butterfly image	*Grow & Turn* (Entrance)	None	*After Previous*	*02.00*
7	Graphic	*Wipe* (Entrance)	*From Left*	*After Previous*	*02.50*
11	Text "Make it memorable"	*Bounce* (Entrance)	*As One Object*	*After Previous*	*02.00*
12	Success shape	*Grow/Shrink* (Emphasis)	*Both, Larger*	*After Previous*	*02.50*

5. Prepare speaker notes on two slides. In the notes for slide 9, apply bullets and indent the bulleted text (Figure 3-92).
   a. *Slide 2*: Never underestimate the importance of a first impression
      If possible, welcome people as they arrive for your presentation
   b. Slide *9*: Be careful with how you use humor
      - Use humor only if it is appropriate
      - Avoid jokes—you could unintentionally offend someone

      Humor works best when it fits the presentation and seems natural
      - Break the ice

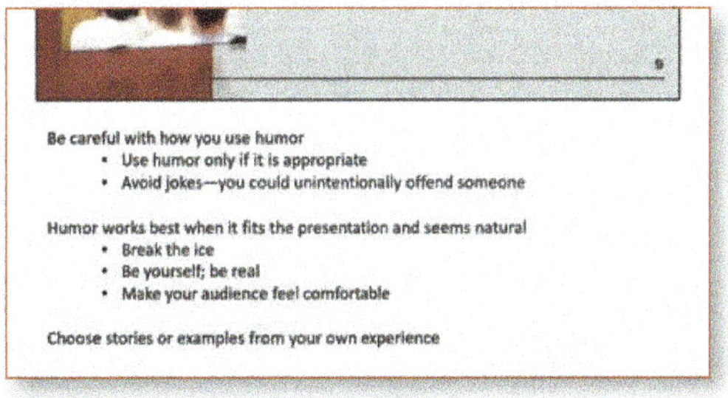

3-92 Notes with bullets and indents

- Be yourself; be real
- Make your audience feel comfortable

Choose stories or examples from your own experience

6. Print notes pages for slides 5, 6, and 7.
7. Hide slide 8.
8. Review the presentation to check transitions and animations.
   a. Select the *Transitions* tab and deselect **On Mouse Click**.
   b. Change *After* to **00:03:00** seconds.
   c. Click **Apply To All**.
   d. Start your slide show from the beginning and review all slide movements.
9. Use *Presenter View* to review your presentation.
   a. Deselect **Use Timings** [*Slide Show* tab, *Set Up* group] so you can advance through the slides at your own pace.
   b. Select **Use Presenter View**.
   c. Begin the presentation. If you have one monitor, right-click and select **Show Presenter View**.
   d. Navigate through slides using the **Advance to the next slide** and **Return to the previous slide** buttons.
   e. Click the **See all slides** button and click thumbnails to move to different slides.
10. Use *Presenter View* to add annotations on the following slides using the **Pen** with **Blue** ink. If you are not satisfied with your markings, then use the **Eraser** to remove them and try again.
    a. *Slide 2*: Circle the words "**Be professional**."
    b. *Slide 4*: Draw a rectangle around the words "**Eye Contact**" and "**Smile**" (Figure 3-93).

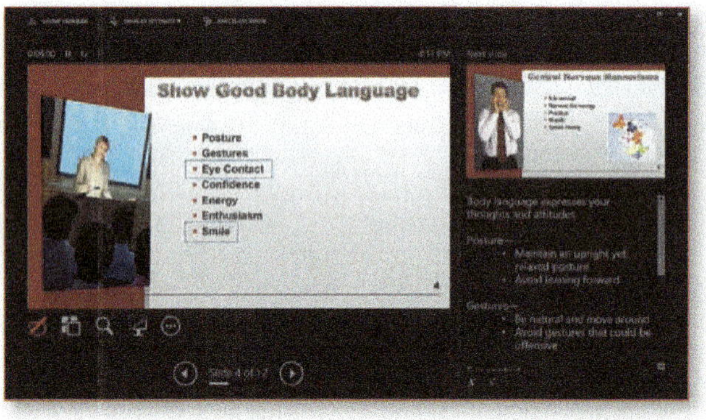

3-93 ***Presenter View* showing ink annotations**

    c. *Slide 7*: Circle the words "**Avoid monotone**."
    d. *Slide 10*: Circle "**End on time**."
    e. Click **Keep** at the end of the presentation to save annotations.
11. Record a slide show with narration if you have a microphone on your computer. If you don't have a microphone, practice the following steps.
    a. Print notes pages for additional slides where you need reminders about what to discuss.
    b. Click the *Slide Show* tab, click the **Record Slide Show** list arrow and select **Start Recording from Beginning** to open the *Record Slide Show* dialog box.
    c. Select both **Slide and animation timings** and **Narrations, ink, and laser pointer**. Click **Start Recording**.
    d. Speak clearly into your microphone as each slide displayed.
    e. Save and close your presentation (Figure 3-94).

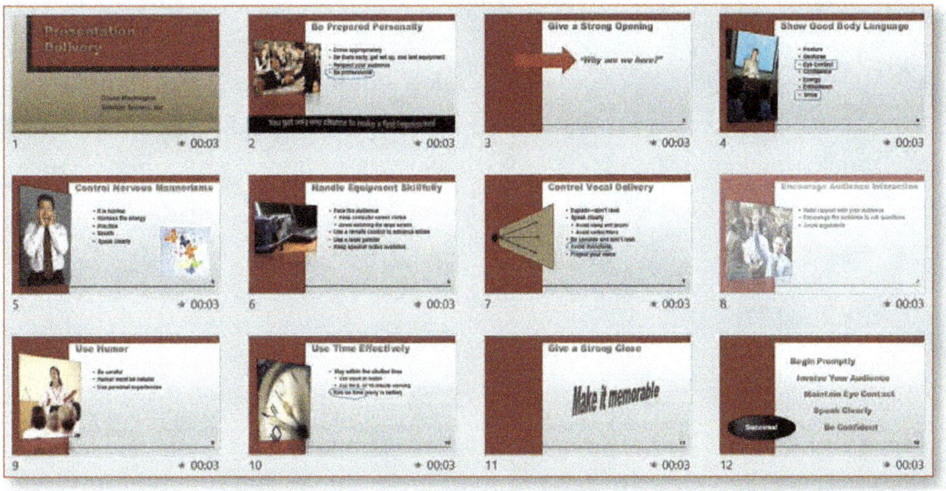

3-94 PowerPoint 3-5 completed

Independent Project 3-6

At the Hamilton Civic Center (HCC), classes are offered for a variety of fitness activities. For this project, you complete a presentation to promote the water aerobics classes at several community events. It will also be used as a self-running presentation at the HCC front desk.
[Student Learning Outcomes 3.1, 3.2, 3.3, 3.4, 3.5, 3.6, 3.8]

File Needed: ***WaterAerobics-03.pptx*** *(Student data files are available in the* Library *of your SIMnet account.)*
Completed Project File Name: ***[your initials] PowerPoint 3-6.pptx***

Skills Covered in This Project

- Create custom theme colors.
- Modify background fill colors.
- Change object colors on selected slides.
- Apply animation and effect options.
- Change to a widescreen slide size.
- Hide and reveal a slide.
- Use slide show navigation tools, keyboard shortcuts, and blank slides.
- Link to an online video.
- Prepare a kiosk presentation.

---

1. Open the ***WaterAerobics-03*** presentation from your student data files. This presentation is saved in the **Standard (4:3)** format (Figure 3-95).
2. Click the **Slide Size** button [*Design* tab, *Customize* group] and click **Widescreen (16:9)**. The slide size has changed from 10" to 13.33" wide.
3. Save the presentation as [your initials] PowerPoint 3-6.
4. Adjust objects to better fit the widescreen format:
   a. *Slide 1*: Increase the picture size (*Height* **4"** and *Width* **6"**).
   b. *Slide 4*: Resize the text box on the right so the text fits on four lines (Figure 3-96). Align it to the slide on the right.

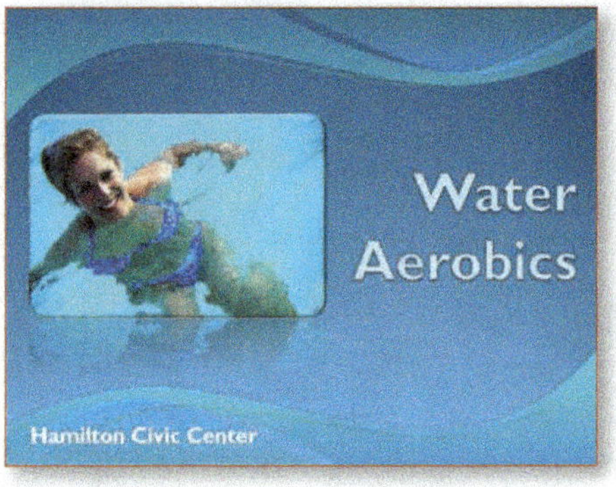

3-95 Title slide in standard slide size

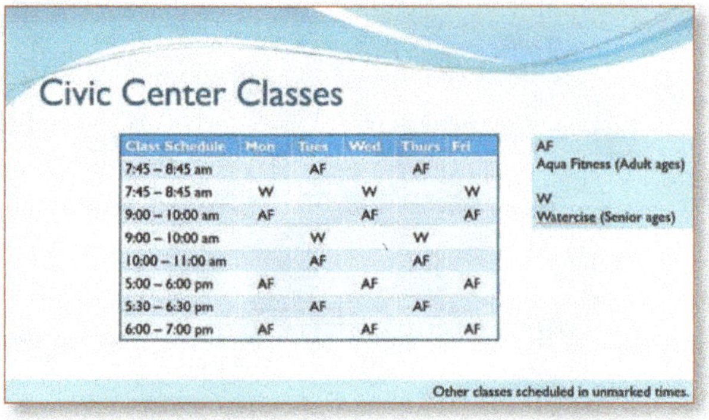

3-96 Text boxes adjusted

c. *Slide 4*: Right align the text box at the bottom of the slide then extend the left end of the box to fit across the bottom of the slide.
d. *Slide 5*: Repeat the same alignment and size increase process for the text box at the bottom of the slide.

5. Use the *Create New Theme Colors* dialog box (Figure 3-97) to create a custom theme. Change four colors according to the *Red, Green,* and *Blue* numbers shown in the following table. Name the custom theme Water and save it.

	Text/ Background - Dark 2	Accent 1	Accent 3	Accent 5
Red	7	53	16	255
Green	55	151	89	51
Blue	99	241	100	153

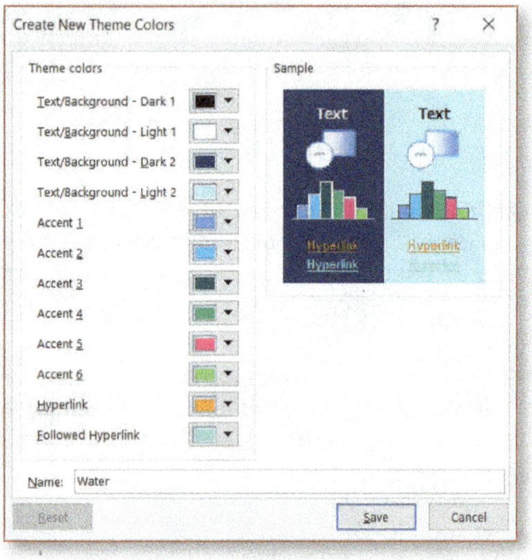

3-97 *Water* theme colors

6. Change the background colors.
   a. Click the **More** button [*Design* tab, *Variants* group] and select **Background Styles**. Click **Style 2** so a light blue is applied to the background of all slides in the presentation.
   b. Select slide 1. Use the *Format Background* pane to change the background fill. Select **Solid Fill** and choose **Dark Blue, Text 2**.
   c. Change the font color for "Hamilton Civic Center" to **White, Background 1** (Figure 3-98).
   d. Select slide 8 and change to the same background and text colors (steps 6 b – c).

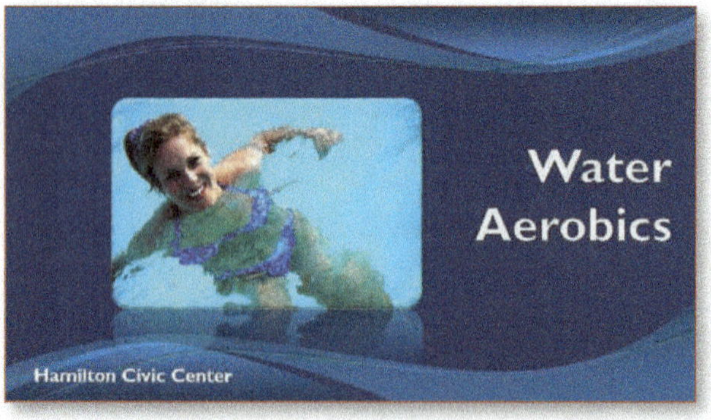

3-98 Title slide in widescreen slide size and *Water* theme colors

7. Change the color for the following two objects to **Pink, Accent 5**.
    a. *Slide 3*: *Text Fill for* "Fun"
    b. *Slide 4*: *Shading* for the table heading row
8. Apply the **Ripple** transition with the **From Top-Left** effect option. Apply this transition to all slides.
9. Apply animation on three slides and change options as shown in the following table. Some settings will appear by default.

Slide	Object	Animation Effect	Effect Options	Start	Duration
2	Bulleted list	*Fly In* (Entrance)	*From Bottom-Right, By Paragraph*	*After Previous*	01.00
3	Bulleted list	*Fly In* (Entrance)	*From Bottom, As One Object*	*After Previous*	01.00
3	*WordArt* "Fun"	*Bounce* (Entrance)	*As One Object*	*After Previous*	02.50

10. Hide slide 6.
11. Practice the following features using *Slide Show* view:
    a. Click **Next** and **Previous** in the control bar to change slides.
    b. Click the **See all slides** button in the control bar to see slide thumbnails; click a thumbnail to go to a different slide.
    c. Click the **Zoom into the slide** button in the control bar to magnify the "To Wear" list on slide 8.
    d. Click the **More slide show options** button in the control bar, select **Screen,** and then select **Black Screen**. Click the screen to return to the same slide.
    e. Go to the hidden slide 6.
12. Use the *Insert Video* dialog box to find and insert an online video.
    a. Display slide 5. Use the search words water aerobics exercises and select an appropriate video. For referencing purposes, write down the name of the video and online source from the lower left of the dialog box. Click **Insert**.
    b. Increase the video size if the quality remains acceptable.
    c. Below the video, insert a text box for a source note with the name of the video and online address.
    d. Test the video in *Slide Show* view to be sure it plays correctly.
13. Use *Presenter View* to review the presentation.
    a. Select **Presenter View** on the *Slide Show* tab.
    b. Select slide 1 and begin the presentation. If you have one monitor, right-click and select **Show Presenter View**.
    c. Advance through the presentation and review the speaker notes that appear in *Presenter View*.
14. Apply timings to advance each slide after 5 seconds.
15. Use the *Set Up Show* dialog box to select the following settings for a kiosk presentation.
    a. *Show type*: **Browsed at a kiosk (full screen)**
    b. *Show options*: **Loop continuously until 'Esc'** (automatically selected)
    c. *Show slides*: **All**
    d. *Advance slides*: **Use timings, if present** (automatically selected)

16. Save and close the presentation (Figure 3-99).

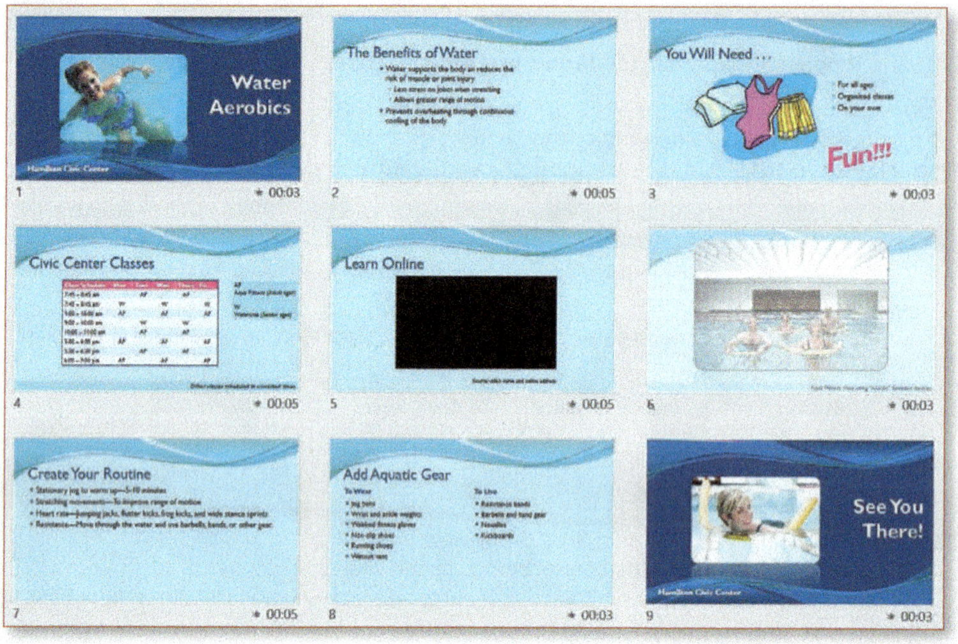

3-99 PowerPoint 3-6 completed

Improve It Project 3-7

Delivering news that employees may perceive as bad news is a difficult task. Olivia Hudson with Solution Seekers has been working to convert a formerly text-only presentation to one that is more visual. She is using pictures with brief text and transferring listed information to notes pages she will use during her presentation. She has asked you to complete a notes page, convert a list to a *SmartArt* graphic, apply custom theme colors, and add animation.
[Student Learning Outcomes 3.1, 3.2, 3.4, 3.8]

File Needed: ***Announcement-03.pptx*** *(Student data files are available in the* Library *of your SIMnet account.)*
Completed Project File Name: ***[your initials] PowerPoint 3-7.pptx***

Skills Covered in This Project

- Create custom theme colors.
- Modify slide content with *SmartArt.*
- Create and print notes pages.
- Apply appropriate transitions.
- Apply animation and effect options.
- Use *Presenter View.*
- Prepare a kiosk presentation.

1. Open the ***Announcement-03*** presentation from your student data files.
2. Save the presentation as [your initials] PowerPoint 3-7.
3. Create custom theme colors using the name Announce. Change five colors as shown in the following table.

	Text/Background - Dark 2	Text/Background - Light 2	Accent 1	Accent 2	Accent 3
Red	38	255	255	124	204
Green	19	230	153	26	236
Blue	0	193	0	26	255

4. Make the title slide text more distinctive.
   a. Display slide 1 and apply bold to the title and subtitle.
   b. Increase the title font size to **66 pt**. and "Big" to **96 pt**.
   c. Change the title font color to **Orange, Accent 1, Lighter 40%**.
   d. Increase the subtitle text to **32 pt**. and "You" to **48 pt**.
   e. Resize the subtitle placeholder on the left so the text fits on one line (Figure 3-100).

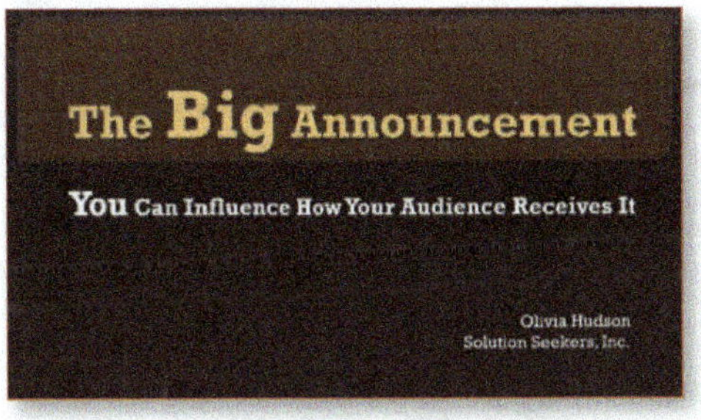

3-100 Revised title slide

5. Use the existing bulleted text to create a notes page.
   a. Display slide 2. If the *Notes* pane is not available below the slide in *Normal* view, click the **Notes** button on the *Status* bar. Increase the size of the *Notes* pane so you can work in both panes.
   b. Copy the existing bulleted text on the slide and paste it in the *Notes* pane. Arrange this text neatly (Figure 3-101).
   c. Click the **Notes** button again to hide the *Notes* pane.

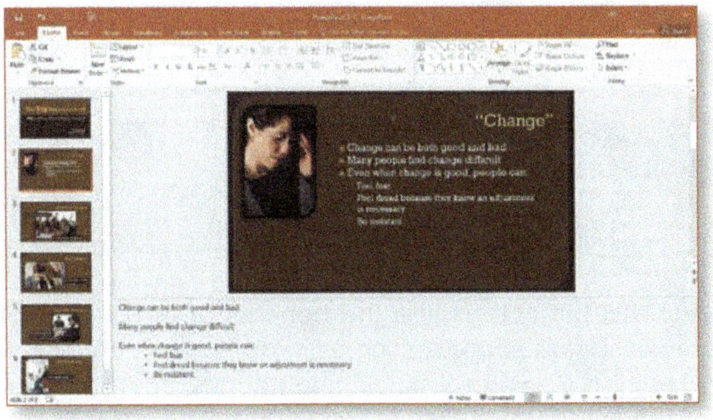

3-101 *Notes* pane expanded

6. On slide 2, modify and reposition the bulleted text.
   a. Replace the bulleted text with three words:
      - Fear
      - Dread
      - Resistance.
   b. Resize the body placeholder and move it to the lower right.
7. Insert a *SmartArt* graphic to show that "change" can be perceived as both good and bad.
   a. Insert the **Opposing Arrows** layout from the *Relationship* category.
   b. Type the text Good and Bad.
   c. Apply the **Inset** *SmartArt* Style.
   d. Resize *SmartArt* objects and position them as shown (Figure 3-102).

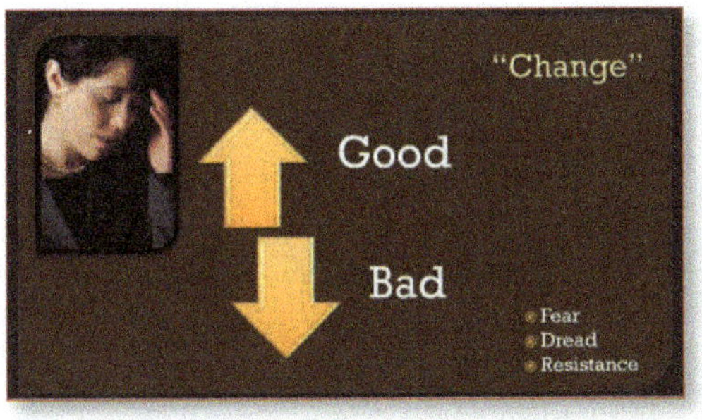

3-102 Slide 2 revised

8. Animate a text box on slides 3-5.
   a. Display slide 3. Select the "**Do**" text box.
   b. Apply the **Wipe** animation with the **From Left** effect option.
   c. Repeat this animation for the "**Do**" text boxes on slides 4 and 5.
9. Apply the **Gallery** transition to all slides.
10. Review the presentation and speaker notes using *Presenter View.*
11. Modify the transitions by entering 00:03:00 for *After* seconds and apply the change to all slides.
12. Set up the slide show for a kiosk presentation.
13. Save and close the presentation (Figure 3-103).

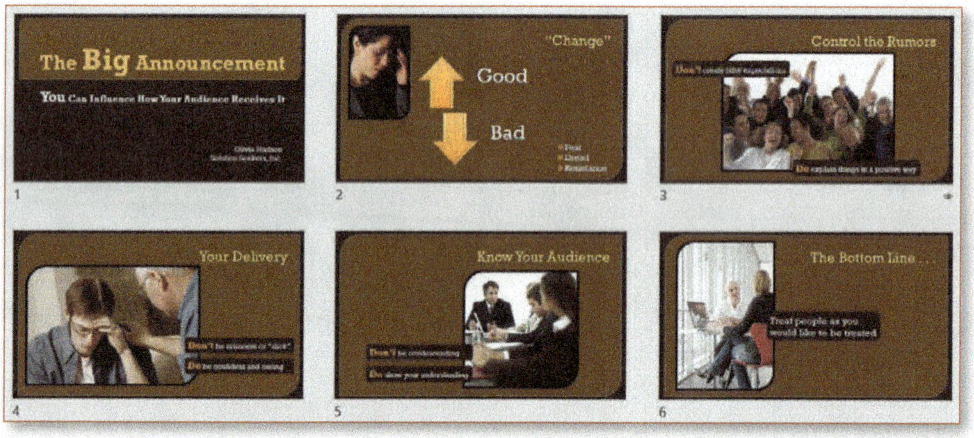

3-103 PowerPoint 3-7 completed

Challenge Project 3-8

For this project, explain the benefits of tablet computing and factors to consider when purchasing a tablet. Using sources such as www.pcmag.com, list some of the top-rated products and their prices. Describe common features, applications, and accessories.
[**Student Learning Outcomes 3.1, 3.2, 3.3, 3.4, 3.5, 3.9**]

File Needed: None
Completed Project File Name: ***[your initials] PowerPoint 3-8.pptx***

Create a new presentation and save it as [your initials] PowerPoint 3-8. Modify your presentation according to the following guidelines:

- Select an appropriate theme and create custom theme colors for a high-tech appearance.
- Change to a widescreen format, if necessary.
- Include pictures from www.pcmag.com or other sources and credit the source below each picture.
- Animate approximately three objects for emphasis and apply appropriate effects.
- Rehearse the presentation and save timings.
- Link to an online video.
- Prepare a slide listing your references and include it as the last slide in your presentation.
- Use *Package Presentation for CD* to save the presentation to a folder.

Challenge Project 3-9

Prepare a presentation to promote a student or civic organization. Use pictures and very brief text to convey the purpose of the organization. Consider using an organization chart to illustrate the officer or committee structure. Apply styles and text treatments consistently.
[Student Learning Outcomes 3.1, 3.2, 3.3, 3.4, 3.6, 3.9]

File Needed: None
Completed Project File Name: ***[your initials] PowerPoint 3-9.pptx***

Create a new presentation and save it as [your initials] PowerPoint 3-9. Modify your presentation according to the following guidelines:

- Select an appropriate theme then prepare custom theme colors for your topic.
- Modify backgrounds by applying a gradient fill to all slides and a picture fill to one slide.
- Design slides with a variety of illustration techniques and minimal text.
- Add transitions and animations with appropriate effects.
- Create and print notes pages.
- Include an online video if one is available and credit your source.
- Prepare a slide listing your references and include it as the last slide in your presentation.
- Rehearse the presentation and use a variety of navigation techniques.
- Use *Package Presentation for CD* to save your presentation to a folder.

Challenge Project 3-10

Create a presentation about living green. Focus on ways to conserve water and other resources. Use references such as www.mygreenside.org and others. Prepare a slide listing your references and include it as the last slide in your presentation.
[Student Learning Outcomes 3.1, 3.2, 3.3, 3.4, 3.6, 3.7, 3.8]

File Needed: None
Completed Project File Name: ***[your initials] PowerPoint 3-10.pptx***

Create a new presentation and save it as [your initials] PowerPoint 3-10. Modify your presentation according to the following guidelines:

- Select an appropriate theme then prepare custom theme colors that fit the "green" topic.
- Modify backgrounds and use at least one picture fill.
- Design slides with a variety of illustration techniques and minimal text.
- Add transitions and animations with appropriate effects.
- Create and print notes pages.
- Include an online video about "green" living and credit your source.
- Hide one or more slides.
- Rehearse the presentation, use the pen to circle key points, and save timings
- Modify timings as needed for a kiosk presentation.
- Prepare a kiosk presentation with looping.

Appendices

appendices

APPENDIX A

Office 2016 Shortcuts

Using Function Keys on a Laptop

When using a laptop computer, function keys perform specific Windows actions on your laptop, such as increase or decrease speaker volume, open Windows *Settings*, or adjust the screen brightness. So when using a numbered function key in an Office application, such as **F12** as a shortcut to open the *Save As* dialog box, you may need to press the ***function key*** (**Fn** or **fn**) on your keyboard in conjunction with a numbered function key to activate the Office command (Figure Appendix A-1). The function key is typically located near the bottom left of your laptop keyboard next to the *Ctrl* key.

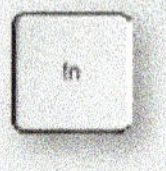

Appendix A-1 Function key

Common Office 2016 Keyboard Shortcuts

Action	Keyboard Shortcut
Save	**Ctrl+S**
Copy	**Ctrl+C**
Cut	**Ctrl+X**
Paste	**Ctrl+V**
Select All	**Ctrl+A**
Bold	**Ctrl+B**
Italic	**Ctrl+I**
Underline	**Ctrl+U**
Close *Start* page or *Backstage* view	**Esc**
Open *Help* dialog box	**F1**
Activate *Tell Me* feature	**Alt+Q**
Switch windows	**Alt+Tab**

Word 2016 Keyboard Shortcuts

Action	Keyboard Shortcut
File Management	
Open a new blank Word document	**Ctrl+N**
Save	**Ctrl+S**
Open *Save As* dialog box	**F12**
Open an existing document from the *Backstage* view	**Ctrl+O**
Open an existing document from the *Open* dialog box	**Ctrl+F12**
Close a document	**Ctrl+W**
Editing	
Toggle on/off *Show/Hide*	**Ctrl+Shift+8**

Action	Keyboard Shortcut
Copy	**Ctrl+C**
Cut	**Ctrl+X**
Paste	**Ctrl+V**
Bold	**Ctrl+B**
Italic	**Ctrl+I**
Underline	**Ctrl+U**
Double underline	**Ctrl+Shift+D**
Small caps	**Ctrl+Shift+K**
All caps	**Ctrl+Shift+A**
Left align text	**Ctrl+L**
Center text	**Ctrl+E**
Right align text	**Ctrl+R**
Justify text	**Ctrl+J**
Single line spacing	**Ctrl+1**
Double line spacing	**Ctrl+2**
1.5 line spacing	**Ctrl+5**
Left Indent	**Ctrl+M**
Remove Left Indent	**Ctrl+Shift+M**
Undo	**Ctrl+Z**
Repeat/redo	**Ctrl+Y**
Insert line break	**Shift+Enter**
Insert page break	**Ctrl+Enter**
Insert column break	**Ctrl+Shift+Enter**
Insert non-breaking space	**Ctrl+Shift+spacebar**
Copy formatting	**Ctrl+Shift+C**
Paste formatting	**Ctrl+Shift+V**
Increase font size	**Ctrl+Shift+. (Ctrl+>)**
Decrease font size	**Ctrl+Shift+, (Ctrl+<)**
Insert an endnote	**Alt+Ctrl+D**
Insert a footnote	**Alt+Ctrl+F**
Update field	**F9**
Open Panes and Dialog Boxes	
Print area on the *Backstage* view	**Ctrl+P**
Open *Font* dialog box	**Ctrl+D**
Open *Spelling and Grammar* pane	**F7**
Open *Thesaurus* pane	**Shift+F7**

(continued)

Action	Keyboard Shortcut
Open *Navigation* pane	**Ctrl+F**
Open *Find and Replace* dialog box with the *Replace* tab selected	**Ctrl+H**
Open *Find and Replace* dialog box with the *Go To* tab selected	**Ctrl+G or F5**
Open *Insert Hyperlink* dialog box	**Ctrl+K**
Open Word Help dialog box	**F1**
Selection and Navigation	
Select all	**Ctrl+A**
Turn selection on (continue to press F8 to select word, sentence, paragraph, or document)	**F8**
Move the insertion point to the beginning of the document	**Ctrl+Home**
Move the insertion point to the end of the document	**Ctrl+End**
Move the insertion point to the beginning of a line	**Ctrl+left arrow**
Move the insertion point to the end of a line	**Ctrl+right arrow**
Switch window	**Alt+Tab**

Excel 2016 Keyboard Shortcuts

Action	Keyboard Shortcut
File Management	
Open a new blank workbook	**Ctrl+N**
Open an existing workbook from the *Backstage* view	**Ctrl+O**
Open an existing workbook from the *Open* dialog box	**Ctrl+F12**
Close	**Ctrl+W**
Save	**Ctrl+S**
Move to cell A1	**Ctrl+Home**
Next worksheet	**Ctrl+Page Down**
Previous worksheet	**Ctrl+Page Up**
Editing	
Cut	**Ctrl+X**
Copy	**Ctrl+C**
Paste	**Ctrl+V**
Undo	**Ctrl+Z**
Repeat/redo	**Ctrl+Y**
Underline	**Ctrl+U**
Bold	**Ctrl+B**
Italics	**Ctrl+I**
Open *Format Cells* dialog box	**Ctrl+1**

Action	Keyboard Shortcut
Edit mode (insertion point appears within the cell)	F2
Manual line break in a cell	Ctrl+Enter
Toggle between formula view and results view	Ctrl+~
Customizing Sheets	
Hide row	Ctrl+9
Hide column	Ctrl+0
Unhide row	Ctrl+Shift+(
Insert dialog box (cell, row, or column)	Ctrl+plus sign (+)
Insert worksheet	Shift+F11
Insert chart object	Alt+F1
Formula Creation	
Open *Insert Function* dialog box	Shift+F3
Insert a plus sign	Shift+=
Insert a multiplication sign	Shift+8
Insert an exponent sign	Shift+6
Insert an open parenthesis	Shift+9
Insert a closed parenthesis	Shift+0
Insert the *SUM* function	Alt+=
Absolute symbol toggle	F4
Open *Paste Name* dialog box (insert range name)	F3

Access 2016 Keyboard Shortcuts

Action	Keyboard Shortcut
Database File Management	
Open a new blank database	Ctrl+N
Open an existing database	Ctrl+O
Editing	
Cut	Ctrl+X
Copy	Ctrl+C
Paste	Ctrl+V
Working with Objects	
Open or close *Navigation Pane*	F11
Open selected object in the default view	Enter
Open selected object in *Design* view	Ctrl+Enter
Save a database object; if first time saving the object, opens the *Save As* dialog box	Ctrl+S

(continued)

Action	Keyboard Shortcut
Open the *Save As* dialog box	**F12**
Open shortcut menu for the selected object	**Shift+F10**
Working with Text and Data	
Move to next field in a table, query, or form	**Tab**
Move to preceding cell in a table, query, or form	**Shift+Tab**
Insert line break when entering data in a *Short Text* or *Long Text* field	**Ctrl+Enter**
Undo changes to current field. Undoes all changes if more than one field on current record has been changed.	**ESC**
Switch between *Edit* mode (insertion point displayed) and *Navigation* mode	**F2**
Select current column (works in *Navigation* mode only)	**Ctrl+spacebar**
Increase selection to add adjacent column to the right	**Shift+right arrow**
Increase selection to add adjacent column to the left	**Shift+left arrow**
Open *Find and Replace* dialog box	**Ctrl+F**
Open *Find and Replace* dialog box with the *Replace* tab selected	**Ctrl+H**
Find next	**Shift+F4**
Working in Design View	
Open *Expression Builder* dialog box	**Ctrl+F2**
Open *Zoom* window	**Shift+F2**
Open or close the *Properties* window for the selected control	**F4**
Show or hide *Field* list	**Alt+F8**
Switch to *Form* view from *Design* view	**F5**
Print Preview Shortcuts	
Open *Page Setup* dialog box from *Print Preview* view	**S**
Open *Print* dialog box from *Print Preview* view	**P** or **Ctrl+P**

PowerPoint 2016 Keyboard Shortcuts

Action	Keyboard Shortcut
File Management	
Open a new blank presentation	**Ctrl+N**
Open an existing presentation from the *Backstage* view	**Ctrl+O**
Open an existing presentation from the *Open* dialog box	**Ctrl+F12**
Open *Save As* dialog box	**F12**
Save	**Ctrl+S**
Editing	
Cut	**Ctrl+X**

Action	Keyboard Shortcut
Copy	**Ctrl+C**
Paste	**Ctrl+V**
Duplicate slides	**Ctrl+D**
Undo	**Ctrl+Z**
Redo	**Ctrl+Y**
Soft return, causes text to word wrap to the next line	**Shift+Enter**
Slide Movement in Normal View	
Move to first slide	**Home**
Move to last slide	**End**
Move to next slide	**Page Down** or **down arrow**
Move to previous slide	**Page Up** or **up arrow**
Move from the slide title to the body placeholder	**Ctrl+Enter**
Slide Movement in Slide Show View	
Start a presentation slide show from the beginning	**F5**
Open *Presenter View* and start a slide show	**Alt+F5**
Advance to the next slide	**N**, **spacebar**, **right arrow**, **down arrow**, **Enter**, or **Page Down**
Go to the previous slide	**P**, **Backspace**, **left arrow**, **up arrow**, or **Page Up**
Go to a particular slide	Slide number, **Enter**
Go to a particular slide by opening *All Slides* dialog box and selecting a slide title	**Ctrl+S**
Go to a hidden slide	Slide number, **Enter** or **H** if the next slide is hidden
Blanks the screen to black	**B** or **period**
Blanks the screen to white	**W** or **comma**
Zoom in	**Plus sign**
Zoom out	**Minus sign**
Stop or restart an automatic show	**S**
Ink Markup in Slide Show View	
Change pointer to pen	**Ctrl+P**
Change pointer to arrow	**Ctrl+A**
Change pointer to eraser	**Ctrl+E**
Show or hide ink markup	**Ctrl+M**
Erase markings on the screen	**E**

APPENDIX B

Business Document Formats

Common Types of Business Documents

There are three main types of business documents, and each has a specific use for professional communication. The following table lists the different types of business document and their uses:

Types of Business Documents

Business Document	Purpose
Memorandum (Memo)	Used for intra-office or intra-organization communication. Most communication within an organization is done using email, but memos are still regularly used for formal business communication.
Business letter	Used by businesses and organizations to communicate with those outside of their organization. Business letters are sent to other companies or individuals. Business letter are typically printed on company letterhead stationery.
Personal business letter	Used for communication from an individual to a business or another individual. A job application letter (cover letter) is the most common type of personal business letter.

Parts of Business Documents

Most business documents have similar parts. The following sections describe the common parts of memorandums, business letters, and personal business letters.

Memorandums

The following table lists and describes the standards parts of a memorandum:

Parts of a Memorandum

Part	Description
Title	The title "MEMORANDUM" or "MEMO" is typically centered at the top of the page. Sometimes the title is omitted on memos.
Memo heading	Memo heading guidewords begin at the left and are typed in all caps followed by a colon. The following are the memo heading guidewords and a description of each: **TO:** Recipient(s) of the memo **FROM:** Writer of the memo **DATE:** Date of the memo **SUBJECT:** Brief description of the content of the memo Information after each guideword is typically lined up at 1" using a left tab stop.
Body	The body of a memo is single spaced. Include a double space (press **Enter** twice) after each body paragraph. Each paragraph begins at the left margin, no tab or indent is used.
Reference initials	Used when someone else types the letter for the writer of the letter. Reference initials are typed in lower case letters with no spaces or punctuation between (e.g., rn) and a double space (press **Enter** twice) after the last body paragraph. Reference initial are omitted if the writer of the memo also types the memo.
Enclosure or attachment notation (if needed)	Used when something is enclosed with or attached to the memo. The attachment can be an itinerary, meeting agenda, or any supplemental information. If you include an attachment or enclosure, type the words "Enclosure" or "Attachment" below the reference initials or last body paragraph. If there is more than one enclosure or attachment, the number of enclosures or attachments can be included in parentheses (e.g., Enclosures (3)).

Business Letters

The following table lists and describes the standards parts of a business letter:

Parts of a Business Letter

Part	Description
Date line	Type the date of the letter in the following format. January 15, 2015
Inside address	This typically includes the letter recipient's full mailing address, including name, company name (if applicable), street address, and city, state, and ZIP code. Typically, use a courtesy title (e.g., Mr., Mrs., Ms., Dr.), first name, and last name. Use standard USPS address. Mrs. Cammie Speckler Hartford Specialty 4788 Market Street, Suite A205 San Francisco, CA 95644
Salutation	This is the formal greeting to the recipient of the letter. The salutation typically includes "Dear", a courtesy title (e.g., Mr., Mrs., Ms., Dr.), and the recipient's last name. Dear Mrs. Speckler The punctuation that follows the salutation is determined by the type of punctuation style used in the letter: *mixed* or *open*. The different types of punctuation are discussed in the *Types of Business Letter Punctuation* section of this appendix.
Subject line (optional)	A brief description of the content of the letter. The subject line is optional. The subject line typically begins with "SUBJECT:", "Subject:", or "RE:" followed by a brief description of the subject of the letter.
Body	The body of a letter is single spaced. Include a double space (press **Enter** twice) after each paragraph.
Complimentary close	Used to conclude the letter. The complimentary close is typically "Sincerely," "Sincerely yours," "Best regards," "Cordially," or "Cordially yours." The punctuation that follows the complimentary close is determined by the type of punctuation style used in the letter: *mixed* or *open*. The different types of punctuation are discussed in the *Types of Business Letter Punctuation* section of this appendix.
Writer's name and title	The writer of the letter and his or her title. The writer's name and title can be typed on the same line as the close or on separate line. Sometimes the writer's company name is included below the writer's name and title.
Reference initials	Used when someone else types the letter for the writer of the letter. Reference initials are typed in lower case letters with no spaces or punctuation between (e.g., rn) and a double space (press **Enter** twice) after the last body paragraph. Reference initial are omitted if the writer of the memo also types the letter.
Enclosure notation (if needed)	This notation is included when something is enclosed with or attached to the memo. An attachment can be an itinerary, meeting agenda, or any supplemental information. If you include an attachment or enclosure, type the words "Enclosure" or "Attachment" a single space below the reference initials. If there is more than one enclosure or attachment, the number of enclosures or attachments can be included in parentheses (e.g., Enclosures (3)).
Copy notation (if needed)	Use as a notation to list others who are receiving a copy of the letter. Type a lower case "c" and type the name(s) of those receiving a copy of the letter. c Taylor Mathos
Postscript (if needed)	Used to include a note at the end of the letter. Type "P.S." and the information to be included. P.S. An updated itinerary will be emailed to you later this week.

MORE INFO

The punctuation after the salutation and complimentary close can vary depending on the type of business letter punctuation used. Types of business letter punctuation are covered later in this appendix.

Personal Business Letters

In a personal business letter, the writer's address is included below the writer's name (rather than the writer's title, as it is in a business letter) and reference initial are omitted since the writer of a personal business letter is also the one who types the letter. The following table lists and describes the standards parts of a business letter:

Parts of a Business Letter

Part	Description
Date line	The date of the letter is typed in the following format: January 15, 2015
Inside address	This typically includes the recipient's name, company name (if applicable), street address, and city, state, and ZIP code. Typically, use a courtesy title (e.g., Mr., Mrs., Ms., Dr.), first name, and last name. Use standard USPS address. Mrs. Cammie Speckler Hartford Specialty 4788 Market Street, Suite A205 San Francisco, CA 95644
Salutation	This is the formal greeting in the letter. The salutation typically includes "Dear", a courtesy title (e.g., Mr., Mrs., Ms., Dr.), and last name. Dear Mrs. Speckler The punctuation that follows the salutation is determined by the type of punctuation style used in the letter: *mixed* or *open*. The different types of punctuation are discussed in the *Types of Business Letter Punctuation* section of this appendix.
Subject line (optional)	A brief description of the content of the letter. The subject line is optional. The subject line typically begins with "SUBJECT:", "Subject:", or "RE:" followed by a brief description of the subject of the letter.
Body	The body of a letter is single spaced. Include a double space (press **Enter** twice) after each paragraph.
Complimentary close	Concludes the letter. The complimentary close is typically "Sincerely," "Sincerely yours," "Best regards," "Cordially," or "Cordially yours." The punctuation that follows the complimentary close is determined by the type of punctuation style used in the letter: *mixed* or *open*. The different types of punctuation are discussed in the *Types of Business Letter Punctuation* section of this appendix.
Writer's name and address	The writer of the letter and his or her address. Use standard USPS address.
Enclosure notation (if needed)	This notation indicates that something is enclosed with or attached to the memo. The enclosure can be a résumé, job application, or any supplemental information. If you are including an enclosure, press **Enter** twice (double space) after the writer's name and address and type "Enclosure" or "Attachment." If there is more than one enclosure or attachment, the number of enclosures or attachments can be included in parentheses (e.g., Enclosures (3)).

Part	Description
Copy notation (if needed)	This notation lists any others who are receiving a copy of the letter. Type a lower case "c" and type the name(s) of those receiving a copy of the letter. c Taylor Mathos
Postscript (if needed)	Used to include a note at the end of the letter. Type "P.S." and the information to include. P.S. I completed the job application online.

Business Letter Formats

There are two commonly-used formats for business letters: *block* and *modified block*. You can use either block or modified block format on business and personal business letters.

- ***Block format:*** All parts of the letter begin at the left margin.
- ***Modified block format:*** The date line, complimentary close, and writer's name and title (or return address on a personal business letter) begin at the horizontal midpoint (text is not centered but begins at the center). Set a left tab stop at the horizontal midpoint and press tab to begin these lines at the horizontal midpoint.

Types of Business Letter Punctuation

There are two types of business letter punctuation that you can use on business and personal business letters: ***mixed punctuation*** and ***open punctuation***. Mixed or open punctuation can be used on either block or modified block formats. This punctuation only applies to the punctuation after the salutation and complimentary close.

- ***Mixed punctuation:*** Use a colon after the salutation and a comma after the complimentary close.
- ***Open punctuation:*** Omit the colon after the salutation and the comma after the complimentary close.

Margins on Business Documents

Memos are usually typed using the default margins (1" top, bottom, left, and right). For average length business letters, place the date line approximately 2" from the top margin and use the default left and right margins. The objective is to balance the letter vertically on the page. Longer letters have less space above the date line, while shorter letters have more space above the date line. You can change the amount of space before the date line using the following methods:

- *Change top margin*: For a letter that is average length, set a **2"** top margin.
- *Change the* Before *paragraph spacing on the date line*: For an average length letter, use **72 pt.** *Before* paragraph spacing on the date line. This option is best when typing a multipage business letter.
- *Press* **Enter** *before the date line*: For an average length letter, press **Enter** five times before typing the date line.

Examples of Business Documents

The examples provided here illustrate the standard format for each of the different types and formats of business documents. Realize that a given company might use a format that varies slightly from those shown on the following pages.

The spacing provided after each part on the following examples is based upon a document with single line spacing (1.08 line spacing is the default in Word 2016) and 0 pt. *After* paragraph spacing.

Note: You can use paragraph spacing to provide a similarly spaced business document. For example, you might use 10 or 12 pt. *After* paragraph spacing to provide space after each body paragraph rather than pressing **Enter** twice (double space; DS) after each body paragraph. If you use paragraph spacing in your document, you can insert line breaks (**Shift+Enter**) to omit the *After* paragraph spacing in the inside address and writer's name and title (or address on a personal business letter).

The following table lists abbreviations that are used to describe spacing after parts of business documents. Also included is the equivalent *After* paragraph spacing that can be used in lieu of pressing *Enter* between parts.

Spacing after Parts of Business Documents

Abbreviation	Spacing	Number of Times to Press Enter	Blank Lines between Typed Lines	Equivalent *After* Paragraph Spacing
SS	Single	One	None	0 pt.
DS	Double	Two	One	12 pt.
TS	Triple	Three	Two	24 pt.
QS	Quadruple	Four	Three	36 pt.

Memorandum

Memo guidewords are typed in all caps followed by a colon.

Memo title is centered and typed in all caps.

TS or **DS** after title.

MEMORANDUM

¶
¶
TO: All ARCC Club Members

Information after the guidewords lines up at **1"**. Set a **1"** left tab stop if necessary.

DS after each line.

¶
FROM: Taylor Mathos, ARCC Coach
¶
DATE: January 12, 2018
¶
SUBJECT: Heart Rate Training

TS or **DS** after subject line. Spacing should be consistent with the spacing after the title.

¶
¶
What is **Maximum Heart Rate**? The maximum heart rate is the highest your pulse rate can get. To calculate your predicted maximum heart rate, use this formula:

SS body paragraphs with a **DS** (two *Enters*) after each paragraph.

¶
220 - Your Age = Predicted Maximum Heart Rate
(Example: a 40-year-old's predicted maximum heart rate is 180.)
¶
Your actual maximum heart rate can be determined by a graded exercise test. Please note that some medications and medical conditions might affect your maximum heart rate. If you are taking medicines or have a medical condition (such as heart disease, high blood pressure, or diabetes), always ask your doctor if your maximum heart rate/target heart rate will be affected.
¶
You gain the most benefits and decrease the risk of injury when you exercise in your **Target Heart Rate Zone**. Usually this is when your exercise heart rate (pulse) is 60 percent to 80 percent of your maximum heart rate. Do not exercise above 85 percent of your maximum heart rate. This increases both cardiovascular and orthopedic risk and does not add any additional benefit.
¶
yoi

DS after last body paragraph and type reference initials.

Typist's initials are typed in lower case with no spaces or punctuation.

Omit if the writer is also the typist.

Block Format Business Letter with Open Punctuation

> ***Date line***: Use **72 pt.** *Before* paragraph spacing or **2"** top margin for an average length business letter.
>
> **QS** after date line.

September 1, 2017
¶
¶
¶
Mrs. Cammie Speckler
Hartford Specialty
4788 Market Street, Suite A205
San Francisco, CA 95644
¶

> ***Inside Address***: **SS** each line and **DS** after the last line. Use proper USPS format for the address.

Dear Mrs. Speckler
¶

> ***Salutation***: Use courtesy title and last name. **DS** after.
>
> ***Open Punctuation***: No color after the salutation.

RE: Valley Custom Manufacturing
¶

> ***Subject Line***: Optional. **DS** after.

Central Sierra Insurance has insured **Valley Custom Manufacturing (VCM)** since 1992. We changed co[...]inal underwriters and/or branch managers left and the [...] to study the risk. In both cases, renewal numbers were offered but were not competitive. In all cases, in every year with all three companies, this risk has been very profitable.
¶

> ***Body***: **SS** body paragraphs with a **DS** after each paragraph.

Valley Custom Manufacturing are best known as a m[...] ment. Your loss control people have visited VCM several times, and I'm told the reports are very good. Expiring combined premiums are around $525,000. I expect we'll see some inflation for the January renewal.
¶
Thank you for your careful [...]eting to discuss this renewal. Plea[...] may be of any assistance.
¶

> ***Complimentary Close***: **DS** after body to type the complimentary close. **QS** after.
>
> ***Open Punctuation***: No comma after the complimentary close.

Sincerely
¶
¶
¶
Jennie Owings
Vice President
¶

> ***Writer's Name and Title***: Name and title can be typed on the same line or separate lines. Company name can also be included after title. **DS** after last line.

yoi
Enclosures (2)
c Bob Lingle
¶
P.S. Last year's policy will be faxed to y[...]

> ***Reference Initials***: Use lower case letters and no punctuation.
>
> ***Enclosure Notation***: If needed. **SS** before.
>
> ***Copy Notation***: If needed. **SS** before.
>
> ***Postscript***: If needed. **DS** before.

Modified Block Format Business Letter with Mixed Punctuation

> ***Modified Block***: Set left tab stop at the horizontal midpoint (3.25" when using 1" default left and right margins).
>
> ***Date line***: Use **72 pt.** *Before* paragraph spacing or **2"** top margin for an average length business letter.
>
> **QS** after date line.

September 1, 2017

¶

¶

¶

Mrs. Cammie Speckler
Hartford Specialty
4788 Market Street, Suite A205
San Francisco, CA 95644

> ***Inside Address***: **SS** each line and **DS** after the last line. Use proper USPS format for the address.

¶

Dear Mrs. Speckler:

> ***Salutation***: Use courtesy title and last name. **DS** after.
>
> ***Mixed Punctuation***: Colon after the salutation.

¶

SUBJECT: Valley Custom Manufact

¶

> ***Subject Line***: Optional. **DS** after.

Central Sierra Insurance ring **(VCM)** since 1992. We changed companies tw ers and/or branch managers left and the new personnel did not take the time to study the risk. In both cases, renewal numbers were offered but were not competitive. In all cases, in every year with all three companies, this risk has been very profitable.

¶

> ***Body***: **SS** body paragraphs with a **DS** after each paragraph.

Valley Custom Manufacturi of nut harvesting equipment. Your loss control pec and I'm told the reports are very good. Expiring combined premiums are around $525,000. I expect we'll see some inflation for the January renewal.

¶

Thank you for your careful consideration. Please note tha to discuss this renewal. Please review the enclosed inform be of any assistance.

¶

> ***Complimentary Close***: **DS** after body.
>
> ***Modified Block***: **Tab** to the horizontal midpoint. **QS** after.
>
> ***Mixed Punctuation***: Comma after the complimentary close.

Sincerely,

¶

¶

¶

Jennie Owings
Vice President

> ***Writer's Name and Title***: **Tab** to the horizontal midpoint. **DS** after last line.

¶

yoi

> ***Reference Initials***: Use lower case letters and no punctuation.

Enclosures (2)

> ***Enclosure Notation***: If needed. **SS** before.

c Bob Lingle

> ***Copy Notation***: If needed. **SS** before.

¶

P.S. Last year's policy will be faxed t

> ***Postscript***: If needed. **DS** before.

Block Format Personal Business Letter with Mixed Punctuation

Date line: Use **72 pt.** *Before* paragraph spacing or **2"** top margin for an average length business letter.

QS after date line.

March 22, 2018
¶
¶
¶
Ms. Geneva Song
Central Sierra Insurance
5502 Ridley Way
Cameron Park, CA 94463
¶
Dear Ms. Song:
¶

Inside Address: **SS** each line and **DS** after the last line. Use proper USPS format for the address.

Salutation: Use courtesy title and last name. **DS** after.

Mixed Punctuation: Colon after the salutation.

I am interested in the position of Marketing Director listed on Career Finder. I will be receiving my bachelor's degree in Business Communication and Computer Science in May 2018. I also have internship and educational experience in sales, sales analysis, graphic design, event planning, customer service, and distribution logistics.
¶

Body: **SS** body paragraphs with a **DS** after each paragraph.

As a small business owner, I have direct sales experience. I have de grams to increase sales among existing customers and to expand the c flyers, and brochures are still useful, but a company website is the strongest path to connect with customers. Web sites offers exceptional flexibility in reaching a target audience with a message. My training in the most current and effective methods of web development and business communication will benefit your company and customers.
¶
The combination of actual work experience and contemporary and relevant education makes me a candidate who is very suitable to be your marketing director. My resume is enclosed. I look forward to meeting you in person to further discuss this opportunity. Feel free to schedule an appointment at your conver
¶
Sincerely,
¶
¶
¶
Mark Dillard
6784 Akers Road
Sacramento, CA 95841
¶
Enclosure

Complimentary Close: **DS** after body to type the complimentary close. **QS** after.

Mixed Punctuation: Comma after the complimentary close.

Writer's Name and Address: **SS** after each line. Use proper USPS format for the address.

Enclosure Notation: If needed. **DS** before.

Modified Block Format Personal Business Letter with Open Punctuation

March 22, 2018

Modified Block: Set left tab stop at the horizontal midpoint (3.25" when using 1" default left and right margins).

Date line: Use **72 pt.** *Before* paragraph spacing or **2"** top margin for an average length business letter.

QS after date line.

¶
¶
¶
Ms. Geneva Song
Central Sierra Insurance
5502 Ridley Way
Cameron Park, CA 94463

Inside Address: **SS** each line and **DS** after the last line. Use proper USPS format for the address.

¶
Dear Ms. Song

Salutation: Use courtesy title and last name. **DS** after.

Open Punctuation: No colon after the salutation.

¶
Subject: Marketing Director

Subject Line: Optional. **DS** after.

¶
I am interested in the position of Ma[...] be receiving my bachelor's degree in Busines[...] lay 2018. I also have internship and educational experience in sales, sales analysis, graphic design, event planning, customer service, and distribution logistics.

¶
As a small business owner, I have direct sales experience. I[...] programs to increase sales among existing customers and to e[...] media, flyers, and brochures are still useful, but a company website is the strongest path to connect with customers. Web sites offers exceptional flexibility in reaching a target audience with a message. My training in the most current and effective methods of web development and business communication will benefit your company and customers.

Body: **SS** body paragraphs with a **DS** after each paragraph.

¶
The combination of actual work experience and contempo[...] me a candidate who is very suitable to be your marketing[...] I look forward to meeting you in person to further disc[...] schedule an appointment at your convenience (mdillard@[...]
¶

Sincerely

Complimentary Close: **DS** after body to type the complimentary close. **QS** after.

Modified Block: **Tab** to the horizontal midpoint. **QS** after.

Open Punctuation: No comma after the complimentary close.

¶
¶
¶
Mark Dillard
6784 Akers Road
Sacramento, CA 95841

Writer's Name and Address: **SS** after each line. Use proper USPS format for the address.

Modified Block: **Tab** to the horizontal midpoint.

¶
Enclosure

Enclosure Notation: If needed. **DS** before.

glossary

3D cell reference A cell address in another worksheet in the same workbook.

3D Rotation Style effect option that includes parallel, perspective, and oblique options to create an illusion of depth.

.docx The file format of a Word 2016 document.

A

absolute cell reference A cell address with dollar signs such as $B$2.

Action Center A menu that displays on the right side of the Windows desktop and lists notifications, such as new email, upcoming calendar items, and software updates and notifications. The *Action Center* also contains buttons at the bottom of the menu to quickly access other Windows commands, such as *All settings, Tablet mode,* and *Airplane mode.* Click the *Action Center* button on the *Taskbar* to display the *Action Center* menu.

active cell Cell that is ready for editing, surrounded with a solid border.

adjustment handle Yellow circle used to change shape curves or points.

Advanced Filter Filter process that uses a criteria range and an optional output range.

aggregate function Function that performs calculations on a group of records such as *Avg, COUNT,* and *SUM.*

alignment Vertical and horizontal position of text, data, and objects.

All apps An area of the *Start* menu in Windows 10 that displays all app (applications) on the computer.

***All Markup* view** The *Display for Review* view that displays all tracked changes and comments in a document.

***Allow Additions* property** Form property that controls whether the form allows users to enter data into the database.

***Allow Deletions* property** Form property that controls whether the form allows users to delete a record from the database.

***Allow Edits* property** Form property that controls whether the form allows users to change data in the database.

alternate row colors Formatting option to define alternating colors for adjacent rows.

alternative text (alt text) Information tag that appears when a reader places the pointer on a table or graphic object; also used with screen readers to accommodate those with visual impairments.

***AND* logical operator** Operator that requires that a record meet all of the individual conditions to be included in the results.

animation Movement of objects on a slide.

app Short for application; software program or Windows application or accessory.

append row Last row in a table, indicated by an asterisk; enter data values into the fields in the append row to add a new record into the table.

argument Cell reference, value, or other element required for a function.

array Range of cells in a row or a column.

Arrows Line style that provides arrowheads or other shapes for both ends of a line.

ascending order Sort order that arranges data from lowest to highest for a numeric field or from A to Z for a text field.

aspect ratio The ratio of width to height; affects slide, picture, and other object sizing.

attribute Setting or property for a cell.

AutoCalculate Status bar area that displays calculations for selected cells.

AutoComplete Feature that fills in the complete day, month, or date as you type.

***AutoComplete* tag** The notation that displays and predicts what will be typed, such as a day, month, or date. When the tag appears, press *Enter* to automatically insert the text.

AutoCorrect Feature that automatically corrects commonly misspelled words.

***AutoCorrect Options* smart tag** Tag that appears by a word that has been automatically corrected.

AutoFilter Arrow in a header row used for sorting or filtering data.

AutoFit Formatting option that automatically adjusts column width or row height to reveal all the contents within a column or row; also referred to as *AutoFit Column Width.*

AutoFormat Feature that controls the formatting of items such as numbered and bulleted lists, fractions, ordinal numbers, hyphens and dashes, quotes, indents, and hyperlinks.

***AutoNumber* data type** Data type used to store a unique number, automatically assigned by Access.

AutoOutline Excel summary sheet that inserts groups based on formula locations.

axis title Chart element that names the horizontal and vertical axes using placeholders or text boxes.

B

Background Style Option that changes slide background and text colors to light or dark variations.

Backsolve Analysis in which the result is known and a value necessary to reach that result is determined.

***Backstage* view** Area of an Office application where you perform common actions (such as *Save, Open, Print,* and *Share*) and change application options; document properties are displayed here.

balloon The object where comments display.

bar tab stop Tab that inserts a vertical line at the tab stop.

Bevel Style effect option that applies light and dark areas to create a dimensional appearance so objects and text look raised or inset.

bibliography List of the sources used in a report.

bibliography style Style that determines the formatting of sources and citations in a report.

Blank desktop database Command used to create a new database from scratch.

block format letter All parts of the letter begin at the left margin. No lines are indented or centered. Block format can be used on either business or personal business letters.

block layout Report layout option available when grouping records that displays the fields in a row and column format with the field names displayed as column heads; the grouped field displays in the left-most column but on the same row as the first record for the grouping.

bookmark Location in a document that is electronically marked and can be linked to a hyperlink or cross-reference.

border Line around text, paragraph, page, cell, table, or graphic object.

bound control Control that gets its value from a field in a table.

bound form Form that is directly connected to a table or query as the data source.

bulleted list Unordered list of items; a bullet symbol precedes each item, and a left and hanging indent controls left alignment.

business intelligence Tools, applications, and processes used to analyze data.

button Use to apply a command or open a dialog box in Office applications.

Button control Control on a form or report that performs an action when clicked; also knows as a *Command Button* control.

C

calculated control Control that gets its value from an expression.

calculated field Field that gets its value from a calculation instead of a value that is entered into the field.

caption Descriptive text that appears above or below a graphic.

caption property Field property used to create a caption that displays in the column header in datasheet view of a table and in the labels on forms and reports; captions often include spaces and multiple words and are more readable than a field name.

Cap type Line option that controls the look of the ends of lines; usually applied to single lines or arrows.

Cascade Delete Related Records Referential integrity option that allows you to delete a record from a table even if there are matching records in related tables; also deletes all matching records from related tables.

Cascade Update Related Fields Referential integrity option that allows a primary key value to be changed in a record in one table and automatically updates the foreign key values in matching records in related tables.

case Typographic term for capitalization; small letters are lowercase and capital letters are uppercase.

category axis (X-axis) Describes data shown in a chart; the horizontal axis in a column chart and the vertical axis in a bar chart.

category label Text label that describes a data series in a chart.

cell Intersection of a column and a row.

cell address Column letter and row number that identifies location of cell or range; also referred to as cell reference.

cell style Set of formatting elements for data in a cell.

center tab stop Tab that centers text at the tab stop.

Change Case Button used to change text from the case shown to a different case such as uppercase to lowercase.

Change Colors Gallery that displays different color combinations for SmartArt layouts that are based on theme colors.

character spacing Space between letters and words.

chart A visual representation of numeric worksheet data.

chart area Background rectangle area for a chart.

chart element Separate, selectable, editable object or part in a chart.

chart floor Area at the bottom of a 3-D chart.

chart layout Set of charts elements and their locations.

chart object Selectable chart with clickable elements located on the worksheet.

chart sheet Chart displayed in its own tab or sheet in a workbook.

chart style Combination of colors and effects for a chart and its elements.

chart title Name or main label for a chart.

chart wall Vertical background for a 3D chart.

check box Box that allows you to choose one or more from a group of options.

Check Box control Control on a form or report used to display data for a field with a *Yes/No* data type; when used on a form, it can also accept data when a user enters a value.

circular reference Formula error in which the formula refers to the cell in which it is located.

citation Abbreviated source information in the body of the report that credits the source of information referred to in a document.

Clear Formatting Command that removes formatting from selected text and formats the text in *Normal* style.

Clipboard Location where multiple copied items from an Office file or other source such as a web page are stored.

***Clipboard* pane** Pane that displays the contents of the *Clipboard*.

Color Saturation Option that controls the intensity of the colors in a picture; colors that are vibrant are highly saturated and colors that are muted have a low saturation level.

Color Tone Option that controls temperature values to make a picture's colors more cool or warm.

Colorful Chart option that provides varied colors for *Chart and SmartArt Styles*.

column break Formatting option that ends a column and pushes subsequent text to the next column.

Column chart Chart type that shows a comparison of values or data changes over time.

columnar layout Form or report layout that displays the fields in one column with the field names displayed to the left of the field.

Combo chart Chart type that combines two charts such as a column chart with a line chart.

comments Notations attached to text used to provide feedback or notes when reviewing a file.

Command Button control Control on a form or report used to perform an action such as *Close Report* or *Open Form*.

Command Button Wizard Tool that guides you through the steps of creating a command button control and assigning an action to the button.

Compact & Repair Database Database utility that removes unused space from a database to help improve performance; can be used to repair a database in which some objects have become corrupted.

completeness rule Data integrity rule that ensures a value is entered if required.

compound criteria Criteria used in filters or expressions that combine more than one value using the *AND* and *OR* logical operators.

Compound type Line option that provides outlines with two or more lines that vary in thickness.

Compress Pictures Command that reduces presentation file size by reducing picture resolution.

concatenated key Primary key made up of more than one field; also known as a composite key.

concatenation Combine multiple parts of an equation together into one piece; often used in an expression to combine several fields together.

conditional formatting Format settings that are applied based on rules, rankings, or other criteria.

connection Identifier and a link to external data in a workbook.

consistency rule Data integrity rule that ensures a value in one field is consistent with a value in another field.

constant A value used in a formula.

content control field Word field in which you type custom information such as the date or year.

context menu Menu of commands that appears when you right-click text or an object.

context-sensitive Describes menu options that change depending on what you have selected.

contextual tabs Ribbon tabs that becomes available when working on different tasks.

continuous section break Formatting option that divides a document into different sections on the same page so sections can be formatted independently of each other; can also be used at the end of columns to balance column length.

control Item on a form or report such as a text box, label, or command button; used to enter, edit, or display data, or perform tasks in the database.

control layout Structure that helps to align the different controls on a form or report.

Control Wizards Tool that directs Access to launch an available wizard when adding controls to an object in the database; for example, the *Control Wizards* tool must be turned on for the *Command Button Wizard* to activate.

Copy Duplicate text or other information.

Cortana The help feature in Windows 10 that responds to both keyboard and voice commands. *Cortana* searches not only the computer but also the Internet and displays search results in the *Cortana* menu.

criteria range Two or more rows of data used to specify advanced filter conditions.

criterion (pl. criteria) Expression entered into a query to limit and focus results.

crop Trim unwanted areas of a selected picture.

cropping handles Black handles that appear on the corners and sides of pictures that you can drag to remove part of the picture.

crosshair Plus sign pointer used to draw a shape.

cross-reference Note in a document that directs readers to another location in a document.

custom dictionary Location in Office where words that you add are stored.

Cut Remove text or other information.

Cycle *SmartArt* layout type used to illustrate a continuing sequence or concepts related to a central idea.

D

Dash Type Line option that displays lines made with various combinations of dots and dashes.

Dashes Line styles that combine dots and dashes to make different patterns.

***Data Entry* property** Form property that determines whether existing data in the database is displayed on the form.

data format rule Data integrity rule that ensures a value entered into a field matches the data type of the field.

data integrity rules A set of rules that ensures data in a database is accurate and consistent.

data label Object that displays value for each data marker in a chart.

data marker Bar, column, slice, or other object used to graph a value in a chart.

data point A single value graphed in a chart.

data series A group of related values graphed by columns, bars, slices, or other objects in a chart.

data table Columnar display of values for each data series in a chart located below the chart.

data type Field property that determines the type of data that can be entered in a field, what properties can be manipulated, and how that field can be used.

data visualization Formatting that uses colored bars, color variations, or icons based on rules or rankings.

database An organized collection of integrated and related tables.

database management system (DBMS) Software that allows a user to create a database; manage the data in the database by adding, deleting, and updating records; sort and retrieve data; and create queries and reports relating to that data.

Database Properties Details and information about the database.

datasheet layout Form layout that displays the fields in *Datasheet* view.

Datasheet view View option that allows you to enter, modify, view, or delete data; available in a table, query, or form.

Date function Function that obtains the current date from your computer.

decimal tab stop Tab that aligns text at the decimal point at the tab stop.

default Setting that is automatically applied by an application unless you make specific changes.

***Default Value* property** Field property that sets a value to automatically be entered into a field.

Delay Animation timing command used to make an animation begin at a specified time.

delimited File that separates data into columns with a special character.

delimiter Character used to separate columns.

dependent Cell that is affected by the active cell.

descending order Sort order that arranges data from highest to lowest for a numeric field or from Z to A for a text field.

***Design* view** View option that allows you to build or modify the basic structure or functionality of a database object.

destination cell Cell location for pasted data.

dialog box Window that opens and displays additional features.

Different First Page Formatting option that displays first-page header or footer content that differs from the other headers and footers in a document.

Different Odd & Even Pages Formatting option that displays headers and/or footers that differ on odd and even pages.

dimension Number of row and columns in an array.

Display for Review The drop-down list used to select how tracked changes display.

Distribute Columns Table option that evenly distributes column width.

Distribute Rows Table option that evenly distributes row height.

document properties Information recorded in a file such as title, author name, subject, creation date, etc.

document property field Word field that displays the document property contents in the body, header, or footer of a document.

drag and drop A method to copy or move select text or an object.

drop-down list List of options that displays when you click a button.

duplicate Create a copy of an object or a slide.

duplicate row Record in a table with the same content as another record in one or more columns.

Duration Length of time; controls the speed of transitions and animations in a slide show.

dynamic Describes results that adjust in real time to data changes.

E

***Edit* link** A hyperlink used when sharing a file with others that allows users to edit the shared file.

Effect Formatting feature such as shadow, glow, or soft edges added to Wordart, shapes, or pictures.

Effect Option Command that controls the direction of slide transitions and animation movement.

embedded TrueType fonts Embedded TrueType fonts Option that saves presentation fonts for display on a different computer.

Emphasis Animation effect that calls attention to an object that remains on the slide.

endnote Reference, citation, or other text that appears at the end of a document.

Entrance Animation effect that occurs when an object appears on the slide.

Error Bar Chart element that shows margin of error or standard deviation amounts.

Excel *Start* page Opening screen when Excel is started.

Excel table Excel data formatted with a header row followed by data rows.

Exit Animation effect that occurs when an object leaves the slide.

expression Type of formula used to write validation rules, perform calculations, create query criteria, control macros, and group and sort data in a report.

***Expression Builder* dialog box** Window that provides easy access to tools used to create expressions.

exporting Saving or copying data for use in another program or application.

external data Data that originated in another program or format.

extract Create a regular folder from a zipped folder.

extract range One row of labels for results of an advanced filter.

Eyedropper Feature in PowerPoint used to match colors.

F

field Collection of characters that describes one aspect of a business object or activity (a single unit of data).

field handle Area to select a document property of content control field.

field name Label in a header row.

field properties Description of the specific details of each field in a table; basic field properties include the *Field Name, Data Type and Field Size.*

field width Side to side measurement of a column; controls how much content displays in a field.

File Explorer Window where you browse for, open, and manage files and folders (formerly called Windows Explorer).

file name extension A series of letters automatically added to a file name that identifies the type of file.

fill Color or pattern used as a background.

Fill Handle Small black square at lower right corner of a cell or range used to complete a series or copy data.

Filter Feature that limits the data records that display in a datasheet.

Filter by Selection Filter option that displays only the records that match the value in specific fields you have selected.

Find Feature that searches a file to locate specific text and/or formatting.

first line indent Horizontal space between the first line of a paragraph and the left margin.

fixed width Specific number of characters assigned to a field or column.

Flash Fill Excel feature that completes column data based on the first entry.

folder A Windows feature used to store and organize files in a specific location.

font Named design of type for characters, punctuation, and symbols.

font color The color applied to selected text.

font face Specifies the shape of text.

font size Specifies the size of text.

font style Formatting applied to create bold, italics or underlined text.

footer Displays content at the bottom of a document page, slide, or object.

footnote Reference, citation, or other text that appears at the bottom of a page.

foreign key Field in one table that is also the primary key in another table; used to create relationships between tables.

form Database object used to enter, modify, view, or delete data from a table.

Format Painter Command that copies formatting from selected text, shapes, or pictures, and applies these changes to another selection.

***Format* property** Property that indicates the way a field displays in a table.

***Form* button** Tool that allows you to quickly create a form; no options are provided during the initial creation process.

formula A calculation in a cell that displays a result.

formula auditing Process of reviewing formulas for accuracy.

Formula AutoComplete Feature that displays a list of function and range names after a character is typed.

***Formula* bar** Bar below the Ribbon that displays active cell contents.

***Form* view** View option used to enter and view data.

Form Wizard Tool that guides you through the steps to create a form.

function A built-in formula.

function keys The numbered command keys (i.e., F1, F2, etc.) located near the top of the keyboard. Function keys can perform both Windows and Office application commands. Some laptops require the user to press the *function key* (*Fn* or *fn*) on the keyboard in conjunction with a numbered function key to activate an Office command.

G

gallery Group of options on a tab.

Glow Style effect option that provides a colored area around an object that fades into the background color.

Go To The feature that moves the insertion point to a specific location in a file, such as a page, bookmark, footnote, comment, or heading level.

Gradient Option that blends two or more colors or light and dark variations of the current fill color in different directions.

graphics Visual objects such as pictures, clip art, shapes, *SmartArt*, charts, and *WordArt*.

grayscale A range of shades of black in a display or printout.

Gridlines Lines that visually frame rows and columns; in PowerPoint, lines that appear behind chart elements such as columns or bars or that can be displayed on a slide as an aid to alignment.

group Area on a tab that contains related commands and options; option used to organize data in a report so that similar records appear together; and feature used to combine selected objects.

H

Handout Feature that prints 1–9 slides on a page.

hanging indent Additional horizontal space between second and carryover lines of a paragraph and the left margin.

header Displays content at the top of a document, slide handout, or object.

Header Row First row of a table.

hidden worksheet Worksheet whose tab is not visible.

Hierarchy SmartArt layout type used to illustrate a decision tree or top-to-bottom relationship such as an organization chart.

hierarchy of data Organization of data in a database from the smallest to largest grouping of data.

Highlighter *Highlighter* Tool used to write or draw on a slide in Slide Show view.

Histogram chart Chart type that shows the distribution of data grouped by frequencies.

horizontal alignment Content positioning option that aligns material in relation to the left, center, right, or middle (justified) of the page or slide; can also refer to the position of objects in relation to each other.

hyperlink Text or an object that a reader can click to be taken to another location in the document, to a web page, or to a different file.

I

import Transfer data from an application or browser into an application.

indent Increase the distance between the cell contents and the left boundary of the cell.

ink annotations Markings that call attention to information you mark by writing or drawing on slides.

***Input Mask* property** Property used to specify the format for data entered into a field.

Input Mask Wizard Tool that guides you through the steps to define an input mask; only available on *Short Text* or *Date* fields.

insert control Button that allows you to quickly insert a row or column into a table.

IntelliSense Tool that suggests a list of possible values when you enter an expression.

J

Join type Line option that controls the look of the connection point where two lines meet, such as the corner of a rectangle.

junction table Table created to link the two tables in a many-to-many relationship; also known as an intersection table.

justified alignment Content positioning option that aligns material with both the left and right margins.

justified layout Form or report layout option that displays the fields in a horizontal, justified layout with field names displayed above each field.

K

Kerning Space between letters in a proportional font.

keyboard shortcut Key or combination of keys that you press to apply a command.

kiosk presentation Self-running slide presentation that automatically loops.

L

label Text data in a worksheet that is not used in calculations.

Label control Control on a form or report that displays the content of the caption property of a field.

***Landscape* orientation** Page layout option in which the page is oriented so it is wider than it is tall.

laser pointer *Slide Show* feature that displays a small dot on the screen during a presentation; also available on remote control devices.

launcher (dialog box launcher) A small square in the bottom right corner of some groups on the *Ribbon*. When a launcher is clicked, a dialog box with more options opens.

Layout Controls the position of placeholders on a slide.

***Layout* view** Form or report view option used to make design changes to the object and see the effects of the changes in real time.

leader Series of dots or characters that fills the blank space between text and a tab stop.

left indent Horizontal space between a paragraph and the left margin.

left tab stop Tab that aligns text at the left of the tab stop.

legend Descriptive text or key that describes a data series and identifies it by color.

line break Formatting option that controls where lines begin and end, which can be used to keep lines together in a bulleted or numbered list.

line spacing Amount of space between lines of text within a paragraph.

List SmartArt layout type used to illustrate non-sequential or grouped information in a graphical list.

live preview Display option that allows you to temporarily apply and view a style or formatting feature.

Lock Aspect Ratio Command used to maintain proportion when entering object height or width sizes.

Lock Drawing Mode Feature used to draw more than one of the same shape.

***Long Text* data type** Data type used to store alphanumeric data longer than 255 characters or text containing rich text formatting.

lookup field Field used to display a list of data values that users can select to store in the field.

loop Cycle continuously in a slide show from beginning to end and automatically repeat.

M

macro Database object used to attach code to objects and controls in a database.

many-to-many relationship Relationship between tables in a database where many rows of data in one table can be associated with many rows of data in a related table.

margin Blank space at the top, bottom, left, or right of a document; in a text box, the space between the outside of the box and the text within the box; in a table, the space between a cell border and the cell text.

marker Data point in a sparkline.

***Markup* area** The area at the right side of a Word document that displays comments and certain tracked changes.

Master Views Group of commands that are used to make global changes to a presentation: *Slide Master, Handout Master,* and *Notes Master.*

mathematical order of operations Sequence of arithmetic operations in a formula.

Matrix SmartArt layout type used to illustrate the relationship of four parts to the whole.

maximize Increase the size of the window of an open Office file so it fills the entire computer monitor.

mean Value determined by adding all values in a range and dividing by the number of values.

Merge Cells Command that combines two or more cells in a row or column.

metadata Document properties stored with the file.

Microsoft Access The database software in the Microsoft Office suite of applications.

Microsoft account Free account that gives you access to an email account, *SkyDrive* online storage area, and Office Web Apps.

Microsoft Excel The spreadsheet software in the Microsoft Office suite of applications.

Microsoft Office 2016 The suite of Microsoft productivity software that typically includes Microsoft Word, Excel, Access, PowerPoint, OneNote, and Outlook.

Microsoft Office 365 The subscription version of Microsoft Office where users pay a monthly or yearly fee to install and use the Microsoft Office applications on a computer.

Microsoft OneNote The note-taking software in the Microsoft Office suite of applications.

Microsoft Outlook The personal information management software in the Microsoft Office suite of applications that includes email, calendar, contacts, and tasks.

Microsoft PowerPoint The presentation software in the Microsoft Office suite of applications.

Microsoft Publisher The desktop publishing software in the Microsoft Office suite of applications.

Microsoft Store The online store where users can purchase and download a variety of apps (applications).

Microsoft Word The word processing software in the Microsoft Office suite of applications.

mini toolbar Toolbar listing formatting options that appears when you select text or right-click.

minimize Place an open Office file on the taskbar so it is not displayed on the desktop.

mixed cell reference A cell address with one dollar sign such as $B2 or B$2.

mixed punctuation Use a colon after the salutation (e.g., "Dear Ms. Vasquez:") and a comma after the complimentary close (e.g., "Best regards,"). Mixed or open punctuation can be used on either business or personal business letters.

modified block format letter Type the date line and closing lines [complimentary close, writer's name, writer's title, and return address (on personal business letters)] beginning at the horizontal midpoint. Typically, set a left tab stop at 3.25". Modified block format can be used on either business or personal business letters.

Monochromatic Color combinations containing only shades of one color; color option for Chart Styles.

multilevel list Customized list that includes a combination of numbers, letters, or bullets.

N

***Name* box** Area in Formula bar that displays cell address of the active cell.

***Navigation* bar** Area at the bottom left corner of a table that contains buttons used to move among table records in *Datasheet* view.

***Navigation* menu** Contains category and group settings that control the display of objects in the *Navigation Pane*.

***Navigation Pane* (Access)** Displays all objects contained in a database.

***Navigation* pane (Windows File Explorer)** The area on the left side of a *File Explorer* window that displays the different storage areas of the computer.

***Navigation* pane (Word)** The pane at the left side of the Word window when the Find command is selected. The *Navigation* pane displays headings, pages, and search results.

***No Markup* view** The *Display for Review* view that displays the final document with changes applied.

non-breaking space Formatting option that keep words together so they are not separated by word wrap at the end of a line.

***Normal* template** Predesigned and ready-to-use document that includes default fonts, font sizes, line and paragraph spacing, styles, and margins; new blank document.

Normal View Default view option where you enter the content of slides and move between slides as you develop them.

Notes Page View Option that displays each slide on a page with space below the slide where you can type speaker notes.

null Value in a field that indicates that nothing was ever entered in that field.

***Number* data type** Data type used to store numbers in fields that are used in mathematical calculations.

numbered list List that arranges items in order; a number or letter precedes each item, and a left and hanging indent controls left alignment.

***NumPages* field** Word field that lists the number of pages in a document.

O

object Major component in an Access database.

Office Clipboard Storage location for cut or copied data shared by all Office applications.

Office desktop apps The version of Microsoft Office that users download and install on a PC or Apple computer.

Office Online The online version of Microsoft Office that is available through a web browser.

Office universal apps The version of Microsoft Office that users download and install on tablets or mobile phone devices.

OneDrive Online storage area that is a part of your Microsoft account where you can store and access documents from any computer with an Internet connection.

***OneDrive* folder** An online storage location connected to a user's Microsoft Account that displays in the *File Explorer* window.

one-to-many relationship Relationship between tables in a database where a row of data in one table can be associated with many rows of data in a related table.

one-to-one relationship Relationship between tables in a database where a row of data in one table can be associated with only one row of data in a related table.

open punctuation Punctuation after the salutation and complimentary close are omitted. Mixed or open punctuation can be used on either business or personal business letters.

operating system Software that makes a computer function and controls the working environment.

***OR* logical operator** Operator that requires that a record meet at least one individual condition to be included in the results.

***Original* view** The *Display for Review* view that displays the original document with none of the tracked changes applied.

outdent Negative indent that lines up information outside the left or right margins.

outline Border around selected element.

outline layout A report layout available when grouping records. Displays the grouped field and its label on a separate row at the start of each grouping. The field names are displayed as column heads above the first row of data in each grouping.

Outline View Option that expands the pane at the left of the slide area to show slide titles and bulleted text.

P

Package Presentation for CD Feature that saves a presentation and related files to a CD or a folder.

page borders A border that applies to an entire page rather than selected text or paragraph.

page break Formatting option that controls where text on a page ends.

Page Break Preview Worksheet view that shows printed pages with dashed or dotted lines to mark where new pages start.

Page Layout Worksheet view that opens header and footer areas, indicates margin areas, and shows rulers.

page number field Word field that lists the page number.

page orientation The direction of the page. The two different orientation options are *Portrait* and *Landscape*.

paragraph alignment Formatting option that determines how a paragraph is positioned horizontally on the page.

paragraph break Formatting option that you insert when you press **Enter** at the end of a word, line, or paragraph.

paragraph spacing Amount of spacing before and after a paragraph.

paragraph symbol Icon that indicates a paragraph break.

parameter Specific phrase (entered in the *criteria* box of a query field) that displays in the *Enter Parameter Value* dialog box when a parameter query is run.

parameter query Query that asks a user to enter a specific criterion value.

Paste Place text or other objects that have been stored on the *Clipboard* in a new location.

Paste Options Gallery of choices for how data is copied.

***Pattern Background* color** Color used with a foreground color to create a pattern.

Pattern Fill Shape Fill option that applies a mixture of two colors in various dotted or crosshatch designs.

***Pattern Foreground* color** Color used with a background color to create a pattern.

PDF (portable document format) File format used to convert a file into a static image.

Pen Tool used to write or draw on a slide in Slide Show view; also used in Normal view to draw tables and edit border lines.

Picture SmartArt layout type used to show pictures as integral parts of many different diagrams.

Picture Fill *Shape Fill* option that fills the *WordArt* or shape with a picture from a file or from the Office.com clip art collection.

Picture Effects Command used to apply effect options, such as *Shadow* or *Glow,* to pictures.

PivotChart Summary chart built from a PivotTable or a range of data.

PivotTable Summary report for a range of data with interactive field and filter buttons.

pixel Abbreviated term for picture element, a single unit of information about color.

placeholder In PowerPoint, the area of a slide where you can add text, tables, charts, and pictures. In Word, text that temporarily marks a spot in a document where a citation is missing and needs to be completed.

plot area Chart element bounded by the horizontal and vertical axes.

points Font measurement of 1/72 of an inch.

***Portrait* orientation** Page layout option in which the page is oriented so it is taller than it is wide.

Position A character-spacing option that raises or lowers text by a designated number of points.

precedent Cell that contributes to a formula's result.

Presenter View Option that displays slides and features helpful for a speaker; can be displayed on one monitor or with a second monitor or projector that shows the presentation at full-screen size.

primary key Field that contains a unique value for each record in a table; allows one record to be distinguished from another.

print area Defined range of cells that prints.

Print Preview Print option that allows you to see how a document, spreadsheet, or database object will look when printed and to make changes to the printing options before printing.

Print Settings Options to control what and how printing occurs.

print title Row or column that prints on each page.

Process *SmartArt* layout type used to illustrate sequential steps in a process or workflow.

product Result of a multiplication formula.

program options Area in each Office application where you can make changes to the program settings.

Protected View Status of a workbook opened or copied from an Internet source.

Pyramid *SmartArt* layout type used to illustrate proportional or interconnected relationships.

Q

query Database object used to find data in a database.

Quick access (Windows File Explorer) The area at the top of the *Navigation* pane in a *File Explorer* window that displays folders or locations on a computer so users can quickly access these item. Users can pin folders or locations on a computer to the *Quick access* area of a File Explorer window.

***Quick Access* toolbar** Area located above the *Ribbon* with buttons you use to perform commonly used commands.

Quick Analysis Tool that displays for a selected cell range with suggested command groups.

R

radio button Round button you click to choose one option from a list.

range Rectangular group of cells such as A1:B3.

Range Finder Feature that highlights and color-codes a formula cell range in Edit mode.

range name Label assigned to a single or a group of cells.

range rule Data integrity rule that ensures a value in a field falls within an established range of acceptable values.

Reading View Option that displays a slide show at full-screen or alternate window size determined by the viewer.

Real-time collaboration The Word 2016 feature that allows multiple users to simultaneously edit a shared filed stored in an online location, such as OneDrive.

Recolor Option that changes picture colors to different monotone color variations.

record Collection of related data fields.

record validation rule Validation rule that compares fields in the same table; entered into the *Validation Rule* property of a table.

Recycle Bin Location where deleted files and folders are stored.

Redo Repeat an action.

reference marker Number, letter, or symbol that marks a footnote or endnote in the body of a document.

referential integrity The quality of consistency in data entered into related tables; enforcing referential integrity prevents a record in one table from referencing a record that does not exist in a related table.

Reflection Style effect option that shows a mirror image below an object.

Rehearse Timings Feature that helps you to judge the pace of the presentation.

relational database Database in which data is organized into a collection of related tables.

Relationship *SmartArt* layout type used to illustrate concepts that are connected such as contrasting, opposing, or converging.

***Relationships* window** (Access) Used to create, edit, and view the table relationship in a database.

relative cell reference A cell address such as B2.

remote control Device that enables a speaker to control a slide show when he or she steps away from the computer during a presentation.

Reorder Animation Animation timing command used to adjust animation sequence.

Repeat The command to automatically repeat the previous command used.

Replace Feature that searches a file to locate specific text and/or formatting and replace it with specified replacement text and/or formatting.

report Database object used to view and print data in a database.

***Report* view** Report view option that shows all of the data contained in the report; displays in a continuous layout, which does not separate the data into separate pages.

Report Wizard Tool that guides you through the steps to create a report.

***Required* property** Field property that indicates whether a value must be entered into a field or if it can be skipped and left blank.

Reset Picture Command used to restore a picture's original characteristics and dimensions.

resize pointer Pointer used to change the size of a graphic object or a table column or row.

restore down Decrease the size of the window of an open Office file so it does not fill the entire computer monitor.

***Reviewing* pane** The pane at the left or bottom of the document that displays tracked changes and comments.

RGB model Typically used for computer displays; colors are formed by blending values for Red, Green, and Blue.

Ribbon Bar that appears at the top of an Office file window and displays available commands.

Ribbon Display Options A button is the upper right corner of an Office application window that controls how the *Ribbon* displays. The options include *Auto-hide Ribbon, Show Tabs,* and *Show Tabs and Commands.*

right indent Horizontal space between a paragraph and the right margin.

right tab stop Tab that aligns text at the right of the tab stop.

rotation handle A circular arrow used to turn an object in different directions.

row Horizontal grouping of cells.

row height Top to bottom measurement of a row.

row selector Pointer that selects a row of a table.

***row selector* (Access)** Box at the left of a table row. When checked it selects that row. Also called a record selector.

ruler Vertical or horizontal guide that displays measurements within the margins of a document.

S

sans serif font One of several font typefaces with letters that do not include structural details (flair).

Scale Character-spacing option that changes spacing by a designated percentage.

scope A worksheet set as the location for a range name.

ScreenTip Descriptive information about a button, drop-down list, launcher, or gallery selection that appears when you place your pointer on the item.

Search Feature that allows you to look for specific data values.

section break Formatting option used to break a document into different sections so sections can be formatted independently of each other.

select method Technique of selecting cell addresses to create a formula.

select query Query that locates, or selects, data in a database.

selection handle Four-pointed arrow that selects and moves objects.

serif font One of several font typefaces with letters that feature structural details (flair).

serial number Value assigned to a date.

series List of labels or values that follow a pattern.

Set Transparent Color Feature that removes one color from a picture; used to remove solid backgrounds.

Settings (Windows 10) The area of Windows 10 used to customize computer settings. The *Settings* area in Windows 10 is similar to the *Control Panel* in previous versions of Windows.

shading Fill color applied to text, paragraph, page, cell, table, or graphic object.

Shadow Style effect option that provides dimension by inserting a shadow behind or below an object.

shape Graphic object that can be drawn, such as a line, arrow, circle, or rectangle.

shape adjustment handle Yellow circle that changes the contour of a shape.

Shape Effects Command used to apply effect options, such as Shadow or Glow, to objects.

shape fill Color that fills a shape or graphic object.

shape outline Border around a graphic object.

shape style Set of built-in formats for shapes that include borders, fill colors, and effect components.

Share (Windows 10 *File Explorer*) The feature in a File Explorer window that allows users to share files stored online with other users.

***Share* pane** The pane at the right side of the Word, Excel, or PowerPoint window that displays options to share a file.

SharePoint server Web platform designed for collaboration via the Internet.

***Short Text* data type** Data type used to store alphanumeric data; the maximum length is 255 characters.

***Show* check box** Box in *Design* view of a query that indicates whether a field used in a query displays in the query results.

Show/Hide Button that displays or hides paragraph breaks, line breaks, spaces, tabs, and other formatting symbols in a document.

Shutter Bar Open/Close Button Opens and closes the *Navigation Pane* in Access.

Simple Markup view The *Display for Review* view that displays the document with all tracked changes applied and a line at the left side of the document indicating where changes are made.

Simple Query Wizard Tool that guides you through the steps to create a query.

sizing handles White circles on the corners and sides of an object that are used to resize the object.

Slide Master Feature that stores information about slide backgrounds, layouts, and fonts for each theme.

Slide Show View Option that displays slides in sequence at full-screen size for audience viewing.

Slide Sorter View Option that displays slides as thumbnails.

Smart Lookup The feature that displays the definition and additional information from the Internet of a selected word or words.

Smart Lookup pane The pane on the right side of the Office application window that displays the definition and additional information from the Internet of a selected word or words when the *Smart Lookup* feature is used.

SmartArt graphics Diagram layouts used to illustrate concepts such as processes, cycles, or relationships.

SmartArt Styles Gallery that displays different effects for emphasizing shapes within SmartArt layouts.

Snap Assist The Windows feature that allows users to fill half or a quarter of the computer screen with an open application or window and select another open application or window to fill a different half or quadrant of the computer screen.

Soft Edges Style effect option that creates a feathered edge, which gradually blends into the background color.

soft page break Formatting option that allows text to flow to the next page when it reaches the bottom margin of a page.

Sort Feature that arranges text, table rows, or records in alphabetical or numerical order.

source Complete bibliographic reference for a book, journal article, or web page.

source cell Cell data that is copied or cut.

source data Cell range with values and labels graphed in a chart.

sparklines Miniature charts embedded in a worksheet cell.

speaker notes Reminders to help the speaker present that are entered into the *Notes* pane and are visible in *Notes Pane* view.

Spelling Feature that identifies misspelled words and gives the user word choice options to correct spelling.

split button Use to apply a command or display a drop-down list of additional commands depending on where you click the button.

Split Cells Command that divides a single cell into two or more cells.

Split Form Option that allows you to view data two different ways at the same time; the top section of the form displays a columnar layout and the bottom section of the form displays a datasheet layout.

splitter bar Horizontal or vertical gray bar that divides a worksheet into panes.

spreadsheet In PowerPoint, data displayed in columns and rows to create a chart.

stacked layout Control layout that organizes the data vertically.

Standard Slide size option in PowerPoint that uses a more square 4:3 aspect ratio; the default size in earlier PowerPoint versions.

Standard colors Ten colors that are not affected by *Theme Color* changes.

Start Animation timing command that controls when animation begins.

Start button (Windows 10) The button located on the left of the Windows Taskbar that opens the Windows Start menu.

Status bar The area at the bottom of an Office application that displays certain file information and application commands.

stepped layout Report layout option available when grouping records; displays the fields in a row and column format with the field names displayed as column heads; the grouped field displays in the left-most column.

structured reference Name assigned to specific parts of an Excel table.

style Set of built-in formats, which include a variety of borders, shading, alignment, and other options.

style gallery Collection of preset effects for text, shapes, pictures, or other objects.

Subtotal Summary row for grouped data.

SUM *Math & Trig* Function that adds cell values.

summary query Query that analyzes a set of records and displays summarized results.

Sunburst chart Hierarchy chart similar to a pie chart with concentric rings for each level in the hierarchy.

syntax Required elements and the order of those elements for a function.

T

tab Area on the *Ribbon* that lists groups of related commands and options.

tab scrolling buttons Buttons to the left of tab names used to move through all worksheet tabs.

table Shows data in an organized, easy-to-read format with information arranged in columns and rows; in Access, database object that stores a collection of related records.

table of contents List of topics in a document; lists headings in the document and related page numbers.

table selector handle Handle that appears at the upper left of a table when the pointer is on a table.

Table Style Options The feature used to apply table style formatting to certain parts of a table, such as the header row, first column, or banded rows.

Table Styles Gallery of built-in table formats which include a variety of borders, shading, alignment, and other options.

tab selector Button at the top of the vertical ruler where you select the type of tab stop you want to set on the ruler.

tab stop Marker that controls where the insertion point stops when *Tab* is pressed.

Tablet mode The Windows feature that optimizes the computer for use with a touch screen.

tabular layout Form or report layout option that displays the fields in a row and column format with the field names displayed as column heads.

target frame Window where a reader is directed when a hyperlink document or web site opens.

task pane Area at the left or right of an Office application window where you can perform tasks.

Task View The feature in Windows 10 that displays all open windows as tiles on the desktop, and users can select an item to display as the active window on the desktop.

Taskbar Horizontal area at the bottom of the Windows desktop where you can launch programs or open folders.

Tell Me The new help feature in Office applications that displays both application commands and information about commands.

template Predesigned and ready-to-use document, workbook, database, or slide presentation that includes formulas, formatting, viewing options, and sample content.

test data A set of data created to test a database application to ensure that the system performs as desired.

text box Area where you can type text.

Text Box control Control on a form or report used to display data; when used on a form, it can also accept data when a user enters a value.

Text Effects Command used to apply effect options, such as *Shadow* or *Glow*, to text.

text files Files such *as* .txt (text) documents, .csv (comma separated values) files, and .prn (printer) files.

Text Pane Area where you enter text for *SmartArt* shapes.

text wrapping Formatting option that controls how text wraps around a graphic.

Texture Fill *Shape Fill* option that applies an image such as woven fabric or wood.

Theme Collection of fonts, colors, and effects that you can apply to an entire document, workbook, or presentation; provides consistent background graphics.

Theme Colors Set of background and accent colors.

Theme Fonts Pair of fonts used for a presentation's headings and body text.

Thesaurus Resource tool that lists synonyms for a selected word.

thumbnail Small picture of an image or layout.

tick marks Small lines on a chart axis to guide in reading values.

Tile picture as texture Option to format a slide background with a picture that is repeated to fill the slide.

Total row Table Style option showing color and text emphasis; in Access, row added in Design view of query that specifies the aggregate function to perform.

Touch Mode The Office applications feature that optimizes the software for use with a touch screen.

Track Changes The reviewing feature that marks changes made to a file.

Transform Style effect option used to change the shape of words.

transition Visual effect that occurs when one slide changes into another slide.

Transparency Color setting that is adjusted by percentage to allow the background to show through objects.

trendline Chart element that averages and forecasts chart data.

U

unbound control Control that is not linked to a data source.

unbound form Form that does not have a connection to a data source.

Undo Reverse an action.

***Unique Records* property** Query property that directs Access to display only records that do not include duplicated values; checks all fields in the table, whether or not they have been included in the query.

***Unique Values* property** Query property that directs Access to display only records that do not include duplicated values in the fields included in the query.

V

***Validation Rule* property** Property used to set limits on acceptable values that can be entered into a field.

***Validation Text* property** Property used to enter a custom message that displays when a validation rule is violated.

value Number that you type in a cell for numbers, currency, dates, and percentages, and can be used for calculations.

value axis Shows the numbers in a chart; the vertical axis in a column chart and the horizontal axis in a bar chart.

Variants Theme designs showing different color combinations.

vertical alignment Content positioning option that aligns material in relation to the top, bottom, or middle of the page or slide; can also refer to the position of objects in relation to each other.

***View-only* link** A hyperlink used when sharing a file with others that allows users to only view or download a shared file.

volatile Description for function results that depend on the date and time set in the computer.

W

Waterfall chart A chart that depicts a running total based on the negative and positive values.

Weight Thickness of an outline measured in points.

white space Blank space around text and objects in a document; improves the readability of a document and prevents the document from appearing cluttered.

Widescreen The PowerPoint default slide size option that uses a 16:9 aspect ratio; a 16:10 aspect ratio is available.

wildcard character Symbol used in an expression in a query to find records that match, or in a validation rule to require data being entered to match a specific character, number, or pattern.

Windows 10 Operating system software that controls computer functions and the working environment.

Windows desktop Working area in Windows.

Windows *Start* menu Menu that displays when the *Start* button in the bottom left corner of the screen is clicked. Open applications and Windows features from the *Start* menu.

word wrap Formatting option that ensures that text automatically continues to the next line when a line ends at the right margin.

WordArt Displays text as a graphic object with preset text effects that can be modified.

workbook Saved Excel file that contains worksheets.

worksheet Individual page or sheet in a workbook.

worksheet tab Identifier at the bottom left of a worksheet that displays the name of sheet.

Wrap Text Formatting tool that enables you to display the contents of a cell on multiple lines.

X

.xlsx Excel file format for workbooks.

Z

zip The Windows feature that combines files and/or folders into one compressed folder. Also, called a compressed folder.

zipped (compressed) folder Folder that has a reduced file size and can be attached to an email.

Zoom Change file display size.